Dictionary of World Biography

The 20th Century

Dictionary of World Biography

Dictionary of World Biography

Volume 8
The 20th Century

Go-N

Frank N. Magill, *editor*

Christina J. Moose, *managing editor*

Alison Aves, *researcher and bibliographer*

Mark Rehn, *acquisitions editor*

FITZROY DEARBORN PUBLISHERS
CHICAGO • LONDON

SALEM PRESS
PASADENA • HACKENSACK, NJ

Dictionary of World Biography is a copublication of Salem Press, Inc. and Fitzroy Dearborn Publishers

For information, write to:
SALEM PRESS, INC.
P.O. Box 50062
Pasadena, California 91115

or

FITZROY DEARBORN PUBLISHERS
919 N. Michigan Ave., Suite 760
Chicago, Illinois 60611
USA

or

FITZROY DEARBORN PUBLISHERS
310 Regent Street
London W1R 5AJ
England

Library of Congress Cataloging-in-Publication Data
Dictionary of world biography / editor, Frank N. Magill ; managing editor, Christina J. Moose ; researcher and bibliographer, Alison Aves ; acquisitions editor, Mark Rehn.
   v. cm.
   A revision and reordering, with new entries added, of the material in the thirty vols. comprising the various subsets designated "series" published under the collective title: Great lives from history, 1987-1995.
   Includes bibliographical references and indexes.
   Contents: v.8. The twentieth century.
   ISBN 0-89356-322-6 (v. 8 : alk. paper)
   ISBN 0-89356-320-X (v. 7-9 set : alk paper)
   ISBN 0-89356-273-4 (vol. 1-10 set : alk. paper)
   1. Biography. 2. World history. I. Magill, Frank Northen, 1907-1997. II. Moose, Christina J., 1952-   . III. Aves, Alison. IV. Great lives from history.
CT104.D54   1998
920.02—dc21   97-51154
                                                                                                         CIP

British Library Cataloguing-in-Publication Data is available.
Fitzroy Dearborn ISBN 1-57958-047-5

First Published in the U.K. and U.S., 1999
Printed by Sheridan Books

Cover design by Peter Aristedes.

First Printing

CONTENTS

LIST OF ENTRANTS

JEAN-LUC GODARD

Born: December 3, 1930; Paris, France

Area of Achievement: Film

Contribution: Godard, along with his colleagues in the Nouvelle Vague (New Wave) of postwar French film, expanded the possibilities of cinematic expression so that traditional narrative patterns could no longer be regarded as limits and was instrumental in locating film at the center of postmodern aesthetics, establishing the cinema as the equal of any form of artistic expression.

Early Life

Jean-Luc Godard was born in Paris in 1930. His father, Paul Godard, was a prosperous doctor, and his mother, Odile Monod, was the daughter of a family that had been established in the banking profession in Switzerland for generations. The family moved to Switzerland in 1940 to escape the war and lived in Nyon until 1945. After the war, they returned to Paris, where Godard continued his education at the prestigious Lycée Buffon, a school specializing in the physical and biological sciences. His parents were divorced in 1946, and Godard moved into a hotel room a few blocks from the center of Montparnasse, one of the artists' quarters of the city. He describes himself as a casual filmgoer until 1948, but in that year he discovered Travail et Culture, a Left Bank film club run by the distinguished film theorist André Bazin, and attended lectures at the Ciné-Club du Quartier Latin, where he met Eric Rohmer and François Truffaut, soon to be fellow members of the New Wave. He was enrolled in the Sorbonne in 1950 and worked toward a degree in ethnology, attending lectures by Ferdinand de Saussure, the founder of semiology, and received a certificate in 1952. Between 1949 and 1951, Godard recalls that "I saw every film I could see," and, although he was planning to become a journalist, drawn to writing partly by the prestige that the word carried in the existential ethos of Paris in the 1950's, he was already committed to film as a means of exploring and expressing his creative impulses.

In 1954, he returned to Switzerland to work briefly as a construction laborer and made his first film in 35 millimeter, a twenty-minute documentary on the building of the Grande-Dixence Dam, where he was employed. He had been writing essays on film since 1950, when he, Rohmer, and Jacques Rivette founded *La Gazette du cinéma*

(which lasted for five issues) and when Bazin founded *Cahiers du cinéma* in April, 1951, a journal that quickly became the most influential film magazine in the world; Godard began to publish essays there as well. In 1956, he assisted Rohmer and Rivette on their early productions and began to think of himself as a film artist who could comment on films by making other films. During 1957, he began to write film scripts, discussing his work with producers as well as working as a publicist for Twentieth Century-Fox studios.

Pierre Braunberger, a producer of shorts, commissioned Godard to direct *Tous les garçons s'appellent Patrick* (1957; *All the Boys Are Called Patrick*), another twenty-minute short. The discursive nature of the narration, the verbal density of its texture, and Godard's postproduction dubbing of the main character's voice are all characteristics of Godard's work, and, although the film was rejected by the Tours Festival for "nonprofessionalism," Godard dismissed these critics as people "for whom the cinema is comprehended only by its past."

Life's Work

As the sixth decade of the twentieth century drew to a close, the motion picture industry was relatively moribund and static throughout the Western world. American studio films were increasingly formulaic, and European productions were generally also confined by conventions and expectations. The relative tranquillity of the 1950's and the caution induced by the Cold War and the fear of nuclear destruction were about to be shattered by the explosion of suppressed energy of the next decade, and Godard's first feature film, *à Bout de souffle* (1960; *Breathless*), both reflected and directed many of that decade's most characteristic patterns. Its story about a girl studying at the Sorbonne and her relationship with a young gangster who has adopted a style fashioned after American film heroes (particularly Humphrey Bogart) was presented with a dazzling, innovative structure and very creative editing, which projected the rhythms of an emerging generation. The lack of traditional linear connections, the self-referential nature of the narration, the anarchic, almost nihilistic attitude of the street-smart young man, and the feeling of spontaneity that the film expressed had an enormous impact on film-goers and filmmakers. Godard was

Jean-Luc Godard in the 1980's film First Name: Carmen.

immediately made the subject of fierce support and enraged condemnation as artists of every variety saw opportunity either created or demolished.

Godard himself was too intent on making films to be especially concerned about the critical furor. His next film, *Le Petit Soldat* (1961; *The Little Soldier*), was made "to catch up with the realism I had missed in *Breathless*." The film was a meditation on the French colonial situation in Algeria, and Godard was interested in what he called the "moral repercussions" of war. The French government banned the film until 1963, but by then Godard had gone on to direct *Une Femme est une femme* (1961; *A Woman Is a Woman*), a comedy that Godard called "my first real film." He also made *Vivre sa vie* (1962; *My Life to Live*), a twelve-part, proto-feminist examination of prostitution, in which Godard attacked the use of people as products in a consumerist society. Becoming steadily more specific about his politics, Godard directed *Les Carabiniers* (1963; *The Riflemen*), a consideration of the specific nature of war, which confounded most

of the critics, who could not see Godard's deconstruction of the standard presentation of warfare in films. Adverse critical reaction caused the film to be withdrawn.

One of Godard's favorite cinematic techniques was the Brechtian concept of alienation, in which the audience is compelled to recognize and regard its own responses to the action on the screen. While Godard purposely interrupted the expected course of the narrative with jump-cuts, asides, quotes, and shifts in time, he realized that he was progressively distancing himself from his characters as well, and his next film, *Le Mépris* (1963; *Contempt*), was designed to restore what he called his "movie-loving attitude." Using international stars such as Jack Palance, Brigitte Bardot, and the director Fritz Lang (as himself), the film was ostensibly about "men cut off from the gods, cut off from the world," but the presence of Bardot in particular detracted from Godard's attempt to render a Homeric conception in which the filmmaker was like the poet in ancient Greece—a storehouse of the wisdom of his time. Continuing to work so that he did not exclude "one aspect of the cinema in the name of another aspect of the cinema," Godard followed *Contempt* with *Une Femme mariée* (1964; *The Married Woman*), an examination of bourgeois expectations for a marriage shot in a pop-art, surface-against-surface approach; *Bande à part* (1964; *Band of Outsiders*), a romantic recollection of the moods of the American gangster film and a comment/analysis on the conventions of that genre; and *Alphaville* (1965), a vision of a postmodern world where a detective/hero carries his hardboiled sensibility into a surrealistic, mechanized landscape in a clash of an out-moded past and an inhuman future.

In *Pierrot le fou* (1965) and *Masculin-féminin* (1966), Godard moved closer to his own feelings, revealing some of his deepest personal responses through his characters. He even cast his own wife, Anna Karina, in *Pierrot le fou*. In *Masculin-féminin*, Godard attempted to come to terms with his own youth and with the excitement that he had felt in Paris as he learned about life in the city of light, about the art of film itself, and about the mysterious nature of feminine reality. Although the film employs many of Godard's now familiar devices (words dissected on the screen, interior monologues, interviews amid the narrative action, a randomness of sequences), there are many scenes of lyric intensity in which an emotional and subjective point of view transcends the witty social commentary.

Concluding a decade of exceptional cinematic activity, Godard directed *Le Week-end* (1967; *Weekend*), a raucous, explosive tableau of the modern world as a long, winding, insane highway replete with blatant sexual displays, comic violence, and people devoured by their own selfishness; *Le Gai Savoir* (1968; *The Joy of Learning*), an examination of philosophic responses to contemporary situations; and *One Plus One* (released as *Sympathy for the Devil* in 1968), a quasi-documentary examination of pop culture including the band the Rolling Stones. Then, after a decade of influential and prolific filmmaking, Godard disappeared from view. This disappearance was actually a refusal to continue to make films and distribute them in the familiar manner of the film industry. The political events of 1968 (assassination and murder, Vietnam, the student revolts in Paris) led Godard to form a production group named for the Soviet filmmaker Dziga Vertov, in which he collaborated with the theorist Jean-Pierre Gorin on specifically ideological films, using politically oriented celebrities such as Yves Montand and Jane Fonda to try to mix commercial filmmaking and social criticism. In 1972, Godard shifted entirely into the realm of video technology to try to avoid completely the strictures of commercial control over his efforts, moving to Switzerland in order to set up a production facility in which he and Anne-Marie Miéville, his partner, could be fully responsible for their work. While the films and television features Godard made during this time have their admirers, many people believe that much of the work was largely inaccessible to all but the most dedicated film scholars.

A third phase of Godard's career began in 1979, further confounding the critics who had dismissed him as a has-been. Still living in Switzerland, Godard directed *Sauve Qui Peut (La Vie)* (1979; *Every Man for Himself*), an effort which Godard called his "second first film." In a story of three people, two women and a man, the characters' lives connect, interact, and finally diverge. The film is another critique of modern society, and, while it tends to be episodic, the lives of the people whom the film follows are presented in powerful and sympathetic fashion. Although Godard does not quite connect everything, scene after scene resonates with Godard's arresting use of the camera to direct the viewer's attention. This film was followed by others, including *Je vous salue, Marie* (1985; *Hail Mary*), a bizarrely ironic recounting of the Nativity story, featuring a modern Virgin Mary appearing completely nude. Godard knew that the official religious publications would attack his work as blasphemous, but what interested him was trying to place the archetypal events in both a modern and unfamiliar context. Much of the film is obscure, but much of it is also witty and pointed, mixing the carnal with the spiritual in an unpredictable manner. That same year, he also directed *Detective*, a reprise of 1940's *film noir* styles in a kind of comic murder mystery. In 1987, Godard produced his first film entirely in English, a very eccentric version of *King Lear*, featuring Norman Mailer, Woody Allen, Molly Ringwald, and Godard himself, and at the Cannes Festival in 1990, his typically controversial film *Nouvelle Vague* premiered. In his fourth decade of filmmaking, he produced *For Ever Mozart* (1996) and *Hélas pour moi* (1993; *Oh, Woe is Me*), among others.

Summary

It has been said that D. W. Griffith gave the cinema its alphabet, that Sergei Eisenstein gave the cinema its intellect, and that Charles Chaplin gave it its humanity. Perhaps it is a bit presumptuous to include Jean-Luc Godard in this exalted pantheon, but it is not unreasonable to say that Godard, by subverting all of its conventions, gave the cinema its freedom. Even now that his work is relatively familiar, there is a bold, imaginative quality to a Godard film that is remarkably refreshing even when the director's idiosyncrasies make the film frustrating in some ways.

Specifically, Godard mixes various cinematic modes to arrive at new possibilities that work because he knows film history so well. His use of sight and sound is like a sensory assault that prevents the viewer from watching with a mind on automatic pilot. Escape is impossible, engagement unavoidable. Godard takes as his primary challenge the problem of how to communicate what is "real" when nothing is real except the projected celluloid on the screen at any moment. His examination of shifting realities has led him (and his audience) to a new understanding of the nature of perception itself, time and space ordered and reordered by the artist and the observer. One of his primary fields of experimentation is in the area of editing, in which Godard rejects the classical theory of montage and substitutes his own style. It is the excitement of discovery that makes Godard's work so compelling, the singularity of his vision that makes it so provocative, and the demands that he makes on the audience that prevent it from ever being ordinary cinema.

Bibliography

Brown, Royal S., ed. *Focus on Godard*. Englewood Cliffs, N.J.: Prentice-Hall, 1972. An anthology containing essays, reviews, and an interview with Godard covering his Dziga Vertov period. There is a careful textual analysis of his early films by Marie-Claire Ropars.

Collet, Jean. *Jean-Luc Godard: An Investigation into His Films and Philosophy*. Translated by Ciba Vaughan. New York: Crown, 1970. Several revealing interviews with the director as well as perceptive commentary on the social conditions surrounding Godard's work.

Dixon, Wheeler W. *The Films of Jean-Luc Godard*. Albany: State University of New York Press, 1997. The only book to cover objectively Godard's entire career as a filmmaker; includes his television productions and his ethnographic work in Africa. Well-researched and including forty-six rare photographs, this is the definitive overview of Godard's work.

Gaggi, Silvio. *Modern/Postmodern: A Study in Twentieth Century Arts and Ideas*. Philadelphia: University of Pennsylvania Press, 1989. Comparisons between works in the theater, film, painting, and literature to demonstrate relationships among different forms of contemporary art and philosophy. Places Godard in a larger aesthetic and philosophical context.

Giannetti, Louis. *Godard and Others: Essays on Film Form*. Rutherford, N.J.: Fairleigh Dickinson University Press, 1975; London: Tantivy Press, 1976. An especially lucid essay on *Masculin-féminin* and many other incisive comments on Godard's work in relation to other films.

Godard, Jean-Luc. *Godard on Godard*. Edited and translated by Tom Milne. 2d ed. New York: Da Capo Press, 1989. Godard's comments and reactions concerning a very wide range of films and filmmakers. An excellent companion to the director's films, capturing the flavor of Godard's wit and insight. Milne's translations are adequate, although John Kreidl believes that they are weak in the area of film theory.

Kreidl, John. *Jean-Luc Godard*. Boston: Twayne, 1980. An intense, engrossing full-length study of Godard's films and ideas through the first two decades of his career. Written in a style that attempts to approximate the structure of Godard's films, the book is a bit eccentric but very intelligent. Thorough notes and references, an accurate filmography, and a very useful annotated bibliography.

MacCabe, Colin. *Godard: Images, Sounds, Politics*. London: Macmillan, and Bloomington: Indiana University Press, 1980. An intellectual and personal defense of the period when Godard removed himself from conventional film-distributing patterns. Detailed and analytical, with many illustrations, sketches, and photographs. Designed for the serious student but not inaccessible. Interviews with Godard follow each chapter.

Monaco, James. *The New Wave*. New York: Oxford University Press, 1976. A lengthy discussion of Godard's work in relation to the other filmmakers of the Nouvelle Vague. Competent and thorough.

Mussman, Toby. *Jean-Luc Godard*. New York: Dutton, 1968. A critical anthology containing some very interesting interviews by Godard near the beginning of his career, critical essays on the first films, and some commentary by other filmmakers.

Roud, Richard. *Godard*. 2d ed. London: Thames and Hudson, and Bloomington: Indiana University Press, 1970. A clearly written analysis of Godard's career from its inception through the conclusion of the first phase. Roud concentrates on form and shows the connective threads in the films of the 1960's.

Silverman, Kaja, and Harun Farocki. *Speaking about Godard*. New York: New York University Press, 1998. Collection of eight dialogues between a feminist film theorist and an avant-garde filmmaker on Godard's work spanning his entire career.

Simon, John. *Movies into Film*. New York: Dial Press, 1971. Simon's essay on *La Chinoise* (1967) is a representative example of the kind of criticism that unsympathetic commentators applied to Godard's work. It is a testament to the power of the work that it has evoked such wide-ranging responses.

Sterritt, David. *Jean-Luc Godard: Interviews*. Jackson: University Press of Mississippi, 1998. A selection of interviews with Godard by scholars, journalists, and critics between 1960 and the 1990's. Topics include the character and impact of film, his thoughts on aging, and the significance of language.

Leon Lewis

ROBERT H. GODDARD

Born: October 5, 1882; Worcester, Massachusetts
Died: August 10, 1945; Baltimore, Maryland
Area of Achievement: Rocketry
Contribution: As the deviser of the first successful liquid-fuel rocket and as a tireless explorer of the theoretical and practical problems of rocketry decades before the subject gained substantial support in the United States, Goddard stands as the great American pioneer of space travel.

Early Life

Robert Hutchings Goddard was born on October 5, 1882, in the central Massachusetts industrial city of Worcester. Nahum Goddard, then a bookkeeper for a manufacturer of machine knives, and his wife, the former Fannie Louise Hoyt, moved to Roxbury, Massachusetts, when Robert was only an infant but continued to spend considerable time at the family homestead until fifteen years later, when Mrs. Goddard's health dictated their return to Worcester. Various bronchial ailments plagued their only son, who, because of frequent absences from school, was not graduated from high school until his twenty-second year.

Like many boys of his time, Goddard devoured such prototypes of science fiction as Jules Verne's *From the Earth to the Moon* (1865) and H. G. Wells's *The War of the Worlds* (1898). Goddard dated the discovery of his vocation, however, from an experience which, like the story often told of George Washington, involved a cherry tree—but a story whose authenticity is not in doubt. On October 19, 1899, shortly after his seventeenth birthday, he climbed a cherry tree on the family property and, while in its branches, imagined a spaceship that might travel to Mars. He later claimed that when he descended from the tree, he was "a different boy," and for the remainder of his life he would solemnly celebrate the date as "Anniversary Day." Whenever possible, he visited the tree on October 19, as long as it stood.

Single-minded in his dedication to the idea of space flight, he entered the local engineering college, Worcester Polytechnic Institute, in 1904. Although he pondered space travel in his spare time, the nature of his collegiate work suggested to his physics professor the likelihood of a career in radio engineering. Upon graduation in 1908, he continued his study of physics at Clark University, also in Worcester; Clark had been founded as a graduate school and emphasized the natural and social sciences. Goddard taught physics briefly at Worcester Polytechnic Institute, but, upon receipt of his Ph.D. in physics in 1911, he accepted a research fellowship at Princeton University, realizing that his aptitude for research exceeded that for teaching.

In March of 1913, he learned that he had contracted his mother's illness, tuberculosis, and physicians gave him little chance to survive. He spent a year at home recuperating, and by 1914, was well enough to conduct a series of experiments with tiny rockets propelled by a smokeless powder of his own devising. The struggle with disease, however, had exacted its toll, leaving him nearly bald in his early thirties. He remained thin and frail throughout his life, and he developed a stoop while relatively young. The young scientist was of average height, his two most prominent facial characteristics being a trim brown mustache and expressive brown eyes under dark brows.

Rejecting offers from Princeton and Columbia, which he feared might not leave him sufficient time for research, he accepted a position as instructor in physics at Clark, an association which would last the remainder of his life.

Life's Work

The two world wars bounded, and greatly influenced, Goddard's working life. Of the 214 patents issued to him, the first two came in the summer of 1914, as World War I was beginning. One, for a cartridge-feeding mechanism, turned out to be impractical in rocketry; the second, for a liquid rocket-fuel, presaged his greatest accomplishment, still more than a decade of hard work away from fruition. Whereas science fiction had fired his imagination early, Goddard invariably approached his investigations in a matter-of-fect way and never seems to have wasted time on romantic but scientifically dubious schemes for space travel. At his time, weaponry, not space flight, occupied the American military, and Goddard, aware that the Germans had pursued applications of the Wright brothers' great invention more quickly than had Americans, and anxious that they not take the lead in rocket development, wrote to the United States Navy about his experiments. Although he provoked some interest, President Woodrow Wilson's declaration of American neutrality discouraged research in military rockets.

Furthermore, despite his success at sending his tiny powder rockets nearly five hundred feet into the air over Worcester by 1915, Goddard had not yet developed a suitable liquid fuel. When his university salary proved inadequate to support his research, he obtained a five-thousand-dollar grant from the Smithsonian Institution, and by the fall of 1918, he had devised a rocket which was capable of being fired from a trench and of delivering a payload three-quarters of a mile away. In November, he demonstrated his rockets at the army's proving grounds at Aberdeen, Maryland. Impressed that these rockets outperformed existing trench mortar, the army agreed to appropriate money for production. A few days later, however, Germany surrendered. It would require another global conflict to revive high-level interest in Goddard's rockets.

Returning to his first love, the goal of space travel, Goddard, under the auspices of the Smithsonian, published in 1919 a treatise explaining how rockets might ascend to the moon. This work, *A Method of Reaching Extreme Altitudes*, brought him unwelcome publicity as an eccentric professor, and references to him in the popular press as "moon man" stung this serious investigator. He was fortunate in his academic affiliation, however, for Clark granted him leaves of absence when necessary, and his work proceeded steadily. Between 1920 and 1923, he conducted experiments at the navy ordnance facility at Indian Head, Maryland. Back in Worcester in 1923, he was appointed director of laboratories at Clark in addition to his professorship. Goddard took time out, in 1924, to marry Esther Kisk, who proved a devoted helpmate; after his death his widow would spend years editing his voluminous papers.

On March 16, 1926, on a farm in nearby Auburn, Goddard achieved his greatest success. The ten-foot rocket he sent up that day traveled for only two and one-half seconds and flew only 184 feet. His sponsor at the Smithsonian, Dr. Charles G. Abbot, was not impressed, for Goddard had talked in terms of hundreds of miles, and this rocket had attained a maximum altitude of forty-one feet. In retrospect, however, this short flight looms as momentous as that of the Wright brothers' airplane twenty-three years earlier at Kitty Hawk, North Carolina. This first successful flight of a liquid-propellant rocket established the feasibility of the spectacular space ventures that Goddard did not live to see.

His experiments having outgrown New England pastures, Goddard received the assistance of Colonel Charles A. Lindbergh, whose 1927 transoceanic flight had earned for him international fame. In 1929, Lindbergh talked philanthropist Harry Guggenheim into granting Goddard fifty thousand dollars for research on a larger scale. This largess enabled Goddard to spend much of the following decade at Roswell, New Mexico, improving his rockets. Clark issued another monograph on his work to date in 1936, but not until after his death would his major publication, *Rocket Development: Liquid-Fuel Rocket Research* (1948), appear. Unlike Hermann Oberth, his younger German contemporary, who independently achieved results comparable to Goddard's, the Clark professor shunned publicity and avoided joint projects with other scientists. As a consequence, he spent the latter part of his career laboring in obscurity while Oberth's work led directly to the V-1 and V-2 rockets of World War II.

During the war, Goddard worked for the navy in Maryland but found the required teamwork uncongenial. As the war dragged on, declining health and the knowledge that German rocketry was outdistancing that of the United States seized Goddard, and the American government's decision to concentrate on atomic research left him in a military backwater. In May of 1945, a few weeks after Germany's surrender, a physician detected a growth in Goddard's throat. Despite two operations at the University of Maryland Hospital in Baltimore, Goddard continued to fail. On August 10, 1945, America's rocket pioneer died; his body was returned to Worcester and buried on August 14—the day of Japan's surrender.

Summary

Assessing Goddard's achievement later that year, *Science* magazine credited him with investigating virtually every principle vital to the theory and practice of jet propulsion and rocket guidance. Nevertheless, most Americans did not know him until the early 1960's, when the successes of the American space program provoked interest in its historical background, and publications describing Goddard's life and work began to appear.

When his story was told, it was often with an emphasis on the solitariness and obscurity of his endeavors. His biographers have tended to depict him as a lonely hero, obliged to endure at first scorn and later neglect. Historians of rocketry and

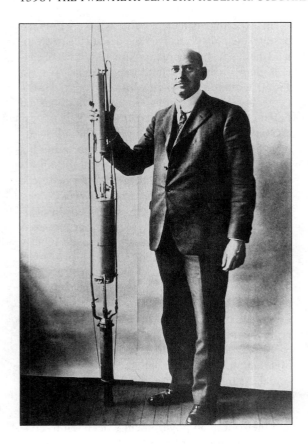

space travel, however, have pointed out the extent to which he imposed his plight upon himself. Retiring by nature, Goddard appears to have been driven further inward by the facetious tone of early journalistic accounts of his research. He conducted his experiments in a secretive and possessive manner, sharing his discoveries with only a few trusted assistants. Although a true scientist, Goddard evinced an inventor's interest in protecting his work by patent much more often than a scientist's desire to share his discoveries with fellow scientists in scholarly monographs. Pursued by both professional and amateur societies in his field, he generally remained aloof. As a result, it is likely that he fell behind other researchers in the 1930's and 1940's.

One of Goddard's biographers has noted that his brown eyes could radiate warmth and friendliness at times and turn cold and austere at others. Many anecdotes testify to his congeniality when at ease and among friends, but he seems to have been a man who coveted and cherished his professional isolation. Whatever the explanation of his proprietary attitude toward his work, he was a true pio-

neer in rocketry. He made original discoveries in many aspects of his subject, producing innovative igniters and carburetors, pumps and turbines, gyroscopic stabilizers and landing controls, jet-driven propellers and variable-thrust engines. His ceaseless dedication and the thoroughness of his research and testing complemented his sheer brilliance. Robert H. Goddard's legacy, so little recognized at the time of his death, is now manifest in the space age.

Bibliography

Bainbridge, William Sims. *The Spaceflight Revolution: A Sociological Study.* Seattle: University of Washington Press, 1976; London: Wiley, 1977. Useful for its systematized information about the personal characteristics of space pioneers and for its insights into how and why the movement succeeded, this study stops short of explaining the often puzzling pattern of Goddard's professional behavior.

Braun, Wernher von, and Frederick I. Ordway III. *History of Rocketry and Space Travel.* 3d ed. New York: Crowell, 1975. This well-illustrated volume gives careful consideration to Goddard's achievements in relation to those of earlier and later theorists and practitioners. Contains a five-page chronology of Goddard's rocket tests from 1915 to 1941.

Dewey, Anne Perkins. *Robert Goddard: Space Pioneer.* Boston: Little Brown, 1962. A short, popular, illustrated life. Based on diaries and interviews with the scientist's widow, this book will serve the purposes of those seeking an intimate portrait of Goddard at home.

Goddard, Robert H. *The Papers of Robert H. Goddard.* Edited by Esther C. Goddard and G. Edward Pendray. 3 vols. New York: McGraw-Hill Book, 1970. Meticulously assembled from thousands of manuscript pages, this work is a highly competent chronological account of Goddard's career in his own words. Indispensable to the serious student of Goddard's life and work.

Hunley, J. D. "The Enigma of Robert H. Goddard." *Technology and Culture* 36, no. 2 (April, 1995). Examines the factors affecting Goddard's life and development of the rocket, including his education, an interest in mysticism, and his battle with tuberculosis.

Kernan, Michael. "The Object at Hand." *Smithsonian* 20, no. 8 (November, 1989). An entertaining and informative discussion of Goddard's first successful rocket experiment.

Lehman, Milton. *This High Man: The Life of Robert H. Goddard*. New York: Farrar Straus, 1963. Easily the best-written and most thorough of Goddard biographies. Gives some attention to the scientific context in which Goddard worked. Does not interpret Goddard but supplies most of the important facts in a well-constructed and readable narrative. The standard life until someone plumbs the wellsprings of his character.

Stoiko, Michael. *Pioneers of Rocketry*. New York: Hawthorn, 1974. For readers wishing a profile of Goddard, this book offers the chance to compare his career with those of four other pioneers, including the Russian Konstantin Tsiolkovsky and the German Hermann Oberth.

Winter, Frank H. *Prelude to the Space Age: The Rocket Societies, 1924-1940*. Washington, D.C.: Smithsonian Institution Press, 1983. The best source for Goddard's relations, or lack of them, with others who shared his interests. Suggests that Goddard's work would have been less often misunderstood and misinterpreted had he cultivated such relationships.

Robert P. Ellis

EDWIN LAWRENCE GODKIN

Born: October 2, 1831; Moyne, Ireland
Died: May 21, 1902; Brixham, England
Area of Achievement: Journalism
Contribution: As editor of *The Nation* and, later, of the *Evening Post*, Godkin was one of the most influential voices in post-Civil War American politics.

Early Life

Edwin Lawrence Godkin was born in Moyne, Ireland, on October 2, 1831, to Sarah Lawrence and James Godkin. The elder Godkin was a Protestant clergyman, journalist, and political activist of some note, a prominent figure in the Irish independence movement.

Godkin attended a series of Irish and English schools and in 1846 entered Queens College in Belfast, Ireland. There, he was introduced to the works of the Utilitarian philosophers Jeremy Bentham and John Stuart Mill, whose political and economic theories did much to shape Godkin's own views. Particularly attractive to Godkin was the Utilitarians' belief in *laissez-faire*, private property rights, and economic law as the basis for sound government. The young Godkin was also captivated with the idea of American democracy, though this view was always tempered by a distinctly aristocratic streak in his thought.

Upon his graduation in 1851, Godkin moved to London, where after a brief flirtation with law study, he began his journalism career as subeditor of *The Workingmen's Friend*, an entertainment magazine published by John Cassell. Godkin's first book, *The History of the Hungary and the Magyars:* From the Earliest Times to the Close of the Late War, was published in 1853.

Hired as a special correspondent in Turkey for London's *Daily News*, Godkin covered the Crimean War from 1853 to 1855. The young correspondent's dispatches from the Turkish front, sharply critical of perceived incompetence in the British and Turkish military leadership, exhibit the penchant for faultfinding and polemics that marks his later writings. After his return to Great Britain, Godkin spent two years lecturing on the war and contributing articles to the liberal Belfast newspaper *The Northern Whig*.

Life's Work

In October, 1856, at the age of twenty-five, Godkin sailed to America, settling in New York. One of Godkin's first acquaintances in the United States was Frederick Law Olmsted, the distinguished writer, landscape architect, and political activist. Olmsted's liberal political opinions were close to those of Godkin, and the two men began a long friendship. Inspired in part by Olmsted's writings on the American South, Godkin traveled through the region in the fall of 1856. Reporting his experience in the London *Daily News*, Godkin expressed his dislike of the South—which he found rude and backward—and his aversion to slavery on both moral and economic grounds.

Returning to New York, Godkin studied law for a time and began contributing reportage to *The New York Times* and the *Evening Post*. His pieces offered perceptive, sometimes witty and biting commentary on American political affairs, usually taking a position intermediate between conservatism and radicalism.

On July 29, 1859, Godkin married Frances Elizabeth Foote, a member of a prominent New England family that included the writer and ecclesiastic Henry Ward Beecher and the novelist Harriet Beecher Stowe. A son, Lawrence, was born to the Godkins in 1860. The family spent two years in Europe, from 1860 to 1862, during which Godkin did little writing. When the Godkins returned to the United States, they found a country in a great upheaval. The Civil War had broken out, and President Abraham Lincoln had issued the preliminary Emancipation Proclamation. Godkin sided with the Union cause, though he criticized Lincoln for military inactivity in the early years of the conflict. For the next several years, Godkin wrote for a number of American newspapers, including Charles Eliot Norton's *North American Review*.

One of Godkin's more important essays, "Aristocratic Opinions on Democracy," was penned during this period. In it, Godkin argued that many of America's shortcomings, such as its people's coarseness of manners, could be attributed to the movement of populations to and from the country's less civilized frontier.

Godkin and Olmsted had for years sought to start their own periodical, free from the biases of the daily press. In 1865, their plan was realized.

With the aid of a number of liberal and abolitionist financial backers, including Norton, the weekly New York-based newspaper *The Nation* was launched, with Godkin as its editor in chief. The first issue was published on July 6, 1865.

A journal of politics, literature, science, and the arts, *The Nation* was founded by its stockholders in part to promote the rights and societal assimilation of the newly freed slaves. Always fiercely independent, Godkin soon diverged from the goals of the paper's more liberal owners, opposing black suffrage and state support of the poor. On the reconstruction of the South, he took a moderate position between the mild policies of President Andrew Johnson and the more sweeping reforms proposed by the radicals. Godkin's disagreements with *The Nation*'s more radical stockholders produced a battle for control, and he assumed principal ownership of the paper in 1866.

Under Godkin's leadership, *The Nation* became one of the most influential publications of its era, distinguished by its superior writing and broad international scope; the paper won a large following among the country's scholars and decision makers. *The Nation*'s staff and contributors included many of the best-known historians, writers, and thinkers of nineteenth century America, among them Norton and Olmsted, the journalist John R. Dennett, the philosopher Charles Sanders Pierce, and the novelist Henry James and his brother, William, the philosopher and psychologist.

Godkin's own editorials set the tone of the paper, mixing astute observation and persuasive argument with humor, sarcasm, invective, and a sharp eye for governmental misconduct. Although Godkin is often remembered as liberal and progressive, his highly individual positions make him difficult to classify. He held government's true aim to be the promotion of virtue and culture, and he was therefore mistrustful of American democracy and popular rule, which he saw as leading to cultural vulgarization and political mediocrity. He pressed for civil-service reform, seeking to free the system from political favoritism, but opposed suffrage for blacks, women, and many immigrant groups. He resisted American territorial expansionism, but for reasons seemingly more economic than moral.

Godkin's personality and editorial style earned for him as many enemies as friends. He has been described by some contemporaries as mean-spirited and icy and by others as jovial and good-na-

tured. Physically he was thick-set and of medium height. Pictures from his middle years depict a man of stately bearing, with chiseled features, full beard, and mustache.

Throughout its first decade, *The Nation* rose steadily in circulation, reaching a peak of about thirteen thousand in the mid-1870's. Circulation declined thereafter, a consequence to some extent of several unpopular political stands the paper had taken, including support for the presidential candidacy of Republican Rutherford B. Hayes.

On April 11, 1875, Godkin's wife, Frances, died, following a long illness. Godkin's younger daughter Elizabeth (born 1865) had died in 1873, and an infant son, Ralph, had died shortly after his birth in 1868. Grief-stricken, Godkin left his home in New York and moved to Cambridge, Massachusetts, relinquishing many of his editorial responsibilities at *The Nation*.

When Godkin moved back to New York several years later, *The Nation* was in severe financial difficulty. In 1881, Godkin was sold to the *Evening Post*, to be published as that paper's weekly edition. Godkin joined the *Evening Post* as associate editor under its new owner, Henry Villard, and editor in chief, Carl Schurz. Relations between Schurz and Godkin were strained, and Godkin eventually used his influence with the paper's owners to unseat Schurz and replace him as top editor in 1883. *The Evening Post* under Godkin in many ways resembled the *The Nation* of years previous: outspoken, independent, and reformist.

Godkin focused much of his editorial scrutiny during this period on American foreign policy, opposing the "annexation fever" and jingoism of the 1880's and 1890's. Godkin opposed American territorial expansion in a number of regions, including the Philippines, Cuba, Santo Domingo, Hawaii, and Samoa. He decried the United States' aggressive posture in disputes with Chile, Great Britain, and Spain.

Another target of Godkin's criticism was the New York City and State Democratic leadership at Tammany Hall, which was implicated in numerous corruption scandals during the latter part of the century.

In 1884, Godkin, a Republican of long standing, broke with the party and joined a number of independents (dubbed Mugwumps) in supporting Democratic presidential candidate Grover Cleveland. Godkin had been a vocal critic of the Republican presidential nominee, the congressman James G. Blaine, whom he accused of using political office for personal gain. The *Evening Post* continued to espouse the Mugwump cause throughout the decade.

Godkin was married in 1884 to Katherine B. Sands, of a wealthy and prominent New York and London family. In late 1899, in failing health and declining mental ability, Godkin was relieved of his duties with the *Evening Post*, staying on officially until January 1, 1900. Godkin traveled regularly to Europe in his later years and, in 1901, moved to England for good. He died there, at Brixham, on May 21, 1902.

Summary

Though it could hardly be called nonpartisan, Godkin's *The Nation* did set a new standard for independence and incisiveness. The publication's literary quality was virtually unrivaled. Among its other accomplishments, the paper's book reviews and literary notices were especially highly regarded.

Godkin himself influenced an entire generation of political thinkers and writers. He pressed doggedly for higher standards of governmental and municipal conduct, attacking corruption and cronyism wherever he perceived abuses. Godkin's forceful writings helped spur many regulatory reforms and served as an inspiration for twentieth century muckraking journalism. As an opponent of American militarism overseas, Godkin had a moderating effect on many international disputes. Yet he was not a pacifist or anti-imperialist. He believed, instead, that territorial annexation would disrupt free trade. He asserted, furthermore, that the absorption of new, non-Anglo-Saxon populations would contributed to the nation's moral decline.

While Godkin's reformist bent has earned for him the reputation of a progressive, he was in many ways conservative, looking back to older, more genteel traditions. The elevation of American manners and mores was perhaps his most cherished goal, an ideal that was often at odds with the values of an egalitarian society.

Bibliography

Armstrong, William M. *E. L. Godkin: A Biography.* Albany: State University of New York Press, 1978. An authoritative, well-written, and thoroughly researched work, the first full-scale Godkin biography since Ogden's work (below). Armstrong presents a variety of original material, painting Godkin in a less flattering light than have earlier biographers.

———. *E. L. Godkin and American Foreign Policy: 1865-1900.* New York: Bookman, 1957. A well-written account of Godkin's political milieu and his role in the key foreign policy debates of the day. Introduces many of the biographical themes explored more fully in Armstrong's later study of Godkin.

Fridlington, Robert. "Frederick Law Olmsted: Launching the Nation." *The Nation* 202 (January 3, 1966): 10-12. A useful summary of Olmsted's career, his social philosophy, and his relationship with Godkin. Describes the two men's efforts in founding *The Nation* and offers an insightful analysis of their shared political views.

Keller, Morton. *Affairs of State: Public Life in Late Nineteenth Century America.* Cambridge, Mass.:

Belknap Press of Harvard University Press, 1977. An excellent overview, thoroughgoing and well documented, of Godkin's era, its issues, and major figures. Numerous references to Godkin and *The Nation*.

Ogden, Rollo. *Life and Letters of Edwin Lawrence Godkin*. 2 vols. New York and London: Macmillan, 1907. Godkin's authorized biography, by his younger colleague at the *Evening Post*. Deferential and uncritical, this study is short on serious scholarship, but it has provided source material for many subsequent works.

Vanderbilt, Kermit. "Norton and Godkin: Launching *The Nation*." *The Nation* 200 (February 15, 1965): 165-169. Good background on the creation of *The Nation*. Useful description of Godkin's long relationship with his ideological ally and financial backer Charles Eliot Norton, one of *The Nation*'s founders and primary contributors.

Robert Pollie

JOSEPH GOEBBELS

Born: October 29, 1897; Rheydt, Germany
Died: May 1, 1945; Berlin, Germany
Areas of Achievement: Government and politics
Contribution: Goebbels was the propaganda master of the Nazi regime and Adolf Hitler's minister of culture during the twelve-year Third Reich. One of the few intellectuals in the Party leadership, Goebbels was largely responsible for the success of the Nazi program.

Early Life

Paul Joseph Goebbels was born into a strict Catholic working-class home, but his surprisingly fine intellect, combined with frail health, rescued him from a drab life of farming or factory work and pointed him toward higher education. Following early training at a Roman Catholic school, where he considered the priesthood, young Goebbels went on to study literature and history at a string of universities: Bonn, Freiburg, Würzburg, and Munich. He finished his studies in 1921 at the University of Heidelberg. Money was scarce, and Goebbels survived on odd jobs and generous loans from the Catholic Albertus Magnus Society (which he never repaid). Ironically, considering his lifelong virulent anti-Semitism, Goebbels studied under a renowned Jewish literary historian, Friedrich Gundolf, from whom he eventually earned a doctorate degree in history. Goebbels was rejected for military service in World War I, since a childhood bout with polio had left him with a crippled leg and a weak constitution. The frustration of having missed participation in the searing experience of his generation tormented him for the rest of his life. In fact, he usually lied about serving in the war and implied that his lameness was the result of a battle wound. He overcompensated by his worship of the blond, blue-eyed Nordic type (borrowed from Nietzsche) and became an early and ardent supporter of Marxism and later National Socialism.

In 1922, Goebbels joined the Nazi Party (NSDAP), in which his keen political instincts, shameless opportunism, and genuine charisma propelled him to the top. The "little doctor," as he was called behind his back, blossomed in the new movement. He discovered a remarkable ability to sense the moods of his audiences and to sway them. By many accounts, Goebbels was a better orator than Hitler himself. In 1925, he was made business manager of the NSDAP in the Ruhr Valley. The Nazi Party was still far from monolithic, and Goebbels made one of his few political errors by joining the wrong faction. Goebbels threw his lot in with the Strasser brothers, Otto and Gregor, who controlled the social-revolutionary North German wing of the Party. He was enamored of their proletarian socialism and went so far as to join the Strassers in a call for Hitler's expulsion from the NSDAP before his political instincts warned him that it was time to switch sides. In 1926, Goebbels deserted the Strasser brothers and joined Hitler, for which he was rewarded with the leadership (*Gauleiter*) of the Berlin Party section.

Life's Work

Berlin was a formidable challenge and not much of a prize. The Party apparatus was in disarray, the Strasser brothers had seriously eroded Hitler's support among the cadres, and the streets belonged to the Communists and the Socialists. Goebbels proved to be equal to the task. He founded a weekly newspaper, *Der Angriff* (the attack), through which he hammered at the Jews, the Weimar Republic, and wayward members of his own party. The "little doctor" was everywhere: He designed the posters, organized the street brawls, and created the editorial campaigns. He directed every aspect of the Party's efforts, from the cartoons in his newspaper to beatings, bombings, and assassinations. The Party structure was modeled after the Catholic church, whose discipline, order, and splendor both he and Hitler admired.

In many respects, Goebbels created Hitler and defined the Nazi Party's platforms, methods, and goals. Women, newly enfranchised after World War I, were encouraged to leave the marketplace and have babies; the Weimar Republic, blamed for Germany's defeat in 1918, was pilloried at every opportunity; and the Jews were likened to a virus attacking a healthy Aryan body and were destined for isolation. The Nazi vision of education was a Spartan life-style punctuated by political and military training, polished by a stint in the labor service or armed forces, not the university. Hitler distrusted and despised intellectuals (Goebbels being an exception) and free thought. The purpose of education—indeed, life itself—was to produce healthy, obedient servants of the state. Most important, Goebbels portrayed Hitler as a new Christ—the answer to Germany's problems and the defender of the mythical Aryan race. Goebbels left little doubt about the identity of Christ's messenger to Berlin.

In 1928, Goebbels was elected as a deputy to the Reichstag, representing the NSDAP. In 1929, Hitler was so impressed with Goebbels' overall success in Berlin that he named him the Party's minister of propaganda. In October of that year, the disastrous stock market crash in the United States reverberated across Europe and plunged the West into the Great Depression. Hitler's party capitalized on the crisis and within a year garnered almost 6.5 million votes, and 107 seats in the Reichstag. The result largely of Goebbels' hugely successful propaganda efforts, the NSDAP was the third strongest party in Berlin (after the Communists and the Social Democrats). It was at a Nazi rally that Goebbels met a twenty-nine-year-old divorcée, Magda Quandt, wealthy, bored, and in search of a cause. Goebbels was a surprisingly romantic figure, and, whether for love, money, or social connections, they were married on the Quandt estate on September 19, 1931. Hitler was a witness at the ceremony. Their luxury Berlin apartment became the center of Hitler's social life. Although Goebbels maintained a string of mistresses, usually flashy showgirls, Magda remained with him, often at Hitler's urging.

The continuing Depression was the ideal setting for Goebbels' propaganda. He organized as many as three thousand meetings a day, and distributed millions of posters, handbills, pamphlets, brochures, and newspapers. He made films of Hitler's speeches, which were distributed to cinema owners and projected against the sides of large buildings on warm summer nights. Hitler was a candidate for national office and by November, 1932, was assured of a position in the government. He demanded to be named chancellor, and on January 30, 1933, the bewildered President Paul von Hindenburg gave in. Recognizing Goebbels' crucial contribution to his success, Hitler named him the Reich's minister for public enlightenment and propaganda on March 13, 1933.

Goebbels was now in charge of Germany's news media, cinemas, art, music, and culture, and, at thirty-five, he was the youngest member of Hitler's cabinet. The works by such immortal painters as Pablo Picasso, Marc Chagall, Paul Gauguin, Henri Matisse, and even Vincent van Gogh were no longer to be shown; the same for such German luminaries as Paul Klee, Georg Grosz, Otto Dix, Ernst Ludwig Kirchner, and Lovis Corinth. A similar decimation of culture took place in every other area of German art, journalism, opera, publications, and films. Many of the nation's finest writers were expelled, and hundreds of other scholars and artists left Germany on their own.

Through the creation of his Reich Chamber of Literature, Goebbels succeeded in achieving a strong degree of centralization. First came newspapers. When Hitler became chancellor, Germany had nearly 4,700 newspapers, many with long traditions and worldwide reputations. Of these the Nazis controlled only 121 dailies and periodicals. On October 4, 1933, the new Nazi government passed a law promoting the position of newspaper editor to an official post. Editors were now subject to strict regulations. They were bound by law not to print anything that criticized Germany or her government. Jews, like everywhere else, were to be immediately dismissed. Faced with punishment for breaking these laws, the majority of newspapers soon fell into line. Free opinion in Germany had become illegal.

Among all the artistic sections under his ministry, Goebbels felt closest to the film division. The films were a virtual obsession. In each of his three private homes, he had a cinema installed, where he watched one or two films every evening. He was particularly interested in foreign films, and a continuous supply was obtained through neutral countries even at the height of the war. Final control over the film industry came with the Film Law of February 16, 1934. The government introduced a bureau of censorship that determined if any film violated religious, moral, or National Socialist beliefs. Simultaneously, the regime created a Film Credit Bank that provided money for new films—but only those approved by the government censors. Goebbels gloried in his success and even presented the reading public with his blueprint by publishing a book composed of his copious diary entries between January 1, 1932, and May 1, 1933.

Goebbels was not without enemies in the Party. One in particular was Alfred Rosenberg, the powerful Nazi ideologue. Rosenberg's task was to analyze all published or cinematic works to evaluate their ideological trustworthiness. Goebbels and Rosenberg clashed over a number of issues, generally film projects, with no clear winner overall. Another occasional opponent, to Goebbels' horror, was Hitler, who sometimes overruled his propaganda minister.

Germany's attack on Poland in September 1, 1939, and the beginning of World War II saw Goebbels and the propaganda machine move into high gear. Although he argued against the war in secret meetings with Hitler prior to 1939, Goebbels quickly became the war's fiercest defender. It was no longer merely a case of politics; propaganda now trumpeted nationalism, patriotism, sacrifice, and total participation. To be anti-Nazi was now to be anti-Germany, and the punishment for treason was death. Goebbels mobilized every means at his disposal to exhort the population to greater sacrifice. Radio broadcasts, newspapers, broadsides and posters, even postage stamps were utilized to rally the public against Germany's various enemies. After the Allies called for unconditional surrender, Goebbels turned it to his advantage by convincing his audiences that there was no alternative to victory but destruction.

His propaganda was so filled with untruths that it often backfired. For example, when German forces discovered, in the spring of 1943, the buried corpses of several thousand murdered Polish officers near the Polish town of Katyn, the world was horri-fied and refused to believe Berlin's (truthful) explanation that the Soviets had committed the brutal crime. The German public was told on three separate occasions during the war that the Soviets had surrendered. By the end of the war, only the most devoted followers of Hitler believed the official news. Still, the propaganda mills continued to grind out stories of nonexistent secret weapons, chaos in their enemies' camps, and the arrival of heroic German armies who would turn the tide. There can be little doubt that Goebbels and his ministry, together with Heinrich Himmler's shadow army of informers and Gestapo agents, held the home front together as the war progressed, and that, on at least one occasion, he saved Hitler's regime.

Goebbels chose his end as the war closed in on Berlin. Like Hitler, he was enraptured by the glory of a final apocalypse, and, as Berlin crumbled before the Red Army, Goebbels decided to commit suicide. Disregarding Hitler's last will and testament, which named him as the new Reich chancellor, Goebbels and Magda had their six children poisoned by lethal injection and ordered their own executions at the hands of a Schutzstaffel (SS) orderly on May 1, 1945.

Summary

Joseph Goebbels, was a master of theater. Driven by demons stemming from his diminutive size, club foot, and intellectual isolation, Goebbels found a unique ability to sway people. Being the Party propagandist and cultural dictator, Goebbels, in essence, created the play and its players. Hitler became his god, the source of his power and, eventually, his reason for life. At the same time, Goebbels was a brazen liar, a man without scruple, obsessed with a desire for power. He manipulated public opinion against the hapless Jews. Indeed, the nationwide attack on the Jews of Germany on November 10, 1938, the so-called *Kristallnacht*, was largely orchestrated by Goebbels' propaganda ministry. Goebbels later introduced the measure requiring all Jews to wear yellow stars or armbands, thus making them daily targets for further discrimination and terror. Millions died as a result. Yet, for all his professed love of the German people, Goebbels had a profound disdain for the public, whom he continued to exhort and deceive until the very end. Like Hitler, he played his part until the final curtain, and with his devoted family, considered by Hitler nearly his own, the "little doctor" died with his creation.

Bibliography

Culbert, David. "Joseph Goebbels and His Diaries." *Historical Journal of Film, Radio and Television* 15, no. 1 (March, 1995). Discusses Goebbels' 80,000-page diary, its accounts of German high command decisions, Goebbels' battle with osteomyelitis, and his comments on film production and critique.

Hornshoj-Moller, Stig, and David Culbert. " 'Der ewige Jude' (1940): Joseph Goebbels' Unequaled Monument to Anti-Semitism." *Historical Journal of Film, Radio and Television* 12, no. 1 (March, 1992). Examines the most infamous propagandistic film of the anti-Semitic movement in Nazi Germany, "Der ewige Jude."

Meissner, Hans-Otto. *Magda Goebbels: The First Lady of the Third Reich.* Translated by Gwendolen Mary Keeble. London: Sidgwick and Jackson, and New York: Dial Press, 1980. A bit dramatic in the English edition, but a fascinating look into the private and social lives of the Nazi leadership.

Reimann, Viktor. *Goebbels.* Translated by Stephen Wendt. New York: Doubleday, 1976; as *The Man Who Created Hitler: Joseph Goebbels,* London: Kimber, 1977. An excellent and objective history of both the man and the Nazi era, based on detailed and authoritative sources.

Semmler, Rudolph. *Goebbels: The Man Next to Hitler.* London: Westhouse, 1947; New York: AMS Press, 1981. An interesting diary, kept by one of Goebbels' aides. Although it is somewhat lavish in its judgment about the Goebbels ministry, this diary is an important insight into the man and the movement.

Sington, Derrick, and Arthur Weidenfeld. *The Goebbels Experiment: A Study of the Nazi Propaganda Machine.* London: Murray, 1942; New Haven, Conn.: Yale University Press, 1943. This is an excellent analysis of both Goebbels and his propaganda ministry. It is filled with the passion of wartime writing, and, despite some minor inaccuracies, it is an outstanding source on the topic.

Zeman, Z. A. B. *Nazi Propaganda.* 2d ed. London and New York: Oxford University Press, 1973. The standard text on the topic, this fine volume examines the art of propaganda in the hands of the Nazis, while simultaneously painting the backdrop of events between 1933 and 1945.

Arnold Krammer

GEORGE WASHINGTON GOETHALS

Born: June 29, 1858; Brooklyn, New York
Died: January 21, 1928; New York, New York
Area of Achievement: Engineering
Contribution: Goethals was chief engineer of the Panama Canal, which revolutionized maritime transportation and commerce.

Early Life

George Washington Goethals was born on June 29, 1858, in Brooklyn, New York. His parents were Dutch immigrants of modest means. Goethals attended public schools in Manhattan and Brooklyn prior to matriculation (at the age of fourteen) at City College. Three years later, in 1876, he won appointment to the United States Military Academy at West Point. He was commissioned a second lieutenant in the Army Corps of Engineers in 1880, having been graduated second in his class. (He was later upgraded to honor man when the actual honor man was convicted by court-martial of embezzlement.) Goethals valued his West Point education highly. Many years later, when he was offered a civilian job at an enormous increase over the salary that he had earned in the army, Goethals would decline, saying that all of his training and education had been at the public's expense and that he intended to serve his country, hoping thereby to repay that investment, as long as he was needed by his country.

Following commissioning, he was assigned to the United States Advanced Engineering School and then, in 1882, to Cincinnati to improve the Ohio River channel for navigation. This detail provided him with practical experience in lock and dam construction. A variety of engineering assignments followed. For example, he was in charge of the construction of the Muscle Shoals Canal on the Tennessee River. In this construction he designed and successfully completed a lock within a hydraulic system with a lift of twenty-six feet—an unprecedented height. He was chief engineer for a similar canal-hydraulic system near Chattanooga, Tennessee. In 1894, he was appointed assistant to the chief of engineers. During the Spanish-American War he was promoted to lieutenant colonel of volunteers (regular army major) and assigned as chief engineer of the Puerto Rican Army of Occupation. After that war he served in New England assisting in the design and construction of harbor defenses. His most important contribution related to the specific design for the fortifications near Newport, Rhode Island. Goethals was later made a member of the General Staff and was graduated from the United States Army War College.

Goethals married Effie Rodman of New Bedford, Massachusetts, in 1884, shortly before a stint as an instructor at West Point. She was the daughter of Captain Thomas R. Rodman. She bore him two sons—George R. and Thomas R. Goethals. George went on to a successful military career (rising to the rank of colonel) and Thomas became a physician.

Life's Work

Goethals will always be remembered as the man who "built" the Panama Canal. While his distinguished assistants were as numerous as a regiment, it was Goethals who was ultimately responsible for recruiting and inspiring the huge army of workers; for conceiving the overall project; for laying out the many tasks; and for organizing, planning, and carrying through the work against the many obstacles posed by man, government, and nature. It was Goethals, for example, who fought to make the Panama Canal a lock canal and not a sea-level one. The problem of sanitation was mastered—with the invaluable help of William Crawford Gorgas—where earlier efforts had failed. Under Goethals, the Canal Zone was transformed from the vast graveyard it had been under Ferdinand de Lesseps and the French into a place where men could work and thrive.

The first work on the Panama Canal was begun in 1881 by the Panama Canal Company, a French chartered and financed business, under the direction of de Lesseps. De Lesseps had earlier been chief engineer for the Suez Canal project. De Lesseps had planned to construct a sea-level canal with no locks at a cost of 128 million dollars. Because of obstacles he could not overcome, his efforts ended with the bankruptcy of the French company and a major scandal in government. Only a small amount of work was actually accomplished. There followed over the next several years attempts to complete de Lesseps' plans for a sea-level canal. All failed. Matters stood at this point until the United States government determined to undertake the project.

The history of the United States' acquisition of the French company's charter to construct a canal and of the political complications that arose is fairly well-known and need not be recounted. It is sufficient to state that the United States in 1903 acquired the right to dig a canal across a new nation—Panama. President Theodore Roosevelt, well versed in the arguments among the supporters of a sea-level and the supporters of a lock canal, selected then Major George Goethals (junior to scores of other army engineers) to head the project. Goethals favored a lock canal. That Roosevelt came to the conclusion that a lock canal was superior to a sea-level canal reflects Goethals' persuasive arguments. Originally civilian engineers had been charged with the task. The planning and work of that group, especially of John Frank Stevens, proved to be extremely valuable to Goethals and to the Army Corps of Engineers. Goethals never failed to praise the work of his subordinates or, in this case, his predecessors— even when he found the hydraulic systems, the locks, dams, and spillways (all Goethals specialities) to be either as yet unplanned or flawed in design. When Goethals and the Army Corps of Engineers took over in 1907, he found that an awesome amount of work needed to be accomplished. The enormity of the task of digging the canal was far more staggering than were the technological difficulties which had to be overcome.

The Panama Canal as it was finally constructed works by raising a ship from the Caribbean Sea or from the Gulf of Panama in a lock chamber (of which there are twelve) eighty-five feet. Each chamber is 110 feet wide, built to accommodate the largest ship the navy had on the drawing boards, and one thousand feet long but capable of division into two chambers—one six and the other four hundred feet. These chambers are built in pairs so as to accommodate two-way traffic. Once raised, a vessel travels over Gatun Lake—a man-made, one-hundred-seventy-square-mile body of water eighty-five feet above sea level—to the opposite side of the isthmus. There it is lowered to sea level via the same process in reverse.

Completion of the canal took until 1914. The task called for the tearing away of the mountains in the canal channel, which involved moving hundreds of millions of cubic yards of earth. Creating Gatun Lake involved not only the damming of the Chagres River in order to control it but also the filling of the valleys with earth and water to a depth of eighty-five feet in many places. Building the enormous locks of concrete and steel was the most

monumental task man had ever attempted. It was George Washington Goethals who made it a reality. He coordinated all the factors involved—sanitation, excavation, housing, commissary, labor, design, and construction. A man of great force and personality, he inspired complete confidence in the entire organization and brought it together in harmony. This effort served for years as a model of efficient labor and industrial harmony as well as sound engineering. Upon completion, Goethals received the formal thanks of the United States Congress for "distinguished service in constructing the Panama Canal."

President Woodrow Wilson appointed Goethals the first civil governor of the Panama Canal Zone. Following a two-year term, he was named state engineer for New Jersey. He resigned that post to accept recall to active duty with the United States Army when World War I erupted. During the war he was acting quartermaster general and director of purchase, storage, and supplies. As such he was responsible for the supply and transportation of all United States troops at home and abroad.

In 1919, he retired from active service and opened George Goethals and Company, a consultant engineering firm with offices in New York City. Among the major clients was the City of New York. Goethals and his company made a major impact upon the projects of the Port of New York Authority. He offered his expertise to help complete and operate the Holland Vehicular Tunnels under the Hudson River; the then-proposed George Washington Bridge, spanning the Hudson River; and the Goethals Bridge.

During his lifetime General Goethals was the recipient of many honors from educational and scientific institutions, including the National Geographic Society, the Civil Forum of New York, and the National Institute of Social Science. Goethals died after a prolonged illness in New York City on June 21, 1928. In his honor, flags in the Canal Zone were flown at half mast.

Summary

Goethals will always be remembered as the engineer who saw the Panama Canal become a reality. He is the most famous engineer ever to wear the uniform of the United States Army and one of the best-known graduates of West Point since the Civil War. His ability as director of the massive construction operations in Panama and as director of purchase, storage, and supplies in the United States Army in World War I is indicative of his greatness as an administrator as well as an engineer. His place in American and world history is secure.

Bibliography

Baker, Ray S. "Goethals the Man and How He Works." *Technical World Magazine* 21 (July, 1914): 656-661. Praises Goethals and describes his techniques in the administration of the entire range of the construction project that produced the Panama Canal.

Cameron, Ian. *The Impossible Dream: The Building of the Panama Canal*. London: Hodder and Stoughton, and New York: Morrow, 1972. Contains facts and figures concerning the magnitude of the actual construction efforts—down to the number of tons of concrete poured as well as where it was poured.

Fast, Howard. *Goethals and the Panama Canal*. New York: Messner, 1942. One of the best examinations of Goethals' achievements in Panama. It should be consulted by the serious student.

McCullough, David. *The Path Between the Seas: The Creation of the Panama Canal, 1870-1914*. New York: Simon and Schuster, 1977. Extremely reliable account of the construction of the Panama Canal. McCullough's tale of the pre-United States efforts are detailed and accurate. The role of the Army Corps of Engineers and of Goethals is placed in its proper perspective.

Mack, Gerstel. *The Land Divided: A History of the Panama Canal and Other Isthmian Canal Projects*. New York: Knopf, 1944. Perhaps the single most valuable work on the construction of the canal from inception to completion. Goethals' role is well detailed. Gives much credit to Goethals' predecessors, especially John Stevens.

Pepperman, W. L. *Who Built the Panama Canal?* London: Dent, and New York: Dutton, 1915. An older source yet very useful on the personnel involved in the undertaking. Gives major credit to Goethals as the man who orchestrated a seemingly impossible task.

Richard J. Amundson

EMMA GOLDMAN

Born: June 27, 1869; Kovno, Lithuania
Died: May 14, 1940; Toronto, Canada
Area of Achievement: Social reform
Contribution: A leading member of the anarchic
  Left in the early twentieth century, Goldman was
  a critic of both capitalism and socialism and an
  advocate of women's rights.

Early Life

Emma Goldman was born on June 27, 1869, in Kovno (now Kaunas) in Lithuania, which was then part of the Russian Empire. Her parents, Abraham Goldman and Taube Binowitz Zodikow, were already rearing two daughters, Helena and Lena, from Taube Goldman's first marriage (she was a widow when she entered into an arranged marriage with Goldman). Beaten frequently by her father and denied comfort by her mother, Emma was unable to find either emotional or financial security in the Goldman household. For a time, she lived with relatives in Königsberg, a city in the northeastern corner of Germany. Her experience in her uncle's household was, if anything, worse, and Emma returned to her parents, who themselves moved first to Königsberg and then, in 1881, to St. Petersburg in Russia.

Emma did find some satisfaction in life. She was able to attend school in Königsberg, where a young teacher befriended Emma and introduced her to music and literature, both of which became lifelong sources of pleasure for her. In St. Petersburg, however, the family's economic privation meant that Emma had to abandon her hopes of continuing her education and becoming a doctor (her father could not understand why a woman needed an education) in order to work in factories that made gloves and corsets.

Rebelling against her father's authority and the Jewish religious and cultural traditions in which she was raised, Emma became fascinated with radicalism. An avid reader, she found inspiration in Vera Pavlovna, the heroine of Nikolai Chernyshevsky's radical novel *What Is to Be Done?* (1863), who defied authority and convention. Especially meaningful to Emma, whose father suggested arranging a marriage for her, was Pavlovna's rejection of that practice as the auctioning of a sex object. Emma also admired the martyred young women who had been active participants in the 1870's Russian radical movement, the People's Will.

Emma sought immediate relief from her despair by emigrating to the United States, the land of hope, departing Russia with Helena late in 1885. They intended to live with their sister Lena, who was married and living in Rochester, New York. To Emma's dismay, she soon seemed trapped in Rochester by the very things she wished to escape: monotonous, low-paying work in a clothing factory, further talk of an arranged marriage, and the presence of her parents, who followed their daughters to the New World.

Again, Emma found inspiration in the story of martyred radicals: four men executed (a fifth committed suicide) in November, 1887, for the bomb murder of several Chicago policemen during a mass workers' meeting at the Haymarket Square in Chicago the previous year. What especially angered Emma was that the authorities never ascertained who threw the bomb, making it seem clear that the men who had been arrested were really being tried for their beliefs. If injustices similar to those that occurred in Russia could also take place in the United States, reasoned Emma, it was time for her to align herself with the opponents of capitalism and of its tools, the state and the church.

Emma had one more personal crisis to endure before making a commitment to activism. In her early teens, Emma had had her first sexual experience, a humiliating and painful one, with a young man she had considered her friend. She was still able to develop emotional attachments with men, however, and in Rochester she fell in love with a fellow worker, the handsome and seemingly intellectual Jacob Kersner, whom she married in February, 1887.

The marriage seemed to offer escape from familial pressures but did not succeed. Kersner proved to be impotent and took comfort in gambling with his cronies. For a time, Emma tried to avoid the stigma of divorce, but at age twenty, she divorced Kersner and moved to New Haven, Connecticut. She briefly returned to Rochester, remarried Kersner, divorced him a second time, and moved to New York City.

Life's Work

Among the new friends Emma Goldman made in the immigrant neighborhoods of New York's Low-

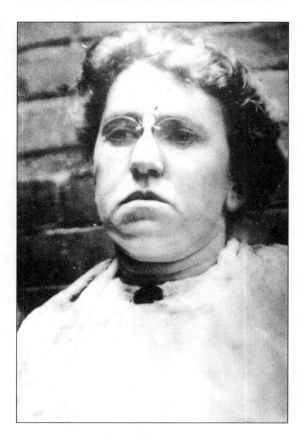

er East Side, two stood out: Alexander Berkman, who became her lover, and Johann Most, an older man who had made a name for himself in Germany and became a leading figure among anarchists in the United States. Although she was familiar with socialist thought, she regarded it as menacing to individual freedom because it accepted large state-owned industry as positive. Anarchism, in contrast, promised a society based on justice and reason and opposed both the centralization of the corporation and the centralization of the state.

Schooled by Most in both anarchist theory and public speaking, Goldman made her first speaking tour in 1890 and was delighted to realize that she had the power to sway people with the spoken word. She also came to realize, however, that the words she was speaking were not hers but Most's, and she repudiated his mentorship. Converts to anarchism and to the communal living that Goldman and Berkman advocated were disappointingly few, and the two thought of returning to Russia.

In 1892, a pressing new cause kept them in the United States: planning the assassination of tycoon Henry Clay Frick, who had violently suppressed a strike at the Homestead steelworks of Pittsburgh. They decided that Berkman would shoot Frick, while Goldman, who helped him plan the assassination attempt, would explain his actions. The affair went awry. Berkman merely wounded Frick, and other radicals, including Most, distanced themselves from Berkman and from assassination as a political weapon.

Goldman had now come to another turning point in her life. She thought of herself not as an exile from Russia but as a woman who could have a meaningful future fighting for change in the United States. Although she escaped prosecution for her role in Berkman's attack on Frick, she was arrested in 1893 and sentenced to a year in Blackwell's Island prison for her activities at a protest demonstration in New York's Union Square.

On her release, Goldman met a new lover, the Austrian-born anarchist Ed Brady, who wished to marry her. She rejected marriage, but did heed his suggestion to find another outlet for her compassion and sympathy for the downtrodden. To support herself, she was already working as a practical nurse (a skill she had learned in the prison hospital), and she went to Vienna to earn certificates in nursing and midwifery. During her year in Vienna (1895-1896) and another year in Paris (1899-1900) she also immersed herself in avant-garde literature and drama.

For some time, Goldman hoped to have two careers: the first as a nurse and midwife among the downtrodden in New York, the second as a radical lecturer. The two careers were not necessarily compatible, however, for as a lecturer she was attracting increasing fame as an opponent of war in 1898, of organized Christianity, and of conventional sexual morality. She became widely known as an advocate of free love, a term that added to her notoriety as "Red Emma." In using the expression "free love," Goldman meant not indiscriminate sexual activity but love without a legally recognized marriage, which she regarded as one of many devices society used to exploit women.

Goldman again faced prison in 1901 when she was arrested following the assassination of President William McKinley. She was not involved in the crime and was not held for trial, but with her characteristic defiance she could not resist asking Americans to show compassion for the condemned assassin, Leon Czolgosz. Public outrage made it impossible for her to book a lecture hall, and she was further embittered when radicals repudiated

Czolgosz. For a while she retreated from public view. Using the pseudonym E. G. Smith, she tended to the poor in New York's slums.

By 1903, however, she was ready to resume lecturing. In 1906, she undertook a second commitment, that of publisher of a new periodical that she founded and named *Mother Earth*. She chose the name to suggest that the earth should provide the opportunity for all humankind to lead free and productive lives. *Mother Earth* would serve as a forum not only for anarchism but also for the issues of the Lyrical Left—personal liberation, freedom of artistic expression, and equality in sexual relations.

The journal, however, did not sell well enough to support Goldman—after one year it had two thousand subscribers—so she had to lecture more than ever. Often traveling with her new lover, Ben Reitman the hobo doctor, who acted as her booking agent, Goldman gave hundreds of speeches a year, reaching out to the "psychologically stifled middle class" as well as to the impoverished. Small of stature, she impressed listeners with her intensity and with her command of humor and sarcasm. In the question-and-answer sessions that usually followed her talks, she also showed a mastery of many subjects that came from countless hours of reading. English had long since become Goldman's primary language, but although her most publicized lectures were to American audiences, she insisted on making separate lectures in Yiddish.

From 1906 to 1916, Goldman continued to write and lecture on the sins of capitalism and also on art, drama, literature, and women's issues. She addressed the topic of birth control, criticized the institution of marriage, denounced the corset, and dared women to have more sexual experiences. Much of what she said infuriated social conservatives, but for good measure she also condemned suffragists as single-issue reformers. Ethical and social conventions, she maintained, were bigger obstacles to women's emancipation than were suffrage restrictions and other external barriers.

From 1914 on, World War I became an issue she had to address. As long as the United States remained neutral, Goldman could freely oppose the war, but even when the United States entered the war in 1917 she remained uncompromising in her opposition to it. No pacifist, she regarded war as more capitalist exploitation. The conscription law that the Wilson administration endorsed in 1917 was both repressive and illogical, she asserted, since it meant Prussianizing America in the name

of democratizing Germany. Although she did not explicitly advocate resistance to the draft, she and Berkman (who had been released from prison in 1906 and was the editor of *Mother Earth*) were arrested on June 15, speedily tried, and sentenced to prison terms of two years. In a separate action, the government stopped the publication of *Mother Earth*.

In 1919 Goldman, Berkman, and more than two hundred other radicals of foreign birth were deported from the United States to Soviet Russia, but life there proved intolerable for her. Goldman did have an interview with communist leader Vladimir Lenin, but she soon concluded that a new era of statist repression was dawning.

She left Russia in 1921 and proceeded to relate her observations in lectures and in two books that were condemned by other leftists. At various times she lived in Sweden, England, France, and Canada, writing her memoirs and carrying on a large correspondence with many friends and members of her family with whom she had long before reconciled. In 1934, she was allowed to return to the United States, where she desperately wished to live, just long enough to make a speaking tour. In her last years, she expressed contempt for both Nazism and Stalinism, but when World War II began in September, 1939, she refused to make a choice between the evil of war and the evil of a dictatorship. An individualist to the last, she died in Toronto in 1940.

Summary

During Emma Goldman's lifetime, anarchism never became a mass creed. If anything, it declined in the United States because of government actions against radicalism, the growing appeal of trade unions, and because communism, especially after the Leninists had gained power in Russia, was able to win more converts. Nevertheless, Goldman was of major importance in the history of American radicalism, for her success lay not in contributing to the demise of capitalism or the state but in alerting people to issues involving personal liberation and self-fulfillment.

Unlike most members of the political left, who argued that the advent of the socialist state would emancipate women, Goldman demanded that women's issues be addressed immediately. Jeered, arrested, and threatened on many occasions, she won admirers among many middle-class Americans who might not have become converts to her causes but who believed in her right to advance them. She herself became a major spokesperson for free speech. It is therefore in the cultural history of twentieth century America that Goldman has most significance, for the issues she had raised prior to 1918 were issues that again seemed relevant in the 1960's, when a new generation of American dissenters and feminists rediscovered Goldman and celebrated her as a symbol of defiance and liberation.

Bibliography

Chalberg, John. *Emma Goldman, American Individualist*. Edited by Oscar Handlin. New York: HarperCollins, 1991. Written as part of an ongoing series of brief biographies of eminent Americans, this book provides the best introduction to Goldman's life.

Drinnon, Richard. *Rebel in Paradise*. Chicago: University of Chicago Press, 1961; London: University of Chicago Press, 1982. Especially helpful for its explanation of the historical and social context in which Goldman lived. Shows the maturation of Goldman from youthful enthusiast to spokesperson for a cultural revolution.

Falk, Candace Serena. *Love, Anarchy, and Emma Goldman*. Rev. ed. New Brunswick, N.J. and London: Rutgers University Press, 1990. Falk concentrates on explaining the relationship between Goldman's various loves and her thinking on social and moral issues. Previously undiscovered correspondence between Goldman and Reitman helped give Falk new insights.

Frankel, Oz. "Whatever Happened to 'Red Emma'? Emma Goldman, from Alien Rebel to American Icon." *Journal of American History* 83, no. 3 (December, 1996). Looks at Goldman's life and autobiography.

Goldman, Emma. *Living My Life*. 2 vols. New York: Knopf, 1931; London: Duckworth, 1932. Written while Goldman was residing in St. Tropez, France, this memoir is inaccurate and misleading in many areas but is still the best source for information about Goldman's childhood.

————. *Nowhere at Home: Letters from Exile of Emma Goldman and Alexander Berkman*. Edited by Richard Drinnon and Anna Maria Drinnon. New York: Schocken, 1975. This topically organized compilation reveals much about Goldman's thoughts on communism and on the approach of World War II. Thoughtful editorial notes are included.

Shulman, Alix Kates. *To the Barricades: The Anarchist Life of Emma Goldman*. New York: Crowell, 1971. This book for juvenile readers provides a lucid introduction to Goldman's life and thought.

Solomon, Martha. *Emma Goldman*. Boston: Twayne, 1987. Solomon analyzes Goldman's rhetorical style in both her written and spoken words. Provides insight into Goldman's thought, especially her evaluations of early twentieth century literature and drama.

Waldstreicher, David. *Emma Goldman*. New York: Chelsea House, 1990. This thoughtful book for young readers does an excellent job of presenting the main themes and events in Goldman's crowded life.

Wexler, Alice. *Emma Goldman: An Intimate Life*. London: Virago, and New York: Pantheon, 1984. In this three-hundred-page work, Wexler challenges many views of Goldman and seeks to explain the contradictions between the public Goldman and the private Goldman.

————. *Emma Goldman in Exile*. Boston: Beacon Press, 1989. Wexler concludes her study of Goldman with this assessment of her last twenty years.

Lloyd J. Graybar

SAMUEL GOLDWYN
Samuel Goldfisch

Born: August 27, 1882; Warsaw, Poland
Died: January 31, 1974; Beverly Hills, California
Area of Achievement: Motion pictures
Contribution: Working as an independent Hollywood producer with his own company and studio, Goldwyn made films that were known for their high quality and good taste, despite his own impoverished upbringing and limited education.

Early Life

Samuel Goldwyn was born as Samuel Goldfisch on August 27, 1882, in the Jewish ghetto in Warsaw, Poland. His parents, Abraham and Hannah Goldfisch, were Orthodox Jews who lived in poverty. It is not known how they earned a living.

Goldwyn's schooling stopped at age eleven, when he was put to work as an office boy in a Warsaw banking firm, earning five zlotys (one dollar) a week. An early encounter with anti-Semitism—in which a policeman called him "a dirty little Jew" and then beat him up, and robbed him of his money—impelled Goldwyn to escape from Warsaw at the age of twelve. He eventually made his way to the home of an aunt and uncle in England, where he worked at various jobs, until he was able to raise enough money to pay for a steerage ticket to the United States.

Arriving in New York in 1896, where an immigration official changed the spelling of his name from Goldfisch to Goldfish, Goldwyn was recruited to work in a glove factory in Gloversville (near Albany), New York. He began by sweeping floors, then became a glove-cutter, often working at the same bench for sixteen to eighteen hours a day, until at the age of sixteen, he was able to convince his employers to let him travel on the road as a glove salesman.

Goldwyn enjoyed great success as a salesman. Although he never entirely lost his Polish-Yiddish accent, and although he was neither well-read nor well educated, Goldwyn was a most convincing and energetic speaker who refused to take no for an answer. In addition, he had a winning smile and an impressive physical appearance—about six feet tall, slim, and always proudly erect—augmented by suits that were precisely tailored. In later years, Goldwyn became extremely vain about his wardrobe and appearance. He refused to carry anything—money, keys, or pens—in his pockets, so as not to mar the fit of his clothes.

As a result of Goldwyn's charm and tenaciousness, he was soon earning close to fifteen thousand dollars a year as a glove salesman. He became a sales manager in 1909 but was eager to improve himself further. Seeking to marry the boss's niece, Bessie Ginzberg, he lost out to Jesse L. Lasky, a vaudeville entrepreneur. Bessie, however, introduced Goldwyn to Lasky's sister, Blanche, whom he married in 1910.

Following the 1912 election of Woodrow Wilson, who promised to repeal the restrictive tariffs on imported products, Goldwyn became afraid that American-made gloves would be threatened by cheaper foreign competition. Looking for a new line of work, he saw potential in motion pictures.

Life's Work

At a time when most motion pictures were one- and two-reelers, lasting not much more than fifteen minutes, Goldwyn was one of a small group of people who believed that motion pictures had more to offer. Using his best salesmanship skills, Goldwyn convinced his brother-in-law, who had extensive contacts in show business, to establish the Jesse L. Lasky Feature Play Company. Goldwyn hired the actor Dustin Farnum to play the title role in a film adaptation of *The Squaw Man* (1914), a popular play about an Englishman in the Wild West. Lasky knew a young playwright, Cecil B. DeMille, who was eager to direct.

After much trial and error, *The Squaw Man* was released in February, 1914, and was an immediate hit, making a profit of roughly $200,000. More successes followed for the Lasky Company, which merged in June, 1916, with Adolph Zukor's Famous Players, to form the Famous Players-Lasky Company. Yet there was not room enough in the new company for both Goldwyn and Zukor. Lasky was forced to choose, and—perhaps because his sister had divorced Goldwyn in 1915—he chose Zukor. Famous Players-Lasky went on to become Paramount Pictures: Goldwyn, with the $900,000 he received as a settlement, went on to start a new company with Edgar and Arch Selwyn, two Broadway producers.

Looking for a new company name, Goldwyn (whose name then was still Goldfish) and the Selwyns thought of combining their two surnames. Sel-fish was one possibility, but Gold-wyn was more practical. The result was the Goldwyn Pictures Corporation, the sound of which was so pleasing to the company's president and chief stockholder (Samuel Goldfish) that in 1918 he legally changed his own name to match it: one of the few instances in which a man was named after a corporation, rather than vice versa.

The major reason that Goldwyn had been unable to work with Zukor and Lasky was that he was fiercely independent and accustomed to having things done his own way. It was inevitable, therefore, that Goldwyn would clash with his business partners in the Goldwyn Pictures Corporation. In March, 1922, for the second time in six years, Goldwyn was forced to resign from a company he had helped establish. The Goldwyn Pictures Corporation went on to merge with Marcus Loew's Metro Pictures Corporation in 1924, later becoming known as Metro-Goldwyn-Mayer. Samuel Goldwyn, having received one million dollars for his stock in Goldwyn Pictures, decided that he could not tolerate further partnerships and started his own company, known as Samuel Goldwyn Presents, in 1923.

Two years later, on April 23, 1925, Goldwyn married Frances Howard McLaughlin, a former actress, twenty-two years his junior. They moved from New York to Hollywood the next day, where they remained for the remainder of their lives. Goldwyn's wife was the only person in whom he seemed to have complete trust and confidence. She became his unofficial assistant producer and story consultant. Their only child, Samuel Goldwyn, Jr., later became a motion-picture producer himself.

From 1923 to 1959, Goldwyn independently produced eighty motion pictures. This output may be divided into three stages: the first, from 1923 to 1935, when he produced forty-one pictures, more than half of his life's work; the second, from 1936 to 1946, when he produced twenty-seven pictures, many of them enduring classics; and the third, from 1947 to 1959, when he produced only twelve pictures.

During the first period, from 1923 to 1935, Goldwyn's productions ranged from love stories (Ronald Colman and Vilma Banky were his most successful screen couple) to musical comedies (six of which starred Eddie Cantor) to sophisticated dramas, such as *Arrowsmith* (1931) and *Cynara* (1932). None of these films is acclaimed as a classic, but as a group they established Goldwyn's reputation in Hollywood as a producer who always aimed for top quality, regardless of cost.

The films produced during Goldwyn's second period, from 1936 to 1946, include those for which he is best known. He worked with screenwriter Lillian Hellman to make *These Three* (1936), based on a Hellman play which had been thought unproducible in Hollywood, and *The Little Foxes* (1941), nominated for eight Academy Awards. He adapted classic novels, such as Emily Brontë's *Wuthering Heights* (1847), in 1939, which helped make a star of Laurence Olivier, as well as more current literature, such as Sinclair Lewis' *Dodsworth* (1929), in 1936, and Sidney Kingsley's *Dead End* (1935), in 1937. As always, Goldwyn worked with many of Hollywood's best directors, including Howard Hawks in *Come and Get It* (1936) and *Ball of Fire* (1942) and John Ford in *The Hurricane* (1937). His own favorite director seemed to be William Wyler. Wyler and Goldwyn worked together eight times, culminating in Goldwyn's greatest success, *The Best Years of Our Lives* (1946), which won seven Academy Awards and the Irving Thalberg Memorial Award for Goldwyn.

During Goldwyn's final period, from 1947 (when he turned sixty-five) to 1959, fewer pictures were made, none of them particularly memorable. Included were several starring Danny Kaye, notably *The Secret Life of Walter Mitty* (1947) and *Hans Christian Andersen* (1952), and Goldwyn's final two productions, both of them musicals adapted from successful stage shows, *Guys and Dolls* (1955) and *Porgy and Bess* (1959).

The failure of *Porgy and Bess* was a great disappointment to Goldwyn. After 1959, he ceased making pictures on his own and began renting his studio to other film and television producers. He suffered a stroke in 1969, which left him partially paralyzed. He died at his Beverly Hills home on January 31, 1974.

Summary

In spite of Goldwyn's success as a producer of high-quality motion pictures, he may be best known for his fractured phrases, unintentionally humorous, which have become known as Goldwynisms. Goldwyn is even included in Bartlett's *Familiar Quotations* for such memorable sayings as "Include me out" and "In two words: im-possible."

Yet Goldwyn's real achievements are of a different order. Even if most Goldwynisms are not apocryphal—and there is good reason to believe that many of them are—he ought to be judged not by what he said, but by what he put on the screen: There, his talents are indisputable. At a time when the major Hollywood studios regularly filled their yearly quotas with films of low quality, Goldwyn insisted on producing nothing but the very best. He did not always succeed in doing so, but it was never for lack of trying.

From the 1920's through the 1950's, the motion-picture industry was controlled largely by a handful of Hollywood studio heads who oversaw all aspects of a film: from production, to distribution, to exhibition. As an independent, Goldwyn ran counter to this trend. In so doing, however, he pioneered the way for the independent producer of the post-1960's New Hollywood.

For Goldwyn, being independent meant that he did not have to answer to anyone—bankers, stockholders, company officers—other than the public. It may sound peculiar that an uneducated, Jewish immigrant from Poland could have understood so well what the American public wanted to see. Goldwyn's artistic instincts, however, combined with a shrewd business sense, made him one of the most successful creators of one of the most distinctively American enterprises: the Hollywood motion picture.

Bibliography

Aberbach, David. "The Mogul Who Loved Art." *Commentary* 72 (September, 1981): 67-71. A balanced assessment of Goldwyn's career, noting his unusual combination of artistic taste and business shrewdness. There is also an attempt by Aberbach at a psychological interpretation of Goldwyn's accomplishments.

Berg, A. Scott. *Goldwyn: A Biography.* London: Sphere, and New York: Knopf, 1989. Moving biography with behind-the-scenes stories and a feeling for the historical context of Goldwyn's life and career.

Easton, Carol. *The Search for Sam Goldwyn.* New York: Morrow, 1976. This biography contends that Goldwyn, embarrassed by his humble origins, tried to hide them with elaborate (and deceitful) publicity.

Epstein, Lawrence J. *Samuel Goldwyn.* Boston: Twayne, 1981. This is the only book that examines Goldwyn's films in an analytic and thematic, rather than simply chronological manner. According to Epstein, Goldwyn deserves to be taken seriously as a film auteur.

Goldwyn, Samuel. *Behind the Screen.* New York: Doran, 1923; London: Richards, 1924. These memoirs, surely ghostwritten, cover Goldwyn's first ten years in the motion-picture business but have little to do with Goldwyn himself. There is no mention, for example, of his birth in Poland or his marriage. Instead, the focus is on Goldwyn's famous Hollywood friends.

Griffith, Richard. *Samuel Goldwyn: The Producer and His Films.* New York: Museum of Modern Art Film Library, 1956. Published in conjunction with a series, "The Films of Samuel Goldwyn," at the prestigious Museum of Modern Art, this book gives a quick overview of the "Goldwyn touch," followed by a chronological examination of Goldwyn's work through 1955.

Harrison, K. "Like Father, Like Son." *Forbes* 148, no. 10 (October 28, 1991). Profile of Goldwyn, including his life in the shadow of a famous father.

Johnston, Alva. *The Great Goldwyn.* New York: Random House, 1937. As indicated by the title, this is a flattering portrait of Goldwyn. The Goldwyn touch is defined, and Goldwyn's search for quality is seen as comparable to that of Gustave Flaubert. Originally published in *The Saturday Evening Post* (May-June, 1937).

Marill, Alvin H. *Samuel Goldwyn Presents.* South Brunswick, N.J.: Barnes, 1976. This provides the most detailed examination (with complete credits, plot summaries, and critical reception) for all eighty of Goldwyn's independent productions, taken in chronological order.

Marx, Arthur. *Goldwyn: A Biography of the Man Behind the Myth.* New York: Norton, 1976. As a Hollywood insider (Marx is the son of Groucho Marx), the author has written the most authoritative biography of Goldwyn. The book is especially good on Goldwyn's career within the larger context of the American film industry.

James I. Deutsch

BENNY GOODMAN

Born: May 30, 1909; Chicago, Illinois
Died: June 13, 1986; New York, New York
Area of Achievement: Music
Contribution: A superb jazz clarinetist, Goodman led a series of outstanding dance bands that shaped the character of American swing music between 1935 and 1950.

Early Life

Benjamin David Goodman's parents were poverty-stricken Jewish immigrants who settled in Chicago, Illinois, in 1903. His father, David, worked in the stockyards and the garment business. His mother, Dora, stayed at home and cared for the couple's twelve children.

When Goodman was about twelve years old, his father arranged for him and two brothers to take music lessons and join a band sponsored by their synagogue. Goodman began to learn the clarinet. He progressed to a band sponsored by Hull House and to private lessons from Franz Schoepp, one of the best clarinet teachers in the country. He helped give Goodman, whose extraordinary talent was quickly evident, a thorough grounding in the fundamentals of the instrument.

At that time, jazz music was rising in popularity, spurred by the Original Dixieland Jass Band, which began producing phonograph records in 1917. Goodman was impressed by recordings by clarinetist Ted Lewis and his band and liked to imitate Lewis's distinctive (and sometimes humorous) style. Jazz music stressed a strong and steady beat with improvised variations around the simple chord patterns of popular songs or the blues. Goodman quickly became a skilled improviser but could also read music far better than most of his musical associates.

By age fourteen, Goodman was finding as much paid work as he could handle with pickup groups playing dance music and jazz. He quit school and earned enough money to contribute substantially to the family income. In 1925 he was recruited into Ben Pollack's orchestra, a jazz-oriented dance band in which Goodman worked with such jazz notables as Glenn Miller, Jimmy McPartland, Bud Freeman, and Jack Teagarden. Beginning in late 1926, the Pollack band was recording for Victor Records, with Goodman featured on jazz solos. By 1928 he was also recording with many pickup jazz groups, sometimes under his own name, playing saxophone and clarinet.

Life's Work

Goodman left the Pollack band in 1929. For the next few years he lived and worked in New York City, where there was a lot of well-paid work for musicians in radio as well as local clubs and shows. In 1932 he organized and briefly managed a dance band fronted by pop singer Russ Columbo.

By 1934, perhaps because freelance earnings were skimpy and his temperament was not well suited to working under other people's direction, Goodman organized a real dance band under his own name. The band was booked into the recently opened Billy Rose Music Hall. Just as their engagement ended in October, the band successfully auditioned for a three-hour, three-band Saturday night national network radio series entitled *Let's Dance*. The terms provided the band with a generous allowance to pay for new arrangements. *Let's Dance* premiered in December, 1934, with a large live audience as well as the radio broadcast. By then the band featured Helen Ward, the first of Goodman's female vocalists, and included drummer Gene Krupa and jazz trumpet star Bunny Berigan. Goodman rapidly acquired a book of fine arrangements by Spud Murphy, Fletcher and Horace Henderson, Jimmy Mundy, Edgar Sampson, and many others.

In 1935, Goodman's band was signed by the Music Corporation of America (MCA), which was the nation's largest booking agency at the time. This came just in time because the radio show, although very popular, was terminated in May, 1935. Fortunately the band's recordings for Victor Records were selling well. Noteworthy was the July, 1935, version of "King Porter Stomp," a showpiece for Berigan's trumpet. The band's growing popularity also reflected their ability to enhance undistinguished pop songs with good arrangements and swinging performances.

In an engagement at the new Palomar Ballroom in Los Angeles, California, in August, 1935, the band's popularity suddenly exploded. After two months, they moved back to a Chicago hotel ballroom, an engagement that was extended by popular demand for six months. The band was featured in a motion picture entitled *The Big Broadcast of 1937* (1936), signed a new radio contract, and produced a steady flow of new recordings. In addition to recording the full band, Goodman also experimented with small jazz groups. As early as 1935, he began to feature a trio, using Krupa and black pianist Teddy Wilson. In 1936 Goodman also recorded with a quartet, adding black vibraphonist Lionel Hampton. In doing so, Goodman helped promote racial integration in the music business.

From the beginning, Goodman's bands experienced a high rate of turnover. The dance-band business was full of stress. Bands were often on the road for extended periods, and hours were late and irregular. Furthermore, Goodman was not easy to work for because he was a perfectionist. In addition, his musicians complained that he would develop an animosity toward someone for no apparent reason. Musicians also quit on their own initiative as other job opportunities became abundant. At any rate, Goodman was eager to hire the best talent available, and much of that talent had high respect for Goodman's playing and for his band's musicianship. After Berigan left the band, Goodman added Ziggy Elman and Harry James to his trumpet section in early 1937.

In March, 1937, the band was booked into the Paramount Theater in New York. By 7:00 A.M. the following day, hundreds of fans were lined up for tickets. The crowds overflowed onto the stage. The swing era was in full bloom. Rival big bands were being organized, following many elements of Goodman's style, particularly the mixing of fast and slow, hot and sweet, all with a strong, danceable beat. Artie Shaw and Woody Herman started bands in 1936; Shaw's lush-toned clarinet solos soon established him as a rival to Goodman. In 1937, bands headed by Glenn Miller, Bunny Berigan, and Larry Clinton appeared. Jimmy and Tommy Dorsey divided forces to create separate bands. The sales of dance-band records increased. Coin-operated jukeboxes turned many eating and drinking establishments into dance parlors.

Excitement over Goodman and his band continued through 1937. They were featured in major magazines such as *Life*, *The New Yorker*, and *The Saturday Evening Post*. Goodman was reported to be earning $100,000 per year, a huge sum at that time. On January 16, 1938, Goodman's band presented a concert at Carnegie Hall in New York City, which was normally a citadel of classical music. The music generated wild excitement for a packed house. The high spot was the extended performance of "Sing, Sing, Sing," featuring Krupa,

James, and pianist Jess Stacy. The concert was recorded live (a rare event in 1938) but was not released until 1950, when it could be presented on long-playing vinyl. The recording itself caused a sensation and became one of the best-selling jazz records of all time.

Soon after the performance, Krupa left to start his own band, followed by James, and Goodman began recording with Columbia Records. Despite the loss of exciting soloists, he soon released new recordings such as "Honeysuckle Rose," "Scarecrow," and "Stealin' Apples," all distinguished by their driving rhythms and top-notch solos by Goodman and trumpeter Elman. An exciting and very innovative soloist named Charlie Christian became a member of a rejuvenated sextet. Christian, who was African American, was a pioneer on electric guitar.

In the middle of 1940, Goodman was afflicted with a very painful spine disorder. He suspended operations and laid off all but seven of his musicians. Hampton left to start his own band. After resting for a couple of months, Goodman was ready to rebuild. He was able to engage Cootie Williams, whose growling trumpet solos had been a feature with Duke Ellington. Other new soloists were tenor saxophonist George Auld, pianist Mel Powell, and trombonist Lou McGarity. Sophisticated arranger Eddie Sauter produced several distinctive numbers such as "Superman," which became a showpiece for Williams. One of the band's biggest hits was "Why Don't You Do Right?," sung by Peggy Lee.

World War II disrupted the music business after the draft was initiated in 1940. Goodman's medical condition kept him out of military service, but he lost many musicians to the draft. In August, 1942, the musicians' union imposed a ban on new recordings in order to pressure the recording companies to pay royalties to musicians. The ban lasted until 1944.

Goodman's reign as king of swing probably ended early in the war, eclipsed as much as anything by the sentimental sounds of Glenn Miller, Harry James, and Tommy Dorsey, which seemed more soothing to the wartime audience. However, Goodman continued to produce good swing, aided in part by his willingness to rehire some of his stalwarts of the past such as Krupa, Wilson, Arthur Rollini, and Vernon Brown. In March, 1944, he dismissed the band, rested, played a few pickup dates, and waited.

Early in 1945 Goodman organized a new band that included many fresh, young musicians such as Sonny Berman, Kai Winding, and Stan Getz. Unfortunately, the material they were playing was not innovative or interesting. By then leadership in big-band creativity had passed to people like Stan Kenton, Boyd Raeburn, and Woody Herman. Furthermore, the big-band era itself was coming to an end, partly because consumer demand was not sufficient to employ so many live musicians. The most creative jazz was being played by bebop innovators such as Charlie Parker and Dizzy Gillespie.

Goodman dismissed his band late in 1946, moved to the West Coast early in 1947, and signed a recording contract with Capitol Records. He assembled a recording band that included many of his old sidemen but also quite a few with some bebop inclinations. This was especially true for his small groups that, in 1948, included tenor saxophonist Wardell Gray and trumpeter Red Rodney. A reorganized big band played for President Harry S. Truman's inauguration in January, 1949. In October of 1949, however, Goodman dismissed this group. Thereafter Goodman periodically assembled bands for special purposes, such as a trip to the Soviet Union in 1962.

A motion picture entitled *The Benny Goodman Story* was released in 1955, with Steve Allen playing the title role. Goodman again assembled a band for the sound track. He continued to perform frequently, including occasional classical concerts. Although his days as an effective big-band organizer were over, he continued to play until his death in June, 1986.

Summary

Benny Goodman was one of the best jazz clarinet players of all time. He could play at breakneck speed, invent new melodies, and perform in a wide variety of styles. Goodman's genius was also expressed in his groups, both the big bands and the smaller ensembles. He chose the musicians and the material, set the tempos, and drove the music. His legacy of recorded swing is now recognized as an exceptional contribution to American culture.

Bibliography

Collier, James Lincoln. *Benny Goodman and the Swing Era*. New York: Oxford University Press, 1989; Oxford: Oxford University Press, 1991. Collier puts Goodman's life and work into a full musical and historic context. Includes detailed analysis of many recordings and capsule biographies of many of the important people in Goodman's career.

Connor, D. Russell. *Benny Goodman: Listen to His Legacy*. Metuchen, N.J.: Scarecrow Press, 1988. An encyclopedic discography of Goodman's recordings with comments on many of the sessions and participants.

Firestone, Ross. *Swing, Swing, Swing: The Life and Times of Benny Goodman*. London: Hodder and Stoughton, 1993; New York: Norton, 1994. A social historian's view of Goodman's often-rocky career and life based on extensive research and interviews with the musician's contemporaries. Accounts of Goodman's performances, his integrated bands, his conflicts with music industry executives, and his support of Gene Krupa after the drummer's conviction on a drug charge.

Goodman, Benny, and Irving Kolodin. *The Kingdom of Swing*. New York: Ungar, 1939. Goodman's autobiography, issued at the height of his popularity, conveys his attitudes and many anecdotes about his early career.

Schuller, Gunther. *The Swing Era: The Development of Jazz 1930-1945*. New York and Oxford: Oxford University Press, 1989. Chapter 1, devoted to Goodman, stresses his technical virtuosity and commercial instincts but is skeptical about his jazz solos. Schuller, a composer and arranger, gets pretty technical in spots.

Simon, George T. *The Big Bands*. 4th ed. New York: Schirmer, and London: Macmillan, 1981. Simon reviewed big bands for a magazine and writes from much personal exposure and interviews. Goodman is featured at pages 204-222 and 524-528.

Teachout, Terry. "Swinging with Benny Goodman." *Commentary* 105, no. 5 (May, 1998). Profile of Goodman's life and career. Includes a discography.

Paul B. Trescott

MIKHAIL GORBACHEV

Born: March 2, 1931; Privolnoye, Soviet Union
Areas of Achievement: Government and politics
Contribution: Gorbachev, as general secretary of the Communist Party and also President of the Soviet Union, made efforts to implement major improvements in the economy and society, underscoring his genuine belief in the need for long-overdue reforms. The revisions and adjustments in Soviet foreign policy that occurred during the Gorbachev era are noteworthy.

Early Life

Mikhail Sergeyevich Gorbachev was born on March 2, 1931, in the village of Privolnoye, in the Stavropol Territory of the Soviet Union. This agricultural region, located north of the Caucasus Mountains, lies between the Black and Caspian seas. Gorbachev came from several generations of farmers. He was baptized in the Orthodox Church but is not a Christian. During World War II, the area where he lived was occupied by Nazi military forces. Following the war, he continued his education and worked summers (1946-1950) in local farming. He was awarded (1949) the Order of the Red Banner of Labor at age eighteen and was graduated second in his high school class.

Gorbachev entered Moscow State University in the fall of 1950, graduating with a degree in law in 1955. During this period, he joined the Communist Party (1952) and married Raisa Maximovna Titorenko (1954). Following graduation, he returned to the Stavropol area where he spent the next twenty-three years in Communist Party service.

Gorbachev's initial responsibilities were in the Komsomol (Young Communist League). He became first secretary of the Stavropol City Komsomol organization in 1956, holding this position until 1958. Between 1958 and 1962, he worked in the Komsomol Committee for the Stavropol Territory (Krai) and eventually became first secretary of the group. By 1962, he was responsible for choosing party members for promotion, and also headed a production board supervising collective and state farms. In 1963, Gorbachev became head of the agricultural department for the entire Stavropol region.

In 1966, Gorbachev moved into full-time party administration as First Secretary of the Stavropol City Communist Party Committee. Two years later, in August, 1968, he became second secretary of the Stavropol Territory Communist Party Committee.

In April, 1970, at age thirty-nine, Gorbachev was selected as first secretary of the Stavropol Territory Communist Party Committee and held this post until 1978. During these years he made several official foreign trips: to East Germany (1966), Belgium (1972), West Germany (1975), and France (1976). He also was elected to membership in the Central Committee of the Communist Party in 1971.

Life's Work

His competence, honesty, and effective administration, as well as the support given by party leaders (Yuri Andropov and Mikhail Suslov), eventually brought Gorbachev to national attention. A front-page interview in *Pravda* (1977) and a brief meeting with General Secretary Leonid Ilich Brezhnev in September, 1978, culminated in his assignment in November, 1978, to Moscow as the Party's agricultural expert in the secretariat. He held this position from 1978 to 1983. Although Gorbachev was known for his administrative skills and agricultural expertise, Soviet agriculture did not improve during his tenure. Gorbachev was elected in 1979 to the Party's ruling Politburo as a candidate member and was raised to full membership in October, 1980. At the age of forty-nine, Gorbachev was the youngest member of a powerful group dominated by very senior party leaders.

Yuri Andropov succeeded Brezhnev in November, 1982, and shifted Gorbachev's responsibilities to personnel evaluation and selection. Upon Andropov's death in early 1984, Gorbachev nominated Konstantin Chernenko as general secretary. During the brief Chernenko interlude, Gorbachev provided important party leadership and gained stature among his colleagues. During the post-Brezhnev period, he also led Soviet delegations to Canada (1983) and Britain (1984). In April, 1984, he became Chairman of the Foreign Affairs Commission in the Supreme Soviet of the Soviet Union. With Chernenko's death on March 10, 1985, the party elite immediately elected Gorbachev as general secretary.

A priority for Gorbachev was to replace government and party personnel at all levels. New appointments to the ruling party Politburo started in April, 1985, with other major changes in 1987 and 1988. More than half of the regional party secretaries and the Council of Ministers were replaced. A new prime minister was selected in 1985, as well as a new foreign minister. Andrei Gromyko was named president in 1985 and served in that role until Gorbachev replaced him in the fall of 1988 by taking that office himself. The Congress of People's Deputies, under the revised parliamentary system, elected Gorbachev chairman of the Supreme Soviet in May, 1989. Extensive changes in the Central Committee occurred in April, 1989, as senior members were replaced. Gorbachev showed effective control and leadership of major party and government meetings, especially the Twenty-seventh Communist Party Congress (1986), the Nineteenth Communist Party Conference (1988), and the Congress of People's Deputies (1989).

The Soviet economy was recognized as a problem for years in its lack of productivity, cumbersome bureaucracy, waste, poor growth rates, supply bottlenecks, and reduced worker output. Improving the economy was seen as the fundamental key to Gorbachev's ultimate success or failure. His calls for greater labor effort, reduction of alcohol abuse among workers, and more flexibility of economic planning yielded mixed results. Some new experiments promised the potential for improvement, but productivity remained low. New policies introduced to spur the economy included the cooperative system (some limited free enterprise), economic accountability (enterprises must make a profit or face closure), and provision for private ownership or long-term leases in agriculture.

These steps were part of Gorbachev's policy known as *perestroika* (restructuring). The results proved to be initially inadequate, and Gorbachev's economic advisers publicly predicted no substantial improvement of the economy from the implementation of these policies until 1992 at the earliest. Unemployment was expected to rise, creating further problems. Consumer goods, promised regularly, were in even shorter supply for many in 1989. Some food rationing was invoked. Ideology and reform blended in Gorbachev's Marxist orientation and his efforts to make improvements. He rejected changing the fundamental organizations and institutions of the nation and opposed a multiparty political system. Nevertheless, he called on the Communist Party and the public to be more efficient and active. Several constitutional changes occurred, altering the national government's structure and powers. Gorbachev's economic reforms cut sharply at the ideological patterns of seven decades.

Foreign policy during the Gorbachev era reflected more flexibility in meeting Soviet defense needs and addressing competition with the United States and other states. Gorbachev and United States President Ronald Reagan met in five summits (1985, 1986, 1987, and two in 1988). Some arms control agreements were reached (notably the INF Treaty of 1987), and others were negotiated. Gorbachev undertook a nuclear testing moratorium for a lengthy period, called for the end of nuclear weapons by the year 2000, and, in December, 1988, made a significant address to the United Nations. His trips to other nations were remarkable for their effects and implications. Major trips in 1989 included West Germany, France, and China. Improvements in relations with allies and opponents became a prominent aspect of the Gorbachev years. The Soviet military leadership was extensively revised after Gorbachev came to power (from the chief of the general staff and the minister of defense down), and the Soviet Union's extensive participation in the Afghanistan war, starting in 1979, ended in early 1989 with the withdrawal of Soviet combat forces.

While Gorbachev's international popularity was at its height, however, his reputation at home was rapidly deteriorating. His policies resulted in both political openness and polarity, and his economic reforms were disastrous. Serious and substantial problems broke into the open in 1988 and 1989. Nationality discontent expanded to affect at least half of the nation's fifteen republics. Violent outbursts led to increasing deaths and injuries. Political activists, charging that Gorbachev was moving too slowly, attempted to create alternative political reform agendas and even called for a multiparty political system. Growing labor unrest, especially among striking Soviet coal miners in the summer of 1989, threatened economic stability. Anti-Semitism and ethnic antipathies, suppressed under previous regimes, re-erupted, and both the eastern bloc countries and Soviet republics began breaking away. In 1989, the Soviet Union collapsed, and Gorbachev was soon succeeded by his protégé Boris Yeltsin. Gorbachev formed a research foundation and remained politically active, but his career and reputation were ruined.

Summary

Soviet society and culture saw significant changes during Gorbachev's tenure. The concept of *glasnost* (openness) was reflected in more candid com-

ment in the Soviet press and public opinion. Film, drama, and art became more experimental and outspoken in subject matter and approach. *Glasnost* went far beyond previous decades of Soviet rule, but limits remained. The primary purpose was to admit old problems and work for solutions. Gorbachev encouraged this behavior, so long as it did not undermine national unity and security or his *perestroika* efforts. Soviet law and human rights issues also saw some improvement after late 1986. More citizens, especially Jews, were allowed to emigrate. Several punitive laws were not used as they had been in the past to punish those who criticized the lack of human rights in the Soviet Union. Andrei Sakharov, for example, banished to Gorky by Brezhnev in early 1980, was permitted by Gorbachev to return to Moscow in December, 1986.

Time, however, worked against his reform program. Gorbachev and his advisers admitted that the problems were greater than originally identified. Public inertia, the stifling ideological system, and the bureaucratic opposition to *perestroika* proved too difficult to overcome. In the meantime, the quality of life for many citizens became worse, and they increasingly blamed Gorbachev for their discomfort. The public admission of problems in the era of *glasnost* further heightened frustration and anti-Gorbachev feeling. The Soviet superpower was ultimately reduced to an assortment of struggling, underdeveloped nations, and Russia's devastation was laid largely at the feet of its reform-minded former leader.

Bibliography

Brown, Archie. *The Gorbachev Factor.* Oxford and New York: Oxford University Press, 1997. The author, one of the foremost authorities on Gorbachev, provides a detailed account of Gorbachev's rise and fall including perceptive analysis of his policies and beliefs. Profiles of Soviet leaders such as Brezhnev, Yeltzin, and Andropov are presented.

Butson, Thomas G. *Gorbachev: A Biography.* New York: Stein and Day, 1985. A readable biography of the Soviet leader from early years to his selection as general secretary in 1985. Contains some information based on interviews not found in other sources. An adequate description and assessment.

Gorbachev, Mikhail. *Perestroika: New Thinking for Our Country and the World.* New York: Harper, 1987; London: Fontana, 1988. A well-known account by the Soviet leader of the challenges his country faces. This candid assessment of strengths and weaknesses, with a minimum of rhetorical camouflage or self-serving defense, reveals the man and his outlook.

McCauley, Martin. *Gorbachev.* London and New York: Longman, 1998. The first major study of Gorbachev's career. Objective analyses of the politician, his goals, the reasons for the failure of his reforms, and his mishandling of the nationalities question. Questions the self-serving aspects of Gorbachev's memoirs.

Medvedev, Zhores A. *Gorbachev.* Oxford: Blackwell, and New York: Norton, 1986. A careful biography by a noted Soviet intellectual and former dissident now living in Great Britain. Penetrating assessment of Gorbachev's values and priorities, with predictions of the success or failure of Gorbachev's reform efforts.

Morrison, Donald, ed. *Mikhail S. Gorbachev: An Intimate Biography.* New York: New American Library, 1988. Very readable and complete biography, taking the story to the Washington summit in December, 1987. Gorbachev's personality and leadership style are effectively presented. An important source for the general reader. Illustrated.

Murarka, Dev. *Gorbachev: The Limits of Power.* London: Hutchinson, 1988. An important and useful biography by an Indian journalist stationed in the Soviet Union for many years. Reveals independent judgment about Gorbachev and his nation. Includes his rise to power with emphasis on the first several years in office, attempted reforms, and results.

Schmidt-Häuer, Christian. *Gorbachev: The Path to Power.* London: Pan, and Topsfield, Mass.: Salem House, 1986. A readable account of Gorbachev's life with the focus on the 1980's. Relates Gorbachev's reform efforts to Peter the Great and others. Very good coverage and assessment of his political leadership and policies as general secretary. Includes helpful appendices.

Zemstov, Ilya, and John Farrar. *Gorbachev: The Man and the System.* New Brunswick, N.J.: Transaction, 1989. The most current and thorough analysis of Gorbachev as general secretary, in a detailed presentation. A daunting source to read but very illuminating. Excellent charts, chronologies, and appendices. Focus is on 1985 to 1987.

Taylor Stults

NADINE GORDIMER

Born: November 20, 1923; Springs, near Johannesburg, South Africa

Area of Achievement: Literature

Contribution: Through her writings, Gordimer has illuminated the troubled history of South Africa with unparalleled clarity, sensitivity, honesty, and art.

Early Life

Nadine Gordimer's father was an impoverished watchmaker who emigrated from Lithuania to Springs, a small mining town on the East Rand about thirty miles from Johannesburg, South Africa, shortly before the Boer War. Her mother was born and grew up in London. Although both parents were Jewish, Gordimer and her only sibling, an elder sister, were sent to a local convent school run by Dominican nuns; the family had little involvement with the local Jewish community. Her father benefited from the increasing prosperity of the town and became proprietor of a jewelry store, thus securing a middle-class living for his family. Gordimer's father had no interest in civic affairs, but her mother took an active role in the community, particularly associating with the Scots Presbyterians. In an essay recalling her childhood, Gordimer describes the strange landscape of the East Rand, the richest gold-mining region in the world. It is a bleak and eerie scene with its manmade mountains of waste material, cyanide sand hills, and smoldering coal dust dumps. The town was equally barren, causing Gordimer to observe: "We children simply took it for granted that beauty—hills, trees, buildings of elegance—was not a thing to be expected of ordinary, everyday life."

Not only was Gordimer's environment strange but also her childhood was unusual. Between ages eleven and sixteen she was kept out of school and from participation in normal activities by her mother, who became convinced that Gordimer had a serious heart condition, a condition that Gordimer subsequently learned was a very minor ailment. Although she was sent to a tutor for three hours a day, her contacts with others her own age were severed. Her sister went away to the university which left Gordimer as constant companion of her parents, particularly of her mother, who took Gordimer with her everywhere. Socializing only with adults in a world of tea parties and trivia,

Gordimer became, as she said, "a little old woman." In her isolation and loneliness, she retreated into herself, read voraciously, and thereby discovered an alternative world more to her liking—the world of ideas.

Although Gordimer attended the university for one year at age twenty-one, she largely educated herself. Through her early and as she acknowledges indiscriminate reading (devouring children's books and Burton's *The Anatomy of Melancholy*, 1621, with equal enjoyment), she prepared herself to be a writer. Perhaps Gordimer would have become a writer even without her unusual childhood; her interest in reading and writing predated her illness; in fact, she wrote her first poem at age nine. There is little doubt, however, that her enforced isolation accelerated the process. At age thirteen, she began writing for the children's page of the Johannesburg *Sunday Express*. At fifteen, she published her first short story in *The Forum*, a South African journal. In 1949, her first volume of short stories, *Face to Face*, was published in South Africa. The following year, she began publishing stories in *The New Yorker*, and soon thereafter her writing began appearing in other American journals, such as *Virginia Quarterly Review* and the *Yale Review*. Her first novel, *The Lying Days*, was published in 1953. By that time, she had married, was divorced, and had an eighteen-month-old baby to support.

Her early short stories, those written before 1953, focus on the daily lives of the poor white class and show little political consciousness. In fact, Gordimer acknowledges that her full awareness of black Africans and their paradoxical position in their own country (particularly after the Afrikaner Nationalist government assumed power in 1948 and instituted its repressive apartheid laws) developed with incredible slowness. Perhaps this is unsurprising considering the life she led among white middle-class colonials, whose very existence depended on the pretense that blacks do not exist, except as a permanent underclass of servants and laborers. Yet, the politics of South Africa, particularly its apartheid and censorship laws, became the central concern of her writing and of her life. Her writing constitutes a merciless scrutiny of that society and of her own developing consciousness and role within that society.

Life's Work

During her year at the University of Witwatersrand, Gordimer met for the first time white people (writers, painters, and actors) who defied the color bar and associated with blacks. This was the beginning of her political education, although she was still not interested in politics. Her attitude at this time was humanistic, individualistic, and optimistic: "I felt all I needed, in my own behavior, was to ignore and defy the color bar. In other words my own attitude toward blacks seemed to be sufficient action." It seemed to her that an "inevitable historical process" was taking place that eventually would demolish racial barriers, an attitude reflected in both of her novels of this period, *The Lying Days* and *A World of Strangers* (1958). The hope of ending apartheid by personal relationships across the color bar became much more difficult to sustain following the Sharpeville massacre of 1960 and the subsequent draconian measures against blacks initiated by the government: prohibition of all right to peaceful protest and banning of the best black writers. Gordimer's next two novels, *Occasion for Loving* (1963) and *The Late Bourgeois World* (1966), reflect the paralysis and frustration that she undoubtedly felt. Her characters seem unable to act, unable to connect with people and situations, and unable to do more than observe and record.

A Guest of Honour (1970) and the novels that follow reveal Gordimer exploring alternatives to the failed Forsterian liberal humanism. Ultimately, she finds it necessary to give up her identification with white European culture in favor of an African-centered consciousness, a change in perspective which resulted in her new, unorthodox definition of African literature: work by those "of whatever skin color who share with Africans the experience of having been shaped, mentally and spiritually, by Africa rather than anywhere else in the world." In apartheid-era South Africa, where literature and culture were regarded as the exclusive property of an educated, white, European-centered minority, such a definition had revolutionary implication.

The shift from Eurocentric to African culture seems to have been a liberating one for Gordimer. In her fiction, she developed greater freedom in form and style (for example, her use of multiperspective narration) and in content a broader, more diverse cast of characters, including many blacks and Indians. At the same time that she became interested in African culture, she also became convinced that "inspirational" literature is superior to the ironical or the satirical, and this seems to have made some difference in the tone of her writing. Although most critics had praised her scrupulous powers of observation and analysis, a frequent criticism of her fiction had been that it lacked warmth and feeling. Some critics had speculated that the cool detachment of her earlier fiction was a consequence of the political situation in South Africa itself, which "'dehumanises' even the artist." Her novels *Burger's Daughter* (1979) and *July's People* (1981) impressed even her sterner critics with their warmth, energy, and commitment.

The relationship between literature and politics is a subject to which Gordimer has necessarily given considerable thought, and her views are complex. She has stated unequivocally the two absolutes in her life:

> [O]ne is that racism is evil . . . and no compromises, as well as sacrifices, should be too great in the fight against it. The other is that a writer is a being in whose sensibility is fused . . . the duality of inwardness and outside world, and he must never be asked to sunder this union.

On one hand, she believes that "art is on the side of the oppressed," and she calls on the South African writer, whether black or white, to be a revolutionary as well as a prophet. On the other hand, she remains wary of the writer as proselytizer and the ways that art can deteriorate into propaganda. A writer has the freedom not to write propaganda, even for the "right" cause. She believes that a writer must confront the reader with a situation in such a way that he can no longer ignore it. Ultimately, her view of the writer's responsibility is paradoxical: The writer must at the same time stand apart and also be fully involved. It is the tension that arises from this objective/subjective vision that makes a writer, according to Gordimer.

Gordimer regards herself as intensely loyal to South Africa, her home. She concedes that life in Europe would be more comfortable for her, but she remains in South Africa, where she courageously continues to attack the twin evils of racism and censorship. Gordimer is a much honored writer who has achieved world recognition. Among her many awards are the W. H. Smith award in 1961 for *Friday's Footprints;* the James Tait Black Memorial Prize for *A Guest of Honour* in 1972; the Booker Prize for *The Conservationist* (1975) in 1975; the Grand Aigle d'Or in 1975; and an honorary D.Litt. degree from the University of Leuven in 1980. She is an honorary member of the American Academy of Arts and Sciences and of the American Academy of Literature and Arts.

Summary

Gordimer's fiction is above all an attempt to awaken people from the slumber of habit, to reveal the corruptions that racism brings, including the subtle corruptions of whites. To enlarge the reader's apprehension of South Africa's troubling history, to write of it with honesty and objectivity, succumbing neither to the self-pity of whites nor to the romanticizing of blacks, and yet to retain the necessary passion of commitment—these are the high and difficult aims of Gordimer's art.

Bibliography

Clingman, Stephen. *The Novels of Nadine Gordimer: History from the Inside.* 2d ed. Amherst: University of Massachusetts Press, 1992; London: Bloomsbury, 1993. Correlates Gordimer's fiction with events in South African history. Gordimer's historical consciousness, the way in which she has responded to the history of her society, makes her a particularly valuable writer. Clingman regards South Africa as an unusually extreme and therefore clear case of the class, racial, and cultural struggles occurring in the world at large today.

Cooke, John. *The Novels of Nadine Gordimer: Private Lives/Public Landscapes.* Baton Rouge: Louisiana State University Press, 1985. Traces Gordimer's development as a writer. Identifies a private theme in her fiction (the rebellion of daughters against possessive mothers) which gradually assumes a more political character (liberation from oppressors). Contains a valuable bibliography.

Gordimer, Nadine. *The Essential Gesture: Writing, Politics and Places.* Edited by Stephen Clingman. London: Cape, and New York: Knopf, 1988. This collection of twenty-three essays written between the early 1950's and 1985 allows a reader to trace Gordimer's development as person and as writer.

————. "A South African Childhood: Allusions in a Landscape." *New Yorker* 30 (October 16, 1954): 121-143. Descriptions and anecdotes of daily life, including vacations at Durban and excursions to Cape Town and Kruger National Park. Her early, learned, racist responses to African and Indian people reveal how pervasive such attitudes are.

Head, Dominic. *Nadine Gordimer.* Cambridge and New York: Cambridge University Press, 1994. Detailed analysis of each of Gordimer's novels, focusing on their depictions of the real world. Suggests how the body of Gordimer's works relates to other literature challenging apartheid.

Hurwitt, Jannika. "The Art of Fiction LXXVII: Nadine Gordimer." *Paris Review* 88 (Summer, 1983): 83-127. The most comprehensive and revealing interview that the usually reticent Gordimer has granted. Of particular interest is the account of her early "illness," her relationship with her mother, her beginnings as a writer, and her attitude toward feminism and toward masculine and feminine writing.

JanMohamed, Abdul R. *Manichean Aesthetics: The Politics of Literature in Colonial Africa.* Amherst: University of Massachusetts Press, 1983; London: University of Massachusetts Press, 1984. In a chapter devoted to Gordimer entitled "The Degeneration of the Great South African Lie," the author discusses the ways in which the contradictions of life for a white liberal writer in an apartheid society are reflected in her major fiction.

McEwan, Neil. *Africa and the Novel.* London: Macmillan, and Atlantic Highlands, N.J.: Humanities Press, 1983. In this examination of "the best work of African novelists since 1950," McEwan considers Gordimer an "outsider," that is, one who writes about apartheid primarily for a world of readers outside South Africa. He selects Gordimer's novel *July's People* for extended analysis.

Yelin, Louise. *From the Margins of Empire: Christina Stead, Doris Lessing, and Nadine Gordimer.* Ithaca, N.Y.: Cornell University Press, 1998. The author examines how three authors' nationalities affect their works and the issues they raise about the roles of white women in politics and culture.

Karen A. Kildahl

ALBERT GORE

Born: March 31, 1948; Washington, D.C.

Areas of Achievement: Government and politics

Contribution: Gore has been involved in national government for more than twenty years. He has gained a reputation as an able legislator and effective executive. His particular policy contributions have been in the areas of nuclear disarmament, environmental improvements, government efficiency, and government policy with regard to electronic communications.

Early Life

Albert Arnold Gore, Jr., was born to U.S. Representative (later Senator) Al Gore, Sr., and Pauline Gore. He was raised in Carthage, Tennessee, and Washington, D.C. The family home was in Carthage, but with his father in Congress, Gore spent most of the time in Washington. He attended the elite St. Alban's School for Boys in Washington, where he was an honors student and captain of the football team. He met his future wife, Mary Elizabeth "Tipper" Aitcheson, at a school dance during his senior year. Upon graduation from St. Albans, Gore attended Harvard University. He graduated as an honor student in 1969 with a major in government. His senior thesis was titled "The Impact of Television on the Conduct of the Presidency, 1947-1969."

Gore was drafted into the Army after he graduated from college, and he enlisted despite his opposition to the war in Vietnam. His decision to enlist was made in part because a failure to do so might reflect negatively on his father but also because Gore thought it unfair for others to go in his place. In Vietnam, he served as a reporter for *Stars and Stripes* near Saigon. He sent copies of the stories he wrote to his wife, whom he had married after college graduation. She forwarded some of the stories to the Nashville *Tennessean*, where they were published. When Gore's tour of duty in Vietnam ended, he went to work for the *Tennessean* from 1971 to 1976. He reported on stories of local interest, including local politics. A series of articles he wrote during 1974 led to the conviction of several local politicians for corruption and bribery. During this time, Gore, a devout Baptist, studied religion at Vanderbilt University's Graduate School of Religion. For two years, he studied at Vanderbilt Law School.

Gore had grown up in a political family in which both of his parents had been active in his father's career. Gore was seen by many as a natural political leader. However, like many of his generation, Gore shunned politics early in his adult life. Perhaps it was because of the Vietnam War, which he had opposed, or perhaps it was because of his father's bitter loss of his Senate seat in 1970. Whatever the reason, Gore seemed destined for a career outside of electoral politics during the years after his departure from the Army.

Life's Work

In February, 1976, when incumbent U.S. representative Joe L. Elvins of Gore's district announced that he would not seek reelection, Gore suddenly decided to follow in his father's footsteps and run for Congress. He defeated eight opponents in the Democratic primary and won against only token opposition in the general election. His campaign themes were to place higher taxes on the rich, to create more public jobs, and to spend less on defense. He became a distinguished member of the House, and he focused particularly on nuclear disarmament. While serving on the House Intelligence Committee, he published a comprehensive report on disarmament in the February, 1982, issue of *Congressional Quarterly*. A few months later, when U.S. arms experts visited Moscow, the Soviets wanted to discuss "the Gore Plan."

Gore also became interested in the subject of toxic waste, holding the first congressional hearing on the topic and helping bring to light toxic waste problems near Memphis, Tennessee, and in the Love Canal neighborhood in Niagara, New York. Technology was also of interest to Representative Gore, and he pressed to have House proceedings televised. When that campaign was successful, it was Gore who delivered the first televised speech in March of 1979. He served four terms in the U.S. House of Representatives. During that time, he had the voting record of a moderate liberal.

When Senator Howard Baker, Jr., the Republican majority leader in the Senate, announced that he would not run for reelection in Tennessee in 1984, Gore quickly became the likely Democratic nominee for the seat. He easily won election against a split Tennessee Republican party, a victory made all the more impressive since it came during a presidential election in which President

Ronald Reagan was reelected in a landslide. Gore won reelection in 1990, carrying each of the ninety-five counties in Tennessee. He became an expert in the area of environmental policy, where he advocated reducing the number of pollutants in the air through government regulation. Opponents of Gore have charged that he is "an environmental extremist," but Gore argues that a stringent environmental policy is necessary to stem the "global environmental crisis." His vote to support President George Bush in the Persian Gulf during the prelude to that war was a boon to the Republican president and demonstrated that Gore was neither universally liberal nor bound entirely by party affiliation. In both the Senate and the House, Gore earned a reputation as one of the hardest-working people on Capitol Hill. He was a quick study on policy issues and was particularly able to understand policy issues on a high intellectual plane.

From the beginning of his political career, Gore appeared to have aspirations beyond Congress, and, in 1988, he ran for the Democratic nomination for president. Although he had some success during the primary campaign, he eventually lost the nomination to Massachusetts governor Michael Dukakis. He won more votes in the southern primaries than did his opponents, and although he lost the nomination, he was seen by many as a serious candidate for the 1992 nomination. However, in 1991, Gore announced that he would not become a candidate for president in 1992, citing family concerns. Some thought that his decision not to run was more likely because of the fact that incumbent president Bush seemed invincible at the end of the Persian Gulf War. When Bill Clinton became the Democratic candidate for president in 1992, he asked Gore to be his running mate. The choice was unconventional because Clinton and Gore were of similar ages, of similar ideologies, and from the same part of the country. However, Gore brought to the ticket a great talent as a campaigner, and he helped Clinton greatly in his election bid. Gore's performance in the vice presidential debate with Republican candidate Jack Kemp was thought by most to be outstanding. He was inaugurated as vice president on January 20, 1993.

As vice president, Gore became a close advisor and partner to President Clinton, perhaps because of the affinity they developed for one another during the 1992 campaign. Another asset he brought to the Clinton White House was experience in the nation's capital, which President Clinton lacked. That became evident early in the Clinton years when Gore was of great assistance in the drive to pass the North American Free Trade Agreement (NAFTA). His performance in a nationally broadcast debate against Texas businessman H. Ross Perot was seen as a turning point in the passage of the agreement. His National Performance Review presented a comprehensive plan to cut costs and eliminate waste in government, helping redefine the Clinton administration as one that was committed to a new approach to government rather than the "old" liberal ways of the Democratic Party. Gore continued to be involved in attempts to help the world's environment by representing the United States for President Clinton in that arena. He was also involved in nearly all of the major decisions made by the Clinton administration.

In 1997, Vice President Gore was criticized for his role in Democratic Party fund-raising. It was alleged that he had used the telephone in his government office to raise those funds, a practice that many saw as unethical. The charges threatened to damage Gore's reputation as a clean and honest politician, but they have not been substantiated. As vice president, Gore was seen as a likely candidate for the Democratic nomination for president in the year 2000 since President Clinton could not run for another term.

Gore's reputation as a family man was enhanced in 1989 when his son Albert was hit by a car and critically injured as he was leaving a baseball game. The experience, Gore said, "changed me forever," and he canceled all of his appointments for a month to be with his son, who made a full recovery. His reputation as a strong family man was particularly helpful to the Democrats in 1992 since the Republicans wished to discredit the party as not being committed to "family values."

As a politician, Gore has gained a reputation for being boring, even "wooden." He has made fun of himself and that image, but he has also parried it into a reputation as a person of solemn rectitude. His distinguished bearing makes others take his expertise seriously, and the reputation seems to hide the fact that Gore is an engaging and extremely able campaigner. Indeed, Gore seems to have a complex personality that allows him to be animated and engaging one moment, and quiet and circumspect the next.

Summary

Al Gore is one of the leaders of the generation of Americans known as the "baby boomers," those born in the years following World War II. He has, in many ways, been a representative of that group. He grew to question the national government during the Vietnam War and engaged in behaviors, such as smoking marijuana, that were abhorrent to the previous generation. As a result, he, along with President Clinton, has touched a chord of popularity with the voters.

His successes as a politician stem from his exceptional campaigning abilities and from his talent for understanding complex political problems and proposing solutions to them. In the areas of arms control policy, environmental policy, government efficiency, and electronic communications, Vice President Gore has earned a reputation as a political leader of substance.

Bibliography

Barone, Michael. *Almanac of American Politics 1992.* Washington, D.C.: National Journal, 1991. This gives a detailed summary of the political experiences of Gore prior to his election to the vice presidency, particularly with reference to Tennessee politics.

Gore, Albert, Jr. *Earth in the Balance: Ecology and the Human Spirit.* Boston: Houghton Mifflin, and London: Earthscan, 1992. In this book, Gore discusses his views on environmental policy.

"Gore, Albert, Jr." *Current Biography* (1987): 211-214. This is the most complete treatment of Gore's early life and early congressional career.

Jones, Alex S. "Al Gore's Double Life." *New York Times Magazine* (October 25, 1992): 40-44, 76-77. This is an insightful profile of the vice president written during the 1992 campaign that shows the complexity of his personality.

Menand, Louis. "After Elvis: Is There a Future for a Politician Whose Ideas Are Almost as Big as His Ambitions?" *New Yorker* 74, no. 33 (October 26, 1998). Interview with Gore covering his approach to change in the Democratic Party, his philosophy, and his ideas on government and politics.

National Performance Review. *Access America.* Washington, D.C.: Government Printing House, 1997. This is the final report of Vice President Gore's National Performance Review.

James W. Riddlesperger, Jr.

WILLIAM CRAWFORD GORGAS

Born: October 3, 1854; Toulminville, Alabama
Died: July 4, 1920; London, England
Area of Achievement: Public health
Contribution: Gorgas, a dedicated humanitarian, led the effort that eliminated yellow fever as one of the major epidemic diseases throughout the world. This feat was accomplished through the diligent and practical application of scientific discoveries concerning the disease.

Early Life

William Crawford Gorgas was born October 3, 1854, in Toulminville, Alabama. His father, Josiah Gorgas, was an officer in the United States Army and a Northerner; his mother, Amelia (Gayle) Gorgas, was a Southerner. The sectional strife in the late 1850's caused Josiah Gorgas considerable anxiety, for both marriage and experience inclined him to the Southern side. Eventually, he resigned his commission and offered his services to the Confederacy. The family was soon living in Richmond, where Josiah was serving as chief of ordnance with the rank of general. His son, known as Willie while a child and W.C. as an adult, spent his early formative years intoxicated with the military romanticism of the rebellion. He never stopped wanting to be a soldier or wishing that the rebels had won.

When the war ended, the family settled in Brierfield, Alabama, where Josiah Gorgas invested his small remaining capital in a blast furnace. Willie got what schooling was available and was in fact fortunate that his father's business quickly failed. When the senior Gorgas obtained a position at the University of the South in Sewanee, Tennessee, his son entered as a preparatory student. In 1870, the young Gorgas went as a volunteer to fight a yellow fever epidemic in New Orleans, an experience that started his lifelong interest in the disease. He still wanted to be a soldier, and when he was graduated, his father, who wanted him to study law, reluctantly and unsuccessfully tried to get him an appointment to West Point. Gorgas decided to get into the army via the medical corps. In 1876, he entered Bellevue Hospital Medical College in New York. Although he had felt no initial call to the profession, he found that medicine fascinated him. After graduation and a year of internship at Bellevue Hospital, he realized his longtime ambition by becoming in June, 1880, a first lieutenant in the United States Army.

Gorgas was tested both physically and spiritually during his first two decades in the army. He was stationed at out-of-the-way posts in Texas, North Dakota, and Florida, where, as the only doctor in the area, he worked long hours serving the local civilian population as well as keeping up with his military duties. His small frame and frail appearance belied his toughness, and his devotion to military life never dimmed. He charted his own future course when in 1883, while stationed at Fort Brown, Texas, he violated orders by working with victims of a yellow fever epidemic. Having been exposed, he was kept at the task, and he met his future wife, Marie Doughty; she was the sister of the post commander, whom he treated and with whom, after contracting the disease himself, he convalesced. Gorgas and Miss Doughty were married the next year. His illness not only afforded him a bride, but also deepened his interest in yellow fever, which he continued to study over the next few years. Gorgas was soon recognized as an expert on the disease, though he was not impressed with the mosquito transmission theory which was gaining more and more attention. Little did the hardworking small-post army doctor know it, but yellow fever was about to become the center of his life.

Life's Work

When, in 1898, the Spanish-American War put large numbers of American soldiers into the Caribbean, the medical corps proved ill-prepared to handle the inevitable outbreaks of tropical disease. Already known for his work with yellow fever, Gorgas was assigned to the yellow fever camp at Siboney, near Havana. His best advice was the burning of everything that might have been in contact with victims—even buildings. Later in 1898, Major Gorgas was appointed sanitary officer of Havana. The city was littered with sewage and filth and was a pool of yellow fever infection, exporting the disease with trade goods to American ports. Gorgas went to work on the needed cleaning only to find that, contrary to expectations, yellow fever became increasingly common. This was, of course, a result of the arrival of more and more nonimmunes. At first the bitterly disappointed Gorgas seemed headed for failure, but the solution to his problem was at hand.

An American medical commission headed by Walter Reed had come to Cuba to study the problem of yellow fever. With Gorgas as fascinated observer, the Reed Commission combined past discoveries with new experiments to answer the question of transmission. A number of investigators—most recently Carlos J. Finlay—had suggested mosquitoes as the carrier, but no one had actually been able to show such a transmission. Henry Rose Carter in Mississippi had, however, established that there was a period of development for the germ in the mosquito's system before it could be passed along. The Reed Commission was able to show conclusively that the mosquito had to bite an infected person within three days of the initial infection and that the mosquito itself was not dangerous for at least ten days. It was also determined that the carrier was the *Stegomyia fasciata* (called today *Aëdes aegypti*). This proved the vital information.

Despite the efforts of the Reed Commission, Gorgas remained dubious. The only real test, he believed, was to rid the city of the mosquito and see what happened. Reed agreed but believed that such an extermination was impossible. Gorgas first tried for a vaccine, but soon focused his attack on the insect. Studying its habits, he found that it preferred to live in and around human habitations and lay its eggs in fresh water held in artificial containers. It also had a fairly limited range. Dividing the city into zones, Gorgas assigned teams to eliminate or put a film of kerosene on all open water. Windows were screened and houses, especially those where a case of yellow fever had occurred, were fumigated. Civilian objections to such intrusions were gently but firmly put aside. The result was that October, 1901, was the first October in the recorded history of Havana without a case of yellow fever. A happy side effect of the campaign was that malaria cases were reduced by fully three-quarters as well. The surgeon general of the army recognized Gorgas' efforts by deciding that he should become the army expert on tropical diseases. In 1902-1903, he was sent to attend the world conference on tropical medicine at Cairo and to have a look at the antimalaria work done at Suez. He was also promoted to colonel.

These assignments were to help prepare him for a job in the planned construction of a canal across the Isthmus of Panama. The American Medical Association lobbied for his appointment to the Canal Commission, headed by Admiral John G. Walker, but he was merely appointed chief sanitary officer. Problems caused by disease had played a substan-

tial part in the failure of the French effort to construct a canal in Panama, and Gorgas believed that he could prevent such problems. Admiral Walker and the other commissioners, however, considered the idea of mosquito transmission of disease foolish and were much more concerned with economy and avoidance of even the appearance of graft than with sanitation. Indeed, the sanitary staff was hopelessly inadequate in number, and its requests for supplies were often denied or reduced to a fraction of the amount requested. Pay scales were set so low that qualified medical personnel were uninterested in the positions.

Gorgas protested as strongly as his sense of military hierarchy and his courtly Southern demeanor would allow, but to no avail. During the first yellow fever season, the disease was at low ebb, but Gorgas knew that, as in Havana, the influx of nonimmunes would provide the raw material for an epidemic. In the spring and summer of 1905, the number of cases began to increase rapidly, and official reaction was to blame Gorgas. Fortunately, the American Medical Association sent Dr. Charles A.L. Reed to investigate and report to Secretary of

War William Howard Taft. The report, which was made public, supported Gorgas totally, and in addition to other studies led President Theodore Roosevelt to reorganize the Canal Commission. The new chairman, however, Theodore P. Shonts, also rejected the mosquito transmission theory and tried to get rid of Gorgas. Although inclined to agree with Shonts and other doubters, the president sought the advice of several prominent physicians, all of whom maintained that Gorgas was the best man for the job and that mosquito transmission had been proved. Roosevelt ordered that Gorgas be given full support.

Gorgas quickly began to apply the lessons learned in Havana. By November, 1905, he had four thousand men, and although earlier his entire budget had been fifty thousand dollars a year, he was able to order ninety thousand dollars' worth of window-screen wire alone. Panama City and Colón were fumigated house by house, piped water was supplied to end the need for open household cisterns, and pools of standing water which could not be drained were regularly sprayed with kerosene. By the end of 1905, yellow fever was under control. Other diseases that had threatened, such as cholera and bubonic plague, were gone, and malaria was much reduced. Health care for workers was very good generally, and death rates would have been acceptable in virtually any American city. The arrival in April, 1907, however, of George W. Goethals as chief engineer, proved a beginning of renewed frustration for Gorgas. Goethals had been given extremely broad powers and used them dictatorially. His efforts at economy, Gorgas feared, would weaken the sanitary effort. The two rarely found common ground personally or professionally, but the sanitary foundation had been laid and morbidity rates did not increase.

Gorgas' success in the canal zone led to numerous honors. In 1907, he received the Mary Kingsley Medal and in 1908 was elected president of the American Medical Association. He was also granted many honorary degrees. An invitation came in 1913 to consult on the problem of pneumonia among miners in South Africa, and with the canal nearing completion, he received permission to accept. Although his visit was cut short in February, 1914, by his appointment as surgeon general of the United States Army—with promotion to the rank of brigadier general—his report proved the basis for a program that improved the miners' situation significantly.

As surgeon general, Gorgas was responsible for reforms that prepared the Army Medical Corps for World War I. He encouraged doctors to join the service and helped develop the Medical Reserve Corps which supplied many of the physicians needed when the United States entered the war in 1917. Between the beginning of American participation and the armistice, the number of doctors in the military service increased by more than thirty times its original amount. Sanitation in military camps proved a problem, and at times Gorgas faced strong criticism. He was able to defend himself by pointing out failures to follow basic regulations through ignorance or more often through pressure to enlist and train an army before the British and French were overwhelmed. He also became involved in a controversial political struggle over provision of higher rank for American medical officers and eventually saw the necessary legislation through Congress. On October 3, 1918, Gorgas turned sixty-four, and despite protests from friends and admirers, had to retire from active duty. He spent the rest of his life working on behalf of the Rockefeller Foundation trying to eliminate the remaining pockets of yellow fever in the world. After getting the program started in South America, he died in London on July 4, 1920, while on a journey that had been intended to take him to West Africa, where yellow fever was still often epidemic. King George V visited the hospital to bestow on Lieutenant General William C. Gorgas, the only son of a Confederate general officer to achieve a similar rank in the United States army, the Order of St. Michael and St. George. It was a high and fitting last honor.

Summary

Two quintessentially American qualities are the hallmarks of William Crawford Gorgas' career: practicality and hard work. Although he made none of the basic scientific discoveries needed to end the scourge of yellow fever, when those discoveries were made he took advantage of them. His dogged and eventually successful struggle to get the necessary support for his sanitation program saved thousands of lives among the work force that built the canal and was a key factor in making construction possible. He proved that controlling the mosquitoes that spread the disease would prevent epidemics. These lessons, when applied throughout the world, saved countless thousands more.

Gorgas' work as surgeon general of the army was also extremely successful. The American Expeditionary Force in World War I suffered almost twice as many combat deaths as deaths from disease. The army as a whole had fewer than twenty-five percent more deaths from disease than in battle. While to modern ears the latter may not sound like success, it was unprecedented for its day.

A gentle, soft-spoken man, Gorgas was widely admired and often loved. Although a brasher man might have gotten things done in a shorter time, his very courtesy made it very difficult to turn him away, and his gentleness masked an iron determination. His achievements helped to establish modern standards of public health, standards which have improved the quality of life in almost every part of the globe.

Bibliography

Duffy, John. *Sword of Pestilence: The New Orleans Yellow Fever Epidemic of 1853*. Baton Rouge: Louisiana State University Press, 1966. Although its subject predates Gorgas' activity, this short book gives an excellent picture of what a yellow fever epidemic meant before modern public health brought the disease under control.

Gibson, John M. *Physician to the World: The Life of General William C. Gorgas*. Durham, N.C.: Duke University Press, 1950. The most recent and scholarly biography of Gorgas, it contains some anecdotes of dubious authenticity and is flawed by racial and ethnic stereotypes.

Gorgas, Marie D., and Burton J. Hendrick. *William Crawford Gorgas: His Life and Work*. New York: Doubleday, 1924. Written by Gorgas' daughter, this biography is overly kind to its subject but does contain interesting personal observations.

Gorgas, William Crawford. *Sanitation in Panama*. New York and London: Appleton, 1915. Gorgas' own account of his program in the canal effort, this book, while not the easiest of reading, is the best source of information about Gorgas' ideas while he was working on the canal.

McCullough, David. *The Path Between the Seas: The Creation of the Panama Canal, 1870-1914*. New York: Simon and Schuster, 1977. Well-written study of the canal with a chapter on Gorgas' life and the problems of sanitation woven throughout. Excellent background for anyone interested in Gorgas or the canal.

Martin, Franklin H. *Fifty Years of Medicine and Surgery*. Chicago: Surgical Publications, 1934. A colleague and admirer of Gorgas, Martin supplies the observations of a trained colleague as well as personal commentary.

Fred R. van Hartesveldt

HERMANN GÖRING

Born: January 12, 1893; Rosenheim, Germany
Died: October 15, 1946; Nürnberg, Germany
Areas of Achievement: The military, government, and politics
Contribution: Göring, a highly decorated fighter pilot in World War I who cultivated contacts with conservative-nationalist elements in Germany before 1933, contributed to Adolf Hitler's rise to power and played a major role in his consolidation of power. After 1935, Göring directed both the massive rebuilding of the German air force and economic efforts to prepare Germany for war. One of the most powerful leaders of the Third Reich until 1942, and Hitler's designated successor, Göring was tried and convicted at Nürnberg in 1946 for his part in the crimes of the Third Reich.

Early Life

Hermann Wilhelm Göring was born in Rosenheim, Bavaria (Germany), on January 12, 1893, the fourth child of Franziska Göring. Franziska was the second wife of Heinrich Ernst Göring, a former Prussian provincial judge and German consul-general in Haiti at the time of young Göring's birth. After Franziska returned to her husband in Haiti, Göring was reared during the first three years of his life by a friend of his mother in Fürth, Bavaria. Following the return of Göring's father to Berlin, shortly before his retirement from government service in 1896, the boy was reunited with his parents. In 1901, the family moved into castle Veldenstein, Bavaria, which was only thirty miles from Fürth, where young Göring had started elementary school the previous year. The castle belonged to Hermann Göring's godfather, Ritter von Epenstein, who was also the lover of Göring's mother. Ironically, Epenstein, a Catholic, was of Jewish descent. Göring's experience at Veldenstein stimulated his interest in pageantry and implanted a romantic attachment to Germany's medieval past. Both interests were ostentatiously displayed during the Third Reich at Karinhall, Göring's huge estate twenty-five miles north of Berlin. Following a year of unsatisfactory academic performance at a boarding school in Ansbach, Bavaria, Göring was enrolled as a cadet at a military school in Karlsruhe, Baden, in 1905. He thrived in this atmosphere, and, after completing his military education at the prestigious advanced cadet school in Grosslichterfelde,

near Berlin, he received a commission as a second lieutenant in June, 1912. He was soon posted with a regiment in Mühlhausen, Alsace. During the first months of World War I, Göring saw action as an infantry officer in Alsace until he was hospitalized in late 1914 with rheumatism. At the hospital, Bruno Loerzer, a pilot, recruited him for the air force. Göring's career as a fighter pilot was so successful that he was awarded the coveted Pour le Mérite award on June 2, 1918, and given command of the famous Manfred von Richthofen fighter squadron on July 6, 1918.

After Germany's defeat, Göring was discharged from the army with the rank of captain. Like many nationalistic officers, he could not accept the new Weimar Republic and blamed Marxists and Jews for Germany's defeat. In early 1919, Göring left Germany and for the next two years earned a living in Denmark and Sweden as a pilot and salesman for aircraft companies and parachute manufacturers. In the winter of 1920, he met the Swedish baroness Carin von Kantzow, who became a major influence on his life until her death in 1931. In 1921, she left her husband and son and followed Göring to Germany, where they were married on February 3, 1922. With no regular income and an uncertain future, Göring was enrolled at the University of Munich in 1921 to prepare for a new career at the age of twenty-eight.

Life's Work

After Göring's first meeting with Hitler in October, 1922, he joined the Nazi Party and soon was given command of the Sturm Abteilung (SA), the party's paramilitary organization. Hitler welcomed the services of a highly decorated former officer. After less than a year as commander of the SA, Göring's new career ended abruptly when he was wounded during Hitler's abortive attempt to seize power in Munich on November 9, 1923. Sought by the authorities, Göring and his wife fled to Austria and later Italy. Not until 1925 did Göring return to the safety of Sweden, where he was hospitalized and cured of addiction to morphine between September and November of that year. Disillusioned with the Nazi Party, and with no serious prospects for the future, Göring had little contact with the Hitler movement for the next two years.

Following a general amnesty, Göring returned to Germany in November, 1927. He established himself in Berlin as a representative of the Bavarian Motor Works, and he renewed his contacts with Hitler. The Nazi leader placed Göring on the party's election slate in May, 1928. Elected as one of twelve Nazi delegates to the Reichstag, Göring became the president of this legislative body after the spectacular Nazi success in the election of July 31, 1932. Between 1928 and 1932, Göring was little involved in the Nazi Party's day-to-day organizational and administrative work, although he did act as Hitler's representative in Berlin. Indeed, Göring never held a leading party post either before or after 1933. Prior to that year, Göring was mainly useful to Hitler in helping to foster contacts with conservative-nationalist interests in Germany. Göring visited the former Kaiser in Holland in 1931 and 1932, and he maintained cordial relations with the crown prince August Wilhelm. Beginning in the fall of 1930, Hitler used Göring's residence in Berlin for negotiations with political, economic, and military spokesmen.

As president of the Reichstag after July, 1932, Göring used his powers to further Nazi interests and to disrupt effective parliamentary action. During the crucial discussions in January, 1933, which led to Hitler's appointment as chancellor, Göring played a major role. In that fateful month, Göring was able to inform Hitler that President Paul von Hindenburg, after repeated refusals, had finally agreed to appoint Hitler Chancellor of Germany.

Through his control of key state offices and the information obtained from the Forschungsamt, a secret intelligence gathering office, Göring contributed significantly to the Nazi consolidation of power in 1933. As Reichstag president, he guided the Enabling Act of March, 1933, through that legislative body. Although he had been appointed Reich Minister without portfolio on January 30, 1933, Göring's real power rested on his position as Prussian Minister of Interior and later as Minister President of Prussia. In these capacities, Göring was able to use the Prussian police against the enemies of the Nazis, particularly after the suspicious Reichstag fire of February 27, 1933. In 1933, Göring established the first state-controlled concentration camps, and he organized the dreaded Gestapo. Finally, in the summer of 1934, Göring helped Hitler consolidate his power in the Nazi Party by directing the purge of suspected supporters of Ernst Röhm in Prussia.

After Göring relinquished his control of the Gestapo and the concentration camps to Heinrich Himmler's Schutzstaffel (SS) in 1934, he focused his interests primarily on the air force (Luftwaffe), German economic preparations for war, and Eastern Europe. Although Göring had been appointed Reich commissioner for air transport in January, 1933, it was not until March, 1935, when Hitler announced Germany's official establishment of the Luftwaffe, that Göring was named commander in chief of the air force. Göring was committed to a massive rearmament program in anticipation of a major conflict by the mid-1940's. He was appointed director of the Office of Raw Materials and Foreign Exchange in April, 1936, to deal with Germany's foreign currency crisis. Named head of the Four Year Plan on October 18, 1936, Göring supported a policy of autarchy that would permit massive German rearmament free from foreign economic pressures. In June, 1937, the first "Reichswerke Hermann Göring," a state-controlled iron and steel complex, was opened in Salzgitter, Braunschweig.

Göring also took advantage of the official anti-Jewish pogroms in November, 1938, to exclude Jews completely from the economy and to expropriate their property. His repeated trips to Eastern and Southeastern Europe and his key role in the German annexation of Austria in March, 1938, helped to increase Germany's economic power. By 1938, Göring controlled nearly two thirds of industrial investments in Germany. After the outbreak of war in 1939, the "Reichswerke Hermann Göring" were used to expand Göring's economic power in Europe.

Göring accumulated a plethora of titles between 1933 and 1940, ranging from Master of the Hunt and Reichs Forest Manager to Reich Marshal, the highest military rank in Germany. Göring failed to gain the post of Minister of War after he had helped to engineer the purge of both General Werner von Blomberg and General Werner von Fritsch in early 1938. Nevertheless, by 1938 Göring was at the height of power and prestige and, unlike many other Nazi leaders, he was enormously popular with the public. Though he held no major party position, Göring was named Hitler's successor in a secret decree on December 19, 1934, an appointment that was publicly acknowledged on September 1, 1939, and again on June 29, 1941. Together with his second wife, the actress Emmy Sonnemann, whom he had married on April 11, 1935, Göring hosted many of the official state ceremonies of the Third Reich. To complete his person-

al triumphs, on June 2, 1938, his only child, Edda, was born.

Göring participated in the negotiations leading to the Munich Agreement in September, 1938, but he was not consulted before the German occupation of Prague in March, 1939, or later during the preparations leading to the Barbarossa Plan for the invasion of Russia. Once war erupted in September, 1939, however, Göring was named Chairman of the Ministerial Defense Council. He expanded his economic empire into Eastern Europe, signed orders on October 7, 1939, giving Himmler special powers in the East, and in July, 1941, delegated to Reinhard Heydrich the task of finding a so-called final solution to the Jewish problem. For his personal enjoyment, Göring cleared the population from parts of the forest of Bialowiez to establish a personal hunting reserve and looted and purchased art treasures from all parts of Europe.

The failure of the Luftwaffe between 1940 and 1942 at Dunkirk, during the Battle of Britain, and at Stalingrad, undermined Göring's position with Hitler. The inability of the Luftwaffe to protect German cities from massive Allied air attacks, the appalling transportation system, and the totally inadequate armament production caused Hitler to lose all confidence in Göring. Even an enemy spy organization, the Red Orchestra, was discovered operating out of the Air Ministry in late 1942. Beginning in early 1942, Hitler began to relieve Göring of control over both armament production and the transportation system and assigned these tasks to Albert Speer. No longer an intimate part of Hitler's entourage and scolded by Hitler in August, 1944, for being lazy, the increasingly obese Göring, who consumed paracodeine pills daily, retreated to his self-indulgent private life at Karinhall and castle Veldenstein. Before seeking refuge in Bavaria, Göring visited Hitler in Berlin for the last time on April 20, 1945. Three days later, after informing Berlin of his intentions to assume command in Germany, Göring was stripped of all of his titles and arrested by the SS. In his last testament on April 29, 1945, Hitler expelled Göring from the Nazi Party. Arrested by the Americans in May, 1945, Göring was tried and convicted at Nürnberg for his part in the war crimes committed by the Third Reich. Although Göring reasserted some of his old confidence and mental agility during the trial, he committed suicide on October 15, 1946, and so escaped the hangman.

Summary

Both cunning and brutal in furthering his egotistical interests, Hermann Göring could charm people and present a good-natured, jovial image to the public. His personality was certainly influenced by the unusual family situation he experienced as a child, but his attraction to the Nazi movement was typical of many former German junior officers whose military careers had been disrupted by Germany's defeat in 1918. Göring detested Marxism but he was not a doctrinaire anti-Semite like Himmler. He did not hesitate to expropriate Jews, and he delegated the task of finding a solution to the "Jewish problem" to the dreaded Heydrich.

Göring was completely loyal to Hitler, who, in turn, valued his advice during domestic and international crises between 1932 and 1938. Never a leading party functionary, Göring totally depended on Hitler for his state powers in the Third Reich. He was neither a conservative nor a moderating influence on Hitler. Indeed, his military and economic policies threatened the influence of both private industry and traditional military elites in Germany.

Göring shared Hitler's goal of world power, even if he was apprehensive when war broke out in 1939. The failure of the Luftwaffe and armament production after 1939 was a result of Göring's ineffective leadership. Like Hitler, he disliked a routine work schedule, and he never committed himself to details. Overwhelmed by his numerous offices, Göring delegated responsibility for the implementation of general plans to subordinates who were either weak or unqualified. For both public and private reasons, Hitler allowed Göring to remain his appointed successor until April 23, 1945, when the bond between these two men was finally severed.

Bibliography

Davidson, Eugene. *The Trial of the Germans.* New York: Macmillan, 1966; London: University of Missouri Press, 1997. Chapter three is devoted to Göring's role in the Third Reich, his complicity in the Nazi crimes, and his behavior and defense at Nürnberg.

Gilbert, G. M. "Hermann Goering, Amiable Psychopath." *Journal of Abnormal and Social Psychology* 43 (April, 1948): 211-229. The author relies on his experiences as prison psychologist at Nürnberg in 1945 and 1946. He reviews Göring's personal history and concludes that by the time Göring reached his early adolescence he was a psychopath with "infantile ego-drives."

Gritzbach, Erich. *Hermann Goering: The Man and His Work.* Translated by Gerald Griffin. London: Hurst and Blackett, 1939; New York: AMS Press, 1973. The official biography of Göring, written by his personal chief of staff. Well illustrated, each chapter is devoted to one specific aspect or activity of Göring's life.

Irving, David. *Göring: A Biography.* London: Macmillan, and New York: Morrow, 1989. The author of several popular biographies of leaders and soldiers of the Third Reich, Irvin blames Epenstein for the weaknesses of Göring's character. The book offers a wealth of information about Göring's personal life, but the conclusion that Göring was unaware of the mass murder of Jews is rejected by scholars.

Lee, Asher. *Göring: Air Leader.* London: Duckworth, and New York: Hippocrene, 1972. This is a short but well-illustrated book by a former Royal Air Force intelligence officer. Although the author praises Göring's understanding of tactical air power, he argues that Göring failed to understand strategic air power.

Mosley, Leonard. *The Reich Marshal: A Biography of Herman Goering.* London: Weidenfeld and Nicolson, and New York: Doubleday, 1974. The author of this wordy biography, which is aimed at the general reader, was a British correspondent in Berlin in 1938. This is not a political biography but rather an attempt to discover Göring's "true identity" by emphasizing personal details of Göring's life and his entourage.

Overy, Richard, J. *Goering: The 'Iron Man.'* London and Boston: Routledge, 1984. This is the best and most reliable scholarly work in English on Göring's role in the Third Reich. The notes, bibliography, and illustrations are immensely valuable.

Steinhoff, Johannes. *The Last Chance: The Pilots' Plot Against Göring 1944-1945.* Translated by J. A. Underwood. London: Hutchinson, 1977. Steinhoff was a highly decorated German fighter pilot in World War II. He describes his experiences as a pilot and a wounded prisoner of war between October, 1944, and September, 1945. Most interesting is his discussion of the unsuccessful attempt of some fighter pilots to have Göring removed as leader of the German air force in late 1944.

Swearingen, Ben. E. *The Mystery of Hermann Goering's Suicide.* San Diego: Harcourt Brace, 1985; London: Hale, 1987. The author refutes the official findings of October, 1946, which concluded that Göring had hidden poison in the toilet in his prison cell. Swearingen argues that the American lieutenant Jack Wheelis was so charmed by Göring that he allowed him to go to the baggage room and retrieve a vial of poison from his personal luggage.

Johnpeter Horst Grill

MAXIM GORKY
Aleksey Maksimovich Peshkov

Born: March 28, 1868; Nizhni Novgorod, Russia
Died: June 18, 1936; Gorki, near Moscow, U.S.S.R.
Areas of Achievement: Literature and social reform
Contribution: Gorky is recognized as the founding father of Soviet literature, influencing the development of the Soviet short story and the proletarian novel and drama. His reminiscences of both Anton Chekhov and Leo Tolstoy give valuable, insightful observations about two older contemporaries. Equally important is his contribution to the Bolshevik revolutionary movement as one of its chief supporters and journalists. Because of his close associations with Vladimir Ilich Lenin, Leon Trotsky, and Joseph Stalin, he became the official cultural spokesman for the new government.

Early Life

Aleksey Maksimovich Peshkov was born on March 28, 1868, in Nizhni Novgorod, a city which once expelled him but which Stalin later renamed Gorki in honor of its most famous son. Gorky's father, an upholsterer, died of cholera when Gorky was only four, and his mother took him with her to live with her parents, the Kashirins. From his earliest days, young Gorky suffered the harshest and most brutal experiences. The Kashirins were cantankerous, depraved, and mercenary. His life with them was a miserable nightmare. Except for his grandmother, the household radiated hostility. At times his grandfather beat him until he was unconscious. This youthful suffering implanted in him a lasting empathy for the pain and misfortunes of others.

When he was nine, his mother died, and his grandfather drove him from the household, telling him that he must go out into the world and make his own way. For fifteen years he wandered through Russia supporting himself by working in a boot shop and as an office boy, a railway porter, dishwasher on barges along the Volga, longshoreman, janitor, and laborer in a basement bakery.

While with the Kashirins, he had received his only formal education. He sought to continue to educate himself by reading voraciously and experimenting with writing. During those years, mixing with outcasts who were seeking to eke out their existence through the most degrading work, he became disillusioned with the whole social structure. Life was unfolding before him as an unending chain of hostility and cruelty. He was distressed at the sordid, unceasing struggle by so many for worthless objects. Yet through these observations, his personal experiences, and his reading he was growing mentally and gaining a greater self-assurance.

At one point, however, when only nineteen, he became so despondent that he unsuccessfully attempted suicide. For weeks he was in the hospital recuperating from a wounded lung, perforated by the bullet. This experience was the turning point in his life. He left the hospital consumed by a radical rebellion against the social order. The next year he joined a subversive Marxist group and was arrested while involved in their activities. From that point on, he was under police surveillance. In 1892, he published his first short story, "Makar Chudra," in a local newspaper, using his pseudonym, Maxim Gorky, which means "Maxim the Bitter One." In 1895, another story, "Chelkash," was published by a prominent journal in St. Petersburg. Three years later an anthology of his stories appeared. Immediately the two foremost living Russian authors, Tolstoy and Chekhov, recognized that a new young literary talent had joined their company.

Life's Work

The publication in 1898 of the first volume of his stories, *Ocherki i rasskazy* (partial translation, *Selected Short Stories*, 1970), was a tremendous success. He had depicted characters even lower on the social scale than Fyodor Dostoevski's city dwellers: the peasant, the workingman, downtrodden tramps, factory workers, and social outcasts, living in terrible squalor and dwelling on the fringe of society. His stories concerned the most elemental passions and the struggle for survival. They were written in the language of the proletariat. The public received them with rapture, and it was natural that he should become the spokesman for the rising proletariat.

Gorky was also interested in the theater. In 1898, he had established a rustic theater in the Ukraine. He had also developed a warm relationship with Chekhov and through him was introduced to Kon-

stantin Stanislavsky of the Moscow Art Theatre, who urged him to write a drama concerning the proletariat, something completely new for his theater. The result was *Na dne* (1902; *The Lower Depths*, 1906). After radical cuts, the czarist government permitted its production, thinking it would fail. Rather, it was received with enthusiastic applause, an enthusiasm that spread throughout Europe and across the Atlantic.

Shortly after his attempted suicide in 1888, Gorky came under the influence of Mikhail Antonovich Romas, the Populist revolutionary who influenced his social and political views. Because of his involvement in subversive Marxist activities, he was arrested and imprisoned a number of times. In 1899, he became the literary editor of the Marxist newspaper *Zhizn* (life), in which he expressed his concerns about social injustice. After the success of *The Lower Depths*, he had become a national hero and was elected to the Imperial Academy of Sciences. At the request of Czar Nicholas II, the appointment was withdrawn. In objection to this insult to Gorky, both Vladimir Korolenko and Chekhov resigned from the academy. In 1905, Gorky assisted Father George Gapon in the abortive revolution for which he was imprisoned in the Peter and Paul Fortress. During that year, he first met and began a lifelong friendship with Lenin. In December, he was the moving spirit behind the barricade fighters in their armed rising in Moscow.

Gorky's growing fame led to a triumphal tour through Europe and an enthusiastic reception in New York City, where he had been sent to raise funds for the Bolshevik cause and to undermine the czar's efforts to procure a loan. The United States turned on him, however, when his enemies revealed that his companion, the actress Maria Fyodorovna Andreyevna, was not his wife. He retaliated by denouncing New York as "the city of the yellow devil" and by writing several articles against American capitalism. While in the United States, he also began work on his most famous novel *Mat* (1906; *The Mother*, 1906), which, because of its excellent propaganda for socialism, was later acclaimed as the model for Socialist Realism.

In 1907, when Gorky returned to Europe because of his trouble with the czarist regime, he settled on Capri as a political émigré. Until 1913, his Villa Serafina was to be a center for revolutionary activities. Lenin and Leon Davidovich Trotsky were his guests. There he trained writers and politicians sympathetic to the Bolshevik cause, used his income to further the revolutionary movement, and helped to train its leaders.

Gorky returned to Russia in December, 1913, after the czar granted amnesty to seditious writers. During the next four years, he was hard at work producing propaganda to undermine Russia's involvement in World War I and to support the revolution that followed. After the revolution, he assisted in shaping and spreading the official philosophy. With several others in 1917, he began publishing *Novaya zhizn* (new life), a newspaper devoted to propaganda for socialism that was extremely popular among the Russian intelligentsia. His friendship with Lenin continued, but Gorky was growing deeply concerned about the ruthlessness of some of the Bolshevik leaders. Once he criticized Lenin's "Communist hysteria" and Lenin himself as "the mad chemist." At this time, Lenin and Trotsky became concerned about Gorky's more moderate approach to socialism. Finally, in 1918, the new government forced *Novaya zhizn* to close, and, fearing for Gorky's safety, Lenin in 1921 encouraged him to leave Russia to recuperate from a serious lung ailment.

By 1920, Gorky was beginning to admire Lenin as a world revolutionary and to reestablish his friendship with him, but many of the Bolshevik leaders still distrusted Gorky. Much of the time from 1921 until 1928 he was abroad, primarily in Sorrento. Yet, because of his association with Lenin and later with Stalin, he had a considerable influence on the cultural and literary life of Russia during the turbulent years of the Revolution and the following two decades. As early as 1919, he edited the publication of a series of masterpieces of world literature and in 1923 objected to the removal from libraries of certain Western classics that were considered counterrevolutionary. He headed a cultural committee to protect Russia's museums and works of art and presided over commissions to improve the living conditions of artists, scholars, and writers. Many of these and others who belonged to the intelligentsia owed their survival to his intervention during the Stalin purges. He was especially encouraging to the Serapion Brothers, a fellowship of young authors, several of whom acknowledge his influence on their careers.

At Stalin's invitation, Gorky returned to Russia in 1932 as the entire nation joined in a jubilee to celebrate the fortieth anniversary of his first publication. Numerous honors were heaped upon him, including the coveted Order of Lenin. The Literary Institute of Moscow was renamed for him, as were numerous libraries, theaters, and schools. In 1934, he received the first membership in the Union of Soviet Writers and presented the opening address. He was the moving spirit behind the union's adoption of Socialist Realism, which became the approved official method for all Soviet writers. The union used his works as the chief models for their new literary theory.

Although Gorky was at first optimistic about Stalin as the leader of the Soviet Union, he became increasingly fearful of him and refused to write a laudatory eulogy about him, as he had done for Lenin. In secret, he used his influence, when possible, to moderate the brutalities of Stalin's dictatorship. Stalin, in turn, became distrustful of Gorky and in 1935 refused to grant him permission to travel to Italy for his health. From that time on, Gorky's freedom of movement was strictly controlled. At the time of his death on June 18, 1936, it was rumored that he was a victim of Stalin's purges. Although this rumor has been disputed, it was seemingly verified in a treason trial in 1938. Notable figures of the state were present for the funeral in Red Square—Stalin, Vyacheslav Molotov, and Nikita S. Khrushchev—and his ashes were sealed in the Kremlin wall. For more than ten years, he had been at work on his most enthusiastic work, *Zhizn Klima Samgina* (1927-1936; *The Life of Klim Samgin*, 1930-1938), a four-volume epic set in Russia from the assassination of Czar Alexander II to the death of Lenin. He left it unfinished at his death.

Summary

At the time of his death, Maxim Gorky was considered the dean of Soviet literature, the writer with the greatest influence upon other Russian authors. This influence outlived him and even extended beyond the Russian borders. For example, in 1932, while developing his own dramatic style, Bertolt Brecht adapted Gorky's *The Mother* for the stage. Also it is usually conceded that *The Iceman Cometh* (1946), which ushered in Eugene O'Neill's last and most powerful period, was influenced by *The Lower Depths*. In the West, however, only a few of his creative works remain influential—several short stories, such as the immortal "Dvadtsat'shest' i odna" (1899; "Twenty-six Men and a Girl," 1902), and *The Lower Depths*, which retains a significant position in the Western theatrical repertoire. His autobiographical writings and his literary portraits of his contemporaries—Tolstoy, Chekhov, and Aleksandr Blok—are considered his supreme achievements.

His compassion for the downtrodden and belief in their ability to win through a greater dignity and worth not only permeated his works but also motivated his revolutionary activities. This compassion and faith also stirred him to use his influence to denounce the Bolshevik excesses, to improve the lot of starving artists during the first decade of Soviet rule, and to moderate, when possible, the Stalin purges. It is likely that his continuing reputation will rest upon his role in preparing for the Revolution and his efforts to temper the excesses of the new regime during the aftermath of the Revolution. Chekhov, who first recognized Gorky's worth as an author, foresaw such a future reputation for Gorky and wrote: "It seems to me that a time will come when Gorky's works will be forgotten, but he himself will hardly be forgotten in a thousand years."

Bibliography

Borras, F. M. *Maxim Gorky the Writer: An Interpretation.* Oxford: Clarendon Press, 1967. Analyzes Gorky's ideas and outlook; discusses his works according to genre; studies the appeal of Gorky's works to both the Soviet and Western mind; includes a biographical chronicle and the chronology of Gorky's principal works.

Clark, Barrett H. "Maxim Gorky." *Intimate Portraits.* New York: Dramatists Play Service, 1951. The first chapter is a memoir of the author's visit with Gorky in 1923. It presents Gorky's views about his own works, Tolstoy, and American writers, including O'Neill, whom he found interesting but "a little bit too Russian."

Clowes, Edith W. *Maksim Gorky: A Reference Guide.* Boston: Hall, 1987. The definitive bibliographical study of Gorky in English. Includes primary and secondary works with brief notes on the secondary. Introduction studies the ambivalent aspects of Gorky's art and life. Organized chronologically with an excellent index according to author and subject.

Figes, Orlando. "Maxim Gorky and the Russian Revolution." *History Today* 46, no. 6 (June, 1996). Examines allegations that Stalin may have ordered Gorky's death.

Gorky, Maxim. *Autobiography of Maxim Gorky.* Translated by Isidor Schneider. New York: Citadel Press, 1949. Covers the first twenty-odd years of his life and gives insights into the formative experiences and people that prepared him to become the spokesman for the proletariat.

Habermann, Gerhard E. *Maksim Gorki.* New York: Ungar, 1971. Emphasizes in particular the factors contributing to Gorky's political development and to his involvement in social causes. Concludes with a chronology of his life and significant contemporary events in Russia.

Kaun, Alexander. *Maxim Gorky and His Russia.* New York: Cape, 1931; London: Cape, 1932. Useful early biography of Gorky up to 1929. Based on Gorky's autobiographical materials and long interviews with Gorky. Appendices include an essay on Gorky's visit to the United States and a letter from Trotsky about his concerns about *Novaya zhizn,* for which Gorky was an editor.

Levin, Dan. *Stormy Petrel: The Life and Work of Maxim Gorky.* New York: Appleton, 1965; London: Muller, 1967. Studies the cultural, social, and political aspects of Gorky's life and gives personal reactions to Gorky's works, including works frequently overlooked. Contains a helpful index of references to Gorky's writings.

Muchnic, Helen. "Maxim Gorky." In *From Gorky to Pasternak: Six Writers in Soviet Russia.* New York: Random House, 1961; London: Methuen, 1963. Discusses Gorky's humanistic presentation of truth and reality, a contrast between "a truth that 'saved' and a truth that 'killed.' " Evaluates his portraits drawn from life as superior to his creative work. Sympathetic analysis of Gorky's literary strengths and weaknesses.

Segel, Harold B. *Twentieth-Century Russian Drama: From Gorky to the Present.* New York: Columbia University Press, 1979. Most detailed study of Gorky as a dramatist. Includes two chapters on Gorky's plays, those before the Revolution and those of the Soviet period. Contrasts the development and techniques of Chekhov and Gorky as dramatists.

Wolfe, Bertram D. *The Bridge and the Abyss: The Troubled Friendship of Maxim Gorky and V. I. Lenin.* London: Pall Mall Press, and New York: Praeger, 1967. Contrasts the political views of Gorky and Lenin as well as their relationships. Epilogue discusses Gorky's three portraits of Lenin. Includes selected bibliography of both Lenin and Gorky.

James Smythe

BILLY GRAHAM

Born: November 7, 1918; near Charlotte, North Carolina

Areas of Achievement: Diplomacy, and religion and theology

Contribution: Friend and confidante of presidents, popes, and world figures, Billy Graham stands as the twentieth century's best-known and most effective evangelist as well as a rigorous, though unofficial, diplomat. His mass meetings, attended by hundreds of thousands of individuals and televised to reach millions more, have presented the tenets of Christianity on a worldwide scale.

Early Life

The first of four children, William Franklin Graham, Jr., was born November 7, 1918, on a dairy farm just outside Charlotte, North Carolina, to William Franklin and Morrow Coffey Graham. As a boy, Graham crackled with nervous energy and fought a slight stutter. By age twelve the thin, wiry youth stood a head taller than fellow students, with deep-set and intense blue eyes, sharp and jutting features, and thick, wavy blond hair. His upbeat personality made him a favorite with peers and adults alike.

William and Morrow raised their children in the Southern Presbyterian Church. Although young Graham memorized the shorter catechism and attended church every Sunday, he did not feel particularly religious. In school, the extremely likeable young man appeared to be an indifferent student, to the point that one of his teachers declared to Morrow that "Billy Frank will never amount to a thing."

The year that Graham turned sixteen, traveling evangelist Mordecai Ham set up his revival tent in Charlotte. Although young Graham gave little credence to evangelists, believing that they merely played with people's emotions, he accepted when one of his father's employees asked him to attend the revival. He went back every night thereafter. In one of the last revival meetings, the young man acknowledged his vital transformation: He responded to Reverend Ham's invitation to give his life to the Lord. Later Graham noted that he felt no emotion and shed no tears but went home and made a simple declaration on his knees that he wanted to dedicate his life to Christianity.

Graham spent the summer after high school graduation as a door-to-door salesman for the Fuller Brush Company, capturing the company's award for top sales in North and South Carolina. Graham said later that evangelism and sales had certain parallels, among them the presentation of the product.

In September, 1936, Graham enrolled at Bob Jones College in Cleveland, Tennessee, lasting one semester at the ultraconservative school before transferring to the more relaxed atmosphere of the Florida Bible Institute in Tampa. He graduated in 1940 as an ordained Baptist minister with several years of preaching behind him and enrolled as a second-semester freshman at Chicago's Wheaton College. In his first year he met and courted fellow student Ruth McCue Bell, daughter of Southern Presbyterian missionaries to China. Graham graduated from Wheaton in June, 1943, with a bachelor's degree in anthropology and married Ruth Bell in November of that year.

Life's Work

At the end of 1944, Graham joined the staff of the fledgling organization Youth for Christ (YFC), whose evangelistic teams visited high school and college campuses across the United States and Europe. In 1948 Graham accepted the invitation of W. B. Riley to succeed him as president of Northwestern Schools in Minneapolis, Minnesota, making Graham the youngest college president in the United States at that time. He held the post until February, 1952.

While at Northwestern Schools, Graham conducted evangelistic meetings in Los Angeles, California, and several New England cities. His 1949 Los Angeles crusade made Graham a national figure. As the legend goes, newspaper publisher William Randolph Hearst ordered a reporter to "puff Graham." The resulting publicity made the young evangelist front-page news in Hearst's national newspaper chain. He appeared on the cover of the November 14, 1949, issue of *Time* magazine. Billy Graham Films (renamed World Wide Pictures) was incorporated to film the crusades and Christian-oriented drama. (Graham had already turned down a major picture contract with Paramount.) After Los Angeles, Graham contracted to conduct major crusades in Portland, Oregon; Atlanta, Georgia; and Minneapolis. By December, 1950, cumulative crusade attendance figures had passed 1.5 million. Monthly crusades filled 1951 and 1952.

As attendance at evangelistic crusades mounted and Graham's weekly radio program, *The Hour of Decision*, went on the air, Graham had to address the issue of disbursing the substantial donations from crusades and his growing radio audience. On the advice of Northwestern Schools' financial officer, the Billy Graham Evangelistic Association (BGEA) incorporated in late 1950 in St. Paul, Minnesota, for the purpose of negotiating contracts and receiving donations. The first BGEA directors—Cliff Barrows, Grady Wilson, George Wilson, and Graham—separated themselves from crusade funding by becoming salaried employees of the BGEA with salaries comparable to those of ministers of large city churches. To underscore the Graham organization's integrity, BGEA made its financial records public.

After the 1949 Los Angeles Crusade, Graham and his team accepted President Harry S. Truman's invitation to visit the White House. In 1952, Graham met Dwight D. Eisenhower and helped persuade him to run for president. Thereafter Graham and Eisenhower frequently played golf together during Eisenhower's two terms of office. The tradi-

tion of the Washington, D.C., National Prayer Breakfasts began during Eisenhower's presidency.

In 1954, the nationally known Graham team planned a crusade in response to an invitation from the Evangelical Alliance of Britain. The London organizing committee secured Harringay Arena, a twelve-thousand-seat stadium north of London, for three months. The English press, predicting failure on a grand scale, ridiculed the Americans who "came save to Britain." However, for nearly four months, thousands of Britons filled Harringay night after night; hundreds made their way forward daily at Graham's invitation to "receive Christ." Relenting, the press became friendly, and church attendance climbed. Winston Churchill invited Graham to 10 Downing Street for tea and conversation. As the London crusade ended, invitations to hold crusades poured in from cities on every continent: Harringay had catapulted Graham to worldwide notice. After the Harringay Crusade came a rapid tour through Europe: Helsinki, Stockholm, Copenhagen, Amsterdam, and Berlin. Thousands crowded stadiums to hear Graham speak. Tremendous publicity accompanied the crusades, some of it favorable, some not. However, all the critics found the crusades newsworthy.

For the rest of 1954 and 1955, the Graham evangelistic team worked in Scotland and continental Europe. In 1956, they traveled to Asia: India, the Philippines, Hong Kong, Formosa, Japan, and Korea. Stadiums continued to fill. In most countries, heads of state and business and religious leaders requested that Graham and his team visit for informal, off-the-record meetings. News from crusade sites, both religious and political, became familiar and customary to millions of readers and viewers; Graham became an "ambassador at large" for his religion and for his country.

Along with receiving worldwide crusade coverage, Graham began writing as well. His syndicated newspaper column, entitled *My Answer*, reached a daily circulation exceeding twenty million readers. In 1953, Graham published *Peace with God*, an immediate best-seller that sold millions of copies and was translated into fifty languages. In 1956, Graham launched the highly respected *Christianity Today* magazine. *Decision* magazine followed in 1960. Other publications include more than one dozen books, among them *The Secret of Happiness* (1955), *World Aflame* (1965), *Angels: God's Secret Agents* (1975), *How to Be Born Again* (1977), *Approaching Hoofbeats* (1983), *Storm Warning*

(1992), and *Just As I Am: The Autobiography of Billy Graham* (1997).

From 1957 through 1960, Graham and his evangelistic team held invited crusades in New York City and then in Australia. Between the Australian and succeeding crusades throughout Africa, the Grahams met Queen Elizabeth II in Buckingham Palace for tea. As sovereign, the queen expressed deep interest in descriptions of Australian crusades. After 1958, a nonstop schedule of crusades faced the team, which had expanded to include many more ministers and lay people than the original four. They visited countries in the Caribbean, returned to hold meetings in Chicago, then turned their attention to South America. Later in the 1960's, Graham and his team visited the Soviet Union as tourists, but no invitations to mount a crusade materialized. However, in 1967, at the request of the Yugoslavian Protestant Churches, Graham preached for the first time in a Communist country.

As preceding presidents had done, both President John F. Kennedy and Vice President Lyndon B. Johnson invited Graham's counsel. Graham's friendship with Johnson continued after Johnson left office, with Graham eventually speaking at Johnson's funeral. Probably the closest and most remarked of Graham's presidential relationships was with Richard M. Nixon. Because Graham had known Nixon's parents, his friendship with Nixon predated Nixon's 1968 presidency. Graham maintained that friendship during the Watergate crisis and Nixon's resignation. As he had done for Johnson, Graham spoke at Nixon's funeral. In their turns, Presidents Gerald Ford, Jimmy Carter, Ronald Reagan, George Bush, and Bill Clinton extended White House hospitality to the Graham family and invited Graham's counsel and prayers.

Summary

Billy Graham, twentieth century evangelical Christianity's most visible figure, took literally the biblical mandate to preach the Gospel to all the world. As he did so, his name became a household word. Late in the 1990's, Graham bequeathed the management of the BGEA to his oldest son, William Franklin Graham, III. As of 1995, the BGEA had 525 employees, revenues of eighty-eight million dollars, and a mailing list of 2.7 million active donors. The BGEA's highly effective follow-up program for converts, in addition to its advance organization of crusade personnel, funding, and locations, has long been recognized as part of Graham's legacy to world evangelism.

Bibliography

Cornwell, Patricia. *Ruth, A Portrait.* New York: Doubleday, 1997; London: Hodder and Stoughton, 1998. Written by family friend and popular mystery author Patricia Cornwell, this book traces Ruth Graham's life with Billy Graham and presents a very personal picture of the evangelist. The volume includes illustrations and an index.

Eskridge, Larry. "'One Way': Billy Graham, the Jesus Generation, and the Idea of an Evangelical Youth Culture." *Church History* 67, no. 1 (March, 1998). Considers Graham's attempts to bridge the gap between parents and children in the 1970's through his endorsement of the Jesus movement.

Frady, Marshall. *Billy Graham: A Parable of American Righteousness.* London: Hodder and Stoughton, and Boston: Little Brown, 1979. This biography is written by a journalist from a secular point of view and is probably the least flattering of the biographical volumes available.

Graham, Billy. "Billy Graham's Challenge for the Third Millennium: Recovering the Primacy of Evangelism." *Christianity Today* 41, no. 14 (December 8, 1997). Discusses Graham's beliefs regarding the factors that will take evangelism into the twenty-first century, including overcoming denominational differences to present a united front against the growth of non-Christian religions.

————. *Just As I Am: The Autobiography of Billy Graham.* London and New York: HarperCollins, 1997. Graham's own view of his life and accomplishments contains personal anecdotes, accounts of his relationships with famous world figures, and an almost daily record of his many crusades. The 760 pages include illustrations, a detailed table of contents, an index, and a complete list of crusades.

Martin, William. *A Prophet With Honor: The Billy Graham Story.* New York: Morrow, 1991. This volume is organized by subject areas of interest to the author.

Pollock, John. *Billy Graham: The Authorized Biography.* New York: McGraw-Hill, 1966. This straightforward, objective chronology was written in Graham's forty-seventh year as his worldwide influence began to solidify. It includes an index and illustrations.

———. *Billy Graham, Evangelist to the World: An Authorized Biography of the Decisive Years*. San Francisco: Harper, 1979. Pollock continues the biographical account from 1970 to 1979. This illustrated volume mainly covers crusades and Graham's political acquaintances.

Wirt, Sherwood Eliot. *Billy: A Personal Look at Billy Graham, the World's Best-Loved Evangelist*. Wheaton, Ill.: Crossway, 1997. This illustrated, annotated, and indexed book was written by a long-time Graham acquaintance who also edits *Decision* magazine.

Barbara C. Stanley

KATHARINE GRAHAM

Born: June 16, 1917; New York, New York
Areas of Achievement: Publishing and journalism
Contribution: The only woman to serve as publisher of a major American newspaper during the twentieth century, Graham built *The Washington Post* into a national institution and helped bring down an American president.

Early Life

Katharine Meyer was born on June 16, 1917, into financial power, social privilege, and public life. The fourth child of Eugene Meyer and Agnes Ernst Meyer, Katharine had almost limitless options when she graduated from the University of Chicago in 1938 after spending her first two years of college at Vassar. By numerous accounts, her father was one of the more remarkable Americans of his time—a man who consciously chose to marry a white Anglo-Saxon Protestant (WASP) so his children would not have to fight the anti-Semitism that stung him at an early age; a man who had amassed a fortune of more than $50 million in careers in merchandising and in investment by 1917, when he liquidated his holdings to embark on government service; and a man who had successfully pursued more than a half-dozen different careers by 1933, when at fifty-seven years old, and almost as a hobby, he purchased at a bankruptcy sale a discredited newspaper, *The Washington Post*.

As her father pursued the task of bringing the *Post* to a level of journalistic respectability, Katharine—alone among the Meyer children—chose journalism as a career, working initially as a reporter on the *San Francisco News* for a year before joining *The Washington Post* in 1939. According to Carol Felsenthal's biography of Katharine Graham, her father had mailed her daily issues of the *Post* throughout her stay at the University of Chicago, where she had gone to pursue her interest in journalism after two unchallenging years at Vassar College. The year on the West Coast served as something of a first and last apprenticeship before joining the *Post*.

Although Katharine's entry in *Who's Who in America* indicates that she served on the editorial staff of *The Washington Post* from 1939 to 1945, and although she did throw herself wholeheartedly into that job upon her arrival there, Felsenthal maintains that her interest in a career in journalism ended the moment she met her future husband, Philip L. Graham, one of Washington's most eligible bachelors and a man endowed with a commanding presence who could also be engagingly charming. They married on June 5, 1940, within six months of their first meeting. Katharine Meyer had found a mainline WASP to marry. More important, in Philip Graham, a former editor of *The Harvard Law Review*, she had also found a man to whom her father would turn to manage the *Post*.

Life's Work

Her marriage lasted for nearly a quarter of a century, but few of those years appear to have been easy ones for Katharine Graham. Her husband was allegedly capable of thinking of her and his father-in-law in terms of vile ethnic slurs even as he loved the one and respected the success of the other. Over time, he became a philanderer, separated from his wife only to return to her later, took over the *Post* and expanded its operations by opening overseas bureaus in 1957, and threw himself increasingly into national politics as an undisguised booster of Lyndon Johnson in the latter's struggle with John Kennedy for the Democratic Party's 1960 presidential nomination. Bouts of depression and self-doubt increasingly injected themselves into his otherwise often manic lifestyle to the point that he was finally willing to seek institutionalized treatment.

For her part, Katharine Graham concentrated on retiring from her involvement in the paper and into private life, and on rearing their four children, a daughter, Elizabeth, and sons Donald, William, and Stephen. Then, on August 3, 1963, Philip Graham checked out of the Chestnut Lodge treatment center to spend a day with his wife, played tennis with Katharine in the morning, and killed himself while she took an early afternoon nap. Katharine Meyer Graham in that moment became the head of *The Washington Post*.

As the newspaper's publisher, president (1963-1973, 1977), chairman of the board (1973-1993), and chief executive officer (1973-1991), Katharine Graham ran the *Post* for most of the next thirty years. During those decades, she continued and improved upon the efforts of first her father and then her husband to build the *Post* into a great journalistic institution and, eventually, into a profitable *Fortune 500* company. The task required consider-

able physical and emotional effort. As Kenneth Berents, a respected newspaper analyst, observed in *The New York Times* article (of September 10, 1993) covering Graham's formal retirement as the *Post*'s chairman of the board, Graham often spoke of herself as "an oddity [in a world dominated by men], and looked upon as such." Breaking down gender bias took time and diligence; however, as that time passed, she gained confidence in both her ability to manage the newspaper and in the men she chose to run it. By the time she began cutting back on her involvement in the operations of the *Post* and turned the publisher and chief executive responsibilities over to her son Donald (in 1979 and 1991, respectively), *The Washington Post* had become not only a world-class newspaper but also the centerpiece in a respected media conglomerate including the *International Herald Tribune* (on which Graham served as cochairman), *Newsweek* magazine, and cable and broadcast television properties. Not surprisingly, during those years—in Berents' words—Graham herself came to be viewed as "one of the industry's great ladies." Indeed, she had become the only woman to head a major

American newspaper. In 1998 she won a Pulitzer Prize for her autobiography *Personal History.*

Summary

Just as Katharine Graham broke new ground as a woman heading a media empire, so her newspaper constantly broke new ground in covering the news under her steadying influence, care in selecting the *Post*'s management team, and willingness to support her subordinates even when under tremendous pressure to do otherwise.

To write of these developments is to relive the America covered by the *Post* during Katharine Graham's directorship. The years following Graham's succession to the newspaper's leadership were turbulent ones for the United States, with Washington serving as the center stage in a changing America. Only months after her husband committed suicide, President John F. Kennedy was assassinated in Dallas. Then came the Lyndon Johnson-Barry Goldwater campaign of 1964 and the buildup of American military forces in Vietnam the following year. Civil rights marches declined, antiwar protests commenced, and the cities began to explode. The Tet offensive in Vietnam in early 1968 persuaded President Johnson not to seek re-election; Robert Kennedy was killed in June campaigning for the Democratic Party's nomination to succeed him. In between, Martin Luther King, Jr., was also assassinated, and the Washington riots that followed his assassination provided *The Washington Post* with a fast-breaking story quite literally on its doorsteps, complete with photo opportunities of machine-gun emplacements on the steps of the Capitol. Its coverage of the event was perhaps the key moment in the *Post*'s emergence among the elite national newspapers in the United States.

The Post remained in that company with its openly critical coverage of the Johnson and Nixon administrations' conduct of the Vietnam war and its publication in June of 1971 of "The Pentagon Papers." In fact, and much to the annoyance of Ben Bradlee, Graham's hand-picked editor of *The Washington Post*, *The New York Times* broke the story two days before the *Post* obtained its own copy of the documents chronicling America's often governmentally choreographed entry into the Vietnam war. By the time the case reached the Supreme Court to test the government's ability to squelch the publication of the documents on the grounds of national security considerations, *The Washington Post* had become an equal party to the action.

Graham's greatest impact on the newspaper and public affairs, however, was still to come—in the *Post*'s investigative coverage of a minor break-in conducted in the early morning hours of June 17, 1972, at the headquarters of the Democratic National Committee. *The Washington Post* would stay with that story long after other news organizations and newspapers had abandoned it. Requests to drop the story would come from such important personages as Secretary of State Henry Kissinger. Veiled and not-so-veiled threats of action against the *Post* and its media empire came from the offices of President Nixon's special counsel, Charles Colson, and from former Attorney General John Mitchell. Still, with the same determination she would elsewhere show in facing down strikers at her newspaper, Graham never wavered in her support of her staff. In the end, the trail led from Watergate to the White House, the affair cemented *The Washington Post*'s growing reputation for journalistic respectability and independence, and the *Post*'s coverage of the Watergate affair made celebrities out of Katharine Graham as well as

Ben Bradlee and the reporter team of Bob Woodward and Carl Bernstein. It was President Richard Nixon who would have to resign from office in disgrace, not the publisher of the *Post*.

Bibliography

Bernstein, Carl, and Bob Woodward. *All the President's Men.* New York: Simon and Schuster, and London: Secker and Warburg, 1974. No study of Katharine Graham and the *Post* would be complete without this rendition of the Watergate affair. The crucial decisions at the newspaper were not made by Mrs. Graham so much as by the executives she trusted and by whom she stood throughout their pursuit of the story.

Childs, Kelvin. "Kay Graham's Side of the Story." *Editor and Publisher* 130, no. 46 (November 15, 1997). Presents Graham's comments at the 1997 Southern Newspaper Publishers Association convention on her treatment by condescending executives and other topics.

Davis, Deborah. *Katharine the Great: Katharine Graham and Her "Washington Post" Empire.* 3d ed. New York: Sheridan Square Press, 1991. The third edition of a work that originally appeared in 1979, this book has been updated to cover Graham's years in the quasi-retirement that followed her 1979 decision to turn her publisher's duties over to her son Donald.

Diamond, Edwin. "Oh, Kay: The Unauthorized Graham." *New York* 26, no. 8 (February 22, 1993). Focuses on the unauthorized biography of Graham, which was published in 1992 despite her efforts to discourage the author.

Felsenthal, Carol. *Power, Privilege, and the "Post": The Katharine Graham Story.* New York: Putnam, 1993. Something of an unauthorized biography on Katharine Graham. Reputedly published without interviews with Graham (who was working on her memoirs), it was published shortly before her official retirement from *The Washington Post.*

Gilbert, Ben W., and the staff of *The Washington Post. Ten Blocks from the White House: Anatomy of the Washington Riots of 1968.* New York: Praeger, 1968; London: Pall Mall, 1969. The 1968 riots provided the *Post* with a major story several years before the flaps over the Pentagon Papers and the Watergate affair. This work provides a good account of how Graham's newspaper covered that story.

Sussman, Barry. *The Great Coverup: Nixon and the Scandal of Watergate*. New York: New American Library, 1974. A well-crafted, readable outsider's account of the Watergate scandal and the role of the *Post* and its management in the downfall of the Nixon administration.

Ungar, Sanford J. *The Papers and the Papers: An Account of the Legal and Political Battle over the Pentagon Papers*. New York: Dutton, 1972. An outstanding analysis of the struggle over the Pentagon Papers, this reprint of the 1972 book released by E. P. Dutton captures some of the drama behind the decision of both *The New York Times* and *The Washington Post* to publish the secret documents concerning the Vietnam War. The focus is on *The New York Times* as a party in the court case arising from the publication of the Pentagon Papers.

The Washington Post Staff. *The Fall of a President*. New York: Delacorte Press, 1974. An excellent collection of the *Post*'s coverage of the Watergate affair, from its early, limited reporting on the Watergate break-in to the House of Representatives' consideration of Articles of Impeachment against President Richard Nixon.

Joseph R. Rudolph, Jr.

MARTHA GRAHAM

Born: May 11, 1894; Allegheny, Pennsylvania
Died: April 1, 1991; New York, New York
Area of Achievement: Dance
Contribution: Graham is generally accepted as the greatest single figure in American modern dance.

Early Life

Although her name is virtually synonymous with modern dance, Martha Graham did not have a single dance lesson until she was twenty-two years old. Her father, George Graham, was a doctor who specialized in nervous disorders and, consequently, was intrigued by physical movement. He warned his daughters never to be dishonest because he would know they were lying by the tension in their bodies. Although he would not allow Martha to study ballet because of the social taboos of the era and on the pretext that it would interfere with her schoolwork, Martha credits her father with being her first dance teacher, for he taught her the importance of the body's language and of honesty.

George Graham was the son of an Irish immigrant, while Martha's mother, Jane Beers Graham, could trace her heritage back to Miles Standish and the *Mayflower.* Martha's upbringing consisted of a strict Puritan code of ethics, and she and her two younger sisters were required to attend church and daily prayers. As an outlet for their mischievousness, however, the sisters were permitted to play "dress up" and to create their own plays. Because she was a physically plain child, this early role playing gave Martha a means of escape as well as a means of channeling her explosive temper. As an adult, she would create her own brand of glamour, but the temper and the subsequent tantrums would only become more pronounced.

The young Martha was a voracious reader who appeared to be mesmerized by the drama of life and called to reveal its mysteries. One of these mysteries was the impact of ritual, and when the Grahams hired a nanny, Lizzie Pendergast, who took the girls with her to Catholic mass, Martha was fascinated by the ceremony and the music.

When Martha Graham was in her teens, her sister Mary was diagnosed with asthma, and, in an effort to seek a better climate, Jane Graham moved with the girls to Santa Barbara, California. Martha immediately acclimated to her new environment and was drawn to the pageantry of the Asian population in the area. This pageantry, coupled with the recollected Catholic mass, would eventually become the root of her creations.

Although she was still not allowed to study dance formally, Martha was active in other areas; in high school, she edited the literary magazine, acted in the school play, and played basketball. Many of these interests decreased in importance, however, when in 1911, Martha saw her first ballet, a performance by Ruth St. Denis at the Mason Opera House in Los Angeles. Martha memorized some of the moves, tried them at home, and sealed her fate. Even though her parents would not give their blessings to this chosen profession, Martha took her first step toward her career by giving up sports in order not to injure her legs.

In 1913, Martha enrolled in an arts-oriented junior college, the Cumnock School. With her father's reluctant assent, she studied acting, play writing, and dance. During her years at the Cumnock, two events took place which affected the course of her future. In 1914, George Graham died, leaving enough investments for his daughters to finish their educations, and, in 1915, Martha's idol, Ruth St. Denis, and her husband Ted Shawn opened a dance school in Los Angeles.

Immediately after being graduated from the Cumnock School, Martha auditioned for and was accepted to the Denishawn School. Denishawn was the most innovative training available, because St. Denis believed in teaching holistic dance, not merely ballet. Although Martha adored St. Denis, the feeling was not reciprocated, and she was sent to study with Ted Shawn. While working with Shawn, she performed the lead in *Serenata Morisca,* memorizing the steps after seeing them demonstrated only four times, and it became her trademark piece, transforming her from a student into a professional.

By 1918, she had become Shawn's principal teacher, and a dance he created especially for her marked her entry into modest fame. The dance was *Xochital,* about an assault on an Aztec maiden. Putting her emotional being into the performance, Graham was a terrifying figure of wildness and fury in defending her virtue, and often her partners were bleeding as they came off stage. She performed the number from coast to coast for two years, until it was scheduled for a European tour and St. Denis appropriated the role for herself.

Because of their artistic and temperamental differences, Martha Graham and Ted Shawn came to despise each other, and Martha looked for a way out. In spite of the animosity, she studied and worked as a teacher and principal dancer with Denishawn for almost eight years until an offer to return to New York in 1923 permitted her to strike out on her own.

Life's Work

The liberating offer was from the Greenwich Village Follies, a vaudeville revue. At long last, Martha Graham was encouraged to create her own dances within the exotic parameters of glamour required by the Follies management. Although the position garnered her a certain amount of fame and financial comfort, she knew it was not her life's work. She felt destined to be an "artist," which in her view translated as "worker"; in 1925, she left Broadway to teach and, more important, to learn in the newly created dance department of the Eastman School of Music in Rochester.

Founded by George Eastman, the inventor of the Kodak camera and a patron of the arts, the school became the launching pad for the creative genius of Martha Graham. Since she was given autonomy, she threw out the old, standardized modes of teaching dance and began to experiment with and through her students.

Using several of her most gifted disciples as a company, the true Martha Graham emerged in 1927 with *Revolt*, which related man's injustice to man, followed closely by *Heretic* and *Vision of the Apocalypse*. Discarding the traditional flow of ballet, her dancers used spastic jerks, trembling, and falls to the floor to illustrate their themes. The press and the public were shocked. This was not entertainment, they believed; this was disturbing, which was exactly the response Graham had hoped to elicit.

In 1929, beginning with her former Eastman students, Martha initiated her own company, the Martha Graham School of Contemporary Dance. From that point, she was unfailingly experimental and uncompromising, and she was frequently the source of bewilderment and angry resistance. People were rarely indifferent to her, and she was surrounded by debate throughout her career. Whether it was adoration or disgust, it was impossible to view one of her performances without experiencing a definite emotional reaction. Known for her tyranny and her temper, she nevertheless instilled

hero worship in her students, who followed her in a cult-like procession. They knew that although she demanded perfection and absolute obedience, she could also be genuinely kind, caring, and surprisingly sentimental.

Thematically, Martha Graham delved into every dark corner of the human mind through physical expression. She was fascinated by rituals, psychological conflicts, and mythology, a subject she considered the ancestor of psychotherapy. Throughout her career, she composed more than one hundred dances and choreographed more than one hundred eighty works, each of which was extremely complex in terms of symbolic meaning and literary allusion.

Although condemned by some for her use of the body and her frank acknowledgment of human sexuality, Graham proclaimed she was tracing the genealogy of the soul of humanity, that she wanted to "chart the graph of the heart." Holding her work-worn hands skyward and performing in bare feet, she moved to themes that dealt with archetypes and rituals so old that humankind could not understand them because it had forgotten them. Her fame led to world tours, and she traveled extensively in both Europe and Asia. She became an honorary ambassador for the United States and was courted by both the Nazi party in 1936 and the communists in the 1950's. She rejected both groups.

Although she excelled as a choreographer, Graham insisted that she was primarily a performer. Thus, when she was forced to retire from the stage in 1969 at the age of seventy-five, the media and her company expected her to wither away. After a cycle of hospitalization and convalescence, Martha recovered, thanks, in part, to the encouragement of a young photographer, Ron Protas, who adored her. Through his care, she regained her will to live, and in her eighties, Martha Graham staged a comeback, including tours of the United States and the Far East and a full return to teaching.

In 1991, after completing a fifty-five-day tour of the Far East with her troupe, Martha Graham contracted pneumonia. Two months later, on April 1, she died of cardiac arrest. She was ninety-six years old.

Summary

Frequently ranked with Pablo Picasso, Igor Stravinsky, and James Joyce for developing a form of expression that broke the traditional mold, Martha Graham is generally accepted as the greatest single figure in American modern dance and the symbol of it in the popular mind. She invented a new and codified language of dance and began a whole fashion with respect to stage design and costuming, symbolic props, and mobile scenery. During her long career, she won virtually every honor an artist can receive, including the Presidential Medal of Freedom and the French Legion of Honor. She performed for heads of state and was granted honorary degrees from Harvard and Yale, among other universities.

Despite the acclaim, it was her ground-breaking style, her refusal to compromise, and her depiction of the American woman on the threshold of a new life for which Martha Graham will be remembered. Seeking the key to woman's present dilemma, Graham laid bare the mythos surrounding the feminine role and in the process created such memorable pieces as *Primitive Mysteries*, for which she was awarded a Guggenheim Fellowship, *Appalachian Spring*, which won a Pulitzer Prize for Aaron Copland's score, and *Letter to the World*, which depicted the inner and outer life of poet Emily Dickinson and was considered by some to be Graham's masterwork. She was also the first choreographer consistently to employ African American and Asian dancers and to incorporate the spoken word into her dances.

Because it deals with myth, ritual, and the unconscious, the substance of her work is intangible and cannot be analyzed; it involves a total sensory impression that can only be experienced. Martha Graham shall remain, in the words of her biographer, Agnes de Mille, the "most startling inventor and the greatest performer who trod the native stage."

Bibliography

Anderson, Jack. *Dance*. New York: Newsweek, 1974. This work is a brief overview of the entire range of ballet history. It includes biographical information on dancers, including Graham, and a selected bibliography.

Balanchine, George. *Balanchine's New Complete Stories of the Great Ballets*. Edited by Francis Mason. New York: Doubleday, 1968. Written by one of the great masters in dance, this work includes plot summaries of ballets, including those devised by Martha Graham. A chronology of significant events in ballet history, an annotated list of recordings, and a selected bibliography are included.

Bird, Dorothy, and Joyce Greenberg. "Bird's Eye View. (Part 1)" *Ballet Review* 24, no. 4 (Winter 1996). Accounts of dancer Dorothy Bird's experiences with Graham in the 1930's. Graham's choreography of several pieces is discussed. Explanation of Bird's split with Graham in 1937 over the choreographer's autocratic style.

Burt, Ramsay. "Dance, Gender and Psychoanalysis: Martha Graham's 'Night Journey'." *Dance Research Journal* 30, no. 1 (Spring 1998). Focuses on Graham's choreography of "Night Journey," the story of Oedipus from his mother/wife's point of view, with emphasis on gender representation.

de Mille, Agnes. *Dance to the Piper*. London: Hamilton, 1951; Boston: Little Brown, 1952. Although this book is de Mille's autobiography, much information on Graham is included. The two were contemporaries and friends, and de Mille eventually became Martha Graham's biographer.

————. *The Life and Work of Martha Graham*. New York: Random House, 1991; London: Hutchinson, 1992. This biography of Graham was written by one of the greatest figures in twentieth century dance, an artist who is ideally qualified to discuss Graham and her work.

Greenberg, Joyce. "Bird's Eye View. (Part 2)" *Ballet Review* 25, no. 2 (Summer 1997). Continuation of part 1 of this article (see Bird, above).

Lloyd, Margaret. *The Borzoi Book of Modern Dance*. New York: Knopf, 1949. Biographical information on Martha Graham and a discussion of her work are included in this volume. Additionally, the book contains information on the conversion of classical ballet into legitimate theater.

Terry, Walter. *Frontiers of Dance: The Life of Martha Graham*. New York: Crowell, 1975. Written by a former student of Graham's, this book depicts the life and work of Martha Graham from the early years through the initial stages of her comeback.

Joyce Duncan

ANTONIO GRAMSCI

Born: January 23, 1891; Ales, Sardinia, Italy
Died: April 27, 1937; Rome, Italy
Areas of Achievement: Government, politics, and political science
Contribution: Gramsci gave modern social and political theory and the study of history a new method of social analysis with his writings on culture and hegemony. He was one of the first European communists to establish the theoretical foundations for a Western Marxism free of reliance on the Soviet Union. Gramsci was himself an active revolutionary who produced his most influential work during an eleven-year imprisonment under Benito Mussolini.

Early Life

Antonio Gramsci was born in Ales, a small agricultural village in Sardinia, on January 23, 1891. His family lived on modest means, supported by a father who was a clerk in the Italian state bureaucracy. The family moved frequently between several villages during much of Gramsci's youth. At the age of four, Gramsci severely injured his spine; he remained a hunchback and suffered from poor health for the rest of his life.

Gramsci was a gifted student and an avid reader even as a young boy. He was graduated from elementary school early, at age ten. In 1908, he left home to attend secondary school, studying languages in Cagliari, the capital city of Sardinia. In 1911 he won a scholarship to study at the University of Turin. It was in Turin that Gramsci developed as an intellectual and political figure. He abandoned linguistics for the study of society and philosophy. Interested in the social questions of a new, industrial society, and particularly those of a mass working-class, Gramsci entered the youth movement of the Italian Socialist Party in 1914. Soon after Italy's entry into World War I in 1915, Gramsci withdrew from the university, convinced that the moment had arrived to change and not merely to study society.

Gramsci displayed a remarkable talent for writing and contributed articles to the Socialist press throughout the war years. From Italy, Gramsci praised Vladimir Ilich Lenin prior to the Bolshevik Revolution and even more strongly afterward. Gramsci himself never ceased to struggle with the question of how to make a revolution in Italy. He supported the formation of workers' councils and in 1919 helped launch a new Socialist newspaper, *Ordine nuovo* (new order), which promoted these councils and rapidly became the most influential paper in the Turin area. In January, 1921, Gramsci formed the Communist Party of Italy and adopted a revolutionary program for Italy.

From 1921 to 1922, Gramsci suffered from poor health, depression, and even a nervous breakdown. In 1922, while in Russia, he met Giulia Schucht; they married shortly afterward and had two sons. Gramsci was in Vienna when he was elected as a deputy to the Italian Parliament in 1924. He took advantage of his parliamentary immunity from arrest to return to Fascist Italy in May, where he became an outspoken opponent of Mussolini. In November, 1926, Gramsci was arrested by the Fascists and charged with six counts of treason. The prosecutor noted that the state had to "prevent this brain from functioning for twenty years." Gramsci began his prison sentence near Bari. He would remain in jail for a decade, until his death in 1937.

Life's Work

It was during his prison years that Gramsci produced his most important work—a series of notebooks entitled *Quaderni del carcere* (1948-1951; partial translation, *Selections from the Prison Notebooks of Antonio Gramsci*, 1971). He wrote these volumes under the most difficult of conditions, with little, if any, access to primary sources or secondary literature. The scrutiny of prison censors forced Gramsci to adopt an elliptical writing style and to employ code words (for example "philosophy of praxis" instead of the more direct "Marxism") in order to have his works pass outside the prison walls. The result is a collection of writings that is incomplete and often ambiguous. Nevertheless, *Quaderni del carcere* stands as one of the most important revisions of social and political theory in the twentieth century.

The principal question that Gramsci set himself during the prison years was how best to explain the failure of Communism in Italy immediately after World War I. Marxists maintained that revolution would first take place in the most advanced capitalist societies. Italy certainly did not fit that description, but neither did Russia—both countries were economically and socially backward, and Gramsci,

with firsthand experience of peasant Sardinia, had already written extensively on the "Southern Question" before incarceration. Why had Bolshevism triumphed in Russia—the "East" in Gramsci's prison code—and not elsewhere? The search for an answer led Gramsci to the first of many important insights: his assertion that there was more to revolution than the mere seizure of the state. Gramsci began to explore the question of power in modern societies in a new fashion.

Power, Gramsci maintained, needed to be considered under two, related aspects: coercion and consent. The coercive element of power lay in the direct control over society that the state exercised through its political institutions—police, army, and legislature. According to Gramsci, coercion was the primary form of power in less advanced societies, where control was maintained directly by a repressive state. Czarist Russia was the best European example of a coercive state, and Lenin's tactic of a frontal assault (Gramsci's "war of maneuver") was the correct strategy in such conditions.

In Western Europe, however, the issue of power was more complex. Alongside the state and its co-

ercive strength lay the power derived from the citizens' recognition of the state's right to rule. This was "consent," and, according to Gramsci, this kind of power was even more important in the West than pure coercion. Consent, though, was not spontaneous; rather, it was taught by the many institutions—schools, church, family, and others—of what Gramsci termed "civil" or "private" society. All of these institutions passed along certain ideas, reinforced a way of thinking, and instilled a set of values, thereby creating a dominant culture that tended to reinforce the state and confer legitimacy on its rule.

For Gramsci, culture then played an important social role in educating consent; its conservative function lay in restricting one's ability to view critically the present and imagine (and act on) a vision of a substantially different future. The label Gramsci gave to this phenomenon was "hegemony": the power of a dominant way of thinking to reinforce the social status quo. The concept of hegemony and its orgins in civil society were Gramsci's greatest theoretical contributions.

If revolution had failed in Italy (and elsewhere in the West) after World War I, Gramsci believed it was the result of a failure to understand the power of culture and the strength of consent. Gramsci also took up the issue of how to counter the hegemony of contemporary bourgeois culture over consciousness and action. He noted the need to substitute for the Eastern "war of maneuver" a different tactic for social change in the West, what he termed the "war of position."

Two ideas were central to Gramsci's thinking on Western revolution. The first was the creation of a separate awareness that would act as a counterconsciousness to the dominant strains of thought in bourgeois society. Gramsci called for the articulation of a working-class culture with its own ideas and ethos which would gradually spread and acquire hegemony in certain areas of society. This undertaking would be the work of individuals who could apply their intelligence and organizational abilities to questions of culture. The revolutionary character of their work would be guaranteed only when these individuals came from the working class itself and not from traditional intellectual elites. Gramsci gave the term "organic intellectuals" to these people, who—very much like himself—had working-class origins and turned their energies to the articulation of an alternative consciousness and culture. Therefore, organic intellectuals, fighting for ideas and culture, would play a key role in the revolutions in the West.

Gramsci's second idea for the "war of position" was the creation of a new kind of political party, which he called the "Modern Prince." Drawing inspiration from Niccolò Machiavelli, Gramsci declared that the complexity of modern societies required that revolution become the business of an organized group and not a single ruler. Hence, in the twentieth century, the Modern Prince must be the political party. In his writings on the revolutionary political party, Gramsci openly accepted the distinction between "leaders" and "led." His Modern Prince was a reformulation of Karl Marx's Communist Party as the "vanguard of the proletariat"—a revolutionary elite acting to inspire and direct a potentially revolutionary population. Though the goal of the Modern Prince was the elimination of the difference between "leaders" and "led," there is little in Gramsci's writings on politics to show how he proposed to avoid a concentration of power in the hands of his "organic intellectuals." Indeed, Gramsci remained too enthusiastic a supporter of Lenin to consider critically Russian events after the November Revolution; later, he was too isolated in prison (and his Italian comrades often misrepresented events in the Soviet Union) to be aware of developments in Stalinist Russia in the 1930's.

Ill health plagued Gramsci throughout the years of his incarceration. By 1935, his physical condition had deteriorated so greatly that Fascist officials transferred Gramsci to a private clinic in Rome. A year and a half later, in April, 1937, Gramsci died. The *Quaderni del carcere* found their way through clandestine channels from Fascist Italy to Moscow, where they were kept until after World War II. It took nearly thirty years until a complete, definitive edition was published in 1975.

Summary

Antonio Gramsci's contribution to European communism was a significant one. In his analysis of East and West, the state and civil society, and coercion versus consent, Gramsci provided the foundations for a Western Marxism substantially different from that of the Soviet Union. His focus on culture, hegemony, and ideology allowed contemporary Marxists to emphasize the role of consciousness in the process of changing societies. Gramsci's work thereby aided in the rediscovery of an earlier, humanist Marxism that had been lost between evolutionary socialism, Fascism, and Stalinism.

Gramsci's greatest influence, however, lies outside strictly political circles. His writings on hegemony and culture have influenced virtually every other field of study of human society. Gramsci inaugurated the tendency to view culture not as an abstract body of knowledge, beliefs, or habits but as a social construction. Society's institutions are now understood as contributors to the creation of well-articulated worldviews, with profound effects on human consciousness and action. Scholars influenced by Gramsci's terms and analysis may be found in all branches of the humanities: anthropology, history, linguistics, political science, religious studies, sociology, and the study of ideas. Few other thinkers have worked under such difficult conditions; fewer still have made as significant a contribution to such a wide range of disciplines.

Bibliography

Cammett, John M. *Antonio Gramsci and the Origins of Italian Communism.* Stanford, Calif.: Stanford University Press, 1967. One of the best books on Gramsci, this is the text that introduced his work to an English audience. Cammett treats Gramsci's life up to his arrest in great detail and concludes with a general overview of the principal concerns in *Quaderni del carcere.*

Clark, Martin. *Antonio Gramsci and the Revolution That Failed.* New Haven, Conn.: Yale University Press, 1977. This book's concerns are the postwar revolutionary years, the rise of workers' councils, and the period of factory occupation. It highlights Gramsci's role and the theoretical insights developed between 1919 and 1920.

Davis, John A., ed. *Gramsci and Italy's Passive Revolution.* London: Croom Helm, and New York: Barnes and Noble, 1979. A collection of essays by various authors who adopt Gramscian concepts and analysis to examine Italian society, economy, and politics in the fifty years following unification.

Femia, Joseph. *Gramsci's Political Thought.* Oxford: Clarendon Press, 1981; New York: Oxford University Press, 1987. One of the most thorough discussions of Gramsci's work, which develops in some detail his ideas on hegemony, organic intellectuals, and the role of the modern political party. Femia also indicates the areas in which Gramsci has had a strong influence on the thinking of contemporary Italian communists.

Finocchiaro, Maurice A. *Beyond Right and Left: Democratic Elitism in Mosca and Gramsci.* New Haven, Conn.: Yale University Press, 1999. The author presents the first comprehensive study of the connection between Mosca and Gramsci, arguing that they share a basic belief in democratic elitism.

Fiori, Giuseppe. *Antonio Gramsci: Life of a Revolutionary.* London: New Left Books, 1970; New York: Dutton, 1971. The most complete treatment of Gramsci's life written by one of the foremost Italian specialists on Gramsci.

Gramsci, Antonio. *Letters from Prison.* Selected, translated, and introduced by Lynne Lawner. New York: Harper, 1973; London: Cape, 1975. A selection from among the 450 letters Gramsci sent to family and friends during his ten-year imprisonment. The letters contain interesting insights into Gramsci's thinking on politics and society and reveal the man behind the theory.

———. *Selections from the Prison Notebooks of Antonio Gramsci.* Edited and translated by Quintin Hoare and Geoffrey Nowell Smith. London: Lawrence and Wishart, 1971; New York: International, 1972. This book is the best English translation of Gramsci's most important prison writings. Hoare's extended introduction to Gramsci's life and works is a valuable addition to the volume.

Joll, James. *Antonio Gramsci.* Edited by Frank Kermode. New York: Viking Press, 1977; London: Penguin, 1978. An excellent, brief biography of Gramsci. In passing, Joll offers a few comments on the nature of Gramsci's work in different periods.

Kolakowski, Leszek. *Main Currents of Marxism.* Vol. 3, *The Breakdown,* translated by P. S. Falla. Oxford: Clarendon Press, 1978; New York: Oxford University Press, 1981. In chapter 6, Kolakowski manages to present an impressive, critical evaluation of Gramsci's work and contributions to Marxist thought, concluding with a revealing account of Gramsci's place in the history of European Marxism.

Sassoon, Anne Showstack, ed. *Approaches to Gramsci.* London: Writers and Readers, 1982. A collection of essays by leading scholars from many different disciplines on Gramsci, his life and work, his commitment to revolution and the cultural applications of his theories.

Williams, Gwyn A. *Proletarian Order: Antonio Gramsci, Factory Councils and the Origins of Italian Communism, 1911-1921.* London: Pluto Press, 1975. The best English-language treatment of the formative years in Gramsci's political development: 1915-1920. Williams locates the stimulus to Gramsci's later thinking in the revolutionary two years in Turin that followed World War I.

David Travis

GÜNTER GRASS

Born: October 16, 1927; Danzig, Germany
Area of Achievement: Literature
Contribution: Grass is to be considered one of the leading figures of German literature since 1945. His writings address social and political issues in a unique manner, and he has consistently stressed the relationship between the artist and society.

Early Life

Günter Grass was born in the free city-state of Danzig (Germany), today the Polish city of Gdańsk, on October 16, 1927. His parents were middle-class merchants of German-Polish descent. The free state of Danzig was occupied by the Nazis when Grass was eleven years old, and, by the age of fourteen, he had become, as did most boys his age, a willing member of the Hitler Youth. From 1944 to 1945, he served in the German army but was wounded in April, 1945, and then sent to a hospital in Czechoslovakia, where he was captured by the Americans. Taken one day by his American captors to the Nazi concentration camp of Dachau (outside Munich), Grass could not believe that such atrocities could have taken place, and he thought it was a hoax perpetrated by the Americans. When the Nürnberg trials on Nazi war crimes were held, he finally realized the truth of the historical record.

After the end of the war, Grass worked for a while as a farm laborer, and in 1947 he became a stonemason's apprentice, spending time in a mine. He also performed in a jazz trio. He married Anna Schwarz, a dancer, in 1954. These various jobs did not suit his artistic nature, and from 1949 to 1956 he studied drawing and sculpture in Düsseldorf. In 1955, his wife submitted, without his knowledge, one of his poems to a poetry contest, and he won third prize. He then spent several years in Paris and worked on his writing projects and his graphic art. Grass has given exhibitions and published collections of his etchings.

Life's Work

During the early 1950's, Grass wrote a number of surrealistic poems, which he illustrated himself and which were published under the title *Die Vorzüge der Windhühner* (1956; the advantages of windfowl). He also wrote several plays that suggest the love of the grotesque and bizarre that figures in so many of his later writings. *Noch zehn Minuten bis Buffalo* (1954, 1958; *Only Ten Minutes to Buffalo*, 1967) is one of the better-known plays from this early period. In 1958 the young author was asked to read at the prestigious Group 47 annual meeting of German writers and was awarded first prize.

The epic novel *Die Blechtrommel* (1959; *The Tin Drum*, 1961) was his first commercial success, and it generated much public controversy. It is the grotesque and, at times, licentious story of Oskar Matzerath, a precocious dwarf, and his picaresque adventures before, during, and after World War II. Oskar—part Grigory Rasputin, the madman, and part Johann Wolfgang von Goethe, the poet— struggles in the course of the novel to find his true identity amid the chaos of his family life and the social and political upheavals of Germany during the Nazi era. The text incorporates many of Grass's memories of and reflections on his youth in Danzig. Because of the novel's often open attitude toward sexuality, it scandalized many of the more conservative elements in German society at that time. The city government of Bremen, for example, refused to grant him the literary prize that the committee had awarded him.

The surrealistic style of *The Tin Drum* marks Grass, at least in part, as the heir to a well-known Prague writer of the early twentieth century, Franz Kafka. As in the latter's dreamlike stories, emotional states of mind are treated as if they were external events. Oskar, for example, distrusts, as a child, the adult world, and so he refuses to grow up. He wills himself into not growing and retains the physical stature of childhood. When he is angry or upset, he screams, as does any child, but, in the novel, Oskar's vocalizations have the unique ability to shatter glass. The effect of such a writing style is of an altered or miraculous "reality" in which subjective feelings become objective occurrences.

After the success of this initial novel, Grass was awarded the Berlin Critics Prize in 1960, and he moved from Paris to Berlin, where he has resided since. His first marriage ended in divorce; he married again in 1979. An outspoken and independent-minded liberal, Grass rejected the materialistic consumer society of West Germany, refusing to own a car, television, or telephone.

Grass's first novel became part of a series of narrative texts that has been called "Die Danziger Trilogie" (the Danzig trilogy). The second work of the set, *Katz und Maus* (1961; *Cat and Mouse*, 1963), is a novella that describes the youth and early adulthood of the Christ-like figure Joachim Mahlke, as related by his childhood friend and eventual betrayer, Pilenz. Mahlke, a Danzig youth, is an overachiever who has an overly prominent Adam's apple. He feels he must exceed the accomplishments of his fellows and thereby earns both their admiration and resentment. He becomes a superior swimmer and diver and eventually, in his pursuit of social acceptance, a war hero. In this story, as well as in *The Tin Drum*, Grass levels criticism at the German involvement with the phenomenon of Nazism. Grass, along with his contemporary Heinrich Böll, is part of Germany's postwar attempt to come to some kind of moral and social reckoning with the terrible events of the past. The third novel of the trilogy, *Hundejahre* (1963; *Dog Years*, 1965), also takes place in Danzig and picks up thematic elements as well as characters present in the first two works. It utilizes three narrators—Eddi Amsel,

Harry Liebenau, and Walter Matern—who offer a colorful and bizarre portrait of modern Germany and the horrors of the Nazi era. In 1966, Grass published a play, *Die Plebejer proben den Aufstand* (*The Plebeians Rehearse the Uprising*, 1966), which takes a critical look at the revolutionary theater of Bertolt Brecht and the discrepancies between artistic production and the realities of social and political change. *Örtlich betäubt* (1969; *Local Anaesthetic*, 1969) deals with issues of both World War II and the Vietnam conflict. It is a novel about the high school student Philipp Scherbaum, who seeks to protest against the hypocrisy of the adult world and his teacher, Eberhard Starusch, himself a former rebel. A nameless dentist, who treats both student and teacher, offers commentary and wisdom to both his patients.

During the 1960's and into the 1970's, Grass became more involved with the German political scene, campaigning and writing speeches on behalf of the liberal Social Democratic Party. The semifictional text *Aus dem Tagebuch einer Schnecke* (1972; *From the Diary of a Snail*, 1973) chronicles his political involvement during the 1969 West German election campaign and develops several fictional strands as well. The image of the snail comes to represent the steady but slow nature of social change and historical progress.

The 1970's saw the emergence of the feminist movement in the United States and Europe, and Grass's next novel, *Der Butt* (1977; *The Flounder*, 1978), takes a satiric look—from a decidedly male perspective—at some of the more controversial issues. The story begins with a version of the "Fisherman and His Wife" fairy tale. In Grass's book, the flounder—the archetype of the male—is caught by three German feminists who put him on public trial for crimes against humanity. It presents a series of chapters that examine in a humorous and outrageous manner the relationships of men and women throughout history. After this text, Grass worked in a more serious historical context in the novel *Das Treffen in Telgte* (1979; *The Meeting at Telgte*, 1981). The plot involves a fictitious meeting of German writers and artists toward the end of the exceedingly destructive Thirty Years' War (1618-1648). The novel looks at a typical concern of its author: the success or failure of the "humanizing" role that art and literature play in the "real" world of politics, greed, and war.

Grass's next novel, *Kopfgeburten: Oder, Die Deutschen sterben aus* (1980; *Headbirths: Or, The*

German Are Dying Out, 1982), again makes use of both diary material and fictional invention. The fictional plot involves two German schoolteachers, Harm and Dörte Peters, who are traveling throughout Asia and in the process of deciding whether they should have a child or not. At that time, Grass himself traveled in Asia, and his diary observations on cultural and political differences between Germany and the East make up a major part of the text. His next novel, *Die Rättin* (1986; *The Rat*, 1987), is a sobering tale of Europe after the nuclear holocaust, narrated by a female rat who is one of the sole survivors. The novel reflects Grass's pessimistic attitudes about the future of mankind amid the failed attempts to limit nuclear proliferation between the superpowers in the 1980's.

Although Grass is known primarily as a novelist, he has published a wide variety of work in other literary forms. Several of his plays have already been noted; he has also published a number of poetry collections in the course of his career. *Gleisdreieck* (1960), *Ausgefragt* (1967; *New Poems*, 1968), and *"Ach Butt, dein Märchen geht böse aus": Gedichte und Radierungen* (1983) present a variety of poems and illustrations that take up the same themes present in his narrative texts.

Some of Grass's works elude generic classification. One such book is *Zunge zeigen* (1988; *Show Your Tongue*, 1989), based on a trip that Grass and his second wife, Ute, took to India between October, 1986, and January, 1987. Combining journal entries, poems, and drawings, this text takes up many of the themes that have preoccupied Grass in his later work, particularly his apocalyptic vision of the contemporary world.

Summary

The playful sense of the absurd and grotesque that informs many of Günter Grass's works has given him a unique presence in the literary history of postwar Germany. He must be considered a consummate narrative artist who possesses a wild and decidedly Rabelaisian imagination. His surrealistic style appears at times as a forerunner of the "magic realism" found in the later works of Latin American authors such as Gabriel García Márquez. The often bizarre characters that populate his fiction are highly entertaining and yet offer a singular and disturbing perspective on the historical and political events around them.

These grotesque and absurd elements in Grass's work comprise a major dimension of the satiric thrust that fuels his sharp social and political criticism. His intent is to raise—through satire, humor, and outrage—the reader's consciousness concerning politics and society. Grass's work represents in this regard what the French philosopher and author Jean-Paul Sartre called *une littérature engagée*, a literature that directly addresses the pressing concerns of society. This author's active participation in the political issues of West German society has been an extension of the import of his writings. For future generations, Grass will be remembered as a highly talented artist who sought to take a stand on the problems that confronted his nation.

Bibliography

Cunliffe, W. Gordon. *Günter Grass*. New York: Twayne, 1969. An overview of Grass's major works as of the late 1960's. Provides a good introduction to major themes in early Grass. Contains notes and bibliography.

Hayman, Ronald. *Günter Grass*. London and New York: Methuen, 1985. An excellent critical introduction to Grass's writings up to the early 1980's. Contains notes and a bibliography.

Hollington, Michael. *Günter Grass: The Writer in a Pluralist Society*. London and Boston: Boyars, 1980. This is a scholarly study that examines the sociopolitical themes of Grass's writings and personal life. Contains notes and a bibliography.

Jameson, Frederic, "Ramblings in Old Berlin." *South Atlantic Quarterly* 96, no. 4 (Fall 1997). Discusses Grass's novel *Ein Weites Feld* and German postunification literature. Jameson draws a parallel between the sterility of the characters' conversations and the lack of conflict that has resulted from unification.

Leonard, Irène. *Günter Grass*. New York: Harper, and Edinburgh: Oliver and Boyd, 1974. This is an introductory monograph on Grass's works up to the early 1970's. Contains notes and a bibliography.

Miles, Keith. *Günter Grass*. London: Vision Press, and New York: Barnes and Noble, 1975. This is a scholarly study of Grass's major texts (up to the early 1970's) that presents reasonable critical discussions of important themes and issues. Contains notes, a bibliography, and an index.

Preece, Julian. "Sexual-Textual Politics: The Transparency of the Male Narrative in 'Der Butt' by Gunter Grass." *Modern Language Review* 90, no. 4 (October, 1995). Analysis of Grass's novel

Der Butt, which has received significant criticism from feminists.

Reddick, John. *The "Danzig Trilogy" of Günter Grass: A Study of "The Tin Drum," "Cat and Mouse," and "The Dog Years."* London: Secker and Warburg, and New York: Harcourt Brace, 1974. An excellent scholarly study of Grass's well-known novel trilogy. Contains notes and a bibliography.

Tank, Kurt Lothar. *Günter Grass.* New York: Ungar, 1969. An introductory study that is dated but still useful. Contains a bibliography.

Willson, A. Leslie, ed. *A Günter Grass Symposium.* Austin: University of Texas Press, 1971. An excellent collection of scholarly articles that explore various aspects of Grass's work up to the late 1960's. Contains notes and a bibliography.

Thomas F. Barry

GRAHAM GREENE

Born: October 2, 1904; Berkhamsted, Hertfordshire, England
Died: April, 1991; Vevey, Switzerland
Area of Achievement: Literature
Contribution: Combining a fascination with the
nature of good and evil in the contemporary
world and a masterful ability to develop exciting
plots about complex yet believable characters
caught in real-life situations, Greene created a
body of fiction which enjoys a critical and popular appeal unique in twentieth century literature.

Early Life

Graham Greene was born October 2, 1904, in
Berkhamsted, Hertfordshire, England, the fourth of
six children in a large upper-middle-class Edwardian household. His father, Charles Henry Greene,
was a history and classics master who, in 1910, became the headmaster of the Berkhamsted School.
In his memoir, *A Sort of Life* (1971), Greene recalls
his early childhood as pleasant. Although he appears to have seen little of his father and mother, he
enjoyed the company of a large number of aunts,
uncles, and cousins who lived nearby.

In 1912, Greene was enrolled in Berkhamsted
School where he was to spend the next ten years.
His adolescence, however, was marked by the passage from a state of security and joy into one of
fear and depression. At age thirteen, Greene entered the senior part of his father's school. Now required to board in the "hated brick barracks" of the
English public school with the older boys, he was
bitterly unhappy. His manic-depressive tendency
became acute during this period. Feeling homesick
and betrayed, tormented by conflicting loyalties—
the headmaster's son was cruelly shunned by the
other boys—Greene was plagued by nightmares;
he developed a terror of birds and bats and an obsessive fear of drowning which survived as a recurrent motif in his fiction. By 1920, Greene's behavior was so eccentric and suicidal that his father sent
him to London for psychoanalysis. The treatment
was moderately successful, and Greene returned to
Berkhamsted with renewed self-confidence, but his
horror of living among strangers and enemies endured, later influencing the characterization of the
protagonists of his novels.

In 1922, Greene entered Oxford University to
study history. By 1923, his depression had returned, and on six occasions he played a deadly

game: Slipping a bullet into his brother's revolver,
he would spin the chamber, point the gun into his
right ear and pull the trigger. In this gratuitous
gambling with his life, Greene found what he
called "an extraordinary sense of jubilation" which
assuaged his terrible feeling of emptiness. Although he soon gave up these suicidal experiments,
his desperate need to experience danger in his
"life-long war against boredom" persisted. His later excursions into Africa, Mexico, and Vietnam in
the midst of wars and revolutions may owe something to this compulsion.

After leaving Oxford, Greene embarked on a career in journalism. In 1926, he became an unpaid
film reviewer for the Nottingham *Journal*. He also
met Vivien Dayrell-Browning, a Roman Catholic.
They were married in 1927 and later had two children. Greene himself was formally received into
the Catholic Church in 1926, the same year he left
the Nottingham *Journal* for *The Times*, where he
worked for the next four years as a subeditor. In
1929, the distinguished publisher William Heinemann accepted Greene's first novel, *The Man Within* (1929). Although the novel did well in England,
selling more than eight thousand copies, a remarkable success for a first novel, it failed in the United
States. Still, Heinemann was sufficiently pleased to
offer Greene six hundred pounds a year for three
years in return for a promise of three more novels.
On the strength of this encouragement, Greene
gave up his position at *The Times* to pursue a career
as a novelist.

Life's Work

The first two novels in Greene's Heinemann contract, *The Name of Action* (1930) and *Rumour at
Nightfall* (1931), were awkward and undeveloped
action stories which Greene later withdrew from
his bibliography. In the 1930's, he began to distinguish between entertainments and novels. The novels were serious works in which the characterization was both complex and ambiguous. The
entertainments were conceived as thrillers designed to satisfy his publisher and generate an income for his growing family. *Stamboul Train*
(1932) was just such an entertainment. Published
in the United States as *Orient Express*, the book
catapulted Greene to popular success. The English
Book Society chose it as a selection, thereby ensuring sales of at least ten thousand copies, and Twen-

tieth Century-Fox purchased the film rights. Most notable among the entertainments that followed were *A Gun for Sale* (1936), which appeared in the United States as *This Gun for Hire*; *The Confidential Agent* (1939); and *The Ministry of Fear* (1943).

A prolific writer, Greene was already at work on his next book before *Stamboul Train* had been published. *It's a Battlefield* (1934) was not well received. Undaunted, Greene wrote *England Made Me* (1935), later reissued as *The Shipwrecked* (1953), a pessimistic portrait of a doomed society. While employed as the film critic for *The Spectator* from 1935 to 1939, Greene produced books that were heavily influenced by cinematic effects. Indeed, a measure of Greene's success is the great number of his novels which have been made into films.

A tireless traveler, Greene ranged widely in Africa, Mexico, Asia, and South America during his lifetime. In the winter of 1934-1935, he undertook an arduous walking tour of Liberia with his cousin Barbara Greene; he published an account of this experience as *Journey Without Maps: A Travel Book* (1936). At about the same time, Greene began work on the novel, *Brighton Rock* (1938), that was to mark a significant watershed in his career: It established him as a major novelist and signaled, to some readers, that he was a Catholic writer. Although Greene had been a Catholic since his conversion in 1926, *Brighton Rock* was the first of his religious novels—which include *The Power and the Glory* (1940), *The Heart of the Matter* (1948), *The End of the Affair* (1951), and, to a lesser extent, *A Burnt-out Case* (1961)—in which Catholicism was both a significant narrative principle and an object of scrutiny. Commissioned to report on the persecution of Catholics in Mexico, Greene spent the winter of 1938 in the provinces of Tabasco and Chiapas, Mexico. The record of his observations was published as *The Lawless Roads: A Mexican Journal* (1939), appearing in the United States as *Another Mexico*. The Mexican expedition also provided him with the background and inspiration for one of his most compelling novels, *The Power and the Glory*. Published under the title *The Labyrinthine Ways* in the United States, the novel is considered by some to be his best. In 1941, it was awarded the prestigious Hawthornden Prize. Because of wartime economy measures, the first edition was limited to thirty-five hundred copies. Only two thousand copies of *The Labyrinthine Ways* were sold in the United States. After 1945,

however, the novel was a huge success in France, in part the result of the enthusiastic praise of the novelist François Mauriac. The American director John Ford made the novel into a film titled *The Fugitive* (1947), with Henry Fonda in the leading role, and by the 1950's the novel had won wide critical acclaim in the United States. The story of the "whiskey priest" with the illegitimate daughter, however, also brought a strong condemnation from the Vatican.

In 1941, Greene joined the British Secret Service and spent much of the next five years in Africa. Among both Europeans and Americans, Greene's reputation as a Catholic novelist was spreading quickly. When he published *The Heart of the Matter* in 1948, his first serious novel in eight years, Catholic critics debated whether its hero, Major Scobie, was saved or damned. A married middle-aged police officer in British West Africa, Scobie falls in love with a nineteen-year-old girl and finally, because of a series of events, decides to commit suicide. For years after the novel appeared, Greene was hounded by the religious public on both sides of the Atlantic for his counsel on marital or spiritual questions. Greene said that he had grown weary of the "reiterated arguments in Catholic journals on Scobie's salvation or damnation."

As a novelist and a journalist, Greene was particularly active in the 1950's and 1960's, often accepting dangerous assignments to visit regions of political or civil unrest. After publishing *The End of the Affair* in 1951, he traveled to Malaya for *Life* magazine. Between 1951 and 1955, he spent winters in Vietnam covering the French Wars for the *Sunday Times* and *Le Figaro*, and he also reported from Kenya at the height of the Mau Mau uprising for the *Sunday Times*. He subsequently traveled to Stalinist Poland, Cuba, the Belgian Congo (to study life in a leper colony), and Haiti. The journeys inspired at least four novels: *The Quiet American* (1955), *Our Man in Havana* (1958), *A Burnt-out Case* (1961), and *The Comedians* (1966).

In the 1970's, Greene visited Chile, Argentina, and Panama. The significant novels of the decade included *The Honorary Consul* (1973) and *The Human Factor* (1978), the latter based on the sensational defection to the Soviet Union of Kim Philby, Greene's former boss in the British Secret Service. With the publication of *The Human Factor*, Greene, now seventy-four, assumed his "writing days were finished." Then, on Christmas Day, 1978, in Switzerland, a new book came to him. He published that book, the bizarre novel *Dr. Fischer of Geneva: Or, The Bomb Party* (1980), another volume of autobiography, titled *Ways of Escape* (1980), *Monsignor Quixote* (1982), a short novel about a priest who journeys across Spain in the company of his friend, a Communist ex-mayor, and *The Tenth Man* (1985).

Summary

Graham Greene was one of the most remarkable writers of the twentieth century. His novels won for him enormous popularity among Catholic and non-Catholic readers, both in America and elsewhere, as they dramatize in contemporary political settings such universal themes as the struggle of innocence against evil and the hope of redemption in a fallen world. For example, his fiction offers vivid pictures of the Mexican religious persecutions of the 1930's, the demise of French power and the growing involvement of the Americans in Vietnam of the early 1950's, and the horror of life in Haiti under François "Papa Doc" Duvalier. Although Greene's reputation rests principally on his novels, he contributed to a wide variety of genres; his canon includes short stories, travel books, essays and literary criticism, autobiography and biography, children's books, plays, and film scripts.

Greene had an undeniable impact on the shape of American fiction and film (all the major American film companies have made films from his novels), yet his relationship with America was characterized by mutual ambivalence. In 1954, Greene was refused a visa to enter the United States because of his brief association with the Communist Party when he was an undergraduate at Oxford University thirty years before. The following year, he published *The Quiet American*, which portrays the true villains of the French colonial war in Vietnam as neither the French nor the Vietnamese but the covertly interfering Americans. The novel was attacked by American reviewers for its anti-Americanism, and Greene was accused of caricaturing Pyle, a young idealistic American, through the eyes of Fowler, a British journalist, in order to express his antipathy for America. Yet in 1961, Greene was named an honorary member of the American Institute of Arts and Letters. A year after the appearance of *The Comedians* in 1966, in which Greene presented a somewhat unflattering portrait of the Americans Mr. and Mrs. Smith and their naïve politics, he wrote in a letter to *The Times* that if he were forced to choose between life in the Soviet Union and life in America, he would choose the Soviet Union. In 1970, Greene resigned from the American Institute of Arts and Letters to protest American involvement in Southeast Asia.

Greene's political views, however antipathetic to American foreign policy, do not detract from his accomplishments as a novelist. A consummate storyteller of outstanding technical ability, he wrote of fear, pity, violence, and man's restless search for salvation in a highly readable prose which offers moments of poignant intensity.

Bibliography

Adamson, Judith. *Graham Greene and Cinema.* Norman, Okla.: Pilgrim, 1984. A study of the transformations of Greene's novels and entertainments into films as well as a consideration of Greene's own film criticism. Includes a useful appendix listing all the films in which Greene had a hand to 1983.

Allain, Marie-François. *The Other Man: Conversations with Graham Greene.* New York: Simon and Schuster, 1981; London: Bodley Head, 1983. An indispensable aid to any serious study of Greene. The novelist is witty and charming as he answers questions about his craft.

Boardman, Gwenn R. *Graham Greene: The Aesthetics of Exploration*. Gainesville: University of Florida Press, 1971. A sensitive discussion of Greene's interest in the theme of lost innocence in the major novels before 1967.

De Vitis, A. A. *Graham Greene*. Boston: Twayne, 1964, rev. ed. 1986. A lucid survey of Greene's books and the major themes, although with a bias to read Greene principally as a religious novelist.

Gordon, Hayim. *Fighting Evil: Unsung Heroes in the Novels of Graham Greene*. Westport, Conn.: Greenwood Press, 1997. Discusses the heroes of Greene's novels, their battles with evil, and can be learned from them.

Greene, Graham. *A Sort of Life*. London: Bodley Head, and New York: Simon and Schuster, 1971. The first volume of Greene's autobiography, from his childhood to the 1930's. Most interesting for the insights which it provides to the mind of the mature writer as it describes the peculiar mix of joy and pain which characterized Greene's childhood and adolescence.

———. *Ways of Escape*. London: Bodley Head, and New York: Simon and Schuster, 1980. The best criticism available on Greene is his own. This fascinating if somewhat circumspect volume continues the memoirs of *A Sort of Life* and offers excellent musing on Greene's work, politics, and travels.

Kelly, Richard. *Graham Greene*. New York: Ungar, 1984. A workmanlike study of both the man and the major writings. Attempts more biographical information than other sources, although it draws heavily on Greene's two published autobiographical volumes.

Malamet, Elliott. *The World Remade: Graham Greene and the Art of Detection*. New York: Lang, 1998. Examines the narration, themes, and philosophical meanings in Greene's mysteries.

Smith, Grahame. *The Achievement of Graham Greene*. Brighton, Sussex: Harvester Press, and Totowa, N.J.: Barnes and Noble Books, 1985. Close studies of individual works as well as analysis of the major themes. Argues that Greene's appeal to a wide popular audience is a crucial part of his success as a serious writer. Attempts to shift attention away from Greene as a religious writer by focusing on his involvement with politics.

Spurling, John. *Graham Greene*. London and New York: Methuen, 1983. A short but useful examination of the mind of the novelist as it is revealed in the published writings. A good general introduction to Greene's fiction.

Stratford, Philip. *Faith and Fiction: Creative Process in Greene and Mauriac*. Notre Dame, Ind.: University of Notre Dame Press, 1964. Examines the works of Greene and Mauriac individually and then considers the religious milieus from which these authors drew their fictions. A scholarly study of the relation of religious faith to the act of writing fiction.

Richard Butts

ALAN GREENSPAN

Born: March 6, 1926; New York, New York

Areas of Achievement: Economics, government, and politics

Contribution: As chairman of the U.S. Federal Reserve Board, Alan Greenspan has worked to balance economic growth, employment rates, and inflation.

Early Life

Alan Greenspan was born in New York City, the only son of Herman Herbert and Rose Goldsmith Greenspan. The couple divorced when Alan was six. From then on, he was reared by his mother, a furniture store salesperson; Rose and her son moved in with her parents, Russian Jewish immigrants, in the Washington Heights section of New York.

Alan attended the city's public schools and, eventually, the renowned Juilliard School, where he studied saxophone and clarinet. After two years, he dropped out and toured the country with the Henry Jerome swing band. After a time, however, he decided that he could not excel in music professionally, and he left the ensemble. His insatiable love of figures and economics prompted him to enroll in New York University's School of Commerce. There he earned a bachelor's degree in economics, graduating summa cum laude in 1948. He was to obtain a master's degree from the same institution in 1950 and, much later, a doctorate in 1977 after a stint at Columbia University. While there, he met the noted economics professor and public official, Dr. Arthur F. Burns.

Greenspan proved to be more than merely an academic economist. Together with a bond trader William Townsend, he formed the economic consulting firm of Townsend-Greenspan; he became the firm's director following Townsend's death in 1958. Greenspan maintained this connection until 1987, advising scores of the most important corporate entities on economic trends. He prospered as a business economist.

The year 1952 was a watershed in Greenspan's life. That year, he met Joan Mitchell, a landscape painter, to whom he was to be married for a year. Although their marriage was brief, she introduced him to one of the greatest influences in his life—the best-selling novelist and social philosopher Ayn Rand. The writer described her first meeting with

Greenspan: "He impressed me as very intelligent, brilliant and unhappy. He was groping for a frame of reference. He had no fundamental view of life." Assisted by Rand, the author of such works as *The Fountainhead* (1943) and *Atlas Shrugged* (1957), Greenspan seemed to have found that frame of reference, at least in his professional life. He subsequently espoused Rand's objectivist philosophy of individual freedom from interference, including government interference. According to this doctrine, unmitigated "rational selfishness"—and its economic adjunct, sweeping laissez-faire capitalism—would lead to the best of all worlds. Greenspan has acknowledged that Rand persuaded him that capitalism is not only efficient and practical but also moral.

Life's Work

Greenspan first became connected with official Washington in 1968, when he was named the director of domestic policy research for Republican presidential candidate Richard M. Nixon. After Nixon's election, Greenspan served on other occasional assignments. Yet he did not accept a regular government appointment until July, 1974, when President Nixon—who was soon to resign as a result of the Watergate scandal—made him chairman of the Council of Economic Advisers. True to his conservative colors, Greenspan urged Nixon's successor, President Gerald R. Ford, to make curbing inflation his administration's top economic priority. To Greenspan, keeping price levels low was more important than keeping economic growth and employment rates high. When Democrat Jimmy Carter won the 1976 presidential election, however, Greenspan returned to his consulting firm in New York.

Following Republican Ronald Reagan's presidential victory in 1980, Greenspan once again began receiving assignments from Washington. His most notable public service during this period was as chairman of the bipartisan National Commission on Social Security Reform in 1982 and 1983. This fifteen-member advisory panel recommended measures to prevent the bankruptcy of the Social Security system. He also appeared on lecture circuits and was recruited to serve on the boards of a number of corporate giants, including Alcoa, General Foods, and Mobil Oil.

Paul A. Volcker's unexpected resignation as chairman of the Federal Reserve Board as of June 1, 1987, provided the opportunity for Greenspan's appointment as Volcker's successor. His anti-inflation approach and "hands off" philosophy harmonized well with Reagan's policies, and he came highly recommended by Volcker, Secretary of the Treasury James A. Baker, and the business community. His nomination, announced on June 2, was easily confirmed by the Senate. On August 11, 1987, he was sworn in as head of the Federal Reserve System, making him director of America's central bank and giving him primary responsibility for the Reagan Administration's monetary policy.

Greenspan thus assumed a major role in manipulating money and credit in the U.S. economy, taking actions that would have important effects on the nation's income levels, interest rates, prices, and employment. His overarching goal was to keep the money supply at a level sufficient to support the total amount of goods and services produced by the economy without generating excessive inflation. To achieve this objective, the Federal Reserve Board has a number of tools at its command, such as discount rates and the commercial banks' reserve requirements.

How did Greenspan and his fellow governors on the board fare in achieving these contradictory goals? That is, did they on the whole choose an appropriate level of tradeoffs between economic growth and employment, on one hand, and inflation, on the other?

The response of the American public, as measured by a *Fortune* magazine poll in 1996, was that Greenspan had called the shots accurately, that he had set the monetary thermostat at the approximately correct reading during much of his decade in office. There were, however, a few bumps along the way. Greenspan's first test came early in his tenure as head of the "Fed." On October 19, 1987, the Dow Jones Industrial Average, a measure of prices in the New York Stock Exchange, dropped by 508 points. That drop represented 22 percent of the value of stocks traded on that exchange. By then, Greenspan had already raised the interest rate that the Fed charges its member banks once, from 5.5 to 6 percent. Following the crash and under Greenspan's impetus, the Fed quickly relaxed its anti-inflationary brake and added money to the economy to prevent further asset deflation. It reversed directions when Wall Street recovered and

inflation, flowing from the federal government's growing budget deficit, threatened once more.

The next year, 1988, was a presidential election year. Incumbent presidents or their hand-picked successors—George Bush in 1988, Bill Clinton in 1996—typically try to run in an expansionary, job-creating economic climate reflecting a good rate of growth and employment. Off-the-record pressures on the Fed were reported in both years and were generally denied. Disagreement exists as to whether Greenspan gave in to any such pressures and steered the economy in the direction desired by the president.

An unusual bank-induced "credit crunch" in 1990 and the Persian Gulf War in 1991 led to a recession that lasted from 1990 to 1992. Considering George Bush's defeat in that year, critics hold that the Fed on this occasion was not fast enough in creating an economically "winning" climate. Even though the business cycle was on an upswing by the election date in November, 1992, the electorate's perception—especially in the light of the extensive corporate downsizing under way—was that things were bad. Presidential candidate Bill Clinton's slogan "It's the economy, stupid!" played to wide and receptive audiences.

By 1994, the business community itself was openly critical of Greenspan's characteristic tight money policy, especially in the absence of conclusive indicators suggesting overheating of the economy. Disagreements on inflation levels and thus on appropriate interest rates were now connected with other fundamental structural matters. For example, increasingly permeable borders and globalism raised the question of whether the U.S. economy was less subject to inflationary pressures from domestic sources, given greater exposure to the world economy. Economists had long held that a growth rate of 2.5 percent per year could be sustained without inflation. Was that rate still realistic? No one knows for sure. Greenspan tended to answer these and other economic questions conservatively, arguing that monetary growth must be kept slow. He was not, however, a hard-boiled ideologue. On his earlier appointment to the Council of Economic Advisers in 1974, he had described himself as "not a Keynesian . . . not a monetarist . . . [but] a free enterpriser." Even though he was one of Ayn Rand's early enthusiasts, he concedes that her utopia may be impossible to achieve. Although early profiles of Greenspan played up his conservatism, later ones accented his pragmatism; for example, a March 18, 1996, *Fortune* article about Greenspan summarized his policies as heading for "no recession, no inflation, and no voodoo."

In December, 1996, in the face of a steadily rising, record-breaking stock market, then again in February, 1997, in blunter and more detailed language, Greenspan warned the investing community against "irrational exuberance." The stock market responded with decreases in the Dow Jones Industrial Average, but it was not immediately clear to what extent the expected "Greenspan effect" had cooled the stock market's frenetic rise, which continued unabated, if volatiley, in the following months.

Despite the pressures of his job with the Clinton Administration, Greenspan continued to find time to maintain a personal life. In April, 1997, he was married a second time, to television reporter Andrea Mitchell.

Summary

During his tenure as chairman of the Federal Reserve Board, Greenspan was judged generally successful in juggling the various and often contradictory aggregates of monetary policy. This assessment reflects his democratic management style, which gave others, even junior advisers, a voice in the decision-making process. As a former Wall Street economist, Alan Greenspan may be seen as more sensitive to the need for protecting the value of investors' assets than maintaining, through government action, a high level of economic growth and employment.

Greenspan's relatively consistent anti-inflationary stance sensitized several administrations, both Republican and Democratic, to the value of putting a reasonable brake on growth in the interest of a more balanced government budget and the resulting stability of the economy. Greenspan himself, in an interview with Alfred L. Malabre, Jr., of *The Wall Street Journal*, offered the following perspective on his achievements: "[T]here is a vague disillusionment with economists; we are not going out of style, but we are retrenching from what had been an unrealistic position about what we could accomplish." This encapsulates Greenspan's oftenvoiced opinion that a painless solution to economic woes is beyond the means of any economic theory or individual.

Bibliography

Andrews, Suzanna. "Other People's Money." *Mirabella*, December 1991, pp. 92-96. A rare profile of Greenspan's personal side, including his early family life, his weakness for glamorous women, his love of tennis, and his drive to please.

Branden, Barbara. *The Passion of Ayn Rand*. New York: Doubleday, 1986; London: Allen, 1987. A provocative and highly personal profile of author-philosopher Ayn Rand, whose libertarianism greatly influenced Greenspan. He weaves in and out of the narrative as a member of Rand's early inner circle. Includes photographs.

Greenspan, Alan. "Antitrust," "Gold and Economic Freedom," and "The Assault on Integrity." In *Capitalism: The Unknown Ideal,* by Ayn Rand. New York: Signet, 1966. A collection of essays on the desirable moral aspects of capitalism. Greenspan's contributions echo Rand's Objectivist philosophy of unrestricted economic freedom yielding not only maximum efficiency but also honesty and trust.

————. "Is There a New Economy? The Effect of Human Psychology on the Market." *Vital Speeches* 64, no. 24 (October 1, 1998). Transcript of a speech by Greenspan on the "new economy" and whether the gains seen since 1991 could be maintained.

————. "The Crisis in Emerging Market Economies: The Global Marketplace." *Vital Speeches* 65, no. 1 (October 15, 1998). Transcript of a speech by Greenspan concerning the need for stability in international financial markets to offset crises in emerging market economies.

Jones, David M. *The Politics of Money: The Fed Under Alan Greenspan*. New York: New York Institute of Finance, 1991. An economist's widely read critical evaluation of Greenspan's monetary policies at the Federal Reserve Board. The notes contain bibliographical references.

Norton, Rob. "In Greenspan We Trust." *Fortune*, March 18, 1996. A laudatory assessment of Greenspan's past record and future prospects following his second reappointment as chairman of the Federal Reserve Board, this time by Democratic President Bill Clinton and again to the applause of corporate America. The article profiles both the chairman and his colleagues on the board.

Rosen, Isaac. "Alan Greenspan: Chairman of the Federal Reserve Board." *Newsmakers 1992*. Detroit, Mich.: Gale, 1992. Based primarily on newspapers and periodicals; nevertheless includes, in user-friendly style, material found in such standard reference works as *Who's Who*, *Current Biography*, and *The Concise Dictionary of American Jewish Biography*. The article plays up Greenspan's intermediating skills in the various administrations but also discusses his success in achieving consensus among colleagues who espouse sharply conflicting economic theories.

Peter B. Heller

SIR EDWARD GREY

Born: April 25, 1862; London, England
Died: September 7, 1933; Fallodon, Northumberland, England
Areas of Achievement: Government and politics
Contribution: As foreign secretary for more than a decade, Grey set the course of British policy before and during the early years of World War I.

Early Life

Edward Grey was born on April 25, 1862, in London, the eldest of seven children in a prominent English family. His father, Colonel George Henry Grey, had left his career in the army by the time Edward was born and managed the family estates in Fallodon, Northumberland, where the boy grew up. When his father died suddenly in 1874, Edward's grandfather, Sir George Grey, second baronet, became the most important influence on him. Sir George had been a Member of Parliament who had held cabinet offices in several governments.

Grey was sent to preparatory school in 1871, first to a small school in Northallerton, then to Temple Grove, a more distinguished school at East Sheen. He went to Winchester, one of the country's elite public schools, in 1876, and then to Balliol College, Oxford, in 1880, where he became active in outdoor sports and a variety of other concerns but not in his studies. He was expelled from the university in 1884.

Grey did not lack the means to support himself once he left Oxford. When his grandfather died in 1882, he had inherited the family estates and title. He energetically pursued activities which were to dictate the course of his later life. One was the study of nature. A dedicated fisherman and bird fancier, he pursued his interests actively. The other field was public affairs, and he was able to begin an apprenticeship in it in July, 1884, as private secretary to Sir Evelyn Baring, later Lord Cromer. In October, 1885, Grey married Dorothy Widdrington, the daughter of a neighboring squire from Northumberland, who shared his enthusiasm for country pursuits.

Life's Work

Grey's career as a Liberal politician was launched in 1885, when he was chosen to stand for election to his grandfather's old seat in Berwick-on-Tweed. His victory at the age of twenty-three made him the youngest member of the House of Commons.

Under the influence of his rector, Mandell Creighton, Grey had adopted fairly progressive views on domestic reform. He took an especially intense interest in the most divisive issue of the day, home rule for Ireland. Like the colleagues in the House with whom he worked most closely, Herbert Asquith—later prime minister—and Richard Haldane, Grey backed home rule but was critical of the way party leader William Ewart Gladstone had handled it.

The Liberal Party, divided by the Irish question, was out of office during Grey's first years in Parliament. When they returned to power in 1892, he was made a parliamentary undersecretary in the Foreign Office. Serving first under Lord Rosebery and then Lord Kimberley, he was able to achieve some unusual prominence in the post. Because both of his foreign secretaries sat in the House of Lords, he had to speak for his department in the Commons. This he did most effectively. It was his duty in 1895 to deliver one especially important statement, "the Grey declaration," warning the French against encroaching on the upper waters of the Nile River.

Grey may have been fairly radical on some domestic issues; he was a supporter of free trade and the educational rights of religious Nonconformists. Yet in the foreign policy area which was now his specialty, he was emerging as a strong imperialist. Out of office when the Liberals left power in 1895, Grey became an ardent supporter of the Boer War (1899-1902). In the struggle for leadership of the Liberal Party, he shifted his allegiance at first toward and then away from Lord Rosebery, the choice of the more conservative wing of the party, but never backed Sir Henry Campbell-Bannerman, Rosenbery's rival and party leader.

It was by no means certain, then, that Grey would be invited to join the cabinet when the Liberals came back into office in 1905. Another factor, a rather unusual one for a rising politician, mitigated against his assuming high office: It was unclear whether he really wanted to serve. Coupled with his ambition there was always a certain reluctance which made him a rather puzzling figure to his contemporaries. He genuinely loved the world of nature and appeared to be so devoted to it that he resented time spent away from bird-watching and fishing. His classic book *Fly Fishing* had appeared in 1899, and his later *The Charm of Birds* (1927) showed his expertise in these fields. Moreover, Grey's wife, who was to die in an accident in 1906, was not interested in politics and preferred not to live in London.

When the call came, Grey hesitated and needed some convincing from his friends, but he finally went to the Foreign Office to serve Prime Minister Campbell-Bannerman. Despite his protestations that he would really like to be elsewhere and his frequent retreats to Fallodon or another country house closer to London, he stayed for eleven years, an unusually long and eventually crippling period of service at Whitehall. His policies, such as support of closer ties to France, became those of his country.

He was able to implement that policy during his first weeks in office in dealing with a major crisis which had erupted over Morocco. Germany had raised objections to French plans to annex that North African country, posing the question of how firm Great Britain's commitments to France were. Many Liberals, including Rosebery, had spoken out against the Conservative government's policy of entente with France, so there were doubts about which way Grey would take Great Britain.

Grey made it clear from the start that he intended to continue a bipartisan policy of support for France, the United States, and the Anglo-Japanese Alliance. This position made him popular with opposition Conservatives, who lauded him as more of a statesman than a politician. Back-bench Liberals were unhappy with this direction but unable to do much about it. They criticized Grey as being too insular to be foreign secretary because he had not traveled or lived abroad and could speak French only haltingly. Grey had no personal following as a politician, but Liberal leaders and the general public found him a reassuring figure to keep at Whitehall, in part because he was so purely English. Moreover, the suspicion of Germany which was at the heart of his policies was something they shared. The German thrust onto the center of the world stage, and especially her building a fleet which could challenge British supremacy at sea, was deeply resented.

Great Britain's firm support of France in the aftermath of the Moroccan crisis caused Germany to back down somewhat. Grey was able to use the support of President Theodore Roosevelt of the United States in opposing excessive German demands. He cultivated the relationship with Roosevelt, another keen naturalist, as part of his broader policy of Anglo-American cooperation. He also secured an agreement with Russia in 1907, which strengthened the entente and further isolated Germany. Friendship with the repressive Russia of the czars was a bitter pill for English Liberals to swallow, but Grey was able to get his way.

In the succession of crises which paved the way to war in 1914, Grey stuck to his course of backing the entente. Ultimately, this policy led to the creation of two rival alliance systems in Europe, which allowed a small incident to escalate into a major war. If only the entente had been less threatening to Germany, his critics argued, she might not have pursued the aggressive policies which caused war. Alternately, if Grey had only made it clear that the entente was an alliance, that Great Britain would necessarily line up with France in the event of a German attack, Germany might have held back. Yet it is doubtful whether the surge of German nationalism could have been contained by any British policy, no matter how astute. Grey can perhaps be blamed for not appreciating the military imperatives of foreign policy better. He clearly did not understand how Great Britain's diplomatic options were limited by the military conversations which were held between Great Britain and France after 1906.

When the assassination of Austrian Archduke Francis Ferdinand triggered the crisis of 1914, Grey played a pivotal role. He tried to urge settlement of the dispute through European arbitration, only to have his suggestion rejected by Austria and Germany. When the German plan to attack France through Belgium unfolded, Grey convinced a wavering British cabinet of the need to enter the war with her entente partners. Grey, making clear his revulsion to war and the sadness of the moment, was able to strike the right note to convince the British public that the right course was being pursued. That Belgian neutrality was being violated gave him a high-minded and understandable issue around which to rally the nation. In fact, the nation learned only later about the extent of its military commitment to protect France against aggression.

Grey's record as a wartime foreign secretary was mixed. His health, and in particular his eyesight, was failing by then. He was able to maintain some of the policy priorities he had set fairly well: He kept good relations with the United States by limiting the imposition of the blockade. A less successful part of his policy was the conclusion of the secret Treaty of London, signed in April, 1915, which bought Italy's entry into the war for the entente with the promise of territory on the Dalmatian coast. This and other secret treaties he signed in 1915 were later widely criticized.

When his old friend H. H. Asquith was forced out as prime minister in 1916, Grey finally left Whitehall. He was given a peerage, assuming the title Viscount Grey of Fallodon. His prestige remained high; hence, the support he gave to the League of Nations movement was critical. Increasing blindness limited his role in politics in the last years of his life. He led a mission to the United States in 1919, attempting in vain to get Americans into the League. In 1928, he was elected Chancellor of Oxford, the university which had expelled him years before. He died at Fallodon on September 7, 1933.

Summary

Sir Edward Grey was not a great statesman, but it would be unfair to place too much stress on his limitations as foreign secretary. In routine administration, he was competent, and it is doubtful if anyone else put in his place could have averted World War I. Once the war came, he was clearly not the right person to have in control at Whitehall, and his conduct of affairs was open to criticism.

In at least two other roles, Grey's contribution was noteworthy. As a writer on nature, he won a wide and devoted following. As an internationalist, in the years after he left office in 1916, he made important contributions to the establishment of the League of Nations. This world body represented for him, as for most British liberals, the path away from international anarchy and toward disarmament and peace. His leadership of the League of Nations Union gave that society the prestige it needed to build widespread support for the League in Great Britain.

Bibliography

Birn, Donald S. *The League of Nations Union, 1918-1945.* Oxford: Clarendon Press, and New York: Oxford University Press, 1981. A study of the voluntary organization to bolster support for the League of Nations. Grey founded this group and was its president until his death.

Egerton, George W. *Great Britain and the Creation of the League of Nations: Strategy, Politics, and International Organization, 1914-1919.* Chapel Hill: University of North Carolina Press, 1978; London: Scolar Press, 1979. A scholarly study of the founding of the League of Nations which contains a discussion of Grey's role.

Grey, Viscount of Fallodon. *Twenty-five Years: 1892-1916.* 2 vols. London: Hodder and Stoughton, and New York: Stokes, 1925. Not a complete autobiography, but a useful memoir of Grey's career in politics. It is a dated but still invaluable perspective on Grey's contribution.

Robbins, Keith. *Sir Edward Grey: A Biography of Lord Grey of Fallodon.* London: Cassell, 1971. A reliable and well-documented scholarly biography with a balanced perspective on Grey's career.

Steiner, Zara S. *Britain and the Origins of the First World War.* London: Macmillan, and New York: St. Martin's Press, 1977. A balanced account of British foreign policy during the period of Grey's stewardship at the Foreign Office. It contains many useful observations on his approach to policy-making.

Trevelyan, George Macaulay. *Grey of Fallodon.* London and New York: Longman, 1937. A very readable but somewhat oversympathetic account of Grey's life by an eminent historian.

Donald S. Birn

D. W. GRIFFITH

Born: January 22, 1875; Floydsfork, Kentucky
Died: July 23, 1948; Hollywood, California
Area of Achievement: Motion pictures
Contribution: A genius in the exposition of complex plots through revolutionary filmmaking techniques, Griffith was the foremost figure in the development of the American film as an expression of American values and as a commercially successful medium.

Early Life

David Wark Griffith was born January 22, 1875, in the family farmhouse at Floydsfork in Oldham County, Kentucky, the second youngest of seven children. His mother, née Mary Oglesby, was the daughter of a wealthy Kentucky farmer who provided his daughter and her husband with a cottage and employment on his farm. David's father, Jacob Griffith, who claimed descent from Virginia planter aristocracy, was a romantic ne'er-do-well who, although he died when David was only seven years old, had a profound influence on his young son. Jacob Griffith had a checkered career. He had left his home in Virginia as a young man and gone to Kentucky, where he studied medicine as an apprentice for two years and briefly practiced it in Floydsburg. Unsuccessful and easily bored, he went off to fight in the Mexican War. He then returned to Kentucky, married, and, in 1850, left his wife and three children to escort a wagon train from Missouri to California toward the end of the Gold Rush. After returning home, in 1853-1854, he served in the Kentucky legislature. His glory days, however, lay ahead. At the outbreak of the Civil War he became a colonel under General Thomas "Stonewall" Jackson. He was wounded on several occasions, and one of these wounds, improperly treated, contributed to his later semi-invalidism and death. His most unusual wartime experience was to lead a victorious cavalry charge from a buggy since his wounds prevented him from riding a horse.

After the war, the Griffith family lived in the genteel poverty common among many of their station at the time. Jacob Griffith dabbled again briefly in Kentucky politics but spent most of his time regaling his family with tales of his heroic experiences and of the Lost Cause. He also convinced the young and impressionable David of his descent from Welsh kings. He read to his family in his deeply resonant voice from Edgar Allan Poe, Sir Walter Scott, and William Shakespeare and took his children to a magic-lantern show which made a deep impression on the young David. By 1882, Jacob Griffith was dead, a victim of his wartime wounds and heavy drinking. It was during David's childhood years that his outlook was to be developed: He became a romantic imbued with a sense of Southern gentility and convinced of his destiny to make his name in the literary and artistic world.

After the colonel's death, the family eventually moved to Louisville, where the young Griffith's mother opened a rooming and boarding house. Griffith took a variety of menial jobs to supplement the family's income. Most significant, he worked in the bookstore run by Bernard and Washington Flexner, members of a remarkable family of Jewish intellectuals. The shop was a gathering place for many local writers, including James Whitcomb Riley. David's literary appetite was further whetted by this experience. He also attended, as means would allow, this river town's numerous theaters and developed that intense interest so characteristic of youth. He was soon convinced that his destiny was to become a playwright, an American Shakespeare. He also developed an interest in acting as the means by which he could best learn stagecraft. By his early twenties, he had a job as an actor in a touring group of amateur players, much to his mother's dismay. In deference to his mother, he took the name Lawrence Griffith and began his theatrical career.

By the late 1890's, when Griffith began his theatrical career, he had developed the physical appearance he was to retain for most of the remainder of his life. Tall and thin with an aquiline nose, high forehead, and a moderately wide, thin-lipped mouth, he conveyed an aristocratic mien well suited to the stage actor. Later in life, he always wore a wide-brimmed hat.

Acting then, as ever, was an insecure profession. There were always more actors than roles, and anticipating the changing tastes of a fickle public was difficult. Thus, although Griffith acted, he took numerous other jobs as well. He worked in a steel mill and on a ship that carried lumber along the West Coast. He rode a freight train across country and begged for food. These experiences were important, however, for they acquainted the son of Southern aristocrats with the variety and conditions of men. In 1905, in San Francisco, he met a

young actress, Linda Arvidson, who was to become his first wife. After the marriage, a year later in Boston, the two continued to act intermittently and maintained a hand-to-mouth existence. Griffith continued to write plays and sold one, *A Fool and a Girl*, in 1907 for seven hundred dollars. He also sold a poem and a short story for considerably lesser amounts and got an occasional acting role. In his early thirties, however, he was essentially a failure as an actor and writer. Yet his passion for both did not abate, and a chance meeting in 1908 which enabled him to utilize his talents successfully ignited a spark that was to develop into an obsession: a career in the fledgling motion-picture industry.

Life's Work

In the spring of 1908, in New York City, Griffith ran into an old friend, a fellow actor he had not seen for several years. As each recounted his experiences to the other, Griffith told his friend of the financial straits in which he and his wife then found themselves. The friend told Griffith that the motion-picture industry had been a lifesaver to him and suggested Griffith contact some of the numerous studios then operating in New York. Although Griffith knew little about this rapidly growing new industry, he took his friend's suggestion and found employment at the Edison Company. In his only film for Edison, Griffith worked under cinematographer-director Edwin S. Porter, the creator of the famous "chase" film *The Great Train Robbery* (1903). Griffith was to use the device of the chase in many of his own films, including *The Birth of a Nation* (1915), *Intolerance* (1916), *Way Down East* (1920), and *Orphans of the Storm* (1922). Griffith also learned from Porter the rudiments of the trick-shot or special effect, which he later incorporated into his films. At that time interested primarily in scriptwriting, Griffith turned to American Biograph Studios, where he and his wife then found employment, she as an actress and he as a writer and actor. Within weeks, however, Griffith was given his first opportunity to direct. Having found what, in combination with writing, proved to be his calling, Griffith started to work, immediately choosing the cast and crew of his first film, *The Adventures of Dollie* (1908). His most important choice was his cameraman, Billy (G. W.) Bitzer, who worked closely with Griffith throughout the heyday of the director's career.

Thus, in 1908, Griffith began his five-year tenure at Biograph, a period during which he developed his craft as a technician and storyteller, built up a talented crew of technical personnel headed by Bitzer, and created a stock company of players including Mary Pickford, Lionel Barrymore, Henry B. Walthall, Mae Marsh, Robert Harron, and, most important, the Gish sisters, Dorothy and the luminous Lillian—who was, for Griffith, the embodiment of virginal innocence and his favorite and most talented performer. During his years at Biograph, Griffith made more than four hundred films, none longer than two reels and of varying quality. Moving his operations to California and establishing his fame inside and outside the industry, Griffith became dissatisfied with Biograph's financial and creative restrictions. In October, 1913, he left Biograph, taking with him his players and certain technical and business personnel, and joined the recently allied Reliance-Majestic production company and the Mutual distributing company, for whom he made four films in 1914. Within less than a year he started to work on the first and best remembered of his masterpieces, *The Birth of a Nation*, the film which elevated the motion picture to art.

The Birth of a Nation is about two families, one from the South, the other from the North, during the Civil War and Reconstruction. Based upon two books by Thomas Dixon, an avowed racist, the scenario by Griffith was significantly different, less racist. The film, which when first shown ran two hours and forty-five minutes, is nevertheless pro-Southern, and its leading villains, especially in the section dealing with Reconstruction, are white abolitionists and carpetbaggers, blacks, and mulattoes. Indeed, it is the Ku Klux Klan, under the leadership of the film's Southern hero, which eventually prevails. For this reason, the film was at the time and has continued to be widely criticized. Nevertheless, it was the greatest film of its time and is considered one of the major films in history because of its impact on later filmmakers. Griffith's Civil War battle scenes, based on his study of the photographs by Matthew Brady, have never been improved upon. His attention to historical accuracy in set construction was also remarkable, and he set a standard few filmmakers have reached since. The film is also important for Griffith's ability to develop three-dimensional characters in what is essentially a spectacle film. Technically the film was far ahead of its time, and every film director since has been consciously or unconsciously influenced by it. Many of the features found separately in earlier

Griffith films are found together in *The Birth of a Nation*: the close-up, the fade-out, the wide landscape shot, the use of moving cameras attached to vehicles in action scenes, and the action close-up of horses' hooves. Most important, Griffith was the first director-producer-writer to master the art of editing, enabling him to switch rapidly from place to place and character to character in a long, complex narrative and maintain the interest of the viewer. The film, which President Woodrow Wilson described as "history written by lightning," was a great critical and popular success, even as it was simultaneously attacked, vindicating Griffith's solicitation of additional financing when Reliance-Majestic ran short of funds. Unfortunately, Griffith enjoyed his greatest success with this, one of his very first feature films. At the peak of his creativity, he soon was to find that he was artistically and intellectually far ahead of his audience.

The success of *The Birth of a Nation* led Griffith to undertake immediately his magnum opus, *Intolerance*, which many film historians regard as the greatest film ever made, but which, at the time of its release in 1916, was a commercial failure. The theme is essentially the same as that of *The Birth of a Nation*: the damage wrought by hypocritical do-gooders who attempt to remold society in the image of what they think it should be without regard for the pain and suffering they cause. The scope of the film is, however, much larger, and this is what confused audiences. Griffith moves rapidly from twentieth century industrial America, to ancient Babylon, to Palestine at the time of Jesus, to sixteenth century France during the wars of religion. The segments of the film are bridged by a recurring scene of the universal mother forever rocking the cradle, reflecting Griffith's conviction of the endurance of love even during periods of evil and destruction. The spectacle of the film is revolutionary, especially the scenes of the walls and public buildings of Babylon. All the revolutionary technical innovations found in Griffith's first great film are here as well. In *Intolerance*, however, the subject matter was too obscure for the average viewer, and Griffith's editing confused more than excited.

Griffith continued to make films, though none of the scope and expense of *The Birth of a Nation* and *Intolerance*, with the partial exception of *Orphans of the Storm*, set during the French Revolution and notable for its action sequences, such as that of the storming of the Bastille. After 1916, Griffith became less independent because of the financial failure of *Intolerance* and found his creativity often stifled by the studios, even by United Artists, which he founded jointly with Douglas Fairbanks, Mary Pickford, and Charles Chaplin. One very significant additional film, however, was made. It was far more intimate than the aforementioned films and was made almost entirely on interior sets. This was *Broken Blossoms* (1919), a tragic tale set in the slums of London about the corruption and destruction of the virtuous and good.

Griffith reached the apex of his career by his early forties. From 1921 on, he found himself the prisoner of studio heads and their accountants. The independence which had fostered his creativity—his ability to work as director, producer, writer, and editor—was lost. He made his last film in 1931, a forgettable one called *The Struggle*. From that time until his death, Griffith was lost. He returned to Kentucky for several years, married a woman thirty-five years his junior (his first marriage had broken up during his Biograph days, although he did not get a divorce until 1936), and then returned to Hollywood in the late 1930's to work for Hal Roach on *One Million B.C.* (1940). When that film was completed, Griffith's name was mysteriously excluded from the credits. During the 1940's, he was a lonely, embittered man, often the recipient of praise and awards but unable to find employment in the city whose success he, more than any other, had assured; he was merely tolerated by many who had appropriated his innovations to their own use. Divorced for a second time in 1947, Griffith suffered a cerebral hemorrhage in the small hotel where he lived. He died at Temple Hospital on July 23, 1948.

Summary

D. W. Griffith was the foremost creative figure in the history of motion pictures. He developed the motion picture, America's greatest contribution to the arts, into a viable commercial and artistic medium. His influence on the evolution of the medium is incalculable, and it was recognized by many during his time, especially in the years during which he was ignored. He is a tragic figure in the history of American art. Beginning his career in an age when men of creative genius were allowed freedom in the application of their directorial, literary, and technical talents, he fell victim to the cupidity and timidity of an industry which he, more than any other, helped to create. To the end the Southern gentleman, he was unable to sacrifice his uncommon ideals to the demands of a medium which often has flourished on the trivial and the banal.

Bibliography

Croy, Homer. *Star Maker: The Story of D. W. Griffith*. New York: Duell Sloan, 1959. An anecdotal account of Griffith by a man who himself was active in the film industry in its early years. Not always accurate, it is engagingly written and provides a satisfactory introduction to the subject.

Gish, Lillian, and Ann Pinchot. *The Movies, Mr. Griffith and Me*. London: Allen, and Englewood Cliffs, N.J.: Prentice-Hall, 1969. A delightful autobiography by the actress most loved and admired by Griffith, and who reciprocated in affection and admiration for him.

Griffith, D. W. *The Man Who Invented Hollywood: The Autobiography of D. W. Griffith*. Edited by James Hart. Louisville, Ky.: Touchstone, 1972. The subject's own account of his life, essential for the serious student.

Henderson, Robert M. *D. W. Griffith: His Life and Work*. New York: Oxford University Press, 1972.

————. *D. W. Griffith: The Years at Biograph*. New York: Farrar Straus, 1970; London: Secker and Warburg, 1971. Readable and authoritative accounts of Griffith's life by a man who has come to be recognized as the leading authority on the film pioneer.

Mast, Gerald. *A Short History of the Movies*. 6th ed. Boston: Allyn and Bacon, 1996. Includes a valuable evaluation of Griffith and his films within the context of the entire history, national and international, of filmmaking.

O'Dell, Paul, and Anthony Slide. *Griffith and the Rise of Hollywood*. New York: Barnes, 1971. A brief but useful volume in the International Film Guide Series. O'Dell emphasizes Griffith's artistic contributions to motion pictures, contributions he believes have been ignored by those who have concentrated only on his technical innovations.

Schickel, Richard. *D. W. Griffith: An American Life*. New York: Simon and Schuster, 1984. A massive biography that includes virtually every bit of information one could want to know about Griffith. Schickel, the film critic for *Time* magazine, has written numerous books on American film and the personalities prominent in its development. Though packed with information, this book is highly readable and incorporates more up-to-date material on Griffith.

Simmon, Scott. " 'The Female of the Species.' D.W. Griffith: Father of the Woman's Film." *Film Quarterly* 46, no. 2 (Winter 1992). Discusses Griffith's groundbreaking direction of films focusing on women's interests.

————. *The Films of D.W. Griffith*. Cambridge and New York: Cambridge University Press, 1993. This study places Griffith and his work in the context of film history and focuses on perceptions of him as both a cinematic genius and a creator of racist films. *The Birth of a Nation* and *Intolerance* are analyzed.

Williams, Martin. *Griffith: First Artist of the Movies*. New York: Oxford University Press, 1980. A fine, brief treatment of Griffith and his films, this book provides the reader with an ideal introduction to the subject.

J. Stewart Alverson

JUAN GRIS
José Victoriano González

Born: March 23, 1887; Madrid, Spain
Died: May 11, 1927; Boulogne-sur-Seine, France
Area of Achievement: Art
Contribution: Despite a relatively short professional career, Gris was one of the founding fathers and most influential artists of the cubist movement in art in the early twentieth century.

Early Life

José Victoriano González, later known as Juan Gris, was born in Madrid, Spain, on March 23, 1887, the thirteenth of fourteen children. His father, Gregorio Gonzalez, was a prosperous businessman. According to one of his sisters, he began drawing around the age of six or seven. In 1902, Gris was enrolled at Madrid's Escuela de Artes y Manufacturas (School of Arts and Industries), where he studied mathematics, engineering, science, and physics. He soon developed an interest in painting. He began to send sketches to the Madrid papers *Blanco y Negro, Madrid Comico,* and others, though he was paid little. In 1904, he entered the studio of José Moreno Carbonero to study painting, but the experience was not a happy one. Carbonero was later to tutor Salvador Dalí. Gris also began to associate with foreign painters in Madrid during this period.

In 1906, Gris illustrated *Alma América, Poemas indo-españoles* (1906) by the Peruvian poet José Santos Chocano; one illustration is signed "J. Gris," the first known use by the artist of his pseudonym. Gris's future style is evoked in a startling manner in this early work. There is considerable speculation as to why he chose the pseudonym "Gris" (in both French and Spanish it means "gray") for his work; the most frequent theory is that he chose to exhibit his independence from his background and that the name Gris seemed most clearly neutral. While Gris continued to contribute to Madrid's journals, he decided that his artistic development necessitated a move to Paris.

Life's Work

Gris was nineteen when he decided to go to Paris and sold all of his possessions to be able to do so. He arrived in Paris nearly penniless in September, 1906, having only sixteen francs in his pockets. A friend, a painter from his Madrid days named Daniel Vasquez Diaz immediately introduced him to a fellow Spaniard, Pablo Picasso, and he moved into the same building at 13 rue Ravignand, a studio he was not to abandon completely until 1922. Gris had not done his military service prior to his departure, and this would later hamper his efforts to obtain a passport for foreign travel.

Gris met many of Paris' literary and artistic avant-garde, including Guillaume Apollinaire, Max Jacob, André Salmon, Georges Braque, and Maurice Raynal. A new artistic spirit was evolving, one that combined sources as diverse as African art and French poetry. Picasso, six years older than Gris, was to serve as a "big brother," and Gris was both to acknowledge his debt and to admire his fellow Spaniard for the rest of his life. While he carried on his work for the illustrated papers, he began to work on projects that followed his own interests. It was nearly four years before Gris decided to exhibit his paintings.

Gris was quite poor during the next six years; his major source of income was selling satirical drawings to French and Spanish publications. In the winter of 1907, Gris was befriended by Daniel-Henry Kahnweiler, who opened a gallery and later represented Gris. Besides rough drawings and some still-life drawings, only one painting, *Siphon and Bottles,* dated 1910, remains from these early years. It seems likely that Gris destroyed much of his work done before 1910; he would later throw out paintings that dissatisfied him and request his agent and wife to destroy all preparatory sketches. He began to paint in the cubist style in 1911-1912. Gris's works from this period have an analytical style and metallic sheen; one work from this period capturing these characteristics is his *Portrait of Picasso* (1912). Gris was totally absorbed in his work during this period; Max Jacob later related that Gris said, "I only stroke dogs with my left hand so that if I am bitten I shall still have my right hand to paint with."

In April, 1909, Lucie Belin, Gris's mistress, had a son, who was named Georges Gonzalez Gris; after Gris and Belin separated, the child was sent to Madrid, where he was reared by relatives. Georges did not return to Paris until 1926, at his father's request, to continue his studies in chemical engineering.

In the spring of 1910, Gris exhibited his cubist paintings at the Salon des Indépendants. Later that year, his paintings were included in a "Section d'Or" society exhibition, which included Fernand Leger, Marcel Duchamp, Jacques Villon, and Louis Dunnoyer de Segonzac, all cubist painters. Shortly thereafter Gris's works began to be bought by collectors, and his financial difficulties eased considerably.

In January, 1912, Gris had his first exhibition at Sagot's gallery. In September, Gris began to experiment with the *papier collé* technique, following the earlier efforts of Picasso and Braque. Later that month, he signed with Kahnweiler for the agent to represent his work, which meant that he no longer participated in salon exhibitions. Kahnweiler wrote, "I became convinced that in this painter, whose development I had been watching for some time, I had in fact discovered an artist as great as I believed. . . ." The friendship would last until Gris's death.

In August, 1913, Gris and his new wife, Josette Herpin, moved to Ceret, where a number of other cubist painters had taken up residence. They remained there until November. While at Ceret, Gris further experimented with the *papier collé* (collage) technique. Throughout 1914, Gris worked almost exclusively in the *papier collé* method. The same year, Gris spent time with Henri Matisse at Collioure. With the outbreak of World War I in August, 1914, the cubist movement was dispersed. Kahnweiler had returned to Germany the previous month, because of persecution. Many artists, including Apollinaire, Braque, Derain, Leger, and Raynal, entered military service. Gris's finances were hard hit by Kahnweiler's absence, and Gertrude Stein sent him two hundred francs. Attempts by other dealers to represent Gris's works fell through because of Gris's loyalty to Kahnweiler. Gris returned to Paris in 1915 and remained there until the end of the war.

During the war years Gris's style continued to evolve. His cubist works became more ordered, with architectural elements in their design becoming more prominent. Gris himself referred to his paintings from this period as "flat, coloured architecture." In 1917, Gris produced his only sculpture, *Harlequin*, now in the Philadelphia Museum of Art.

Cubism began to decline as a style after World War I; in 1920, Gris participated in the last exhibition by cubists as a group, the Salon des Indépendants. That autumn Gris's health began to falter, and he wintered at Bandol. While at Bandol in April, 1921, Gris was contacted by Sergei Diaghilev, impresario of Les Ballets Russes, to do sets and costumes for an upcoming production. Gris went to Monte Carlo to discuss the project, but it was later abandoned. Diaghilev and Gris later collaborated on several ballets, among them *La Colombe*, *Les Tentations de la Bergère*, and *L'Éducation Manquée*. His last work for Diaghilev was an architectural work for a Red Cross fête held on May 28, 1924.

Gris also strove to reveal his theories behind his art. In 1921, he attempted to explain his attempts to inject warmth into the rigid, mathematical elements of cubist style by stating, "I consider that the architectural element is mathematics, the abstract side; I want to humanize it." Despite his adherence to cubist ideals, he saw himself squarely within the Western European classical tradition, remarking, "I cannot break away from the Louvre. Mine is the method of all times, the method used by the old masters." On May 15, 1924, he read "Les Possibilités de la Peinture" (on the possibilities of painting) to the Society of Philosophic and Scientific Studies at the Sorbonne. The paper was later widely published in German, French, Spanish, and English journals, and Gris became widely known.

Gris was constantly ill during the last two years of his life. While stoically bearing his suffering, Gris was forced by his ill health to move frequently, in search of a climate more conducive to his being. Gris died on the evening of May 11, 1927, from uremia. He was buried two days later in Boulogne-sur-Seine. Among the mourners were his son Georges, Jacques Lipchitz, Raynal, Kahnweiler, and Picasso.

Summary

Despite his death at an early age, Juan Gris belongs to a select group of artists who created and refined cubism, an artistic style that echoes through the present. Gris's entire painted output was completed between his twenty-third and fortieth birthdays. Unlike Picasso, who quickly moved on from the cubist style after initial experimentation, Gris continued to create in that genre until his death. Along with Picasso, Braque, and Leger, Gris is considered one of the giants of the cubist style. While cubism lasted less than a decade as an avant-garde style practiced by many artists, its influence has continued to make itself felt. Cubism's influence was felt in fields beyond painting. For Gris's ability there was an increasing admiration; Gertrude Stein, a friend of both Gris and Picasso, called Gris "a perfect painter."

Shortly after Gris's death, Picasso was standing in front of one of Gris's canvases and observed, "it's grand to see a painter who knew what he was doing." Gris himself had a very clear notion of what he was trying to achieve in his art, once observing, "I start with an abstraction in order to arrive at a true fact. Mine is an art of synthesis, of deduction. . . ." Traces of his style can today be seen everywhere from the graffiti in the New York subways to the gigantic Soviet propaganda placards.

Bibliography

Cooper, Douglas, and Gary Tinterow. *The Essential Cubism: Braque, Picasso, and Their Friends, 1907-1920.* London: Tate, 1983; New York: Braziller, 1984. This is a catalog with commentary on a cubist exhibition held at the Tate Gallery in London in the spring of 1983. It is a very useful work for setting Gris in the context of his contemporaries; the reproductions are excellent, with many in color.

Gaya-Nuño, Juan Antonio. *Juan Gris.* Translated by Kenneth Lyons. Boston: New York Graphic Society, 1975. This translation of a Spanish work contains not only numerous black-and-white and color reproductions of Gris's work but also an extensive text and annotated bibliography on Gris.

Green, Christopher. *Juan Gris.* London: Whitechapel Art Gallery, and New Haven, Conn.: Yale University Press, 1992. Study of the works of Gris in the context of his cultural, political, and intellectual times.

Gris, Juan. "On the Possibilities of Painting." Parts 1/2. *Transatlantic Review* 1 (June/July, 1924): 482-488, 75-79. An explanation by Gris of the concepts involved in his art, from color to aesthetic technique. Gris concludes that "the essence of painting is the expression of certain relationships between the painter and the outside world," and that a painting is the 'intimate association' of these relationships on the painted surface."

Kahnweiler, Daniel-Henry. *Juan Gris: His Life and Work.* Translated by Douglas Cooper. London: Humphries, and New York: Curt Valentin, 1947. The English translation of Kahnweiler's work is a very useful source for information on Gris. The author represented the artist's work in Paris and was a close personal friend of the artist.

Kaufman, Jason Edward. "Juan Gris, Cubism's Great Theorist." *World and I* 8, no. 7 (July, 1993). Profile of Gris including biographical information, his contributions to Cubist painting, and a review of a Gris exhibition at the Whitechapel Art Gallery in London.

Rosenthal, Mark. *Juan Gris.* New York: Abbeville Press, 1983. A catalog and critique with reproductions published on the occasion of an exhibition of Gris's work displayed in Berkeley, California, Washington, D.C., and New York City. The text contains a fairly standard biography of Gris but includes many color reproductions of his work that are hard to find elsewhere. A useful bibliography of writing by Gris is included as well as a listing of works illustrated by him and monographs covering aspects of his life.

Soby, James Thrall. *Juan Gris.* New York: Museum of Modern Art, 1958. This work was published to coincide with an exhibition of Gris's work held at the Museum of Modern Art in the spring of 1958. Most of Gris's major works are represented, and the text is very informative, though rather sparse on the painter's early years in Spain.

John C. K. Daly

WALTER GROPIUS

Born: May 18, 1883; Berlin, Germany
Died: July 5, 1969; Boston, Massachusetts
Area of Achievement: Architecture
Contribution: Considered one of the founders of modern architecture, Gropius worked to make architecture and art responsive to the needs of an urbanized and industrialized society. His major projects were in urban and industrial architecture and in industrial design. He designed educational programs in both modern architecture and industrial design.

Early Life

Walter Adolph Gropius was born into a family with an architectural and artistic tradition. His father was an architect involved in city planning. His great uncle was an architect of distinction, a student and colleague of the classical architect Karl Friedrich Schinkel. The young Gropius always knew he wanted to be an architect. Gropius was deeply influenced by two developments he witnessed firsthand: the rapid expansion of Berlin from a city of 800,000 in 1871 to one of nearly three million in 1914 and the emergence of Germany as Europe's greatest industrial power. Everywhere, Gropius saw the problems created by rapid urbanization and industrialization: dark, inefficient factories; squalid, unsanitary housing; household and industrial products shoddy in construction and ugly in design. The problem, as Gropius saw it, was that architecture and the architect had become divorced from engineering, science, and technology; art and the artist had become separated from design and craftsmanship. For Gropius, they were inseparable and should be reunited.

Finding the curriculum at the Technical Institute in Berlin irrelevant, Gropius continued his architectural training in Munich but failed to take the degree. He always maintained he learned more from reading, observing, and working in the studios of architects than he did from formal studies. Gropius was fortunate in obtaining a position in the studio of Peter Behrens, one of the outstanding architects of the time.

Life's Work

Two innovative designs, modern in the sense of being free of eclecticism and ornamentation, established Gropius as one of Europe's outstanding young architects. The first, a factory building completed in 1911, used glass and steel in an innovative way. Gropius reduced the walls to screens of glass suspended from a steel frame, thereby emphasizing their nonstructural function; he cantilevered the floors, thereby eliminating the traditional corner supports. A definitive resolution of architectural design and engineering technique, the building was of amazing lightness but at the same time sturdy, handsome, and functional. Gropius' other design, a model, combining factory, garage, and administration building and using the same innovative techniques, including cantilevered stairs dramatically encased in transparent glass silos, was a major attraction in an exhibition held in 1914 in Cologne.

The 1914-1918 war, in which Gropius served with distinction, interrupted his career but gave him the opportunity to reconsider his goals. For Gropius, the war had destroyed the old order not only in politics but also in architecture and art. It was a time for new beginnings. Gropius' opportunity came as early as 1915, when the Grand Duke of Saxe-Weimar asked him to head the Weimar School of Arts and Crafts. Gropius accepted the post in 1919 and shortly thereafter combined the school with the Weimar Academy of Fine Arts to create the Bauhaus—a great educational invention with far-reaching effects on art, architecture, and design. The Bauhaus, which can be translated as "house of creative constructions," was primarily an idea. Gropius sought to reunite architecture with technology and science, and art with design and handicraft. Because of the troubled economic conditions in Germany which precluded expensive architectural creations, the major emphasis was on art, industrial, and product design.

Gropius refused to see technology, science, and the machine as enemies. His answer to modernity was more modernity. The machine had become the great medium of artistic creation. The task of the architect and artist was not only to understand but also to master and utilize all three. To his school Gropius attracted some of the greatest names in modern art—artists such as Paul Klee, Wassily Kandinsky, Lyonel Feininger, and László Moholy-Nagy. Students could work in a wide number of areas, from typography and poster design to ceramics, metals, and fabrics. All students had to take introductory courses in the structure and creative possibilities of basic materials such as stone, fiber, glass, or wood and in the logical structure of an artistic creation. All students worked alternately under the supervision of a craftsman and an artist. All students had to produce a design suitable for mass production.

Considering its short life, the production of the Bauhaus was considerable, and many of its designs, such as the tubular steel chair, are now commonplace. Finding the atmosphere at Weimar increasingly hostile, Gropius moved the Bauhaus to Dessau in 1925 and designed for it an integrated group of buildings considered among the finest examples of modern architecture. Gropius always believed buildings to be the supreme artistic creation—a combination of architecture, art, painting, sculpture, and design. The Bauhaus buildings were palpable evidence.

Gropius created a variety of product designs from spoons to automobile bodies, but his first love was always architecture. During the Bauhaus period, in addition to the buildings of the school, he designed low-cost workers' housing utilizing prefabricated panels, a plan for the Chicago Tribune Tower that was not adopted, and an imaginative design for a "total theater" in which the proscenium arch was eliminated, thereby eliminating too the barrier between actors and audience. Movable panels enabled the theater to be turned into one with a deep or narrow stage or to become a theater-in-the-round.

Facing increased opposition from the rising tide of right-wing fanaticism in Germany, Gropius left the Bauhaus in 1928 to work as an independent architect in Berlin. Continuing his work in urban housing and planning, Gropius developed slab apartment houses—long, narrow high-rises placed in parklike settings at angles designed to maximize the availability of light and air. Gropius disliked the peripheral design of traditional city blocks with their lightless airshafts and rear courts, with one side never receiving sunlight. For workers, Gropius designed less expensive but equally pleasant row, or ribbon, housing, one apartment wide and two or three stories high. In addition to light and air, he planned for trees, flowers, and greenery, of which ordinary workers were usually deprived. Gropius also worked on developing prefabricated parts that could be utilized to produce individualized, creative housing.

The Nazi takeover of power in 1933 ended Gropius' career in Germany. The new totalitarian state could not tolerate a free spirit such as his. Us-

ing a theatrical conference in Italy as a pretext, Gropius and his wife in 1934 left for Rome and from there went to England as exiles.

Gropius' stay in England was short but productive. His design for a college became the prototype for much of England's post-World War II academic architecture. In 1937, he accepted an invitation to become professor of architecture at Harvard University. The following year, he became chairman of the department of architecture at the Graduate School of Design. He now embarked on the second most important phase of his career, again involving education.

Gropius turned the Harvard architectural school into the most influential in the world. The major emphasis was on social commitment, social criticism, teaching, and counseling. His objective was to foster free spirit and creative thinking. Gropius had no desire for disciples or smaller editions of himself. As in the Bauhaus years, he found time for architectural designs. As he had done throughout his career with the exception of the Bauhaus buildings, Gropius always worked with other architects as well as artists, engineers, and builders.

Most of his projects in the United States were done working with The Architects Collaborative (TAC), an organization that included some of his former students

Gropius always asked what the social and economic utility of a projected design would be. Many of Gropius' admirers believed that because of collaboration and social commitment, the creative aspect of his work suffered. Gropius, however, deplored the egotism of some of his better-known colleagues and maintained that if it were a question of the importance of the container or the contained, the latter must take precedence. He conceived of a building not as a monument but as an impersonal instrument, a receptacle for the flow of life. Probably his most important design of the Harvard years was that of the Harvard Graduate Center.

Gropius' work inevitably inspired copyists, and styles called "International" or "Bauhaus" developed and were attributed to him. Gropius deplored the trend and repeatedly stated that introducing a definitive style was not his intention, but rather a methodology or ideas that would fulfill a need or resolve a problem as effectively and as expeditiously as possible.

Gropius left Harvard in 1952, again to devote himself to architecture. Major projects that resulted were the Grand Central City Building in New York, the American Embassy in Athens, and the spectacular University of Baghdad in Iraq. True to the work ethic of his Prussian background, Gropius worked to the last. He helped design a glass factory in 1968; he died the following year. Gropius was married twice. His first marriage, to Alma Schindler Mahler, ended in divorce. He was survived by his second wife, the former Ise Frank.

Summary

Walter Gropius' greatness must be seen in context with what he called collaborative, or total, architecture—that is, architecture involved with technology, science, other arts, economic and social utility, and the environment. To this should be added the psychological element, for Gropius was convinced that art or beauty was part of the human psyche, as was a relationship to nature. Gropius saw the gap not only between architecture, science, and technology, between art and craftsmanship, but also between human beings and the environment. Gropius was an environmentalist before the word came into common usage. Narrowing

that gap was the objective of his professional work and social commitment. He submerged his own creative talents by collaborating with others; he sacrificed fame and monetary rewards in favor of teaching; and he disavowed architectural dogma and style in favor of methodology. Gropius should be remembered as much for his humanity as for his architecture.

Bibliography

Bayer, Herbert, Walter Gropius, and Ise Gropius, eds. *Bauhaus, 1919-1928*. New York: Museum of Modern Art, 1938; London: Secker and Warburg, 1975. This is both a guide to and overview of the important exhibit the museum mounted in 1938 on the work of the Bauhaus. In addition to informative essays by authorities in the field, of particular value are the many detailed illustrations that give some indication of the wide scope of Bauhaus work and design.

Dornberg, John. "Rebirth of the Bauhaus." *ART-news* 92, no. 8 (October, 1993). Discusses the Bauhaus School and Gropius' collection.

Fitch, James Marston. *Walter Gropius*. New York: Braziller, 1960; London: Mayflower, 1961. This short book is probably the best general introduction to Gropius and his work. Succinct and readable, it covers Gropius' career in his capacities as educator, architect and designer, and social critic. The many annotated illustrations cover both Gropius' completed projects and his designs.

Gay, Peter. *Art as Act: On Causes in History: Manet, Gropius, Mondrian*. New York: Harper, 1976. A distinguished historian, as part of a lecture series, analyzes Gropius from the viewpoint of a "cause" in history. Entitled "Imperatives of Crafts," Gay supports Gropius' thesis of the need for the reuniting of art and craft. Of particular interest is the relation of Gropius' work to earlier architects such as Schinkel and to contemporaries such as Ludwig Mies van der Rohe and Le Corbusier. Completed after Gropius' death, the essay covers his entire career.

Giedion, Sigfried. *Walter Gropius: Work and Teamwork*. London: Architectural Press, and New York: Reinhold, 1954. Probably the most comprehensive book in English on Gropius, prepared by a professional and obvious admirer. The book is divided into two parts: text and illustrations. The text is comprehensive and covers

Gropius' career from its beginning to 1953 and includes all of his major projects. Detailed illustrations cover not only completed projects and designs but also many of his industrial and product designs.

Gropius, Walter. *Scope of Total Architecture.* New York: Harper, 1955; London: Allen and Unwin, 1956. A relatively short but important collection of essays, speeches, and reviews on architectural education, the contemporary architect, housing, and what is meant by total architecture. What becomes evident is Gropius' great breadth of interest, the strength of his convictions, and his combative assertiveness. Of particular interest is the essay "The Architect—Servant or Leader?"

Gropius, Walter, and Arthur S. Wensinger. *The Theater of the Bauhaus.* London and Baltimore: Johns Hopkins University Press, 1996. First published in English in 1961, this is the reproduction of the fourth of the fourteen Bauhaus Books. Includes photographs, drawings, and four essays: "U-Theater" by Farkas Molnar; "Man and Art Figure" and "Theater (Butane)" by Oskar Schlemmer; and "Theater, Circus, Variety" by Laszlo Moholy-Nagy.

Nis Petersen

HEINZ GUDERIAN

Born: June 17, 1888; Culm, Germany
Died: May 15, 1954; Schwangau bei Füssen, West
  Germany
Area of Achievement: The military
Contribution: Guderian was the tactical innovator
  who created the modern armored division, using
  tanks with motorized support as a battle formation. He led German panzers with great success
  in the early years of World War II.

Early Life

Heinz Wilhelm Guderian was born June 17, 1888,
at Culm, Germany (now Chełmno, Poland), eldest
son of Friedrich Guderian, a Prussian officer and
later a general, and Clara Kirchoff. The families
were more junker gentry than officer in background. Heinz attended the Karlsruhe Cadet
School at Baden from 1901 to 1903, the Cadet
School at Gross-Lichterfelde, Berlin, from 1903 to
1907, and the War School at Metz in 1907. He became an ensign in February, 1907, and a second
lieutenant in January, 1908, in the Tenth Hanoveri-
an Jäger Battalion, then under his father's command. Fairly short, broad-faced with a light brown
mustache, and stockily built but trim, Guderian
was an outdoorsman, though equally fond of dancing parties. He was also studious, serious, and ambitious; his sometimes introspective diary noted:
"To run with the mob is nothing to be proud of"
and "If only I could find a friend." This friend was
to be Margarete Goerne, whom he married on October 1, 1913; they had two sons.

Guderian's first year at the Berlin War Academy
was interrupted by the outbreak of war in August,
1914, and his immediate assignment—first lieutenant, wireless operations—was on the Western
Front, where he spent the war. Promoted to captain in 1915, Guderian completed a staff officers'
course in occupied Sedan and in 1918 gained a
place on the general staff. At war's end, he did
staff work on Eastern defenses plus volunteer service in the Baltic area. Although he apparently acquired some of the *Freikorps* bitterness against the
Weimar Republic as well as the Versailles Treaty,
Guderian's assignments kept him within the small
army (four thousand officers plus ninety-six thousand other ranks) which was headed by Colonel-
General Hans von Seeckt.

In 1922, Guderian accepted a chance to return to
general staff work and was assigned to the Motorized Transport Department, pursuing Seeckt's
"mobility" gospel with trucks but forbidden by
Versailles to have tanks or tracked vehicles. With
no knowledge of tanks, Guderian educated himself
largely from British publications, reading General
John Frederick Charles Fuller's writings on "deep
penetration" and becoming a disciple of Captain
Basil Henry Liddell Hart.

Life's Work

Guderian's first hands-on experience with tanks in
Sweden in 1929 convinced him that tanks alone or
with regular infantry divisions could never achieve
decisive importance. Instead, he proposed a radical change in division operations as well as tank
use: Instead of distributing tanks to support or lead
infantry divisions, those tanks could be concentrated into a special division under a tank commander. The combat units would then have to have
armor (*Panzer*), and the whole division would
have to be motorized. The division general, in a
forward tank (*Panzerkampfwagen*), would radio
commands to engineers, tanks, mobile artillery,
airplanes, and all the motorized support for a continuing penetration and disorganization of the enemy's defense structure.

In a *Reichswehr* (German army) with only ten
divisions altogether, a shortage of large engines,
and little faith in the mechanical reliability of
tanks, Guderian's ideas made slow progress until
Adolf Hitler began preparatory remilitarization in
1933. "That's what I want!" was Hitler's quick verdict on Guderian's vehicles, and, in 1935, the first
three panzer divisions started training.

Guderian was a tactician rather than a mechanical expert, but he contributed tank design ideas to
the Ordnance Department. The 1933 two-man light
trainer (Panzerkampfwagen I) and 1934 three-man
variant (PzKw. II) were already essentially set, but
Guderian pushed his three-man turret in a five-man
tank idea for the 1936 medium PzKw. IV and the
1937 PzKw. III "tank killer." These excellent vehicles were initially weakened in armor and gunpow-
er by being kept within the 24-metric-ton weight
limit of German bridges. The 1942 heavies, PzKw.
V "(Panther)" and VI ("Tiger"), more nearly embodied Guderian's ideas.

Guderian popularized his ideas in articles and a
1937 book, *Achtung! Panzer! (Attention! Tanks!,*
1937) while enjoying rapid promotions, becoming

lieutenant-colonel in 1931 and General of Panzer Troops in 1938. Not surprisingly, he was enthusiastic about the dictator who made it possible. Like most officers, he had found the Republic "unlovable" and saw the Third Reich in generally positive terms, although he did not join the Nazi Party and was disquieted by the power of Heinrich Himmler's Schutzstaffel (SS). Hitler's successes in the Rhineland, Spain, Austria, and Czechoslovakia confirmed Guderian's faith in the Führer, and, while he reacted more soberly to war on the Polish question in 1939, he was encouraged that the Hitler-Stalin pact had secured Russia's cooperation.

The September, 1939, Polish campaign vindicated Guderian's tactics, and, as a close-to-the-action commander of the 19th Army Corps of Panzer Group Kleist, he showed how boldness against a weak defense could carry enemy positions without wasting men. In the 1940 Blitzkrieg in the West, Guderian's 19th Army Corps, with three panzer divisions, spearheaded Panzer Group Kleist's breakthrough at Sedan on May 13-14. Cutting across northern France according to the Manstein Plan, they reached Abbeville on May 20, forcing the

British to evacuate at Dunkirk and leading to the surrender of France on June 22. This thunderclap breakup of Anglo-French defenses in a matter of days established Guderian's fame as a military wizard whose tanks were the new "kings of battle," at least in journalistic accounts. More prosaically, tank concentration had been a strategic and tactical factor, as had Guderian's use of the speed and superior handling of German tanks, to cut around French strength rather than attacking it directly.

Guderian's proposals for a Mediterranean campaign in 1941 were ignored, and he found himself commanding an enlarged corps under Field Marshals Günther von Kluge and Fedor von Bock, for Barbarossa, the invasion of Russia that Hitler launched on June 22, 1941. Guderian, from his 1932 visit to the Soviet Union, believed that the Führer's high command, creating panzer divisions with only half the tanks needed, underestimated the scale of Russian distances, people, and production.

Starting on June 22 from west of Brest-Litovsk, Guderian's forces crossed the Berezina River on July 1 and took Smolensk on July 16, a spectacular advance of more than four hundred miles in twenty-five days. Yet the infantry was far behind, Guderian's tanks were choked up with dust, and his repair facilities were at least five hundred miles away on incompatible rail gauges and with a supply system in chaos. The next two hundred miles to Moscow did not look easy. The center group commanders all wanted to take Moscow, but each wanted even more not to be blamed for failing to take it. Guderian's superiors set him up for a headquarters presentation of the Moscow case to Hitler, who had already decided to shift Guderian's forces southward to pressure Kiev for a time and then return them for the fall drive on Moscow. The accusation that Guderian betrayed them by finally giving in to Hitler's decision hardly becomes the superiors who had cast him for the scapegoat role. The December Russian counteroffensive at Moscow forced Guderian to retreat in defiance of Hitler's orders, and he was among the thirty-five generals dismissed in the winter of 1941-1942.

Invalided by heart trouble in 1942, Guderian, in March of 1943, was made Inspector General of Armored Troops. He reorganized panzer formations around the new Panthers, but these tanks were not mechanically ready when thrown into Hitler's July offense against the strong defenses of the Kursk salient. The mutual slaughter of attrition was less affordable to Germany than to Russia. Guderian resumed a less active role.

Hitler named Guderian to succeed Kurt Zeitzler as chief of staff after the July 20, 1944, generals' attempt to assassinate the Führer. Guderian took the post to preserve unity, defend the Eastern Front, and protect the army from the SS, but he was no longer vigorous and probably never had the talents needed for a chief of staff. His collaboration with Albert Speer increased the output of weapons, but Hitler used these against the Western Allies, in order that a Russian occupation might teach Germany the real meaning of defeat. Himmler's deterioration reduced the threat of an SS takeover of the army, and Guderian's shouting matches with Hitler led to the general's final retirement on March 28, 1945.

Imprisoned without charge by the Allies from 1945 to 1948, Guderian composed his memoirs, which achieved international success. After his release, he authored two books questioning West German defense policy. Guderian died May 15, 1954, at Schwangau bei Füssen, Bavaria, and was buried at Goslar, West Germany.

Summary

Heinz Guderian's work as a military innovator reinforced the lesson that new technology often requires new methods. Just as the elder Helmuth von Moltke had geared the Prussian army to railways, so Guderian geared the armored division to the tank and a radio command system. Equally important was Guderian's principle of using the armored division's shock capacity against weak sectors in order to accomplish the deep penetrations that would cut off the enemy's stronger defense units.

Colonel-General Guderian also achieved success as a great field commander. His reputation as a difficult subordinate seems to have been well earned but so also was his popularity as an inspiriting and fair chief for those who served under him. Clearly, he could win a battle and move an army while doing so, which cannot be said of all generals, even in World War II. In broader strategic and military terms, Guderian's shortcomings are clear. Although neither a Nazi nor a war criminal, he served Hitler in increasingly important roles virtually to the end. In separating the idea of a "good Hitler" from the crimes of Hitler's rule, Guderian credulously accepted the Nazi propaganda that made service to Hitler the sole test of German loyalty. The narrow view produced by this sleight of hand denied the general any real understanding of the great world coalition of moral opinion and military strength assembled against Nazi Germany. An inventive tactician and good soldier, Guderian as chief of staff failed to prevent his master from losing the war.

Bibliography

Clark, Alan. *Barbarossa*. London: Hutchinson, and New York: Morrow, 1965. A readable analysis of the highlights and controversies of the Russian war. Somewhat impressionistic, but well organized and easy to follow.

Goerlitz, Walter. *History of the German General Staff, 1657-1945*. London: Hollis and Carter, and New York: Praeger, 1953. The best generally available account of Guderian's tenure as chief of staff. Gives the agenda of problems more clearly and comprehensively than do Guderian's memoirs.

Guderian, Heinz. *Panzer Leader*. Translated by Constantine Fitzgibbon. London: Joseph, and New York: Dutton, 1952. This work is readable, insightful, exciting, persuasive, and informative as history and autobiography.

Horne, Alistair. *To Lose a Battle*. London: Macmillan, and Boston: Little Brown, 1969. While told from the French view, this detailed but well-organized and readable chronology is unequaled as a handy guide to 1940 operations.

Keegan, John. *Guderian*. New York: Ballantine, 1973. The brief text gives little biographical information not in Guderian's account, but provides interesting analysis. Includes a good collection of photographs.

Liddell Hart, B. H. *The German Generals Talk*. New York: Morrow, 1948. The author's interviews with other generals are pertinent, and the book gives a useful context for Guderian's ideas.

McKenzie Jr., Kenneth F. "Guderian: The Master Synchronizer." *Marine Corps Gazette* 78, no. 8 (August, 1994). Examines the importance of synchronization in Guderian's May, 1940 campaign.

Macksey, Kenneth John. *Guderian, Panzer General*. London: MacDonald and Jane's, 1974; Meackpole, Pa.: Greenhill, 1997. The only full-scale biography of Guderian in English so far. Essential as the only systematic corrective to Guderian's memoirs.

Mellenthin, F. W. von. *German Generals of World War II*. Norman: University of Oklahoma Press, 1977. Largely secondhand, by an officer under Rommel, but some additional insights are here.

Rothbrust, Florian K. *Guderian's XIXth Panzer Corps and the Battle of France: Breakthrough in the Ardennes, May 1940*. New York: Praeger, 1990. Hailed as "the definitive work" in English on the Battle of France, this volume offers information on the six-month planning process, the preparation, and the execution of this successful military engagement. It includes the only day-to-day account of German activities during the battle's first five days, several appendices, and biographical sketches of the key individuals.

K. Fred Gillum

CHE GUEVARA

Born: June 14, 1928; Rosario, Argentina
Died: October 9, 1967; La Higuera, Bolivia
Areas of Achievement: The military, government, and politics
Contributions: Guevara is best known as a theorist and practitioner of revolutionary guerrilla warfare in Latin America. Guevara's writings and his ill-fated military experience in Bolivia have influenced Latin American revolutionary strategy as well as created posthumously a heroic international symbol for those who share his political ideals.

Early Life

Ernesto Guevara de la Serna was born in Rosario, Argentina, on June 14, 1928, to politically conscious upper-middle-class parents. In spite of a severe asthmatic condition that persisted throughout his life, Ernesto became an active youth with adventurous personality traits. The young Guevara demonstrated leadership capabilities in sports requiring much physical endurance and skill, and was an enthusiastic hiker and traveler. Guevara undertook his most ambitious journey in 1952, when he was one year short of finishing an M.D. degree at the University of Buenos Aires. Guevara and a student companion motored and hitchhiked northward over the continent from Chile to Caracas, Venezuela.

After returning to complete his medical degree, Guevara again set out in the same direction, observing social conditions in a number of countries. In 1954, Guevara reached Guatemala, where he became a sympathetic witness to the radical reform program of Jacobo Arbenz's government. When rebels sponsored by the American Central Intelligence Agency (CIA) overthrew this regime in late 1954, Guevara, who had endangered himself by attempting to organize support for Arbenz, received asylum in the Argentine Embassy. In early 1955, Guevara arrived in Mexico City. There he joined a group of Cuban revolutionaries under Fidel Castro who were seeking to overthrow the dictatorship of Fulgencio Batista. Following clandestine military training, Guevara, now known to his colleagues by the Argentine nickname "Che," participated in the contingent's landing by boat on the coast of Cuba's Oriente Province in early December, 1956. During the next two years, Guevara distinguished himself in military actions and reached the rank of major with command of his own guerrilla column.

Life's Work

Guevara emerged from the victorious armed struggle as an important leader in Castro's July 26th Movement and a trusted adviser to the Cuban revolutionary chief. On January 9, 1959, the revolutionary regime bestowed Cuban citizenship upon the Argentine-born revolutionary. Guevara soon became one of the best-known figures associated with Castro's regime. Guevara undertook numerous diplomatic and commercial missions on behalf of the new government. Between 1959 and 1965, Guevara held several important posts in the areas of economic planning and finance. Guevara headed the Department of Industry within the National Institute of Agrarian Reform (1959), managed the National Bank (1959-1961), and served as minister of industry from 1961 to 1965. Guevara represented the most radical tendency within the Cuban revolutionary regime. Through his writings and speeches, he came to be regarded as the leading Castroist theorist on socialist economic development and revolutionary warfare. While his views were clearly Marxist and even communist in a broad sense, Che's views were frequently at odds with those of the Soviet leadership and the Moscow-oriented Latin American Communist parties.

In his administrative posts, Guevara promoted a program of accelerated industrialization to diversify the Cuban economy. When it became clear that this overambitious project was failing and adversely affecting agricultural output, Soviet advisers recommended that the Cubans put aside this goal and return to the country's traditional emphasis on the production and export of sugar. Although Guevara was forced to adopt this policy in 1963, he refused to abandon the long-term goal of industrialization and insisted that the Soviet Union had a moral obligation to finance Cuba in this effort. Guevara's advocacy of moral rather than material incentives to stimulate worker productivity and create the new communist man coincided with the Maoist position in the Sino-Soviet dispute.

Guevara's ideas on revolutionary strategy and tactics also put him in conflict with the Soviets and their allied Communist parties in Latin America. The Argentine's concepts on revolutionary struggle are found in his now famous *La guerra de guerril-*

las (1960; *Che Guevara on Guerrilla Warfare*, 1961) and in a 1963 article entitled "Guerrilla Warfare: A Method." Guevara projected the Cuban example of hit-and-run tactics by small, highly mobile, rural-based partisan bands as the proper path to revolutionary transformations in Latin America. Armed struggle based in the countryside, Guevara asserted, was a more effective means of creating a revolutionary attitude in the masses than the long-term political tactics advocated by the urban-based Communist parties. Revolutionaries need not wait until all the conditions for revolution were present. The insurrectionary guerrilla *foco* (center) itself could create them.

Guevara asserted that a small nucleus of properly trained and politically dedicated fighters could establish and consolidate a guerrilla *foco* in any Latin American country if they obtained the cooperation of local inhabitants and possessed a knowledge of the terrain superior to that of the enemy. The struggle would be long and protracted, passing through several tactical phases as the guerrilla force gained in strength and recruits and expanded the scope of its operations.

In Guevara's scheme, the revolution unfolded without the direction of the Communist parties. The fighters, through their direct revolutionary experience and involvement with the local citizenry, acquired a political education and revolutionary commitment superior to that provided by textbook theories and rigid ideological formulations.

In 1964, the relationship between Guevara and Moscow-style communism deteriorated further as he publicly criticized the Soviets for insufficient support of the new underdeveloped nations and Third World revolutionary movements. Later, in March of 1965, Guevara suddenly disappeared from public view. Castro's explanation that Guevara had chosen to serve the revolutionary cause somewhere in another capacity did not silence speculation on other reasons behind his absence. Some charged that Guevara was purged or removed because his views on economic development and foreign policy threatened to alienate Moscow. Guevara had encountered strong opposition from Old Guard Communists within the Cuban government. There were also unsubstantiated reports about a possible mental or emotional collapse.

It is probable that Guevara became dissatisfied with the bureaucratic routines of his administrative duties and disappointed with the results of his

industrialization drive. On several occasions, Guevara confided to friends his desire to return to direct involvement with revolutionary struggle, particularly in Latin America. Although in sympathy with many of Guevara's views, Castro was not willing in 1965 to embark on a course totally independent from Moscow and accepted his friend's resignation. Yet the Cuban leader did agree to back Guevara in his desire to advance the cause of revolution abroad. Between July, 1965, and March, 1966, Guevara, with Castro's assistance, secretly took a contingent of Cubans to the Congo to aid a revolutionary movement against the pro-Western regime. After a frustrating experience, Guevara withdrew from the Congo when the Chinese, who were now feuding with Castro, pressured the Congolese rebel movement to dispense with the Cubans.

Guevara, whose whereabouts and fate remained a mystery, returned to Havana and began to prepare a project for which he had long shown an interest—the establishment of an insurrectionary *foco* in the Andean or southern cone region of South America. Bolivia was finally selected as the site to begin operations because of its strategic central location as a country bordering on most other states of the continent. In his plan for spreading insurrection to other countries, Guevara described his strategy as one of creating many Vietnams; he envisioned that American intervention to defeat these uprisings would tie down and exhaust the Yankee colossus and also provoke anti-imperialist reactions leading to revolutionary successes.

Guevara's ideas had now gained ascendency in Havana. With Castro's help, Guevara assembled a mixed force of Cuban and Peruvian revolutionaries who entered Bolivia in late 1966, establishing a secret base in the heavily wooded Ñancahuazú River Valley of southeastern Bolivia. Guevara's Bolivian affair was jeopardized by mistakes from the beginning. Ironically, Guevara violated many of his own rules for successful guerrilla warfare. Guevara's haste to get on with his plans and the group's carelessness resulted in a premature start of combat in March, 1967, before the necessary preparations and groundwork for support inside Bolivia were arranged. The Bolivian Communist Party refused to cooperate with this venture, and the site of operations was also poorly chosen. Throughout this campaign the guerrilla force remained hopelessly isolated without logistical, political, or mass support. After some initial victories over inexperienced army recruits, the guerrillas' position became increasingly perilous. The Bolivian army, which became more formidable as it benefited from American counterinsurgency training and equipment, closed in on the guerrilla band. On October 8, a government ranger unit wounded and captured Guevara. A Bolivian army officer executed the famous revolutionary leader the following day in the village of La Higuera.

Summary

Che Guevara's impact on his times became a heated topic after the sensational termination of his exciting career in Bolivia. Nevertheless, Guevara merits a place in the history of twentieth century Latin American social and political thought. The revolutionary leader's book on guerrilla warfare is still considered a classic work in this field. Guevara's ideas inspired many radical groups in Latin America to go off to the countryside or mountains in an effort to follow and apply the Cuban example.

After his death, Guevara also became a popular hero and legendary symbol on a worldwide scale; he was particularly a heroic cult figure for the rebellious youthful generation and New Left groups in the 1960's. The Cuban government proceeded to hold forth "El Che" as a model for schoolchildren to study and emulate. Guevara's idealism, revolutionary dedication, and courage in giving his life for his political ideals are traits most frequently cited by his admirers. On the other hand, Guevara's detractors attempt to depict him as a bloodthirsty, mentally unstable, or psychopathic adventurer and a failure in everything he undertook.

Guevara's major contribution to Latin American revolutionary movements may be the lessons drawn from studying his unsuccessful Bolivian campaign. This experience indicates that regular troops trained in counterinsurgency tactics are likely to defeat isolated rural guerrilla forces. Revolutionary warfare based in the countryside requires cooperation from local rural inhabitants and the existence of a national organizational apparatus for providing both material and political support. Guerrilla warfare should be combined with other forms of struggle waged throughout the country.

Bibliography

Debray, Régis. *Che's Guerrilla War.* Translated by Rosemary Steed. London and Baltimore: Penguin, 1975. A detailed analysis of what went wrong with Guevara's Bolivian campaign. The author is a French Marxist intellectual who collaborated closely with Castro and Guevara to further elaborate their theories on revolutionary struggle; he also was a firsthand witness to Guevara's experience in Bolivia.

González, Luis J., and Gustavo A. Sánchez Salazar. *The Great Rebel: Che Guevara in Bolivia.* Translated by Helen R. Lane. New York: Grove Press, 1969. One of the most objective accounts of this subject. The authors interviewed officials, soldiers, and captured guerrillas, and had access to tape recordings of prisoner interviews.

Guevara, Ernesto. *The Complete Bolivian Diaries of Che Guevara and Other Captured Documents.* Edited by Daniel James. Rev. ed. New York: Stein and Day, 1970. Guevara's daily notations and observations from the time of his arrival in Bolivia in late 1966 up to his capture. Also included are the shorter but useful diaries of three Cuban personnel who took part in this episode.

Harris, Richard. *Death of a Revolutionary: Che Guevara's Last Mission*. New York: Norton, 1970. A very interesting and accurate analysis of Guevara's experience in Bolivia. The introductory chapter summarizes Guevara's early life. The author is sympathetic to his subject but strives for objectivity.

————. "Reflections on Che Guevara's Legacy." *Latin American Perspectives* 25, no. 4 (July, 1998). Analyzes the primary sources on Guevara plus his own diaries, which provide valuable information on his politics, thoughts, and revolutionary spirit.

Ryan, Henry Butterfield. *The Fall of Che Guevara: A Story of Soldiers, Spies, and Diplomats*. New York: Oxford University Press, 1998. The author, a retired U.S. Foreign Service officer, provides a well-written, in-depth, and accurate account of Guevara's fatal foray in Bolivia with emphasis on the roles of the Green Berets and U.S. government agencies. Ryan's book is based on analysis of new source information concerning the CIA, Department of State, and others, made available through the Freedom of Information Act.

Sauvage, Léo. *Che Guevara: The Failure of a Revolutionary*. Translated by Raoul Frémont. Englewood Cliffs, N.J.: Prentice-Hall, 1973. This book tries to answer questions about what really happened to Guevara in terms of his relations with Castro and in terms of his death. Includes an index.

David A. Crain

DANIEL GUGGENHEIM

Born: July 9, 1856; Philadelphia, Pennsylvania
Died: September 28, 1930; Port Washington, New
  York
Areas of Achievement: Business and philanthropy
Contribution: Through daring business risks and
  tight family control over his ventures, Guggenheim created one of the first multinational corporations and went a long way toward his goal of
  controlling the mineral wealth of the entire
  world.

Early Life

Daniel Guggenheim was born July 9, 1856, in Philadelphia, Pennsylvania. His father was the greatest
single influence in his life. Meyer Guggenheim had
emigrated from Switzerland in 1848 to escape the
restrictions placed on Jews in that country at that
time. Daniel was the second of seven sons. When
Daniel was born the family was still struggling.
Meyer was a peddler who had gone into the manufacture and sale of stove polish and coffee essence.
He made a large sum of money as a wholesaler
during the Civil War. By the 1870's, Meyer had
branched into the making of lye for domestic soap,
had speculated in railroad stock, and had formed
the firm of Guggenheim and Pulaski to import lace
and embroideries from Switzerland and Saxony.
Meyer was determined to earn enough money to
provide for his family even after his death. His
children were given a lax religious upbringing. His
goal was that they should receive as good an education as could be had, so Daniel and his brothers
were sent to a Catholic school.

Academically, Daniel did not shine; like his father, he was more concerned with things practical.
At seventeen, he was sent to Switzerland to perfect
his German and to study the embroidery business;
he stayed there ten years. In 1877, M. Guggenheim
and Sons was founded. Two years later, Meyer's
worth was estimated at around $800,000. In 1881,
he bought an interest in two lead and silver mines
in Colorado. It was a gamble that was to set the
course of Daniel's subsequent career (and those of
his brothers) because the mines proved to be enormously rich. Daniel was recalled to man the New
York office and all seven sons went into the mining
business. By 1889, the entire Guggenheim family
had moved to New York, the financial capital of the
nation. From 1890 to 1923, it was Daniel, the most

energetic and ambitious of the brothers, who directed the affairs of the Guggenheim interests.

In 1890, at the age of thirty-four, Daniel
Guggenheim stood barely more than five feet tall.
He was quick and very agile, bold and adventurous, possessed of truly demonic energy, and a born
general. His manner was European; he was polished and self-assured. He believed in the essential
virtue and inevitability of material progress. In his
eyes there was an expression of such intensity that
it appeared he was forever about to explode. His
mania was for profits. Even at the end of his life,
Guggenheim worked a sixteen-hour day. He was
independent, autocratic, dynamic, and forward-
looking. Morally, he was the typical Victorian—a
devoted family man (he married in 1884), puritanical, and not in the least interested in society. His
view of industrial management was unabashedly
feudal.

Life's Work

The two Guggenheim mines in Colorado were followed by the construction of a smelter at Pueblo.
As a result of favorable federal legislation which
served to boost silver prices, a harsh labor policy,
selective stockpiling, and the attainment of cheap
railroad freight rates, profits from the smelter
alone ran at five million dollars. Guggenheim's
control over the Guggenheim interests, now all in
mining, occurred as a result of a further piece of
legislation, the McKinley Tariff Act of 1890. This
placed a heavy duty on imported ores and motivated the Guggenheims to lease or buy mines in Mexico and to build smelters there. Guggenheim was
sent to obtain the necessary concession from the
Mexican government. It was the first, and by no
means the last, occasion when the Guggenheims
were able to use their industrial power to control
poor countries. The result of Guggenheim's negotiations with President Porfirio Diaz was not only
the right to operate in the country but also exemptions from import duty on machinery and from all
municipal and state taxes. On his return to New
York, Guggenheim was chosen to oversee the entire mining and smelting business and to plan future expansion.

The rise of the Guggenheims had excited the interests of others in the mining business. In 1889,
Henry Huttleston Rogers, with the principal backing of William Rockefeller, began to form a huge

trust to monopolize the smelting business in America. In 1898, the new trust became known as the American Smelting and Refining Company (ASARCO). The Guggenheims were invited to join but they refused. Guggenheim was convinced that his family's business was now too big to be squeezed out. By 1900, through a series of well-planned, astute moves, and aided by a two-month strike of ASARCO workers, the Guggenheims were able to flood the world market with cheap lead and silver, drive down prices and thus the value of ASARCO shares, and buy up those shares at low prices. Following merger negotiations and a series of court battles, Guggenheim emerged as chairman of the board and president of ASARCO, his brother Solomon became treasurer, three other brothers were board members, and the Guggenheims and their allies controlled fifty-one percent of the stock. Daniel Guggenheim was now firmly in control of mining and smelting in America.

In 1906, Guggenheim formed what came to be called the Alaska Syndicate with John Pierpont Morgan and Jacob Schiff. The discovery of Kennecott Creek, the richest copper deposit in the world at that time, excited the Guggenheims and their partners to the extent that they were willing to build the necessary two-hundred-mile railroad and the new harbor and acquire a steamship line to get the ore to the Guggenheim smelter at Tacoma, Washington. The necessity of buying coal mines to supply power to machinery and forests for construction purposes led the syndicate to attempt control over all the natural resources of Alaska. This led to the first great public controversy over Guggenheim business practices. Despite the efforts of Gifford Pinchot, chief of the United States Forestry Service, and others who argued that natural resources should belong to the nation as a whole, the conservationists got nowhere. Guggenheim had too many friends in the Administration and his brother Simon, United States senator from Colorado, also worked effectively for M. Guggenheim and Sons. Between the completion of the railroad in 1911 and the end of 1912, Kennecott paid three million dollars in dividends. By 1918, it had yielded more than seventy-two million dollars.

During this same period, the Guggenheim interests, with the aid of their consulting engineer, John Hays Hammond, bought up more mines in Mexico, constructed more smelters there, acquired Esperanza, the richest gold mine in Mexico, formed the Yukon Gold Company to dredge the gold-bearing

sands of the Klondike and, after 1916, transferred the equipment to Malaya to dredge for tin; and got over the disaster of investment in Nipissing silver. The same period too, saw Daniel Guggenheim in partnership with Thomas Fortune Ryan and King Leopold of Belgium with exclusive rights to prospect for and develop all minerals in the Congo (modern Zaire), where gold and especially diamonds were found. Back in the United States, the Guggenheims bought Bingham Canyon, in Utah, which became the first open cast copper mine and the biggest copper operation in the world. Fully under way in 1910, the mine was run as a virtual slave-labor camp with specially imported cheap labor, and backed by the Utah state militia. Guerrilla warfare broke into open warfare between workers on the one side and company security men and state militia on the other. Some reforms followed, and, by 1935, profits from Bingham Canyon alone were estimated at $200 million. The year 1910 also saw the purchase of the Chuquicamata copper mine in Chile, nine thousand feet up in the Andes. It proved to be greater and richer than either Kennecott or Bingham Canyon. To exploit it, Guggenheim had to build a modern port, a road from the sea to his new mining town, an electric power plant, and fifty-five miles of aqueduct to bring in the nearest water.

By 1915, the Guggenheims controlled seventy-five to eighty percent of the world's silver, copper, and lead, and could dictate prices. Their mines were in full production to fill war orders. From 1915 to 1918, their copper interests alone paid $210 million in dividends. Public criticism of the Guggenheims as war profiteers grew until President Woodrow Wilson forced them to peg copper prices. Their reputation was not enhanced when, in a short strike at Kennecott, the company evicted striking workers from their bunkhouses into bitter thirty-below-zero weather.

Guggenheim's power in the industrial world was recognized by President Wilson in May, 1917, when he was chosen as one of two representatives of capital, the other being John D. Rockefeller, Jr., to meet the representative of labor to discuss industrial peace for the duration of the war. Guggenheim's public embrace of Samuel Gompers, the head of the American Federation of Labor, and his public endorsement of unionism, however, did not alter the policies of Guggenheim companies around the world.

The huge success of the Guggenheims was based on a business strategy devised by Daniel Guggenheim. First, they always went in for big development when the business barometer was low. Second, they used the cheap labor and raw materials of underdeveloped countries to depress their own country's wages and prices until they were so cheap that they could afford to buy them up and place them within their own monopoly. Third, in the metals industry, Guggenheim felt that there was no use competing unless one owned everything from mine mouth to finished product.

In 1922, Guggenheim was sixty-six years old. In that year, the board of ASARCO accused the Guggenheims of milking the company to further their own separate family interests. It voted the family out of control at a stockholders meeting. Not long after, Guggenheim retired and Simon, the ex-United States senator, became president of ASARCO, assisted by Guggenheim's son-in-law Roger Straus. The following year, Chuquicamata was sold by the family to Anaconda Copper.

During the next few years, Guggenheim and his brothers devoted their energies to redeeming the family image through philanthropy. In 1924, the Daniel and Florence Guggenheim Foundation was created for "the promotion, through charitable and benevolent activities, of the well-being of men throughout the world." Guggenheim's son, Harry, a World War I naval pilot, persuaded him to promote the neglected science of aeronautics; in 1925, the foundation granted $500,000 to New York University to establish the first school of aeronautics in the United States. The following year, the Daniel Guggenheim Fund for the Promotion of Aeronautics was established with $2.5 million. By 1930, the fund, almost single-handedly, had placed American aviation on a firm footing and had converted the public from apathy to enthusiastic support. Finally, convinced by Charles Lindbergh, the aviator, Guggenheim supported the experiments of an obscure physics professor in New England, Robert Hutchings Goddard. Following an initial grant from the foundation, the Daniel Guggenheim Fund for the Measurement and Investigation of High Altitudes enabled Goddard to establish the first United States rocket testing ground at Roswell, New Mexico.

When Guggenheim died, September 28, 1930, he had achieved not only a great reputation as a powerful industrialist, but also the admiration and affection of many.

Summary

Daniel Guggenheim was the head of an extraordinary industrial dynasty. Guided in the first instance by his father, he and his brothers developed a modest one-million-dollar fortune into one worth perhaps three hundred times that sum. The Guggenheims were a team, but, even though the contribution of his brothers is often much underrated, it was the driving ambition, ruthlessness, and boldness of vision provided by Daniel which, together with his undoubted ability and autocratic methods, made the Guggenheims into the controllers of most of the world's exploited mineral resources by 1915. It was said that, with one telegram, Daniel had the power to topple governments.

Bibliography

Baruch, Bernard. *My Own Story.* New York: Holt Rinehart, 1957; London: Odhams Press, 1958. The "boy wonder of Wall Street" was closely associated with Daniel Guggenheim for many years, and in this book he leaves portraits of Daniel and all of his brothers.

Bernstein, Marvin D. *The Mexican Mining Industry, 1890-1950*. Albany: State University of New York Press, 1965. A comprehensive account of the development of the industry. Concentrates heavily on the Guggenheim interests and operations.

Cleveland, Reginald M. *America Fledges Wings: The History of the Daniel Guggenheim Fund for the Promotion of Aeronautics*. New York: Pittman, 1942. A good account of the "foster father of United States aviation" stage of Guggenheim's life though, naturally, there is more material on Guggenheim's son Harry, who actually ran the fund.

Davis, John H. *The Guggenheims: An American Epic*. New York: Morrow, 1978. A well-balanced and informative account of the family to 1978. Daniel is dealt with in parts 1 and 2 and chapter 3 of part 3.

Glines, C.V. "The Guggenheims." *Aviation History* 7, no. 2 (November, 1996). Profiles Daniel and Harry Guggenheim and their efforts in support of aeronautics, including the establishment of the Daniel Guggenheim Fund for the Promotion of Aeronautics and the construction of the first American school of aeronautics.

Lomask, Milton. *Seed Money: The Guggenheim Story*. New York: Farrar Straus, 1964. A work for a popular audience devoted largely to the philanthropic ventures of the family. Daniel is dealt with in chapters 2, 3, 6, and 8. Published by his grandson.

Marcosson, Isaac F. *Metal Magic: The Story of the American Smelting and Refining Company*. New York: Farrar Straus, 1949. A detailed account of the smelting and refining trust set up by Rockefeller to break the Guggenheims on the path to domination of metals in America but taken over by Daniel and his brothers in 1900. Published by Daniel's grandson.

O'Connor, Harvey. *The Guggenheims: The Making of an American Dynasty*. New York: Covici, Friede, 1937. Written by a socialist, labor journalist, and writer who also wrote about the Rockefellers, Astors, Mellons, and Carnegies. It takes a caustic view of Guggenheim business practices, favoring unions, independent miners, and smelter owners. It is the product of careful research and is in no way personally vicious. A good balance to Davis or Lomask.

Williams, Gatenby, and Charles Monroe Heath. *William Guggenheim*. New York: Lone Voice, 1934. Gatenby Williams was the pseudonym of William Guggenheim, youngest brother of Daniel, who left the company in 1901 and was forced to divorce his first wife, a California divorcée, by Daniel. His scholarly, contemplative temperament was overshadowed by the aggressiveness of his elder brothers, but his autobiography contains useful insights into the workings of the Guggenheim partnership and the building of its mining empire in the United States and Mexico.

Stephen Burwood

CHARLES-ÉDOUARD GUILLAUME

Born: February 15, 1861; Fleurier, Switzerland
Died: June 13, 1938; Sèvres, France
Area of Achievement: Physics
Contribution: Measurements, and the standards on which they are based, are the foundation of the physical sciences. During his long tenure as assistant director and director of the International Bureau of Weights and Measures at Sèvres, Guillaume was indefatigable as researcher and administrator in refining instruments and methods of measurement to the greatest possible precision, and in publishing to the world the current status of metricization and metric standards. For his efforts, he received the Nobel Prize in Physics in 1920.

Early Life

Charles-Édouard Guillaume was born on February 15, 1861, in Fleurier, in the canton of Neuchâtel in western Switzerland, about eighty-five kilometers from Geneva. His father and grandfather were watch and clock makers. Guillaume attended the local schools, then the *Gymnasium* in Neuchâtel, and entered the Technical University in Zurich at the age of seventeen. He received his doctorate five years later, in 1883, with a thesis on electrolytic capacitors. In the same year, after a few months as an artillery officer, he entered the International Bureau of Weights and Measures at Sèvres, France, where he would spend his entire scientific career (retaining his Swiss citizenship until his death).

The first task that the bureau gave him was the study of the mercury-in-glass thermometer, its calibration and its stem correction (the correction necessary when the thermometer is only partially immersed in the medium whose temperature is to be measured). This innocuous-sounding assignment resulted in the ninety-two-page *Études thermométriques* (1886; studies in thermometry), later expanded as the *Traité pratique de la thermométrie de précision* (1889; practical manual of precision thermometry), which became the standard textbook in the field. During these early years in the bureau, Guillaume met and married A. M. Taufflieb; they had three children.

Another early research by Guillaume upset one of the defining standards of the metric system. The kilogram was originally declared to be the mass of one cubic decimeter (one thousand cubic centimeters) of water at its temperature of greatest density,

4 degrees Celsius. Guillaume determined that a kilogram of water at this temperature in fact occupies 1,000.028 cubic centimeters, a finding that caused physical scientists thereafter to express volumes in milliliters, leaving the cubic centimeter to their less exacting medical colleagues. The units were declared equal in 1964, but the distinction persists.

Life's Work

The research that occupied more than three decades of Guillaume's life, for which he was specifically awarded the Nobel Prize, began as a fairly straightforward activity of the International Bureau of Weights and Measures. In 1889, the bureau decided to distribute prototype standards of length and weight to the nations of the world that subscribed to the metric system. The platinum-iridium standards used by the bureau were too expensive for wholesale replication, and by 1891 Guillaume hit upon pure nickel as a relatively cheap, noncorrosive, machinable metal for meter and kilogram prototypes. Thus, the distribution of these standards to the bureaus of standards in various countries was solved, and laboratory and industrial measurements could be referred to the local standards without the inconvenience of crossing oceans or international boundaries.

Yet one important type of measurement was overlooked: geodesy, or the precision measurement of land areas, distances, and directions. Geodesy standards at the turn of the century were clumsy, four-meter bars with scribed lines at each end, aligned by microscope, and protected in the field from weather and temperature changes (which changed the bars' lengths) by portable huts. The baselines measured with these bars could be kilometers long, and the measuring teams numbered as many as sixty skilled workers, who could work for days at a single baseline. For simplicity and decreased expense, new methods were obviously needed.

New methods developed, in Guillaume's hands, from new materials. For manufacturing reasons, the nickel of the smaller standards could not be used in the long rods of geodetic measurement. Other materials were required. In 1895, Guillaume began the study of nickel-iron alloys, or nickel steels, with nickel content of 25 percent and above. Long and painstaking studies (literally thousands of alloy bars and rods were tested) showed that nickel steels containing 35.8 percent nickel exhibited a thermal expansivity (change of length with temperature) less than one tenth that of nickel or iron by itself. Moreover, treatment in finishing the nickel steel (forging and controlled-temperature cooling) could reduce temperature expansivity to almost zero. The alloy of this composition was given the name "invar," because of the invariability of its length with changes in temperature. Invar's application in geodesy was quickly found. Guillaume produced a twenty-four-meter invar wire for E. Jäderin, leader of the Spitzbergen (surveying) Expedition of 1899-1900, which could be carried in a coil and used without temperature precautions or microscopic alignment. Jäderin reported measurement of a baseline more than ten kilometers long with an error of less than nineteen millimeters. In subsequent years, geodetic measuring devices converted completely to invar.

Measurement of time also yielded to invar. Pendulum chronometers were the standard of the day. The period of a pendulum is dependent on its length, and ordinary metals such as brass or steel change length with temperature, requiring that precision instruments be kept in a temperature-controlled environment. Pendulum arms made of invar freed these devices from that requirement and took time measurement out of the laboratory and into factories and government offices.

Uses for invar were also found outside measurements and standards. Railway switches at the time were operated by hand levers in a switch tower that was sometimes hundreds of meters from the switches themselves. The connecting cables could contract enough in very cold weather to throw a switch, or slacken enough in heat to make the switch inoperable. The use of invar cables eliminated this problem.

If invar could be made with zero temperature expansion, nickel steels of slightly different composition could be made with any desired expansivity—specifically, that of glass. Light bulbs of the time were made with their electrical leads sealed into glass bases, requiring that the metal of the leads have the same temperature-expansion behavior as glass to preserve a gas-tight seal. The only metal that possessed this property was platinum. Mass commercial application of electric light was impossible with expensive platinum, but a nickel steel of the required expansivity was developed and made light bulbs available to all.

Nickel steels in the range of 25 to 35 percent nickel also show interesting magnetic anomalies: At low temperatures, they are magnetic, but above a certain temperature they are nonmagnetic. Below this transition temperature, they are again magnetic. This finding led to the construction of thermostats based on magnetic coils. These were fixed-temperature devices, not variable like house thermostats, because the percentage of nickel was fixed; yet any given temperature could be chosen initially, because the transition temperature varied with the nickel content.

In the course of developing invar, Guillaume evaluated ternary alloys and discovered one, containing about 12 percent chromium in addition to the iron and nickel, that showed zero (or even negative) change in elasticity with temperature change. This combination was named elinvar, and it completed the revolution in horology and chronometry that had begun with the invar pendulum. The accuracy of chronometers depends upon the constancy of size of pendulum, balance wheel, and other parts, but also on the constancy of elasticity of the hairspring mechanisms of the balance wheel.

The designs of the time used complex pairings of metals (mostly steel and brass), whose changes in length and elasticity offset each other so long as temperature changes were not too great. Elinvar at one stroke eliminated the need for this kind of design and brought chronometry to the peak of mechanical perfection that yielded, finally, only to electronic measurement. Elinvar was so successful and inexpensive, in fact, that within a very few years mass-produced watches used nothing else for hairsprings.

In all of these researches on alloys, it was Guillaume, the standards-of-measurement man, who directed Guillaume, the metallurgical investigator. Standards of the time were material and mechanical—bars with scribed lines, carefully adjusted masses of metal, carefully adjusted physical volumes, and the like. Modern standards are determined by optical and electronic methods—length and time through wavelengths and frequencies of light, for example. At the turn of the century, however, improvements in standards had to come not from improvements in circuitry but from improvements in methods and materials.

Summary

Charles-Édouard Guillaume knew exactly what he wanted his materials to do, and exactly how to apply the properties of those materials when he found what he wanted. This is the story behind the discovery of invar and elinvar and not merely a happy accident that turned out to have useful consequences. Guillaume's was a determined search for exactly the right materials for the task at hand—measurement. Guillaume reported his findings in more than half a dozen book-length publications from 1897 to 1927, as well as in numerous papers in research journals.

The final reason for Guillaume's importance in science was his determination to communicate not only his own research but also the status of metric research and the metric system worldwide to the scientific community and all interested laymen. His earliest work in this line, *Unités et étalons* (units and measures), appeared in 1893, when he was still a staff member of the bureau. Other works appeared when he was assistant director and director, including the series of biennial reports, *Les Récents Progrès du système métrique* (recent advances in the metric system), that were published from 1907 through 1933, many as books. Guillaume took his position as director of the bureau seriously and was a tireless propagandizer, in the best sense of the word, for the metric system. To those who knew his work, he represented the International Bureau of Weights and Measures and the metric system. He continued in this position until he retired as director in 1936. Even as honorary director, he remained active until he died on June 13, 1938.

Bibliography

Chaudron, Georges. "Charles Édouard Guillaume." In *Dictionary of Scientific Biography*, edited by Charles Coulston Gillispie, vol. 5. New York: Scribner, 1981. A rare biographical treatment of Guillaume that includes a bibliography of his works.

Guillaume, Charles-Édouard. Interview in *Scientific American Monthly* 3 (February, 1921): 105-109. This article describes the activities of the International Bureau of Weights and Measures. Includes photographs and Guillaume's own work.

"Obituary: Dr. C.-E. Guillaume." *Nature* 142 (August 20, 1938): 322-323. Gives a brief biographical account and discusses Guillaume's scientific achievements.

Robert M. Hawthorne, Jr.

H. D.
Hilda Doolittle

Born: September 10, 1886; Bethlehem, Pennsylvania
Died: September 27, 1961; Zurich, Switzerland
Area of Achievement: Literature
Contribution: The works of H. D., the first great modernist poet, formed the true core of Ezra Pound's Imagist movement and exercised an extraordinary influence on modern poetics. She explored images taken from classical mythology from a profoundly feminine and personal perspective in spare, taut poems.

Early Life

Hilda Doolittle—better known by the nickname "H. D.," given her by Ezra Pound—was born September 10, 1886, in Bethlehem, Pennsylvania, into a world of mystical pietism. Her father was a noted astronomer, her mother was artistic and musical, and the family as a whole was deeply involved in the social and religious life of Bethlehem, stronghold of the Moravian Brotherhood. The profound and eccentric Christianity of Moravianism was to remain an interest of H. D.'s throughout her life. In 1895, the Doolittle family moved to Philadelphia, leaving the close-knit world of the Brotherhood for the more cosmopolitan academic sphere: H. D.'s father became Flower Professor of Astronomy and founder of the Flower Observatory at the University of Pennsylvania.

In 1901, H. D. met Ezra Pound, who was then a student at the university. She was fifteen and he was barely a year older, but he already cut a striking figure in his romantic green robe with his green eyes and golden hair. H. D. herself had, in the words of William Carlos Williams, "a loose-limbed beauty." The relationship between H. D. and Pound, nourished by Pound's suggestions for H. D.'s reading (William Morris, William Blake, Henrik Ibsen), led to their engagement in 1905.

H. D. published short stories in two newspapers between 1901 and 1905, but her account of her relationship with Pound was to come much later: "Mr. Pound it was all wrong," she wrote in *End to Torment.* "You turned into a Satyr, a Lynx, and the girl in your arms (Dryad, you called her), for all her fragile, not yet lost virginity, is Maenad. . . ." In her account, the tone of their encounter is Greek, pagan.

Pound was, almost predictably, less than faithful to his dryad, and his 1908 trip to Europe resulted in a fascination with troubadour lyrics—and with the ideal of adulterous love that they embodied. By 1909, Pound had published *A Lume Spento* and *Personae,* and he was meeting William Butler Yeats, Ford Madox Hueffner (Ford), and other literary lights in London. In 1911, H. D. joined him there.

Since 1908, Pound had been discussing a new style of poetry, one that would cut away trite or stilted language by focusing on the "thing," by using no word that fails to contribute to "the presentation," and by writing "in sequence of the musical phrase," not according to a metronomic beat. The new style was called "Imagisme." H. D. was to be its avatar.

The January, 1913, issue of *Poetry* contained three poems by H. D., which Pound had sent to the editor with a warm commendation, after editing them slightly—and signing them for her "H. D. *Imagiste.*" His manifesto for Imagism (written with F. S. Flint) followed two months later. The Modernist era had begun.

Life's Work

Ancient Greece was the magnet of H. D.'s poetic mind: Her first published poem was entitled "Hermes of the Ways," and it is a Greek simplicity that she strives for and that Pound turns to his own purposes by calling it Imagism. People thought that H. D. looked Greek: "her features were Greek, they suggested a hamadryad," Louis Wilkinson wrote in *The Buffoon* (1916), and indeed her leggy beauty was admirably suited to the tastes of a world bent on escaping the confining corsets of its Victorian past. Her "Grecianness" was not, however, merely a myth woven about H. D. within her circle of friends; it was a serious (if not utterly scholarly) pursuit.

After H. D.'s marriage in 1913 to Richard Aldington, the couple spent time in Paris, where they met Henry Slominsky, a young philosopher who had recently published *Heraclit und Parmenides,* and spent many evenings with him ("noctes Atticae," Aldington called them) discussing Homer and Aeschylus, Pythagoras and Plato. In the Diocletian Gallery in Rome, H. D. discovered a little statue of the Hermaphrodite, which she would visit each time she returned to the eternal city; and on a short visit to Capri—her first true taste of the Grecian world—she believed she saw the god Pan.

The result of this immersion in the Greek spirit was the invention or discovery of a peculiarly modern and personal mythic Greece that was to dominate her poems. More directly, she began work on translating some choruses from *Iphigenia in Aulis*. Her Greek was not scholarly: She once commented to a friend on the word "freesia," saying it was an example of a beautiful Greek word, only to be told the flower had been named for F. H. T. Freese. Douglas Bush claims that her "self-conscious, even agonized, pursuit of elusive beauty is quite un-Greek."

If H. D. indulged at times in false etymologies, that has always been the prerogative of a poet, and T. S. Eliot was to say of her translations of Euripides that they were, "allowing for errors and even occasional omissions of difficult passages, much nearer to both Greek and English" than those of Gilbert Murray, the dean of Greek translators. Writing of her poem "Hermes of the Ways," Hugh Kenner would capture to a nicety the curiously Greek yet un-Greek, ancient yet modern tone of so much of H. D.'s work: "We do not mistake the poem for the imagined utterance of some Greek, nor do we hear a modern saying 'I feel as if. . . .' "

Within her Greek matrix, H. D. presented her own struggles and betrayals, her own erotic ambiguities and creative anxieties. H. D. published *Sea Garden*, her first book of verse, and *Choruses from the Iphigenia in Aulis* in 1916: Her early collections all contain translations from—and works inspired by—Sappho, Meleager, and Euripides. *Hymen* (1921), *Heliodora and Other Poems* (1924), and *Red Roses for Bronze* (1929) followed.

H. D. lived in England through World War I. Her marriage to Aldington was virtually over by 1917. In 1918, she met Bryher (Winifred Ellerman), who was to be her lifelong companion; she had a daughter, Perdita, by Cecil Gray, in 1919. Meanwhile, and she had appeared in numerous Imagist anthologies, had formed friendships with D. H. Lawrence and other creative artists, and had traveled in Greece and Egypt. *Collected Poems of H. D.* was published in 1925.

During the 1920's, H. D. began to write prose fiction. *Palimpsest* (1926) is set in classical Rome, London between the wars, and the Egypt of the archaeologists. *Hedylus* (set in ancient Alexandria)

followed in 1928. She also wrote several works with specifically lesbian content, which were not published during her lifetime: *Pilate's Wife*, *Asphodel*, and *Her* (published as *Hermione* in 1981).

In 1933, H. D. went into analysis with Sigmund Freud. If her poetry was of the realm of the gods, dryads, and maenads of Greek myth, his technique of psychoanalysis was no less rooted in Greek mythology—the myth of Oedipus—in language, and in a notion of self-uncovering for which he himself used the metaphor of archaeology. Indeed, H. D.'s title *Palimpsest* could also stand as metaphor for Freud's sense that there are layers upon layers of meaning within human consciousness, inscribed upon one another in the same way that writing is layered upon writing in a palimpsest.

"I am on the fringes or in the penumbra of the light of my father's science and my mother's art—the psychology or philosophy of Sigmund Freud," H. D. would write later. Freud told her she was a perfect example of the bisexual and that she had "two things to hide, one that you were a girl, the other that you were a boy."

Freud and H. D. were in some ways perfectly matched: It is no surprise that her first account of her analysis, *Tribute to Freud* (1956), was described by Freud's biographer Ernest Jones as "surely the most delightful and precious appreciation of Freud's personality that is ever likely to be written." An expanded version was published in 1974.

After her Freudian analysis, World War II was the next major influence on H. D.'s writing—it was also the only time that H. D. and Bryher lived together for an extended period—the two strands coming together in her long poetic sequence *Trilogy* (published posthumously in one volume in 1973), comprising *The Walls Do Not Fall* (1944), *Tribute to the Angels* (1945), and *The Flowering of the Rod* (1946).

The poems of *The Walls Do Not Fall* are remarkable, written in a time of bombs falling, magnesium flares, houses torn open: "there is zrr-hiss,/ lightning in a not-known,// unregistered dimension;/ we are powerless,// dust and powder fill our lungs/ our bodies blunder// through doors twisted on hinges. . . ." Like the *Four Quartets* of T. S. Eliot ("The dove descending breaks the air/ With flame of incandescent terror"), these poems of war carry war into apocalypse. It is the spiritual dimensions, the possibility that H. D. calls "spiritual realism," in which the ancient past merges with the present, that H. D. is after: "possibly we will reach

haven,/ heaven." No less remarkable are the poems that make up *Tribute to the Angels*, which H. D. herself called a "premature peace poem."

In December, 1946, aged sixty, H. D. moved to Lausanne, Switzerland, and what was arguably the most fertile period of her life began, in which she published *By Avon River* (1949), a tribute to Shakespeare; *Bid Me to Live* (1960), a novel; *Helen in Egypt* (1961), a poem about Helen of Troy; and *End to Torment* (1979), a memoir of her long friendship with Ezra Pound.

H. D. died in Zurich on September 27, 1961, having become the first woman to receive the Award of Merit Medal for Poetry of the American Academy of Arts and Letters the year before.

H. D. summed up her life and writings, from "Hermes of the Ways" to her final poetic sequence, in this taut phrase: "H. D.—Hermes—hermeticism and all the rest of it." *Hermetic Definition* (1972), her final sequence of poems, was published posthumously.

Summary

Long thought of as Pound's protégé or as the quintessential early Imagist—and thus a minor figure of note in a largely male poetic history—H. D. can be seen as more in the light of a feminist rewriting of critical history. Imagism itself becomes the cult of H. D., and modern poetics begins with her at least as much as with Pound.

In addition, she brings (as does her friend and colleague Marianne Moore) a uniquely feminine vision to her poetry. Judy Grahn is among those poets who have followed H. D. in the exploration of feminine myth, in such works as *The Queen of Wands* (1982) and *The Queen of Swords* (1987).

Writing in 1993 of Gertrude Stein, Marianne Moore, and H. D., Margaret Dickie noted, "Because they were considered marginal figures even by their friends among the male Modernists, these women were free to experiment long after their male contemporaries were moved to consolidate and conserve. . . . They have waited almost a century for the readers that they have today because they were at least that far ahead of their times."

Bibliography

Dickie, Margaret. "Women Poets and the Emergence of Modernism." In *The Columbia History of American Poetry*, edited by Jay Parini. New York: Columbia University Press, 1993. A sensitive essay offering an extended treatment of H. D., Marianne Moore, and Gertrude Stein.

Gregory, Eileen. *H. D. and Hellenism: Classic Lines*. Cambridge and New York: Cambridge University Press, 1997. Focuses on H. D.'s fascination with Hellenic literature, art, and mythology and Hellenism's relationship to her work. The author's analysis highlights various allusions to the classics found in H. D.'s works.

Guest, Barbara. *Herself Defined: The Poet H. D. and Her World*. New York: Doubleday, 1984; London: Collins, 1985. An excellent biography of H. D., tracing the many strands that, woven together, constitute the complex life of a woman whose work was always autobiographical, always rooted in the concrete event as it flowered in symbolic and mythic thought. A bibliography and an index are included.

H. D. *Tribute to Freud*. Oxford: Carnacet Press, 1971; Boston: Godine, 1974. H. D.'s own account of her psychoanalysis with Freud, which provides an entrance into the understanding of her life and mode of work, besides being a fascinating account of both Freud and psychoanalysis. Widely recommended as the first book of H. D.'s to read. An appendix of letters from Freud to H. D. is included.

Laity, Cassandra. *H. D. and the Victorian Fin de Siecle: Gender, Modernism, Decadence*. Cambridge and New York: Cambridge University Press, 1996. The author argues that H. D. legitimized the expression of female desire in poetry, challenging contemporary male modernist themes of androgyny and homoeroticism.

Robinson, Janice S. *H. D.: The Life and Work of an American Poet*. Boston: Houghton Mifflin, 1982. Another excellent biography of H. D. Includes notes, a bibliography, and an index.

Stock, Noel. *The Life of Ezra Pound*. London: Routledge, and New York: Pantheon, 1970. A biography of the poet who was H. D.'s first love and mentor in poetry, and from whose shadow she has only recently begun to emerge. Provides essential background on Imagism and early modernism. Index.

Charles Cameron

FRITZ HABER

Born: December 9, 1868; Breslau, Silesia
Died: January 29, 1934; Basel, Switzerland
Area of Achievement: Chemistry
Contribution: Haber developed a synthetic process, now named for him, for manufacturing ammonia directly from elemental nitrogen and hydrogen. This made the commercial production of artificial fertilizers possible and has had a profound effect on global agriculture and food production.

Early Life

Fritz Haber was born on December 9, 1868, in what is the modern Polish city of Wrocław, which at that time was under Austrian control and known as Breslau. His father was the owner of a successful merchandising company that dealt in oils, resins, and natural dyestuffs, and was one of Germany's largest importers of indigo. His mother died in childbirth, and young Fritz was reared by relatives until he was nine, when his father remarried. He showed an early interest in experimentation and was allowed by his father to work in the family attic. He entered the University of Berlin in the fall of 1886 and soon became interested in chemistry, taught there by Professors Hermann von Helmholtz and August Wilhelm von Hoffmann. As was then the vogue, Haber attended several universities as a student. He stayed in Berlin for one semester and then went to Heidelberg University for one and a half years. There he was influenced by the intensely practical and factual chemistry professor Robert Bunsen and also developed interests in physics and mathematics. He returned to Breslau for compulsory military service for one year and then entered the Charlottenburg Technische Hochschule in Berlin, the largest engineering college in Germany. There Carl Liebermann, one of the synthesizers of the dye alazarin, introduced him to chemical research, and his first study, done for Liebermann, became his first publication. He earned his doctorate in 1891. After several brief routine jobs outside Germany, Haber decided to enter the Federal Polytechnical School in Zurich, Switzerland, in 1892 in order to study with Georg Lunge, a very respected analytical chemist and teacher. This move was unusual, for few chemists of the time engaged in postdoctoral study. During his one semester there, he studied and experimented with the current chemical technology in dyes, metallurgy, and textiles. After a brief but stormy period working in his father's business, he became an assistant in Ludwig Knorr's laboratory at the University of Jena. Under the system of that day, he had little latitude for personal creativity and applied for a position as assistant in the Department of Chemical and Fuel Technology at the Karlsruhe Technische Hochschule, which he obtained in 1894. This marked the start of his long, broad, and productive career as a teacher, mentor, researcher, and industrial consultant.

Life's Work

Haber was among the first to explore and define the newly developing discipline that would be called physical chemistry and to link university research with industrial production. His scientific interests were broad, but the main themes were the study of combustion processes, chemical phenomena at electrode surfaces, and catalysis. His practical bent was evident throughout his career and distinguished him from those academics of the time who considered practical applications beneath them. His first studies at Karlsruhe were on the breakdown of hydrocarbons by heating, which has become a very important process in the world's oil industry for producing gasoline (thermal cracking). His third book, published in 1905 on the thermodynamics of gas reactions, showed how theoretical calculations could be used by industry and established both his reputation as a preeminent authority on science and technology and his academic career. His early papers dealt with fundamental chemical processes that occur during combustion of coal and gasoline, and the accompanying energy releases. He studied the complex chemical reactions of numerous materials burning in air or oxygen throughout his career.

In the 1890's, Hans Luggin, a close friend of Haber who had studied with the Swedish scientist Svante Arrhenius, suggested that he investigate the new field of electrochemistry. Electrochemistry thus became one of Haber's main interests, such that he became one of the preeminent German names in electrochemistry along with Wilhelm Ostwald. He studied fuel cells for the direct conversion of chemical energy into electricity, the electrochemistry of organic compounds, and the electrochemical conversion of atmospheric nitrogen into useful chemicals, and he did early studies on the electrical production of aluminum metal, at that time an exotic material. This interest continued throughout his career, and he published more than fifty papers on electrochemistry, singly and with various coauthors.

There were forecasts at that time (1905) of an impending world shortage of nitrate fertilizer, and Haber was hired to study nitrogen fixation by several companies. Based on work he saw during an American tour in 1901, he tried various chemical and electrical experiments at increasingly higher temperatures and pressures. Numerous scientists had studied various ways to combine the elements hydrogen and nitrogen directly to form ammonia, with little success. Walther Nernst, a very influential physical chemist, had made small amounts of ammonia using very high pressures, which were impractical for commercial use, and announced publicly that Haber's early experiments were wrong. Haber redoubled his lab efforts, and, with the help of a talented staff, devised the necessary high-pressure apparatus and found a suitable catalyst which made the process a commercial success. He found the right combination of the two opposing variables of temperature and pressure, succeeding where others had failed. The first commercial ammonia plant started production in 1910 in Oppau. His ideas for pressure apparatuses and catalysts were also very useful contributions and were applied by others in several industrial processes.

In the first decade of the twentieth century, Haber's chemistry laboratories at Karlsruhe enjoyed the reputation of being the best equipped in the world and employed more than forty researchers from around the world. He consulted with industry continuously and had several offers of employment in business and at other universities. His success in solving the ammonia-synthesis problem brought an unprecedented offer: The owner of a chemical company, being unable to hire Haber as director of research, offered to help build a research institute on the sole condition that Haber be appointed as its head. Haber accepted. Thus, the Kaiser Wilhelm Institute for Physical Chemistry and Electrochemistry, located in Berlin, was started in 1911. During the tumultuous years of World War I, Haber continued his research with ammonia and chemical oxidation, and also developed and patented a whistle that miners could use to detect the presence of explosive mixtures of methane in the coal mines. Haber consulted for the German War Office. He found a method to prevent gasoline from freezing

and, although he personally abhorred war, devised the chlorine-gas weapon first used at Ieper, Belgium, in April, 1915. His motivation was his belief that it would end the current stalemate caused by trench warfare, and he shared the belief of many of his countrymen that the war would end quickly. He supervised Germany's war effort with chemical weapons, an effort which led to the suicide of his wife, Clara Immerwahr, and which caused his later selection for the Nobel Prize to be contested. He was awarded the prize for the synthesis of ammonia from its elements, which was recognized as "an exceedingly important means of improving the standards of agriculture and the well-being of mankind" by the Swedish Royal Academy.

He worked in the 1920's on behalf of Germany's efforts to make reparation payments to other countries. He tried to obtain gold from seawater, based on estimates of its concentration by others, but abandoned the effort after careful and innovative analytical work showed the earlier estimates to be too large. The Kaiser Wilhelm Institute in 1933 was one of the world's foremost research and training centers and hosted colloquia for such notables as Niels Bohr, Otto Warburg, Peter Debye, Albert Einstein, and others. Haber resigned his directorship that year, when the Nazis came to power, stating that he would not choose his collaborators ". . . on the basis of their grandmothers," and thus created a significant split between government and science. After making detailed arrangements for positions for all of his staff, he briefly moved to Switzerland, then to the University of Cambridge in England. There he occupied the laboratory of his friend of many years Sir William Jackson Pope (who developed the mustard-gas weapon for Great Britain). Before going to England, he had earlier accepted a position at the Daniel Sieff Research Institute in Palestine, offered by the chemist and first President of Israel, Chaim Weizmann. He left England, whose weather he did not find agreeable, for Israel in January, 1934, and, in failing health, stopped for a brief holiday in Switzerland and the Riviera with his sister and a son. He died in his sleep in Lugano (Basel), Switzerland, on January 29, 1934, of coronary sclerosis.

Summary

Fritz Haber was a kind, humorous, dramatic man who regarded his friends and associates as a larger family. His patriotism derived from faith and devotion to Germany, not politics. As one example, during the dire times of 1919, he organized the Emergency Society for German Science, which was created to save the country's scientific research institutions. This organization united the government, the technical societies, universities, and the Kaiser Wilhelm Institute into one national body to foster science and distribute supporting funds. Haber loved an intellectual challenge and had an extremely wide range of interests: He was an innovative scientist, an excellent administrator, an extraordinary organizer, a soldier, an outstanding public speaker and conversationalist, and was well versed in economics, politics, human affairs, and the classics. As he was a talented leader, his laboratory produced many outstanding physical chemists. He was unprecedented in his efforts to foster links between academic and industrial research, and in the industrial application of theory. His scientific life parallels and reflects the main developments in the early years of physical chemistry. His contributions were quite varied, and included the ammonia synthesis for agricultural chemistry, thermal cracking for petroleum chemistry, new instruments for the measurement of gas concentrations and acidity (pH), heterogeneous catalysts for industrial chemistry, new standards for electrical cell measurements, new processes for textile dying, and new dyestuffs. He worked tirelessly to use science to assist technological advance in Germany and, as his international reputation grew, expanded this work to other countries.

Bibliography

Appl, Max. "The Haber-Bosch Process and the Development of Chemical Engineering." In *A Century of Chemical Engineering*, edited by William F. Furter. New York: Plenum Press, 1982. A historical view of the industrial implementation of Haber's ammonia process and its place in the development of the chemical industry.

Coates, J. E. "The Haber Memorial Lecture." *Journal of the Chemical Society*, November, 1939: 1642-1672. Perhaps the best English-language summary of Haber's life and scientific accomplishments. Revealing insights are given into Haber's character and career as a scientist and public figure. His contributions are placed in clear scientific perspective and linked to other concurrent developments in chemistry. For the technical reader.

"The Curious Fate of Fritz Haber." *Scientific American* 277, no. 1 (July, 1997). Profile of Haber. Includes speculations on his work and life.

Goran, Morris. "The Present Day Significance of Fritz Haber." *American Scientist*, July, 1947: 400-403, 406. This article, written as a communication, explains to the post-World War II audience the general importance of Haber's scientific works and addresses criticisms of his involvement in chemical-weapons development.

———. *The Story of Fritz Haber.* Norman: University of Oklahoma Press, 1967. This biography gives many details of Haber's personal life and places his scientific achievements in the historical context of the world events of his time. His personal character is emphasized, and his chemical achievements are summarized in a nontechnical manner.

Haber, L. F. "Fritz Haber and the Nitrogen Problem." *Endeavour* 27, no. 102 (1968): 150-153. An article for the general science reader, describing the chemical problems Haber faced in devising the ammonia synthesis.

Medeiros, Robert W. "Of Swords and Plowshares." *Chemistry* 48 (July, 1975): 12-14. A short article for the student, relating the history of the development of the Haber process for producing ammonia.

Nachmansohn, David. *German-Jewish Pioneers in Science, 1900-1933.* New York: Springer-Verlag, 1979. A brief cameo of Haber's life and main contributions is given. This book covers Jewish notables in the fields of chemistry, physics, and biochemistry at a time when Germany was the leading center for the development of science and technology. Provides information about many scientists who knew Haber and gives highlights of the people and the tremendous scientific activity of that period.

Stock, John T. "Fritz Haber (1868-1934) and the Electroreduction of Nitrobenzene." *Journal of Chemical Education* 65 (April, 1988): 337-338. A short biographical sketch that outlines Haber's work in electrochemistry for the student reader.

Travis, Tony. "The Haber-Bosch Process: Exemplar of 20th Century Chemical Industry." *Chemistry and Industry,* no. 15 (August 2, 1993). Short profiles of Haber and Carl Bosch and the history of their landmark experiments.

Willstätter, Richard. *From My Life: The Memoirs of Richard Willstätter.* Edited by Arthur Stoll. Translated by Lilli S. Hornig. New York: Benjamin, 1965. Willstätter was a Nobel laureate in organic chemistry and one of Haber's best longtime friends and neighbors. He offers personal insights about the life and work of Haber and gives firsthand accounts of the intellectual development, excitement, and aspirations in the European scientific community.

Wolfenden, John H. "The Role of Chance in Chemical Investigation." *Journal of Chemical Education* 44 (May, 1967): 299-303. An article for students that describes how scientists, including Haber, have used unexpected results or unforeseen events to make advances for mankind.

William Van Willis

OTTO HAHN

Born: March 8, 1879; Frankfurt am Main, Germany
Died: July 28, 1968; Göttingen, West Germany
Areas of Achievement: Chemistry and physics
Contribution: A pioneer in understanding the nature of radioactivity, Hahn (with his colleague Fritz Strassmann) is credited with having discovered nuclear fission as well as certain radioactive isotopes and elements. He was awarded the 1944 Nobel Prize in Chemistry and played a major role in reestablishing German science after World War II.

Early Life

Otto Hahn was born into a prosperous middle-class family of Rhenish and northern German ancestry, the youngest of four boys. His father was a glazier and businessman in Frankfurt. Hahn had a happy childhood and lacked for nothing materially. Hahn was a good student but not outstanding. Yet it was during this time that his deep and abiding interest in chemistry began to develop. He attended some adult-oriented lectures on chemistry, conducted some experiments, and began reading about chemistry on his own. Hahn's father, Heinrich, wanted his son to become an architect. Yet the younger Hahn decided to pursue formally the study of chemistry. In 1897, he was graduated from the equivalent of high school and entered the University of Marburg.

Hahn indicates that he was not always a diligent student, sometimes spending more time with beer and friends than with books and lectures. Because it was customary in his day to change one's university a number of times before graduating, Hahn went to the University of Munich in 1898 for two terms. There, he attended classes of another future chemistry Nobel Prize winner, Adolf von Baeyer. Yet Hahn's attention to chemistry was again distracted by other lectures (on such topics as Rembrandt and Peter Paul Rubens) and by extracurricular activities.

Ultimately, Hahn returned to Marburg to complete his work in organic chemistry under the supervision of Theodor Zincke. In 1901, Hahn was awarded the degree of doctor of philosophy magna cum laude at the age of twenty-two. During the summer of that year, he prepared his thesis for publication. It was recognized as an important contribution to the field of organic chemistry for many years after its appearance. Indeed, the future looked bright at the turn of the century for a well-trained organic chemist.

Life's Work

Hahn's fame and greatest achievement came not as a result of his research in organic chemistry but as a result of his pioneering work in the newly evolving field of radiochemistry during the 1930's. Looking over the events which had carried him along the course of his illustrious career, Hahn himself ascribed his direction and success in large measure to what he called a series of lucky accidents.

Following one year of military service after the completion of his degree, Hahn returned to Marburg for two more years as assistant to his mentor, Zincke. This was not only a coveted post for anyone (Zincke's recommendation would secure a position with almost any of the large chemical companies in Germany) but also particularly fortuitous for Hahn at that time. Zincke was able to obtain for Hahn a place in Sir William Ramsay's laboratory at University College, London, while Hahn was in England to learn the English language in preparation for promised employment with an international chemical company.

Hahn's association with Ramsay was of tremendous importance at this stage in his professional life. Ramsay guided Hahn into the realm of research on radioactivity. While with Ramsay, Hahn discovered the previously unknown radioactive element, radiothorium, when he extracted radium from barium using the Curie method.

Because of Ramsay's kindness and his connections, Hahn was able to establish ties that helped him advance his knowledge of and research on radioactivity. Ramsay believed that such research ability as Hahn possessed would be wasted in industry and so encouraged him to accept a position that Ramsay secured for him with the Chemical Institute of the University of Berlin. Hahn's interest in organic chemistry by now was quickly fading in the face of the excitement of radioactivity.

Before going to Berlin, Hahn traveled in September, 1905, from England to McGill University in Montreal, Canada, to work with Ernest Rutherford, who was at that time the best source of information on radioactivity in the world. Hahn spent a year at McGill, during which time he discovered another new radioactive element, radioactinium, and helped determine the process or chains of radioactive decay.

In October, 1906, Hahn arrived in Berlin. At the Chemical Institute, he felt quite alone, since he was the only person at the celebrated organic chemist's institute who knew anything of significance about radioactivity and one of only three there who seriously regarded research on the subject. Yet Hahn's diligent work ultimately brought the respect of some of his colleagues as well as the discovery of another isotope, which he called mesothorium. He was also acquiring, in the course of his studies, something which would prove to be of the greatest help later in discovering the fission process: namely, a thorough familiarity with methods of separating radioactive substances.

Hahn was not long at the institute before Lise Meitner, the most important physicist to have entered his life, came to Berlin from Vienna to do some postgraduate work in theoretical physics under Max Planck at the Institute of Physics. She arrived in the fall of 1907, already possessing some experience in the field of radioactivity. The Hahn-Meitner association blossomed into a thirty-year collaboration, which only terminated in the summer of 1938 because of the Nazi regime.

In October, 1912, the new Kaiser Wilhelm Institute for Chemistry opened its doors, and Hahn was afforded the opportunity to become the head of a small but independent radiochemistry department. He invited Meitner to join him in continuing their work together examining beta radiation, the decay products of radioactive isotopes, and the measurements of extremely weak radioactive substances (rubidium and potassium), since their new laboratory was as yet uncontaminated. Over the years, this small department developed into two large departments—one for radiochemistry under Hahn's direction and one for nuclear physics under Meitner. The new position at the institute also afforded Hahn some degree of financial security so he could think of marriage. He married Edith Junghans on March 22, 1913.

Hahn's work at the institute was interrupted by World War I, during which he served as a chemical-weapons specialist in the gas-warfare corps. He was directly involved with the research, development, testing, manufacture, and use of new gas weapons. Occasionally he had to go to Berlin or Döberitz, usually to test the efficiency of gas masks by observing how long it took poison gas to penetrate them. On one of those trips to Berlin in 1917,

he arranged his time to do some research with Meitner on one of the projects on which they had been working. This resulted in their discovery of a new radioactive substance, element 91, which they named protactinium.

After the war, Hahn returned to the institute with Meitner to work on various problems, including the decay processes of protactinium, uranium, and uranium isotopes. Yet because all the natural radioactive nuclides were known by that time, he increasingly turned his attention (over the next ten years) to applied radiochemistry. He started a new kind of experiment that resulted in the development of the emanation method to study changes in the surfaces and formation of surfaces in certain precipitates. While Hahn became successful with his professional research, his personal life was enriched by the birth of a son and only child on April 22, 1922. In 1928, Hahn became director of the Kaiser Wilhelm Institute for Chemistry.

In 1932, a breakthrough in radiochemistry was achieved when the English physicist Sir James Chadwick discovered the neutron. Immediately, the Italian physicist Enrico Fermi recognized the value of this electrically neutral particle for conducting experiments. Fermi discovered that, by bombarding the elements of the periodic table up to uranium with low-energy neutrons, almost all of them were transformed into radioactive isotopes of the element with the next highest atomic number. When he bombarded the heavy nuclei of uranium, atomic number 92, with neutrons, Fermi concluded that he had produced a transuranium element with an atomic number of 93.

In 1934, Hahn and Meitner decided to repeat Fermi's experiments. They were joined by Fritz Strassmann, who had been at the institute since 1929. The three at first believed that they had verified Fermi's results, although the evidence looked very complicated and confusing. For the next four years, Hahn and his associates examined transuranium elements, their chemical and physical properties, and their decay patterns.

In July, 1938, Meitner was forced to flee Nazi Germany, but Hahn and Strassmann continued their research. The neutron bombardment of uranium seemed to produce several radioactive substances whose chemical properties indicated either radium isotopes or barium. Since the prevailing views of physics at the time made barium production from uranium out of the question, radium was the only reasonable conclusion. Yet when it became impossible to separate the radium, Hahn and Strassmann began to realize that, under the action of the neutrons, the uranium had split into two parts of unequal weight, the most accessible of which was barium. The two scientists confirmed their findings using differing procedures, although they could scarcely believe in the transmutation of uranium to barium.

Hahn sent news of his findings to Meitner in Sweden. With her nephew, Otto Frisch, she correctly interpreted the phenomenon as a splitting of the uranium nucleus and named it "fission." Shortly after the publication of this revolutionary information, Hahn and Strassmann announced the discovery of the second product of uranium fission, the rare gas krypton. Thus, the true picture was complete. When bombarded with slow neutrons, uranium (nuclear charge 92) divided into two fractions, yielding barium (nuclear charge 56) and krypton (nuclear charge 36), with a release of energy.

Hahn was not interested in exploring the practical use or development of his discovery. As war erupted again, he was allowed to continue with his own research, which included investigation of the products of uranium fission. When the chemical institute was destroyed in an air raid, he moved his usable equipment to southern Germany and resumed work there.

In the spring of 1945, he, along with several nuclear physicists and chemists, was arrested by Allied troops and interned in England for more than six months. There, he learned that he had been awarded the 1944 Nobel Prize in Chemistry for his discovery of the fission of heavy nuclei; at the same time, he was profoundly shaken when he also heard that his discovery had led to the production of atom bombs, which had been detonated over Hiroshima and Nagasaki. Normally a man of dry, underplayed wit, Hahn conceived his personal responsibility to be so great that his colleagues feared that he might commit suicide. He became a firm opponent of and spokesman against nuclear weapons and in 1957 refused to cooperate in a planned West German manufacture of such weapons.

Upon his release and return to Germany in 1946, Hahn accepted leadership of the Kaiser Wilhelm Society, which was renamed the Max Planck Society for the Advancement of Science following the death of Planck in 1947. From 1948 to 1960, Hahn directed the policy of that society as its president. Accordingly, he played a major role in the revival

of science and scientific institutions in Germany after World War II. In the 1950's, the quick and successful rebuilding of a series of important research institutes was largely his work.

Grief came again to Hahn in 1960, when his son and daughter-in-law were killed in an automobile accident. His wife never recovered from this shock, and when he died in 1968 at age eighty-nine, she survived him by only two weeks.

Summary

Otto Hahn has justly been called the father of atomic fission. His was a life of tremendous scientific achievement and historic significance. His careful experimentation and discovery of phenomena previously thought to have been impossible led to the practical conversion of matter into energy and helped usher in the atomic age. Hahn's work turned theory into practice.

On a different level, Hahn's personal impact was great, as he held the unlimited trust and confidence of all who knew him. This was of no small help in restoring German science in the postwar years to some semblance of its former greatness.

Of his original publications, only one was a full-size scientific text, consisting of his 1933 Baker Lectures at Cornell University and entitled *Applied Radiochemistry* (1936). Yet Hahn was prolific in the recording of his reminiscences about various developments in the evolution of radiochemistry (especially the discovery of nuclear fission), believing, perhaps, that the personal touch was just as needful in the communication of scientific information as chemical equations and raw data.

The winning of a Nobel Prize is a tremendous accomplishment and is a profound statement of the significance of one's life's work. Yet the magnitude of Hahn's accomplishments is all the more emphasized by the awards which continued to come to him in later life. In 1966, he shared, with Lise Meitner and Fritz Strassmann, the prestigious Enrico Fermi Award, issued by the United States Atomic Energy Commission. It was the first time the award went to foreign citizens and, thus, seems to lend credence to the idea that Hahn's great discovery marked the beginning of a new epoch in history.

Bibliography

Asimov, Isaac. "Otto Hahn." In *Asimov's Biographical Encyclopedia of Science and Technology*. Rev. ed. Newton Abbott: David and Charles, and New York: Doubleday, 1972. This short article presents the essential events of Hahn's life, especially those associated with the discovery of fission. Its strength lies in its references to most of the important colleagues with whom Hahn had contact.

Badash, Lawrence. "Otto Hahn." In *Dictionary of Scientific Biography*, edited by Charles C. Gillispie, vol. 6. New York: Scribner, 1972. This article presents in concise fashion an overall biography of Hahn beginning with his childhood and ending with his involvement in the 1950's warning against nuclear weapons. Though it omits some important details of Hahn's later life, the article's strength consists of its extensive bibliography, including some foreign-language entries.

Crawford, Elizabeth, et al. "A Nobel Tale of Wartime Injustice." *Nature* 382, no. 6590 (August 1, 1996). Discusses the controversy over the decision-making process involved in the awarding of the 1944 Nobel Prize for the discovery of nuclear fission. The author states that the award should have been shared by Hahn, Lise Meitner, and Fritz Strassmann, but was given to Hahn alone.

Graetzer, Hans G., and David L. Anderson. *The Discovery of Nuclear Fission: A Documentary History*. New York: Reinhold, 1971. This short volume is an invaluable source on the context of Hahn's greatest discovery.

Hahn, Otto. "Otto Hahn: Autobiographical Notes." *Bulletin of the Atomic Scientists* 23 (March/April, 1967): 19-24, 22-28. This two-part article is a much scaled-down version of *Otto Hahn: A Scientific Autobiography*. Its value is its brevity and accessibility.

————. *My Life, the Autobiography of a Scientist*. Translated by Ernst Kaiser and Eithne Wilkins. New York: Herder, 1970. Translated from an original German version, this volume represents one of the most complete pictures available on Hahn's life. It presents all aspects of his life, whether humorous, scientific, or (as some might consider) ordinary.

Heisenberg, Werner. "Otto Hahn, Discoverer of Nuclear Fission, Dies." *Physics Today* 21 (October, 1968): 101-102. Written by the then-director of the Max Planck Institute and a younger associate of Hahn, this expanded obituary emphasizes Hahn's scientific accomplishments and pays tribute to his kind and winning personality.

Stehling, Kurt. "Fission's Chemist." *World and I* 12, no. 6 (June, 1997). A profile of Hahn that includes his education, family, achievements in physics, and his collaboration with others.

Andrew C. Skinner

HAILE SELASSIE I
Tafari Makonnen

Born: July 23, 1892; near Harer, Ethiopia
Died: August 27, 1975; Addis Ababa, Ethiopia
Areas of Achievement: Government and politics
Contribution: During his long rule as emperor (1930-1974), Haile Selassie instituted programs for unification and modernization at home, while striving to open up Ethiopia to the world outside its formidable borders.

Early Life

Haile Selassie I was the last in a long line of emperors of Ethiopia which, according to the legendary history, originated with Menelik I, the son of Makeda, the Queen of Sheba, and King Solomon. He was born Tafari Makonnen on July 23, 1892, near Harer, Ethiopia. His father, Ras (duke) Makonnen, was the governor of Harer and adviser to his cousin, Emperor Menelik II. Young Tafari, born as he was in one of the oldest Christian domains, was baptized while only a few days old and, according to custom, given a Christian name, Haile Selassie (power of the trinity)—a name he would use in church and later as ruler.

Tafari was reared in the Coptic Christian faith and educated by European tutors. His father, an important influence on Menelik II and, finally, on young Tafari, had traveled to Rome on state business, and this exposure helped convince him that Ethiopia could benefit from education, modernization, and development. He died in 1906 before he could complete Tafari's political education, which he had only recently begun. He had, however, made Tafari a district governor in Harer province in 1905, giving him the title *dejazmatch* (count). Passed over by Menelik to succeed his father as governor of Harer because of his youth and inexperience, Tafari stayed instead at the palace at the emperor's request. During this eight-month period, he observed much, learning the ways of rulers and much about palace intrigue. His political education advanced rapidly, even without his powerful father. Tafari spent the next year continuing his education in Addis Ababa.

In 1908, Tafari was made governor of Darassa, a subprovince of Sidamo. He moved there with three thousand troops and several trusted officers. In April, 1909, he returned to Addis Ababa because Menelik, who had suffered a minor stroke in 1908,

experienced a more crippling one in January, 1909. As his condition worsened, Empress Taitu's power increased, but so did the plotting by some powerful rases against her. Aware of intrigues by various factions against various members of the royal family, Tafari managed to remain on good terms with all. In 1910, Taitu, who had gained more power following Menelik's third and worst stroke in October, 1909, was overthrown, and Lij Iyasu, Menelik's grandson and Tafari's cousin, assumed power. Taitu had promoted Tafari to governor of Harer, and Iyasu confirmed the appointment. Tafari entered Harer on May 12, 1910, and began to restore the reforms begun by his father.

In 1911, Tafari married Waizero Menen, a wealthy, attractive woman of twenty-two who, as it happened, was the crown prince's niece. The crown prince, meanwhile, was creating problems for his rule even before the death of Menelik II in 1913, favoring Islam in this historically Christian country and not fully tending to the affairs of his office. Tafari, who had been undercut by some of Iyasu's policies, was at the center of a plot to overthrow the crown prince. The coup came in September, 1916. Iyasu was removed from power, Menelik's daughter, Zauditu, was named empress (October, 1916), and Tafari, at age twenty-four, was made ras, heir presumptive, and regent. He was also invested with the Grand Cordon of the Order of Solomon.

Life's Work

Tafari proved to be an able and progressive ruler. Even early in his regency he showed his interest in modernization and reform, despite the more conservative and religious preoccupations of the empress. These early efforts were capped by the seating of Ethiopia in 1923 in the League of Nations. Resistance to accepting Ethiopia was based on objections to its slavery and slave trade. Tafari promised to abolish the slave trade, which he did the next year and then began implementation of a program for the gradual emancipation of Ethiopia's slaves.

Tafari became the first Ethiopian ruler to go abroad when in 1924 he traveled to Rome, Paris, and London, among other European capitals. This trip only increased his determination to bring

change and modernization, however gradual, to Ethiopia upon his return.

Ruling Ethiopia, once a group of separate kingdoms, was made difficult not only by the extremes of terrain, the ethnic diversity, and the primitive communication and transportation facilities, but also by the continuing independence of a number of its provinces. In the mid-1920's, Tafari began to move to exert more control over these provinces. In 1926, he took control of the army and by 1928 had increased his authority while the power of Empress Zauditu and of a number of the provincial governors had lessened. On October 7, 1928, amid much pomp and ceremony, Tafari was crowned negus (king).

In late March, 1930, Ras Gugsa Wolie, the estranged husband of Zauditu, led a coup attempt against Tafari. Wolie was killed in a battle at Ankim on March 31, 1930, and the coup died with him. Zauditu died suddenly the next day. Tafari, with an endorsement by the archbishop, declared himself negusa nagast (king of kings) and took his baptismal name, Haile Selassie. Then, in a grand ceremony on November 2, 1930, to which world leaders and monarchs specifically were invited, Haile Selassie was crowned His Imperial Majesty Haile Selassie I, King of Kings of Ethiopia, Conquering Lion of Judah, and Elect of God. The event and the refurbishing of Abbis Ababa to host it were, among other things, calculated to symbolize Haile Selassie's determination to bring modernization and reform to Ethiopia and to open it up to the rest of the world.

In July, 1931, he proclaimed a new constitution. The "constitutional monarchy" that was established vested all final power and authority in the emperor. It also increased the power of the central government in an attempt to unify what had been little more than a collection of interacting provincial governments. Haile Selassie then began his efforts at modernization, introducing programs for road building, public works, education, and public health.

These long-overdue changes would be abruptly halted by actions taken against Ethiopia by Italy from bases it had established in Somalia and Eritrea. Benito Mussolini had designs on the horn of Africa, and the conquest of Ethiopia was crucial to the realization of those designs. Haile Selassie was not unaware of the threat that Italy represented but trusted in the League of Nations to protect Ethiopia against aggression. On October 3, 1935, Mussolini

telegraphed instructions to open the attack against Ethiopia. The league did nothing. Haile Selassie led his warriors against the invading Italian army. They fought bravely but were gravely overmatched. The Italians, using planes, poison gas, and sophisticated weapons, crushed the Ethiopian resistance, capturing Addis Ababa on May 5, 1936. Haile Selassie fled his country, living in exile, ultimately, in England. This represented the first loss of national independence in Ethiopian recorded history.

On June 30, 1936, Haile Selassie addressed the League of Nations. A decade earlier, protests to that body opposing some 1926 Anglo-Italian accords which infringed on the sovereignty of Ethiopia had fallen on deaf ears. Now Haile Selassie's personal appeal for military sanctions to help stop Italy's aggression brought similar results. His warning that "God and history will remember your judgment" struck a chord but produced no immediate result. Only mild sanctions were voted and were never really enforced. By late 1938, the horn was being recognized as Italian East Africa.

When World War II broke out and Italy joined the Axis Powers, Great Britain recognized Haile Selassie as an ally, then, in January, 1941, joined with him and his army in exile in Sudan. They, with the assistance of freedom fighters still in the country, drove the Italian army out of Ethiopia. On May 4, 1941, Haile Selassie reentered Addis Ababa. By November, he once again ruled Ethiopia, now with a new set of circumstances and problems. His absence and the struggle against the Italians at the local level had revitalized some provincial power bases. At the same time, the Italians had constructed roads, bridges, and a bureaucracy that would facilitate unification. Haile Selassie moved quickly to reassert his authority, extending his administrative and military control over the country by regulating the church, the government, and the finances of the nation. He also put down uprisings in Gojjam and Tigre provinces. Unification as he envisioned it would not be easy, nor would the establishment of proper relations with foreign nations. Haile Selassie wanted foreign assistance in the development of Ethiopia but not interference in its internal affairs. In fact, however, Great Britain, then other Western nations including the United States, especially while World War II raged, were deeply involved in Ethiopia's modernization and, almost necessarily, its internal affairs.

In 1947, Haile Selassie began to press for annexation of Eritrea. Arguing that it had been a part of Ethiopia before the 1890's, that Eritreans shared with Ethiopia a common language, dress, and set of social customs, and adding Ethiopia's need for a Red Sea port (Mesewa), Haile Selassie took his case to the United Nations. In December, 1950, the United Nations General Assembly voted to federate an "autonomous Eritrea" with Ethiopia "under the sovereignty of the Ethiopian crown." This arrangement would remain, Eritrea's objections notwithstanding, until Ethiopia absorbed Eritrea in 1962. Eritrea's struggle for independence would present problems for Haile Selassie for the rest of his rule.

In 1954, Haile Selassie, who would be among the most widely traveled of world leaders, visited the United States, Canada, and Mexico. He was an overnight guest of President Dwight D. Eisenhower at the White House, he addressed a joint session of Congress, and he received honorary degrees from Howard, Columbia, and Montreal universities. He was less fortunate during another series of state visits in December, 1960. While he was in Brazil, a number of important and highly placed individuals attempted to overthrow Haile Selassie's government. His supporters managed to defeat the conspirators, but the very challenge to his authority suggested the growing tensions in the changing if still delicately balanced society.

Haile Selassie would continue to keep a high profile in his country, on the continent, and in the world. In 1963, he helped found the Organization of African Unity, whose headquarters opened that year in Addis Ababa. He helped mediate disputes on the continent, such as the Algerian-Moroccan Border War (1963), and continued his rounds of state visits. By 1970, he seemed more involved in foreign affairs than in domestic concerns. In February, 1974, a military coup, this time successful, was mounted against Haile Selassie's government. On September 12, a provisional military government was established and Haile Selassie was deposed and made a prisoner in his own place. Crown Prince Asfa Wossen was named king-designate, but then in March, 1975, the military rulers issued a proclamation abolishing the monarchy entirely. Haile Selassie died in Addis Ababa on August 27, 1975.

Summary

During his rule first as regent and then emperor, Haile Selassie I sought to unify and modernize Ethiopia and involve it in the larger world. This meant moving, within the period of his rule, from an isolated, preindustrial, feudal society, still with the institution of slavery, to a unified nation-state growing in wealth and exercising influence throughout the continent and the world. His efforts at unification, based on control of a standing army, the institution of a centralized fiscal system, and the reorganization of provincial governments under a more powerful "constitutional monarchy," were successful, unleashing new forces less easily controlled. The same result was obtained through his efforts at modernization. Foreign aid was sought but not foreign intrusion. For a time the Italians provided the most and worst of both, but even friendly nations would leave their stamp. For Haile Selassie modernization included three priorities, which he articulated in 1950: expansion of education, development of communications, and secure employment for all Ethiopians. Progress in these areas, which would involve restructuring Ethiopian society and the creation of an intelligentsia, would also give rise to groups less content to live under the limitations and restrictions of Haile Selassie's autocratic rule. It seemed inevitable that the forces of change unleashed in Ethiopia should one day challenge the ancient system of rule that had first set them in motion. It is a tribute to Haile Selassie that he was able to balance competing claims and remain in power for as long as he did.

Bibliography

Greenfield, Richard. *Ethiopia: A New Political History.* London: Pall Mall Press, and New York: Praeger, 1965. Another survey, and a good one, this study emphasizes the complexities of Ethiopian politics, especially in the twentieth century, all building toward the 1960 coup attempt. Greenfield devotes a quarter of the book to the failed coup and makes no effort to hide his sympathy for it.

Hess, Robert L. *Ethiopia: The Modernization of Autocracy.* Ithaca, N.Y.: Cornell University Press, 1970. This is a good introductory survey of prerevolutionary Ethiopia, including some two thousand years of history. The second two-thirds of this book, which includes a good bibliography, concentrates on the rule of Haile Selassie.

Marcus, Harold G. *Haile Sellassie I: The Formative Years, 1892-1936.* Berkeley: University of California Press, 1987. The first of a three-volume biography, this is an excellent account of

Haile Selassie's life up to the time of the Italian occupation. It is illustrated and includes an extensive bibliography.

Mosley, Leonard. *Haile Selassie: The Conquering Lion.* London: Weidenfeld and Nicolson, 1964; Englewood Cliffs, N.J.: Prentice-Hall, 1965. A generally sympathetic book by a British journalist who covered the liberation of Ethiopia and who knows his subject well. Illustrated.

Spencer, John H. *Ethiopia at Bay: A Personal Account of the Haile Selassie Years.* Algonac, Mich.: Reference Publications, 1984. A detailed study of Haile Selassie's Ethiopia written in the first person by an American who was an adviser to that country's government during the Italian invasion and who later served as principal adviser to the Ethiopian Ministry of Foreign Affairs for much of the period 1943-1974. Though its maps and illustrations are welcomed by the general reader, its prose and detail make it more appropriate to the specialist.

David W. Moore

HALIDE EDIB ADIVAR

Born: 1884; Istanbul, Ottoman Empire
Died: January 9, 1964; Istanbul, Turkey
Areas of Achievement: Literature, government, politics, and women's rights
Contribution: Adıvar was a leading Turkish nationalist, writer, and social reformer. She played a prominent role in the Young Turk Revolution of 1908-1909 and an even more important part in the Nationalist Revolution, led by Mustafa Kemal (Atatürk) between 1919 and 1924. As such she was one of the first Turkish women to take an active, indeed militant, interest in national politics. She was the first Turkish graduate of the American College for Girls in Istanbul, and she is credited with writing the first novel in Turkish.

Early Life

Halide Edib Adıvar's life spans a critical period in the history of modern Turkey—from the twilight of the Ottoman Empire under Sultan Abdülhamid II until the aftermath of the first military coup in the early 1960's. These eighty years brought momentous changes and upheavals to Turkish society; Adıvar participated actively in those changes, influencing the course of her country's social and political evolution. She was born in the ancient, imperial capital of Istanbul, then the center of the Ottoman Empire. Her family lived in the neighborhood of Beshiktash, on a hill overlooking the Sea of Marmara, not far from the Yildiz Palace, which served as the residence of the Ottoman ruler. Adıvar's father, Mehmed Edib Bey, enjoyed an important government office, the position of first secretary to the sultan's privy purse, which made the family part of the inner circle of the ruling elite. Her mother, Bedrfem Hanim, died of tuberculosis when Adıvar was quite young, and her father remarried sometime before her fourth birthday.

Because of her father's admiration for the English and for British ways of bringing up children, Adıvar's early childhood was quite different from that normally accorded upper-class Turkish Muslim girls. She was dressed, reared, and even fed in the English manner and sent to a nearby kindergarten run by Greek Christians. A childhood illness ended her first experience with modern, Western-type education, and Adıvar was sent to live with her grandmother. In her grandmother's more traditional household, the young girl was introduced to popular lore, folk medicine, and literature, as well as the milieu of conservative Turkish Muslim women. Later she would draw upon this fund of popular beliefs and lore in her writings. A local Islamic teacher—the *imam* of the nearby mosque-school—taught her to read and write as well as instructing her in the Koran. All of this changed when Adıvar was eleven, for her father enrolled her for a year in the American College for Girls in Istanbul, where she studied English, eventually becoming remarkably fluent in the language. Until 1899, she continued her studies under an English governess as well as several well-known Turkish tutors, then reentered the American College for Girls, where she was the only Turkish student. In 1901, she was graduated and married her former tutor, a mathematician named Salih Dheki Bey, with whom she had two sons.

Life's Work

The first decade of the twentieth century was a tumultuous era in Turkish history, and, during this time, Adıvar read widely not only in classical Ottoman literature but also in European classics such as those of William Shakespeare and Émile Zola. In 1908 came the Young Turk Revolution, which represented a turning point in the centuries-old Ottoman system of rule, because the autocratic power of the sultan was limited, the constitution of 1876 was restored, and a new political elite eventually came to power. It was during the events of 1908 that Adıvar became a political essayist and writer, publishing articles in the daily newspaper *Tanin* that pressed for social and educational reforms along Western lines. Among the things that she advocated were gradual educational changes and the emancipation of women. Her writings brought her instant literary fame as well as arousing the opprobrium of more reactionary elements in society.

Less than a year later, a counterrevolutionary attempt by those supporting the *ancien régime* occurred in Istanbul during the spring of 1909. Fearing repression, Adıvar traveled in disguise with her two young sons to Egypt and then went to England for several months. While in England, she experienced two things that she later regarded as instrumental in the formation of her own Turkish nationalism—a stay in Cambridge, where she heard a debate on the matter of Irish home rule, and a visit to Parliament, which she says "inspired me almost with pious emotion." In addition, she met with prominent female suffragists, then campaigning for expanded political and legal rights.

In October of 1909, Adıvar returned to Turkey, since the counterrevolutionary movement had been suppressed. Caring for her son during his bout with typhoid, Adıvar composed her first novel during nighttime vigils. Entitled *Seviye Talip* and published in 1910, the book "exposed social shams and conventions," and, while immensely popular, it also encountered severe criticism. At that time, Adıvar was invited to join the teaching staff of the Women Teachers' Training College, where she collaborated with another leading educational reformer, Nakiye Elgün, in modernizing the institution's curriculum and administration. The year 1910 also brought personal distress to Adıvar, since her husband married a second wife—polygamy not yet being outlawed in Turkey—and thus she divorced him. At this time, Adıvar became involved in a new cultural ideology, known as Turkism, and she wrote a second novel, *Yeni Turan* (1912; the new Turan), which was influenced by this movement.

Resigning her post at the Women Teachers' Training College, Adıvar next accepted a position as inspector general of the *Ewkaf* (religious) schools, then in the process of being modernized. In addition, she was active in a new women's association, The Women's Club, which was involved in various community services. Both of these activities exposed her to popular social classes very different from her own background; later these experiences would furnish material for her novels as well as heighten her social consciousness.

Late in 1914, the Ottoman Empire entered the war on the side of Germany and Austria, a decision that ultimately resulted in the empire's demise. During the difficult war years, Adıvar pursued her work of educational reform, organizing orphanages and the Red Crescent (Turkish Red Cross) not only in Turkey but also Syria. In 1917, she was married a second time to Dr. Adnan Adıvar, who was a prominent member of the ruling Committee of Union and Progress. The Ottoman defeat by the Allies in 1918 brought political chaos to Turkey as well as foreign occupation and the Greek invasion of 1919. While the victorious powers met in Versailles throughout 1919 to decide Turkey's fate, armed resistance to the Greek army erupted in Anatolia, as did mass protests against the partition of the country by the Allies.

In these expressions of popular opposition to European imperialism, Adıvar played once again a leading role, even addressing a huge crowd in Istanbul's great square, Sultan Ahmed Square, on May 23, 1919. By then, public speaking was not new to Adıvar. A decade earlier she had given the commencement speech at the American College, the first time ever that a Turkish woman had formally addressed a male-female audience in public.

While an ardent nationalist, Adıvar was opposed to violence to achieve Turkish independence, and she even attempted to arrange for an American mandate in Turkey between 1919 and 1920 to avoid further clashes between the European forces and the Turkish army, then under the command of Mustafa Kemal (Atatürk). In 1920, she and her husband were forced to flee Istanbul to avoid arrest by the Allied powers. They took refuge in the Anatolian countryside and, after a journey full of hardships, reached Ankara, where the provisional Turkish government had been established to fight for the country's independence. The difficulties of escape and the couple's desperate flight across rural Anatolia formed the core of her 1923 novel, *Ateştan gömlek* (*The Shirt of Flame*, 1924), which was later made into a Turkish film by the same title. As was true earlier when she worked among the poor classes of Istanbul, her experiences among the peasantry made Adıvar painfully aware of the unfavorable conditions suffered by rural peoples.

Once in Ankara, where she and her family resided in a mud hut, Adıvar devoted her energies fully to the nationalist cause. She worked for the Agricultural School, for the Anatolian news agency, and contributed articles to the daily newspaper. Her pivotal importance as a nationalist figure is attested by the fact that she was admitted to Mustafa Kemal's circle of political intimates and also was condemned to death *in absentia* by the sultan's government in Istanbul. During the Turkish-Greek wars, Adıvar was instrumental once again in organizing women, relief works, and the Turkish Red Crescent, even laboring as a nurse in a provincial hospital. Thus, while moving in the highest male-dominated nationalist organizations—Adıvar was even made a sergeant major in the army—she did not abandon her feminine and feminist concerns and goals.

With the nationalist victory in November of 1922, the Adıvars returned to Istanbul, since Adnan had been named as the representative of the Ministry of Foreign Affairs to the former capital, Ankara now being the seat of government. The next few years witnessed deep divisions within the ranks of the nationalists. Because the Adıvars held firm to their liberal ideological stance, as opposed to the more radical position of the Turkish Republic's first president, Atatürk, they were unjustly accused of plotting against the increasingly authoritarian president. Finally, Adıvar and her husband left Turkey in 1924 for Europe, where they spent the next fourteen years in exile.

During those years, the couple resided first in England and then in France for nearly a decade since Adnan was appointed to a teaching position at the École des Langues Orientales Vivantes in Paris. While in England between 1924 and 1928, Adıvar wrote her memoirs; even today she remains one of the few Middle Eastern women ever to write an autobiography, another genre borrowed from the West. Published in two volumes, her memoirs appeared in 1926 and 1928 under the titles of *Memoirs of Halide Edib* and *The Turkish Ordeal*. In 1929, she traveled to the United States to give a series of lectures at various American universities and returned for the 1931-1932 academic year to teach at Columbia University as a visiting professor. Adıvar later toured the Indian subcontinent to give lectures devoted to political and cultural/religious changes in the Turkish Republic, which greatly interested Muslims all over the world. At the same time, she continued to produce novels, composing her only work of fiction in English, *The Clown and His Daughter*, which appeared in 1935.

Atatürk's death in 1938 meant that the Adıvars could return to Turkey for good the next year. There Adıvar was made the chair of the newly created department of English at the University of Istanbul. Between 1950 and 1954, she served as a member of Parliament. Because of her husband's death in 1955 and her increasingly delicate state of health, she retired from public life. Adıvar died on January 9, 1964, at the age of eighty in a suburb of Istanbul, greatly mourned by her countrymen.

Summary

Although her style has often been criticized by the literary establishment, Halide Edib Adıvar remains one of the most widely read authors of her generation. Her creative output is staggering. In addition to twenty novels, she published short stories, essays, literary criticism, plays, memoirs, articles pressing for a wide range of social reforms, and translations from European languages into Turkish. Not content with the pen as an instrument for needed social changes, Adıvar lived passionately what she advocated in her writings. It is difficult to find among her feminist peers, whether in the Middle East or in Western Europe, a woman or man who matches Adıvar in terms of courage, vitality, and devotion to national as well as internationalist causes. She merits well the sobriquet of the "Joan of Arc of Turkey."

Bibliography

Adıvar, Halide. *Memoirs of Halide Edib*. New York and London: Century, 1926. This is an absolutely indispensable as well as fascinating account of the author's life from early childhood until the end of her educational mission in Syria in 1917. It represents a precious source of information for historians of this period in Turkish history.

———. *The Turkish Ordeal*. New York and London: Century, 1928. This is the subsequent volume of Adıvar's memoirs dealing with the nationalist era from 1918 to 1922. It provides insights not only into her own activities but also into those of an entire generation of Turkish nationalists.

———. *The Shirt of Flame*. New York: Duffield, 1924. One of her novels (1923) which belongs to her second phase of writing devoted to the Turkish war of liberation. It draws upon her personal experiences and was regarded as a pioneering work in the period.

Iz, Fahir. "Khālide Edīb." In *The Encyclopedia of Islam*, edited by G. van Donzel, B. Lewis, and Ch. Pellat, vol. 4. Rev. ed. Leiden: Brill, 1978. This is the fullest English-language treatment of Adıvar's life and work. It synthesizes much research in Turkish on Adıvar which is otherwise inaccessible to English-speaking audiences.

Kinross, Lord. *Atatürk: A Biography of Mustafa Kemal*. New York: Morrow, 1965. Kinross' biography of the father of modern Turkey is the definitive work in English. Essential to an understanding of the nationalist and early Republican periods, the work also contains information regarding Adıvar's contribution to the Turkish independence movement.

Lewis, Bernard. *The Emergence of Modern Turkey*. 2d ed. London and New York: Oxford University Press, 1968. While Lewis only mentions Adıvar in passing, this is the essential background text for understanding the culture and society in which she lived and the historical changes she not only experienced but also helped to shape.

Julia A. Clancy-Smith

WILLIAM F. HALSEY

Born: October 30, 1882; Elizabeth, New Jersey
Died: August 16, 1959; Fishers Island, New York
Area of Achievement: Military affairs
Contribution: "Bull" Halsey was a colorful and offensive-minded fighter who went by the slogan "hit hard, hit fast, hit often." A proponent of naval aviation and an avowed risk taker, he epitomized the aggressive spirit of the United States Navy during World War II.

Early Life

William Frederick Halsey, Jr., was born in Elizabeth, New Jersey, the son of a former naval captain. Like his father, he attended the Naval Academy in Annapolis, Maryland, and he graduated as a midshipman in 1904. He served on several ships before joining the battleship *Kansas* as part of President Theodore Roosevelt's Great White Fleet, which steamed around the world from 1907 to 1909. Halsey rose steadily through the ranks and, during World War I, commanded the destroyers *Shaw* and *Benham* while on escort duty in Queenstown, Ireland. Fine seamanship garnered him the Navy Cross in 1918, and he spent the next twenty years holding down various assignments on ship and ashore.

Following several tours in Berlin, Germany; Copenhagen, Denmark; and Stockholm, Sweden, as a naval attaché, Halsey attended the Naval and Army War Colleges before turning his attention to naval aviation. The invention of the aircraft carrier held the potential for revolutionizing naval warfare, and Halsey envisioned opportunities for advancement in this new and untested field. Undeterred by advanced age and poor vision, he received flight training at the Naval Aviator's School at Pensacola, Florida, in 1935 and won his wings at the age of fifty-two. Halsey then transferred to the carrier service by commanding the *Saratoga* and distinguished himself during various fleet training exercises up through 1937.

In terms of naval tactics, Halsey was no traditionalist and made a name for himself by demanding greater roles for naval aviation. This view was advocated at the expense of the "battleship admirals," who saw airplanes as little more than scouts for the battle fleet. Furthermore, Halsey deliberately cultivated a "fighting sailor" image. When his promotion to vice admiral arrived in June, 1940, Halsey took charge of Carrier Division 2, consisting of the *Enterprise* and the *Yorktown*, and deployed them in the Pacific. War with Japan seemed imminent to Halsey, and on December 1, 1941, while ferrying fighter aircraft to Wake Island, he took the unprecedented measure of placing the ships on a war footing. His premonitions were justified six days later when Japanese carrier aircraft dealt a devastating blow to the U.S. battle fleet at Pearl Harbor, Hawaii.

Life's Work

Halsey personified aggressive leadership, and he quickly emerged as one of the United States' earliest wartime heroes. In January, 1942, Admiral Chester W. Nimitz ordered him to conduct the Navy's first offensive of World War II by launching air strikes against the Gilbert and Marshall Islands. The following month Halsey also struck Wake and Marcus Islands before embarking on one of the most audacious raids in military history. That April Halsey commanded a task force that escorted Captain Marc A. Mitscher's carrier *Hornet* to within bombing distance of Japan. On board were sixteen Army Air Force B-25 Mitchell bombers under veteran aviator Colonel James H. Doolittle. Despite a stealthy, northern approach to within 620 miles of the enemy homeland, the Americans were discovered by a Japanese picket vessel the day before the launch was scheduled. With characteristic boldness, Halsey and Doolittle decided to move up the launch date by one day, anticipating that the Japanese now expected a raid by short-range naval aircraft. On April 18, 1942, the bombers were launched against Tokyo and other targets, which completely surprised the defenders. Little material damage was inflicted and all the aircraft subsequently crash-landed in China, but Doolittle's raid provided tremendous lift to American morale.

In Halsey's absence, elements of the U.S. carrier fleet fought a large Japanese task force to a draw at the Battle of Coral Sea in May, 1942. This was the first time in history that two opposing battle fleets traded shots without ever sighting each other. An impending Japanese invasion of Port Moresby, New Guinea, was thwarted, but Japan countered with an ambitious amphibious attack against Midway Island. The intention of Admiral Isoroku Yamamoto was to lure the three remaining U.S. carriers into battle at a numerical disadvantage and destroy them. It was a scenario tailor-made for

Halsey's daredevil leadership, but fate intervened when he was sidelined by a skin rash. While he recuperated in Hawaii, the Americans fought and won the decisive victory at Midway Island in June, 1942. Halsey missed the greatest carrier clash in history, but his efficiently trained staff was present and contributed greatly to the battle's successful outcome.

Halsey had no sooner recovered in October, 1942, when he was dispatched to the Pacific on an extremely urgent mission. In the wake of Midway Island, the United States staged its first amphibious offensive of the war by landing marines on Guadalcanal in the Solomon Islands in August, 1942. The Japanese responded with a ferocious land, sea, and air offensive intended to drive them out. Over the next few weeks, the U.S. Navy took heavy losses at the hands of the Japanese navy and was withdrawn from the area. This left the marines stranded on Guadalcanal without support and open to attack from the sea. The Navy Department, dissatisfied by the timid leadership of Admiral Robert L. Ghormley, replaced him with Halsey in an attempt to stave off disaster. As commander of the South Pacific Force, he infused all hands with an offensive spirit and issued one standing order: Attack! Halsey then sailed forth to engage the enemy, fighting the Japanese to a draw near the Santa Cruz Islands on October 26-28 and decisively defeating them off Guadalcanal on November 12-15. Victory proved costly in terms of men and ships, but the tide had turned. Within three months the Japanese had abandoned Guadalcanal and the Allies were free to expand their offensive strategy.

As a reward for his fighting leadership, Halsey received promotion to full admiral and was entrusted with clearing out the Solomon Islands. In this endeavor he was forced to cooperate with another leader of tremendous ability and ego, General Douglas MacArthur. Happily, the two headstrong, aggressive commanders agreed on a number of strategic and tactical priorities. They realized that any advance up the Solomons would eventually encounter the powerful Japanese stronghold on Rabaul at the northernmost end of the island chain. Rather than risk their few remaining carriers to aerial assault, Halsey and MacArthur decided to seize lightly defended areas around the bastion, construct airfields, and isolate it with air power. Thus a costly invasion of the island became unnecessary. As the U.S. steamroller continued westward and into the Gilbert and Marshall Islands, Halsey

and MacArthur decided that the heavily fortified island of Truk could be bypassed in identical fashion. Consequently, many lives were spared and two sizable enemy garrisons were neutralized without a shot being fired. By March, 1944, the South Pacific region was firmly in Allied hands and U.S. leaders turned their attention to the bigger objective of recapturing the Philippines.

In October, 1944, Halsey relieved Admiral Raymond A. Spruance as commander of the Third Fleet (Task Force 38) and made preliminary dispositions for cooperating with MacArthur's army. Up to this point, he enjoyed a reputation as the Unites States' leading naval fighter. However, the impending Philippine campaign was a huge, multifront endeavor combining the resources of many fleets and objectives. The sheer scope of operations, combined with a wily adversary, seems to have gotten the better of Halsey, and his reputation suffered. His initial operations against the original target, the southern island of Mindanao, revealed very weak Japanese air defenses, suggesting that it was also weakly held. Halsey then brilliantly suggested that it be bypassed altogether, an act that would move up the intended invasion of Luzon, the main island, by two months.

Subsequent operations, however, taxed Halsey's abilities to the limit. He was entrusted with the dual responsibility of shielding MacArthur's intricate landings at Leyte Gulf, while simultaneously seeking out the remaining Japanese carriers and destroying them. The October, 1943, landings succeeded, but the Japanese countered with a three-pronged naval offensive that confused the U.S. high command. Unaware of the larger picture, Halsey predictably pursued Admiral Jisaburo Ozawa's ships and sank his last four carriers. In doing so, he ignored repeated suggestions from his staff that Ozawa was probably a decoy sent to lure Halsey away from Leyte. In fact, this is exactly what happened. In Halsey's absence, two other Japanese strike forces penetrated the Surigao Strait unopposed and briefly menaced the landing zones. Fortunately, the enemy turned back after meeting heavy resistance from an inferior force of escort carriers and destroyers at Samar Island and disaster was averted. Japanese losses during the Battle of Leyte Gulf were crippling and were achieved at relatively little cost to U.S. forces. Nonetheless, Halsey endured considerable criticism for charging after Ozawa and leaving the beachheads undefended.

In December, 1944, Halsey made another controversial decision by riding out a typhoon that sank three destroyer escorts and damaged his fleet far more than the enemy had. The final months of the war saw Task Force 38 making wide sweeps through the China Sea, Formosa, Okinawa, and the Chinese coast, decimating the remnants of enemy sea and air power. That June he elected to ride out another typhoon, again with appreciable damage to the fleet. By July, 1945, Halsey's aircraft were ranging the Japanese home islands at will, while his ships bombarded installations on shore. Following Japan's capitulation in August, 1945, the official surrender ceremony was concluded aboard Halsey's former flagship, the battleship *Missouri*. In three and one-half years of combat, the old admiral was responsible for sinking more enemy warships than any other naval commander. After the war, Halsey turned over the Third Fleet to Admiral Howard Kingman and returned home to become a five-star fleet admiral. He then performed several months of special duty with the secretary of the Navy before formally retiring in April, 1947. Halsey, one of the most popular sailors in U.S. history, died at the Fishers Island Country Club in New York on August 16, 1959.

Summary

Halsey, dubbed "Bull" by the press for his aggressive swagger, was a proven fighter and a brilliant naval tactician. Given a short-term objective, no matter how daunting, he invariably assembled the means for attacking and proceeded relentlessly until victorious. In this sense, his approach to war reflected the eighteenth century British school epitomized by Lord Horatio Nelson: a single-minded determination to seek out, engage, and destroy the enemy fleet through decisive action. However, his highly individualistic leadership style was more appropriate to this earlier setting and was anachronistic given the mounting complexities of modern naval warfare in which teamwork, analysis, and managerial skills proved paramount.

In truth, Halsey stumbled badly at Leyte and, had the Japanese displayed more aggressive leadership, the ensuing disaster might have compromised MacArthur's invasion. Furthermore, his decision to twice expose the Third Fleet to the ravages of typhoons cost seven hundred lives, several ships, and scores of aircraft, and it called into question his competency as a sailor. Throughout the war, detractors raised legitimate points about his limitations, but the Halsey's public popularity and combat record shielded him from recriminations. No other admiral could have made his mistakes and survived. Nevertheless, he enjoyed a lengthy, controversial, and ultimately successful career and is rightly credited with turning the tide of battle in the Pacific. Halsey's efficacy as one of naval warfare's most determined and colorful practitioners is secure and unmatched by any admiral of the twentieth century.

Bibliography

Adamson, Has C., and George F. Kosco. *Halsey's Typhoons: A Firsthand Account of How Two Typhoons, More Powerful Than the Japanese, Dealt Death and Destruction to Admiral Halsey's Third Fleet*. New York: Crown, 1967. As the title implies, the book provides an eyewitness treatment of the Third Fleet's terrible beating at the hands of nature. The admiral is highly criticized.

Cutler, Thomas J. *The Battle of Leyte Gulf, October 23-26, 1944*. New York: Harper, 1994. Cutler's analysis of the controversial victory credits Halsey with winning the battle. The most extensively researched book available.

Halsey, William F., and J. Bryan III. *Admiral Halsey's Story*. New York: McGraw-Hill, 1947. This book contains a journalistic and anecdotal account of high command that suffers from an unabashed lack of objectivity.

Merrill, James M. *A Sailor's Admiral: A Biography of William F. Halsey*. New York: Crowell, 1976. An exciting and popular account that focuses almost entirely on the war years.

Potter, E. B. *Bull Halsey*. Annapolis, Md.: Naval Institute Press, 1985. This well-researched, engagingly written account is somewhat limited by the author's refusal to criticize Halsey's more questionable decisions.

Roddewig, Robert. "Bull Session." *American Heritage* 48, no. 5 (September, 1997). The author discusses a personal experience with Admiral Halsey.

John C. Fredriksen

DAG HAMMARSKJÖLD

Born: July 29, 1905; Jönköping, Sweden
Died: September 18, 1961; near Ndola, Northern
   Rhodesia
Area of Achievement: Diplomacy
Contribution: As secretary-general of the United
   Nations from 1953 to 1961, Hammarskjöld vast-
   ly increased both the influence and the prestige
   of the United Nations (U.N.). He oversaw the ex-
   plosive growth of the organization among Third
   World nations, prevented the U.N. from becom-
   ing a pawn of the major Cold War rivals, and ini-
   tiated the U.N.'s peacekeeping role.

Early Life

Dag Hjalmar Agne Carl Hammarskjöld grew up in
a home dominated by the ideals of public service
and faith in one's own convictions. The youngest
of four sons, he watched his father, a former prime
minister of Sweden, sacrifice his political career by
defending Sweden's neutrality during World War I.
Certainly his father's subsequent devotion to the
principles of the League of Nations, the world's
first genuine collective-security organization, influenced the young Hammarskjöld's later career. His
mother's influence was less apparent, although her
skepticism of rational thought can be discerned in
his later poetry and religious writings.

Educated at the University in Uppsala, Hammarskjöld first studied social philosophy and French
literature, later turning to the fields of economics
and political economy, in which he did exceedingly well. In 1927, he studied at the University of
Cambridge under the great English economist John
Maynard Keynes, receiving his degree the following year and a doctorate in economics from the
University of Stockholm in 1933. After teaching
for a year, he went into government service. First
employed on the staff of the National Bank of
Sweden, he then became permanent undersecretary
of Sweden's Ministry of Finance. During World
War II, he combined this latter post with service as
board chairman of the Swedish National Bank, retaining that position until 1948.

When the war ended in 1945, Hammarskjöld
left the Ministry of Finance for the cabinet, in
which he served as an adviser on financial issues.
This was an exciting period for a young economist, for the Swedish government was breaking
new ground in shaping a socialist economy. Ham-

marskjöld thrived in an atmosphere in which he
could emphasize practical measures rather than
economic theory and soon achieved a genuinely
national reputation.

It was shortly after the war that he entered the
field of diplomacy. As a cabinet adviser, he helped
to shape many of Sweden's trade and financial
policies in negotiation with foreign governments.
In 1949, he became the Swedish delegate to the
Organization of European Economic Cooperation
and served on its executive committee, a post that
launched his work in the field of international organization.

Life's Work

Hammarskjöld's reputation would be forged in the
world of diplomacy, not economics. Between 1947
and 1953, however, the future secretary-general of
the United Nations straddled both the economic
and the diplomatic worlds. Becoming under secretary for economic affairs in the Foreign Ministry in
1947, Hammarskjöld supervised Sweden's role in
discussions leading to the Marshall Plan for the
economic reconstruction of Europe. Two years later, he became secretary-general of the Foreign Office, and, in 1951, he received a cabinet appointment as minister without portfolio in which he
specialized in economic matters. Characteristically, Hammarskjöld thought of himself as a civil servant and not as a politician. Even after he entered
the cabinet, he refused to join a political party, believing that his only real loyalty other than to Sweden should be to the ideal of public service. In this
he shared the attitude of many men in the professional foreign services. The principle of public service also proved to be central to the U.N., chartered in June, 1945, to keep the world from again
fighting a world war.

When Trygve Lie of Norway, the first secretary-
general of the U.N., found himself crippled in
office by Soviet opposition to his support for
the U.N.'s role in the Korean War, and by anti-
Communist American supporters of Senator Joseph McCarthy, who denounced the U.N. as a hotbed of Communist activity, he announced his retirement. The Security Council in a compromise
vote then selected Hammarskjöld as his successor.
The new secretary-general was still not well known
outside economic circles, his U.N. experience lim-

ited to once having served as head of Sweden's U.N. delegation. Nevertheless, neither his lack of reputation nor his inexperience interfered with his desire to reinvigorate the United Nations secretariat. Retaining the best of Lie's aides, he surrounded himself with an exceptionally able group of subordinates and quickly addressed issues that affected the morale of U.N. employees. He asserted successfully the independence of the U.N. as an international civil service when he protected American employees against efforts to subject them to political tests by the Dwight D. Eisenhower administration. In the process, Hammarskjöld would gain the respect of the previously demoralized secretariat, increasing both his prestige and his authority.

After addressing internal U.N. matters, Hammarskjöld turned to the more complex rivalries among the great powers. It was there that the relatively unknown Swede first displayed his extraordinary negotiating skills. After months of frustrating effort, he helped gain the release in August, 1955, of seventeen American flyers held prisoner by the new Communist government in China. Having proved himself to skeptical officials in both power blocs, he thereafter became a major factor in international diplomacy.

In 1956, Hammarskjöld encountered two of his three most challenging crises as secretary-general. The emotional and historic rivalries in the Middle East pitting Israelis against their Arab neighbors erupted in full-scale war in November, a situation complicated when British and French paratroopers wrested control of the Suez Canal from Egypt's President Gamal Abdel Nasser, who had recently nationalized that international waterway. The crisis combined colonial politics with ethnic hatreds. Reestablishing peace between Israel and Egypt would have tested Hammarskjöld's talents in the best of times. With both Great Britain and France possessing a permanent veto on the Security Council, a peaceful settlement looked all the more remote. Taking advantage, however, of the opposition of both the United States and the Soviet Union to the Suez invasion and skillfully implementing the proposal of Canada's Lester Pearson for the creation of an international peacekeeping force (the U.N. Emergency Force), Hammarskjöld not only helped to resolve the crisis but placed the U.N. into a much more active and creative role than its founders had ever anticipated.

Unfortunately, Hammarskjöld was much less successful when seeking to moderate the effects of a Soviet invasion of Hungary that occurred at the same time. A revolutionary anti-Soviet government in Budapest sought to withdraw from the Warsaw Pact, the Soviet security system in Eastern Europe, and the Russians responded by sending in their tanks. The Hungarian situation exposed the real limits of U.N. action, for there was no possibility of challenging a superpower squarely within its own geographical sphere of influence. Moreover, the General Assembly's action appeared to make Hammarskjöld personally responsible for the failure of the organization's efforts. As observers credited him with the Suez success, so he had to absorb criticism (most of it unjustified) for the Hungarian failure.

From 1957 to 1960, Hammarskjöld's tenure as secretary-general witnessed a number of lesser successes (as in Lebanon, where he succeeded in using the U.N. to minimize the intrusion of foreign powers) and failures (as in Laos where a civil war introduced great power rivalries). Yet his greatest challenge came after the Congo received its independence from Belgium in the summer of 1960. There he extended the authority of his office far beyond its original parameters, conveying to observers the creative possibilities as well as the dangers of U.N. initiative. His efforts helped to stabilize an extremely dangerous situation that threatened to convert central Africa into a Cold War minefield, but he paid a high price. The Soviet leader Nikita S. Khrushchev called for Hammarskjöld's resignation and demanded a "troika" system to weaken the secretary-general (it would have effectively allowed an East-West veto of the secretary-general's action), while France's President Charles de Gaulle joined the Soviet Union in refusing to pay its U.N. assessment. More important, it was during the Congo Crisis that Hammarskjöld tragically died in a plane crash when seeking to end the secession of mineral-rich Katanga province in September, 1961. He was posthumously awarded the Nobel Peace Prize of 1961.

Summary

Although the U.N. Charter made the secretary-general's office nonpolitical, Dag Hammarskjöld after 1953 converted it into a dynamic and highly political instrument. In the process, he injected new life and controversy into a U.N. seriously weakened by the Cold War rivalry between the United States and the Soviet Union. The timing

was right, for he took advantage of the diplomatic thaw that followed the death of Joseph Stalin and the end of the Korean War. By the same token, he made the most of his extraordinary intellect, his great confidence, and his phenomenal endurance. Hammarskjöld came to symbolize unusual integrity, singlemindedly devoting his energies to the U.N. Even his harshest political critics, such as Khrushchev and Israel's David Ben-Gurion, personally held him in high esteem. Virtually all observers understood that his imaginative use of both his own office and the U.N. in general by creating U.N. peacekeeping forces and a U.N. "presence" in troublespots made the organization into a major factor in international political life.

Bibliography

Cordier, Andrew, and Wilder Foote, eds. *The Quest for Peace: The Dag Hammarskjöld Memorial Lectures*. New York: Columbia University Press, 1965. Essays by many of the leading personalities at the U.N. Contains much rhetoric but much useful information as well.

Cruise O'Brien, Conor. *The United Nations: Sacred Drama*. London: Hutchinson, New York: Simon and Schuster, 1968. An insightful and somewhat controversial history of the United Nations by an Irish official deeply involved in the Congo operation. Highly critical of Hammarskjöld's political activity.

Gibbs, David N. "Dag Hammarskjöld, the United Nations, and the Congo Crisis of 1960-1: A Reinterpretation." *Journal of Modern African Studies* 31, no. 1 (March, 1993). The author offers a new slant on the events surrounding the death of Hammarskjöld and presents evidence of a connection between the crash and Belgian mining interests in Katanga.

Hammarskjöld, Dag. *Markings*. London: Faber, and New York: Knopf, 1964. A meditative, even religious, work that provides great insight into the author's mind, though offering no direct comment about his political activity.

Jordan, Robert S., ed. *Dag Hammarskjöld Revisited: The U.N. Secretary-General as a Force in World Politics*. Durham, N.C.: Carolina Academic Press, 1983. Recent scholarship on the secretary-general, including an excellent bibliographical article by B. L. S. Tractenberg.

Kelen, Emery. *Hammarskjöld*. New York: Putnam, 1966. Organized topically rather than chronologically, Kelen's book is lively though sometimes inaccurate. The author headed television services for the U.N.

Lash, Joseph P. *Dag Hammarskjöld: Custodian of the Brushfire Peace*. London: Cassell, and New York: Doubleday, 1961. Based mainly on published sources, this is an admiring though superficial biography.

Lipsey, Roger. "Blessed Uneasiness: Dag Hammarskjöld on Conscience." *Parabola* 22, no. 3 (Fall, 1997). Examines Hammarskjöld's practice of objective self-observation and its basis in Christian mystic teachings. Hammarskjöld's journal is used as a basis for analysis.

Rosio, Bengt. "The Ndola Crash and the Death of Dag Hammarskjöld." *Journal of Modern African Studies* 31, no. 4 (December, 1993). Discusses the controversy surrounding Hammarskjöld's death. Covers the questions that still exist with respect to the plane's loss of altitude and the seeming indifference of the authorities in mounting a rescue effort.

Urquhart, Brian. *Hammarskjöld*. New York: Knopf, 1972; London: Bodley Head, 1973. The most important study of Hammarskjöld, written by his Undersecretary-General for Special Political Affairs. Sympathetic yet not uncritical.

Van Dusen, Henry P. *Dag Hammarskjöld: The Statesman and His Faith.* Rev. ed. New York: Harper, 1969. A somewhat superficial biography by a leading Protestant theologian.

Zacher, Mark W. *Dag Hammarskjöld's United Nations.* New York: Columbia University Press, 1970. A bit dull, but plenty of good analysis of Hammarskjöld's strategy and tactics for settling disputes.

Gary B. Ostrower

OSCAR HAMMERSTEIN II

Born: July 12, 1895; New York, New York
Died: August 23, 1960; Doylestown, Pennsylvania
Area of Achievement: Theater
Contribution: Working with such composers as Herbert Stothart, Jerome Kern, Sigmund Romberg, and especially Richard Rodgers, Hammerstein wrote books and lyrics which transformed the American musical into an integrated dramatic form and created a number of classics.

Early Life

Oscar Greeley Glendenning Hammerstein, named for his famous grandfather, Horace Greeley, and the minister who married his parents, was born in New York City on July 12, 1895, into a comfortable, middle-class environment. His father, William, was the son of the noted impresario Oscar Hammerstein and his first wife, Rose Blau. His mother, Alice Nimmo, was the daughter of Scottish immigrants, Janet and James Nimmo. Even though William Hammerstein managed the Victoria Theater, a leading vaudeville house, for his father, young Oscar saw very little of the flamboyant grandfather whose name he bore.

His interest in the theater began in 1902 when he made his debut in a Christmas entertainment at Public School No. 9; he began piano lessons at the age of nine. A happy childhood was marred by his mother's death in 1910. In 1912, Hammerstein entered Columbia University to prepare for a law career in accordance with his father's wishes. He joined the Pi Lamba Phi fraternity, played baseball, and maintained the grades he had always achieved. In 1914, his father died, but this bereavement did not affect him as deeply as the loss of his mother, to whom he had been devoted.

The following fall he joined the Columbia University Players, assuring his father's brother Arthur that this involvement would be strictly extracurricular. That same year he made his acting debut as a song-and-dance comic in the annual Columbia University Varsity Show. In his fourth year, he dutifully enrolled in Columbia Law School, attaining his B.A. at the end of the year. In 1916, he met the then fourteen-year-old Richard Rodgers, who later described Hammerstein at this time as "a very tall, skinny fellow with a sweet smile, clear blue eyes and an unfortunately mottled complexion."

Hammerstein's involvement with the Columbia Players continued even after he left the university

and law. The 1917 varsity show, *Home James*, was written by Hammerstein and Herman Axelrod, but the *New York Herald* reviewer singled out young Hammerstein for his acting ability. The year 1917 was truly momentous in Hammerstein's life: He left law school, he was turned down by his draft board for being too thin, and he was able to persuade his uncle Arthur to give him employment as an assistant stagehand. In late summer, he married Myra Finn, and the following year their first child, William, was born. In 1919, he wrote two songs with Richard Rodgers for the Columbia Players and yet another in 1920. They were not to work together again for twenty-three years.

Life's Work

Hammerstein's career as a Broadway lyricist and librettist began, however, in 1920, when he wrote the book and lyrics for *Always You* (1920) to Herbert Stothart's music. More important, that year marked the beginning of a collaboration with Otto Harbach, whom he described as "the best play analyst I have ever met . . . and [a] born teacher." It was Harbach who taught him the importance of integrating all the elements of a show. Their musical, *Tickle Me* (1920), set to Stothart's music, was soon followed by such shows as *Daffy Dill* (1922), *Wildflower* (1923), and *MaryJane McKane* (1923). Their 1924 show, *Rose Marie*, set to Rudolf Friml's tuneful music, was in a number of ways a break from the standard musical comedy formula of the day: "song, cue, song, cue." The songs now served to further the story, which even contained a murder, and the play ended with only two persons onstage instead of the usual assemblage of singers and dancers. It enjoyed a record-breaking run of one year, four months, and seven days. In 1925, Hammerstein and Harbach joined with composer Jerome Kern to create the first Hammerstein-Kern collaboration, *Sunny* (1925), which opened to good reviews. The following year, Hammerstein and Harbach wrote the lyrics to Sigmund Romberg's *Desert Song* (1926). During these productive years, the Hammerstein-Harbach collaboration gave birth to a series of highly popular songs, including "Who?," "The Desert Song," "The Riff Song," "One Alone," and "The Indian Love Call."

The Hammerstein-Kern collaboration attained its height in 1927 when they brought out *Show Boat*. Based on Edna Ferber's novel of the same title and set in the American South, it was the first really successful American musical play on a strictly American theme. The reviews were wildly enthusiastic, praising its "exceptionally tuneful score" and "gorgeous pictorial atmosphere." Hammerstein had written a folk play with characters and dialogue true to life, social problems mixed with humor, and lyrics that advanced the story line. Considered by many to be his masterpiece, it featured such songs as "Can't Help Lovin' Dat Man," "Make Believe," "Why Do I Love You," and notably "Ol Man River"—among the finest ever written for American musicals.

He followed it the next year with *The New Moon*, perhaps best remembered for the beautiful "Lover Come Back to Me" and the stirring "Stout-hearted Men," set to Sigmund Romberg's music. *Sweet Adeline*, written to Jerome Kern's score in 1929, was virtually a family affair, produced by uncle Arthur Hammerstein, directed by brother Reginald, and played at Hammerstein's Theater, a vast neo-Gothic structure recently built by Arthur.

While Hammerstein was becoming increasingly successful, his marriage to Myra was falling apart. Despite the birth in 1921 of a second child, Alice, the couple lived more or less separate lives, largely because of Myra's numerous affairs. She finally consented to a divorce in 1928. On May 13, 1929, Hammerstein married Dorothy Blanchard Jacobson, whom he had met en route to England. The new household at first consisted of Hammerstein, Dorothy, and her daughter Susan, who in 1950 would marry the actor Henry Fonda; Myra in time relinquished custody of Alice and Billy. Hammerstein disliked young children, but as they grew older he gave them stability and love, and they came to adore him. In March, 1931, a son, James, named for James Nimmo and James Blanchard, Dorothy's father, was born.

Generally speaking, the 1930's were comparatively unproductive years for Hammerstein. With the exception of *Music in the Air* (1932), a collaboration with Kern which produced the charming "I've Told Every Little Star," he spent most of this decade writing films. *Very Warm for May* (1939), written with Kern, was a Broadway failure, remembered only for one hit song, "All the Things You Are." His foray into English stage production turned out to be a mistake; his adaptation of a play staged at the Drury Lane Theater in London was a failure. Forsaking London, a rich Metro-Goldwyn-Mayer contract in hand, Hammerstein moved his family to Hollywood. The song "When I Grow Too Old to Dream," set to Romberg's music, was one of his very few lasting contributions as a Hollywood writer.

It was, however, during this period that Hammerstein's social conscience became manifest. Events in Germany convinced him of the evil of Nazism and, in 1936, he was one of the founders of the Hollywood League Against Nazism, becoming chairman of its cultural commission, which evolved the following year into an interracial commission. Throughout his life, he maintained an active interest in promoting understanding among persons of different races. His broad sympathies appear in *Show Boat*, in *Carmen Jones* (1942), in which he transplanted Georges Bizet's opera *Carmen* (1875) to the American South and substituted American blacks for Spanish Gypsies, in *South Pacific* (1949), in which he wrote against racial prejudice, and in *The King and I* (1951), set in nineteenth century Siam.

The fall of Paris in 1940 saddened him, recalling scenes of the city as he had known it as a small boy traveling with his family, as an adolescent, and as an adult living there for a few months in 1925. Now he composed a love poem to the captive city, which became the much-loved song "The Last Time I Saw Paris," which received the Motion Picture Academy Award after it was incorporated in the film *Lady Be Good* (1941). Kern wrote the music to Hammerstein's lyrics, one of the first times that the words preceded the composition of the music. In commenting on this practice later, however, Hammerstein said it seemed to make little sense. It had always been the other way around: score, then lyrics. Setting words to music was an almost infallible formula, and, when Hammerstein joined forces once more with Richard Rodgers in 1943, it became their regular mode of work.

The lean years ended in 1942 when Hammerstein's adaptation of Bizet's opera *Carmen*, retitled *Carmen Jones* and played by an all-black cast, was greeted enthusiastically by New York critics. *Variety* commented that "Hammerstein is now at the peak of his career." Little could the critic know what was to follow: in 1943, *Oklahoma!*, with 2,212 performances that year, a record that lasted for fifteen years; in 1945, *Carousel*, of which there were 890 performances; in 1945, the film *State Fair*; in 1947, *Allegro*, of which there were 315 performances; in 1951, *The King and I*, with 1,246 performances; in 1953, *Me and Juliet*; in 1955,

Pipe Dream; in 1958, *Flower Drum Song*, of which there were 600 performances; and finally, in 1959, *The Sound of Music*, with 1,443 performances. The song "It Might as Well Be Spring" from *State Fair* also won an Academy Award (1945). From the Rodgers and Hammerstein collaboration came five musicals which are considered classics: *Oklahoma!, Carousel, South Pacific, The King and I*, and *The Sound of Music*.

Hammerstein died of cancer at the age of sixty-five on August 23, 1960, at his home in Doylestown, Pennsylvania. In tribute to him the lights on Broadway were blacked out for one minute at 9:00 P.M. the night of September 1. As taps were sounded in Duffy Square, a crowd of five thousand stood with bowed heads.

Summary

Hammerstein's contribution to the American musical theater is almost legendary. As early as 1932, his effort to transform the musical was recognized. In reviewing *Music in the Air*, Brooks Atkinson wrote in *The New York Times*, "At last the musical drama has been emancipated. . . . Without falling back into the cliches of the trade, Hammerstein has written sentiment and comedy that are tender and touching." Hammerstein was creating a new art form, removed from the trivial albeit melodious light opera or operetta, cohesive in form, no longer a parade of disconnected songs and dances interspersed with comedy routines but peopled with characters an audience could care about, expressing a concern for human beings of all races and persuasions, often tender, both sad and happy and never tasteless. The Pulitzer Prize committee in 1944 gave a special citation to Rodgers and Hammerstein for *Oklahoma!*

Hammerstein was expert in adapting the writings of others to the new form: *Show Boat* from the novel of the same title, *Oklahoma!* from Lynn Riggs's *Green Grow the Lilacs* (1931), *Carousel* from Ferenc Molnár's *Liliom* (1909), *South Pacific* from James Michener's *Tales of the South Pacific* (1947), *The King and I* from Margaret Landon's *Anna and the King of Siam* (1944), and *The Sound of Music* from a German film about the von Trapp family.

Even his critics acknowledged that Hammerstein was a consummate craftsman. He labored over his writing, usually working in a standing position at a portable, "stand-up" writing desk. Hammerstein changed the course of the musical, its content and its form, turning it from the revue and chorus into the musical play. His lyrics dwelt on themes of racial tolerance, human dignity, joy, suffering, love, and the fraternity of all mankind. They were warm, charming, human, poetic, and quintessentially American.

Bibliography

Fordin, Hugh. *Getting to Know Him: A Biography of Oscar Hammerstein II*. New York: Random House, 1977. The best available account, based in large part on interviews with Hammerstein's widow, Dorothy, and children, this biography also has an introduction by Hammerstein's protégé, Stephen Sondheim.

Green, Stanley, ed. *Rodgers and Hammerstein Fact Book: A Record of Their Works Together and with Other Collaborators*. New York: Day, and London: Allen, 1963. An invaluable compendium of facts, including casts of both Broadway and other companies, numbers of performances, and excerpts from reviews.

Hammerstein, Oscar, II. *Lyrics*. New York: Simon and Schuster, 1949. This volume contains only lyrics which the author wrote alone. It has besides a preface by Richard Rodgers a valuable autobiographical note on lyrics by Hammerstein.

Hurley, Joseph. "Broadway a Permanent Home to Rodgers and Hammerstein." *Variety* 363, no. 4 (May 27, 1996). Short evaluation of the continuing worldwide interest in the musicals of Rodgers and Hammerstein.

Rodgers, Richard. *Musical Stages: An Autobiography*. New York: Random House, 1975; London: Allen, 1976. This autobiography of Hammerstein's most successful collaborator contains some reminiscences of note.

Rodgers, Richard, and Oscar Hammerstein II. *The Rodgers and Hammerstein Song Book: The Stories of the Principal Musical Plays and Commentary by Newman Levy*. New York: Simon and Schuster and Williamson Music, 1958. The title almost speaks for itself; this book is a mine of source material.

Sheean, Vincent. *Oscar Hammerstein I: The Life and Exploits of an Impresario*. Preface by Oscar Hammerstein II. London: Weidenfeld and Nicolson, and New York: Simon and Schuster, 1956. The life of the grandfather of Hammerstein II with a note by the grandson. Written by a noted author, the book has a special value from interviews with the niece of Hammerstein I.

James A. Rawley

KNUT HAMSUN
Knut Pedersen

Born: August 4, 1859; Lom, Norway
Died: February 19, 1952; Nørholm, Norway
Area of Achievement: Literature
Contribution: The author of more than twenty novels, six plays, and numerous essays, poems, and short stories, Hamsun is widely considered to be Norway's greatest novelist. He was the recipient of the Nobel Prize in Literature in 1920.

Early Life

Knut Hamsun was born Knut Pedersen in the agricultural area of Lom, Gubrandsdal, Norway, on August 4, 1859. When he was four years old, his impoverished family moved to the farm of a wealthier uncle in Nordland, one hundred miles north of the Arctic Circle. Life was easier for the family there, but debts continued to mount. At nine, Knut was sent to live with another uncle, Hans Olsen, working in Olsen's post office to pay off a family debt. For five years, Knut worked for his uncle, who starved and beat him. Once Knut had finished his schooling, however, he was able to escape, beginning at the age of fourteen a life of wandering and searching for work.

For the next five years, Hamsun roamed northern Norway, working as a store clerk, an itinerant merchant, a shoemaker's apprentice, a sheriff's deputy, and a schoolteacher. Throughout these years he sharpened his writing skills, and he published his first novel, *Den gaadefulde* (the mysterious one), in 1877. In 1878, he published a poem, "Et gjensyn" ("A Reunion"), and another novel, *Bjoerger.* The two novels were transparently autobiographical accounts of the loneliness and frustrations of Hamsun's own life. None of these minor works has been translated into English.

In 1879, Hamsun traveled south again, working as a member of a road crew. The pay was poor, and he nearly starved, but he continued his education and his literary pursuits, reading everything he could find in local libraries and offering himself as a lecturer on literary topics. He emigrated to the United States in 1882, expecting to find literary success and prosperity there. Instead, he found a life of hardship and illness, and he returned to Norway in 1884.

Upon his return, he published an article on Mark Twain, using the pseudonym Knut Pedersen Hamsund ("Hamsund" being the name of his family's farm). The printer accidentally omitted the "d," and the writer was thereafter known as Knut Hamsun. Over the next few years, Hamsun delivered more lectures and traveled again to the United States, this time finding employment as a streetcar conductor in Chicago and as a journalist in Minneapolis. Yet literary fame continued to elude him there, and upon settling in Copenhagen in 1888 he began a series of anti-American lectures and writings.

Life's Work

With his first major novel, *Sult* (1980; *Hunger,* 1920), Knut Hamsun established himself as an original talent. Until his appearance on the literary stage, most Norwegian literature of the time tended toward themes of "social problems," focusing on the evils of society at large, and involving complicated plots. *Hunger* focuses instead on the inner workings of one man.

Like Hamsun's earlier novels, *Hunger* is largely autobiographical. Based on Hamsun's miserable years on the road crew, it is the story of a starving young writer who works diligently at his art, sustained only by his yearning for literary success. *Hunger* brought Hamsun the fame and respect he had long sought. In this novel, Hamsun unveiled techniques that he would develop throughout his career: the interior monologue, flashbacks and other jumps in time, and the interruption of narrative by episodes of fantasy. Hamsun's work with interior monologue was perhaps the most influential, leading the way for James Joyce's development of stream-of-consciousness. Indeed, many of Hamsun's techniques, which seem rather commonplace to the modern reader, were quite new to readers in the nineteenth century.

Hunger also ushered in a period during which Hamsun focused on gifted and isolated men—men like Hamsun himself—who struggle to nurture their talents but who are unable to form lasting family or romantic attachments or become a part of the society in which they live. These heroes live steadfastly according to their own beliefs, making no attempt to modify themselves in order to adapt to society's demands. The novels written in this vein are some of Hamsun's greatest: *Mysterier* (1892; *Mysteries,* 1927), *Pan, of Loeitnant*

Glahn's papirer (1894; *Pan*, 1920) and *Victoria: En kaerligheds historie* (1898; *Victoria*, 1923). During this period, Hamsun also wrote short stories, essays, plays, and poetry reflecting his new ideas about literature.

Hamsun's work underwent a marked change after the turn of the century. While the gifted but isolated hero continued to appear in his novels, Hamsun's attention turned from the inner workings of the individual to the environment in which he lived; the novels themselves were no longer interior monologues but became more conventionally plotted social novels with omniscient narrators. Hamsun became increasingly critical of cities and of urban people, seeing in Norwegian cities the same cultural mediocrity and the same lack of individuality that he had found in the United States. Hamsun owned a farm himself and began more and more to consider himself a farmer as well as a writer; for him, the earth was an important source of power, strength, and inspiration.

In the early 1900's, Hamsun produced a series of humorous novels dealing with simple folk in northern Norway. The first of these was *Svaermere*

(1904; *Dreamers*, 1921), the story of a slightly foolish telegraph operator who realizes his dream of marrying the beautiful daughter of the town's most important citizen. Like *Benoni* (1908; *Benoni*, 1925) and *Rosa, af student Parelius' papirer* (1908; *Rosa*, 1925), *Dreamers* features broadly painted comical characters, including overzealous civil servants, unscrupulous businessmen, romantic and unreliable artists, homespun and hardworking laborers, and sharp-tongued women. His novels of this period have in common an affectionately satiric attitude toward simple rural folk and depictions of people from the cities as grasping and untrustworthy.

With *Boern av tiden* (1913; *Children of the Age*, 1924) and its sequel *Segelfoss by* (1915; *Segelfoss Town*, 1925), Hamsun tells a more serious tale of an old estate growing to be an industrial center, and of the economic and social problems caused by this growth. These novels are peopled with dozens of characters; instead of focusing on the fate of one man, they depict the disintegration of an entire society.

Hamsun the writer/farmer continued to examine the effects of modernization in northern Norway, holding up as his ideal the pioneer farmer who resists society and embraces nature, carving out a place for himself through his own strength and know-how. *Markens groede* (1917; *Growth of the Soil*, 1920), which was instrumental in winning for Hamsun the Nobel Prize in Literature, is the story of a rugged farmer who suffers every hardship that nature can throw in his path, but who nevertheless endures. This book makes clearer than any other the nuances of Hamsun's attitude toward nature. He did not revere nature because it is kinder than the powers of mankind or society, but because it is greater. Those who choose to grapple with nature have a difficult life, and they must face death and loss, but, Hamsun believed, their life is the only spiritually and emotionally satisfying one.

Hamsun produced several more novels, including the important August trilogy, comprising *Landstrykere* (1927; *Vagabonds*, 1930), *August* (1930; *August*, 1931) and *Men livet lever* (1933; *The Road Leads On*, 1934). August is a wandering musician who travels from village to village upsetting convention and habit, and he was the last major character Hamsun created. By this time, Hamsun was in his seventies, and, by all accounts, he had not aged gracefully. Throughout his life he had been unyielding and opinionated. His first marriage had been brief, and his second was not harmonious. Hamsun took his pleasure from his farm and from his writing; but as he aged, his strength and creative abilities began to fail him. His reputation suffered greatly, as well, when in 1940 he wrote newspaper editorials welcoming the Nazis and encouraging his fellow citizens to lay down their arms and accept Nazi rule. So firmly did he believe in the Nazi cause that he met personally with Adolf Hitler and presented his Nobel Prize medal to Joseph Goebbels.

In 1945, Hamsun was arrested and charged with collaborating with the Nazis. He was held for months in various hospitals and old-age homes awaiting trial, because it was felt that his age and mental condition made him unfit for trial. During this confinement, he wrote his celebrated memoir, *Paa gjengrodde stier* (1949; *On Overgrown Paths*, 1967), a lyrical and clearly written work which he intended in part as a defense against the charge of mental incompetence. Nevertheless, he was judged incompetent, fined, and released. He never wrote again and died three years later.

Summary

Widely accepted as Norway's greatest novelist, Knut Hamsun has also been called the father of modern literature. Regardless of whether this claim exaggerates his importance, it cannot be denied that many of the techniques and themes of the so-called modern writers appear in some form in Hamsun's early works. He was certainly one of the first important writers to develop the psychological novel, using interior monologue, memory, fantasy, and flashback to probe the inner workings of a central character.

For some twenty years after World War II, most criticism of Hamsun's work focused on his controversial political beliefs, attempting to find even in his earliest works hints of totalitarian leanings. Yet Hamsun will not be remembered chiefly as a political writer. He did find much to approve of in Nazi Germany—a reliance on manly strength over intellectual ability, the subjugation of women, the glorification of the peasant—but his attraction was intellectual rather than political; his ideas had been formed well before the new Germany arrived on the scene.

Hamsun's greatest legacy lies in his lyrical depictions of nature, his skillful characterization, and his demonstration of the possibilities inherent in focusing on the individual instead of society and on the inner man rather than on the outer one. Because of his humorous tales, his glorious scenic depictions, his love stories, and his rejection of materialism, Hamsun will always have a place in popular literature. And because of his influence on modern writers in more than thirty languages, he will always have a place as an important literary figure.

Bibliography

Buttry, Dolores. "Pursuit and Confrontation: The Short Stories of Knut Hamsun." *Scandinavian Studies* 70, no. 2 (Summer, 1998). Examines the themes of Hamsun's short stories, which mirror the author's personal frustrations, especially in the area of the public's perceptions of him personally, and of his work.

Ferguson, Robert. *Enigma: The Life of Knut Hamsun.* London: Hutchinson, and New York: Farrar Straus, 1987. An excellent, unflinching look at the ambiguities and complexities of Hamsun's life. This illustrated biography falls into three parts: Hamsun's picaresque early life, the middle period with its back-to-the-earth emphasis, and the later years of Hamsun's involvement with Hitler. Includes a bibliography (only a handful of the entries are in English) and a chronological list of Hamsun's works.

Gustafson, Alrik. "Man and the Soil: Knut Hamsun." In *Six Scandinavian Novelists.* Minneapolis: American-Scandinavian Foundation, 1940. An admiring and sentimental look at Hamsun's life before World War II, with a generous look at the early years and a novel-by-novel account of Hamsun's greatest works.

Hamsun, Knut. *Overgrown Paths.* Translated by Carl Anderson. New York: Eriksson, 1967; London: MacGibbon and Kee, 1968. A memoir writen between 1945 and 1948, while Hamsun was interned on suspicion of aiding the Nazis. As he awaits his trial, Hamsun reflects on his life, his politics, his books, and his importance as a writer.

Larsen, Hanna Astrup. *Knut Hamsun.* London: Gyldenal, and New York: Knopf, 1922. A very readable but dated biography dealing with the first half of Hamsun's life. By uncovering the writer's "artistic personality," Larsen identifies Hamsun with the lonely figure featured in many of his novels. Includes four photographs of Hamsun.

Næss, Harald. *Knut Hamsun.* Boston: Twayne, 1984. A solid overview of Hamsun's life and works, countering the common view that his creative powers diminished after the middle period. Includes a chronology and an extensive bibliography.

————. "Who Was Hamsun's Hero?" In *The Hero in Scandinavian Literature*, edited by John M. Weinstock and Robert T. Rovinsky. Austin: University of Texas Press, 1975. A clear and convincing description of how Hamsun's own life as an individualist and social outsider was reflected in the heroes he created.

Naess, Harald, and James McFarlane, eds. and trans. *Knut Hamsun: Selected Letters,* vol. 2, *1898–1952.* Norwich: Norvik Press, 1998. This collection of letters does much to clarify the tragedies of Hamsun's later years. The entries are separated into four time periods and are prefaced with biographical information outlining the major professional, political, and personal events that affected Hamsun during each period.

Cynthia A. Bily

LEARNED HAND

Born: January 27, 1872; Albany, New York
Died: August 18, 1961; New York, New York
Area of Achievement: Law
Contribution: During a career on the federal bench spanning more than half a century, Hand became one of the most respected and honored jurists in America. His commitment to tolerance and rigorous thought helped transform and modernize American law in the twentieth century.

Early Life

Billings Learned Hand was born in Albany, New York, on January 27, 1872. The second of two children born to Samuel and Lydia Coit Hand, Billings Learned (he dropped the "Billings" when he was thirty as being too "pompous") came from a distinguished legal family. His paternal grandfather, Augustus Cincinnatus, was a prominent New York attorney, active in the Democratic Party in the late nineteenth century. His older cousin, Augustus, was a lawyer and judge and served for many years on the same federal bench as Hand. Hand's father served a term on the highest state court in New York, the Court of Appeals.

Hand received his early education at a small private school, the Albany Academy, in New York. In 1889, following his cousin Augustus by two years, he enrolled at Harvard College. There he studied philosophy under one of the most distinguished groups of scholars of that time—men such as George Santayana, Josiah Royce, and William James. His intellectual and literary gifts were evidenced by his election to Phi Beta Kappa and by his being chosen commencement orator at his baccalaureate in 1893. He stayed on at Harvard for another year, receiving a master's degree in philosophy.

Though strongly attracted to an academic career in philosophy, Hand again followed his cousin, entering Harvard Law School in 1894. At this time the law school was in the midst of what has been described as its "Golden Age": Teachers such as Christopher Langdell, James Bradley Thayer, and James Barr Ames were revolutionizing the study of law through their casebook approach, and in the process were laying the foundation for the transformation of many traditional legal doctrines. In this atmosphere of intellectual ferment, Hand flourished, becoming one of the first editors of the *Harvard Law Review* and being graduated with honors.

Following his admission to the New York bar, Hand practiced law in Albany for the next five years. In 1902 he moved to New York City, where he spent the next seven years in what he described as the "dull and petty" work of a New York law firm. His move to New York City was perhaps also motivated by the fact that he now had a family to support. On December 6, 1902, Hand married Frances Amelia Fincke, a graduate of Bryn Mawr College. They had three daughters: Mary Deshon, Frances Lydia, and Constance.

Hand's lifelong love of the outdoors and hiking (including walking to work every day until his death) was reflected in his looks and physique. Of medium height and stockily built, he had a large, noble head highlighted by rugged features, bushy eyebrows, and dark, piercing eyes. On the bench, he was known for his quick temper, but appropriate apologies were made just as quickly. He did not suffer fools gladly, yet few jurists could be more tolerant. His demeanor was serious, but not solemn, and while he craved company and good conversation, he would also have periods of melancholy and brooding. Hand also had a streak of playfulness—he enjoyed dressing up as an Indian chief for his grandchildren's amusement, expertly mimicking William Jennings Bryan, and singing ribald sea chanteys or Gilbert and Sullivan melodies.

Life's Work

Hand began his judicial career in 1909. President William Howard Taft was eager to improve the quality of the federal judiciary, and upon the recommendation of Attorney General George W. Wickersham and a number of prominent New York attorneys, Hand was appointed to the federal District Court for Southern District of New York, the lowest level of the court system. Five years later, Hand was joined on this court by his cousin Augustus. During his tenure on the district court, he became a skilled trial judge and an expert on the intricacies of commercial and corporate law.

In 1912, while serving on the federal bench, Hand ran for, and lost, the position of chief judge of the New York Court of Appeals. It was of dubious propriety for a sitting judge to seek an elective office, and Hand compounded this mistake by running as a Progressive (in the election that year, Hand supported Theodore Roosevelt's unsuccessful bid for the presidency on the Progressive, or

Bull Moose, Party ticket). In so doing he incurred the wrath of the regular Republicans and their leader, Taft. Taft never forgave Hand his political apostasy, and during the 1920's Taft, as Chief Justice of the Supreme Court, used his considerable influence to prevent Hand's elevation to the High Court.

Hand's judicial accomplishments were, however, at last recognized in 1924, when President Calvin Coolidge appointed him to the United States Court of Appeals for the Second Circuit (including New York, Connecticut, and Vermont), replacing Judge Julius M. Mayer. During Hand's tenure on the Second Circuit, he served with some of the most distinguished jurists in the nation. Thomas Walter Swan and Charles Edward Clark were both former deans of Yale Law School, and Jerome Frank headed the Securities and Exchange Commission during the New Deal. Clearly Hand's greatest pleasure, though, was being joined once again by his cousin and closest friend, Augustus, on the same court in 1927.

Over the next twenty years, the Second Circuit Court of Appeals became one of the busiest and most respected federal tribunals in the nation. The measure of Hand's influence was the fact that, by the 1930's, the court was being referred to as "Learned Hand's Court." Unlike the Supreme Court, which could choose which cases to hear and therefore dealt with far fewer cases, the circuit court would handle an average of some four hundred appeals a year, involving a wide range of public (constitutional) and private law issues. The latter would involve questions concerning copyright law, patent law, antitrust regulation, admiralty law, contracts, torts, and trusts and estates (among others).

Given the relative obscurity of most of the work done by the federal judiciary below the Supreme Court level, it was not suprising that Hand's leadership and legal influence were recognized mainly by the bar and bench. In May, 1944, however, he was invited to give an address at the annual "I am an American Day" celebration in Central Park. His short speech "The Spirit of Liberty" was greeted with tremendous enthusiasm. Reprints of the work appeared nationwide, and glowing articles in newspapers and magazines introduced Hand's wisdom and style to the general public. During these years, he was also active in a number of professional organizations: He was one of the founders and early leaders of the American Law Institute. The institute was created to simplify segments of the vast body of American law by codifying and restating the thousands of state and federal court rulings, along with relevant legislation, in order to provide "model" codes of law for future legislative bodies and judges. Hand's specific contributions to the institute included his work on the *Model Penal Code* and the *Restatement of Conflicts of Law, Restatement of Torts*.

Throughout his career, Hand was proposed and considered for elevation to the Supreme Court, but never nominated. Why this was so will never be known with absolute certainty. He had the support of the nation's bar, and at least three Supreme Court justices—Oliver Wendell Holmes, Jr., Harlan F. Stone, and Felix Frankfurter—all strongly thought that Hand should join them. Taft's hostility probably accounts for the 1920's. After that it seemed to be a combination of factors—geography, politics, and age—that prevented his appointment. In 1951, Hand officially retired from the Court of Appeals, though in fact he continued to sit on the court off and on for the next ten years. In 1952, a collection of his writings and speeches was published under the title of his 1944 address, *The*

Spirit of Liberty. This and the publication of his 1958 Holmes lectures at Harvard University on the Bill of Rights helped spread his fame to the general public even further. Three years later, on August 18, 1961, Judge Hand died of heart failure in New York City.

Summary

It is difficult to assess fully a judicial career that lasted more than half a century. In large part, Learned Hand's achievement was his work: more than two thousand opinions, along with his articles and speeches. His role on the middle level of the federal judicial pyramid gave him the freedom and scope to apply his vast erudition and wisdom, but precluded as well any major impact on American constitutional development. Yet from his work a number of themes emerge that reflect both the man and the times. Of immense importance was his contribution to the transformation of private law (contracts, torts, and so on) in the twentieth century. Like his friend Justice Holmes, Hand believed that the law did and should reflect changing social and economic conditions. Industrialization in America in the late nineteenth and early twentieth centuries brought with it not only increased business and commercial activity but also expanded governmental authority, as well as a host of social and economic problems. Hand's opinions speak to the necessity of the law to adjust to these changes—for the betterment of society. In this essentially optimistic vision, he shared many of the beliefs common to the Progressive reform movement that appeared during the first part of the twentieth century.

Another element of Hand's legacy was his passion for tolerance and his commitment to the protection of the human liberties embodied in the Bill of Rights. He believed that freedom to express different thoughts and ideas, even unpopular ones, and respect for all persons were both essential to the preservation of democracy. In this, Hand mirrored (and led, to the extent possible for a lower federal court judge) the growing concern by the judiciary for civil liberties and civil rights issues that began in the 1920's and reached its zenith with the landmark decisions of the Supreme Court under Chief Justice Earl Warren in the 1950's and 1960's.

Finally, Hand's opinions and writings reflected the ambivalence within both the legal community and American society concerning the role and function of judges. The dilemma, simply put, was how to balance on one hand the recognition that judges can, and possibly should, actually make law, and on the other the necessity for a judiciary that is independent yet responsive to the citizenry. While Hand accepted the necessity and freedom of judges to adapt the law to fit changing times and circumstances, he spoke for that school of thought which first appeared in the early part of the twentieth century (and which became more popular in the 1970's) that urged judicial "restraint," especially when dealing with some legislative action or constitutional interpretation. In so doing, he was embraced by liberals and conservatives, judicial activists and restraintists, alike. That he could be so many things to so many people is a mark of his greatness.

Bibliography

Gilmore, Grant. *The Ages of American Law.* New Haven, Conn.: Yale University Press, 1977. A brief and extremely readable survey of the development of American law. A useful introduction to the context of legal thought and practice within which Hand worked.

Griffith, Kathryn P. *Judge Learned Hand and the Role of the Federal Judiciary.* Norman: University of Oklahoma Press, 1973. A detailed and critical analysis of Hand's judicial and legal philosophy. Griffith's early chapters on Hand's life and his world are probably the best introduction to these aspects.

Gunther, Gerald. *Learned Hand: The Man and the Judge.* New York: Knopf, 1994. In this comprehensive study, Gunther merges the judge and the man to create what critics hail as a judicial biography without equal.

Hand, Learned. *The Bill of Rights.* Cambridge, Mass.: Harvard University Press, 1958. The Oliver Wendell Holmes, Jr., Lectures delivered by Hand at Harvard in 1958. Constitutes Hand's most complete statement of his view of the judicial process and the necessity for judges to exercise restraint in their role as guardians of individual and human rights. One of the classic statements of the "judicial restraint" philosophy.

———. *The Spirit of Liberty.* Edited by Irving Dillard. New York: Knopf, 1952. A collection of Hand's extrajudicial writings and speeches, including his famous speech "The Spirit of Liberty." The introduction by Dillard is indeed a "personal appreciation"—rather uncritical, indeed almost worshipful.

Schick, Marvin. *Learned Hand's Court.* Baltimore: Johns Hopkins University Press, 1970. A detailed and brilliant study of the Court of Appeals for the Second Circuit during the years that Hand sat on the court. Focuses on the work of the court, the relationships among the judges, the impact of the CA2, as it came to be known, other federal courts, and most important, how Hand's brilliance was able to influence the other judges.

Schwartz, Bernard. "Holmes versus Hand: Clear and Present Danger or Advocacy of Unlawful Action?" *Supreme Court Review* (Annual, 1994). Compares the stances of Hand and Oliver Wendell Holmes with respect to whether speech promoting illegal action is protected by the First Amendment.

Shanks, Hershel, ed. *The Art and Craft of Judging: The Decisions of Judge Learned Hand.* New York: Macmillan, 1968. A collection of forty-three decisions taken from Hand's almost two thousand opinions written on the bench. Most of the forty-three deal with public law issues. The introduction by Shanks is interesting because it includes details not generally known about Hand (for example, that his close friends called him "B," not for the Billings name that he dropped, but for "Bunny").

White, G. Edward. "Cardozo, Learned Hand, and Frank: The Dialectic of Freedom and Constraint." In *The American Judicial-Tradition.* New York: Oxford University Press, 1976; Oxford: Oxford University Press, 1978. This chapter is part of a larger study of important American judges and is especially interesting in linking Hand with his friend Benjamin Cardozo.

Robert M. Goldman

LORRAINE HANSBERRY

Born: May 19, 1930; Chicago, Illinois
Died: January 12, 1965; New York, New York
Area of Achievement: Literature
Contributions: A writer and an activist, Lorraine Hansberry was the first African American woman to win the New York Drama Critics' Circle award.

Early Life

Lorraine Vivian Hansberry was born on May 19, 1930, into a middle-class family on the south side of Chicago, Illinois. The youngest of four siblings, she was seven years younger than Mamie, her older sister. The oldest were two boys, Carl, Jr., and Perry.

Lorraine's father, Carl Augustus Hansberry, the son of two teachers, was a former U.S. deputy marshal who worked as a banking accountant and later founded his own bank. His real success, however, came in the real estate business, where he earned the name "Kitchenette Landlord" for buying properties and converting them into kitchenettes. Lorraine's mother, Nannie Hansberry, the daughter of a bishop, who had attended Tennessee State University, became a teacher and later a ward committeeman of the Republican Party.

Hansberry was born in the Depression era, but lived in affluence as a result of her father's wealth. Nevertheless, her middle-class background did not insulate her from the racism and segregation of the time. Living in a ghetto community, she attended Betsy Ross Grammar School, a crowded public school. Fortunately, her enlightened father had a library of classic books, encyclopedias, and the works of black writers. In addition, Carl Hansberry was an avowed nationalist and a member of the National Association for the Advancement of Colored People (NAACP) and the Urban League. Prominent black figures such as W. E. B. Du Bois, Langston Hughes, Paul Robeson, Duke Ellington, and Jesse Owens were regular visitors to the Hansberry home. Lorraine met them all.

By age ten, Lorraine had read most of the books in her father's library and had developed a consciousness that was unusual for children of her age group. Her uncle, William Leo Hansberry, a professor of African history at Howard University and a renowned Africanist for whom a college was named at the University of Nigeria in Nsukka, had a lasting influence on her. From him, she learned of the greatness of Africa and its ancient civilizations, such as old Ghana, Mali, and Songhai. She also heard about colonialism in Africa and its impact on the people. She drew a parallel between the exploited Africans and the subjugated African Americans. These early influences were clearly reflected later in Hansberry's works.

Hansberry also witnessed history. At age eight, she watched her defiant father buy a house in a white neighborhood and challenge the restrictive covenants that promoted segregation by taking his case to court. When the lower court ordered him to vacate the residence, he appealed to the U.S. Supreme Court and won, in the *Hansberry v. Lee* decision of 1940. His victory did not, however, grant him immunity from bigotry and hostility. As he was contesting his case in the court, a mob attacked his family, hurling stones and bricks at them. Carl Hansberry, who also campaigned for a Republican seat in Congress in 1940 but lost, became disillusioned by racism and with the American justice system. He bought a house in Polanco, Mexico, to settle there permanently with his family, but died shortly afterward, at the age of fifty-one.

The segregational experience left an indelible mark in young Hansberry's mind which was manifested in her future works, particularly in her award-winning play *A Raisin in the Sun* (pr. 1959). When Hansberry was graduated from Englewood High School in 1948, she attended the University of Wisconsin. It is not known why she chose a white college, considering her orientation and her family's choice of black schools. Her sister Mamie attended Howard University. It seems likely that Hansberry had a global vision and did not deem attending a white school a betrayal or an abdication of her black causes.

Hansberry spent three years at the University of Wisconsin. Her freshman courses included physical geography, drawing, and fine arts. Her concern about racism and the general plight of black people found expression in her drawings and sketches. A drawing of herself on the help wanted page of a newspaper followed by the drawing of a man being lynched served as an indication of a war that she would later wage in newspapers, public speeches, and literature.

When Hansberry saw a production of Sean O'Casey's *Juno and the Paycock*, she was captivat-

ed by the story and performance. She identified with the plight of Irish men as portrayed in the play. Going to the theater became one of her favorite activities.

While testing the artistic waters by drawing and going to the theater, she experimented with politics, becoming a supporter of Henry Wallace and campaigning for him. Although she attended a white school, Hansberry's interest in black experience continued; while taking her regular courses, she continued to immerse herself in black history, literature, and culture. Unsustained by the school's curriculum, she bid goodbye to her friends and left for New York in 1950.

Life's Work

Lorraine Hansberry continued her education at the New School for Social Research and settled on a career in journalism. After writing briefly for the Young Progressives of America, she went to work for *Freedom*, a monthly magazine published by Paul Robeson. With contributors such as W. E. B. Du Bois, Charles White, and Alice Childress writing on black and Pan-African issues, *Freedom* was

a natural choice for Hansberry. Her interests in arts, African history, and politics found outlets in the magazine, and concern for women's rights was also articulated. Distinguishing herself as a versatile writer of "consciousness," she soon rose from the position of staff writer to become associate director of *Freedom*. In five years, she contributed more than twenty-two articles, and several reviews of books and plays.

Among her articles were "Child Labor Is Society's Crime Against Youth," "Negroes Cast in Same Old Roles in T.V. Shows," and "Gold Coast's Rulers Go: Ghana Moves to Freedom." While writing, she participated in different protest movements, picketed, spoke on street corners, and demonstrated against segregation by helping evicted African Americans move their furniture back to their apartments. When the U.S. government denied Paul Robeson a passport to attend the intercontinental Peace Congress in Montevideo, Uruguay, Hansberry risked reprisal from the government and took a treacherous flight to Uruguay to represent Robeson. The experience broadened her interest in people of color and in world issues.

While still working for *Freedom*, Hansberry developed an interest in creative writing. She wrote stories, poetry, and plays. One of her sketches was performed during a commemoration of *Freedom*'s first anniversary.

While on an assignment in 1951, Hansberry met Robert Nemiroff, a white Jewish graduate student and a communist, at a picket line protesting the exclusion of African American students from the New York University basketball team. After less than two years of courtship, they married in 1953, to the chagrin of black nationalists, who felt betrayed by Hansberry's interracial marriage. Although he was a Jewish American, Nemiroff shared the same social consciousness as Hansberry, and both loved arts and creativity. Marriage to Nemiroff was in no way a contradiction to Hansberry, who had a broad concept of life and a vision for humanity.

After the marriage, the young couple struggled for a couple of years. Hansberry, who had resigned her position with *Freedom* in 1953 to concentrate on her writing, wrote drafts of three plays while working temporarily as a typist, hostess, store clerk, camp program director, and teacher. Their fortune changed when Nemiroff wrote a successful hit song, "Cindy, Oh Cindy," in 1956. Hansberry became a full-time writer. It was at that time that she completed *A Raisin in the Sun*, a play that was to bring her fame. It received its title from Langston Hughes's poem "Harlem," which posed the question, "What happens to a dream deferred? . . . Does it dry up like a raisin in the sun? . . . Or does it explode?"

Hansberry provided the answer. Set in a ghetto in Chicago, *A Raisin in the Sun* centers on a black widower, Lena, who at age sixty harbors her grown son, Walter Lee, Jr., his wife, Ruth Younger, their son, Travis, and her youngest daughter Beneatha in a cramped kitchenette. They live in abject poverty but have dreams and aspirations for a better life. When a long-awaited life insurance check of $10,000 for the death of Lena's husband, Walter, Sr., arrives, the family sees it as a means of escape. Walter wants to buy a liquor store; Beneatha wants to use her share for medical tuition; Lena wants a house and surprises everyone when she reveals that she has made a down payment on one in all-white Clybourne Park. Walter, Jr., does not approve, but when a representative of the white neighborhood tries to dissuade the family from moving into their new house by suggesting monetary compensation, Walter joins his mother and family in rejecting the offer. They move to the bigger home triumphantly, their dream fulfilled.

A Raisin in the Sun is not only about dreams; it is about culture, black identity, and black pride. It is also about feminine strength, as exemplified by Lena, a strong matriarch who keeps her family together, offering love and care without compromising discipline. Since the play affirms the human spirit, it has a universal appeal and offers hope to all struggling people.

One of the first people to read Hansberry's *A Raisin in the Sun*, Phil Rose, Nemiroff's friend and music associate, optioned it for Broadway production. Unfortunately, Broadway producers were not eager for a realistic and positive black play, but Ross was not discouraged. With the help of a co-producer, David S. Cogan, money was raised from different sources, and a production directed by Lloyd Richards toured New Haven and Philadelphia, receiving astounding reviews. The play moved to Chicago, and an agreement was reached to produce it on Broadway.

On March 11, 1959, *A Raisin in the Sun* opened at Broadway's Barrymore Theater and received rave reviews from such influential critics as Brooks Atkinson of *The New York Times* and Walter Kerr of the *New York Herald Tribune*. Superb casting

and fine acting by the original cast, Sidney Poitier, Diana Sands, Ruby Dee, and Claudia McNeil, helped to make the play a success. In April, the play won the New York Drama Critics' Circle Award for Best Play of the Year, making Hansberry the first black playwright and the fifth woman to win the prestigious award. At age twenty-nine, she was also the youngest person to achieve that honor.

An instant celebrity, Hansberry was courted by producers from Hollywood. In 1960, she was commissioned to write the opening segment for a television series on the Civil War. When she finished her segment on slavery, *The Drinking Gourd*, it was considered controversial and was not produced. In 1959, Columbia Pictures bought the film rights to produce *A Raisin in the Sun* for the screen. After the film script underwent several rewrites, the film opened in 1961.

Hansberry worked on several scripts following the success of *A Raisin in the Sun*. She started research on *The Sign in Sidney Brustein's Window* in 1959 and completed the play in 1961. *The Sign in Sidney Brustein's Window*'s protagonist is a Jewish intellectual, and the play is based on the people Hansberry knew while living in Greenwich Village. Hansberry used the play as an appeal for intellectuals to pay attention to social and international issues. In 1962, Hansberry completed *What Use Are Flowers?*, a play on the Holocaust and its devastating effects, and embarked on another project, *Les Blancs*. She continued to write articles for newspapers and to make public appearances and talk about causes in which she believed. She talked about black oppression in America and about peace and justice. She wrote essays and articles on black history, art, and culture, and on racism, women, and homophobia. One of her major articles serves as her manifesto today. The article "The Negro Writer and His Roots," was delivered to a black writers' conference on March 1, 1959. Hansberry used it to call on black intellectuals to become involved in world affairs.

Another unpublished article, "Simone de Beauvoir and the Second Sex," expressed concern regarding the status of women and homophobia. As Hansberry worked feverishly in 1963 to complete multiple projects, she became ill. She was to die a slow and painful death from cancer of the pancreas. In the same year, she and Nemiroff obtained a divorce. The divorce was unknown to most of their friends, since the two maintained an intimate and professional relationship. The last two years of

Hansberry's life were to be spent in and out of the hospital. She continued to write, to make public appearances, and to revise *Les Blancs* and *What Use Are Flowers?* She also attended meetings and rehearsals for the production of her play *The Sign in Sidney Brustein's Window.*

When *The Sign in Sidney Brustein's Window* opened at the Longacre Theater on October 15, 1964, it was not as well received as *A Raisin in the Sun* had been. Critics who were baffled by Hansberry's choice of a Jewish subject and the intellectual complexity of the play responded unfavorably. In spite of mixed reviews and relatively low attendance, Hansberry's friends and contemporaries rallied around the producers, ensuring that the play was moved to Henry Miller's theater when Longacre was about to close its doors. Both the play and its playwright were struggling to survive.

On January 12, 1965, Hansberry drew her last breath. *The Sign in Sidney Brustein's Window* was closed for the night in Hansberry's honor as thousands mourned her death.

Summary

Lorraine Hansberry lived for not quite thirty-five years, but she accomplished a full lifetime's work. As Martin Luther King, Jr., predicted in his letter of eulogy to her, her life and work have remained "an inspiration to generations yet unborn."

Her former husband and literary executor edited, produced, and published most of her uncompleted scripts. Among them are *To Be Young, Gifted, and Black*, an autobiographical text, and *Les Blancs: The Collected Last Plays of Lorraine Hansberry.* The latter volume includes *Les Blancs*, *The Drinking Gourd*, and *What Use Are Flowers?* *To Be Young, Gifted, and Black* was adapted for the stage, and it became the longest-running drama of the time when it was produced Off-Broadway in 1968 and 1969. A film based on the play was released in 1972.

Other uncompleted scripts were "Mary Wollstonecraft"; an adaptation and a film version of *Masters of the Dew*, by the Haitian author Jacques Roulmain; a musical adaptation of the novel *Laughing Boy*, by Oliver La Farge; an adaptation of *The Marrow of Tradition*, by Charles Chestnut; *Achanron*, a play about an Egyptian pharaoh; and *Toussaint*, which was published in 1968 in an anthology of plays by black women edited by Margaret B. Wilkerson.

Nemiroff also polished and promoted Hansberry's existing works. *A Raisin in the Sun* was adapted as a musical and was produced on Broadway in 1972. In 1987, a television production of which Hansberry would have been proud was released by the Public Broadcasting System. The script included original segments that had been omitted in earlier productions. Committed to a better world, Hansberry represented different causes and advocated social and political changes in the United States and throughout the world. She also pressed for the rights of women, whom she described in an interview with Studs Terkel as "the most oppressed group of any oppressed group." She saw a link between racism, homophobia, and the oppression of women, and she envisioned a world in which men and women could unite in a fight for human rights. Hansberry should be remembered as a writer of remarkable talent and as a dedicated humanitarian.

Bibliography

Carter, Steven R. *Hansberry's Drama: Commitment Amid Complexity.* Urbana: University of Illinois Press, 1991. Carter begins his analysis of Hansberry's works with an overview of her commitment in life as expressed in her actions and her nonliterary as well as literary writings.

Cheney, Anne. *Lorraine Hansberry.* Boston: Twayne, 1984. This book is an intimate biography of Hansberry and an analysis of her plays. One chapter is devoted to black nationalists, such as W. E. B. Du Bois, who had a significant influence on the playwright.

Domina, Lynn. *Understanding "A Raisin in the Sun": A Student Casebook to Issues, Sources and Historical Documents.* Westport, Conn.: Greenwood Press, 1998. A collection of commentary from a range of disciplines, and forty-five primary sources. This volume is designed to enhance the reader's appreciation of the social and historical context of *A Raisin in the Sun.*

Hansberry, Lorraine. *Les Blancs: The Collected Last Plays of Lorraine Hansberry.* Edited by Robert Nemiroff. New York: Random House, 1972. Published posthumously, this collection of Hansberry's plays *Les Blancs*, *The Drinking Gourd*, and *What Use Are Flowers?* contains a critical introduction by Robert Nemiroff and an introduction by Margaret B. Wilkerson.

———. *The Movement: Documentary of a Struggle for Equality.* New York: Simon and Schuster,

1964. This photo-essay examines the history of the Civil Rights movement.

———. *A Raisin in the Sun*. London: French, and New York: Random House, 1959. This work, Hansberry's first play, describes an African American family whose dream of escaping poverty and living a better life is fulfilled when the female protagonist makes a down payment on a house in an all-white neighborhood.

———. *The Sign in Sidney Brustein's Window*. New York: Random House, 1965. Hansberry's second play, which deals with a Jewish intellectual and his circle of friends, examines the role of intellectuals in politics.

———. *To Be Young, Gifted, and Black: Lorraine Hansberry in Her Own Words*. Adapted by Robert Nemiroff. Englewood Cliffs, N.J.: Prentice-Hall, 1969. This book contains materials from Hansberry's speeches, essays, journals, memoirs, interviews, letters, and various unpublished works. Includes a foreword by Robert Nemiroff and an introduction by James Baldwin.

Leeson, Richard M. *Lorraine Hansberry: A Research and Production Sourcebook*. Westport, Conn.: Greenwood Press, 1997. A reference guide to the career of Hansberry. Includes a short chronology of her life; entries for all her plays with plot summaries and commentary; and an annotated bibliography.

Whitlow, Roger. *Black American Literature*. Chicago: Nelson-Hall, 1973. In the section devoted to Lorraine Hansberry, Whitlow gives a brief biographical account of Hansberry and analyzes *A Raisin in the Sun*.

Nkeonye Nwankwo

WARREN G. HARDING

Born: November 2, 1865; Caledonia, Ohio
Died: August 2, 1923; San Francisco, California
Area of Achievement: Government and politics
Contribution: As president of the United States from 1921 to 1923, Harding adopted compromise politics in economics and foreign affairs in an attempt to guide the nation through readjustment to great social and economic changes.

Early Life

Warren Gamaliel Harding was born on November 2, 1865, in Caledonia (modern Blooming Grove), Ohio. His father, George Tryon Harding, was a homeopathic doctor who practiced for a few years in the town of Caledonia before moving the family to Marion when Warren was sixteen. His mother, Phoebe (Dickerson) Harding, after bearing eight children, attended the same Cleveland homeopathic institute as her husband and joined him in practice in Marion. Harding's youth was occupied with family chores and working for nearby farmers. After ascending the grades in the one-room schoolhouse in Caledonia, he attended Ohio Central College, an academy a few miles from Caledonia, graduating from the two-year institution in 1882. He was quick-witted and did well in school, although he was never studious. Following graduation, he taught school for a single term, a period long enough to convince him of an aversion to teaching, just as a few months of reading law were sufficient to dispel interest in the legal profession.

When Harding moved to Marion, it was a growing town with a booster mentality. Harding contributed to the city's reputation by playing in the local brass band at nearby towns and in Chicago, an excursion he arranged. With financial assistance from his father, he acquired the failing *Marion Daily Star* in 1884. Two young friends from Caledonia who had entered this venture with him left the enterprise within a few months. By hard work, attention to detail, modernization of the production facilities, and constantly supporting civic progress in Marion, Harding built the *Marion Daily Star* into a successful paper by 1890. In addition, he joined an array of civic and service organizations and was among the best-known citizens of the town by the time he married the widow Florence Kling DeWolfe in 1891.

As the town of Marion and the *Marion Daily Star* grew apace, Harding's political influence also increased. He was a leader in the Marion County Republican organization during the 1890's and entered politics as a candidate for the Ohio Senate in 1899. He won that election and subsequent reelection in 1901; in 1903, he was elected as lieutenant governor under Governor Myron T. Herrick. He was a popular figure in Ohio Republican circles from the outset, as his political style of conciliation and persuasion appealed to leaders of a party that was rancorous and bitterly divided for three decades prior to World War I. From 1905 to 1910, Harding left the political arena to run the *Marion Daily Star*, which now assumed statewide importance because of the reputation of the owner. He lost as the Republican gubernatorial candidate in 1910, largely because of the emerging rift between Progressives and regular Republicans. He achieved national recognition two years later, when he nominated William Howard Taft at the Republican National Convention, although he alienated many of the Progressives forever by derisive references to Theodore Roosevelt. In 1914, he handily defeated both Democratic and Progressive candidates in the election for the United States Senate; off to Washington, he left behind a reputation for amiability and achievement.

Life's Work

Harding was not an outstanding senator. He did not make any memorable speeches during his term, he introduced no legislation of national importance, and he had one of the highest absentee rates on roll-call votes. He continued to make friends, however, including another freshman senator, Albert B. Fall of New Mexico, and the wealthy Ned and Evalyn McLean, owners of The Washington Post. His prestige within the party increased following his keynote address at the Republican convention in 1916. He generally supported Woodrow Wilson's wartime legislation but voted after the war with Senator Henry Cabot Lodge's strong reservationists against the League of Nations. His political strategy on Prohibition, a popular issue in Ohio, was to vote in favor of the amendment, while acknowledging that he was a "wet" who thought that the people in the states had the right to decide the issue.

Harding announced his presidential candidacy in 1919, at the urging of several of his friends, and, on the advice of political ally Harry M.

Daugherty, he set forth with a cautious strategy to win support. When the Republican National Convention of 1920 became deadlocked between Governor Frank O. Lowden of Illinois, General Leonard Wood, and Senator Hiram Johnson of California, Harding received the nomination for several reasons—he was from the key state of Ohio, he was well-known, if not distinguished, he was not associated with strong stands on controversial issues, and he was acceptable to most elements within the party; he was, in the political parlance, "available." Harding made an effective campaigner. Speaking mainly from his front porch in Marion, the handsome candidate with classic features and silver hair looked statesmanlike. He promised a return to "normalcy" and had little trouble defeating the Democrat, James M. Cox, as he received the greatest majority of popular votes of any preceding presidential election.

As president, Harding launched the era of normalcy by supporting financial initiatives which posed an alternative to the prewar Progressive policies of Woodrow Wilson. His appointment of Pittsburgh banker Andrew Mellon as secretary of the treasury presaged a conservative financial program, which included cuts in government spending, higher tariff rates (the 1922 Fordney-McCumber Tariff), and corporate tax reduction. Shortly after entering office, Harding signed the Budget and Accounting Act, which created a Bureau of the Budget accountable to the president; bureau director Charles Dawes immediately implemented a program to reduce government expenditures. As a fiscal conservative, Harding vetoed the 1922 soldier's bonus bill, a plan designed to pay a cash bonus to veterans of World War I. A compromise tax reduction plan emerged from Congress as the Revenue Act of 1921, which Harding signed. Secretary of Agriculture Henry C. Wallace successfully pressed for the passage of farm relief legislation in 1921 and 1922.

The implementation of much of Harding's program for normalcy was a result of strong cabinet members and Harding's tendency to allow much latitude to congressional leaders. His conciliatory approach to presidential-congressional relations, however, was unsuccessful in some areas. Midwestern senators and congressmen, who formed the so-called Farm Bloc, fought the Administration's agricultural policies and urged stronger measures; Progressives in both parties opposed the Fordney-McCumber Tariff and repeal of the ex-

cess-profits tax. Harding's defense of Truman Newberry, accused of gross overspending in his Senate race in 1918, also stirred controversy. By early 1923, Harding was more often a congressional antagonist than mediator.

In foreign policy matters, Harding for the most part followed the lead of his legalistic-minded secretary of state, Charles Evans Hughes, and the Senate leadership. Following a general policy of nonintervention in matters under consideration by the League of Nations, the Administration nevertheless assembled the Washington Disarmament Conference in 1921, which dealt boldly with problems of naval development in the Far East. In addition, the Administration settled some remaining problems from World War I, such as peace treaties with Germany, Austria, and Hungary, and adopted a noninterventionist policy toward Latin America.

The Harding Administration is, unfortunately, best remembered for its improprieties, notably the Teapot Dome Scandal, in which Secretary of the Interior Albert B. Fall improperly leased government oil reserves in Teapot Dome, Wyoming, and Elk Hills, California, to private interests. While

Harding himself was not directly linked to the wrongdoing, he bears much of the blame, owing to his appointments of the men responsible for these affairs—Fall, a former Senate colleague and friend; Veterans' Bureau director Charles Forbes, who bilked his agency until discovery by a congressional investigating committee; and Harry M. Daugherty, Harding's attorney general, who was accused of selling government favors, along with his and Harding's "Ohio gang" friends, from the infamous "little green house on K Street." Harding had a penchant for appointing his cronies to these and other positions, which were well beyond their abilities.

Accusations about these scandalous affairs and a subsequent Senate inquiry drove a tired Harding from Washington in June of 1923. With other government officials and Mrs. Harding, he took a train across the country to look into developments in the Alaska territory. After a hectic trip to Alaska, the party came back via California; Harding suffered what was later diagnosed as a mild heart attack on the train but seemed much improved upon arrival the next day in San Francisco. He died a few days later, however, on August 2, while resting in his hotel. His body was taken to Washington for funeral services on August 8, and to Marion for burial on August 10.

Summary

Harding's career was a reflection of Midwestern life in the nineteenth century. A product of a small town in Ohio, he adopted the virtues for success in that environment. He demonstrated his sense of civic responsibility by joining merchants and businessmen in local organizations, and he used the columns of the *Marion Daily Star* to boost Marion's economic growth. He was popular, both socially and as a speaker, although his forceful speeches were often ponderous. His success in this narrow arena, as well as his likable personality, helped lead to political success. As he ascended the ladder of Ohio politics, his availability for national office became apparent. Yet in the larger context of national politics, Harding lacked the intellect and training to understand and deal adequately with the forces for change, which propelled many of his contemporaries into the prewar reform movement.

In some ways, though, Harding's administration compared favorably to that of his predecessor, Woodrow Wilson. For example, aside from miscalculated choices of friends for some appointments, Harding did surround himself with men of high caliber in his Cabinet. Herbert Hoover, as secretary of commerce, was the liberal of the Cabinet and was instrumental in organizing the Unemployment Conference of 1921; Henry C. Wallace, secretary of agriculture, was a friend of the farmers, who thoughtfully pursued progressive agricultural policies during the farm crisis of the early 1920's; Charles Evans Hughes, secretary of state, fashioned a better record in Latin American policy than did his predecessors; and Andrew Mellon, secretary of the treasury, John W. Weeks, secretary of war, and James J. Davis, secretary of labor, were all competent men.

The policies of normalcy represented a somewhat old-fashioned response to the upheavals of war and economic and social change; while Harding pursued his policies as an adjustment to these changes, his program was carried on by Calvin Coolidge and, to a lesser extent, Herbert Hoover. In pressing policies to allow for economic expansion and economy in government, Harding applied his political talents for compromise and melioration to assuage congressional opponents. While some historians have pointed to his growth in office and more effective leadership of the nation by early 1923, he did not live to develop any newfound talents. Had he lived, he undoubtedly would have been hamstrung by the scandals that broke shortly after he died. Hampered by his background and limitations, he did his best in a difficult time. Unfortunately, this was an area where his availability could be of no use.

Bibliography

Adams, Samuel Hopkins. *Incredible Era: The Life and Times of Warren Gamaliel Harding*. Boston: Houghton Mifflin, 1939. An early biography of Harding, based on the author's interviews with Harding family members, associates of the president, and journalists of the Harding era. Mainly concentrates on the sensational aspects of the time, including scandals, amorous affairs, and the rumor of Harding's black ancestry.

Anthony, Carl Sferrazza. "The Most Scandalous President." *American Heritage* 49, no. 4 (July-August, 1998). A reassessment of Harding's presidency and life.

Buckley, Thomas H. *The United States and the Washington Conference, 1921-1922*. Knoxville: University of Tennessee Press, 1970. Ably assesses the major foreign policy event of the Harding years. Describes the Four-, Five-, and Nine-Power Treaties as necessary first steps in achieving lasting peace, which later administrations failed to follow up.

Downes, Randolph C. *The Rise of Warren Gamaliel Harding, 1865-1920*. Columbus: Ohio State University Press, 1970. An extremely detailed, lengthy (640-page) study of Harding's early career. Valuable for its coverage both of Harding's rise in Ohio politics and of the issues and strategies of the election of 1920.

Frederick, Richard G., comp. *Warren G. Harding: A Bibliography*. Westport, Conn.: Greenwood Press, 1992.

Grieb, Kenneth J. *The Latin American Policy of Warren G. Harding*. Fort Worth: Texas Christian University Press, 1976. Indicates that Harding was active in promoting goodwill in United States-Latin American relations through a commercial approach rather than the armed intervention of previous administrations.

Murray, Robert K. *The Harding Era: Warren G. Harding and His Administration*. Minneapolis: University of Minnesota Press, 1969. The major revisionist work on the Harding era: Attempts to evaluate the Harding presidency objectively by examining major policies and events apart from the scandals and Harding's sometimes indecorous personal life. The best-researched and most detailed of the works dealing with the Harding presidency.

———. *The Politics of Normalcy: Governmental Theory and Practice in the Harding-Coolidge Era*. New York: Norton, 1973. Analyzes and interprets the approach of Warren G. Harding to the presidency and to national affairs. Murray stresses the positive aspects of the Harding Administration and demonstrates Harding's growth in office, especially in congressional relations.

Potts, Louis W. "Who Was Warren G. Harding?" *Historian* 36 (August, 1974): 621-645. Examines the historical writing on Warren G. Harding from the time of his death until the early 1970's. Shows that the textbook writers and other generalists have usually described Harding in the worst terms, while students of his life and administration have responded more favorably in analyzing his accomplishments.

Russell, Francis. *The Shadow of Blooming Grove: Warren G. Harding in His Times*. New York: McGraw-Hill, 1968. A lengthy biography which tends to be anecdotal rather than analytic, particularly in treating the presidential years. Well detailed in the sections on Harding's amorous affairs.

Sinclair, Andrew. *The Available Man: The Life Behind the Masks of Warren Gamaliel Harding*. New York: Macmillan, 1965; London: Macmillan, 1967. Sinclair was the first researcher to publish a book based on the Harding papers opened by the Ohio Historical Society in 1964. He questions many of the myths surrounding Harding's career and is particularly adept at explaining the times as well as the life of Warren G. Harding.

Trani, Eugene P., and David L. Wilson. *The Presidency of Warren G. Harding*. Lawrence: Regents Press of Kansas, 1977. A review of the Harding Administration based almost entirely on published sources. The authors conclude that the achievements of the Harding Administration were short-term, stopgap measures during a time made difficult by transitions in American life. Harding, they assert, had no real strength as president and failed to achieve any personal stature.

Richard G. Frederick

ALFRED HARMSWORTH and HAROLD HARMSWORTH

Alfred Harmsworth (First Viscount Northcliffe)

Born: July 15, 1865; Chapelizod, Ireland

Died: August 14, 1922; London, England

Harold Harmsworth (First Viscount Rothermere)

Born: April 26, 1868; Hampstead, England

Died: November 26, 1940; Hamilton, Bermuda

Areas of Achievement: Journalism and politics

Contribution: The Harmsworth brothers' innovative approach to newspaper publishing revolutionized the practice of journalism, and both became adept at translating their business acumen into an effective force in the political arena.

Early Lives

Alfred Charles William Harmsworth was born on July 15, 1865, in Chapelizod, Ireland, and his brother Harold was born on April 26, 1868, in Hampstead, England They were the first and second sons of their parents. Their mother, née Geraldine Maffett, was the daughter of an Irish land agent; their father, Alfred Harmsworth, was an unsuccessful barrister whose poor health contributed to his difficulties in providing a living for his family. His death in 1880 meant that both his eldest sons had to cut short their schooling and begin earning a living while still in their teens.

Young Alfred attended Stamford Grammar School, where he edited a school magazine that featured a controversial gossip column. Only fifteen when his father died, he began to write freelance articles for children's publications and newspapers, and by 1882 his work was appearing in the *Globe, The Morning Post*, and *The St. James's Gazette.* A bout of ill health forced him to leave London, but by 1885 he had secured a good position with a publishing firm in Coventry. Harold attended St. Marylebone Grammar School but left before graduating to become a clerk in the Inland Revenue Office.

Alfred, by far the more ambitious and energetic of the two, founded his own publishing company in 1887. Within a year, he had induced Harold, whose financial expertise he sorely needed, to join him in publishing a variety of periodicals that included the very successful *Answers*. Each of the brothers made a good marriage: Alfred to Mary Milner in 1888, and Harold to Mary Shore in 1893. By the early 1890's, their company, The Amalgamated Press, seemed assured of a respectable if by no means remarkable future.

The two brothers presented contrasting images as they began their careers. As a youth, Alfred had followed a vigorous program of bicycle riding to develop his physique. By the age of sixteen, his presence had become commanding: His golden blond hair, hypnotically fascinating eyes, and boldly prominent facial features made for a striking appearance. More critical observers noted that he found it difficult to relax and bit his fingernails until they bled, and they were not surprised when he proved prone to serious nervous disorders. Harold's much shyer disposition—most photographs of him show hands shoved firmly into pockets—was somewhat belied by a robustly ruddy complexion and bushy eyebrows and mustache; he was often described as the stable, composed half of the brothers Harmsworth. It would have been difficult to invent a more sharply contrasting set of characteristics for two men who were shortly to turn the world of newspaper publishing on its head.

Life's Work

The acquisition of two major newspapers was the first step in the foundation of the new publishing empire. The purchase of the *Evening News* in 1894 and the *Daily Mail* in 1896 permitted the Harmsworth brothers to implement the ideas they had developed during their business apprenticeship. Under Alfred's immediate direction, the two newspapers were revitalized in terms of both appearance and tone: Concise, easily readable stories were presented with attractive illustrations and eye-catching layout, and the aggressive support of new inventions and dramatic feats of exploration brought readers a heady dose of daily drama. Under Harold's skillful financial management, the resultant rise in circulation was translated into greatly increased advertising revenues.

By 1900, the Harmsworth empire had grown to include *Home Chat*, a magazine for women, *Comic Cuts* and *Illustrated Chips*, two comic papers for boys, the adventure story magazine *Marvel*, and several other weeklies. Like the *Evening News* and *Daily Mail*, all turned a substantial profit. In the years leading up to World War I, further acquisitions and honors followed: Both brothers were made baronets—Alfred in 1903 and Harold in 1910—and the *Daily Mirror* (1903), *The Observer* (1905), and *The Times* (1908) came under their control. The flagship *Daily Mail* had the largest circulation of any newspaper in the world, and by acquiring *The Times* the brothers had gained access to the most powerful figures in English society.

The outbreak of World War I in 1914 made both brothers into prominent public figures. Alfred's strong convictions regarding the right way to fight the war produced a series of campaigns conducted in the columns of his newspapers: He agitated for the removal of Lord Haldane from office, criticized Earl Kitchener for an alleged shortage of artillery shells, and urged the creation of coalition governments. Harold had also assumed a more prominent role in public life, which culminated in his being named minister for air in 1917; the deaths of his two eldest sons in battle devastated him, however, forcing him to resign his position shortly after accepting it. In 1917, Alfred went on an official war mission to the United States at the request of Prime Minister David Lloyd George. He was made first Viscount Northcliffe when he returned.

With the end of the war, Alfred expected to take a major role in the peace negotiations, but he was rebuffed by Lloyd George in a speech in the House of Commons. Alfred's worsening health limited his public appearances, but he still exercised great influence through his newspapers; he was instrumental in promoting the Irish Treaty of 1921, and he could still make or break most politicians with a well-timed editorial. In 1922, he embarked upon an around-the-world tour, but his increasingly erratic behavior, now characterized by fits of wild impulsiveness and paranoia, forced him to return home before it had been completed. He died on August 14, 1922, disappointed in his political ambitions but inarguably a distinguished newspaper proprietor who had done much to change the course of English journalistic history.

Harold's services during the war were recognized when he was made first Viscount Rothermere in 1919. After Alfred's death he assumed sole control of their publishing enterprises and became more involved in the kinds of political questions that had absorbed his older brother. In 1919, he joined his fellow press magnate Lord Beaverbrook in crusading for free trade within the British Empire, and he campaigned vigorously for a stronger

air force. Harold also became a notable benefactor of institutions such as the Middle Temple and Foundling Hospital and donated many works of art to smaller municipal galleries. In 1940, he was asked by Lord Beaverbrook, then minister of aviation, to go on a confidential mission to the United States, but on the journey there his health failed him, and he died in Bermuda on November 26, 1940. Although Harold was a much less flamboyant figure than his brother Alfred, his more focused support for the causes that caught his interest was in its different way just as effective, and he could certainly take pride in the financial ability which made possible the success of the Harmsworth publications.

Summary

The activities of Alfred and Harold Harmsworth revolutionized the practice of journalism in England. Appearing upon a scene in which the major papers offered tediously long articles directed at society's upper crust, the Harmsworths fashioned news organs which attracted and held a mass readership. Although this practice earned for them much criticism from those who cherished a more gentlemanly tradition of publishing, it is probably fairer to say that the Harmsworths simply introduced into journalism the kinds of democratic changes that by the turn of the century were about to invade every aspect of social life. The Harmsworths were among the first to perceive and take advantage of these forces, but they can hardly be held responsible for creating them.

As well as their important contribution to modern journalism, both Alfred and Harold used their positions as successful businessmen to lobby for practical political ends. In the pre-Harmsworth era, newspapers had expressed views on political issues, but the Harmsworths undertook the mobilization of their readers' attitudes as a method of increasing both their political power and the circulation of their publications. Thus, they forged the kind of influential mirror and molder of public opinion that is the modern newspaper. The Harmsworths also made the owners and editors of major newspapers into prominent public figures, as those who controlled the production of the news became news themselves. Although their actual accomplishments, in terms of the political results achieved, were not seminal in themselves, the Harmsworths were at the center of seminal events in that history of the media which constitutes one of the central themes of contemporary experience.

Bibliography

Brendon, Piers. *The Life and Death of the Press Barons*. London: Secker and Warburg, 1983. A somewhat racy but essentially sound treatment of Alfred Harmsworth, Lord Beaverbrook, William Randolph Hearst, Joseph Pulitzer, and other important journalists. Concentrates on the daily routines and contextual milieu of early twentieth century newspaper operation.

Falk, Bernard. *Five Years Dead*. London: Book Club, 1938. The memoirs of an experienced British journalist. Chapter 13 provides an extensive portrait of Harold Harmsworth in his own words. The absence of his definitive biography makes this a necessary as well as flavorfully contemporary source.

Lee, Alan J. *The Origins of the Popular Press, 1855-1914*. London: Croom Helm, and Totowa, N.J.: Rowman and Littlefield, 1976. Lee traces the economic and technical changes that brought about journalism for the masses. He concentrates upon the relationships between the press and political leaders and offers much interesting detail regarding the dollars-and-"sense" aspect of newspaper production.

Pound, Reginald, and Geoffrey Harmsworth. *Northcliffe*. London: Cassell, and New York: Praeger, 1959. The first full biography, and in many respects still the best. The authors make extensive use of Alfred's letters and memoranda in constructing a psychologically convincing portrait of a man driven by forces over which he had little control, and they also have worthwhile things to say about the generally neglected Harold.

Taylor, A. J. P. "The Chief." In *Politics in Wartime, and Other Essays*. London: Hamilton, and New York: Atheneum, 1964. One of the most important British historians offers a succinct but cogent summation of Alfred's career. Essential for an understanding of his attempts to influence the politics of his day.

"Up to a Point, Lord Rothermere." *Economist* 338, no. 7951 (February 3, 1996). A short history of *The Daily Mail*.

Williams, Keith. *The English Newspaper: An Illustrated History to 1900*. London: Springwood, 1977. A large-format, copiously illustrated volume that provides a detailed discussion of Alfred's innovations in design and layout, accompanied by many reproductions of period newspaper pages. Gives the reader an excellent idea of why these changes appealed to contemporary newspaper readers.

Paul Stuewe

ADOLF VON HARNACK

Born: May 7, 1851; Dorpat, Estonia, Russian Empire

Died: June 10, 1930; Heidelberg, Germany

Areas of Achievement: Religion, theology, and scholarship

Contribution: Harnack's writings on the history of early Christianity remain the standard for all work done in this field. Harnack became an absolute master of the literature of the early Christian era and definitively shaped the perception of this era and its literature not only through his interpretation of the texts but also by his careful editing of the sources.

Early Life

Adolf von Harnack was born in 1851 in Dorpat, Estonia. His father, Theodosius Harnack, was a professor of practical theology at the University of Dorpat. In 1853, the family moved to Erlangen when the father was named to the faculty at the University of Erlangen but returned to Dorpat in 1866 when Theodosius rejoined the faculty at the university. Adolf attended the *Gymnasium* in Dorpat, where he initiated his study of church history and began his university studies at the University of Dorpat. In 1872, Adolf left Dorpat to attend the University of Leipzig, where he completed his studies for the doctorate in church history in 1873 and his thesis on Apelles the Gnostic in 1874.

The University of Dorpat surrounded Harnack with a faculty that was Lutheran, strongly devotional, and passionately committed to issues relating to Christology. His decision to focus his studies on church history put him under the tutelage of Moritz von Engelhardt. Engelhardt proved to have a determinative influence on Harnack's later life. Engelhardt inspired in Harnack a conviction about the role of history as the means for recovering and liberating the core of the Christian religion. Engelhardt is also the source of Harnack's commitment to a method of study that began with a critical text and grounded all conclusions in a thorough examination of the original sources.

Harnack's years at Leipzig brought him into contact with the work of Albrecht Ritschl. Ritschl's influence on nineteenth century German Protestant theology was profound, leading to the establishment of the so-called Ritschlian School with which Harnack is often associated. Ritschl wanted to ground Christian theology in history and practice and remove it from the realm of the speculative, the mystical, and the metaphysical. In concert with sixteenth century Reformers, Ritschl emphasized justification and reconciliation, the corporate and historical nature of the Christian community, and that the Christian religion is a way of life, a manner of living which expressed a set of ethical convictions. Harnack absorbed much of this and later reflected it in his historical, nondogmatic approach to Christian theology and his insistence on the ethics as the core of the Christian proclamation.

After the completion of his studies at Leipzig, Harnack began his long and illustrious career as a professor of church history. His first faculty appointment was at Leipzig in 1876, and this was followed by brief tenures at Giessen and Marburg. While at Marburg, Harnack met and married the daughter of Professor Hans Thiersch.

Life's Work

William II appointed Harnack to the University of Berlin's chair in church history in 1888. The appointment caused considerable controversy, as Harnack's writings had earned for him a number of critics in ecclesiastical circles. The appointment was upheld, but the friction between Harnack and the members of the ecclesiastical establishment remained and served as a source of sadness and alienation for Harnack throughout his career.

Harnack remained at the University of Berlin until his death in June of 1930. His career is vivid testimony to a man with extraordinary intelligence, energy, and organizational skills. Besides having to his credit more than one thousand publications, Harnack was the editor and founder (or co-founder) of *Patrum apostolicorum opera, Theologische Literaturzeitung*, and the series entitled *Texte und Untersuchungen zur Geschichte der altchristlichen Literatur*. In addition, Harnack was elected to the Prussian Academy of Sciences and asked to write the history of the academy in connection with the celebration of its two hundredth anniversary in 1900. In 1906, Harnack was appointed Director General of the Royal Library in Berlin, and in 1911 he was given the post of the president of Kaiser Wilhelm Gesellschaft. Harnack's service to the state was recognized by the award of the Order of Merit in 1902, and in 1914 Kaiser Wilhelm raised him to the hereditary nobility.

Harnack's writings and scholarly career revolved around two intricately related poles. On the one hand, he was deeply committed as a scholar to the task of providing critical editions of the texts of early Christian authors and to using these primary sources as the basis for his theories about the rise and development of Christian thought. On the other hand, Harnack as Protestant churchman, was driven by the idea that through the reading and analyzing of these texts he could offer to the church "the inner form of Christian truth," the true Gospel of Christ. The interrelationship of these two poles had ensured a powerful and enduring legacy. While Harnack's theories about the Gospel of Christ were controversial and have often been challenged, they rested upon solid and seemingly unimpeachable scholarship. To render Harnack inconsequential, one would have to master the primary sources at the same level as Harnack—a task no one has managed to accomplish.

Harnack's classic work, *Lehrbuch der Dogmengeschichte* (seven volumes, *History of Dogma*, 1896-1899), was first published between 1886 and 1890. It was followed by a one-volume summary, *Grundriss der Dogmengeschichte*, which was published in two parts between 1889 and 1891. The study follows the development of Christian doctrine to the Reformation, giving exhaustive treatment to the earliest period. The work displays Harnack's extensive familiarity with and control of the sources and exposes his conception of the historian's task and his theological standpoint. For Harnack, the historian has the responsibility of revealing, through historical research, how the Gospel of Jesus Christ became absorbed into authoritative ecclesiastical doctrines and thereby transformed from that "which awakened in men's hearts the certainty that God rules heaven and earth and is Judge and Redeemer," to dogmatic propositions to which one gave simply intellectual assent. This tragic transformation began when ancient Christians attempted to translate the Gospel into thought forms comprehensible to a Hellenistic worldview. By the fourth century, the simple Gospel of Christ had been replaced by a complex set of propositions protected by a rigidly authoritarian institution. The liberation of the Gospel from this morass had begun with the Reformation in that "the Reformation obtained a new point of departure for the framing of the Christian faith in the Word of God and it discarded all forms of infallibility. . . . In this way that view of Christianity from which dogma arose was

set aside." Harnack envisioned his own work as bringing this aspect of the Protestant Reformation to its completion.

The ideas woven into the *History of Dogma* were distilled and presented in a more accessible form in Harnack's second major work, *Das Wesen des Christentums* (*What Is Christianity?*, 1901), which was first published in 1900. This work was enormously popular, receiving fourteen printings, and equally controversial. The early chapters attempt to define the Gospel of Christ. As in his previous work, the Gospel is characterized as "simple" (that is undogmatic), offering a set of moral precepts combined with a proclamation about the power and love of God. The later chapters test the different forms of Christianity against this definition. It was Harnack's hope that this procedure would not only further clarify the central characteristic of the Gospel but also demonstrate its persistence by locating it within the manifold manifestations of the Christian religion.

A significant portion of Harnack's later life and work was preoccupied by New Testament research. In a series of studies entitled *Beitrage zur Einleitung in das Neue Testament* published in four parts between 1906 and 1916 (*Luke the Physician*, 1909), he dealt at length with the question of the interrelationship of the first three Gospels (the Synoptic problem) and the dating and authorship of Acts. Harnack supported the widely held theory of the priority of the Gospel of Mark, and he agreed with the supposition of the existence of an independent source for Matthew and Luke. Harnack broke from the academic mainstream by assigning a very early date for the composition of the Synoptic Gospels and by claiming that Acts was written by Luke during the time of Paul's Roman captivity.

Summary

Adolf von Harnack's extensive list of publications and record of service to the academic community and the state readily attests his talent and energy as a scholar and administrator. For Harnack himself, however, the measure of success was the cause of Protestantism. Harnack frequently referred to himself as one who had been given the task to reawaken and complete the efforts begun by the Reformers of the sixteenth century. The tools learned and used in the academy, especially the tool of historical criticism, were to be used to consummate the

Protestant revolt against the dogmatic authoritarianism of the Roman Catholic church.

While Harnack's theological standpoint has been challenged and to a large extent displaced (ironically) by the Protestant dogmatist Barth, his stature as a scholar of Christian literature remains at the highest level. Harnack's quest for the Gospel of Jesus Christ resulted in such an extraordinary grasp of the early Christian literature that he continues to be recognized as the standard against which all work in the literature of the early Christian era is compared.

Bibliography

Glick, G. Wayne. *The Reality of Christianity: A Study of Adolf von Harnack as Historian and Theologian.* New York: Harper, 1967. A thorough examination of Harnack's theological and historical studies. The work is especially useful for detailing the influences of Harnack's father and Harnack's teachers at Dorpat and Leipzig.

Jenkins, Finley Dubois. "Is Harnack's *History of Dogma* a History of Harnack's Dogma?" *Princeton Theological Review* 21 (July and October, 1923): 389-428, 585-620. A detailed attack on Harnack's claim to have rescued the simple Gospel of Christ from Christian dogma. Jenkins argues that Harnack operated from a nave view of historical research which blinded him to his own theological bias.

Pauck, Wilhelm. *Harnack and Troeltsch: Two Historical Theologians.* New York: Oxford University Press, 1968. This is a brief summary of the life and work of Harnack with special attention given to Harnack's *History of Dogma.* The book includes Harnack's moving funeral address given for Troeltsch.

————. "The Significance of Adolf von Harnack's Interpretation of Church History." *Union Seminary Quarterly Review,* January, 1954: 13-24. An article written in defense of Harnack's interpretation and conception of Christianity as a historical phenomena and against "the Barthian and neo-confessional theologies . . . which neglect the historical dimensions of the Christian faith."

Richards, George W. "The Place of Adolph von Harnack among Church Historians." *Journal of Religion* 11 (July, 1931): 333-345. This article has a brief biographical sketch, a summary of the important works of Harnack, and a comparison of the work of Harnack with that of Baur and Ritschl.

C. Thomas McCollough

WILLIAM AVERELL HARRIMAN

Born: November 15, 1891; New York, New York
Died: July 26, 1986; Yorktown Heights, New York
Area of Achievement: Diplomacy, government and politics
Contribution: One of the chief architects of the containment policy in the 1940's, Harriman lent valuable continuity to American policy toward the Communist world during his nearly forty years of government service.

Early Life

William Averell Harriman was born on November 15, 1891, in New York City. His father, Edward Henry Harriman, was one of late nineteenth century America's richest men; he controlled a railroad empire extending from Chicago to the Pacific. His mother, Mary (Averell) Harriman, was famous for her charities. When William Averell was seventeen, his father died, leaving him a fortune of close to $100,000,000.

After graduating from Yale, the young Harriman went to work for the Union Pacific Railroad, where he had already been working during the summers as a clerk and section hand. Although primarily a railroad executive, Harriman had other business interests as well; he entered the shipping business and also became involved in various foreign investment ventures. One of his less successful ventures, an attempt made in the 1920's to secure a manganese concession in Bolshevik Russia, provided the young Harriman with experience that was to prove of great value to him later.

In 1932, Harriman became chairman of the board of the Union Pacific Railroad. He proved to be a worthy son of his late businessman father. At a time when the national economy was suffering from the effects of the Great Depression, the young Harriman managed not only to turn a profit through modernization of service and clever merchandising but also to maintain exceptionally good labor-management relations. Through Harriman's efforts as a developer, the famous Idaho ski resort, Sun Valley, was opened for business. Yet it would not be as a businessman, but rather as a public servant, that Harriman would win a lasting place in history.

In 1928, at a time when most big businessmen were Republicans, Harriman became a Democrat. This decision seems to have been partly a result of the influence of Harriman's older sister Mary, who had an acute social conscience, and partly a result of Harriman's own blossoming friendship with the then Democratic governor of New York, Alfred E. Smith. Above all, Harriman appears ultimately to have tired of the race to make money. Although he would throughout his life have a reputation for being careful with money to the point of stinginess, the mere amassing of an ever-greater fortune was probably not enough challenge for him.

In 1932, Franklin D. Roosevelt, with whom Harriman had been acquainted since his preparatory school days, was elected president on the Democratic ticket. The connection with Roosevelt brought Harriman into government service after Roosevelt's inauguration in 1933. As an administrator under the National Recovery Act, as a member of the Business Advisory Council of the Department of Commerce, and, from 1937 through 1939, as chairman of that Business Advisory Council, Harriman acted as a mediator between the Roosevelt Administration and an often suspicious business community. Harriman's active involvement in the carrying out of New Deal policies sharply distinguished him from most members of his social class during these years.

Life's Work

As a still-neutral United States began to prepare for the possibility of war with Nazi Germany, Harriman finally found his true niche. Appointed chief of the raw materials branch of the Office of Production Management in May, 1940, he did much to speed up arms production. Once Harriman had shown his ability in this crucial area where business and government overlap, he was appointed, in February, 1941, to be "defence expediter" in London, the capital of an England still standing alone against Nazi Germany. Harriman's job under the Lend-Lease Act was to do as much as possible to match British arms needs with American arms production.

After the German invasion of the Soviet Union in June, 1941, Harriman traveled to that country in late September of the same year, accompanied by the British prime minister's representative, Lord Beaverbrook. Harriman's mission was to find ways of extending Lend-Lease aid to the now-beleaguered Soviet state. In August, 1942, Harriman accompanied British prime minister Sir Winston Churchill on another trip to Moscow, where the question of an Allied second front against Nazi Germany was discussed. On October 1, 1943, Harriman, who had already twice met Soviet leader Joseph Stalin, was appointed ambassador to the Soviet Union by President Roosevelt. Harriman's long career as an expert on Soviet affairs was about to begin.

In 1943, Harriman, although well into middle age, still had a youthful appearance; he was a tall, slender, handsome man with thick, dark hair. His spouse, the former Marie Norton Whitney, was his second wife; his first marriage, to Kitty Lanier Lawrence, had ended in divorce in 1930. In his spare time, Harriman was an accomplished skier and polo player.

A patient negotiator, Harriman possessed in ample measure (perhaps as an inheritance from the social milieu in which he had been brought up) the charm and tact necessary for effective diplomacy; he instinctively knew how to be firm without being rude when dealing with foreign statesmen. Although not a snob in the usual sense, Harriman would, throughout his life, demonstrate a kind of power snobbery; he would instinctively gravitate, in any situation, to those who had the power to make crucial decisions. As ambassador to the Soviet Union, Harriman would attack his tasks with great zeal, driving both himself and his subordinates to work their hardest. A man who worked under him at this time, the later foreign policy theorist George Frost Kennan, would remember with great admiration his former boss's concentration and attention to detail.

At first Harriman was very optimistic about the prospects for future good relations with the Soviet Union. Harriman's initial optimism reflected the general enthusiasm then prevailing in the Western democracies of Great Britain and the United States for the active role the Soviet Union was playing in the military struggle against Nazi Germany.

As time wore on, however, Harriman became increasingly suspicious of Stalin's intentions; these suspicions were heightened by the Warsaw Uprising of August-October, 1944, during which Russian troops stood idly by a short distance from the Polish capital while the German army suppressed a rising by anti-Communist Polish patriots within the city. Harriman came more and more to fear that Stalin would try to dominate all of Europe after the war was over. As early as September, 1944, Harriman was sending cables to Washington urging a stiffer policy toward the United States' trouble-

some ally. American policy, Harriman urged his superiors, should demand, in a "firm but friendly" way, a *quid pro quo* from the Soviets. The threat of the withdrawal of American aid, Harriman believed, could be used as a bargaining chip to gain concessions from Stalin.

Despite his high regard for Harriman, President Roosevelt did not accept the ambassador's recommendations. At the end of 1944, Nazi Germany, although on the defensive, still had considerable fighting strength left; nobody had any idea when Japan would be conquered. Roosevelt seems to have believed that Great Britain and the United States needed the Soviet Union more than the Soviets needed them. It was not until the death of President Roosevelt on April 12, 1945, that Harriman's hard-line point of view began to become influential within the inner councils of government. The surrender of Germany in May of 1945 and of Japan in September of that year, which removed the threat of enemies which the United States and the Soviet Union had in common, further strengthened the position of those who argued for a tougher American policy toward the Soviet Union.

The new American president, Harry S Truman, proved much more willing to listen to Harriman's advice concerning the Soviets than Roosevelt had been. In May, 1945, Lend-Lease aid to the Soviet Union was cut off, albeit more abruptly than Harriman would have liked. By the time Harriman's stay as ambassador to the Soviet Union had come to an end, in February, 1946, the United States government was beginning to take diplomatic steps to oppose the growing Soviet domination of Eastern Europe. In March, 1947, the president, asking Congress for military aid to a Greece torn by Communist insurgency and a Turkey threatened by Soviet territorial demands, promulgated the Truman Doctrine, pledging United States help to any country threatened by external pressures or internal subversion. The Cold War had begun.

Even after leaving his post in Moscow, Harriman continued to help shape the new American policy of containing Russian expansion by all means short of all-out war. After a brief stint as ambassador to Great Britain, Harriman was appointed secretary of commerce in September, 1946, replacing Henry Agard Wallace. As secretary of commerce, Harriman, through his testimony in Congress, did much to win appropriations for the Marshall Plan, President Truman's program of helping Western Europe rebuild its war-shattered industrial base. In the spring of 1948, Harriman was appointed special representative in Europe for the organization set up to administer Marshall Plan aid. The aid Harriman disbursed, although limited in advance to the years 1948 to 1951, provided a much-needed impetus to European economic recovery, thus helping to check the further spread of Communism. From 1950 to 1951, Harriman was special assistant to the president on foreign affairs; in 1951, he was American representative on a committee studying Western European rearmament; from 1951 to 1953, he was director of the Mutual Security Agency, which disbursed military aid to American allies in Western Europe.

Since the Republican administration of Dwight D. Eisenhower, elected in 1952, chose not to make use of his considerable talents, there was, in the 1950's, a hiatus in Harriman's diplomatic career. Harriman. tried in 1952, and again in 1956, to win the Democratic nomination for president; both times, he failed. Elected governor of New York by a narrow margin in 1954, he failed to secure reelection in 1958. With his patrician manner, Harriman never acquired enough of the common touch to win lasting popularity among the voters; his speaking style, moreover, remained wooden and uninspiring.

A return to the old life of government service as a diplomat, where Harriman so obviously excelled, did not come until the election of John F. Kennedy to the presidency in 1960; in 1961, Harriman was appointed Ambassador at Large. Although old and slightly deaf, Harriman proved to be as mentally and physically vigorous as ever. Gaining influence rapidly within the new administration, he gained the nickname "Crocodile" for his impatient habit at meetings of brusquely cutting short those whom he believed were illogical or long-winded in their arguments.

Under the Kennedy Administration, Harriman showed that although he was a realist in his attitudes toward the Soviet Union, he was no rigid Cold War ideologue. The man who had once rung the warning bells for the policy of containment now strove for peaceful solutions to the major sore points in Soviet-American relations. Harriman succeeded, against some opposition from military circles within the Administration, in hammering together the fourteen-nation Geneva Accords of July 23, 1962. These agreements temporarily took the Southeast Asian state of Laos out of the Cold War by giving it a government of national union that all warring factions within that country—neutralist, Communist, and anti-Communist—could accept. Harriman was promoted first to undersecretary of state for Far Eastern Affairs, then, in April, 1963, to undersecretary of state for political affairs. As head of the American negotiating team, Harriman, with his characteristic mixture of restraint and toughness, played a crucial role in winning the signature of the Soviet Union to the treaty of August 5, 1963, which banned above-ground nuclear testing.

On November 22, 1963, President Kennedy was assassinated. Under Kennedy's successor, Lyndon B. Johnson, Harriman, although retaining office, had considerably less influence over policy. After Johnson decided, in July, 1965, to commit American combat troops to the war against the Communists in South Vietnam, Harriman, as roving ambassador, defended the policy and pleaded (in vain) in Moscow for Soviet diplomatic pressure on Communist North Vietnam. Within the councils of the Administration, however, Harriman's was a voice for moderation, for negotiations, and for a halt to the bombing of North Vietnam. In March, 1968, in a dramatic policy turnaround, Johnson appointed Harriman chief of the United States delegation to the Paris peace talks with North Vietnam. The beginning of serious negotiations was frustrated by disagreements between the United States and the South Vietnamese ally; by the time Johnson had ordered a complete bombing halt in order to facilitate negotiations, his term as president was rapidly coming to a close.

Republican President Richard M. Nixon, elected in 1968, made no further use of Harriman's service; Nixon's lingering distrust of the liberal Democratic establishment was partly responsible for this failure to make use of Harriman's talents in the still-lingering Vietnam peace talks, which would not be successfully concluded until January, 1973. During the frustrating Vietnam negotiations of 1969-1973, Harriman publicly urged both a fixed timetable for American withdrawal and the exertion of greater pressure on South Vietnam. Expressing these views aroused Nixon's displeasure but won Harriman popularity with the growing American antiwar movement, even even though the elder statesman had not originally sympathized with the movement's demands.

Up to the end of his life, Harriman strove for better Soviet-American relations and for increased mutual understanding between the two superpowers. In June, 1983, as a private citizen, he visited then Soviet leader Yuri Andropov, concluded that the Soviets wanted peace, and urged a return by the administration of President Ronald Reagan to what Harriman considered to be the traditional American policy of peaceful coexistence. In the autumn of 1982, Harriman endowed the W. Averell Harriman Institute for Advanced Study of the Soviet Union at Columbia University, to encourage a younger generation of Americans to devote themselves to the study of the politics, economics, society, and culture of the Soviet Union.

In 1970, Harriman's second wife died, and the following year, he married Pamela Digby Hayward, the former wife of one of Sir Winston Churchill's sons; Harriman had first met her during his World War II years in London. On July 26, 1986, Harriman, who had been in failing health for some years, died at the age of ninety-four.

Summary

In the course of his long life of public service, Harriman held a greater number of public posts than any American since John Quincy Adams. Although he had been one of the key architects of the early Cold War policy of containment of a Soviet Union led by Joseph Stalin, Harriman had come, by the end of his life, to urge greater efforts to achieve peaceful relations with Stalin's successors. Harriman was sometimes accused of being a warmonger, and at other times was charged with being an appeaser who was soft on Communism. Harriman viewed the policy that he advocated as a steadfast attempt to preserve both the freedom of the Western democracies and the peace of the world, in an era in which the possession of nuclear weapons by both the Soviet Union and the United States had made another world war unthinkable.

In Harriman's life, one also sees that adherence to the principle of *noblesse oblige* that has so animated some Americans born to wealth and privilege; the same phenomenon can be seen among the later generations of the Rockefeller dynasty. Despite his inherited wealth, Harriman did not live the life of the idle rich; instead, he devoted himself unstintingly to the pursuit of the common good, like other beneficiaries of the Ivy League education who also made their way in American diplomacy of this time.

Throughout his life, Harriman was fueled by burning ambition, not to acquire wealth, but to be at the center of the decision-making process. Perhaps this open hunger for power repelled the voters when it became apparent in the domestic scene. In the realm of diplomacy, such ambition could be harnessed to give the United States the best possible representation abroad. In the best sense of the word, Harriman truly was an American aristocrat.

Bibliography

Bird, Kai. "Disinterring Truth in a Dungeon." *New York Times* 148, no. 51362 (December 5, 1998). Article on the author's discovery of several documents in Harriman's dungeon, including a top-secret 1962 document concerning the Vietnam War.

Chandler, Harriette L. "The Transition to Cold Warrior: The Evolution of W. Averell Harriman's Assessment of the U.S.S.R.'s Polish Policy, October 1943: Warsaw Uprising." *East European Quarterly* 10 (Summer, 1976): 229-245. Argues that Harriman was at first sympathetic toward the Soviet position on Poland and adopted a stiffer attitude only after observing Soviet response during the Warsaw Uprising.

Cooper, Chester L. *The Lost Crusade: America in Vietnam*. New York: Dodd Mead, 1970. Written by a man who worked as an aide to Harriman during the Johnson years, this book contains some interesting material on Harriman's work as chief American negotiator in Paris in 1968. Asserts that Harriman was more impatient for progress in negotiations with Communist North Vietnam, even over possible objections from the United States's South Vietnamese ally, than was President Johnson.

Halberstam, David. *The Best and the Brightest*. New York: Random House, and London: Barrie and Jenkin, 1972. This controversial book, based on interviews with unnamed governmental officials, contains, among other things, a fascinating analysis of the role played by Harriman within both the Democratic Party and the two Democratic administrations during the years 1961-1969. Halberstam sees Harriman as part of the group within the Kennedy Administration which effectively threw its weight against large-scale American military involvement in Vietnam. Ascribes the escalation of the war in 1965 partly to Harriman's loss of influence following Johnson's ascent to the presidency in 1963; Harriman had failed to cement his relationship with Johnson when the latter was Kennedy's vice president.

Herring, George C., Jr. *Aid to Russia, 1941-1946: Strategy, Diplomacy, the Origins of the Cold War*. New York: Columbia University Press, 1973; London: Columbia University Press, 1976. A valuable monograph on the issue of Lend-Lease aid to the Soviet Union. The author concentrates on the struggle within the United States government between advocates of unconditional aid and those who wanted the United States to demand a political price for such assistance.

Hogan, Michael J. "American Marshall Planners and the Search for a European Neocapitalism." *American Historical Review* 90 (February, 1985): 44-72. Deals with Harriman's ideas, not with Harriman the man. Argues that such men as Harriman wanted to see established in Europe, as part of the reconstruction process, a new, reformed capitalism, in which free-enterprise economic principles would be modified by close cooperation between business, government, and labor.

Kennan, George Frost. *Memoirs: 1925-1950*. Boston: Little Brown, 1967; London: Hutchinson, 1968. Kennan, an influential foreign policy thinker from the late 1940's onward, served under Harriman during the latter's years as ambassador to the Soviet Union. The book gives valuable insights into Harriman's personality and methods of work during those years.

Larsh, William. "W. Averell Harriman and the Polish Question, December 1943-August 1944." *East European Politics and Societies* 7, no. 3 (Fall, 1993). Discusses the papers of Harriman covering U.S.-Soviet relations and meetings with Soviet Commissar for Foreign Affairs V.M. Molotov on the reconstruction of the Polish government.

Larson, Deborah Welch. *Origins of Containment: A Psychological Explanation*. Princeton, N.J.: Princeton University Press, 1985. A stimulating and original study of Cold War origins, in which Harriman is seen as one of the four principal architects of the containment policy during the years 1944 through 1947 (the others, according to the author, were Secretary of State James F. Byrnes, Undersecretary of State Dean Acheson, and President Harry S Truman himself). Larson stresses how tentative and gradual was the American journey from cooperation to Cold War; even Truman himself did not fully share Harriman's fears.

Rust, William J. *Kennedy in Vietnam*. New York: Scribner, 1985. Relying on government documents that became available to the public in the early 1980's and on oral history interviews, the book provides (among other things) fascinating bits of information on Harriman's role in shaping Indochina policy at this time. Harriman is shown as having pressed for United States approval in advance of the coup that toppled controversial South Vietnamese leader Ngo Dinh Diem in 1963.

Schlesinger, Arthur M., Jr. *A Thousand Days: John F. Kennedy in the White House*. Boston: Houghton Mifflin, and London: Deutsch, 1965. This book, the memoirs of a man who was special assistant to the president in the Kennedy years, gives the reader an insider's description of Harriman as New Frontier diplomat. Contains a good account of how Harriman achieved his two major triumphs: the Geneva Accords on Laos and the Atmospheric Nuclear Test-Ban Treaty. Fairly sympathetic to Harriman.

Seaborg, Glenn T. *Kennedy, Khrushchev, and the Test Ban*. Berkeley: University of California Press, 1981. This book, written by the man who was chairman of the Atomic Energy Commission during the Kennedy years, contains a detailed account of the role played by Harriman in the negotiations for an atmospheric nuclear test ban in 1963. The author has a high regard for the skill with which Harriman led the American team during these talks.

Paul D. Mageli

LORENZ HART

Born: May 2, 1895; New York, New York
Died: November 22, 1943; New York, New York
Areas of Achievement: Theater and musical comedy
Contribution: The first musical-comedy lyricist to receive equal billing with the composer, Hart was among a small group of early musical-comedy writers who led the way in combining diverse theatrical traditions of romance, spectacle, satire, and musical revue into a distinctly American art form.

Early Life

Lorenz Milton Hart was born May 2, 1895, in the Lower East Side of New York City. His parents, Frieda Isenberg and Max Hertz, were Jewish German immigrants. Max, who changed the spelling of his name in the United States, was an outgoing, free-spending businessman with political links to Tammany Hall. Frieda was a frustrated actress. Besides Lorenz, or Larry, as he was called, the Harts had one other child, Theodore Van Wyck Hart, who as Teddy Hart became a well-known actor in theatrical comedy.

Sparked by Frieda's love for the theater, the Harts began taking the boys to plays and shows when they were quite young, and the children responded by writing and acting comedy skits at home and in school. Larry attended Columbia Grammar and DeWitt Clinton schools and the summer camp-schools the Weingart Institute and Paradox Lake Camp. There, he was active in literary societies, as editor, literary reviewer, and humorous essayist for the school papers, and as actor and writer of school dramatics. One summer, Larry, a voracious reader, brought to camp a trunk full of books, including a fifteen-volume set of the works of William Shakespeare. He also loved music, listening eagerly to opera, light opera, and vaudeville, but especially to operettas by W. S. Gilbert and Arthur Sullivan and the new musical shows by Jerome Kern, P. G. Wodehouse, and Guy Bolton.

At the camps, Hart and his friends joked that the size and weight of his brain prevented his body from growing. He never grew taller than about five feet, and his head was somewhat too large for his body. Although he was not dwarfish in this disproportion, he was sensitive about his appearance, especially in regard to its effect on women. His face, however, was intelligent, lively, and animated, highlighted by intense, dark eyes. In photographs, he often gazed at the camera from under rather straight, dark eyebrows, as though totally absorbing whatever he perceived. In later years, his hairline receded, increasing the impact of the intelligent eyes and forehead. His other facial features were also regular and handsome. He moved quickly, laughed easily and heartily, and frequently rubbed his hands together in a characteristic nervous but gleeful gesture. He is most often described as dynamic, charismatic, restless, witty, and generous. With his charm and liveliness, he was usually the center of attention, and people often overlooked his small size completely.

When Hart was twenty-three and Richard Rodgers sixteen, a friend brought the two together to work on a fund-raising benefit. By this time, Hart had attended Columbia University, primarily to participate in the varsity shows program there. (At that time, the university varsity shows were somewhat like Off-Broadway shows later. They were publicly performed in hotel meeting rooms and little theaters and were reviewed by professional critics seeking new talent.) Hart had also written some comedy routines for minor vaudeville entertainers but was making little headway in his career. Within an hour of their meeting, Rodgers and Hart knew that they had compatible ideas about music and that they would work together as composers. Their fund-raiser was successful, and one of its songs, "Any Old Place with You," was purchased by Lew Fields for inclusion in a Broadway musical, their first professional success.

When Rodgers enrolled at Columbia, he and Hart continued their collaboration in the varsity shows *Fly with Me* (1920) and *You'll Never Know* (1921), both of which were moderately successful. In these amateur productions, the two were perfecting their theatrical skills and learning to complement each other's talents. Altogether, they wrote about twenty-five amateur shows before the brilliant success of *The Garrick Gaieties* of 1925. This was a fund-raiser for the Theater Guild, intended for only two performances, but the cheers of the audience and the rave reviews by the critics prompted the guild to give it a regular run, and it became the hit of the 1925 theatrical season, continuing for 211 performances. From this revue came "Manhattan," Rodgers and Hart's first major hit song. On the strength of this success, they were able to get backing for the professional production of their musical comedy *Dearest Enemy* (1925). With Herbert Fields as librettist, they had written this show several years earlier but could not find a backer. The story was based on a Revolutionary War incident, and producers were afraid that the public would be cool toward a comedy by unknown writers and based on history. The production of *Dearest Enemy* was the professional debut of the songwriting team of Rodgers and Hart.

Life's Work

The year 1926 was busy for the new team. *Dearest Enemy* was followed by three more highly popular and profitable shows, which established Rodgers and Hart as commercially successful writers well worth the investment of major Broadway producers such as Billy Rose, Florenz Ziegfeld, and Charles Dillingham. The three shows were *The Girl Friend*, with its hit song "The Blue Room," *The Garrick Gaieties* of 1926, featuring "Mountain Greenery," and *Peggy-Ann*. The striking fact about these four shows was their diversity. Rodgers and Hart wanted to avoid becoming stereotyped in a particular form of comedy, and they actively sought out stories and shows that offered fresh opportunities. These four shows of 1926 were a light operatic period piece, a bright, contemporary romantic comedy, a satirical revue, and a somewhat surrealistic fantasy based on Freudian dream theories and violating most of the traditions of staging, lighting, and use of chorus. *Peggy-Ann* received high praise from critics for its originality. Also produced in 1926 were three other, less successful, shows, two in London. From the 1926 shows came the songs "The Blue Room," "Mountain Greenery," and "My Lucky Star."

A Connecticut Yankee (1927) confirmed Hart's preeminence as a lyricist. In his youthful, exuberant shows, he delighted in unexpected and unconventional rhymes, especially feminine, approximate, and run-on rhymes, as in "We could find no cleaner re-/ Treat from life's machinery/ Than our mountain greenery/ Home." Although most critics and audiences welcomed this sophisticated and witty departure from the moon/June clichés, others considered such cleverness too facile or too heavy-handed and forced. Some complained, too, that Hart's satirical tendency was too brittle, too pervasive, that he could write nothing else. In *A Connecticut Yankee*, Hart proved that he was not simply a facile rhymer. He showed his linguistic

deftness and his ear for dialect in songs such as "Thou Swell" which mixed Shakespearean words with New York slang and New England cadences. The result was delightful. He also proved his ability to handle simple rhymes and tender sentiment in the graceful love ballad "My Heart Stood Still."

Following *A Connecticut Yankee* came an unhappy period. Some good songs came out of 1928 and 1929: "My Lucky Star," "You Took Advantage of Me," "Spring Is Here," "With a Song in My Heart," "Ten Cents a Dance," "Dancing on the Ceiling"; nevertheless, the next seven shows ranged from average to failure. Hart's father died in 1928. The stock market crash in 1929 substantially halted Broadway musical production for several years. During the Great Depression of the early 1930's, Rodgers and Hart spent five years in Hollywood, writing first for Warner Bros. and then for Paramount, United Artists, and Metro-Goldwyn-Mayer films. Although they were unhappy working under the unaccustomed filming conditions and studio contract restrictions, some of their memorable songs were introduced in motion pictures, most notably those written for Maurice Chevalier: "Isn't It

Romantic?," "Mimi," "Maxim's," and "Girls, Girls, Girls." Also "Lover," "You Are Too Beautiful," and "Blue Moon" came from the Hollywood period, as did Hart's lyrics to Franz Lehar's music for the film *The Merry Widow* (1934), "Vilia" and "The Merry Widow Waltz." Writing music for films taught Rodgers and Hart some new techniques for background music, integration of songs with action, and rhythmic dialogue leading into songs.

As the Depression began to ease, Rodgers and Hart returned to Broadway to write the songs for Billy Rose's *Jumbo* (1935), including "The Most Beautiful Girl in the World," "Little Girl Blue," and "My Romance." It was after the success of this venture that the pair wrote the books, as well as the songs, to four of their productions: *On Your Toes* (1936), *Babes in Arms* (1937), *I Married an Angel* (1938), and *By Jupiter* (1942). These years of 1936 through 1942 were the prime years of Rodgers and Hart's creative genius, as it seemed that everything they did turned to gold. Although the books they wrote were fairly trivial entertainments, both these shows and others for which they wrote only the lyrics were so innovative that they helped change the whole course of Broadway musicals. *On Your Toes*, for example, introduced George Balanchine and serious ballet to the musical comedy with "Slaughter on Tenth Avenue." Although *Babes in Arms* was a traditional revue, its varied and wonderful music represented song writers at the peak of their creative powers. "The Lady Is a Tramp," "Johnny One-Note," "My Funny Valentine," "Where or When," and "I Wish I Were in Love Again" all came from that one show. *I'd Rather Be Right* (1937) took the unprecedented step of satirizing an American president still in office. *I Married an Angel* adapted a drama with serious social satire and psychological insight into the Broadway production techniques of lavish scenery and costuming, setting a pattern for the semiserious musical theater of the next three decades. *The Boys from Syracuse* (1938) adapted Shakespeare's *The Comedy of Errors* (1592-1594) to the musical tradition, establishing a new standard of literacy for musical comedy and paving the way for later great classical adaptations such as *Kiss Me, Kate* (1948), *Man of La Mancha* (1965), and *Candide* (1956). Besides the songs already mentioned, other great songs from this period include "There's a Small Hotel," "Spring Is Here," "Falling in Love with Love," "This Can't Be Love," "It Never Entered My Mind," and "Ev'rything I've Got [Belongs to You]."

After two mediocre productions, *Too Many Girls* (1939) and *Higher and Higher* (1940), Rodgers and Hart wrote the songs for the musical drama that is now considered their masterwork and a turning point in the musical theater—*Pal Joey* (1940). This was the first musical to feature unromanticized, gritty realism in its plot and characters. The story concerned the moral and intellectual fiber of the small-time entertainment world. Its two big hits were "I Could Write a Book" and "Bewitched, Bothered and Bewildered." These became popular as conventional love songs, but in the play the first was an ironic line of seduction and the second so explicitly sexy that the lyrics were revised for popular broadcasting. The play and songs received mixed critical reaction, from derision of the low-life characters and disgust at the explicit sexuality to raves for the satiric bite and uncompromising characterization. *Pal Joey's* first run was not as highly applauded as other Rodgers and Hart musicals from this brilliant period in their careers, but when it was revived twelve years later, it received universal praise. The world was ready for it in 1952, and it received the New York Drama Critics Award for best musical and eleven out of sixteen Donaldson Awards.

Hart never married. He did propose to several women, but none accepted him. This hurt him deeply, and he became increasingly morose. He probably considered himself physically unattractive to women, but that was never the reason those women gave for refusing his proposals. To the contrary, most women found his small size and disproportion insignificant compared to his enormous wit, warmth, and generosity, and he had numerous female friends and several serious relationships. His genius, however, was intimidating and his nervous energy overwhelming. His work was his obsession. He was a compulsive spender and socializer, and he had a major problem with alcoholism. Women no doubt recognized him to be a poor marriage risk. Upon meeting Hart in his early twenties, Rodgers' mother had predicted that he would be dead within a few years. Rodgers himself considered Hart self-destructive.

By the 1940's, Hart's drinking was seriously interfering with his work. His behavior became more and more erratic. He was late to appointments, or never showed up, and had to be tracked down and made to finish his lyrics. He began to experience blackouts. World War II depressed him greatly; he tried to enlist but was rejected. Most of his friends had married and settled down, and he felt cut off from his former society. He became a worry to his family and a problem to his friends. He was hospitalized several times for his alcoholism but never stayed confined long enough to complete treatment or restore his health. Although his writing was still brilliantly creative in the book and lyrics for *By Jupiter* and in new songs for the 1943 revival of *A Connecticut Yankee*, he had become so unreliable that Rodgers had already found a new partner in Oscar Hammerstein, anticipating Hart's incapacity or death. On the opening night of the revival of *A Connecticut Yankee*, Hart caught pneumonia and died in New York City, on November 22, 1943.

Summary

Lorenz Hart's impact on the development of the American musical theater was almost immeasurable. He and a handful of other musical and literary geniuses made it what it is: a blend of the bawdy and satirical comedy of burlesque, the singable songs of folk music and Tin Pan Alley, the spectacle and dance of musical revue, the wit and wordplay of Gilbert and Sullivan operetta, combined with the story tradition of European opera. The earliest truly American musical comedies were the work of the brilliant team of Jerome Kern, Guy Bolton, and P. G. Wodehouse. Their shows were a revelation to a generation of writers and composers, including Rodgers and Hart among the first, as well as George and Ira Gershwin, Herb and Dorothy Fields, Cole Porter, Irving Berlin, Oscar Hammerstein, Arthur Schwartz, and Howard Dietz.

Hart's particular contributions were his witty and imaginative rhymes, his poetic ability to use the rhythm and melodic phrases of music as punctuation for the lyrical line, and his youthfully buoyant sense of humor, which appealed to the people of the United States when they most felt, and later most needed to feel, youthfully buoyant themselves. Besides these lyrical talents, he had a restless innovative spirit which led him into breaking the molds of whatever came before, including his own successes. He and Rodgers seldom did the same sort of musical twice; they were always experimenting with new subjects, such as historical events, Freudian theory, plucky and independent heroines, adult love, political satire, or classical literature. Hart was the first lyricist whose work was so integral to the success of the music that his name appeared on theater marquees with equal status to that of the composer.

His contributions were not limited, however, to the lyrics of songs. He had an unerring sense of the theater, and he and Rodgers were involved in all aspects of theatrical production: the inclusion and exclusion of stage business, the timing of action, the rewriting of dialogue, the introduction of new techniques such as rhythmic dialogue lead-ins to songs, the integration of music to plot and character, the selection of performers. No records are kept of the individual working contributions of members of a theatrical production team, so the extent of Hart's influence can only be inferred from the comments of his colleagues. One after another, they praised the value of his quick and instinctive decisions about what would be right, what would work well on stage.

Hart also brought to the musical comedy his extensive knowledge of literature and classical music. Perhaps more than any other single figure in early musical comedy, he contributed to raising the artistic standards of musical shows to those of musical drama. To his lyrics, he brought knowledge of and sensitivity to poetic theory and dialect; to his books, an awareness of plot structure, character delineation, and natural dialogue; and to the music and dance, a natural aesthetic taste richened through years of attending opera and ballet. He continually supported artistic innovations to appeal to a viewing public that he believed had been underestimated. It was this faith in the intelligence and taste of the American theatergoer which motivated Hart in shaping a uniquely American art form. Even though the shows for which he wrote are mostly passé and unrevivable for today's audiences, the songs and the tradition survive. Rodgers-Hart songs are still performed all over the world, and it would be difficult to imagine the successes of Betty Comden and Adolph Green, Jule Styne, Alan Jay Lerner and Frederick Loewe, Abe Burrows, Stephen Sondheim, Leonard Bernstein, and Kurt Weill, without the precedent of lyrical literacy and excellence set in the 1920's and 1930's by Lorenz Hart.

Bibliography

Ewen, David. *Men of Popular Music*. Chicago: Ziff-Davis, 1944. A brief critical assessment of Rodgers and Hart's importance to the development of popular music in the United States.

———. "Rodgers and Hart." In *The Complete Book of the American Musical Theater*. Rev. ed. New York: Holt, 1959. Brief biographies with production and critical notes on thirteen of the team's major theatrical productions.

Green, Stanley. "Richard Rodgers and Lorenz Hart." In *The World of Musical Comedy*. 4th ed. San Diego: Barnes, and London: Tantivy Press, 1980. A concise, professional biography with brief comments on the plots and the critical reception of twenty-six of Rodgers and Hart's forty-one stage and film productions. An objective account of the twenty-five-year partnership of the composers.

Hart, Dorothy, ed. *Thou Swell, Thou Witty: The Life and Lyrics of Lorenz Hart*. New York: Harper, 1976; London: Elm Tree, 1978. The primary source of biographical information about Hart, this book-length biography contains intimate memoirs, sketches, and tributes by twenty-one people who lived and worked with him. It also contains photographs of Hart at all ages, pictures from most of the plays and films, production notes and lyrics from most of the productions, reproductions of several letters and reviews, and a complete list of the musical comedies and songs in which he collaborated as lyricist or librettist.

Nolan, Frederick. *A Poet on Broadway: The Life and Lyrics of Lorenz Hart*. New York: Oxford University Press, 1994. A sensitive, sympathetic yet balanced biography of Hart. The author attempts to explain the mysteries of Hart's often lonely and secretive life, sorting gossip from what is known to be true. Includes anecdotes and interviews and is cross-referenced for personalities and events.

Rodgers, Richard. *Musical Stages*. New York: Random House, 1975; London: Allen, 1976. Although primarily an autobiography, the sections on the years 1918-1943 contain much on the personality of Hart, the nature of the collaboration, and the personal contributions of each member of the partnership. Anecdotes about sources of inspiration, periods of stalemate, and difficulties in production give considerable insight into the nature of the musical-comedy theater.

————. *The Rodgers and Hart Song Book*. New York: Simon and Schuster, 1951. Admiring assessment of the artistry of Hart's lyrics, with comments on his phonetic and rhythmic intentions and skills.

Smith, Cecil. *Musical Comedy in America*. 2d ed. New York: Theater Arts Books, 1981. This history of the musical comedy explains the contributions of each of the major artists in the field. In Hart's case, it emphasizes his wit and satire, his leadership in sophisticated rhyme and rhythms, and the relationship between his work and the social history of the 1920's, the Depression, and the war years.

Carol I. Croxton

NICOLAI HARTMANN

Born: February 20, 1882; Riga, Latvia
Died: October 9, 1950; Göttingen, West Germany
Area of Achievement: Philosophy
Contribution: Hartmann successfully vindicated ontology as worthy of a scientific study of being to his contemporaries who treated it cavalierly.

Early Life

Nicolai Hartmann was born at Riga, Latvia, on February 20, 1882, to Karl August, a merchant, and Helene, daughter of a pastor. His father died early. His mother founded and directed a German private school in Riga. Her educational undertakings and the moral rigors of her father's personality must have strengthened the pedagogical propensities and austerity of thought that Hartmann displayed later in his life.

His education started at a *Gymnasium* in St. Petersburg, a vibrant center of European intellectual activity in those days. After graduation from the *Gymnasium*, he studied medicine in Dorpat in Estonia and, later, classical philology and philosophy in Marburg, a university town in Hesse, Germany. It was in Marburg that Hartmann came under the influence of Herman Cohen, the founder of the Marburg school of Neo-Kantianism, and his outstanding pupil Paul Natorp—an influence that stayed with Hartmann in one form or another for the rest of his life. His juvenilia bustles with Neo-Kantian idealism. Even in his more mature works, Hartmann is often seen conducting a dialogue with Immanuel Kant while moving away from him.

Life's Work

In 1907, Hartmann was graduated from the University of Marburg with a Ph.D. He was made a privatdocent in philosophy in 1909, joined the army, experienced battle on the Russian front, and in 1920 became professor of philosophy at Marburg, a profession that helped him think dispassionately and analyze philosophically his dehumanizing experiences of war. Consequently Hartmann wrote a three-volume work on the ethos of mankind called *Ethik* (1926; *Ethics*, 1932), criticizing the Kantian ethics of categorical imperatives, thereby giving a message to the world that it is possible to put humanity back onto the right track in spite of the wounds of war. Hartmann agreed with Kant that moral imperatives or values are a priori and objective, but he disagreed with Kant's idea that their objectivity issues from human reason, probably, arguing the possible reasons of a war. Hartmann saw the objectivity of moral imperatives in their unique ontological existence, "an existence in themselves, independent of all imagination and longing. It means consciousness of them does not determine values, but the values determine the consciousness of them."

If values exist so independent of human consciousness, one wonders how they get actualized in it unless they stick to it as barnacles do to the bottom of the ship. Hartmann believed that values are endowed with almost an innate and an irresistible urge to come into being, which they do through the human agency. Once values are embedded in human consciousness, they shape its ethical consciousness with the same power as the physiological structure of the eye, which determines for the owner of the eye the shape of things he sees with that eye. The owner of the eye cannot choose to see what the eye does not permit.

These values harbor in them innate antinomies much like the antinomic nature of Aristotle's "virtue." For example, happiness, a so-called good value, is not without its antinomic bad. As Hartmann comments, "even in happiness there lurks a hidden disvalue," which makes "anyone who is spoiled by happiness . . . shallow." Because of the antinomic nature of value, punctiliously analyzed by Hartmann in the second volume of his *Ethics*, it is clear that humans have the moral freedom to choose between two antinomic goods of a given value. This concept of moral freedom or freedom of will is explored in greater detail in the third volume of *Ethics* through an analysis of man's sense of responsibility and the working of guilt in him. Hartmann's ethics projects a picture of a moral world that is free from the determinisms of all kind: Kantian, teleological, and axiological. It is not a chaotic world of the nihilist, because of the presence in it of a healthy reaction between its own world and the world of human consciousness.

In spite of a lesson in moral values, Hartmann, like many of his contemporaries, must have been uncomfortable at the uneasy truce following the war and the impending danger of the global destruction of a possible second war. Eschewing politics completely, as most of the intellectuals of his days did, Hartmann sublimated his inherent fears in an ontological investigation of being in four books that can loosely be described as an ontological quartet: *Zur Grundlegung der Ontologie* (1935; on the foundations of ontology), *Möglichkeit und Wirklichkeit* (1938; possibility and reality), *Der Aufbau der realen Welt* (1940; structure of real world), and *Neue Wege der Ontologie* (1949; *New Ways of Ontology*, 1952). "Quartet" is an appropriate description of these works not only because they form a chain of four books on one subject but also because the various problems of the subject of being are discussed in a stereophonic way, creating a Platonic commingling of the conceptually formal with the aesthetically beautiful.

Ontology is the study of really, truly existing things, described as being-in-itself, among other terms. Hartmann's term for this is *Ansichsein*, which is consistently translated as being-in-itself in this article. This being-in-itself, as Hartmann explores it in the first volume of his quartet, is a being of everything—not only the being of humans—displaying not the generality of a genus as color is the genus of red, blue, and yellow, but the generality of a *summum genus*, a generality that is not a species of anything. This being is transcendental in the sense that it is beyond the grasp of any consciousness. At the same time it is real because it exists the way two-and-two-makes-four exists, going beyond space and time. What saves it from being a nothing and makes it ontologically viable is its structure.

In spite of a convincing argument for the ontological viability of the being-in-itself, one cannot help wondering if it is ever possible to understand it. This question of possibility led Hartmann to an investigation of the modality of being-in-itself in the second and the most difficult volume of the quartet, *Möglichkeit und Wirklichkeit*. In ordinary language, possibility is discussed as if it were on the same footing with the real (*Wirklichkeit*). For example, when a television commercial says, "It is possible that you will be the winner of this lottery," it is assumed that the reality of winning or not winning exists in a disjunct yet a copresent way. That is, if winning is considered real, not winning becomes a disjunct reality, a ghostlike presence and vice versa. Hartmann argues that in real life there is nothing like a disjunctive presence, a ghostlike reality. According to his argument, for something to be a real possibility (*reale Möglichkeit*) it has to meet all the conditions that make it necessary. Once it meets the necessary conditions, it is also meeting the conditions for being real. Therefore, real possibility is also inevitable reality (*Wirklich-*

keit). Extrapolating on this finding, it is not difficult to see how a being-in-itself that has been convincingly argued in the preceding work of the quartet to be possible will be real enough for the consciousness to understand it.

Der Aufbau der realen Welt, the third member of the quartet, replays its music in fragmented tunes. It explores the categories of being-in-itself, which is an enunciation of the being-such-and-such, *Sosein*, the equivalent of a law, a structure, a theoretical formulation of a modus operandi. In this study, Hartmann devises a hierarchy or a chain of being-such-and-such, with matter at the lowest level and life, consciousness, and spirituality standing on it in that order, the lower one controlling the one immediately above it in that the lower one is the necessary condition for the one above to exist. Thus, life is not possible without matter, consciousness without life, spirituality without consciousness. In spite of the mechanistic rigidity of the system, it offers scope for innovation, as *New Ways of Ontology*, the last member of the quartet, demonstrates. The last volume of the quartet gives a final touch to the various tunes of the other works and ends on a happy note.

Summary

Nicolai Hartmann is remembered in the history of philosophy for the outstanding example that he set to encourage philosophy to change from system-building to problem-solving through a revival of aporetics. It is the ancient Greek philosophical method that tries to unravel the problem into its strands. The solution emerges in this unraveling, not in the building of a system. Socrates in the early dialogues of Plato asks a series of questions, raising many objections without providing answers, without putting all his effort into creating a system.

Hartmann's first important work, *Grundzüge einer Metaphysik der Erkenntis* (1921), primarily explains the futility of system-building instead of using an existing system to solve a specific problem, although a system may emerge in the process. Hartmann himself freely used the insights of Aristotle, Kant, Georg Wilhelm Friedrich Hegel, and Edmund Husserl and at times can be seen unintentionally building what can be described as a system. His main focus, however, has been to bring out the contradictions in a systematic solution and resolve them aporetically. It is not a method but a rainbow of methods. The history of philosophy will remember Hartmann for the rainbow he left in it.

Bibliography

Cadwallader, Eva H. "The Continuing Relevance of Nicolai Hartmann's Theory of Value." *Journal of the Value Enquiry* 18 (1984): 113-121. Not only good for understanding Hartmann's contribution to axiology but also useful in understanding the contemporary American moral scene, especially its polarization into the moral majority and the new morality.

————. *Searchlight on Values: Nicolai Hartmann's Twentieth Century Value Platonism.* Lanham, Md. and London: University Press of America, 1984. As the subtitle suggests, it is mostly a study—a critical one at that—of Platonic theory of value. The Anglo-American reader will find it more interesting because of the inclusion of G. E. Moore, an influential philosopher of the twentieth century.

Heiss, Robert. "Nicolai Hartmann: A Personal Sketch." *Personalist* 42 (October, 1961): 469-486. One of Hartmann's students pays glowing tributes to his teacher.

Hook, Sidney. "A Critique of Ethical Realism." *The International Journal of Ethics* 40 (January, 1930): 179-210. Hartmann was introduced to the English-speaking world through this article written by a tough critic who mostly disagrees with Hartmann but pays some of the best compliments to his analytical acumen.

Kuhn, Helmut. "Nicolai Hartmann's Ontology." *The Philosophical Quarterly* 1 (July, 1951): 289-318. An excellent introduction to the most difficult subject of Hartmann's work, explaining his ontology in the light of influences such as Aristotle and Husserl.

Mohanty, Sri Jitendra Nath. *Nicolai Hartmann and Alfred North Whitehead: A Study in Recent Platonism.* Calcutta, India: Progressive, 1957. Though published in India, this book is held by many libraries in the United States. The chapter on Hartmann is very useful in understanding his idealism, even if the reader is not interested in Whitehead. The author's strong base in Husserl and the phenomenological movement helps in appreciating Hartmann.

Samuel, Otto. *A Foundation of Ontology: A Critical Analysis of Nicolai Hartmann.* Translated by Frank Gaynor. New York: Philosophical Library, 1953. This work is specifically intended to introduce Hartmann to American readers. The result is questionable; it is both a digest and a critical commentary on Hartmann's *Zur Grundlegung der Ontologie.* The digest part is confusing, but the commentary is insightful.

Abdulla K. Badsha

HATOYAMA ICHIRŌ

Born: January 1, 1883; Tokyo, Japan
Died: March 7, 1959; Tokyo, Japan
Areas of Achievement: Government and politics
Contribution: Hatoyama was the architect of the postwar conservative coalition which has ruled Japan as the Liberal Democratic Party (Jiyu-Minshuto) since 1955.

Early Life

Hatoyama Ichirō was the son of Hatoyama Kazuo, who was graduated from Kaisei Gakko (now Tokyo University), studied at Columbia and Yale universities, and returned to Japan to pursue a distinguished career in diplomacy and party politics, being elected to the Diet in 1892 and rising by 1896 to become Speaker of the House. Hatoyama's mother, Haruko, was a leading educator of women who founded Kyoritsu Joshi Shokugyo Gakko (now Kyoritsu Women's University) and served as the school's president from 1922 until her death. Hatoyama's younger brother, Hideo, represented Japan at the League of Nations, served in the Diet like his father and brother and was a respected legal scholar. The family was wealthy and well-positioned to make significant contributions to the development of modern Japan.

Life's Work

Hatoyama was graduated from Tokyo Imperial University in 1907 with a specialty in English Law. In 1915, he was first elected to the Diet as a member of the Seiyukai Party. As a protégé of Tanaka Giichi, he served as chief cabinet secretary from 1927 to 1929, when Tanaka was prime minister. Hatoyama became embroiled in controversy when, as Tanaka's cabinet secretary, he helped draft legislation applying the death penalty to anyone proposing changes in the *kokutai*, or "national polity," the term used to denote Japan's prewar political system, thus foreshadowing the thought control characteristic of the 1930's. This early display of conservatism was followed in the 1930's by several additional incidents that came to haunt him for the rest of his life.

In 1930, after the government of Prime Minister Hamaguchi Yuko agreed to a new round of naval arms reductions at the London Naval Conference, Hatoyama emerged as a vocal member of the Seiyukai opposition by demanding an end to the government's bargaining with the West over the security of Japan. By arguing that the Hamaguchi cabinet had violated the principle of autonomous command for the navy—the principle that the navy itself should determine its requirements without being subject to cabinet control—Hatoyama took a position which was later used by other rightists throughout the 1930's to defeat civilian control of the military. Hamaguchi himself was wounded in an assassination attempt and had to resign in 1931.

From December, 1931, until March, 1934, as Minister of Education under Prime Ministers Inukai Tsuyoshi and Saitō Makoto, Hatoyama further established his reputation as an arch-conservative by instituting curbs on freedom of speech and ordering the revision of textbooks to reflect the prevailing nationalist ideology. In May, 1933, he ordered the dismissal of Takigawa Yukitoki, a professor of law at Kyōto Imperial University, for harboring "dangerous thoughts" which Hatoyama believed were detrimental to the *kokutai*. Takigawa had argued that society bore some responsibility for the acts of criminals and had criticized the relegation of women to inferior social and legal status. Takigawa's dismissal sent shock waves across Japan. The president and thirty-six members of the Kyōto University faculty resigned in protest. A subsequent search for more "dangerous thoughts" among state employees led to more dismissals and arrests of teachers at all levels. In 1934, Hatoyama himself was forced to resign after being charged with bribery and tax evasion.

Hatoyama's prewar public positions were not always antidemocratic. He is remembered for having opposed the military's removal of Saito Takeo from the Diet in 1940 for giving an antimilitary speech on the floor, his refusal to join the Imperial Rule Assistance Association, the combined party of wartime Japan, and his candidacy in the 1942 election as a supporter of constitutional government.

The more common view of Hatoyama, however, is that he remained committed to the policy first expressed by Tanaka in the late 1920's, to promote Japan's special destiny on the mainland of Asia—the so-called positive policy toward Manchuria and China. In 1937, he toured the United States and Europe as Prime Minister Konoe Fumimaro's personal representative to explain Japan's objectives in the war. In 1938, he wrote a book in which he commented favorably on Nazism and compared it with Japanese *bushido*. He also recommended Nazi-style labor controls for Japan. These activities associated him with Japanese militarism in the eyes of the occupation authorities after 1945, when they accused him of having "aided the forces of obscurantism, reaction and militarism" and of having paid only lip service to democracy.

With Japan's defeat in 1945, Hatoyama organized his followers into the Jiyuto, the "Liberal Party," and together they won a 140-seat plurality (out of 466 contested seats) in the Diet election of April, 1946. It was at that point, on the eve of his assuming the prime ministership, that the American occupation authorities stepped in and removed him from the political arena by labeling him a "militarist and ultranationalist." In his place, Yoshida Shigeru, a wartime peace advocate and foreign minister under the liberal leader Shidehara Kijuro, became prime minister. Hatoyama was allowed to resume public life in 1951, in the waning months of the occupation. His supporters, who had been temporarily in Yoshida's camp, now returned to him and became the nucleus of the Democratic Party. Their defection cost Yoshida his majority in the Diet, and he was forced to resign in December, 1954.

Hatoyama became the next prime minister, but his Democratic Party proved unable to win an absolute majority in the Diet. Consequently, he was forced to engineer a merger of his party, which won 185 seats in the election of February, 1955, with the Liberals, who had 112, forming the Liberal Democratic Party (LDP), the conservative coalition that has ruled Japan since November, 1955. As prime minister, Hatoyama had two major objectives: the pursuit of an independent foreign policy and the revision of the constitution. The first involved a readjustment of Soviet-Japanese relations and the seecond entailed an effort to have Article IX, the famous "no more war, no more military forces" article, removed from the constitution. He started talks with the Soviet Union, and, though the talks nearly foundered over the issue of ownership of the Kuril Islands, Hatoyama was able to conclude a peace treaty with the Soviets during a trip to Moscow in October, 1956, thereby normalizing relations. Trade and fisheries agreements followed. Ironically, it was the right wing in postwar Japan that attacked Hatoyama at the end of his career for dealing with the Soviet Union, and there were vociferous patriotic demonstrations against the agreements.

There were three Hatoyama cabinets between 1954 and 1956. Being based on the Liberal Democratic coalition, his governments were perhaps more democratic than those of Yoshida, but they were also weaker. For example, he strongly opposed the diffusion of political authority that had taken place under the occupation and fought to reassert central government control over such functions as local administration, civil service appointments, police, and education. Powerful opposition from within the LDP and the bureaucracy forced him to accept many compromises in the area of administration. He was successful, however, in centralizing the police and broadening their powers to include internal security and in getting the Ministry of Education to appoint local school committees instead of having them elected. He also asserted government control over the content of school textbooks.

In December, 1956, Hatoyama resigned because of ill health and was succeeded by a journalist, Ishibashi Tanzan, who also fell ill, and then by Kishi Nobusuke, who served until 1960. Although Hatoyama and Kishi were arch-conservatives and sought to restore much power to the central government, what they accomplished was more on the order of adjustments to the massive reforms already effected by the occupation. Many of the reforms could not be undone. For example, despite Hatoyama's sentiments against universal suffrage, including voting rights for women, most Japanese supported it. The old-fashioned values reflected in the conservatism of Hatoyama and Kishi, together with their records of service to militarist governments before the war, made them ideal targets for charges by the Socialists that they were trying to take Japan back to the repression of the 1930's. Prime ministers who followed Kishi's resignation in 1960 and who had not served in government before 1941 were much less vulnerable to that kind of criticism.

Summary

Hatoyama Ichirō was one of several Japanese political leaders whose careers survived World War II. His contributions were in the area of party politics, and the postwar history of Japan owes much to the way Hatoyama forged the conservative factions in postwar Japan into an effective political force. Yet his actions at key moments during the Japanese government's rightward drift in the 1930's associated him with the curse of militarism and handicapped his postwar governments by denying him the full measure of legitimacy necessary for strong leadership. Personal ties, therefore, were his stock-in-trade and have been the key to understanding Japanese politics ever since the end of the American occupation.

Bibliography

Baerwald, Hans. *The Purge of Japanese Leaders Under the Occupation*. Berkeley: University of California Press, 1959. The basic source on the purge that robbed Hatoyama of the prime ministership in 1946.

Dower, John W. *Empire and Aftermath: Yoshida Shigeru and the Japanese Experience, 1878-1954*. Cambridge, Mass., and London: Harvard University Press, 1979. A basic book on Prime Minister Yoshida, especially useful for comparisons of the way Yoshida and Hatoyama were seen by the American occupation authorities.

Fukui, Haruhiro. *Party in Power: The Japanese Liberal-Democrats and Policy-Making*. Berkeley: University of California Press, 1970. A detailed study of the inner working of the LDP factions, useful for understanding the political genealogies of modern Japanese leaders before and after the war.

Gayn, Mark. *Japan Diary*. New York: Sloane, 1948. Events in occupied Japan from the point of view of an outstanding journalist. Especially useful for the election of 1946 and the events surrounding Hatoyama's purge.

Hellmann, Donald C. *Japanese Foreign Policy and Domestic Politics*. Berkeley: University of California Press, 1969. A basic study useful for Japan's alignment with the United States and Hatoyama's attempts to settle the peace treaty negotiations with the Soviet Union.

Masumi, Junnosuke. *Postwar Politics in Japan, 1945-1955*. Translated by Lonny E. Carlile. Berkeley: Center for Japanese Studies, University of California, 1985. Includes a detailed account of Hatoyama's political career after the war, from the purge through his election as prime minister.

Morris, Ivan I. *Nationalism and the Right Wing in Japan: A Study of Postwar Trends*. London and New York: Oxford University Press, 1960. A discussion of the continuities in Japanese politics between the pre- and postwar eras.

Thayer, Nathaniel. *How the Conservatives Rule Japan*. Princeton, N.J.: Princeton University Press, 1969. The classic work on the coalition of conservatives that formed the LDP in 1955.

Yoshida, Shigeru. *The Yoshida Memoirs*. Translated by Kenichi Yoshida. London: Heinemann, 1961; Boston: Houghton Mifflin, 1962. Prime Minister Yoshida's own version of political events before and after the war, with surprisingly gentle treatment of his rival Hatoyama.

Donald N. Clark

MOHAMMAD HATTA

Born: August 12, 1902; Bukittinggi, Sumatra, Dutch East Indies
Died: March 14, 1980; Djakarta, Indonesia
Areas of Achievement: Government and politics
Contribution: Hatta directed the nationalist movement leading to the independence and final transfer of power to Indonesia at the end of 1949. He consolidated the independent nation's government, military, and economy based on democratic means.

Early Life

Mohammad Hatta was born on August 12, 1902, in Bukittinggi in Sumatra, one of the islands of the archipelago of the Dutch East Indies (now called Indonesia). He is from a family of the Minangkabaus, a group of indigenous Sumatran Muslims known for their matriarchal social structure and sharp business acumen. Hatta's father, Haji Mohammad Jamil, an Islamic scholar in the mystical tradition of the Sufist *tarekat*, died when Hatta was eight years old. So the young Hatta was mostly reared in Padang by his mother's family, a family better known for its business than for its scholarship in religion.

In spite of their interest in business, his family provided Hatta with the best possible education. After his initial schooling in Sekolah Melayu in Bukittinggi, he was sent to Europeesche Lagere school, a Dutch-language elementary school in Padang, the capital of West Sumatra, which accepted only a handful of Minangkabau students. While still in elementary school, the precocious Hatta passed the examination that qualified him for entrance into the Dutch-language secondary school in Batavia (modern Djakarta), a city on the island of Java. His mother was not ready to part from her young son, however, so she decided to send him to the junior secondary school in Padang.

The school in Padang gave Hatta time to become the chairman of the school's soccer association, which brought him in touch with people interested in politics, and to assume the treasurer's office of the Jong Sumatranen Bond (young sumatra league). After his graduation in 1919, Hatta moved to Batavia. In 1921, he completed his senior high school education with distinction at Prins Hendrik School, a school with emphasis on commerce. In Batavia, Hatta continued to hold the treasurer's office of the Jong Sumatranen Bond.

Life's Work

Hatta took a major step toward his self-actualization when he left for The Netherlands in 1922 to pursue higher education at the Rotterdam School of Commerce. After ten years of course work in economics, he succeeded in finishing the requirements for his doctorate except for the dissertation, which he never finished because of his intense involvement in politics through the Perhimpunan Indonesia (Indonesian Association), an Indonesian nationalist student organization in The Netherlands. Hatta became the treasurer of the Perhimpunan from 1922 to 1925 and, later, its chairman until 1930. During this period, Hatta was the Perhimpunan's delegate to the first and second congresses of the League against Imperialism and for National Independence in Brussels (1927) and in Frankfurt (1929), acts for which he was arrested and imprisoned for six months.

The political insights that Hatta actualized through his political activities in The Netherlands made him very valuable to the nationalist movement at home when he returned to Indonesia in 1932. He found the leading nationalist political party of Indonesia, Partindo (an acronym for Partai Indonesia, meaning "Indonesian Nationalist Party"), repeating the mistake that the banned Partai Nasional Indonesia (PNI) had made, namely, trying to create nationalism in the masses through the charismatic leadership of a few key political figures who could easily be controlled by the colonial rulers in order to crush the movement. Instead, Hatta wanted to build a significant nucleus of well-educated, well-trained, and self-reliant personnel who could progressively expand until Indonesia could lift itself out of the colonial control and become free for good. The plan was somewhat elitist, yet Hatta incorporated it in his newly created party, the PNI Baru. The plan could not go too far because from 1934 to 1941 Hatta was put in prison, exiled, and interned, until the pandemonium created by a Japanese attack released him in 1942.

The Japanese invasion gave an interesting turn to Hatta's struggle for freedom. For one, it created a unique symbiosis of the ruler and the ruled because of the presence of a common enemy, the Dutch. The Japanese needed Hatta and Sukarno to guide them with the rounding up process of the Dutch. Hatta and Sukarno used this need of the Japanese to bargain for their early retirement from Indone-

sia. Further, it brought together the otherwise divergent personalities of Sukarno and Hatta into a healthy *dwittunggal* (two-in-one) symbol of complementary fulfillment; Sukarno's charming flamboyance of a born leader complemented Hatta's studied deliberateness of an inveterate diplomat-administrator. Also, the Javanese Sukarno working in harmony with the non-Javanese Hatta symbolically created a unity in the diversity of Indonesia. Such a symbol of unity gave the nationalist movement a sense of pride and self-confidence that went a long way in making them take advantage of the Japanese surrender to the Russians in Manchuria and usher in the revolutionary proclamation of Indonesia's independence on August 17, 1945. The revolutionary government of the republic named Sukarno its president and Hatta its vice president.

The gestalt energy of the *dwittunggal* further helped the revolutionary republic, inexperienced in war as it was, fight successfully against the British in 1945 and 1946. It also succeeded in warding off the military efforts of the Dutch to reassert their power—especially the two police actions on July 20, 1947, and December 18, 1948—besides crushing the domestic left-wing rebellion of Tan Malaka in 1946 and the communist revolt, called the Madiun Affair, of September, 1946. While engaged in defensive military acts, Hatta on behalf of the republic continued to carry on dialogue with the Dutch on the issue of transfer of sovereignty to an independent United States of Indonesia beginning December, 1949.

After the transfer of power in 1949, Hatta became prime minister for a period of about eight months, went back to the vice presidency in 1950, and stayed in the position until his resignation in 1956. During his time in office, Hatta noticed the power of *dwittunggal* diminishing. The frequent changes of cabinets did not please Hatta. Without making it explicit, Hatta did his best to remind his country of the dangers of losing democracy. He also knew that, without a sound economic base, democracy would be unattainable. Hatta therefore promoted cooperatives in order to improve the economic conditions of small business. In spite of his busy schedule, he found time to lecture at Gadjah Mada University in Jogjakarta and at the Army Command and Staff College in Bandung.

Sukarno, on the other hand, moved more and more toward authoritarianism. He became increasingly critical of democracy and decided to introduce *demokrasi terpimpin* (guided democracy), which in effect was authoritarian control. Hatta found it hard to cooperate with Sukarno's new concept of democracy. He resigned on December 1, 1956.

After his resignation, Hatta carried a low profile, even discontinuing his lectures at Gadjah Mada University and the Army Command and Staff College. When Suharto came to power in 1966, however, Hatta was pleased at the economic reforms that Suharto promised. He even offered to be the president of the country and served on a committee on controlling corruption. Apart from these public events, Hatta lived mostly a private life. He did resume his public educational activity, however, through lecturing at universities in Indonesia and abroad and publishing pamphlets on topical issues until his death on March 14, 1980.

Summary

Mohammad Hatta is a unique example of an East-West synthesis, which made him comfortable with both camps but cozy with neither. The West introduced him to the concept of democracy, *Kadaulatan rakyat* (peoples' sovereignty) as he called it.

He was attracted to the socialist slant in communism, although its atheistic slur made his soul squirm. The East gave him Islam. Hatta brought a synthesis of the two by purging communist socialism of its atheistic overtones and internalizing Islamic values more as character-building guides than as norms for passing judgments on others. This point of view helped him be a devout Muslim and at the same time follow the principles of *Panca sila*, the five secular principles of good government, one of them being respect for all religions. His public life, however, was different. He was too Islamic for Indonesia's Communist party, the Partai Komunis Indonesia (PKI), and too liberal for the Islamic-oriented Masjumi Party. Later in life, Hatta succeeded in blending the two in the profile of his political creation, Partai Demokrasi Islam Indonesia. Understandably, the party did not get the approval of Suharto's "New Order" regime, which probably was afraid that Hatta's party would release the stored-up anger of the banned liberal and religico-political parties of Indonesia. If an individual has to be evaluated more for the example that he presents to the world than the precepts or theoretical frameworks he preaches, then Hatta stands out as a shining star.

Bibliography

Feith, Herbert. *The Decline of Constitutional Democracy in Indonesia.* Ithaca, N.Y.: Cornell University Press, 1962. This is a good source that comes alive because of the author's personal experience in Indonesia, although it covers a limited period.

Hatta, Mohammad. *Mohammad Hatta, Indonesian Patriot: Memoirs.* Edited by C. L. M. Penders. Singapore: Gunung Agung, 1981. A very readable book that stops with the transfer to power to the Indonesians. Contains some photographs that illustrate Hatta's life.

———. *Portrait of a Patriot: Selected Writings.* The Hague: Mouton, 1972. Herein Hatta discusses Indonesian and world politics. This work not only provides understanding of the times of Hatta but also provides good specimens for research topics defining "orientalism."

Lewis, Reba. *Indonesia: Troubled Paradise.* London: Hale, 1962; New York: McKay, 1963. An account of the author's experiences in the three years of her stay in Indonesia (1957-1960). The author has the eye of a keen observer, the inquisitiveness of a historian, and the narrative style of a novelist. Refreshing to read.

Palmier, Leslie H. *Indonesia.* London: Thames and Hudson, 1965; New York: Walker, 1966. Contains brief but solid biographical information on Hatta and shows how he fits into the history of Indonesia. There are many photographs, including one of Hatta, notes, a select bibliography, a section of "who's who" in Indonesia, and an index.

Rose, Mavis. *Indonesia Free: A Political Biography of Mohammad Hatta.* Ithaca, N.Y.: Cornell Modern Indonesia Project, 1987. Complete in its coverage of Hatta's life, this work, being the result of the author's research for a Master of Philosophy thesis, is well-documented.

Zainu'ddin, Ailsa. *A Short History of Indonesia.* 2d ed. North Melbourne: Cassell Australia, 1980. This book is a general work on Indonesia by a non-Westerner. Contains a useful index and a glossary that a beginner cannot help appreciating.

Abdulla K. Badsha

STEPHEN W. HAWKING

Born: January 8, 1942; Oxford, England

Areas of Achievement: Astronomy and physics

Contribution: Many consider Hawking to be the greatest physicist of the late twentieth century. His work combines the two primary developments of early twentieth century physics—general relativity and quantum mechanics—to explain the origins and structure of the universe.

Early Life

Stephen William Hawking was born on January 8, 1942, on the three hundredth anniversary of the death of one of the greatest physicists of all time, Galileo Galilei, who is generally credited with proving that the earth revolves around the sun. Hawking's birth was also only four days after the three hundredth birthday of another great physicist, Isaac Newton, who developed a mathematical model to explain the structure of the universe that was essentially unchallenged for over two hundred years. Hawking was born in Oxford, England, where both of his parents had attended Oxford University. However, the Hawkings had only recently returned to Oxford to escape the likelihood of London being bombed during World War II.

Hawking's father, Frank, was a physician who had the same ambition for his son. However, Hawking did not find medicine and biology theoretically rich enough and instead decided to major in physics at Oxford. By his own admission, Hawking averaged barely one hour per day of studying at Oxford and decided to concentrate on theoretical physics as a way to avoid the busy work of memorizing facts. After graduating from Oxford, Hawking had hoped to study at Cambridge University with Fred Hoyle, who had developed "steady-state" cosmology, which argues that the structure of the universe remains relatively constant over time. However, his acceptance to Cambridge was contingent upon his receiving honors from Oxford. Because of his lack of studying, his final examination scores at Oxford were only borderline for an honors degree. In an interview, he then told his examiners that if they gave him honors, he would go to Cambridge. Otherwise, he would stay at Oxford. They gave him honors.

Upon reaching Cambridge, Hawking was disappointed to learn that he would not study with Hoyle but Dennis Sciama, another steady-state cosmologist unfamiliar to Hawking. However, Sciama turned out to be much more available and open to students developing their own alternative perspectives than Hoyle would have been. Within a few months of arriving at Cambridge, Hawking faced a far more serious disappointment. Never robust or athletic, Hawking was becoming increasingly clumsy. At his mother's insistence, he saw a doctor. He was diagnosed with amyotrophic lateral sclerosis (ALS; called Lou Gehrig's disease in the United States), a degenerative condition causing the patient to gradually lose control of all muscles, including those necessary to move, gesture, speak, and swallow. Hawking was told he might only live another two years and underwent a deep depression as he contemplated the futility of trying to complete his doctorate. Sciama persuaded him to continue but refused to lower his standards. As his condition worsened, Hawking came to need a cane, then a wheelchair, and then an artificial speech synthesizer. However, he has survived for many years since he was diagnosed with a terminal condition.

Through Sciama, Hawking met Roger Penrose, a mathematician who had developed the idea of a "singularity," a point at which the laws of mathematics and science break down. Hawking earned his doctorate by proposing that singularities could be used to understand the structure of the universe. He has since come to rethink the concept of singularity and argue that the laws of physics are continuous throughout the universe.

Life's Work

Early in the twentieth century, Newton's physics faced two challenges: relativity, conceived by Albert Einstein, and quantum mechanics, which had several founders. Although Einstein contributed to the development of quantum mechanics, he was uncomfortable with it. What most disturbed him was the uncertainty principle of Werner Heisenberg, which suggests that not everything is knowable and measurable. Because Einstein's relativity insists that everything can ultimately be determined, a position that it shared with Newtonian mechanics, Hawking calls it a "classical theory." One implication of relativity that Einstein himself shunned was that large stars could collapse into black holes, single points with such overwhelming gravitational strength that nothing, including light, can escape. Penrose considered black holes to be

singularities and thought that since they emitted no signals, they were unknowable by the laws of physics as scientists understood them.

In the 1920's, astronomers began to believe that the universe was expanding. Hoyle's steady-state cosmology was one model of an expanding universe. However, a rival cosmology emerged to account for the expanding universe, which Hoyle disparagingly dismissed as the "big bang." The big bang theory proposes that billions of years ago the entire universe was compressed into a single point that exploded. The energy released from that explosion gave birth to the four forces that govern the universe (gravity, electromagnetism, strong nuclear force, and weak nuclear force), elementary particles, atoms, galaxies, stars, and planets. The initial explosion was so strong that it continues to cause the universe to expand to the present day. The big bang hypothesis suggests that residual radiation from that explosion should pervade the cosmos even now. Around the time Hawking wrote his doctoral dissertation, the radiation was discovered. This caused most physicists to reject Hoyle's steady state. In his dissertation, Hawking suggested that the entire universe was originally a singularity like a black hole and that the big bang could be understood by comparing the universe to a star collapsing into black hole. Hawking's analogy reversed the time sequence of a compressing star: The universe explodes from a singularity rather than imploding into one.

One of the most serious problems in twentieth century physics is that its two main theories, relativity and quantum mechanics, appear to be incompatible. Black holes are predicted by relativity, which implies that they should emit no energy. In the 1970's, Hawking began to wonder if he could reconcile relativity and quantum mechanics by applying quantum mechanics to black holes. He found that according to quantum mechanics, black holes would indeed emit energy and would eventually explode. Hence, if the universe prior to the big bang was analogous to a black hole, it would one day burst like a black hole; therefore, the big bang could be explained by combining relativity and quantum mechanics. This means that the primordial universe as well as black holes can be understood by laws of mathematics and science and neither are really singularities. Hawking came to believe that the universe was continuous and governed by a single set of laws. This would not mean

that all events were predictable because a comprehensive theory of the universe would still contain Heisenberg's uncertainty principle. Hawking cautions that even if humans knew all the laws that underlie the operation of the universe, an account of all possible occurrences would require knowing the history of every particle, something clearly impossible within finite time.

Twentieth century physics believes the universe is governed by four forces: gravity (which binds the planets, stars, and galaxies together), electromagnetism (which binds the atom together), the strong nuclear force (which holds the atomic nucleus together), and the weak nuclear force (which is necessary to account for radioactive decay). Einstein spent his later years unsuccessfully searching for a "grand unified theory," a single set of equations that would account for all four forces. Hawking is convinced that Einstein failed because he did not incorporate quantum mechanics. According to Hawking, the place to look for the grand unified theory is during the big bang, when Hawking and other physicists believe the four forces were one.

The universe assumed the shape it did because of the particular way energy happened to have been distributed at the time of the big bang. With slight differences, the galaxies and stars may never have developed. Indeed, the big bang may have produced regions where space, matter, and energy assumed different forms. Hawking proposed that the result could be an infinite number of "baby universes" and that the universe in which humans live may be only one of many possibilities.

The ultimate fate of the universe may depend upon how much matter it contains. If it contains only the matter that astronomers can see with visible light, then the universe should expand forever. If there is more matter, the universe will eventually contract and ultimately collapse into a single point. Hawking hypothesizes that black holes may have formed not only out of imploding stars but also from residues of the big bang. If that is true, black holes may pervade the universe, and there may be enough invisible matter to one day reverse its expansion. Long after the universe again congeals into a single point, it will again explode and expand. Hence, the universe would have a continual history whose broad outline is predictable. If Hawking is correct, then the dream of physics, a single set of laws to explain the development of the universe and all its contents, is indeed attainable.

Summary

Stephen Hawking considers his own work incomplete. However, as Hawking himself suggests, science is never complete. It is supposed to be self-critical and forever subject to revision. Even if Hawking's work leads to a reassessment of Einstein, it will not diminish Einstein's greatness. Einstein caused a rethinking of Newton's theory, which had served as the foundation of physics for over two centuries. Hawking would have never developed his model had Einstein not preceded him, nor would Einstein have produced relativity without Newton's prior framework. The ideal of scientists is to build on each other. Today's truth may become tomorrow's error, but it is also the foundation of tomorrow's truth. As Newton admitted, "I can see far because I stand on the shoulders of giants." Most likely, Hawking will prove to be another layer in a pyramid of giants.

There are critics who charge that Hawking is simply one of a number of scientists trying to unify physics and explain the development of the universe and that his disability is the primary reason he has received so much attention from the media. Even if that were true, the fact that anyone can produce such acclaimed work with an affliction such as his should serve as an inspiration to both the handicapped and the able-bodied. Albert Einstein, Bertrand Russell (who revised mathematics and worked for world peace), and Linus Pauling (who won Nobel Prizes in Physics, Chemistry, and Peace) are remembered not only as great scientists but also as great humanitarians. The same will very likely be true of Stephen Hawking.

Bibliography

Boslough, John. *Stephen Hawking's Universe.* New York: Morrow, and London: Collins, 1985. An introduction to twentieth century cosmology, relativity, quantum mechanics, and Hawking's contribution to them.

Hawking, Stephen. *A Brief History of Time.* New York and London: Bantam, 1988. A popular book that Hawking wrote to explain his own work as part of the development of twentieth century physics. It set a record for the number of weeks on *The New York Times* Best-Seller List.

———. *Black Holes and Baby Universes.* New York and London: Bantam, 1993. A collection of popular essays written by Hawking. They discuss his life, his philosophy of science, the possibility of science knowing everything, and the origin, structure, and fate of the universe.

Hawking, Stephen, and Roger Penrose. *The Nature of Space and Time.* Princeton, N.J.: Princeton University Press, 1996. This is the published edition of a series of debates between Hawking and his former mentor and collaborator, Roger Penrose. They contrast their opinions about black holes, the origin and fate of the university, and the philosophy of science.

McEvoy, J. P., and Oscar Zarate. *Introducing Stephen Hawking.* New York: Totem, 1995. A comic-book presentation of Hawking's life and work that is particularly good at mixing graphics and text. In the process of explaining Hawking, it offers an amusing but informative history of twentieth century physics.

White, Michael, and John Gribbin. *Stephen Hawking, A Life in Science.* London and New York: Penguin, 1992. A biography of Hawking that shows how his personal history impacted upon his scientific discoveries.

Zycinski, Joseph M. "Metaphysics and Epistemology in Stephen Hawking's Theory of the Creation of the Universe." *Zygon* 31, no. 2 (June, 1996). The author argues that Hawking's theories on the creation of the universe are consistent with Christian theism.

Yale R. Magrass

VÍCTOR RAÚL HAYA DE LA TORRE

Born: February 22, 1895; Trujillo, Peru
Died: August 2, 1979; Lima, Peru
Areas of Achievement: Government and politics
Contribution: Haya de la Torre was the founder of the Alianza Popular Revolucionaria Americana (APRA), an inter-American, democratic political movement that stimulated parties to modernize the old elitist orders in Peru and throughout Latin America.

Early Life

Víctor Raúl Haya de la Torre was the eldest of five children born to Raúl Edmundo Haya and Zoila María de la Torre. Though not wealthy, both parents claimed to be part of the criollo (Spanish descent) elite that controlled Peru's economic and political fortunes. Haya de la Torre attended local private schools, and at age eighteen he was enrolled in Trujillo's University of La Libertad. While pursuing a law degree, he joined an avant-garde literary club and student government. When his first play, a comedy, was performed, Haya de la Torre became convinced that his future lay in politics, not the fine arts.

In 1917, Haya de la Torre attended a meeting of the newly formed National Student Federation in Lima. While there, he visited Manuel González Prada, the aging founder of Peruvian *indigenismo* (Indianism). Since the 1880's, González Prada had been urging the Peruvian elite to reverse its centuries-old practice of despising Indian culture, and the Indians themselves, by integrating the Indians into society. Shortly after the convention, the prefect of Cuzco, a kinsman, hired Haya de la Torre as his secretary. Haya de la Torre moved to the capital of the ancient Inca empire in August, 1917, and traveled widely in the highland Indian communities of southern Peru. The poverty of the Indians and the labors of Protestant missionaries greatly impressed the pretentious criollo. After being in Cuzco only a few weeks, Haya de la Torre inherited a sizable sum of money from an uncle. He left the mountains, was enrolled in the University of San Marcos at Lima, and submerged himself in extracurricular activities.

Haya de la Torre joined the university reform movement that was sweeping Latin America, and he persuaded the student federation to support the textile workers' strike for an eight-hour day. The participation of the students proved to be decisive, and in January, 1915, the grateful workers elected Haya de la Torre president of the newly formed Federation of Peruvian Textile Workers. Although flattered, Haya de la Torre turned the presidency over to a worker and devoted his energies to organizing a free university for urban workers and Indian migrants to the city. Students and professors from San Marcos taught classes at no charge in a variety of disciplines to the poor with the hope of bringing the lower classes of Peru into the mainstream of the national culture. This work with organized labor and the popular universities from 1918 to 1923 laid a foundation for Haya de la Torre's political activity for the next five decades.

When President Augusto Leguía planned to dedicate Peru to the Sacred Heart of Jesus in May, 1923, Haya de la Torre led students and workers in a massive protest march. After police fired into the crowd and killed two marchers, the president canceled his plans. In October, 1923, Leguía charged Haya de la Torre with sedition and imprisoned him. When Haya de la Torre embarked on a protest hunger strike, Leguía deported him to Panama and suppressed the new labor unions and popular universities.

Life's Work

The exile lasted until 1931. In those eight years, Haya de la Torre traveled widely and studied at first hand the newly emerging government systems in Mexico, the Soviet Union, and Europe. When he left Peru, he considered himself a Marxist, and, after working briefly with the education minister of revolutionary Mexico, José Vasconcelos, Haya de la Torre went to the Soviet Union in 1924. He interviewed many of the high-ranking Communists, including Leon Trotsky. From Bolshevik Russia he went to Fascist Italy and liberal England. He was enrolled in the London School of Economics and the University of Oxford and thrived in the Socialist milieu of England's universities of the 1920's. In 1927, he attended the Communist-dominated World Anti-Imperialist Congress in Brussels and declared that Soviet Socialism was nonexportable. Calling himself a revisionary Marxist, he earned the hostility of the Communists that lasted until his death.

From Europe he traveled to the United States and then went on a speaking tour through Central America. When he reached Panama, the government—at the request of Peru—deported him to Germany. He spent the remaining three years of his exile as a student, author and journalist, observer of the growing National Socialist Party, and nursemaid to a Latin American movement he had founded in 1924.

While in Mexico City, Haya de la Torre had announced to university students the formation of the Alianza Popular Revolucionaria Americana (the American Popular Revolutionary Alliance, or APRA). Referring to America south of the Rio Grande as Indo-America—to stress the importance of the indigenous populations—Haya de la Torre urged all nations to integrate all races and classes and to break free of the imperialist influence of the United States. Small Aprista movements began in the European exile communities of Latin Americans, and a few began in Latin America. Haya de la Torre's labor and student followers in Peru formed the Partido Aprista Peruano (PAP) and prepared for the end of the Leguía dictatorship and the restoration of electoral politics.

Military coups in 1930 and 1931 permitted Haya de la Torre to return to Peru and take personal control of PAP and campaign for the presidency in the October, 1931, election. With Haya de la Torre at the helm, PAP became the focal point of a mass movement, not merely a political party. Although he diagnosed Peru's ills in Marxist terms, Haya de la Torre prescribed a corporatist remedy. Discarding class conflict and a revolutionary vanguard, Haya de la Torre called for class cooperation, social unity, and the democratic process. He organized Aprista clubs in all social groups and promised to establish a parliament composed of functional groups. PAP called for the nationalization of industry, the inter-Americanization of the Panama Canal, and resistance to imperialist—that is, U.S.—influence. PAP added workers' restaurants, recreation halls, and medical centers to the revived popular universities. Uniformed youth cadres led massive rallies in marches, songs, and chants that virtually idolized Haya de la Torre. The party slogan was "Only Aprismo will save Peru," and melodramatic photographs gave the party's *jefe máximo* (greatest chief) heroic proportions.

Actually, Haya de la Torre was short—just over five feet tall—and had a stocky build that got chunkier with age and oversized features on a large head—thick eyebrows, a powerful aquiline nose, and stirrup-shaped ears. The lifelong bachelor governed party affairs with a firm, autocratic hand. He

could be spellbinding whether speaking to thousands in the Plaza de Acho bullring or to one or two individuals in an intimate setting.

Haya de la Torre's principal rival was Luis M. Sánchez Cerro, the officer who had toppled Leguía. Sánchez Cerro led a mass movement that appealed to the nonunion workers and *cholos* (Indians adapting to Western culture), who readily identified with the dark-skinned military hero with Indian features. When election officials announced the results of the most spirited, bitterest campaign in Peruvian electoral history, Apristas cried fraud. Sánchez Cerro had won by a comfortable margin.

In December, 1931, militant Apristas rose in rebellion in several places in Peru and began a sixteen-month period of violence that ended with the assassination of Sánchez Cerro on April 30, 1933. When the rebellion began, the government imprisoned and tortured Haya de la Torre charging him with masterminding the revolt. Then and thereafter, Haya de la Torre affirmed his commitment to nonviolence. Sánchez Cerro's successor, General Oscar R. Benavides, released Haya de la Torre and hundreds of other Apristas in a general amnesty.

One year later, the Benavides government outlawed PAP and arrested thousands of party members. Haya de la Torre eluded the dragnet and chose to stay in Peru rather than flee. For the next ten years, he was an internal exile, providing leadership to his warring clandestine party while staying constantly on the move to avoid arrest. Benavides barred PAP from the 1939 elections, and his successor, Manuel Prado y Ugarteche, continued the ban.

As World War II neared its end, Benavides persuaded Prado to legalize PAP in exchange for Haya de la Torre's promise to refrain from running in the 1945 election. Benavides' change in attitude may be partly attributed to Haya de la Torre's moderation of his anti-North American rhetoric. He saw in the Good Neighbor Policy a fundamental change in the United States' Latin American policy. The nightmare of Nazism prompted Haya de la Torre to reduce the similarities of his program to European corporatism, and he concluded that, to progress, Peru would have to embrace rather than repudiate international capitalism.

In 1945, Haya de la Torre and his followers joined a coalition that elected José Luis Bustamente y Rivero president, but the coalition fractured when Bustamente's nominations slighted the Apristas. In retaliation, the Aprista-dominated par-

liament deadlocked the operations of government. In October, 1948, Aprista cadres in the navy rebelled but were swiftly quelled. General Manuel A. Odria ousted Bustamente and ferociously attacked the APRA movement.

Haya secured political asylum in the Colombian embassy in January, 1949, and he remained there until April, 1954, because the Odria government would not grant him safe passage to leave the country. A compromise with Mexico, after two inconclusive decisions of the World Court, enabled Haya de la Torre to go again into exile, this time for three years.

Odria permitted APRA participation—without fielding candidates—in the election of 1956, but in 1962 PAP was allowed to participate fully. Haya de la Torre's principal opponent was Fernando Belaúnde Terry, who headed Acción Popular. Haya de la Torre won 32.98 percent of the necessary 33 percent of the vote. His old nemesis, the military, seized power, annulled the election, and promised a new, honest election in June, 1963. In that election, Belaúnde captured 39 percent of the vote to Haya de la Torre's 34 percent. Bitter over the sto-

len election and defeat, Haya de la Torre entered into a parliamentary coalition with the same Odria who had sought his arrest and execution a dozen years earlier. The APRA-controlled parliament severely hampered Belaúnde's government for the next five years. As Belaúnde's term neared its end, his Acción Popular was in disarray, and Haya de la Torre appeared positioned to win the presidential sash he had been pursuing since 1931; the military, however, intervened once again. A leftist reform military government ruled for the next twelve years. Within six years the government's domestic programs and foreign policy strikingly resembled APRA's goals of the 1930's. When the regime decided to return political power to civilians, it permitted APRA to participate in the constitution-writing process.

In the 1978 elections to the constituent assembly, Aprista candidates won 35 percent of the vote and had the largest delegation. The assembly elected Haya de la Torre its president, and the aging Aprista served as the ceremonial President of Peru during the transition from military to civilian rule. In 1979, his party nominated him for president and supporters secured his nomination for the Nobel Peace Prize.

These honors were final tributes to APRA's founder, now known in Peru as "El Personaje," the personage. Haya de la Torre suffered from a blood disease, a heart condition, and lung cancer. Three weeks after signing Peru's new constitution, he succumbed to his ailments and died on August 2, 1979, at age eighty-four. Peru and Venezuela declared a day of national mourning, and two million people attended his funeral procession.

Summary

Many political observers were convinced that PAP was dependent upon the magnetism and leadership of Víctor Raúl Haya de la Torre, but the party did not dissolve at the death of its founder. The party's candidate, Alán García, won the national election in 1985, and PAP has proved to be one of the most durable parties in Peru's highly volatile political environment. The APRA movement has had enduring influence outside of Peru. APRA sunk strong roots in pre-Castro Cuba and permanent roots in Costa Rica, Bolivia, Puerto Rico, and Venezuela. Haya de la Torre's many books and hundreds of articles found a ready audience throughout Latin America during the nearly six decades of his career. His introduction of mass politics to Latin

America, his programs of fundamental social reform, and his commitment to democratic processes made him one of the most important political philosophers in twentieth century Latin America.

Bibliography

Alexander, Robert J. *Prophets of the Revolution.* New York: Macmillan, 1962. One chapter is dedicated to Haya de la Torre. Alexander is an admiring, but not uncritical, student of Haya de la Torre and APRA. He claims that all major revolutionary movements in Latin America have been influenced by Haya de la Torre.

Beals, Carleton. *Fire on the Andes.* Philadelphia and London: Lippincott, 1934. Beals met Haya de la Torre in Mexico and described his movement as the first in Peru based on principles rather than on personalities and greed. Beals feared Haya de la Torre was too Mussolini-like but believed that APRA would renew antiquated Peru.

————. *Latin America: World in Revolution.* London and New York: Abelard-Schuman, 1963. In this book, Beals bitterly assails Haya de la Torre for betraying his principles and selling out to the United States.

Haya de la Torre, Víctor Raúl. *APRISMO: The Ideas and Doctrines of Víctor Raúl Haya de la Torre.* Edited and translated by Robert J. Alexander. Kent, Ohio: Kent State University Press, 1973. This major English-language collection of Haya de la Torre's writings is prefaced by a scholarly biographical sketch.

Kantor, Harry. *The Ideology and Program of the Peruvian Aprista Movement.* Berkeley: University of California Press, 1953.

Klarén, Peter F. *Modernization, Dislocation, and Aprismo: Origins of the Peruvian Aprista Party, 1870-1932.* Austin: University of Texas Press, 1973. Excellent study of Haya de la Torre's early years and the conditions that gave rise to the Aprista movement.

Stein, Steve. *Populism in Peru: The Emergence of the Masses and the Politics of Social Control.* Madison: University of Wisconsin Press, 1980. Careful analysis of the campaign and election of 1932. Concluded that Haya de la Torre lost fair and square. Most other students assume that Sánchez Cerro stole a landslide victory from APRA.

Werlich, David P. *Peru: A Short History.* Carbondale: Southern Illinois University Press, 1978. Best survey of Peru in print. Traces Haya de la Torre and APRA through the decades. Concludes that Haya de la Torre's convoluted philosophy accommodated itself rather easily to changing events.

Paul E. Kuhl

HELEN HAYES

Born: October 10, 1900; Washington, D.C.
Died: March 17, 1993; Nyack, New York
Area of Achievement: Theater and drama
Contribution: In more than sixty years on stage and screen, Hayes became the "first lady of the American theater."

Early Life

Born Helen Hayes Brown on October 10, 1900, in Washington, D.C., Helen was the granddaughter of Patrick and Ann Hayes, who emigrated from Ireland to the United States during the potato famine. Her great aunt, Catherine Hayes, was a famous Irish singer (the "Swan of Erin") who entertained large crowds in London as well as "forty-niners" in America. Helen's mother, Catherine "Essie" Hayes, an aspiring but unsuccessful actress, directed her early career. Helen's father, Francis Arnum Brown, was a wholesale meat salesman.

Like many "stage mothers," Catherine Hayes brought her child into the world of drama. Essie took Helen to her first theater experience: Franz Lehar's *The Merry Widow*. Nicknamed "the white mouse" by her family, Helen immediately acquired a strong affection for the theater. Shortly thereafter, she gave her first performance, as Peaseblossom, in *A Midsummer Night's Dream*.

Helen's early education enhanced her theatrical ambition. First at Holy Cross Academy, then later at Sacred Heart Convent, Helen came under the influence of Roman Catholic nuns who encouraged her interests in acting and music. She also attended Minnie Hawke's School of Dance, which sponsored several musicals in which the young girl could sing and dance. Since Helen's singing was better than her dancing, she concentrated on the latter, resulting in her first professional performance in *The Prince Chap*.

At the age of eight, Helen accompanied her mother to a New York audition for Broadway's Lew Fields. Fields, impressed with Helen's singing, signed her for a leading role in Victor Herbert's 1909 presentation *Old Dutch*. This began a series of stage performances in Fields's presentations.

Despite Helen's youthful successes, her childhood was not without its heartaches. Her mother began to drink excessively, and Helen, like many children of alcoholics, believed that somehow it was her fault. Caring for a drunken mother was not easy for the young girl and her father. Eventually, it became too much for Francis Brown. Although the Browns never divorced, they separated for life.

Helen's stage career also produced its share of difficulties. In 1918, following her exceptional performance in *Dear Brutus*, she received her first starring role on Broadway as a flapper in *Bab* (1920). The latter was a growing experience. By her own admission, she suffered from poor posture and an inability to relax on stage. Her shrill voice bothered critics, including one who dismissed her performance as an unsuccessful effort to get by on her cuteness.

Although these criticisms bruised Helen's youthful ego, she resolved to develop sufficient discipline to correct all of her major weaknesses, and she did. Improving her posture and relaxing the tenseness (by curling her toes), Helen entered the world of light comedy, in which she quickly excelled. In 1926, her performance in *What Every Woman Knows* not only restored Helen to the critics' good graces but also made the play one of her signature presentations, and she repeated it in 1938 and 1954.

Helen's subtlety and power in *What Every Woman Knows* so impressed producer Jed Harris that he cast her for the leading role in *Coquette* (1927), in which she played an aristocratic Southern belle who commits suicide after becoming pregnant by a poverty-stricken young man. Although veteran Broadway observers doubted the wisdom of casting a light comedienne in such a dramatic role, the critics raved and the audience gave her sixteen curtain calls.

Coquette established Hayes's Broadway career. The distinguished British writer Noël Coward, who was not known for giving out compliments, summarized Helen's performance as "astonishingly perfect. . . . She ripped our emotions to shreds." At the age of twenty-seven, Hayes was now a full-blown star.

Hayes's personal life also reached fruition during these formative stages. In 1925, while preparing for *Caesar and Cleopatra*, she met a Chicago newspaper reporter and aspiring playwright named Charles MacArthur. It was love at first sight. Over the protests registered by Helen's mother and both of MacArthur's parents, and despite the fact that he was married (although separated) at the time, the mutual attraction was overwhelming. Their marriage followed shortly after his successful collaboration with Ben Hecht in *The Front Page* (1928). With professional and personal foundations established, Hayes embarked on one of the most remarkable careers in American theater.

Life's Work

Following her wedding and the birth of her daughter Mary in February, 1930, Helen Hayes entered the most productive phase of her career. Although *Mr. Gilhooley* (1930) produced little praise, and *Petticoat Influence* (1930) and *The Good Fairy* (1931) fared only slightly better, Hayes entered Hollywood's cinematic world with a flourish, attaining instantaneous national stardom in *The Sin of Madelon Claudet* (1931), which won for her an Academy Award for Best Actress.

Madelon Claudet's amazing success was made even more remarkable by the fact it was not only her first Hollywood film but also her first talking picture. Editing problems (preview audiences booed during private screenings) nearly prevented the film's release. Producer Irving Thalberg saw brilliant potential and saved the film by making only slight alterations. Helen's performance as Madelon, a French mother forced into prostitution through her efforts to save her illegitimate son, left audiences weeping all over America.

Since winning an Oscar established Hayes's cinematic reputation, her film career immediately scaled new heights. First, she played opposite Ronald Coleman in Sinclair Lewis' *Arrowsmith* (1931); next came a costarring appearance with an emerging young actor named Gary Cooper in another American classic, Ernest Hemingway's *A Farewell to Arms* (1932). Her next film, which paired Hayes with the "King of Hollywood," Clark Gable, was *The White Sister* (1933). Still not finished, Hollywood exploited Hayes by featuring her in four more films in less than two years.

When Hayes returned to New York in 1933 to play *Mary of Scotland*, her reputation as a film celebrity preceded her. Helen's box-office appeal was so great that she played to packed houses for several months. Although the actress stood only five feet tall, she somehow managed to capture the six-foot queen's essential spirit and presence.

The techniques that Helen employed in *Mary of Scotland* served as a successful basis for her tour de force performance of *Victoria Regina* in 1935. It was this portrayal of the great English monarch that won for her the medal awarded by the Drama League of New York for the best stage achievement by an actress that year. *Victoria Regina* probably was Hayes's most famous role in her long career.

Audiences and critics alike applauded her contribution to American culture. The play enjoyed a run of 969 performances in front of America's toughest crowds. The acting challenge was formidable, requiring Hayes to age more than fifty years throughout the evening—complete with sagging face and swelling cheeks. Reflecting first youth, then maturity, and finally old age required talent rarely seen even on the New York stage. So successful was her depiction of the aging queen that some members of the audience did not even recognize her.

The play went on the road throughout the United States. For millions of Americans, Hayes was Queen Victoria. In Washington, D.C., Eleanor Roosevelt saw the play three times and "could not stop clapping." Invited to the White House by the first lady, Hayes met President Franklin D. Roosevelt, who inquired, "And how is your majesty?" *Victoria Regina* left an indelible imprint upon the history of acting in America.

Hayes never again matched the heights she achieved in *Victoria Regina*, although memorable stage and screen performances followed during her long career. In 1938, Hayes and MacArthur adopted a seven-month-old son, James MacArthur, who later spent twelve years playing detective Danny "Danno" Williams on the television show *Hawaii Five-O*. In the late 1930's, Hayes and her husband strongly supported America's entry into World War II, which was already raging in Europe. After the Japanese attack on Pearl Harbor on December 7, 1941, Charles MacArthur volunteered his services to the military, while Helen sold war bonds.

Hayes's stage and screen career flattened out during the war years until she succeeded in 1943 with *Harriet*, a historical play based on Harriet Beecher Stowe's classic *Uncle Tom's Cabin* (1852). Hayes's great concern with civil rights for African Americans undoubtedly accounted for the emotional commitment that she made to this work. Critics also praised her work in *Happy Birthday* (1946).

Tragedy struck Hayes in 1949, when polio claimed the life of her nineteen-year-old daughter Mary MacArthur, a budding actress who had just appeared with her mother in *Good Housekeeping*. Hayes later wrote that "nothing is more difficult to accept than the death of a child."

More adversity followed Mary's death. First, Hayes's alcoholic mother, Catherine Hayes Brown,

died shortly after her granddaughter's death. Then, Charles MacArthur, also an alcoholic, began drinking incessantly because he was unable to cope with the loss of his daughter. According to Hayes, her husband "set about killing himself. It took seven years, and it was harrowing to watch." MacArthur died in 1956.

Coping with the loss of three of the people she loved most dearly became Hayes's greatest challenge. After first believing that she had caused her husband's death, Hayes came to understand that only MacArthur could have sought help for himself. When she accepted that fact, she was able to go on with her future. With grim determination, Hayes turned to her son and her profession for solace. She also returned to the Roman Catholic church, which had excommunicated her following her marriage to the divorced MacArthur. Together, her faith, her son, and her profession sustained her throughout her remaining years.

Although Hayes had not undertaken a significant film since *Vanessa, Her Love Story* in 1935, friends urged her to make *Anastasia* (1956) with Ingrid Bergman and Yul Brynner. The result might have pleased other actresses, but for Hayes it represented only an average performance.

Hayes also returned to Broadway with renewed vigor. Four plays in four years followed: *The Skin of Our Teeth* (1955), *The Glass Menagerie* (1956), *Time Remembered* (1957), and *A Touch of the Poet* (1958). Hayes also took to television in her later years. Television viewers enjoyed her performances in *The Snoop Sisters* (1972), *Victory at Entebbe* (1976), *Murder Is Easy* (1982), *A Caribbean Mystery* (1983), and *Murder with Mirrors* (1985).

Hayes appeared in several films near the end of her career, and in 1971 Hollywood gave her a second Academy Award (Best Supporting Actress) for her role in *Airport* (1970). She retired from the stage following her performance in Eugene O'Neill's *Long Day's Journey into Night* (1972). Helen Hayes died of heart failure at the age of ninety-two on March 17, 1993.

Summary

Helen Hayes was one of the great stars within the American theatrical firmament. Although her talents came to her naturally, it was her great determination, durability, and many years of toiling under the lights that made her one of America's consummate troupers. Work, "plain hard steady work," was the most satisfying thing in her life.

No task was too great or small for this diminutive woman who threw herself into all areas of theatrical performance. On Broadway and in Hollywood, on radio and television, her willingness to work hard without complaining complemented the great natural talent she displayed in rising to the top of her profession.

Hayes suffered through her share of disappointments, but when tragedy seemed to block her way, she never gave up hope or faith. Life's setbacks never deterred her from her ultimate goals. Reared by unhappy parents, rejected by the church of her childhood, married to an increasingly alcoholic husband whom she loved, staggered by the tragic death of her only biological child, Hayes more than persevered in the face of sometimes overwhelming adversity—she triumphed.

Her achievements were many, both in and out of the acting profession. Two Academy Awards and the New York Drama League Medal symbolized the contributions of this actress who was honored as the "first lady of the American theater." In August, 1988, President Ronald Reagan presented her with the National Medal of Arts award for artistic excellence. There was more: Hayes was president of the American Theater Wing and the American National Theater and Academy, chairwoman of the March of Dimes, and the winner of the Catholic Interracial Council of New York's award for her civil rights activities.

Although Hayes was more than America's leading theatrical actress, acting remained her greatest achievement. *The New York Times* called her one of the three great women of the American theater. When she died, the lights of Broadway dimmed in honor of the little lady who bestrode the theatrical world like a colossus.

Bibliography

Eames, John Douglas. *The MGM Story.* Rev. ed. London: Octopus, and New York: Crown, 1979. Since Helen Hayes did a number of films for Metro-Goldwyn-Mayer, this collection of articles and photographs makes a solid contribution toward an understanding of her film career.

Hayes, Helen. *On Reflection.* New York: Evans, 1968; London: Allen, 1969. Hayes's autobiographical contributions are always valuable primary sources, and this is no exception. Hayes is refreshingly self-analytical and self-critical. Her honest analyses, however anecdotal and impressionistic, usually are very helpful in assessing the strengths and weaknesses of her career and life.

Hayes, Helen, with Lewis Funke. *A Gift of Joy*. New York: Evans, 1965. Written nine years after her husband's death, this deeply penetrating memoir is an excellent philosophical, psychological, and spiritual exposition of Hayes's professional and personal life. Includes Hayes's favorite poetry and some speeches and quotations that inspired her.

Hayes, Helen, with Katherine Hatch. *My Life in Three Acts*. San Diego: Harcourt Brace, 1990; London: Owen, 1991. Hayes's final work is more revealing than previous efforts, particularly in areas deemed controversial or painful. This autobiography is especially helpful in understanding the pitfalls of being the child of an alcoholic and being married to an alcoholic.

Houghton, Norris. *Advance from Broadway*. New York: Harcourt Brace, 1941. Houghton traveled 19,000 miles to observe America's theatrical patterns. In the process, he discovered the incredible impact that Hayes exerted on the general public in the "sticks."

Johnson, Jill. "Transformation: A Memory of Helen Hayes." *American Heritage* 44, no. 6 (October, 1993). The author recalls one of Hayes' performances in Korea in 1966.

Murphy, Donn B., and Stephen Moore. *Helen Hayes: A Bio-Bibliography*. Westport, Conn.: Greenwood Press, 1993. This volume includes a biography; a chronology of major events in Hayes' life and career; sources separated into sections on stage, radio, television, and film; and includes reviews, synopses, cast listings, and more.

Robbins, Jhan. *Front Page Marriage*. New York: Putnam, 1982. A fine study of the relationship between Hayes and her husband, Charles MacArthur.

J. Christopher Schnell

LE LY HAYSLIP

Born: December 19, 1949; Ky La, Vietnam

Areas of Achievement: Literature and social reform

Contribution: Advocating forgiveness and healing on both sides in the wake of the Vietnam War, Le Ly Hayslip created the East Meets West Foundation to build clinics, schools, and rehabilitation centers in Vietnam with the assistance of American veterans and other donors.

Early Life

Phung Thi Le Ly was born the sixth child of Vietnamese peasants in the village of Ky La (later Xa Hoa Qui) near Danang, where she lived until the age of fifteen. A premature baby who survived against great odds, she was called *con troi nuoi* (she who is nourished by God) by the villagers. From her father, Phung Trong, she learned to revere her family, her ancestors, and Vietnamese tradition. Her mother, Tran Thi Huyen, taught her humility and the strength of virtue. Le Ly attended a village school through the equivalent of the third grade, her formal schooling cut short by the Vietnam War. From the age of twelve, she supported and worked for the Viet Cong against the American and South Vietnamese (ARVN) armies. Her two brothers also served Ho Chi Minh: Bon Nghe as the leader of a North Vietnamese Army reconnaissance team and Sau Ban as a soldier killed in the South by an American mine.

In her autobiography, *When Heaven and Earth Changed Places*, Le Ly describes how the people of her village were forced to labor for government soldiers by day and assist the Viet Cong by night. Such a schizophrenic existence led to Le Ly's imprisonment and torture by the ARVN as well as a traumatic death sentence and rape at the hands of the Viet Cong.

Forced to flee her village, Le Ly first took a job as housekeeper for a family in Danang and then went with her mother to Saigon, where her sister Lan was living. There, Le Ly and her mother found positions as servants to Anh, a wealthy textile factory owner. Giving in to Anh's affection, sixteen-year-old Le Ly became pregnant with her first child, James (Hung), born in 1967. Anh paid for their return trip to Danang, where Le Ly, with her baby and mother, lived with Lan, who worked as a bar girl.

Le Ly's father, Phung Trong, remained in the village to keep watch over ancestral land and shrines, but he became more and more depressed over the war's effects on the village and his family, particularly his daughters. Lan by then was earning money as a prostitute, while Le Ly hawked cigarettes and drugs on the black market. When Le Ly's father committed suicide, the family risked their lives to give him a traditional funeral. In a moment of shame, Le Ly accepted $400 to have sex with a soldier, but did so knowing that the money would support her family for a year. She worked as a nurse's aide at the Nha Thuong Vietnamese Hospital in Danang and later as a cocktail waitress at a Korean-owned nightclub.

Life's Work

Le Ly Hayslip sprang to national prominence with the publication of her first book, *When Heaven and Earth Changed Places* (1989), in which she chronicled her life as a peasant girl during the Vietnam War in and around her village of Ky La near Danang. One of the first publications to give expression to Vietnam experiences in the ten-year-old war, her book stunned Americans of all political persuasions with the truth that many villagers were tortured and oppressed by both sides in the war. A second book, *Child of War, Woman of Peace*, appeared in 1993, chronicling her arrival in the United States as the wife of an American much older than herself, a second marriage, and fulfillment of her long-held dream to create the East Meets West Foundation to fund projects that would assist both her own people and the American veterans who were still suffering from their war experiences.

Le Ly Hayslip's life in the United States began when she married Ed Munro, a sixty-year-old construction worker who sought a young Asian-born wife who would care for him in his old age. Attracted by his promise of education for Jimmy and the opportunity to escape from Vietnam, Le Ly consented. Her second son, Tommy, was born before they left.

Arriving in the United States in 1970, Le Ly adjusted with difficulty to life in San Diego, California, with her in-laws. When Ed's job prospects failed, they returned to Vietnam and Ed took a construction job at An Khe. There, Le Ly fell in love with an American officer, Dan, who was instrumental in helping her and her children to flee An Khe during a major battle in 1972. Shortly afterward, Ed and his family returned to the United States, where he died of pneumonia.

After the death of her first husband, Le Ly hoped to find happiness with Dan. Because Dan was reluctant to divorce his wife, however, Le Ly married Dennis, who made a heroic trip to Vietnam to rescue her sister Lan and her children as South Vietnam was falling to the Communists in 1975. Unfortunately, Dennis manifested an unstable personality, which found an outlet in fundamentalist Christianity and compulsive gun collecting. During this time, Le Ly began to turn more frequently to Buddhism in search of spiritual comfort and enlightenment. Angered by her resistance to Christianity, Dennis kidnapped their son Alan, Le Ly's third child, and threatened her life. Following a court order which banned him from his wife's household, Dennis died accidentally while burning charcoal in a closed van. After his death, Le Ly sought to pacify his angered spirit through Buddhist rituals and find peace of her own. Her thoughts turned to the possibility of returning to her family in Vietnam.

Terrified of the Communists and fearful of right-wing Vietnamese in the United States, yet resisting efforts of the CIA to co-opt her as a spy, Le Ly Hayslip traveled to Vietnam in 1986 to visit her family. She found a desperately poor country where people were still starving and the war was still going on in the hearts and minds of everyone there. Although her brother Bon would not eat the American food she had brought, her mother and sister welcomed her lovingly. Nevertheless, it was Anh, the father of her first son, who encouraged Le Ly not to settle down again in Vietnam, as she contemplated, but to "help people overcome the pain of war—to learn trust where they feel suspicion; to honor the past while letting go of it; to learn all these things so that they, in turn, may teach."

After returning to the United States, Le Ly went to Hawaii to marry Dan, who was by that time divorced from his wife. Once she arrived, she discovered that he intended to become an arms merchant and had little in the way of personal assets. The marriage never took place, since Le Ly refused to be allied with anyone who marketed weapons and was so obviously interested in her money. Through taking community college courses, workshops, and attending spiritual retreats, Le Ly had educated herself and gained considerable business acumen. Her financial knowledge had accrued from her experiences in various settings: an assembly-line position at National Semiconductor, an aborted attempt at starting her own delicatessen, a partnership in an Oriental restaurant, real estate transactions, and experimentation with the stock market. Yet it was in meeting and talking with American veterans who flocked to the restaurant that Le Ly realized how desperately in need of healing they were.

Determined to use her assets to build a clinic in Quang Nam province, Le Ly acquired licences from the U.S. State Department, assembled medical equipment and supplies, and established the East Meets West Foundation in 1987. She was assisted in her efforts by Cliff Parry, a wealthy individual later convicted as a professional swindler. Having been disillusioned once again, Le Ly resolved no longer to center her life on a man, and instead set about making humanity the love of her life. She worked with writer Jay Wurtz to publish *When Heaven and Earth Changed Places* and also traveled to the Soviet Union with Youth Ambassadors of America to learn about communism and the Cold War. Returning to Vietnam, Le Ly talked with Hanoi officials about her project, burned incense at her father's shrine in Ky La, and visited various assistance projects supported by Vietnam Veterans of America.

On her return to the United States, she enlisted the aid of Veterans-Vietnam Restoration Project, endured the wrath of some individuals in the Vietnamese American community, and earnestly began to raise money for the clinic. On a third trip, she won permission to build a clinic at Ky La. A public announcement by Vietnamese officials eased relations between Le Ly's mother and villagers suspicious that she was hiding money from her "American" daughter. On a fourth trip, accompanied by an American news crew, Le Ly took her sons with her, allowing Jimmy to meet his father Anh, for the first time. With the financial help of film director Oliver Stone, who became interested in Le Ly's story and her project, the Mother's Love Clinic was opened near Ky La in 1989. In her speech to the assembled crowd, Le Ly stated that "America made me a citizen and has let me come back with these presents which she gives you freely and without reservations. What she wants more than anything, I think, is to forgive you and be forgiven by you in return."

A second project of the East Meets West Foundation was the creation of a twenty-acre rehabilitation center for the homeless and handicapped at China Beach, the site where 3,500 Marines landed in Vietnam to begin the American buildup in 1965. A full-service medical center and a school are among the center's efforts to break the circle of vengeance that has kept the countries of Vietnam and the United States, as well as individuals, locked in paralyzing ha..ed. Her vision is one of reconciliation and spiritual connection. In adapting Le Ly Hayslip's first two books for the screen, Oliver Stone's film *Heaven and Earth* (1993) tells her story as the third film in his Vietnam trilogy (the first two films were *Platoon* [1986] and *Born on the Fourth of July* [1989]). Sadly, this film fails to convey the transformative vision by which she has healed her own painful war memories and enabled thousands more to regain spiritual energy through love, mutual understanding, and cooperation.

After settling in San Francisco, Le Ly Hayslip continued to serve as executive director of the East Meets West Foundation, a charitable relief and world peace organization that funds health care and social service projects in Vietnam. She has devoted much of her time to raising money for the foundation through lecture tours, book signings, and newsletters that keep donors apprised of projects completed and needs still to be met. Working together to coordinate the foundation's efforts with those of other grass-roots organizations offering material assistance to Vietnam, Hayslip has also encouranged veterans to help with various privately funded assistance projects in that country.

Summary

Out of the chaos, hardship, and upheaval of her early life, Le Ly Hayslip developed courage and self-reliance that allowed her to launch her efforts to heal the physical and emotional wounds left by the Vietnam War at a time when such efforts were viewed with great suspicion. Drawing upon her own reserves as a survivor, Hayslip has written two autobiographical memoirs to document the war experience from a Vietnamese perspective. Although her memoirs had a mixed reception among the highly political and polarized Vietnamese community in the United States, Hayslip struck a sympathetic chord among many American veterans of the Vietnam War. In forming the East Meets West Foundation, Hayslip managed to build a bridge between her native country and her adopted country— one that would allow individuals in Vietnam and the United States to understand one another more completely and to effect a more lasting reconciliation than could be provided by diplomatic agreements.

Bibliography

Abramowitz, Rachel. "The Road to 'Heaven.'" *Premiere* 7 (January, 1994): 46-50. A feature story on the making of Oliver Stone's film *Heaven and Earth*, this article includes a personal profile of Le Ly Hayslip and the contributions she made in helping to create an authentic portrait of her life during the Vietnam War.

Hayslip, Le Ly. "A Vietnam Memoir." *People* 32 (December 18, 1989): 147-150. In this autiobiographical profile, which appeared shortly after the publication of *When Heaven and Earth Changed Places*, Hayslip discusses her life and the impact that the Vietnam War continued to have upon her long after the conclusion of the fighting.

Hayslip, Le Ly, and James Hayslip. *Child of Peace, Woman of War.* New York: Doubleday, 1993; London: Pan, 1994. This second autiographical volume chronicles Hayslip's difficult life in the United States as the foreign-born wife of an American citizen and provides a detailed account of her efforts to return to Vietnam and establish various rehabilitation projects there.

Hayslip, Le Ly, and Jay Wurtz. *When Heaven and Earth Changed Places.* New York: Doubleday, 1989; London: Pan, 1991. One of the few accurate descriptions of life in rural Vietnamese villages during the Vietnam War, this autobiography also interweaves the narrative of Hayslip's astonishing return to her native country in 1986.

Klapwald, Thea. "Two Survivors Turn Hell into 'Heaven and Earth.' " *New York Times* 143 (December 19, 1993): H22. A dual portrait of Oliver Stone and Le Ly Hayslip and their collaborative efforts on the film *Heaven and Earth*. Includes a discussion of their individual efforts to heal the wounds that remain in the wake of the Vietnam War.

Mydans, Seth. "Vietnam: A Different Kind of Veteran and Her Healing Mission." *New York Times* 139 (November 28, 1989): A10. A biographical profile of Hayslip written shortly after the publication of her first book. Gives details about her work on behalf of refugees in the United States and in her native country.

Truaong, Monique Thuy-Dung. "The Emergence of Voices: Vietnamese American Literature 1975–1900." *Amerasia Journal* 19, no. 3 (Fall, 1993). Analysis of Vietnamese literature including Hayslip and Wurst's "When Heaven and Earth Changed Places."

Janet M. Powers

RITA HAYWORTH

Born: October 17, 1918; Brooklyn, New York
Died: May 14, 1987; New York, New York
Area of Achievement: Film
Contribution: A dazzling film star, Hayworth was renowned worldwide as one of the favorite pinup queens of American servicemen during World War II.

Early Life

Rita Hayworth was born Margarita Carmen Cansino in Brooklyn, New York, on October 17, 1918, the first child of Eduardo Cansino, a Spanish-born vaudeville dancer, and Volga Haworth, a showgirl. Although Haworth was herself a dancer with a promising career, her husband preferred to keep together his own successful act, the Dancing Cansinos. In it he and his sister Elisa starred. Volga Cansino gave up all thought of resuming her career when her daughter Margarita was born, to be followed soon by two sons.

Margarita was eight when the family rented a home in New York City and she was finally able to attend school and play with other children. Until then, she had traveled constantly from one theatrical hotel to another while the family was on the road with the Dancing Cansinos. Vaudeville was nearing its end, however, and Cansino moved his family to California in 1927 so that he could try to break into films at the start of the sound era. He never achieved success in films, and in 1931 Cansino revived the Dancing Cansinos. His daughter Margarita, who had been dancing since she was four, became his partner.

Her education again became secondary to the needs of the Dancing Cansinos. Since California law forbade minors from performing in clubs where alcohol was served, the act was booked in offshore gambling ships and in clubs in Tijuana, Mexico, near San Diego. Margarita was exploited in every possible way: She was removed from school and denied any chance of having a normal education and friends her age, was made to perform in nightclubs while she was several years underage, was required to learn how to be sexually alluring onstage, and (according to biographer Barbara Leaming) was forced to have sexual relations with her father.

Two Margarita Cansinos had begun to emerge: a shy, insecure girl who was denied the chance to be a normal teenager, and a sensuous young dancer.

After she had been dancing professionally for about two years, Eduardo Cansino decided that his daughter should have a career in films. She failed her first screen test at the age of fifteen, but in 1934 Fox pictures signed her to a contract. She now served two masters, her father and the studio, which required her to slim down through exercise and dieting, to take dancing, acting, and riding lessons, and to change her name to Rita.

Rita Cansino soon began to find out that a young actress received many offers from older men claiming they could do something for her career. She did begin to pay attention to Edward Judson, a thirty-nine-year-old wheeler-dealer who approached her through her father. As usual, Eduardo Cansino was trying to control his daughter's career and hoped to use Judson's interest in her to his advantage. She, in turn, was willing to use Judson to revive her career (her contract had been dropped when Fox was taken over by Twentieth Century) and to liberate herself from Eduardo Cansino's domination. Judson did succeed in getting Rita small roles as a freelance performer in several minor detective and Western films. Early in 1937, Columbia Pictures put her under contract, and Rita, her career once again on track, married Judson.

Life's Work

Judson, who was living mainly on his wife's income, began to pay even more attention to creating a star. Rita Cansino had to walk as he wanted, take voice and diction lessons, and undergo over a two-year period the painful treatment of electrolysis to alter her eyebrows and her hairline. She also took riding and tennis lessons so that she would be able to behave properly when she met the right people. To see that she did meet such people, Judson squired her to clubs where she could meet Hollywood's power brokers, hired a publicist for her, and apparently even suggested that she offer her sexual favors to the right men.

Columbia officials also had a hand in molding their new property, and to help break with the Latin image she had developed in her early days in films, they changed her name from Rita Cansino to Rita Hayworth. The "y" was added to clarify the pronunciation and to anglicize the name. Ambitious herself, the actress also spent countless hours with makeup and wardrobe specialists to improve her appearance, and she dyed her brown hair auburn.

The actress got her first good role in a major film when she was cast as the other woman in the 1939 adventure *Only Angels Have Wings*, which starred Cary Grant and Jean Arthur. Harry Cohn, the Columbia mogul, now replaced Judson as Hayworth's prime image maker. Cohn wanted her brought along slowly, casting her in good parts in several low-budget films and lending her to other studios such as Warner Bros., for whom she appeared in *The Strawberry Blonde* (1941) with James Cagney and Olivia de Havilland. That same year Hayworth also acted in Twentieth Century-Fox's *Blood and Sand*. Although Linda Darnell had the female lead, Hayworth stole the film with a scene in which she seduced leading man Tyrone Power.

The Columbia publicity specialists then went to work in earnest, sending out innumerable photos and thousands of stories on Hayworth. The buildup achieved its goal when *Life* magazine featured Hayworth in a black lace and white satin negligee on the cover of its August 11, 1941, issue. The photo became one of the popular pinups on the walls of servicemen's quarters during World War II. More than five million copies of it were eventually distributed.

Although she had again played a Latin "femme fatale" in *Blood and Sand*, the Rita Hayworth of 1941 could project another image as well—one more likely to appeal to wartime film audiences. The image was that of a beautiful and desirable woman who was undeniably American. It was this Hayworth that Columbia teamed with dancing great Fred Astaire in *You'll Never Get Rich* (1941), the first of two pictures they did together. Both critics and Astaire praised Hayworth's dancing. Hayworth's own favorite film of this period was *Cover Girl*, a 1944 release in which she danced superbly with costar Gene Kelly. In it she wore contemporary clothing as well as lavish costumes that showcased her beauty. As in her other musicals, Hayworth's songs were dubbed.

Hayworth made news on and off the screen. Her marriage was in trouble, partly because Hayworth was questioning Judson's handling of her income and partly because she and Judson both had other romantic involvements. Hayworth wanted a divorce, and when acrimony and negative publicity threatened to erupt, Columbia attorneys stepped in to end matters as quietly as possible.

On the day the divorce became final in September, 1943, Hayworth married actor Orson Welles, then regarded as a prodigy for his *Citizen Kane*

(1941). Partly because she became pregnant, Hayworth starred in only one film, the musical *Tonight and Every Night* (1945), between her marriage and the end of the war. She did make numerous visits to training camps and military hospitals and did volunteer work at the Hollywood Canteen, where servicemen could relax while on leave. To the studio's relief, the birth of her daughter, Rebecca Welles, late in 1944 did not detract from her image of sensuality.

In 1946, Hayworth had her greatest screen success: *Gilda*. Although the plot was convoluted, the film was a box-office hit that returned Hayworth's screen image to that of temptress. Despite the dress and language codes that then governed the film industry, Hayworth performed a remarkably sensuous dance and uttered such lines as "If I'd have been a ranch they would have called me the Bar Nothing." Her sexual allure was so compelling that *Life* soon did a feature on her in which Hayworth was acclaimed as the "love goddess."

By this time, Hayworth's second marriage was in trouble. Shy and insecure, the actress did not readily fit into Welles's world, which was filled with intellectuals and politicians. Both began drinking, and Welles was openly involved with other women.

The one project they undertook together was *The Lady from Shanghai*, filmed in 1946 but not released for two years. For it, Welles got Hayworth to cut her hair and bleach it blonde, a vivid contrast with the Hayworth that fans had come to know. The film failed at the box office, but critics would later consider it a minor classic. Before the film was even released, Hayworth left Welles, taking their daughter with her.

Soon Hayworth was involved in another affair, became pregnant, and had an abortion. She took pains to keep news of it out of the media. Her next romance was with Prince Aly Khan, heir to one of the largest fortunes in the world. Their affair attracted enormous publicity, much of it negative, since Aly Khan was still legally married and since Hayworth globetrotted with Aly Khan, keeping Rebecca with her. When his divorce became final in 1949, Hayworth and Aly Khan were married. Hayworth and Aly Khan had one daughter, Princess Yasmin Khan, but fatherhood did not keep Aly Khan from becoming involved with other women. The couple divorced in 1951.

Hayworth was still under contract to Columbia, and in 1952 the studio teamed her with Glenn

Rita Hayworth in Gilda.

Ford, her leading man from *Gilda*, in *Affair in Trinidad*. Her first film in four years, it was a hit at the box office. The following year Hayworth starred in *Miss Sadie Thompson*, a role that emphasized her sensuality but required her to portray the character of Sadie as aging and somewhat weary.

Her personal problems continued. Hayworth had numerous affairs and was married twice more, to singer Dick Haymes and to producer James Hill. The marriage to Haymes was especially troubled and also cost Hayworth much of her money, which she squandered on Haymes's unwise film projects and in paying for assorted legal problems.

By the time she played Sadie Thompson, Hayworth had also begun to have the problem that many actresses face: how to cope with aging when their film success had been built on glamour and beauty. Perhaps hoping to put the love goddess image behind her, she apparently handled the transition with grace, becoming more selective of her roles. In 1957, she appeared as a well-to-do older woman in *Pal Joey*, a musical in which Frank Sinatra leaves her for Columbia's youthful new sex object Kim Novak. Hayworth then appeared in *Separate Tables* (1958) and *They Came to Cordura* (1959). In the latter film, a twentieth century Western costarring Gary Cooper, Hayworth did not even wear makeup. A worn, weary look was called for. *Variety* called her performance in that film the best of her career.

Hayworth performed infrequently during the 1960's and had no screen successes. She began to make television appearances and twice was to have been in Broadway shows: *Step on a Crack* in 1962 and, a few years later, *Applause*. The transition to the unfamiliar routines of stage acting, however, caused her great anxiety. Rehearsals became such an ordeal for her that she could not perform in either show.

At the time, no one understood why such an experienced actress had such problems, but even in films—her last film was in 1972—she began to have trouble with her lines. Later evidence indicated that she might have already begun to suffer from Alzheimer's disease, an affliction that can cause sharp mood swings and difficulty in remembering. Consumption of alcohol (which she apparently gave up about ten years before her death) can aggravate these problems. Eventually, the disease robbed her of control over her body functions and of her ability to think. Medical experts had little understanding of the disease until the 1970's and did not diagnose Hayworth's disorder until 1980. During her last years, she was placed under the guardianship of her daughter Yasmin, who used the media attention paid to her mother's plight to raise money for research into the causes and treatment of Alzheimer's disease.

Summary

Rita Hayworth once seemed to have everything—beauty, glamour, and financial success. The height of Hayworth's fame came during and immediately after World War II. Even though she starred in only half a dozen major films prior to *Gilda*, her screen magnetism, her good performances (primarily in musicals), the studio's media blitz, and the needs of servicemen to escape the stress of war through pinups and other reminders of home combined to establish the Hayworth legend.

Perhaps more than any of her film contemporaries—even Lana Turner and Betty Grable, who vied with her in popularity as World War II pinup queens—Hayworth transcended reality to become an icon of popular culture, the "love goddess," an image largely created before the war and fixed by her performance in the otherwise undistinguished film *Gilda*. Her public, however, was unaware that years of work by Hayworth and by professional publicists had preceded the creation of the love goddess figure. As she aged, publicists would no longer labor to create a new image appropriate to a woman in her forties. She would have to make the difficult transition unaided, for by the 1950's the publicity mill was at work trying to create new love goddesses—Kim Novak, Jayne Mansfield, and Marilyn Monroe.

Many of Hayworth's anxieties and problems undoubtedly derived from her childhood experiences and from the early onset of Alzheimer's disease. Hayworth's career also exacted its costs, however, which provides a clear example of the difficulties that can arise from the needs of the American people to have larger-than-life heroes and heroines—in Hayworth's case, the love goddess—and the need of the rare performer who is elevated to this status to have privacy and a life apart from the image.

Bibliography

Brady, Frank. *Citizen Welles: A Biography of Orson Welles*. New York: Scribner, 1989; London: Hodder and Stoughton, 1990. A detailed account of the legendary Welles, Hayworth's second husband and one of the many men who manipulated her career.

Edwards, Anne. "The Goddess and the Playboy." *Vanity Fair* 58, no. 6 (June, 1995). Discussion of Hayworth's affair with and eventual marriage to Ali Khan. Mentions her history of sexual abuse as a child, the effect of the marriage on Khan's status, and Hayworth's marriage to Orson Welles.

Hill, James. *Rita Hayworth: A Memoir*. London: Robson, and New York: Simon and Schuster, 1983. Hill, an acclaimed motion picture producer, married Hayworth in 1958. In writing this memoir of their years together, Hill tries to provide insight into the woman he knew while correcting the public image of the star.

Kobal, John. *Rita Hayworth: The Time, the Place, and the Woman*. London: Allen, 1977; New York: Norton, 1978. Interviews with Hayworth and many of her coworkers give this book special value. One wonders, however, whether the author, who emphasizes her inner strength, was overprotective of Hayworth.

Leaming, Barbara. *If This Was Happiness: A Biography of Rita Hayworth*. New York: Viking Press, and London: Weidenfeld and Nicolson, 1989. The fullest account of Hayworth, this is the first study to say that she was the victim of incest as a child. Also includes many interviews.

McLean, Adrienne L. " 'I'm a Cansino': Transformation, Ethnicity, and Authenticity in the Construction of Rita Hayworth, American Love Goddess." *Journal of Film and Video* 44, no. 3–4 (Fall-Winter, 1992). Examines the transformation of Margarita Carmen Cansino into Hollywood's Hayworth, including her background and the impact of her Latin heritage on her eroticism and popularity.

Morella, Joe, and Edward Z. Epstein. *Rita: The Life of Rita Hayworth*. New York: Delacorte Press, 1983. This brief volume offers nothing new but has many illustrations and a filmography.

Parish, James Robert, and Don E. Stanke. *The Glamour Girls*. New Rochelle, N.Y.: Arlington House, 1975. Hayworth is only one of nine actresses profiled in this book, but the lengthy account of her is valuable for its efforts to assess her career in the context of the studio system. Includes a filmography.

Ringgold, Gene. *The Films of Rita Hayworth: The Legend and Career of a Love Goddess*. Secaucus, N.J.: Citadel Press, 1974. Provides a brief synopsis of each of Hayworth's films, a description of her role in each film, a selection from the reviews, and an abundance of illustrations, many rarely seen.

Stanke, Don E. "Rita Hayworth." *Films in Review* 23 (November, 1972): 527-545. In this valuable overview of Hayworth's career, Stanke shows clearly how a Hollywood legend was created.

Thomas, Bob. *King Cohn: The Life and Times of Harry Cohn*. London: Barrie and Rockliff, and New York: Putnam, 1967. A useful biography of the Columbia Pictures magnate who controlled Hayworth's career during its peak. An index makes it easy to find the material bearing directly on Hayworth.

Vincent, William. "Rita Hayworth at Columbia, 1941-1945: The Fabrication of a Star." In *Columbia Pictures: Portrait of a Studio*, edited by Bernard F. Dick. Lexington: University Press of Kentucky, 1992. A fascinating attempt to show how Hayworth's managers and Columbia Pictures combined to create a sultry star from a young, insecure woman.

Lloyd J. Graybar

WILLIAM RANDOLPH HEARST

Born: April 29, 1863; San Francisco, California
Died: August 14, 1951; Beverly Hills, California
Area of Achievement: Journalism
Contribution: By a paradoxical combination of sensationalism, support for reform, and innovative design, Hearst changed the fashion in which American newspapers reported and influenced the news. He made essential contributions to journalism but clouded these contributions when reporting the news fell second to advancing his own interests.

Early Life

William Randolph Hearst was the only son of George and Phoebe Apperson Hearst and grew up enjoying his mother's total devotion and his father's considerable wealth. Although personally shy, young Hearst had a passion for outlandish pranks; both the shyness and the desire for public sensation were traits he retained throughout his life. Other characteristics were his imperious desire to have his way in all things immediately, a nature that seemed both sentimental and cynical, and a passion for collecting.

George Hearst had come to California during the 1849 gold rush. Enjoying a combination of geologic skill and innate good fortune, he discovered or was a partner in some of the largest mines in the nation, including the Comstock Load (silver) in Colorado and the Anaconda (copper) in Wyoming. From these would flow wealth that seemed inexhaustible—until William Randolph Hearst began to spend it.

George Hearst's enterprises grew to include vast land holdings in California and Mexico; almost his entire attention was on mining, and later, politics; he left young William entirely to his doting mother. Eventually, George Hearst realized his ambition with his election as United States Senator from California. To further his political career, he also acquired a small, struggling newspaper in San Francisco, the *Examiner.*

Young Hearst was given an extensive, if incomplete, education. He was sent east to a boy's school but was asked to leave after two years, probably because of a prank. In 1882, he entered Harvard but was expelled during his junior year for sending his professors silver chamber pots, with their names engraved inside. For a while, he drifted through various jobs, including a stint with Joseph Pulitzer's New York *World.*

Hearst was a tall man—six feet, two inches—and his large frame carried his weight with grace and agility; he was an excellent dancer and often surprised friends and associates with vaudeville steps during conferences or conversations. His eyes were gray, and he had the disconcerting habit of staring unblinkingly. His voice was surprisingly high-pitched and soft; he had himself carefully coached in speaking during his long political career.

Life's Work

As a young man, William Randolph Hearst declined a position with any of his father's mining or ranching operations. In 1887, after several requests, he was given control of the San Francisco *Examiner,* and he immediately began to spend money and attention on the paper. He initiated a series of promotional efforts, joining articles advocating serious reform with those that were wildly sensational. He launched an attack on the powerful Southern Pacific Railroad, the first of many battles he would have with big business and monopolies. Hearst's efforts on behalf of municipal ownership of utilities and other services began with the *Examiner;* in San Francisco, they earned for him the title of "Socialist" among the well-to-do, but circulation of the *Examiner* soared. Hearst would continue this same basic pattern with his newspapers for the remainder of his long career.

In 1891, George Hearst died, leaving all of his money to his widow. Phoebe Hearst would frequently complain about her son's spending, but she continued to provide him with funds. In 1895, she gave him $7.5 million; this was to finance Hearst's attack on New York journalism.

At that time, the New York *World* was the predominant newspaper in the nation's largest city. Purchased by Joseph Pulitzer in 1883, the *World* used sensational techniques: blaring headlines, promotional stunts, and popular crusades had established its large circulation and consolidated its power. The *World* was Hearst's target.

His paper, the *Journal,* lagged far behind. Always impatient, Hearst wanted a huge circulation immediately and was prepared to pay for it. He increased the paper's size, dropped its price, and splashed even larger and more startling headlines on the front page. He began raiding Pulitzer's staff,

attracting them with the lure of higher salaries; at one point, he hired away the entire staff of the Sunday *World*. Pulitzer won them back with a raise, but Hearst topped that offer the next day. This time the staff stayed bought.

Hearst and Pulitzer battled it out daily. The *Journal* coaxed the artist of a popular comic strip, "The Yellow Kid," into leaving the *World*. Pulitzer immediately hired a new artist and continued to run the feature, and so "yellow journalism" was born. Aspects of the practice included a reliance on sensational stories, chiefly involving crime, sex, and political corruption; the growth of comics, pictures, and features at the expense of hard news; crusades for the good of the public, especially against big business; and countless gimmicks, such as contests, fireworks displays, and giveaways.

The most blatant form of yellow journalism was the hysteria the two newspapers whipped up over Cuba. Then a Spanish possession, Cuba had been struggling for independence for years. In 1897, Hearst turned his interest to the revolt, and the *Journal* carried stories about Spanish atrocities and Cuban heroics. The Hearst papers also attacked the United States government in general, and President McKinley in particular, for not taking action. One article by the satirist Ambrose Bierce went so far that it seemed to encourage McKinley's assassination. The main target of the *Journal*, however, was the Spanish presence in Cuba; in effect, Hearst personally had declared war on Spain. He admitted as much when the artist Frederick Remington, sent to Cuba to sketch the revolt, asked to return because the island was quiet. The reply came quickly: "You furnish the pictures and I'll furnish the war."

The destruction of the United States battleship *Maine* in Havana harbor led to the Spanish-American War long sought by Hearst. At the same time, the circulation of the *Journal* rose to more than one million daily. Clearly, yellow journalism had its results.

One result was increased political power for William Randolph Hearst. With the *Journal* the strongest Democratic Party paper in New York, Hearst easily won election to the House of Representatives in 1902. Already he had his eye fixed on the supreme prize, the White House; his newspaper empire expanded, providing him with a power base for the campaign. By 1903, he had seven papers in major cities across the country.

In 1903, he married Millicent Willson, a chorus girl. She was twenty-two, Hearst was forty. Even-

tually there would be five sons born to the Hearsts. Despite this fact, Hearst's detractors, and there were always many, said that the marriage was designed primarily to improve his political image.

His career did advance with furious intensity. In 1904, he was only a first-term congressman, but he mounted a determined effort to win the Democratic presidential nomination. His campaign was surprisingly strong, and the obvious power of his newspapers impressed regulars in the Democratic Party. Still, while they needed the support of the Hearst press, they feared losing control of the party to the publisher, who had clearly shown that he could never be satisfied with less than total dominance. In addition, Hearst had already displayed his lifelong tendency first to embrace, then to denounce politicians.

Hearst easily won reelection to the House in 1904, but the next year, he launched a drive for the office of mayor of New York City. He had fallen out with the powerful Tammany machine and, characteristically, challenged it head-on. Hearst came within three thousand votes of winning the election, and there is strong evidence that he would have won an honest contest. In 1906, Hearst was a candidate once again, this time for the office of governor of New York. Once again, the powerful Hearst press and a liberal platform gave considerable momentum to his candidacy. At the last moment, President Theodore Roosevelt came out against Hearst, reminding voters of the violent attacks against President McKinley before his assassination: Hearst lost.

Hearst would be an official candidate only one more time, in 1909, when he again ran for mayor of New York. His political career, however, was far from finished; it simply moved behind the scenes. The Hearst papers supported a bewildering variety of candidates: Republicans, Democrats, independents, and third-party nominees. Typically, Hearst would support a candidate, then repudiate the man once he was in office for not following the Hearst line. Doubtless, Hearst believed that he could have done the better job had he been chosen by the voters. Until the 1930's, Hearst retained considerable political influence, especially within the Democratic Party. He was pushed aside, however, when he lost a bitter struggle with New York governor Al Smith. Hearst had his revenge in 1932, when he helped swing the Democratic nomination to Franklin Roosevelt; characteristically, he later became one of Roosevelt's most implacable opponents.

The Hearst newspaper empire became one of the largest in the world. At its height, it had twenty-six daily papers, fifteen Sunday papers, seven magazines in the United States and two more in England; all this made Hearst the single largest user of paper in the world. He branched out into radio stations, news services, and newsreels; he also attempted to become a motion-picture mogul.

Part of the reason for his interest in film was Marion Davies (born Douras), an actress whom he met in 1915. At the time, she was eighteen and Hearst was fifty-one. Although Hearst and his wife were never divorced (despite his repeated attempts to do so), Hearst and Marion Davies remained inseparable for the remainder of his long life. He attempted to fashion a brilliant cinema career for her, spending millions on her motion pictures and promoting those films in his many newspapers. While Davies was talented, she was never the star Hearst believed she should be—another example of Hearst wanting something immediately and believing he could grasp it through his money and influence.

Hearst was a fanatic and eclectic collector of art. He spent millions upon paintings, statuary, furniture, and decorations, which remained crated in warehouses, and some of which Hearst himself never saw. He bought an entire medieval Spanish cloister and had it shipped to the United States; it remained in a Bronx warehouse. Other treasures included paintings by the old masters, antique furniture, and entire rooms from Renaissance manor houses. The setting for much of this treasure was the palatial estate of San Simeon, begun in 1919 and never finished. Hearst's massive California castle was a highly personal combination of styles and periods, a baroque mingling that accurately reflected the complicated personality of its owner.

That personality and Hearst's accomplishments were the inspiration for the 1941 film *Citizen Kane*, which marked Orson Welles's Hollywood debut. A brilliant collaborative effort, *Citizen Kane* was a thinly veiled but acutely accurate portrait of Hearst and marked a milestone in American film. Although critically acclaimed, the film was a commercial failure, in part because of pressure from the Hearst papers, including a total advertising ban.

Hearst's empire was weakened by his massive purchases, his lavish expenditures on Davies' pictures, and his newspaper promotional schemes. The onslaught of the Great Depression forced a crisis; unthinkable as it was, Hearst and his corporations were on the verge of bankruptcy. Removed from direct financial control, Hearst watched in agony as stringent economy measures were taken: Radio stations were sold; production of feature films was halted; salaries were cut and employees were fired; worst of all, newspapers were consolidated or closed, including the New York *American*, Hearst's flagship paper. The drastic efforts, joined, ironically enough, with federal spending ordered by President Roosevelt, helped save the Hearst corporations. By 1945, Hearst had maneuvered himself back into control.

His operations were still massive by any standards. At his death, Hearst was in command of sixteen urban newspapers, with a total circulation topping five million. His King Features, which included the most popular comic strips in the world, had fifty-two million readers. There were still the magazines, the International News Service, the radio and television stations.

Hearst attempted to continue guiding his far-flung enterprises himself, but time had caught up with him. Weakened by age and illness, he was forced to leave his beloved San Simeon, still unfinished. He died on August 14, 1951, in Beverly Hills, California.

Summary

Hearst is best known as a journalist, but he was more interested in promoting causes than in presenting the news. His papers were a strange mixture of ideas and sensationalism. In many ways, he was more of a publicist and showman than a newspaperman.

His crusades could be noble: He fought for municipal ownership of utilities long before that concept was popular; he supported the rights of workers when labor unions were not yet powerful; and he opposed American entry into World War I, even though it brought him infamy as a pro-German "traitor."

On the other hand, his papers could preach cheap sentiment and sometimes violent hatred. He was a primary cause of the Spanish-American War; his papers attacked politicians with a vehemence that went beyond public issues and into their private lives; as he grew older, he turned against organized labor and the liberal causes of his youth. Above all, the Hearst press was notorious for its love of sensation and disregard for fact.

Hearst was a paradox, an enigma. Although he literally bought many of his staff from other papers, most of them remained loyal to him throughout their careers. Personally, he was a kind, shy man, capable of great generosity; publicly, he inspired mistrust, dislike, and downright hatred. Indisputably, he was one of the greatest press lords in history, but whether for good or ill is a question that continues to be debated.

Bibliography

Carlson, Oliver, and Ernest Sutherland Bates. *Hearst, Lord of San Simeon.* New York: Viking Press, 1936. Didactic psychological approach to Hearst, portraying all of his activities as the result of acute megalomania and lifelong immaturity. Distinctly unfavorable to its subject.

Chaney, Lindsay, and Michael Ciepley. *The Hearsts: Family and Empire.* New York: Simon and Schuster, 1981. Brief but helpful summary of life and career of William Randolph Hearst; major concentration is on the fortunes of the Hearst family business dealings since the death of the founder.

Coblentz, Edmond D., ed. *Newsmen Speak: Journalists on Their Craft.* Berkeley: University of California Press, 1954. Contains several illuminating passages from Hearst on what journalists do and how newspapers should be run. One memorable line: "I think promotion is absolutely essential to success."

Hearst, William Randolph. *William Randolph Hearst: A Portrait in His Own Words.* Edited by Edmond D. Coblentz. New York: Simon and Schuster, 1952. A collection of Hearst's writings on various topics, personal and public, brought together by one of his chief lieutenants and editor of the New York *American.*

Neuzil, Mark. "Hearst, Roosevelt, and the Muckraker Speech of 1906: A New Perspective." *Journalism and Mass Communication Quarterly* 73, no. 1 (Spring, 1996). Focuses on the battle between Hearst and Theodore Roosevelt. Discusses Roosevelt's "muckraker" speech of 1906, its political impact on Hearst, and its more wide-ranging effect on all such journalism.

Procter, Ben. *William Randolph Hearst: The Early Years, 1863–1910.* New York: Oxford University Press, 1998. The most accurate and authoritative of the biographies of Hearst's early years. Adds information on the power and innovation of Hearst's papers to the usual accounts of "yellow journalism."

Swanberg, W. A. *Citizen Hearst.* New York: Scribner, 1961; London: Longman, 1962. Still the best biography of Hearst, a well-researched, in-depth, and generally fair presentation of a difficult, enigmatic character. Strong on information from Hearst's contemporaries.

———. *Pulitzer.* New York: Scribner, 1967. Several good chapters on the relationship between Hearst and Pulitzer and their influence on each other. Especially interesting for the circulation war between the *World* and the *Morning Journal.*

Tebbel, John. *The Life and Good Times of William Randolph Hearst.* New York: Dutton, 1952; London: Gollancz, 1953. Brisk general biography of Hearst.

Michael Witkoski

EDWARD HEATH

Born: July 9, 1916; Broadstairs, Kent, England

Areas of Achievement: Government and politics

Contribution: Rising through the ranks of the Conservative Party to become Prime Minister of Great Britain, Health led his country into partnership with Europe by achieving British admission to the European Economic Community.

Early Life

In 1965, Edward Health was elected Leader of the Conservative Party, the youngest to be so since the days of Benjamin Disraeli. Five years later, upon becoming prime minister, he achieved his ultimate ambition. In a sense Heath's life has been a preparation for high office. At every turn—at university, in the civil service, in journalism and banking—he has readied himself to lead the political nation. Careful preparation has always been his forte, and this characteristic helped to carry Heath to 10, Downing Street. Once there, though, he experienced difficulties which forced him from office in less than four years. So much time and so much effort were devoted to acquiring power; so little time was permitted to exercising it. This is the irony of the professional life of Edward Heath.

Heath was born at Broadstairs in Kent in 1916, the first of two sons. Heath's forebears, originally from the West Country, had moved to Kent at the beginning of the nineteenth century. Heath's grandfather was first a dairyman, then a porter. Heath's father, a carpenter by trade, eventually acquired his own business as a local builder. At Broadstairs, Edward attended a free primary school and later, at age ten, won a scholarship to Chatham House, the area's leading grammar school. Heath was a good student, though not exceptional. His reputation was based primarily on serious-mindedness and hard work. Indeed, in his final year Heath received Chatham House's most prestigious prize, awarded, interestingly, for personal character.

In 1935, Heath was admitted to Balliol College, Oxford, where he read philosophy, politics, and economics. Above average height, Heath was a handsome young man whose sensitive eyes revealed intelligence and alertness. Once at Balliol, he won in open competition the Balliol organ scholarship and was soon active in university concerts and dramatic productions. Love of music notwithstanding, Heath's passion was politics. Al-

ready he was a self-proclaimed Tory. It was not long before he became a significant figure in college politics. Eventually, he was elected president of the junior common room at a time when Balliol boasted some of Oxford's brightest political stars. He also joined the Oxford Union, distinguished himself in debate, and made a name for himself by backing an anti-Chamberlain, antiappeasement foreign policy.

Academically Heath performed respectably, but only a notch above average. He took a solid second-class degree, more a sign of industry than of brilliance. Unlike many students, though, Heath seemed to know precisely what he wanted out of Oxford. These were exciting times in Europe for a student of politics. Heath visited troubled Spain, and during one summer vacation he lived in Germany as an exchange student. There he witnessed for three days Adolf Hitler and the Nazi demonstrations at Nuremberg, an experience which strengthened his opposition to totalitarianism. In his final year, Heath achieved his crowning glory at Oxford, the office of President of the Union, which afforded him administrative experience and knowledge of how to handle others. At Oxford, Heath was neither particularly popular nor was he a sportsman, an important part of Oxford life. Yet he was politically successful and, what is more, a person of consequence.

Life's Work

After serving as an army officer during World War II, Heath returned home eager to prepare himself for a political career. He passed the civil service exam and spent a year at the Ministry of Aviation. For two years he worked as a church journalist, after which he trained for another year in the City, learning the intricacies of merchant banking.

In 1947, the Conservative Association at Bexley, Kent, selected Heath as its candidate; Heath was pleased. Since Bexley was near his hometown, he would be viewed as a local boy. Further, Bexley was composed largely of white-collar workers, many of whom owned property. Heath's belief that the Conservatives could unseat Labour was confirmed in February, 1950, when he defeated the incumbent, Ashley Bramall, a contemporary of Heath at Oxford, by a slender margin of 133 votes.

By February of the next year, Heath had been selected as an Assistant Whip at a time when Clement Attlee's Labour government was on the verge of collapse. A new election in October, 1952, resulted in both a Conservative victory under Winston Churchill and an increase in Heath's majority at Bexley. Churchill made Heath a member of government, a Lord Commissioner of the Treasury. From this junior position, Heath rose steadily to become Leader of the Party and would not return to the back-benches again for another twenty-two years.

Sir Anthony Eden replaced the aging Churchill in 1955, and Eden appointed Heath Chief Whip. Here Heath became known as a thorough organizer with a taste for administrative detail. As Chief Whip, more so than if he had been a cabinet member, Heath enjoyed personal contact with every Tory Member of Parliament.

Eden's early resignation, owing to the Suez debacle, cleared the way for a happier period for Conservatives. Under the leadership of Harold Macmillan, Heath's position improved as well. He became Macmillan's confidant, meeting with the prime minister each weekday. His office at 12, Downing Street was connected to that of Macmillan's by a passage. Over the next seven years, Heath's loyalty and competence were rewarded with promotion. His appointments included Minister of Labour, Lord Privy Seal, Secretary of State for Industry, Trade and Regional Development, and President of the Board of Trade. During these years, he distinguished himself, especially when, in 1964, Heath, against opposition within his own party, abolished resale price maintenance, by which manufacturers fixed the prices of their goods. Heath believed that this practice stifled competition and thus undermined a free market. Economics aside, Heath's battle to pass his Resale Prices Act was viewed, not least of all by himself, as a test of his prime-ministerial ability. It was a test Heath was determined to pass.

Macmillan's retirement in 1963 created uncertainty within the party at a time when Labour was becoming more assertive and confident under Harold Wilson's leadership. In 1964, Wilson sent the Conservatives to defeat. Tory partisans felt the need for a vigorous leader who could match Wilson. Macmillan's aristocratic successor, Lord Home, stepped down under pressure. Heath, with characteristic efficiency, mounted a determined campaign which led to a slender victory over his nearest rival, Reginald Maudling, a former Chancellor of the Exchequer.

Upon his accession as Tory leader, Heath set about revitalizing the party. Despite a chilling Labour victory in 1966, Heath pressed forward, creating a specialized Shadow Cabinet and encouraging more than thirty study groups to formulate policy. At the Selsdon Park Hotel conference in 1970, Heath summarized his philosophy: belief in the European Economic Community, incentives for industry, legislation on industrial relations, and reduction of taxation. In 1970, lagging far behind in the polls, the Conservatives won the general election, surprising the pollsters, Wilson, and perhaps Heath himself.

Heath served as prime minister for nearly four years, during which time the country struggled with severe social and economic problems. Entry into the European Economic Community took place early in 1973. At home, though, industrial disputes threatened the government. When the coal miners went on strike for more pay, Heath was forced to return to the statutory incomes policy of Wilson's Labour government. This reversal, the famous "U-turn," made him vulnerable to criticism from all sides.

By October, 1973, against the backdrop of the Arab-Israeli War and rising oil prices, the miners' demands resulted in another strike. This time Heath went to the country. In 1974, he was defeated. Wilson seized the initiative later in the year by calling another election in order to increase his majority. Heath struggled to survive politically by calling for a coalition, a government of national unity, to combat the national emergency facing Great Britain. This was a risky, desperate maneuver, and one which, in the end, failed badly.

Wilson's victory in October, 1974, returned Labour to power for nearly the rest of the decade, and it removed Edward Heath from power for the remainder of his career. By February of the following year, an election for leadership of the party was held in which Heath finished second, eleven votes behind Margaret Thatcher, a woman he had never considered seriously as a rival.

Summary

There have been several Conservative prime ministers who have not come from the privileged orders of British society—Robert Peel, Andrew Bonar Law, and Stanley Baldwin come to mind. Yet the rise to power of Edward Heath does seem something of a turning point as the Conservative Party approaches the twenty-first century. For nearly a quarter of a century, Conservatives have been led by a man and a woman whose backgrounds are similar, each well educated, industrious, and ambitious. Both come from self-employed, property-owning families; Heath's father owned his own business; Thatcher's father was an independent grocer. Both Heath and Thatcher were the first leaders of the party to be elected by Tory Members of Parliament. Heretofore, leaders emerged mysteriously from what has been called the "magic circle." It will be interesting to see if this "democratization" of the party continues.

Heath's politics of consensus—as evidenced by his "U-turn" and his strategy for "national unity"—has been superseded by Thatcher's more uncompromising version of conservatism. This has been difficult for him to accept, and for years Heath refused to concede defeat. Heath has never been a popular statesman, even during his most successful years. A disdainful attitude toward his successor has done little to enhance his reputation among many of the party's faithful.

Still, Edward Heath's single-minded pursuit of British entry to the European Economic Community remains a great achievement. From the outset of his career, Heath has been a committed European. Europe fires his imagination. Great Britain's future, he believes, lies with Europe. Once a great island power, Great Britain now must reach outwardly. In a changing world, Great Britain must think in Continental terms. In this way she will find a new role and new meaning; of this he is convinced. The wisdom of Great Britain's marriage to Europe is the final question on which Edward Heath is to be judged.

Bibliography

Ball, Stuart, and Anthony Seldon. *The Heath Government 1970–1974: A Reappraisal.* London and New York: Longman, 1996. The authors examine the Heath government's goals and achievements in all areas including immigration, social reform, the economy, and more. Based on analysis of the archives of the Conservative Party and the TUC, and interviews with high-ranking government officials.

Buckley, William F. "There'll Always Be an England." *National Review* 39 (March 27, 1987): 63. An interesting assessment of the contest for Chancellor of Oxford in which Heath is a candidate.

Campbell, John. *Edward Heath: A Biography.* London: Cape, 1993. Extensive biography, highlighting Heath's personality and many talents.

Gale, George. "The Private Anger of Edward Heath." *New Statesman*, October 11, 1974: 494-496. An analysis of Heath's leadership on the eve of the October, 1974, election.

Heath, Edward. *Old World, New Horizons.* London: Oxford University Press, and Cambridge, Mass.: Harvard University Press, 1970. An important book by Heath in which he discusses the political situation in Europe prior to Great Britain's entry into the European Economic Community. It also conveys his enthusiasm for British participation in the Community.

Hutchinson, George. *A Personal and Political Biography.* London: Longman, 1970. A colorful account of Heath's early life and rise to power in the Conservative Party, although it stops short of his actual victory in 1970.

Iremonger, Lucille. "Edward Heath." In *British Prime Ministers in the Twentieth Century*, edited by John P. Mackintosh, vol 2. London: Weidenfeld and Nicolson, and New York: St. Martin's Press, 1977. An assessment of Heath's record as prime minister, his policies, and his personality. Generally balanced and very useful.

Johnson, Paul. "Harold Wilson's Best Friend." *New Statesman*, October 3, 1975: 395-396. This article is an investigation into Heath's motivations a year following his final defeat by Wilson. It is an interesting piece which sheds light on divisions within the Conservative Party.

Laing, Margaret. *Edward Heath: Prime Minister.* London: Sidgwick and Jackson, and New York: Third Press, 1972. Laing's approach is chronological; she provides a critical analysis of Heath's career and concentrates on Heath's rise to power rather than his administration.

William M. Welch, Jr.

MARTIN HEIDEGGER

Born: September 26, 1889; Messkirch, Germany
Died: May 26, 1976; Messkirch, West Germany
Area of Achievement: Philosophy
Contribution: Though within the Continental tradition of philosophy known as existentialism,
Heidegger strove to free philosophy from what
he claimed were its millennia-old metaphysical
shackles. Using complex and arcane terminology, he sought to penetrate the nature of the confrontation of the human being with being itself
and to clear a way for the answer to the age-old
question of why there is something rather than
nothing.

Early Life

Martin Heidegger was the son of Friedrich Heidegger, a Catholic sexton at Messkirch, a small village
in the Black Forest region of southwestern Germany, and Johanna (Kempf) Heidegger. Martin, the
elder of the couple's two sons, attended public
school in Messkirch and then entered the *Gymnasium* at Constance, with an intention to study for the
Jesuit priesthood. In 1909, after three years of
study at the *Gymnasium* at Freiburg, he entered the
University of Freiburg. Unable to pursue the priesthood because of poor health, Heidegger's study of
Christian theology and medieval philosophy—after
courses in physics and mathematics—drew him toward a lifelong devotion to philosophy.

Heidegger's doctoral dissertation in 1913, *Die
Lehre vom Urteil im Psychologismus* (the doctrine
of judgment in psychologism), published the next
year, took issue with the kind of simplistic reduc-
tionism that would collapse speculative philosophy
into mere psychology. Heidegger acknowledged
the influence of Edmund Husserl, the father of phenomenology, who called for the critical examination of the phenomena of consciousness on their
own terms. Heidegger continued his studies even
after the outbreak of World War I in 1914, his poor
health leading to a quick discharge from military
service.

By 1916, a second book-length work, on the
doctrine of categories of the medieval Scholastic
philosopher John Duns Scotus, enabled Heidegger
to teach philosophy at Freiburg as a privatdocent
(an unsalaried lecturer paid out of students' fees).
Elfriede Petri became Heidegger's wife in 1917;
the couple had two sons, Jörg and Hermann.

In 1916, Husserl went to Freiburg, and by 1920
Heidegger had become his assistant, though
Heidegger began to be uncomfortable with the
kind of analysis of the "things" of consciousness
promoted by Husserl. Heidegger believed that the
ancient Greeks, especially the pre-Socratics, had
had an experience of being itself—that is, the "is-
ness" of all things—something Husserl's epistemology, or theory of knowledge, merely obscured.

From 1923 until 1928, when he returned to
Freiburg to succeed Husserl in the chair of philosophy, Heidegger taught as an associate professor at
Marburg, where he was exposed to influences to
which he would owe much in the shaping of his
ontology (or theory of being). A new friendship
with the theologian Rudolf Bultmann introduced
Heidegger to the work of another theological writer, Karl Barth. That opened the way to a study of
Martin Luther and existentialist Søren Kierkegaard. It was at Marburg that Heidegger published
the first volume of his masterpiece, *Sein und Zeit*
(1927; *Being and Time*, 1962).

Life's Work

Being and Time was Heidegger's attempt to start
philosophy over again, to return to the pre-Socratic
insights into being lost with the advent of the rationalistic metaphysics of Plato. Heidegger was convinced that the pre-Socratics—true "thinkers" such
as Parmenides and Heracleitus—had stood astonished before the presence of being: that which was
manifested in all the actually existing beings of the
universe. For Heidegger, authentic human being
was an openness to exactly this same astonishment, obscured by centuries of forgetfulness of being, of neglect of the most important question:
Why is there something rather than nothing? By
an extraordinary etymological analysis of the pre-
Socratics, Heidegger detected evidence of this primordial awareness of being. Heracleitus said "One
is all" (*panta ta onta*), and for Heidegger this was
precisely the insight that "all being is in Being."

The questioning of being is Heidegger's task in
Being and Time. This questioning is what gives humanity to man, who in his human being is a "being-in-the-world" (*In-der-Welt-Sein*), a finite creature bounded by death. Time and being are
inextricably linked, contrary to Western metaphysical thought, which had attempted to ground its theories in some notion of the eternal. Human being

(Heidegger's *Dasein*) is open to its "thrownness" into the world with no reference except to that of "no-thing-ness," or death. Yet *Dasein* often fails to respond to its being-in-the-world and instead, says Heidegger, becomes an alienated "they," mass man, with the incessant chatter of words drowning out the speech through which being expresses itself. *Dasein* does not listen. Only with the experience of an existential angst, or dread—the realization that one's being-in-the-world is an open question—can the voice of being be heard once again.

There is no easy way to achieve authenticity in one's human being, for one's very existence means being-with-others and a falling away from true self-possession. Yet the uncanny feeling of homelessness in the world, elicited by one's angst, serves to shatter complacency and allow the human being to see that his authenticity must come in the caring for being, in the answering to being. This insight allows Heidegger to commend, in his later writings, those who care for the earth by working with it, and to condemn the technological rapacity of both the Soviet Union and the United States. *Dasein* is a being-toward-death, and this future inevitability must mark how man perceives his past as well as his present. It must be the same for whole peoples: History is a working out or working with the destiny that will come to all. It is here that *Being and Time* abruptly ends.

Despite the book's convoluted German coinages and abstract analysis, Heidegger's fame grew. Returning to Freiburg in 1928, he replaced Husserl at the elder philosopher's retirement; Heidegger's inaugural address, published as *Was ist Metaphysik?* (1929; "What Is Metaphysics?" 1949), represents, in the estimation of some scholars, a *Kehre* (or turning) from the thought expressed in his magnum opus. He sought not to repudiate his central insights into being, but to deemphasize the anthropocentrism of his work, in which the truth of being "uncovers" itself through *Dasein*; the truth comes not by way of man but by language itself.

On May 27, 1933, Heidegger gave another inaugural address, this time as the newly elected rector of the university. Entitled *Die Selbstbehauptung der deutschen Universität* (published in 1934; the self-determination of the German university), it affirmed the autonomy of the university (in the face of National Socialist pressure, as Heidegger later maintained) and the *Führerprinzip* by which Heidegger would take control of the school, by-

passing its senate. In the speech, Heidegger glorified the historical mission of the German people, though he was not clear on the exact nature of that mission. Regardless, the rector must guide students and teachers alike into the "spiritual mission of the *Volk*," the destiny of the German people. Elsewhere, Heidegger was not so ambiguous; on November 3, 1933, he told students that "the Führer alone is the present and future German reality and its law."

Heidegger had joined the Nazi Party, reluctantly or not, but he apparently never resigned. He did resign the rectorate in 1934, disillusioned with the grand promise of National Socialism—not the "inner truth and greatness of the National Socialist movement" but with the "works that are being peddled about nowadays as the philosophy of National Socialism." Heidegger had appeared at official Nazi functions wearing National Socialist insignia and as rector had secretly denounced several colleagues and students as having unsuitable philosophy. In November, 1944, with the end of the war approaching, Heidegger ended his lectures at the university; the next year, the Freiburg denazification committee issued its report on Heidegger, charging him with holding significant Nazi office and of Nazi propaganda, with introducing the *Führerprinzip*, and with inciting students against certain professors. Heidegger's health broke in 1946, and he spent three weeks at a sanatorium. The denazification hearings dragged on into 1949, when Heidegger was declared a Nazi "fellow traveler" and forbidden to teach until 1951; subsequently, he participated in periodic university seminars and continued to speak elsewhere, especially in France.

During the war years, Heidegger had taught several courses on Friedrich Wilhelm Nietzsche, who had also called for the death of Western metaphysics; yet Heidegger contended that Nietzsche's "will to power" was merely the culmination of Western metaphysical nihilism and not its overcoming. Power was a manifestation of all that was wrong in European civilization—the need to exert human will over the forces of nature, to bend and shape nature into human design. The conception of truth, that of a correspondence between statements and states of affairs, encouraged this imposition of man's will upon the world, shaping it to "correspond" with what his power willed. Heidegger returned to the early Greeks for his understanding of truth. Man does not pursue truth, truth pursues man and opens itself up to him. *Dasein* must be open to the truth; man must be a mediator, not a calculator. The survival of civilization depended on it.

In his *Über den Humanismus* (1947; *Letter on Humanism*, 1962), Heidegger disdained any affinity with French existentialist Jean-Paul Sartre, though Sartre himself was much influenced by Heidegger. Sartre's form of humanism, as all humanisms, only recast man's relation to other beings, not to being itself; Sartre's dictum that existence precedes essence was still a metaphysical construct. Such "language under the dominance of the modern metaphysics of subjectivity . . . still denies us its essence: that it is the house of the truth of Being." In *Being and Time*, Heidegger had spoken of the resoluteness to choose authenticity in order to encounter being; now he said the guardianship of being lay in language, and in the greatest poets of the language. True thinking was an openness to being as it disclosed itself to and in man. Man was the trustee, or shepherd, of being; his must be an active readiness to receive the disclosure. Great art, especially poetry, brought Being to man in a way that no metaphysical construct, concerned as it is with beings, could do. Great art was no mere imitation of something eternal; it housed being, as all human creations should. Technology, said Heidegger, alienated man from nature, and in turn nature alienated man from being.

Heidegger was enamored of the countryside, turning down opportunities in the 1930's of a professorship in Berlin to remain near the Black Forest and his ski hut above Todtnauberg near Freiburg. In his later years, the stocky Heidegger, with piercing eyes, mustache, and thinning hair, often affected the garb of a Swabian peasant for his ascetic and contemplative life.

Summary

Martin Heidegger exerted a profound influence on the development of existentialism, especially through Jean-Paul Sartre. Additionally, his reflections on language and the way in which it disclosed the truth of being were central to the French deconstruction movement, notably to Jacques Derrida. Theologians such as Bultmann have been deeply influenced by Heidegger's ambiguous depiction of man's fallenness "into the world." The hermeneutic movement, associated with former student Hans-Georg Gadamer, built on Heidegger's work in textual criticism; psychoanalysis, especially the schools of existentialist therapy and phenomenological psychology, also benefited from Heidegger. In philosophy, the Marxists warmed to Heidegger's critique of technology, and Ludwig Wittgenstein's analysis of language showed some affinity with that of Heidegger.

Heidegger's thought has been praised as offering a revolutionary way back to being and has been excoriated as obscurantist and almost meaningless, based on fanciful etymological interpretations. Above all, in the years since his death both friends and foes of Heidegger have wrestled with the fact that, whatever the quality of his thought, he was also a Nazi. Some have seen an organic connection between Heidegger's thought and National Socialism in Heidegger's sense of German destiny and narrow nationalism; others have excused him as one among many who were caught up in Hitlerism. Most vexing of all was Heidegger's determined silence about the Holocaust; despite his critique of the perversions of technology, he refused to make any public statement about the death camps. Heidegger's lifelong questioning of being would endure to challenge future philosophers; some of the "answers" he chose to endorse would endure as a warning.

Bibliography

Biemel, Walter. *Martin Heidegger: An Illustrated Study*. Translated by J. L. Mehta. New York: Harcourt Brace, 1976; London: Routledge, 1977. Biemel, a student under Heidegger, elucidates Heidegger's concern for being and truth in an accessible analysis of seven works, including *Being and Time*. Dozens of black-and-white photographs of Heidegger and his contemporaries, a five-page chronology, and a twenty-page bibliography (including English translations and important secondary works) contribute to this essential introduction to Heidegger's thought.

Coltman, Rodney. *The Language of Hermeneutics: Gadamer and Heidegger in Dialogue*. Albany: State University of New York Press, 1998. The first study in English of the relationship between Gadamer and Heidegger, based on analysis of their readings of Plato, Aristotle, Holderlin, and Hegel.

Derrida, Jacques. *Of Spirit: Heidegger and the Question*. Translated by Geoffrey Bennington and Rachel Bowlby. Chicago: University of Chicago Press, 1989. "The question" is that of Heidegger and Nazism, and in this slim volume

Derrida seeks to distinguish Heidegger the philosopher from Heidegger the man yet caught up in the false humanisms of the world. Derrida's work, though burdened with deconstructionist rhetoric, is a compassionate attempt at a (partial) explanation.

Farías, Victor. *Heidegger and Nazism.* Edited, with a foreword, by Joseph Margolis and Tom Rockmore. Translated by Paul Burrell and Gabriel R. Ricci. Philadelphia: Temple University Press, 1989. An indictment of Heidegger's philosophy through a study of Heidegger the man. Farías, a Chilean who studied under Heidegger, claims Heidegger's involvement in Nazism was both more extensive and more consistent with his philosophy than previously acknowledged.

Heidegger, Martin. *Basic Writings.* Edited by David Farrell Krell. Rev. ed. London: Routledge, and San Francisco, Calif.: Harper, 1993. Krell provides a generally sympathetic introduction to Heidegger's life and philosophical concerns, as well as concise introductions to each of nine key essays by Heidegger along with Heidegger's own introduction to *Being and Time.* A three-page bibliography lists other of Heidegger's works in English.

Naess, Arne. *Four Modern Philosophers: Carnap, Wittgenstein, Heidegger, Sartre.* Translated by Alastair Hannay. Chicago: University of Chicago Press, 1968. A lucid presentation of the facts of Heidegger's life and the essence of his philosophy. A brief bibliography of Heidegger's major works in German is included in this accessible semitechnical study.

Steiner, George. *Martin Heidegger.* New York: Viking Press, 1978; London: Penguin, 1980. Intended for the general reader, Steiner's short work, published soon after Heidegger's death, intertwines a short biography of the philosopher and an exposition of *Being and Time,* with a nod toward Heidegger's later works. Clarifies the central themes of Heidegger's philosophy. A brief chronology of Heidegger's life, a short bibliography of English titles, and an extensive index supplement a helpful text.

Young, Julian. *Heidegger, Philosophy, Nazism.* Cambridge and New York: Cambridge University Press, 1997. Examines Heidegger's involvement with Nazism and argues that this political involvement does not alter his philosophy or commitment to liberal democracy.

Dan Barnett

ERNST HEINRICH HEINKEL

Born: January 24, 1888; Grünbach, Germany
Died: January 30, 1958; Stuttgart, West Germany
Area of Achievement: Aeronautics
Contribution: Heinkel was a major figure in the development of European military and commercial aviation in the first half of the twentieth century, noted for advanced designs and the first practical jet- and rocket-propelled aircraft.

Early Life

Ernst Heinkel was the son of the local plumber in the small south German town of Grünbach. As a child he showed a disposition toward mechanical pursuits. In 1907, Heinkel enrolled in the engineering program at the Technische Hochshule in Stuttgart, from which institution he eventually received several advanced degrees.

Heinkel shared with many in his generation a fascination for the achievements of early aviation. Shortly after he began studies at the Technische Hochshule, Heinkel witnessed one of the tragic incidents of that era when lightning struck a Zeppelin lighter-than-air dirigible, then regarded as the epitome of aviation technology, turning the hydrogen-filled balloon into a deadly inferno. For Heinkel, the explosion was a turning point: He became convinced that the future of aviation lay with heavier-than-air craft. The rest of his education, and his career, would be devoted to perfecting that technology.

Heinkel's early experiments were less than successful. The prototype of his first aircraft design, patterned closely after the styles used by Wilbur and Orville Wright, crashed on its first test flight in 1910. During the succeeding year, however, several of his designs proved themselves in the air. Heinkel, like many European aviation pioneers, was deeply interested in developing aircraft that could take off from water rather than land, and several of his early models were so designed. His efforts attracted the financial support of Jacques Schneider, a Swiss industrialist, who enabled Heinkel to form his first modest aircraft company. Heinkel's experiments culminated in 1913 in construction of the *Albatross*, a monoplane with advanced fuselage and wing design.

Life's Work

In 1914, shortly before the start of World War I, Heinkel received an offer to become technical director of the Hansa Aircraft Company. A few months later, he was invited to head the important Brandenburgischer Flugzeugwerke, which had just been purchased by a consortium led by Camillo Castiglioni, an Austrian millionaire and aviation enthusiast. In this favorable environment, Heinkel produced hundreds of aircraft designs for the war effort. The light Brandenburg reconnaissance plane, soon to be armed with machine guns, became the scourge of the English Channel for the first two years of World War I. By the end of the conflict, Heinkel had established himself among a tiny handful of leading aircraft developers in Europe.

His career, however, fell upon hard times after the war. International treaties severely limited the size and flexibility of the German military aircraft industry, and serious commerical aviation was still in its infancy. Anticipating these conditions, Castiglioni closed the Brandenburgischer Flugzeugwerke and dismissed the employees. Heinkel had to find work as a mechanic and automobile salesman until he could raise the funds to start a new aircraft company on his own.

Heinkel's fortunes revived quickly as other governments sought his advice. In 1921, he signed contracts to design and build seaplanes for the navies of Sweden and the United States, a specialty for which he already had an international reputation. In December, 1922, Heinkel realized a lifelong dream by founding his own company, the Ernst Heinkel Flugzeugwerke, located at Warnemünde, near the northern coast of Germany. The firm was immediately successful in landing contracts from the Japanese air force. Throughout the 1920's, the Heinkel firm supplied seaplanes and other aircraft to more than a dozen governments as well as many private companies throughout the world.

With his aircraft company financially secure, Heinkel returned in the mid-1920's to his first love: experimental design. It was in this capacity that he revealed himself as a genius of aeronautics. In 1925, his company produced the prototype of the stunning He-70, a revolutionary, four-passenger transport that was nothing less than a leap into the future. The He-70 featured the streamlined, solid fuselage and large, elliptical forward wings that would become standard aircraft design for decades. The He-70 could reach air speeds of 355 kilometers per hour, nearly triple the average speed of World War I aircraft.

During the 1920's, Heinkel also pioneered the technique of launching aircraft by steam catapult, all the while continuing the development of award-winning seaplane designs. In 1929, with aid and encouragement from Lufthansa and German steamship lines, he combined seaplanes and catapults to create an international air mail service long before the appearance of aircraft with transatlantic range. In one version of his method, steamships making the Atlantic crossing catapulted small mail planes into the air while still hundreds of miles from land, thus reducing the delivery time for overseas mail by several hours at each end of the crossing. Later, seaplanes launched many hours after the departure of transatlantic liners were used to catch up with the ships and deliver late mail.

By 1931, Lufthansa, using Heinkel seaplanes, developed all-aircraft international mail routes from Germany to the United States and Latin America. Small ships placed at regular points along the transatlantic routes served as fuel tenders and way stations. The seaplanes carrying the mail flew to each tender and landed on the water, were winched aboard, refueled, and then launched by catapult to the next ship hundreds of miles away. It was a kind of oceanic Pony Express, capable of delivering mail across the Atlantic in less than one third of the time required by the fastest steamship.

The ambitious military expansion program of the German government in the mid-1930's transformed priorities in the Heinkel Flugzeugwerke, by now one of the largest aircraft plants in Europe. It quickly provided the highly successful He-111, an upgraded, much-enlarged version of the standard-setting He-70. The twin-engined He-111 was a versatile design easily converted into a commercial airliner, military transport, or bomber. In the latter guise, it appeared in the Spanish Civil War in 1936, helping decide the outcome on behalf of the German-supported Loyalists.

In 1935, Heinkel met Wernher von Braun, a brilliant aeronautical engineer obsessed with the possibilities of rocket-powered flight. Heinkel already had sensed that the technology of propeller-driven aircraft, using reciprocating piston engines, was approaching its theoretical performance limits, and that revolutionary thinking about new power plants and methods of propulsion was necessary for the industry to advance. He and von Braun began a fruitful collaboration. Heinkel specialized in pro-

pulsion design while von Braun developed aircraft structure. By 1937, their tests demonstrated the feasibility of power flight without propellers.

The following year, Heinkel and von Braun established themselves at a new test site at Peenemünde, on the Baltic Sea, destined to be the birthplace of future German military rocket programs. In June, 1939, they tested the world's first successful rocket plane, the He-176, which reached the then astonishing speed of 800 kilometers per hour. By the end of 1939, Heinkel and von Braun also had tested their first turbojet aircraft, the He-178, as well as ramjet vehicles of the sort that later would be developed as the V-1 "buzz bomb" used against London and other British cities.

The outbreak of World War II in September, 1939, was, for Heinkel, the beginning of a period of irony and frustration. Materially the contributions of the Heinkel Flugzeugwerke to the German war effort were enormous. Thousands of He-111's rolled off the assembly lines, together with huge numbers of the highly successful He-162 "Volksjager" fighter-bombers. Yet these were perfected aircraft; the promising work with von Braun, which might have resulted in timely technological innovations crucial to the war effort, encountered only political roadblocks. While Heinkel awaited government support, his competitor and bitter rival, Willy Messerschmitt, developed practical ramjet and turbojet power plants and by 1942 brought them into production.

From the beginning, Heinkel had difficulty convincing the German general staff of the potential of rocket planes and jet aircraft. In July, 1939, he demonstrated the He-176 rocket plane to an official audience, including Adolf Hitler, Hermann Göring, and a host of high-ranking officers. The plane performed flawlessly; the pilot even buzzed the onlookers at near-supersonic speed. Strangely, Hitler was unimpressed; he left the demonstration without a word. Göring, despite being in charge of the Luftwaffe, only expressed concern for the safety of the pilot. At a later demonstration of the He-178 turbojet, Göring displayed no interest whatsoever. When the government finally did turn to Heinkel, he embarked on a crash program resulting in the first production-line jet fighter, the He-280. It was, however, too little, too late. Only a few could be produced before Germany surrendered in April, 1945.

Administrative obstinacy—no doubt combined with the success of Messerschmitt—drove Heinkel into a position of outspoken criticism for Luftwaffe leadership in the waning months of World War II, which served only to remove him further from official favor. In 1944, Heinkel casually associated with the anti-Hitler clique led by Admiral Wilhelm Canaris, former chief of German counterintelligence. Although nothing came of this contact during the war, when Heinkel was brought before an Allied tribunal in 1948, charged with aiding the German war effort, his involvement with Canaris was instrumental in winning acquittal.

The division of Germany devastated Heinkel's industrial complex. Most of his plants and equipment, as well as some of the most important technicians, ended up in East Germany and the Soviet Union. Heinkel himself, though in West Germany, was reduced once more to trivial pursuits. In 1950, he and his son opened a small factory for bicycles, motorcycles, and midget automobiles. Heinkel was determined that this experience, like that of the early 1920's, would be only a temporary setback. By 1955, he was back in aviation as a codirector of the Fokker aeronautics combine. In January, 1958, he joined forces with his old rival Messerschmitt in a new venture to manufacture antiaircraft missiles and modern jet aircraft. The day following announcement of this enterprise, Heinkel died.

Summary

Ernst Heinrich Heinkel was a man of two different generations. Like the Wright brothers, Alberto Santos-Dumont, Louis Blériot, and many others, he was a gritty pioneer of early aviation who designed his own aircraft and often risked his life testing them. Unlike some of these pragmatic, intuitive tinkerers, however, Heinkel possessed a singular genius that enabled him to perceive technological frontiers far beyond his time. His work with catapult launches, for example, helped make possible the modern aircraft carrier. His rocket plane experiments were the basis of jet-assisted takeoff (JATO), which made it possible to store combat aircraft in widely dispersed bunkers without runways. Above all, his conception of the limitations of propeller-driven craft presaged not only the jet age but also the first steps in modern rocket development.

It was not only some of his colleagues in aviation whom Heinkel eclipsed in foresight. The outcome of World War II may have been determined, in part, by the fact that Heinkel was far more the visionary than any of the German political or military leaders who professed to be so fond of novel weapons.

Bibliography

Galland, Adolf. *The First and the Last: The Rise and Fall of the German Fighter Forces, 1938-1945.* Translated by Mervyn Savill. New York: Holt, 1954; London: Fontana, 1970. A fascinating account of the interplay among politics, strategy, personalities, and technological developments in the Luftwaffe, written by an officer in the German Condor Legion attached to the Spanish Loyalists, later a staff officer in the German Air Ministry. Galland's account justifies much of Heinkel's bitterness about decision making in the government.

Hanniball, August. *Aircraft, Engines, and Airmen: A Selective Review of the Periodical Literature, 1930-1969.* Metuchen, N.J.: Scarecrow Press, 1972. More than eight hundred pages of annotations and summaries of technological and biographical histories during the period when Heinkel flourished.

Josephy, Alvin M., Jr., ed. *The American Heritage History of Flight.* New York: American Heritage, 1962. Typical of many general histories of aviation organized to emphasize the overall development of industry and technology rather than the careers of individuals.

Sunderman, James F., ed. *Early Air Pioneers, 1862-1935.* New York: Watts, 1961. Deals with the careers of many early aviators, arranged so that the interconnections among these figures are stressed. Particularly useful for its international perspective on technological developments.

Taylor, John W. R., and Kenneth Munson. *History of Aviation.* 2d ed. London: New English Library, and New York: Crown, 1978. Heavily illustrated and detailed accounts both of major milestones in aviation technology and of contributors to early aviation. One of the best organized sources of biographical accounts.

Ronald W. Davis

WERNER HEISENBERG

Born: December 5, 1901; Würzburg, Germany
Died: February 1, 1976; Munich, West Germany
Area of Achievement: Physics
Contribution: Heisenberg is considered to be one of the most important scientists of the twentieth century, mainly as a result of his creation of quantum mechanics, a theory that has dominated the development of nuclear and atomic physics since 1925.

Early Life

Werner Heisenberg always claimed that the events of his childhood and youth, and the ideas nurtured in the course of them, were the most fundamental and strongly influential forces in his life. Born in the Rhine town of Würzburg on December 5, 1901, he lived his early life in the time of imperial Germany and the kingdom of Bavaria. Heisenberg's mother, Annie Wecklein, was the daughter of the headmaster at Munich's Max-Gymnasium. She was a blend of intelligence, naïveté, and gentleness, and she helped pave the way for a happy childhood for both of her sons. Heisenberg's father, August Heisenberg, had an unusual career. After studying classical languages, he became a secondary school teacher in Würzburg and then was offered a post at the University of Munich, where he occupied the only chair for Byzantine studies existing in Germany at the time. He held this position for the rest of his life. Thus, during his early years Heisenberg felt secure in the environment of a stable family.

When Heisenberg was eight years old, the family moved to Munich, which became his home from that point on. The move concluded the first phase of young Heisenberg's life; a new, more independent and expansive phase was to follow, one that introduced new people and new stimuli for his inquisitive mind as well as new interests and projects. He enjoyed building things. He also quickly achieved a certain level of accomplishment on the piano, and during these years he often considered becoming a musician.

The path of Heisenberg's future life, however, had already been charted for him, since he felt most comfortable and most fascinated moving about in the realm of scientific ideas. When he was fourteen years old, for example, he prepared a friend of the family for the mathematical examination required for a doctorate in chemistry. Heisenberg had always been intensely involved with mathematical questions, but soon his casual interest became philosophical. At the University of Munich, he studied theoretical physics under Arnold Sommerfeld and received his doctorate in physics in 1923, writing a dissertation on turbulence in fluid streams.

Life's Work

Interested in Niels Bohr's work on the planetary model of the atom, Heisenberg went to the University of Göttingen to study physics under Max Born and mathematics under David Hilbert. Later, in the fall of 1924, Heisenberg traveled to the University Institute for Theoretical Physics in Copenhagen to study under Bohr. This was a time of great excitement and confusion in the field of physics. Bohr, in 1913, had used the quantum theory of Max Planck and Albert Einstein as the basis for a new atomic theory that would account for the emission spectra of elements. Essential to Bohr's atomic model was the concept of energy levels that could not be occupied by the electrons orbiting the atom's nucleus. The discrete atomic spectral emission lines were, according to Bohr, caused by electrons "jumping" from one permitted energy level to another of lower energy and, in the process, emitting a quantum of energy that equaled the difference between the initial and final energy levels.

Bohr's critics were anxious to determine the position of the electron during the jump, since the electron, according to his theory, could not occupy the space between permitted orbits. This problem and others arising from Bohr's adherence to an easily schematized atomic model prompted Heisenberg to adopt the revolutionary attitude that led to the birth of quantum mechanics (the science that describes discrete energy states and other forms of quantized energy) in 1925. In discarding all models, he was rejecting a method that had led physicists to success after success for two centuries.

In his article "Über quantentheoretische Umdeutung kinematischer und mechanischer Beziehungen" (1925; about the quantum-theoretical reinterpretation of kinetic and mechanical relationships), Heisenberg offered a reinterpretation of the basic concepts of mechanics. Physical variables were to be represented by matrices of numbers and would treat only observable or measurable quantities. Heisenberg and other promi-

nent physicists subsequently used the new quantum mechanics to interpret many atomic and molecular spectra, ferromagnetic phenomena, and electromagnetic activities. In 1926, variations on the new quantum theory were proposed by Erwin Schrödinger and Paul Dirac.

In 1927, Heisenberg announced his famous "uncertainty (or indeterminacy) principle," which clarified the theoretical limitations imposed by quantum mechanics upon certain pairs of variables that constantly interact with each other, such as position and momentum. He asserted that in their new classifications as conjugate observables (an interrelated pair of measurable quantities), indeterminacy dictated that no quantum mechanical system could simultaneously possess an exact position and exact momentum. Although indeterminacy affects all phenomena, large and small, its significance is usually confined to subatomic particles.

Bohr and Heisenberg subsequently developed a philosophy of complementarity to take into account the new physical variables, each of which would be relative to an appropriate measurement process on which it depends. This innovative conception of the measurement process in physics emphasized the active role of the scientist, who, in the act of making measurements, interacts with the observed object and thus causes it to be revealed not as it is in itself but as a function of how it is measured. Many physicists, however, including Einstein, Schrödinger, and Louis de Broglie, rejected the philosophy of complementarity.

From 1927 to 1941, Heisenberg served as professor of theoretical physics at the University of Leipzig. It was during this period, in 1937, that Heisenberg married Elizabeth Schumacher, a union that would eventually produce seven children. After 1941, Heisenberg was director of the Kaiser Wilhelm Institute for Physics in Berlin for four years. During World War II, he collaborated with Otto Hahn, one of the discoverers of nuclear fission, on the development of a nuclear reactor. Although Heisenberg never took a public position opposing the Nazi regime, he was critical of its policies and attempted to prevent Germany from developing effective nuclear weapons. After the war, he organized and became director of the Max Planck Institute for Physics and Astrophysics at Göttingen and later moved to Munich, along with the institute, in 1958.

Heisenberg began working on a universal nonlinear spinor equation (a nonlinear differential equation for complex vectorlike entities, representing all possible states of matter) for particulate systems that would exhibit the basic set of universal symmetries (relative to possible observer viewpoints in nature) and yet be able to explain the assortment of elementary particles generated in high-energy collisions. He exhibited strong opposition to the logical positivism developed by philosophers in Vienna in his writings on the philosophical implications of quantum mechanics. In his theory of quantum physics, he emphasized the active role of the observer and replaced the absolute objects of classical science with relativized observational situations. Quantum mechanics implies that on the subatomic level the traditional idea of scientific causality needs broadening, since the behavior of particles can be predicted only on the basis of probability, and that Isaac Newton's laws concerning the motion of bodies in space and time are not applicable to the basic processes within the atom. Yet, in Heisenberg's view, classical physics remains valid for a wide range of macroscopic phenomena.

Although primarily known as a physicist, Heisenberg continued in the classical tradition of philosophy, constantly seeking a new solution to the ancient problem of unity and multiplicity. In addition to receiving the Nobel Prize in Physics in 1932, such honors as the Max Planck Medal, the Matteucci Medal, and the Barnard College Medal of Columbia University were bestowed upon him.

Summary

Werner Heisenberg, physicist and philosopher, in helping to establish the modern science of quantum mechanics, managed to destroy the familiar world of physics that the nineteenth century had carefully created and defended. He contributed significant refinements to a conceptual understanding of the atomic nucleus, ferromagnetism, cosmic rays, and elementary particles, and he conceived of a Platonic central order, consisting of a set of universal symmetries that are exhibited in all natural phenomena. Moreover, in his view, these symmetries constitute the rationale for a mathematical equation that can be applied to all systems of particulate matter. Heisenberg's work has continued to stimulate many questions in the philosophy of science involving the certainty and probability of scientific knowledge.

Bibliography

Carazza, Bruno, and Helge Kragh. "Heisenberg's Lattice World: The 1930 Theory Sketch." *American Journal of Physics* 63, no. 7 (July, 1995). Examines Heisenberg's unpublished "lattice world" theory (originally outlined in a letter to Neils Bohr).

Heelan, Patrick A. *Quantum Mechanics and Objectivity: A Study of the Physical World of Werner Heisenberg.* The Hague: Nijhoff, 1965. Heelan's informative analysis of the philosophical context of Heisenberg's physics is the only critical study of Heisenberg's philosophy of science in English.

Heisenberg, Elisabeth. *Inner Exile: Recollections of a Life with Werner Heisenberg.* Translated by S. Cappelari and C. Morris. Boston: Birkhäuser, 1984. Heisenberg's wife gives a detailed and interesting inside look at her husband's life as a man and as a scientist under a regime of dictatorship and oppression, even though Heisenberg was not a direct victim of the system. She describes the complexity of the compromises Heisenberg had to make in order to save what he considered to be most important.

Heisenberg, Werner. *Physics and Beyond: Encounters and Conversations.* Translated by Arnold J. Pomerans. London: Allen and Unwin, and New York: Harper, 1971. This autobiographical memoir, or "intellectual history," of Heisenberg's early life is important in that it sheds a unique light on some of the twentieth century's most outstanding scientists and their impact on the life and work of Heisenberg. Extensive quotations from dialogues and discussions with these men demonstrate Heisenberg's belief that science is a cooperative enterprise.

Jammer, Max. *The Philosophy of Quantum Mechanics: The Interpretations of Quantum Mechanics in Historical Perspective.* New York: Wiley, 1974. This is the most complete historical study of Heisenberg's contribution to the development of quantum mechanics. It views the progression of ideas that led to Heisenberg's discoveries and illustrates how his discoveries revolutionized existing physical theories of his time.

Logan, Jonothan. "The Critical Mass: As Allied Scientists Established the Feasibility of an Atomic Bomb, Germany's Leading Theorist Came to a Mistaken Conclusion." *American Scientist* 84, no. 3 (May-June, 1996). Discusses the German fission project, its eventual stagnation, and the mistaken estimations Heisenberg made with respect to critical mass.

Price, William C., and Seymour S. Chissick, eds. *The Uncertainty Principle and the Foundations of Quantum Mechanics: A Fifty Years' Survey.* New York: Wiley, 1977. This series of essays is a unique tribute published to commemorate the fiftieth anniversary of the formulation of quantum mechanics, quantum theory, and Heisenberg's uncertainty principle. In addition to various essays about Heisenberg's work, an insightful essay by Heisenberg entitled "Remarks on the Origin of the Relations of Uncertainty" is included.

Wolf, Fred Alan. *Taking the Quantum Leap: The New Physics for Nonscientists.* San Francisco: Harper, 1981. This work presents both the history and the concepts of the new physics (quantum physics) for an audience with very little mathematical or scientific expertise. In several sections of the book, Wolf discusses Heisenberg's contribution to the discovery of quantum mechanics as well as the uncertainty principle in easy-to-understand language. The book includes extensive footnotes, a bibliography, and simple diagrams.

Genevieve Slomski

LILLIAN HELLMAN

Born: June 20, 1905; New Orleans, Louisiana
Died: June 30, 1984; Martha's Vineyard, Massachusetts
Areas of Achievement: Literature and film
Contribution: A leading American playwright and important screenwriter, Hellman published memoirs in the 1960's and 1970's that advanced the growing interest in women's lives and in autobiography.

Early Life

Lillian Florence Hellman was born in New Orleans, Louisiana on June 20, 1905, the daughter of Max Hellman, a shoe salesman, and Julia Newhouse, an Alabama native whose family had succeeded in several business enterprises, including banking. As a child, Lillian was acutely conscious of the power the Newhouses' money gave them; financial speculation and chicanery would become the theme of her most powerful plays. When her father's New Orleans shoe business failed, he moved his family for six months of each year to New York City while he traveled as a salesman. Five-year-old Lillian found it difficult to adjust to two different cultures and school systems; her record as a student was erratic. Nevertheless, she acquired a diversity of experience that stimulated her precocious imagination and provided many of the themes of her plays and memoirs.

Hellman was an only child, doted on by her parents, who indulged her whims and gave her room to experiment in the heady, vibrant atmosphere of New York City in the 1920's. Hellman attended classes at New York University and then at Columbia, but she did not earn a degree. Instead she worked briefly for the innovative New York publisher, Horace Liveright, where she met important writers and celebrities, including her future husband, Arthur Kober, whom she married on December 21, 1925. Kober wrote plays and stories for *The New Yorker*, and he helped Hellman obtain various jobs as a script reader and publicity agent for theatrical producers. She had ambitions to write, but her early attempts at fiction fizzled, and she accompanied her husband to Hollywood, where he had a contract to write screenplays.

Hellman was hired in Hollywood as a script reader. Her job was to summarize books that might make good films. She found her work dull, but she made friends with writers and film actors, eventu-

ally meeting Dashiell Hammett, the handsome and successful writer of hardboiled detective stories. With the marriage to Kober failing (they were divorced in 1932), she became romantically involved with Hammett, who suggested that she write for the stage. He even provided the plot, based on a true story, for her first successful play, *The Children's Hour* (1934). Despite many problems, the relationship with Hammett would endure until his death in 1961 and become an important theme in her memoirs.

Life's Work

For *The Children's Hour*, Lillian Hellman updated the story of two teachers who had been accused of lesbianism in nineteenth century Edinburgh. She shifted the setting to twentieth century New England and made the teachers, Karen and Martha, victims of an accusation leveled against them by a malevolent child, Mary, who refuses to be disciplined and who strikes back by suggesting to her grandmother, a powerful member of the community, that her teachers have an "unnatural" love for each other. Karen and Martha are not lovers, but Martha kills herself when she realizes that she does have sexual feelings for Karen. The two teachers are the targets of the blind hysteria of society, which tends to take the word of authority figures and to be swayed by the emotional impact of a shocking accusation. An enormous success (the play ran for more than seven hundred performances on Broadway), *The Children's Hour* established Hellman as a promising playwright with a keen eye for both individual and social psychology.

Hellman's success as a playwright brought an offer from Samuel Goldwyn to write screenplays. Throughout the 1930's, Hellman worked for Goldwyn, producing superior scripts for *The Children's Hour*, retitled *These Three* (1936), and for *Dead End* (1937) as well as working in collaboration on other projects. She had unusual creative control over her own scripts and a reputation in Hollywood for independence. She was instrumental in forming the Screen Writers Guild and became involved in leftist politics, briefly becoming a Communist Party member from 1938 to 1940.

Hellman is perhaps best known for her third play, *The Little Foxes* (1939), a classic of the American theater, set in the South just after the Civil War. The play's main character, Regina Hub-

bard Giddens, holds her own with her brothers, Ben and Oscar Hubbard, in capitalizing on the family business. Although the play is susceptible to a political reading and can be analyzed as a critique of capitalism, it is equally the story of a family, each member struggling for dominance and individuality. One of the most striking features of this play is its lack of sentimentality, a hardheadedness Hellman herself exemplified in the pursuit of her career and which she attributed to her mother's family in *An Unfinished Woman: A Memoir* (1969) and *Pentimento* (1972).

In *Watch on the Rhine* (1941), Hellman focuses on the innocence of Americans and their blindness to the appeasement of fascism that had gone on throughout the 1930's. In Kurt Müller, a German anti-Fascist fighter seeking momentary refuge in the United States, she creates a vulnerable hero, a fragile man with broken hands who is constrained to strangle a foreign national who threatens to reveal Kurt's presence and to expose the network of anti-Fascist groups Kurt supports. That Fanny Farrelly, the mother of Kurt's American wife, Sarah, must condone this killing in her own household and allow Kurt to escape, accomplishes the playwright's aim in bringing home to Americans the fact that they are implicated in the world's evils and must take some responsibility for combating them, even at the price of losing their innocence.

Although Hellman managed to complete a second successful play on the Hubbards, *Another Part of the Forest* (pr. 1946, pb. 1947), she began to sense that her resources as a playwright were diminishing. Her final plays—*The Autumn Garden* (1951), *Toys in the Attic* (1960), and an adaptation of a novel, *My Mother, My Father, and Me* (1963)—show that she was moving toward the form of the memoir as more flexible and more open than her tightly wound melodramas.

Called on to explain her career in numerous interviews, and energized by the contentious campus life of the 1960's (she taught at Harvard, Yale, and other colleges), it seemed incumbent on Hellman to present some record of herself. In her memoirs, Hellman dedicated herself not only to explaining the origins of her work but also to revealing to a later generation what it was like growing up in the 1920's, making her way among the writers and the politics of the 1930's and 1940's and coping with being blacklisted in the 1950's for her leftist sympathies.

Hellman's first two volumes of memoirs, *An Unfinished Woman* and *Pentimento*, were an enormous success, garnering her the best reviews of her life. She became a cult figure, lionized by young people, especially women, who saw in her a role model who had held her own in a man's world while remaining feminine. There was criticism of her long-term relationship with Hammett—some women viewing Hellman as the subordinate partner—but on the whole she was praised for confronting the temper of her times with magnificent courage and candor. The style of the memoirs, particularly *Pentimento*, was much admired, for her chapters read like short stories, especially her account of her childhood friend, Julia, who had become part of the anti-Fascist underground in Europe and whom Hellman had aided at considerable risk to herself.

When Hellman's third memoir, *Scoundrel Time* (1976), appeared, it was initially greeted with rave reviews. Eventually, however, the tide turned as her enemies of the 1930's and 1940's emerged to dispute her accounts. In an article published in *The Paris Review* in 1981, Martha Gellhorn, Ernest Hemingway's third wife, ridiculed the contradictions and inaccuracies of *An Unfinished Woman* and made a compelling case for Hellman's having lied about many incidents to aggrandize her own life. Other attacks followed, pointing up the self-serving quality of *Scoundrel Time* and its deficiencies as history. The culmination of this criticism came in Mary McCarthy's allegation on national television that every word Hellman wrote was a lie.

Hellman received little sympathy when she decided to sue McCarthy for libel. Having built her reputation on candor, the likelihood that the stories in *Pentimento*, especially Julia's, were fiction came as devastating news to Hellman's readers, and Hellman did not deign to reply to the charges. When she died on June 30, 1984, the suit against McCarthy was still pending, but Hellman's reputation had been significantly damaged.

Summary

Several of Lillian Hellman's plays—*The Children's Hour, The Little Foxes, Another Part of the Forest, The Autumn Garden, Toys in the Attic*—are regularly revived and are likely to remain a part of the American repertory. The quality of the writing in her memoirs is high, although their final place in the canon of American literature remains to be determined, as does the precise nature of her political views and the extent to which those views must be considered in an analysis of her writing.

Hellman's life represents a challenge and an inspiration to women's studies. On the one hand, she was a product of her moment—especially of the 1930's—when her writing reflected the need of many writers to engage in some form of political engagement. She chose to pursue the hardboiled creed of her mentor, Dashiell Hammett, never excusing or rationalizing her actions. On the other hand, her memoirs and plays provide ample criticism not merely of male chauvinism but of her characters and of herself. She knew that she was "unfinished," and that many of her actions were contradictory. The very terms she used—such as pentimento—suggest that she recognized that human identity, and especially a woman's identity, entailed constant revision and remaking—similar to the artistic process of repenting, in which an artist makes changes and paints over his or her work. This dynamic process of self-creation is what accounted for the tremendous success of Hellman's memoirs, and it is what is likely to repay study in considering Hellman's status as a woman of achievement.

Bibliography

Dick, Bernard F. *Hellman in Hollywood*. Rutherford, N.J.: Fairleigh Dickinson University Press, and London: Associated University Presses, 1982. The only complete study of Hellman's screenwriting career, based not only on archival sources but also on interviews with her coworkers. Notes, bibliography, and index.

Feibleman, Peter. *Lilly: Reminiscences of Lillian Hellman*. New York: Morrow, 1988; London: Chatto and Windus, 1989. An effective memoir of his close association with Hellman, which provides important details on the last years of her life.

Horn, Barbara Lee. *Lillian Hellman: A Research and Production Sourcebook*. Westport, Conn.: Greenwood Press, 1998. Thorough coverage of Hellman's career including an overview of her life, a chronology of her accomplishments, plot summaries and critiques of her original plays, and more.

Lederer, Katherine. *Lillian Hellman*. Boston: Twayne, 1979. A sound introductory study, including a chapter on her biography and discussions of her major plays and memoirs. Contains notes, chronology, bibliography, and index.

Mahoney, Rosemary. *A Likely Story: One Summer with Lillian Hellman*. New York: Doubleday, 1998. Memoirs of the author, who spent the summer of 1978 as Hellman's housekeeper.

Newman, Robert P. *The Cold War Romance of Lillian Hellman and John Melby*. Chapel Hill: University of North Carolina Press, 1989. An important contribution to an understanding of Hellman's politics and her personal life, concentrating on her relationship with Melby, an American foreign service officer dismissed from his position in the 1950's because of his love affair with Hellman.

Rollyson, Carl. *Lillian Hellman: Her Legend and Her Legacy*. New York: St. Martin's Press, 1988. A full-length biography that discusses all of Hellman's major work as autobiographer, screenwriter, and playwright. There is also an extensive discussion of her politics and sketches of the main characters in her life. Useful footnotes, bibliography, and index.

Spacks, Patricia Meyer. *The Female Imagination*. New York: Knopf, 1975; London: Allen and Unwin, 1976. Contains a searching and highly critical discussion of Hellman's memoirs.

Triesch, Manfred, comp. *The Lillian Hellman Collection at the University of Texas*. Austin: University of Texas Press, 1966. An important census and discussion of Hellman's manuscripts in the most important depository of her work.

Wright, William. *Lillian Hellman: The Image, The Woman*. New York: Simon and Schuster, 1986; London: Sidgwick and Jackson, 1987. A full-length biography concentrating on Hellman's life. Wright is less concerned with her plays and memoirs than with her politics, which he treats in a fairly objective manner. Notes and index.

Carl Rollyson

ERNEST HEMINGWAY

Born: July 21, 1899; Oak Park, Illinois
Died: July 2, 1961; Ketchum, Idaho
Area of Achievement: Literature
Contribution: Hemingway was one of the most influential writers in the twentieth century, both as a much-imitated stylist and as a larger-than-life celebrity.

Early Life

Born into a conservative, upper-middle-class family in Oak Park, Illinois, an affluent suburb of Chicago, Ernest Hemingway spent much of his life and early literary career trying to break away from the constraints of his youth. Hemingway's father, Clarence Edmonds Hemingway, was a physician who had a great interest in hunting and fishing. The young Hemingway, whose father hoped that his son would eventually join him in his medical practice, became an avid outdoorsman at an early age.

During long holidays spent at the family's summer home on Walloon Lake in northern Michigan, Ernest, who was not healthy as a youth, pushed himself to the limits of his physical endurance, as he did throughout much of his later life. He became an enthusiastic sportsman.

Grace Hall Hemingway, Ernest's mother, was a cultivated woman, much interested in music. She dominated her husband, and Ernest realized early that his father was henpecked. Until her death, Grace Hemingway never had a positive word to say about her son's work. She regarded Ernest's writing as an embarrassment to the family because it dealt with a side of life that Grace considered seamy. Never able to win from his mother the approbation that he wanted, Hemingway was early attracted to older women who appreciated his work and who appreciated him. Three of his four wives were considerably older than he, and his first serious romantic encounter was with Agnes von Kurowsky, a nurse who tended him in Italy and was eight years his senior.

Hemingway completed high school in 1917, just as the United States was being drawn into World War I. He had no wish to go to college and was eager to serve his country. His defective vision precluded his serving in the armed forces, so after a summer at Walloon Lake, Hemingway, drawing on his experience in writing for his high school newspaper in Oak Park, went to Kansas City as a reporter for the *Star*, a celebrated daily newspaper of that

era. He was to return to Oak Park only five or six times in his entire life after he made the initial break. In Kansas City, Hemingway served an intense journalistic apprenticeship for seven months before he left for Italy as a Red Cross ambulance driver in May, 1918.

Hemingway had been in Italy for less than six weeks when he was wounded at Fossalta di Piave on Italy's boundary with Austria. Despite his wounds, he dragged an injured solider from the front line to safety. For this act of heroism, he was decorated.

After spending some time in an Italian hospital near Milan recovering from his wounds, Hemingway was sent home, where he was looked upon as a hero. He reveled in his newly won celebrity. After he regained his strength at Lake Walloon, Hemingway went to Chicago, where he held a variety of menial jobs. Soon he married Hadley Richardson, eight years older than he, and sailed with her for France, where he served as a foreign correspondent for the *Toronto Star*. He arrived in Paris just as the city was reaching a postwar zenith of intellectual ferment and literary activity, and there he was to remain for the better part of the next decade, coming to know well such influential literary figures as F. Scott Fitzgerald, Gertrude Stein, Ford Maddox Ford, Ezra Pound, and James Joyce.

Hemingway, handsome with his animated eyes, his ready smile, and his dark mustache, was soon the darling of Parisian literary society. His good looks and amiability won for him a legion of friends, many of whom ultimately came to see the darker side of his highly complex and often bewildering personality. Aside from his journalistic commitments, he began in Paris to work assiduously on his short stories and on a novel about the aimless postwar expatriates who lived a somewhat undirected existence in France and Spain. On a personal level, Hemingway was able to give purpose to his own life by writing about the aimlessness that characterized many of the Americans of his generation who lived in Europe at that time. He came to deplore the term he had popularized (borrowed from Gertrude Stein): the "lost generation."

Hemingway's first book, a collection of short stories interspersed with imagistic reflections, *In Our Time* (1924), was recognized by the literati as a work of considerable promise. Although the book was not a resounding commercial success, it was

clearly the work of a serious author who had begun to master his craft.

Life's Work

Hemingway's first novel, *The Sun Also Rises* (1926), established him as an author of considerable significance, just as *In Our Time* had established him as an author of considerable promise. *The Sun Also Rises*, a book that was right for its time, depicts dislocated members of the postwar generation. Set in Paris and Pamplona, Spain, it featured Hemingway's first extended treatment of one of his lifelong fascinations: the art of the bullfight. It was not merely the timeliness of *The Sun Also Rises* that established Hemingway as a serious artist; it was also the meticulous control that he exercised over his material and the care and authenticity of his spare descriptions that made both readers and literary critics realize that he was an author of extraordinary stature.

The Sun Also Rises was followed by *A Farewell to Arms* (1929), which was published in the year that Hemingway divorced his first wife, Hadley, who had borne him one son, John. The protagonist of *A Farewell to Arms* is an American disenchanted with a society that could let something such as World War I happen. He finally deserts the Italian army, in which he has been serving and which is in disarray. His disenchantment is intensified by the death of his lover in giving birth to their child.

In the years following *A Farewell to Arms*, Hemingway became an increasingly romantic figure, a rugged outdoorsman who spent much time attending bullfights in Spain, hunting big game in Africa, and fishing the waters off Key West, Florida, where he bought a home in which he resided when he was not traveling. Out of this period were to come such books as *Death in the Afternoon* (1932), an extended discourse on bullfighting in which Hemingway gives valuable insights into his own creative processes, and *Green Hills of Africa* (1935), which remains one of the most sensitively written books about big game and those who hunt it.

Out of Hemingway's Key West experience came his novel *To Have and Have Not* (1937), a mediocre book whose action takes places in Cuba and Key West during the Great Depression. Hemingway's next book, *For Whom the Bell Tolls* (1940), is an optimistic novel that calls for the unity of humankind. The book is set in Spain during the Civil War, which Hemingway had seen at first hand as a correspondent with strong Loyalist sympathies.

For Whom the Bell Tolls was to be Hemingway's last novel for ten years, after which he published *Across the River and into the Trees* (1950), an overly sentimental novel of little distinction.

Meanwhile, in 1940, Hemingway divorced Pauline Pfeiffer, his second wife and the mother of his sons Patrick and Gregory, after thirteen years of marriage. He married Martha Gellhorn, a writer, almost immediately and was married to her until 1945. Then he married Mary Welsh, also a writer, to whom he remained married for the remainder of his life.

When Hemingway returned from covering the Spanish Civil War, he bought Finca Vigía, a quite modest estate not far from Havana, Cuba, and this was to be his home until 1959, when the political situation under Fidel Castro forced Hemingway out of the country. He then bought a home in Ketchum, Idaho, where he was to spend the remaining years of his life.

During World War II, Hemingway first served as a correspondent in China, then, from 1944 until the end of the war, as a correspondent in Europe, crossing the English Channel on D-Day with the Twenty-second Regiment of the Fourth Infantry Division, with which he saw considerable combat in Normandy and later at the Battle of the Bulge. He also devised the Crook Factory, which, in 1943, undertook some ill-conceived and abortive missions on his boat, *The Pilar*, to try to destroy German submarines in the waters off Cuba.

Hemingway's excursion into drama was with a play about the Spanish Civil War, *The Fifth Column* (1938). It was published in *The Fifth Column and the First Forty-nine Stories* (1938), a collection which includes such celebrated stories as "The Killers," "The Snows of Kilamanjaro," and "The Short Happy Life of Francis Macomber."

Hemingway had a writing slump after World War II that plagued him for the remainder of his life. *Across the River and into the Trees* brought vitriolic reviews, and some critics thought that this book marked the end of Hemingway's literary career. He published *The Old Man and the Sea* (1952) two years later, however, and this short, tightly controlled novel about Santiago, an old fisherman who almost dies during a three-day encounter with a marlin, helped to salvage his deteriorating reputation. In 1953, this book won for Hemingway the Pulitzer Prize and was also instrumental in his being awarded the Nobel Prize in Literature in 1954.

The Old Man and the Sea was Hemingway's last novel, although two earlier, unfinished novels, *Islands in the Stream* (1970) and *The Garden of Eden* (1986), were published posthumously. The last of these was constructed by Scribner's editor Tom Jenks from more than fifteen hundred manuscript pages that Hemingway left on his death. Also published posthumously was *A Moveable Feast* (1964), a memoir which details Hemingway's life in Paris during the 1920's and which has much of the power and grace of his early work.

Hemingway began to suffer increasingly from depression and anxiety after World War II, and he was twice hospitalized at the Mayo Clinic for electric shock therapy. On July 2, 1961, after returning to Ketchum from his second hospitalization, Hemingway ended his life with a shotgun blast.

Summary

At a time when much writing was florid and verbose, Ernest Hemingway stripped language to the bare essentials for expressing fundamental thoughts and rendering the most accurate descriptions possible. Although he dealt with complex thoughts and emotions, Hemingway labored to achieve directness and simplicity of expression. From Gertrude Stein, he learned the effectiveness of verbal repetition as a means of achieving the rhythms of language. From Ezra Pound and from his early experience as a journalist, he learned to write exactly, using accurate verbs and nouns, depending little on adjectives and adverbs.

Hemingway's best work demonstrates careful control, close observation, accurate depiction, and the highest level of artistic integrity. It glorifies the dignity in life as seen in the works that deal with bullfighting, big-game hunting, fishing, war, drinking, brawling, and camaraderie. Hemingway's concept of courage as grace under pressure underlies his finest writing.

As the fourth American author to be awarded the Nobel Prize for Literature, Hemingway brought renewed attention to his country as a source of fine writing. Often a deeply troubled person, Hemingway went through life trying to demonstrate a courage that perhaps he was not convinced he really possessed. His increasing need to project a macho image stemmed from deep psychological sources which were intimately connected to his artistry.

Bibliography

Baker, Carlos. *Ernest Hemingway: A Life Story.* London: Collins, and New York: Scribner, 1969. Focuses on the origin, development, and reception of Hemingway's writing. Information drawn largely from primary sources, including more than twenty-five hundred letters. Written at the invitation of Scribner's, Hemingway's publisher since 1926. Deals more with events than with ideas.

————. *Hemingway: The Writer as Artist.* 4th ed. Princeton, N.J.: Princeton University Press, 1972. A solid consideration of Hemingway's literary technique. Baker is knowledgeable but detached and objective. One of the better books on Hemingway.

Burgess, Anthony. *Ernest Hemingway and His World.* London: Thames and Hudson, and New York: Scribner, 1978. Although a pictorial biography, this book contains some remarkable literary insights and acute critical analysis. Shows how Hemingway introduced a new standard of language, one of "nerves and muscle."

Eby, Carl P. *Hemingway's Fetishism: Psychoanalysis and the Mirror of Manhood.* Albany: State University of New York Press, 1998. Focuses on the use of fetishism in the life and works of Hemingway. Based on new archival research.

Grebstein, Sheldon N. *Hemingway's Craft.* Carbondale: Southern Illinois University Press, 1973. The book emphasizes technique and literary motivations. Shows sequential development to 1940, followed by a seeming diminution in Hemingway's literary abilities.

Griffin, Peter. *Along with Youth: Hemingway, The Early Years.* New York: Oxford University Press, 1985; Oxford: Oxford University Press, 1987. Focuses on Hemingway's life from birth until his marriage to Hadley Richardson and his departure for Paris. Prints for the first time a number of Hemingway's poems and early contributions to his high school newspaper.

Hanneman, Audre, ed. *Ernest Hemingway: A Comprehensive Bibliography.* Princeton, N.J.: Princeton University Press, 1967; *Supplement*, 1975. These volumes, which again need updating, are the most comprehensive and reliable bibliographies of Hemingway's work and of scholarship related to Hemingway.

Meyers, Jeffrey. *Hemingway: A Biography.* New York: Harper, 1985; London: Macmillan, 1986. Well written and intriguing. Meyers clearly demonstrates that Hemingway's life was as interesting as the lives of any of his protagonists. Presents trenchant insights into Hemingway's view of women, particularly as his view was shaped by his early relationship to his mother.

Rovit, Earl H. *Ernest Hemingway.* Rev. ed. Boston: Twayne, 1986. A useful overview which is now somewhat dated. Well researched although a bit hampered by the restrictions of length and format imposed by the series of which it is a part.

Wagner-Martin, Linda. *Ernest Hemingway: Seven Decades of Criticism.* East Lansing: Michigan State University Press, 1998. A collection of critical essays on Hemingway's works, concentrating on criticism written in the 1980's and 1990's.

Young, Philip. *Ernest Hemingway: A Reconsideration.* Rev. ed. University Park: Pennsylvania State University Press, 1966. This second edition of Young's superb critical study, first published in 1952, adds an interesting preface telling of the author's difficulties with Hemingway over the publication of the book. Young hypothesizes that Hemingway's heroes were modeled on himself and that his life in turn was modeled on the heroes of earlier American classics, particularly those of Mark Twain.

R. Baird Shuman

SONJA HENIE

Born: April 8, 1912; Kristiania (now Oslo),
Norway
Died: October 12, 1969; in an airplane bound for
Oslo, Norway
Areas of Achievement: Sports and acting
Contribution: Henie is the only female figure
skater to win gold medals in three consecutive
Olympics—1928, 1932, and 1936. By combin-
ing graceful dance movements with her athletic
ability, Henie was largely responsible for creat-
ing the huge international interest in figure
skating.

Early Life
Sonja Henie was born in Kristiania, Norway, on
April 8, 1912. Her father, Wilhelm, had inherited a
successful fur business and the family's wealth enabled Sonja to pursue whatever interests struck her
fancy. At age five, Sonja began to perform elaborate, if awkward, costume dances for her family
and friends. When it became evident that her interest in dance was more than a childhood whim, her
indulgent parents, Wilhelm and Selma, arranged
for her to receive ballet lessons from Love Krohn,
a well-known Oslo dance instructor who had once
taught famed ballerina Anna Pavlova. Shortly after
Krohn took her on as a student, Sonja, inspired by
her brother, Leif, ventured on to ice skates. Within
a year of her first tentative strides, she was encouraged to enter a children's competition. At seven
years old, she was competing against youngsters
who were much bigger and much older, but Sonja
won. From that moment, Sonja and her parents
were consumed by a passion to make her the best
female skater in the world.

By the age of eight, Sonja had settled into a
highly disciplined routine that required her to practice at least five hours every day. Her father hired a
series of academic tutors so that she would not
need to attend school and a succession of skating
instructors to help her refine her performance. For
the next several years, she won a number of junior
championships. With each victory, the expectations
of Sonja and her parents were raised to a new level.
By the time she was ten, her family had built a "ritual of living" around her skating.

Although the ice was now her first love, Sonja
did not completely neglect her dancing. She and
her parents were well aware that the grace of
movement when displayed on the ice owed much
to her ballet instruction. From time to time she returned for lessons with Krohn and other well-
known instructors. Her skating had also taken on
new dimensions with training sessions in various
European locales, particularly those with indoor
skating surfaces. Sonja's mother was her constant
companion in these years and directed all of her
activities.

Having won all the competitions offered in Norway by age eleven, Sonja, with the concurrence of
her family and Norwegian officials, entered the
1925 Winter Olympics in France. Although not expected to triumph over mature and experienced
skaters, Sonja, and especially her father, were disappointed when she finished last. Wilhelm berated
Olympic officials for not giving enough consideration to the free-skating portion of the program, the
portion in which everyone agreed that Sonja excelled. This was the only time that Sonja participated in any competition that she did not expect to
win. Her preparation was complete. For the next
twelve years (1925-1937), she won every major
competition that she entered.

Life's Work
Henie's unparalleled string of victories began with
the 1927 World Championships held in her hometown, Oslo. At fourteen, she was the youngest
competitor, but she was now physically strong
enough to carry her jumps and spins smoothly. Her
success in Oslo propelled her to enormous popularity in Norway and throughout Scandinavia. To
win a World Championship, a skater had to excel
in the school figures, required of all competitors,
and to perform as flawlessly as possible in the free-
skating segment. Henie built her reputation on giving a solid performance in the required figures and
then thrilling the audience and the judges with a
graceful, yet daring, free skating routine. In all, she
won ten consecutive World Championships from
1927 through 1936.

These first-place finishes were her most remarkable achievement, but her performances in
the 1928, 1932, and 1936 Olympics made Henie
an international celebrity. Not only did she win
the gold medal in each of these competitions but
she also completely changed the perception of female figure skaters. Henie's free-skating programs included a number of daring jumps and fast

Sonja Henie on the ice with a German master skater, Arthur Vieregg.

skating steps that were unlike anything attempted by her predecessors. Moreover, she introduced elaborate and skimpy (for the times) costumes. Her brilliantly colored outfits were often bedecked with furs and sequins. She wore ever shorter skirts to show off her well-developed legs, which Henie considered her best physical feature. This was quite a departure from the long skirts worn by earlier competitors.

During her years at the top of the amateur skating world, Henie maintained a regimen of diet and practice that kept her physically and mentally sound. Henie feared only two things: falling on the ice and losing. She was fastidious about her skates, her costumes, and the condition of the ice. Her skates were meticulously sharpened before every event, and her many assistants regularly checked the ice for hairpins and other objects that might pose a hazard.

After the 1936 Olympics, Henie retired from amateur skating. Her great popularity, which now extended to the United States, made her an enter-tainment commodity. Henie knew that she could sustain a long career by skating in revues, but her ambition was Hollywood. That ambition was realized when she attracted the attention of Darryl Francis Zanuck of Twentieth Century-Fox Motion Pictures. Within weeks, Henie, her mother at her side, signed a contract with Zanuck. In all, she completed eleven motion pictures between 1936 and 1948, nine of them for Twentieth Century-Fox. In her first two films, she was paired with Tyrone Power.

As a film star, Henie proved to be as demanding as she was when performing on the ice. Her relationship with Zanuck was often stormy, but her films for Twentieth Century-Fox all made money, and the company continued to extend her contract. In motion pictures, Henie was perceived as an older Shirley Temple. With the story lines always very thin, Henie's films were filled with music and skating. The best of her eleven films was *Sun Valley Serenade* (1941), in which she starred with John Wayne, Glenn Miller, Milton Berle, and Joan

Davis. The film featured black ice, which was used to create an appealing mirror effect. Interest in the film musical waned in the post-World War II United States and so did Henie's career in films.

During the entire time that she made films, and for some years after, Henie toured in her highly successful ice revues. Her boundless energy, her incomparable costumes, and her flair as a performer never failed to charm her audiences. She appeared on television in the 1950's, but she kept these appearances to a minimum for fear of draining appeal from her touring shows.

Henie's work ethic and showmanship brought her acclaim and wealth (she earned more than forty-five million dollars), but they did not protect her from criticism and personal disappointment. During World War II, she was accused of having an overly friendly relationship with Adolf Hitler and the Nazis. Henie was a favorite with Hitler and was his guest on more than one occasion. At one point she made the mistake of skating onto the ice in Berlin, stopping in front of Hitler's box, and giving the Nazi salute with a loud "Heil Hitler." Later, when Nazi troops invaded Norway, some of her countrymen questioned her loyalty. Although her brother Leif said that Henie shared Hitler's views on race, she appears to have been essentially apolitical.

With her arrival in California, Henie's private life became more public as she broke free from her mother's direct influence and threw herself into a Hollywood life-style. Her sexual exploits became legendary. Her most publicized affair was with Tyrone Power, whom she met on the set of her first film, *One in a Million*. Henie was married three times: first to Dan Topping (1940-1946), then to Winthrop Gardiner (1949-1956), and finally to Niels Onstad (1956-1969). She had no children.

In later years, Henie gained the reputation for being an astute businesswoman; in fact, much of her financial well-being came as a result of investments made by her business manager, Arthur Wirtz. For her part, Henie's main interest was in collecting fine jewelry and, with Niels Onstad's guidance, modern paintings.

Although she continued to enjoy celebrity status, Henie's revues declined in popularity in the mid-1950's. Competition from other ice shows and poor performances from Henie quickly brought her professional skating career to an end. Now in her early forties, Henie began to lose her enthusiasm and her timing.

Her last years were spent in relative obscurity with her husband, Onstad. Together they established (1968) a center for modern art at Blommenholm, outside Oslo. For the last twenty years of her life, Henie was estranged from her brother, Leif. The two, once close, had argued about financial considerations. In 1968, Henie began to train for what she had hoped would be a successful return to the ice. Within weeks after she resumed training, Henie was diagnosed as having a virulent leukemia. She was never told the true nature of her illness. On October 12, 1969, Henie died on an airplane en route from Paris to Oslo, where she was going for medical treatment.

Summary

Sonja Henie, more than any other individual, was responsible for creating an international audience for ice skating. She accomplished this in amateur and professional realms. By bringing ballet movements into her skating routines and by wearing daring costumes, she made figure skating appear glamorous and graceful. So much did she overwhelm audiences that judges were forced to give more weight to the free-skating portions of international competitions. Her gold-medal performances in three successive Olympics set the standard by which future female figure skaters would be judged.

International ice-skating competition could never be the same, especially for women, after Henie. Future stars on the ice would have to emulate her single-minded devotion to conditioning and practice, and they would have to learn to cope with celebrity status. Simply being a splendid skater no longer guaranteed success.

On the professional level, Henie's revues simulated the staging of a Broadway production. Other ice shows quickly adopted her production standards. Since the late 1940's, traveling ice shows have been a staple in American and European entertainment. Henie had less impact on Hollywood. Her motion pictures were basically old-fashioned musicals on ice, and she never had the opportunity to develop as a serious actress.

Bibliography

Gelman, Steve. *Young Olympic Champions*. New York: Norton, 1964. This book is a compendium of uncritical sketches of Olympic champions. The chapter on Henie emphasizes the importance of dance to her success.

Henie, Sonja. *Wings on My Feet*. New York: Prentice-Hall, 1940. This is Henie's own account of her life to 1940. In the second half of the book, Henie provides instructions for young skaters. Includes many photographs of Henie.

"Ice Wars: The Prequel." *Sports Illustrated* 80, no. 6 (February 14, 1994). Discusses the feud between Olympic skaters Henie and Viv-Anne Hulten in the 1930s.

Johnson, William O. *All That Glitters Is Not Gold: The Olympic Game*. New York: Putnam, 1972. Johnson's work is a general and irreverent examination of the Olympic Games in the twentieth century. It emphasizes the commercialism and materialism generated by the games. He notes that no one used the games more effectively in this regard than Henie.

Lussi, Gustave, and Maurice Richards. *Championship Figure Skating*. New York: Ronald Press, 1951. Lussi, a well-known skating instructor, notes the impact of Henie in popularizing ice skating, particularly in the United States. Most of the book provides a lesson in skating.

"Remembering Sonja Henie." *Films in Review* 47, no. 7-8 (July-August, 1996). Interview with Bill Griffin, a skater who worked with Henie. Touches on her failed marriages, temperament, and more.

Strait, Raymond, and Leif Henie. *Queen of Ice, Queen of Shadows: The Unsuspected Life of Sonja Henie*. Briarcliff Manor, N.Y.: Stein and Day, 1985. This is the only English-language biography of Henie. The book relies heavily on *Wings on My Feet* in discussing Henie's early years. It is essential reading, but Strait and Leif Henie have produced an unflattering account of Henie's life. Readers should be wary of the book's many unsubstantiated contentions.

Ron Huch

HANS WERNER HENZE

Born: July 1, 1926; Gütersloh, Germany
Area of Achievement: Music
Contribution: Henze is one of the most prolific European composers of the postwar era, with a catalog of published compositions numbering more than 150 works in almost every medium. His success as a modern operatic composer is unique.

Early Life

The first of six children, Hans Werner Henze was born in the small Westphalien town of Gütersloh on July 1, 1926. His father Franz, a schoolteacher with strong Fascist views, found his eldest son's artistic inclinations objectionable and discouraged him from serious musical study. Finally, in an attempt to prove to him the uselessness of a musical career, Franz allowed his son to leave the privileged *Gymnasium* and to become enrolled in a much less prestigious local trade school for instrumentalists. There Henze studied piano and percussion.

In 1944, the eighteen-year-old Henze was drafted into the Germany army. Although he was intended for service in an armored division in Poland, Henze was transferred to a unit charged with the production of Nazi propaganda films (an item that Henze omitted from his official 1980 autobiographical sketch). Captured by the advancing British in May, 1945, Henze was released in mid-July. Returning home, he found himself the head of his household, for his father had yet to be released by the Allies. To support his mother and five siblings, Henze first worked for the British occupation forces as a transport laborer. Within a few months, he took another job as a rehearsal pianist in the reopened Bielefeld municipal theater.

Henze's shame in being German, which grew eventually into animosity toward German culture in general, had an enduring effect on his character and music. Armed with forged papers that allowed him entry into the American occupied zone, in early 1946 Henze left his family in Bielefeld to study in Heidelberg. There, at the Institute for Church Music, Henze studied counterpoint and fugue with Wolfgang Fortner, one of Germany's leading composers and teachers. During his two years in Heidelberg, Henze wrote his first symphony, violin concerto, and string quartet. The Darmstadt performance of "Kammerkonzert," for piano, flute, and strings, in 1946 (his first publicly performed composition) resulted immediately in a publishing contract with Schott.

By the close of the 1940's, Darmstadt, West Germany, had become the focal point for the European avant-garde. Founded in 1946 by Wolfgang Steinecke, the Internationale Ferienkurse für Neue Musik (international summer course in new music) drew to Darmstadt musicians from all over Europe. Henze participated in the very first session, in which he conducted an adaptation of Bertolt Brecht's *Das Badener Lehrstück vom Einverständnis* (1929; *The Didactic Play of Baden: On Consent*, 1960). Returning the following summer, Henze attended lectures by René Leibowitz, a friend of Arnold Schoenberg and a highly articulate apologist for both his music and twelve-tone compositional method. Henze returned to Darmstadt again in 1948, this time studying privately with Leibowitz. Although he immediately began incorporating twelve-tone techniques in his writing (the "Variations for Piano" being his first twelve-tone work), Henze never became the kind of doctrinaire dodecaphonist for which Darmstadt became famous.

Life's Work

At a time when most composers are only ready to make their first steps toward a professional career, by 1950 the twenty-four-year-old Henze was already an established artist. This unusual success was a result of both Henze's high productivity and the support of what the composer called "angels." He had been taken up by the professional music world. Yet Henze realized that, as well as benefits, such patronage posed hazards. "Perhaps slowly, and without your recognizing it you begin to repress from your music what you wanted but which others thought inappropriate."

Thus sustained (and, potentially, inhibited), Henze produced a body of works unequaled by his contemporaries in their quantity, number of professional productions, and stylistic diversity. In 1949, he completed his Second Symphony. In 1950, he finished both his Third Symphony and First Piano Concerto. The year following, the city of Düsseldorf awarded him the Robert Schumann Prize. That same year, Henze premiered two dramatic works, the radio opera *A Country Doctor* and the lyric drama *Boulevard Solitude*. In 1955, Henze completed his first full-length opera, *König*

Hirsch. Its premier the following September at the West Berlin State Opera established what was to become a tradition with Henze's first performances: critical accolades mixed with political scandal. The conductor, Hermann Scherchen, was dubbed the "red dictator" for his politics by the orchestra, and the first night's performance was repeatedly interrupted by catcalls, the noise twice halting the third act altogether.

By 1953, Henze had abandoned Germany for Italy, further life in his homeland becoming intolerable for two reasons. First, the composer believed that he saw the legacy of German fascism neither repudiated nor expiated by the "new" Germany, but rather readopted in subtle forms. Second, Henze believed that his isolation as a homosexual would be less severe among the Italians than among his fellow Germans. Never seeking to conceal his sexual orientation, Henze had been increasingly harassed for it. Apparently his "angels" feared the effect that public knowledge of his homosexuality might have upon the public reception of his music (and its marketability). Arrested from his home with a lover in the winter of 1948-1949, Henze avoided a trial and possible imprisonment only by denying his sexual orientation—an act he found odiously deceitful.

Selling almost all of his belongings, Henze hired a car and drove into Italy, intending fully to begin a new life. He settled first on the island of Ischia, renting a two-room house. There he came under the spell of Italian folk song and would thereafter seek to synthesize popular music traditions with his own, highly artificed, style. In 1955, Henze moved to Naples, where he wrote *Four Poems for Orchestra* (1955), *Five Neapolitan Songs* (1956), the ballet *Ondine* (1957), the three-act opera *The Prince of Homburg* (1958), and the pantomime *L'usignolo dell'imperatore.* In 1961, Henze moved again, this time to the Roman resort village Castelgandolfo. That year he saw the premier of yet another opera (*Elegy for Young Lovers*, begun in 1959 with a libretto by W. H. Auden and Chester Kallman) and the awarding of the Arts Prize of the City of Hannover. He also began work on an oratorio, *Novae de infinito laudes*, commissioned by the London Philharmonic Society (because the society found the piece too expensive to perform, it was premiered in 1963 in Venice at the Biennale).

Henze first came to the United States in 1963 to hear the premiere of his Fifth Symphony by the New York Philharmonic led by Leonard Bernstein.

He returned in 1967 to teach as a visiting professor at Dartmouth University and again in 1968 for the first American performance of his opera *The Bassarids* in Santa Fe (the opera had been premiered earlier that year at Milan's La Scala). During his 1967 stay, he witnessed at first hand the race riots that erupted in Washington and Newark and asked himself what his contribution would be in these times. He wondered what music could do, and this question quickly came to dominate Henze's work. He read works by Karl Marx and Vladimir Ilich Lenin and was deeply influenced by Brecht. He became active in the German Socialistischer Deutscher Studentenbund (SDS), attended the Vietnam Congress, and joined the East German Academy of Arts as a corresponding member. He grew convinced that music and theater not only could but should advance the spread of world communist revolution.

Although such a stance had been implicit in many of Henze's earlier works, the first composition in which it was explicit was *The Raft of the Medusa*, an oratorio that Henze described as a requiem for Che Guevara. Its scheduled premiere in Hamburg on December 9, 1968, was a political event in its own right. At the performance's beginning, the hall was invaded by protesters who showered the audience with thousands of anticonsumer culture leaflets (an event staged, with the composer's blessing, by music students with the Hamburg and Berlin SDS). When a poster of Guevara, which had been mounted on the podium, was torn up by the event's producer, Henze himself replaced it with a red flag. Part of the chorus refused to sing in the presence of the revolutionary banner and walked off the stage. While Henze, the producer, and Radio Hamburg's lawyer were negotiating some sort of compromise that would allow the work's performance, in came fully equipped riot police who began arresting the protesters. Amid such pandemonium a performance was impossible. Henze responded to the brouhaha the next year with a work for narrator, brass quintet, and chamber orchestra that he called *Essay on Pigs.*

Probably Henze's masterpiece of the period was the dramatic song cycle *El Cimarrón.* Composed after visits to Fidel Castro's Cuba in 1969 and 1970, the hour-and-a-half work is scored for bass-baritone, flute, guitar, and one percussionist. This setting of the rather dubious autobiography of the 101-year-old ex-slave Esteban Montejo gave Henze an ideal form for both creating a work of riveting theater and presenting an icon of proletarian liberation. Using a largely graphic-style notation, which allowed his performers opportunities for improvisation, Henze's work moved through Montejo's reminiscences of slavery, his escape, and his lovers, climaxing in his participation in the revolutionary battle of Mal Tiempo. Throughout, Henze juxtaposed Caribbean popular song to aleotoric and atonal techniques.

In 1975, the council of the impoverished Tuscan town Montepulciano wrote Henze for advice after they had failed to establish a music festival. Believing that music could raise the town's moral, economic, and social standards, Henze began a musical program to strengthen the town's cultural life. Thus bettered, Henze thought, the citizens would be able more fully to participate in the establishment of a progressive communist *italiaità*, music here being a tool of the class struggle. In October of that year, Henze brought to Montepulciano a group of composers (the best known of whom was Peter Maxwell Davies). Together they worked on a collective opera (*The Oven*) and discussed plans for the festival. The Cantiere, as the festival was called, was born. In 1978, it included production of a play written by town intellectuals, another play written and performed by children, performances by a visiting band from Yorkshire, and concerts by a choir from Cambridge.

While much of his energy was devoted to the Montepulciano Cantiere, Henze continued to receive and fulfill commissions. In 1976 (the year of the first festival), Henze completed his third and fourth string quartets. A fifth followed the year after. In 1979, he returned to the medium of the song cycle with the theater piece for mezzo-soprano and ensemble, *The King of Harlem*. In 1980, Henze began began teaching at the Cologne Musikhochschule, and in 1983 he published the opera *The English Cat*. His *Seventh Symphony* followed in 1984.

Summary

In 1969, Hans Werner Henze wrote,

> I can conceive of utopian possibilities only in socialism. Utopia is defined by the absence of capitalism . . . the liberation of art from its commercialization. I visualize the disappearance of the musical elite and of globe-trotting virtuosi. . . . I could envisage composing becoming something that all people can do, simply by taking away their inhibitions. . . . Music would then be something that belongs to all, that is not alien but a part of people's lives. People will no longer be alienat-

ed, but will be able to develop; they will be able to open themselves to all the beauties of life.

Music, for Henze, was both a means with which he glorified past proletarian revolutions and a tool by which he effected revolutionary acts. Its impact was primarily political and only secondarily aesthetic. He borrowed freely from many sources—folk song, jazz, atonal and aleotoric practices—using whatever best suited his immediate purpose. Yet Henze's strong compositional craft and vivid imagination ensured that his political views were consistently presented in musical settings of utmost artistry and theatric power.

Bibliography

Austin, William W. *Music in the Twentieth Century*. London: Dent, and New York: Norton, 1966. Although dated, Austin's text is an excellent source for the student interested in understanding the developments upon which recent composers have built their own styles. Henze is discussed briefly in the context of other, post-World War II, German composers.

Baker, Theodore. *Baker's Biographical Dictionary of Musicians.* 7th rev. ed. New York: Schirmer, and Oxford: Oxford University Press, 1984. This brief biography of Henze is followed by a work list helpful in both its completeness and in its listings of both dates of works' completion and their premiere.

Clinch, Dermot. "Hans Werner Henze: Profile." *New Statesman* 125, no. 4289 (June 21, 1996). Short discussion of the works of Henze.

Henderson, Robert. "Hans Werner Henze." In *New Grove Dictonary of Music and Musicians.* Edited by Stanley Sadie. 6th ed. London and New York: Macmillan, 1980. Henderson's six-and-a-half-page article on Henze is the best general source on the composer in English. Although the book provides much useful material, Henderson's enthusiasm for the composer's work borders on hagiography.

Henze, Hans Werner. *Music and Politics: Collected Writings 1953-81.* Translated by Peter Labanyi. Ithaca, N.Y.: Cornell University Press, and London: Faber, 1982. Any study of Henze's work should begin with this translation of Henze's essays and selected letters. Helpful in understanding the cultural climate of Germany immediately following the Nazis' defeat, this volume also contains a useful chronology of Henze's life and works.

James, Jamie. "Pacific Overture." *Opera News* 56, no. 5 (November, 1991). Interview with Henze, who discusses his adaptation of Yukio Mishima's "The Sailor Who Fell from Grace with the Sea."

Machlis, Joseph. *Introduction to Contemporary Music.* 2d ed. New York: Norton, 1979; London: Dent, 1980. Machlis is one of his generation's best writers on music. His concluding "dictionary," which presents brief biographies of several hundred contemporary composers, including Henze, is helpful.

Salzman, Eric. *Twentieth Century Music: An Introduction.* 3d ed. Englewood Cliffs, N.J.: Prentice-Hall, 1988. Salzman discusses Henze briefly within a chapter devoted to musical theater.

Michael Linton

KATHARINE HEPBURN

Born: May 12, 1907; Hartford, Connecticut

Area of Achievement: Film

Contribution: With a career spanning most of the twentieth century, Katharine Hepburn has, from her early career days, embodied wit, independence, and charm to the American public. Hepburn was one of the first actresses to break down Hollywood's stereotype of women, and she has served as a model of grit and beauty throughout her career.

Early Life

Katharine Houghton Hepburn was born on May 12, 1907 (despite conflicting reports that have dogged her since her first Hollywood film), the second of the six children of Katharine "Kit" Hepburn and Thomas Hepburn. Her mother was part of a well-known New England family, the Houghtons. Encouraged by her dying mother to acquire an education for herself and her sisters, Kit Houghton eventually earned a bachelor's degree from Bryn Mawr (1899) and a master's degree from Radcliffe (1900). Houghton's upbringing encouraged her to value independence, education, and social responsibility, three qualities that dominated her life. Because of her mother's interests, Katharine Hepburn had a childhood that was characterized by her family's deep involvement in many social causes of the day: the suffrage movement, the presence of brothels in their home city of Hartford and the associated spread of venereal disease, and the efforts to provide safe birth control to women (the latter cause was ably headed by Margaret Sanger, a friend of the Hepburns.) The Hepburn family's social conscience was not, however, guided solely by Kit Hepburn. Thomas Norval Hepburn was a young medical student when he first met Kit Houghton, and his sense of social awareness was as acute as hers. He chose to specialize in urology, an unmentionable subject in the polite society of that time. His practice led him to understand the horrors of syphilis, which was devastating the populations of all social classes. He chose to speak out about this unmentionable disease, at one point even paying for the printing and distribution of a play (*Damaged Goods*, by French dramatist Eugène Brieux) on the subject.

Another feature of Hepburn's childhood was her family's emphasis on physical activity. From ice cold baths to swinging on a homemade trapeze strung from the trees to playing tennis and golf, the family's active life was the result in large part of Thomas Hepburn's belief that a sluggish body led to a sluggish mind.

This closely knit family did suffer one early tragedy that also shaped Hepburn's growth: the accidental death by hanging of the oldest child, Tom, who was especially close to his sister Katharine. Soon after this time, Hepburn and her four siblings formed the Hepburn Players, an assortment of neighborhood children who put on performances with their own staging and direction. Even here, the family's social consciousness dominated: All proceeds from the production of *Beauty and the Beast* went to benefit the children of the Navajo Indians in New Mexico. (Hepburn herself played the beast.)

Like her mother and grandmother before her, Hepburn attended Bryn Mawr College, where she took part in many of the school theatricals: Her parts ranged from playing a young man in one performance to playing Pandora in *The Woman in the Moone* [sic]. These experiences seem to have led to her decision to become an actress; just before the end of her senior year, she approached Edwin H. Knopf, a director of a local theater company, armed with a letter of introduction and asking for work.

Life's Work

In 1928, just before her graduation from Bryn Mawr, Katharine Hepburn's persistence overrode Knopf's objections, and he hired her to play one of six ladies-in-waiting in a production of *The Czarina* (1928). Hepburn's early years on the stage were marked by many struggles and ups and downs. She was, as she later said, "a quick study": She could read a part wonderfully and impress the director. When she was hired, however, she lacked the training and experience to carry through a full performance.

In 1932, Hepburn played the supporting role of Antiope, an Amazon warrior, in the Broadway production of *The Warrior's Husband*. Her entrance staggered Broadway: Wearing a short tunic, a helmet, a breastplate, and leggings, and carrying a dead stag over her shoulder, Hepburn leapt down a steep ramp and onto a platform, where she hurled the stag at Hippolyta's feet. This performance led

Katharine Hepburn and Douglas Fairbanks, Jr. in the 1930's film Morning Glory.

to an offer of a screen test for Hepburn. On the basis of this screen test, Hepburn was awarded her first role in Hollywood, playing Hillary Fairfield in the 1932 film *A Bill of Divorcement* with the famous John Barrymore. This role led to Hepburn's instant fame, although her second film in Hollywood, *Christopher Strong*, was neither a popular nor a critical success. Hepburn's popularity returned after her third picture, *Morning Glory* (1933), for which she was awarded her first Academy Award for Best Actress. Hepburn's next film role, Jo in *Little Women* (1933), was critically acclaimed, but she was not to be part of another popular film until *Stage Door* in 1937.

After she received her Academy Award, Hepburn's appeal was so great that she was offered the lead in the stage production of *The Lake* (1934). The play began disastrously, with a hard director apparently trying to browbeat Hepburn into buying out her contract. Hepburn stuck to her work, however, and struggled so hard to improve each performance that, by the time the play closed, she was

turning in excellent performances. Soon after this experience, Hepburn returned to Hollywood.

In 1938, Hepburn's second film with the talented Cary Grant, *Bringing up Baby,* was released. Though it was not enormously popular upon first release, *Bringing up Baby* later came to be considered the finest of the "screwball comedies" that were so popular during the 1920's and 1930's.

Despite her successes in dealing with Hollywood on her own terms and her previous difficulty with *The Lake*, Hepburn often returned to the stage. One of her most successful theatrical runs was in *The Philadelphia Story* (1939). As well as starring in the play, Hepburn was involved in all aspects of its production, from writing to casting to arranging financing. Hepburn was as deeply involved in the writing and production of the film version of *The Philadelphia Story* (1940), in which she repeated her role from the stage version.

In 1942, yet another Hepburn film, *Woman of the Year*, was released. This picture marked Katharine Hepburn's first screen work with the superb actor

Spencer Tracy, and it initiated what became the longest screen partnership in history as well as a legendary Hollywood romance. Hepburn and Tracy worked together until 1967, when their last film together, *Guess Who's Coming to Dinner*, was completed shortly before Tracy's death. Hepburn's work in this film earned for her a second Academy Award, which she believed must have been meant for both Tracy and herself.

The African Queen (1951), made with Humphrey Bogart on location in Africa, saw the transition in Hepburn's career from a young Hollywood actress whom the studios had tried to portray as a starlet to the mature Hepburn, who was able to show film audiences the confidence and competence she had possessed all along. As one of her biographers, Sheridan Morley, explained, with the role of the missionary Rose Sayer, Hepburn transcended the "battle-of-the-sexes . . . comedies . . . and the old high- society romps" of her early career to become a great dramatic actress. This picture (for which Bogart won the Academy Award for Best Actor) was a critical and financial success for all concerned. Another Hepburn film that received great critical acclaim was *Long Day's Journey into Night* (1962), in which she gave a compelling performance of a woman sinking into the depths of drug addiction. According to many critics, this performance was the pinnacle of her career, a review that seems a bit premature, since Hepburn continued to work. She won her next two Academy Awards for Best Actress for her portrayal of Eleanor of Aquitane in *The Lion in Winter* (1968) and for her portrayal of Ethel Thayer in *On Golden Pond* (1981). These two films clearly demonstrated to the studios and critics that the American public would not only pay to see but also relish quality films starring mature, competent actors.

Summary

Throughout her career, Katharine Hepburn has pushed herself to explore the limits of her ability and of the motion picture medium. Her frequent stage work, from her struggles with *The Lake* to her success in *The Philadelphia Story* to her frequent Shakespeare roles, bears testimony to her determination not to rest on her laurels. Her four Academy Awards for Best Actress attest her talent as an actress and the admiration of her colleagues. Although audiences initially did not know what to make of her early performances (which were far from the typical Hollywood stereotypes of women) and despite more than her share of critical attacks, Hepburn eventually came to epitomize honesty, independence, and intelligence, and she has been idolized by millions of filmgoers. Hepburn's biographer, Gary Carey, quoted Richard Watts of the *Herald Tribune* as saying, "Few actresses have been so relentlessly assailed by critics, wits, columnists, magazine editors, and other professional assailers over so long a period of time, and even if you confess that some of the abuse had a certain amount of justification to it, you must admit she faced it gamely and unflinchingly and fought back with courage and gallantry."

Bibliography

Andersen, Christopher. *An Affair to Remember: The Remarkable Love Story of Katharine Hepburn and Spencer Tracy*. New York: Morrow, 1997. Examines the twenty-six year love affair between Hepburn and Tracy. Includes information on their other affairs and Tracy's darker side.

———. *Young Kate*. London: Macmillan, and New York: Holt, 1988. Based on conversations with Hepburn, this book chronicles her parents' lives, vividly recounts what it was like to grow up in the Hepburn family, and provides a detailed family chronology as well as a bibliography of supplementary references.

Britton, Andrew. *Katharine Hepburn: Star as Feminist*. New York: Continuum, 1995. Comprehensive discussion of Hepburn's career and her inability to defeat the sexist attitudes of Hollywood. Includes a number of photographs, a filmography, and a bibliography.

Bryson, John. *The Private World of Katharine Hepburn*. London: Gollancz, and Boston: Little Brown, 1990. Primarily a fine collection of photographs taken by the author (a professional photographer) of Katharine Hepburn over the years, this work also provides complementary text (based on discussions with Hepburn) that relates many stories about her family, her life, and her career.

Carey, Gary. *Katharine Hepburn: A Hollywood Yankee*. New York: St. Martin's Press, 1983. After a brief discussion of her childhood and college years, this book provides a general survey of Hepburn's career from her first theater job through her work in the early 1980's and a chronology of her films from her first film in 1932 to *On Golden Pond* in 1981.

Edwards, Anne. *A Remarkable Woman: A Biography of Katharine Hepburn*. New York: Morrow, 1985. Although it seems to relate a romanticized version of Hepburn's life, this biography includes detailed theater, film, radio, and television chronologies, a list of all of Hepburn's Academy Award nominations, and a long bibliography that lists many good references about Hepburn and about Hollywood and the theater in general.

Hepburn, Katharine. *The Making of The African Queen: Or, How I Went to Africa with Bogart, Bacall, and Huston and Almost Lost My Mind*. London: Century, and New York: Knopf, 1987. This is Hepburn's writing at its best as she recalls the making of *The African Queen* from her first awareness of the project through the trials of the location work in Africa, the completion of the film in the studio, and Bogart's Academy Award.

———. *Me: Stories of My Life*. New York: Knopf, and London: Viking Press, 1991. This book lives up to its title, providing stories of Hepburn's life from childhood through 1990. Written in a warm, readable, almost telegraphic style, the book discusses her career, her films and plays, and her family in a personal manner. Many photographs are included.

Kanin, Garson. *Tracy and Hepburn*. New York: Viking Press, 1971; London: Angus and Robertson, 1972. This very personal chronicle of the work and lives of Hepburn and Spencer Tracy is based on the author's long friendship with both and tells many stories of their lives together, both privately and professionally.

Morley, Sheridan. *Katharine Hepburn*. London: Pavilion, and Boston: Little Brown, 1984. This thorough retrospective of Hepburn's career, written by the son of one of Hepburn's former colleagues, provides detailed information about the progress of Hepburn's career and each of her pictures. Fourteen pages are devoted to a filmography, which provides thorough documentation about her films through 1984, her television work, and her stage work.

Katherine Socha

AILEEN CLARKE HERNANDEZ

Born: May 23, 1926; Brooklyn, New York

Areas of Achievement: Labor relations, social reform, and women's rights

Contribution: As president of the National Organization for Women (NOW), director of the International Ladies' Garment Workers Union, and commissioner of the Equal Employment Opportunity Commission, Aileen Hernandez has represented the interests of women and minorities in the forefront of social reform.

Early Life

Aileen Clarke was reared in Brooklyn by her parents Charles and Ethel Clarke, who had emigrated from Jamaica in the British West Indies and eventually became American citizens. Her mother was a costume maker and seamstress in the New York theater district, and her father worked in the art supply business. Aileen and her brothers were taught to cook and sew, since her parents believed that no gender distinctions should be made in employment. They also emphasized people should not be treated differently regardless of race or gender. This family value left an indelible mark on Aileen that would deeply influence her life and career. She was graduated from Bay Ridge Public School as valedictorian, and in 1943 from Bay Ridge High School as class salutatorian. Aileen received a scholarship to attend Howard University in Washington, D.C. She served as editor and writer for the campus paper *The Hilltop*, and wrote a column for the *Washington Tribune*. In 1946, she received honors in Kappa Mu Society, Howard's counterpart to Phi Beta Kappa.

Her political philosophy was molded by her college years in Washington, D.C., during the postwar period. She joined the student chapter of the National Association for the Advancement of Colored People (NAACP) and demonstrated against racial discrimination of the National Theatre, Lisner Auditorium, and the Thompson Restaurant chain. Her decision to participate in these early pickets stemmed largely from living as an African American in the United States. Venturing south for her college years at Howard, she experienced even more distinct discrimination as she traveled by train and waited for the segregated taxis in Washington, D.C., which were always the last in line. Believing that "democratic government requires full participation by all citizens," she supported equal rights for black World War II veterans returning to an unchanged segregated America.

After graduating magna cum laude from Howard University in 1947, with a degree in sociology and political science, Aileen Clark traveled to Norway as part of the International Student Exchange Program and studied comparative government. From 1947 to 1959, she attended New York University, the University of California at Los Angeles, and the University of Southern California. In 1959, she was awarded a master's degree in government, summa cum laude, from Los Angeles State College. In 1979 Southern Vermont College granted her an Honorary Doctorate in Humane Letters.

Life's Work

While attending New York University Graduate school, Aileen Clarke accepted an internship to the International Ladies' Garment Workers Union (ILGWU) Training Institute. She was hired in 1951 and transferred to the ILGWU Pacific Coast Region in California as an organizer. Eventually she served for eleven years in the ILGWU's West Coast office at Los Angeles as education director and public relations director. Her duties ranged from organizing social affairs to mobilizing strikes, pickets, and legislative lobbies. She was also responsible for naturalization classes for foreign-born union employees. In 1957, she married Alfonso Hernandez, a Mexican American garment worker whom she had met in Los Angeles. They were later divorced in 1961.

In 1961, her career shifted from union work to politics, managing a victorious campaign for Alan Cranston, as state controller. She was appointed assistant chief of the California Division of Fair Employment Practice Commission (FEPC), in 1962. In this position she supervised a staff of fifty in four field offices. While serving with the FEPC, she initiated a Technical Advisory Committee (TACT). The TACT report was a comprehensive analysis of industrial testing as it affects the hiring of minorities.

By this time she had acquired experience and recognition for her work in labor relations and fair employment practices. With the recommendation of California Governor Edmund G. "Pat" Brown, President Lyndon B. Johnson appointed her the first woman to the five-member commission of the Equal Employment Opportunity Commission. Her

duties included coordinating the activities of state and local commissions with the National EEOC. During her term on the Commission, commercial airlines overturned their traditional policy of terminating female flight attendants when they married. After eighteen months of service, she resigned from the EEOC because she felt that the commission lacked any power to enforce its own policies. In 1966, she established her own consulting firm in San Francisco, Hernandez and Associates, to advise businesses, government, labor, and private groups in urban affairs, and for the purpose of hiring minorities and women.

Aileen was present in 1966 at the Third National Conference of the State Commissions on Women in Washington, D.C. Betty Friedan, author of the 1963 best-seller *The Feminine Mystique*, was also there and they spoke of the necessity to establish a civil rights movement for women. At that conference, the National Organization for Women (NOW) was created and Friedan was chosen as its first president. In 1967, NOW appointed Aileen vice president of the Western region. In 1971 she succeeded Friedan as president of NOW. Her lead-

ership, and articulation of the women's movement were a real asset. Until 1971 many African American women viewed the women's movement as the elitist preserve of white middle-class women with nothing better to do. Aileen Hernandez considered NOW as an extension of the Civil Rights movement for all women. In one interview, Hernandez addressed the issue head on: "Until women, black as well as others, gain a sense of their own identity and feel that they have a real choice in society, nothing is going to happen in civil rights. It's not going to happen for Blacks; it's not going to happen for Mexican-Americans; it's not going to happen for women."

Summary

Aileen Hernandez's contributions to labor relations, the women's movement, equal opportunity, political activism, and community service compose an extensive list of accomplishments. Her dedication to public service has made her both a national and an international figure. She has represented the State Department abroad in Latin America, where she toured six countries, Argentina, Chile, Colombia, Peru, Uruguay, and Venezuela, lecturing in English and Spanish on trade unions, minorities, and the political system of th United States.

As president of NOW in 1973, she chaired the summer meeting in Boston of the International Feminist Planning Conference, bringing together women from thirty countries. At the invitation of the U.S. State Department and the Konrad Adenauer Foundation, in 1975 she attended the International Conference in Bonn, Germany, on *Minorities and the Metropolis*. She traveled to the People's Republic of China with an American Rights group in 1978. That same year, with the National Commission, she made a fact-finding tour of South Africa with the National Commission. The report of that regional study by the Commission published in 1981 entitled, *South Africa: Time Running Out*, received praise for its analysis of apartheid and U.S. policy in South Africa. She has also received international visitors on behalf of the United States from Japan, South Africa, Australia, New Zealand, Norway, Germany, Bangladesh, Belgium, Nigeria, and Sweden.

The numerous awards in recognition of her public service are impressive. She was chosen as Woman of the Year in 1961 by the Community Relations Conference of Southern California. Howard University honored its distinguished alumna in 1968 for Distinguished Postgraduate Achievement in the Fields of Labor and Public Service, and that same year she received the Charter Day Alumni Post Graduate Achievement in Labor and Public Services Award. *The San Francisco Examiner* named her one of the Ten Most Distinguished Women of the San Francisco Bay Area in 1969. The Bicentennial Award was granted to her in 1976 by the Trinity Baptist Church of San Mateo County. Equal Rights advocates commended her in 1981 for her service to the women's movement, and in 1984, the Friends of the San Francisco Commission on the Status of Women honored her. In 1985, The San Francisco League of Women Voters named her among the Ten Women Who Make a Difference, the National Urban Coalition recognized her service to urban communities, and the San Francisco Black Chamber of Commerce presented her with the Parren J. Mitchell Award for

dedicated service to the African American community. The Memorial United Methodist Church commended her services to humanity in 1986 and Gamma Phi Delta Sorority made her an honorary member. She has also received awards in appreciation from the National Institute for Women of Color in 1987, and the following year from the Western District Conference on the National Association of Negro Business and Professional Women's Clubs as well as the San Francisco Convention and the Visitor's bureau. The Northern California American Civil Liberties Foundation conferred the Earl Warren Civil Liberties Award in 1989.

Bibliography

Banner, Lois W. *Women in Modern America: A Brief History*. 3d ed. Fort Worth, Tex.: Harcourt Brace, 1995. A survey of the women's rights movement from the 1890's to 1984 that places Hernandez in the context of the formation of NOW.

Christmas, Walter. *Negroes in Public Affairs and Government*. Vol. 1. Yonkers, N.Y.: Educational Heritage, 1966. This specialized study, although dated, recognizes the work of Hernandez in the EEOC, labor relations, and NOW.

Dreyfus, Joel. "Civil Rights and the Women's Movement." *Black Enterprise* 8 (September, 1977): 35-37, 45. Includes Hernandez as the first African American woman to hold a national office and her vision of the women's movement as part of the larger Civil Rights movement.

Hartmann, Susan M. *From Margin to Mainstream: American Women and Politics Since 1960*. New York: Knopf, 1989. Hartmann's study of women who emerged on the American political scene between 1960 and 1980 assesses their impact on public policy.

Lewis, Ida. "Conversation: Ida Lewis and Aileen Hernandez." *Essence* 1 (February, 1971): 20-25, 74-75. An interview with Hernandez during her presidency of NOW in which she speaks about her role and the issues of the women's movement, civil rights, and equal opportunity.

Emily Teipe

ÉDOUARD HERRIOT

Born: July 5, 1872; Troyes, France
Died: March 26, 1957; Lyons, France
Areas of Achievement: Government and politics
Contribution: One of the most important French statesmen of the first half of the twentieth century, Herriot served nearly four decades in the French parliament, headed three governments between 1924 and 1933, held posts in six other cabinets between 1916 and 1936, was mayor of Lyons (France's second-largest city) from 1905 to 1957, and was leader of the Radical-Socialist Party for much of his career.

Early Life

Édouard Herriot was born into a humble provincial family less than two years after republican rule returned to France. Education was the key to his personal success. While both of his parents came from military backgrounds, none of his relatives was prominently connected or wealthy; consequently, the young Herriot had to rely on native intellectual ability and scholarship grants to gain educational opportunities. Tutored at an early age by a village priest, Herriot at age fifteen received a scholarship to a prestigious Paris *lycée* from a local official whom he happened to impress. Four years later, he won admission to the École Normale Supérieure, where he received training as a teacher. In 1905, he completed his doctorate at the Sorbonne.

Herriot's rich educational experience instilled in him a deep commitment to rational investigation and inspired him to work throughout his political career to expand educational opportunity for all Frenchmen. It also cultivated a love of literary pursuits, which made him one of the most brilliant orators and prolific writers of his day. Before he died, Herriot published nearly fifty books and articles—historical and political tracts, literary essays, works based on his own travels abroad, and memoirs. He composed his first scholarly treatise, *Philon le Juif* (1898), a study of the important Hebrew philosopher who was a contemporary of Jesus Christ, in the barracks at Nancy while completing his mandatory military service in 1898. In 1947, his writings would win for him election to the Académie Française.

Herriot's early and enduring affiliation with the Radical-Socialist Party at the municipal and national levels followed naturally, in his view, from his concern for the defense of basic human rights and his faith in the power of rational thought. As he wrote in 1931: "Radicalism appears as the political application of rationalism." It was also, Herriot believed, the best embodiment of France's democratic tradition. Herriot's political philosophy solidified at the time of the Dreyfus affair and the vicious anticlerical campaign that followed it. A spirited Dreyfusard and anticlerical himself, Herriot claimed to have entered public life under the patronage of Émile Combes, the Radical prime minister from 1902 to 1905 who spearheaded the controversial separation of church and state. Herriot first gained public office by winning election to the Lyons city council in 1904. The following year, he was elected mayor of Lyons (at thirty-three, he was the youngest mayor in the country), and, as chief executive of France's second largest city, he gained a voice in Radical politics at the national level. In 1912, he began a seven-year term as France's youngest senator, and, in 1919, he won election to the Chamber of Deputies. In the latter year also, he was chosen president of the Radical-Socialist Party, and his career as a statesman was under way.

Life's Work

Herriot's life's work focused on city hall in Lyons and the cabinet rooms and legislative chambers of Paris. In the first setting, Herriot's disposition toward social activism may be most easily seen. As mayor, he improved hospitals and schools, expanded housing for working-class citizens, enhanced libraries and museums, constructed numerous public buildings, renovated and enlarged port facilities, and undertook municipal beautification programs. Despite the heavy responsibilities of national office for most of his career, Herriot emphasized that nothing was as important to him as Lyons and said once: "I loved Lyons as one adores a woman."

His service in Lyons and the publication of a collection of his lectures earned for Herriot recognition by the national leadership and resulted in his first appointment to ministerial office in December, 1916, in the cabinet of Aristide Briand. He held the post of minister of public works, transports, and supplies for barely four months, however, and his decision to ration bread and limit the number of courses allowed in restaurant meals was not popular despite its importance to the war effort. Herriot did not hold governmental office again until 1924, when he was named prime minister after the ruling center-right majority was overthrown in national elections by a coalition of left-wing parties (Cartel des Gauches), in which his own Radical-Socialist Party constituted the largest group.

It was as head of the government from June, 1924, to April, 1925, that Herriot established himself as an important national leader. During this brief term, Herriot directed the end of France's Ruhr Valley occupation, the implementation of the Dawes Plan, and the preliminary negotiations to the Locarno Pact. In all of this, he manifested a more conciliatory approach to Germany and a significant change in tone from earlier postwar French foreign policy. In 1924, he became the first head of a French government to address the League of Nations in Geneva, an occasion he later termed "the most solemn moment" of his life. He also established full diplomatic relations with the Soviet Union in 1924, a move paralleled by Great Britain's Labour government in the same year. In 1925, Herriot became the first minister of any major European government to advocate publicly some form of European federation. His domestic agenda favored the standard left-wing (though non-Marxist) program of social insurance, educational reform, reorganization of the tax structure, and reduction of the length of military service. The conservative senate ended his premiership when he tried to enact a tax on capital. Herriot's colleagues in the Chamber of Deputies, however, rewarded him with the presidency of the lower house when his government was overthrown, and he held this post—generally viewed as the third-highest office under the French republics—on several occasions during the next quarter-century.

Herriot's appointment as Minister of Public Instruction in July, 1926, led to his most enduring achievements in cabinet politics. As a trained teacher of humble origins, Herriot appreciated the importance of equal educational opportunity for all Frenchmen regardless of their wealth or social status. He also believed that the democratic state had an obligation to finance and universalize public education in the interest of creating an informed citizenry. Accordingly, among Herriot's accomplishments as minister in the 1920's were laws admitting students to primary and secondary schools without charge, equalizing instruction for girls and boys, and standardizing course content nationwide. Perhaps his greatest triumph in educational reform may be seen in the preamble to the constitution of the Fourth Republic, which he helped to frame in 1946, which guaranteed "equal access of children and adults to education, professional training and culture" and affirmed as "the duty of the State to provide free, secular, public education at all levels."

In the 1930's, Herriot headed one more government and sat in four others. His major accomplishment as premier in 1932 was a nonaggression pact with the Soviet Union, which paved the way for a full-scale anti-Fascist alliance with Moscow four years later. During this troubled decade, Herriot held such influential positions as president of the Radical-Socialist Party, president of the Chamber of Deputies, and president of the Foreign Affairs Committee of the Chamber of Deputies. After 1936, however, he was excluded from cabinet posts and was opposed to the official policy of appeasement of the Fascist dictators.

The fateful year of 1940 found Herriot, as presiding officer of the chamber, in the midst of events surrounding national defeat and the dissolution of the Third Republic. Herriot became one of the most outspoken defenders of parliamentary rights during the authoritarian Vichy regime. He was arrested in 1942 and spent the remainder of the war in captivity, ultimately in Germany. After the defeat of Adolf Hitler and Herriot's own liberation by Russian troops, he returned to France, resumed his mayoral duties in Lyons, and restored himself and his Radical-Socialist Party to national prominence. With so many French politicians discredited by collaboration with the Nazis, Herriot's example of passive resistance to the wartime tyranny won vast public admiration. He emerged during the postwar years as a primary shaper of France's new republican regime and served as president of the National Assembly from 1947 to 1953. These years also afforded Herriot the opportunity to champion another of his long-standing goals: European federation. In November, 1948, he became president of the international study commission for European unity, and, when the Council of Europe was founded as the first common political institution for Europe in 1949, Herriot delivered the inaugural address in Strasbourg.

Summary

Édouard Herriot's life coincided with one of the most tumultuous periods of French history. Born two years into the Third Republic, itself the offspring of catastrophic defeat in the Franco-Prussian

War, Herriot became one of the most important leaders of the last three decades of that regime. His first ministerial post came in the midst of one world war; his tenure as president of the Chamber of Deputies ended with France's defeat at the beginning of the next. His death preceded by one year the end of the Fourth Republic, a regime he had helped to found. While his specific political and literary achievements speak for themselves, Herriot's ultimate contribution may lie in what he symbolized. His rise from ordinary beginnings to extraordinary prominence bore witness to republican France's emphasis on careers open to talents. As a statesman, he confronted the problems of war and recovery on two momentous occasions. Above all, Herriot stands out for his unyielding commit-ment to parliamentary government, the ideals of the French revolutionary heritage, and international harmony. For his defense of these principles, he fell momentary victim to the Nazi tyranny. Once vindicated, he regained the opportunity to move his nation toward the elusive vision of "liberty, equality, and fraternity." In the aftermath of World War II, Herriot became to many "the patriarch of the Republic" and the symbol of what was best in France's entire political tradition.

Bibliography

De Tarr, Francis. *The French Radical Party: From Herriot to Mendès-France.* London and New York: Oxford University Press, 1961. Contains an entire chapter on Herriot as the "symbol of Radicalism" and is especially informative on Herriot's importance as party leader after World War II.

Herriot, Édouard. *In Those Days.* Translated by Adolphe de Milly. New York: Old and New World, 1952. An English translation of the first volume of Herriot's memoirs covering to the outbreak of World War I. Offers useful insights into Herriot's formative years as a writer and a politician.

Jessner, Sabine. *Édouard Herriot, Patriarch of the Republic.* New York: Haskell House, 1974. The only full-length Herriot biography in English. Based solidly on Herriot's own writings and the wealth of scholarly literature about him in the French language.

Larmour, Peter J. *The French Radical Party in the 1930's.* Stanford, Calif.: Stanford University Press, 1964. A scholarly treatment of radicalism that provides extensive material on Herriot's role in the Radical-Socialist Party during the turbulent decade before the outbreak of World War II.

Talbott, John E. *The Politics of Educational Reform in France, 1918-1940.* Princeton, N.J.: Princeton University Press, 1969. Contains a good summary of Herriot's achievements in the field of education.

Thomas H. Conner

GUSTAV HERTZ

Born: July 22, 1887; Hamburg, Germany
Died: October 30, 1975; Berlin, East Germany
Area of Achievement: Physics
Contribution: Hertz and his colleague James Franck received the Nobel Prize in Physics in 1926 for their spectroscopic experiments on mercury vapor when bombarded with electrons. Their results were some of the first to confirm empirically the accuracy of Niels Bohr's model of atomic structure as well as the hypothesis of Max Planck and Albert Einstein that atoms absorb energy in discrete quanta rather than continuously.

Early Life

Gustav Ludwig Hertz was born in Hamburg, Germany, on July 22, 1887. His parents were Auguste Hertz, née Arning, and the lawyer Gustav Hertz, brother of the famous expert on electromagnetic waves Heinrich Hertz. Little has been written about Hertz's childhood, but it is known that Hertz attended the Johanneum School in Hamburg and at age nineteen began his studies at the University of Göttingen. He seems to have chosen a career as a scientist early in life, although it is not known to what extent the example of his distinguished uncle influenced his decision. The atomic scientist Arnold Sommerfeld probably had a more direct and significant impact as Hertz's teacher when Hertz attended the University of Munich during the 1907 academic year.

After military service in 1908, Hertz went to Berlin to continue his studies and received a doctorate at the University of Berlin in 1911, after which he began working with another young scientist from Hamburg, James Franck. They experimented with, among other things, electron bombardment on mercury vapor. The spectroscopic results of their experiments were interpreted in several publications, and eventually the scientific community would recognize the significance of their work, as evinced by the selection of Hertz and Franck as recipients of the Nobel Prize in Physics in 1926.

Both Franck and Hertz left the University of Berlin at the outbreak of World War I and served in the army. Hertz was severely wounded in 1915 and recovered slowly. In 1917, he returned to Berlin as a privatdocent, or lecturer, at the university. As applied physics was his exclusive field of interest,

Hertz did not hesitate in the following years to leave academic physics for private industry, although he would periodically return to Berlin to teach and to pursue research at one of the academic institutions there. In 1919, at the age of thirty-two, he married Ellen Dihlmann.

Life's Work

When Hertz returned to the University of Berlin after World War I, he resumed work in the study of electron bombardments and the quantized energy exchanges that accompany them, and began to experiment with X-ray spectroscopy as well. Hertz was first and foremost a meticulous laboratory scientist. In 1920, he began a five-year sojourn as a researcher in Eindhoven, the Netherlands, at the Philips Incandescent Lamp Factory, which was one of the first industrial laboratories where basic research was pursued. Hertz devoted most of his time and energy to the problem of the separation of gases, that is, to obtaining pure forms of a given gas by diffusion.

In 1925, Hertz was asked to serve as director of the Physics Institute of the University of Halle; he accepted and remained there for three years. In these years, his work with Franck had become extremely well known, one result being an invitation in 1928 to return to Berlin as director of the Physics Institute at the Technische Hochschule of Berlin-Charlottenburg. In the early 1930's, Hertz perfected a highly successful method for separating gaseous isotopes of helium and neon by diffusion. This technique, known as a diffusion "cascade," was based on principles applicable to all types of isotopes. Hertz's successes in this field would become especially important in the following decades, as he and other scientists began to investigate the uses of uranium isotopes in the creation of nuclear energy. Scientists in the United States used the method in developing the first atom bombs.

Hertz refused to take a Nazi loyalty oath in 1934 and resigned his academic post to accept a position as chief physicist for Siemens Corporation in Berlin. Had it not been for his usefulness to Siemens, his future in Germany, as well as that of his wife, who was vocally pro-Allies, doubtlessly would have been far worse, since he was part Jewish. At Siemens, Hertz was encouraged to continue his work on the separation of isotopes, particularly heavy neon (neon 22).

As the decade of the 1930's drew to a close, Hertz's interest was consumed—in spite of the growing necessity to oversee conventional weaponry projects at Siemens—by problems associated with the actual creation of nuclear energy. The importance of Hertz's method of separating isotopes was augmented considerably when a refugee from Austria, Lise Meitner, announced in 1939 in Sweden that she and her former collaborator in Germany, Otto Hahn, had split the atom, thus setting the stage for the possible creation of a chain reaction with uranium 235.

While Hertz had been indeed tolerated by Nazi authorities (he was a productive scientist with an impressive military record), the war years nevertheless were not free of tragedy. Ellen, his wife of twenty-two years, died in 1941. Their two sons, both of whom became professional scientists, would survive the war. In 1943, Hertz married Charlotte Jollasse. When the Red Army entered Berlin after World War II, Hertz agreed to join a research team in the Soviet Union. At first, it was reported that he had been coerced by the Soviets, but Werner Heisenberg revealed to the press in Febru-

ary of 1947 that Hertz and about two hundred other German scientists had joined the Soviet project willingly, accepting a stipend of six thousand rubles per month. Hertz and several of his colleagues and former pupils were given a manor house near Stochi on the Black Sea in which they constructed a laboratory for nuclear research and began planning for production of radioactive isotopes on a large scale.

In 1949-1950, when the Soviet Union acquired essential technical information for the construction of its own atom bomb, Hertz's skills were employed directly in the construction of nuclear weapons; he did not return to Germany until 1954, when he moved to Leipzig to teach experimental physics and serve as director of the Physics Institute. By 1957, it was widely known in the West that Hertz was one of the key minds behind the Soviet Union's atomic weapons program, although little was known about the details of his work.

As a teacher at the University of Leipzig, Hertz saw the need for good textbooks on the specialized field of atomic physics and subsequently devoted much of his seemingly limitless energy to consolidating and compiling his knowledge of the structure of the atom. In 1957, he published a book on the principles and methods of nuclear physics (*Grundlagen und Arbeitsmethoden der Kernphysik*), which was followed by a three-volume compendium of nuclear science in 1958-1962 (*Lehrbuch der Kernphysik*). In 1961, Hertz withdrew from his post as director of the Physics Institute and began a much-deserved retirement. He died on October 30, 1975.

Summary

Meticulous laboratory work and cautious analysis of experimental data were Gustav Hertz's métier; his contributions were not characterized by breathtaking originality but rather by painstaking accuracy and reliability. He helped to fill in the edifice of modern atomic theory. His scientific career was his life, and he managed, despite his religious background and political opinions, to remain in Germany and continue his work during the tribulations of the Nazi period. Moreover, he was able at the end of World War II to arrange for nearly ideal working conditions by going to work in the Soviet Union. Unlike his former colleague Franck, who fled Germany as early as 1933 and later worked on the first U.S. atom bomb, Hertz never made known any problems he might have had with the political and ethical implications of a military use of nuclear power.

Hertz is often credited with leading the team that built Germany's first cyclotron in the 1930's. With this "atom-smashing" device, he wished to extend his early investigations on energy transfer in elastic collisions of electrons and atoms to inelastic collisions, that is, collisions in which an elementary particle fired at the atom is not absorbed but actually causes the breakup of the nucleus. The Nazi government did little to discourage his work in private industry. In time, he made considerable advances in the development of a method for the separation of the volatile isotope uranium 235.

After his retirement, Hertz was honored by his colleagues with a ceremony and *Festschrift* in celebration of his eightieth birthday in 1967. At that time, he was praised for the discovery of laws governing discrete energy transfer in electron collisions and for the invention and continual refinement of methods for separating isotopes, without which the use of nuclear power would have been impossible. In addition to the Nobel Prize shared with Franck, Hertz by the end of his life had received many other professional awards, including the Lenin Prize of the Soviet Union in 1955. He was a member of most scientific academies in the Eastern Bloc, as well as the Göttingen Academy of Sciences in the West.

Bibliography

Barwich, Heinz, and Efi Barwich. *Das rote Atom.* Munich: Scherz, 1967. Because of the paucity of materials on Hertz, this German book is noted here, since it is a standard work on the otherwise obscure history of atomic research in the Soviet Union following World War II. Barwich was a student of Hertz who also went to the Soviet Union after World War II. He fled the Eastern Bloc in 1962.

Franck, James. "A Personal Memoir." In *Niels Bohr: A Centenary Volume*, edited by Anthony P. French and P. J. Kennedy. Cambridge, Mass.: Harvard University Press, 1985. This reminiscence by Hertz's colleague gives an interesting account of the experimental work that earned for them the Nobel Prize. Franck explains why he and Hertz were slow to realize the significance of their results for the tenability of the Bohr theory of the atom.

Heathcote, Niels Hugh de Vaudrey. *Nobel Prize Winners in Physics, 1901-1950.* New York: Schuman, 1953. This valuable collection contains a straightforward treatment of the electron experiments of Hertz and Franck, based on selections from their Nobel Prize lectures.

Hermann, Armin. *The Genesis of Quantum Theory, 1889-1913.* Cambridge, Mass.: MIT Press, 1971. Contains a useful discussion of contributions to quantum theory by Hertz and Franck. The author's historical approach is intended not only for the physicist but also for the reader with a basic knowledge of science.

Holton, Gerald. "On the Recent Past of Physics." *American Journal of Physics* 29 (1961): 805-810. This article, published in the year of Hertz's retirement, mostly describes early reactions to Bohr's atom model but briefly discusses the work of Franck and Hertz.

Mark R. McCulloh

HERMANN HESSE

Born: July 2, 1877; Calw, Germany
Died: August 9, 1962; Montagnola, Switzerland
Area of Achievement: Literature
Contribution: Writing in the tradition of Romantic individualism, Hesse produced novels and novellas that brought him literary acclaim. Highly autobiographical and confessional, his prose works employ modernist thought and aesthetic principles to narrate the development of existential protagonists.

Early Life

Hermann Hesse was born on July 2, 1877, in Calw, a village on the edge of Germany's Black Forest. His parents, Johannes and Marie (née Gundert), were German Pietists, and his maternal grandfather was a distinguished Indologist. In Hesse's youth, the family lived for six years in Basel, Switzerland, where his father taught at a mission school. His own youth and schooling were marked by years of unhappiness, primarily because of conflict with his father and other authority figures. After experiencing severe depression in a Protestant seminary at Maulbronn, he entered a *Gymnasium* but remained only briefly. Subsequent service as an apprentice in a tower clock factory in Calw was similarly dispiriting. Employment in bookstores, first in Tübingen and later in Basel, enabled him to develop his intellect through reading. With the success of his first novel, *Peter Camenzind* (1904; English translation, 1961), he resolved to devote his life to literature.

The personal and psychological strife and unhappiness of his early life persisted through most of his writing career, at least until his third marriage, when he was in his fifties. Following the failure of his first marriage in 1916, he suffered a mental breakdown. Disillusioned with German militarism even before World War I, he became a Swiss citizen in 1923. After settling in Montagnola, Switzerland, in 1919, and particularly after his marriage to Ninon Auslander in 1931, his life assumed a measure of stability.

Life's Work

Hesse's literary career spanned more than six decades, and over that period he drew his ideas, themes, and narrative techniques from rich and eclectic sources. Among German Romantic writers, the influence of Johann Wolfgang von Goethe,

Jean Paul, Novalis, and others was so extensive that critics have placed Hesse in the tradition of Romantic individualism. Among philosophers, Immanuel Kant, Arthur Schopenhauer, and Friedrich Wilhelm Nietzsche impressed him most deeply. Further, he was steeped in Eastern philosophy and religious thought, including classical Chinese poets, the Upanishads, and the Bhagavad Gita. The historian Jakob Burckhard, the psychologists Sigmund Freud and Carl G. Jung, and the Russian novelist Fyodor Dostoevski also exerted strong influence on his thought and art. From the individualism of the Romantics with their emphasis on intuition, from the psychology of the will in Schopenhauer and Nietzsche, and from the depth psychology of Freud and Jung, Hesse developed a Romantic individualism akin to modern existentialism—one that escapes the sentimentality of earlier German Romanticism. His writing, confessional and highly autobiographical, is essentially concerned with the development of the individual through what he termed an inward journey.

Hesse's artistic production was also exceptionally varied. His first book was a collection of lyric poems, and throughout most of his life he continued writing verse—hundreds of lyrics in all. Moreover, he produced essays, articles, book reviews, and short stories in abundance. He mastered watercoloring and illustrated some of his volumes. His major literary achievement, however, lies in the novels and novellas produced during the period spanned by the two world wars, from *Demian* (1919; English translation, 1923) to *Das Glasperlenspiel: Versuch einer Lebensbeschreibung des magister Ludi Josef Knecht samt Knechts hinterlassenen schriften* (1943; *Magister Ludi*, 1949; also as *The Glass Bead Game*, 1969).

Individual development, Hesse believed, was thwarted by two major forces: nationalism and technology. Because he considered these obstacles to be dehumanizing, Hesse consistently rejected their standardization and regimentation and portrayed characters who transcended them in order to reach the highest level of self-expression. In his early *Künstlerromans*, such as *Klingsor* (1920; *Klingsor's Last Summer*, 1970), he presents the view that to excel one must escape middle-class conformity through either asceticism or sensuality. Hesse's protagonists usually engage in these extreme forms of self-denial or self-assertion.

Highly autobiographical and unendingly confessional in form, Hesse's novels belong to literary genres originating with Jean-Jacques Rousseau in which confession becomes an avenue to self-justification. Yet the prized inner journey implied more than a Romantic celebration of individualism. It meant the development of individual talent and capacity through an effort of will in a Schopenhauerian sense, an essentially existential emphasis. Hesse's protagonists are engaged in a journey; they are seekers who, unable to control reality outside themselves, strive for individual development, fulfillment, and meaning.

Accompanying this individual quest centered in the self is a set of assumptions about the outside world. Hesse's orientalism treats Asia as a source of renewal, both personal and spiritual, but it also reflects his view that Europe is in decline because of spiritual and intellectual bankruptcy. This theme surfaces boldly in *Klingsor's Last Summer*. In an almost Spenglerian pessimism, Hesse endorses the decline of Europe, and much of his later fiction is influenced by this perceived reality. Often presenting external decline through expressionistic techniques, Hesse has his protagonists view external events as grotesquely distorted and chaotic. Avenues of their escape are isolation, which Siddhartha attempts; sensuality, Harry Haller's means in *Der Steppenwolf* (1927; *Steppenwolf*, 1929); or projection into the future where an ideal society replaces a failed one, as in *The Glass Bead Game*. Hence, the plight of the individual soul enmeshed in a declining civilization sets the conflict for the major prose fiction.

Hesse's first novel, a *Bildungsroman, Peter Camenzind*, a story of adolescent friendship and poignant young love based upon his own early life and schooling, is rich with descriptions of nature and the idyllic mountain valleys he knew as a child. The second novel, another *Bildungsroman, Unterm Rad* (1906; *The Prodigy*, 1957; also as *Beneath the Wheel*, 1968), is more darkly pessimistic. Its title comes from a statement of the schoolmaster to the young protagonist Hans Giebenrath admonishing him to keep up in his studies to avoid falling beneath the wheel. The novel is based on Hesse's unhappy experience at Maulbronn, with a lengthy account of life in a boarding school and work in the Calw clock factory. It introduces a theme significant in Hesse's later fiction—adolescent friendship as a preface to romantic heterosexual love.

With the publication of *Demian*, Hesse received recognition as a major voice in modern literature. Another *Bildungsroman* and highly influenced by Hesse's experience with psychoanalysis, *Demian* shows the protagonist Emil Sinclair developing through three stages. In the first, he is secure in childhood innocence and family warmth. In the second, he departs in order to establish his own identity and thereby incurs guilt and sorrow. In the third, he accepts a spiritual point of view that combines and unites good and evil, symbolized in the novel by the gnostic deity Abraxas. Heavily dependent upon dreams and symbols, *Demian* portrays a divided and conflicted psyche that develops through transforming experiences. Sinclair's growth is aided by friends and role models who guide and inspire him, the Christlike Demian being the most significant.

The quest for spiritual development appears subsequently as the primary theme in *Siddhartha* (1922; English translation, 1951), a novella set in India. Here, the Nietzschean division between the Apollonian and Dionysian spirits emerges when the protagonist first becomes a Hindu holy man and then turns to a life of sensuality, finally becoming a ferryman at a river crossing and experiencing spiritual growth. Siddhartha finds that he must seek to know himself before he can pursue a transcendent ideal; the novel suggests that self-knowledge grows out of sensuality, which in turn must be transcended. In the role of ferryman, he learns through revelation that love is a greater force than knowledge. Like Sinclair in *Demian*, Siddhartha has a close friend in the more spiritually oriented Govinda, who follows the Eastern principles of asceticism. Unlike Sinclair, however, Siddhartha has to discover the way suitable for himself rather than following a role model.

The theme of self-discovery through Dionysian sensual experience is more fully developed in Hesse's best-known novel, *Steppenwolf*. The protagonist, Harry Haller, an essentially alienated hero, forsakes middle-class values to become either a saint or a sinner. Abandoning his career as a writer, he experiences sensual pleasure through a romantic attachment to Hermine, a symbolic as well as real heroine. From this experience he proceeds into a surrealistic fantasy world of violence and homosexuality. Haller thus transforms his life by encountering and transcending sensual experience.

Narziss und Goldmund (1930; *Death and the Lover*, 1932; also as *Narcissus and Goldmund*, 1968), set in the turbulent German Middle Ages, returns to the theme of two chief male characters, presenting like *Siddhartha* a conflict between asceticism and sensuality. Narcissus is a clergyman, and Goldmund, his close friend, is a sensualist and restless artist who justifies his existence through a life of struggle, artistic creation, and varied experience. His diverse experiences enrich even the life of his ascetic friend Narcissus.

In *Die Morgenlandfahrt* (1932; *The Journey to the East*, 1956), a novella with another individualistic protagonist, H. H., Hesse anticipates his greatest work and longest novel. Both *The Journey to the East* and *The Glass Bead Game* explore the relationship of their protagonists and organizations, a mystic and elusive order in *The Journey to the East* and a larger ideal society in the later novel. In *The Glass Bead Game*, set four centuries into the future, the society of Castalia has achieved admirable order based upon mathematics and music. Its hero, Joseph Knecht, is impelled to leave society at the end of the work to become a seeker instead of remaining in the Utopian world of Castalia. Essentially a work of Utopian fiction and a *roman à clef*, the novel represents Hesse's most complex fictional work.

Writing in the tradition of Romantic individualism, Hesse was highly influenced by modern intellectual currents and developments, both in content and in technique. He was among the first novelists to grasp the potential for character portrayal using Freudian psychology, although he reveals a greater debt to Jung than Freud. In his fiction, Hesse places significant emphasis upon Eastern religious thought, an important strand in his intellectual perspective. He employs the narrative technique known as mirroring, in which an image is transformed before the eyes of the protagonist. This often suggests the importance of symbols of transformation in the sense that Jung used the term. In addition, Hesse makes heavy use of symbols and recurrent motifs to enrich the texture of his narratives. As for the description of the external world, he follows the expressionistic movement in art to describe the world of reality as chaotic and at times grotesque.

Once he had settled in Montagnola, Hesse lived as a reclusive man of letters. He seldom traveled, though the need to publish in Germany made occasional trips to his native land mandatory. Throughout most of his career, he remained little known outside German-speaking nations. Following World War II, his fame began to spread worldwide, and he was awarded the Nobel Prize in Literature in 1946. After a long struggle with leukemia, Hesse died at Montagnola on August 9, 1962.

Summary

Hermann Hesse's inclination to lead a reclusive life meant that during his lifetime he remained a shadowy figure. He once attended a meeting of a local Hesse society without anyone there recognizing him. Further, he was out of sympathy with the society that published his works because of his opposition to German militarism and the National Socialist movement. Although he raised objections in letters and comments, his opposition, unlike Thomas Mann's, was muted because of his awareness that his works needed to be accessible to his main audience, the German-speaking public. Following the award of the Nobel Prize in 1946, his works became much more popular worldwide, and their impact extended beyond the German-speaking world.

Even during his lifetime, Hesse's critics placed him within the tradition of German Romanticism. His emphasis upon individualistic protagonists whose lives are a journey of self-discovery, who live in remote or exotic settings, and who experience angst reflects the conventions of a long tradition of Romantic literature. Like the Romantic heroes, his protagonists live at an extremely high level of intensity, not by performing great feats but by experiencing intense emotions and transforming experiences that enable them to develop as individuals. Yet Hesse advances the tradition by including in his works modern intellectual and aesthetic developments such as analytic psychology and expressionism.

The emphasis upon individual growth and definition made Hesse's writing highly popular in the West during the period of existentialism from about 1950 until the early 1970's. Following their translation into numerous languages, the novels were widely read as accounts of personal development. With the decline of existentialism, Hesse's works lost some of their popularity, yet he remains one of the most widely read German authors of his era, and his works appear destined to endure.

Bibliography

Baumer, Franz. *Hermann Hesse.* Translated by John Conway. New York: Ungar, 1969. A brief and readable introductory overview, the book provides a biographical account and an assessment of Hesse as a writer. Baumer relies heavily on a personal interview with his subject. The book is especially informative about the judgments of Hesse's contemporaries and, through judicious use of quotations, reflects Hesse's own view of his achievement.

Boulby, Mark. *Hermann Hesse: His Mind and Art.* Ithaca, N.Y.: Cornell University Press, 1967. A study of the major novels, the book concentrates on themes of Hesse's fiction. More than other critics, Boulby relates Hesse's themes in the prose fiction to those of his poetry and of the Germanic tradition of letters that preceded Hesse. Boulby finds a high degree of consistency in Hesse's thought and characters. He draws upon the poetry, the letters, and the minor works to explicate the themes of the novels.

Field, George Wallis. *Hermann Hesse.* New York: Twayne, 1970. A one-volume critical analysis of Hesse's entire literary achievement, with a helpful bibliography. Field clarifies themes of the novels, drawing frequently on Hesse's autobiographical writing, letters, and criticism. He places earlier critics into perspective, providing an analysis of their work.

Freedman, Ralph. *Hermann Hesse: Pilgrim of Crisis.* New York: Pantheon, 1978; London: Cape, 1979. A fully developed biography of Hesse, giving a thorough account of his literary career. The book advances the thesis that during his life Hesse confronted numerous personal and public crises that led to his contemplation and dedication to creative work. Illustrated.

Hesse, Hermann. *The Fairy Tales of Hermann Hesse.* Introduction and trans. by Jack Zipes. New York: Bantam, 1995. English translations of the fairy tales written by Hesse between 1900 and 1933. Includes an introduction with analysis by Zipes.

Mileck, Joseph. *Hermann Hesse: Life and Art.* Berkeley: University of California Press, 1978. Mileck's critical biography identifies major stages in Hesse's development and accounts for the works produced. The book clarifies Hesse's views on controversial issues such as war and peace, racism, and the role of the artist. It explores Hesse's development as an artist. Illustrated.

Otten, Anna, ed. *Hesse Companion.* Albuquerque: University of New Mexico Press, 1977. The volume begins with a lengthy overview of Hesse's literary career and then includes reprinted essays dealing with the major novels exclusive of *Demian,* with two chapters devoted to *The Glass Bead Game.* The final section, by Joseph Mileck, provides an assessment of Hesse's poetry.

Stelzig, Eugene L. *Hermann Hesse's Fictions of the Self: Autobiography and the Confessional Imagination.* Princeton, N.J.: Princeton University Press, 1988. A penetrating analysis of autobiographical elements in Hesse's fiction. Stelzig clarifies the intellectual influences on Hesse's work and explores the author's conflicted personality.

Tusken, Lewis W. "A Mixing of Metaphors: Masculine-Feminine Interplay in the Novels of Hermann Hesse." *Modern Language Review* 87, no. 3 (July, 1992). A study of duality in the works of Hesse from a Jungian perspective.

Ziolkowski, Theodore. *The Novels of Hermann Hesse: A Study in Theme and Structure.* Princeton, N.J.: Princeton University Press, 1965. A study of Hesse's major novels, it concludes that he stands intellectually between Romanticism and existentialism. The interpretation emphasizes the genesis of each novel, its similarities to novels by other writers, and, most important, the intellectual currents that inform each novel.

Stanley Archer

GEORG VON HEVESY

Born: August 1, 1885; Budapest, Hungary
Died: July 5, 1966; Frieburg im Breisgau, West
   Germany
Areas of Achievement: Chemistry, physics, biolo-
   gy, and medicine
Contribution: Hevesy pioneered the use of radio-
   active isotopes to study chemical processes. For
   this work, he was awarded the Nobel Prize in
   Chemistry in 1944 and the Atoms for Peace
   Award in 1959. He is also known for his discov-
   ery in 1923 of the element hafnium.

Early Life

Georg von Hevesy was born in Budapest, Hungary,
on August 1, 1885, into a family of wealthy Jewish
industrialists and landowners. He was educated at a
Roman Catholic school in Budapest and was expected to enter one of the professions. The young
Hevesy decided to become a scientist instead. He
was enrolled in the Technical High School in Berlin with the aim of becoming a chemical engineer,
but his studies there were cut short when he contracted pneumonia in 1905 and had to move to
Freiburg, Germany, for the milder climate.

At the University of Freiburg, Hevesy studied
chemistry and physics. In 1908, under the direction of Georg Meyer, he completed his doctorate
there on the interaction of metallic sodium with
molten sodium hydroxide. Because of his family's
wealth, Hevesy was free to pursue postdoctoral
studies wherever he wished. He traveled first to
Switzerland to study the chemistry of molten salts
with Richard Lorenz and then to the Karlsruhe
laboratories of Fritz Haber, where he investigated
the emission of electrons during the oxidation of
sodium-potassium alloys.

In 1911, on Haber's advice, Hevesy went to
Manchester to study the technique of radioactive
measurement that had been developed by Ernest
Rutherford. It was a decisive move for him, not
only because his research at Manchester would
form the basis for the work which many years later
would earn for him the Nobel Prize but also because there he met and became lifelong friends
with Niels Bohr.

Much of the research in physics and chemistry at
this time was concerned with the phenomenon of
naturally occurring radioactivity. Rutherford set
Hevesy the task of chemically separating radioactive radium D, with which Rutherford was interest-

ed in experimenting, from lead. Hevesy worked on
the problem for two years without success. It is
now known that chemical separation is impossible
because radium D is an isotope of lead. Turning his
apparent failure to advantage, Hevesy used this
very property of radium D—that it is inseparable
from lead—to label lead and thus to indicate its
presence by measuring the radioactivity imparted
to it by its isotope, radium D.

Hevesy returned to Hungary in 1912 and spent
the next year traveling between Budapest and Vienna to collaborate with Friedrich Paneth at the Institute of Radium Research. Paneth had also been
trying, unsuccessfully, to separate radium D from
lead. Hevesy proposed to Paneth that they use radium D not only to label lead but also to trace it
through a series of chemical reactions. Hevesy had
been quick to realize the significance of the fact
that radioactive atoms behave chemically and
physically like their stable counterparts, but with
the important difference that they can be traced, or
tracked, by measuring the radiation they emit. Using radium D and a Geiger counter, the two men
successfully applied the tracer method to the investigation of the solubility of lead chromate in water
at various temperatures.

Hevesy planned to return to England to study
with Henry Moseley, who was then working in X-
ray spectroscopy at the University of Oxford. Yet
World War II erupted, and he returned instead to
Vienna to continue his research with Paneth on the
tracer method, applying it to the study of the phys-
icochemical properties of heavy metals and their
inorganic salts. Judged unfit for military service
because of his frail health, Hevesy spent the war
as a supervisor in an electrochemical plant. After
the war, in 1919, he received a one-year appointment to lecture on experimental physics at the
University of Budapest. Yet the revolution in Hungary left his financial and professional future in
that country uncertain, and within the year he decided to emigrate.

Life's Work

Bohr had invited Hevesy to Copenhagen to work at
Bohr's newly established Institute of Theoretical
Physics. Hevesy's tenure there, from 1920 to 1926,
was to be one of the most creative periods of his
career. Bohr was then working on explaining the

periodic table of elements. Based on his theories of atomic structure and the X-ray studies of Moseley, he had identified six elements that had not yet been discovered. It was generally assumed that the element corresponding to atomic number 72 was chemically similar to the rare earth elements. Bohr thought otherwise. He suggested to Hevesy that he look for the undiscovered element 72 in the ores of metallic zirconium. Hevesy accepted Bohr's challenge with the help of Dirk Coster, an expert in X-ray spectroscopy. In 1923, while investigating zirconium minerals using X rays, the two men discovered the new element, which they called hafnium, for *Hafnia*, the Latin name for Copenhagen. Hafnium is a lustrous, silvery metal, whose chemical properties are almost identical to zirconium. Hevesy proceeded to separate successfully hafnium from zirconium and conducted extensive investigations on the chemical nature of the new element. He lectured widely on the subject and wrote numerous papers, as well as a book, *Das Element Hafnium* (1927).

It was generally expected that Hevesy and Coster would be awarded the Nobel Prize for their work, but several British as well as French chemists also laid claim to the discovery of element 72. The controversy that followed confused the issue to the extent that the Nobel Committee was unable to agree on honoring Hevesy and Coster, although the two men were eventually recognized as the legitimate discoverers of element 72.

During this time, Hevesy returned to the use of radioactive isotopes as tracers, which he now applied to the field of botany. In 1923, using a radioactive isotope of lead, he traced the absorption and distribution of lead in bean plants. In the same year, his book on radioactivity, *Lehrbuch der Radioaktivität* (1923; *A Manual of Radioactivity*, 1926), which he wrote with Paneth, was published. The following year, Hevesy used the tracer method to study the circulation in animals of bismuth, then being used to treat syphilis, and lead salts, which were of interest in cancer therapy.

In 1926, Hevesy left Copenhagen to accept the chair of physical chemistry at the University of Freiburg. He had married Ria Riis in Denmark in the fall of 1924, and their first of four children had been born. The position in Freiburg, which Hevesy held for eight years, offered him economic security and prestige, although apparently not the inspiration that had produced the remarkable achievements of the previous years. Hevesy did very little

work on radioactive indicators during this time. Instead, he concentrated on studying the occurrence of various chemical elements in rocks and meteorites using quantitative X-ray analyses. His book, *Chemical Analysis by X Rays and Its Applications* (1932), was published several years later.

In the early 1930's, Hevesy began experimenting again with his radioactive tracer technique, applying it more widely to biological studies. Until this time, his biological research had been limited because the heavy metals he had to work with, such as lead, were extremely toxic to biological organisms. This changed in 1931 with Harold Urey's discovery of deuterium, an isotope of hydrogen. Using deuterium, Hevesy was able to measure the rate of exchange of hydrogen in animals as well as the elimination of water from and the total water content of the human body.

In July, 1934, in response to the growing threat of Nazism, Hevesy resigned his position at Freiburg and, again at Bohr's invitation, returned to Copenhagen to work at the Institute of Theoretical Physics. His stay there, which was to be an extremely productive one, lasted from 1935 to 1943. In 1933, Enrico Fermi had discovered that radioactive isotopes could be formed by bombarding a stable element with neutrons. This discovery, which made it possible to produce radioactive isotopes for the common elements artificially, was to broaden significantly the scope of Hevesy's research. The production in 1934 of an unstable isotope of phosphorus made it possible for him to investigate phosphorus metabolism in animals. Hevesy also used the isotope to trace the movement of phosphorus in the human body. His work revealed that the formation of the bones is a dynamic process and that the mineral constituents of the skeleton are constantly renewed, a finding that challenged the prevailing views. This was perhaps the single most important discovery Hevesy was to make using the tracer method. Hevesy also experimented on the soft tissues of the body, which he showed were likewise dynamic in nature, and went on to study the lifespan of the red and white blood cells as well as the biochemistry of nucleic acids. His research received the intellectual support of Bohr, the financial support of the Rockefeller Foundation, and eventually the acclaim of the scientific and medical research communities.

In 1943, Hevesy was forced to flee German-occupied Denmark. He sought asylum in Sweden, where he became a professor at the Institute of Or-

ganic Chemistry at the University of Stockholm. While there, he was awarded the 1943 Nobel Prize in Chemistry for his discovery and development of radioactive tracing. Along with the prize, Hevesy accepted Swedish citizenship.

For some time after World War II, Hevesy traveled between Stockholm and Copenhagen, where he continued to work on the movement of radioactive isotopes in living material. Yet as his health began to fail, he confined his research efforts to Stockholm, primarily focusing on the effect of X rays on biochemical processes in animals. While gradually cutting back on his experimental work, Hevesy continued to be a prolific writer. During this time, he wrote his classic book on the use of radioisotopes as tracers, entitled *Radioactive Indicators: Their Application In Biochemistry, Animal Physiology, and Pathology* (1948). In 1959, Hevesy received the Atoms for Peace Award for the medical application of radioisotopes. The award was presented to him by Dag Hammarskjöld, secretary-general of the United Nations. In 1962, Hevesy published a two-volume collection of what he considered to be his most important papers, entitled *Adventures in Radioisotope Research: The Collected Papers of George Hevesy.*

Bohr, Hevesy's closest friend and greatest source of inspiration, died in the fall of 1962. Shortly thereafter, Hevesy was diagnosed as having lung cancer. His condition quickly deteriorated, and he was moved to a clinic in Freiburg, where he died on July 5, 1966, at the age of eighty.

Summary

Georg von Hevesy's genius is perhaps best exemplified in the way he turned failure into success. His inability to separate radium D from lead led to his discovery of radioactive labeling and the development of the use of radioactive isotopes as tracers. Though his discovery, first made in Manchester and applied in Vienna in 1912, did not receive much attention at the time, Hevesy continued to develop and expand the technique over the next several decades, applying it not only to problems in chemistry but also to physics, biology, and medicine. In time, Hevesy's tracer method was recognized as one of the most important research tools of modern science. It has been used to study the nocturnal activity of bats, the assimilation of carbon dioxide and water by green plants, the fixation of iodine by the human thyroid gland, and the physiological fate of medicines and poisons. In industry, the tracer method is used to test the wear and corrosion of mechanical components and even to monitor and control the entire operation of an industrial plant. Yet perhaps the greatest impact of Hevesy's pioneering work has been in the field of medicine, where radioactive isotopes are used in the diagnosis and treatment of diseases. Radioisotopes are now routinely used in cancer research and detection, most notably in the scanning techniques used to locate tumors in the brain.

Bibliography

Cockcroft, John D. "George de Hevesy." *Biographical Memoirs of Fellows of the Royal Society* 13 (1967): 125-166. Based almost entirely on the extensive notes that Hevesy turned over to Cockcroft shortly before his death, this article is, in effect, an autobiographical account by Hevesy of his own life and work. It is filled with personal insights, political observations, and affectionate, often amusing anecdotes about Hevesy's associates and friends. Includes a six-page bibliography of Hevesy's scientific work.

Hevesy, George de. "A Scientific Career." *Perspectives in Biology and Medicine* 1 (1958): 345-365. An autobiographical essay by Hevesy for the layperson. Contains reminiscences of some of Hevesy's distinguished colleagues and contemporaries, including Rutherford, Bohr, Moseley, Albert Einstein, and Marie Curie, as well as a discussion of the controversy surrounding the discovery of the element hafnium.

Levi, Hilde. *George de Hevesy: Life and Work.* Bristol and Boston: Hilger, 1985. A short biography of Hevesy written by his assistant in Copenhagen from 1934 to 1943. Based on Hevesy's letters, notes, and manuscripts, the book focuses on the personal aspects of Hevesy's life. His scientific achievements are viewed in the context of his family background and early training as well as the times in which he lived. The book includes photographs, a list of references, a glossary, an index of names, and a complete bibliography of Hevesy's considerable output.

————. "George de Hevesy: 1 August 1855-July 1966." *Nuclear Physics* 98 (1967): 1-24. A tribute to Hevesy written shortly after his death. The essay gives a clear and concise summary of Hevesy's scientific work and its impact on modern science as well as a short biographical sketch. Includes a bibliography of Hevesy's papers and books.

————. "George Hevesy and His Concept of Radioactive Indicators-In Retrospect." *European Journal of Nuclear Medicine* 1 (1976): 3-10. Originally presented at the University of Copenhagen as the Georg von Hevesy Memorial Lecture, this essay traces the development of Hevesy's major contributions to science over a twenty-year period. Describes in some detail, and with photographs, the scientific instrumentation, such as the early Geiger counters, that made it possible for Hevesy and his co-workers to carry out their experiments using radioisotopes as tracers.

Myers, William G. "Georg Charles de Hevesy: The Father of Nuclear Medicine." *Journal of Nuclear Medicine* 20 (1979): 590-594. Given as the first Hevesy Nuclear Pioneer Lecture in 1979 by the historian of the Society of Nuclear Medicine, this address acknowledges Hevesy as the father of nuclear medicine and pays tribute to his discovery of the tracer method of analysis and its application to the field of biomedicine.

Spence, R. "George Charles de Hevesy." *Chemistry in Britain* 3 (1967): 527-532. A chronological and complete overview of Hevesy's work. The essay is an abridged version of a lecture given in Hevesy's honor. Includes photographs of Hevesy, Bohr, Rutherford, and Moseley.

Nancy Schiller

THOR HEYERDAHL

Born: October 6, 1914; Larvik, Norway

Areas of Achievement: Anthropology, archaeology, and exploration

Contribution: Heyerdahl undertook several successful sea voyages using prehistoric type of craft to demonstrate that early man was skilled in navigation on ocean currents and thus, by transpacific and transatlantic crossings, was able to migrate. He has written numerous books, both popular and scientific, about his voyages and diffusionist theories.

Early Life

Thor Heyerdahl was born in Larvik, Norway, on October 6, 1914. He had numerous siblings by his mother's two previous marriages and his father's previous wife, but as they left home early Thor was reared like an only child. His father had inherited money because of the rather early death of his own father and thus was able to establish a successful brewery business. Thor's mother sheltered his life so that he was allowed few playmates in his early years. In 1933, Heyerdahl entered the University of Oslo to study zoology, and his mother took an apartment there.

Heyerdahl married Liv Coucheron Torp on Christmas Eve, 1936. She had agreed to live with him in the Marquesa Islands, and his father was to finance the venture. Leaving Norway in January, 1937, they went to live on Fatu Hiva but developed medical problems and eventually problems with the natives. In March, 1938, they returned to Norway, where in September their son, Thor, was born.

Heyerdahl's interest now shifted to primitive peoples. With his family, he traveled to the coast of British Columbia, Canada, to study the Bella Coola Indians, who in many ways resembled the Polynesians on Fatu Hiva. Heyerdahl's early book *På jakt efter paradiset: et år på en sydhavsø* (1938); *Fatu-Hiva: Back to Nature*, 1974) provided the finances for this expedition. Trapped in British Columbia by the German invasion of Norway, and with funds exhausted, Heyerdahl had to work as a manual laborer to support his family, now with a second son, Bjorn. In 1942, he volunteered as a guerrilla with the Free Norwegian Forces and became a lieutenant. He was assigned to train in Nova Scotia and then in Scotland. He did not reach active duty in northern Norway until very shortly before the end of the European front of World War II in May, 1945.

Life's Work

Early people, their navigational possibilities in terms of ocean currents, and their possible migrations and cultural contacts have been the focus of Heyerdahl's scientific work. His historic voyage from the coast of Peru to eastern Polynesia, recounted in *Kon-Tiki ekspedisjonen* (1948; *Kon-Tiki: Across the Pacific by Raft*, 1950), made him world famous. Subsequently, he sailed from the west coast of Morocco to the West Indies and then from the foot of Iraq through the Persian Gulf, to Asia, and on to Africa, where he was blocked by political turmoil. These voyages involved the use of replicas of prehistoric vessels. Heyerdahl's concern was to demonstrate that early peoples using their type of craft could so migrate. The navigation out of the Persian Gulf indicated that the ancient Sumerians could thus have had contact with numerous other early civilizations.

With the end of World War II, Heyerdahl returned to civilian life. He formulated theories about the origins of the peoples of the Pacific Islands in contrast to the standard perspective that their ancestors had come directly from southeastern Asia. Heyerdahl noted that when Europeans first came to the Pacific Islands, they found some natives with white skins, beards, red or blond hair, and almost Semitic faces; they were said to be descended from the first chiefs of the islands. The ruling family of the Incas also had fair skin, beards, and (for some) red hair. Their ancestors had been there before the Incas became rulers. According to native tradition, in a battle at Lake Titicaca in the high Andes Mountains, the fair race was massacred, but the leader and some others escaped to the Ecuadorian coast and vanished into the Pacific Ocean.

When Heyerdahl's theories were ignored in academic circles, he decided to sail on a duplicate of a prehistoric raft in order to establish the feasibility of the journey. Locating financial backers and a crew of fellow Norwegians (only one of whom was a trained seaman), he built the raft and set sail on April 28, 1947. The vessel was constructed of logs, which were lashed together allowing the mountainous seas that poured onto it simply to run through the cracks. A cabin on top was built like a jungle dwelling and thus offered a psychological sense of security. A large sail and prehistoric navigational equipment enabled the *Kon-Tiki*, as the vessel was named, to move in the desired direction, primarily propelled by the powerful ocean currents.

Narrow escapes resulting from uncanny good judgment, courage, confidence, and self-sacrifice led to the sighting, on July 30, of land, an island in the Tuamotu group of the South Sea Islands, but the raft drifted past. Eventually, they were shipwrecked on the reef of an uninhabited island; no lives were lost, and the raft was soon salvaged with the help of natives. By radio, a schooner was sent to bring them to Papeete in Tahiti. There a large Norwegian steamer took them and the *Kon-Tiki* back to the Western world. The *Kon-Tiki* is now in a museum at Oslo, Norway, as is the *Ra II* from a subsequent voyage.

A book by Heyerdahl narrating the *Kon-Tiki* experiences appeared in Norwegian in 1948. In 1949, a translation into Swedish established a publishing record in its first year. In 1950, an English translation appeared in London and Chicago, where for months it was on the best-seller lists. By 1969, it had been reprinted in sixty different languages, thirty million people had seen a film of the voyage in theaters, and 500 million had seen the film on television.

Shortly after Heyerdahl's return home from Tahiti, he and his wife decided to separate. In the early summer of 1949 in Santa Fe, New Mexico, where he was doing research on North American Indians, he was married to Yvonne Dedekam-Simonsen, who had spent her early years in Oslo. Three daughters, Anette, Marian, and Elisabeth, were born of this union.

In 1952, Heyerdahl published, in London, Chicago, and Stockholm, *American Indians in the Pacific: The Theory Behind the Kon-Tiki Expedition*. He noted that fishhooks of the Polynesians were almost identical to those of ancient civilizations of North and South America. Yet there was opposition from other scholars, who espoused an isolationist, nondiffusionist viewpoint. Heyerdahl argued that from the mainland of southeast Asia there was an ocean current that ran via the extreme north Pacific via northwest America to Hawaii.

In 1953, Heyerdahl visited the Galapagos Islands off the west coast of South America and found four habitation sites, predating the European period. A book about this appeared in 1956. In

1954, Heyerdahl visited Lake Titicaca in the Andes and formulated the theory that natives from this area were the founders of the Easter Island culture. In 1955, Heyerdahl, his wife, two-year-old Anette, and five archaeologists spent substantial time on Easter Island. His book *Aku-Aku: Paaskeoeyas Hemmelighet* (1957; *Aku-Aku: The Secret of Easter Island*, 1958), a popular narrative, discusses their work and propounds that the island was originally settled by two races, the long-ears and the short-ears: The long-ears left their center near Lake Titicaca and landed on Easter Island. Heyerdahl had located archaeological evidence of occupation that had occurred one thousand years earlier than scientists had previously assumed. The scientific account, *Archaeology of Easter Island*, was published in 1961.

In 1958, in Norway, Heyerdahl suffered influenza with inflammation of the brain. Subsequently, he renovated a home on the Italian Riviera near the mountains. His scientific reputation had been rising for many years. On the 150th anniversary of Oslo University in 1961, an honorary doctorate was bestowed upon him.

In 1969, Heyerdahl made a sea voyage, to investigate where ancient Egyptians could have crossed the Atlantic Ocean. An ancient-style, papyrus-reed boat was built. As with the *Kon-Tiki*, it also was named in honor of a sun god, in this case the Egyptian Ra. With an international crew of seven, the craft sailed twenty-seven hundred miles in eight weeks but began to collapse about six hundred miles from Barbados in the West Indies. The following year, a new vessel, the *Ra II*, sailed from the Atlantic coast of Morocco and reached Barbados safely. The book *Ra*, detailing these adventures, was published in 1970 as was the English translation, *The Ra Expeditions*.

In 1977, Heyerdahl undertook a third major voyage. The ancient Sumerian people of the third millenium B.C. developed an outstanding civilization. Heyerdahl employed Iraqi marsh Arabs aided by Indians from Lake Titicaca to construct a vessel from the Mesopotamian reed, berdi, and with a crew of eleven sailed down the Tigris River through the dangerous Persian Gulf to Oman, to Pakistan, and then over the Indian Ocean to Djibouti at the opening of the Red Sea. This voyage demonstrated that the ancient Sumerians could have made similar voyages and thus benefited from extensive cultural contacts in developing their extraordinary civilization. In 1982-1983, Heyerdahl organized and led two archaeological expeditions to the Maldive Islands in the Indian Ocean to investigate the prehistoric Maldives regarding global trade.

Summary

Thor Heyerdahl's significance lies, first, in his practical demonstration, using prehistoric vessels, that various early peoples could have successfully navigated several lengthy sea routes. Second, on the basis of these voyages and on archaeological evidence, Heyerdahl has argued for various diffusionist theories. He believed that Polynesians did not come directly from the Asian mainland but that some followed the north Pacific current and stopped along the Pacific coast of British Columbia, and of this group some moved via Hawaii to other Pacific islands. For Heyerdahl, a different group of migrants left the Peruvian coast and eventually reached Easter Island and Polynesia. Heyerdahl also demonstrated the feasibility of early man crossing the Atlantic Ocean to the West Indies, again by using the prevailing ocean currents. He argued that these migrants might have contributed to the development of the great American civilizations of the Aztecs and the Incas.

Further, Heyerdahl studied the Sumerians, the brilliant developers of the first great civilization of early Mesopotamia, upon which Western biblical culture is based. Heyerdahl argued that the Sumerian culture was not an isolated one but that, because of his demonstration of the capability of their sailing vessels, they could have traveled as far as Egypt as well as to the important Indus River civilization. Thus, the Sumerian civilization could have grown in part because of these cultural contacts.

Therefore, Heyerdahl has brought into focus the important role that sea voyages could have played in the diffusion of early peoples and the development of their cultures. This aspect of ethnography had not received this much prominence prior to Heyerdahl's work.

Bibliography

Emory, Kenneth P. "Easter Island's Position in the Prehistory of Polynesia." *Journal of the Polynesian Society* 81 (March, 1972): 57-69. This article presents arguments against Heyerdahl's theories. Emory claims that early Polynesians had the maritime capability to reach Easter Island and to build the giant statues. Also, he believes that the Easter Islanders are descendants of an early offshoot of the Polynesians.

Golson, Jack. "Thor Heyerdahl and the Prehistory of Easter Island." *Oceania* 36 (Summer, 1965): 38-93. Golson challenges some of Heyerdahl's hypotheses, using data provided by the Heyerdahl expedition. He argues that the Easter Island script is equally likely to be post-European.

Heyerdahl, Thor. "Feasible Ocean Routes to and from the Americas in Pre-Columbian Times." *American Antiquity* 28 (April, 1963): 482-488. This article discusses three possible routes of aboriginal overseas arrivals to the New World and two of departure. Also, studies of plant life demonstrate that some form of transoceanic contact has occurred. Includes a bibliography.

———. *Green Was the Earth on the Seventh Day.* New York: Random, 1996; and London: Abacus, 1998. Heyerdahl's account of the year he and his wife spent studying the animals on Fatu-Hiva Island in the Marquesas and the manner in which the species arrived on the island.

————, et al. *Pyramids of Tucume: The Quest for Peru's Forgotten City.* London and New York: Thames and Hudson, 1995. A straightforward account of the archaeological excavation of Tucame by Heyerdahl and his team and the discoveries linked to their work.

Jacoby, Arnold. *Señor Kon-Tiki.* Chicago: Rand McNally, 1967; London: Allen and Unwin, 1968. This clearly written, lengthy, and sympathetic biography is by a close friend of Heyerdahl and covers Heyerdahl's life from a discussion of his early family background until the mid-1960's. It fills in the gaps between Heyerdahl's own accounts.

Schumacher, William. "On the Linguistic Aspects of Thor Heyerdahl's Theory: The So-Called Non-Polynesian Number Names from Easter Island." *Anthropos* 71 (May/June, 1976): 806-847. This article discusses linguistic factors in relation to Heyerdahl's theory about the migrations from the Americas to Polynesia. Includes an extensive bibliography.

E. Lynn Harris

SIR EDMUND HILLARY

Born: July 20, 1919; Auckland, New Zealand
Areas of Achievement: Exploration and mountaineering
Contribution: Hillary and his Sherpa guide Tenzing Norgay were the first men to reach the top of Mount Everest. Hillary also was the first man to drive a land vehicle across Antarctica to the South Pole.

Early Life

Edmund Percival Hillary was born in Auckland, New Zealand, on July 20, 1919. He was the son of Percival Augustus Hillary and Gertrude Clark Hillary, who had a daughter older than Edmund, and who would later have a second son. Like many New Zealanders, Hillary's parents had their roots in England. On his mother's side, Edmund's great-grandmother had emigrated to New Zealand from Yorkshire in England. Edmund's grandfather Clark had come to New Zealand in the mid-1800's, also from Yorkshire. Percival Hillary's father had been a watchmaker who settled in New Zealand in the early 1880's; Percival's mother, Ida Fleming, had been an Irish governess with an English family who had come to New Zealand.

Edmund Hillary's relationship with his father was not an easy one. He describes his father as an unusual combination of a moral conservative who also had much pride and independence, an intelligent man who hated the poverty in which he had been reared. Percival Hillary managed a small newspaper outside Auckland in the years after he served in World War I. He kept a close eye on his three children and supervised all of their activities very strictly; Edmund grew to resent this treatment. By his teenage years, he argued frequently with his father. Edmund credits his mother with giving him the affection and support he needed as he matured.

Hillary attended the Tuakau Primary School for his first grades. Since his mother had been a teacher, she also educated him at home. He was a good student and was able to finish his primary grades by age eleven instead of the usual age of thirteen. He next attended the Auckland grammar school, commuting there by train to save the boarding expenses. He did this for more than three years, until his family moved to Auckland. At this time, Hillary's father gave up journalism to become a beekeeper. At age sixteen, Edmund would put all of his time not spent on school into his father's busi-

ness. Once, however, during some free time, Hillary went on a ten-day skiing trip with some friends. He discovered then that he loved the snow.

Although Hillary entered college, he stayed for only two years, as he felt uncomfortable there. Despite being an avid reader, he was unhappy because he did not socialize easily. When he left college, he became a full-time beekeeper, working long hours for his father.

In the summer of 1939-1940, Hillary and some friends took a trip to the Southern Alps in New Zealand, where he climbed his first snow-covered peak, Mount Olivier. Hillary found the experience to be exhilarating, experiencing an intense feeling of freedom. It was an experience he wanted to have again.

When World War II began, Hillary continued at first to work as a honey farmer at his father's request. By 1944, however, he was restless and was glad to be called up by the Royal New Zealand Air Force, for which he had previously applied. During his basic training, Hillary continued to climb mountains for his amusement on weekends. He scaled Mount Tapuae at 9,465 feet. During his special training as a navigator, he climbed Mount Egmont at 8,260 feet. Next he climbed a series of mountains at about this same height, including Mount Sealy at 8,600 feet.

After the war, in January of 1946, Hillary tested the knowledge of mountaineering techniques which he had acquired through his reading. He scaled Malte Brun in the Southern Alps at 10,000 feet. After this, he saved all of the money he could to buy proper climbing equipment. In the summer of 1947, he climbed Mount Cook at 12,349 feet, thereby fulfilling his first major ambition as a climber.

In April of 1950, when his family visited England for his sister's wedding, Hillary first saw the European Alps. He spent time climbing in both Austria and Switzerland and reached the top of the Jungfrau at 13,642 feet and Aletschhorn at 13,784 feet.

Life's Work

On his return to New Zealand from Europe, Hillary prepared for his trip to the Himalayas. He was a member of a four-man New Zealand group, the first of their country to make a Himalaya expedition alone. This group included George Lowe, who had climbed with Hillary before and who would become a lifelong friend and climbing companion. This expedition left New Zealand in May of 1951. After traveling by boat, then through India to the Himalayas, they were ready to begin a climb in early June. On June 8, they reached the Kuari Pass at 12,400 feet, which offered the men an excellent view of the major Himalayan mountains. When the group scaled Mukut Parbat at 23,760 feet, it was Hillary's first time at more than 20,000 feet.

While in the Himalayas, Hillary read that the British explorer Eric Shipton was planning to study the area around Mount Everest in the next few months. Hillary excitedly wrote to the explorer, asking if he or his New Zealand friends could accompany Shipton. On August 25, a telegram arrived for Hillary, stating that he was chosen to go on Shipton's reconnaissance mission. Hillary was elated at this news.

In September, he was back in Nepal near the base of Everest. It was an extremely treacherous mountain that men had been attempting to scale for the previous thirty years (some dying in the effort). No one had yet been successful. Shipton's group was on the southern side of Mount Everest in Nepal, where they were studying a feasible approach to the summit. Most earlier climbers had used a northern route that began in Tibet. During the month of October, Hillary aided Shipton personally in investigating the southern side of Everest. The worst hazard from that approach seemed to be a dangerous ice fall.

Although Hillary returned to beekeeping after this mountaineering mission, the return was short-lived. He was back in Nepal in 1952 on premission training for the British Everest Expedition that would begin in 1953. On this trip, the men scaled Cho Oyu at 26,870 feet, the seventh highest peak in the world.

When the British expedition started out in 1953, Hillary and his friend Lowe were both included, but the leadership was given to John Hunt, not Eric Shipton. Hunt, a military man, seemed to have the extra drive, determination, and discipline necessary to reach the top of Everest. Hillary also met for the first time on this expedition Tenzing Norgay, a Sherpa climber. Hillary has recalled his feelings as the expedition began its preparations: He felt restless (a mood he always experienced just before a climb); he also felt competitive and somewhat argumentative (he always strove to control his rather quick temper). Those were the very qualities that

were to help Hillary reach the top of Everest. He always drove himself hard physically (even at beekeeping), and he often relied on his own judgment in climbing situations; he admits that he was never a man who could take orders well. In May of 1953, Hillary, paired with Norgay, experimented with an open-circuit oxygen system that they would need at the high altitudes near the top of Everest, where the air is too thin for efficient breathing. During May, a series of support camps was built along the approach to the summit; the route had seven camps along it, the highest at 24,000 feet. Lowe, an experienced trail cutter, dug into the ice and snow on the approach. On May 28, Hillary and his support crew established a camp at 27,900 feet. The temperature there was about -27° Centigrade, and three liters of oxygen were consumed by each man per minute. On the morning of May 29, Hillary and Tenzing moved out of camp toward the summit. They took a snow-covered route to avoid the icier areas, and at about 9:00 A.M. they reached the peak of the South Summit, below a dangerous ridge. Tenzing was feeling somewhat sluggish, but since they were consuming oxygen at a safe, steady rate, the two men continued climbing. At 11:30 A.M. they were standing on the top of Mount Everest—the first men ever to do so. They shook hands and took some photographs for about fifteen minutes, then they descended. The highest peak in the world had been conquered by men.

Hillary finished this expedition thin, exhausted, and suddenly famous. The Queen of England immediately knighted Hillary and John Hunt. Hillary became pressed by newsmen and photographers for the rest of 1953. He has a rugged appearance in pictures from this era, with his long, thin face with a large, toothy smile, a sturdy nose, and bright eyes, along with a tuft of thick, unruly hair. At six feet, three inches, he presented a tall, lean figure.

In all the confusion of sudden fame, Hillary was certain of one thing: He wished to marry Louise Mary Rose, a music student whom he had known in Auckland. They were married on September 3, 1953, which was Louise's twenty-third birthday. Her openness and enthusiasm helped the shy and softspoken Hillary through the numerous receptions in his honor.

Hillary quickly became restless for more challenges, and he found an opportunity for action in the middle of 1955; then he was asked to aid Vivian Fuchs in leading an expedition to Antarctica to cross that continent through to the South Pole.

Both Hillary and Lowe were to support Fuchs in this effort. Hillary was to establish bases where Fuchs and his crew would stop for food and fuel. Hillary took with him to Antarctica for his own travel use reconditioned farm tractors. On December 21, 1956, he left New Zealand and would be away for the next sixteen months. After Hillary and his men had established and supplied the support bases, his customary restlessness set in. He became convinced that he could cross the South Pole at about the same time that Fuchs did; thus, he set out to do so on his farm tractors. Hillary left from the last supply depot, some five hundred miles from the South Pole, on December 20. On January 4, 1958, Hillary had reached the pole several days before Fuchs did.

On his return to New Zealand, Hillary was happy to spend some time with his wife and their three young children. He would have other wilderness adventures in the coming years but none as famous as those at Mount Everest and the South Pole. Tragedy would also touch him in 1975, when his wife and their youngest child died in an airplane crash.

In 1960, Hillary led an expedition of scientists and climbers to Nepal, where they studied two phenomena: the existence of the Yeti (or Abominable Snowman) and the effect of high altitudes on men and their ability to acclimatize. The first of these studies proved that the Yeti is only a legend; the second demonstrated the life-threatening aspects of high altitude when Hillary suffered a cerebral vascular accident at more than 21,000 feet. Other climbers on this expedition did reach 27,000 feet without oxygen, but could go no farther. On his return to recuperate in Nepal, Hillary decided on his next Himalayan project—to build a school for the children of Khumjung (the home village of the Sherpa climbers who were on the major Everest expedition).

Summary

Sir Edmund Hillary is more than a climber and explorer; he is a humanitarian. His concern for the welfare of the Sherpas goes far beyond making mere token gestures on their behalf. He works hard to improve their lives in a spirit of genuine friendship and true compassion.

Once Hillary began building much-needed modern facilities for the Sherpas, it became a lifelong mission. In the early 1980's, Hillary spent four months of each year in Nepal, four months living in New Zealand, and four months on lecture tours raising money for his projects in Nepal. By about 1984, twenty-five schools had been built for the Sherpa children. Other projects Hillary funded and worked on built airfields, hospitals, clinics, and water pipelines. When he became concerned about any detrimental effects of the modernization of Nepal (including an influx of tourists and climbers), Hillary also helped plan and establish in 1976 the Sagarmatha National Park of 480 square miles, including Mount Everest.

Bibliography

Dowling, Claudia Glenn. "Death on the Mountain." *Life* 19, no. 9 (August, 1996). Story of the May, 1996, deaths of eleven climbers in a sudden storm on Mount Everest. Includes a related piece on Hillary's views on commercial climbing trips.

Fuchs, Vivian, and Edmund Hillary. *The Crossing of Antarctica: The Commonwealth Trans-Antarctic Expedition, 1955-1958.* Boston: Little Brown, and London: Cassell, 1958. This is a detailed account of the famous South Pole expedition. There is a helpful glossary of terms included, as well as appendices explaining airplane and land vehicle specifications. The Antarctic landscape comes alive here in numerous pages of photographs, many in splendid color. A very interesting book.

Hillary, Edmund. *From the Ocean to the Sky*. London: Hodder and Stoughton, and New York: Viking Press, 1979. This book records Hillary's travel up the Ganges River from its mouth to its source in the Himalayan mountains. A chronological chart is included, along with a glossary of terms. Hillary describes the areas he travels through and their people with clarity and interest (especially in the case of the Hindus of India).

————. *High Adventure*. London: Hodder and Stoughton, and New York: Dutton, 1955. Hillary writes here of his climbing expeditions prior to that of Mount Everest. He gives a fine account of the 1951 reconnaissance and climb of Cho Oyu. The book vividly demonstrates the dangers of climbing such treacherous peaks. It has many excellent explanatory illustrations and maps, as well as stunning pictures.

————. *Nothing Venture, Nothing Win*. London: Hodder and Stoughton, and New York: Coward McCann, 1975. This is Hillary's autobiography; it is written with an honesty and sincerity that are hallmarks of his character. His style is simple and direct. He covers more of his personal life here than in his other books and describes his developmental years in detail.

————. *Schoolhouse in the Clouds*. London: Hodder and Stoughton, and New York: Doubleday, 1964. The mission Hillary describes here is less related to climbing and more explicit about his work to improve the Sherpas' existence. Many fine illustrations bring to life this highest region of the world. A glossary of terms is included, along with a roster of the expedition members.

Hillary, Edmund, and Desmond Doig. *High in the Thin Cold Air*. New York: Doubleday, 1962; London: Hodder and Stoughton, 1963. This book records the events of the Himalayan Scientific and Mountaineering Expedition of 1960-1961, in which Hillary and his party searched for the Yeti and studied high-altitude acclimatization by men. It is an interesting narrative that relates much about Sherpa life. Much space is given to the search for the Yeti.

Hunt, John. *The Conquest of Everest: With a Chapter on the Final Assault by Sir Edmund Hillary*. London: Hodder and Stoughton, and New York: Dutton, 1954. Hunt provides all the details of the work and preparations necessary for the famous expedition. The final chapter, about the actual climb to the summit, is a firsthand account written by Hillary. The narrative throughout is written simply and is enhanced by numerous photographs (many in color) and very detailed maps.

Salkels, Audrey. "South Side Story." *Geographical Magazine* 65, no. 5 (May, 1993). The six surviving members of the first team to scale Mount Everest meet in Nepal and remember their historic trip.

Patricia E. Sweeney

HEINRICH HIMMLER

Born: October 7, 1900; Munich, Germany
Died: May 23, 1945; Lüneburg, Germany
Areas of Achievement: The military, government, and politics
Contribution: As Reich leader of the Schutzstaffel (SS) and chief of the German police, Himmler controlled the entire security apparatus of the Third Reich. Entrusted by Adolf Hitler with the implementation of the so-called final solution, Himmler became the principal organizer of the killing of nearly six million Jews.

Early Life

Heinrich Himmler was born on October 7, 1900, into a conservative, upper-middle-class family in Munich. His father, a onetime tutor to Prince Heinrich of Wittelsbach, served as a teacher of classical languages at several prestigious secondary schools in southern Bavaria. The young Himmler, by all accounts a model student, was, like many others of his generation, deeply affected by the news from the battlefields of World War I and was eager to see combat. Although he was accepted as an officer candidate in December of 1917, his plans to obtain a commission were cut short by the war's end.

Upon completion of his secondary education, Himmler was enrolled in an agronomy program at the Technische Hochschule in Munich, where he earned a diploma in August of 1922. During his student days, he had joined several patriotic organizations as well as a dueling student fraternity. His intense dislike of the Weimar Republic and his growing identification with Nazi Party causes led to his increasing involvement in right-wing politics. Although a practicing Catholic, he began to question his religious beliefs as he immersed himself in racist and anti-Semitic literature.

Unable to find suitable employment as a manager of an agricultural estate and still hoping for a military career, Himmler became a follower of Captain Ernst Röhm, the later chief of the paramilitary Sturm Abteilung (SA), and joined the National Socialist German Workers' (Nazi) Party in August of 1923. After Hitler's failure to overthrow the Bavarian government in November of the same year and the subsequent ban on paramilitary organizations, Himmler left Munich for the city of Landshut in Lower Bavaria, where he attached himself to Gregor Strasser, one of the leaders of the National Socialist Freedom Movement. With Hit-

ler's release from prison, the refounding of the Nazi Party in 1925, and the subsequent subordination of Strasser's group to the Hitler movement, Himmler became an official of the Nazi Party. Always the loyal follower, he was now fully committed to Hitler's cause. His considerable organizational and administrative skills as well as his adroit political maneuvering soon bore fruit: In 1929, he was appointed Reich leader of the relatively small SS, and a year later he was elected as a deputy to the German Reichstag.

Life's Work

Central to Himmler's view of the world was his firmly held belief that the Germanic race was inherently superior to all other races and that the fate of Germany depended on the extent to which its racial purity could be preserved. Germany's political, social, and economic difficulties during the 1920's convinced him that the restoration of German power required not only a political reorientation but also an effective racial policy. To that end, Himmler pursued a variety of policies which, in keeping with Hitler's general objectives, envisioned the removal and eventual elimination of entire peoples considered to be racially inferior; in addition, Himmler favored the elimination of the congenitally ill and of other individuals who for various reasons were considered to be a threat to the racial health of the nation.

To assure Germany's future, Himmler furthermore envisioned the creation of a racial elite, represented by the SS, whose members had to meet certain physical requirements and to submit proof that they (and their spouses) were of pure Aryan descent. While encouraging his SS men to have large families, he also provided institutional support for unwed mothers and their offspring if their racial characteristics met his standards. Perhaps the most extreme measure along these lines was Himmler's order to kidnap children with desirable racial features in the conquered territories and to have them reared in Germany.

Along with the creation of a racial elite, Himmler sought to replace the Judeo-Christian system of values with what he understood to have been the ethical beliefs of the pre-Christian Germanic peoples. Unquestioning loyalty and obedience to the leader, racial pride, and service to the Germanic people would be at the core of the new Nazi ethic. Mindful

Heinrich Himmler (right) with Nazi führer Adolf Hitler.

of the power of religious practices and symbols, Himmler even created quasi-religious rituals complete with Germanic symbols for use within the inner circles of the SS. While such practices as well as his moralizing tone and his schoolmasterly demeanor did little to increase his popularity among the Nazi hierarchy, his leanings toward mysticism and the occult met with Hitler's angry disapproval. Still, he was determined to find evidence to substantiate various racial and historical fantasies. To that end, he created and lavishly endowed special SS research institutions, whose findings, however, lacked all scientific merit.

The principal instrument for carrying out Himmler's ambitious plans was the SS, whose phenomenal increase in membership to some thirty thousand by 1933 was largely the result of his tireless recruiting efforts. Following the murder of Röhm in the bloody purge of June 30, 1934, the SS became independent of the SA. Two years later, Himmler, now as Reich leader of the SS and chief of the German police, had won control of the entire security and police apparatus of the Third Reich. In October, 1939, he was appointed Reich Commissar for the Strengthening of Germanism; in 1943, he became minister of the interior and a year later was made commander in chief of the Replacement Army, even though he had no military experience to speak of.

With the German conquests and annexations in the East, Himmler was at last in a position to realize his cherished vision of an expanded German living space by removing native populations and settling the area with peasants of German descent. By the time Germany attacked the Soviet Union, a million Poles had already been driven from their homes with their property distributed among ethnic Germans. Having been entrusted by Hitler with the implementation of the so-called final solution, Himmler proceeded to expand the system of concentration camps by establishing additional camps in the German-occupied territories. Although the increasing demands for laborers in the German armaments industry persuaded Himmler to permit some utilization of Jewish laborers in German industries, his policies nevertheless resulted in the murder of nearly six million Jews.

In addition to the various security agencies and the armed units of the SS, the Waffen SS, Himmler created a giant economic and administrative agency that would eventually control about twenty concentration camps and 165 labor camps. As early as 1939, the SS already controlled commercial enterprises in such diverse areas as food production, textile and leather goods, and building materials. In the years to come, the SS was to establish a monopoly in the mineral water business and acquire a hefty share in the furniture-making industries. At the same time, Himmler sought to create an armaments industry that would make the SS independent of the ever-suspicious regular armed forces.

Although Himmler had carved out for himself an extremely powerful position, the rivalries between the various power centers in the Third Reich prevented him from gaining a position of dominance. At bottom a timid man, Himmler was forever fearful of incurring Hitler's wrath and of the intrigues of the Party, the SA, and the armed forces. The failed attempt to assassinate Hitler on July 20, 1944, and the subsequent elimination of much of the German resistance movement clearly strengthened Himmler's position, even though his security agencies had failed to prevent the assassination attempt. With Germany's military situation worsening, however, he also faced growing disaffection and even outright insubordination by senior commanders of the Waffen SS in the West.

Himmler's brief tenure as a military commander, first on the Upper Rhine Valley and then as commander in chief of Army Group Vistula, was an unmitigated fiasco and ended in his being relieved of all military duties. Realizing Germany's increasingly hopeless military situation, he secretly opened negotiations with the Western Allies, while seeking to maintain the public image of Hitler's "faithful Heinrich." On April 18, 1945, however, Hitler learned of Himmler's negotiations and in his last will and testament expelled him from the Party and from all offices.

Equipped with false papers bearing the name of Heinrich Hitzinger and wearing the uniform of a sergeant in the field security police, Himmler was arrested by the British near Lüneburg in northern Germany on May 23, 1945. Shortly after his arrest, he committed suicide by swallowing a vial of cyanide.

Summary

Heinrich Himmler's entire political career exemplifies National Socialism in its purest and most uncompromising form. His place in the history of the Third Reich is unique. As the architect and principal administrator of one of the most efficiently organized and most brutally operated police states in history, he translated the ideology of the Third Reich into reality and enabled National Socialism to assert itself on virtually all levels of society. As the principal organizer of the so-called final solution, Himmler directed the wholesale murder of millions of people in the service of an ideology that viewed genocide of supposed racially inferior peoples as a positive, though admittedly stressful, act of political necessity.

The overriding ambition of this outwardly unimpressive, timorous, sickly, and puritanical man was to restore and enhance Germany's greatness by eliminating the racially or genetically inferior and by vigorously supporting the growth of racially superior Germanic elements. As carriers of superior racial characteristics and as missionaries of a new morality, untainted by Christianity, his SS, like a latter-day Order of Teutonic Knights, was to show the path to Germany's future.

There is no doubt that the immense coercive powers at Himmler's disposal and the comparative secrecy shielding his most barbaric programs help account for the relative ease with which his plans could be implemented. Still, Himmler's success in carrying out programs of truly unimaginable horror in a nation counted among the most civilized and advanced countries of Europe raises some very disturbing questions about the nature and strength of a civilization's values.

Bibliography

Fest, Joachim C. *The Face of the Third Reich: Portraits of the Nazi Leadership.* Translated by Michael Bullock. London: Weidenfeld and Nicolson, and New York: Pantheon, 1970. One chapter in this collection of essays on the leading figures of the Third Reich focuses on Himmler. The author sees Himmler's lack of realism as a major determinant in his life. Includes extensive notes, excellent documentation, a bibliography, and an index.

Frischauer, Willi. *Himmler: The Evil Genius of the Third Reich.* London: Odhams Press, and Boston: Beacon Press, 1953. A fairly accurate, although dated, general portrayal of Himmler's career and his beliefs, based in part on interviews with several former associates. The volume also describes the development and the functions of the SS. Contains a brief bibliography, several excellent photographs, and an index, but no footnotes.

Gingerich, Mark P. "Waffen SS Recruitment in the 'Germanic lands,' 1940-1941." *Historian* 59, no. 4 (Summer 1997). Discusses Himmler's recruiting efforts and methods during World War II.

Goldin, Milton. "Financing the SS." *History Today* 48, no. 6 (June, 1998). The author discusses schemes used by the Nazis to finance Himmler's SS "state within a state" with stolen Jewish assets.

Höhne, Heinz. *The Order of the Death's Head: The Story of Hitler's SS.* Translated by Richard Barry. London: Secker and Warburg, 1969; New York: Ballantine, 1971. The most comprehensive work on the development and function of the SS for the general reader. Offers a thorough and well-documented analysis of Himmler's various functions. Contains several appendices, featuring a glossary, tables, maps, and a very useful organizational chart of all agencies under Himmler's control. Includes an extensive bibliography, footnotes, and an index.

Kersten, Felix. *The Kersten Memoirs, 1940-1945.* Translated by Constantine Fitzgibbon and James Oliver, with a foreword by H. R. Trevor-Roper. London: Hutchinson, 1956; New York: Macmillan, 1957. This work contains selections from the diaries of Kersten, who served as Himmler's personal physician during World War II. The entries provide interesting insights into the private Himmler. Covers the negotiations between Himmler and representatives from Sweden concerning the release of prisoners held by the Nazis. Contains an index.

Manvell, Roger, and Heinrich Fraenkel. *Heinrich Himmler.* London: Heinemann, and New York: Putnam, 1965. A well-documented and lucidly written biographical study based on interviews with many of Himmler's former associates and on extensive archival research. The authors focus on the contradictions in Himmler's character and see him as a weak personality hiding behind his offices. Includes excellent notes, an index, appendices, and a useful bibliography.

Reitlinger, Gerald. *The SS: Alibi of a Nation, 1922-1945.* London: Heinemann, 1956; New York: Da Capo Press, 1957. This is the first comprehensive, scholarly study of the SS. The author emphasizes that Himmler's work and that of the SS would not have been possible without the cooperation of the German bureaucracy. Contains a useful list of the major figures of the period, maps, a bibliography, a glossary, and an index.

Smith, Bradley F. *Heinrich Himmler: A Nazi in the Making, 1900-1926.* Stanford, Calif.: Hoover Institution Press, 1971. This work is concerned with the young Himmler, his family background, the social milieu of his early years, and the reasons for his career choice as a Nazi Party official. Himmler's early years offer no satisfactory explanation for his later involvement in mass exterminations. Includes excellent scholarly apparatus and an appendix featuring Himmler's reading list.

Helmut J. Schmeller

PAUL HINDEMITH

Born: November 16, 1895; Hanau, Germany
Died: December 28, 1963; Frankfurt am Main,
West Germany
Area of Achievement: Music
Contribution: Hindemith, a neoclassicist, used
forms that were popular during the seventeenth
and eighteenth centuries. He sought to redefine
and assert the principles of tonality in the twentieth century in his writings and to reflect those
principles in his compositions.

Early Life

Paul Hindemith was born in Hanau, Germany, on
November 16, 1895. Paul was the eldest of three
children born to Robert Rudolph Hindemith and
Marie Sophie Warnecke. There is evidence that
Paul's childhood was not altogether a happy one,
because of poor family finances and his father's
running the household in such a strict and authoritarian manner. There appears to have been little affection between father and son for this reason. In a
series of moves over several years, the father finally relocated the family to Frankfurt am Main sometime in 1902 in search of a better job.

The father, a lover of music and an amateur musician himself, saw to it that his three children received professional musical instruction beginning
at an early age. It was there, in Frankfurt am Main,
that Paul began the serious study of the violin at
the Hoch Conservatory under the supervision of
Anna Hegner, a violinist of some accomplishment.
Undoubtedly young Hindemith's extraordinary talent attracted attention, and, when Hegner left the
conservatory a short time later, Hindemith continued his study of the instrument with Adolph Rebner, also associated with the conservatory and a violinist of considerable reputation. Later,
Hindemith came to play second violin in Rebner's
string quartet and became concertmaster of the
Frankfurt Opera Orchestra in 1915, no small accomplishment for a young man who had not yet
reached his twentieth birthday.

It was sometime during his association with the
conservatory, which lasted until 1917, that Hindemith began to reveal to Rebner his interest in
composition. He first studied composition with
Arnold Mendelssohn at the conservatory and then,
when Mendelssohn left the conservatory, with
Bernard Sekles. Both men were to produce a different but profound and lasting impression on the

young Hindemith, although he finally came to regard the academic environment at the conservatory to be too repressive to continue his study of
composition.

World War I claimed Hindemith in 1917, when
he was drafted. He spent his military service as a
member of a regimental band, in which he played
the bass drum. His commanding officer respected
his talent and treated Hindemith more as an equal
than as an enlisted man. He made it possible for
Hindemith to form a string quartet and to give
concerts.

The years immediately following the war were
professionally and personally important ones for
Hindemith. With the end of the war, he returned to
Frankfurt am Main and resumed his association
with the Rebner Quartet and the Frankfurt Opera
Orchestra, this time as a violist. He soon left the
Rebner Quartet and in 1921 formed the Amar
Quartet, in which he continued to play the viola
and in which his brother Rudolph played the cello
for a time. The quartet came to be recognized as
one of the leading quartets in Europe. Later, partly
because of the performance activities of the quartet
and also his desire to find more time for composition, Hindemith left the orchestra.

Hindemith, with Sekles' encouragement, submitted several compositions for consideration to
the Schott and Sons publishing house. The acceptance of these early pieces by the firm began a lifelong association with the Schott firm and with the
two Strecker brothers, who owned and operated the
business upon the death of their father. The success
of his early published compositions did much to
advance young Hindemith's reputation as a talented composer.

Hindemith became a member of the planning
committee of the Donauschingen Festival in 1922.
The festival was active in the promotion of contemporary music, and Hindemith played a major
role on that committee, which further advanced his
reputation and position in the music committee.
The festival brought young and old composers,
representing a diversity of styles, together in the
spirit of friendship and cooperation. In his later
years, Hindemith would speak highly of his experiences at the Donauschingen Festivals that were
held in the early 1920's.

Hindemith married Gertrud Rottenberg in 1924.
She was the daughter of the conductor of the Frank-

furt Opera. She was trained as a musician, but she never pursued a career in music. Instead, she increasingly became the manager of Hindemith's career, handling his correspondence and carefully controlling other people's demands on her husband's time. The role she played in assisting Hindemith in his career cannot be overestimated.

Life's Work

Hindemith's early postwar compositions were experimental in nature. Among several works surrounded in controversy were three one-act operas: *Mörder, Hoffnung der Frauen*; *Sancta Susanna*; and *Das Nusch-Nuschi*. Particularly scandalous was the opera *Sancta Susanna*, which dealt with the sexual fantasies of a nun. These three operas, among other works, reflect Hindemith's fleeting interest in expressionism and atonality.

Beginning with the seven works entitled *Kammermusik* that were composed from 1922 to 1927, Hindemith moved toward a style that has been described as neoclassic or perhaps more appropriately neo-Baroque, so called because of his interest in contrapuntal texture, reminiscent of Johann Sebastian Bach, and also his interest in Baroque forms. The emphasis was on the linear movement, and, though decidedly dissonant, his use of the music material was rooted in tonality. Hindemith continued to refine his technique but maintained this essential style throughout his career.

Hindemith left Frankfurt am Main to accept a position as professor of composition at the Berlin Staatliche Hochschule für Musik in 1927, a position that he held for ten years. His decision to enter academe turned out to be a good one. The contact with students challenged him to articulate his philosophy of composition and stimulated him in his own compositional activity as he attempted to construct a theory that reflected his own compositional practices. The natural outgrowth of the process was his book entitled *Unterweisung im Tonsatz* (*The Craft of Musical Composition*), which was published in Germany in 1937, appearing in English translation in 1941. Criticized by some and hailed as a major contribution by others, the first volume was followed by two additional volumes, the last being published posthumously.

Hindemith's professional good fortune gradually began to change when the Nazi Party came to power in 1933. His music was held in low esteem by the Nazi authorities, who viewed it as decadent.

Hindemith, reluctant to abandon the country of his birth, initially attempted to work within the repressive guidelines of the Third Reich. In 1935, he accepted an invitation by the Turkish government to reorganize the music and music education systems in that country. Hoping for a change of attitude from the German government in his absence, Hindemith busied himself with the Turkish project, which often saw him out of Germany, until its completion in 1937. Hindemith finally tired of waiting for the Nazi regime to change its mind and resigned his position at the Hochschule in 1937; after a brief time in Switzerland, he went, in 1940, to the United States, where he was to remain for the next thirteen years.

Ironically, the opera *Mathis der Maler*, one of his finest and most popular works, was composed in 1934 during this period of Nazi harassment. The subject of the opera, which involved the sixteenth century painter Matthias Grünewald, proved to be politically too sensitive, and the Nazi regime banned the opera's performance. A symphony based on the themes from the opera was performed in that same year and was enthusiastically received. The opera was not to be performed until 1938 in Zurich, Switzerland.

Hindemith accepted a professorship at Yale University in 1940. His thirteen-year tenure at Yale yielded only a handful of graduates under his supervision. While attracting a number of the brightest students that the United States had to offer, he also acquired the reputation of being a rigorous and exacting, if enthusiastic, taskmaster. Hindemith had long had an interest in the generally neglected works of great composers of the medieval and Renaissance periods. Having the rich resources of talented musicians and materials at his disposal while at Yale, he assumed an active role in the performing and conducting of early music.

He continued to produce important works in what was to become his adopted country in 1946, when he became an American citizen. Most notable was *Ludus Tonalis* for piano in 1942, a masterful exercise of the composer's contrapuntal skill. The *Symphonic Metamorphosis of Themes by Carl Maria von Weber*, composed in 1943, was, perhaps, his most popular work. It was for an orchestra and implemented several themes taken from works by the early nineteenth century composer of the title. Finally, the requiem he composed in 1945 in response to the death of Franklin D. Roosevelt remains one of his most expressive and heartfelt compositions. The work was based on Walt Whitman's poem on the death of Abraham Lincoln, "When Lilacs Last in the Dooryard Bloom'd."

Hindemith surprised everyone when he elected to leave his newly adopted country in 1953 and return to Europe, where he settled in Switzerland. The major work of this last decade of his life was his opera *Die Harmonie der Welt*, which was based on the life of the astronomer Johannes Kepler. He devoted much of the time from these last years to traveling and making guest appearances as a conductor. He died in Frankfurt am Main, West Germany, in 1963 following a brief illness.

that could be used by performers of varying levels of maturity. One such piece, for example, was Hindemith's opera to be performed by children, *Wir bauen eine Stadt*, which was first performed in 1930. He also composed a series of challenging sonatas for a number of the orchestral instruments. He treated the orchestral instrument and the piano in these works as partners in the sharing of the music material. Hindemith intended these to be learning pieces that would be appealing to the performers involved and also appealing to the audiences who had to listen to them. This basic concept has been referred to as *Gebrauchsmusik*, or functional, utilitarian, music.

The idea also relates to the composer/audience relationship that had been on a collision course since the early nineteenth century, when the composers had gradually begun to disassociate themselves from the opinions of audiences and patrons. As the musical language became more complex throughout the nineteenth century and into the early twentieth century with the emergence of expressionism and atonality, the distance between composer and audience was greater than ever. Hindemith was one of those composers in the twentieth century who attempted to reverse that trend by writing music that would be more appealing and understandable to audiences.

Hindemith was a performer and a composer who was driven to share his ideas with fellow musicians who were less accomplished or knowledgeable, as Bach had done in his day. In Hindemith's role as teacher, the emphasis was always on practical performance. He was constantly involving his students in the performance problems of music, ancient and modern, and sometimes this even led to the learning of a new instrument. Hindemith did not see his roles as performer, composer, teacher, or music consumer as being separate from one another. To him, they were all part of being a twentieth century musician.

Summary

Paul Hindemith's attitude toward music was essentially Baroque, and it manifested itself in various ways that are identifiable. First, he believed that the composer should be writing music for a specific function or purpose, not simply for the sake of inspiration. He was very sensitive about the relationship between composer and performer and believed that the composer should compose music

Bibliography

Hindemith, Paul. *A Composer's World: Horizons and Limitations*. Cambridge, Mass.: Harvard University Press, 1952. Based on the six Charles Eliot Morton lectures he presented at Harvard, this book provides interesting insights into Hindemith's private thoughts about music. It is a good source for the general reader.

Kemp, Ian. "Paul Hindemith." In *New Grove Dictionary of Music and Musicians*, edited by Stanley Sadie, vol. 8. 6th ed. New York: Macmillan, 1980. Kemp provides an excellent overview of Hindemith's life. He divides Hindemith's creative work into three periods and discusses each period. Contains a list of Hindemith's works and writings at the end of the article, along with an excellent bibliography.

Machlis, Joseph. *Introduction to Contemporary Music.* New York: W. W. Norton, 1979. Contains some biographical information on Hindemith. Machlis briefly discusses Hindemith's music and compositional style. This book is an excellent survey of the twentieth century and is intended for the general reader.

Neumeyer, David. *The Music of Paul Hindemith.* New Haven, Conn.: Yale University Press, 1986. Neumeyer's book discusses Hindemith's compositional theories. He establishes an analytical procedure for the purpose of describing the technical features of Hindemith's music. Contains an excellent appendix that provides a dated chronological listing of Hindemith's works, including city where composed, performance time, and publisher.

Richter, Eckhart. "Paul Hindemith as Director of the Yale Collegium Musicum." *College Music Symposium* 18 (1978): 20-44. This article provides an excellent insight into Hindemith, the practicing musician who was active in the study and performance of early music while he was at Yale.

Rockwell, John. "The Artist's Dilemma." *Opera News* 60, no. 3 (September, 1995). Discusses Hindemith's opera *Mathis Der Maler,* its themes, and the composer's later music.

Skelton, Geoffrey. *Paul Hindemith: The Man Behind the Music.* London: Victor Gollancz, and New York: Crescendo, 1975. Skelton's book is a thorough and detailed historical account of Hindemith's life. Contains a chronological listing of his works and a discography of recordings involving Hindemith as performer or conductor. This is an excellent book for the general reader.

———, ed. and trans. *Selected Letters of Paul Hindemith.* New Haven, Conn.: Yale University Press, 1995. A collection of nearly two hundred of Hindemith's letters revealing his personality and approach to his work.

Michael Hernon

PAUL VON HINDENBURG

Born: October 2, 1847; Posen, Prussia
Died: August 2, 1934; Neudeck, Germany
Areas of Achievement: The military, government, and politics
Contribution: During the years 1916-1918, Hindenburg commanded Germany's armed forces. As the second President of the Weimar Republic, Hindenburg attempted to manage a Germany that was beset by extreme political, economic, and social disorder. As a result of this instability, Hindenburg presided over the rise of Nazi power. On January 20, 1933, he appointed Adolf Hitler as Chancellor of Germany, despite his personal dislike of the man, thereby legally giving Hitler power.

Early Life

Paul Ludwig Hans Anton von Beneckendorff und von Hindenburg was born on October 2, 1847, in Posen, Prussia, into an old Prussian Junker family devoted to military service of the Prussian state. In 1858, when he was eleven years old, Hindenburg entered the Prussian Cadet Corps. In April, 1865, Hindenburg was subsequently appointed a second lieutenant in the Prussian Third Guard Infantry Regiment. His battle experience was not long in coming. In the summer of 1866, Hindenburg fought in Prussia's war against Austria. He was eager for combat, remarking, "It is high time the Hindenburgs smelt powder again." At the Battle of Königgrätz, he was slightly wounded in the head and earned a citation for bravery, along with the Order of the Red Eagle with Crossed Swords, an honor normally reserved for officers of the rank of major and higher.

In August, 1870, Hindenburg fought in the Franco-Prussian War, again with the Prussian Third Guard Infantry Regiment. Hindenburg again distinguished himself in battle and was present at St. Privat, later called "the graveyard of the Prussian Guard," where the Prussians had a casualty rate of more than 40 percent. Hindenburg was also present at the climactic Battle of Sedan, for which William II awarded him the Iron Cross. Hindenburg then served with the army besieging Paris and represented his regiment at the ceremony on January 18, 1870, at Versailles, where the German Empire was proclaimed.

Following his return from France, Hindenburg began his higher military education. Hindenburg pursued military studies from 1873 to 1876 at the Kreigsakademie, after which in 1878 he was made a member of the German General Staff, through which he came into contact with Field Marshals Helmuth von Moltke and Count Alfred von Waldersee. His personal life was enriched by his marriage in 1879 to Gertrude Wilhemine von Sperling, the daughter of a military officer. The Hindenburgs eventually had three children; their one son also entered military service.

Life's Work

Hindenburg's assignments provided the basis of his future greatness; in 1881, he was assigned to Königsburg in East Prussia, where in 1914 his superior knowledge of the geography of the area would allow him to achieve his great victories against the armies of the Russian czar. In 1883, he was transferred to Berlin, where he served under Moltke's successor, General Count Alfred von Schlieffen, whose war plan was utilized in 1914. Schlieffen's doctrine was based on a swift German attack on its enemies to overcome the threats of a two-front war against both France and Russia. According to Schlieffen, German armies would advance rapidly through Belgium and engage French forces on the Franco-Belgian frontier; having defeated them, the military would use its superior railway network to transfer German forces to the Eastern Front, where they could then confront the more slowly mobilizing Russian forces in turn.

Hindenburg spent the next few years passing through the system on the basis of bureaucratic seniority. In 1889, Hindenburg was transferred to the War Office. Four years later, he was promoted to colonel and given command of the Ninety-first Infantry Regiment based at Oldenburg. He remained at Oldenburg until 1896, when he was transferred to the Seventh Army Corps, based in Koblenz, having been promoted to major-general. Three years later, Hindenburg took over command of the Fourth Army Corps at Magdeburg, where he served until his retirement in 1911. Upon retiring he moved to Hannover.

With the outbreak of World War I in August, 1914, Hindenburg wondered if he would be recalled to active service. On August 23 he received a telegram asking if he was ready to return to active service. Hindenburg was immediately appointed commander of the Eighth Army, stationed in East

Prussia. General Erich von Ludendorff was appointed his chief of staff.

Hindenburg's immediate problem was to blunt the thrust into East Prussia being made by Russian forces. Given Russian difficulties, Hindenburg's forces on August 14-16 were able to score a crushing victory against the invaders at Tannenberg. Russian casualties were immense. Hindenburg then shifted his forces and twelve days later fought and won the Battle of the Masurian Lakes. Russian losses in less than a month totaled more than 250,000 killed, wounded, and captured. Hindenburg's victories ended Russian dreams of a swift offensive into Germany that would relieve pressure on their French allies in the West. For his victories, Hindenburg received the rank of colonel general, the Iron Cross first class, command of all the German forces on the Eastern Front, and the adulation of the nation.

The magnitude of Hindenburg's victories caused the German High Command to reconsider their policy of remaining on the defensive on the Eastern Front. The possibility of supporting their Austrian allies in a campaign in Russian Poland caused the authorities to appoint Hindenburg to the command of an army group that contained the Eighth and Ninth armies. By October, 1914, the German forces had pushed to the outskirts of Warsaw. A flanking movement by Austrian forces failed, however, and, in order to cover their flanks, Hindenburg's forces retreated to the Masurian Lakes, stalemated for the winter. Hindenburg was promoted to field marshal for his efforts and in 1916 made chief of staff of the army. The High Command again turned its attention westward and left the region quiescent until August, 1916, when Romania entered the war on the Allies' side, an event that threatened to turn the Austrian flank.

With the fall of the Russian monarchy in March, 1917, effective Russian resistance largely came to an end. Hindenburg and Ludendorff had pressed the Kaiser to authorize unrestricted submarine warfare, however, despite the pleadings of many politicians. The Kaiser overruled the fainthearted in his government, and unrestricted submarine warfare began on February 1, 1917, hastening the United States' entry into the war in April. Following the collapse of Central Power forces on the Balkan fronts, Hindenburg realized that Germany could not triumph over such a coalition and in September, 1918, pressured the government to seek an armistice. On November 9, 1918, the Weimar Repub-

lic was declared; the armistice followed two days later. In June, 1919, Hindenburg retired from active service and in 1920 published his memoirs, *Aus Meinem Lieben* (*Out of My Life*, 1920), a modest account of his activities. Following his retirement, Hindenburg lived quietly.

The immediate postwar years were hard for Germany; racked by massive inflation in 1922-1923 and the punitive terms of the Versailles Treaty, with its infamous "war guilt" clause, Germany had to bear the indignity of both foreign occupation of the Rhineland and the payment of reparations. In the chaotic postwar environment, many looked back with increasing nostalgia to the one national institution that had comported itself with honor, only to be "stabbed in the back" at home by defeatists: the army. As the former head of the army, Hindenburg was increasingly viewed as above politics. Even before the death of President Friedrich Ebert in February, 1925, Hindenburg was being sounded out as to his willingness to serve as president. Despite his age, Hindenburg agreed to be the candidate of the united parties of the Right. On April 26, 1925, Hindenburg was elected president with

14,655,766 votes, as opposed to his nearest opponent's 13,751,615.

Much to his supporters' and opponents' surprise, the new president followed a path of dignified simplicity in executing the duties of his office and continually stressed the need for unity. Hindenburg was not entirely free of the imperial past; he had actually communicated with the former kaiser, seeking his permission to accept the presidency. The political Left was not impressed with Germany's new president. Under the centrist governments, however, Germany's economic instability began to subside; yet Germany's equilibrium was still fragile.

When the Allies evacuated the Rhineland in July, 1930, five years ahead of schedule, Hindenburg was triumphantly acclaimed. Such nationalist triumphs could not, however, mask the worsening economy. The German economy had begun to feel the aftershocks of the October, 1929, stock market crash, and unemployment began to soar. In such an environment, political extremism flourished. Hitler's National Socialists were the major beneficiaries of this extremism; in the September, 1930, Reichstag elections, the National Socialists' number of delegates increased from 12 to 170.

In 1932, Hindenburg's seven-year term of office expired, and he again ran for president. The old general was four-tenths of a percent short of a majority and needed to stand in a runoff election. As one of the more popular nationalist parties, Hitler's Nazis battled Communists and leftists in increasing street violence. Hindenburg called on Franz von Papen as chancellor to form a coalition government, but this proved to be a temporary measure. In the election on November 6, the Nazis actually lost votes for the first time since 1928. Despite such a volatile political atmosphere, Hindenburg still hesitated to make Hitler chancellor. Under increasing pressure, Hindenburg gave way, and on January 30, 1933, Hitler became chancellor. Hitler moved swiftly to consolidate his power. Two days after becoming chancellor, Hitler dismissed the Reichstag. A suspicious fire gutted the Reichstag building on February 28, and Hitler persuaded Hindenburg the same day to issue a "Decree for Protection of People and the State," which effectively suspended the constitution.

Despite his weakening health and increasing frailty, Hindenburg made sporadic attempts to restrain Hitler. In June, 1934, the president threatened to impose martial law if Hitler did not restrain the more radical elements of the Nazis. Hindenburg's health rapidly worsened, and on August 2, 1934, he died. The same day, Hitler took over the office of president as well as that of chancellor.

Summary

Paul von Hindenburg was a pivotal figure in Germany's transition from a loose confederation of states headed by Prussia through the height of empire to Nazi Germany. As a military leader he was competent, though hardly outstanding. Having proved his personal courage in conflicts with Austria and France, he subsequently led the typical life of an average staff officer. Called from retirement by World War I, Hindenburg was fortunate in being assigned Ludendorff as his chief of staff. As a team they achieved striking victories against the Russians in 1914, in distinct contrast to their colleagues on the Eastern Front.

As head of the army from 1916 to the end of the war, Hindenburg made no innovative decisions and more than one ill-considered one. The German offensive that captured Poland ruled out the possibility of a separate peace with the Russian Empire, while Hindenburg's forceful advocacy of unrestricted submarine warfare, when implemented, brought the United States into the war.

Hindenburg was largely out of his depth when he assumed the presidency of the Weimar Republic in 1925. While his immense prestige provided stability to the government, his adherence to an officer's code of honor and political naïveté made him blind to the true threat that Hitler and his Nazis represented. As an ill and befuddled old man of eighty-six, he appointed Hitler chancellor, which ended the Weimar Republic and made increased friction with Western democracies inevitable. With Hindenburg's death, Germany quickly sank into the nightmare of Hitler's totalitarianism, which took World War II to overthrow.

Bibliography

Dorpalen, Andreas. *Hindenburg and the Weimar Republic.* Princeton, N.J.: Princeton University Press, 1964. A well-balanced, scholarly account of Hindenburg's early dealings with the Weimar Republic and his two subsequent terms as president.

Dupuy, Trevor N. *The Military Lives of Hindenburg and Lundendorff.* New York: Watts, 1970. A paired set of biographies by an outstanding military historian emphasizing the campaigns and strategies of Hindenburg and Ludendorff during the World War I.

Goldsmith, Margaret, and Frederick Voigt. *Hindenburg: The Man and the Legend.* London: Faber, and New York: Morrow, 1930. This account is a balanced but mostly favorable narrative of Hindenburg's career as both a military man and politician. It does not deal with the Nazis' rise to power.

Hindenburg, Paul von. *Out of My Life.* Translated by F. A. Holt. London and New York: Cassell, 1920. Hindenburg's own soldierly, modest record of his life up to the end of World War I and the beginnings of the Weimar Republic.

Wheeler-Bennett, John W. *The Nemesis of Power: The German Army in Politics 1918-1945.* 2d ed. London: Macmillan, and New York: Viking Press, 1964. This brilliant, thorough work draws extensively on German primary and secondary sources and attempts to fit Hindenburg and the Prussian military tradition into the larger picture as it groped to find its place in the changed circumstances of Weimar and Nazi Germany.

———. *Wooden Titan: Hindenburg in Twenty Years of German History, 1914-1934.* London: Macmillan, and New York: Morrow, 1936. Wheeler is one of the best British historians working on modern Germany; this is an eminently readable, scholarly account of both Hindenburg's military service in World War I and his subsequent role as reluctant politician.

John C. K. Daly

HIROHITO

Born: April 29, 1901; Tokyo, Japan
Died: January 7, 1989; Tokyo, Japan
Areas of Achievement: Government and politics
Contribution: Hirohito, in an unprecedented action, made the decision that ended World War II in the Pacific. Thereafter, he provided the symbolic leadership that facilitated the recovery of Japan from the devastation of the war, while first renouncing a divine status for himself and then promulgating the new democratic constitution for his nation.

Early Life

Hirohito was born barely three decades after the fall of the Tokugawa system that had ruled Japan from 1603 to 1867. His grandfather, posthumously known as the Emperor Meiji, was the symbol of the new order that succeeded the feudal Tokugawa regime. As with emperors and heirs apparent of the time, the newborn was given the suffix "hito" (benevolence) and a name by which his reign would be known posthumously: Showa (Enlightened Peace). Again following custom, only a few months after birth, the infant was placed in the care of a trusted aristocratic family—and eventually, a second.

Showa, as he should now be called, had an elitist education. In 1906, a private school was organized for him, his younger brother, and selected classmates. In 1908, he was sent to the Gakushuin or Peers' School, an elementary school for aristocratic offspring, similar to Britain's Eton. There, he came under the influence of Count Marusuke Nogi, a naval hero and Hirohito's first role model. Yet the direct influence was short-lived: In 1912, on the eve of Emperor Meiji's funeral, Nogi and his wife committed ritual suicide to express their grief. This had a lasting impression on Hirohito and was said to be an important factor in leading him to question traditional military values.

After six years, Hirohito was graduated from the Gakushuin and became the sole pupil at a special school created for him. Although efforts were made to imbue him with military values, he gradually spent more time on science, especially marine biology, and while a teenager he discovered a new species of marine life.

By this time, his father (then known as Yoshihito, but subsequently as Emperor Taisho) was demonstrating erratic behavior, a result of mental illness, that would lead to his retirement from public life and in 1921 to the appointment of Hirohito as Prince Regent, assuming the duties of his father. These new responsibilities came soon after he returned from his 1921 tour abroad—the first by a Japanese heir apparent. Years later, he would say his visit to Great Britain was the happiest time of his life.

In 1918, his engagement to Princess Nagako was announced. Despite her being the explicit choice of her fiancé, who customarily would not be consulted, and his mother, her selection was opposed by leaders of the Choshu clan, who expected to have one of their own be the empress-designate. The Choshu circulated information that Nagako had a genetic tendency for colorblindness, grounds for which the engagement could be terminated. Yet the Prince Regent and his supporters were insistent, and Nagako became his bride on January 26, 1924. Since the imperial line, in modern times, could only pass through the male side, disappointment was widespread when four daughters were born. Pressure grew that the emperor consider a concubine, but that issue was resolved when in 1933, a son, Akihito, was born. Later a second son and a fifth daughter joined the family, and Japan had its first deliberately monogamous emperor.

Life's Work

At Emperor Taisho's death, December 25, 1926, his eldest son immediately succeeded him, although the formal ceremony of enthronement did not occur for nearly two years. During Taisho's life, Japan had moved from a feudal society, similar to that of Europe centuries before, to a modern one, ranking just below the United States and Great Britain in many measures of industrial development. Major efforts were made to provide mass education, to generate capital for economic investment, and to organize a system whereby private and public management could be coordinated in pursuit of priorities established by the government. As would be the case throughout the twentieth century, the benefits of this modernization were dispersed unevenly among the population. Especially in rural areas, hardship continued to be common.

A principal motive for this drive to modernize was the desire not to be humiliated by the Western powers, as China and other Asian nations were.

Japanese leaders were convinced that military prowess was essential to dissuade the occidental nations from exploiting Japan. Japan had achieved remarkable success in creating a modern military apparatus. One indication of that was manifested in the naval conferences of the 1920's, wherein Japan's naval power was recognized as falling into a category just below that of the United States and the major European powers, excluding Germany, which was denied rearmament by the Treaty of Versailles. Yet Japanese military leaders were offended that their nation had not been placed in the highest category.

Unmistakably in the 1920's and continuing into the 1930's, advocates of militarism, glorifying Japanese successes in the Sino-Japanese War of 1894-1895 and the Russo-Japanese War of 1904-1905, promoted larger military expenditures and aggression on the Asian mainland. China was the main target of those ventures as Japanese militarists fabricated one "incident" after another with the intention of provoking the Japanese people to support a vengeful retaliation.

Thus, the new emperor Hirohito was confronted with a rising militarism that would eventually bring devastating destruction to his nation. His position was paradoxical: Symbolically, he had unlimited powers as a god-ruler, but, throughout most of recorded history, Japanese emperors had rarely exercised power. Instead, the power had been used in their name by various other officials, the Shogun of the Tokugawa being an excellent example. Until the Meiji Restoration, emperors had for centuries resided in Kyōto, while effective governmental authority was wielded at Edo (now Tokyo), hundreds of miles away. It was customary before the Meiji Restoration for emperors to abdicate while relatively young men and bestow the office upon their, in many cases, minor sons. With Meiji, the emperor became more visible and increasingly informed about affairs of state. Whether the 1889 Meiji Constitution made Japan a constitutional monarchy is debatable. The document gave the nation the appearance of a parliamentary system, but Taisho certainly did not decide governmental policy. No emperor has wielded the powers attributed to Hirohito by British and American propaganda during World War II.

Hirohito, while a retiring personality, was aware of major actions leading up to and during World War II. Prince Kimmochi Saionji, who was for years the chief imperial adviser, concurred with Hirohito's advice of moderation to the military. In several instances, Hirohito reportedly expressed reservations and even anger about actions taken or planned by the military. Given the imperial tradition, it is nearly inconceivable that the emperor would have directly countermanded decisions of duly authorized officials, although he did move swiftly to halt the attempted military coup of 1936. In August, 1945, after two atomic bombs had been dropped on Japan and faced with the inevitable invasion of the Japanese islands, the war cabinet deadlocked. Only then did the emperor decisively move to stop the war.

At the close of World War II, there was considerable sentiment in the victorious nations to try Hirohito for war crimes. Others contended that at least he should abdicate. These positions were founded on the view that even if he was not directly responsible for Japan's military aggression, he was morally responsible. In his famous visit to General Douglas MacArthur of September, 1945, Hirohito voluntarily assumed responsibility for the war. The relative positions of the two men were dramatized in the photograph of the emperor in formal Western dress standing beside MacArthur in casual military attire with an open-shirt collar.

MacArthur chose not to bring Hirohito to trial or have him abdicate. It is unlikely that MacArthur did this because of a profound comprehension of the actually limited powers of Japanese emperors. Rather, MacArthur's decision was motivated by his desire to use the emperor to develop popular support for conversion of the Japanese governing system and for rebuilding the economy. To have punished the emperor might have fomented widespread opposition to occupation programs.

The end of the war did not complete Hirohito's remarkable efforts. In 1971 and 1975, he and the empress traveled abroad, to Europe and to the United States, respectively. These precedent-setting events, combined with his 1921 tour, secured his place as the first emperor to have direct knowledge of foreign nations. The wide television coverage of the later imperial tours abroad gave the Japanese far greater exposure to the royal family than was conceivable for any of his predecessors on the Chrysanthemum Throne. This was in line with a policy that Hirohito pursued with the end of World War II to make the imperial office more accessible to the Japanese populace. The reticent emperor was uncomfortable in his initial efforts to move among his subjects shortly after the war, but he persisted.

The intention was not to make the imperial office as visible as the British monarch but to emphasize its human rather than divine status. Once that was established, imperial walkabouts were cut back. In later years, Hirohito's public appearances were largely restricted to formal occasions, such as opening the 1964 Olympic Games in Tokyo. Hirohito thus continued as the symbol of the Japanese nation but with a human face and with far less mystery and reverence than his office accrued before Japan's surrender.

Until near the end of his life, Hirohito pursued his youthful enthusiasm for marine biology, being recognized as an authority on the hydroza. Of the more than one dozen books that he published, some translated into English, four dealt with that topic.

Hirohito's final years were occupied with the heavy ceremonial functions of his office, many of which dated from his earliest ancestors; presiding at the renowned New Year's poetry reading, initiated by his grandfather; following sumo wrestling; and in general being a father figure for his people. He retained some distinctly non-Japanese habits for his generation, such as his love of golf and a daily breakfast of toast and eggs, two by-products of his 1921 visit to Great Britain. His funeral, however, was a reminder of the elaborate ritual associated over the centuries with the direct descendant of the Sun Goddess.

Summary

Hirohito lived longer and reigned longer than any of his 123 predecessors. Neither of these, however, was the major achievement of his reign—that was his transformation of the imperial office. In transforming that role, he continued to be not only a primary symbol of Japanese nationhood but also a manifestation of the democratic principles of the postwar regime imposed by the occupation under MacArthur. Ironically, rather than using the democratic mechanism of a referendum to enact the new constitution, MacArthur had the emperor announce it. Years before, Hirohito had quietly indicated his preference for a more liberal system, reservations about imperial divinity, and an envy of the less restrictive manner of royal rule that he had observed in Great Britain. Yet with the firm emphasis on duty and tradition in which he had been trained, he would never have initiated these changes. His duty was to serve.

Bibliography

Bergamini, David. *Japan's Imperial Conspiracy.* London: Heinemann, and New York: Morrow, 1971. Bergamini, born in Japan and a prisoner of war in the Philippines, presents a massive (1,277-page) book that purports to demonstrate that Hirohito was the driving force behind Japanese militarism in the 1930's and 1940's. Few Japanologists concur.

Bix, Herbert P. "Inventing the 'Symbol Monarchy' in Japan, 1945-52." *Journal of Japanese Studies* 21, no. 2 (Summer 1995). Discusses the "symbol monarchy" invented by Hirohito and General MacArthur, and its function and ultimate demise after the U.S. withdrawal.

Irokawa, Daikichi. *The Age of Hirohito: In Search of Modern Japan.* Translated by John K. Urda and Mikiso Hane. New York: Free Press, 1995. Critical assessment of Hirohito and Japanese society that does not attempt to justify the emperor's activities based on his stature as a figurehead, suggesting instead he could have stopped the war.

Kanroji, Osanaga. *Hirohito: An Intimate Portrait of the Japanese Emperor.* Los Angeles: Gateway, 1975. Kanroji was an imperial attendant for seventy years, retiring in 1959, and a classmate of Taisho at Peers' School.

Manning, Paul. *Hirohito: The War Years.* New York: Dodd Mead, 1986. Focuses on the planning, conduct, and immediate aftermath of World War II. Assumes that Hirohito had a commanding role in that event. Appendix has a list of key figures who advised him.

Mosley, Leonard. *Hirohito: Emperor of Japan.* London: Weidenfeld and Nicolson, and Englewood Cliffs, N.J: Prentice-Hall, 1966. Perhaps the most readable and detailed biography in English, but misses the final quarter century of the subject's life.

Packard, Jerrold M. *Sons of Heaven: A Portrait of the Japanese Monarchy.* New York: Scribner, 1987; London: Macdonald, 1988. The last 250 pages concern Hirohito. Contains a seven-page bibliography, a list of all Japanese rulers, various documents pertaining to the imperial office, and the preface to a 1977 scientific paper by Hirohito.

Severns, Karen. *Hirohito.* New York: Chelsea House, 1988. Part of the World Leaders: Past and Present series, this work was written for young adults but is useful for a broad audience. There are photographs or other graphic material on nearly every page. Names are given in Oriental fashion: family name first. An excellent starting point to examine Hirohito's life.

Takeda, Kiyoko. *The Dual-Image of the Japanese Emperor*. London: Macmillan, and New York: New York University Press, 1988. In less than two hundred pages, this book examines American, British, Canadian, Australian, and Chinese views of the Japanese emperor from 1942 to 1952. Also contains a chronology of this period.

Thomas P. Wolf

ALGER HISS

Born: November 11, 1904; Baltimore, Maryland
Died: November 15, 1996; New York, New York
Areas of Achievement: Diplomacy and law
Contribution: Hiss was a U.S. diplomat accused of being a Communist spy and became the defendant in two notorious trials that heightened the public's fear of communist infiltration in the government.

Early Life

Alger Hiss was born on November 11, 1904, in Baltimore, Maryland, the son of Mary and Charles Alger Hiss. Raised in an upper-middle-class atmosphere, Hiss possessed an eagerness for knowledge and excelled at his studies. He enjoyed being read to by an aunt who lived in the Hiss household after Charles died when Alger was just two years old. As a youth, Hiss attended Baltimore public schools; after graduating from high school at Baltimore City College in 1921, he attended Powder Point Academy in Massachusetts. Hiss glided through college and law school with honors and scholarships, graduating from Johns Hopkins University in 1926 and Harvard Law School in 1929. He was a protégé of Felix Frankfurter (a future U.S. Supreme Court justice) and later clerked for Justice Oliver Wendell Holmes.

After practicing law in Boston, Massachusetts, and New York City from 1930 to 1933, Hiss began his career in Washington, D.C. He held several New Deal posts in President Franklin Delano Roosevelt's administration, including the Agricultural Adjustment Administration (AAA), the major New Deal agency concerned with farming. In July, 1934, Hiss shifted from the AAA to a new post on the legal staff of the Nye Committee, which was investigating the arms manufacturers of World War I. Hiss then worked briefly for the Department of Justice before transferring to the Department of State on September 1, 1936, where he served in various capacities, including assistant to the adviser on political relations, assistant to the director of the Office of Far Eastern Affairs, and deputy director for the Office of Special Political Affairs.

Hiss's hard work and dedication enabled him to rise quickly through the ranks of the State Department. He was appointed executive secretary to the Dumbarton Oaks Conference in 1944, at which the blueprint of the United Nations Charter was approved. The following year, Hiss accompanied President Roosevelt to the Yalta Conference as a member of the U.S. delegation. He then participated in the founding of the United Nations as the temporary secretary general of the United Nation's organizing conference in San Francisco, California, in April, 1945. After returning from the meeting and delivering a copy of the U.N. Charter directly to President Harry S. Truman, who praised his work, Hiss settled into his new responsibilities as director of the Office of Special Political Affairs. Hiss continued to impress his superiors and, as a result, attended the first meeting of the United Nations General Assembly in London, England, as a principal adviser for the U.S. delegation in January, 1946. One year later, at the age of forty-two, Hiss left the State Department to become the president of the Carnegie Endowment for International Peace.

After joining the Roosevelt administration, Hiss had experienced swift and remarkable career advancements. He seemed headed for a great future, yet his many accomplishments occurred at a time when the United States was engaged in an ideological struggle between the forces of capitalism and the forces of communism. The Cold War extended beyond foreign policy and reached into the spirits of the United States and the Soviet Union. As tensions heightened, Communist infiltration in the government became a serious concern. Many soon began to doubt Hiss's allegiance to the United States, suspecting him of Communist sympathies. While Hiss's public career had been that of a brilliant bureaucrat and model New Dealer, his notoriety derived from the accusations leveled against him in the late 1940's. The events that transpired would change his life forever.

Life's Work

In the summer of 1948, the country was electrified to learn that Hiss, president of the Carnegie Endowment for International Peace, had been identified as a member of an underground Communist Party cell in Washington, D.C., during the 1930's. The fascinating drama began on August 3 when a former Communist named Whittaker Chambers, a senior editor of *Time* magazine, appeared before the House Committee on Un-American Activities and accused Hiss of having been a Communist spy while working for the State Department in 1937 and 1938. The charge was shocking. The tall,

handsome, and elegantly dressed Hiss seemed to be the model U.S. citizen. Hiss demanded the right to refute the charges; forty-eight hours later, in a masterful performance in front of an audience of supporters, he seemingly put the accusations to rest by insisting that he had never met Chambers and did not even recognize a picture of him. Hiss received a standing ovation from Congress as he ended his testimony. There was one Congressman, however, who remained unconvinced. Richard Nixon, a freshman from California, harbored doubts about Hiss's veracity.

Under the eyes of the country, an exciting drama of confrontation developed between Hiss and Chambers. Hiss challenged Chambers to repeat his charge without the protection of legal immunity. Chambers did so on *Meet the Press*, and Hiss sued him for libel. Hiss's defense lawyers became thoroughly committed to the task of destroying Chambers' credibility. To defend himself, Chambers produced microfilm copies of sixty-five classified State Department documents that he claimed Hiss had passed to him in the mid-1930's to give to the Soviets. These secret documents,

hidden in a hollowed-out pumpkin behind Chambers' Maryland farm, have been known ever since as the Pumpkin Papers. Although the documents possessed little secret value, the American public's preoccupation with the infiltration of Soviet influence into the U.S. government allowed the revelation to discredit Hiss. As a result, Hiss resigned as president of Carnegie Endowment on December 13, 1948. Two days later he was indicted for perjury, since the statute of limitations on espionage had expired. Hiss was tried twice, his first trial having ended with a hung jury. After the second trial, which began on November 17, 1949, Hiss was found guilty and sentenced to five years in prison. He served forty-four months in the Lewisburg Federal Penitentiary in Pennsylvania.

Hiss was released from prison on November 27, 1954. Unable to return to a normal lifestyle, he devoted the rest of his life to establishing his innocence. He identified himself as the victim of a larger evil—Cold War hysteria and antagonism toward the New Deal—and emphatically insisted that he was the subject of a frame-up. In his two books, *In the Court of Public Opinion* (1957) and *Recollections of a Life* (1988), Hiss continued to present himself as an American innocent. His reputation made a partial comeback in public esteem when the Watergate scandal forced Nixon to resign the presidency. The judgment that Hiss was guilty beyond a reasonable doubt, however, has been upheld in the face of repeated appeals to the highest courts. In 1978, using newly acquired government documents obtained under the Freedom of Information Act, Hiss petitioned the United States Supreme Court for a third time in an attempt to get a new trial. On October 11, 1983, the Court refused to hear his case. Yet Hiss remained determined to demonstrate his innocence.

Following the breakup of the Soviet Union and the end of the Cold War, Hiss requested information from Soviet sources to clear his name. After extensive research, General Dimitri Volkogonov, head of the Russian military intelligence archives, announced in October, 1992, that "not a single document" substantiated the allegation that Hiss collaborated with the Soviet Union intelligence. Pressured by the American Right, Volkogonov qualified his finding, stating that while he had found no evidence against Hiss in KGB files, he could not speak for other Soviet intelligence agencies nor could he comment on the many documents that had been destroyed. In 1993, Hungarian historian Maria Schmidt divulged material from Communist Hungarian secret police files that seemed to suggest Hiss's guilt. Another piece of evidence also became available in 1996 when the Central Intelligence Agency (CIA) and the National Security Agency released several thousand documents of decoded cables exchanged between Moscow and Communist agents in the United States from 1939 to 1957. These materials were part of a secret intelligence project called "Venona." A cable, dated March 30, 1945, referred to an agent code-named "Ales." An anonymous footnote, dated more than twenty years later, suggested that Ales was "probably Alger Hiss." Hiss issued a statement denying this allegation. Never ceasing to maintain his innocence, Hiss died on November 15, 1996, at the age of ninety-two.

Summary

The Hiss-Chambers case emerged in 1948 at a pivotal moment in Cold War America. The controversial and well-publicized case dramatized the emerging political and cultural implications of the Cold War. Hiss's conviction, more than any other domestic event, convinced millions of Americans that there was truth to the often-made Republican charges that Roosevelt and Truman had not been sufficiently alert to the dangers of Communist infiltration, subversion, and espionage. Over the years, the Hiss-Chambers controversy was transformed from an argument over the facts of the case to a struggle between the United States' patrician liberal establishment and its populist opponents. For many Americans, the contest was an elemental struggle between good and evil, between leftist New Dealers and right-wing anti-Communists. It divided the nation and set off widespread fears that the State Department was infiltrated by Soviet agents. Hiss's conviction also gave prominence to a fledgling Congressman, Richard Nixon, who used the notoriety to help win a Senate seat in 1950 and the vice presidency in 1952. Furthermore, the case boosted the anti-Communist crusade in the United States and legitimated Senator Joseph McCarthy's reckless attacks on the Truman and Eisenhower administrations.

The Alger Hiss case continues to ignite controversy within political and cultural circles. While some evidence suggests that Hiss was guilty, his unrelenting declarations of innocence have allowed historians, journalists, and political figures to continue to debate the case. Interestingly, an ironic twist occurred in the Hiss saga. The metal box used by Hiss to transport the United Nations Charter back to President Truman in 1945 now contains the infamous Pumpkin Papers, which are stored at the National Archives II in College Park, Maryland.

Bibliography

Breindel, Eric. "The Faithful Traitor: Alger Hiss's Refusal to Recant Helped Create the Myth of His Innocence." *National Review* 49, no. 2 (February 10, 1997). Discusses Hiss's refusal to recant his denials that he was a Russian agent.

Chambers, Whittaker. *Witness*. New York: Random House, 1952. This memoir constructs a portrait of Chambers's early years.

Hiss, Alger. *In the Court of Public Opinion*. London: Calder, and New York: Knopf, 1957. In this subjective account, Hiss takes his case to the court of public opinion and details the evidence and arguments that he believes establish his innocence.

————. *Recollections of a Life*. London: Unwin Hyman, and New York: Seaver, 1988. The eighty-three-year-old Hiss offers an intriguing narrative that serves as both a memoir and a final declaration of his innocence.

Nixon, Richard M. *Six Crises*. London: Allen, and New York: Doubleday, 1962. This memoir details the various crises confronted by Nixon and his response to them. Chapter 1 is Nixon's personal account of the Hiss case.

Oshinsky, David M. *A Conspiracy so Immense: The World of Joe McCarthy*. London: Macmillan, and New York: Free Press, 1983. Oshinsky offers a comprehensive narrative of the rise and fall of Joseph R. McCarthy with extensive interviews and archival research. Recreates the Cold War melodrama. Includes selective bibliography, footnotes, and photos.

Romerstein, Herbert. "Hiss: Still Guilty." *New Republic* 215, no. 27 (December 30, 1996). Discusses Czech documents supporting Hiss's guilt. The document indicates that Hiss was named as a Russian agent by another field agent who was interrogated by Hungarian police.

Smith, John Chabot. *Alger Hiss: The True Story*. New York: Holt Rinehart, 1976; London: Penguin, 1977. Smith portrays Hiss as the victim of a conspiracy in which Chambers played the central role. A spectrum of conspiracy theories find expression within this single volume.

Tanenhaus, Sam. *Whittaker Chambers: A Biography*. New York: Random House, 1997. An exhaustive 638-page biography by a freelance journalist that provides a sympathetic portrait of Chambers while sustaining Hiss's guilt. This well-written and compelling work makes an invaluable contribution to the history of American communism and anticommunism.

Weinstein, Allen. *Perjury: The Hiss-Chambers Case*. London: Hutchinson, and New York: Knopf, 1978. This extensively researched work uses previously classified documents obtained under the Freedom of Information Act and is supplemented with numerous personal interviews. Weinstein began working on the book convinced of Hiss's innocence but concludes that he is guilty.

Zeligs, Meyer A. *Friendship and Fratricide*. New York: Viking Press, and London: Deutsch, 1967. Zeligs offers a 476-page psychoanalytic study of Hiss and Chambers. Based on numerous interviews, legal records, and personal writings, the book attempts to explain the unconscious motives that determined their actions.

Heather L. Shaffer

ALFRED HITCHCOCK

Born: August 13, 1899; Leytonstone (now in London), England
Died: April 29, 1980; Bel Air, California
Area of Achievement: Film
Contribution: In a film career that lasted more than fifty years, Hitchcock directed numerous thrillers that explored the psychological depths of the human condition. In the process, he created some of the most memorable and influential films of the modern era.

Early Life

Alfred Joseph Hitchcock was born in Leytonstone, part of what is now called the Cockney area of London, on August 13, 1899. He was the third and last child of William and Emma Hitchcock and spent his early years with his brother William and sister Ellen Kathleen in a staunchly middle-class and Catholic environment. His father was a hardworking, moderately successful grocer and, at least to Hitchcock, a somewhat intimidating figure. Hitchcock's Catholic background marked him as an outsider in Anglican England, and his education at a Jesuit school, St. Ignatius College, reinforced not only his habits of discipline bred at home but also his overall sense of worry, guilt, and fear, qualities that proved to be integral to his creativity, to the intense concentration in his career, and to the world of disorder and pain envisioned in his films.

After leaving school, Hitchcock continued on with occasional courses and workshops at the University of London, but when his father died in 1914, he suddenly needed to support himself and went to work for the Henley Telegraph and Cable Company as a technical clerk. His skill as a draftsman led him to the advertising department, where the layouts he designed prepared him for the most momentous step in his life. His fascination for technical as well as visual details was well suited to the newly developing cinema, and he soon found a place at Famous Players-Lasky Corporation, a studio on the rise that welcomed his energy and many talents.

After assisting on several films, Hitchcock was finally trusted to direct on his own. In 1925 he traveled to Germany to direct his first two films, *The Pleasure Garden* (1925) and *The Mountain Eagle* (1926). Among his coworkers was Alma Reville, an experienced editor and assistant director. They would marry on December 2, 1926 (their only child, Patricia, was born on July 7, 1928), and continue to work together on films for more than fifty years.

Hitchcock made nine silent films between 1925 and 1929. He spoke of *The Lodger* (1926) as the first true Hitchcock film, and it indeed captured in an early form his lifelong fascination with attractive murderers, lovely blonde women who provoke dangerous passions, and the threat of chaos and unpredictable disruptions that lurk beneath not only gloomy and mysterious settings but ordinary everyday locales as well. Other early works showed his versatility and include literary adaptations, a boxing film, and several of what might be called moral tales showing young men and women at risk in a precarious modern world. Linking all these films is a constant sense of experimentation with cinematic techniques, including some startling camera angles and expressionist effects (such as shadows, mysterious characters, and distorted images), and the beginning of what came to be known as "the Hitchcock touch": an instantly recognizable blend of cinematic inventiveness and wry—and sometimes shocking—explorations of the deeper reaches of the human psyche and society. For Hitchcock, these early silent motion pictures were the cradle of "pure cinema" recalled in many of his later films where pivotal scenes are shot without any dialogue.

Life's Work

The British period of Hitchcock's career reached its height in his first sound film, *Blackmail* (1929), and in the key films of the 1930's that established him as a master of the genre that he was most often associated with, the thriller. *Blackmail* was begun as a silent picture, but Hitchcock shrewdly realized that the industry was about to change over to the newly developed sound technology and planned his film accordingly, integrating not only spoken dialogue but also startling sound effects into his tale of a woman tormented by guilt as well as by a blackmailer who threatens to reveal to her police detective "boyfriend" that she killed a man who sexually assaulted her. *Blackmail* was a great commercial and critical success, not only because of its novelty as Britain's first "talkie" but perhaps also because viewers appreciated Hitchcock's ability to tell an exciting and suspenseful story via fast-paced, visually interesting, and innovative cinematic techniques.

These qualities reached full expression in the series of films he made for Gaumont-British Pictures between 1934 and 1938, each of which crystallized a recurrent Hitchcock theme or motif. For example, *The Man Who Knew Too Much* (1934) throws an innocent family on holiday into the middle of an assassination plot that jeopardizes their daughter as much as a government official. As the title suggests, knowledge is dangerous in Hitchcock's world. *The 39 Steps* (1935) is structured around what Hitchcock once defined as the "core of the movie," the chase, in this instance a double chase as an innocent man, wrongly accused, is pursued by the police even as he is pursuing the spy organization. This film also highlights the device called the "MacGuffin," the term Hitchcock used to describe whatever it is that sets the plot in motion. Interestingly, Hitchcock was not concerned with the particulars. His real focus was on the ripple effect, the disturbances and complications caused by the pursuit of something that is important but never really specified.

One final key element of Hitchcock's developing technique that was refined in this series of thrillers was his notion of suspense. While he often made good use of sudden dramatic action, he typically worked for the more sustained tension and involvement created by letting his audience in on what was happening. *Sabotage* (1936) contains one of the classic examples of Hitchcock's use of suspense: He shows viewers a young boy carrying a bomb that they know is set to go off at a quarter to the hour; thus, instead of a ten-second shock effect created by a sudden bomb blast, he creates ten minutes of excitement as viewers anticipate the inevitable.

By the end of the 1930's, Hitchcock was contemplating a move to Hollywood, California, not only to capitalize on his popularity and increase his audience but also to take advantage of the tremendous technological facilities available in Hollywood studios. His American period began when he signed with film producer David Selznick in 1939 and left England to make *Rebecca* (1940), a costume melodrama that in some ways seems markedly different from his previous work but in other ways shows his skill at making domestic as well as espionage thrillers. Throughout his career, he showed tremendous imagination in expanding the form of the thriller, using it to examine psychological and interpersonal themes as well as broader action-adventure themes.

Not surprisingly, several of his films of the early 1940's revolved around World War II: *Foreign Correspondent* (1940) urged an end to U.S. neutrality, *Saboteur* (1942) warned of the danger of subversive fascism within the United States, and *Lifeboat* (1944) reminded audiences that the enemy was well organized, disciplined, and resourceful, and could only be defeated by unified and committed action. However, his best films of this period were psychological and personal as well as political and historical. *Shadow of a Doubt* (1943) presents a haunting analysis of the violence and pathology that lie just beneath the surface of "normal" American life. Uncle Charlie is one of Hitchcock's most memorable charming villains, alerting filmgoers to the fact that they face dangers not only from outside but also from within the family and the psyche. *Notorious* (1946) blends an exciting anti-Nazi tale with a stunning analysis of a relationship between a man and a woman driven apart by the clash of love and duty, but also by the demands of love. Although these conflicts are resolved by the end of *Notorious*, Hitchcock increasingly turned his attention to the irresistible but dangerous and destructive force of human passions and desires, including love.

Hitchcock was remarkably ambitious, productive, and successful throughout his working life, but the years from the early 1950's to the early 1960's may legitimately be called his "major" phase. During this period he consolidated and expanded his international reputation by continuing to make films that were both entertaining and artistically well crafted and by paying ceaseless attention to marketing and self-promotion. Hitchcock created a highly visible persona for himself by appearing in a brief cameo role in each of his films, regularly writing and giving interviews about how he made his films, attaching his name to a series of mystery story anthologies and a magazine, and hosting an enormously successful television series. Beginning in 1955, *Alfred Hitchcock Presents* brought him into millions of homes, and his memorable appearance as a short, overweight, simultaneously inviting and menacing host confirmed his image as the master of suspense and the macabre.

Despite his activities in other areas, though, it was the films of this period that mark it as his major phase. Even lesser efforts, including *Strangers on a Train* (1951), *I Confess* (1953), and *The*

Wrong Man (1957), are fascinating and shed important light on his lifelong interest in not only the dramatic but also the moral and metaphysical aspects of guilt, particularly the way guilt is shared or exchanged, literally passed from one person to another. His entertainment vehicles such as *Dial M for Murder* (1954) and *To Catch a Thief* (1955) are witty, diverting, thoroughly appealing, and culminate in his most masterful blend of action, adventure, suspense, and romance, *North by Northwest* (1959), which for all its excitement also evokes a sense of anxiety about the instability of one's self in a chaotic and overwhelming environment.

Finally, Hitchcock's best films of this period are among the finest achievements of cinematic art. He often cited *Rear Window* (1954) as his example of what he meant by "pure cinema" because it uses visual means and skillful editing to create powerful emotional effects and tell a story of murder and romance, but perhaps also because it is in many ways a fable about making and watching motion pictures. The main character in the film, a photographer confined to a wheelchair, is primarily a voyeur, and Hitchcock's examination of his "peeping Tom" mentality applies equally to the guilty pleasures of the audience watching a film. *Vertigo* (1958) is in many ways Hitchcock's most haunting film, studying a man's obsession with and subsequent loving and brutal manipulation of a woman. The title of the film describes not only a medical but also an existential condition, and the main character's fear of heights, which he ultimately overcomes, is only one aspect of a much broader disorientation of a human soul living in a world of corruption, chaos, and powerful emotional drives that are not so easily overcome. *Psycho* (1960) is one of Hitchcock's most terrifying and influential works. Shot in black and white and on a low budget, in many ways it represents Hitchcock's final statement on the horrors that lie just off the well-traveled roads, just beneath the surface of apparently normal and harmless individuals—horrors that cannot be understood, avoided, or erased. Hitchcock conveys this horror visually by using evocative, even symbolic, set design, off-center and unsettling camera framing, and stunning montage effects, including one of the most celebrated sequences in all of film history, the murder in the shower.

Hitchcock continued to work almost until the end of his life, but clearly in decline. *Torn Curtain* (1966) and *Topaz* (1969) are uninspired spy thrill-

ers, and his last two films, *Frenzy* (1972) and *Family Plot* (1976), show only occasional flashes of the Hitchcock touch. Slowed by health problems, old age, and perhaps a sense that he was incapable of keeping up with the demands of a new audience and a new filmmaking environment, he reluctantly closed his office. His last few months, though marked by tributes to his lifelong achievements and concerned attention by his longtime friends, were difficult and painful. It may have been a great relief when he died on April 29, 1980.

Summary

Alfred Hitchcock's achievements, popularity, and influence are enormous. Like William Shakespeare, Charles Dickens, and D. W. Griffith, figures whose works he knew well, he was an entertainer and entrepreneur as well as an artist, a shrewd businessman with an uncanny knowledge of his audience. He knew how to attract, move, and manipulate this audience and, especially in his most characteristic works, please and satisfy even as he was frightening and otherwise disturbing them. This ability, coupled with his economical shooting style, skills as a producer and director, and relentless concern for marketing and self-promotion, allowed him a relatively high degree of independence and control in an industry that often operated, in the words of D. W. Griffith, as though it was simply cranking out sausages.

Commercial concerns, though, were not incompatible with his deeply felt responsibilities to his art, and part of what made him so captivating to viewers and influential on other filmmakers was his constant experimentation with film form, his attempt, as he put it, always to avoid the cliché and find new ways to mobilize the visual resources of cinema. For many modern viewers, Hitchcock is the ultimate auteur, a director's director whose vision is imprinted in every film he ever made. It is this vision, not so much of the art of cinema as of the world, that may account for Hitchcock's appeal. He presents a landscape of unaccountable humor and horror, an often nightmarish but instantly credible world in which peace is fragile, love is dangerous, violence is inevitable, and moral action is always compromised. Hitchcock often claimed that the shocks he administered were ultimately therapeutic, even pleasurable, helping viewers to make sense of and perhaps master what otherwise might be the overwhelming facts of life. Whether or not he is one of the great healers, he is unquestionably one of the great visual artists of the modern world.

Bibliography

Freedman, Jonathan, and Richard H. Millington, eds. *Hitchcock's America*. Oxford and New York: Oxford University Press, 1999. Study of Hitchcock's films as responses to changes in U.S. society between the 1940's and the 1960's.

Hitchcock, Alfred. *Hitchcock on Hitchcock: Selected Writings and Interviews*. Edited by Sidney Gottlieb. Berkeley: University of California Press, and London: Faber, 1995. Includes important and otherwise inaccessible autobiographical comments and descriptions of Hitchcock's theories and working methods.

Phillips, Gen D. *Alfred Hitchcock*. Boston: Twayne, 1984; London: Columbus, 1986. A very readable and authoritative overview of Hitchcock's life and career.

Samuels, Robert. *Hitchcock's Bi-Textuality: Lacan, Feminisms, and Queer Theory*. Albany: State University of New York Press, 1998. A psychological study of Hitchcock's films based on analysis of the films, Lacan's theory of ethics, and theories of feminine subjectivity and queer textuality.

Spoto, Donald. *The Art of Alfred Hitchcock: Fifty Years of His Motion Pictures*. 2d ed. London: Fourth Estate, and New York: Doubleday, 1992. Chronological, film-by-film commentary on Hitchcock's work. Knowledgeable and extremely readable background information, summaries, and brief analyses. Many illustrations.

————. *The Dark Side of Genius: The Life of Alfred Hitchcock*. London: Collins, and Boston: Little Brown, 1983. A thoroughly researched biography emphasizing the personal background of many of the tensions and horrors in Hitchcock's films.

Truffaut, Francois, with Helen G. Scott. *Hitchcock*. Rev. ed. New York: Simon and Schuster, 1984; London: Paladin, 1986. This essential work captures Hitchcock's reminiscences and observations on virtually his entire career. Many illustrations.

Wood, Robin. *Hitchcock's Films Revisited*. London: Faber, and New York: Columbia University Press, 1989. Arguably the best and most influential critical study of Hitchcock, stressing the unity and artistic greatness of the films. Contains specific essays on twelve key films and other broadly focused essays on such topics as Hitchcock and feminism, the star system, and homosexuality.

Sidney Gottlieb

ADOLF HITLER

Born: April 20, 1889; Braunau am Inn, Austro-Hungarian Empire
Died: April 30, 1945; Berlin, Germany
Areas of Achievement: Government and politics
Contribution: As leader of the National Socialist German Workers' Party in Germany and as dictator of the Third Reich, Hitler was responsible for many of the events that led to World War II. His belief in Teutonic racial superiority and his anti-Semitism also resulted in the Holocaust.

Early Life

Adolf Hitler was born on April 20, 1889, at Braunau am Inn, which is near Linz, in the Austro-Hungarian Empire. His father, Alois, was a customs agent whose primary concerns were his work, his status, and himself. When he was forty-seven, Alois married Klara Pölzl, his third wife. Even though eight children were born of his marriages, he took little interest in his family, preferring to devote his time to his work. He was a rigid and taciturn man who was especially severe to his sons. Klara, on the other hand, was an indulgent and loving mother, whose children and stepchildren loved and respected her deeply. Alois's position in the petite bourgeoisie provided the family with a good income and a secure standard of living. Even after his retirement in 1895, the family was able to live comfortably on his pension and inheritances.

Young Adolf was a sickly child who was overprotected by his mother. His father became a direct influence in his son's life only after he retired, for he then determined to impose his ideals on his children. When Adolf finished the *Volksschule* in 1900, Alois decided that the boy should attend the *Realschule* and prepare for a career in the civil service. The son rebelled at this treatment, for he considered himself to be an artist, not a member of the bourgeoisie. His father forced him to attend the *Realschule*, and Adolf's grades, which had been excellent, became quite poor. The boy became sullen, resentful, uncooperative, and withdrawn, both at home and at school.

During this period, the boy became enamored of Germanic myths, especially those presented in Wagnerian opera and in historical romance. It was not an unusual interest for boys of that era, as Austria-Hungary was greatly divided over various issues of nationality. German nationalists believed fervently that all German people should be bonded together in a single German Reich. The schools of the time were a place where Teutonic national superiority and an emphasis on social Darwinist views of the "survival of the fittest" were constantly taught. By the age of sixteen, Hitler had become what he was to be until his death—a fanatical German nationalist.

In 1903, Alois died, leaving an adequate income for his family. His son did complete the *Realschule* in 1905, although he did not receive a certificate of graduation. In 1906, he moved to Vienna but twice failed to gain entry into the Imperial Academy of Fine Arts. For several years he eked out a precarious, solitary existence in Vienna by painting postcards or advertisements, drifting from one men's home to another.

The Vienna in which he lived was a veritable hotbed of anti-Semitism. Hitler read widely, but shallowly, preferring to read that which buttressed his own opinions about life. During this time he manifested many of his later characteristics: a quick temper that erupted when he was contradicted, an inability to form ordinary relationships with others, a passionate hatred of non-Germans and Jews, the use of violent rhetoric to express himself, and a tendency to live in a world of fantasy in an effort to escape his own poverty and failure. In 1913, he left Vienna for Munich, hoping to gain admission to the art academy there. Again he met with failure. He was twenty-four, with no marketable skills and little prospect for the future.

Life's Work

With the outbreak of World War I in August, 1914, Hitler immediately volunteered for and was accepted into the Sixteenth Bavarian Reserve Infantry Regiment. He served on the Western Front as a dispatch runner in the frontline throughout the war. That he served courageously is evidenced by his decorations for bravery. He received the Iron Cross, Second Class, in December, 1914, and he was awarded the Iron Cross, First Class (a rare distinction for a mere corporal), in August, 1918. He was wounded in October, 1916, and was gassed in October, 1918. The war was critical for his development, for it gave to him a sense of purpose, of comradeship, and of discipline. It also confirmed in him his belief in the heroic nature and necessity of war as well as his belief in the need for an authoritarian form of government.

Adolf Hitler stands in front of the Eiffel Tower in Paris, June 23, 1940.

War's end found him convalescing from his gassing. As there were few jobs available in postwar Germany for a young man of thirty with few skills, Hitler remained in the army. Serving in the army's political department, his primary job was the political education of soldiers. Hitler quickly learned that he could control large audiences with his oratorical skills. His other job was that of spying on various Bavarian political groups that the army wanted controlled. In September, 1919, he visited one such group, the German Workers Party, a violently anti-Semitic group. Finding that his ideas closely matched those of the group, he resigned from the army and began working with the party. Within a year, he had become its chief propagandist and, soon thereafter, its leader. In 1920, the renamed National Socialist German Workers' (or Nazi, a shortened form of the German name) Party issued its program: the union of all Germans in a greater German state, the expulsion of Jews from Germany, the revocation of the Treaty of Versailles, and "the creation of a strong central power of the State." Hitler introduced the swastika as the symbol of the party and created a private army of brown-shirted storm troopers. Force and violence quickly became a trait of the new party.

The double shock of military defeat and economic humiliation had left many Germans prepared to listen to anyone who promised a better national future. To be sure, Hitler's earliest adherents were the poor and dispossessed, but his message was also appealing to many middle-class Germans. In 1923, during the French occupation of the Ruhr Valley, which had resulted in the collapse of the German economy, Hitler attempted to overthrow the Bavarian government. This Beer Hall Putsch was a fiasco, for the army remained loyal to the government. Hitler was sentenced to five years' imprisonment, of which he served nine months. While in prison, he dictated *Mein Kampf* (1925-1927; English translation, 1933), an autobiographical account of his life and his political philosophy.

Mein Kampf is a rambling, turgid statement of Hitler's biases, of which there were many. To Hitler, the goal of the National Socialist German Workers' Party was to create a highly centralized state of and for the master race, that is, the Germans. The *raison d'être* for this state was the rectification of the injustices perpetrated upon the German people by the decadent Western powers at Versailles. Only through war, Hitler believed, could the illegalities of that imposed settlement be erased. In this state, his racial policies would result in the rooting out of those who were not of Aryan blood. His most venomous statements were reserved for the Jews. To them he ascribed the blame for all of Germany's misfortunes, especially the loss of World War I. Jews, and their underlings, the Bolsheviks, were internationalists bent on destroying the purity of the German race. These "malignant tumors" had to be eradicated.

By the time Hitler was released from prison, economic and political conditions in Germany had improved dramatically. Gustav Stresemann, the Weimar Republic's chancellor, made the government more respectable, both at home and internationally. The Dawes Plan and currency reform resulted in German economic stability. Moreover, without Hitler's leadership, the Nazi Party had virtually disintegrated. Hitler himself was forbidden to speak publicly in Bavaria until 1929. As a result, the Nazi Party played an insignificant role in German politics until the Depression caused German economic and political instability once again.

Between 1929 and 1933, the Nazi Party grew from one of the smallest to the largest single party in Germany. Hitler made alliances with the army, with the magnates of business and industry, and with other conservative elements in German society. Still, the Nazis would not have been victorious had not Hitler's speeches regarding the future of Germany struck a responsive chord in the German electorate. Hitler's demagogic tactics and the failure of the Weimar government to mount effective opposition resulted in his being named Chancellor of Germany in January, 1933.

The Reichstag fire of February, 1933, led to the destruction of the German Communist Party and to decrees that limited personal freedom in Germany. Hitler was given virtually unlimited power. Hitler's rearmament program quickly stimulated the German economy and put Germans back to work. Hitler and his minions thus restored German confidence and power at the expense of the democratic liberalism of the Weimar Republic. Those who opposed him were ruthlessly eliminated. Concentration camps were established to incarcerate enemies of state, especially Bolsheviks and Jews.

Hitler himself was not as interested in creating a totalitarian state as he was in establishing German hegemony in Europe. In October, 1933, Germany walked out of the international disarmament conference in Geneva as well as left the League of Nations. Two years later, Hitler proclaimed Germany's repudiation of the disarmament clauses of the Treaty of Versailles and began rearming. In 1936, he further repudiated Versailles by remilitarizing the Rhineland. In 1938, after witnessing Italian successes in Ethiopia, Japanese successes in China, and Francisco Franco's success in Spain, Hitler ordered an Anschluss with Austria. This too was successful. In September, 1938, at Munich, further appeasement by the Western democracies left Czechoslovakia truncated, with the Sudetenland being given to Hitler.

Hitler had now achieved, through bluff and diplomacy, part of the program set forth in *Mein Kampf.* In March, 1939, Germany dismembered the rest of Czechoslovakia, thereby shattering the myth of appeasement. Hitler then shrewdly maneuvered a Nazi-Soviet Nonaggression Pact, which neutralized the threat of a two-front war. On September 1, 1939, the war that Hitler had wanted and for which he had planned erupted. Success quickly followed success as Poland, Denmark, Norway, the Low Countries, and France were defeated by the German juggernaut. The Blitzkrieg resulted in German domination of Central and Western Europe. When German forces were unsuccessful in swiftly conquering Great Britain, Hitler's attention quickly turned to the East. First Yugoslavia, then Greece were annexed. Finally, it was the turn of the Soviet Union. In June, 1941, in a massive surprise attack, Hitler launched his attack on Bolshevism. Despite enormous early victories, the size and weather of the Soviet Union prevented an outright German victory.

While the war was being waged, Hitler concerned himself primarily with military matters, leaving domestic policies to his subordinates. These henchmen continued implementing the Nazi totalitarian program as well as creating for themselves powerful bases. To many Nazis, the domestic issue that was of greatest concern was the so-called final solution of the Jewish question. Before the war, Jews had been allowed to emigrate or had been expelled; war ended this option. The next stage was concentration, and numerous concentration camps and ghettos were established to hold the Jews of occupied Europe. This, however, was viewed as only a temporary measure; extermination was to be the final solution. Some six million Jews were systematically eliminated during the Holocaust. In addition, millions of others perished in concentration camps or labor camps, or as the result of Nazi activities or atrocities.

Hitler himself became ever more preoccupied with the running of a war that was quickly becoming unwinnable. As the Allies could outproduce Germany six to one, Germany could make do only by relying upon slave labor and total mobilization of the German population for war. Hitler became increasingly irrational during 1943 and early 1944, as Allied armies in North Africa, Italy, and the Soviet Union pushed German armies backward. Hitler's vegetarian diet and his living conditions led to a precipitous decline in his health. His personal physician, Theo Morell, prescribed huge doses of medication that resulted in a marked deterioration of Hitler's nervous system. The assassination attempt of July 20, 1944, merely accelerated the physical decline of the Führer.

As the Allies closed in from Italy, France, and the East, Hitler completely lost touch with reality. He sincerely believed that secret weapons would save Germany and that a rupture of the Grand Alliance was merely a matter of time. Even the Battle of the Bulge, which was merely a recapitulation of the 1940 offensive against France, resulted in the shattering of the German forces on the Western Front. Early 1945 found Hitler maneuvering nonexistent armies on maps in his bunker and issuing orders that could not be carried out. Finally, when the Russian guns were within firing distance of the Reichs-Chancellery in Berlin, Hitler realized the finality of the situation. On April 30, 1945, he and Eva Braun, his mistress whom he finally married, committed suicide. It was ten days after his fifty-sixth birthday. Hitler's Thousand Year Reich survived him by only eight days. It had lasted for only twelve years and four months.

Summary

The appalling statistics from the end of World War II can only begin to itemize the legacy of Adolf Hitler. To Germany he bequeathed more than 6.5 million dead and more than twice that number as refugees. Germany itself was in ruins, partitioned, and occupied. The European balance sheet was similar. The total number of civilian and military dead from World War II probably exceeded fifty million. Direct and indirect costs from the war are virtually impossible to calculate. Europe was prostrate, both economically and politically. War damage was in the trillions of dollars, and most governments were either unstable or nonexistent because of the dislocations of war. While Germany in particular and Europe in general rebuilt themselves with the aid of the Marshall Plan and through the European Community, the scars of war and fears of Nazism/Fascism remain. Despite denazification, fear of a strong Germany continues to temper the attitudes of European neighbors toward a revitalized Germany. Germans fear that they will never be forgiven for the nightmare that was Hitler.

The destruction of Germany and the impact of the war on other European powers left a weak Western and Central Europe overshadowed by the military power of the Soviet Union and the United States. The Cold War that emerged from the ashes of World War II stemmed from two sources. The memory of Munich in 1938 left a fear of appeasement of the Soviet dictator by the West and resulted in a hard-line policy of containment of communism. The Cold War was also a competition between the United States and the Soviet Union over control of the Europe that had been devastated by Hitler's war. The artificial barrier, the so-called Iron Curtain, that separated Eastern and Western Europe resulted in dislocation and scarcity as well as political instability. Hostile alliances and competition between the superpowers along the line of 1945 continue to exist.

One final significance of Hitler would be an understanding of totalitarianism. The totality of defeat for the Third Reich in 1945 meant that the state documents of the Third Reich fell into the hands of the victors. This documentation was used initially to prosecute war criminals at Nürnberg and elsewhere. It has since been used to study the megalomania of the Nazi leaders. No other dictator has ever been so well documented or studied. An understanding of the situation that brought Hitler to power as well as an understanding of the forces that drove the man could help in dealing with future threats of his type. Although Hitler was, perhaps, the greatest megalomaniac in history, it does not mean that he was or will be the only one.

Bibliography

Bracher, Karl Dietrich. *The German Dictatorship: The Origins, Structure, and Effects of National Socialism.* Translated by Jean Steinberg. New York: Praeger, 1970; London: Weidenfeld and Nicolson, 1971. This is the best introduction to the theory and practice of National Socialism.

Bullock, Alan. *Hitler: A Study in Tyranny.* Rev. ed. London: Penguin, 1962; New York: Harper, 1964. This biography is a solid account of the life of Hitler that combines excellent research with lucid writing. With an emphasis on political narrative, it remains one of the best single-volume accounts of Hitler's life.

Carr, William. *Hitler: A Study in Personality and Politics.* London: Arnold, 1978; New York: St. Martin's Press, 1979. This study of Hitler focuses upon the interrelationship between Hitler and the social forces that existed in Germany between World War I and World War II.

Fest, Joachim C. *Hitler.* Translated by Richard Winston and Clara Winston. London: Weidenfeld and Nicolson, and New York: Harcourt Brace, 1974. This German biography is considered by many to be the standard biography of Hitler from the German point of view.

Hamann, Brigitte. *Hitler's Vienna: A Dictator's Apprenticeship.* Translated by Thomas Thornton. Oxford and New York: Oxford University Press, 1999. Hamann studies Hitler's Vienna years and their impact on the development of his ideology and career.

Langer, Walter C. *The Mind of Adolf Hitler: The Secret Wartime Report.* New York: Basic, 1972; London: Secker and Warburg, 1973. In 1943 psychoanalyst Langer wrote a psychological profile of Hitler for the Office of Strategic Services. This long-classified work was finally released in 1972 and is considered to be the best psychohistory of Hitler.

Marrus, Michael Robert. *The Holocaust in History.* Hanover, N.H.: University Press of New England, 1987; London: Weidenfeld and Nicolson, 1988. As literature pertaining to the Holocaust is considerable, this work provides a broad survey of the causes and events of the Holocaust as well as a bibliography of literature about the Holocaust.

Redlich, Franz. *Hitler: Diagnosis of a Destructive Prophet.* New York: Oxford University Press, 1999. The first Hitler biography to make use of his medical records. Redlich outlines how Hitler's physical and mental health affected his behavior.

Shirer, William L. *The Rise and Fall of the Third Reich: A History of Nazi Germany.* London: Secker and Warburg, and New York: Simon and Schuster, 1960. Written by a journalist who covered the Third Reich during the 1930's, this single-volume account of the period is one of the best and most readable introductions to the many issues and personalities of National Socialism.

Smith, Bradley F. *Adolf Hitler: His Family, Childhood, and Youth.* Stanford, Calif.: Hoover Institution on War, Revolution, and Peace, 1967. There is little primary material extant that pertains to Hitler's formative years, but Smith attempts to provide a background for Hitler's development prior to World War I. It is primarily a chronological narrative.

Toland, John. *Adolf Hitler.* New York: Doubleday, 1976. While there is little new in this biography of Hitler, Toland achieves an intensity lacking in other biographies, perhaps because of the 250 oral interviews with personalities closely associated with Hitler, which gives a new perspective to the personal nature of the dictator.

William S. Brockington, Jr.

HO CHI MINH
Nguyen That Thanh

Born: May 19, 1890; Kim Lien, Vietnam, French
Indochina
Died: September 3, 1969; Hanoi, North Vietnam
Areas of Achievement: Government and politics
Contribution: Ho was the chief architect, founder,
and leader of the Indochinese Communist Party
(1930), an organizer of the Viet Minh (1941), and
President of the Democratic Republic of Vietnam
(North Vietnam) from 1945 until his death. An
ardent proponent of his country's independence,
Ho was recognized as one of the twentieth centu-
ry's greatest anticolonial revolutionaries and
most influential Communist leaders.

Early Life

Ho Chi Minh was a native of the village of Kim
Lein, in the province of Nghe An, in central Vietnam (then part of French Indochina), an area long
noted for its poverty, rebellious spirit, antiforeign
leaders, and anticolonial activity. He was originally
named Nguyen Sinh Cung and called by several
others, before adopting the name Ho Chi Minh in
the early 1940's. Ho's father, Nguyen Sinh Sac
(sometimes Nguyen Sinh Huy), was a Mandarin
and man of letters like his father before him. Nguy-
en Sinh Sac was dismissed from his civil service
post for anti-French activities and nationalist leanings. Ho's mother, Hoang Thi Loan, was the eldest
daughter of a village scholar with whom Ho's father studied as a young man.

Ho was the youngest of three surviving children.
Like both his brother, Khiem, and his sister, Thanh,
Ho espoused anticolonial ideas in his youth. He
was sent initially to a public school to study the
Vietnamese and French languages in addition to
Chinese ideograms. At the age of nine, Ho, his siblings, and his mother, who had been charged with
stealing French weapons for rebels, fled to Hue,
the imperial city. Ho's father had left for Saigon,
where he earned a meager living by practicing Oriental medicine.

Ho's stay in Hue was short. His mother died suddenly, and the young boy (age ten) found himself
back in Kim Lien. Also, at age ten, according to
custom, Ho's birth name was changed to Nguyen
That Thanh (Nguyen who is destined to succeed).
At age fifteen, Ho started attending Quoc Hoc Secondary School studying *Quoc Ngu* (the romanized

form of Vietnamese) and French. The school was
then considered the best in the country. While
there, he was involved in some insurrectional
movements that swept across central Vietnam in
1908. After four troubled and disappointing years
of study, Ho headed southward to the town of Phan
Tiet, where he taught French and Vietnamese at an
elementary school.

After several months Ho went to Saigon, was enrolled in a vocational school, and then decided to
leave Vietnam after the first Chinese Revolution
broke out in October of 1911. Under the name of
Ba, he took work on a French steamer. He was a
seaman for more than three years, visiting ports in
France, Spain, North Africa, and the United States.
At the outset of World War I, Ho gave up his seafaring career and took up residence in London. In
1917, he moved yet again. When he set foot on
French soil toward the end of World War I, he saw
his future mapped out before him.

Life's Work

Ho's life was dedicated to improving conditions in
his own country, working to force colonial regimes
to introduce reform, and promoting revolution (ultimately worldwide revolution) against imperialism. Adopting the new name of Nguyen Ai Quoc
(Nguyen the patriot) in Paris, Ho immediately took
up the struggle for the political rights of the Vietnamese people, a struggle which lasted five decades. During the six years Ho spent in France
(1917-1923), he became an active socialist, and
then a communist. In 1919, he organized a group
of Vietnamese living in France and, with others,
drafted an eight-point petition addressed to the
Versailles Peace Conference that demanded that
the Vietnamese people be given legal equality with
the French colonials; freedom of assembly, press,
speech, and emigration; better educational facilities; and permanent Indochinese representation in
the French parliament. He also requested a general
amnesty for political detainees. There was, in the
modest document, no explicit mention of independence or of self-determination.

Because the petition brought no response, except
to make Ho a hero among certain Vietnamese, he
took more drastic measures. In 1920, he became a
founding member of the French Communist Party.

He then began to denounce the evils of British and French colonialism in his new French journal, *Le Paria* (the outcast). The journal was the voice of the Intercolonial Union founded in 1921 to acquaint the public with the problems of the colonial people. When Ho went to Moscow at the end of 1923, his friends considered him a thoroughgoing revolutionary. He participated in revolutionary and anti-imperial organizations and took an active part in the Fifth World Congress of the Communist International. Under the name of Nguyen Ai Quoc, Ho was the first of a series of Vietnamese revolutionaries to attend Moscow University for Oriental Workers, studying political theory. Although throughout his life Ho considered theory less important than revolutionary practice, he felt at home at the university as his emotional ties with the Soviet Communists grew stronger.

In December, 1924, Ho's first visit to Russia ended when he departed for the southern Chinese port of Canton. This area was a hotbed of agitation and a center of Vietnamese nationalist activities. There he organized the Vietnamese Revolutionary Youth Association known as the Thanh Nien. Almost all of its members had been exiled from Indochina because of anticolonial beliefs and actions against the French. Canton became the first real home of organized Indochinese nationalism.

After expulsion from China at the hands of Chiang Kai-shek, Ho sought refuge in the Soviet Union. In 1928, he was off again to Brussels, Paris, and finally Siam (Thailand), where he spent two years as the Southeast Asian representative of the Communist International Organization. In February of 1930, Ho was brought back from Siam to Hong Kong to preside over the founding of the Indochinese Communist Party. Ho's achievement was his unification of three separate Communist groups into one organization. Ho, still using the name of Nguyen Ai Quoc, summarized and published the results of his and others' efforts by issuing a call for support of the new Communist Party among the workers, peasants, soldiers, youth, and students of Vietnam. This document also contained Ho's first demand for the complete political independence of Indochina.

In the summer of 1930 there occurred the first mass revolutionary uprising in Vietnam brought about by the peasants (something Ho had advocated earlier). It followed on the heels of a less successful rebellion in February of 1930 and originated in the provinces of Ha Tinh and Nghe An (where Ho was born). The French reacted brutally, executing without trial some seven hundred anticolonials and torturing others. Though Ho was outside the country during the summer rebellion and his role was probably nil, the French condemned him to death in absentia. In June, 1931, Ho was arrested in Hong Kong, where French officials arranged with the British to have him extradited. He was finally released, but not before he had spent one year in prison and had contracted tuberculosis.

In 1934, Ho returned to Moscow, and in 1935 he participated in the Seventh Congress of the Communist International as chief delegate for the Indochinese Communist Party. The congress sanctioned the idea of the Popular Front (an alliance of leftist organizations to combat Fascism), which Ho had advocated for some time. Relations eased in 1936 between Communists in Indochina and the French because of the formation of Premier Léon Blum's Popular Front government in France. With the fall of the Blum government in 1937, however, French repression in Indochina returned, and Ho's era of relative quiet (1934-1938) came to an end.

In 1938, Ho returned to China, stayed with Mao Tse-tung for a time, and traveled throughout the land. With the German defeat of France in 1940, and Japan's attempt to occupy and rule Indochina, Ho returned to his homeland for the first time in thirty years in January, 1941. With the help of his lieutenants, Vo Nguyen Giap and Pham Vam Dong, Ho organized in May, 1941, the League for the Independence of Vietnam, better known as the Viet Minh.

This new organization promoted Vietnamese nationalism with renewed zeal. In June, 1941, Ho issued the clarion call for national insurrection and liberation. In an important letter published at that time to all Vietnamese, Ho pledged his modest abilities to follow them in their revolutionary efforts. Although the concrete results of the June appeal were not immediately apparent—the Viet Minh had few guns—the events of 1941 were the most important in Vietnamese revolutionary history. For Ho, who had celebrated his fifty-first birthday on the day of the founding of the Viet Minh, those events meant the end of thirty years of leadership of revolution from outside his own country, with the exception of some time he spent in a Chinese prison. Ho's new organization sought help from China in 1942. When Ho crossed the border in the summer of 1942, he had already taken the name of Ho Chi Minh (Ho who enlightens). Be-

cause Chiang Kai-shek distrusted Ho, the latter was imprisoned for eighteen months. During this time, he wrote his famous prison diary as friends were arranging his release.

In 1945, Ho established his first contacts with Americans and began to collaborate with them against the Japanese who had overrun Indochina and imprisoned or executed all French officials. At the same time, Giap and his commandos, under Ho's direction, moved against Hanoi, the Vietnamese capital. The moment Ho had been waiting for finally came following Japan's surrender to the United States after the atomic bombings in August. On September 2, before an enormous crowd gathered in Ba Dinh square, Hanoi, Ho declared Vietnam independent and proclaimed the inauguration of the Democratic Republic of Vietnam, which included the entire country. The declaration, drafted by Ho himself, opened with words intended to garner United States support. After September 2, 1945, Ho became more than merely a revolutionary, he became a statesman. Nationwide elections held on January 6, 1946, conferred the presidency on Ho. In July, 1946, a liberal constitu-

tion was adopted, modeled in part on the United States Constitution.

France, under the leadership of Charles de Gaulle, did not accept Vietnamese independence, nor did the Chinese. The Chinese were supposed to replace the Japanese and occupy Vietnam north of the sixteenth parallel. Ho persuaded the French, who were attempting to reassert their authority over Vietnam, to force the withdrawal of the Chinese; he then began negotiating with the French to secure Vietnam's autonomy and unification. After many months, negotiations broke down when a French cruiser opened fire (November 20, 1946) on the town of Haiphong after a clash between French and Vietnamese soldiers. Almost six thousand Vietnamese were killed. On December 20, 1946, Ho declared a national war of resistance and called on his countrymen to drive out the French colonialists and save the fatherland. Ho sought refuge in northern Vietnam while the first Indochinese war was fought. Finally, in May of 1954, the French were thoroughly defeated at Dien Bien Phu and had no choice but to negotiate. The meeting between representatives of eight countries in May-July,

1954, yielded the Geneva Accords, in which it was finally concluded that Vietnam was to be divided at the seventeenth parallel into northern and southern sections. The north was to be led by Ho, the south by Bao Dai (later Ngo Dinh Diem), until elections could be held in 1956 and a unified government be established by the vote of the people.

In September, 1955, Ho, who had been both President and Premier of North Vietnam, relinquished the premiership to Pham Van Dong. He continued to be recognized as the real leader of North Vietnam (still officially called the Democratic Republic of Vietnam). The 1956 elections that were to guarantee the country's reunification were postponed by the United States and by South Vietnam, which was created on a de facto basis at that time. In September, 1960, Ho was reelected president of his country, and a new constitution, adopted that year in the north, gave him unlimited power and placed greater emphasis on Communist principles.

Ho never lived to see the fulfillment of his vision—a unified, autonomous, peaceful Vietnam. In 1959, there emerged in South Vietnam the Communist-oriented Viet Cong guerrilla force supported by Ho and the North Vietnamese government. They began conducting an armed revolt against the American-sponsored regime of Ngo Dinh Diem. In response, the United States sent military aid to South Vietnam. The conflict escalated to full-fledged war which lasted until 1975, when the Vietnamese Communists unified their country as a totalitarian state. Ho had died six years before, on September 3, 1969, at the age of seventy-nine.

Summary

Ho Chi Minh was a man of many facets: a shrewd calculator, a consummate actor, a patient revolutionary, and a relentless agitator. Above all, he was a successful leader. He did not hesitate to resort to any means to achieve his political objectives, but his popularity seems never to have waned. Throughout the villages of North and South Vietnam he was referred to as Uncle Ho, a name symbolic of the affection he engendered in the public mind. Behind the scenes, he ruled increasingly with an iron fist and, for reasons of state, ultimately silenced forever half a million adversaries during the infamous period of land reform in North Vietnam (1953-1956).

Ho was not the intellectual genius that some of his admirers claimed him to have been. Rather, he worked to improve his knowledge of men and things as part of the pursuit of his ideal. Being in the company of international revolutionary theorists (in France, Russia, and China) made him keenly aware of his shortcomings. While in France (1917-1923), he suffered from his relative lack of education (because of a wretched childhood) and sought to correct this by reading the works of William Shakespeare and Charles Dickens in English, Lu Hsün in Chinese, and Victor Hugo and Émile Zola in French. His favorite author became Leo Tolstoy. Ho's ability to create and motivate groups and organizations was surpassed only by his ability to continue to influence them, as was demonstrated in 1954 when he persuaded the Viet Minh radicals to accept, for a time, the Geneva Accords. His death in 1969 ruined chances for an earlier settlement of the Vietnam War.

Ho was one of the most important leaders of the twentieth century. His continual battle against foreign control of Vietnam caused grave crises in two of the West's most powerful countries, France and the United States. As one of the leading Communists internationally, he emphasized the role of the peasantry in the success of revolutionary struggle.

Bibliography

Bradbury, Steve. "New Translations from Ho Chi Minh's 'Prison Diary'." *Boundary* 23, no. 3 (Fall, 1996). Examines the poetry written by Ho Chi Minh during his imprisonment in China.

Fenn, Charles. *Ho Chi Minh: A Biographical Introduction.* London: Studio Vista, and New York: Scribner, 1973. As a correspondent and friend of Ho, the author brings an important perspective to his work. This book attempts synthesis rather than completeness by culling, from previous biographies, scholarly studies, and personal knowledge, essential information on the life of Ho. It presents to the reader extensive quotations from these other sources.

"Ho Chi Minh: He Married Nationalism to Communism and Perfected the Deadly Art of Guerrilla Warfare." *Time* 151, no. 14 (April 13, 1998). Discusses the career and activities of Ho Chi Minh.

Huyen, N. Khac. *Vision Accomplished? The Enigma of Ho Chi Minh.* New York: Macmillan, 1971. A native of Indochina, Huyen lived under Ho's regime for seven years. The book represents a scholarly contribution to the literature on Ho. It is well documented and contains appendices, a bibliography, and an index which are helpful to the researcher or serious student. Written from the perspective of respect for Ho, it nevertheless attempts a balanced view.

Karnow, Stanley. *Vietnam: A History.* 2d ed. New York and London: Penguin, 1991. Written by a distinguished journalist who reported on Southeast Asia during his career, this extensive volume covers the first (1946-1954) and second (1959-1975) anticolonial Indochinese wars. Three introductory chapters trace the history of Vietnamese nationalism and help the reader to understand the context of Ho's nationalistic ideas.

Lacouture, Jean. *Ho Chi Minh: A Political Biography.* Translated by Peter Wiles. London: Allen Lane, and New York: Random House, 1968. Originally published in French in 1967, this is one of the best-known biographies of Ho written by French journalist Lacouture two years before the leader's death. Its style is popular rather than scholarly and focuses on the political activities of Ho and how they had been viewed up to the time of the book's publication.

Neumann-Hoditz, Reinhold. *Portrait of Ho Chi Minh: An Illustrated Biography.* New York: Herder, 1972. This volume presents the essential events of Ho's life, with special attention given to his early political training in France and his visits to China and Russia. Written in an engaging style, the book contains many informative photographs as well as extensive quotations taken from the translated writings of Ho Chi Minh. It does not say much about Ho's activities from 1954 through 1969.

Sainteny, Jean. *Ho Chi Minh and His Vietnam.* Translated by Herma Briffault. Chicago: Cowles, 1972. This work tells of Ho's life from the standpoint of a noted French diplomat who engaged in negotiations with the Vietnamese leader and became his close personal friend. It is an easy-to-read translation of a succinctly written study.

Andrew C. Skinner

OVETA CULP HOBBY

Born: January 19, 1905; Killeen, Texas
Died: August 16, 1995; Houston, Texas
Area of Achievement: Government and politics
Contribution: As army officer, cabinet member, and business leader, Hobby was a pioneer for American women in many areas of public life.

Early Life

Oveta Culp was born on January 19, 1905, to Isaac William Culp and Emma Hoover Culp. Her father was an attorney who was first elected to the Texas state legislature in 1919; her mother was a housewife who was active in the woman suffrage movement. From her earliest childhood, Oveta's father took a personal interest in her training and schooling. Isaac Culp instilled an interest in public life in Oveta and convinced her that her gender did not constitute a barrier to any ambition she might have had. It was still somewhat unusual for a woman of her day, even one of the educated classes, to attend college. Not only did Oveta complete her undergraduate work at Mary Hardin-Baylor College, but she also studied law at the main campus of the University of Texas.

At a very young age and only partly through the influence of her father, Oveta Culp began securing positions in the law, business, and government matrix of Texas. At the age of twenty, she was working as assistant city attorney in Houston. For several years, she served as parliamentarian, or chief clerk, for the lower house of the Texas state legislature, a position that enabled her to make extensive contacts in Texas politics. She made some use of these contacts when she decided to run for the legislature as a Democrat in 1929. Despite her efforts, she was not elected; women in electoral politics were to be more truly a phenomenon of her children's generation. On February 23, 1931, Oveta took a more conventional step when she married William P. Hobby, a man some thirty years her senior who was the publisher of the Houston *Post* and a former governor of Texas.

Life's Work

Marriage, however, did not mean retirement to domesticity and obscurity for Oveta Culp Hobby, as it did for many women of the period. Hobby immediately threw herself into both the business and ed-itorial aspects of her husband's newspaper business. Starting out as a research editor, she moved steadily up the hierarchy of the newspaper until 1938, when she was named executive vice president. These were not ceremonial positions; Hobby's husband, busy managing other sectors of his extensive business interests, delegated much of his responsibility for the *Post* to his wife.

Houston during the 1930's was a much smaller city than it became later in the century, and the *Post* was in many ways a small, regional newspaper. Hobby made efforts to modernize the newspaper and bring it to the level of sophistication achieved by dailies on the East Coast. She placed a premium on intelligent coverage of women's issues, adding a woman editor to the staff to cover the activities and interests of women. Aside from her newspaper work and her devotion to her children, Hobby was particularly active within the Texas chapter of the League of Women Voters.

Hobby first attained national prominence with the beginning of American involvement in World War II. The United States government realized immediately after the onset of the war that this conflict would be more "total" than previous ones. It would affect not only soldiers fighting the war but also civilians living and working on the home front. Realizing that women would be more actively involved in the war effort than before, the government sought the assistance of recognized women leaders to help coordinate this involvement. Hobby was recruited to be the head of the women's division of the War Department's Bureau of Public Relations. This mainly involved liaison work between the army and female family members of servicemen, and therefore fell short of giving women full equality in the war effort. The War Department soon realized the inadequacy of this situation, and, in the spring of 1942, the Women's Auxiliary Army Corps (WAAC) was established to mobilize the talents and energy of women. Because of her work with Army Chief of Staff George C. Marshall to plan the WAAC, Hobby was the natural choice to head this corps and, as such, was given military rank, first as a major, and then, more appropriately considering the status of her role, as colonel.

World War II was one of the great watersheds in the democratization of American society. Most, if not all, of this democratization was unintentional. The government did not set out to use the war to

enfranchise women and African Americans. Yet its need for manpower compelled the government to make use of their talents to serve the war efforts. Hobby's tenure at the WAAC saw the most thorough emergence of American women into the public sphere in history. Once it was realized that the contribution of women was indispensable to the war effort, their social marginalization was far less viable. The increasing significance of women was recognized when the "auxiliary" was dropped from the name of the corps in the middle of the war. By 1945, Hobby's efforts with the WAC had become nationally known, and, next to Eleanor Roosevelt, she became the second most important woman in the American war effort.

After the war, Hobby returned to her duties at the Houston *Post*, but her interest in Washington affairs continued. In 1948, she advised the commission headed by former President Herbert Hoover on reducing waste in government bureaucracy. Surprisingly, her continuing interest in politics was no longer centered on the Democratic Party. In the Texas of Hobby's girlhood, it had been culturally mandatory for a Texan to be a Democrat, since

Texas, like many southern states, was dominated by a virtual one-party system. During her years in Washington, D.C., however, Hobby was increasingly drawn to the Republican Party, especially after its transformation under the leadership of Thomas E. Dewey. Under Dewey, the Republicans accepted most of Franklin D. Roosevelt's New Deal social policies, while being more friendly to the free market and to capitalist initiative than were the Democrats. Hobby, a businesswoman as well as a liberal, was particularly sympathetic to this point of view. In addition, since they did not depend as heavily on the political influence of southern conservatives and urban party bosses, as did the Democrats, the Republicans could theoretically be more responsive in alleviating the oppression of African Americans. As a result, although she continued to support local Democratic candidates, Hobby actively campaigned on behalf of Republican presidential candidates in 1948 and again in 1952.

Although Dewey suffered an upset loss in his 1948 presidential race against incumbent Harry Truman, the Republicans won in 1952 with the election of former general Dwight D. Eisenhower. By this time, Hobby was solidly in the Republican camp. When it came time for the new president to make his appointments, Eisenhower remembered Hobby's wartime service and asked her to be the director of the Federal Security Agency. This agency coordinated the various government efforts directed at securing the health and comfort of American citizens. Socially concerned Democrats had long wanted to give this agency cabinet-level status, but it was the Eisenhower Administration, often attacked for its conservativism, that presided over the agency's elevation as the Department of Health, Education, and Welfare (HEW). After her appointment as secretary of this department was approved in 1953, Hobby became the second woman to serve in the cabinet. (Frances Perkins, Secretary of Labor in the Roosevelt Administration, was the first.)

Hobby had enormous ambitions for her department, not all of which were realized during her tenure. She considered plans for overhauling the nation's medical insurance system, proposing legislation that would have established a federal corporation to provide financial backing for private low-cost medical plans. Although her proposals were defeated as a result of staunch opposition by the American Medical Association and fiscal conservatives in Congress, many elements of her plan received renewed attention during the 1990's under President Bill Clinton. Hobby also wished to focus more attention on the plight of the disadvantaged and economically subordinated, a highly unpopular cause during the prosperous 1950's. So much of the budget was being spent on Cold War defense projects that funding for the projects Hobby wished to undertake was simply not available.

Despite these difficult challenges, Hobby performed her job with dynamism and diligence. She was particularly instrumental in the widespread distribution of Jonas Salk's polio vaccine. As one of the few highly visible women in public life in the 1950's, she made a decided impression on young women growing up at the time. She seemed responsible, capable, optimistic, someone equipped for the challenges of the political world. Although she had only been in office for two years when she resigned to take care of her ailing husband on July 13, 1955, Hobby had made important contributions during her tenure at the HEW.

Hobby did not rest on her laurels after her retirement from government. Taking over the executive reins at the Houston *Post*, she presided over its development into a large metropolitan daily, acquiring the latest in technological equipment to help the paper keep pace with the exponential growth of Houston itself. She also oversaw the expansion of the *Post* media empire into the new realms of radio and, especially, television. She served as cofounder of the Bank of Texas and was invited to serve on the boards of several corporations, including the Corporation for Public Broadcasting. Hobby also developed more interests in the cultural sphere, accumulating an impressive collection of modern art, including paintings by Pablo Picasso and Amedeo Modigliani. Although Hobby did not pursue public office herself, she did have the satisfaction of seeing her son, William, Jr., elected as lieutenant governor of Texas in 1972 and serve twelve years in that position. In 1978, she became the first woman to receive the George Catlett Marshall Medal for Public Service from the Association of the United States Army in recognition of her contributions during World War II.

Hobby continued to be a prominent and much-beloved figure on the local Houston scene. In the later years of her life, Hobby's business success and family fortune made her one of the richest women in the United States. She could look back on a remarkable and unmistakably American life.

Summary

It is difficult to isolate one specific mark Oveta Culp Hobby made on American history, if only because her long life saw her excel in so many pursuits. Her wartime service helped pave the way for the promotion of women to a position of full equality in the military as well as in civilian society. Her business success proved that women not only could direct a large corporate concern but also could transform and expand that concern at an age when many business executives typically settled into retirement.

Nevertheless, it was arguably in her cabinet role as the first secretary of Health, Education, and Welfare that Hobby made her most enduring contribution. Hobby started her cabinet position off on a good footing, helping institutionalize it so that it (and, more important, the concerns it represented) became a Washington fixture. The Eisenhower cabinet of which Hobby was a member was derided at the time as consisting of "eight millionaires and a plumber," but it was in fact composed of many remarkable personalities, four of whom survived well into the 1990's: Attorney General Herbert Brownell, Secretary of Agriculture Ezra Taft Benson, Attorney General William Rogers, and Hobby herself. Perhaps slighted by the Democratic bias of many historians, the Eisenhower cabinet was, especially in terms of domestic policy, a progressive force. Hobby's presence was crucial in shaping this tendency.

Hobby's cabinet service also firmly established the tradition of women being present in the cabinet. Under Roosevelt, the Democratic Party had been most associated with the equality of women. Hobby's presence in a Republican cabinet meant that drawing upon the abilities of Americans of either gender became a bipartisan concern. Every future woman cabinet member owed her position, in a way, to the achievement of Oveta Culp Hobby.

Bibliography

Beasley, Maurine H., and Sheila J. Gibbons. *Taking Their Place: A Documentary History of Women and Journalism*. Washington, D.C.: American University Press, 1993. This book provides an impression of the history of women in journalism before, during, and after Hobby's newspaper years.

Clark, James Anthony. *The Tactful Texan: A Biography of Governor Will Hobby*. New York: Random House, 1958. This biography of Hobby's husband provides information on Hobby's early career.

Eisenhower, Dwight D. *The White House Years: Mandate for Change, 1953-1956*. New York: Doubleday, and London: Heinemann, 1963. The first volume of Eisenhower's presidential memoirs makes frequent mention of Hobby in her role as head of the HEW.

Howes, Ruth, and Michael Stevenson, eds. *Women and the Use of Military Force*. Boulder, Colo.: Rienner, 1993. This book considers the theoretical issues accompanying women's service in the military.

Lyon, Peter. *Eisenhower: Portrait of the Hero*. Boston: Little Brown, 1974. Emphasizes Hobby's role as the nation's top health-care official.

Margaret Boe Birns

LEONARD T. HOBHOUSE

Born: September 8, 1864; St. Ive, England

Died: June 21, 1929; Alençon, Normandy, France

Areas of Achievement: Sociology, political theory, and philosophy

Contribution: Hobhouse helped develop the theoretical basis of modern liberalism and was the founder of sociology as an academic discipline in Great Britain.

Early Life

Leonard Trelawny Hobhouse was born in the small fishing village of St. Ive on the east coast of Cornwall, England, on September 8, 1864. His paternal grandfather, Henry Hobhouse, a member of the landed gentry, was permanent Undersecretary of State at the Home Office. Leonard's father, Reginald, was the Rector of St. Ive. Leonard's mother, Caroline Trelawny, was the daughter of the eighth baronet of Trelawny, Cornwall. Her family was prominent in Liberal politics; Caroline's brother, John, was a Radical Liberal Member of Parliament for twenty-two years.

The young Hobhouse's formal education was typical of British upper-class families. After attending a preparatory school at Exmouth, he went to a prominent public school, Marlborough College, from 1877 to 1883. While at Marlborough, his political opinions changed from Conservative to Liberal. This change may have been precipitated by the emergence of his uncle, Arthur Hobhouse, whose criticisms of the Conservative government's expansionist policy in Afghanistan brought him to prominence as a Liberal political figure. Leonard's father, however, was a staunch Conservative and was shocked by the shift in his son's views. He was even more disturbed when he discovered that Leonard had broken away from his High Church Anglicanism and was claiming that he was an agnostic, an avowal that directly affected Leonard's college career. Although members of the Hobhouse family had traditionally gone to Balliol College, Oxford, Reginald encouraged Leonard to apply at the more conservative Corpus Christi College at Oxford because he feared that the intellectual atmosphere at Balliol would strengthen Leonard's unorthodox religious opinions.

During his four years at Corpus Christi College, Hobhouse was an exceptional student. His course of study was based on the classics and involved intensive study of ancient Greek and Roman history and philosophy. Hobhouse's study of classical Greece had a lasting influence on his ethical and political theories; he became convinced, for example, that the ancient Greek city-state was the ideal of what a true moral community should be like.

After receiving a first-class honors degree for his superior academic performance at Corpus Christi, Hobhouse was awarded a prize fellowship to do graduate study in philosophy at Merton College, Oxford. While at Merton from 1887 to 1890, Hobhouse studied under two of the outstanding nineteenth century British philosophers, both of whom were prominent figures in the British Idealist movement: William Wallace and F. H. Bradley. Hobhouse's work at Merton was sufficiently impressive that in 1890 he was appointed a fellow of that college, and he taught philosophy there until 1894, when he became a fellow of Corpus Christi College. Although he later became a critic of Idealism, it should not be surprising, given his close contact with the leading spokesmen for British Idealism over a seven-year period, that Hobhouse incorporated important Idealist doctrines into his own philosophical system.

In addition to his academic interests, Hobhouse was deeply involved in several groups which comprised the political Left at Oxford in the late nineteenth century. He was a member of the Russell Club, an organization of Radical Liberals, and of two groups established by T. H. Green's devotees: the Oxford Economic Society and the Inner Ring. Both societies shared Green's conviction that economic problems could not be divorced from ethical considerations and attempted to apply Green's theories to specific social problems. Hobhouse soon became involved in Toynbee Hall, the East London settlement house, and in efforts to organize Oxfordshire agricultural laborers into a union. He also became acquainted with the leading left-wing intellectuals of that time. Although he did not become a Fabian, he was favorably impressed with Sidney Webb following a long discussion with him, while the founder of the Oxford University Fabian Society, Sidney Ball, became one of his closest friends.

Life's Work

Hobhouse's first book, *The Labour Movement*, was published in 1893 and established his reputation as Green's successor at Oxford. It reflected Hobhouse's conviction that traditional Liberalism had become an obstacle to social improvement. In its place Hobhouse proposed a type of Liberal Collectivism; his book was intended to provide the theoretical basis for this new movement. Although parts of his theory were influenced by Fabian economics, Hobhouse's central philosophical analysis consisted of a refinement of Green's concept of positive freedom. Like Green, Hobhouse believed that state intervention was necessary in order to increase individual liberty, even if that meant the coercion of some individuals in order to enlarge the scope of freedom for others.

Hobhouse taught philosophy at Oxford for seven years, and even after he moved into other areas of employment he continued to think of himself as a philosopher. He published three essays in *Mind*, a leading philosophy journal, in 1891, and in the following year he was invited to join the prestigious Aristotelian Society. In 1891, he married an Oxford student, Nora Hadwin; they had several children, and it appeared that he would spend the rest of his life teaching philosophy at Oxford. Yet his initial efforts to establish his reputation as a philosopher brought him into conflict with Great Britain's leading philosopher, Bradley, and this left Hobhouse despondent about continuing to teach at Oxford.

The publication in 1896 of Hobhouse's first philosophical work, *The Theory of Knowledge*, was a critical turning point in his chosen career. It attempted to refute the Idealist theory of knowledge as presented by its most eloquent spokesman, Bradley, at a time when Idealism was the dominant philosophical system at Oxford. In arguing that the intentionality of consciousness proved the existence of an extraconscious reality, Hobhouse's critical realism anticipated the direction which the reaction against Idealism would take later in the twentieth century. William James was impressed with Hobhouse's book and believed that he had succeeded in refuting Bradley's theory of relations, but within Oxford the book received a cold response. Hobhouse was so hurt by this reaction that he resolved to leave Oxford if the opportunity arose. When C. P. Scott, the editor of a prominent Liberal newspaper, the *Manchester Guardian*, late in 1896 offered Hobhouse a position as an editorial writer for the paper, Hobhouse quickly accepted.

In retrospect, Hobhouse regarded the years from 1897 to 1902 that he spent in Manchester as a writer for the *Manchester Guardian* as the most satisfying in his life. While at Oxford he had been unhappy about his inability to influence national politics, but as a political writer for the *Manchester Guardian* he was able to reach a wider audience of Liberal and independent readers with his application of liberal theory to day-to-day political issues. Scott was so impressed with Hobhouse's judgment and his ability to articulate Liberal principles in a journalistic style that he came to trust Hobhouse in a way that went beyond his feelings toward other members of the staff. In 1911 he had Hobhouse appointed to the paper's board of directors, the first person outside the Scott family to hold such a position, and in later years when he was away on vacation he would leave Hobhouse in charge of the paper.

While he was in Manchester, Hobhouse's attitude toward Fabian socialism underwent significant modification. Although never a member of the Fabian Society, he had previously assumed that Fabianism was closely related to the Liberal Collectivism he had been fashioning in the 1890's. Yet in his 1898 essay "The Ethical Basis of Collectivism," Hobhouse insisted that Fabian socialism was inconsistent with Liberalism because it viewed state intervention as an end in itself. Liberals, according to Hobhouse, should support state action only when it facilitated ethical ends, such as increased liberty.

The Boer War of 1899-1902 increased Hobhouse's concern about the amoral nature of Fabian socialism. Hobhouse believed that the British government had behaved immorally in seeking war with the Boer states in order to incorporate them into the British Empire. His criticism of the government's policy in the *Manchester Guardian* contributed to its reputation as the leading antiwar newspaper. When the Fabian Society published a pamphlet, largely written by George Bernard Shaw, defending the seizure of the Boer states, this seemed to confirm Hobhouse's suspicions that the Fabians were opportunists whose policies lacked any moral basis.

Hobhouse also became disenchanted with those Liberal Imperialists, such as Herbert Asquith, who endorsed the government's behavior. This sense of disillusionment was a factor in his decision to resign from the *Manchester Guardian* in 1902. Although not narrowly partisan, it was a Liberal paper, and Hobhouse found it increasingly difficult to defend a party in which imperialist sentiment was so significant. Also, while working for the

Manchester Guardian, Hobhouse had been allowed to spend one-half of each day continuing his work in philosophy. Thus, he was able to complete *Mind in Evolution* in 1901. The strain of carrying on both lines of work simultaneously left him exhausted and believing that he must choose one or the other. When he finally resigned in 1902, he informed Scott that philosophy had first claim on his services.

Although he intended to devote himself to philosophy, Hobhouse's need for a regular income brought him back into journalism. He wrote frequently for a Liberal weekly, *The Speaker*, and for the Free Trade Union, a Liberal Party organization which employed Hobhouse from 1903 to 1905. When *The Tribune*, a new Liberal newspaper, was established in London in 1905, Hobhouse became its political editor, with responsibility for editorials and the political line of the paper. Under his direction, *The Tribune* became an exponent of advanced Liberalism, urging the new Liberal government to introduce old-age pensions, women's suffrage, and work programs for the unemployed. *The Tribune*, however, was not a financial success, and when, in January, 1907, the owner placed a Conservative in charge of the paper's political line, Hobhouse resigned.

Hobhouse's continued preoccupation with scholarly social research even while employed as a journalist enabled him to publish an important study on social development, *Morals in Evolution*, in 1906. This may account for his selection in 1907 to the newly created Martin White Chair in Sociology at the London School of Economics, a position he retained until his death in 1929. Hobhouse is often referred to as the founding father of sociology in Great Britain, in part because he was the first person to hold a position as professor of sociology in that country. He played a leading role in the development of sociology as an academic discipline in Great Britain, continued to publish in this area, and in 1908 became the editor of Great Britain's major scholarly journal in that field, the *Sociological Review*.

Yet even while deeply involved in sociology, Hobhouse continued his political journalism. After its establishment in 1907, *The Nation*, a Liberal weekly, became the main organ for the dissemination of New Liberal political opinion. Hobhouse had been considered for the editorship of the journal and became an important member of its staff. He was a frequent participant at the weekly *The Nation* luncheon meetings at which the editorial line of the paper was debated; when the editor, Henry Massingham, was not present, Hobhouse chaired these meetings.

Hobhouse's reputation among Liberals by 1909 is suggested by an invitation from the Northampton Liberal Party to become their candidate for Parliament at the next election. Since it was a safe seat, Hobhouse would have been almost certain of election, but he declined on the grounds that he did not wish to become subservient to party discipline. His invitation to write the volume *Liberalism* (1911) in a series on modern political ideologies is more consistent with his reputation as one of the leading theorists of the New Liberalism. The book is considered a classic statement of modern Liberal theory and established Hobhouse's reputation as the successor to Green and John Stuart Mill among Liberal theoreticians. It was published in 1911, during a period in which the Liberal government was initiating important new social policies which some consider the origin of the British welfare state. Within the context of contemporary political debate it was important for its explanation of how state intervention would further liberal ends. Hobhouse indicated that the provision of old-age pensions, minimum wages, and unemployment insurance by the state were desirable because they would enhance individual liberty, as well as for other reasons.

When World War I broke out in 1914, Hobhouse's first reaction was to join the British Neutrality Committee, which attempted to keep Great Britain out of the war. Yet after the German invasion of Belgium, he reversed his position and accepted that British security required the defeat of Germany. He attributed Germany's aggression to the influence of Idealist political theory, and in 1918 he published a scathing critique of it in *The Metaphysical Theory of the State*. During the last two years of the war, Hobhouse became convinced that the pursuit of total victory over Germany was transforming Great Britain into a "Prussian" state, and he became a prominent advocate of a negotiated peace.

World War I was a tremendous blow to Hobhouse, for most of his philosophical writings were rooted in a belief in social progress and the increasing rationality of mankind. The intense class conflict of the postwar years also threatened his belief in social harmony. He became convinced that the setting of wages by an independent body such as the Trade Boards could reduce conflict arising out of wage issues. Prime Minister David Lloyd George appointed him chairman of several Trade Boards, and Hobhouse became one of their leading defenders. Yet the disappointing record of the Liberal and Labour parties in the 1920's left him discouraged about the possibility of social improvement through political action. His sense of depression during his later years was deepened by ill health following a severe attack of phlebitis in 1924, and by the death of his wife, Nora, in 1925. He traveled to France each summer for medical treatment, and while receiving care he unexpectedly became ill and died suddenly on June 21, 1929.

Summary

During the decade prior to World War I, British Liberalism was changed from a movement which viewed the state as a threat to individual liberty to one which recognized that the state could be a weapon for increasing the amount of freedom in society. Leonard T. Hobhouse was a prominent member of the group of Liberal intellectuals who helped bring about this transformation. He was especially important in elaborating the social and political theory upon which this New Liberalism was based, and for this reason is considered to be the successor to John Stuart Mill and T. H. Green among Liberal theorists.

Hobhouse also made important contributions to philosophy and sociology. He always considered himself primarily a philosopher; his critical studies of Idealist philosophy helped stimulate the reaction against that system in Great Britain. His most significant role as an academician was to establish sociology as an academic discipline in Great Britain.

Bibliography

Abrams, Philip. *The Origins of British Sociology: 1834-1914*. Chicago and London: University of Chicago Press, 1968. A standard work on the intellectual history of sociology in Great Britain; demonstrates Hobhouse's crucial contributions to the field.

Ayerst, David. *The Manchester Guardian: Biography of a Newspaper*. London: Collins, and Ithaca, N.Y.: Cornell University Press, 1971. An important study of the newspaper with which Hobhouse was associated from 1897 to 1929.

Clarke, Peter. *Liberals and Social Democrats*. Cambridge and New York: Cambridge University Press, 1978. The most thoroughgoing study of the group of New Liberal intellectuals to which Hobhouse belonged.

Collini, Stefan. *Liberalism and Sociology: L. T. Hobhouse and Political Argument in England, 1880-1914*. Cambridge and New York: Cambridge University Press, 1979. A major study of the relationship between Hobhouse's political theory and his work in sociology. Contains the best critical evaluation of his theories.

Freeden, Michael. *The New Liberalism*. Oxford: Clarendon Press, 1978; New York: Oxford University Press, 1986. A valuable discussion of New Liberal ideas, treating them as an important development in political theory.

Hobhouse, L. T. *L. T. Hobhouse: Liberalism and Other Writings*. Edited by James Meadowcroft. Cambridge and New York: Cambridge University Press, 1994. A new edition of Hobhouse's classic *Liberalism,* with commentary.

Hobson, John, and Morris Ginsberg. *L. T. Hobhouse: His Life and Work*. London: Allen and Unwin, 1931. An important source of biographical information written by two of Hobhouse's closest friends. Contains information no longer available from other sources.

Smith, Harold L. "World War I and British Left-Wing Intellectuals: The Case of Leonard T. Hobhouse." *Albion* 5 (Winter, 1973): 261-273. Makes extensive use of Hobhouse's unpublished correspondence in presenting the fullest account of the shifts in his views during World War I.

Studholme, Maggie. "From Leonard Hobhouse to Tony Blair: A Sociological Connection?" *Sociology* 31, no. 3 (August, 1997). Compares the work of Hobhouse and Anthony Giddens, a prominent sociological theorist.

Harold L. Smith

DAVID HOCKNEY

Born: July 9, 1937; Bradford, Yorkshire, England
Area of Achievement: Art
Contribution: In the forefront since the mid-1960's, his work immensely popular worldwide, Hockney brings to postmodern art a freshness and originality that, although modern, harks back to traditional art sources, employing figurative and narrative elements.

Early Life

David Hockney was born in Yorkshire, England, in the northern industrial working-class town of Bradford, on July 9, 1937. He was the fourth child in a family of four boys and one girl. On scholarship, he attended Bradford Grammar School, where he was "terribly bored," relieved only by making posters for school events and cartoons and drawings for the school magazine. At eleven, he knew that he wanted to be an artist, but when he announced that to the headmaster, he was told that there was plenty of time to pursue art later. As a youngster, Hockney went with his father to the Alhambra Theatre every Saturday, regardless of the fare, and from the age of ten to twenty, he went to a concert two or three times a week during the concert season. This early introduction to lively arts, however provincial, would stand him in good stead later, when he would be asked to design sets for theater and opera.

In 1953, at age sixteen, Hockney managed to convince his parents to send him to Bradford Art School, finances being their only consideration; there he majored in painting, supposedly so that he could teach (the only other alternative was to become a commercial artist). He worked between twelve and sixteen hours a day at whatever he was told to do—such as perspective or anatomy exercises—immensely relieved to be away from the stifling, anti-art atmosphere of grammar school. At the end of four years, he began to question whether he had learned or done anything of value, only vaguely aware of contemporary art and unsure of his own relationship to it. He had visited London for the first time at nineteen, and then and only then did he have a chance to look at a wide variety of art, especially non-British contemporary art.

Beginning in 1957, Hockney did national service as a conscientious objector and little art, working instead in hospitals, one in Bradford and one in

Hastings, and reading Marcel Proust. In 1959, he was accepted for entrance into the Royal College of Art, where he became part of the pop art scene along with classmates Ron Kitaj, Allen Jones, Joe Tilson, and Peter Blake. There, he experimented with abstract expressionism but found it barren, spending the next years searching not only for his style but also for his subject. It was Kitaj, an American studying abroad on the G.I. Bill, who urged him to paint what interested him. After that, Hockney's art became more figurative, although it was still abstract. For example, he wrote the word "Ghandi" on a very abstract picture of the Mahatma Ghandi in the painting *Myself and My Heroes* (1961). While other members of the Royal College avant-garde, such as Jones, were being thrown out for their "dangerous," left-leaning, abstract art, Hockney was left alone because of his considerable drawing ability, which continued to be his clearest link to the traditional art world.

In January, 1961, the Young Contemporaries Exhibition created quite a stir, what with its paintings of toothpaste tubes and the like; it was in this context that Hockney sold his first works. Also, in 1961, a work by Hockney, along with one by Kitaj, received recognition and a small prize of three pounds from Richard Hamilton, an artist and teacher in the Royal College of Interior Design. From that time on, the staff stopped dismissing Hockney's paintings.

Also around 1961, the dark-haired, slouch-shouldered, bespectacled Hockney dyed his hair blond, reinventing himself as it were, on a trip to New York City, where he got the idea of doing his own version of William Hogarth's engraving *The Rake's Progress* (1735), that by Hockney, titled *A Rake's Progress*, set in New York and based on his experiences there. Also, around a year earlier, Hockney began to declare openly his homosexuality, something which he claims made his work more honest and relevant, as evidenced in *Doll Boy* (1960-1961), a painting loosely about the British pop singer Cliff Richard, and *We 2 Boys Together Clinging* (1961), the title taken from a Walt Whitman poem. Finally, in 1960 Hockney saw a large exhibition of Pablo Picasso's work at London's Tate Gallery eight times and became deeply enthralled with it, particularly with Picasso's draftsmanship and the range of styles.

Life's Work

In 1963, the London *Sunday Times* invited Hockney to travel to Egypt to do some sketches for them, none of which they used. This trip produced *Shell Garage*, with its interesting commingling of styles. With the money he had earned from *A Rake's Progress*, Hockney went to California to live for a year in 1964, in Los Angeles, a place he thought very Mediterranean and sexy; Los Angeles was a venue which suited him well, for he would live on and off there for the next decade doing some of his most famous works, flattened and shadowless, with the Los Angeles lifestyle either as subject or background as in *A Bigger Splash* (1967) and *American Collectors* (1968). There he would meet English expatriate author Christopher Isherwood.

In 1964, Hockney had a one-man exhibition of prints at New York Museum of Modern Art, and in 1965 his first collector, John Kasmin, organized a group exhibition of paintings in London titled "The New Scene," Hockney representing London. From 1964 to 1967, Hockney taught at various American universities, the first being the University of Iowa.

There he would complete the painting *Boy About to Take a Shower* (1964) from a sketch made in Los Angeles, the shower, like the swimming pool, being for Hockney a representative image of California.

In 1966, Hockney was asked to design the set for the English absurdist play *Ubu Roi* (1896) by Alfred Jarry, something which consumed his energies for three months; he then flew back to California in 1967 to teach at the University of California at Los Angeles, where he met Peter Schlesinger, who would become his companion. In 1968, with his painting *Christopher Isherwood and Don Bachardy*, he would begin his well-known explorations of twosomes and their psychodynamics; most of the subjects were his friends, some of them famous in their own right. These pictures are more naturalistic, and many are loosely taken from photographs.

Deciding that he had gone as far with naturalism as he wanted to go with the painting *Mr. and Mrs. Clark with Percy* (1970-1971), Hockney started on a series of etchings based on the tales of the Brothers Grimm, most of which he etched spontaneously onto the plate. Commuting from England to California, he finished these in 1969.

In 1973, Hockney moved to Paris and had a retrospective of his work from 1961 to 1974 shown at the Louvre. There he worked with Aldo Crommelynck, Picasso's master printer, on a series of etchings in Picasso's honor. In 1974, he designed the costumes and set of Igor Stravinsky's *The Rake's Progress* (1951) for the Glyndebourne Festival Opera in England. He would later do the same for productions of Ronald Petit's new ballet *Septentrion* (1975) and, in 1977, Lev Ivanov's ballet *The Magic Flute* (1893). In 1978, the Tate Gallery, where Hockney had first seen Picasso's work, had a major exhibition which circulated over America and Europe.

In the late 1970's and early 1980's, Hockney experimented with Polaroid collages in a cubistic tribute to Picasso which Hockney said captured the way people see: in separate, disparate glimpses. The collages would also improve upon the photograph, because they could illustrate the concept of a subject in time and be much more than something caught in a thousandth of a second. He would later use the Pentax thirty-five-millimeter camera to make his photocollages; he called this technique drawing with a camera. There were several exhibitions of these collages in 1982, the largest in the George Pompidou Center in Paris. In 1987, AT&T agreed to underwrite a Hockney retrospective at the Los Angeles County Museum of Art and the Los Angeles Music Center Opera's production of *Tristan und Isolde*, for which Hockney designed sets and costumes. The exhibition coincided with the artist's fiftieth birthday, and was called "UK/ LA '88." Hockney's 1998 exhibition of drawings at the Los Angeles Louver illustrated Hockney's ability to blend caricature and homosexuality with remarkable color and life.

Summary

According to Henry Geldzahler, art collector, critic, and curator of the New York Museum of Modern Art, David Hockney has conducted his education in public. He has gone from style to style and from subject to subject, exploring his options, trying to make his meaning clear with each new style, while never letting style dominate or become academic. He calls himself a narrative painter, and in that sense he is clearly within the tradition of English art, but his means are his own, not a reaction against tradition or abstraction, but a unique blend of the two. Since 1966, Hockney has affirmed that he is competing not with artists of his own generation but with the history of art itself. His wish is to be more than a popular, eccentric figure in English art.

Hockney's art is popular and accessible, partly because of his skill as a draftsman and portrait painter and partly because his subject matter strikes a chord within the audience: a show-within-a-show, emotion buried beneath a calm façade—indifference hiding the real attachment, the frozen moment, the familiar made into the fabulous, the story beneath the surface. As demonstrated in his art from the 1950's to the 1990's, his work reveals a knowing innocence, a cool detachment masking and, therefore, highlighting, passion, a powerful technical ability, and a deep understanding of art.

Bibliography

Adam, Peter. *David Hockney and His Friends.* New York and Bath, Somerset: Absolute Press, 1997. Written by one of Hockney's friends, this volume presents an honest account of the artist's life—including his sexual orientation, friends, and lovers—and his work, paying particular attention to the artist's gay erotica.

Beadleston, William. *David Hockney in America.* Introduction by Christopher Finch. New York: Beadleston, 1983. Enjoyable book with a witty, well-written introduction focusing on Hockney's American themes: swimming pools, building façades, subtopias.

Clothier, Peter, and Michael Glover. " 'Well, I'll Paint the Dogs': David Hockney Muses about Court TV, Cyberspace, and Painting His Dogs." *ARTnews* 95, no. 8 (September, 1996). Interview with Hockney in which he comments on cyberspace and his views on future methods of communication.

David Hockney: Paintings and Drawings. Introduction by Stephen Spender. Interview by Pierre Resnay. Paris: Museum of Decorative Arts, 1974. Interesting compilation of paintings and drawings from 1960 to 1974 with a lyrical introduction by the poet, Hockney's friend Stephen Spender, who compares Hockney to William Blake in his love of "minute particulars."

David Hockney: Prints. Introduction by James Mollison. Canberra, Australia: Australian National Art Gallery, 1976. Mollison's introduction is moderately interesting in that it and the compilation focus only on Hockney's prints, especially the ones illustrating fairy tales by the Brothers Grimm.

David Hockney: Prints and Drawings. Introduction by Gene Baro. Washington, D.C.: International Exhibitions Foundation, 1978. A compilation of various prints and drawings from 1960 to 1978. Baro writes of Hockney's accessibility and wit. A very interesting, lucid analysis of his style and what he terms the artist's essentialization.

Friedman, Martin, and John Dexter. *David Hockney Paints the Stage.* London: Thames and Hudson, and New York: Abbeville Press, 1983. Well-written, authoritative commentary on Hockney's stage work by Friedman and others, including Stephen Spender and Hockney. Elucidates Hockney's commitment and absorption in his projects. Also provides interesting background material on Hockney.

Hockney, David. *David Hockney.* Edited by Nikos Stangos. Introduction by Henry Geldzahler. London: Thames and Hudson, 1976; New York: Abrams, 1977. A fascinating, thorough, and conversational book that sheds considerable light on Hockney's process as an artist. Very important reading. Insightful introduction by art dealer and critic Henry Geldzahler.

Hockney, David, and Lawrence Weschler. *Cameraworks.* London: Thames and Hudson, and New York: Knopf, 1984. Hockney compiled the photography and Weschler, a writer for *The New Yorker* magazine, supplied the text, which is largely from interviews with Hockney. An important book for the understanding of his photo techniques. Beautiful full-color reproductions.

Livingstone, Marco. *David Hockney.* Rev. ed. London: Thames and Hudson, 1987; New York: Thames and Hudson, 1988. A rather academic critical overview of Hockney's work, largely written as a defense because of his enormous popularity. Dry and a bit self-important, it is thorough and sometimes critical of Hockney. The only source that does not rely primarily on Hockney's own analysis of his work.

Sandra Christenson

BILLIE HOLIDAY

Born: April 7, 1915; Philadelphia, Pennsylvania
Died: July 17, 1959; New York, New York
Area of Achievement: Music
Contribution: One of the most influential jazz singers ever recorded, Billie Holiday created the standards by which jazz singers continue to be judged. Her life reflected the racism of a white entertainment industry and the sexism within a male-dominated jazz world.

Early Life

Although she is known as a hometown celebrity in Baltimore, Billie Holiday was actually born in Philadelphia, Pennsylvania, on April 7, 1915. Much about her early life is unknown. Much of what is said about her comes from her autobiography, which is known to be inaccurate in many respects. Her autobiography, *Lady Sings the Blues*, written with the help of author William Dufty, represented Holiday's early years as pitiful and worthy of sympathy. This account has Billie Holiday starting life as Eleanora Fagan, born to thirteen-year-old Sadie Fagan and eighteen-year-old Clarence Holiday. A second, more accurate account by Robert O'Meally, author of *Lady Day*, has established the ages of her mother and father as nineteen and seventeen, respectively. Billie Holiday said that she took on the Holiday name when her parents married three years later and moved to a home on Durham Street in East Baltimore, but O'Meally could never establish that that marriage took place or that her parents had ever lived together. He concluded that the move from Philadelphia to Baltimore was her mother's attempt to start over. In Baltimore, Holiday's mother worked as a maid to support the two of them. The autobiography explained that Eleanora became "Billie," a name she took from her screen idol, Billie Dove. This source also noted that her father was drafted during World War I, was sent to Europe, and suffered lung damage from inhaling poisonous gas. While recovering in Paris, he learned how to play the guitar, and he played professionally when he returned home to the United States, a career that required much traveling and family separation. He toured as a musician with the jazz band of Fletcher Henderson and soon abandoned his family, leaving Sadie struggling to make a living. Eventually, the couple divorced. Whatever the reason, young Holiday lived a solitary life as a child.

Her mother left Holiday with relatives in Baltimore while she went to New York seeking better wages. Holiday stayed with a physically abusive cousin, Ida, her maternal grandparents, her great-grandmother, and Ida's two children, with whom Holiday had to share a bed. The great-grandmother told stories about her life as a slave on the plantation of Charles Fagan, the father of her sixteen children. Holiday was traumatized when her great-grandmother died after lying down with Eleanora for a story and a nap. According to the autobiography, Holiday awoke and could not loosen the dead arms, which had to be broken to remove them from her small body.

According to *Lady Sings the Blues*, Holiday spent her early years in extreme poverty, working at six as a babysitter and a step scrubber. She finished the fifth grade in the Baltimore schools. She performed household chores for Alice Dean, a brothel owner, ran errands for the prostitutes, and listened to the jazz that was played on the record player in the parlor of the brothel. As the records played, she sang along. By 1925, mother and daughter had saved enough money to move to a house on Pennsylvania Avenue in northern Baltimore, where the mother met a dockworker named Philip Gough, who became her husband. Within a short time, his sudden death brought the family to poverty again. An attempted rape of young Holiday by a forty-year-old neighbor led to more terror when she was put in jail to ensure her testimony and then was placed in a home for wayward girls until she reached twenty-one years of age. The judge assumed that her mature appearance had brought on the rape. Robert O'Meally found that Holiday was sent at age ten to the House of the Good Shepherd, a Catholic home for African American girls. Their records indicated that she had no guardian and was on the streets at this time. Her mother, unable to help young Holiday, again went North seeking better wages.

Holiday wanted to be with her mother, who managed to reverse the judge's ruling and bring her daughter to New York to work as a maid in 1927. From that time, Holiday and her mother remained close throughout her lifetime. Holiday boarded in a Harlem apartment owned by Florence Williams, a well-known madam. Billie became a twenty-dollar call girl to earn money. The profession led to arrests and a four-month prison term when her moth-

er testified that her daughter was eighteen (she was thirteen) years old so that she could avoid another term in a home for wayward girls. Holiday returned to prostitution after her release, and both mother and daughter could afford to move to an apartment on 139th Street in 1929. It was not long before the effects of the Great Depression touched the Holiday women.

Life's Work

Not until she received an eviction notice in 1930 did Billie Holiday launch her career as a singer. To avert her forthcoming eviction, she sought work as a dancer at *Pod's and Jerry's*, a Harlem speakeasy. Since she was no dancer, she asked to sing. Jerry Preston, the owner, was so impressed with her presentation that he offered her the job. From that point on, Holiday enjoyed recognition as part of a floor show featuring tap dancer Charles "Honi" Coles and bassist George "Pops" Foster. In 1933, when Prohibition was repealed, the speakeasies became legitimate jazz clubs, and jazz enthusiast John Hammond heard Holiday perform in *Monette's*, a jazz club on 133rd Street. He noticed her exquisite phrasing and manipulation of lyrics, which led him to give her a rave review in the magazine *Melody Maker*. He brought influential musicians and managers to hear her sing, and soon organized her first recording session, which launched her public career. A few days after her twentieth birthday, Billie Holiday appeared for her first performance at the Apollo Theater. That same year, she recorded with some of the finest jazz musicians of the time under the direction of Teddy Wilson. These recordings built Holiday's reputation as a jazz singer. She toured with the bands of Fletcher Henderson, Count Basie, and Artie Shaw.

During the 1930's, she continued to record and perform. She played a small part in a radio soap opera. She appeared briefly in a musical film, *Symphony in Black*, in which she played a prostitute. When she appeared outside Harlem, she was criticized for not being "jazzy" enough or for singing too slowly. She had a bad temper, and stories about her throwing an inkwell at a club manager and similar tantrums spread throughout the business. She used the money she earned to buy a restaurant for her mother, and the two of them lived in the upstairs apartment. She sang and waited on tables. She refused to accept tips unless they were handed to her, a practice that led the other women to call

her "a lady." When jazzman Lester Young found a rat in his hotel room, he moved in temporarily with Holiday and her mother. During this time, the tenor saxophonist and the women gave nicknames to each other. He called Billie "Lady Day," a title that remained with her, and her mother "Duchess," the mother of a lady. In turn, they called him "the President," or "Pres," because he was the commander-in-chief of the saxophone players. Together, the two performers produced some of the finest music of Holiday's career.

Holiday was essentially a jazz singer who put the blues feeling into every word she sang. During her entire career, however, she included only a dozen blues songs in her repertoire, preferring instead to use popular songs as the vehicles of her art. She learned her art from blues queen Bessie Smith. One of her best-known songs, "Billie's Blues," was a distinctive, original blues that demonstrated her total control of her music, a control she never had in her life. Holiday strung her songs together in ways characteristic of African speech, and she invested her music with a blues feeling that contained not only sadness but also honesty and directness of expression. Like the best blues artists, she created music that transcended trouble and pain.

She took subtle liberties with melodies, improvising in the same way that jazz musicians improvised with their instruments. Moreover, Holiday could sing mundane lyrics and make them sound significant and urgent. Her sophisticated approach to singing yielded a novel effect. Whereas popular singers only entertained audiences, Holiday both entertained and communicated with her listeners. She conveyed to them in song what she knew about a life of pain and disillusion. The songs she sang lent themselves to improvisation and metaphorical protest. With the release of her song "Strange Fruit" in 1939, Holiday became a celebrity. Her record was based on Lewis Allen's poem, which recounted lynchings in the American South. The "strange fruit" was the bodies of the lynched blacks hanging from the branches of the trees. "Strange Fruit" as sung by Holiday became a powerful condemnation of racism and her signature song. Perhaps the pain expressed in the song replicated her sense of the injustice of her father's death in March of 1937. Her father's weak lungs, inability to find a black hospital to treat his pneumonia, and rejection by white Jim Crow hospitals in the South led to his death in a Dallas veterans' hospital.

As the bands with which Holiday sang toured the South, they experienced Jim Crow segregation at hotels, theaters, restaurants, and public restrooms. Band members survived through mutual support and accommodation to segregation. When she was told that her skin was too light to play with the band, Holiday put on special makeup to darken her face so that the audience would not think she was white under the lights. Her song "God Bless the Child" captured the response of the black community to segregation. When she joined the Artie Shaw Orchestra, an all-white band, the touring problems were worse. In order to avoid finding her a segregated hotel room, Artie Shaw painted a red dot on her forehead, making the hotel management think she was an East Indian. This technique succeeded occasionally. In the North, her performances at *Cafe Society*, the only unsegregated nightclub outside of Harlem, made her a star and broke down racial barriers. By the early 1940's, she was the highest-paid performer in jazz. The versatile Holiday was at home in both the swing and the bebop eras of jazz, a rare feat among jazz musicians. Her subtle phrasing and imagination enabled her to approximate what jazz instrumentalists did with their instruments.

The success of her career was not duplicated in her personal life. In 1941, Holiday married James N. Monroe, whose brother owned the *Uptown House*, a nightclub. She started to use heroin. James Monroe smoked opium, and he soon shared his habit with his wife. Within a year, their marriage disintegrated, and Holiday began a relationship with a heroin addict, Joe Guy. When her mother died in 1945, Holiday felt alone. She was voted best singer in the *Esquire* Jazz Critics Poll (1944), was named *Metronome* Vocalist of the Year (1946), and had a role in the film *New Orleans* (1946), but these successes did not stem the tide of her drug addiction. The addiction sapped her strength, made her late to performances, and created an unending need for more money. In 1947, she checked herself into a sanatorium to beat the habit. When she returned to the stage, however, she started to use heroin again. Arrested several times, she served time in prison rather than undergo rehabilitation. By 1949, she was released but was denied a license to perform in New York; she slowly slipped back into addiction.

Holiday experienced both setbacks and successes during the 1950's. Her contract with Decca records lapsed in 1950. In 1952, she signed with the Verve label and recorded more than a hundred songs. In 1954, she received a special award from *Down Beat* as "one of the all-time great vocalists in jazz," and in 1956, she married Louis McKay, her manager, had her autobiography published by Doubleday, and was again arrested for possession of narcotics. Following her rehabilitation, she turned to alcohol. Ultimately, the drug and alcohol addiction took its toll. McKay and Holiday separated in 1957. The following year, she recorded her last album, *Lady in Satin*, backed by the string arrangements of Ray Ellis. When her longtime friend Lester Young died in 1959, Holiday was hospitalized for cirrhosis of the liver and heart failure. She was arrested in her hospital bed for drug possession. She died on July 17, 1959, of congestion of the lungs and heart failure, leaving a bank account of seventy cents and a small dog as her family. The forty-four-year-old jazz singer was buried in Saint Raymond's Catholic Cemetery in the Bronx, New York City.

Summary

Billie Holiday commands attention because of the unique blues-inspired jazz singing that she contributed to American music. Her renditions, phrasing, pitch, and timing still move audiences and continue to influence singers and instrumentalists. Her career brought jazz from Harlem into cafe society, breaking down racial barriers. Billie Holiday expressed the dynamic tradition of black independence in a unique and powerful voice. In her art, she found the power and control that eluded her in other areas of her life.

Bibliography

Burnett, James. *Billie Holiday*. Tunbridge Wells, Kent: Spellmount, and New York: Hippocrene, 1984. A standard work on Holiday's career which devotes considerable attention to her personal relationships.

Chilton, John. *Billie's Blues: Billie Holiday's Story, 1933-1959*. London: Quartet, and New York: Stein and Day, 1975. In his biography, Chilton focuses primarily on Holiday's musical career. The work contains an extensive bibliography and a discography.

Davis, Angela Y. *Blues Legacies and Black Feminism: Gertrude "Ma" Rainey, Bessie Smith, and Billie Holiday*. New York: Pantheon, 1998. The author examines the manner in which Rainey, Smith, and Holiday expressed social consciousness in their music.

Holiday, Billie, with William Dufty. *Lady Sings the Blues.* New York: Doubleday, 1956; London: Sphere, 1973. Holiday's autobiography, written with Dufty, provides details but is often chronologically and factually inaccurate.

Kliment, Bud. *Billie Holiday.* New York: Chelsea House, 1992. This biography, written for juvenile readers, provides an introduction to Holiday's career as a singer. Unfortunately, the work repeats many of the inaccuracies included in Holiday's autobiography. It does, however, contain useful appended material, including a selected discography, a chronology, and a bibliography.

Nicholson, Stuart. *Billie Holiday.* London: Gollancz, and Boston: Northeastern University Press, 1995. A factual approach to the life and music of Holiday. Full-blown analysis of her music coupled with an account of her rise and fall.

O'Meally, Robert. *Lady Day: The Many Faces of Billie Holiday.* New York: Arcade, 1991. This book corrects many of the errors of previous biographical sources and illuminates the various facets of Holiday's personality and career.

White, John. *Billie Holiday: Her Life and Times.* Tunbridge Wells, Kent: Spellmount, and New York: Universe, 1987. White's book does a fine job of placing Holiday within the historical framework that shaped her life and music.

Dorothy C. Salem

OLIVER WENDELL HOLMES, JR.

Born: March 8, 1841; Boston, Massachusetts
Died: March 6, 1935; Washington, D.C.
Area of Achievement: Jurisprudence
Contribution: Holmes helped set the stage for the development of modern American jurisprudence.

Early Life

Oliver Wendell Holmes, Jr., was born in Boston on March 8, 1841. He was the son of the famous poet and writer Dr. Oliver Wendell Holmes, who would influence him greatly, although their relationship would be strained. His mother, Amelia Jackson, came from a well-known New England family, members of which were involved in the region's commerce, banking, and law; her father was a judge on the Supreme Judicial Court of Massachusetts. Young Oliver had a sister, Amelia, and a brother, Edward.

At age ten, Holmes began study at the Private Latin School. The headmaster, Mr. Epes S. Dixwell, a graduate of Harvard College, had been a legal apprentice in the law office of Holmes's maternal grandfather. Holmes studied Latin, Greek, ancient history, and mathematics. In addition, he read on his own, having a strong interest in poetry and in the historical novels of Sir Walter Scott. An important part of Holmes's education took place outside his formal schooling. His father was at the center of the literary and intellectual life of New England. Dr. Holmes was well traveled, and he was well-known in Europe as well as in America. Through his father, Holmes became acquainted with literary figures, philosophers, historians, jurists, and scientists.

Holmes entered Harvard College in the fall of 1857. He was more than six feet tall and was extremely thin. His dark, straight hair dipped over his forehead and deep-set, blue-gray eyes. While in the army, he grew a flaring mustache which he maintained until his death.

At Harvard, Holmes's interest in poetry, philosophy, and science grew, as did his intellectual curiosity. Like his father before him, he was the class poet. He also supported reformist causes such as antislavery and wrote articles for the *Harvard Magazine*. When the Civil War began, however, Holmes left Harvard and enlisted in the Fourth Battalion of Infantry. After he was graduated, Holmes received a commission as first lieutenant in the Twentieth Massachusetts Regiment of Volunteers, which was later mustered into the United States Army.

His war service was brutal, bloody, and painful. Memories of the war strongly shaped his thought and especially his feeling about his government. Yet Holmes was proud of his service; according to Holmes, the war experience "touched with fire" the hearts of those who served. He often referred to his army days throughout his life and writings.

In the battle of Ball's Bluff, on October 21, 1861, Holmes was hit in the stomach with a spent bullet and was knocked to the ground. He got up, urging his men forward, and was shot in the chest, the bullet passing through his body. His wound led to a long convalescence at home in Boston. In March, Holmes returned to his regiment and was soon promoted to captain. On September 17, 1862, he was shot through the neck, the bullet just missing the spinal cord and the carotid artery. After a period of convalescence, he again returned to active duty. He was to be wounded again: On May 3, 1863, in the battle of Chancellorsville, he was injured in the heel. From this point onward, Holmes suffered from battle fatigue.

On January 3, 1864, Holmes returned to his regiment as a lieutenant colonel. On January 29, he was assigned to the staff headquarters of General H. G. Wright, completing his term of enlistment in July of that year.

The fall of 1864 found Holmes at Harvard Law School. The Harvard law faculty reflected the fundamental traits of American jurists of the time. Legal thinkers were not given to searching for a unified philosophy on which to base decisions; rather, they sought to solve particular practical problems.

After he was graduated from law school in 1866, Holmes traveled to Europe. There, he exchanged ideas with some of the world's great minds: Sir Frederick Pollock, Sir Henry Maine, John Stuart Mill, and Benjamin Jowett, among others. With Sir Frederick Pollock, Holmes kept a lifelong friendship.

Life's Work

After his return from Europe, Holmes was admitted to the practice of law. He entered the law office of Robert Morse and then the office of Chandler, Shattuck and Thayer. Later, he joined forces with George O. Shattuck and William A. Munroe to form his own firm. On June 17, 1872, he married Fanny Bowditch Dixwell, who was the eldest daughter of his former schoolmaster, E. S. Dixwell.

Holmes's early legal career included a time as editor of the *American Law Review* from 1870 to 1873. He also edited James Kent's *Commentaries on American Law*, published in 1873. His early writings show the further development of his philosophy of American law. He rejected the idea that law basically consists of logical deduction from given principles. Holmes saw the need for a philosophical structure as the basis for legal decisions, since logic itself rested on a philosophical base. Many of Holmes's ideas came together in 1881, when he published *The Common Law*, which had a tremendous impact on American jurisprudence. Its basic thesis stood directly against the prevailing legal thought. Holmes boldly stated that "the life of the law has not been logic: it has been experience." According to Holmes, the prevailing attitudes, values, assumptions, "even the prejudices" of judges had more to do with governing men than did logic.

In *The Common Law*, Holmes looked to history and, in some degree, to utilitarianism—the doctrine that the greatest good for the greatest number should be the determining consideration of conduct—for a philosophical system to support the law. "The law," he wrote, "embodies the story of a nation's development through many centuries . . . ." He also noted that "the substance of the law at any given time pretty nearly corresponds . . . with what is then understood to be convenient." He pointed out, however, that "its form and machinery" is dependent "very much upon its past." Holmes's philosophy was thus moving toward a legal science. His legal philosophy showed the influence of thinkers such as Herbert Spencer, Henry Buckle, John Stuart Mill, and Auguste Comte.

Holmes's growing reputation led to an offer to join the Harvard Law School faculty. In January, 1882, he became Weld Professor of Law. In December, 1882, he was appointed to the Supreme Judicial Court of Massachusetts. In 1902, President Theodore Roosevelt appointed him associate justice of the United States Supreme Court. As associate justice, he dealt with the fundamental issues of the Constitution, in particular the problem of how constitutional law is concerned with the conflict between the powers of Congress and those of the state legislatures, and issues concerning the rights and freedoms of the individual and the extent to which the federal government can limit those free-

doms. Holmes was a strong advocate of judicial restraint, and his decisions deeply influenced the philosophical underpinnings of American law.

Before he came to the Court, Holmes had taken the stance that legal principles did not resolve all issues. His study of history and philosophy had made him skeptical about the existence of absolute truths. While he recognized the value of the doctrine of utilitarianism, he saw law as being affected by the prevailing attitudes, values, and assumptions of the community. He believed that legislative bodies, not courts, must make laws. Within constitutional bounds, people have a right to whatever laws they want. This sort of freedom, a long-range freedom which he sought to preserve in his legal interpretations, was, for Holmes, critical to social growth. For Holmes, the most important principle of the Constitution is that of freedom of thought—not only for those with whom one agrees but also "for the thought that we hate." Thus, Holmes developed the concept of "clear and present danger" as the only justification for curtailing the right of free speech: "The most stringent protection of free speech would not protect a man in falsely shouting fire in a theatre and causing a panic."

Yet on no issue did Holmes take an unalterable, absolute position. During the Red Scare of 1918-1919, in *Abrams v. U.S.* (1919), he defended free speech in opposing the Sedition Act of 1919. In *Schenck v. U.S.* (1919), however, he argued that free speech is limited if it created "a clear and present danger." His dissent in *Lochner v. New York* (1905) attacked unrestricted economic rights, declaring that the Fourteenth Amendment "does not enact Mr. Herbert Spencer's *Social Statics*."

At the same time, Holmes argued that judges should limit their actions to declare legislative acts unconstitutional. In *Otis and Gassman v. Parker* (1902), for example, he pointed out that judges should allow "for differences of view" and that "conditions which this court can know but imperfectly" should make the justices cautious. In a child labor issue, *Hammer v. Dagenhart* (1918), and in an issue involving women's wages, *Adkins v. Children's Hospital* (1923), he argued against the absolute right of contract, writing that the Constitution did not prevent reasonable laws controlling wages and hours.

Summary

Holmes's contribution to American jurisprudence was both deep and long-lasting. His view that the

law was experience, that the law was shaped by a degree of utilitarianism and that it should be subjected to a legal science, deeply affected Anglo-American jurisprudence. These ideas sent jurists and scholars inquiring into the conditions that surround the law and helped develop a sociology of law.

Holmes was the first Anglo-American jurist to probe seriously the subconscious mind, seeking further understanding of legal decision-making. In this regard, he predated European pioneers in the psychology of the subconscious.

Holmes sought the meaning of words in history, taking the view that dictionary definitions are inadequate. He recognized that words have a life history and that the meanings of words can differ depending upon their historical context.

Holmes built a reasoned, scientifically oriented philosophy of law that broke American law free from the stagnated condition in which he found it when he first began his legal studies. He set the stage for a maturing of American law.

Holmes does not fit any fixed category. To say that he represented the liberal wing of the Court at the time when *laissez-faire* concepts dominated much of legal thought overlooks his skepticism. He urged caution before declaring laws unconstitutional: People, through their legislatures, had the right to create the society that they saw fit to create. For Holmes, the Court should respect that right in its deliberations. This view mirrored Holmes's view of law. Holmes has been called the greatest legal mind in the history of Anglo-American jurisprudence. When he died in Washington, District of Columbia, on March 6, 1935, he left his considerable wealth to the United States with no letter of explanation.

Bibliography

Biddle, Francis. *Justice Holmes, Natural Law and the Supreme Court.* New York: Macmillan, 1961. The author takes a rather uncritical view of Holmes, but he does discuss an important part of Holmes's thought.

Bowen, Catherine Drinker. *Yankee from Olympus: Justice Holmes and His Family.* Boston: Little Brown, 1944; London: Benn, 1949. A popular biography written in an easy, colorful, and interesting style. Holmes is placed in the historical context of his times.

Frankfurter, Felix. *Mr. Justice Holmes and the Supreme Court.* 2d ed. Cambridge, Mass.: Belknap Press of Harvard University Press, 1961. Written by a Supreme Court justice who served with Holmes on the Court, the book is favorable to Holmes and presents him as a great jurist. Frankfurter gives insights into the interior workings of the Court and the thinking of Holmes.

Holmes, Oliver Wendell. *The Common Law.* Edited by Mark Dewolfe Howe. Cambridge, Mass.: Belknap Press of Harvard University Press, 1963. A classical work in American jurisprudence. Howe is a leading Holmesian scholar.

————. *Touched with Fire: Civil War Letters and Diary of Oliver Wendell Holmes, Jr., 1861-1864.* Edited by Mark Dewolfe Howe. Cambridge, Mass.: Harvard University Press, 1946. An interesting set of documents that aid in understanding Holmes, the man.

Howe, Mark DeWolfe. *Justice Oliver Wendell Holmes: The Shaping Years, 1841-1870.* Cambridge, Mass.: Harvard University Press, 1957.

————. *Justice Oliver Wendell Holmes: The Proving Years, 1870-1882.* Cambridge, Mass.: Harvard University Press, 1963. This two-volume work is a first-rate intellectual biography of Holmes with a favorable point of view.

Meyer, Edith P. *That Remarkable Man: Justice Oliver Wendell Holmes.* Boston: Little Brown, 1967. The title establishes the author's view of Holmes.

" 'The Path of the Law' After One Hundred Years." *Harvard Law Review* 110, no. 5 (March, 1997). Includes the text of Holmes' speech "The Path of the Law" along with commentaries by noted modern legal scholars.

Pohlman, H. L. *Justice Oliver Wendell Holmes and Utilitarian Jurisprudence.* Cambridge, Mass., and London: MIT Press, 1984. Pohlman develops aspects of the origin of Holmes's thought that others have failed fully to develop. A thoughtful and useful book.

John Aiken

SOICHIRO HONDA

Born: November 17, 1906; Iwata-gun, Japan
Died: August 5, 1991; Tokyo, Japan
Areas of Achievement: Business and industry
Contribution: Honda's career provides an authentic rags-to-riches story. From the humblest of beginnings as a mechanic and with only the scantiest of formal education, he became an inventor, innovator, and manufacturer in one of the most competitive industries in Japan. The motorcycles and automobiles produced by the company which bears his name are sold throughout the entire world.

Early Life

Soichiro Honda was born into the family of a blacksmith in a small town in Shizuoka Prefecture not far from Tokyo. Bicycles were only then gaining popularity in Japan, and Soichiro's father, Gihei, expanded the family business by purchasing used bicycles in Tokyo and then repairing them for resale. From his earliest years, Soichiro helped out with his father's business and gradually became adept at mechanics. At the age of fifteen, he was sent as an apprentice to an automobile repair shop in Tokyo. It was not long before Soichiro, still a teenager, had developed his skills to the point at which he was able to build his own racing car; it was the beginning of a lifelong fascination with automobile and motorcycle racing. He not only built but also drove racing cars and in fact set a Japanese speed record in 1936 that remained unbroken for many years.

In the meantime, from the age of twenty-one, Honda was in the auto repair business for himself in the city of Hamamatsu. In the decade of the 1930's, Honda's career led him in several directions, from creating a successful car repair shop to experimenting with inventions (including cast metal spokes for a wheel). At the age of thirty-one, he returned to part-time study at the Hamamatsu High School of Technology, though he never received a diploma, because he failed to take the examinations. Much later in his career, after his automobiles had gained international recognition, he would be awarded numerous honorary doctorates from universities in Japan and the United States.

During the war years, 1937-1945, Honda's company, Tokai Seiki, prospered as military demands for the company's products, including piston rings and metal aircraft propellers, accelerated. In the final year of the war, after the factory took direct hits in a bombing raid and was further damaged in an earthquake, Honda sold what was left of Tokai Seiki's assets to Toyota.

Life's Work

In October, 1946, after the end of the war, Honda established the Honda Technical Research Institute, the forerunner of the Honda Motor Company, in the city of Hamamatsu. The organization's main project was refitting small wartime surplus engines to bicycles. This project soon led Honda to manufacture his own bicycle engines. The fuel-efficient models that he built sold well at the time, when the economy was still impoverished and when fuel was especially scarce and expensive.

In 1948, Honda teamed up with Takeo Fujisawa, an investor and businessman, to launch the Honda Motor Company, with Honda as the president. One year later, the twenty-man firm produced its first prototype. This "Dream Type D" motorcycle, boasting a 98cc, two-stroke engine capable of a maximum output of three horsepower, went into full-scale production at a new factory in Tokyo in 1950. At that time there were about two hundred firms engaged in manufacturing motorcycles in Japan, but the Honda models quickly earned a reputation for sturdiness and reliability that enabled them to prevail over the competition. By 1952, at a time when the company was capitalized at only about forty-one million dollars, sales had reached about nineteen million, and the company controlled 70 percent of the domestic motorcycle market in Japan. By 1967, only four companies manufactured motorcycles in Japan, and Honda accounted for slightly more than half of the total production.

Honda contributed in a personal and direct way to quality control by frequently appearing on the factory floor, wrench in hand, to oversee operations. A bolt that had been tightened by a young factory hand, it was said, could always be tightened by two more turns when the company president took over. At the same time, Honda encouraged employee improvement of work-floor design and methods, a feature of the Honda style that became formalized in 1970 with "idea contests," which occur every eighteen months and which conclude with daylong picnic celebrations at which workers present their ideas.

A trip abroad in 1951 proved to Honda that Japanese mechanical technology was woefully behind the West. He persuaded Mitsubishi Bank to extend a $1.25 million loan of scarce hard currency to his company to buy the most up-to-date machine tools available. He was convinced that the future success of his company depended on making a motorcycle that could compete successfully in the most demanding international races. After several presentable showings in European events in the late 1950's, Honda's racing machines won the first five positions in both the 125cc and 250cc class at the prestigious Isle of Man contests in 1961. By that date, Hondas had already achieved the distinction of being the largest selling motorcycles in the world. The establishment of the American Honda Motor Company in 1959 and Honda Germany in 1961 accelerated sales in the West. When Honda Motor opened Honda Benelux in Belgium in 1962 to assemble mopeds, it marked the first time that a Japanese manufacturer had directly invested in the establishment of a factory in an advanced Western nation. Twenty-five years later, Honda operated fifty plants in thirty-three countries around the world.

Honda delayed entry into automobile production in part because the government of Japan discouraged smaller companies from challenging the industry's giants, Nissan and Toyota. Smaller firms such as Honda Motor were supposed to remain content with supporting roles. Honda, however, took an unusually aggressive posture in his relationship with government authorities, and by the early 1960's his company could no longer be held back. In 1962, a lightweight truck was introduced, and in the following year a sports car made its appearance. Honda's first lightweight passenger car was marketed in 1967. The big breakthrough, however, especially in overseas markets, came in 1973, when the Civic model was launched. Intended to compete in North America with Germany's Volkswagen, this popular model possessed a compound vortex controlled combustion engine system, which gained a quick marketing advantage over the competition by being the first to meet the 1975 emission standards set forth by the United States Clean Air Act.

This stunning technical achievement, all the more noteworthy because it came at a time when the "Big Three" automakers of Detroit were pleading for a postponement of the implementation of the standards, was directly attributable to the emphasis placed on research and development by both Honda and his partner Fujisawa. This emphasis was formalized in the creation in 1961 of Honda R and D Company, with Honda as president. In order to ensure that independent-minded researchers be kept free from interference by the main company's bureaucracy, Honda R and D was given an entirely independent and autonomous status—the first such instance in the Japanese auto industry. Funding for the research operations comes from a guaranteed annual flow of 2.5 percent of all parent-company sales.

Another watershed event in the Honda Motor Company's history, though it happened after Honda had retired from the presidency, was the establishment of a factory in 1978 to produce motorcycles in the United States. This move was followed four years later, in 1982, by the opening of an automobile assembly line in Marysville, Ohio. Despite many studies that warned that such a move, using American labor, would not be profitable, the venture proved to be a shrewd investment for Honda and a boon for the Ohio economy. Business analysts give the Ohio operation special credit for the way in which it managed to involve workers in the affairs of the company, a legacy of the Honda style. By the mid-1980's, more than one quarter of the Honda automobiles sold in the United States were being produced in the Marysville facility. Before long, the other two big Japanese auto manufacturers, Toyota and Nissan, followed Honda's example by building their own plants in the United States.

In October, 1973, both Honda and the company cofounder, Fujisawa, retired. A longtime associate, Kiyoshi Kawashima, hired by Honda as an engineer in 1947, became president of the Honda Motor Company. Honda continued to take a role in company affairs with the title of "supreme adviser." The early retirement of Honda and Fujisawa (Honda was only sixty-two years old and Fujisawa was four years younger) was a striking exception to customary Japanese practice in which senior executives are often in their seventies or even eighties before stepping down. Honda explained the decision by saying that it was necessary to allow younger leaders the opportunity to explore new ideas and strategies unhampered by the tendency to defer constantly to the cofounders. Honda's early retirement was seen by Japanese observers as one more example of his maverick style. Following retirement, Honda devoted much of his energy to two foundations: the International Association of Traffic and Safety Sciences (privately funded by Honda and Fujisawa), which conducts research and holds symposia on traffic safety, and the Honda Foundation (funded primarily by Honda himself), which was established in 1977 and is devoted to finding solutions to environmental problems created by modern technology. In October, 1989, Honda became the first Japanese automobile manufacturer to be named to the American Automotive Hall of Fame.

Summary

The Honda Motor Company is the only Japanese automobile firm that does not have any connection to a prewar auto manufacturer. The success of the company and its dozens of overseas affiliates is not entirely the result of Soichiro Honda's efforts. The company's cofounder, Fujisawa, and Kawashima have made enormously important contributions. Still it is not surprising that the company bears the name of Honda, for his talents, both technical and entrepreneurial, and the bold racing-car-driver spirit that he projected, made indelible impressions on the Honda Motor Company. Perhaps the most important contribution he made was to impart an egalitarian spirit to his work force—in large measure by the example he set. He told a New York Times reporter:

> The worst kind of president is the person who eats in fancy restaurants, smoking a fat cigar and thinking well of himself while employees work in a dirty factory with their hands dirty. If you're like a god, people will respect you, but they won't come close. So employees should feel that the president has made some mistakes.

Bibliography

Cameron, K. "Soichiro Honda." *Cycle World* 30, no. 11 (November, 1991). Short profile of Honda including his background and career, his innovative marketing strategies, and Honda's entrance into the U.S. automobile market.

Cusumano, Michael A. *The Japanese Automobile Industry: Technology and Management at Nissan and Toyota.* Cambridge, Mass. and London: Harvard University Press, 1985. Although primarily about Honda's competitors, this scholarly study includes much valuable information and important statistical data about the Japanese auto industry in general.

Gibney, Frank. *Miracle by Design: The Real Reasons Behind Japan's Economic Success.* New York: Times Books, 1982. Honda and his company are frequently discussed in this book which is a major interpretive examination of Japan's "economic miracle" written by an American scholar who was also for ten years the guiding force behind his own company's swift expansion in Japan.

Kamioka, Kazuyoshi. *Japanese Business Pioneers.* Union City, Calif.: Heian, 1988. In addition to general comments on characteristics of business and management styles in Japan, this book includes chapters devoted to eight corporate leaders of Japan, including Honda.

Kodansha Encyclopedia of Japan. New York: Kodansha International/USA, 1983. Contains brief but valuable entries for Honda and for the Honda Motor Company.

Sakiya, Tetsuo. *Honda Motor: The Men, the Management, and the Machines.* New York: Kodansha International/USA, 1982. This is a major source of information on both Honda and the Honda Motor Company. It manages to be both a very scholarly and a very readable business history. Contains numerous interesting photographs as well as a valuable fifteen-page chronology, which is made more useful by incorporating pictures of motorcycle and automobile models.

John H. Boyle

HERBERT HOOVER

Born: August 10, 1874; West Branch, Iowa
Died: October 20, 1964; New York, New York
Area of Achievement: Government and politics
Contribution: As the president whose presidency
ushered in the Great Depression, Hoover has long
been castigated as a failure. Nevertheless, his career both before and after his presidency and the
accomplishments of his administration give final
judgment of Hoover as a great American.

Early Life

Herbert Clark Hoover, or "Bertie" as he was
known to his family, was born in West Branch,
Iowa, on August 10, 1874. He had an older brother,
Tad (Theodore), and a younger sister, May (Mary).
His father, Jesse Hoover, was a businessman who
worked as a blacksmith and operated a farm implement store. He died in 1880, at the age of thirty-
four. Herbert's mother, Hulda Minthorn Hoover,
worked as a seamstress to pay the family's debts
after the death of her husband and was vigorously
active in the Quaker Church, speaking at meetings
throughout the area. She died of pneumonia in
1884, at the age of thirty-five.

The three orphaned children were separated and
parceled out to other family members. Herbert
stayed briefly with his uncle Allan Hoover and his
aunt Millie before moving to Oregon at the age of
eleven to live with Laura and John Minthorn. John
Minthorn was a medical doctor and a businessman,
and the family provided a more cultured environment for young Hoover than he had found in Iowa.
In 1891, Herbert became the youngest member of
the first class to attend the newly established Stanford College in California. Nearly six feet tall, thin,
and muscular, with thick, light hair, Hoover had the
brusque, retiring manner which also characterized
him as an adult. Even as a youth he had the plumb
cheeks, which, as an adult, became the familiar
jowls that dropped down to the stiff white collars
he wore, long after they had gone out of style. He
worked his way through the University, where he
met his future wife, Lou Henry, who, like Hoover,
was majoring in geology.

Hoover was graduated in 1895 and the following year left for a mining job in Australia, where
he began a highly successful career in mining. In
1899, he married Lou Henry, who accompanied
him to China, where they were both actively involved in aid for those civilians caught in the Box-

er Rebellion. Hoover moved up the ladder of success, returning to Australia and then to London,
where his son Herbert, Jr., was born in 1903, followed by another son, Allan, in 1907. By 1908,
Hoover had built a home in Palo Alto, California,
developed mines in Burma, and established a consulting business which allowed him to exercise his
managerial and organizational talents as well as
enlarge the fortune he had already earned. In
1909, Hoover published his *Principles of Mining*,
which was the standard textbook in the field for
many years. In 1912, he was named a trustee of
Stanford University, an institution to which he was
always loyal. He later established the Hoover Institute on their campus.

Hoover was in Europe at the outbreak of World
War I and immediately plunged into the organization of Belgian relief. His committee was credited
with saving more than several hundred thousand
persons from death. After the United States entered
the war, Hoover turned his organizational talents to
directing the United States Food Administration
with remarkably effective results. He next accompanied President Woodrow Wilson to Paris, where
Hoover acted as head of the European Relief Program and as one of Wilson's economic advisers at
the Paris Peace Conference.

Life's Work

At the end of World War I, Hoover had both a national and an international reputation. As the Great
Humanitarian and as the Great Engineer, Hoover
seemed to combine the best of both worlds, a practical idealist. In 1920, both the Democrats and the
Republicans considered him to be a presidential
possibility. When he declared himself to be a Republican, he allowed friends to pursue his possible
candidacy, but the Republican leadership was cool,
and he did not do well in early primaries. In 1921,
he accepted the position of secretary of commerce
in the cabinet of President Warren G. Harding, and
he remained there under President Calvin Coolidge
as well. He was an activist secretary, certainly one
considered a Progressive in the context of the
1920's.

Under Hoover's direction the Commerce Department made major gains in gathering and distributing information on a wide variety of subjects of interest to the business community. Hoover was also
reasonably sympathetic to labor unions. He effec-

tively used two tactics which had served him well in his earlier activities—voluntary cooperation and widespread publicity for his goals. Once again responding to crisis, Hoover directed relief efforts for victims of the 1927 Mississippi River flood. In that program, and throughout the Commerce Department, Hoover began an effective program of racial desegregation.

When Calvin Coolidge chose not to run again in 1928, Hoover became a candidate for the Republican nomination—which he received and accepted on his fifty-fourth birthday. His campaign focused on progress through technology and, on major issues, differed little from that of his Democratic opponent Alfred E. Smith. Hoover, his reputation enhanced by his Cabinet years, and the country ready to continue the prosperity which seemed tied to Republican leadership, was a comfortable winner in 1928.

As president, Hoover was more progressive than most contemporaries recognized. He supported both civil liberties (as a good Quaker should) and civil rights. The Wickersham Commission on Crime and Prohibition gave a mixed report on the constitutionally mandated abstinence from alcohol. Hoover chose to enforce the law, though he was apparently not in full agreement with it. Although Lou Hoover would tolerate no alcohol nor, while in the White House, would the Hoovers attend functions where alcohol was served, after leaving the presidency, Hoover was partial to one martini after dinner. Hoover, as president, supported conservation of natural resources, aid to the economically distressed farmers, and, in 1930, supported the Hawley-Smoot Tariff. A high tariff had long been a Republican tradition, but the Hawley-Smoot Tariff became highly policitized as the Democrats charged that it had helped to spread the Depression.

Hoover had little opportunity to initiate a program before the Stock Market Crash of 1929 launched the Great Depression. He had been concerned about the speculative fever of the stock market before he took office and, after the initial crash, worked closely with the nation's major banks to alleviate the crash. Hoover believed that the decline would, like the other panics in America's past, be relatively brief in duration. The idea that prosperity was "just around the corner" (actually said by Vice President Charles Curtis, though often attributed to Hoover) quickly proved false, and the nation rejected Hoover both

for the crash itself and for what was perceived to be false optimism.

Hoover endeavored to follow the pattern of his earlier success—voluntary activity and publicity. Despite his holding biweekly press conferences and participating in ninety-five radio broadcasts during his four years in office, Hoover never was able to restore public confidence. His bland, unemotional voice conveyed neither his genuine concern for the suffering caused by the Depression nor his underlying confidence in America and in her people. Voluntary action similarly proved to be inadequate in the face of the ever-worsening Depression.

In spite of a philosophy and a personal experience which emphasized individualism, Hoover did provide active leadership to meet the emergencies of the Depression. In 1932, he encouraged the establishment of the Reconstruction Finance Corporation (RFC) to provide economic aid for the banks, which Hoover believed would then "trickle down" to help provide funds for business and thus jobs for the unemployed. Hoover, throughout his Administration, feared direct relief on the part of the federal government, believing that it would damage the concept of local self-government as well as deprive the recipients of the desire to work. The RFC was maintained and expanded by the New Deal; indeed, many of the concepts held by Hoover became part of the New Deal. Franklin D. Roosevelt, however, carried many ideas further and faster than Hoover could have tolerated.

In foreign policy, Hoover was something of a pacifist. He met face-to-face with British prime minister Ramsay MacDonald and French premier Pierre Laval. He supported the World Court and continued the pursuit of disarmament at the 1930 London Naval Conference and, in 1932, at the Geneva Peace Conference. He opposed the kind of "dollar diplomacy" which led to intervention in Latin America, anticipating here the Good Neighbor Policy of his successor, Franklin D. Roosevelt. The Japanese invasion of Manchuria produced the Stimson Doctrine, which provided nonrecognition of such aggression. The Hoover Moratorium in 1931 suspended payment for one year of both the Allied war debts and the German reparations from World War I. The continuing downward spiral of the economy had the result of making the suspension of payments permanent.

In 1932, Hoover was renominated by the Republicans but without noticeable enthusiasm. The

Democrats chose New York Governor Franklin D. Roosevelt, who promised the nation a "new deal." The two men were of dramatically different personalities, which made them seem further apart in philosophy than they often were. Hoover appeared even more aloof from the problems of the common man as he failed to repudiate the excessive actions of General Douglas MacArthur in driving the Bonus Army (World War I veterans who marched to Washington to seek early payment of their promised bonus) out of the Capitol. The outcome of the election was easily predicted—a Democratic victory.

Hoover and his wife briefly returned to their home in Palo Alto, California, but in 1934, moved permanently into a suite in the Waldorf-Astoria Hotel in New York City. Hoover wrote many books, traveled to Europe, and, over the years which made him the longest lived former president except John Adams, collected eighty-five honorary degrees and 468 awards. With the outbreak of World War II, he once again raised funds for relief. He opposed United States participation in the Korean War in spite of a growing and rigid anti-Communist outlook. President Harry S Truman brought Hoover back into government to do what he had always done best—organize and manage. Hoover chaired the 1947 Committee on the Organization of the Executive Branch of Government and brought much needed reform and coherence to that branch of government. At the age of eighty, he chaired a second committee to which he was appointed by President Dwight D. Eisenhower. He died at his home in New York at the age of ninety.

Summary

Throughout his long life and varied career, Hoover's outlook was dominated by his Quaker heritage. He believed in an orderly universe and in the beneficial results of cooperation among men of goodwill. He also held strongly to the belief, grounded in experience, in individualism. It was a self-help philosophy tempered by his belief in cooperative action. His engineering background gave him a strong faith in technology and statistics. His many humanitarian activities reveal a deep and abiding concern for his fellow man—revealed also in his opposition to foreign intervention and his desire for peace.

In any other time, Hoover would have been a superior president. He had abundant leadership and managerial skills, but, unfortunately, few political talents. His pompous physical appearance, his dry wit, and undynamic demeanor were suitable for the chairman of the board, not for an elected executive who on occasion needed to persuade both the Congress and his countrymen of the value of his policies. Generally nonpolitical (he had never voted for president before 1920, because he was so often out of the country), Hoover never acquired the skills which came so easily to Franklin D. Roosevelt (and which made the contrast between the two of them so painfully denigrating to Hoover).

Hoover's experience and philosophy limited the extent to which he could involve the government in the lives of citizens. Yet when it was clear that voluntary and local relief had failed, Hoover first set the federal government on the path of response to the public need—down which it traveled so much more rapidly under the New Deal. In the context of the 1920's Hoover was a classic Progressive in the programs he supported; it was the Depression and the vigorous activism of Roosevelt which made him seem to be a conservative.

Hoover lived long enough to see himself rehabilitated in public esteem. He advised many presidents, and his enormous managerial skills were again used for the national good under Truman and Eisenhower. In spite of his stalwart anti-Communist stance, he never supported the excesses of Senator Joe McCarthy during the Red Scare of the 1950's (nor had he tolerated the similar excesses of the 1920's). He was a good man, indeed a great man, who was overpowered by the awesome circumstances of the Great Depression. Unable to articulate and communicate his concern for the people and his optimism for the future, Hoover's reputation, like the stock market, plunged down—and, like the economy, eventually revived.

Bibliography

Best, Gary Dean. *The Politics of American Individualism: Herbert Hoover in Transition, 1918-21.* Westport, Conn.: Greenwood Press, 1975. An excellent work on Hoover's early public service. Best has also written on Hoover's postpresidential years, and his excellent research is useful in rounding out the story of this president.

Burner, David. *Herbert Hoover: A Public Life.* New York: Knopf, 1979. Probably the best single biography among the many available on Hoover. It covers his entire life and career admirably and strikes a balance between admiration and criticism.

Emerson, Edwin. *Hoover and His Times*. New York: Garden City Publishing, 1932. A useful book with a valuable immediacy of views concerning Hoover's presidency. Like several books published soon after Hoover left office, it suffers from a lack of perspective.

Fausold, Martin L. *The Presidency of Herbert Clark Hoover*. Lawrence: University Press of Kansas, 1985. One of the most valuable books on the presidency of Hoover. It does not do justice, nor does it attempt to do justice, to the other areas of Hoover's career.

Hoff-Wilson, Jean H. *Herbert Hoover: Forgotten Progressive*. Boston: Little Brown, 1975. Another relatively brief account of Hoover's entire career, focusing on the basically progressive character of Hoover and the many ways in which his ideas did, in fact, anticipate the New Deal. An interesting and provocative account.

Liebovich, Louis W. *Bylines in Despair: Herbert Hoover, the Great Depression, and the U. S. News Media*. Westport, Conn.: Praeger, 1994. Liebovich traces Hoover's relationship with the media and discusses how his negative attitudes helped to aggravate a number of issues. Based on the diaries of Hoover aides, oral histories of journalists, news and magazine stories, public documents, and more.

Lyons, Eugene. *The Herbert Hoover Story*. Washington, D.C.: Human Events, 1947. A very favorable book in support of Herbert Hoover. Originally entitled *Our Unknown Ex-President*, its interest comes especially from the personal viewpoint of the author, who, in his youth, was sympathetic toward Communism until a visit to Russia thoroughly disillusioned him. His philosophical travels from Left to Right provide an interesting perspective from which to view Hoover.

Smith, Richard N. *An Uncommon Man: The Triumph of Hoover*. New York: Simon and Schuster, 1984. Another excellent biography of Hoover, taking its title from one of Hoover's own inspirational articles on being uncommon. Smith picks up a theme many writers have used, that Hoover did triumph over the Depression, and that a dispassionate view of his administration will reveal this fact.

Walch, Timothy M., and Dwight Miller. *Herbert Hoover and Franklin D. Roosevelt: A Documentary History*. Westport, Conn.: Greenwood Press, 1998. A collection of historical materials including telegrams, letters, and reports highlighting the relationship between Hoover and Roosevelt.

Warren, Harris Gaylord. *Herbert Hoover and the Great Depression*. New York: Oxford University Press, 1959. A relatively brief and easily read book covering the major facets of Hoover's life and concentrating on the Depression years.

Carlanna L. Hendrick

J. EDGAR HOOVER

Born: January 1, 1895; Washington, D.C.
Died: May 2, 1972; Washington, D.C.
Area of Achievement: Government and politics
Contribution: Head of the Federal Bureau of Investigation for forty-eight years (from 1924 to 1972), Hoover was one of the most controversial figures in American politics, the first and most durable leader of the anti-Communist movement that ruled American public life for much of the century.

Early Life

John Edgar Hoover was born to a family of civil servants in Seward Square, Washington, D.C., a few blocks behind the Capitol. Educated in the District of Columbia public schools, Hoover showed early signs of the drive and the leadership abilities that would make him one of the most powerful bureaucrats in American history. At Washington's elite Central High, he was a leader of the student cadet corps and a champion debater; at the Old First Presbyterian Church, he was a teacher in the Sunday school. Photographs of him show a sword-slim figure of suppressed nervous energy, his expression one of intense determination. The values he absorbed from Seward Square, from Central High, and from the Old First Church were his guiding principles throughout his life: absolute assurance that his middle-class Protestant morality was the essential core of American values, and a deep distrust of alien ideas and movements that called those certainties into question.

Life's Work

After receiving his bachelor's and master's degrees in law from George Washington University's night school, Hoover joined the Justice Department as a clerk on July 26, 1917, four months after the beginning of World War I. Hoover spent the war working for John Lord O'Brian's War Emergency Division in the Alien Enemy bureau, administering the regulations that governed the hundreds of thousands of German and Austro-Hungarian aliens interned or supervised by the department.

While Hoover was wrapping up the affairs of the expiring Alien Enemies Bureau after the November 8, 1918, armistice, the Bolshevik Revolution was breaking out of Russia and spreading across central Europe to Germany and Hungary; general strikes in Vancouver and Seattle seemed to be the opening shots in an American class war. A sense of crisis took hold of the country as the Comintern, organized in Moscow on March 4, 1919, predicted a worldwide proletarian revolution by the end of the year. Forever after, Hoover would see Communism through a perspective colored by the crisis of 1919, when the world seemed on the brink of a Communist revolution.

A series of bombings in the spring of 1919, including an explosion at the Washington home of Attorney General A. Mitchell Palmer, gave rise to irresistible demands for action against radicals. Palmer, a candidate for the 1920 Democratic presidential nomination, decided to respond with a Justice Department drive that would concentrate on aliens, since they could be deported *en masse* administratively without the protection of legal due process. Hoover's experience dealing with aliens brought him to the attention of Palmer, who put the twenty-four-year-old attorney in charge of the antiradical campaign.

As leader of the 1919-1920 antiradical drive, Hoover became the government's first expert on the Communist movement. He established an "antiradical division" in the Justice Department and then, when the American Communist and Communist Labor parties were established in the late summer of 1919, prepared briefs arguing that their alien members were subject to deportation under the immigration laws. Hoover planned a raid of the headquarters of the anarchist Union of Russian Workers in November, 1919; on December 21, 1919, he put 249 radicals, including Emma Goldman and Alexander Berkman, two of the most noted radicals of the day, on a ship for the Soviet Union. Then, on January 2, 1920, Hoover led a nationwide roundup of alien Communists, arresting more than four thousand. The Justice Department was hoping to use the arrests to spur passage of a peacetime sedition bill that would have outlawed expression of revolutionary opinions by citizens, but widespread abuses of the prisoners' rights and the overbearing behavior of the Justice Department stirred up the opposition of liberals and civil libertarians who brought the drive to a halt. Hoover, however, emerged with an enhanced reputation as an expert on radicalism and an organizational genius.

Hoover served as assistant director of the Bureau of Investigation from 1921 to 1924, when he was placed in charge of the scandal-plagued bureau. Acting quickly to bring his agents, previously loosely supervised, under tight control, Hoover turned the bureau's newly acquired (1924) fingerprint collection into a national law enforcement resource, and, in the spirit of the progressivism of Herbert Hoover (no relation), made the bureau a force for professional standards and scientific methods.

During the 1930's, Hoover and his men became national heroes as the result of a series of sensational hunts for gangsters such as John Dillinger, Pretty Boy Floyd, and Baby Face Nelson. FBI agents, "G-men," were celebrated by Hollywood, radio, and the adventure magazines; their exploits convinced the public that the New Deal had the determination necessary to restore the national unity and morale that had been weakened by the Depression. Meanwhile, as part of his secret defense preparations, Roosevelt had Hoover rebuild and expand the domestic intelligence system that had been dismantled during the 1924 reorganization of the bureau.

With the coming of war, Hoover's widely heralded successes against Nazi spies in the United States reassured the public that the "home front" was secure. Hoover was also notably successful in countering the Axis underground in South America.

After the war, as Cold War tensions heightened between the Soviet Union and the United States, Hoover interpreted the post-World War II international conflicts as a prelude to a war with the Soviet Union; this meant the bureau would have to be prepared to counter sabotage and subversion and to round up domestic Communists. Hoover quickly lost confidence in Harry S Truman's resolve to deal effectively with the issue of Communists in the government and broke with the Administration in 1947, siding with such congressional Republicans as Richard M. Nixon of the House Committee on Un-American Activities and Senator Joseph R. McCarthy. As part of his assault on domestic Communists, Hoover's bureau pursued the investigation of Alger Hiss that discredited the domestic security policies of the Truman Administration, and uncovered the alleged atom spy conspiracy of Klaus Fuchs, Harry Gold, and Julius and Ethel Rosenberg. In 1949, Hoover's bureau provided the evidence for the Smith Act convictions of the top leadership of the American Communist Party, effectively destroying American Communism.

During the late 1950's, Hoover's bureau shifted to a counterintelligence program (COINTELPRO) of covert harassment of the remnants of the American Communist Party. Under Lyndon Johnson, who indefinitely deferred Hoover's mandatory retirement, which should have taken place in 1965, when he turned seventy, Hoover extended COINTELPRO to include harassment and disruption of the Ku Klux Klan at first, and then the black militant and antiwar movements, the Black Panthers, and the Students for a Democratic Society in particular. By this time, Hoover, with his pronouncements in favor of traditional Americanism and his denunciations of civil rights and antiwar protests as Communist-inspired, had gained a sacrosanct position as the hero of the anti-Communist Right; his public attacks on Martin Luther King, Jr., Robert Kennedy, and Ramsey Clark confirmed liberals and the Left in their conviction that Hoover was a dangerous and malevolent force on the American political scene.

During the Nixon Administration, Hoover's acute political instincts told him that the bureau's illegal investigative techniques (including wiretapping and microphone surveillance) and its programs of political harassment (COINTELPRO) could no longer be concealed and would no longer be tolerated; he radically curtailed them and had to resist the strenuous efforts of the White House to enlist the FBI in the comprehensive drive against dissent called the Huston Plan.

Hoover's state funeral in 1972 was a final gathering of the standard-bearers of Cold War anti-Communism. After his death, post-Watergate investigations of the bureau's abuses of civil liberties, together with releases of FBI files made possible by the Freedom of Information Act, all but destroyed his reputation; within a few years, public opinion about Hoover had so shifted that the mention of his name was enough to conjure up the image of a government at war with the rights and liberties of its citizens.

Summary

The broad sweep of Hoover's unusual career has been obscured, not to say eclipsed, by the revelations of FBI abuses of civil liberties, particularly his vendetta against Martin Luther King, Jr., who was recognized after his assassination as one of the true moral leaders of the nation. Hoover's most tangible and lasting achievement was to mold the FBI into a progressive force that pro-

moted professional standards and scientific techniques for American law enforcement. His real historic significance, however, is of the sort that afterward cannot be measured accurately: the day-to-day leadership he furnished over so many years as a spokesman for traditional values and a reassuring symbol of stability for millions of Americans who were frightened by change and international tensions.

That he did, on many occasions, misuse this trust is undeniable, and he eventually came to see any criticism of himself or his bureau as an attack on the nation's security. Any assessment of Hoover's achievement, therefore, must combine respect for his political judgment, bureaucratic skills, and leadership abilities with a condemnation of his willingness to take unto himself the roles of judge, jury, and executioner when he saw a danger to the country, instead of relying on the legal process and confining himself to open and constitutional methods. Even in his worst excesses, however, it is essential to see Hoover's career not as an anomaly but as an expression of American opinion and values during a trying and crisis-filled half-century.

Bibliography

Breuer, William B. *J. Edgar Hoover and His G-Men*. Westport, Conn.: Praeger, 1995. This glowing biography of Hoover's career through World War II concentrates on the 1920's and 1930's. Ignores criticism of Hoover and lacks objectivity.

Demaris, Ovid. *The Director: An Oral Biography of J. Edgar Hoover*. New York: Harper's Magazine Press, 1975. An indispensable collection of interviews with the people who knew Hoover best.

Felt, W. Mark. *The F.B.I. Pyramid: From the Inside*. New York: Putnam, 1979. The autobiography of the man who was Hoover's top aide during his last years. Invaluable source of information on Hoover's relationship with the Nixon Administration.

Garrow, David. *From Solo to Memphis: The FBI and Martin Luther King, Jr.* New York: Norton, 1981. An exemplary investigation, based on FBI files, of the most disgraceful episode in Hoover's career: his attempt to destroy the leader of the Civil Rights movement.

Lowenthal, Max. *The Federal Bureau of Investigation*. New York: Sloane, 1950; London: Turnstile Press, 1951. A caustic review of bureau abuses over the years, written by a friend of Harry S Truman. Based on the public press and congressional reports.

Navasky, Victor. *Kennedy Justice*. New York: Atheneum, 1971. An analysis of the conflict between Hoover and the Justice Department of Robert Kennedy.

O'Reilly, Kenneth. *Hoover and the Un-Americans: The FBI, HUAC, and the Red Menace*. Philadelphia: Temple University Press, 1983. Based on FBI files, a study of Hoover's relationship with congressional anti-Communists that surveys a broad spectrum of Hoover's assaults on political dissent.

Powers, Richard Gid. *G-Men: Hoover's FBI in American Popular Culture*. Carbondale: Southern Illinois University Press, 1983. A study of Hoover's public role as a symbol of patriotism and law enforcement, with particular attention to his reputation and the function of the FBI in American popular entertainment.

―――. *Secrecy and Power: The Life of J. Edgar Hoover*. New York: Free Press, and London: Macmillan, 1986. A comprehensive study of Hoover's career, based on interviews, FBI records, and official documents.

Preston, William. *Aliens and Dissenters.* 2d ed. Urbana: University of Illinois Press, 1994. One of the best treatments of Hoover's role in the 1919-1920 anti-Communist campaign.

Radosh, Ronald, and Joyce Milton. *The Rosenberg File: A Search for the Truth.* 2d ed. New Haven, Conn.: Yale University Press, 1997. The definitive investigation of the case, which endorses the FBI's conclusions regarding the spy ring.

Sullivan, William C. *The Bureau: My Thirty Years in Hoover's FBI.* New York: Norton, 1979. A vitriolic portrait of Hoover by the man who headed the bureau's domestic intelligence programs during the 1960's. Factually unreliable but valuable for its insights.

Theoharis, Athan. *Spying on Americans.* Philadelphia: Temple University Press, 1978. A brilliant investigation of Hoover's surveillance and disruption of the Left, based on FBI files and records in presidential libraries.

Unger, Robert. *The Union Station Massacre: The Original Sin of J. Edgar Hoover's FBI.* Kansas City, Mo.: Andrews and McMeel, 1997. Examines Hoover's use of a shooting incident in Kansas City to build FBI status. Suggests that intimidation, wire taps, and falsified evidence were used to railroad Adam Richetti, who was executed for his alleged participation.

Weinstein, Allen. *Perjury: The Hiss-Chambers Case.* London: Hutchinson, and New York: Knopf, 1978. The definitive investigation of one of Hoover's most important cases, an exoneration of the FBI's investigation.

Whitehead, Donald. *The FBI Story.* New York: Random House, 1956; London: Muller, 1957. An authorized history of the bureau, often an earnest defense of Hoover in his controversies. Nevertheless, a well-organized account of a complex subject, extremely accurate as far as facts are concerned.

Richard Gid Powers

HARRY HOPKINS

Born: August 17, 1890; Sioux City, Iowa
Died: January 29, 1946; New York, New York
Area of Achievement: Government and politics
Contribution: A superb administrator, Hopkins led the United States in combating unemployment during the Great Depression in the 1930's and the menace of Fascism during World War II.

Early Life

Harry Lloyd Hopkins was born August 17, 1890, in Sioux City, Iowa, and grew up in Grinnell, Iowa, where, after several moves, his family settled in 1901. His father, David Aldona Hopkins, was a moderately successful traveling salesman and merchant who imparted to Harry his competitive, good-natured character and his loyalty to the Democratic Party, while his strictly religious mother, née Anna Pickett, impressed on him values of honesty and moral rectitude. Two other early influences were Grinnell College, from which he was graduated in 1912 and which emphasized Social Gospel Christianity, stressing one's responsibility to help the underprivileged, and his sister Adah, who preceded him at Grinnell College and entered professional social work.

Upon graduating from college, Hopkins went to New York City, where he became a social worker and rose rapidly in the Association for Improving the Poor. From 1915 to 1930, he held various high positions in social work in which he was responsible for instituting new programs: pensions for widows with children, relief for the families of servicemen during World War I, and coordination of health services in a major "demonstration" project. He helped to organize the American Association of Social Workers, his profession's first national society, and served a term as its president. In 1924, he became director of the New York Tuberculosis and Health Association, which he developed into the major health agency in New York City.

In these years of early achievement, Hopkins was a handsome man, six feet tall with features that in different moods varied from sharp to boyishly rounded. In his later years, ill health caused him to become gaunt, hollow-cheeked, and round-shouldered. Consistently, however, people were drawn by his large, dark brown eyes, which conveyed sympathy, eagerness to learn, and a merry delight in life.

In 1913, Hopkins married Ethel Gross, who shared his interest in social reform. They had three sons. In 1931, the marriage ended in divorce when Hopkins fell in love with Barbara Duncan, a secretary at the Tuberculosis and Health Association. They were married shortly after his divorce became final and had one daughter.

Life's Work

Although Hopkins achieved notable success as a social worker, his greatest accomplishments came as a member of President Franklin D. Roosevelt's administration. Hopkins became known to Roosevelt during the early years of the Great Depression when, as governor of New York, Roosevelt appointed him to manage and then to direct the Temporary Emergency Relief Administration to help New York State's unemployed. When Roosevelt became president in 1933, he brought Hopkins to Washington to head the Federal Emergency Relief Administration, which granted money to states for unemployment relief. Hopkins set to work rapidly, stressing the duty of the states to set up professionally competent relief organizations and to appropriate funds that matched the federal contribution. The prospect of an unemployment crisis for the winter of 1933-1934 caused Hopkins to recommend that the federal government establish its own relief program. Roosevelt followed his advice and created the Civil Works Administration, which Hopkins administered until it was ended in the spring of 1934. The persistence of unemployment caused Roosevelt to recommend a large federal program which Congress approved and which developed into the Works Progress Administration (WPA) under Hopkins' supervision. By 1936, the WPA had become the administration's major effort to combat the Depression.

Roosevelt appointed Hopkins to these positions because Hopkins demonstrated a genius for emergency administration. Drawing on his years of experience in developing innovative social work programs, Hopkins appointed an able staff (which included Aubrey Williams, Jacob Baker, and Ellen Woodward) and gave them inspiring leadership that emphasized the need for creative ideas, hard work, and practical results. One new idea that fit the practical realities of the Depression was work relief—that the unemployed should earn government support by doing socially useful work. This approach rejected the belief—common to American society at large and to many social workers—that persons on relief suffered from character defects that caused them to fail as useful workers. Hopkins emphasized instead that the unemployed were simply victims of economic circumstances that were beyond their control.

Politically popular because it relieved local officials from having to cope with unemployment, WPA enriched American society by building thousands of miles of streets, roads, bridges, and grade separations, laying out parks and playgrounds, and constructing schools, airports, and other public buildings. WPA also provided jobs for artists, who decorated buildings with murals, and for musicians and actors, who formed local orchestras, choirs, and theatrical groups. One of WPA's most notable contributions was the American Guide series. Produced by a program for unemployed writers, the series contained volumes that combined state and local history and culture with tourist information.

Although WPA involved the federal government more heavily than ever before in unemployment relief, Hopkins operated it in a decentralized fashion. State and local governments proposed and supervised projects that WPA approved and funded, making it possible for localities to define their own needs and giving local politicians the chance to claim some credit for local improvements. This latter feature of WPA involved Hopkins in Democratic Party politics, especially with such big-city bosses as Edward J. Kelly of Chicago and Frank Hague of Jersey City.

Hopkins' alliance with state and local politicians and the national prominence of the WPA led him to develop the ambition to succeed Franklin D. Roosevelt in 1940, an ambition which Roosevelt encouraged. Yet Hopkins' dreams soon turned to ashes. In 1937, he underwent surgery for cancer of the stomach. The surgery cured his cancer but left him with a digestive disorder that condemned him to a weakened state. In 1939, Roosevelt appointed him secretary of commerce, but Hopkins was not strong enough to work effectively in the job and, in 1940, he resigned, apparently to return to private life. He did so facing a bleak personal future, because, in the meantime, his wife had died of cancer.

By the time Hopkins resigned, however, the aggressive actions of the Fascist powers Germany and Italy had brought war to Europe, and the Nazi blitzkrieg had isolated Great Britain. Committed to aiding the British, Roosevelt responded to a plea from Prime Minister Winston Churchill by sending Hopkins as his personal representative to London while he pressed Congress for legislation to expand American aid by a method he called lend-lease. When Congress passed the legislation, Roosevelt appointed Hopkins to supervise the program. Operating as he had during his relief days, Hopkins recruited an able staff that included General James H. Burns, W. Averell Harriman, and Edward R. Stettinius. He also became familiar with all aspects of defense mobilization, deepened his warm personal friendship with Churchill, whom he had impressed on his visit to London, and won the respect of Chief of Staff General George C. Marshall, whom he boosted with President Roosevelt. After Germany invaded the Soviet Union, Roosevelt sent Hopkins to Moscow to confer with Joseph Stalin to begin aid to that country. When the United States entered the war in December, Hopkins was the one American best informed about the details of his country's war-making capability.

World War II marked the high point of Hopkins' service. Soon after United States entry, he emerged and remained the point at which both domestic and allied interests converged. Hopkins balanced and harmonized these interests by winning the personal confidence of various war leaders, to get them to state their objectives clearly and then to bring them to a compromise with their competitors in the war establishment. Through it all, he emphasized that everyone should devote himself to the single task of winning the war.

A strong supporter of General Marshall, Hopkins pushed hard for the chief of staff's plan to invade France in 1942. When the British opposed the plan, he played a key role in arranging for agreement on an invasion of North Africa. Later, however, he suspected that the British would never approve a cross-channel attack and advocated closer cooperation with the Soviet Union to counter British influence. Indeed, he and many others in the Roosevelt Administration believed that the United States' interests would be best advanced during and after the war if the United States and not the British were the Soviet's most trusted ally.

As the war progressed, Hopkins' role in diplomacy increased. At the Casablanca Conference in January of 1943, he managed an agreement that strengthened ties between the United States and the Free French forces under General Charles de Gaulle. At Tehran in December, he acted in place

of Secretary of State Cordell Hull. Early in 1944, his health seriously declined, and he was out of Washington until July. After he returned, he helped the new Secretary of State Edward R. Stettinius to reorganize the department and to form a team for the upcoming Yalta Conference with Churchill and Stalin. Because of his efforts, Yalta was the best planned and organized of the wartime conferences. At the meeting, Hopkins supported the United States' objectives of organizing a postwar United Nations to keep the peace and on other issues, putting the United States in the mediator's role between Great Britain and the Soviet Union. He continued to work for these objectives after President Roosevelt's death, when President Harry S Truman sent him to Moscow to resolve issues that had postponed the formation of the United Nations and were creating mistrust between the Americans and Soviets over the postwar government of Poland, where the Soviets were installing a puppet regime. Hopkins' discussions on the Polish issue revealed the tension that existed between his desire for the wartime allies to continue their cooperation and the American desire that the people of liberated nations choose their own government. Still, his efforts resolved the issues over establishing the United Nations and, for the moment, eased tensions on the Polish question, and President Truman hailed Hopkins' mission as a success.

When Hopkins returned from Moscow, his health was bad, and although President Truman asked him to remain in the government, he decided to retire to private life. In 1942, he had married for the third time, to Louise Macy, and they moved to New York, where he planned to write his memoirs. His health failed rapidly, however, and, on January 29, 1946, little more than six months after leaving government service, he died.

Summary

Harry Hopkins was one of the truly important men of twentieth century American history; few men have better served their country in critical times. Hopkins' career in social work and his experience in establishing innovative programs enabled him to act creatively during the Great Depression. His work projects gave hope, dignity, and a measure of security to millions of Americans and in the process bolstered their faith in representative government at a time when fascism and communism seemed to be the waves of the future. Hopkins instinctively realized that administrative leadership depended less on well-established channels of authority and systematic procedures than on recruiting and supporting hardworking, imaginative people and having the courage to make controversial decisions. A democratic leader, Hopkins sought agreement and common effort and operated by persuasion rather than assertions of authority. His years in Washington were characterized by many friendships and, amazingly for one so highly placed, few long-lasting enmities.

Hopkins' wartime service was the pinnacle of his career. His ability to win others' confidence was vital in holding together the wartime alliance and making the American war machine function effectively. His ability to understand others was vital both to this end and to his task of carrying out President Roosevelt's policies. Although Hopkins revered Roosevelt, he recognized that the president was a temperamental executive, given occasionally to snap decisions or to periods of inactivity. Hopkins was able to compensate for Roosevelt's shortcomings, calming the anger and frustration of those affected by them. His sensitivity to others also enabled him to understand what others most desired in a particular conference and to follow a discussion carefully enough to pinpoint the essential issues. His ability to do this, which inspired Prime Minister Churchill to propose naming him Lord Root of the Matter, made him especially valuable at wartime conferences, when so many vital decisions had to be made in a short time. After the war, General Marshall expressed the opinion that Hopkins had personally shortened the conflict by two or three years. That Hopkins was able to perform such service while chronically ill serves as powerful testimony to his courage as well as his ability.

Bibliography

Adams, Henry H. *Harry Hopkins: A Biography*. New York: Putnam, 1977. A well-written biography that follows the outline of Sherwood's volume, cited below, but more successfully clarifies events. Primarily a narrative account that fails to discuss Hopkins' historical importance. Its most serious shortcoming is the failure to utilize the wealth of primary source material that was available.

Burns, James M. *Roosevelt: The Lion and the Fox*. New York: Harcourt Brace, and London: Secker and Warburg, 1956.

————. *Roosevelt: The Soldier of Freedom*. New York: Harcourt Brace, 1970; London: Weidenfeld and Nicolson, 1971. These two volumes by Burns constitute the best political biography of Franklin D. Roosevelt. Indispensable for understanding the political and personal circumstances in which Hopkins operated.

Charles, Searle F. *Minister of Relief: Harry Hopkins and the Depression*. Syracuse, N.Y.: Syracuse University Press, 1963. A brief but insightful account of Hopkins' administration of federal relief. Strong in outlining the problems Hopkins faced and in evaluating his success. Less detailed than one might expect in showing Hopkins' day-to-day activities and the larger context of New Deal policies.

Harvey, Philip. *Securing the Right to Employment: Social Welfare Policy and the Unemployed in the United States*. Princeton, N.J.: Princeton University Press, 1989. Looks at the contemporary relevance of Hopkins' programs of job creation.

Hopkins, Harry. *Spending to Save: The Complete Story of Relief*. New York: Norton, 1936. Written to explain and to justify federal relief policies during President Roosevelt's reelection campaign. Contrasts the accomplishments of Roosevelt's policies with the failures of Republican efforts under President Herbert Hoover. Still, the book provides valuable insights into how Hopkins perceived his job and his sense of the risks he took in performing it.

Kurzman, Paul A. *Harry Hopkins and the New Deal*. Fair Lawn, N.J.: Burdick, 1974. A brief account of Hopkins' role in unemployment relief, stressing how the policy of work relief rejected previous assumptions that the unemployed suffered from character defects that made them poor workers. Inadequately researched and less comprehensive than the Charles volume.

Leighton, Richard M., and Robert W. Coakley. *Global Logistics and Strategy*. 2 vols. Washington, D.C.: Office of the Chief of Military History, 1955. A comprehensive account of military supply activities during World War II. Although written to evaluate the army's administrative performance, the volumes contain numerous references to Hopkins and provide necessary detail for understanding his wartime role.

Schwartz, Bonnie Fox. *The Civil Works Administration, 1933-1934: The Business of Emergency Employment in the New Deal*. Princeton, N.J.: Princeton University Press, 1984. An excellent study of a brief experiment that goes beyond its subject's limited historical importance to explore fundamental issues of federal work relief. Shows the administrative development of the program, judiciously assesses its accomplishments, and compares it to the larger and more significant Works Progress Administration.

Sherwood, Robert E. *Roosevelt and Hopkins: An Intimate History*. Rev. ed. New York: Harper, 1950. A prizewinning study that remains a classic in the history of the Roosevelt era. Sherwood wrote shortly after Hopkins' death, had access to his voluminous papers, and was able to interview dozens of persons who had worked with Hopkins. Partially a memoir—Sherwood knew Hopkins personally—the book emphasizes the war period, follows a chronological format that occasionally confuses the reader, and breaks up the flow of Sherwood's prose with large extracts from documents. For its time, however, it was a triumph of scholarship and is the standard source for understanding Harry Hopkins.

George McJimsey

EDWARD HOPPER

Born: July 22, 1882; Nyack, New York
Died: May 15, 1967; New York, New York
Area of Achievement: Art
Contribution: Hopper is widely acknowledged as one of the most significant twentieth century American realist painters. His deceptively simple but striking images of the loneliness and alienation of city life have become icons of American popular culture.

Early Life

Edward Hopper was born in the small seafaring town of Nyack, New York, on July 22, 1882. Hopper's father, Garrett Henry Hopper, was of English and Dutch descent. His mother, Elizabeth Griffiths Smith, was English and Welsh. Garrett owned and operated a dry-goods store in Nyack. Both Hopper and his sister, Marion, were introduced to the arts during childhood by their mother, who encouraged them to draw. Rather shy and quiet as a child, Hopper developed a penchant for solitude that remained with him for the rest of his life. He also developed a love for the sea and the nautical life—later reflected in his work—and spent much of his boyhood at the Nyack shipyards.

Hopper attended a local private school for the primary grades. After graduating from Nyack Union High School in 1899, Hopper decided to become a fine artist. His parents, however, persuaded him to study commercial illustration—which, they believed, offered a more secure income than did painting—at the Correspondence School of Illustrating in New York City. Dissatisfied with illustration, Hopper transferred the following year to the New York School of Art, where he remained for the next six years studying under William Merritt Chase, Kenneth Hayes Miller, and Robert Henri. Henri, Hopper's most influential teacher at the New York School of Art, was a major proponent of the so-called ashcan school. This group of radical American artists sought to paint the harsher, more urban qualities of contemporary life, while retaining elements of the impressionist style. Hopper later stated that it took him years to "get over" Henri's influence.

Between 1906 and 1910, Hopper traveled to Europe, supporting his journeys through illustration, a profession he detested but relied upon during his years as a struggling artist. Introduced to the works of the French Impressionists, including Alfred Sis-

ley, Pierre-Auguste Renoir, and Camille Pissarro, Hopper experimented with the Impressionist style during this period. After returning to New York in 1910, however, his palette began to darken, and he painted in a style closer to that of his former teacher, Robert Henri, and other contemporary realists.

Hopper never returned to Europe. He spent the rest of his life in New York and New England. The years immediately following his return home were financially difficult, and Hopper once again supported himself as a commercial illustrator. He also began exhibiting his paintings. Although these early paintings met with little critical success, Hopper experienced much artistic growth as an artist during this period.

In 1915 Hopper was introduced to etching. By the early 1920's, his etchings contained several key elements characteristic of his more mature work: unusual vantage points, harshly lit scenes of city life at night, themes of alienation and loneliness, and the solitary female figure near a window.

Life's Work

The year 1924 marked a turning point in Hopper's professional life: He had his first one-man show. In 1923 Hopper had given up etching and taken up watercolors. What interested him about watercolors was not the creation of textures or the manipulation of the medium but the exploration and recording of light. In an uncharacteristically bold move, Hopper took some of his watercolors to Frank K. M. Rehn, an art dealer in New York, in 1924. Impressed by the works, Rehn not only became Hopper's first dealer but also arranged a one-man show in his gallery. All eleven watercolors that were shown, as well as five additional pieces, were sold. The show was also a critical success. Aside from illustrations and prints, Hopper had only sold two other paintings up to that point: *Sailing* (1912 or 1913), an oil, at the Armory Show in New York in 1913; and *The Mansard Roof* (1923), a watercolor, to the Brooklyn Museum in 1923. After 1924 Hopper had the financial freedom to give up illustrating and devote himself entirely to his art.

Hopper's personal life also changed in 1924 when he married Josephine Verstile Nivison, a fellow student from the New York School of Art with whom he had kept in touch over the years. Although they never had children, the couple was in-

separable for the next forty-three years. "Jo," as Hopper called her, promoted her husband's work, managed most of his affairs, and was his only female model after their marriage.

An oil painting called *House by the Railroad* (1925) marked the period of Hopper's mature style. In this work, Hopper resolved a number of important influences, from French Impressionism to contemporary American realism, to create a personal style. In this skillfully crafted composition, a mansard-roofed Victorian house stands alone against railroad tracks. The subtle diagonal of the tracks, one of the most enduring symbols of American art, endow the space with depth and power. By 1925, this solitary house recalled America's more innocent past—a simpler time that had been irrevocably engulfed by the complexities of modern urban life and rootlessness. Hopper had finally found his personal vision as well as some recognition. Henceforth, little of significance changed in his art or in his life. He and his wife continued to live at 3 Washington Square North in Manhattan and spent nearly every summer on the New England coast. Also, the subjects that Hopper explored were almost entirely variations on themes that had fascinated him in the past.

Throughout his lengthy career, however, Hopper did often shift his approach to investigating certain subjects. Although Hopper's art was not overtly political or social, he was profoundly fascinated by mood and human interaction. Many critics have observed a sense of loneliness, sometimes even boredom, in much of Hopper's work. Hopper's paintings, which appear to represent ordinary scenes of everyday life, are in fact intensely personal, complex narratives. He infused commonplace subjects with hints of eroticism, feelings of absence, and, late in life, the foreboding sense of loss and death.

In examining Hopper's figural works, it is significant that his wife was not only his only female model but also joined her husband in naming and fantasizing about the characters in his paintings. Thus she played a crucial role in developing his dramatic imagination and assisted him in transforming her image into one of his fantasy.

In conveying the mood of disenchantment, Hopper turned to dusk and imbued it with melancholy. *Cape Cod Evening* (1939) depicts a man beckoning to a distracted dog from the doorstep with a pensive-looking woman standing in front of the window. The couple appears disconnected: She is detached and in a world of her own, and he is attempting to communicate with a dog, which ignores him. In the painting *Summer Evening* (1947), the time of day also plays a symbolic role in the couple's relationship. The young couple represented in the painting appears absorbed in an unpleasant discussion while they lean against the wall of a porch with a bright electric light glaring above them. The woman's facial expression and stance is defensive; the man's left hand is on his chest, as if in protest. As in *Cape Cod Evening*, dusk symbolizes the melancholy of lost connection and desire, a frequent theme in Hopper's mature paintings.

Just as Hopper associated erotic despair to the melancholy of dusk, he also associated erotic tension with the night. This mood can be found in works ranging from an early etching, *Night on the El Train* (1918), to his later oil paintings *Night Windows* (1928), *Office at Night* (1940), and his masterpiece, *Nighthawks* (1942). In *Nighthawks*, three of Hopper's most significant themes—sexuality, solitude, and death—are linked. The man and woman, almost touching hands in the sinister atmosphere of the diner at night, are contrasted to the solitary man seated across the counter, suggesting sexuality as a means of easing the loneliness of night. Critics have pointed out that this painting in both setting and mood evokes a short story by Ernest Hemingway entitled "The Killers" (1927), a story Hopper admired. Yet it has been noted that the setting of the painting also conveys a certain innocence and vulnerability.

In exploring the theme of solitude, Hopper depicted scenes devoid of human presence in locations where people might be expected to congregate: a street, a park, or a room. In *Hotel Room* (1931), for example, a tall, slender, pensive woman sits on a bed, her eyes cast downward toward a piece of yellow paper in her hand. The stark vertical and diagonal bands of color and sharp contrast convey an intense nighttime drama with an open interpretation.

In his old age, Hopper, pessimistic by his own admission, increasingly focused on death, the ultimate escape. As his preoccupation with death increased, he made it the theme of some of his last paintings. At the age of eighty-three, he painted *Two Comedians* (1965), which he intended as a sort of personal farewell. As his wife later confirmed, the painting of the two figures on stage represented Hopper and his wife gracefully bowing out of their earthly existence. Hopper would die less than two years later, and his wife followed one year later.

Summary

A pioneer in borrowing subjects from everyday life to make high art, Edward Hopper is regarded as one of the greatest twentieth century representational American artists. He was a modernist with a distaste for abstraction, the dominant mode of modernism. Instead of following current trends, he used the force of his imagination to find his own psychologically and artistically powerful means of responding to contemporary life. Although the style he chose was traditional, his radical content expressed an alienation from much of modern life, ultimately making his work modern. Hopper's art continued to resonate for successive generations of artists; his genius and imagination provided deep insight and symbols that both inspired and challenged viewers.

The impact of Hopper's work has been felt not only in artistic circles but also in popular culture. Although Hopper detested commercial illustration, the artist's images, particularly *Nighthawks*, have found their way into advertisements, posters, T-shirts, and greeting cards. The universal appeal of Hopper's art and its powerful and disturbingly truthful portrayal of the American psyche have raised his works to the status of cultural icons that have remained relevant and accessible to a wide audience.

Bibliography

Berkow, Ita G. *Edward Hopper: A Modern Master.* New York: Smithmark, 1996. This thoughtful, eighty-page overview of the early development, maturity, and late works of Hopper contains full-color reproductions and index.

Goodrich, Lloyd. *Edward Hopper.* New York: Abrams, 1971. This informative chronological discussion of the artistic and personal development of Hopper includes statements by Hopper, a biographical note, full-color illustrations, and an index.

Iversen, Margaret. "In the Blind Field: Hopper and the Uncanny." *Art History* 21, no. 3 (September, 1998). Discusses the unsettling paintings of Hopper and the techniques used in creating them, including his use of shadows, darkness, the pale skin of his subjects, and their rigid postures.

Levin, Gail. *Edward Hopper.* New York: Crown, 1984. A respected authority on Hopper writes that Hopper's work demonstrates that realism is not merely a literal or photographic copy of what one sees but rather an interpretive rendering. Examples of all aspects of Hopper's career, including oil paintings, watercolors, drawings, etchings, and commercial illustrations, are reproduced and discussed in this volume. Contains a chronological biography, a list of principal exhibitions, and list of illustrations.

Lyons, Deborah, and Adam D. Weinberg. *Edward Hopper and the American Imagination.* New York: Norton, 1995. This volume contains fifty-nine of Hopper's most important works in full color as well as original works by fiction writers and poets who pay homage to, or make reference to, the ways in which Hopper represented America. The work celebrates the impact of Hopper's imagery on contemporary culture and is dedicated to a fuller understanding of Hopper's place in the American psyche.

Strand, Mark. *Hopper.* Hopewell, N.J.: Ecco Press, 1994. Strand, a poet, approaches Hopper's work with a fresh eye, exploring the aesthetic principles behind twenty-three of Hopper's most important works. He cites aesthetic reasons for Hopper's continuing ability to deeply move people in an America that has grown considerably more complex, both politically and socially, since the 1950's. Includes black-and-white illustrations.

Genevieve Slomski

KAREN HORNEY

Born: September 16, 1885; Eilbek, near Hamburg,
Germany
Died: December 4, 1952; New York, New York
Area of Achievement: Psychology
Contribution: Horney was a leading psychologist
who contributed to understanding the psychology of women, emphasized the role of sociocul-
tural factors in producing neurosis, and
developed a new noninstinctivist psychoanalytic
theory.

Early Life

Karen Clementina Theodora Danielsen was born in
Eilbek, Germany, on September 16, 1885. She was
the daughter of Berndt Henrik Wackels Danielsen,
a sea captain with the Hamburg-American Lines,
who was a Norwegian by birth but later became a
naturalized German, and Clothilde Marie Van Ron-
zelen Danielsen, of Dutch background. Clothilde,
or "Sonni," was sixteen years younger than her
husband when she married him. Danielsen had
four grown children from a previous marriage who
did not like his new wife and the new children that
came later. Berndt Danielsen, an intensely religious man, believed in a patriarchal family structure with women in subservient roles. His emotional presence in the home was felt by everyone.
Sonni was a religious freethinker, was more educated, liberal, and cultured than her husband, and
advocated a greater independence for women.

Karen Danielsen was born as Hamburg was
coming into the industrial age. Just ten years after
her birth, Hamburg Harbor became the third largest
international port in the world. Karen traveled with
her father and experienced life in different cultures,
which added to her understanding of human nature. She was an avid reader, and her life was greatly augmented and embellished by her own imagination. It may have been her imagination that led
her to envision a path for herself that was not common for any German female of her time. In her
imagination, she thought of herself as Doctor
Karen Danielsen, even though, in 1899, there was
not one university in Germany that admitted wom-
en. Germany was, however, changing quickly
enough to accommodate her. She attended the first
Gymnasium for Girls in Hamburg in 1900. In the
spring of 1906, Karen graduated from the Gymnasium, and on Easter Sunday of the same year, she

boarded a train bound for the University of
Freiburg to begin university life and her medical
studies. The University of Freiburg became the first
university in Germany to graduate a woman, even
though female professionalism was considered unnatural. On October 30, 1909, while still a medical
student, Karen married Oskar Horney, a student of
political science and economics. Oskar was that
rare man in Berlin who was able to tolerate ambition in a wife. They had three daughters, Brigitte
(born in 1911), Marianne (born in 1913), and
Renate (born in 1915). Karen received her M.D.
from the University of Berlin in 1915.

Life's Work

After passing her medical exams, Karen Horney
worked for the influential Berlin psychiatrist Hermann Oppenheim, as an assistant in his clinic. It
was there that she learned of psychoanalysis and
began analysis with Karl Abraham, the only
trained Freudian analyst in Berlin. Once Horney
had discovered psychoanalysis, it became the intellectual and emotional focal point of her life. Unfortunately, psychoanalysis was frowned upon by the
medical establishment. Understanding the stigma
associated with psychoanalysis, Horney continued
to specialize in psychiatry during the day, but after
hours she pursued Freudian psychoanalysis as a
patient and a student. She was decidedly cautious
about discussing Freud's ideas in and around Berlin and in the psychiatric clinics where she trained.
While writing her doctoral dissertation, she was
extremely careful not to discuss Freudian ideas.
Everything about her dissertation suggests that she
was a faithful and serious disciple of her psychiatric profession. Upon receiving her medical degree
in 1915, she was from that point on a psychoanalyst. She was no longer hesitant to discuss Freudian ideas. She became more controversial and even
more convinced of the therapeutic value of psychoanalysis. She took her first patients in psychoanalysis in 1919 and became actively involved with the
Berlin Psychoanalytic Clinic and Institute for the
next twelve years.

The relationship between Karen Horney and her
husband became strained and began deteriorating.
Their lifestyle had been prosperous, but with the
economic crisis of 1923, Oskar was forced to declare personal bankruptcy. He later developed a se-

vere neurological illness that caused a radical change in his personality. The Horneys separated in 1926 and were divorced in 1937. After her divorce, Karen channeled most of her energy into professional writing. Over the next six years, she was to publish a total of fourteen professional papers. The years between 1926 and 1932 were among the most productive of her life. Her friends, busy practice, and active involvement in institute affairs made Karen Horney a central figure in the beginnings of the Berlin Institute. Her most important contribution to the future of psychoanalysis grew out of her teaching role. She was a member of the education committee at the institute and a member of the education committee of the International Psychoanalytic Association beginning in 1928.

Horney made contributions to feminine psychology over a thirteen-year period from 1923 to 1936. She did not like the tenets of Freudian psychology, which described female development from a male-oriented, phallocentric viewpoint and made it appear that women had an inferior status. She put emphasis on interpersonal attitudes and on social influences in determining women's feelings, relations, and roles. Six of her papers on marital problems were published between 1927 and 1932.

In 1932, Horney accepted the position of associate director of the new Chicago Institute for Psychoanalysis, offered to her by its director, Franz Alexander, a former Berlin colleague. She looked forward to the United States and greater freedom of expression than she was allowed in Berlin. She remained in Chicago for only two years because she clashed with Alexander and the practices he was introducing at the institute. She had already begun to emphasize cultural factors in female psychology, which departed from Freud's original ideas. Alexander regarded her departure from orthodox Freudianism as revolutionary. In 1934, she moved to New York City, built an analytic practice, and taught at the New York Psychoanalytic Institute and the New School for Social Research. During this time, she produced her major theoretical works, *The Neurotic Personality of Our Time* (1937), which discussed the role of social practices in causing neuroses, and *New Ways in Psychoanalysis* (1939), spelling out her differences with Freudian theory. Horney had a strong personality, and she tended to resist all attempts at control and regulation. These traits, combined with her expressed desire that the New York Psychoanalytic

Institute should become a progressive institution instead of a rigid teaching institution, caused friction between her and the institute's president, Lawrence Kubie. He did not like her departure from Freud's original ideas, and in the end he and others required that she return to Freud or teach her ideas elsewhere. She was singled out as a troublemaker and demoted from instructor to lecturer.

Shortly after this demotion, in April of 1941, she and four other analysts offered their letters of resignation to the secretary of the New York Psychoanalytic Society. These five then started their own organization, the Association for the Advancement of Psychoanalysis. The first volume of the organization's journal, the *American Journal of Psychoanalysis*, listed fifteen "charter members" in New York and a handful in other cities. The organization offered thirteen courses for students and interested physicians. The curriculum was to train psychiatrists for clinical practice in psychoanalysis. Horney's third book, *Self-Analysis*, was published in 1942. After her break from the New York Psychoanalytic Institute and Freudian orthodoxy, she found herself in enormous demand as a psychoanalyst. *Self-Analysis* was ignored or reviled by every popular and psychoanalytic publication. Many did not review it at all, an indication of the power of the New York Psychoanalytic Society. Her last two books, *Our Inner Conflicts* (1945) and *Neurosis and Human Growth* (1950), were also not reviewed. Karen Horney's new alternative institution never gained official national recognition. Her work continued to be overlooked and minimized within psychoanalysis because of this split.

In her later years, Horney took to religion, especially Zen Buddhism. She met with D. T. Suzuki, the author of *Zen Buddhism and Its Influence on Japanese Culture* (1949). She, Suzuki, and some of her friends planned a trip to Japan to experience Zen life at first hand. The trip to Japan was to be one of the happiest adventures in Karen Horney's life. Suzuki led Horney and her friends for a month on a tour of some of the most important Zen monasteries in Japan. Within two months after her return, she suddenly became ill and was admitted to Columbia Presbyterian Hospital. She was diagnosed as having cancer of the gall bladder. During her second week in the hospital, her condition rapidly worsened. On December 4, 1952, Karen Horney died. She was buried in Ferncliff Cemetery in Ardsley, a quiet suburb of Westchester, north of New York City.

Summary

Karen Horney disputed the basic principles of Sigmund Freud, his psychoanalysis theories, and the therapeutic results of the application of these theories. She believed that neuroses and personality disorders were the results of environmental and social conditions, not of biological drives. She challenged Freud's libido theory and his theories of psychosexual development. She also contended that feminine psychology could not be understood unless the masculine bias in psychoanalysis and other fields were lifted. There was a clear need to formulate a masculine and feminine psychology to prepare the way for her whole-person philosophy. Horney was considered an early feminist, although she was not allied with any political movement. She fought for the equality of the sexes and praised women for being homemakers and mothers. She also stated that women should have the freedom to have careers. Since her death, many of her followers have continued to praise her theories and to apply them to new problems and conditions. Her ideas have entered the mainstream of psychology and some have been rediscovered and appropriated by other schools. Her theories regarding the causes and dynamics of neurosis and her later revision of Freud's theory of personality have remained influential. Her analysis of humankind allowed for a broader scope of development and coping than did the determinism of Freud. Her influence on American readers has been far-reaching.

Bibliography

Alexander, Franz, Samuel Eisenstein, and Martin Grotjohn, eds. "Karen Horney: The Cultural Emphasis." In *Psychoanalytic Pioneers*. New York: Basic, 1966. This work tells the histories of the pioneers in psychoanalysis and describes their work and its influence.

Kelman, Harold, ed. *Feminine Psychology*. London: Routledge, 1967; New York: Norton, 1993. A collection of Karen Horney's papers on women, many of which were previously unavailable in English.

Paris, Bernard J. "Introduction to Karen Horney." *American Journal of Psychoanalysis* 56, no. 2 (June, 1996). Discusses Horney's sometimes-controversial theories, which challenged Freud's ideas on female development.

———. *Karen Horney: A Psychoanalyst's Search for Self-Understanding*. New Haven, Conn.: Yale University Press, 1994. Examines Horney's emotional struggles and their effect on the development of her ideas. The author argues that her need for men led her to self-analysis, which, in turn, led her to her insights on human nature.

Quinn, Susan. *A Mind of Her Own: The Life of Karen Horney*. New York: Summit, 1987; London: Macmillan, 1988. The first full-scale biography of Karen Horney, this is a fine source that covers the full range of Horney's life and work.

Rubins, Jack L. *Karen Horney: Gentle Rebel of Psychoanalysis*. New York: Dial Press, 1978; London: Weidenfeld and Nicolson, 1979. Examines the life story of Karen Horney from the persecution of the Jewish psychoanalysts during the early Nazi period to the analytic classes in Chicago and New York.

Sayers, Janet. *Mothers of Psychoanalysis: Helene Deutsch, Karen Horney, Anna Freud, Melanie Klein*. New York: Norton, 1991. The mother-centered view of psychoanalysis constituted a direct challenge to the discipline, which was once patriarchal and phallocentric. The story of the revolution in psychoanalysis is told here through the biographies of its first women architects.

Westkott, Marcia. *The Feminist Legacy of Karen Horney*. New Haven, Conn.: Yale University Press, 1986; London: Yale University Press, 1988. Westkott presents a social-psychological theory that explains women's personality development as a consequence of growing up in a social setting in which they are devalued.

Darlene Mary Suarez

VLADIMIR HOROWITZ

Born: October 1, 1903; Berdichev, Russia (now Ukraine)
Died: November 5, 1989; New York, New York
Area of Achievement: Music
Contribution: Horowitz was the foremost twentieth century exemplar of the Russian school of Romantic pianists.

Early Life

The youngest of four children, Vladimir Horowitz was the son of Simeon and Sophie Horowitz, upper-middle-class Jews who, shortly after Vladimir's birth, moved to a comfortable apartment on Music Lane in Kiev, the capital of the Russian province of the Ukraine. Each of his siblings were musical and received their earliest training from their mother, but it was Vladimir who showed such precocious talent that his parents enrolled him in the Kiev Conservatory just before his eighth birthday. Over the next eight years he studied with Vladimir Puchalsky, Sergei Tarnowsky, and Felix Blumenfeld, mastering the techniques and much of the repertoire that would mark him as unique and controversial. Even his posture at the piano was unconventional. Slumping low on the bench and playing with low wrists and flat fingers, Horowitz defied the high upright carriage, elevated wrists, and curved fingers of standard piano pedagogy.

Although initially more interested in composition than performance, Horowitz began performing publicly in May, 1920, to help support his family. Hard times descended when Bolshevik revolutionaries confiscated his father's electrical supply business, evicted the Horowitzes from their home, and confiscated their bank accounts. During the next difficult year, Vladimir built a reputation by playing about one dozen concerts in Kharkov, Odessa, Tiflis, and Moscow. The tempo of his appearances increased until, in 1924 and 1925, he played as many as seventy recitals, twenty-three in Leningrad. His audiences had rarely heard octaves and scales played with greater velocity and clarity; moreover, such was his strength, belied by his frail Chopinesque build, that his thundering fortissimos often broke strings. Sometimes paid in food and clothing, he became increasingly celebrated in the Soviet Union as his life there became ever more intolerable. In 1925 he applied for and, to his amazement, received a visa to leave the country for six months, ostensibly to study with pianist Artur Schnabel in Germany. At the age of twenty-two and with his shoes stuffed with money to evade the restriction on leaving the country with more than $500, Horowitz departed the grim nation of his birth, not to return for sixty-one years.

Life's Work

The cultural vitality of Weimar Germany delighted its latest Russian émigré. Horowitz began playing recitals to mixed notices, as neither his flamboyant Russian Romanticism nor his Jewish identity endeared him to the Berlin critics. However, a performance of Peter Ilich Tchaikovsky's First Piano Concerto in Hamburg, an assignment accepted on less than one hour's notice, won over critics and audience alike, and Horowitz's reputation outside of Russia took root. He moved to Paris in March, 1926, where the French embraced his playing as well as his whimsical personality. From there he booked sixty-nine concerts throughout Western Europe during the next year. In early 1928 he began his conquest of the United States. In New York he met his hero and fellow expatriate Sergei Rachmaninoff and, in January, made his U.S. debut at Carnegie Hall under the direction of English conductor Sir Thomas Beecham, also making his U.S. premiere. Again the critics were of divided mind, but the audience adored him. Guided by Arthur Judson of Columbia Artists Management, Horowitz toured extensively in American small towns and large cities during the early 1930's. For the first time his fees were sufficient to allow him to indulge his fondness for fine automobiles (Studebakers) and elegant clothing—he eventually boasted a collection of six hundred bow ties.

In New York Horowitz met the legendary Italian conductor Arturo Toscanini, with whom he played Ludwig van Beethoven's Fifth Piano Concerto in March, 1933. Although intimidated by Toscanini's musical stature and cowed by his volcanic temper, Horowitz made bold to court his daughter Wanda, whom he married on December 21. In October, 1934, the couple presented Toscanini a granddaughter, Sonia, who was destined to a life of almost operatic drama and despair smothered between the two towering geniuses who were her father and grandfather and emotionally impaired by two quarrelsome and monumentally heedless parents.

In the Soviet Union, meanwhile, the Bolsheviks were seeing to the ruination of the Horowitz family. During the civil war, Horowitz's brother Jacob died in the ranks of the Red Army. Not long thereafter, his brother George committed suicide while under psychiatric care. Most devastating of all, his beloved mother Sophie died of peritonitis after incompetent treatment for appendicitis. Around the time of Sonia's birth, Horowitz's father visited Paris, promising a prompt return to the Soviet Union. Happy amid the splendors of the French capital and desperate to remain with his son, Simeon tore himself away to spare his new wife an unthinkable punishment if he failed to keep his bargain. Arrested anyway when he crossed the border into the Soviet Union, he was condemned to a gulag and died miserably several years later. Only Horowitz's sister Genya survived. Understandably, Horowitz never dared return to the Soviet Union during Genya's lifetime despite the assurances of Joseph Stalin's government that he could come and go freely.

The heartbreaking destruction of his family combined with the pressures of overwork, a stormy marriage, colitis, and professional frustrations to bring on the first of several breakdowns and retirements that punctuated the remainder of Horowitz's career. His mastery of the piano notwithstanding, he was always prone to the paralyzing self-doubts that left him incapacitated between 1936 and 1938. With a family to support and a censorious father-in-law to mollify, he struggled back to the stage in the fall of 1938 and performed until the fall of 1939, when World War II began.

The war prompted an exodus of some of Europe's finest musicians to the United States, among them Rachmaninoff, Toscanini, and Horowitz himself. In the United States, the musical public resumed its love affair with its favorite Russian; obligingly, he began every concert with his own version of "The National Anthem" and closed many with his transcription of John Philip Sousa's "Stars and Stripes Forever." On Easter Sunday, 1943, he played a war bond rally that raised over ten million dollars, the largest sum ever collected at a musical benefit to that date. Granted U.S. citizenship in 1942, he bought a large townhouse in New York City on Fifty-ninth Street near Central Park, which he appointed with great works of art bought as investments and which he later sold when he tired of their insurance costs.

After the war Horowitz kept up his demanding schedule of concerts and recordings, but as his career expanded, his marriage collapsed. Unsuited for marriage in almost every way, especially in his sexual preference for men, Horowitz shared with Wanda his intense ambition, avarice for fame and fortune, and single-minded musical perfectionism. Without her, moreover, he was nearly helpless in the day-to-day business of life. She was the tough, uncompromising mediator between the childlike Horowitz and the world outside their Manhattan townhouse. Nevertheless, in 1949 they separated and, except for brief reconciliations, lived apart until 1953, when Horowitz endured his second and longest breakdown. Under his wife's close ministrations, he gradually recovered, took a few students, and resumed recording. During this period, Horowitz's deeply troubled daughter was nearly killed in a traffic accident in Italy and was left with lasting brain injuries.

Thanks in part to electric shock treatments, Horowitz resumed concertizing on May 9, 1965. The night before tickets went on sale, more than 1,500 people lined up reverentially in a rain storm to insure their place in the hall. Next morning Wanda sent Horowitz's shivering devotees hot coffee, but when only three hundred made it to the ticket booth before the concert sold out, the remainder left distressed and irate. Half of the 2,700 available seats had been reserved for the press, record company executives, officials of the Steinway company (whose pianos he played exclusively), and others who had not stood patiently through the rain-drenched vigil. The concert was a gala affair, one of the most celebrated concerts in the history of Carnegie Hall, with, among others, Leonard Bernstein, Leopold Stokowski, Richard Tucker, Rudolf Nureyev, and Igor Stravinsky attending.

Tired and dispirited after four more years of concerts, including a television special in 1968, Horowitz retired yet a third time, his depression so grave that he eschewed the piano for eight months during 1973 and 1974. After more shock treatments, he resurfaced to play at Cleveland's Severance Hall on May 10, 1974. Then, in January, 1975, his daughter Sonia died, apparently by her own hand, in Geneva. In the aftermath, the sixty-nine-year-old pianist engaged in a whirlwind of concerts for which promoters paid him 80 percent of ticket sales plus expenses. Cantankerous about his accommodations and personal comforts, he had always been anxious before performances, arriving at the last moment and insisting that no one talk to him before going on stage. On occasion he had to

be nudged toward the piano. Regardless of the enormous fees, he often canceled dates at the last moment. The eccentric pianist Oscar Levant, himself notorious for the same maddening predilection, once quipped that he and Horowitz should have placed an advertisement in *Musical America*: "Vladimir Horowitz and Oscar Levant available for a limited number of cancellations."

By the mid-1980's, communism was crumbling in the enfeebled Soviet Union, and Horowitz, then over eighty, felt safe to go home. In 1986 blissful Russian audiences wept at the return of their prodigal son and sent him back to the United States buoyed and musically reawakened. He played and recorded steadily over the next three years until, on November 5, 1989, he suffered a fatal heart attack only four days after his last recording session. Ironically, his wife buried him not in Russia with his own family nor in the United States, which had adopted him so lovingly, but in the Toscanini family plot in Milan, Italy, near the father-in-law who had terrified him and close by his daughter, whose funeral fourteen years earlier he had neglected to attend.

Summary

Vladimir Horowitz was the last great representative of nineteenth century Romantic pianists and among the foremost interpreters of Franz Liszt, Robert Schuman, Frédéric Chopin, and Sergei Rachmaninoff. Small wonder, then, that he played the music of most Baroque and classical composers indifferently, Giuseppe Domenico Scarlatti and Muzio Clementi excepted. Obsessed with opera, he overcame the naturally percussive quality of the piano to wrest a singing tone from taut metal strings. This passionate lyricism came, in part, from his uncanny ability to combine pedaling and dynamics to coax unexpected colors from his instrument.

Contending that the music lay "behind the notes" and impressing his own personality on the score to produce unique interpretations, he avoided literal decoding of notes on a page and rarely played a piece twice in the same manner. To the horror of purists, he sometimes rewrote music, such as Modest Mussorgsky's Kartinki s vystavki (1874; Pictures at an Exhibition) and Franz Liszt's Hungarian Rhapsodies (1851-1886). He was, consequently, out of step with mainstream twentieth century pianists such as Arthur Rubinstein, Arthur Schnabel, and Rudolf Serkin, who stressed fidelity to the composer's intentions and aimed at interpretations consistent with historically authentic performance practices. While no one doubted Horowitz's astounding technical ability and his unmatched virtuosity (indeed, many regarded him as the greatest pianist of the century), influential critics such as Virgil Thomson, B. H. Haggin, and Irving Kolodin questioned his musical judgement, condemned his cavalier rejection of the composer's authority, and decried his self-conscious showmanship.

Bibliography

Dubal, David. *Evenings with Horowitz: An Intimate Portrait.* London: Robson, 1992; New York: Carol, 1994. Gossipy recollections of private moments and conversations by one of Horowitz's most uncritical admirers.

———. *Remembering Horowitz: 125 Pianists Recall a Legend.* New York: Schirmer, 1993; London: Prentice Hall, 1995. Mainly hagiographic but useful for understanding Horowitz's technique and his approach to turning notes into music.

Horowitz, J. "Letters from New York: The Transformation of Vladimir Horowitz." *Musical Quarterly* 74, no. 4 (Winter 1990). Focuses on the life and career of Horowitz.

Kennicott, P., and D. Regen. "Have Piano, Will Travel." *Musical America* 111, no. 6 (November-December, 1991). Focuses on Horowitz's nine-foot Steinway piano, which accompanied him on all his tours. Examines its current condition and why it is special.

Mach, Eleyse. *Great Pianists Speak for Themselves.* New York: Dodd Mead, 1980; London: Robson, 1981. Horowitz's observations on teaching, his retirements from public performance, and his views on the performer's relationship to the printed score and the composer's intentions.

Plaskin, Glenn. *Horowitz: A Biography of Vladimir Horowitz.* London: Macdonald, and New York: Morrow, 1983. A book-length biography of Horowitz's career to 1982. Written without Horowitz's cooperation and generally unsparing. Includes bibliography and discography.

Schonberg, Harold C. *Horowitz: His Life and Music.* New York and London: Simon and Schuster, 1992. Schonberg's book, the first book-length biography of Horowitz's entire career, is based on six weeks of recorded conversations with Horowitz. More sympathetic than Plaskin's account but less than Dubal's. An entirely satisfying biography is yet to be written. Includes bibliography and discography.

David Allen Duncan

GODFREY NEWBOLD HOUNSFIELD

Born: August 28, 1919; Newark, Nottinghamshire, England

Areas of Achievement: Engineering, invention, technology, and medicine

Contribution: Hounsfield invented computed tomography, a method of producing detailed images of internal body tissues that provides physicians with much more information than ordinary X rays can supply. Computed tomography pioneered the development of other advanced methods of medical imaging in the late twentieth century.

Early Life

Godfrey Newbold Hounsfield was born on August 28, 1919, in Newark, Nottinghamshire, and was raised on a farm in the nearby town of Sutton-on-Trent in a rural area of central England. His father, Thomas Hounsfield, had previously worked as an engineer in the steel industry but had turned to farming after World War I because of failing eyesight. Another relative, Leslie Hounsfield, was a noted inventor who had designed an automobile known as the Trojan in 1910. As the youngest of five children, Hounsfield was often left out of the activities of his older siblings. He amused himself by figuring out how his father's farm equipment worked and soon revealed a talent for engineering. As an adolescent, he built phonographs, radio sets, and gliders.

Hounsfield attended the Magnus Grammar School in Newark, where he excelled in science and mathematics. Although he did not do well enough in other subjects to attend a university, he studied radio communications at City and Guilds College in London. He also worked as a draftsman for a local builder and joined the Voluntary Reserve of the Royal Air Force. When World War II broke out in 1939, Hounsfield was called to active duty. Because of his engineering skills, he was assigned to the military's radar school. Radar, a newly developed technology, was a military secret and vital to the British war effort. Hounsfield did so well as a student at this school that he was soon made an instructor. When the war ended in 1945, he was awarded a Certificate of Merit from the Royal Air Force.

After leaving the military in 1946, Hounsfield won a government grant to attend Faraday House Electrical Engineering College in London, where he studied electrical and mechanical engineering. Upon graduating in 1951, Hounsfield began working for Electrical and Musical Instruments Limited (EMI), where he spent the rest of his professional life.

Life's Work

Because of his experience in the military, Hounsfield began his career at EMI by working on radar systems. He later started working on computer design. From 1958 to 1959, he led a design team that developed the EMIDEC 1100, the first large British computer to be built with transistors instead of vacuum tubes. Hounsfield's most important contribution to this project was the use of small magnetic cores within the computer that enabled the transistors to work much more quickly.

Hounsfield next began working on computer memory systems. He developed a method of storing information on large, thin, grooved sheets of copper coated with a magnetic substance. Although Hounsfield was able to prove that this technique was feasible, EMI abandoned the idea as unprofitable. EMI allowed Hounsfield to submit several ideas for his next project. Eventually it was agreed that he would work on the problem of pattern recognition. Hounsfield's assignment was to develop methods that would allow machines to correctly interpret information presented in the form of characters, such as the letters of the alphabet.

In 1967, during one of the long walks through the countryside that made up his favorite form of recreation, Hounsfield began thinking of ways to combine his experience with radar, computers, and pattern recognition to develop a new method of using X rays for medical diagnosis. Traditional X-ray photography produced excellent images of bones and good images of air-filled organs such as the lungs but much less information about other tissues.

In the 1920's and 1930's, a method known as tomography was developed that allowed X rays to produce a sharply focused image of a thin section of a patient's body while blurring the image of the tissues surrounding it. This was done by moving the source of the X rays and the photographic film in opposite directions parallel to the patient's body. Tomography revealed more information about in-

ternal organs than ordinary X-ray images, but Hounsfield realized that it could be greatly improved. His basic idea was to project X rays through a patient's body to a detector. The X-ray source and the detector would then be moved to new positions, and the process would be repeated several times. The data recorded by the detector would then be processed by a computer to produce an image. EMI patented the idea in 1968 and made arrangements with the National Health Service of the British Department of Health and Social Security for Hounsfield to develop a working model. The National Health Service was particularly interested in producing images of the brain, which conventional X-ray photography did very poorly.

Although Hounsfield independently conceived of this method of producing images, which came to be known as computed tomography (CT, also known as the CAT scan), previous researchers had envisioned similar systems. The American physician William Oldendorf built a small model of such a device in 1960 but lacked the computers needed to process the data it produced. The South

African-born American physicist Allan Cormack had worked on the mathematical theory of a similar system in the 1950's and 1960's but had failed to interest physicians in the possibilities of such a device.

Hounsfield's engineering skills, combined with financial support from EMI and the National Health Service, allowed him to build a practical device that could be used on real patients. Although Oldendorf and Cormack would later be honored for their work, Hounsfield is generally considered to be the true inventor of CT. His earliest experiments involved a source of gamma rays and a detector placed on opposite sides of a plastic box filled with water and pieces of metal and plastic. The box, known as a "phantom," represented a patient's body. The source and the detector were moved sideways, one-eighth of an inch at a time, across the phantom. The intensity of the gamma rays after they passed through the phantom was recorded at each position. The phantom was then rotated 1 degree, and the process was repeated. After the phantom had been rotated 180 degrees, the resulting measurements were processed by a computer to produce an image. The entire process took nine days of measurements and more than two hours of computer time. The success of this slow but inexpensive demonstration allowed Hounsfield to move on to more powerful X rays instead of gamma rays, reducing the measurement time to nine hours.

Instead of phantoms, Hounsfield worked with tissues from freshly slaughtered animals and preserved samples of human tissue. In 1971 a prototype CT machine was installed in Atkinson Morley's Hospital in Wimbledon, a suburb of London. The first patient to undergo CT was a woman with a suspected brain tumor. After fifteen hours of taking measurements and two days of processing the information, an image of the patient's brain was produced with the location of the tumor clearly visible, allowing surgeons to remove it. The dramatic success of the first clinical use of CT encouraged EMI to announce the availability of the technology in 1972. Hospitals in the United Kingdom and the United States soon began installing CT devices despite the fact that each machine cost about $500,000.

Over the next few years, Hounsfield continued to work on improvements in CT. In addition to greatly reducing the time needed to produce an image, changes in the way that X-ray sources and detectors moved allowed an image of a patient's entire body to be produced. By 1977 more than one thousand CT units had been installed around the world.

Hounsfield was named head of medical systems at EMI in 1972. He continued to research medical imaging systems for the company, turning his attention to a method known as nuclear magnetic resonance, which used magnetism instead of X rays. Hounsfield was promoted to chief staff scientist in 1976, senior staff scientist in 1977, and consultant to laboratories in 1986. Among the many honors awarded to Hounsfield for his invention were the MacRobert Award, the highest British engineering award, in 1972, and the Lasker Award, a prestigious American award for medical research, which he shared with Oldendorf in 1975. Hounsfield shared the Nobel Prize in Physiology or Medicine with Cormack in 1979 and was knighted in 1981.

Summary

The invention of CT was the most important advance in the use of X rays for medical imaging since they were first discovered by the German physicist Wilhelm Conrad Röntgen in 1895. Initially controversial because of the expense involved, CT soon became accepted as a method of diagnosis. The ability of CT to produce detailed images of body tissues made it a valuable tool in the diagnosis of brain diseases, which formerly required difficult and dangerous exploratory surgery. CT proved to be useful in producing images of other soft organs, such as the liver, heart, and kidneys. CT has also been used to produce images of the interiors of ancient artifacts and fossils.

CT went through numerous improvements after Hounsfield's initial demonstration. The time required to produce an image was reduced from several hours to a few minutes. By 1985, some CT units could produce an image in less than .1 second, allowing images to be made of the heart between beats. In 1989, spiral CT was introduced, producing images that could be viewed from any angle. The success of Hounsfield's invention paved the way for the development of other methods of medical imaging, including magnetic resonance imaging (MRI) and positron emission tomography (PET). Although MRI and PET did not use X rays, they both used computers to translate complex data into visible images in ways similar to CT.

Bibliography

Fullerton, Gary D., and James A. Zagzebski, eds. *Medical Physics of CT and Ultrasound: Tissue Imaging and Characterization.* New York: American Institute of Physics, 1980. Two sections of this book are of particular interest. William R. Hendee provides a clear account of the invention of CT and how the technology rapidly advanced in the 1970's in "History of Computed Tomography." The history of the theory behind CT is described in "Development of the CT Concept" by Allan Cormack, who shared a Nobel Prize with Hounsfield in 1979.

Hounsfield, Godfrey N. "Computed Medical Imaging." *Science* 210 (October 3, 1980): 22-28. This transcription of Hounsfield's Nobel Prize lecture includes a description of his early experiments with CT and several photographs of the equipment he used and the results he obtained.

Kevles, Bettyann Holtzmann. *Naked to the Bone: Medical Imaging in the Twentieth Century.* New Brunswick, N.J.: Rutgers University Press, 1997. Kevles provides a detailed history of the technology used to produce images of the interior of the human body. Included in the chapter "The Perfect Slice: The Story of CT Scanning" is an extensive discussion of Hounsfield's contributions. The book also contains a large bibliography and a useful time line.

Sochurek, Howard. *Medicine's New Vision.* Easton, Pa.: Mack, 1988. This book is intended for a general audience and includes a chapter called "Computed Tomography," which discusses the advances made in CT technology from the beginning to the 1980's. Includes numerous colorful photographs illustrating the uses of CT.

Susskind, Charles. "The Invention of Computed Tomography." In *History of Technology Sixth Annual Volume.* Edited by A. Rupert Hall and Norman Smith. London: Mansell, 1981. This essay is a lengthy and extremely detailed account of Hounsfield's invention of CT. Includes extensive information on the inventor, the company he worked for, the device itself, and its influence on the practice of medicine.

Rose Secrest

FÉLIX HOUPHOUËT-BOIGNY

Born: October 18, 1905; Yamoussoukro, Ivory
Coast
Died: December 7, 1993; Yamoussoukro, Ivory
Coast
Areas of Achievement: Government and politics
Contribution: Houphouët-Boigny began serving as
President of the Ivory Coast in 1960. Through
his guidance and close ties with France, the Ivo-
ry Coast became one of the most economically
and politically stable nations of Africa.

Early Life

Félix Houphouët-Boigny, often known as *"le
vieux"* ("the old man"), was born in Yamoussoukro village in 1905. He is a member of the Akwe
clan of the Baule ethnic group. His father and his
uncle were cantonal chiefs, and he himself was
named chief at the age of five, when his father
died. His mother served as chief regent. He married a woman whose mother's side descended from
the Agni royalty of Ghana. Houphouët-Boigny attended primary school at Yamoussoukro village
and at Bingeville School in the Ivory Coast. The
relative wealth and influence of his cocoa-planting
family allowed him to be enrolled as a high school
student at the École Normale William Ponty, on
Gore Island, in Dakar, Senegal. From there he entered the Dakar École de Médecine, from which
he received his African Medical diploma in 1925.
Thereafter, until 1940, he served as a doctor at
several posts within the Ivory Coast. Although little has been written about his younger years,
Houphouët-Boigny's experience as a son of a
wealthy farmer who faced many obstacles posed
by colonialism—discrimination, forced labor, and
taxation without representation—and the fact that
he was one of the few highly educated Ivory Coast
natives who understood the workings as well as
the vulnerability of the French colonial system explain his rise to prominence in the colony and in
the French metropolis itself. Houphouët-Boigny
was so determined to play a role in the colonial
system that he refused at first to become chief of
the Akwe in 1932, offering the position to his
younger brother (who died in 1939).

In December, 1940, Houphouët-Boigny could no
longer decline his chiefly calling following the
death of his uncle, chief of the Akwe: He assumed
the position of Chef de Canton of his clan. Concerned about the plight of the farmers even before

becoming Chef de Canton, Houphouët-Boigny began organizing the Abengorou African cocoa and
coffee farmers in 1933. In 1940, he not only became chief but also inherited, as is traditional
among the matrilineal Baule, a large tract of land
following the death of his uncle. In his capacity as
chief, the then-celebrated medical doctor organized
the Association of Traditional Chiefs to prevent the
erosion of African chiefly powers, prestige, and social status. "Short and stocky," as one writer described his physical stature, Houphouët-Boigny
availed himself of all opportunities that the French
colonial system offered. Houphouët-Boigny never
disguised his admiration for and love of French
civilization and traditions, something his adversaries used against him, or neglected the people he
chose to represent. As he entered the decade of the
1940's, Houphouët-Boigny's activities had already
earned for him from the French the label of "radical," while many Africans considered him to be either a conservative or a reactionary African politician on account of his ties to the French
establishment and his love for France.

Life's Work

During the 1944-1945 period, Houphouët-Boigny
launched in earnest his career as a politician and
statesman who would take very popular positions
at home but quite often controversial ones in the
metropolis and in colonial and independent Africa.
In the end, however, he remained the winner on all
fronts. In 1944, for example, he was elected president of the Syndicat Agricole Africain (SAA), an
African trade union that he had founded. In this capacity, he demanded fair prices for the crops of the
African farmers, treatment equal to that of their
white counterparts in the colony, and exemption
from forced labor for all cocoa and coffee planters.
His effort paid off, as the price of African farm
products rose dramatically.

In October, 1945, Houphouët-Boigny won a
seat on the first French Constituent Assembly, a
victory that took him to Paris. Subsequently, at a
Bamako Conference of October, 1946, attended
by more than eight hundred delegates from
French-speaking Africa, Houphouët-Boigny inspired the establishment of the interterritorial Ras-
semblement Démocratique Africain (RDA), of
which he became the first president, represented in
the Ivory Coast by the Parti Démocratique de la

Côte d'Ivoire (PDCI), a political organization he had founded the previous year.

As a candidate of his party for the French National Assembly in 1946, Houphouët-Boigny won a landslide victory that propelled him deeper into French domestic and overseas politics for the next fourteen years. He subsequently accepted a position in the French cabinet from 1956 to 1958. From his new political "pulpit," Houphouët-Boigny fought for his platform: the abolition of forced labor, an end of the *indigénat*, fair prices for African farmers, a measure of autonomy for the colonies, and African political participation. In spite of his Catholic upbringing and his conservative views, Houphouët-Boigny did not hesitate to forge an alliance with the leftist blocks in France, particularly the French Communist Party. From his position as a minister in the cabinet and his influence as a member of the National Assembly, and using his diplomatic skills, Houphouët-Boigny won victory after victory on almost all fronts: Forced labor was abolished without debate in April, 1946 (by a law known as the Houphouët-Boigny Law); the infamous dual college was eliminated by the Loi-Cadre (Enabling Act) in 1956; and the Framework Law of 1957 gave the colonies a large measure of autonomy. These victories were extremely significant to the Africans. While the Loi-Cadre created and strengthened the power of territorial assemblies, created executive councils, instituted universal suffrage, and stressed the Africanization of the bureaucracy and economic development programs for each one of the colonies as well as for the region, the Framework Law ensured that French Africa would remain within the French Community but with complete autonomy. It promised increased French assistance, but it also noted that Africans could opt to become separate independent states.

A nagging political problem, however, forced Houphouët-Boigny to repudiate some of his organized political support. His alliance with the communists, who had become a permanent opposition to the government, and the radically perceived activities of the PDCI in the colony brought about severe reprisals from the colonial state against outspoken PDCI leaders. The situation became so threatening to Houphouët-Boigny and to the very survival of his own party that, in 1950, he declared a split with the French Communist Party and instead allied himself with centrist elements in France and cooperated with the establishment in the Ivory Coast. Subsequently, he took complete

control of the PDCI and embarked upon a campaign for economic self-sufficiency for the Ivory Coast, even if this move meant a break with his fellow African leaders. Meanwhile, his political career was reaching new plateaus. In 1956, he was elected the first Mayor of Abidjan and was appointed to serve as a minister in the French cabinet. In 1957, he was reelected to the French National Assembly. During the 1957-1958 period, he became President of the Grand Council of French West Africa (the "legislative" body of the artificial Federation of West Africa created by the French government) as well as President of the Territorial Assembly of the Ivory Coast. When the French government gave a choice to the colonies to become either independent states or republics within the French Community, in 1958, Houphouët-Boigny, by then Charles de Gaulle's most trusted adviser on African affairs, convinced his people at home to remain within the community, fearing the economic consequences of a rupture with the French government and the mother country. As a necessary move, he resigned his position as minister of state in the French cabinet in Paris and became premier of the new Republic of the Ivory Coast on May 1, 1959.

Realizing, however, that by remaining within the French Community the potentially vast resources of his country would have to be shared with other members of the community and the poorer French West African Federation states such as Senegal and Mali, and sensitive to the criticism that he was willing to sacrifice the total independence of his people to safeguard his love and admiration for France and her culture, Houphouët-Boigny, to the dismay of the French, made an about-face and led his country to independence on August 7, 1960. In November of that year, without opposition, Houphouët-Boigny was elected president of the new republic.

As president, Houphouët-Boigny embarked upon achieving four major objectives: assurance of continued financial and technical assistance from France; accelerated economic growth for his country as a national priority; assurance of a prominent role for his country and himself within the Francophone African states; and the creation of, at all cost, political "stability" at home. The attainment of the first objective would rely on close cooperation with France on the diplomatic, cultural, and the economic front. The second would muster the country's assets to achieve self-sufficiency in food production, to explore natural resources (timber, coffee, cocoa), to improve the country's infrastructure and industry through the pursuit of liberal Western investments and to adopt a slow Africanization process within the bureaucracy. The last would be achieved through Houphouët-Boigny's role as mediator and spokesman of the new Francophone states, while becoming the promoter of the concept of loose federations such as the Conseil d'Entente, which had brought together, in 1959, several African nations in an effort somehow to coordinate foreign policy and defense and facilitate trade through a customs union and joint economic ventures. To this end, Houphouët-Boigny was instrumental in convening meetings of the twelve Francophone states, including Madagascar, at Abidjan and Brazzaville in 1960 and 1961 respectively. It was from these meetings that the establishment of the Organisation Africaine et Malgache de Coopération Économique and the Union Africaine et Malgache came about.

Houphouët-Boigny then tackled his fourth objective (political stability at home) by declaring his country a single-party state under the banner of the PDCI. As a consequence of this act, he did not hesitate to imprison or coopt his opponents, arguing that parties (except the PDCI), as manifested in the republic, would always be ethnically based and thus prove themselves detrimental to national unity. In 1963, for example, he claimed to have uncovered an attempted coup, which was followed by the arrest of nearly two hundred people, including cabinet ministers, all of whom were secretly tried at Yamoussoukro and given long jail sentences or sentenced to death. Three years later, Houphouët-Boigny lessened the penalties to be paid by those involved. He cushioned his continued mild repressive measures against his opponents by preventing the rise to prominence of any politician who could challenge his authority or be perceived as the most likely to succeed to the presidency.

A combination of an authoritarian regime, the cultivation of a fatherly image, and the Ivory Coast's "economic miracle" guaranteed the unopposed and "overwhelming" reelection of the president in 1965, 1970, 1975, 1980, and 1985. In the 1965 reelection, he is reported to have captured 99.99 percent of the vote. In later years, however, the voluntary departures from power of Julius Nyerere, Ahmadou Ahidjo, and Léopold Senghor fueled speculation among the political experts that Houphouët-Boigny would soon follow their example.

Paradoxically, notwithstanding an active public life, details of Houphouët-Boigny's private life remain sketchy at best. He is said to have had simultaneously at least three wives and to have fathered several children. His fortune was unknown, although in 1983 he admitted to having billions of francs in a Swiss bank as well as in Ivory Coast financial institutions. He owned property in France and in the country. He was harshly criticized for his extravagant lifestyle, particularly at his birthplace, Yamoussoukro, which was declared the country's new capital by the National Assembly in March, 1983. The president was quick to point out to his critics that he was creating a place for people to live (there are 100,000 people in the new capital today) and initiating a history and a tradition for his young motherland. Overall, therefore, it seems that Houphouët-Boigny was almost impervious to criticism of his public or private life.

Nevertheless, he did agree to hold multi-party elections in 1990. He was re-elected to a seventh term and died in office in 1993.

Summary

The Ivory Coast is one of the most economically developed countries in Africa. The rate of its economic growth was estimated at an average of 7 percent per year during the 1970's. In spite of the fact that its natural resources, particularly mineral deposits, are not as abundant there as in other African countries (although oil has been discovered lately), the per capita income of the citizens is close to fifteen hundred dollars—therefore much higher than that of most Sub-Saharan Africans. Abidjan has been called the Paris of Africa, while industrial growth has increased fourfold during the past thirty years. This indisputable economic development in the country has resulted from the vision and the determination of its leader, Félix Houphouët-Boigny. Sarcastically, however, some analysts have called the Ivory Coast's economic progress "growth without development" and have, instead, given all credit to France. Understandably, Houphouët-Boigny was harshly criticized for his close ties to France and labeled by "radicals" as "the French African puppet." Houphouët-Boigny, however, ignored every criticism and continued to court French loans, French technicians, and French businessmen, while welcoming French citizens and Western entrepreneurs who wish to invest or live in the Ivory Coast. Although he maintained lukewarm relations with the communist world, Houphouët-Boigny preferred to deal with the West and coordinated most of the country's foreign policy with France. As the "dean" (doyen) of the Francophone leaders, Houphouët-Boigny, the elder statesman, enjoyed great respect from his Francophone colleagues and other African statesmen, notwithstanding their honest disagreement about the best methods and strategies to improve Africa's overall conditions.

Houphouët-Boigny's behind-the-scenes diplomacy, his unending meetings (some secret) to resolve some of Africa's most pressing problems, such as the Congo crisis of the 1960's and the Angolan tragedy following independence, and the emphasis he put on resolving South Africa's racial conflict peacefully demonstrated the extent of his involvement in international affairs and his determination to follow his own instincts, irrespective of resulting criticism. Thus, he did not hesitate to meet with South African leaders and to maintain trade relations with the apartheid regime. Evidently, his unpopular positions won for him praise in the West but only scorn from intellectuals in many African capitals and abroad. It is clear, nevertheless, that, although not a charismatic leader, Houphouët-Boigny remained a national hero for his countrymen—a man who led their country to independence and who gave it a prominent place on the world map.

Bibliography

Italiaander, Rolf. *The New Leaders of Africa.* Translated by James McGovern. Englewood Cliffs, N.J.: Prentice-Hall, 1961. Italiaander characterizes Houphouët-Boigny in this early and incomplete study of emerging African leaders as "a politician and statesman who talks a lot about democracy but, like many of the new leaders in Africa, a rather autocratic ruler."

Jackson, Robert H., and Carl G. Rosberg. *Personal Rule in Black Africa: Prince, Autocrat, Prophet, Tyrant.* Berkeley: University of California Press, 1982. Jackson and Rosberg demonstrate their excellent analytical skills in African politics and portray Houphouët-Boigny as an efficient autocrat able to deliver, without the use of political "brokers," the "goods" that placate and coopt his opponents and generate popular support.

Melady, Thomas P. *Profiles of African Leaders.* New York: Macmillan, 1961. In this critical biographical survey of the African leaders of the time, Melady takes a positive view of Houphouët-Boigny.

Mundt, Robert. *Historical Dictionary of the Ivory Coast (Côte d'Ivoire).* 2d ed. Lanham, Md.: Scarecrow Press, 1995. This is an excellent and comprehensive survey of the Ivory Coast and provides an objective portrait of the country's leader.

Siriex, Paul-Henri. *Félix Houphouët-Boigny: L'Homme de la paix.* Paris: Seghers, 1975. Siriex presents an extremely sympathetic image of Houphouët-Boigny in his role as a political stabilizer and as an international peacemaker.

Ungar, Sanford. *Africa: The People and Politics of an Emerging Continent.* Rev. ed. New York: Simon and Schuster, 1986. This volume deals with several African states and their leaders and is therefore a useful overview of the Ivory Coast.

Widner, Jennifer. "Two Leadership Styles and Patterns of Political Liberalization." *African Studies Review* 37, no. 1 (April, 1994). A comparison of the leadership styles of Houphouët-Boigny and Kenya's Daniel Arap Moi.

Woods, Dwayne. "The Politicization of Teachers' Associations in the Cote d'Ivoire." *Afri-*

can Studies Review 39, no. 3 (1996). Discusses the role played by teachers and their unions in the fall of Houphouët-Boigny's single-party government.

Woronoff, Jon. *West African Wager: Houphouet versus Nkrumah.* Metuchen, N.J.: Scarecrow Press, 1972. A comparative study of Ghana and the Ivory Coast and their two leaders. The author avoids taking sides but holds the view that, on balance, the winner was Houphouët-Boigny.

Zolberg, Aristide R. *One-Party Government in the Ivory Coast.* Rev. ed. Princeton, N.J.: Princeton University Press, 1969. An essential source of information on the politics of the Ivory Coast and the personal rule of Houphouët-Boigny.

Mario Azevedo

BERNARDO ALBERTO HOUSSAY

Born: April 10, 1887; Buenos Aires, Argentina
Died: September 21, 1971; Buenos Aires, Argentina
Areas of Achievement: Physiology, biology, and medicine
Contribution: Houssay was the first South American to receive the Nobel Prize in Physiology or Medicine. He was awarded the prize in 1947 for his discovery of the relation between the pancreas and the pituitary gland. This important work paved the way for further studies of diabetes.

Early Life

Born on April 10, 1887, in Buenos Aires, Bernardo Alberto Houssay was the son of Alberto Houssay and Clara Laffont. His parents had emigrated to Argentina from France in 1870, and they were married in 1879. Alberto Houssay was a practicing attorney, who also taught literature at the National College of Buenos Aires. He was a well-read man with a love of the classics and a remarkable memory. One of eight children (four girls and four boys), Bernardo was something of a prodigy, completing his secondary school studies by the age of thirteen. Because of his age (and perhaps because his three older brothers had been educated in Europe), it was necessary for Bernardo to obtain special permission from the principal to enter the Colegio Britanico in Buenos Aires. It was at this time that Bernardo announced to his father his intention to pay all of his own expenses. Bernardo had obtained a post at the dispensary of a hospital and throughout his college career worked as a pharmacist in various hospital clinics. In this way, he became accustomed to the austere lifestyle that he practiced the rest of his life. In 1904, at the age of seventeen, he received his degree in pharmacy. In 1907, he was appointed to the faculty of medicine at the University of Buenos Aires as a laboratory assistant in physiology. He was awarded a doctorate in medicine in 1910 and became certified as a physician in 1911. Initially choosing internal medicine as his field of study, he entered the medical department at Alvear Hospital in Buenos Aires. He became chief physician of a ward at the hospital in 1913. Houssay later resigned this post to dedicate his full attention to physiological research.

Houssay was a severe and exacting taskmaster who demanded more of himself than of others. Physically he was a small man, measuring five-feet, nine-inches tall and weighing less than 150 pounds. He spoke French and English fluently.

Houssay was married to Maria Angelica Catan, herself a doctor of chemistry, on December 22, 1920. The couple had three sons, Alberto Bernardo, Hector Emilio José, and Raul Horacio, all of whom went on to earn medical degrees of their own. Maria, who, in Houssay's words, had always been "an efficient and unostentatious helpmate," died on March 12, 1962.

Life's Work

Until 1915, Houssay headed the physiology section at the University of Buenos Aires, when he was named laboratory chief of the Bacteriological Institute of the National Department of Hygiene. From 1910 to 1919, Houssay, a professor of physiology on the faculty of agronomy and veterinary medicine, taught classes at the University of Buenos Aires. In 1919, Houssay was given the chair of physiology on the faculty of medicine at the university. He held this post until his ouster, for political reasons, in 1943. During this period, Houssay established a laboratory for the study of biological chemistry, physiology, biochemistry, pharmacology, and experimental medicine. The laboratory soon became renowned in scientific circles, attracting students and scientists from around the world.

Houssay held a number of other posts, including, at the university, counselor of the faculty of medicine, vice dean, and member of the superior council of the university as well as being a member of the National Commission on Climatology and Mineral Waters and vice president of the Permanent Pharmacopoeia Commission.

Although Houssay did make important discoveries in his experiments on snake and spider venoms, his best-known work was with the pituitary gland. He performed a series of experiments on this gland from 1924 to 1937. He found that removing the anterior lobe of the pituitary made laboratory animals more sensitive to insulin and that subsequently adding anterior pituitary extract decreased insulin sensitivity. Through this series of tests, he showed that giving doses of the extract to normal animals could produce diabetes. Because diabetes is caused by a failure of the isles of Langerhans in the pancreas to produce enough insulin, Houssay's discovery would prove crucial in the treatment of the once-fatal disease.

Houssay then revealed the relationships of many other organs in the body to the pituitary gland. He discovered that insulin, rather than effecting the oxidation of sugar, merely acted against chemicals from the pituitary or adrenal glands that block the effective burning of oxygen.

In 1943, Houssay was one of 150 educators who were dismissed from their posts by Argentina's dictator Juan Domingo Perón for signing a petition opposing Argentina's relationship with Nazi Germany and demanding a return to constitutional government in Argentina as well as solidarity with other American nations. Perón's actions brought a public outcry and offers of university positions for Houssay from around the world. Not wishing to abandon his country in what he saw as its hour of need, Houssay remained in Buenos Aires and helped to establish the privately financed Institute of Biology and Experimental Medicine, of which he became the director. In 1945, Perón's actions were declared illegal, and Houssay was reinstated at the University of Buenos Aires, only to be asked to retire in 1946 for what were widely believed to be political reasons. Houssay's popularity was evidenced by a subsequent boycott of physiology classes by many students and the resignations of many staff members of various Argentine universities. In 1955, Perón was exiled, and Houssay was reinstated at the university by the revolutionary government.

Physiologie humaine (1950; *Human Physiology,* 1955) was the first Latin American scientific work to be translated into English for worldwide distribution; it was hailed as the finest physiology text then written. Houssay published many books dealing with scientific and educational topics, his first being a doctoral thesis in 1916. More than fifty papers on medical studies of snake, spider, and scorpion venoms have appeared in his name, and more than five hundred scientific papers and several books containing his discoveries, including those regarding diabetes, have been published.

Houssay received many scientific honors during his life, including election to the National Academy of Sciences in Buenos Aires in 1937, receipt of the Charles Mickle Fellowship of Toronto in 1945, the Banting Medal of the American Diabetes Association in 1946, the research award of the American Pharmaceutical Manufacturers Association in 1947, and the Baly Medal in 1947 from the Royal College of Physicians of London. He held honorary doctorates in medicine from, among others, the

Universities of Paris, Montreal, Lyons, and Geneva. He held honorary doctorates in science from such universities as Harvard, São Paulo, and Oxford. He was named Hitchcock professor of physiology at the University of California, and he was one of the founders and onetime president of the Argentine Association for the Advancement of Science. He was awarded the Nobel Prize in Physiology or Medicine for his discovery of the part played by the hormone produced by the anterior lobe of the pituitary gland in the metabolism of sugar. He shared the prize with Carl F. Cori and Gerty T. Cori, whose works revealed the mechanism by which the hormone produces the above effect.

Houssay died on September 21, 1971, at the age of eighty-four.

Summary

Bernardo Alberto Houssay's discoveries regarding diabetes mellitus were a turning point in the treatment of the disease. His conclusions regarding the oxidation of sugar provided the key to possible insulin substitutes in the case of depleted supplies in the human body. These experiments also showed how the balance of opposing hormones can control specific types of metabolism.

Steeped as he was in scientific studies, the husband and father of other scientists, Houssay did not insulate himself from political and social concerns. When Houssay was awarded the Nobel Prize, the controlled Argentine press complained that it was a politically motivated act aimed at Perón. Houssay responded that one must not confuse small things, meaning Perón, with big things, meaning the Nobel Prize. Houssay later summarized his own code of belief: love of country, defense of freedom, respect for justice, and love of family and friends.

Houssay's teachings instituted a new era in Argentine medicine. He was responsible for the initiation of modern scientific techniques, not only in Argentina but also around the world. He strongly advocated training students to achieve independent thought, fearing as he did the undue influence of propaganda on the young. He often preached the need for fundamental reform in Argentine education, affirming that a nation that does not contribute to scientific knowledge is a parasite. Throughout his lifetime, Houssay was well respected by both students and colleagues.

Bibliography

Aaseng, Nathan. *The Disease Fighters: The Nobel Prize in Medicine.* Minneapolis: Lerner, 1987. Although this book gives no information on Houssay, it provides an overview of the history of the study of diabetes mellitus. Includes the discovery of insulin by Sir Frederick Grant Banting and Charles Best. Intended for primary school readers but can be useful for older students as well. Contains a glossary and an index.

Cori, Carl Ferdinand, et al., eds. *Perspectives in Biology: A Collection of Papers Dedicated to Bernardo A. Houssay on the Occasion of His Seventy-fifth Birthday.* New York: Elsevier, 1963. This collection includes one of Houssay's own papers—a study of hair growth in mice. As a preface, the editors have included a lengthy biographical sketch of the scientist. College-level material.

Ludovici, Laurence James, ed. *Nobel Prize Winners.* London: Arco, and Westport, Conn.: Associated Booksellers, 1957. Gives biographies of fourteen well-known Nobel Prize winners, including such contemporaries of Houssay as Albert Einstein, Sir Alexander Fleming, and Thomas Hunt Morgan. Helpful in placing Houssay's life in a historical context.

Roethe, Anna, ed. *Current Biography: Who's Who and Why, 1948.* New York: Wilson, 1949. This annual publication provides detailed biographies of people in the news for the previous year. Written in clear language for a general audience.

Schück, H., et al. *Nobel: The Man and His Prizes.* 2d rev. ed. New York: Elsevier, 1962. A comprehensive account of the Nobel Prizes in Literature, Physiology or Medicine, Chemistry, Physics, and Peace. Surveys each discipline and details the justification for the individual prizes. Includes a biography of Alfred Nobel and an index. College-level material.

Sourkes, Theodore L. *Nobel Prize Winners in Medicine and Physiology, 1901-1965.* London and New York: Abelard-Schuman, 1966. Sixty-five years of Nobel Prize winners, their lives, and the works which won for them the award. Some of the material is somewhat technical, but the biographical information can be valuable to all.

Maureen Connolly

DOLORES HUERTA

Born: April 10, 1930; Dawson, New Mexico

Area of Achievement: Trade unionism

Contributions: Cofounder of the United Farm Workers Association with César Chávez, Huerta became renowned throughout the labor movement as a tireless and effective negotiator and organizer. Her role as a Chicana labor leader in the male-dominated culture of southwestern farmworkers has made her a champion of the women's movement in the 1970's and beyond.

Early Life

Dolores Huerta was born Dolores Fernández in the mining community of Dawson, New Mexico, in 1930. Her father, Juan Fernández, was of Native American and Mexican heritage; her mother, Alicia Chávez Hernández, was a second-generation New Mexican. Dolores' parents were divorced while she was quite young, and she was reared by her mother in Stockton, California. Her mother worked in a cannery and saved enough to buy a small hotel and restaurant while establishing her household in an integrated working-class community. Dolores, along with her two brothers, grew up assuming that women and men were equal, drawing on the example of her mother, who never favored her sons above her daughter and who became a business entrepreneur on her own. Dolores grew up in a racially mixed neighborhood of farmworkers and other laborers of Chinese, Latino, Native American, Filipino, African American, Japanese, and Italian descent. As a result, she learned to appreciate the rich diversity of a range of ethnic cultures at a young age. This absence of sexual or cultural discrimination, in combination with her egalitarian family background, contributed to Dolores' leadership style in later life. Because she suffered no sense of inferiority at home and subsequently no acceptance of a secondary role in life or in her later career, Dolores came to maturity convinced that she was not required to accept the traditional feminine role of women as submissive domestic partners. Instead, she rebelled against conventional restraints upon women and competed directly with her male colleagues.

After graduating from an integrated high school in Stockton, Dolores married her high-school sweetheart, Ralph Head, in 1950. The marriage ended in divorce after the birth of their daughters Celeste and Lori. Dolores' mother took care of the children while Dolores studied for a teaching degree at Stockton College. Although she eventually received a provisional teaching credential, she became dissatisfied with a career as a teacher. A dawning awareness of the pervasiveness of social injustice confronting the Mexican American community and other ethnic minorities led Dolores in a new direction in 1955.

In that year, Dolores met Fred Ross, an organizer for Saul Alinsky's Industrial Areas Foundation who was trying to encourage the growing political consciousness of members of Mexican American communities throughout California. Ross started the Community Service Organization (CSO), a self-help association that led voter registration drives, pushed for more Chicanos on the police forces, lobbied for Spanish-speaking staff at hospitals and government offices, and campaigned for sewers and community centers in the barrios. Because of her newfound civic activism and devotion to the work of the CSO, Dolores' marriage to her second husband, Ventura Huerta, also ended in divorce.

Life's Work

It was through her activities with the CSO that Dolores Huerta eventually became active as a labor organizer among migrant workers in California's San Joaquin Valley. She first came in contact with César Chávez when she was introduced to him by Fred Ross in 1955 when both were working for the CSO. By that time, Huerta was a full-time lobbyist for the CSO in Sacramento, pressuring the legislature for disability insurance, unemployment insurance, and minimum wage bills for farmworkers. Although she was instrumental in securing the passage of bills that extended social insurance and welfare benefits to farmworkers and aliens, she was convinced that these workers could never escape poverty through the CSO strategy of pressure-group politics. What they needed was a union. At approximately the same time, César Chávez was reaching the same conclusion. By 1962, Chávez had presented the CSO with a program outlining strategy for the unionization of farmworkers. When this program was rejected, he left the organization. While his wife Helen worked in the fields to support their family of eight children, Chávez organized small meetings of workers sympathetic to the idea of a union of agricultural laborers. The

Farm Workers Association (FWA), a precursor of the United Farm Workers (UFW) union, was founded in Fresno, California, in September, 1962, at a convention attended by about three hundred delegates—practically the entire membership. It was organized primarily by César Chávez, but the first person he called upon to work with him organizing the Mexican American farmworkers into a union was Dolores Huerta, who promptly left her post with the CSO to help Chávez.

When Dolores Huerta began her labor organizing efforts, she was pregnant with the seventh of her eleven children (she had two by her first husband, five by her second, and four by her live-in lover, Richard Chávez, the brother of César). Because of the demands of her work, Huerta was frequently absent from home, and her children spent much of their childhood in the care of her friends or family. Her union work was always her first priority, to the consternation and outrage of the more traditional adherents to Latin culture. Huerta clearly loved her children and was loved by them in return, but she refused to allow motherhood to deter her from her work. Even her colleague César Chávez disapproved of Huerta's divorces, her decision to live with his brother, and her seemingly chaotic way of raising her children. Nevertheless, he understood that the union was the center of her life—just as it was for him.

The foundation of the United Farm Workers union was laid during the bitter Delano Grape Strike of 1965-1970. The farmworkers of the 1960's often lived in mind-numbing poverty and toiled under inhumane conditions. The bulk of the workforce spoke little English, was often of illegal residency status, could not vote, and was poorly educated. As a result, they were easily exploited by the powerful growers in the agribusiness industry of California. The growers often used deadly pesticides, primarily DDT, in the fields, ignoring the devastating health effects these chemicals had on both the workers and their unborn children. Pickers were paid by the bushel or basket rather than the hour. A field over-staffed with pickers, therefore, could result in a day's labor with little or no pay for the worker. There were no health and welfare benefits, no medical insurance, and no low-cost housing for the mainly transient workforce. Workers were forced to live in cars, shacks, and tents; many workers had no other place to sleep than the chemical-laden fields in which they had worked earlier in the day.

The grape-growing industry was perhaps the worst offender in terms of working conditions and pesticide use in all of California. Because of this, it became the logical site of the 1965 United Farm Workers (UFW) battle known as the Delano Grape Strike with César Chávez and Dolores Huerta at the forefront. The strike began at dawn, when the workers moved out into the fields around Delano. The pickets met them carrying NFWA banners with the union's symbol of a black Aztec eagle on a red flag with the single Spanish word "Huelga" (strike). The pickets led the workers off the fields of Delano and the five-year battle began. Before the strike ended in 1970, Huerta was arrested eighteen times.

As quickly as the UFW pickets pulled work crews out, these laborers were replaced by scabs, or strikebreakers, trucked in from Mexico and Texas by the growers. The union's pickets and organizers were harassed and arrested continually by local police, under the influence of the powerful growers. Support for the farmworkers was growing, both within the labor movement and on a national level. Senator Robert Kennedy embraced their cause and became their champion. Powerful unions, including the United Auto Workers (UAW), Amalgamated Clothing Workers, and the Packinghouse Workers rallied behind the striking grape pickers and provided relief in the form of fresh pickets, food, and money. It was against this backdrop of national labor and political support that Chávez and Huerta made the decision to escalate the strike to a nationwide struggle by declaring a universal consumer boycott. This boycott initially targeted individual growers and products, but eventually led to the boycott of all California-grown grapes. Hundreds of workers were delegated throughout the country to promote and organize the boycott, while Huerta herself organized in New York City. She was an eloquent and powerful public speaker, and her speeches expressed the deep desires and struggles of all poor and dispossessed peoples, not just those who worked the fields.

The UFW boycott was successful. Trade unionists across the country joined forces with the farmworkers, and a new consciousness of the Chicano in the United States was born as a result of the Huelga, as the strike was commonly known. On May 30, 1970, the first table grapes bearing a union label—a black eagle on a red flag—were shipped to market. The grapes came from seven growers who, unable to withstand the effects of the boycott, had signed contracts with the UFW. On July 29, twenty-six Delano growers filed into the UFW union hall to sign the contracts that ended the bitter five-year battle. As negotiated by Huerta, the workers received an hourly wage of $1.76, a guaranteed yearly increase of fifteen cents per hour, and a twenty-five-cent bonus per box picked. In addition, the growers were required to contribute to a health and welfare plan and to low-cost housing for their workers. Most importantly, the growers agreed not to use certain pesticides, and DDT was banned forever from California vineyards. Huerta's skills as a negotiator were entirely self-taught. In fact, before the strike she had never even read a union contract. Besides negotiating the UFW's first contracts, Huerta had organized for the strike in the fields, in boycott offices, and in union election halls as well as serving as a picket herself. In retrospect, however, it was her skill, tenacity, combativeness, and cunning as a negotiator that truly separated Dolores Huerta from her peers in the labor movement. Her contract negotiations with the California growers was the crowning achievement of one of the greatest victories ever in the history of American workers.

Dolores Huerta continued to serve in the UFW as negotiator and vice president into the 1990's. She became notorious in the union for her fervor and tenacity; stories are told of growers begging to face anyone at the negotiating table except Huerta. Huerta and Chávez continued their aggressive style of Chicano trade unionism through periodic use of the consumer boycott, most notably against Gallo Wine, the Dole Company, and California table grapes. In the wake of Chávez's death in 1993, Huerta, in her sixties, continues to be an eloquent and frequent speaker and organizer on behalf of workers, Mexican Americans, and women.

Summary

As a leading figure in the Chicano trade union movement, Dolores Huerta has found union organizing to be an enjoyable, creative process that has provided her personal and intellectual fulfillment. All of her work has been based on four philosophical axioms: first, to establish a strong sense of identity; second, to develop a sense of pride; third, to maintain always the value of services to others; and fourth, to be effective and true to oneself. Huerta was convinced of the necessity to lead others through persuasion and personal example, rather than by intimidation. Ideas are vital and criticism is necessary, but for Huerta, action through responsible commitment and moral choice is the key to creating a just society. More than a liberal, ethnic unionist, Huerta has taken additional pride in her stance as a feminist, a Chicano activist, and, above all, a humanist. Huerta's cause has transcended the narrow scope of unionism. As Huerta herself stated at an organizing rally at Santa Clara University in 1990: "I would like to be remembered as a woman who cares for all fellow humans. We must use our lives to make the world a better and just place to live, not just a world to acquire things. That is what we are put on the earth for."

Bibliography

Coburn, Judith. "Dolores Huerta: La Passionaria of the Farmworkers." *Ms.* 5 (November, 1976): 10-16. An interview with Dolores Huerta during a union election dispute in Sacramento, California, in 1975.

"Dolores Huerta." *Current Biography* 58, no. 11 (November, 1997). Profile of Huerta and her successful opposition to California agricultural interests in the 1960's and 1970's.

Fink, Gary M. *Biographical Dictionary of American Labor.* 2d ed. Westport, Conn., and London: Greenwood Press, 1984. A listing of biographical data on important people in the history of the American labor movement.

Foner, Philip. *Women and the American Labor Movement: From World War I to the Present.* New York: Free Press, 1980; London: Macmillan, 1982. A historical overview of the entire American labor movement since World War I with an emphasis on the roles of women, both as labor leaders and as workers.

Garcia, Richard A. "Dolores Huerta: Woman, Organizer and Symbol." *California History* 71 (Spring, 1993): 57-71. This article, appearing in the journal of the California Historical Society, explores the philosophical and ethical underpinnings of Dolores Huerta's activism.

Loya, Gloria Ines. "Considering the Sources/ Fuentes for a Hispanic Feminist Theology." *Theology Today* 54, no. 4 (January, 1998). Discusses the origins of "Mujerista Theology," or Hispanic feminist theory, including the contributions of Huerta, Sor Juana Ines de la Cruz, and Malintzin-La Malinche.

Meier, Matt S. *Mexican American Biographies: A Historical Dictionary, 1836-1987.* New York: Greenwood Press, 1988. Meier, an expert on Mexican American history, includes a profile on Huerta in this biographical dictionary. Although brief, the sketch on Huerta does provide a fine summary of her activities on behalf of "la causa."

Rose, Margaret. "Dolores Huerta." In *Notable Hispanic American Women*, edited by Diane Telgen and Jim Kamp. Detroit: Gale Research, 1993. A thorough biographical profile of Huerta that traces her activism from the 1950's up through her injury at a 1988 demonstration in San Francisco protesting various Bush Administration policies.

Derrick Harper West

CHARLES EVANS HUGHES

Born: April 11, 1862; Glens Falls, New York
Died: August 27, 1948; Osterville, Massachusetts
Area of Achievement: Law, government and politics
Contribution: Hughes served America's public interests as secretary of state and chief justice of the United States. He combined reforming zeal with brilliant administrative skills, and few Americans have demonstrated such commitment to the national good.

Early Life

Charles Evans Hughes was the only child of David Charles Hughes, an evangelical Baptist minister, and Mary Catherine Connelly, a woman who combined intelligence with pious discipline. When Charles was six years old, he convinced his parents that he should be educated at home because he was impatient with his slower classmates at school. By the time he was ten, however, he was back in public school, and in 1876 he entered Madison University (Colgate). Two years later, finding Madison too provincial for his interests, he transferred to Brown University, from which he was graduated at the top of the class in 1881. In 1884, he was graduated from Columbia University Law School. He married Antoinette Carter in 1888. She was the daughter of one of the partners in a New York law firm for which Hughes worked after leaving Columbia. The couple had four children; the eldest was the only boy.

After graduation from law school, Hughes devoted himself to the practice of law for twenty years. He became a law partner by the time he was twenty-five, and within a few years he had made himself financially secure. During this period he gave no thought to public life, but in 1905 he came to the public's attention when he accepted a position as special counsel to the New York legislature investigating the unfair rates of gas and electricity and insurance fraud. Hughes's investigative reports brought him almost unanimous praise from New York City newspapers. Indeed, he became so popular that, in an attempt to shore up the popularity of the Republican Party, President Theodore Roosevelt pushed party members to nominate Hughes for mayor of New York City. Hughes declined the nomination, thereby causing a rift between himself and Roosevelt which would last the rest of Roosevelt's life. Yet as a result he was estab-lished as a prominent, albeit reluctant, public figure. In his early forties, Hughes was launched on a career of public service that would occupy the rest of his life.

Life's Work

In 1906, the Republican Party desperately needed a popular figure to run for governor of New York against the powerful, ambitious journalist William Randolph Hearst. The Republicans sought a candidate who, in contrast to the ruthless Hearst, would be perceived as committed to principled government. They chose Hughes, and this time he accepted—and by the narrowest of margins defeated Hearst. He proved to be an effective, popular governor. He was responsible for reform legislation that was to have a long-term effect on the state of New York. He established, for example, public service commissions that regulated utilities and railroads. As a result, service became better and more impartial and rates fairer, while employees for the first time were able to secure safety provisions in their contracts. The eight-hour workday gained acceptance, and the first workers' compensation laws were established.

Again, with this progressive record as governor, Hughes had attracted the attention of the national Republicans, particularly that of the Republican president, William Howard Taft. Taft nominated Hughes for a seat on the Supreme Court of the United States, and Hughes accepted and was confirmed as a justice on the Court in 1910.

He came to the bench when the country was struggling with the issue of constitutional centralization, and he was to play a significant role in settling that issue. Centralization meant placing more power in the hands of the federal government while taking it from the states. Among other factors, the increased complexity of commerce made centralization a necessity, and Hughes's legal decisions were decisive in establishing the limits of state and federal control. Ostensibly, he used the federal authority of interstate commerce to defend decisions that produced Progressive policies. He wrote and supported opinions that regulated working hours, equal accommodations on railroads for black citizens, nonwhite representation on trial juries, equal access to employment for nonnative citizens, trials in locations free from community passions, and numerous other liberal opinions.

Hughes remained on the Court for six years. While on small matters he might render a conservative opinion, on large issues he supported the expansion of federal powers in defense of individual liberties. He did not hesitate in striking down state statutes that he perceived to be in conflict with the Bill of Rights. By 1916, Hughes's brilliant reputation on the Supreme Court had become so distinguished that the Republican Party once again prevailed upon him to run for office, this time for president of the United States. He resigned from the bench and ran against the popular incumbent, Woodrow Wilson. Hughes lost. It is fair to say that this was the least satisfactory episode in a distinguished career; Hughes was not a good campaigner, lacking the intense partisanship necessary to run for the presidency. He had no success in moving masses of people to follow him. He had a weak and internally feuding political organization. Most important, the Progressive wing of the Republican Party under Theodore Roosevelt's leadership was only lukewarm in its support.

Four years later, the nation elected the Republican Warren G. Harding as president. Hughes became Harding's secretary of state. The stolid, provincial Harding had no coherent foreign policy of his own; as a result, responsibility for such decisions fell squarely on Hughes. Clearly, he was up to the task. Few secretaries of state in the history of the United States can be called his equal. None was more intelligent. Few possessed his imagination, his administrative skills, or his genuine idealism. Indeed, many diplomatic scholars consider Hughes to be one of the three top secretaries of state the nation has ever had. His influence was indelible, even though lesser individuals were left to implement his goals.

Hughes's long-term influence was most noteworthy in four areas: disarmament, reparations and war debts, and the United States' relationships with the Soviets and with Latin America. In November of 1921, Hughes invited representatives of the world's nations to Washington, D.C., to consider ways of reducing national tension in the Western Pacific. The conference became known as the Washington Conference on Naval Disarmament. It was Hughes's plan to reduce tensions around the world, particularly in the Western Pacific, by getting the governments of Great Britain, Japan, and the United States to reduce the size of their naval forces. In an opening speech that both astonished and pleased the delegates to the conference, the

secretary of state presented a specific plan for this reduction. In addition to setting limits on tonnage levels for the navies of the world (the French proved the most reluctant to concede on this score), Hughes sought to reduce the militarization of various islands in the Pacific controlled by the national powers. He also pushed for the sovereignty and integrity of China, its right to commercial equity, and Japan's abandonment of expansionism on the Asian mainland. Within fifteen years, all the treaties that resulted from the Washington Conference were either being ignored or abrogated, but for a brief moment in history Hughes's "noble experiment" had influenced international relations.

The matter of reparations and war debts, which was closely related to disarmament in Hughes's mind, also required his attention. After the close of World War I, the victorious Allies (and in particular the French) were seeking huge financial reparations from Germany for losses suffered in the war. Hughes convinced the European Allies that they neither would, nor could, get Germany to pay such reparations, and that continued insistence on these payments would only exacerbate the volatile and unstable condition of postwar Europe. In order to balance the various claims against the German government, Hughes proposed a more realistic payment schedule and the acquisition of an international loan for Germany that would enable it to stabilize its currency and generate the money necessary to meet reparation payments. At the same time, he convinced Congress that it was necessary to extend the payment schedule and reduce the interest requirements on debts owed the United States by its allies. These reparation and refunding policies lasted for only a few years between World War I and World War II, but they did bring a more rational, tranquil policy to an otherwise chaotic situation.

In Russia, the Communists came to power in 1917, but the United States refused to recognize the Soviet government as a legitimate regime. Many in the United States Senate, however, argued that it was in the United States' interest to resume diplomatic relations with Moscow. It was, they argued, the *de facto* regime, and as such should be recognized; moreover, recognition would encourage the resumption of trade and promote the United States' commercial interests. Hughes held fast against recognition, arguing that the Soviet revolution was on *prima facie* grounds both illegal and immoral, because its coming to power abrogated international *bona fide* agreements between legally established governments. What is more, he held, any assumed economic advantage is problematic, and at best hazardous. As long as the Communists make and encourage worldwide revolution among legally constituted governments, he argued, the United States has a responsibility not to participate in policies that could legitimate the revolution. As long as Bolsheviks refused to recognize international legal obligation, recognition of this regime can only be a disservice to legitimate democratic governments that continue to meet their international responsibilities.

The last, and in many ways the most important, policy in Hughes's tenure as secretary of state was initiated when he first entered office and lasted throughout his term as secretary. Working together with Sumner Welles, he forged an American policy toward Latin America that was much less interventionist than the policies of administrations that had preceded him. This policy was the beginning of what was later to be called the Good Neighbor Policy. Essentially, the Good Neighbor Policy meant fewer American marines controlling United States interests in Latin America. "I utterly disclaim as unwarranted," he declared, "[superintending] the affairs of our sister republics, to assert an overlordship, to consider the spread of our authority beyond our domain as the aim of our policy and to make our power the test of right in this hemisphere. . . . [Such assertions] belie our sincere friendship, . . . they stimulate a distrust . . . [and] have no sanction whatever in the Monroe Doctrine." In reality, however, such intervention was only partially implemented under Hughes's leadership. The marines were withdrawn from Nicaragua and the Dominican Republic, but not from Haiti and Panama, where the secretary argued that in the latter two countries it was premature and contrary to the United States' "special interests."

Hughes stepped down from his position as secretary of state in 1925; three years later he was a judge on the Court of International Justice, and in 1930 he accepted his last important public position as chief justice of the United States under Herbert Hoover's presidency.

Constitutional scholars are almost unanimous in assessing Hughes as one of the greatest chief justices in Supreme Court history. He served for eleven years, and during that time his legal leadership was dynamic and progressive, never static and protective. Some of his opinions on economic matters were conservative, but on matters of citizens' welfare his positions represented progressive activism. He argued in support of the government's right to determine an equitable balance between the interests of business and the interests of labor. Expressly, he defended the right of Congress to regulate collective bargaining agreements in interstate commerce. The benchmark decision on this issue was the Wagner Labor Relations Act, which paved the way for supporting legislation on the matter of minimum wages and the hours of work required per day. In addition, Hughes led a unanimous court in declaring President Roosevelt's National Recovery Act (NRA) unconstitutional (the Court argued that the act allowed code-fixing; that is, it allowed independent nongovernmental agencies to set wages, prices, and working hours). In other words, Roosevelt's NRA appointments from business and industry were prevented from setting codes of competitive commerce between the states, and Congress could not turn over its legislative responsibility to the executive branch of government in this area, Hughes argued.

As a general rule, Hughes supported the expansion of federal power as an instrument for the protection of personal liberty. He upheld, for example, the right of states to fix prices (*Nebbia v. New York,* 1934), the right of the federal government to regulate radio frequencies (*Federal Radio Commission v. Nelson Bros.,* 1933), the right of women to the same minimum wage afforded men (*Morehead v. Tipaldo,* 1936), and the right of citizens to set aside private contracts under certain hardship constraints.

In the arena of civil liberties, the chief justice was no less supportive of the government's constitutional right to intrude where it can be shown that the Bill of Rights has been abrogated. He argued that the state of Alabama had denied due process to a black man because he had been denied an attorney (*Powell v. Alabama,* 1932). He supported the reversal of the notorious *Scottsboro* decision (a case of rape against a group of young black men) by declaring that blacks cannot be excluded from jury service merely by virtue of their color (*Norris v. Alabama,* 1935, and *Patterson v. Alabama,* 1935). He maintained that such exclusion denied "equal protection of the laws" as provided in the Fourteenth Amendment. And in a case anticipating by sixteen years the famous *Brown v. Board of Education* (1954) school desegregation case, he held that qualified black students must be granted admission to an all-white law school (*Missouri ex rel. Gaines v. Canada,* 1938). As in *Brown,* the Hughes Court declared that separate facilities for blacks was not equal; that is, separate is not equal, and the plaintiff Gaines had not received "equal protection of the laws."

Over the course of Chief Justice Hughes's term on the bench, he supported legal decisions that provided constitutional protection for suffrage (voting rights), the freedom of speech, the freedom of religion, the freedom of the press, and the right to political dissent. Hughes's record on civil liberties can only lead one to agree with Samuel Hendel's observation that he had a "greater fondness for the Bill of Rights than any other Chief Justice."

Summary

The magnitude of Charles Evans Hughes's service to the country was so widespread and pervasive that it is difficult to know just where the emphasis should be placed. In fact, the wise course is to avoid placing undue emphasis on any specific aspect of his numerous accomplishments, but rather to review the traits of character that he brought to every public position he held. His strong sense of social interest led him throughout his life to fight institutional dishonesty in all of its forms. He was never reluctant to employ the legal leverage of the judiciary against what he perceived to be the injustices of institutional forms of government, business, and industry. On the bench he was always reluctant to impede social reform with a "judicial veto." His conception of a justice's role was as a principled libertarian; in particular, a member of the judiciary must be prepared to employ the law in defense of the citizen's individual rights against the inevitably unfair advantages of powerful national institutions. Understandably, corporations, industry, and government will exercise the initiative necessary to make their efforts worthwhile and successful. In return, individual citizens have the right, through their legislative representatives, to see to it that they do not fall victim to the aspirations of these powerful organizations. It is the role of the judiciary to establish a balanced fairness between collective interests and public liberties.

Hughes not only had the role of jurist; he also represented the most powerful of all institutions, the government itself. In this role, however, he acted with restraint and with an eye to the common good. Because he was an individual with a scrupulous moral sense, an unshakable commitment to fidelity and honor, and the intellectual powers to match, he was never willing to sacrifice long-term ideals for short-term expediencies. Thus, it seems proper to argue that Hughes was a "futurist" and as such endures as one of America's most gifted and distinguished secretaries of state.

Bibliography

Friedman, Richard D. "Switching Time and Other Thought Experiments: The Hughes Court and Constitutional Transformation." *University of Pennsylvania Law Review* 142, no. 6 (June, 1994): 1891-1984.

Glad, Betty. *Charles Evans Hughes and the Illusions of Innocence: A Study in American Diplomacy.* Urbana: University of Illinois Press, 1966. In this study of American diplomacy between the two world wars, Hughes is the centerpiece. Schooled in mainstream nineteenth century American culture, Hughes formulated American foreign policy throughout the era. It is

Glad's contention that Hughes's moral puritanism often led to optimistic illusions. Glad's ideological generalizations are not always convincing.

Hendel, Samuel. *Charles Evans Hughes and the Supreme Court.* New York: King's Crown Press, 1951. This is a case-by-case study of Charles Evans Hughes's judicial career, a careful, detailed assessment and evaluation that has become a sourcebook for much legal scholarship on Hughes's Supreme Court opinions.

Hughes, Charles Evans. *The Autobiographical Notes of Charles Evans Hughes.* Edited by David J. Danelski and Joseph S. Tulchin. Cambridge, Mass.: Harvard University Press, 1973. It is difficult for writers not to sketch Hughes as larger than life. Reading his own notes affords an opportunity to assess his own words; this work reveals the man both directly and indirectly.

————. *Our Relations to the Nations of the Western Hemisphere.* Princeton, N.J.: Princeton University Press, 1928. Hughes's analysis of the United States' relationship to Canada and Latin America: his assessment of the Monroe Doctrine, the recognition of governments, and the United States' role in honoring Central American treaties and supplying military arms and financial loans to foreign powers. Particularly interesting is the section in which he sets forth the conditions that he believes justify intervention in Latin American affairs.

————. *The Supreme Court of the United States.* New York: Columbia University Press, 1928. A historical account of the role of the United States Supreme Court. Ostensibly, the Court's task as the "supreme tribunal" is to interpret the intentions of the nation's legislatures. Hughes argues that it is the Court's role to balance state and national priorities and to determine the rights of citizens against common social interests.

Perkins, Dexter. *Charles Evans Hughes and American Democratic Statesmanship.* Boston: Little Brown, 1956. This is a smoothly written account of Hughes's political and legal career from his start in New York City to his retirement from the post of chief justice of the U.S. Supreme Court. Throughout, Perkins attempts to portray Hughes as a brilliant, principled individual striving to balance the ideals of liberalism and conservatism in the art of statesmanship.

Pusey, Merlo J. *Charles Evans Hughes.* 2 vols. New York: Macmillan, 1951. One of the best and most exhaustive works on Hughes. Beginning with his childhood in Glens Falls, New York, and ending with his fight against Franklin D. Roosevelt's attempt to "pack the Supreme Court" in 1938, it is a standard text on Hughes. Especially valuable for its interviews with Hughes at the end of his illustrious career: Pusey had the good fortune to interview him many hours a week over a two-and-a-half-year period.

Donald Burrill

LANGSTON HUGHES

Born: February 1, 1902; Joplin, Missouri
Died: May 22, 1967; New York, New York
Area of Achievement: Literature
Contribution: While Hughes's greatest achievement was his poetry, which related and celebrated the African American experience, he was also a novelist, dramatist, short story writer, and journalist, making him one of the most versatile black American writers to grow out of the Harlem Renaissance of the 1920's and 1930's.

Early Life

James Mercer Langston Hughes was born in Joplin, Missouri, in 1902 to parents who would soon separate. His father, contemptuous of racist barriers that kept him from achieving his professional goals, settled in Mexico, where he prospered as a lawyer and landowner. His mother, refusing to accompany her husband, moved wherever work was available. She had an interest in the arts that she conveyed to her young son. She also valued a good education and, while living in Topeka, Kansas, insisted that her son be enrolled as a first grader in a white school rather than a black school. In 1909, when economic necessity demanded that she seek employment elsewhere, she took the seven-year-old child to live with his grandmother in Lawrence, Kansas.

A solitary child, Hughes spent his early years reading and listening to his grandmother's stories about the black people's heroic quest for freedom and their noble, unflinching determination to achieve liberty and justice. After her death in 1914, Hughes moved to Lincoln, Illinois, to live with his mother and stepfather. He finished elementary school and, as the elected class poet, read his first poem at his graduation ceremony. He then moved with his family to Cleveland, Ohio, where he attended high school. Hughes read voraciously, developed a keen interest in poetry, music, and art, and served as editor of the class yearbook.

In 1920, Hughes went to live with his father in Mexico where he taught English to the children of wealthy Mexicans. In spite of fact that his materialistic father had little regard for his son's artistic aptitude and wanted him to go abroad to continue his education, Hughes began to publish in National Association for the Advancement of Colored People (NAACP) periodicals. When his poem "The

Negro Speaks of Rivers" appeared in *The Crisis* in 1921, the young writer became more determined than ever to grow both intellectually and aesthetically. Compromising with his father, he enrolled in Columbia University in 1921, only to leave after one year because of the bigotry he experienced there.

Hughes continued to write as he worked in a series of menial jobs while living in Harlem in Manhattan to help support himself and his mother. In 1923, he shipped out on a freighter bound for West Africa as a cabin boy, a journey that also took him throughout Europe, where he met such writers as Theodore Dreiser, Zora Neale Hurston, Richard Wright, Lillian Hellman, Ernest Hemingway, and Pablo Neruda. Upon returning to the United States in 1924, Hughes lived with his mother in Washington, D.C., where he served as a research assistant for black historian Carter G. Woodson. More important, while working as a hotel bus boy, he was "discovered" by noted poet Vachel Lindsay, who publicly hailed him as the "bus boy poet."

With his experiences abroad and in Harlem (where he would have a permanent residence from 1947 until his death in 1965), his intimate sense of the joys and agonies of his fellow African Americans, and his love for the music and mood of African American language, Hughes was primed to began creating some of his most enduring literature.

Life's Work

Hughes began to publish poems with the same passionate language and rhythms contained in the jazz and blues music he had heard in Harlem and Paris nightclubs. He started to win literary prizes for his work, which brought him the praise of critic Carl Van Vechten, who helped him publish his first book of verse, *The Weary Blues* (1926). The poems in the collection convey the musical and heated nightlife of Harlem, as well as the agonies of racial conflict and poverty.

After enrolling in Lincoln University in Pennsylvania in 1926 and graduating in 1929, Hughes continued to write not only poetry but also short stories and essays for black publications. In 1927, he and some other black writers founded *Fire!*, a literary journal of African American culture. In that same year a second volume of poetry, *Fine Clothes to the Jew* (1927), appeared. This book contained

poems depicting the harsh, often violent underside of Harlem life, and its realism brought Hughes the financial patronage that allowed him to complete his first novel, *Not Without Laughter* (1930).

In 1932, Hughes went to the Soviet Union, where he worked as a journalist. During this time he read D. H. Lawrence's stories and was inspired to write more of his own. After returning to the United States, he published *The Ways of White Folks* (1934), his first collection of stories. However, Hughes's most notable achievements in short fiction are the morality sketches dealing with the joys and sorrows of black life in the United States that also satirize the hypocrisy and foibles of all Americans and human nature in general. These stories originally appeared in the *Chicago Defender*, an African American publication. Their initial compilation into book form was, perhaps, inspired by Hughes having to testify before the House Committee on Un-American Activities, which found him apologizing for some of his own early prosocialist writings. Over the years these stories were collected and published in *Simple Speaks His Mind* (1950), *Simple Takes a Wife* (1953), *Simple Stakes a Claim* (1957), and *Simple's Uncle Sam* (1965).

Hughes was also involved in the theater. He wrote such plays as *Mulatto* (1935), *Little Ham* (1935), and *Tambourines of Glory* (1963). His dramas dealt with the economic and social difficulties inherent in modern, urban black life as well as the abiding dignity of African Americans and their tenacious will to survive. The plays also exhibited Hughes's sensitivity to and appreciation for African American culture and language and were often staged in nontraditional ways.

Hughes also wrote operas. *The Barrier* (1950) was based on some of his earlier writings, including his play *Mulatto*, and was produced on Broadway in 1950. Another opera, *Esther* (1957), was brought to the stage by Boston's New England Conservatory. His light musical, *Simply Heaven* (1957), based on the sketches in *Simple Takes a Wife*, also had a run on Broadway. However, some viewers were disappointed in the musical's popularized portrayal of Simple as an entertaining fool rather than the wily folk philosopher of the stories. During these years, Hughes also founded the Harlem Suitcase Theatre, the Skyloft Players of Chicago, and the New Negro Theatre in Los Angeles so that black playwrights and actors would have opportunities to perfect their crafts.

In addition, Hughes wrote two autobiographies. The first, *The Big Sea* (1940), recounts how he strove to overcome the racism that pushed hard to stifle his and other African Americans' creativity. Among other things, it relates how the young Hughes rejected his materialistic father's attempts, with the lure of wealth and security, to persuade his son to give up the idea of becoming a poet of his people. It also tells how Hughes again resisted the temptation of being artistically controlled when he rejected the easy financial patronage offered by a person who sought, in the bargain, to interfere with what and how Hughes wrote. He preferred to be a poor wanderer, free to live and write as he wished.

Hughes's second autobiography, *I Wonder as I Wander* (1956), further recounts his seemingly rootless, wandering life, from his trip to Africa in 1923 through his travels in Europe and his exposure to many great modern writers and artists. Like *The Big Sea*, the book was also nonconfessional in the sense that little was revealed about Hughes's very private life. Why he remained unmarried is never really discussed, and no significant intimate relationships are recounted, leaving the question of Hughes's sexuality unanswered and leading some to speculate that he was homosexual.

Hughes's greatest achievement was in poetry, and he continued to publish collections. *Montage of a Dream Deferred* (1951) pictured a Harlem life that had changed drastically from its renaissance years of jazz and vibrant life in the 1920's and 1930's to a postwar ghetto of violence and blighted poverty. Stylistically, the velvety rhythms of the blues that permeated his earlier poetry were often replaced by angular rhythms of sharp contrast like those emanating from a modern bebop jazz session. The poems in *Ask Your Mama: Or, Twelve Hoods for Jazz* (1961) explore the issue of segregation and, among other things, picture a time when Martin Luther King, Jr., is governor of Georgia and a former white segregationist governor has been relegated to the position of caretaker "mammy" for little black children.

Hughes's last collection of poetry, *The Panther and the Lash: Or, Poems of Our Times* (1967), was published posthumously and contained harsh criticisms of the state of race relations in the United States and abroad. The works are, in part, a response to the black power movement in an era of change wherein the desirability of integration, long held essential by black people of Hughes's generation, was questioned by some African Americans.

Summary

During his phenomenally creative life, Langston Hughes published seventeen books of poetry, seven short story collections, twenty-six dramatic works, two novels, and two autobiographies. He also edited anthologies and translated works of other writers.

While some criticize Hughes for remaining limited by his persistent focus on the folkways, language, and basic issues surrounding lower-class African Americans and regret that his portrayals of common black life sometimes failed to present a progressive view of his race, Hughes himself always insisted that he was an honest, social poet who did not know enough about upper-class black people to write about them. He felt that while the poor black residents of Harlem may not have worn shined shoes, been to Harvard, or listened to classical music, "they seemed to me," he said, "good people" who possessed a life force, survival instinct, and dignity worthy of his artistic efforts and personal sympathy.

Also criticized by a new, more militant generation for supposedly not successfully addressing the issues and politics of black power, Hughes's writings, nonetheless, continue to speak to readers who value his clear, vividly rendered, and honest vision of his people. They value his celebration of their language, culture, and spirit so beautifully permeated, in his most memorable poems, by the rhythms of blues and jazz. Hughes's rich, sensitive rendering of an authentic black voice and his fatherly role as mentor for a whole generation of aspiring African American literary artists assure his place as one of the most influential African American poets and writers of the twentieth century.

Bibliography

Berry, Faith. *Langston Hughes: Before and Beyond Harlem*. Westport, Conn.: Lawrence Hill, 1983. Solid critical biography of Hughes covering his education, politics, involvement in the Civil Rights movement, and his many books and pamphlets. Contains extensive chapter notes.

Dace, Tish, ed. *Langston Hughes: The Contemporary Reviews*. Cambridge and New York: Cambridge University Press, 1997. The first book of contemporary reviews (1926-1967) of the works of Hughes.

Emanuel, James A. *Langston Hughes*. Boston: Twayne, 1967. An overview of Hughes's life and art, including critical readings of his poetry, drama, and fiction. Contains a selected bibliography and life chronology.

McLaren, Joseph. *Langston Hughes: Folk Dramatist in the Protest Tradition, 1921-1943*. Westport, Conn.: Greenwood Press, 1997. Analysis of Hughes' plays and discussion of his participation in community drama groups such as the Karamu Theatre in Cleveland. Deals with the playwright's radical and post-radical periods.

Miller, R. Baxter. *The Art and Imagination of Langston Hughes*. Lexington: University of Kentucky Press, 1989. An examination of Hughes's development as a poet focusing on his autobiographical, apocalyptic, lyrical, political, and tragicomic imaginations. Includes extensive chapter notes and a selected bibliography.

Mullen, Edward J., ed. *Critical Essays on Langston Hughes*. Boston: Hall, 1986. Includes essays on Hughes's poetry, prose, and drama, as well as reviews of his works.

Ostrom, Hans. *Langston Hughes: A Study of the Short Fiction*. New York: Twayne, 1993. Includes critical analyses of Hughes's short fiction; excerpts from his essays and speeches on his life, racial issues, and writings; and remarks from critics on his works. Contains a life chronology and selected bibliography.

Rampersad, Arnold. *The Life of Langston Hughes*. 2 vols. Oxford and New York: Oxford University Press, 1988. The definitive biography of Hughes, tracing his life and work from 1902 to 1967. Deals extensively with his personal, political, public, and artistic concerns and accomplishments.

Trotman, C. James, ed. *Langston Hughes: The Man, His Art, and His Continuing Influence*. New York: Garland, 1995. A fine collection of essays dealing with such topics as the Harlem Renaissance, "Race, Culture, and Gender," and Hughes's continuing influence on poetry, fiction, and drama.

Richard M. Leeson

WILLIAM MORRIS HUGHES

Born: September 25, 1862; London, England
Died: October 28, 1952; Sydney, New South Wales, Australia
Areas of Achievement: Government and politics
Contribution: Trade union organizer and wartime leader, Hughes was the first prime minister to put Australia's case on the international scene, especially winning concessions from a reluctant President Woodrow Wilson at the Paris Peace Conference (1919).

Early Life

William Morris Hughes was born on September 25, 1862 in London. His mother, née Jane Morris, a farmer's daughter, worked as a domestic servant. Welsh-speaking and a deacon of the Particular Baptist Church, his father, William Hughes, was a carpenter at the Houses of Parliament. On the death of his mother, young Hughes, an only child, went to live with family members in Wales. At the age of twelve, he returned to St. Stephen's School, Westminster, where as a pupil-teacher he later came under the influence of poet and critic Matthew Arnold.

A short, slight, but energetic and adventurous young man, at twenty-two Hughes sailed for Queensland as an assisted migrant. After two years of rough life in the outback, he settled in Sydney—living, by 1890, in the suburb of Balmain with a wife, née Elizabeth Cutts, and two children. Their little shop distributed political tracts and provided a meeting-place for young Socialists who discussed the theories of Karl Marx and Henry George while helping to lay the foundation for the Australian Labor Party.

Elizabeth Hughes died at age forty-two on September 1, 1906, survived by six children. In 1911, Hughes was married again, to Mary Ethel (née Campbell); he was fifty-three when their beloved daughter, Helen, was born.

Life's Work

Seeking parliamentary representation for Labor, in 1894 Hughes won the seat of Lang. After revitalizing the Sydney wharf-laborers' union and becoming its secretary, he became organizer and president of the Trolley, Draymen and Carters' Union. Although preferring a constitution that gave greater powers to the Commonwealth, he saw the federation's advantages and in 1901 joined those elected to the first parliament. His seat of West Sydney incorporated Lang and an adjoining waterside precinct, so he was well placed to organize and become president of the Waterside Workers' Federation. Industrial relations proved to be his forte. A believer in the arbitration system, he used the courts with spectacular success; Hughes gained increased wages and shorter working hours for his members, while qualifying (1903) as a lawyer.

In the first, short-lived federal Labor government (1904), led by John C. Watson, he became minister for external affairs. The dominant figure in this and in the Labor governments of Andrew Fisher (1908-1909, 1910-1913, 1914-1915), in which he served as attorney general, Hughes began to carry out many of Fisher's duties even before the prime minister resigned in October, 1915, for health reasons.

Great Britain had been at war with Germany since August, 1914. Fisher, then briefly in opposition, promised to stand by the mother country to the "last man and the last shilling"; a large contingent of volunteers with the Australian Imperial Force had departed for England on November 1, 1914; on resuming the position of attorney general Hughes had pressed for economic sanctions against enemy interests. Fearful of Germany's proximity in New Guinea and of Japanese intentions (even though the latter was an ally), he invited himself to London, where his speeches (published in 1916 as *"The Day"—And After: War Speeches*) met with amazing success. He attended meetings of the British cabinet and the War Committee, represented Australia at an allied conference in Paris, and visited his nation's troops at the front.

Hughes returned from Europe ready to follow the lead of Great Britain (and New Zealand) by conscripting men for overseas service. The Senate blocked the legislation so instead he held a referendum. Most people undoubtedly supported the war, but on October 28, 1916, they narrowly voted against compelling young men to fight. The Labor Party split over the issue: Conscriptionists, considered to have contravened the spirit of the party platform, were expelled. Among them was the prime minister.

No longer acceptable to West Sydney voters, Hughes sought a base in Victoria which, along with Tasmania and Western Australia, had voted for conscription. On May 5, 1917, he carried the seat of Bendigo and his "Win the War" Nationalist Party won government. He had, however, given an election promise to call another referendum should volunteers fall short, which they did. Affected partly by mounting casualty figures, recruiting numbers dropped from 11,520 in October, 1916, to an average of 3,180 per month from January, 1917. The second referendum campaign was even more divisive, especially in Victoria, the stronghold of one of conscription's most virulent opponents, Archbishop Daniel Mannix, who used the issue to press for independence for his native Ireland. A majority of voters on December 20, 1917, again were opposed, and this time Victoria changed sides.

The United States having entered the conflict in April, 1917, eventual victory seemed certain, but the war continued to be Hughes's consuming interest. He attended meetings of the Imperial War Cabinet and Imperial War Conference during 1918; he also vigorously represented Australia at the Paris Peace Conference the following year, returning from Versailles to a triumphant welcome. Twenty-five thousand pounds were subscribed in 1920 in recognition of his services to Australia and the British Empire, but the "Little Digger," as soldiers called him, gradually fell from favor. With a majority of only one in the House of Representatives, he called an early election. Not only was he opposed by the Labor Party, but the Country Party and the dissident Nationalists also campaigned against him. Unable to form a government, he was forced to resign and Stanley M. Bruce, his former treasurer, arranged a coalition with Sir Earle Page of the Country Party. In 1922, at age sixty, Hughes was merely the member for North Sydney. His parliamentary career, however, lasted almost another three decades.

Always distrustful of coalitions, Hughes was surprised to see it win on "law and order" on November 14, 1925, the first election at which voting was compulsory. He began to criticize Bruce's handling of industrial relations, immigration, and the economy. The coalition fared less well in 1928 and lost office in October, 1929, through a motion moved by Hughes on the Maritime Services Bill. His biographer, Professor L. F. Fitzhardinge, discerns in his motive not merely revenge on Bruce for confining him to the backbench but also "a shrewd premonition of impending catastrophe, political consistency, and even a measure of disinterested patriotism." Nationalist efforts to oust him

from North Sydney failed, in an election in which even Bruce lost his seat.

Expelled from the Nationalist Party, Hughes briefly supported the Labor government of James H. Scullin. After an abortive attempt to help establish an Australian Party, he then swung his support to the United Australia Party led by Joseph A. Lyons, a former Scullin minister who broke with the Labor Party over its fiscal policies during the depression. In an "amazing metamorphosis," as Hughes described it, he served first as vice president of the executive council and minister for health and repatriation and then as minister for external affairs, a position only recently reinstated after he abolished the department in 1915. Always concerned about national security, alone among the cabinet he was dismayed at the Munich Agreement (1938). The extrenal affairs portfolio gave him very little influence, the real power resting with the prime minister. He was, however, also a member of the Council of Defence, and Lyons, once a vigorous opponent of Hughes's conscription referenda and still a pacifist, asked him to take charge of a volunteer recruitment campaign.

After some uncertainty and much intrigue, Robert G. Menzies became prime minister when on April 7, 1939, Lyons died unexpectedly. Then, on September 3, 1939, Great Britain declared war on Germany. Australia was also at war. Hughes was again member of a wartime government, staying on as attorney general and minister for industry, and then as attorney general and minister for the navy under Menzies' successor, until John Curtin took power on October 7, 1941. Later in the war, in 1944, at his request Hughes resumed his seat on the Advisory War Council after the United Australia Party withdrew its members. For the third time the now-shrunken, almost totally deaf, but still indomitable and always immaculately dressed Hughes was expelled from a political party. He now settled down to write two volumes of memoirs: *Crusts and Crusades* (1947) and *Policies and Potentates* (1950).

Hughes loved children and idealized motherhood, but his restless striving infringed on the lives of his own children and their mothers. As his career progressed, he was absent from his first family for weeks at a time. He did, however, see that his children had a good education and when his two younger sons enlisted, he asked a ministerial colleague to watch out for them. In later years, following the death of their daughter in 1937, Dame Mary (since 1922 a Dame Grand Cross of the Order of the British Empire) increasingly became the butt of his dyspeptic bad humor. Because of her nursing skills, however, she was always indispensable to his comfort, especially on overseas trips.

Hughes died at his home in Lindfield, Sydney, on October 28, 1952, having been in Parliament for so long he seemed an intrinsic part of that institution. For two days, Australians came to pay their last respects as his body lay in state at St. Andrew's Anglican Cathedral.

Summary

In 1916, William Morris Hughes was hailed by the British press, the United States ambassador reported to President Wilson, as a Moses, touring the United Kingdom from end to end. Fifty thousand women were so impressed that they signed a petition urging his continued presence in the Imperial War Cabinet. He returned in 1918 at a disadvantage because, unlike the other prime ministers from the British dominions of Canada (Robert L. Borden), New Zealand (William F. Massey), and South Africa (Jan Christian Smuts), he had been unable to be in England during 1917. Like them he was critical of the management of the war which consumed so many lives—including sixty thousand Australians. Then, through what he and his aides saw as another blunder, in November the armistice was signed with Germany without his having been consulted on the Fourteen Points governing peace conditions. The British prime minister (David Lloyd George) offered representation to the dominions at the Paris Peace Conference the following year through rotating membership in the British Empire delegation; Hughes, supported by Borden, held out for separate representation and they achieved both.

President Wilson, whom Hughes dubbed "Heaven-born," was determined to establish the League of Nations through the Treaty of Peace. Hughes came to Paris equally as determined to protect Australia's interests: He successfully argued for war reparations, control over German New Guinea, and the right for a member country to set its own immigration code.

A brilliant and imaginative wartime leader, achieving a voice for his nation on the conduct of the Great War and postwar events, Hughes remains, however, a controversial figure. He is looked on as an unprincipled opportunist by some. Others would agree with Dame Enid Lyons, the first woman to enter the House of Representatives, who wrote in 1972 that of all the prime ministers to that date, through his early work in the Labor movement "he had the greatest influence on the developing pattern of Australian life."

Bibliography

Booker, Malcolm. *The Great Professional: A Study of W. M. Hughes.* New York: McGraw-Hill, 1980. A provocative account of Hughes's career to 1923 by a former private secretary (1940-1941) and career diplomat.

Edwards, P. G. *Prime Ministers and Diplomats: The Making of Australian Foreign Policy, 1901-1949.* New York: Oxford University Press, 1983. Providing a useful sequel to Neville Meaney's book (see below), Edwards demonstrates how Australia's foreign policy was conducted almost exclusively by Hughes during his prime ministership.

Fitzhardinge, L. F. *William Morris Hughes: A Political Biography.* 2 vols. Sydney: Angus and

Robertson, 1964-1979. A scholarly work, commenced with Hughes's approval and written with sole access to his papers during its long gestation. The post-1923 years, however, receive inadequate attention.

Hughes, W. M. *The Case for Labor.* Sydney: Worker Trustees, 1910. Described by R. G. Menzies as a masterpiece of political polemics, this work collects twenty out of more than two hundred articles written for the Sydney *Daily Telegraph.*

————. *The Splendid Adventure: A Review of Empire Relations Within and Without the Commonwealth of Britannic Nations.* London: Benn, 1929. Part 1 has often been drawn on by writers of textbooks on the Commonwealth.

MacIntyre, Stuart. *The Succeeding Age, 1901-1942.* New York: Oxford University Press, 1986. A good general survey of the period.

Meaney, Neville. *The Search for Security in the Pacific, 1901-1914.* Sydney: Sydney University Press, 1976. An original, well-documented study, providing the background to Australia's development of an independent national defense and foreign policy.

Whyte, W. Farmer. *William Morris Hughes: His Life and Times.* Sydney: Angus and Robertson, 1957. Although not always reliable, a useful biography by a journalist long associated with Hughes.

Annette Potts
E. Daniel Potts

CORDELL HULL

Born: October 2, 1871; Overton County, Tennessee
Died: July 23, 1955; Bethesda, Maryland
Area of Achievement: Diplomacy, government and politics
Contribution: Serving as secretary of state longer than any man in American history, Hull shaped the world of diplomacy along the lines of his Jeffersonian and Wilsonian principles. His commitment to Woodrow Wilson's dream of a world organization helped make the United Nations a reality.

Early Life

Cordell Hull's boyhood was spent in the lovely Cumberland Mountains of Tennessee. Born in 1871 at the dawn of the industrial era, he absorbed the values of individualism and entrepreneurial activity. His father, William Hull, made a sizable fortune as a merchandiser and a supplier of logs. His mother, the former Elizabeth Riley, imbued him with strong religious (Baptist) and humanitarian sentiments.

Both parents encouraged Cordell and his two older brothers to obtain a formal education. A combination of private tutoring and local schooling eventually led him to normal schools at Bowling Green, Kentucky, and the National Normal University at Lebanon, Ohio. In 1889, illness ended his general education. He did, however, read law on his own, and he became an attorney after completing a ten-month course (in five months) at Cumberland Law School. His next step was into politics.

Before his twentieth birthday, Hull had already become the Democratic Party chairman of his county, entering the Tennessee state legislature two years later. His debating skills served him well. Hull enlisted in the army when the Spanish-American War began in 1898, although the war ended before he saw battle. By 1903, the young lawyer had been appointed to a Tennessee judicial seat (he would be called Judge for the remainder of his life), and he moved to Congress three years later.

By age thirty-six, when he moved to Washington, Hull had exhibited his ambition, his devotion to law and public life, and his principled approach to politics. Even his critics recognized his abilities. He possessed a fine intelligence and a courtly appearance, both of which served as important political assets. He was more reserved than most of his colleagues appreciated, and he combined a strong ethical sense with the moralistic outlook typical of the Progressive period. He was one of the best lawyers in Congress by the time he arrived in 1906, but he was also legalistic in ways that would later inhibit his political effectiveness.

Life's Work

Hull spent a quarter of a century in Congress. He served in the House of Representatives from 1907 until 1930 (except for a two-year period from 1921 to 1923), and then in the Senate until President-elect Franklin D. Roosevelt offered him the post of secretary of state. As a congressman, he sat on the Ways and Means Committee, where he specialized in tax and tariff matters during a period when federal spending soared. Hull fought for an income tax even before the ratification of the Sixteenth Amendment to the Constitution, and he became one of President Woodrow Wilson's chief congressional allies in the pursuit of a low tariff.

Indeed, the horrors of World War I helped to fix Hull's attention on low tariffs for the remainder of his public career. Like many others in his Progressive generation, Hull believed that the chief cause of war was economic injustice, which he ascribed to tariff barriers that inhibited international commerce. Combined with his faith in the sanctity of law and respect for written agreements and treaties, Hull's approach to international affairs had largely crystallized by the time Germany surrendered in 1918.

It was Hull's tenure as secretary of state, though, that secured his place in history. Hull was a compromise candidate for that post following Franklin D. Roosevelt's victory in 1932. He had already earned Roosevelt's gratitude following his outspoken support for United States' entry into the League of Nations when Roosevelt ran for the office of vice president in 1920, and he ably chaired the Democratic National Committee for the next three years while serving on that body during most of the decade. Hull had few enemies. After 1930, his articulate opposition to the Smoot-Hawley Tariff Act, which disastrously raised rates to the highest levels in American history, guaranteed him national prominence.

Hull's long service as secretary of state obscures the degree to which his record was decidedly mixed. He came to his post with many assets, in-

cluding an excellent relationship with Congress, a conscientious attitude toward his work, and genuine respect for the professionals in the State Department and the Foreign Service. Yet he was handicapped by his moralistic rigidity in a field which placed a premium on compromise, by his limited experience in foreign policy, and by his somewhat formal and distant relationship with the president. Consequently, Hull never achieved the influence in the foreign policy area that he desired. Roosevelt often relied upon friends and personal envoys rather than upon his secretary of state. The president even bypassed the department entirely at certain critical moments, leaving Hull uninformed and embarrassed. This sort of thing plagued Hull as early as 1933, when Roosevelt undermined his efforts at international cooperation at the London Economic Conference, and as late as 1944, when the secretary of the treasury, but not the secretary of state, joined Roosevelt and Winston Churchill at the Second Quebec Conference to formulate the famous Morgenthau Plan. Bitterly opposed by Hull, the plan aimed to turn post-World War II Germany into an agricultural society.

Indeed, Hull's chief assistants in the State Department were Roosevelt loyalists, who had been appointed largely without consulting the new secretary in 1933, and Roosevelt often relied on Secretary of the Treasury Henry Morgenthau, Jr., or Undersecretary of State Sumner Welles in formulating foreign policy. Hull's memoirs occasionally reflect his dismay at these arrangements. The fact of the matter is that Roosevelt devalued Hull's contributions. Like his cousin Theodore before him, Roosevelt insisted on being his own secretary of state, particularly during the period after 1939, when the line between diplomatic and military affairs was blurred.

Nevertheless, Hull rarely considered resignation from an administration for which, in fact, he had only limited ideological sympathy. His optimism, loyalty, congeniality, and fascination with power kept him in the Cabinet. He often lamented the influence of those whom he considered radicals and extreme New Dealers. His Jeffersonian suspicion of large government kept him something of an outsider in the Administration. Despite this fact, he continued to have a cordial, if not close, relationship with the president, and he had an excellent working relationship with conservative Cabinet members such as Henry Stimson in the War Department and Frank Knox in the Navy Department.

Hull may have had limited influence within the Roosevelt Administration, but his long tenure in the State Department resulted in some notable successes. Perhaps most important was his sponsorship of the Reciprocal Trade Agreements Act, which Congress passed in 1934. Hull's support for this measure—which permitted the president to negotiate lower tariffs on a bilateral basis—stemmed from his belief that lower rates would contribute to both international peace and economic recovery. Based on this act, the secretary helped to negotiate twenty-one agreements that moderated rates from the high Smoot-Hawley levels of the Hoover years. Moreover, the measure shifted tariff authority from the Congress to the executive, a change congenial to Hull, who was very much influenced by the Progressive movement of the early twentieth century.

Hull's two other chief accomplishments centered on improving relations with Latin America and strengthening the framework of international organizations. He was a prime mover behind Roosevelt's Good Neighbor Policy, which sought to reverse years of American bullying in Central and South America. Hull continued the policy enunciated in the Clark Memorandum of 1930, which renounced the use of military intervention in Latin America. Much of Hull's work was formalized at a series of conferences, the most dramatic of which was held in Montevideo, Uruguay, in 1933. Hull eventually strengthened the relationship of the United States with all Latin American nations except Argentina. He relaxed the heavy hand of American economic imperialism in the hemisphere, and he built a basis for military cooperation during World War II.

Hull was in every sense a Wilsonian in supporting international cooperation through a world organization. He strongly supported the United States' entry into the International Labor Organization in 1934, and he deeply regretted the Senate's rejection of World Court membership for the United States the following year. His most gratifying work as secretary of state was his effort to create a successor organization to the League of Nations. He helped to author the Charter of the United Nations, and he was instrumental in sidetracking regional agreements as a substitute for a genuine world organization. Moreover, Hull's political skills helped to prevent the Republicans from making the United Nations into a partisan issue during the presidential campaign of 1944. He had learned the lessons of 1919.

These successes must be balanced against his most significant failure, for Hull and Roosevelt did little to prevent the drift toward war in 1939. Partly handcuffed by the degree to which most Americans were preoccupied with the economic crisis, Hull maintained a policy toward the future Axis powers that relied excessively on a rigid repetition of moral principles that he assumed to be the universal basis for international conduct. He never understood the degree to which Axis leaders held his principles in contempt, nor the degree to which American interests in distant areas might justifiably be compromised to prevent war.

Summary

For all of Hull's success in such areas as trade, international organization, and good-neighbor relations, his service as secretary of state was marked more by failure than success. His approach to world affairs had been shaped excessively by the moralistic attitudes of the Progressives. Adolf Hitler and Benito Mussolini were unimpressed by his moral pronouncements. Hull's genuine fear of war contributed to lukewarm support for the pre-1939 appeasement policy of Great Britain and France. Hull was more assertive toward Japan, but without the support of the Allied powers, he was unwilling to take any action of a decisive nature before 1940, and neither was Roosevelt. American policy was neither courageous nor distinguished before World War II.

Once the Japanese attacked Pearl Harbor, Hull's influence further declined. Roosevelt utilized personal envoys such as Harry Hopkins to sidestep the State Department during the war. The president cultivated a personal relationship with Allied heads of state such as Joseph Stalin and Winston Churchill, therefore diluting the contributions of his secretary of state. By the time that Hull left office for health reasons in November, 1944, the center of foreign policy decision was no longer in the State Department. Cordell Hull must accept his share of responsibility for this development.

Bibliography

Butler, Michael A. *Cautious Visionary: Cordell Hull and Trade Reform, 1933-1937*. Kent, Ohio: Kent State University Press, 1998. Butler, a career diplomat, discusses Hull's contributions to U.S. diplomacy during Franklin Roosevelt's first administration. Contends that influence of Hull's belief in a link between economics and security survives to this day.

Drummond, Donald F. "Cordell Hull." In *An Uncertain Tradition: American Secretaries of State in the Twentieth Century*, edited by Norman Graebner, 184-209. New York: McGraw-Hill, 1961. This is the most skillful short study of Hull. The author admires Hull's opposition to Fascism but believes that his rigid emphasis on principle often rendered his diplomacy ineffective.

Gellman, Irwin F. *Secret Affairs: Franklin Roosevelt, Cordell Hull, and Sumner Welles*. Baltimore: Johns Hopkins University Press, 1995. Gellman examines the relationships among Roosevelt, Hull, and Welles, concentrating on the feud between Welles and Hull. Critics observed a lack of objectivity and a tendency toward censorship on the part of the author.

Hull, Cordell. *The Memoirs of Cordell Hull*. 2 vols. London: Hodder and Stoughton, and New York: Macmillan, 1948. Hull's own highly detailed and somewhat dull account of his public life. These volumes gloss over the rivalry for influence within the Roosevelt Administration, but they nevertheless offer a wealth of valuable information.

Jablon, Howard. "Cordell Hull, His 'Associates,' and Relations with Japan, 1933-1936." *Mid-America* 56 (1974): 160-174. The author argues that Hull's policy toward Japan was merely an extension of Henry Stimson's Non-Recognition Policy. Hull, says Jablon, relied excessively on his advisers and an approach which elevated principle over any serious assessment of Japanese interests.

Pratt, Julius. *Cordell Hull: 1933-44*. New York: Cooper Square, 1964. The best and most comprehensive study of Hull as secretary of state. Pratt is often uncritical of Hull, but, like most other historians, he faults Hull's excessive moralism. The book is organized topically.

Gary B. Ostrower

HUBERT H. HUMPHREY

Born: May 27, 1911; Wallace, South Dakota
Died: January 13, 1978; Waverly, Minnesota
Area of Achievement: Government and politics
Contribution: In the tradition of philosophical pragmatism and New Deal liberalism in the twentieth century, Humphrey became one of the most innovative and effective legislators in United States history.

Early Life

Hubert Horatio Humphrey, Jr., was born on May 27, 1911, in Wallace, South Dakota, of Yankee pioneer and Norwegian immigrant stock. He was the second of four children. His autobiography reveals that his life on the northern plains was difficult. During the 1920's, his family lived on the edge of poverty, buffeted by agricultural hard times after World War I, grasshopper infestations, drought, and the national economic collapse of 1929-1939. His father, a pharmacist and liberal Democrat, exerted the greatest impact upon his life. Young Hubert absorbed his father's Midwestern populism and Wilsonian moralism.

In spite of economic hardship, Humphrey's home life was serene and loving. He debated political issues with his father, sold newspapers, played football and basketball in high school, participated in drama and debates, and maintained a high scholastic average. The Humphreys lived with the threat of bankruptcy throughout this period and had to sell their home in Doland, South Dakota, to pay their bills.

Even so, Hubert entered the University of Minnesota in 1928, but, lacking funds, he was compelled to leave the university and enroll in Capital College of Pharmacy in Denver. By 1933, he had received his pharmacist's diploma and was working in his father's drugstore in Doland. He became active in politics and joined the Young Democrats. He was an ardent New Dealer who believed that strong government was a positive force in society. He argued that government had a responsibility to protect the weak and allow for the fullest expression and development of the individual.

In 1936, he married Muriel Buck, daughter of an agricultural wholesaler; they would have four children. In 1937, he resumed his studies at the University of Minnesota, joined the debating team and Phi Beta Kappa, and was graduated magna cum laude. In 1939-1940, Humphrey received his master's degree in political science at Louisiana State University. While living in Baton Rouge, he was profoundly shocked by the state's segregationist system.

Life's Work

During the summer of 1940, Humphrey returned to Minnesota to earn his doctorate. He also found a position with the Works Progress Administration (WPA) in Duluth and then headed the WPA Workers Education Program in Minneapolis. These positions introduced Humphrey to influential labor, civic, and political leaders of the city and state. After World War II began, Humphrey liquidated the WPA state apparatus. In 1943, he campaigned for mayor of Minneapolis against a corruption-tainted incumbent. Although he lost by five thousand votes, Humphrey learned valuable campaign lessons which he utilized successfully in his mayoralty bids of 1945 and 1947. Critical to his success, however, was his role in negotiating the fusion of the Democratic and Farm Labor parties in 1944. The Democratic-Farm Labor Alliance (DFL) has been a dominant force in Minnesota politics ever since.

Humphrey's two terms as mayor of Minneapolis were reformist and liberal in character. He promoted a housing program for returning veterans and the disadvantaged; he hired a tough, no-nonsense police chief to root out gamblers and racketeers; he fostered closer religious and racial relations through a Human Relations Board; and he obtained a permanent Fair Employment Practices Commission to end job discrimination. Meanwhile, he led the fight to expel Communists from DFL leadership, and in 1947, he helped organize the Americans for Democratic Action (ADA) to unite anti-Communist liberals on domestic and foreign affairs issues. In 1949, he chaired the ADA.

In 1948, Humphrey declared his candidacy for the United States Senate. Perhaps the highlight of his career occurred in the 1948 Democratic National Convention when he successfully pushed through a strong civil rights plank in the platform. That stand led Southern Democrats to bolt the party and unite under the banner of the States Rights Party. Along with the left-wing Progressive Party of America, this defection promised to make 1948 a banner Republican year. Ironically, Humphrey's civil rights plank proved to be a major Democratic

issue and contributed significantly to President Harry S Truman's upset victory.

Humphrey's senatorial victory in 1948 made him one of many freshman liberal faces in national affairs. His early years in the Senate were frustrating. Southern Democrats nursed a grudge for his role in the nominating convention, and his long-winded oratory did not endear him to his colleagues. Instead of maintaining a low profile as a freshman senator, he introduced bill after bill on a wide range of issues that reflected the liberal agenda for the 1950's and 1960's, but little action was taken on them. The nadir of his senatorial career came when he violated Senate protocol by attacking Harry F. Byrd of Virginia while the latter visited his ailing mother. Byrd's response was crushing, and Humphrey regretted the incident for the remainder of his life.

He overcame that debacle largely because of the rehabilitative efforts of Lyndon B. Johnson, an ambitious Texan and perhaps the greatest Senate majority leader in history. Humphrey gave Johnson access to liberals, civil rights groups, and labor; Johnson gave Humphrey respectability and

brought him within the folds of the Senate establishment. Consequently, Humphrey acquired the knowledge and skills to become one of the most successful legislators in history. Among his accomplishments were the National Defense Education Act, Food for Peace, Job Corps, Peace Corps, Vista, Foodstamps, the Nuclear Arms Control and Disarmament Agency, Nuclear Test-Ban Treaty of 1963, and the Civil Rights Act of 1964. Another Humphrey achievement was the Medicare bill of 1965, which he had promoted since his arrival in the Senate.

Humphrey had long been interested in the presidency. His membership on the prestigious Foreign Relations Committee enabled him to establish credentials in foreign affairs. In 1958, for example, he held meetings with world leaders, including the celebrated eight-hour meeting with Soviet Premier Nikita S. Khrushchev. In 1956, Humphrey supported Adlai Stevenson's nomination for president and believed that he had the latter's commitment for the vice presidency. As it turned out, Stevenson allowed the convention delegates to select his running mate, who was Senator Estes Kefauver of Tennessee. In 1960, he made an ill-fated bid for the presidency, only to be crushed by the Kennedy juggernaut in the Wisconsin and West Virginia primaries.

As Senate majority whip during the John F. Kennedy and Lyndon B. Johnson administrations (1961-1965), Humphrey became the central player in the legislative enactment of their programs. In 1964, Johnson, who had become president following Kennedy's assassination in 1963, sought election in his own right. To create some interest in the nominating convention, he dangled the vice presidency before Humphrey and his Minnesota colleague, Eugene McCarthy. Both men endured this humiliating manipulation in the months before the convention as Johnson pushed one, then the other, to the forefront. He ultimately selected Humphrey with the expectation that Humphrey would be completely loyal to his program.

As vice president (1965-1969), Humphrey's loyalty to the administration was unquestioned in spite of increasing unpopularity of United States adventures in South Vietnam. This loyalty earned for Humphrey the disgust and contempt of many antiwar liberals. One of these liberals was Senator McCarthy, who challenged Johnson's bid for renomination in 1968. McCarthy's surprising strength in the New Hampshire primary forced Johnson to withdraw from the campaign.

The removal of Johnson from the presidential contest gave Humphrey his best opportunity to capture the White House. While his opponents, McCarthy and Senator Robert F. Kennedy of New York, bloodied each other in primary contests, Humphrey began to pull away in delegate strength by relying on the support of the traditional New Deal coalition. His theme was the "politics of joy," a phrase turned against him by the Tet offensive in South Vietnam, political assassinations, race riots, and violent antiwar protests in the streets. It appeared to many Americans that their country was coming apart. Although Humphrey won the presidential nomination in Chicago, the political cost was high, and his image was tarnished further in the public mind by televised scenes of Chicago police beating youthful protestors during his acceptance speech.

From that moment, Humphrey's campaign had nowhere to go but up. His opponents were Richard M. Nixon for the Republican Party and Alabama Governor George C. Wallace for the American Independent Party. Nixon had resurrected himself from political oblivion following successive defeats for president in 1960 and for California governor in 1962. Far ahead in the polls, he waged a careful and controlled media campaign based on law and order and honorably terminating American involvement in South Vietnam. Wallace's appeal was racist, anti-bureaucracy, and anti-Communist, and he sought to win the Southern states and the Northern blue-collar vote. For his part, Humphrey entered the campaign late, with a bitterly divided party behind him, a weak national campaign organization, no money, and plagued by a public perception of him as a Johnson clone. Protestors also made it difficult for him to present his ideas coherently to the voters.

On September 30, 1968, Humphrey's fortunes reversed when he pledged to halt the bombing of North Vietnam before receiving conciliatory gestures from the enemy. This subtle breach with Johnson quieted the antiwar movement, which slowly and grudgingly returned to the Democratic fold—a return symbolized by McCarthy's tepid endorsement late in the campaign. Simultaneously, the traditional blue-collar voter also returned to the Democratic Party, and public opinion polls reflected a dramatic surge in Humphrey's popular support. By election day, 1968, polls indicated that the race had concluded in a virtual dead heat. Although momentum was clearly with him, Humphrey narrowly lost the election by approximately 500,000 votes. In the electoral college, Nixon won with 301 votes to Humphrey's 191 and Wallace's 46.

Humphrey returned to Minnesota, to teach and to write his memoirs, but, in 1970, he was elected to the Senate when McCarthy declined to seek reelection. Two years later, he made another determined bid for the presidential nomination, but he could not overcome his association with Johnson and Vietnam. His campaign ended in California, where he was defeated by Senator George McGovern of South Dakota. In 1974, he found that he had cancer, which became a factor in his decision not to make another presidential effort. On January 13, 1978, Hubert Humphrey died in his Waverly, Minnesota, home, and he was replaced in the United States Senate by his wife, Muriel.

Summary

Hubert Humphrey's life reflected the Horatio Alger myth. Born in humble circumstances, he worked hard all of his life and came agonizingly close to achieving the highest office in the land. Yet, in spite of all of his efforts, he failed to achieve that prize. Those who knew him well do not doubt that he would have made an excellent president, and one must wonder how the history of the United States would have been altered if he had emerged triumphant in 1968. His was an ebullient personality, the "happy warrior" who sought to heal the divisiveness and wounds of the body politic.

Still, there was something in Humphrey's makeup that denied him his greatest hopes. Some believed that he lacked the instinct for the political kill, that he was not ruthless enough, that he was too emotional, too talkative, and that he was simply too nice a human being to become president. There may be some truth to this theory. Humphrey was an eternal optimist; he believed in the idea of progress, that man was reasonable and good, and he lived his life—public and private—in harmony with these attitudes. His failure lay in his overwhelming need to be liked; he could never say no. Thus, he allowed himself to be so dominated by Lyndon B. Johnson that he lost his public persona, and he was not to regain his separate identity until late in his career.

Humphrey was a New Deal liberal, and he believed in the social welfare state. The Great Depression of the 1930's taught him that "rugged individualism" was anachronistic in twentieth century economic and political life. Alone, the citizen was defenseless against concentrated sources of private and public power. Government, he believed, was not an enemy to be despised, but a friend to protect one from disasters beyond one's control and to allow one to live freely. Humphrey was a pragmatist and a believer in New Deal experimentation. As much as any man of his time, he fulfilled the promise inherent in Franklin D. Roosevelt's program during the New Frontier and Great Society days of the 1960's.

Bibliography

Berman, Edgar M. D. *Hubert: The Triumph and Tragedy of the Humphrey I Knew.* New York: Putnam, 1979. A memoir by a Humphrey confidant who emphasizes the latter's pragmatic, liberal philosophy. Explores Humphrey's vice presidency and blames Johnson for Humphrey's 1968 defeat.

Cohen, Dan. *Undefeated: The Life of Hubert H. Humphrey.* Minneapolis: Lerner, 1978. A useful biography by a political veteran in Minnesota. Emphasizes Humphrey's early life and career, particularly Minnesota politics during the 1930's and 1940's. Full illustrations, background material, and anecdotes, reflecting Humphrey's character and personality.

Eisele, Albert. *Almost to the Presidency: A Biography of Two American Politicians.* Blue Earth, Minn.: Piper, 1972. Written by a newspaperman and close observer of the careers of Humphrey and McCarthy. A study of contrasts: Humphrey representing the politics of consensus and McCarthy symbolizing the politics of change.

Garrettson, Charles Lloyd. *Hubert H. Humphrey: The Politics of Joy.* New Brunswick, N.J.: Transaction, 1993. Somewhat disappointing biography focusing on defense of Humphrey's Vietnam policies and his 1968 campaign for president.

Griffith, Winthrop. *Humphrey: A Candid Biography.* New York: Morrow, 1965. Written by a Humphrey aide. Focuses on Humphrey's political philosophy, character, personality, and Senate career.

Humphrey, Hubert Horatio. *The Education of a Public Man: My Life and Politics.* Edited by Norman Sherman. New York: Doubleday, and London: Weidenfeld and Nicolson, 1976. A superior political autobiography. Candid but remarkably free from bitterness. A very revealing look into Humphrey's character and personality, particularly his relationship with Johnson.

————. *The Political Philosophy of the New Deal.* Baton Rouge: Louisiana State University Press, 1970. Published version of Humphrey's master's thesis. Written from a partisan perspective. Defends the New Deal as an attempt to establish economic democracy and as being part of a democratic trend in American politics that dates back to Thomas Jefferson.

Ryskind, Allan H. *Hubert: An Unauthorized Biography of the Vice President.* New York: Arlington House, 1968. A critical biography of Humphrey. Denounces virtually all aspects of his public life, presenting him as a hypocritical pleader for the social welfare state.

Solberg, Carl. *Hubert Humphrey: A Biography.* New York: Norton, 1984. The most recent, complete, and objective study of this Minnesota liberal. Places Humphrey in the tradition of William Jennings Bryan, George W. Norris, and Robert M. La Follette. An often absorbing analysis of Humphrey's life and career.

Thurber, Timothy. *Politics of Equality: Hubert Humphrey and the African American Freedom Struggle, 1945-1978.* New York: Columbia University Press, 1999. The author examines Senator Humphrey's policies on racial justice, which were based on the achievement of racial equality through economic reforms. Humphrey's career is the basis for exploration of the clashes among race, class, and politics in the second half of the twentieth century.

Stephen P. Sayles

ZORA NEALE HURSTON

Born: January 7, 1891; Eatonville, Florida
Died: January 28, 1960; Fort Pierce, Florida
Area of Achievement: Literature
Contribution: The most accomplished African American woman writing in the first half of the twentieth century, Zora Neale Hurston was a major writer of the Harlem Renaissance and an important influence on later generations of women writers.

Early Life

Zora Neale Hurston's hometown was Eatonville, Florida, a self-governing all-black town that allowed her to develop a sense of individuality. One of eight children, she was urged to "jump at de sun" by her mother, who tried to preserve her high spirits so that she would not become, in Zora's words, "a mealy-mouthed rag doll." Her father, however, feared that her audacious spirit would not be tolerated by white America and often punished her for impudence. A minister and three-term mayor of Eatonville, John Hurston was something of a hero among the townsfolk, and Zora would devote a novel (*Jonah's Gourd Vine*, 1934) largely to his life story. Yet she was also fascinated by her mother, who molded John Hurston into the successful public man that he became. Lucy Ann Potts Hurston was perhaps the only person in town who did not regard her husband with awe. As Zora described their relationship in her autobiography, "the one who makes the idols never worships them, however tenderly he might have molded the clay." Zora observed with keen interest how Lucy Ann, with a few simple words, could confound the very arguments for which townsfolk or church members praised John.

Zora read widely, preferring adventure stories such as *Gulliver's Travels*, Norse mythology, and the Greek myth of Hercules to stories that urged little girls to become dutiful and domesticated. Eatonville gave her a strong sense of herself, but she was also impatient with small town restrictions. "My soul was with the gods and my body in the village. People just would not act like gods. . . . Raking back yards and carrying out chamber-pots, were not the tasks of Thor. I wanted to be away from drabness and to stretch my limbs in some mighty struggle."

Hurston's world fell apart when her mother died. When John Hurston remarried, Zora's stepmother had no use for her and her siblings, and Zora had to leave home. She was passed from relative to relative, was unable to attend school, and badly missed the close family environment in which she had grown up. She was also poor and had to work as a nanny and housekeeper, although she really wanted to read and dream. Tired of poverty and dependence, she was hired as a wardrobe girl by a young actress in a traveling troupe who performed Gilbert and Sullivan musicals. She was well-liked and, in turn, she enjoyed the camaraderie and adventure of traveling.

Life's Work

Zora Neale Hurston's writing career began not long after she left home. After graduating from night school at Morgan Academy in Baltimore in 1918, she attended Howard University. While there, she wrote a story that caught the attention of the founder of *Opportunity* magazine, Charles S. Johnson, who sponsored literary contests and was instrumental in the development of the black arts movement of the 1920's known as the Harlem Renaissance. Johnson published her next two stories, "Drenched in Light" (1924) and "Spunk" (1925), and she suddenly found herself among the Harlem Renaissance's prominent writers.

Both these stories and her play *Color Struck* (1926) were based on the folk life she had observed in Eatonville. In her autobiography *Dust Tracks on a Road* (1942), Hurston describes the importance of Joe Clarke's general store, a repository of the rich African American oral tradition. There she heard the "lying sessions"—that is, exaggerated folk tales featuring talking animals such as Brer Rabbit, Brer Fox, and Buzzard—that she eventually used in her finest writings. In an age in which many blacks believed that fitting into America meant showing that they could conform to middle-class values just as well as whites, Hurston concentrated on the black masses and their values. Far from being ashamed of the lower classes, she knew that their expressions—black folklore, blues, and spirituals—were those of a people who were healthy minded and who had survived slavery through their own creative ingenuity.

Hurston's talent as a writer attracted the interest and friendship of several benefactors, including Fannie Hurst, a best-selling white author who befriended Hurston and hired her as a secretary, and

Annie Nathan Meyer, who secured a scholarship to Barnard College for Hurston.

Two other benefactors helped to show Hurston that the folk culture of Eatonville had anthropological, as well as literary, interest. A paper she wrote at Barnard caught the eye of Franz Boas, the noted Columbia University anthropologist, and she was invited to study with him. He urged her to regard the Eatonville folklore as a continuation of African oral storytelling and suggested that she return to the South and collect it. Another person who encouraged her to do so was Charlotte Osgood Mason, who was nicknamed "Godmother" for her maternal characteristics and perhaps also because of her godlike behavior (she liked to sit on a throne-like chair when her "godchildren" visited her). She was a wealthy white patron of the arts who wished to preserve "primitive" minority cultures—in other words, cultures free of the civilized pretensions of modern life. She provided Hurston with money, a movie camera, and an automobile with which to collect folklore in the South. *Mules and Men* (1935), a masterly collection of southern black

folktales, was the eventual result of Hurston's efforts in that area.

Although Hurston was pressured to adapt her novels to a prescribed theme about struggles against racism, she believed that such a theme would be a limitation. She preferred to concentrate on those indigenous elements of black community life that survived racism intact.

Her first novel, *Jonah's Gourd Vine* (1934), is the story of a Baptist minister who delivers powerful sermons but who upsets his congregation by following his own natural impulses and entering into adulterous relationships that his parishioners cannot reconcile with his role as minister. *Their Eyes Were Watching God* (1937), Hurston's masterpiece, explores a black woman's three marriages, her frustrations, and her aspiration to become a fully autonomous human being. *Moses, Man of the Mountain* (1939) is an ambitious allegory about the "hoodoo man" Moses, who tries to inspire in an enslaved people a group identity. To dispel the idea that black writers were limited to black subjects, Hurston devoted her last novel, *Seraph on the Suwanee* (1948), to the subject of poor southern whites.

Richard Wright criticized *Their Eyes Were Watching God* because it did not protest racial oppression, but Hurston disagreed with the attitudes of protesters, whom she called "the sobbing school of Negrohood." In *Dust Tracks on a Road*, she insisted that all individuals had it in their power to determine their fates and that an appeal to racial uniqueness was the refuge of the weak. Believing that "skins were no measure of what was inside people," Hurston ridiculed anyone "who claimed special blessings on the basis of race." In spite of the fact that it was criticized—most notably by Arna Bontemps—her autobiography won the Anisfield-Wolf Award for its contribution to better race relations.

Hurston's devotion to writing and collecting left her little time for sustained relationships. She states in her autobiography that *Their Eyes Were Watching God* was written in Haiti in an attempt to come to terms with a love affair she had had in New York with a young college student of West Indian descent. She left him for the same reason that she had divorced her first husband, Herbert Sheen, in 1931. She wished to be free to pursue her career, and her relationships with men did not allow her that freedom. As she writes about her young lover: "My work was one thing, and he was all the rest";

to him, however, it was "all, or nothing." A second attempt at marriage, with Albert Price III in 1939, ended in divorce a year later.

In 1948, Hurston was arrested and charged with molesting the ten-year-old son of a woman from whom she had rented an apartment in New York. Although she proved that she could not have committed the act because she was out of the country at the time, the story was sensationalized in the African American press. She felt betrayed and wrote, "My race has seen fit to destroy me without reason."

After the 1948 publication of *Seraph on the Suwanee,* Hurston never published another book. In her last decade, she worked as teacher, librarian, reporter, and maid. She also became active as a political conservative. She supported the 1946 campaign of Republican Grant Reynolds against Adam Clayton Powell, Jr., in Harlem, and in the primary elections of 1950, she opposed the liberal Claude Pepper. In "I Saw Negro Votes Peddled" (1950), she attributed to a lack of self-esteem black complicity in vote-buying schemes perpetrated by the Pepper campaign. In 1954, she opposed the Supreme Court's decision in *Brown v. Board of Education,* which ordered school desegregation. She viewed it as a matter of self-respect. She could get little satisfaction from a law that forced associations between persons who did not want to associate and that assumed that blacks could not develop properly unless they associated with whites.

After suffering a stroke in 1959, she died on January 28, 1960, in a nursing home in Fort Pierce, Florida. Her grave remained unmarked until the 1970's, when Alice Walker located it and erected a stone that reads, in part:

Zora Neale Hurston
"A Genius of the South"
Novelist, Folklorist, Anthropologist

Summary

To Alice Walker, who documented her discovery of Zora Neale Hurston in the collection of feminist essays *In Search of Our Mothers' Gardens,* Hurston represented an artistic foremother whose achievements and defiance of conventional roles for women were inspiring. Hurston's efforts to preserve, nurture, and transmit African American folk culture were based on her belief that folklore was the common person's art form and that black folklore provided America with its greatest cultural wealth. Her ability to capture the sounds of folk speech and to retell the imaginative stories of African Americans was the foundation of her talent as a writer of fiction. Living most of her life in obscurity and buried in an unmarked grave, Hurston lived and wrote with a confidence and self-acceptance that made her a favorite model for later generations of writers.

Bibliography

Bloom, Harold, ed. *Modern Critical Views: Zora Neale Hurston.* New York: Chelsea House, 1986. This book of essays about Hurston includes contemporary accounts by those who knew her, as well as modern critical appraisals.

Davis, Rose P., comp. *Zora Neale Hurston: An Annotated Bibliography and Reference Guide.* Westport, Conn.: Greenwood Press, 1997. A guide to the body of work on Hurston produced in the last seventy-five years. Includes annotated entries for dissertations, books, articles, and more.

Glassman, Steve, and Kathryn Lee Seidel, eds. *Zora in Florida.* Orlando: University of Central Florida Press, 1991. This book of critical essays examines Hurston's lesser-known works and is particularly concerned with the influence of her native Florida on her work.

Hemenway, Robert E. *Zora Neale Hurston: A Literary Biography.* Urbana: University of Illinois Press, 1977; London: Camden Press, 1986. The strength of this scholarly biography is its placing of Hurston's literary achievements in the context of American and African American literary history.

———, ed. "Introduction." In *Dust Tracks on a Road: An Autobiography,* by Zora Neale Hurston. 2d ed. Urbana: University of Illinois Press, 1984; London: Virago, 1986. Despite its unfortunate attempt to discredit the conservative views expressed in Hurston's autobiography, this essay does provide useful information about the political context in which the book was written and confirms that Hurston's birth year was more likely 1891 than the oft-cited 1901.

Holloway, Karla F. C. *The Character of the Word: The Texts of Zora Neale Hurston.* New York: Greenwood Press, 1987. An analysis of Hurston's use of language in her writings.

Howard, Lillie P., ed. *Alice Walker and Zora Neale Hurston: The Common Bond.* Westport, Conn.: Greenwood Press, 1993. Eleven African-American scholars consider the relationship between Hurston and Alice Walker including Hurston's influence on Walker and Walker's use of Hurston's views and thoughts.

————. *Zora Neale Hurston.* Boston: Twayne, 1980. A useful overview of Hurston's life and works in an accessible format including a bibliography.

Hurston, Zora Neale. *Dust Tracks on a Road: An Autobiography.* 2d ed. Urbana: University of Illinois Press, 1984; London: Virago, 1986. Hurston's autobiography is a chronicle of an independent woman. She discusses her earliest childhood impressions, her involvement in the Harlem Renaissance, and her thoughts on the racial problem in the United States.

————. *Their Eyes Were Watching God.* Philadelphia and London: Lippincott, 1937. Hurston's compelling novel about a woman's search for love and self-actualization is a masterpiece of African American literature. Hurston states that it had an autobiographical basis.

Walker, Alice. "Zora Neale Hurston—A Cautionary Tale and a Partisan View." Foreword to *Zora Neale Hurston: A Literary Biography*, by Robert E. Hemenway. Urbana: University of Illinois Press, 1977; London: Camden Press, 1986. This partisan defense of Hurston's work is written by the person most responsible for engineering a revival of interest in Hurston. The essay emphasizes Hurston's value to feminists and views her poverty as a cautionary story from which other women writers can learn.

William L. Howard

HUSSEIN I

Born: November 14, 1935; Amman, Transjordan
Died: February 7, 1999; Jordan
Areas of Achievement: Government and politics
Contribution: Holding power longer than any other world leader, Hussein, King of Jordan, maintained the autonomy of Jordan, contributed to Arab unity, and served as a stabilizing force in the Middle East.

Early Life

Hussein I (born Hussein ibn Talal) of Jordan is considered a direct descendant of the Prophet Mohammed and the head of the "first family" of Islam, the Hashemites. The eldest of four children born to Crown Prince Talal and Princess Zein, he was born in Amman, the capital of Transjordan (now Jordan), on November 14, 1935. At that time, Jordan was a poor, feudal, Bedouin state, mostly desert, and even the royal family lived frugally. Hussein grew up in a five-room house in Amman, where, by his own account, he learned to mend his clothes and even sold his bicycle at one point to help with family finances.

Hussein's father suffered from mental illness, and his grandfather, King Abdullah, took a special interest in young Hussein's upbringing and exerted a significant influence on his character. Under his grandfather's supervision, Hussein was reared as an Arab prince and educated in both English and Arabic. At age five, he was enrolled in kindergarten in Amman, where he also attended the Islamic College. At age eight, he was sent to Victoria College in Alexandria, Egypt.

The Hashemites had played a key role in ending the Ottoman rule over the Arab states. As his reward, Abdullah was recognized by the British as Emir of Transjordan, created as an adjunct of the British Mandate in Palestine in 1921, and received a British subsidy to maintain security and establish a central government over the Bedouin tribes. In 1946, Abdullah established the independent Hashemite Kingdom of Transjordan, with continued support and collaboration from the British. When the termination of the British Mandate in Palestine on May 14, 1948, resulted in the creation of Israel and the Arab-Israeli War, King Abdullah took control of areas of eastern Palestine on the West Bank of the Jordan River and was proclaimed King of United Transjordan and Palestine (or the Hashemite Kingdom of Jordan) in December, 1948.

Hussein frequently accompanied his grandfather on his official duties. In July, 1951, on a trip to Jerusalem, King Abdullah was assassinated by a Palestinian extremist at El Aqsa Mosque (the Mosque of the Rock), and Hussein narrowly escaped death himself when he tried to capture the assassin and a medal on his uniform deflected a bullet. Witnessing his grandfather's murder and the panic that ensued among his loyal followers made a profound impression on the young prince. His firsthand experience with political assassination and the unreliability of the king's followers taught Hussein the risks of political life at an early age and instilled in him a determination to live purposefully and to be ready for death whenever it comes.

Crown Prince Talal, who had been receiving treatment in a mental hospital in Switzerland, was crowned king in September. Hussein, now crown prince, was sent to complete his studies at Harrow in England, where his cousin, Faisal II, heir to Iraq's throne, was also a student. When Talal suffered a relapse and was asked to step down from the throne in August, 1952, Hussein was declared king three months before his seventeenth birthday. He took a six-month accelerated course at the Royal Military Academy at Sandhurst, England, while the regency council exercised control of Jordan until his eighteenth birthday.

Life's Work

Hussein was crowned King of Jordan on May 2, 1953. His strong autocratic rule, strength of character, and personal charisma make it difficult to extricate his personal history from the history of the state of Jordan. Despite his youth and lack of political experience, he was able to survive multiple internal and international challenges during the economic and political instability of the early years of his reign. His commitment to Arab nationalism, his desire for peace in the Middle East, his search for a solution to the Palestinian problem, and his democratic ideals were not always compatible with consistent political decisions.

Jordan's incorporation of the West Bank under King Abdullah resulted in a sudden increase in population that strained the small country's resources. Some 750,000 Palestinians, including an

influx of more than 500,000 refugees from Israeli-occupied Palestine, outnumbered the Jordanians almost two to one. Although Jordan was the only Arab state to grant the Palestinians citizenship and participation in parliamentary and municipal elections, they were bitter and resentful. They resented Jordan's financial dependence on Great Britain, British influence on the Jordanian government and armed forces, and the parliament's token participation in government.

Jordan's desire for accommodation and peace with Israel, given its extended border with that country, contrasted dangerously with the demands for all-out war from the other Arab states. Left-wing Middle Eastern extremists, led by Egyptian President Gamal Abdel Nasser, fanned the fires of Palestinian resentment and labeled Hussein "a tool of the West." Confronting the first urban unrest and agitation in Jordan, Hussein yielded to demands for political liberalization and relaxed restrictions on the press, measures that temporarily enhanced his popularity but unfortunately only served to increase the turmoil.

When the British insisted in 1955 that Jordan join the Baghdad Pact, part of a general Middle East defense system against the Soviet Union, riots followed. The king dissolved parliament, and the Arab Legion (the Jordanian armed forces), commanded by an Englishman, John Bagot Glubb, had to suppress the mobs. Hussein announced his unwillingness to join either the Baghdad Pact or the Egyptian-Syrian-Saudi Arabian Bloc, but the demands for a scapegoat on whom to blame the disturbances resulted in his dismissal of Glubb in March, 1956; one of Glubb's replacements was Lieutenant Colonel Ali Abu Nuwar, the leader of the movement to eliminate foreign influence in Jordan. Relations between Great Britain and Jordan cooled. In October, 1956, Hussein agreed to join the Unified Arab Command (UAC), a mutual defense pact, and in January, 1957, Egypt, Syria, and Saudia Arabia agreed to provide Jordan with financial support, replacing the British subsidy. The 1948 Anglo-Jordanian treaty was terminated in March, 1957; Great Britain's involvement in the Israeli attack of Egypt, October, 1956, made Hussein's break with Great Britain inevitable. By September, 1957, the last British troops had left Jordan.

Meanwhile, the Jordanian elections of October, 1956, led to a coalition government under Suleyman an-Nabulsi, the leader of the National Social-ists. The king, aware of an-Nabulsi's Soviet leanings, demanded his resignation, suppressed all political parties, and imposed martial law. An attempted coup, allegedly instigated by Nuwar, head of the armed forces, followed; the king escaped being overthrown only through a courageous appeal to loyal Bedouin troops. Nuwar, together with leaders of the coalition, was exiled.

Egypt and Syria, now firmly aligned with the Communist bloc, had not fulfilled their financial commitments to Jordan, and their relations with Jordan worsened when Hussein accepted American aid. In February, 1958, they merged to form the United Arab Republic (UAR). In response, Hussein and his cousin, King Faisal II of Iraq, formed a federation between their two countries. That summer, Faisal and his family were massacred in a coup and Hussein narrowly escaped a military takeover by Nasser supporters. The armies of Iraq, Syria, and Israel threatened Jordan, and only the arrival of British troops, in response to Hussein's appeal, averted the collapse of his kingdom.

During the next two years, Hussein enjoyed relative peace and the financial support of the United States. He took a firm stand against communism but in August, 1959, renewed diplomatic relations with the UAR (broken off in July, 1958), in spite of frequent incidents on the Syrian border. In 1960, Prime Minister Hazza al-Majali, labeled "an imperialist agent" by Egyptian and Syrian sympathizers, was murdered. After his death, there were several attempts on the king's life, a succession of prime ministers, and cycles of repression, relaxation, and riots.

Relations with Israel were tense. Major issues included the future of the refugees, Israel's plan to divert the Jordan waters, and the future of Jerusalem. At the Second Arab Summit in August, 1964, Hussein mended relations with Nasser, recognized the Palestinian Liberation Organization (PLO), and agreed to the creation of a unified Arab military command. From the summer of 1965, however, border raids by the PLO increased, and in July, 1966, Hussein banned the organization in an attempt to stop Israeli counterattacks. A massive Israeli reprisal raid in November, 1966, led to violent demonstrations in Jordan. Worsening relations with Syria resulted in border clashes and calls by Syria and the PLO for Jordanians to revolt against Hussein.

Jordan boycotted the next meeting of the Arab Defense Council. Yet, concerned about an imminent war with Israel, Hussein signed a defense agreement with Egypt and joined forces in the June, 1967, Six-Day War. The war was disastrous for Jordan. It cost Hussein his entire air force, fifteen thousand troops, and all Jordanian territory on the West Bank, including the old city of Jerusalem. Refugees poured into the East Bank. Realizing that Jordan would bear the brunt of any war with Israel, Hussein helped to draft the United Nations' resolution calling on Israel to give up occupied territory in exchange for Arab recognition ("land for peace") following the war.

The PLO, supported by Syria, increased its presence within Jordan (a "state within a state"), threatening Jordan's internal security. Bloody confrontations between guerrilla organizations and the official government increased between 1968 and 1970. Finally, in September, 1970 ("Black September"), after an assassination attempt on King Hussein and the hijacking of four Western airliners, Hussein drove the guerrillas from Amman. By August, 1971, the last of the PLO had been ousted from Jordan.

In 1972, again trying to resolve the Palestinian problem, Hussein proposed a United Arab Kingdom, a federation of autonomous Jordanian and Palestinian regions, united under the king and a federal council of ministers. Other Arab states criticized the plan and Hussein's handling of the PLO problem, and he was not apprised of Egypt and Syria's plans for the fourth Arab-Israeli War in October, 1973. Therefore, Jordan's involvement in the war was limited, although Hussein received credit from the other Arab states for going to Syria's assistance.

In another move to regain political standing in the Arab world, Hussein agreed to the 1974 Arab Summit resolution, which recognized the PLO as the only legitimate representative of the Palestinian people, thereby virtually abandoning his claim to the West Bank. In 1978, he denounced the Camp David Accords that led to a peace treaty between Egypt (by then under Anwar el-Sadat) and Israel. Enjoying improved relations with the Arab states, in November, 1978, he received pledges of renewed support from oil-rich countries at the Baghdad Summit Conference.

By 1982, the United States was supporting the creation of a Palestinian state on the West Bank in confederation with Jordan, but Hussein met with repeated failures in his attempts to persuade the PLO to support a joint Jordanian-Palestinian nego-

tiating team. Hussein maintained that he would not negotiate a separate peace. He called for an international conference to be attended by all concerned parties, including the PLO, requiring Israel to accept the principle of "land for peace" and giving the Palestinians the right to self-determination regarding the proposed confederation. His proposal was temporarily supported by Yasir Arafat, head of the PLO, but it did not gain the support of the Arab states or Israel.

Meanwhile, Hussein attempted to create a Palestinian constituency on the West Bank and introduced in 1986 a five-year development plan for the region. In December, 1987, following the Amman Summit, which agreed to support an international peace conference if the PLO was recognized as "the sole legitimate representative of the Palestinian people," there was a spontaneous uprising (intifada) on the West Bank, despite brutal security measures by Israel. At the Extraordinary Arab Summit called in Algiers in June, 1988, in support of the uprising, Hussein denied any ambition to rule the West Bank, and, on July 28, 1988, he severed Jordan's legal and administrative ties with the West Bank, dissolving the Jordanian House of Representatives, where the West Bank occupied thirty of sixty seats; laying off about twenty thousand teachers and public servants; and terminating the West Bank Development Plan. This move placed the responsibility for peace negotiations and the administration of the West Bank squarely on the PLO and Israel. While persevering in his efforts to support any movement toward peace in the Middle East, Hussein devoted more time to internal affairs, responding to serious problems in the economy and a call for political reform. The first elections in Jordan in more than twenty years were held in November, 1989.

The 1990 Persian Gulf War forced Hussein to choose between allies. While his relationship with the United States cooled when he expressed support for Iraq's Saddam Hussein, relations with the Palestinians and with his own people were improved. By 1994 he had cultivated good diplomatic ties with both the West and the Arab nations, signing a formal peace treaty with Israel that awarded him custodianship of the Muslim holy sites in East Jerusalem. Frequently operating as a moderating influence in the Israeli-Palestinian peace process, his contribution to stability in the Middle East cannot be underestimated.

In 1998 Hussein went to the United States for cancer treatments. When he returned briefly to Jordan in early 1999, he altered Jordan's political future by announcing that his younger brother Hassan was no longer the heir to the throne. He returned to the United States for further treatment, leaving his eldest son and new heir, Prince Abdullah, in charge of the country.

Summary

Hussein I was thrust onto the stage of world politics at the age of eighteen, when he came to the throne of Jordan, which occupies an important strategic position in the Middle East. His remarkable survival—he has survived numerous assassination attempts, attempted coups, and four Arab-Israeli wars—is accredited to his undeniable courage and strength of character. He has enjoyed an immense popularity within his own country and is respected throughout the world. Although he maintains the real authority in Jordan, he is committed to democratic ideals, and his anticommunist, moderate stance has set him at odds with other Arab states during most of Jordan's turbulent political history.

Hussein is committed to preserving the state of Jordan and the Hashemite throne. His vision has literally shaped the destiny of the nation. Although by the late 1980's the economy was burdened by foreign debt and a growing trade deficit (the result of the failure of some Arab states to give the financial assistance they pledged), Hussein has brought about impressive economic progress in the country. Illiteracy has markedly declined, electrical power supplies were developed, irrigation projects multiplied, agricultural production increased, new roads were built, a national airline was created, and tourism increased during his reign. This progress is all the more remarkable considering that Jordan is a small state, poor in natural resources and dependent on foreign aid.

Hussein's policies have been dictated by his commitment to Arab nationalism and, in part, by his desire not to alienate the Palestinians, who represent a considerable threat to political stability in Jordan. While attempting to integrate the Palestinians and to forge a national consciousness among the people of both the East and West Banks, he has affirmed the Palestinians' rights to self-determination and to their own homeland. Many world leaders have come and gone during Hussein's reign. He remains one of the foremost spokesmen for peace in the Middle East, respected worldwide for his statesmanship and integrity.

Bibliography

Bailey, Clinton. *Jordan's Palestinian Challenge 1948-1983: A Political History.* Boulder, Colo.: Westview Press, 1984. Bailey focuses on the problems that the Palestinian nationalists have posed for the Hashemite monarchy since 1984 and concludes that Hussein's policies were dictated, for the most part, by his desire not to alienate the Palestinian majority in his country. Bailey sees Hussein's survival as a remarkable achievement in the light of PLO, Israeli, and Egyptian schemes to topple the king.

Dann, Uriel. *King Hussein's Strategy of Survival.* Washington, D.C.: Washington Institute for Near East Policy, 1992. A study of King Hussein's rule during four decades of trying circumstances within and outside of Jordan.

Hussein, King of Jordan. "A Bold Peace: Partners in Shaping the Future." *Vital Speeches* 60, no. 21 (August 15, 1994). Transcript of a speech by King Hussein to a joint session of Congress in 1994 concerning Jordan's path toward peace with Israel.

———. *Uneasy Lies the Head: The Autobiography of His Majesty King Hussein I of the Hashemite Kingdom of Jordan.* London: Heinemann, 1962. Hussein begins by recounting the details of his grandfather's assassination, then discusses his early life, including his school days of Harrow and Sandhurst, and devotes most of the volume to the turbulent years following his inauguration as king. His account of the many attempts on his life is presented against a political context in which communism and Zionism are regarded as the chief obstacles to peace and to Arab nationalism.

Hussein, King of Jordan, with Vick Vance and Pierre Laver. *My "War" with Israel.* Translated by June P. Wilson and Walter B. Michaels. London: Owen, and New York: Morrow, 1969. The book consists, for the most part, of conversations with Hussein and the king's radio broadcasts and speeches. Hussein reveals his attitudes toward Israel and the Palestinians and provides his account of the events preceding, during, and following the June, 1967, war.

Lunt, James. *Hussein of Jordan: A Political Biography.* London: Macmillan, and New York: Morrow, 1989. A comprehensive, well-documented biography of Hussein, Lunt's book reflects the author's long experience in Jordan and his personal knowledge of the king. Lunt provides a sympathetic, though not uncritical, view of the Arab character and Jordanian history. Lunt's scholarly biography is augmented by an extensive bibliography.

Moritz, Charles, ed. *Current Biography Yearbook.* New York: Wilson, 1986. The entry on Hussein is this rather general series is very helpful in offering introductory biographical information and an assessment of Hussein's career to the date published.

Mutawi, Samir A. *Jordan in the 1967 War.* Cambridge and New York: Cambridge University Press, 1987. An account by an Arab journalist of the 1967 war with Israel, "the most shattering event in recent Arab history." The book discusses the causes of the war, exploring the motives behind King Hussein's decision to enter the war, inter-Arab rivalries, the events of the war itself, and Jordan's position in the postwar period. An extensive bibliography is included.

Seccombe, Ian J. *Jordan.* World Bibliographical Series. 55. Oxford and Santa Barbara, Calif.: Clio Press, 1984. More than eight hundred critical annotated entries on works from the nineteenth century to modern times, dealing with key aspects of Jordan's history, geography, economy, politics, culture, and social organization. Many entries provide invaluable background information for a study of Hussein's life. A comprehensive cross-referencing system and thorough author, subject, and title index are provided.

Snow, Peter John. *Hussein: A Biography.* London: Barrie and Jenkins, and Washington, D.C.: Luce, 1972. Though it is of the "popular" variety, Snow's biography, which is anecdotal rather than scholarly, is readable and persuasive about both Hussein and the Middle East situation. Snow is sympathetic toward Hussein, whom he presents in the complex political context that includes Zionism, the PLO, Arab nationalism, and Western ties.

Sparrow, Gerald. *Hussein of Jordan.* London: Harrap, 1960. The first English-language biography of Hussein, Sparrow's relatively short book is highly anecdotal and extremely sympathetic toward the king. Though it has been superseded by Lunt's biography, Sparrow's book provides a valuable early assessment of the king's early life until 1959.

Edna Quinn

EDMUND HUSSERL

Born: April 8, 1859; Prossnitz, Moravia, Austrian Empire

Died: April 21, 1938; Freiburg im Breisgau, Germany

Area of Achievement: Philosophy

Contribution: Husserl is known as the founder of phenomenology, regarded by many as one of the most significant movements of the twentieth century.

Early Life

Edmund Husserl was born on April 8, 1859, in Prossnitz, Moravia (then part of Austria), to a German-speaking Jewish family. (The Jewish connection would become a liability later on, even though Husserl had become an Evangelical Lutheran in 1886; throughout his life he remained deeply moral and religious, but not within the framework of a particular sect.) He passed the *Gymnasium* examinations in 1876 and studied in Leipzig, Berlin, and Vienna, concentrating on mathematics and science as well as philosophy. He gained his Ph.D. in 1882 from Vienna with a thesis in mathematics. After several years of study with the Catholic philosopher Franz Brentano, he moved to Halle, where in 1887 he qualified himself as a privatdocent (unpaid lecturer) and where he remained until 1901. The years at Halle were years of doubt and difficulty, but gradually, through his struggles with the problems of mathematics and logic, he developed his own distinctive system of ideas. It was during this period that he married Malvine Steinschneider, his ever-loyal wife; they had three children, one of whom was killed at the Battle of Verdun.

Life's Work

In 1900, Husserl published his first important work, *Logische Untersuchungen* (logical investigations). In 1901, he was invited to the University of Göttingen as an *ausserordentlicher Professor.* Husserl's position in the university was not an entirely happy one; his colleagues in the other faculties did not appreciate his work. He owed his promotion to the rank of *ordentlicher Professor* to the intervention of the Prussian minister of education. By this time, however, the new discipline of phenomenology was proving appealing not only to German students but also to foreigners, and Husserl is said to have had as many as twelve nationalities in his seminar at once.

In defining the term "phenomenology," it must be kept in mind, first of all, that Husserl's thought was still evolving at his death; he left behind an enormous amount of manuscript that has gradually been edited and published. His ideas are difficult and sometimes invite confusion with trains of thought that they superficially resemble or that they are connected with historically, such as existentialism. His battlecry "to the things themselves" is deceptive, since it suggests materialism, which he was trying to refute; his "bracketing" might be wrongly taken to suggest the rejection of the things bracketed. Finally Husserl was an inspiring but not an authoritarian teacher, so that, although he had numerous disciples, they do not necessarily reproduce his thought.

Phenomenology can be considered as a philosophy, some would say the only true philosophy, but also can be considered as a method, perhaps simply one among many, suitable for the solution of some philosophical problems but not of others. Phenomenology begins with the analysis of consciousness or experience—they come to the same thing in the end, for consciousness is always intentional, pointing to something outside the ego. While this analysis is going on, the philosopher "brackets" all irrelevant considerations, such as the operations of empirical science and the conjectures of metaphysics about the reality of the material world. These latter are not pronounced meaningless as by the positivists; they are bracketed, put aside for the moment, perhaps to be used on another occasion or by another thinker, but not to be allowed to confuse the present investigation.

Husserl eloquently describes the "stream of consciousness" (or experience) in which from time to time the ego singles out some "thing" (which is most easily conceived as an object but could be a memory or a mood) for special attention, viewing it from various aspects, so that eventually some "essence" emerges that is not identical with any specific perception. Note, however, that phenomenology does not deal with a shadow or symbol or illusion of some Kantian *Ding-an-sich* (thing-in-itself) that is supposed to be the ultimate reality; experience is real enough in itself, and the *Ding-an-sich* has been bracketed. While the stream of experience must include feelings and emotions as they enter into experience, and while the things of experience are given intuitively, this world is also

the world of logic and mathematics. In the end, Husserl acknowledges that the only absolute reality is the pure ego and its life; all the external world, including other egos, is "contingent" and might turn out not to exist after all. In practice, however, Husserl treats the world and other egos as confirmed by experience.

In 1916, Husserl was called to an ordentlicher professorship at Freiberg. In spite of the grief and disillusionment caused by the war, he was now at the peak of his authority and prestige. Even in the aftermath of the war, he had invitations to lecture abroad, first in London and later in Amsterdam and Paris. His philosophy, however, was changing. Even before the war, some of his disciples feared that he was becoming "transcendental" in his attempts to found a universal philosophical science on a foundation of phenomenology. Now he was becoming moralistic, hoping that phenomenology would establish the ethical autonomy of man. After his retirement in 1928, he would face further disappointments.

When Husserl retired in 1928, his position went to Martin Heidegger, whom he regarded as his chief disciple and logical successor. Yet the works that Heidegger was publishing at the time seemed to point in an entirely new direction—Heidegger would eventually be hailed as an existentialist. Husserl was deeply hurt, but worse was to come. Adolf Hitler came to power in 1933, and, for a time at least, Heidegger supported him. Husserl was excluded from the university and silenced in Germany; many of his associates believed it necessary to distance themselves from him and his ideas. Others were still loyal, and there were some final triumphs. As late as 1935, Husserl was still able to lecture in public and did so with great force and eloquence in Vienna and Prague, which had not yet fallen to Hitler. In 1937, Husserl's health began to fail, and he died on April 21, 1938.

Summary

Husserl's ultimate position in the history of philosophy is uncertain. His editors complain of the "partisan reception" of his posthumous material and the "uneven character of its discussion"; a survey capturing the full breadth of his achievement is yet to be written. The phenomenon of phenomenology is believed to be important, but the nature of the importance is hard to define.

A scholar of Husserl's eminence is expected to end his career in a flurry of banquets and *Festschrifts*. Husserl's end better fits his character. His years of unrewarded toil as a privatdocent, his Puritanical devotion to his work, and the uncompromising standards of clarity and logic by which he judged his own work find a fitting culmination in the final defiant lectures that he delivered in the shadow of Hitler and of world war. If he could not establish ethical autonomy for man, he could at least establish it for himself.

Bibliography

Barrett, William, and Henry D. Aiken, eds. *Philosophy in the Twentieth Century: An Anthology.* New York: Random House, 1962. Volume 3 contains a very useful introduction to phenomenology and existentialism by Barrett as well as a series of selections from Husserl that should be meaningful even to the beginning student.

Bello, Angela Ales. "The Space of the Goddess." *International Review of Sociology* 6, no. 3 (1996). Discusses Husserl's work in the area of phenomenological inquiry.

Edie, James M. *Edmund Husserl's Phenomenology: A Critical Commentary.* Bloomington: Indiana University Press, 1987. Edie believes that phenomenology teaches philosophers "how to distinguish what is *properly philosophical* in their wide-ranging investigations from the rest" and that it is "the conscience of philosophy."

Farber, Marvin. *The Aims of Phenomenology: The Motives, Methods, and Impact of Husserl's Thought.* New York: Harper, 1966. Farber gives a more extensive analysis of Husserl than does Barrett and also comments on his influence. Includes some moderately informative biographical material.

————. *Philosophical Essays in Memory of Edmund Husserl.* Cambridge, Mass.: Harvard University Press, 1940. Given the circumstances of Husserl's death, a standard memorial volume could hardly be expected; not a single German institution is represented, and the authors are said to be "a fair sample of those who . . . reacted to Husserl's teaching." The volume can give the reader an idea of the various reactions to phenomenology.

Husserl, Edmund. *Husserl: Shorter Works.* Edited by Peter McCormick and Frederick A. Elliston. Brighton, Sussex: Harvester Press, and Notre Dame: University of Notre Dame Press, 1981. The first two items—the Inaugural Lecture and the encyclopedia article—represent two attempts by Husserl to give a brief summary of phenomenology. Some readers may find the first at least as useful as the commentators. Contains extensive bibliographies of Husserl, including posthumous works and English translations; extensive commentaries and annotations; and a very helpful glossary of terms.

Kockelmans, Joseph J. *A First Introduction to Husserl's Phenomenology.* Pittsburgh: Duquesne University Press, 1967. This work gives a relatively clear and concise overview of the main themes and topics in Husserl's philosophy.

Sawicki, Marianne. "Empathy Before and After Husserl." *Philosophy Today* 41, no. 1 (Spring 1997). Examines Husserl's views on empathy in cultural context, including the impact of Theodore Lipps on Husserl's work.

John C. Sherwood

ROBERT M. HUTCHINS

Born: January 17, 1899; Brooklyn, New York
Died: May 14, 1977; Santa Barbara, California
Areas of Achievement: Education and social criticism
Contribution: By working to reform higher education, directing foundation programs, and heading study centers, Hutchins helped preserve, during the twentieth century, the Jeffersonian concept of an educated citizenry in a participatory democracy.

Early Life

Although born in Brooklyn, Robert Maynard Hutchins was descended on both sides from old New England families. In his introduction to *Freedom, Education, and the Fund* (1956), Hutchins states that his father, William James Hutchins, a Presbyterian minister (and later president of Berea College), came from "a long line of Connecticut doctors and ministers" and that his mother, Anna Laura Murch Hutchins, came from "a long line of sea captains from Maine." Thus he was born into the sturdy New England tradition of independence and individuality.

In young Hutchins the family tendencies were given further impetus by Oberlin College, where his father became a professor of theology when Hutchins was eight. Oberlin College, then "a Puritan island in the Middle West," prided itself on its abolitionist past, its nonconformist spirit, and its dedication to "poverty, work, service, and . . . Rational Living." "We seriously believed," Hutchins continues, "that the greatest thing in the world was to lay down your life for your principles." These principles were rigorously debated on campus and within the family circle.

After attending Oberlin for two years, Hutchins, at eighteen, enlisted in the United States Army. He served with the United States Ambulance Corps in Italy, receiving the Italian Croce di Guerra in 1918. He continued his education at Yale University, taking a B.A. with honors in 1921. In that same year he married the sculptress Maude Phelps McVeigh. He taught history and English at Lake Placid School in New York (1921-1923), served as secretary of Yale University (1923-1927), and meanwhile studied at Yale for his law degree. Extremely bright, articulate, confident, and handsome (his slightly wavy brown hair then parted in the middle according to the fashion, emphasizing his high

brow, brown eyes, regular features, and cleft chin), Hutchins received his LL.B. degree magna cum laude in 1925 and began his precocious rise in higher education. Teaching in the Yale Law School after graduation, he became a full professor in 1927 and was also appointed acting dean. In 1928 he was confirmed as dean. Then in 1929, at the age of thirty, he became president of the University of Chicago, founded in 1891 and already a leading university, arguably one of the nation's two best.

Life's Work

Inspired by classical ideals going back to Plato and Aristotle, Hutchins believed that education should above all prepare people to think and to exercise responsible citizenship. He therefore advocated a strong liberal arts education and opposed that which stood in the way of a well-rounded academic education—overspecialization, vocationalism, emphasis on social life and athletics, lockstep methods, and a fragmented curriculum. He had already indicated his directions at Yale Law School, where he had widened the law curriculum to include other social sciences, raised entrance requirements and academic standards, started an honors program, and helped found the Yale Institute of Human Relations. At Chicago he used his preeminent position in American higher education to launch a reform program, starting with Chicago, whose example Hutchins hoped other colleges and universities would follow.

Dubbed "the Boy Wonder" (with various meanings depending on who was speaking), Hutchins set to work immediately. In 1930, he consolidated Chicago's academic departments into five bodies: a college of general studies, covering the first two years of undergraduate work, and four divisions— the biological, physical, and social sciences, and the humanities—covering the next two years and graduate programs. The Chicago Plan for undergraduates began to emerge. It required yearlong courses in all four academic areas, plus freshman composition, mathematics, and competency in a foreign language, for a total of fourteen courses to graduate. It also emphasized discussion rather than lectures, abolished required class attendance, and gave credit for passing course examinations, administered at various convenient times by a special examining board. Chicago also used entrance and placement examinations. The system of examinations enabled students to progress at their own rate and, in some cases, to graduate from the university in less than four years.

Hutchins' changes aroused excitement but also controversy. A number of Chicago faculty members resigned in protest. In 1939, when the university cut its intercollegiate football program, alumni howled. Hutchins' most controversial reform, however, was a major redefinition of the bachelor's degree. In 1937, the university decided to admit high school students after their sophomore year, provided they could pass the entrance examination. The students entered a four-year liberal arts program in the college of general studies and eventually earned a B.A. degree. Many educators deplored this somewhat mislabeled "two-year degree," and some universities refused to recognize it. Yet the degree covered approximately the same material and the same examinations as before. Hutchins merely wanted to cut out high school and college duplication and, on the model of the German gymnasium and university, to define clearly the different missions of the American college and university: the college should provide a strong, integrated liberal arts background and the university should concentrate on specialization and research.

Hutchins did not confine his efforts to University of Chicago undergraduates. The university's graduate and professional schools adopted broader, theoretical approaches which attempted to integrate their disciplines with the liberal arts. A program of adult education offered courses in the "Great Books," out of which grew the monumental fifty-four-volume publishing venture of which Hutchins was editor-in-chief, *Great Books of the Western World* (1952). Hutchins also served as chairman of the board of editors of Encyclopædia Britannica, and carried his message to the world via numerous articles, speeches, and lectures, which he collected and published in such books as *No Friendly Voice* (1936), *The Higher Learning in America* (1953), and *The University of Utopia* (1953).

Eventually Hutchins' influence in higher education led to his activity in other areas. Before World War II he was a public spokesman for American noninvolvement, but once the United States was involved he strongly supported the cause. The University of Chicago was one of the main sites where scientists gathered to develop the atomic bomb. They conducted the first nuclear chain reaction in the university's football stadium on December 2, 1942. The university's science programs, already

outstanding, benefited tremendously from the influx of government money and scientists, some of whom joined the university after the war and established new institutes. These benefits did not prevent Hutchins from becoming an advocate of world government and international control of nuclear energy after the war. In 1945, he headed the Committee to Frame a World Constitution.

The postwar period marked a time of change in Hutchins' life, perhaps a kind of middle-age crisis. In 1948 he and his first wife were divorced after twenty-seven years of marriage and three daughters; the following year Hutchins married Vesta Sutton Orlick. In his public life Hutchins began gradually to move away from higher education. He switched from president to chancellor of the University of Chicago in 1945, took a leave of absence in 1946, and in 1947 chaired the Commission on the Freedom of the Press, which issued a thoughtful report. Always an exponent of academic freedom, Hutchins became more interested in the issue of freedom as the postwar anti-Communist movement heated up and led to government investigations, loyalty oaths, and purges (the University of Chicago was investigated repeatedly). Like many public figures, sometimes including even the conservative president Dwight Eisenhower, Hutchins felt that the anti-Communist movement, exemplified by McCarthyism and Hooverism, posed a greater threat to American freedom than did Communism.

Thereafter Hutchins devoted his career to programs more directly concerned with democracy, the conditions favoring it, and its defense. In 1951, he left the University of Chicago to become an associate director of the Ford Foundation. There, in 1952, he was instrumental in creating the Fund for the Republic, which addressed the challenge of McCarthyism by providing financial support to organizations defending civil liberties. The fund also supported civil rights organizations in the South. In 1954 Hutchins became president of the Fund and in 1959 established the Center for the Study of Democratic Institutions, in Santa Barbara, California. The Center sponsored resident scholars, conferences, and publications that debated the issues of democracy, social justice, and the conditions affecting these in the modern world. Hutchins was associated with the center as president (1959-1969, 1975-1977) and senior fellow until his death in 1977.

Summary

Hutchins died thinking that he was a failure. His educational reforms did not become widespread: Not many schools dropped football or adopted the Chicago Plan. Some of his reforms were dropped even at Chicago after he left. Meanwhile, from Hutchins' perspective, higher education continued to deteriorate, with fragmentation, overspecialization, and vocationalism during the 1970's causing a drop in academic standards. With education in decline, a fertile field was being prepared for future demagogues similar to Senator Joseph R. McCarthy.

Yet the demagogic senator from Wisconsin had been finally defeated and McCarthyism itself thrown into disrepute, the word becoming a synonym for "witch hunt." Through the Fund for the Republic and his outspoken opposition, Hutchins played a significant part in bringing down McCarthyism and inoculating the Republic against future outbreaks. In other areas, too, Hutchins' successes were partial but highly significant. The Center for the Study of Democratic Institutions exercised an intangible but nevertheless strong influence both in the United States and abroad. In higher education, Hutchins' reforms were not totally rejected. A few colleges—most notably St. John's in Annapolis, Maryland—were inspired to build programs around the "Great Books" (whose richly bound volumes also found their way into aspiring households). Many other schools imitated or adopted variations of Chicago's general studies curriculum; hence, the most obvious tribute to Hutchins' influence is the liberal arts program college freshmen and sophomores are generally still required to take.

Hutchins had the greatest impact, however, in the world of ideas. He was an eloquent and controversial figure who stirred things up and got people to think. Regardless of whether his particular educational reforms took hold, Hutchins showed the need for reform. He also articulated an educational ideal, just as he helped define the various American freedoms. He did so in language that was simple, direct, witty, and sometimes caustic—unlike the educationese of many fellow educators. Hutchins was a powerful public speaker, and his books continue to preserve the force of his language.

Bibliography

Ashmore, Harry S. "Robert Maynard Hutchins: *The Higher Learning in America.*" *Society* 33, no. 5 (July-August, 1996). Profile of Hutchins and his sometimes controversial contributions to education, including the first liberal arts program.

Botstein, Leon. "Wisdom Reconsidered: Robert Maynard Hutchins' *The Higher Learning in America* Revisited." In *Philosophy for Education,* edited by Seymour Fox. Atlantic Highlands, N.J.: Humanities Press, 1983. Reconsiders Hutchins' classic work in the light of conditions between 1970 and 1980. Says the liberal education advocated by Hutchins is needed now more than ever, with democracy threatened and career education promoted as a way to extinguish radicalism and questioning.

Boucher, Chauncey Samuel. *The Chicago College Plan.* Chicago: University of Chicago Press, 1935. A detailed description of the "Chicago Plan" by the dean of the college, complete with official documents, sample student schedules, and statistics.

Cohen, Arthur A. "Robert Maynard Hutchins: The Educator as Moralist." In *Humanistic Education and Western Civilization: Essays for Robert M. Hutchins,* edited by Arthur A. Cohen. New York: Holt Rinehart, 1964. A summing up of Hutchins' thought and career, showing the connections between his concerns for law, education, and freedom.

Geiger, Roger L., and Karen Paulson. "Robert Maynard Hutchins and the University of Chicago." *American Journal of Education* 101, no. 2 (February, 1993). Examines Hutchins' fight for liberal arts education programs while at the University of Chicago.

Harris, Michael R. *Five Counterrevolutionists in Higher Education*. Corvallis: Oregon State University Press, 1970. The chapter on Hutchins summarizes the abstract theory, especially concerning reason and democracy, underlying Hutchins' philosophy of education. It also briefly treats Hutchins' efforts to apply the philosophy at the University of Chicago.

Hutchins, Robert M. *Freedom, Education, and the Fund: Essays and Addresses, 1946-1956*. New York: Meridian, 1956. A collection of miscellaneous statements on the Bill of Rights, academic freedom, freedom of the press, democracy, education, and the Fund for the Republic, this book is the best introduction to Hutchins' thought in general. Hutchins' introduction to the book itself is also a key autobiographical statement.

————. *The Higher Learning in America*. New Haven, Conn.: Yale University Press, and London: Oxford University Press, 1936. This series of lectures at Yale is Hutchins' classic statement on the restructuring of college and university studies around liberal education in order to combat specialization, anti-intellectualism, vocationalism, and what Hutchins sees as triviality.

————. "Locksley Hall in 1988-89." In *What Is a College For?*, by John D. Millett et al. Washington, D.C.: Public Affairs Press, 1961. An example of Hutchins' wit: a tongue-in-cheek report on a perfect college—with all of Hutchins' requirements—in a mythical state, Rancho del Rey, which now leads the world in intellectual achievement.

————. *The State of the University, 1929-1949*. Chicago: University of Chicago Press, 1949. Hutchins' official report on the achievements of the University of Chicago during his administration.

Kelly, Frank K. *Court of Reason: Robert Hutchins and the Fund for the Republic*. New York: Free Press, and London: Macmillan, 1981. A detailed but rambling account of the fund's second phase, when it was converted into the Center for the Study of Democratic Institutions. The author is a former officer of the fund who saw Hutchins on a daily basis for nineteen years.

Reeves, Thomas C. *Freedom and the Foundation: The Fund for the Republic in the Era of McCarthyism*. New York: Knopf, 1969. An absorbing account of the fund's activist, controversial first phase, particularly its confrontation with McCarthyism. Well written and analytical, the narrative also includes biographical background on Hutchins.

Harold Branam

ALDOUS HUXLEY

Born: July 26, 1894; Laleham, near Godalming, Surrey, England
Died: November 22, 1963; Los Angeles, California
Area of Achievement: Literature
Contribution: Through far-sighted, iconoclastic thought and prolific, diverse writings, Huxley not only recorded but also transcended his age, greatly enriching intellectual life for the twentieth century and beyond.

Early Life

Aldous Leonard Huxley, the third son of Leonard Huxley and Julia Frances Arnold, descended from two distinguished families: one known for high achievement in the sciences and the other equally renowned for contributions to education and literature. On his father's side, Thomas Henry Huxley, the eminent biologist and popularizer of English naturalist Charles Darwin's theory of evolution, was Aldous's grandfather. On his mother's side, Dr. Arnold of Rugby was his great-grandfather, Matthew Arnold (poet and educator) was his great uncle, and the novelist Mrs. Humphrey Ward was his aunt. His schoolmaster father became an editor of the *Cornhill Magazine*, and his mother founded a very successful school for girls.

Huxley attended Hillside Preparatory School and then was sent to Eton at age fourteen. He was an intellectually precocious youth who had already almost reached his full height of 6 feet 4 inches. A few months later Huxley suffered the first of three losses that deeply affected him. In November of 1908, his much-loved mother died of cancer at age forty-five. Years later, he expressed some of the devastation he experienced in *Eyeless in Gaza* (1936), perhaps his most autobiographical novel.

In 1911 came another life-altering trauma. He contracted a serious eye disease that resulted in near blindness for eighteen months, forced him to leave Eton, and left him visually handicapped for the rest of his life. Not knowing whether he would ever see again, Huxley faced this crisis with courage and patience by teaching himself to read Braille. Although he eventually recovered some sight, his visual impairment caused him to abandon his plan to become a doctor.

A third tragedy occurred in 1914 when his older brother, Trevenen, committed suicide at age twenty-four, a victim of depression over his failure to achieve first-class honors at Oxford University and a place in the Civil Service. An unhappy love affair may have been an additional factor, but Huxley believed it was "just the highest and best in Trev— his ideals—which have driven him to his death." Failure to achieve academic distinction might be a disappointment for an ordinary person, but to be a Huxley was to be aware that one is not ordinary, and Trevenen, a particularly sensitive young man, was destroyed by his failure to live up to his brilliant promise. Huxley's other brother, Julian, achieved eminence as a biologist and a writer.

These early shocks left their mark on Huxley: His visual impairment caused him to turn toward literature rather than science, and much of the literature he created reflected a concern with physical suffering, malignant disease, decay, and death. Additionally, his brother's death seemed a demonstration of the potentially tragic conflict between ideals and reality and of the way that ideals can take on a life of their own and even kill if held too rigidly or unrealistically. It is unsurprising to find that skepticism about conventional social values as well as pleas for agnosticism, tolerance, and pacifism became characteristics of his works.

Despite the need to read with a magnifying glass, Huxley attended Balliol College, Oxford, where he wrote and published poems and short stories, finished with first honors in English, and won the Stanhope Historical Essay Prize. His allowance ended when he graduated from Oxford, and his lack of money prevented him from marrying Maria Nys, a young Belgian he had met at Lady Ottoline Morrel's country house, Garsington Manor. A brief, unhappy stint as a schoolmaster at Eton and Repton from 1916 to 1919, during which time he continued to write, convinced him that the only way remaining to make a living was to become a professional writer. After his marriage to Maria at Bellem, Belgium, in 1919, Huxley began working as a literary journalist for various publications, at the same time working on his novels, short stories, and essays. Finally, after the publication of three works of fiction (*Limbo*, 1920; *Chrome Yellow*, 1921; and *Mortal Coils*, 1922), three collections of poems (*The Burning Wheel*, 1916; *The Defeat of Youth*, 1918; and *Leda*, 1920), and a book of essays (*On the Margin*, 1923), Huxley signed the first of many three-year contracts with Chatto & Windus Publishers (an arrangement that continued throughout his life), which finally provided financial security for Aldous, Maria, and their three-year-old son, Matthew. Huxley eventually produced forty-seven books of fiction, nonfiction, poetry, and plays.

Life's Work

Huxley's satirical novels of the 1920's established him as a major, although controversial, writer. Critics attacked *Antic Hay* (1923), *Those Barren Leaves* (1925), and *Point Counter Point* (1928) for promoting attitudes of sexual permissiveness, emotional detachment, postwar disillusionment, cynicism, brutality, and even hatred of existence. They complained that his characters lacked depth and were unsympathetic. (A few of his friends, such as D. H. Lawrence and Lady Ottoline Morrell, recognized themselves in the novels and were not pleased). The perennial issue became Huxley's whole approach to the craft of fiction: his tendency to be discursive, to be more interested in ideas than in telling a story. The lack of a central, unified consciousness in his novels and their formlessness were further transgressions against the novelist's art as practiced by such masters as Henry James.

If Huxley had detractors, he also acquired a large number of admirers who appreciated his witty, brilliant style and who were not in the least put off by his failure to observe the conventions of fiction. Such readers saw in these novels not heartlessness or cruel reveling in human foibles, but clear-eyed exposure of a hollow age much in need of liberation from sham and outmoded Victorian and Edwardian ideas.

Huxley's best-known work, the antiutopian novel *Brave New World* (1932), provoked a bewildering array of reactions. In Australia it was banned for four years because it was perceived to be obscene. Writers such as H. G. Wells and Wyndham Lewis attacked it as "an unforgivable offense to Progress," while other reviewers dismissed it as a "thin little joke." Still others, totally missing the satire, thought Huxley was actually recommending this dystopia as a solution to social problems. A few discerning readers, such as the philosopher Bertrand Russell and writer Rebecca West, saw the novel's meaning and understood its relevance, which has increased to an uncanny degree in the years since it was written. Huxley's vision of the future as a nightmare of efficiency controlled by the most advanced scientific and technological means (test-tube babies, behavioral conditioning to stunt intellect and emotion, and the mindless pur-

suit of pleasure through total sexual freedom and the drug Soma) became a specter ever more haunting as the twentieth century wore on.

Despite an obviously superior intelligence and vast erudition—an effortless command of science, art, history, languages, philosophy, and religion—Huxley was no ivory tower intellectual. It delighted him to know that ordinary people read his books, and his graciousness and charm were legendary. He was unaffected by even his harshest critics, perhaps in part because he seldom read criticism of his work, whether good or bad. However, he was passionate about some issues of his day, such as the pacifist movements following World War I. He also cared greatly about some issues that his own age was too myopic to see but that have since emerged as major problems, such as overpopulation and environmental degradation.

Inevitably, Huxley's bold advocacy of unpopular views, particularly his pacifism, caused still more controversy. In *What Are You Going To Do About It?* (1936) and *Ends and Means* (1937), he argued for the view that war is not a biological necessity but an avoidable evil that humans are morally obligated to resist, a view that was dismissed as naïve and unrealistic. Then, as war clouds gathered over Europe, Huxley, with his wife and child, left England in 1937 for the United States, eventually settling in Southern California. In England, as elsewhere in Europe, Huxley's change of residence provoked some resentment and charges of leaving home to avoid a war. It was pointed out that crossing the Atlantic was not one of his acceptable answers to the question posed in his pamphlet, *What Are You Going To Do About It?* Huxley said his purpose was to place his son in an American school, but the fact remains that the United States became Huxley's permanent home, although he continued his habit of wide and frequent travel throughout the world.

In the 1940's Huxley's interests turned toward mysticism (*Grey Eminence: A Study in Religion and Politics*, 1941; *Time Must Have A Stop*, 1945; and *The Perennial Philosophy*, 1945), a development that astonished his many followers but that reflected his need to move beyond reason and the philosophy of humanism in his explorations toward the unfathomable mystery of life. More shocking was his much-publicized interest in and medically supervised use of the hallucinogenic drugs lysergic acid diethylamide (LSD) and mescaline as an aid to visionary experience during the

last eleven years of his life. Needless to say, Huxley's attitude toward hallucinogenics remains problematic, but it seems unfair to bracket him with the infamous popularizer and high priest of psychedelic drugs Timothy Leary, whom Huxley had met at Harvard University and whose irresponsible behavior Huxley deplored. Huxley's view was that some drugs may be useful to some people on some occasions, if used intelligently. He did not claim they were essential to or would necessarily produce positive mystical visions, nor did he approve of their hedonistic, frivolous, or "recreational" use. In *The Doors of Perception* (1954), he described his experiences and explained their value: "To be shaken out of the ruts of ordinary perception, to be shown for a few timeless hours the outer and the inner world, not as they appear to an animal obsessed with words and notions, but as they are apprehended, directly and unconditionally, by Mind at Large—this is an experience of inestimable value."

Huxley's wife Maria died of cancer in 1955. One year later he married Laura Achera, a psychotherapist and longtime friend. Although he continued to write, much of his time was taken up giving lectures at major universities and institutes and attending conferences throughout the world. In 1961 his Los Angeles home, along with his library and all of his papers, was destroyed by a brush fire, an irreparable loss not only for him but also for students of literature and biographers. Aldous noted, "there is no more tangible link with the past" but gamely added, "It is an interesting challenge and I hope I shall be able to cope with it properly." However, little time to cope remained. In 1962 he suffered a recurrence of a cancer believed to have been cured two years earlier. This time neither cobalt nor radiation treatments availed. His death on November 22, 1963, was overshadowed by the death of President John F. Kennedy a few hours earlier.

Summary
No summary can convey the significance of the astonishingly diverse achievement of Aldous Huxley nor do justice to his mercurial, complex, paradoxical nature—a nearly blind man who became a seer, who tried to reconcile the competing claims of flesh and spirit, science and humanism, and Eastern and Western philosophy. Despite a life lived at the center of intellectual and artistic circles and frequently in a glare of publicity, he remains elusive, one who will continue to fascinate. His works will continue to draw readers who, like him, are not afraid of shedding light "in dark places," who wish to explore many worlds, who want always to experience and learn more.

Bibliography
Bedford, Sybille. *Aldous Huxley: A Biography.* London: Chatto and Windus, 1973; New York: Knopf, 1974. The only complete biography of Huxley, by a novelist who knew him. Draws on his letters and diaries as well as interviews with friends to give a full account of his life. Includes forty-four photographs, a detailed chronology, and an index.

Clark, Ronald W. *The Huxleys.* London: Heinemann, and New York: McGraw-Hill, 1968. Chronicles the Huxley family of geniuses, beginning with T. H. Huxley. Valuable in understanding the intellectual heritage and the expectations it imposed. Three chapters are devoted to Aldous. Includes a select bibliography and an index.

Dunaway, David King. *Aldous Huxley Recollected: An Oral History.* New York: Carroll and Graf, 1995. A collection of excerpts from interviews conducted by Dunaway while researching another book on Huxley, this volume offers insight into Huxley's personality that has been lacking in past biographies. Interviewees include his second wife, Laura, other family members, friends, and his literary agent.

Firchow, Peter. *Aldous Huxley: Satirist and Novelist.* Minneapolis: University of Minnesota Press, 1972. Discusses Huxley's poems and novels, and concludes that despite mystical leanings, Huxley belongs with the empiricists. Considers *Point Counter Point* (1928) a pivotal work separating the earlier "destructive" satire and the later "constructive" satire that affirms positive values. Index.

Keulks, Gavin. "Aldous Huxley: A Centenary Bibliography (1978-1995)." *Journal of Modern Literature* 20, no. 2 (Winter 1996). An addition to previous Huxley bibliographies. This piece is divided into fourteen themes such as "Huxley and Shakespeare" and "Huxley and Mysticism." English and non-English works are separated.

Thody, Philip. *Aldous Huxley: A Biographical Introduction.* London: Studio Vista, and New York: Scribner, 1973. By connecting the major themes in the literature with relevant biographical facts,

Thody provides an insightful, integrated overview of Huxley and his work, which his biographer did not attempt. Selective index.

Watt, Donald, ed. *Aldous Huxley: The Critical Heritage*. London and Boston: Routledge, 1975. A compilation of representative critical reviews of Huxley's works (chiefly fiction) from 1920 through 1962. Essential for anyone interested in Huxley's historical situation, his reading public, and the shifting winds of literary taste.

Karen A. Kildahl

HAYATO IKEDA

Born: December 3, 1899; Yoshina, Hiroshima Prefecture, Japan

Died: August 13, 1965; Tokyo, Japan

Areas of Achievement: Government and politics

Contribution: As Prime Minister of Japan from 1960 to 1964, Ikeda succeeded in restoring Japan's prestige in the eyes of the world after the riots and unrest attending the 1960 renewal of the United States-Japan Security Treaty. Ikeda brokered a cooperative effort between his political party and the bureaucracy, which produced the widely supported Income Doubling Plan and resulted in a high-growth economic pattern that has been maintained ever since.

Early Life

Hayato Ikeda was the second son of an old and wealthy family of rice wine brewers, born in Yoshina, Hiroshima Prefecture, on December 3, 1899. He studied law and economics at Kyōto Imperial University. After graduation in 1925, he managed his own brewing business for a short time but in 1927 began what was to be a twenty-three-year career in the Ministry of Finance. He began as an administration officer in Tokyo, then worked for a period as chief of taxation offices in the small cities of Hakodate, Utsunomiya, and Tamazukuri. In the early 1930's. Ikeda suffered a rare skin disease that kept him bedridden for the better part of five years. He then headed tax bureaus in Kumamoto and Tokyo. By 1945, he was overall director of the national tax bureau of the Ministry of Finance.

In the course of his bureaucratic service, Ikeda developed an impressive knowledge of Japan's financial structure and its problems. In fact, he was later to write several books on financial subjects, including taxation, cost accounting, balanced budgeting, and tax law. He also developed close relations with many of Japan's leading industrialists. He survived the bureaucratic purges of the American occupation (he was not yet high enough in rank) and between 1945 and 1952 was to render valuable assistance to the occupation in its effort to hold the line against postwar inflation, becoming in the process a strong advocate of the strict anti-inflationary policy of Joseph M. Dodge, the economic adviser to the occupation authorities.

In 1949, Ikeda decided to shift into elective politics. Winning a seat in the House of Representa-

tives and repeating his success in four elections following, he drew close to then-Prime Minister Shigeru Yoshida. Named finance minister, head of the agency for which he had worked so long, he continued to espouse a strong anti-inflationary stance. He also helped negotiate the United States-Japan Peace Treaty as well as the accompanying bilateral Security Treaty, which placed Japan under an American defense umbrella, in 1951. Meanwhile, he moved up in the Liberal Party, serving as secretary-general in 1952. When the Liberal Party merged with the Democratic Party in 1955, Ikeda was again appointed finance minister, helping to push through a tax cut.

Life's Work

Ikeda served in subsequent Liberal-Democratic Party (LDP) cabinets under Prime Minister Nobusuke Kishi as Minister for International Trade and Industry. In 1960, Kishi pushed for renewal of the United States-Japan Security Treaty in a particularly high-handed way in the face of violent demonstrations and strikes by a variety of antigovernment elements. It was clear to many of the factions that made up the LDP coalition that the opposition, particularly the Socialist Party, had been handed a popular issue that tapped many aspirations of average Japanese people. It was also clear that, while the treaty would have to be swallowed for the sake of relations with the United States (and was ratified in a stormy parliamentary session), Kishi would have to go if the conservative LDP wanted to maintain national power.

After much maneuvering among the LDP factions, Ikeda was elected party president and prime minister on July 18, 1960. He faced the immediate problems of restoring harmony among the divided LDP factions, of gaining some cooperation from opposition parties, of reassuring the United States that Japan was a responsible ally without appearing unduly subservient, and of beginning economic policies that would bring together a majority of Japanese interests. He was to succeed in a general way in all of these endeavors.

Within the LDP, nine personally led factions vied with one another for appointive posts in the cabinet and party. Whereas Kishi had penalized opposing factions by denying their members good positions, Ikeda distributed appointments more equitably. The result was to make LDP factions more supportive of the prime minister. While sacrificing some of his direct decision-making control, he gained party harmony and personal popularity. As factional infighting decreased, the LDP parliamentary majority went up from 283 of 467 seats to 296. For the next two decades, the LDP acquired such a permanent dominance in the parliament that it was said that Japanese politics was a one-and-one-half-party system.

In the aftermath of the Security Treaty blowup, which had caused Kishi's downfall, Ikeda shifted his government's priorities to domestic matters, specifically to economic growth. In what came to be called the Income Doubling Plan, Ikeda proposed that the government stimulate the economy by means of public works and central planning initiatives to an average 7.2 percent annual growth (doubling the gross national product in ten years). He did this in spite of advice from many within his party to restrain the economy in the face of an expected international economic slowdown. Ikeda's solution to this was to stimulate Japanese consumer demand through government expenditure. The 1961 budget was accordingly 24 percent higher. Since this outpaced the gross national product (GNP) growth, Ikeda hoped that increases in revenues would offset any deficits. At first it appeared that bonds would have to be issued to finance public construction, but, at Ikeda's request, the finance ministry escalated its estimates of revenues to bring them into line with the proposed expenditure. A New Industrial Cities Plan targeted twelve regions with upgraded transportation links, harbors, landfills, and public service improvements. Development corporations were established, combining private and government capital.

Ikeda's stated objectives in putting forward this plan were to begin to build "social capital," from which the average Japanese could improve his standard of living. He hoped to obtain a structural reform of business, promote foreign trade and technical cooperation, cultivate human resources, and equalize the uneven pace of development in the different segments of society and the economy. His vision created a consensus in the LDP and in Japan as a whole built around the notion of high growth and of managed growth. The LDP came to have more influence in budget making as the party rank and file seized more of the initiative in what had been the wholly bureaucratic preserve of the finance ministry. Ikeda was crucial in this process insofar as the finance ministry trusted and cooperated with one of their own alumni. He knew their procedures, could persuade through personal contacts and made skillful use of advisers. Moreover, Ikeda's personal popularity invited expanded newspaper coverage and stimulated a public consciousness of a "culture of growth," which has characterized Japanese politics ever since.

The results of the Income Doubling Plan exceeded all expectations. The annual GNP growth rate in 1961 was 15.5 percent, then it dropped to 7.5 percent in 1962 and 1963, then rose to 13.8 percent in 1964. Instead of ten years, Japan's doubling of GNP had occurred by 1965. The 1962-1965 budgets all ran ahead of the economy but continued to be funded without tax increases or bond sales. Annual per capita national income more than tripled.

In view of his predecessor's difficulties in surviving politically while attempting to align Japan closely with the United States, Ikeda set a new low-profile foreign policy direction with an emphasis on self-reliance and greater sensitivity to neutralist or pacifist feelings. Therefore, while relying implicitly on the Security Treaty, he resisted the John F. Kennedy administration's pressure to increase the Japanese military, for closer military cooperation with the United States, and for closer ties with South Korea. As the Cold War heated up, Ikeda paid lip service to resistance to world communism but played to pacifist opinion by paying equal lip service to the United Nations.

Ikeda managed to draw broad public support for his foreign policy by, as he put it, "separating politics from economics." This was clear in his approach to Taiwan and the People's Republic of China. Resisting American calls for containment of Communist China, Ikeda adopted instead a two-Chinas policy of increasing trade with Communist China while beginning economic aid for (and continuing to trade with) Taiwan. He hoped to reduce American tariffs on Japanese exports through vigorous personal diplomacy. While there were no substantial American concessions in the short term, Ikeda did succeed in creating a Joint Trade and Economic Affairs Committee, which considerably enhanced Japan's status and voice in bilateral trade matters.

One month after the Tokyo Summer Olympic Games of 1964, which showcased Japan's growing position in the world, Ikeda developed a throat tumor and resigned in October, 1964. He died of postoperative complications on August 13, 1965.

Summary

Hayato Ikeda played an important role in the transition of Japan from a defeated nation to the front rank among economic powers. The five years of the Ikeda premiership can be viewed as the triumph of economics over politics. It is no surprise, therefore, that the man who presided over this introduction of the politics of high-growth prosperity was trained as an economist and functioned through most of his career as a bureaucrat rather than as a politician. As a bureaucrat, he was well known for speaking his opinions bluntly and frankly without much regard for public opinion. Yet, as a politician in the last stage of his life, he certainly proved that he could master the first principles of Japanese politics—to listen to the opposition and then to devise the broadest possible consensus.

His policies of promoting a self-sustaining economic growth by a managed stimulation of the private sector and by coordinated planning grew naturally out of his own unique ability to bridge the gap between the political party and the professional career bureaucracy. As an activist prime minister willing to transcend factionalism, he drew his party into the economic decision making. As a trusted bureaucrat, he tapped the planning expertise of the finance agencies. The result was to associate both in the vastly popular endeavor of raising the GNP and standards of living. For decades thereafter, the LDP dominance would remain bound with its association with prosperity, and the partnership between elected politicians and the bureaucratic planning agencies would sustain the Japanese "economic miracle."

Bibliography

Campbell, John C. *Contemporary Japanese Budget Politics.* Berkeley: University of California Press, 1977. Treats budget making from 1954 to 1974. This is an especially crucial area for the study of any country's politics and is especially important for the Ikeda administration. Campbell's approach is one of a political scientist. Based largely on firsthand observations and interviews or on primary materials, he develops insights into the Ikeda domestic policies mainly in chapter 9. He details the shift from bureaucratic monopoly over budgeting to an LDP-Ministry of Finance partnership, which required much behind-the-scenes maneuvering.

Curtis, Gerald L. *The Japanese Way of Politics.* New York: Columbia University Press, 1988. The most comprehensive general treatment of Japanese politics since Thayer (see below), including the 1986 elections. Based entirely on Japanese sources, it describes the whole three decades of LDP dominance and thus gives us a sense of perspective on Ikeda's place in the context of post-World War II political history. Shows how the Income Doubling Plan, for example, was attempted in different guises by later prime ministers. Shows the problems and questions that have emerged since the Japanese "economic miracle."

Langdon, Frank C. *Japan's Foreign Policy.* Vancouver: University of British Columbia Press, 1973. Treats foreign policy by looking at two case studies—the Ikeda administration (1961-1964) and the Sato administration (1965-1972)—showing the contrasts between them. Ikeda's policies are cautious, conciliatory, and nationalistic, whereas Sato's are more pro-United States and, therefore, confrontational at home in facing opposition parties. About a third of the book concerns Ikeda's foreign policy, which evidently set the paradigm for Japanese foreign policy following Nakasone.

Scalapino, Robert, and Junnosuke Masumi. *Parties and Politics in Contemporary Japan.* Berkeley: University of California Press, 1962. Describes the political situation at the time of Ikeda's takeover. The last chapter is a detailed case study of the foreign policy crisis of 1960 in which the Kishi administration was brought down. It details the factional setup, behind-the-scenes maneuvers, and voter behavior, which the authors view as a transition from traditional to more "modern" politics. As a backdrop for Ikeda's consensus building and shifting priorities, it serves to highlight his legacy to later politics.

Thayer, Nathaniel B. *How the Conservatives Rule Japan.* Princeton, N.J.: Princeton University Press, 1969. This is one of the earliest standard surveys on postwar Japanese politics. It is based entirely on Japanese written sources or on interviews with LDP politicians. Focusing as it does on the ruling party and the organs and processes of government, it mentions less about the Ikeda administration as such than the other works mentioned. As a source for how Japanese politics worked during Ikeda's time, it is unsurpassed.

David G. Egler

İSMET İNÖNÜ

Born: September 24, 1884; Smyrna (now İzmir), Ottoman Empire (now Turkey)
Died: December 25, 1973; Ankara, Turkey
Areas of Achievement: Government and politics
Contribution: İnönü served as the first prime minister of the Turkish Republic from 1923 to 1937 and as its second president from 1938 to 1950. During this time, he worked to maintain his nation's neutrality in international affairs and oversaw its transformation into a modernized state.

Early Life

İsmet Pasha was born into a middle-class family in Smyrna (now İzmir). From an early age, his education was directed toward entering the military, which was a key vehicle for social advancement during the waning years of the Ottoman Empire. İsmet graduated from the Ottoman Army Staff College in 1906. As a junior officer posted with the Second Army in the European Turkish city of Adrianople, İsmet became one of the youngest members of a group of junior military officers determined to revitalize the decaying Ottoman realm. When some of them took power in 1908 as the Young Turks, İsmet became more politically conscious.

İsmet began to develop strategic friendships with his fellow young officers, particularly the charismatic Mustafa Kemal, who was to be İsmet's close friend all his life. İsmet and Kemal admired the principles of the Young Turk regime but felt that the new leaders were not fully committed to rapid modernization. Thus the two friends were regarded with growing suspicion by the regime. Nonetheless, İsmet rose through the ranks. He served in the Ottoman army during World War I, helped suppress an Arab revolt in Yemen (where, incongruously, he discovered the delights of Western classical music and glimpsed for the first time the European way of life), and fought in the Caucasus Mountains, where, as chief of staff to Kemal, he forged a close working relationship with his comrade. İsmet, whose stability, humorous and compassionate temperament, and mastery of detail were the natural complement to Kemal's mercurial temperament and visionary talent, emerged as the perfect second-in-command. He was then assigned to command an army corps in Syria, where he was again working under Kemal, who shared his resentment of Turkey's German allies. By the time the war ended in a humiliating defeat for Turkey in 1918, İsmet had been raised to the rank of colonel and was stationed in the war ministry. Appalled by the inaction of the sultan's government when Turkey was threatened with complete dismemberment by the victorious Allies, in late 1919 İsmet left Constantinople (now Istanbul) for the Anatolian heartland to join Kemal in his struggle of national resistance.

Life's Work

İsmet soon arrived in Ankara, the seat of the resistance. His intelligence and good sense were badly needed in January, 1921, because the Greek army, allowed a more or less free hand by the Allies occupying Constantinople, were advancing rapidly into Anatolia. Commanding a hastily recruited group of soldiers, İsmet managed to hold off the Greeks at the town of İnönü (from which he later derived his surname). This victory gave the Turkish forces both internal confidence and credibility in the eyes of foreign powers, who henceforth treated the nationalist movement with more respect. Undaunted, the Greeks again attempted to pass through İnönü in late March of 1921. Once again, İsmet stymied them, partially through wise management of reserve personnel. Some observers felt, though, that his role in the battle was overplayed for propagandistic reasons. İsmet continued to play a major role in the remainder of the war, in which Kemal's forces eventually triumphed, establishing a nationalist Turkish regime whose borders were acknowledged in the Treaty of Lausanne, signed in 1923. During treaty negotiations, İsmet was the chief of the Turkish delegation.

Kemal inevitably became president of the new state, and İsmet became prime minister. Despite the republican character of the constitution, the new Turkey was an authoritarian regime where there was only really one party, the Republican People's Party (Cumhuriyetçi Halk Partisi, or CHP). Opposition was only intermittent and was never allowed to coalesce. Other than a brief dismissal in 1924 for political reasons, İsmet served as prime minister through most of Kemal's presidency. The new regime introduced massive changes in Turkey. Islamic law yielded to European civil codes, the Arabic alphabet gave way to the Latin, and the Turks were encouraged to adopt Western-style manners, mores, and even surnames. Kemal took the name of Atatürk ("Father of the Turks"), while İsmet took that of İnönü, after the scene of his triumphs. İnönü took an energetic role in propagating the new social model by personally conducting classes in the new alphabet in the city of Malatya, where, with blackboard and chalk, he taught the common people how to write a language whose expression was finally made accessible to them.

Ironically, İnönü and Atatürk, close friends for so many years, had a falling out shortly before Atatürk's death in 1938. During a meeting, İnönü had called attention to Atatürk's alcoholism in a rather brusque manner and had also evinced disagreements over economic and military policy. Nonetheless, shortly before his death Atatürk designated İnönü as his successor because he realized that no one else was willing or competent to carry on his legacy. İnönü was elected president, as well as head of the CHP, which enabled him to be the sole ruler of Turkey. İnönü's administration was the political continuation of Atatürk's, with the same stress on nationalism, modernization, and centralized control of the economy; if anything, İnönü was more of a state-oriented planner than his predecessor. He also exercised form control over the press and over public discussion of political issues.

Like John Adams when compared to George Washington, his predecessor as president of the United States, İnönü never managed to transcend partisan divisions and serve as a symbol of the nation's unity in the manner achieved by Atatürk. The potential for political factionalism in Turkey, however, was quelled by the swift approach of World War II. The Turkish military felt that they had been betrayed by German promises into entering World War I to the severe detriment of their nation and were determined not to ally with Germany or any other nation in the upcoming conflict. Turkey thus professed a strict neutrality at the outbreak of the war, although it was most afraid of Italy and the Soviet Union. Turkey was of value to both sides not only because of its size, population, and strategic position straddling Europe and Asia but also because of its large reserve of natural resources such as chrome and other minerals. As a neutral country, Turkey became a hotbed of spies, agents, and refugees, including some Jews seeking harbor from Nazi persecution.

İnönü's policy of neutrality did not preclude an ongoing dialogue with Great Britain, particularly

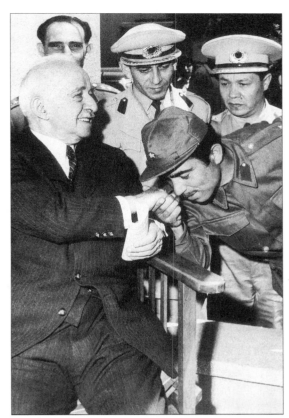

İsmet İnönü (left) with members of the Turkish military in 1960, after a military coup toppled the government of Adnan Menderes.

after Winston Churchill became prime minister. Churchill, once an adversary of Atatürk, had become an admirer of his in the 1920's and spent much time trying to persuade İnönü to actively enter the war on the Allied side. While teasing Churchill and the Allies with ambiguous pledges to enter the war at some later date, İnönü refrained from actually doing so, partially because his protests about the Turkish army being unprepared for war were mostly true and partially because İnönü felt that Turkey's interests were best served by staying out of the war as long as possible. After Germany invaded the Soviet Union in 1941, there was some fear among the Allies that Turkey would join Germany in order to avenge itself upon its Russian enemy. These rumors were lent corroboration when Turkey sold chrome to Germany in 1942 and when İnönü's foreign minister, Numan Menemencioglu, seemed to evince pro-German sentiments. In 1944, however, when the war began to go against Germany, economic ties with Germany were severed and Menemencioglu was dismissed. İnönü formally entered the war against Germany in 1945 so Turkey could be a founding member of the United Nations and because İnönü desired British and American military support against Germany and the Soviet Union, against which Turkey finally sought protection as a member of the American-led North Atlantic Treaty Organization (NATO).

İnönü realized that one-party rule was no longer tenable. His wartime economic measures (especially increased taxes and inflation) had made him unpopular, and İnönü judged that Turkey was finally mature enough to have an opposition party. In 1946, the Democrat Party, led by Adnan Menderes and Atatürk's former financial adviser Celal Bayar, was founded and quickly became popular. To maintain his political position, İnönü announced in 1947 that as president he was not a partisan figure and thus tried to dissociate himself from the CHP. İnönü also tried to regain popularity by relaxing restrictions on Islam (imposed by Atatürk to try to engender a secular national unity) and permitting labor unions to function freely for the first time in modern Turkey. However, these concessions were not enough to prevent İnönü from being turned out of office in May, 1950. Some of İnönü's military officers wanted the president to agree to an army coup in order to stay in control, but İnönü refused and acceded to a democratic turnover of power to the opposition.

İnönü led the CHP in opposition for ten years, occasionally feeling the bite of the other party's control, as when his son-in-law, Metin Toker, was arrested in 1955 and when his partisans were harassed. İnönü, increasingly concerned that the Democrats were jeopardizing the secular legacy of Atatürk by giving too much leeway to Islamic influences, acceded to the military coup that overthrew the Democrats in 1960. In the ensuing 1961 elections, İnönü's CHP won a narrow victory but was able to secure a consensus by İnönü's pledge not to be vindictive to his former opponents, a pledge that had the individual impact of sparing the life of Bayar, his old adversary and comrade, who would have been executed if not for a reprieve granted him by İnönü.

Though nearing eighty, İnönü served as prime minister in several CHP governments during the 1960's, providing a striking example of continuity and infusing the spirit of modern Turkey's founding and of Atatürk himself into its latter-day ad-ministrations. After friction broke out between Turkey and Greece over Cyprus in 1964, İnönü tried to distance Turkey from an exclusive reliance on U.S. support in foreign affairs, seeking out relationships with a diverse group of other nations. By this point, the CHP, always statist in economic terms, had become a doctrinally left-wing party, and İnönü was increasingly giving way as its most prominent figure to the young Bülent Ecevit. The final break between İnönü and Ecevit occurred when İnönü allowed some CHP ministers to serve in a government established after another, more informal, military coup in 1971. Ecevit protested and wrested control of the CHP from İnönü at the 1972 party convention. İnönü, nearing ninety, resigned from the CHP and accepted a nonpartisan appointment in the Turkish senate.

Summary

İsmet İnönü died in December, 1973, having played a distinguished role in his country's public life for over sixty years. His son Erdal, educated as a nuclear physicist, entered into Turkish politics and remained prominent through the 1990's.

Bibliography

Deringil, Selim. *Turkish Foreign Policy During the Second World War : An "Active" Neutrality.* Cambridge and New York: Cambridge University Press, 1989. Good account of the foreign policy of İnönü's presidency from the viewpoint of diplomatic history.

Kinross, Lord (Patrick Balfour). *Atatürk: A Biography of Mustafa Kemal, Father of Modern Turkey.* New York: Morrow, 1964. This definitive and stylishly written biography of Atatürk sheds light on İnönü's role in the war for independence as well as his complex relationship with Atatürk. The author was a friend of İnönü and interviewed him for the book.

Lewis, Bernard. *The Emergence of Modern Turkey.* 2d ed. London and New York: Oxford University Press, 1968. This survey, easily available but a bit dated, essentially sees Atatürk and İnönü as Westernizers and modernizers.

Pope, Hugh, and Nicole Pope. *Turkey Unveiled: Atatürk and After.* London: Murray, 1997; Woodstock, N.Y.: Overlook Press, 1998. An unusually thorough and comprehensive history of twentieth century Turkey written in a literate and topical style. Covers İnönü's wartime and presidential years, his motives in maintaining neutrality during World War II, as well as his postpresidential years, including relations with allies and adversaries such as Bulent Eçevit and Celal Beyar. The best book for the beginning student seeking a general survey.

Rubin, Barry. *Istanbul Intrigues: Espionage, Sabotage, and Diplomatic Treachery in the Spy Capital of World War II*. New York: McGraw-Hill, 1989. An evocative and informative survey of Turkey during World War II; sees İnönü's inclinations as essentially pro-Allied.

Zürcher, Erik. *Turkey: A Modern History*. Rev. ed. London: Tauris, and New York: St. Martin's Press, 1997. This responsible but sometimes inaccessibly written survey places İnönü's career within an ideological context usually scanted by other historians.

Nicholas Birns

EUGÈNE IONESCO

Born: November 26, 1912; Slatina, Romania
Died: March 28, 1994; Paris, France
Area of Achievement: Literature
Contribution: One of the greatest playwrights of the twentieth century, Ionesco helped develop and popularize the genre of Theater of the Absurd through his then-experimental plays, which expose the emptiness of societal institutions.

Early Life

Eugène Ionesco was born on November 26, 1912, about one hundred miles west of Bucharest in the Romanian town of Slatina. His father, a lawyer, was Romanian, and his mother was French. The following year, Ionesco's sister was born, and in 1914 the young family moved to Paris. His brother was born in 1915, and a year later, when Ionesco was four, the infant died as a result of meningitis. Against the tragic setting of his brother's demise, Ionesco witnessed his parents' hysterical and inane quarreling, caused by the loss of their youngest child. Following this the family moved no fewer than four times in one year, Ionesco staying with his mother while his sister went to live in a home for infants and his father took an apartment to prepare for his French law examinations.

In 1917, following Romania's loss of neutrality in World War I, Ionesco's father went back to his homeland to join the army. Ionesco's mother was obliged to work in a factory to support her children when, after hearing no news from his father, she assumed that he had been killed in action. In 1921, the nine-year-old Ionesco developed anemia, and his mother took him and his sister to a small country village in the Mayenne. This village, La Chapell-Anthenaise, came to play an important part in Ionesco's private mythology and appears in several of his writings, theatrical and nontheatrical. It was in this bucolic setting that he spent many happy months, perhaps the first such of his life. Back in Paris the following year, Ionesco soon discovered literature through reading Gustave Flaubert's "Un Cœur simple" in *Trois Contes* (1877; *Three Tales,* 1903). Inspired, he began to write poems, a patriotic play, his memoirs, and sketches that would end with children destroying the family property and throwing their parents out the windows.

Ionesco's father had not been killed in the war. He had merely discontinued communication with his family, and, after the war, joined the Romanian police. He returned to Paris in 1925 when, after divorcing his wife, he won custody of both children and took them back to Romania. There Ionesco's patriotic French play became Romanian, but despite this and his brilliant success as a student in his new language, he considered himself an outsider and a foreigner in the country of his birth. His father remarried, but the two children did not get along with their new stepmother, and Ionesco's sister was soon obliged to return to France. Ionesco stayed until he was seventeen, when he fled domestic strife to pursue French studies at the University of Bucharest in 1929.

Throughout the early to middle 1930's, Ionesco pursued his studies in Romania while he published poems and literary critiques in Romanian reviews and magazines. He published a collection of essays entitled *Na* (no) in 1934, in which he first attacked and then reinstated several fashionable Romanian writers, creating a fusion of opposites that revealed an ability to present both sides of an issue without pronouncing judgment in favor of either side. This is an early sign of an affinity for revealing a situation while leaving the resolution up to the auditor that was to find itself at the heart of his theater. As political strife throughout Europe began to lead to World War II, Ionesco's father was exercising a political flexibility that equaled his son's own literary objectivity. As the Romanian government progressed treacherously toward Fascist alliance with a rising Nazi Germany, the elder Ionesco maneuvered his way along the slippery path of Balkan politics, always managing to find himself on the side of the government in power, while Ionesco found himself in increasing opposition. To his horror, it seemed that not only his own father but also all around him were throwing in their lot with the collective madness of bigoted and military nationalism.

Ionesco's mother died in 1936, and in the following year Ionesco married a young philosophy student, Rodica Burileano. In 1938, he received a scholarship from the French government to go to Paris to write a thesis on the themes of sin and death in French poetry since Charles Baudelaire. He discontinued his research with the advent of World War II and the German occupation of France. During the war, the Ionescos lived in Marseilles, where Eugène eked out a meager living for them both as an editor for a publishing house. In 1944, a daughter, Marie-France Ionesco, was born to them. The war ended in 1945, and Ionesco's father made a timely conversion to Romanian communism. Three years later, while trying to learn English, Ionesco stumbled upon the first of many devices that was to provide the inspiration and absurdity of his revolutionary theater.

Life's Work

Attempting to learn English at home with the aid of a self-teaching manual, Ionesco was struck by the arbitrary and inane example conversations that were given in the text for the student to repeat. As the fictional characters in the lesson book bluntly stated obvious and inconsequential facts about themselves and each other, what was trivial became important, and what was important became trivial, with the end result that the language itself began to lose all meaning. Ionesco himself lost all interest in learning English as he began to use his English lessons as the basis for writing down his ideas about the loss of meaning in language. As he wrote, his writing, to express his intent, began to take the form of a play, and Ionesco found himself writing for a medium that he had shunned since his initial childhood efforts for what he perceived as its dishonesty.

Ionesco was introduced to Parisian theater director Nicolas Betaille, and the two men began reworking and rehearsing the new piece. On May 11, 1950, it premiered at the Théâtre des Noctambules as *La Cantatrice chauve* (*The Bald Soprano*, 1956). As the play opens Mr. and Mrs. Smith, an average middle-class English couple, sit chatting in clichés about everyday trivia. The pointlessness of their dialogue reaches its most absurd point as they begin to discuss the triumphs and misfortunes of a very large family of their acquaintance whose every member, regardless of age or sex, is named Bobby Watson. The Martins enter. Only vaguely familiar to each other at the outset, they discover, as they talk to each other, that they are indeed man and wife and have been so for quite a while, being the parents of the same child and having shared everything for a number of years. The clock strikes seventeen and the doorbell rings to admit no one. The fire chief rushes in, in a hurry to extinguish all the fires in the city, but he gets delayed as he recounts one seemingly interminable anecdote after another. He exits and the two couples talk, but their language disintegrates into meaningless sounds.

Finally the Martins are left alone and, using the same dialogue with which the Smiths opened the play, they seem to begin the action anew as the curtain falls. The play, the language of which exists only to uphold daily banalities, was not an immediate success. The senseless and empty routine of the automaton-like characters on the stage was too appallingly familiar to the people in the audience.

Ionesco, initially reluctant, soon embraced his métier, and in a short time the public and critics alike applauded his efforts. During the next five years, he wrote and produced no fewer than five new plays. While the words of his first play are shown to have no meaning, the language of his second play, *La Leçon* (1951; *The Lesson*, 1955), was given, quite literally, a point. A student is being tutored in preparation for her "total doctorate" examination. Meek at the outset, the professor, a philologist, gains confidence as he speaks because he speaks, and drowns his pupil, in highly stylized rhetoric that brings to mind the propaganda of the previous two decades. Impatient with his student's seeming inadequacy, the professor begins to discuss the word "knife" and stabs the student to death with a knife, having apparently forged a deadly weapon with his very words.

With *Les Chaises* (1952; *The Chairs*, 1958), Ionesco put on the stage the futility of life and human endeavor. An Old Man and his his contentious wife fill the stage with chairs for an invisible audience that will gather to hear a speech by the Old Man that represents the culmination of his life's work and will save mankind. Leaving an Orator to deliver the message, the couple jump out the windows into the sea, but the Orator cannot deliver the message, as he is mute. This play initially played to empty houses, but an article in its defense appeared in a magazine and was signed by Samuel Beckett and Arthur Adamov among others, giving Ionesco new recognition and attention.

Ionesco was beginning to reveal to larger audiences the Theater of the Absurd. He was showing how a world turned upside-down had been emptied of its meaning, leaving hollow institutions and behaviors to which people still clung in their daily routines. He employed a wide range of accepted theatrical conventions at the same time that he stripped them of all but their barest mechanical functions. He does not indicate a path; he merely shows his audience how ridiculous they are, leaving it up to them to reinvent and reinvigorate themselves. With success came controversy, and in its wake Ionesco began to write more complicated and more personal works.

Beginning in 1956, the influential theater critic Kenneth Tynan, an early champion of Ionesco, began attacking the seeming pointlessness of his plays, criticizing him for not taking a firmer and more pointed political stand to help answer the profound questions that he seemed to be asking. There ensued lively literary debate when Ionesco himself took up the challenge in articles and speeches with the support of other French writers, such as Jean Anouilh and André Breton.

Rhinocéros (1959; *Rhinoceros*, 1959) was produced first in Düsseldorf, and with it Ionesco gave a nod to Tynan's demands while refusing to take more than a very personal, individual stand by introducing the Ionesco Everyman, Bérenger. Average and unconcerned, Bérenger does not take notice that everyone in the city is turning into a rhinoceros until his friend and the girl he loves become transformed too. In the end, Bérenger takes up a gun and decides to defend his humanity. While this drama is clearly antitotalitarian, Ionesco has plainly drawn on his personal experiences from the nightmare world of his father's Romanian politics, and by so doing avoids standing on a soapbox to proclaim any specific political dogma.

In *Le Roi se meurt* (1962; *Exit the King*, 1963), Ionesco confronts most directly and most simply a theme that was to have increasing importance in his works: man's inability to accept his own death. Here Ionesco has crowned his Everyman King Bérenger I, and the story of his life is essentially the story of humanity with specific references to the history of Europe. Having lived for centuries, Bérenger has personally built all Europe's great cities and ghostwritten William Shakespeare's plays, among other things. At the play's opening, one of his wives, Queen Marguerite, announces that the king will die within the next hour and a half (the duration of the play), and the action covers a stage life of twenty years. Bérenger laments and rails against his inevitable demise, accepting everyone else's death but his own, begging to be remembered forever, even though he, wiser than his predecessor the Old Man, knows that he will be forgotten. In the end he disappears (dies), his final moments of life unchanged by the death he knew to be approaching.

In many ways his simplest and most direct, *Exit the King* is Ionesco's most important work, and, perhaps, his best. Man knows he will eventually die, and, despite even the greatest of life's achievements, he will be forgotten and his work left undone. Life is presented in the face of death, the ultimate absurdity. If analysis indicates that this is Ionesco's harshest play, the universality of the human plight of the characters on stage makes the drama his most affecting and moving to witness. This is achieved not with sentimental manipulation but with the honest and simple way that the playwright reveals the humanity of his audience by the characters on his stage.

Barely a decade after his astonishing debut, Ionesco was an accepted institution, the kind of *monstre sacré* that he so enjoyed debunking in his theater. This is perhaps the greatest irony and the greatest absurdity in the life of one of the greatest absurdists. In 1971, he applied to and was accepted as a member of that most conservative of French literary institutions, the Académie Française.

Summary

Deliberate and provocative, Eugène Ionesco's theater has, since its first appearance, been the subject of lively discussion and debate, with the playwright himself as his own most outspoken defender. In addition to the stage works for which he is best known, he also published stories, poetry, autobiographical articles, and criticism. In the hour or so that his comedies take to present themselves, Ionesco's theater reveals itself entirely with each work. Such self-definition gave the public something that was at once revolutionary and neatly packaged, which accounts for the rapid acceptance of a worldview so shocking and profoundly disturbing. While such cool demonstrations of human absurdity can be alienating, the audience is drawn in because, above all, Ionesco uses the theater as a metaphor for life. Unobscured by the mannerisms and speech he is so brilliantly exposing, his nonsense on stage makes a direct appeal to the audience in the house.

Bibliography

Coe, Richard N. *Ionesco.* New York: Barnes and Noble, 1961. A good introductory criticism and analysis of Ionesco's first ten years as a dramatist.

Esslin, Martin. *The Theatre of the Absurd.* 3d ed. London and New York: Penguin, 1980. An early look at the Theater of the Absurd as a genre. Ionesco is put into the context of the theater of his time alongside great contemporaries such as Beckett and Adamov.

Hayman, Ronald. *Eugène Ionesco.* London: Heinemann, 1972; New York: Ungar, 1976. Beginning with an interview with the playwright, this study explains and analyzes Ionesco's oeuvre play by play.

Issacharoff, Michael, and Lelia Madrid. "Between Myth and Reference: Puig and Ionesco." *Romantic Review* 87, no. 3 (May, 1996). Discusses how Manuel Puig and Ionesco use disruption of time as a technique for unsettling readers.

Kluback, William, and Michael Finkenthal. *The Clown in the Agora: Conversations about Eugène Ionesco.* New York: Lang, 1998. A collection of fabricated conversations and other encounters based on the philosophies of Ionesco.

Lamont, Rosette C., ed. *Ionesco: A Collection of Critical Essays.* Englewood Cliffs, N.J.: Prentice-Hall, 1973. A collection of important critical essays dealing with Ionesco's theater, here is a wide range of interpretations that demonstrates the stimulating variety of thought and ideas that his works provoke.

Lewis, Allan. *Ionesco.* New York: Twayne, 1972. Part of the Twayne World Authors series, this work includes general biographical and critical information on Ionesco. Also contains a chronology, a bibliography, and an index.

Wagner, Walter, ed. *The Playwrights Speak.* London: Longman, and New York: Delacorte Press, 1967. A more personal glimpse of Ionesco in his own words is included in this compilation of essays and interviews by celebrated modern playwrights.

Pavlin Lange

CHARLES IVES

Born: October 20, 1874; Danbury, Connecticut
Died: May 19, 1954; New York, New York
Area of Achievement: Music
Contribution: Using experimental techniques that disregarded traditional musical theories, Ives wrote compositions which expressed American experiences and feelings.

Early Life

The most important influence upon the life and career of the American composer Charles Ives was his father, George Edward Ives. The elder Ives, himself an extremely talented and innovative musician, was the youngest bandleader in the Union Army during the Civil War, and, after the war, was a tireless experimenter in novel musical forms and techniques in his hometown of Danbury. These experiments would reappear years later in Charles Ives's own compositions, which involved intentional dissonance, bold new harmonics, and other deliberate violations of musical tradition.

In addition to this experimental tendency, the father gave his son a solid foundation in basic musical theory and a wide knowledge of traditional American musical forms such as church hymns, camp-meeting tunes, and patriotic marches and airs. Charles was an avid and quick student, and by the age of fourteen he was the youngest professional church organist in Connecticut. He had already begun composing, and his earliest extant piece "Slow March" (c. 1887), uses one of his favorite devices, that of "quotations" from other musical works, especially popular music. By 1894, Ives had finished his first serious work, a setting to the Psalms; this work also relied on quotations and on extensive use of dissonance, polyphony, and contrasting rhythms.

From 1894 to 1898, Ives attended Yale University, where he studied at the newly formed department of music. From his father, Ives had already learned a distaste for the European musical traditions as transplanted to the United States; both men felt them to be weak, effeminate, and unimaginative. Ives's experiences at Yale confirmed this belief: His professors were either amused or disdainful of his original compositions and required him to "correct" dissonances and resolve harmonics according to standard—that is, European—musical theory and training. Although Ives spent much

time writing music at Yale, he was known mainly for his tune "The Bells of Yale" (1903), a highly traditional work frequently performed by the university's glee club.

Life's Work

Upon graduation, Ives moved to New York, where he lived with a number of Yale men in a tenement known as Poverty Flat. He took a position with the Mutual Insurance Company but continued to compose at night and during weekends. He sometimes showed his works to friends in the building but seldom consorted with professional musicians.

In 1899, Ives and a friend, Julian Myrick, transferred to an insurance agency associated with Mutual. Together they developed new and more effective methods of selling insurance. In working out these techniques, Ives displayed the humanitarian, benevolent side of his personality, a side allied with the Transcendentalist philosophy espoused by such New England thinkers as Henry David Thoreau and Ralph Waldo Emerson. In a remarkably short time, Ives and Myrick became quite wealthy because of their success in the insurance business; at one point, their own company had the largest volume of sales in the country.

While becoming a successful businessman, Ives did not neglect his composition—although he made little effort to have his more innovative works performed. Some pieces, such as *The Celestial Country* (1902), were presented at Central Presbyterian Church in New York, where Ives worked as organist; his more daring work, however, remained in his desk, unheard.

These unperformed works advanced along the experimental lines suggested by Ives's father. Old tunes were quoted, changed, and transmuted as Ives pitched instrument against instrument and tempo against tempo, defying traditional concepts of music. In doing this, he was working entirely on his own, since his self-imposed isolation from professional musicians left him unaware of the work of contemporary composers.

In works such as his Third Symphony (1904), known as "The Camp Meeting" and based largely on traditional organ tunes and popular songs, he was exploring new musical territory. Often in his works, Ives attempted to use musical form to express nonmusical situations or ideas. This was a recurrent and dominant focus of his career; in essence, Ives was a composer of ideas of situations rather than forms. For example, his work *All the Way Around and Back* (1906) illustrated a baseball play—a runner at first base advances to third on a foul ball and then must return to first.

Ives was also a humorist, both in his concepts and in his titles. One of his most famous works, composed in 1906, is entitled "I. A Contemplation of a Serious Matter: Or, The Unanswered Perennial Question. II. A Contemplation of Nothing Serious: Or, Central Park in the Dark In the Good Old Summer Time." This work demands two separate orchestras performing independently yet simultaneously.

Shortly after his graduation from Yale, Ives had been introduced to Harmony Twichell, the sister of a college friend. After a long courtship, the two were married by Harmony's father in June, 1908. The couple first lived in Manhattan, but Ives's uncertain health and aversion to company led them to purchase a farm in the Connecticut countryside near West Redding. The Iveses had no children of their own, but in 1915 they adopted Edith Osborne Ives, a young girl who had first come to West Redding through the Fresh Air Fund, which sponsored country vacations for poor city children.

The years up to 1918 were the productive period of Ives's career. In 1909, he finished *Washington's Birthday* and the First Piano Sonata; the year 1912 saw the creation of the *Concord* Sonata, which embodied the spirit of New England Transcendentalism, and *Fourth of July*, a glorious mixture of program music, popular tunes, and nostalgia for a vanished, bucolic America. That same year produced the work for which Ives is perhaps most respected, *Three Places in New England* (1912). This work is a musical evocation of the Boston Common, of Putnam's Camp, a Revolutionary War site in Connecticut, and of the Housatonic River at Stockbridge, Massachusetts. In passages of strong yet touching lyric and melodic beauty, Ives created musical landscapes that were distinctly American in both subject and style. With this work and his cumulative Fourth Symphony (1911-1916), Ives succeeded in his life's ambition of writing vigorous compositions that sprang naturally from the American experience and which were unfettered by the artificial constraints of European tradition.

Ives had been troubled by heart problems as early as 1906, and in 1918 he had a serious attack. There would be other health complications as he aged, diabetes and cataracts chief among them. His creative period ended in 1918; ironically, he was still almost completely unknown as a composer.

In the early 1920's, Ives put together his thoughts on music in the book *Essays Before a Sonata* (1920). He also collected much of his music itself, compiling a book of 114 songs and the *Concord* Sonata, which he had privately printed and mailed free to musicians and critics across the country. The innovative, starkly original works evoked bewilderment and derision from many, but a discerning few were captivated. By 1926, musicians such as Henry Cowell and Nicholas Slonimsky were champions of Ives. Cowell printed Ives's scores in his magazine *New Music*, while Slonimsky conducted the Boston Symphony Orchestra in *Three Places in New England* during a 1931 tour of the United States, Havana, and Paris. The following year, Slonimsky presented Ives's *Fourth of July* in Paris, Berlin, and Budapest.

Music written decades before was being heard for the first time, and young American composers were intensely excited. Aaron Copland included seven of Ives's songs in the 1932 Yaddo Festival, held at Saratoga Springs, New York. In 1933, the first Ives broadcast was conducted by Bernard Herrmann, who later wrote the highly original score for the film *Citizen Kane* (1941). The culmination of this growing recognition came in 1947 when Ives was awarded the Pulitzer Prize for his Third Symphony, which he had composed forty-three years before.

Throughout, Ives steadfastly avoided public association with professional musicians, refusing even to attend performances of his own works. He did help finance musical journals and other activities, but this involved his money and not his time or person. For Ives, music remained a supremely important yet never quite revealed preoccupation, and he seemed at once proud and embarrassed to be known as a great American composer.

Since Ives's death from a stroke in 1954, his musical reputation has continued to advance, and his compositions have become more available to the listening public. This accessibility is largely through recordings, which are nearly essential for adequate presentation of his difficult scores. Improved audio equipment and techniques make it possible for musicians and engineers to capture the complicated, subtle conditions Ives demanded, while stereophonic sound allows the listener to appreciate fully the variations in location of instruments as well as harmonics which Ives employed

in his works. The fact that Ives's music adapts so well to recordings—and in fact needs recording for best impact—is yet another indication of his originality and genius.

Summary

While having *Fourth of July* professionally copied, Ives was forced to write the following message on the manuscript: "Mr. Price: Please don't try to make things nice! All the wrong notes are *right*. Just copy as I have—I want it that way."

The note is appropriate to Ives's musical compositions and career. His bold, innovative works displayed techniques and devices that disregarded or openly defied accepted musical conventions. He used dissonance and discordance, even cacophony, to present his images. His works demanded that orchestras disrupt their normal seating arrangements or that the pianist play the instrument with a strip of wood. Because he was not a professional, musicians regarded him as an ignorant eccentric, while the public dismissed him as a wealthy crank.

Still, even from the first, there were those who heard the true notes of originality and power in

Ives's music. His dissonance, for example, was an integral part of his musical structure, and actually served to reinforce the unity of his compositions. He was a master of melody and variations, and a work such as *Fourth of July* is a musical metamorphosis which takes as its subject all of America and America's music.

It was as a composer of specifically American music that Ives was most successful and influential. He rejected the European tradition and sought to replace it with a tough, vital, American musical heritage. This heritage he equated with musical experimentation akin to the political experimentation which formed the nation. In forging a new musical idiom for a new world, Ives became a uniquely and unmistakably American composer.

Bibliography

Burkholder, J. Peter. *The Ideas Behind the Music*. New Haven, Conn.: Yale University Press, 1985; London: Yale University Press, 1987. Traces the development of Ives's unique aesthetics of composition, which is particularly important for his innovative and individual style and his use of musical forms to portray essentially nonmusical items, such as sports or philosophical ideas.

Cowell, Henry, and Sidney Cowell. *Charles Ives and His Music*. London and New York: Oxford University Press, 1955. Written by a friend and associate of Ives, this was the first full-length study to appear and presents a generally well-rounded biography and musical exposition.

Hitchcock, Hugh Wiley. *Ives*. London and New York: Oxford University Press, 1977. This slim volume, number 14 in the "Oxford Studies in Composers" series, concentrates on the techniques of composition employed by Ives. At least a basic knowledge of music is required to understand this work.

Lambert, Philip. *The Music of Charles Ives*. New Haven, Conn.: Yale University Press, 1997. The first comprehensive study of Ives' major works, examining the composer's artistic vision and techniques.

Lambert, Philip, ed. *Ives Studies*. Cambridge and New York: Cambridge University Press, 1997. A collection of essays by ten noted scholars covering Ives' choral, chamber, and symphonic music.

Perlis, Vivian. *Charles Ives Remembered: An Oral History*. New Haven, Conn.: Yale University Press, 1974. A collection of conversations and interviews with friends and associates of Ives from his boyhood through adult life. The book is divided into sections on family life, the insurance business, and his musical career. Provides an excellent portrait of the composer as an individual person.

Rossiter, Frank R. *Charles Ives and His America.* New York: Liveright, 1975; London: Gollancz, 1976. A well-researched examination of Ives's life and career, placing him within the cultural and social conditions of his times. Rossiter is especially acute in discussing the tension between Ives's business life and his creative activities.

Michael Witkoski

JESSE L. JACKSON

Born: October 8, 1941; Greenville, South Carolina
Areas of Achievement: Civil rights, government, and politics
Contribution: Jesse Jackson became one of the most influential, eloquent, and widely known African American political leaders in the United States during the decades after the death of Martin Luther King, Jr.

Early Life

Jesse Louis Jackson was born on October 8, 1941, in a six-room house in the textile-mill town of Greenville, South Carolina. His mother, Helen Burns, was a student at Greenville's Sterling High School when she became pregnant with Jesse. His father, Noah Robinson, was married to another woman; the Robinsons lived next door to the Burns family. Two years after Jesse's birth, on October 2, 1943, his mother married Charles Henry Jackson, who bestowed his last name on the boy and formally adopted him in 1957.

The young Jesse Jackson apparently learned the circumstances of his birth sometime during elementary school. Other children who had heard rumors of the small-town scandal taunted him. When Jesse was nine, Noah Robinson began seeing the boy standing in the Robinsons' backyard, peering through a window. The hardships and insecurities did not, however, discourage Jesse. At any early age, he became a high achiever, determined to prove his own worth.

When he was nine, Jesse, whose mother and stepfather were devout Baptists, won election to the National Sunday School Convention in Charlotte, South Carolina. By the time he reached high school, his teachers knew him as a hardworking student, and he excelled at athletics. After he was graduated from Sterling High School in Greenville in 1959, Jackson won a football scholarship to the University of Illinois.

In Jackson's freshman year, however, a white coach told him that blacks were not allowed to play quarterback for the University of Illinois team. Stung by this example of segregation outside the South, the young man transferred the next year to a black college, the North Carolina Agricultural and Technical College in Greensboro, North Carolina. The decision to return to the South was fateful, since Greensboro was a center of the student sit-in movement to integrate lunch counters and other public facilities. Jackson threw himself into the movement and became known as an energetic and outspoken young civil rights activist.

Life's Work

From his Greensboro years onward, Jackson's life revolved around political struggles for civil rights. On June 6, 1963, he was arrested for the first time, on charges of inciting a riot while leading a demonstration in front of a municipal building. At one sit-in, he met his future wife, Jacqueline Lavinia Davis, whom he married after his graduation in 1964. He became active in the Congress of Racial Equality (CORE), and during his last year at North Carolina Agricultural and Technical College, he was appointed field director of CORE's southeastern operations.

At the same time that Jackson was deeply involved in protests and civil disobedience, he was also displaying an interest in mainstream politics. For a short time during his student days in Greensboro, he worked for North Carolina Governor Terry Sanford. Sanford, recognizing the young man's promise, sponsored him as one of the first African American delegates to the Young Democrats National Convention in Las Vegas. Electoral politics absorbed Jackson to the point that he almost entered law school at Duke University, with the goal of using legal qualifications as a political springboard. Instead, however, he decided to enter the ministry.

After receiving a bachelor's degree in sociology, Jackson enrolled in the Chicago Theological Seminary. His stay in Chicago was brief, as the call to struggle for civil rights proved to be more compelling. In 1965, he left the seminary to return south. During the celebrated march in Selma, Alabama, Jackson came to know the Reverend Dr. Martin Luther King, Jr. Most of Jackson's biographers have concluded that King became a revered father figure for the young man who had looked longingly through his natural father's window. King, in turn, was impressed with his follower's abilities.

Jackson quickly became a part of the inner circle of the organization headed by King, the Southern Christian Leadership Conference (SCLC). In 1966, King asked him to take over the Chicago operations of Operation Breadbasket, an SCLC-sponsored organization designed to pressure businesses into hiring African Americans. A year later, King appointed him Operation Breadbasket's national director.

Jackson was with King in Memphis, on April 4, 1968, the day that King was assassinated. Other close associates of King have cast doubt on Jackson's claim to have been the last one to have spoken with the dying leader. Some were also critical of Jackson's dramatic television appearance on the *Today Show*, wearing a sweater that had supposedly been stained with King's blood, immediately after King's death.

On June 30, 1968, still without a theological degree, Jackson was ordained as a minister by two famous pastors, the Reverend Clay Evans and the Reverend C. L. Franklin. Instead of taking over a church, however, he continued to head Operation Breadbasket, although his independence brought him into conflict with the leaders of the SCLC. In particular, tensions emerged between Jackson and Ralph D. Abernathy, King's successor as head of the SCLC.

On December 12, 1971, Jackson submitted a formal resignation from the SCLC and from Operation Breadbasket. At the same time, he used the personal following he had built in Operation Breadbasket to form Operation People United to Save Humanity (PUSH). PUSH was a personal power base for Jackson, but he used it to agitate for greater black employment in American businesses and to promote the economic interests of African Americans. At the same time, PUSH operated self-esteem programs for disadvantaged young blacks and encouraged them to excel academically. During the years that Jackson led PUSH, the slogan he urged young people to adopt, "I am somebody," became a well-known motto of self-reliance.

As early as 1980, Jesse Jackson was announcing the need for an African American presidential candidate. As the nation approached the 1984 election, Jackson announced on the television program *60 Minutes* that he would run for the office. African Americans continued to be his electoral base, but he attempted to broaden his political program to include other Americans who had little power or representation in the American political system. He appealed to what he called a "Rainbow Coalition" that included poor people, small family farmers, gays, and others who might be sympathetic to a progressive agenda. He advocated government programs for full employment and a freeze on military spending, as well as a renewed commitment to civil rights. Thus, while conservatism had become a dominant force in American political life as President Ronald Reagan approached his second term, Jackson became a major spokesman for liberal causes.

Jackson's reputation, and his campaign, received a boost at the end of 1983 and the beginning of 1984. Robert Goodman, an African American military pilot, was shot down over the Syrian-controlled area of Lebanon. In December, Jackson flew to Damascus, Syria, to meet with Syrian president Hafez al-Assad. The Syrian leader arranged for Goodman's release, and in early January, Jackson and the freed hostage flew home together.

In January, 1984, Jackson also made one of the most serious blunders of his political career. His support for the Palestinian Liberation Organization and his connections to Arab nations had aroused the suspicions of some Jewish Americans. Jackson also had ties to Nation of Islam leader Louis Farrakhan, whom many people accused of being anti-Semitic. During a conversation with reporters at the beginning of 1984, Jackson referred to New York City as "Hymietown," a slang reference to the city's large Jewish population that was widely viewed as offensive. Although he apologized for the remark, the incident contributed to tensions between Jews and African Americans, and many observers speculated that Jackson's comments indicated an unspoken prejudice against Jews.

Although Jackson did not win the Democratic nomination, his strong showing demonstrated that an African American could compete at the highest levels of American politics. His showing in his second presidential campaign, in 1988, was stronger still. By this time, his Rainbow Coalition had become well organized. Jackson himself had also refined his positions and developed a comprehensive and consistent platform. He advocated a national health-care program, an increase in the tax rate on the highest incomes, and the adoption of comparable-worth policies to combat gender inequalities in pay. Although he again failed to win the Democratic nomination, he did receive approximately 7 million—out of 23 million—votes cast in primaries. His strong showing helped to establish him as a national leader, not simply among African Americans but among all Americans. In the 1992 presidential election, Democratic candidate Bill Clinton actively sought Jackson's endorsement, which Jackson withheld until the final weeks of the campaign.

Summary

The Civil Rights movement of the 1960's helped secure legislation to ensure and protect basic freedoms for African Americans; among the most important of these was the right to vote. Jackson played a large part in consolidating this achievement by acting as a symbol and voice for African American political aspirations. As the country moved to the right politically in the 1980's, he continued to use his powerful oratory in the service of liberal causes, broadening and deepening the American political dialogue.

Jackson became a symbol of black political power, perhaps the most widely recognized African American leader since Martin Luther King, Jr. Numerous politicians, including President Clinton, have sought his support, providing testimony to the importance of African Americans in the American political process.

Both Operation Breadbasket and Operation PUSH resulted in jobs and economic opportunities. To all of his organizational activities, Jackson brought a moral energy that instilled a sense of self-esteem in many disadvantaged people. He directed his moral message toward young people in particular. While working to expand the opportunities available to them, he also exhorted them to make the most of the opportunities they had. In compelling speeches, he urged young people to avoid drugs and to devote themselves to academic excellence. As a result of his efforts, many were able to avoid being dragged down by the social and economic forces plaguing the inner cities.

Bibliography

Barker, Lucius J., and Ronald W. Walters, eds. *Jesse Jackson's 1984 Presidential Campaign: Challenge and Change in American Politics.* Urbana: University of Illinois Press, 1989. Contains eleven articles that offer an in-depth look at Jackson's first presidential campaign. Describes the political context of the campaign, the mobilization of the black community behind Jackson, his appeal to voters in general, the convention, and the campaign's political and social impact.

Colton, Elizabeth O. *The Jackson Phenomenon: The Man, the Power, the Message.* New York: Doubleday, 1989. A detailed but readable examination of Jackson's second run for the presidency in 1988. Also examines earlier events in his life as background for his role in the election.

Frady, Marshall. *Jesse: The Life and Pilgrimage of Jesse Jackson.* New York: Random House, 1996. A thorough and perceptive biography of Jackson that presents its subject as both an ambitious opportunist and a morally courageous visionary. Frady argues that Jackson's accomplishments have been driven by a loner's need to reinvent himself and that Jackson's slogan, "I am somebody," has always been directed at himself as much as at others.

Haskins, James. *I Am Somebody! A Biography of Jesse Jackson.* Hillside, N.J.: Enslow, 1992. Written primarily for older children and young adults, this biography presents an account of Jackson's life, accomplishments, and goals. Treats the flaws in Jackson's character as well as his strengths. Contains an extensive bibliography.

Hertzke, Allen D. *Echoes of Discontent: Jesse Jackson, Pat Robertson, and the Resurgence of Populism.* Washington, D.C.: Congressional Quarterly Press, 1993. Discusses the role of religion in American politics by comparing the 1988 presidential campaigns of Jesse Jackson and Pat Robertson. Describes the importance of the churches associated with these two candidates and examines how the two brought different types of religious activism into electoral politics. Includes an examination of Jackson's move from leadership of Operation PUSH to political campaigning.

Reynolds, Barbara A. *Jesse Jackson: The Man, the Movement, the Myth.* Chicago: Nelson-Hall, 1975. An early biography of Jackson, covering the period from his childhood to his work as leader of PUSH. Particularly informative on the goals and achievements of PUSH. Also contains an essay by Jackson on how people in low-income minority communities can achieve control over their own economic resources.

Stanford, Karin L. *Beyond the Boundaries: Reverend Jesse Jackson in International Affairs.* Albany: State University of New York Press, 1997. Examines Jesse Jackson's activities in the international arena. Based on interviews, 1984 campaign documents, and press coverage.

Carl L. Bankston III

FRANÇOIS JACOB

Born: June 17, 1920; Nancy, France
Areas of Achievement: Biology, biochemistry, and genetics
Contribution: Jacob shared the 1965 Nobel Prize in Physiology or Medicine with André Lwoff and Jacques Monod, for their collaborative discoveries concerning the genetic control of enzyme and virus synthesis. These studies were a landmark in the evolving area of molecular biology. They spanned virology, biochemistry, and microbiology.

Early Life

The Nobel Prize-winning French molecular biologist François Jacob was born in Nancy, the only child of Simon Jacob and Thérèse (née Franck) Jacob. Jacob was reared in the Jewish religion. In his autobiography, he reminisces about the great contrast between his father's orthodox family and the relaxed Judaism of his mother's family and its effects on the development of his character.

Simon Jacob, a partner in a prosperous real estate firm, sent his son to excellent schools, beginning with elementary school in Nancy and followed by the Lycée Carnot in Paris. Jacob was an excellent student. Yet, during this period of his life, he considered himself a loner who had "companions but no friends." He dreamed fervently of becoming a surgeon, after falling in love with the "race against death and the precision" perceived upon viewing an operation. He was encouraged toward this career by a physician uncle, Henri Jacob, and enrolled in the Sorbonne with that goal in mind. With his superb grades, he quickly joined the student elite. Jacob also developed an interest in research here, from his interaction with his anatomy professor André Hovelacque. His first love, however, remained surgery.

Jacob's studies ended abruptly when the German *Wehrmacht* invaded France. He escaped to London, where he joined the Free French Army in Exile. At first, Jacob was in the artillery. A shortage of doctors led him to join the medical corps. Throughout World War II, he saw action all over North Africa as a medical officer with General Paul Leclerc. During the Normandy invasion, he served with the American Second Armored Division.

In 1944, near Le Mans, Jacob was wounded severely while trying to help an injured officer. The resulting hand and arm injuries ended his chances of becoming a surgeon. His valorous war record won for him the French War Cross and the Companion of the Liberation, two of the highest French War medals. Returning to Paris, Jacob had great difficulty in readjusting to civilian life. His family helped him to heal mentally and physically during this troubled period. As a result of his intelligence and diligent study, Jacob passed rigorous second-year medical examinations and decided to switch to medicine, after unsuccessful attempts to continue his training as a surgeon. He did well there but felt trapped and briefly attempted careers in freelance journalism, politics, and civil service. Yet none of these professions held his interest.

Jacob next became involved in study of the antibiotic tyrothricin at the National Penicillin Center. Bored with medicine and very restless, he developed an interest in a career in biological research. Yet at age twenty-eight he considered himself to be too old and perhaps inadequate to meet the challenges of the required career change. Meeting and marrying Lise Bloch led him to that career in an interesting way. Conversation with Lise's cousin, Henri Marcovich, a physician turned biological researcher, led Jacob to realize that he had the ability to go in that direction too. Jacob decided that genetics was the area for him, because it dealt with "quantitative biology" and sat at the "core of things."

Life's Work

Jacob's life's work may be described as the investigation of the cellular genetics of bacteria. His contributions to the area are many and varied. He began by seeking a research fellowship at the National Research Center and the National Hygiene Institute, where he was rejected by Émile-Florent Terroine and Louis Bugnard, directors of the two agencies. Finally, Jacques Trefouel, director of the Pasteur Institute, offered Jacob a fellowship beginning in October, 1949. There, he did his doctoral work with the well-known geneticist André Lwoff, whose scientific virtuosity Jacob attempted to emulate.

Jacob bloomed there, in an environment that included frequent encounters with internationally reputed scientists. He completed his Ph.D. thesis, under Lwoff, in 1954. His efforts stemmed from Lwoff's study of lysogenic bacteria. Such bacteria

are not destroyed immediately after infection with bacterial viruses (bacteriophages). Yet when they are subjected to external stimuli, such as ultraviolet light, lysogenic bacteria are destroyed through multiplication of the viruses in the cell and release of the viral progeny. The overall process is called "lysogeny."

Lwoff had shown that the bacteriophages in lysogenic cells initially existed as noninfectious prophages. Jacob's doctoral research extended understanding of lysogenic bacteria and prophage, carrying Lwoff's efforts forward. It included the concept that prophage was hooked into the bacterial chromosome as one of its genetic elements. Jacob later proved this to be correct, but at the time of his thesis defense it was not entirely acceptable to the scientific community.

Immediately after completion of his doctoral thesis, Jacob began collaborating with Elie Wollman in study of the genetics of bacterial chromosomes. This work was made possible by the discovery that bacteria were sexually differentiated into males and females, which mated by attaching themselves together with a conjugation tube. As

soon as this tube forms, the male passes its genetic material through it and into the female.

The experiments that Jacob and Wollman conducted using mating bacteria showed that bacterial chromosomes are circular deoxyribonucleic acid (DNA) molecules, which contained genes arranged in an ordered array that could be mapped experimentally. These chromosomes, attached to the cell membrane, proved always to have their genes arranged in the same consecutive order from this point of attachment. Bacterial variants exhibiting loss of genetic attributes were found to have portions of the chromosome missing. Those exhibiting new genetic characteristics were found to contain additional chromosomal material.

Next, Jacob collaborated with Jacques Monod in the discovery of messenger ribonucleic acid (RNA), making a giant step toward understanding the cellular genetics of bacteria. As a result of their efforts and those of others, it is known that there are three main types of RNA in cells: ribosomal RNA, messenger RNA, and transfer RNA. These RNAs cooperate in protein synthesis, the means by which the hereditary information in the chromosome is actualized. Ribosomal RNAs are structural components of the ribosomes on which proteins are synthesized. Messenger RNAs are copies of genes, and each contains the blueprint for synthesis of a protein. Transfer RNAs carry amino acids, the building blocks of proteins, to the ribosomes.

In their examination of the genetics of protein synthesis, Jacob and Monod also discovered that chromosomal DNA contains structural and regulatory genes. Structural genes are copied to produce messenger RNA blueprints for the production of proteins that cause observed genetic characteristics. Messenger RNAs, produced from regulatory genes, are blueprints for repressor proteins. These proteins combine with chromosomal operator sites and turn off messenger RNA production from structural genes.

Jacob and Monod hypothesized that cellular chromosomes were divided into units called "operons." An operon is defined as a portion of a chromosome composed of a regulatory gene, an operator site, and several structural genes. The operon hypothesis indicates how cells adapt to environmental changes. Among the phenomena it explains is enzyme induction, the rapid production of enzymes (biological catalysts) needed to respond to a sudden change in the supply of a food (for example the sugar lactose) given to bacteria. Jacob and

Monod hypothesized that this process occurred because the food combines with the repressor protein to inactivate it. Repressor protein inactivation was proposed to allow the operon to function well, producing its enzymes via action of its structural genes. The hypothesis stated that when the food was exhausted the repressor protein became functional again and turned off the operon. Numerous repressor proteins have been isolated, and their properties validate the hypothesis.

In the course of this work, Jacob and his coworkers also showed that lysogeny, which had occupied Jacob's doctoral work, was a result of addition of the viral genome to the chromosome of the host bacteria. This was accomplished by a process that prevented viral replication because of the action of a repressor. Therefore, the reproduction of a bacteriophage in lysogenic bacteria behaved like the expression of an operon. Ultraviolet light and other factors were viewed as the inducers that led to this reproduction and to the destruction of the host cell that followed.

Great things began to happen to Jacob in 1960, when he became chief of the department of cellular genetics at the Pasteur Institute. In 1964, the Collège de France established a chair in cellular genetics for him. Then, in 1965, he shared the Nobel Prize in Physiology or Medicine with Lwoff and Monod, for "discoveries concerning the genetic control of enzyme and virus synthesis," including the operon hypothesis. This research is viewed by most scientists as the wedge that opened up the field of molecular biology by explaining how genetic information is converted into chemical processes. Jacob continued to contribute to molecular biology after the prize, completing, developing, and editing important concepts about molecular genetics. Among his major interests has been proof of the viral theory of human cancer production.

Throughout his life, Jacob has remained a family man, fathering four children, Henri, Laurent, Odile, and Pierre. Professionally, his honors have included membership in the French Academy of Sciences, the Royal Society of London, and the American Academy of Arts and Sciences.

Summary

François Jacob has always been known as a man of probity, an idealist imbued with respect for the law and for honesty, decency, character, and respect for other people. In his autobiography, he attributed these characteristics to his father, from whom he must have gained them. He is also recognized as a superb scientist with a love for scientific research. He has made exceptional contributions to molecular biology. Working in a defined area, he made it quantitative, where before it was mostly speculative. His efforts have greatly enriched the reputation of the Pasteur Institute, helping to keep it in the forefront of research in the area. Before the seminal research to which he contributed so greatly, it was not understood how expression of the genetic information was accomplished.

Jacob, as a scientist and as a person, has demonstrated bravery and determination. Deprived of his dreams of surgery, he rallied and chose another career in which he not only succeeded but also excelled. Willingness to strive is a lesson he has passed on to all of his students. It is an important exemplar for today.

Bibliography

Hayes, William. *The Genetics of Bacteria and Their Viruses.* 2d ed. Oxford: Blackwell, and New York: Wiley, 1968. Describes the state of the art in bacterial and viral genetics at the time. Also deals with lysogeny and with the contributions of Jacob and his coworkers to the area.

Jacob, François. *The Logic of Life: A History of Heredity.* Translated by Betty E. Spillman. Princeton, N.J.: Princeton University Press, 1993. A concise history of biology that considers how approaches have changed over time. Discusses the discovery of the functions of cells, organs, DNA, and genes.

———. *Of Flies, Mice, and Men: On the Revolution in Molecular Biology, by One of the Scientists Who Helped Make It.* Translated by Giselle Weiss. Cambridge, Mass.: Harvard University Press, 1998. Jacob examines biology from a historical perspective focusing on the ways in which biologists work and the role of the scientist in society.

———. *The Statue Within.* New York: Basic, and London: Unwin Hyman, 1988. This intriguing autobiography, funded by the Sloan Foundation, gives important insights into Jacob, his contemporaries, and the development of molecular biology. Contains many interesting anecdotes about the environment and the scientists of the Pasteur Institute.

Jacob, François, and Jacques Monod. "Genetic Regulatory Mechanisms in the Synthesis of Proteins." *Journal of Molecular Biology* 3 (1961): 318-356. This important, insightful article describes the messenger-RNA concept and the function of repressors, operators, and structural genes.

Jacob, François, and Elie Wollman. *Sexuality and the Genetics of Bacteria.* Rev. ed. New York: Academic Press, 1961. This valuable book describes the development of bacterial genetics, the existing knowledge about sexual conjugation in bacteria, the use of this sexual conjugation to in-

vestigate problems in cellular genetics, and the genetic aspects of lysogeny.

Stent, Gunther. *Molecular Biology of Bacterial Viruses.* San Francisco: Freeman, 1963. An excellent compilation of many historical issues in the development of the molecular biology of bacteriophages. Includes sections on infection of bacteria, growth and reproduction of viruses, genetic recombination, lysogeny, transduction, and expression of hereditary information.

Sanford S. Singer

ROMAN JAKOBSON

Born: October 11, 1896; Moscow, Russia
Died: July 18, 1982; Cambridge, Massachusetts
Areas of Achievement: Literature, language, and linguistics
Contribution: A prominent and founding member of the linguistic circles of Moscow and Prague, Jakobson was instrumental in the European development of structuralism in linguistics and in literary theory. Arriving in the United States in 1941, he brought extensive knowledge of European linguistics to the American scene, and, through his teaching at Columbia and Harvard universities and his prolific scholarship, he profoundly influenced Slavic studies, poetic analysis, and the development of American phonology.

Early Life

Born to Anna Volpert Jakobson and the chemist Osip Jakobson in 1896, Roman Osipovich Jakobson grew up in the intellectual circles of Moscow, where French and Russian were the normal languages of the intelligentsia and conversation often focused on poetry and art. By the time he entered high school at the Lazarev Institute of Oriental Languages in Moscow in 1906-1907, he was already engaged in writing and analyzing poetry. The curriculum at the institute included studies of Russian folk poetry and folklore, as well as literary theory, French poetry, and Russian grammar.

Jakobson's friends were the young painters and poets of Moscow, and he saw in the emerging Russian Futurist poetry relationships to French Postimpressionism and cubism. Jakobson exchanged writing and ideas with the poets Velemir Khlebnikov and Aleksei Kruchonykh, and the latter eventually published three experimental "supra-conscious" poems that Jakobson wrote in 1914 under the pseudonym Alyagrov.

Entering the University of Moscow in 1914, Jakobson was enrolled in the Department of Slavic and Russian of the Historico-Philological Faculty, where linguistics was a required subject. His earliest readings in linguistics were a recent study of Russian vowels by Lev Vladimirovich Shcherba, a book not approved by his teachers because of its departure from traditional Russian linguistics, and a forgotten work on sound alternations from 1881 by the Polish linguist Mikołaj Kruszewski. Although dissatisfied with the orthodoxy of the Mos-

cow linguistic school, Jakobson was very much interested in his studies of Old Russian language and literature, particularly in folk poetry. In 1914, with six other students from the faculty, he drafted the statutes of the Moscow Linguistic Circle; young Moscow linguists began meeting in spring 1915, combining insights from linguistics, poetics, and metrics for the analysis and discussion of the verse of Russian folk epics (*byliny* in Russian).

The Moscow Linguistic Circle remained Jakobson's intellectual home until he left for Prague in 1920. At meetings of the circle, he tested his analysis of Khlebnikov's verse, and that analysis in turn was the beginning of his lifelong work on phonology, the structure of sounds in human language. A draft of his first book, *Noveshaya russkaya poeziya* (1921; recent Russian poetry), a slim volume of sixty-eight pages published in Prague, was read in 1919 at the Moscow Linguistic Circle.

Life's Work

Linguistics, the science of human language, is at the core of Jakobson's life work. His most significant contributions to the discipline involved phonology, but he was far from a narrow specialist. In fact, perhaps more than any other linguist of the twentieth century, Jakobson brought to the field a wide range of perspectives, from poetry and folk literature to acoustic science, medicine, and child language acquisition. He also extended linguistics into other fields—Slavic history and culture, literary criticism, and semiotics. Many of these interests were already present in his Moscow years, but others evolved during his two decades in Czechoslovakia (1920-1939), two years in Scandinavia (1939-1941), and finally throughout his forty years of teaching and research in the United States (1941-1982).

Heading for Prague in 1920, on a boat between Tallin and Stetin, Jakobson passed the time reading Czech poetry. Intrigued by elements that he encountered in the verse, he decided to conduct a study comparing Czech and Russian verse from the medieval period to the avant-garde. What he sought was a universal theory of metrics, applicable to all human languages. Jakobson came to view metrics not only in the traditional terms of stress, length, and syllable but also in terms of the phonetic properties of consonants and vowels and the presence and absence of the boundaries between words. Indeed, his studies of poetry expanded over the years to grammatical, as well as metrical, analysis, and by the end of his career he had published essays on poetic texts from more than a dozen languages with poetic traditions spanning a thousand years. Jakobson brought linguistic analysis to poetry and poetry to linguistic analysis.

Complementing Jakobson's interests in poetry was his continuing study of both modern and ancient sound systems and how they are structured. From work on the phonology of Czech and Russian, conducted in Prague during the 1920's, Jakobson developed in the 1930's a theory that phonemes (the sounds of a language) are not unanalyzable entities, but rather are composed of features, each of which might serve to distinguish one phoneme from another. As in poetry, here too Jakobson sought a universal framework that could be applied to all languages. Much of this work was carried out in Prague with his friend and fellow Russian expatriate Nikolai S. Trubetzkoy, but it was Jakobson who established that the distinctive features of languages are binary; each exists as a two-way opposition (for example, English *b* is distinct from *p* by the opposition voiced/voiceless, whereas *b* is distinct from *m* by the opposition oral/nasal). Almost twenty-five years later in his career, as Cross Professor of Slavic Languages and Literatures at Harvard University (a position he held from 1949 until his retirement in 1967), Jakobson worked with two colleagues, Gunnar Fant and Morris Halle, to determine the acoustic and articulatory bases of the distinctive features. Their landmark book *Preliminaries to Speech Analysis: The Distinctive Features and Their Correlates* (1952) established the foundation for the development of generative phonology in the United States.

Jakobson's early work on distinctive features was interrupted by the German invasion of Czechoslovakia. In 1939, he fled north, first to Denmark, then to Norway, and finally to Sweden, where in Stockholm he turned to yet another aspect of phonological study. With access to the medical libraries of the Swedish capital, Jakobson established what he termed a "mirror-image relationship" between the acquisition order of distinctive oppositions in sounds by children and the loss of those oppositions in victims of aphasia. He pointed out important relationships between these orders and the types of historical changes that had been observed in the sound systems of a number of different languages. *Kindersprache, Aphasie und allge-*

meine Lautgesetze (1941; *Child Language, Aphasia and Phonological Universals,* 1968) was a pioneering work, and although details of Jakobson's findings have been challenged, the book is a classic in both aphasia studies and child language acquisition.

Jakobson arrived in New York in June, 1941. Although he had held a professional position in Russian philology at the Masaryk University in Brno, Czechoslovakia, and served as a visiting lecturer in Russian and linguistics at universities in Copenhagen, Oslo, and Uppsala, it was not until the fall of 1946 that he received a regular appointment at an American university—professor of Czechoslovak studies at Columbia University. In the interim, Jakobson taught, primarily in French, at the École Libre des Hautes Études, a "university-in-exile" established in 1942 in New York City by Belgian and French scholars who had fled the war in Europe.

At the École Libre des Hautes Études, Jakobson's first lectures were on the relationship between phonology and semantics (meaning), and he framed much of the discussion in terms of his agreements and disagreements with the theories of the Swiss linguist Ferdinand de Saussure. Jakobson brought to the United States the broad scope of European linguistics at a time when American linguistics was becoming increasingly isolated, narrow, and behavioristic. As a champion of flexibility and with a philosophical concern for explanation and universals in the study of language, Jakobson was at odds with much of what his American contemporaries of the 1940's viewed as the proper scope of the discipline. His dynamic personality, his excellence as a teacher, and his prolific publications influenced several generations of students, and in 1956, only fifteen years after his arrival and four years after his naturalization as a United States citizen, Jakobson was elected president of the Linguistic Society of America.

Still at the École Libre des Hautes Études, Jakobson worked with Byzantine scholar Henri Grégoire on the authenticity of the *Slovo o polku Igoreve* (*The Lay of Igor's Host*), a medieval Russian epic. When Jakobson joined the faculty of Harvard University in 1949, he continued his lectures on the Russian language and on Slavic mythology and folklore. His influence on Slavic studies in the United States is unparalleled.

In 1957, Jakobson was appointed visiting institute professor at the Massachusetts Institute of

Technology (MIT), concurrently with his Harvard appointment in Slavic studies. By 1960, his Harvard professorship had been extended to general linguistics, and the MIT appointment had become permanent; he continued his active MIT affiliation until 1970. This period coincides in the United States with the development and dominance of generative grammar, a theory which Jakobson never adopted. His influence on American linguistics declined, and, during the last quarter-century of his life, Roman Jakobson focused increasingly on poetics and semiotics; he became widely viewed as a founder of structuralism in literary theory.

Summary

Roman Jakobson's influence on twentieth century linguistics and literary studies comes from the energetic force of his personality as much as from his scholarship.

One of the most prolific scholars of his time, Jakobson's *Selected Writings* (1962-1985) initially constituted seven volumes, most more than seven hundred pages in length. Yet he produced not a single major book-length study, and some of his work has been described as "dilettantish." Many of his most effective publications were produced in collaboration with other scholars: the work on the *The Lay of Igor's Host* with Grégoire; a major analysis of the poem "Les Chats" by Charles Baudelaire co-authored with the structural anthropologist Claude Lévi-Strauss, published in 1962 in *L'Homme;* the acoustic and articulatory bases of distinctive features with Fant and Halle; and, with his wife of twenty years, Krystyna Pomorska, a professor of Slavic studies at MIT, *Dialogues* (1983).

A major catalyst in the establishment of important organizations of linguists, Jakobson was a co-founder of the Moscow Linguistic Circle, serving as president until his departure for Prague in 1920. As the first vice president of the Prague Linguistic Circle in 1926, he played a major role in the Prague school until he left Czechoslovakia in 1939. In New York, too, he was a charter member of the Linguistic Circle, vice president from its founding in 1943 until he went to Harvard in 1949.

Jakobson lectured throughout the world, reaching an unusually wide audience through visiting professorships and participation at national and international conferences; he received honorary degrees from more than two dozen universities in the United States, Great Britain, and Europe. His international reputation and influence were surely related to his fluent speaking knowledge of six languages and his ability to read twenty-five.

Bibliography

Armstrong, Daniel, and C. H. van Schooneveld, eds. *Roman Jakobson: Echoes of His Scholarship.* Lisse, The Netherlands: Peter de Ridder Press, 1977. An excellent and extensive overview of Jakobson's contributions to numerous fields of study. Of particular interest are essays by Umberto Eco on semiotics, Morris Halle on phonology, A. R. Luria on aphasia, and Krystyna Pomorska on the new poetics.

Bradford, Richard. *Roman Jakobson: Life, Art and Literature.* London and New York: Routledge, 1994. The author summarizes Jakobson's theories on poetic language and argues that his work offers much to contemporary studies on language and poetry.

Drake, James. "The Naming Disease." *TLS,* no. 4979 (September 4, 1998). Considers postmodernism and its genesis in Jakobson's essay "Two Aspects of Language and Two Types of Aphasic Disturbances."

Holenstein, Elmar. *Roman Jakobson's Approach to Language: Phenomenological Structuralism.* Translated by Catherine Schelbert and Tarcisius Schelbert. Bloomington: Indiana University Press, 1976. An account of the philosophical and methodological principles of Jakobson's work and the tenets of his comprehensive theory of language. Includes a brief historical introduction, an accurate biographical outline, and a selected bibliography through 1975.

Jakobson, Roman, and Krystyna Pomorska. *Dialogues.* Cambridge: Cambridge University Press, and Cambridge, Mass.: MIT Press, 1983. The record of a remarkable dialogue on Jakobson's thought and work. First published in French, this book is highly autobiographical and provides particularly good insights into Jakobson's intellectual life.

Pomorska, Krystyna, Elżbieta Chodakowska, Hugh McLean, and Brent Vine, eds. *Language, Poetry and Poetics: The Generation of the 1890s: Jakobson, Trubetzkoy, Majakovskij.* New York: Mouton de Gruyter, 1987. Especially valuable for the essays on Jakobson's work with the Russian poet Vladimir Mayakovsky, his philosophical base drawn from Georg Wilhelm Friedrich Hegel, Edmund Husserl, and Charles

Sanders Peirce, his cooperative work on phonology with Nikolai Trubetzkoy, and Pomorska's discussion of Jakobson's attitudes toward his own life, "The Autobiography of a Scholar."

Waugh, Linda R. *Roman Jakobson's Science of Language.* Lisse, The Netherlands: Peter de Ridder Press, 1976. Waugh worked closely with Jakobson during the last decade of his life, coauthoring his final monograph on phonology *The Sound Shape of Language* (1979). Here she delineates the invariant organizing principles of language that Jakobson developed over his lifetime.

Julia S. Falk

LEOŠ JANÁČEK

Born: July 3, 1854; Hukvaldy, Moravia, Austrian
Empire
Died: August 12, 1928; Ostrava, Czechoslovakia
Area of Achievement: Music
Contribution: As the originator of a unique method
of musical composition utilizing Moravian
speech patterns and folk music, Janáček created
the ideal medium for the musical expression of
Czech folk culture and aspirations, and became
one of the few composers to integrate folk art
into formal European music.

Early Life

Leoš Janáček was born on July 3, 1854, in the tiny
village of Hukvaldy, Moravia, which is today in
central Czechoslovakia. He was the fifth of nine
children born into an extremely poor family which,
nevertheless, had a long tradition in the music profession: his father, grandfather, and several other
ancestors were all music teachers. At age eleven,
he, too, was sent to begin preparation for this profession at the choir school of the Augustinian monastery in Brno, then the capital of Moravia. He received his lodging, food, and training in return for
playing organ and singing in the choir. An important formative influence on Janáček was the conductor of the choir, Moravia's leading composer
and music teacher, Pavel Krizkowsky.

In 1866, Janáček's father died, leaving the family in even deeper poverty. Since going home would
have added another mouth to feed, the boy stayed
in school, earning a state scholarship to the Czech
Teachers' Institute in September, 1869. An outstanding pupil, Janáček was graduated with honors
in music, history, and geography in July, 1872, and
went on to serve the compulsory two years of unpaid service in one of the schools of the institute.
Already, he had begun to display the phenomenal
energy that characterized his entire life, for, in addition to his unpaid service, he succeeded Krizkowsky at the Brno choir school when the latter
was transferred. The following year, he was also
appointed choirmaster for a workingmen's choral
society, the Svatopluk, for which he wrote his first
secular compositions, four-part settings of folk
texts. In the autumn of 1874, he was granted leave
from his positions to begin a three-year course of
study at the Prague Organ School, but he was so
poor that he could not even afford to rent a piano

on which to practice. Even so, he composed several choral and organ works during this time.

Completely destitute, Janáček returned to Brno
in 1874 and resumed all of his previous duties
there. His first published work was an offertory,
Exaudi Deus, written for the monastery choir.
Soon, he acquired yet another appointment, becoming conductor of a middle-class choral society,
the Beseda. In this position, as in all the others,
Janáček successfully strove both to improve the
quality of performance and to broaden the repertoire of the group. He also championed the works
of Antonín Dvořák, the first, and best-known, of
the three great Czech nationalist composers. Janáček and Dvořák became friends, and the two went
on a walking tour of Bohemia together in 1877. It
is likely that Dvořák's Serenade for Strings was the
inspiration for Janáček's Suite for String Orchestra
(1877) and Idyll for Strings (1878).

In 1879, Janáček returned to school, first to the
Leipzig Conservatory, then in Vienna. He was once
more mired in poverty, and, though he polished his
composition technique during this period, he was
extremely unhappy. Perhaps the most important
reason was that, being without money, he could not
afford to marry his fiancé, one of his own piano pupils. In May, 1880, he was (finally) certified by the
Ministry of Education as a fully qualified teacher
of music, and, returning to Brno to resume all of
his former activities, he was able to get married in
July, 1881.

Life's Work

It is difficult to determine exactly where Janáček's
youth ends and his adulthood begins: He started
working very early in life and continued almost to
the moment he died. In December, 1881, he founded the Brno Organ School, with which he was associated as director and teacher for nearly forty
years. From 1886 to 1902, he also taught at the
Brno Gymnasium (secondary school) and continued to expand and improve the Beseda, establishing singing, violin, and piano classes, and even
adding a permanent orchestra. In 1884, he founded
and edited a journal to review the productions of
the new Provisional Czech Theater, which had just
opened in Brno. Overburdened by these responsibilities, he stopped composing for about four
years, but, in 1885, he resumed with a series of
choral works, some of which demonstrated the

startling changes of key which later often characterized his music.

It was not until 1887 that Janáček began working on his first opera, *Šárka*, using a verse libretto based on Czech mythology by Julius Zeyer. Unfortunately, Janáček did not seek Zeyer's permission to use the text until after he had composed the music. Since Zeyer had intended the libretto for Dvorák (who did nothing with it), he refused to release it to Janáček, and *Šárka* was not staged until 1925.

The following year marked an important juncture in Janáček's career: He accepted the invitation of another teacher at the Brno Gymnasium to visit northern Moravia to collect folksongs for publication. Collecting and publishing folksongs was very popular among nineteenth century composers, many of whom used elements of them in their works. For the next three years, Janáček not only helped edit several volumes of the folksongs of his native land but also composed a group of popular works based on them. These included the *Lachian Dances*, the Suite for Orchestra, a folk ballet, and a one-act opera entitled *The Beginning of a Romance*, which had a modestly successful production in 1894.

Janáček's work with folksongs, as well as the positive reception given *The Beginning of a Romance*, inspired him to begin what is regarded as his greatest work, a serious opera in a Moravian folk setting entitled *Janůfa*. Unlike Janáček's other works, *Janůfa* required an extremely long gestation, nearly nine years (1894-1903), during which Janáček gradually transformed his whole approach to composition. In about 1897, he began to formulate a theory of melodic structure based upon the speech patterns of the peasantry of Moravia. Coming himself from a village background of poverty, Janáček identified strongly with the attitudes, problems, and struggles of his people, perhaps especially with their desire for a nation of their own.

Moravia, as well as its western neighbor Bohemia, were at this time parts of the polyglot Austro-Hungarian Empire, ruled by the Habsburg monarchy and dominated by ethnic Germans and Hungarians. The many Slavic groups of the empire had long chafed under Habsburg rule. In the nineteenth century, the success of nationalism as an ideology and unifying force in France, Italy, and Germany led Moravians and Bohemians to hope that they, too, could form an independent nation. Patriotic composers such as Dvořák and Bedřich Smetana had both reflected and encouraged this feeling

through works that incorporated folk elements and created powerful musical images of Bohemia and Moravia. Janáček now took this process a large step further through a theoretical analysis of the speech patterns of the Moravian language and their relationship with the words and melodies of Moravian folk music.

In a series of articles on music theory, Janáček insisted that this relationship must be reflected in the works of Moravian composers, and he apparently spent much time reworking *Janůfa* so that it would reflect this relationship. He created several new techniques, including the use of short, highly dramatic motifs, rather than the long, well-developed themes of most European romantic music of the time. Emphasizing the tonal colors of individual instruments within the orchestra, he used them to produce maximum heightening of expression. Perhaps most powerfully, he employed both vocal and instrumental repetition to build the musical tension toward great emotional climaxes.

As a result of Janáček's new approach, *Janůfa*, a powerful story of lust, hypocrisy, and murder set in a Moravian peasant village, was significantly different from his earlier works. He was unable to persuade the Prague National Opera to present it, so the premiere took place in Brno in 1904, where it was fairly well received. Over the next twelve years, Janáček composed several additional operas as well as a large number of instrumental works and choral pieces. Throughout this period, he continued to integrate folk elements into his personal style. These included not only themes from folk music but also settings and stories, as well as the linguistic inflections and rhythms of the Moravian peasantry. By 1914, when World War I began, he was well respected in Brno and had finally gained at least a moderate level of prosperity. Outside Moravia, however, he was still virtually unknown.

Janáček generally avoided involvement in the war, though his pro-Russian sympathies were expressed in a three-movement tone poem for orchestra, *Taras Bulba*, based on the novel by Nikolai Gogol. Like many of his fellow Slavs, Janáček looked to Russia for liberation from the Habsburgs. Toward the end of the war, the declining fortunes of Austria-Hungary increased the probability that an independent Czechoslovakia would be created, and Janáček began to write music specifically intended to endorse this idea. In 1918, his patriotic opera *Mr. Brouček's Excursion to the Fifteenth Century* was dedicated to Tomaš Masaryk, the first president of the new Czechoslovak republic.

By this time, Janáček had become a celebrity, for, through the influence of some of his friends, *Janůfa* had finally been staged by the Prague National Opera in 1916. It was an immense success and was soon produced in cities throughout Europe and the United States. Finally assured of a broad audience, Janáček concentrated primarily on opera, and, from 1919 to 1925, he composed three of his finest works in this genre: *Kat' a Kabanova* (1921), *The Cunning Little Vixen* (1923), and *The Makrapoulos Affair* (1925). At the same time, he demonstrated his awareness of current trends in instrumental music by incorporating some elements of the methods of Arnold Schoenberg, Igor Stravinsky, and Claude Debussy in symphonic works such as *The Danube* (1923) and *Sinfonietta* (1926). His groundbreaking First String Quartet was written in a few days in 1923, and a Concertino for Piano and Chamber Ensemble in the spring of 1925. All this creative energy came from a man in his late sixties.

On his seventieth birthday, Janáček was awarded an honorary doctorate from Masaryk Universi-

ty in Brno, a distinction that he cherished for the rest of his life; he was also honored at a special concert of his works given in London the following year. That summer, he wrote perhaps his finest choral work, the powerfully dynamic *Glagolitic Mass*. At seventy-one, he finally retired from the Brno Organ School, but he continued to teach master classes in composition at the Prague Conservatory. His fame continued to grow, and his prodigious energy remained undiminished. In 1927, he began work on *From the House of the Dead*, an opera based on Fyodor Dostoevski's account of life in prison. Though he took three weeks off in January, 1928, to write another string quartet, the new opera occupied most of his time. At the end of July, while working in the cottage he had recently purchased in his home town of Hukvaldy, he contracted pneumonia. On August 10, he was moved to the hospital at Ostrava, where he died on August 12. His funeral, held three days later in Brno, was one of the largest public events in Czech history. *From the House of the Dead*, which had been nearly completed, received some finishing touches from two of Janáček's students and was produced in 1930. It is regarded generally by critics as one of his finest works.

Summary

It has been said that Leoš Janáček left no unsolved problems for other composers; his work is complete in itself. No other composer has so completely integrated folk art—which is unconscious, improvisational, and organic in its development—into a consciously developed style. Thus, Janáček left no "school" or "movement" to follow him. Music critics have often likened Janáček to the Russian composer Modest Mussorgsky, who also tried to evolve his melodies out of the inflections, cadences, and rhythms of his native tongue. Though Janáček, as a Czech national composer, is often grouped with Dvořák and Smetana, his method, and the attitudes underlying it, were fundamentally different. Both Dvořák and Smetana created music that was folk-oriented, but their approaches to both melody and harmony remained within the formal principles of the Western tradition as it developed in the nineteenth century. For Janáček, the use of folk tunes and peasant speech patterns was not simply a device to be adapted to a previously existing system. As a Czech patriot and a man of peasant origins himself, he believed that Czech music must find its own unique medium of expression. He regarded the structure of Western music as alien to the Czech experience, and, as a result, created his own theory of musical forms appropriate to that experience.

In practice, this meant the use of short musical phrases, heavily ornamented, that were shaped into asymmetrical groups rather than smoothly developed melody lines. These were frequently repeated, using different instruments, and were combined with abrupt shifts, unconventional rhythms, and extreme variations of tempo, volume, and tone color. In many of Janáček's works, the result is often a highly dramatic structure of immense emotional power. Because these methods are most clearly exhibited in Janáček's operas and later vocal music, he is usually grouped with twentieth century composers. Unlike the works of many of these, however, Janáček's music has remained popular with concert audiences all over the world. It should also not be forgotten that he created a very large body of work before the Prague premiere of *Janůfa*, and some of his most pleasant pieces, such as the Suite for Strings, were composed long before he became a figure of international renown. In a career that spanned more than six decades, Leoš Janáček crafted a unique musical style, one that effectively communicates the spirit of Moravia to listeners far removed from it.

Bibliography

Deri, Otto. *Exploring Twentieth-Century Music.* New York: Holt Rinehart, 1968. A well-written text that attempts to aid the listener in understanding and appreciating twentieth century music by explaining how its aesthetic principles and materials evolved. Though brief, the section on Janáček offers a cogent analysis of his career and music. Extensive bibliography and discography.

Ewen, David. *The World of Twentieth Century Music.* 2d ed. London: Hale, 1991. An encyclopedic sourcebook of brief articles on all the major composers, musicians, movements, and other aspects of modern music. The essay on Janáček contains a short biographical section as well as an analysis of some of his major works. Readers should take care not to confuse this work with others on twentieth century music by the same author, which are much less helpful.

Hartog, Howard, ed. *European Music in the Twentieth Century.* London: Routledge, and New York: Praeger, 1957. A book of essays by specialists. Focuses on several specific composers but also includes a group of articles classified by country, which allows for enlightening comparisons between different composers from the same country.

Hollander, Hans. *Leoš Janáček.* Translated by Paul Hamburger. London: Calder, and New York: St. Martin's Press, 1963. The only full-length biography of Janáček in English. An extremely well-written study, unusual in that its analyses of Janáček's music do not require extensive background knowledge in music theory. Extensive use of Janáček's letters and theoretical works provides helpful insights into the composer's personality and attitudes.

Machlis, Joseph. *Introduction to Contemporary Music.* 2d ed. London: Dent, and New York: Norton, 1979. An essential work for general readers interested in twentieth century music. Introduces modern music through comparison and contrast with earlier periods, creating a painless introduction to music theory. European and American composers are grouped by types; each receives a concise biographical treatment and analysis of important works. Includes an excellent bibliography, discography, and texts and translations of vocal works.

Tyrell, John. "Leoš Janáček." In *Iacobus-Kremlin.* Vol. 9 in *The New Grove Dictionary of Music and Musicians*, edited by Stanley Sadie. London: Macmillan, 1980. Though articles in *The New Grove Dictionary of Music and Musicians* are often too technical for those without musical training, this essay on Janáček is probably the best brief source available, especially because the section on Janáček himself is clearly separated from the technical discussion of his style and works. Contains an extensive bibliography.

Tyrrell, John, ed. and trans. *Intimate Letters, Leoš Janáček to Kamila Stosslova.* London: Faber, and Princeton, N.J.: Princeton University Press, 1994. A collection of previously suppressed letters between Janáček and Stosslova spanning their eleven-year affair. Provides valuable insight into Janáček's personality, loneliness, and creativity.

Wingfield, Paul. *Janáček: Glagolitic Mass.* Cambridge and New York: Cambridge University Press, 1992. The first comprehensive study of one of Janáček's most important works. Includes a full synopsis and interpretations.

Thomas C. Schunk

PIERRE JANET

Born: May 30, 1859; Paris, France
Died: February 24, 1947; Paris, France
Area of Achievement: Psychology
Contribution: Janet is best known for his work in bringing together clinical psychiatry and academic psychology. He integrated his systematic observations of neurotic disorders, in the description of which he coined the term "subconscious," with more general psychological concepts concerning behavior patterns and thought processes. He has had a considerable impact not only upon French psychiatry but also upon psychiatry as a whole through his influence on Carl Jung, Alfred Adler, and, to some extent, Sigmund Freud.

Early Life

Pierre Janet was born on May 30, 1859, in Paris, the city which was his spiritual and cultural home, and, except for seven years of his life, his geographic home as well. He came from an upper-middle-class Parisian family, which included among its members a number of influential lawyers, engineers, and scholars. Pierre was the eldest of three children born to Fanny and Jules Janet. His mother, for whom he developed a deep and lifelong affection, was a warm and sensitive woman and a devout Catholic. His father, apparently a very kind but shy and seclusive man, worked most of his life as a legal editor. Another notable family influence was Pierre's uncle Paul Janet, who became a prominent philosopher and who provided Pierre with a model of professional orientation and achievement.

During his childhood, Janet became very interested in the natural sciences, especially botany, and at an early age showed an enthusiasm for collecting plants. As he commented in an autobiographical article many years later, "this passion determined my taste for dissection, precise observation, and classification, which should have made a naturalist or physiologist of me." Other tendencies were also working in him, however, ones which precluded a single-minded pursuit along the path of pure science. Perhaps in part through the influence of his mother, Janet displayed an intense interest in religious questions and concerns. A period of depression through which Janet suffered at the age of fifteen was in part a religious crisis, and religious motivations molded much of his life's work.

Janet pursued his philosophical interests at the École Normale Supérieure from 1879 until 1882. Yet though the primary focus of his education there was philosophy, he studied science and medicine in his spare time, benefiting from the guidance and encouragement of his uncle Paul, who always urged him to combine medical and philosophical studies. The integration of these interests led him naturally to the study of psychology.

Life's Work

At the age of twenty-two, Janet was appointed professor of philosophy at the Lyceum in the city of Le Havre, where he taught for more than six years. During this period, he also continued his informal studies of scientific subjects by doing volunteer work at the hospital in Le Havre and by pursuing independent psychiatric research. Through this research, Janet was hoping to find a topic upon which to write his doctoral thesis and had settled on the subject of hallucinations and their relation to the processes of perception. He approached a well-known Le Havre physician with the idea, hoping that this doctor might know of a suitable patient for him to study. Though the doctor was not aware of any patients at that time who were suffering from hallucinations, he suggested that Janet could study another patient, whose case was considered far more interesting. This patient's name was Léonie, and she was known to possess powers of clairvoyance and mental suggestion, as well as the ability to be hypnotized from a distance.

Janet's experiments with Léonie began in 1885 and continued for several years, attracting the interest of both the scientific community and the popularizers of psychic phenomena. The latter group interpreted his findings irresponsibly, to Janet's chagrin, while the former group recognized and respected Janet's careful experimental methods. During the course of these investigations, Janet had realized the necessity of taking copious and meticulous notes on everything that happened and that was said, both by his patient and by himself, during the experimental sessions. He continued this practice throughout all of his future clinical work; he relied so heavily on his written notes, distrusting any speculations or unwarranted generalizations that departed from them, that he dubbed his psychology the "psychology of the fountain pen." This research, along with his studies of hysterical

women conducted at the Le Havre hospital, formed the basis of his thesis entitled *L'Automatisme psychologique* (1889; psychological automatism), for which he received his doctorate in philosophy from the Sorbonne in 1889 and which had a significant impact upon psychiatric thinking. It was in this work that Janet introduced the term "subconscious" to describe those thought processes that reveal themselves in the delayed and automatic performance of posthypnotic suggestions.

Janet realized, however, that he would not be able to pursue his research in psychopathology professionally unless he obtained the M.D. degree. He therefore undertook medical studies between 1889 and 1893, during which time he continued teaching philosophy in Paris. In 1890, Jean Martin Charcot, in an effort to incorporate experimental psychology into the research program of his world-renowned neurological clinic at the Salpêtrière Hospital, established a psychological laboratory and selected Janet as its supervisor. There Janet studied many patients suffering from hysteria and attempted to organize the multitude of clinical facts he had collected into a systematic whole. This

work resulted in his medical thesis, *L'État mental des hystériques* (1892-1894; *The Mental State of Hystericals*, 1901), for which he was awarded the M.D. and which became his best-known book. The year after his graduation, Janet married Marguerite Duchesne, a Le Havre native who had since settled in Paris. They had three children, Hélène, Fanny, and Michel.

Janet continued to teach philosophy until 1898, having published a textbook of philosophy in 1894. As a result of his increased qualifications and reputation in psychology and psychiatry, he also began to assume teaching responsibilities in these fields. He was asked by Théodule Ribot, who is considered the founder of French psychology, to replace him temporarily as professor of experimental psychology at the Collège de France from 1895 to 1897, and again in 1900 and 1901. Then, in 1902, Janet was appointed Ribot's successor in the chair of psychology, a position he held until 1935.

As Janet remarked in his autobiography, the circumstances of his professional responsibilities placed him between philosophers and physicians. This rather unusual positioning was the source of a certain frustration for him because he noticed that these two groups were speaking such different theoretical languages that it was difficult for him to converse on professional matters with both of them at the same time, and almost impossible for them to understand each other. The gulf that existed between the world of philosophy and the world of science and medicine became even more obvious to Janet during his early years of teaching psychology, the field which he thought should represent a unification of these realms. Whereas Ribot's teaching of experimental psychology and psychopathology had been almost purely theoretical, with little basis in clinical experience, one of Janet's primary concerns was to ground all discussions of psychology and psychiatry in the data of carefully recorded clinical observations. He also worked to develop a terminology through which the more theoretical and purely academic teachers of psychology could be united, or at least engage in fruitful communication with, the more practical and clinical practitioners.

Janet's efforts at synthesis and unification are evident in his system of psychology, which he described as a "psychology of conduct." He believed that in order for psychology to be truly scientific it must be based on externally observable facts. He therefore considered visible behavior the fundamental phenomena and saw intellectual operations as internal forms of behavior. By his emphasis on behavior, Janet hoped to construct a conceptual system that would encompass all types of psychological processes, from the lowest and most simple to the highest and most complex. (His psychology differed from the behaviorism developed in the United States by its recognition of the existence and importance of consciousness.) Janet proposed, therefore, that if action is taken as fundamental, thinking, for example, can be considered inner language—an economical reduction and reproduction in consciousness of language behavior that was originally action in the external world.

Janet's theories of personality and psychotherapy were also informed by the concept of action. He proposed that the human personality consists of a dynamic interplay of "tendencies," or dispositions to perform particular actions, which exist in a stratified order revealing their phylogenetic and ontogenetic evolution from the more primitive processes such as pain, anger, and sex to the higher and more recent processes such as thinking and believing. The lower tendencies are endowed with a large amount of energy, while the higher tendencies possess less energy but more of what Janet termed "psychological tension," a cohesive force that reflects the degree of integration of the psychological operations. Personality is thus seen as a shifting and dynamic organization of forces, and psychological well-being as based on a balance between psychological energy and psychological tension. Psychotherapy, then, is a means of establishing, or regaining, this balance. The emphasis Janet placed on the present distribution and organization of energy in the personality, and on the integrating and illuminating function of the higher mental tendencies, serves to distinguish his approach to psychopathology from that of Freud, who focused on the influence of past experience and on interpreting the veiled messages of the lower, unconscious processes.

During the last decades of his life, Janet continued to develop and to publish in a number of books the details of his psychology of conduct, always being careful to let the data of clinical observations guide the development of his theories. He presented sparkling and spirited lectures in numerous countries, speaking several times in the United States, and his influence was felt around the world. He died on February 24, 1947, at the age of eighty-seven, leaving unfinished a book on the psychology of belief.

Summary

Pierre Janet occupied, both by historical accident and by personal inclination and professional training, a position at the convergence of a variety of streams of thought. The diversity of his interests is revealed in the range of his writings, which cover, in addition to the topics mentioned above, everything from alchemy and alcoholism to "social excitation in religion" and the psychology of time. Yet he was not content to deal with these topics in isolation from one another; he always sought a way of understanding and acting that would bring a measure of order and unity to the apparent diversity of the world. His mind was fertilized with the ideas of evolution, of neurology and physiology, and of unconscious processes. When these intellectual seeds took hold in the soil of Janet's deep metaphysical tendencies, they blossomed into a unified yet variegated system of thought.

The immense scope of the synthesis Janet was trying to accomplish prohibits any easy categorization of his work and has perhaps served to diffuse its impact. Many great psychologists, however, including Freud, Jung, and Adler, have mentioned their indebtedness to particular aspects of Janet's work, and though the name of Janet is often forgotten amid the success surrounding these men's systems, he stands with them at the threshold of modern dynamic psychiatry.

Bibliography

Boring, Edwin Garrigues. *A History of Experimental Psychology*. 2d ed. New York: Appleton-Century-Crofts, 1950. A standard account of the development of experimental psychology. Discusses Janet's and his colleagues' contributions.

Brown, Paul, and Onno van der Hart. "Memories of Sexual Abuse: Janet's Critique of Freud, a Balanced Approach." *Psychological Reports* 82, no. 3 (June, 1998). Consider's Janet's work in which he challenges Freud's theories on sexual trauma and explains his own theories on the subject.

Ellenberger, Henri F. *The Discovery of the Unconscious: The History and Evolution of Dynamic Psychiatry*. London: Allen Lane, and New York: Basic, 1970. A substantial and detailed study of the development of dynamic psychiatry. Chapter 6 is devoted to Janet and provides perhaps the most extensive and up-to-date discussion of his life and personality, his philosophical and psychological work, his intellectual precursors and contemporaries, and his influence. Contains many illustrations of the major figures in the history of modern psychiatry.

Ey, Henri. "Pierre Janet: The Man and His Work." In *Historical Roots of Contemporary Psychology*, edited by Benjamin B. Wolman. New York: Harper, 1968. Written by a leading French psychiatrist and former student of Janet, this chapter provides good summaries of Janet's major works and a discussion of his principal psychological and psychopathological concepts.

Janet, Pierre. "Autobiography." In *A History of Psychology in Autobiography*, edited by Carl Murchison, vol. 1. Worcester, Mass.: Clark University Press, 1930. Janet's reluctant autobiographical article outlines some of the formative influences and significant events of his life.

Leys, Ruth. "Traumatic Cures: Shell Shock, Janet, and the Question of Memory." *Critical Inquiry* 20, no. 4 (Summer 1994). Discusses Janet's theories on memory and forgetting and the treatment of psychic trauma with hypnosis.

Mayo, Elton. *Some Notes on the Psychology of Pierre Janet.* Cambridge, Mass.: Harvard University Press, 1948. Intended as a guide to Janet's views on selected subjects, such as psychopathology and social study, hysteria and hypnosis, and the psychology of adaptation, especially as they relate to problems in social and industrial psychology.

Taylor, W. S. "Obituary of Janet." *American Journal of Psychology* 60 (October, 1947): 637-645. This article gives an overview of Janet's life and work and includes a list of his varied publications.

Gordon L. Miller

KARL JASPERS

Born: February 23, 1883; Oldenburg, Germany
Died: February 26, 1969; Basel, Switzerland
Areas of Achievement: Philosophy and medicine
Contribution: In his early career, Jaspers played an important role in establishing the foundations of clinical psychiatry, and in his mature years he was one of the major philosophers to lay the groundwork for the existential movement. After World War II, he attempted to develop a world philosophy which would promote human unity based on freedom and tolerance.

Early Life

Born and reared near the North Sea in Oldenburg, Karl Theodor Jaspers was the eldest of three children in an upper-middle-class family whose ancestors had lived in northern Germany for generations. His father was a successful lawyer who served as President of the City Council as well as a bank director. Never in good health, during childhood Jaspers suffered from serious diseases which developed into a chronic dilation of the bronchial tubes, and this led to cardiac decompensation (the heart's inability to maintain normal circulation). These severe health problems meant that Jaspers had limited energy for physical activity, leading him to think seriously about the significance of human existence.

In his early years of school, Jaspers was not an especially outstanding student, but he did gain a reputation for a spirit of independence. Having a strong dislike for discipline and regimentation, during his high-school years he was in constant conflict with the school authorities. In 1901 and 1902, he studied law at the Universities of Heidelberg and Munich, but, not finding this field compatible with his interests, he decided to study natural science to learn as much as possible about the universe. Between 1902 and 1908, he studied medicine at the Universities of Berlin, Göttingen, and Heidelberg. After passing the state examination to practice medicine, he wrote his dissertation *Heimweh und Verbrechen* (1909; nostalgia and crime). In 1909, he took a job as a volunteer research assistant at the psychiatric clinic of the University of Heidelberg, a position that he held for six years; in 1910, he married Gertrud Mayer, an attractive German Jew who was the sister of his closest friend.

Life's Work

At the Heidelberg clinic, Jaspers chose to work in his own way, at his own pace, and with his own choice of patients. He was allowed this independence because he agreed to work without a salary. Jaspers was very dissatisfied with the conditions of clinical psychiatry, especially the emphasis on organic medicine, the limited attempts at therapy, and the failure to consider individual differences. In his clinical work, Jaspers was influenced by Edmund Husserl's method of phenomenology—the direct observation and description of phenomena with the attempt not to depend upon causal theories. His first published book, *Allgemeine Psychopathologie* (1913; *General Psychopathology*, 1963), was one of the first serious attempts to present a critical and systematic synthesis of the modern methods available in psychiatry, making Jaspers one of the best known of the psychiatrists of Germany.

In spite of this success, Jaspers' interests were moving in the direction of general philosophy; the same year that he published his book he was able to enter the philosophical faculty as the specialist in empirical psychology at Heidelberg. Although his work was not appreciated by Heinrich Rickert and other philosophers at the university, his academic advance was rapid. By 1921, he was a full professor of philosophy, and in 1922 he occupied the second chair of that field.

Jaspers' intellectual development was reflected in his published lectures *Psychologie der Weltanschauungen* (1919; psychology of worldviews). In this work, Jaspers investigated the limits of the philosophical knowledge of humankind, and he anticipated all the major themes of his later works. Emphasizing the differences between philosophy and science, he argued that the latter was based on empirical data, providing objective facts that are apodictically certain. In contrast, Jaspers considered philosophy to be directed at subjective insight into the nature of being, using intuitive methods that resembled Oriental mysticism. His system, while founded on belief, recognized the validity of modern science, seeking for a philosophy that would transcend scientific knowledge while remaining free of any dogmatism. Jaspers believed that human existence was the center of all reality, and he argued that in contrast to inanimate objects, human existence included the freedom for self-determination.

Jaspers developed these germinal ideas during the 1920's and early 1930's, and during these years he worked in association with Ernst Mayer and Martin Heidegger. In 1932, he published his three-volume work, *Philosophie* (*Philosophy*, 1969), which was his most systematic account of the so-called existential philosophy. Jaspers argued that philosophy was primarily an activity in which a person gains illumination into the nature of his existence, and that content and doctrines are relatively unimportant—not to be considered as objectively true or false. Influenced by Søren Kierkegaard, he used the term "existence" to refer to a sentient subject (or soul) possessing self-awareness and freedom. Although rejecting theism and divine revelation, Jaspers sought for a vague form of transcendence which was not knowable by empirical data, with the individual finding hints of this reality through symbolic "ciphers" as found in myths or religious teachings. In the realm of ethics, Jaspers focused on the goal of "authentic existence," which primarily meant to seek truth and to stand by one's convictions.

Jaspers seriously underestimated the appeal of National Socialism, and he was taken by surprise when Adolf Hitler assumed power in 1933. Unlike many academicians, he made no concessions to the Nazi government, and, unwilling to forsake his Jewish wife, he became an enemy of state. Until 1937, he was allowed to teach and publish, and his book *Vernuft und Existenz* (1935; *Reason and Existenz*, 1955) developed the key concept of "the encompassing," which referred to the spiritual and material reality which surrounds human existence. When removed from his professorship at Heidelberg, he was allowed to present a final group of lectures, published·in the short book *Existenzphilosophie* (1938; *Philosophy of Existence*, 1971). While emphasizing metaphysics, these lectures did contain anti-Nazi implications in the defense of individualism, the advocacy of seeking truth, and the focus on spirituality.

In 1942, Jaspers received permission to emigrate to Switzerland, but his wife would have been required to remain behind. He refused to leave without her, and she was soon forced to hide in the home of friends. If arrested, both of them had decided, they would commit suicide. In 1945, he learned that his deportation was scheduled for the middle of April, but fortunately American troops occupied Heidelberg two weeks before the appointed date. Although disillusioned by the Nazi period, Jaspers used this time to write a revision of the *General Psychopathology* and to complete his large book on logic, *Von der Wahrheit* (1947; of truth).

After the German surrender, Jaspers spent most of his energies in trying to provide a theoretical basis for the rebuilding of the universities and in helping to promote the moral and political rebirth of the nation. In the book *Die Idee der Universität* (1946; *The Idea of the University*, 1959), he called for the complete denazification of the teaching staff and for the return of the autonomous university of the years before 1933. Believing that an acknowledgment of national guilt was necessary for a moral rebirth, in *Die Schuldfrage* (1946; *The Question of German Guilt*, 1947) Jaspers argued that those who actively participated in crimes against humanity were morally guilty, while those Germans who passively tolerated Nazi crimes were only politically responsible. He hoped that the German people would accept this sense of collective guilt and responsibility, allowing for a higher level of democracy and moral sensitivity. Jaspers was disappointed when his writings did not appear to have any impact on the emerging society, and thus in 1948 he accepted a professorship in philosophy in Basel, Switzerland. Many Germans bitterly resented his emigration.

Jaspers was convinced that the modern developments in science and nuclear weapons meant that nationalism had become a dangerous anachronism and that it was necessary for humankind to strive for a new unity based on a world confederation, a project which was elaborated in *Die Atombombe und die Zukunft des Menschen* (1958; *The Future of Mankind*, 1961). This utopian dream would be accomplished gradually through democratic means, and in the short term Jaspers supported the United Nations and decolonization. Radical change would require a new mode of thinking, to which Jaspers referred as "world philosophy," with the fundamental ideas developed in *Der philosophische Glaube angesichts der Offenbarung* (1962; *Philosophical Faith and Revelation*, 1967). Since all thinking ultimately relies on faith, Jaspers looked to humanity's commitment to a common transcendence approached through the ciphers of various cultures, resulting in a new attitude of tolerance.

In formulating his world philosophy, Jaspers took a renewed interest in the history of philosophical thinking, writing the erudite book *Die grossen Philosophen* (1957; *The Great Philosophers*, 1966). In the work *Vom Ursprung und Zeit der Geschichte* (1949; *The Origin and Goal of History*, 1953), one of Jaspers' most important contributions was the concept of the axial period (from 800 to 200 B.C.), during which time the religious and philosophical foundations of the existing civilizations came into being.

With his ambitious aspirations for humanity, Jaspers was disappointed with developments of the postwar world, especially with the conservative climate in Germany. He wrote a bitter critique of German democracy in *Wohin treibt die Bundesrepublik?* (1966; *The Future of Germany*, 1967), a book that was widely criticized in West Germany. In response, Jaspers returned his German passport and applied for Swiss citizenship. In 1968, his physical condition deteriorated rapidly, and he died early in 1969, three days after his eighty-sixth birthday.

Summary

Although Karl Jaspers rejected the label of "existentialism," he was one of the philosophers who had a great influence on this diverse movement in the postwar period. As a popular teacher for a long period of time and as author of thirty books, Jaspers inspired large numbers of students to think about the meaning of human existence and to engage in the act of philosophizing. Never attempting to establish a school of thought or to argue the truth of particular doctrines, Jaspers is not remembered for particular ideas as much as for a general style and mood in metaphysical speculation.

Authorities agree that much of Jaspers' thought was rather vague and ambiguous—at times contradictory. Since he emphasized the subjectivity of the individual thinker, not making a clear distinction between truth and knowledge about the truth, his philosophy can be classified as a form of idealism, and he was a strong critic of materialism, positivism, and scientism. Although not committed to any particular religion, he expressed a mystical temperament, appearing to be overwhelmed by a generalized spirituality that he considered to be the ground of being. He tended to use common words, such as "existence," in a specialized sense, and some of his favorite words (for example, "the Encompassing") are open to multiple connotations and interpretations. When Sebastian Samay once asked Jaspers what he thought about some of his commentators, Jaspers replied: "Their work is excellent, but you know, they are much too clear. They have tried to do away with many of my ambiguities." In the postwar years, however, Jaspers' works in philosophy and government are more readable and cogently argued, reflecting his growing concern for the social values of reason, justice, and democracy.

Although Jaspers always insisted that he was not a hero during the Nazi era, he clearly demonstrated much moral courage in standing by his wife and refusing to renounce his convictions. In like manner, he demonstrated considerable strength of character in doing productive work in spite of a weak physical condition. As much as for his philosophical and psychological writings, Jaspers deserves to be remembered for these personal characteristics.

Bibliography

Ehrlich, Leonard. *Karl Jaspers: Philosophy as Faith.* Amherst: University of Massachusetts Press, 1975. An analysis of the importance of belief in Jaspers' thought, emphasizing the themes of freedom, ciphers, and the transcendental ground of being.

Erickson, Stephen A. "The Image of Socrates in the Mirror of Jaspers." *Philosophy Today* 38, no. 3 (Fall 1994). Considers Jaspers' belief that the state of philosophy can be determined by examining current views of Socrates.

Jaspers, Karl. "Existenzphilosophie." In *Existentialism from Dostoevsky to Sartre*, edited by Walter Kaufmann. New York: Meridian, 1956; London: Thames and Hudson, 1957. Contains three concise essays by Jaspers: "On My Philosophy," "Kierkegaard and Nietzsche," and "The Encompassing."

Reinhardt, Kurt. *The Existentialist Revolt.* 2d ed. New York: Ungar, 1960. An interesting and readable summary of the major ideas of Jaspers and five other thinkers who are classified as existentialists.

Samay, Sebastian. *Reason Revisited: The Philosophy of Karl Jaspers.* Notre Dame, Ind.: University of Notre Dame Press, 1971. A critical interpretation of Jaspers' thought, emphasizing that Jaspers does not usually provide answers for the questions he asks. Samay is especially critical of his use of reason and logic.

Schilpp, Paul Arthur, ed. *The Philosophy of Karl Jaspers.* New York: Tudor, 1957. Following Jaspers' "Philosophical Autobiography," the book contains twenty-four critical essays with Jaspers' "Reply to My Critics." This is perhaps the most important scholarly source available in English.

Wallraff, Charles F. *Karl Jaspers: An Introduction to His Philosophy*. Princeton, N.J.: Princeton University Press, 1970. The best introductory study of Jaspers' life and thought, including a critical analysis of his terminology and a useful bibliography.

Wisser, Richard. "Karl Jaspers: The Person and His Cause, Not the Person or His Cause." *International Philosophical Quarterly* 36, no. 4 (December, 1996). Compares and contrasts Jaspers and Martin Heidegger based on their views on the biographical element in philosophy.

Thomas T. Lewis

MOHAMMED ALI JINNAH

Born: December 25, 1876; Karachi, India
Died: September 11, 1948; Karachi, Pakistan
Areas of Achievement: Government and politics
Contribution: Jinnah led the movement that resulted in the establishment of Pakistan as a Muslim-majority state when the British granted the Indian subcontinent home rule in 1947. Jinnah served briefly as Pakistan's governor-general, and as Qā'īd-e A'zam (supreme leader) he represented the Muslim voice in British Indian affairs as Mahatma Gandhi had represented the Hindus.

Early Life

Mohammed Ali Jinnah was born into a wealthy Shi'ite Muslim family in Karachi, India. Although his first school record shows his birthdate as October 20, 1875, he later claimed to have been born on December 25, 1876, the official birthdate celebrated throughout Pakistan. The Arabic name Jinnah means "wing," as of a bird or army. He adopted this form of his family name Jinnahbhai while in London in 1893. Jinnah was the eldest of seven children, and his family belonged to a minor sect within Islam, the Khojas, representing a successful merchant community in South Asia. He early realized that he was part of the Muslim minority in India, which made up about 20 percent of that British colony's population.

As a young man, Jinnah was not a diligent student, and his tolerance for formal education was never high, but his natural intelligence caught the attention of one of his father's British business associates, Sir Frederick Leigh Croft. Croft recommended Jinnah for an apprenticeship at the Douglas Graham and Company home office in London. Barely sixteen, Jinnah left for England in January, 1893, after a hastily arranged marriage demanded by his mother. Both his bride and his mother died before his return from London.

The drudgery of his apprenticeship caused Jinnah to apply for admission to Lincoln's Inn during the spring of 1893. There he completed the process of legal certification and on May 11, 1896, at the age of twenty, was admitted to the bar as a barrister welcome to practice in any British court.

While in London, Jinnah had almost followed a theatrical career and also became fascinated by the glamorous world of politics. Because of this political exposure, he returned to India as a Liberal nationalist. He enrolled as a barrister in Bombay's high court on August 24, 1896, and joined advocate-general John M. MacPherson's firm in 1900 as the first native Indian lawyer. He sat on the municipal bench for a six-month interim term in 1901.

Life's Work

Involvement in India's congress politics was an integral by-product of his flourishing legal career. He favored Indian home rule through a gradual, constitutional process which would ensure unity of the various communities, especially Hindu and Muslim. Jinnah attended the twentieth Indian Congress in December, 1904. At this point, he opposed the formation of the Muslim League in 1906 and was a leading moderate voice during the nine years between 1907 and 1915 when congress divided into angrily conflicting parties, all claiming to be the heir to India's nationalist movement.

On January 25, 1910, Jinnah took his seat on the expanded sixty-member legislative council, which offered a voice to the Indian public regarding British colonial policy. Jinnah finally joined the Muslim League in 1913 but insisted that it did not overshadow his larger loyalty to an independent, unified India. He understood but did not share the Muslims' apprehension about their role in a Hindu majority population when self-government on Western parliamentary lines came to India. Jinnah was confident that he could safeguard the future of the Muslims by constitutional provisos.

It was during this period, at the beginning of World War I, that Jinnah met Mahatma Gandhi, who returned to India in 1915. From the very beginning, their relationship was one of deep tensions and mistrust underlying superficially polite manners. Jinnah believed that Gandhi's Hindu ideology could never support a common Indian nationalism. In the push for Hindu-Muslim unity, Jinnah supported the general demands of congress for reforms from the British raj. These reforms focused on equal military treatment, extension of self-government, and development of local commerce and industry. It was during this period that Jinnah was able to negotiate with congress the 1916 Lucknow Pact, which guaranteed separate electorates and weighted representation for the Muslims in any future constitution. Hindu-Muslim unity declined when Gandhi supported British recruitment of Indian soldiers for World War I, and Jinnah opposed such a move without guarantees of

Mohammed Ali Jinnah, second from left, governor-general of Pakistan with Louis Mountbatten (center) in Karachi, Pakistan, in August, 1947, the month India and Pakistan were granted independence from England.

equal citizenship in the empire. Nevertheless, there was a brief honeymoon between congress and the Muslim League after World War I.

During the World War I era, between 1916 and their marriage on April 19, 1918, Jinnah courted the young daughter of a wealthy Parsi merchant. Ratanbai Petit was eighteen and Jinnah more than forty when they wed. The marriage lasted until her death in February, 1929, but it caused her to be disowned by her family; during the last five years of Ratanbai's life, she was virtually estranged from Jinnah as well. A daughter, Dina, was born to the union, and she, like her mother, married outside her family's religious community. The marriage of Dina to a Parsi who had converted to Christianity led to an almost complete break between her and Jinnah. Fatima Jinnah, Jinnah's adoring spinster sister, served as housekeeper, hostess, and nurse to Jinnah until his death.

A period of discontent and withdrawal began for Jinnah in 1919 and lasted until 1934, when he undertook leadership of a reconstituted Muslim League and moved toward acceptance of the idea of Pakistan. During the 1920's, the Rowlatt Act, the Amritsar Massacre, the Khilafat Pan-Islamic movement, and Gandhi's growing following for nonresistance, satyagraha, caused division over methodology among advocates of home rule. Therefore, Jinnah's earlier successes at Lucknow and the desire for moderate nonconfrontational programs were rejected, and he withdrew from not only the Legislative Council but also the Muslim League and congressional leadership. Jinnah's goal was to bring independence to India through a unified Hindu-Muslim state, so he led a Muslim League faction that opposed the radical Khilafat movement. He gradually regained positions of prominence in political circles and went to London in 1930 to participate in the Round Table conferences on India. These conferences ended without tangible results. Disillusioned over the failure to achieve communal unity in India or even unity among his Muslim colleagues, Jinnah moved to England in 1930 and transferred his law practice entirely to appeals before London's Privy Council, the highest court in the empire. Jinnah returned to Bombay in 1934 and began to help rebuild the Muslim League, planning appeals to congress to support Muslim demands and to present a common front against the British.

These unity efforts failed, and in October, 1937, Jinnah moved toward leadership of the All-India Muslim League and set off on a path that would lead to the formation of Pakistan. At this point, he became known as Qā'īd-e A'zam, changed to native dress, and soon adopted the black Persian lamb cap that would be known throughout the world as a "Jinnah cap." By the spring of 1940, in an address at Lahore, Jinnah lowered the final curtain on any prospect for a united India. This early advocate of unity had transformed himself into Pakistan's great advocate and became the father of that nation based on Muslim solidarity.

For the next seven years, until success came in August, 1947, Jinnah devoted himself to the establishment of Pakistan and the division of India. He resisted all compromise, whether offered by the British, the Hindus, or his fellow Muslims. He determined Pakistan a necessity, because he feared Muslims would be excluded from power or prospects of advancement in the close-knit structure of

Hindu social organization and their majority state. Even during World War II, there was constant vying for position so that home rule for the Indian subcontinent would be quickly granted afterward. Jinnah upheld Muslim demands for Pakistan and bitter communal struggle characterized the whole process. With few options left, the British and Hindus acquiesced, and Pakistan was born, a divided state with the Bengali area in the east and the larger region on the western border.

With independence, Jinnah was the supreme authority and the symbol of the new state. He was governor-general of the dominion, while uniting in himself the ceremonial functions of a head-of-state and the effective power of a chief executive. He often presided over the deliberations of the cabinet or sent it directives and was president of the Constituent Assembly as well as its legal adviser. Provisions in the India Independence Act of 1947 and the Government of India Act of 1935 were adapted to give his office wide powers of discretion and special responsibility. Jinnah's leadership, however, lasted only thirteen months, and during that time he was seriously ill. He died September 11, 1948, in Karachi, the place of his birth, but now the city was a part of the state of Pakistan, carved from the India of the British raj for its Muslim citizens.

Summary

The founding of Pakistan as a Muslim majority state was the crowning glory of Mohammed Ali Jinnah's life. He first devoted himself to the goal of an independent, unified India with communal harmony achieved between Hindus and the various minorities by constitutional guarantees. Eventually he realized that his professional success as a leading barrister in colonial India and the high economic and social position he thus achieved would never allow him to participate fully in the Indian congress movement, because his status as a Muslim always provided an invisible barrier.

Jinnah's logical, precise, and self-controlled mind rejected communal violence and supported constitutional guarantees for all Indians. By 1940, however, Jinnah had determined that those guarantees would not protect Muslim interests in a Hindu-dominated state and that separate states must be formed when the British granted India home rule. Jinnah's position reflects the use of religious identification as a foundation of nationalism, a major force in the modern world. The rise of Islam as a nationalistic unifier was early evidenced in the Indian struggle. Although not particularly devout himself, Jinnah became the Qa'id-e A'zam of Pakistan and headed a nationalistic movement that succeeded in dividing the Indian subcontinent based on religious identification. The bitter struggle and communal hatred engendered by that division has had long-lasting political and diplomatic repercussions.

Pakistan's founding in August, 1947, gave Jinnah the task of guiding the infant state through its earliest difficulties. He had devoted so much effort to the struggle for independence that a detailed plan of action for the new government had to be formulated after the fact. He survived only thirteen months, but he affixed his own indelible seal to the ideals of the new nation as he advocated law and order, elimination of bribery and corruption, and equal rights for all citizens regardless of religion. Achieving these goals presented problems for Pakistan, and the internal conflict that resulted in the eastern Bengali region, now Bangladesh, seceding from Pakistan have altered the dream he had for the future.

Jinnah spent his life as a freedom fighter: first, for freedom from British colonial rule; then, for civil freedom for the Muslim minority in India; and, finally, for guaranteed freedoms in the new state of Pakistan. He used his skills as a barrister to serve as the Muslim voice in India, to found the nation-state of Pakistan, and to build its early structure as the first governor-general. He is revered today as Pakistan's founding father, and he alone retains the title of supreme leader, Qā'īd-e A'zam.

Bibliography

Ahmad, Jamil-ud-Din, comp. *Historic Documents of the Muslim Freedom Movement.* Lahore, Pakistan: Publishers United, 1970. The documents in this collection focus on the resolutions, speeches, and writings of the Islamic Indian community. They are organized in chronological order and provide an overview of the move toward home-rule and partition.

———, comp. *Quaid-i-Azam, as Seen by His Contemporaries.* Lahore, Pakistan: Publishers United, 1966. Jinnah's work, personality, and influence are examined from several points of view by former associates. The recollections are generally positive but provide telling personal insights that reveal the man and his relationships.

Ahmed, Akbar S. "Jinnah and the Quest for Muslim Identity." *History Today* 44, no. 9 (September, 1994). The author traces Jinnah's development from advocate of Hindu-Muslim unity to Muslim nationalist.

Ali, Chaudhri Muhammad. *The Emergence of Pakistan.* New York: Columbia University Press, 1967. This historical study of the creation of Pakistan focuses on 1946-1948, but it also provides an examination of the social, economic, and political background. Jinnah is portrayed as a calm, logical, astute politician protecting Muslim rights, while the role of Hindus and Sikhs is criticized.

Collins, Larry, and Dominique La Pierre. *Freedom at Midnight.* Rev. ed. London: HarperCollins, 1997. A series of anecdotes and highly descriptive accounts depict the transition of power from British control to independence. The focus is on Gandhi and India with a negative presentation of Jinnah and the Pakistan movement as key hindrances to Indian unity.

Edwards, Michael. *The Last Years of British India.* London: Cassell, and New York: World, 1963. Beginning before the turn of the century, major forces that allied with the congress and the Muslim League are identified. The key factor in partition is depicted as Muslim determination for autonomy led by the dedicated guidance of Jinnah. Evidence of a less than positive opinion is evidenced when Jinnah is compared to Adolf Hitler.

Ispahani, M. A. H. *Quaid-i-Azam Jinnah as I Knew Him.* 3d ed. Karachi, Pakistan: Forward Publication Trust, 1976. The memoirs of one of Jinnah's closest personal friends represent the wealthy commercial and financial voice of Calcutta and the Bengali faction of the Muslim League. Jinnah's role in the East Pakistan region is particularly explored.

Merriam, Allen Hayes. *Gandhi vs. Jinnah: The Debate Over the Partition of India.* Columbia, Mo.: South Asia, 1980. The leading figures in the Indian independence movement evidence the differing philosophies, conflicting methodology, and tense antagonism between the two who are heroic figures within their own communities.

Pandey, Bishwa Nath. *The Breakup of British India.* London: Macmillan, and New York: St. Martin's Press, 1969. This study analyzes the origins of nationalism in the British raj and then examines the growing movement of Muslim separatism. There is a focus on religious and social issues while noting the strong influence of the leaders on each side.

Wolpert, Stanley A. *Jinnah of Pakistan.* New York: Oxford University Press, 1984. This objective, well-documented, comprehensive biography of the life of Jinnah portrays the complexity of his personality and his dedication to the Muslim voice in India. While always acknowledging his role as a major leader in twentieth century Indian affairs, his enigmatic character is evidenced.

Zaidi, Zafar H., ed. *Quaid-I-Azam Mohammed Ali Jinnah Papers.* First series, volume 3: *On the Threshold of Pakistan, July 1 - July 25, 1947.* Oxford: Oxford University Press, 1994. Includes four hundred documents dated between July 1 and July 25, 1947, illustrating the development of the Partition Plan and the Indian Independence Act.

Frances A. Coulter

JOSEPH-JACQUES-CÉSAIRE JOFFRE

Born: January 12, 1852; Rivesaltes, France
Died: January 3, 1931; Paris, France
Area of Achievement: The military
Contribution: Joffre was the chief of staff of the French armies facing the armies of the German Empire in August, 1914. His armies halted the German tide at the First Battle of the Marne, and his actions between August 25 and September 5, 1914, enabled other commanders to blunt, disrupt, and eventually turn back the invading Germans.

Early Life

The future Marshal of France was born in Rivesaltes, France, near the eastern edge of the Pyrenees Mountains on January 12, 1852. He was one of eleven children, his father a manufacturer of barrels and casks. Joseph-Jacques-Césaire Joffre very early showed an aptitude for mathematics and science and at the age of seventeen was enrolled in the École Polytechnique. A year later, he entered the army as a junior lieutenant in the military engineers during the Franco-Prussian War of 1870-1871 and endured the Siege of Paris in one of the outer forts. After the war, Joffre returned to the École Polytechnique, graduating in 1876 and receiving a commission as a captain in the army engineers. He was first involved in the construction of fortifications along France's eastern frontier until 1885, the year that his wife died.

On the death of his wife, Joffre requested colonial service and was given assignments over the next fifteen years in Vietnam, Africa, and Madagascar. During this time, he served for three years as the chief military engineer in Hanoi, organizing the defenses throughout the upper Tonkin area. In 1888, he returned to Paris in the Engineering Directorate with later service at the War College at Fontainebleau as a professor of fortifications. Further service in the early 1890's was spent building railroads in West Africa. It was serendipity that Joffre was called upon in 1894 to lead a French relief expedition to rescue the French position against the native Touaregs. He ended by securing the entire region for France. A hero in a country starved for heroes in the 1890's, Joffre was promoted to lieutenant colonel. In 1896, he was recalled to France as the secretary of the Military Commission on Inventions but was almost immediately posted to Madagascar.

It was in Madagascar that Joffre made his reputation as a military engineer under the command of General Joseph Gaillieni. He managed the construction of the defenses for the new French naval base at Diego-Suarez. Joffre's rise to the top ranks of the army was fairly rapid, particularly with Gaillieni's patronage. In 1900, returning to France, he became a brigadier general in command of the Nineteenth Artillery Brigade, stationed at Vincennes.

In 1905, Joffre was promoted to major general and served in the Ministry of War as director of engineers. One year later, he assumed command of the Sixth Infantry Division and by 1910 was the corps commander for the Second Corps at Amiens, becoming a member of the Supreme War Council. The council served as an advisory board to the minister of war during peacetime. From the ranks of the Supreme War Council in time of war would come the chief military commanders for the armed forces.

Life's Work

In 1911, in what was a surprise compromise choice, Joffre was appointed the chief of the Army General Staff. General Gaillieni again played a key role in shifting support toward Joffre, who was believed to be apolitical and a loyal republican with few aristocratic or ultra-Catholic associations. In the aftermath of the Dreyfus affair, Joffre's reputation, therefore, particularly earned for him the support of the parties of the Left. Joffre's age, fifty-nine at this time, also recommended him as one who could provide continuity at the top of the command structure for a reasonable period of time. In his new position, General Joffre also served as vice chair of the Supreme War Council.

Joffre realized that he lacked both operational command and general staff experience. He appointed General Noël de Castelnau as his deputy chief. They devised a strategy to be used in the event of war with Germany. This so-called Plan Seventeen, in combination with frontal offensive tactics devised by the operations branch, was to prove disastrous. Plan Seventeen envisioned a French offensive crashing through Lorraine and pushing back the German forces. Both Joffre and Castelnau were aware of the possibility of a German attack through Belgium and unsuccessfully attempted to station French troops in Belgium in

1912. The British government, particularly, while advocating closer cooperation with the French, was loath to acquiesce in such a move. Plan Seventeen did provide for what was thought to be sufficient French forces centered on Sedan to prevent a successful German attack through Belgium. What Plan Seventeen failed to imagine was the size, scope, and the force of the German attack through this region. The strategy also called for the French to send two of their armies up through the Ardennes to disrupt a German offensive.

When war broke out in August, 1914, and to stem the German tide sweeping through Belgium, Joffre, in support of the British position, moved the French Fifth Army into Belgium to hold the sector around the Meuse and Sambre rivers on the outer flank of the British Expeditionary Force. The French and British position in Belgium then collapsed under the weight of the German advance, while the French forces advancing through Lorraine ground to a halt. At this point Plan Seventeen simply fell apart, and Joffre was compelled to begin a general retreat, which continued until his armies were fighting in the suburbs of Paris.

It was during the retreat that Joffre showed his greatest attribute as a military commander. Through his calm, cool, and collected leadership, he rallied the defeated French forces. Joffre kept his armies in good order and prevented the retreat from becoming a rout. Joffre was everywhere visiting the troops. He replaced failed commanders and broke one hundred generals in a week, replacing some of his oldest friends and comrades. Joffre restored and reinvigorated the command structure, and without question his actions between August 25 and September 5 enabled others to play decisive roles at the critical hour, as Joffre prevented his armies from being encircled by the Germans.

On September 6, 1914, Joffre's finest hour arrived. The French forces turned on the enemy, launching a splendid counterattack that slowed and then halted the German attack at the Battle of the Marne. Joffre had moved the French armies from their positions in Lorraine and, acting with other forces, including those sent to the front by Gaillieni, blunted and reversed the German advance. This moment was the high point of Joffre's success as a military commander.

Soon after the First Battle of the Marne, the Western Front settled into the debilitating trench warfare that was to exhaust and bleed in a protracted way both sides for the remainder of the war. It

was a stalemate, and, despite attempts around Artois and Champagne in 1915, Joffre could not break through the German lines. As the heavy losses mounted and as troop morale plummeted, Joffre came under increasingly severe criticism in the parliament. In late 1915, it was clear, with changes in the war ministry and a revamping of the general staff, that Joffre's days were numbered.

The year 1916 proved to be disastrous for Joffre and his forces. In February, the Germans began their powerful and prolonged attack against Verdun, resulting in heavy loss of life on both sides over the course of the year. The month of July was another bitter time for the French troops, who, in support of the British, launched an attack along the Somme River. The loss of life among the French and British forces was appalling, and the resulting gains in territory could be measured in yards rather than miles.

The state of affairs was too much for the French government, and on December 13, 1916, the premier, Aristide Briand, dismissed Joffre by pretending to promote him. Joffre was made commander in chief of the French Forces and was to act as a technical adviser to the French government. By December 27, it was clear that Joffre had definitely been removed from active command, and the government promoted him to Marshal of France.

Marshal Joffre continued to serve France and in 1917 headed a mission to the United States to spark American enthusiasm for the war. After the armistice, he became the chief of a military mission to Japan. In 1918, Joffre was elected a member of the prestigious French Academy and spent the remainder of his years with loyal staff members writing his memoirs. Joffre died in Paris on January 3, 1931.

Summary

Joseph-Jacques-Césaire Joffre has been faulted for many things. Certainly, he was neither an aggressive leader nor an innovative thinker. Whatever strategic concepts he had, Plan Seventeen was heavily flawed, and the tactics devised by the general staff were absurd, particularly in the face of the bitter and protracted trench warfare along the Western Front. Nevertheless, at the critical point in the initial German advance, Joffre remained calm, replaced many military commanders, selected the generals who ultimately won the war, and restored the morale of the French forces. So it was at the Battle of the Marne that Joffre prevented France from falling to the forces of the German Empire. Thereafter, although much admired by both his peers within the French Army and the opposing German commanders, Joffre simply did not have the imagination, the training, and the broader vision needed to find a way out of the bloody stalemate that plagued the French nation until 1918.

Bibliography

Dutton, David. "The Fall of General Joffre: An Episode in the Politico-Military Struggle in War Time France." *Journal of Strategic Studies of Great Britain* 1 (1978): 3. Dutton's work is an excellent analysis of Joffre's fall from power in reaction to the politicians' unhappiness with the military conduct of the war.

Horne, Alstair. *The Price of Glory: Verdun 1916.* London: Macmillan, and New York: St. Martin's Press, 1962. Another well-written work setting forth the story of Joffre's involvement with the bloodshed of Verdun.

Isselin, Henri. *The Battle of the Marne.* Translated by Charles Connell. London: Elek, 1965; New York: Doubleday, 1966. This work details Joffre's involvement in his finest achievement of the war. It is a fair analysis of Joffre's leadership.

Joffre, Joseph J. C. *The Personal Memoirs of Joffre, Field Marshal of the French Army.* Translated by T. Bentley Mott. 2 vols. New York and London: Harper, 1932. This account covers French prewar planning and Joffre's role as French commander from 1914 to 1916. Surprisingly, it is a generally accurate and even account.

King, Jere Clemens. *Generals and Politicians: Conflict Between France's High Command, Parliament, and Government.* Berkeley: University of California Press, 1951. A detailed, well-researched account of the struggle between the military and civilian leadership in France.

Liddell Hart, Basil H. *Reputations: Ten Years After.* Boston: Little Brown, 1928. Liddell Hart clearly believes Joffre was to blame for the flawed strategy of the French during World War I. He refers to Joffre as "a national nerve sedative." Not a balanced analysis.

Ralston, David B. *The Army and the Republic: 1871-1914.* Cambridge, Mass.: MIT Press, 1967. Ralston analyzes Joffre's role in the command structure in France between the wars. This work includes the effects of the Dreyfus affair and the relationship between the parliament and the army, which became nonpolitical, forging an entente with the politicians.

Singer, Barnett. "Mon General." *American Scholar* 65, no. 4 (Fall 1996). Profile of Joffre focusing on his ego, character disorder, self-concept, and political actions.

Williamson, Samuel R., Jr. *The Politics of Grand Strategy: Britain and France Prepare for War, 1904-1914.* Cambridge, Mass.: Harvard University Press, 1969. This work reviews Joffre's limited role in forging the Entente Cordiale. This work is a detailed study of a world of bureacratic politics.

Fred W. Hicks

JOHN XXIII
Angelo Giuseppe Roncalli

Born: November 25, 1881; Sotto il Monte, Italy
Died: June 3, 1963; Vatican City, Italy
Areas of Achievement: Church government and church reform
Contribution: John called the Second Vatican Council, which would modernize the Catholic church, and guided the early planning of the council, which helped ensure its achievements.

Early Life

Angelo Giuseppe Roncalli, the future Pope John XXIII, was the fourth of ten children in a poor, devout tenant farmer family in a small Lombard village. Unusually for the time period, when illiteracy was still common in rural villages, Angelo was sent to a nearby village to be educated by the priest. Although not a brilliant student, Roncalli was admitted to the diocesan seminary (a prep school for those who hoped to study for the priesthood later) at age fourteen. Roncalli enjoyed the regimen at the seminary, and he became one of the better students of his class. Because of this improvement, he was chosen to finish his studies at the pontifical Seminary of the Apollinare in Rome in 1901, and he entered the priesthood in August, 1904.

After he had finished his first mass, Roncalli was introduced to Pope Pius X, who was from the same area of Italy. Roncalli had already been selected by one of the rising members of Pius' household, Monsignor Radini-Tedeschi, as a young man who knew his home diocese of Bergamo well. When Radini-Tedeschi was made bishop of Bergamo in 1905, Pius approved Roncalli's becoming his secretary. Radini-Tedeschi remained bishop until his death in 1914, and Roncalli became a well-known individual within the Italian clerical establishment because of his connection.

Roncalli spent just more than a year teaching in the local seminary and producing works on the sixteenth century saint Charles Borromeo (which brought him into close contact with the librarian Monsignor Achille Ratti, later Pope Pius XI) and an autobiography of Radini-Tedeschi. Soon after Italy entered World War I, however, Roncalli became a chaplain in the Italian army. When the war ended, he spent a year preparing Church organizations in Bergamo to help returning veterans and

students cope with economically depressed postwar Italy.

Roncalli moved up the Church ladder the next year to a position in the Vatican. From 1919 through 1925, he was the director of the Society for the Propagation of the Faith as well as a parttime instructor at the Lateran Pontifical Seminary. Pius XI also entrusted most of the arrangements for the 1925 Holy Year celebrations to Roncalli and, in 1925, chose Roncalli to become the papal representative to the small Catholic population in Bulgaria, thus starting nearly thirty years of work in the Vatican diplomatic service. It also marked Roncalli's elevation to the rank of bishop.

Roncalli worked hard to make Catholics of the Eastern Rite, who outnumbered Roman Rite Catholics in Orthodox Bulgaria, feel more welcome within the Church, a mission that he would include in the work of the Second Vatican Council. When he left in 1934, Roncalli had become one of the most popular members of the diplomatic corps. He left to become the apostolic delegate to both Greece and Turkey, and it was in these posts that Roncalli started to achieve international notice.

Life's Work

The first few years of Roncalli's work centered mostly on Turkey, which was still undergoing a secularization process, controlled by the political leaders of the young republic. Neither Turkey nor Greece had large Catholic populations, and in both cases native Catholics were often treated as social outcasts. Roncalli worked hard to improve relations with the local political and religious leaders and so exert some pressure for his widespread flock, and he was moderately successful.

It was World War II that truly made Roncalli's work vitally important. He was a vital link in various Catholic attempts to help refugees from Adolf Hitler's regime, including large numbers of Jews. At the same time, Roncalli was able to satisfy the Turkish officials that their country's neutrality was not being violated, help bring aid into occupied Greece, and make certain that most of that aid actually reached the Greek people.

Because of his work in Greece and Turkey, Pope Pius XII appointed Roncalli to become his papal nuncio to France in December, 1944. The Catholic

Pope John XXIII (center) addressing reporters covering the Ecumenical Council at the Vatican in 1962.

church, like all other institutions in France, was divided. Some Church officials had collaborated with the Nazis while France was occupied from 1940 to 1944, others had worked with various resistance movements, but most, again reflecting the nation, had done neither. It was the new nuncio's duty to help heal the wounds left by World War II and the occupation within the Catholic community. As he had been in Bulgaria and Greece, Roncalli was soon one of the most popular members of the diplomatic community.

In late 1952, it was announced that Roncalli would become a cardinal the next January. Soon after his elevation, the new cardinal was named the new patriarch (archbishop) of Venice. Roncalli was soon working as hard in his new job as he ever had, in spite of his age. The archdiocese had not had a leader as interested in the everyday affairs of the area since Giuseppe Sarto had left to become Pope Pius X in 1903. After the death of Pius XII in October, 1958, Angelo Roncalli was elected his successor, despite his advanced age of seventy-seven, be-

coming the second of three twentieth century popes who had been patriarch of Venice before his election (the third was Pope John Paul I).

Roncalli chose John for his name, the first Pope John in more than five hundred years. John also quickly showed the style that had endeared him to the common people of Bulgaria, Greece, Paris, and Venice even more than it had made him popular with diplomats and journalists. John became a common sight in the workshops, grounds, and less frequented parts of the Vatican, talking with the workers. He was also seen visiting the poor and children in hospitals as well as prisons in and around Rome, showing that he was a true Bishop of Rome as well as pope. He was quickly called "good Pope John" by the people of Rome, who were more accustomed to going to see the pope than having the pope come to see them.

John quickly enlarged the College of Cardinals, adding more of the world's important archbishops so that it would be a better reflection of the Church, including the first black African in 1960. He also quickly announced, in January, 1959, that he was calling an ecumenical council, a general meeting of the world's bishops and other Catholic church leaders. There had only been twenty called in this manner, the first in 325, all to settle some major problem or doctrine and only one since the Reformation. John had called this new one, known as the Second Vatican Council or Vatican II, not to fight a heresy but to redefine the Church in terms of the modern world, or as he is said to have phrased it, "to open a window and let in some air."

John would spend much of the rest of his life making certain the same "fresh air" was indeed let into the open discussions at the Second Vatican Council, blocking attempts of the Church's central administration, known as the Curia, to control the council. John also made certain that representatives of the non-Roman Rite portions of the Church were well represented, and he also had observers invited from other Christian churches, other religions, and the world's press. Although John only lived to see the first session of the council (October through December, 1962), the other three sessions (which would last through the end of 1965) reflected the concerns that John had raised; the council produced sixteen documents that today define the role of the Catholic church in the modern world and the way that the Church is run, as well as update the teaching authority of the Church.

John not only relied on the council to get his points across but also gave more direct evidence of his concerns in his encyclicals. His 1961 encyclical *Mater et magistra* (English translation, 1962) restated in postwar terms the social encyclicals of Leo XIII and Pius XI, while his most famous was the 1963 *Pacem in terris* (English translation, 1963). This last sought to define the role of the state and the rights of the individual. Both encyclicals try to ensure the rights and dignity of every person in the face of modern economic and political systems, which often claim superiority over the individual.

John fell ill soon after the end of the council's first session. He worked as hard as he could during the last six months of his life. Around noon on June 3, 1963, he went into a coma, and he died a few hours later.

Summary

John XXIII was elected as a short-term "caretaker," but he was determined, in the light of all he had seen since he was a chaplain during World War I, to bring the Catholic church into a closer understanding with the twentieth century, which the Second Vatican Council accomplished. He also brought areas of the Church that might have been considered on the periphery into closer communion with the central Church, particularly between the Eastern and Uniate Rites. Moreover, by increasing the College of Cardinals, John brought the national leadership of the world's larger non-European countries into a more powerful position within the Church and so started the trend of the Church's leadership being less Eurocentric (and especially less Italian).

Bibliography

Daughters of St. Paul. *Popes of the Twentieth Century.* Boston: St. Paul Editions, 1983. A short work which serves as a favorable introduction to the twentieth century popes, laying out the salient facts of each one's biography and life's work.

Hales, E. E. Y. *Pope John and His Revolution.* London: Eyre and Spottiswoode, and New York: Doubleday, 1965. Early but excellent study on John's policies, especially on the social concerns that the pope brought to his pontificate and the manner in which he brought attention to them.

Hatch, Alden. *A Man Named John.* New York: Hawthorn, 1963. Written in the last months of John's pontificate, this book is a good, general biography, even if the praise is a bit overwhelming at times. Most interesting is a memorial section added after John's death, describing his death and funeral.

Hebblethwaite, Peter. *Pope John XXIII, Shepherd of the Modern World.* New York: Doubleday, 1985. An excellent biography of the pontiff, with very good endnotes that often offer interesting additional material. Contains a bibliography with short annotations and an appendix of the Roman Curia officials at the start of the council, which helps identify the behind-the-scenes players mentioned in the text.

———. "Roncalli Sainthood Cause to Survive Letters: John XXIII Critics 'Make Meal of Scraps'." *National Catholic Reporter* 30, no. 7 (December 10, 1993). Discusses the uproar over the publication of more than one hundred letters written by Roncalli before he became pope. The author argues that the letters must be viewed in the historical context of the era.

John XXIII, Dorothy White, trans. *Journal of a Soul*. London: Chapman, and New York: McGraw-Hill, 1965. John started keeping a spiritual diary in 1895, after he had finished his work in the junior seminary in Bergamo, and he added to it, especially when he was on retreats, through 1962. Some of his written prayers and letters and his spiritual testament are also included.

Murphy, Francis X. *The Papacy Today.* London: Weidenfeld and Nicolson, and New York: Macmillan, 1981. A concise history of the internal and external political evolution of the papacy during the first eighty years of the twentieth century.

Trevor, Meriol. *Pope John.* London: Macmillan and New York: St. Martin's Press, 1967. An easily read, well-documented general biography, which concentrates more on John's personality and reactions to events than on John as a Church administrator or on his policies. Contains a bibliography with some annotations.

Terrance L. Lewis

AUGUSTUS JOHN

Born: January 4, 1878; Tenby, Wales

Died: October 31, 1961; Fordingbridge, Hampshire, England

Area of Achievement: Art

Contribution: A talented portrait painter, an accomplished etcher, and a notorious bohemian, John became one of the best-known British artists in the twentieth century.

Early Life

Augustus John was born on January 4, 1878, in Tenby, Wales, the third child (out of five) of Edwin William and Augusta (née Smith) John. His mother died six years later, and because his father, a lawyer, was preoccupied with his legal practice, John suffered a lonely and unhappy childhood. He attended a few local schools without much enthusiasm until, in 1894, he became determined to be an artist and left Wales for the Slade School of Art in London.

John originally impressed his teachers as a hardworking and methodical pupil but not a particularly outstanding one. In the summer of 1897, however, he received a head injury while swimming and returned to school the following fall a man transformed. His work began to demonstrate a brilliance that had not been apparent earlier, and he rapidly became a near legend among his teachers and fellow students. His rising stature was confirmed in 1898, when he won a school-wide competition in composition with a work entitled *Moses and the Brazen Serpent*.

He used the money he won in this contest to travel to Amsterdam in the autumn of 1898 to visit a Rembrandt exhibition. This was the first of several trips to the Continent that John would make during his formative years. The next year, 1899, he used the money he had earned from his first public exhibit at the Carfax Gallery in London to finance a journey to France, where he spent time at Vattetot-sur-mer and Paris. In the French capital, he studied the work of Honoré Daumier and devoted his days at the Louvre to intense reflection on the work of the masters. The influence of such masters as Rembrandt was apparent in his work at the time and prompted one of his contemporaries to comment that his work was the best since the Renaissance.

It was during this trip to Paris that John began to cultivate the bohemian image he would retain for the rest of his life. Influenced by the eccentric fashions of French artists and by his interest in Gypsies, he cultivated quite a striking appearance. People who knew him at the time have described a tall, graceful young man with long hair and large violet eyes. He frequently wore earrings, a sailor's shirt, and a large, floppy hat, and, in general, impressed acquaintances as a flamboyant and charismatic individual. One did not soon forget a meeting with this colorful and interesting young man.

In 1901, John married Ida Nettleship, the daughter of the painter John Trivett Nettleship. Before she died in 1907, she bore John five sons. He had also met Dorothy (Dorelia) McNeil in 1903, and she had one son by John before Ida's death and two daughters by him afterward. John would produce several more illegitimate children by other women during the course of his life, but he would nevertheless retain a very close relationship with Dorelia until his death.

Life's Work

John worked as an art instructor at the University of Liverpool during 1901 and 1902. During this short period, John developed several interests that would remain with him for the rest of his life. For example, John began to etch while he was at Liverpool. Heavily influenced by the Rembrandt tradition, the subjects of his etchings ranged from Gypsies and slum dwellers to well-known individuals such as William Butler Yeats. He also began his portrait practice during this time and produced one of his most famous works in this genre in 1902, *Merekli* (a portrait of his wife, Ida). This portrait established the tradition of the "John girl" (a dark haired and vivacious woman draped in a bright-colored and provocative dress), one that would reappear many times in his later paintings. John also met Dr. John Sampson, an expert in Gypsy lore, at Liverpool and, through him, cultivated what would prove to be a lifetime interest in Gypsies and their customs. He mastered their difficult language, adopted their fashions, used them as the subjects of numerous paintings and etchings, befriended many of them, and often acted as their advocate when they ran afoul of the authorities. In recognition for his long and passionate attachment to the Gypsies of England, John was elected president of the Gypsy Lore Society in 1937.

In 1903, John and his family moved to Matching Green in Essex and began his famous habit of launching "caravans," consisting of himself and assorted friends and family members, into the British countryside in search of Gypsies, landscapes, and other interesting subjects to draw and paint. These caravans rapidly assumed an international character as John and his ever changing entourage explored southern France, Spain, and Italy as well as every corner of Great Britain and Ireland. As he wandered around England and the Continent, his artistic reputation continued to soar. Exhibitions of his etchings and paintings, such as the one held at the Chenil Gallery in Chelsea during 1908, attracted national attention and portrait commissions literally poured in from individuals from all walks of life. Although academic critics had yet to be won over (and many never would be), the general British public idolized him for his romantic appearance and life-style, his simple and powerful drawings, and his colorful, eye-catching paintings.

John was rejected for active military service during World War I for physical reasons, but he obtained the position of official artist for the overseas Canadian forces and achieved the rank of major. In this capacity he produced a design for the Canadian War Memorial and many portraits of various allied political and military leaders, including Prime Minister David Lloyd George of Great Britain. He also received an invitation to attend the postwar Versailles Peace Conference in 1919 and painted portraits of most of the important participants. At about the same time, he provided most of the illustrations for the original edition of T. E. Lawrence's *Seven Pillars of Wisdom* (1926), including a portrait of Lawrence himself.

Several authorities argue that the quality of John's work declined after World War I. Perhaps some of his paintings from the postwar period, such as *In Memoriam Amedeo Modigliani* (1920), do not compare favorably with his earlier work, but others, such as *Joseph Hone* (1932) and *Sir Matthew Smith* (1944), are powerful and striking portraits and are as good as anything he produced during his long career. John's artistic production had always been erratic in terms of quality, and this characteristic merely seems to have become more pronounced after 1918.

It does not, however, seem to have affected his public reputation to any degree. Following an extraordinarily successful show at the Alpine Club Gallery in London in 1921, John was elected an associate member of the Royal Academy and, in 1928, was promoted to full membership. He resigned in protest in 1938 when the Academy refused to allow his friend and fellow artist Wyndham Lewis to show a painting in the Academy's annual exhibit. In February, 1940, however, the Academy reelected him as a member, only the third time in its history that it restored a resigned member. In this period, he also was a member of the New English Art Club; a Fellow of University College, London; president of the Society of Mural Painters; and trustee of the Tate Gallery (1933-1961). He received the Order of Merit in 1942.

In addition to continuing his artistic work, John also began to publish some nonfiction in the 1930's. He contributed articles to the *Journal of the Gypsy Lore Society* and several short pieces on painting to various British art journals. He also wrote a two-volume autobiography. The first volume, entitled *Chiaroscuro: Fragments of Autobiography*, appeared in 1952 while the second, *Finishing Touches*, was published posthumously in 1964.

Although he continued to paint portraits of both the famous (King Faisal, Queen Elizabeth, and many others) and the anonymous, John became increasingly interested in what he called "imaginative painting." This attempt to paint without any reference to visual nature went against John's natural talents as an observer of reality and did not produce any notable results. In fact, John abandoned his planned grand culmination of this phase, a huge triptych entitled *Les Saintes-Maries de la Mer with Sainte Sara l'Egyptienne* in 1961, after recognizing that it would never work. John died soon thereafter, on October 31, 1961, at his home, Fryern Court, in Fordingbridge, Hampshire.

Summary

Augustus John's reputation during his lifetime appears in retrospect to have been a bit inflated. He was an outstanding draftsman and portraitist, but his expeditions into other realms of artistic expression failed to impress knowledgeable critics. Yet within the boundaries of his expertise, he was a master. His portraits, for example, are brilliantly designed and produce a free and forceful, yet sensitive, appreciation of their subjects. Nor did he limit his talents to individuals with fat checkbooks. Some of his best work portrayed humble people who caught his interest, such as his numerous Gypsy paintings or the series of West Indian slum-dweller portraits he presented at a show at Arthur Tooth's Gallery in 1939.

John's fame also rested as much on his personality and public image as it did on his actual work. His colorful dress and personal life presented the image of the eccentric artist that many members of the general public seemed to desire. His generous nature also contributed to his popularity. For example, when Professor Oliver Elton retired from the University of Liverpool in 1926, his literature students wanted John to paint the beloved professor's portrait. They did not, however, have the money to meet John's standard fee, so he accepted the small amount of cash they did manage to raise and painted the portrait anyway. The finished product was one of John's best. This combination of eccentricity and generosity, along with his talent for producing the type of art that the public loves best—portraits and landscapes—contributed to the creation of his near-legendary reputation during his lifetime. If it has diminished somewhat since his death, one can attribute the change, at least in part, to the natural revision that legends in all fields undergo over the course of time.

Bibliography

Earp, T. W. *Augustus John*. London: Nelson, 1934. This book, written while John was still alive, deals largely with his work to 1920. Biographical details are scanty and its assessment of John's art is highly favorable.

Finch, Christopher. "20th-Century British Portraits: Incisive Renderings by Modern Masters." *Architectural Digest* 51, no. 7 (July, 1994). Discusses the works of John and others who have resisted modernism and continued in portraiture.

Gaunt, William. *A Concise History of English Painting*. London: Thames and Hudson, and New York: Praeger, 1964. Although the section on John is very brief, it accurately summarizes the major achievements in his career and places him within the context of British art during the twentieth century.

Harris, Frank. *Contemporary Portraits: Third Series*. New York: Author, 1920. This book contains a short, impressionistic chapter on John which serves as a good source for information on the artist's personality and eccentric characteristics.

Holroyd, Michael. *The Art of Augustus John*. London: Secker and Warburg, 1974; Boston: Godine, 1975. A scholarly and balanced treatment of John's work by the foremost authority on the artist living today.

John, Augustus. *Chiaroscuro: Fragments of Autobiography*. London: Cape, and New York: Pellegrini and Cudahy, 1952.

———. *Finishing Touches*. London: Cape, 1964. The above two volumes make up John's autobiography and are similar, in many ways, to his artistic work: parts of them are beautifully written and intelligent; other parts are ponderous and confused.

———. *The Drawings of Augustus John*. Edited by Stephen Longstreet. Alhambra, Calif.: Borden, 1967. An excellent collection of John's pen and pencil drawings, this collection shows the artist at his best.

Rothenstein, John. *Augustus John*. London: Phaidon Press, and New York: Oxford University Press, 1944. A generally critical study of John's work by the former director of the Tate Gallery. The author makes the point that John's reputation with the public was based more on his colorful image than on his abilities.

Christopher E. Guthrie

JOHN PAUL II
Karol Jozef Wojtyła

Born: May 18, 1920; Wadowice, Poland

Area of Achievement: Church government

Contribution: John Paul II is the 264th pope of the Roman Catholic church and the first non-Italian pope since 1522. The first Slav to be named pope, the first pope from a communist country, and the youngest pope in modern times, John Paul II has a history of political involvement that predates even his religious vocation, having fought attempts first by Nazi Germany and later by the Soviet Union to weaken the power of the Church in Poland. During his reign as pope, he has sought to bring the Church back to some of the traditional values that he believed were lost after the Second Vatican Council.

Early Life

Karol Jozef Wojtyła, the future Pope John Paul II, was born on May 18, 1920, to Karol and Emilia (Kaczorowska) in Wadowice, a small town near Kraków, Poland. "Lolek," as he was affectionately known, was delivered by a midwife in the Wojtyła family apartment, a three-room residence on the second floor of a house across from the village church. The Wojtyła family originally came from Czaniec, a village near Andrychow. Wojtyła's paternal grandfather, Maciej, was a tailor who had settled in Biala Krakowska. Wojtyła's father, Karol, married in Wadowice and decided to settle there. The elder Karol Wojtyła had been a staff officer with the Twelfth Infantry Regiment of the Polish Army. While Wojtyła was growing up in Wadowice, his father was retired, and the family subsisted on a meager army pension.

Wojtyła learned to speak German from his mother, Emilia, whose family had come from Silesia. Emilia died from a heart ailment when Wojtyła was nine years old. Four years later, Edmund, Wojtyła's only surviving sibling, a doctor, died after contracting scarlet fever from a patient. This left Wojtyła and his father, a stern but warmhearted man, alone. While Wojtyła went to high school, his father took care of the apartment. As time went on, Wojtyła's father became all but a recluse, with only his son to keep him company. As a result, the two became very close.

The younger Wojtyła was devout even as a boy, stopping each morning at the church to pray. His gifts for the humanities were evident early; he excelled in religion, Latin, Greek, German, and philosophy. Even in grammar school, he demonstrated a fierce enthusiasm for the theater and frequented the cinema. He also wrote poetry and took second prize reciting poems at a local speech festival. He loved the outdoors, especially enjoying skiing, hiking, and kayaking. Accounts of his youth reveal an irrepressible personality, a young man with a prankish disregard for authority, and a skilled raconteur. Naturally, he was likable, and he was popular even with the young girls. Like most of his teenage friends, he had a steady girlfriend. Wojtyła was graduated from high school with distinction in 1938, and he and his father moved to Debniki Krakowskie, a district of Kraków. There they lived in a cramped, dark, cold, basement apartment, which was nicknamed the "catacombs."

Life's Work

Wojtyła was enrolled at Kraków's Jagellonian University to study for a degree in Polish literature. Always enthusiastic and energetic, the young student joined the Polish Language Society, a group of students who wrote poetry, held literary meetings, and went to the theater. He also joined the newly established Theatrical Fraternity. His first year of college completed, Wojtyła spent the summer of 1939 in military training, which was compulsory for all Polish young men. Before the fall term began, the Blitzkrieg offensive against Poland was launched. On September 1, 1939, Kraków, along with other Polish cities, was bombed by Adolf Hitler's army. While most of the citizens of Kraków sought cover from the bombing, Wojtyła spent that morning assisting the vicar in saying Mass. When the city fell to German forces a few days later, one of the first things that the occupying army did was to close the university and to make it illegal for Poles to seek a university education. The handful of teachers who had managed to avoid arrest were to establish an underground university by the end of the year. Wojtyła was immediately enrolled as a second-year literature student in one of the secret cells.

To support himself and his father, and to acquire the *Arbeitskarte* needed to avoid arrest by the Nazis, Wojtyła was able to secure a job at a quarry, breaking and hauling rocks. Later he worked at a water purification factory. During this time, he continued writing poetry, kept up his secret university studies, and even began studying French with a family friend. Because the Polish theater was outlawed, Wojtyła and his friends started an underground theater. Later, Wojtyła joined the clandestine Rhapsody Theater as an actor and coproducer. This small group was able during the war to give more than twenty performances of plays by Polish writers. Most of these plays were presented in the apartments of friends. One play was performed immediately after a Gestapo search. Wojtyła's daring extended beyond the theater, and he was eventually blacklisted by the Gestapo for providing many Jews with new identities and hiding places.

Wojtyła's father died of a stroke in the spring of 1941. Several months later, Wojtyła was enrolled at the clandestine theological seminary in Kraków. He distinguished himself academically at the seminary, where he finally moved in 1944, for safety, along with the other seminarians, under the orders of the archbishop. The end of World War II brought little in the way of political reprieve for the Poles, for Poland was immediately occupied by Joseph Stalin's Soviet army. The schools, however, were no longer outlawed, and Wojtyła was permitted to complete his education.

Karol Wojtyła was ordained on November 1, 1946, by the metropolitan Archbishop of Kraków, Prince Adam Sapieha. Wojtyta was sent to Rome to study at the Pontifical University Angelicum under the Dominican Fathers. There he resided at the Belgian College, where he was able to further refine his knowledge of the French language. His studies first focused on the Spanish mystic Saint John of the Cross; later, he would concentrate on Saint Thomas Aquinas. He became a doctor of divinity, magna cum laude, on April 30, 1948.

Upon his return from Rome, Wojtyła was made pastor of a poverty stricken parish in the small country village of Niegowic. He soon became very popular with the young people there. He organized a theater group and took many of the youth with him on hiking and kayaking trips. In less than a year, much to the disappointment of Niegowic's inhabitants, Wojtyła was transferred to the important parish of St. Florian, in Kraków. Again he gave much of his time to the youth of the parish, risking arrest by the Soviet-backed government, which had its own ideas about to which groups the Polish young people should belong. At this time, Wojtyła

was also lecturing on Thomistic philosophy and Max Scheler at the Catholic University of Lublin.

In 1958, he was consecrated Auxiliary Bishop of Kraków. He officially became archibishop in 1964 and was elevated to the cardinalate by Pope Paul VI on May 29, 1967. Throughout his career, Wojtyła was a chief advocate of greater concessions by the communistic state toward the people. His main concerns have been human rights, better education, improved access to the mass media, the abolition of censorship and atheistic propaganda, and religious freedom, including freedom of religious instruction.

On October 16, 1978, Wojtyła was chosen pope by the Conclave of Cardinals. He chose the name John Paul after his immediate predecessor and began his reign by declining coronation, preferring to be installed simply during a pontifical Mass in St. Peter's Square on October 22, 1978.

In June, 1979, Pope John Paul II landed at Warsaw airport for a historic visit to his homeland of Poland. His trip stimulated processes of reform that almost certainly contributed to the fall of the communist regime in Poland ten years later. Relations with the communist leaders of Poland were quite tense during the visit. Two years later, in May of 1981, John Paul survived an assassination attempt by a Turkish terrorist in Vatican City's St. Peter's Square.

One of the many ways in which John Paul II has distinguished himself as pope is in his travels. He has been to Latin America, Ireland (becoming the first pope ever to go there), the United States, the Philippines, Brazil, and other countries, including his beloved homeland. During his first American tour, he addressed the United Nations on world problems, especially peace and disarmament. He confronted Church leaders and dissidents in the United States, listening patiently to their complaints. He admonished the Catholics in the United States to beware of excesses and wished for a more equitable share of wealth in the world. Throughout his American tours, he stressed the sanctity of unborn life, the Church's opposition to artificial means of birth control, and the sacredness of the marriage bond. His call for an end to the death penalty is credited with saving the life of a convicted murderer whose sentence was commuted following John Paul's visit to the U.S. in January, 1999. The pope has called for Christian unity but does not want to dilute the Church's essential doctrine or compromise essential practices. When Anglican leaders expressed an interest in intercommunion, John Paul refused, saying that fundamental differences needed to be resolved first.

With the fall of communism in the early 1990's, John Paul II focused on different threats to the dignity of humankind in the form of Western commercialism, liberalism, materialism, secularism, and hedonism. He increased his efforts to confront those who called for relaxation of Catholic norms regarding the use of birth control, the practices of abortion and euthanasia, priestly celibacy, and the ordination of women. To impose greater order in the Church, John Paul II issued a new *Catechism of the Catholic Church* in 1993. He also issued many encyclicals, including *Veritatis Splendor* (1993) and *Evangelium Vitae* (1995). *Evangelium Vitae* (gospel of life) seeks to clarify Catholic Church teachings concerning abortion, euthanasia, and the death penalty. In the encyclical John Paul stresses that respecting the dignity of the person calls for the respect of life as a gift of God.

Summary

John Paul II's enrollment at the secret university, his assistance to Kraków's Jewish population, and

his affirmation of faith in the face of an atheistic government are the direct result of the environment in which he was reared, as are his traditionalist views concerning morality. As pope, John Paul has asked for less permissiveness in faith. His reign reflects a return to conservativism after the liberalism of Vatican Council II. In contrast to Paul VI, who laicized two thousand priests each year, John Paul II has reaffirmed the permanence of priestly vows and has refused to dispense a single priest. Despite the growing demand in the United States and elsewhere for the admittance of women into the episcopate, the pope stands firm on the side of an all-male priesthood.

John Paul II is, paradoxically, a sociopolitical liberal. He believes strongly in the inalienable rights of the individual and the peaceful coexistence of church and state. He is steadfastly opposed to Communism. A savvy diplomat and sophisticated intellectual, he can hold his own in debate with Marxists. For these reasons, he is respected by friends and enemies alike. He is in constant contact, often physical, with his congregation and has traveled to more countries than any pope before him, thus expanding his visibility and modernizing his position. He has also canonized more saints than any other pope.

Bibliography

Beigel, Gerard. *Faith and Social Justice in the Teaching of Pope John Paul II.* New York: Lang, 1997. Examines John Paul II's theories on the relationship between Christian faith and social justice.

Blazynski, George. *Pope John Paul II.* London: Sphere, and New York: Dell, 1979. Although its prose suggests that the author's first language is not English, this biography is packed with accurate information on the pope's early life. Blazynski provides the reader with the social and political backdrop of John Paul's Poland. Suitable for a general audience.

Fox, Thomas C., and Arthur Jones. "Pope John Paul II: The First 20 Years." *National Catholic Reporter* 34, no. 44 (October 16, 1998). A collection of quotes from the pages of the National Catholic Reporter covering the period between John Paul II's election as pope in 1978 through 1998.

Gronowicz, Antoni. *God's Broker: The Life of Pope John Paul II.* New York: Richardson and Snyder, 1984. Gronowicz skillfully weaves a portrait of John Paul from interviews with the pope himself and others who know him well. This book makes excellent reading, offering humorous and dramatic insight into the life and mind of the pope. Illustrated and indexed.

Korn, Frank. *From Peter to John Paul II: An Informal Study of the Papacy.* Canfield, Ohio: Alba, 1980. Written by a Fulbright scholar, this volume, as its title suggests, covers more than two thousand years of papal history. It is illustrated and contains a useful chronological listing of all the popes.

Moritz, Charles, ed. *Current Biography Yearbook, 1979.* New York: Wilson, 1980. A comprehensive biographical reference, written in an easy-to-read style, this book provides information on people in the news. Published annually, it is illustrated and indexed.

National Catholic News Service, eds. *John Paul II: "Pilgrimage of Faith."* New York: Seabury Press, 1979. Pictorial account of the first year of John Paul's reign, with an emphasis on his October, 1979, visit to the United States. An appendix contains the texts of his major addresses and homilies.

Joyce M. Parks

LYNDON B. JOHNSON

Born: August 27, 1908; near Stonewall, Gillespie
County, Texas

Died: January 22, 1973; en route to San Antonio,
Texas

Area of Achievement: Government and politics

Contribution: An astute, skilled, and compassionate professional politician, Johnson advanced the
cause of civil rights and expanded the government's role in social welfare through his Great
Society programs.

Early Life

Lyndon Baines Johnson, the thirty-sixth president
of the United States, was born August 27, 1908, the
first of five children of Rebekah Baines and Sam
Ealy Johnson, Jr. His mother, a graduate of Baylor
University, taught school briefly before her marriage to Sam Johnson, a Gillespie County tenant
farmer, realtor, and politician. A frontier Populist,
Sam Johnson demonstrated political courage as a
member of the Texas legislature. During World
War I, when anti-German sentiment ran to extremes, he rose to oppose a bill aimed at German-
Americans. Later, he joined forces with Governor
James Ferguson to oppose the Ku Klux Klan in
Texas. A further claim to remembrance lies in the
fact that he introduced in the legislature the bill
that saved the Alamo from demolition. Johnson's
gregarious and extroverted father represented a
contrast to his sensitive and introspective mother.

Johnson began his education at age four in a
country school near his home along the Pedernales
River in the Texas hill country. Later, he attended a
school in the small community of Albert and then
transferred to high school in nearby Johnson City,
where his parents had moved. He served as president of his six-member graduating class of 1924.
After high school, Johnson, then fifteen years old,
had not decided on a career for himself. He left
with a group of friends to travel to California,
where for two years he worked at odd jobs. Returning home, he worked as a laborer before deciding
to enroll in college, as his mother had desired. She
selected Southwest Texas State Teachers College
in San Marcos, about sixty miles from his home.
Johnson worked throughout his entire college career, for a time as the college president's assistant.
He left college for one year to teach school at Cot-

ulla in the South Texas brush country, where he encountered for the first time the struggles and depri-
vations of the Hispanic Texans whom he taught.
Despite his year of teaching, he completed his B.S.
in history (1930) in three and a half years. The following year, he taught secondary public speaking
and debate at Sam Houston High School in Houston, where his first-year debate team went to the
state finals. His career as a teacher ended abruptly
when Richard M. Kleberg of the King Ranch family won an off-year congressional election in 1931
and selected Johnson as his secretary.

In Kleberg's Washington office, Johnson became, in effect, the manager. He mastered the operations of federal institutions and bureaucracies,
took care of Kleberg's constituents, made as many
influential contacts as he could, and found federal
jobs for Texas friends and associates. A workaholic
for whom the sixteen- or eighteen-hour day was
normal, he set the pattern of diligence, commitment, and loyalty that he would later expect from
his own staff. After the 1932 presidential election
brought in the New Deal of Franklin D. Roosevelt,
Johnson worked on behalf of the new programs
and often influenced a reluctant Kleberg to support
them. While a member of Kleberg's staff, he established several important working relationships
with experienced political leaders who served him
well later, the most significant being a fellow Texan, Sam T. Rayburn, later to become a powerful
Speaker of the House of Representatives.

More important, following a whirlwind courtship, he married Claudia Alta (Lady Bird) Taylor
on November 17, 1934. The daughter of a businessman and landowner from Karnack, Texas, she
became a valued adviser, supporter, and counselor,
as well as a gracious hostess and often his most effective personal representative.

After leaving Kleberg's staff in 1935, Johnson
was selected by Roosevelt to head the Texas
branch of the National Youth Administration, a
New Deal organization designed to help young
people remain in school during the Depression,
largely through providing public works jobs in
summers. In this office, Johnson came to understand the power of government programs to help
needy people, including minorities. Continuing his
torrid pace of work, he gained national recognition
as an effective leader.

Life's Work

By the time Johnson enrolled in college, he was reasonably sure that his life's work lay in politics, though he was unsure as to how it would develop. His career in political office lasted thirty-two years and included every elective office within the federal government. It began with a congressional election in 1937, to fill an unexpired term in the Tenth District of Texas, which included the state capital of Austin and Johnson's home region. He ran on a platform of all-out support for Roosevelt. A tireless campaigner but not always an inspiring speaker, Johnson often included in his campaign catchy or novel elements that his opponents found corny. In 1937, his slogan, "Franklin D. and Lyndon B.," succeeded in identifying him with the popular president.

As a congressman, Johnson formed a close working relationship with Roosevelt, supporting the president's programs while looking out for his own district and the economic interests of Texas. More quickly than many others in Congress, he realized that the nation was on a course toward war and strongly supported the president's rearmament efforts. He took time out in 1941 to run for the Senate against Texas Governor W. Lee O'Daniel, losing the race by a narrow margin. During World War II, he served briefly in the navy before Roosevelt summoned all congressmen in military service back to Washington.

Following the death of Roosevelt in 1945, Johnson realized that world conditions had changed considerably since the early days of the New Deal. Employment levels were high, and a victorious nation was prosperous once again. Perceiving the major challenge confronting the United States to be Communist expansionism, he supported President Harry S Truman's efforts to rebuild the armed forces. Formerly a strong supporter of labor, Johnson cast his vote in favor of the restrictive Taft-Hartley Act.

When the opportunity came for another Senate race in 1948, Johnson ran against Governor Coke Stevenson, campaigning throughout the state in a helicopter, then a novel mode of transportation. With the support of the National Democratic Party, he won the primary by a narrow margin, and in the one-party state that Texas then was, this was tantamount to victory.

He selected as his Senate mentor Richard Russell, the Democrat from Georgia, whose guidance helped Johnson to advance quickly to positions of power and prominence. Senate Democrats chose him as party Whip in 1951, minority leader in 1953, and majority leader in 1955. Through his total commitment to success, his boundless energy, his own abilities as an organizer and leader, and his grasp of Senate operations and traditions, he became perhaps the strongest senatorial leader in American history. As a leader, his primary watchwords were: pragmatism, compromise, reason, bargaining, and consensus. During deliberations, he preferred face-to-face discussion and debate, including bargaining, for in this mode he usually held the advantage. Almost six and a half feet tall, long limbed with a broad forehead, large nose and ears, and prominent cheekbones, Johnson commanded a formidable presence. A complex man of many moods, known for homely language and abundant anecdotes, he was highly persuasive.

As Senate leader, Johnson forged the consensus that enabled passage of the Civil Rights Act of 1957, the first legislation of its kind in eighty-seven years. In foreign policy, he persuaded Democrats in the Senate to adopt a bipartisan approach in support of President Dwight D. Eisenhower. He believed that the opposition party should operate in a constructive manner, especially in foreign affairs.

In 1960, he sought his party's nomination for the presidency but lost in the primaries and at the convention to Senator John F. Kennedy. Kennedy chose the powerful Johnson as his running mate, hoping to carry the South, which had defected almost wholesale to Eisenhower in the two previous presidential elections. Despite his record on civil rights, Johnson had respect and strong support in the South and succeeded in swinging enough votes to win.

As vice president, Johnson undertook important missions and responsibilities. He represented the president in travels abroad, oversaw the high priority national space program, and pressed hard, with reasonable success, for equal opportunity employment. He gave speeches on foreign policy, indicating that he understood that many conflicts are regional or local, not the result of the East-West confrontation. Yet where Southeast Asia was concerned, he clearly perceived the conflict in the context of the larger ideological struggle. He accepted the view, a legacy of the Eisenhower years when John Foster Dulles as secretary of state shaped American policy, that the fall of one Southeast Asian nation would precipitate the fall of all the others—the Domino Theory.

Following the assassination of President John F. Kennedy in Dallas on November 22, 1963, Johnson became the thirty-sixth president and led the shocked nation along the course charted by his predecessor. Perhaps no other vice president was better prepared to assume the powers of the presidency. With a long career of public service behind him and with his energy undiminished, he undertook enormous efforts on both domestic and foreign fronts. The overwhelming support he received in the 1964 national election against the conservative Senator Barry Goldwater gave him a mandate to proceed with his own programs. He declared war on poverty and vowed to end it. He brought forward important legislation in almost every area on the domestic front, a cluster of programs together known as the Great Society. In health care, the environment, housing, inner cities, education at all levels, and, above all, civil rights, he proposed new and important legislation. The nation had not experienced anything like the amount of new domestic legislation since Roosevelt's first term.

In foreign policy, he continued to regard the East-West conflict as paramount. He met with So-viet Premier Aleksei Kosygin to explore avenues of agreement. Yet the main foreign policy preoccupation remained the war in Vietnam. In an effort to secure a non-Communist South Vietnam, Johnson increased the level of American commitment to half a million men. Casualties mounted, little progress was discernible, the war became increasingly unpopular at home, and the president felt obliged to seek a negotiated peace that did not come until long after his term had ended.

Having decided not to seek a second full term, Johnson left the White House in January, 1969, to return to his Texas ranch in retirement. He died there, within a mile of his birthplace, on January 22, 1973.

Summary

In the assessment of historians, Lyndon B. Johnson's legacy will be limited primarily to his presidency. Early responses suggest that he will be included among the strongest of American presidents. Placed in the larger context of American post-World War II foreign policy, his failure in Vietnam will become more understandable. In domestic affairs, it will be apparent that his influence has endured. His Great Society was in essence a continuation of Roosevelt's New Deal. It sprang from Johnson's deepest sympathies and concerns for the underprivileged, a reflection of his Populist roots.

The Civil Rights Act of 1964 and the Voting Rights Act of 1965 assured fundamental rights to millions previously denied them. Johnson championed federal support for education, from the pre-school Head Start program, to job training programs and federal programs for higher education. Medicare and increased Social Security benefits brought greater financial security to older Americans; Medicaid and increased welfare appropriations improved the lot of those in need. Although some Great Society programs had limited or mixed results—housing and urban projects among them—the Great Society effectively extended the benefits of an affluent society to a larger number of people.

The tribute by Ralph Ellison at the time of Johnson's death appears valid: "When all of the returns are in, perhaps President Johnson will have to settle for being recognized as the greatest American President for the poor and for the Negroes, but that, as I see it, is a very great honor indeed."

Bibliography

Bechloss, Michael R. "The Johnson Tapes: LBJ Secretly Recorded the Private Moments in an Era of War and Riot. An Exclusive Glimpse at How Power Really Works." *Newsweek* 130, no. 15 (October 13, 1997). Excerpts from Johnson's tapes. Topics include Kennedy's assassination, the Vietnam War, and partisan politics.

Bornet, Vaughan Davis. *The Presidency of Lyndon B. Johnson*. Lawrence: University Press of Kansas, 1983. Bornet attempts a balanced assessment of Johnson's programs and his overall impact on the nation, including the economic cost of the Great Society and the Vietnam War. He includes a useful annotated bibliography.

Caro, Robert A. *The Years of Lyndon Johnson: The Path to Power*. New York: Knopf, 1982; London: Collins, 1983. A lengthy assessment of Johnson's early career down to 1948. Develops the thesis that Johnson's actions and decisions were calculated to increase and enhance his power.

Dallek, Robert. *Lone Star Rising: Lyndon Johnson and His Times, 1908-1960*. New York: Oxford University Press, 1991. A well-balanced study of Johnson from childhood through his election as vice president under John Kennedy.

Dugger, Ronnie. *The Politician: The Life and Times of Lyndon Johnson, the Drive for Power from the Frontier to Master of the Senate*. New York: Norton, 1982. Traces Johnson's views on government to his family background and myths of the frontier. Emphasis upon Vietnam in Johnson's experience and political life.

Kearns, Doris. *Lyndon Johnson and the American Dream*. London: Deutsch, and New York: Harper, 1976. The book contains a poignant account of Johnson's early family life. The author provides an account of his career and an assessment of his strengths and weaknesses as a leader.

Miller, Merle. *Lyndon: An Oral Biography*. New York: Putnam, 1980. Miller presents a chronological biography through the words of those who knew Johnson, recorded in interviews and arranged in sequence with little additional comment and explanation. The author interviews those who knew him best, from secretaries to cabinet members. A lively, multifaceted portrait of a complex subject.

Valenti, Jack. *A Very Human President*. New York: Norton, 1975. A sympathetic view of the Johnson presidency by a prominent member of the White House staff. It includes a perspective on the decision-making process, discussion of important issues, and an insider's account of the president's interaction with the staff.

White, William S. *The Professional: Lyndon B. Johnson*. Boston: Houghton Mifflin, 1964. A favorable retrospective of Johnson's career, beginning with his accession to the presidency. White attempts to shed light on Johnson's personality, political views, goals, and methods.

Stanley Archer

FRÉDÉRIC JOLIOT and IRÈNE JOLIOT-CURIE

Frédéric Joliot

Born: March 19, 1900; Paris, France   *Died:* August 14, 1958; Paris, France

Irène Joliot-Curie

Born: September 12, 1897; Paris, France   *Died:* March 17, 1956; Paris, France

Area of Achievement: Chemistry

Contribution: The Joliot-Curies continued the work which Irène's parents, Pierre and Marie Curie, had begun on radioactivity. Frédéric and Irène received the Nobel Prize in Chemistry in 1935 for having discovered the possibility of artificial radioactivity. The resulting new radiosotopes could then be used in research and medicine far more economically than could the rare and expensive radium.

Early Lives

Irène Curie was delivered by her paternal grandfather on September 12, 1897, in Paris, France. Her mother, Marie Curie, marked the event of her daughter's birth by recording in her household accounts that on that day unusual expenses, for champagne and for telegrams, had occurred.

By the time of his daughter's birth, when he was in his late thirties, Irène's father was well recognized as a brilliant research scientist. Pierre Curie had had an unusual upbringing, and the same was to be true for his children. His own father, active in research as well as in the practice of medicine, tutored Pierre at home so that the young boy's obvious genius could thrive, and Pierre had proved the wisdom of this decision when by age eighteen he had already earned his master's degree in physics.

Irène's mother, Marie, was the brilliant and studious daughter of a professor of physics and mathematics. In November of 1891, she had arrived in Paris from her native Poland to study at the Sorbonne for her master's degree in physics. In Paris, she met and married Pierre, and the couple soon became known throughout the world for their achievements in scientific research. Irène was the elder of their two daughters.

Irène's early life was dominated by the professional lives of her parents. She was born just prior to her mother's discovery of radium, and she developed an early affinity for the laboratory environment. Her unorthodox education, which was similar to that which her father had been afforded and which was influenced by her grandfather, allowed

her to explore and experiment on her own. Irène and her contemporaries who were children of the colleagues of Pierre and Marie were taught for a time by their parents in a cooperative school which most believed was far superior to the public schools. Irène earned her bachelor's and master's degrees at the Sorbonne.

Irène accompanied her mother to Stockholm when in 1911 Marie Curie was awarded a second Nobel Prize—in Chemistry—for the preparation of pure radium. Irène traveled with her mother whenever she went abroad in order to receive recognition. There was little doubt that Irène, like her mother, would make a life for herself in laboratory research.

Jean Frédéric Joliot was the sixth child born to Émilie and Henri Joliot. His birth, in Paris on March 19, 1900, was special to his parents because of their earlier loss of two sons. Frédéric's father, a successful wholesaler in textiles, loved the outdoors, and he spent much time with his son on long walks in the woods, where the young boy developed a profound respect for and curiosity regarding nature. His interest in science came also from his mother, who always expressed interest in reports of new discoveries. She also influenced her son in the areas of politics and social movements, contributing, perhaps, to Frédéric's interest in and eventual membership in the French Communist Party.

Frédéric attended a number of small, private schools. He was active in sports, and he frequently performed independent experiments in chemistry. Performing well in mathematics, chemistry, and physics, Frédéric was admitted to the Paris technical school, the École de Physique et de Chimie Industrielle de la Ville de Paris, where students obtained practical laboratory experience. This was where the Curies had performed their research in radioactivity. Founded in 1882, it was a remarkable technical school with a fine faculty.

Required to make a choice between chemistry and physics, Frédéric finally decided upon the latter. He soon proved his brilliance and was appointed to work with Marie Curie as an assistant in the laboratory at the Institut du Radium. Frédéric had admired the Curies since he was a small child, and he recognized the wonderful opportunity he had been given. He studied hard, learning about radioactivity in the laboratory while working toward first his bachelor's and then his master's degree, the latter qualifying him as a teacher.

Frédéric and Irène, having met while both assisted in the Radium Institute, had much in common. Apart from their scientific interests, each was fond of sports and of the outdoors. They spent time together in the laboratory and in many other activities. Finding themselves inseparable, they were married in a civil ceremony in Paris on October 9, 1926.

Life's Work

That Frédéric and Irène should carry on the work of Irène's parents was to be expected. They had worked together in the radium laboratory, one of the few in the world, and had studied closely with Marie. From the beginning of the young couple's partnership, they worked diligently, taking pleasure in meeting the challenges which were presented them. For the first several years of their marriage, while Frédéric completed his academic degrees, the couple set about enhancing the resources which they would need for their work and becoming more expert at experimentation. With state financial aid in the form of grants, they were able, after 1930, to proceed with their research, which was almost entirely in the new field of atomic physics.

Polonium, a decay product of uranium, had been discovered by Marie and so was available for use by the Joliot-Curie team. Their supply of the naturally radioactive material made them well equipped in the essential source of alpha particles. The team had trained themselves to make photographs using the Wilson cloud chamber, in which the paths of alpha particles, having passed through a gas, can be made visible. By using the Geiger counter, they could detect the passage of particles through a gas. They were ready, by late 1931, to proceed with a study of the effects produced on the nuclei of the lighter chemical elements, such as beryllium, when bombarded with alpha particles from polonium. A year earlier, German physicists Walther Bothe and H. Becker had reported experiments of a similar nature in which, much to their surprise, beryllium emitted radiation similar to that of radium.

This unexplained result was what the Joliot-Curies determined to duplicate. From their preliminary studies, the neutron was revealed by Sir James Chadwick and was further confirmed by follow-up work done by the Joliot-Curies. From subsequent studies using the same type of experiment on boron, this time observing the action of the positron, Frédéric and Irène concluded that the emission of positive electrons persisted for more than half an hour after the source of irradiation was removed. They had induced radiation, or created it artifically, and they were also able to produce the same effect using magnesium and aluminum. The production of artificial radioactivity was confirmed by chemical tests, and on January 15, 1934, the official announcement of the discovery was made. The Joliot-Curies had opened a new path of research which eventually led to the final splitting of the atom.

They accepted their Nobel Prizes in Stockholm on December 12, 1935. Irène, in her speech, emphasized that their experiments had been done jointly, her purpose being to respond in advance to those who might attempt to give her husband only secondary credit—the same treatment unjustly

dealt her father. Frédéric mentioned in his speech the pride which Marie Curie had expressed when they had presented her with a sample of the physical evidence of their achievement. (Marie had died before she could hear of the awarding to her daughter and son-in-law of the Nobel Prize.) The monetary prize of about forty-one thousand dollars afforded the couple the possibility of paying for their new home at Parc de Sceaux, near Paris.

In 1933, the Joliot-Curies had been awarded the Henri Wilde Prize, and in 1934 the Marquet Prize of the Académie des Sciences was theirs as well. Meanwhile, the Joliot-Curies continued atomic physics research. In February, 1940, they were among the first scientists to achieve the chain reaction in nuclear fission. In 1940, they were the recipients of the Barnard Gold Medal for Meritorious Service to Science, a prize awarded only every five years. In the same year, Frédéric joined the French Communist Party, to which Irène was not unsympathetic. Active in the Resistance against the Nazi occupiers of his country, he saw the Communist Party as the only salvation for France, and he gave as his reason for membership his intense patriotism. Nevertheless, his politics were to have a negative effect on his attempts, after World War II, to be of service to the world scientific community.

During the war, Frédéric served in the rank of captain in the French artillery. He was assigned to coordinate the atomic research being conducted at the Université de Paris, the Collège de France, and the Centre National de la Recherche Scientifique, and to see that the research being done was geared toward war. Early in this effort, Frédéric dispatched a negotiator to Norway with the mission to attempt to buy Norway's supply of heavy water, a substance required in atomic research. Norway lent the material to France, but when his country fell to Germany, Frédéric managed to have the heavy water smuggled to England for use by the Allied effort. Frédéric also managed, after having endured a twelve-hour ordeal with the Gestapo, to dissuade the Nazis from taking the only cyclotron as well as the radium supply out of France.

After the war, it was learned that Frédéric had supervised the production of explosives and radio equipment while pretending (for the benefit of Nazi scientists near whom he was forced to work) to do atomic research. When the Nazis became suspicious of some of his Resistance activities, Frédéric went into hiding while Irène fled with their children to Switzerland.

After the war, Charles de Gaulle named Frédéric head of the Atomic Energy Commission of France. He was removed, however, in 1950 because of his membership in the Communist Party. He was awarded the Stalin Peace Prize in 1951. In May of 1958, he made his sixth and last visit to Moscow. He reported that in his meeting there with Nikita Khrushchev, attended only by the two of them, a Khrushchev colleague and an interpreter, they discussed the necessity for a movement toward world disarmament and peace.

Irène died in 1956 of the same disease which had caused her mother's death. They each had developed leukemia as a result of their contact in the laboratory with radioactive materials. Frédéric died two years later, as a result of hepatitis, from which he had suffered for years. The couple had two children, Pierre and Hélène.

Summary
Within a few years of Frédéric Joliot and Irène Joliot-Curie's discovery of artificial radioactivity, atomic-energy research was well under way.

Their discovery had not only been of immediate interest and value to the scientific community but also had been an important step in that rapid chain of events which gave the world its most controversial scientific achievement.

They had barely missed discovering the neutron but had contributed to its discovery through their research. Chadwick, who is credited with its discovery, gave considerable credit to the couple, stating that it had been their preliminary research that had laid a foundation for the hypothesis of the existence of the neutron. Theirs had been a major contribution to the work of Chadwick and others.

Bibliography

Biquard, Pierre. *Frédéric Joliot-Curie: The Man and His Theories.* Translated by Geoffrey Strachan. London: Souvenir Press, 1965; New York: Eriksson, 1966. Relates the friendship between the author and Frédéric, which began during their student years. Useful information on Frédéric's life.

Cotton, Eugénie. *Les Curie.* Paris: Seghers, 1963. The author, a family friend of the Curies, offers recollections of Irène, Frédéric, Marie, and Pierre. Assesses their scientific achievements.

Giroud, Françoise. *Marie Curie: A Life.* New York: Holmes and Meier, 1986. While the subject of the biography is the famous mother of Irène, included are many references to Irène and her sister, Eve, and their education and upbringing. Included are quotations from letters exchanged between mother and daughter, giving insight into the relationship between Marie and Irène. Chapter 25 provides a few sentences with regard to Marie's opinion of Frédéric.

Goldsmith, Maurice. *Frédéric Joliot-Curie: A Biography.* London: Lawrence and Wishart, 1976. Contains appendices listing honors and decorations awarded the subject and a list of his scientific publications, his own and those published jointly with his wife. The bibliography contains secondary sources in book form as well as those published in journals. Scientific drawings are included in the reference notes, which are extensive. The index is comprehensive. Excellent.

McKown, Robin. *She Lived for Science: Irène Joliot-Curie.* New York: Messner, 1961; London: Macmillan, 1962. This book, intended for juvenile readers, is one of the few (if not the only) available English-language volumes written primarily about Irène. Contains 192 pages.

P. R. Lannert

BOBBY JONES

Born: March 17, 1902; Atlanta, Georgia
Died: December 18, 1971; Atlanta, Georgia
Area of Achievement: Sports
Contribution: Jones climaxed his career in amateur golf in 1930 by winning in a single year the "Grand Slam," the four major American and British open and amateur championships, an achievement still unmatched by the late 1980's. He went on to found the Augusta National Golf Club and the Masters Tournament.

Early Life

Robert Tyre "Bobby" Jones, who was named after his grandfather, was born March 17, 1902, in Atlanta, Georgia, the son of Robert Purmetus and Clara Thomas Jones. He received his early education at Woodbury School and Tech High School in Atlanta. He later took a degree in mechanical engineering at the Georgia Institute of Technology in 1922 and one in English literature at Harvard in 1924. He also attended Emory University Law School between 1926 and 1927 and was admitted to the Georgia bar in 1928.

Jones's golfing career began at the age of five, when he played with clubs (which had been cut down for his size) over a five-hole "course" that he and a neighbor boy had laid out in his front yard. Jones's father decided at that time to move from the city to the town of East Lake, where the Jones family lived on the fringes of the East Lake Country Club. Young Jones was not a robust youngster, because of a digestive problem that kept him from eating properly, and it was thought that living in the suburbs would be good for his health.

Jones learned the game by imitating the swing of Stewart Maiden, who came to the job of head professional at East Lake from Carnoustie, Scotland. Jones was six years old at the time. Maiden was never to give Jones a formal lesson, but in the years ahead he would coach him informally; he was the only teacher Jones would ever have.

At the age of seven, Jones was given permission to play at East Lake on any day but Saturday or Sunday. He did so after school in the afternoon, often taking a capful of balls to practice at the thirteenth green, which was located just behind his house. Jones's first tournament victory came at the age of nine, in 1911, when he won the junior championship cup of the Atlanta Athletic Club. At the age of thirteen, Jones won, among other titles, the

club championships of both East Lake and the Druid Hills Country Club.

Life's Work

In 1916, then the Georgia Amateur tournament champion, Jones played in his first national championship, the United States Amateur, in which he was a quarterfinalist. Thus began a fourteen-year career on a national and international level which was to end in 1930 with the Grand Slam, a sweep of the four major American and British open and amateur championships.

Jones was an amateur golfer who achieved his success mostly during the years when he was a university student. For most of the years in which he played competitively, he was in school. Jones experienced a limited tournament schedule, an average of less than four tournaments per year. The greatest number of tournaments he ever played in a single year was eight, in 1920, when he was eighteen. Later, as a young attorney and father (following his marriage in 1924 to Mary Malone and the subsequent births of their three children), his family and his law practice would take precedence in his mind.

Although Jones came immediately into the public eye as a fourteen-year-old at his first United States Amateur, he was not an immediate winner on the national scene. For seven years, Jones was without a national title, although he won such tournaments as the Southern Amateur and other regional events. During that time, he was the runner-up in the United States Amateur (1919), at the age of seventeen, and semifinalist in that event in both 1920 and 1922. In 1920, Jones had his initial experience in a national open championship when he played in the United States Open; his first British Open followed in 1921. In his first United States Open at the Inverness Club in Toledo, Ohio, he tied for eighth place. His first tournaments in England were not happy ones. After being eliminated in the fourth round of the British Amateur at the Royal Liverpool Golf Club at Hoylake, Jones entered the British Open at the Old Course of St. Andrews in Scotland. For years, Jones had had a violent temper that led him to throw clubs following errant shots. In time, he curbed that tendency, but at St. Andrews, he withdrew after the eleventh hole after having played the first nine in forty-six shots, taking a double-bogey six at the tenth and missing his

first putt after being in a sand bunker at the eleventh. Jones hated St. Andrews, even though it is conceded to be the founding place of the game, but later came to regard the Old Course as his favorite.

Jones's period of dominance in the game finally began two years later, in 1923, when he won the United States Open at the age of twenty-one. Jones and Bobby Cruickshank tied over the seventy-two holes of the championship with a score of 296. Jones won the playoff with a score of seventy-six to Cruickshank's seventy-eight.

Starting in that year, Jones held one or more major titles every year for eight years, for a total of thirteen. His championships included the United States Amateur title in 1924, 1925, 1927, 1928, and 1930; the United States Open title in 1923, 1926, 1929, and 1930; the British Open title in 1926, 1927, and 1930; and the British Amateur title in 1930.

Jones's dominance from 1923 to 1930 was such that he either won or tied for the lead in six of eight United States Opens, finishing second and eleventh in his other two tries. In the United States Amateur, Jones won five of the seven he entered, losing once in the finals and once in the first round. He won all three British Opens in which he played during those years, having failed to win only in his first one, from which he withdrew. The British Amateur was the most difficult, as he was victorious in only one of three. During those eight years, Jones won seventeen of the twenty-eight tournaments he entered and was second six times. In addition, Jones played in the Walker Cup competition, held between the leading amateurs of the United States and Great Britain, a total of five times. The American side was victorious in each instance, and Jones was a hero.

Jones was not an imposing physical specimen, standing only five feet, eight inches tall and weighing about 165 pounds at the time he was accomplishing his greatest golfing feats. His clean-cut, boyish appearance had much to do with his almost unparalleled popularity as a 1920's sports figure.

In 1930, Jones finished second in his first tournament of the year, the Savannah Open. He won the other six in which he played, the Southeastern Open, the *Golf Illustrated* Gold Vase, the British Amateur, the British Open, the United States Open, and the United States Amateur. Ironically, he won the British Amateur title on the same St. Andrews course on which he had withdrawn in disgust. (He had also set the British Open record at St. An-

drews, where he won that tournament with a seven-under-par 285 in 1927.) Jones's victim in the final match of the British Amateur in 1930 was Roger Wethered, the 1923 British Amateur champion, who was closed out on the thirtieth hole, seven and six. In the British Open at Hoylake, Jones's four-round score of 70-72-74-75-291 was two strokes better than that of Leo Diegel and Macdonald Smith, who shared second place. In the United States Open at Interlachen Country Club in Minneapolis, Smith was again second as Jones won with 71-73-68-75-287, one under par. Jones thus became the first man in history to break par in the United States Open. In the United States Amateur at Merion Cricket Club in Philadelphia, Jones never had to play the last four holes in any of his matches, and he defeated Eugene V. Homans, eight and seven, in the championship finale.

It was fitting that Jones should win what was to be his final tournament of serious competition at Merion, the same club where he had begun his national championship career at the age of fourteen. He also won his first United States Amateur title on that course.

On November 18, 1930, Jones announced his retirement from tournament golf with a letter to the United States Golf Association, surrendering at the same time his amateur status so that he could earn money from the fame he had won on the golf course. Not mentioned by Jones in the letter was the fact that tournament golf was taking its toll on him. Although his demeanor before tournament galleries was outwardly calm, inside he was extremely nervous. He would be sick to the point of vomiting on occasion and would lose as much as eighteen pounds during a tournament.

After retirement, Jones made a series of instructional films seen by an estimated twenty-five million people. He designed the first set of iron golf clubs to be numbered and sold as a matched set for A. G. Spalding and Brothers. Jones wrote newspaper and magazine articles and narrated an instructional series for radio. He also worked for his father's law firm, concentrating on business contracts.

In July, 1931, Jones and Clifford Roberts, a New York City investment broker, announced plans to build the Augusta National Golf Club at Augusta, Georgia. The club opened in the spring of 1933. Building the course was the culmination of Jones's desire to design a course of his own, which he did, with the help of golf architect Alister Mackenzie.

Also in that spring, it was suggested that the Augusta National be the site of the United States Open. When it was decided not to offer the course for the open, Roberts suggested that the club hold its own invitational tournament. Roberts, from the beginning, thought that the event should be called the Masters Tournament. Jones disagreed, believing such a title presumptuous. Instead, the event was officially called the Augusta National Invitation Tournament. By 1938, even Jones had agreed, long after the press, that the tournament was the Masters.

Jones was prevailed upon by Roberts to play in the new Masters Tournament, but Jones was never a threat to win it. His best finish, in fact, was in the inaugural 1934 event, when he played the four rounds in 76-74-72-72-294, good enough to tie for thirteenth place.

From that beginning, the Augusta National Golf Club grew in reputation, while the Masters became one of the four tournaments considered the modern Grand Slam, along with the United States and British opens and the American Professional Golfers Association Championship.

Jones continued to play in the Masters through the 1948 tournament. After a back operation, undertaken that same year to correct an injury thought to have occurred in his youth, Jones announced in advance of the 1949 tournament that he would no longer take part.

For a time, it was rumored that the increasing deterioration of Jones's health was because either the 1948 operation or another in 1950 was not a complete success. It was not until 1956 that it was discovered that Jones was suffering from an extremely rare disease called syringomyelia, which attacked Jones's central nervous system and damaged it to such an extent that he could no longer turn the pages of a book. He finally died of an aneurysm, on December 18, 1971.

Summary

Perhaps the most striking aspect of Jones's unparalleled success as a golfer was the fact that he accomplished it with apparent ease. Jones spent an average of only three months a year playing golf, for he regarded his family and his legal profession as having greater priority in his life than golf. Yet his technique was exceptional: Jones's golf swing was smooth and effortless, and he could drive a golf ball farther than the great majority of his opponents; his secret was his superb timing. As a result, he was able to distinguish himself with the record of having won four major tournaments in a single year, in 1930—a record still unbroken by the late 1980's.

Jones may also serve as an inspiration to young golfers for his character. Although he had his struggle with a great temper early in his career, Jones overcame it and never appeared unnerved during a tournament. Jones was consistently considerate of both his opponents and the onlookers. Yet his inward turmoil, perhaps a result of the fierce concentration needed to perform as a golfer, took its toll and was a major contributing factor in his retirement from competition at the age of twenty-eight.

Jones contributed to golf and American sports with works other than his exquisite swing. He wrote four books on golf: *Down the Fairway* (1927), *Golf Is My Game* (1960), *Bobby Jones on Golf* (1966), and *Bobby Jones on the Basic Golf Swing* (1969). The last two had to be authored by dictation because of his ailment.

Sometime before his death, it was made known to Jones that some individuals were considering the erection of a monument to him on the grounds of the Augusta National Golf Club. Ever modest, he immediately vetoed the idea; he said that the club itself would be monument enough. Indeed, the Augusta National Golf Club has become perhaps the best-known modern course in the world, and its tournament, the Masters, one of the four most important events in the life of professional golfers every year. The Augusta National is truly a fitting and lasting tribute to Bobby Jones.

Bibliography

Fimrite, Ron. "The Emperor Jones." *Sports Illustrated* 80, no. 14 (April 11, 1994). Profile of Jones, including his moral and ethical character and how he was viewed by others.

Jones, Bobby. *Secrets of the Master: The Best of Bobby Jones.* Edited by Sidney L. Matthew. Chelsea, Mich.: Sleeping Bear Press, 1996. A collection of fifty newspaper columns written by Jones during the 1920's. Includes instruction on the game of golf, plus commentaries on other golfers of the period.

Keeler, Oscar Bane. *The Bobby Jones Story.* Edited by Grantland Rice. Atlanta: Tupper and Love, 1953. A complete account of the golfing career of Bobby Jones.

Price, Charles. *A Golf Story: Bobby Jones, Augusta National and the Masters Tournament.* New

York: Atheneum, 1986. The story of Bobby Jones's golfing career and his involvement in the founding of the Augusta National Golf Club and the Masters Tournament.

Roberts, Clifford. *The Story of the Augusta National Golf Club.* New York: Doubleday, 1976. A history of the Augusta National Golf Club, the involvement of Bobby Jones, its members and the relationship of President Dwight D. Eisenhower with the club.

Taylor, Dawson. *The Masters.* New York: Barnes, and London: Yoseloff, 1973. A concise history of the Masters Tournament and its founding, with a year-to-year listing of the top twenty-four finishers and ties in the event, including a brief account of each tournament.

Wind, Herbert Warren. *The Story of American Golf: Its Champions and Its Championships.* 4th ed. Cincinnati, Ohio: Old Golf Shop, 1986. A comprehensive history of golf in America with chapters devoted to the career of Bobby Jones and the atmosphere in which his feats were accomplished.

Al Ludwick

MARY HARRIS "MOTHER" JONES

Born: May 1, 1830; Cork, Ireland
Died: November 30, 1930; Silver Spring, Maryland
Areas of Achievement: Social reform and trade unionism
Contribution: As a labor organizer and fiery orator, Mother Jones inspired workers and breathed life into union organizing efforts in the early twentieth century.

Early Life

The birth date of Mary Harris "Mother" Jones is in dispute as are other critical facts about her early life. This uncertainty is not unusual for poor and working-class people whose lives are often not recorded in traditional ways. Even births, deaths, marriages, and work history may not be documented.

In her autobiography, Jones herself gave 1830 as her birth year, but she gave other dates in interviews throughout her life. Most historians agree on 1830, although one cites 1839 and another 1843. Her father migrated to the United States from Ireland and worked as a laborer building canals and railroads. The family followed and settled initially in Toronto, Canada, where young Mary Harris went to school, graduating in 1858 or 1859. Little is known of her father and mother or her siblings.

Mary Harris taught school in Michigan in 1859, worked as a dressmaker in Chicago in 1860, and again taught school in Memphis, Tennessee. In Memphis, she met George Jones, a member of the Iron Workers' Union, and in 1861 they were married. George Jones and all the couple's children died in the yellow fever epidemic of 1867. In her autobiography, Mother Jones claims to have had four children, but some evidence exists to suggest it may have been one or three. No one disputes the fact that Jones was alone after 1867 with no family and no permanent home.

Mother Jones left Memphis in 1867 to return to Chicago, where she resumed working as a dressmaker for the wealthy. In 1871, she was burned out of her home and lost all of her possessions in the great Chicago Fire. Following the fire, she began attending nightly lectures at the Knights of Labor building, which was located near the place where many homeless refugees from the fire were camping out. Records of these years of her life are scarce, but it is known that Mother Jones traveled during the 1870's and 1880's from one industrial area to another speaking and organizing, usually in connection with the Knights of Labor. In 1877, she was in Pittsburgh for the first nationwide industrial strike, that of the railroad workers. In 1886, she was in Chicago, active in organizing for the eight-hour work day. In 1890, when the Knights of Labor District 135 and the National Union of Miners and Mine Laborers merged to form the United Mine Workers of America (UMWA), Mary Harris Jones became a paid organizer for the union. She was approximately sixty years old and about to enter the national stage. She was thought of as "the Miner's Angel," the most dangerous woman in the country, or America's most patriotic citizen, depending upon the point of view of the different people who encountered her.

Life's Work

Until her health failed in the late 1920's, Mother Jones traveled the nation speaking and organizing not only for coal miners but also for textile, railway, and steel workers. She figured in most major strikes in the United States in the early 1900's, but was repeatedly drawn to the coalfields of Pennsylvania, Colorado, and West Virginia. For a time, she was active in Socialist Party politics, particularly in the campaigns of Eugene V. Debs. She supported Mexican revolutionary Francisco "Pancho" Villa in his fight for better wages and living conditions for Mexican workers, who were often used as strike breakers, particularly in Western mines. She did not support woman's suffrage or other social reform efforts of her era that were not founded solely on working-class rights.

Her speeches reveal that Mother Jones saw herself as an agitator and educator charged with the tasks of teaching the American working class about the nature of capitalism and mobilizing an international working-class movement. In 1909, she told the national convention of the UMWA that she was there to "wake you up." At a UMWA district convention in 1914 she explained, "I hold no office only that of disturbing." In 1920, near the end of her public speaking career, she summarized her mission: "I am busy getting this working man to understand what belongs to him, and his power to take possession of it."

Mother Jones was so effective at "disturbing" workers that corporate and government officials often went to great extremes to keep her from speak-

"Mother" Jones meets with President Coolidge in the fall of 1924.

ing. She was arrested many times, imprisoned, and forcefully escorted out of strike zones where she had been called to help organize. Her success as an educator is less easily documented, but her speeches and audience responses reveal a talented, tireless woman who was able to move people to action while instructing them about the nature of their conflicts and their place in history.

Conditions in mines and mining communities in the early 1900's were stark. Wages were low; mines were unsafe; rates of deaths and disabling injuries were very high; children were often employed. Miners lived in company-owned housing and were often paid in scrip, a substitute currency that could be redeemed only at company stores. If miners tried to improve their conditions through union organizing, they and their families were evicted from houses, and armed guards (often from the Baldwin-Felts detective agency) were hired by the companies to fight the organizing efforts.

In the face of these conditions Mother Jones devised a wide array of organizing strategies, as the

1897 UMWA strike at Turtle Creek near Pittsburgh illustrates. She spoke to ten thousand miners and sympathizers urging them to fight. Then she organized farmers in the region to provide food to strikers and escorted the farmers and their wagons to strike headquarters where the food was distributed. She called on neighborhood women to donate a "pound" of something to the cause and urged factory workers to come to miners' meetings and donate. As in many other strikes, Mother Jones made certain that women and children were actively involved and featured in national news coverage of the conflicts. At Turtle Creek, she organized wives of miners into groups of pickets and demonstrators and positioned the children of miners at the front of parades. In one parade fifty little girls marched with homemade banners, one of which read "Our Papas Aren't Scared."

Mother Jones was often in West Virginia in these early years of the twentieth century. In 1902, she worked in the southern coalfields, but she was successful in organizing only in the Paint Creek and

Cabin Creek areas near Charleston, the state capital. While trying to organize the northern part of the state, she was arrested and briefly imprisoned. For several years she traveled across the country to protest child labor, organize miners in the West, and support striking brewery workers, textile workers, copper miners, and smelter workers. Then in 1912 and 1913, once again working as a UMWA organizer, Mother Jones returned to West Virginia's southern coalfields. She faced down armed mine guards in order to allow union meetings and threatened to encourage West Virginia miners to arm themselves and fight back. She was imprisoned again, tried by a state military militia court, convicted of a charge of conspiracy to commit murder, and sentenced to prison for twenty years. She served eighty-five days, passing her eighty-fourth birthday in jail, before national public outcry and the promise of a congressional investigation prompted that state's newly elected governor to free her.

In her final organizing effort with West Virginia miners, Mother Jones attempted to halt the spontaneous 1921 march of thousands of miners on Logan. It was an unusual role for the aging firebrand, and she was not able to stop the march, later known as the "Battle of Blair Mountain." That bloody confrontation left many dead and injured. The determined coal miners proved powerless in the face of armed Baldwin-Felts detectives, the state militia, and the six thousand federal troops and twenty military airplanes sent by President Warren Harding to support the coal operators and prevent the union men from marching into non-union territory. The battle halted organizing efforts in West Virginia until national legislation authorized collective bargaining in 1932.

Organizing miners in Colorado was as difficult as in West Virginia. Mother Jones made her first visits there in 1903 soon after John D. Rockefeller, Sr., bought control of Colorado Iron and Fuel Company and the Victor Fuel Company. These early organizing efforts were not successful and led to a split between Jones and the UMWA leadership over organizing strategy. She did not return to the UMWA payroll until 1911.

In 1913, miners in southern Colorado went on strike for higher wages; an eight-hour day; coal weighing to be monitored by miners; free choice of stores, schools, doctors and boarding houses; enforcement of Colorado laws; and abolition of the mine guard system. Although most of these provisions were already law in Colorado, the state did not implement them in the southern fields. When the miners went on strike, they were evicted and lived in tent cities through the bitter cold Colorado winter.

Mother Jones joined the striking miners there in the fall of 1913, and returned in December and again in January. Between January and March of 1914, Jones, then in her early eighties, was arrested many times and spent more than a month in basement jail cells in Colorado. Refusing to be silenced, she smuggled out an open letter to the American people that was read and published across the country. She was not in Colorado in April when the state militia attacked the family tent camp, killing thirty-two, including many women and children. Subsequent state and national investigations into this incident, known as the Ludlow Massacre, were extremely critical of the actions of the governor, the state militia, and Colorado Iron and Fuel Company.

When Mother Jones wrote about her life she always identified her cause with the miners. After her death on November 30, 1930, she was buried as she had requested at the Miners Cemetery in Mount Olive, Illinois. A choir of coal miners sang her final tribute.

Summary

Mother Jones is remembered as a great labor agitator and a tremendously effective public speaker. Stories of her visits to coal camps, leadership at rallies and demonstrations, and confrontations with company and government officials are part of a living oral history of resistance in mining communities. Her memory continues to inspire the labor movement. When women mobilized in a 1989 UMWA strike against the Pittston Coal Group, they identified themselves as the "Daughters of Mother Jones" as they carried out actions in her name, such as occupying company headquarters and holding vigils outside jails where union officials were imprisoned.

The message of Mother Jones's life is that ordinary people, indeed unlikely people, can make important contributions to improving workers' lives. She was homeless and alone; she was poor and sometimes in prison; yet Mary Harris Jones used the resources she had—mind, voice, wit, spirit, and energy—to influence conditions for workers in America.

Bibliography

Fetherling, Dale. *Mother Jones, the Miners' Angel: A Portrait.* Carbondale: Southern Illinois University Press, 1974. This first full-scale biography on Jones presents a sympathetic yet balanced portrait.

Jones, Mother. *The Autobiography of Mother Jones.* Edited by Mary Field Parton. 3d ed. Chicago: Charles Kerr, 1974. First published in 1925; later editions (1972, 1974) add useful introductions. Insights into coal strikes, early twentieth century labor leadership, and Jones's spirit and personality; marred by inaccuracies and serious omissions.

————. *The Correspondence of Mother Jones.* Edited by Edward M. Steel. Pittsburgh: University of Pittsburgh Press, 1985. A collection of all known letters, notes, and telegrams (eight communications are added in Steel's 1988 collection of Jones's speeches and writings). Illustrates development of her political views over the course of her life.

————. *Mother Jones Speaks: Collected Writings and Speeches.* Edited by Philip S. Foner. New York: Monad Press, 1983. The most comprehensive work and best reference source in conveying the full range of Jones's intellect and activities. Includes speeches, testimony before congressional committees, articles, interviews, letters, an extensive bibliography, and historical background information.

————. *The Speeches and Writings of Mother Jones.* Edited by Edward M. Steel. Pittsburgh: University of Pittsburgh Press, 1988. Collection of thirty-one speeches believed to have been accurately recorded and transcribed in their entirety; also includes seventeen articles Jones penned for newspapers and socialist periodicals. A helpful "Biographical Notes" section identifies people in her speeches. A good introduction to her life with historical context for her speeches and activities.

Long, Priscilla. *Mother Jones, Woman Organizer: And Her Relations with Miners' Wives, Working Women, and the Suffrage Movement.* Boston: South End Press, 1976. Examines Jones's position as a female leader in the labor movement and her relationships with working class women and with women's rights organizations of her era.

Stepenoff, Bonnie. "Keeping It in the Family: Mother Jones and the Pennsylvania Silk Strike of 1900-1901." *Labor History* 38, no. 4 (Fall 1997). Examines Jones' participation in and impact on the Pennsylvania silk mill strike of 1901.

Tonn, Boor. "Militant Motherhood: Labor's Mary Harris 'Mother' Jones." *Quarterly Journal of Speech* 82, no. 1 (February, 1996). A case study of Jones that examines the relationship between radical labor union tactics and the symbolism of motherhood as employed by female labor leaders.

Sally Ward Maggard

JANIS JOPLIN

Born: January 19, 1943; Port Arthur, Texas
Died: October 3, 1970; Hollywood, California
Area of Achievement: Music
Contribution: Janis Joplin, one of the prime movers in the evolution of rock 'n' roll, demonstrated that white women were capable of singing with as much emotional intensity as that of great black singers such as Bessie Smith.

Early Life

Janis Joplin was born in Port Arthur, Texas, on January 19, 1943. Her father worked as a mechanical engineer and her mother was a registrar at a business college. In spite of her conventional family background, Janis was a rebel from an early age. As a teenager, she withdrew from high-school social life and spent much of her time listening to the music of black artists such as Leadbelly, Bessie Smith, and Odetta. Her taste in reading, like her taste in music, set her apart from her peers.

Port Arthur is in the heart of the Texas Bible Belt. Janis acquired such a reputation in this ultraconservative community that the citizens were still speaking of her in horrified whispers years after her death. Even while still in junior high school, she scandalized the townspeople with her sexual promiscuity. Her classmates rejected her and called her filthy names; they threw pennies at her as a way of symbolizing that they considered her a whore. Janis felt badly hurt by this rejection, but she built a façade of individualism and indifference which was to remain her outstanding characteristic.

It is evident that Janis was overcompensating for feelings of inferiority resulting in part from being overweight, feeling physically unattractive, and being harshly criticized by her mother. Janis had an insatiable craving for love and belonging which was partly responsible for her legendary sexual promiscuity in later life as well as her consumption of liquor, marijuana, and heroin.

At seventeen, she left home with the intention of earning a living with her voice. She hitchhiked around the country, scraping up money by getting short-term jobs as a folksinger. Eventually, she made it to California, where she attended several colleges but was never graduated. In California, she lived in hippie communes, indulged in group sex, and was introduced to new kinds of drugs.

This was the very beginning of the 1960's, which will always have a place in American history as a period of youthful rebellion against the beliefs and traditions of older generations. At first, Janis found the undisciplined lifestyle of California too much for her, and she returned to Texas to try to live a conventional life. She realized, however, that she had outgrown Port Arthur completely, and she went back to the West Coast.

The most important event in her life occurred when she was asked to become the "chick singer" with a new San Francisco rock 'n' roll group called Big Brother and the Holding Company.

Life's Work

Big Brother and the Holding Company has its place in popular music history because of its connection with the dynamic Janis Joplin. Her first public appearance with this group was at the Avalon Ballroom in San Francisco on June 10, 1966. She was twenty-three years old but had done more living than many people do in their lifetimes.

Partly because of her early adulation of the great Bessie Smith, Joplin had developed the ability to put her heart and soul into her singing. She was also gifted with a voice that had an enormous range and variety of tones. Big Brother and the Holding Company's instrumentalists helped her to discover her true niche as a singer, and in turn she helped the musicians to define themselves as a group.

Joplin's performance at the Monterey Pop Festival in the summer of 1967 is legendary. She electrified the huge audience with the intensity of her performance. Older, much better known groups were totally overshadowed by the dynamic new sound. Music critics were unanimous in their enthusiastic praise of this new female vocalist.

Joplin attained national stardom in 1968 with the release of *Cheap Thrills*, her second album with Big Brother and the Holding Company. The album hit number one on the best-seller charts and stayed there for eight weeks. Janis made a clean sweep of *Jazz and Pop* magazine's awards, winning the International Critics Poll for Best Female Vocal Album and Best Female Pop Singer as well as the magazine's Reader's Poll for Best Female Pop Singer. Yet Joplin had developed an insatiable lust for success. She was no longer satisfied with the musicians who were backing her up, and she announced that she was leaving them to form her own backup group.

Janis was a victim of a scourge that has destroyed the lives of many popular musicians. When musicians speak of the rigors of the "music scene," they are referring not only to the music but also to the destructive lifestyle that goes with it, including drinking, drugs, and association with a criminal element that is attracted to nightclubs and bars. Among these criminals are those who make their living selling illicit drugs, and they are forever trying to recruit new customers. At first, Janis used heroin because she thought it inspired her to be more creative and uninhibited. Ultimately, she was killed by her use of the same drug that destroyed the lives of such great musicians as Charlie Parker and Elvis Presley.

Joplin was one of the star attractions of the Woodstock Music and Art Fair in 1969, and she had a huge success when she toured Europe. At the end of 1969, she won *Jazz and Pop* magazine's International Critics Poll, which named her Best Female Pop Singer for the year. Ironically, as her career skyrocketed, she became more and more depressed and self-destructive.

Just a few days before her death, Joplin attended a reunion of her high-school class at Port Arthur. She expected to return in triumph to the people who had made her so unhappy as a teenager; however, she found that most of the narrow-minded townspeople were unimpressed by her success and still despised her for her hedonistic lifestyle. This disappointment had a powerful impact on the singer and may have led to her death. On Sunday, October 3, 1970, her body was discovered in the Landmark Hotel in Hollywood. The autopsy confirmed the story that was already apparent from the hypodermic needle marks all over both of her arms: She had died of an overdose of heroin.

Janis Joplin's best and most successful record album, *Pearl* (her nickname), was released shortly after her death. It immediately placed number one on the *Billboard* chart. Her rendition of "Me and Bobby McGee," written by Kris Kristofferson, was also released as a single and reached number one in that category as well. It remains her most famous song. The royalties from those two records would have made her a millionaire if she had lived.

Eighteen years after Joplin's death, her picture appeared on the cover of *Time* magazine. The *Time* article states, "Janis Joplin expressed one side of 1968 fairly well: ecstatic and self-destructive simultaneously, wailing to the edges of the universe." Janis was to become the symbol of the "sixties generation" in her music, her lifestyle, her language, her clothing and hairstyle, and unfortunately in her self-destructive use of drugs and alcohol.

Summary

In her short lifetime, Janis Joplin was one of the foremost personalities in defining the so-called sixties generation, a generation that made a more powerful impact on popular culture than has any other generation before or since. She was one of a very few women to make it to superstardom in the male-dominated world of popular music. Called "the high priestess of the rock scene," Joplin was a leader in asserting women's right to sexual freedom. She helped to popularize a new kind of liberated music—a fusion of blues, country-western, and other styles—that has since become the leading wave of popular music around the world. Millions of young women imitated her behavior and her highly individualistic clothing styles, outraging their parents and forcing the older generation to re-examine its traditional attitudes.

Joplin, like many of her youthful contemporaries, was opposed to the undeclared war the United States was waging in Vietnam because it involved ecological devastation and indiscriminate slaughter of women and children. She hated racial discrimination and regarded American involvement in Vietnam as a form of neocolonialism.

The unrest of the 1960's was largely a result of the feeling that the world was doomed to inevitable destruction by atomic holocaust and that the war in Vietnam was only a prelude to the final disaster. The United States and the Soviet Union continued adding to their atomic arsenals until both nations possessed enough of the weapons to destroy humanity several times over. As one of the leaders of the so-called youth rebellion of the 1960's, Joplin was instrumental in forcing the federal government to look for a way out of a conflict that was tearing the country apart.

One of Joplin's greatest contributions to the cause of women was that she demonstrated that women not only could be electrifying performers but also could lead bands, create new and innovative styles, and generate huge incomes, all while living the lifestyles they wished to live. After Joplin's tremendous success, record companies became more willing to give promising women the opportunity to achieve a high level of commercial success and artistic control.

Unfortunately, the fun-loving, high-spirited young singer also set a bad example for millions of young women with her use of drugs and alcohol. This bad influence went all the way down through high school and even affected junior high school students, who erroneously believed that the drinking and drug abuse were somehow connected with the music they loved.

Joplin's death from an overdose of heroin served as an object lesson to many of her admirers; the consumption of heroin in the United States decreased dramatically after her death. Like the deaths of other folk heroes of the period, including comedian Lenny Bruce, Janis Joplin's death served as a grim reminder that substance abuse destroys youth and talent without pity. "If you think you need stuff to play music or sing, you're crazy," said Billie Holiday, one of America's greatest singers. "It can fix you so you can't play nothing or sing nothing."

Bibliography

Amburn, Ellis. *Pearl: The Obsessions and Passions of Janis Joplin.* New York: Warner, 1992; London: Warner, 1994. This is the best available full-length biography of Joplin. Discusses her early childhood, her development as a vocalist, her numerous love affairs with both men and women, and her self-destructive lifestyle. Contains an excellent bibliography. Thoroughly indexed. Contains many photographic illustrations of Joplin and friends, including one famous picture of Joplin in the nude.

Caserta, Peggy, as told to Dan Knapp. *Going Down with Janis.* Secaucus, N.J.: Lyle Stuart, 1973; London: Futura, 1975. An intentionally shocking book about Janis Joplin's private life, especially her use of drugs and her lesbian sexual activities, written by a woman with whom she had a long-term relationship.

Dalton, David. *Piece of My Heart: The Life, Times and Legend of Janis Joplin.* New York: St. Martin's Press, 1985; London: Sidgwick and Jackson, 1986. A collection of interviews and personal impressions by a friend who accompanied Joplin on many of her tours. Written in the informal, expressionistic style characteristic of "New Journalism."

Echols, Alice. *Scars of Sweet Paradise: The Life and Times of Janis Joplin*. New York: Holt/Metropolitan, 1999. A well-balanced, in-depth look at Joplin's life, based on primary sources and interviews with survivors of her turbulent times.

Friedman, Myra. *Buried Alive*. New York: Morrow, 1973; London: Allen, 1974. An early biography written by a woman who was Joplin's press agent and close personal friend. This deeply moving work explains Joplin's manic, self-destructive behavior as a compensation for the fact that the singer believed she was ugly and unlovable (she had been nominated for "Ugliest Man on Campus" at the University of Texas).

Joplin, Laura. "Love, Janis." *Rolling Stone*, no. 638 (September 3, 1992): 55-57. An article based on a collection of letters written by Janis Joplin to members of her family during the 1960's. Laura Joplin is Janis' sister.

Marshall, Jim. "Red Hot Mama." *Harper's Bazaar*, no. 3446 (January, 1999). A profile of Joplin that includes her views on her life and career.

Wakefield, Dan. "Kosmic Blues." *Atlantic* 232 (September, 1973): 108-113. A highly intelligent, eulogistic article about Janis Joplin based on a review of two published biographies: *Going Down with Janis* and *Buried Alive*.

Wolf, Mark. "The Uninhibited Janis Joplin." *Down Beat* 56 (September, 1989): 65-66. A good profile of Janis Joplin that covers her life from her childhood in Port Arthur up to the time she joined Big Brother and the Holding Company in San Francisco. Contains illustrations of historical interest.

Bill Delaney

BARBARA JORDAN

Born: February 21, 1936; Houston, Texas

Died: January 17, 1996; Austin Texas

Areas of Achievement: Government and politics, law, and education

Contribution: The first African American elected to the Texas Senate since Reconstruction, Barbara Jordan went on to become a member of the U.S. House of Representatives. She mesmerized the nation during televised coverage of the House Judiciary Committee's investigation considering the impeachment of President Richard Nixon.

Early Life

On February 21, 1936, Barbara Charline Jordan was born to Benjamin Jordan, a warehouse clerk and part-time clergyman, and his wife, Arlyne Patten Jordan, in Houston, Texas. Barbara was raised in a time of segregation and Jim Crow laws. She lived with her parents, her two older sisters, Bennie and Rose Marie, and her grandfathers, John Ed Patten and Charles Jordan.

Barbara's outlook on life as well as her strength and determination can be attributed to the influence of her maternal grandfather, John Ed Patten, a former minister who was also a businessman. While assisting him in his junk business, Barbara learned to be self-sufficient, strong-willed, and independent, and she was encouraged not to settle for mediocrity. Her determination to achieve superiority was quickly demonstrated in her early years.

Barbara spent most of her free time with her grandfather Patten, who served as her mentor. They would converse about all kinds of subjects. His advice was followed and appreciated by the young girl, who adoringly followed him every Sunday as he conducted his business. He instilled in her a belief in the importance of education. Every action, every aspect of life, he stated, was to be learned from and experienced.

With her grandfather's advice in mind, Barbara embraced life and education. She showed herself to be an exemplary student while attending Phillis Wheatley High School in Houston. A typical teenager, Barbara was active in school clubs and other extracurricular activities. She also led an active social life during her years at Phillis Wheatley. It was during her high school years that Barbara was inspired to become a lawyer. She was drawn to the legal profession during a career day presentation by the prominent African American attorney Edith Sampson. Moved by Sampson's speech, Barbara became determined to investigate law as a possible area of study.

Barbara received many awards during her high school years, particularly for her talent as an orator. Her skill in this area was rewarded in 1952, when she won first place in the Texas State Ushers Oratorical Contest. As part of her victory package, she was sent to Illinois to compete in the national championships. She won the national oration contest in Chicago that same year.

The year 1952 began a new stage in Barbara Jordan's education. She was admitted to Texas Southern University after her graduation from high school. It was here that she truly excelled in oration. She joined the Texas Southern debate team and won many tournaments under the guidance and tutelage of her debate coach, Tom Freeman. He was also influential in urging her to attend Boston University Law School. At law school, she was one of two African American women in the graduating class of 1959; they were the only women to be graduated that year. Before 1960, Jordan managed to pass the Massachusetts and Texas Bar examinations. Such a feat was an enviable one. She was offered a law position in the state of Massachusetts, but she declined the offer.

Jordan's impoverished background seemed far behind her. With the continued support of her parents and grandfathers, she opened a private law practice in Houston, Texas, in 1960. She volunteered her services to the Kennedy-Johnson presidential campaign. She organized the black constituents in the black precincts of her county. Her efforts were successful. The voter turnout was the largest Harris County had ever experienced. Jordan's participation in such a history-making event demonstrated her talents for persuasion and organization. These skills, coupled with her education and intellect, were to become her assets in all her future endeavors. The political career of Barbara Jordan was born as a result of the Kennedy-Johnson victory of 1960.

Life's Work

The decade of the 1960's witnessed Barbara Jordan's emergence in the political arena. The 1960's were a period of transition and hope in American history. With the election of the first Catholic president and the epic changes brought on by the Civil Rights movement, it was a time of change. Jordan was determined to be part of that change. After becoming the speaker for the Harris County Democratic Party, she ran for the Texas House of Representatives in 1962 and 1964. She lost on both occasions. Undeterred, Jordan ran for a third time in the newly reapportioned Harris County. She became one of two African Americans elected to the newly reapportioned eleventh district. Jordan was elected to the Texas state senate. She became the first black since 1883 and the first woman ever to hold the position.

Jordan impressed the state senate members with her intelligence, oration, and ability to fit in with the "old boys' club." She remained in the state senate for six years, until 1972. During her tenure, she worked on legislation dealing with the environment, establishing minimum wage standards, and eliminating discrimination in business contracts. She was encouraged to run for a congressional seat. She waged a campaign in 1971 for the U.S. Congress. While completing her term of office on the state level, Jordan achieved another first: In 1972, she was elected to the U.S. House of Representatives. Jordan served briefly as acting governor of Texas on June 10, 1972, when both the governor and lieutenant governor were out of the state. As president pro tem of the Texas senate, it was one of her duties to act as governor when the situation warranted. Despite his being present for all of her earlier achievements, Jordan's father did not live to see her take office as a member of the U.S. House of Representatives. He died on June 11, 1972, in Austin, Texas. His demise spurred Jordan to continue her work.

Having already caught the attention of Lyndon B. Johnson while a member of the Texas state senate, Jordan sought his advice on the type of committees to join. She became a member of the Judiciary and the Ways and Means committees. Little did she know that the Judiciary Committee would evolve into a major undertaking. Jordan's membership in the House of Representatives was to be one of the many highlights of her political career.

The 1974 Watergate scandal gave Jordan national prominence. Her speech in favor of President Richard Nixon's impeachment was nothing short of oratorical brilliance. Her eloquence was considered memorable and thought-provoking. Her expertise as an attorney was demonstrated in 1974

when she spoke about the duty of elected officials to their constituents and the United States Constitution. Despite her personal distaste for an impeachment, Jordan insisted that President Nixon be held accountable for the Watergate fiasco. A Senate investigation, she believed, was warranted. Her televised speech was the center of media attention and critique for days to come. She sustained her reputation for eloquence during the 1976 Democratic National Convention. During her tenure in the House, she introduced bills dealing with civil rights, crime, business, and free competition as well as an unprecedented plan of payment for housewives for the labor and services they provide. Jordan's popularity was at its zenith when talk of her running for the vice presidency was rampant among her supporters. She shrugged off the suggestion, stating that the time was not right.

It was discovered in 1976 that Jordan suffered from knee problems. The ailment was visible during her keynote address when she was helped to the podium to give her speech. She admitted that she was having problems with her patella. The cartilage in one knee made it difficult and painful for her to walk or stand for long. Her brilliant oration was not hampered by her muscle weakness during the delivery of her speech in 1976. She opted not to run for reelection in 1978 and entered the educational field.

During his presidency, Jimmy Carter offered Jordan a post in his cabinet. Political rumor persists that she would have preferred the position of attorney general to Carter's suggestion of the post of secretary of the Department of Health, Education, and Welfare. Since Carter was firm in his offer, Jordan opted to refuse the offer rather than settle for something she did not want. Such an attitude is indicative of her childhood training and upbringing.

Jordan was offered and took a teaching post at the University of Texas in Austin. She taught at the Lyndon Baines Johnson School of Public Affairs. In addition to her instructional duties, she also held the positions of faculty adviser and recruiter for minority students. She continued to hold these positions into the early 1990's. In addition, Governor Ann Richards of Texas appointed her to serve as an adviser on ethics in government.

Barbara Jordan received innumerable honorary degrees. Universities such as Princeton and Harvard bestowed honorary doctorates upon her. She received awards touting her as the best living orator. She was one of the most influential women in the world as well as one of the most admired. She was a member of the Texas Women's Hall of Fame and hosted her own television show. At the 1988 Democratic National Convention, Jordan gave a speech nominating Senator Lloyd Bentsen as the party's vice presidential candidate. She delivered the speech from the wheelchair she used as a result of her battle with multiple sclerosis. In 1992, she received the prized Spingarn Medal, which is awarded by the National Association for the Advancement of Colored People (NAACP) for service to the African American community.

Summary

Barbara Jordan's rise from poverty to prominence through diligence and perseverance in the fields of law, politics, and education is a model for others to follow. During an interview on the Black Entertainment Television channel in February of 1993, Jordan maintained that circumstances of birth, race, or creed should not inhibit an individual from succeeding if he or she wishes to achieve greatness. As an individual who was born poor, black, and female, Jordan demonstrated the truth of her assertion, and her life is a portrait of success highlighted by a series of significant "firsts" and breakthroughs.

In 1984, Jordan was voted "Best Living Orator" and elected to the Texas Women's Hall of Fame. Her honorary doctorates from Princeton and Harvard substantiate her dedication to education and excellence. As a black female from the South, Jordan broke one barrier after the other. She maintained her integrity and dignity while in political office. Her defense of the U.S. Constitution during the Watergate era as well as her dedication to the field of education continues to be an example to those entering the field of law and education.

Jordan denied that her life's achievements were extraordinary. Her modesty was part of her upbringing. She endeavored to live a life that she believed would benefit the country. One of the reasons she refused to run for reelection in 1978 was her need to serve more than a "few" constituents in her district. She wished to serve them in addition to the masses. As she stated in her resignation: "I feel more of a responsibility to the country as a whole, as contrasted with the duty of representing the half-million in the Eighteenth Congressional District." She maintained that anyone may succeed with the proper attitude. Early in her political career, she made a conscious choice not to marry. Like Susan B. Anthony, Jordan believed that marriage would be a distraction from the cause to which she was drawn. In 1978, Jordan believed that her legislative role and effectiveness had ceased and that her most effective role in the global community was in the field of instruction. A new challenge presented itself, and Jordan was eager to confront it.

Despite the effects of her long illness, Jordan demontrated that race, socioeconomic status, and societal barriers may be overcome and dispelled as roadblocks to success. She gave interviews, lectures, and commencement addresses almost up to the time of her death in 1996.

Bibliography

Browne, Ray B. *Contemporary Heroes and Heroines.* Detroit: Gale Research, 1990. A collection of biographical profiles on men and women who have made major contributions to American life. Includes a fine piece on Barbara Jordan and her career.

Famous Blacks Give Secrets of Success. Vol. 2 in *Ebony Success Library.* Chicago: Johnson, 1973.

A collection documenting the lives and achievements of black luminaries. The excerpt on Barbara Jordan traces her political achievements through 1973.

Jordan, Barbara, and Shelby Hearn. *Barbara Jordan: A Self-Portrait*. New York: Doubleday, 1979. Jordan's autobiography traces her life from childhood to her political career in the U.S. House of Representatives.

Moss, J. Jennings. "Barbara Jordan: The Other Life." *Advocate*, no. 702 (March 5, 1996). Discusses Jordan's secret life as a lesbian and the difficulties she encountered as a result.

Ries, Paula, and Anne J. Stone, eds. *The American Woman: 1992-93*. New York: Norton, 1992. This book is one in a series of reports documenting the social, economic, and political status of American women. Includes profiles and articles on Jordan as well as female political contemporaries such as Governor Ann Richards of Texas and Senator Nancy Kassebaum of Kansas.

Rogers, Mary Beth. *Barbara Jordan: American Hero*. New York: Bantam, 1998. Inspiring biographical study of Jordan by Rogers, a colleague of Jordan's at the Lyndon B. Johnson School of Public Affairs in Austin, Texas.

United States House of Representatives. Commission on the Bicentenary. *Women in Congress, 1917-1990*. Washington, D.C.: Government Printing Office, 1991. Compiled to honor the bicentennial of the U.S. House of Representatives, this work provides biographical sketches of the various women who have served in Congress, beginning with Jeannette Rankin in 1917 and continuing through the women serving in 1990.

Annette Marks-Ellis

JAMES JOYCE

Born: February 2, 1882; Dublin, Ireland
Died: January 13, 1941; Zurich, Switzerland
Area of Achievement: Literature
Contribution: Author of the germinal modernist novels *Ulysses* and *Finnegans Wake*, Joyce played a central role in the development of the mystique of the inaccessible artist and helped define the course of twentieth century culture.

Early Life

Although James Joyce spent his adult life in self-imposed exile, his sensibility and writing remained firmly grounded in Ireland. Born in Dublin on February 2, 1882, Joyce experienced the tensions of Irish culture and politics in his immediate family. In addition to a politically motivated distrust of the clergy, John Joyce imparted to his son a gift for storytelling, a tendency toward excessive drinking, and an inability to cope with financial matters. In contrast, Mary Murray Joyce, a devout Catholic, provided the oldest of her ten children with a consistent source of love which was particularly important given the decline in family finances, accompanied by frequent changes of residence, which was to continue throughout his childhood. The tensions within the Joyce family came to a head over the Home Rule movement headed by Charles Stewart Parnell, who was denounced from the pulpit after being accused of adultery. What both father and son saw as Parnell's betrayal— Joyce was to identify strongly with the fallen leader throughout his life—inspired Joyce's first literary production, a political satire which his father distributed to friends.

With the exception of a brief stay at the Christian Brothers' School, Joyce was educated almost entirely by Jesuits, at Clongowes Wood College, at Belvedere College, and finally at University College, Dublin, from which he was graduated in 1902. Although he was to reject most of the specific teachings of his Jesuit masters, Joyce maintained a respect for their intellectual rigor. The broad-based knowledge of classical authors—particularly the aesthetic speculations of Saint Thomas Aquinas—and the knowledge of languages which Joyce first developed under the Jesuits were to prove essential to his literary development. Of equal importance were the long walks which provided the encyclopedic knowledge of Dublin geography, and social life, so important to his later works.

During Joyce's youth, Dublin had developed an important literary community revolving around slightly older writers including William Butler Yeats, George Moore, Æ (George Russell), and Lady Gregory. Joyce was both interested in and aloof from what came to be known as the Irish Literary Renaissance. Following the riots over Yeats's play *The Countess Cathleen* (1892) in 1899, Joyce defended Yeats against the widespread Catholic and nationalist outrage. Nevertheless, distancing himself from what he saw as the mysticism and the provincialism of the Irish Literary Renaissance, Joyce chose to model his own early work after the example of Continental realism, particularly the work of Norwegian playwright Henrik Ibsen. Although the dialogue may be apocryphal, Joyce was widely believed to have told Yeats on their first meeting (which Joyce instigated) in 1904, "You are too old for me to help you." A similar confidence emerges in a letter to Ibsen on his seventy-third birthday in which Joyce cryptically announces himself as a new presence waiting to assume the master's role in European letters.

Beginning in 1902, Joyce began to prepare for the physical exile he found essential to a clear vision of his native country. Both photographs and descriptions dating from this period portray a tall, thin young man who maintains a somewhat distant and aloof expression. His first trip to Paris, where he was ostensibly studying medicine, was brought to an end by his mother's terminal illness. Asserting his artistic independence from strictures of religion, nation, and family, Joyce refused to honor his mother's deathbed wish that he take communion. Remaining in Dublin through most of 1904, Joyce began work on his first published literary works. The year was marked by several personal events of immense importance to his later development. A brief residence at the Martello Tower with his friend and rival Oliver St. John Gogarty—the Buck Mulligan of Joyce's fiction—provided a substantial amount of the material incorporated into *Ulysses* (1922). The story of a single day, *Ulysses* takes place on June 16, 1904, the day of Joyce's first extended meeting with Nora Barnacle, who was to be his lifelong companion and the mother of his two children. Armed with his chosen weapons of "silence, exile, and cunning" and accompanied by

Nora (whom he was not to marry legally until 1931), Joyce set off in late 1904 to pursue his literary destiny on the Continent.

Life's Work

Two interrelated themes—one aesthetic, the other financial—dominate Joyce's career. Even as he wrote the books that established him as a major modernist author, he struggled with only intermittent success to provide a comfortable level of support for his family. With the exception of brief stays in Pola (1904-1905) and Rome (1906-1907), Joyce spent the first decade of his exile in Trieste, an Austrian port city with Italian traditions and sympathies. There, Joyce taught English both privately and in association with the Berlitz School. With the aid of his brother Stanislaus, Joyce managed to maintain his growing family; a son Giorgio was born in 1905, a daughter Lucia in 1907. Stanislaus also served as an underappreciated, but invaluable, intellectual foil and critic for the drafts of *Dubliners* (1914) and *A Portrait of the Artist as a Young Man* (1916), which were written primarily in Trieste. An essentially realistic portrayal of Dublin life, *Dubliners* was accepted for publication in 1906, but objections from editors and printers delayed publication until 1914. Although there is little in any of Joyce's books likely to outrage late twentieth century taste, Joyce expended a large amount of energy throughout his life resisting attempts to censor his writing. The skirmishes over *Dubliners* anticipate the landmark American trial of *Ulysses*, which John M. Woolsey cleared of charges of obscenity in 1933, thus supporting the right of artists to treat material which in some contexts might be deemed obscene.

The recognition of Joyce as a significant writer can be dated to 1913, the beginning of a valuable, if not always smooth, friendship with the American poet Ezra Pound. Instrumental in furthering Joyce's career both aesthetically and financially, Pound initiated a correspondence and shortly thereafter established contacts between Joyce and *Egoist* editor Dora Marsden, who accepted *A Portrait of the Artist as a Young Man* for serial publication, and Harriet Weaver, who provided Joyce with an extraordinary amount of financial patronage and intellectual support over nearly four decades. By the time his family was relocated to Zurich, where they would remain throughout World War I, Joyce was on the verge of his first real literary success. *Dubliners* had finally been published;

A Portrait of the Artist as a Young Man was received favorably when it was published in late 1916. When the first chapters of *Ulysses* began appearing in reviews in 1918, Joyce was widely recognized as something more than an interesting experimental writer on the fringes of a diffuse literary movement.

His celebrity increasing even before the appearance of *Ulysses* in book form, Joyce moved to Paris in 1920. In addition to fighting the charges of obscenity which again delayed publication, Joyce expanded his literary contacts in a milieu which brought together disaffected artists from throughout Europe and the Americas. Bolstered by the positive responses of French writers such as Valéry Larbaud, who delivered one of the first public lectures on his work, Joyce actively encouraged detailed critical examination of his work. Over the next two decades, he would encourage, and at times direct, Stuart Gilbert, Frank Budgen, and Herbert Gorman in the writing of books which established the "Joyce mystique" in its early form. Sometime in 1923, Joyce also began work on *Finnegans Wake* (known prior to publication as "Work in Progress"), a project which would command his attention for the next fifteen years and would finally be published in 1939.

Despite his literary celebrity and a degree of financial security derived primarily from Weaver's patronage, the years following the publication of *Ulysses* were on the whole difficult for the Joyce family. Plagued from childhood by poor eyesight, Joyce's health problems worsened steadily. In Zurich, he had undergone the first of a continuing sequence of operations to protect his remaining sight and relieve the pain which would sometimes render him incapable of working for extended periods. In addition, Joyce's literary career did not develop smoothly. Responding to the widespread perception that *Finnegans Wake* was little more than a literary curiosity unworthy of the author of *Ulysses*, Joyce quarreled with Pound, Wyndham Lewis, and others. His growing sense of isolation was exacerbated by the severe mental problems of his daughter Lucia, who was ultimately institutionalized for schizophrenia. Intensely devoted to his daughter, and apparently seeing her difficulties as a reflection of his own genius, Joyce refused to acknowledge the severity of her problem and quarreled with friends who refused to endorse his interpretation of events. Ultimately, Joyce broke even with Weaver, whom he accused without justification of having

withheld support from Lucia and from his work. Taking place under the gathering shadows of World War II, which diverted attention from aesthetic events in 1939, the long-awaited publication of *Finnegans Wake* was something of an anticlimactic event for Joyce. Despite his general disdain for political issues, Joyce was inevitably affected by political events. Having aided several Jews, including the novelist Hermann Broch, in their escape from Nazi territory, Joyce finally succeeded in relocating his family to Zurich shortly after the fall of Paris in 1940. There, Joyce died unexpectedly of a perforated ulcer early in 1941.

Summary

The defining aspect of James Joyce's immense influence on the development of twentieth century literature is its diffuse nature. Particularly in *Ulysses* and *Finnegans Wake*, Joyce provided sufficient material to fuel passionate attacks and defenses from nearly every position on the aesthetic and/or political spectrum. Rather than attempt to communicate a specific determinate vision of "reality," Joyce shifted attention to the complexity of aesthetic processes. Anticipating central concerns of a wide range of later experimental expression—Joyce has fascinated composers and visual artists as well as writers—Joyce contributed directly to a far-reaching redefinition of the relationship between audience, artist, and the work of art.

Joyce's personal example both complements and contradicts the contents of his books. Grounded in the semiautobiographical portraits in *A Portrait of the Artist as a Young Man* and *Ulysses*, Joyce's personal mystique has been cited as inspiration by many later writers, particularly in their phases of youthful rebellion. As a result, the image of the writer as a distinctly aloof, frequently arrogant "priest of the eternal imagination" has attached itself strongly to the public perception of Joyce. Combined with the stylistic complexity of his work, this image reinforces the common perception of avant-garde art as irrelevant and/or indifferent to daily life.

The irony of this image emerges when it is juxtaposed to the content of *Ulysses* and *Finnegans Wake*, both of which celebrate aspects of reality—including physiological processes such as eating and defecating—which, prior to Joyce, had been dismissed as too trivial to command the attention of the serious artist. The story of a single day in Dublin, *Ulysses* focuses on the external wanderings and internal thoughts of three central characters, none of whom emerges as more important or valuable than the others: the "Joycean" artist Stephen Dedalus; the outwardly undistinguished middle-class Dubliner Leopold Bloom; and his wife, Molly, who is committing adultery, probably for the first time. Joyce's exhaustive treatment of the Dublin landscape—almost every location can be verified—and internal consciousness pushed preexisting literary tendencies to extremes, establishing an imposing point of reference for later writers. Of equal importance was Joyce's use of what T. S. Eliot called the "mythic method." Suggesting an underlying parallel between the lives of his characters and those of the classical heroes, Joyce was the most important early exemplar of a technique which has been employed widely in both "serious" and "popular" culture. Again blending extreme erudition and "trivial" ephemera, Joyce intended *Finnegans Wake* as a "night book" dealing with the subconscious dream life subordinated in his "day book," *Ulysses*. Noteworthy for its multilingual puns—any inventive style of speech is still likely to be labeled "Joycean"—*Finnegans Wake* has been viewed both as an incomprehensible nightmare of self-indulgence and as a liberating, and hilarious, statement of human unity. Just as *Ulysses* provided a central reference for the "symbolic" approach to literary studies which dominated the 1960's, *Finnegans Wake* has emerged as a central text in the continental theoretical movements which seek to "deconstruct"—to reveal the limitations and arbitrariness of—"normal" modes of interpretation or expression. It is part of the paradoxical nature of Joyce's achievement that his books have repeatedly been summoned as evidence by both sides in a continuing sequence of heated cultural battles over the nature and heritage of modernism.

Bibliography

Bowen, Zack, and James F. Carens, eds. *A Companion to Joyce Studies.* Westport, Conn.: Greenwood Press, 1984. A collection of essays by a range of established critics summarizing various aspects of Joyce studies. Since Joyce has attracted a vast amount of critical attention, this volume provides a valuable starting place for work on specific topics.

Brown, Malcolm. *The Politics of Irish Literature: From Thomas Davis to W. B. Yeats.* London: Allen and Unwin, and Seattle: University of

Washington Press, 1972. Provides a clear overview of the Irish context of Joyce's writing. More important for its comments on Joyce's contemporaries and on the Irish political tradition than for its direct commentary on his writing.

Ellmann, Richard. *James Joyce*. Rev. ed. Oxford and New York: Oxford University Press, 1982. One of the great literary biographies. Ellmann provides an exhaustive record of the events of Joyce's life, which provides the groundwork for all serious scholarship concerning his major works. Particularly valuable for its insights into Joyce's relationship with Ireland and with his literary contemporaries.

Gilbert, Stuart. *James Joyce's "Ulysses": A Study*. Rev. ed. London: Faber, and New York: Vintage, 1952. Written under Joyce's personal supervision, this idiosyncratic study provides much of the raw material on which later interpretations have been based. Notable for the detailed development of the "scheme" of correspondences underlying the surface details.

Kenner, Hugh. *The Pound Era*. Berkeley: University of California Press, 1971; London: Faber, 1972. The best overall presentation of the dynamics of the part of the modernist movement with which Joyce was most closely associated. A respected critic who has written several books specifically on Joyce, Kenner highlights the subtle differences, as well as the general connections, between Joyce and his contemporaries.

Lawrence, Karen R., ed. *Transcultural Joyce*. Cambridge and New York: Cambridge University Press, 1998. Several noted scholars evaluate the place of Joyce's work in a multinational context. Includes analysis of Joyce's impact on literature and discussion of the difficulty involved in translating his works into other languages.

Levin, Harry. *James Joyce*. Rev. ed. London: Faber, and New York: New Directions, 1960. The first comprehensive scholarly study of Joyce's career, Levin's book remains the best overall introduction. Stresses the polarity between the artist and the city as the crucial tension explored in diverse ways in Joyce's four works of fiction.

Peake, Charles H. *James Joyce: The Citizen and the Artist*. Stanford, Calif.: Stanford University Press, and London: Arnold, 1977. A balanced overview of the tension between Joyce's sense of artistic autonomy and his sense of civic responsibility. A good contemporary synthesis of previous critical insights.

Riquelme, John Paul. *Teller and Tale in Joyce's Fiction: Oscillating Perspectives*. Baltimore: Johns Hopkins University Press, 1983. An intelligent and reasonably accessible application of contemporary critical theory to Joyce's work. Examines the implications of the narrative devices employed in each of the major works.

Vanderham, Paul. *James Joyce and Censorship: The Trials of Ulysses*. New York: New York University Press, 1997; London: Macmillan, 1998. An entertaining study of the Ulysses trials that includes important analysis of the impact the decisions have had on the law itself.

Craig Werner

CARL JUNG

Born: July 26, 1875; Kesswil, Switzerland
Died: June 6, 1961; Küssnacht, Switzerland
Area of Achievement: Psychology
Contribution: Jung, the founder of analytic psychology, is probably best known for his descriptions of the orientations of the personality, "extroversion" and "introversion." His theories of universal symbolic representations have had a far-reaching impact on such diverse disciplines as art, literature, filmmaking, religion, anthropology, and history.

Early Life

Carl Gustav Jung was descended from a long line of physicians and theologians. His father, Johann Paul Achilles Jung, was a pastor of the Swiss Reformed church, as were eight of his uncles. His mother, Emilie Preiswerk, suffered from a nervous disorder which often made her remote and uncommunicative; his father was reportedly irritable and argumentative. Since his parents were of little comfort or support to him as a child, and since his sister, Johanna Gertrud, was born nine years after he was, Jung spent much of his childhood alone. Jung's adolescence was a time of confusion and probing, especially about religious matters. His religious conflicts, however, were eventually supplanted by other intellectual interests. Before concentrating on the study of medicine at the University of Basel in 1895, he explored biology, archaeology, philosophy, mythology, and mysticism, subjects which laid the foundation for the wide-ranging inquiries he undertook throughout his life.

After receiving his degree in medicine, Jung decided to specialize in psychiatry. Consequently, in 1900 he went to the Burghölzli, the mental hospital and university psychiatry clinic in Zurich, where he studied under the famous psychiatrist Eugen Bleuler. While working at the Burghölzli, Jung published his first papers on clinical topics, as well as several papers on his first experimental project—the use of word-association tests (free association). This was a project which he pioneered and which later gained for him worldwide recognition. Jung concluded that the word-association process could uncover groups of emotionally charged ideas that often generated morbid symptoms. The test evaluated the patient's delay time between introduction of the stimulus and the response, the appropriateness of the response word, and the patient's behavior. A significant deviation from normal denoted the presence of unconscious affect-laden ideas. Jung coined the term "complex" to describe this combination of the idea with the strong emotion it aroused.

In 1906, Jung published a study on dementia praecox which was to influence Bleulet when the latter designated the term "schizophrenia" for the illness five years later. In this work, Jung hypothesized that a complex produced a toxin which impaired mental functioning and caused the contents of the complex to be released into consciousness. Thus, the delusional ideas, hallucinatory experiences, and affective changes of the psychosis were to be viewed as more or less distorted manifestations of the originally repressed complex. Jung, in essence, was venturing the first psychosomatic theory of schizophrenia; although he subsequently abandoned the toxin hypothesis in favor of disturbed neurochemical processes, he never relinquished his belief in the primacy of psychogenic factors in the origin of schizophrenia.

Life's Work

By the time that Jung first met Sigmund Freud in Vienna (1907), he was well acquainted with Freud's writings. As a result of their meeting, the two men formed a close association which lasted until 1912. In the early years of their collaboration, Jung defended Freudian theories and Freud responded to this support with enthusiasm and encouragement.

In 1910, Jung left his position at the Burghölzli to focus on his growing private practice. It was during this time that he began his investigations into myths, legends, and fairy tales. His first writings on this subject, published in 1911, manifested both an area of interest which was to be sustained for the rest of his life and a declaration of independence from Freud in their criticism of the latter's classification of instincts as either self-preservative or sexual. Although Jung's objections to conceiving the libido in primarily sexual terms was already apparent at this early stage, the significance of these objections became clear only much later in his studies of the individuation process. It was not only intellectual disagreements, however, that led to the rupture between Freud and Jung. Jung objected to Freud's dogmatic attitude toward psycho-

analysis, his treating its tenets as articles of faith, immune from attack. This attitude diminished Jung's respect for Freud (although Jung's writings reveal that he, too, was prone to dogmatic assertions). Thus, while Freud worked to establish causal links extending back to childhood, and in so doing posited a mechanistic account of human behavior, Jung attempted to place human beings in a historical context which gave their lives meaning and dignity, which ultimately implied a place in a purposeful universe. In their later writings, both men became increasingly concerned with social questions and expressed their ideas in more metaphysical terms. Hence Freud weighed the life-instinct against the death-wish, and Jung discussed the split in the individual between the ego and the shadow (animal side of the psyche).

After breaking with Freud, Jung underwent a prolonged period of inner turmoil and uncertainty about his theories. Like Freud, he used self-analysis (dream interpretations, specifically) to resolve his emotional crisis. Yet this was also a time of creativity and growth, leading to Jung's unique approach to personality theory. Both a milestone in Jung's career and the signal of his break with Freudian psychology, *Wandlungen und Symbole der Libido* (1912; *Psychology of the Unconscious*, 1916) was the book in which his own point of view began to take definite shape. In this work, Jung interprets the thought processes of the schizophrenic in terms of mythological and religious symbolism.

The theme which unifies most of Jung's subsequent writings is individuation, a process which he viewed as taking place in certain gifted individuals in mid-life. While he believed that Freud and Alfred Adler had many valuable insights on the problems encountered during the maturation process, he considered their investigations limited. Jung's particular concern was with those people who had achieved separation from their parents, an adult sexual identity, and independence through work, people who nevertheless underwent a crisis in mid-life. Jung viewed individuation as a process directed toward the achievement of psychic wholeness or integration. In characterizing this developmental journey, he used illustrations from alchemy, mythology, literature, and Western and Eastern religions, as well as from his own clinical investigations. Particular signposts on the journey are provided by the archetypal (universal) images and symbols which are experienced, often with great

emotion, in dreams and "visions," and which as well as connecting the individual with the rest of mankind signify his or her unique destiny. In his writings on the "collective unconscious" and the archetypal images which are its manifestation, Jung maintained that cultural differences cannot wholly account for the distribution of mythological themes in dreams and visions. He writes of many patients who, while completely unsophisticated in such matters, describe dreams that exhibit striking parallels with myths from many different cultures.

It has been pointed out, however, that there appears to be a basic ambiguity in Jung's various descriptions of the collective unconscious. At times, he seems to regard the predisposition to experience certain images as comprehensible in terms of some genetic model. At other times, he emphasizes the numinous quality of these experiences, maintaining that archetypes demonstrate communion with some divine or world consciousness.

The latter part of Jung's life was relatively uneventful. He lived in Zurich, where he pursued private practice, studied, and wrote. Unfortunately, he left no detailed accounts of his clinical activities, although throughout his works there are scattered anecdotes from his professional experience as a psychotherapist. His great interest in religious questions is often treated as an embarrassment by practicing psychotherapists, and the problems with which he struggled are viewed as esoteric. Nevertheless, his popularity as a thinker derives from precisely this subject matter and from his belief that life is a meaningful journey. He studied Eastern religions and philosophy but saw himself as inescapably belonging to the Judeo-Christian tradition, although he was in no sense an orthodox believer. In a late work, *Antwort auf Hiob* (1952; *Answer to Job*, 1954), he pictures Job appealing to God against God and concludes that any split in the moral nature of man must be referred back to a split in the Godhead. The book is often obscure, but Jung asserts that in contemplating the future he became more inclined to view the division in man as an expression of divine conflict.

In his memoirs, written shortly before his death, Jung appears more detached and agnostic and denies having any definite convictions. He concludes the book with a statement about his own feelings of uncertainty, maintaining that the more uncertain he felt about himself the more he felt a kinship with all things. It seemed to him as though the alienation which separated him from the world was transferred to his own inner world and revealed an "unexpected unfamiliarity" with himself.

Summary

Although Carl Jung's theories have widened the scope of thinking about the human mind, his effect on therapeutic practice has been relatively minimal. Jung has been ardently attacked on a number of grounds, especially by Freudian analysts. They claim that archetypes are metaphysical constructs whose existence cannot be proved, and that the idea of the collective unconscious violates accepted principles of psychology and evolution. He is also criticized for his failure to offer any coherent model of personality development and for resurrecting an outdated concept of the unconscious. Others simply dismiss him as a mystic or ignore his work because he does not offer experimental evidence for his observations.

Whatever the opinion about his theories, however, Jung's impact on the field of modern psychology has been extensive. For example, the word-association test has become a standard instrument of clinical psychology; a number of rating scales have been devised for testing the introversion-extroversion dimension of personality; his concept of individuation has been incorporated into some of the most renowned theories of personality development; and finally, the comparative studies of mythology, religion, and the occult which he undertook in his search for archetypes have shed new light on the universal aspects and dynamics of human experience and have influenced psychological thinking about humans as symbol-using beings.

Bibliography

Faber, M. D. *Synchronicity: C. G. Jung, Psychoanalysis and Religion.* Westport, Conn.: Praeger, 1998. The author discusses Jung's theory of synchronicity and explains the psychoanalyst's approach to human behavior.

Fordham, Frieda. *An Introduction to Jung's Psychology.* 3d ed. London and Baltimore: Penguin, 1966. This brief (159 pages) but excellent work, along with the works listed by Hall and Jacobi, is considered to be one of the best introductions to Jungian psychology available. In it, Jung's major theories are clearly outlined. Fordham also includes a short autobiographical sketch by Jung.

Hall, Calvin S., and Vernon J. Nordby. *A Primer of Jungian Psychology.* New York: New American Library, 1973; London: Croom Helm, 1974. This is a standard (and thorough) introduction to the basic Jungian concepts of the structure, dynamics, and development of the normal personality.

Jacobi, Jolande. *The Psychology of C. G. Jung.* 8th ed. Translated by Ralph Manheim. New Haven, Conn.: Yale University Press, 1973. In this introductory work, consisting of a profile of Jung's major theories, Jacobi broadens the scope of her *Der Weg zur Individuation* (1965; *The Way of Individuation,* 1967) to give an overview of Jung's contributions to the field of analytic psychology.

Jung, Carl. *Jung on Mythology.* Continued by Robert A. Segal. London: Routledge, and Princeton, N.J.: Princeton University Press, 1998. Examines Jung's theories on myth based on his writings on the subject and those of Erich Neumann, James Hillman, and Marie-Louise von Franz.

Mattoon, Mary Ann. *Jungian Psychology in Perspective.* London: Macmillan, and New York: Free Press, 1981. This book not only offers an insightful overview and brief discussion of the major concepts of Jung's psychology but also attempts to evaluate those concepts. It gathers, for the first time, the results of empirical studies in which Jungian hypotheses have been tested. It also includes a comprehensive bibliography of works on Jungian psychology.

Progoff, Ira. *Jung's Psychology and Its Social Meaning.* London: Routledge, and New York: Julian Press, 1953. Progoff's study is a comprehensive statement of Jung's psychological theories and an interpretation of their significance for the social sciences. It sets the specialized concepts of Jung's psychology specifically into the context of his whole system of thought and, more generally, considers Jung's work in its historical context.

Genevieve Slomski

FRANZ KAFKA

Born: July 3, 1883; Prague, Austro-Hungarian
   Empire
Died: June 3, 1924; Kierling, Austria
Area of Achievement: Literature
Contribution: Kafka's unique style of narration
   and the intensely psychological and existential
   nature of his fiction, letters, and diaries have
   made him one of the most influential authors of
   the twentieth century.

Early Life

Franz Kafka was born on July 3, 1883, in the city
of Prague, which at that time was part of the huge
Austro-Hungarian Empire and which is today the
capital of Czechoslovakia. His father, Hermann,
was a prominent merchant in the Josefstadt, the
Jewish ghetto section of Prague. A crude, uneducated man, Hermann Kafka had worked his way up
from very poor and humble beginnings. Like many
such men, he was a domineering husband and father. A lifelong conflict between father and son developed early and remained a pivotal issue in Kafka's fiction. His mother, Julie, was a more
accommodating individual and often served as the
family peacemaker. Kafka also had three younger
sisters, Elli, Valli, and Ottla, who later perished
during the Nazi Holocaust.

Kafka graduated from secondary school in 1901
and began his studies at the German University of
Prague with a major in law. In 1902 he met another
student, Max Brod, who would later become his
close friend and confidant. Kafka completed his legal program in 1906; after a law practicum, he
found a job with the Workers' Accident Insurance
Institute.

During these early years, Kafka had begun to
write fiction, and by 1911 he had published a number of short prose pieces. His writing fulfilled an
inner desire that he would increasingly come to see
as the one true vocation in life. This vocation, however, later became the focus of major psychological conflicts. The tension between the bourgeois
life—career, marriage, and children—valued by
society and the solitary and marginal social existence necessary to the artist's creative ability came
to tear at Kafka's psyche. During his lifetime, he
kept a number of diaries that contain details of the
emotions and ideas that motivated his writing. The
thematic issues of Kafka's fiction are in many essential respects intimately bound to the personal
conflicts he experienced.

Life's Work

During the night of September 22-23, 1912, the
then twenty-nine-year-old Kafka wrote a story entitled *Das Urteil* (1913, 1916; *The Sentence*, 1928;
better known as *The Judgment*, 1945), and this
short text marked the breakthrough to the unique
style of his mature fiction. This dreamlike story of
Georg Bendemann, his bizarre confrontation with
his aging father, and Georg's suicide upon his father's condemnation was precipitated by Kafka's
meeting with a young woman, Felice Bauer, the
month before. He soon began a correspondence
with her, and, in his mind, the possibility of marriage soon arose. The demands of his father for a
married son and a successful businessman clashed
with the son's need to write, and Kafka seemed to
be paralyzed by a tense and debilitating ambivalence. The complex psychological conflict apparently engendered by this meeting led to this unusual text as well as to several other of Kafka's more
famous stories.

Die Verwandlung (1915; "The Metamorphosis,"
1936) undoubtedly remains the best known of the
author's short texts, and it illustrates the unique
quality of his writing. Composed during the
months of November and December, 1912, this
story also reflects the psychic tensions occasioned
by Kafka's relationship with Felice Bauer. Gregor
Samsa, a traveling salesman, awakes one morning
to find that he has been transformed into a huge insect. Kafka's narrative conveys the nightmarish
horror of this transformation with such convincing
detail that it all seems plausible. His approach
transforms the subjective nature of dreams and inner emotional experience into the concrete reality
of the everyday. Kafka's prose manages to attain a
unique balance between subjective and objective in
what has been termed a style of "narrated monologue." He tells a story from the subjective perspective of the protagonist—as if it were a first-
person monologue—but he does so using the traditional third-person narrative form. The effect is one
which recalls the logic and quality of dream experience. As in *The Judgment*, a conflict between father and son develops in "The Metamorphosis,"
and again the central character perishes. A variant

of this father-son conflict occurs in the well-known story *In der Strafkolonie* (1919; "In the Penal Colony," 1941), written in November, 1914. In this latter text, however, the father figure begins to assume the dimensions of an institutional authority.

In June, 1913, Kafka, apparently yielding to the inner and outer pressures that demanded he adopt a proper middle-class life, proposed marriage to Felice, and she accepted. Their engagement was officially announced in April of 1914. In the following July, however, he met with Felice and her parents in a Berlin hotel and broke off the planned marriage. He noted in his diary that the entire episode made him feel as if he were being put on trial. This notion was the germ for a novel, *Der Prozess* (1925; *The Trial*, 1937), which he began in July of 1914 but never completed. Much of the text, however, is finished in rough-draft form. It deals with the fate of Josef K., a bachelor, who is arrested one morning as he awakens and spends much of his time attempting to defend himself before the vague instance of the "Court." He finally accedes to the judgment of the Court and willingly goes to his execution. This novel, as well as the other stories Kafka wrote during the period of 1912-1914, all deal with complex psychological issues of guilt and judgment; the court ultimately exists within Kafka's mind. The crime is one of ambivalence, as is made clear in the parable told to Josef K. by the priest in *The Trial*. In this parable, a man from the country seeks admittance to the "Law" through a doorway that is guarded by a large man. Seemingly intimidated by the guard, the man waits for permission and spends his whole life waiting. He dies a pitiful death. Kafka was unable to accept the demands of his family and society to choose a bourgeois life and equally unable to reject them in order to embrace the path of the artist. In this wavering state of mind, he sinned, he believed, against both life and the spirit. At this point in his life, he was preoccupied with thoughts of suicide, seemingly the only release from the tensions he suffered.

In July, 1916, Kafka became unofficially engaged to Felice for a second time, and they made it formal in July the following year. By December, 1917, however, they had quarreled several times, and the engagement was again terminated. During these years, Kafka was plagued by increasing ill health, and in August, 1917, he suffered a lung hemorrhage that was the first sign of tubercular infection. In his diary, he interpreted his illness as a

symbol of Felice and the inner conflict that tormented him.

Kafka's relationship with his father and the kind of life the latter represented to the son formed the major issue of the writer's existence. In November, 1919, at the age of thirty-six, Kafka wrote a long and involved letter to his father. Later published as *Brief an den Vater* (1953; *Letter to His Father*, 1953), the document represents Kafka's attempt to justify his personality and art to his father. It is both an attempt at reconciliation and an attack on his father's treatment of him. He describes, for example, an incident when, as a very young child, his father locked him out of the apartment, and he stood waiting before the door for the "big man" to let him in. Kafka claims that all his writing is merely a kind of "sobbing" at the breast of the man before whom he had so much fear. Again the psychological basis of Kafka's writing is evident in such documents. He gave this letter to his mother so that she would pass it on to his father, but she never did.

Kafka's tubercular condition gradually grew worse over the following years, but he continued to write. In 1919, a woman named Milena Jesenská-Polak wrote to Kafka asking for permission to translate his published works into Czech. They began a brief love affair and a correspondence that lasted until shortly before his death. In 1920, he began the first sketches for a planned novel entitled *Das Schloss* (1926; *The Castle*, 1930), which would involve a land surveyor named K. who seeks admittance to the higher bureaucratic authorities of a castle town. Another of his well-known short texts, *Ein Hungerkünstler* (1922; "A Hunger Artist," 1945), was also written during this period. In June, 1922, ill health forced Kafka to apply for retirement from his job. Knowing that he would not live much longer, he instructed his friend, Max Brod, to destroy all of his manuscripts, including his unfinished novels, after his death. Brod was well aware of Kafka's immense talent and never carried out his friend's orders. He later edited and published these texts.

In July of 1923, Kafka met a young Jewish woman, Dora Dymant, a student who was half his age, and in September he moved with her to Berlin. His condition worsened, however, and in March of 1924 he returned to Prague and moved in with his parents again. By April his health had deteriorated to such a degree that he was forced to enter a sanatorium near Vienna. Suffering from advanced tuberculosis of the larynx and therefore unable to eat or drink, Kafka died during·the morning of June 3, 1924.

Summary

Franz Kafka's impact has been primarily within the area of literature. Much of modern and postmodern narrative fiction is unthinkable without the Prague author's body of texts. Modern writers as varied as Alain Robbe-Grillet, Peter Handke, Thomas Bernhard, Philip Roth, and Gabriel García Márquez—to name only a few—have acknowledged a profound debt to his surreal and disturbing prose. The unique ability of Kafka's writing to capture the logic and ambience of dream reality has been a formative influence on fiction in a decidedly post-Freudian universe. Kafka's writing and Freud's depth psychology as well are the natural extensions of nineteenth century Romantic literature and thought. The Romantic exploration of the inner dimensions of human experience generated a questioning of the nature of objective meaning and subjective perception, and it is in precisely such a universe that Kafka's characters move.

Kafka's depiction of the individual who is alienated from his own unconscious and from the experience of those around him has been regarded as a seminal rendering of the existential condition of twentieth century man. The struggles of Josef K. against the anonymous authority of the Court and the efforts of the land surveyor K. to gain entrance to the Castle have been seen by many readers as an image of the estranged individual facing the impersonal bureaucracies of modern society. Kafka was gifted with an artistic talent that enabled him to transform his personal dilemmas into literary texts that have universal significance and appeal.

Bibliography

Boa, Elizabeth. *Kafka: Gender, Class and Race in the Letters and Fictions.* Oxford: Clarendon Press, and New York: Oxford University Press, 1996. Study of Kafka's use of gender stereotypes in his writings.

Brod, Max. *Franz Kafka: A Biography.* Translated by G. Humphreys Roberts and Richard Winston. 2d ed. New York: Schocken, 1960. The first Kafka biography, written by his friend and literary executor. Though dated, this firsthand account remains indispensable. Includes a chronology.

Emrich, Wilhelm. *Franz Kafka: A Critical Study of His Writings.* Translated by Sheema Z. Buehne. New York: Ungar, 1968. An English translation of a major scholarly study originally published in German. Contains notes and a bibliography.

Hall, Calvin S., and Richard E. Lind. *Dreams, Life, and Literature: A Study of Franz Kafka.* Chapel Hill: University of North Carolina Press, 1970. A brief interpretation of the author's life and works with a distinct emphasis on Freudian approaches. Contains appendices, bibliography, and index.

Hayman, Ronald. *Kafka: A Biography.* New York: Oxford University Press, 1982. An excellent critical biography which draws on previously unpublished material. Contains notes, a bibliography, and an index.

Mailloux, Peter. *A Hesitation Before Birth: The Life of Franz Kafka.* Newark: University of Delaware Press, 1989. The fullest account of Kafka's life available in English, complemented by a thorough analysis of his works. Illustrated; includes a bibliography, notes, and an index.

Politzer, Heinz. *Franz Kafka: Parable and Paradox.* Rev. ed. Ithaca, N.Y.: Cornell University Press, 1966. One of the first extended critical interpretations of the author's writings. Contains notes, an index, and a bibliography.

Shulman, Ernest. "Franz Kafka's Resistance to Acting on Suicidal Ideation." *Omega* 37, no. 1 (August, 1998). A study of self-preservation in those with suicidal tendencies, using Kafka's writings as a basis for analysis.

Sokel, Walter H. *Franz Kafka.* New York: Columbia University Press, 1966. A brief but excellent introduction to Kafka's life and texts by one of the foremost scholars. Contains a selected bibliography.

Sussman, Henry. *Franz Kafka: Geometrician of Metaphor.* Madison, Wis.: Coda Press, 1979. A scholarly interpretation of Kafka's use of language which utilizes aspects of poststructuralist literary theory. Contains notes.

Thomas F. Barry

WASSILY KANDINSKY

Born: December 4, 1866; Moscow, Russia
Died: December 13, 1944; Neuilly-sur-Seine, near
   Paris, France
Area of Achievement: Art
Contribution: Both for the quality and influence of
   his works and for the influence of his theoretical
   and pedagogical writings, Kandinsky was the
   most significant figure in the development of
   nonrepresentational abstract art in the first half
   of the twentieth century. He was the pioneer
   among those artists whose aim was not to reproduce the expressive qualities of objects and
   events in nature but to exploit the intrinsic expressive attributes of artistic materials, particularly pigments, without reference to natural
   appearances.

Early Life

In 1871, Wassily Kandinsky's family moved from
Moscow to Odessa in the Crimea for the sake of
the father's health; Kandinsky spent his childhood
there. His father, born in eastern Siberia, was a successful tea merchant and always encouraged his
son's artistic gifts, sending him, at age seven, to a
special drawing teacher. His father generously supported him for many years. Kandinsky's mother,
Lydia Tikheeva, came from Moscow but was half
Baltic. One of his great-grandmothers is said to
have been a Mongolian princess, and people who
knew Kandinsky noticed a certain Asiatic cast to
his features.

The young Kandinsky drew, wrote poems, and
played the piano and cello. In 1886, he went to the
University of Moscow, where he studied law and
political economy, and in 1893 he was appointed
as a lecturer there in the faculty of law. Yet it was
not until 1895, when he visited an exhibition of the
French Impressionists in Moscow, that a painting
by Claude Monet had a lasting effect on him and
revealed to him his true vocation. In Monet's paintings, the subject matter played a secondary role to
color, and reality and fairy tale were intertwined.
These qualities were also essential to Kandinsky's
early work, which was based on folk art. Even his
later works were influenced by folk art, although
on a more intellectualized level.

Kandinsky decided to abandon his legal career in
1897 and went to Munich to devote himself entirely to painting. He studied with Anton Azbé, and he
later studied under Franz von Stuck, a teacher at
the Munich Academy and a founding member of
the Munich Sezession. At this time, the prevailing
avant-garde in Munich was Art Nouveau or, as it
was called, *Jugendstil*, and Kandinsky familiarized
himself with this style. Kandinsky's early Impres-
sionist-inspired paintings as well as those of his
Jugendstil period are strong in color; color continued to dominate his landscapes of Murnau. In
1901, Kandinsky became one of the founders of
the avant-garde exhibiting association Phalanx. His
first marriage, to his cousin, Ania Chimiakin, ended in divorce in 1911; in 1912, he took up with
Gabriele Munter, who had been his pupil before
becoming his companion during his Munich years,
until he broke with her in 1916.

After traveling throughout Holland, Tunisia, and
Italy, he settled for a year (beginning in June,
1906) at Sèvres, near Paris. In 1909, after returning
to Munich, he helped to found, together with Alexei Kubin, the Neue Künstlervereingung (the new
artist union). From his meeting with Franz Marc in
1911, the Blaue Reiter (blue rider) movement was
born; the two exhibitions of this expressionist
group proved to be major events in the development of modern German painting.

Life's Work

After 1909 emerged Kandinsky's series of "Impro-
visations" and "Compositions," which were alternately figurative and nonfigurative, the latter possessing a remarkable degree of invention. The year
1910, however, was crucial for Kandinsky as well
as for world art. It was in 1910 that, with a thoroughly abstract watercolor, Kandinsky emerged as
an initiator of nonrealistic art. About that time he
also wrote *Über das Geistige in der Kunst, insbe-
sondere in der Malerei* (1912; *Concerning the
Spiritual in Art, and Painting in Particular*, 1912),
a prophetic treatise on the artist's inner life. Soon
the naturalistic elements disappeared from Kandinsky's work and were replaced by turbulent lines
and vehement colors clashing together in a passionate, romantic disorder. Abandoning himself to
lyricism, he subsequently produced some of the
most masterly and original compositions in the history of abstract art.

World War I coincided with a break in the development of Kandinsky's art; the painter of *Black
Arc* (1912) and the great *Fugue* (1914) accepted
the discipline of the objective, rational, and severe

style that became the trademark of the Bauhaus. The romantic effusion of his previous style was replaced by a colder, more thoughtful, more calculated conception that produced geometric forms and architectural structures in which it is tempting to see a certain tribute to the constructivism of Kandinsky's rival, the Dutch painter Piet Mondrian. Kandinsky set about translating his mental schemes into combinations of lines, angles, squares, and circles, and flat applications of color, but with an excitement and animation of rhythm that are absent from Mondrian's more austere works. The Bauhaus period also accentuated Kandinsky's didactic tendencies: In his essay *Punkt und Linie zu Fläche* (*Point and Line to Plane*, 1947), published in 1926, it is as a theoretician that he constructs a set of limitations to creative freedom.

With the outbreak of World War I, Kandinsky was forced to return to Russia. In 1917, he married Nina Andreewsky (to whom he remained married until his death). During the Russian Revolution, the artist occupied a prominent position at the Commissariat of Popular Culture, and in 1921 he founded the Academy of Arts and Sciences. At the end of that year, however, he left Soviet Russia, since he rebelled at the reign of Socialist Realism. He then settled in Germany, first at Weimar and later at Dessau, becoming one of the most prominent teachers at the Bauhaus School from 1922 to 1933. His art from about 1920 to 1924 has been referred to as his "architectural period." The shapes are more precise than before; there are points, straight or broken lines, single or in groups, and snakelike, radiating segments of circles; and the color is cooler, more subdued, with occasional outbursts of earlier expressionist tonality. This period is exemplified by the work *Composition VIII* (1923). From 1925 to 1927, Kandinsky accentuated circles in his paintings, as can be seen in *Several Circles* (1926). When the Bauhaus was closed by the Nazis in 1933, Kandinsky took refuge in Paris.

Together with his paintings, Kandinsky produced woodcuts and drawings, designed the settings and costumes for Modest Mussorgsky's *Pictures at an Exhibition* (1928) for the Friedrich Theater at Dessau, and executed frescoes for a music room at the International Exhibition of Architecture in Berlin (1931). In December, 1933, he took up permanent residence at Neuilly-sur-Seine, a suburb of Paris. During this time, his style underwent yet another change: His forms abandoned their geometric aspect, became suddenly more

concentrated, and evolved again into indecipherable hieroglyphs and ornamental motifs. His works demonstrated an opulent and balanced maturity that often exhibited an extraordinary, almost un-European character of form and color, which some critics have attributed to his Mongolian ancestry. Some of the paintings of the late 1930's and 1940's displayed a serene exuberance combined with a vital energy, giving them the quality of genuine masterpieces. The works of this period contain a Russian richness of color, a plenitude of formal invention, and a charming humor. In addition, Kandinsky's work communicated the presence of a spiritual world, as in *Composition X* (1939) and *Tempered Elan* (1944)—both in the collection of Nina Kandinsky.

Summary

Wassily Kandinsky was one of the first painters to realize more thoroughly than others that the naturalistic traditions in art were exhausted. He staunchly adhered to a belief in the artist's right to express the imaginings of his inner world and, in so doing, created an art as far removed from the pure abstraction of Mondrian as were the poetic images of Paul Klee or the biting sensuality of Robert Delaunay. Because it is simultaneously that of a precursor, an inventor, and a master, Kandinsky's work is of such richness that its effect on the development of art cannot yet be fully calculated.

From early childhood, Kandinsky was unusually sensitive to the emotional associations of colors and had strongly developed powers of synesthesia. Finding it impossible to reproduce in painting the colors that moved him so profoundly, he reached the conclusion by some inner conviction that art and nature are two separate worlds with different principles and different aims. From this conviction, Kandinsky came to his belief in the autonomy of art—the belief that a work of art stands or falls by inherent aesthetic principles, not by any resemblance to the external world.

With the disappearance of geometric perspective along with the abandonment of representation, Kandinsky organized his picture space by a very precise manipulation of the more abstruse sensory properties of colors and shapes. Unless it has abandoned composition altogether, nearly all expressive abstraction subsequently has based itself on Kandinsky's new picture space. His other most important contribution was in the creation of virtual movement without the representation of moving things. From about 1920 on, he was able to impart virtual movement to his canvases in a manner and to a degree which had not been hitherto realized. Although a forerunner of expressive abstraction, he was a master of composition and did not participate in the more spontaneous, improvisational, formless ideals of abstract expressionism and informal art.

Bibliography

Barnett, Vivian E., and Josef Helfenstein, eds. *The Blue Four: Feininger, Jawlensky, Kandinsky and Klee in the New World*. Cologne: Dumont, and New Haven, Conn.: Yale University Press, 1998. Documents Galka Scheyer's friendship with and promotion of the expressionist art of the Blue Four. Includes 200 black-and-white and 140 color illustrations of these artists' works. The catalog of the 1998 spring/summer exhibition at the Kunstmuseum in Bern and at the Kunstsammlung Nordrhein-Westfalen in Düsseldorf.

Conil-Lacoste, Michele. *Kandinsky*. Translated by Shirley Jennings. New York: Crown, 1979. In this well-written book, Conil-Lacoste argues that Kandinsky's work is not altogether free from incomprehension and misunderstanding. She discusses his life and his art, focusing especially on the Munich period. The book is brief and contains many color plates, a chronology of the artist's life, and a bibliography of primary and secondary works.

Grohmann, Will. *Wassily Kandinsky: Life and Work*. Translated by Norbert Guterman. New York: Abrams, 1958; London: Thames and Hudson, 1959. This is still the standard and most comprehensive biography of Kandinsky. The work is lengthy and contains numerous color and black-and-white plates, a catalog of reproductions, a bibliography, a list of exhibitions, and copies of original signatures. The author discusses the artist as a painter and thinker, since relatively little was known about the man, and does not offer a detailed analysis of his painting.

Long, Rose-Carol Washton. *Kandinsky: The Development of an Abstract Style*. Oxford: Clarendon Press, and New York: Oxford University Press, 1980. This informative book is about Kandinsky's struggle to resolve the battle between the personal desire for abstraction and the public desire for representation in his art. Extensive color and black-and-white plates and notes are included.

Overy, Paul. *Kandinsky: The Language of the Eye*. London: Elek, and New York: Praeger, 1969. Overy believes that most books on Kandinsky have traced his development toward abstraction. His book, on the other hand, is mainly concerned with other, more important aspects of his work. Part 1 discusses the artist's visual imagery, reason and intuition, allegory, and language; part 2 discusses the artist's color theory, figure and ground, time, place, point and line, and the life of forms. The books contain a brief bibliography and extensive color and black-and-white plates.

Weiss, Peg. *Kandinsky in Munich: The Formative Jugendstil Years*. Princeton, N.J.: Princeton University Press, 1979. Since the author's conviction is that art history must be viewed from a broad cultural perspective, Kandinsky's Munich experience is examined in all its cultural manifestations. This excellent book includes a bibliography, an index, black-and-white and color plates, and a chronology of the artist's life and work.

———. *Kandinsky and Old Russia: The Artist As Ethnographer Shaman*. New Haven, Conn., and London: Yale University Press, 1995. A significant reinterpretation of Kandinsky's work, this volume supports the view that his modernism was in part based on mysticism.

Genevieve Slomski

PYOTR LEONIDOVICH KAPITSA

Born: July 9, 1894; Kronshtadt, Russia
Died: April 8, 1984; Moscow, U.S.S.R.
Areas of Achievement: Physics, invention, and technology
Contribution: Kapitsa was both an experimental physicist and a brilliant designer of investigative and industrial equipment. As a tribute to the importance of his research at very low temperatures, he was awarded a Nobel Prize in Physics for his discovery of the superfluidity of liquid helium and for his invention of apparatuses for the liquefaction of helium and air.

Early Life

Pyotr Leonidovich Kapitsa was born into a family with a strong intellectual background. His father was a military fortifications engineer, and his mother was a well-known member of literary circles in nearby St. Petersburg who specialized in folklore and children's literature. Following his early education in Kronshtadt, Kapitsa studied at the Petrograd Polytechnical Institute under the famous physicist Abram Joffe. In 1914, his academic life was interrupted by World War I, and he spent two years as an ambulance driver at the Polish front. He then returned to the Polytechnical Institute and was graduated in 1918 amid the chaotic conditions accompanying the Russian Revolution of the previous year.

He remained at the institute as a lecturer until 1921, but his work had lost its appeal after personal tragedy struck in 1919. Following the death of his son from scarlet fever, his father, his wife, and his newborn daughter all died during an epidemic of Spanish influenza. To help allay his grief, Kapitsa joined a Soviet-sponsored scientific trade delegation organized by Joffe. Although several countries were on the planned itinerary, England turned out to be the only country to grant Kapitsa a visa. The contingencies of international politics thus brought about a major turning point in Kapitsa's career. He soon convinced the famous and influential English physicist Ernest Rutherford that he should be allowed to work under Rutherford's supervision at the famous Cavendish Laboratory at Cambridge. Kapitsa remained at Cambridge for thirteen years, and it was with Rutherford's guidance that his unique style of scientific creativity first flowered.

Several of Kapitsa's characteristic work habits became established during these early years of research in England. First, although Rutherford was a nuclear physicist and initially set Kapitsa to work on problems in that field, Kapitsa soon became more interested in the design and operation of new apparatuses than in nuclear theory as such. Subsequent transitions in Kapitsa's research interests can usually be traced to his desire to explore new domains with apparatuses originally designed to test established theory. For example, his interest in very high magnetic fields and very low temperatures came about in this way. Kapitsa thus sympathized with Rutherford's rather brusque emphasis on experimental physics rather than highly formalized theory. Kapitsa also adopted Rutherford's straightforward administrative style. Both men tried to keep administrative complications in their laboratories at a minimum. They also encouraged their students to stay in close touch with the experimental grounding of their science and to explore their intuitions by constructing and operating their own apparatuses whenever possible.

Life's Work

The major transitions in Kapitsa's career were brought about by political interventions. In 1934, he was detained after a visit to his mother in the Soviet Union, and he was not allowed to travel outside his native country again until 1965. The strategic and industrial demands of World War II required a move from Moscow to Kazan and an emphasis on the production of liquid oxygen. After the war, Kapitsa's refusal to work on nuclear weapons resulted in his banishment from the Institute for Physical Problems, of which he had been director, and he was restricted to his own home, a restriction that amounted to virtual house arrest. In 1955, following Joseph Stalin's death, Kapitsa was reinstated in the Soviet scientific establishment, and his work once again received state support. Because of Kapitsa's experimental orientation, these fluctuations in his working conditions considerably influenced his research; his fascination with precise measurement remained his mainstay through what were often extremely trying circumstances.

Although the low-temperature research for which Kapitsa eventually won the 1978 Nobel Prize in Physics was primarily carried out in the 1930's, shortly after his detention in the Soviet

Union, his interest in this subject began during his years with Rutherford at the Cavendish Laboratory. Rutherford initially set Kapitsa to work on an important topic in nuclear physics, the curvature of the trajectory of alpha particles in strong magnetic fields. These positively charged particles are emitted by radioactive nuclei, and Kapitsa was the first to photograph their curved trajectories during the short period of time in which they pass through experimental apparatuses. Kapitsa invented new equipment to produce the strong magnetic fields required, and this project quickly shifted his attention away from nuclear physics. He began studying how very strong magnetic fields alter the electrical properties and dimensions of magnetized materials; the discovery of unexpected results at very low temperatures then instigated the research that produced his most famous discoveries.

As early as 1913, Heike Kamerlingh Onnes had discovered that when helium gas becomes a liquid at the very low temperature of 4.2 Kelvins, it becomes a superconductor and presents no resistance to the flow of an electric current. This discovery suggested the exciting possibility that technology could eventually utilize powerful electric currents without the usual limitations caused by resistive heating effects. Furthermore, these currents could be used to create powerful magnetic fields with innumerable applications in transportation and industry. Kapitsa's contributions to low-temperature physics thus should be understood as part of one of the most important scientific investigations of the twentieth century, an investigation that appealed to Kapitsa's practical interest in engineering problems.

This is particularly true, for example, of Kapitsa's work on the liquefaction of gases such as hydrogen, helium, atmospheric air, and oxygen. Readily available supplies of low-temperature liquids are essential to the study of the properties of other materials at these temperatures. While still at the Cavendish, Kapitsa and John Cockcroft improved upon existing methods for the liquefaction of hydrogen. In 1933, with Rutherford's support, Kapitsa became an internationally acknowledged leader in low-temperature physics as director of the new Royal Society Mond Laboratory. He soon perfected a new method for the liquefaction of helium which later became the basis for the commercially successful Collins liquefier.

Kapitsa's detention in the Soviet Union in 1934 was a serious disruption of his research for several

years. He had remarried in England, and the stability he had achieved within the social and scientific world of Cambridge made it difficult for him to relocate his family in Moscow. Furthermore, his fierce sense of independence made him bridle at the thought of perhaps having to produce science according to a preset agenda. The blow was softened somewhat when, with the help of Rutherford and other friends, Kapitsa's equipment was sold to the Soviet Union and shipped to the new Institute for Physical Problems which he had been appointed to direct.

By 1938, he had accomplished one of his most important investigations, the demonstration of the superfluidity of liquid helium II. Helium II is a phase of helium that exists only below the extremely low temperature of 2.2 Kelvins. Kapitsa designed ingenious experimental apparatuses to demonstrate that the reason helium II is such a good conductor of heat is its vanishingly low viscosity, a property for which he coined the term "super-fluid." He also encouraged his associate at the institute, Lev Davidovich Landau, to develop what became a widely accepted quantum-mechanical explanation for this phenomenon. This research in low-temperature physics was Kapitsa's most creative and influential work, and it was cited as the reason for his Nobel Prize in Physics in 1978.

During World War II, Kapitsa made important contributions to the industrial base for the Soviet war effort. He invented a new turboexpansion machine for the liquefaction of air. Because oxygen is the first component of air to pass into the liquid phase as the air is cooled, Kapitsa's invention was of great value for the production of pure oxygen.

Following the end of the war in 1945, Kapitsa fell out of favor with Stalin by refusing to contribute to nuclear-weapons projects. He was dismissed from the institute he had organized and directed and was restricted to his own home until 1954. During this period, he continued to do research on a smaller scale and made important contributions to the design of microwave generators. After returning to the Soviet scientific establishment in 1955, he became increasingly interested in plasma physics, the study of matter at very high temperatures, comparable to those in the interior of stars. Inspired by his study of ball lightning and bolstered by his production of energy discharges in helium using his own power generators, Kapitsa began investigating a new method of producing nuclear energy through controlled thermonuclear fusion of deuterium atoms. Although he remained enthusiastic about the potential of his technique until his death in 1984, there was little favorable response on the part of other nuclear physicists. Fusion research during the 1980's continued to be dominated by methods that required high-temperature plasmas to be confined by strong magnetic fields. The general consensus was that this was one case where Kapitsa's unique combination of theoretical and practical intuitions led him astray.

Summary

Pyotr Leonidovich Kapitsa's most important scientific accomplishments were in the domain of low-temperature physics. His rare combination of theoretical insight and engineering skills resulted in his ingenious design of precise measuring apparatuses and industrial equipment of great practical value. He is thus an important member of the large group of twentieth century physicists responsible for the gradual realization of the technological potential of low-temperature materials.

Kapitsa is a significant and symbolic figure for reasons other than his technical accomplishments.

Few scientists have achieved his level of success under both Western and Soviet systems of government. Both in England and, to a much greater extent, in the Soviet Union, Kapitsa made an impact not only through his own research but through his direction of the research of others as well. Furthermore, in spite of the oppression he experienced under Stalin, Kapitsa retained the independence and iconoclasm that had endeared him to Rutherford. He wrote and spoke extensively about the Soviet system of education and scientific training. As might be expected from someone with Kapitsa's broad cultural experiences, he repeatedly called attention to the dangers of an overly narrow emphasis on technical training in any one specialty. His fondness for Western art and literature was a typical example of his conviction that creative and beneficial science flourishes best under the stimulating conditions of a rich and argumentative culture. He openly expressed his scorn for political attempts to place restraints upon the free exchange and debate of scientific ideas.

Finally, in addition to his resistance to Cold War barriers to scientific progress, Kapitsa represents the tension between good and evil that haunts twentieth century nuclear physics. His refusal to work on nuclear-weapons projects apparently was unflinching, and following his release to travel abroad in 1965 he became an active member of the Pugwash movement, an international group of scientists dedicated to bringing about nuclear disarmament and the peaceful application of scientific knowledge. His final work on controlled nuclear fusion as a means of relieving the increasing demands upon global energy sources thus was an attempt to practice his commitment to the scientific enhancement of the human condition.

Bibliography

Badash, Lawrence. *Kapitza, Rutherford, and the Kremlin.* New Haven, Conn. and London: Yale University Press, 1985. After a brief but accurate description of the early years of Kapitsa's career, Badash provides a detailed and well-documented description of the 1934 detention of Kapitsa in the Soviet Union and the unsuccessful diplomatic efforts by Rutherford and other scientists in response. Includes a valuable collection of Kapitsa's letters during the transitional period between 1934 and 1936.

Kapitsa, Petr. *Collected Papers of P. L. Kapitza.* 3 vols. Edited by D. ter Haar. New York: Macmillan, 1964-1967. The first volume of this three-volume collection includes a succinct summary of Kapitsa's scientific accomplishments up to 1955.

Lifshitz, Eugene M. "Superfluidity." *Scientific American* 198 (June, 1958): 20. Written by a brilliant student and colleague of Kapitsa, this usefully illustrated article provides a thorough firsthand account of Kapitsa's discovery of the superfluidity of helium II and the subsequent experimental confirmations of Landau's theoretical explanation.

Shoenberg, D. "Piotr Leonidovich Kaptiza." *Biographical Memoirs of Fellows of the Royal Society* 31 (1985): 327-374. Kapitsa was elected to the prestigious Royal Society of London in 1929, and this article is the official biographical sketch commissioned by the society. It is written by a knowledgeable physicist who was one of Kapitsa's research students at Cambridge. The article thus is both scientifically accurate and based upon personal knowledge of Kapitsa's work habits. Includes a very thorough bibliography.

Spruch, Grace Marmor. "Pyotr Kapitza, Octogenarian Dissident." *Physics Today* 32 (September, 1979): 34-36. Written by a professor of physics at Rutgers University, this article provides a brief survey of Kapitsa's career. Relying upon Nikita Khrushchev's published memoirs, Spruch provides evidence for Kapitsa's refusal to contribute to Soviet military projects.

Trigg, George L. *Landmark Experiments in Twentieth Century Physics.* New York: Crane Russak, 1975; London: Constable, 1995. In chapters 4 and 5, Trigg provides a fairly detailed discussion of the research into the low-temperature physics of helium during the three decades after 1908. His discussion includes extensive quotations and illustrations from the original publications, including Kapitsa's 1938 account of his discovery of superfluidity. These chapters thus provide a useful survey of the context in which Kapitsa's most original Nobel Prize-winning research took place.

James R. Hofmann

HERBERT VON KARAJAN

Born: April 5, 1908; Salzburg, Austro-Hungarian Empire
Died: July 16, 1989; Anif, Austria
Area of Achievement: Music
Contribution: Karajan, the finest conductor of the postwar period, was the conductor of the Berlin Philharmonic Orchestra and was named conductor for life of that organization in 1955. He was also the head of the Vienna State Opera, of the Salzburg Festival, and of the Philharmonia Orchestra of London.

Early Life

Herbert von Karajan was born on April 5, 1908, in Salzburg, Austria (then part of the Austro-Hungarian Empire). Salzburg enjoys a rich musical history as the home of Wolfgang Amadeus Mozart, Joseph Haydn, Ludwig van Beethoven, and many other composers of orchestral and opera literature. Because of this musical heritage, great performers, composers, and conductors were relatively common in Austria. Great music, performed with technical grace and interpretation, seemed always just around the corner for the young Karajan.

Karajan, who would someday be considered a virtuoso conductor, and one of the last Austro-German traditionalists, began his career as a young piano prodigy. His first public performance came before the age of eight, and, although he soon left the piano keyboard for the baton, his piano skills were always of great value to him as he studied and prepared conducting scores. He first began studying conducting at the Vienna Conservatory of Music, where his teacher was Franz Schalk, who is remembered primarily for his recordings of Beethoven's Sixth and Eighth Symphonies. From Schalk, Karajan learned many conducting techniques to enhance the natural flow of the music as well as refinement and lyricism. His first conducting post was with a small group of musicians in Ulm, but he soon left that position for a post as conductor of the orchestra at Aachen, where he remained for seven years.

In addition to his life of exciting musical experiences with many orchestras and opera companies, Karajan was a daredevil racecar driver, an accomplished yachtsman, an expert pilot, and a downhill ski racer. He was known as one of the best amateur skiers in Europe. Karajan lived a fast-paced life of excitement, which may have had an effect on his married life, as he was married three times. Many people, some much younger than he, found it difficult, if not impossible, to keep up with him. He was as much at home climbing mountains or racing automobiles as he was at the conductor's podium.

Life's Work

In 1933, while conductor of the Berlin Opera, Karajan joined the Nazi Party as a method of furthering his career and in hope of being in the favor of the ruling influences. Hermann Göring was a strong supporter of Karajan's assuming the position of permanent conductor at the Berlin Opera, which set Karajan in opposition to Wilhelm Furtwängler, who was being supported by Joseph Goebbels for the same position. Later, as Karajan saw the full impact of Nazi domination, he became very ashamed that he had counted himself among the Nazis and tried to break all connections with the Nazi Party. Although he was never known to speak of his Nazi past, it was evident throughout his life that the decision to join the Nazi Party haunted him.

It was after the war that Karajan's rapid ascent as a conductor began. There was something about this short, slim, handsome, dynamic conductor that seemed to make musicians beat a path to his door. For many years he was the supreme conductor in Europe and was equally popular in other parts of the world. He had the reputation in the United States of being a virtuoso conductor, and, when he conducted the Berlin Harmonic in New York in 1955, the music critics saw him as a conductor whose gestures were restrained and tasteful and who was completely objective in his interpretations. This surprised many people, who considered that a man of Karajan's lifestyle, one who loved to climb mountains, ski in racing events, and the like, would show passion in his conducting gestures. Many people expected to see a choreographic onslaught of emotion and reckless energy, but what they really found was a man of conducting efficiency and tender restraint. Karajan indeed was flying high and in so many directions by 1960 that he seemed to be a one-man airline, or at least he was wealthy enough to own one. He was simultaneously head of the Vienna Staatsoper, of the Salzburg Festival, and of the Berlin Philharmonic; he was also one of the chief conductors at La Scala and conductor of the Philharmonia Orchestra in London.

For a while it appeared that Karajan was going to seize all of musical Europe and challenge the rest of the world. In anything he did, he had the compulsive desire to excel, to dominate, to command, and to perfect. There are more than eight hundred recordings to his credit with many major symphony orchestras of the world as well as with his beloved Berlin Philharmonic. He was considered by many critics and professional musicians to be arrogant, at times flamboyant, and rather expensive to have around. His seeming inability to make and keep associations followed him wherever he traveled.

Karajan was known as demanding in every aspect of a production and was often criticized for his insistence on total direction of a production, including staging, lighting, music, and scenery. Although he was considered by many not to be a good administrator in production affairs, he still knew tremendous successes at the podium.

The Austro-German school of conducting, which Karajan seems to represent the best, incorporates styles that have been held in common by all German, Austrian, and Hungarian conductors, even though conductors may have varied individually in expression of those styles. The Austro-German school features a tradition that has its roots in the nineteenth century. Karajan is considered to have been the last of the Austro-German school as well as a bridge into a whole new tradition of conductors. This school is so new, in fact, that it has yet to be fully defined or named.

The Austro-German school taught Karajan that musical essence is the key to successful understanding, by musician and listener alike. Karajan, like other postwar conductors, was noted for taking very seriously—often arrogantly—his responsibility as musical representative of the country that produced the great, unbroken line of master musicians from Johann Sebastian Bach to Gustav Mahler. Because of this serious attitude, rehearsals conducted by Karajan were often considered intense and one-sided. He was interested in one basic musical element—making music as authoritatively, as honestly, as unostentatiously as possible. His conducting gestures always had an extraordinary degree of finish and, often, power. He strove to serve the wishes of the composer in the reproduction of his music. Study of the score, knowledge of related pieces,

and understanding the composer's life, times, and musical form and structure were mandatory for Karajan, even before rehearsals began. When beginning a new piece of music with the orchestra, Karajan always tried to achieve rehearsal perfection, striving for complete mastery of detail and mechanization. Next, he would usually suggest that the musicians play with a certain amount of freedom in the performance so that they could feel the sensation of making music by individual means. Through technical perfection and freedom of expression, a level of emotion was shared by the orchestra and conductor together.

To Karajan, conducting was more of a communication of feelings than a keeping of beat. He boasted to his students that he could have both wrists tied to his sides, and the orchestra would still feel his beat. Like the famous conductor of the classical period Gasparo Spontini, Karajan used to say that he could conduct an orchestra with his eyes alone. He was a firm believer that rhythm is a mysterious force that goes out in pulses from the conductor to the performers. It is this inner rhythm that is more important to musical flow than that conveyed through arm and body movement.

Karajan resigned the Berlin post in April, 1989, because of failing health. He died in Anif, Austria, an area very near to his childhood home of Salzburg, on July 16, 1989.

Summary

Herbert von Karajan, although in constant demand with European orchestras, conducted only fifteen performances at the Metropolitan Opera in New York. Yet few as they were, they were of great importance, if only because Karajan almost never came to the United States as a guest conductor and only rarely appeared there with the orchestras with which he was so involved all of his life in Europe—the Berlin and Vienna philharmonics. If Karajan's history in the United States is sparse, his impact upon classical music and opera in the United States, as well as throughout the world, is nevertheless beyond calculation. His recorded legacy is his performance legacy, and, to at least two generations of music lovers, his recordings were the keys that unlocked the riches of the repertory. First with the Philharmonia Orchestra in London and later with the Berlin and Vienna philharmonics, Karajan recorded and often rerecorded that legacy.

It is doubtful that there will be anyone to fill the vacancy left by Karajan: He was considered the

general music director of the world for many years, and his nearly six hundred recordings are left as textbook examples of the efficacy of rehearsal, casting control, and overall structural vision. For that reason, Karajan's contributions to music in the later twentieth century are engraved permanently in memory.

During his thirty-five years at the helm of the Berlin Philharmonic, which he molded into the most commanding symphony in the world, Karajan won acclaim as a master musical architect, achieving a remarkable fusion of precision and power. He lived an intensely passionate lifestyle. He made a goal for himself never to fritter away one moment of his life, and he achieved that goal.

Bibliography

Green, Elizabeth A. H. *The Dynamic Orchestra.* Englewood Cliffs, N.J.: Prentice-Hall, 1987. This book discusses how the conductor prepares, inspires, and interacts with the orchestra. Many examples of Karajan's leadership and short stories of his conducting are included.

Hurd, Michael. *The Orchestra.* New York: Facts on File, 1980; Oxford: Phaidon Press, 1981. Written from the orchestra member's point of view, this book describes the relationship of performer and conductor with various examples of Karajan and others who have made an impression upon the conducting profession in modern times.

"Maestro Deflated." *Economist* 324, no. 7775 (September 5, 1992). Discusses the end of Karajan's career and the factors leading to his fall, including his connections to Nazi Germany.

Matheopoulos, Helena. *Maestro: Encounters with Conductors of Today.* London: Hutchinson, and New York: Harper, 1982. The text is written in the style of an interview with Karajan, providing insight into his views of the role of conductor.

Schonberg, Harold C. *The Great Conductors.* New York: Simon and Schuster, 1967; London: Gollancz, 1968. A life sketch of Karajan including his schooling, early career, and life accomplishments.

Stuckenschmidt, H. H. *Germany and Central Europe.* London: Weidenfeld and Nicolson, and New York: Holt Rinehart, 1980. Although chiefly about composers, the book details the Austro-German school of conducting and how it relates to the music of Europe. Karajan is mentioned in his relationship to the music of composers such as Mahler.

Tharichen, Werner, and Henry Pleasants. "Furtwangler and Karajan as Conductors." *Opera Quarterly* 11, no. 1 (Fall 1994). Reviews the opera stylistics of Karajan and Wilhelm Furtwangler and their contributions to the Berlin Philharmonic Orchestra's worldwide acclaim.

Robert Briggs

YASUNARI KAWABATA

Born: June 11, 1899; Osaka, Japan
Died: April 16, 1972; Zushi, Japan
Area of Achievement: Literature
Contribution: Kawabata was the first Japanese writer to be awarded the Nobel Prize in Literature. Considered to be among the most Japanese of Japanese writers, he served as a critic and as a mentor for other writers as well.

Early Life

Yasunari Kawabata was born in Osaka, Japan, on June 11, 1899. His father, a physician, was interested in Chinese poetry, and Kawabata himself was at first more drawn to painting than to literature in his youth. In middle school, however, he decided to be a writer and had some pieces published in magazines and local newspapers while still a schoolboy. Entering Tokyo Imperial University in 1920, Kawabata first was enrolled in the English literature department and then moved to the Department of Japanese Literature; he was graduated in 1924.

Some doubt remains regarding the date of Kawabata's first work, an account of twelve days in May, 1914, a short time before the death of his grandfather. The piece, *Jurukosai no nikki* (diary of a sixteen-year-old), was published in 1925, at which time Kawabata wrote an afterword describing his discovery of the diary that he had kept eleven years before. Some scholars cite stylistic evidence to argue that it was written much later. This dispute over the dates of composition of Kawabata's first work may be of interest to the general reader as a memorable foreshadowing of the way Kawabata composed so many of his pieces, many of which were published serially, some of which were continually revised, and still more never completed.

The aspect of Kawabata's early years most significant to understanding his fiction is the tragic loss of so many members of his family: When he was two years old, his father died; a year later, his mother died. The maternal grandmother who took him in died when Kawabata was seven, and two years later, his only sister died. By the time he was nine, Kawabata only had a grandfather left.

Later in life, Kawabata was cast into the position of mourner several times as well, penning eulogies for his close friends. Critics note as well the romantic loss that may have indelibly marked Kawabata's youth. When he was about twenty years old, Kawabata was jilted by the young girl he had hoped to marry. This early loss of love may account for Kawabata's pessimistic attitudes toward love and happiness, which are so eloquently evoked in his writing.

Life's Work

The sad events in Kawabata's personal life did not, fortunately, mirror his professional life. Rather, with his very first published story, *Shokonsai ikkei* (1921; a scene of the memorial service for the war dead), Kawabata attracted the attention of a powerful literary figure, Kikuchi Kan, who introduced him to other writers. One of these, Riichi Yokomitsu, was a lifelong friend and among the twenty writers who founded a literary magazine, *Bungei jidai* (literary age), which became the center of a short-lived but influential literary group called the Shinkankaku-ha (Neo-Perceptionist or Neo-Sensationist group). Initially, Kawabata made his name as a literary theorist and critic by vigorously espousing the goals of this movement. Modeled on European modernists, this group of writers sought to break away from established ways of expression and valued new ways of recording what could be perceived through the senses. Newness was valued for itself, a goal that naturally tended to result in manneristic writing.

Even Kawabata's doomed love affair served him professionally. Heartbroken by his failed engagement, Kawabata joined a group of itinerant entertainers while on a walking tour of the Izu Peninsula in 1918 and, in 1922, wrote an account of his travels. Though he never published that work, he used it as the basis for one of his earliest successes, *Izu no odoriko* (1926; *The Izu Dancer*, 1955). Ironically enough, this brief story of the narrator's attraction to a dancer and his subsequent loss of desire when he discovers that she is but a child is not particularly distinguished by any new modes of expression at all. So popular was this tale of unfulfilled adolescent love that it was filmed as early as 1933 and several times subsequently.

The Izu Dancer is important to understanding Kawabata's later works, for it introduces the motif of attraction to young, virginal women, which some critics have found central to Kawabata's fiction. In the much later work, *Nemureru bijo* (1960-1961; "The House of the Sleeping Beauties," in *The House of the Sleeping Beauties and Other Stories*, 1969), this motif appears again in the much more perverse story of an impotent old man who frequents a house of assignation to sleep next to drugged, naked young girls. A recurring theme in Kawabata then is that love is unattainable, even if physically consummated, resulting in what critics see as nihilism in his work.

Throughout his life, Kawabata wrote very short stories which he referred to as "stories that fit into the palm of one's hand." These 146 stories, written intermittently from 1921 to 1972, were for Kawabata the essence of his art. They show his "preference for the miniature and for the half-spoken wisp of a plot." The publishing history of his acknowledged masterpiece *Yukiguni* (1935-1937, 1947; *Snow Country*, 1957) illustrates much about Kawabata's modus operandi. The genesis of the novel was a short piece published in a literary magazine in 1935; thereafter, over twelve years, other portions were published as separate pieces. Kawabata gathered the distinct portions and revised and published them to prize-winning acclaim in 1937; even then he added two more chapters in 1939 and 1940, revised them, and then finished it again in 1947.

The inevitably episodic quality of the work is not only a result of the serial approach to novel writing so common among Japanese writers but a key to the worldview in Kawabata's work. Indeed, it is one of the major aspects of his works that is identifiably Japanese. One obstacle for Western readers of Japanese novels is the de-emphasis, or, perhaps more accurately, lack of concern for plot or even individual character in Japanese literature. The closest equivalent in Western terms might be to distinguish the lyrically poetic from the novelistic mind-set. *Sembazuru* (1952; *Thousand Cranes*, 1958), another of Kawabata's better-known works, is even more illustrative of this mind-set. Its extremely short paragraphs remind the reader to approach it as a series of perceptions, rather than looking for meaning in a sustained narrative structure. The semblance of a plot concerns Kikuji, an orphaned young man, who is caught up with three women. Two of them were his father's mistresses; the third is the daughter of one of the mistresses. There is a strong suggestion that there are intrigues among the three women to win the male character, but, since the point of view is his and since he, like other male figures in Kawabata's fiction, tends to be a remote, detached figure, it is never clear exactly what actions are actually occurring. Rather, the reader is treated to suggestive ruminations about

the significance of antique tea bowls and minute observations, such as the pattern of a thousand cranes on a young woman's scarf, that apparently lead nowhere but are the essence of the novel.

Kawabata's sad childhood may, as some critics have argued, account for the detached quality of his work. It comes as a surprise, therefore, to note that Kawabata was not the total recluse in his private life that his fiction might suggest. Even after he decided to stop writing as a critic, Kawabata engaged in public activity in sporadic fits. In the 1930's, he was on the staff of several magazines and was selected by government authorities to be part of a group officially designated to revitalize Japanese literature. He supported younger writers, and one of his novels, *Meijin* (1942-1954; *The Master of Go*, 1972), for example, is even based on a series of actual matches between the master of the game at the time and a young challenger in 1938. During World War II, Kawabata continued to write, mainly about his childhood, but those years, so troubling to Japan's pride, increased the scope of his recollections of the past to include a renewed interest in his country's past as well. Japan's defeat affected him as deeply as the rest of his countrymen; he expressed his concern for preserving his heritage by collecting traditional Japanese art, particularly from the eighteenth century. After the war, he became the president of the Japanese PEN Club and in that capacity traveled all over the world and met other writers. The Nobel Prize in 1968 only increased his public exposure.

Toward the end of his life, Kawabata was still performing his childhood role as chief mourner at funerals. Particularly affecting for him was the suicide in 1970 of Yukio Mishima, a writer whom he had championed several years earlier. As late as 1971, Kawabata was active publicly, campaigning for an unsuccessful political candidate. When, on April 16, 1972, he left his house, went to his office, and killed himself by inhaling gas, this productive writer left no note and no explanations. The reasons for his suicide remain a mystery.

Summary

Yasunari Kawabata started many more projects than he ever finished. It is all the more remarkable then that he produced so steadily and for so wide a public. It is very difficult to classify Kawabata's output into the conventional categories of lowbrow, middlebrow, or highbrow fiction, because he published in popular magazines throughout his career. In the 1930's, when there was much debate about the renaissance of literature in Japan, Kawabata declared that such a revitalization could only occur in "works that are at once of pure literature and aimed at a mass audience." One of his own longest works, *Tokyo no hito* (1955; Tokyo people), was published serially more than five hundred times and, like some of his other pieces, made into a film.

The ultimately nihilistic nature of Kawabata's point of view may have been one reason that he was not overly protective of his literary reputation. Or perhaps like so many writers, he published where he could for the most money. He himself believed that he could only write when pushed to a deadline, and perhaps writing serially for periodicals was the only way he could write. Whatever the reason, his writing reached beyond literary circles to the reading public. His countrymen were delighted but surprised when a Japanese writer so difficult for the Japanese to comprehend was appreciated by foreigners, but Kawabata was perhaps appropriately selected for such international renown. Although, like many twentieth century Japanese writers, Kawabata was drawn to Western literature and learned from its major practitioners, he, like many of his contemporaries, believed himself first and foremost a Japanese writer. His Nobel Prize speech emphasized his appreciation of Japanese culture. It is no easier to say of Kawabata than it is of any great writer what is typical of his culture or uniquely his own vision. Fortunately, the legacy of his written words, his distinctive appreciation of the subtleties and fragility of love and beauty, speaks to all thoughtful readers.

Bibliography

Keene, Donald. "Kawabata Yasunari." In *Dawn to the West: Japanese Literature of the Modern Era, Fiction.* New York: Holt Rinehart, 1984. One of the most comprehensive books on modern Japanese literature. The critical/biographical approach provides an excellent extended introduction to Kawabata and his work. Includes notes, an index, and a selected bibliography.

Kimball, Arthur G. "The Last Extremity." In *Crisis in Identity and Contemporary Japanese Novels.* Rutland, Vt.: Tuttle, 1972. Author approaches several major writers thematically, from a Western point of view. Includes notes, a bibliography, and a syllabus for a suggested reading course.

Metevelis, Peter. "Translating Kawabata's 'Thenar Stories'." *Japan Quarterly* 41, no. 2 (April-June, 1994). Assesses the difficulties in translating the subtlety, moods, and beauty in Kawabata's "Thenar Stories."

Miyoshi, Masao. "The Margins of Life." In *Accomplices of Silence: The Modern Japanese Novel.* Berkeley: University of California Press, 1974. Specific discussions of *Snow Country* and *Yama no oto* (1949-1954; *The Sound of the Mountain,* 1970). Preface provides an excellent discussion of some differences between Japanese and Western novels. Includes notes and an index.

Petersen, Gwenn Boardman. "Kawabata Yasunari." In *The Moon in the Water: Understanding Tanizaki, Kawabata, and Mishima.* Honolulu: University Press of Hawaii, 1979. Extensive discussions intended for the general reader. The list of works available in English and the partial chronology at the end of each section are particularly helpful. Includes a general bibliography and an index.

Rimer, J. Thomas. "Kawabata Yasunari: Eastern Approaches." In *Modern Japanese Fiction and Its Traditions: An Introduction.* Princeton: Princeton University Press, 1978. Extended discussion of

Snow Country. The introduction offers an interesting discussion of structural principles in Japanese narrative fiction. Includes appendices, a bibliography, and an index.

Tsuruta, Kinya, and Thomas E. Swann, eds. "Kawabata Yasunari." In *Approaches to the Modern Japanese Novel.* Tokyo: Sophia University, 1976. Intended for undergraduates, this collection of essays on fifteen Japanese novels devotes three essays to Kawabata's best-known works. Includes a preface and notes on contributors.

Yamanouchi, Hisaaki. "The Eternal Womanhood: Tanizaki Jun'ichiro and Kawabata Yasunari." In *The Search for Authenticity in Modern Japanese Literature.* Cambridge and New York: Cambridge University Press, 1978. A brief critical/biographical approach comparing the two writers. Includes notes, a bibliography, and an index.

Shakuntala Jayaswal

FIRST BARONET KAY-SHUTTLEWORTH
James Phillips Kay

Born: July 20, 1804; Rochdale, Lancashire, England
Died: May 26, 1877; London, England
Areas of Achievement: Education and public administration
Contribution: One of the earliest civil servants appointed to office in the reformed British government, Kay-Shuttleworth helped to shape both the nature of elementary education and the methods of nineteenth century public administration.

Early Life

James Phillips Kay (he added his wife's surname upon marrying) was born July 20, 1804, in Rochdale. His parents, Robert and Hannah Phillips Kay, were middle-class textile manufacturers, Congregationalist in faith. After studying at home, Kay clerked in a relative's bank; nevertheless, both young James and his mother harbored aspirations for a more distinguished career. Kay entered the University of Edinburgh's medical school, then considered to be the best in the English-speaking world, in 1824, and received the M.D. degree in 1827.

Kay practiced medicine in Manchester, the capital of the textile industry and London's rival as an intellectual center, from 1827 to 1835. Although he published several articles and a book on medical experiments, his practice languished and he failed to receive appointments to several hospitals. He had become involved in the Manchester Statistical Society, a pioneering social research organization; and he played a small role in the political turmoil over the movement to reform Parliament from 1830 to 1832. The parliamentary Reform Act of 1832 led to reforms in other areas of British government (such as factory inspection and poor relief) and increased the need for civil servants to administer governmental activities. Kay left medicine and Manchester in 1835, being appointed an assistant Poor Law commissioner (traveling inspector) with special responsibility for East Anglia.

Kay's work as a physician and civil servant opened doors, both personal and professional, which led to high bureaucratic office, marriage to an heiress, and a title. In the course of his work, he met Whig politicians such as Joseph Hume, the Marquess of Lansdowne, and Lord John Russell; his circle expanded to include more gentlemen and aristocrats after he joined the Reform Club. He married Janet Shuttleworth in 1842; her family had held an estate in Lancashire since the 1300's; her fortune included stock in railroads and coal mines. Simultaneously, he drifted away from the Congregationalism that his family had followed since 1662. At some point between 1834 and 1839, he started attending Church of England services. His marriage and conversion transformed him from a middle-class urban Nonconformist into an Anglican country gentleman, a transformation symbolized by his adoption of his wife's surname.

Life's Work

Kay-Shuttleworth's work as assistant Poor Law commissioner brought him into contact with farm laborers, the new industrial proletariat, and domestic outworkers. He came to the conclusion that the New Poor Law, which in its conception was solidly rooted in the Benthamite principles of efficiency, simplicity, uniformity, and self-regulation, was the cure for poverty. He understood that circumstances beyond workers' control—market fluctuations and the social dislocation caused by the transition from the domestic system to the factory system—contributed to their poverty, but he also believed that their ignorance, improvidence, immorality, and lack of self-discipline prevented them from freeing themselves from poverty, exacerbated their economic condition, and made them potential revolutionaries. The way around these perceived problems was education, which would rehabilitate children by teaching them marketable skills and middle-class social values.

Kay-Shuttleworth's educational reports led to his transfer to London in 1837, and in 1839 he was appointed the first permanent secretary of the newly created Education Department. An ambitious man, Kay-Shuttleworth sought to expand the role of his department, and thereby his own importance. The Education Department in 1839 operated no schools: It could only issue grants to build schools, and it had the right to inspect schools receiving state aid. Kay-Shuttleworth proposed an elaborate system of tax-supported education, but the fact that the elementary schools were connected with religious denominations (especially the Church of England), jealous of their independence and suspicious of state control, meant that such a scheme had no chance of passing through Parliament. Kay-Shuttleworth then turned to bureaucratic methods to expand the Education Department's role. He tried to use the department's inspectorial powers to impose a uniform curriculum on the schools and on teacher-training colleges, but again the religious issue thwarted his schemes.

The 1830's and 1840's were years of intense religious conflict in British history. Nonconformists (mainly Baptists, Congregationalists, Presbyterians, and Methodists) were militant and wanted to eliminate the legal privileges and special access to tax revenues enjoyed by the Church of England; mostly middle-class, the Nonconformists associated Anglican privileges with their political enemies, the landed gentry. During the same period, Roman Catholics had become militant, spurred by ultramontanism (the belief that the Papacy should be the supreme power in the Church) and triumphalism (the belief that the Church should attempt to convert England); they wanted a share of state funds for their schools. The Nonconformists, who hated Roman Catholicism for doctrinal reasons, objected. In reaction, the Church of England also became militant, insisting on its prerogatives as the national church established by law.

All these religious groups believed that education had to have a religious component; they disagreed as to the nature of that component. The governments of the day, whether Liberal or Conservative, tried to pursue an evenhanded policy, for they did not wish to alienate powerful institutions. Hence the politicians responsible for overseeing the Education Department (the Lord President of the Privy Council and the Home Secretary) restrained Kay-Shuttleworth's schemes, removed the making of policy from his hands, and limited him to routine administrative tasks. These limitations frustrated him, for his educational ideas were mixed together with his own desire for upward social mobility. He suffered fainting spells and temporary paralytic attacks in 1848; these maladies, attributed at the time to overwork, but probably psychosomatic symptoms of an emotional breakdown, forced his resignation in 1849. He was created a baronet as reward for his administrative work.

Kay-Shuttleworth spent the rest of his life in retirement, administering his wife's Lancashire estates. (Shortly after his retirement, his wife also suffered paralysis. The couple eventually agreed upon a permanent separation.) Kay-Shuttleworth died at his London home on May 26, 1877.

Summary

James Kay-Shuttleworth belongs to a select group of early Victorian civil servants who enjoyed high public visibility and who were pioneers in the creation of the modern British bureaucracy. Along with men including Edwin Chadwick at the Poor Law Commission, Charles Trevelyan at the Treasury, John Simon at the Board of Health, and James Stephen at the Colonial Office, Kay-Shuttleworth has the reputation of being a master civil servant, a statesman in disguise (as the historian George Kitson Clark called these bureaucrats), an administrator who made governmental policy in the name of politicians who were his ostensible, but not real, superiors.

In fact, Kay-Shuttleworth, as well as the other civil servants of his era, provided a useful function for the politicians. Experts on technical matters relating to their areas of administrative expertise, they helped make departments of state operate efficiently. They could be relied upon to carry out expeditiously the policies that politicians had decided upon. Moreover, their prominence in the public eye meant that those who opposed the policies of departments of state attacked them, not the politicians, in Parliament and in the press.

Equally as important, Kay-Shuttleworth's career illustrates an important theme in the history of Victorian Britain: the opportunities for upward social mobility for the middle classes that the expansion of the bureaucratic state provided.

Bibliography

Arnstein, Walter L. *Britain Yesterday and Today: 1830 to the Present.* 7th ed. Lexington, Mass.: Heath, 1996. A very readable survey of English history; useful for background.

Brown, Lucy M., and Ian R. Christie. *Bibliography of British History, 1789-1851.* Oxford: Clarendon Press, 1977. The most recent bibliography of writings on British history for this period. Organized by subject and well indexed.

Hurt, John. *Education in Evolution: Church, State, Society, and Popular Education, 1800-1870.* London: Hart-Davis, 1971. A well-written and interesting account which provides an excellent introduction to the history of English elementary education in the nineteenth century.

Johnson, Richard. "Educational Policy and Social Control in Early Victorian England." *Past and Present* 49 (November, 1970): 96-119. An analysis of the state's involvement in teacher training, an important policy initiative commonly attributed to Kay-Shuttleworth.

Kitson Clark, G. " 'Statesmen in Disguise': Reflexions on the History of the Neutrality of the Civil Service." *Historical Journal* 2 (1959): 19-39. Shows how early Victorian civil servants attempted to advance their political and economic views.

MacDonagh, Oliver. *Early Victorian Government, 1830-1870.* London: Weidenfeld and Nicolson, 1977. A good introduction to the history of Victorian public administration.

Paz, D. G. "The Limits of Bureaucratic Autonomy in Victorian Administration." *Historian* 49 (1987): 167-183. Compares Kay-Shuttleworth's administrative record with those of chief servants in the Home Office, Admirality, and Colonial Office, and argues that politicians limited and controlled their activities.

———. *The Politics of Working-Class Education in Britain, 1830-50.* Manchester: Manchester University Press, 1980. An account of the origins and early development of the Education Department, in the contexts of Victorian political, religious, administrative, and educational history.

———. "Sir James Kay-Shuttleworth: The Man Behind the Myth." *History of Education* 14 (1985): 185-198. How Kay-Shuttleworth's socioeconomic background, religious faith, family relationships, and ambitious personality affected his public bureaucratic career and his private life.

Selleck, R. J. W. *James Kay-Shuttleworth: Journey of an Outsider.* London and Portland, Ore.: Woburn Press, 1994. A perceptive biography based on significant research based on both primary and secondary sources. Helpful in understanding Victorian Britain.

Smith, Frank. *The Life and Work of Sir James Kay-Shuttleworth.* London: Murray, 1923. Laudatory, uncritical, and outdated, but the only book-length biography.

D. G. Paz

NIKOS KAZANTZAKIS

Born: February 18, 1883; Heraklion, Crete
Died: October 26, 1957; Freiburg, West Germany
Area of Achievement: Literature
Contribution: The best-known, most successful, and most controversial Greek writer of the twentieth century, Kazantzakis has written several of the most absorbing and enduring works of his time.

Early Life

On February 18, 1883, Nikos Kazantzakis was born on the island of Crete, the son of a poor farmer and feed supplier. His early life, spent in rural surroundings, brought him into close contact with the common people who feature so largely in his books. At this time he also developed a fascination with the land, weather, and sea of the Mediterranean region, the images of which resonate and take on a mystical intensity in his writing. When Kazantzakis was fourteen, native Cretans rose in rebellion against their Turkish rulers. To keep Kazantzakis away from the fighting, his father sent him to the island of Naxos, where there was a private school operated by Franciscan monks. For the first time, the young Kazantzakis encountered the intellectual traditions of Western civilization, and he was fascinated. The concept of spiritual development, especially in its mystical and ascetic aspects, gripped him.

This fascination never left him. From this point his life became a quest for the ideal spiritual role model, which led him from one great historical figure to another. After high school, he won a scholarship to the University of Athens, where he studied philosophy. Following graduation, he traveled to Paris to study with the philosopher Henri Bergson, at that time developing his central theme of creative intelligence as the means of man's liberation from the bondage of matter. Under Bergson's direction, Kazantzakis came to admire the writing of Friedrich Wilhelm Nietzsche and Oswald Spengler, both of whom viewed history as dominated and directed by great spiritual principles. Leaving France, Kazantzakis attempted a spiritual experiment: He retreated to a Greek Orthodox monastery on Mt. Athos in Macedonia, where he lived and meditated in an isolated cell for six months. Solitary meditation proved not the secret for him; he felt further removed from God at the end. Instead, he decided to follow the doctrine of Nietzsche, who taught that man elevated himself by spiritual struggle. According to Nietzsche, man had the capacity to transform himself into a superman by actualizing spiritual energy. This could be accomplished by fusing the opposed principles of reason and passion, embodied in the Greek gods Apollo and Dionysus. Nietzsche became the first of a series of spiritual guides for Kazantzakis, each of whom incorporated the values of earlier members.

Life's Work

At this point in his life, Kazantzakis decided to pursue one pole of the Nietzschean opposition: the Dionysian ideal of ecstatic action, of losing oneself enthusiastically in a cause, as opposed to the Apollonian ideal of restrained, detached contemplation. Because of this ideology of action, he identified with and supported a series of revolutionary movements promising to liberate the oppressed. He was first moved by the Cretan and Greek nationalist revolutionaries, but the Russian Revolution broke out in 1917 when he was on the point of leaving for Greece. This inflamed his imagination, for he instinctively found his own aspirations reflected in the spectacle of the common man seizing power by sheer force of numbers. Still, he found himself unable to join the revolution immediately and felt committed to Greece. There, far from joining in a revolution, he was appointed to a succession of offices by the government. As part of his duties, he took part in a Peloponnesian mining operation with an activist named George Zorbas, who struck him as the embodiment of his concept of the Nietzschean ideal. That impression remained with him. Later he would transform it into the image of the superhero in his novel *Vios Kai politela tou Alexe Zormpa* (1946; *Zorba the Greek*, 1953).

Around 1920 Kazantzakis modified his ideal, or reinterpreted Nietzsche. Now he became convinced that struggle was the important element rather than attainment; man realized himself by tension, by harboring opposites. Suddenly he felt compelled to project this theme in literature. He began writing and producing a series of verse plays that focused on his developing image of the hero. He also translated works by Bergson, Charles Darwin, Johann Peter Eckermann, William James, Maurice Maeterlinck, Nietzsche, Plato, and Dante, all of whom seemed to him to reconcile the opposed principles of contemplation and action.

Eventually he developed his ideal of what he called the "Cretan glance," which focuses the conflicting forces in a tense crucible.

In 1922, Kazantzakis moved to Vienna, where he encountered the teaching of Buddha, whose doctrine of renunciation helped him reconcile himself to the desolation and loss of the desperate post-World War I period. Following that inspiration, he began to compose an integrated statement of his beliefs, which after several revisions became *Salvatores Dei: Asketike* (1927; *The Saviors of God: Spiritual Exercises*, 1960). By that time he had grown far beyond the Buddhist origins of his ideas; few Buddhists would find such a celebration of creative energy congenial. The work does, however, embody the basic values developed in his later works. For the next few years, Kazantzakis took advantage of several opportunities to travel to the Soviet Union, where for a while he identified Vladimir Ilich Lenin as a new savior and vowed to promote the Leninist system. After close exposure to the practice rather than the theory of Leninism, however, he became disillusioned. While traveling through Russia, supposedly to gather materials for publicizing Leninism, he found himself repeatedly preoccupied with the figure of Odysseus and with the values he seemed to incarnate.

For the next ten years—during which he published two novels, both written in French—Kazantzakis worked and reworked what would eventually become *Odysseia* (1938; *The Odyssey: A Modern Sequel*, 1958). This modern epic continuation of Homer's poem runs to 33,333 lines in an obscure and difficult verse form and incorporates extensive research into ancient Greek history and archaeology. This monumental verse narrative, ostensibly setting forth the experiences and reflections of Odysseus after his return to Ithaca from the Trojan War, actually centers on projecting Kazantzakis' ideal of purposive action, of a spiritually informed energy directed toward a goal.

Kazantzakis' political beliefs, motivated primarily by a desire to liberate the common man, caused him to select certain specific formal and linguistic patterns—thus the extensive number symbolism, the elaborate verse, and the use of demotic (common) rather than formal Greek. As a result, his work is finally quite un-Homeric, and his Odysseus rather different from the original. Still, Kazantzakis did not intend to imitate Homer; in fact, he claimed to transcend him. The liberties he took with the Homeric materials and characters,

with history and with the literary language, antagonized and irritated both traditional and modernist Greeks. For these reasons, the book has not been well received in its native culture, though the energy and art of the narrative, the audacity of the ideas, and the accuracy of antiquarian details would seem to compel recognition. This work may be one of the few great works of world literature appreciated better in translation than in its original language.

His next major work, *Zorba the Greek*, is the single work by Kazantzakis to gain critical recognition both at home and abroad; it also was adapted successfully to the screen, becoming an extremely successful motion picture. Yet, like all of his work, it seems appreciated most for qualities that he did not intend, or did not intend to be central. The novel is particularly remarkable for an innovative use of technical point of view. What happens is related by an anonymous observer, precisely because experiencing the events moved him from a state of despair to one of acceptance, from believing that significant human action was impossible to acting with serenity. The narrator enters a state of calm indifference, though again able to act, in the end; this state is what Kazantzakis intended to induce. He creates a novel in which the enclosing frame finally takes precedence over the enclosed narrative. The novel, however, is usually praised because of the dynamic energy of the main character, whose zest for life is so infectious that it persists even in disaster. In this image of self-realization through action, Kazantzakis carries further his concept of the Cretan glance, of resolution by fusion of opposites. Zorba begins at the lowest point of despair but comes to discover that he must still act in defiance of despair, which is what being human means.

The work by which Kazantzakis is best known today, *Ho teleutaios peirasmos* (1955; *The Last Temptation of Christ*, 1960), represents a further stage in the evolution of his hero. That stage is incarnate in the figure of Jesus Christ, depicted as a man tormented by the fear that God has singled him out to be the Messiah. This concept of the heroic Christ is entirely heterodox; the writer makes him subject to temptations of the flesh as well as obsessed with ungodlike fears. The book's publication resulted in Kazantzakis' excommunication from the Greek Orthodox church in 1961; a generation later, in 1988, a filmed version by Martin Scorsese provoked a widespread boycott and threats of reprisal from conservative Christian churches.

In both cases these reactions seem based on misunderstanding, for the image of Christ presented in this book is truly heroic, truly human, truly admirable and inspiring. It is the humanity with which Kazantzakis endows him that causes the problem: He displays a Christ who is frail, imperfect, only gradually discovering the godhead immanent in himself, and—as the title indicates—susceptible to temptation, as indeed the biblical Christ seems to have been. Theology aside, this is a compelling, riveting novel, full of brilliantly imaginative solutions to the problems facing anyone attempting to realize the sketchy narrative of the Gospels.

Kazantzakis himself certainly identified with this ideal of self-actualization. Following *The Last Temptation of Christ*, he continued to add depth and dimensions to his image of the hero. In *Ho phtochoules tou Theou* (1956; *Saint Francis*, 1962), he showed how a Christian mystic and ascetic could recapitulate the self-sacrificial experience of Christ in his own person. The following year, though suffering from leukemia, he seized the opportunity to visit China. There he developed an infection from a smallpox inoculation, and he died shortly after his return on October 26, 1957. The Greek church interfered with plans to bury him with the honors due a hero; as a banned writer he was refused burial in consecrated ground.

Summary

Nikos Kazantzakis is a curiosity among twentieth century writers. During his lifetime, he rarely received the kind of critical reception that he deserved, particularly among his own countrymen. Yet in many respects he deserves to be ranked with the accepted giants of twentieth century literature: D. H. Lawrence, James Joyce, and Thomas Mann, for example, all provide illuminating parallels. In fact, not even his detractors have ever denied the power of his creations, or his capacity to irritate nonreaders with his radical or innovative theories.

To an extent the success of Kazantzakis' ideas—or his fidelity to them—may have brought about his failure with literary critics. Like Rudyard Kipling, Hermann Hesse, and Lawrence, Kazantzakis believed that writers were primarily moralists, obligated to mold and motivate the beliefs and behavior of their readers. His writings are consciously didactic; this in turn means that his characters and plots are highly predetermined and controlled. This approach runs counter to the prevailing temper of twentieth century fiction, which has tended to follow the more objective, independent approach typified by Joyce. Further, readers who for whatever reason find Kazantzakis' ideas uncongenial are likely to notice only the artifice and believe that he is attempting to manipulate them. In truth, some of his books fail to integrate his visions with his technique, and in these the seams show. At his best, however, his visions are realized as brilliantly as any in literature.

Bibliography

Bien, Peter. Afterword to *The Last Temptation of Christ*, by Nikos Kazantzakis. New York: Simon and Schuster, 1960; London: Faber, 1975. This eight-page note surveys the life, ideas, and works of Kazantzakis more clearly and effectively than any other single source.
———. "Kazantzakis and Politics." In *The Politics of Twentieth Century Novelists*, edited by George A. Panichas. New York: Hawthorn, 1971. In this twenty-page article, Bien explores an interesting question: What connection might there

be between Kazantzakis' political activities—he held several offices—and his evolving image of the hero?

———. *Kazantzakis and the Linguistic Revolution in Greek Literature.* Princeton, N.J.: Princeton University Press, 1972. This is the single major scholarly work on Kazantzakis in English, but it focuses primarily on his use of language. Still, this has the most detailed account of his leading themes to be found and has the best bibliography available.

———. *Nikos Kazantzakis.* New York: Columbia University Press, 1972. Part of the Columbia Essays on Modern Writers series, this short book is the best general introduction to Kazantzakis' work available in English. It focuses primarily on the leading themes and provides relatively little information about his life. The bibliography is good.

Dillistone, F. W. *The Novelist and the Passion Story.* London: Collins, and New York: Sheed and Ward, 1960. This is a useful survey of works published up to the late 1950's of representations of the passion of Christ in fiction, a surprisingly popular topic in the first half of the century. The discussion of Kazantzakis' work in this context is quite interesting.

Dombrowski, Daniel A. *Kazantzakis and God.* Albany: State University of New York Press, 1997. The first book-length study of Kazantzakis's religious vision through analysis of his work in numerous genres.

Friar, Kimon. Introduction to *The Odyssey: A Modern Sequel,* by Nikos Kazantzakis. London: Secker and Warburg, and New York: Simon and Schuster, 1958. In much more than the standard introduction, Friar presents a thirty-page survey of Kazantzakis' work and ideas, with particular reference to the *The Odyssey: A Modern Sequel.*

Journal of Modern Literature 2, no. 2 (Winter, 1971-1972). This issue, devoted entirely to Kazantzakis, collects a number of useful essays, including efforts by Peter Bien (on the influence of Nietzsche), Adele Black (on Kazantzakis' use of masks), Joseph C. Flay (on erotic stoicism), Morton P. Levitt (on the influence of Cretan culture), and others.

Kazantzakis, Helen. *Nikos Kazantzakis: A Biography Based on His Letters.* Oxford: Cassirer, and New York: Simon and Schuster, 1968. An extraordinary assemblage of letters edited to shed light on different periods of Kazantzakis' life and aspects of his character, this work by his second wife presents that life as unusually consonant with his ideas. It calls for a more balanced, objective account.

Kazantzakis, Nikos. *Report to Greco.* Translated by Peter A. Bien. Oxford: Cassirer, and New York: Simon and Schuster, 1965. This posthumously published autobiography offers the author's own insights into his life. Some sections are fascinating, but it is fragmentary and incomplete.

Middleton, Darren J. N. "Apophatic Boldness: Kazantzakis's Use of Negation and Silence to Emphasize Theological Mystery." *Midwest Quarterly* 39, no. 4 (Summer 1998). Discusses Kazantzakis's description of God in his work *The Last Temptation of Christ.*

Stanford, W. B. *The Ulysses Theme: A Study in the Adaptability of a Traditional Hero.* 2d ed. Oxford: Blackwell, 1963; New York: Barnes and Noble, 1964. This book contains some valuable insights into Kazantzakis' poem, particularly with reference to his concept of the hero. Only some twenty pages are given to his work, however, mostly in comparison with Joyce.

James Livingston

HELEN KELLER

Born: June 27, 1880; Tuscumbia, Alabama
Died: June 1, 1968; Westport, Connecticut
Areas of Achievement: Social reform and education
Contribution: Blind and deaf since early childhood, Keller exemplified by her life of activism
the full empowerment potential of disabled persons who receive appropriate adaptive education. She served as a spokesperson and fund-
raiser for the benefit of deaf and blind people.

Early Life

Helen Adams Keller was born in a small town in
northern Alabama to Kate Adams Keller and Captain Arthur Keller, a Confederate Civil War veteran. At nineteen months, Helen suffered an illness
that left her blind, deaf, and eventually mute. She
remained locked in this lonely state of sensory deprivation until she reached the age of six, when her
family employed Anne Sullivan, the twenty-year-
old daughter of working-class Irish immigrants, as
her tutor. Sullivan herself was visually impaired.

With Sullivan's devoted, creative, and stubborn
help, Helen soon rediscovered the concept that
concrete things are associated with linguistic symbols—in her case, the letters of the manual alphabet spelled into her hand. Once that breakthrough
was made and communication was reestablished,
the young girl worked quickly to master manual
lip-reading, handwriting, typewriting, Braille, and
basic vocal speech. Helen's recovery of communication was aided by the residue of language skills
that had developed before she went deaf, by a stim-
ulus-rich home environment, by the early age at
which her adaptive education began, and by her
own remarkable intelligence and perseverance. Accompanied and assisted by her tutor, Helen attended the Perkins Institution for the Blind (Boston),
the Horace Mann School of the Deaf (New York),
the Wright-Humason School for the Deaf (New
York), and, eventually, Gilman's preparatory Cambridge School for Young Ladies and Radcliffe College (both in Cambridge, Massachusetts), from
which she was graduated with honors.

While she was still a schoolgirl, Keller began her
lifelong career of philanthropic fund-raising, collecting contributions for the education of a destitute blind and deaf boy when she was eleven, giving a tea to benefit the kindergarten for the blind
when she was twelve, and campaigning for money

to start a public library in Tuscumbia when she was
thirteen.

She also began her career as a writer early. In her
childhood, she published several short pieces, but
those early successes were also accompanied by
what she later referred to as "the one cloud in my
childhood's bright sky." In 1892, she wrote a short
story called "The Frost King," which she sent as a
birthday present to Michael Anagnos at the Perkins
Institution for the Blind, who published it in one of
the Institution reports. The story was discovered to
be remarkably similar to Margaret T. Canby's "The
Frost Fairies." The twelve-year-old child was accused of willful plagiarism and was interrogated
for many hours. The experience traumatized her so
deeply that, although she loved stories, she never
wrote fiction again, remaining anxious and uncertain about which were her own ideas and which
were impressions she had gathered from other
writers. Helen's literary creativity turned toward
autobiography.

When she was a sophomore at Radcliffe, she was
asked by the editors of *Ladies' Home Journal* to
write her life story in monthly installments. With
the help of John Macy, a Harvard English instructor, and Sullivan (who eventually married Macy),
Keller completed the project, which was later published in 1902 as *The Story of My Life*.

Life's Work

After her 1904 graduation from Radcliffe with
honors in German and English, Helen Keller continued to write. *The World I Live In* was published
in 1908; *The Song of the Stone Wall*, in 1910; and
Out of the Dark, in 1913. She also wrote a number
of magazine articles, primarily inspirational pieces.
Some critics objected to the visual and auditory
imagery in her work, criticizing it as mere "hearsay" or even offering it as evidence of outright
fraud. As time went by, however, the disbelief with
which some people greeted Keller's accomplishments gradually faded. This widening public estimation of what was possible for the deaf and blind
significantly enlarged the field of opportunities
available to all disabled people after Keller.

Sullivan married Macy soon after Keller's graduation, but the partnership between the two women
continued into Keller's adulthood. (Keller never
married; her engagement at age thirty-six to Peter

Fagan was thwarted by her family.) The two women began to lecture together. Keller would speak her lectures and, because Keller's voice was still very difficult for strangers to understand, Sullivan would interpret. Their lectures served to increase public comprehension of the life of the perceptually impaired.

As Keller gained experience, moving through the world on Sullivan's arm, her scope of interest enlarged from human limitations caused by visual and auditory impairment to include human limitations caused by gender, by class, and by nationalism. She began to see the welfare of all people as being interdependent. She worked for woman suffrage. A pacifist to the core, she spoke against the vast amount of money her country poured into military expenditures. She read Marx and Engels, and in 1909 she joined the Socialist Party, of which John Macy was also a member. At the advent of World War I, she became a member of the Industrial Workers of the World. She wrote and lectured in defense of socialism, supported the union movement, and opposed the United States' entry into World War I. She remained sympathetic toward socialist causes all of her life, but in 1921 she decided to focus her energies on raising money for the American Foundation for the Blind.

Around the time of World War I, the advent of modernism in literature caused Keller's sentimental, rather flowery prose to seem less fashionable. An assertive and political single woman in her middle years, Keller was less comprehensible to the American public than she had been as a child. Her income from her writing diminished, and, after years of refusing it, she finally accepted a yearly stipend from the great archcapitalist Andrew Carnegie. Financial issues became more and more important as Sullivan's health deteriorated and Macy descended into alcoholism.

Financial pressure prompted Keller and Sullivan to venture into vaudeville. Between 1920 and 1924, their lectures were a great success on Harry and Herman Weber's variety circuit. Besides further deepening public understanding of blindness and deafness, their years of vaudeville gave them the opportunity to meet and develop friendships with many of the famous people of the day, including Sophie Tucker, Enrico Caruso, Jascha Heifetz, and Harpo Marx. Throughout her life, Keller's extensive acquaintance with influential people was part of the power she wielded in the world. (She was received in the White House by every American president from Grover Cleveland to John F. Kennedy.)

During the 1920's, Keller and Sullivan also traveled frequently on fund-raising tours for the American Foundation for the Blind, an agency that Keller supported until her death. She also continued to write. In 1927, she published *My Religion*, an explanation of her understanding of the alternative reality described by the eighteenth century visionary Emanuel Swedenborg. In 1930, *Midstream: My Later Life* appeared as well.

The 1930's saw more of Keller's books produced: *Peace at Eventide* was brought out in 1932, and *Helen Keller's Journal* was published in 1938. Keller deplored the rise of the Nazis and supported John L. Lewis' union strikes. Anne Sullivan died in 1936. After the death of her primary life-partner, Keller relied mainly on Polly Thompson, a Scots immigrant who had been assisting her since 1915. They remained together until Thompson's death in 1960.

In 1955, Keller published *Teacher*, a biography of Anne Sullivan Macy. She continued to be active on behalf of the blind and deaf until around 1962. In 1964, Keller was awarded the Presidential Medal of Freedom, the country's highest civilian honor. She died quietly in her sleep at the age of eighty-seven.

Keller's life was filled with activity: writing, lecturing, studying, and traveling. Her significance was not simply based on her untiring work on behalf of the constituency that a childhood misfortune and her own choice selected for her. By all accounts, she was a woman of great spiritual authority. Religious faith, the self-mastery needed to overcome tragedy, and a powerful and loving teacher produced in Keller one of the spiritually radiant figures of her time, whose power was not simply based on what she did or who she knew, but also on who she was and the direct effect of her presence on those whose lives she touched.

Summary

Helen Keller worked her entire life for the betterment of the disabled. She wrote. She lectured. She exerted her considerable influence over public institutions and powerful people. She raised funds for a number of agencies serving the disabled. She acted as a catalyst for the organization of state commissions for the blind. She helped to educate the American public about the prevention of gonorrheal blindness in newborn babies. The work that she did earned for her numerous humanitarian awards and citations.

The fruits of Keller's work were important, but what is even more important is that she did that work at all. She came into a world that had extremely limiting ideas about what was possible for a deaf and blind woman to accomplish. The disabled were seen as less than fully human; deaf and blind people were still being locked away in mental asylums in the world into which Helen Keller was born. In that world, the mere existence of a powerful, educated, assertive figure such as Keller was profoundly significant. Each lecture she gave, each article she wrote defied stereotypes and served to change the attitudes and expectations of her society. Her public life as an active deaf and blind woman truly altered the intellectual horizons around her. When she died, she left a world that had been radically changed by her life.

Bibliography

Einhorn, Lois. *Helen Keller, Public Speaker: Sightless but Seen, Deaf but Heard.* Westport, Conn.: Greenwood Press, 1998. This is the first full-length study of Keller's career as a public speaker. Includes the text of several speeches, analysis, a chronology of her speeches, and a bibliography.

Gibson, William. *The Miracle Worker.* New York: Bantam, 1965. The original play that examined the early years of the relationship between Helen Keller and Anne Sullivan.

Houston, Jean. *Public Like a Frog: Entering the Lives of Three Great Americans.* Wheaton, Ill.: Quest, 1993. Concise biographical sketches of Emily Dickinson, Thomas Jefferson, and Helen Keller, highlighting their spirituality. This work is unique in that the biographies are interspersed with personal growth exercises that invite the reader's imaginative participation in crucial moments of the subjects' lives.

Keller, Helen. *Midstream: My Later Life.* London: Hodder and Stoughton, and New York: Doubleday, 1929. The story of Keller's life from around 1904 until 1927. Describes her work for the blind, her lecturing and writing career, her experiences in Hollywood, and her relationships with some well-known public figures, including Mark Twain, Alexander Graham Bell, and the Carnegie family.

———. *The Story of My Life.* London: Hodder and Stoughton, 1958; New York: Macmillan, 1972. The best-known of Keller's autobiographical works, this book tells the story of her first two decades and includes a selection of letters that illustrate the development of her language skills from the age of seven to adulthood. Contains a useful short introduction by Lou Ann Walker.

———. *Teacher: Anne Sullivan Macy.* New York: Doubleday, 1955; London: Gollancz, 1956. Keller's respectful and loving account of Anne Sullivan's life. Seeks to redress what Keller saw as an imbalance between excessive public attention on herself and neglect of Sullivan's accomplishments.

Lash, Joseph P. *Helen and Teacher: The Story of Helen Keller and Anne Sullivan Macy.* Radcliffe Biography Series. London: Allen Lane, and New York: Delacorte, 1980. This long dual biography acknowledges the long, fruitful relationship between Keller and Anne Sullivan.

Donna Glee Williams

JOHN F. KENNEDY

Born: May 29, 1917; Brookline, Massachusetts
Died: November 22, 1963; Dallas, Texas
Area of Achievement: Government and politics
Contribution: Combining intelligence with personal charm, Kennedy became a model to millions around the globe, inspiring them to seek new goals and to work toward those goals with self-confidence.

Early Life

John Fitzgerald Kennedy was born May 29, 1917, in Brookline, Massachusetts, an inner suburb of Boston. He was the second son of Joseph P. Kennedy, a businessman rapidly growing wealthy, and Rose Fitzgerald Kennedy, daughter of former Boston mayor John F. "Honey Fitz" Fitzgerald. He was educated at Choate School in Connecticut and was graduated from Harvard in 1940. While his earlier years were plagued by illness, and his grades were often mediocre, he revealed himself to be an original thinker. His senior thesis was published as *Why England Slept* (1940), largely by the efforts of Joseph Kennedy's friends. John Kennedy was able to travel widely in Europe in 1937 and 1938 and to spend the spring of 1939 in Britain, where his father was United States ambassador. Still there when World War II began in September, he assisted in caring for American survivors of the first torpedoed passenger ship, gaining a sense of realism about war.

As United States entrance into the war became likely, he entered the United States Navy as an ensign, September, 1941, six feet tall but extremely thin and looking younger than his years. A thatch of often rumpled, sandy hair added to his boyish appearance. He was sent to the South Pacific where he commanded PT 109, a patrol torpedo boat. The boat was sunk in action on August 2, 1943, and Kennedy not only rescued survivors but also swam for help though badly injured. Awarded the Navy and U.S. Marine Corps medal, he briefly commanded another boat but soon went on sick leave and was discharged for disability as a full lieutenant in December, 1944. Because of his injury, coming in the wake of earlier illnesses, he was often a sick man.

Life's Work

Kennedy had thought of writing as a career and covered the United Nations Conference at San Francisco, April-July, 1945, and the 1945 British elections for the New York *Journal-American*. His older brother, Joseph, Jr., slated to be the family's political success, had been killed in the war in Europe, and John took up that task. In 1946, he ran for the House of Representatives from the Eleventh District of Massachusetts, narrowly gaining the Democratic nomination but winning the November election with 72.6 percent of the vote. The district sent him to Washington for three terms, during which time his record was mixed. In favor of public housing and an opponent of the then reactionary leadership of the American Legion, he was friendly with Senator Joseph McCarthy of Wisconsin, whose "red-baiting" began in 1950. Plagued by a painful back, he was diagnosed in 1947 as having Addison's disease also, then usually fatal, and was often absent from the House. He showed more interest in national issues than local ones and became deeply interested in foreign policy. He rejected his father's isolationism, supported the Truman Doctrine and the Marshall Plan, but joined right-wing critics of the so-called loss of China to Mao Tsetung. In 1951, he toured Europe and Asia for several weeks and returned better balanced regarding a Russian threat to Western Europe and the significance of Asian anticolonialism.

Unwilling to spend many years gaining seniority in the House, in 1952, Kennedy ran against Henry Cabot Lodge for the United States Senate. Despite illness, explained to the public as wartime injuries or malaria, he campaigned effectively, helped by family money and friends, building his own political organization. He won 51.5 percent of the vote and would be easily reelected in 1958.

He married Jacqueline Lee Bouvier on September 12, 1953, and they had two children, Caroline, born November 27, 1957, and John, Jr., born November 26, 1960. A third child, Patrick Bouvier Kennedy, born in August, 1963, lived only a few hours. Jacqueline Kennedy's beauty, charm, and linguistic skills helped the future president on countless occasions.

As a senator, Kennedy gained national publicity by working to cure the economic ills of all of New England. He continued to speak out on foreign policy, often against French colonialism in Indochina or Algeria. He finally turned away from McCarthy as the Senate censured the latter. During one long illness, he put together another book, *Profiles in*

Courage (1956), based heavily on others' research, winning a Pulitzer Prize and good publicity. One result of Kennedy's growing national reputation was his almost becoming Adlai Stevenson's running mate in the 1956 presidential election. While older politicians often regarded him as a rich young man with no serious intentions, his popularity was growing among voters.

Kennedy began, in 1956, to work for the 1960 Democratic presidential nomination. His brother Robert observed the Stevenson campaign, and afterward, the brothers began building a national organization. Finding his health improving, thanks to the use of cortisone, Kennedy made speeches throughout the country and created a "brain trust" of academic and other specialists who could advise him on policy. To win the nomination and then the 1960 election, Kennedy had to overcome anti-Catholicism and his own image as too young and inexperienced. Campaigning hard both times, he convinced millions of voters that he was intelligent and prepared for the office as well as a believer in the separation of church and state. He named as his running mate Lyndon B. Johnson of Texas, Democratic majority leader in the Senate, who was strong where Kennedy was weak, especially in the South. In televised debates with his opponent, Vice President Richard M. Nixon, Kennedy appeared competent and vigorous; Nixon, exhausted from campaigning, did poorly. Kennedy won the election by 303 electoral votes to 219, with a popular vote margin of only 119,450 out of 68,836,385, so narrow a victory that it limited his political strength. He named a Cabinet representing all factions of the Democratic Party and including two Republicans. Despite the Administration's New Frontier label, it was balanced between liberals and conservatives.

As president, Kennedy sought a constant flow of ideas of all shades of opinion. He held few Cabinet meetings, preferring the informality of task forces on various problems. To reach the public, he used "live" televised press conferences. A handsome face, no longer gaunt and pained, the thatch of hair, plus Kennedy's spontaneity and wit, captivated millions. His inaugural address had promised boldness, especially in the Cold War, and he acted on that in agreeing to a Central Intelligence Agency plan for an invasion of Cuba to overthrow Fidel Castro. When the CIA fumbled and the Cuban exile invaders were killed or captured at the Bay of Pigs, Kennedy publicly took the blame and found

his popularity rising. He went to Europe to meet French president Charles de Gaulle, who warned against American involvement in Vietnam, and also Nikita Khrushchev of the Soviet Union, finding the Communist leader tough, belligerent, and unwilling to help solve any problems.

In domestic matters, Kennedy accomplished little during his thousand days in office. He sought and obtained minor increases in the minimum wage and Social Security coverage, plus money for public housing, and forced a temporary rollback in steel prices. Jacqueline Kennedy supervised a notable redecoration of the White House in Early American style. Only late in his brief term did Kennedy take up the issue of civil rights, because of increasing violence in some Southern states. He took executive action where he could and proposed an anti-poll tax amendment to the Constitution, which passed the Congress while he was still president. He also called for increased federal power to enforce voting rights and a major civil rights act to include the opening of public accommodations and an end to job discrimination.

Kennedy was more active in foreign affairs. Concerned about Soviet moves in the Third World, he founded the Peace Corps and the Alliance for Progress. After the Bay of Pigs and his encounter with Khrushchev, he became "hard line," appointing such militant anti-Communists as John McCone as CIA director and General Curtis LeMay as commander of the Air Force. He also vowed that the Western powers would remain in West Berlin.

The major event of Kennedy's foreign policy was the crisis that arose when Khrushchev tried to establish nuclear missiles in Cuba in 1962. Using all of the information and ideas he could get from another task force and forcing his advisers to debate their ideas in his presence, he chose to blockade Cuba and threaten Khrushchev, keeping in reserve an air attack on the missile sites. Khrushchev withdrew the missiles and countless millions around the world were relieved that no nuclear war took place.

Kennedy learned from the missile crisis. Afterward he was interested in "peace as a process," as he put it in the spring of 1963; the United States and the Soviet Union had to find ways to end the nuclear threat. Kennedy established a "hot line" for communication between the White House and the Kremlin and negotiated a treaty which stopped American and Russian outdoor nuclear tests, reducing radioactivity in the atmosphere. It is this,

Kennedy's admirers say, that indicates how he would have acted in a second term. Yet Kennedy also listened to advisers who insisted that the United States send troops to Vietnam to go into combat and show the South Vietnamese army how to fight. Skeptical, Kennedy agreed, saying that if this did not work he could change his mind and withdraw the American forces.

Tragically, he did not live to follow that plan. In Dallas on a trip to heal a split in the Texas Democrats, he was assassinated on November 22, 1963.

Summary

Kennedy represented a new generation in American politics, for whom World War II and the Cold War were the major events, rather than the 1920's and the Depression of the 1930's. He brought with him a style different from that of Presidents Harry S. Truman and Dwight D. Eisenhower, a contemporary style without formality and with wry, self-deprecatory humor. While his actual accomplishments were limited largely to proposing domestic legislation and to steps toward detente in foreign policy, he inspired millions in the United States and abroad to reach toward new goals in a spirit of confidence that they could make a difference. As did another assassinated president, Abraham Lincoln, he left a legacy of legend, in this case of Camelot or a new King Arthur's court of brave men and beautiful ladies engaged in serving good ends.

Bibliography

Fairlie, Henry. *The Kennedy Promise: The Politics of Expectation.* London: Methuen, and New York: Doubleday, 1973. The expectations created and left unfulfilled by John and Robert Kennedy.

Manchester, William. *One Brief Shining Moment.* Boston: Little Brown, 1983; London: Joseph, 1984. The best of the memorials, with superb pictures and a moving text.

May, Ernest R., and Philip D. Zelikow, eds. *The Kennedy Tapes: Inside the White House During the Cuban Missile Crisis.* Cambridge, Mass.: Harvard University Press, 1998. This volume contains the full, authenticated transcripts of Kennedy's audio recordings of the discussions of the National Security Council during the Cuban Missile Crisis.

Miroff, Bruce. *Pragmatic Illusions: The Presidential Politics of John F. Kennedy.* New York: McKay, 1976. An incisive reassessment, showing the reality of Kennedy's presidency rather than the myth.

Parmet, Herbert S. *Jack: The Struggles of John F. Kennedy.* New York: Dial Press, 1980. The closest there is to a definitive biography, well balanced and based on exhaustive research; the story to 1960.

————. *JFK: The Presidency of John F. Kennedy.* New York: Dial Press, 1983; London: Penguin, 1984. The second volume of the best biography is also the best balanced view of Kennedy as president.

Schlesinger, Arthur M., Jr. *A Thousand Days.* Boston: Houghton Mifflin, and London: Deutsch, 1965. An admiring tale of Kennedy's presidency by a friend and aide.

Sorensen, Theodore C. *Kennedy.* New York: Harper, and London: Hodder and Stoughton, 1965. Even more admiring memoirs by Kennedy's closest aide.

————. *The Kennedy Legacy.* New York: Macmillan, 1969; London: Weidenfeld and Nicolson, 1970. An early and favorable attempt to assess Kennedy's presidency.

Walton, Richard J. *Cold War and Counterrevolution.* New York: Viking Press, 1972. Harshly critical of Kennedy as a "cold warrior."

White, Mark J. *Kennedy: The New Frontier Revisited.* New York: New York University Press, 1997. White attempts to provide a balanced analysis of the Kennedy years in the White House by examining such principle issues as the Vietnam War, the Cuban Missile Crisis, trade policy, and space exploration. A significant reappraisal.

Robert W. Sellen

ROBERT F. KENNEDY

Born: November 20, 1925; Brookline, Massachusetts

Died: June 6, 1968; Los Angeles, California

Area of Achievement: Government and politics

Contribution: Kennedy served his brother President John Kennedy as an able and active attorney general; he passionately advocated justice and equality for minorities and the poor in the United States.

Early Life

Robert Francis Kennedy was born on 131 Naples Road in Brookline, Massachusetts, on November 20, 1925. He was the seventh of nine children born to Joseph Patrick and Rose Fitzgerald Kennedy; both of Robert's parents came from distinguished Irish Catholic families of Boston. Rose's father had been the mayor of Boston, and Joseph Kennedy himself was an able financier who earned millions of dollars while still a young man.

When Robert was four, the family moved to the New York City area, where Joseph, Sr., believed that he could be more in touch with financial dealings than he was in Boston. Robert first attended school in Bronxville, New York, where he was remembered as a nice boy, but not an outstanding student. A constant admonition from his mother in his youth was to read more good books—a suggestion he followed. From his father's advice and guidance in Robert's boyhood, the youngster learned values to which he would firmly adhere all of his life. Joseph, Sr.'s goal was for his children always to try their hardest at whatever they were doing. The father could abide a loser, but he could not abide a slacker.

Robert's position as the seventh child in his family also affected the development of his personality. His older brothers, Joseph P. Kennedy, Jr., and John F. Kennedy, were ten and eight, respectively, when Robert was born. After these oldest boys' births, the Kennedys had had four daughters. Robert, although friendly and playful with his sisters, sought the attention and approval of Joe, Jr., and John. To this end, the little boy developed himself as an athlete, mostly by determination, because he was of small stature. Even as a grown man, Robert was considerably shorter than his brothers. Robert attained a height of five feet ten inches, but his slightly stooped carriage sometimes made him look even smaller. He also appeared somewhat frail, although he was muscular and physically active all of his life. Robert had also inherited the Kennedy good looks; he had deep-blue eyes, sandy-brown hair, and handsome, angular facial bones. He was also shy as a boy.

The Kennedys reared their children as Roman Catholics; of all the boys, Robert was the most religious as a youth and as a man. He served as an altar boy in St. Joseph's Church, Bronxville.

In 1936, Joseph, Sr., was named by President Franklin D. Roosevelt as ambassador to the Court of St. James (London, England), and the family moved abroad. The number and physical beauty of the Kennedy children caused them to be public favorites in England. They all received press coverage, were presented to royalty, and attended British schools.

When World War II began in 1939, Joseph, Sr., sent his family home for their safety. Robert then attended preparatory schools, including Milton Academy, in order to gain admission to Harvard; although his grades were not extremely high, he was admitted in 1944. Robert distinguished himself most at Harvard on the football squad. He was too small to be an outstanding football player, but by hard practice and a will to succeed, he did make the varsity team. Among his teammates, he found friends, several of whom he kept throughout his life. These men attest that Robert was always deeply loyal to his friends.

With the United States' entry into World War II, Robert joined the Navy but did not see battle because of the combat death of his brother, Joe, Jr., a pilot. When he was discharged from the service, Robert finished his interrupted Harvard education and entered the University of Virginia Law School.

While in law school, Robert was introduced to his sister Jean's college roommate, Ethel Skakel. Ethel came from a wealthy Catholic family and was also a vibrant, athletic young woman. She and Robert were married in June of 1950, while he was still a law student. The marriage would produce eleven children, the last of whom was born after Robert's death in 1968.

Life's Work

Robert's political career dates from 1946, when he helped manage his brother John's congressional campaign in Massachusetts. In 1952, when John ran for the Senate, his younger brother was his campaign manager. Between these campaigns, Robert also worked in the federal government. He served as a legal assistant to Senator Joseph McCarthy in 1953, when congressional inquiries were being made into un-American activities. McCarthy's investigations focused on subversive, Communist activities in the United States. Robert also served, in 1954, on the John McClellan Committee of the United States Senate, which was investigating organized crime in the United States. Among the groups under the committee's scrutiny was the powerful Teamsters' union, headed by Jimmy Hoffa. Robert displayed relentlessness in questioning Hoffa and in his determination to uncover the corruption in the Teamsters' Union. Some of the press viewing the committee's hearings believed Robert to be too rude and harsh in his persistent examination of witnesses, especially Hoffa. The term "ruthless" became attached to Robert's name; it was, his closest friends and advisers believed, a misnomer. Robert's aggressiveness in the Senate hearings demonstrated his strong desire for success and meaningful achievements in public service.

Robert achieved more national recognition when he managed his brother John's campaign for the presidency in 1960. Robert worked feverishly on John's behalf; he passionately believed in John's ideas for the United States. When the campaign ended after a long night of waiting for election returns, Robert was exhausted but exuberant. He was thirty-five years old, and his brother had just been elected the first Catholic President of the United States.

In announcing his cabinet members in the weeks following his election, John Kennedy wished to include his brother Robert as the attorney general. In private discussions, Robert showed reluctance; he feared that people would charge John with nepotism. Finally, John and Joe, Sr., convinced Robert to accept the cabinet position.

Robert proved himself to be a good choice for attorney general. He was John's close adviser in many critical instances. The two worked on controlling the volatile civil rights demonstrations that came close to tearing the United States apart in the early 1960's. Some lives were lost in the blacks' battle for freedom of education, public accommodations, and voting rights in the South, but more may have been sacrificed if the Kennedy Administration had not intervened with negotia-

tions (and sometimes with federal troops) at critical junctures.

Another tension-fraught moment during which Robert aided his brother was the Cuban Missile Crisis. In October of 1962, United States surveillance had determined that Soviet nuclear missiles were being established on secret bases in Cuba. For thirteen days, President Kennedy, his cabinet, and his advisers met to discuss their possible reactions to these missiles, for they could not let them be fully installed. While some cabinet members and military leaders advocated an invasion of Cuba and/or bombing the island, John Kennedy was determined not to begin a war that could easily lead to a nuclear confrontation. During these thirteen days, Robert Kennedy was one of the leading proponents of a naval quarantine of Cuba. This was the method of protest that John did follow. The result of the quarantine was that Soviet ships, bringing in more missiles and installation equipment, turned back. The United States also removed some of its own missiles from Turkey to appease the Soviets. President Kennedy was greatly relieved that his advisers advocating war had not convinced him.

Tragedy then entered the Kennedy presidency: John was assassinated on November 22, 1963, in Dallas, Texas. Many Americans suffered and mourned, but none so deeply as Robert. His associates in the Justice Department noted his sullenness and depression in the months following John's death. Robert had spent almost all of his political career working on John's campaigns and projects; Robert had never held an elective office at this point in his life. He was spiritually allied to John's plans for the United States, and he was lost without his brother.

At first, Robert remained attorney general under President Lyndon B. Johnson, to ease the transition of administrations. In 1964, however, when a Senate seat was vacant in New York, Robert decided to seek that office. His running was welcomed by people who believed that he would continue John's work. Yet some New Yorkers were upset by the fact that Robert was a Massachusetts' native seeking office in their state. To those people opposed to Robert's campaign, his supporters reviewed his life as a boy in New York. The campaign was a success; Robert Kennedy became a United States senator when he defeated the Republican Kenneth Keating. When Robert took the oath of office to begin his work as a senator, his younger brother, Edward, was present as a senator from Massachusetts.

Robert proved to be an energetic and outspoken senator (a role not usually assumed by a freshman). He worked hard to see that his late brother John's civil rights legislation was passed. Robert also toured in many nations during the first years after John's death. Robert was always greeted with great enthusiasm and admiration wherever he went. In these travels abroad, as well as in his extensive touring throughout the United States, Robert was astonished at the deep poverty and endless discrimination under which many people suffered. He began to advocate more strongly legislation providing government aid and training for such groups as rural blacks, inner-city blacks, migrant farm workers, and American Indians. Some people who disliked Robert Kennedy accused him of visiting the poor for his own publicity, but many of those who traveled with him said that he was genuinely moved by and truly sympathetic to the plight of the lower classes in the United States. He often said that he knew he had been born into the privileges of a wealthy family, and he felt a real obligation to help those so much less fortunate than he.

In 1966, American opinion of the expanding conflict in Vietnam supported President Johnson's policy to fight hard and subdue the Communists. Robert Kennedy, however, began to advocate negotiations and political compromises as the only sensible way of bringing the war to an end. He more openly opposed President Johnson's policies in the months that followed, when American forces heavily bombed North Vietnam. The years 1966 to 1968 (and beyond) were marked by intense domestic debate, particularly centering on opposition to the increasingly bloody and costly war in Vietnam. Robert Kennedy became involved in the effort to negotiate quickly an honest and just settlement of the war. To this end, he struggled for several months with the decision of whether to run for the presidency. Kennedy believed that President Johnson's military escalation to defeat North Vietnam was a doomed and tragically wrong policy. Roundly criticized both by political opponents and by large numbers of citizens, Johnson decided not to run for reelection; he announced this decision to the American people on March 31, 1968. Robert Kennedy had declared that he would seek the Democratic Party's nomination to run for president earlier that same month.

With Johnson out of the race, Kennedy began to campaign intensely for an office which he believed he could win. His one formidable opponent was the Democratic senator Eugene McCarthy of Minnesota, also an antiwar activist. McCarthy defeated Kennedy in an Oregon primary for Democratic voters in late May. Kennedy, however, surged back with a win in the California primary, held in the next week. As Kennedy left a platform after thanking his campaign workers for his California success, he was assassinated. He died in a Los Angeles hospital on June 6, 1968, at age forty-two.

Summary

Robert Kennedy's untimely and tragic death robbed the United States of one of its most dedicated and compassionate public officials. In office or not, Kennedy was always passionately advocating equal rights, a decent education, adequate housing, and freedom from hunger for all Americans. He particularly befriended migrant farm workers and American Indians, at a time when few national leaders were speaking on behalf of these minorities. Kennedy showed deep personal sympathy for the poor people he visited across the nation and vowed to end their degradation and suffering.

Robert Kennedy did not live to see an end to suffering among America's poor or to see an end to the tragic war in Vietnam. Yet he left behind him many scores of admirers who believed in his social policies and who advocated justice and decent lives for all Americans. Robert Kennedy's greatness lies not only in the struggles he entered during his lifetime but also in the inspiration he gave people to help their fellow Americans in need.

Bibliography

Halberstam, David. *The Unfinished Odyssey of Robert Kennedy.* New York: Random House, 1969. A very detailed account of Robert Kennedy's pursuit of the Democratic Party's nomination for the presidency. Halberstam begins with Kennedy's opposition to Johnson's war policies and proceeds to the night of his assassination, ending rather abruptly and inconclusively.

Kennedy, Rose F. *Times to Remember.* London: Collins, and New York: Doubleday, 1974. A mother's clear and detailed remembrances of her married life and her nine children. Rose Kennedy is candid on the childhood faults of Robert, as well as his admirable traits. She also deals openly with the assassinations, how she learned of them, and their effect on her family.

Moldea, Dan E. *The Killing of Robert F. Kennedy: An Investigation of Motive, Means, and Opportunity.* New York: Norton, 1995. Moldea, an investigative journalist, presents the results of his mission to discover the truth about Kennedy's assassination and the suggestion that the investigation was botched and important evidence suppressed. A well-researched piece including Moldea's own theories on this event.

Newfield, Jack. *Robert Kennedy: A Memoir.* New York: Dutton, 1969; London: Cape, 1970. An account by a journalist who traveled in Kennedy's press entourage and became close to him. Newfield includes many details that only an insider could report. He clearly admired Kennedy; here, he endorses Kennedy's policies and defends him against defamers.

Plimpton, George, ed. *American Journey: The Times of Robert Kennedy.* New York: Harcourt Brace, 1970; London: Deutsch, 1971. A fascinating book of candid interviews on Kennedy's personal life and political career. Plimpton and Jean Stein interviewed the mourners aboard Kennedy's funeral train; included are recollections by relatives and political allies, as well as spectators watching the train pass by.

Schlesinger, Arthur M. *Robert Kennedy and His Times.* Boston: Houghton Mifflin, and London: Deutsch, 1978. An extensive account of Kennedy's entire life, filled with countless details of his work and recreation. Emphasizes Kennedy's work with Senate committees in the 1950's and his tenure as attorney general in the early 1960's. Schlesinger especially wishes to refute critics of Kennedy's methods and policies.

Shesol, Jeffrey. *Mutual Contempt: Lyndon Johnson, Robert Kennedy, and the Feud That Shaped a Decade.* New York: Norton, 1997. The author uses memoirs, biographies, personal interviews, and previously unavailable recordings to examine the relationship between Kennedy and Lyndon Johnson.

Sorensen, Theodore C. *The Kennedy Legacy.* New York: Macmillan, 1969; London: Weidenfeld and Nicolson, 1970. Sorensen, a leading American historian and Kennedy adviser, thoroughly outlines Kennedy's political stances and plans for action, most of which he supports. The author also compares John and Robert Kennedy, analyzing their similarities and differences.

Vanden Heuvel, William, and Milton Gwirtzman. *On His Own: Robert F. Kennedy, 1964-1968.* New York: Doubleday, 1970. Both authors were close friends of their subject, and theirs is a powerful, forceful study of the man. They also show much of the inner workings of American politics. They fully present Kennedy as an unselfish proponent of justice for all Americans.

Witcover, Jules. *Eighty-five Days: The Last Campaign of Robert Kennedy.* New York: Putnam, 1969. Like Halberstam, Witcover describes Kennedy's last run for public office—the presidency. Unlike Halberstam, however, Witcover continues through the assassination and the funeral (perhaps because he was at both events). The author tries to maintain a balance between Kennedy's strong points and his shortcomings.

Patricia E. Sweeney

JOMO KENYATTA
Kamau Ngengi

Born: c. 1894; Ichaweri, British East Africa
Died: August 22, 1978; Mombasa, Kenya
Areas of Achievement: Government and politics
Contribution: Kenyatta wrote the first scholarly
book on indigenous African culture from an African perspective, entitled *Facing Mount Kenya:
The Tribal Life of Gikuyu* (1938). He became the
first Prime Minister of the Republic of Kenya
and the symbol of national unity.

Early Life

Jomo Kenyatta was born around 1894 in Ichaweri
near Nairobi. He belonged to the Kikuyu tribe. The
Kikuyu are Kenya's largest tribe and form 20 percent of the population. Kenyatta's father died when
he was very young, and his grandfather, Kungu,
reared Kenyatta and his brother Kongo. Kenyatta
became independent and self-reliant at an early
age. He was enrolled in the Thogoto Presbyterian
mission school. He learned English, carpentry, and
other skills that benefited him throughout his life
and allowed him to serve as a bridge between African and Western culture. Kenyatta sought to blend
the best of both worlds into a new world—modern
Africa.

After Kenyatta completed grammar school, he
moved to Nairobi. In 1920, he married Grace
Wahu, and the couple had a son, Peter Muigai Kenyatta, at their small home in Dagoretti. That same
year, Kenyatta began helping Subchief Kioi wage a
legal battle to save his land, and Kenyatta became
painfully aware of the discrimination faced by his
people. From this point on he took an active interest in public affairs, especially the restoration of
Kikuyu land. The injustice of British settlers toward Kikuyu land ownership rights hurt Kenyatta
deeply. To the Kikuyu, land is life; taking the
Kikuyu's land was equivalent to condemning them
to starvation and death. As a result, he fought land
cases with a personal passion.

By 1924, Kenyatta had joined the Kikuyu Central Association (KCA); he drafted their letters and
correspondence. As early as 1928, Kenyatta became editor of the KCA newspaper *Muigwithania*
(the reconciler, or the unifier). Kenyatta wrote numerous articles on Kikuyu culture and urged his
people to seek education and adopt modern agricultural techniques so that they could prosper. He

began the long fight to improve the material and
spiritual welfare of his people by preaching a gospel of modernization without the loss of African
identity. In 1929, the KCA sent Kenyatta to England to argue its case of the restoration of Kikuyu
land before the Hilton Young Commission. He won
some compensations for a few Kikuyu families,
but huge areas remained set aside for whites only.
The KCA was pleased, but Kenyatta was not. He
stayed in England for nearly sixteen years to continue his original mission. The grievances of his
people were Kenyatta's main agenda during his
stay in Europe. When the British ignored his constant petitions, he turned to the Soviet Union. He is
said to have taken classes at the Lenin School in
Moscow in 1932 and later to have attended Moscow University. Joseph Stalin, however, alienated
Kenyatta and other African nationalists when he
declared racial struggles a form of "petit bourgeois
nationalism."

In 1936, Kenyatta began studying anthropology
under Bronisław Malinowski at the University of
London. Malinowski was impressed by Kenyatta's
insight into African culture. Malinowski edited
several of Kenyatta's papers and arranged for their
publication as a book entitled *Facing Mount Kenya*. This book won for Kenyatta a diploma in anthropology. In Africa the work was hailed as a patriotic statement of African nationalism. This was
one of the first "inside" glimpses that the world had
had of African culture. Celebrated as a literary figure, Kenyatta was emerging as a spokesman for
Africa and not merely for the Kikuyu. Kenyatta
wrote other books and articles and helped William
Edward Burghardt Du Bois and Kwame Nkrumah
organize the 1945 Fifth Pan-African Congress,
which added to Kenyatta's stature as a spokesman
for all blacks. He was called a champion of the African people, and his fiery oratory earned for him
the Kikuyu name Jomo, or "burning spear."

Life's Work

In 1946, when Kenyatta returned to Kenya, James
Gichuru, the leader of the Kenya African Union
(KAU), stepped down so that Kenyatta could become the leading voice for all Kenyan African people. From his position as head of KAU, he began
demanding freedom for Africans and independence

Kenyan premier Jomo Kenyatta (left) welcomes U.S. federal judge Thurgood Marshall to Nairobi in 1963.

for Kenya. Kenyatta asked Africans to rise above narrow tribal loyalties and unite to win their freedom. There would be no easy walk to freedom, especially for many young Africans who were born and reared in cities such as Nairobi. These people were dedicated to the future and to rapid change. They were "New Age" Africans and, like Kenyatta, men of two worlds. Many young African men were drafted by the British Army. They fought bravely to defend freedom and democracy in Burma and elsewhere. Exposure to people and ideas outside Kenya made them acutely aware of how oppressed they were. When they returned to crowded city slums and were forced to accept menial jobs or unemployment, they became frustrated. These "marginal" men saw Kenyatta as their savior and took up his call for freedom.

Neither the settlers nor the colonial government easily gave in to African demands. Settlers defeated each request forwarded by Kenyatta. Africans began to grow impatient and started to form secret societies. African unemployment began reaching

the 20 percent mark, while white officers were being granted big estates as rewards for loyal service to Great Britain. Tension began mounting, and everyone knew that a social explosion was inevitable. It came in the form of the Mau Mau Rebellion in 1952. The origin of the Mau Mau Rebellion remains a mystery, and no one has ever conclusively either confirmed or denied Kenyatta's role as its instigator. What is clear is that the Mau Mau Rebellion caused Great Britain to use brutal tactics similar to those used by the Nazis in a vain attempt to deny Africans freedom.

The settler philosophy of white supremacy caused great suffering for Africans. A United Nations Special Survey of 1953 revealed that the average annual income of Africans in Kenya was approximately one tenth of the Asians' annual income and one twenty-fourth of white income. Kenya was run for the good of the rich, who were exclusively white, and Africans were angry. The Kikuyu began taking nonviolent biblical oaths of unity in 1947, shortly after Kenyatta returned from

England and after the government refused to recognize Kikuyu grievances and sided with the settlers. With every refusal, Kikuyu oaths gradually became more violent and secretive. After Kenyatta was arrested, the killing oath appeared in Mau Mau ceremonies, and white settlers died in *panga* (a short broad blade sword) attacks. Between 1952 and 1959, Mau Mau insurgents took the lives of 32 white settlers and 167 security officials; however, 11,503 Mau Mau were killed in battles and 1,000 were hanged during this period known as the Mau Mau Emergency. Hundreds of thousands of Africans were arrested, and many were tortured and often died. Unwilling to admit that racial discrimination and the color bar caused these problems, the colonial government convicted Kenyatta of sedition in 1952. He was imprisoned and banished to the countryside for seven years. These events prompted many Africans to strike a blow for freedom, even when this meant death.

Kenyatta emerged from this conflict as the unchallenged leader of the African community and the only person capable of saving Kenya from disaster. Kenyatta's name became a household word. KAU became KANU, or the Kenya African National Union, and its members elected Kenyatta as their president in absentia in 1960. In response to constant pressure from almost every quarter of Kenya society, Kenyatta was released in August, 1961. The man whom white settlers had once called the "leader to darkness and death" was given a jubilant reception by thirty thousand cheering Africans from all tribes at a rally for him in Nairobi.

On December 21, 1963, Kenyatta, with a smile on his face, watched as the British flag was taken down and the black, green, and red flag of independent Kenya was raised on high. Born during the first years of British rule, he lived to see the end of British colonialism in Kenya. The slogan for the new Kenya became *harambee*—"let us pull together." Kenyatta vowed to work not only for the Kikuyu but also for all Africans and Kenyan citizens. In 1963, Kenyatta declared: "People of different races, colors, and religions can walk together to build a new Kenya, a new nation." White farmers were not driven out of Kenya; rather, they were encouraged to stay, and East Indian citizens were allowed to keep coveted businesses. Although Kenyatta had personally suffered, he fought for reconciliation without rancor. He asked people of all races to "stay and cooperate."

Through a program of Africanization, Africans were brought into the administration of the country in large numbers. A mix of scholarships and on-the-job training prepared them for their new responsibilities. Eventually this policy placed Africans in top business positions and helped them to gain control of many firms. Kenya and Great Britain jointly financed a "million acre" land purchase scheme in the fertile, formerly white highlands of Kenya. This permitted whites owning huge tracts of land to sell them to Africans on a "willing seller, willing buyer" basis. Most white farmers were aware that land was the major grievance of African Kenyans and that land hunger was acute, so they sold their farms. Many stayed in Kenya and went into manufacturing or tourism. Some of the Africans who bought this land secured large loans and bought vast estates. These individuals became commercial farmers, and their estates often stretched across thousands of acres. Others bought estates ranging from twenty-five to two hundred acres in size. They became small-scale employers and small commercial farmers, often growing cash crops such as coffee. Finally, Africans with few resources formed cooperatives with government help and bought farms that were later subdivided into small plots that provided for their subsistence. They produced a modest surplus to pay their children's school fees as well as to buy clothing for their families. These schemes and others are the cornerstones of the stability that Kenyatta achieved for Kenya.

Kenya became a model of racial harmony, where personal freedoms were protected and the economy flourished. Kenyatta vowed to eradicate ignorance, disease, and poverty. He asked his Kenyans to beat their swords into plows. Loans, improved hybrid seeds, insecticides, herbicides, and modern technical advice were made available to small farmers as well as large. All Kenyans were encouraged to grow cash crops, and, as a result, agricultural output dramatically increased. Primary education, once a privilege for elite children only, became free for all Kenyan children. Kenyatta spent nearly one-third of Kenya's budget on education, because he believed that this was the key to modernization. Since he also believed that good health is the foundation for all other activities, Kenyatta offered Kenyans free medical service.

In its first decade, Kenya's economy grew at an amazing rate of 7 percent a year. Kenya's coastal resorts, with their world-class hotels, fine restaurants, and international airports, attracted hundreds of thousands of tourists from all over the world. Foreign companies began establishing businesses in Kenya because they had faith in Kenyatta. Under his direction, Africans began to modernize without destroying their own culture. Kenyatta transformed Kenya into a model for Africa and the world to emulate.

Kenyatta died peacefully on August 22, 1978, and Kenyans, saddened by his death, mourned their loss. It is a tribute to Kenyatta that Daniel Arap Moi, a Kalenjin, not a Kikuyu, was elected to succeed Kenyatta as President of Kenya. The election was orderly and the transition was democratic and peaceful. Kenyatta suffered greatly for his people, but he lived to lead a stable and prosperous nation into the modern era.

Summary

Under Jomo Kenyatta's leadership, Kenya became a showcase for capitalistic development in Africa. This phenomenon has attracted capital from abroad, fueling impressive growth. Low levels of military spending allowed Kenyatta to make dramatic improvements in the health and education of millions of Kenyans. His policies have created peace and prosperity for modern Kenya. Kenyatta provided modern agricultural advisers, fertilizers, herbicides, pesticides, credit, and improved seeds to African farmers. They responded by boosting commercial production of cash crops, such as coffee, tea, and pyrethrum to record high levels. He simultaneously improved roads all over Kenya, making it easier for farmers to market their crops while still fresh. Cattle and sheep ranches have expanded and now supply many European, Middle Eastern, and Asian countries with high-quality beef. Preservation of vast wildlife reserves and game parks has assisted the expansion of tourism. Many modern luxury hotels can be found throughout Kenya, and tourism is the third largest source of foreign exchange.

Foreign investment was encouraged, resulting in the vigorous growth of industry. Kenya now assembles American, British, German, and Japanese cars as well as heavy vehicles. It manufactures textiles, electronic products, chemicals, paper, pharmaceuticals, and processed agricultural goods. Technical institutes are springing up in every province of Kenya to supply skilled technicians to manage existing and future industries. Kenya is poised for economic takeoff, thanks to Kenyatta's policies. Kenyatta brought freedom, racial harmony, peace, political stability, and prosperity. His policies were so successful that his successor, Daniel Arap Moi, named his own policies *nyayo*, or footsteps, suggesting that Kenyans wish to continue Kenyatta's policies. No greater tribute could be offered to anyone.

Bibliography

Berman Bruce J., and John M. Lonsdale. "The Labors of 'Muigwithania': Jomo Kenyatta as Author, 1928-45." *Research in African Literatures* 29, no. 1 (Spring 1998). Discusses Kenyatta's writing career and his development as a political historian.

Delf, George. *Jomo Kenyatta: Towards Truth About "The Light of Kenya."* New York: Doubleday, and London: Gollancz, 1961. The first major portrait of Kenyatta that was sympathetic prior to independence. One of the first authors to paint a picture of Kenyatta as a political healer, rather than a terrorist.

Holmquist, Frank W., et al. "The Structural Development of Kenya's Political Economy." *African Studies Review* 37, no. 1 (April, 1994). Examines Kenya's political economy, the democratic ideology of which is based on the desires of the urban middle class.

Kenyatta, Jomo. *Harambee! The Prime Minister of Kenya's Speeches, 1963-1964.* New York: Oxford University Press, 1964. A collection of Kenyatta's political speeches and philosophy. He explains his self-help philosophy, or *harambee*, and encourages his countrymen to donate time, effort, and money to improve their communities.

Murray-Brown, Jeremy. *Kenyatta.* 2d ed. London and Boston: Allen and Unwin, 1979. An in-depth portrait of Kenyatta. He is accurately portrayed as the leader of the independence struggle and the architect of postindependence modernization, economic growth, and prosperity. Brown shows how Kenyatta used a combination of control over ethnic group leaders and charisma to rule Kenya.

Slater, Montagu. *The Trial of Jomo Kenyatta.* 2d ed. London: Secker and Warburg, 1956. This book shows how white settlers blamed the Mau Mau Emergency on Kenyatta, even though they had no conclusive evidence proving that he led the movement.

Wepman, Dennis. *Jomo Kenyatta*. New York: Chelsea House, 1985; London: Burke, 1988. An excellent account of Kenyatta's formative years, his education, and his foreign travel. Provides a good account of the struggle for independence but little information on postindependence Kenya.

Dallas L. Browne

ALEKSANDR FYODOROVICH KERENSKY

Born: May 2, 1881; Simbirsk (now Ulyanovsk), Russia

Died: June 11, 1970; New York, New York

Areas of Achievement: Government and politics

Contribution: Kerensky was the leading figure in the short-lived Provisional Government that replaced the deposed Czar Nicholas II and was in turn displaced by the Bolshevik (Communist) Party of Vladimir Ilich Lenin during the Russian Revolution of 1917. He attempted unsuccessfully to establish a liberal democratic government in Russia.

Early Life

Born in Simbirsk (now Ulyanovsk), Russia, on May 2, 1881, Aleksandr Fyodorovich Kerensky was the eldest son of Fyodor Mikhailovich Kerensky, a schoolteacher and administrator, and his wife, Nadezhda Aleksandrovna (née Adler), the daughter of a prominent military officer and topographer. During their son's earliest years in Simbirsk, the Kerenskys' social and professional circle undoubtedly included Ilya Nikolaevich Ulyanov, another local school official, and his son Vladimir Ilich, who, under the pseudonym Lenin, was later to become Aleksandr's chief antagonist during the stormy days of the Revolution of 1917. Since, however, the future Lenin was more than ten years older than young Aleksandr, there is no evidence that the two were at all acquainted as children.

In 1889, Fyodor Kerensky moved his family from Simbirsk to the frontier city of Tashkent in distant Central Asia, where he had been appointed head of the Turkestan educational administration. Eleven years later, having completed his basic education in Tashkent, Aleksandr traveled to the then capital of Russia and enrolled in the faculty of history and law at St. Petersburg (now Leningrad State) University. As a student, young Kerensky came under the influence of the famous philosopher N. O. Losskii and the liberal jurist L. I. Petrazhitskii and became affiliated with the liberal constitutionalist movement, although his sympathies were more truly drawn to the radical populist Party of Socialist-Revolutionaries (PSR).

Upon graduation from the university in 1904, Kerensky married Olga Lvovna Baranovskii, the offspring of a distinguished military family and cousin of several active Socialist-Revolutionaries. Thereupon, swept up in the turbulent events of the abortive Revolution of 1905, Kerensky soon joined the PSR, became editor of its newspaper, and even attempted, though unsuccessfully, to join the so-called Fighting Organization, the terrorist wing of the PSR. As a result of these activities, the young revolutionary was arrested and exiled from St. Petersburg for a period of some six months.

Returned to the capital in late 1906, Kerensky began a brief but sensational career as a defense lawyer in a series of highly publicized political trials. Beginning in 1906, Kerensky's legal activities attracted widespread attention throughout Russia and finally culminated in two celebrated cases in 1912: the first, involving the largely successful defense of the Armenian Dashnak Party, held before a special tribunal of the Imperial Russian Senate (supreme court), and the other, even more famous, embracing the official investigation and condemnation of the czarist government's mishandling of the tragic Lena Goldfields massacre. The notoriety gained by Kerensky in these two episodes set the stage for his brief but spectacular career in Russian politics.

Life's Work

In late 1912, taking advantage of the favorable publicity surrounding his legal exploits, Kerensky was elected to the Fourth State Duma (Parliament), representing the Volsk district of Saratov Province. Elected as a member of the Trudoviki (Laborite) Party, an amalgam of moderate Socialists loosely associated with the PSR, the young legislator at once became the leading spokesman for the Duma's radical opposition. Meanwhile, behind the scenes, Kerensky also joined the ranks of Russian Freemasonry, a secret but highly influential political movement dedicated to the creation in Russia of a republican government under liberal direction.

In 1914, Kerensky received an eight-month prison sentence for sponsoring a protest against the czarist government's support for the disgraceful trial of Mendel Beilis, a Ukrainian Jew who had been unjustly accused of ritual murder. Saved from incarceration by his parliamentary immunity, Kerensky continued his radical activities in 1914 by leading the Trudoviki refusal to support unconditionally Russia's entry into World War I. By 1915, Kerensky's deepening disgust with czarism drove him to the advocacy of a political revolution in Russia though, as yet, without success. Untracked by serious illness in early 1916, Kerensky returned to the Duma later in that year and began at once to agitate for the overthrow of the monarchy, including, if necessary, the assassination of Czar Nicholas II.

In March, 1917, the unexpected coming of the revolution thrust the youthful Kerensky into a position of political leadership during an eight-month period of more or less continual revolutionary chaos. For its part, to fill the vacuum created by the removal of the czar, the Duma promptly established a so-called provisional government headed by a cabinet made up entirely of middle-class liberals with the exception of Kerensky, who, as minister of justice, became the new government's sole representative of political radicalism. At the same time, the popular Kerensky was also elected vice chairman of the powerful Petrograd (formerly St. Petersburg) Soviet of Worker's and Soldiers' Deputies, an unofficial body representing the interests of political radicals and the poor. In these circumstances, the young revolutionary became the only common member of the two bodies, which had effectively replaced the fallen monarchy.

As minister of justice in the original provisional government, Kerensky introduced a broad program of civil rights in Russia, including the ending of ethnic and religious discrimination as well as the abolition of capital punishment and the long-established exile system. On the other hand, in late April and in May, Kerensky also became embroiled in a fierce debate with Foreign Minister P. N. Miliukov regarding Russian war aims, in particular the latter's alleged insistence upon Russian acquisition of Constantinople and the Straits of the Dardanelles. In the end, confronted by hostile street demonstrations, Miliukov was forced to resign from the cabinet, in which action he was soon joined by the minister of war, Aleksandr Guchkov.

As a result of the resignations of Miliukov and Guchkov, the provisional government was reorganized on May 18. Arranged by Kerensky and his Masonic "brother" Nikolai Nekrasov, the new cabinet included a combination of liberals and Socialists and was thus called the Coalition, the first of three such reorganizations that were destined to occur over the next several months. As minister of war in this new cabinet, Kerensky became convinced that the government's declared goal of a "general democratic peace" could be achieved only by the undertaking of one last great Russian military offensive that would demon-

strate the nation's continued military strength and thereby pave the way for successful peace talks. With this in mind, the war minister at once departed for the front, where he soon earned the title "Supreme Persuader-in-Chief" in token of his fiery speeches seeking to convince the Russian soldiery to support his planned offensive. Finally launched in early July, the so-called Kerensky Offensive, after some initial success, quickly turned into a disastrous rout, following which the Russian Army began rapidly to disintegrate.

On July 16, prompted by the failure of the Kerensky Offensive, popular demonstrations, led first by disaffected workers, soldiers, and sailors and later by the Bolsheviks, erupted in the capital city of Petrograd. In response to this "July Days" crisis, Kerensky assumed the prime ministership of Russia on July 20. Having defused the Petrograd uprising by releasing documents purporting to show that Lenin and the Bolsheviks were really German agents, Kerensky at length organized a new, second Coalition, which again consisted of a shaky combination of liberals and Socialists. Thereupon, in late August, in an effort to reconcile all the contending factions in Russia, the new prime minister summoned the Moscow State Conference, which instead of arresting the country's deteriorating political situation merely emphasized its hopelessness.

Finally, in early September, the climax of the Kerensky era was reached in the form of the famous Kornilov Revolt. In this confusing episode, the prime minister became convinced that General Lavr Kornilov, the commander in chief of the army, had concocted a plot to overthrow the provisional government and establish a military dictatorship in Russia. Whatever the truth of this charge, which was never substantiated, Kerensky responded by ordering the commander in chief's dismissal and arrest. More important, to defend the government from the alleged danger posed by Kornilov's troops (who, in fact, were easily disarmed), Kerensky also ordered the relegalization and arming of the Bolsheviks, who had been proscribed and in hiding since the July Days. In the wake of these developments, no expedient, including the organization in mid-September of still another, third Coalition in which Kerensky served as both prime minister and commander in chief, or the convocation in October of a so-called Council of the Republic (or Pre-Parliament) was sufficient to save the situation. Instead, on November 7, 1917, the Kerensky regime was overthrown in an easy, almost bloodless, revolution engineered in Petrograd by Lenin and his Bolshevik (later Communist) Party.

For his part, having escaped the capital on the eve of the revolution and led a brief, futile effort by a small band of Cossack troops to dislodge the new rulers, Kerensky was forced to flee Russia in May, 1918, never to return. Arriving in Paris, the former prime minister tried to convince the Western allies to support his return to power in Russia by military action. Having failed in this effort, Kerensky began more than fifty years of political exile, living first in Western Europe and later in the United States. During this long period, the former Russian leader engaged in a variety of anticommunist (and antifascist) activities and supported himself by writing and lecturing, much of the subject matter of which was devoted to the justification of his behavior in 1917.

In 1927, Kerensky visited the United States and published the first version of his memoirs, entitled *The Catastrophe* (1927). From 1928 to 1933, he worked in Paris and Berlin, where he edited the émigré journal *Dni* (days). In 1939, he divorced his first wife and married Lydia Ellen Tritton, the daughter of a prominent Australian industrialist. Having narrowly escaped the Nazi occupation of Paris in 1940, Kerensky moved to the United States, where he lived for the rest of his life, though not without frequent, often lengthy, visits to Western Europe. From 1956 to 1961, together with the American historian Robert P. Browder, Kerensky worked in the Hoover Institution at Stanford University, where he prepared for publication a large collection of documents on the provisional government that finally appeared in three volumes in 1961. In 1965, he published a second version of his memoirs, grandiloquently entitled *Russia and History's Turning Point* (1965). He died of cancer in New York City on June 11, 1970.

Summary

In addition to its enormous historical significance, the Bolshevik Revolution of 1917 was a great watershed in the life of Aleksandr Fyodorovich Kerensky. Thus, before the revolution, Kerensky's career represents an all but unbroken tale of personal and public accomplishment. Based on a philosophical commitment to liberal democracy combined with a kind of populist dedication to improving the welfare of the Russian people, Kerensky's early legal career, as well as his service in the State Duma, was devoted to the defense of individual rights and the struggle for a better society in the face of a corrupt and tyrannical state.

In 1917, however, primarily because of his great reputation as an implacable foe of czarism, Kerensky was abruptly thrust into a position of political leadership in conditions of revolutionary chaos. In these circumstances, although his personal magnetism and great oratorical skills enabled him for a time to hold his own, his essential political moderation was soon outstripped by the deepening radicalism of the revolution. In the end, therefore, insufficient ruthlessness and a stubborn refusal to sacrifice democratic principles to radical expedience spelled Kerensky's political doom.

Following the revolution, although he retained his faith in democracy and fought adamantly against both Soviet and, later, Fascist authoritarianism, Kerensky's always considerable ego caused him to spend much of his long time in exile defending his conduct in 1917 and developing various conspiratorial, almost paranoid, explanations for his failure. As a result of this inability to perceive that his fate was really the consequence of powerful social and economic forces largely beyond his capacity to control, the former prime minister alienated his friends, aggravated his enemies, and died in a state of splendid political isolation.

Bibliography

Abraham, Richard. *Alexander Kerensky: The First Love of the Revolution.* London: Sidgwick and Jackson, and New York: Columbia University Press, 1987. This is the only full-length biography in English. Based on Kerensky's official papers as well as materials supplied by his family, the treatment is sympathetic but not uncritical.

Browder, Robert P. "Kerensky Revisited." In *Russian Thought and Politics*, edited by Hugh McLean et al. Cambridge, Mass.: Harvard University Press, 1957. A positive reevaluation of Kerensky, particularly his role in the early period of the Revolution.

Elkin, Boris. "The Kerensky Government and Its Fate." *Slavic Review* 23 (1964): 717-736.

———. "Further Notes on the Policies of the Kerensky Government." *Slavic Review* 25 (1966): 323-332. Articles hostile to Kerensky and the provisional government in practically every area of their endeavor. Written by a close associate of Miliukov, the treatment is especially critical of Kerensky's alleged submission to the radical leaders of the Petrograd Soviet.

Flora, James. "The Interview." *American Heritage* 48, no. 1 (February-March, 1997). Describes the author's personal encounter with Kerensky.

Katkov, George. *The Kornilov Affair: Kerensky and the Break-up of the Russian Army.* London and New York: Longman, 1980. This slender volume constitutes an exhaustive analysis of perhaps the pivotal episode in Kerensky's political career. Based in part on interviews with Kerensky in 1963; the author places most of the blame for the Kornilov disaster on Kerensky.

Kerensky, Alexander F. *Russia and History's Turning Point.* New York: Duell Sloan, 1965; London: Cassell, 1966. These are Kerensky's memoirs. In addition to his interpretation of events, Kerensky contends that he and Russian democracy were betrayed by virtually everyone, including the parties of the Left, Right, and center as well as the Germans and the Allies.

Vishniak, Mark. "A Pamphlet in the Guise of a Review." *Slavic Review* 25 (1966): 143-149. This article is a rejoinder to the above criticisms of Elkin. The author's support of the provisional government is more an attack on Miliukov than a defense of Kerensky.

John W. Long

JACK KEROUAC

Born: March 12, 1922; Lowell, Massachusetts
Died: October 21, 1969; St. Petersburg, Florida
Area of Achievement: Literature
Contribution: Kerouac was one of the major figures of the Beat movement in the United States, a literary and cultural reaction against Cold War America. Although Kerouac viewed himself as a naturalistic novelist in the tradition of Thomas Wolfe and William Faulkner, literary and social critics generally view him as one of the more dramatic examples of American countercultural artistic expression, especially in novels such as *On the Road* and *The Dharma Bums.*

Early Life

Jean Louis Lebris de Kerouac was born in the French-Canadian section of Lowell, Massachusetts, known as Pawtucketville, the second son and third child of Leo Alcide Kerouac and Gabrielle Ange Levesque Kerouac (whom Kerouac called "Memere" to the end of his life). Kerouac's parents, especially his mother, were devout Catholics, and the memory and imagery of a distinctly Catholic altarboyhood in an impoverished northern factory town informed much of Kerouac's fiction. When Kerouac was five, his older brother Gerard died, and Kerouac remained obsessed throughout his life with the memory of a religiously devout and spiritual older brother who was iconized by parish nuns into a figure of superhuman rectitude. This became a source of great guilt in Kerouac's personal life that was expressed repeatedly in his fiction, especially in *Doctor Sax* (1959) and *Visions of Gerard* (1963).

Despite his average stature, Kerouac was a standout athlete at Lowell High School in football and track in the late 1930's and earned a scholarship for a postgraduate year at the Horace Mann School in New York in order to prepare for Columbia University the following year. Although knee injuries limited Kerouac's football heroics to a single punt-return touchdown at Columbia, Kerouac's short, two-year stay at the university introduced him not only to the literary interpretations of Professor Mark Van Doren but also and especially to fellow classmate and future Beat poet Allen Ginsberg, as well as to future Beat writer William Burroughs and Lucien Carr, among others.

Through Ginsberg, Kerouac became acquainted with the bohemian fringe of students and artists in Greenwich Village, Soho, and Morningside Heights and also became acquainted with various members of the "subterranean" fringe that would soon introduce him to such disparate figures as Neal Cassady and Gary Snyder. The friendship between Kerouac and Ginsberg would survive for the next twenty-five years, but it was tempered on Kerouac's part by a deeply held anti-Semitism nurtured in Depression-era Lowell and by a deeply held ambivalence toward homosexuality (despite Kerouac's own experimentation in that area in the 1940's with both Ginsberg and Cassady). The friendship between Kerouac and Cassady was more unalloyed than that between Kerouac and Ginsberg but was undermined by Cassady's wanderlust as well as his need to cycle through multiple sets of friends and experiences.

Perhaps Kerouac's ultimate statement of friendship toward Cassady was expressed through making him the absolute hero of Kerouac's most important text, *On the Road* (1957). Sal Paradise, the narrator, is sometimes at a loss for direction or words, but Sal's friend, Dean Moriarty, is the very personification of energy, excitement, and living for the moment, all characteristics that seemed rare and even unlawful in the United States during the 1950's. The experiences that comprise *On the Road* largely occurred in the late 1940's, and evidence suggests that an essentially final manuscript of *On the Road* was completed in 1951, the year following the publication of Kerouac's first novel, *The Town and the City* (1950). However, *On the Road* remained unpublished until 1957, and the novelist who confronted the critical acclaim of publication in the late 1950's was a thirty-five-year-old politically conservative and somewhat paranoid mama's boy, not a young adventurer in the ilk of Dean Moriarty or even Sal Paradise.

Life's Work

Kerouac expressed and defined the Beat movement in literature, espousing at least two parallel and consistent understandings of the word "beat": beaten down, in the sense of being tired and downtrodden; and beatific, in the sense of being blessed and full of spiritual joy. The enduring controversy over the term and over Kerouac's place in the movement increased rather than lessened after Kerouac's death in 1969. Analysis of Kerouac's literary works have often included societal commentary on the

author and the lifestyles depicted in the text. In a similar vein, prose pieces on beatniks and later on hippies often included evaluative references to Kerouac's prose output. Therefore, Kerouac's literary output, especially his prose fiction, has not always received the sort of extended close readings separate from societal context that serious fiction deserves.

Kerouac's juvenalia, as well as his first published novel, *The Town and the City*, were comparatively traditional works of fiction. Although Kerouac's first novel received some critical approval, poor sales compelled his publisher, Harcourt Brace, not to exercise an option on a second novel. The next seven years served as an informal literary apprenticeship period for Kerouac as he travelled to New York City, Denver, San Francisco, and Mexico City, with side trips to Lowell and Rocky Mount, North Carolina, to visit family. Kerouac's periods of travel alternated with periods of literary productivity, supported in part by Memere's indulgent largesse. Kerouac was also stockpiling experiences that he would use in his later fiction.

Although critical commentary differs on the issue, it seems likely that Kerouac speed-typed a complete first draft of *On the Road* during three weeks in New York City in 1951 on a stolen teletype roll. Kerouac was a quick and accurate typist who was often frustrated by the task of replacing typewriter paper every time the 11 inches were filled. Foolscap paper provided only an additional three inches, but Lucien Carr's theft of a teletype roll provided Kerouac with a seamless roll of paper on which his ideas could be quickly transferred to the page. During this period, Kerouac began to develop a theory of poetics that he called "spontaneous prose" in which he thought of an idea and developed it by writing without stopping or editing. Despite protestations to the contrary, however, there is evidence that Kerouac continued to tinker with the text until 1956, when it was finally accepted for publication in the following year.

Meanwhile, in 1951 and 1952, Kerouac wrote much of *Visions of Cody* (1960), a more extended attempt to put Cassady into a literary form worthy of his personality. The text was not published in any form until 1959 and not in completed form until 1972, but it belongs strongly to immediate postwar America, where it moves the characters of Jack Duluoz and Cody Pomeray through a subterranean landscape of the highways, diners, and flophouses of which Kerouac was enamored.

Despite William Burroughs's accidental lethal shooting of his wife, Joan, in Mexico City in September, 1951, Kerouac wrote *Dr. Sax* there during the winter of 1951-1952. He subtitled the eclectic text *Faust: Part 3* and used the book as an opportunity to remember the radio mysteries of his childhood. Travelling later in the year to San Francisco and to North Carolina (where his mother had moved), Kerouac began compiling his *Book of Dreams* (1961), a transcription of dreams that he kept by his bedstead in order to recall and transcribe the otherwise inchoate meanderings of his subconscious.

Kerouac's productivity continued in New York City in 1953 as he composed manuscripts that continued to chronicle the Beat movement (*The Subterraneans*, 1958) at the same time that he also extended the Jack Duluoz legend (*Maggie Cassidy*, 1959), this time replete with small-town football games and homecoming queens. A return trip to Mexico City in 1955 caused Kerouac, now toying with Zen Buddhism (partly because of Gary Snyder's and Allen Ginsberg's separate influences), to become infatuated with an Indian woman named Esperanza, who would become the model for *Tristessa* (1960). During his stay in Mexico City, Kerouac also composed the "242 Chants" that comprise *Mexico City Blues* (1959), Kerouac's only extended foray into poetry during his adult years.

A 1955 Christmastime visit to his mother in North Carolina extended into 1956 as Kerouac wrote *Visions of Gerard* with his mother in the house to coax recollections about the boy who had died three decades earlier. In the summer of 1956, Kerouac worked for the National Park Service as a fire lookout in Mount Baker National Forest near Marblemount, Washington. Kerouac's lookout point was 12 miles south of the Canadian border near the top of Desolation Peak, and it was there that he wrote the first section of what would later become *Desolation Angels* (1965).

The publication of *On the Road* in 1957, especially Gilbert Millstein's September 5, 1957, *New York Times* review of the novel ("the writing is of a beauty almost breathtaking. . . . *On the Road* is a major novel"), catapulted Kerouac to instant international fame, a responsibility and a burden that Kerouac rather gracelessly carried with him during the final twelve years of his life.

Although Kerouac's publication record throughout the period remained fairly constant, much of the work had been written earlier, and the work composed after 1957 is generally considered to be second-echelon Kerouac (*The Dharma Bums*, 1958; *Big Sur*, 1962; *Satori in Paris*, 1966; *Pic*, 1971). Kerouac also dabbled in film (*Pull My Daisy*, 1961) and religious writings (*The Scripture of the Golden Eternity*, 1960), but he remained, both in the public eye and to himself, primarily a prose writer. Increasingly isolated from his friends and finding it more difficult to write as time went on, Kerouac died of a hemorrhage in 1969 at his mother's home in St. Petersburg, Florida.

Summary

The legacy of Jack Kerouac ultimately lies in his status as a spokesperson for the Beat movement through his book *On the Road* and, to a lesser extent, the essay "The Essentials of Spontaneous Prose." Selected passages from *On the Road* have entered popular culture and remain as vital and expressive comments on the place of youth, art, and longing in American culture. Videotape of a shy yet personable Kerouac on the Steve Allen Show, as well as existing photographs have made him a cultural icon of the young even as new generations come of age. Kerouac's characters, especially those in *On the Road*, were on a neoreligious quest for personal understanding and fulfillment. Those needs and that sort of quest are common to all eras and generations.

Bibliography

Amburn, Ellis. *Subterranean Kerouac: The Hidden Life of Jack Kerouac*. New York: St. Martin's Press, 1998. Amburn, Kerouac's editor for Desolation Angels, uses the author's archives to support Kerouac's claim that his novels were autobiographical. Amburn ties Kerouac's major works to specific events in the author's unsettled, self-destructive life.

Cassady, Neal. *The First Third: A Partial Biography and Other Writings*. San Francisco: City Lights, 1971. This posthumous collection of Cassady's prose includes the three extant chapters ("the first third") of an unfinished autobiography, six brief narrative prose pieces, and two lengthy letters, one to Jack Kerouac and one to Ken Kesey.

Charters, Ann. *Kerouac: A Biography*. London: Deutsch, and New York: Warner, 1974. This is the earliest critical biography and remains a benchmark for Kerouac biographical criticism.

French, Warren. *Jack Kerouac*. Boston: Twayne, 1986. This text, composed for a scholastic audience, focuses on the Duluoz legend (*Maggie Cassidy, Visions of Gerard, Vanity of Duluoz, Doctor Sax*) as Kerouac's version of a collective *Bildungsroman* analogous to James Joyce's Stephen Daedalus novels or Marcel Proust's *À la recherche du temps perdu* (1913-1927; *Remembrance of Things Past*, 1922-1931, 1981).

Kerouac, Jack. *On the Road*. Edited by Scott Donaldson. New York: Viking, 1979. This is a scholarly edition with significant critical articles, position pieces by Kerouac himself, and various useful appendices, including a section on "Topics for Discussion and Papers."

———. *The Portable Jack Kerouac*. Edited by Ann Charters. New York: Viking, 1995. This relatively inexpensive text provides selections from Kerouac's principal works as well as biographical background and critical commentary.

Knight, Arthur, and Kit Knight, eds. *Kerouac and the Beats: A Primary Sourcebook*. New York:

Paragon, 1988. This collection includes interviews, personal recollections, and other primary source material relevant to an understanding of Kerouac's significance to the Beat movement.

Miles, Barry. *Jack Kerouac: King of the Beats—A Portrait.* London: Virgin, and New York: Holt, 1998. A psychological biography of Kerouac.

Nicosia, Gerald. *Memory Babe: A Critical Biography of Jack Kerouac.* New York: Grove Press, 1983; London: Penguin, 1985. This lengthy and amply documented biography divides Kerouac's life into three principal periods. It includes forty-four pages of sources and notes as well as a comprehensive index.

Tytell, John. *Naked Angels: The Lives and Literature of the Beat Generation.* New York: McGraw-Hill, 1976. This eminently readable text considers the origins and development of a Beat sensibility within the cultural context of the 1950's. There are worthwhile discussions of most major Beat texts, including *On the Road* as well as Allen Ginsberg's poem *Howl* and William S. Burroughs's novel *Naked Lunch*.

Richard Sax

ALBERT KESSELRING

Born: November 20, 1885; Marktsteft, Germany
Died: July 16, 1960; Bad Nauheim, West Germany
Area of Achievement: The military
Contribution: Kesselring was one of Germany's more effective military commanders during World War II, particularly during the 1943-1944 Italian Campaign. He was instrumental in building the *Luftwaffe* into a viable component of the German war machine.

Early Life

Albert Kesselring was born in the Kingdom of Bavaria, part of Otto von Bismarck's German Empire, at Marktsteft on November 20, 1885. His family was Protestant and of middle-class origin. Kesselring's father was a state employee holding a post as a school supervisor. At the age of nineteen, Kesselring entered the Bavarian officer corps. By the outbreak of World War I, he had risen to the rank of captain in the artillery and had seen action on the Western Front. During the course of the war, he was promoted and served first on a divisional staff and, later, on the staff of corps. Kesselring was one of the bright officers of the General Staff, who during the Weimar Republic drew up secret plans for the establishment of the German air force. This planning during the 1920's for the *Luftwaffe* was forbidden by the Treaty of Versailles, but Kesselring carried forward his plans while posted to the training section of the *Truppenamt*, which was part of the old General Staff. It was during this service that he acquired a reputation as an able planning and operations officer. Not politically active, Kesselring nevertheless welcomed the rearmament stance of the Nazi Party. When Adolf Hitler and the Nazis were called upon to form a government in 1933, Kesselring, now a colonel, responded to a call from Hermann Göring to accept a post as chief of administration in the air ministry under the direction of Erhard Milch, the state secretary of the department.

Life's Work

Kesselring was now ready in 1933 to participate fully in the rearmament of Nazi Germany. At first, outwardly holding a civilian appointment, he turned his attention to putting his ideas concerning a *Luftwaffe* into practice. Officially resuming his military rank when Hitler renounced the Treaty of Versailles in 1935, Kesselring found his relations strained with Milch. Kesselring favored an air force of fighters and ground support aircraft over a *Luftwaffe* weighted in favor of a strategic heavy bomber force. His views brought him into conflict with some members of the military high command. After the death of General Walther Wever, in May, 1936, Kesselring was appointed the first chief of staff of the Air Force. As the chief, he submitted his conceptual views for the utilization of a modern air force to his colleagues and superiors, as he rapidly expanded the *Luftwaffe*. As chief of staff, Kesselring sent units of the air force to participate in the civil war in Spain in November, 1936. The members of the Condor Legion, as the units were named, gained invaluable combat experience in support of the Spanish Fascist forces. Kesselring's ideas did not meet with approval, and, as a result of deteriorating relations with Milch, Kesselring was transferred, in 1937, to an operational command. As matters grew worse, he resigned. His period of resignation was brief, and Kesselring was soon reappointed to operational command, with his concepts subsequently approved in February, 1939.

When war broke out in September, 1939, Kesselring was in command of Air Fleet I in action against Poland. Acting in close concert with the panzer groups, the *Luftwaffe* gave an added dimension to the *Blitzkrieg*, or lightning war. It was Kesselring who ordered the heavy bombing of Warsaw, destroying much of the old city center. After the rapid fall of Poland, Kesselring's command was transferred to Air Fleet II. It was Kesselring who led the *Luftwaffe* in its action against the Dutch, Belgians, French, and British in the dark days for the Allies of May and June, 1940. Kesselring again demonstrated his closely coordinated use of the air force in support of the fast-moving panzer divisions. He ordered the destruction of Rotterdam to break the will of the Dutch and commanded the air force in its attack on the British forces retreating across the Channel at Dunkerque, although failing to prevent their escape. In recognition of his success and leadership in the invasion of the West, Kesselring was promoted to general field marshal of the air force on June 30, 1940.

After the surrender of France, still in command of Air Fleet II, Field Marshal Kesselring led the *Luftwaffe* in offensive operations during the Battle of Britain, from August to October, 1940, in an intensive campaign against the enemy's air bases in

southeast England and aircraft production centers throughout the British Isles. As Göring and the German High Command shifted their strategy to inflicting maximum bombing on London, the *Luftwaffe* began to suffer high losses.

When Hitler's attention shifted to the Soviet Union, Kesselring was transferred to command the *Luftwaffe* in the central region in support of the invading German armies in the summer of 1941. After the initial success of German arms in Russia, Kesselring and the air fleet under his command were transferred to the Mediterranean area in December, where the field marshal was appointed commander in chief of the German armed forces in the southern region.

Kesselring, who was a thorough planner and had exceptional skill in managing people, now was called upon to use all of his considerable diplomatic abilities to cajole and motivate the Italians to maximize their efforts. Considering his poor opinion of the condition of the Italian armed forces, this was no mean feat. In particular, the field marshal was able to charm the Fascist leaders, including Benito Mussolini, and tried to bolster Italian re-

solve against the British and later the Americans. Kesselring was also able to develop a positive working relationship with Field Marshal Erwin Rommel. Rommel, as the highly successful commander of the Afrika Army Corps, was technically under Kesselring's control but largely independent. Kesselring attempted to sustain Rommel's troops by heavy air attacks on the stragetic island of Malta and by ferrying troops by air across the Mediterranean. When the German forces retreated out of Libya into Tunisia and Rommel had been recalled, Kesselring assumed command as the Germans evacuated their African beachhead. It was during this period, 1942-1943, that Kesselring became commander in chief of all German forces along the European periphery of the Mediterranean.

After the Allied invasion of Sicily and Italy in the summer of 1943, Kesselring took direct control of efforts to stop the advance of the British and Americans up the peninsula of Italy. His forces, particularly after Italy's surrender, fought a series of brilliant defensive actions for much more than a year. The Allied advance to the North was slowed particularly before Monte Cassino, as Kesselring's troops fought tenaciously and resourcefully. Using what planes he had and his armor to great advantage in the rugged terrain of Italy, he superbly slowed the Allied advance to a crawl. Kesselring was named the supreme commander in Italy in October, 1943, after the fall of Rome.

In October, 1944, Kesselring was injured and for several months of recuperation was out of action. Upon recovery of his health, Kesselring was transferred from Italy to command the collapsing German front in February, 1945, and succeeded Field Marshal Gerd von Rundstedt as commander in chief in the West and southern region of Germany in March, 1945. He surrendered his command to the Allies on May 7, 1945, loyal to his soldier's oath to Hitler to the end.

Following the war, Kesselring was tried, convicted, and sentenced for his part in the shooting of several hundred Italian hostages in the Ardeatine Caves near Rome in 1944. This action, ordered by Kesselring in retaliation for attacks on German forces by Italian partisans, resulted in a death sentence by a British court in Venice in May, 1947. Clemency was granted, his sentence was commuted to life imprisonment, and he was released on grounds of ill health in October, 1952. Kesselring, upon his release from custody, was elected president of the Stahlhelm, a German veterans' organization. He was actively involved in veterans' affairs until his death in Bad Nauheim in July, 1960, at the age of seventy-four.

Summary

Albert Kesselring was well respected by his peers, who were his opponents. He was a military leader who believed that excellent results could only come through proper planning. Kesselring was open to innovation and showed considerable resourcefulness in developing strategies for the specific use of the air force in support of the ground forces and in the general use of air power to terrorize his opponents, including the disruption of enemy communications and transportation networks. The field marshal was a tenacious commander and made use of whatever resources were at hand. Loyal to a fault, despite entreaties from Hitler's opponents he fought on, even when the German cause was hopeless. Kesselring was a worthy opponent and demonstrated considerable ingenuity in the defense of the German position in Italy.

Bibliography

Ansel, Walter. *Hitler and the Middle Sea.* Durham, N.C.: Duke University Press, 1972. Chapter 26 examines Kesselring's role in the Mediterranean campaign in late 1941 and early 1942. The entire book is a well-written study.

Higgins, Trumbull. *Soft Underbelly: The Anglo American Controversy over the Italian Campaign, 1939-1945.* New York: Macmillan, 1968. This work, as its title implies, covers the debate over what strategy to use against Hitler's fortress Europe. It analyzes the American and British view of Kesselring's efforts to impede their military efforts in Italy.

Jackson, William Godfrey F. *The Battle for Italy.* London: Batsford, and New York: Harper, 1967. Written by General Jackson, it is a balanced account of the fight for Italy. Sets forth the Allied view of Kesselring's tenacious efforts to prevent the Allied advance up the Italian boot.

Kesselring, Albert. *The Memoirs of Field-Marshal Kesselring.* Translated by Lynton Hudson. London: Kimber, 1953. Published after his release from prison, Kesselring's remembrances are a fairly straightforward account of his participation as a military commander of both air and ground forces during World War II.

MacDonald, Charles B. *The Last Offensive: The United States Army in World War II.* Washington, D.C.: Center of Military History, United States Army, 1973. An excellent account for the student of military history. From the American perspective, it reviews Kesselring's efforts to stem the Allied advance in the last days of the War.

Macksey, Kenneth. *Kesselring: The Making of the Luftwaffe.* London: Batsford, and New York: McKay, 1978. This work details Kesselring's role in the development and buildup of the German air force. It is a well-written analysis of the pivotal leadership brought by Kesselring to the building of Germany's air fleets.

Westphal, Siegfried. *The German Army in the West.* London: Cassell, 1951. An excellent account of German military action. It gives a good overview of this sector of the fighting.

Fred W. Hicks

JOHN MAYNARD KEYNES

Born: June 5, 1883; Cambridge, England
Died: April 21, 1946; Tilton, Sussex, England
Area of Achievement: Economics
Contribution: Keynes's seminal work, *The General Theory of Employment, Interest, and Money,* created a school that dominated economic thought in the mid-twentieth century and that continues to exercise a potent influence. Concern for world economic health, however, made him equally important in the arena of public affairs from World War I to the creation of the International Monetary Fund and World Bank after World War II.

Early Life

John Maynard Keynes was born June 5, 1883, in Cambridge, England. His mother, Florence Ada Brown, came from a family of Scots whose relatives included the poet Robert Burns. His father, John Neville Keynes, a Pembroke Fellow lecturing in logic and political economy at Cambridge, traced his lineage to land grants in Cambridgeshire from the time of William the Conqueror (1066). John Maynard was the first child; a sister, Margaret, and brother, Geoffrey, completed the family by 1887.

His quick mind showed at age three, when Keynes mastered the alphabet. Before age nine, he was enrolled in a day school where he impressed few except in mathematics and vocabulary. By age eleven, however, he was first in his class. Although his family was constantly concerned about his health, Keynes participated in various physical activities, including daring bicycle riding (which resulted in a finger injury over which he was self-conscious throughout his life). In 1897, to the delight of his parents, Keynes won a scholarship to Eton with a first in mathematics. Following his graduation from Eton, Keynes entered King's College, Cambridge, in October, 1902, and completed his exams in June, 1906. He then worked on currency and finance in the India Office until returning to Cambridge as a lecturer in economics in 1909. He was awarded a fellowship in 1910, which he retained until his death. A Cambridge undergraduate, Charles R. Fay, was impressed by Keynes's appearance—his mustache and striking waistcoat—the day they met. Keynes's penchant for fancy dress was evident even at Eton, where he acquired a purple coat and regularly wore a lapel flower. The mustache was a trademark until his death. In August, 1925, Keynes married Lydia Lopokova (1891-1981), a Russian ballerina, who helped ease the pain of his illnesses and the stress of his multifaceted persona and career.

Life's Work

In October, 1911, Keynes became the editor of the *Economic Journal,* a position that he would hold for thirty-three years and one that permitted him to support the work of numerous young economists. His first major published work was *Indian Currency and Finance* (1913). This work resulted from his experience in the India Office during his brief absence from Cambridge from 1906 to 1909.

The path to international fame began in early August, 1914, when Keynes was consulted about the gold standard three days before British entry into World War I. Both David Lloyd George, Chancellor of the Exchequer, and Herbert Asquith, the prime minister, utilized Keynes's ideas in setting national fiscal policy during the war. In 1915, Keynes was hired by the Exchequer to join its finance team. In that role, he consulted and negotiated with Great Britain's allies on matters of loans, currency, and economic planning during the war and made his first trip to the United States. For his efforts, Keynes was made a Commander of the Bath (K.C.B.) in 1919. He also acquired his permanent London residence, located in Bloomsbury, at 46 Gordon Square.

The British Treasury named Keynes its chief representative to the Versailles treaty negotiations in 1919. He was not part of the reparations commission, although he did negotiate food for Austria and Germany in exchange for merchant ships and gold. The rejection of his proposal for an international fund for rebuilding, rather than punitive reparations, led to his resignation in June. In early December, he published *The Economic Consequences of the Peace* (1919). The book criticized the self-defeating economic policies of the Versailles treaty such as the reparations payments demanded of Germany and other Central Powers and restrictions on merchant fleets. Keynes predicted that other countries would not permit the Germans, for example, to sell the products of their industry without tariff restrictions. Therefore, the money to pay reparations would not be readily available. *The Economic Consequences of the Peace* was an instant,

worldwide success. Within a short time, it was translated into German, French, Flemish, Danish, Italian, Romanian, Russian, and Japanese, among other languages, and sold more than 140,000 copies by 1924.

In 1923, Keynes was nominated for a Nobel Peace Prize as a result of his efforts in the area of peaceful international economic cooperation. Such activities included advising Carl Melchior, German finance director, on monetary policies, and British and German officials on inflation; reporting on the Genoa economic conference for *The Manchester Guardian* (1922); and publishing a sequel book on Versailles, *A Revision of the Treaty* (1922), and *A Tract on Monetary Reform* (1923), in which he argued for managed currencies.

His two-volume *A Treatise on Money*, the most scholarly of Keynes's writing, was published late in 1930. The seven books into which he divided the treatise are filled with insights, but the whole is nearly impossible to comprehend. It nevertheless contains hints of the ideas that later came to encompass Keynesian economics. In the treatise, he noted the effect of the Depression on investments: Lost profitability caused money to be saved, not invested. He thus proceeded to seek a more general economic theory.

After six years of drafting, seeking the advice and criticism of others, and revising his ideas, Keynes published *The General Theory of Employment, Interest, and Money* (1936). This work effectively destroyed the classical capitalist idea that economies automatically function optimally by arguing that unequal income distribution in a period of growth produces more saving and less investment, which then result in underconsumption and unemployment. The solution, for Keynes, was to have government use its taxing and spending powers to manage the level of investment and savings for the purpose of maintaining full employment and a stable economy.

Although a heart attack in 1937 affected his health, Keynes hardly reduced his activities. He engaged in extensive debate over his theory, wrote and spoke to general audiences on the Depression, and began focusing on war financing, publishing *How to Pay for the War* in 1940. This pamphlet had first appeared as a series of articles in *The Times*. Keynes recommended tax increases to discourage consumer buying when a nation is at war. He also argued for deferred income for workers in order to provide for postwar buying demands. He

also urged low interest rates as a means of stimulating industrial investment in war production. Ultimately, Great Britain used these fiscal tools to help pay for the costs of World War II, and it can be said that they were Keynes's most significant contribution to national policy. Throughout the war years, Keynes was an unpaid counselor to the British Exchequer as well as the most influential spokesman for economic issues. He had access to Prime Minister Winston Churchill through the leader's advisers and through his writings, especially in the *Economic Journal*, which often became position papers for official policies on trade, rationing, social surveys, allied loans, currency exchange, and finance.

Even in his sixties, enfeebled by recurrent illnesses, Keynes continued to pursue many activities. By 1944, he was involved with efforts to plan for economic cooperation after the war. He believed that the best approach would be through multilateral trade and exchange programs. He represented Great Britain at the Bretton Woods Conference, in New Hampshire, in 1944. Keynes dominated the representatives of the forty-four nations participating. His prescription for healthy international trade was a managed international monetary system, including stable currency exchange rates. In March, 1946, at Savannah, Georgia, Keynes served as the British delegate at the creation of the International Monetary Fund and World Bank. Afterward, he was to be the British member of the board of each organization, although he was prevented from serving by his death in April, 1946. His final public contribution was steering the loan repayment agreement with the United States through Parliament.

Keynes was not only an economist, writer, and policy adviser but also a book and art collector, magazine owner (Nation and Athenaeum), principal backer of the Cambridge Arts Theatre, investor/investment adviser, insurance company board member, Cambridge University investment portfolio manager, biographer, generous financial backer of friends, recipient of numerous honorary degrees, a member of the House of Lords as of 1942, and, days before his death, a Fellow of the Royal Society.

Summary

A man whose mature life spanned the first half of the twentieth century, John Maynard Keynes was involved in many significant events and developments, with numerous persons. He was a part of the Bloomsbury Group, which included Lytton Strachey (critic and biographer), writers Leonard and Virginia Woolf, and artist Duncan Grant. His university colleague mentors included the economist Alfred Marshall, the philosopher Alfred North Whitehead, and the mathematician and philosopher Bertrand Russell. At Versailles, he worked with such Americans as John Foster Dulles, Walter Lippmann, and Felix Frankfurter, as well as the South Africans General Jan Smuts and Louis Botha. Keynes personally advised (on Depression and wartime finances) three American presidents, four British prime ministers, and several other heads of state. He was involved in World War I, the Versailles Settlement, the Great Depression, World War II, and the post-1945 arrangements as a financial expert. His ideas dramatically altered economic thought, and because he advocated government activism as a principle, he brought political decisions into both alliance and opposition with economists. Within economics, however, *The General Theory of Employment, Interest, and Money* led to specialized studies and models that in turn led to the public perception of mass confusion among the "experts."

Bibliography

Bateman, Bradley W. *Keynes's Uncertain Revolution*. Ann Arbor: University of Michigan Press, 1996. Bateman considers the interest economists have shown in a possible relationship between the ideas outlined in the *Treatise of Probability* and those in the *General Theory of Money, Interest and Employment*. The author concludes that it is impossible to understand the connection without considering Keynes' perceptions of financial markets and his approaches to controlling them.

Drucker, Peter F. "Schumpeter and Keynes." *Forbes* 131 (May 23, 1983): 124-128. Drucker, a respected management scholar, was asked by the editors to do this essay upon the hundredth anniversary of the birth of the two great economists. His analysis is that Keynes was too short-term oriented in his thinking while Schumpeter understood long-term effects. Drucker contends that, while the latter was a more pedestrian economist, his wisdom was greater.

Felix, David. *Keynes: A Critical Life*. Westport, Conn.: Greenwood Press, 1999. The first critical biography of Keynes that takes into account Keynes' own archives. Considers his sexuality, his marriage and its impact on his political and social stability, and his self-confidence.

Harrod, Roy F. *The Life of John Maynard Keynes*. London: Macmillan, and New York: Harcourt Brace, 1951. A sympathetic account by a devoted student. Less prone to confront the intimate personal side and more inclined to deal with the influential "ruling class" composition of Keynes's circle. Also, there is more emphasis on economic ideas.

Heilbroner, Robert L. *The Worldly Philosophers: The Lives, Times, and Ideas of the Great Economic Thinkers*. 6th ed. New York: Simon and Schuster, 1986. Contains sketches of a number of economic contributors, from Adam Smith through Keynes.

Hession, Charles H. *John Maynard Keynes: A Personal Biography of the Man Who Revolutionized Capitalism and the Way We Live*. New York and London: Macmillan, 1984. A revealing, readable account that seeks to explain the man through insights borrowed from many disciplines, such as the psychology of homosexuality. Also, places Keynes's accomplishments in the broader context of historical development and ideas in the realm of execution.

Keynes, John Maynard. *Essays in Biography*. London: Macmillan, 1933; New York: Norton, 1963. A collection of fifteen sketches beginning with his immediate analysis of the four major participants at Versailles. There is an essay on Lloyd George, written in 1919 but omitted from *Economic Consequences of the Peace* (London: Macmillan, 1919), in which Woodrow Wilson and Georges Clemenceau were critically sketched.

Keynes, Milo, ed. *Essays on John Maynard Keynes*. Cambridge and New York: Cambridge University Press, 1975. Twenty-eight essays by distinguished acquaintances. The first eight deal with personal subjects; part 2 contains ten accounts of Keynes's economic ideas and influence. The last ten essays deal with Keynes's contributions in areas such as art, education, philosophy, international negotiations, and biography.

Lekachman, Robert. "A Keynes for All Seasons." *The New Republic* 3(June 20, 1983): 21-25. Lekachman, author of *The Age of Keynes* (1966), presents a review of Keynes's ideas and their application since the 1930's. Although Keynesianism was downgraded after the OPEC oil increases in 1973, the solutions offered by supply-siders and monetarists are seen to have produced other dilemmas or to have worked only as subliminal Keynesianism.

Schumpeter, Joseph A. *Ten Great Economists, from Marx to Keynes*. New York: Oxford University Press, 1951; London: Allen and Unwin, 1952. Author of the highly respected *A History of Economic Analysis* (1954), Schumpeter attempts a portrait of both the man and the economic theorist. He notes that Keynes was skilled in mathematics yet shunned mathematical (scientific) economics, was politically interested in applying his measures, and devised a theory that rested on simplified short-run phenomena.

Skidelsky, Robert. "The Economist as Prince: J. M. Keynes." *History Today* 33 (July, 1983): 11-20. Poses the issue of Keynes as creator of twentieth century economic policies that produced great prosperity yet seemingly brought the kernel of destruction: inflation. A personality sketch underscores Keynes's unwavering belief in individualism, his opposition to authoritarianism (Marxist economics), and his presumed willingness to accept a new general theory if faced with post-1970 problems.

————. *John Maynard Keynes*. Vol. 1, *Hopes Betrayed (1883-1920)*. London: Macmillan, 1983; New York: Viking Press, 1986. The first volume of a projected two-volume account. Emphasis on early life and the young man's search for truth and ways to live out those findings. Because of Skidelsky's focus on Keynes's circle of friends and lovers, there is less room for discussion of his work on finance at the India Office and economics in general.

Lance Williams

RUHOLLAH KHOMEINI

Born: November 9, 1902; Khomein, Iran
Died: June 3, 1989; Tehran, Iran
Area of Achievement: Religion, government, and politics
Contribution: Arguably the most famous postmedieval Muslim religious leader anywhere, Khomeini directed the Iranian Revolution of 1978 and 1979, established the Islamic Republic of Iran in April, 1979, and ruled the country thereafter for ten years. His legacy also includes inspiring fundamentalist Muslim activism throughout the world.

Early Life

Ruhollah Khomeini was born in the small town of Khomein to a local Shi'i cleric who was killed a year later in a quarrel with employees of an absentee landlord. Ruhollah was reared at an aunt's house, there apparently being insufficient money or room at home for him. At an early age, he began traditional religious education, partly under the tutelage of an elder brother. In 1919, shortly after the deaths of his aunt and his mother, Ruhollah went to the city of Arāk to continue his theological studies. There Ruhollah joined the group around Shaykh 'Abdolkarim Ha'eri Yazdi and in 1920 followed Ha'eri to Qom, where he completed his basic theological education in 1926.

Meanwhile, in Tehran a military officer called Reza Khan participated in a 1921 *coup d'état* against the central government and later emerged as the strongest political actor on the national scene. In 1924, Reza Khan visited Ha'eri in Qom, which the latter was molding into a leading Shi'i theological center. Shi'i clerics, wary of Reza Khan's Persian nationalism, blocked a plan to replace the Qajar monarchy with a republic. In 1925, Reza Pahlavi deposed Ahmad Shah and brought the Qajar Dynasty to an end. A year later, he crowned himself *shahanshah* (emperor) and embarked on ambitious programs of Westernization and secularization, which made the Pahlavi monarchy Khomeini's lifelong arch enemy.

In 1930, returning from a pilgrimage to the Shi'i shrine at Mashhad, Khomeini visited Tehran and married a prominent cleric's daughter called Batul, who was ten years old at the time. In 1932, Khomeini's first son, called Mostafa, was born. Khomeini's second son, Ahmad, was born in 1936.

By this time, Khomeini was an established instructor of Islamic jurisprudence in Qom and had even conducted some of the recently deceased Ha'eri's advanced theology classes. In 1937, Khomeini made the hajj, or pilgrimage to Mecca.

In the fall of 1941, upon the arrival of British and Russian occupation forces, Reza Shah Pahlavi was forced to abdicate the Iranian throne. The Allies allowed his son, Mohammad Reza Shah Pahlavi, to succeed him, despite efforts by Shi'i clerics to persuade the British to put an end to the monarchy.

By 1946, Ayatollah Mohammad-Hussein Borujerdi emerged as the leading Shi'i cleric and proceeded to advocate an apolitical course. Khomeini became a Borujerdi aide and taught in the Qom theological school system. At a 1949 meeting of leading clerics, while Borujerdi advocated withdrawal by leading clerics from active participation in politics, Khomeini sided with clerics advocating political activism. Later, these activists played a role in events that led in August, 1953, to an American-orchestrated *coup d'état* that toppled the nationalist prime minister Mohammad Mosaddeq and reestablished Mohammad Reza Shah Pahlavi on the throne. In 1955, now a very prominent instructor of Islamic sciences, Khomeini supported, and Mohammad Reza Pahlavi allowed, the persecution of the Baha'is.

In 1960, Borujerdi and other clerics opposed a land reform law, which Mohammad Reza Shah Pahlavi was consequently obliged to have annulled. In 1961, Khomeini, now an ayatollah, published *Tawzīh al-masā'il* (*A Clarification of Questions*, 1984). When Borujerdi died in the same year, no single ayatollah was recognized as his successor as the chief Shi'i leader, although Khomeini received support from clerics advocating, as he did, political activism on their part.

Life's Work

By 1962, Khomeini was being referred to by the title "grand ayatollah." In January, 1963, he published an attack on a government land redistribution proposal. In March, he was arrested after speeches in which he ordered the Shi'i faithful not to celebrate *Nowruz* (Iranian New Year). In April, Mohammad Reza Shah Pahlavi went regally to Qom and castigated the clergy. Then on June 3, which coincided with the anniversary of Shi'i

Imam Husayn ibn 'Alī's death at Karbala in 680, Khomeini again preached against the government, calling the Shah an agent of Israel. After his arrest two days later, riots ensued. Khomeini remained in jail in Tehran for three months and was thereafter kept under house arrest. In October, he was again arrested, this time for advocating a boycott of elections. In April, 1964, by now the leading opposition figure, Khomeini was allowed to return to Qom. In November, Khomeini gave a speech protesting an Iranian/American bill that would extend diplomatic immunity to American military personnel in Iran and asserting the Shah's subservience to the American government. Again arrested, Khomeini was this time exiled to Turkey. In January, 1965, Khomeini settled in Najaf, Iraq, where he was forced and allowed to go after protesting Western dress codes in Turkey. On January 20, Prime Minister Hasan 'Alī Mansur was assassinated at the behest of Khomeini aides, after a secret Islamic court condemned him to death. The social reformer Kasravi had been similarly assassinated by Shi'i activists in 1946, as had Prime Minister Haj 'Alī Raz-Mara in 1951.

In June, 1967, after Israel defeated the Arabs in the Six-Day War, Khomeini discussed clerical political rule for Iran and an Islamic holy war against Israel. In 1968, Khomeini resumed his teaching of theology and thereafter implored Iranians to overthrow the Pahlavi monarchy. Based on that teaching, Khomeini's *Hokumat-e-Eslami* (*Islamic Government*, 1979) was published in 1971. In it, while arguing that Muslim jurisprudents were uniquely qualified to govern societies, he predicted the overthrow of the Pahlavi monarchy and the establishment of an Islamic state. About this time, Khomeini met the prominent Arab religious leader Musa Sadr, whose niece had become Ahmad Khomeini's wife. In 1975, Khomeini called for a boycott of the newly formed Rastakhiz Party, the basis for the Shah's new, one-party state.

In October, 1977, Khomeini's son Mostafa died in suspicious circumstances in Iraq. In December, students in Tehran demanded that Khomeini be allowed to return to Iran. In January, 1978, an article planted by the government in a national daily newspaper slandered Khomeini. A series of protests, clashes with the government, and memorial services ensued throughout that spring. In July, the Rex Cinema in Ābādān burned down, with hundreds of people locked inside. Clerical involvement in the tragedy was assumed, but Khomeini blamed the Shah's security forces. In October, expelled from Iraq and denied entry to Kuwait, Khomeini traveled to Paris, from which, via television, he became a household name throughout the world. Demonstrations in Tehran in December, coinciding with the anniversary of Husayn ibn 'Alī's death, called for Khomeini to return to lead Iran. The magnitude of the demonstrations made it obvious that the Shah would not survive politically.

On February 1, 1979, Khomeini returned triumphantly to Tehran, two weeks after the abject departure of the Shah. In March, the Islamic Republic of Iran was established, with Khomeini as its leader. The execution of hundreds of Pahlavi government officials followed. Sensing the strict theocratic basis of the new social order, tens of thousands of educated, secular-minded Iranians began leaving the country. In November, 1979, a group of Iranians identifying themselves as followers of "the Imam's line" seized the American Embassy in Tehran and held some fifty hostages until January, 1981. Khomeini orchestrated the release of the hostages to take place the moment that Ronald Reagan was sworn in to succeed Jimmy Carter as President of the United States.

In September, 1980, Iraq invaded Iran, and a war commenced that served to unite some elements of the Iranian population behind Khomeini. By the time hostilities had ended inconclusively in mid-1989, it had cost hundreds of thousands of Iranian lives and devastated the economy.

In 1981, a longtime supporter of Khomeini called Sheik Mohammad Saduqi declared that Baha'i blood might be legally spilled. In June of that year, Islamic Republic's president, Abolhassan Bani-Sadr, was deposed as mullahs grew more powerful. A hundred or more clerical leaders and officials died in a bombing at a party headquarters in June, for which the subsequently outlawed Mujahedeen-e-Khalq-e-Iran (People's Combatants of Iran) claimed responsibility. In 1982, former Khomeini supporter and foreign minister Sadeq Ghotbzadeh was executed for plotting Khomeini's overthrow. In 1983, leaders and thousands of members of the Tudeh Party of Iran were arrested. An assembly of experts was charged in 1984 with planning for Khomeini's successor. His will and testament were deposited in a safe at the Parliament Building for publication the moment he died. In 1988, Khomeini declared edicts on governmental prerogatives which are binding for Shi'is. Early in 1989, Khomeini called for the death of India-born, British author Salman Rushdie because of the latter's alleged insults to Islam in a novel called *The Satanic Verses* (1988).

Khomeini died on June 3, 1989. Millions of Iranians mourned his death and attended his funeral, one of the largest in history. The chant "Death to America" was an integral part of the proceedings. In late July, former Parliament speaker Hashemi Rafsanjani was elected President of the Islamic Republic of Iran, thereafter consolidating his position as Iran's most powerful political figure and sending signals that he might harmonize Islamic teachings with modern realities.

Summary

From his early adult years until 1979, Ruhollah Khomeini labored to achieve two ends, the collapse of the Pahlavi monarchy and the installation of an Islamic government. Incorruptible, ascetic, religious, single-minded, and self-confident in pursuing these goals, Khomeini proceeded in 1979 to show the world an authoritarian, autocratic leadership style (as an arguably traditional Iranian patriarch), intense xenophobia against the West and Israel, and ignorance of things beyond the pale of Islam. In asserting that American president Jimmy Carter was a manifestation of Satan and consequently deserved assassination, and that women should be in their husbands' homes by the time they menstruate for the first time, among other things, Khomeini presented a challenge to the nonfundamentalist Muslim world and to the non-Muslim world: how to deal with a leader whose perspectives and thought processes are very different and who does not believe in compromise.

As the leader of one of the world's great revolutions, as the architect of a successful fusion of theology and politics in the establishment of perhaps the first "fundamentalist" Islamic republic in the history of Islam, as the implementor of a historical alternative to secular misrule, and as a successful thwarter of Western values, Khomeini stands as an almost uniquely successful political leader in the short term. As a pan-Islamic activist who argued for the substitution of the notion of the Islamic community for the Iranian nation or Iranian nationalism, Khomeini offers a political vision with serious consequence in the long term for nation-states with significant Muslim populations. History alone will tell how lasting his vision and influence will ultimately prove to be.

Bibliography

Abdelnasser, Walid M. "Islamic Organizations in Egypt and the Iranian Revolution of 1979: The Experience of the First Few Years." *Arab Studies Quarterly* 19, no. 2 (Spring 1997). Discusses the different Islamic groups in Egypt and their support for the Islamic unity called for by Iran after the Iranian Islamic Revolution.

Arjomand, Said Amir. *The Turban for the Crown: The Islamic Revolution in Iran*. New York: Oxford University Press, 1988. A sociologist's explanation of the Islamic revolution of 1979 in Iran and "assessment of its significance in world history," this study details Khomeini's role as a chief actor in the Iranian political arena, compares him with other famous revolutionary leaders, and demonstrates the success of his Islamic revolutionary ideology.

Ferdows, Adele. "Shariati and Khomayni on Women." In *The Iranian Revolution and the Islamic Republic of Iran*, edited by Nikki R. Keddie and Eric Hooglund. Syracuse, N.Y.: Syracuse University Press, 1986. A discussion of a most sensitive issue in modernizing Muslim societies today, that of the continuing relegation of women in Islam, according to feminist observers, to inferior social status. Khomeini's conservative views receive treatment along with those of the Western-educated and anti-Pahlavi social reformer Ali Shariati.

Fischer, Michael M. J. "Imam Khomeini: Four Levels of Understanding." In *Voices of Resurgent Islam*, edited by John L. Esposito. New York: Oxford University Press, 1983. A biographical sketch and an analysis of Khomeini's public persona in an attempt to account for his success as a charismatic religious and political leader.

Kazemazadeh, Masoud. "Review Essay." *Middle East Policy* 4, no. 3 (March, 1996). The author argues that Khomeini's philosophies, which are customarily portrayed as rigid and conservative, are actually quite modern and adaptable. Considers the changes that occurred in Khomeini's beliefs between 1940 and 1989.

Mottahedeh, Roy. *The Mantle of the Prophet: Religion and Politics in Iran*. New York: Simon and Schuster, 1985; London: Chatto and Windus, 1986. Intended for the "intelligent general reader of Middle Eastern history" and in the context of "an extended reading of Iranian culture," including historical interchapters, this study traces the life of a prominent contemporary Iranian Shi'i Muslim cleric given the pseudonym Ali Hashemi. Although not the explicit focus of the presentation, Khomeini figures prominently in it because Hashemi's life revolves around Khomeini's political activism and role in Iranian affairs as of the late 1970's.

Rose, Gregory. "*Velayat-e Faqih* and the Recovery of Identity in the Thought of Ayatullah Khomeini." In *Religion and Politics in Iran: Shi'ism from Quietism to Revolution*, edited by Nikki Keddie. New Haven, Conn.: Yale University Press, 1983; London: Yale University Press, 1984. A sympathetic treatment of Khomeini's response to what he perceived as the Muslim world's identity crisis and pervasive alienation. With a review of the history of the concept of authority or governance of the Muslim jurisprudent over the affairs of the Muslim community, the essay describes Khomeini's view that Shi'ite Islam needs to be a revolutionary ideology.

Taheri, Amir. *The Spirit of Allah: Khomeini and the Islamic Revolution.* London: Hutchinson, 1985; Bethesda, Md.: Adler and Adler, 1986. Although not a sympathetic portrait and not inclusive of Khomeini's last three years, this is the fullest and most informative treatment to appear.

Michael Craig Hillman

NIKITA S. KHRUSHCHEV

Born: April 17, 1894; Kalinovka, Russia
Died: September 11, 1971; Moscow, U.S.S.R.
Areas of Achievement: Government and politics
Contribution: Khrushchev ruled the Soviet Union for a tumultuous decade, during which he began de-Stalinization and released millions of his countrymen from the Siberian Gulag. In foreign affairs, the Sino-Soviet split, the suppression of the Hungarian Revolution of 1956, and the Cuban Missile Crisis characterized his time in power.

Early Life

Nikita Sergeyevich Khrushchev was born in Kalinovka, Kursk Region, Russia, on April 17, 1894. He started working in factories and mines of the Ukrainian Donets Basin when he was fourteen years old. In 1918, he joined the Communist Party and fought in the Russian Civil War. By the mid-1920's, he had become a local Party secretary, and he held various Party jobs in the Ukraine over the next decade. In 1935, he became first secretary of the Moscow Communist Party. In 1938, he returned to the Ukraine as first secretary in that republic. In 1939, he became a full member of the Politburo. During World War II, Khrushchev was a member of the Military Council on the Southern Front.

When Stalin died on March 5, 1953, Georgi Malenkov became the senior Communist Party secretary and head of the Soviet government. Khrushchev, while one of the Party secretaries, was still a secondary figure. Eight days after Stalin's death, Malenkov miscalculated. He had a picture of the signing of the 1950 Sino-Soviet Treaty cropped to show only Joseph Stalin, Mao Tse-tung, and himself, and published the picture. Malenkov's colleagues interpreted this maneuver as a bid for sole power. They forced him to relinquish his position as head of the Party, although he remained the dominant governmental figure. The Party leaders subsequently made Khrushchev the senior Party secretary, apparently assuming that Khrushchev would pose no serious threat to their own power positions.

Life's Work

In March of 1953, Lavrenty Beria, the head of the secret police, was generally regarded as the second most powerful man in the Soviet Union, after Malenkov. Beria inspired both loathing and fear. In an action of notable courage, Khrushchev went secretly to his colleagues and convinced them that Beria was plotting a supreme power-grab that might bring a terror worse than that of Stalin. Beria was arrested in July of 1953 and executed in December. When Khrushchev was asked after his fall what his greatest achievement had been, he answered that it was the saving of his country from Beria.

The balance of power between Khrushchev and Malenkov shifted gradually in Khrushchev's favor. In the autumn of 1954, an open policy dispute erupted between them, with Malenkov advocating consumer goods and Khrushchev favoring heavy industry and military strength. Khrushchev won, and Malenkov was forced from his position as head of government on February 8, 1955.

It was not long before Khrushchev began to cut a wide swath in foreign affairs. In late 1954, Khrushchev visited Mao in Peking, and the Chinese pressed unsuccessfully for the return to China of Mongolia, then a Soviet puppet state, and for other concessions. When Khrushchev returned to Moscow, as he reports in his memoirs, he told his colleagues that "conflict with China is inevitable." In Europe, Khrushchev visited Yugoslavia and tried unsuccessfully to undo the 1948 Stalin-Tito break. West Germany was moving toward participation in the North Atlantic Treaty Organization (NATO) in 1954, and Khrushchev tried to convince the Germans that neutrality might open the door to German reunification. Perhaps as an example, he agreed to a neutral, unified Austria, and the withdrawal of Soviet forces. Khrushchev also gave up the Porkkala Peninsula naval base in Finland. Vyacheslav Molotov opposed these concessions and was later forced out as foreign minister. West Germany did enter NATO, however, and the Warsaw Pact was the East Bloc's response. In 1956, twin crises erupted in Poland and Hungary. The Poles, led by Władysław Gomułka, faced down Khrushchev in a tense Warsaw confrontation and achieved half the loaf of their national autonomy. In Hungary, the crisis resulted in the crushing of the Hungarian Revolution by Soviet tanks and troops. In the Suez crisis, which broke out at the same time, Khrushchev waited until the worst was over before he threatened to support Egypt's Gamal Abdel Nasser with rockets.

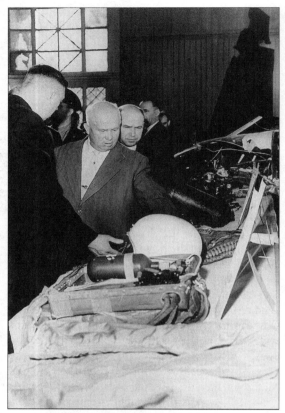

Soviet premier Nikita S. Khrushchev inspecting wreckage from the American U2 spy plane shot down over the Soviet Union in May, 1960.

In domestic affairs, Khrushchev encouraged a "thaw" and permitted greater literary freedom. Works by nonconformist writers, such as Aleksandr Solzhenitsyn, were published. Khrushchev was also notably, if not always consistently, liberal with cultural figures and scientists. In February of 1956, at a closed session of the Twentieth Congress of the Soviet Communist Party, Khrushchev delivered his "Secret Speech" denouncing Stalin's crimes. De-Stalinization swept the land, and statues and portraits of Stalin disappeared. Khrushchev followed up with an amnesty, which led to the release of millions of Soviets from the Siberian Gulag. In addition, Khrushchev restored national autonomy to Caucasian and other peoples whom Stalin had deported, and allowed most survivors to return to their homes. He launched a program to build apartments everywhere and more than doubled annual housing construction during his time in office.

In agricultural policy, Khrushchev abolished the machine and tractor stations that had served both as mechanized service units and centers of political control in the countryside. He transformed many collective farms into state farms (state-run factories in the countryside). He pushed a drive to plant corn for fodder with such vigor that underlings forced plantings where the corn would not grow. He also launched the Virgin Lands Program in Kazakhstan and Central Asia, forcing the planting of vast stretches of prairie in wheat. By 1956, Soviet wheat production had risen by 50 percent, but bad years, such as 1958 and 1963, reflected emerging dust bowl conditions. Khrushchev promised that the Soviet Union would soon overtake the United States in the production of milk, meat, and butter, but that program faltered.

In 1957, Khrushchev's opponents in the Communist Party Presidium (Politburo) combined against him. His opponents included Malenkov and Molotov (for reasons already indicated), Old Stalinists, and ambitious careerists. Khrushchev's adversaries formed a majority to oust him. Khrushchev appealed the decision to the Party Central Committee. Marshal Georgi Zhukov, the minister of defense and a World War II hero, helped Khrushchev fly in Central Committee supporters from distant places, and the Presidium vote was overturned. Key members of the Presidium majority were then publicly branded as an "anti-Party Group." Molotov was sent off as ambassador to Mongolia, and Malenkov became manager of an electric power station in Semipalatinsk. Khrushchev removed his erstwhile ally Zhukov in October.

Khrushchev decreed a system of rotation in Party jobs and limits to incumbency. Later he split the Communist Party leadership in each region, constituting a separate agricultural and industrial party organization, to the deep resentment of many local party chiefs. Khrushchev reformed education, forcing adolescents to interrupt their academic studies to work in factories and farms. He launched an antireligious drive that resulted in the closing of more than 40 percent of the Russian Orthodox churches in the country. He turned from support of heavy industry to consumer goods, scrapped Navy cruisers and destroyers, reduced the Red Army by more than a million men, and cut the perquisites of military and police officers. Many of these initiatives made for Khrushchev new enemies in the establishment.

Relations with China worsened as the Great Leap Forward of 1957-1958 produced turmoil and failure. In 1959, Khrushchev scrapped the Sino-Soviet arms aid agreement and supported India during Chinese-Indian border hostilities. In 1960, the Soviet Union withdrew its technicians from China and sent Chinese students home. In Moscow in October of 1961, the Sino-Soviet split became public. Chou En-lai laid a wreath at Stalin's bier in the Red Square mausoleum and went home. Eight days later, Khrushchev had Stalin's body removed, cremated, and buried by the Kremlin wall.

With respect to the West, Khrushchev issued a six-month ultimatum on Thanksgiving Day of 1958 to get out of Berlin. He let the ultimatum slide, however, as preparations went forward for a two-week visit to the United States in September, 1959. The visit proved a success, and President Dwight D. Eisenhower hoped that a planned return visit and the Paris Summit of May, 1960, would bring important new arms control agreements. The shooting down of Francis Gary Powers and his U-2 "spy plane" dashed these hopes. When Eisenhower refused to apologize, Khrushchev broke up the Paris summit. In the autumn of 1960, Khrushchev returned to New York for the United Nations General Assembly, banging a shoe on his desk in protest during a debate about the suppression of the Hungarian Revolution.

John F. Kennedy was inaugurated in January of 1961, and a series of incidents convinced Khrushchev that Kennedy was weak. First, there was an American humiliation in Laos. In April, there was the Bay of Pigs. In June, there was the Khrushchev-Kennedy summit in Vienna, where Khrushchev was able to browbeat Kennedy. In August, there was the erection of the Berlin Wall. All this no doubt influenced Khrushchev in his decision to place intermediate-range nuclear missiles in Cuba. The Cuban Missile Crisis ensued and, in Dean Rusk's words, Khrushchev blinked first. While the settlement guaranteed that the United States would not invade Cuba, the identity of the loser was clear. Nevertheless, Khrushchev did not withdraw into sullen isolationism but responded to Kennedy's initiative the next year and negotiated the Atmospheric Nuclear Test Ban Treaty—a blessing to the health of the world.

The seeds of discontent had produced dense thickets of opposition in the Soviet Union by the summer of 1964. Aleksandr Shelepin, Chief of the Party-State Control Commission, reportedly argued with other Presidium members that Khrushchev would soon purge them. The head of the secret po-lice Komitet Gosudarstvennoi Bezopasnosti (KGB), Vladimir Semichastny, joined the plotters. There was discontent among army and navy officers. The bad harvest of 1963 had produced bread rationing, and the Cuban Missile Crisis had been a humiliation. The shoe-banging had not helped. Old Stalinists smoldered, Party bureaucrats grumbled, and defense-minded advocates of heavy industry fumed. Many blamed Khrushchev for the break with China. Perhaps the last straw was the knowledge in Communist Party circles that Khrushchev intended a new shake-up when he returned from his 1964 Black Sea vacation.

Leonid Ilich Brezhnev telephoned Khrushchev on October 13, 1964, and convinced him to cut short his vacation for an important meeting in Moscow. When Khrushchev drove to the nearby airport, he found an unfamiliar plane. In Moscow he found a different car, driver, and bodyguards, and he was met by KGB Chief Semichastny. When Khrushchev arrived at the Kremlin, he found the nine other members of the Presidium waiting. Mikhail Suslov, from a current copy of *Pravda* and one from Stalin's day, showed Khrushchev that he had promoted his own "personality cult," as Stalin had. As in 1957, Khrushchev demanded a Central Committee meeting. His colleagues, anticipating this, had already assembled a hand-picked quorum, the members of which had already waited for days in the Kremlin incommunicado, watching films to while away the time. Khrushchev was led to the meeting and obliged to resign.

Khrushchev retired to his country house in Petrovo-Dalnee, near Moscow. He planted a vegetable garden and began to dictate his memoirs into a tape recorder. The tapes were smuggled to the West and published. It is said that the ensuing pressure on Khrushchev to repudiate the memoirs hastened the two heart attacks that resulted in his death on September 11, 1971.

Summary

Nikita S. Khrushchev's flamboyant style left a residue of amusement, admiration, outrage, and fear. In some ways, Khrushchev did better by his country then either his countrymen or the world appreciated. The monument over his tomb displays a dramatic juxtaposition of black-and-white marble, as the sculptor correctly proclaims that Khrushchev's life was a contrasting mixture of darker deeds and gleaming white ones. He was a forerunner of Gorbachev and his policies, including *pere-*

stroika (economic restructuring) and *glasnost* (openness).

Bibliography

Crankshaw, Edward. *Khrushchev: A Career.* New York: Viking Press, 1966. This work by one of the foremost experts of the Soviet Union covers Khrushchev's career in its entirety. Includes a chronology, notes, and an index.

Geller, Mikhail, and Aleksandr Nekrich. *Utopia in Power.* London: Hutchinson, and New York: Summit Books, 1986. Two prominent dissident émigrés have written a critical history of Soviet rule. They include about a hundred pages of description and commentary on the Khrushchev period, when they were intellectual leaders in the Soviet Union.

Gorlizki, Yoram. "Anti-Ministerialism and the USSR Ministry of Justice, 1953-56: A Study in Organizational Decline." *Europe-Asia Studies* 48, no. 8 (December, 1996). Discusses Khrushchev's move against Soviet bureaucracy in the 1950's and the eventual elimination of several ministries, including the Ministry of Justice.

Khrushchev, Nikita S. *Khrushchev Remembers.* Edited and translated by Strobe Talbot. Boston: Little Brown, 1970; London: Deutsch, 1971.

———. *Khrushchev Remembers: The Last Testament.* Edited and translated by Strobe Talbot. Boston: Little Brown, and London: Deutsch, 1974. These are Khrushchev's own memoirs, spoken into a tape recorder after his fall from power. They represent more than eleven hundred pages of fascinating and indispensable commentary on Khrushchev's time in power.

Medvedev, Roy A. *Khrushchev.* Oxford: Blackwell, 1982; New York: Anchor Press/Doubleday, 1983. Medvedev has long been recognized as the leading dissident Communist historian working in Moscow. His book has discerning judgments and much information about Khrushchev's period of rule.

Richter, James G. *Khrushchev's Double Bind: International Pressures and Domestic Coalition Politics.* Baltimore: Johns Hopkins University Press, 1994. Richter examines Khrushchev's attempts to solidify support for his policies in the Soviet Union while maintaining his credibility internationally.

Serov, Alexei, ed. *Nikita Khrushchev: Life and Destiny.* Moscow: Novosti Press Agency, 1989. This small volume brings together reminiscences by members of Khrushchev's family, a colleague on the Politburo in Khrushchev's time, and other prominent Soviet writers and political figures.

Shevchenko, Arkady N. *Breaking with Moscow.* London: Cape, and New York: Knopf, 1985. Shevchenko became the senior Soviet diplomat at the United Nations Secretariat before he defected. Much of his diplomatic career was spent under Khrushchev, and his unvarnished account is rich in anecdotes and insights.

Nathaniel Davis

JEAN-CLAUDE KILLY

Born: August 30, 1943; Saint Cloud, France
Area of Achievement: Sports
Contribution: Killy dominated men's international Alpine skiing competitions from 1965 through 1968. He will also be remembered as the second skier in Olympic history to sweep the Alpine events.

Early Life

Jean-Claude Killy was born on August 30, 1943, in Saint Cloud, near Paris, while his father was flying as a combat pilot for the Allies. Killy, whose family name was originally Kelly, is a descendant of an Irish mercenary who fought with Napoleon. Longing for the quiet life, Killy's father moved his family from Paris to Val d'Isère, 6,037 feet high in the French Alps. For the next fifteen years, Killy's family struggled while his father operated a sporting goods store and, later, a restaurant. Killy began skiing at the age of three, and within a year he became a familiar sight in his baggy pants on the slopes outside town. As a student in the parochial grade school, Killy customarily went skiing with his friends instead of going to catechism.

Killy began competing well before adulthood. He won his first competition—a jumping contest—when he was eight years old. At the age of nine, Killy won his chamois medal, an award that most boys earn when they are thirteen or fourteen. That same year, Killy was skiing slalom only one second behind the instructor. His skiing career was interrupted temporarily by a bout of tuberculosis, which sent him to a sanatorium at the age of fourteen. He displayed enough ability later that year to be picked for the French team that competed at Cortina d'Ampezzo in Italy. By his own admission, Killy took too many chances and suffered the first of two broken legs.

At the age of sixteen, Killy dropped out of school, a decision that he was to regret years later. He spent the next three years competing and training. In 1962, shortly before the world championships, Killy broke his right leg in a downhill race—again at Cortina. Shortly thereafter, Killy joined the military and was transferred to Algeria. At the age of twenty, he left the military and resumed his skiing career. Underweight and undertrained, he fell in two races and managed a creditable fifth in the giant slalom. During the Olympics, Killy began his close friendship with Jimmy Heuga, who encouraged Killy's unruly behavior and assisted him in committing pranks such as pushing a Volkswagen into a hotel lobby during a pre-Olympic race stop and disrupting an awards ceremony by shooting seltzer bottles at his fellow recipients.

Life's Work

The promise that Killy had shown in 1964 was fulfilled the following year. Killy's first year of stardom was undoubtedly 1965. He won most of the major competitions in Alpine skiing at Kitzbühel, Megeve, Davos, and Valie, as well as several minor meets known as the Coupe des Pays Alpins. By the end of the year, Killy rated first in slalom, first in giant slalom, and sixth in downhill. Even though Killy had not yet won the final proof of his ability—an Olympic or Fédération Internationale de Ski (FIS) gold medal—he had fully developed his skiing ability.

Killy continued to dominate slalom competition in Europe and the United States, but the talented Karl Schranz from Austria continued to pace the downhill events. At the beginning of the 1965-1966 season, Killy was still known chiefly as a clownish racer with a flair for spectacular saves, even though the American skier Billy Kidd and Killy had traded off victories. Killy gained this reputation from his practice of "psyching out" his competition by performing outrageous acts at exhibition. For example, three nights before the Lauberhorn races began, Killy jumped off a small one-hundred-foot hill and pulled down his pants to make the Austrians think that he did not take skiing seriously. Then, Killy injured an ankle at Kitzbühel and was out of the winter competition.

During the summer of 1966, Killy redeemed himself at the world championships, which were held at Portillo, Chile. After Kidd shattered his leg practicing for the downhill, Killy handily won the downhill and placed well enough in the other two races to win the combined title and the championship. At Portillo, Killy perfected his unconventional skiing techniques. Instead of tucking tightly into the aerodynamic "egg position" favored by most skiers on the downhill run, Killy changed position constantly to compensate for rough spots in the surface. In the slalom, Killy used his poles as little as possible and strove for speed by skating through the gates—a technique that requires phenomenal balance.

After Portillo, Killy and his fellow team members trained in the fall at a special center in St. Tropez, where they built up their ankle and calf muscles by running, bicycling, and playing soccer and volleyball. During this lull in the competition, Killy avoided sweets and the legions of snow bunnies who shrieked his name at the finish line; instead, he indulged his interest in fast cars. Killy drove the way he skied—recklessly—wrecking six different cars by 1966. That summer, he entered Sicily's Targo Florio sports-car race, his first serious motoring competition, and finished first. He also cultivated an interest in bullfighting, spending a week in Nîmes in the south of France loitering with many of Spain's finest matadors.

After Portillo, Killy also worked intensely to prepare himself for the 1966-1967 season. He became so painstakingly selective about his skis that he tried more than forty pair before he found a pair that suited him. In addition, his valet, Michel Aprin, spent at least ninety minutes waxing the skis before every Killy race.

In the 1966-1967 season, Killy finally began to win world recognition for his talent. After winning all the big races in the Alps of Switzerland, Austria, France, and Italy, he promptly won three more in the White Mountains of New Hampshire. He then went to Vail, Colorado, and won the slalom, the giant slalom, and the downhill, leading the French to victory over the competition. His first-place finish in the Vail Trophy giant slalom gave him a perfect score in the World Cup competition which was awarded by the FIS for finishing most consistently among the leaders in a series of international races. His remarkable box score for the season showed that he had captured seven out of eight downhills, four out of five giant slaloms, and four out of eight slaloms. In the summer of 1967, ski officials from the United States traveled to Europe in a futile attempt to disqualify Killy for having driven with professionals in a car race in Sicily.

As if being World Champion was not enough proof of his ability, Killy set out in 1968 to show that he was even better than that by winning the gold at the Olympics. Before the start of the Olympics, Killy almost made a fatal mistake by stripping half the wax off his skiis in a preparatory run for the downhill race. Lacking time to rewax, Killy raced wildly down the upper half of the course and barely beat out his teammate, Guy Perillat, by eight one-hundredths of a second. Compared with that, the giant slalom was easy. He overpowered runner-up Willi Fuvre of Switzerland by the crushing margin of 2.22 seconds. To match the record set by Tony Sailer in 1956, Killy had to win the toughest event: the special slalom. In a heavy fog that reduced visibility to 250 yards, Killy came in third behind Norway's Haakon Mjoen and Austria's Karl Schranz. Miraculously, Mjoen and Schranz were disqualified for skipping a few gates, and Killy won the gold medal after all. Because of changes in the rules, Killy's triple is considered by many to be far more impressive than that of Tony Sailer.

Killy had no sooner made sports history than his victory was tarnished by scandal. In the first week of March, 1968, France's most exclusive newspaper accused him of selling an exclusive story about himself to the weekly magazine *Paris-Match* for seven thousand dollars. Other stories circulated later that Killy had paid a ski manufacturer six thousand dollars to keep quiet about an endorsement fee that he had been paid and that he had received as much as seventy-five thousand dollars annually for skiing. Killy responded to these charges by accusing the Olympics itself of hypocritical behavior. By calling the Olympics an "Evian World Cup event," Killy was referring to the name of the co-sponsor, Evian, which sold bottled water. Although the FSI had considered banning him from international competition, it was in full retreat by the end of the week. In spite of the controversy, Killy won the World Cup giant slalom at Meribel, France, and the Roch Cup Races in Aspen, Colorado, later that month.

Having finally realized his lifelong goal, Killy retired from skiing in the closing months of 1968. After driving professionally in a few automobile races, Killy branched into acting. In 1971, Killy traveled to the Swiss Alps to star in a motion picture entitled *The Great Ski Caper*. During the filming, Killy also became engaged to the French actress Daniele Gaubert, who had been married to the youngest son of President Rafael Trujillo Molina of the Dominican Republic. Later that year, Killy also starred in his own television show in France.

In 1972, at the age of twenty-nine, Killy briefly came out of retirement. Even though he was by this time a millionaire who owned a splendid villa overlooking Lake Geneva, Killy became a professional skier, racing not for medals but for money. Despite his reputation, Killy did poorly in his first professional race at Aspen, losing to Harold Stuefer, a nonentity who had never won a World Cup race in six years of international competition. Aside from the fact that professional skiing was entirely different from World Cup runs, Killy was out of shape after four years of relative inactivity. Although he performed better in the following races, his primary concern was not the money he was drawing every two weeks. His manager, Mark McCormack, persuaded Killy to turn professional to regenerate interest in him with equipment sponsors. In addition to the fifteen-thousand-dollar appearance money that Killy was guaranteed for appearing at the races, he received even more money in fresh endorsements. After a short career as a professional racer, Killy retired once again to spend his time racing cars, endorsing products, and making personal appearances.

Summary

Like many other great athletes, Jean-Claude Killy can be said to have made a significant contribution to sports simply by setting records. Although many of Killy's records for speed racing have been broken, his Olympic performance in 1968 has not been equaled since. Thus, Killy's performance continues to inspire athletes who also would like to become world champion skiers.

Aside from setting records, Killy helped to increase the popularity of skiing in the 1960's. Young people who were attracted to his irreverent behavior turned him into one of the many antiheroes who were popular at that time. In a decade weary of war news and counterculture protests, Killy's achievements were welcomed by many others as a breath of fresh air. Consequently, magazines that had never paid much attention to sports figures before, such as *Life* and *The Saturday Evening Post*, ran four- and five-page features on him. Because of Killy's tremendous sex appeal and boyish good looks, women's magazines such as *Ladies' Home Journal* were running articles on Killy's love life, his involvement with a kindergarten ski clinic, and his preference in ski attire.

In the final analysis, Killy's most enduring legacy will probably be the legend that he has left behind. During his brief career, Killy ignited so much nationalistic fervor that he continues to be revered as a hero of France. In addition, his flamboyant life-style added a spark of glamour, both to his name and to the sport of skiing itself, that has not yet diminished.

Bibliography

Flower, Raymond. *The History of Skiing and Other Winter Sports.* New York: Methuen, 1976. This general history of skiing contains a foreword by Killy and is important for understanding the sport in which Killy made his mark.

"In Search of Killy." *Skiing* 44, no. 5 (January, 1992). Detailed profile of Killy including his part in bringing the Olympic Winter Games to France, his retirement from racing, and more.

Jenkins, Dan. "Skiing's Darling of Derring Do." *Sports Illustrated* 24 (February 21, 1966): 20-22. In the first of many articles that appeared on Killy in *Sports Illustrated*, Jenkins gives the best biographical information about Killy's early years that is available. Jenkins also provides a detailed account of Killy's victories in 1966.

Johnson, W.O. "A Man and His Kingdom." *Sports Illustrated* 72, no. 6 (February 12, 1990). In-depth profile of Killy.

Johnson, William. "Back Again, Booming His Way into Your Hearts." *Sports Illustrated* 37 (December 18, 1972): 26-28. The only magazine article written about Killy's career as a professional skier. Johnson speculates as to why Killy came out of retirement.

Killy, Jean-Claude, with Al Greenberg. *Comeback.* New York: Macmillan, 1974. An autobiographical memoir of Killy's racing days, retirement days, comeback, and thoughts on his experiences. Includes several photographs.

"King Killy." *Time Magazine* 91 (February 23, 1968): 56. This article not only provides a detailed account of Killy's Olympic victories but also includes a short biography, an explanation of Killy's skiing technique, and several photographs.

Ress, Paul, and Gwilym S. Brown. "A Tale of Two Idols." *Sports Illustrated* 28 (March 18, 1968): 22-24. This is the most detailed account of the scandal that plagued Killy after his Olympic victories.

Skow, John. "Winter Olympics: Has Anybody Here Seen Killy?" *Saturday Evening Post* 241 (February 10, 1968): 66-71. In this article, written shortly before Killy's victories in the Olympic Games at Grenoble, Skow traces Killy's career in detail from 1966-1968.

Alan Brown

BILLIE JEAN KING

Born: November 22, 1943; Long Beach, California
Area of Achievement: Sports
Contribution: In addition to being a superb tennis player, Billie Jean King has been a driving force for the recognition and improvement of women's tennis. Her victory over Bobby Riggs in September, 1973, established her as the preeminent advocate of equity for women tennis players in every phase of their sport.

Early Life

Billie Jean Moffitt was born in Long Beach, California, on November 22, 1943. Her father, Willard J. Moffitt, was an engineer with the city's fire department, and her mother, Betty Moffitt, was a housewife and receptionist at a medical center. Her parents were not affluent, but they encouraged Billie Jean and her younger brother Randy to take part in sports. Randy Moffitt became a major league pitcher with the San Francisco Giants and other teams.

Billie Jean's tennis career began at the age of eleven, when her father allowed her to take tennis classes. She immediately displayed an aptitude for the game and a burning desire to excel. She told her parents that she wanted to compete in the Wimbledon tournament. She worked at odd jobs to buy a tennis racquet and devoted long hours daily to exercise and practice.

When Billie Jean was fifteen, Alice Marble, the great women's player of the 1930's and early 1940's, became her coach. Billie Jean stood only five feet, three inches tall at that stage of her life, and Alice Marble remembered that her student was "short, fat, and aggressive." It was also evident that Billie Jean had the clear makings of a champion because of her positive attitude toward the sport.

Billie Jean's first tournament victory came in the Southern California championship, when she was fourteen, and she made steady progress in junior girls' tournaments for the next several years. By the time she was eighteen, she and Karen Hantze won the women's doubles title at Wimbledon, the youngest pair ever to do so. In 1962, she and Hantze won again. In the singles, Billie Jean defeated top-seeded Margaret Smith of Australia, 1-6, 6-3, 7-5, in one of the most stunning upsets in the history of the British grass-court classic. Billie Jean lost in the quarterfinals, but the victory over

Smith signaled that she was on her way to the top of women's tennis. During these years, she also attended Los Angeles State College (later known as the California State University at Los Angeles).

She returned to Wimbledon in 1963 and reached the finals before losing to Margaret Smith. Her game improved during 1964 and 1965, but she was not successful in the Grand Slam tournaments that she entered. In 1964, she became engaged to Larry King, and they were married on September 17, 1965. By the end of the year, she was the number-one-ranked women's player in the United States. Her breakthrough to the top of women's tennis would come in 1966.

Life's Work

Billie Jean King achieved impressive international triumphs in 1966, when she led the Americans to victory over the British in the Wightman Cup competition and three weeks later defeated Maria Bueno in the Wimbledon final, 6-3, 3-6, 6-1. She faltered at the U.S. Open later in the summer but came back in 1967 to win Wimbledon for the second time. She beat Ann Jones of Great Britain, 6-3, 6-4, in the final, and she also captured the women's doubles and mixed doubles crowns. She triumphed at the U.S. Open without losing a single set in the competition. She bested Ann Jones, 11-9, 6-4, in an exciting final.

For the next sixteen years, Billie Jean King was a major star in women's tennis. She became a professional in 1968 and won seventy-one tournaments during her career. She was the first woman to win more than $100,000 in a single year of competition. Her prize money totaled $1,966,487. She won the Australian and French Opens each on one occasion, but won the United States Open singles title four times and the Wimbledon singles title six times. She won twenty Wimbledon titles in singles, doubles, and mixed doubles.

The grass courts of Wimbledon were the scene for many of Billie Jean's most memorable matches. She lost in the final in 1970 to Margaret Court, 14-12, 11-9, in a contest that both players called one of their all-time best. In 1973, she beat Chris Evert, 6-0, 7-5, for her fifth title. Two years later, King won her last Wimbledon singles crown with a 6-0, 6-1, victory over Evonne Goolagong Cawley. King played her final match at Wimbledon in 1983, when she lost in the semifinals to Andrea Jaeger.

King's success as a tennis player rested on her absolute unwillingness to lose. Standing five feet, four inches tall, with knees that often ached and several times required surgery, she drove herself around the court. She talked to herself during matches, exhorting her body to the athletic extremes that she demanded of herself. She would say, "Oh, Billie, think!" or "You've got the touch of an ox." She resented those who wanted to keep tennis a clubby sport, and she sought to "get it off the society pages and onto the sports pages." She attacked the ball, the net, and her opponents with relentless energy and a shrewd brain for the fine points of the game. Spectators and foes never knew what Billie Jean King might do on the court, but her energy and fiery spirit made her fascinating to watch.

Her sense of outrage at obvious unfairness in her sport made her a leader for the cause of women's tennis during the 1960's and 1970's. After open tennis came along in 1968, Billie Jean could not understand why men should receive more prize money and attention than their female counterparts did. She was instrumental in organizing the women players to start their own tour and to challenge the supremacy of the United States Lawn Tennis Association. She helped to found the Women's Tennis Association, and she served as its president from 1973 to 1975 and from 1980 to 1981.

The event that made Billie Jean King an international celebrity and forever identified her with the cause of rights for women athletes was her match with the male tennis player Bobby Riggs in 1973. Riggs had been an excellent tennis star during the 1930's and 1940's. By the 1970's, he had a well-deserved reputation as a "hustler" on the court who could win even when giving his opponents an advantage in advance. In 1973, Riggs loudly claimed that he could easily defeat any of the star women players of that day, even though he was fifty-eight years old. He challenged Billie Jean King and other women to televised matches on that basis. At first, Billie Jean ignored his sexist taunts lest she give him free publicity.

In May of 1973, however, Riggs defeated Margaret Court in a nationally televised match on Mother's Day. Riggs renewed his challenge to Billie Jean King and said that he wanted to play her as the "Women's Libber Leader." King agreed to meet Riggs. The match was held at the Houston Astrodome on September 20, 1973. The event drew a crowd of almost 31,000 spectators, and the televi-

sion audience was estimated to be more than thirty million. The match was seen in thirty-six foreign countries via satellite. A circuslike atmosphere prevailed. Billie Jean King came into the stadium on a gold litter that four male athletes carried. Tickets for courtside seats sold for $100.

The match was a total victory for Billie Jean King. She outplayed Riggs in every phase of the game on her way to a three-set victory, 6-4, 6-3, 6-3. Rather than rely on her usual attacking game, Billie Jean kept the ball in play, mixed up the speed of her strokes, and relied on her accuracy and stamina to wear down the older and slower Riggs. After the first set, she was in total command of the match, and the result was in the end no contest at all. For all his bravado, Riggs did not have the shots or the talent to keep up with Billie Jean King at the top of her form.

Since her retirement in 1984, Billie Jean King has been active as a tennis coach, television commentator, and organizer of Team Tennis. She has written her autobiography and an engrossing history of women's tennis. During the early 1990's, she was active in charitable events that raised money for AIDS research. Billie Jean King will be a significant presence in the sport of women's tennis for many years and a continuing inspiration to the younger players who have followed her.

Summary

Billie Jean King was a great champion on the tennis court, especially at Wimbledon, where she dominated for so many years. Her aggressive, attacking style helped popularize women's tennis in the 1960's and 1970's. Off the court, she established the structure of women's tennis that brought the sport to great heights of popularity and international appeal. Without her energy and resourcefulness, it would have taken much longer for women's tennis to have made the gains that it did. The match with Bobby Riggs, although it was a media event rather than a serious athletic contest, had great symbolic and cultural importance in providing credibility for women's athletics at a time when restrictive male attitudes still predominated. As a result of that match, Billie Jean King became more than a famous athlete. She emerged as one of the leaders in the movement for equal rights for women that transformed American society during the last quarter of the twentieth century.

Bibliography

Brown, Gene, ed. *The Complete Book of Tennis.* Indianapolis: Bobbs-Merrill, 1980. A compilation of stories from *The New York Times,* this book contains accounts of most of the significant matches of Billie Jean King's career.

Danzig, Allison, and Peter Schwed, eds. *The Fireside Book of Tennis.* New York: Simon and Schuster, 1972. This compilation of newspaper and magazine accounts of important tennis players and matches has several important essays that deal with Billie Jean King's rise to prominence in tennis during the 1960's.

Drucker, Joel. "The Once and Future King." *Women's Sports and Fitness* 14, no. 8 (November-December, 1992). Discusses King's views on men and women working together to improve tennis and her perspectives on women coaches.

Fleming, Anne Taylor. "The Battles of Billie Jean King." *Women's Sports and Fitness* 1, no. 11 (September-October, 1998). Interview with King. Topics include her views on sexuality in sports and her thoughts on her career.

King, Billie Jean, with Frank Deford. *Billie Jean.* London: Granada, and New York: Viking Press, 1982. A candid autobiography in which King discusses the controversial aspects of her career as an athlete and public figure.

King, Billie Jean, with Cynthia Starr. *We Have Come a Long Way: The Story of Women's Tennis.* New York: McGraw-Hill, 1988. A history of the sport which contains Billie Jean King's own comments about her career and the players with whom she competed. An essential book for understanding her impact on the game.

Lumpkin, Angela. *Women's Tennis: A Historical Documentary of the Players and Their Game.* Troy, N.Y.: Whitson, 1981. This overview of women's tennis is a good guide to what has been written about the sport, and it has references to many articles concerning Billie Jean King.

Marble, Alice, with Dale Leatherman. *Courting Danger.* New York: St. Martin's Press, 1991. Marble was Billie Jean's coach, and the book has comments about the impression Billie Jean made on her.

Tinling, Ted. *Love and Faults.* New York: Crown, 1979. The memoirs of the noted designer of tennis dresses and court attire contain some insightful observations on his friendship with Billie Jean King and her role in the sport.

Wade, Virginia, with Jean Rafferty. *Ladies of the Court: A Century of Women at Wimbledon.* London: Pavilion, and New York: Atheneum, 1984. One chapter deals with Billie Jean King's outstanding record as a champion at Wimbledon and her important impact on the tournament.

Karen Gould

MARTIN LUTHER KING, JR.

Born: January 15, 1929; Atlanta, Georgia
Died: April 4, 1968; Memphis, Tennessee
Area of Achievement: Civil rights
Contribution: As founding president of the Southern Christian Leadership Conference, King spearheaded the nonviolent movement that led to the 1964 Civil Rights Act and the 1965 Voting Rights Act.

Early Life

Martin Luther King, Jr., was born in Atlanta, Georgia, on January 15, 1929, the second child of the Reverend Michael Luther and Alberta Williams King. He was originally named Michael Luther King, Jr., but after the death of his paternal grandfather in 1933, King's father changed their first name to Martin to honor the grandfather's insistence that he had originally given that name to his son in the days when birth certificates were rare for blacks. Nevertheless, King was known as M. L. or Mike throughout his childhood. In 1931, King's father became pastor of the Ebenezer Baptist Church on Auburn Avenue, only a block away from the house where King was born.

King's father was both a minister and a bold advocate of racial equality. His mother was the daughter of the Reverend Adam Daniel Williams, who had preceded King's father as pastor of Ebenezer and had established it as one of Atlanta's most influential black churches. Both of King's parents believed in nonviolent resistance to racial discrimination. He grew up under the strong influence of the church and this family tradition of independence.

King was a small boy, but vigorously athletic and intellectually curious. He enjoyed competitive games as well as words and ideas. Intrigued by the influence of his father and other ministers over their congregations, young King dreamed of being a great speaker. Lerone Bennett noted:

> To form words into sentences, to fling them out on the waves of air in a crescendo of sound, to watch people weep, shout, *respond*: this fascinated young Martin. . . . The idea of using words as weapons of defense and offense was thus early implanted and seems to have grown in King as naturally as a flower.

King excelled as a student and was able to skip two grades at Booker T. Washington High School and to enter Morehouse College in 1944 at age fifteen. At first he intended to study medicine, but religion and philosophy increasingly appealed to him as the influence of Morehouse president Dr. Benjamin E. Mays and Dr. George D. Kelsey of the religion department grew. Mays, a strong advocate of Christian nonviolence, sensed in King a profound talent in this area. In 1947, King was ordained a Baptist minister, and after graduation the following year he entered theological studies at Crozer Theological Seminary in Pennsylvania.

During his studies at Crozer and later in a doctoral program at Boston University (1951-1954), King deepened his knowledge of the great ideas of the past. Especially influential upon his formative mind were the Social Gospel concept of Walter Rauschenbusch, the realist theology of Reinhold Niebuhr, and above all, the nonviolent reformism of Mohandas K. Gandhi. In Gandhi, King found the key to synthesizing his Christian faith, his passion for helping oppressed people, and his sense of realism sharpened by Niebuhrian theology. Later King wrote:

> Gandhi was probably the first person in history to lift the love ethic of Jesus above mere interaction between individuals to a powerful and effective social force on a large scale. . . . It was in this Gandhian emphasis on love and nonviolence that I discovered the method for social reform.

King realized that nonviolence could not be applied in the United States exactly the way Gandhi had used it in India, but throughout his career King was devoted to the nonviolent method. In his mind, Gandhi's concept of *satyagraha* (force of truth) and *ahimsa* (active love) were similar to the Christian idea of *agape*, or unselfish love.

In Boston, King experienced love of another kind. In 1952, he met Coretta Scott, an attractive student at the New England Conservatory of Music. They were married at her home in Marion, Alabama, by King's father the following year. Neither wanted to return to the segregated South, but in 1954, while King was finishing his doctoral dissertation on the concepts of God in the thinking of Paul Tillich and Henry Nelson Wieman, he received a call to pastor the Dexter Avenue Baptist Church in Montgomery, Alabama. Their acceptance marked a major turning point in their own lives, as well as in American history.

By then King was twenty-five years old and still rather small at five feet, seven inches. With brown

skin, a strong build, large pensive eyes, and a slow, articulate speaking style, he was an unusually well-educated young minister anxious to begin his first pastorate. As the Kings moved to the city which had once been the capital of the Confederacy, they believed that God was leading them into an important future.

Life's Work

King quickly established himself as a hardworking pastor who guided his middle-class congregation into public service. He encouraged his parishioners to help the needy and to be active in organizations such as the NAACP. Montgomery was a rigidly segregated city with thousands of blacks living on mere subsistence wages and barred from mainstream social life. The United States Supreme Court decision of 1954, requiring integration of public schools, had hardly touched the city, and most blacks apparently had little hope that their lives would ever improve.

An unexpected event in late 1955, however, changed the situation and drew King into his first significant civil rights activism. On December 1, Rosa Parks, a local black seamstress, was ordered by a bus driver to yield her seat to a white man. She refused, and her arrest triggered a 381-day bus boycott that led to a United States Supreme Court decision declaring the segregated transit system unconstitutional. King became the principal leader of the Montgomery Improvement Association, which administered the boycott, as thousands of local blacks cooperated in an effective nonviolent response to legally sanctioned segregation.

Quickly, the "Montgomery way" became a model for other Southern cities: Tallahassee, Mobile, Nashville, Birmingham, and others. In January, 1957, King, his close friend Ralph David Abernathy, and about two dozen other black ministers and laymen met at the Ebenezer Baptist Church to form a Southwide movement. Subsequent meetings in New Orleans and Montgomery led to the formal creation of the Southern Christian Leadership Conference (SCLC), which King used as the organizational arm of his movement.

From this point onward, King's life was bound with the Southern nonviolent movement. Its driving force was the heightened confidence of thousands of blacks and their white supporters, but King was its symbol and spokesman. He suffered greatly in the process. In 1958, while promoting

his first book, Stride Toward Freedom (1958), an account of the Montgomery boycott, he was stabbed by a black woman. He was frequently arrested and berated by detractors as an "outside agitator" as he led various campaigns across the South. By early 1960, he had left his pastorate in Montgomery to become copastor (with his father) of the Ebenezer Baptist Church and to give his time more fully to SCLC.

Not all of King's efforts were successful. A campaign in Albany, Georgia, in 1961 and 1962 failed to desegregate that city. At times there were overt tensions between King's SCLC and the more militant young people of the Student Nonviolent Coordinating Committee (SNCC), which was created in the wake of the first significant sit-in, in Greensboro, North Carolina, in February, 1960. King supported the sit-in and freedom ride movements of the early 1960's and was the overarching hero and spiritual mentor of the young activists, but his style was more patient and gradualist than theirs.

King's greatest successes occurred from 1963 to 1965. To offset the image of failure in Albany, the SCLC carefully planned a nonviolent confrontation in Birmingham, Alabama, in the spring of 1963. As the industrial hub of the South, Birmingham was viewed as the key to desegregating the entire region. The campaign there was launched during the Easter shopping season to maximize its economic effects. As the "battle of Birmingham" unfolded, King was arrested and wrote his famous "letter from a Birmingham Jail" in which he articulated the principles of nonviolent resistance and countered the argument that he was an "outside agitator" with the affirmation that all people are bound "in an inextricable network of mutuality" and that "injustice anywhere is a threat to justice everywhere."

The Birmingham campaign was an important victory. Nationally televised scenes of police chief Eugene "Bull" Connor's forces using fire hoses and trained dogs to attack nonviolent demonstrators stirred the public conscience. The Kennedy Administration was moved to take an overt stand on behalf of civil rights. President Kennedy strongly urged the Congress to pass his comprehensive civil rights bill. That bill was still pending in August, 1963, when King and many others led a march by more than 200,000 people to Washington, D.C. At the Lincoln Memorial on August 28, King delivered his most important speech, "I Have a Dream," calling upon the nation to "rise up and live out the true meaning of its creed 'that all men are created equal.'"

After the March on Washington, King reached the height of his influence. Violence returned to Birmingham in September when four black girls were killed at the Sixteenth Street Baptist Church. In November, President Kennedy was assassinated. Yet in July, 1964, President Lyndon B. Johnson signed into law the Civil Rights Act that ended most legally sanctioned segregation in the United States. Later in 1964, King was awarded the Nobel Prize for Peace. Increasingly, he turned his attention to world peace and economic advancement.

In 1965, King led a major campaign in Selma, Alabama, to underscore the need for stronger voting rights provisions than those of the 1964 Civil Rights Act. The result was the 1965 Voting Rights Act, which gave the federal government more power to enforce blacks' right to vote. Ironically, as these important laws went into effect, the ghettos of Northern and Western cities were erupting in violent riots. At the same time, the United States was becoming more deeply involved in the Vietnam War, and King was distressed by both of these trends. In 1966 and beyond, he attempted nonviolent campaigns in Chicago and other Northern cities, but with less dramatic successes than those of Birmingham and Selma.

King's opposition to the Vietnam War alienated him from some of his black associates and many white supporters. Furthermore, it damaged his relationship with the FBI and the Johnson Administration. Many observers have seen his last two years as a period of waning influence. Yet King continued to believe in nonviolent reform. In 1968, he was planning another march on Washington, this time to accentuate the plight of the poor of all races. In April he traveled to Memphis, Tennessee, to support a local sanitation workers' strike. On the balcony of the Lorraine Motel on April 4, he was shot to death by James Earl Ray. King's successor, Ralph David Abernathy, carried through with the Poor People's March on Washington in June. King was survived by Coretta and their four children: Yolanda Denise (Yoki), Martin Luther III (Marty), Dexter, and Bernice Albertine (Bunny). Soon Coretta established the Martin Luther King, Jr., Center for Nonviolent Social Change to carry on, like the SCLC, his work.

Summary

Martin Luther King, Jr., embodied a number of historical trends to which he added his own unique contributions. He was the author of five major books and hundreds of articles and speeches. His principal accomplishment was to raise the hopes of black Americans and to bind them in effective direct-action campaigns. Although he was the major spokesman of the black movement, he was modest about his contributions. Just before his death he declared in a sermon that he wanted to be remembered as a "drum major for justice." Essentially, he is. The campaigns he led paved the way for legal changes that ended more than a century of racial segregation.

Above all, King espoused nonviolence. That theme runs through his career and historical legacy. He left a decisive mark on American and world history. His dream of a peaceful world has inspired many individuals and movements. In 1983, the United States Congress passed a law designating the third Monday in January a national holiday in his honor. Only one other American, George Washington, had been so honored.

Bibliography

Ansbro, John J. *Martin Luther King, Jr.: The Making of a Mind.* Maryknoll, N.Y.: Orbis, 1982. The best study of King's intellectual and spiritual development, based on extensive primary material from King's student days as well as later writings. Ansbro sees King in positive terms, focusing on the pivotal role of nonviolence based on *agape* in his social theology. Moral premises of nonviolence are skillfully analyzed. Organization, which is more thematic than historical, is at times complex.

Bennett, Lerone, Jr. *What Manner of Man: A Biography of Martin Luther King, Jr.* 8th ed. Chicago: Johnson, 1992. Originally published in 1964 while King was still living, this well-written volume captures the meaning of King's personality and faith. Bennett, a fellow graduate of Morehouse College and distinguished black historian and editor of *Ebony*, shares many details of King's childhood and intellectual development. Although less thoroughly documented than some later biographies, Bennett's account is stronger than some in presenting King as a man driven by ideals and willingness to sacrifice.

Brauer, Carl M. *John F. Kennedy and the Second Reconstruction.* New York: Columbia University Press, 1977. Indispensable reading for understanding King's political impact and the setting within which the Civil Rights movement developed. Brauer traces in detail, and with thorough documentation, the development of Kennedy's civil rights advocacy and the role of King in shaping the political culture of the 1960's.

Garrow, David J. *Bearing the Cross: Martin Luther King, Jr., and the Southern Christian Leadership Conference, a Personal Portrait.* New York: Morrow, 1986; London: Cape, 1988. The most thorough recounting of the life of King, with extensive material on SCLC as well. Garrow carefully documents King's personal life, the origins and progress of his movement, and does so with specific attention to the famous leader's internal struggles. In particular, King's struggle with sexual temptations, and his sometimes agonizing awareness that his life was at risk, come through powerfully in this well-researched account. In places, brief on interpretation and perspective, but a highly valuable source on King, the movement, and the FBI's probing of them.

———. *The FBI and Martin Luther King, Jr.: From "Solo" to Memphis.* New York: Norton, 1981; London: Penguin, 1983. Garrow has established impressive authority in analyzing King's public career. This work examines the roots and nature of the FBI's opposition to King and SCLC and demonstrates that serious efforts were made to discredit King as a national leader. Well documented, although to some degree limited by lack of access to the FBI tapes on King's personal life.

King, Coretta Scott. *My Life with Martin Luther King, Jr.* Rev. ed. New York: Holt, 1993. Written shortly after King's death, this book is a valuable personal account of the King family, the Montgomery bus boycott, and several later SCLC campaigns. Its chief value lies in what it shares about Coretta's own thinking, her husband's personal trials and accomplishments, and the human reality of the civil rights story. It needs to be balanced by scholarly accounts of the campaigns and King's biography.

King, Martin Luther, Jr. *Stride Toward Freedom: The Montgomery Story.* New York: Harper, 1958; London: Gollancz, 1959. Not only King's first book, but the best as a source of his intellectual pilgrimage. Shares many internal details of his own development as well as the origins and nature of the boycott. The last part is a comprehensive analysis of the Church's role in race relations.

King, Martin Luther, Sr., with Clayton Riley. *Daddy King: An Autobiography.* New York: Morrow, 1980. A refreshing addendum to the scholarly accounts of King and his family. Reflects a proud father's view of his famous son, as well as the struggles and suffering of the King family. The theme of unrelenting commitment to nonviolence comes through clearly. Contains a foreword by the late Benjamin E. Mays and by Andrew J. Young.

Lewis, David Levering. *King: A Critical Biography.* 2d ed. Urbana: University of Illinois Press, 1978. A reprint with some modifications of the 1970 edition, this book is a useful account of the evolution of King's public career. Hampered by lack of certain documents available after the 1970's, it is nevertheless valuable reading. Lewis sought to write a critical biography rather than a eulogy of King. The casual use of first names detracts somewhat from the overall objectivity of the book's coverage. Particularly incisive on the Birmingham campaign of 1963.

Lischer, Richard. *The Preacher King: Martin Luther King, Jr. and the Word That Moved America.* New York: Oxford University Press, 1997. Drawing almost exclusively on King's personal, unpublished materials including speeches and sermons, Lischer considers King's life, his passion for his ideals, and his oratory.

Oates, Stephen B. *Let the Trumpet Sound: The Life of Martin Luther King, Jr.* New York: Harper, 1982. Prepared by a professional biographer as part of his trilogy on Abraham Lincoln, Nat Turner, and Martin Luther King, Jr. Although there are few new conclusions about King, his personal life and struggles are more frankly treated than in any previous biography. Well documented, including references to numerous interviews of people who knew King.

Peake, Thomas R. *Keeping the Dream Alive: A History of the Southern Christian Leadership Conference from King to the 1980s.* New York: Lang, 1987. The first comprehensive history of SCLC, with considerable biographical information on King. Based on a wide variety of sources, including many interviews. Analyzes SCLC's organizational history, the nature of King's social dream, and the continuity of King's ideas and influence after 1968.

Walton, Hanes, Jr. *The Political Philosophy of Martin Luther King, Jr.* Westport, Conn.: Greenwood Press, 1971. A thoroughly documented account of King's political beliefs and problems. Somewhat weak on the changing strategy of King's movement, but a valuable guide to his linkage of faith and political practice.

Ward, Brian, and Tony Badger. *The Making of Martin Luther King and the Civil Rights Movement.* London: Macmillan, and New York: New York University Press, 1996. A collection of essays on the history and changing focus of the civil rights movement. Topics include the essential centers of African-American life, influential leaders, and incorrect assumptions regarding the genesis of the movement.

Thomas R. Peake

STEPHEN KING

Born: September 21, 1947; Portland, Maine
Areas of Achievement: Film and literature
Contribution: Through his storytelling abilities and vivid imagination, as demonstrated in his novels, short stories, and films, Stephen King has done much to move the horror genre into the forefront of popular literature. He has modernized many gothic or horror themes and techniques.

Early Life

Stephen Edwin King was born on September 21, 1947, at Maine General Hospital in Portland, Maine, the second son of Donald Edwin and Nellie Ruth King. His brother David had been born two years earlier. When King was only two years old, his father, a captain in the merchant marines, deserted the family and never saw them again. This desertion placed hardships upon the young family, forcing them to move often in order for Nellie to provide for her two sons. In their search for a place to call home, the family lived in Maine, Massachusetts, Illinois, Wisconsin, and Indiana. Finally, when King was six years old, the family settled in Stratford, Connecticut, where they lived for six years.

King became interested in the horror genre early in life. He listened to suspenseful radio dramas and eventually came under the spell of good storytelling such as in Robert Louis Stevenson's *Treasure Island* (1883) and *Dr. Jekyll and Mr. Hyde* (1886) and horror films such as *The Creature from the Black Lagoon* (1954). The real potential of other worlds came into young King's life in 1957 with the launch of the Soviet satellite Sputnik I. King's teachers reported that one of his greatest passions was writing stories of his own, an activity that began when he was six years old.

In 1958, when King was eleven years old, his family moved to Durham, Maine. It was here that the future writer discovered that he had something in common with his absent father when he discovered an old trunk in the attic of his aunt and uncle's garage that contained a box of his father's books, including some by New England horror writer H. P. Lovecraft and some of Donald's own early attempts at writing short stories.

King continued his interest in writing throughout his public education and, after graduating from Lisbon Falls High School, entered the University of Maine in Orono in 1966. At the University of Maine he pursued a degree in English, wrote the "King's Garbage Truck" column for the campus newspaper, *The Daily Maine*, and submitted short stories to whatever publications he thought might be interested. In 1967, King made his first sale as an author with the purchase of his short story "The Glass Floor" for thirty-five dollars by *Startling Mystery Stories*. Even with his first sale, King continued his college education and filled empty hours by working campus jobs, writing, protesting local situations, and courting his future wife, fellow University of Maine student and library worker Tabitha Spruce.

King graduated from the university in 1970 and accepted a position as an English teacher at Hampden Academy in Hampden, Maine, in 1971. In this same year, King married the recently graduated Tabitha, who would eventually become a novelist in her own right. The young couple lived in a small mobile home and held second jobs, King in an industrial laundry and Tabitha in a donut shop, to supplement King's meager teaching salary of $6,400 per year. During this time they began their family.

Life's Work

Although his early married life proved to be taxing, King did not forego his drive to write. Often the small amounts that his short stories brought were used to purchase medicine for his children or finance the repair of a major appliance. When he was not teaching or working in the laundry, King produced several manuscripts, often typed in the furnace room of the Kings' mobile home. He would freely throw away pieces in which he saw no real potential. One such effort was saved from the garbage by Tabitha, who saw more than her husband did in the discarded germ of an idea. She argued that there was something of value to be found in the fragment that he had thrown away and that he should complete what he had begun. Following his wife's encouragement, King finished the manuscript that was eventually published as *Carrie* (1974). With the sale of *Carrie* to Doubleday for a $2,500 advance (he later sold the paperback rights for $400,000 and saw the novel turned into an award-winning motion picture with Sissy Spacek), King knew that he could earn his way as a writer and gave up his teaching position to write full-time.

The books that followed *Carrie* were received with varying degrees of acceptance. After King published his modernized vampire tale *Salem's Lot* (1975) and proposed that his third book, *The Shining* (1977), would be a ghost story, his agent feared that the young writer from Maine would be typecast, but King had no fear of failing at his craft or in his chosen genre. His later publication successes proved him correct.

In 1981, King published *Danse Macabre* to explore the horror film genre and to illuminate his fascination with both motion pictures and literature based upon investigations of humanity's darker emotional and psychological sides. In producing his own works of horror, King soon found that the clearest way for him to approach a piece of fiction in progress would be to seek an answer to the question, "what if?" From his earlier works on, this question has been central to each of King's works, and he answered it as it related to how individuals would act following almost total annihilation of humanity in *The Stand* (1978), to actions of obsessive fans in *Misery* (1987), the effect extraterrestrial visitors might have on a community in *The Tommyknockers* (1987), and to the reactions of various individuals to capital punishment in the six-part *The Green Mile* (1996).

In addition to his many novels, King also wrote numerous successful short stories that eventually appeared in collections, including "The Body" (*Different Seasons*, 1982), "The Woman in the Room" (*Night Shift*, 1978), and "Word Processor of the Gods" (*Skeleton Crew*, 1985). In addition, he produced six novels under the name Richard Bachman in order to publish works that did not quite fit the Stephen King persona and to allow him to publish more than one book per year. The true identity of Bachman, under whose name King published *Rage* (1977), *The Long Walk* (1979), *Roadwork* (1981), *The Running Man* (1982), *Thinner* (1984), and *The Regulators* (1996), was eventually made public because of the curiosity and research of a bookstore clerk.

King's audience grew even larger as film and television versions of his works and original screen- and teleplays by King caught the attention of viewing audiences. Many of these versions have been passed off as weak at best; however, some have received rave reviews as well as major awards. The motion pictures with King ties that are generally considered the best are *Carrie* (1976), *The Dead Zone* (1983), "The Body" spinoff *Stand*

by Me (1986), *The Shining* (1980), and *Misery* (1990). Among the King television movies and miniseries were *Salem's Lot* (1979), *It* (1990), *The Tommyknockers* (1993), *The Stand* (1994), and *The Shining* (1997).

The name of Stephen King became familiar even to those who had never read any of his works. King maintained a high public profile and at the same time tried to maintain some degree of privacy for himself and his family. King made television spots for a major credit card and for a national publicity drive for library usage. He also visited many of the top network talk shows and appeared as a contestant twice on *Jeopardy*. Perhaps he gained the most attention with his 1994 cross-country motorcycle trip during which he touted his novel *Insomnia* and independent bookstores over the big chain stores.

Summary

Because of his vast audience and his high public profile, Stephen King became more than merely one who wrote scary stories. His works entered legal proceedings when defendants contended that they were encouraged to carry out their crimes after having read a particular King work. King has been condemned because of the use of evil in his works even though the works argue that the evil must be confronted. His residence in Bangor, Maine, was even invaded by a distraught and mentally unbalanced man from Texas who threatened to destroy the house.

The greatest contentious confrontations came, however, when critics and reviewers debated the significance and quality of King's fiction. Many thinkers willingly passed him off as just an author who met the prurient curiosity of the reading masses. In contrast, other writers have compared King to Charles Dickens and Edgar Allan Poe and have considered him to be among the best of modern storytellers. Two entities who did not seem to be overly concerned with this ongoing critical battle were King himself and his fans.

Throughout his career, King approached his work with all seriousness, writing almost every day of the year. King also realized that he had led a charmed life and went out of his way to share his good fortune with others. He and his wife's philanthropy was enjoyed by such diverse causes as the recreation program of their hometown of Bangor, Maine; various educational institutions, most noticeably the University of Maine; library rebuilding programs such as one in Old Town, Maine; and individual needy students whom they heard about from various sources.

In addition to their separate writing careers and their philanthropic gestures, King and his wife put most of their efforts into rearing their three children, Joseph, Naomi, and Owen. As in King's fiction, one of his driving impulses was to ensure that his children had a normal, loving family life.

Bibliography

Beahm, George, ed. *The Stephen King Companion.* Rev. ed. Kansas City, Mo.: Andrews and McMeel, 1995. Beahm presents a comprehensive introduction to the works of King through analyses of the works, interviews with the authors, and comments by others.

———. *The Stephen King Story.* Kansas City, Mo.: Andrews and McMeel, 1991; London: Little Brown, 1993. This is the most complete book-length story of King's life.

Docherty, Brian, ed. *American Horror Fiction: From Brockden Brown to Stephen King.* London: Macmillan, and New York: St. Martin's Press, 1990. This collection of essays places King's works into context with other American horror writers.

Heller, Terry. *The Delights of Terror: An Aesthetics of the Tale of Terror.* Urbana: University of Illinois Press, 1987. Heller provides an in-depth discussion of the artistic and psychological foundations of horror fiction. This discussion will lead the reader to a fuller understanding of the structures and themes appearing in King's fiction.

Herron, Don, ed. *Reign of Fear: Fiction and Film of Stephen King.* Los Angeles: Underwood and Miller, 1988; London: Pan, 1991. The essays in this collection discuss the significance of film in the development of King's reputation.

King, Stephen. *Danse Macabre.* New York: Everest House, and London: Macdonald, 1981. Although this work is a history of the horror film genre, it provides insight into King's development as a student of all things horror.

Lant, Kathleen Margaret. "The Rape of Constant Reader: Stephen King's Construction of the Female Reader and Violation of the Female Body in 'Misery'." *Journal of Popular Culture* 30, no. 4 (Spring 1997). Links King's *Misery* to the author's brushes with harassment and harm at the hands of fanatic readers. Lant draws a parallel between King's treatment of the character Annie Wilkes in this novel and his feelings toward overwrought fans.

Magistrale, Tony. *The Moral Voyages of Stephen King.* Mercer Island, Wash.: Starmont, 1989. In this rather brief work, Magistrale attempts to clarify the underlying moral structures found in King's fiction.

Reino, Joseph. *Stephen King: The Second Decade, "Danse Macabre" to "The Dark Half."* Boston: Twayne, 1992. Reino discusses the second ten years of King's writing career.

———. *Stephen King: The First Decade, "Carrie" to "Pet Sematary."* Boston: Twayne, 1988. Reino introduces the works that began King's writing career.

Schroeder, Natalie. "Stephen King's 'Misery': Freudian Sexual Symbolism and the Battle of the Sexes." *Journal of Popular Culture* 30, no. 2 (Fall 1996). Examines King's *Misery* and its themes. The author argues that although there are no sexual scenes in the novel, Freudian metaphors can be noted.

Singer, Mark. "What Are You Afraid Of?" *New Yorker* 74, no. 26 (September, 1998). Profile of and interview with King. King comments on his love of storytelling and his move to Scribner after years with Viking Press.

Underwood, Tim, and Chuck Miller, eds. *Kingdom of Fear: The World of Stephen King*. New York: New American Library, 1986. This is perhaps the single best collection of essays discussing King's works. These essays are written by individuals who look at his works as perceptive critics and not as fans.

Thomas B. Frazier

WILLIAM LYON MACKENZIE KING

Born: December 17, 1874; Berlin, Ontario, Canada
Died: July 22, 1950; Kingsmere, Quebec, Canada
Areas of Achievement: Government and politics
Contribution: King helped organize Canada's Department of Labour and was the first Canadian political leader concerned with industrial exploitation of workers. As prime minister, he established an independent Canadian policy in world affairs.

Early Life

William Lyon Mackenzie King was born December 17, 1874, in Berlin (modern Kitchener), Ontario, Canada. His mother, née Isabel Grace Mackenzie, was the daughter of the rebel William Lyon Mackenzie. His father, John King, was a lawyer.

Young King attended the University of Toronto, where he received a B.A. in 1895 and, while working as a journalist, an L.L.B. in 1896 and an M.A. in 1897. He studied at the University of Chicago (residing at Hull House) and completed his education at Harvard, where he obtained another M.A. in 1898 and, in 1899, completed course work on a Ph.D. In September, 1899, King received a Harvard traveling fellowship to study industrial conditions in Europe. At Rome, in the fall of 1900, he received a cable from Sir William Mulock, a family friend and the Canadian postmaster general, who was organizing a labor department. He offered King editorship of the *Labour Gazette*. After first turning down the offer in favor of a teaching position at Harvard, King reconsidered and accepted.

Returning to Ottawa, King became deputy minister of labour. Canada's population was increasing and manufacturing industries were expanding and increasing in number. While King traveled about the country settling industrial disputes—solving more than forty of great importance—his former Toronto classmate and close friend, Henry Albert Harper, was in charge of the department. One time, while en route back to Ottawa, King learned that Harper had drowned in December, 1901, in the Ottawa River. Four years were needed for him to get over the shock, and then only by writing a memoir, *The Secret of Heroism* (1906).

King conferred with the British government in 1906 and secured legislation in their Parliament prohibiting "importation" of British strikebreakers into Canada. In the winter of 1906, he settled a potentially dangerous miners' strike in the southern Alberta coalfields. King used his friendship with Sir Wilfrid Laurier, the Liberal prime minister, who was thirty years his senior, to ensure his election in 1908 to the Canadian House of Commons. Laurier sent him to Asia to talk to government officials in India, China, and Japan about restricting immigration of their people into Canada as laborers. He was successful. While in Shanghai, he served as one of the British delegation of the International Opium Commission.

On King's return from Asia, the Department of Labour became a separate organization. King, the first labor minister, continued to mediate industrial disputes. He successfully arbitrated the Grand Trunk Railway strike in 1910. As a direct result of that labor dispute, King convinced Parliament to pass legislation greatly restricting economic free enterprise and introducing government regulation over Canadian businesses.

King lost his parliamentary seat—and his ministry—when Laurier's government was defeated in the 1911 general election on the issue of tariff reciprocity with the United States. The Conservatives equated free trade with American annexation of Canada. King spent the next three years, from 1911 to 1914, as the Liberal Party's information officer, reorganizing the party and editing its journal, *The Liberal Monthly*. He also wrote, lectured, and read political economy.

When he took over the directorship of the Rockefeller Foundation's new Department of Industrial Research in June of 1914, King's first duty was to bring about an end to the two-year strike in Rockefeller mining properties in Colorado. He persuaded the aloof John D. Rockefeller, Jr., to witness the poor working conditions that management had provided. Despite the circumstances, Rockefeller and King became lifelong friends. In 1948, Rockefeller gave King an outright gift of $100,000 to ensure his comfortable retirement.

While King was still working for the Rockefeller Foundation, his sister Bell died, and so, in the following year, did his father. In 1917, while King was campaigning for a seat in Parliament (which he did not win), his mother died. The loss of his mother, to whom he was extremely close, was especially painful, coming so soon after the death of his sister and father.

When King's foundation work ended in February, 1918, he became a freelance industrial relations consultant. He developed the labor-management plans for General Electric Company, Youngstown Sheet and Tube Company, and International Harvester. In 1918, King published *Industry and Humanity*. It summarized his work as an industrial conciliator and his philosophy of industrial relations. He believed that an elaborate program of social services was necessary if unemployment and poverty were to be eliminated.

King, a short, well-built man, was no showman. He was modest, shunned the limelight, and was likely to underestimate his importance on the political scene. He felt extremely insecure and was a man of contradictions. In character, he was described as proper, colorless, and Gladstonian. King, a pragmatist, could anticipate the needs of his government and of his country. His guiding principle once he was in a position of power would be national unity.

Life's Work

In 1919, King returned to Ottawa, and in February, the grand old man of Canadian politics, Sir Wilfrid Laurier, died. The Liberal Convention in August of that year elected King Liberal Party leader, both because he was Laurier's protégé and because his ideas for social reform won the support of the younger generation of party members. In October, in a by-election, King was returned to Parliament.

King's first task as leader was to unify the party: The conscriptionists had broken away, and many farmers in Ontario and western Canada now supported a new agrarian party, the Progressives. King would successfully return the conscriptionists to the party and retain the political support of Quebec throughout his career. He let his deputy, Ernest Lapoint (who was later succeeded by Louis St. Laurent), deal with administrative problems involving Quebec. The general election of December, 1921, returned the Liberals to political power, though without a decisive majority. King took office as prime minister for the first time on December 29. In the spring of 1922, personal tragedy again struck him; his brother died in early March.

In his first administration, King acted cautiously. He tried to maintain Progressive support by reducing tariffs and freight rates. In external affairs, helped by Canada's isolationist attitude, King reversed his country's usual support of England and asserted Canada's independence within the Commonwealth. At his first imperial conference (in London, in 1923), King again opposed the principle of a uniform Commonwealth foreign policy. At the 1926 Imperial Conference, King sometimes acted as mediator to bring about a satisfactory definition of the dominions within the British Commonwealth. According to the Balfour Declaration, the dominions were to be equal in status within the British Commonwealth of Nations. The Statute of Westminster (1931), confirming the Balfour Declaration and the dominions' relations with England, came out of the London Imperial Conference (1931), in which King played a major role.

King and several of his fellow Liberals had lost their seats in the 1925 general election. While a safe seat was soon found for King, Governor-General Lord Byng thought that King should resign and allow the Conservatives to form a government. Holding fewer seats than did the Conservatives, King's government nevertheless received a vote of confidence, but within only six months, another crisis had struck: Customs officials were accused of smuggling bootleg liquor across the border. Rather than have his government face a vote of censure, King asked Lord Byng to dissolve Parliament and call an election. Byng refused and King resigned. On behalf of the Conservatives, Arthur Meighen accepted office. At the proper moment, King, leader of the opposition in the House of Commons, attacked Meighen for naming only acting heads of cabinet positions and for overriding a law requiring appointed ministers to be confirmed in a by-election. In the vote of confidence that followed, Progressive votes defeated the Conservative government. When Meighen resigned, Lord Byng called for an election. Even though Lord Byng had acted correctly, King used the constitutional issue to divert attention away from the customs scandal. King's Liberal Party benefited from the attention given to economic issues during the election as well as from the alliance in several constituencies between Liberals and Progressives. For the first time, King and the Liberals had an absolute majority in Parliament.

As long as the Canadian economy prospered, King's government remained essentially true to his promises of social reform. In addition to enacting an old-age pension law, he increased subsidies to the western provinces, lowered taxes, and used government surpluses to reduce the public debt. By late 1929, however, King had not recognized that an economic depression was imminent. He refused to help the provinces in programs of unemployment relief or to help them in road construction.

The result was that in the 1930 general election, King and his government met defeat.

Early in 1931, the Liberals were accused of having accepted a large campaign contribution from the Beauharnois Power Corporation in return for navigation rights. King replied that his party had not promised anything in return. As opposition leader in the years from 1931 to 1935, King accepted the Conservatives' social legislation but questioned its constitutionality. He attacked the government's high tariff policy and its authoritarian methods. He reorganized the Liberal Party and adopted a platform of moderate welfare legislation.

The 1935 general election results were affected by the continued Depression, aggravated by western crop failures. Campaigning under the slogan "King or Chaos," King was returned as prime minister for his third term in office. From that time until he retired in 1948, King was the dominant figure in Canadian public life. He continued to make federal grants to the provinces for emergency relief, to subsidize housing, and to assist farm rehabilitation. He enacted a new form of unemployment insurance and signed tariff agreements with both Great Britain and the United States.

As the Canadian economy slowly recovered, Europe again was on the brink of war. To preserve Canada's autonomy and to avoid domestic conflict over foreign policy, King refused to enter into international agreements. He remained neutral when Benito Mussolini invaded Ethiopia, when Adolf Hitler sent troops into the Rhineland, and when the Spanish Civil War erupted. He supported Prime Minister Neville Chamberlain's appeasement policy, believing that Canada's interests were the same as England's. In violation of his appeasement policy, however, King increased Canada's defense appropriations and worked for closer Anglo-American relations.

One week after Great Britain's declaration, Canada declared war on Germany, on September 10, 1939. To get the country solidly behind his government, King called a general election for March, 1940; King won by an even larger margin than in 1935. With France's fall in June, 1940, the opposition demanded full mobilization. A mobilization bill was introduced and passed by Parliament. When Montreal mayor Camillien Houde advised his people not to comply with the law, King imprisoned him. King now became dedicated to the war effort. King stated his position in *Canada at Britain's Side* (1941) and *Canada and the Fight for*

Freedom (1944). To control the Canadian war economy, King established the Wartime Prices and Trade Board. During the war, King went to London many times to confer with the British prime minister, Winston Churchill (whom he did not like), and other war leaders. In England, he met with Canadian soldiers, but because of his opposition to conscription, they were hardly cordial.

Before the war, King began to develop a close relationship with the American president, Franklin D. Roosevelt (whom he greatly admired). The two became even closer once war was on the horizon, and cooperation between the two countries increased. As early as 1937, King and Roosevelt engaged in joint defense talks. Roosevelt declared that the United States would not remain neutral if Canada were threatened with aggression. That commitment was formalized between the two leaders by the Ogdensburg Agreement in 1940. The next year, King accepted the Hyde Park Declaration, which provided collaboration in defense production, and a joint board of defense was established. Sales of Canadian manufactured equipment to the United States increased considerably, helping to alleviate Canada's American exchange problem. In December, 1941, King, Churchill, and Roosevelt met on a ship off Newfoundland to plot their common cause. When announcing the United States' Lend-Lease plan to Parliament, King stated, "We in Canada may feel more than just a little pride in the share we have had in bringing about closer relationship between the United States and the British Commonwealth." A few months before the war ended, King reached a wartime agreement with the United States on military transport routes.

On the domestic front, King concentrated on his country's industrial and mobilization efforts in helping the Allies win the war, maintaining his country's precarious political unity, and ensuring his continuance in office as prime minister. The conscription issue loomed large. Quebec was against the draft. Beginning in 1940, King committed his government to an enlarged military without conscription. Once Canadian forces were engaged on the European continent, however, casualties increased, and there were insufficient volunteers for replacements. In English Canada, conscriptionist sentiment rose to the fore, even manifesting itself in King's cabinet. King agreed to a series of compromises, finally putting the issue before the people in a plebiscite in 1942. In the country as a whole, the majority voted in favor of a draft, but Quebec's voters remained solidly opposed. Conscripts were called up, but only for home defense. The great crisis came after the Normandy invasion on June 6, 1944, when a shortage of infantry reinforcements developed. Most of the home conscripts ("Zombies") did not want to volunteer for overseas service. King agreed to partial conscription for overseas service. Since he had delayed and evaded conscription for such a long time, French Canadians accepted the decision.

Once the war ended, King called an election in 1945. King and his government won, but only because of Quebec's support. King avoided a postwar slump by instituting a number of social security measures such as unemployment insurance and family allowances (the baby bonus), thereby creating the welfare state. He did not take any steps toward a national health plan, however, until he was close to retirement. A system of federal payments to the provinces was put into effect to allow even the poorest ones to maintain a minimum of services. King's great achievement in the postwar period was to arrange for Newfoundland's entrance as the tenth province into the Dominion in March, 1949, after King's retirement.

In external affairs, King served as chairman of the Canadian delegation at the 1945 San Francisco conference to draft the charter for the United Nations and headed the one in attendance at the peace conference (1946). Along with President Harry S. Truman and Prime Minister Clement Attlee, he signed the Washington Declaration on Atomic Energy. One of King's last official duties was to attend the 1948 Commonwealth Prime Ministers' Conference, in London. Returning to Canada, he resigned as prime minister on November 15, 1948. He had dominated Canadian politics for more than thirty years, twenty-one of them as prime minister. King died at his much-loved Kingsmere estate, near Ottawa, on July 22, 1950, and was buried in Toronto.

Summary

William Lyon Mackenzie King was accused of having been an opportunist, and many considered him ambiguous, evasive, and overcautious. Even though it cannot be doubted that he was masterful at compromise and procrastination, most Canadians admired him for his tenacity and his calm nature. One critic stated that though his methods might have been frustrating to many, he maintained national unity in a difficult federal system. In his time, Canadians became politically astute and, henceforth, maintaining national unity was to be much more difficult.

After King's death, his diaries—written over a period of fifty-seven years—disclosed that in his early adult life he was enamored of nurses and that the longtime bachelor was not the solitary, lonely man the public believed he was. He had many relationships with women, many of them short-term, but three of them definitely not. The diaries also disclosed his visitations with spiritualists in order to contact his dead relatives.

Kingsmere, which he acquired in 1901, became synonymous with King. It was also his monument. He left it and Laurier Place (his Ottawa residence, which had been willed to him by Mrs. Laurier) to the people of Canada.

Bibliography

Esberey, Joy E. *Knight of the Holy Spirit: A Study of William Lyon Mackenzie King*. Toronto: University of Toronto Press, 1980. This work is psychobiography and challenges the accepted view that King led a double life. The author relates the traumas and insecurity of King's early life, his search for security, and his temporary release from his psychic tensions by his success on the Canadian political scene. This work gives a good insight into King's personality and how it related to his political behavior.

Hutchison, Bruce. *The Incredible Canadian: A Candid Portrait of Mackenzie King.* London and New York: Longman, 1953. A highly readable biography that not only acquaints readers with King's background, his family, his education, and his nongovernmental activities but also details his entire political career. Hutchison makes the point that King possessed his country's confidence but never its affection.

Ludwig, Emil. *Mackenzie King: A Portrait Sketch.* Toronto: Macmillan, 1944. This is a sympathetic, interview-like, idealized study of King dealing with his ancestry, the highlights of his life, and his political career to 1944.

Martin, Joe. "William Lyon Mackenzie King: Canada's First Management Consultant?" *Business Quarterly* 56, no. 1 (Summer 1991). The author, a partner with Deloitte and Touche Management Consultants, looks at King's development of management practices.

Stacey, C. P. *A Very Double Life: The Private World of Mackenzie King.* Toronto: Macmillan, 1949. This work deals primarily with King's private, personal, and intimate life, a life that was unknown to the mass of Canadians. It is told mostly in King's own words, extracted from his diaries.

Kathleen E. Dunlop

ALFRED CHARLES KINSEY

Born: June 23, 1894; Hoboken, New Jersey
Died: August 25, 1956; Bloomington, Indiana
Areas of Achievement: Zoology and sex research
Contribution: The greatest pioneer in sex research since Sigmund Freud, Kinsey revolutionized the study of human sexual behavior by applying to it the methodology of scientific empiricism.

Early Life

Alfred Charles Kinsey was born June 23, 1894, in Hoboken, New Jersey, to a self-made, forceful man, Alfred Seguine Kinsey, who became a professor of engineering at Stevens Institute of Technology. His mother, Sarah Ann, was extremely shy. The family had few friends and entertained sparingly. Alfred, Jr., was close neither to his parents nor to his younger brother, Robert. During his first ten years, he was troubled by rickets, a weak heart, and typhoid fever; the aftereffects of the last-named disease exempted him from military service in World War I.

The family moved to South Orange in 1903, and the frail boy developed a passionate, lifelong love for the out-of-doors, becoming an Eagle Scout and organizing his own troop. While in high school, he published his first article, "What Do Birds Do When It Rains?" based on hours of meticulous observation in fields and forests and presaging his penchant for detailed and precise analysis. Kinsey's other compelling interest was the piano.

To please his overbearing father, Kinsey studied engineering for two years at Stevens Institute of Technology but then decided to attend Bowdoin College and major in biology. The father, outraged at his son's defiance, refused him any financial aid once he had enrolled at Bowdoin. (The two were to meet only rarely in subsequent years.) Kinsey was a serious student who kept apart from most campus social activities; for relaxation, he played the piano, hiked in the woods, or starred on the debating team; he never dated.

After graduating magna cum laude in 1916, he entered Harvard's distinguished Bussey Institute, majoring in taxonomy and serving as an instructor in biology and zoology while working for his Sc.D. degree, which he received in 1920. While at Bussey, Kinsey began collecting thousands of gall wasps, which fascinated him as living evidence of evolution. As he ranged over the country in his search for the insects, he encountered simple country residents with whom he developed empathy; in his later sex research he was to prove singularly skilled in interviewing people of rudimentary formal education. Moreover, he developed an intricate shorthand system for recording his findings concerning the galls; this system anticipated his intricate coding device for noting detailed sexual histories on a single sheet.

Indiana University offered Kinsey an assistant professorship in zoology, starting in the fall term of 1920. His decision to accept this bid over others was influenced by his having encountered, on the occasion of his job interview, a chemistry major named Clara Bracken McMillen. They married in June, 1921, had four children, and were harmoniously matched in their interests—she was also fascinated by insects and joined him on his gall-wasp hunts. The Kinseys took pride in building their own home and cultivating a garden that many visitors considered Bloomington's most beautiful.

Kinsey climbed the academic ladder smoothly, achieving a full professorship in 1929. He became the world's leading authority on gall wasps, measuring and cataloging 3,500,000 specimens. He wrote a high school biology textbook, *An Introduction to Biology* (1926), which sold nearly half a million copies. In the 1930's, he wrote three more biology texts and about twenty scholarly articles. Then came what proved the turning point of his career: He was asked by university administrators to coordinate a marriage course, initially to be taught in the summer of 1938. Kinsey was surprised to find no reliable statistical evidence regarding human sexual conduct. He decided that the empirical, taxonomic approach he had successfully used for his gall wasps and biology classes might also work well for sex research. He therefore began, in July, 1938, to take the sexual histories of those of his marriage course students who were willing to provide them.

Within a year, Kinsey had amassed 350 histories but in the process had aroused opposition among a few colleagues and within the conservative Bloomington community. The university's president, Herman Wells, offered Kinsey the choice of continuing either the marriage course or his case-history project. As a trained research scientist, Kinsey naturally preferred to pursue his investigative studies, and he resigned from the course. He had found a second career that was to make this unassuming, modest Midwesterner world-famous.

Life's Work

Prior to the late 1930's, little knowledge had been factually established regarding human sexuality. Sigmund Freud (1856-1939), the founder of psychoanalysis, had studied the sexual lives of largely upper-class Viennese women. Havelock Ellis (1859-1939) had corresponded concerning sexual behavior with upper-class British men. In 1915, an American physician, M. J. Exner, had sent one thousand male college students questionnaires about their sex lives. By 1938, nineteen different studies on human sexual behavior had been reported, all of them sketchy in their topics and inadequate in their methodology.

Kinsey was particularly appalled by Freud's moralistic judgments regarding masturbation, which the Austrian condemned as infantile and neurotic. Instead, Kinsey made one principle clear above all others throughout his sexual investigations: As a scientist, he registered no objection to any kind of sexual behavior in which a subject might be involved. This written statement to a student was typical:

> I am absolutely tolerant of everything in human sex behavior. It would be impossible to make an objective study if I passed any evaluation pro or con on any sort of behavior. . . . Moreover, . . . I have absolutely preserved the confidence of all individual records. . . .

In the early 1940's, Kinsey recruited three able assistants for what was to be incorporated as the Institute for Sex Research. His chief aide was Wardell Pomeroy, a psychologist trained in penal work, who conducted approximately eight thousand sex history interviews to Kinsey's eighty-five hundred. The group's statistician was Clyde Martin, recruited from Kinsey's biology laboratory. Last to be added was anthropologist Paul Gebhard, who often chafed at what he considered Kinsey's excessively autocratic control of the project. Yet all three lieutenants shared an intense devotion to their arduous work and an admiration for Kinsey's integrity, energy, and intelligence.

Pomeroy recalls Kinsey as being remarkably warm and generous, radiating sympathetic understanding to interviewees and buying thoughtful and elaborate gifts for staff and their children. He literally worked himself to death, usually beginning his active day by seven in the morning and ending it at

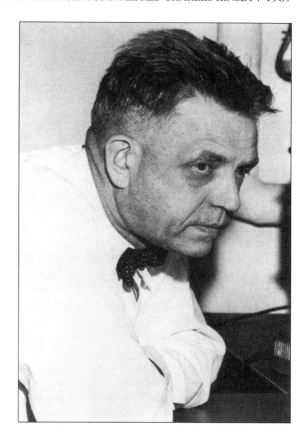

midnight or later, six and sometimes seven days a week. He never took a vacation. Of sturdy, stocky build, with his sandy hair like a shock of Kansas wheat, and with extraordinarily penetrating gray-blue eyes, Kinsey often made a profound impression on people. He was never selfish, shallow, cynical, petty, or malicious. He held his staff to the most stringent standards yet found himself unable to delegate important work, even after doctors had warned him of his need to ease the tremendous stress to which his ambitious undertaking subjected him. His grand dream was to establish the truth about people's sexual lives through the statistical evidence of 100,000 histories; he had to settle for eighteen thousand. Pomeroy concludes: "We were working for a genius who maddened us, delighted us, drove us to the point of exhaustion, but most of all inspired us to share something of his total dedication."

Beginning in 1941, the Rockefeller Foundation granted Kinsey's project financial support which increased from an initial sixteen hundred dollars to forty thousand dollars by 1947—this figure remaining constant until the foundation severed its subsidy in mid-1954. By the end of 1942, Kinsey had collected thirty-four hundred histories, and Clyde Martin had devised one of Kinsey's most scientific and controversial contributions: a zero to six scale measuring a subject's homosexual behavior. Two hieroglyphic codes were devised: one for taking down case histories, the other for identifying them in the files. Neither was put on paper; both were taught, by rote, to Kinsey's trio of key assistants. Each history covered a minimum of 350 items, a maximum of 521. The order of asking questions varied according to the subject's social background, age, and educational level. Interviewers were trained to assume that their subjects had engaged in every possible sexual activity; they began by asking when their subjects had done it rather than whether. They were taught to look their subjects directly in the eyes and ask their questions as rapidly as possible. Interlocking questions were used to cross-check for accuracy. Among eighteen thousand persons, fewer than ten refused to complete a history they had begun.

The questions were grouped under nine major rubrics: social and economic data, marital histories, sex education, physical and physiological data, nocturnal sex dreams, masturbation, heterosexual history, homosexual history, and animal contacts. Each of these sets had subdivisions and subsections. The category of masturbation, for example, provided for information on twenty-nine points under seven subheads.

By the mid-1940's, Kinsey felt ready to begin writing the first institute volume, on male sexual activity. He insisted that all income derived from this and subsequent books, as well as all lecturing fees he or his staff would receive, be returned to the institute. Kinsey did the actual writing of both *Sexual Behavior in the Human Male* (1948) and *Sexual Behavior in the Human Female* (1953). He solicited suggestions from his staff but did not hesitate to override their judgments. He placed publication of both books with an old, respected medical house, W. B. Saunders; most unusual, he refused advance royalties on either text, submitted an entire typescript, ready for copyediting and the press, and made virtually no changes on the page proofs.

On January 5, 1948, *Sexual Behavior in the Human Male* was published. Even though the book's prose was deliberately dry and academic and its accompanying charts and tables highly technical and specialized, the work sold more than 200,000 copies in its first two months and had eleven printings by Kinsey's death eight years later.

The sample for *Sexual Behavior in the Human Male* covered fifty-three hundred American whites, sixty-three percent of whom were college graduates. These were some of its most significant findings: Eighty-three percent had had sexual intercourse before marriage; fifty percent had had extramarital relations; early-maturing adolescents maintained higher sexual frequencies than late adolescents for thirty-five to forty years; socially upper-level males tended to rationalize their sexual behavior on the basis of morality, while lower-level males rationalized their behavior on what they considered natural or unnatural; and ninety-six percent engaged in masturbation, to no apparent ill effect. Perhaps of greatest interest was the conclusion that thirty-seven percent of males had or would have at least one homosexual experience to the point of orgasm between adolescence and old age. Probably of greatest importance was the discovery that sexual conduct differed enormously from one individual to another and from one social level to another, with petting, for example, largely an upper-class preoccupation, while lower-class males minimized foreplay prior to intercourse.

The general public's response to Kinsey's investigation was overwhelmingly favorable: According to a 1948 Gallup Poll, only ten percent were hostile. Yet the scientific and lay professional reactions were far more mixed: Some moralists, such as Henry Van Dusen, president of Union Theological Seminary, were displeased that the study had been done, in the first place, and that the Rockefeller Foundation had supported it, in the second. Some psychologists, such as Stanford's Lewis Terman, thought that they could infer, behind Kinsey's stance of empiric neutrality, a slanting of the evidence "in the direction of implied preference for uninhibited sexual activity." An endless debate arose over the validity of the institute's interviewing samples. Were homosexuals and college graduates overrepresented? Were devout Roman Catholics and orthodox Jews underrepresented? Why were blacks excluded? Why were the subjects not evenly distributed geographically? After all, Kinsey had to take his volunteers where he could find them. He responded that his sampling was stratified rather than proportional, "in order that we shall have enough cases even in the less common groups to make a good statistical calculation." Possibly the most far-reaching objection was related to the social consequences of scientific inquiry. Kinsey's response was,

> I think there is wisdom in keeping a research investigation rather separate from clinical or social application. When one becomes interested primarily in the application of data, it is too liable . . . to play too large a part in the decision as to what ends of the research should be undertaken.

The eagerly awaited companion volume, *Sexual Behavior in the Human Female*, was published September 14, 1953. Five chapters of this text compared male and female reactions (the female sample comprised 5,940 American whites) in the areas of anatomy, physiology of sexual response and orgasm, psychological factors in sexual response, neural mechanisms of sexual response, and hormonal factors in sexual response. As in *Sexual Behavior in the Human Male*, the core of the book covered types of sexual activity. The institute found that frigidity was far less common among women than folklore had supposed, that ninety percent of the subjects were orgasmic by the age of thirty-five. Kinsey contradicted many psychoanalysts by stating that the areas involved in females' sensory responses were the clitoris and labia—and not the vagina; William H. Masters and Virginia E. Johnson's research, presented in *Human Sexual Response* (1966), has since confirmed this claim. The institute further found that women's sexual responsiveness peaked in their late twenties and could then be maintained at or near top level to old age, while men's maximum responsiveness was in their late teens and then inexorably declined. About fifty percent of females had premarital sex; about twenty-six percent had extramarital sex; three out of five single women had had sex by the age of forty. Female homosexuality was considerably lower than males', ultimately reaching twenty-eight percent. Three-fourths of the females who had experienced premarital or extramarital sex had no regrets regarding their conduct. Females responded to orgasm as quickly as males—some females even more rapidly.

This time the cannonading of adverse criticism was even more intense, though it represented a small minority of scientific opinion. (In one survey, ninety-five percent of respondents among members of the American Psychological Association considered Kinsey's project worthwhile.) Clerical condemnation of *Sexual Behavior in the Human Female* ranged from organized pressure by the National Council of Catholic Women to individual denunciations by Billy Graham and Reinhold Niebuhr. Dr. Karl Menninger, who had championed *Sexual Behavior in the Human Male*, now pronounced himself "disappointed" by the later book. Dr. Franz Alexander vehemently urged his fellow psychiatrists to reject every conclusion reached in both volumes.

Worst of all for the institute, a number of angry protest letters from moralistic critics caused a powerful right-wing congressman, Carroll Reece, to open an investigation into tax-exempt foundations. Reece was determined to discredit two targets with one attack: Kinsey and the Rockefeller Foundation. Without giving Kinsey a hearing, the foundation withdrew its financial support from the institute in August, 1954. Indiana University took up as much of the support burden as it could but lacked the means to replace most of the foundation funding.

Kinsey's spirit was severely depressed, with his increased anxiety and tension reflected in deteriorating health. He had difficulty sleeping, often felt exhausted, yet kept working at a compulsively furious pace. In June, 1956, he suffered a minor heart attack, was ordered by his physician to restrict his daily work schedule to no more than four hours, but disobeyed his doctor. He died on August 25, 1956, of a cardiac embolism complicated by pneumonia.

After his death, the institute published two more of the texts he had planned but had not lived to write: *Pregnancy, Birth and Abortion* (1958), by Gebhard, Pomeroy, Martin, and Virginia Christenson, and *Sex Offenders: An Analysis of Types* (1965), by the same authors. After 1965, the institute changed its structure to that of a coordinating umbrella organization, sheltering a number of researchers pursuing a diversity of sexual studies, such as sexual deviance, the personalities of child molesters, and homosexuals in the military forces. Kinsey's most direct descendants have been the sexual physiologists Masters and Johnson, in *Human Sexual Response* and *Human Sexual Inadequacy* (1970).

Summary

Alfred Kinsey and his coworkers compiled and published a monumental amount of information regarding sexual behavior in the United States. Despite some dubious sampling techniques and perhaps an overweighting of homosexual histories, his work became the standard achievement in the empirical investigation of human sexual patterns. The tremendous scale of the research opened previously closed doors of a culture constrained by Puritan and Victorian inhibitions. Alfred Kinsey took sex research out of the realm of subjective speculation and placed it on a scholarly and respectable scientific foundation.

Bibliography

Brecher, Edward M. *The Sex Researchers*. Boston: Little Brown, 1969; London: Deutsch, 1970. This is a clearly written, popular account of the contributions made to the knowledge of human sexual behavior from Richard von Krafft-Ebing (1840-1902) to Masters and Johnson. It dispenses much important information in direct, plain prose.

Christenson, Cornelia V. *Kinsey: A Biography*. Bloomington: Indiana University Press, 1971. Christenson was a research associate at the Institute for Sex Research from 1950 to 1967, where she became a friend not only of Kinsey but also of Gebhard. Her style is pedestrian, but the book includes a number of superb photographs and other illustrations.

Jones, James. *Alfred C. Kinsey: A Public/Private Life*. New York: Norton, 1997. Stunning biography of Kinsey. Jones makes use of previously undisclosed information to clarify Kinsey's interest in sexuality as an attempt to counter his own psychological trauma, which resulted from a tortured childhood and emotional and sexual repression.

Kinsey, Alfred C., Wardell B. Pomeroy, and Clyde E. Martin. *Sexual Behavior in the Human Male*. Philadelphia: Saunders, 1948.

———. *Sexual Behavior in the Human Female*. Philadelphia: Saunders, 1953. These two volumes have been described in the body of this essay. They have helped transform the nature of contemporary culture.

Pomeroy, Wardell B. *Dr. Kinsey and the Institute for Sex Research*. London: Nelson, and New York: Harper, 1972. This is a splendid biocritical study by Kinsey's closest associate. Pomeroy writes both knowledgeably and admiringly of his mentor, without hiding such warts as Kinsey's controlling and occasionally thin-skinned character. The prose is lucid, compact, and assured. An indispensable source on its subject.

Trilling, Lionel. "The Kinsey Report." In *The Liberal Imagination*. New York: Viking Press, 1950; London: Secker and Warburg, 1951. A distinguished critic of culture and literature analyzes Kinsey's *Sexual Behavior in the Human Male* and worries that it may "do harm by encouraging people in their commitment to mechanical attitudes toward life." He insists that the report is by no means as objective as it proclaims to be, since it is biased in favor of quantitatively measuring sexuality, thereby reducing sex to no more than the discharge of physical tensions. An elegant statement of the antiempiricist position.

Gerhard Brand

ERNST LUDWIG KIRCHNER

Born: May 6, 1880; Aschaffenburg, Germany
Died: June 15, 1938; near Davos, Switzerland
Area of Achievement: Art
Contribution: Kirchner was one of the founders and a leading artist of German expressionism—a major early twentieth century art movement whose basic ideas effectively challenged the then-dominant Impressionistic art and influenced contemporary literature, music, drama, and film.

Early Life

Ernst Ludwig Kirchner was born May 6, 1880, in Aschaffenburg, Germany. His father was a chemical engineer; his mother came from a merchant family. On his father's side, Kirchner was descended from a long line of scholars and professionals. His father once had wanted to be an artist. Therefore, when the son at the age of four demonstrated a precocious talent for art, he was encouraged by his parents, who hired private tutors in drawing and watercolors. The young Kirchner was high-strung and impressionable, and the many moves necessitated by the father's changes in employment had a pronounced effect on the boy's artistic development. In Frankfurt am Main, for example, Kirchner was exposed to big-city life and to the works of Flemish primitives and German Renaissance artists in the city museum.

Further moves involved Switzerland. In 1890, his father secured a professorship at the Technical Institute of Chemnitz (Karl-Marx-Stadt), and the traveling ceased. In 1898, Kirchner visited Nuremberg and became acquainted with the works of the German Renaissance master Albrecht Dürer, who became a guiding influence in his life. Kirchner was especially impressed by the woodcuts, whereby strong messages could be conveyed by the sparing use of bold lines and colors.

At eighteen, Kirchner was determined to become an artist, although his parents advised him to train in a more secure profession, reserving art as an avocation. Largely to satisfy his parents, Kirchner in 1901 enrolled in the Dresden Technical Institute to study architecture. In 1903-1904, he visited Munich, Germany's artistic capital, and took conventional courses in life drawing and color theory. He spent time in Munich's museums examining the works of German Renaissance masters and the drawings of Rembrandt, which

inspired him to learn the art of sketching from life. At the time, Kirchner visited an exhibition of the best in modern German art heavily influenced by French Impressionism and sadly noted the contrast between these pallid works and the vigor of early German art as well as the pulsating life of contemporary Munich. Kirchner received his degree in architecture in 1905. The filial obligation completed, he now devoted his life to art. He never practiced architecture.

Life's Work

By this time, Kirchner had formed his theory on art, from which he never deviated. His chief aim was to bring life and art into harmony. He would put aside bourgeois constraint and the deadening influence of the academician. He would create from nature and life and, through the innovative, imaginative use of line and color, give the viewer not only recognition and truth about life but also heightened awareness, greater appreciation, and deeper understanding of the subject material. Reality would be distorted in order to communicate inner visions.

Kirchner found three like-minded colleagues. In 1905, they formed a group called Die Brücke (the bridge), taking the name from a work by Friedrich Wilhelm Nietzsche to the effect that man is not an end in himself but a "bridge." The artist is to be the creative bridge between the viewer and the work of art.

The year 1905 was also pivotal for European art. In Paris a group of renegade artists in protest against the controlled theories and methodology of French Impressionism showed works so violent in the use of color, so unconventional in form and line, that they were called the "fauves," or "wild beasts." Die Brücke similarly rebelled against prevailing German art that they believed to be infused with philistine prejudice and bourgeois morality. In a manifesto, Kirchner called for a new generation of creators from among the young and told them: "We want to create for ourselves freedom to move and to live. . . . He belongs with us, who renders with immediacy and authenticity that which drives him to creation." Following Kirchner's directive, the group painted from nature or life, using live models. The stress was not on a particular style but rather on the artist's individual creativity.

Kirchner's artistic development can be divided into three periods, each with its dominant style: 1905-1911, the formative Brücke period; 1911-1917, the mature Berlin period; 1917-1938, the Swiss period. The Brücke years were devoted to experimentation and development. His works were often decorative, and many clearly show the influence of other artists. Kirchner carefully studied others' works, and, even though influenced, he was never dominated by them. From the Dutch artist Vincent van Gogh and from his own experimentation, Kirchner learned that the use of color should be emotional and intuitive rather than "scientific" and rational. He became skilled in its effective use. A typical Kirchner work of the period is *Emmy Frisch with Red Flowers* (1906). Even though Kirchner's creation, this painting shows the influence of the French Impressionists.

More important to Kirchner's artistic development during the Brücke years was his mastery of media and development of work habits. He learned woodcutting, lithography, and engraving. He had always drawn or sketched in pencil, crayon, pastels, and pen and ink and became a master draftsman. He was totally absorbed in his work, and, despite his relatively short life, his output was formidable—his oils numbered in the hundreds; his drawings and graphics numbered in the thousands. Despite the volume of his work, he was always a perfectionist. Works that did not meet his exacting standards were either reworked or destroyed.

In 1911, Die Brücke moved to Berlin, hoping to find in the German capital a wider audience and greater tolerance. In 1912, Kirchner met the dancer-model Erna Schilling, who became his common-law wife and life-long companion. His work in the city alternated with painting nudes in bucolic settings on the Baltic Sea island of Fehmarn. In 1912, Kirchner believed that he was completely developed as an artist.

In 1913, Die Brücke was dissolved. The temperaments of its members had become too disparate for the artists to continue working as a group. Kirchner now focused his attention on what many consider to be his greatest artistic achievement—capturing the spirit of a great metropolis in his street scenes. Kirchner was fascinated by the city: its pulsating life, in which he found a strong erotic element; its deceptive glitter; its amorality; and its alienation. He also realized that it was an indispensable part of the life of modern man. Typical of his work of this period was *Street, Berlin* (1913). This work is uniquely Kirchner: discordant colors, bold outlines, distorted perspective, a sense of instability achieved by the use of inverted triangles. A "truth" made patently clear is the public condemnation of and the private attraction to the streetwalker.

The coming of the war in 1914 was devastating to Kirchner both mentally and physically. What Kirchner especially hated was the dehumanizing element of the military—its destruction of the individual. Art became a form of protest such as his *Self-Portrait as a Soldier* (1915). Kirchner is in uniform, but his eyes are those of a dully uncomprehending robot. In the background is a waiting model and an unfinished painting. His right arm is upraised but the hand—the painting hand—has been amputated. He is useless both as an artist and as a soldier. Kirchner, who never saw service, suffered both a physical and a mental collapse. After time spent in sanatoriums, he found his way in 1917 to Switzerland, where, except for short trips to Germany, he remained for the rest of his life.

The ruggedly beautiful Alpine area as well as the ministrations of the kindly peasants gradually restored Kirchner's shattered health. He now began his third and last period, this one dominated by his Alpine scenes. These scenes were the closest the mature Kirchner would get to representative art, but these were not postal card scenes. Their structure was monumental and architectural; the use of color was often unconventional. A typical work is *View of Basel and the Rhine* (1935).

Kirchner's Alpine pictures were influenced by his working in tapestry design. He found an experienced tapestry weaver, and together they created a number of tapestries. Kirchner also sculpted and carved in wood, and he designed furniture, jewelry, and theater sets. He continued working as an expressionist, and his work now was influenced by the Surrealists and Pablo Picasso. Kirchner became a major influence in the development of Swiss art, training several prominent Swiss artists and starting the Blue-Green School of Swiss Art.

Kirchner's artistic works were increasingly appreciated in turbulent but tolerant Weimar Germany. A series of important exhibitions of his works were held not only in Germany but also in Switzerland and the United States. In 1931, Kirchner was belatedly elected to the Berlin Academy of Plastic Arts. Because of the troubled financial situation in Germany, which was his chief market, the sale of his artworks remained small. Kirchner was never to know affluence.

The Nazi seizure of power in 1933 was more devastating to Kirchner than the war. He was designated a "degenerate" artist; his works could be neither displayed nor sold, and 639 of his paintings were removed from German museums and either destroyed or sold for pittances. The most crushing blow came in 1937, when a traveling exhibit of "degenerate art," including twenty-five of Kirchner's works, was organized by the Nazis. The public humiliation was more than the sensitive artist, already broken in health, could bear. On June 15, 1938, leaving an unfinished work on his easel, Kirchner went into a quiet field beside his cabin and shot two bullets into his heart.

Summary

The greatness of Ernst Ludwig Kirchner as an artist lies principally in his single-minded purpose of giving "expression" and honest subjective meaning to his art. Toward achieving this end, he became a master of most artistic media, utilizing in an innovative and creative way color, form, line, perspective, and symbols. Kirchner contributed to making expressionism a major art movement whose influence was felt in literature, music, and film. Expressionism, international in scope, has emerged in the 1980's as "neo-expressionism," involving the works of artists such as Jackson Pollock, Picasso, Georg Baselitz, and Anselm Kiefer.

Bibliography

Foster, Hal. "'Primitive' Scenes." *Critical Inquiry* 20, no. 1 (Fall 1993). The author provides a psychoanalytic interpretation of works involving gender subversion by Kirchner, Picasso, and Gauguin.

Gordon, Donald E. *Ernst Ludwig Kirchner.* Cambridge, Mass.: Harvard University Press, 1968. Donald Gordon is considered an authority in English on Kirchner. The book contains an account by periods of Kirchner's artistic career; color plates of his best known works with accompanying criticisms; locations of the works; and black-and-white productions of 240 of the artist's works arranged in chronological order.

———. *Expressionism: Art and Idea.* New Haven, Conn.: Yale University Press, 1987. This book provides a clear account of the development of expressionism, from its inception at the turn of the century to the 1980's. Kirchner is seen as a major influence.

Joachimides, Christos M., Norman Rosenthal, and Wieland Schmied, eds. *German Art in the Twentieth Century.* London: Weidenfeld and Nicolson, and New York: Neues Publishing, 1985. A handsomely illustrated volume with color plates of the works of fifty-two German artists from Kirchner to Kiefer. The continuing influence of expressionism is clearly visible. Kirchner is extensively discussed in two essays and a short biography. His association with "degenerate art" is covered in a separate essay.

Myers, Bernard S. *The German Expressionists.* New York: Praeger, 1957. Although not as comprehensive as Gordon, Myers gives a highly readable account of the development of German expressionism, including a separate essay on Kirchner. Contains numerous color and black-and-white plates.

Zigrosser, Carl. *The Expressionists: A Survey of Their Graphic Art.* London: Thames and Hudson, and New York: Braziller, 1957. For many, the greatness of Kirchner is expressed in the graphic arts. The work contains thirty-five graphic works of the Brücke artists, including twelve by Kirchner with a fine accompanying text.

Nis Petersen

JEANE KIRKPATRICK

Born: November 19, 1926; Duncan, Oklahoma
Areas of Achievement: Diplomacy, government and politics, and women's rights
Contributions: The first woman to serve as American Ambassador to the United Nations (1981-1985), Kirkpatrick also wrote one of the first books on women and American politics, giving that new field of scholarship legitimacy.

Early Life

Jeane Duane Jordan was born in Duncan, Oklahoma, a small town forty miles from Texas where her father was an oil business contractor and her mother kept books for the family business. She was born November 19, 1926; her brother Jerry was born eight years later. Like most Oklahomans, the Jordans were Democrats and avid supporters of Franklin D. Roosevelt. Jeane's grandfather Jordan, a Texas justice of the peace, had a collection of law books that Jeane found fascinating. Jeane's mother loved to read and inspired her daughter's lifelong love for reading and writing.

When Jeane was twelve, the family moved to Illinois. By the time she entered high school, Jeane had become an accomplished pianist and had developed a love for literature. She was a straight "A" student at Vandalia High School, edited the school newspaper, and acted in plays. In her senior year, she wrote an essay about George Eliot, the British nineteenth century woman writer who used a male name in order to publish her work. Although Jeane's mother encouraged her daughter to pursue whatever goals she chose, her father wanted her to get married. She chose college.

Jeane embarked on her college years with enthusiasm, focusing on the liberal arts courses at Stephens College in Columbia, Missouri, then moving on to be graduated in 1948 from Barnard College in New York with a degree in political science. She told friends that her goal in life was to be a spinster teacher at a women's college. Her favorite author was Virginia Woolf. Then, daring to do what was quite untraditional at the time, she completed a master's degree from Columbia University and would have continued with doctoral studies had her father not decided it was time for her to support herself. She went to the nation's capital, political science degrees and references in hand, seeking a job. The doctorate would come later.

Jeane was successful in finding jobs in Washington, D.C., including one at the State Department, where she met Evron Kirkpatrick. She also won a fellowship that enabled her to spend a year studying communism in France, and a research position at George Washington University gave her an opportunity to explore Chinese communism while developing research techniques she would use later in life. At the Economic Cooperation Administration, she helped to write a book about the Marshall Plan. Her satisfaction in the work was marred by the author's failure to acknowledge her contributions.

By 1955, Jeane and Evron Kirkpatrick had been dating for about five years. The two intellectuals married, spending their honeymoon at a political science convention near Chicago. Jeane continued working at George Washington University until the first of her three sons was born in 1956. At that point, based on her motto "refuse to choose," she combined motherhood with her career.

During the early 1960's, Kirkpatrick combined her at-home academic work with Democratic Party politics. She and her husband actively supported John F. Kennedy's candidacy in 1960. In 1962, their youngest son entered nursery school and Kirkpatrick took a part-time teaching position at Trinity College, a small women's college near Washington, D.C. While teaching there, she completed her first book, *The Strategy of Deception: A Study in World-wide Communist Tactics*, a collection of essays that analyzed the rise of communist governments outside the Soviet Union.

In 1968, Kirkpatrick completed her Ph.D. at Columbia University. Her dissertation about Perónist politics in Argentina was later published by the MIT Press. Deciding that her children were old enough for her to return to full-time teaching, she applied for and won a position in Georgetown University's political science department. She was to become only the second woman in the university's history to win tenure. It was the beginning of an illustrious career that spanned the academic, political, and journalism professions.

Life's Work

Jeane Kirkpatrick's disillusionment with the Democratic Party began during the late 1960's. During that period, riots took place following the assassinations of Martin Luther King, Jr., and Robert F.

Kennedy, a 1968 presidential candidate. It was a time of extreme frustration, violence, and urgent demands for change in cities and on campuses around the nation. Some of the worst violence took place at the August, 1968, Democratic Party Convention in Chicago. Students demonstrated at Columbia University, too, making it difficult for Kirkpatrick to deliver her dissertation to Columbia's library.

Kirkpatrick supported Hubert Humphrey's Democratic Party candidacy in 1968, which he lost to Richard Nixon. In 1972, however, she voted against Democratic challenger George McGovern. In the first of many articles she would write for the journal Commentary, she argued that McGovern represented a set of counterculture values that most Americans, herself included, rejected. Nixon, however, established himself as a supporter of traditional American values and as a fervent opponent of communism. The strategy won him Kirkpatrick's vote and a landslide victory over McGovern.

Kirkpatrick's studies of totalitarian governments led her to advocate an anticommunist foreign policy that came to be known as the Kirkpatrick doctrine. It advocated support for right-wing authoritarian leaders if that support would weaken left-wing totalitarianism. It was a policy that the Reagan Administration was to apply to its relations with Central and Latin American governments in the 1980's.

Following the 1972 election, Kirkpatrick became associated with neoconservative thought, which combined opposition to communism and belief in a strong military with liberal views on social issues. Kirkpatrick was very concerned, for example, about the obvious absence of women in government. Her research about that concern led to the publication in 1974 of America's first major book about women in government. *Political Woman* gave Kirkpatrick new recognition outside of academia and gave legitimacy to the emerging study of women in politics. Acclaimed as an expert on the topic, she was asked to represent the United States at a 1975 International Women's Year conference held in West Africa.

In 1976, Kirkpatrick wrote *The New Presidential Elite: Men and Women in National Politics*. Whereas *Political Woman* had focused on state government, the new book studied women at the national level of government. In addition to being well received, the second book also won Kirk-

patrick an invitation to join the staff of the American Enterprise Institute (AEI), one of Washington's oldest think tanks. She spent 1977 working full-time at the institute, then returned to Georgetown University while continuing part-time work at the AEI. At the Institute, Kirkpatrick became the first woman to serve as a senior scholar.

During the Jimmy Carter Administration, Kirkpatrick wrote one of her most influential articles for *Commentary* magazine. In "Dictatorships and Double Standards," she argued that Carter failed to appreciate communism's threat and reiterated her belief that the United States sometimes needed to fight totalitarianism by supporting authoritarian regimes. At issue was Carter's support for leftist Sandinistas in Nicaragua. Carter thought that the Sandinistas were more likely to evolve toward democracy than the corrupt Somoza government was. Kirkpatrick pointed out that no communist system in the past had ever become democratic.

Kirkpatrick's article won her the admiration of 1980 presidential candidate Ronald Reagan, who made her foreign policy adviser during his campaign and in 1981 appointed her Ambassador to the United Nations; she was the first woman to hold the latter position. The president won considerable acclaim for his Reagan doctrine, which was an adaptation of the proposal Kirkpatrick presented in "Dictatorships and Double Standards."

As head of her country's U.N. delegation, Kirkpatrick earned a reputation as a capable, if not always popular, negotiator. Her first victory was a difficult compromise she negotiated in response to Israel's 1981 bombing of Iraq's nuclear reactor. President Reagan called her handling of the incident heroic, and Iraq's foreign minister was so impressed that he commented, "One Kirkpatrick was equal to more than two men. Maybe three." That kind of positive response was unusual, however, in the male-dominated United Nations. Ambassador Kirkpatrick often had to cope with sexism among her colleagues.

In addition to sexism, Kirkpatrick had to deal with anti-American attitudes at the United Nations. She developed a theory about why the United States had had difficulty influencing General Assembly decisions since the 1970's. In her view, the United States failed to adapt to a system of coalitions that emerged when dozens of newly independent developing nations became United Nations members starting in the 1960's. Because it refused to participate in any of the new coalitions, the United States lost its ability to influence decisions. During her four years at the United Nations, Kirkpatrick worked to strengthen America's position there while also focusing on the dangers of communism in Central and Latin America.

Early in 1985, Kirkpatrick resigned her U.N. position to return to family and scholarly responsibilities. She continued her association with Georgetown University and the American Enterprise Institute, resuming a heavy schedule of writing that included books, articles, and a syndicated *Los Angeles Times* column on post-Cold War developments. She assumed positions on various foreign-policy related associations, including the Defense Policy Review Board and the Council on Foreign Relations.

Only after her U.N. resignation did Kirkpatrick officially change her voting registration to Republican, prompting discussion of her potential as a 1988 presidential candidate. Although she decided not to run, she had the support of an unusual coalition of conservatives, who appreciated her foreign policy positions, and feminists, who appreciated her stand on women's issues. She had always supported passage of the Equal Rights Amendment, and she generally advocated gender equity.

Summary

Commenting on her years at the United Nations, Kirkpatrick once pointed out that she had been the only woman in history who sat in regularly at top-level foreign policy-making meetings. Those kinds of meetings, she said, had historically been closed to women in most countries. In her view, it matters very much that women have been so excluded. "It's terribly important," she said, "maybe even to the future of the world, for women to take part in making the decisions that shape our destiny."

As a mother of three sons who grew up during the Vietnam War years, Kirkpatrick came to believe that force should be used to resolve conflict only in the most extraordinary circumstances. She believed fervently in using diplomatic negotiation as the primary method for resolving international disputes, and she will be remembered primarily as the first woman to serve as America's principal negotiator at the United Nations. Her scholarly work will also stand as a testament to her commitment to the intellectual analysis of international relations.

Kirkpatrick's advice to women was to "refuse to choose" between motherhood and career. Although many women will not have that luxury, Kirkpatrick is nevertheless an inspiration to those women who want to take control of their own lives so that they can at least expand their range of opportunities. She is especially important as a model for young women who hope to lead productive, satisfying lives.

Bibliography

Crapol, Edward P., ed. *Women and American Foreign Policy: Lobbyists, Critics, and Insiders.* London and New York: Greenwood, 1987. This scholarly volume analyzes women's roles in the historical development of U.S. foreign policy. Judith Ewell's chapter seeks explanations for Kirkpatrick's limited impact on U.S. foreign policy.

Harrison, Pat. *Jeane Kirkpatrick.* New York: Chelsea House, 1991. Part of the American Women of Achievement youth series, this short, illustrated biography describes Kirkpatrick's personal and political life in positive, anecdotal terms.

"Jeanne Kirkpatrick: A Critical Appraisal." *Harvard International Review* 17, no. 4 (Fall 1995). An interview with Kirkpatrick. Comments are included on the current purpose of the United Nations, the United Nations' stand on the civil war in Bosnia, and more.

Kirkpatrick, Jeane. *Political Woman*. New York: Basic, 1974. A project of Rutgers University's Center for the American Woman and Politics, this study of women serving in state governments was the first major scholarly examination of women in politics.

————. *The Withering Away of the Totalitarian State—and Other Surprises*. Washington, D.C.: American Enterprise Institute Press, 1990. In this collection of columns written between 1985 and 1990, Kirkpatrick analyzes post-Cold War events in the Soviet Union.

LeVeness, Frank P., and Jane P. Sweeney, eds. *Women Leaders in Contemporary U.S. Politics*. Boulder, Colo.: Rienner, 1987. Naomi B. Lynn's chapter on Kirkpatrick's rise from political science professor to participant in international politics is based on analysis of Kirkpatrick's written work, on interviews with Kirkpatrick, and on interviews with people who have known her.

Selle, Robert. "Diplomat and Mother." *World and I* 13, no. 8 (August, 1998). Discusses Kirkpatrick's fourteen-year hiatus from her diplomatic career to raise her children.

Susan MacFarland

HENRY A. KISSINGER

Born: May 27, 1923; Fürth, Germany

Area of Achievement: Diplomacy, government and politics

Contribution: Both in theory (in his writings as an academic) and in practice (serving as national security adviser and secretary of state), Kissinger advocated a new conception of American foreign policy more closely akin to traditional European balance-of-power politics than to the reformist model to which Americans had become accustomed.

Early Life

Heinz (later Henry) Alfred Kissinger was born in the small town of Fürth, located in the south German province of Franconia near Nuremberg, on May 27, 1923. His father, Louis, was a professor at a local high school, while his mother, Paula, was a housewife. The setting was a typical middle-class German one, except for one factor: The Kissingers were a Jewish family in a Germany that was on the brink of Nazism. Heinz and his younger brother Walter were often beaten by anti-Semitic Hitler youths on their way to and from school; finally, they were expelled and forced to attend an all-Jewish institution. Their father was eventually forced to resign his position, and after years of social ostracism, the Kissinger family was fortunate to be able to immigrate to the United States in 1938. Such early experiences were formative; they led Kissinger to distrust the opinion of the moment and to a lifelong concern for the conditions conducive to the preservation of social stability and an abhorrence of revolution and all social upheaval.

The Kissinger family settled, as did many refugees from Nazism, in the Washington Heights section of New York City, where Louis found employment as a bookkeeper and Paula worked as a cook in the homes of wealthy families. Perhaps because he was already fifteen in 1938, the youth never entirely lost his German accent and usually impressed Americans as being rather European in manner and appearance. He was graduated from George Washington High School in 1941 with a straight-A average and began to prepare himself for a career as an accountant, taking evening courses at City College. The United States' entry into World War II changed all that, expanding his horizons and presenting unforeseen opportunities.

In 1943, Kissinger was drafted into the United States Army and became a naturalized American citizen. His language abilities and high scores on aptitude tests soon catapulted this bespectacled and rather unprepossessing (he was only five feet, eight inches tall and intellectual rather than athletic in appearance) young man into important positions. He became German interpreter for his commanding general and worked his way up to the position of staff sergeant in army intelligence. After the war, Kissinger was given the task of reorganizing municipal government in the town of Krefeld and became a district administrator with the Occupation government.

In September, 1946, he entered Harvard College under a New York State scholarship and embarked on what was quickly to become a very distinguished academic career. Majoring in government, he came under the tutelage of William Yandell Elliott. He wrote an extremely ambitious 377-page senior honors thesis entitled "The Meaning of History: Reflections on Spengler, Toynbee and Kant" and was graduated with highest honors. The study of international relations at the graduate level was a new and burgeoning field in the early 1950's, and Kissinger rode this new academic wave. While still a graduate student, he served as executive director of the Harvard International Seminar and as editor of the journal *Confluence: An International Forum.* Kissinger received his Ph.D. in 1954, on the basis of a doctoral dissertation which earned for him the Sumner Prize and which was later published as *A World Restored: Metternich, Castlereagh, and the Problems of Peace, 1812-1822* (1957). It was history written from a presentist perspective and with a purpose: Kissinger looked at the conservative statesmen of an earlier age in order to develop a blueprint for how best to reintegrate revolutionary powers into the international system.

Life's Work

Kissinger stayed on at Harvard as an instructor and received a big break when he was appointed study director of an important Council on Foreign Relations research program which sought to explore means short of all-out nuclear war of coping with Soviet challenges as an alternative to the "massive retaliation" doctrine of Secretary of State John Foster Dulles. The end result was Kissinger's first major published work, *Nuclear Weapons and Foreign Policy* (1957), which argued persuasively that strategy must shape weaponry rather than the reverse but which also provoked considerable controversy in that Kissinger seemed to believe that it might prove possible to fight a limited or tactical nuclear war. The book was widely read, met an obvious need, and gave Kissinger an international reputation as one of the country's leading "defense intellectuals."

Thereafter, his academic and public-governmental careers advanced in tandem, and Kissinger became a frequent traveler on the Boston-New York-Washington corridor. Kissinger became a lecturer in government at Harvard University's Center for International Affairs in 1957. He was named associate professor of government in 1959 and professor in 1962. For ten years, from 1959 to 1969, he also served as director of Harvard's Defense Studies program. Meanwhile, he served as a consultant on defense and foreign policy matters, first in the Eisenhower Administration and then in those of John F. Kennedy and Lyndon B. Johnson. In the !atter administration, he also served as President Johnson's secret emissary in efforts to bring the North Vietnamese to the peace table. He somehow also managed to find the time to write prolifically on the subject of international relations, producing scores of articles and, in the 1960's, several penetrating books: *The Necessity for Choice: Prospects of American Foreign Policy* (1961), *The Troubled Partnership: A Reappraisal of the Atlantic Alliance* (1965), and *American Foreign Policy: Three Essays* (1969).

Kissinger's work for the Council on Foreign Relations early brought him to the attention of Nelson Rockefeller, and by the time Rockefeller made his unsuccessful bid for the Republican presidential nomination in 1968, Kissinger had been serving him as a foreign policy adviser and speech writer for some years. In 1968, Kissinger helped draft Rockefeller's platform and was especially influential in devising the governor's relatively dovish plank on Vietnam. Kissinger and Rockefeller were both personally and ideologically compatible, liberal on most domestic matters but profoundly suspicious of the Wilsonian strains in the Democratic Party's approach to the conduct of foreign policy, and Kissinger viewed Rockefeller's defeat by Richard M. Nixon with considerable dismay. Nevertheless, after his victory, Nixon invited Kissinger to become his principal foreign policy adviser. The choice was not as unusual as it first appeared; Nixon was well acquainted with Kissinger's writings, had reason to want to improve his standing with liberal Republicans, and, moreover, knew that Kissinger had frequently in the past taken a hard-line, anti-Soviet position similar to Nixon's own.

Kissinger took a leave of absence from Harvard and assumed the position of assistant to the president for national security affairs in January, 1969. There was a certain irony in the fact that a man who had spent his life studying the conditions and policies most conducive to the achievement of international stability should have arrived at a position of power and influence at a time when the United States was in turmoil and when the American public was particularly divided over foreign policy issues, especially over the war in Vietnam, and at a time when the United States' power and ability to influence events abroad were in decline.

Over the first few years, Nixon and Kissinger gradually pieced together a new strategy that tried to address both problems. Instead of looking at the world as a bipolar contest of blocs, Kissinger saw in international politics an emerging multipolar system to be structured and regulated by the balance of power. Instead of relations of total enmity or total friendship, both inimical to diplomacy, there would again be those fluctuating mixes of common and divergent interests characteristic of eighteenth and nineteenth century European diplomacy. Such a strategy not only matched trends already apparent in the world but also seemed to correspond to the psychological conditions of the United States after Vietnam. Instead of a universal American presence on the front lines, the new strategy, the so-called Nixon Doctrine, promised restraint. It also held out the possibility of maintaining the essence of the American world position on the cheap—of substituting Kissinger's adeptness at diplomacy for declining military strength. After the colossal strains of engagement, it pointed the way to some disengagement. Perhaps most important of all, after the delusion or dream of an American world mission, after the pretense of being the only nation with a sense of world responsibility, the new strategy proclaimed that henceforth self-interest would be the guiding principle of American foreign policy, not the activist idealism that led first to empire and then inevitably to disillusionment.

Once the philosophy underlying this approach is acknowledged, it becomes much easier to under-

stand why the Nixon Administration's foreign policy was marked by so many dramatic reversals of previous policy and why the Administration's flexibility led to some rather stunning successes. Those events are chronicled in considerable detail in two volumes of memoirs that Kissinger has published, *White House Years* (1979) and *Years of Upheaval* (1982), the latter volume covering the period after he became secretary of state in 1973.

Kissinger's role was in the early years usually shrouded in secrecy but was no less vital than it was when it later became more public. He conducted numerous secret meetings with representatives from North Vietnam in Paris in 1970 and 1971, talks which eventually led to more formal negotiations. In July, 1971, he undertook his now-celebrated trip to Peking to arrange for a presidential visit to mainland China that was to bring about a marked reversal of past policies and greatly improve relations between the People's Republic of China and the United States. Equally noteworthy was the inauguration of a policy of détente with the Soviet Union, which began with a secret visit to Moscow in April, 1972, again to smooth the way

for a visit by President Nixon. Though both Nixon and Kissinger had reputations as hardliners when it came to the Soviet Union, they operated from the assumption that the Soviet Union was becoming a more conservative power and that, consequently, there existed the possibility of reintegrating that power into a more stable international system. Though Kissinger would later admit that détente had not been altogether successful, he always believed that the effort was worth making, that a way had to be found to lend greater stability to superpower relations in the interest of preventing the disaster of nuclear conflict.

Kissinger was also deeply involved in efforts to find a compromise solution to the Arab-Israeli conflict, frequently exhausting himself in rapid trips (so-called shuttle diplomacy) back and forth between Tel Aviv and the Arab capitals. Some of his other efforts won for him less credit, but his role was no less prominent in the president's controversial decision to label India the aggressor in its war with Pakistan and in the overthrow of the government of Salvador Allende in Chile.

Yet no aspect of the foreign policy of the Nixon Administration was or remains so controversial as its approach to the war in Vietnam. For years, Kissinger promoted a policy of Vietnamization aimed at effecting the withdrawal of American forces from Indochina without causing the collapse of the government of South Vietnam. This policy did not, however, mean military inactivity. Indeed, it was accompanied at times by such military actions as the invasion of Cambodia and the bombing of Hanoi and Haiphong harbor, actions which seemed to threaten an escalation of the conflict and which provoked widespread criticism. In the end, but only after the conflict had dragged on for years, Kissinger, after the most protracted of negotiations, was able, in 1973, to effect a settlement of the conflict that earned for him and for his North Vietnamese counterpart the Nobel Peace Prize. The peace did not hold, however, for in 1975, the regime in Hanoi launched a successful invasion of the South which culminated in the fall of Saigon. Much controversy still surrounds the question of whether Kissinger thought the 1973 agreement was capable of leading to a lasting settlement or whether he was simply buying time so as to effect a total American withdrawal as gracefully as the difficult circumstances permitted.

After Nixon's resignation, Kissinger continued to serve as secretary of state in the administration of Gerald Ford. He then returned to private life but remained an important figure both as a consultant on international politics and as a frequent commentator on the course of American foreign policy.

Summary

Henry Kissinger brought to the attention of the American public a whole new approach to the conduct of foreign policy. The title Bruce Mazlish chose for his book on Kissinger is particularly apt, *Kissinger: The European Mind in American Policy* (1976). Both in his writings as an academic and in his service as national security adviser and secretary of state, Kissinger sought, not always successfully, to wean Americans away from their missionary approach to the conduct of foreign policy and to devise a policy based on calculations of national interest and on a preoccupation, stemming therefrom, with achieving a high degree of stability in international relations. This goal introduced a long absent and much needed new development into the debate over the goals of American foreign policy. Kissinger's endeavor to return to the European balance-of-power politics of the eighteenth and nineteenth centuries led initially to many a notable success, but, as one commentator, Stanley Hoffmann, put it, the real question was whether the balance of power would balance at home—that is, whether the American people would be satisfied with a policy based on calculations of relative power rather than on such long-standing American goals as the spread of democracy and the achievement of international justice.

Bibliography

Graubard, Stephen R. *Kissinger: Portrait of a Mind.* New York: Norton, 1973. The best account of Kissinger's intellectual development and of his writings as an academic. Very useful but devoid of critical analysis.

Hersh, Seymour M. *The Price of Power: Kissinger in the Nixon White House.* London: Faber, and New York: Summit Books, 1983. A well-written but vitriolic account of Kissinger's role as national security adviser and secretary of state. Disappointing in its lack of historical perspective.

Kissinger, Henry A. "A World We Have Not Known." *Newsweek* 129, no 4 (January 27, 1997). Kissinger examines the challenges currently facing the United States in foreign affairs. Several scenarios are presented.

———. "Continuity and Change in American Foreign Policy." *Society* 35, no. 2 (January-February, 1998). Discusses the ingredients necessary for a successful foreign policy.

Mazlish, Bruce. *Kissinger: The European Mind in American Policy.* New York: Basic, 1976. A biography by a prominent psychohistorian. Though the interpretation is occasionally heavy-handed, it also contains considerable insight into Kissinger's highly complex personality.

Morris, Roger. *Uncertain Greatness: Henry Kissinger and American Foreign Policy.* New York: Harper, 1977. A rather critical but revelatory account written by someone who worked on Kissinger's staff. Morris' responsibility was African affairs, and the book is soundest on that aspect of American foreign policy.

Rust, Michael. "All the President's Men Were Not Team Players." *Insight on the News* 13, no. 23 (June 23, 1997). Short discussion of Kissinger's possible involvement in leaks during the Watergate scandal.

Shawcross, William. *Sideshow: Kissinger, Nixon and the Destruction of Cambodia.* 2d ed. London: Hogarth, 1986; New York: Simon and Schuster, 1987. A rather sensational and tendentious account of Nixon and Kissinger's approach to the war in Vietnam. Shawcross blames them directly for the atrocities which Pol Pot perpetrated on the Cambodian people.

Sheehan, Edward R. F. *The Arabs, Israelis, and Kissinger: A Secret History of American Diplomacy in the Middle East.* New York: Reader's Digest Press, 1976. A highly readable account of Kissinger's Middle Eastern shuttle diplomacy written by a prominent and knowledgeable journalist.

Starr, Harvey. *Henry Kissinger: Perceptions of International Politics.* Lexington: University Press of Kentucky, 1984. Written by a political scientist, this book brings some of that discipline's newer analytical tools and approaches to bear on Kissinger and his policies. The results are somewhat uneven.

Stoessinger, John G. *Henry Kissinger: The Anguish of Power.* New York: Norton, 1976. Probably the best book yet written on Kissinger. Stoessinger not only tries to understand why Kissinger proceeded as he did but also presents some trenchant criticism.

William C. Widenor

LORD KITCHENER

Born: June 24, 1850; near Listowel, County Kerry,
Ireland
Died: June 5, 1916; off the Orkney Islands, Scotland
Area of Achievement: The military
Contribution: Kitchener held many military and
imperial positions throughout the Middle East
between 1874 and 1899. He was commander in
chief of British forces in the South African War,
1900-1902. He served as the secretary of state
for war during World War I and was regarded as
a symbol of Great Britain's will to victory.

Early Life

Horatio Herbert Kitchener was born June 24, 1850,
near Listowel, County Kerry, in Ireland. His father,
Lieutenant-Colonel Henry Horatio Kitchener, had
retired from the military because of his wife's failing health. The family lived a solitary life, and the
children were educated by private tutors. From his
father, a martinet, the young Kitchener learned a
code of discipline and honor that would guide him
for the rest of his life. His father also taught him to
believe in English superiority to other groups and
races. When Kitchener was thirteen, his mother's
health necessitated a move to the Alps. There, for
the first time, he attended a formal school where,
through hard work, he excelled in mathematics and
French.

Kitchener's military career began in 1868 when
he entered the Royal Military Academy at Wool-
wich, England. He was commissioned in the Royal
Engineers in 1871, and three years later he was
posted to the Middle East. His various postings and
tasks included the surveying of Palestine (1874-
1878), the surveying of Cyprus (1878-1882), military command and action with the Egyptian army
(1882-1883), the surveying of the Sinai Peninsula
(1883), action against the Sudanese (1884-1885),
governor-generalship of the Eastern Sudan (1886-
1888), and adjutant generalship in Egypt (1888-
1892).

During these formative years, Kitchener developed the talents that made him the leader he became. His early assignments were often lonely and
dangerous, yet his honor required that he perform
tasks to the best of his ability. Kitchener was fascinated by the peoples of the Middle East; his linguistic facility enabled him to learn Arabic and to
work closely with natives, particularly Egyptians.

He was courageous and never asked his men to do
anything that he would not himself do. Indeed,
Kitchener often disguised himself as a native in order to obtain intelligence for military needs. On the
negative side, he seldom took others into his confidence and was rarely willing to delegate authority.
Still, his successes ensured Kitchener's reputation
as an authority on Arabic customs and as a brave
and able soldier.

Life's Work

In 1892, Kitchener was appointed sirdar (commander in chief) of the Egyptian army; under his
leadership, it became a credible fighting force.
When the British government learned of French
interests in the upper Nile region, Kitchener was
ordered to invade the Sudan. For two and a half
years, Kitchener's Anglo-Egyptian army methodically moved up the Nile. Finally, in September,
1898, he and his army arrived at Omdurman,
across the Nile from Khartoum. In a fierce battle,
the Sudanese forces were annihilated, thereby
ending the River War. With a strong detachment
of troops, Kitchener continued southward along
the Nile to Fashoda, where Major Jean-Baptiste
Marchand had raised the French flag. There, in December, he diplomatically dealt with Marchand,
thereby allowing London and Paris to defuse the
international crisis. For his various military successes, he was created Baron Kitchener, of Khartoum, and was appointed Governor-General of the
Sudan.

Following the outbreak of the South African War
in October, 1899, British forces suffered numerous
military disasters at the hands of the Boers. Field
Marshal Sir F. S. Roberts was appointed commander in chief of the British forces sent to the area.
Kitchener was appointed his chief of staff. His prodigious energy swiftly resulted in the reorganization of the transport system, which increased the
mobility of the British forces. Within a year, Roberts and Kitchener defeated the organized Boer
forces and occupied the major Boer cities. Roberts,
believing the war to be won, returned to London,
leaving Kitchener to end it.

In reality, the war had only entered a new phase.
The major Boer leaders were still at large, and the
loss of their major cities freed them from the restraints of conventional warfare. Kitchener imme-

diately appreciated the task facing him. He believed that guerrilla warfare could be combatted only through denial of supplies to the guerrilla. He therefore ordered all Boer women and children to be collected in secure camps (called concentration camps), all farms and supplies to be burned or destroyed, defensive positions to be constructed across the veldt, and mobile columns to pursue without pause the Boer commandos. For eighteen months, this bitter and ugly phase of the war continued; the Boers were finally forced to surrender. Yet, as brutal as he had been in warfare, his patience and moderation in the peace negotiations led to the successful Peace of Vereeniging in May, 1902. Kitchener was now regarded by the average Briton as a national hero.

Upon his return to England from South Africa, Kitchener was awarded a viscountcy and then was posted to India. As commander in chief of British forces in India, Kitchener reorganized the Indian army. As in Egypt, his changes transformed a moribund colonial army into a vital military force. This was to prove invaluable, as India was to provide substantive military assistance to Great Britain during World War I. Kitchener departed India in 1909 and was promoted to field marshal. After serving as a member of the Committee of Imperial Defense, he was appointed Consul-General of Egypt (1911-1914), where he devoted himself to social reforms and economic development. He received an earldom in 1914.

With the outbreak of World War I, Kitchener was appointed secretary of state for war. There was no one more qualified or who commanded more public respect than he. His awareness of the military capabilities of the British Empire was second to none, and his lifetime of military experience had prepared him for the necessities of mobilizing an army. Although few agreed with him, he believed that the war would last at least three years, and he worked to triple the size of the army and to provide for it. As he had spent most of his life away from Great Britain, however, he was ill-prepared either to work with government departments or to relate to politicians. Kitchener preferred to keep his own counsel and to oversee everything. This was to result in his undertaking too much responsibility, as well as friction with those in power. Moreover, his methods often lacked system. Kitchener knew what had to be done, but frequently he did not know how to do it (then again, no one else did, either).

Despite Kitchener's efforts to supply the needs of the army, there were numerous shortages in France. This led to a waning of his influence in the War Cabinet. His authority over war production was shifted to others in 1915, and his control over strategy was removed in 1916. Although privately made the scapegoat for the military failures of those years, Kitchener himself continued to behave with dignity and purpose. He offered to resign and to return to field command, but the politicians realized that public opinion would never have permitted it. Instead, his prestige was utilized to improve relations with Great Britain's allies, especially France. On June 5, 1916, he embarked on a mission to Russia. On June 5, 1916, his ship, HMS *Hampshire*, struck a German mine off the Orkney Islands and sank. Kitchener was drowned.

Summary

Lord Kitchener's death provoked an immediate outpouring of national grief. He had been a symbol of national unity and purpose; indeed, a stylized portrait of Kitchener, replete with bushy mustache, on a recruiting poster, was the single most visible reminder to the war generation of their duty to serve king and country. As the war dragged on, however, and as the Kitchener volunteers were decimated in the trenches of Flanders, this symbolism was tarnished. After the war, the nation preferred to forget the man who had presided over the national sacrifice. Kitchener's reputation also suffered at the hands of his political enemies. Eager to blame the appalling costs of the war on others, numerous self-serving memoirs reviled the dead Kitchener as having been a prime cause of the failures during the war. Furthermore, as the empire crumbled, symbols of imperial greatness were also discarded. Thus, within a few years of his death, Kitchener had become at best a footnote and at worst a scapegoat. A study of Kitchener's life, however, offers insight into the dynamic forces affecting the Great Britain of the late nineteenth and early twentieth centuries.

As one of the great builders and shapers of late Victorian British imperial greatness, Kitchener epitomized the winning and maintaining of empire. At Omdurman, he fought and won a colonial war; in South Africa, he was the architect of victory of the first modern war of the twentieth century. As a peacemaker, his efforts at Fashoda and Vereeniging demonstrated not only ability but also compassion and common sense. As an administrator in the Sudan, in Egypt, and in India, he was sincere in his desire to improve that which he found and to build a better British world. Yet in each of these tasks, Kitchener was free to make decisions imperially, that is, he was accountable to no one but himself. His inability to delegate and his hesitancy to communicate were not major handicaps in areas where his word was law.

When Kitchener was chosen to administrate Great Britain's efforts in World War I, he was a military man among politicians. His imperial demeanor led to tension and friction which ultimately undermined his effect. That he accomplished what he did is a real testament to his genius. Under his direction, Great Britain produced its first mass army of volunteers. His strategy was global in nature, while most politicians could see only the Western Front. Most significantly, he developed the system which provided the army with the supplies needed to fight a war of unprecedented scale. Kitchener was the architect for Great Britain's victory in World War I. He died before the structure he designed was completed.

Bibliography

Cassar, George H. *Kitchener: Architect of Victory.* London: Kimber, 1977. A balanced, comprehensive, analytical study of Kitchener. This work is particularly significant for its analysis of Kitchener's contributions to the war effort in World War I.

Churchill, Winston S. *The River War.* 2 vols. London and New York: Longman, 1899. A long, egoistic overview of the British war in the Sudan as written by a participant. Churchill was somewhat critical of Kitchener as commander, but his description of the campaign is picturesque.

Kruger, Rayne. *Goodbye Dolly Gray.* London: Cassell, 1959. A generally balanced overview of the Boer War. Although there have been several histories of the Boer War published since this work, it is still the most readable available. See also *The Boer War* by Thomas Pakenham, published in 1979 in New York by Random House.

Magnus, Philip. *Kitchener: Portrait of an Imperialist.* London: Murray, 1958; New York: Dutton, 1959. Primarily a chronological and favorable study of Kitchener's life. Although it utilizes much source material, the work is lightly footnoted and lacks a bibliography.

Robertson, Sir William. *From Private to Field-Marshal.* London: Constable, and Boston: Houghton Mifflin, 1921. Provides an inside look at managing the war effort. Robertson, a chief of the British General Staff during World War I, was well qualified to discuss Kitchener's talents in his own autobiography.

Royle, Trevor. *The Kitchener Enigma.* London: Joseph, 1985. A clear, concise, well-documented biography of an extraordinarily complex man. Although the public life of Kitchener is well studied, the forte of this work is its analysis of the man himself.

Spies, S. B. *Methods of Barbarism?* Capetown: Human and Rousseau, 1977. A study of Kitchener's strategy and its impact on civilians in the second phase of the Boer War. The work is particularly concerned with the conduct of the war according to then-accepted rules of war.

Warner, Philip. *Kitchener: The Man Behind the Legend.* London: Hamilton, 1985; New York: Atheneum, 1986. A popular and quite readable biography. Warner is particularly concerned about the development of Kitchener's public image.

William S. Brockington, Jr.

PAUL KLEE

Born: December 18, 1879; Münchenbuchsee, near Bern, Switzerland
Died: June 29, 1940; Muralto-Locarno, Switzerland
Area of Achievement: Art
Contribution: Klee was one of the most brilliant, varied, and complex artists of the twentieth century. Klee, whose paintings and graphics were always rooted in physical reality, invented symbols for the formative process of nature. As a teacher and theoretician, he was able to provide significant insights into the meaning of art. His writings include the most complete principles of design devised by a modern artist.

Early Life

Paul Klee was the son of Hans Klee, a German music teacher, and Ida Maria Frick of Basel. In 1880, the family moved to Bern, where Paul attended primary school and in 1898 was graduated from the *Literarschule* (humanities program) of Bern Gymnasium (secondary school). As a young boy, he displayed unusual talent both as a violinist and as a draftsman. In 1898, he began his *Tagebücher* (diaries), which he maintained until 1918.

In October, 1898, he moved to Munich, and there, until 1901, he studied first at the painting school of Heinrich Knirr and later with Franz von Stuck at the Munich Academy. In Munich, he took courses in art history and anatomy and learned etching. Also at this time, his interest in music, which he had inherited from his family, was strengthened, and for a long time he was undecided in his choice of careers. When he chose to pursue the visual arts, music continued to inspire him in developing his theories of visual design; they were formed to a great extent by analogies with musical theory. His favorite composer was Wolfgang Amadeus Mozart, but he also appreciated Claude Debussy, Arnold Schoenberg, and Bruno Walter. Titles of many subsequent paintings referred to his musical interests.

In October, 1901, Klee traveled to Italy, returning in May, 1902, to Bern, where he remained for financial reasons with his parents until 1906. In April, he traveled to Germany and saw the Centenary Exhibit in Berlin, works by Matthias Grünewald at Karlsruhe, and works by Rembrandt at Kassel. On September 15, he married Lily Stumpf, a Munich pianist whom he had known since 1899. They settled in Schwabing, the artists'
quarter of Munich, where they lived until 1920. In November, 1907, Felix, their only child, was born.

During the early Munich years, Klee devoted himself more to drawing and graphics than to painting, in the hope that he could earn enough to survive as an illustrator. Unfortunately, the couple's sole source of income until the start of the war was from the music lessons given by Lily. From 1902 to 1912, Klee struggled with black-and-white compositions in etchings, charcoals, watercolors, and glass paintings, with which he explored methodically the possibilities of line, tone, and chiaroscuro. From 1903 to 1905, Klee etched his first original works, the ten *Inventions*, which he exhibited at the 1906 Munich Sezession. Exhibitions of the art of Vincent van Gogh in 1908 and of Paul Cézanne in 1909 gave Klee the opportunity to study these masters. In the Munich Pinakothek, he also studied prints of William Blake, Francisco de Goya, and James Ensor.

Life's Work

In 1910, the Bern Kunstmuseum housed the first exhibition of Klee's collected works. In the spring of 1911, he began a catalog of his own works, retroactively recording work dated as far back as 1883, and maintained it until his death.

Klee was intimately involved with the ferment of modern art in the early decades of the century, absorbing the tenets of cubism, Dada, and Surrealism without relinquishing his own slowly developing sense of direction. In the autumn of 1911, through his friend Louis Moilliet, he met Wassily Kandinsky, Franz Marc, August Macke, Alexey von Jawlensky, and Gabrielle Münter, who composed a group called Der Blaue Reiter (the blue rider). He joined this avant-garde group and in February, 1912, participated in their second Munich exhibition. The group stimulated Klee's interest in cubism, and in April he went to Paris, where he met Robert Delaunay, in whose painting he saw for the first time an attempt to free color from reference to precise objects. Klee then carefully developed from cubism a set of pictorial principles that permitted him to construct his art in such a way that he could reject art derived from outward appearances in favor of one dependent solely on the inherent principles of pictorial organization. It did not matter to Klee if references to reality appeared in the work as long as they did not interfere with the primary requirement of obeying the rules of pictorial structure.

Klee's art, which evolved slowly until 1914, was predominantly in black and white. Full maturity of his painting occurred during the trip he made to Tunisia in April with Macke and Moilliet. Then the range of pictorial devices in Klee's painting, especially color, expanded dramatically. Exquisite watercolors such as *Before the Gates of Kairouan* (1914) demonstrated his ability to free color from representation. The painting, constructed of simple overlapping color planes, is practically abstract. Although it was painted from nature, internal pictorial concerns rather than fidelity to natural appearances regulated its construction.

By the time Klee was recruited into the German Army in March of 1916, his friends Macke and Marc had been killed. Since he was never sent to the front, he continued to draw and paint whenever possible. He expanded his vocabulary to include arrows, letters, numbers, exclamation points, heavenly bodies, eyes, and hearts in his compositions. He made a number of poem-paintings that attempt to fuse painting compositionally with poetry; one of these is the luminous watercolor *Once Emerged from the Gray of Night . . .* (1918).

The period immediately after the war was particularly productive for Klee, and the scope of his activities increased. In 1918, he wrote an essay on the formal elements of the graphic arts, which was published as part of his *Schöpferische Konfession* (1920; *Creative Credo*, 1959). By 1921, three monographs on the artist were published. In October, 1920, Walter Gropius invited Klee to teach in Weimar at the Bauhaus. Gropius required strict collaboration among faculty, and this brought Klee into close association with his friend Kandinsky and with Lyonel Feininger.

Until 1933, instruction and theory were major concerns for Klee. He felt a strong need to define that which he had previously done instinctively. A conscientious teacher, he prepared his lessons in advance and recorded them meticulously. His theoretical work and his teaching, like his art, relied on the careful study of the creative and structural principles of nature. Yet theory was always placed at the service of his creative activities. In 1925, his *Pädagogisches Skizzenbuch (Pedagogical Sketchbook*, 1953) was published as second in the series of Bauhaus Books.

At the Bauhaus, Klee experimented continually with new techniques and unusual combinations of media. A favorite method of Klee was the transfer drawing, in which he used oil or ink to trace a drawing onto a new sheet to which watercolor was added. The process produced random smudges that cue the viewer to the method of creation. The stains also add an ambiguity to spatial relations on the composition. The famous *Twittering Machine* (1922) is a fragile example in which sensitive lines connect birds to a mechanical contraption which holds them and forces them to sing in an atmospheric haze of delicate color.

Through the Bauhaus, Klee came to know such artists as Kurt Schwitters, Amédée Ozenfant, and Albert Gleizes. The 1923 Bauhaus Exhibition afforded him the opportunity of talking with such notable musicians as Igor Stravinsky and Paul Hindemith. In 1925, Klee organized a one-man show at the Galérie Vavin-Raspail in Paris and took part in the first Surrealist exhibition at Paris' Galérie Pierre. By 1929, he achieved international acclaim, and his fiftieth birthday was marked by a one-man show at the Flechtheim Gallery in Berlin. In 1930, this show was exhibited in New York's Museum of Modern Art.

On April 1, 1931, Klee left the Bauhaus to take a professorship at the Düsseldorf Art Academy, a position that he held for two years. When the Nazis came to power, he was dismissed from the academy, and, shortly before Christmas, 1933, he and his wife left Germany for good and returned to Bern. In 1935, the Bern Kunsthalle held a large Klee retrospective.

From 1933 to 1937, Klee's creative activity diminished, and in 1935 he began to suffer from the incurable illness scleroderma. In 1937, more than one hundred of his works were confiscated from German museums by the Nazis, and seventeen pieces were included in Hitler's Degenerate Art Exhibition. Yet, despite increasingly failing health, Klee's productivity suddenly exploded in an intense outpouring of drawings and paintings. In 1937, Pablo Picasso, Georges Braque, and Kandinsky all visited him in Bern.

During his last three years, Klee worked in unorthodox media and larger formats. Many pieces of 1939-1940 are full of presentiments of his own death. Painted only months before his death, *Death and Fire* (1940) consists of an ashen death mask being ferried toward the sunset on its final trip to the next world. The simple black lines form letters from his own name. Thus, Klee, with courageous humor, confronted his own death in a touching requiem. He continued to create until six weeks before his death.

On January 7, 1940, Klee submitted an application to Bern city officials for Swiss citizenship, but it was never granted. In February, a large Klee exhibition was held at the Zurich Kunsthaus. On May 10 he entered the sanatorium, where he died on June 29. Soon after his death, large retrospectives of his work were held in Bern, New York, Basel, and Zurich.

Summary

Paul Klee's importance as an artist lies in his ability to transcend the abstract elements of pictorial composition in order to achieve a parallel with creation. The creative process itself, not the finished forms of nature, was his point of departure. He sought to transform and not merely to imitate nature in his attempt to make visible the essence that lies behind visible things.

Klee's art possesses a wide range of allusions to music, poetry, and Eastern philosophy. His travels to North Africa help to explain similarities in his art to that of the Islamic world in the interweaving of figures, animals, and plants, and the ambiguity of figure-ground relationships. Although Klee believed in a clear separation of the arts, his work has many points of contact with music. He always began a piece with a small pictorial motif, which was then developed as a composer develops a musical theme. There are works that have a distinguishable polyphonic character, such as *Ad Parnassum* (1932), a major piece done in the pointillist technique. Its color harmonies develop from superimposed planes, one of colored dots, the other of squares. Each plane further consists of two layers, the first in white, the second a glaze of color. Visual tension is conveyed from the contrast between the elaborate surface of shimmering color and the insistent lines that suggest images that can be read several ways: mountain, pyramid, gateway, heavenly body, dynamic crescendo. The title refers to Mount Parnassus, home of Apollo and ideal of art. It may also recall the title of a baroque treatise on musical counterpoint. The painting can even be viewed as a highly varied intricate polyphony of voices.

It is difficult to trace Klee's stylistic development even after 1914, since he continually reexamined themes in his attempt to come to grips with the creative process. His methods of creation enabled him to invent images in painting of an unprecedented originality. He was a poet, and the associational titles he gave to his pictures show a highly inventive use of language. Finally, it is difficult to select masterpieces from Klee's body of work, since almost everything he made is of the same high quality.

Bibliography

Bauschatz, Paul. "Paul Klee's Anna Wenne and the Work of Art." *Art History* 19, no. 1 (March, 1996). Analysis of two of Klee's paintings, "Schaufenster fur Damenunterkleidung" and "Ein zentrifugales Gedenkblatt," both of which include the name Anna Wenne. Discusses the use of the verbal in art.

Fineberg, Jonathan. *The Innocent Eye*. Princeton, N.J.: Princeton University Press, 1997. Fineberg considers the cliché that modern art resembles the art of a child and explores the importance of child art held in collections of modernist masters such as Klee and Picasso.

Grohmann, Will. *Paul Klee*. New York: Abrams, and London: Humphries, 1954. Monumental biographical volume on Klee by an author who knew him personally for twenty years. Contains a wealth of material on the artist's personality and much instructive information on his art and career, including pertinent references to Klee's writings. Includes color and black-and-white reproductions.

Klee, Paul. *The Diaries of Paul Klee 1898-1918*. Translated by R. Y. Zachary and Max Knight. Berkeley: University of California Press, 1964; London: Owen, 1965. Intimate, all-encompassing autobiographical picture of Klee's many sided interests, including his views on painting, sculpture, drawing, poetry, architecture, theater, dealings with others, and, above all, music. Includes black-and-white reproductions of drawings and photographs.

————. *Paul Klee*. Edited by Carolyn Lanchner. New York: Museum of Modern Art, 1987. Comprehensive catalog of the extensive Klee retrospective held at the Museum of Modern Art in the spring of 1987. Contents include four essays with new material on various aspects of the artist's career, influences, and historical significance. Includes excellent color plates and bibliography.

————. *Paul Klee: His Life and Work in Documents*. Translated by Richard Winston and Clara Winston. New York: Braziller, 1962. This authoritative, varied volume supplements the diaries with Klee's posthumous writings and unpublished letters to and from the artist. Includes black-and-white illustrations and photographs.

—————. *Pedagogical Sketchbook*. Translated with an introduction by Sibyl Moholy-Nagy. New York: Praeger, 1953; London: Faber, 1959. This major document of twentieth century art theory is a simple introduction to the nature of Klee's inductive vision. Many large illustrations accompany brief statements about the nature of line, dimension, curve, and energy.

—————. *The Thinking Eye: The Notebooks of Paul Klee*. Edited by Jürg Spiller. Translated by Ralph Manheim. Vol. 1. New York: Wittenborn, 1961; London: Humphries, 1964. Includes Klee's early lecture notes from the Bauhaus as well as such seminal theoretical documents as *The Creative Credo*, "Wege des Naturstudiums" (1923: "Ways of Nature Study," 1961), and the Jena lecture *Über die moderne Kunst* (1924; *On Modern Art*, 1947). Contains extensive color and black-and-white reproductions, and diagrams.

—————. *The Nature of Nature: The Notebooks of Paul Klee*. Edited by Jürg Spiller. Translated by Heinz Norden. Vol. 2. New York: Wittenborn, 1970. This is a continuation of the artist's meticulous Bauhaus lectures on design, color, and form. Contains extensive color and black-and-white reproductions, and diagrams. Includes a very comprehensive bibliography on Klee.

John A. Calabrese

HELMUT KOHL

Born: April 3, 1930; Ludwigshafen am Rhein, Germany

Areas of Achievement: Government and politics

Contribution: Kohl strengthened Germany's international position during the late twentieth century, and, in 1990, he aggressively pursued German reunification.

Early Life

Helmut Michael Kohl, the son of a German civil servant, was born in Ludwigshafen am Rhein. Kohl was only three years old when the Nazis assumed power; therefore, his early years were heavily influenced by Adolf Hitler's regime. After experiencing the trauma of World War II, Kohl, like many of his European political counterparts, became a leading proponent of European unity.

In 1958, Kohl earned a doctorate in politics from Heidelberg University and began a career with a business association. However, his political activity started in 1947, when he became a leader in the youth political organization of the newly formed Christian Democratic Union (CDU). The CDU, West Germany's conservative political party, was then under the leadership of Konrad Adenauer, the former mayor of Cologne who would later preside over West Germany's postwar economic "miracle." By the end of the 1950's, Kohl was ready to assume a more active role in West German politics.

Life's Work

In 1959, Kohl was elected a member of the state assembly of the province of Rhine-Palatinate. In this role, he was able to continue to build a network of friends and supporters within the CDU. In 1966, he was elected the Rhine-Palatinate state chair of the CDU. A major career advancement came three years later when Kohl was elected minister-president of his province. The minister-president, the chief executive officer of the state government, also has important responsibilities in the German national government. In this office, Kohl not only presided over the affairs of his province but was also given a seat in the upper house (Bundesrat) of the West German parliament. Although Kohl was reelected minister-president in 1975, he resigned his office in order to become the leader of the opposition in the lower house (Bundestag) of parliament.

As leader of the opposition, Kohl led the Christian Democrats in the 1976 election against

Chancellor Helmut Schmidt. Schmidt, the leader of the Social Democratic party, was heir to the legacy of former Chancellor Willy Brandt, who ushered in a fundamental change in West German foreign policy. In 1969, Brandt's policy, dubbed "Ostpolitik," focused on changing Germany's position in Eastern Europe. From Ostpolitik came a more friendly relationship among West Germany, Poland, and East Germany. After Germany's division following World War II, it became difficult for families split between East and West Germany to maintain contact. Brandt's policy increased the contact between the two Germanys. Nevertheless, Kohl nearly defeated the Social Democrats, and Chancellor Schmidt's political position was greatly weakened. Although the CDU lost the election, Kohl remained the party leader. During his tenure as party head, the CDU gained political strength.

In 1982, Chancellor Schmidt's Social Democrats formed a coalition government with the much smaller Free Democratic Party. The Free Democrats, although a small political party, were necessary for Schmidt to remain as chancellor. In 1982, the Free Democrats deserted Schmidt's government and voted to make Kohl the West German chancellor. In 1983, West German voters approved the parliament's decision as the CDU and the Free Democrats won a majority in the legislative body.

Kohl pursued conservative policies, including closer military ties with the United States. He supported the deployment of U.S. nuclear missiles on West German soil, a decision that was controversial in Germany and Europe and that helped spawn an antinuclear movement in Western Europe and a "nuclear freeze" movement in the United States. Domestically, Kohl faced strikes in key German industries, such as engineering and metal, during 1984. Although Kohl's first term as chancellor was difficult, he was reelected in 1987. Still, the CDU-Free Democrat coalition lost seats in the parliament.

Mikhail Gorbachev's reforms in the Soviet Union changed the political conditions in Eastern Europe, including East Germany. The East German government, an old-style communist regime, resisted the changes emanating from Moscow. Eventually, the pressure for change forced the resignation of the hard-line East German leadership and paved the way for German reunification.

Since a united Germany threatened to alter the European balance of power, Kohl had to overcome stiff European opposition. The four powers with responsibilities in West Berlin (France, Great Britain, the Soviet Union, and the United States) were involved in the discussions about how German reunification would occur. Among the issues discussed were the presence of North Atlantic Treaty Organization (NATO) forces in West Germany and Soviet troops in East Germany, the question of the 1945 borders, and financial considerations.

German reunification took place in October, 1990, and in December, 1990, East and West Germans voted in the first all-German election since 1933. The elections produced a victory for Kohl's CDU and provided his government with the political strength to implement reforms in eastern Germany. The most pressing issue confronting Kohl was the disparity in income and living standards in the two Germanys. Moreover, Kohl's cabinet was responsible for changing the East German socialist economy into a free market system. This task proved to be extremely difficult, and Germany continued to struggle with integrating its eastern sec-

tion with the more affluent western sections. As a result of the free market reforms, unemployment increased in eastern Germany, and the German economy entered a period of slow growth. Without Kohl's strong victory in 1990, it would have been difficult for a German chancellor to pursue an aggressive policy.

In addition to economic troubles, Kohl, as the first chancellor of the reunited Germany, faced problems with the rise of extremist political groups and immigration. The right-wing Republican Party of Germany made a strong showing in the Berlin city elections. Moreover, Kohl's government was forced to deal with right-wing violence in German cities. As economic conditions in reunited Germany worsened, violence against foreign workers intensified.

Reunification also influenced Germany's treatment of Germans living in Eastern Europe and the former Soviet Union. Germans had settled in Russia during the reign of Catherine the Great, and they remained a part of Russia's ethnic background into the twentieth century. Having suffered persecution from the Soviet government, these Russian-Germans were eager to leave for Germany. Millions of them did leave, and the German government offered substantial financial help to integrate them into German society. Complicating the issue has been the continuing immigration of Germans from Poland and Rumania. Given the austere conditions of postreunification Germany, many Germans have looked with disdain at the government's policy this question.

Indeed, Kohl tried to negotiate an agreement with Russian president Boris Yeltsin regarding the establishment of a special geographical area in Russia for Russians of German descent. There have been many difficulties in securing such an agreement, but the German government has provided funds for the support of German culture and schools in the Russian Republic. In September of 1998, German voters rejected Kohl after sixteen years as chancellor. He was defeated in the elections by Gerhard Schröder, a Social Democrat who signaled the beginning of a new era in a Europe now dominated by center-left politics.

Summary

Helmut Kohl became the first chancellor of the post-World War II reunited Germany. Perhaps of equal importance was his long tenure in office: He served as chancellor for a period of time longer than the entire history of the post-World War I Weimar Republic. In foreign affairs, Kohl worked hard at creating European unity. He renounced any German territorial claims in Poland, and his government developed a close relationship with the Polish government. This connection with Poland was a new direction for German foreign policy. Germany and Poland have historically had very troubled relations. In this respect, Kohl performed a role similar to West Germany's first chancellor, Konrad Adenauer. Under Adenauer's leadership, Germany and France became close partners in European integration. Following Germany's reunification in 1990, France, Germany, and Poland began the process of forming a new partnership in European affairs. These changes, partially coming under Kohl's chancellorship, transformed the contours of European politics.

Kohl also supported a common European currency, the formation of closer military ties between France and Germany, and a more active role for Germany in world politics. Although Kohl reduced the size of the German military, this action was made possible by the enhanced security that Germany and Europe achieved under his chancellorship.

Bibliography

Adenauer, Konrad. *Memoirs 1945-1953*. Translated by Beate Ruhn von Oppen. London: Weidenfeld and Nicolson, and Chicago: Regnery, 1962. This work contains the views of West Germany's first chancellor concerning Germany's defeat during World War II and the creation of the West German state. As such, it provides important background information on German politics.

Braunthal, Gerard. *The West German Social Democrats Since 1969*. 2d ed. Boulder, Colo.: Westview Press, 1994. This book provides crucial information about the appointment of Willy Brandt as chancellor, the policy of Ostpolitik, the chancellorship of Helmut Schmidt, and the events leading to Kohl's appointment as chancellor.

Dragnich, Alex N., and Jurgen S. Rasmussen. *Major European Governments*. 9th ed. Belmont, Calif.: Wadsworth, 1994. This volume provides excellent coverage of the powers of the chancellor, historical background, and German political parties, and also provides information on Kohl.

Griffith, William E. *The Ostpolitik of the Federal Republic of Germany*. Cambridge, Mass.: MIT Press, 1978. An excellent synoptic overview of the German policy of Ostpolitik. The work uses a historical approach to studying this question.

Livingston, Robert Gerald. "Life after Kohl? We'll Always Have Germany." *Foreign Affairs* 76, no. 6 (November-December, 1997). Considers Kohl's prospects for the future and his capabilities with respect to handling Germany's problems.

Nyrop, Richard F., ed. *The Federal Republic of Germany: A Country Study*. 2d ed. Washington, D.C.: American University Press, 1982. This volume contains information regarding the political and social systems of the former West Germany.

Omestad, Thomas. "Is Helmut Kohl Kaput? Many Germans No Longer Feel Grateful for Reunification." *U.S. News and World Report* 125, no. 10 (September 14, 1998). Examines Kohl's chances for re-election in 1998 Germany in the face of unemployment and falling popularity.

Wilson, James Q., and John J. DiIulio. *American Government*. 6th ed. Lexington, Mass.: Heath, 1995. This volume provides an excellent comparison of different procedures and powers available to the U.S. president and European leaders, including the German chancellor.

Michael E. Meagher

OSKAR KOKOSCHKA

Born: March 1, 1886; Pöchlarn, Austro-Hungarian
  Empire
Died: February 22, 1980; Villeneuve, Switzerland
Area of Achievement: Art
Contribution: Although he was reluctant to be
  identified with any art movement, Kokoschka is
  generally considered one of Europe's finest expressionist painters. Excelling at psychologically
  oriented portraiture, he also produced striking allegorical compositions, lithographs, landscapes,
  posters, and half a dozen plays.

Early Life

Oskar Kokoschka was born in the Austrian village
of Pöchlarn on the Danube River, thirty miles west
of Vienna. The Kokoschkas moved to Vienna
when Oskar was four, subsisting marginally on the
feckless father's poor wages as a clerk. From an
early age, Oskar considered himself the virtual
head of the family, generously providing for his
parents, sister, and younger brother once his paintings sold. At school, bored by his courses, he read
unassigned classics under his desk. In 1904, he received a scholarship to the School of Arts and
Crafts, whose faculty was dominated by members
of the "Secession" group, which sought to vitalize
Vienna's formalist art. One of his teachers, Carl
Czeschka, encouraged Oskar to plan a career as an
artist, not merely as an art instructor. Although
Kokoschka received no formal training in painting, he began doing oils and lithographs in 1907
that were immediately notable for their wild fantasy, violent rocking effects, undulating lines, and
glowing colors.

In 1908, Kokoschka had a number of entries accepted at the annual *Kunstschau,* a widely reviewed, municipally sponsored exhibition. His illustrated book, *Die traeumenden Knaben* (the
dreaming youths), published in 1917, shocked
most of the conservative critics, who quickly labeled him an *enfant terrible.* Kokoschka's work attracted the fascinated admiration of the architect
Adolph Loos, who became his lifelong friend, patron, adviser, and agent. Loos bought at the exhibition a polychrome head in clay, the first of what
were to be frequent Kokoschka self-portraits. Loos
welcomed Kokoschka's individualistic rejection of
romantic ornamentalism, considering Kokoschka's art, like his own architecture, a rebellion
against sham and hypocrisy.

In 1909, Kokoschka again sent a group of works
to the *Kunstschau,* but this time critics concentrated
their attack, not on his paintings, but on his single-
scene, expressionist play: *Mörder Hoffnung der
Frauen* (murder hope of women). In it, a man,
threatened by an assaultive woman's sexual desire,
renews the strength she has sapped from him by
killing her. A riot erupted among the first-nighters;
Kokoschka's school immediately dismissed him.

Life's Work

Kokoschka's boldly provocative art and whimsical personality won for him, by his early twenties,
the friendship of some of Vienna's leading avant-
garde luminaries, including not only Loos but
also the poet Peter Altenberg and the scorchingly
satirical journalist Karl Kraus. They formed a witty, sophisticated circle in which Kokoschka felt
proud to be included. Loos commissioned him to
paint portraits of Kraus and Altenberg. Impressed
by his talent, Loos made this arrangement with
Kokoschka: Loos would search out people prepared to sit for the gifted young artist. Should the
subject then decide to refuse the result, Loos obligated himself to buy the painting. Loos's generosity was put to a quick test when, in the autumn of
1909, Kokoschka drew the great Swiss zoologist
Auguste Forel. The scientist rejected his portrait,
complaining that it made him appear as though he
had suffered a stroke. Two years later, Forel had a
stroke. Loos was convinced Kokoschka possessed
prophetic vision.

In 1910, Kokoschka, always restless, moved to
Berlin. Where Vienna was ancient, leisurely,
beautiful, and accustomed to being the center of
an empire, Berlin was comparatively young,
brash, ugly, and dynamic. Kokoschka found its
modernity stimulating, particularly contact with
such expressionist artists as Emil Nolde, Ernst
Ludwig Kirchner, Erich Heckel, and Max Pech-
stein. These and other painters and sculptors proclaimed the direct rendering (hence, "expression") of emotions as the primary purpose of art,
subordinating to that goal all considerations of
line, form, and balance. They were willing to dis-
tort representational design in order to convey
sensations forcibly. Kokoschka found himself
clearly identified with the expressionist movement by his use of agitated lines, sonorous colors,
and heavily psychological themes.

Kokoschka was fortunate enough to attract two enthusiastic patrons in Berlin: Paul Cassirer and Herwarth Walden. Cassirer, wealthy and well connected, owned a highly successful gallery. In 1910, he showed twenty-seven of Kokoschka's oils, then acted as his publicist for several years. Walden founded an influential weekly magazine of the arts, *Der Sturm* (the storm). Kokoschka became its deputy editor and contributed at least one drawing to every issue. Kokoschka did a superb portrait of Walden, stressing the contrast between his generally academic, gaunt appearance and thick, sensual mouth in a spidery, scratchy sketch.

In 1911, Kokoschka returned to Vienna for an exhibition featuring twenty-five of his paintings. To his disappointment, the reviewers' response was even more hostile than it had been in 1909; one writer excoriated his work as putrescent, calcified, and depraved. Hurt and humiliated, Kokoschka developed considerable paranoia toward a city which seemed to insist on rejecting the most talented Austrian painter of his generation.

By 1912, Kokoschka was twenty-six, tall, blond, thin, and taciturn, his eyes a remarkably deep blue, and confident that, despite Viennese derogation, he had already attained a significant place in contemporary art. He had had no serious romantic involvement. On April 14, 1912, however, he met and instantly fell in love with perhaps Vienna's most celebrated woman: Alma Mahler, then thirty-three. Herself a painter's daughter, Alma had wide knowledge of the arts and was erotically drawn to men of talent. She had married the great composer-conductor Gustav Mahler in 1902, even though he was twenty years her elder. She became an ambitious hostess, met many men, and had many affairs. One was with the German architect Walter Gropius, whom she had pursued assiduously; another was with a famed biologist. Her stepfather asked Kokoschka to paint her portrait. According to her (often unreliable) memoirs, he was so overcome by her magnetism at the first sitting that he rushed out of the studio, wrote a passionate declaration of love, and sent it to her within the hour.

They made a curious couple: Alma was a grande dame, socially expert and poised; Kokoschka was a fledgling, shy and insecure; not surprisingly, she dominated their turbulent romance. Whereas Kokoschka surrendered wholly to the pains and pleasures of Eros, Alma, while attracted to his raw energy, often held her feelings and person in check and regularly left Vienna without him, presumably for trysts with other lovers. For more than three years she drove him to distraction. Their liaison inspired some of Kokoschka's best work. He painted her in diverse madonna or whore guises, himself as a suffering Christ. In what may be his greatest picture and is certainly his most ambitious, *Die Windsbraut* (the tempest), the clearly identifiable lovers lie in a boat resembling a gigantic seashell, shrouded in the swirling mists of another world, their bark floating above a moonlit, mountainous landscape, their love perhaps too powerful to remain earthbound. The dominant color is, however, a subdued, cold blue-green.

The June, 1914, assassination of the Austrian Archduke Francis Ferdinand ignited World War I by late August. Kokoschka decided on a grand gesture: In early 1915, he sold *Die Windsbraut* for enough money to buy a mare and joined a cavalry regiment usually receptive only to the sons of nobility or wealth. On the eve of his enlistment, he painted a superb self-portrait, *Der irrende Ritter* (the knight errant), with himself as a wounded warrior, clad in full armor, on the verge of death, prostrate in an attitude of surrender to stormy elements. Attending him are what may be an angel of death and also a half-bestial woman resembling Alma. The portrait proved, like many of his portraits, premonitory.

As soon as Kokoschka had enlisted, Alma revived her affair with Gropius. She and Kokoschka corresponded through early July, 1915; nevertheless, she married Gropius on August 18 and bore him a daughter by October. Meanwhile, Kokoschka's regiment saw hard combat on the Eastern Front. On August 29, he was shot in the head, then bayonetted in the chest by a Russian soldier, barely escaping death. The head injury, damaging his inner ear, affected Kokoschka's sense of balance for the rest of his life. Volunteering for frontal duty again in 1916, he was seriously shell-shocked in Italy. Deeply scarred both emotionally and physically, Kokoschka decided in 1918 to accept an art professorship in Dresden, Germany.

Mentally confused and vulnerable, he retreated into a world of imagery and fantasy. He had a life-size doll made in Alma's image, then made drawings of it and carried it into restaurants and theaters with him. At a party given in the doll's honor, a guest decapitated it. Next morning the police came, investigating the report of a headless corpse in Kokoschka's garden. Gradually Kokoschka recovered his emotional balance, helped by the challenge of

his teaching duties at Dresden's Academy of Art. His painting became less adventurous and intense as he turned his attention increasingly to undisturbing cityscapes. As his work lost wildness, it gained in popularity: He had well-received exhibitions throughout the 1920's, particularly at Venice in 1921 and Zurich in 1927.

When the academy wanted to name him its rector, Kokoschka flinched from such an administrative burden and reasserted his nomadic urges. From 1924 to 1934, while usually maintaining an apartment in Paris, he roamed most of Europe, North Africa, and the Near East. Some critics dubbed him "the Cook's Tour painter." The landscapes that he produced during this period tended to avoid difficult aesthetic problems while concentrating on picturesque motifs.

After the Nazi Party came to power in Germany in January, 1933, anti-Semitic campaigns were immediately organized. One early consequence was the expulsion of Max Liebermann from the presidency of the Prussian Academy of Arts, which he had held for twelve years. Within days, in May,

1933, Kokoschka, himself Catholic, wrote a warm letter in Liebermann's behalf. When Kokoschka's mother died in 1934, he moved to Prague, whose political atmosphere he preferred to that of either Germany or Austria. There he painted what became his most famous portrait: an allegorical depiction of Czechoslovakia's head of state Tomáš Masaryk. On Masaryk's left stands the philosopher Comenius, pointing to a chart illustrating the five senses.

In Germany the propaganda against modernism in the arts reached its apex with a 1937 exhibition of "degenerate art" in Munich. Nine of Kokoschka's portraits were shown. He responded by painting himself in an oil that he entitled *Self-portrait of a Degenerate Artist.*

In 1935, Kokoschka met the woman who was to become his only wife. Olda Palkovska, daughter of a Prague art connoisseur, was much younger than he but unusually mature, courageous, imaginative, and practical. She ideally complemented his impulsive, eccentric nature. It was Olda who insisted that, with Germany threatening Czechoslovakia's independence, they flee to England in October, 1938.

Although his reputation on the European continent was by now immense, Kokoschka found himself still unheralded in England; London art circles tended to lag behind in recognizing advanced styles. During World War II, he produced a number of patriotic, politically symbolic paintings, such as the 1941 *Red Egg* and the 1943 *What We Are Fighting For.* Critics generally dismiss these works as conventional and uninspired. In 1947, he became a British subject, repudiating his right to Austrian citizenship.

Kokoschka's innovative, indeed revolutionary, years as an artist were now far behind him. He painted portraits and landscapes for another generation of his long life but broke no new ground. He did, however, extend his subject matter to classical mythology and designed the sets for several operatic productions, including a celebrated 1955 Salzburg staging of Wolfgang Amadeus Mozart's *The Magic Flute.* By all counts his proudest post-World War II achievement was the establishment of an art academy in Salzburg, Die Schule des Sehens (the school of seeing), in which he taught summer classes from 1952 to 1962. From 1953 onward, he and Olda resided in the village of Villeneuve, near Montreux, Switzerland. After his death, Austria, which had so often belittled his talents, established an Oskar Kokoschka Prize for outstanding achievement in the visual arts.

Summary

Oskar Kokoschka is indisputably Austria's foremost modern painter; whether his achievement is distinguished enough to rank him with such world masters as Pablo Picasso, Henri Matisse, Joan Miró, Georges Braque, and Willem de Kooning is, however, highly dubious. His outstanding success lies in his frequently profound exposition of the inner life of his subjects. In his often brilliantly perceptive portraits, particularly those he did before World War I, he realized the vital roles of dreams and fantasies in releasing the loneliness, broken hearts, and other sorrows that often afflicted his personages.

Bibliography

Hodin, John Paul. *Oskar Kokoschka: The Artist and His Time*. London: Cory Adams, and Greenwich, Conn.: New York Graphic Society, 1966. A distinguished art historian and critic, Hodin was a close friend of Kokoschka who worked intermittently on this text for twenty years. He considers his subject a profound artist and sage; nowhere does he note any of Kokoschka's limitations.

Hoffman, Edith. *Kokoschka: Life and Work*. London: Faber, 1947. Herself a Central European refugee residing in London, Hoffman has written a perceptive study of Kokoschka's art. Her biographical material is, unfortunately, sometimes curtailed: Kokoschka insisted that she not describe his three-year liaison with Alma Mahler or his involvement with several other women.

Kokoschka, Olda, and Alfred Marnau, eds. *Oskar Kokoschka: Letters 1905-1976*. London and New York: Thames and Hudson, 1992. This volume includes letters covering subjects such as Kokoschka's education, his love affairs as a young man, and his World War II military service. Includes notes, biographical sketches of those to whom he wrote, and a chronology of his life.

Kokoschka, Oskar. *My Life*. Translated by David Britt. London: Thames and Hudson, and New York: Macmillan, 1974. The artist was eighty-five when he dictated these reminiscences of his life. While he occasionally confuses his fantasies with factual evidence, Kokoschka is unfailingly interesting as he evokes, through many anecdotes, his richly eventful career.

Selz, Peter. *German Expressionist Painting*. Berkeley: University of California Press, 1957; London: University of California Press, 1974. Selz's text is the most authoritative account in English of the expressionist movement, which branched off into such schools as the Bridge, Blue Rider, and Vienna Secession. While Selz devotes only about fifteen pages to Kokoschka, his analysis of his development is trenchant.

Whitford, Frank. *Oskar Kokoschka: A Life*. London: Weidenfeld and Nicolson, and New York: Atheneum, 1986. A British lecturer in the history of art, Whitford writes smoothly and gracefully. He focuses on Kokoschka's biography, covering essentially the same ground that *My Life* did, and undertakes surprisingly little interpretation of the painter's work.

Gerhard Brand

KÄTHE KOLLWITZ

Born: July 8, 1867; Königsberg, East Prussia
Died: April 22, 1945; Moritzburg, Germany
Area of Achievement: Art
Contribution: Kollwitz was one of the most talented and renowned graphic artists of the early twentieth century. While her art was clearly social and political in meaning, her mastery of light and form resulted in a purely aesthetic statement that has seldom been equaled in the graphic arts.

Early Life

Born in Königsberg, East Prussia, Käthe Schmidt Kollwitz was the fifth child of well-educated parents. Her mother, Katherina, was the daughter of Julius Rupp, a nonconformist Lutheran minister who left the state church to found the first Free Congregational Church in Germany, a group that emphasized rationalism and ethics. Kollwitz's father, Karl Schmidt, was a lawyer, a follower of Karl Marx, and an activist in the Social Democratic Workers' Party who, finding his socialist beliefs in conflict with the militaristic regime of Otto von Bismarck, gave up the practice of law to become a master mason and a successful builder. Kollwitz's later reminiscences of her childhood recall the warmth, the social and moral idealism, and the mutual respect for the rights and freedom of others that characterized her family's thinking and that strongly influenced her own development.

Karl Schmidt was an enlightened father who encouraged his daughters to develop their individual talents, looking beyond the traditional female roles of wife and mother. An avid reader, the young Käthe was drawn especially to the works of Émile Zola, Henrik Ibsen, Leo Tolstoy, Fyodor Dostoevski, Gerhart Hauptmann, and Johann Wolfgang von Goethe—naturalistic works which dealt with the social problems of contemporary society. Another author who contributed to her intellectual development was August Bebel, whose pioneering treatise on the social and economic emancipation of women, *Die Frau und der Sozialismus* (1879; *Woman Under Socialism*, 1904), argued that capitalism had enslaved women and only socialism could free them from their second-class status. This, combined with her father's influence, did much to shape Kollwitz's own socialist outlook on life as a woman and as an artist.

At an early age, Kollwitz also evidenced an interest in the visual arts and a talent for drawing. Her father, determined to develop this potential, provided her with the best training available. Since women were denied admission to the Königsberg Academy of Art, she studied privately with the engraver Rudolf Mauer and later with Émile Neide, a local painter of some renown. In 1885-1886, she studied with Karl Stauffer-Bern at the Art School for Women in Berlin, and then, in 1888-1889, she worked with Ludwig Herterich at the Women's School of Art of the Munich Academy. As her taste in the visual arts matured, it paralleled her taste in literature; she was primarily drawn to artists whose work reflected the problems of contemporary life—Rembrandt, Francisco de Goya, William Hogarth, and Honoré Daumier. She was also excited by Max Klinger's graphic series, particularly *Ein Leben* (1883; a life), which is an indictment of the moral hypocrisy of the double standard held against women.

Life's Work

In 1891, Käthe Schmidt married Karl Kollwitz of Berlin, despite the disapproval of her father and of her former colleagues at the Women's School of Art in Munich, who looked upon marriage as a betrayal of one's commitment to art. Kollwitz, however, never doubted her ability to combine her role as an artist with that of wife and mother and had wisely realized that she would have more freedom as a wife in Berlin than as an unmarried woman in her father's home in provincial Königsberg. She was fortunate that, throughout their long marriage, her husband shared her socialist beliefs, encouraged her independence, and was supportive of her work.

Her husband's medical practice in a Berlin working-class neighborhood gave Kollwitz an immediate and intense experience of the problems and hardships of the lower classes, and this experience began to interact with her art, which she now perceived as an effective instrument to help achieve the political changes that she believed would result in a better society with equality and justice for all. Disdaining the idea of art for art's sake, she proclaimed that her art had a social function, that she wanted to be effective in a time when people were so helpless and destitute, Throughout her career, she drew her subjects from the same sources that had inspired Rembrandt, Goya, and Daumier—the downtrodden, the poor, and the oppressed. She had, however, a greater awareness of the particular responsibilities, sorrows, and joys of women in the lower classes.

Early in her career, Kollwitz chose to work in the graphic media—prints and drawings—rather than painting. She was undoubtedly influenced by Klinger, whose depictions of workers victimized by social forces beyond their control illustrated his belief, as stated in a treatise written in 1885, that graphic artists tend to criticize while painters idealize the world. He emphasized that beauty, optimism, and glorification of the world relate to painting but that the graphic arts express all the resignation, weakness, nonfulfillment, and misery of poor creatures struggling between will and ability. Kollwitz realized that the graphic medium was best suited to the creation of an art with social content and would also allow her to reach a broader audience.

In 1897, Kollwitz completed the first of her many print cycles, *A Weavers' Revolt*, which was inspired by a play by Hauptmann about a workers' revolt in 1844. Her other notable graphic cycles include *The Peasant War* (1902-1908), *War* (1922-1923), *Proletariat* (1925), and *Death* (1934-1935), all of which express the moral and ethical issues so central to her work.

Kollwitz sometimes used the past to interpret the present, as in *A Weavers' Revolt* and *The Peasants' War*, which is thematically related to the sixteenth century exploitation of German peasants. A significant innovation in this latter cycle is her interpretation of woman as revolutionary. The romantic concept of woman as a muse or an allegorical figure inspiring revolution was traditional in Western art; in this series, however, Kollwitz depicted a flesh-and-blood woman actually leading the revolt.

In other instances, Kollwitz's art was more directly related to current events, as in *War* and *Proletariat*, which were generated by her son Peter's death in World War I and the subsequent unstable political conditions in Germany. She also expressed her strong socialist, and now pacifist, beliefs in other themes that appeared with variations in numerous prints, drawings, and sculptures—mothers and children, whom she frequently depicted as the helpless and abandoned victims of war.

Despite initial governmental opposition to her critical social content (Kaiser Wilhelm labeled it "gutter art"), Kollwitz gradually gained recognition for her work. She exhibited regularly at the Berlin Free Art Exhibition from 1893 until 1936, when her work was banned by the Nazis, and she won a gold medal in Dresden in 1899 for *A Weavers' Revolt*. In 1898, she was appointed to the faculty of the Berlin School for Women Artists and also joined the Berlin Secession. In 1907, she received the Villa Romana Prize, enabling her to study in Italy, and by 1909, her drawings were being published in the journal *Simplicissimus*. In 1919, she was the first woman elected to membership in the Prussian Academy of Arts and was director of graphic arts there from 1928 to 1933, resigning with the advent of the Nazi era. In 1926, she was one of the founders of the Society for Women Artists and Friends of Art, a group dedicated to bringing women's art before the public.

In 1904, Kollwitz made her first trip to Paris, studying sculpture at the Académie Julien and visiting August Rodin's studio in Meudon. When she took up sculpture in 1910, Rodin's influence was apparent. From 1914 to 1932, much of her creative effort was devoted to *Mourning Parents*, a sculpture originally conceived as a tombstone for her son, Peter, but finally executed as a public monument symbolizing all bereaved parents and commemorating all victims of war. Additionally, the many small bronzes that she created from 1933 to 1943 constitute some of her most powerful statements about the misery, suffering, and anguish brought on by war.

After 1933, Kollwitz was silenced by the Nazis, making the last years of her life difficult ones. Earlier, in the brief period of the Weimar Republic, Kollwitz had achieved a public recognition that enabled her to carry on a meaningful dialogue with her audience. Now, however, her work having been labeled "degenerate," she lost her studio and teaching position at the academy, and she was not allowed to exhibit or publish; thus her art was literally banned from public view, and she suffered an isolation that was more complete and restrictive than that of the Wilhelminian era. Nevertheless, she continued to work in her studio in Berlin until she was evacuated to Moritzburg in 1944. She had lost both her husband (1940) and her grandson Peter (killed in battle in 1942) as well as the home in Berlin that she had occupied all of her married life. She died on April 22, 1945, at age seventy-seven, only a few weeks before World War II ended in Europe.

Summary

If Käthe Kollwitz's themes were often controversial, her style and technique were not. She was never interested in the stylistic and technical innovations that occupied so many early twentieth century artists. That does not mean that her style was stagnant, with no growth or development. Her early works were in a naturalist style, using traditional spatial and compositional arrangements with careful attention to detail, although, even then, she avoided the merely descriptive and anecdotal. As her style matured, she grew increasingly aware of the expressive possibilities of reduced forms and simplified composition, and, as she sought greater simplicity in her work, she learned, as had Titian, Rembrandt, and Frans Hals, that "less is more." Therefore, the expressive power of her mature work comes not only from its emotional subject matter but also from light playing on its concentrated, monumental forms arranged in simple compositions.

Throughout her long career, Kollwitz created more than ninety self-portraits, and these certainly constitute one of her most lasting contributions to the world's art. Not since Rembrandt had an artist accomplished such an intimate self-revelation. These self-portraits chart her development as an artist and as a woman, revealing through line, form, and light her moods, her joys and sorrows, her doubts, and her convictions.

Bibliography

Herzog, Melanie. "Art as Expression: Käthe Kollwitz." *School Arts* 93, no. 6 (February, 1994). Profile of Kollwitz including her major works, her techniques, and her preferred media.

Kearns, Martha. *Käthe Kollwitz: Woman and Artist*. Old Westbury, N.Y.: Feminist Press, 1976. The first biography of Kollwitz written from a contemporary female perspective. Kearns's major resources were Kollwitz's own writings, such as her many letters and her diary, parts of which were printed here for the first time in English.

Klein, Mina C., and H. Arthur Klein. *Käthe Kollwitz: Life in Art*. New York: Holt Rinehart, 1972. Contains many excellent reproductions of Kollwitz's graphic works and sculpture. Intending the book for the general reader, the authors avoided a formal, art-historical analysis of Kollwitz's work. A very readable biography, with especially good coverage of the years after 1933.

Kollwitz, Käthe. *Kaethe Kollwitz*. Introduction by Carl Zigrosser. New York: Bittner, 1946. Contains reproductions of seventy of Kollwitz's works, including the complete cycles: *A Weavers' Revolt*, *Peasant War*, *War*, *Proletariat*, and *Death*. The accompanying monograph is informative but often patronizing.

————. *Prints and Drawings of Käthe Kollwitz*. Edited by Carl Zigrosser. New York: Dover, 1969. A revised and enlarged version of Zigrosser's 1951 publication. The quality of the reproductions was much improved and several important works were added. The text itself remained basically unchanged, however, with the author's bias of sex and class still apparent.

Nagel, Otto. *Käthe Kollwitz*. Translated by Stella Humphries. London: Studio Vista, and Greenwich, Conn.: New York Graphic Society, 1971. This book's most valuable feature is its extensive catalog of Kollwitz's works. The fact that Nagel was acquainted with Kollwitz from 1920 on leads one to expect a greater wealth of new information and a more perceptive analysis of her work than is actually the case.

Winkler, Mary G. "Walking to the Stars: Käthe Kollwitz and the Artist's Pilgrimage." *Generations* 14, no. 4 (Fall 1990). Presents Kollwitz's self-portraits as steps along the road to self-knowledge and spirituality.

LouAnn Faris Culley

SERGEI KOROLEV

Born: December 30, 1907; Nerzhin, Ukraine, Russian Empire
Died: January 14, 1966; Moscow, U.S.S.R.
Area of Achievement: Aeronautics
Contribution: Korolev, known as the "chief designer of rocket-cosmic systems" in the Soviet Union, was the father of the Soviet space program of the 1950's and 1960's. He designed the rocket boosters, the first unmanned Sputnik satellites, and the manned Vostok, Voskhod, and Soyuz spacecraft.

Early Life

Much of the information about Sergei Pavlovich Korolev is speculative and, in many cases, apocryphal. Korolev's name was not even released to Western authorities until years after his death in 1966. To all but those directly involved in the Soviet space program, he was known simply as the "chief designer of rocket-cosmic systems," the title given to him by Nikita Khrushchev, the first secretary of the Communist Party and the leader of the Soviet Union during the 1950's and early 1960's.

Korolev was born in the Ukrainian town of Nerzhin on December 30, 1907, to Pavel and Maria Korolev. Shortly after his birth the Korolevs moved to the Ukrainian city of Zhitomir. Unfortunately, the Korolevs' marriage soon failed, and Maria decided to take the young child to stay with her parents in Nerzhin while she returned to school in Kiev. It is believed that Korolev stayed with his grandparents (where his mother visited often) until the age of sixteen, when his mother married an engineer, Grigori M. Balanin. Balanin moved his new family to the city of Odessa on the Black Sea.

Korolev is known to have been an intelligent child with an intense interest in aeronautics and flight. While still a teenager in the Odessa First Construction School, where he studied roofing, Korolev built his first gliders and received his introduction to the principles of aeronautics. This interest led him to the prestigious Bauman Higher Technical School in Moscow in 1926. It was during this period that Korolev came in contact with some of the pioneers of Russian aeronautics and rocketry who would influence his own life's work. At the Bauman Technical School, Korolev met Andrei Tupolev, the famous Russian aircraft designer (for whom he would later work), and built his first

experimental rocket-powered glider, a forerunner to the jet-propelled aircraft. Later, at the age of twenty-five, Korolev met the father of modern astronautics, the Russian schoolteacher turned rocket theorist Konstantin Tsiolkovsky.

In 1931, Korolev joined with Frederick A. Tsander, also a pioneer in Soviet rocketry, to form the Moscow Group for the Study of Reactive Propulsion. This group, which later, after several incarnations, is believed to have become the Jet Scientific Research Institute, experimented with liquid-fueled rockets and jet aircraft through the mid-1930's. It was also during the mid-1930's that he married his first wife, Xenia Vincentini. In 1935, Korolev's daughter was born. Reputedly, Xenia denounced Korolev when he was later placed in prison. Upon gaining his freedom, Korolev divorced his first wife and married Nina Kotenkova in 1947.

Events in Korolev's life are sketchy from about 1937 until his reappearance as the chief designer of the Soviet space effort. It is known, however, that for at least a portion of this time, and possibly on two separate occasions, he was arrested during Joseph Stalin's purges of the country's intelligentsia and placed in a gulag, or Soviet prison. While in the gulag, where he suffered considerable torture and degradation, Korolev was put to work with Tupolev and other scientists designing and building Soviet aircraft for World War II.

Life's Work

Korolev's life's work was rocketry and the pursuit of the dream of spaceflight. It can be said that, even while researching, designing, and testing jet- and rocket-propelled aircraft, he pursued this goal through the many stages of his existence until finally achieving it with the launch of Sputnik 1 in 1957.

In 1946, while still in prison, as part of a special work group of scientists, Korolev was sent to Germany as part of a team to recover V-1 and V-2 rockets, as well as several of the former Nazi scientists and engineers who built them. These German scientists were brought back to the Soviet Union and pressed into service as part of the fledgling Soviet missile-research program. As in the United States in the late 1940's and early 1950's, Soviet advances in rocketry were made to develop unmanned

missiles that would be able to deliver nuclear weapons over great distances, what would later be called intercontinental ballistic missiles (ICBMs). Korolev (after his second arrest in 1947) quickly rose to a leadership position in this effort.

Korolev's increasing value to the Soviet military gained for him more freedom and respect as the Soviet missile program progressed. Once, during this period, he is even said to have conducted a personal briefing of Stalin himself on the missile efforts. In 1947, the Soviets, under Korolev's leadership, successfully launched their first ballistic missile. It was not until 1953, after Stalin's death, that Korolev was released from the gulag and offered full membership in the Communist Party. That same year, he was selected as a corresponding or associate member of the Soviet Academy of Sciences, the most elite and influential scientific body in the Soviet Union (in 1958, after Sputnik, he was elected to full membership in the academy; at the time only 150 or so scientists in the Soviet Union were so honored). It was also at this time that the new Soviet leadership, under the direction of

Khrushchev, officially endorsed and committed substantial funds to the development of Korolev's missiles.

In 1955, Korolev supervised the construction of what would later become the Baikonur Cosmodrome near the village of Tyuratam in the Soviet Republic of Kazakhstan. By early 1957, he had conducted the first unsuccessful tests of the R-7 rocket. (The Soviets and the United States use different designations for the same Soviet rockets. In the West, this was called the SS-6, or Sapwood rocket.) As part of the International Geophysical Year (a period running from 1957 through 1958 in which several nations committed to making significant scientific advances), the Soviet Union and the United States both announced intentions to place man-made satellites in orbit around Earth. Korolev, because of his work with the Soviet missile program, was given operational control of the fledgling space effort. Overall authority was under Field Marshall Mitrofan Nedelin, commander of the Soviet military Strategic Rocket Forces.

In 1956 and early 1957, Korolev's missile program is said to have experienced numerous launch failures similar to those that occurred in the United States at the same time. Because the Soviet Union was a closed society and this was a classified program, however, the Western world knew little of the progress of the Soviet effort. Finally, after announcing to the world the frequency at which its radio would transmit after launch, Sputnik 1 (which is the Russian word for "satellite") was placed into orbit on October 4, 1957. The 80-kilogram metal sphere contained a radio transmitter, four antennae, and simple electronic equipment, but its appearance shocked the world.

After Sputnik, when Khrushchev saw how deeply the event affected the Westerners, he personally assumed control over Korolev's program. The scientist could undertake no launch or research effort without first receiving the approval of the Soviet leader. Khrushchev's interest in space research, however, was dictated more by his desire for propaganda successes in the West than by an understanding of the value of space research. Because of this limitation, Korolev was not allowed to conduct the kind of redundant tests that usually occur in an experimental program. He was instead pressured to make new inroads with each launch, and his launches were timed to accommodate the Soviet leader's political agenda. This was especially evident with the launching of Sputnik 2, a larger satellite that contained the first living being placed in space, a dog named Laika. The Soviet program had not yet developed a reentry capability, so Laika died in orbit after a week in space.

Two of Korolev's goals in the early days of the Soviet space effort were to send a satellite to the moon and to launch a man into space and, again, eventually place him on the moon. This would fulfill one of the boldest predictions of his idol, Tsiolkovsky, about the potential for rocket travel beyond Earth. Again after several failed efforts, Korolev succeeded in the launching of Luna 2 in September, 1959. Luna 2 became the first man-made object to come into contact with another celestial body when it crashed into the moon at the Sea of Tranquillity. Luna 3, which followed soon after, orbited the moon and took the first pictures of that body's dark side, the side that is not visible to Earth.

The launch vehicles Korolev designed and built were far more powerful than their American counterparts because of the inability of Soviet industry to miniaturize the warheads for their ICBMs, hence the need to carry larger, heavier payloads. This heavier lift capability gave Korolev the hardware he would need to place a man into Earth orbit. Khrushchev, realizing the potential propaganda value of putting men into space, supported Korolev's effort enthusiastically. On March 14, 1960, the first group of twenty cosmonauts began training for the Vostok spaceflights.

Korolev actually held three jobs in the Soviet program. He was chief designer of rocket-cosmic systems, head of the teams that built the spacecraft and launch vehicles, and director of launch operations at the launch pad. He even had constructed near the launch facility a small cottage for his own use so that he could sleep near his rockets and work longer hours.

In October of 1960, Korolev narrowly escaped death after the worst disaster in the history of space exploration, the explosion of a rocket on the launch pad (several Western experts believe that the rocket carried an unmanned probe bound for Mars) that took the lives of dozens of Soviet space scientists and engineers. To meet Khrushchev's demand for continued propaganda success, Korolev began test-launching spacecraft called "Korbul-Sputniks." These vehicles were unmanned versions of the Vostok capsules that would carry men into Earth orbit. On April 12, 1961, Vostok 1, with Yuri A. Gagarin on board, circled Earth once and began the

movement of mankind into space. Korolev had achieved his dream.

The remaining five Vostok missions for which Korolev received approval were longer in duration but dictated in content by political considerations. Korolev, for example, was forced to launch a woman, a parachutist named Valentina Tereshkova, into space on Vostok 6, in order to be allowed to fly Vostoks 3 and 4 at the same time to conduct the first rendezvous attempts in orbit.

Further pressure came when the Americans announced Project Gemini, a two-man program to develop many of the techniques that would be necessary on lunar landing missions. In order to outdo the Americans, Khrushchev ordered Korolev to launch three men into space before Gemini could begin. Voskhod, an upgraded version of the Vostok capsule, was created and two missions were flown in 1964 and 1965. Voskhod 1 was manned by three cosmonauts. Voskhod 2, in reaction to the announced intention of the Americans to attempt an extravehicular activity, or space walk, featured a space walk by Alexei Leonov. Other planned Voskhod missions were canceled when Khrushchev was deposed and replaced by a new leadership in the Kremlin.

During the Voskhod period, Korolev was occupied with the development of the Soyuz spacecraft, the craft that would be the centerpiece of the Soviet lunar landing program. He was also concerned with the creation of a large launch vehicle called the "Proton." His efforts were cut short, however, by his untimely death at the age of fifty-eight on January 14, 1966, the result of improperly executed surgery in Moscow. His body was cremated and given a hero's burial in the Kremlin wall.

Summary

Few, if any, efforts are so identified with the twentieth century's technological revolution as is mankind's movement into space. Sergei Korolev was one of the first and most important pioneers in that effort. Although unknown to most of those he affected, he was, indeed, one of the most influential figures in the latter half of the twentieth century. The space age he helped create reshaped the mind and imagination of a generation and set his nation and the world on a new course in human history. Korolev's leadership in his country's space program, as well as the influence his success had on American space efforts, helped advance computer science, engineering, electronics, communications technology, and numerous other disciplines. In many ways, he was a spark that ignited a bonfire of discovery in his time.

He is said to have been a compelling figure to those with whom he worked. The space program certainly suffered with his loss. Two of the missions that followed shortly after his death ended in the deaths of four of his cosmonauts, and the moon landings he envisioned were canceled altogether after the American success of Apollo 11. The Soviet space program, while continuing to move steadily and well, has lacked the clear vision and purpose it once had under Korolev's leadership.

Bibliography

Clark, Phillip. *The Soviet Manned Space Program: An Illustrated History of the Men, the Missions, and the Spacecraft.* London: Salamander, and New York: Orion, 1988. Clark is one of the acknowledged Western experts on the Soviet space program, and this is one of the most comprehensive books on the subject.

Daniloff, Nicholas. *The Kremlin and the Cosmos.* New York: Knopf, 1972. This book, by a noted American journalist, gives an insightful look at the early days of the Soviet space program. For its time, it was a landmark effort and is still worthy of note. A seminal work.

Furniss, Tim. *Manned Spaceflight Log.* Rev. ed. London: Jane's, 1986. A concise, fact-filled listing of the primary mission objectives and results from all manned spaceflight up to Soyuz T-15, this book provides a broad overview of the progress made in space exploration. One of the best books for the beginning space enthusiast.

Golovanov, Yoroslav. *Sergei Korolev: The Apprenticeship of a Space Pioneer.* Translated by M. M. Samokhvalov and H. C. Creighton. Moscow: MIR, 1975. Written in the Soviet Union, this is a fanciful and not wholly accurate account of Korolev's life. It reads like a melodramatic novel and fails to address many important questions about key facets of Korolev's life and works.

McAleer, Neil. *The Omni Space Almanac: A Complete Guide to the Space Age.* New York: World Almanac, 1987. A compendium of information about the major developments of the space age, with emphasis on the later years and their import for the future.

Oberg, James. E. *Red Star in Orbit: The Inside Story of Soviet Failures and Triumphs in Space.* London: Harrap, and New York: Random House, 1981. Oberg is one of the West's leading experts on the Soviet space program. In this, his most famous book, he carefully details the development of the cosmonauts' march to space in an entertaining and informative format. A must for the beginning student.

———. *Uncovering Soviet Disasters: Exploring the Limits of Glasnost.* New York: Random House, 1988; London: Hale, 1989. Two chapters in this book are dedicated to examining the secretive nature of the Soviet space program and debunking the rumors that have sprung up in the West over supposed space tragedies. Again, Oberg opens the door to the layperson with concise, interesting descriptions and fast-paced storytelling.

Penkovskii, Oleg. *The Penkovskiy Papers.* Translated by Peter Deriabin. London: Collins, and New York: Doubleday, 1965. This work, reported to be the memoirs of one of the most important Western spies ever to operate in the Soviet Union, discusses many aspects of the Soviet system, including the earliest formulation of the missile and space programs.

Eric Christensen

LEE KRASNER

Born: October 27, 1908; New York, New York
Died: June 19, 1984; New York, New York
Area of Achievement: Art
Contribution: Lee Krasner was a leader in the abstract expressionist movement in the United States. She spoke out for women's rights and became an example of a woman who took her work seriously within a movement that was dominated by males.

Early Life

Lenore "Lena" Krassner was born in Brooklyn, New York, on October 27, 1908. She was the fourth of five children born to Russian parents who had immigrated to the United States. Lenore's parents were Orthodox Jews who owned and ran a produce store in Brooklyn.

As a girl, Lenore was drawn to the visual arts. From 1922 to 1925, she attended Washington Irving High School in Manhattan, the only secondary school that allowed females to study art. From 1926 to 1929, Lenore attended the Woman's Art School of the Cooper Union for the Advancement of Science and Art in New York. In 1929, Lenore enrolled at The National Academy of Design in New York, a traditional art school, where she studied life drawing, painting, and techniques of the Old Masters. It was also during this year that Lenore was first introduced to the more radical, experimental art of modern European artists such as Henri Matisse and Pablo Picasso. The work of both of these artists was to be highly influential in the development of Lenore's own art.

Because of the ensuing Depression economy, Lenore dropped out of art school in 1932 and began working as a waitress. She also attended City College of New York, working toward a high school teaching credential, but she soon realized that she had no interest in teaching. By this time, Lenore Krassner had become dedicated to living her life as an artist; although she had taken many years of traditional art training, she was becoming increasingly interested in more modern, experimental art.

Life's Work

Lee Krasner's career as a professional artist began in 1935, when she was hired by the WPA (Works Progress Administration) Federal Art Project.

Krasner was hired as part of the mural division of this government-subsidized project, which had as its goal the decoration of public spaces with large-scale realistic, socially conscious painting. Krasner worked for the WPA until 1943, making murals, posters, and displays for department store windows. During this period, Krasner began calling herself Lee and dropped an "s" from her last name.

Although Krasner's work for the WPA was primarily realistic, her personal style was becoming more abstract. In 1937, Krasner entered the Hans Hofmann School of Fine Arts in New York. Hans Hofmann was a German artist who immigrated to New York in 1932 and became an influential exponent of modern European art in the United States. He served as a link with major artists such as Picasso and Matisse, and he taught their ideas and techniques at his school. He emphasized the tenets of cubism, spatial tension, and all-over composition. Hofmann believed in painting subjects from nature but emphasizing energy, tension, form, and color rather than detail and scientific accuracy.

Lee Krasner had already become interested in Hoffman's ideas. At Hofmann's school, Krasner studied the cubist style and began creating in a more abstract style that emphasized form, color, line, and rhythm. She retained subject matter but presented it in a simplified, abstract, and geometric manner. Her focus became self-expression rather than the duplication of particular subjects.

By 1937, Krasner had read *System and Dialectics of Art* by the writer and artist John Graham, who was to become a major inspiration to the abstract expressionists. Graham promoted the idea that pure feeling could be represented on canvas through automatic, spontaneous movement of the brush. He emphasized psychological content, emotionality, and drama in painting. Graham's concepts appealed to Krasner, since she was already moving away from the more intellectual, analytical thought of Hans Hofmann. She was searching for a means of painting that would be more directly emotional, spiritual, and psychological in nature.

In 1940, Lee Krasner began to exhibit with the American Abstract Artists (AAA). She participated in the "First Annual Exhibition of the American Modern Artists," held at Riverside Museum in New York (1940), and the "Fifth Annual Exhibition of the American Abstract Artists," which was organized by the WPA and traveled throughout the

United States in 1941. At that time, Krasner was showing abstract paintings with thick black outlines, bright colors, and heavily impasted oil paint. Many of her paintings from this period were based on subjects from nature or still lifes, others were nonrepresentational (without recognizable subject matter).

John Graham invited Krasner to show her work in an important exhibition he organized in 1942, entitled "French and American Painting," in which the work of young modern American artists would be shown alongside that of famous modern French artists, including Matisse and the cubist painter Georges Braque. Jackson Pollock, who was to become one of the most famous modern American painters, was also invited to participate in the exhibition. It was at this time that Krasner and Pollock met. They were married in 1945 and purchased an old farmhouse in Springs, East Hampton, Long Island, where they both had studios.

Both Krasner and Pollock are identified as leaders in the first wave of the abstract expressionist movement, which was the first major modern art style to originate in the United States. Abstract expressionism is a nonrepresentational style in which line, form, and color are spontaneously arranged on a canvas or painting surface. Paint is brushed, swirled, dripped, or poured onto the surface in an automatic, gestural manner. The goal is to express one's inner spirit. Many of the abstract expressionists, including Krasner and Pollock, were influenced by the writings of Carl Jung, Eastern religions, and mystical religious traditions in general. The movement stressed the spontaneous expression of the self, emotion, and the spiritual, through color, line, form, and gesture.

Although Lee Krasner's career was less public than Pollock's, she has been recognized as one of the pioneers of the American abstract expressionist movement and as an artist who continually expanded and created innovative forms. While she was married to Pollock, Krasner was inspired by him, dedicated to him, and overshadowed by him. The public most often viewed her simply as Jackson Pollock's wife. The Krasner-Pollock relationship was, however, based on mutual support and encouragement. Krasner was influenced by Pollock, but he was also influenced by her, and much of Krasner's work presents ideas and techniques that are very different from Pollock's.

In 1946, Krasner made two mosaic tables that may have been the inspiration for a series of paintings she executed between 1946 and 1950, called the "Little Image" paintings. On a series of small-to medium-sized canvases, she brushed, scraped, and dripped oil paint into dense arrangements of small rhythmic images encompassing the entire canvas surface and resembling hieroglyphics or intricate webbings.

Cyclical change is one of the hallmarks of Krasner's career: She changed her subject matter, format, and technique every few years, but would often return to ideas that had interested her in the past. In the early 1950's, Krasner made large-scale paintings based on mysterious figural and floral forms. Her technique was automatic drawing done directly on canvas with oil paint. Large, graceful forms moved rhythmically across the canvas, as in her *Blue and Black* (1951-1953). Krasner worked regularly throughout the 1950's, but because the abstract expressionist movement was becoming increasingly male-dominated and because of her association with Pollock, she was not receiving much recognition from the galleries or the press.

Few paintings from Krasner's earlier periods survive. Some were destroyed by fire; others she destroyed herself or cut up to use in collages. During the 1950's, she began including bits of paper and parts of her old canvases in her new paintings. Continuing her interest in expressive, nonrepresentational paintings and nonillusionistic (without perspective) space, Krasner incorporated and overlapped abstract painted forms with frayed, torn, and cut areas of paper and old canvases. These collage paintings, which are among Krasner's most innovative works, were exhibited at Eleanor Ward's Stable Gallery in New York in 1955.

In July of 1956, Krasner took her first trip to Europe. It was there, in August, that she was informed that Pollock had been killed in a car accident. She returned to New York immediately. After Pollock's death, Krasner painted large canvases with brightly colored, intensely energetic abstract compositions based loosely on natural forms such as flowers, fruit, and the human body.

Krasner returned to the medium of mosaic again in 1959, when she executed two large mosaic murals for the exterior of the Uris Brothers office building in New York. In 1959, she also began her series of huge, powerful umber and off-white paintings, which she worked on until 1962. These paintings were shown in solo exhibitions at the Howard Wise Gallery in New York between 1960 and 1962.

After 1962, Krasner returned to a more vibrant color scheme that included brilliant greens, raspberry, yellows, and oranges. Her forms were essentially nonrepresentational, but their organic and flowing quality suggests birds, flowers, and plants boldly surging across the canvases in joyous, lyrical moods. In 1965, Krasner was given a retrospective exhibition at the Whitechapel Art Gallery in London, England, which included these works. In 1966, she joined the Marlborough Gallery in New York.

During the early 1970's, Krasner created several huge canvases in a more hard-edged style, composing crisp, spare geometric designs that seem to explode from the canvas, as in *Rising Green* (1972). Throughout the later 1970's, she made another series of collage paintings, this time incorporating cut-up sections of her old charcoal drawings and combining fragments of figural forms with forceful abstract painted forms. In these works, she deconstructed past ideas, reworked them, and brought them into a new realm and into new paintings with titles that play on the idea of time, such as *Past Conditional* (1976) and *Imperfect Indicative* (1976).

Although Krasner was still not taken as seriously as the male artists of the abstract expressionist movement, she began to receive much more attention by the 1970's. In 1974, she was awarded the Augustus St. Gaudens Medal by the Cooper Union Alumni Association and the Lowe Fellowship for Distinction from Barnard College. In 1976, she joined the prestigious Pace Gallery in New York, and in 1978 she was the only woman included in the major exhibition "Abstract Expressionism: The Formative Years," which was shown at the Herbert F. Johnson Museum of Art at Cornell University, the Whitney Museum of American Art in New York, and the Seibu Museum in Tokyo, Japan.

During the early 1980's, Lee Krasner continued to paint and exhibit. She joined the Robert Miller Gallery, New York, in 1981. In 1982, she was awarded the Chevalier de l'Ordre des Arts et des Lettres by the French Minister of Culture. She traveled to Houston, Texas, in 1983 for a major retrospective exhibition of her work which was given at the Museum of Fine Arts. Lee Krasner died in New York on June 19, 1984. She left funds and paintings to create a foundation for needy artists, and she asked that the house in Springs be given to a charitable institution. It was opened as the Pollock-Krasner House and Study Center in 1988.

Summary

Although Lee Krasner is recognized as one of the pioneers of the American abstract expressionist movement and is identified as a member of the first wave, or first generation, of that movement, she has never received as much attention or serious study as the male members of that movement have. Although women were involved in it, the abstract expressionist movement has most often been viewed as a male- oriented phenomenon. For this reason and because of her close association with Jackson Pollock, Krasner has been overshadowed by the male artists of the movement.

Krasner herself was aware of this situation and often spoke out for women's rights. She believed in equality for women and in women's right to express themselves. She took her own work extremely seriously. Although she was married to Pollock and admired his work, her art was experimental and innovative, and her artistic explorations were most often very different from those of Pollock. In 1972, she picketed the Museum of Modern Art in New York because it was not showing enough work by women artists. She received an honorary award from the Long Island Women Achievers in Business and the Professions in 1977, and in 1980 she was presented with the Outstanding Achievement in the Visual Arts Award by the Women's Caucus for Art.

Lee Krasner was a leader in the development of abstract, nonrepresentational, experimental art styles in the United States. She was one of the first artists in the country to explore the use of color, form, line, and gesture to express inner psychological, spiritual, and emotional realities. She was also one of the first artists in the United States to explore widely diverse painting techniques such as automatism, dripping, and collage. For these reasons, Krasner's importance in the history of modern American art cannot be overestimated. The ideas that Krasner brought forth in her art became some of the hallmarks of many modern artists in America in the twentieth century. In particular, her art, as well as the art of the other first wave abstract expressionists, was a direct and profound influence on the second wave of abstract expressionists, including Joan Mitchell and Helen Frankenthaler.

Bibliography

Gibson, Ann. "Universality and Difference in Women's Abstract Painting: Krasner, Ryan, Sekula, Piper, and Streat." *Yale Journal of Criti-*

cism 8, no. 1 (Spring 1995). Gibson discusses the meaning of abstraction as it applies to Krasner and four other artists of the era.

Hobbs, Robert. *Lee Krasner*. New York: Abbeville Press, 1993. This well-written book chronicles Krasner's life and career from childhood to death, with a focus on the development of her art. Includes ninety-three black-and-white and color illustrations as well as a chronology, a bibliography, list of exhibitions, and "Artist's Statements."

Landau, Ellen G. *Lee Krasner: A Catalogue Raisonne*. New York: Abrams, 1995. This volume covers all of Krasner's drawings, paintings, prints, and collages with exhibition histories, insight into and interpretations of the works, and a bibliography.

————. "Lee Krasner's Early Career." Parts 1-2. *Arts Magazine* 56 (October/ November, 1981). This two-part article is extremely important. It thoroughly documents Krasner's early career, from her childhood to the 1950's. The focus is on her education, influences, and the "Little Images" paintings. Includes twenty-three illustrations—among them some of the rarely shown early works—and footnotes.

Munro, Eleanor. *Originals: American Women Artists*. New York: Simon and Schuster, 1979. Twenty pages of this book are dedicated to a discussion of Krasner's life and career. The book also addresses the situation of twentieth century women artists in the United States and views Krasner in the context of "Women of the First Wave: Elders of the Century." Includes a bibliography and five illustrations.

Rose, Barbara. *Lee Krasner: A Retrospective*. New York: Museum of Modern Art, 1983. An extremely detailed, important work written in conjunction with Krasner's 1983 retrospective in Houston. Documents Krasner's life and career from childhood to 1983, focusing on her education, work for the WPA, influences, marriage, and philosophy. Includes more than 155 black-and-white and color illustrations, a chronology, and a bibliography.

Tucker, Marcia. *Lee Krasner: Large Paintings*. New York: Whitney Museum of American Art, 1973. A brief but very informative discussion of the development of Krasner's painting and collage styles and techniques, focusing on her work from the 1930's through the 1960's. Addresses the issues of Krasner's philosophy, influences, and education. Includes eighteen color and black-and-white illustrations of paintings, a chronology, and a bibliography.

Nannette Fabré Kelly

AUGUST KROGH

Born: November 15, 1874; Grenaa, Denmark
Died: September 13, 1949; Copenhagen, Denmark
Areas of Achievement: Physiology and zoology
Contribution: Krogh won the 1920 Nobel Prize in Physiology or Medicine for his investigations into how the capillaries regulate the flow of blood, and thus oxygen, in the body. He also made important advances in the understanding of how the lungs exchange oxygen from the air into the bloodstream.

Early Life

Schack August Steenberg Krogh was born in the town of Grenaa in Jutland on November 15, 1874. His father, Viggo, had been a shipbuilder, but the time of the large wooden ships was past. By the time of August's birth, he had bought a small brewery. In this business, he supported his wife, Mimi Drechman Krogh, and his six children, August being the eldest. Money was never in abundance for the Kroghs, and August learned early to be frugal; even later, when large funds were available to him in his research, he still used scraps of paper for his notes.

In his schooling, August exhibited an independent nature. He found formal schooling boring but pursued his interests in nature and physics outside school, watching the behavior of insects and spiders for hours. One teacher, Carl Nilsson, recognized the potential of the frustrated student and gave him the individual attention he needed. In a letter to his future wife, August recounted how he and Nilsson spent an afternoon together with a new telescope the boy had received for his confirmation. They took the instrument apart and studied how the lenses worked. They discovered that the ocular could be used as a small microscope, and soon August had made a wooden holder for it and began studying everything within reach.

Another strong influence that helped August in finding his profession was a friend of the family, William Sorensen. Sorensen, a zoologist, spent many summer vacations in Grenaa with his friend Viggo. August, in his youth, enjoyed walking with him, scouring the fields. On entering the University of Copenhagen in 1894, he took Sorensen's advice and attended a class taught by Christian Bohr (father to Niels Bohr), an eminent physiologist. After the first lecture, on quantitative methods for determining the blood volume of the human body, August decided that such studies appealed to him most. He became Bohr's student but held his earlier interest, zoology, and was graduated in that subject in 1899.

Life's Work

Krogh is best known for his work on capillaries, but respiration and the exchange of oxygen in the body was the unifying theme of his endeavors. For his doctoral research, under Bohr's supervision, he investigated the respiration of the frog. He concluded that the animal took in oxygen through the lungs, but that the more diffusible carbon dioxide escaped through the moist skin.

In 1905, Krogh married, and he and his wife Marie started the research that would cut Krogh's ties to Bohr. Bohr believed that the lungs secreted oxygen into the bloodstream using cells controlled by the nervous system. For a time, Krogh followed this theory but agreed that conclusive evidence to support it was lacking. To answer the question of whether gas exchange in the lungs was passive or active, Krogh used his microtonometer, a small gas-analyzing apparatus he designed for work on insect respiration. The microtonometer could measure the air pressure of an air bubble of only about ten cubic millimeters, or about the size of a pinhead. With this instrument, Krogh could measure the oxygen tension of the blood and compare it to that of the lung alveolus. In 1909, in seven papers that the Kroghs later called "the seven small devils," they published their results. They concluded that Bohr was wrong and that oxygen passed into the bloodstream by diffusion alone. This work led Krogh to believe that gas transport throughout the body relied on diffusion, and this belief proved an important factor in his subsequent studies on capillaries.

In 1910, Krogh started working with a professor of gymnastics, Johannes Lindhard, on muscular work in man. Their experiments on the circulatory system showed the enormous increase in the total circulation rate induced by muscular activity. It also revealed that the increase in oxygen consumption occurred mainly in the working muscles. These results led him to question how the same circulatory system could satisfy the high oxygen demand of the body at work and the relatively low demand at rest.

The current theory on capillaries hypothesized that as the heartbeat quickened, the rising blood pressure forced open more and more capillaries in the muscles. Krogh found this theory unacceptable. During physical exertion, this system would open capillaries throughout the body, even where extra oxygen was not needed. Krogh started with the idea that every capillary, by supplying blood, supplied oxygen to the surrounding tissue by diffusion. He then asked how the capillary network could be sufficient for the body's needs for oxygen during work without being wasteful during periods of rest. One day, while he was at the library, a solution occurred to him: If a local lack of oxygen in the muscle forced the opening of the nearest capillary, and a relative surplus allowed the capillary to close, the capillaries would open or close in alternation. This would allow for increased oxygen supply only where and when needed, serving equally well in times of relaxation or intense activity.

Now that he had a theory, Krogh had to determine if it was worthwhile to make an experimental test of it. He later said that nothing short of experimentation helped more to clarify his ideas than discussion with a sympathetic colleague. Thus, that evening he went home to discuss his theory with his wife. Marie decidedly influenced her husband's studies; Krogh himself described her as "always my nearest colleague."

To test his hypothesis, Krogh needed to determine if increased oxygen demand did indeed result in the opening of more capillaries. He observed the tongue of a frog and found that, when stimulated, many more capillaries became visible as a result of being filled with blood. To answer the question of whether only the capillaries of stimulated muscles opened, however, he needed an alternative method; the capillaries from many parts of the tongue needed to be observed simultaneously. To do so, Krogh used an India-ink solution injected into the bloodstream shortly before death. Any open capillaries, filled with the mixture of blood and ink, would then appear as black lines. He found that capillaries of the skin, liver, and brain, organs that are constantly active, were always open. The empty stomach and intestine had only a small number of open capillaries. The muscles varied, with inactive muscles relatively white, while the ones stimulated before stopping circulation appeared almost black from the large number of injected capillaries. Obviously, then, the capillaries themselves had the ability to open or close

as needed, allowing oxygen through their walls by diffusion, as Krogh had hypothesized.

Krogh published his findings in 1918. The significance of his work was understood surprisingly soon, and he received the Nobel Prize in Physiology or Medicine in 1920. Yet while the publicity from this award attracted many scholars anxious to work with him, Krogh himself remained in the background. Therefore, his students received the lion's share of recognition from their researches, something in which Krogh strongly believed. In 1922, Krogh published a review of the research done by himself and his students, *The Anatomy and Physiology of Capillaries*, which represents his major contribution to medical science. After this, though his guidance was actively sought, and if rejected was done so foolishly, Krogh's contributions to human physiology became secondary.

In his later years, Krogh returned to zoophysiology, his first love. In 1941, he published *The Comparative Physiology of Respiratory Mechanisms*, returning to his original work on oxygen exchange, but now including the insect world. Even after his retirement in 1945, Krogh remained active, beginning an investigation into the flight of insects. Only Krogh's death in 1949 stopped his studies.

Summary

With the recognition that came with the Nobel Prize, August Krogh's laboratory attracted scholars from all over the world, especially the United States. At least twenty Americans spent time under Krogh's direction, and in 1951, two years after his death, the faculty of Harvard University included eight professors who had studied with him. His students often remarked that their love for him was excelled only by their respect for his scientific ability.

The implications of Krogh's research with oxygen diffusion through the capillary walls proved wide-ranging. The lymph system and the kidneys are affected by diffusion through the capillaries. Diffusion also accounts for inflammatory symptoms, such as allergy, edema (the swelling of tissues by fluid retention), and surgical and wound shock (hemorrhage). These areas and many more fell to Krogh's students to pursue.

Krogh also used his fame to further humanitarian concerns. When in the United States in 1922 to deliver a series of lectures on his work on capillaries, Krogh acquainted himself with the preparation of the newly discovered insulin. On his return to Denmark, he organized its production and convinced the producer that it should be manufactured without profit. Thus this lifesaving substance could be obtained in his homeland at a much lower price than elsewhere—only one of the many ways that Krogh advanced scientific studies in his native Denmark.

Bibliography

Drinker, Cecil K. "August Krogh: 1874-1949." *Science* 112 (July 28, 1950): 105-107. Written by one of Krogh's students, this recollection fondly describes what it was like to work in the Krogh laboratory. Krogh's kindly direction and concern for his students are noted.

Hill, A. V. "Schack August Steenburg Krogh, 1874-1949." *Obituary Notices of Fellows of the Royal Society* 7, no. 19 (November, 1950): 221-237. An obituary by a scientific organization of which Krogh was a member. It includes a portrait of Krogh, a complete listing of his publications (almost three hundred entries), and excerpts from the speech given when he was awarded the Nobel Prize.

Krogh, August. *The Anatomy and Physiology of Capillaries*. 2d ed. New Haven, Conn.: Yale University Press, and London: Oxford University Press, 1929. Contains a reminiscence of capillary studies that Krogh delivered in 1946, explaining the influences that directed the research that resulted in his receiving the Nobel Prize. It also includes an annotated bibliography on capillary research.

————. *The Comparative Physiology of Respiratory Mechanisms*. Philadelphia: University of Pennsylvania Press, 1941. Reveals the research interests that most compelled Krogh, the combination of oxygen exchange, and the respiratory systems of lower-order animals, especially insects. Includes illustrations of the exchange systems of many different animals, a listing of all animals investigated in the book, and an annotated bibliography.

Rehberg, Brandt P. "August Krogh: November 15, 1874-September 13, 1949." *Yale Journal of Biology and Medicine* 24 (1951): 83-102. Written by Krogh's research associate, this article is a wide-ranging account of Krogh's career. Of note is its review of Krogh's zoophysiological pursuits, especially in the years after he won the Nobel Prize, and his approach to laboratory work.

Schmidt-Nielson, Bodil. "August and Marie Krogh and Respiratory Physiology." *Journal of Applied Physiology* 57 (August, 1984): 293-303. One of the Kroghs' daughters recounts the Krogh family life, especially the close working relationship between her mother and father. She deals most extensively with Krogh's childhood and the early years of his research. The seven papers that proved Krogh's oxygen-diffusion theory for the lungs are dealt with at length. Includes photographs.

Wayne, Randy, and Mark P. Staves. "The August Krogh Principle Applies to Plants." *BioScience* 46, no. 5 (May, 1996). Considers application of Krogh's animal research theories in the world of botany.

James Owen

ELISABETH KÜBLER-ROSS

Born: July 8, 1926; Zurich, Switzerland

Area of Achievement: Psychiatry

Contribution: A leading researcher in the field of thanatology (the study of death), Kübler-Ross is most widely recognized for having identified five stages in the process of dying that have provided a framework for further work by professionals in the area of counseling the terminally ill and their families. Her work has helped remove former taboos from the subject of death and brought a compassionate and humane approach to the care of the dying.

Early Life

Elisabeth Kübler, daughter of Ernst and Emmy (Villiger) Kübler, was the first-born of triplet girls. Although Elisabeth and one of her sisters weighed barely two pounds, the triplets survived as a result of their mother's diligent care. The close-knit Kübler family was dominated by a father who was a firm disciplinarian yet who also sang songs with his children around the parlor piano and led them on summer nature hikes at the family's Swiss mountain retreat in Furlegi. These trips instilled in young Elisabeth a lasting love and respect for nature. Never a religious person in the traditional sense, Elisabeth favored a sort of pantheism and exhibited compassion for all living creatures. As a child attempting to escape from the constant company of her sisters, she chose a secret place atop a flat rock in the woods near her home to which she returned even as an adult when in need of solace.

Elisabeth struggled for personal identity since her childhood was spent with very few belongings or activities that were different from those of her sisters. This situation was further complicated by the fact that she was physically identical to Erika, for whom she was often mistaken. Elisabeth developed a fascination for African history that became the source of the first personal possession she later recalled was not shared by her sisters. As a reward for recovering from a near fatal case of pneumonia, Elisabeth's father bought her an African rag doll for which she had been yearning. This fascination with a culture that differed radically from her own resulted in the creation of a sort of tribal nonsense language used by the imaginative triplets that only they understood.

Although their older brother, Ernst, was educated to enter the business world, the girls were sent to local schools with the objective that they be properly prepared for marriage. The basics bored Elisabeth, who longed for more challenge and saw education as her doorway to important work. She soon discovered a passion for science. Because Elisabeth received no parental support for her goals, her educational pursuits beyond secondary school were entirely self-motivated.

Several events in Elisabeth's youth were key factors in determining the direction of her life and her profession. The peaceful death of her hospital roommate when Elisabeth was five, the release from the suffering of meningitis of a young girl in her hometown, and memories of a neighboring farmer with a broken neck calmly preparing his family for his death were never forgotten. These early experiences with death intensified the belief that later became the crux of her professional credo—that death is only a stage of life and people should be able to face death with dignity and the support of those they trust.

September 1, 1939, marked in some ways the most crucial day in her life. When Elisabeth heard on the radio that the Germans had invaded Poland, she made a vow to go help the Polish people as soon as she was able. First, she was involved with refugees sent to the Swiss hospitals where she worked as a laboratory assistant during the war. She joined the International Volunteers for Peace in 1945 hoping to have found the right avenue to reach the Polish people. In intervals between her laboratory work, she worked on the French-Swiss border and in Sweden before her dream of being sent to Poland was finally realized in 1948. She worked at numerous jobs, including those of camp cook, gardener, carpenter, and nurse, as she assisted war victims in rebuilding.

These postwar experiences, combined with poignant memories of butterfly signs of hope left on barrack walls at Maidanek concentration camp, made it clear to Elisabeth that her purpose in life was to channel her energy and compassion into the healing of human minds as well as bodies. She worked tirelessly to complete her preliminary medical school exams in two years instead of the usual three while meagerly financing her studies working as a lab assistant in an eye clinic. In 1951, she was admitted to the University of Zurich Medical School and she embarked upon the winding trail that led her to the field of psychiatry. Having come to believe without question that people's bodies often achieve healing only after their minds and souls are healthy and free, Elisabeth was convinced that psychiatry offered the perfect venue for the combination of her special instincts and intellect.

Life's Work

Elisabeth Kübler was graduated from the University of Zurich in 1957 and practiced for a few months as a Swiss country doctor. On February 7, 1958, she married Emanuel Robert Ross, a fellow medical student to whom she was wed for eleven years. Elisabeth Kübler-Ross came to the United States with her new husband, a native New Yorker, and they were able to secure internships at Community Hospital in Glen Cove, Long Island. This experience was followed by a three-year residency in psychiatry at Manhattan State Hospital in Ward's Island and a concurrent year at Montefiore Hospital in the Bronx. Even patients with the most severe psychoses seemed to respond to Kübler-Ross's compassionate yet persistent and simple way of communicating with them. The lack of humane concern in psychiatric hospitals was appalling to the young doctor, and the more freedom she was given to work in her own way, the more successful were her treatments.

The couple felt a need to leave the city environment after the arrival of their new child, Kenneth. In 1962, they accepted positions at the University of Colorado School of Medicine in Denver. Kübler-Ross was given a fellowship in psychiatry and the next year became an instructor at Colorado General Hospital. In 1965, the family, with the addition of a daughter Barbara, moved to Chicago, where Kübler-Ross became an assistant professor of psychiatry and assistant director of psychiatric consultation and liaison services at the University of Chicago Medical School. All through her working years, she had been disturbed by the attitude of avoidance that existed in dealing with the anxiety of terminally ill patients. She found the situation the same almost universally and began to quietly develop her own methods for recognizing the anxiety of the dying and also guiding them in expressing their feelings. It was in Chicago that fame for her work in thanatology began. Against administrative pressures to bring as little attention to her work as possible, she networked with nurses, willing doctors, priests, and seminarians to further her studies of the counseling of the dying. She held weekly seminars that attracted overflow crowds.

These seminars were eventually canceled by administrators who were concerned about public reaction to discussions about death rather than recovery of patients.

In these seminars, dying patients were interviewed by Kübler-Ross behind a one-way glass through which those who attended could observe. Kübler-Ross viewed death as the final stage of life and began to identify five stages in the process of dying that she found all patients to experience, though not necessarily in the same order. The five stages were denial, anger, bargaining, depression, and acceptance. These stages and other conclusions were the subject of many guest lectures and of her best-selling work *On Death and Dying* (1969). The book became a standard resource for counselors, physicians, and laymen as they helped patients, friends, and relatives deal with the issue of death. *Life* magazine published an article on November 21, 1969, that related to the public for the first time the boldness with which Kübler-Ross approached the issue of death with patients and their open dialogue with her. The public response was overwhelming, and Kübler-Ross saw this as a turning point in her career. Her work turned solely to assisting dying patients and their families.

In 1977, she established "Shanti Nilaya" ("Home of Peace"), a healing center for dying persons and relatives in the hills north of Escondido near San Diego, California. She moved her residence there from Chicago, and profits from her lectures and books supported the center. In 1990, she moved the Elisabeth Kübler-Ross Center to her own 200-acre farm in Headwater, Virginia, where she had retired in 1984. Kübler-Ross continued to keep abreast of current issues and attempted in 1986 to establish a hospice for babies with acquired immune deficiency syndrome (AIDS); because of heated community dissent, however, she abandoned the idea. Nevertheless, the center was enormously successful in its efforts to offer assistance to professionals and laypersons in dealing with terminally ill patients. The center is supported by proceeds from Kübler-Ross's workshops and lectures and by volunteer help.

Since the advent of *On Death and Dying*, Kübler-Ross has published a number of other books based on her studies, including *Questions and Answers on Death and Dying* (1974), *Death: The Final Stage of Growth* (1975), *To Live Until We Say Good-bye* (1978), *Living with Death and Dying* (1981), *Working It Through* (1982), *On*

Children and Death (1983), *AIDS: The Ultimate Challenge* (1987), and *On Life After Death* (1991).

Over the years, Kübler-Ross has been recognized for her selfless devotion and tireless efforts by numerous organizations, including the Teilhard Foundation (1981) and the American Academy of Achievement (1980). She was named a "Woman of the Decade" by *Ladies' Home Journal* in 1979. She was one of the founders of the American Holistic Medical Association and is a member of other major medical and psychological associations. Honorary degrees have been bestowed upon her by Smith College, University of Notre Dame, the Medical College of Pennsylvania, Albany Medical College, Hamline University, and Amherst College. In 1998 she published *The Wheel of Life: A Memoir of Living and Dying*, which she has said will be her last book.

Summary

Elisabeth Kübler-Ross is almost solely responsible for the humanitarian focus on the care of the dying patient which currently exists. Her workshops and lectures continue and she assists where she is needed. She responds also to individual pleas and has flown to the bedside of patients in their final stages of life to listen and give comfort to them and their families. Elisabeth Kübler-Ross's name has become synonymous with the idea of respect for the dying. Over the years, her work has literally revolutionized for doctors and patients the world over the area of psychology dealing with death and dying.

Bibliography

Bartlett, Kay. "No Stranger to Death, Kübler-Ross Turns Her Attention to AIDS." *Los Angeles Times*, May 10, 1987, sec. 1, p. 25. Kübler-Ross discusses her feelings about the after-life of the human spirit and the application of her thanatological research to the counseling of children and adults suffering with AIDS.

Gill, Derek. *Quest: The Life of Elisabeth Kübler-Ross*. New York: Harper, 1980. The first full-length biography of Kübler-Ross. An intimate volume that contains an epilogue by Kübler-Ross and covers her life through 1969, the year that *On Death and Dying* was published and her attentions turned solely to work with the terminally ill.

Goleman, Daniel. "We Are Breaking the Silence About Death." *Psychology Today* 10 (September, 1976): 44-47. Kübler-Ross discusses her work and traces the path of her career. The article includes an interview about dealing with the death of children, the difficult subject of much of her recent writing.

Kübler-Ross, Elisabeth. *On Death and Dying*. New York: Macmillan, 1969. Kübler-Ross's first work and the one in which she defines her famous "five stages" in the process of death. The best-known treatise in the field, this work set the standard for later research.

————. *The Wheel of Life: A Memoir of Living and Dying*. New York: Scribner, 1997; London: Bantam, 1998. An autobiography that describes Kübler-Ross's early years in Switzerland, her struggles to become a physician, and negative reactions to her decision to study death and dying. Surprising discussion of her visits from spirit guides.

Rosen, Jonathan. "Rewriting the End: Elisabeth Kübler-Ross." *New York Times Magazine* (January 22, 1995). Discusses Kübler-Ross's feelings about her own death and her motivation for writing her books on the terminally ill.

Wainwright, Loudon. "Profound Lesson for the Living." *Life* 67 (November 21, 1969): 36-43. This was the first article addressed to a general audience that publicized Kübler-Ross's controversial Chicago seminars on dying. Her unorthodox method of working is revealed in his observation of an emotional interview between the doctor and a twenty-two-year-old leukemia patient.

Sandra C. McClain

KUO MO-JO

Born: November 10 or 16, 1892; Shawan, China
Died: June 12, 1978; Peking, China
Areas of Achievement: Government, politics, and literature
Contribution: Historian and novelist, poet and propagandist, Kuo was perhaps the most prolific Chinese intellectual of the twentieth century. After the founding of the People's Republic of China in 1949, he served in a variety of government posts, including that of President of the Chinese Academy of Sciences. He survived the purges of the Anti-Rightist Campaign (1957) and the Cultural Revolution era (1966-1976) and continued publishing through the 1970's.

Early Life

Kou Mo-jo, like many of the leaders of revolutionary China, was born during the tumultuous last decade of the nineteenth century. Born Kuo K'ai-chen in November, 1892, to a well-to-do merchant family in the interior province of Szechwan, he received the foundation of a classical education at a time of sweeping educational reform. The near collapse of the Ch'ing Empire in the wake of the 1894-1895 war with Japan, the abortive One Hundred Days of Reform in the summer of 1898, and the Boxer Rebellion of 1900 spurred an unprecedented overhaul of the curriculum required for admission to the bureaucracy. Thus, Kuo studied Chinese and Western subjects at a school in Chiating from 1906 to 1909.

During the revolution of October, 1911, Kuo received his secondary education in the provincial capital of Ch'eng-tu. Upon completion of his studies there, he decided to pursue additional modern courses in Japan. He completed an accelerated preparatory course of study for Chinese students and in 1915 was enrolled in pre-medical studies at Okayama. For the next half-decade, he labored to finish his medical studies while increasingly devoting himself to literary interests. The tensions involved in resolving this dilemma of direction taxed his family life as well as his inner muse and would play a crucial role in his later work.

Kuo had submitted to an arranged marriage in 1912 but remained estranged from his wife almost from the beginning. During his medical studies in Japan, he met Satō Tomiko, a Japanese Christian, and soon moved in with her. Their liaison would eventually produce five children, though Kuo refused to marry her for fear of offending his parents.

Kuo's literary interests during this period, which coincided with the development of the new vernacular literature advocated by Ch'en Tu-hsiu, Hu Shih, Li Ta-ch'ao, and the "Literary Renaissance" at the University of Peking, already displayed a surprising eclecticism and showed evidence of an early search for cross-cultural synthesis. Sources as varied as the idealist philosopher Wang Yang-ming, the Western Romantics and the poetry of Johann Wolfgang von Goethe, Walt Whitman, and Rabindranath Tagore dominated his studies.

In the autumn of 1919, amid the furor of the May Fourth Movement, Kuo's poems were published for the first time in the *Hsih-hsih hsin-pao* (the China times), and he soon determined, over Tomiko's desperate protests, to leave his medical studies and pursue writing as a career. With his colleagues Yu Ta-fu, T'ien Han, and Chang Tzu-p'ing, he formed the Creation Society and in the early 1920's founded the *Ch'uang-tsao chi-k'an* (creation quarterly), as well as a weekly and a daily. Kuo and his fellow creationists, for the most part, followed a Romantic aesthetic—a belief in pantheism, the primacy of intuitive knowledge and emotion, the heroism of individual action, and the need for rebellion. With the breakup of the group in 1924, however, he increasingly turned his attention to the momentous political events that would initially unite China, then plunge the nation into civil war.

Life's Work

Like many Chinese intellectuals during the May Fourth period, Kuo had initially been receptive to a wide variety of novel Western ideas. As early as the publication in 1921 of his poetry collection *Nü-shen* (partial translation, *Selected Poems from "The Goddesses,"* 1958), he had announced his interest in communism. The Bolshevik experiment in Russia, Vladimir Ilich Lenin's renunciation of czarist claims in China, and the Comintern-inspired United Front of Chinese Communists and Kuomintang (Nationalists) drew the admiration of many patriotic Chinese, and by 1924, Kuo had written of his conversion to Marxism-Leninism, though he did not join the party until 1927. His influences during this period included the Japanese Marxist Hajime Kawakami, Friedrich Nietzsche,

Goethe, and Ivan Turgenev, and he produced translations of works from all of these writers. True to the catholicity of his interests, he also managed to publish, during a time when he was increasingly dedicating himself to remaking the social order, a series of vernacular translations of classical poetry and a romantic novel.

The next three years, which encompassed Chiang K'ai-shek's Northern Expedition to unite China under the Nationalists and his bloody purge to eliminate the Communists in 1937, saw Kuo involved in the reforming of the Creation Society, heading the literature department of Sun Yat-sen University in Canton, and leading the propaganda section of the National Revolutionary Army's political department. Yet, in a move that would earn for him the enmity of Chiang, Kuo secretly informed the Communists of Nationalist plans and in March, 1927, wrote an attack on Chiang urging the Party to execute him. Chiang's "White Terror" against the Communists began less than two weeks later.

In the confused internecine conflict between Chiang's right-wing Kuomintang forces and the left wing and their Communist allies, Kuo participated in a number of unsuccessful insurgencies but eventually fled to the International Concession of Shanghai and finally to Japan. His stay in Japan would last ten years and would span the momentous period of struggle between the Nationalists and Mao Tse-tung's Communist guerrillas, as well as the accelerating Japanese incursion into China. Kuo, now in the frustrating position of living in an increasingly hostile country and trying to aid a revolution from which he was far removed, turned to writing a series of Marxist interpretations of ancient Chinese history. He also worked on translations of Karl Marx's *Zur Kritik der politischen Ökonomie* (1859; *A Contribution to a Critique of Political Economy*, 1904) and *Die deutsche Ideologie* (1845-1846; *The German Ideology*, 1938). Continuing his lifelong interest in Russian literature, he also translated a section of Leo Tolstoy's *Voyna i mir* (1865-1869; *War and Peace*, 1886).

Kuo's decade-long exile ended in the spring of 1937, when, in the wake of the Second United Front between the Communists and the Nationalists, he was invited to work for the new coalition. Received by Chiang Kai-shek in Nanking, he refused an offical position but agreed to propagandize for the war against Japan. During the epic Nationalist retreat up the Yangtze to the wartime capital of Chungking, Kuo served in a number of capacities and frequently assisted in relief work. Tomiko and Kuo's children had remained in Japan when war broke out, and during this period he formed a liaison with Yü Li-ch'un, the younger sister of a Chinese acquaintance from Tokyo.

After 1940, when he was removed from a briefly held post in the Military Affairs Commission, he worked closely with Chungking Communists and produced his most famous play, *Ch'ü Yüan* (1945; English translation, 1953). True to Kuo's role as a propagandist, the play is an allegorical attack on the Nationalists—as well as the Japanese—through the freely interpreted life of the poet and minister Ch'ü Yüan. He also continued his researches in ancient Chinese paleography.

With the end of the war, Kuo participated unsuccessfully in the attempts at reconciliation between Communists and Nationalists, and, with the outbreak of civil war, he moved briefly to Hong Kong. In November, 1948, with Communist victory imminent, he came back to China. In 1949, he chaired the All-China Congress of Writers and Artists for the new regime and through the 1950's served in such positions as chairman of the Committee on Cultural and Educational Affairs, vice president of the World Peace Council, and president of the Chinese Academy of Sciences.

Despite his status as China's leading intellectual and his years of service to the Party, he was not immune to the periodic upheavals of the Maoist interval. He adroitly weathered the Anti-Rightist purges of 1957, even traveling with Mao to the Soviet Union, and his *Mo-jo wên-chi* (collected literary works), totaling seventeen volumes, was published from 1957 to 1963. Yet Mao's calls for attacks on intellectuals during the Great Poletarian Cultural Revolution in 1966 subjected him to ritual abuse, threats of violence, and forced recantation of his works and ideas.

Still, by 1971 he was considered rehabilitated, and his publication of *Li Pai yü Tu Fu* (1971) marked the first classical studies done since the onset of the Cultural Revolution. Despite the often violent disfavor in which ancient Chinese culture was held during Mao's last years, Kuo continued to publish studies of paleography and poetry. By 1975 his reemergence on the national stage was complete when he was made a member of the standing Committee of the National People's Congress. In 1978, at the age of eighty-five, he died in Peking.

Summary

Kuo Mo-jo has been called "the most versatile Chinese intellectual of our day," and it is within this extraordinary range of abilities and interest that his significance lies. Like a number of the May Fourth period intellectuals who had sampled widely, but not deeply, of Western thought, he was enamored of the possibility of finding in it complementary aspects of Chinese philosophy. Unlike many of them, however, he lived long enough to develop a sophisticated grasp of the strengths and limitations of these foreign sources.

Kuo pursued simultaneous researches in both classical Chinese and Western literature, sometimes with startling synthetic results. The cosmology of the Taoist Chuang-tzu and the idealist philosophy of Wang Yang-ming—with their emphasis on the spiritual unity of man and universe—had, he believed, achieved many of the same insights as had Buddhism, the Vedic literature of India, and, in the West, the philosopher Baruch Spinoza and the Romantics. The urge to synthesize, to unify, permeates his writing, and, ultimately, Marxism comes to represent the means of achieving the material ends of this unity.

This breadth of interest—as well as his longevity—coupled with the constant intrigue of his life as a party functionary and propagandist, has led to criticism of Kuo as an intellectual and political opportunist. Notwithstanding this controversy, he remains one of the most prolific writers of the twentieth century in any language. His studies of ancient Chinese scripts and attempts to translate them into vernacular represent important pioneering efforts. His poetry marked the beginning of the modern era of Chinese verse and is considered some of the best of the May Fourth period. Above all, he epitomizes the role of the intellectual as propagandist.

Bibliography

Chesneaux, Jean, Françoise Le Barbier, and Marie-Claire Bergère. *China from the 1911 Revolution to Liberation*. Translated by Paul Auster and Lydia Davis. New York: Pantheon, 1977; Hassocks: Harvester Press, 1978. In one of the most complete accounts of the tumultuous years of China's fragmentation and reconstitution, Chesneaux traces the evolution of the literary movement within the broader context of the Nationalist/Communist struggle.

Goldman, Merle. *Literary Dissent in Communist China*. Cambridge, Mass.: Harvard University Press, 1967. A somewhat dated but extremely useful work tracing the literary trends of Chinese Communism from the Yenan period of the 1940's to their climax in the Hundred Flowers and Anti-Rightist campaigns of the late 1950's. Kuo's activities during this era, and particularly his works of the late 1950's, are well documented.

Hsu, Kai-yu, ed. *Literature of the People's Republic of China*. Bloomington: Indiana University Press, 1980. Perhaps the most complete volume of songs, poetry, and short prose works of the Communist era. Contains an excellent short summary of Kuo's career.

Roy, David Tod. *Kuo Mo-jo: The Early Years*. Cambridge, Mass.: Harvard University Press, 1971. One of the few works available on Kuo's life in English. Carefully stressing the role of Chinese sources, Roy provides a nuanced account of the intellectual influences that shaped Kuo's career up to his 1924 conversion to Marxism.

Schwarcz, Vera. *The Chinese Enlightenment: Intellectuals and the Legacy of the May Fourth Movement of 1919*. Berkeley: University of California Press, 1986. In a revisionist look at intellectual trends in twentieth century China, Schwarcz views the May Fourth Movement as the beginning of a decades-long "Chinese Enlightenment" rather than an isolated nationalist incident. She provides a sophisticated contextual background of Kuo's times and the evolving concerns of China's intelligentsia.

Charles A. Desnoyers

FRANTIŠEK KUPKA

Born: September 23, 1871; Opočno, Bohemia, Austro-Hungarian Empire
Died: June 24, 1958; Puteaux, France
Area of Achievement: Art
Contribution: Kupka painted what were probably the first abstract modern paintings, beginning around 1911. He was also a talented illustrator of books and magazines and an important theorist of abstract art.

Early Life

František Kupka was the eldest and brightest of Václav Kupka's five children, but the family lacked the money needed to send him to high school. This lack of formal education was a source of regret and humiliation for Kupka for years thereafter. He was instead apprenticed to a local saddler. He hated the profession, but the saddler introduced him to spiritualism, and Kupka grew into a talented medium. Kupka began his formal study of art at age seventeen, with Alois Strudnica, who was interested in ornamental abstraction. Strudnica had his students draw and work with geometric forms, rather than constantly copy from models as many conservative teachers did. Strudnica also introduced Kupka to the Nazarenes, an early nineteenth century art movement whose followers wanted to return art to the spirituality of the late medieval German artists. Kupka's own tendencies found resonance in the Nazarene belief that contemplation should be a principal source of artistic inspiration. He moved to Prague in 1888 to attend the Prague School of Fine Arts, becoming the star pupil and supporting himself by working as a medium. He lived in abject poverty, experiencing several mental breakdowns as a result. Kupka's extreme sensitivity led to the debilitating bouts of depression from which he suffered for the rest of his life.

In 1892, Kupka moved to Vienna and attended the Vienna Academy of Fine Arts. The artistic and intellectual milieus that he found during his four years in Vienna were an important influence on his work. The Jugendstil decorative arts movement was in full flower in Vienna; its influence, combined with the simple geometry of Viennese architects such as Otto Wagner and the Czech folk art to which he was exposed as a child, helped push Kupka onto the long and twisting path toward abstraction. Kupka also read voraciously in Vienna, studying the German philosophers and theosophy and becoming fascinated by the interrelation of color and music. He became interested in the vivid colors of stained glass and studied Greek and Gothic architecture, which confirmed his belief that mathematics could be related to art. He achieved some artistic success in Vienna, executing portraits of the Empress Elizabeth and others in the court. In 1894, he became involved with the Danish clothes designer Maria Bruhn, for whom he did fashion designs.

Life's Work

In 1896, Kupka moved to Paris, looking for broader artistic horizons, and quickly became a successful illustrator for several socialist and anarchist periodicals. He was a first-class draftsman and produced excellent drawings, etchings, and lithographs in a detailed, dramatic style influenced by the Symbolist and Art Nouveau currents flowing through Paris at the time. Kupka also had a good eye for satire; his journalistic illustrations were exhibited in Paris and Czechoslovakia. By 1905, he was a sought-after book illustrator, working on "The Song of Songs," contemporary French poetry and fiction, and the Greek myths. In 1906, Kupka married Eugénie Straub, and the couple moved to the village of Puteaux on the outskirts of Paris, where the rent was low and Kupka had the isolation that he needed to work. Kupka continued to paint during this time, becoming a member of the Salon d'Automne in 1907 and regularly exhibiting there for years.

Kupka's training had been in the academic tradition and so had his style, but he wanted to go further, to express things that representational art could not express. He believed that the painting of such objects from nature as trees was pointless when one could see "better ones in reality." In Paris, Kupka was exposed to the same French preoccupation with the formal means of painting that led to cubism, and it opened his eyes to new possibilities. Starting around 1905, his work underwent a rapid evolution, becoming increasingly abstract, concentrating on color and motion. In 1908, Kupka painted "Girl with a Ball," inspired by his stepdaughter's playing with a red and blue ball in his garden. He was frustrated with the inability of traditional painting methods to depict the motion that he saw. When he finished this painting, he continued doing sketches, trying to draw motion. He ended up with studies that look like interlocking curves and arcs, barely recognizable as a human body or a ball. Kupka continued to experiment in this direction, and soon his canvases bore no resemblance to external reality.

In *Newton's Discs* (1911-1912), Kupka paid tribute to Sir Isaac Newton's experiments with color and motion. Newton discovered that, if a disc is painted with every color of the spectrum and then spun, the colors merge to form white. Kupka painted a series of interlocking discs, concentric circles of motion spreading out from them. The motionless disc at the top of the painting is bright red, like a miniature sun. The colors become cooler and more dilute as the motion increases, until the final, rapidly spinning disc at the bottom of the painting is grayish white. He applied what he had learned from this work to his studies of the girl and ball and came up with *Amorpha, Fugue in Two Colors* (1912), sinuous lines of motion in red and blue on a black-and-white background. Many art historians believe that the painting's exhibition later that year was the first public appearance of a work without an objective subject, and the public reaction was predictably that of bewilderment and outrage.

Kupka, however, received admiration from other artists. He met regularly with Marcel Duchamp, Jacques Villon, and Francis Picabia, all of whom admired math and science as much as Kupka and were influenced by his work. The poet Guillame Apollinaire defended Kupka's brand of painting, labeling it "Orphism." Soon other artists, notably Robert Delaunay, were exhibiting paintings in a similar style. Many critics lumped Kupka's work with that of the cubists, but Kupka vigorously denied that cubism had any similarity with or influence on his own work. He became paranoid, believing that others were stealing his ideas, and acquired a reputation as a difficult and taciturn man.

World War I ended this period of Kupka's life. As a foreign national, he was under no obligation to join the war effort, but he did so anyhow, serving at the front and becoming ill as a result. After the war, Kupka began painting again and intensified work on his theoretical writings started in 1910. He finished his volume of theory on the plastic arts around 1919, but it did not appear until 1923, and then only in Czech, though it was originally written in French. The only theoretical work on abstract painting to be published earlier was Wassily Kandinsky's *Über das Geistige in der Kunst insbe-*

sondere in der Malerei (1912; *Concerning the Spiritual in Art and Painting in Particular*, 1912).

His work continued to evolve, sometimes looking more geometric, sometimes more organic, but always full of sweeping, cosmic motion that has reminded many viewers of music. *Animated Lines* (1921) depicts semicircles in browns and grays falling from all sides down a whirlpool to a point near the bottom left of the canvas, while huge arcs of green and blue come shooting back out again. The effect is like the climax of a Romantic symphony.

In 1921, Kupka had his first one-man exhibition in Paris. It was a critical success but unfortunately an economic failure. Kupka had been impoverished again for some time but was named resident professor of the Prague Academy in Paris in 1922, which somewhat eased his financial situation. During the late 1920's, he did a series of abstractions of imaginary machines. Starting in the 1930's, he did hard-edged paintings of geometric shapes— lines, rectangles, trapezoids, and circles—arranged in bold compositions. Once again he suffered from health and financial problems. He also endured relative artistic obscurity, though the Jeu de Paume in Paris devoted an entire exhibition to Kupka and his friend Alphonse Mucha, an Art Nouveau illustrator, in 1936.

Kupka spent World War II in Beaugency, on the Loire River, painting very little because of poor health. After the war, his artistic fortune took a turn for the better. In 1946, the Museum of Modern Art in New York bought a number of his paintings, on the advice of Marcel Duchamp, and a major exhibition was organized in Prague to celebrate his seventy-fifth birthday, after which the government of Czechoslovakia bought twenty of his paintings. His work appeared in many other major exhibits during the following years, and, in 1951, he signed his first contract with a gallery. In 1956, the Museum of Modern Art bought more of his works, and he donated many of his preparatory drawings to them. After his death in Puteaux on June 24, 1958, the Musée National d'Art Moderne, in Paris, organized a major retrospective of his work and bought several paintings.

Summary

František Kupka was unquestionably a pioneer, and his work influenced many of his contemporaries; his exact place in twentieth century art is, however, still being debated. Much argument has taken place about whether Kupka was the first abstract artist. Many art historians believe that he was, while others award that prize to Robert Delaunay or Wassily Kandinsky. Many critics believe that Kupka was not as consistent as these other artists, or that he stumbled into abstraction, while other artists got there along a clearly recognizable path. His work does not resolve itself into tidy patterns and therefore receives far less critical attention than that of other artists. Another criticism is that his abstractions were too decorative, deriving as they did from the spirit of ornamentation, while the work of the other early abstract artists is considered more "rational." For whatever reason, his work has never been as fashionable as that of other pioneers of twentieth century art. No doubt his own reclusive tendencies contributed to this status, as did his belief that an artist's mission is cosmic— a view considered to be out of touch with twentieth century currents. Few, however, doubt Kupka's importance to the evolution of twentieth century abstract art, and not many painters have come close to his ability to depict motion. His work continues to go through periods of renewed interest, which often coincide with major Kupka exhibits.

Bibliography

Boice, Bruce. "Problems from Early Kupka." *Artforum* 19 (January, 1976): 32-39. Boice focuses on Kupka's earliest abstractions and the disputed dates at which they may have been painted, attempting to assess Kupka's contributions to abstract art relative to that of his contemporaries.

Fauchereau, Serge. *Kupka.* Translated by Richard-Lewis Rees. New York: Rizzoli, 1989. Contains fairly extensive passages from his theoretical writings. The text is short but informative, and the 137 high-quality color reproductions are indispensable.

Galloway, David. "František Kupka." *Art News* 94, no. 9 (November, 1995). A review of an exhibition of Kupka's work at the Gmurzynska Gallery in Cologne, Germany.

Kupka, František. *František Kupka, 1871-1957: A Retrospective.* New York: Solomon R. Guggenheim Foundation, 1975. Contains several scholarly articles, written to accompany a large exhibition of Kupka's work, as well as an excellent chronology and a biographical essay. Probably the best introduction to Kupka's work.

————. *Kupka: Gouaches and Pastels.* Text by Jean Cassou and Denise Fédit. Translated by Robert Erich Wolf. New York: Abrams, 1964. Kupka's gouaches and pastels show the intermediary stages through which his work went on the way to abstraction. The authors present succinct essays on Kupka's rapid evolution, concentrating on his exploration of the formal means of art.

Vachtová, Ludmila. *Frank Kupka.* Translated by Zdeněk Lederer. London: Thames and Hudson, and New York: McGraw-Hill, 1968. Perhaps the most thorough biography of Kupka, containing many facts not available elsewhere. Vachtová was not allowed to leave Czechoslovakia to do research, so this book lacks some information on Kupka's work in Paris as well as an understanding of what other artists were doing in Paris at the time.

Scott Lewis

IGOR VASILYEVICH KURCHATOV

Born: January 12, 1903; Sim Mill, in the Ural
Mountains, Russia
Died: February 7, 1960; Moscow, U.S.S.R.
Area of Achievement: Physics
Contribution: Kurchatov was the father of atomic
power in the Soviet Union. He played a pivotal
role in the introduction and advancement of
atomic energy as a peaceful source of power in
that country and was a leader in the development
of the Soviet Union's atom bomb in the late
1940's.

Early Life

Igor Vasilyevich Kurchatov was born on January
12, 1903, at the village of Sim Mill, in the Ural
Mountains, in Russia. His father, Vasili Alek-
seevich, was, at different times in his career, a surveyor and a forester's assistant. Igor's mother,
Mariya Vasilevna Ostyroumeya, was the daughter
of the local parish priest in Sim Mill. Igor was the
second of three children born to Vasili and Mariya;
his sister, Antonina, was the eldest and his brother,
Boris, the youngest.

In 1909, Igor's formal education began when his
family moved to the town of Simbirsk to allow him
to attend the Simbirsk *Gymnasium*, an acclaimed
regional primary school. Three years later, he
transferred to the Simferopol *Gymnasium*, after his
family moved to the Crimean town for his sister's
health. Igor excelled in virtually every subject in
his early education, but it was not until his teens,
after reading a book on engineering and physics,
that he chose physics as what would later be his
life's work. In 1920, after working days and going
to school at night, Igor was graduated from the
Simferopol *Gymnasium* with a gold medal for
scholastic achievement. He went on the same year
to attend the Tavricheski University in Simferopol.

Kurchatov was one of the first class of seventy in
the university's physics and mathematics department. As a result of his academic achievements,
Kurchatov and another student were placed in
charge of the university's physics laboratory and
allowed free rein to conduct experiments to advance their studies. From these early experiments,
Kurchatov was to gain an important understanding
of the value of practical evidence to support a scientific precept that would benefit him in his later
research. By 1923, Kurchatov was graduated from

Tavricheski University with a degree in physics,
completing the four-year course of study in three
years.

Moving to the city of Petrograd shortly after
graduation, he was enrolled in postgraduate work
in nautical engineering at the polytechnic institute
there. As in Simferopol, Kurchatov had to work to
support himself. He became a supervisor at the
electrical pavilion of the Magnetometeorological
Observatory in Pavlovsk, a position that allowed
him both to earn a living and to advance his professional interests. As his work at the observatory
grew in importance, Kurchatov fell behind in his
studies at the institute and was dropped from the
nautical engineering program in his second semester. Thereafter, Kurchatov decided to focus his efforts on physics.

After working as a researcher at the Baku Polytechnical Institute in 1924-1925, Kurchatov was
selected to work as a physicist at the Physico-
Technical Institute in Leningrad, the central facility for studies into advanced engineering and physics in the Soviet Union at the time. During the
same period, including the time of his marriage in
1927 to Marina Dmitrievna Sinelnikov, Kurchatov
also worked as an instructor in the mechanical
physics department of the Leningrad Polytechnical Institute and of the Teachers' Institute in the
same city. In these positions, Kurchatov would
spend his most active years and make some of the
most important discoveries of his career.

Life's Work

During the late 1920's and early 1930's, Kurchatov
was fascinated with the study of what was termed
ferroelectricity, the study of the properties and
characteristics of different materials as affected by
the introduction of electrical currents. These studies led to the development of electron semiconduc-
tors and moved Kurchatov's attention to nuclear
physics in the early 1930's. After conducting some
initial experiments on beryllium radiation and corresponding and meeting with nuclear physics pioneer Frédéric Joliot in 1933, Kurchatov began his
seminal studies into harnessing the power of the atom. Working with other researchers, including his
brother Boris, Kurchatov made pivotal breakthroughs in the discovery and study of isometric
nuclei, atomic nuclei—in Kurchatov's case radio-

active bromine isotopes—that have the same mass and composition but that possess different physical characteristics. This work led to significant advancements in the understanding of the structure of the atom within the Soviet scientific community.

During the same period, 1934-1935, Kurchatov worked with scientists at the Soviet Radium Institute (a facility for research and education patterned after similar institutes started by radiation pioneer Marie Curie in France and Poland) on the study of the neutron, a neutral subatomic particle about which very little was known at the time. Highly charged neutrons are used to bombard the nucleus of a radioactive atom such as uranium to split the nucleus and release high levels of energy in a nuclear reaction.

In the 1930's, researchers such as Joliot, Enrico Fermi, J. Robert Oppenheimer and others in the United States, Germany, and elsewhere began to realize that the nuclear reaction, if properly harnessed, could be used to create a bomb of unparalleled explosive power. Kurchatov, as one of the Soviet Union's leading nuclear physicists, was considered one of the de facto leaders of research and experimentation in the field in his country. Because of a variety of factors, including a scarcity of resources and the politically repressive atmosphere of the Stalinist regime at the time, the Soviet Union lagged behind the rest of the world in the race to master atomic energy.

In the late 1930's, Kurchatov and his team of researchers in Leningrad made advances in nuclear fission in radioactive isotopes of thorium and uranium. In 1940, two of Kurchatov's physicists discovered an incident of spontaneous fission in a uranium isotope and, under Kurchatov's direction, wrote a brief article about it to the American scientific publication *Physical Review*. *Physical Review*, at the time, was the world's leading scientific journal, publishing articles about progress in nuclear research.

After several weeks of waiting for a reply from the journal, Kurchatov initiated a search of current scientific publications for news about nuclear fission experimentation. The study showed that, after the middle of 1940, all American scientific journals had stopped publishing news of nuclear fission. This observation of sudden, uncharacteristic silence on the part of the American scientific community led Kurchatov to report to the Soviet political leadership that the United States, in reaction to the increasing threat of global war with the Axis powers of Germany, Italy, and Japan, was probably increasing its effort to build an atom bomb. That led to a corresponding increase in the research being conducted in the Soviet Union. Kurchatov's Leningrad laboratories became a major focus of that effort.

The advance of German troops into Soviet territory in July of 1941 drained resources from all sectors of the Soviet Union, including the scientific community. Many of Kurchatov's researchers and physicists were reassigned to assist the war effort, with Kurchatov himself being put to work in the shipyards of Sevastopol, training sailors to degauss ships. Degaussing is a process in which metallic coils are placed around a ship to demagnetize it as a defense against magnetic mines.

By 1942, Soviet espionage efforts in the United States had confirmed the fact that the Manhattan Project was making significant advances in the development of an American atom bomb. At the urging of other scientists and politicians, Kurchatov was recalled from Sevastopol and named chief designer of the facility that would be charged with developing a sustained, controlled nuclear reaction. This facility would later form the heart of the Soviet Atomic Energy Institute.

At the institute, Kurchatov's team built a cyclotron and other equipment necessary to operate a nuclear pile, or nuclear reactor. After the United States successfully tested and used atom bombs at the end of World War II, the Soviet Union increased its effort to counter what it perceived as an American nuclear threat. Kurchatov was a central figure in that controversy. On December 27, 1946, Kurchatov and his team created the first nuclear reactor in Europe. From the reactor, Kurchatov was able to develop the plutonium isotope necessary for the atom bomb. On September 29, 1949, the Soviet Union officially joined the nuclear age with the successful test explosion of an atom bomb. This feat was followed in November, 1952, by the test detonation of an American hydrogen bomb—a weapon many times more powerful than an atom bomb—and, on August 12, 1953, by a similar Soviet achievement.

After the development of the atom and hydrogen bombs, Kurchatov was instrumental as a leader in the movement within the Soviet scientific community to use nuclear power for peaceful purposes. He helped design and construct the first nuclear power plants in his country. In 1951, he organized one of the first major conferences on nuclear power in the Soviet Union and, later, was part of the team that put into operation the first nuclear-powered electrical generating stations in the Soviet Union on June 27, 1954.

Kurchatov was a highly regarded figure within the power structure of the Soviet government. In addition to serving the presidium (ruling body) of the Academy of Sciences of the Soviet Union, he was three times named a Hero of Soviet Labor, was a deputy to the Supreme Soviet, and was a respected politician in addition to his reputation as an outstanding scientist. It is believed that his political acumen, almost as much as his scientific ability, enabled him to lead successfully the increasingly complex organizations that accomplished his appointed objectives.

Beyond his role in the internal development of nuclear physics in his own country, Kurchatov was viewed as a pioneer by his peers in the international community of scientists. Frédéric Joliot of France, the husband of Irène Joliot-Curie and corecipient of the Nobel Prize for his seminal work in nuclear physics, shared a long correspondence with Kurchatov. In the late 1950's, Kurchatov participated in international conferences on atomic energy and joined other scientists in calling for a worldwide ban on nuclear weapons. In the late 1950's, he was a strong advocate for a ban on the atmospheric testing of atomic weapons, a concept on which the United States and the Soviet Union later agreed in the Nuclear Test Ban Treaty of 1963. Moving into semiretirement after two strokes in 1956 and 1957, Kurchatov continued to involve himself in the continuing developments in nuclear physics and in the design and construction of several nuclear power plants in the Soviet Union. On February 7, 1960, in Moscow, he died, presumably of heart failure.

Summary

Igor Vasilyevich Kurchatov's achievements go beyond the projects to which he dedicated his life. His theoretical work, while of considerable importance, only paralleled—and usually lagged behind—that of other nuclear pioneers of the early twentieth century. It is, rather, in the application of the theories he helped discover that his work takes on immeasurable importance.

Kurchatov flourished under the oppressive and technologically stifling atmosphere of the regime of Joseph Stalin. Kurchatov was able to assemble teams of outstanding scientists under grueling and arduous conditions and, moreover, to motivate those scientists to build a working, productive community. He managed to stay in favor—and out of prison—during Stalin's several purges of the nation's scientific and political leadership and to advance his objectives at the same time. He was, by all accounts, a dedicated scientist who believed that the laboratory was the place to develop and test theories of physics. Because of this practical perspective, he encouraged a whole generation of Soviet physicists to put their principles and concepts to the test throughout the creative process. He served as a mentor to many of his country's greatest scientific figures, including nuclear physicist Andrey Sakharov.

Kurchatov also helped his country move into the technological age of the last half of the twentieth century by shaping a dual course of development for atomic energy in the Soviet Union. Had he focused entirely on the development of nuclear weapons, the peaceful applications of atomic energy—electrical generating plants—might not have had a powerful champion to guide them to reality as early as occurred.

Bibliography

Golovin, I. N. *I. V. Kurchatov: A Socialist-Realist Biography of the Soviet Nuclear Scientist.* Translated by William H. Dougherty. Bloomington, Ind.: Selbstverlag Press, 1968. This book is one of the only biographies produced in the Soviet Union on Kurchatov that has been translated into English. As with many Soviet works, there is a strong propagandist cast to the narrative, but the information is well organized. It is interesting reading, both as a means to learn about Kurchatov and as a view into the mindset of the Soviet system of government.

Kurchatov, Igor. Article in *Pravda*, February 28, 1958. *Pravda* was the official daily newspaper of the Soviet Union. The article appearing under Kurchatov's byline outlines his views on the need for useful exchanges and dialogue between the world's scientists to advance international cooperation in the development of nuclear power.

Rhodes, Richard. *The Making of the Atomic Bomb.* New York: Simon and Schuster, 1986. This expansive compendium of information about the West's development of the atom bomb includes brief listings of information about Kurchatov himself but explores in greater depth the time and sociopolitical atmosphere in which both the United States and the Soviet Union raced to develop mankind's most destructive weapon.

Eric Christensen

AKIRA KUROSAWA

Born: March 23, 1910; Tokyo, Japan
Died: September 5, 1998; Tokyo, Japan
Area of Achievement: Film
Contribution: Throughout his long career as one of the greatest directors in the history of the cinema, Kurosawa explored a humane and profound vision of existence with a brilliantly inventive use of the art of film.

Early Life

Akira Kurosawa was the youngest of seven children born to a family that recognized its rural roots but prided itself on being Edokko, or third-generation dwellers in Tokyo. In Kurosawa's youth, Japanese country life was slow and peaceful and the culture of the city was just beginning to absorb ideas from the outside world. Kurosawa's father was a graduate of a school for training army officers and was a severe disciplinarian who valued the varieties of experience that a man might encounter; his devotion to the ancient code of the samurai, Bushido, was an important influence on his son, both as a model and as a rigid pattern against which to react. Kurosawa was also deeply impressed with his mother's quiet strength and iron will and by his darkly sardonic and brilliantly perceptive elder brother Heigo, whose suicide in 1933 led him to become "impatient with my own aimlessness."

As a student in primary and secondary school, Kurosawa concentrated on the art and literature courses that he liked and ignored his required studies in math and science. He treasured teachers who taught with imagination and creativity, despised those who operated by rote, substituted reckless behavior for a lack of physical dexterity, and failed every aspect of military training he was required to take. Although his father was a noted figure in army society, he was not a military fanatic; he taught Kurosawa both calligraphy and poetry as a child and did not complain when Kurosawa decided to become a painter after graduation from middle school in 1927.

When Kurosawa was rejected by the army in 1930 as physically unfit, he joined several leftist political organizations, as much for the fascination of new experience as for his genuine sympathy for the people in Tokyo slums, and while working as a courier for underground political organizations, he spent his leisure time among friends of his brother, who had become a noted narrator of silent films. Kurosawa was gradually becoming involved in the avant-garde world of theatrical and artistic creativity, but his own career had not progressed at all. After his brother's suicide, he worked as a commercial artist ("illustrations of the correct way to cut giant radishes") to earn money to buy canvases and paints, but he was becoming anxious about his inability to find a real calling. In 1935, he noticed an advertisement announcing openings for assistant directors at the newly established studio Photo Chemical Laboratory (PCL). Kurosawa had been an avid filmgoer since elementary school; his test essay on the fundamental deficiencies of Japanese films was accepted, and he joined the studio. Although he found his first assignment routine and trivial, his father persuaded him to stay on, saying that anything Kurosawa tried "would be worth the experience." His next assignment was with the director Kajirō Yamamoto, "the best teacher of my entire life," and his life's work had begun.

Life's Work

Kurosawa joined PCL immediately after the "2-26 Incident" of February, 1936, in which young army-officer extremists assassinated cabinet ministers whose policies they found too moderate. Kurosawa recalled that the studio was a true "dream factory" in those days, making films "as carefree as a song about strolling through fragrant blossoms." Kurosawa was assigned to the group headed by his mentor, "Yama-san," advancing from third assistant director to chief assistant director, concentrating on editing and dubbing from 1937 to 1941, as PCL grew into the huge Tōhō company, the single largest film studio in Japan. While the studio tried to avoid political issues, the severity of the censors led to increasing tension between the creative artists and the wartime government. When Kurosawa turned to screenwriting after spending a year with the second unit on *Uma* (1941; *Horses*), his second effort, "Shizuka nari" (all is quiet), won the Nihon Eiga contest for best scenario but was not filmed, nor were his next two scripts, which were "buried forever by the Interior Ministry censorship bureau," a group Kurosawa viewed as "mentally deranged." Two of Kurosawa's lesser scripts, about the aircraft industry and boy aviators, were filmed by others in 1942, but, when he read the story of a rowdy young judo expert, he had an intuition that "This is it." After convincing the studio to buy rights, he wrote the script for *Sugata Sanshiro* (1943; *Sanshiro Sugata*) in one sitting. The censors regarded his initial effort as a director as too "British-American," but Yasujiro Ozu argued for its release, and although some critics believed that it was too complicated, the film was a success.

Realizing that he would not be permitted to make any films that did not contribute to the war effort but reluctant to support a government that he despised and alert enough so that, by 1943, it was clear to him that Japan was going to be defeated, Kurosawa wrote a script about a group of women working in a precision optics factory. *Ichiban utsukushiku* (1944; *The Most Beautiful*) was intended to illuminate the beautiful spirit (*kokoro*) of the young women struggling under trying conditions. This film introduced Takashi Shimura, an outstanding actor who went on to work with Kurosawa in many subsequent films.

Between 1945 and 1950 Kurosawa made nine films. Some of these were clearly apprentice works, but several—including *Yoidore tenshi* (1948; *Drunken Angel*) and *Nora-inu* (1949; *Stray Dog*)—show his increasing mastery and retain their interest. *Drunken Angel* is also notable as the first of many Kurosawa films to feature the great actor Toshiro Mifune. Later in the same year that saw the release of the relatively weak film *Shubun* (1950; *Scandal*), which marks the end of this period, Kurosawa completed the film that first brought him international recognition.

Working with a cast and crew he knew and trusted, Kurosawa adapted a story about an incident in a forest in eleventh century Japan, told from four points of view. The theme, according to Kurosawa's explanation to a somewhat befuddled cast, was that "human beings are unable to be honest with themselves about themselves." In a rare fusion of superb cinematography, exceptional music, inspired acting, and a perfect location coalescing through a director's guidance, *Rashomon* (1950) delighted its participants and won the Grand Prix at the Venice Film Festival, a most prestigious award at the time, as well as the American Academy Award for Best Foreign Language Film. Kurosawa's next project was *Hakuchi* (1951; *The Idiot*), based on the novel by Fyodor Dostoevski. The film was more than four hours long in its original version and was a commercial failure in all of its released forms. Kurosawa clashed frequently with

the studio about its production and remarked in retrospect on the film's failure, "One should be brave enough to risk this kind of 'mistake.'" According to Donald Richie, "Without the trials, disappointments, mistakes and uncertainties of *The Idiot*," the films that followed, among them some of the true masterpieces of cinematic art in this century, "might not have appeared at all."

Beginning with *Ikiru* (1952), Kurosawa reached his productive prime. Now in the middle years and conscious of his mortality ("Sometimes I think of my death . . . of ceasing to be"), he shows an anonymous clerk—a cipher, a brick in a huge wall—who is told that he has six months to live. In his remaining time, the clerk becomes intensely aware of the value of life, escaping from the bureaucratic prison that bedevils modern Japan. *Ikiru* is a compassionate affirmation of existence, still contemporary and tremendously moving decades after its production, and it was both a commercial and critical success, Kurosawa's first real triumph in Japan. It was followed by an even greater success, *Shichinin no samurai* (1954; *The Seven Samurai*), which Richie calls "perhaps the best Japanese film ever made"—a judgment with which many critics have concurred.

The Seven Samurai is a penetrating examination of the old samurai code as well as an epic action-film in the grand style of the American Western. With the insight accumulated from his own experience as the son of a soldier combined with his knowledge of Japanese history, Kurosawa explores the nuances and complexities of self-expression and self-submission embodied in the warrior's code, rescuing the true samurai spirit from its debasement in numerous Japanese exploitation films. The temporal glory of the warrior is presented in contrast to the eternal grandeur of farmers struggling through the testing cycles of the seasons, and although the film is one of the most dramatically and visually exciting ever made, it is also a marvelous, detailed study of character and society. It was the most expensive production attempted by Tōhō to that time, and it took more than a year to make.

Continuing to alternate between modern and period work, Kurosawa next turned to a theme that had been tormenting Japan since atom bombs had been dropped on Hiroshima and Nagasaki. The nuclear tests of 1954 and the resulting fallout on Japanese islands led to Kurosawa's *Ikimono no kiroku* (1955; *I Live in Fear*; also known as *Record of a Living Being*), a film about an industrialist with two separate families by wife and mistress who is being driven insane by nuclear phobia and wants to move all of his dependents to Brazil—theoretically out of danger. The film is sprawling and emotional, but Kurosawa put so much into it that he said at its completion, "When the last judgment comes upon us, we could stand up and account for our past lives by saying proudly: 'We are the men who made *Ikimono no kiroku.*'"

Working steadily, Kurosawa then directed *Kumonosu-jo* (1957; *Throne of Blood*), his adaptation of *Macbeth* (1606) and possibly the best visual correlative to a Shakespeare play ever filmed. The supernatural elements, the psychology of Macbeth and Lady Macbeth, the mood of violence and the extraordinary ending are highlights of a powerful, gripping production. After three more films in rapid succession, Kurosawa made one of his most popular works, the vastly entertaining *Yojimbo* (1961).

Another homage to the Western, but with a twist, it is the story of a man who cleans up a corrupt town; unlike a typical American lawman, however, he is cynical, amoral, and convulsively funny. Mifune at his best played the wandering, disenfranchised ex-samurai and then extended the conception in a demonstration of what a real sequel can be in *Sanjuro* (1962). Here the protagonist is ten years older as well as wider, deeper, broader, and stranger; his singular stylistic gestures now become bizarre expressions of eccentricity. The aging samurai is a man out of place and time who still grudgingly maintains a set of realistic principles that structure his actions.

Returning to the present, Kurosawa directed *Tengoku to jigoku* (1963; *High and Low*), an incisive examination of life in upper- and lower-class sections of modern Yokohama, presented in the form of a detective story. Then, in the culmination of his greatest period of productivity, he worked with Mifune for the last time in *Akahige* (1965; *Red Beard*). Set at the end of the Tokugawa period, it is the story of a young apprentice physician who learns how to become a real doctor (and a real man) through his training in a rural clinic with an experienced older physician known as Red Beard. Embodying the essential core of Kurosawa's philosophy, Red Beard has a kind of rage for good but is fully realistic about the evil in human nature. His anger helps him to avoid cynicism and inspires the young doctor to become a man worthy of the profession.

After filming *Akahige*, Kurosawa observed that "a cycle of some sort has concluded," and he began to work less frequently. He did not make another film until *Dodesukaden* (1970), a story of slum dwellers in the modern era told in episodic form. The film is a sincere but somewhat diffuse effort, lacking the energy and transcendent vision of Kurosawa's best work. It was his first color film, but, aside from some striking individual scenes, there is no real sense of a coordinated palate. The commercial failure of *Dodesukaden* and his problems with the American producers of *Tora! Tora! Tora!* (1970), who hired him to work on the Japanese sequences of the attack on Pearl Harbor, drove Kurosawa to despondency and a suicide attempt at the age of sixty-one. In Japanese culture, an artist's suicide in his sixties is an acknowledgment of declining powers and an homage to his craft, but Kurosawa was probably driven more by personal frustration at the difficulty of getting financing for his work. Consequently, he accepted a Mosfilm project to film *Dersu Uzala* (1975), set in the Siberian wilderness. The film was almost more of an exploration of landscape than a study of character, but it showed Kurosawa's increasing facility with color.

The real indication of Kurosawa's enduring power as a filmmaker was his direction of *Kagemusha* (1980; *Kagemusha: The Shadow Warrior*), a film with the epic sweep of his finest period studies, the character penetration of his most compelling work, and a real mastery of color cinematography. The funding for the production was raised by the American directors Francis Coppola and George Lucas. Although the film ends on a bleak, even desolate note, its scenes are alive with passion and its effect is ultimately of the world of men viewed from the perspective of time and history, neither judgmental nor falsely optimistic. This philosophical position was continued in *Ran* (1985), a rather loose adaptation of the King Lear legend, replete with violence, strife, treachery, confusion, and death. The clan of rulers is wiped out by the film's end, but other rulers arrive to replace them; life goes on.

Continuing to work as a filmmaker in his late seventies, Kurosawa concluded the 1980's with a nine-episode film based on some of the central images of his lifetime, tentatively entitled "Akira Kurosawa's Dreams." The film was financed by Steven Spielberg and George Lucas and is a kind of lament for what Kurosawa calls the loss of human goodness. "I am nostalgic for a good environment and good hearts," he said in describing his motivation. In 1990, Kurosawa was awarded the Academy Award for Lifetime Achievement.

Summary

Akira Kurosawa introduced the Western world to the full richness of Japanese film and, in turn, to the beginning of an understanding of the range and complexity of Japanese history and culture; at the same time, he introduced the Japanese people to a deeper understanding of their own traditions and heritage. Through his inventive mastery of all the elements of filmmaking, he commented on the central moral issues of modern times and examined the eternal questions of the mystery of existence for all times. "I think of the earth as my home," he said, and like all great artists, he tried to celebrate the richness of life on that home for all human beings who can appreciate its vast gifts. At the same time, he understood the contradictory forces within human nature which often make that home an uninhabitable hell and tried to dramatize the importance of recognizing reality and overcoming illusion as a crucial step in the process of reconciling human beings to the tragic grandeur of life. Like William Shakespeare, one of his own masters, Kurosawa dealt with the largest questions humanity must confront but never forgot that the traditional elements of narrative, character, and language are the fundamental blocks upon which any serious artistic statement must be built.

Bibliography

Braudy, Leo, and Morris Dickstein, eds. *Great Film Directors: A Critical Anthology.* New York: Oxford University Press, 1978. This volume contains four essays on Kurosawa, including one by Akira Iwasaki which offers a commentary on Kurosawa's work from the perspective of a Japanese critic.

Desser, David. *The Samurai Films of Akira Kurosawa.* Ann Arbor, Mich.: U.M.I. Research Press, 1983. An informative if somewhat academic examination of the Japanese cultural history which underlies the samurai film, including a detailed discussion of Kurosawa's work in this area as well as a consideration of the influence of Kurosawa's films on both Japanese and American filmmakers.

Erens, Patricia. *Akira Kurosawa: A Guide to References and Resources.* London: Prior, and Boston: Hall, 1979. While the biographical background and survey of Kurosawa's work are rather pedestrian, the synopses of the films themselves and the list of articles about Kurosawa are thorough and accurate. A useful resource.

Hogue, Peter. "The Kurosawa Story." *Film Comment* 35, no. 1 (January-February, 1999). Considers the films of Kurosawa, emphasizing plots, settings, imagery, and characters, as well as the director's views on society.

Kurosawa, Akira. *Something Like an Autobiography.* Translated by Audie E. Bock. New York: Knopf, 1982. An extremely revealing, candid, and analytical account of the director's life up to the release of *Rashomon* in 1950. Ably translated, it is interesting and highly readable and provides much information about the author as well as the Japanese film industry and about Japan in the decades before World War II.

Maxfield, James. "'The Earth Is Burning': Kurosawa's *Record of a Living Being.*" *Literature Film Quarterly* 26, no. 2 (1998). Examines the experiences of Kurosawa during the filming of *Record of a Living Being,* the film's poor reception, and the visual presentation of the film.

Mellen, Joan. *Voices from the Japanese Cinema.* New York: Liveright, 1975. Includes an overview of Kurosawa's work by an expert on Japanese films and a good interview with the director himself.

———. *The Waves at Genji's Door: Japan Through Its Cinema.* New York: Pantheon, 1976. Covers many of Kurosawa's important films and includes an essay on "Kurosawa's women," examining one of the more controversial aspects of the director's work.

Richie, Donald. *The Films of Akira Kurosawa.* 3d ed. Berkeley: University of California Press, 1996. Indispensable for the student of Kurosawa's work, and one of the finest books ever written about any film artist. Richie provides detailed discussion of each film, combined with extensive background information, many illustrations, and a filmography.

Wilmington, Michael. "Akira Kurosawa 1910-1998." *Film Comment* 35, no. 1 (January-February, 1999). Profile of Kurosawa including the themes of his films, his directorial style, and violence in films in general.

Leon Lewis

ROBERT M. LA FOLLETTE

Born: June 14, 1855; Primrose, Wisconsin
Died: June 18, 1925; Washington, D.C.
Area of Achievement: Government and politics
Contribution: As governor of Wisconsin and United States Senator, La Follette combined a strong sense of social justice with an intense commitment to principles as a leader of the reform movement in politics from 1900 to 1925.

Early Life

Robert Marion La Follette was born June 14, 1855, in Primrose township, Dane County, Wisconsin, a few miles from Madison. His father, Josiah, died before Robert was a year old; in 1862 his mother, née Mary Ferguson, married John Z. Saxton of Argyle, a prosperous merchant and Baptist deacon. La Follette attended school in Argyle until 1870, when he returned with his family to the La Follette family farm in Primrose, where he assumed much of the responsibility for operating the farm. In 1873, a year after his stepfather's death, he began preparatory courses at the Wisconsin Academy in Madison and entered the University of Wisconsin in 1875. He did not distinguish himself in academics but built a reputation as a brilliant speaker and a popular student who financed his education by purchasing and publishing the student newspaper, the *University Press*. Following graduation, he took law courses at the University, read in a Madison attorney's office, and courted his University of Wisconsin classmate Belle Case, whom he married in December, 1881.

La Follette established a legal practice in Madison in 1880; he entered politics the same year with his election to the office of district attorney for Dane County. His warm personality and speaking ability made him popular, and he was easily reelected in 1882. He was elected to the first of three consecutive terms in the United States House of Representatives in 1884, even though he did not have the backing of Republican state bosses. The youngest member of Congress when he entered the House in 1885, La Follette was a fairly regular Republican during his three terms there. He strengthened his political hold on his congressional district by supporting legislation he saw as beneficial to farmers, including assiduous support of the McKinley Tariff of 1890. In spite of his strong political base, he was the victim of an imbroglio over a law requir-ing English-language instruction in Wisconsin schools. While La Follette had nothing to do with the state law, he was caught in a backlash against Republicans and was defeated in 1890.

La Follette returned to his legal practice in Madison. The clean-shaven, square-jawed lawyer with piercing eyes and upswept, bushy dark hair (which added inches to his five-foot, five-inch frame) built a reputation for dynamism in jury trials. At the same time, he strove to fulfill his political ambitions by establishing, within the Republican Party in Wisconsin, an organization to challenge the control of state bosses, notably United States Senators John C. Spooner and Philetus Sawyer. By 1897, the La Follette organization had adopted a popular program which grew out of the economic depression which began in 1893: corporate regulation, equity in taxation, and the democratization of the political system through direct primary elections. Refused the gubernatorial nomination by state Republican conventions in 1896 and 1898, La Follette persevered in winning support; in 1900 he was elected governor of Wisconsin and assumed office in January, 1901.

Life's Work

As governor for two full terms and part of a third, La Follette successfully converted Wisconsin into a so-called laboratory of democracy. The transformation, however, did not take place immediately. When he entered office with the intention of redeeming his campaign pledges of a direct primary law and railroad tax legislation, he encountered persistent opposition from the state legislature. The lack of reform accomplishments in his first term led to a sweeping campaign in 1902 not only for his own reelection but also for the election of state legislators who would follow his program. In subsequent sessions, the legislature passed the primary election and railroad tax laws and set up a railroad rate commission. Moreover, La Follette so firmly established the direction of reform politics in Wisconsin that his followers would control state offices for years after he left the governorship. A few weeks after the legislature convened in January, 1905, La Follette was elected to the United States Senate. He left Wisconsin at the end of the year, after securing passage of the railroad rate commission law, and was sworn into the Senate on January 4, 1906.

La Follette made an immediate impact on the Senate. Although unsuccessful in promoting major reform legislation in early sessions, he received widespread attention for pressing for more stringent regulation of railroads and for his attack on the "Money Trust" while filibustering against a monetary bill proposed by Senate Republican leader Nelson W. Aldrich. His national reputation was further enhanced by his frequent Chautauqua speaking tours around the country (which began while he was governor of Wisconsin) and by the attention accorded him by reform journalists such as David Graham Phillips and Lincoln Steffens; the latter proposed a La Follette presidential campaign in 1908 on an independent ticket. While eschewing such a campaign, La Follette successfully assisted Progressive candidates in several states in their congressional races, thus establishing a solid core of reform-minded colleagues for the ensuing Congress. To publicize his causes (and with the hope of a solid financial return), he initiated *La Follette's Weekly Magazine* in January, 1909; he would continue the venture until his death, although it was more a financial liability than a success and was reorganized as a monthly in 1914.

La Follette and his new Senate allies challenged the Taft Administration on several important issues and effectively established themselves as an insurgent wing of the Republican Party. By leading Senate Progressives in opposition to the 1909 Payne-Aldrich Tariff and in pressing for conservation measures and a program of direct democracy, La Follette earned the hostile attention of President William Howard Taft, who worked hard to unseat the Wisconsin senator in his 1910 bid for reelection. La Follette won easily and returned to Washington in 1911 determined to reconstruct the Republican Party along liberal lines. As much as any individual, he was responsible for the ideological split in the GOP which led to the formation of the Progressive Party in 1912. He was not the presidential nominee, however, as most of his supporters in the National Progressive Republican League (which he had founded in January, 1911) deserted him to support the popular ex-president Theodore Roosevelt; his candidacy was further impaired by a temporary breakdown he suffered while delivering a speech in February, 1912, before the annual banquet of the Periodical Publishers' Association in Philadelphia. He refused to endorse any candidate in 1912, but his speeches and magazine articles were generally supportive of the Democrat Woodrow Wilson.

La Follette's influence declined in the Democratic-controlled Senate of the early Wilson Administration. While he supported some Wilson labor measures and managed to steer his La Follette Seamen's Act through Congress in 1915, he was critical of the president's blueprint for the Federal Reserve System, appointments to the Federal Trade Commission, and policy on racial segregation in the federal government. His greatest opposition to Wilson came in the area of foreign policy. Sharply critical of Wilson's increased military spending in 1915-1916, La Follette argued that such expenditures increased the profits of corporations at the expense of taxpayers and, ultimately, American security interests. Using the same argument, he voted against American entry into World War I and remained a leading antiwar spokesman throughout. He also led fights for free speech and against censorship laws, and proposed new taxes on war profits to pay for the prosecution of the war. He voted against the Versailles Treaty in the Senate, characterizing it as reactionary in its treatment of the Soviet Union and in reinforcing colonialism in Ireland, India, and Egypt.

In the conservative Republican era that followed the war, La Follette fashioned a new political constituency among the farm and labor groups that emerged in political affairs in the early 1920's. Reacting to an agricultural depression and what many saw as an antilabor atmosphere, groups such as the American Federation of Labor, the railroad brotherhoods, the Nonpartisan League, and the American Farm Bureau Federation formed an alliance which resulted in the Conference for Progressive Political Action in 1922 and the Progressive Party in 1924. In a zealous campaign against Republican "normalcy," La Follette and Burton K. Wheeler, Progressive candidates for president and vice president, respectively, polled 4.8 million votes, approximately one in every six cast. La Follette's health was poor during this campaign, which was his last. He died of a heart attack on June 18, 1925, and was buried at Forest Hill Cemetery in Madison four days later.

Summary

La Follette's campaigns, full of vitriol directed against "the interests" as opposed to "the people," largely reflected the Populist roots of Midwestern Progressivism. In La Follette's view, the most obvious villain was large-scale corporate capitalism; his ideal was an open, competitive economic sys-

tem—he consistently championed the cause of individuals as voters, consumers, and small businessmen. His political solutions included a roster of Populist planks: the direct election of United States senators, direct primary elections, the graduated income tax, and public ownership of railroads, among others.

In opposing corporate growth, La Follette fought a losing battle against modernization; he was also responsible, however, for labor and agricultural programs that eased the adjustment of some groups to modern conditions. In addition, an important facet of the "Wisconsin Idea" he initiated as governor was the modern use of expert panels and commissions to make recommendations on legislation and regulatory activities. His reliance on faculty members of the University of Wisconsin (such as economists John Commons and Richard Ely) not only enhanced the university's reputation but also served as an example to reformers in other states.

Nicknamed "Fighting Bob" La Follette, the senator possessed notable personal characteristics which made him a symbol of the movement he led. His dynamic, aggressive style was complemented by a fearless quality which enabled him to challenge the leadership of his own party and to risk his career in opposing World War I. When engaged in a cause, his intensity was so great that he suffered several physical breakdowns during his political career. This combination of qualities contributed to a remarkable Senate career; in 1957, the Senate voted to recognize La Follette as one of the five outstanding members in Senate history.

Bibliography

Burgchardt, Carl R. *Robert M. La Follette, Sr.: The Voice of Conscience*. Foreword by Bernard K. Duffy. New York: Greenwood Press, 1992. A unique rhetorical biography that provides texts of key speeches along with analysis, a chronology of major speeches, and a bibliography.

La Follette, Belle Case, and Fola La Follette. *Robert M. La Follette: June 14, 1855-June 18, 1925*. 2 vols. New York: Macmillan, 1953. Written by La Follette's wife and daughter. As an "insiders'" account, the book naturally tends to lack objectivity, but it is strengthened by the authors' intimate understanding of the subject. In addition, the book is meticulously researched and ably written with a wealth of detail.

La Follette, Robert M. *La Follette's Autobiography: A Personal Narrative of Political Experiences*. Madison, Wis.: Robert M. La Follette, 1913. Originally published by La Follette as a campaign document for the 1912 presidential election. La Follette provides a detailed narrative of his political thought and activities, as well as his antagonism toward Theodore Roosevelt.

Margulies, Herbert F. *The Decline of the Progressive Movement in Wisconsin: 1890-1920*. Madison: State Historical Society of Wisconsin, 1968. Margulies finds that the Progressive movement in Wisconsin was well into decline before World War 1. He details how internal divisions among the Progressives (largely over La Follette's political tactics) led to their defeat by conservatives.

Maxwell, Robert S. *La Follette and the Rise of the Progressives in Wisconsin*. Madison: State Historical Society of Wisconsin, 1956. The author finds the roots of Progressivism in Midwestern farm problems. He emphasizes the achievements of Wisconsin Progressives, including direct primaries, expert commissions, and comprehensive insurance code, pointing out that the strengths and weaknesses of the Progressive movement in Wisconsin reflected those of La Follette.

Thelen, David P. *The Early Life of Robert M. La Follette, 1855-1884*. Chicago: Loyola University Press, 1966. A brief examination of La Follette's formative years in Wisconsin, to his 1884 election to Congress.

————. *The New Citizenship: Origins of Progressivism in Wisconsin, 1885-1900*. Columbia: University of Missouri Press, 1972. Demonstrates how La Follette came into a movement already under way in Wisconsin in the late 1890's. The book is particularly good in its treatment of the social and political milieu in which reform ideas grew, largely out of issues of the 1893-1897 depression; these issues caused a "new civic consciousness" to develop among politicians and voters of diverse backgrounds.

————. *Robert M. La Follette and the Insurgent Spirit*. Boston: Little Brown, 1976. Incisively relates La Follette's career to the course of Progressive insurgency in the Republican Party from the late 1890's to the 1920's. Thelen clearly delineates La Follette's positions and contrasts them with those of regular Republicans and Wilsonian Democrats.

Richard G. Frederick

HENRI-MARIE LA FONTAINE

Born: April 22, 1854; Brussels, Belgium
Died: May 14, 1943; Brussels, Belgium
Areas of Achievement: Diplomacy, government, politics, and law
Contribution: La Fontaine was a leader in the European popular peace movement and was awarded the Nobel Peace Prize in 1913. In addition to being an influential pacifist, he was an outstanding jurist, dedicated professor, Belgian senator, social reformer, and prolific author.

Early Life

Henri-Marie La Fontaine was born in Brussels, Belgium, on April 22, 1854. He studied law at the Free University of Brussels, received his doctorate when he was twenty-three, and was admitted to the bar in 1877. He maintained a successful private law practice for the next sixteen years, during which he became an authority on international law. In 1893, he was appointed professor of international law at the Université Nouvelle in Brussels.

Throughout his early legal career, La Fontaine developed a sharp intellect and compassion that would be the trademark of his future peace work. La Fontaine's legal career led him into politics, first nationally and later internationally. He became an active though moderate Social Democrat and was a founding member of the socialist political newspaper *La Justice.* His enthusiasm for reform issues and his talent for organization were perfectly suited for a political career. He was elected senator to the Belgian parliament in 1895 and served for thirty-six years, eventually becoming the vice president of the senate. While a senator, he was active in education and labor reform, foreign affairs, and economic issues.

Life's Work

La Fontaine is most widely known as a spokesman for world peace. He first became active in 1889 in the loosely organized international peace movement, when he was asked by the English pacifist Hodgson Pratt to organize and operate the Société Belge de l'Arbitrage et de la Paix (Belgian Society of Arbitration and Peace), which was to be modeled after Pratt's London organization. La Fontaine's insight and ability to mobilize and manage followers for the peace movement soon proved invaluable to the cause. He organized the Universal Peace Congress held at Antwerp in 1894 and pre-

pared the report of its proceedings. La Fontaine was soon recognized as a leader of the peace movement and a tireless advocate for world peace.

La Fontaine was a founding member and a staunch supporter of the International Peace Bureau (Nobel Peace Prize recipient in 1910). The bureau, located in Berne, Switzerland, was conceived in 1882 by Élie Ducommun (Nobel Peace Prize corecipient in 1902) as a clearinghouse for international peace information. La Fontaine worked as a bureau commissioner and, in 1907, succeeded Frederik Bajer as its director. Through his association with the bureau, La Fontaine played an active role in arranging the Hague Peace Conferences of 1899 and 1907.

La Fontaine's election to the Belgian senate in 1895 entitled him to a seat in the Interparliamentary Union, an organization created in 1888 by Frédéric Passy and William Cremer (Nobel Peace Prize recipients in 1901 and 1903, respectively) and dedicated to ending international war. The union encouraged members of parliaments from many nations to meet regularly and resolve international disputes before the antagonists became so passionately involved in their own positions that arbitration would be impossible. La Fontaine served as chairman of its juridical committee prior to 1914 and served on two other committees that drafted a model treaty for arbitration and created a world parliament model. Moreover, La Fontaine worked outside officially sponsored peace activities to create informal peace associations among diverse private organizations in order to build international social interdependence, which he believed was a necessary element of a unified world.

Prior to his senatorial election and direct participation in the Interparliamentary Union, La Fontaine observed and criticized union affairs for leading periodicals and was acutely aware of the union's limitations. He believed that the union was only the first step toward a world government that would be the ultimate arbitrator of international disputes. Though La Fontaine was a visionary, he was also realistic enough to know that a true world state was possible only in the distant future.

In 1895, La Fontaine established, with the help of his friend Paul Otlet, the Institut International de Bibliographie, or the "House of Documentation." This immense bibliographical scheme was an attempt to index, collate, and provide information on significant scientific works written in all languages, aimed at the unprecedented task of cataloging all written material in the world. At the same time, Otlet and La Fontaine created a universal information classification system and produced several reference works, especially bibliographies of the social sciences and peace. This work reflected La Fontaine's conviction that institutionalized international culture and achievement was a significant step toward world harmony.

Another related body that La Fontaine and Otlet founded was the Union of International Associations, located in Brussels. Established in 1910, the union's purpose was to coordinate international nongovernmental organizations and enable them to operate effectively in international affairs. In 1951, with the United Nations Social Council and in 1952 with the United Nations Educational, Scientific, and Cultural Organization (UNESCO), the union was granted consultative status, and it remains today the only organization in the world devoted to the research, promotion, and documentation of international organizations.

In 1913, La Fontaine was awarded the Nobel Peace Prize and was heralded by the Nobel committee as "the true leader of the popular peace movement in Europe." One year later World War I began, and La Fontaine fled first to Great Britain and then to the United States. It was during the war that he wrote his best-known work, *The Great Solution: Magnissima Charter* (1916). In this work, La Fontaine proposed a number of measures to prevent future war among nations. He sought to influence traditionally isolationist nations, especially Great Britain and the United States, into accepting his concept of a union of nations; he proposed a set of principles for international organization; and he sketched the rough outline of a federal world constitution that would eventually be incorporated into a world government. He stressed the need for international courts and provisions for collective military sanctions to enforce international court judgments. He proposed the creation of an international language, institutions such as a world school and university, library, parliament, bank, and sources for labor, immigration, and trade statistics. Also during the war, La Fontaine wrote *International Judicature* (1915), an article outlining the basics for a world supreme court.

At the end of the war, out of respect for his vision of postwar world organization, La Fontaine was appointed technical adviser for the Belgian delegation to the Paris Peace Conference of 1919. In 1920 and 1921, he was a delegate to the First Assembly of the League of Nations, at which he pressed for obligatory armed intervention against aggressor nations that violated the rules of the League. Many of the ultimate weaknesses of the League, primarily its inability to enforce its rules with collective military force, were anticipated by La Fontaine in *The Great Solution* and other writings. Some of La Fontaine's ideas were incorporated into the postwar peace scheme, such as his Centre Intellectual Mondial (world intellectual center), which evolved into the League's Institute of Intellectual Cooperation.

After the war, La Fontaine continued his peace efforts. He endorsed the Kellogg-Briand and Locarno pacts and supported disarmament. He worked with the Carnegie Endowment for International Peace, the Interparliamentary Union, and the International Peace Bureau. Until 1940, he continued to teach international law at the Free University of Brussels. He lectured on international disputes, disarmament, world government, the League of Nations, and the relationship between politics and morality. La Fontaine continued to attend peace conferences and meetings of the International Peace Bureau. He lived long enough to see his homeland invaded a second time and the world plunged once again into war. He died in Brussels in 1943 at the age of eighty-nine, working for the cause of world peace almost until his death. La Fontaine left a prodigious written legacy of hundreds of articles, pamphlets, and books, including a manual on the laws of international peace and arbitration, a sourcebook of 368 documents on international arbitration written between 1794 and 1900, and a bibliography on international arbitration containing 2,222 entries.

Throughout his life, La Fontaine displayed a wide scope of interests. He supported reforms in the Belgian bar to allow women to practice law and was a lifelong advocate for women's rights. He was an avid mountain climber and drafted a two-volume mountaineering bibliography. He published respectable translations of the operas of Richard Wagner and lectured on such diverse topics as modern art and his personal impressions of the United States.

Summary

The cause of world peace was a popular preoccupation among educated people, especially prior to

World War I. Henri-Marie La Fontaine was at the heart of the international peace movement as both an organizer and an inspiration. He was an advocate of a world state that would prevent international disputes and war through the operation of law and arbitration. He was one of the first to recognize the emergence of an international culture in the industrial age and attempt to make it understandable and give it an institutional form. He was a visionary whose ideas proved prophetic, though they were all too often ignored by politicians. La Fontaine was a devoted but moderate Socialist rather than a revolutionary and was concerned with far-reaching social reforms, not solely with reforming the working class. He was the only Socialist among the international peace movement leaders of the era and was unique in that he was active in all social classes of the peace internationalists as well as with the Socialist Party.

Bibliography

Abrams, Irwin. *The Nobel Peace Prize and the Laureates: An Illustrated Biographical History, 1901-1987.* Boston: Hall, 1988. This illustrated work presents a historical overview of all the Nobel Peace Prize laureates of the twentieth century. Each article is concise, with an excellent bibliography. It is a good starting point for a general understanding of La Fontaine.

Chatfield, Charles, and Peter van den Dugen, eds. *Peace Movements and Political Cultures.* Knoxville: University of Tennessee Press, 1988. This collection of essays provides solid background for understanding the international peace movement. Included are works on the First Hague Peace Conference and the International Peace Bureau.

Davis, Hayne, ed. *Among the World's Peacemakers.* New York: Progressive Publishing, 1907. Michael Lutzker wrote an insightful new introduction for the Garland edition that helps to put the international peace movement into perspective. Chapter 30 is based on an interview with La Fontaine.

Gray, Tony. *Champions of Peace.* New York: Paddington Press, 1976. This presentation of the Alfred Nobel story also contains biographies of the prize-winners and highlights the Nobel Prize committee's reasons for making their award to La Fontaine. Included are some interesting statistics on La Fontaine's publications.

Hull, William I. *The Two Hague Conferences and Their Contributions to International Law.* Boston: Ginn, 1908. This two-volume work is the most detailed account of the two Hague conferences. It is valuable because it provides a contemporary, optimistic view of the events and the peace movement.

Josephson, Harold, ed. *Biographical Dictionary of Modern Peace Leaders.* Westport, Conn.: Greenwood Press, 1985. The book includes an exhaustive list of biographies of many diverse pacifists. Each article is written by an authority on a particular figure; in the case of La Fontaine, the article was written by Nadine Lubelski-Bernard after review of the original La Fontaine papers.

Eric Wm. Mogren

FIORELLO HENRY LA GUARDIA

Born: December 11, 1882; New York, New York
Died: September 20, 1947; New York, New York
Areas of Achievement: Government and politics
Contribution: Using boundless energy, La Guardia, the son of immigrants, served the public during a thirty-year career that included several terms as a U.S. congressman and three terms as mayor of New York City. He was the first Italian-American elected to these positions.

Early Life

Fiorello Henry La Guardia was born in New York City, the first son and second child of Achille and Irene La Guardia, Italians who had immigrated to the United States in 1880. Although identified with New York City, La Guardia spent most of his youth away from the city. His father, a musician, had difficulty finding work in early 1880's New York and enlisted in the United States Army when Fiorello was three years old. Achille became the chief musician of the Eleventh Infantry Regiment posted on the frontier, first in Dakota Territory and later in Arizona Territory.

The La Guardias spent almost six years at Whipple Barracks, near Prescott, Arizona. Several biographers note that during his political career, La Guardia regarded Prescott as his hometown, regularly wearing Stetson hats to emphasize his western "roots." In Prescott, he was introduced to many of life's truths. For example, he learned that a boundary existed between officers and enlisted men on a military post. Officers and their families received more privileges and better accommodations. The distinction between officers and enlisted men extended down to the children on the post. La Guardia did not choose to follow the rules and regularly engaged in fights with officers' sons. Economic uncertainty was also on display as miners and laborers in nearby towns went long periods without employment.

La Guardia's tendency to scuffle with other children can be attributed largely to his short stature, his Italian name, and his swarthy looks. As the son of Italian immigrants, he had to endure many racial slurs. In addition, he had a high-pitched voice, described by some contemporaries as a falsetto and by others as a screech.

In 1898, Achille took his family back to Italy. The bandmaster had been a casualty of the "embalmed beef" sold to the Army by profiteers during the Spanish-American War. He did not recover from the poisoning and was discharged from the Army shortly after the war. Since he could not find work in New York City, Achille decided to return to Trieste, Italy.

La Guardia was a teenager when he arrived in Italy. In 1900, he found work as a clerk in the American consulate in Budapest. Despite his lack of a high school education, he displayed a command for languages. La Guardia used his gift to help the growing number of people in the Austro-Hungarian Empire emigrate to the United States. In 1906, La Guardia decided to return to New York City. He found work as a translator and interpreter, eventually working at Ellis Island, the entry point for most immigrants into the United States in the early twentieth century. While working, he completed a high school equivalency diploma and earned a law degree.

Life's Work

La Guardia's main achievement, serving the residents of New York City as a congressman and mayor, culminated a career that started when he completed a law degree at New York University. His clients primarily were immigrants who could not pay large fees. He also developed a specialty in labor law. La Guardia's goal as a lawyer was not to get rich; rather, he worked to build a base of supporters for future ventures into politics. He also developed an interest in aviation and eventually earned a pilot's license.

After one unsuccessful congressional campaign, La Guardia was elected to the U.S. House of Representatives in 1916. He was a Republican candidate in a district considered a stronghold of the Tammany Hall Democrats. He became the first Italian-American elected to Congress. Shortly after he took office, the United States entered World War I. La Guardia, while continuing his service in Congress, joined the Army Air Corps. He was stationed in Italy where he worked to keep Italy in the war. After the war, La Guardia, now a major, resigned his commission. He was reelected to Congress in 1918.

In an effort to position himself for a mayoral campaign, La Guardia successfully sought the presidency of the city's Board of Aldermen in 1920. The largely ceremonial position, the second highest post in the city, provided him with a seat on the Board of Estimate, the city's executive committee. He also served as acting mayor in the absence of the mayor. La Guardia used his position to learn about city government with the expectation that he would be a candidate for mayor in 1921. His candidacy, however, was a victim of backroom deals among the leadership of the New York Republican Party.

In 1922, after the deaths of his daughter and wife, La Guardia again sought a congressional seat. He ran as a Progressive reformer and was elected. During his tenure, he allied with such Progressives as Senators Robert LaFollette of Wisconsin and George Norris of Nebraska. Working for the "little guy," La Guardia became known as "America's most liberal congressman" for supporting social welfare legislation, opposing strike breaking, and calling for the repeal of Prohibition. Ever a showman, La Guardia concocted illicit beer in his congressional office using ingredients purchased at a drugstore.

While he was happy to serve his New York neighbors in Washington, D.C., La Guardia wanted to be mayor. He ran for the post in 1929, challenging the Tammany Democrat James J. Walker. La Guardia described Walker as corrupt and incompetent, but he was defeated handily in a city in which there were two Democrats for every Republican voter. Shortly after the election, the nation was rocked by the Stock Market Crash and the onset of the Great Depression. Walker also had to endure an ethics investigation that eventually forced him from office before completing his term.

La Guardia's political career suffered as well. By 1932, the character of his congressional district had changed. New residents, primarily Puerto Ricans, moved in to replace older immigrants who were moving to other parts of the city. Even Italian-Americans were changing through the process of "Americanization." La Guardia did not recognize these changes in time, and he was defeated in his reelection bid. By 1933, he was out of public service for the first time in fifteen years.

The energetic politician would not be out of office for long. As a lame duck during President Franklin Roosevelt's first one hundred days, Representative La Guardia spearheaded many of the reform measures proposed by the new president. La Guardia attracted the attention of influential members of Roosevelt's "brain trust," many of whom were New Yorkers. Working with local political leaders, the brain trusters were able to enter

La Guardia's name on the 1934 mayoral ballot as the Fusion candidate. His platform included various proposals to end corruption in city government and institute a more rational, nonpartisan administration. La Guardia was elected with 40 percent of the vote, becoming the city's first Italian-American mayor. Upon taking office, La Guardia attacked the problems faced by New York City with characteristic energy. He was an activist mayor at a time when the city needed active leadership. As he had done during his earlier career, La Guardia saw the mayoralty as a tool to help people in his city. He was not in office for the money.

La Guardia, while a popular politician, was not without his faults. Thomas Kessner, in *Fiorello H. La Guardia and the Making of Modern New York* (1989), argues that the mayor ran the city's administrative establishment personally and autocratically. For example, city residents would not be surprised to see Mayor La Guardia dashing to a fire with the city fire department. He even utilized an obscure provision in the city charter to occasionally sit as a judge. Many of his commissioners cringed when informed that the mayor wanted to see them.

La Guardia was successful in pulling New York City out of the Depression with some assistance from the federal government. By the end of his second term, the mayor was seeking greater challenges. He wanted a national office. Unfortunately, President Roosevelt sought a third term in 1940, and La Guardia could not run against an ally. La Guardia's requests for an appointive office were rebuffed by Roosevelt's aides, who believed that La Guardia lacked the temperament to serve in the cabinet. The mayor's request for a military post also was rejected.

While focusing on national offices during his third term, his administration began to deteriorate. Petty corruption crept into government. He was challenged by civil libertarians who did not like his treatment of people he considered racketeers. Sensing that his era was over, La Guardia did not seek reelection in 1945. After leaving office in January of 1946, La Guardia had one last chance in public service. He was appointed director general of the United Nations Relief and Rehabilitation Administration. La Guardia resigned from the position after the United States withdrew support of the agency at the end of 1946. By 1947, few people were listening to La Guardia, an old man who was seen as being out of touch with modern times. In September, 1947, the reforming mayor and longtime public servant died.

Summary

Unlike his predecessors as mayor, Fiorello La Guardia wanted to help people. Reforming municipal government in New York City involved getting city services to as many residents as possible. Sometimes the reforms required that Mayor La Guardia take unilateral action without consulting other elected city leaders or state officials in Albany. On occasion, he had to seek those leaders' approval for his actions.

His motives were clearly different than those of his predecessors. At his death, La Guardia's second wife inherited an estate of $8,000 in war bonds and a house. Like his early career as a lawyer, public service did not make La Guardia a rich man. His goal was to serve the people of New York. The measure of his success in reaching this goal comes every election year when New Yorkers hope for "another La Guardia."

Bibliography

Angell, Roger. "Ink: Boy Scribes Inflame Little Flower." *New Yorker* 75, no. 1 (February 22, 1999). The author recounts his interview of La Guardia at age fifteen for his school newspaper. La Guardia discussed public versus private school quality at length.

Elliott, Lawrence. *Little Flower: The Life and Times of Fiorello La Guardia.* New York: Morrow, 1983. This biography, written for a popular audience, is a complete examination of La Guardia's youth and career before becoming mayor, with a brief discussion of his tenure in office. Includes bibliography and illustrations.

Friedman, Andrea. " 'The Habitats of Sex-Crazed Perverts': Campaigns against Burlesque in Depression-Era New York City." *Journal of the History of Sexuality* 7, no. 2 (October, 1996). Examines the efforts of La Guardia and the Catholic church to emphasize morality and control male sexual behavior through an attack on burlesque, which was viewed as a cause of the rise in sex crimes during the Depression.

Heckscher, August. *When La Guardia Was Mayor.* New York: Norton, 1978. This strong narrative account of La Guardia's career as mayor of New York City provides some criticism of his abilities to manage the city.

Kessner, Thomas. *Fiorello H. La Guardia and the Making of Modern New York.* New York: McGraw-Hill, 1989. Kessner's definitive and lengthy biography of La Guardia from birth through death draws upon a wealth of evidence to identify La Guardia's impact on the government of New York City. Includes illustrations and footnotes but no bibliography.

Mann, Arthur. *La Guardia: A Fighter against His Times.* Philadelphia: Lippincott, 1959. The first of two volumes, this work is a scholarly examination of La Guardia's life before running for mayor of New York. Includes bibliography.

————. *La Guardia Comes to Power: 1933.* Philadelphia: Lippincott, 1965. The second of two volumes, this book analyzes the mayoral campaign of 1933, La Guardia's first successful campaign for the office.

Sayre, Wallace S., and Herbert Kaufman. *Governing New York City: Politics in the Metropolis.* New York: Russell Sage, 1960. This classic scholarly examination of New York City government evaluates all aspects of municipal government and assesses the performance of mayors including La Guardia. Includes diagrams, maps, tables, and chapter bibliographies.

Zinn, Howard. *La Guardia in Congress*. Ithaca, N.Y.: Cornell University Press, 1959. This book is a detailed evaluation of La Guardia as a member of the U.S. House of Representatives. Includes a bibliography.

John David Rausch, Jr.

RUDOLF LABAN

Born: December 15, 1879; Poszony, Austro-Hungarian Empire
Died: July 1, 1958; Weybridge, England
Area of Achievement: Dance
Contribution: In Germany Laban is recognized as the father of the Expressive Dance (Ausdruckstanz) Movement. In England his Effort theory has vitally influenced the educational system. In the United States, dance acquired literacy through his system of notation (Labanotation).

Early Life

Rudolf Laban was born Rudolf Jean-Baptist Attila Marquis de Laban de Varalja in Poszony, Austro-Hungarian Empire (now Bratislava, Czechoslovakia). Nobility, having preceded him, formed his aesthetic, wit, charm, intellect, and vision, attributes he possessed in glowing colors. Leban's father, who was a general in the Austro-Hungarian military, envisioned his son in the military, while his mother encouraged him to develop his athletic abilities. Rudolf, a namesake of the reigning house of Habsburg, attended military school for one year but withdrew to follow his visualizing mind through the arts of painting and sculpture. These disciplines were not his final expression; they did not capture the festive spirit that had magnetically drawn the youthful Laban as he traveled with his father to a variety of celebrations: parades, rituals, folk dances, whirling dervishes, and military ceremonies. The artistry that captured the totality of his zealous mind was the dance of human motion and space celebrating the spirit of humankind. Laban's career choice reinforced his parents' worst fear: He would become a family outcast similar to his stage artist uncle, Adolf Mylius, who as a direct result of his career choice was forbidden to continue to use the family name. Laban broke from traditional family nobility of aristocratic service to serve the magic of human motion and space that impelled his imaginative and scientific mind.

Having broken from the expectations of his family by deciding to follow his artistic instincts, Laban had to take full responsibility for the direction and sustenance of his life. He never returned to his father's house. He chose Paris to set his vision in motion; there he managed to support himself through his natural talents in graphic arts. He dabbled in the art scene of Paris to become familiar with the broader spectrum of his interests. He studied ballet with Monsieur Morel, a student of François Delsarte, and at the École des Beaux-Arts he studied architecture. While in Paris it is reasonable to assume that Laban became familiar with the notation system of Raoul-Auger Feuillet, to whom Laban later made reference. From these influences, he began to formulate a system of movement and a design for a theater that would demonstrate his vision of motion in space.

Laban learned the rudiments of life and art from several master teachers. As a schoolboy, Laban gained a proper respect for craftsmanship from an old friend, a painter, who taught him to discipline his imagination by, among other tasks, the cleaning of paint brushes. Laban conceived the staging of dance as living sculpture (*tableaux vivants*) while serving as an apprentice. These moving poses developed into group-dance scenes and later into movement choirs, a form that became Laban's stylistic signature.

Life's Work

Dance, for Laban, was the expression of man's festive being, a celebration that grew out of the community and culminated in a common identity and purpose. His new dance was not intended to teach new laws of nature or new rules of conduct, but rather to foster the recognition of humankind's vigilance for the observance of laws and rules: He pontificated a global community in celebration of its individual and collective festive natures as far superior to a global community intent on arsenals and killing fields. The new dancer was created out of a world of "thinking-feeling" and willing, not as isolated parts of the psyche but as harmonic interchange of these elements. Dance was the ideal art to integrate the isolated elements, since words were formed from body sounds, which, in turn, were formed from body movement: *Tanz-Ton-Wort* (dance-song-word), a phrase coined by Laban, represented a basic triadic function in his theory of movement.

These ideas were developed during his summers at a dance farm in Ascona, Switzerland, and during his winters (1908-1919) with his dance company and school in Munich, Germany. At the dance farm, he explored the rhythms of the moving body (motion with force or strength, time or duration, space or direction) moving in the open air space. He worked with a dedicated group of students who came together each summer to study with him. The most prominent among them included Mary Wigman, Suzzanne Perrottet, Maja Lederer, and Dussia Bereska. His book *Die Welt des Tänzers* was published in 1920 and set forth his basic structure for the theory of free dance.

Subsequent years found Laban choreographing, teaching, organizing festivals, and writing. In 1921, he served as the ballet master at the Mannheim National Theatre where he created *Die Geblendeten, Epische Tanzfolge*, and the *Bacchanalia* in conjunction with Richard Wagner's performance of *Tannhauser.* In 1923, he opened the Zentralschule Laban and Kammertanzbuhne Laban (school and small studio stage) in Hamburg. The Zentralschule Laban became important for its emphasis in the training of movement choirs. They presented new works by Laban entitled *Lichtwende, Agamemnon's Tod, Dammernde Rhythmen*, and *Titan.* His choreography for the stage included *Der Schwingende Tempel, Faust Part II, Prometheus, Die Gaukelei, Casanova, Don Juan, Die Nacht, Narrenspiegel*, and *Ritterballet.* Laban continued to organize the layman for the festivals of community life. He was invited to thousands of these celebrations, ranging from small funerals to the Festzug des Handwerkes und der Gererbe in Vienna. The latter festival exhibited a moving snake seven kilometers in length and ten thousand participants.

Being involved with the world of dance from a variety of perspectives, Laban was concerned with the low position that dance held in relation to the other arts. He credited dance's lack of equality to its nonpermanent, "now you see it, now you don't" status. He believed that a system of notation was as important to literacy in dance as it was to literature and music. Whenever he was choreographing, he was also working on a way to notate his movements: In 1928, *Titan* became his first notated score that proved to him it could be done.

Laban continued to open the traditional boundaries in dance, created primarily by the existent codes in ballet. By his constant search for the natural laws of movement and their prosodic relation to "dance-song-word," he developed a language of dance that strengthened the five positions of ballet and expanded the field of dance and movement to new possibilities and applications. His theories of dance were published in two books that have become germinal to English-speaking students of Laban. *Choreutics* (1966) gives the framework for Laban's space harmony, and *The Mastery of Move-*ment on the Stage* (1950) also contains his thesis for human movement. Predecessors to *Choreutics* are the German publications *Choreographie* (1926) and *Gymnastik und Tanz* (1926) by Laban.

With the reign of the Nazis in Germany, it became difficult for Laban to continue his role in the organization of dance for festivals and concerts. The Eleventh Olympic Games, in Berlin, brought the rising tensions to a head. Laban was given responsibility for the dance section but was never allowed to perform his premier, *Vom Tauwind und der neuen Freude*, for the occasion. He was placed in exile but escaped to England, where he joined two of his previous students, Kurt Jooss and Lisa Ullmann. Through the influence of Ullmann, Laban designed a course of study in dance for education. The course has had wide acceptance in England and culminated in the publication of *Modern Educational Dance* (1948).

While in England, Laban met F. C. Lawrence, who was interested in the application of Laban's movement concepts to the performance efficiency of industrial workmanship. This collaboration created a divergent path for the application of Laban's thesis on the qualities of human effort. It resulted in the publication of *Effort* (1947), coauthored by Laban and Lawrence.

In 1953, Laban settled permanently in England in the community of Addlestone, Surrey, near London. He established the Laban Art of Movement Centre and wrote one more book before his death on July 1, 1958, in Weybridge, Surrey.

Summary

In the Western world, the impact of Rudolf Laban's ideas has led to the founding of several centers: in London, the Laban Center for Movement and Dance, and in New York, the Laban Institute of Movement Studies and the Dance Notation Bureau. Labanotation is a common inclusion in the graduate dance curriculum of American universities. The movement scholarship in dance therapy is deeply reliant on the science of movement as Laban has written it.

Human movement embodied the qualities of the mind, in the thinking of Laban; therefore, to study the natural rhythms of ebb and flow in movement might be the most tangible way to explore the nature of harmony itself. His idea of community and festive events as the greatest pleasure of dance was to deepen humankind's understanding of the harmonious structure provided by nature. He did not view this structure as a balance of parallels but as a dynamic tension existent in polarity.

Laban's life work has indicated another way to view human nature and life. From the perspective of human movement in three-dimensional space, a kinship is formed. Experiencing movement and space as a kinship relationship creates an alternative to the common acceptance of space and movement as isolated entities. Laban's discovery of laws of affinity in human movement and space as illustrated in his scales of movement have become as important to the art of dance as the laws of harmony are to music. Much of this material he could only set into motion but did not have time to complete. It was his ardent wish that his "methods might be developed, or better forms might be found."

Bibliography

Foster, John. *The Influences of Rudolph Laban.* London: Lepus, 1977. A thorough book that contains a good biographical section and that discusses influences on Laban and Laban's influence. Includes appendices, references, and an index.

Green, Martin. *Mountain of Truth.* Hanover, N.H.: University Press of New England, 1986. A comparative study of three artists, of which Laban was one, who passed through the Italian-Swiss village of Ascona between 1900 and 1920. Their personalities and ideas on art and culture are compared within a social critique.

Groff, Ed. "Laban Movement Analysis: Charting the Ineffable Domain of Human Movement." *Journal of Physical Education, Recreation and Dance* 66, no. 2 (February, 1995). Examines Laban's movement analysis theory, which is taught at the university level.

Hutchinson, Ann. *Labanotation.* New York: New Directions, 1954. This work is a fairly easy to follow explanation of Labanotation. Includes a foreword by Laban himself.

Laban, Rudolf. *A Life for Dance.* Translated by Lisa Ullmann. London: Macdonald, and New York: Theatre Arts, 1975. Laban's autobiography in a unique format that combines his artistic, personal, and imaginative life with his work.

———. *Modern Educational Dance.* 4th ed. Plymouth, Devon: Northcote House, 1988. A guide for teachers and parents who wish to use the basic movement themes to develop the expressive qualities of children.

Laban, Rudolf, and F. C. Lawrence. *Effort.* 2d ed. London: Macdonald and Evans, and Boston: Plays, 1974. A concise presentation of Laban's Effort theory as it related to industrial workers.

Maletic, Vera. *Body—Space—Expression.* New York: Mouton de Gruyter, 1987. The most comprehensive development of Laban's movement and dance concepts to date. His concepts, works, publications, and life are placed in chronological order, showing the roots and development of his system.

Schwartz, Peggy. "Laban Movement Analysis: Theory and Application." *Journal of Physical Education, Recreation and Dance* 66, no. 2 (February, 1995). Discussion of Laban's movement interpretation technique, which is designed to improve execution of physical education, dance, and leisure activities.

Ullmann, Lisa, ed. *A Vision of Dynamic Space.* London: Falmer Press, 1984. A compilation of Laban's sketches, drawings, and words, not all originally intended for publication. Gives insight into the visual and visionary aspects of the man.

Lois M. Trostle

JACQUES LACAN

Born: April 13, 1901; Paris, France
Died: September 9, 1981; Paris, France
Areas of Achievement: Psychology, philosophy, language, and linguistics
Contribution: Lacan was the single most important figure in the development of psychoanalysis in twentieth century France. His powerful rereading of Freud's work and rethinking of Freud's fundamental concepts made him a key figure in French intellectual life from the 1950's until his death.

Early Life

Jacques Marie Émile Lacan was born on April 13, 1901, into an upper-middle-class Parisian family. His academic training focused first on medicine, then on psychiatry. He studied with the distinguished French psychiatrist Louis-Nicholas Clérambault, receiving his doctorate in 1932 with a thesis on the relationship of paranoia to personality structure. While still working as a psychiatrist, Lacan began psychoanalysis with the distinguished Freudian analyst Rudolf Loewenstein and in 1934 became a member of the Paris Psychoanalytic Society.

During the 1930's, a complex set of influences helped form the mind of the young Lacan, laying the foundation for the mature work that would make him a leading luminary in the febrile Parisian atmosphere of the decades following World War II. In addition to his growing absorption in the thought and teaching of Sigmund Freud, Lacan associated closely with the Surrealist circle of artists and writers and contributed essays and poems to Surrealist publications. This Surrealist connection attests his lifelong fascination with language and its power to shape human life.

Lacan was also strongly influenced, as were many others of his generation, by the teaching of the Russian émigré thinker Alexandre Kojève. It was primarily through Kojève's lectures at the École Normale Supérieure on Georg Wilhelm Friedrich Hegel between 1933 and 1939, with particular emphasis on the *Phänomenologie des Geistes* (1807; *The Phenomenology of Spirit*, 1931), that the work of the great German philosopher first made a major impact on French thought. Thus, at the same time that he was immersing himself in Freud's theories, Lacan attended Kojève's lectures emphasizing the Hegelian account of the problems for the development of human self-consciousness. This complex of Lacan's interests in the 1930's—psychiatry, Freud, Surrealism, Hegel—typifies what would always mark his work: a breathtaking catholicity of scope buttressed with remarkable erudition, reminiscent of Freud himself.

Lacan's position as an important thinker within Freudian psychoanalysis was first established for an international audience in 1936, when he spoke at the Fourteenth Congress of the International Psychoanalytic Association. In this address, Lacan presented his theory of the mirror stage. He argued that the earliest development of the human ego (somewhere between six and eighteen months) occurred on the basis of the infant's imagined relationship with its own body as first perceived in a mirror and with that of the significant others—typically the mother—in its life. Lacan's conclusion was that the human ego is never a coherent entity, even from its very inception. This moment—1936—at which Lacan chose to present his developing theory is significant, for it was at this time that Freud's daughter Anna and others following her lead were beginning to argue for the coherence of the ego and to elaborate its varied mechanisms of defense and adaptation. Thus Lacan's first step onto the international psychoanalytical stage veered toward possible schism from the keepers of Freudian orthodoxy, thereby prefiguring the series of rifts and splits within the psychoanalytic movement that Lacan would repeatedly provoke later in his career.

Life's Work

Lacan was a dominant intellectual presence in French cultural life for three decades prior to his death, and his influence radiated far outward from its psychoanalytic base into disciplines such as philosophy, literary criticism, and linguistics and into broader interdisciplinary fields such as feminism and some variants of Marxism. The extent of Lacan's impact both within and beyond psychoanalysis highlights what he himself considered to be his primary purpose as analyst and writer: to revivify psychoanalysis by a radical return to Freud's work and to do so by putting Freud's thought in touch with the latest developments in contemporary thought. For Lacan, these two intentions were inextricable, and together they define both the originality of his contribution to twentieth century thought and the breadth of his influence.

Lacan's published work consisted primarily of essays, the most important of which were collected and published as *Écrits* (1966; *Écrits: A Selection*, 1977). Yet his most immediate impact on the French intellectual public came not from his writings but rather through the biweekly seminars (actually public lectures) that he conducted for more than three decades, very few of which appeared in print during his lifetime. Lacan's verbal brilliance, personal flamboyance, and intellectual charisma fused in lectures that became veritable performances to which important thinkers from many fields in French culture came at one time or another.

The impact Lacan had on French psychoanalysis was pervasive as well as divisive. No one escaped his influence, but that influence provoked repeated divisions and splits. In 1953, Lacan and several colleagues broke with the Paris Psychoanalytic Society, the official French branch of the International Psychoanalytic Association, and formed a new Societé Française de Psychoanalyse. Then in 1964 Lacan reformed his analytic society, calling it L'école Freudienne de Paris, only to dissolve it in 1980 to create a new organization he called La Cause Freudienne. These schismatic moves bear witness to Lacan's growing worry that his teachings were becoming too institutionalized and thereby overly rigid and narrow, a fear similar to Freud's earlier concern that the professionalization of psychoanalysis as a branch of medicine would unduly constrict its applicability in the broad arenas such as education, where Freud hoped his science's impact would be most profound. Lacan's ambitions for his own rethinking of Freud's work were equally far-reaching.

Lacan's protean thought defies summary, but certain emphases within it can be isolated as indicative of major currents within his work. He always stressed that the core of Freud's vision lay in *Die Traumdeutung* (1900; *The Interpretation of Dreams*, 1913) and the works that immediately followed it. There the core concepts of psychoanalysis—the unconscious and sexuality—were first developed and elaborated. Lacan argued that Freud perceived that the unconscious could be understood as having a structure. In his own reworking of Freud, this was one of the places where Lacan turned to contemporary thinkers to elaborate upon a core Freudian insight, typified by his most fre-

quently quoted phrase: "The unconscious is structured like a language." Twentieth century linguists such as Ferdinand de Saussure and Roman Jakobson had argued that when human beings acquire the use of speech they are subsumed into a symbolic order that preexisted them as individuals and that could be shown to have a systematic structure. Since the unconscious makes itself visible and audible primarily through speech (as well as symptoms, dreams, and involuntary acts of omission and commission), Lacan emphasized that the unconscious has a structure like that of language and hence can be systematically examined.

In a related vein, and with important cues taken from the work of the anthropologist Claude Lévi-Strauss on kinship structures and totemic relationships, Lacan theorized that the human subject is situated within different orders, or planes of existence, which he called the Imaginary, the Symbolic, and the Real. The Imaginary evolves out of the mirror stage but extends into adult life; it is the realm of all false or fantasized identifications that a human subject makes with an Other. The Symbolic is the realm of social and cultural symbolism and of language. Entrance of the child into the domain of the Symbolic with the acquisition of language means that the laws of language and society come to dwell within him or her, thus laying the foundation for social, mediated relationships with others that are different from the self-centered but alienating relationships of the Imaginary. This constituted Lacan's reworking of Freud's fundamental concept of the Oedipus complex. Finally, the Real for Lacan was everything that was neither within the Imaginary nor the Symbolic; hence, in a typical Lacanian paradox, the Real was what could not be known directly about a human subject.

Lacan's unorthodox approach to psychoanalytic training was as provocative and disturbing as his revisions of Freudian theory on the basis of linguistic concepts or his attempts to reevaluate the status of psychoanalytic knowledge in the light of the new directions emerging from other disciplines. The classic psychoanalytic session lasts fifty minutes, but Lacan introduced shorter sessions of varying length, some lasting only a few minutes. This tampering with a cornerstone of psychoanalytic practice was a key factor in helping to precipitate Lacan's break with the Paris Psychoanalytic Society in 1953. From Lacan's point of view, sessions of variable length better perserve the overall movement of a patient's discourse during the course of an analysis, while adherence to the standard length session is constraining and rigid for both patient and analyst.

Over and over again, both in his theoretical work and in his practice as a psychoanalyst, Lacan sought to challenge the limits to psychoanalysis, which he thought had been created by Freud's disciples. He sought to recapture the radical core of Freud's vision in his own work and to transmit it to his audiences with the aid of what he took to be the best tools available in the intellectual milieus with which he was familiar. His achievement was similar but far more extensive than that of his early mentor Kojève. Just as the Russian philosopher was almost singlehandedly responsible for the widespread impact of Hegel's thought on French intellectual life after the 1930's, so Lacan was the single most important figure in the rather belated reception of Freud into twentieth century French cultural life.

Summary

With the publication of *Écrits* in 1966, Jacques Lacan became not only a thinker known in French intellectual circles but also an intellectual presence of major impress on Western culture. Practitioners of a variety of the intellectual disciplines which the French call the human sciences found inspiration in Lacan's work, and his influence spread beyond Western Europe to various parts of the world. There was widespread interest in Lacanian ideas in South American psychoanalytic circles. His work proved to be a fertile source for new approaches in cinema criticism and literary studies in England and the United States as well as on the European continent. Especially after his 1972-1973 seminar *Encore*, in which he turned his attention to the place of love and sexuality in psychoanalysis with particular attention to female sexuality, his thought became a focus of much critical attention by European and American feminist theorists. As Malcolm Bowie has noted, part of the reason for Lacan's profound impact on European thinking after World War II was that "his writing proposes itself consciously as a critique of all discourses and all ideologies." For Lacan, as for Freud before him, psychoanalysis was to be the basis for a self-critique of Western culture itself, not merely of individuals within it, although, like his great predecessor, Lacan never abandoned the idea that the fundamental basis of Freud's science was the spoken dialogue between analyst and analysand.

The implications of Lacan's work were always disturbing. His thought can be seen as part of a broader twentieth century critique of the notion of a unified human subject, thus placing his work alongside that of his Parisian contemporaries. Where Lacan's peculiar originality lay was in his understanding of the radicality of Freud's discoveries and in his desire to push the consequences of those discoveries to their logical limits. In doing so, he may indeed have become, as the philosopher Ellie Ragland-Sullivan writes, "the most important thinker in France since René Descartes and the most innovative and far-ranging thinker in Europe since Friedrich Nietzsche and Sigmund Freud."

Bibliography

Benvenuto, Bice, and Roger Kennedy. *The Works of Jacques Lacan: An Introduction.* London: Free Association, and New York: St. Martin's Press, 1986. A straightforward, chronologically oriented discussion of Lacan's key writings from his early years until his death.

Bowie, Malcolm. "Jacques Lacan." In *Structuralism and Since: From Lévi-Strauss to Derrida,* edited by John Sturrock. Oxford and New York: Oxford University Press, 1979. This essay provides a brief introduction to Lacan's thought and is a good place to begin reading about him.

Bracher, Mark. *Lacanian Theory of Discourse: Subject, Structure, and Society.* New York: New York University Press, 1994. A collection of thought on Lacan's theories regarding the relationships among language, society, and subjectivity.

Clément, Catherine. *The Lives and Legends of Jacques Lacan.* Translated by Arthur Goldhammer. New York: Columbia University Press, 1983. Originally published in France in 1981, this book by a former disciple of Lacan is a provocative meditation on the meaning and significance of his life and work in and for contemporary culture.

Felman, Shoshana. *Jacques Lacan and the Adventure of Insight: Psychoanalysis in Contemporary Culture.* Cambridge, Mass.: Harvard University Press, 1987. This complex book explores the implications of Lacan's work for the practice of reading and interpretation in contemporary culture.

Gallop, Jane. *Reading Lacan.* Ithaca, N.Y.: Cornell University Press, 1985. A series of powerful psychoanalytic readings of Lacan's work by a literary critic. This book both demonstrates the importance of Lacan's thought for work in the humanities disciplines in general and is a representative instance of the impact Lacan's thought has had on feminist theory.

Muller, John P., and William J. Richardson. *Lacan and Language: A Reader's Guide to Écrits*. New York: International Universities Press, 1982. Extensive commentary on each of the nine essays included by Lacan in the English translation of *Écrits*.

Nasio, Juan-David. *Five Lessons on the Psychoanalytic Theory of Jacques Lacan*. Translated by David Pettigrew and Francois Raffoul. Albany: State University of New York Press, 1998. The first English translations of Nasio's classic text on Lacan's theories.

Ragland-Sullivan, Ellie. *Jacques Lacan and the Philosophy of Psychoanalysis*. London: Croom Helm, and Urbana: University of Illinois Press, 1986. Important effort to probe the philosophical implications of Lacan's thought.

Schneiderman, Stuart. *Jacques Lacan: The Death of an Intellectual Hero*. Cambridge, Mass.: Harvard University Press, 1983. The core of this work is the author's account of his experience of psychoanalysis with Lacan.

Turkle, Sherry. *Psychoanalytic Politics: Freud's French Revolution*. 2d ed. London: Free Association, and New York: Guildford Press, 1992. Lacan is the central figure in this account of the reception of Freud and psychoanalysis in French culture in the decades after 1945.

Wilden, Anthony. "Lacan and the Discourse of the Other." In *Speech and Language in Psychoanalysis*, by Jacques Lacan. Translated by Anthony Wilden. Baltimore and London: Johns Hopkins University Press, 1981. An excellent wide-ranging introduction to and critique of Lacan's work and its place in the broader currents of twentieth century intellectual life.

Michael W. Messmer

SELMA LAGERLÖF

Born: November 20, 1858; Mårbacka, Sweden
Died: March 16, 1940; Mårbacka, Sweden
Area of Achievement: Literature
Contribution: Lagerlöf was the first woman to receive the Nobel Prize in Literature (1909) and the first woman to be elected to the Swedish Academy (1914). During her lifetime, she was loved throughout the world because of both her gift for storytelling and her idealism, which was a welcome change from the pessimistic realism dominating her period. Since her death, she also has been increasingly recognized as a preserver of the folkways and traditions of rural Sweden.

Early Life

Selma Ottiliana Lovisa Lagerlöf was born at Mårbacka in rural Värmland, Sweden, on November 20, 1858, the fourth of five children. Her father, a navy officer, and her mother often read to the children, old sagas, for example, and the fairy tales of Hans Christian Andersen. From travelers, from workmen, from an old housekeeper, from an aunt, and above all, from her grandmother, Lagerlöf heard folktales and legends told with such convincing detail that the children could not deny their truth.

When she was three, Lagerlöf was paralyzed, evidently by an attack of infantile paralysis. Although she later became able to walk again, she was lame throughout her life. In an attempt to find a cure, she was sent for two winters to relatives in Stockholm. There she saw the world of power and fashion, so unlike Mårbacka; there, too, in her uncle's library, she discovered the great romantic writer Sir Walter Scott, whose fascination with the lives and the traditions of humble rural people may well have influenced Lagerlöf's own attitudes toward the rich material of Mårbacka.

From the age of seven, Lagerlöf had intended to be a writer. When her father died, leaving only debts, which eventually necessitated the sale of her beloved Mårbacka, Lagerlöf's road to higher education was blocked. It was a chance encounter with the feminist Eva Fryxell which sent Lagerlöf on to school. After Fryxell heard one of Lagerlöf's occasional poems read at a wedding, Fryxell advised the talented young girl to become enrolled in a teachers' college. It was during her time there, when Lagerlöf was twenty-two, that she suddenly found her material: the stories of Värmland that she had heard in childhood and, in particular, the saga of the Värmland cavaliers. She worked on this story at first tentatively, then, settling into a poetic prose that was very different from the popular analytical, realistic style, she knew that she had found her voice. During her final years at college and her first years in the classroom, Lagerlöf continued work on the cavaliers' story. In 1890, she submitted five closely related chapters in a novella contest and won first prize for her entry. As a result, a patron and friend arranged for her to have a year's leave of absence from teaching. During that time, Lagerlöf completed *Gösta Berlings Saga* (1891; *The Story of Gösta Berling*, 1898; also as *Gösta Berling's Saga*, 1918), the novel that brought her popular and critical success.

Life's Work

Gösta Berlings Saga was the story of a group of appealing but rascally rogues led by a defrocked pastor, Gösta Berling. These rogues have descended upon Ekeby Manor as permanent guests, to the dismay of the mistress of the manor, who believes in hard work, frugality, and responsibility. Like an epic, the work develops episodically; each of the twenty-three chapters relates a different adventure. The work is unified, however, by the central conflict between the free spirits, directed by the devil, and the strong woman, who must order her world.

Even though the public liked the work, critics carped about the fanciful material and the poetic style, which suggested a return to Romanticism, which had become thoroughly unpopular. Not until two years after the publication of the novel, when the influential Danish critic Georg Brandes wrote a review praising it, was Lagerlöf's reputation really established in her native country. The next year, a collection of short stories sold well, and, in 1895, *Gösta Berlings Saga* went into a second edition. Now Lagerlöf could quit her teaching job and devote herself to her chosen profession.

With a stipend from King Oscar II, Lagerlöf was able to travel, and, as she went through Europe, to Italy, and later to Jerusalem, she was always alert to ideas for future works. In Italy, she heard a story about peasants' veneration of a counterfeit figure, and the result was her second novel, *Antikrists mirakler* (1897; *The Miracles of Antichrist*, 1899). In 1897, she moved to Dalecarlia, an area near Värmland; there she was told of a group of peas-

ants who the preceding year had become convinced that the end of the world was at hand, had sold all of their belongings, and had moved to Jerusalem, where many of them had died. Curious about the episode, Lagerlöf traveled to Jerusalem with her best friend, Sophie Elkan, and interviewed the survivors. The result was a two-volume work, *Jerusalem I:I Dalarne* (1901; *Jerusalem*, 1915) and *Jerusalem II:I det heliga landet* (1902; *The Holy City: Jerusalem II*, 1918).

While she was writing these complex works, Lagerlöf was also bringing forth simpler short novels as well as collections of short stories, perhaps the most popular of which was *Kristuslegender* (1904; *Christ Legends*, 1908), a collection of stories about Christ, which brought Lagerlöf to the attention of Americans. In 1906, she ventured into children's literature at the request of the Swedish National Teachers' Society, who hoped with her help to interest children in Swedish geography and history. Interestingly, it was the work produced as a result of this request, *Nils Holgerssons underbara resa genom Sverige* (2 volumes, 1906-1907; *The Wonderful Adventures of Nils*, 1907, and *The Further*

Adventures of Nils, 1911), for which she was to be most famous. The story is of a boy who for his misdeeds is turned into an animal and who then travels the length of Sweden on the back of a wild goose, noting the scenery and reforming his character as he flies; the story was eventually translated into forty languages.

Honors began coming to Lagerlöf with regularity. She received a gold medal from the Swedish Academy in 1904, an honorary doctorate from the University of Uppsala in 1907, and the Nobel Prize in Literature in 1909, the first woman to receive the world's highest honor in that field. In 1914, she became the first woman member of the Swedish Academy. Probably more important to her than all these honors was the fact that with the profits from her writings she was able to buy back her childhood home, Mårbacka, in 1907, and with her Nobel Prize money she purchased the entire estate. There she was to spend the rest of her life, functioning as an active landowner.

Evidently Lagerlöf's return to her ancestral home stimulated her creative powers. Now when she heard the old tales, she had a double vantage point, the childhood memories and the adult perspective. Year after year, the works poured forth—short stories, novellas, and novels. Among the latter was a book based on her grandmother's life, *Liljecronas hem* (1911; *Liliecrona's Home*, 1914), and the poignant *Kejsaren av Portugallien* (1914; *The Emperor of Portugallia*, 1916), the story of a father rejected by the daughter whom he loves above all else in the world.

Lagerlöf was also stimulated by her friendships with some of the most interesting men and women of her time. Among her closest friends were Valborg Olander, a teacher of Swedish, and the friend of her later years, the Baroness Henriette Coyet. In a sense, these relationships took the place of marriage; at a time when single women were circumscribed, they provided Lagerlöf with the emotional warmth and the companionship that she would otherwise have lacked.

During the 1920's, Lagerlöf wrote a trilogy tracing one family's history from 1700 to 1830, *Löwensköldska ringen* (1925-1928; *The Ring of the Löwenskölds: A Trilogy*, 1928), and began her three-volume autobiography with *Mårbacka* (1922; English translation, 1924) and *Ett barns memoarner* (1930; *Memories of My Childhood*, 1934). In 1932, she published the third book, *Dagbok, Mårbacka III* (*The Diary of Selma Lagerlöf*,

1936), an invaluable story of her early years, told in the form of a journal. The following year saw the publication of the writer's complete works.

In her final decade, Lagerlöf was deeply concerned about the loss of freedom and the rise of anti-Semitism in Nazi Germany. Her opposition to the regime cost her many of her German readers. Unfortunately, Lagerlöf did not live to see the triumph of the forces of freedom. She died on March 16, 1940, at Mårbacka, the scene of her happiest memories and the major source of her material and her inspiration.

Summary

In an age that had spurned Romanticism, with its interest in humble people and in the supernatural and with its tendency to idealism, in favor of a realism that often stressed the worst traits in humanity and even suggested that there was no hope for improvement either in human beings or in their lot, Selma Lagerlöf developed a unique kind of prose. Although she created realistic characters and placed them in rural settings with which she was intimately familiar, she included in her stories episodes and creatures whose reality depended on the tales passed down in Värmland and Dalecarlia from generation to generation. There was no academic superiority in her attitude toward these tales; instead, there was a willing suspension of disbelief, or perhaps a real belief, which carried Lagerlöf's readers along with her.

If they loved her for her magic, Lagerlof's readers also loved her for her idealism. She was not judgmental. One reason for the success of her works is that she never underrated the appeal of vice or folly. From her cavaliers to disobedient Nils to the wrongdoers in her so-called Ring trilogy, all of her imperfect characters are understandable, and, similarly, many of her most moral characters, like the leaders of the Dalecarlian exodus, are either mistaken or rigid. As she explores the human heart, Lagerlöf makes it clear that finally one must choose the right course and choose wisely, even at the cost of seeming dull.

It is this insistence that the world is divinely ordered that explains Lagerlöf's power to fuse the ordinary and the magical. In remote Värmland, humble people fight demons no different from those in Stockholm; the difference is that the Värmlanders are strengthened by the wisdom of their traditions, by stories that, if not factual, have the validity of myths. The lasting popularity of Lagerlöf in Sweden and throughout the world can be attributed not only to her power as a storyteller and her powerful, lyrical prose but also to the fact that she assured her readers that the world was and had always been patterned in ways revealed by the myths of its people and that those myths must be remembered and understood, lest human beings and humanity itself move forward to destruction.

Bibliography

Berendsohn, Walter A. *Selma Lagerlöf: Her Life and Work*. Translated by George F. Timpson. London: Nicholson and Watson, 1931; New York: Doubleday, 1932. A major study of Lagerlöf, emphasizing her poetic achievement and pointing out her departure from the realism and naturalism of her period.

Björkman, Edwin. "Selma Lagerlöf: A Writer of Modern Fairy Tales." *American Review of Reviews* 41 (February, 1910): 247-250. Written after Lagerlöf had received the Nobel Prize, this article assesses her work up to that time. Important for its reflection of early critical opinion.

Danielson, Larry W. "The Uses of Demonic Folk Tradition in Selma Lagerlöf's *Gösta Berlings Saga*." *Western Folklore* 34 (July 3, 1975): 187-199. An analysis of the character of the devil, Sintram, who dominates the cavaliers in Lagerlöf's first work, showing how he developed from folk materials into fiction.

Edström, Vivi. *Selma Lagerlöf*. Translated by Barbara Lide. Boston: Twayne, 1984. Part of Twayne's World Authors series, this concise and accurate book is invaluable. After providing a detailed chronology and a brief biography, the author proceeds to clear, thoughtful chapters on the major works of Lagerlöf. The final chapter, "Selma Lagerlöf and the Role of Writer," is one of the best summaries available. Includes an extensive bibliography.

Gustafson, Alrik. *Six Scandinavian Novelists*. Minneapolis: University of Minnesota Press, 1940. Helpful both for the fifty-page analysis that focuses on *Gösta Berlings Saga* and for the general introduction to the book, where Gustafson establishes Lagerlöf's position among the writers of her native region.

Johannesson, Eric O. "Isak Dinesen and Selma Lagerlöf." *Scandinavian Studies* 32 (February, 1960): 18-26. A fascinating comparison of Dinesen's *Out of Africa* (1937) and Lagerlöf's *Mårbacka*. In addition to contrasting their approaches to autobiography, this article includes comments on the philosophical differences between the two women, which the author sees as explaining the difference in the extent of their influence upon later writers.

Lagerlöf, Selma. *The Diary of Selma Lagerlöf.* Translated by Velma Swanston Howard. New York: Doubleday, 1936. Although it was written when Lagerlöf was in her seventies, this illustrated third volume of the autobiography recaptures the outlook of the naïve teenage girl who loved Mårbacka but found her first love and her vocation as a writer when she journeyed to Stockholm. Essential for any study of Lagerlöf.

Larsen, Hanna Astrup. *Selma Lagerlöf.* New York: Doubleday, 1936. A study of Lagerlöf as a superbly imaginative writer. A full analysis of each work, with special attention to the various collections of short stories.

Monroe, N. Elizabeth. "Provincial Art in Selma Lagerlöf." In *The Novel and Society: A Critical Study of the Modern Novel.* Chapel Hill: University of North Carolina Press, 1941. One of the best studies of Lagerlöf in comparison to other modern writers. Directed specifically toward defining her uniqueness, both in form and in matter. Highly recommended for all readers.

Nylander, Lars T. "Psychologism and the Novel: The Case of Selma Lagerlöf's *Goesta Berlings Saga.*" *Scandinavian Studies* 67, no. 4 (Fall 1995). Critique and analysis of *Goesta Berlings Saga.*

Todorov, Tzvetan. "The Labor of Love." *Partisan Review* 64, no. 3 (1997). Discusses Lagerlöf's novel *The Emperor of Portugallia*, focusing on the story's basis and issues of human identity.

Rosemary M. Canfield Reisman

FREDERICK WILLIAM LANCHESTER

Born: October 23, 1868; Lewisham, London, England
Died: March 8, 1946; Birmingham, England
Area of Achievement: Technology
Contribution: With an intuitive genius, Lanchester designed and built the first truly British motorcar, owing nothing to previous production of a horseless carriage and little or nothing to the pioneering designs of the French and Germans whose works were copied or adapted by other British inventors. In addition, Lanchester developed, ten years before the first heavier-than-air flight, the principles of powered flight and aircraft design.

Early Life

Frederick William Lanchester was born the fourth child in a family of eight to Henry Jones Lanchester, architect, and his wife, the former Octavia Ward, a onetime teacher, on October 23, 1868, in Lewisham, a fashionable suburb in the south of London. Before he was six years old, the family moved some fifty miles to the south of London to the seaside town of Hove. From nursery school, Frederick was sent to a preparatory boarding school in neighboring Brighton. By this time in England, despite the provision of elementary education for all laid down in the Forster Education Act of 1870, the English middle and upper classes provided for their children in public schools (the equivalent of private schools in the United States), which usually separated children from their families except during school vacations and which trained them to rule the country and the Empire. The preparatory school was designed to socialize younger children to the life-style and expectations of the public school.

It quickly became clear that Frederick would not easily follow the path laid down for him. The public school curriculum was heavily slanted in favor of the classics and the new social sciences of history and geography, with huge doses of English language and literature. The architect's son showed exceptional ability at mathematics and science but always found English difficult. At the age of fourteen, his parents sent him to Hartley College in Southampton, at that time the best place anywhere in the south of England for scientific and technical training. Within two years, Frederick won a national scholarship to study for a degree at the Normal School of Science in London (subsequently the Royal College of Science, then Imperial College, University of London).

Lanchester was a full-time student for three years. He left without taking his final examinations and therefore without any formal educational qualifications. It was not a result of failure on his part. By the end of two years, Lanchester was determined to become an engineer but became frustrated by the lack of applied engineering in the curriculum or of any course work on mechanical engineering, his chosen field. He therefore spent his last year in the library reading everything he could on mechanical engineering and his evenings at the Finsbury Technical College learning workshop practice.

At this time, 1889, the number of engineering graduates in England was extremely small compared to the twentieth century and with Germany in the same year. In addition, many English engineering graduates left the country for long periods to work on projects worldwide, constructing docks, harbors, and railroads. There was no official realization that industrial and technical training should be a priority. In contrast, the German government was actively engaged in sponsoring both training and research at all levels. The British perspective was that the system of apprenticeship, supplemented by evening classes at a small number of institutions such as the Finsbury Technical College after a full day's work, was the best training of all. This extremely partial and ad hoc arrangement serves well to illustrate a lack of commitment to innovation and industry and gives one clue as to why Germany and the United States outpaced Great Britain industrially by 1900 and why Great Britain failed to respond. Within such a context, it is easy to understand why Lanchester remained unappreciated for so long.

Lanchester's first invention was made while he was still a student. He developed an accelerometer to measure and record the acceleration and deceleration of a vehicle. A second invention, which he also made while he was still a student, was a fixture on slide rules which could be used for rapid calculations in thermodynamics. Both inventions were later further developed and manufactured.

Lanchester's first job on leaving the Normal School was as a low-paid draftsman. This was a consequence of his lack of formal qualifications.

During this time, he took out his first patent. He invented a draftsman's tool for hatching, shading, and geometrical design.

Through the good offices of an uncle, Lanchester's second job offered him more scope. In 1889, he began work as assistant works manager for the small firm of T. B. Barker and Company, makers of the Forward gas engine. The factory was in a very poor section of Birmingham, a large manufacturing city in the English Midlands well-known for its hundreds of small manufacturing businesses. The company serviced, maintained, and manufactured Otto engines. Within one or two years, Lanchester overhauled the engine designs and constructed engines ranging from two to sixty horsepower. At the age of twenty-one, in 1890, he was made works manager. There quickly followed two important inventions. First, Lanchester developed a pendulum governor which replaced the previous centrifugal governor used in all such engines. Next, as a safety feature following a number of fatalities, he invented an engine starter. Both innovations were almost universally applied to gas engines within the next twenty years.

At twenty-three, Lanchester resigned his job to visit the United States and sell his patents. Though the trip was a financial failure, Lanchester learned much about American manufacturing methods.

Life's Work

Shortly after his return to England, Lanchester determined to design and make his own motorcar. At that time, car building and design was at a very rudimentary stage. Lanchester had seen a Daimler at the Paris Exhibition. There was also the work of Gottlieb Daimler's fellow German Carl Benz, and of Armand Peugeot of France. Although, during the rest of the 1890's, other German and French companies arrived on the scene, British car manufacturers were reduced to importing, assembling, copying, or adapting Continental models. In addition, designs were based on the model of horse-drawn carriages, with the horses simply replaced by an engine and the bodywork undertaken by traditional companies of coach-builders. Finally, there was little incentive to British pioneers. An act of Parliament passed in 1865 provided that horseless vehicles should be restricted to a maximum speed of four miles per hour and be preceded at a distance of twenty yards by a man carrying a red flag. The Red Flag Act was still in effect until 1896, when the speed limit was raised to fourteen miles per hour and the red flag was discontinued. Even then, low-performance vehicles had to remain the norm if the law were to be respected.

Lanchester's first experimental car appeared in 1895. It was completely original. His was the first motorcar to be designed and thought out as such. The first Lanchester was built around the driver, and for comfort. It was a five-seater with a single-cylinder, air-cooled engine of five horsepower. Unlike most early inventors, Lanchester used a system of electrical ignition of his own invention. Other original features included a Lanchester carburetor, his own transmission system, and an epicyclic gearbox combined with a chain drive. In February, 1896, Lanchester and his brother George took the car on its first run. While it ran smoothly, they found it underpowered, since they had to push the vehicle up hills. Following an eighteen-month period of reconstruction work, the car reappeared, this time with a twin-cylinder, aircooled engine of eight horsepower; a special counterbalancing mechanism to achieve a balanced engine; and a new kind of worm drive replacing the chain drive. On the road in 1897, the Lanchesters drove the car at speeds of up to twenty-eight miles per hour, in an early-morning foray to avoid the police. A second car, with even more original features, appeared in 1898. It was famous in its day and won a special gold medal for design and performance at trials arranged by the Automobile Club of Great Britain and Ireland.

In 1899, the Lanchester Engine Company was founded, and this Gold Medal Phaeton was its first production model. The balancing of the engine allowed for higher piston speeds than thought possible at the time; a splined shaft and Lanchester's own roller bearings were introduced into the gearbox; a pedal accelerator was used for the first time; ignition was achieved through a magnetic generator; and cantilever springs at the forward end of the chassis were used for the first time. The result was a nearly smooth, noiseless glide, a great contrast to its competitors, and a high speed of twenty-eight miles per hour.

In the early years of the twentieth century, motorcar driving was still the preserve of the rich. The luxury car market was therefore the only outlet for car manufacturers. Unfortunately, most early car designers were badly undercapitalized. Lanchester was no exception. His first financial backers were the family Pughs, the successful bicycle financiers. From 1901 to 1905, the armaments company Vickers and Maxim provided money to exploit the Lanchester motor patents. As a result of cash-flow problems, however, the company went into receivership in 1904. Lanchester was forced to resign as general manager when the company was reorganized as the Lanchester Motor Company. He even failed to raise enough capital to remain a director of the company that bore his name. He finally resigned all connection with the company in 1914, remaining thereafter on the periphery of motor manufacture.

To compensate for the loss of his company, Lanchester accepted the offer in 1910 of Edward Manville, Chairman of the Daimler Motor Company, to become its consulting engineer. He remained in that capacity, part of a multitalented prewar team, until his dismissal in 1930 at a time when managers were desperately seeking to save the company. Ironically, Daimler was saved in large part by its acquisition of the Lanchester Motor Company in 1931, which offered it a better engine design and performance and an opportunity to move into the middle-class market which had developed since 1920.

Remarkable though Lanchester's career in motor design was, however, it was not his only career. As early as 1890, he is said to have confided to a friend that he would like to build an engine for an aircraft. Given that no heavier-than-air machine had ever flown at that time, his friend sagely advised him to forget the idea as his reputation as a sane engineer would be ruined. While he did not build his engine, Lanchester remained deeply interested in powered flight. When he worked at the Forward engine works, he used his spare time in many experiments with model gliders launched from his bedroom window and in the meadow behind his house; he studied the flight of birds, took up shooting to examine the wings and body structure of birds, and took up fishing to study the streamlining of fish. By 1894, Lanchester had made a great discovery in aerodynamics. His vortex theory explained the lift which sustains aircraft in flight. A paper on the subject was rejected by the prestigious Royal Society and was given instead, in 1895, to the Birmingham Natural History and Philosophical Society. He could not get it published. Later expanded, Lanchester's findings and theories were published as *Aerial Flight* in two volumes—*Aerodynamics* (1907) and *Aerodonetics* (1908). In Great Britain, his work was ignored for many years. It was not until after World War I that English and French scientists accepted his theories. Only in Germany was Lanchester taken seriously and justly famed, an irony that would be amusing were it not so tragic for English and French fliers.

Toward the end of his most outstandingly creative period in 1901, Lanchester was a big man in appearance, of heavy build, with strong features framed by a thick, dark beard. He was as commanding personally as he was physically. He was not a man to minimize his own achievements and was often intolerant of people whose minds did not work as quickly as his own. He could be cruelly sarcastic. He loved opera and classical music; he sang; he even wrote and published a book of poetry. He was married in 1919 to Dorothea Cooper, a clergyman's daughter. They had no children. Lanchester died penniless at the age of seventy-eight on March 8, 1946, at his home in Birmingham.

Summary

Frederick William Lanchester was an intuitive genius. His work was rarely appreciated when it first appeared precisely because he was so original and innovative. Though he is now called by many modern writers the "father of the British motorcar," the remarkable technique and performance of his machines did not lead to widespread recognition. His pioneering aeronautical work suffered an even worse fate. It was ignored in his home country for twenty-five years. Only then did his *Aerial Flight* become the textbook for aircraft designers, as it had already years before in Germany. Frederick Lanchester has still not been accorded that renown which should be his due. For a brief while, a new university was named for him in Coventry, the center of the British car industry. By the 1980's, it had altered its name to the Coventry Polytechnic.

The lack of recognition embittered Lanchester even though appreciation eventually did come. In 1919, Birmingham University awarded him an honorary degree. In 1922, he was finally elected a fellow of the Royal Society. He was made an honorary fellow of the Institutions of Mechanical Engineers and Automobile Engineers. In 1926, Lanchester was made an honorary fellow and awarded the gold medal of the Royal Aeronautical Society. In 1931 came the Daniel Guggenheim gold medal. Lanchester in 1941 was recognized by the Institution of Civil Engineers with its Alfred Ewing gold medal, and, finally, in 1945, came the James Watt international medal, the highest award of the Institution of Mechanical Engineers.

In his lifetime, Lanchester took out more than four hundred patents for his inventions. Most remarkable of all, Lanchester rarely received financial backing and worked alone with few resources.

Bibliography

Church, Roy. *Herbert Austin: The British Motor Car Industry to 1941*. London: Europa, 1979. An interesting examination of one of Lanchester's more successful rivals, the book shows well the early trials and tribulations of the British car industry and is particularly good on the interwar period. The introduction by Neil McKendrick provides a stimulating polemic on the subject of British hatred for industry, machines, technology, and those associated with them, especially self-made businessmen.

Kingsford, P. W. *Engineers, Inventors, and Workers*. London: Arnold, and New York: St. Martin's Press, 1964. A well-written small book covering many aspects of the Industrial Revolution in Great Britain based mainly on short biographical sections making up each chapter. Chapter 11 contains an interesting and informative section on Lanchester.

————. *F. W. Lanchester: The Life of an Engineer*. London: Arnold, 1960. The standard, as well as the only, biography of Lanchester. Enormously informative.

Lanchester, George. "F. W. Lanchester, L.L.D., F.R.S., His Life and Work." *Newcomen Society Transactions* 30 (1957). A retrospective vindication of the great inventor by his brother and associate.

Landes, David S. *The Unbound Prometheus: Technological Change and Industrial Development in Western Europe from 1750 to the Present*. Cambridge: Cambridge University Press, 1969. One of the standard accounts of the Industrial Revolution in Europe. It discusses well the kinds of handicaps faced by Lanchester, the context within which he worked, and the attitudes that surrounded him. The author criticizes Great Britain for its lack of regard for entrepreneurial spirit during this time.

Penrose, Harald. *British Aviation: The Great War and Armistice, 1915-1919*. London: Putnam, and New York: Funk and Wagnalls, 1969. Good on Lanchester mainly through omission. It shows that the founder of the vortex theory of flight was largely ignored by aircraft designers and military planners.

Richardson, Kenneth. *The British Motor Industry, 1896-1939*. London: Macmillan, and Hamden, Conn.: Archon, 1977. The author taught at the then Lanchester (Coventry) Polytechnic. The book is mainly about the Daimler Company, but it is very good on the early period and on Lanchester's efforts.

Rolt, R. T. C. *Victorian Engineering*. London: Allen Lane, 1970; Baltimore: Penguin, 1974. Excellent for the context out of which Lanchester emerged. Chapter 10 deals with Lanchester, and the book contains photographs of Lanchester and his car.

Thoms, D., and T. Donnelly. *The Motor Car Industry in Coventry Since the 1890's*. London: Croom Helm, and New York: St. Martin's Press, 1985. Interesting on this city in the early period of car design and manufacture. Good on Lanchester's association with Daimler and the problems all carmakers faced.

Stephen Burwood

LEV DAVIDOVICH LANDAU

Born: January 22, 1908; Baku, Azerbaijan, Russian Empire
Died: April 1, 1968; Moscow, U.S.S.R.
Area of Achievement: Physics
Contribution: Landau contributed to the development of quantum mechanics and its applications to the physical world. Among his major achievements are the development of the theory of phase transitions and his explanation of the behavior of quantum liquids such as liquid helium in the superfluid state. Landau's contributions to the theory of quantum liquids were recognized by the award of the Nobel Prize in Physics in 1962.

Early Life

Lev Davidovich Landau was born in Baku, on the Caspian Sea, on January 22, 1908. His father, David Llovich Landau, was the chief engineer at an oil field in Baku. His mother, Lyubov Veniaminovna Garvaki-Landau, was a physician and a teacher. When Landau finished high school at the age of thirteen, he wanted to go to the University of Baku to study mathematics. Landau's father wanted him to have a career in finance or administration and so sent Landau to the Baku Economics Technicum. Landau refused to continue his studies there after the first year, and so in 1922 his father sent him to the University of Baku. There, Landau studied chemistry, physics, and mathematics. At the age of sixteen, Landau went to Leningrad State University, where he studied physics. Landau published his first scientific paper at the age of eighteen on the spectra of diatomic molecules. While Landau was a student at the university, he had a research scholarship at the Leningrad Röntgen Institute, where he worked on the developing science of quantum mechanics.

In 1929, Landau received a traveling fellowship from his own government and a Rockefeller Fellowship, which enabled him to travel in Western Europe for eighteen months. During that time he met and worked with many of the developers of quantum mechanics and himself became an outstanding and renowned theoretical physicist. This trip marked the beginning of Landau's scientific career.

Landau spent some of his time in Copenhagen at Niels Bohr's Institute for Theoretical Physics, where much of the theory of quantum mechanics was being developed. Landau came to admire Bohr and regarded him as his teacher. In fact, the theoretical seminar that Landau ultimately developed was strongly reminiscent of the way in which Bohr worked. Landau worked on a variety of problems at the institute. While Landau was at the institute, he collaborated with Rudolf Peierls; this collaboration led to a joint paper that pointed out some problems in quantum electrodynamics. It was with this work that Landau's international reputation began to grow.

Life's Work

On his return to the Soviet Union in 1931, Landau returned to Leningrad, then still the center of Soviet physics, and became a researcher and professor at his former university. Landau had returned to Leningrad with definite ideas about the way in which theoretical physics should be taught, but as a professor in the department where he had so recently been a student, he encountered difficulties in the implementation of his program. In 1932, he was appointed head of the Theoretical Physics Division of the Ukrainian Physicotechnical Institute, which was established by Leningrad State University in Kharkov. It was at Kharkov that Landau put his methods into practice and developed his own way of doing theoretical physics.

At Kharkov, Landau devised a program for the education of theoretical physicists known as the theoretical minimum. This eventually led to the multivolume textbook on theoretical physics, written with Evgenii Lifshitz, a student of Landau at Kharkov. This work had a significant effect on the way in which advanced physics is taught all over the world, and as a result Landau influenced the research style of a generation of theoretical physicists. At Kharkov, Landau developed a reputation as a problem solver—he solved many problems in experimental physics that were brought to his attention, and as a result worked in a variety of fields. Landau published numerous studies in this period; they dealt with low-temperature physics, acoustics, superconductivity, the photoelectric effect, and a wide range of other topics. Also at Kharkov, Landau first organized his theoretical seminar, in which Landau's students and coworkers reported on their own work and on the latest work of other researchers appearing in scientific journals. These seminars covered a wide range of topics and became Landau's chief source of scien-

tific information for his own research; the seminars were also a valuable teaching tool, as Landau's students were able to observe the way in which Landau approached problems. Two other important events took place in the time Landau was at Kharkov. He was awarded a doctorate by Leningrad State University in 1935; he also met his future wife, Concordia (Cora) Drobantseva, at Kharkov, where she was an engineer in a chocolate factory. They were married in 1937.

Also in 1937, Pyotr Leonidovich Kapitsa invited Landau to become the head of the theoretical division of the Institute for Physical Problems in Moscow. The institute had been recently formed by Kapitsa, who had, in 1934, been prevented by Joseph Stalin from returning to his Cambridge laboratory where he had worked with Ernest Rutherford. Landau remained at this institute for the rest of his active career, with the exception of the time during which he was imprisoned by Stalin and when he was evacuated with the rest of the institute during World War II.

In 1937, Kapitsa had resumed the work he had been pursuing at Cambridge on low-temperature

physics and was investigating the superfluid properties of liquid helium at low temperatures. Landau then began his work on quantum liquids, for which he was to win the Nobel Prize in 1962. As a result of the findings of Kapitsa's experiments, Landau realized that the behavior of liquid helium at these low temperatures had features in common with the onset of the superconducting state, and that the properties that liquid helium exhibited at low temperatures were the result of large-scale quantum behavior. In the course of this work, Landau began to develop his theory of phase transitions, that is, the study of matter as it changes from one state to another, such as from solid into liquid.

In 1938, Landau was sentenced to be imprisoned for ten years for espionage. The allegation was that he was a German spy (that he was of Jewish descent would seem to make this a ridiculous charge). Landau remained in prison for almost a year, even after Stalin signed a treaty with Adolf Hitler. Landau was eventually released when Kapitsa interceded with Vyacheslav Molotov on his behalf, and he returned to his work at the institute. On his return, he was, along with many other leading scientists, involved with war work; after the war, he published several papers on the detonation of explosives.

At the end of the war, Landau was his country's leading theoretical physicist and began to receive many honors. In 1946, he became a full member of the Academy of Sciences. In 1951, he became a member of the Danish Royal Academy of Sciences; in 1956, he became a member of the Netherlands Royal Academy of Sciences; and in 1960, he became a foreign member of the Royal Society. In these years he also received two Orders of Lenin and three state prizes and was a Hero of Socialist Labor. In 1962, he was awarded the Lenin Prize as well as the Nobel Prize.

In the postwar years, Landau worked on a wide variety of problems, making fundamental contributions to nuclear physics, quantum electrodynamics, and fluid dynamics. He continued his work on liquid helium and on other quantum liquids as well. Landau was also interested in education at all levels, and he planned to write textbooks to educate physicists.

The scientific career of Landau came to a tragic end in 1962, when he was involved in a serious traffic accident. On January 7, 1962, Landau was a passenger in a car being driven by the physicist Vladimir Sudakov on the ice-covered roads of

Moscow on his way to Dubna. The car was struck by a truck. Landau's injuries were severe: He had nine fractured ribs, three fractured pubic bones, and a fractured left femur. His left lung was completely collapsed, he had suffered internal injuries, and brain damage was suspected. That Landau ever survived to be awarded the Nobel Prize was a miracle; he was still in the hospital a year after it was awarded. Landau did eventually leave the hospital. His memory returned to him, and he seemed to retain his complete mastery of theoretical physics. Nevertheless, he was never to work creatively again. Landau's constant pain rendered him unable to concentrate on theoretical problems. He lived for six years after his accident but never again performed any research.

Summary

Lev Davidovich Landau was one of the greatest physicists of the twentieth century. His contributions are of enduring importance. Few physicists have been so diversely talented, fewer still have been able to make fundamental contributions in such a wide variety of fields. His greatest contribution to physics, however, may well have been his teaching. Landau was one of the major figures involved in the rise of Soviet physics: His former coworkers and pupils have included many of the leading Soviet theoretical physicists, and his textbooks have had a worldwide impact on the teaching of theoretical physics. Unfortunately, Landau's writings are inaccessible to all but professional physicists and advanced students of physics. The simpler works, *Kurs obshchei fiziki* (1965; *General Physics*, 1967) and *Physics for Everyone* (1974), were largely written by his coauthors and do not reflect the full power of Landau's ability to communicate physical ideas.

Landau's contributions to physics have shown that a mastery of the mathematical structure of theoretical physics can enable a physicist to work creatively on a variety of different problems; his textbooks, which are his legacy to the world, have shown how seemingly different problems can be solved by the same methods. Landau has continued the tradition of the great physicists from Isaac Newton to Albert Einstein and has shown that the key to scientific progress is to identify the parts of the problem that are fundamental and to ignore the rest. His contributions to the world beyond physics lie in the engineering developments of his theories and in the example of his heroic grasp on life after his unfortunate accident. In the end Landau's was a career that was tragically shortened.

Bibliography

Akhiezer, Alexander I. "Recollections of Lev Davidovich Landau." *Physics Today* 47, no. 6 (June, 1994). Recollections of one of Landau's colleagues.

Cline, Barbara L. *Men Who Made a New Physics.* New York: New American Library, 1965. A historical study of the development of the quantum theory and its developers. This book is written for the general reader and provides an adequate introduction to the theoretical framework in which Landau worked.

Dorozynski, Alexander. *The Man They Wouldn't Let Die.* New York: Macmillan, 1965; London: Secker and Warburg, 1966. This is the most complete biography of Landau available. A major part of the book is devoted to telling the story of Landau's accident and of his long recovery. The account of Landau's earlier life was compiled from secondary sources. Offers a complete account of Landau's life. One of the chapters is devoted to the development of the Soviet nuclear weapons capability.

French, Anthony P., and P. J. Kennedy. *Niels Bohr: A Centenary Volume.* Cambridge, Mass.: Harvard University Press, 1985. This volume is primarily devoted to Niels Bohr, but it contains other interesting material. In particular, the way in which quantum physics and its Copenhagen interpretation developed is discussed. Contains some information about Landau's time at the institute.

Gamow, George. *Thirty Years That Shook Physics: The Study of Quantum Theory.* New York: Anchor, and London: Constable, 1966. An introduction to quantum mechanics written by a great expositor and an early colleague of Landau. This book contains the text of a quantum mechanical Faust performed at Niels Bohr's institute. A good starting point for someone completely unfamiliar with modern physics.

Gorelick, Gennady. "The Top-Secret Life of Lev Landau." *Scientific American* 277, no. 2 (August, 1997). Discusses Landau's efforts to publish an anti-Stalin manifesto and his part in the creation of the first Soviet thermonuclear bomb.

Hey, Tony, and Patrick Walters. *The Quantum Universe.* Cambridge and New York: Cambridge University Press, 1987. An excellent second book on quantum concepts written for the general reader. Useful for the reader interested in more applications than are provided by Cline and Gamow. The explanations are pictorial rather than mathematical.

Lifshitz, Evgenii. "Lev Davidovich Landau." In *Mechanics*. 3d ed. Oxford and New York: Pergamon Press, 1976. Provides a thorough introduction to Landau's life and work. Probably the best source for the mathematically educated reader. The nonmathematical reader would do better to consult the book by Dorozynski.

Livanova, Anna. *Landau: A Great Physicist and Teacher.* Translated by J. B. Sykes. Oxford and New York: Pergamon Press, 1980. This is a biography in the Soviet tradition; care should be taken when using Soviet sources, since all embarrassing facts are omitted. As an example, Landau's imprisonment by Stalin is unmentioned. This book provides a readable account of Landau's scientific work. The period following Landau's accident is not mentioned.

Stephen R. Addison

FRITZ LANG

Born: December 5, 1890; Vienna, Austro-Hungarian Empire
Died: August 2, 1976; Los Angeles, California
Area of Achievement: Film
Contribution: Lang was a pioneer in twentieth century filmmaking. The silent films that he directed in Germany in the 1920's established his reputation as a creative innovator and skilled cinematic craftsman. His sound films in the early 1930's and Hollywood films of the 1940's and 1950's demonstrated his remarkable ability to adapt to changing technical and cultural settings without sacrificing cinematic integrity.

Early Life

Fritz Lang was born in Vienna on December 5, 1890. His father was the municipal architect, and Lang followed in his father's footsteps, studying engineering and architecture at Vienna's technical university (1908-1910). Though he grew increasingly disenchanted with conventional middle-class life and finally broke with his father and family to study modern art in Munich and Paris, he never lost the architect's eye for space, light, and alignment.

In the years before World War I, Lang lived a bohemian existence. He traveled to Asia, North Africa, and the South Seas, exotic places that figured occasionally in later films. Even more important for his subsequent development as a director was his immersion in prewar expressionism, a German cultural revolt that challenged most existing standards. Like other youthful artists in this movement, Lang repudiated the urban bourgeois values of his parents' generation, turning in his case to the orient, the works of Friedrich Wilhelm Nietzsche, Karl May Westerns, and the occult in search of a new worldview. By 1913, he was back in Paris painting and selling postcards and cartoons.

Interned at the outbreak of World War I, Lang soon escaped and returned to Vienna, where he joined the Austrian army. He rose to the rank of lieutenant during the war and was decorated several times. He was wounded three times, including one injury that left him blind in his right eye. It was during a year of hospitalization at the end of the war that Lang wrote and sold his first screenplays to a leading German filmmaker. While convalescing he also took a small part in a patriotic war play; in the audience was a representative of Berlin's

Decla Film Company, who invited Lang to Berlin as soon as he recovered.

Life's Work

Lang arrived in Berlin at an opportune moment in early 1919. While most Germans were trying to cope with the chaotic consequences of military defeat and political revolution, the infant German film industry was struggling to satisfy surging public demand for escapist entertainment. It was in this turbulent setting that Lang made his directorial debut in *Halbblut* (1919), a low-budget thriller about two men destroyed by their love for a half-caste woman. Lang's early silent films were distinguished by their expressionist stylization, simplification, and exaggeration. Lang's imaginative use of lighting, fantasy, Freudian symbolism, and oversize corridors, stairways, and doorways reflected the influence of expressionist theater. This style is clearly visible in his first popular film, *Der müde Tod* (1921; *Destiny*). Here names such as "the Man" are utilized to universalize characters in the expressionist manner. In *Dr. Mabuse der Spieler* (1922; *Dr. Mabuse the Gambler*), Lang's silent classic about a master criminal out to dominate the world, the young director utilized expressionist sets with painted shadows on the walls. In *Metropolis* (1927), an overly simplistic study of class and moral conflict in a futuristic city, he introduced stylized workers enslaved to gigantic expressionistic machines. The expressionist element in Lang's films gave way to greater realism in the late 1920's, but reminders of this appeared in many later films.

Lang's silent films were also notable for their extraordinary technical innovation and creativity. *Destiny*, for example, so impressed Douglas Fairbanks, Sr., that he purchased the American rights to the film in order to copy its flying carpet scene and other special effects for his 1924 production of *The Thief of Bagdad*. *Die Niebelungen* (1924), a two-part epic based on the Siegfried saga, contained an eerie artificial forest guarded by a seventy foot fire-breathing dragon—another cinematic first. Later, in *Metropolis*, Lang introduced the first "transformation" scene in film history, turning a machine into a lifelike woman. Finally, in his first sound film, the unforgettable classic *M* (1931), Lang utilized sound creatively to intensify audience anxiety as police and criminals pursue a child murderer. Lang's fifteen films, all studio-produced in Berlin, created cinematic images that have been copied by film directors ever since.

As one of Universium Film's foremost directors, Lang enjoyed considerable public and artistic attention. Yet like many intellectuals and artists of the time, he displayed little concern for the democratic values indispensable to artistic freedom. Indeed, his films often reflected and reinforced German society's widespread antidemocratic attitudes. In *Die Niebelungen*, for example, Lang reinforced traditional German prejudices about Eastern Europe by presenting the Russian Huns as primitive, barbaric people, incapable of organized activity or civilized feelings. *Metropolis*, Lang's most expensive and memorable silent film, ends with the calculating factory owner and rebellious, easily manipulated workers united harmoniously by a new leader, a man who seems to foreshadow Adolf Hitler.

Shortly after the Nazi takeover in 1933, Propaganda Minister Joseph Goebbels asked Lang to make films for the Third Reich. Apparently Hitler had been impressed by Lang's earlier epics. Surprised by this offer but aware that filmmaking in Nazi Germany was changing and that his mother's Jewish origins might present serious problems, Lang packed what few things he could carry and took the night train that evening to Paris. His wife, Thea von Harbou, with whom he had collaborated on all his scripts since 1920, elected to stay in Nazi Germany and make films for the Third Reich.

In Paris, Lang directed one film, *Liliom* (1934), before being hired by Metro-Goldwyn-Mayer's David O. Selznick to make films in Hollywood. Lang's transition to the United States was not easy. It required not only a change in language and cultural orientation but also subordination to front office decisions, box-office demands, and meddling censors. For a director accustomed to absolute control over every phase of film production, from script selection to crew selection and final editing, Hollywood proved endlessly frustrating.

Yet Lang adjusted. He learned colloquial English, became a citizen in 1935, and slowly won the industry's respect by making carefully crafted films on time and within budget. His first Hollywood film, the critically acclaimed psychological thriller *Fury* (1936), probed one of Lang's favorite themes, mob violence, but this time in a uniquely American setting. Later films explored social issues such as the mistreatment of society's unfortunate, *You Only Live Once* (1937), the impossibility of escaping fate, *Man Hunt* (1941), and the good man misled by the promiscuous woman, *The Woman in the Window* (1944) and *Scarlet Street* (1945). Some of his early American films were deliberately critical of American society, most followed conventional Hollywood themes, but each was stamped with Lang's unique visual style and exacting attention to detail.

Lang also made three interesting Westerns. In *The Return of Frank James* (1940), his first color film, this German exile examined man's struggle against frontier injustice. Lang's favorite was *Western Union* (1941), a technically accurate but historically fictionalized film about the building of the transcontinental telegraph. His last film in this genre, *Rancho Notorious* (1952), was memorable for the first use of theme music and for Marlene Dietrich's sparkling performance. During World War II, Lang directed several anti-Nazi films. They hint at the naked brutality of the Third Reich but do not explain the real character or dangers of National Socialism.

In the 1950's, the House Committee on Un-American Activities blacklisted Lang for his liberal views and association with leftist exiles such as Bertolt Brecht. He was still able to film a number of detective, or criminal, thrillers, but none was as compelling as his earlier films and several exhibited growing disillusionment with American society. Lang's favorite American film was the next to last, *While the City Sleeps* (1956), another story of a frantic manhunt for a pathological killer. He had so much trouble making this film that he decided to retire from Hollywood filmmaking. After returning to West Germany in 1959 to make two mediocre films, Lang retired to the privacy of his comfortable Beverly Hills home, emerging occasionally when declining health permitted to attend retrospectives honoring his work or to speak with film historians. He died on August 2, 1976.

Summary

Fritz Lang was one of the twentieth century's most creative film directors. A product of pre-1914 expressionism and World War I, he came to film with an aesthetic and intellectual background rarely found among early direcition. In forty-two films spanning five decades and two continents, he spawned many firsts in cinematography.

Lang's German films attracted the greatest popular acclaim. Visually powerful and intellectually provocative, they often focused on the struggle between good and evil, the dark struggle, and they earned for him international recognition long before he moved to Hollywood. That he made the transition to America better than most cultural exiles from Nazi Germany resulted in part from his own talent and resilience and in part from the unique nature of film, which relies more on visual images than on language. It was in the visual dimension of filmmaking that Lang excelled in both Berlin and Hollywood. Yet Lang always seemed out of place in Hollywood. His strong German accent, Viennese monocle, and serious approach to making film reminded many of his pre-1933 origins. He may have directed the United States' most famous stars in his twenty-eight Hollywood films, Spencer Tracy to Joan Bennett and Henry Fonda, but Lang always remained an outsider in the United States. It was this perspective, however, that added a unique touch to his Hollywood films.

Film critics and historians were slow to recognize Lang's achievements. The political ambiguity in his early German films produced sharp criticism in the 1940's and 1950's that clouded his reputation in both the United States and Europe. With the international film revival of the 1960's, critics began to discover the extent to which this prickly, elusive man had creatively expanded the dimensions of film in both its technical possibilities and psychological power.

Bibliography

Armour, Robert A. *Fritz Lang*. Boston: Twayne, 1978. This is the best film biography of Lang available. It analyzes Lang's career and most important German and American films, emphasizing the importance to Lang of the struggle between good and evil.

Bogdanovich, Peter. *Fritz Lang in America*. London: Studio Vista, 1968; New York: Praeger, 1969. Bogdanovich introduces American audiences to the French auteur perspective that looks at the works of an author as a whole. Bogdanovich sees all of Lang's films as forming a unified whole, united by visual style and thematic continuity.

Dolgenos, Peter. "The Star on C.A. Rotwang's Door: Turning Kracauer on its Head." *Journal of Popular Film and Television* 25, no. 2 (Summer 1997). Analysis of Lang's controversial film *Metropolis*.

Eisner, Lotte H. *Fritz Lang*. Edited by David Robinson. Translated by Gertrud Mander. London: Secker and Warburg, 1976; New York: Oxford University Press, 1977. A film biography by a friend of Lang, who allowed the director to comment on the book before completion. Provides important personal insights, a brief autobiographical statement by Lang, and a list of unrealized projects.

Hall, Jeanne. " 'A Little Trouble with Perspective': Art and Authorship in Fritz Lang's *Scarlet Street*." *Film Criticism* 21, no. 1 (Fall 1996). Analysis of Lang's film *Scarlet Street* and the questions it raises with respect to artists and art critics.

Jensen, Paul M. *The Cinema of Fritz Lang*. New York: Barnes, 1969. This is the first thorough discussion of Lang's cinema that provides detailed descriptions and analyses of his German and American films. Its focus is more on the cinematic character and innovations than political or public impact of Lang's films.

Kaplan, E. Ann. *Fritz Lang: A Guide to References and Resources*. Boston: Hall, 1981. An indispensable reference to writings about Lang and his films to 1980. Contains a brief biographical introduction, valuable discussion of Lang's changing place in film criticism, detailed information on each of Lang's films, and a list of archival sources.

Ott, Frederick W. *The Films of Fritz Lang*. Secaucus, N.J.: Citadel Press, 1979. Nicely illustrated text based on research in American and German film archives and institutes; includes information from interviews with Lang.

Rennie W. Brantz

K. D. LANG

Born: November 2, 1961; Edmonton, Alberta, Canada

Area of Achievement: Music

Contribution: A songwriter and Grammy-winning singer, Lang has achieved success in the genres of country-western and alternative pop music while challenging stereotypes of female popular entertainers.

Early Life

Kathryn Dawn "K. D." Lang was born on November 2, 1961, in Edmonton, and was reared with her three older siblings in Consort, a town of almost seven hundred people in the eastern central plains of Alberta, Canada. Her father, Fred, purchased and operated the town pharmacy, and her mother, Audrey, taught elementary school.

Supported by her parents, especially her mother, Lang began to sing at local music festivals when she was five years old, and she continued to perform at school shows and weddings until she finished high school. At the age of seven, she started weekly piano lessons in the town of Castor (about an hour's drive from Consort), but after three years she switched to playing the guitar. Throughout her childhood, she listened to a wide variety of musical genres, ranging from classical music to Broadway tunes to rock and roll.

Lang's parents also taught her to challenge gender stereotypes. She actively participated in sports as a javelin thrower and volleyball player. Although her father left the family when Lang was twelve, she had a close relationship with him prior to his departure, and from her father she learned how to ride motorcycles and target shoot. She also exhibited a nonconformist sense of fashion, wearing leather pants and favoring "hippie" headbands and sunglasses.

Life's Work

When she was eighteen, K. D. Lang left Consort to study music and voice at Red Deer College, ninety miles south of Edmonton, but the combination of her frustration with academic requirements and job opportunities in Edmonton led her to quit college and pursue a career as an entertainer. Her early work was eclectic and included performance art, but increasingly she defined herself as a country-and-western singer.

This identity was strengthened in 1981, when Lang appeared in Edmonton in a musical, *Country Chorale*, playing a part loosely modeled on American country singer Patsy Cline, who died in a plane crash in 1963. Lang felt strongly drawn to Cline as an artistic role model and especially appreciated the pain-filled songs of lost love for which Cline had been famous.

Lang also continued to defy traditional gender stereotypes and to develop her own distinctive style. She began to use her first and middle initials instead of Kathy Dawn, and to spell her name entirely in lower-case letters. She also drew attention with her unusual stage costumes, which might combine heavy socks and boots with long square-dance skirts or false sideburns with a cowboy hat.

In 1982, Lang auditioned for and received a job as vocalist for an Edmonton country swing group, but when the band folded after one public performance, she decided to form her own group. With the help of Larry Wanagas, an Edmonton recording studio owner who became her manager, Lang created "The Reclines" and began to appear with this band at Edmonton nightclubs.

In 1984, K. D. Lang and the Reclines released *A Truly Western Experience* on the independent Bunstead label and toured Canada to promote the album. Initially, Lang and the Reclines appeared in smaller Canadian cities. Her act combined an exotic blend of country crooning and rockabilly with vigorous dancing and light-hearted clowning. These elements, plus her gender-bending appearance (enhanced by a new, close-cropped hairstyle), seemed to puzzle audiences. Some wondered if Lang's performances were serious efforts at country music or humorous spoofs of the genre. In Toronto, however, she and her band found enthusiastic audiences and received good reviews. Based on this success in a major urban center, Lang and the Reclines were booked in 1985 at The Bottom Line, a well-known New York City nightclub. After watching Lang perform, Seymour Stein of Sire Records, famous for his interest in offbeat musical performers, signed her to a recording contract.

Angel with a Lariat (1986), Lang's first album with Sire, sold more than 460,000 copies and brought her a Juno Award as Canada's best Country Female Vocalist. On that album and her next for Sire, *Shadowland* (1988), Lang offered mixtures of country music standards (rearranged to feature her energetic "cowpunk" style) and tunes cowritten by Lang and Ben Mink, a member of the Reclines. She also paid homage to Patsy Cline with deeply emotional torch songs and through her choice of Owen Bradley, Cline's longtime producer, as the producer of *Shadowland*. The torch songs enabled Lang to use her rich voice to full advantage and to develop a romantic quality in her performances.

Lang began to win both a large audience and praise from much of the music industry. *Shadowland* sold more than a million copies and won praise from numerous critics, as did her next Sire album, *Absolute Torch and Twang* (1989). Lang also won the Grammy award for Best Country Vocal Collaboration in 1988, for her duet with Roy Orbison on a remake of his hit song "Crying," and the 1989 Grammy for Best Country Female Vocal Performance for *Absolute Torch and Twang*.

Yet such success did not translate into full acceptance in the ranks of country-and-western music. Centered in Nashville, Tennessee, the country music industry did not respond with uniform enthusiasm to Lang's willingness to combine country tunes with blues, rock, and punk music. Her unwillingness to conform to industry standards of feminine appearance also drew criticism, as did her growing reputation as a model of female independence and strength. Although individual country performers (including Minnie Pearl, Brenda Lee, and Loretta Lynn) did embrace Lang and work with her, few country radio stations would play her songs. Despite this lackluster response from mainstream country-and-western supporters, Lang continued to expand her base of fans, especially among enthusiasts of alternative pop music and from critics writing for publications such as *Rolling Stone* and *The New York Times*. She toured widely in North America and Europe to promote her albums, and developed a strong reputation as a live performer. Her appearances with Sting and Bruce Springsteen on the Amnesty International Tour of 1988 helped to cement her position as a favorite with rock-and-roll audiences.

The year 1990 brought new levels of acclaim and new criticisms for Lang. Although the Country Music Awards continued to ignore her, Lang won a 1990 Grammy for Best Female Country Vocalist. She also recorded a television commercial at the request of People for the Ethical Treatment of Animals (PETA). In the commercial, Lang spoke strongly against the beef industry and meat-eating. A longtime vegetarian, Lang referred to her own upbringing in the cattle country of Alberta and bluntly stated, "Meat stinks." Furor over the advertisement developed before its planned release, and although it aired only on news programs, Lang became notorious for her statements.

Although her animal rights activism did not seem to damage Lang's reputation with most of her fans and won strong approval from some, it did give country music another reason to reject Lang. Many country radio stations in Canada and the United States announced that they would no longer play her music (even though most never had).

Rather than run from such condemnation, Lang took new paths in her career and life. In 1991, she released *Harvest of Seven Years (Cropped and Chronicled)*, a compilation of her videos and taped performances since 1984. She tried dramatic acting in *Salmonberries* (1992), a film directed by Percy Adlon and set in Alaska and Berlin. Lang played an Inuit woman in love with a German widow, and while the film was only released in theaters in Europe and then appeared once on Canadian television in 1993, Lang's performance won praise. In her fifth album, *Ingenue* (1992), Lang abandoned most of her country sound and instead featured her voice in ten yearning and introspective love songs, all cowritten by Lang and Ben Mink.

Both *Salmonberries* and *Ingenue* increased rumors about Lang's sexual orientation, since she portrayed a lesbian in the former and sang of unrequited passion in the latter. Although Lang had never denied her sexual orientation, in an interview in the summer of 1992 she eliminated the rumors by clearly stating that she was a lesbian. She explained that her earlier reticence reflected her concern that her mother, who had been targeted by hate mail following Lang's PETA advertisement, would suffer an additional round of attacks.

Lang's openness about her sexual orientation did not have a negative effect on her popularity as a singer and songwriter. In 1993, she won a Grammy for Best Female Pop Vocal on "Constant Craving," a single from *Ingenue*. The album achieved platinum status in sales, and "Constant Craving" reached the Top Ten on *Billboard*'s Adult Contemporary chart and Top 100 Singles chart. Lang and Ben Mink also wrote the soundtrack for *Even Cowgirls Get the Blues* (1994).

Summary

K. D. Lang is renowned for her commitment to musical innovation and her ability to fuse a wide variety of musical styles in her songwriting and performances. Her work drew new listeners to country-and-western music, and alongside artists such as Lyle Lovett, Lang successfully broadened the image of country performers. With her song "Constant Craving," Lang also established herself as a popular alternative pop artist and ballad singer. Her performance in *Salmonberries* also indicated her ability as a dramatic actor, and Lang expressed interest in developing a film career as a complement to her musical work.

Beyond her contributions to popular music, Lang has challenged gender stereotypes and proved that female performers can draw fans and praise without conforming to a particular model of appearance or behavior. From the onset of her career, she playfully tested and teased the established, rather demure style of many female country singers, even as she clearly demonstrated her respect for her colleagues' choices of style and appearance. Although Lang considers herself to be a musician first and a social activist second, her advocacy of animal rights and openness about her sexual orientation remain significant aspects of her public image. In the latter decades of the twentieth century, as a number of women challenged the limits placed on female entertainers, K. D. Lang became one of the most prominent examples of a female artist committed to honesty and independence in both her work and her public life.

Bibliography

Bufwack, Mary A., and Robert K. Oermann. *Finding Her Voice: The Saga of Women in Country Music*. New York: Crown, 1993. This comprehensive history and analysis of women in the country music industry includes a thorough assessment of Lang's impact in the 1980's and since. References to Lang's work with other female country performers and to her performances of classic country songs are also offered. This work, the best source available, analyzes Lang's place in the history of female country artists.

Gillmor, Don. "The Reincarnation of Kathryn Dawn." *Saturday Night* 105 (June, 1990): 27-35. A detailed examination of Lang's life and career, with discussions of her childhood, her early studies in music, and the various stages of her career development. Brief interviews with Lang, her family, and her fellow musicians are included.

Gore, Lesley. "Lesley Gore on k.d. lang." *Ms.* 1 (July-August 1990): 30-33. This transcript of a lengthy conversation between Lang and pop singer Gore provides information about the musical influences in Lang's career, the reception given to women in popular music in the late twentieth century, and Lang's methods as a songwriter.

Johnson, Brian D. "A Lighter Side of Lang." *Maclean's* 108, no. 45 (November 6, 1995). Interview with Lang, who talks about her personal life and the effects of fame.

Klam, Julie. "K.D. Lang." *Rolling Stone*, no. 773 (November 13, 1997). Interview with Lang that examines her sexual orientation, those who have influenced her music, and other topics.

Robertson, William. *k.d. lang: Carrying the Torch*. Toronto: ECW Press, 1992. This biography of Lang is the first book devoted entirely to her life and career. It is an honest, detailed account, and is written for a general audience.

Udovitch, Mim. "k.d. lang." *Rolling Stone*, no. 662 (August 5, 1993): 54-57. This article briefly summarizes Lang's musical career and more extensively discusses her public image and iconoclastic style. It includes an interview with Lang and comments on reactions to her open status as a lesbian.

Beth Kraig

DOROTHEA LANGE

Born: May 26, 1895; Hoboken, New Jersey
Died: October 11, 1965; San Francisco, California
Areas of Achievement: Photography and social reform
Contribution: Considered by many to be the country's most distinguished documentary photographer, Dorothea Lange brought her photographic vision to bear most memorably on the living conditions of Depression America's rural poor and Japanese Americans detained in World War II internment camps.

Early Life

Dorothea Lange was born Dorothea Margaretta Nutzhorn on May 26, 1895, in Hoboken, New Jersey. She was named for her father's mother, Dorothea Fischer. Later in her life, she would drop her middle name and the surname Nutzhorn, using instead her mother's maiden name, Lange. Her father was Heinrich (Henry) Martin Nutzhorn, a lawyer and the son of German immigrant parents. Her mother, Joanna (Joan) Caroline Lange, also of German heritage, enjoyed music and worked as a clerk or librarian until the birth of Dorothea, her first child.

In 1902, Dorothea Lange suffered poliomyelitis, an ailment for which there was not yet a vaccine. As a result, Dorothea had limited mobility in her right leg, particularly from the knee down. This condition caused her to walk with a limp, and she was teased throughout childhood. In her own accounts, Lange described the experience of illness and subsequent paralysis as being formative in her life. She found people's reactions to be both humiliating and instructive, and Lange claimed never to have gotten over this experience. Later in life, though, she did report that her physical disability inspired photographic subjects to be open with her.

When Dorothea was twelve years of age, her father left his wife and children. Details remain uncertain, but it is widely speculated that his departure represented flight from some criminal offense. Throughout her life, however, Dorothea Lange spoke little of her father. In 1907, Joan Nutzhorn took her children to live with her mother in Hoboken. Joan Nutzhorn began work at the New York Public Library on the Lower East Side.

By traveling to New York with her mother and posing as a New York resident, Dorothea was able to attend Public School No. 62, also on New York's Lower East Side. On February 5, 1909, Dorothea Lange enrolled at Wadleigh High School in Harlem; later, she attended the nearby New York Training School for Teachers. When Wadleigh failed to hold Dorothea's interest, which proved to be often, she would explore the city—attending concerts, viewing museum exhibits, and the like. Before launching her career as a photographer, Dorothea also accompanied her mother on home visits in her new capacity as investigator for a juvenile court judge. Dorothea Lange's sensitivity to the plight of others likely had its roots in her exposure to New York's poverty and its immigrant ghettos. As a result of her experiences in the New York area, Lange knew well the adverse conditions in which many people were forced to live, and her mind filled with these vivid images.

Life's Work

At about the time of her high school graduation, Dorothea Lange informed her mother of her plans to become a professional photographer. At that point in her life, however, Lange had never taken a photograph. She began work in the studios of several New York City photographers, though, and one of her first positions was with studio photographer Arnold Genthe. Genthe taught Lange the basic techniques of photography, and Lange continued her photographic apprenticeship in 1917 and 1918 by studying at Columbia University under photographer Clarence H. White. She also worked with a variety of other portrait photographers in the vicinity. Lange abandoned her teacher-training school at this point, finding her experiences in teaching displeasing, and devoted herself to a life in photography.

At age twenty, Dorothea Lange started to travel, selling photographs along the way to help finance her journey. When her money ran out, Lange found herself in San Francisco, California, where she settled and opened her own portrait studio in 1916. On March 21, 1920, she and the painter Maynard Dixon were married. She spent the 1920's in San Francisco, working as a society photographer. She and Dixon became known within San Francisco's bohemian circles. On May 15, 1925, Dorothea gave birth to her first child: Daniel Rhodes Dixon. The couple's second child, John Eaglefeather Dixon, arrived on June 12, 1928. After the stock market crash of 1929, Lange and her family ventured

Dorothea Lange, with her camera, is propped above a crowd of Japanese Americans being evacuated in April, 1942.

to a Taos art colony presided over by writer Mabel Dodge Luhan. On their return trip, Lange and her family observed America's homeless, unemployed, and migrant workers.

Upon returning to California, Lange could not reconcile studio work for those who could afford professional portraits with the poverty she saw around her. In 1932, she left the comfort of her portrait studio and began to make photographs of the social conditions she observed, including soup kitchens and breadlines. A 1933 image of this kind, "White Angel Bread Line," went a long way toward establishing Lange's reputation as a documentary photographer. With her images, Lane also made an extensive and change-making chronicle of the plight of California's migrant workers. Similar images of migrant labor and poverty would later be rendered in fiction by John Steinbeck in the novel *The Grapes of Wrath* (1939).

When one of Lange's photographs of an "agitator" was chosen to accompany a *Survey Graphic* article by economist Paul Schuster Taylor, Lange

and Taylor began a close association. In 1935, Taylor was asked by the Division of Rural Rehabilitation to design a program to assist migrant workers. His first decision was to secure Lange's services as project photographer, although for official purposes, she was listed on the payroll as a typist. Lange and Taylor were married a short time later, two months after Lange and Dixon divorced. In that same year, Taylor and Lange presented a monograph of their findings in Southern California, entitled *Notes from the Field* (1935). After a copy of this report arrived in Washington, D.C., it was forwarded by Columbia University economist Rexford Guy Tugwell to Roy Stryker, head of the photographic section of the Resettlement Administration, later renamed the Farm Security Administration (FSA). Upon seeing Lange's potential, Stryker hired her to produce government photographs of Depression America.

Lange worked chiefly in the southern and southwestern United States. She began government photography in 1935, and her images for the FSA featured California, New Mexico, and Arizona. At times, she photographed as many as five states a month, sometimes traveling from Mississippi to California in a month's time. Lange used a Berkeley darkroom to hasten the availability of her images, although it was general policy for exposed film to be returned to Washington, D.C., for filing and processing at national headquarters. Lange's insistence on retaining this California darkroom allowed her to direct immediate aid through the Emergency Relief Administration to Nipoma Valley pea pickers, such as the woman who became the subject of one of her signature photographs, "Migrant Mother." Lange remained on the staff of the FSA until budgetary concerns led to her firing in October of 1936. By January of 1937, Lange was rehired, released, and rehired again in October of 1938. Her last photographs in the government photographic files date from 1939. In that same year, Lange and Taylor published a collaborative volume entitled *An American Exodus: A Record of Human Erosion* (1939).

Lange's release from the FSA did not curtail her productivity. On February 1, 1940, not long after the end of Lange's association with the FSA, she was hired as head photographer for the Bureau of Agricultural Economics, another division of the U.S. Department of Agriculture. In 1941, she was offered a Guggenheim Fellowship to make photographic studies of rural communities in the United States. Her proposed work concentrated on the Mormons of Utah, the Hutterites in South Dakota, and the Amana society in Iowa. Before Lange reached the Mormon community, war conditions changed her plans. In the wake of the Japanese attack on Pearl Harbor, Lange opted to photograph the relocation camps where Japanese Americans were being detained. For a time, she photographed internees for the government's War Relocation Authority. She then did photographic work for the Office of War Information. After World War II, she completed numerous photo-essays for *Life* magazine, including "Mormon Villages" and "The Irish Countrymen." Her work focused on cooperative religious communities, such as the Shakers, and other dimensions of agrarian America. She also photographed delegates to United Nations conferences.

Illness kept Lange from photography for a few years during the 1940's. In 1951, she returned to active work as a photographer. She spent the 1950's creating photo-essays, including some collaborative work with Ansel Adams, and consulting on exhibition designs. She also began teaching seminars in photography. In the late 1950's, she took photographic trips to Egypt and the Far East. Dorothea Lange died of cancer on October 11, 1965, a short time before a one-woman show of her work was to open at New York's Museum of Modern Art.

Summary

The Women's Book of World Records and Achievements lists Dorothea Lange as "The United States' Greatest Documentary Photographer." She was the first woman to earn distinction within the field of documentary photography, the first woman to receive a photography grant, and the first woman to be honored with a photographic retrospective at the Museum of Modern Art. Perhaps her best-known image, and arguably the most widely recognized of the 270,000 photographs presented by the FSA's photographic team, "Migrant Mother," was published throughout the world. In addition to raising awareness of the plight of the poor, this particular photograph proved to be instrumental in raising funds for medical supplies. Whether working in conjunction with the Farm Security Administration, California's Emergency Relief Administration, or the War Relocation Authority, Dorothea Lange produced striking and memorable images that bore poignant testimony to the historical events she witnessed. With these images, she reached a wide audience of viewers who otherwise would have been unfamiliar with the arduous lives of other Americans. Lange's photographs became evidence for needed reforms as well as valuable historical documents. Her career in documentary photography has inspired women photographers in their efforts not only to chronicle conditions but also to change them.

Those wishing to find out more about the career of Dorothea Lange may explore a variety of archival sources. The Dorothea Lange Collection, including both photographs and writings by Lange, is housed by the Oakland Museum's Prints and Photographs Division in Oakland, California. Other photographs and notebooks may be found in the Library of Congress and the National Archives.

Bibliography

Becker, Karin E. *Dorothea Lange and the Documentary Tradition.* Baton Rouge and London: Louisiana State University Press, 1980. Although

Becker does not engage in very much close analysis of specific Lange photographs, she has much to say about Lange's role within the emerging genre of documentary photography.

Curtis, James. *Mind's Eye, Mind's Truth: FSA Photography Reconsidered*. Philadelphia: Temple University Press, 1989. The third chapter of this historical treatment of FSA images is devoted to Lange's most recognized photograph: "Migrant Mother." Curtis includes a thorough account and critique of the photograph's origin and reception.

Davidov, Judith Fryer. " 'The Color of My Skin, the Shape of My Eyes': Photographs of the Japanese-American Internment by Dorothea Lange, Ansel Adams, and Toyo Miyatake." *Yale Journal of Criticism* 9, no. 2 (Fall 1996). Examines the photographs of Japanese-American interns taken by Lange, Adams, and Miyatake. Lange's photographs focus on the inhuman treatment of the interns.

Dorothea Lange. New York: The Museum of Modern Art, 1966. This exhibition catalog urges viewers to read Lange's images closely and to return to them for successive viewings. It comments in some detail on specific photographs, comparing Lange's portrait work favorably to the streetscapes and architectural photographs of fellow photographer Walker Evans.

Fisher, Andrea. *Let Us Now Praise Famous Women: Women Photographers for the U.S. Government, 1935-1944*. London and New York: Pandora Press, 1987. Fisher argues that Lange is as important to the documentary tradition as her male FSA colleague Walker Evans, and she explores the implications of Lange's reputation as the mother of documentary photography.

Guimond, James. *American Photography and the American Dream*. Chapel Hill: University of North Carolina Press, 1991. This volume is especially helpful in its discussion of Lange's later life, particularly her photographs in internment camps, her blacklisting as a member of the Photo League in the late 1940's, and her impact on the design of photographer Edward Steichen's landmark 1955 exhibition "The Family of Man."

Meltzer, Milton. *Dorothea Lange: A Photographer's Life*. New York: Farrar Straus, 1978. Meltzer supplies a thorough and well-researched biography, including a bibliography of archival sources, writings by Lange, and writings concerning Lange. Of particular interest is the incorporation of Lange's reflections about her experiences and images, culled from interviews and oral histories.

Mullins, Gerry. *Dorothea Lange's Ireland*. London: Aurum, and Washington, D.C.: Elliot and Clark, 1996. Documentation of Lange's 2,400 photographs of Irish agricultural life in 1954.

O'Neal, Hank. *A Vision Shared: A Classic Portrait of America and Its People, 1935-1943*. New York: St. Martin's Press, 1976. This volume features thirty-one well-reproduced Lange photographs from the FSA years and includes a brief but solid biographical sketch of the photographer. A helpful introductory section discusses the Farm Security Administration's Photographic Division.

Linda S. Watts

SUSANNE K. LANGER

Born: December 20, 1895; New York, New York
Died: July 17, 1985; Old Lyme, Connecticut
Areas of Achievement: Philosophy and education
Contribution: A leading American philosopher in an historically male-dominated field, Langer was one of the major influences on twentieth century thought in the fields of philosophy and aesthetics. Her work in the realm of "symbolic transformation" helped to establish logical philosophical framework for art and social science, areas not formerly thought to adhere to any ordered system of ideas.

Early Life

Susanne Katherina Knauth was born to Antonio and Else M. (Uhlich) Knauth on the Upper West Side of New York City just before the turn of the century. Along with her two brothers and two sisters, Susanne was surrounded by a rich German heritage of academic and artistic influences. Her father, a lawyer from Leipzig, was an accomplished pianist and cellist. One of his fondest diversions was to invite friends to his home to play chamber music in the evenings. The children all played musical instruments. Susanne was a pianist, but later, as an adult, she became a proficient cellist.

Else Knauth instilled a love of poetry in her children, and as a young child, Susanne often created and recited her own verses. Later, her creative flair extended to drama, and she wrote pageants drawn from classical subjects that she and her siblings presented to family and friends. A wealthy family, the Knauths had a vacation retreat at Lake George in upstate New York, where they spent many happy summers. A love of nature and of the natural sciences was born here that was evident in all aspects of Susanne's later life and writings.

Else Knauth never became easily fluent in English, so German became the preferred language at home. This had its disadvantages when Susanne attended school, and as a result, much of her learning was self-motivated, with reading constituting a large portion of her activity. Her childhood thirst for knowledge of all subjects was prodigious: In a 1960 *New Yorker* interview with Winthrop Sargeant, she spoke of having read Louisa May Alcott's *Little Women* and Immanuel Kant's *Critique of Pure Reason* simultaneously as a teenager. In

spite of the respect for knowledge in the home, Susanne's father hated what he interpreted as masculine qualities in females and would not agree to send any of his daughters to college. After his death, however, Susanne enrolled at Radcliffe College with the encouragement of her mother. Out of her broad early education arose an interest in philosophy, and she received her bachelor's degree in the field in 1920. In 1921, Susanne was married to William Leonard Langer, a Harvard graduate student of history, and the couple spent a year studying in Vienna, Austria. Upon their return to Massachusetts, Susanne began graduate studies in philosophy and earned a master's degree in 1924 and her Ph.D. from Harvard in 1926. For the next fifteen years, she served on the Radcliffe faculty and taught occasionally at Smith and Wellesley Colleges as well, while her husband was a respected professor of history at Harvard from 1936 to 1964.

Life's Work

Susanne Langer's ventures as a published writer began not with philosophical works but with a volume entitled *The Cruise of the Little Dipper, and Other Fairy Tales* (1924). The book was illustrated by Helen Sewell, an artist who was a lifelong friend and upon whom Langer depended later for critique of her writing about aesthetics. Since childhood, Langer had been fascinated by the world of myth and fantasy. The subject carried over into her later work as myth became a central focus in her study of the human formulation of symbols. At Radcliffe, Langer was in contact with the major philosophical minds of the age, and their influence can be traced throughout her work. Her professors—Alfred North Whitehead, the English mathematician and philosopher, and Henry Sheffer—were largely the catalysts for her writing.

The Practice of Philosophy (1930), Langer's first philosophical treatise, contained a preface by Alfred North Whitehead. The book discusses the purposes and methods of philosophy and the importance of symbolic logic in contemporary thought. The book's premise was that training in logic frees the mind. Henry Sheffer's influence on Langer is most obvious in her second book on philosophy, *An Introduction to Symbolic Logic* (1937). She employed his methods of symbolic logic to create a textbook on the subject and an essay on logic.

Langer defined philosophy as the clarification and articulation of concepts. She saw the purpose of philosophy as making explicit what is implicit in people's beliefs and actions. An awareness that modern society seemed to function without a defined philosophical base was always of major concern to Langer. In 1942, she published *Philosophy in a New Key: A Study in the Symbolism of Reason, Rite, and Art*. The book, which was dedicated to Whitehead, established Langer as a leading figure in the field of aesthetics.

The most direct influence on her thinking at this time was the German philosopher Ernst Cassirer, whose 1925 book *Sprache und Mythos* was translated into English as *Language and Myth* by Langer in 1946. His work in the philosophy of symbolism served as a framework for Langer's formulation of "new key" concepts. This book had varied reception among scholars in the field, but was nevertheless a landmark. Langer expounded upon the idea that there are things inaccessible to language that have their own forms of conception. She refused to accept the common premise that language represented the limits of rational experience. It was in this book that she delved into what she considered the human need for "symbolic transformation"—that man is constantly creating new symbols for different areas of life and thought. Langer intended to create a frame of mind that would lead people to treat with the same seriousness as is given to the sciences, areas such as art and social sciences that had previously not been thought to lend themselves to philosophical logic. The book laid the groundwork for Langer's work on the larger problem of the structure and the nature of art, a subject that became the focus of her continued writing.

In what Langer termed a sequel to *Philosophy in a New Key*, she wrote *Feeling and Form: A Theory of Art* (1953), in which she further developed her theories of symbolism and logic. Dedicated to the memory of Ernst Cassirer, *Feeling and Form* is the application of her theories to each of the arts separately. She defined such words as expression, creation, symbol, and intuition in such a way that art might be better understood in those particular terms. The book was not intended to further the cause of such things as criticism of artistic masterpieces nor was it to help in the creation of art. The expressed purpose was to define simply the logical and philosophical basis on which art rests and the relationship of art to feeling. Langer's *Problems of*

Art followed in 1957 and remained true to the concepts set forth in her previous book. She maintained that art is not an expression of the artist's own feeling, but is rather an expression of his knowledge of feeling in nondiscursive terms (symbols). It is an expression not possible to the same extent by verbal means and for which art provides humans with a set of symbols whose meanings may vary as necessary. Langer believed strongly that the importance of this concept was that once an artist is supplied with a secure framework in logic and symbolism, it is possible for his knowledge to exceed even the limits of his own experience.

Langer had left Radcliffe in 1942 and spent a year teaching at the University of Delaware in Newark before teaching from 1945 to 1950 at Columbia University. With the support of the university and a Rockefeller Foundation Grant, she wrote *Feeling and Form*. She continued to work as a guest lecturer and to contribute articles and chapters to books in the area of art and aesthetics. In 1954, she was made chair of the Department of Philosophy at Connecticut College in New London, Connecticut. She remained there until her retirement in 1962, when she was named a professor emeritus and a research scholar in philosophy. In 1956, with a grant from the Edgar J. Kaufmann Charitable Trust of Pittsburgh, Langer began the project that was to be the pinnacle of her career. The depth of the work was such that she committed herself totally to the writing and in 1967, the first volume of *Mind: An Essay on Human Feeling* was published. Two more volumes were to follow; the second in the series was published in 1972 and the final installment appeared in 1982. These products of Langer's latest years assumed a certain familiarity with the earlier suppositions she advanced in *Philosophy in a New Key* and *Feeling and Form*. Langer examined in great detail the course of development of human feeling as it departed from the level of the animal who possesses feeling without intellect. The work was the culmination of her understanding of philosophical symbolic logic as applied to abstract areas of human existence.

Langer was recognized by a number of disciplines for her work through the years. Equally comfortable lecturing to educators, philosophers, artists, or scientists, she was a frequent guest at conventions and conferences. In 1950, she was the recipient of the Radcliffe Alumnae Achievement Award and in 1960, she was elected to the American Academy of Arts and Sciences. Honorary doctorate degrees were bestowed upon her by Wilson College, Wheaton College, and Western College for Women.

Upon her retirement from Connecticut College, she remained in her colonial home in Old Lyme, retreating when necessary to the solitude of an old farmhouse in Ulster County, New York, where she avoided all modern conveniences including electric lights and especially the telephone. Fiercely independent, she organized her life to suit her needs. Communing with nature, quiet time spent writing and thinking, and occasionally playing chamber music with friends filled her days with favorite activities. After her husband died in 1977, her children and grandchildren provided companionship during their welcome visits as did her lifelong friends from her professorial days. Langer died in 1985 at her Connecticut home at the age of eighty-nine.

Summary

Susanne Langer entered a field in which few women had ever achieved serious recognition and her work had a profound effect on philosophical thought of the twentieth century. Her hunger for knowledge and experience in almost every realm of human existence from the most scientific fields to simple, as well as sophisticated, artistic forms of expression provided a rich backdrop for her ideas. From her thinking emerged some of the most scholarly work which exists in the fields of philosophy and aesthetics. Her contributions to education in these fields and her influence on the approach to philosophy and education brought about a distinct change in the framework of the logic upon which human feeling and art are interpreted.

Bibliography

Ahlberg, Lars-Olof. "Susanne Langer on Representation and Emotion in Music." *British Journal of Aesthetics* 34, no. 1 (January, 1994). An analysis of Langer's theories on emotion and representation in music, with comparison to theories by others.

Danto, Arthur C. "Mind as Feeling, Form as Presence; Langer as Philosopher." *The Journal of Philosophy* 81 (November, 1984): 641-646. Danto follows the progression and development in philosophical thought that occurred in Langer's literary career. The article is one of three in this special issue that formed the basis of a symposium entitled "The Philosophy of Susanne K. Langer" for the American Philosophical Society in December, 1984.

de Sousa, Ronald B. "Teleology and the Great Shift." *The Journal of Philosophy* 81 (November, 1984): 647-653. The "great shift" from animal to human behavior and its philosophical implications are explored by de Sousa based on Langer's *Mind: An Essay on Human Feeling.*

Hagberg, Garry. "Art and the Unsayable: Langer's Tractarian Aesthetics." *British Journal of Aesthetics* 24 (1984): 325+. Hagberg reconsiders Langer's theory that art is a creation of forms that symbolize human feeling, picking up where language ends.

Langer, Susanne. *Philosophy in a New Key.* 3d ed. Cambridge, Mass.: Harvard University Press, 1979. This book, with a preface by the author, is the treatise upon which all Langer's later writing in the area of philosophy and aesthetics is based. Her basic tenets about the importance of symbolic logic as applied to human expression are detailed.

———. "Why Philosophy?" *The Saturday Evening Post* 234 (May 13, 1961): 34-35. Langer discusses her personal life and career and major factors which influenced the direction of her philosophical thought. Her views about the lack of apparent philosophical framework in modern society are also presented.

Morawski, Stefan. "Art as Semblance." *The Journal of Philosophy* 81 (November, 1984): 654-662. Morawski grapples with Langer's theories of symbolic logic in aesthetics and Langer's role as a pivotal philosophical figure in the 1950's.

Sargeant, Winthrop. "Philosopher in a New Key." *The New Yorker* 36 (December 3, 1960): 67-68. In a lengthy and intimate interview, Sargeant questions Langer about her life and career, revealing information about her method of working and lifestyle not available in a formal biography.

Watling, Christine P. "The Arts, Emotion, and Current Research in Neuroscience." *Mosaic* 31, no. 1 (March, 1998). Examines Langer's theories on art and how the results of contemporary studies support them by establishing that music and literature can affect moods.

Sandra C. McClain

FIFTH MARQUESS OF LANSDOWNE
Henry Charles Keith Petty-Fitzmaurice

Born: January 14, 1845; London, England
Died: June 3, 1927: Newtown Anmer, Clonmel, Ireland
Area of Achievement: Government
Contribution: Lansdowne was instrumental in forming major alliances with Japan in 1902 and with France in 1904.

Early Life

Henry Charles Keith Petty-Fitzmaurice was born on January 14, 1845, in Lansdowne House, Berkeley Square, London. His father, the fourth marquess, was at that time known as the Earl of Shelburne because the third marquess was still alive. The Petty-Fitzmaurices had long been prominent in Anglo-Irish affairs but had spent little time in Ireland for the past century. Petty-Fitzmaurice's father, who became the fourth earl in 1863, sat in Parliament and held the chairmanship of the Great Western Railway but was generally content to occupy positions rather than build on them. His mother, Emily, the fourth earl's second wife, had inherited large estates in Scotland from her mother.

The young Lord Clanmaurice (as he was known until his father succeeded to the marquessate in 1863, at which point he became Lord Kerry) was educated at a private school until the age of thirteen, when he entered Eton. There he was anything but a devoted student, concentrating mainly on rowing. His parents removed him for a year prior to his taking the entrance exams for Balliol College, Oxford. He entered Balliol in 1864 and studied earnestly but was only able to take a second when he left in 1867.

Petty-Fitzmaurice's father, the fourth marquess, died in 1866, while Petty-Fitzmaurice was still studying at Balliol. The new Marquess of Lansdowne found it ordained that he should enter politics, and, because he was the leader of a great Whig family and one of the largest landowners in the country, the way was paved for him. Perhaps because he had shown no interest in politics, his bearing was not such as would stimulate confidence in oratorical abilities. His reserved character, coupled with a long head and large nose sitting atop a slight body, led many to doubt that his tenure in public life would be a long one. Lansdowne remained devoted to his mother until her death in 1895, writing

to her at least once each week, pouring out to her his worries and fears. In 1869, Lansdowne married Lady Maud Hamilton, the youngest daughter of the Duke of Abercorn, and by her he had two daughters and two sons, the elder, Henry, succeeding him as sixth marquess and the younger, Charles, being killed in action in 1914.

Life's Work

In 1869, the year of his marriage, Lansdowne was appointed a junior lord of the treasury, being transferred in 1872 to the position of under secretary of war. In 1874, however, William Ewart Gladstone's government fell, and it was not until the Liberals again gained power in 1880 that Petty-Fitzmaurice took a post in government, this time that of under secretary of state for India. Circumstances intervened at this juncture, however, to separate Lansdowne and the Liberal leader. Gladstone initiated his new Irish policy and Lansdowne as one of the largest landowners in Ireland, felt compelled to oppose him. He therefore resigned his post, thus becoming the target for Irish agitators. This opposition he felt keenly. He also believed it unjust, as he could not be labeled an absentee landlord, having for several years made his principal seat at Derreen. Nevertheless, a concerted and successful attempt by his tenants to withhold rents soon placed him in financial difficulties and necessitated his return to public life.

In 1883, Gladstone again offered Lansdowne a position, that of Governor-General of Canada. Lansdowne's tenure in that post was relatively undisturbed, broken only by Louis Riel's abortive rebellion in 1885 and the completion of the Canadian Pacific Railway in 1886. In 1887, the Conservative Lord Salisbury asked Lansdowne to succeed Lord Dufferin as Viceroy of India, and Lansdowne took up the reins of government there late in 1888. Again, his term in office was remarkably quiet despite the formation of the Indian National Congress and various minor frontier disturbances. Lansdowne returned to England in 1894.

Lansdowne was named secretary of war in Lord Salisbury's government in 1895, chiefly in an attempt to take advantage of his well-known tact. The onerous task of retiring the seventy-six-year-old Duke of Cambridge from the post of commander in chief demanded the velvet touch that all admitted belonged to Lansdowne. The delicate job completed, he was then faced with the Boer War. Criticism of the secretary of war mounted with British defeats, although Lansdowne could not be blamed for the incompetence of British field commanders. Nevertheless, he stepped down in 1900.

Lord Salisbury immediately offered him the office of foreign secretary. Initially, Lansdowne was a tremendous success in the post. In 1901, he met with the Japanese ambassador, Count Hayashi, and the two career diplomats produced the Anglo-Japanese treaty of 1902, in which each country pledged to maintain the status quo in the Far East against the aggressive moves of Germany, France, and Russia. The treaty assured Japan that Great Britain would come to its aid if Japan were attacked by two of the Great Powers. This promise helped Japan immeasurably in the Russo-Japanese War.

During his time as foreign secretary, Lansdowne also faced problems in Persia and Venezuela. British influence in the Shah's domains was on the wane and the Russians were in the ascendant. The outbreak of war between Japan and Russia, however, temporarily distracted the czar's ministers. Lansdowne again received criticism in 1902 for a proposed joint Anglo-German blockade of Venezuela as a response to piracy and misgovernment. The American government threatened to intervene by force to prevent the seizure of Venezuelan assets, and British public opinion was overwhelmingly critical of any alliance with Germany.

Again, Lansdowne triumphed just when it seemed his public career was over. From 1902 to 1904, Lansdowne and members of the French government were engaged in talks designed to reduce tensions arising from imperial conflicts. By 1904, the Anglo-French entente was a reality. The French recognized British rights in Egypt, and their effective control over Morocco was also acknowledged. The basis of the anti-German alliance had been laid.

In 1903, Lord Salisbury died and Lansdowne became the Conservative leader in the House of Lords. As such, he coordinated the opposition to the 1909 budget and to the emasculation of the Lords' veto power. He was unsuccessful in both attempts but continued to lead the Lords until 1916. After that year, he withdrew more and more from public life. In 1919, an attack of rheumatic fever signaled the beginning of a decline in his health. He died on June 3, 1927, while at the house of his youngest daughter at Newton Anmer, Clonmel, Ireland.

Summary

The fifth Marquess of Lansdowne was not personally ambitious, but the position into which he was born compelled him to be politically active. Aloof, soft-spoken, and more interested in sport than society, he nevertheless served his country for more than fifty years. His social connections perhaps stood him in better stead than his administrative abilities, but it would be wrong to underrate his service in India and Canada simply because little took place while he was in office.

It was as secretary of war and as foreign secretary that Lansdowne made his greatest contributions. While he may be to blame in part for the fiasco of the Boer War, there is little doubt that his experience with German policy during the crisis led to his desire to begin to take Great Britain out of its political isolation. The Japanese and French alliances helped to set the stage for the debacle of World War I, although these were regarded at the time as major steps forward in stabilizing world affairs.

Lansdowne took a great interest in Ireland, and his defection from the Liberal Party over Gladstone's Irish policy was certainly a great blow to the Whigs, not so much because of his talents but because the Lansdowne name was one to take seriously. The onset of the Irish troubles also reduced his personal revenue to almost nothing, and that, as much as anything else, was responsible for his accepting the posts in Canada and Ireland.

Finally, Lansdowne's dilemma was that of the traditional landowning peer in the late nineteenth century. The vulnerability of an income based on land rents was revealed, and the hostility toward landlords, which resulted in the burning of Lansdowne's estate at Derreen in 1922, revealed to the aging marquess that not only his time but also the time of his class was passing.

Bibliography

Barker, Dudley. *Prominent Edwardians*. London: Allen and Unwin, and New York: Atheneum, 1969. A biographical sketch which is at times hilariously irreverent and at other times simply scurrilous. The chapter on Lansdowne contains almost no dates, although the general outline of the marquess' career is clear. Reads easily and should be used to balance Lord Newton's hagiography.

Dangerfield, George. *The Damnable Question: One Hundred and Twenty Years of Anglo-Irish Conflict.* Boston: Little Brown, 1976; London: Constable, 1977. Covers Anglo-Irish relations from 1800, with special attention to the years of World War I. Lansdowne's role in the formation of Irish policy is documented. Good account of the conflict that in many ways lay at the center of Lansdowne's life.

Jenkins, Roy. *Mr. Balfour's Poodle: An Account of the Struggle Between the House of Lords and the Government of Mr. Asquith.* London: Heinemann, 1954. Highly focused account of the constitutional struggle of 1911-1912. Well researched and entertaining; important for understanding the swan song of Lansdowne's career.

Joll, James. *The Origins of the First World War.* 2d ed. London and New York: Longman, 1992. This short introductory survey to the origins of World War I places Lansdowne's policies while foreign secretary into the greater context of European politics and diplomacy. Very clearly organized and written.

Wodehouse, Thomas, and Lord Newton. *Lord Lansdowne: A Biography.* London: Macmillan, 1929. An older work which nevertheless contains much information vital to an understanding of Lansdowne's career. Biased in favor of Lansdowne in the sense that his reluctance to make decisions is portrayed as an asset.

Thomas C. Thompson

HAROLD J. LASKI

Born: June 30, 1893; Manchester, England
Died: March 24, 1950; London, England
Areas of Achievement: Political science and education
Contribution: Laski combined a strong commitment to social democracy with an equally strong faith in education; his career as a professor at the London School of Economics provided him with the opportunity to develop his political theory while also enabling him to influence the intellectual debate about the Labour Party program of the 1930's and 1940's.

Early Life

Harold Joseph Laski was born June 30, 1893, in Manchester, the son of affluent Jewish parents who were among the leaders of the city's Jewish community. At an early age, Laski showed a penchant for academic achievement, the precursor of his own academic career. Laski attended New College, Oxford, where he studied history and politics and received a variety of intellectual influences, particularly the scholarship of Frederic Maitland and Otto von Gierke. After graduation in 1914, Laski's frail physique prevented him from service in the armed forces. Laski possessed a slight build, dark eyes that gave him the appearance of an inquisitor, and large glasses that invested him with the air of a university don. Laski was estranged from his family for a long period because of his marriage at eighteen to a woman six years his senior. This marriage survived all obstacles until Laski's death. Denied his father's financial support, Laski secured a position as lecturer in history at McGill University in Canada.

Laski remained at McGill for two years and then moved to Harvard University in the United States in 1916 through the agency of Felix Frankfurter. The precocious young man from Oxford made a strong impression at Harvard, by virtue of his devotion to scholarship, generosity to his students, and the atmosphere of omniscience he exuded. During this period, he formed friendships with several notable Americans, especially Justice Oliver Wendell Holmes. His American experience gave Laski a deep affection for the United States and led in later life to his frequent visits on vacation and lecture tours. The Boston police strike of 1919, and Laski's public advocacy of the strikers' position, made his future at Harvard uncertain. Personal at-tacks on his politics and ethnicity convinced him that his academic ambitions would best be served by an appointment in England. In June of 1920, Laski returned to England to accept a position at the London School of Economics, where in 1926 he became professor. This homecoming inaugurated the process by which Laski became perhaps the most renowned academic in Great Britain.

Life's Work

Laski's initial success stemmed from his academic publications. Between 1917 and 1925, Laski wrote the "big four" scholarly works that made his scholarly reputation. These works were *Studies in the Problem of Sovereignty* (1917), *Authority in the Modern State* (1919), *The Foundations of Sovereignty, and Other Essays* (1921), and *A Grammar of Politics* (1925). The central themes of these works included an attack on the traditional bases of state authority, the nature of legal and political obligation, and his attempt to provide a theory of political pluralism that made possible corporate pillars of authority other than the state to which the individual citizen could give allegiance. The fundamental point was to establish that the individual needed protection from the omnipotence of the state. Subsidiary organizations such as trade unions and religious groups provided relief from the excesses of a capitalist society. By 1925, Laski's analysis stipulated that individual conscience must judge the legitimacy of state action. Associations inferior to the state were better able to meet the material and spiritual needs of citizens.

After 1925, Laski turned increasingly to a more pragmatic examination of social and political problems. Initially, Laski had indulged in a flirtation with guild socialism, a form of British socialism that stressed the role of unions in the transition to socialism. Laski turned away from his early infatuation with corporate entities and faced more systematically the challenges posed by a capitalist social order. Laski became more concerned with practical problems and spent less and less time on his scholarly writing.

By the end of the 1920's, Laski conceived his primary task to serve as an intellectual spokesman for the Labour Party, the only organization committed to those changes in capitalism that would provide a better life for the individual. Political events helped turn Laski's views in a radical direc-

tion. Dramatic episodes such as the General Strike in 1926 and the (to Laski) suspicious circumstances surrounding the fall of the Labour government in 1931 forced Laski to reassess his political values. It became clear to him that the transition from capitalism to socialism would not occur easily. The revolution by consent that he had always envisioned would not happen spontaneously.

In the 1930's, therefore, Laski's political thought acquired a militant, Marxist veneer. Laski did not advocate violent revolution, as critics often charged, but he did argue that a major change in economic and social foundations, for the benefit of the individual, might well require a greater degree of government coercion than he had supposed. Though frustrated in a practical realization of his hopes in the 1930's, Laski saw in the eventual victory of Great Britain during World War II the great opportunity for reconstruction he had always sought. Though his hopes for a British society in line with his political theories did not materialize completely, he had the satisfaction of seeing in the welfare state after 1945 many of the social services

that would ensure a life of dignity and justice for ordinary people.

As his political views changed, Laski became a more visible political personality. He never ran for elective office, but his frequent appearances at party meetings, and his newspaper contributions made him a famous advocate of the Labour Party. Laski often played the political insider, although in retrospect his influence in politics was never as great as he pretended. Laski gained a certain notoriety for the militancy of his views; in the general election of 1945, he became an issue because the *Daily Express* charged that he had endorsed revolution by violence at a public meeting. He filed suit for libel against the newspaper, but a jury found against him, a lack of public vindication that marred his last years.

Laski's other great area of contribution was as professor at the London School of Economics. In this position, Laski taught students from around the world, combining technical mastery of subject matter with a personal interest in his students to exert a formidable influence on several generations of pupils. Laski possessed the special skill as educator to draw the best from his students, even from those who differed politically and intellectually with him, while maintaining rigorous standards for doctoral work. As a result, his students carried fond remembrances of his tutelage to every part of the world. He did not found a coterie of students to imitate his work but was content to train them and permit them to follow their own inclinations. The best record of his professional influence remained in the intellectual achievements of his many students.

Finally, Laski represented one element of the many connections that bound Great Britain to the United States in the twentieth century. In 1948, Laski published *The American Democracy: A Commentary and Interpretation*, a work comparable to James Bryce's *The American Commonwealth* (1888). Although Laski's book did not acquire the reputation of Bryce's, it remains a powerful analysis of American life at mid-century. Laski hoped for appointment as ambassador to the United States, but the position eluded him. Frequent lecture tours to the United States made Laski a familiar figure in American academic circles, the most famous British academic of his generation. His affection for the United States never waned. Laski died, on March 24, 1950, while planning yet another visit to the country he loved.

Summary

The political theories espoused by Harold J. Laski helped shape the programmatic outlook of the Labour Party prior to its triumph in 1945. Although specific positions cannot be attributed directly to Laski, his writings generated debate at a time when the intellectual focus of the party seemed in doubt. If Laski never had the influence on party decisions that he wished, nevertheless his legacy remains in the definition of socialism as social justice, a commitment to the dignity of each individual.

In his academic work, Laski brought the London School of Economics to a pinnacle of fame never again reached. His visibility both in and out of academic life made the school a center of learning and sometimes of controversy. His facility in lecturing and personal interest in his students made him a beloved figure for graduate and undergraduate students alike. Laski set a standard of university instruction equalled by few and surpassed by none.

Bibliography

Cosgrove, Richard A. *Our Lady the Common Law: An Anglo-American Legal Community, 1870-1930.* New York: New York University Press, 1987. Emphasizes Laski's role as an Anglo-American figure, particularly the influence his experiences in the United States had upon the development of his political theory.

Deane, Herbert A. *The Political Ideas of Harold J. Laski.* New York: Columbia University Press, 1955. Deane is the best overall guide to Laski's political philosophy. The book offers little context for the circumstances that shaped his theories.

Eastwood, Granville. *Harold Laski.* London: Mowbrays, 1977. A personal memoir by a friend that stresses the private life of Laski as husband, father, and teacher. It is not a formal analysis of his political thought.

Ekirch, Arthur A. "Harold J. Laski: The Liberal Manque or Lost Libertarian." *Journal of Libertarian Studies* 4 (Spring, 1980): 139-150. An interesting essay that stresses Laski's concern for the individual as he went from Liberalism to socialism. Laski retained a humanistic interest in the individual even as his political ideology changed.

Gupta, Ram Chandra. *Harold J. Laski.* Agra, India: Ram Prased, 1966. A popular work that accents Laski's work as a teacher, especially of international students. It conveys some of the affection that Laski generated in his students.

Laski, Harold J., and Paul Q. Hirst. *Harold Laski: Collected Works.* London and New York: Routledge, 1997. A collection of ten works by Laski, including *A Grammar of Politics and Communism.*

Martin, Kingsley. *Harold Laski (1893-1950): A Biographical Memoir.* New York: Viking Press, 1953; London: Cape, 1969. The best life of Laski, written by a longtime friend. Martin wrote with a sympathetic attitude toward his subject but was not blind to mistakes and foibles. Written with affection.

Newman, Michael. "Harold Laski Today." *Political Quarterly* 67, no. 3 (July-September, 1996). Discusses Laski's theories and their place in contemporary politics.

Zylstra, Bernard. *From Pluralism to Collectivism: The Development of Harold Laski's Political Thought.* Assen, the Netherlands: Van Gorcum, 1968. An excellent, incisive examination of the topic. Zylstra focuses on the early part of Laski's life in seeking to explain his political theory. Should be read in conjunction with Deane.

Richard A. Cosgrove

JULIA C. LATHROP

Born: June 29, 1858; Rockford, Illinois
Died: April 15, 1932; Rockford, Illinois
Areas of Achievement: Government and politics and social reform
Contribution: As the first woman to head a federal agency, the U.S. Children's Bureau (1912-1921), Lathrop identified and shaped significantly twentieth century public policy for children.

Early Life

Julia Clifford Lathrop was born on June 29, 1858, in Rockford, Illinois. She was the first of five children, two girls and three boys, born to Sarah Adeline Potter Lathrop and William Lathrop. Her mother was graduated as valedictorian from the first Rockford Seminary (later renamed Rockford College) class in 1854. An enthusiastic woman suffrage advocate, Sarah Lathrop also urged the creation and maintenance of art and cultural organizations in her community. William Lathrop was a prominent attorney and one of the founders of the Illinois Republican Party. Elected to the state general assembly and Congress, William Lathrop was a reform-minded politician who supported civil service legislation, woman suffrage, and various social welfare issues.

Julia Lathrop attended her mother's alma mater for one year before transferring to Vassar College, where she earned a degree in 1880. During the next ten years, Lathrop worked in her father's law office and as a secretary for two local manufacturing companies. In 1890, she moved to Chicago, where she joined Rockford College graduates Jane Addams and Ellen Gates Starr at their recently established Hull House settlement. Lathrop remained at Hull House for twenty years.

Life's Work

Julia Lathrop's association with Hull House placed her in contact with one of the most significant social reform networks of the Progressive Era. In addition, beginning in 1893, she began volunteer work as a Cook County agent visitor. Assigned to investigate relief applicants living within a ten-block radius of Hull House, Lathrop had the opportunity to observe the desperate circumstances of many ordinary people in an increasingly industrial and urban America. Many of her findings were published two years later in *Hull-House Maps and Papers* (1895). Her work came to the attention of

reform governor John P. Altgeld, who appointed Lathrop to the Illinois State Board of Charities in 1893. In this capacity, she visited each of the state's 102 county poorfarms and almshouses. Particularly appalled by the grouping of children, the elderly, the mentally handicapped, and the sick in the same institutions, Lathrop spent the next twelve years lobbying for the creation of separate facilities for these constituencies. As a result of her efforts and those of other prominent activists, Illinois built new state hospitals for the insane and, in 1899, established the nation's first juvenile court system in Cook County. In 1901, Lathrop resigned her state appointment in protest when Altgeld's successor circumvented the board's authority by giving jobs to political supporters rather than adhering to the state's civil service laws.

Lathrop believed that the political spoils system resulted in the appointment of poorly qualified staff. From 1903 to 1904, she and another member of the settlement house network, Graham Taylor, devised and implemented courses designed to produce trained individuals for careers in social work. Educators Edith Abbott, Sopho-nisba Breckinridge, and others later joined Taylor and Lathrop in this effort. Their "college" was incorporated in 1908 as the Chicago School of Civics and Philanthropy (made part of the University of Chicago in 1920). In the meantime, newly elected Governor Charles Deneen had reappointed Lathrop to the State Board of Charities, where she served from 1905 to 1909. She also became one of the founders of the Illinois Immigrants' Protective League (1908) and continued to work as a trustee for that organization until her death.

These years also brought Lathrop deeper into child welfare work. In 1909, she attended the first White House Conference on the Care of Dependent Children. At that meeting, participants heartily endorsed a proposal to establish a federal children's bureau. New York's Henry Street Settlement founder Lillian D. Wald and the National Consumers' League's Florence Kelley had first suggested the idea for a federal bureau mandated to investigate and report on American children as early as 1903. In 1905, the National Child Labor Committee (NCLC) made the creation of such an agency its highest legislative priority. The measure received little attention, however, until the 1909 White House meeting. Over the next three years, supporters lobbied Congress on the proposal's behalf.

On April 9, 1912, President William Howard Taft signed legislation establishing the U.S. Children's Bureau in the Department of Commerce and Labor. The next step was to find a Children's Bureau chief who would be acceptable to all concerned. Taft asked the NCLC for advice. In response, members of the NCLC board met with President Taft on April 15 and named Julia Lathrop as their first choice. Although she was well known to most social welfare reformers in Illinois, Lathrop was not a nationally recognized children's rights advocate. NCLC board member Jane Addams lobbied strongly on her behalf. A year earlier, Lathrop had published a report on public schools in the Philippines after completing a trip around the world with her sister Anna Case. This study, combined with the NCLC's recommendation, Lathrop's experience in Illinois, and assurances from Attorney General George Wickersham that there was no legal restriction to appointing a woman, led Taft to name her as Children's Bureau chief on April 17, 1912. Although national woman suffrage was not made a part of the constitution for another seven years, many Americans believed that child welfare work was a proper domain for women. Therefore, Lathrop became the first woman to head a federal bureau.

Under Lathrop's direction, the Children's Bureau hired a staff, selected fields of work, and designed and implemented a program for the "whole child." The U.S. Children's Bureau was the first national government agency in the world created solely to consider the problems of children. Limited by a paltry appropriation of $25,640 and a staff of only fifteen, Lathrop was determined that financial obstacles should not hinder the bureau's beginnings. She built on statistical work already completed by other government agencies and supplemented her staff with volunteers from the General Federation of Women's Clubs and other private organizations. This tactic proved to be a valuable source of public support for the agency.

The chief also made an astute choice of infant mortality as the bureau's first subject of original investigation. Although its institution was generally a popular idea, some individuals believed that the Children's Bureau might violate parental and states' rights as well as serve as a wasteful duplication of federal activities. The American Medical Association complained that the Public Health Ser-

vice should deal with child health issues. Other critics questioned the suitability of a childless "spinster" for such a job. Sensitive to such criticism, Lathrop realized that the study of infant mortality was probably the least debatable topic under the Children's Bureau's mandate. The United States lagged far behind many other countries in the collection and analysis of such data. Furthermore, no branch of the federal government, including the Public Health Service, had investigated why so many babies died before their first birthday.

The Children's Bureau found that the United States' 1913 rate of 132 deaths per 1,000 live births ranked behind seven comparable nations. The effort to save babies' lives became the flagship issue for the Children's Bureau. The popularity of this work enabled Lathrop and her staff later to address more controversial issues, such as child labor regulation, juvenile delinquency, and mothers' pensions. Although her political prowess is often overlooked, Lathrop was an astute politician as well as a competent administrator.

During her tenure as chief, the Children's Bureau's budget increased tenfold and the effort to reduce the nation's high infant mortality rate resulted in passage of the pioneering 1921 Sheppard-Towner Maternity and Infancy Act. In addition, the agency was given the responsibility for enforcing the first federal child labor law, the 1916 Keating-Owen Act. Lathrop brought former Hull House resident Grace Abbott to Washington to head the bureau's Child Labor Division. Although the Supreme Court declared the Keating-Owen law unconstitutional in 1918, this legislation and the Sheppard-Towner Act served as blueprints for the children's programs included in the 1935 Social Security Act and the 1938 Fair Labor Standards Act. Thousands of mothers wrote the bureau for advice, and the chief and her staff carefully answered every letter. Overall, Lathrop's strategy firmly established the Children's Bureau as the major source of information and advocate for America's children. By 1921, Julia Lathrop was one of the most popular and well-known federal bureaucrats. Her election to presidency of the National Council of Social Work in 1918 also shows her status as a political insider who had contacts with a vast reform network. Confident that the Children's Bureau was a permanent part of the federal bureaucracy, Lathrop resigned as Children's Bureau chief in August, 1921. Ill with a hyperthyroid condition but not wanting to jeopar-

dize the pattern of work she had established, Lathrop convinced President Warren G. Harding to appoint Grace Abbott as her successor.

For the remainder of her life, Lathrop lived in Rockford with her sister. During these years, she remained active and served as president of the Illinois League of Women Voters (1922-1924), as an assessor for the League of Nations' Child Welfare Committee (1925-1931), and as an adviser to a presidential committee examining conditions at Ellis Island (1925), and she continued to work for the rights of minors. Two months before her death, Lathrop orchestrated a campaign to keep Russell Robert McWilliams, a seventeen-year-old Rockford boy convicted of killing a motorman, from execution under Illinois' death penalty. McWilliams was granted a reprieve after Lathrop's death. Lathrop died in Rockford on April 15, 1932, at the age of seventy-three.

Summary

Although Julia Lathrop never married or had children of her own, her legacy is most important in the field of child welfare. In its first decade of work, the U.S. Children's Bureau identified major issues and designed the blueprint according to which federal child welfare policy has developed. Furthermore, even though she did not seek the appointment of chief and actually had little to do with the effort to establish the bureau, Lathrop's acceptance of the job and the strategy she implemented secured a role for women in child welfare policy development and implementation. Her appointment also set a precedent that was not broken until President Richard M. Nixon appointed the Children's Bureau's first male chief in 1973. Although Lathrop's "whole child" philosophy did not survive federal restructuring in 1946, which reduced the agency's influence, the Children's Bureau's first decades of work highlighted the vulnerability of children and opened public debate on how best to preserve "a right to childhood." Julia Lathrop's ability to act as "statesman" as well as politician made her a successful bureaucrat who helped to legitimize the notion that the federal government's responsibilities include the welfare of its youngest citizens.

Bibliography

Addams, Jane. *My Friend, Julia Lathrop.* New York: Macmillan, 1935. To date, the only biography of Lathrop's life. This work focuses on her life to 1912.

Ladd-Taylor, Molly. *Mother-Work: Women, Child Welfare, and the State, 1890-1930.* Urbana: University of Illinois Press, 1994. This work underscores the role of women in the development of the American social welfare system and includes a discussion of Lathrop's part in this process.

———, ed. *Raising a Baby the Government Way: Mothers' Letters to the Children's Bureau, 1915-1932.* New Brunswick, N.J.: Rutgers University Press, 1986. An edited collection of letters sent to the U.S. Children's Bureau asking for advice or other assistance. Includes some of Lathrop's responses and an overview of the bureau's early work.

Lathrop, Julia, et al. *The Child, the Clinic and the Court: A Group of Papers by Jane Addams, C. Judson Herrick, A. L. Jacoby, and Others.* New York: New Republic, 1925. An excellent source of Lathrop's opinions concerning the role of the state in child welfare.

Meckel, Richard A. *"Save the Babies": American Public Health Reform and the Prevention of Infant Mortality, 1850-1929.* Baltimore: Johns Hopkins University Press, 1990. While focusing on the national effort to reduce infant mortality, this work includes an examination of the Children's Bureau's role in the effort to save babies' lives.

Muncy, Robyn. *Creating a Female Dominion in American Reform, 1890-1935.* New York: Oxford University Press, 1991. An important work examining how Julia Lathrop and Grace Abbott worked to keep child welfare policy as a proper domain for women.

Parker, Jacqueline K., and Edward M. Carpenter. "Julia Lathrop and the Children's Bureau: The Emergence of an Institution." *Social Service Review* 55 (March, 1981): 60-77. An excellent brief overview of the Children's Bureau and its work under Lathrop's tenure.

Kriste Lindenmeyer

SIR WILFRID LAURIER

Born: November 20, 1841; St. Lin, Canada East
(now Quebec, Canada)
Died: February 17, 1919; Ottawa, Ontario, Canada
Areas of Achievement: Politics and government
Contribution: By transforming Canadian Liberal-
ism and shifting its base to Quebec, Laurier
made possible the subsequent dominance of fed-
eral politics by the Liberal Party. As the first
French-Canadian to become Prime Minister of
Canada (1896-1911), he presided over an era of
expansion, general prosperity, and increasing
Canadian self-awareness.

Early Life

Sir Wilfrid Laurier was born November 20, 1841,
in St. Lin, Quebec, a small village north of Montreal. His father, Carolus Laurier, a farmer and land
surveyor, was a seventh-generation descendant
from one of the first French settlers of Montreal,
and his mother, Marcelle Martineau, came from
another old French-Canadian family. Laurier, an
only son, received an unusual education, proceeding from the local Catholic parish school to a Scottish Presbyterian school which opened the door to
the English language and English culture. His love
of reading developed early and lasted throughout
his life. At age twelve, he went to college at L'As-
somption for seven years and then studied law for
three years at McGill University. With law degree
in hand, he began to practice in Montreal in 1864
in the office of Rodolphe Laflamme, a founder of
the Institut Canadien, home of the advanced liberal
and anticlerical views sponsored in politics by the
liberal party Les Rouges. Laurier's family revered
the radical Louis Joseph Papineau, leader of the
Patriotes, who had rebelled against Great Britain in
1837, and in school young Laurier's ideas had
alarmed his clerical teachers, so it was not surprising that he now joined the Institut and Les Rouges.

Bronchial problems impelled Laurier to move in
1866 to the village of L'Avenir and then to Artha-
baska, where he edited the liberal paper *Le Dé-
fricheur.* He followed the Rouges line, opposing
the project for Canadian Confederation then being
pushed by the Conservative (Bleu) leader, George
Étienne Cartier, a fervent supporter of the Catholic
church and a friend to railroads and big business.
Cartier's political alliance with John A. Macdonald, the English-Canadian Conservative leader,
seemed to threaten the future of Liberalism. More-

over, in the new and larger Dominion of Canada,
the French would become a still smaller minority.
Laurier, however, after a token fight, could see no
point in resisting the inevitable and soon accepted
confederation when it became a reality on July 1,
1867.

A picture of Laurier in 1869 shows a handsome
youth, tall and slender, with wavy reddish-brown
hair, a prominent nose, and captivating eyes. He
never exercised, seldom even taking a long walk,
but he retained his erect carriage and trim figure
into old age. In his youth, he worried much over
his health, but, when finally assured that he did not
have tuberculosis in 1868, he married Zoë, the
daughter of G. N. R. Lafontaine of Montreal. The
union, though childless, was happy and reached its
golden anniversary. Laurier was never rich and for
many years was quite poor, but he lived simply, returning every summer to his much-loved Arthabas-
ka, and only in his later years enjoying a comfortable upper-middle-class home in Ottawa.

Life's Work

Laurier entered the Quebec legislature in 1871 as a
Liberal member for Drummond-Arthabaska, despite clerical opposition. Not especially interested
in local questions, he was glad to move up to the
Canadian House of Commons in the Liberal landslide of 1874. His intelligence and personality, together with his skill as an orator in both French and
English, soon made him the leading Quebec Liberal on the federal stage.

His real rise dates from his celebrated speech at
Quebec City in 1877 (published that year as *A Lecture on Political Liberalism*). By distinguishing
political Liberalism from Catholic Liberalism, a
movement within the Church which the hierarchy
had condemned, Laurier sought to put any taint of
Les Rouges behind him and to identify his party
with moderate British Liberalism. Unless he could
distance his party from the anticlerical revolutionary tradition of France, Canadian Liberals would
never become acceptable in Quebec. Although the
Catholic bishops were not at once appeased, the
new Pope Leo XIII (1878-1903) accepted the distinction, and Laurier's liberalism gradually became
respectable in Quebec. The basis for a great political change was set.

In 1877, Laurier's increasing importance led
Prime Minister Alexander Mackenzie to appoint

him minister of inland revenue, but the job did not last long, for the Liberals and Laurier were swept to defeat in 1878. Laurier quickly found himself a new seat for Quebec East, which would sustain him in Parliament until his death more than forty years later. In 1880, Edward Blake took over as Liberal leader with Laurier as his chief lieutenant, and when Blake retired in 1887 after two electoral defeats, he named Laurier to succeed him. Despite his ambition, Laurier was hesitant because of his health and finances and also because some English-Canadian Liberals resented his outspoken support for Louis Riel, leader of the rebellion in Saskatchewan in 1885. The execution of Riel aroused Laurier's deepest French instincts, and his emotional speeches alienated English Canada. Yet, in the absence of any outstanding English-Canadian Liberal alternative, Blake prevailed and Laurier became Liberal leader.

Laurier's first bid for power in 1891 failed on the Liberal proposal for free trade with the United States, sometimes called "continentalism." Old Prime Minister Macdonald, fighting his last fight, successfully portrayed the Liberal plan as an entering wedge for annexation to the United States while playing up Canadian loyalty to the old flag of Great Britain. Laurier's only consolation in defeat was continued Liberal progress in Quebec.

The Liberals now dropped the controversial issue of closer ties with the United States and watched the Conservatives flounder in the years after Macdonald's death. In 1896, the major issue was an act of the Manitoba legislature closing French Catholic schools. The Conservative government saw this as unconstitutional. Laurier stood to gain by picking up supporters of provincial rights; on the other hand, Quebec might resent his disappointing French Catholics in Manitoba. Gambling that he himself, as a French-Canadian, would be the issue in Quebec, he catered to the foes of Catholic schools as quietly as possible by simply declaring his belief that confederation was based on provincial rights. The strategy worked: Quebec stood by him despite the fulminations of reactionary bishops, and elsewhere provincial rightists rounded out his victory on June 27, 1896.

Prime minister at last, Laurier was now fifty-four. The hair which had disappeared from the crown of his head was now compensated by an impressive mane, soon to be completely white, flowing out to back and sides. His natural elegance and fastidious dress gave him an increasingly dignified

and stately appearance as he grew older. He stood out in any crowd, even at Queen Victoria's Diamond Jubilee. As great an actor as the stage itself could offer, he never failed to convince journalists, back-benchers, and constituents of his personal concern. Always the great gentleman, his warmth, courtesy, and charm were legendary, but for all of his cordiality, he was reserved and formal, and he had very few close friends.

As a politician he was essentially pragmatic in the Macdonald tradition. Admittedly lazy, he disliked detail and sometimes failed to act in time to prevent political problems. Although much given to compromise, he often displayed an iron will and usually mastered his cabinet. His first cabinets were the ablest; in time some of the stronger personalities such as Clifford Sifton and Israel Tarte were replaced by more obliging colleagues. Like many another leader long in power, Laurier heard only what he wanted to hear. In his best days, however, he accomplished much, winning over many adversaries with his "silver tongue" and "sunny ways." For example, he quickly compromised with Manitoba on the school question, recognizing provincial authority but winning concessions for after-hours religious teaching and for instruction in the French language, where numbers warranted.

The Tariff of 1897 revealed Laurier's practical side. Despite years of Liberal talk about lower duties, there were few reductions in the general tariff. It did provide, however, a preferential treatment for Great Britain which greatly stimulated British imports. Such a move not only erased earlier suspicions of Liberal drift toward the United States but also won support from Canadians still strongly attached to the imperial tie. Laurier, however, at the Colonial Conference of 1897 (which met during the Diamond Jubilee), resisted calls for imperial unity. Like Macdonald ten years earlier, he envisioned what the British Commonwealth later became: a galaxy of free states freely associated. In any case, his assurances of Canadian loyalty were warmly received and Laurier himself was knighted.

French and English Canadians divided over the question of assistance to Great Britain during the Boer War (1899-1902). Laurier's compromise was to pay transport costs for volunteers who would then be maintained at British expense. This minimal action, insufficient for Ontario "imperialists," aroused opposition in Quebec (led by Henri Bourassa), but most Quebecois, sensing that the Conservatives would be decidedly pro-British, stayed with Laurier, who rewarded their trust by steadily resisting over the next decade all British appeals for financial help in the naval race with Germany. He also signaled Canada's growing independence by setting up the Department of External Affairs in 1909.

The early 1900's were the great years of expansion and prosperity. An energetic program to recruit immigrants from overseas brought in millions of immigrants until World War I intervened. From 1901 to 1911, Canada's population showed a net increase of 1,832,212. The majority went to the West, producing an agricultural boom and making possible the creation of two new provinces, Alberta and Saskatchewan, in 1905. Other immigrants went to the cities and became vital cogs in urban and industrial development. As elsewhere in the first phase of industrialization, labor was often exploited. The Laurier government made some efforts to help, setting up a Department of Labour and producing schemes for conciliation and arbitration, but no real protection for unions was forthcoming. Some believed that Laurier was more in-terested in providing a cheap labor force for industry and railroad construction.

Railway building was especially close to Laurier's heart. In 1903, he unveiled plans for a new transcontinental line to be built from Winnipeg to the Pacific by the privately owned Grand Trunk Pacific, and from Monckton, New Brunswick, to Winnipeg, by the government, which would then lease its track to Grand Trunk. Despite other sweeteners in the deal, the enterprise was popular at first, but cost overruns and rumors of graft began to dim its luster. Competition, not only from the existing Canadian Pacific but also from a third line, the Canadian Northern, undermined it further. It was all too much, and later both lines had to be taken over by the Canadian Government—a costly legacy of Laurier's optimism.

Meanwhile, Laurier's efforts to avoid racial schism were running into trouble. In 1905, there was a great row when he tried to procure for Catholics in the new provinces the same rights which they had obtained in Manitoba. The English won, provoking Bourassa and the Quebec nationalists and losing a good chance to create the kind of cultural dualism Laurier had always wanted. Then in 1910, when he decided to build a small Canadian navy as a way of pacifying Canadian "imperialists" intent on aiding Great Britain, he alienated not only Bourassa but also enough Quebecois voters to ensure his defeat in the election of 1911.

The main reason for Laurier's defeat, however, was the revival of the dream of reciprocal trade with the United States, this time on American initiative. Laurier, whose tour of the West in 1910 had revealed strong antitariff sentiment among farmers, accepted eagerly, but opposition arose among worried manufacturers and lovers of the Empire who feared that East-West ties would be replaced by a North-South connection. As in 1891, prophecies of an American annexation, seemingly confirmed by speeches and newspapers in the United States, weakened Laurier considerably. In the election, Ontarians deserted in droves, and that, coupled with Bourassa's inroads in Quebec, put an end to Laurier's rule.

Although nearly seventy, Laurier remained as leader of the Liberal Party until his death. A brief dose of Conservative imperialism, highlighted by an effort to give Great Britain money for three battleships, soon rallied all Quebec behind Laurier once again. While he supported Canada's entrance into the war in 1914 and even encouraged voluntary enlistments in the struggle to save civilization, Laurier opposed conscription. In part, it went against his concept of civil liberty, but his main fear was that it would wreck the fragile French-English unity that he had always worked to preserve. Abandoned by most English-speaking Liberals, he fought a losing battle in the bitter election of 1917. He was reviled as a traitor and his political base was for the most part reduced to Quebec, although he did win forty percent of the vote nationally and won twenty seats outside Quebec. It was a sad end to his career. Death soon followed, on February 17, 1919, and Canada quickly awoke to the realization that one of her giants was gone.

Summary

Sir Wilfrid Laurier had the good fortune to preside over an age of expansion, confidence, and optimism, epitomized by his own prophecy that, just as the nineteenth century had been the time of the United States, so the twentieth century would belong to Canada. As the plains filled, immigration swelled, and industry grew, it was easy to believe in this prophecy and to ignore the pockets of discontent. The prevailing impression was of progress and promise, and Laurier's reputation benefited accordingly. The man of silver tongue and sunny ways seemed perfectly matched with his hour.

Politically, he won for Quebec a dominant voice in one of the two great national parties, and that was essential to prevent the disintegration of Canada along ethnic lines. He also ensured that the Liberal Party, with its solid base in Quebec, would dominate federal politics for decades to come. Only in 1958 and 1984 has Quebec departed from its Liberal allegiance, a remarkable turnabout from the Macdonald era when Quebec regularly sent large Conservative majorities to the federal parliament. From 1896 to 1984, Liberals dominated in Ottawa three-fourths of the time. What Liberalism meant is, however, another question. Until the 1960's, the Liberals, like Laurier himself, were not distinguished for their record on social reform. Laurier, and successors such as W. L. Mackenzie King and Louis St. Laurent, had many ties to big business and the railroads. Laurier opposed regulation of railroad rates, did not favor public ownership or collectivism in any form, and believed that reforms should be left to the opposition. While he was in part inhibited by constitutional provisions which left many subjects to the provinces, he was also influenced by the laissez-faire notions of British Liberalism. He showed inconsistency, however, in using government to promote new railroads and, contrary to campaign rhetoric, to protect Canadian industry.

Although Laurier has been celebrated for his dream of a unified Canadian nation, his real goal was the harmonious cooperation of the French and English communities. He opposed all appeals to racial and religious emotions, and his compromises were designed to hold Canada together in a period of radical change and cultural clash. Like all men in the middle, he antagonized extremists on both sides, but had it not been for World War I and the conscription issue which divided the two peoples so seriously, his efforts might have been more durable. The fact that he never became a hero to Quebec nationalists or separatists—then or later—confirms his often-expressed devotion to Canada: "I love France which gave me life; I love England which gave me liberty; but the first place in my heart is for Canada, my home and native land."

Bibliography

Arnold, Abraham. "Sir Wilfrid Laurier and Canada's Jews." *Beaver* 78, no. 5 (October-November, 1998). The author offers an account of Jewish history in Canada in the early 1900s, including Prime Minister Laurier's promise to give part of Manitoba to the Jews.

Clippingdale, Richard. *Laurier: His Life and World.* Toronto: McGraw-Hill, 1979. A fine introduction to Laurier. Handsomely and profusely illustrated, the book focuses on the years of Laurier's premiership (1896-1911), successfully evoking the social and cultural atmosphere of the turn of the century. Unusually comprehensive and perceptive for a brief work. Includes a useful bibliographical essay.

Cook, Ramsay, and R. Craig Brown. *A Nation Transformed: Canada, 1896-1921.* Toronto: McClelland and Stewart, 1974. Part of the Canadian Centenary Series, written by two first-class scholars. Much broader in scope than a mere biography, yet Laurier is covered extensively and his work is placed in perspective.

Dafoe, John W. *Laurier: A Study in Canadian Politics.* Toronto: McClelland and Stewart, 1922. Dafoe, a longtime Liberal editor of the Winnipeg *Free Press,* stoutly supported Laurier until the conscription crisis of 1917. Dafoe here briefly suggests that Laurier "had affinities with Machiavelli as well as with Sir Galahad."

Neatby, H. Blair. *Laurier and a Liberal Quebec: A Study in Political Management*. Toronto: McClelland and Stewart, 1973. Originally a doctoral dissertation written in 1956 and published later. A scholarly monograph which helps explain Laurier's methods and success, emphasizing the importance of Quebec as a bastion of Liberalism.

Robertson, Barbara. *Wilfrid Laurier: The Great Conciliator*. Toronto: Oxford University Press, 1971. One volume in a series of brief lives with emphasis on character, anecdote, and social history. A good introduction to Laurier. Illustrated.

Schull, Joseph. *Laurier: The First Canadian*. New York: St. Martin's Press, 1965. The longest and most detailed biography, making use of source material and providing detail not published elsewhere. Still, as the title indicates, this is a hymn of praise.

Skelton, Oscar Douglas. *Life and Letters of Sir Wilfrid Laurier*. 2 vols. New York: Century, and London: Milford, 1922. This is an "authorized" biography, written by a wholehearted admirer. The first work to be based on Laurier's correspondence.

Stanley R. Stembridge

PIERRE LAVAL

Born: June 28, 1883; Châteldon, France
Died: October 15, 1945; Paris, France
Areas of Achievement: Government and politics
Contribution: An opportunistic and controversial politician, Laval held eighteen ministerial offices and was premier of France four times. Following France's early defeat in World War II, he led the Vichy French government in a policy of collaboration with Germany.

Early Life

A small, stocky man with thick, straight, black hair and heavy eyelids who almost always wore a black suit, white shirt, and characteristic white silk tie, all of which accentuated teeth blackened by a lifetime of chain smoking, Pierre Laval presented an ideal character for political cartoonists to lampoon as a trickster politician. His historical role, however, does not lead to simple characterization.

Pierre Laval was born in Châteldon in the northern part of the Auvergne region of France on June 28, 1883, the fourth child of an innkeeper-butcher who also served as local postman. Raised to follow in his father's businesses, Laval instead continued his education. In 1903 he joined the Socialist Party. Following one year service in the army, he was relieved of duty because of varicose veins, a disability that exempted him from active duty during World War I. Laval went on to study law. He was admitted to the Paris bar in 1909, the same year he married the daughter of the mayor of Châteldon. Two years later, his daughter and only child was born.

Laval's early practice of law focused on defending trade unionists, socialists, and anarchists. His legal talents lay in manipulation and compromise to keep cases from going to trial. A rising star in the Socialist Party, Laval won election to French parliament in May, 1914, to represent the working-class Paris suburb of Aubervilliers. During World War I, Laval worked hard in the parliament to bring about a negotiated peace to a war he detested. At the end of the war, he voted against the Treaty of Versailles as being too harsh on Germany.

As French postwar politics drifted to the Right, Laval became an independent politician. In April, 1925, he was appointed to his first cabinet post as minister of public works. One year later, he was appointed as minister of justice and in 1927 was elected to the senate as a representative of the Department of the Seine. In 1930, he became minister of labor for the conservative government of André Pierre Gabriel Amédée Tardieu, gaining fame for passage of a social insurance law. In 1931, Laval climbed to the top rungs of political power by becoming the premier of France.

Life's Work

As premier of France, Laval introduced a new element to the office: personal diplomacy. He travelled to Berlin, Germany, and Washington, D.C., in the United States to meet with government leaders. Although he gained notoriety as the first French premier to visit either capital on official business, he failed in bringing his persuasive powers to bear to effect any policy changes. In February, 1932, Tardieu again became premier, replacing Laval but keeping him as the new minister of labor. Two years later, Laval moved to the position of minister of colonies. By this time, Adolph Hitler had come to power, steering Germany on a path of increased militancy. In response, the dynamic French foreign minister, Jean-Louis Barthou, moved France toward an alliance with the Soviet Union. However, in October, 1934, Barthou was assassinated at Marseilles, France, opening the opportunity for Laval to take his place as foreign minister. Continuing Barthou's alliance with the Soviets, Laval concluded the Franco-Soviet Pact of Mutual Assistance in 1935. The pact, however, was a watered-down version of the one that Barthou had originally envisioned.

In June, 1935, Laval again became premier and tried to move France closer to an alliance with fascist Italy. The problem was that Italy had been branded as an aggressor by the League of Nations for its invasion of Ethiopia. Laval's solution was to invite British foreign secretary Samuel Hoare to Paris, where they worked out a plan to offer Italian leader Benito Mussolini two-thirds of Ethiopia if Italy would terminate the invasion. The secret Hoare-Laval Agreement was leaked to the British press, raising a public outcry. When the British government disassociated itself from Hoare's work, a humiliated Laval saw his cabinet collapse.

From 1936 to 1940, the embittered Laval remained a member of the senate but had no role in any major affairs. He became identified with forces seeking an agreement with Hitler's Germany. With the outbreak of World War II, he remained steadfast in his opposition to a declaration of war on Germany. As France was falling to Hitler's forces, he vehemently opposed continuing the war from French North Africa, arguing that the government could not save France by leaving it.

On June 16, 1940, eighty-four-year-old Philippe Pétain was invited to form a new French government. He immediately sought an armistice with Germany, which was ultimately signed on June 22. The next day, Laval was appointed minister of state. He immediately launched into terminating the Third Republic, giving Pétain exceptional constitutional powers. France was transformed into an authoritarian regime ruled from Vichy, a small town in the center of France known only for the name of its mineral water. While Laval did not work for his nation's defeat, the fall of France served to resurrect his political career. It also convinced him that France should collaborate with Germany and seek the best terms for a partnership in a new world order.

In October, 1940, seemingly without Pétain's knowledge, Laval had a personal meeting with Hitler in the French village of Montoire about arranging a summit meeting with Pétain. The problem was that Hitler had little interest in collaboration or in making concessions about such issues as the return of French prisoners of war, ending the zone of occupation, lowering French reparation payments, or returning Alsace-Lorraine. The only sympathetic ear Laval obtained was that of Otto Abetz, Germany's foreign ministry representative in Paris. Hitler's meeting with Pétain was mainly a photo opportunity for the German propaganda machine. Laval's failure to gain concessions caused Pétain to dismiss Laval on December 13, 1940, and place him under house arrest. Intervention by Abetz, accompanied by armed German guards, gained Laval's release to Paris and the Occupied Zone of France. Meanwhile, Abetz worked furiously to move Hitler to demand Laval's return. Consequently, on April 27, 1942, Laval resumed his former role but in a very different world. Great Britain had survived the German onslaught, and the Soviet Union and the United States had joined the war against Germany. Hitler's new order now appeared less than certain.

Given these conditions, Laval incorrectly reasoned that French collaboration would be even more valuable to Germany, thus giving him needed leverage to gain concessions. Knowing Germany's need for factory workers, Laval tried to negotiate a one-to-one exchange of factory workers for French prisoners of war. Instead, the Germans agreed to return one French prisoner of war for every three workers sent to Germany. By 1944, 700,000 workers had been sent to Germany, but this did not put a damper on Hitler's demand for one million more. Failure to get volunteers to work in Germany ultimately caused Laval to conscript workers. No single act did more to drive Frenchmen to join the Resistance. The German reaction to the Resistance was not only to shoot individual Resistance members but also to hold their families and townspeople hostage. To avoid this, Laval set up special police and special courts to deal with saboteurs.

In June, 1942, Hitler demanded that France participate in the so-called final solution and turn over all of its Jews. Laval resisted but then agreed to turn over all foreign Jews residing in France. He defined foreign Jews as both refugees and Jews who became naturalized French citizens after 1930. Although the Germans only demanded adult Jews, Laval insisted that children should not be separated from their parents. In all, over 76,000 Jews in France were rounded up by French police in both the Occupied and Unoccupied Zones and delivered for extermination.

Although Laval resisted military participation in the war, he did everything else to show his sincere support for the German war effort. In his famous radio speech of June, 1942, he told the French people that "to avoid communism establishing itself everywhere, I wish for a German victory." Later, Laval would claim that he uttered these words only as a ploy to convince Hitler of his sincerity. By 1944 it was evident that Germany would not win the war. Laval, who by now was seriously distrusted by Hitler, hoped for a peace negotiated by the United States. In August, 1944, the Germans decided to transport Laval to Belfort, on the Franco-German border, and then to a castle in Germany. On May 2, 1945, Laval was flown by a German aircraft to Barcelona, Spain, but Spanish dictator Francisco Franco decided to arrest him instead of granting him refuge. In July, Laval was returned to the French Provisional government. It had been a year since he last set foot in France.

Laval was tried before three hostile judges and even more hostile jurors, who hurled invectives at him when he spoke. A guilty verdict was returned, and a death sentence was imposed. On the morning of October 15, 1945, the day of his execution, Laval swallowed cyanide powder, but swift medical attention revived him. As Laval stated in his suicide note, he wanted to die with dignity by his own hand like the ancient Romans rather than be brutally murdered by a France he had dutifully served. Helped into his suit and last white silk tie by a nun, he was brought before the firing squad, barely alive, and tied to a post. As the command "aim" was given, he uttered his last words: "Vive la France!"

Summary

Pierre Laval's political career shifted from the far Left to the far Right, a phenomenon not uncommon in the Third Republic. His survival ability was uncanny, but his successes were few and far between. His persuasive powers did not work in either Washington, D.C., or Berlin in 1931, and the Hoare-Laval Agreement of 1935 produced the opposite effect that he hoped for, including the wrecking of his effective role in politics. He grew bitter against the Third Republic and served as its grave digger in 1940 when Hitler's conquest of France provided yet another opportunity. Following a policy of collaboration to construct a Franco-German partnership in a new world order, Laval succeeded only in leaving a name associated with treason and an image that came to symbolize the essence of the Vichy regime. In 1940 and again in 1942, he failed to convince Hitler of the value of French collaborationism.

Historians are still debating whether Laval should be given some credit for saving three-quarters of France's 300,000 Jews or condemned for sending 76,000 to their death, whether he should be praised for bringing home French prisoners of war or castigated for sending so many French workers to an uncertain future in Germany, whether his collaborationist machinations protected France from a harsher treatment by Germany or added to its suffering, and whether he was the creator of or scapegoat for the policies of the Vichy government. What is more certain is that Laval's adherence to Germany until the last days of the war is indicative that, above all other concerns, his own career stood paramount. It is also quite evident that he greatly overrated his powers of persuasiveness and the importance of his own intervention in shaping important matters. As a statesman, he left only policy disasters in his wake and was extremely shortsighted. As a Frenchman, he became one of the most hated individuals in France, leaving behind a legacy that the French would like to forget.

Bibliography

Cole, Hubert. *Laval: A Biography.* London: Heinemann, and New York: Putnam, 1963. Cole provides a readable portrayal of Laval's life and career that relies heavily on memoirs and rests more on description than analysis.

Laval, Pierre. *The Unpublished Diary of Pierre Laval.* London: Falcon Press, 1948. Laval wrote little except for this diary written while in prison in which he portrays himself as a tireless worker for the best interests of France.

Paxton, Robert. *Vichy France: Old Guard and New Order.* London: Barrie and Jenkins, and New York: Knopf, 1972. Based on archival materials, this seminal study takes a hard look at the men and policies operating the Vichy regime.

Thomson, David. *Two Frenchmen: Pierre Laval and Charles de Gaulle.* London: Cresset Press, 1951; Westport, Conn.: Greenwood Press, 1975. This analytical biography of Laval's career reveals his Machiavellian opportunism in trying to salvage his own political fortunes as well as those of France.

Warner, Geoffrey. *Pierre Laval and the Eclipse of France*. London: Eyre and Spottiswoode, 1968; New York: Macmillan, 1969. This book is a comprehensive scholarly study of Laval amid the background of the Third Republic and Vichy. It is the best source dealing with the subject.

Weisberg, Richard. "Cartesian Lawyers and the Unspeakable: The Case of Vichy France." *Tikkun* 7, no. 5 (September-October, 1992). Assessment of Laval's persecution of the Jews, sanctioned by the Vichy government.

Irwin Halfond

ROD LAVER

Born: August 9, 1938; Rockhampton, Queensland, Australia

Area of Achievement: Sports

Contribution: An outstanding world tennis player, Laver won the grand slam of tennis in 1962 and in 1969, the first time as an amateur and the second time as a professional. The grand slam of tennis involves winning the four major world singles' titles in the same year: the American, Australian, British, and French championships. Laver is the only player to have accomplished this feat twice, the first to have won the grand slam since the American John Donald Budge in 1938, and the first professional player ever to have won the grand slam.

Early Life

The son of Roy Stanley and Melba (Roffey) Laver, Rodney George Laver was the third of four children. His parents, his older brothers, Trevor and Robert, and younger sister, Lois, were also tennis players. Roy Laver raised cattle in Rockhampton, Queensland, and constructed a tennis court to encourage his three sons to play tournament tennis. He was also instrumental in starting a tennis school in Rockhampton, where young Rodney enrolled. All three sons won a number of trophies in regional play in the early 1950's.

Rod Laver's first coach was Charlie Hollis, who taught him the backhand and the topspin service when Laver was but ten years old. At age eleven, when he was not spearfishing in the Pacific, Laver began to play tournament tennis and won his first tennis trophy two years later when Hollis entered him in the under-fourteen state championships at Brisbane. The next year, Laver met two people who were to have enormous influence on his career: Roy Stanley Emerson (two years his senior), with whom he played his first tennis match, and Harry C. Hopman, the former captain of the Australian Davis Cup team. Following an illness, young Laver dropped out of school that year to devote more time to the game. He was hired as a clerk in Brisbane by the Dunlap Rubber Company, for which he later performed public relations services after he became an amateur star.

Hopman persuaded Laver to go to the United States, where, at age seventeen, he won the United States Junior Championship to launch his world tennis career. Following a year in the Australian

army in 1957, Laver went to England, where his first major victory was a defeat of American star Barry Bruce MacKay in the Queen's Club Tournament in London. By then his powerful service had earned for him the sobriquet "Rocket."

Although slight of build, the left-hander boasted of a powerful service forearm measuring thirteen inches around, a full inch larger than his other forearm. He is said to have been the first left-hander to possess a strong backhand stroke. Laver stands five feet, nine inches, and weighed 155 pounds in his playing days. He has blue eyes, red hair, and a freckled face. A member of the Church of England, he was known throughout his career as a free-spirited, beer-drinking, music-loving figure who would sometimes play golf in the free time available during important tournaments.

Life's Work

Many Australian tennis players of world-class caliber were ranked much higher than Laver in the 1950's, but in 1959, Laver was chosen for the Australian Davis Cup team, joining Emerson and Neale Andrew Fraser. The Australians defeated the Americans three matches to two as Laver lost twice. His second loss was a marathon contest of sixty-six games to Alex Olmedo, a Peruvian-American. Later that year, the bowlegged Laver lost to Olmedo again, this time in the finals of the United States men's singles' contest at Forest Hills, New York. In the following year, Laver won the Australian title when he defeated Fraser in five sets. Fraser then came back to defeat Laver in the Wimbledon and Forest Hills finals later in 1960. At Wimbledon, Laver won his first English title when, teaming with Darlene Hard, they won the mixed doubles championship in 1959 and duplicated the triumph in 1960. In December, 1960, Laver teamed with Fraser to win the Davis Cup finals over Italy.

In 1961, Laver failed to fulfill the expectations of the press when he lost to Emerson in the American finals at Forest Hills in three sets. Nevertheless, Laver's brilliance was demonstrated at Wimbledon when he won his first All-England singles title by defeating Chuck McKinley of the United States in the final round in three short sets. Both Emerson and Laver (Fraser was injured in 1961) then rejected offers from Jack Albert Kramer to join the professional circuit. He finished the year by leading Australia to the Davis Cup with another victory over Italy. For the first time since 1909, a Davis Cup team had won the best of five series without losing a set to any opponent.

Laver's greatest year as an amateur was in 1962. He began the year by defeating Emerson for the Australian title, followed by a much-heralded victory in the French championships in Paris. He defeated Emerson again for the title in the Queen's Club Tournament in London just prior to his Wimbledon victory, where he defeated another countryman, Martin F. Mulligan, in less than one hour in the final contest. When Laver won the United States title two months later at Forest Hills, over Emerson in four sets, he completed the sweep of the four major world titles, commonly called the grand slam in tennis. Laver was the first player in twenty-four years to accomplish this feat. Another redhead, American star Don Budge, had won the grand slam in 1938, the year of Laver's birth. In September, 1962, *Time* magazine described Laver's "vicious ground game and the cunning way he masks his shots." Laver, who also won the Norwegian, Dutch, Irish, German, Italian, and Swiss singles titles that year, and won the United States Tennis Association Indoor doubles title with Charles R. McKinley and the Italian doubles title with John Fraser, finished his near-perfect year by teaming with Emerson to gather Australia's eleventh Davis Cup title in the previous thirteen years. The Australian team swept Mexico 5-0.

In late December, Laver, noted already for his popular broad-brimmed Australian sun hat, acceded to blandishments from the professionals and signed a three-year contract for a $110,000 guarantee with the International Professional Tennis Association. In truth, he had reached every goal attainable by an amateur player. Yet his introduction to the professional ranks was something of a surprise. On January 5, 1963, he lost to Australian Lewis A. Hoad, 6-8, 6-4, and 8-6. When he lost to another Australian professional, Kenneth R. Rosewall in four sets in April, he had yet to win a match as a professional in four attempts. Laver lost nineteen of his first twenty-one professional matches, mostly to Hoad and Rosewall. In his book, *Education of a Tennis Player* (1971), Laver wrote of repeated nosebleeds he suffered during this period, as well as the difficulties of long travel. He wrote of matches in La Paz, Bolivia, and Khartoum, Sudan, often on nonregulation-size courts.

Yet Laver persevered and broke Rosewall's string of four straight professional world singles'

titles from 1960-1963. Laver was the world titleholder from 1964 to 1967 and again in 1970. Teaming with Earl H. Buchholz, Jr., in 1965 and with Andres Gimeno in 1967, Laver won the world professional doubles crown.

In 1968, English officials relented to pressures from the professionals and opened competition at Wimbledon for the first time to both amateur and professional players. Laver remarked that his only regret was that the new players would never realize the sense of elation that the professionals felt at being recognized as respectable again. Laver celebrated by winning the Wimbledon title in his first year back. Next year, he won his second grand slam, the first professional player to win. After winning the Australian, English, American, and French titles in 1969, Laver was at the peak of his career. Analysts noted that except for boxing, no athlete dominated his field the way Laver did tennis. In 1969, he won thirty-one consecutive tournament contests at the age of thirty-one.

Laver continued to play superior tennis for several years. He won the United States Professional Indoor title at Philadelphia in 1969, 1970, 1972, and 1974. He won the professional world singles title again in 1970 and was runner-up in 1971. Laver added other championships to his list, winning the Canadian and South African titles in 1970 and teamed with Emerson to capture the Wimbledon doubles crown in 1971. He also won the Italian singles championship for the second time in 1971. His earnings began to decline in 1972, but Laver remained among the top world-class players through 1975. Two of his most famous matches were losses. His 1972 World Championship Tennis circuit (WCT) final with Rosewall in Dallas lasted three hours, thirty-four minutes, and was picked by *Tennis Magazine* as the fifth greatest match in history. At age thirty-six, Laver met the American Jimmy Connors for the first time in Las Vegas as part of the WCT. Although coached by his old rival, Emerson, Laver lost to his younger opponent 6-4, 6-2, 3-6, 7-5 in a televised match amid publicity compared to a boxing match. He was frequently playing with injuries by this time but still managed to become Rookie of the Year in world team tennis, while playing for the San Diego Friars in 1976.

In 1966, Laver had married an American woman, Mary Benson, with whom he had one son, Rick. Laver, who was awarded the MBE (Member of the Order of the British Empire), maintains a family residence in Newport Beach, California.

Summary

The two grand slam achievements of 1962 and 1969 have earned for Rod Laver a prominent place in sports history. Including competition in both doubles and singles, he won twenty titles in the four major world tournaments, a mark below only those of Emerson (twenty-eight), John Newcombe (twenty-five), and Frank Sedgman (twenty-two); his twenty titles tie him with William T. Tilden. The *London Daily Telegraph*'s annual rankings placed Laver among the top ten players in the world twelve times from 1959 to 1975. He was ranked first in 1961, 1962, 1968, and 1969; second in 1960; third in 1971; and fourth in 1970 and 1972.

"The Rocket" also played in one of the longest matches in tennis history when he defeated Anthony Dalton Roche of Australia 7-5, 22-20, 9-11, 1-6, 6-3 in a semifinal contest of the Australian Open in Brisbane in 1969. For three straight years, he led the professional ranks in earned prize money: in 1969 with $124,000; in 1970 with $201,453; and in 1971 with $292,717. Laver was the first tennis professional to earn more than one million dollars in prize money. In 1981, he was elected to the International Tennis Hall of Fame in Newport, Rhode Island.

Bibliography

Asinof, Eliot. "Why Rocket Is Better than the Best." *The New York Times Magazine* 119 (November 30, 1969): 58-80. An excellent review of Laver's early life in Australia and his tutors, training, and unique style.

Bartlett, Michael, and Bob Gillen, eds. *The Tennis Book*. New York: Arbor House, 1981. Reprints of articles by and about Laver and other tennis stars from the past.

Berry, Elliot. "Love-50: Rod Laver and Ken Rosewall on Tennis Techniques for the Rest of Your Life." *Forbes* 153, no. 10 (May 9, 1994). Laver and Rosewall discuss tennis techniques for players in their fifties.

Jares, Joe. "A Two-Armed Bandit Hits the Jackpot." *Sports Illustrated* 42 (February 10, 1975): 18-22. Jares describes the much-heralded match between Laver and Connors, televised from Las Vegas in 1975.

Laver, Rodney George, with Bud Collins. *Education of a Tennis Player*. London: Pelham, and New York: Simon and Schuster, 1971. Reminiscences of famous matches between Laver and his rivals. Especially important are his observations about Emerson's background and his own marathon match with Roche to begin his second grand slam.

Laver, Rodney George, with Jack Pollard. *How to Play Championship Tennis*. London and New York: Macmillan, 1965. The first of Laver's books on technique shortly after he turned professional. In it, he demonstrates how a left-hander can master the backhand.

"The Respectable Rocket." *Time* 98 (July 5, 1971): 57. Describes the difficult transition Laver made to the professional tour and how his perseverance led to a second grand slam.

"The Rocket's Slam." *Time* 80 (September 21, 1962): 57. Reviews Laver's first grand slam of tennis and his other titles in that same year.

Shannon, Bill, ed. *Official Encyclopedia of Tennis*. Rev. ed. New York: Harper, 1979. Lists complete records in Laver's two grand slam matches. Also contains statistics about all major tournaments in which Laver participated.

John D. Windhausen

BONAR LAW

Born: September 16, 1858; Kingston, New Brunswick, Canada
Died: October 30, 1923; London, England
Areas of Achievement: Government and politics
Contribution: As leader of the Conservative Party between 1911 and 1923, Bonar Law reorganized the party's structure, thereby creating the modern Tory Party organization. He was a major force in the coalition government of David Lloyd George during and after World War I, and was Prime Minister of Great Britain, 1922-1923.

Early Life

Andrew Bonar Law was born September 16, 1858, in Kingston, New Brunswick, Canada. His father, the Reverend James Law, was a Presbyterian minister from Ulster, and his mother, Elizabeth, though from Nova Scotia, was the daughter of an iron merchant from Glasgow, Scotland. Bonar Law was the youngest of four brothers and a sister; his mother died when he was two years old. Life in Nova Scotia was spartan and isolated, and it was there that he developed his lifelong habits of hard work and simple tastes.

At the age of twelve, he was brought to Scotland by his mother's family. After four years of formal education at Glasgow High School, he began working at his cousins' merchant banking firm, where he was an apprentice for ten years. In 1885, at the age of twenty-eight, he joined the iron merchant firm of William Jacks and Company as a junior partner. His keen business acumen, as well as his phenomenal ability to recall figures, resulted in a highly successful business career. A firm believer in self-improvement, he read voraciously and attended lectures at Glasgow University. In 1891, he married Annie Pitcairn Robley, and together they had six children. A teetotaler, he derived no pleasure from activities such as dancing or dining. His interests included chess and golf.

From an early age, Bonar Law was interested in politics. His cousins were staunch Conservatives, and they frequently hosted local and national Tory politicians. For many years after 1878, the young man was active in the Glasgow Parliamentary Debating Society, which was closely patterned after the British House of Commons. Despite this interest, financial independence was requisite for British politicians of that era. He therefore concentrated on developing a successful business as a base for his later political activities. Having accomplished this, in 1900, at the age of forty-two, he ran as a Conservative candidate and was elected to the British House of Commons.

Life's Work

That Bonar Law would be a force in the Conservative Party is evidenced by his selection as parliamentary secretary to the Board of Trade after only eighteen months as a Member of Parliament. His political and economic background led to his strong support for Joseph Chamberlain's tariff reform program. With the Conservative Party divided over the issue, the Liberal Party won an overwhelming victory in the general election of 1906. When Chamberlain suffered a career-ending stroke in 1906, Bonar Law became a leading spokesman for tariff reform. The magnitude of the 1906 Liberal victory, however, rendered the tariff reform issue moot.

For five years, under the patrician leadership of Arthur Balfour, the Conservative Party attempted to block Liberal legislation by using the House of Lords, a tactic which ultimately resulted in the Parliament Act of 1911. Conservative failures during the period left the party demoralized and disunited. Bonar Law had played only a minor role in the events between 1906 and 1911, but he was recognized as an excellent campaigner, debater, and party man. His tireless efforts on behalf of Conservatism made him acceptable to party rank and file. When Balfour resigned, Bonar Law was elected Conservative Party leader in the House of Commons. His immediate task was the revitalization of the party.

Bonar Law's first action was the reorganization of the party and the implementation of strict party discipline. When the Liberal Party introduced an Irish home rule bill in 1912, the party was reunited as it had not been in a decade. Although Bonar Law was himself no religious bigot, he empathized with the fears of the Ulster Protestant minority. He also knew that home rule was anathema to all factions of Conservatism. For two years, he used every parliamentary and party tactic, including vituperative public attacks on the Liberal leadership, especially Prime Minister H. H. Asquith, to weld the party together in an effort to defeat the Liberal Party. Unfortunately, the home rule campaign of 1912-1914 evinced party hatreds as well as Irish passions, and by 1914, Bonar Law had led his united party to the brink of civil war over Ulster. Yet when general European war intervened in 1914 he quickly committed himself and his party to support of Great Britain.

Prior to World War I, the issues of tariff reform and Ulster had dominated Bonar Law's political actions. When war came, he cast aside personal and party considerations and placed his country first. He supported the Liberal government war policy until Conservative dissatisfaction with the war effort compelled him to request a coalition government. Placing harmony during wartime ahead of personal ambition, he accepted the modest post of secretary for the colonies. This coalition, in which Conservatives played a relatively minor role, lasted until December, 1916. Again at the instigation of Bonar Law, the government was replaced by a coalition, this time headed by Lloyd George.

The political marriage between the sober Bonar Law and the flamboyant Lloyd George resulted in one of the most successful war ministries in British history. While Lloyd George directed the war effort, Bonar Law directed the home front as Chancellor of the Exchequer and as Leader of the House of Commons. At the treasury, he utilized the skills gained from years in business by revolutionizing the financing of the war. His six war budgets increased revenue through taxation, and his long-term, low-interest war loans effectively raised needed money at much reduced rates. In marked contrast to his prewar speeches, his wartime public appeals were measured calls for sacrifice by all Britons. His own losses (two of his four sons were killed during the war) made his appeals all the more convincing. He was also an outstanding leader of the Commons. His ability to manage, in addition to his integrity, allowed him always to know what was or was not acceptable in the Commons.

At the end of war in November, 1918, a general election was held. Bonar Law considered a continuation of the alliance with Lloyd George to be best for the country, and the so-called Coupon Election resulted in an overwhelming victory for the coalition. After the election, while Lloyd George concerned himself primarily with foreign and imperial affairs, Bonar Law served as the surrogate prime minister at home. This he preferred, although he did sign the Peace Treaty of Versailles. His primary concerns were the mobilizing of parliamentary approval for the peace treaty, the demobilizing of a state that had endured four years of total war, and the settling of the Irish question. For two years, he worked incessantly on these tasks. In March, 1921, wearied from years of overwork and from illness, he retired from public life.

Eighteen months later, his loyalty to the Conservative Party ended this premature retirement. Growing disenchantment with Lloyd George within the Conservative ranks had resulted in a plea for Bonar Law to return as party leader and to terminate the coalition. With the resignation of Lloyd George, on October 23, 1922, Andrew Bonar Law became Prime Minister of Great Britain. He immediately pronounced "tranquillity and stability" to be his major goals, but it was not to be. His brief tenure as prime minister was occupied with the problems of reparations and the Ruhr crisis, the British war debt, and economic depression at home. After only seven months as prime minister, he was again forced by illness to retire. He died in London, on October 30, 1923, and was buried in Westminster Abbey.

Summary

If greatness is measured by concrete achievements, then Bonar Law could not be regarded as great. He sponsored no bills of enduring significance. He was in opposition for most of his political career, holding cabinet-level office for only four years and the office of prime minister for only 209 days. At his funeral, Asquith, his longtime Liberal adversary, referred to him as "the Unknown prime minister." This apparent lack of accomplishment, however, is deceiving. Bonar Law should best be described as a man of quiet ambition who never actively sought the limelight, preferring to serve only when called upon. His contemporaries admired and respected him greatly, and a true picture of his significance must concentrate on the intangibles of leadership, courage, and integrity.

When Bonar Law first rose to political leadership, he was different from anyone who had been Conservative Party leader before. He was first and foremost a working politician. The party was his first loyalty, and, except for wartime, Conservatism came before all else. He had none of the aristocratic or school connections that had been requisite for Tory political leadership. His background as a businessman provided him with the managerial skills that the Conservative Party needed. He reorganized and unified the party, making it into a formidable political weapon. These reforms laid the foundations for the modern Conservative organization. Before him, the party was a gentleman's club; after him, the party was a machine designed to reach the electorate.

Greatness can be achieved only by those who can transcend parochialism. When war erupted in

1914, Bonar Law's attitude toward politics was profoundly altered. Tariff reform and home rule were set aside because of the greater need—the preservation of his country. In the first coalition of 1915, he subordinated himself for the good of the whole. When he was finally offered high office in 1916, he became a great war leader, albeit one who preferred the background. The political alliance between Lloyd George and Bonar Law has been called "the most perfect partnership in political history." After the war, Bonar Law continued to put Great Britain first. Indeed, he ended the Lloyd George coalition for that very reason, for Bonar Law always believed that Conservatives ruled Great Britain best. His place in history, then, is that of a great public servant who served his country and his party quietly and capably.

Bibliography

Adams, R. J. Q. "Andrew Bonar Law and the Fall of the Asquith Coalition: The December 1916 Cabinet Crisis." *Canadian Journal of History* 32, no. 2 (August, 1997). The author assesses Law's role in the 1916 cabinet crisis and the manner in which he has been perceived historically.

Beaverbrook, first Baronet. *Politicians and the War, 1914-1916*. 2 vols. New York: Doubleday, and London: Butterworth, 1928. Beaverbrook was Bonar Law's closest friend, and the portrait of the Conservative leader during this period is very favorable. Beaverbrook's later volume, *Men and Power, 1917-1918*, published in 1956 in London by Hutchinson, continues the narrative through the end of the war.

Blake, Robert. *The Unknown Prime Minister: The Life and Times of Andrew Bonar Law, 1858-1923*. London: Eyre and Spottiswoode, 1955. This official biography combines excellent research with lucid writing. Despite its age, it remains the best single book on Bonar Law's life.

Law, Andrew Bonar. *The Fiscal Question*. London: National Review Office, 1908. This collection of five speeches delivered by Bonar Law in 1907 and 1908 offers insight into one of the driving forces of his early political career. These speeches are also useful because they illustrate his forceful oratorical style.

Rowland, Peter. *Lloyd George*. London: Barrie and Jenkins, 1975; as *David Lloyd George*, New York: Macmillan, 1976. As Lloyd George's memoirs are too self-serving to be accurate, a good biography is preferred. Rowland's biography is one of the best, and his analysis of the relationship between Lloyd George and Bonar Law is excellent.

Smith, Jeremy. "Bluff, Bluster and Brinkmanship: Andrew Bonar Law and the Third Home Rule Bill." *Historical Journal* 36, no. 1 (March, 1993). Considers Law's position with respect to Home Rule and his attempt to force Prime Minister Asquith into a general election as opposed to civil war.

Taylor, A. J. P. *Beaverbrook*. London: Hamilton, and New York: Simon and Schuster, 1972. The closeness of Bonar Law and Beaverbrook throughout Bonar Law's career warrants inclusion of this favorable biography of the press magnate. Taylor focuses on Beaverbrook's character, which lends insight into Bonar Law's own character.

Taylor, H. A. *The Strange Case of Andrew Bonar Law*. London: Paul, 1932. This biography relies heavily on interviews with those who knew Bonar Law personally. The title refers to Bonar Law's extraordinary achievements, most of which were behind the scenes. It is useful for contemporary information and observations.

William S. Brockington, Jr.

D. H. LAWRENCE

Born: September 11, 1885; Eastwood, Nottinghamshire, England
Died: March 2, 1930; Vence, France
Area of Achievement: Literature
Contribution: Combining brilliant descriptive
powers with compelling evocations of natural
settings and basic human drives, Lawrence expanded the limits by which romantic-erotic situations could be portrayed in fictional settings.

Early Life

Circumstances and situations from David Herbert
Lawrence's early life are important as background
to his literary works. In many instances, biographers and critics have been able to trace the development, seemingly on parallel tracks, of
Lawrence's childhood and youth and the progress
of his later fictional creations. The fourth child of
Lydia Beardsall and Arthur Lawrence, he was born
on September 11, 1885, in Eastwood, a mining village situated in a coal-producing region of Nottinghamshire. Early in life, Lawrence preferred diminutive versions of his middle name, and later he was
known from his writing simply by his initials and
surname. His father was a common collier, evidently a handsome and well-formed man, who had
great difficulty in expressing his thoughts and often
seemed completely inarticulate. He was also prone
to prolonged periods of drunkenness which sometimes culminated in physical onslaughts against his
wife and family members. The mother was a
schoolteacher from a modest social background
who sought to instill her Congregationalist faith in
her offspring. In turn, her children felt a greater attachment to their mother and tended to side with
her during household disputes. During his early
years, Lawrence was considered shy and physically weak. He often took it upon himself to advance
his learning by borrowing numerous books from libraries in the area. He was uncannily aware of the
stark contrasts that industrial growth had spawned
amid the once-verdant landscapes of the Midlands,
and as the years went by, divergent forms of class
consciousness, notably between miners and owners, became apparent to him. In his youth he
learned to distinguish regional dialects (which he
later used in his fiction) in contrast to the genteel
usage preferred by the upper classes. Lawrence's
academic aptitude and promise were recognized
with the award of a county scholarship which allowed him to attend Nottingham High School from
1898 to 1901.

When he was fifteen years old, Lawrence became friends with Jessie Chambers, and in the
course of a protracted courtship they were engaged
for a time. Lawrence's first letters of importance
for literary scholars date from 1901. Expanding
upon his schoolboy efforts, Lawrence turned his
hand to poetry and also drafted portions of what
were to become his first prose works. He also pursued painting as an avocation, by which he advanced his own interpretations on canvas of human
figures and natural scenery. For a certain period, he
was employed by a dealer in artificial limbs and
also served for four years as a pupil-teacher in
Eastwood. In 1906, Lawrence resumed his formal
education when he entered Nottingham University
College, and in 1908 he received a teacher's certificate. During the next three years, he was employed at a local boys' school.

In 1907, one of Lawrence's short stories was
published in a local newspaper, and two years later,
his first poems appeared in print. His ardor for
Jessie Chambers faded markedly, and Lawrence
ended by breaking off their engagement in 1910. In
December of that year, one of the mainstays of his
early life was lost when his mother, to whom he
was inordinately devoted, died of cancer. Relationships with other women, including Helen Corke, a
schoolteacher, and Louise Burrows, in the end
seemed to him fruitless and unsatisfying. Nevertheless, his literary career proceeded apace; an important landmark was reached early in 1911, when
a London publisher brought out his novel *The
White Peacock* (1911). This study of the dissolution of a youthful romance, and the changes
wrought over time and distance as leading characters take leave of one another, exhibited variations
on themes featured in Lawrence's later offerings.

Life's Work

Problematical romantic relationships with those
from his native region were set aside in a rather
dramatic fashion when Lawrence unexpectedly
turned to a new love interest: He was attracted beyond measure to Frieda von Richthofen Weekley,
the wife of a professor of French at the university
in Nottingham. Although she was six years older
than he, and already had three children at home,
she responded readily to his overtures in situations

that suggested amorous intrigue. She left her family behind and traveled abroad with him, primarily in her native Germany and in Italy. It was with some difficulty that the legal travails attendant upon a divorce in England could be resolved. When, finally, in 1914 she became free to marry him, Lawrence had to assume lawyers' fees as well as the responsibility of sustaining her in their new household. As a wife, Frieda was helpful and supportive at times, but could also be demanding. Much of the time she relegated certain domestic chores as well as their routine bookkeeping to her husband. They quarreled often enough (indeed, once she hit him over the head with a stone plate), but each also had a deep and instinctive empathy for the other's cares. It has been maintained by some critics that she inspired a fictional counterpart, Ursula Brangwen, one of the major characters in *The Rainbow* (1915) and *Women in Love* (1920).

Promising beginnings to Lawrence's literary career were followed by acute, and in some ways unanticipated, difficulties with the authorities. His second novel, *The Trespasser*, was published in 1912; it is an uneven work dealing with the conflict between cerebral and sensual love, in which the protagonist finally hangs himself. Far more important was *Sons and Lovers*, which was received as a major work soon after its publication in January, 1913. This work's autobiographical origins became evident at many turns. The protagonist, Paul Morel, and the mother and father closely resemble the young Lawrence and his family. Miriam Leivers, who attracts Paul for a time but then repels him by her overly possessive stance, was probably modeled from Jessie Chambers. In the novel, deeply felt but ultimately restrictive ties between Paul and his mother are broken finally when the son administers morphine pills to terminate the mother's fatal illness. Lawrence's sensitive depiction of the conflict between nature and industry in the Midlands also won the notice of some critics.

The first of Lawrence's plays was published in 1914, but to little effect. Though he dabbled occasionally in drama, it was not a genre in which Lawrence felt comfortable. Lawrence also published several short stories during this period. Though he published *The Rainbow* in 1915, it was almost immediately suppressed. Agents of the Crown contended that its frank physical descriptions and suggestive passages, in which sexual themes were brought into the open, precluded fur-

ther distribution in its original form; unsold copies were confiscated.

The years of World War I were difficult for Lawrence. Although he was not a pacifist in any strict sense, he felt no particular enthusiasm for the war effort. He was examined and twice rejected for military service because of health problems. He paid little heed, however, to the early signs of tuberculosis. He was more concerned with whether, in an atmosphere that discouraged efforts thought to be subversive of public morals, he could continue to publish his books. Lawrence was also having problems with the authorities because his wife, Frieda, was a descendant of German aristocrats; among others, she was distantly related to Manfred von Richthofen, the celebrated war pilot. Even while in England, she did little to conceal her cultural sympathies, and indeed during the middle of the war, she performed German songs. For a time, the Lawrences lived in Cornwall, but in October, 1917, police officers, afraid that they were in a position to make contact with enemy seacraft, cited suspicion of espionage as grounds for ordering them to leave the area. Although he saw no fighting whatsoever, the war left Lawrence with the unshakable conviction that conflict and suffering had permanently changed society and indeed civilization at large; gloomy, brooding memories of descent into a moral abyss are recorded when characters in his later works recall wartime events.

Lawrence managed to bring out various collections of his poems, as well as his first travel study, *Twilight in Italy* (1916). One of his most important novels, *Women in Love*, was written for the most part in 1916, though it did not actually appear in print until 1920. There Lawrence shows how complementary and conflicting romantic ends affect the destinies of major characters. The quest for sexual primacy takes place in an atmosphere charged with suggestions of struggle in various forms; marriage and death ultimately resolve the situations of certain protagonists. Like the novel which preceded it, this work was roundly condemned in the popular press.

The pictures and portraits of Lawrence from this period show a man of a slight build. He had straight reddish brown hair, which he generally combed to one side. His lean, slightly pinched features with sunken cheeks were offset by a prominent, blunt nose; he also had large, flattish ears. To many, his forthright blue eyes seemed direct and penetrating. During early manhood, Lawrence had grown a mustache, and about the time of his marriage, he added a full beard, which his admirers considered a mark of distinction; his detractors likened him to a bearded satyr.

During the autumn of 1919, Lawrence left England; he and Frieda traveled about in various parts of the Continent, particularly in Italy. In addition to a general sense of restlessness, for a time there was some uncertainty about the direction of his work as a writer. *Sea and Sardinia* (1921), which contains some of his more impressive travel commentary, was composed shortly after the novel *The Lost Girl* (1920) appeared. Lawrence's travels in Italy affected the plot of *Aaron's Rod* (1922), which, like Lawrence's other novels, drew to a marked extent from the surroundings where its final portions were written. The last, which concerns a musician who leaves his wife and family behind for a wandering existence in various parts of Italy, probably reflected Lawrence's view that old social values had given way while new standards remained to be found. Another work, *Movements in European History*, which appeared in 1921 under a pseudonym and was published under the author's actual name four years later, recorded some highly subjective judgments on the main currents of cultural developments in the West. Although in many quarters Lawrence was reproached for his unabashed and unsparing treatment of sexual drives, he developed a sharp antipathy toward the psychological theories of Sigmund Freud; he announced his opposition to this school of thought in *Psychoanalysis and the Unconscious* (1921) and *Fantasia of the Unconscious* (1922). At different times, Lawrence also tried his hand at translation. His most important contributions in this area probably were his renditions of works by the Italian writer Giovanni Verga.

Evidently persuaded that European civilization was foundering, Lawrence traveled on to Ceylon and then to Australia. His brief visit to the island continent provided the setting for *Kangaroo* (1923), possibly the most forgettable of his novels. After reaching San Francisco in September, 1922, Lawrence and his wife settled for a while in Taos, New Mexico. For some years, Lawrence had harbored vague visionary hopes of establishing a new social order, beginning with the foundation of an experimental utopian colony. On various occasions he had proposed sites in the New World. During a visit to England and Europe in the winter of 1923-1924, Lawrence again took up such notions with certain friends, but his doctrine of "Rananim,"

based upon authoritarian leadership principles within a basic return to natural surroundings, received little firm support. Some time after they went back to the United States, the Lawrences moved south to Oaxaca, Mexico, where further complications began to undermine the author's health. In addition to chronic struggles with tuberculosis, Lawrence caught malaria, and for a certain period in 1925, it was thought that he might die. As a concession to his weakened condition, he later left for Europe, where it was thought his health might improve in a more hospitable climate. Among the works that appeared during this period were *Birds, Beasts, and Flowers* (1923), an important collection of poetry, and *Studies in Classic American Literature*, which also came out in 1923. His production of narrative fiction continued with *St. Mawr: Together with the Princess* (1925), a curious and imperfectly realized short novel which contrasts the diminished vital forces of male and female characters with the seemingly untamed powers of a stallion. *The Plumed Serpent* (1926), which has a political theme of sorts, depicts the new and positive directions opened in leading characters' lives as Mexico repudiates socilism and Catholicism equally; a new national order symbolized by ancient Indian emblems then comes into being.

Lawrence's last years were troubled by the struggle against prevailing attitudes of propriety. Much of the time, he and Frieda lived in Italy. Much of his effort was spent drafting or revising the novel that became known as *Lady Chatterley's Lover* (1928), which, in addition to stating more forthrightly themes presented in earlier works, openly challenged the standards of that day with his explicit sexual descriptions. When it appeared, the novel was suppressed almost immediately in Great Britain and the United States, and later it was published in expurgated versions; the entire work could not appear legally in the United States until 1959, while in 1960, a celebrated trial established that it could appear openly in Great Britain. Indeed, a number of episodes seemed to heighten the association with scandal that had grown up around Lawrence. In January, 1929, British police seized a manuscript version of *Pansies* (1929), a collection of his light verse. About six months later, a public display of Lawrence's paintings in London was closed after police raided the exhibition. A book showing facsimile reproductions of his visual art was suppressed as well. In a series of essays, Lawrence set forth his own interpretations of pornography and obscenity: He contended that his conception of art and literature, by bringing hitherto forbidden subjects into the open, differed in its intent from the more cynical forms of exploitation with which his work was often classified. His contempt for mere convention, however, took on further dimensions in *The Escaped Cock* (1929; published as *The Man Who Died* in 1931), a short novel in which a figure resembling Jesus Christ comes back to life with the realization that the needs of men for women take primacy over religious martyrdom. All the while that Lawrence was writing, it became increasingly evident that he could not struggle much longer against the disease which had settled for so long in his lungs. By 1928, he had moved toFrance; for a time he traveled about and continued with his literary production. Some articles and poems were prepared as the end of his life drew near. In spite of valiant efforts, he was unable, however, to stave off the ravages of tuberculosis, and on March 2, 1930, he died finally at a sanatorium in Vence, France.

Summary

D. H. Lawrence never had serious ambitions outside literature and art; once he had taken up his calling, he worked diligently and with consistent dedication to his creative efforts. He had great versatility. While his prose works early established his reputation and later were cited both by his admirers and by those who condemned him as indecent, his activity in many genres was noteworthy. Indeed, at various times later scholars have suggested that further understanding of his work may also be approached through the reading of his poetry or his literary criticism. Occasionally, there has been some revival of interest in his drama. His letters, of which several thousand remain, are of interest not merely for literary researchers but also for the commentary that they offer on major literary controversies. It is probably fair to say that some of Lawrence's political and social views have come to be regarded as curious and unfortunate manifestations of the undeveloped side of an essentially aesthetic temperament. Throughout all of his efforts, however, there are common elements which lend an essential unity to the entire body of his work. In all of his fictional offerings, Lawrence stressed the primacy of feeling, and a sense of emotional directness is communicated both in passages presenting natural descriptions and in his evocation of human relations. On a subjective level, sensations and intuitions are recaptured vividly in many places, though it may be contended that this very tendency produced inexactitude and lapses at times into a repetitive style. Lawrence also had little patience for the development of plot; the structure of some major works may appear arbitrary or disjointed in some ways. On the other hand, many of his protagonists possess a vitality and intrinsic appeal that have made them memorable to many readers.

In a related sense, Lawrence's work was important for the audacity with which he evoked human sexual drives within a much wider romantic context. To be sure, such episodes are not particularly frequent and are remarkable primarily for the frank and explicit manner in which they are rendered, yet in no instances do such interludes seem contrived or out of place. Much of the romantic and erotic imagery associated with natural settings performs a symbolic function which complements the briefer but more graphic descriptive passages that aroused such controversy when his major works first appeared. Because of Lawrence's insistence on the explicit handling of sexual issues, in some quarters his work was originally not regarded seriously. The enduring appeal of his major novels and stories, however, which seems to have transcended the vicissitudes of changing mores, points to the deeper forms of artistry that inspired him and were uniquely his own.

Bibliography

Balbert, Peter, and Phillip L. Marcus, eds. *D. H. Lawrence: A Centenary Consideration*. Ithaca, N.Y.: Cornell University Press, 1985. Eleven essays are presented here in commemoration of the one hundredth anniversary of Lawrence's birth; some contributors deal with thematic and doctrinal issues affecting the writer's work, while others consider the influence and reactions of other important literary figures.

Chambers, Jessie. *D. H. Lawrence: A Personal Record*. 2d ed. London: Cass, and New York: Barnes and Noble, 1965. As Lawrence's first major love interest, the author almost certainly was the real-life counterpart of Miriam Leivers in *Sons and Lovers*. Her account of the affair diverges from other versions, both actual and fictional; some bitterness at her ultimate rejection is apparent in the latter portions of this biography.

Cowan, James C., ed. *D. H. Lawrence: An Annotated Bibliography of Writings About Him*. 2 vols.

De Kalb: Northern Illinois University Press, 1982-1985. This reference work, an essential research tool for serious or specialized scholarship, contains 4,627 entries dealing with publications in fifteen languages between 1909 and 1975. In addition to the main subject, there are a number of comparative studies discussed at various points.

Delavenay, Émile. *D. H. Lawrence, the Man and His Work: The Formative Years, 1885-1919.* Translated by Katharine M. Delavenay. London: Heinemann and Carbondale: Southern Illinois Press, 1972. The most thorough and discerning study of Lawrence's early career, this work skillfully traces the intertwined elements of his personal life, intellectual development, and efforts in several genres to elucidate the sources of his first major works.

The D. H. Lawrence Review. This periodical, which commenced publication in 1968 on the University of Arkansas Press, Fayetteville, under the editorship of James C. Cowan, subsequently, from 1984, has been issued by the University of Delaware Press, Newark, with Dennis Jackson as editor. A number of important articles by recognized critics and scholars have appeared here, and this journal is useful as a measure of ongoing research in this field.

Lawrence, D. H. *The Letters of D. H. Lawrence.* Edited by James T. Boulton et al. Cambridge and New York: Cambridge University Press, 1979-1993. This comprehensive collection is useful particularly where it illuminates Lawrence's personal relationships and the development of his literary ideas. For any comparable period it supersedes in accuracy and breadth any previous editions of Lawrence's correspondence. By 1987, four volumes, covering the period from 1901 to 1924, had been published.

Lawrence, Mrs. Frieda (von Richthofen). *"Not I, but the Wind . . ."* New York: Viking Press, 1934; London: Heinemann, 1935. This posthumous tribute rendered to Lawrence by his widow records the positive aspects of their relationship during his courtship and their married life. There are some poignant passages concerning Lawrence's declining health and eventual death; the darker side of his character is not dealt with to any great extent.

Meyers, Jeffrey, ed. *The Legacy of D. H. Lawrence: New Essays.* London: Macmillan, and New York: St. Martin's Press, 1987. The topical concerns discussed by the seven contributors to this volume include the English and American contexts in which Lawrence's works were produced. In addition to poems and novels, Lawrence's travel works and his overall cultural impact are also considered.

Nehls, Edward H., ed. *D. H. Lawrence: A Composite Biography.* 3 vols. Madison: University of Wisconsin Press, 1957-1959. An important compilation of firsthand accounts, including many by Lawrence which have been selected to provide a chronological narrative of his life. This work is valuable particularly for the diversity of sources upon which it draws, and casts light upon its subject's work from many points of view.

Sagar, Keith. *D. H. Lawrence: Life into Art.* Athens: University of Georgia Press, and London: Viking Press, 1985. A major literary biography, this work demonstrates the relationship between the stages through which Lawrence's life passed and the themes that developed in turn through his major writings. The origins of certain novels and collections of poetry are discussed on the basis of original materials depicting his personal concerns and aspirations during the creative process.

Scherr, Barry J. *D. H. Lawrence's Response to Plato: A Bloomian Interpretation.* New York: Lang, 1995. Scherr offers new readings of several Lawrence classics and applies Harold Bloom's "anxiety of influence" theories in his analysis.

Worthen, John, et al, eds. *The Cambridge Biography of D. H. Lawrence.* Cambridge and New York: Cambridge University Press, 1991. A three-volume set of this acclaimed biography of Lawrence.

J. R. Broadus

ERNEST ORLANDO LAWRENCE

Born: August 8, 1901; Canton, South Dakota
Died: August 27, 1958; Palo Alto, California
Area of Achievement: Nuclear physics
Contribution: The inventor of the cyclotron, Lawrence used this particle accelerator to explore the atomic nucleus and became one of America's most influential scientific statesmen during and after World War II.

Early Life

The son of a prominent South Dakota educator, Ernest Orlando Lawrence grew up in Canton and Pierre, South Dakota, where he experimented with crystal radio sets with another future nuclear physicist, Merle Tuve. He was educated in South Dakota public schools, at St. Olaf's College, and at the University of South Dakota, where, under the influence of Dean Lewis Akeley of the College of Electrical Engineering, he turned from an early interest in medicine to one in physics. He pursued his graduate education with W. F. G. Swann, whom he followed from the University of Minnesota to Chicago and Yale, where he received the Ph.D. in 1925.

Lawrence showed great promise as an experimental physicist during his graduate studies and succeeded in winning a National Research Fellowship to continue his researches at Yale with Swann. His experiments with Jesse Beams on measuring very short time intervals and the characteristics of light quanta brought him renown and an assistant professorship at Yale. The University of California succeeded in wooing Lawrence away with an associate professorship in 1928. Two years later, Lawrence became the youngest full professor in the history of the university.

Lawrence was brash, enthusiastic, and ambitious and attracted many admirers, including the daughter of the dean of the medical school at Yale, Mary Kimberly Blumer, whom he married in 1931. At Berkeley, he gathered around him a coterie of graduate students interested in studying the photoelectric effect and other aspects of light quanta.

Life's Work

In the spring of 1929, Lawrence ran across a description of a particle accelerator devised by Rolf Wideröe to accelerate electrons by repeatedly passing them through gaps between cylindrical electrodes carrying an accelerating voltage. If the elec-trodes were properly spaced, the electrons traveled faster in each gap. Lawrence saw that such an accelerator would have to be very long to reach energies that might be useful in investigations of the atomic nucleus. Ernest Rutherford had proposed such investigations, and a number of physicists throughout the world were seeking suitable ways of accelerating charged particles to penetrate the electrostatic force that surrounded atomic nuclei.

Lawrence saw, however, that if the charged particles could be deflected so that they passed through the same electrode gaps over and over, a device might be built to accelerate them to high voltages without having to use high voltages. An electromagnet would serve to cause protons or electrons to travel in a spiral and, if the strengths of the magnetic field and the accelerating voltage were properly related to each other, the times at which the particles would cross the gaps between the electrodes would always be the same. To this idea he gave the name "magnetic resonance accelerator." It later came to be known as the "cyclotron."

Lawrence set one of his graduate students, Niels Edlefsen, to building a primitive cyclotron in the spring of 1930. Although the first cyclotrons gave ambiguous indications of working, Lawrence announced his invention in September, 1930, and set another graduate student, Milton Stanley Livingston, to building a better model. At the same time, he asked David Sloan, whom he had recruited from the General Electric Laboratories, to build a linear accelerator similar to Wideröe's for the acceleration of positive ions. It was characteristic of Lawrence to tackle two or more difficult experimental projects at once, and his reputation was built on the fact that he often succeeded, despite the odds.

Livingston's cyclotron gave unequivocal evidence of acceleration, and Lawrence aspired to build a larger one. He succeeded in locating a giant electromagnet and in obtaining financial backing. Frederick Gardner Cottrell, the founder of the Research Corporation, provided seed money and taught him how to make his way about philanthropic foundations.

In order to attract medical funding, Lawrence developed, in collaboration with Sloan, a high-voltage X-ray machine which could be used for cancer therapy and industrial radiography. The discovery of the neutron in 1932 provided an alternative bullet to aim at cancer tumors, and Lawrence was soon investigating neutron production with the cyclotron. Enthusiasm for these and other medical applications grew. The discovery of artificially radioactive materials such as radio-sodium paved the way to radioisotope therapy using substances that could be produced in quantity by the cyclotron. Support for the machine increased, and Lawrence built larger and larger cyclotrons throughout the 1930's. Many other cyclotrons were built in the United States and abroad. Although many were used for medical purposes, all were used to explore nuclear physics.

The application of the cyclotron to scientific problems led to the development of new specialties: nuclear chemistry, which was developed by Jack Livingood and Glenn Theodore Seaborg in Lawrence's "Radiation Laboratory" in the late 1930's; nuclear medicine, which was developed by Lawrence's brother, Dr. John Hundale Lawrence, in the Radiation Laboratory, the Crocker Laboratory, and the Donner Laboratory in the late 1930's and 1940's; and nuclear engineering, which William Brobeck and other engineers who built the giant cyclotrons of the late 1930's pioneered. Among the many isotopes discovered in the Radiation Laboratory was carbon-14, which opened up the field of radioactive tracing and radiocarbon dating.

In 1939, Lawrence's achievements were recognized with the award of the Nobel Prize for Physics for the invention of the cyclotron and the work done with it. Lawrence was able to parley the award into support for a cyclotron costing $1.5 million from the Rockefeller Foundation. This cyclotron, 184 inches in diameter and weighing forty-five hundred tons, was begun in 1940.

The advent of World War II, however, drew Lawrence and many other American physicists into war research. After the discovery of fission in 1939, Lawrence's associates in the Radiation Laboratory discovered that in some cases, rather than fissioning, uranium atoms produced heavier elements which had not been found in nature. In 1940, Edwin M. McMillan discovered element 93, neptunium, and Seaborg found plutonium in 1941. When British studies indicated that a small mass of uranium-235 ought to make an effective nuclear explosive, Lawrence and his associates turned to the production of machines that would separate this isotope, a very small fraction of natural uranium, from the heavier uranium-238, which made up most of the remainder of the material. Using elec-

tromagnetic techniques to whirl atoms of the element through a magnetic field, Lawrence believed that enough of the lighter isotope might be separated to make an atom (fission) bomb. His colleague at Berkeley, J. Robert Oppenheimer, who had often advised Lawrence on theoretical aspects of nuclear physics, was enlisted to help design such a weapon and eventually went to New Mexico to create and lead the Los Alamos laboratory to this goal. Lawrence's "calutrons" succeeded well enough to produce most of the uranium used in the atom bomb dropped on Hiroshima, while plutonium was made in large enough quantities by Enrico Fermi's nuclear reactors to make up the bomb tested at Trinity and the one dropped on Hiroshima.

Lawrence's success in scaling up the electromagnetic process of isotope separation and his leadership in other phases of the wartime atomic effort solidified his position at the top of America's scientific hierarchy after World War II. Rather than taking on extensive advisory positions as did Oppenheimer, however, Lawrence chose to enlarge his laboratory at Berkeley, which began to sprawl across the hills behind the University of California campus, and to support the development of the Atomic Energy Commission Laboratories at Los Alamos and, later, at Livermore, where Lawrence and Edward Teller founded a second nuclear weapons laboratory in the early 1950's.

On the national scene, Lawrence exerted great influence through his associates on the Atomic Energy Commission and its General Advisory Committee. In the controversy over the development of the hydrogen bomb, he parted company with Oppenheimer, who had left the University of California for Princeton, and sided with Lewis Strauss, the chairman of the Atomic Energy Committee who launched the hearings which deprived the theorist of his clearance in 1954. Here, again, Lawrence worked through his associates Teller, Luis Alvarez, and Wendell Latimer rather than testifying personally against Oppenheimer. His increasingly conservative political stance in the 1950's made him a favored scientist in the Eisenhower Administration, where he fought moves to end nuclear testing and, at the very end of his life, was appointed to negotiate with Soviet technical representatives at Geneva for a means of verifying compliance with a proposed test ban.

The Radiation Laboratory saw an efflorescence of peacetime particle accelerator development after the war, thanks to Lawrence's ability to win federal funding for his machines. The 184-inch cyclotron was completed and, by using the technique newly invented by McMillan to modulate the frequency of the accelerating voltage, produced the first manmade mesons, previously found only in cosmic rays, in 1948. Luis Alvarez invented a linear accelerator of protons which was developed for production of radioactive materials in the early 1950's and which was later used in many larger accelerators. McMillan also invented a frequency-modulated electron accelerator, the synchrotron, in 1945, which became a major tool of high-energy physics.

During the 1950's, Lawrence's laboratory continued its leadership in nuclear and high-energy physics, building the 6.2 billion-volt Bevatron, a proton synchrotron, by 1954, a strong-focused cyclotron for nuclear chemistry by 1958, and a heavy-ion linear accelerator by the end of that decade. These machines made possible much new work in nuclear sciences, including the discoveries of many new transuranium elements, including one which was named in honor of Lawrence.

After traveling to Geneva in the summer of 1958 to negotiate with Soviet scientists, Lawrence was taken ill and rushed back to California, where he died after surgery to relieve a severe ulcerative colitis. After his death, he was honored by the Regents of the University of California, who founded a science education research center as his memorial and named both the Berkeley and Livermore Radiation laboratories after him.

Summary

Ernest Orlando Lawrence's institutional legacy is matched by the influence he had on the politics of American science and upon the development of nuclear science in the United States. Large particle accelerators of the types he pioneered now probe the hearts of the protons and neutrons he studied, revealing scores of subatomic particles. Although the Lawrence Berkeley Laboratory could not maintain the leadership in high-energy physics that it held until 1959, every high-energy accelerator in the world owes much to Lawrence's inventive and organizational skills, and his own laboratories have found new avenues for service to the nation. In many ways, Lawrence was the father of modern Big Science and, in combining American technological know-how with pioneering scientific research, he proved a distinctly American genius.

Bibliography

Childs, Herbert. *An American Genius: The Life of Ernest Orlando Lawrence.* New York: Dutton, 1968. This official biography of Lawrence was commissioned by the Regents of the University of California and is the most detailed exposition of Lawrence's life and career.

Davis, Nuel Pharr. *Lawrence and Oppenheimer.* New York: Simon and Schuster, 1968; London: Cape, 1969. Although less detailed and less accurate than other biographies, Davis' captures, in the words of Lawrence's associates, a variety of views about the physicist.

Kevles, Daniel J. *The Physicists: The History of a Scientific Community in Modern America.* New York: Knopf, 1978. This is still the best treatment of the development of the profession of physics in the United States and places Lawrence's career and contributions in the broadest historical perspective.

Livingston, M. Stanley. *Particle Accelerators: A Brief History.* Cambridge, Mass.: Harvard University Press, 1979; London: Harvard University Press, 1995. This short account, written by the coinventor of the cyclotron, places Lawrence's contributions to particle-accelerator design in the context of the history of accelerator technology.

Seidel, Robert. "Accelerating Science: The Postwar Transformation of the Lawrence Radiation Laboratory." *Historical Studies in the Physical Sciences* 13, no. 2 (1983): 375-400. Lawrence's success in building the first great high-energy physics laboratory in the postwar era is recounted to show how he was successful in converting wartime support for military research to funding for peacetime fundamental physics research.

Robert W. Seidel

T. E. LAWRENCE

Born: August 16, 1888; Tremadoc, Caenarvon-
shire, Wales
Died: May 19, 1935; Bovington, near Clonds Hill,
Dorset, England
Areas of Achievement: The military and literature
Contribution: Lawrence introduced striking innovations when he directed the operations of Arab
irregular forces during the desert campaigns of
World War I in 1917 and 1918; he then captured
the imagination of much of the world by describing his exploits in memoirs that have been called
"one of the greatest modern epics in the English
language."

Early Life

The second of five sons, Thomas Edward
Lawrence was born in Tremadoc, Wales, on August
16, 1888, into a household sustained by what char-
itably could be called a bigamous union. His father, Thomas Robert Tighe Chapman, from a landed family in Ireland, had previously married
another woman, by whom he had four daughters,
before he decided that life with her was insuffer-
able. After a time, he ran off with Sarah Junner, the
family's governess; over the years they took up residence at various locations. The father sometimes
used the surname "Lawrence," and it was chosen
for each of their children when birth certificates
were prepared. It remains unclear precisely when
any of the boys learned of the irregular circumstances surrounding their origins; certainly when it
came, the knowledge was a burden to them in later
life. It would seem that whatever influence was exerted by the parents came largely from their mother, who attempted with limited success to instill her
religious precepts in her children.

A somewhat greater semblance of settled family
life was achieved when they moved to Oxford in
1896. As a boy Lawrence received much of his early education at Oxford High School; evidently, he
was also fond of strenuous exercise and liked
pranks of every sort. He further conceived an interest in castles and military architecture, and beginning in 1906 he spent parts of three summers in
France, where he went about by bicycle to visit
historical sites. In 1907, he entered Oxford University, where he read modern history. Persuaded that
the examples set by fortifications in Western Europe had influenced the development of such constructions farther east, he proposed a thesis on this

topic, and in 1909 he traveled alone to Syria, Palestine, and other parts of the Middle East. In 1910, he
was awarded first-class honors in his chosen field;
in 1936, his thesis, with letters and other materials,
was posthumously published in two volumes as
Crusader Castles. He received a grant to facilitate
further research and travel in conjunction with an
archeological expedition supported by the British
Museum. He also worked with Charles Leonard
Woolley, an important specialist on the ancient
Near East; much of their time was spent at a site on
the northern course of the Euphrates, where artifacts of Hittite settlements were coming to light.
Other work farther south was carried out under the
auspices of the Palestine Exploration Fund. Two
volumes on work at these locations, published in
1914 and 1915, listed Lawrence as a coauthor.
Much of the time, when he was not attending to ex-
cavations, Lawrence explored the countryside; at
times he amused himself by devising odd provoca-
tions to arouse the suspicions of Ottoman officials
and German agents in the region. Along the way,
he acquired a passable knowledge of conversational Arabic, enough to make himself understood,
though not with the fluency or grace of a native
speaker.

Except in certain notable but indefinable respects, Lawrence did not present an imposing figure. He was about five feet, five inches, and seemed
yet more diminutive as his head was disproportionately large in relation to his body. He had light
blond hair and a fair complexion, which eventually
became a reddish brick hue from prolonged exposure to the Levantine sun. He had a strong, pronounced jaw and a broad, curved nose; his lips
were thick and sensuous. Many observers, however, testified to the uncanny character of his clear
blue eyes, which at times suggested visionary or
hypnotic qualities. On the other hand, he had a
high-pitched voice which often turned into a sort of
nervous giggle. Curiously enough, regardless of
whether he ever actually was taken for an Arab, he
was able to win acceptance among the peoples of
the area with his seemingly indomitable stamina
and his extraordinary aptitude for leadership.

Life's Work

After the outbreak of World War I in Europe, the
Ottoman Empire entered the conflict on the side of
the Central Powers, and in November, 1914, Great

Britain and France declared war on the Ottoman state. British officials in Egypt established contact with al-Husayn ibn 'Ali, the Grand Sharif of Mecca, and offered to support some form of Arab national sovereignty in lands then under Ottoman control. In June, 1916, Husayn cast his lot with the British after he raised a force of Arab soldiers that expelled Ottoman troops from the holy city. The insurgents also achieved some advances on the coast. Their opponents held Medina, however, while efforts to dislodge them from other inland cities, or positions to the north, seemed to pose a daunting task.

At the outset of the war Lawrence obtained a commission in the Geographical Section of the War Office; he then worked with military intelligence in Egypt, where for a time he was involved in drawing up maps of the Sinai peninsula. The further effects of the world conflict were brought home to him when two of his brothers were killed in France in 1915. His work with Arab forces began in October, 1916, when with a British colleague he met 'Abdallah ibn al-Husayn, the Sharif's second son, at Jiddah on the Red Sea.

Lawrence traveled on to the camp of Faysal ibn al-Husayn, the third son of their Arab ally; though the prospects there seemed far from hopeful, he counseled against the transfer of British ground forces to the region. Instead, Lawrence offered to act as an adviser and liaison officer alongside Faysal's men.

There were other British personnel who at times had parts to play in the Arab campaigns; among the more notable were Colonel Pierce C. Joyce, Lawrence's immediate superior, and Colonel Stewart F. Newcombe. Others assisted the Arabs by providing munitions and modern weapons. Nevertheless, it is probably fair to say that Lawrence consistently exercised leadership both in devising operations plans and in actually directing the efforts of Arab guerrillas in the field. Some of his accounts are of doubtful veracity, and it has been contended that Faysal and other Arab leaders in the end took many of the decisions that gave some coherence and shape to the desert campaigns. On the other hand, the tactical innovations employed against Ottoman forces bore the stamp of Lawrence's conception of guerrilla warfare. Moreover, he believed that by appearing in Arab dress he would win acceptance more readily, and this additional, characteristic touch, preserved in many later portraits of Lawrence, further enhanced the impression he created among his followers. In January, 1917, he was on hand as Faysal's soldiers surrounded and captured al-Wajh, on the Red Sea; Lawrence also was involved in plans for the Arab armies' march on 'Aqaba, opposite the Sinai peninsula, which was captured in July, 1917. As Ottoman forces obdurately continued to hold out in Medina, Lawrence supervised a series of demolition raids on the Hijaz Railway, to interrupt communications and transport. During the autumn, attacks on Ottoman positions were planned, so far as was possible, to coincide with the advance of Allied forces into Palestine under the command of General Sir Edmund Allenby. In certain instances Lawrence himself set dynamite charges or other explosives on bridges or along railroad tracks; even with valiant efforts, however, he and his men failed to destroy a strategically located structure over the Yarmuk River in southern Syria.

Lawrence later gave out several different accounts of a visit to Dar'a, a city south of Damascus; in all of them he maintained that, while reconnoitering the area, he was apprehended by Ottoman soldiers and brutally misused in the presence of the local governor. Some versions of the story suggest homosexual rape by various parties. Turkish materials, and the evidence provided many years later by others who were then in the area, cast doubt upon Lawrence's story, though not to the extent that such an episode could be ruled out. It would seem that, reticent as he was on such a painfully sensitive issue, Lawrence had fewer reasons for exaggeration or the exercise of his imagination than in discussing his military exploits. Whatever happened, it is known that he returned to friendly forces and was present at General Allenby's entry into Jerusalem, in December, 1917. In January of the next year, Lawrence led troops in a victorious pitched battle at Tafila, southeast of the Dead Sea. During the spring various raids succeeded in cutting the Hijaz Railway entirely at certain points.

The last phases of the desert campaigns, for which he held high hopes, were marred first during an engagement at Tafas, in southwestern Syria. There, according to Lawrence, he and his followers exacted bloody vengeance against enemy prisoners in retribution for Ottoman atrocities against the local population. On October 1, 1918, the day after Arab insurgents had begun to take power within the city, Lawrence arrived in Damascus and was confronted with the daunting task of establishing public order in some form. Moreover, charges that even while encouraging the Arab revolt Great Britain had acted in bad faith could not be put to rest. He had taken no part in the secret agreement negotiated in 1916 between Sir Mark Sykes and François Georges-Picot, which on behalf of Great Britain and France had divided much of the Middle East into zones of direct and indirect influence. Still, Lawrence felt a morbid sense of guilt for what he regarded as a betrayal of the cause for which many Arabs had sacrificed and endured much. The Balfour Declaration of 1917, by which Great Britain had pledged its support for the establishment of a Jewish national home in Palestine, probably was a lesser matter to him; Lawrence was by no means anti-Zionist. Lawrence's own political outlook was subject to varied oscillations. Nevertheless he was disquieted by the air of perfidy which had come to be associated with Anglo-French planning for the Middle East. He acted as Faysal's adviser at the Paris Peace Conference of 1919, where his beliefs and expectations were focused upon the specific problem of restricting French influence in the Levant. He repeatedly lob-

bied against the ultimate award of mandatory powers in Syria and Lebanon to France but was unable to obtain recognition for Faysal's Arab claims. In 1921, Lawrence became an adviser to the Middle Eastern Department of the British Colonial Office, and thus took some part in the decisions by which Faysal was made the King of Iraq, which was maintained as a British mandatory state. In a similararrangement 'Abdallah became the king of mandatory Trans-Jordan. While later Lawrence had nothing to do with ongoing concerns in the Middle East, he was disheartened to learn that Husayn, the original leader of the Arab revolt, had been displaced in Arabia by Ibn Sa'ud, the founder of the Saudi kingdom.

Lawrence's war record had created a distinctive image and aura. In 1919, London newspapers referred to him as "Lawrence of Arabia"; the American journalist Lowell Thomas, who had met Lawrence while reporting on the war in the desert, supplied yet further publicity. A lecture-documentary show was produced, which appeared first in New York and then in London. Evidently, this kind of presentation appealed to Lawrence's instinctive flair for showmanship—indeed he attended several performances—but he also recoiled from the public attention that began to surround him. Thomas' stage account was not overly accurate, but it captivated audiences with its portrayal of a heroic modern Arabian knight, and ever since, semilegendary connotations have in many ways been part of the general public's conception of T. E. Lawrence.

On the other hand, determined to present matters from his point of view, Lawrence began work on an account of his own, *Seven Pillars of Wisdom: A Triumph*. He added touches of mystification and some oddly exaggerated claims which if anything seemed to make any dispassionate assessment of his role in the Arab campaigns yet more difficult. A trial version of this work was published in 1922, and subscribers' copies were produced in a limited edition of 1926. An abridged version of the main work appeared in 1927 as *Revolt in the Desert*. The release of *Seven Pillars of Wisdom* in a commercial edition in 1935, shortly after Lawrence's death, was a major publishing event; the work baffled readers as much as it enlightened them. While it was received as a major landmark in the literature of World War I, historians were hard put in some instances to distinguish between those episodes which could be taken as historical fact—though there were enough of those—and the improbable claims Lawrence willfully was prone to make. Its evocation of the grim majesty and horrors of war, however, was achieved in an oddly individual writing style which seemed peculiarly suited for its subject. There are a number of morbid and openly shocking passages. In addition to Lawrence's account of detention and torture at Dar'a, there are descriptions of his killing a wounded Arab, to preclude a more gruesome end at the hands of the Ottomans; the grim massacre at Tafas, where, as Lawrence would have it, enemy prisoners were summarily killed, is followed somewhat later by grisly descriptions of Ottoman dead decaying in the hospitals of Damascus. Odd and improbably humorous sequences are interspersed about the work. Some readers have been struck by curiously lyrical descriptive passages, which appear even in the midst of battle scenes. Lawrence's own narrative, then, stood somewhere between historical autobiography and literature; in time it also contributed to the semimythical image that was gowing up around the historical man.

Nervous strain left over from the war years, unatoned guilt over the peace settlement, growing reticence in the face of mounting public attention, and various personal and/or sexual traumas have been cited in explanation for the next, bizarre stages in Lawrence's career. Although he had been promoted to colonel during his service in the Middle East and later had been offered various responsible positions in government, he seemed to prefer a simpler existence in some of the newer branches of the armed forces. In August, 1922, he enlisted as a private in the Royal Air Force under the assumed name John Hume Ross. After his presence there was revealed by London newspapers, he was released the following January, but two months later he joined the Royal Tank Corps, where he signed up as T. E. Shaw; he took this name legally through a deed poll in 1927. Much of the time he was stationed in England—indeed he acquired a cottage in Dorsetshire, which he named Clouds Hill, in 1923—and during this period he evidently suffered odd crises affecting his emotional life. He never married, and while claims that he voluntarily engaged in homosexual relations have found no substantiation, there are documents to indicate that at times he hired others to administer ritual flagellation to him. In 1925, he was transferred to the air force once more. For about two years he was stationed in India, but persistent, though unfounded, rumors about his intrigues in neighboring Afghani-

stan compelled the authorities to recall him in 1929. By this time he had completed a draft of *The Mint*, a semifictional study of his enlistment and training as a private in the armed forces. Because of its explicit and at times purposely shocking depiction of the seamy underside of military life, this effort was not published until 1955; an unexpurgated commercial edition appeared only in 1973. During his later period of military service, he worked on literary translations; the most notable of these was his rendition of Homer's *Odyssey*, which appeared in 1932. He also worked with seaplanes and produced a technical manual on the use of advanced military seacraft. When he left the Royal Air Force in February, 1935, he had some hopes of resuming his literary pursuits; at other times he seemed oppressed by a sense of pervasive pessimism. Over the years, he had been fascinated by speed and motor vehicles; he often would race about the countryside on a custom-built motorcycle. On May 13, 1935, while traveling near his home, he swerved abruptly to avoid two boys on bicycles and was thrown violently forward onto his head. He was found in a coma; he never regained consciousness, and after six days he died at last at the Bovington Camp hospital in Dorsetshire.

Summary

Although much of his life was shrouded in mystery, which indeed he acted to heighten when he could, T. E. Lawrence left a twofold legacy which safely could be regarded as embracing his enduring achievements. His doctrine of guerrilla warfare, summarized in various of his writings, has served many later commanders as stating tactics by which irregular operations may be implemented. Lawrence's grasp of the need to gain the sympathy and confidence of peoples among whom military efforts would have to be directed was matched by his understanding of the means by which opposing forces might be harassed by actions against which they could put up no effective defense. In an entirely different sense, Lawrence also left the world a vivid and perhaps inimitable example of the literary uses of military memoirs, which, sometimes in lurid terms, depict the storm and shock of battle. His recorded reactions to killing and responsibility for violent death are among the most sharply and poignantly stated treatments of this theme in any printed form. In addition to its somewhat uncertain historical value, *Seven Pillars of Wisdom* portrays the violent, the exotic, and the personal aspects of war in the desert in a manner which has proved fascinating to several generations of readers; in many ways it anticipated other literary accounts of the horror and suffering of war during the twentieth century.

In other ways, Lawrence's life and exploits remain enigmatic. For one thing, it is rather difficult to measure his contribution to the campaigns fought during the Arab revolt; for that matter the extent to which Arab operations contributed to the final defeat of Ottoman armies is not easily assessed, particularly when they are compared with the efforts of the main Allied Armies under General Allenby. The qualities that made Lawrence an effective leader were uncanny and seemed to elude precise definition. Many of his fellow combatants testified to his remarkable ability to instill in his men confidence in the success of what otherwise seemed to be highly perilous undertakings. Other sides of Lawrence's character also pose questions, particularly as over the years the legend that grew up around him took on a life of its own; on the other hand, details about the darker side of his personal life were learned only many years after his death. Behind these contrasting images lurk the essential complexities of Lawrence's nature. The contrast between self-promotion and self-abnegation was in evidence throughout most of his adult life. Nevertheless it is instructive that most later biographies, however they have handled his personal traumas, have accorded him a secure place in history both for his wartime activities and for his literary accomplishments.

Bibliography

Kaplan, Carola M. "Conquest as Literature, Literature as Conquest: T.E. Lawrence's Artistic Campaign in *Seven Pillars of Wisdom.*" *Texas Studies in Literature and Language* 37, no. 1 (Spring 1995). Discussion and analysis of Lawrence's *Seven Pillars of Wisdom,* in which he writes about his experiences and failures in the Arabian campaign.

Lawrence, T. E. *Seven Pillars of Wisdom: A Triumph.* London: Cape, and New York: Dell, 1935. A work which for anyone concerned with the Middle Eastern campaigns can neither be ignored nor accepted in its entirety. As history, it provides the most accessible source for some otherwise murky episodes; it is also probably a fair statement of the effects war had on Lawrence, and of his own conception of his unusual mission.

Liddell Hart, Basil Henry. *"T. E. Lawrence" in Arabia and After.* London: Cape, 1935; Westport, Conn.: Greenwood Press, 1979. This sympathetic portrait by one of Great Britain's most important military historians accords Lawrence a place as one of the great captains of history. There are some inaccuracies owing to an overly literal acceptance of some early stories. Lawrence himself assisted in the original composition of this work. An American edition exists as *Colonel Lawrence, the Man Behind the Legend.*

Mack, John E. *A Prince of Our Disorder: The Life of T. E. Lawrence.* London: Weidenfield and Nicolson, and Boston: Little Brown, 1976. This major biography by an academic psychiatrist provides a thorough and searching account of Lawrence's military and political efforts while discussing his personal life on the basis of interviews and documents pertinent to such matters. Explanations of Lawrence's character traits are balanced and persuasive. This work was awarded the Pulitzer Prize for Biography.

Musa, Sulayman. *T. E. Lawrence: An Arab View.* Translated by Albert Butros. London and New York: Oxford University Press, 1966. An important critical study, based in part on Arabic publications and some interviews with veterans of the desert war. In his zeal to overturn claims that Lawrence led and Arab notables followed him, the author may have understated the importance of the British officer.

Stewart, Desmond. *T. E. Lawrence.* London: Hamilton, and New York: Harper, 1977. A well-researched critical study which has some interesting observations on British intelligence work during World War I. On certain issues, the author has gone beyond British records and consulted German documents as well as some Arabic materials. On some points, Stewart contests Lawrence's veracity in a most severe fashion.

Tabachnick, Stephen E., ed. *The T. E. Lawrence Puzzle.* Athens: University of Georgia Press, 1984. This collection of critical essays affords varying perspectives on the relationship between Lawrence's literary efforts and the diverse facets of his military and political work. Among the contributors are important scholars whose work otherwise has appeared primarily in France, Germany, or Israel.

Thomas, Lowell. *With Lawrence in Arabia*. London: Hutchinson, and New York: Century, 1924. An account by the correspondent who made Lawrence an international celebrity, this work is often uncritical and lacking in historical perspective. Yet it is vital for an understanding of the image that began to envelop the British officer in the public mind.

Weintraub, Stanley, and Rodelle Weintraub. *Lawrence of Arabia: The Literary Impulse*. Baton Rouge: Louisiana State University Press, 1975. An analysis of Lawrence's literary ambitions which demonstrates the common concerns that ran through his major works and his other efforts. Here as in other areas Lawrence had complex, not easily reconciled notions of his ultimate purpose.

Yardley, Michael. *T. E. Lawrence: A Biography*. London: Harrap, 1985; New York: Stein and Day, 1987. This sprightly work is based in part upon newspaper accounts from the period as well as British military and diplomatic archives. The author concludes with an assessment of past writing on his subject and a discussion of the numerous means, including film and drama, through which Lawrence's exploits have been made a continuing source of fascination for many.

J. R. Broadus

HALLDÓR LAXNESS
Halldór Kiljan Guðjónsson

Born: April 23, 1902; Reykjavík, Iceland
Died: February 8, 1998; near Reykjavík, Iceland
Area of Achievement: Literature
Contribution: Laxness, in a period when Iceland was reawakening to its history, became a spokesman for that history and renewed the distinctive art of Icelandic narrative. He received the Nobel Prize in Literature in 1955, a fitting tribute to his contribution to world literature.

Early Life

Born Halldór Guðjónsson on April 23, 1902, Halldór Laxness was the son of Guðjón Helgi Helgason and Sigríður Halldórsdóttir. Laxness' parents moved from Reykjavík into the country to become farmers when Laxness was still very young. By the time he was seven years old, Laxness had begun to write stories and poems. He began his writing career in 1918, the same year that Iceland gained its independence from Denmark.

In 1919, Laxness published his first book, *Barn náttúrunnar* (child of nature), and left for Europe without having received his high school diploma. In his travels over the next few years, Laxness observed the devastation of World War I; his writing from this period is deeply pessimistic. In 1923, he entered a monastery in Luxembourg and converted to Catholicism. Some of his works that directly followed this conversion—*Nokkrar sogus* (1923; some stories), the novel *Undir helgahnuk* (1924; under the holy mountain), and a defense of Catholicism entitled *Kapólsk viðhorf* (1925; a Catholic point of view)—reflected his new perspective.

Life's Work

As Laxness departed for Rome, where he planned to continue his studies and enter the priesthood, his course appeared to be set. In fact, he was about to undergo another transformation. Instead of Rome, he found himself in Sicily, where he wrote his first fully developed novel, *Vefarinn mikli frá Kasmír* (1927; the great weaver from Kashmir). Depicting a symbolic conflict between good and evil, the book dramatizes the spiritual struggles that culminated in Laxness' disillusionment with Catholicism.

Laxness next traveled to the United States, where he sought work in the film industry, without success. His impressions of Hollywood and of American life are recorded in two bitterly critical articles. During this time Laxness became friends with the novelist Upton Sinclair, whose influence played a part in Laxness' commitment to radical socialism.

Returning to Iceland in 1929, Laxness married Ingibjörg Einarsdóttir in 1930; they had one child, a son. Laxness decided to settle in Reykjavík, although he continued to travel widely.

The 1930's were fruitful for Laxness. He won immediate praise for his two-part novel *Þu vinviðour hreini* (1931) and *Fuglinn í fjörunni* (1932), translated together as *Salka Valka: A Novel of Iceland* (1936), which established him as Iceland's leading novelist. In both its tone—a distinctive mixture of detached cynicism and compassion for struggling humanity—and its specifically Icelandic subject matter, *Salka Valka* set the pattern for Laxness' subsequent works. His next major work, another two-part novel, *Sjálfstætt folk* (1934-1935; *Independent People*, 1946), was a popular as well as a critical success, even becoming a best-seller in the United States after being featured as a selection of the Book-of-the-Month Club.

It is the tetralogy *Heimsljos* (1937-1940; *World Light*, 1969), however, that many critics regard as Laxness' greatest achievement. Written in part while Laxness was traveling in South America and the Soviet Union, the tetralogy is based on the life of a historical figure, the turn-of-the-century Icelandic folk poet Magnús Hjaltason. In transforming this figure into the fictional character Olafur Kárason, Laxness demonstrated his ability to infuse the individual with universal significance. Critics acknowledged as well Laxness' mastery of language, evident in the stylistic range of the four novels in the cycle. In the same year in which he completed the tetralogy, Laxness divorced his first wife; in 1945 he married Auður Sveinsdóttir, with whom he had two daughters.

In his next cycle of novels, the trilogy *Íslandsklukkan* (1943-1946; Iceland's bell), Laxness reached further back in Iceland's history. The trilogy is set in the eighteenth century, a period during which Iceland suffered under Danish domination. The story had contemporary relevance for Laxness' readers, for in 1944 Iceland dissolved its

lemic characteristic of his style are increasingly muted in favor of a more contemplative stance.

Readers who know Laxness only in translation are unlikely to be aware of the variety of his work. While his reputation rests on his novels, he was active throughout his career in many other genres, producing stories, essays, poems, plays (in his later years, he turned to experimental, symbolic drama), and travel books in rich abundance; in addition, he translated into Icelandic works by writers as diverse as Voltaire and Ernest Hemingway. It is thus as a powerful and manifold presence in Icelandic letters as well as a novelist of international repute that Laxness' achievements must be reckoned.

Bibliography

Einarsson, Stefán. *A History of Icelandic Literature.* New York: Johns Hopkins University Press, 1957. This work includes a brief but helpful summary of Laxness' life and the significance of some of his literary works within a historical perspective.

———. *History of Icelandic Prose Writers: 1800-1940.* Ithaca, N.Y.: Cornell University Press, 1948. The life and writings of Laxness are discussed at some length in this work. The biographical information is interesting and informative, and the analysis of Laxness' literary development is insightful and succinct.

Hallberg, Peter. *Halldór Laxness.* Translated by Rory McTurk. New York: Twayne, 1971. Part of the Twayne World Authors series, this is an introductory critical study of Laxness' life and works. Contains relevant historical information, a biographical chronology, and an extensive bibliography. Overall a valuable reference for analysis of individual works and Laxness' literary career.

Hallmundsson, Hallberg. "Halldor Laxness and the Sagas of Modern Iceland." *Georgia Review* 49, no. 1 (Spring 1995). Examines Laxness's works and his unusual assortment of women characters.

Magnússon, Sigurður A. "Halldór Kiljan Laxness: Iceland's First Nobel Prize Winner." *American Scandinavian Review* 44 (March, 1956): 13-18. This article describes Laxness' development as a writer and the significance of the tribute of the Nobel Prize. A personal appraisal—at times highly laudatory, at times quite critical—of Laxness' works and his public political statements.

———. "The World of Halldor Laxness." *World Literature Today* 66, no. 3 (Summer 1992). Dis-

union with Denmark and became an independent republic. Laxness adapted parts of the trilogy for a dramatic production that enjoyed great success when the National Theater of Iceland opened in 1950.

After a satiric novel with a contemporary setting, *Atómstöðin* (1948; *The Atom Station*, 1961), which objected to the continuing American military presence in Iceland, Laxness turned again to a historical subject. His long, ambitious novel *Gerpla* (1952; *The Happy Warriors*, 1958), based on the Norse sagas, is at once a merciless deflation of their heroic ethos and a tribute to their style. Laxness' significant achievements as a novelist and man of letters were honored in 1955, when he received the Nobel Prize in Literature.

Summary

Halldór Laxness continued to write in the years following the award of the Nobel Prize, although none of his later works has been judged the equal of masterworks such as *World Light.* A change of tone is noticeable in his later works, as the satire and po-

cussion of the themes and techniques used by Laxness and the issues that influenced the subject matter of his works.

Nobel Prize Library. *Halldór Laxness, Maurice Maeterlinck, Thomas Mann.* Del Mar, Calif.: CRM, 1971. Focusing on the awarding of the Nobel Prize, the Laxness section of this work contains the presentation address by Elias Wessén, Laxness' acceptance speech, and an analysis of the political background of the decision to award Laxness the Nobel Prize. Also includes a brief review of Laxness' life and works.

Jean Thorleifsson Strandness

GUSTAVE LE BON

Born: May 7, 1841; Nogent-le-Rotrou, France
Died: December 13, 1931; Marnes-la-Coquette,
   France
Areas of Achievement: Anthropology, medicine,
   and sociology
Contribution: Although Le Bon is known primarily
   for his unique work in crowd psychology, he is
   still remembered by some—not always favorably—for his work on the unconscious mind, his
   writing in medicine, his controversial theories of
   race, his books on anthropology and archaeology, his treatise on the training of horses, his explorations into black light and the equivalence of
   matter and energy, and his writing on the composition of tobacco smoke.

Early Life

Gustave Le Bon was born into a bourgeois family
of civil servants in the farming town of Nogent-le-
Rotrou, not far from Chartres. As a boy, he vowed
not to follow in the footsteps of his father and
grandfather, as his brother George was to do, but
rather to escape what he considered the deadening
rural atmosphere of his native town. By the time he
was nineteen, his *lycée* education at Tours behind
him, Le Bon moved to Paris and never returned.

After six years as an intern at the Hôtel Dieu in
Paris, Le Bon was granted his license to practice
medicine, a vocation for which he had slight enthusiasm. Between 1862 and 1873, nevertheless, he
published seven medical books that dealt with topics ranging from fevers and heredity to physiology
and urology. His medical interest began to focus on
pathology, and inevitably he formed connections
between pathologies of the body and pathologies
of society. Le Bon's books, which enjoyed a considerable vogue in the France of his day, usually
went into multiple editions; by 1875, Le Bon had
enough money from them that he no longer had to
work.

Le Bon, a handsome man with a high forehead
and intense dark eyes, aspired to acceptance into
Parisian society but was repeatedly shunned, even
after his books and accomplishments had attracted
considerable attention. Although he was something
of a lady's man, he never married, possibly because his deep-seated pessimism and his views
about the inferiority of women interfered with his
relationships.

During Le Bon's formative years, intellectual
France was applying scientific principles to everything, resulting in such outcomes as Émile Zola's
modeling his theory of literature, *Le Roman ex-
périmental* (1880; *The Experimental Novel*, 1964),
on Claude Bernard's *Introduction à l'étude de la
médecine expérimentale* (1865; *Introduction to the
Study of Experimental Medicine*, 1927), a book
that was influential to Le Bon as well. Using experimental methods to study cranial characteristics of
people from various races as well as to train horses, Le Bon began to transfer his ideas from such diverse areas to his notions about race.

Life's Work

Once he had achieved financial independence, Le
Bon indulged in his lifelong passion of traveling,
going through Europe extensively and to parts of
Africa as well. Between 1880 and 1895, he published significant books on the civilizations of the
Arab countries and of India, as well as one on how
to apply photographic principles to cartography.
His most impressive books of this period, however,
were *L'Homme et les sociétés: Leur Origines et
leur histoire* (1881), *Les Lois psychologiques de
l'évolution des peuples* (1894; *The Psychology of
Peoples*, 1898), and *Psychologie des foules* (1895;
The Crowd: A Study of the Popular Mind, 1896).

Besides inventing apparatuses for use in various
branches of medicine, Le Bon invented apparatuses for making cranial measurements at anthropological sites. As he measured the skulls of various
peoples, he reached generalizations about the
seeming correlation between intelligence and head
features. These generalizations led to his theorizing that some races are superior to others, although
Le Bon used the word "race" to indicate nationality
rather than confining its meaning to its more accepted anthropological definition. In the three
books cited above, he articulated some of his most
influential theories about race.

Le Bon became extremely interested in the unconscious mind of humans. Freudianism was in the
air, although Le Bon's theories in many respects
put one in mind of the collective unconscious of
Carl Gustav Jung, whom Le Bon predates, more
than of Sigmund Freud. Le Bon denied the idea of
rationality in the affairs of societies. He held to a
theory of mental contagion that works constantly
on the unconscious mind, an insight he developed

when he was working on training horses and which he applied to the human race.

So powerful did the unconscious mind appear to Le Bon that he believed both individuals and whole societies respond to it rather than to more rational means of meeting problems or crises. When Le Bon applied his mechanistic view of human behavior to the behavior of crowds, he raised questions of intense interest to those who would manage people. Such political figures as Adolf Hitler, Benito Mussolini, and Vladimir Ilich Lenin admired Le Bon. Hitler's *Mein Kampf* (1925-1927) reflects both the language and philosophy of *The Crowd*. Particularly appealing to revolutionaries is Le Bon's contention that crowds, in destroying the old order, prepare for the emergence of the new.

The Crowd presented the fullest statement of Le Bon's ideas about mob behavior. According to its assessment of crowd characteristics, people *en masse* act with unanimity; anyone who deviates is no longer a part of the crowd, and the consequences for such a deviation are often drastic, particularly at times of national hysteria. The major products of crowd unanimity are intolerance and a sense of absolute rightness. Le Bon believed that crowds assume a life of their own, one often detached from the individual ideas of their members. As crowd momentum accelerates, its energy is fueled by a perception of colossal power.

A second characteristic of crowd behavior is emotionality. This is what Le Bon designates as the feminine characteristic of crowds. It results in sudden action, can change without warning, and is usually based on a one-sided rather than a balanced view of the matters that have led to crowd action. Because in his hierarchy of the superiority of people Le Bon places women, children, the deranged, socialists, and the sexually perverse toward the bottom, it is not surprising that he labels the emotional characteristics of crowds as feminine.

The third characteristic that Le Bon presented is that crowd behavior is purely mechanical and that it grows from a fundamental reaction of the unconscious. The unconscious mind makes members of crowds extremely receptive to leadership that can stir them to the sudden actions that evolve from the second characteristic, emotionality. Le Bon contended that crowd psychology applies both to disorderly mobs aroused by an issue and to such bodies as legislatures, religious groups, regional groups, and entire nations. The crowd reinforces individuals' tentative beliefs and lends them a strength based on primitive reactions rather than rationality.

Le Bon applied his theories to understanding the psychology of World War I. In *Enseignements psychologiques de la guerre européenne* (1915; *The Psychology of the Great War*, 1916), he tried to sustain his earlier observations by noting that soldiers who become separated from their units lose their value because they lose the crowd mentality required for motivation. He observed further that such isolated servicemen usually regained their value when they were united with their own groups but that it did not return when they joined other, less familiar groups, presumably because the latter were impelled by a different unconscious.

Although Le Bon believed that under some circumstances individuals can be transformed into a crowd acting with a collective mind, he nowhere specified what these circumstances are. One might speculate on the behavior of people faced with imminent danger, such as people on a sinking ship, or of people drawn into some action, such as a gang rape, that might not reflect accurately the behavior patterns of every individual in the group.

The Psychology of Peoples, in which Le Bon establishes his hierarchies that set the Anglo-Saxon race (Le Bon's use of the word is narrow) above Latins, has appeal for racists. In his hierarchy of the sexes, Le Bon places males well above women. Prior to the publication of this book, Le Bon had examined and measured the skulls of forty-two famous men collected in the Museum of Natural History in Paris. This research indicated to him that the brightest, most successful men had the largest skulls. He noted that the skull of one general who was frequently defeated measured 1,510 centimeters, whereas the skull of one who was nearly always victorious was 1,725 centimeters. He tried to generalize about criminal behavior from examining the skulls of criminals, finding that the backs of criminal skulls, where the passions are supposedly centered, were overdeveloped.

Summary

Gustave Le Bon died just as Nazism was on the rise in Germany, and it is impossible to deny that the theoretical base of this devastating political movement had some of its roots in Le Bon's opinions and others like his. Nevertheless, much of Le Bon's writing was the product of a highly ordered mind much affected by the positivist sociology of Auguste Comte, the experimental approach to medicine of Claude Bernard, the evolutionary theories of Charles Darwin, and the new psychology of Sigmund Freud.

Le Bon wrote twenty-eight books during his lifetime and was actively writing until the year of his death, when his final study, *Bases scientifiques d'une philosophie de l'histoire* (1931), was published. The range of his interests is truly remarkable, as is the level of accomplishment he achieved in such a broad variety of subjects.

Le Bon's overall misanthropy, demonstrated even in his early childhood, was intensified by the social rejection he suffered when he finally left his native community for Paris. Le Bon died an isolated man, despite his correspondence with such notables as Albert Einstein, Henri-Louis Bergson, Jean-Gabriel de Tarde, and others. Pictures of Le Bon in later life show a balding man with a scraggly beard extending halfway down his chest; he is poised as though he is looking down upon the whole of humanity.

Bibliography

Clemenceau, Georges. *France Facing Germany: Speeches and Articles*. Translated by Ernest Hunter Wright. New York: Dutton, 1919. Despite its age, Clemenceau's book provides interesting insights into the effect upon society of Le Bon's theories about World War I. The notions of racial superiority and of the effect of social isolation on people, particularly on servicemen, as detailed by Le Bon had a profound influence on Clemenceau.

Maury, Lucien. "Mob Violence and War Psychology." *The New Republic* 16 (August 3, 1918). This article illustrates the seriousness with which Le Bon's theory and his books in 1916 and 1917 about the psychology of World War I were taken. The perspective is far to the Left of Le Bon's, but it cannot repudiate extensively the inherent logic of much that Le Bon had written about the topic.

Nye, Mary Jo. "Gustave Le Bon's Black Light: A Study in Physics and Philosophy in France at the Turn of the Century." *Historical Studies in the Physical Sciences* 4 (1974). This article shows Le Bon, when classical physics was in decline, dealing with some of the problems of light and thermodynamics that others such as Max Planck found intriguing at about the same time. The article reveals Le Bon's incredible thirst for knowledge and relates him to events in the French society of his day that served to shape his thinking.

Nye, Robert A. *The Origins of Crowd Psychology: Gustave Le Bon and the Crisis of Mass Democracy in the Third Republic*. London and Beverly Hills, Calif.: Sage, 1975. Nye's treatment of Le Bon remains the fullest presentation in English. It is a carefully documented study, much of it based on manuscript resources held by two branches of Le Bon's family in France. Although Nye concentrates on crowd psychology, he realizes that this theory is so intimately intertwined with Le Bon's earlier work that his discourse is quite complete and extensive.

————. "Two Paths to a Psychology of Social Action: Gustave Le Bon and Georges Sorel." *Journal of Modern History* 45 (1973). Nye shows the irony of the misalliance between Sorel, a vociferous representative of the Left, and Le Bon, an equally vociferous representative of the Right. Although they approached France's basic problems from completely opposing perspectives, the two men assessed the problems similarly, particularly as they considered matters such as the psychology on which French religiosity is based.

R. Baird Shuman

LE CORBUSIER
Charles-Édouard Jeanneret

Born: October 6, 1887; La Chaux-de-Fonds, Switzerland

Died: August 27, 1965; Cap Martin, France

Area of Achievement: Architecture

Contribution: Charles-Édouard Jeanneret was one of the most creative, bold, and controversial architects of the twentieth century. He also wrote passionately and powerfully about the nature and configuration of the modern city, thus making him a pioneer in the field of urban planning.

Early Life

Charles-Édouard Jeanneret was born in La Chaux-de-Fonds, Switzerland, on October 6, 1887. In his adult life, he would adopt the somewhat theatrical pseudonym Le Corbusier, the family name of one of his ancestors from the south of France. La Chaux-de-Fonds was associated with the watch-making industry, which provided employment for his parents, who engraved watch-cases. Upon leaving elementary school at age thirteen, he was admitted to the local art school, which was actually a technical school preparing students for manual vocations. There he learned engraving, chiseling, and goldsmith work, and this type of hands-on experience proved valuable later in his career. One of his teachers was Charles L'Éplattenier, who encouraged him in the direction of architecture and advised him to travel extensively. In 1906, he began his so-called knapsack period, traveling through Central Europe, the Balkans, and along the Mediterranean, visiting famous cities, sites, and buildings, constantly sketching or jotting down notes. Occasionally, his travels were interrupted for extensive periods when he would work in some of the great ateliers or studios of Europe, including the Paris studio of Auguste Perret, an engineer-architect who had pioneered in the use of reinforced concrete, and the Berlin studio of Peter Behrens, a famous architect of industrial design. It was during these travels, especially along the Mediterranean, that he learned much about light, nature, and form.

By the end of World War I, Le Corbusier was once again in Paris, eventually becoming a French citizen in 1930. Perret introduced him to Amédée Ozenfant, the Purist painter, who in turn encouraged Le Corbusier to paint. Over his lifetime, Le Corbusier produced perhaps as many as three hundred canvases, and undoubtedly this activity helped to crystallize some of his views on architecture. In 1920, the two men, along with Paul Dermée, founded an avant-garde journal, *L'Esprit nouveau.* It was a stimulating venture, with articles on the cutting edge of not only architecture but also art, technology, and the social sciences. It reflected the infatuation that many of the intellects of the period had with machinery and science. Architects such as Le Corbusier were enthusiastic about how the new technologies opened up rich possibilities for their craft, particularly in regard to prefabrication, modular construction, and mass production. Modernity and the new machine civilization held no terrors for him.

Le Corbusier's early life, then, was essentially one of self-education. Neither the product of a famous university nor a celebrated mentor, he learned from a variety of sources—his teachers, his travels, his work in the great ateliers of Europe—as well as from friends and colleagues. Now his own creativity and boldness of vision would begin to assert themselves.

Life's Work

What distinguishes Le Corbusier from many great architects is that he never isolated architecture from urban planning and housing, but regarded them as all part of the same challenge. Indeed, his views on the city and urban planning appear to have matured more quickly than those on architecture. At the Salon d'Automne in 1922, he unveiled his plan for a "Contemporary City for Three Million Inhabitants," and in 1925, he presented his famous "Voisin Plan" for Paris, a project that would have placed several skyscrapers on the Right Bank of that city. Throughout his career, he was constantly producing plans for the renewal of cities, including Barcelona, Algiers, Stockholm, Antwerp, Berlin, and São Paulo. His views on the subject were further enunciated in a series of books, including *Urbanisme* (1924; *The City of Tomorrow and Its Planning,* 1929) and *Quand les cathédrales étaient blanches: Voyage au pays des timides* (1937; *When the Cathedrals Were White: A Journey to the Country of Timid People,* 1947), the latter written after a celebrated trip to the United States.

By the mid-1930's, then, Le Corbusier's views on the city were fairly well established. He rejected the linear city, with its haphazard growth, urban sprawl, and distant suburbs, which collectively constituted a great waste of space, raw materials, and commuter traveling time. Instead, he proposed that cities be built upward, the so-called vertical city. These cities would be characterized by office skyscrapers and high-rise apartment buildings. If people could work and live under densely populated circumstances, a vast amount of space would be liberated for parks, gardens, and recreational purposes. There would be a complete separation of pedestrian and vehicular traffic, the latter running below ground level or on elevated freeways. Thus, the vertical city would enable the masses, not only the few, to live in dignity amid light, space, and nature.

Simultaneously, Le Corbusier's views on architecture were advancing, as can be seen in his epoch-making work *Vers une architecture* (1923; *Towards a New Architecture*, 1927). By the late 1920's, however, he had built comparatively little, mostly villas and mansions. It is a tribute to his reputation, then, that when he entered the competition to construct a new palace for the League of Nations at Geneva, his entry was seriously considered but apparently rejected only on a technicality. Shortly afterward he received several important commissions. In 1928, he began work on one of the most famous houses in architectural history, the Villa Savoye, Poissy, France; the house, essentially a white square cube of reinforced concrete and glass resting upon stilts, reflected his commitment to the cubist and Purist traditions. About the same time, he received a commission to build the Centrosoyus in Moscow, a building eventually used by the Soviet Ministry for Light Industry. Between 1930 and 1932, he constructed the Swiss Pavilion, University City, Paris. It is a rectangular "slab-block" dormitory, elevated and resting upon stilts (*pilotis*), made of reinforced concrete, with a flat roof and southern façade made almost entirely of glass. The purpose of the *pilotis* was to lift the structure off the ground, thus freeing space for pedestrians, foliage, and sun. He also was an important consultant on the Ministry of Education and Health building, started in 1936, in Rio de Janeiro, Brazil. This building featured one of his most notable innovations, the sun-break (*brise-soleil*), concrete fins or panels attached to the exterior facade alongside windows. Their positioning was closely coordinated with the trajectory of the sun on the horizon, the purpose being to minimize the heat and glare of the sun in summer and maximize it in winter.

After World War II, Le Corbusier resumed his career with an astounding burst of energy and creativity. He received a commission from the French Ministry of Reconstruction to build his famous complex in Marseilles, the Unité d'Habitation (1946-1952). Perhaps this project, more than any other, encapsulates the theories and innovations of Le Corbusier. It is a high-rise apartment complex, built on the now familiar *pilotis*. The building's reinforced concrete is not simply exposed but flaunted and celebrated. Windows run across much of the façade, leaving few dark or gloomy interior spaces. It has a flat roof, upon which is located a garden and leisure complex, including a pool, a children's play area, and a three-hundred-meter running track. To relieve the monotony of the façade, he introduced a polychromatic scheme, coloring the panels that separated the balcony apartments with vivid pastels. Each apartment within the building contains two levels, the "work areas," such as the kitchen, bath, and bedrooms, being half as high as the spacious living room fronting the balcony. Included in the building were the necessary shops and services. What Le Corbusier did, in effect, was to tilt the linear city into a vertical one. In other words, at the bottom and top of the building are the green spaces and recreational areas, with "the city" in between. Scarcely any wonder then that Le Corbusier and his disciples referred to elevator shafts and stair wells as "vertical streets." Other Unités d'Habitation were constructed in France at Rezé-les-Nantes, Briey-en-Forêt, and Firminy, and in Berlin as well.

One of the most expansive projects of Le Corbusier's career involved the creation of an entirely new city for the capital of the Punjab, at Chandigarh, India. Begun in 1951, the entire city was planned, special emphasis given to lovely pools and pedestrian walks. Le Corbusier was deeply involved in the construction of several governmental buildings, including the High Court, the Secretariat, and the Legislative Assembly Hall. It was an extraordinary achievement for a man who by 1957 had reached his seventieth birthday. His touch of genius is particularly noticeable in the remarkable Chapel Notre-Dame-du-Haut (1950-1955) at Ronchamp, France. Many critics view this building as one of his greatest works. While the familiar con-

crete and geometric shapes are present, there is a plasticity and rhythm to this building not seen in his other works. The basic shape is that of a prow of a ship, and the roof sweeps upward in a fluid, graceful, almost lyrical fashion. Ironically, Le Corbusier built little in the very country most closely associated with modernity and progress, the United States. The Carpenter Center for the Visual Arts at Harvard University, completed in 1963, stands as his only work of consequence in the United States.

In addition to his professional accomplishments, he was forced for much of his life to act as a vigorous advocate and polemicist for his views. While close friends experienced his warmth and friendship, his public posture was often perceived as aggressive, arrogant, and argumentative. In defense of Le Corbusier's annoying didacticism, it must be said that, since his opinions and works were so controversial, he was often forced by his opponents to defend his views with a belligerence and hyperbole that the less talented were spared. Given the vigor and dynamism of his mind and personality, it is something of a blessing that his death came swiftly. He died while swimming near his cabin

home on the French Riviera at Cap Martin on August 27, 1965.

Summary

Le Corbusier's towering reputation is well deserved. He coined much of the modern architectural vocabulary. He demonstrated the rich potential of certain raw materials, such as concrete and stone, especially if their true, raw, primitive qualities were exposed. He pioneered many techniques, or took existing ones and used them with flair and imagination. He left behind not only a rich legacy of architecture but also an integrated vision concerning the nature of the city and the relationship of architecture to it.

Le Corbusier has had his critics, however, and they claim that his dreams have turned into urban nightmares. He is accused, fairly or not, of being godfather to a school of architecture that is characterized by huge, ugly, concrete high-rises, often situated amid a hostile environment of vast empty windswept spaces. His functionalism was said to be the enemy of beauty and comfort and that in the final analysis he never really did understand people and their needs, hopes, and aspirations when it came to city living. His defenders, in turn, claim that much of what was built in his name is only a cruel parody of what he intended. Undoubtedly, controversy will always swirl about his reputation, but none will deny his genius and the immense influence that he exerted upon the course and shape of modern architecture.

Bibliography

Besset, Maurice. *Who Was Le Corbusier?* Translated by Robin Kemball. Geneva: Skira, 1968. A useful introduction into the life, ideas, and works of Le Corbusier. The book is well indexed and heavily illustrated, contains photos of every building that he designed, and has a valuable synoptic table that chronologically compares events in Le Corbusier's life to other events transpiring in the larger world of art and architecture.

Blake, Peter. *The Master Builders.* London: Gollancz, and New York: Knopf, 1960. Written by an architect and former editor of *Architectural Forum*, this book is in effect a lengthy essay intended for the more mature student. While a trifle adulatory, it is particularly good at placing Le Corbusier's work within the larger context of architectural trends in the modern epoch. The book also contains essays of similar length on Mies van der Rohe and Frank Lloyd Wright.

Brooks, H. Allen. *Le Corbusier's Formative Years: Charles-Edouard Jeanneret at La Chaux-de-Fonds.* Chicago: University of Chicago Press, 1997. Brooks examines Le Corbusier's formative years. Based on twenty years of research, the author offers a glimpse into Le Corbusier's personality and the factors that made him a great designer. Well illustrated.

Choay, François. *Le Corbusier.* London: Mayflower, and New York: Braziller, 1960. Written while Le Corbusier was still alive and active, the book has an excellent though brief summary of his life and work up to that point. The book's real strength is the eighty-seven carefully selected plates that are skillfully coordinated with the text. Strongly recommended for the novice who wants a quick visual introduction to Le Corbusier's style.

Le Corbusier. *Final Testament of Père Corbu: An Interpretation and Translation of Le Corbusier's "Mise au point."* Edited and translated by Ivan Zaknic. New Haven, Conn.: Yale University Press, 1997. This is the first English translation of Le Corbusier's *Mise au point,* which was originally published posthumously. Zaknie places the work in context within the architect's life, especially his troubled final years.

———. *The Ideas of Le Corbusier on Architecture and Urban Planning.* Edited by Jacques Guiton. Translated by Margaret Guiton. New York: Braziller, 1981. This book makes an outstanding contribution, collecting the ideas of Le Corbusier from a variety of his books and articles and organizing them into logical topics and categories.

———. *Le Corbusier.* Edited by Willy Boesiger. London: Thames and Hudson, and New York: Praeger, 1972. A condensed edition of Boesiger's multivolumed collected works of Le Corbusier, it was done at the request of Le Corbusier, who wanted an inexpensive survey of his work made available to poor students.

———. *Le Corbusier: Creation Is a Patient Search.* Introduction by Maurice Jardot. New York: Praeger, 1960. Translated by James Palmes. While the narrative and captions are a trifle eccentric and offer no systematic biographical information, this book contains an exceptional collection of plates covering all aspects of Le Corbusier's work. Within the covers of this one volume are assembled his sketches, drawings, paintings, models, and urban plans, as well as first-rate photographs of the exteriors and interiors of his most famous buildings.

David C. Lukowitz

EVA LE GALLIENNE

Born: January 11, 1899; London, England
Died: June 3, 1991; Weston, Connecticut
Area of Achievement: Theater and drama
Contribution: A leading actress of classical plays, Le Gallienne also founded a repertory company with which she introduced dramas by Anton Chekhov and Henrik Ibsen to American audiences. Hoping to build an audience, she drastically reduced the price of theater tickets, which was an innovation in its day.

Early Life

Eva Le Gallienne was born on January 11, 1899, to an English father of French extraction and a Danish mother. Her father, Richard Le Gallienne, was a successful poet and novelist, the friend of such writers as Irish playwright George Bernard Shaw and Irish poet William Butler Yeats. Her mother, Julie Norregaard, was a correspondent for a well-known Danish newspaper, *Politiken*, and a friend of such distinguished English actors as Constance Collier and William Faversham.

When Eva was about seven, her parents separated and her mother took her to live in Paris, where she studied at the Collège Sévigné. They attended theater and ballet performances, and Eva was privileged to see the fabled French actress Sarah Bernhardt in some of her most popular roles. The experience made a deep impression on her, and she was determined to make the stage her career.

Life was difficult for mother and daughter, since Richard Le Gallienne contributed almost nothing to their support. (The couple's divorce became final in 1911). When her newspaper efforts did not bring in enough money, Julie Le Gallienne opened a dress shop in Paris, which became moderately successful thanks to her good taste and to the patronage of her eminent acquaintances. Every summer, mother and daughter returned to England to stay with friends. One of them, actress Constance Collier, noticed Eva's interest in theater and volunteered to give her acting lessons. In 1914, Collier invited Eva to take the role of a page in Belgian dramatist Maurice Maeterlinck's *Monna Vanna* (1902), and Eva's career was officially launched at the age of fifteen.

Feeling the need for more formal training, Eva enrolled in Herbert Beerbohm Tree's Academy for actors. Tree was one of the best-known actor-managers in England, and at his school Eva took classes in dancing, fencing, voice production, and elocution. In 1915, she had a role in playwright George Du Maurier's *Peter Ibbetson* (1891), and soon the young actress was besieged with offers to do other plays. Some came from overseas. Eva, worried that the war, which had just broken out, might cause the curtailment of theater in England, decided to accept an offer from Broadway.

When Eva Le Gallienne, accompanied by her mother, arrived in New York, she found that the so-called little theaters—groups committed to producing plays for their artistic merit rather than for their financial rewards—were in full swing. The Neighborhood Playhouse, the Provincetown Players, and the Washington Square Players were offering dramas by such new writers as Eugene O'Neill, as well as the work of Germany's Georg Kaiser, Hungary's Ferenc Molnár, and Russia's Leonid Andreyev. This discovery gave Eva Le Gallienne a taste for the kind of theater she would prefer and would come to champion in later years. From 1915 to 1920, however, she appeared in a number of negligible plays, most of them opening in New York and touring the country as far as San Francisco. Her employment was steady but her roles were unsatisfactory until she was cast as Julie in Ferenc Molnár's *Liliom* (1921), when play and player came together to make Le Gallienne a name in the theater.

Life's Work

The producers of *Liliom*, whose group had developed from the Washington Square Players into the Theatre Guild, were uneasy about the play, which had failed at its Budapest opening in 1909. (Many years later, it found another life as the successful Broadway musical *Carousel*.) The script possessed such charm and the acting, notably Eva Le Gallienne's, was so powerful that both critics and audiences were captivated by it. Eva Le Gallienne's performance was judged perfect: One critic noted that she was not poetic but was sheer poetry. Her early training at the Academy and her experience had prepared Le Gallienne for this moment; she enriched the role of a waiflike character whose love transcends tragedy with her attention to realistic detail, her imagination, and her perfectionism. Above all, her admiration of French actress Sarah Bernhardt had given way to her worship of Italian actress Eleonora Duse, because Bernhardt projected her own personality on to the part she was playing, while Duse submerged her personality in the role. These are two entirely different approaches to interpretation: One proclaims the star; the other, the actor. As she grew in her understanding, Le Gallienne chose the second, truer way.

After *Liliom* concluded its successful run, it was sent on tour with the company; again, when she was free to perform, Le Gallienne appeared in a few more mediocre plays, good scripts always being difficult to find. In 1923, however, another Molnár play, *The Swan* (1914), was offered to her, and she took the leading role of a princess who for a moment falls in love with her brother's tutor but knows that she may not marry him because she is destined to be a queen. Although it is a slight comedy, the play is full of rueful charm. At the end of the play, the audience gave Le Gallienne a standing ovation (much rarer then than it is now), and the critics all agreed that she had surpassed her performance in *Liliom*. Le Gallienne gave full credit to the art of Eleonora Duse, saying that it would have been easy to stress the play's winsome quality, but by bringing a sturdy reality to the part she was able to make the princess not only believable but also sympathetic. *The Swan* ran for more than a year in New York and then toured for the entire 1924-1925 season.

The next year, Le Gallienne decided to take a new play by Mercedes de Acosta, *Jeanne d'Arc*, to Paris, her background in French making the occasion a major event. American designer Norman Bel Geddes directed the play, but he so overwhelmed it with spectacle and the play itself was so lacking in power (George Bernard Shaw's 1923 *Saint Joan* made every other portrait of the Maid of Orléans seem faded), that the result was a resounding failure. Le Gallienne returned to New York to appear in a play by Viennese dramatist Arthur Schnitzler, *Call of Life* (1925); this time, the critics believed that the role of a young woman who poisons her father and runs away with her lover was an unsuitable vehicle for Le Gallienne. She was beginning to experience the difficulty that every prominent actor (and every playwright) undergoes: excessive praise followed by damnation that is not always justified but is dependent on the mood of an audience and the atmosphere of the times. Le Gallienne began to think about starting her own theater, where she could pick the scripts she preferred, rehearse them in the time she required, and present them to an audience at an affordable price. Before she could realize her dream, however, she had to find the financial backing necessary for such a project.

To her great good fortune, she was offered the role of Hilda Wangel in Henrik Ibsen's *The Master Builder* (1892) in 1925, which was a busy year for her. It opened at the Maxine Elliott Theatre in New York for an announced run of four matinees, but it was such a resounding success that the engagement was extended. The critics once more sang her praises, because the role seemed tailor-made for her. It is probably true that Le Gallienne achieved her best effects playing women of strong character; she was never at home in the lighter pieces that were so popular in the commercial theater. The success that Le Gallienne enjoyed in playing Hilda Wangel, who defies convention, challenges authority, and would even storm the ramparts of Heaven, made her realize that she had to make her own place in the theater.

Because she was again the darling of the critics, Le Gallienne was able to raise money for her project, and such patrons of the arts as banker Otto Kahn, who almost single-handedly rescued the Metropolitan Opera in its early days, gave her his enthusiastic support, both verbal and financial. Le Gallienne took a lease on a building in the lower part of Manhattan, on 14th Street, and she called it the Civic Repertory Theatre. She knew that there were many good young actors who would be willing to work with her in classical plays because there were so few opportunities to do so on Broadway; she also knew that there were dedicated people who cared more for art than for money. If they could make a living from their work, they had no need for riches. Fired with such idealism, she was able to attract a good company and to present plays unfamiliar to the public which would later prove to be theatrical landmarks: The dramas of Ibsen and, especially, Russia's Anton Chekhov would form the basis of her repertory.

On October 25, 1926, the newly refurbished theater, which seated eleven hundred and which offered tickets for a top price of $1.50 (comparable Broadway tickets at that time cost at least five times as much), opened with Jacinto Benavente y Martínez's *Saturday Night* (*La noche del sábado*, 1903), chosen because it needed a large cast that Le Gallienne wished to introduce to her audience. It was received with hostility: England's favorite actor-playwright, Noël Coward, announced that "Eva was terrible, the production awful, and the play lousy." Fortunately for Le Gallienne, however, the repertory system which made it possible to produce several plays in one season and alternate them in the course of a week, saved her. The next evening, Chekhov's *The Three Sisters* expunged the previous night's disaster: Le Gallienne was praised for her acting, for her directing, and for her determination to create an ensemble company instead of a collection of stars. Soon, William Shakespeare's *Twelfth Night* and Carlo Goldoni's *La locandiera* (*The Mistress of the Inn*, 1753) were added to the list. Although all the productions were artistic and critical successes, they did not find favor with audiences; the playhouse was operating only at 60 percent of its capacity. Gregorio Martinez Sierra's *The Cradle Song* (1921), however, turned the tide: It was a genuine triumph, and all fifty-six performances sold out. Le Gallienne was urged to take the play uptown to Broadway, where she could make more money, but she refused, noting that by raising the price of the tickets she would be defeating the purpose of her "mission." She would not compromise.

By the end of her first season, Le Gallienne had won enough acclaim to be convinced that she could make a success of the enterprise, even though she had barely broken even at the box office. The *Nation* magazine chose her for its Roll of Honor, along with Eugene O'Neill and novelist Ernest Hemingway, among others. She received an honorary degree, the first of many, from Tufts University in Massachusetts and was awarded a gold medal by the Society of Arts and Sciences for her contributions to the theater. The second season at the Civic was less impressive: Only Henrik Ibsen's *Hedda Gabler*, with Le Gallienne in the title role, was well received. The next two seasons, however, were profitable as well as artistically satisfying, with such plays as Chekhov's *The Cherry Orchard* and *The Sea Gull*, Molière's *The Would-Be Gentleman*, James Barrie's *Peter Pan*, and Alexandre Dumas' *Camille*, with Le Gallienne in the lead. *Camille* was the greatest box-office success in the Civic's short history. In 1931, Le Gallienne decided to close her theater for one year, to rest and map out plans for the future, which looked grim because the stock market had crashed, play attendance was falling everywhere, and even bankers with seemingly limitless funds could no longer subsidize the arts.

In June of 1931, while she was in the basement of her home in Connecticut trying to light the hot-water heater, the heater exploded, engulfing Le Galli-

enne in fire. Her entire body was burned, and for a week it was believed that she would not live. Part of her face and both of her hands were severely burned. Yet within a year, despite great pain and innumerable operations, Le Gallienne was back. She reopened the Civic in 1932, repeating some of the productions she had presented before and adding an adaptation that she and actress Florida Friebus had made of Lewis Carroll's *Alice's Adventures in Wonderland* (1865). The play, which was extremely successful, was moved uptown to Broadway.

Growing financial pressures forced Le Gallienne to lease out her theater and take her company on the road with some of the plays that had done well. By 1936, it was clear that the Civic could not survive. Le Gallienne disbanded the company, allowing its members to go their separate ways and find work wherever they could. In the ensuing years, she appeared on Broadway sporadically but spent most of her time in the hinterlands playing in the classics. Gradually, she fell out of favor with the public, which was becoming more interested in American playwrights such as Arthur Miller and Tennessee Williams. For a brief time in 1946, Le

Gallienne, director Margaret Webster, and producer Cheryl Crawford banded together to form the American Repertory Theatre, presenting plays by Shaw, Ibsen, Chekhov, and Shakespeare, playing in New York and on the road. Financial problems doomed their efforts. Yet Le Gallienne kept touring, convinced of the rightness of her cause. In 1975, a new company headed by Ellis Rabb and Rosemary Harris invited Le Gallienne to appear in a revival of a 1927 comedy, *The Royal Family*, by Edna Ferber and George Kaufman. Both Le Gallienne and the production were successful. A new generation discovered Le Gallienne and listened to what she said about the theater. In 1986, she was awarded the National Medal of the Arts by President Ronald Reagan in recognition of her service to the drama. Gradually, her strength began to ebb, and she died in her ninety-second year.

Summary

When Eva Le Gallienne first made her mark on the American stage, audiences were not prepared for her concept of theater. She believed in producing plays that had stood the test of time and in holding down ticket prices so that nonaffluent audiences would not be driven away. To her, the theater was a necessity; no one should be kept from it because of cost. She believed in a repertory system that would keep actors fresh in their roles because they would not be performing the same piece night after night. She believed that actors should have a permanent place in which to work, a theater that belonged to them, such as existed in Paris, Berlin, and Moscow. She believed that a theater should be supported by the government, just as public schools and libraries were supported. Above all, she believed in improving the taste of the audience, not because of snobbery, but because people deserved the best.

Although her Civic Theatre failed, Le Gallienne's dream did not. In subsequent years, professional groups have formed throughout the United States. Actors are engaged on a more permanent basis, the classics as well as new plays are produced, local audiences are loyal in their attendance, and the best companies are now supported not only by ticket sales but also by local, state, and even federal monies.

Bibliography

Brown, John Mason. *Upstage*. New York: Norton, 1930. The drama critic of the *New York Post* discusses the structure and contributions of the Civic Repertory Theatre and analyzes the character of its founder. He mentions Le Gallienne's strength in the face of adversity and her enjoyment in doing battle for her principles.

Le Gallienne, Eva. *At Thirty-three*. New York: Longman, and London: Bodley Head, 1934. This is Le Gallienne's own account of her early years and the beginning of her work to establish the Civic Repertory Theatre. The photographs are particularly valuable.

———. *With a Quiet Heart*. New York: Viking Press, 1953. This book continues the story of the Civic, detailing Le Gallienne's attempts to keep it open. It also deals with her later venture, the American Repertory Theatre, and its problems. Excellent photographs.

Middleton, George. *These Things Are Mine*. New York: Macmillan, 1947. An account of the Civic by a playwright who studied acting with Le Gallienne. He also discusses her detailed study of Eleanora Duse's acting technique.

Schanke, Robert A. *Eva Le Gallienne: A Bio-Bibliography*. New York: Greenwood Press, 1989. This comprehensive annotated bibliography of the actress covers her articles, reviews by critics, and records of her performances. A photograph of Le Gallienne as Hedda Gabler is included. An invaluable reference work.

———. "Images of Eva Le Gallienne: Reflections of Androgyny." *Theatre Survey* 34, no. 2 (November, 1993). Schanke examines the manner in which Le Gallienne was photographed in order to disguise her lesbianism. Touches on the scandal she underwent and the problems she endured as a result of her sexual identity and her treatment by the press.

———. *Shattered Applause: The Lives of Eva Le Gallienne*. Carbondale: Southern Illinois University Press, 1992. This exhaustive biography of the actress discusses both her career and her troubled personal life. The author based his book on many interviews he had with Le Gallienne. Many excellent photographs, a complete record of the actress' performances, and a short bibliography are included.

Sheehy, Helen. "Missing Le Gallienne." *American Theatre* 14, no. 1 (January, 1997). Profile of Le Gallienne and her unusual and interesting life.

Mildred C. Kuner

L. S. B. LEAKEY

Born: August 7, 1903; Kabete, Kenya
Died: October 1, 1972; London, England
Area of Achievement: Paleoanthropology
Contribution: Leakey's lifelong examinations of the fossil remains near Lake Victoria and in the Olduvai Gorge in East Africa have provided clues as to the origin of the human species among prehistoric primates. This work, as well as his later support of the study of animal behavior in the wild, has significantly advanced understanding of both how evolution occurred and how prehistoric humans managed to survive and eventually to prevail.

Early Life

Louis Seymour Bazett Leakey was born on August 7, 1903, in Kabete, Kenya, then a tiny Anglican missionary station in the East African Protectorate established by the British in 1894. His mother, Mary Bazett, was the daughter of a colonel in the Indian army, and his father, Harry Leakey, was an Anglican priest who had been born in France. Drawn to missionary work in Africa by inclination, training, and experience, the Leakeys set out, at the turn of the century, to Christianize the Kikuyu, a group that constituted the predominant tribe in the area where their mission station was located. Young Leakey began life there as something of a celebrity, for he was the first white child the Kikuyu had ever seen. The boy learned the Kikuyu language before he learned English, and until his family returned to England in 1910, his only playmates had been his sisters and Kikuyu boys. Leakey spent his boyhood hunting, trapping, exploring the countryside, and absorbing information about the flora and fauna of East Africa; indeed, Leakey always considered himself an African rather than an Englishman.

The boy's education was perforce not what it might have been had the family lived in England. A governess, Miss Broome, tended to the basic education of the Leakey children, and she provided them with a solid grounding in the subjects, particularly mathematics, that were to prove most useful to Leakey in his career. An aunt in England sent young Leakey a book on the Stone Age in the British Isles, and it was this gift which kindled his lifelong passion for prehistory. He received his formal education in England, first at Weymouth College in Dorset and later at Cambridge University. Neither experience was especially gratifying to Leakey. At Weymouth College, he found himself alienated from the English boys, who seemed to him to be immature and incomprehensibly different from the Kikuyu youths with whom he had spent his formative years. Accordingly, he was never really integrated into the English public school system and later seemed to take a certain pride in managing to remain uncorrupted by that system. In any case, Leakey found Cambridge more congenial than Weymouth, and even though he was considered peculiar by some, he made a reasonable adjustment to university life.

While he was playing rugby in October, 1923, Leakey was kicked twice in the head in the course of a match. The resulting headaches and loss of memory were so severe that he had to leave Cambridge for a year. During that time he spent several months looking for the remains of dinosaurs in East Africa. In January, 1925, he returned to Cambridge to finish his education. After further difficulties, in part caused by his head injury, he won a first in modern languages, in French and Kikuyu. He then went on to win another first, a noteworthy distinction, in the second part of the tripos, in anthropology and archaeology. While some later cast doubt on the languages first—asserting that he had examined himself in Kikuyu, which in any event his critics did not consider a modern language—no one could gainsay his first in anthropology and archaeology. It was just as well, for it was in those disciplines that Leakey was to make his most remarkable contribution.

Life's Work

To a great extent, Leakey's career was shaped by the fact that he was not the scion of a wealthy English family. Sons of missionaries do not ordinarily have very much money, and he was no exception. Indeed, if most of his energy was expended on advancing the frontiers of paleoanthropology, then whatever energy he had left was devoted to raising the money to finance his field expeditions. In order to secure funding for his research in Africa during the decades after he left Cambridge, Leakey won fellowships and grants, wrote essays and books that produced modest royalties, gave lectures for minuscule fees, and even bartered African curios for such necessities as clothing. He also proved to be an excellent salesman for his beloved discipline, unfailingly persuading private benefactors, foundations, and such organizations as the National Geographic Society that his research was worthwhile and would deepen and broaden man's understanding of the human prehistoric past. As a result of drive, skill, and luck in finding and displaying to greatest effect the artifacts he found in East Africa, Leakey managed to keep himself in the field.

After leaving Cambridge, Leakey soon began to concentrate on the two fossil sites that would make his international reputation. One was at Lake Victoria, where his discoveries of the fossil remains of various apes—at the time not thought to be of much importance—have subsequently been hailed as a vastly underrated achievement. The other, and more famous, site was at Olduvai Gorge in what is now Tanzania. It was at Olduvai that Leakey spent most of his time, and it was also there that he and his team discovered the fossilized remains of hominids that brought him worldwide renown.

The road to fame was not, however, a smooth one. Before he achieved stature as an anthropologist, Leakey suffered from two scandals that were to plague him through much of his career. One was personal but proved to have far-reaching professional overtones. The other was entirely professional and could well have destroyed the career of anyone less gifted and resilient than Leakey. The personal scandal involved the well-publicized divorce of Leakey from his first wife, Frida—which deeply disturbed his family and shocked English colonial society in East Africa—and Leakey's public affair with a young student, Mary Nicol, whom he had met in 1933. After the divorce, the two were married and formed the most famous paleoanthropological team in history, a team whose work continues under the direction of their son Richard. In contrast, the professional scandal stemmed from Leakey's tendency to let his enthusiasm overcome his caution, causing him to claim too much without thoroughly analyzing the evidence and carefully building a case to support his claims. Specifically, when Leakey discovered two hominid fossils, one consisting of pieces of a skull exhibiting a smooth forehead and the other the infamous "Kanam jaw," he leapt to the conclusion, which he confidently asserted to the international scientific community, that he had discovered a representative of the true line from which modern man descended. His assertion was soon demolished by geologist Percy Boswell, who had earlier proved that Leakey's estimate of the age of a fossil was absurdly exaggerat-

ed. In an article in the prestigious journal *Nature*, Boswell refuted Leakey's claim to have discovered man's oldest ancestor. Although Leakey was wounded by the critique and well aware of the damage it had done to his credibility, his stubbornness was such that even though he could not defend his claim for the "Kanam jaw," he never relinquished his claim that the prehistoric source of *Homo sapiens* would be found in one of his fossil sites.

In time, Leakey decided to concentrate his attention on Olduvai Gorge rather than the Lake Victoria site. What attracted the Leakeys to Olduvai was the great abundance there of very primitive stone tools. They understandably reasoned that very basic stone tools located in geological formations of great age must have been made by very primitive humans or human ancestors. In consequence, they spent more than thirty years, beginning in the mid-1930's, collecting tools and searching methodically for the remains of those creatures who had made and used the tools. During that time, they suffered great privations, for that area of East Africa was very remote, and their ability to work depended entirely on the amount of supplies they could take with them to the site. Accompanying the privation, which neither Louis nor Mary seemed to mind, was the frustration, year after year, of finding virtually everything at Olduvai except the fossils for which they were searching. They found tools in abundance, and they also found notable deposits of the fossils of extinct animals, many of which were unknown before the Leakeys unearthed their remains, but the human ancestor for which Leakey sought eluded them.

They did, however, become thoroughly familiar with the geology of the Olduvai area, and Leakey continued to attract scientific attention and financial support by publicizing his discoveries, which were by no means inconsequential. World War II proved to be no more than an inconvenience to Leakey's work, for while he was limited in the extent of his researches, he played an important role in the British war effort in the African interior by working for the African Intelligence Department, where he assisted the British government in curtailing German influence and activity in East Africa. Because of his African background and connections, he was able to make a contribution to the war effort that few could have made. Similarly, when the Mau Mau emergency erupted in Kenya in the early 1950's, Leakey proved to be an invaluable intermediary between the leadership of the movement among the Kikuyu and British government authorities. While it is doubtful that officialdom appreciated Leakey's part in ending the emergency—he tended to favor the formation of an independent Kenya under the leadership of Jomo Kenyatta, at whose trial he acted as interpreter—Leakey proved to be invaluable in ending the crisis, despite the fact that members of Leakey's family were among those Europeans killed by Mau Mau terrorists.

At the end of World War II, Leakey, who had done voluntary work for the National Museum at Nairobi since the beginning of that conflict, became the museum's director at a modest salary. The salary was small, but it was nevertheless important, for it ensured that the Leakeys would be able to finance annual field expeditions. Throughout the 1940's and into the 1950's, Leakey and his wife returned to Olduvai in search of the elusive evidence of a hominid toolmaker which could explain the presence of the primitive tools at Olduvai and shed light on the evolutionary process that has produced modern *Homo sapiens*. In 1959, the long search finally came to a triumphant end, bringing the Leakeys international recognition for their work.

Toward the end of the 1959 expedition to Olduvai, when Leakey was in his tent, ill with the malaria that periodically plagued him, Mary went into the field alone. While there, she discovered what had eluded them for nearly three decades, the skull of what appeared to be an Olduvai toolmaker. One account of Leakey's response when Mary told him of her find is that he leapt out of bed despite his fever, overcome by the magnitude of the long-sought discovery. Another account has it that he was disappointed to see that the skull was a robust *Australopithecene* and not a *Homo*, which would have vindicated his oft-repeated assertions that the evolutionary ancestor of man had lived in East Africa more than one million years ago. Regardless of which account is true, there can be no disputing that the find made Leakey's reputation and also made him something of a celebrity. He dubbed the skull *Zinjanthropus boisei*, the "boisei" in honor of Charles Boise, who had contributed funding at a crucial juncture in Leakey's career, and soon came to refer to the skull privately as "Dear Boy," while "Nutcracker Man" was a more common appellation because of the very large molars of the skull. Although it clearly is not a direct ancestor of mod-

ern man, but rather a dead end in the primate evolutionary process, "Zinj" (which means East Africa in Arabic), as it came to be called, remains the best example of its type ever discovered. First displayed at the Fourth Pan African Conference on Prehistory held at what was then Leopoldville, it proved a sensation, and it ensured Leakey's stature as a premier paleoanthropologist.

"Zinj" was a first in many ways. It was, for example, not only the first more or less complete skull of its kind but also the first to be accurately dated by the now-standard potassium-argon dating process. Tests performed using that technique developed by Italian scientists indicated that "Zinj" was approximately 1.8 million years old, far older than had been estimated using less reliable scientific methods. An entirely new era had begun for physical anthropology and the study of prehistory.

Despite his age and the infirmities which plagued him toward the end of his career, Leakey remained active both in the field and on the lecture circuit. The discovery of "Zinj" in 1959 was followed by what was in some ways an even more significant find in 1962. Then, Leakey announced to the world in his inimitable fashion the discovery of what he claimed were true *Homo* fossils, and very ancient ancestors of modern man indeed, that were dated at 1.75 million years, fully three times what was then estimated as the age of *Homo*. These creatures came to be called *Homo habilis*, or "handy man," at the suggestion of Raymond Dart, who had first brought to light the Australopithecenes in South Africa. There were four such partial skulls, named Johnny's Child, Cindy, George, and Twiggy, and although their condition was fragmentary, that did not stop Leakey from insisting, primarily on the grounds that their brain capacity was estimated at 642 centimeters, that they were *Homo* and not merely hominid. Leakey's insistence that the fossils were those of true ancestors of man provoked controversy that remains largely unresolved; in any case, the discovery served to confirm Leakey's place in modern paleoanthropology.

After the discoveries of *Zinjanthropus boisei* (subsequently renamed *Australopithecus boisei*) and *Homo habilis*, Leakey, who was by then in ill health, turned his attention to the study of living creatures. Too ill to engage in field observation of primates, he encouraged and supported work by others, and the results have been nearly as important as the work he did earlier in his career on prehistory. Leakey supported and encouraged the work of Dr. Cynthia Booth, who with Leakey founded the Tigoni Primate Research Center to study monkeys. At approximately the same time, Leakey hired a young woman, Jane Goodall, as his secretary at the museum, and she went on, through his support, to become an international authority on the behavior of chimpanzees in the wild. Toward the end of his life, Leakey also encouraged Dian Fossey in her arduous study of mountain gorillas in their natural habitat at some twelve thousand feet of elevation. It was also toward the end of his career that Leakey's earlier work at Lake Victoria on prehistoric monkeys came to be recognized by scientists as of equal importance to his discoveries of "Zinj" and *Homo habilis*, for those Miocene apes provided as much information about the evolution of modern apes as the fossil discoveries of hominids revealed about human origins.

Leakey's physically demanding life caught up with him in London on October 1, 1972. He had traveled there from Nairobi, en route to the United States for one of his perennial lectures, when he found himself so tired that he could not meet a commitment to speak on the British Broadcasting Corporation airwaves. While dressing on the morning of Sunday, October 1, 1972, Leakey suffered a heart attack. He died within hours. His body was returned to Kenya for interment, and he was buried beside his parents at Limuru.

Summary

L. S. B. Leakey was not a practitioner of one of the more traditional sciences such as physics, biology, or chemistry; thus, it is more difficult to assess the significance of his contribution to the advancement of knowledge. Much of what he discovered, particularly the hominid fossils unearthed at Olduvai Gorge, for which he made extravagant claims, cannot be compared reasonably or accurately to discoveries that lend themselves to more precise scientific definition. Still, Leakey's long career as a field paleoanthropologist has undoubtedly produced the answers to many questions thought unanswerable when he began his work. Knowledge of both prehistoric man and animals, as well as many living creatures, has been dramatically expanded through his efforts. A volatile individual whose genius lay as much in his power to inspire others as it did in his ability to perform outstanding scientific feats, Leakey both advanced anthropology as a discipline and brought it to the public attention in a way that had never been done before. He was an almost perfect blend of entrepreneur and serious scientist.

Bibliography

Cole, Sonia Mary. *Leakey's Luck: The Life of Louis Seymour Bazett Leakey.* London: Collins, and New York: Harcourt Brace, 1975. This is the only full-scale biography of Leakey. Written by a friend and colleague at the request of Mary Leakey, it is scarcely the panegyric that might be expected from someone so close to the subject. Forthright, well written, frequently witty, and quite clear about Leakey's limitations as well as his virtues, this work stands as a model for biographies. A tendency on the part of the author to assume more detailed knowledge of paleoanthropology than is likely to be encountered in the average reader is counterbalanced by an accessible portrait of Leakey as a thoroughly human, understandable character.

Johanson, Donald C., and Maitland A. Edey. *Lucy: The Beginnings of Humankind.* London: Granada, and New York: Simon and Schuster, 1981.

While focusing on Johanson's discovery of the "Lucy" fossilized skeleton remains and its implications for the course of human evolution, this book is valuable for the context it offers for the earlier work of Leakey. Leakey's achievements are duly recorded, and a professional analysis is offered. Gives an admirable summary of the work of the Leakeys.

Leakey, Louis S. B. *White African*. London: Hodder and Stoughton, 1937; Cambridge, Mass.: Schenkman, 1966. An autobiographical account of the first thirty years of Leakey's life. Despite its obvious and expected inclination to explain and vindicate the actions of the author, it is well worth reading for the wealth of information it provides about colonial and missionary life in East Africa, as well as for what it reveals about the author's perceptions of himself during the formative years of his life.

————. *By the Evidence*. New York: Harcourt Brace, 1974. The second installment of Leakey's autobiography, covering the period from 1932 to 1952. Published posthumously, this volume does not include Leakey's views on the discoveries at Olduvai for obvious reasons of chronology. It does, however, have much information about his activities during World War II and provides an excellent base for understanding the importance of the unique position he held in East Africa.

Ronald L. Pollitt

LEE KUAN YEW

Born: September 16, 1923; Singapore
Areas of Achievement: Government and politics
Contribution: Lee became one of the longest-rul-
ing, freely elected prime ministers in the world.
His popularity came from his ability to rule fairly, to unite a multiracial society, and to make
Singapore, which is only 224 square miles in
area with 2.6 million people, into the second
busiest port in the world with the third largest oil
refinery and a standard of living second only to
that of Japan in all of Asia.

Early Life

Lee, whose given name, Kuan Yew, means "light
that shines," was born in the British colony of Singapore on September 16, 1923. His parents saw to it
that he would have the best education that the British could provide. Lee excelled in school, but he had
to postpone his admission to an English university
because war broke out in Europe. He won a scholarship to Raffles College in Singapore, where he studied English literature, mathematics, and economics.
He was determined to write and speak English well.
To accomplish the latter, he joined the debating
team and honed his skills as a public speaker.

Lee's education was interrupted by the Japanese
conquest and occupation of Singapore in 1942. By
age twenty, he had learned enough Japanese to
work in the Japanese news agency Domei. He experienced Japanese cruelty and atrocities and saw
the humiliation of the British colonial masters by
the new conquerors. After Japan's defeat, Lee left
Singapore for the University of Cambridge in
1946. There he distinguished himself as an honor
student. He also found time to discuss independence with other Malayan students and helped
formed the Malayan Student Forum, several of
whose members became prominent political leaders in both Malaysia and Singapore. Lee was graduated from Cambridge with high distinction in law,
and he returned to Singapore in 1950. In the same
year he married Kwa Geok Choo, who was also a
recipient of a distinguished law degree from Cambridge. Besides running the successful law firm of
Lee and Lee, the couple produced three children—
two boys and a girl.

Life's Work

Lee entered politics when he helped form the People's Action Party (PAP) and became its first sec-

retary general in 1954. Lee's goal was independence from Great Britain, which afforded Malaya
complete independence in 1957 but agreed to provide Singapore with only internal self-government
in 1959. This meant that Singapore would have a
fully elected legislature with domestic control,
while Great Britain was in charge of external affairs. Lee and PAP ran for elections and won forty-three of the fifty-one seats. As head of the majority party, PAP, Lee became the first Prime
Minister of Singapore.

Lee knew that complete independence for Singapore could only come about by merging with
Malaya. He also knew that Malaya, like Singapore,
was made up of three dominant races of Malay,
Chinese, and Indians, with the Malays having a
slight majority. The Malays would never accept
Singapore, which has a majority of Chinese who
could tip the delicate racial balance against them.
This dilemma was solved in 1961 when Tunku Abdul Rahman, the first Prime Minister of Malaya,
proposed a new Federation of Malaysia that would
include Malaya, Singapore, Sabah, Sarawak, and
Brunei. This formula was favorable for Malaya because Malays would form a majority race. Lee was
satisfied simply to have a Singapore independent
from the British and to be able to play a larger political role in a broader political stage. The British
agreed, because they were ready to relinquish their
empire east of Suez.

Thus, on Lee's fortieth birthday, September 16,
1963, the Federation of Malaysia was formed.
(Brunei opted not to join.) Lee aggressively challenged the other political parties with the slogan a
"Malaysian Malaysia," implying that the old racial politics, which favored the Malays, was "un-
Malaysian." This challenge aroused ethnic, religious, and racial confrontations; compounding
such divisive democratic electioneering was the
military threat from Sukarno of Indonesia, who
saw the federation as a British trick to deprive Indonesia of its rights to Sabah and Sarawak, which
share common boundaries with Indonesia on the
big island of Borneo.

In order to avoid racial turmoil in Malaysia and
destabilize the area of Sukarno's expansionist policy, Lee accepted Tunku Abdul Rahman's suggestion that Singapore leave the federation on August
9, 1965. Cast adrift, the new independent Republic
of Singapore was like a ship with no port. Sin-

gapore has no natural resources—even its drinking water has to be piped in from Malaya. Yet Singapore had well-trained, highly motivated, and industrious citizens. With such human assets, Lee embarked on a course inspired by countries such as Israel and Switzerland. The former is a nation of tough and resourceful immigrants surrounded by enemies, and the latter is a well-established multi-ethnic society of excellent craftsmen and service industry workers. Lee resolved that Singapore would adopt the best from both. First, Lee believed that Singapore must have security and stability. Lee and his associates went on a mission to win friends from around the world. Friendships with Afro-Asian leaders were cultivated, and the members of the North Atlantic Treaty Organization (NATO) were made aware of Singapore's geographical importance.

The Vietnam War and the downfall of Sukarno proved favorable for Singapore. After all, the war was to check the spread of communism, and Lee was a staunch anticommunist. What was more important, to gain cooperation and respect from immediate neighbors, Lee had Singapore join the Association of Southeast Asian Nations (ASEAN) and worked closely with fellow members—Thailand, Malaysia, Indonesia, Brunei, and the Philippines. Diplomacy and alliances formed one leg of Singapore's security. The other was the development of a formidable military that was trained by Israel. This was necessary to bring to fruition Lee's military concept of "poison shrimp" strategy—that is, no other nation could swallow tiny Singapore without itself being destroyed.

With security and stability accomplished, Lee forged a domestic agenda that would make Singapore a global city, a nation that would tap into the postindustrial grid of prosperous Japan and the United States. Singapore recognizes four racial groups; the 1980 census showed that 76.9 percent of the population was Chinese, 14.6 percent was Malay, 6.4 percent was Indian, and 2.1 percent were "other." Four official languages are recognized: Mandarin, English, Malay and Tamil. Lee ensured that every student would be at least bilingual. English became the de facto first language and the language of administration and international commerce.

Education became the cornerstone for building an economically viable, internationally competitive Singapore. To this end, students are streamlined early, with the top 8 percent going to special preuniversity schools, the most famous of which is the National Junior College, which was inspired by Lee's personal investigation and readings about Eton in England and Philips Exeter and St. Paul's in the United States. Lee's eldest son was in the first graduating class of National Junior College, and from there he went on to Cambridge.

The elitist system of education provided Singapore with the requisites of "problem-solvers and creators" as well as the needed technicians and skilled workers in the electronic and light industries. To ensure that Singapore would offer good jobs and pride of citizenship, Lee embarked on an ambitious program of government subsidized housing and the establishment of industrial zones, of which Jurong Industrial Estate is the largest in Southeast Asia. Self-contained housing estates, with schools, and green parks near to industrial sites are enjoyed by 80 percent of the citizens.

With education, housing, and employment secured, Singapore prospered. Lee, however, became worried that the best-educated class was bearing the fewest offspring. He saw moral deterioration in the leisure class, which was also drifting away from the industrious, Confucian, and rugged society that he had envisioned. As a remedy to such problems, Lee experimented on social engineering. Schools must teach religion and ethics, the young must be imbued with respect for elders and law and order, and women, especially those with university degrees, must be encouraged to marry and produce children. To help graduates find compatible mates, the government established free computer matching and ran socials and outings, some of which won the sobriquet "love-boat." Lee's pro-marriage program was also backed by financial incentives of tax deductions and the ease of employing housemaids and servants from abroad—mostly from the Philippines. Much opposition to social engineering came from parents and teachers, who saw children being forced to compete in school and facing an anxiety-filled childhood of constant studying and private tutoring. Yet Lee persisted on his "nature and nurture" policies, and the economic success of Singapore and the constant victories in general elections by Lee and his PAP legitimized such policies to many.

Internationally, Lee worked with ASEAN to force Vietnam out of democratic Kampuchea. He also backed President Corazon Aquino of the Philippines whenever her legitimacy was challenged. He maintained close ties with Prime Minister Mo-

hammad Mahathir of Malaysia and President Suharto of Indonesia. He always had the respect of British prime ministers, and Margaret Thatcher was no exception. The constant travel and contact with foreign leaders made Lee very visible and accessible for consultations. Even Deng Xiaoping of China sought Lee's help on the establishment of free trade zones and inexpensive but stylish public housing.

Declining health prompted Lee to step down as prime minister in 1990. He assumed the role of senior minister of Singapore and continued to advise Prime Minister Goh Chok Tong, while his son, Lee Hsieng Loong, was named deputy prime minister and head of Singapore's central banking authority.

Summary

Lee Kuan Yew's life has been one of success in international and domestic politics and economics. His brand of nationalism, of building a Singaporean identity from such diverse racial and ethnic groups, has come about without any threat of political opposition. His achievements in making Singapore stable and prosperous are formidable and the envy of the Third World.

Such successes come with the price. Singapore is run in a relatively authoritarian way. Lee's opponents, whether the press, opposition party members, or dissidents from the church, can come under the surveillance of the special branch of the Criminal Investigation Department. Unfavorable newspapers and magazines have been censored, and critics, journalists, and social critics as a group have been made *personae non gratae*.

Lee has tried to groom a successor from the younger members of his cabinet. He even announced in an interview that he would step down, but he also said that he would run for election as President of Singapore. In any event, Lee's successors will work under his shadow for many years to come.

Bibliography

Drysdale, John. *Singapore: Struggle for Success.* Singapore: Times Books, 1984. This volume covers in detail the political history of Singapore from 1945 to 1965. Much of Lee's operative style and his concept of political leadership are shown from his recollections about this crucial period in Singapore's history.

Gardels, Nathan. "America is No Longer Asia's Model." *New Perspectives Quarterly* 13, no. 1 (Winter 1996). Interview with Yew detailing his views on China's status going forward to the year 2020.

George, T. J. S. *Lee Kuan Yew's Singapore.* London: Deutsch, 1973. A detailed study of Lee's politics and achievements. The author's analyses of Lee's methods reveal an expedient leader who exercised dictatorial means to make Singapore the prosperous global city that it is today. Too much speculation and hearsay mar this interesting book to make it a fair study of Lee.

Hon, Joan. *Relatively Speaking.* Singapore: Times Books, 1984. Although the author's father, Hon Sui Sin, is the major study of this book, it is an important contribution to the study of Lee because Hon Sui Sin was Lee's finance minister and personal friend. Provides a glimpse of the private life of the rather reclusive Lee.

Josey, Alex. *Lee Kuan Yew.* Rev. ed. Singapore: Times Books, 1989. Counters some of the unfavorable writings in George's work. This work is important because it contains most of the major speeches made by Lee. Since Josey had been a confidant and golfing partner of Lee, many personal details of the prime minister's life were included. Twenty-two photographs of Lee with world leaders and with his family appear in the book.

Minchin, James. *No Man Is an Island: A Study of Singapore's Lee Kuan Yew.* Sydney and Boston: Allen and Unwin, 1986. A balanced study of the man and his dreams. Singapore's success from the 1960's to the present is well covered. This is a good attempt to answer how one man and a tiny, prosperous island-state can play such a global role. One chapter covers Lee's efforts to groom a second generation of leaders to guide Singapore into the twenty-first century.

Tanzer, Andrew. "Asia Will Rise Again." *Forbes* 161, no. 6 (March 23, 1998). Interview with Yew in which he offers analysis of future problems in Japan and China and looks at East Asian economic reform.

Vasil, Raj K. *Governing Singapore.* Singapore: Eastern Universities Press, 1984. The political methods and the institutions of government as practiced in Singapore are detailed in this work. A rare recording of a series of conversations with Lee in 1969 provides an interesting look into his ways of thinking and running a government.

Peng-Khuan Chong

FERNAND LÉGER

Born: February 4, 1881; Argentan, France
Died: August 17, 1955; Gif-sur-Yvette, France
Area of Achievement: Art
Contribution: Léger was known primarily for his depictions of people as machinelike creatures. He was an avid admirer of things modern and strove to reconcile the significance of modern art with an image of the industrial machine society.

Early Life

Fernand Léger, son of a cattle breeder, was born in Argentan, Normandy, where he spent his earliest years. His father was an imposing figure, athletically built and resolute in his conviction that Fernand was to become an architect. Had it not been for his father's untimely death, Léger's life might have taken a different path. Fernand was sent to Caen at the age of sixteen to serve as an apprentice in an architect's office, where he learned to draw plans and blueprints. It was during these two years at Caen that Léger, somewhat impulsively, decided to become a painter. This decision was less than wholeheartedly supported by his mother and uncle, who believed that the profession lacked respectability.

When he arrived in Paris in 1900, Léger applied for admittance to the École des Beaux-Arts. Failing to pass the rigorous entrance examination, he was admitted instead to the École des Beaux-Arts Décoratifs and the Académie Julian, but he chose to attend classes as an unenrolled student in the Beaux-Arts studios of Leon Gérôme and Gabriel Ferrier. Because of his miserable living conditions, Léger fell ill in 1905—the same year that the Fauves were creating a stir with their use of strong pure color—and spent the winter recuperating in Corsica. His Corsican paintings were derivative of Impressionism, which by this time had ceased to be a progressive style.

It was with some difficulty that Léger freed himself from the pull of Impressionism, but he realized that the harmonious style of the Impressionists was at odds with the realities of his own time. Léger was influenced most by Paul Cézanne's style during his early years, and the great Cézanne retrospective of 1907 at the Salon d'Automne was a revelation for him. He credited Cézanne with understanding what had remained unresolved in the painting of the past. He saw Cézanne's art as providing a foundation for the adoption of a revolutionary new painting vocabulary, one which emphasized form and color.

Life's Work

After securing a studio in the Montparnasse district of Paris in 1908, Léger came into contact with the flourishing circle of avant-garde writers and artists who inhabited the cafés of prewar Paris. He developed a lifelong friendship with the poet Blaise Cendrars, with whom he was to collaborate on several projects throughout his career. He also met Henri Rousseau, whose paintings exhibited a hardness of form and simplicity of conception that he greatly admired.

Through his association with Robert Delaunay and the writers Guillaume Apollinaire and Max Jacob, Léger was introduced to the work of Pablo Picasso and Georges Braque, whose cubist experiments boldly rejected traditional perspective and the single viewpoint of the Renaissance. Influenced by Cézanne's new method of depicting volume and space by exploiting planes of color, rather than line or shade, their work was characterized by a dense clustering of spatial planes.

Léger's *Les Nus dans la forêt* (nudes in the forest) of 1909-1910 was the artist's first contribution to the development of modern art and assured for him a place in the Parisian avant-garde. This painting created a sensation when it was exhibited at the Salon des Indépendants in 1911 alongside works by Albert Gleizes, Jean Metzinger, Marie Laurencin, and Delaunay. It was because of this exhibit that the term "cubism" found its way into the popular media. The sheer force with which Léger's forms confront each other creates a clashing quality that sets it apart from cubism and Cézanne's late work and testifies to the individuality of his adaptation of cubist ideas.

In the 1913 essay "The Origins of Painting," Léger asserted that the most powerful tool available to painting was that of contrast. The inherent conflict between flatness and volume, curved and straight lines, realism and abstraction, and the contrast of color formed the basis of his formal experiments for the remainder of his life. The development of this idea can be seen as early as 1913 in his series of paintings entitled *Contrasts of Forms*. This series produced some of the first totally abstract paintings ever painted. The machinelike forms are depicted in a thoroughly modern context.

Like the Italian Futurists and many other artists and writers who began their careers just before the outbreak of World War I, Léger idolized all things modern and believed in the possibility of a glorious new world based on the power of the machine.

Serving as a stretcher bearer, Léger experienced the horrors of World War I at first hand; he was gassed at Verdun and cashiered from the army as an invalid. His years spent working alongside ordinary working-class men had a profound effect on both the direction of his art and his perception of his role as an artist in society: A sense of social responsibility and a desire to reach out to the ordinary citizen began to take an important place in Léger's work.

Another effect of the war on Léger was the almost revelatory experience of the inherent beauty in the forms of war machinery. He began to depict flat, rather than volumetric, shapes, and his color became simpler, pure, and bold. *Les Disques* (the disks) of 1918 and *Éléments mécaniques* (mechanical elements) of 1918-1923 demonstrate Léger's infatuation with the workings of machines, whose forms he borrowed and recombined to create dynamic images of the modern world.

The 1920's were a decade of intense and diverse artistic activity for Léger. Besides producing paintings and drawings, he designed sets and costumes for ballet and theater productions, became involved in experimental cinema, collaborated with architects, and taught painting at the Académie Moderne. *Le Grand Déjeuner* of 1921 is one of his major works from this period. It is one of many monumental compositions in which solemn, ponderous figures are the predominant image. The great figure compositions of this time derive from his admiration of the classic French tradition of Jean-Auguste-Dominique Ingres, Nicolas Poussin, and Jacques-Louis David, whose restraint and serenity are combined with a completely modern treatment of the grand figure style. Léger's work came closest to abstraction when designed for an architectural context. He believed that those paintings which were designed to function as part of an architectural unit had specific objectives and problems apart from those of easel paintings.

In 1924, Léger directed an experimental film entitled *Le Ballet mécanique*, in which close-ups of isolated objects celebrate the aesthetic beauty of ordinary things. Soon after directing this film, he produced a series of paintings that he called his "objects in space." Images of everyday manufac-

tured objects such as pipes, lamps, or keys were isolated and suspended in space. Unlike the Surrealists, who used quotidian objects in strange juxtapositions for symbolic purposes, Léger created ojects that were themselves the subjects of his paintings.

During the 1930's, Léger made three trips to the United States, where he exhibited at the Art Institute of Chicago and at the Museum of Modern Art in New York, where he also decorated an apartment for Nelson Rockefeller. He was impressed with the vivacity of American cities and called New York "the greatest spectacle on earth." A vocal antifascist, Léger fled Nazi-occupied Europe in 1940 and spent the next five years living and working in the United States. Several of his last great series of paintings were executed during this period of the 1940's, including *Les Plongeurs* (the divers), *Les Trois Musiciens* (the three musicians), and several paintings of bicycle and circus subjects—themes that interested him for the remainder of his career.

Upon his return to France after the war, Léger completed a series of paintings called *Les Constructeurs* (the builders), based on his impressions of the rebuilding of war-ravaged Europe. It is noteworthy that Léger concentrated on this optimistic theme in the face of the devastation of war.

At the age of seventy-three, Léger painted the final version of the monumental, nine-by-thirteenfoot, *La Grande Parade* (the great parade). This painting was the climax of ideas which had occupied the artist for the past fifteen years. His art was intended for a mass audience rather than for the artistic intelligentsia. Fernand Léger won the Grand Prize at the Third São Paulo Biennale in 1955, just before he died on August 17 of that year at Gif-sur-Yvette.

Summary

In an age when it was fashionable for artists to respond to their world with either nihilism or narcissism, Fernand Léger did neither. He eschewed both sentimentality and "good taste" in art: He preferred bold, forthright statements. His color and form create their own reality by asserting a physical presence through his forceful manipulation of pictorial elements.

Léger's open-minded attitude and diverse intellectual curiosity allowed him to be affected by most of the major art movements of his day without ever losing hold of his personal vision. With his sense of visual and intellectual freedom, Léger expanded much of the theoretical doctrine of twentieth century art and provided a link between the early pioneers of modern art and those of later generations.

Léger embraced the industrial components of twentieth century life with an unswerving faith that the machine would create a better world for mankind. His conception of art was a moral one, and he felt that collective society could derive a positive benefit from contact with the power of painted images. When, in his most mechanical phase, his painted figures take on the appearance of machines, it is his supreme compliment; this signifies that man is a perfectly tuned and ordered being, in complete harmony with his environment. When, in his late works, figures are depicted as robust peasant types, they signify his vision of the common man as modern hero—full of the vigor of life and in full control of his destiny.

Bibliography

De Francia, Peter. *Fernand Léger*. New Haven, Conn.: Yale University Press, 1983. De Francia's 275-page book explores the entire scope of Léger's artistic production, providing an indepth look at the artist's involvement with film and theater as well as painting. The importance of social and political factors to Léger's creative contributions is emphasized. The book features 162 illustrations, 63 in color.

Feaver, William. "Skyscrapers and Cocktail Shakers." *ARTnews* 97, no. 1 (January, 1998). Short discussion of Leger's work and its dependence on machines and other modern objects as subject matter.

Green, Christopher. *Léger and the Avant-garde*. New Haven, Conn.: Yale University Press, 1976. A 350-page exploration of Léger's work in the context of his relationship with the leading poets, thinkers, architects, musicians, and artists of his day. This book discusses the specific influences of the ideas of such important members of the avant-garde as Le Corbusier, Gino Severini, and Cendrars on Léger's development. The book features 2,013 illustrations, 8 of them in color.

Léger, Fernand. *Fernand Léger*. New York: Abbeville Press, 1982. Published as the exhibition catalog of the exhibit of Léger's work held at the Albright-Knox Gallery in 1982, this 160-page book contains three essays on specific aspects of Léger's career. A chronology of Léger's life with 120 illustrations (76 in color) of the exhibited works is also included.

Schmalenbach, Werner. *Fernand Léger*. New York: Abrams, 1976; London: Thames and Hudson, 1991. This 173-page monograph contains seventy-seven black-and-white illustrations; forty-eight color plates of Léger's most important paintings with a critical discussion of each work and its relationship to his artistic development; and a biographical outline. A large number of Léger's drawings also illustrate the text, which is clearly and concisely written.

Verdet, André. *Léger*. New York: Hamlyn, 1970. This is the most personal summary of Léger's life and achievements, written by an obvious champion of the man himself. This ninety-six-page book contains a biographical outline, sixty-six illustrations, forty-three in full color, a list of exhibitions and catalogs, and an extensive bibliography.

Vetrocq, Marcia E. "Leger's Popular Mechanics." *Art in America* 86, no. 6 (June, 1998). Discusses Leger's desire to merge human experience with the industrial ethic in keeping with the avant-garde art theory of the early twentieth century.

William V. Dunning

GEORGES LEMAÎTRE

Born: July 17, 1894; Charleroi, Belgium
Died: June 20, 1966; Louvain, Belgium
Areas of Achievement: Physics, mathematics, and astronomy
Contribution: Building on evidence and theories adduced by several physicists, mathematicians, and cosmologists whose work, like his own, focused upon the provenance and character of the universe, Lemaître, through brilliant synthesis, formulated what has become the generally accepted scientific explanation of the universe's origin, namely, the big bang theory.

Early Life

Little is known of Georges Abbé Lemaître's early life. He was born on July 17, 1894, in the commercial, mining, and industrial center of Charleroi, Belgium, where as a youth, he commenced studying civil engineering at the local technical university. Eruption of World War I ended his engineering studies, and from 1914 until 1918 he served as an artillery officer with the remnants of the Belgian Army holding the extreme left flank of the Allied armies on the Western Front. His experiences there led him in the war's aftermath to enter the Mechelen (Belgium) Seminary in preparation for a Catholic priesthood, his ordination following in 1923. In addition to learning his priestly vocation during his years as a seminarian, Lemaître, in 1920, procured a doctorate in mathematics and physics—fields of scientific inquiry immensely stimulated by the implications of Albert Einstein's theory of relativity and its relation to regnant Newtonian physics. Already having familiarized himself with Einstein's general theory of relativity while studying at Mechelen, Lemaître, among many other aspiring scientists, was particularly intrigued by Einstein's cosmology, that is, his suggestion that the totality of the universe is fixed in its dimensions, that it is not expanding, though indeed it is full of motion and is undergoing rapid evolution.

Further pursuing the cosmological implications of Einstein's work, Lemaître, encouraged by his superiors, spent 1923 and 1924 in England at the University of Cambridge's solar physics laboratory. There he worked under the aegis of Sir Arthur Stanley Eddington. Eddington had contributed significantly to an understanding of the internal composition of stars and to knowledge of their motion and evolution. Equally important for Lemaître's specific curiosities, Eddington also ranked as an early and foremost champion of Einstein's general theory of relativity. Maintaining his contacts with Eddington, Lemaître subsequently moved on, further to satisfy his astrophysical inquiries, to the United States from 1925 until early 1927.

This too proved an exceedingly fruitful experience, for he was able to work both at the Massachusetts Institute of Technology (MIT) and at the famed Harvard Observatory. Between MIT and Harvard, he became acquainted with two of the world's most prominent astronomers, Harlow Shapley and Edwin Powell Hubble, each of whom was engaged variously in unraveling the structure of the universe. Lemaître, toward the end of his American studies, met Hubble during a notable conference in Washington, D.C., at which he announced his discovery of cepheids (pulsating stars) in the Andromeda nebula. Thus, having enjoyed four years abroad in touch with the world's foremost cosmologists, astronomers, and physicists, Lemaître returned to a professorship in astrophysics at the University of Louvain (Belgium) and the formal launching of his own scientific career.

Life's Work

For scientists such as Lemaître who were obsessed with questions about the structure and origins of the universe, the 1920's was a propitious time, for both the available theories and instrumentation were undergoing significant advances. Hubble's discoveries, for example, owed much to the new one-hundred-inch telescope. Similarly, the appearance of Einstein's general theory of relativity in 1917 dramatically raised the level of cosmological inquiry by proposing a finite yet unbounded universe—a theory in turn suggesting lacunae in Newtonian physics and cosmology.

Yet Einstein's "static" model of the universe, as good theory should, not only sketched fresh lines of inquiry but also revealed discrepancies of its own. How, for example, could the definite "flight" of extragalactic nebulae—confirmed by astronomers' detection of the "red shift" characterizing their light signatures—be explained? Evidently these nebulae were rapidly moving away from our solar system and often from one another, in which case the universe apparently was expanding: infinitely perhaps. Confronted with such novel and mounting evidence, Newton's mechanics, with their presumed universal applicability, as well as Einstein's general theory, invaluable as they were, prompted development of other cosmological models or hypotheses. Thus, although his theory remained unnoticed for several years, Alexander Freedman, a brilliant Russian mathematician, in 1922 had modeled a relativistic universe, which, while expanding, was also curving back upon itself. Similarly, the Dutch astronomer and devotee of Einstein's general theory, Willem de Sitter, whose work directly engaged Lemaître's attention, tried to demonstrate in 1917 that Einstein's universe, while apparently static, was expanding—if certain calculations were ignored. Add to these theories those of Eddington and Shapley, among others, and the intense focus of astronomers, astrophysicists, mathematicians, and cosmologists becomes apparent. This spate of new hypotheses—Lemaître's included—was not surprising, for Einstein was shortly to acknowledge that his proposal of a static universe and of a cosmological constant (which kept it static) was his worst mistake. General relativity, in sum, failed to account adequately for the flight of extragalactic nebulae, for the red shift, or for complex aspects of magnetism as it operated through vast reaches of space.

It was in this fecund intellectual environment that Lemaître, between 1925 and 1927, began advancing his own hypothesis. In a note published in the *Journal of Mathematics and Physics* in 1925, he specifically rejected de Sitter's hypothesis and two years later published his report on a universe of constant mass and variable radius and the problem confronting this perspective in view of the radial speed of extragalactic nebulae. Essentially, the position he was assuming in his depiction of expanding space, intellectually, lay somewhere between that of Einstein and that of de Sitter. He was proposing a mathematically sustainable law that linked the speed evinced by the "flight" of extragalactic nebulae with their distance from the earth. In 1929, Hubble's discovery (known as Hubble's law) that the more distant galaxies were, the faster they were receding from the earth, furnished confirmation of Lemaître's concept of an expanding universe.

Conceptualization of an expanding universe provided Lemaître with a matrix for the formulation and advancement of the hypothesis for which he is most noted, namely, that the universe, and the behavior of matter within it, had been produced by the explosion (subsequently dubbed the big bang)

of what he called the "cosmic egg," or the "primitive atom." To accomplish his quantum conceptual shift from the cosmological macrocosm to the atomic microcosm meant that his inquiries were turned primarily from astronomy toward classical physics as well as to the latest developments in that burgeoning field.

From classical physics, Lemaître had to draw upon that part of the law of thermodynamics linking the decay of matter to increasing divisions of energy; drawing upon then recent discoveries in physics, he mathematically probed the characteristics and behavior of light, of cosmic and radioactive rays, as well as the immense releases of energy from disintegrating uranium. Boldly extrapolating both substantive and theoretical intelligence about known characteristics of the universe and those of the heaviest atoms, he proposed that, except in terms of scale, correlations existed between "exploding" or rapidly compacting and disintegrating atoms (or their side effects) and behavior evidenced by the universe and matter within it. To Lemaître, ultrapenetrating rays from space represented the preserved testimony, billions of years old, of the cosmos' primary activity. Like the earth's geological fossil record, these "fossil rays" were signatures of the age of radioactivity that preceded formation of the stars. That age itself resulted, according to Lemaître's calculations, from unimaginably immense concentrations of matter and energy—the world reduced to a single, if gigantic, particle, the "primitive atom"—which, like "observed" stars, exploded, giving birth to the universe.

Lemaître's hypothesis received its first full exposure in 1933 with his *Discussion sur l'évolution de l'univers* (discussion on the evolution of the universe) and *L'Hypothèse de l'atome primitif: Essai de cosmogonie* (1946; *The Primeval Atom: An Essay on Cosmogony*, 1950). Both works are succinct, pioneering presentations of immense and diverse learning ranging through philosophy, physics and astrophysics, astronomy, and mathematics, which left a modern, evidentially substantiable, big bang theory in tolerable congruence with Einsteinian physics. Lemaître's universe, a relativistic one, was finite yet simultaneously unbounded, there being no limits to the motion of matter—whether stars, galaxies, comets, or light—within its curved space.

By the time of Lemaître's death in Louvain, Belgium, on June 20, 1966, his hypothesis, while withstanding several competitors, inevitably had undergone modifications. Indeed, by 1948, the work of George Gamow and two colleagues reversed important aspects of Lemaître's hypothesis. Lemaître, nevertheless, had propounded a theory from which others profitably had taken their own points of departure.

Summary

Cognizant of the wide range of cosmologies propounded in the past, not only those of biblical origin but also those of philosophers and naturalists such as Immanuel Kant, Comte de Buffon, and Pierre-Simon Laplace. Georges Lemaître had a fine sense of the scientific context into which his own hypothesis fit. Like his contemporary cosmologists (astrophysicists, physicists, astronomers, mathematicians, and philosophers), he had inherited a three-dimensional universe, which, thanks to Einstein, had suddenly become four-dimensional. The addition of time, an autonomous and continuous factor, to the cosmological equation was not the sole new complexity to be grappled with. The four-dimensional universe, thanks to discoveries by the twentieth century's new breed of relativist physicists, was fleshed out with puzzling forms of mass and energy. New forms of attraction and repulsion had to be embodied in their calculations. Astronomers, as the red shift clearly indicated, had to reckon with galaxies billions of light years from the earth that were receding at fantastic speeds. Atoms themselves were found to be subdivided into subparticles of their own, each with its discrete or peculiar characteristics. The operation of gravitation had to be unraveled and recalculated. Classic speculations and Newtonian mathematical descriptions of the universe's structure were rapidly and profoundly altering.

Such were some of the baffling, yet immensely exciting, factors that encouraged, if they did not demand, fresh cosmological theorizing. This theorizing was readily forthcoming, though understandably wanting in some respects. Even Einstein was unable to sketch satisfactorily the lineaments of the cosmos. De Sitter's equations proved far less satisfactory, attaining accuracy only if one dealt with space that was empty—devoid of any matter whatsoever. Into this theoretical penumbra, Lemaître inserted his bold, rather elegant schema concerning the cataclysmic origins of the universe, which for years of intense scientific focus upon the cosmos served as a seminal influence upon others.

Bibliography

Einstein, Albert. *Relativity: The Special and General Theory.* Translated by Robert W. Lawson. New York: Holt, 1920; London: Methuen, 1960. Part 3, chapters 20 to 22, "Considerations on the Universe as a Whole," should dispel the notion that Einstein is unreadable, despite the complexities of other areas of the book. This portion of one of the classic works of science is clear and straightforward. It is superb for understanding the background against which Lemaître's hypothesis was developed. There are some notes as well as modest bibliographical references and a brief index.

Gamow, George. "Modern Cosmology." *Scientific American* 190 (March, 1954): 55-63. A superb summation, clearly written and authoritative, by the Russian-born American scientist whose theory supplanted that of Lemaître. Contains illustrations, photographs, and brief bibliographical suggestions.

Hubble, Edwin P. *The Realm of the Nebulae.* London: Oxford University Press, and New Haven, Conn.: Yale University Press, 1936. A delightful, authoritative exposition. It is an elegant description of the intellectual environment in which Lemaître developed his views by a figure who influenced him. Contains a bibliography and an index.

Munitz, Milton, ed. *Theories of the Universe: From Babylonian Myth to Modern Science.* New York: Free Press, 1965. A splendid collection of essays, easily grasped by intelligent laymen. The editor's introductory overview is excellent. Contains illustrations, a brief but good bibliography, and an extensive index.

"Obituary: Georges Lemaître." *Physics Today* 19 (September, 1966): 119. This brief obituary is actually quite revealing about the facts of Lemaître's life.

Sagan, Carl. *Cosmos.* New York: Ballantine, 1980; London: Macdonald, 1981. A best-seller which is a spinoff of the television series, by a distinguished and prolific scholar. There is no mention of Lemaître, though many other major cosmologists and their theories are mentioned. A delightful and instructive work, containing color photographs, graphs, illustrations, two appendices, fine suggested readings, and a very useful and extensive index.

Clifton K. Yearley

VLADIMIR ILICH LENIN
Vladimir Ilich Ulyanov

Born: April 22, 1870; Simbirsk, Russia
Died: January 21, 1924; Gorki, U.S.S.R.
Areas of Achievement: Government and politics
Contribution: Lenin adapted Marxist theory to the
politics of late imperial Russia, creating and
leading the Communist Party, which eventually
seized power in November, 1917. From 1918 until his death in 1924, he was the main architect of
the new socialist state that became the model for
world communism.

Early Life

Vladimir Ilich Ulyanov, better known by his revolutionary name Lenin, was born in the Volga city of
Simbirsk (now Ulyanovsk) on April 22, 1870. His
father was a regional school inspector, a government post that gave the family hereditary noble status. His mother, Maria Aleksandrovna Blank, was
from a family broadly classified as "upper bourgeois." Lenin was their third child and second son
and was followed by the birth of three more children, two girls and another boy. All but two survived to adulthood and became members of the
revolutionary movement.

Lenin's childhood was uneventful. His mother,
the heart of the family, looked after the children's
education, instilling in all a lifelong enjoyment of
learning. The household also enjoyed a certain
amount of individual freedom that allowed the
children to explore the limits of their provincial
world. This serene family life was shattered in
1886 with the sudden death of the father, followed
the next year by the arrest of the eldest son, Aleksandr, in the capital of St. Petersburg, where he
was attending the university. Aleksandr was associated with the terrorist organization The People's
Will, which plotted the assassination of Czar Alexander III. The young Ulyanov, refusing to show
any remorse, was hanged on May 20, 1887. The
family was subsequently ostracized. Although Lenin never admitted any direct impact of his brother's execution on his own radicalization, there is no
doubt that these two shocks played a determining
role in his future career. When Lenin was enrolled
at the University of Kazan to pursue a law degree,
he was soon expelled for associating with an illegal
student demonstration. He was singled out because
of the fate of his brother and used as an example

for the other students. For the next two years, he
lived with his family on their small country estate
on the Volga River, where he first read the works of
Karl Marx. By the early 1890's, he was a dedicated
Marxist revolutionary.

While he studied Marxism, Lenin also continued his private study of law. In 1891, the authorities allowed him to take the law examinations at
St. Petersburg University, where he passed with
high grades. By 1893, he was in St. Petersburg,
where he began propaganda work in local Marxist
circles. Within two years, he was one of the leaders of a small but significant socialist movement in
the capital.

Life's Work

The years 1893 to 1895 mark the foundation of Lenin's subsequent political career. In 1895, he went
abroad, ostensibly for health reasons but actually
to establish a link with the leaders of Russian socialism in exile. For the first time he met the
founders of Russian Marxism, including Georgy
Plekhanov, a veteran of the Russian Populist movement of the 1870's who virtually singlehandedly
introduced Marxism into Russian radicalism.

Upon his return to St. Petersburg late in 1895,
Lenin plunged again into propaganda work, only to
be arrested by the police. After a year in jail, he
was sentenced to three years' exile in Siberia. Because of family connections, he was able to choose
an area in southern Siberia that had a tolerable climate and a good reputation as an exile spot. The
following years were peaceful and productive. The
authorities allowed fellow conspirator and fiancée
Nadezhda Krupskaya to join him as his bride. He
also had access to a fine library where he completed his first major theoretical work, *Razvitiia kapi-
talizm v Rossii* (1899; the development of capitalism in Russia). In this book, which still remains his
most scholarly, Lenin demonstrated that the country was taking enormous strides toward economic
modernization. The peasantry, however, contrary to
the revolutionary thought of the day, was not aspiring to socialism but instead to the bourgeois goal
of private ownership of land.

In 1900, his term of exile completed, Lenin returned to St. Petersburg for a short time, then received permission to go abroad. Between 1900 and

1917, he and Krupskaya lived a lonely existence in European exile. It was during this time that Lenin developed the reputation and party structure that eventually brought him to power in 1917. By 1900, industrialization had given rise to many Marxist and other workers' groups in Russia. The need to coordinate these organizations led in 1903 to the founding of the Russian Social Democratic Workers' Party (RSDWP) at a meeting held in Brussels and attended by the main leadership of the Russian socialist movement in exile, including Plekhanov and Lenin.

In 1902, in anticipation of the upcoming congress, Lenin produced his most important work, a pamphlet entitled *Chto delat?* (1902; *What Is to Be Done?*, 1929). This represents the first clear expression of what later became known as "Leninism," a combination of Russian revolutionary thinking and Marxist economics and sociology. Lenin was concerned that many members in the newly formed RSDWP were more interested in struggling for petty economic reforms than outright revolution. He reminded them that there cannot be a revolutionary movement without revolutionary theory. Furthermore, he argued that the workers by themselves could not develop a revolutionary consciousness. Instead, as capitalism developed, the working class formed unions and bargained for economic gains such as higher wages and improved working conditions, thus losing sight of the revolution. Revolutionary consciousness, therefore, would have to be brought to the workers from outside by means of a tightly knit organization of revolutionaries. This party would have to be composed of a selected membership engaged in full-time revolutionary activities. Finally, the actions of the party would have to be secret and conspiratorial to avoid detection by the czarist police.

At the 1903 meeting, Lenin's ideas became the crux of the organizational dispute that split the party into "Bolsheviks" (Majorityites) and "Mensheviks" (Minorityites). Although Lenin lost the vote on the crucial issue of party membership, his faction did gain a majority on the editorial board of the party newspaper, *Iskra*—thus his claim to represent the majority. Because of his rhetoric and tactics, however, Lenin's popularity was in serious decline by the end of the congress. Recognizing this, he resigned from *Iskra*, not realizing at the time that he had formed the nucleus of an organization that would eventually rule Russia.

When he returned to the Russian capital after the overthrow of czarism in March, 1917, his first address to the crowd outlined the direction that he wanted the Party to take. He called for an end to Russia's participation in World War I, opposition to the provisional government established upon the abdication of the Romanovs, transfer of all power to the Soviets as the most representative new institution of the revolutionary state, nationalization and redistribution of land among the peasants, renaming the Bolsheviks as the Communist Party, and the creation of a new international to lead the world revolution. Thus, this speech, known as the April Theses, established the platform for the renamed Communist Party.

As Russia sank further into anarchy during 1917, the opportunity for the Communists came in October when they achieved a majority of seats in the Soviet. Lenin pushed for an armed uprising against the provisional government, and on the night of November 6-7 the world's first successful workers' revolution took place. Leadership of the country passed into the hands of an elected executive board, the Council of People's Commissars, with Lenin as chairman. The council undertook the task of implementing the Bolshevik program, negotiating peace with Germany, abolishing private land ownership while upholding the peasants' right to use the soil they tilled, and building the first socialist society. In the course of the following years, Lenin and his party defended their new state in a brutal civil war, during which Lenin and his party established the major institutions of the Soviet state, including the political police and the Red Army. Lenin also tightened control of the Communist Party over the society, forbade the existence of opposition political parties, and condemned factions within his own party.

These efforts eventually took a toll on his health. In early 1922, he suffered his first stroke. While he seemed to recover, he had a second, more debilitating stroke later in the year. His health continued to deteriorate through 1923, removing him from any further party activity, and he finally died on January 21, 1924.

Summary

Vladimir Ilich Lenin's last writings reveal an anguished man deeply troubled by the nature of the state structure he had done so much to create. In his earlier writings, Lenin described a workers' state in which the people elected councils that

ruled as a dictatorship, nationalized and centralized the economy, and controlled the population through police terror. Lenin succeeded so thoroughly that the Soviet brand of Marxism is called Marxism-Leninism.

Bibliography

Conquest, Robert. *V. I. Lenin.* New York: Viking Press, 1972. A well-written biography of Lenin aimed at the general reader that analyzes both his thought and his revolutionary career. Emphasis is primarily on the political side of his nature.

Fischer, Louis. *The Life of Lenin.* London: Weidenfeld and Nicolson, and New York: Harper, 1964. A thorough biography of Lenin written by a man who lived in Moscow in the early 1920's and heard Lenin speak on a number of occasions. Emphasis is on Lenin's personal and political struggles to establish the first socialist state.

Lenin, V. I. *What Is to Be Done?* Translated by J. Fineberg and G. Hanna. New York: International, and London: Lawrence, 1929. This 1902 pamphlet argues the necessity of a party of professional revolutionaries for seizing power and is the best overview of Lenin's thought about the nature of revolution in Russia. It remains basic to an understanding of Lenin's contributions to Marxist theory.

Payne, Robert. *The Life and Death of Lenin.* London: Allen, and New York: Simon and Schuster, 1964. Perhaps the most readable of the many biographies of Lenin, it is also the most superficial and sensational, including every story about Lenin without attempts to assess accuracy or impact. An exciting introduction for the casual reader.

Pipes, Richard, et al, eds. *The Unknown Lenin: From the Secret Archive.* New Haven, Conn.: Yale University Press, 1996; London: Yale University Press, 1999. Pipes uses newly available archive materials to create a picture of Lenin, the man unencumbered by myth and Soviet image control. Lenin is portrayed as a manipulative man who used fear and persecution to reach his goals.

Possony, Stefan T. *Lenin: The Compulsive Revolutionary.* Chicago: Regnery, 1964; London: Allen and Unwin, 1965. An important biography by a specialist in the field. It approaches Lenin as a man striving for personal power and using all means as well as people to reach that goal. It also argues that, when Lenin died, his revolu-

would serve as both legislators and executors of the nation's will. These "soviets" would be the instruments of a truly democratic government. The new nation had not evolved that way. Instead, party bureaucrats ruled the people from afar. This system was to harden under Lenin's eventual successor, Joseph Stalin. Lenin also became preoccupied with the problem of choosing a successor. His "testament," dictated in the winter of 1922-1923, revealed his anxiety about the succession but failed to solve this crucial problem. He also began to have second thoughts about the amount of power that Stalin had accumulated. Unfortunately, his health did not allow him to pursue these issues.

Lenin had committed his life to adapting Marxist philosophy to an agrarian Russia and to working for the proletarian revolution. In so doing, he introduced a fundamental change in Marxism by placing greater emphasis on politics than on economics as the means of change. Central to this was the creation of a highly organized, selective, and secretive political party composed of professional revolutionaries to lead the masses into the new egalitarian world that he foresaw. Once in power, this party

tionary dream was subverted by the dictatorship of Stalin.

Service, Robert. *A History of Twentieth-Century Russia*. London: Allen Lane, 1997; Cambridge, Mass.: Harvard University Press, 1998. Critics hail this volume as a lucid, masterful account of a turbulent period in Russia's history. Service makes use of the large volume of documentation that has become available since the late 1980s.

Ulam, Adam B. *The Bolsheviks: The Intellectual and Political History of the Triumph of Communism in Russia*. New York: Macmillan, and London: Secker and Warburg, 1965. A detailed account of Lenin and his times written by one of the foremost scholars of Soviet history. While it spans the revolutionary movement from the Decembrist Revolt of 1825 to Lenin's death in 1924, emphasis is on the period after 1890.

Wolfe, Bertram D. *Three Who Made a Revolution*. Rev. ed. New York: Dial Press, 1964. This highly readable study of the lives of Lenin, Leon Trotsky, and Stalin emphasizes the formative years of Russian Marxism. It has become a classic of its kind and is an excellent introduction to the subject.

Jack M. Lauber

CLAUDE LÉVI-STRAUSS

Born: November 28, 1908; Brussels, Belgium
Areas of Achievement: Anthropology and linguistics
Contribution: Lévi-Strauss, one of the founders of structural anthropology, used his discipline to achieve insights into Western civilization by studying non-Western societies. He challenged basic Western assumptions about politics, history, and culture and became one of the major figures in the intellectual history of the twentieth century.

Early Life

Claude Lévi-Strauss was born on November 28, 1908, in Brussels, Belgium, where his French parents lived, while his father, an artist, painted. When World War I began, his parents took him home to France, where he joined his grandfather, the Rabbi of Versailles. Little is known about Lévi-Strauss' youth, but his formal schooling obviously proved unsatisfactory. He studied law and philosophy at the University of Paris but found both fields sterile and intellectually confining, although he taught philosophy in the early 1930's.

Outside the formal educational structure, Lévi-Strauss had taken what he described as his three intellectual mistresses: geology, psychoanalysis, and Marxism. He found an underlying similarity in these seemingly disparate modes of thought. Each found surface reality to reflect a truer reality beneath. Each turned the surface chaos of experience into an abstract model that made the deeper reality understandable.

These intellectual interests came together around 1934, when Lévi-Strauss read American anthropologist Robert H. Lowie's *Primitive Society* (1920). It freed Lévi-Strauss from the claustrophobic atmosphere of the academic philosophy that he was teaching and thrust him into what seemed to him the clear air of anthropology. In 1934, he accepted a professorship in sociology at the University of São Paulo and in 1936 began to publish in anthropology.

David Pace, in *Claude Lévi-Strauss: The Bearer of Ashes* (1983), found a clear pattern in Lévi-Strauss' life. He was an outsider, never embracing the artistic or Jewish worlds of his parents, disparaging his education in law and philosophy, distancing himself from Marxism and psychoanalysis by turning them into abstract methodologies, and first finding his true calling in American anthropology practiced in Brazil.

Lévi-Strauss left São Paulo and returned to Paris in 1939. He fought in World War II until France surrendered and then fled Vichy France to teach at the New School for Social Research in New York. The rise of Fascism made the political categories of Western society seem meaningless to him. Unlike Jean-Paul Sartre and other major French intellectuals of his generation, Lévi-Strauss rejected any active political role.

When he returned to France after the war, he built on his anthropological work to make himself a central figure in Western intellectual life. He also continued his outsider's role. He had no social life or friends, he said, and spent half of his life in his laboratory and the other half in his office. His world was abstract: "There is nothing I dread more than a too-close relationship with my fellow men."

Life's Work

Lévi-Strauss published his first articles in anthropology in 1936. His first major book was *Les Structures élémentaires de la parenté* (1949; *The Elementary Structures of Kinship*, 1969), and it was followed by *Race et histoire* (1952; *Race and History*, 1958), *Tristes tropiques* (1955; English translation, 1964), and *Anthropologie structurale* (1963; *Structural Anthropology*, 1963). Recognition came quickly, both within the academic world and in the broader intellectual community.

The anthropological world was divided into two broad approaches. One interpretive school was influenced by Marcel Mauss, who searched for crosscultural patterns that would reveal universal truths about the human mind. In the other was Bronisław Malinowski, who studied the totality of a particular culture to determine the functional role of its parts. Lévi-Strauss was concerned with the former, which explored universal truths about the human mind as revealed in the structures of culture that reflected a collective unconscious. Humans are categorizing animals whose brains order the phenomena perceived by the senses. The brains of African Bushmen and Parisian intellectuals order reality in the same logical and systemic way, although the phenomena perceived would differ. The surface patterns of human cultures may appear chaotic, but underneath are common structures. For example, although the thousands of Native American myths seem endless in their variety, all humans confront such contradictions as life and death or male and female, and all minds confronting these contradictions operate similarly. It is in mythology that humans attempt to resolve contradictions that cannot be resolved by reason and logic. Myths reveal the collective unconscious of the human mind and can be scientifically analyzed, for Lévi-Strauss.

In studying cultures regarded as primitive, Lévi-Strauss broke sharply with Malinowski and the functionalists, who believed that each element of a culture had an understandable and rational function. Lévi-Strauss turned to linguistics for his anthropological insights. Just as speech is composed of arbitrary sign systems that are symbolic of a deeper language structure, so social customs reflected a deeper cultural pattern. The first necessity for a society is to bind itself together by rules, and these rules, kinship customs, for example, can be quite arbitrary and nonfunctional in an immediate sense. Their crucial role is to hold societies together in a system of rules that will appear so natural to those within that they will disappear from consciousness. Taboos against incest, for example, can take many arbitrary forms, but the underlying purpose everywhere is to require an exchange of people, binding the social group together.

From the 1960's into the 1980's Lévi-Strauss continued to write his anthropological works: *Le Totémisme aujourd'hui* (1962; *Totemism*, 1963), *La Pensée sauvage* (1962; *The Savage Mind*, 1966), *Mythologiques* (1964-1971; *Introduction to the Science of Mythology*, 1969-1981), *Paroles données* (1984; *Anthropology and Myth*, 1987), and others. His work won for him the highest honors in academia, and a survey of literature in the 1970's revealed that he was the most cited anthropologist in the world.

Yet most of these books are abstract and difficult, even for well-educated laypersons. Lévi-Strauss' impact on the general intellectual community came first with *Tristes tropiques*, a book of spiritual and philosophical meditation, and in his later attempts to reach out of his laboratory to the general public. He spoke to the crisis of twentieth century Western civilization, a crisis reflected in war, ecological disaster, and general malaise.

Lévi-Strauss had a deep sympathy for non-Western people. Anthropology had been dominated by cultural evolutionists, who ranked societies from primitive ones at the bottom to Western civilization at the top. Lévi-Strauss rejected such ethnocentrism. Ranking societies was meaningless,

since they specialized in different activities. If Eskimos devised the scale of measurement, the West might rank at the bottom and appear as a society unchanged since prehistoric times. The West excelled in industrial technology but lagged far behind India in developing philosophical and religious systems, behind the Polynesians in evolving a freer and more generous way of life, behind the aborigines in Australia in elaborating models of kinship, behind the Melanesians in creating art. Human culture was rich in achievement and 99 percent of it had occurred outside the West, Lévi-Strauss believed.

This worldview gave Lévi-Strauss a perspective from which to analyze modern Western society. Western civilization was sick at its very center. The West, unleashing rapid technological change, had unbalanced the harmony between nature and culture. Order and beauty disappeared in a cluttered world that thrust together things that should be separate. Western humanism justified using technology in a destructive way by making humans the center of creation and by legitimating their domination of all other life. The so-called primitives understood true humanism, Lévi-Strauss argued, one that "puts the world before life, life before man, and the respect of others before the love of self."

Lévi-Strauss angered some Westerners by refusing to place their prized achievements on a higher plane than the achievements of Bushmen or Eskimos and by attacking Western conceptions of humanism. He shocked such intellectuals as Sartre by attacking Western conceptions of history. Western intellectual traditions were based on historical reasoning, on the assumption that institutions and ideas could best be understood by studying them over time. Lévi-Strauss argued that history did not evolve along a linear path. History should be regarded as a matrix, not as a linear record of events. For example, the Industrial Revolution did not start in the West because of that region's unique evolutionary development but because the global cultural division of labor captured all the human possibilities through different specialties in different societies. The Western Industrial Revolution incorporated the inventions of all societies: agriculture, pottery, weaving, and the like. Ancient societies made these achievements using the same processes of reasoning and logic as a scientist in the modern Western world. The Industrial Revolution did not result from the genius of Western Europeans but from the operations of the human mind. The Industrial Revolution occurred in the West by chance of historical accident; it would have occurred elsewhere at another time.

Western ethnocentrism, including its culture-bound view of history, combined with its wealth and power to destroy global balance and to threaten all other cultures with destruction. Lévi-Strauss compared Western civilization with a virus, which entered into living cells (cultures) and caused them to reproduce according to its model, the Western model.

This virus threatened the West as well as the non-West. Lévi-Strauss believed that knowledge, including self-knowledge, came through confronting "the other," not through inward examination. Modern Western civilization started when the Renaissance confronted its own classical tradition and continued in the age of exploration, when it encountered other cultures. Today those cultures, infected by the Western virus, are dying. Their death will end the possibility of Westerners' gaining perspective on their own civilization, ending forever the possibility of self-knowledge.

Summary

Claude Lévi-Strauss' daring anthropological work has earned for him the respect of his colleagues. Even those who reject his approach acknowledge the many insights his work has generated. He is also regarded as a major thinker of the twentieth century, although his thought makes many of his fellow Western intellectuals uneasy. Lévi-Strauss dissolved old political concerns, categories, and labels. His work was explosive in its implications for Western civilization's role in the world. He described his own political position as one of "serene pessimism." Western reform, even of the most humane and enlightened sort, was part of the Western virus. He refused to join organizations working to protect human rights, because such bodies engaged in a form of imperialism, with one culture imposing its conception of such rights on others. He rejected the concept of progress, challenged the ethnocentrism of the West, and brought the growing concerns with ecology to a level deeper than mere attention to a clean environment; sanity itself required balance, distance, and self-limitation. Westerners had to preserve the cultures of primitive people and the existence of other species, he believed, not because they had the right to exist but because they possessed a wisdom on which survival of the West depended.

Bibliography

Badcock, C. R. *Lévi-Strauss: Structuralism and Sociological Theory*. London: Hutchinson, 1975; New York: Holmes and Meier Publishers, 1976. This is a study of Lévi-Strauss' structural thought that tries to avoid jargon and to bring his ideas before the lay public in a clear and concise exposition.

Champagne, Roland A. *Claude Lévi-Strauss*. Boston: Twayne, 1987. An excellent work on Lévi-Strauss' contributions to semiotics. It is a clearly written study of a difficult and critical area of his thought.

Henaff, Marcel. *Claude Lévi-Strauss and the Making of Structural Anthropology*. Minneapolis: University of Minnesota Press, 1998. This is Lévi-Strauss's favorite presentation of his work. Henaff presents an accurate and accessible account of Lévi-Strauss's anthropological theory and his contributions to ethics, linguistics, and other related issues.

Johnson, Christopher. "Anthropology and the Sciences Humaines: The Voice of Lévi-Strauss." *History of the Human Sciences* 10, no. 3 (August, 1997). Profile of Lévi-Strauss including his contributions to anthropology and his neolithic approach to his studies.

Leach, Edmund. *Lévi-Strauss*. 4th ed. London: Fontana, 1996. A critical but fair book on Lévi-Strauss' anthropological work, written by a student of Bronisław Malinowski.

Pace, David. *Claude Lévi-Strauss: The Bearer of Ashes*. Boston: Routledge, 1983; London: Ark, 1986. An excellent and provocative study that evaluates the whole body of Lévi-Strauss' work, showing the personal and scholarly sources of his critical evaluation of Western civilization.

Shalvey, Thomas. *Claude Lévi-Strauss: Social Psychotherapy and the Collective Unconscious*. Amherst: University of Massachusetts Press, and Hassocks, Sussex: Harvester Press, 1979. Considers the philosophical implications of Lévi-Strauss' thought and relates it to Sigmund Freud, Karl Marx, Sartre, and others.

William E. Pemberton

C. S. LEWIS

Born: November 29, 1898; Belfast, Northern Ireland

Died: November, 22, 1963; Oxford, England

Areas of Achievement: Literature, religion, and theology

Contribution: Lewis enlarged the understanding of the literature of the Middle Ages and Renaissance. He also composed novels and children's literature of lasting impact and published many insightful books concerning Christianity.

Early Life

Clive Staples Lewis was born in Belfast in Northern Ireland to parents of the professional middle class in 1898. His father, Albert Lewis, was a successful and well-to-do solicitor who nonetheless always felt threatened by poverty. Lewis's mother, Florence Hamilton, was well educated, having a degree in mathematics and logic, and she had talent in the humanities as well. She tutored Lewis in both French and Latin before he was seven. Such early exposure to languages and learning was complemented by the atmosphere at Little Lea, the family house. The place was erratically planned, full of hidden crannies, empty passageways, and piles of books.

Upon the death of Florence in 1908, Albert sent both of his sons, Warnie and Clive (who insisted on adopting the name "Jack"), to the English boarding school of Wynyard. It was a declining and miserable institution with a brutal headmaster. Lewis escaped this institution and won a scholarship to the prestigious public school Malvern College. The school was dominated by the society of athletic snobs, who ridiculed Lewis. He soon begged his father to remove him from the institution. Albert, making a remarkably wise decision, put his son under the tutelage of his former headmaster, W. T. Kirkpatrick, who trained the boy in logical discourse, languages, and literature. His pupil became adept at argumentation and the translation of Greek and Latin literature.

Lewis won a classical scholarship to Oxford and matriculated into University College in April, 1917. World War I put his academic career on hold as he joined the Officer Training Corps and was billeted in Keble College for his military education. There he met "Paddy" Moore; during leaves, he spent much time with Paddy's family, Janie Moore and her daughter Maureen. Shipped to France in November, 1917, Lewis fought in the Battle of Arras and was badly wounded by friendly artillery fire. Albert's peculiar unwillingness to visit his son and the death of Paddy drove Janie Moore and Lewis to take on the roles of mother and son toward each other. Lewis took care of Moore for the next thirty years by financially supporting her and, after his required residency at college, living with her.

Lewis's student career at Oxford can only be characterized as spectacular. He studied classical literature, philosophy, and ancient history. He placed first in his honors finals in 1920 and 1922. He went on to read English Language and Literature and took a first in that in 1923. After winning the prestigious Chancellor's Price for an essay in English, Lewis was well placed to compete for an academic post at Oxford. With the continued financial assistance of Albert and the academic support of his tutors, he succeeded in a fellowship in English at Magdalen College in 1925. His appointment gave him financial security and launched his scholarly career.

Life's Work

It took Lewis ten years to firmly settle into his academic career and publish his first scholarly work, *The Allegory of Love: A Study in Medieval Tradition* (1936), in which he emphasized the importance of the creative power of myth in English literature. It was anything but a popular work, as it dealt with a neglected literary heritage and a difficult area of interpretation, but scholars in the field received it very favorably. Given Lewis's heavy teaching load and the domestic distractions imposed on him by his selfish, erratic, and "adopted" mother Moore, his productiveness was remarkable. He took his tutorials with pupils and his lectures quite seriously although he saw them as generally unprofitable uses of his time. He would often enter a classroom lecturing and continue in his booming voice with enthusiasm and humor. Lewis was physically startling, being somewhat thickly set with a round, reddish face complemented by a hearty laugh and direct manner.

Lewis underwent a conversion experience in 1929 that eventually provided part of the foundation for much of his creative work. Lewis had rejected Christianity early in his life, arguing with his boyhood friend Arthur Greeves that it was only one of many religious myths with no basis in fact. In *Surprised by Joy: The Shape of My Early Life* (1955), Lewis charts his metamorphosis from atheist to Christian. His close friends J. R. R. Tolkien, Owen Barfield, and Hugo Dyson convinced him that Christianity was similar to the classical and Scandinavian traditions with the singular difference that it was true.

Lewis's conversion made more coherent his notion of "joy," which, unlike the conventional idea, was not "happiness" or "pleasure" but rather a sense of longing for transcendent beauty or truth. Lewis, in the late 1930's, began to combine his Christianity with his literary knowledge to create novels of spiritual fantasy and science fiction. The resulting trilogy, consisting of *Out of the Silent Planet* (1938), *Perelandra* (1943), and *That Hideous Strength* (1945), created nothing less than the impression of a new mythology. *Perelandra*, the only overtly theological work, narrated a story of a different Eve in a surrealistic setting on Venus. Lewis's fundamental message was a strong criticism of the view that saw meaning only in the expansion and distribution of the human race in the cosmos. Perhaps his most complex and critically well received novel was *Till We Have Faces* (1956), a variation on the Cupid and Psyche myth.

During World War II Lewis was catapulted into worldwide fame via his forays into theological fantasy and popularized theology. A speech by Nazi leader Adolf Hitler and its almost satanic persuasiveness inspired Lewis to write *The Screwtape Letters* (1942), an uncanny and frighteningly insightful series of letters from a senior devil to a junior devil who attempts to insure the entrance of one young man into hell. It is a sardonic commentary not only on modernism but also on conventional religion and liberal theology. Perhaps because of this book, many of Lewis's academic colleagues could not forgive his popularity nor his trespass into unacademic advocacy. Lewis was, however, not isolated. Oxford was a place of societies and informal groups that provide inspiration and produce work. Such a gathering was the Inklings, a group of scholars and writers who met in Lewis's rooms and pubs from 1930 to 1949. At these meetings Tolkien read *The Hobbit* (1937), and Lewis read his first purely theological work, *The Problem of Pain* (1940).

Christian apologetics was to become an area of some concern for Lewis during World War II. He made a series of broadcasts on the British Broadcasting Corporation (BBC) in which certain essentials of Christianity were distilled and common doctrines among many denominations were described. These talks were called *Mere Christianity* (1952) when they appeared in book form, the term "mere" meaning the essential and central part of Christianity.

After the war, Lewis again became busy tutoring and lecturing as well as pursuing his scholarly work. He finally completed his *English Literature in the Sixteenth Century, Excluding Drama* (1954) in which he rejected the creative primacy of the Renaissance and pointed to continuity between the medieval and modern ages. In the 1950's Lewis also wrote the series of children's books for which he became most well known. The seven Chronicles of Narnia (1950-1956), beginning with *The Lion, the Witch, and the Wardrobe* (1950), were on a level of high fantasy, depicting a struggle between good and evil through powerful but not obvious religious symbols.

In the mid-1950's, two chairs of English literature became vacant at Oxford, but neither went to Lewis, in part because of academic distaste for and jealousy of his popular works. Cambridge was much more tolerant of Lewis's eclectic interests and elected him as professor of medieval and Renaissance English. Lewis took up residence at Magdalene College in 1955. In the same year Lewis published *Surprised By Joy*. The work could be construed to have a double meaning because Lewis had become close friends with Joy Helen Davidman, an American writer. In order to prevent Joy and her two sons from being deported, Lewis consented to a registry marriage, something he perceived as a mere formal legality. Shortly thereafter, Joy tragically fell ill with bone cancer and Lewis, out of pity, married her in the Anglican church according to Joy's wish. With the approach of death, Lewis admitted his love for Joy. Miraculously, the cancer went into remission and for the next three years Joy and Lewis were able to live a normal and happy life together. Yet the disease returned and ended Lewis's few years as a husband. He movingly described his sense of loss in *A Grief Observed* (1961).

Lewis was productive up until shortly before his death in 1963. Before Joy died, he finished *The Four Loves* (1960), which discussed the nature of affection, friendship, eros, and charity. His final academic work, *The Discarded Image* (1964), was an introduction to medieval and Renaissance literature. Despite problems with his prostate and associated complications, Lewis was able to continue his teaching until the spring of 1963. After a heart attack in July, his health rapidly declined. He died in his home, the Kilns, on November 22, 1963.

Summary

C. S. Lewis has been influential in both literature and religion. He is often perceived as a rallying point for those who reject the trends of relativism and deconstruction in literature, as well as a legitimizing force for orthodox Christianity within academic circles. His impact as an antimodernist and conservative in literature, as well as his rejuvenation of medieval literature and seventeenth century English epic poet John Milton as worthy of study continue to be felt. Lewis's creative work is more difficult to evaluate, but its significance should not be understated. His sense of myth as a creative force has made its mark both in the rise of fantasy literature for children and in the genre of science fiction. Lewis's apologies are more problematic. His arguments for a rational faith have only moderate force, yet his later religious books show a greater sensitivity and depth. The works of all genres in which Lewis wrote remain remarkably popular, and his impact on perceptions of faith, beauty, and truth has been quite profound.

Bibliography

Carpenter, Humphrey. *The Inklings*. London: Allen and Unwin, 1978; Boston: 1979. Carpenter relates the life of Lewis in the context of his closest literary friends, J. R. R. Tolkien, Charles Williams, Owen Barfield, and others. Useful for a sense of Oxonian life and society during the early to mid-twentieth century.

Green, Roger Lancelyn, and Walter Hooper. *C. S. Lewis: A Biography*. London: Collins, and New York: Harcourt Brace, 1974. This "authorized" biography is written by a former pupil (Green) and a friend and personal secretary (Hooper).

Hooper, Walter. *C. S. Lewis: Companion and Guide*. London and San Francisco: Harper, 1996. This extremely useful volume contains a 120-page biography, a chronology, summaries of major works, sample reviews, explanations of key ideas, and an exhaustive bibliography of Lewis's works.

Lewis, C. S. *Surprised By Joy: The Shape of My Early Life*. London: Bles, and New York: Harcourt Brace, 1955. Lewis's spiritual autobiography relates the emotional and intellectual roots of his conversion. Essential to any understanding of Lewis's writings and development.

Meilaender, Gilbert. "The Everyday C. S. Lewis." *First Things: A Monthly Journal of Religion and Public Life* no. 85 (August-September, 1998). The author argues that Lewis's theology was, in fact, reflection on ordinary concepts from a religious perspective and that he is widely read due to his clear communication techniques.

Myers, Doris T. *C. S. Lewis in Context*. Kent, Ohio, and London: Kent State University Press, 1994. This readable study in criticism sees Lewis less as an isolated figure and more reflective of his times. Includes a useful works cited section.

Packer, J.I. "Still Surprised by Lewis." *Christianity Today* 42, no. 10 (September 7, 1998). The author, a theologian who attended Oxford during the 1940s, discusses Lewis's influence then and now.

Peter K. Benbow

JOHN L. LEWIS

Born: February 12, 1880; Lucas, Iowa
Died: June 11, 1969; Washington, D.C.
Area of Achievement: Organized labor
Contribution: As president of the United Mine Workers union and founder of the Congress of Industrial Organizations, Lewis dominated the progress of organized labor in the United States from the 1920's through the 1960's.

Early Life

John Llewellyn Lewis was born in Lucas, Iowa, on February 12, 1880. Both his parents, Thomas and Louisa (née Watkins) Lewis, had been born in Wales and had migrated to the United States in the 1870's; John was the eldest of six sons and two daughters. Thomas worked as a coal miner whenever he could find work, but, having been placed on an employer blacklist for leading a miners' strike in 1882, he often had to fill in with other jobs, such as working as a night watchman.

Young John only went as far as the eighth grade before leaving school to supplement his father's meager and irregular income. He sold newspapers in Des Moines, Iowa, for a few years until the abolition of the blacklist in 1897 allowed his father to return to Lucas, where John, then age seventeen, joined him in the coal mines. John worked there until 1901 and then set off on a working tour of Western mining communities, toiling in copper, silver, gold, and coal mines in Montana, Utah, Arizona, and Colorado. Soon after returning to Lucas in 1906, he married Myrta Edith Bell, the daughter of a local doctor. They would have three children: Margaret Mary (who died in childhood), Florence Kathryn, and John Llewellyn II.

Shortly before Lewis' marriage, the Lucas miners elected him as a delegate to the national convention of the United Mine Workers of America (UMW), the largest union affiliated with the American Federation of Labor (AFL). A few years later, in 1909, he moved his family to Panama, Illinois, and continued his union activity. He was selected president of the Panama miners' local union and soon thereafter was appointed state legislative agent for District 12 of the UMW. It was in this capacity that he convinced the Illinois legislature to pass a comprehensive package of mine safety and workmen's compensation laws by exploiting the Cherry, Illinois, mine disaster of 1911 that killed 160 men.

Samuel Gompers (founder and president of the AFL), impressed by Lewis' obvious leadership talents, took the young labor activist under his wing and made him a national legislative representative for the AFL in late 1911. This job took Lewis to Washington, D.C., where he was able to learn valuable lessons regarding the politics and management of labor organization. He also continued his rise through the ranks of the UMW. In 1916, he served as temporary chairman of the UMW's national convention and, in 1917, he was elected vice president of the union.

Lewis had his first taste of national-level labor confrontation when, in 1919, he became acting president of the union for Frank J. Hayes, who had become too debilitated by alcoholism to carry out his duties. Several months after assuming this position, Lewis called for a strike when mine operators rejected the union's demand for a sixty percent wage hike, a six-hour workday, and a five-day workweek. A federal court issued an injunction against the strike, but, in November, 1919, Lewis defied the injunction, ordering 425,000 men out of the mines. The strike lasted two months and, after a face-to-face meeting with President Woodrow Wilson, Lewis was forced to call the miners back to work. They did gain a wage increase of approximately thirty percent, but their other demands went unsatisfied. The rough, bulky, bushy-eyebrowed Lewis did gain a reputation for toughness during the strike, however, and he parlayed this into an official UMW presidency in 1920. He would hold this position until he retired in 1960.

Life's Work

Lewis assumed the presidency of the UMW at a time when the coal industry had begun to experience serious difficulties. Coal output had skyrocketed between 1916 and 1919 to meet wartime needs but, once World War I was over, demand dropped back to more normal levels, causing a glut of coal on the market. In addition, mine owners with union workers faced rising competition from nonunion mines in the South and from "captive" mines owned by steel companies and railroads. In an effort to meet these threats, unionized producers began to lower both prices and miners' wages. Lewis refused to agree to this wage-reduction strategy and, in 1922, he called a strike. Miners did win a wage increase to $7.50 a day as a result of this strike, but many only worked irregularly as the crisis persisted.

In the years that followed, the situation in the coal industry continued to deteriorate. More than three thousand mines shut down during the 1920's and UMW membership dropped from a high of 500,000 in 1922 to 150,000 by 1930. Lewis responded by urging coal operators to increase their productivity and thereby halt the precipitous decline in regular miner employment. He opposed pay cuts that were made to keep unprofitable operations in business and instead favored the closing of these marginal mines and the introduction of increased mechanization in remaining ones in order to make them more efficient and competitive—and thus a stable source of employment for his members. Factions within the UMW opposed Lewis' proposals and organized a series of wildcat strikes to protest his emphasis on mechanization (which they believed would cost even more jobs). This struggle within the UMW, which also contributed to the decline in membership, culminated at the national convention of 1930, where his opponents made a concerted effort to unseat him. Lewis still had enough support within the UMW, however, to resist these attempts and to purge the leaders of this opposition from the union.

As the Depression tightened its grip on the United States after 1930, it also aggravated the problems within the coal industry. Coal sales continued to slump, and thousands of miners lost their jobs. The UMW, in an increasingly weakened position, could do little to resist employer attempts to reduce the wages of miners who managed to keep their jobs. It was at this point that Lewis turned to the national government for help. Although he had been a Republican throughout the 1920's and had even supported Herbert Hoover in 1932, Lewis recognized that the Democrat who defeated his man in that election, Franklin D. Roosevelt, was sympathetic to labor's plight and might come to its aid. Accordingly, Lewis swung to Roosevelt and the Democratic Party and participated actively in the New Deal. He became a labor adviser to the president, a member of the Labor Advisory Board, and a member of the National Labor Board. This close relationship between the UMW and the Roosevelt Administration benefited both parties. Because of the passage of the Guffey and Wagner labor acts and section 7A of the National Industrial Recovery Act, miners received a substantial daily pay raise, a shortened workday, and the right to bargain collectively through their own representatives. The UMW recovered as a result, and, by 1935, its membership was approaching one-half million again. Roosevelt, on the other hand, received the grateful votes of coal miners, relative labor peace in the mines, and large contributions from the UMW to his campaign treasury.

Meanwhile, trouble was brewing in the AFL, and Lewis, as usual, was at the center of it. Lewis had decided that "industrial unionism" (where all workers in a given industry, regardless of their particular trade, would be part of a single union that represented them all) was the best way for workers to fight for their rights, and he tried to convince the AFL, which represented workers by their trade, to adopt this policy. At the AFL national convention of 1935, however, his proposal was soundly rejected. In response, Lewis resigned as vice president of the AFL in November, 1935, and formed a new omnibus labor organization based on industrial unionism, one that eventually became the Congress of Industrial Organizations (CIO). Lewis' UMW led the way in affiliating with this new organization, and it was soon joined by many others. By 1938, the CIO included forty-four unions and more than four million members.

As president of the CIO, Lewis also began the hard struggle to organize automobile and steelworkers and affiliate them with his organization. Employing such tactics as the sit-down strike, he did force the automobile industry to recognize the CIO in 1937. He then convinced the nation's largest steel manufacturer, United States Steel, to accept the CIO (also in 1937). The smaller steel companies, however, such as Bethlehem and Republic Steel, put up strong resistance to Lewis' organizing efforts, forcing him to call a strike against them in May, 1937. Marred by violence, the strike dragged on until late summer of that year, and Lewis ultimately accepted a compromise settlement that fell short of his initial goals.

The strike also provoked a break between Lewis and Roosevelt. Lewis became disappointed and frustrated at the president's lack of support for the so-called Little Steel strike and tried to rally labor behind his Republican opponent, Wendell Willkie, in the election of 1940. Roosevelt nevertheless won easily, but he never forgave Lewis for his defection. Temporarily defeated, Lewis resigned as president of the CIO and devoted his full attention to his UMW.

Lewis opposed American involvement in World War II and stuck to this position right up to the Japanese attack on Pearl Harbor on December 7, 1941. Although he declared his support for the American war effort after this attack, his "noninvolvement" stand up to Pearl Harbor had alienated many of his former allies among the leadership of the CIO. In 1942, therefore, he pulled the UMW out of the CIO and purged CIO sympathizers from his union.

Lewis did not allow the war to stop him from fighting for the coal miners. In 1943, he declared that the wage increase authorized by the War Labor Board was inadequate and called a strike. The conflict lasted nearly a year, and, during its course, the government temporarily took over the nation's mines and Roosevelt even appealed directly to the miners to return to work. In the end, though, Lewis won a two-dollars-per-day pay increase for his men. He called another strike in 1945 and won again, gaining an increase in overtime pay, the establishment of one-hour travel pay to and from work, and paid vacations for miners. Lewis authorized still another strike in March, 1946, which resulted in a small pay increase and, more important, the establishment of a pension and welfare fund for miners, financed by a five cents per ton royalty on all coal produced.

In October, 1946, Lewis called his third strike in fourteen months in an attempt to reduce the miners' workweek to less than fifty-four hours. A federal court judge issued a restraining order against this work stoppage. When Lewis ignored the order, the judge found him to be in criminal and civil contempt and fined him ten thousand dollars and the UMW $3.5 million. The Supreme Court upheld the judge's older, and Lewis had no choice but to call off the strike.

In between the two strikes in 1946, Lewis had reaffiliated the UMW with the AFL. This reconciliation lasted only a year before Lewis, after a disagreement with other AFL leaders over the organization's position regarding the new Taft-Hartley Act, withdrew the UMW again. It would remain unaffiliated with both the AFL and CIO during the rest of his presidency.

Lewis authorized more coal strikes in 1948 and 1949 and, despite court injunctions, fines, and the strict provisions of the Taft-Hartley law, he won further wage increases, a seven-hour workday, and increases in employer contributions to the pension and welfare fund. At the time of Lewis' retirement from the UMW presidency, a post he had held for forty years, miners earned $24.24 a day and possessed a pension fund of $1.3 billion. Lewis also devoted much of his efforts during the 1950's to improving safety in coal mines and played a major role in obtaining the passage of the Federal Mine Safety Law of 1952.

Following his retirement, Lewis served as a trustee for the union's pension and welfare fund; in 1964, he received the Presidential Medal of Freedom from President Lyndon B. Johnson. Lewis died in Washington, D.C., on June 11, 1969, at the age of eighty-nine.

Summary

John L. Lewis transformed the coal industry and the American labor movement. When he became president of the UMW in 1920, miners were paid seven dollars a day, had no travel-time pay, no paid vacations, no welfare and pension fund, they had to supply their own tools, and they received no state compensation for mine accidents. In 1960, after forty years of Lewis' leadership, they made more than twenty-four dollars a day, had an hour's paid travel-time per day, a week's paid vacation, a huge pension and welfare fund, and used tools supplied by their employers. All states paid compensation for miners killed or injured in work-related accidents, and, moreover, Lewis had persuaded the federal government to enact rules regarding mine safety that were enforced by a joint operator-miner committee. Lewis not only had greatly improved the material condition of coal miners in the United States but also had made them partners with their employers in determining conditions inside the mines.

Lewis' influence spread far beyond the coalfields. His partnership with Franklin Roosevelt from 1932 to 1940 played a large role in determining the prolabor stance of the early New Deal and helped forge the alliance with organized labor that served the Democratic Party so well in future decades. Through his founding of the CIO in 1935 and his organizing efforts on its behalf, Lewis not only established industrial unionism on a solid and permanent foundation in the United States but also helped create the powerful United Automobile Workers and United Steel Workers unions. In addition, Lewis shaped the nature of modern collective bargaining between unions and management. By employing such tactics as the sit-down strike and through his willingness to call strikes whenever the interests of his men were threatened, regardless of the powers lined up against him, Lewis made organized labor a force to be reckoned with in the United States, one that insisted that it share in the decisions that affected it.

Lewis could be stubborn, vain, autocratic, and even abusive, given to labeling his opponents as "communists." Yet the organized labor movement in the United States made gigantic gains under his uncompromising leadership, and the American worker, not only the coal miner, is much better off because of him.

Bibliography

Alinsky, Saul. *John L. Lewis: An Unauthorized Biography*. New York: Putnam, 1949. The author was a formidable organizer himself and he appreciates Lewis' talents in this regard. Yet he is also at pains to point out what he sees as weaknesses in Lewis' character, abilities, and tactics. This book is a good, balanced portrait of Lewis the man and Lewis the organizer.

Carnes, Cecil. *John L. Lewis*. New York: Speller, 1936. Published shortly after Lewis founded the CIO in 1935, this book provides a rather colorless account of his career up to that point.

Dubofsky, Melvyn, and Warren Van Tine. *John L. Lewis: A Biography*. New York: Quadrangle, 1977. This book is not only the most comprehensive and well-written study of Lewis; it is also an often brilliant analytical survey of the American labor movement from 1920 to 1960.

Kurland, Gerald. *John L. Lewis: Labor's Strong-Willed Organizer*. Charlotteville, N.Y.: SamHar Press, 1973. A short (one-hundred-page) general examination of Lewis' life and work. It will provide the interested reader with the highlights of Lewis' career but little else.

McFarland, C. K. *Roosevelt, Lewis, and the New Deal, 1933-1940*. Fort Worth: Texas Christian University Press, 1970. A good and concise investigation of the relationship between Lewis and Roosevelt up until their official split during the presidential election in 1940, this book falls a little short in explaining the long-range repercussions of this seven-year partnership.

Preis, Art. *Labor's Giant Step: Twenty Years of the CIO*. 2d ed. New York: Pathfinder Press, 1972. In the course of tracing the first two decades of the CIO, the author also presents a fairly objective portrait of Lewis' role in creating and then almost destroying the organization.

Roberts, Ron E. "The Roots of Labor's Demiurge: Iowa's John L. Lewis." *Journal of the West* 35, no. 2 (April, 1996). Profile of the career of Lewis.

Wechsler, James A. *Labor Baron: A Portrait of John L. Lewis*. New York: Morrow, 1944. Emphasizes Lewis' negative side and downplays his positive achievements.

Christopher E. Guthrie

SINCLAIR LEWIS

Born: February 7, 1885; Sauk Centre, Minnesota
Died: January 10, 1951; Rome, Italy
Area of Achievement: Literature
Contribution: The first American to win the Nobel
Prize for Literature, Lewis at once painstakingly
depicted and satirized previously neglected areas
of middle-American life.

Early Life

The third son of Edwin J. and Emma Kermott
Lewis, Harry Sinclair Lewis was born in Sauk
Centre, Minnesota, on February 7, 1885. His father
was a country doctor, as were his maternal grandfather and, later, his older brother Claude. This association with medicine would help him in the
writing of *Arrowsmith* (1925); it would also give
him a lifelong inferiority complex for not following his father's and brother's profession.

In addition to providing the model for Gopher
Prairie in his fiction, Sauk Centre contributed in
other ways to Lewis' literary career. In the town library, he found the works of Sir Walter Scott and
Charles Dickens, two writers who greatly influenced him. From Dickens, he learned to use literature as a means of social protest. Also Dickensian
is Lewis' sense of humor, evident in his choice of
names for characters whom he dislikes: Capitola
McGurk (*Arrowsmith*), Lowell Schmaltz (*The Man
Who Knew Coolidge*, 1928), Buzz Windrip (*It
Can't Happen Here*, 1935). From Scott, he took the
element of romance that colors not only his short
stories but also his most realistic social commentary. In Sauk Centre, too, Lewis began his career as
a writer, serving as president of his high school's
literary society and contributing articles to the
town's two newspapers.

Already in Sauk Centre, Lewis was revealing
another trait, that of being an outsider. His voracious reading habits marked him as different from
his peers, as did his homely appearance. He was
tall and thin, with blue eyes and red hair. Over the
years, cancer would disfigure an already plain
face, so that his second wife said that he looked as
if he "had walked through flame throwers." Here,
too, Lewis showed the wanderlust that would never let him settle down; instead of attending the
University of Minnesota, he insisted on going east
to college.

At Yale, he was again a misfit. The eighteenth
century scholar Chauncey Brewster Tinker, one of

Lewis' few friends there, said that "the conventions
and restrictions of good society—especially collegiate society—were offensive to him. His abiding
temptation was to undermine them and blow them
at the moon." In 1906, he abruptly left college to
work as a janitor at Upton Sinclair's utopian community, Helicon Hall, near Englewood, New Jersey. After some two months, he abruptly left Helicon Hall.

During this period, Lewis' literary abilities were
as apparent as was his rebelliousness. He was the
only freshman in his class to publish in the *Yale
Literary Magazine*. By his junior year, he had
earned a spot on the editorial board of the magazine, and he was contributing to the local newspapers as well.

For the seven years after his graduation (1908),
Lewis wandered around the country, holding various jobs associated with publishing. During this
period, he produced a book for adolescents, *Hike
and the Aeroplane* (1912), and his first serious novels, *Our Mr. Wrenn* (1914) and *The Trail of the
Hawk* (1915). When he sold four stories to the *Saturday Evening Post* in quick succession, each earning one thousand dollars, he resigned his editorial
position with George H. Doran Company in order
to devote himself exclusively to writing.

Life's Work

The short stories that Lewis contributed to popular
magazines and the five early novels gave no hint of
what was to follow in the 1920's. *Our Mr. Wrenn*
ridiculed radical reformers and arty types; its hero
is a sales order clerk. *The Innocents* (1917) was rejected by the *Saturday Evening Post* as being too
sentimental. In *The Job* (1917), he wrote that business is "that one necessary field of activity to which
the egotistical arts and sciences and theologies and
military puerilities are but servants." *Free Air*
(1919) includes a scene in Gopher Prairie, which
Lewis praises for its small-town friendliness.

Main Street (1920), a scathing attack on that
same village, thus marked a sharp break with
Lewis' previous work. More important, it crystallized a new attitude toward small-town America.
Other writers, such as Edgar Lee Masters and
Sherwood Anderson, had already begun the revolt
from the village by showing that all was not sweet-
ness and light in the Spoon Rivers and Winesburgs
of the Midwest. Yet no one before had so clearly

diagnosed and described what Lewis called "the village virus":

> It is an unimaginatively standardized background, a sluggishness of speech and manners, a rigid ruling of the spirit by the desire to appear respectable. It is . . . the contentment of the quiet dead. . . . It is slavery self-sought and self-defended.

Having attacked one bastion of American life, Lewis turned his attention to another. His next novel, he said, was to be "the story of the Tired Business Man, of the man in the Pullman smoker, of our American ruler." Even though George F. Babbitt lives in Zenith, a city of some 400,000, rather than in a small town, he is no less parochial than Juanita Haydocks, no less a conformist than Jim Blauser of *Main Street*. Like that earlier work, *Babbitt* (1922) shows the shallowness of American life governed by the quest for status, money, and conformity. Babbitt yearns to escape his stultifying world. He dreams of a fairy-child lover and resists the advances of the Good Citizens League, but at last he concedes, "They've licked me, licked me to a finish." Writers had previously criticized the Rockefellers and the Morgans, but no one had so precisely and devastatingly shown the vacuum that was the daily life of the average businessman.

Always a hard worker, Lewis at once began planning his next novel, which he intended as a celebration of a labor leader. In Chicago to interview the union organizer and Socialist Eugene V. Debs, Lewis happened to meet Paul De Kruif, who had recently been forced to leave the Rockefeller Institute for writing *Our Medicine Men* (1922), an exposé of the unscientific methods of some of his colleagues. With his own knowledge of medicine and De Kruif's assistance, Lewis produced *Arrowsmith*. While the book celebrates scientific curiosity, it attacks the spirit of commercialism and the demand for conformity that isolate Martin Arrowsmith.

This novel earned for Lewis a Pulitzer Prize, which he refused. In 1920, the Pulitzer Prize Committee had selected *Main Street* for the award, but the trustees had overruled the choice and given the prize to Edith Wharton's *The Age of Innocence* (1920). Lewis now got his revenge, attacking the whole concept of literary awards as an effort to make American literature "safe, polite, obedient, and sterile."

Lewis followed one of his best books with one of his worst, *Mantrap* (1926), based on his eleven-day expedition into the Canadian woods in 1924. With *Elmer Gantry* (1927), he returned to his hard-hitting criticism of American life, this time attacking religion. He had long been hostile to the established churches; in *Main Street*, his heroine, Carol Kennicott, observed that "the Christian religion in America [was] as abnormal as Zoroastrianism— without the splendor." In *Babbitt*, Lewis had parodied the popular evangelist Billy Sunday in the character Mike Monday. *Elmer Gantry* expands the satire, showing the hypocrisy and commercialism pervading various denominations.

Following the publication of this novel, Lewis went to Europe to work on his next book. *The Man Who Knew Coolidge* uses the vapid monologues of Lowell Schmaltz to reveal the follies of the American business class he represents. While in Europe, Lewis met the recently divorced journalist Dorothy Thompson. On April 16, 1928, Lewis divorced his first wife, Grace Livingstone Hegger, and, the following week, announced his engagement to Thompson. They were married on May 14, 1928.

In *Dodsworth* (1929), Lewis told his version of his first marriage, portraying himself and his first wife as Sam and Fran Dodsworth, Dorothy Thompson as Edith Cortright. Though one of his better novels, and though an attack on American provincialism, it marks a shift in Lewis' attitude toward middle-class America. The hero is a capitalist and a Republican, whom Lewis seems to prefer to the character's more sophisticated, arty wife.

Throughout the 1920's, Lewis' novels had made complacent and comfortable Americans uneasy. In the Depression decade to follow, he seemed inclined to offer solace to a hard-pressed people. Beginning with *Dodsworth*, most of his novels might have been written by Babbitt. One reviewer even suggested that Babbitt had killed Lewis and was merely using Lewis' name for his own books. *Ann Vickers* (1933) favorably portrays the American small town. The hero of *Work of Art* (1934) is a self-confessed "smug, complacent, mechanical, ordinary food merchant," whom Lewis seems to prefer to this man's writer-brother. *The Prodigal Parents* (1938) criticizes reformed-minded children, holding up their conservative, hardworking parents as the ideal. In 1930, Lewis had said that "the world is suffering from too many reformers"; in most of his novels thereafter he reduced that number by one.

Eleven days before he made that pronouncement, though, he took aim yet again at American

closed-mindedness in his Nobel Prize acceptance speech. Throughout the 1920's, his novels had been popular in Europe, and *Ann Vickers* would be translated into thirteen languages immediately upon publication. Whether the Nobel Prize committee chose Lewis because his books confirmed European views of the United States or they regarded him as a great literary artist, the award, the first to an American writer, confirmed America's literary coming of age. In "The American Fear of Literature," Lewis agreed that many fine writers were emerging to give the country "a literature worthy of her vastness," but he added that they had to combat provincialism and a demand for conformity that came not only from the public but also from academia and more timid fellow authors.

In the next decade, Lewis generally retreated from such reformist positions as he took in this address. In 1935, he even accepted membership in the National Institute of Arts and Letters, which he had specifically named in his speech as having a deleterious effect on innovative writing. Yet he could still lash out occasionally, as he demonstrated in *It Can't Happen Here.*

Dorothy Thompson had interviewed Adolf Hitler, and, in *I Saw Hitler* (1932), she speculated on what he might do if he were in the United States. With such demagogues as Huey Long, Charles E. Townsend, and Gerald L. K. Smith, the United States seemed threatened with the same Fascism that was overrunning Europe. *It Can't Happen Here* was Lewis' response to these would-be dictators, showing what could happen if one of them gained control of the government. Charles and Mary Beard called the book the best portrait of "the ideals of democracy pitted against the tyranny of the demogogic dictator." Against mass culture, big business, and conformity, Lewis poses his spokesman, Doremus Jessup, who champions "the free, inquiring, critical spirit" as the only creative force in the world.

Such powerful writing was all too rare in Lewis' last years. In *Cass Timberlane* (1945), he wrote, "Whether Germany and France can live as neighbors is insignificant compared with whether Johann and Maria or Jean and Marie can live as lovers." Only once after *It Can't Happen Here* did Lewis address a contemporary social issue. The attack, in *Kingsblood Royal* (1947), on racism earned *Ebony* magazine's praise for its contribution to racial understanding. Increasingly, though, Lewis retreated into alcoholism, solitude, and romance. His second marriage ended in 1942, and he died in Rome on January 10, 1951, as a lonely exile.

Summary

Shortly before his death, Lewis remarked that he loved America but did not like it. Both the love and the dislike are evident in his best works, most of which appeared in the 1920's. In his dissection of the middle class, he followed such nineteenth century critics of American materialism as Ralph Waldo Emerson and Henry David Thoreau, showing, in the latter's words, "We are provincial . . . because we are warped and narrowed by an exclusive devotion to trade and commerce and manufacture and agriculture and the like." Like the Transcendentalists, Lewis preached the sanctity of the individual against the masses. In works such as *Babbitt* and *It Can't Happen Here*, he showed the terrible price conformity exacts, while in *Arrowsmith*, he pointed out the rewards of, as well as the challenges to, independent thought.

In his criticism of middle America, Lewis introduced a new region and a new type of figure to literature. E. M. Forster said that Lewis had lodged "a piece of the continent in our imagination." He was among the first, and certainly the best, to describe the daily life of the upper Midwest and the small businessmen and farmers who lived there. Lewis, though, was not simply a latter-day local colorist. He recognized that in this area and these characters he was capturing the American spirit. What F. Scott Fitzgerald did for the few who were rich in the 1920's, Lewis did for the many who were simply comfortable.

While exposing the faults of the middle class, Lewis also recognized its potential. Sam Dodsworth and Doremus Jessup represent the best that the country has to offer, as Elmer Gantry and Lowell Schmaltz show the worst. Lewis' finest writing presents the alternatives available at the same time that it reveals how often Americans make the wrong choice.

All too frequently after 1930, Lewis himself succumbed to mediocrity and retreated from the central issues confronting the country, and his later works have damaged his reputation in the years since his death. Still, when he assumed the role of realist and reformer, he served as the conscience of his country, the symbol at home and abroad of an America that, knowing its weaknesses and its potential, was striving to free the human spirit from the shackles of prejudice and greed. For that role he will always be remembered.

Bibliography

Dooley, D. J. *The Art of Sinclair Lewis.* Lincoln: University of Nebraska Press, 1967. Intended as an introduction to Lewis, Dooley's book presents a biographical as well as critical study. The biography relies heavily on earlier works, but Dooley does seek to refute Mark Schorer's judgment that Lewis was "one of the worst writers in modern American literature."

Grebstein, Sheldon Norman. *Sinclair Lewis.* New York: Twayne, 1962. An introductory overview that combines critical study of Lewis' works with a brief account of his life. Especially strong on Lewis' work in the 1920's.

Lewis, Sinclair. *If I Were Boss: The Early Business Stories of Sinclair Lewis.* Edited by Anthony Di Renzo. Carbondale: Southern Illinois University Press, 1997. DiRenzo has brought together fifteen early stories by Lewis, all of which appeared in magazines of the period. The stories are notable because of they foreshadow Lewis's novel *Babbitt,* and also because they expose many contemporary workplace absurdities as being a result of human nature rather than popular management theory.

Light, Martin. *The Quixotic Vision of Sinclair Lewis.* West Lafayette, Ind.: Purdue University Press, 1975. Notes the romantic aspects that recur in Lewis' fiction and that sometimes clash and sometimes support the realistic, reformist tendencies.

Lundquist, James. *Sinclair Lewis.* New York: Frederick Ungar Publishing Co., 1973. Begins with a biography and then treats Lewis as moralist, artist, and essayist. Claims that despite artistic flaws, Lewis' work will survive because of its social criticism.

Morefield, Kenneth R. "Searching for the Fairy Child: A Psychoanalytic Study of *Babbitt*." *Midwest Quarterly* 37, no. 4 (Summer 1997). Morefield addresses Lewis's character of George Babbitt (from the novel *Babbitt*) from a psychoanalytic perspective. The author argues that this has rarely been done, because readers see so much of themselves in the character.

O'Connor, Richard. *Sinclair Lewis.* New York: McGraw-Hill Book, 1971. Treats both the life and the works and stresses Lewis' contribution to the development of American fiction.

Parrington, Vernon Louis. *Sinclair Lewis: Our Own Diogenes.* Seattle: University of Washington Book Store, 1927. Though dated, Parrington's work remains useful for pointing out Lewis' strengths—his acute social criticism and his photographic (and phonographic) ability to record American life.

Schorer, Mark. *Sinclair Lewis: An American Life.* New York: McGraw-Hill, and London: Heinemann, 1961. The definitive biography. Relates Lewis to the culture and history of his time and place, so that it shows both the man and his era.

Joseph Rosenblum

LI PENG

Born: October, 1928; Chengdu, Sichuan, China

Areas of Achievement: Government and politics

Contribution: Cautious and concerned that reforms should not abandon traditional Communist beliefs and values, Li Peng carried out party policy in various governmental offices while providing a balance against excessive reforms that could lead to instability in China.

Early Life

Li Peng was born in October, 1928, in Chengdu in Sichuan Province to Li Shouxun and Zhao Juntao. His father, Li Shouxun, was a Communist activist martyred in 1930 by the Guomintang or Nationalist Party of Chiang Kai-shek. Three-year-old Li was adopted by Chou En-lai, a close friend of his father. While Chou and his wife Deng Yingchao were childless, they cared for about forty descendants or orphans of the Communists, including Li. Chou was aware of the dangers of nepotism and was careful to ensure that his wife and relatives did not enjoy any governmental favors. Li spent his early years in Chengdu and Chongqing. He joined the Communist Party in 1945 and studied for one year at the Yan'an Institute of Natural Science until the victory of the Anti-Japanese War.

At the age of twenty, Li travelled to the Soviet Union to study electrical engineering at the Moscow Power Institute. Upon returning to the young People's Republic of China, he helped build and maintain hydroelectric plants and was chief engineer and deputy director of the Fengman Power Plant. In 1957, he met and married Zhu Lin; they had two sons and one daughter. In 1966, he became acting party secretary at the Beijing Municipal Power Supply Bureau. During the Cultural Revolution, most Soviet-trained intellectuals faced persecution. While Chou could not prevent the widespread upheaval and purges of this period, he rationed his influence to protect some individuals and institutions, including Li.

By the end of the 1970's, Deng Xiaoping had assumed full leadership of the Chinese Communist Party and began economic reforms to move China toward a socialist market economy. In contrast to the aging leadership drawn from revolutionary days, Li was young and well educated. He was also championed by Chun Yun, an older Marxist who had managed China's planned economy in the 1950's.

Life's Work

Li was promoted to vice minister of the electric power industry in 1979 and then minister in 1981. In brief order, he was also made vice minister of water conservancy and electric power (1982-1985), vice premier of State Council (1983-1987), and minister in charge of the State Education Committee (1985-1988). Li was a member and secretary of the Chinese Communist Party Central Committee from 1985 to 1987. (Each five years, the Chinese Communist Party Congress, consisting of two thousand delegates from local party members to the highest leaders, elects the Central Committee to establish party policy over the next five years.)

In contrast to reformers such as Zhao Ziyang, who advocated rapid market change, Li supported reform and opening China to the outside world; at the same time, however, he was concerned that reforms should not abandon traditional Communist values. Deng Xiaoping had expressed the belief that other eastern Communist governments had fallen because they had first resisted reform and then implemented reforms too fast, which resulted in loss of economic and political control. Some political observers believe Li provided a balance to liberals who espoused a reform pace that was too rapid.

Li gained a reputation as an effective government official. He oversaw dam protection during a 1981 Yellow River flood, investigated a 1985 aviation disaster caused by outdated guidance equipment, and, in 1987, investigated the failure to contain a huge forest fire that blackened a large sector of the Hailongjiang province. In 1985, as head of the State Education Commission, he recommended less government management of China's universities and more student choice in courses. In 1987, some college students held protests for democracy, a brief period of turmoil that resulted in the resignation of Communist Party General Secretary Hu Yaobang. Li considered the protests a symptom of too much "bourgeois liberalism" and recommended college students participate in work programs to develop a realistic view of the problems of China. In 1988, Li successfully defused student demonstrations over Japanese imports.

When Zhao became general secretary and resigned as prime minister, Li was appointed acting prime minister in November, 1987; in March, 1988, he was elected premier of the State Council in the Seventh National People's Congress, receiving 99 percent of the votes. By 1988, the government had also moved away from decisions by singular leaders and was relying more on advisors in government research institutes and universities to study problems and develop proposals. At the Thirteenth Congress, many veterans of the Long March retired from the Central Committee, including Deng Xiaoping. However, the new Central Committee kept Deng as the final decision maker on important issues.

Li had travelled to the United States, Eastern Europe, and the Soviet Union several years earlier, where he gained experience in trade arrangements and joint ventures. As China's new prime minister, Li made overseas visits to Thailand, Australia, and New Zealand in 1988. He also visited Thailand, Indonesia, and Singapore in 1990; Egypt, Jordan, and Kuwait in 1991; and Russia, Germany, Kazakhstan, Japan, and Korea in 1994. As premier, he endorsed the plan to promote coastal development but recognized the economic dangers of abandoning the agricultural interior. He also thought that housing should enter the market economy and be bought and sold at market rates. He considered inflation to be a major problem and cautioned against economic policies that produced fast results but were not long lasting. He also kept older communist values in the forefront, warning against worship of money, ultraindividualism, and decadent lifestyles. While many older members were either retiring or dying, some young party members began adopting the values Li espoused.

To Westerners, the most public aspect of Li's career occurred in the spring of 1989. On April 15 of that year, Hu died. Although he had not publicly supported student demonstrators, students felt he was more sympathetic to their concerns. Student demonstrations over the next days mixed grief over the death of a leader with demands for greater press freedom, better treatment of intellectuals, and favorable reevaluation of Hu. In addition, general complaints over inflation and corrupt officials were reminiscent of student demonstrations in 1978-1979 and 1986-1987. Students expanded this to a mass boycott of classes and to sit-in demonstrations in front of the Great Hall in Tiananmen Square in Beijing. Divided leadership opinions, an accommodating attitude toward college students, and the massing of news media in preparation for a major visit by Russian leader Mikhail Gorbachev in mid-May allowed the student demonstrations to grow unexpectedly over the next month. Li asked students to help guard social stability by ending their boycott and returning to school, but students called for the boycott to continue.

The May 4 speech by Zhao to three thousand students at the Great Hall acknowledged the need for reforms. Although he appealed to students on the need for stability, Zhao was obviously sympathetic to the student class strike. Three days before Gorbachev's May 16 arrival in China, three thousand students began a hunger strike in Tiananmen Square. By May 17, more than one million students had gathered in Beijing to join in an unusual event of greater freedom and permissiveness allowed by the Gorbachev visit and the Chinese government's awareness of world press visibility. While large numbers of the students continuously sang communist anthems to indicate their support for the government, others continued to agitate for reforms. On May 18, Li met for one hour with anticommunist student leaders in the Great Hall. Many government officials and television viewers perceived the students as arrogant and insulting, and very little was settled aside from an agreement to transport the hunger strikers to a hospital. During the meeting, one Beijing University student stressed that their movement was no longer in the students' hands, and a wider people's movement might not be "reasonable."

Indeed, large numbers of workers joined in the May 17-18 demonstrations, including illegal worker organizations that handed out leaflets calling for a general strike. Unrest also occurred in Tianjian, Sian, Chengdu, and other major cities. These were not peaceful student demonstrations, and fears of anarchy and chaos were being realized. On May 20, Deng Xiaoping declared martial law, and the offices of Li and President Yang Shangkun were used to carry out the decision. Young units of the People's Liberation Army (PLA) were brought into Beijing. Union leaflets then called for blocking troops from entering the city. Unable to reach the square, the young troops were pulled back. Many Beijing students ended their strike and returned to campus only to be replaced with new student demonstrators, often from other cities. Regional PLA commanders finally dispatched seasoned troops to Beijing on the night of June 3, 1989. The injuries and deaths of both citizens and soldiers were widely viewed on world media.

In spite of predictions that China would now sink back into isolation or abandon market reforms or that conservatives in government would lose their positions, everyday life in China as well as economic development and reforms continued. The Chinese leadership and people were aware of the serious social problems that had occurred when eastern Communist regimes had fallen after adopting both economic and political reforms. In November, 1989, Li admitted that it would be impossible to say these dramatic changes had no effect on China. In April, 1990, several months after the Soviet Communist Party agreed to give up its monopoly in the Soviet Union, Li visited Moscow, where he attended the ceremonial wreath-laying at Lenin's Tomb on Red Square. He was the first top Chinese leader to do so in thirty years.

As prime minister, Li continued to work diligently on internal and external problems. In 1992, local officials and state-owned banks diverted nearly two-thirds of the funds allocated for crops to make loans for development of industry and infrastructure. Thus, local governments lacked cash to pay peasants for contracted grain and used IOUs (white slips) instead. In December of 1992, Li called a televised conference to tell provincial and city leaders to exchange all IOUs for cash before the Lunar New Year. Over $500 million in funds were sent to provinces to defuse the white slip problem. Despite his efforts, Li continued to be closely associated with the Tiananmen Square massacre, and the National People's Congress adopted a resolution in 1992 that forced Li to denounce hard-line political forces in the party.

Summary

At the end of April, 1993, Li Peng suffered a mild heart attack and was hospitalized; he soon recovered and returned to work in mid-June. Li had been in charge of the environmentally controversial Three Gorges Dam or "San Xia" project since 1984, when he was minister of electric power. Proposed in the 1920's by Sun Yat-sen, this massive project was endorsed by Mao Tse-tung in 1958. Lack of money and the political problems of the Great Leap Forward and the Cultural Revolution set the project aside. In 1990, Li revived the planning, and it was approved by two-thirds vote of the National People's Congress in 1992. Having sponsored its development in modern times, Li has been rightly called the Three Gorges Dam's "godfather."

In March, 1998, Li ended his tenure as premier, having completed the maximum two five-year terms in this office. He was followed by Zhu Rongji. However, Li maintained his high ranking in the Politburo and was designated chairman of the National People's Congress. His biography, titled *Son of Yun'an River*, was published in Chinese in 1996 in Hong Kong.

Bibliography

Baum, Richard. *Burying Mao: Chinese Politics in the Age of Deng Xiaoping*. Princeton, N.J.: Princeton University Press, 1994; London: Princeton University, 1996. Baum provides candid descriptions of the major figures in China's politics from 1976 to 1993.

Burstein, Daniel, and Arne de Keijzer. *Big Dragon*. New York: Simon and Schuster, 1998. In this book, economists view Chinese politics in the 1990's and replace Western views and misconceptions with a practical description of policies, actions, and personalities.

Kane, Anthony J., ed. *China Briefing, 1989*. Boulder, Colo.: Westview Press, 1987. This book contains an overview of Chinese events during a critical historical year.

Li Peng. "Li Peng on Press Freedom, Legislation and Political Parties." *Beijing Review* 42, no. 1 (January 4, 1999). Interview with Li Peng in which he discusses the functions of the press and states that press freedom should promote China's development and social stability.

————. "Report on the Work of the Government." *Beijing Review* 41, no. 14 (April 6, 1998). Transcript of a speech by Li Peng concerning China's progress toward modernization since 1993 and the factors that led to its accomplishments.

Meisner, Maurice. *The Deng Xiaoping Era*. New York: Hill and Wang, 1996. Meisner details the political climate and specific events that led to government decisions during the 1980's.

"Premier Li Peng's Family." *Beijing Review* 39 (October 28, 1996): 23. This article contains a biographical overview of Li's Family.

"Profiles of New State Leaders." *Beijing Review* 36 (April 5, 1993): 6-10. This official biography of Chinese leaders is provided for general readership.

Spence, Jonathan. *The Search for Modern China*. 2d ed. New York: Norton, 1999. In this "long view" of modern Chinese history, Li is appropriately portrayed in the midst of the immense complexity of governing China.

Yang, Benjamin. *Deng: A Political Biography.* Armonk, New York: M. E. Sharpe, 1998. Until his death in 1997, Deng was the major policymaker of China. This biography is less laden with documentation and more readable, revealing in sever-al sections the extent to which Li actively functioned to carry out these party policies under new challenges and changing interpretations.

John Richard Schrock

SERGE LIFAR

Born: April 2, 1905; Kiev, Russia
Died: December 15, 1986; Lausanne, Switzerland
Area of Achievement: Dance
Contribution: As a dancer and choreographer, Lifar reestablished the Paris Opéra's leading role in the world of ballet by a series of innovative reforms: enhancing the role of male dancers; bringing modern concepts to the classical repertoire of the Opéra; and making dance the dominant element by emphasizing rhythm independently of music. His ballets are considered modern in subject and decor but classical in structure. In them, he attempts to convey drama through technique and choreography rather than through mime and music.

Early Life

Serge Lifar grew up in Kiev, where he attended the *Gymnasium*, studied violin and piano at the Kiev Conservatory, and practiced dance at the State School under Bronisława Nijinska, sister of the great Vaslav Nijinsky. Lifar says in his autobiography, *Ma Vie* (1965; English translation, 1970), that, although Russian composers bored him, he found consolation in Wolfgang Amadeus Mozart and the great Russian poet Alexander Pushkin. At fourteen, he served in the White Army. When the Red Army occupied the Ukraine in 1920, Lifar fled to the forests, where he learned the *kamarinskaia* and *gopak* dances from the peasants. He returned to Kiev and resumed ballet with Nijinska, but she left Russia to join Sergei Diaghilev's Ballets Russes in Monte Carlo. In 1923, Diaghilev asked her to recruit her five best Russian pupils at the Kiev Opera. When Lifar joined this select group, he was barely seventeen. After Lifar had escaped Soviet Russia and made his way to Monte Carlo, Diaghilev was disappointed in his dancing but agreed to keep him on.

Lifar first studied *Les Noces* of Igor Stravinsky as a member of the ensemble and later was given a small role in Nikolay Rimsky-Korsakov's *Schéhérazade* as the slave, because he had attracted the eye of Aleksandr Benois, Diaghilev's close friend. He also danced the officer in *Les Facheux* (1924), based on Molière's play, with music by Georges Auric and decor by Georges Braque. Again, he was spotted in Darius Milhaud's *Le Train bleu* the same year. Two of Diaghilev's closest collaborators and patrons, Misia Sert and Coco Chanel, insisted that Lifar had talent; Sert and Chanel were later to become Lifar's good friends. Through their influence, Lifar was given a major role in *Cimarosiana*, choreographed by Léonide Massine with decor by Sert. By 1925, Lifar had become Diaghilev's premier danseur and did Borée in Vladimir Dukelsky's *Zephyr et Flore*. He also took leading roles in *Les Matelots* and *Barabau*.

In 1926, Lifar had to pass an examination in order to please Nijinska, which he did brilliantly, and danced opposite the great Tamara Karsavina. Beginning in 1927, he began dancing with another newcomer, Diaghilev's new prima ballerina, Olga Spessivtzeva. Many roles now fell to him: He did a revival of *Romeo et Juliette, La Pastorale,* and *The Triumph of Neptune*. By 1927, he had danced in *La Chatte* for Diaghilev's new choreographer, George Balanchine, with Spessivtzeva. This ballet is famous for its constructivist decor by two émigré Soviet artists, Naum Gabo and Anton Pevsner. Interestingly, in 1927 he also did *Le Pas d'Acier*, Sergei Prokofiev's first score commissioned by Diaghilev.

The years 1928 and 1929 marked the apex of Lifar's career with Diaghilev. He danced the title roles in Diaghilev's most famous productions, *The Prodigal Son* of Prokofiev and *Apollo* of Stravinsky. Also, he did his first choreography for *Le Renard* by Stravinsky. Balanchine choreographed both *Apollo* and *The Prodigal Son*, perhaps the two most important ballets of the twentieth century. These last two years were epochal for ballet, and Lifar was at the center, giving definitive interpretations to each role. In *Renard* Lifar gained some notoriety because of his ingenious idea of having a double cast of dancers with acrobatic doubles dressed and masked alike so that the audience would believe that the cast was doing an amazing range of actions.

His apprenticeship ended with Diaghilev's death on August 19, 1929. It was Lifar who stood vigil at Diaghilev's bedside, ordered the death mask, and made all the funeral arrangements. At that moment it was clear to Lifar that he must not carry on Diaghilev's Ballets Russes but take other opportunities which now presented themselves.

Life's Work

Jacques Rouche, chief of the Paris Opéra, asked Lifar to produce Ludwig van Beethoven's *Creatures of Prometheus* and star in it. Lifar asked

Balanchine to do the choreography, but Balanchine fell sick and Lifar had to do it. He called upon Spessivtzeva to be his partner. Lifar's idea was to make Prometheus the central character, not his creatures, such as Death or Love. The chorus was to be a living backdrop of protagonists. This plastic conception was influenced by Diaghilevism, especially sharply broken lines and abrupt gestures. The success of this production led to his engagement as both *premier danseur* and *maître de ballet* at the Paris Opéra, posts that he retained, with the exception of the two years after the Occupation, until his retirement in 1959. His virtually unchallenged reign at the Opéra conveys the importance of his reputation and achievement. It was there that he raised the ballet company's position to its former excellence.

Lifar produced more than one hundred ballets and revitalized the teaching and reputation of ballet in France. He also created the cult of Diaghilev. In his most celebrated roles, especially ballets created for himself such as *Icare, Joan de Zoarissa*, and *David Triomphant*, or in the revival of classics such as his part as Albrecht in *Giselle*, he became a performer of magnetism and worked with the greatest ballerinas of his time, particularly Yvette Chauvire and Nina Vryubova. He demanded and created at the Opéra an outstanding troupe by using Diaghilev's methods. To choreography he added heroic boldness. He had his dancers work in parallel formation, feet placed in his own invented sixth and seventh positions with sharply held bodies and a brilliant use of beaten steps. To these highly angular positions and staccato movements he added his own rhythms before devising steps. Thus, for Lifar, ballet expresses certain fundamental emotions in choreographic terms and is created out of rhythms dictated not by the composer but by the choreographer himself.

Lifar had to have a first-class troupe, building it up from nothing by turning to the ballet schools of famous Russian émigrés. Out of these ballet schools came such dancers as Alicia Markova and Nina Vyrubova. Furthermore, Lifar tamed the wealthy subscribers to the Paris Opéra by eliminating them from rehearsals. At this time, during the 1930's, Lifar was busy organizing an homage to Diaghilev's memory, and he produced an original ballet for this purpose, *Bacchus et Ariadne*. Lifar did the choreography and danced Bacchus with Spessivtzeva as Ariadne. All of this was dedicated to the aesthetic tradition of Diaghilev's Ballets

Russes. What provoked a storm was Lifar's leap of some eighteen feet into the wings, where he was caught by stagehands. It was at this time that he revived the *Suite de Danses* and *Le Spectre de la Rose*, in which he used Léon Bakst's decors done for Diaghilev.

In the young Lifar's first pieces, he had tried to revive Diaghilevism. Now he began to turn to a new classicism, a return to roots, but with the lessons of modernism having been learned. In 1931 and 1932, he gained a clearer idea of himself and instituted needed reforms at the Opéra. When Spessivtzeva left the Opéra, Lifar was fortunate in replacing her with Camille Bos. It was a time to think through his own theory and style. He was against expressionism and the theories of Kurt Jooss, who presented this alternative. To counter the ideas of Jooss, Lifar created his own. The catalyst for his ideas was a ballet incarnating man's flight, *Icare*, in which dance could emerge independently of music. Lifar realized that dance was, in its purest form, an autonomous art, and to this end he wrote his now famous *Le Manifeste du choregraphe* in 1935.

In this manifesto, Lifar maintained that musical rhythm is born out of the dance's rhythm, not vice versa. He did not assert, as he is widely misinterpreted to have done, that ballet should not be accompanied by music. Rather, what he did maintain was that rhythmic patterns were the true accompaniment of dance, not necessarily music. The choreographer, or, more correctly, the "choreauthor," must compose his own rhythms, be free to invent, and not be bound by a musical framework. Furthermore, he developed the idea that dance at its purest attempts neither to express shades of emotions nor to be a narrative but that it can be an independent art. Though it can be a part of a spectacular production, dance cannot ultimately be used to illustrate another art, for it remains opposed to any kind of a program.

Lifar's credo was "In the beginning was the dance," which he called the alpha and omega of the dance's art. The composer must construct a score in accordance with the rhythms laid down by the choreographer. It is the choreographer and he alone who is the true creator of the ballet. Dance, for Lifar, is built up from definite rhythmic patterns, and a dance movement is inseparable from its rhythm. The choreographer is responsible for the rhythm. Lifar wants the composer to work to the rhythms and patterns created by the choreographer. The ideal situation, he hints, is for the choreographer to be the composer in order to avoid any ambiguity. The next best is to persuade the composer to create a score upon the rhythmic plan of the choreographer.

Mime, to Lifar, is only a legitimate element if used as an integral part of the dance itself. Gestures are of three kinds: unconscious, conscious, and conventional. The first is the best, the second should be used restrictively, and the third used little or not at all. In short, Lifar employs classical technique but distorts it to his own ends, which are to express fundamental emotions choreographically out of the rhythms dictated by the dance itself. Lifar gave these views their ultimate expression in his 1935 ballet, *Icare*. Lifar's new aesthetic was that rhythm formed the link between dance and music but that everything rhythmical was not necessarily danceable. To prove his point, Lifar omitted music from *Icare*. Arthur Honegger orchestrated rhythms for an ensemble of percussion instruments. No music could be sober and austere enough for the Greek myth of flight. For Lifar, the ballet gained in abstraction without music. *Icare* was performed July 9, 1935, and answered affirmatively the question whether a ballet can exist without music.

From 1938 to 1939, Lifar left the Opéra in order to stage a grand homage to Diaghilev. In 1939, France nationalized the ballet. Maurice Chevalier, the popular singer, dubbed Lifar the "Prince of Paris." The onset of World War II, however, saw Lifar trying hard to preserve the Opéra during the Occupation, even if it meant an arrangement with the Nazis. Under the Vichy regime, he was ordered to defend and preserve the national heritage of France. He sought to preserve it from Nazi persecution. His actions were often interpreted as collaboration and meant a two-year suspension after the Liberation. He returned triumphantly in 1947 to the Opéra. His postwar ballets include such outstanding successes as *Lucifer, Endymion, Phèdre, Les Noces fantastiques*, and Prokofiev's *Romeo and Juliet*.

Summary

Most of Serge Lifar's ballets were considered modern but classical in structure, with dramatic themes drawn from mythology, legend, or the Bible. Lifar considered these themes appropriate for a restoration of the prestige of the Opéra, where classical ballet was first developed. Lifar attempted to convey drama through appropriate technique and cho-

reography rather than through mime. His work was inspired by Diaghilev, and he carried on Diaghilev's tradition during his undisputed reign at the Paris Opéra. Nevertheless, the critics believe that, as a choreographer, he did not leave much behind. It is as Lifar the dancer and theorist that he left his ultimate mark. Lifar was a pioneer of modernism and for that he will be remembered.

Bibliography

Anderson, Jack. *Dance*. New York: Newsweek, 1974. A general work on the realm of dance that places Lifar in context. Contains a chronology of dance, a selected bibliography, an index, and numerous photographs and drawings.

Brinson, Peter, and Clement Crisp. *A Guide to the Repertory Ballet and Dance*. London and North Pomfret, Vt.: David and Charles, 1980. This book is good for placing Lifar in the twentieth century world of ballet. It contains an especially enlightening section on him.

Buckle, Richard. *Diaghilev*. London: Weidenfeld and Nicolson, and New York: Atheneum, 1979. Beyond being a superb biography, this book is an excellent history of ballet in the first quarter of the twentieth century. Buckle treats the formative years of Lifar's career with great detail and places Lifar's role into the larger picture.

Franks, A. H. *Twentieth Century Ballet*. London: Burke, and New York: Pitman, 1954. Chapter 5 is an excellent and succinct summary of Lifar's career and a fine analysis of Lifar's famous manifesto.

Garafola, Lynn. "Looking Back at the Ballets Russes: Rediscovering Serge Lifar." *Dance Magazine* 71, no. 10 (October, 1997). Profile of Lifar. Includes a discussion of his art collection.

Grigoriev, S. L. *The Diaghilev Ballet, 1909-1929*. Translated by Vera Bowen. New York: Dance Horizons, 1950; London: Constable, 1953. This personal recollection by Diaghilev's stage manager contains a good, intimate picture of Lifar with an assessment of his strengths and weaknesses as told by a friend.

Lifar, Serge. *Ma Vie*. Translated by James Holman Mason. London: Hutchinson, and New York: World, 1970. This is an English translation with a French title. It is a lively and entertaining autobiography, free of bias and reasonably objective. It is especially good on Lifar's supposed collaboration with the Nazis.

Donald E. Davis

MAYA YING LIN

Born: October 5, 1959; Athens, Ohio
Area of Achievement: Architecture
Contribution: Lin designed the Vietnam Veterans Memorial in Washington, D.C., and the Civil Rights Memorial in Montgomery, Alabama.

Early Life

Architect Maya Ying Lin was born on October 5, 1959, in Athens, a small midwestern town in southern Ohio. Her father, Henry Huan Lin, was a highly respected ceramicist and dean of fine arts at Ohio University. Her mother, Julia C. Lin, was a poet and professor of Asian and English literature. Both of her parents were born to culturally prominent families in China. Maya Lin's grandfather, Lin Changmin, along with Liang Qichao, whom the author Orville Schell calls "China's First Democrat," and Xu Zhimo, the greatest Chinese lyric poet of his generation, worked to establish democratic rule in China in the early 1900's. Her grandfather was also the director of the Chinese League of Nations Association and was stationed in London, England. While in England, the Lin family socialized with many of the brightest intellectuals of the day, a group that included H. G. Wells, Thomas Hardy, Bertrand Russell, and Katherine Mansfield. Lin Changmin's daughter, Lin Huiyin (Maya Lin's aunt), married the son of Liang Qichao, Liang Xucheng. Liang later became China's greatest architectural historian. After marrying, they moved to the United States, where both received degrees in architecture from the University of Pennsylvania. Lin Huiyin then went to Yale University to study architecture and stage design. The Lins eventually returned to China. Following World War II, however, when the communist forces overtook the Nationalists in a bitter civil war, Maya Lin's parents, like many other Chinese, fled the country. Henry Lin left to escape possible death or imprisonment and Julia left to attend Smith College on scholarship. They met for the first time in the United States and later settled in Athens, Ohio.

Maya Lin grew up in a typical middle-class home in a small midwestern university town. Her home environment included art and literature, and she was surrounded by books. An avid reader, she especially liked works by existentialists Jean-Paul Sartre and Albert Camus as well as fantasies such as J. R. R. Tolkien's *The Hobbit* and *Lord of the Rings*. She learned silversmithing, ceramics, and jewelry design, and she worked at McDonald's.

Although she was a loner at school, Maya Lin was an outstanding student. During her senior year in high school, she was covaledictorian of her graduating class. When she enrolled at Yale University in 1977, she had not selected a major. Eventually, she chose to enroll in a program in architecture. During her junior year she studied in Europe. While traveling in Europe, she became interested in cemetery architecture. She was particularly moved by Sir Edwin Lutyens' memorial to those who died in 1916 during the Somme offensive in World War I, called the Great Arch. This structure is considered one of the world's most outstanding war memorials. She received her bachelor's degree in architecture from Yale in 1981 and her master's degree in architecture from Yale in 1985.

Life's Work

After Maya Lin returned from Europe for her senior year at Yale, she enrolled in a class in funerary architecture. As a part of her coursework, she and her classmates were encouraged to enter the nationwide competition for designing a Vietnam Veterans Memorial in Washington, D.C. This competition attracted 1,420 entries, many of them submitted by noted architects and sculptors. It was the largest design competition in U.S. history. The entries were to be judged by a panel of experts, much as the designs for the U.S. Capitol and the Washington Memorial had been. Maya Lin traveled to Washington with two classmates to view the site of the planned memorial in Constitution Gardens near the Lincoln Memorial. Within a half-hour, she chose her design. She saw people gathered in the park and children playing and decided to make a structure that would not destroy the harmony of the park. When she finally completed her sketch for the entry, she was one of the last people to turn her entry in, only five minutes before the deadline. One month later, she received a telephone call informing her that she had won the competition.

The design, like the Vietnam War itself, was very controversial. The design featured a wall consisting of two segments, each 246.75 feet long, that came together to form a "V"-like structure. One segment points to the Washington Memorial; the

Maya Lin leans over her model of the Vietnam War Memorial.

other, to the Lincoln Memorial. Each segment consists of seventy polished black granite panels. The names of the 58,156 soldiers who died in the war, including those missing in action, are inscribed on the panels in the order in which they fell, along with a brief inscription. At the intersection, the highest point, the panels are 10.1 feet high; they taper to a width of eight inches at each end. On the back side, the entire structure is below ground. The front is open so that people can walk by and touch the wall if they choose to. Because of the reflective quality of the black granite, the wall gives back to those who visit images of themselves and the surrounding landscape.

The structure was praised by architects, the judges, and Jan Scruggs, the founder of the Vietnam Veterans Memorial Fund. Several veterans and other prominent figures, however, opposed it. Some of them called it "a black ditch," "an outrage," and the "black gash of shame." Its supporters called the design "moving" and praised its "extraordinary sense of dignity." As the controversy became more heated and opposition and support for the memorial in-

creased, a compromise was reached, and James Watt, secretary of the interior, issued final approval. The memorial was dedicated on November 13, 1982. A bronze statue of three servicemen, sculpted by Frederick Hart, was placed near the wall and dedicated on November 11, 1984.

Maya Lin's second major design, the Civil Rights Memorial in Montgomery, Alabama, was dedicated in the fall of 1989. The inspiration for the project came from a paraphrase of a verse in the biblical Book of Amos that was spoken by the Reverend Martin Luther King, Jr., "We will not be satisfied until justice rolls down like waters and righteousness like a mighty stream." The main idea of the memorial is that water flows over those words and over the names, each carved into the black granite, of forty men, women, and children who were killed during the course of the Civil Rights movement. Like the Vietnam Veterans Memorial, the work invites visitors to touch the names, this time through the water, and therefore bring some part of themselves to the act of honoring the dead.

In the case of the Civil Rights Memorial, Edward Ashworth, a board member of the Southern Poverty Law Center contacted Lin to see if she would be interested in designing it. The center sent her books about the Civil Rights movement and about various hate groups, including the Ku Klux Klan. Maya Lin was deeply moved by the stories of various people who gave their lives for civil rights. She was especially moved by the story of Michael Donald, a black teenager who was lynched by the Klan in 1981, and the successful prosecution by the center of the person guilty of the murder. Like many people in America, Lin had never learned about these people in school and was shocked to discover that many of them had been killed during her lifetime. She readily agreed to design a memorial that would occupy the plaza in front of the center in Montgomery, Alabama.

The Civil Rights Memorial consists of two parts, both of which are made of Canadian black granite. One part is a large nine-foot-tall panel with the carved inscription ". . . until justice rolls down like waters and righteousness like a mighty stream— Martin Luther King Jr." Water cascades down the panel, covering the inscription but allowing it to be read. The second part is a circular tabletop, almost twelve feet in diameter, resting on a pedestal. On the top of the structure are fifty-three brief entries carved into the stone in chronological order. Forty of the entries describe individual deaths; thirteen describe landmark events in the Civil Rights movement. Water comes out of the middle of the tabletop and gently flows over the inscriptions. As envisioned by Morris Dees, the director of the Southern Poverty Law Center, the Civil Rights Memorial has become a teaching tool for those who come and read the inscriptions. It is also a place of quiet reflection where visitors can come to understand that these individuals' deaths influenced history and helped to make things better.

Maya Lin has also excelled in sculpture and various kinds of architectural work during her professional career. Her public artwork includes "TOPO," an environmental sculpture for Charlotte, North Carolina; "Groundswell," the first sculpture commissioned for the Wexner Center for the Arts in Columbus, Ohio; and the "Women's Table," an outdoor sculpture dedicated to women at Yale University, in New Haven, Connecticut. Her architectural work has included the Museum for African Art in the SoHo district of New York City; the Rosa Esman Gallery, also in New York City; and private homes in Santa Monica, California, and in Williamstown, Massachusetts.

She has also pursued her interest in her own studio sculpture, creating human-scaled works made from beeswax, lead, steel, and broken glass. These works have been exhibited in New York, Los Angeles, San Francisco, and Columbus, Ohio.

Like both of her parents, Maya Lin has also taught at the university level. She has taught at Yale University and as a visiting artist at the Yale School of Art. She has also lectured at many museums and educational institutions, including the University of Washington, the Wexner Center for the Arts, the Metropolitan Museum of Art, the San Francisco Museum of Art, Wellesley College, and Qinghua University of Beijing, China.

In addition to doing her professional work, Maya Lin also serves on several community boards. Her interest in environmental issues has led her to serve on the board of the Energy Foundation and on the national advisory board to the Presidio Council in San Francisco. She also serves on the board of the Ohio University Museum of Art and on the advisory board of the Southern Poverty Law Center.

Summary

Maya Lin has made two significant contributions to architecture, a field dominated by males. Lin, a Chinese American, was selected to create two public memorials in the United States that celebrate two of the most important social issues of the past half-century. The Vietnam Veterans Memorial has become the most visited memorial in Washington, D.C., and has been described as "perhaps the most moving war memorial ever built." On November 20, 1984, the U.S. postal service issued a twenty-cent stamp commemorating the Vietnam Veterans Memorial. The Civil Rights Memorial has also received great praise.

She has received the Presidential Design Award, the American Institute of Architects' Honor Award, and the Henry Bacon Memorial Award. She is a recipient of a National Endowment for the Arts visual artists' grant and has received honorary doctoral degrees of fine arts from Yale University, Smith College, and Williams College.

Maya Lin owns a studio in New York City's Bowery district. Early in her career, Maya Lin has already become one of the most celebrated and accomplished architects in the United States. She has proved that women can succeed in architecture and in sculpture and has opened the doors for others to follow.

Bibliography

Abramson, Daniel. "Maya Lin and the 1960s: Monuments, Time Lines, and Minimalism." *Critical Inquiry* 22, no. 4 (Summer 1996). Examines the monuments created by Lin, including the Vietnam Veterans Memorial and others devoted to the civil rights and women's movements.

Ashabranner, Brent. *Always to Remember: The Story of the Vietnam Veterans Memorial*. New York: Dodd Mead, 1988. This book, which is appropriate for middle and high school students, gives a very good background of the controversy surrounding the Vietnam War as well as the memorial itself.

Ezell, Edward Clinton. *Reflections on the Wall: The Vietnam Veterans Memorial*. Harrisburg, Pa.: Stackpole, 1987. A very good account of various positions toward and impressions of the memorial.

Lopes, Sal. *The Wall: Images and Offerings from the Vietnam Veterans Memorial*. New York: Collins, 1987. An excellent pictorial that captures the beauty and emotions of the memorial.

Pedersen, Martin C. "Maya Lin: One Driving Idea." *Graphis* 53, no. 313 (January-February, 1998). Examines Lin's work, including the sculpture "The Wave Field," which stands near the University of Michigan engineering building, and the memorial for those who died in the 1988 movement for the Southern Poverty Law Center in Montgomery, Alabama.

Scruggs, Jan C., and Joel L. Swerdlow. *To Heal a Nation: The Vietnam Veterans Memorial*. New York: Harper, 1985. An excellent overview of the history of the Vietnam Veterans Memorial, including the controversy surrounding the selection of Maya Lin's design for the memorial and the harsh politics of getting a memorial approved.

Spence, Jonathan D. *The Gate of Heavenly Peace: The Chinese and Their Revolution, 1895-1980*. New York: Viking Press, 1981; London: Faber, 1982. Provides an excellent account of Maya Lin's family in China as well as one of the best histories of modern China.

Zinsser, William. "Deeds and Deaths That Made Things Better." *Smithsonian* 22 (September, 1991): 32. An excellent article detailing the background and the impact of the Civil Rights Memorial in Montgomery, Alabama.

Gregory A. Levitt

LIN PIAO

Born: December 5, 1907; Huang-kang District, Hupeh Province, China

Died: September 12 or 13, 1971; in an airplane crash in Mongolia

Areas of Achievement: The military, government, and politics

Contribution: Lin was a military officer who was an early adherent of Mao Tse-tung's armed rural revolution and achieved notable battlefield successes, especially in the Chinese Civil War from 1947 to 1949. Lin Piao was a champion of Mao's Cultural Revolution, and in 1969 he became Mao's designated successor.

Early Life

Lin Piao came from a rural district in China's inland Hupeh Province. His parents had few means but a large family; Lin was the second of four boys. He was sent to a modern school in the inland city of Wu-han, where he and his elder cousins associated with nationalistic young students. That group became an early cell of the Communist movement in China. In 1925, Lin went to Shanghai, and there he joined the Chinese Communist Youth League, whose leaders included his Wu-han school friends. At this time, the Communist and Nationalist parties were cooperating, and Lin entered the Nationalist Party's Whampoa Military Academy in Canton. He received a year of training before becoming a junior officer.

In 1927, Lin participated in the Nationalists' long-planned Northern Expedition, which sought to unite China by military means. Lin served as a junior officer in Communist-led units stationed at Wu-han. After Chiang Kai-shek turned against the Communist movement in April, 1927, the Communists responded to growing Nationalist power, most notably in the Autumn Harvest Uprising at Nan-ch'ang on August 1, 1927. That attack is celebrated today as the founding of the People's Liberation Army (PLA). Lin was numbered among the twenty thousand Communist-led troops in that unsuccessful uprising.

Life's Work

Following the failed Autumn Harvest Uprising, Lin was only twenty years old, yet his decision to remain with the defeated Communist forces brought him into the inner circle of Mao Tse-tung's followers, who have ruled China since 1949. Lin rose steadily in the ranks because of his battlefield prowess and his loyalty to Mao. During the period of the Kiangsi Soviet (1930-1934), Lin commanded the Communists' First Army Corps and became associated with Mao's faction. Lin led this same unit on the Long March and again proved himself as Mao's loyal subordinate. Lin was numbered among the small cadre of Communist leaders who set up the new headquarters in Shansi Province in 1936.

In 1937, when the war with Japan broke out, the Communist forces were reorganized into the Eighth Route Army. Its commanders were Chu Teh and P'eng Te-huai; Lin commanded its 115th Division of fifteen thousand men. In September, 1937, Lin's division had a notable victory against a Japanese force in northeast Shansi Province. Lin became a practitioner and author of the style of guerrilla warfare that the Communists advocated during the Anti-Japanese War (1937-1945).

Lin was a small man, thin and gaunt even in his thirties. He was seriously injured in 1938. First, he returned to the Communist base headquarters of Yen-an and then in 1939 went to the Soviet Union for treatment, remaining there for three years. Upon returning to China in 1942, Lin did not return to the battlefield but took up administrative duties. In 1945, he was named to the Central Committee of the Chinese Communist Party.

Following the Japanese surrender, Lin led an army of 250,000 troops into Manchuria. Initially, in spite of some Soviet assistance, his army was unsuccessful, but in 1947 his enlarged forces achieved a series of victories that destroyed Chiang Kai-shek's control of this crucial region. Then Lin's army moved into North China, where the Nationalist commander of Peking surrendered to him in the winter of 1948-1949. In the spring of 1949, Lin's army, now known as the Fourth Field Army, crossed the Yangtze River and marched to Canton. There Lin assumed command of a huge military region encompassing about one-third of China's total population.

When China entered the Korean War in the fall of 1950, Lin's Fourth Field Army participated, but Lin remained behind because of poor health, which is believed to have been a consequence of tuberculosis. Lin remained largely inactive through 1959, although he continued to hold many prominent titles. In the military, Lin's star was eclipsed by

P'eng, who had led the Chinese Volunteer Forces during the Korean War.

In the summer of 1959, a year after the beginning of Mao's campaign called "The Great Leap Forward," a conference was held to evaluate the situation. P'eng criticized Mao's efforts at a breakthrough in socialist organization and production as wasteful, foolish, and harmful to China's national defense. Mao accepted some criticism but insisted on keeping the newly created communes while demanding P'eng's removal as minister of defense. Lin was appointed in his place.

In the early 1960's, Lin began to play a major role in Chinese politics. He stressed a radically egalitarian, frugal, and selfless style for the PLA. Following Mao's direction, Lin advocated that the PLA lead all of China back to the simple, selfless dedication shown during the war against Japan. That approach, known as "Yen-an Way" after the Communists' wartime headquarters, stressed self-reliance, active participation in physical work, and spontaneous adaptations in difficult circumstances. It opposed detailed planning, bureaucracy, and privileged life-styles for anyone. The whole of

China adopted this approach in the Cultural Revolution (1966-1969). Lin also fed Mao's personality cult, which reached its highest pitch in these years.

As minister of defense, Lin carried through a program of military modernization. In 1964, largely on the basis of their own efforts, the Chinese developed a nuclear bomb. Beginning in 1964, China began relocating defense plants away from the coastal regions and devoting one-half of the state investment to construction of transportation links and defense facilities dispersed widely in the interior. This strategy, now called the "Third Front" approach, was meant to help China survive if it were attacked by its enemies. The "enemy" meant the United States initially, but increasingly in the 1960's the Chinese came to fear the Soviet Union. Lin's programs combined the simple, nontechnological style of the "Yen-an Way" with an emphasis on creating China's own advanced technology. This combination is summed up in the slogan "walking on two legs," reflecting a desire to harness all available resources to create a socialist China. In these efforts, as earlier in his career, Lin was closely guided by Mao.

Lin threw the PLA's weight behind Mao's call for a "Cultural Revolution." Mao began that effort in 1965, but only in the summer of 1966, when the PLA put its resources behind the student Red Guards, did the Cultural Revolution take off. Wild attacks on the Communist Party, the regular government, and most established institutions followed and brought great disruption to China's society and economy. The Cultural Revolution weakened even the PLA, but nevertheless it remained as the last stable institution. As efforts to reconstitute some order began in late 1967 and 1968, the PLA provided the necessary resources to end the struggle and to re-create the governmental structure. Lin had replaced the disgraced Liu Saho-ch'i as Mao's chief lieutenant in 1967 and was designated in the 1969 Communist Party constitution as "Comrade Mao Tse-tung's close comrade-in-arms and successor."

Even at the pinnacle of his power, Lin remained a small, unimpressive public figure, who transmitted neither energy nor vision. His sudden fall in late summer in 1971 is the most astounding political event in the history of the People's Republic of China. Lin was accused of having led a scheme that was hatched by his son Lin Li-kuo and called the "571" project. These numbers, read in standard Chinese, are homophonous with the term "armed uprising." The plot also involved five top generals of the PLA and Lin's second wife, Yeh Chun, in the attempt to assassinate Mao. When the attempt went awry, Lin and his family commandeered a British-made passenger aircraft of the Chinese Air Force and attempted to flee to the Soviet Union. The airplane lacked sufficient fuel and crashed in Mongolia. All the passengers, including Lin, were killed in the crash.

The full story of Lin's death has never been told. Only months after the events occurred did the first public reports appear outside and inside China. The participating generals who survived the coup attempt were kept in jail for nine years before trial. By that time, several were too old to respond coherently to the charges. What happened to the thousands of minor figures implicated in the plot is unknown. Lin's motivation remains cloudy, for he may have sought to kill Mao in order to speed up his own constitutionally mandated succession, or he may have reacted defensively to Mao's displeasure at Lin's own growing influence.

It is noteworthy that the failed coup and Lin's death came within a few weeks of Henry Kissinger's first visit to Beijing, in the summer of 1971. Following that visit, Chou En-lai advocated, with Mao's concurrence, abandoning China's autarkic position in foreign policy in order to protect China better against the possibility of a Soviet attack. Anti-Americanism had been a hallmark of the People's Republic of China's policies since its establishment in 1949, but by 1960 China had fallen out with the Soviet Union also and had adopted a policy of independence from either of the superpowers. Instead, China would ally itself only with the interests of poorer, disadvantaged states. Lin was closely identified with this policy of nonalignment with either superpower.

The opening to the United States in the late summer of 1971 signaled Mao's willingness to change China's foreign policy radically. Lin probably did not approve, and it seems likely that differences over this new foreign policy helped precipitate the Lin Piao affair. There were other issues, however, involving domestic policy also in dispute in 1970 and 1971. Lin's stress on keeping China poised on a wartime footing in fear of an attack from either superpower was no longer acceptable to Mao, in part because it required continuing commitment to military investment that weakened the growth of Chinese socialism. The official story of how Lin plotted to assassinate Mao is cast in terms of Lin's

own dreams of domination; any differences over the redirection of China's foreign policy go unmentioned.

Summary

Throughout his life, Lin Piao was a disciplined, loyal military man, dedicated to Mao and the Chinese Communist Party. With other members of the small Chinese Communist leadership, he considered Mao not so much as an emperor who stood above them as a special comrade whose brilliance made him the core of their movement. They strengthened that core by rallying around him on all issues. Until 1960, Lin was only a third-level figure who contibuted through his competence in military affairs. Only by his elevation to minister of defense after P'eng's disgrace in 1959 did Lin enter into the second rank of Chinese Communist leaders.

Even in the 1960's, though, Lin's prominence appears to have been thrust upon him. As minister of defense, he continued to follow Mao's policy directions. He lacked independent vision of China's socialist future and saw most questions in the limited terms of China's strategic defense. As long as the top leadership of the Chinese Communist Party remained united, Lin was no more than an influential minister of defense, but, in the Cultural Revolution, Mao accused other top leaders of undermining the revolution. Lin, as always loyal to Mao, followed Mao's leadership into the maelstrom of the Cultural Revolution as the Chinese Communist Party split and turned upon itself. When the tumult subsided, Lin was surprisingly left as Mao's designated successor. After 1969, Lin was uneasy in his elevation, for he was better suited to serve than to lead. His status as the constitutionally designated heir to Mao required broad talents, which he lacked.

Ultimately, his role in history depends on the circumstances of his death, and that role is embedded in the full story of the so-called Lin Piao affair. Lin's position changes with whatever version of his death one accepts. In the official version, Lin was an ungrateful traitor to Mao, who, impatient in waiting for Mao to die, plotted to destroy Mao. In a possible alternative, Lin could have reacted defensively against Mao's displeasure and sought to save his own skin. In a third version, a sudden crisis could have boiled up over a foreign policy initiative toward the United States. Lin could have found himself on the losing side. In a final irony, this prosaic military man, by the circumstances of his death, became a figure of mystery whose full role in history remains unclear.

Bibliography

Ebon, Martin. *Lin Piao: The Life and Writings of China's New Ruler.* New York: Stein and Day, 1970. The biographical section was written before Lin's fall and is often wrong on facts, so this outdated source must be used sparingly.

Ginneken, Jaap van. *The Rise and Fall of Lin Piao.* Translated by Danielle Adkinson. London and New York: Penguin, 1976. Emphasizes the last decade of Lin's life including Lin's activities during the Cultural Revolution. Argues that Mao's retreat from Lin on domestic matters preceded their foreign policy differences. Best available general account.

A Great Trial in Chinese History: The Trial of Lin Biao and Jiang "Qing" Counter-revolutionary Cliques. Oxford and New York: Pergamon Press, 1981. A semiofficial summary of the charges against Lin from the trial of his surviving coplotters held in 1980.

Kau, Michael Y. M., ed. *The Lin Piao Affair.* White Plains, N.Y.: International Arts and Sciences Press, 1975. Translations from Chinese of public documents and some secret party materials concerning Lin and his failed coup attempt.

Naughton, Barry. "The Third Front: Defence Industrialization in the Chinese Interior." *China Quarterly* 115 (September, 1988): 351-386. Describes the economic and military strategy associated with the "Third Front" and Lin's close association with that concept.

Yao, Ming-le. *The Conspiracy and Death of Lin Piao.* Translated by Stanley Karnow. New York: Knopf, 1983. Published as an insider's true account, the stories related in these pages make a riveting fictionalization but cannot be accepted as historically accurate.

David D. Buck

CHARLES A. LINDBERGH

Born: February 4, 1902; Detroit, Michigan
Died: August 26, 1974; Hana, Maui, Hawaii
Areas of Achievement: Aviation and conservation
Contribution: Lindbergh's historic New York to Paris solo flight in 1927 was a turning point in aviation history, and he continued to play a major role in both civil and military aviation throughout his life.

Early Life

Charles Augustus Lindbergh was born February 4, 1902, in Detroit, Michigan, the only son of Swedish-born Charles August Lindbergh (not Augustus as sometimes incorrectly cited), a Minnesota congressman, and Evangeline Lodge Land Lindbergh, a Michigan native and chemistry teacher of English-Scotch ancestry. The elder Lindbergh, a Little Falls, Minnesota, lawyer and businessman, served as a Progressive Republican in the United States House of Representatives from 1907 to 1917, where his reform interests included such issues as banking and currency, the Midwestern farmer, and the European war. Charles August and Evangeline Lindbergh were estranged early in their marriage, but young Lindbergh regularly spent time with both parents, thus living primarily in Minnesota and Washington, D.C. The elder Lindbergh had remarried after his first wife's death and young Lindbergh had two half sisters, Lillian and Eva. In his early years, Lindbergh showed his mechanical and scientific bent when, for example, he visited the laboratory of his grandfather Charles Land (a dentist and researcher) in Michigan, and when he drove the car in his father's 1916 campaign for the United States Senate. He was graduated from Little Falls high school in 1918, and, early in the same year, began working the home farm, where he remained until the fall of 1920.

After three semesters at the University of Wisconsin, where he enrolled in the mechanical engineering program and was a member of the rifle team, Lindbergh quit school in early 1922 and became a flying student at the Nebraska Aircraft Corporation in Lincoln, Nebraska. During this period, "Slim" Lindbergh (he was six-foot, three and one half inches tall) gained a reputation as an expert mechanic, parachute jumper, wing-walker, and pilot. He made several swings on the barnstorming circuit in the Midwest and Great Plains with other flying buddies, and, in 1923, he purchased his first airplane, a surplus World War I Curtiss Jenny. In 1924 and 1925, he completed United States Army Air Cadet programs at Brooks and Kelly fields in Texas and was graduated at the top of his class with the rank of second lieutenant.

Lindbergh then moved to St. Louis, Missouri, where he was head pilot for Robertson Aircraft Company and joined the Missouri National Guard unit. In April, 1926, he became one of the early pilots to carry United States mail when he began flying routes to Peoria and Chicago, Illinois, for Robertson. In order to compete for the twenty-five-thousand-dollar Orteig Prize for the first New York-to-Paris flight, Lindbergh then secured financial backing from St. Louis supporters; with engineer Donald Hall, he helped to design the specially built monoplane, *The Spirit of St. Louis*, at Ryan Airlines in San Diego, California. In early May, 1927, he set a transcontinental speed record when he flew from San Diego to New York via St. Louis.

Even at this point in his life, certain characteristics about Lindbergh had emerged: a constantly inquiring mind, a total sincerity, a meticulous attention to detail and accuracy, and a sense of humor. Like his father, the reform-minded congressman and scholar, he also had a stubborn independence, a sense of courage, and a quiet personal nature.

Life's Work

Lindbergh established a milestone in aviation history, when, on May 20-21, 1927, he flew *The Spirit of St. Louis* nonstop from New York to Paris. His historic flight of 3,610 miles in thirty-three hours and thirty minutes was the first one-man crossing of the Atlantic Ocean by air. The flight was followed by an unprecedented and prolonged public response, and, overnight, Lindbergh became a world figure. After receptions in Europe, Lindbergh returned to the United States aboard the cruiser USS *Memphis*, a trip arranged by President Calvin Coolidge, and was honored in many cities. He received numerous honors and awards, including the Congressional Medal of Honor and a promotion to colonel. Lindbergh also made trips to Latin America and to Mexico, where he met Anne Spencer Morrow, the daughter of United States Ambassador Dwight W. Morrow. Lindbergh and Morrow were married in 1929.

During the period of rapidly expanding aviation activity after the famous flight and through the 1930's, Lindbergh served as technical adviser to Transcontinental Air Transport (TAT, later TWA) and Pan American World Airways. In this capacity, he played a major role in the testing of new aircraft, in planning the first transcontinental route for TAT (he flew the last leg in a Ford Tri-Motor), and in developing regular transoceanic routes for Pan American. It was Lindbergh, representing TWA, for example, who demanded that the Douglas DC-1 airplane be able to take off and land safely with one engine. Ultimately, the design resulted in the legendary DC-3. The pioneer aviator was among the first to recommend the use of land planes crossing the oceans, a practice now accepted after the early use of Clipper flying boats. On international route development and mapping, Charles and Anne Lindbergh made several long test flights about the world in his Lockheed Sirius monoplane, the *Tingmissartog*, one of which Anne has described in her book *North to the Orient* (1935). Lindbergh also served as a consultant to the Guggenheim Fund and the United States Bureau of Aeronautics, and, when the air mail crisis occurred in 1934, he stook a stand in opposition to President Franklin D. Roosevelt's decision to allow the United States Army to fly the mail.

The 1930's also brought tragedy to the Lindberghs. In 1932, their first child, Charles Augustus, Jr., was kidnaped and murdered. The extensive publicity which continued during the trail, conviction, and execution of Bruno Richard Hauptmann for the crime was so distasteful to the Lindberghs that they sought refuge in Europe in 1935. They lived in England and on an island off the coast of France, seeking privacy in rearing their family, which came to include five other children: Jon, Anne, Land, Scott, and Reeve. At this point in his life, Lindbergh's interest turned to scientific research; he worked closely with surgeon Alexis Carrel in developing a perfusion pump (frequently referred to as a mechanical heart) which was able to sustain life in animal organs outside the body, and with Robert Goddard, the father of modern rocketry, for whom Lindbergh secured important financial support.

While in Europe, Lindbergh studied European military aviation and made three major inspection trips to Germany between 1936 and 1938. After these visits, convinced of German air superiority, he warned against the growing air power of the Nazi regime. In 1939, Lindbergh returned to the United States and, at the request of General Henry Arnold, assessed United States air preparations.

With the outbreak of war in Europe, Lindbergh began his antiwar crusade. Fearing possible American involvement, he took a public stand for neutrality and later joined the isolationist America First Committee. Because of this controversy, the Lindbergh image was tarnished as political charges were made over his disagreement on American foreign policy with the Roosevelt Administration. Bolstered by his father's adamant stand against Wilsonian policies prior to American entry into World War I, Lindbergh remained firm in his views.

Following the Japanese attack on Pearl Harbor, however, Lindbergh supported his country fully when it entered the war. Only later was it known that the famous aviator, who resigned his military commission in 1941 under political pressure, had personally tested every type of fighter aircraft used by the United States in the South Pacific. Although a civilian, Lindbergh flew some fifty combat missions, passing on technical knowledge which enabled American pilots to save on fuel consumption and shooting down an enemy plane. During the war, he was also a consultant to the Ford Motor Company at the Willow Run plant and made high-altitude chamber tests at the Mayo Clinic in Rochester, Minnesota.

After World War II, Lindbergh continued to be active in commercial and military aviation, but, increasingly, his time was devoted to two other concerns, conservation and writing. The pioneer aviator, continuing his association with Pan American and with his friend Juan Trippe (his TWA affiliation had ended in the 1930's), early advised the introduction of jets and jumbo jets, which opened a new era in air travel. During the postwar years, he served in an advisory capacity on such matters as the Berlin airlift and selection of the United States Air Force Academy site. On a long-term appointment, Lindbergh was a consultant to the Department of Defense, and he was awarded the rank of brigadier general in the Air Force Reserve in 1954 by President Dwight D. Eisenhower. In this role, one of his most important contributions was his involvement with the structuring and implementation of the Strategic Air Command.

Devoted to the idea of world ecology and the preservation of natural resources, Lindbergh came to the conclusion that modern technology endan-

gered the natural environment of the world—a conflict he described as civilization versus the primitive. Thus, his interests moved from science to mysticism and the study of primitive peoples. Lindbergh valued simplicity in life—the earth and sky—perhaps harking back to the roots of the Minnesota farm boy with his exposure to woods and water. Indeed, Lindbergh felt strongly about his Minnesota and Scandinavian background, and he participated in several projects concerning the Minnesota Historical Society, the biography of his father, Charles August, and the proposed Voyageur's National Park in the state.

When Lindbergh became involved with conservation, especially in his work as director with the World Wildlife Fund, he relaxed somewhat his strong aversion to the press. As early as 1948, he had warned, in his brief study *Of Flight and Life* (1948), that the human race could become a victim of its own technology. Further, according to Lindbergh, the overall quality of life should be the paramount goal of mankind. He put it simply when he wrote in 1964: "If I had to choose, I would rather have birds than airplanes." Lindbergh, aviator and technician, thus was complemented by Lindbergh, conservationist and defender of wildlife. While he encouraged the use of the Boeing 747 as an efficient aircraft, for example, he questioned the economic efficiency and environmental impact of the supersonic transport and spoke out against it during the debate in 1970. His struggle with changing values is also seen by his support of American retaliatory power during the Cold War, which was set against his worry that aviation and technology had made all people vulnerable to atomic annihilation.

Lindbergh also spent considerable time in many successful writing efforts. *We* (1927) is a brief account of the famous flight; *The Culture of Organs* (1938), written with Alexis Carrel, is a record of the research on which the two collaborated. Among his many publications in the post-World War II era are his firsthand and thorough account of the 1927 flight, *The Spirit of St. Louis* (1953), which won a Pulitzer Prize; his *Wartime Journals* (1970), drawn from extensive handwritten diaries; *Boyhood on the Upper Mississippi* (1972), an account of boyhood experiences in Minnesota; and, posthumously, *Autobiography of Values* (1977), a reflective statement on his life and concerns.

After World War II, Lindbergh lived with his family in Connecticut and then, later, in Hawaii. He continued in his duties as consultant to Pan American World Airways and to the Department of Defense and served on a number of aeronautical boards. Lindbergh died in Hana, Maui, Hawaii, on August 26, 1974.

Summary

Lindbergh is remembered first for his long and significant contributions to aviation history. From the barnstormers of the 1920's to the jumbo jets of the 1970's, Lindbergh was at the center of the immense changes that characterized aviation and aerospace technology in the twentieth century. Evidence of Lindbergh's superb technical knowledge and substantial leadership is clear, as he participated in numerous crucial decisions affecting its development. It was the 1927 flight which propelled Lindbergh to prominence, and the effects were immediate. For aviation, the historic flight launched a modern era in aviation history. More than any single event, it made the American people aware of the potential of commercial aviation, and there followed a Lindbergh "boom," with a rapid acceleration in the number of airports, pilot licenses, airlines, and airplanes in 1928-1929. While the crush of publicity was overwhelmingly favorable in 1927, Lindbergh soon came to realize that demands on his time and privacy had irreversibly changed his life. He struggled to maintain his privacy for much of the remainder of his life. From an early dislike of expressions such as Lucky Lindy and the Flying Fool, his distrust for the media deepened after the 1932 kidnaping tragedy. Yet the demanding response to Lindbergh was, in part, the history of the 1920's, an age of expanding print and broadcast journalism. Amid the sensationalism and the Prohibition experiment of the Jazz Age, Lindbergh emerged as an authentic hero to many Americans. People responded enthusiastically to the youthful Lindbergh's individualism and modest character as well as to the new technology of the airplane.

Yet Lindbergh's influence includes more than the 1927 flight, significant as it may have been. He was not simply another flyer who set a record. Indeed, his contributions to American life in the forty-seven years between the flight and his death in 1974 included substantial activity in civil and military aviation, scientific research, and conservation. Ultimately, Lindbergh was a man both of science and of philosophical thought. His broad legacy is represented not only in aviation but also in his insistence that, if the planet is to survive, there must be an understanding between the world of science and the world of nature.

Bibliography

Berg, A. Scott. *Lindbergh*. London: Macmillan, and New York: Putnam, 1998. Berg is the first writer permitted by Lindbergh's widow, Anne Morrow, to have full access to Lindbergh's own archives at Yale University. The result is this, the latest Lindbergh biography, which allows a view of his life through his own eyes.

Bilstein, Roger E. *Flight in America, 1900-1983: From the Wrights to the Astronauts*. Rev. ed. Baltimore: Johns Hopkins University Press, 1994. The best general scholarly treatment of American aviation. Although Lindbergh is mentioned only briefly, historian Bilstein provides the necessary framework to understand total aviation and aerospace development. Good twenty-page bibliographical note section.

Cole, Wayne S. *Charles A. Lindbergh and the Battle Against American Intervention in World War II*. New York: Harcourt Brace, 1974. Well-researched, scholarly study of Lindbergh's involvement in the noninterventionist movement prior to World War II. Cole, who also authored a book on the America First Committee, utilized Lindbergh interviews and the Lindbergh Papers in his work.

Crouch, Tom D., ed. *Charles A. Lindbergh: An American Life*. Washington, D.C.: Smithsonian Institution Press, 1977. Brief but informative volume based primarily on lectures delivered at the Smithsonian by John Greierson, Paul Ignatius, Richard Hallion, Wayne Cole, and Judith Schiff. It also includes notes on *The Spirit of St. Louis* by engineer Donald Hall and a reliable, selected fifteen-page bibliography.

Davis, Kenneth S. *The Hero: Charles A. Lindbergh and the American Dream*. New York: Doubleday, 1959; London: Longman, 1960. Popular account of Lindbergh's life by a well-known journalist. As in many such accounts, there are factual inaccuracies regarding Lindbergh history, yet Davis provides a good overview and some insights into Lindbergh's life. Includes an eighty-two-page bibliographical essay.

Larson, Bruce L. *Lindbergh of Minnesota: A Political Biography*. Foreword by Charles A. Lindbergh. New York: Harcourt Brace, 1973. Primarily a scholarly study of Lindbergh's congressman father, who had a very strong influence on the aviator's life and values. References to the younger Lindbergh and family history until the elder Lindbergh's death in 1924. Lindbergh interviews and Lindbergh Papers included in research.

Lindbergh, Anne Morrow. *Bring Me a Unicorn: Diaries and Letters of Anne Morrow Lindbergh, 1922-1928*. London: Chatto and Windus, and New York: Harcourt Brace, 1972.

———. *Hour of Gold, Hour of Lead: Diaries and Letters of Anne Morrow Lindbergh, 1929-1932*. New York: Harcourt Brace, 1973.

———. *Locked Rooms and Open Doors: Diaries and Letters of Anne Morrow Lindbergh, 1933-1935*. New York: Harcourt Brace, 1974.

———. *The Flower and the Nettle: Diaries and Letters of Anne Morrow Lindbergh, 1936-1939*. New York: Harcourt Brace, 1976.

———. *War Within and Without: Diaries and Letters of Anne Morrow Lindbergh, 1939-1944*. New York: Harcourt Brace, 1980. In these five volumes, Anne Morrow Lindbergh, an accomplished and recognized author, provides important documentation of and insights into the Lindbergh story in her firsthand account of the years between 1922 and 1945. Comments on specific portions of Lindbergh history may also be found in several other published works by Anne Morrow Lindbergh.

Lindbergh, Charles A. *Autobiography of Values*. Edited by William Jovanovich and Judith A. Schiff. New York: Harcourt Brace, 1977. Lindbergh is still the best source on Lindbergh. Published posthumously, this study was drawn from extensive manuscript material and notes written over a forty-year period. It touches on virtually all aspects of his varied life and career but strongly emphasizes Lindbergh's growing concern for the natural environment and his plea for a balance between science and nature. An essential work in understanding Lindbergh and his times.

———. *Boyhood on the Upper Mississippi: A Reminiscent Letter*. St. Paul: Minnesota Historical Society, 1972. An outgrowth of several trips to Minnesota aiding various projects on Lindbergh history, Lindbergh responded to Minnesota Historical Society Director Russell W. Fridley's request for Lindbergh data with this long letter. Recounts his boyhood years.

————. *The Spirit of St. Louis*. New York: Scribner, and London: Murray, 1953. Lindbergh's thorough account of the New York to Paris flight in 1927. This literary effort won for him the 1953 Pulitzer Prize for autobiography and biography in 1954. He writes a compelling narrative of the flight and also uses the flashback technique to touch briefly on earlier parts of his life. Lindbergh's book was the basis for the film *The Spirit of St. Louis* (1957).

————. *The Wartime Journals of Charles A. Lindbergh*. New York: Harcourt Brace, 1970. Selected portions from lengthy handwritten diaries which Lindbergh kept during the wartime era between 1938 and 1945. Helpful in clarifying his involvement with the nonintervention movement, relations with the Roosevelt Administration, and his wartime activities after Pearl Harbor.

Lindbergh, Reeve. *Under a Wing: A Memoir*. New York: Simon and Schuster, 1998. Lindbergh's daughter discusses the kidnaping of her older brother and its effect on the family.

Ross, Walter S. *The Last Hero: Charles A. Lindbergh*. Rev. ed. New York: Harper, 1976. Popular account of Lindbergh's life written by an editor and publisher. Contains some factual inaccuracies. Book went through several editions from first publication in 1964. Broad overview for the lay reader, mostly drawn from secondary sources, with an eighteen-page note section on research.

Bruce L. Larson

JACQUES LIPCHITZ

Born: August 22, 1891; Druskieniki, Lithuania
Died: May 26, 1973; Capri, Italy
Area of Achievement: Art
Contribution: Throughout his long career, Lipchitz made immeasurable contributions to the development of twentieth century sculpture. Beginning with his works of 1913-1930, he was one of the most inventive of the cubist sculptors, creating the sculptural equivalent of the ambiguous spaces and volumes in cubist painting. In his later works, he was less concerned with theory, searching instead for a more personal, expressive formal language.

Early Life

When eighteen-year-old Jacques Lipchitz arrived in Paris in 1909 from his native Lithuania, he had received little if any formal artistic training and knew very little of the history of art. He later recalled that, although there were no sculptors in the small town of Druskieniki, where he was born, and he had no idea what sculpture was, he had begun on his own to model in clay. When he went to school in nearby Vilna, he encountered the usual art instruction of copying from plaster casts of classical Greek and Roman statues. Having been convinced by this experience that real sculpture had to be white, he whitewashed his own clay sculpture.

In Paris, anxious to begin his studies, Lipchitz first was enrolled in the École des Beaux-Arts, under the tutelage of Jean-Antoine Ingalbert, but soon transferred to the smaller, more informal Académie Julian, where he worked with Raoul Verlet. These two schools shared many of the same faculty, and methods of instruction were similar: life drawing and modeling classes; assigned compositions on themes taken from history, the Bible, and classical antiquity; and copying from the works of the masters.

One of the most important things Lipchitz learned from Verlet was the traditional concept of the sculpture sketch—the clay or wax model that allows a sculptor to fix an idea immediately and to change it rapidly. Although many twentieth century sculptors have abandoned the preliminary sketch in favor of a direct and immediate experience in the final work, Lipchitz continued the practice throughout his career. More than 150 of his

sketches have survived and are a significant part of his total work.

Verlet also introduced Lipchitz to François Rude's idea that sculpture involved the contrast of planes and round volumes. This elementary theory had a profound effect on Lipchitz's own work as, in his sketches, he not only recorded the idea and outlines of a subject but began to explore fundamental forms and relationships as well. A typical work of this period, *Woman and Gazelles* (1912), was very favorably received when exhibited at the Salon d'Automne in 1913. Additionally, Lipchitz was exhibiting in several small galleries and at the Salon National des Beaux-Arts.

Life's Work

In 1913, dissatisfied with the academic tradition in which he had been working, Lipchitz began to move seriously into what he called his "protocubist" phase. He was already aware of the more recent stylistic and theoretical developments in painting as a result of the Section d'Or Exhibition at the Galerie de la Boétie, featuring the works of Albert Gleizes, Jean Metzinger, Juan Gris, Fernand Léger, Marcel Duchamp, and Aleksandr Archipenko, and the publication by Gleizes and Metzinger of a treatise on cubism. Then Diego Rivera, who was himself painting in the cubist style, introduced Lipchitz to Pablo Picasso, and the two became good friends. Lipchitz, however, had seen almost no sculpture that could be considered cubist. He later recalled having seen several of Picasso's experiments with translating collage into three dimensions, but for the most part, he began working toward cubism in sculpture entirely on his own.

Lipchitz's first tentative steps in the direction of cubism are seen in *Encounter* (1913), in which he experimented with an angular geometry, and in *Woman with Serpent* (1913), a combinaton of the intricate interaction of masses with an implied, almost baroque, sense of linear movement. His interest in the opening up of the voids predicted his later "transparent" sculpture. Another important move in the direction of pure cubism was *Dancer* (1913). Completed after *Woman with Serpent*, this perfectly balanced figure, pivoting around an axis to emphasize its existence in the surrounding space, is composed of simple, massive, and geo-

metric forms. *Mother and Children* (1914-1915) and *Sailor with Guitar* (1914) are further examples of Lipchitz's progression from the curvilinear to a more geometric style and then to cubism. Departing from the circular movement in space of works such as *Woman with Serpent* or *Dancer*, he was now thinking in terms of absolute frontality and strong geometric, architectural, and vertical-horizontal forms. Light had also become important in his work, his having realized (as he later stated) that volume in sculpture is created by light and shadow.

The detachable figures of 1915 (such as *Bather, Dancer*, and *Pierrot*) illustrate that he now had a more complete understanding of the cubist vocabulary as it applied to sculpture. These works, originally made of different materials such as wood, metal, and even glass, were important milestones in the development of modern sculpture because they were some of the first examples of sculpture as construction. These figures also contain evidence of the "machine influence" that occupied so many painters at this time, that is, an interest in the relationship of machine forms to natural forms.

One of the best examples of Lipchitz's early cubist works is *Head* of 1915, consisting of interlocking, opposing planes that create the mass of the head while—to counter the verticality and horizontality of these planes—the eyebrows curve upward in graceful arcs. The powerful simplicity of this work led to the architectural cubist structures in stone or bronze, each of which he titled simply *Sculpture* to indicate his emphasis on sculptural form rather than on subject. The austere, vertical, rectangular purity of these forms, so reminiscent of Gothic cathedrals or modern skyscrapers, led Lipchitz to be concerned that he had pushed cubism all the way to abstraction—a direction he did not want to take since, for him, sculpture must always remain rooted in nature.

In Lipchitz's next several pieces of 1915-1916 (*Half-Standing Figure, Standing Personage*, and *Man with Guitar*), he achieved the balance between the nonfigurative form and figuration for which he had been looking. In these works, he composed the idea of a human figure from the abstract sculptural elements of line, plane, volume, and the contrast of mass with void. In his cubist sculptures from 1916 through the 1920's, Lipchitz explored many different trends, ranging from the highly abstract to a complication of rotating forms and an emphasis on strict frontality, plus some experiments with color. A series of stone reliefs of the early 1920's established Lipchitz's potential for leadership in the field of abstract, architectural sculpture, but he chose not to continue in this direction. Still convinced that sculpture must retain some ties with nature, he looked for a new subject matter and for ways in which to humanize his figures to an even greater extent.

Although elements of cubism persisted in Lipchitz's work through the 1930's—he always declared that he had never ceased to be a cubist—he was now increasingly concerned with a recognizably human emotional response in his figures, emphasizing specific moods such as happiness, weariness, repose, and even mystery. He also experimented with actual motion as a part of the aesthetic statement in works such as *Joy of Life* (1927), a monumental figure which rotates on its base at four-minute intervals.

In 1925, Lipchitz made the first of his "transparents"—works based on the premise that the actual core of a sculpture can be a void, as opposed to the traditional concept of sculpture composed of an integral mass. Liberated from the customary ideas of mass and volume, Lipchitz created a kind of three-dimensional drawing in space. He remained tied to traditional materials, however, casting his transparents in bronze rather than constructing them in cardboard and wire as Picasso and others did later.

Throughout the rest of his career, Lipchitz continued his search for human subject and content in a wide variety of works based on themes as diverse as portraiture, the mother and child, dancers, the embrace, musicians, and characters from the Old and New Testaments and from classical mythology, as well as a group of sculptural "beings" of his own creation, such as *Chimene* (1930) and *Pilgrim* (1942).

In 1941, the German invasion having forced him to leave Paris, Lipchitz arrived in New York. During his years in the United States, he gained even greater recognition, receiving many important commissions from both private and public sources. In 1954, a major retrospective of his work was held at the Museum of Modern Art. When fire destroyed his studio and its contents in 1952, Lipchitz moved to Hastings-on-Hudson. In the early 1960's, he made the first of several visits to Italy

and Israel. In 1970-1971, there were important exhibitions of his work in Berlin and other European centers, in Tel Aviv, and in Jerusalem, and he began work on several monumental commissions, such as *Bellerophon Taming Pegasus* at Columbia University Law School, *Government of the People* at Municipal Plaza, Philadelphia, and *Our Tree of Life* at Hebrew University, Jerusalem. The year 1972 saw a major exhibition of his work at the Metropolitan Museum of Art and the publication of his autobiography, both entitled *My Life in Sculpture*. The following year, Lipchitz died at the age of eighty-one on the island of Capri and was buried in Jerusalem.

Summary

In assessing the total work of Jacques Lipchitz, one fact becomes immediately apparent—he was a sculptor who worked with a seemingly infinite variety of themes and who changed his style and approaches to sculpture at a pace that is potentially confusing to the casual viewer. As several historians have pointed out, most early twentieth century sculptors were "one-image" artists—that is, they chose to make continual variations on a single or limited number of themes, such as the nude (Aristide Maillol), the elongated figure (Alberto Giacometti), or the ovoid (Constantin Brancuși).

Lipchitz, however, like Picasso, often worked simultaneously in different styles. His last cubist sculptures and his transparents both date from the mid-1920's. A close examination of both style and theme reveals that there was a consistency in Lipchitz's work from beginning to end. What seems at first glance to have been random experimentation with different forms, images, and concepts was actually dictated by his own personality, his own philosophical and religious beliefs, and his own strong sense of discipline.

Bibliography

Hammacher, A. M. *Jacques Lipchitz: His Sculpture.* New York: Abrams, 1960; London: Thames and Hudson, 1961. This monograph includes an introductory statement by Lipchitz, quotations from conversations in which he expresses some of his views on art, and excerpts from reviews on his work between 1917 and 1958. Also contains excellent black-and-white reproductions of major works.

Hope, Henry R. *The Sculpture of Jacques Lipchitz.* New York: Museum of Modern Art, 1954. A monograph and also a catalog of the retrospective exhibition of Lipchitz's works at the Museum of Modern Art, the Walker Art Center in Minneapolis, and the Cleveland Museum of Art. Fully illustrated, with a chronology, a listing of exhibitions of Lipchitz's work, and excerpts from reviews.

Lipchitz, Jacques. *Jacques Lipchitz: Sketches in Bronze.* Edited by H. H. Arnason. New York: Praeger, and London: Pall Mall Press, 1969. A complete cataloging of Lipchitz's sculptural sketches, along with Arnason's text, which emphasizes their importance to Lipchitz's total work, and to the tracing of his stylistic development. Includes black-and-white reproductions of the 161 surviving sketches. Also contains a foreword written by Lipchitz.

Lipchitz, Jacques, and H. H. Arnason. *My Life in Sculpture.* New York: Viking Press, and London: Thames and Hudson, 1972. Based on a lengthy series of taped interviews with the artist, this book is the most complete documentation of Lipchitz's life and career and is illustrated throughout with black-and-white reproductions of his major works. Also includes an extensive bibliography compiled by Bernard Karpel, chief librarian of the Museum of Modern Art.

Patai, Irene. *Encounters: The Life of Jacques Lipchitz.* New York: Funk and Wagnalls, 1961. One of the first biographies of Lipchitz published in English, it is now considered to be a somewhat romanticized account of the artist's life and career. As the author states, this is not a critical appraisal of Lipchitz's art but rather an account of the "joys and tragedies" of his life.

LouAnn Faris Culley

WALTER LIPPMANN

Born: September 23, 1889; New York, New York
Died: December 14, 1974; New York, New York
Areas of Achievement: Journalism and political philosophy
Contribution: In a career spanning six decades, Lippmann lucidly analyzed current events, advised statesmen, and was author of more than twenty books which perceptively examined the challenges confronting American democracy.

Early Life

Walter Lippmann was born on September 23, 1889, in New York City, the only child of Jacob Lippmann, a wealthy clothing manufacturer and real estate broker, and Daisy Baum Lippmann, a cultivated graduate of Hunter College. Both parents were American-born, of German-Jewish ancestry. Encouraged to develop an appreciation of the arts, young Lippmann was taken by his parents nearly every summer to Europe, where he frequented the great museums.

When he was six years old, Lippmann entered Dr. Julius Sachs's School for Boys, where he excelled in history, geography, French, and the classics. He also attended Temple Emanu-El, a fashionable Reform Jewish congregation. He was confirmed in 1904, yet his religious training had been minimal; as an adult, he displayed little attachment to his Jewish heritage.

With ambitions of becoming an art critic, Lippmann enrolled at Harvard in 1906. The disastrous 1908 fire in nearby Chelsea awakened Lippmann's social consciousness. He joined volunteers who aided the impoverished victims, and he sought out the political writings of Karl Marx and others. He became the Harvard Socialist Club's first president and wrote articles for undergraduate publications. He also developed personal ties with such distinguished faculty as philosophers William James and George Santayana, as well as visiting lecturer Graham Wallas, a prominent British Socialist. Although dissimilar, each thinker would exercise a profound influence on Lippmann's thought.

Completing his degree requirements in three years, in 1910 he abandoned his Harvard graduate philosophy studies to pursue a career in journalism under the patronage of muckraker Lincoln Steffens. He accepted a position on the *Boston Common*, a small reform weekly published by Ralph Albertson, a Congregationalist minister. (Several years later, in 1917, Lippmann would wed Albertson's beautiful, vivacious daughter, Faye.) Bored by routine tasks, Lippmann persuaded Steffens, then associate editor of *Everybody's* magazine, to engage him as a research assistant. Soon, Lippmann was writing his own articles and by 1911 had attained an editorial position.

Intensely ambitious and anxious for direct political involvement, Lippmann left his job in 1912 to serve as an aide to the Socialist mayor of Schenectady, New York, the Reverend Mr. George Lunn. Within four months, however, he was disenchanted by the pettiness of local politics and resigned. Nevertheless, Lippmann continued his association with the Socialist Party for another two years, although he never fully subscribed to Marxist theory.

Through Steffens, Lippmann became involved with Mabel Dodge Luhan's Greenwich Village salon. There, he mingled with cultural and political radicals, including former Harvard classmate John Reed, anarchist Emma Goldman, and labor leader William Haywood. In some ways, Lippmann was out of place. A brown-eyed, handsome, muscular (though, when young, slightly chubby) man who stood five feet ten inches in height, Lippmann impressed men and attracted women. Yet in demeanor he was cautious, reserved, and even somewhat conventionally prudish. Although capable of displaying a quiet charm and warmth among intimates and important personages, Lippmann often appeared impatient, aloof, and arrogant to others. Within a short time Lippmann would shed his bohemian connections in favor of a more sedate circle that included statesmen, bankers, and distinguished jurists such as Oliver Wendell Holmes, Jr., and Felix Frankfurter.

Life's Work

Upon leaving his Schenectady post, Lippmann wrote his first book, *A Preface to Politics* (1913), which called for bold reform and dynamic, creative leadership to meet the social crises that followed in the wake of rapid urbanization. Very favorably received, the work drew praise from Lippmann's political hero, former President Theodore Roosevelt. Lippmann's second volume, *Drift and Mastery* (1914), optimistically contended that the application of scientific methods would enable Americans to master their social environment. At the age of

twenty-five, Lippmann, together with Herbert Croly and Walter Weyl, became a founding editor of *The New Republic*, one of the prime organs of Progressivism. The new journal quickly gravitated away from Roosevelt's political camp to that of President Woodrow Wilson. With the outbreak of World War I in Europe, Lippmann directed his attention to foreign affairs. Strongly favoring American intervention in 1917, he temporarily left *The New Republic* to serve as assistant to Secretary of War Newton D. Baker. Later that year he was appointed executive secretary of the Inquiry, a secret research body that drafted the territorial provisions of Wilson's Fourteen Points. After brief duty in France as a captain of military intelligence, Lippmann joined the staff of Colonel Edward M. House, Wilson's influential adviser, at the Paris Peace Conference. Distressed by Wilson's willingness to compromise the ideals upon which American involvement in the war was supposedly based, Lippmann left Paris in early 1919 to return to *The New Republic*.

In 1921, Lippmann moved to the liberal New York *World* as an editorial writer under Frank Cobb; upon Cobb's death in 1923, he became editor. Under Lippmann's direction, the newspaper attacked Republican economic policies, fought Fundamentalist efforts to ban the teaching of evolution, and urged more cooperation with the League of Nations. Lippmann actively supported the unsuccessful presidential campaign of Alfred Smith in 1928, and in that same year he conducted a secret diplomatic mission to resolve a calamitous Mexican Church-State dispute that endangered relations with the United States. Yet if Lippmann remained essentially committed to liberal programs during the 1920's, his books revealed a growing conservative tendency. In *Public Opinion* (1922) and *The Phantom Public* (1925), he expressed grave doubts about the people's ability to govern themselves, given their apathy, ignorance, and susceptibility to propaganda, and he recommended more reliance on experts. *A Preface to Morals* (1929) outlined how a "high religion" based on disinterestedness might replace the traditional religious foundations of ethics that were shattered by the "acids of modernity"; the book further maintained that, imbued with this ideal of disinterestedness, the business community was becoming more and more socially responsible (an untimely suggestion in the year of the stock market crash).

When the Great Depression led to the New York *World*'s demise in 1931, Lippmann accepted an offer by the Republican *New York Herald Tribune* to write a regular column, with the understanding that he would enjoy complete independence. Lippmann's "Today and Tomorrow" column, written in his exquisite, graceful prose, soon became a national institution that endured more than three decades. It eventually appeared in more than 275 newspapers across the nation and overseas, and Lippmann became the nation's most highly regarded political analyst, acclaimed for his Olympian objectivity. Yet Lippmann's association with bankers such as Thomas Lamont and his fierce opposition to much of Franklin D. Roosevelt's New Deal (which he had initially supported) led to charges that Lippmann had become a tool of Wall Street interests. Further controversy surrounded the publication of *The Good Society* (1937), in which he, with some exaggeration, likened the New Deal to Communism and Fascism.

In 1938, Lippmann moved from New York to Washington, D.C., following the collapse of his twenty-year childless marriage and his remarriage to Helen Byrne Armstrong, the recently divorced

THE TWENTIETH CENTURY: WALTER LIPPMANN / 2205

wife of Hamilton Fish Armstrong, editor of *Foreign Affairs* and, until that point, a close friend. The move to the nation's capital not only saved the new couple some embarrassment but also allowed the columnist more direct access to leading political figures.

The start of World War II, in 1939, led to a reconciliation with the Roosevelt Administration, as Lippmann lent his support to the president's efforts to help the Allies. Lippmann played a crucial role in arranging the transfer of American destroyers to Great Britain and in promoting Lend-Lease assistance for that nation. Following the United States' entry into the war, he became especially concerned with the nation's postwar responsibilities. In *U.S. Foreign Policy* (1943) and *U.S. War Aims* (1944), Lippmann repudiated the Wilsonian vision of peace upheld by an international organization, instead advocating a balance of power maintained by the major Allies.

Roosevelt's successor, Harry S Truman, ranked low in Lippmann's estimate, and the journalist spurned a State Department offer in 1945 to serve as chief of its information and propaganda activities. Although Lippmann contributed to the formulation of the Marshall Plan that provided economic assistance to war-torn Europe, he took issue with most of Truman's foreign policy. In a series of columns subsequently published as *The Cold War* (1947), he warned that the Truman Doctrine, designed to contain Communism, would overextend the nation's resources, threaten its constitutional system, and make it dangerously dependent on unreliable client states. He similarly voiced misgivings over Truman's decision to send American ground troops to Korea in 1950.

During the early 1950's, Lippmann stoutly condemned Senator Joseph McCarthy and endorsed the 1952 candidacy of Dwight D. Eisenhower, hoping that the popular general would halt the senator's destructive anti-Communist crusade. Eisenhower's failure to provide firmer direction, however, proved disappointing. In *Essays in the Public Philosophy* (1955), Lippmann, distrustful of democracy and the masses, called for a strong executive leadership that possessed the "mandate of heaven." He judged John F. Kennedy's brief presidency as only partially successful but enthusiastically greeted Lyndon B. Johnson's Great Society reform program. Johnson's extension of the United States' military involvement in Vietnam, however, led to a widely publicized feud. Lippmann, whose

advice Johnson had solicited, maintained that he had been deliberately misled by the president, and his columns vehemently denounced the war as a futile, counterproductive enterprise that diverted national attention from more pressing domestic and international concerns.

Lippmann, in 1967, ended his "Today and Tomorrow" column, distributed for the past four years by *The Washington Post* after the *New York Herald Tribune* had ceased publication. He now returned to New York, where he continued to write occasional articles for *Newsweek* until 1971. Pessimistic, he spent his last years preparing a manuscript tentatively entitled "The Ungovernability of Man." He suffered a heart attack and then a stroke in 1973 and died in a New York City nursing home on December 14, 1974, several months after the death of his wife, Helen.

Summary

During his long career as a journalist, Walter Lippmann attained unparalleled prominence and influence. Heralded as the Great Elucidator and as a philosopher-journalist, he produced nearly ten thousand articles and columns which enabled millions of readers to transcend the confusing events of a tumultuous age to find deeper meaning. The recipient of two Pulitzer Prizes (1958 and 1962) as well as the Presidential Medal of Freedom (1964), Lippmann was lionized as was no other journalist.

In his major books, Lippmann forthrightly probed the dilemmas facing modern democracies, in the hope of discovering principles that might lead to some rational control over forces unleashed by revolution and technology. If Lippmann's ideas were more derivative than original, and if he tended to waver between such philosophical extremes as pragmatism and the concept of natural law, his books as a body, perhaps more so than those of any contemporary, reflect the intellectual and political currents of his era. *A Preface to Politics* was the first work to apply Freudian psychology to the realm of politics; *Public Opinion*, notable for its effort to explain how "stereotypes" limit an individual's perception of reality, has become a classic in the field of political science.

Lippmann's shifting political allegiances led to charges of inconsistency and even opportunism, but from the beginning there was always a tendency toward elitism and a predisposition to value order over justice. His pronouncements on such issues as the Cold War and Vietnam proved prophetic, but his insensitivity toward the plight of European Jews in the 1930's, his advocacy of Japanese-American relocation during World War II, and his relative indifference toward civil rights until the disruptions of the 1960's blemished his reputation. Moreover, while his advice was sought, if not always heeded, by presidents from Theodore Roosevelt to Richard M. Nixon, and while he had access to world leaders such as Winston Churchill, Charles de Gaulle, and Nikita Khrushchev, after his Progressive days, Lippmann seemed to lose empathy for the plight of the common people.

Lippmann's faith in democracy steadily eroded, and as an old man he ruefully confessed that he had found no philosophy suitable for the revolutionary period in which he lived. Yet there always remained an underlying commitment to the democratic process—the fundamental right of the people to choose their own leaders—and an appreciation for the responsibilities of the press in a democratic society.

Bibliography

Barnet, Richard J. "A Balance Sheet: Lippmann, Kennan, and the Cold War." *Diplomatic History* 16, no. 2 (Spring 1992). Discusses the views of Lippmann and George F. Kennan with respect to U.S. Cold War policy toward the USSR. Lippmann opposed containment while Kennan supported it.

Blum, D. Steven. *Walter Lippmann: Cosmopolitanism in the Century of Total War.* Ithaca, N.Y.: Cornell University Press, 1984. Rejects the notion that Lippmann can be understood in terms of liberal or conservative labels and maintains that his writings can be best understood as championing a cosmopolitan outlook that challenged American parochialism. Well written, with valuable insights, but the central thesis is sometimes labored.

Childs, Marquis William, and James Barrett Reston, eds. *Walter Lippmann and His Times.* New York: Harcourt Brace, 1959. Excellent collection of six essays commemorating Lippmann's seventieth birthday. Particularly noteworthy are boyhood friend Carl Binger's depiction of the young Lippmann, Arthur Schlesinger, Jr.'s, critique of Lippmann's writings, and Reston's observations on Lippmann's style of life and work.

Forcey, Charles. *The Crossroads of Liberalism: Croly, Weyl, Lippmann and the Progressive Era, 1900-1925.* New York: Oxford University Press, 1961; London: Oxford University Press, 1972. Fascinating but unflattering depiction of Lippmann's years at *The New Republic*, when the young, ambitious editor forged close ties with the Wilson Administration. Demonstrates Lippmann's vulnerability to seduction by men in power, a problem about which he would later write but which he never fully overcame.

Goodwin, Craufurd D. "The Promise of Expertise: Walter Lippmann and the Policy Sciences." *Policy Sciences* 28, no. 4 (November, 1995). Examines Lippmann's belief that an understanding and appreciation of economics was crucial in the creation of policy in nongovernment research organizations.

Luskin, John. *Lippmann, Liberty, and the Press.* University: University of Alabama Press, 1972. A study of Lippmann's career as a journalist, particularly his views on the tension between the journalist's responsibility to inform the public and the necessity of government secrecy.

Schapsmeier, Edward L., and Frederick H. Schapsmeier. *Walter Lippmann: Philosopher-Journalist.* Washington, D.C.: Public Affairs Press, 1969. A satisfactory but not very penetrating account of Lippmann's activities from Harvard to the 1960's. Although it is generally reverent in tone, the authors were uncomfortable with Lippmann's strong condemnation of Johnson's Vietnam policy.

Steel, Ronald. *Walter Lippmann and the American Century.* Boston: Little Brown, and London: Bodley Head, 1980. A detailed, award-winning authorized biography written by the first researcher who was granted access to Lippmann's private papers. Valuable for its examination of its subject's personal life, it also provides a balanced assessment of his public career. Steel's analysis of Lippmann's political philosophy is disappointingly meager. Contains a short annotated bibliography.

Syed, Anwar. *Walter Lippmann's Philosophy of International Politics.* Philadelphia: University of Pennsylvania Press, 1964. A critical study of Lippmann's views on nationalism, the national interest, alliances, and the balance of power, among other issues. Abstract and theoretical but of benefit to those interested in this area.

Weingast, David Elliott. *Walter Lippmann: A Study in Personal Journalism.* New Brunswick, N.J.: Rutgers University Press, 1949. This attempt to evaluate Lippmann's ideological position in terms of a content analysis of "Today and To-morrow" columns during the period from 1932 to 1938 is somewhat simplistic, but the book is helpful in outlining, if not adequately analyzing, Lippmann's views on the New Deal.

Wellborn, Charles. *Twentieth Century Pilgrimage: Walter Lippmann and the Public Philosophy, 1969.* Baton Rouge: Louisiana State University Press, 1969. A brief, sympathetic intellectual biography that traces Lippmann's evolution as a thinker, with particular emphasis on his views on human nature, democracy, and religion. The con-clusions are debatable, but the book contains a valuable discussion of influences on Lippmann's thought and a good bibliography.

Wright, Benjamin F. *Five Public Philosophies of Walter Lippmann.* Austin: University of Texas Press, 1973. A discerning assessment of nine of Lippmann's books on political philosophy. Wright convincingly argues that Lippmann's knowledge of history, economics, and political philosophy was broader than it was deep. Emphasizes his inconsistencies and makes little effort to find unifying themes.

Allen Safianow

MAKSIM MAKSIMOVICH LITVINOV
Meier Moiseevich Wallach

Born: July 17, 1876; Bialystok, Poland, Russian
Empire
Died: December 31, 1951; Moscow, U.S.S.R.
Area of Achievement: Diplomacy
Contribution: Litvinov was the most prominent Soviet diplomat of the interwar period. During the
1920's, he was a leading advocate of world peace
through universal disarmament. In the 1930's, he
negotiated American recognition of the Soviet
Union and became the main spokesman for the
Soviet policy of collective security with the Western powers against German, Japanese, and Italian
aggression prior to World War II.

Early Life

Maksim Maksimovich Litvinov was born Meier
Moiseevich Wallach on July 17, 1876, in the small
city of Białystok in Russian Poland. He was the
son of middle-class Jewish parents; his father,
Moses Wallach, was a successful produce merchant who, while maintaining a traditional religious life at home, was well known in the local
community for his liberal political views. Young
Meier, however, at first showed little interest in either politics or religion and, in 1893, at the age of
seventeen, joined the Russian army in an effort to
escape the tedium of provincial Russian life. While
in the army Meier was slowly converted to Marxism. He was eventually discharged from the army
for a violation of military regulations and traveled
to Kiev, where he joined the local section of the
newly formed Russian Social Democratic Workers' Party (RSDWP).

During the next two decades, the twenty-two-
year-old Wallach would dedicate himself entirely
to the Russian Revolutionary movement. Tall, energetic, single-minded, and intense, he cut all ties
with the past and worked tirelessly as an underground organizer in the laboring districts of Kiev.
It was during this period that he adopted the pseudonym Maksim Maksimovich Litvinov, the name
"Litvinov" being taken from a character in a novel
by his favorite Russian author, Ivan Turgenev. Arrested in 1901, he spent thirteen months in prison
before escaping and, after a brief period of renewed activity in the Kievan underground, fled
abroad to the West. While in exile, Litvinov met
Vladimir Ilich Lenin for the first time in London.

Deeply impressed by Lenin's overall analysis of
the Russian situation, Litvinov supported the Bolshevik faction at the Second Congress of the RSD-
WP in 1903.

Once committed to Bolshevism, Litvinov never
wavered. Never a theoretician, he avoided all party
controversies and followed Lenin's instructions
without question. Lenin, in turn, valued him for his
personal as well as political loyalty. He saw him as
a competent and reliable agent and organizer and
over the years assigned him to some of the party's
most difficult tasks. In 1912, he was appointed the
permanent Bolshevik representative to the International Socialist Bureau in Great Britain and supported Lenin's position on the war in 1914. Two
years later, he married Ivy Low, a novelist and
member of a noted English literary family. The
couple would have two children in England before
their lives were changed forever by the great upheavals in Russia in 1917.

Life's Work

The Bolshevik Revolution marked the beginning of
Litvinov's career as a diplomat and statesman. It
transformed him, within the relatively brief period
of a decade, from an isolated, virtually unknown
revolutionary living in exile into a major actor on
the international stage. In this new role, Litvinov
would become the main spokesman for the Soviet
policy of anti-Fascism and collective security during the 1930's. He would lead a worldwide campaign against German, Japanese, and Italian aggression, head the Soviet delegations to the World
Disarmament Conference and League of Nations,
and secure diplomatic recognition of the Soviet
Union by the United States. By the time of his
death in December, 1951, he would be regarded in
the Soviet Union as a minor hero, and he has remained the symbol of Soviet efforts during the interwar period to establish closer cooperation with
the West.

Initially, however, Litvinov's diplomatic debut
was far from auspicious. In January, 1918, while
still in London, he was appointed the first Soviet
representative to Great Britain. Unrecognized by
the British government, he was arrested for revolutionary agitation in December and, after a brief period of imprisonment, was exchanged for Robert

Bruce Lockhart, a British agent who had been interned in Moscow the same year.

Once back in Russia, however, Litvinov's career progressed rapidly. A man of exceptional administrative skills who had the full confidence of Lenin, his long years of exile in the West had provided him with an excellent knowledge of Western languages and culture. In addition, many Soviet leaders believed that it would be useful to have an "Old Bolshevik" such as Litvinov join the Soviet diplomatic hierarchy in order to monitor the activities of Georgi Vasilievich Chicherin, a born aristocrat and former Menshevik who had replaced Leon Trotsky as people's commissar of foreign affairs in 1918. In April, 1919, therefore, Litvinov was made a member of the collegium of the Soviet Foreign Commissariat (the Narkomindel), and appointed vice commissar of foreign affairs under Chicherin's ostensible leadership the following year. From then on, the two men occupied their positions as thinly veiled rivals. While Litvinov did not possess Chicherin's extraordinary memory or brilliance, he was often shrewder and more resourceful in negotiations and carried greater political weight. In 1926, as Chicherin's health began to fail, Litvinov gradually came to assume effective control over the Narkomindel's daily operations. Four years later, when his erstwhile superior finally retired, he was officially appointed People's Commissar of Foreign Affairs, a position that he was to hold for nine fateful years.

At the time when Litvinov became effective head of the Narkomindel, Bolshevik leaders still regarded Great Britain and France as their main international enemies and the League of Nations as the chief agency of Western imperialism. Indeed, despite Chicherin's successful efforts to achieve diplomatic recognition by most of the world's great powers, the Soviet Union was still looked upon with suspicion by the majority of the capitalist nations and continued to be ignored by many of the Slavic countries of Eastern Europe and the United States. Litvinov, however, proved to be ideally suited to deal with these problems. Flexible and pragmatic, he never seems to have succumbed to the anti-Western xenophobia that permeated much of the Bolshevik hierarchy. In addition, like the leader of the Soviet Union, Joseph Stalin, he had little faith in the prospects for world revolution and preferred, instead, to rely on traditional power politics to guarantee the security of the Soviet state. Litvinov's relationship with Stalin, in fact, was that of

loyal deputy and faithful follower. While he did privately express some concern over the ruthlessness of Stalin's methods, his confidence in the Soviet leader never seems to have been shaken, even when the purges of the mid-1930's decimated Narkomindel personnel.

From the very beginning of his tenure as chief spokesman for Soviet foreign policy, Litvinov's main aim was to ease tensions with the Western powers and to normalize relations with as many of the Soviet Union's neighbors as possible. In 1927, shortly after taking over for the ailing Chicherin, he made a dramatic appearance before the Preparatory Commission of the World Disarmament Conference in Geneva and delivered a ringing call for complete and universal disarmament. The speech, which would be repeated with somewhat different emphasis at the Disarmament Conference itself in 1932, created a sensation in the Western press and gained for him his first international notoriety. Two years later, in 1929, the Soviet Union joined with sixty-five other nations in signing the Kellogg-Briand Pact, which outlawed war as an instrument of national policy. During the negotiations, Litvinov was able to take advantage of the general optimism created by the occasion in order to formulate a separate agreement (the so-called Litvinov Protocol), which applied the pact on a regional basis and was signed by the Soviet Union, Poland, Romania, Latvia, Estonia, Lithuania, Turkey, Persia, and the Free City of Danzig. In 1932, he extended these agreements by concluding nonaggression pacts with France, Finland, Poland, Estonia, and Latvia and, in one of his greatest diplomatic achievements, was able to secure United States recognition of the Soviet Union the following year.

The moderately pro-Western drift in Soviet foreign policy during Litvinov's early years underwent a decided acceleration after the triumph of Adolf Hitler in Germany in 1933. Unlike many of their Western counterparts, Soviet leaders were convinced that Hitler was sincere in his professed aim of attacking the Soviet Union and acquiring *Lebensraum* ("living space") for the German people in the East. Starting in 1934, therefore, Litvinov launched a concerted campaign to isolate the Fascist powers and develop a global system of collective security. In September, the Soviet Union formally joined the League of Nations. During the following year, the Soviet Union concluded treaties of mutual assistance with France and Czechoslovakia, supported sanctions against Italy during the invasion of Ethiopia, and sought to mobilize world opinion against Germany and Japan. Between 1934 and 1938, in fact, Litvinov became the spearhead of Soviet efforts to combat the policy of appeasement. He advocated League action against Germany during the remilitarization of the Rhineland, repeatedly denounced Japanese aggression in China, and tried to forge a common front with the Western powers in defense of the republican government in Spain.

Nothing, however, seemed capable of stirring the democratic powers to action. In September, 1938, the decision of Great Britain and France to exclude the Soviet Union from the Munich Conference on Czechoslovakia seems to have convinced Stalin of the futility of any further effort to pursue a policy of collective security. On May 3, 1939, therefore, Litvinov was dismissed from his position as People's Commissar of Foreign Affairs. A Jew who was closely identified with the Western powers, he was now seen as an obstacle to improved relations with Berlin. On August 23, 1939, Litvinov's successor, Viacheslav Molotov, formally concluded a nonaggression pact with Germany. Nine days later, Hitler attacked Poland, and Europe entered World War II.

The last years of Litvinov's diplomatic career were clearly anticlimatic. During the period when the Nazi-Soviet Pact remained in effect, he lived in Moscow in relative obscurity. In December, 1941, however, after Hitler launched his assault on the Soviet Union, he was appointed Soviet ambassador to Washington, where he worked for a smooth functioning of the Grand Alliance. Recalled to the Soviet Union in August, 1943, he was made vice commissar of foreign affairs under Molotov and retired from governmental service in 1946. During his last five years, he lived in the Soviet capital and died peacefully at the age of seventy-five.

Summary

Maksim Maksimovich Litvinov was the most outstanding figure in Soviet diplomacy during the interwar period. Passionate, persuasive, and eloquent, he came to symbolize the pro-Western, anti-Fascist, and antimilitarist efforts of the Soviet government to promote collective security between 1934 and 1938. During these years, he developed a considerable following among those segments of the Western public opposed to appeasement, and his often inspired oratory at Geneva made him one of the most visible diplomats on the international scene.

Even at the height of his influence, however, Litvinov did not have the power to determine Soviet foreign policy. Soviet policy was made in the Soviet Politburo, not the foreign commissariat. Representatives of the Narkomindel (of which Litvinov was the most important) were often invited to participate in the discussions, but final decisions were left to the Politburo (and presumably Stalin) itself. Indeed, despite his long years of service, Litvinov was never fully admitted to the inner circle of the Party. Although he was elected to the Central Committee in 1934, membership in the Politburo always eluded him, and he often complained of international initiatives taken without his knowledge or over his head.

Nevertheless, despite his limited ability to influence decisions, Litvinov's acumen as an executor of Soviet foreign policy cannot be questioned. He was naturally gregarious and fecund in expedients, and his tactical skill in conducting negotiations with the United States in 1933 and France in 1935 won the begrudging respect of his supporters and detractors alike. His main contribution, however, was as an advocate of collective security and closer cooperation with the West against the Fascist powers. While this policy did not bear immediate fruit during the 1930's, it helped to reintegrate the Soviet Union into the international states system and provided the foundation for the creation of the Grand Alliance during World War II.

Bibliography

Beloff, Max. *The Foreign Policy of Soviet Russia, 1929-1941.* 2 vols. New York and London: Oxford University Press, 1947-1949. A concise and generally dispassionate analysis of Soviet foreign policy during the Litvinov era. Although superseded by a number of later works on specialized topics, Beloff's book is still useful for its general overview of early Soviet diplomacy under Stalin.

Degras, Jane, ed. *Soviet Documents on Foreign Policy, 1917-1941.* 3 vols. New York and London: Oxford University Press, 1951-1953. The standard source for documents on Soviet foreign policy during the interwar period. Degras' three volumes include treaties, decrees, communiqués, articles from leading Soviet journals, and the speeches of major Soviet statesmen.

Fischer, Louis. *Russia's Road from Peace to War: Soviet Foreign Relations, 1917-1941.* New York: Harper, 1969. A scholarly and highly readable book by an author who first went to the Soviet Union in 1922 and knew many of its leaders, including Litvinov, personally. The work contains many insights into Litvinov's personality and offers a convincing summary of Soviet policy as a whole.

Gaddis, John Lewis. *Russia, the Soviet Union, and the United States: An Interpretive History.* New York: Wiley, 1978. This book provides a comprehensive analysis of the interplay of interests and ideology that has characterized Soviet-American relations since the Bolshevik Revolution. The work contains an excellent chapter on the Litvinov-Roosevelt negotiations leading to recognition and an annotated bibliography.

Kennan, George F. *Russia and the West Under Lenin and Stalin.* Boston: Little Brown, 1961. An eloquent and thoughtful assessment of the relationship between the Soviet Union and the major Western powers from 1917 to the end of World War II. Although heavily weighted toward the 1917-1921 period, the book details the phobias and suspicions that helped prevent effective Soviet-Western cooperation in the decade before 1939.

Pope, Arthur Upham. *Maxim Litvinoff.* New York: Fischer, and London: Secker and Warburg, 1943. A sympathetic account of Litvinov's life and career by his American biographer. Pope benefited from several interviews with Litvinov, and his book remains indispensable for its treatment of Litvinov's early years.

Roberts, Henry L. "Maxim Litvinov." In *The Diplomats, 1919-1939,* edited by Gordon A. Craig and Felix Gilbert. Princeton, N.J.: Princeton University Press, 1953. This article provides a thorough analysis of the content of Litvinov's diplomatic policies, his views on the purges and world revolution, and his relationship to the Soviet Politburo.

Ulam, Adam B. *Expansion and Coexistence: Soviet Foreign Policy, 1917-1973.* 2d. ed. New York: Holt Rinehart, 1974. An exhaustive analysis of the personal, political, and ideological factors that helped shape Soviet foreign policy during the country's first six decades. The best survey available in one volume in English.

John Santore

LIU SHAO-CH'I

Born: 1898; Ning-hsiang district, Hunan Province, China

Died: November 12, 1969; K'ai-feng, Honan Province, China

Areas of Achievement: Government and politics

Contribution: An important first-generation figure of the Chinese Communist Party, Liu was an early advocate of Mao Tse-tung's leadership. After 1949, Liu's management skills were critical to the new People's Republic of China. He served as chairman of the government after 1959, as well as a top party leader.

Early Life

Liu Shao-ch'i was the youngest of nine children; his father was a landlord and kept a store in the family's home village in inland central China. He received primary education in his village but went to the provincial capital, Ch'ang-sha, for his middle schooling. While he was away at school, his father died, and his three elder brothers divided the family property.

While at school in Ch'ang-sha, Liu joined a pre-Marxist student group, the New People Society, organized by an older student, Mao Tse-tung. This began a half-century of association between Liu and Mao, both of whom had been born into rural Hunan farming communities. In 1918, Liu went to Peking intending to prepare to study in Europe but became drawn into the first Chinese Marxist student groups during the May Fourth Movement. He never went to France but was chosen to attend university in the Soviet Union in 1921. He disliked the harsh life and his studies there and asked to return to China in 1922.

Liu was a tall, thin, and serious young man. He was considered bookish and later developed into a respected Chinese Marxist ideologue, in spite of his limited formal education. Throughout his life, Liu thrived on hard work. In his fifties and sixties, Liu's spare frame had filled out and he was distinguished by his white hair. Liu married six times. Before 1945, his fifth wife bore two children who figured in their father's disgrace during the Cultural Revolution. His last wife was Wang Kuang-mei, a talented and beautiful woman who came from an elite North China family. She was working as an English translator in Peking when she joined the Communists. She met Liu in Yen-an and married him in 1948. They had two daughters.

Life's Work

From 1922 until 1930, Liu worked to organize trade unions. He also joined the cooperative efforts between the Communist and Nationalist parties from 1923 to 1927. Liu gained wide experience in the major Chinese cities as a party activist, often operating in secret or great danger in so-called white areas controlled by anticommunist warlords, Chiang Kai-shek's Nationalists, or the foreign powers. In 1931, he headed the All China Labor Federation. Yet Liu did not agree with the regular Party leadership, dominated by returned students from Moscow, about the Communists' urban strategy. Liu believed that the Party must be cautious in the face of a strong opposition, while the returned students wanted to be bold and adventurous. Liu left Shanghai and joined Mao in the rural Jui-chin Soviet. There, Liu moved ideologically and organizationally toward Mao.

Liu was first elected to the Central Committee of the Party in 1934. He participated in the Long March and emerged as a close ally of Mao. In March, 1936, Liu took charge of the Communist movement in North China. His responsibilities included the anti-Japanese student movement centered in Peking. Under his guidance, the Communists captured direction of the movement and overshadowed Nationalist Party influence in the area.

In late 1937, Liu returned to Yen-an, where he advocated the Chinese Communists' independence of Moscow. To this end, he stressed Mao's role as an independent Marxist theoretician who had adapted Marxism-Leninism to China. This effort enhanced both the independence of the Chinese and Mao's stature. In 1939, Liu took charge of Communist efforts in the Yangtze River Valley. His task was to bring a large Communist force, called the New Fourth Army, under the control of the Party headquarters at Yen-an. In early 1941, a series of engagements with Nationalist armies broke out, during which the New Fourth Army's leadership was killed or captured. This event greatly reduced the military importance of the New Fourth Army, but through Liu's political skills, the surviving elements became closely integrated with Mao's forces.

In 1942, Liu returned to Yen-an to become a leader in the Rectification Movement, a sustained effort to purify and strengthen the Communists'

Chinese chairman Liu Shao-ch'i (second right) and Soviet premier Leonid Brezhnev (second left) raise their arms at the Soviet-Chinese Friendship Meeting in Moscow in 1964.

ranks. The movement used a combination of Marxist study and the practice of self-criticism to achieve subordination of all members to Party discipline. This movement drew on ideas that Liu had advanced in speeches he made in the late 1930's and early 1940's. The Rectification Movement further consolidated Mao's dominance in the Party, while strengthening Liu's position as Mao's lieutenant.

During the war years, Liu formed a connection with Teng Hsiao-p'ing, who was the political commissar of the Eighth Route Army's 129th Division. After 1949, Liu and Teng became more closely associated in the Peking central government. In retrospect, it can be seen that both men favored hardheaded practical policies that produced tangible results. This meant that these two, and others associated with them, were important to Mao because they developed the means to implement his radical, visionary policies. Yet, on occasion, they advocated retrenchment to reduce the disruption produced by Mao's revolutionary initiatives. The link be-

tween Liu and Teng was of little significance at the time but became a major element in Chinese politics during the Cultural Revolution and again in Teng's reform era after 1979.

At the Seventh Party Congress in May, 1945, Liu was confirmed as a top leader of the Party. In the Civil War period (1946-1949), he undertook the critical tasks of implementing the land reform in North China and engineering the Communist administration of urban areas. The Chinese Communists had been almost exclusively rurally based since 1927, and the prospect of ruling China's large cities was a true challenge. In 1949-1951, Liu formulated the Communist urban policies, which called for moderation in order to restore functioning of the urban economy.

After the establishment of the People's Republic of China in October, 1949, Liu strengthened his position as the Chinese Communists' number two man. He was in full accord with all the early policies of Communist rule, including the Great Leap Forward (1958-1960), in which the Chinese attempted to leave behind the Soviet style of planned development in favor of Mao's calls for a communist society developed by means of populist creativity. In 1959, Liu was named a chairman of the People's Republic of China, while Mao continued as chairman of the Communist Party.

In the wake of the Great Leap Forward, however, a serious domestic crisis appeared in which food shortages, famine, production breakdowns, and lowered morale threatened the achievements of the Communist Revolution. Liu and his associates—including a large number of the government's top managers—advocated a lessening of socialist innovation in favor of recovery. They promoted solidarity of the Chinese people rather than following Mao's emphasis on class struggle. It is doubtful, however, if Liu imagined himself as an opponent of Mao's leadership at the time.

The Cultural Revolution began, not as an attack of Liu, but as an effort by Mao to sustain the Chinese radical tradition by forcing the tempo of revolutionary change. It widened into an attack on anyone who opposed radical revolutionary action, and thus Liu, who was still advocating policies that would produce stability, became a target. Red Guard diatribes from the Cultural Revolution period charged Liu with betrayal of the Communist movement; such allegations warrant no credence.

Some of Liu's former associates became Cultural Revolution targets in early 1966. Then the charges against "capital roaders"—meaning those whose policies Mao believed would lead China on a road back to capitalism—grew to include Liu by the late summer of 1966. By late November, both Liu and Teng had disappeared from public view. In 1966, dramatic events in the Cultural Revolution occurred on the campuses of Peking's universities. Liu's wife, Wang Kuang-mei, and his children participated in the struggle. His wife defended Liu, but his children divided in attacking and defending their father. Mao's wife, Chiang Ch'ing, counterattacked against Wang Kuang-mei, thus giving the Cultural Revolution the atmosphere of a quarrel between the leaders' wives.

Although Liu Shao-ch'i fell from authority in late 1966, it proved difficult to dislodge his views because so many top Chinese leaders believed that Liu's interests were the same as their own. The Maoist radicals, supported by Defense Minister Lin Piao and championed by the so-called Gang of Four led by Chiang Ch'ing, struggled to establish their dominance. Disorder became so rampant that even in 1969 some locations and units remained outside real central control.

Reviled as public enemies, Liu and others like him underwent humiliating struggle sessions and produced abject confessions but were never tried in the courts. Held in confinement, they were sent to rural farms for common labor or made to do menial jobs such as cleaning toilets. They lived under indefinite prisonlike terms, separated from their families and homes. Liu, in his early seventies, was denied necessary medical treatment and died alone in degrading confinement on November 12, 1969.

Summary

Many of Liu Shao-ch'i's associates survived to re-emerge slowly in the early 1970's during Mao's last years. As long as Mao was alive, the Maoist radicals had authority, but the moderates became stronger after Mao's death in September, 1976. In December, 1978, under Teng's leadership, they gained control of the Party and government. In 1979, Teng began a truly major reform of Chinese Communist policies on all fronts. One of his early actions was to rehabilitate Liu.

Throughout the period from 1931 to 1965, Liu was a stalwart supporter of the Chinese Communist Party. Although a strong supporter of Mao's leadership, Liu can be distinguished by his preference for moderate, practical policies and his belief in regular Communist Party leadership in contrast to Mao's preference for radical policies and his faith in spontaneous mass action. Thus, it is difficult to assume that Liu would have supported the many departures that Teng has permitted from accepted Communist economic and political practices since 1979. Still, Teng and many others were as orthodox as Liu until the Cultural Revolution, so it is entirely possible that Liu might have joined in the post-Maoist reform had he survived.

Bibliography

Beijing Review 10 (March, 1980): 3-10. This volume of an official newsmagazine announced Liu's rehabilitation.

Dittmer, Lowell. "The Chinese Cultural Revolution Revisited." *Journal of Contemporary China* 5, no. 13 (November, 1996). Dittmer provides details of the Cultural Revolution in China, the conflict between Mao Tse-tung and Liu, and Liu's impact on the revolution.

————. "Liu Shaoqi." In *Encyclopedia of Asian History*, edited by Ainslie T. Embree, vol. 2. New York: Scribner, 1988, and London: Macmillan, 1988. A brief look at Liu's life that explores his early years, his involvement in China's Communist Party, and his rehabilitation. Also includes a short bibliography.

Li T'ien-min. *Liu Shao-ch'i: Mao's First Heir Apparent*. Taipei: Institute of International Relations, 1975. A short and useful biography by a Nationalist Chinese researcher who marshals information from Chinese-, Japanese-, and English-language sources. Published before the circumstances of Liu's death were known.

Lieberthal, Kenneth. "The Great Leap Forward and the Split in the Yenan Leadership." In *The People's Republic, Part I: The Emergence of Revolutionary China, 1949-1965*. Vol. 14 in *The Cambridge History of China*, edited by Roderick MacFarquhar and John K. Fairbank. Cambridge and New York: Cambridge University Press, 1987. An overview of the split that emerged out of the Great Leap Forward.

Liu, Shao-ch'i. *Selected Works of Liu Shaoqi*. Vol. 1. Beijing: Foreign Languages Press, 1984. This first of a projected two-volume series contains documents from the period 1927 to 1949. This officially sponsored work presents Liu as a fully rehabilitated figure who "was a great Marxist and proletarian revolutionary and an outstanding leader of the Chinese Communist Party and the People's Republic of China."

Oxenberg, Michael. "The Political Leader." In *Mao Tse-tung in the Scales of History*, edited by Dick Wilson. Cambridge and New York: Cambridge University Press, 1977. An excellent analysis of Mao's methods of leadership that helps in understanding Liu's relationship to Mao.

David D. Buck

DAVID LLOYD GEORGE

Born: January 17, 1863; Manchester, England
Died: March 26, 1945; Ty Newydd, near Llanystumdwy, Wales
Areas of Achievement: Government and politics
Contribution: While guiding his country through
   the trials of World War I, Lloyd George ushered
   in a new era: the age of the common man as
   world leader.

Early Life

David Lloyd George was born January 17, 1863, in
Manchester. His father, William George, was a
schoolmaster of Welsh descent; his mother, Elizabeth Lloyd, was the daughter of a Welshman. David soon became acquainted with his roots; after the
death of her husband in 1864, Elizabeth Lloyd took
her two children (another son was born subsequently) to live with her brother in Llanystumdwy,
Wales. From his uncle, Richard Lloyd, a dissenting
Baptist preacher, liberal political activist, and master shoemaker, Lloyd George acquired not only his
distinctive surname but also his talent for oratory,
his passion for social issues, and his characteristic
willfulness.

Most photographs of Lloyd George feature the
prominent shock of flowing white hair and distinctive mustache, and date generally from his tenure
as prime minister during and after World War I.
Other photographs from as late as 1912 show a
much younger-looking man, with darker hair and a
fresher face, harboring the same piercing eyes;
comparison reveals the strain Lloyd George bore
during the nightmarish stalemate of "the war to end
all wars."

Growing up in the Welsh countryside, Lloyd
George learned early of the inherent political, social, and religious conflicts between his neighbors
and their wealthy British landlords. His avid partisanship, the basis for his lifelong defense of the
rights of the common man, was forged early. After
attending the Anglican village school, he was arti-
cled in 1879 to a solicitor's firm in Portmadoc. He
gained attention by speaking eloquently on land
reform and temperance issues, and pleased his uncle by taking a few turns in local Nonconformist
pulpits.

In 1884, Lloyd George passed the law exam and
opened a practice in Criccieth. He became active in
organizing a local farmer's union and in opposing
the Anglican tithe, again showing a marked parti-

sanship. In 1888, he married Margaret Owen, the
future mother of his five children. The same year
saw the creation of the new county council. Lloyd
George's involvement in this agrarian populist politics led to his election in 1890 as a Member of Parliament from Caernarvon Boroughs. He would
hold his seat for the next fifty-five years.

Life's Work

As a newcomer to the House of Commons, Lloyd
George's initial interest was in home rule for
Wales. He showed assertiveness (and stubbornness) in spearheading a revolt against Lord Rosebery's leadership of the Liberal Party in 1894-
1895, and political skill in pushing a bill to dis-
establish the Church of England in Wales. He
risked much in his adamant criticism of the South
African War on both moral and political grounds,
but this joust with the imperial establishment
marked him as one of the most important young
men of his party.

With the return of the Liberals to power in 1905,
Lloyd George became president of the Board of
Trade. Showing himself an able administrator, he
was instrumental in creating the Port of London
Authority, which brought much-needed order (as
well as increased capacity) to London's dock-
yards. He also lobbied successfully for legislation
to clarify Great Britain's confusing patent and
copyright laws, and to expand and upgrade the
merchant marine.

Herbert Asquith became prime minister in 1908,
and Lloyd George was made Chancellor of the Exchequer. Lloyd George's transition from fiery orator to indispensable administrator represents a remarkable personal achievement. He combined
cool, logical organization with boldness bordering
on heresy in promoting his "People's Budget" of
1909. Designed to fund both a massive naval buildup (the arms race with imperial Germany was well
under way) and a progressive program of social
legislation, the budget showed the ruthless precision of its author by drawing on such hitherto un-
touchable sources as property, income, and inheritance. The wealthy landed class, privileged
oppressor of Lloyd George's youth and ancestry,
met its nemesis. The resulting interparliamentary
crisis led to the limiting of the Lords' Veto, a significant step in the progress of British government;
one more link with the past was broken. Lloyd

George went on to introduce the National Insurance Act, and, amid charges of outright socialism, succeeded in establishing a plan of compensation for illness, injury, and unemployment for the working classes. Lloyd George's will, his greatest political asset, had again helped overcome tradition.

The year 1911 brought crisis. Germany, headed by the master sword rattler of his day, Kaiser Wilhelm, sent a gunboat to Agadir in the French colony of Morocco as a show of force. Lloyd George, whose life had been threatened for opposing the South African War, gave a speech warning of Great Britain's intolerance of such interference in French affairs. His popularity rose instantly. In an age of nationalist fervor, the ardent advocate of Wales stepped onto the international stage.

Broad exposure was followed by embarrassment in the form of the Marconi scandal. Lloyd George was one of several ministers who invested in the American Marconi Company just before it received a British government contract to develop the radio-telegraph. He and the others found themselves stigmatized until World War I arrived to absorb the attention of the public and make corruption seem relatively unimportant.

With the German violation of Belgian neutrality in August, 1914, Lloyd George began the restoration of his reputation by voicing strong support for the war effort. This restoration was completed with his success in the new Ministry of Munitions, part of Asquith's equally new coalition government of May, 1915. Since Great Britain, like all the combatants, had foreseen and planned only for a short conflict (popular theories abounded as to how, given the interdependency of modern economies, the war simply could not last more than a few short months), Lloyd George's values as an arbitrator, builder, and organizer can scarcely be exaggerated. Alarming deficiencies in war matériel became surpluses; Great Britain settled in for the long conflict, owing a great debt to Lloyd George's leadership.

When Lord Kitchener was drowned in June, 1916, Lloyd George became Minister of War. This influential position brought him into immediate conflict with members of the British high command over matters of strategy. Lloyd George was one of several prominent individuals (Winston Churchill was another) who advocated finding some sort of "eastern alternative" to the bloody attrition of trench warfare in Belgium and France. British military leaders, notably Sir Douglas Haig, resented this civilian interference in their sphere of influence; this schism hampered the British war effort for two years, culminating in the disastrous Flanders campaign of 1917. Lloyd George's role in this quarrel and in all phases of the war effort increased when he succeeded Asquith as prime minister in December, 1916.

Lloyd George had reached the pinnacle of political success; he had also sown the seeds of his own downfall. By siding with the Conservatives in the rebellion against Asquith's ineffective leadership, he alienated his colleague and much of the Liberal Party, which would adversely affect his postwar career. During the war, however, he was without equal in popularity and influence. Showing characteristic strength of will, Lloyd George united the public much as Churchill would in the next war, and was instrumental in forging such achievements as the creation of a joint Allied command, a personal triumph and a large step toward victory.

At the war's end, Lloyd George and his coalition were overwhelmingly returned. He again demonstrated his talents as a mediator at the peace conference, negotiating between the widely diverging views of Woodrow Wilson and Georges Clemenceau. In 1921, Lloyd George supported the formation of the Irish Free State; this success lost for him the support of the Conservatives. The Turkish crisis of 1922 found Lloyd George and the Conservatives again on opposing sides; his support for the Greeks was soundly rejected. He resigned in October, never again to serve in a ministerial capacity.

The Liberal Party, divided between Asquith and Lloyd George, lost much of its membership to Labour in the decade following the war. Lloyd George failed in an attempted comeback in 1929; his party, as a viable political base, had disappeared.

Lloyd George spent his final fifteen years in relative obscurity. He favored concessions to Nazi Germany, although in his last highly visible act he called for Prime Minister Neville Chamberlain's resignation for supporting a policy of appeasing the Nazis. After his wife's death in 1941, Lloyd George married his secretary of thirty years, Frances Louise Stevenson. On December 31, 1944, he became a peer. He died in Wales on March 26, 1945.

Summary

David Lloyd George was a new kind of politician for a new century. His fiery populism, a position supported more by oratory and cunning than by birth or connection, represented a new and vibrant

force in British politics. His career was full of paradox and contradiction. Though a man of peace, he gained his greatest popularity and met his greatest success in war. Though a fierce individualist, he accomplished much through compromise. His popularity and willingness to compromise led directly to the destruction of his party and the end of his own career. As a result, this man of the people found himself cast aside by the postwar masses, who flocked to socialism and the Labour Party. It is at least arguable that senility was in part responsible for his misreading of Adolf Hitler; willpower may have given way to wishful thinking. Still, Lloyd George was certainly not alone in his opinions, and the thoughts of a man in his seventies should not diminish his earlier accomplishments, which were huge.

Lloyd George led his country through the worst calamity the world had yet known, and set an ex-

ample of social consciousness at the highest level of government. His nation and the democracies of the West remain greatly in his debt.

Bibliography
Campbell, John. *Lloyd George: The Goat in the Wilderness, 1922-1931*. London: Cape, 1977. A study of Lloyd George's unsuccessful attempts to revive the shattered Liberal Party.

French, David. *The Strategy of the Lloyd George Coalition, 1916–1918*. Oxford: Clarendon Press, and New York: Oxford University Press, 1995. Excellent study of World War I.

Grigg, John. *Lloyd George: From Peace to War, 1912-1916*. Berkeley: University of California Press, and London: Methuen, 1985. Focuses on the transition from man of peace to leader of the war effort.

Morgan, Kenneth O. "Lloyd George and Germany." *The Historical Journal* 39, no. 3 (September, 1996). Examines British politician George's opinions about Germany over time including his admiration for its industrial accomplishments and his eventual denunciation of Germany after its invasion of Czechoslovakia.

Rowland, Peter. *Lloyd George*. London: Barrie and Jenkins, 1975; as *David Lloyd George: A Biography*, New York: Macmillan, 1976. The definitive biography.

Scally, Robert J. *The Origins of the Lloyd George Coalition: The Politics of Social-Imperialism, 1900-1918*. Princeton, N.J.: Princeton University Press, 1975. Traces Lloyd George's progress from agitator to coalition builder and world leader. Interesting insights into the man's erratic brilliance.

Sylvester, A. J. *Life with Lloyd George: The Diary of A. J. Sylvester, 1931–45*. Edited by Colin Cross. New York: Barnes and Noble, and London: Macmillan, 1975. A useful secondary source, full of detail.

Tuchman, Barbara W. *The Proud Tower*. New York: Macmillan, and London: Hamilton, 1966. Provides useful background information for study of Lloyd George and of most of his major contemporaries in Great Britain and abroad.

Anthony Tinsley

HENRY CABOT LODGE

Born: May 12, 1850; Boston, Massachusetts
Died: November 9, 1924; Cambridge, Massachusetts
Area of Achievement: Government and politics
Contribution: Combining integrity, acumen, and strong Republican partisanship, Lodge helped shape the nation's political history throughout his thirty-seven-year tenure as a United States congressman and senator.

Early Life

Henry Cabot Lodge entered an environment dominated by wealth and prestige when he began life on May 12, 1850. Often called Cabot or Cabot Lodge by contemporaries, the future senator could claim several noteworthy ancestors. His most famous progenitor, George Cabot, served in the United States Senate and acted as confidant to such notables as George Washington and John Adams. His mother, Anna Cabot Lodge, could trace her lineage through many generations of a distinguished Colonial family. John Ellerton Lodge, Henry's father, continued his family's tradition of success in shipping and other mercantile concerns. Though not as steeped in the nation's past as the Cabots (the Lodges had come to the United States from Santo Domingo in 1781), the Lodges could also count themselves among Boston's finest families at the time of Henry's arrival.

Cabot Lodge matured and received his formal education in the city's blue-blood milieu. Prominent men of the time, Charles Sumner and George Bancroft among others, frequently visited his childhood home. Yet Lodge described his youth as that of a normal boy. He learned to swim and sail in the waters off Nahant on the Atlantic coast of Massachusetts. Later in life, he would make his home in this area, which he came to love above all others. Lodge was a proper although sometimes mischievous child, taking part in the usual juvenile pranks. He maintained an especially close relationship with his mother, and this bond grew even stronger after his father's death in 1862 and continued until Anna's death in 1900. The family—Henry's mother, his sister, her husband, and he—made a grand tour of Europe in 1866. The following fall, he entered Harvard College. His matriculation coincided with the start of Charles W. Eliot's tenure as the institution's president, an exciting period of change and growth. Though never more than an av-erage student, Lodge benefited from his years at Harvard. Specifically, he began a lifelong friendship with one of his mentors, Henry Adams.

Lodge ascended slowly to national prominence. He married Anna Cabot Mills Davis, or Nannie as she was called, a cousin of his mother and member of an equally prominent family, the day after his college graduation in 1871. Lodge's social stratum had felt the impact of the rapid change which occurred after the Civil War, and Lodge, like many others in his social class, wondered about his place in the new order. He first did literary work for the *North American Review* under the tutelage of Henry Adams. Under Adams' prodding, Lodge began to take an active interest in politics. Adams urged him to work for reform. In the 1870's, this meant attempting to elect honest men to office. Political independents first attracted Lodge's attention, but he soon drifted into the Republican Party. He absorbed what happened around him and learned the nuances of the political world. At the same time, he furthered his literary reputation and did graduate study at Harvard. Lodge worked under his close friend Adams, and in 1876 he received his Ph.D. in history—one of the first Americans to gain this degree. He thereafter lectured at his alma mater and published *The Life and Letters of George Cabot* in 1877. Four years later, he published *A Short History of the English Colonies in America* (1881). These major works, supplemented by numerous shorter pieces, established him as a literary scholar of some note. He continued to write and publish throughout his life.

Politics, however, became Lodge's principal concern. In 1879, he secured the Republican nomination to represent Nahant, by then his place of residence, in the state legislature. The candidate showed a marked determination to achieve his goals, a quality he would exhibit throughout his public career. Lodge served two one-year terms and accumulated a respectable record. In 1880, he went as a delegate to his party's national convention. The next year, he lost in his bid for a state senate seat and for a United States congressional nomination. He failed again to secure the latter two years later but distinguished himself through party service. He remained loyal to Republican presidential candidate James G. Blaine, even though he lost several close personal friends because of it. At the same time, he began a friendship with Theodore

Roosevelt; like Henry Adams, Roosevelt would remain a lifelong intimate. In 1886, Lodge's fortunes improved. He won election to the United States House of Representatives and took his seat on December 5, 1887. He would remain in an elected national office until his death in 1924.

Life's Work

Lodge began his congressional tenure by watching, waiting, and learning. He quickly came to understand that a lawmaker must be practical as well as principled. He and Nannie immersed themselves in Washington society. Lodge continued his close association with Roosevelt and Adams, and he developed new friendships, such as that with the British diplomat Spring Rice. In the House, the nascent legislator proved to be an honest, hardworking, and vain combatant. Though an open-minded person, he was a single-minded politician. He established himself as a principled partisan, one who would support the party but who maintained a strong sense of right and wrong. Lodge did not fail to support President Grover Cleveland, a Democrat, when he thought the chief executive had acted

properly. Lodge chaired the House Committee on Elections. He devoted considerable energy to the cause of civil service reform and trying to pass the Force Bill, a forerunner to the voting rights acts of the 1960's. In 1891, the congressman turned his attention to capturing a United States Senate seat. He succeeded when the Massachusetts legislature elected him to the position in 1892.

Lodge held his Senate seat for thirty-two years. The specifics of such a lengthy term are too numerous for individual coverage, but two issues, immigration policy and foreign affairs, deserve special attention. Lodge witnessed the changes in the United States brought on by industrialization and urbanization. One of these was the marked increase in the number of foreign immigrants arriving annually. Their presence was made even more apparent by their propensity to crowd into the slums of the nation's largest cities. There, they seemed to contribute disproportionately to numerous social ills: squalor, labor unrest, crime, pauperism, and disease. In addition, an ever-increasing percentage of the new arrivals came from nontraditional sources of immigrants. Lodge, along with many other Americans, viewed their influx as a threat to the nation's social and political fabric and tried to bring about their exclusion. In the Senate, and earlier in the House, he made numerous speeches on behalf of the literacy test, the most widely advocated means of general restriction. Lodge worked with the provision's other supporters to secure its ultimate passage in 1917. He also served for a time as the chairman of the Senate Committee on Immigration and as a Senate appointee on the United States Immigration Commission from 1907 to 1910.

Lodge earned his greatest reputation in the area of foreign policy. His father's association with shipping influenced him in this field. As a child, he had considered a nautical career. The years of his Senate tenure provided numerous opportunities for him to exercise his knowledge and pursue his interest in world affairs. After 1890, American involvement in foreign events dramatically increased. Lodge was one of many public figures who advocated preparedness for international conflict, a large navy, and an aggressive global policy. He believed, simply, in imperialism and expansion. As senator, he contended that the United States should establish naval superiority over its rivals. Naval supremacy, he believed, would be followed by American dominance of the international marketplace. Yet Lodge balked at entanglement in European alliances.

A number of events from 1892 to 1924 allowed the senator to refine his theories and ideas and put them into use. In 1893, he supported American annexation of Hawaii. Two years later, he stood behind President Cleveland's attempts to enforce the Monroe Doctrine in regard to the Venezuela boundary crisis. Lodge, in this instance, claimed party politics should stop at the water's edge. His active participation in the affair and the strong sense of nationalism which he displayed won for him a place on the Senate Foreign Relations Committee. When the Cuban insurrection of 1895 escalated into war between the United States and Spain, Lodge applauded American involvement. The senator reveled in the subsequent American victory, though he realized it saddled the nation with global responsibility. He saw the acquisition of new territory as expansion, not imperialism. In his mind, the new lands were dependencies, not colonies. The senator used strategic and economic arguments to defend his position, and he worked diligently to solve the myriad problems related to the takeover of former Spanish possessions. Lodge also helped work out an acceptable Isthmanian Canal treaty. In 1902 and 1903, he won acclaim for his service on the Alaskan Boundary Tribunal, which successfully negotiated a settlement of the border's long-disputed location. His praiseworthy effort, however, failed to earn for him the chairmanship of the Foreign Relations Committee.

New foreign policy concerns, as well as many domestic issues, came to the forefront following Woodrow Wilson's election to the presidency in 1912. During the period prior to his victory, Lodge had had to watch his party divide into two camps, one of which broke away to support the candidacy of his close personal friend Theodore Roosevelt. Now the senator found much to dislike about the new chief executive. He believed Wilson had deserted his true convictions for political expediency. This is not to say Lodge never supported the president, but the two men were often at odds. Differing opinions about the conduct of foreign affairs produced the most serious confrontations.

Lodge disapproved of the choice of William Jennings Bryan as secretary of state. He also found fault with Wilson's Mexican policies and his attitudes toward the growing conflict in Europe. While the president tried to adhere to a policy of neutrality in regard to the latter, Lodge and Congressman Gardner championed preparedness. As hostilities in Europe increased and actions by both sides pulled the United States into the conflict, Wilson began to formulate plans for a moderate peace. Lodge thought Germany should be totally defeated and believed the Allies should impose a harsh settlement. He sharply criticized the president's Fourteen Points, and he refused to support the treaty which Wilson helped draft at the Paris Conference in 1919. Lodge thought Congress should have been consulted during the peacemaking process, believed the League of Nations would compromise American sovereignty, and contended certain treaty provisions would infringe on the Senate's foreign policy prerogatives. For these reasons, he led the fight to defeat Wilson's peace plan. When a compromise could not be worked out, the Senate refused to ratify the treaty. Right or wrong, Lodge, by then Foreign Relations Committee chairman, used his power and position to ensure defeat of the president's measure. The senator felt so strongly about his actions that he wrote *The Senate and the League of Nations* (1925) to explain and justify his behavior.

Summary

Friends and associates lauded Lodge's numerous accomplishments following his death in 1924. He was remembered for community service, scholarship, public service, and friendship. Many of those who had known him talked or wrote of his industry and tenacity of purpose. One who paid tribute quoted the senator's campaign speech made at Symphony Hall in Boston in January, 1911: "The record is there for the world to see. There is not a page upon which the people of Massachusetts are not welcome to look. There is not a line that I am afraid or ashamed to have my children or grandchildren read when I am gone." Such is a fitting epitaph. Lodge, statesman, author, lawmaker, and Republican politician, who once wondered about his place in a nation in transition, found it in honestly serving his country for thirty-seven years.

Bibliography

Fromkin, David. "Rival Internationalisms: Lodge, Wilson, and the Two Roosevelts." *World Policy Journal* 13, no. 2 (Summer 1996). Compares the international policies of Lodge, Woodrow Wilson, and both Roosevelts, and the ambiguity that evolved in U.S. policies of that time.

Garraty, John A. *Henry Cabot Lodge: A Biography.* New York: Knopf, 1953. A most complete treatment of Lodge, though Garraty emphasized the senator's foreign policy activities in the coverage of his career after 1900. The work also contains commentary by Lodge's grandson, Henry Cabot Lodge, Jr. The author is generally sympathetic to the subject of his study.

Lawrence, William. *Henry Cabot Lodge: A Biographical Sketch.* Boston: Houghton Mifflin, 1925. Written by the Bishop of Boston, who was a close personal friend of the senator. More of a testimonial than a legitimate history. Still, a useful source.

Link, Arthur S. *Wilson.* 5 vols. Princeton, N.J.: Princeton University Press, 1947-1965. The most complete biography of Lodge's major opponent in foreign policy and other areas. It offers another perspective on some of Lodge's most important legislative struggles.

Lodge, Henry Cabot. *Early Memories.* New York: Scribner, and London: Constable, 1913. An autobiographical account of Lodge's early life. Written many years after the events which it describes, it is very impressionistic. It nevertheless provides insight into aspects of the senator's early life which is not obtainable elsewhere.

———. *Selections from the Correspondence of Theodore Roosevelt and Henry Cabot Lodge, 1884-1918.* 2 vols. New York: Scribner, 1925. Not complete, judicious, or objective, yet the two volumes provide access to the workings of the very close friendship which existed between the two men. Also details both men's thoughts on many issues.

Schriftgiesser, Karl. *The Gentleman from Massachusetts: Henry Cabot Lodge.* Boston: Little Brown, 1944. A good sketch of the senator that covers most of the important events of his life. Written in the immediate post-New Deal era, it tends to be critical of Lodge.

Widenor, William C. *Henry Cabot Lodge and the Search for American Policy.* Berkeley: University of California Press, 1980; London: University of California Press, 1983. Deals primarily with foreign policy matters and foreign affairs. Widenor stresses the importance of understanding the senator's ideas in order to comprehend more fully his actions; he also argues that the senator was every bit as much an idealist as his bitterest foe, Woodrow Wilson.

Zimmerman, Warren. "Jingoes, Goo-Goos, and the Rise of America's Empire." *The Wilson Quarterly* 22, no. 2 (Spring 1998). Examines the roles of Lodge and four others in the United States' entry into imperialism.

Robert F. Zeidel

JACK LONDON

Born: January 12, 1876; San Francisco, California
Died: November 22, 1916; Glen Ellen, California
Area of Achievement: Literature
Contribution: London was one of the main exponents of American literary naturalism, a popular writer of adventure stories, and a crusading journalist, socialist, and political novelist who pioneered the role of the twentieth century activist writer.

Early Life

Born John Griffith Chaney, Jack London spent his early life around the Oakland, California, docks and the San Francisco waterfront. His family was poor, and life was a grim struggle—facts he later used in autobiographical novels such as *Martin Eden* (1909), the story of how a young, poorly educated man teaches himself to become a writer through dogged persistence and ruthless ambition. Born illegitimate, London identified with the downtrodden and the outcasts of society. His father, William Henry Chaney, was a traveling astrologer. When his mother, Flora Wellman, a spiritualist, married his stepfather, John London, a farmer, he took his stepfather's name.

John's farm failed, and the family faced a continual financial struggle. His stepson was bright and energetic—later photographs reveal a vigorous, ruggedly handsome man—and had an intermittent education, which ceased with grammar school at the age of fourteen (except for a few months at the University of California at Berkeley in 1897). At ten, London was already working, selling newspapers and laboring as a pin boy in a bowling alley. At fourteen, he found a job in a cannery. At sixteen, like his fictional heroes, he showed independence and pluck by pitching in with his friends to buy an oyster boat. He became known as an "oyster pirate." At seventeen, he became a sailor employed on a sealing boat that took him to Japan. At eighteen, he turned hobo and toured the United States and Canada.

By 1895, London had embarked on a fierce program of self-education, reading Charles Darwin, Karl Marx, and Friedrich Nietzsche. These three intellectual mentors imbued London with a vision of society as a struggle in which the fittest survived. However, even the very strong could be crushed, given the political structure of society, and the true nature of a human being might not be revealed except in the struggle against nature that makes London's tales of adventure so stirring and challenging.

At twenty-one, London followed the gold rush to the Klondike River in Canada, and two years later he sold his first story, "To the Man on the Trail." Soon he was producing a flood of stories and novels about the individual quest not only for survival but also for triumph over both the elements of nature and the structures of society.

Life's Work

In 1898, London returned to Oakland to continue his career as a professional writer, drawing first on his Klondike experiences. In 1900, he married Bessie Mae Maddern, with whom he had two daughters, Joan (in 1901) and Becky (in 1902). His name will forever be associated with the classic story *The Call of the Wild* (1903). It has never been out of print, and it has been translated into sixty-eight languages. The book not only made London's career as a best-selling author possible, but it also secured his place in American literary naturalism. The story is about a dog, Buck, half-St. Bernard and half-Scottish sheepdog, who is stolen from a comfortable California home and brutalized as a sled dog. Nevertheless, his spirit overcomes adversity—including the challenge of a vicious dog named Spitz—and Buck earns the love of a kind master, Thornton, to whom Buck remains loyal even after his master's death.

The Call of the Wild reflects the suffering, adventuring, and success of London's early life but also includes the ideas of Darwin, Marx, and Nietzsche by demonstrating how overwhelming the odds are against the individual and yet how indomitable the wild spirit—in humans and dogs—can remain. This is the hard world of American literary naturalism, which posits a universe of biological forces and societal constraints. Only individuals who are insulated by wealth and middle-class comforts can escape the struggle for survival—and even then, comfortable bourgeois may find themselves suddenly thrust into the grim world that luxury can cushion but cannot obliterate.

The key to London's success was to make his adventure stories embody his philosophical and political ideas rather than have those ideas explicitly drive the stories. Readers could easily imbibe London's message while apparently only reading a

gripping story. For London, plot itself, the structure of the story, made his political point.

London followed up his initial success with two more short adventure novels, *The Sea-Wolf* (1904) and *White Fang* (1906). In the former, it is not a dog but a wealthy literary critic, Humphrey van Weyden, who is shipwrecked and has to contend with the ruthless Wolf Larsen, captain of the *Ghost*, a sealing schooner. Just as *The Call of the Wild* drew on London's own Klondike experience to present an authentic portrayal of a cold frontier world, *The Sea-Wolf* capitalized on London's memories of rough sea voyages. In each case, he was confronting readers with rugged and life-threatening environments in which individuals must rely on their own inner resources in a way that sedate society never requires. Van Weyden, with his Dutch name, suggests that London is pointing to the intrepid spirit that had settled America but that had, in the course of several generations, become weak. In the course of his conflict with the Viking-like Larsen, van Weyden builds himself up physically and mentally, returning to society as a strong and self-aware man.

White Fang reverses the plot of *The Call of the Wild*, taking a wolf-dog, brutally tamed by its first owner and trained as a ferocious attack dog, and turning it again into the wild, where it is tamed once more—but this time by a sensitive master who disciplines it to be a fearless but faithful companion. More sentimental than *The Call of the Wild*, *White Fang* presages London's gradual deterioration as a writer. At twenty-nine, he was the most famous, most widely read, and wealthiest author in the United States. He would write increasingly for money to maintain his lavish existence of luxury homes and yachts, although he did not forsake his withering view of a harsh world in which men and women had to battle both nature and society.

London's success as a writer strained his marriage, and he eventually separated from his wife. He fell in love with Charmian Kittredge and married her in 1905. The couple settled on a 130-acre ranch in Glen Ellen, California, where he remained until 1907, when he set sail on his boat, *The Snark*, for a voyage around the world. He was forced to curtail the journey in 1909 because of ill health. Much of his remaining work was written at his California ranch, although in 1914 he reported on the Mexican revolution.

Like his contemporary, the great science fiction writer H. G. Wells, London was not content to use the popular genre of the adventure story to convey his analysis of society and history. Just as Wells turned to journalism and novels of social criticism, so too did London, publishing novels such as *Martin Eden*, in which the hero as writer explicitly confronts the complacency of bourgeois society when he finds himself at a middle-class dinner table arguing for his interpretation of existence with the pillars of society—the judges and politicians who hold power and look upon the powerless as unworthy.

Other books such as *The Iron Heel* (1907), the story of a fascist dictatorship destroyed by socialist revolution, and *The War of the Classes* (1905), a collection of lectures and essays, demonstrated that London retained his commitment to social criticism. As a journalist, he wrote about the Russo-Japanese War (1904) for the Hearst papers and about Mexico for *Collier's*. In 1902, he posed as a sailor and investigated the lives of East End slum dwellers in London, England, producing an exposé the next year titled *The People of the Abyss*. His book *Smoke Bellew Tales* (1912) covers the career of a journalist in the Yukon territory in Canada.

Novels such as *The Valley of the Moon* (1913) drew on London's nostalgia for an agrarian life and his dislike of dehumanizing cities. It proposed an unrealistic return to the land. His work increasingly became the prisoner of the very commercial and cutthroat civilization he deplored. His personal deterioration—abetted by drug-taking and dipsomania—is evident in his autobiographical pro-temperance book *John Barleycorn* (1913). *The Cruise of the Snark* (1911), London's account of his effort to cruise the world in his schooner, is an apt example of his over-reaching. His enterprise was overly ambitious, and it ruined him financially. Nevertheless, his evocations of the writer as hero remain a signal achievement, and his broad and intense engagement with society still attracts generations of readers.

Summary

Jack London has had an extraordinary impact on world culture. He was avidly read in the Soviet Union, for example, and taken as the model of a progressive writer. He inspired writers such as George Orwell and Ernest Hemingway to fuse journalism and fiction, pursuing a commitment to the writing life and to literature as a way of interpreting the world. His sheer passion and output have been inspiring, even if, like his hero Martin

Eden, he committed suicide—a burnt-out case at age forty—as some biographers suspect. The circumstances of his death remain ambiguous, with some biographers suggesting that he died of natural causes such as a stroke or heart failure. His death certificate records uremic poisoning and renal colic.

London offered journalists and novelists a vision of the individual writer at war with the world and yet fabulously successful. He did not blink at the realities of society even as he pursued his own ambitious course. Even writers who might seem worlds apart from the aggressive, high-living London—such as the essayist and novelist Susan Sontag—have paid tribute to London's example, ignoring his excesses and honoring his quest to engage the world on his terms.

London has been equally popular, however, with readers of adventure stories who are not devotees of Nietzsche, Marx, or Darwin. For them, it is surely London's ability to describe the world, to place readers in his characters' situations, that is so compelling. London always gave his readers a vivid sense of having been to the same places as his characters.

As a popular writer, London fashioned plots that overwhelm the seeming contradictions in his thinking. Nietzsche and Marx, for example, did not have the same vision of society or of the individual. Nietzsche would have rejected Marx's materialism and his emphasis on the structures of society that militate against individual success. There was no room in Marx's Communism for the superman, or superhero, as in Nietzsche. Neither Marx nor Nietzsche adopted Darwin's biological view of humans as organisms in the evolving natural world. Yet in London, society, nature, and the individual are synthesized in dramatic plots that defy logical analysis. London speaks simultaneously for both the social critic and the social aspirant: individuals who know that the world will crush them but who nevertheless persist in the belief that they can master their misfortunes.

Bibliography

Auerbach, Jonathan. *Male Call: Becoming Jack London*. Durham, N.C.: Duke University Press, 1996. As its title suggests, this biography focuses on how London became a writer and public celebrity as well as an exponent of the masculinized viewpoint that later became the forte of Ernest Hemingway.

Barltrop, Robert. *Jack London: The Man, the Writer, the Rebel*. London and New York: Pluto Press, 1976. A short, well-illustrated biographical and critical study with separate chapters on *The Iron Heel* and the Snark voyage, and the consequences of his fame. Includes notes, bibliography, and index.

Cassuto, Leonard, and Jeanne C. Reesman, eds. *Rereading Jack London*. Stanford, Calif.: Stanford University Press, 1996. A collection of essays that expand the customary range of topics in London critique to include his treatment of different cultures, gender, class, and race.

Doctorow, E. L. *Jack London, Hemingway, and the Constitution: Selected Essays*. New York: Random House, 1993. A long, thoughtful reflection on London's politics and fiction from the point of view of a major novelist who is sympathetic but also critical of London's example.

Kershaw, Jack. *Jack London: A Life*. London: HarperCollins, 1997; New York: St. Martin's Press, 1998. A comprehensive and lively biography that reveals few new facts but retells the story of London's life and career in intimate, revealing details.

Labor, Earle. *Jack London*. Rev. ed. New York: Twayne Publishers, 1994. A useful introduction to London that includes a chronology, notes, and annotated bibliography.

McClintock, James I. *Jack London's Strong Truths*. East Lansing: Michigan State University Press, 1997. Reprint of the classic analysis of the short stories of London. Includes a new introduction and updated bibliography.

Perry, John. *Jack London: An American Myth*. Chicago: Nelson-Hall, 1981. A detailed biography that is especially good on London's early life and his later adventures as sailor and journalist. Lacks illustrations but includes notes, bibliography, and index.

Sinclair, Andrew. *Jack: A Biography of Jack London*. New York: Harper, 1977; London: Weidenfeld and Nicolson, 1978. A comprehensive biography that includes chapters on London's period in Mexico and his later reputation. Includes excellent illustrations, notes, bibliography, and index.

Tavernier-Courbin, Jacqueline, ed. *Critical Essays on Jack London*. Boston: Hall, 1983. Contains a helpful introduction, essays on many aspects of London's life and work, and a bibliography.

Carl Rollyson

HUEY LONG

Born: August 30, 1893; near Winnfield, Louisiana
Died: September 10, 1935; Baton Rouge, Louisiana
Area of Achievement: Government and politics
Contribution: Joining a sincere concern for the economic plight of the common people with an overwhelming desire to realize his ideas and plans, Long fashioned a political career of great accomplishment for both good and ill.

Early Life

Huey Pierce Long, second son of Huey Long, Sr., and Caledonia Tison Long, was born in the family's rural, northern Louisiana home in 1893. Eventually, there would be seven children in the Long family, and all of them would receive at least part of a secondary education, an achievement insisted upon by their mother. The Long family was not poor, as later stories would claim, chief among them told by Huey Long himself. The elder Long was actually a moderately prosperous farmer whose wealth consisted of land, crops, and animals rather than actual cash.

From his earliest days, Huey Long was restless and energetic; he would undertake any prank to be the center of attention. He read widely, chiefly in history, the works of William Shakespeare, and the Bible, but his favorite book was Alexandre Dumas, *père*'s *The Count of Monte-Cristo* (1844-1845); he was impressed by the hero's tenacious quest for power and revenge.

In school, Huey was able and demonstrated early his remarkable memory. He often gained his wishes through sheer boldness and manipulation, as when he convinced the faculty to promote him a grade on his own recommendation. In 1910, Huey left school without graduating. He worked for a while as a salesman, and he met his future wife, Rose McConnell, at a cake-baking contest. They were married in 1913 and had three sons and one daughter. In 1914, Huey entered Tulane Law School in New Orleans as a special student; he did not pursue a formal degree but instead concentrated on the courses needed for the bar exam, which he passed in 1915.

As a lawyer, Long took cases protecting the economic rights of the common folk, such as workers' compensation claims. He became convinced of the need to redistribute wealth and found precedence for this particularly in the Bible, which enjoined the periodic remission of debts and readjustment of riches.

Early in his twenties, Long looked much as he would for the remainder of his life. He was not quite six feet tall and generally weighed around 160 pounds; as he grew older, he had a tendency to become heavier. His face was full, even fleshy, with a round, prominent nose, dark eyes, a wide mouth, and a dimpled chin. Depending on his mood, his appearance could be comical or impressive. His reddish-brown hair was unruly, and he often ran his fingers through it while speaking; one strand usually drooped over his forehead. His most notable characteristic was his unbounded energy: constantly in motion, he ran rather than walked and spoke with an intensity that kept his listeners spellbound.

Long delighted in his courtroom battles, but early in life he had already settled upon the path he intended to follow: state office, the governorship, the Senate, the presidency. In 1918, he decided that he was ready to begin.

Life's Work

In 1918, Louisiana was a state ruled by a few, powerful interests: a handful of large corporations, chief among them Standard Oil; the banks and railroads; and the remnants of the old plantation aristocracy. The average citizen earned little, received few services, traveled on wretched dirt roads, and sent his children to ill-funded schools. This was the situation that Long was determined to change.

He ran for a position on the State Railroad Commission, a regulatory body much like modern public service commissions. A tireless campaigner, Long spoke widely and also began the use of circulars—short, vividly written handbills stating his views and attacking his opponent. He would make brilliant use of this technique throughout his career, always writing the copy himself, using a pithy style that appealed to the voters.

Elected to the Railroad Commission, Long vigorously attacked the dominant force in Louisiana political and economic life, the giant Standard Oil Company. In speeches, commission hearings, and circulars, he detailed the improper influence the company had on Louisiana state government, and, in 1921, Long was found "technically guilty" of libeling the state's governor. His fine was nominal, but his position as champion of the common folk of Louisiana was firmly established. In 1923, he ran for governor.

He had none of the traditional supporters a candidate of that time was careful to recruit: no banks, no sugar barons, no railroads, no corporations, no political machine. The small, elite group which had dominated Louisiana politics for a century was against Long, and Long was fundamentally hostile to their rule. He was opposed by the only large corporation then in the South—Standard Oil—and by the region's only true big city machine—the Old Regulars in New Orleans.

With such a combination against him, it is not surprising that Long lost in 1923, but the size of his vote revealed that Huey Long and his ideas of economic and political reforms had substantial approval across the state. This fact was evident in 1924, when he was reelected to the Public Service Commission (the new name of the Railroad Commission) by an eighty percent majority. When he ran again for governor in 1928, he won decisively, and his victory signaled a new day for Louisiana.

As governor, Long moved to implement programs which would benefit the majority of Louisiana residents: paved roads and highways, public bridges, free textbooks to students (not schools, thus bypassing the Church-State controversy in largely Catholic Louisiana), and increased taxes on corporations and business to pay for these programs. Remarkably, most of his agenda was enacted during his first year in office, a tribute to his own personal magnetism, his brilliant political skills, and his immense popular support. His enemies were repulsed, rather than convinced, by this support. When Long asked the legislature for a tax on the huge profits of Standard Oil, the result was an effort to impeach him in April, 1929. The charges, many of them absurd, were all rejected. After the impeachment fight, Huey Long was stronger than ever; he secured a tax on Standard Oil and expanded the reach of his programs.

It was during this time that his political strength and the efforts of his enemies combined to undermine much of the idealist nature of Long. Realizing that his opponents would use any tactics to destroy him and wreck his programs, he came to believe that he must crush his adversaries, leaving them no option but to join him or face extinction. It was also at this time that the fabled Long machine came into being: a powerful institution that reached into every parish in Louisiana, able to dispense jobs, help friends, harm foes, and, most important, get out the vote. One by one, the existing political factions were absorbed; the last to submit was the once-mighty Old Regular machine in New Orleans, which finally yielded to Long in the mid-1930's.

Long became known as the Kingfish, a name adopted from the popular "Amos and Andy" radio program. It perfectly suited his style of leadership: a combination of low comedy and high political acumen. His opponents sneered at him as a buffoon, only to realize too late that they had underestimated the Kingfish.

In 1930, Long's term as governor ended with an impressive list of accomplishments: paved roads and public bridges, better hospital facilities, the expansion of Louisiana State University into a nationally recognized educational institution, more and better public education, free schoolbooks, improved port facilities and an airport for New Orleans, and, symbolic of it all, a new state capitol building. Typically, the construction was a modern, up-to-date skyscraper, visually demonstrating how Huey Long had brought Louisiana into the twentieth century.

Unable to serve a second term as governor, Long was elected to the United States Senate in 1930, but for the remainder of his life, Long remained the effective, if not official, chief executive of Louisiana, commanding special sessions of the legislature whenever he pleased and ordering passage of the laws he desired. This heavy-handed, unmasked expression of power was the most unpleasant aspect of Long's career; apparently he had reached the conclusion—probably confirmed by the impeachment battle—that his enemies had forced him to employ any means, however questionable or undemocratic, to achieve his high-minded and progressive ideals.

Long used the Senate to espouse with fervent intensity his plans to redistribute wealth in the United States. Pointing out that a minority of the population owned the majority of the riches, Long urged taxes that would limit both earned and inherited wealth and spread the wealth among everyone. Everyman a King was his slogan, and he used it as the title of his 1933 autobiography. Spread the Wealth clubs were organized throughout the country to support the Long program.

Long supported Franklin D. Roosevelt for president in 1932, but the honeymoon with FDR soon ended. The president moved too slowly for Long, and Long was often an annoyance, sometimes a threat to the president, who was trying to hold a Depression-shaken country together. Long made some positive efforts—increasing federal banking insurance, for example—but was generally opposed to Roosevelt's plans as being too timid and too superficial. He grew more open in his plans to defeat Roosevelt in 1936 by supporting a Republican or third-party candidate, then sweeping into office himself in 1940 as the only man who could save the country.

While involved in national affairs, Long remained closely connected with events in Louisiana. He had his selected governor summon sessions of the state legislature to pass bills which Long wrote, rushed through committee, and shepherded through the final vote. His efforts were increasingly aimed at overawing his opponents; during the 1934 mayoral elections in New Orleans, he ordered out the state militia to control the balloting. Such high-handed techniques, combined with his vitriolic attacks on the popular Roosevelt, began to erode his support. Undeterred, he pressed onward. In 1934, he had a series of radical measures introduced into the Louisiana legislature, which were a preview of what he soon hoped to attempt on a national level. His consistent theme had not changed: He urged economic opportunity for all, but his reliance on brute power had greatly increased.

There had always been strong, indeed violent, opposition to Long in Louisiana. He had fought too many entrenched interests and helped too many of the poor and oppressed for it to be otherwise. Now this opposition began to organize and become dangerous. The Square Deal League raised an armed force which seized control of the Baton Rouge jail in early 1935; it dispersed only after a siege by the state militia. Later that year, the Minute Men of Louisiana formed, claiming to have ten thousand members, all ready to end the rule of the Kingfish, by murder if necessary.

It was in such a climate of violence that Huey Long's life and career ended. On the evening of September 8, 1935, Long was confronted in the state capitol by a young doctor, Carl Austin Weiss, who apparently hated Long for both personal and political reasons; there is no evidence that he was part of any organized plot. Weiss fired two shots at Long and was immediately gunned down himself by Long's bodyguards. The wounded Long was rushed to the hospital. An operation to save him

failed, and on September 10, 1935, Huey Long died. His last words were, "God, don't let me die. I have so much to do."

Summary

In his 1928 race for governor, Long gave a speech which so well expressed his political philosophy that he reprinted it later in his biography, *Every Man a King* (1933). He began by referring to Henry Wadsworth Longfellow's poem "Evangeline," and then continued:

> But Evangeline is not the only one who has waited here in disappointment. Where are the schools that you have waited for your children to have, that have never come? Where are the roads and highways that you send your money to build, that are no nearer now than ever before? Where are the institutions to care for the sick and disabled? Evangeline wept bitter tears in her disappointment, but it lasted through only one lifetime. Your tears in this country, around this oak, have lasted for generations. Give me the chance to dry the eyes of those who still weep here!

The bright side of Huey Long's career and legacy was that he answered the needs of the people of Louisiana for the schools, roads, institutions, and services which they so desperately needed. He broke a century-old tradition of rule by the few and wealthy, and he made the government benefit all the people.

On the dark side, however, he turned the state legislature into his personal tool and the state government into an extension of the Long machine. His supporters have insisted that he was driven to these tactics by the implacable opposition of his foes. There is truth to this; Huey Long was intensely despised and feared by many in Louisiana, often for the good which he had done. Long was not the first popular leader to use questionable methods to obtain worthwhile ends.

During his career, Huey Long was passionately loved and hated; he was called both a Fascist and a friend of the common man. His enemies admitted his political brilliance; his friends acknowledged his irregular methods. His many accomplishments have never resolved some basic questions: Was he the best leader to arise in Louisiana, or its worst political disaster? Had he lived, would he have proven to be a national figure of genius or the architect of a homegrown Fascist state? These puzzles have no answer—or too many answers—and the life and career of Huey Long remain an American enigma.

Bibliography

Amenta, Edwin, et al. "Stolen Thunder? Huey Long's 'Share our Wealth,' Political Mediation, and the Second New Deal." *American Sociological Review* 59, no. 5 (October, 1994). Detailed examination from several perspectives of Long's plan for redistribution of wealth.

Brinkley, Alan. *Voices of Protest: Huey Long, Father Coughlin, and the Great Depression.* New York: Knopf, 1982. Helps to place Long in the economic and social situation of the 1930's, when the country was wracked by depression and a number of theories competed with Share the Wealth and Roosevelt's New Deal as solutions to the economic problems of the United States.

Cortner, Richard C. *The Kingfish and the Constitution: Huey Long, the First Amendment, and the Emergence of Modern Press Freedom in America.* Westport, Conn.: Greenwood Press, 1996. Examines Long's conflicts with the press and the resulting U.S. Supreme Court decision that created the foundation for today's press freedoms.

Davis, Forrest. *Huey Long: A Candid Biography.* New York: Dodge, 1935. A contemporary portrait of Long, this biography is more balanced than most produced at the time. Davis had extensive interviews with Long and used them extensively.

Dethloft, Henry, ed. *Huey P. Long: Southern Demagogue or American Democrat?* Boston: Heath, 1967. Part of the Problems in American Civilization series and contains essays and articles by a variety of authors, including Huey Long and historians such as T. Harry Williams and V. O. Key, Jr. A good source for sampling the intense emotions that Long and his program could arouse.

Deutsch, Hermann. *The Huey Long Murder Case.* New York: Doubleday, 1963. While this work concentrates on Long's assassination, it does provide some helpful background on his political career, especially in relationship to the Louisiana legislature.

Hair, William Ivy. *The Kingfish and His Realm: The Life and Times of Huey P. Long.* Baton Rouge: Louisiana State University Press, 1991.

Long, Huey. *Every Man a King.* New Orleans, La.: National Book Co., 1933. Long's 1933 autobiography can be lean on facts and naturally stops with Long in mid-career, but it offers a fascinating glimpse of his energetic personality.

McSween, Harold B. "Huey Long at His Centenary." *The Virginia Quarterly Review* 69, no. 3 (Summer 1993). Profile of Long including references to several books that have been written on his life, and a discussion of his achievements.

Opotowsky, Stan. *The Longs of Louisiana.* New York: Dutton, 1960. A general biography of the Long family and their roles in state, regional, and national politics. It clearly shows that, while Huey Long was the most brilliant politician of his family, others shared some of his gifts.

Schlesinger, Arthur M., Jr. *The Politics of Upheaval.* Boston: Houghton Mifflin, and London: Heinemann, 1960. This study of the Roosevelt Administration and the New Deal contains a well-informed and impartial discussion of Long, his program, and his impact upon the nation. Schlesinger points out the danger implicit in Long's philosophy and tactics but also acknowledges Long's considerable accomplishments.

Williams, T. Harry. *Huey Long.* New York: Knopf, 1969; London: Thames and Hudson, 1970. This is the definitive biography of Long, unlikely to be surpassed. Williams worked extensively with contemporaries of Long, including many members of the Long organization, who spoke remarkably freely. The book is excellently researched and extremely well written; it is a classic of modern American biography.

Michael Witkoski

ANITA LOOS

Born: April 26, 1888; Sissons, California
Died: August 18, 1981; New York, New York
Areas of Achievement: Literature and film
Contribution: A pioneering scriptwriter who developed the use of intertitles during the silent film era, Anita Loos also wrote the famous jazz-age novel *Gentlemen Prefer Blondes.*

Early Life

Corinne Anita Loos was born on April 26, 1888, in Sissons (later Mount Shasta), California, to Minerva and R. Beers Loos. "Minnie" Loos was a proper, patient wife who socially abided the flamboyant, philandering ways of her husband, an itinerant journalist whose wanderlust led him to one small-town California newspaper after another. The wayward father also loved everything theatrical. A self-proclaimed "Edwin Booth of amateur theatre," he opened (and closed) as many drama societies as he did newspapers.

When a San Francisco weekly, *Music and Drama*, went on the market, Anita's father bought it and moved the family once again. San Francisco's frontier spirit and Barbary Coast pleasures fascinated him as he prowled the city's bustling waterfront, often with the diminutive Anita. He introduced Anita and her younger sister Gladys to theater when the youngsters made their dramatic debut in the Alcazar Stock Company's production of *Quo Vadis?* (1894).

The close bond between Anita and her father survived a family tragedy when eight-year-old Gladys Loos died after an emergency appendectomy performed on the family's kitchen table while R. Beers Loos was out on the town. The family's fortunes dipped again when Anita's father's paper failed because of lax supervision. R. Beers Loos next managed the Cineograph in San Francisco's Mexican district, where short one-reel films alternated with vaudeville acts. When that venture failed, the family moved to San Diego, where R. Beers managed the Lyceum, a theater featuring pirated Broadway plays that often starred Anita, who by now was a versatile teenage actress and an increasingly important source of the family's income.

In spite of the promise of a successful theatrical career, Anita Loos concluded that acting was a profession for numbskulls and narcissists and turned her attention to writing. In 1912, after penning gossip items for the local paper, Loos tried the "galloping tintypes." Her target was New York's Biograph Company, the nation's top studio thanks to innovative director D. W. Griffith. Biograph responded to Loos's unsolicited script for *The Road to Plaindale* with a check for twenty-five dollars and a release form. Within months, at age twenty-four, Anita Loos had sold three scripts to Biograph and a fourth to the Lubin Company. One of these, *The New York Hat* (1912), was directed by Griffith as a swan song for Mary Pickford, who was making her final appearance for Biograph. The film was a barometer prefiguring Loos's penchant for satirizing provincialism and busybody moralists.

Life's Work

During the first phase of Anita Loos's career with D. W. Griffith at Biograph and then at Triangle, the attractive four-foot, eleven-inch comedic dynamo churned out more than one hundred scenarios. In the process, she revolutionized the "art" of writing intertitles, the printed snippets of dialogue and expositional narrative that helped audiences follow the melodramatic unfolding of a film's plot and the development of its characters. Typical of her approach was an early film for Lubin in which she identified the antagonist, Proteus Prindle, as "a self-made man who adored his maker." The wittily turned intertitle soon would become her stock-in-trade.

Although Loos had met Griffith briefly in 1914 on one of the director's winter sojourns to shoot under Southern California's sunny skies, their professional relationship did not move from correspondence to direct collaboration until 1915. Griffith, who along with Mack Sennett and Thomas Ince headed one of Triangle's three production units, hired Loos to help the ambitious tripartite studio keep pace with an urgent need for fresh material. At the time, with Europe consumed by World War I, the American film industry was growing at a rapid rate in order to meet growing domestic and international demands for new films. Loos could not have been at a better place (Hollywood) at a better time (1915).

Griffith, keenly aware of his need for smart writing talent, tendered Loos a contract for seventy-five dollars a week plus a bonus whenever one of her scripts was produced. Fresh from his triumph with *The Birth of a Nation* (1915) and preoccupied with his independent production of Intolerance, Griffith turned Loos over to Frank Woods, head of Triangle's script department. The paternal Woods, affectionately known on the Triangle lot as "Daddy," at first kept Loos busy with wise-cracking titles for Sennett's Keystone Kops and rewrites for the progressively longer melodramas, which by 1920 would become standardized at a feature length of one to two hours. Her first major assignment was an adaptation of *Macbeth* (1915) for renowned English actor Sir Beerbohm Tree. It was a "prestige production" for which, thanks to Daddy Woods, she received her first screen credit: "*Macbeth* by William Shakespeare and Anita Loos." She later wrote, "if I had asked, Daddy Woods would have given me top billing."

Loos was soon assigned to one of Triangle's secondary directors, John Emerson, who had been charged with trying to find some way of using former Broadway leading man Douglas Fairbanks. Loos penned *His Picture in the Papers* (1916) for Fairbanks, a project that poked fun at America's love of publicity and instant celebrity. Loos had a field day with the titles, which horrified Griffith, who ordered the picture shelved on the assumption that if audiences wanted to read, they would stay home with a book. A shortage of product prompted the film's release. To Griffith's surprise, *His Picture in the Papers* was a huge hit that made Fairbanks a film star and the intertitle a basic part of film technique. For his part, the savvy Griffith, recognizing Loos's unique talents, hired her to work, uncredited, on the titles for his mammoth production of *Intolerance* (1916).

Meanwhile, Loos and Fairbanks collaborated on nine more pictures for Triangle, most of which were directed by Emerson. Almost all of these films deflated current fads and fashions. In *The Mystery of the Leaping Fish* (1916), Fairbanks' hyped-up Coke Ennyday, "the scientific detective," parodies applied empiricism and cocaine. In *Reaching for the Moon* (1917), Coueism, a then-popular self-help regimen based on an autosuggestive mantra, "Every day in every way I am getting better and better," was cheerfully sent up and shot down. In *Wild and Woolly* (1917), Hollywood itself is mocked. In the process, the Loos-Emerson-Fairbanks team capitalized on Fairbanks' athletic ability, boundless cheer, good humor, and winning smile to fashion one of Hollywood's greatest icons and embodiments of American optimism.

In 1920, Loos married director John Emerson, a relationship that perplexed her friends, who resented the director for putting his name as coauthor on Loos's scripts. Loos seemed to have an affection for domineering, unfaithful men. In her autobiography, *A Girl Like I* (1966), Loos explains that she could not fall in love with an especially ardent suitor because "he gave me full devotion and required nothing in return, while John treated me in an offhand manner, appropriated my earnings, and demanded from me all the services of a hired maid. How could a girl like I resist him?"

In 1925, on sabbatical from Hollywood, Loos wrote the novel *Gentlemen Prefer Blondes* (1925). Loos was praised by literary lions such as H. L. Mencken for "making fun of sex, which has never before been done in this grand and glorious nation of ours." The novel's durable Lorelei Lee, the ditzy gold-digging blonde from Little Rock, first appeared on the silver screen in a silent version directed by Mal St. Clair in 1928. (Howard Hawks's 1953 remake featured the incandescent Marilyn Monroe as Lorelei Lee.)

Loos returned to Hollywood in the late 1920's to work with Irving Thalberg at Metro-Goldwyn-Mayer (MGM). Like her friend and fellow scenarist Francis Marion, Loos negotiated the switch to "talking" pictures smoothly. In *Red-Headed Woman* (1932), for example, the combination of Loos's wise-cracking dialogue and Jean Harlow's gold-digging glamour and genius for comic timing clicked with precision and panache. Among Loos's own favorites was the melodramatic *San Francisco* (1936), set around the earthquake of 1906, starring Clark Gable, Jeannette MacDonald, and Spencer Tracy; Gable's role was based on the great yet unrequited love of Loos's life, Wilson Mizner, the bon vivant she later traced in her book *Kiss Hollywood Goodbye* (1974). Loos also coscripted with veteran MGM writer Jane Murfin a sharp-edged adaptation of Clare Boothe Luce's venomous comedy The Women (1939), which was directed by George Cukor and featured Norma Shearer, Rosalind Russell, Paulette Goddard, and Joan Crawford.

After John Emerson's attempt on her life in 1937 and his subsequent confinement in a sanitarium as an uncurable schizophrenic for the final twenty years of his life, Loos became one of the few Hollywood scriptwriters to move successfully to the writing of plays, novels, and memoirs. She continued to produce various kinds of work for many

years. Anita Loos died in New York in 1981 at the age of ninety-three.

Summary

The name Anita Loos promises to live long as the author of *Gentlemen Prefer Blondes*, whether its form be novelistic, cinematic, or theatrical. Indeed, the golden-haired Lorelei Lee—whose sexual politics are summed up in Leo Robin's and Jule Styne's aphoristic "Diamonds Are a Girl's Best Friend," from the 1949 Broadway musical adaptation of Loos's novel—remains an entertaining though increasingly problematic representation of American womanhood, since it trades heavily on the stereotype of the dumb, submissive blonde bombshell.

In the history of the American film, especially during the silent era, Loos will continue to occupy a prominent place on the strength of her crisp satirizations of American foibles, her innovative exploitation of intertitles, her shaping of Douglas Fairbanks' exuberant screen persona, and her collaboration with D. W. Griffith on the intertitles for the director's masterwork, *Intolerance*.

Critic Marjorie Rosen suggests that although Loos's tender age may have limited the scope of her early scripts, it may also have accounted for their success. "For it is unlikely," Rosen concludes, "that in any other era the thoughts of a teen-aged girl—granted an exceptional one—could have so directly corresponded to the dreams of millions of women who were just beginning to take their moviegoing seriously."

Bibliography

Acker, Ally. *Reel Women: Pioneers of the Cinema, 1896 to the Present.* New York: Continuum, and London: Batsford, 1991. Acker's invaluable set of profiles places Anita Loos under the category "From the Silents to the Sound Era" in the chapter "Reel Women Writers."

Bartoni, Doreen. "Anita Loos." In *International Dictionary of Films and Filmmakers,* edited by Nicolas Thomas, et al. 2d ed. Vol. 4, *Writers and Production Artists.* Detroit and London: St. James Press, 1993. A concise biographical profile supplemented with a useful filmography and bibliography.

Carey, Gary. *Anita Loos: A Biography.* New York: Knopf, 1988. Based on extensive interviews with Loos and a cadre of her associates, Cary's lively and meticulous account is the definitive biography of the writer. Illustrated with fascinating photos from the Loos family collection.

Fraser, Kennedy. "Loos Talk." *Harper's Bazaar* no. 3441 (August, 1998). Profile of Loos including personal information and descriptions of the characters in her novel, *Gentlemen Prefer Blondes*.

Loos, Anita. *Cast of Thousands.* New York: Grosset and Dunlap, 1977. This handsomely produced scrapbook of Loos's memorabilia is crammed with revealing photos, posters, newspaper items, and magazine covers that bring the reader face-to-face with Fairbanks, Emerson, and the other members of the incredible cast that swirled around the diminutive dynamo Anita Loos.

———. *A Girl Like I.* New York: Viking Press, 1966; London: Hamilton, 1967. Loos's autobiography paints a rich picture of Hollywood's golden age and her exotic associates, who paraded through "a life that was never boring."

Rosen, Marjorie. *Popcorn Venus: Women, Movies, and the American Dream.* New York: Coward, McCann and Geoghegan, 1973; London: Owen, 1975. Rosen's groundbreaking survey of women's contributions to the classical Hollywood film includes a concise, penetrating account of Loos's unique talents.

Charles Merrell Berg

HENDRIK ANTOON LORENTZ

Born: July 18, 1853; Arnhem, The Netherlands
Died: February 4, 1928; Haarlem, The Netherlands
Area of Achievement: Physics
Contribution: Lorentz's work on electromagnetic theory paved the way for the development of relativity theory and quantum mechanics. In 1902, he was awarded the second Nobel Prize in Physics. His scientific research and his efforts to create an international scientific community drew the leading physicists of the early twentieth century to Leiden, making it a leading center for theoretical physics.

Early Life

Hendrik Antoon Lorentz was born on July 18, 1853, in Arnhem, The Netherlands. His father, Gerrit Frederik Lorentz, owned a nursery. His mother, Geertruida van Ginkel, died when Lorentz was four. Little is known about his boyhood, except that he excelled in school, especially in mathematics, science, and languages. He developed a reputation with his teachers as being highly gifted. In addition to his regular schooling, Lorentz was allowed to attend a special evening school, where he could work independently on his studies. In many areas, he simply taught himself what he thought he needed to know.

Lorentz's reputation preceded him when he was matriculated at the University of Leiden in 1870, and the physics lectures were revived especially for him. He received his Candidates degree (roughly equivalent to a bachelor's degree) summa cum laude in mathematics and physics in November, 1871. In her reminiscences, his daughter Geertruida de Haas-Lorentz, herself a physicist, notes that the examiner in mathematics passed Lorentz but felt disappointed in his performance. It turned out that he thought Lorentz was being examined for the Ph.D. For his doctoral examination and dissertation, Lorentz wanted to work in the area of electromagnetism and, in particular, on implications of James Clerk Maxwell's electromagnetic theory. Since no one at Leiden—or in The Netherlands—was familiar with Maxwell's work, he returned to Arnhem in February, 1872, to work on his own. He passed his oral examination summa cum laude in 1873 and received his Ph.D. in 1875.

Between 1872 and 1877, Lorentz was an evening-school teacher in Arnhem. In 1877, he was offered the chair for mathematics at Utrecht but declined because he wanted to teach physics. He applied for the post of teacher in the middle school in Leiden and for that of tutor at the university. Instead of these positions, he was awarded the first chair for theoretical physics in The Netherlands at the University of Leiden. On January 25, 1878, at the age of twenty-four, he delivered his inaugural address, in which he set forth what was to be the central problem of his scientific career: how to combine Maxwell's electromagnetic theory with a theory of matter so as to account for all optical and electromagnetic phenomena.

Life's Work

Lorentz began his scientific research on a major unresolved problem of Maxwell's theory: the reflection and refraction of light. His dissertation established the superiority of Maxwell's theory for explaining optical phenomena. Convinced of the great potential of Maxwell's field theory of electric and magnetic actions, Lorentz began trying to combine it with a particle theory of matter. This enterprise culminated nearly thirty years later in a set of lectures on his theory of electrons, delivered at Columbia University in 1906 and published in 1909 in a volume of that name.

The cornerstones of the theory of electrons are small, charged particles—the electrons—and an all-pervasive, immobile ether, which transmits actions between the particles. The nature of the ether-particle interaction is addressed for the first time in "La Théorie électromagnétique de Maxwell et son application aux corps mouvants" (1892; Maxwell's electromagnetic theory and its application to moving bodies). It is in this paper that Lorentz first introduced what he called a startling hypothesis: The charged particles within matter oscillate when struck by light waves. Lorentz was to use this hypothesis in his theoretical explanation of Pieter Zeeman's 1896 discovery of the splitting of the lines of a spectrum when a magnetic field is applied to the source of the spectrum (Zeeman effect). It should be noted that, when Lorentz gave this explanation, electrons had not yet been discovered experimentally. Their discovery in 1897 by Sir Joseph John Thomson was seen as providing evidence for Lorentz's theory. In 1902, Lorentz received the Nobel Prize, along with Zeeman, for his explanation of the Zeeman effect. With the publication of *Versuch einer Theorie der elektrischen und optischen Erscheinungen in bewegten Körpern* (1895; attempt at a theory of electric and optical phenomena in moving bodies), Lorentz's theory was recognized as the most comprehensive and successful electromagnetic theory.

Although Lorentz could be characterized as extending classical physics to its limits, he also broke with it in significant ways quite early in his career. In establishing the nature of the interaction between the ether and the charged particles, he was led to introduce a new force, which does not obey the Newtonian law of action and reaction, that is, the Lorentz force (force with which the ether acts on the particles), into electromagnetic theory. Next, in order to explain the result of an 1887 experiment performed by Albert Abraham Michelson and Edward Williams Morley, he hypothesized that molecular forces interact with the ether. This experiment was designed to detect the effect of the motion of Earth on the propagation of light. It established conclusively that there is no effect, from which Michelson and others concluded that, contrary to Lorentz's hypothesis that it is immobile, the ether must move along with Earth. Shortly after writing the 1892 paper, Lorentz proposed his famous explanation that objects moving through the ether change their dimensions in one direction (later called the contraction hypothesis).

In the penultimate formulation of his theory, "Electromagnetische verschijnselen in een stelsel dat zich met willekeurige snelheid, kleiner dan die van het licht, beweegt" (1904; "Electromagnetic Phenomena in a System Moving with Any Velocity Less Than That of Light," 1904), he used this hypothesis to account for an even wider range of phenomena. An additional feature put the theory of electrons at variance with classical theory. The mass of an electron and of uncharged matter is not constant but depends on its state of motion. Albert Einstein was to derive all the results of Lorentz's theory of electrons in a quite different manner in 1905. Although Einstein's theory is now called the special theory of relativity, until around 1911, it was called the Lorentz-Einstein theory, with few scientists besides Lorentz and Einstein appreciating the significant conceptual differences between the theories.

Although electromagnetism was the focus of Lorentz's scientific research, he did some important work in other areas of physics as well. In the 1800's, he worked on the molecular-kinetic theory of heat. He also made important contributions to

the development of the general theory of relativity and of the early quantum mechanics. In the last years of his life, he did the only applied analysis of his career when he devised a method for calculating storm surge in a network of channels and shoals for the project to build a twelve-mile dike enclosing the Zuiderzee (modern IJsselmeer) in the north of The Netherlands.

For nearly half of his scientific career, Lorentz remained in The Netherlands and sought no contact with the international community of physicists. This behavior changed dramatically after 1897, when he attended a conference in Dusseldorf and realized the value of discussion with colleagues equally knowledgeable in physics. He went on to give many lectures in Europe and in the United States. His linguistic abilities (Lorentz was fluent in German, French, and English) and his talent for dealing with difficult personalities made him the perfect choice to chair the first Solvay conference in 1911 and all subsequent conferences until his death.

In 1912, Lorentz moved to Haarlem to become curator of the Teylers Stichtung Museum. He continued to hold his Monday morning seminar at Leiden but now gave many popular lectures as part of his position at the museum. From 1909 to 1921, he was president of the physics section of the Royal Netherlands Academy of Sciences and Letters. From that position and that of chair of the Committee on International Cooperation of the League of Nations, he tried to restore international science after World War I. In addition to the Nobel Prize, he received the Royal Society's Rumford and Copley medals, was awarded honorary doctorates from the Universities of Paris and Cambridge, and was elected to the German Physics Society and the Royal Society. At the time of his death, Lorentz was a great scientific and cultural figure, both at home and abroad. Thousands of ordinary Dutch citizens lined the route of his funeral procession, and representatives of the Dutch government and the international scientific community attended the funeral.

Summary

When asked his opinion of the legacy of Hendrik Antoon Lorentz to twentieth century physics, Einstein said: "We cannot imagine how it would have gone had not Lorentz made so many great contributions." This is not simply a statement made in homage to a revered colleague and a beloved friend; it is an accurate assessment as well. Although the theory of electrons did not survive, Lorentz's analysis shaped the foundations of modern physical theory. Lorentz pushed classical theory beyond its limits and in so doing exposed the foundational problems modern physics would have to resolve. His intellectual prowess and personal integrity exerted a profound influence on the emergent international community of scientists.

Bibliography

De Haas-Lorentz, Geertruida, ed. *H. A. Lorentz: Impressions of His Life and Work.* Amsterdam: North Holland, 1957. This volume, edited by Lorentz's daughter, commemorates the one hundredth anniversary of his birth. Contains assessments of the man and his work and reminiscences by his daughter. The recollections of his daughter, though sketchy, provide the most extensive information available on Lorentz's life. Most of the articles are nontechnical. The book contains interesting photographs of Lorentz and of other leading scientists of the time.

Lorentz, Hendrik Antoon. "The Theory of Electrons and the Propagation of Light." In Nobelstiftelsen's *Physics, 1901-1921.* New York: Elsevier, 1967. The lecture outlines Lorentz's major scientific problems and accomplishments in electromagnetic theory. The lecture is admirably lucid and requires minimal technical knowledge.

McCormmach, Russell. "H. A. Lorentz and the Electromagnetic View of Nature." *Isis* 61 (Winter, 1970): 459-497. The article analyzes the development of Lorentz's electromagnetic theory and discusses its relationship to the program to reduce all mechanical phenomena to states of an electromagnetic ether.

Nersessian, Nancy J. "Lorentz' Non-Newtonian Aether-Field." In *Faraday to Einstein: Constructing Meaning in Scientific Theories;* edited by Nancy J. Nersessian. Dordrecht, Netherlands, and Boston: Martinus Nijhoff, 1984. The chapter traces the development of Lorentz's theory of electrons in nontechnical language. Places his concept of field within the context of the formation of the electromagnetic field concept from Michael Faraday to Einstein.

———. "Why Wasn't Lorentz Einstein? An Examination of the Scientific Method of H. A. Lorentz." *Centaurus* 29 (1986): 205-242. The article probes the question of why Lorentz never accepted the special theory of relativity, even though it is formally equivalent to the theory of electrons.

Nancy J. Nersessian

KONRAD LORENZ

Born: November 7, 1903; Vienna, Austro-Hungarian
   Empire
Died: February 27, 1989; Altenburg, Austria
Areas of Achievement: Zoology, psychology, physiology, and medicine
Contribution: Awarded a Nobel Prize in Physiology or Medicine in 1973, Konrad Lorenz, initially
   working as a zoologist, became one of the principal founders of the science of ethology through
   his studies correlating patterns of animal and human behavior and their implied common evolutionary origins.

Early Life
Konrad Zacharias Lorenz was born in Vienna, then
part of the Austro-Hungarian Empire, on November 7, 1903. His father, Adolph, had already so distinguished himself as a Viennese surgeon that one
of the city's streets, Adolphlorenzstrasse, honored
him. Unquestionably too, Adolph proved to be an
immensely tolerant parent. If not always happy
about his son Konrad's domestic zoo and aquariums, he bore nobly the droppings of various birds
and fowl that freely roamed the house all by way of
propitiating Konrad's observational passions—passions that would develop into lifelong studies: researches in medicine, physiology, zoology, comparative animal and human studies, psychology,
and the phylogenetic and cultural plight of modern
humankind.

   When Konrad was ten, reading Wilhelm
Bölsche's writings on evolution and his description
of archaeopteryx—an animal with wings like a
bird's but with a lizard's tail, discovered in the
nineteenth century—convinced him that he wanted
to study zoology and paleontology. Yet he obediently followed his father's dictum to pursue a medical education, which, after two years of biology at
Columbia University and several years at the University of Vienna, he did. He was not to practice
medicine, however, until World War II. Instead, he
worked under Ferdinand Hochstetter, a brilliant
professor of comparative anatomy, who was an
even more distinguished comparative embryolo-
gist. Lorenz consequently learned to reconstruct
the genealogical trees of animals by comparing
similar and dissimilar characteristics of modern
and recent forms. In 1935, he abandoned his job at
Vienna's Anatomical Institute for an unpaid lectureship in comparative anatomy and comparative

psychology at the city's Zoological Institute. In
1936, supported by his wife, Margarethe, herself a
doctor specializing in obstetrics and gynecology,
Lorenz completed his Ph.D. in zoology at the University of Vienna, where he remained for a few
years in junior faculty positions, subsequently
moving to the University of Munich and then to the
chairmanship of the University of Königsberg's
psychology department.

   Drafted from his Königsberg professorship into
the German Army in 1941, his medical skills initially were ignored. When it was discovered that he
was a doctor, he was sent to serve in a Poznan military hospital as a psychiatrist and neurologist from
1942 to 1944. With the rank of sergeant, he was
sent as a doctor to the Soviet front, where, after
three months, he was captured in June, 1944, near
Vitebsk. Thereafter, he served as a prison doctor in
thirteen prison camps widely scattered across the
Soviet Union and was not released until 1948,
three years after the war's end.

Life's Work
Repatriated to Vienna in 1948, Lorenz returned to
lines of ethological inquiry that he had begun in the
1920's. His first important publication, an observation of jackdaws, appeared in 1927, followed by
twenty-seven additional professional articles before 1943. Though initially he established a private
institute for the furtherance of his ethological studies, he was soon called upon by the Max Planck
Gesellschaft (association) to move his work to
Westphalia and then in 1955 to Seewiesen, south of
Munich, in a parklike setting at the foot of the Austrian Alps, where he, his colleagues, and students
could observe the behavior and social customs of
greylag geese, shelldrakes, rats, dogs, jackdaws,
Siamese fighting fish, and a variety of other animals in environments as natural as possible.

   Lorenz is regarded as the founder of the novel
science of ethology, simplistically defined as the
comparative study of animal behavior (humans included) in their natural surroundings. Ethology's
observational methods are complex, rigorous, and
ultimately—despite Lorenz's eschewal in his writings of mathematical data or graphs—dependent
on mathematical verification. So while Lorenz has
usually been depicted as a white-haired, bearded
man, invariably with a curved pipe in his mouth
and garbed in corduroy trousers, and farmer's

boots and clothing, spending countless hours standing in ponds, lying in muck, sitting before aquariums, or listening to animal communications and patiently watching their discrete movements, he was far from a mere naturalist observer.

Lorenz was a thoroughgoing Darwinist in his perceptions of phylogenetic processes—that is, the evolutionary history of natural organisms—and an equally profound believer in first taking a Gestalt approach (to view the whole of the organism whether a cichlid fish, a dog, or a human and to try grasping what the sum of its parts are before empirically disassembling it). His humane experiments have amply demonstrated that the behavior of organisms is as adaptive or nonadaptive, as subject to Darwinian natural selection, as are physical characteristics. For Lorenz, behavior in all living things is influenced by two great constructors: mutation, the accidental change in a plant or animal's inherited characteristics, and natural selection. While affirming that humankind is the most highly adaptive and organized creature to appear in the past 500 million years, Lorenz believed that mounting ethological evidence indicates that the behavior patterns of squid, certain fish, geese, birds, rats, or chimpanzees are very greatly simplified versions of some human behavior.

Lorenz, like ethologists generally, concluded that there is a phylogeny of behavior. The novelty of this view is illuminated by the contrasting beliefs of evidential disagreements between two schools of psychologists. Purposive psychologists believe that instincts set the goals of animal behavior, yet still allow individual animals various ways to attain these goals; behavioral psychologists, on the contrary, believe that learning capacities endow individual creatures with their ability to vary behavior. Yet Lorenz believed that instincts and organs have to be studied from the common viewpoint of phyletic descent. As more inherited patterns of behavior—scratching behavior in certain birds, for instance—have been recognized experimentally, they have provided reliable clues to the origins and relationships of large groups of animals; Lorenz entertained little doubt that animals in general inherit certain deeply rooted behavioral traits. These traits reveal themselves clearly in fish and birds, and less clearly in higher animals and in humans, because they may be obscured by learned behavior. Moreover, because biologists have long developed morphologies (histories of animal structure and form), until Lorenz and the development

of ethology, few curiosities were elicited about the histories of various species' behavior.

More specifically, Lorenz earned scientific notoriety for his elucidation of imprinting—that is, the fixation of an animal's innate behavior pattern, the irreversibility of this process, and its occurrence within the first few hours or days of some animals' lives. Not all animals imprint; yet Lorenz's geese, ducklings, and chickens, for instance, when exposed to a "foster parent," human experimenters among them, became sexually fixated upon them, followed them about as if they were real parents, and in many cases would not breed with their own species. From such experiences, Lorenz extrapolated that perhaps human adolescents, skeptical about their parental culture, search for their identity by embracing ideals or causes, which leads to disappointment and ultimate frustration and their future refusal to attach themselves to any ideal or cause.

In addition, Lorenz is identified with developing the concept of releasing mechanisms, which he averred may have been his most significant discovery. Releasing means that the central nervous system consists of a mechanism-generating stimulus and another mechanism-inhibiting stimulus. A cichlid fish, a goose, or a human engaged in intraspecific aggression—fighting with its own kind—for sexual dominance or leadership, often manages to abort its otherwise harmful, even fatal assault produced by the mechanism-generating stimulus by the kicking in of its mechanism-inhibiting stimulus—even redirecting aggressive intent elsewhere. The man who pounds his fist on the desktop when he really wants to punch the fellow across the table is a crude representation of releasing. Lorenz believed that often the inhibiting mechanism works less well in human beings than among other species, and accordingly he explained his views in his famed book *Das Songennante Böse: Zur Naturgeschicte der Aggression* (1963; *On Aggression*, 1966).

Summary

Remarkable for his range of professional skills in medicine, physiology, zoology, psychiatry, and psychology, Konrad Lorenz was the father of the new science of ethology. From 1927 on, he published 145 professional articles and in addition to the books cited above authored seven widely acclaimed, if in part controversial, books, all eminently intelligible scientific expositions quite understandable by laymen. Though his principal heuristic work involved so-called lesser animals than humans, an understanding of the human condition was his principal objective and his chief concern. Born of his own scientific findings and analogizing, Lorenz's immense humanity led him to conclude that overpopulation as well as the swift advance of urbanization and technocratic culture has outrun the slow phylogenetic pace of man's evolution, threatening to erode man's humaneness. Critics—none of them ethologists—have accused Lorenz of excessive anthropomorphism and of inaccurately extrapolating his experience with non-human subjects to depict important aspects of human behavior and culture. Yet in 1973, the Nobel Prize Committee thought otherwise, conferring its first award ever made to a behavioral scientist on Lorenz.

Bibliography

Alsop, Joseph. "Profiles: A Condition of Enormous Improbability." *The New Yorker* 39 (March 8, 1963): 39-93. Written from interviews with Lorenz by a highly respected journalist, this is a first-rate, eminently readable account of Lorenz's life and work. Unfortunately, much of Lorenz's work still lay ahead when this article was conceived, hence other works cited here must be used to update it.

Cavanaugh, Michael. "The Precursors of the Eureka Moment as a Common Ground between Science and Theology." *Zygon* 29, no. 2 (June, 1994). Considers Lorenz's theory on "eureka moments" and its relevance with respect to clarifying the confusion in contemporary epistemology.

Evans, Richard I. *Konrad Lorenz: The Man and His Ideas.* New York and London: Harcourt Brace, 1975. Written in a delightful, authoritative style, this book's format is a series of dialogues with Lorenz, with the addition of four of Lorenz's representative essays. Includes a full chronological list of all Lorenz's major publications, a fine select bibliography, and a good index.

Lorenz, Konrad. *Civilized Man's Eight Deadly Sins.* Translated by Marjorie Kerr Wilson. New York: Harcourt Brace, and London: Methuen, 1974. More philosophical than clinical, this slight volume warns of the functional disorders of living systems, the destruction of the environment, humankind's race against itself, the entropy of feeling, genetic decay, the breakdown of tradition, indoctrinability, overpopulation, and nuclear weapons. The writing is clear, and there is a brief select bibliography.

————. *Here Am I—Where Are You?: The Behavior of the Greylag Goose.* Translated by Robert D. Martin et al. New York: Harcourt Brace, 1991. Quite technical and perhaps not for all laypersons. Entertaining description of an experiment performed by Lorenz and his assistants involving a colony of greylag geese. Compares the behavior of geese and humans.

————. *On Aggression.* Translated by Marjorie Kerr Wilson. New York: Harcourt Brace, and London: Methuen, 1966. Starting with aggressive behavior among laboratory coral fish and proceeding to analyses of the positive side of aggression and eventually to humans and their phylogenetic links to aggression in other animals, Lorenz ends on a note of muted optimism that is somewhat less perceptible in his later works. Includes a bibliography and an index.

Sheehan, Edward R. F. "Conversations with Konrad Lorenz." *Harper's* 236 (May, 1968): 69-77. A lengthy, delightful interview focused on Lorenz's main behavioral findings. Includes a number of photographs of Lorenz with his greylag geese.

Clifton K. Yearley

JOE LOUIS

Born: May 13, 1914; near Lafayette, Alabama
Died: April 12, 1981; Las Vegas, Nevada
Area of Achievement: Boxing
Contribution: World heavyweight boxing champion from 1937 to 1949, Louis was a hero to black
Americans of all backgrounds. Although some
maintained that a boxer should not have been so
celebrated, Louis was perhaps more widely recognized and applauded by the black community
than any other individual prior to the modern
Civil Rights movement.

Early Life

Born May 13, 1914, in a sharecropper's shack in
the Buckalew Mountain region of east central Alabama, Joseph Louis Barrow was the seventh of
eight children of Lillie Reese and Munroe Barrow.
In 1916, Joe's father was committed to a hospital
for the insane. Believing that her husband had died
(in fact, he lived, institutionalized, for twenty more
years), Mrs. Barrow married widower Pat Brooks,
who had five children of his own. The couple had
several more children. The combined families lived
in Brooks's small wooden house in tiny Mt. Sinai,
Alabama.

In 1926, Pat Brooks got a job with the Ford Motor Company in Detroit, and the family moved
north to an ethnically mixed Detroit slum. Joe, already behind in his education because of inadequate schooling in Alabama, was placed in a class
with younger children. He developed a stammer
and became a loner. Officials assigned him to a vocational school, mistaking his difficulties for lack
of mental ability.

Brooks lost his employment during the Depression, and Joe had to do odd jobs to help support
the large family. At that time Joe began boxing at
the Brewster Recreation Center, where he used
the ring name Joe Louis for fear that his mother
would find out he was boxing and insist that he
stop. Instead, his new interest won her approval.
When he quit school to get a job at an auto body
plant, however, he had neither time nor energy to
train properly. He temporarily gave up the sport
after suffering a bad beating at the hands of a
member of the 1932 Olympic team, but, with his
mother's backing, he soon quit his job to concentrate on the ring.

Life's Work

As an amateur light-heavyweight Louis won fifty
of fifty-four fights in the next year and was becoming known in boxing circles by early 1934. In
April, he won the National Amateur Athletic Union
title. Under the guidance of a man from Detroit's
black community, he then turned professional, using part of his earnings to provide for his family.
Louis' color might have delayed his chance to
break into the big time; an earlier black heavyweight, Jack Johnson, had provoked the wrath of
the white public prior to World War I through his
enormous success as a fighter and his life-style
outside the ring. According to Louis' best informed
biographer, Johnson's controversial actions "confirmed the worst stereotypes of black behavior."

Louis' break came in early 1935 when New York
ticket-broker and promoter Mike Jacobs took an
interest in him. Unlike other promoters of the time,
recalled Louis, Jacobs "had no prejudice about a
man's color so long as he could make a green buck
for him." Although Jacobs himself was not knowledgeable about boxing, he sought good advice
about Louis and was impressed with what he saw
and was told. *The New York Times* described Louis
in 1935 thus:

> He has sloping shoulders, powerful arms with sinews
> as tough as whipcords and dynamite in his fists. A slim
> perfectly modeled body, tapering legs, an inscrutable,
> serious face that reveals no plan of his battle, gives no
> sign whether he is stung or unhurt—these are his char-
> acteristics . . . . Louis has about the most savage, two-
> fisted attack of any fighter of modern times. He
> doesn't punch alone with one hand. He destroys with
> either or both.

Jacobs had as silent partners several Hearst
sportswriters; therefore, favorable publicity began
to grow not only in the influential Hearst press but
also in other papers. Remembering the follies of
Johnson, Louis' managers were careful to cultivate
the image of Louis as a model of middle-class propriety. He did not smoke or drink, he read the Bible, he was modest, and he was generous. He was
indeed many of these things; in areas where his behavior was not exemplary—for example, his profli-
gacy with money and his pursuit of women—he
was discreet, and the image his managers sought to
develop remained substantially intact. It was probably not true that John Roxborough, the man who

Joe Louis defeats Max Schmeling in 1938.

first sponsored Louis' professional career, intended all along for Louis to become a racial ambassador, but as Louis' fame grew, he did become one.

After his well-publicized fifth-round knockout of former heavyweight champion Primo Carnera on June 25, 1935, Louis was being ballyhooed as the greatest gate attraction in boxing since Jack Dempsey. Less than three months later, Louis whipped another former champ and gained widespread recognition as the world's best heavyweight, if not yet champion. Also in 1935, he married Marva Trotter, a young Chicago secretary; they had two children.

Louis' march to the title received an unexpected setback on July 10, 1936, when he met the prominent German boxer Max Schmeling, a former titleholder yet a big underdog to Louis. In the fourth round, Louis was knocked down for the first time in his professional career. Schmeling won by a knockout in the fourteenth round.

Much of the white press seemed to be waiting for this chance to rejoice in Louis' defeat. Racism, especially in the South, came through clearly in columnists' analyses of the match, and Louis was now being called just another fighter. In Germany, the Nazi press was ecstatic. Louis' managers scheduled Louis for other fights to keep him from brooding over his defeat. He kept on winning, and Jacobs got Louis a title bout with James Braddock in June, 1937. A journeyman who had held the title since 1935, the underdog Braddock fought gamely in their Chicago match but was clearly weakening by the middle rounds. Louis' corner spotted this, and he was able to knock Braddock out in the eighth. Louis had become only the second black man to hold the heavyweight title and at twenty-three was the youngest champion in his division.

Louis had still to win recognition as a great champion. Erasing the stigma of his loss to Schmeling would help Louis gain this status. The two men met again on June 22, 1938. Since their first battle, Americans had come to understand much more about Nazism, and although Schmeling was not a Nazi himself, he was now seen as the representative of Hitler's Germany. Louis, in contrast, had grown in stature and was perceived as a symbol of freedom. Now the crowd's favorite, Louis at six feet, two inches, was in superb condition, weighing barely less than two hundred pounds.

Louis, the aggressor from the opening moments, pummeled Schmeling thoroughly and was proclaimed the winner by a technical knockout scarce-

ly two minutes into round one. Louis was now acclaimed virtually everywhere, even in the Deep South. He was an unusually active champion, fighting so often that one writer called his schedule the "Bum-of-the-Month Club." Whether his opponents were "bums" in the ring or among the best of a poor lot of heavyweight contenders as Louis believed, Louis met no serious challenger until his eighteenth title defense, when he fought the recent light-heavyweight champion Billy Conn in June, 1941. Nearly thirty pounds lighter than Louis, Conn had public sentiment on his side. He used his superior quickness to outbox Louis through twelve rounds. Rather than fight cautiously (as his handlers were advising in the belief that Conn was winning on points), Conn continued to fight aggressively. Louis staggered Conn with several punches and knocked out the challenger with two seconds to go in round thirteen of what is still remembered as one of the classic heavyweight bouts. The "Brown Bomber" or the "Dark Destroyer," the nicknames by which Louis was most often known, remained heavyweight champion.

World War II came when Louis' skills were at their height. Although he could have claimed deferment from military service as the sole support of his mother and his wife Marva, Louis believed that it was his duty to join. In addition, to seek a deferment in the aftermath of Pearl Harbor might have been disastrous for Louis' image. Jacobs further improved Louis' public standing when he arranged a January 9, 1942, title defense against Buddy Baer, the bulk of the proceeds to go to the Navy Relief Fund. Louis won and promptly enlisted in the United States Army. Praise for Louis was never higher; the white press now viewed him not only as a credit to his race and a great champion but also as a good American. His public statement that the United States would inevitably win because "We are on God's side" became one of the most quoted patriotic phrases of the war.

Louis' role in the army, like that of many other celebrities, was to boost morale. He made goodwill visits to various bases and military hospitals and appeared in a few films, most notably *This Is the Army* (1943), starring Ronald Reagan. He also defended his title in 1942 for the benefit of Army Emergency Relief. From late 1943 to the end of the war, Louis was the star of a touring troupe of boxers that included the young Sugar Ray Robinson and other black fighters. Louis fought ninety-six exhibitions while in the service. In some ways his army experience brought Louis added maturity; away from his managers, Louis had to confront Jim Crow on his own. His approach was that when off-post he would accept local conditions concerning segregation, but when on a military base he would insist on fair treatment for himself and for other black soldiers present.

In other ways, however, Louis remained much the person he had been. He continued his free spending habits, borrowing money from Jacobs and others while a federal tax bill in excess of $100,000 still hung over him. Jacobs' bad advice and Louis' divorce in 1945 compounded his financial problems. Although Joe and Marva Louis were soon remarried, the birth of a son in 1947 (the couple had previously had one daughter) gave Louis added financial responsibility.

By this time Louis' ring skills had begun to erode, and after two title defenses in 1946, the first a much-anticipated but disappointing rematch with Billy Conn in which neither man recaptured his 1941 form, Louis found himself without a challenger who could help draw a profitable gate. After two victorious matches with Jersey Joe Walcott, another aging boxer, Louis, now fighting at about 215 pounds, found his reflexes slowing and announced his retirement early in 1949.

Continued financial problems drew him back into the ring. In September, 1950, he lost to the new heavyweight champion, Ezzard Charles, by a unanimous decision, beat several mediocre opponents, and on October 26, 1951, fought Rocky Marciano, ten years Louis' junior and the most promising heavyweight contender. The clearly lethargic Louis suffered his first knockout since his first match with Schmeling fifteen years before. The Marciano fight was Louis' last, save for a few exhibitions. His financial difficulties remained unsolved. He had outspent his income during his prime years and after the war as well, made poor investments, and by the mid-1950's owed more than one million dollars in back taxes and interest. He made a brief, unfortunate effort to become a professional wrestler, earned some money from promotional appearances, and finally settled with the Internal Revenue Service to pay twenty thousand dollars a year on his back taxes. He never did succeed in paying them, and the IRS, while not forgiving Louis' tax obligation, eventually quit trying to collect.

Louis had other troubles. He and Marva Louis were divorced again in 1949; in 1955, he married Rose Morgan, the prosperous proprietor of a Harlem beauty salon. They separated in 1957, and by mutual consent the marriage was annulled. As before, Louis simply could not settle down but traveled extensively, played golf during the day when at home, and stayed out many nights. In 1959, Louis married Martha Malone Jefferson, the first black woman to be admitted to the California bar. She was bright and compassionate, sacrificing her own career to help Louis through some of his most difficult years. He had affairs with other women, became a cocaine user, and began to suffer paranoid delusions severe enough for him to be confined at the Colorado Psychiatric Hospital for several months in 1970. Martha Louis and Joe Louis Barrow, Jr., his son by his first marriage, agreed on treatment for Louis.

Although he was never completely rid of his delusions, Louis was able to drop his use of cocaine and lived a reasonably normal life in Las Vegas with Martha Louis and several children she convinced him to adopt. He was employed at Caesar's Palace casino as a greeter, provided with a luxurious house and a handsome salary. According to Joe Louis Barrow, Jr., Louis was happy with his job, which consisted largely of being seen, shaking hands, and giving autographs. In 1977, Louis suffered a major heart attack followed shortly by a stroke. He was confined to a wheelchair for the rest of his life but was still able to make appearances at some Caesar's Palace functions. He died at his home on April 12, 1981.

Summary

Joe Louis held the heavyweight boxing championship for twelve years, longer than any other boxer in his division. At his prime as a boxer, before World War II, he won acclaim that endured for decades. His skills were such that he was, arguably, the greatest heavyweight ever. During the 1960's he was perceived by some blacks as an Uncle Tom, but he was recognized even by many civil rights activists as having done much for the cause of blacks in the United States in an earlier day. Boxing in the 1930's had not been totally segregated as major league baseball then was; the mores of white society, however, certainly influenced the way the few prominent black boxers were perceived and made it more difficult for others to become successful professionals. In the white community, Louis won widespread acceptance as an American champion and a man of dignity. To his black contemporaries, who knew little but racism and financial deprivation, he was a symbol of hope and pride. "We all feel bigger today because Joe came this way" stated the Reverend Jesse Jackson in his eulogy.

Bibliography

Astor, Gerald. *". . . And a Credit to His Race": The Hard Life and Times of Joseph Louis Barrow, a.k.a. Joe Louis*. New York: Saturday Review Press, 1974. A well-written book, published when Louis's mental illness made him more newsworthy than he had been in years.

Deardorff, Don, II. "Joe Louis Became Both a Black Hero and a National Symbol to Whites after Overcoming Racism in the Media." *St. Louis Journalism Review* 26, no. 180 (October, 1995). Discusses Louis's problems with the boxing community, which was controlled largely by whites.

Louis, Joe, with Edna Rust and Art Rust, Jr. *Joe Louis: My Life*. New York: Harcourt Brace, 1978. Written in the first person, this book is especially useful for its abundant photographs and supplement listing each bout in Louis' professional boxing career.

Mead, Chris. *Champion: Joe Louis, Black Hero in White America*. New York: Scribner, 1985; London: Robson, 1986. Perhaps the best biography of Louis. Mead views Louis within the framework of American popular culture and places much emphasis on Louis as symbol. Also contains a helpful bibliography.

Miller, Margery. *Joe Louis: American*. New York: Current Books, 1945; London: Mark Geuilden, 1947. This book makes its theme evident in the title.

Nagler, Barney. *The Brown Bomber: The Pilgrimage of Joe Louis*. New York: World Publishing, 1972. This is another book published when Louis's mental illness returned the former champion to the headlines. Written by a longtime boxing writer, it is useful for many phases of Louis's career.

Roberts, Randy. *Papa Jack: Jack Johnson and the Era of White Hopes*. New York: The Free Press, and London: Macmillan, 1983. A study of the great black heavyweight champion whose controversial career burdened Louis's own career. Johnson lived long enough to know and resent Louis.

Van Deusen, John. *"Brown Bomber": The Story of Joe Louis*. Philadelphia: Dorrance, 1940. Written at the height of Louis's career, this book is a study in hero-worship. Van Deusen accepts the press agents' portrayal of Louis without question, but his book is useful for its rather detailed descriptions of Louis's fights.

Wilkinson, R., and K. Light. "With Mandela." *Mother Jones* 15, no. 7 (November-December, 1990). Compares and contrasts public reception of Louis and Nelson Mandela.

Lloyd J. Graybar

JULIETTE GORDON LOW

Born: October 31, 1860; Savannah, Georgia
Died: January 18, 1927; Savannah, Georgia
Area of Achievement: Social reform
Contribution: The principal founder of the Girl Scouts of the United States of America, Low spent the last fifteen years of her life working for an organization which would be similar to, but independent of, the Boy Scouts of America.

Early Life

In the midst of the secession crisis of 1860, Juliette Magill Kinzie Gordon was born in Savannah, Georgia, on October 31, 1860. She was the second of six children and the second of four daughters. Juliette's mother, Eleanor Lytle Kinzie Gordon, a Chicago native, had learned about the frontier experience from her father, who was a government agent to the Indians. Juliette's father, William Washington Gordon II, was a cotton broker who served during the Civil War as an officer in the Confederate army and later served as a general and peace negotiator for the United States in the Spanish-American War.

Full of energy, quick of wit, and blessed with an artistic nature, Juliette Gordon displayed much of the wit and charm attributed to her mother. She early exhibited the strong will and organizational abilities of her father, often taking charge of the childhood activities that she, her sisters, and more than a dozen cousins engaged in every summer at The Cliffs, the home of her aunt in northern Georgia. The Gordon girls and their cousins swam, camped, and sometimes hunted, and they often acted in and wrote several plays. Daisy, as Juliette was called by her family, usually acted several parts in each play.

Juliette attended private schools in Georgia, Virginia, and New York. The private school in New York City, nicknamed "The Charbs" by its students, was a finishing school run by the Charbonnier sisters, two extremely circumspect Frenchwomen who had emigrated to the United States following the Franco-Prussian War. While in New York City, Juliette wrote additional plays, acted in amateur productions, and studied painting. Once her formal education was finished, Juliette Gordon began dividing her time between living in the United States and visiting Britain and Europe, a pattern she would continue until her death.

While on one of her visits to Britain, Juliette Gordon fell in love with William Mackay Low, the son of a wealthy Englishman with Savannah connections. After a four-year courtship, which she attempted to conceal from a doting and protective father who viewed William Low as a social playboy, Juliette Gordon and William Mackay Low were married in Savannah, Georgia, in December of 1886. Juliette Gordon Low became part of the social elite in Britain, where her multimillionaire husband owned substantial property and was a close friend of the Prince of Wales and his entourage. The Lows hunted at their own estate in Scotland and entertained extensively in England and the United States. In addition, Juliette Gordon Low was presented at Court to Queen Victoria.

Beneath the surface, however, all was not well. Increasingly Low was left alone as her husband went throughout the world on game-hunting expeditions and engaged in other gentlemanly pursuits. Kept even from her favorite pursuit of horseback riding by an injury, Low took up sculpting and oil painting to fill the lonely hours. She also carved a mantlepiece for the smoking room at her Warwickshire estate, forged a pair of iron gates for the entrance to the Wellesbourne property, and often traveled without her husband (but always properly with a female companion). When the Spanish-American War began in 1898, Juliette Low helped her mother operate a hospital for soldiers in Miami, Florida.

Meanwhile, Low's marriage continued to disintegrate. In 1902, she consented to a separation and, after her husband's affair with an attractive widow became common knowledge to English society, agreed to begin proceedings for a divorce. William Low died before the divorce was concluded, leaving his estate to his lover. After several months of tense negotiations with estate lawyers, Juliette Gordon Low was granted a settlement of approximately $500,000, making her financially secure for the remainder of her life. Low resumed her active social life, alternating her time between London and Scotland while wintering in Savannah, Georgia, and other parts of the United States.

Life's Work

A turning point in Juliette Gordon Low's life came in 1911, when she met Sir Robert Baden-Powell, the hero of the defense of Mafeking in the Boer

War and the founder of the Boy Scouts. She admitted later that she had disliked Baden-Powell before she met him, believing that he had received public acclaim at the expense of some of her friends who had participated in the rescue of Mafeking during the Boer War, but she and Baden-Powell soon became close friends and quickly discovered they had much in common. She shared with him a book that her mother had written about the frontier experiences of Juliette's maternal grandfather; he introduced her to his sister, who had founded the Girl Guides in England.

Low had found the rewarding service she had been seeking throughout her life. She organized a troop of Girl Guides in Scotland and two troops of Girl Guides in London before deciding to expand the movement to include girls in her native country. Upon her return to the United States, Low established a Girl Guide unit on March 12, 1912, consisting of sixteen young girls in two troops that met in the carriage house in the rear of the garden of her house in Savannah, Georgia. The first Girl Guide was her niece, Margaret Eleanor ("Daisy") Gordon. The young girls, dressed in middy blouses, dark blue skirts, light blue ties, and dark cotton stockings, wearing large black ribbons in their hair, engaged in camping and other sports and were soon the envy of the young girls of Savannah. Juliette Low rapidly moved to make the Girl Guides a national organization.

William Gordon's death, although a serious blow to his worshipful daughter, caused only a slight delay in Low's plans. After a year abroad in England with her mother, Low returned to the United States and resumed her efforts to make the Girl Guides a national organization. At first, she hoped to merge the existing Campfire Girls organization, founded in 1910, with her Girl Guides organization and call the new organization the Girl Scouts, but the merger fell through. Undaunted, Low continued her dream of a national organization. She began organizational efforts in various states, created a national headquarters, and enlisted prominent Americans to serve on the national board. In 1915, the Girl Scouts of the United States of America was incorporated, with Low serving as its first president. By early 1916, more than 7,000 young women in the United States had registered as Girl Scouts.

Although World War I did not appear to affect Low's travels between the United States and Britain, it did take its toll upon her finances. She had been the major financial supporter of the Girl

Scouts before the outbreak of the war; with the increasing success of the organization, however, she discovered that even her substantial finances were insufficient to keep pace with the growth of the organization. She adopted little economies to save money for her Girl Scouts. Her famous teas began to feature cakes that were recycled until either they were eaten or ingeniously disposed of by her guests. She refused to permit the electric lights to be turned on in her home until half past five, regardless of how dark the day might be. Her friends and relatives claimed that she was saving pennies while spending hundreds of dollars on the Girl Scouts. Others suspected that her "economies" were a ruse to encourage donors to give more generously to the cause of Girl Scouting.

With the advent of their nation's entry into World War I, the Girl Scouts performed valuable services for their country, donations increased, and the organization soon grew too large to be staffed by volunteers alone. Juliette Low, recognizing that her responsibilities could be handled by a new generation of leaders, resigned as the president of the

Girl Scouts in 1920, but remained active in her support and was granted the title "The Founder."

Diagnosed with cancer in 1923, Juliette Low continued to demonstrate the energy and will she had exhibited throughout her life. She attended the World Camp of the Girl Scouts in England the following year and soon became involved in plans to hold the World Camp of 1926 in New York state. When told by a friend to wait until 1928 to bring the World Camp to the United States, Juliette Low responded that she would not be around in 1928.

Although she found it difficult to conceal the increasing pain of her illness, Juliette Low summoned the energy to engage in the week-long meeting of the World Camp in New York state in 1926. Following the World Camp's closing, she sailed for England, bidding her farewells to friends who were unaware of her condition, and returned to her beloved Savannah, where she died on January 18, 1927.

Summary

Juliette Gordon Low would not be surprised by the size and importance of the Girl Scout movement today. She had faith in her abilities and the abilities of the young women she attracted to the Girl Scouts. Her indomitable will, boundless energy, and belief that physical challenges, such as her own increasing deafness, only slowed advances, never stopped them, proved to be an inspiration both to the young girls fortunate enough to know her personally and the young women who would follow in their footsteps. The last message that she received from the national headquarters of the Girl Scouts shortly before her death adequately sums up her life: She was, the telegram read, "not only the first Girl Scout," she was "the best Scout of them all."

Bibliography

Choate, Anne Hyde, and Helen Ferris, eds. *Juliette Low and the Girl Scouts: The Story of an American Woman, 1860-1927.* New York: Doubleday, 1928. First published for the Girl Scout organization shortly after Juliette Low's death, this collection of reminiscences by friends and family members is filled with anecdotal information about the eccentricities of the Girl Scout founder. The revised edition, prepared by Ely List, who was the assistant to the director of the public relations department of the Girl Scouts, is an updated and shortened version of the Choate collection.

Kudlinski, Kathleen. *Juliette Gordon Low: America's First Girl Scout.* New York: Viking Kestrel, 1988. Designed for juveniles, this brief book provides a useful introduction to the life of Juliette Low.

Revzin, Rebekah E. "American Girlhood in the Early Twentieth Century: The Ideology of Girl Scout Literature, 1913-1930." *Library Quarterly* 68, no. 3 (July, 1998). Examines the literature published by the Girl Scouts of America and provides information on Low.

Saxton, Martha. "The Best Girl Scout of Them All." *American Heritage* 33 (June/July, 1982): 38-47. Although brief, this article could be used as an introduction to an examination of Juliette Low's life.

Shultz, Gladys D., and Daisy Gordon Lawrence. *Lady from Savannah: The Life of Juliette Low.* Philadelphia: J. B. Lippincott, 1958. Although it does not have either a bibliography or an index and nearly half of it concentrates on the Kinzie and Gordon family histories, this book continues to be useful as the most thorough treatment of the life of Juliette Gordon Low.

Strickland, Charles E. "Juliette Low, The Girl Scouts, and the Role of American Women." In *Woman's Being, Woman's Place: Female Identity and Vocation in American History*, edited by Mary Kelley. Boston: Hall, 1979. Strickland uses Erik Erikson's life-cycle model to analyze the reasons why Juliette Low became the founder of the Girl Scouts of the United States. Although designed for specialists in gender and child development studies, this essay can be read with benefit by the nonspecialist. Contains useful bibliographical references.

Robert L. Patterson

AMY LOWELL

Born: February 9, 1874; Brookline, Massachusetts
Died: May 12, 1925; Brookline, Massachusetts
Area of Achievement: Literature
Contribution: A leading poet of her day and leader of the Imagist movement, Amy Lowell also worked enthusiastically to popularize poetry and the other arts. She supported the work of other writers by editing collections of their works and by giving popular lectures on literature.

Early Life

Amy Lowell was a member of the Lowell family which arrived in America in 1639, twenty years after the arrival of the *Mayflower*, and rose to become one of the leading New England families. (It was the Cabots who spoke only to the Lowells, and the Lowells who spoke only to God.) Amy's older brother Lawrence was president of Harvard University from 1909 to 1933. Amy was the last of seven children, five of whom survived infancy. Amy's mother remained a semi-invalid for all of Amy's life (she suffered from Bright's disease), and Amy was raised mainly by her nurse-governess at Sevenels, the Lowells' home in Brookline, Massachusetts.

Amy did not have the companionship of other children and was often lonely, and as a result she took up the interests that her father and older brothers had. She preferred outdoor games and activities and was considered a tomboy by the age of eight.

Stimulated by the distinguished adults in her family and those who visited the Lowells, Amy was precocious. She became a good conversationalist and could amuse her parents' guests with puns. She liked to write, and at age ten she started a mimeographed magazine called *The Monthly Story-Teller.* Her mother encouraged her to put together a book for sale at a charity bazaar: *Dream Drops.*

She was sent to private schools, but after attending some lectures at Radcliffe College, which she found boring, she left school at the age of seventeen. She educated herself by reading, both at home and at the Boston Athenaeum, a private library founded in 1807. She developed a special fondness for the English poet John Keats and later began a collection devoted to him. Her two older brothers had both published books (Percy on the Orient and astronomy and Lawrence on government), and Amy decided that she too would pursue a writing career. She experimented for several years with various literary forms, including plays, novels, and short stories.

After her mother died in 1895 and her father died in 1899, Amy bought the ten-acre family Brookline estate from her siblings. She created a large library and designed a music room. She had the house electrified, and she bought a summer home in New Hampshire. She joined various civic boards and shocked the local gentry by speaking up in meetings (which was unusual for women in those days).

Amy was plump and had always felt self-conscious about her weight, and in 1897 she may have been jilted by a suitor. She gave up thoughts of marriage and contented herself with friends. In 1912, she met the actress Ada Dwyer, and their friendship grew to such an extent that Ada quit the stage in 1914 to become Amy's full-time secretary-companion until Amy's death.

Amy had made many contacts in the social and political world by meeting and becoming friends with the many guests her family had entertained at Sevenels as she grew up. After the death of her parents, Amy was helped in her endeavors not only by Ada but also by her many friends; for example, Carl Engel, a composer and music publisher. With his encouragement, she put on and acted in plays at Sevenels and organized monthly concerts. At her salons, she introduced her audiences to new music, including that of Béla Bartok, Claude Debussy, and Erik Satie.

Amy's position in a wealthy and influential family (whose wealth came mainly from the cotton mills that its members owned), combined with the support of her parents and older siblings, allowed her to have a larger role in determining the course of her life than many young women of her day had. The death of her parents by the time she was twenty-five relieved her of any need to secure their approval for her plans, and the wealth she inherited permitted her to live as she wished, writing, being a patron of the arts and salon hostess, or traveling wherever she wished. Thus, she was in a position to be much more independent than most other women of her era.

Life's Work

In 1902, when she was twenty-eight, Amy Lowell was inspired by a performance of the European ac-

tress Eleonora Duse to write a poem, and she decided to focus on poetry. Amy's first published poem appeared in *Atlantic Monthly* in August of 1910. She organized her first book of poems and persuaded Houghton Mifflin to publish it. *A Dome of Many-Colored Glass* came out in October of 1912 to tepid reviews. The poems were not seen as very exciting. Amy came across an article by Ezra Pound on a group of poets to which he belonged: the Imagists. She traveled to London to meet the poets in the group and began both to write in the Imagist style and to campaign for the recognition of the group in the United States.

Amy worked hard at selling her work and that of other poets whom she admired. She read her poetry whenever she was asked, and she soon began to be in demand as a lecturer on both poetry and music. Her lectures were well prepared and were usually published, first as magazine articles and then as books (for example, *Tendencies in Modern American Poetry*, 1917). She visited editors of magazines and her publishers, selling them on her poems and ideas for books. She worked at first with local magazines and publishers, such as Houghton Miff-

lin, but soon extended her forays to New York, where she worked with Macmillan. She edited several volumes of poems by Imagists (the first, *Some Imagist Poets*, appeared in 1915) and a volume on six French poets (*Six French Poets*, 1915), followed by several other similar volumes, the royalties from which Amy delighted in dividing into portions and sending to the authors, some of whom desperately needed money.

Soon Amy began to be noticed by the media. She had begun to smoke cigars, and her behavior made headlines in the *New York Tribune*. Amy saw that this kind of publicity would help her establish a public image and contribute to the success of her poetry, so she cultivated the image, even though it was natural for her to behave in the way she did. She smoked, she bullied, and she stayed in bed till past noon, even receiving visitors there. Such behavior was most unusual for a woman of that era, but Amy's financial independence and social position led others to see her actions as interesting rather than shocking.

Her second volume of poems, *Sword Blades and Poppy Seeds*, made a splash in 1914. The poems had varied rhythms and versification, and the reviews came in angry, favorable, or puzzled. No one viewed her work as bland anymore. The criticism, rather than depressing her, made her ready to do battle to convert people to the "new poetry." She hired two full-time secretaries. She wrote letters, ran dinner parties, worked on anthologies, lectured, and continued to write poems and give readings. Eventually, she was speaking to audiences of more than a thousand people at a time throughout the United States.

Although Lowell had suffered from occasional depressions and somatic disorders such as jaundice and gastritis (developed during a trip to Egypt to lose weight), she was not seriously ill until she developed a hernia while attempting to extricate her carriage from mud in 1916. From this time on, her health deteriorated rapidly. The injury and its complications required several operations, none of which satisfactorily resolved the problem (the practice of medicine at the time was severely limited in its treatment of internal problems), and she developed several symptoms of stress, perhaps as a result of the deaths of close relatives and fears of political action by the workers at the Lowell family cotton mills.

In the midst of the series of operations for her hernia, Amy worked on a translation of Chinese poems into English (*Fir-Flower Tablets*, 1920) and on a book of poems about North American Indians (*Legends*, 1921). Critics liked *Legends* but disapproved of *Fir-Flower Tablets*.

She suffered a mild heart attack and retinal hemorrhages, and the hernia broke through again, but she kept working frenetically. In 1922, she determined to finish a biography of Keats she had begun to write, but first she wrote an anonymous spoof of modern poets (including herself), a hoax to which she did not admit for over a year (*A Critical Fable*, 1922). She was upset in 1922 when Edna St. Vincent Millay became the first woman to win a Pulitzer Prize for poetry. (Amy's came posthumously, in 1926.) A final lecture tour was completed in January of 1923. The eleven-hundred-page manuscript on Keats (*John Keats*) finally reached the publisher in November of that year, and the biography was released in February, 1925, to good reviews in America but poor reviews in England, where they seemed to be jealous that an American could write a good biography on Keats.

By March, Amy's weight was down to 160 pounds from a high of 250. (She was only slightly more than five feet tall.) An operation to correct her hernia was scheduled for May, but the day before the operation, on May 12, 1925, Amy had a stroke and died.

Summary

Although only a few of Amy Lowell's poems are considered good enough to merit inclusion in modern anthologies, she was an accomplished poet of her day, if not the leading poet. She received a Pulitzer Prize for poetry in 1926, shortly after her death. In the 1920's, Lowell was one of the most striking figures in American literature. She replaced Ezra Pound as the leader of the Imagist group, and she experimented with form and technique in poetry, becoming especially good at free verse. She is remembered particularly for her enthusiasm for the enterprise of poetry and for her efforts to promote it. She edited collections of works by authors whom she admired and gave lectures to large audiences across the country, attempting to arouse their enthusiasm for the arts. Her published essays established her as a literary critic, and her scholarly biography of Keats was received favorably. Her comfortable financial and social position permitted her a great deal of freedom to act, and she took advantage of that freedom to promote literary causes, including her own poetry.

Bibliography

Benvenuto, Richard. *Amy Lowell*. Boston: Twayne, 1985. This work contains a brief biography of Amy Lowell but consists mostly of a critical appraisal of her work, focusing on her prose, early poetry, narrative poetry, and lyrical works.

Coffman, Stanley K. *Imagism: A Chapter for the History of Modern Poetry*. Norman: University of Oklahoma Press, 1951. Coffman reviews the history and development of the poets who became known as the Imagists, who were led first by Ezra Pound and then by Amy Lowell.

Damon, S. Foster. *Amy Lowell: A Chronicle with Extracts from Her Correspondence*. Boston: Houghton Mifflin, 1935. This is an early biography of Amy Lowell and a review of her work. Unlike later biographies, it contains long extracts from her letters.

Gould, Jean. *Amy: The World of Amy Lowell and the Imagist Movement*. New York: Dodd Mead, 1975. This biography focuses on Lowell's life, providing much information about her personal habits and day-to-day activities. It does not attempt a literary analysis or critical appraisal of her poetry or essays.

Heymann, C. David. *American Aristocracy: The Lives and Times of James Russell, Amy, and Robert Lowell*. New York: Dodd Mead, 1980. This book traces the history of the Lowells in America from their arrival in 1639 but concentrates on the lives of three members of the family, each of whom wrote poetry: James Russell Lowell (1819-1891), Amy Lowell (1874-1925), and Robert Lowell (1917-1977).

McGiveron, Rafeeq O. "Lowell's 'Patterns.'" *The Explicator* 55, no. 3 (Spring 1997). Analysis of Lowell's poem "Patterns," including the poet's depressive state and evidence for this in the rhyme and rhetoric of the piece.

Ruihley, Glenn, R. *The Thorn of a Rose: Amy Lowell Reconsidered*. Hamden, Conn.: Archon, 1975. This work is both a biography and a critical appraisal of Amy Lowell's writing.

David Lester

LU HSÜN
Chou Shu-jên

Born: September 25, 1881; Shao-hsing, China
Died: October 19, 1936; Shanghai, China
Areas of Achievement: Literature, government, and politics
Contribution: One of twentieth century China's great men of letters, Lu Hsün pioneered a new literary tradition in China and offered a defiant indictment of Chinese character and traditions. He is honored by the Chinese Communists for his formative impact on young Chinese intellectuals and the revolutionary movement.

Early Life

Chou Shu-jên (pen name Lu Hsün) was born into a family with commercial and minor official connections in Shao-hsing, China, in 1881. He and his two younger brothers received an early classical Chinese education based on Confucian texts. Although his family's financial situation deteriorated during his early years because of his grandfather's imprisonment for official bribery and the death of his father in 1897, Lu Hsün was able to acquire a solid grounding in traditional Chinese history and literature and studied the illustrious history of his local district. His mother, a literate woman of indomitable character, held the family together during Lu Hsün's first seventeen years and had a powerful influence on him throughout his life.

As was typical of many intellectuals of his generation, Lu Hsün turned to modern learning after his early grounding in Confucianism. After enrolling briefly in the Kiangnan Naval Academy in Nanking in 1898, he transferred to the School of Railways and Mines, graduating in 1901. He then won a government scholarship to study medicine in Japan. After two years of Japanese language study in Tokyo, he entered the Sendai Provincial Medical School in the summer of 1904. After witnessing the humiliation of China in the Russo-Japanese War of 1904-1905, Lu Hsün turned his attention to literature as a means of awakening the Chinese people to the need for revolutionary change. Between 1906 and 1909, he sought to rescue China from its moral and physical ills. Disappointed by the failure of the masses to respond to his writings, however, and discouraged by the failure of the Revolution of 1911 to overthrow autocracy, he abandoned his crusade to change China and spent most of the years 1909 to 1919 publishing studies of traditional Chinese literature and art.

Life's Work

Lu Hsün burst into national prominence during the Cultural Revolution launched by the May Fourth Movement of 1919. Invited by a friend in 1918 to contribute to the leading periodical *Hsin ch'ing-nien* (new youth), Lu Hsün authored his famous story "K'uang-jen jih-chi" ("The Diary of a Madman," 1941). This was a searing indictment of the traditional Chinese family system, using the fantasies of a madman as a literary vehicle. The story epitomized the frustrations of Chinese youth with petrified Confucian social values and conventions and set the basic agenda for a generation of Chinese writers. Based loosely on Nikolai Gogol's story of the same title, "The Diary of a Madman" moved far beyond Lu Hsün's earlier writings, since it was written in Western literary style. Thus launched on a national career, Lu Hsün continued to write short essays on the Chinese public scene for the next few years. His best-known effort, "Ah Q chong-chuan" ("The True Story of Ah Q," 1926) was published in 1921. This story satirizes the Chinese penchant for self-deception. Ah Q, an illiterate peasant outcast in the era of the 1911 Revolution, is constantly humiliated yet believes himself to be the most noble of men. He symbolizes China itself, which lies prostrate in the face of superior Western technology yet still maintains its cultural superiority.

These writings initiated the most creative period of Lu Hsün's life, the years between 1919 and 1926. In these years, he wrote about two dozen short stories designed to stimulate nationalistic consciousness among China's youth. His acerbic, realistic stories were based on his own youth in Shao-hsing and focused on young rebels struggling against the oppression of traditional society. He was extremely popular among young people, and liberal scholars recognized his great talent. He was relentless in his determination to avoid self-delusion and to carve out a new kind of humanistic morality. He launched an even more explicit attack on the evils of the old society in the essays that he wrote in those years. Using an impassioned, witty

style, he called on the Chinese to abandon those elements of traditional society that were preventing China from creating a new, rational order. He called for the abolition of the traditional family system, which enslaved women and youths, and argued that China had to cease venerating the past at the expense of the present and future.

Lu Hsün's convictions led him into political controversies concerning student rights, culminating with his role in the March 18, 1926, incident in which demonstrating students were massacred by the warlord government of Tuan Ch'i-jui. Lu Hsün was forced into hiding after this incident and was listed as a dangerous radical. He fled from Peking to south China, where he briefly taught at Sun Yat-sen University in Canton. He resigned his position there in April, 1927, following the Kuomintang's bloody purge of leftist elements from the Party. Many of his students were killed or arrested by the Kuomintang. Until this incident, he had been convinced that China could move gradually toward a liberal, democratic society. Thereafter, however, he was convined that China would have to take a more radical approach to change.

Lu Hsün moved to Shanghai in October, 1927, and remained there until his death from tuberculosis on October 19, 1936. It was there that he developed his relationship with the political Left. He had apparently concluded during his Canton days that the Communist Party was the driving force of the Chinese revolution, and he took the first two years after he moved to Shanghai to explore Communist ideology and strategies for change. While he never made a completely systematic study of Communist literature, he became convinced by 1929 that China's future lay with the Communists.

By the end of 1929, Lu Hsün began to cooperate with the Communists. Between 1929 and 1936, he engaged in several activities supportive of the Communist cause. In February, 1930, he joined the Freedom League, a group that protested Kuomintang restrictions on freedom of speech. In March, 1930, he helped to establish the League of Left-Wing Writers. Among other pro-Communist activities, he joined the International Union of Revolutionary Writers, headquartered in Moscow. He was acquainted with several important Chinese Communist leaders and supported their causes throughout these years. He never joined the Communist Party. He remained an independent thinker and was always skeptical of Communist motives. He was drawn to the Communists because of his hatred of the Kuomintang dictatorship and his conviction that the Communists meant to bring about a social revolution and free China from foreign oppression. He was not an orthodox Communist, since he did not agree fully with the Communist analysis of China's ills and placed the blame for China's humiliations on China itself rather than on imperialism. He refused to join the party because he believed that revolutionary writers have the obligation to work toward the goals of the revolution free of undue interference from party hacks. His attacks on the increasingly authoritarian Kuomintang regime made him a marked man. He lived in virtual hiding in Shanghai while he continued to revile the Kuomintang's censorship, its campaign of terror against its critics, and its failure to resist Japanese aggression.

Although he did not produce any new creative work during his last years in Shanghai, Lu Hsün had already attained his reputation as China's leading literary figure, and he helped many younger writers become established. During the 1930's, he perfected his essay style, translated foreign fiction and literary theory, wrote classical poetry, and maintained his lifelong interest in traditional Chinese crafts. He was particularly interested in woodblock engravings and published two collections of traditional woodblocks. He hoped to encourage a new national art that would retain its traditional Chinese spirit but that would incorporate new Western techniques.

Summary

Lu Hsün is important for his penetrating insights into Chinese national character, society, and culture. He is noted for the originality of his mind and for the techniques that he used to translate his intellectual and psychological insights into literature. His literary reputation rests on a relatively small body of published work, primarily his short stories and his prose poems. His political reputation relies on his role as a social critic, especially during the last years of his life in Shanghai.

Lu Hsün was a complex man. In public, he projected a self-confident persona, defiantly indicting Chinese character and traditions. He remained unflinching in his criticism of the Kuomintang dictatorship even in the face of obvious official hostility after 1927. A handsome man with penetrating eyes and a full, flowing mustache, Lu Hsün appeared to be a model of revolutionary courage. He always seemed to know precisely what he wanted. The Communist Party has chosen to cultivate this public image and to reduce the complexities of his personality and thought to a simplistic set of heroic traits. In his public life, Lu Hsün sought to develop a new spirit of self-respect and self-confidence in China. This would serve as the basis for national regeneration. In this way, he became a symbol of China's quest for a mature, modernized society.

There was a private side to Lu Hsün, however, which was considerably more complex and problematical. He had a deeply tragic view of life and society, which caused him to feel hemmed in by the forces of reaction and repression and to harbor genuine doubts about the prospects of victory for the revolution. His personal life was filled with spiritual anguish, doubts, and obsession with death. His political commitment to communism grew out of his search for national regeneration and not out of mere ideological conviction. His integrity was based on his determination to avoid self-delusion, combined with his habit of ruthless self-scrutiny. He looked facts fully in the face, and his morality grew out of concrete human situations. His contributions to the political revolution notwithstanding, it is the conflicts and contradictions in his writing that mark his place in modern Chinese history. He will be remembered for his deep insights into Chinese character and for his ability to express his own psychological anguish in literature and poetry.

Bibliography

Goldman, Merle, ed. *Modern Chinese Literature in the May Fourth Era*. Cambridge, Mass.: Harvard University Press, 1977. This volume of essays sets the literary renaissance of the 1920's in perspective. It contains a fine essay on Lu Hsün's educational experiences.

Hsia, Tsi-an. *The Gate of Darkness: Studies on the Leftist Literary Movement in China*. Seattle: University of Washington Press, 1968. Hsia deals with several of the May Fourth era writers in this book. His essay on the power of darkness in Lu Hsün's writings explores the private anguish that Lu Hsün experienced throughout his life.

Huang, Sung-k'ang. *Lu Hsün and the New Culture Movement of China*. Westport, Conn.: Hyperion

Press, 1975. This is a pioneering book on Lu Hsün's impact on the May Fourth generation of writers. It explores his relationship with younger writers who succeeded him.

Lee, Leo Ou-fan. *The Romantic Generation of Modern Chinese Writers*. Cambridge, Mass.: Harvard University Press, 1973. Lee places Lu Hsün in the context of the May Fourth Movement. He and the other writers were part of a conscious social group who practiced literature as an independent profession.

———, ed. *Lu Xun and His Legacy*. Berkeley: University of California Press, 1985. The product of an international conference marking the centennial of Lu Hsün's birth, this volume contains important essays on the many aspects of Lu Hsün's life. It is an indispensable source.

Lyell, William A., Jr. *Lu Hsün's Vision of Reality*. Berkeley: University of California Press, 1976. A good biographical treatment, this book introduces Lu Hsün and his stories to the general reader.

Pusey, James R. *Lu Xun and Evolution*. Albany: State University of New York Press, 1998. A philosophical critique of Lu Hsün, his personal struggles, and the relevance of his work today, sixty years after his death.

Wang, Shiquing. *Lu Xun: A Biography*. Beijing: Foreign Languages Press, 1984. This is probably the best brief biography of Lu Hsün available in English. The book does, however, present the official Chinese Communist appraisal of Lu Hsün.

Yin, Xiaoling. "The Paralyzed and the Dead: A Comparative Reading of 'The Dead' and 'In a Tavern.'" *Comparative Literature Studies* 29, no. 3 (Summer 1992). Compares Lu Hsün's story "In a Tavern" and James Joyce's story "The Dead," both of which involve dealing with loss and paralysis.

Loren W. Crabtree

CLARE BOOTHE LUCE

Born: April 10, 1903; New York, New York
Died: October 9, 1987; Washington, D.C.
Areas of Achievement: Journalism and government and politics
Contribution: As a journalist, playwright, and political appointee, Luce became an eminent example of how women could overcome gender stereotypes that limit their goals.

Early Life

Ann Clare Boothe was born on April 10, 1903, in New York City. Her mother, Ann Clare Snyder Boothe, was the daughter of Bavarian Catholic immigrants and was a former chorus girl. Her father, William F. Boothe, was a Baptist minister's son who played the violin and worked as an executive for the Boothe Piano Company. Young Clare was related to the theatrical Booth family, Edwin and John Wilkes Booth. After the Lincoln assassination, however, some family members changed the spelling of their name to camouflage the relationship.

When Clare was eight, her father abandoned his family and business to become a musician. Clare's mother worked to provide her only child with the kind of education normally given to children of much wealthier families. She lived with friends, put Clare to work as a child actress, and invested in the stock market. Unwilling to let Clare attend public schools, Ann Boothe sent her daughter to private schools when she could afford it. She supplemented her daughter's intermittent formal education with home schooling and with trips abroad, and instilled in her a lifelong love for books. Clare graduated from Castle School in Tarrytown in 1919.

After her graduation, Clare ran off to Manhattan, where she stayed in a boarding house and worked in a candy factory. Having taken the pseudonym Joyce Fair as a child actress, Clare took the name Jacqueline Tanner as a factory worker. An attack of appendicitis forced her to return to her mother's home for surgery. After Mrs. Boothe married a wealthy physician, Albert E. Austin, Clare lived with her mother and stepfather in Sound Beach, Connecticut. In 1919, she left the United States to visit Europe with her parents. On the return voyage, Clare met Mrs. O. H. P. Belmont, a wealthy Manhattan socialite, who introduced her to millionaire George Brokaw. In 1923, Clare Boothe and George Brokaw were married; she was twenty, and he was forty-three.

Life's Work

Clare Boothe's high-fashion Manhattan marriage ended in 1929 when she sued George Brokaw for divorce, claiming mental cruelty. The generous divorce settlement enabled her to move into a fashionable Beekman Place penthouse with three servants and a governess for her daughter. It also enabled her to begin a new life that was to include remarkable success in publishing, playwrighting, politics and diplomacy.

Following her divorce, Boothe went to work in New York's publishing industry. By 1933, she was managing editor of *Vanity Fair*. She also began writing on her own, and after only a year as a *Vanity Fair* editor, resigned to devote her full attention to writing plays. A rapid and prolific writer, Boothe had her first major success with *The Women*, which opened on Broadway on December 26, 1936. Although it was much more successful than her first play, *Abide with Me*, it was not considered great theater by critics. The author herself assessed it modestly, but audiences enjoyed the satire, which features a cast of thirty-eight women. Two motion picture versions and a television special were made of the play, which has been produced throughout the world. Described as a satire about men without a single man in the cast, it also satirizes the pretensions of bored, wealthy women.

Clare Boothe had become a highly successful independent woman by 1935, the year she married Henry Luce, cofounder of *Time* magazine. Together, the couple collaborated in developing *Life* magazine, soon to become one of the world's most popular magazines. Her work in the publishing business prompted Clare Boothe Luce to stay well informed about political developments throughout World War II. Although she had been a supporter of Franklin Roosevelt and the New Deal Democrats, by 1940 she was ready for new leadership in the White House. She decided to support the Republican Party's candidate, Wendell Willkie, making some forty speeches and appearances on his behalf. Although her candidate lost, Luce had gained important experience as a political activist.

In 1941 and 1942, Luce traveled as a *Life* magazine correspondent to China, the Philippines, Egypt and the Far East. Her description and analysis of the war in Europe, *Europe in Spring*, appealed to Republican party leaders, who convinced her to run for Congress in 1942 from Connecticut's

Second District, a seat held previously by her late stepfather, Albert Austin. She won the nomination easily, but had to work hard to oust the Democratic incumbent, using criticism of Roosevelt's handling of the war as her campaign theme.

Although Clare Boothe Luce entered Congress with a reputation for being rich, beautiful, and clever, she relied on intelligence and hard work to get things done. Like all new lawmakers, she learned about the importance of compromise. She wanted a seat on the House Foreign Affairs Committee but settled for the Committee on Military Affairs.

In a celebrated 1943 speech, "American and the Postwar Air World," Luce criticized the Roosevelt Administration's foreign policies, referring to them as "globaloney." The press focused on her cleverly coined word, but failed to discuss her analysis of America's ongoing air policy. It was a pattern that concerned Luce. Journalists tended to emphasize her minor comments, but ignored her major themes. Media coverage of her views was further complicated by her failure to comply consistently with Republican Party platforms. She was independent and unpredictable—characteristics not always appreciated by politicians or journalists.

Luce's policy interests included both foreign and domestic issues. She proposed gender equality in the armed services, affordable housing for veterans, independence for India, and an end to restrictions on immigration from China. She voted against the 1943 anti-labor Smith-Connally Act and was instrumental in developing Senator J. William Fulbright's Resolution of 1943 calling for creation of "international machinery" to establish and maintain a just and lasting peace. That line of reasoning contributed to creation of international agencies such as the United Nations and the North Atlantic Treaty Organization (NATO).

Although Luce opposed isolationism and favored American participation in international organizations, she criticized politicians who expressed sentimental principles instead of developing specific foreign policy goals and objectives. She was particularly critical of the Atlantic Charter, a joint declaration that had been issued by President Roosevelt and British Prime Minister Churchill in 1941. The two leaders proclaimed their commitment to "Four Freedoms": freedom from fear and want, and freedom of speech and religion. Luce called the proclamation wartime propaganda, not real foreign policy.

After winning a close election race in 1944, Luce toured Europe with a congressional delegation. The devastation she saw there bolstered her opposition to America's wartime foreign policy, which she considered incoherent and inconsistent. As the war ended, Luce continued her criticism of the Democratic administration, warning against Soviet aggression in Eastern Europe and condemning Roosevelt for his participation in the Yalta conference. America's foreign policy, in her opinion, was to "drift and improvise."

By 1944, Luce had given Republican leaders ample evidence that she could develop and present ideas forcefully, both in writing and in speeches. They selected her to deliver the keynote address at the Republican National Convention, the first woman of either party to be so honored.

Luce's extensive legislative output during her second term included proposals to rewrite immigration quotas, to help veterans get civil service jobs, to study profit sharing for workers in order to reduce strikes, to permit physicians tax breaks for charity work, to ban racial discrimination in the workplace, to promote scientific research, and to require popular election of U.S. representatives to the United Nations.

In 1945 Luce wrote to Congressman Everett Dirksen describing a plan for helping Europe recover from the war. She did not believe her staff had the expertise to write sufficiently comprehensive legislation, and so she called on Dirksen to do so. Dirksen did, but no immediate action was taken. In 1947, Secretary of State George C. Marshall proposed an almost identical approach to the problem. Although historians have traced the origins of the Marshall Plan to several men, they have generally overlooked Luce's early insight into that foreign policy situation.

In spite of her accomplishments and her interest in a wide range of political issues, Luce did not particularly enjoy the legislative process. In 1946, she decided not to pursue reelection. She continued working for the Republican Party, however, and was particularly forceful in expressing her concern that America's former ally, the Soviet Union, had become a threat to world peace.

In 1952, Luce campaigned for Dwight Eisenhower and was offered a position as secretary of labor in his presidential cabinet. She declined that offer but accepted an appointment as ambassador to Italy, becoming the first woman to represent the United States in a major foreign embassy. She handled the difficult job successfully until 1957. In 1959, Eisenhower asked her to take a position as ambassador to Brazil. She accepted, but when the confirmation process turned into a heated attack on her anti-Roosevelt stance during World War II, she withdrew her name.

Because of her friendship with the Kennedy family, Luce kept a low profile during the 1960 campaign, but in 1964 she worked for Republican Barry Goldwater's candidacy. She moved to Hawaii during the 1970's, then returned to the East Coast to serve on the President's Foreign Intelligence Advisory Board under the Nixon, Ford, and Reagan administrations. She died in 1987, the holder of numerous awards and honors for her contributions to political and cultural life in America.

Summary

Clare Boothe Luce was an intelligent, talented, hard working woman who succeeded in an unusually wide range of endeavors. The term "multivalent" probably describes her best as a person with unusually diverse abilities and ambitions. For American women who want a role model who inspires them to set high goals and to pursue them vigorously, Luce is a good choice. *The Women* will endure as part of America's cultural history. The very different story of Clare Boothe Luce herself as writer, politician and diplomat will also endure as a reflection of America's cultural and political development during the twentieth century.

Bibliography

Harriman, Margaret Case. *Take Them up Tenderly: A Collection of Profiles.* New York: Knopf, 1944. A cleverly written sketch of Luce as congresswoman and playwright. It is a witty, subjective profile rather than an objective analysis of Luce's life and accomplishments.

Luce, Clare Boothe. *Europe in the Spring.* New York: Knopf, 1940. In this analysis of pre-war conditions in Europe, Luce describes the factors that made war virtually inevitable. A popular book, this work was reprinted eight times.

————. *The Women.* New York: Random House, 1937. Popular among audiences, this play depicts upper-class women at their worst. It satirizes relationships between women and those between women and men.

Lyons, Joseph. *Clare Boothe Luce.* New York: Chelsea House, 1989. Written as part of the American Women of Achievement series, this biography is written for juvenile readers. Provides a good introduction to Luce's accomplishments as ambassador, legislator, dramatist, and journalist.

McFadden, J. P. "Clare Boothe Luce Revisited: 'The Woman of the Century.'" *The Human Life Review* 23, no. 3 (Summer 1997). Discusses a letter sent to Luce asking for her support of the movement to legalize abortion and her response to the letter. Luce declined to be associated with the movement and felt such legalization would not help establish women's equality.

Shadegg, Stephen. *Clare Boothe Luce: A Biography.* New York: Simon and Schuster, 1970; London: Frewin, 1973. Based on his friendship with Luce, his correspondence with her and on documents from her files, Shadegg presents a sympathetic yet well-written account of her personal and political life.

Sheed, Wilfrid. *Clare Boothe Luce.* New York: Dutton, and London: Weidenfeld and Nicolson, 1982. Sheed's biography, written with the cooperation of Luce, is notable for its informality and popular appeal. As Sheed himself notes in his preface to the book, many people have deified or demonized Luce, and his own portrait strives for a somewhat objective tone in dealing with the various facets of Luce's personality.

Vidal, Gore. "The Woman behind the Women: Why Did They All Hate Clare Booth Luce?" *The New Yorker* 73, no. 13 (May 26, 1997). Vidal, a long-time friend of Luce, discusses her unusual personality and the reasons she was often regarded with jealousy and mistrust.

Susan MacFarland

HENRY R. LUCE

Born: April 3, 1898; Tengchow (modern P'eng-lai), China
Died: February 28, 1967; Phoenix, Arizona
Area of Achievement: Journalism
Contribution: Luce established a powerful journalistic empire with magazines such as *Time*, which took survey of all the world, and used this power to influence American politics and foreign policy for almost four decades.

Early Life

Henry Robinson Luce was born in China, the son of American Presbyterian missionaries. His early years were spent in the relative isolation of a missionary compound, where he lived with a few dozen Westerners and their Chinese servants. In 1900, the Luce family and other missionaries fled to Korea because of the Boxer Rebellion, an uprising of the Chinese who despised the foreigners because of their negative influence on China and their arrogant attitudes. After European and American troops supressed the outbreak, the Luce family and other missionaries returned to China.

As a boy, Henry was extremely intelligent and remarkably serious. He was an avid student, and all of his life he was a passionate collector of facts and information. Sent to a British boarding school on the Chinese coast, he developed an intense, sometimes belligerent patriotism which he expressed freely and forcefully.

In 1912, young Luce was awarded a scholarship to the Hotchkiss School in Connecticut, where he met Briton Hadden. Hadden, Luce's equal in intelligence, was also popular, charming, and socially graceful—qualities which eluded Luce then and later. Although the two were soon close friends, their relationship held a constant, hardly muted air of fierce competition.

This competition continued when the two entered Yale in 1916. Both coveted positions on the powerful *Yale Daily News*, and both were selected to serve, although Hadden took the more prestigious post of chairman, while Luce ranked below him as editor. On a campus whose older students had already enlisted in World War I, Hadden and Luce early gained considerable authority; both of them clearly enjoyed the experience.

Hadden and Luce planned to start their own magazine following graduation. After working for a series of newspapers, the two moved to New York in 1922 and began raising money. They were aided by their excellent Yale connections—the mother of one classmate invested twenty thousand dollars—and within a relatively short period of time had amassed eighty-six thousand dollars. With this, they launched *Time* magazine, the first issue rolling off the presses on March 3, 1923.

The two young editors were largely responsible for writing the early issues and needed endurance and energy. These were qualities which Luce possessed in abundance throughout his life. Restless, tireless, endlessly curious, he relentlessly interrogated companions, associates, and complete strangers. He was tall and strongly built, with brilliant, piercing blue eyes and shaggy brows. Balding as he grew older, he had hearing problems which increased his tendency to bark out his statements in sharp, powerful staccato. His staff was cowed by his dogmatic assurance and insistent commands.

Life's Work

Time was not completely novel in journalism: There were other newsmagazines which offered a broad survey of national and world activities. The difference was that *Time* presented the week's events in a bright, colorful prose style. Hadden and Luce used newspaper accounts and items from wire services for their content and rewrote these for the magazine. Two devices, introduced by Hadden and perfected by Luce, marked *Time*: the use of epithets and an inverted sentence style.

The first device, which Hadden probably learned in his Greek classes at Hotchkiss and Yale, used highly descriptive adjectives for persons. Those who appeared in *Time* were likely to be beetle-browed, tough-talking, even snaggle-toothed. The second method rearranged the expected order of English sentences to startle and provoke the reader. Its effect was best captured in a parody by Walcott Gibbs when he wrote: "Backward ran sentences until reeled the mind."

While the new, breezy writing style made *Time* pleasurable to read, there was a darker side which became increasingly prominent. *Time* seemed to be objective and factual, but its reporting was carefully loaded to favor Luce's causes. Politicians whom Luce admired were likely to be steely-eyed and firm-talking; opponents were more likely to be

snaggle-toothed or pot-bellied. These and other, more serious, distortions were present in the Luce press from the beginning.

While not an immediate sensation, *Time* soon began a steady upward climb in circulation. Its compressed news stories appealed to businessmen; its clever style was prized by the sophisticated; schools and libraries valued its coverage of cultural and artistic events. By 1926, the magazine was firmly established, the founders were becoming enormously wealthy, and Luce was the youngest man to receive an honorary Yale degree.

In 1928, eager to expand, Luce began drafting ideas for a new magazine to be a celebration of American free enterprise. At first titled *Power*, it would later be known as *Fortune*. Hadden was cool to the idea, but in 1929, he died suddenly from influenza. Luce quickly bought up enough shares to take control of *Time*; he would keep that control until his death.

Once in charge, Luce directed his press into three causes that dominated his entire career: his vigorous support of American interests worldwide; his desire to see China united as a Christian and democratic nation; and his absolute and unalterable hatred of Communism. In a sense, the enormous power generated by his publications was created to accomplish these goals.

As an opponent of Communism, Luce was prepared to overlook the excesses of its opponents. The July, 1934, issue of *Fortune*, for example, was devoted to Italy and showed open admiration for Benito Mussolini and his Fascist regime. In 1935 and 1936, *Time* clearly sided with Mussolini during his brutal invasion of Ethiopia, and *Time* writers mocked Emperor Haile Selassie in terms that were both belittling and racist. During the Spanish Civil War, the Luce press was predictably pro-Franco.

Time's attitude toward Adolf Hitler was colored by the dictator's avowed anti-Communist stance. The German reoccupation of the Rhineland received favorable notice, and when Hitler announced the creation of the *Luftwaffe*, an action specifically forbidden by the Versailles treaty, *Time* lightly compared him to a boy caught sneaking out of a jam closet. It was not until the advent of war that Luce and his publications discovered the full extent of the Nazi menace. By the war's end, Luce had already declared his own cold war against the Soviet Union; he made it clear that he would have preferred open hostilities.

The lifelong obsession with China was a constant theme in *Time* and other Luce magazines. Although Luce did not meet Chiang Kai-shek until 1941, he had been a supporter of the Chinese leader since the mid-1930's. Chiang was a convert to Christianity and a fierce anti-Communist, both essential traits to Luce. *Time* featured Chiang on its cover often, and its articles urged closer American support and greater American aid for Chiang's Nationalist party. Even after the Communists had swept Chiang from mainland China in 1948, Luce still dreamed of and worked for a triumphant return for his hero. In the United States, this meant fierce, often brutal attacks in Luce publications on those responsible for the "loss of China" and any who showed signs of being "soft on Communism."

Luce's third great theme, his intense Americanism, embraced the other two and merged them into a transcendent whole. After World War II, he called for the American Century, in which the United States would have no equal in the world but would be the supreme arbiter of events. Naturally, to Luce, this meant the eventual destruction of Communism, a struggle which he preached with apocalyptic intensity.

To obtain these ends, Luce could call upon an imposing media empire to influence opinion. After *Time* and *Fortune* proved successful, he launched the picture magazine *Life* in November, 1935. An immediate success with the public, *Life* would be a mighty force until vanquished by television and speciality magazines in the 1970's. Until then, however, it had enormous impact on Americans, both public and private.

Other Luce ventures included newsreels ("Time Marches On"), radio programs, and the magazine *Sports Illustrated*. At the height of its power, the Luce press may have reached as many as one-third of the total adult literate population in the United States.

Although Luce was devoted to this empire and its works, there was a personal side to his life. As a reporter in Chicago in 1921, he had met Lila Ross Hotz; they were married in 1923. Nine years later, Luce met and quickly fell in love with Clare Boothe Brokaw, a beautiful, intelligent, sharp-tongued divorcée. Abruptly, Luce informed Lila that he wanted a divorce; in 1935, he remarried.

Clare Boothe Luce, as she is inevitably known, was a remarkable woman: a playwright (*The Women*, 1936), politician (two-term Republican congresswoman from Connecticut), and diplomat (ambassador to Italy after World War II), she matched Luce in intellect and ambition.

Luce also had political yearnings which were never satisfied. Hesitant to seek elective office, despite the massive power of his magazines, he hoped for appointment as secretary of state under a Republican administration. Harry S Truman's stunning upset over Thomas Dewey in 1948 robbed Luce of his best chance for the office. He thereafter offered his forceful advice through the pages of *Time* and *Life* and was a powerful influence in the Republican Party.

Unable to relax, a compulsive chain-smoker, and almost utterly humorless, Luce drove himself all of his life at a relentless pace. In February, 1967, he suffered a coronary occlusion at his home in Phoenix and died immediately.

Summary

For a free press to function in a democratic society such as the United States, there are two requirements: The government must be tolerant and the media must be impartial. Certainly no newspaper or magazine ever published has achieved total objectivity, but all responsible journals strive consistently toward that goal. It was the great failing of the Luce press that it rejected this search for objectivity and instead imposed its own view upon its readers. This was particularly damaging in three ways.

First, the slanting of news was done covertly. *Time* articles seemed to be objective news reports, but their use of adjectives, their turns of phrase, their juxtaposition of quotations—all these built up a carefully designed viewpoint for the reader, without his knowledge. This viewpoint was demanded by Luce, who was passionately convinced of his views and who seemed to believe that the traditional impartiality of the press would only be an impediment to the larger truth as he saw it.

Second, the techniques used were often destructive. Careers, lives, even national events were adversely affected by the Luce press's editorial bias. At home, *Time* supported the activities of Communist-hunters such as Senator Joseph McCarthy, despite the wrecked careers of innocent persons and the dangers to traditional American liberties. Abroad, Luce advocated the forceful extension of American interests. During the Korean War, for example, he called for an open confrontation with Communist China, arguing that this stance would not necessarily mean the commitment of American troops; only the use of nuclear weapons could have achieved this end.

Finally, Luce's media empire was so large and reached such a vast audience that its negative effects were magnified. For millions of Americans, *Time* and *Life* were the sole or major source of news; when this news was slanted or distorted, a huge segment of the American public was robbed of its ability to reflect seriously and decide responsibly on matters of great importance.

Neither Luce nor his press was completely malign. There was much that was good in *Time* and the other publications: a brisk, lively writing style; a wide, if fleeting, review of world events; and greater attention to cultural, artistic, and literary items. *Life* became justly known for the exceptionally high quality of its photography, many of the photographs becoming indelible images of the twentieth century. If, on balance, it must be said that Luce was more concerned with the power of the press to influence, rather than inform, it should be added that he created and sustained a mighty media empire that was capable of both.

Bibliography

Brinkley, Alan. "To See and Know Everything: Henry R. Luce Had an Insatiable Curiosity, with the Drive and Ambition to Match." *Time* 151, no. 9 (March 9, 1998). Profile of Luce, including his development of *Time* magazine with Briton Hadden while attending Yale University.

Elson, Robert. *Time Inc: The Intimate History of a Publishing Enterprise.* 3 vols. New York: Atheneum, 1968-1986. This is the "official, authorized history" of *Time*, as told by staff writers. The three volumes are filled with an enormous amount of detail (especially financial) and a wealth of historical anecdotes (usually favorable) which demonstrate clearly that *Time* was a world-spanning enterprise.

Griffith, Thomas. *Harry and Teddy: The Turbulent Friendship of Press Lord Henry R. Luce and His Favorite Reporter, Theodore H. White.* New York: Random House, 1995. Entertaining volume examining Luce's turbulent relationship with White. Includes anecdotes found in archives and through interviews with White's associates.

Halberstam, David. *The Powers That Be.* New York: Knopf, and London: Chatto and Windus,

1979. A study of the rise and influence of the major news media in the United States during the twentieth century; Luce's empire is placed in perspective alongside such giants as *The New York Times*, *The Washington Post*, and the Columbia Broadcasting System. Extensively researched and excellent in exploring the relationship of the media to American politics.

Kobler, John. *Luce: His Time, Life, and Fortune*. New York: Doubleday, and London: MacDonald, 1968. Although written by a longtime *Time* staffer, this biography retains much of its objectivity and fairness. This book provides a good introduction to Luce's life and career but should be used along with W. A. Swanberg's more complete (and critical) biography.

Shadegg, Stephen. *Clare Boothe Luce: A Biography*. New York: Simon and Schuster, 1970; London: Frewin, 1973. A favorable, even admiring biography of the talented Clare Boothe Luce, interesting in his portrayal of the relationship between husband and wife, with its own undercurrent of competition and rivalry.

Swanberg, W. A. *Luce and His Empire: A Biography*. New York: Scribner, 1972. A lengthy, well-researched biography of Luce and his press which does not shirk from pointing out the many journalistic faults that press had. Swanberg had access to many in the Luce organization and used his sources to give a fascinating review of Luce's career.

Michael Witkoski

ERICH LUDENDORFF

Born: April 9, 1865; Kruszewnia, near Posen,
Prussia (now Poznan, Poland)
Died: December 20, 1937; Munich, Germany
Area of Achievement: The military
Contribution: Ludendorff served as second in
command to Field Marshal Paul von Hindenburg
during World War I and became the most powerful man in Germany from 1916 to 1918. In the
1920's, he was involved with radical nationalist
movements, including the Nazi movement, but
eventually became too radical even for Hitler. By
the mid-1920's, he had lost his influence with
conservative and radical nationalists.

Early Life

Erich Friedrich Wilhelm Ludendorff was born
into an impoverished middle-class landowning
family. His father was a reserve officer in the
Franco-German War (1870-1871). As a student,
Ludendorff had an excellent academic record, especially in mathematics, but showed no interest in
sports and was without close friends. Ludendorff
entered cadet school in 1877, passing his entrance
examination with distinction. Though his academic
performance was superb, there and at the Military
Academy in Berlin, he isolated himself from fellow students. Ludendorff was commissioned in
1885. In 1893, he entered the Kriegsakademie for
advanced training. After service as company commander and staff officer, he was transferred to the
general staff in 1904 and assigned to the crucial
Mobilization and Deployment Section, in which he
played a growing role in war plan preparations, updating the Schlieffen Plan (Germany's plan for a
two-front war). He became head of the section in
1907. Ludendorff strongly supported the planned
attack into France through Belgium.

As war appeared increasingly imminent, with repeated international crises and an intensified arms
race, Ludendorff drafted the Army Bill for 1913,
calling for an increase of 300,000 men. Overly active lobbying for that increase outside regular military channels caused Ludendorff, then a colonel, to
be transferred to a regimental command in January,
1913. When war began in August, 1914, Ludendorff, who had become a major general (one star),
became deputy chief of staff of the Second Army,
part of the thrust through Belgium. He distinguished himself during the capture of the strategically important fortress of Liege, becoming the
war's second Pour le Merite recipient. Liege's early fall was vital to the Schlieffen Plan's success.

Life's Work

On August 22, 1914, Ludendorff was appointed
chief of staff of the Eighth Army, after its commander was dismissed because he had failed to
stop the Russian advance into eastern Prussia.
Shortly thereafter, retired General Hindenburg
was appointed Eighth Army commander, thus creating the Hindenburg-Ludendorff duo, which
played a crucial role in Germany's victories and
its final defeat.

When Hindenburg became Supreme Commander in the East, in November, 1914, Ludendorff, now a lieutenant general (two stars) continued as his chief of staff. In August, 1916,
Hindenburg became chief of the General Staff, replacing Erich Falkenhayn, and the Hindenburg-
Ludendorff team again remained intact; Ludendorff was promoted to general of infantry (three
stars) and given the position of first quartermaster
general, Hindenburg's deputy. Though Hindenburg was nominally in command, Ludendorff became the true power and Germany's "silent dictator." Ludendorff was a master of detail in
planning and execution. Strategically he advocated encirclement, as in the Schlieffen Plan. Even
when the war stalemated, he attempted to retain
operational mobility, as with the strategic withdrawal to the "Siegfried Line" in 1917. This
shortened German supply lines and forced the Allies to launch their 1917 offensive across devastated territory. In the spring of 1918, he supported
introduction of the "Hutier tactics"—the use of
infiltration by specially trained and equipped
storm troopers—finally breaking the stalemate.

Ludendorff's political machinations caused the
removal of Imperial Chancellor Theobald von
Bethmann-Hollweg in July, 1917, and the establishment of a government subservient to the army.
The German economy in particular was tightly
controlled by Ludendorff in order to squeeze the
last ounce of war effort from the country. The year
1917 also witnessed Russia's collapse. By March,
1918, following the harsh Brest-Litovsk Treaty
with the Bolsheviks, Germany was in control of
the East's vast resources. That treaty was an ex-

pression of Ludendorff's concept of economic warfare, which he understood better than did his contemporaries.

In January, 1917, Ludendorff advocated unrestricted submarine warfare, which brought the United States into the war. He recognized that American belligerence would be inevitable but believed that Great Britain could be defeated before significant American aid arrived. With a clear, though short-range, superiority in men and material, the Germans launched their final offensive in March, 1918. Having already lost the gamble on unrestricted submarine warfare, Ludendorff now gambled all on a decisive blow before substantial American troops could arrive to support the exhausted and wavering Allies. The "Ludendorff offensive," however, fell short of its goals. The hard-pressed Allies held, finally launching counteroffensives with the aid of fresh American troops. On August 8, Ludendorff recognized that the war was lost. On September 29, physically and emotionally exhausted and in near panic, he demanded that the civilian government, which he had earlier neutralized, negotiate an immediate armistice before his forces collapsed and the enemy entered Germany. He quickly reversed himself and demanded continuation of the war, hoping to halt the Allies on French soil, delaying the decisive action until 1919. On October 26, 1918, however, Ludendorff was dismissed. Late in the war, Ludendorff was ennobled (entitled to use the "von" with his name), and he was awarded the Grand Cross of the Iron Cross for his part in the March, 1918, offensive.

Following the November armistice, Ludendorff fled to Sweden, where he wrote his memoirs, published in June, 1919. In his writings he placed the blame for defeat on the "soft" civilian government and its unwillingness to rally the people to a final total war effort. In November, 1919, Ludendorff and Hindenburg appeared before the parliamentary commission investigating the reasons for Germany's defeat. Hindenburg popularized the "stab-in-the-back" legend—the argument that the German army was not defeated, and could have continued, but was "stabbed in the back" by the Bolshevik Revolution.

In 1920, Ludendorff joined the disgruntled Free Corps members in the abortive Kapp Putsch against the Berlin government. In November, 1923, he participated in the Nazis' equally ill-fated Munich Beer Hall Putsch, beginning an uneasy relationship with Adolf Hitler. While Hitler was imprisoned for treason, Ludendorff, because of his illustrious war record, was found not guilty. During Hitler's absence, Ludendorff attempted to rally the banned Nazi Party around himself and, in 1924, was elected to the German parliament under the National Socialist label, serving for four years without playing a significant role. Ludendorff rapidly slipped into an increasingly irrational and paranoid, racially based radical nationalism, which even the Nazis found unacceptable. Ludendorff's role in the party ended with Hitler's return in 1925, but not until he had served as the Nazis' presidential candidate, following the death of President Friedrich Ebert. In a field of seven candidates, Ludendorff carried only 1.1 percent of the vote. Since no candidate received the required majority, a second election was necessary, in which Hindenburg, not a candidate initially, was elected.

In 1926, Ludendorff divorced his first wife and married Mathilde von Kemnitz, a doctor. Under her influence, he continued to drift further into an eccentric racism. The two published numerous works in which they argued that "supernational forces," the Jews, the Freemasons, the Marxists, and the Catholic church were responsible for all evil that had befallen the Western world, including the murders of Sarajevo, World War I, the Bolshevik Revolution, and the United States' entry into the war. Ludendorff's growing persecution complex led to his falling out not only with Hitler but also with his wartime colleagues, including Hindenburg. Together with his wife, Ludendorff founded a pseudoreligious movement, the Deutsche Gotteserkenntnis (German understanding of God), based on Germanic pagan traditions. In 1939, Hitler's government officially recognized this movement as a religion.

Following his death in 1937, Ludendorff received a hero's funeral, with Hitler as a prominent mourner. Ludendorff's widow continued her radical racist activities, even after 1945, though without significant influence. In 1961, the Federal Republic of Germany outlawed her "Ludendorff Movement" as a revival of National Socialism.

Summary

Erich Ludendorff was the embodiment of the bourgeois military technocrat in an aristocratic era. Though he adopted aristocratic bearing, Ludendorff did not have the aristocracy's sense of moderation and its desire to avoid politics. In

1912, while heading the Mobilization and Deployment Section of the General Staff, he concluded that future wars would be "total." In a memorandum to Helmuth von Moltke, chief of the General Staff, he wrote, "We once again have to become a people in arms." While confessing to follow Carl von Clausewitz, he in fact inverted Clausewitz's views. While Clausewitz saw war as politics' servant, to remain under civilian control, Ludendorff saw politics as the handmaiden of military needs. He expressed this concept again in 1935, charging that "war is the highest expression of the national will to live, and therefore politics must serve warmaking." Though the general staff rejected his extreme views both times, his views deeply influenced Hitler.

In 1916, when he was in a position to realize his concepts, he pushed for total economic and manpower mobilization under military administration, contributing substantially to the people's physical and emotional exhaustion and final collapse. Yet strangely he did not take the concept of military preeminence to its ultimate conclusion; he did not advocate or establish military-political dictatorship but settled for total economic control. His inability to recognize failure of the 1918 spring offensive—both civilian and military exhaustion—also demonstrates his inability to recognize limits. Consequently, he missed the opportunity of possibly gaining a favorably negotiated peace in the late spring of 1918. His decision to ask for peace negotiations in late 1918 is seen by some as a ploy, designed to rally the German people against unreasonable Allied terms, not recognizing that the bulk of the population was ready for peace at any price.

Ludendorff's inability to question his own judgment led him to seek blame for the lost war elsewhere, and the "stab-in-the-back" legend provided that escape. He was a highly intelligent and capable military leader, but he was also an arrogant and egotistical individual who, for example, bitterly resented the credit that went to Hindenburg for their joint achievements. His increasingly paranoid attitude toward Judaism, Christianity, Marxism, and Freemasonry merged with his inability to accept military defeat. His extremism and his inability to get along even with like-minded persons, his lack of political pragmatism, and his total lack of charisma prevented him from playing a popular role within the conservative, or radical, Right. By the mid-1920's, Ludendorff had lost his earlier credibility.

Bibliography

Falls, Cyril. *The Great War, 1914-1918.* New York: Putnam, 1959. Aimed at the general reader, this is a history of the war, with some discussion of its background and war plans. Also includes some discussion of the home front and wartime diplomacy. Military events are described in detail with frequent references to Ludendorff. Contains a short bibliography.

Goodspeed, D. J. *Ludendorff: Genius of World War I.* Boston: Houghton Mifflin, and London: Hartz Davis, 1966. Though the emphasis is on Ludendorff's wartime career, the author also briefly covers his early life and the postwar period.

Ludendorff, Erich von. *Ludendorff's Own Story, August 1914-November 1918.* 2 vols. New York: Harper, 1919; London: Harper, 1920. Ludendorff's own story, this is a detailed account of his command decisions and campaigns. It is unclear to what extent he utilized official records.

Parkinson, Roger. *Tormented Warrior: Ludendorff and the Supreme Command.* London: Hodder and Stoughton, 1978; New York: Stein and Day, 1979. The author believes that Ludendorff has been ignored by historians and sees Ludendorff as Germany's leading personality. Includes a bibliography.

Wheeler-Bennett, John W. *Hindenburg: The Wooden Titan.* New York: Morrow, and London: Macmillan, 1936. Though Hindenburg is the chief topic, Ludendorff is discussed extensively. Largely based on interviews with personalities of the period. Though the emphasis is on Ludendorff's wartime career, the author does deal with his postwar political involvements.

Frederick Dumin

LORD LUGARD

Born: January 22, 1858; Madras, India

Died: April 11, 1945; Abinger Common, Surrey, England

Areas of Achievement: Exploration and government

Contribution: Employing his impressive military and administrative skills, Lugard played a major role in extending British control over Uganda and Nigeria and developed the administrative system known as "indirect rule."

Early Life

Frederic John Dealtry Lugard, later Lord Lugard, was born in Madras, India, on January 22, 1858. His parents, Frederic Grueber Lugard and Mary Jane Howard, were both children of clergymen and had themselves become missionaries to India. Returning with his mother and sisters to England in 1863, Lugard's early, deep religious convictions were tested by his mother's death in 1864. His schooling at Rossall in Lancashire was not entirely successful. He was a poor scholar and received constant punishment for his violation of school rules. Failing the India Civil Service examination, Lugard passed the army examination in 1877 and entered the Royal Military Academy at Sandhurst.

The threat of war with Russia in 1878 ended his military education, and in 1878, Lugard received a commission in the Royal Norfolk Regiment. Assigned to service in India, in 1879-1880 he participated in the Second Afghan Campaign. In 1885, he served in the Sudan Campaign as a transport officer, a position he also filled with great ability in Burma in 1886 and 1887, receiving the Distinguished Service Order. His apparently successful military career was cut short by a turbulent relationship with a married woman. Following her back to England, Lugard was distraught when she proved as unfaithful to him as to her husband. Deeply depressed, Lugard turned to fighting fires in London as a member of the newly organized Fire Brigade. A handsome, physically strong man sporting a large mustache, Lugard possessed obvious military and leadership abilities. At the age of thirty, however, he was emotionally and professionally confused and without a settled career. In 1888, he left England, almost penniless, for East Africa determined to aid in eradicating the Arab slave trade. His meteoric rise to prominence was something few of his contemporaries could have predicted.

Life's Work

Lugard's first position was with the African Lakes Company, established in 1878 to develop commerce and Christianity in the Lake Nyasa region. Leading a fight against Arab slavers with mixed results, Lugard was seriously wounded and returned to England in 1889. There he participated in the public campaign to persuade the British government to lay claim to Nyasaland, a decision approved by Great Britain in May, 1891. Although regarded by some as impetuous and receiving little credit for his work in Nyasaland, Lugard had found a career in Africa.

Between 1889 and 1894, Lugard worked for Sir William Mackinnon's Imperial East Africa Company, which had received a Royal Charter in 1888. Leading a caravan to Uganda in 1890, Lugard immediately became embroiled in the civil and religious wars plaguing the region. An extensive military campaign resulted in Lugard's establishment of the company's rule over a united kingdom. The violence associated with his campaign, however, caused a diplomatic crisis with France and sullied his reputation for years. In 1892 he returned again to London, where he wrote extensively, defending himself against charges of brutality and urging the desirability of British annexation of Uganda. Lugard was pleased both by the discovery that he had powerful defenders in Great Britain and by Great Britain's annexation of Uganda in 1894.

Lugard's next, and most famous, imperial work was in the region later known as Nigeria, administered for Great Britain by Sir George Goldie's Royal Niger Company. Threatened by French encroachment from the west, Goldie dispatched Lugard on a race to Nikki in Borgu. Arriving only a few days before a French expedition, Lugard obtained a treaty that strengthened British claims to the region. Following a brief period of service (1895-1897) with the British West Charterland Company in the Kalahari Desert in Southern Africa, Joseph Chamberlain, the British colonial secretary, appointed Lugard commander of a new West African Frontier Force with the rank of colonel. This force was assigned the task of retarding French advances on the middle Niger. Lugard's military abilities, firmness, and tact were in large part responsible for the favorable 1898 treaty with France delineating the modern boundaries of Nigeria. In 1898, at the age of forty, he returned once more to England, his decade of adventure in pushing forward the frontiers of British Africa behind him.

The revocation of the charter of the Royal Niger Company placed Nigeria under the control of the British Colonial Office, and in 1900, Lugard became the first High Commissioner for Northern Nigeria. Although now an administrator of an immense area, Lugard's first years necessitated the use of his considerable military talents. In 1902 and 1903, military expeditions succeeded in conquering the ancient emirates of Kano and Sokoto, finally bringing Northern Nigeria under the management of British administration. The remainder of his rule was devoted to establishing a government and administration and the development of his ideas of indirect rule. In 1906, Lugard resigned his position, exhausted from his work and unwilling to be further separated from his wife, Flora Shaw, a prominent female imperialist whom he had married in 1902.

From 1907 to 1912, Lugard served as Governor of Hong Kong. Restive under the constitutional restrictions of his new position, Lugard was never entirely comfortable with his largely ceremonial duties. His principal achievement during these years was the foundation of the University of Hong Kong in 1911. Hong Kong was, however, only an interlude in his African work. In 1912, Lugard was appointed governor of the new united Nigeria. Between 1912 and 1919, when he finally retired from colonial service, Lugard devoted himself to building an administrative structure which combined local autonomy with the maintenance of a centralized administration. The success of his work was confirmed by the constitution which Nigeria adopted when it became independent in 1960. Lugard's work was made more difficult at the time because of the outbreak of World War I in 1914 and his supervision of the conquest of the adjacent German colony of the Cameroons.

Following his retirement in 1919, Lugard remained active in colonial affairs, eventually becoming an internationally recognized authority in this field. Between 1922 and 1936, he served as a member of the League of Nations' commission on the mandate territories. He also served on an international committee studying slavery, advised the British government on colonial education, and participated in a parliamentary study of the union of Great Britain's East African territories. For his past and continuing colonial service and for his writings on colonial administration, Lugard received a peerage in 1928, becoming Baron Lugard of Abinger. He died on April 11, 1945, at the age of eighty-seven.

Summary

Lord Lugard's life and career spanned almost the entire period of British colonial rule in Africa, and in a sense he personified Great Britain's experience in Africa. During his early years, he was often vilified by both British and foreign critics as a ruthless swashbuckler who would stop at nothing to expand the empire and his own reputation and power. His expeditions to Nyasaland, to Uganda, to the French border of Nigeria, to the Kalahari, and finally back to Nigeria displayed a personal frenzy and impatience similar to the larger "scramble for Africa" by the European statesmen of the 1880's and 1890's.

Lugard's reputation changed, however, after 1900, when he assumed administrative control of Northern Nigeria, Hong Kong, and a united Nigeria. Increasingly, he was viewed as an innovative and successful colonial administrator. Most important, he developed and made systematic the concept of indirect rule. Convinced that Africa could develop best under British rule, he nevertheless also believed that as much responsibility as possible should be left with those administrators on the spot. Averse to highly structured bureaucracies on principle and because of temperament, he maintained that European nations should rule through traditional African institutions and rulers. This arrangement would maintain the integrity of African society and also serve as a means of educating Africans in self-government.

Lugard's ideas on colonial administration were most fully developed in his *The Dual Mandate in British Tropical Africa* (1922). Immensely popular and highly regarded, this book was soon recognized as a classic explanation both of what had been done in Nigeria and of what should be done in Africa in the future. As the title of his book indicates, the dual mandate was to be of benefit both to the British and to the Africans they ruled. Entering Africa for reasons other than pure philanthropy, Great Britain had a right to profit from her rule. On the other hand, Great Britain had the responsibility to make her rule beneficial to the Africans by bringing to them the advantages of Western civilization. Both his concept of indirect rule, often seen as retarding African national development, and his idea of a dual mandate, viewed by some as justifying the economic exploitation of Africa, remain controversial. The fact that such debates remain current, however, confirms Lugard's place as the most significant British colonial administrator of the twentieth century.

Bibliography

Lugard, Frederick John Dealtry, Baron. *The Diaries of Lord Lugard*. Edited by Margery Perham. 4 vols. Evanston, Ill.: Northwestern University Press, and London: Faber, 1959-1963. The first three volumes cover Lugard's travels in Uganda; the fourth volume deals with his Nigerian experiences. Essential to an understanding of Lugard's early African tribulations.

————. *The Dual Mandate in British Tropical Africa*. Introduction by Margery Perham. 5th ed. Hamden, Conn.: Archon, and London: Cass, 1965. Lugard's masterful literary monument to his life's work. Gives his views as to Great Britain's role in Africa and discusses in detail his concept of "indirect rule."

————. *Lugard and the Amalgamation of Nigeria*. Edited by A. H. M. Kirk-Greene. London: Cass, 1968. The best study of Lugard's principal administrative achievement, the unification of Nigeria, and his attempted application of indirect rule.

————. *The Rise of Our East African Empire: Early Efforts in Nyasaland and Uganda*. 2 vols. London: Blackwood, 1893. Lugard's exciting description and defense of his actions in East Africa.

Muffett, D. J. M. *Concerning Brave Captains: Being a History of the British Occupation of Kano and Sokoto and the Last Stand of the Fulani Forces*. London: Deutsch, 1964. A fast moving account of Lugard's conquest of Northern Nigeria.

Perham, Margery. *Lugard: The Years of Adventure, 1858-1898*. Hamden, Conn.: Archon, 1956; London: Collins, 1960. The first volume of the standard biography of Lugard. Covers his years of conflict in East Africa and Nigeria.

————. *Lugard: The Years of Authority, 1898-1945*. Hamden, Conn.: Archon, and London: Collins, 1960. The second volume of the standard biography of Lugard. Deals with his various governorships and the development of his ideas on native administration.

Shaw, Flora Louisa. *A Tropical Dependency: An Outline of the Ancient History of the Western Soudan, with an Account of the Modern Settlement of Northern Nigeria*. London: Nisbet, 1905; New York: Cass, 1964. Written by Lugard's wife, the most famous female imperialist of her age. An early defense of Lugard's policies as high commissioner.

Thomson, Arthur A., and Dorothy Middleton. *Lugard in Africa*. London: Hale, 1959. The first major biography of Lugard. Well written and interesting but now supplanted by Perham's work.

Brian L. Blakeley

GYÖRGY LUKÁCS

Born: April 13, 1885; Budapest, Austro-Hungarian Empire
Died: June 4, 1971; Budapest, Hungary
Areas of Achievement: Philosophy and literature
Contribution: Lukács is one of the most outstanding and respected Marxist philosophers and literary critics from Eastern Europe in the twentieth century.

Early Life

György (also known as Georg) Lukács was born in Budapest in 1885, the son of a wealthy Jewish banker. He became interested in the theories of Karl Marx while attending school. He also had an interest in drama and helped to found the Thalia Theater in his native city. In 1906, he received a doctorate in philosophy from the University of Budapest. Later, before World War I, he continued his philosophical studies at the Universities of Berlin and Heidelberg. He became a serious Marxist around 1908 while in Germany. When he returned to Budapest, he joined the Social Democratic Party and fell under the influence of Ervin Szabo, the leader of the party's radical wing. At that stage of his life, Lukács was interested in the sociological theories of Marx. Before the war, he was also influenced by the works of Georg Wilhelm Friedrich Hegel, Georg Simmel, Max Weber, Søren Kierkegaard, and Georges Sorel. Besides Szabo, among Marxists, Rosa Luxemburg had an important effect on him. World War I and the Russian Revolution made a great impression on him, and his hatred of the capitalist system became even stronger. In 1918, he joined the Hungarian Communist Party and in 1919 was the minister for cultural affairs in the short-lived Hungarian Soviet Republic established by Béla Kun. When the republic collapsed, he was arrested but soon released.

Life's Work

Lukács is best known not as a political figure but as a cultural philosopher. He is one of the few, and certainly the best known, of twentieth century Marxist philosophers from Eastern Europe who have been accepted by the political authorities in the Socialist world (although with some reservations) and at the same time have earned the respect of their colleagues in the West. His earliest pre-World War I works were chiefly on literary aesthetics, including *Die Seele und die Formen (Soul and Form,* 1974), published in 1911—his first major work and still regarded as one of his best. In this work, he presented many ideas that he developed later in his life as a Marxist—the universality of experience and the role of the critic, for example. A drama, he wrote, is a play about man and fate—a play in which God is the spectator. In 1911, he wrote *A modern dráma fejlödésének története* (the history of the development of modern drama), and immediately after the fall of the Kun government he published *Die Theorie des Romans: Ein geschichtsphilosophischer Versuch über die Formen der grossen Epik* (1920; *The Theory of the Novel: A Historico-Philosophical Essay on the Forms of Great Epic Literature,* 1971).

After the failure of the Marxist Revolution in Hungary, he was forced to live in exile. He went to Vienna, where he remained until 1929 editing the journal *Kommunismus* (communism). Lukács was not immune to attack from both the left and right wings of the socialist camp, but he still managed to produce valuable philosophical literature and continue participating in the international Marxist debates of the day. While in Vienna, he engaged in political debate with Kun, who sided with the extreme Left in the Communist International. Out of this came Lukács' *Geschichte und Klassenbewusstein: Studien über marxistische Dialektic* (1923; *History and Class Consciousness: Studies on the Marxist Dialectic,* 1971), in which he first developed his own theories of dialectical historicism building on Marxism. He also began to examine the relationships between culture and class in historical development.

In *History and Class Consciousness,* he was heavily influenced by the struggle of the labor faction in the Soviet Party, which had brought its dispute against Vladimir Ilich Lenin and Leon Trotsky to the Communist International. Lukács believed that the greatest contribution of this work was the refutation of those philosophers who saw Marxism exclusively as a theory of society and not of nature, while he himself maintained that nature is a category of society. This deviation is most evident in economics, which he addresses in this treatise. In the new preface to *History and Class Consciousness* in the 1968 edition, he wrote that he specifically rejected the ideas of both Anatoly V. Lunacharsky, Lenin's Bolshevik ally, and the Austrian Marxist Max Adlar, whom he regarded as Kantian in philosophy and a revisionist Social Democrat in politics. The difference between bourgeois and socialist outlooks, Lukács believed, is in the materialist view of nature, and "the failure to grasp this blurs philosophical debate and prevents the clear elaboration of the Marxist concept of praxis."

In 1923, Lukács wrote and published an examination of Lenin's theory and practice entitled *Lenin: Studie über den Zusammenhang seiner Gedanken* (*Lenin: A Study of the Unity of His Thought*, 1971). As an admirer of Lenin, Lukács wished to show how the Soviet leader was able to put his revolutionary theories into practice. In a 1967 edition, he wrote that he was attempting to find the spiritual center of Lenin's personality, to find the objective and subjective forces that made Lenin's action possible. Lukács saw Lenin as a counteraction against the dogmatism that was manifested in the age of Stalin.

In 1929, Lukács moved to Berlin, where he stayed until the advent of Adolf Hitler in 1933. During this period, he also briefly lectured at the Marx-Engels Institute in Moscow, and in 1933 he went back to Moscow to take a post at the Soviet Academy of Sciences' Institute for Philosophy. After World War II, Lukács returned to Hungary, where he worked until his death in 1971. He participated in Hungarian politics as a member of the Hungarian delegation to the World Peace Council. He was also elected to the Hungarian parliament in the Communist-controlled one-slate elections and was a professor of aesthetics and the philosophy of culture at the University of Budapest. In 1956, he joined Imre Nagy's dissident Communist government once more as minister of culture. When the invasion of Soviet troops toppled the government, Lukács was deported to Romania but returned to Budapest in 1957. He then retired to private life and continued writing. He had already begun his major exposition on Marxist aesthetics, which was published from 1963 to 1972. He also wrote a number of works of literary criticism on the works of Johann Wolfgang von Goethe, Hegel, Thomas Mann, and Aleksandr Solzhenitsyn.

Lukács' work has earned much praise but has also provoked much criticism in the West as well as in Eastern Europe. In 1970, he received the Goethe Prize of the city of Frankfurt, but it has been the Frankfurt school that has bitterly attacked his aesthetics. When he first returned to Hungary after World War II, he was attacked by educational bureaucrats such as Joseph Revai. Western critics

such as Morris Watnick have said that Lukács was, despite his Marxism, in fact an elitist. Alfred Kazin agrees, attributing this elitism to his bourgeois birth. Kazin also points out that Lukács did not, in general, analyze Soviet writers; indeed, with the exception of Mann, he was not interested in modern masters. His *Der russische Realismus in der Weltliteratur* (1949; partial translation in *Studies in European Realism*, 1964) contains essays on Honoré de Balzac, Stendhal, Émile Zola, and Leo Tolstoy. These nineteenth century writers were for Lukács not the mere continuation of schools of literature but purveyors of moral philosophy with lessons for their and modern generations.

In his 1969 critique of Solzhenitsyn, he courageously analyzed the dissident Soviet writer without heaping the condemnation upon him that was in vogue with the writers' unions of the Socialist countries or fawning upon him as in the West. He believed Solzhenitsyn to be a writer in the proletarian, but not Marxist, tradition. In *Goethe und seine Zeit* (1947; *Goethe and His Age*, 1969), Lukács defended German culture to show that Nazism was not a natural outgrowth of it. In fact, he believed that an anti-German attitude was not truly an anti-Fascist attitude. He saw Fascism, as well as all developments in Germany, as part of the class struggle and historical dialectic. Most of all, Lukács wished to demonstrate in this work that Goethe was not a reactionary, as many critics had maintained, but a progressive. Of the twentieth century German writers, Lukács' favorite was Mann, an anti-Facist but bourgeois author. Lukács maintained that, with his critique of Mann, he was attempting "to interpret this ideological decay of the bourgeoisie in the work of the last great bourgeois writer." For Lukács, it is the Faust legend as a condemnation of bourgeois society that links Goethe and Mann.

Summary

György Lukács stands as a unique figure in the cultural history of the twentieth century. He was a Marxist scholar who was able to survive the rigors of Stalinist totalitarian thought without compromising his principles and yet continue to make a contribution to his discipline. He was one of the most powerful aestheticists and literary critics of modern times, and his impact is felt in both East and West. He was a committed Marxist and philosophical materialist from his early student days, and his work is noted for its rigorous logic and uncompromising principles. His earliest work in the field of literary criticism led to the classic *Soul and Form*, in which he established the materialist basis of literary categories. During the short-lived Hungarian Soviet government, he played a key role as minister of education and culture and afterward became involved in the factious fighting that split both the Hungarian and international Communist movement. As a supporter of Lenin, he became a defender of the Soviet Union and, because of the threat of Fascism and Nazism, continued to do so even though he disagreed with Stalin's methods. Nevertheless, he attacked Fascism from a class basis and defended German ideology and literature.

As a Marxist professor and editor in Austria, Germany, and Moscow between the wars, Lukács built a solid reputation in the field of philosophy. His reputation continued to grow as a professor in Communist Hungary after the war. Lukács has been pilloried by Socialist authorities for not being ideologically pure and by Western critics for not being a dissident, but his reputation has withstood all attacks. His consistent theme was always the unity of thought and action, theory and practice. All of his ideas proceed from his materialist conception of the universe based on his belief in Marxism. He believed that culture and literature also proceed from a materialist basis. His *History and Class Consciousness* was written to defy those Communists who could not make the transition from coffeehouse intellectuals to molders of history in the real world. It is for this reason that he admired Lenin, who was for Lukács the ultimate practitioner of theory and practice of revolution. It may be true that he could find no author from the Socialist world, save perhaps Maxim Gorky and Bertolt Brecht, whom he could admire and use as examples for his philosophy of culture. Aside from briefly looking at Solzhenitsyn, it was only Mann of twentieth century authors whom he wrote about. Although he admired Mann as writer and an heir to the best in German culture, he still classified him as part of the decadent bourgeoisie. His real heroes in literature were from the eighteenth and nineteenth centuries. The genius of Lukács remains his ability to put theory and practice into his own life—to meet his critics on their own ground. No other Marxist cultural figure from Eastern Europe in the twentieth century has accomplished this to the same degree.

Bibliography

Bahr, Ehrhard, and Ruth G. Kunzer. *Georg Lukács*. Translated by R. G. Kunzer. New York: Ungar, 1972. Part of the Literature and Life series, this work is an excellent short biography and analysis. Includes notes, a bibliography, a chronology, an index.

Fekete, Éva, and Éva Káradi, eds. *György Lukács: His Life in Pictures and Documents*. Translated by Péter Balabán. Budapest: Covina Kiado, 1981. A biography for the general public, chiefly containing pictures of Lukács and his contemporaries. Very useful for those who wish to learn more about the man. Includes illustrations.

Graham, Gordon. "Lukács and Realism after Marx." *The British Journal of Aesthetics* 38, no. 2 (April, 1998). The author discusses Lukács' book *The Meaning of Contemporary Realism* and its ties to the theory of Karl Marx.

Heller, Agnes, ed. *Lukács Reappraised*. New York: Columbia University Press, 1983; as *Lukacs Re-*

valued, Oxford: Blackwell, 1983. A collection of scholarly essays examining Lukács' works and ideas. Includes notes and an index.

Lapointe, François H. *George Lukacs and His Critics: An International Bibliography with Annotations (1910-1982)*. Westport, Conn.: Greenwood Press, 1983. While not listing books by Lukács himself, this is an exhaustive annotated bibliography of books about him in all languages. Includes appendices for cross reference and an index.

Lichtheim, George. *George Lukács*. New York: Viking Press, 1973. Part of the Modern Masters series, this is a scholarly biography emphasizing Lukács' philosophical development. Includes notes, a bibliography, and an index.

Lukács, Georg. *Conversations with Lukács: Hans Heinz Holz, Leo Kofler, Wolfgang Abendroth*. Edited by Theo Pinkus. London: Merlin Press, 1974; Cambridge, Mass.: MIT Press, 1975. A series of conversations between Lukács and contemporary philosophers showing his ideas.

———. *History and Class Consciousness*. Translated by Livingstone Rodney. London: Merlin Press, and Cambridge, Mass.: MIT Press, 1971. An important philosophical work showing Lukács' philosophical development. Includes notes and an index.

Parkinson, George H. R. *Georg Lukács*. London and Boston: Routledge, 1977. An excellent scholarly biography and analysis of Lukács' thought. Includes notes and an index.

Rockmore, Tom. "Fichte, Lask, and Lukács's Hegelian Marxism." *The Journal of the History of Philosophy* 30, no. 4 (October, 1992). Examines Lukács' version of Marxism and his interpretations of German philosophy.

Frederick B. Chary

AUGUSTE LUMIÈRE and LOUIS LUMIÈRE
Auguste Lumière

Born: October 19, 1862; Besançon, France

Died: April 10, 1954; Lyons, France

Louis Lumière

Born: October 5, 1864; Besançon, France

Died: June 6, 1948; Bandol, France

Areas of Achievement: Business, invention, and technology

Contribution: The Lumière brothers introduced many successful innovations to the manufacture of photographic materials and won particular renown for the development of the first commercially viable projected motion pictures and for the introduction of the color photographic medium known as the Autochrome process.

Early Lives

Auguste Marie Louis Lumière was born on October 19, 1862, and Louis Jean Lumière was born two years later, on October 5, 1864. Their father, Claude-Antoine, was born in 1840 at Ormoy, near Besançon, a city in the foothills of the Jura Mountains in southeastern France. Antoine, as he was later known, lost his parents to cholera in 1854, but he was taken in by the painter Auguste Constantin, who taught him drawing. Antoine first took up the trade of sign painting, but by 1860 he established himself as a painter and photographer in Besançon, where he married Jeanne-Joséphine Costille. The couple were to have, in addition to Auguste and Louis, a daughter, Jeanne, and a son, Édouard, who died as an aviator in World War I.

After nearly a decade as the proprietor of his own studio in Besançon, Antoine accepted a partnership with a photographer in Lyons beginning in 1871. Within three years, he had gained recognition for his photography by winning medals in Vienna, Lyons, and Paris. An intelligent and industrious man, Antoine fostered his sons' interest in science and technology. In 1880, Louis placed first in his class at the Martinière Technical School in Lyons during a period in which he was pursuing the improvement of a type of photographic plate known as a gelatin-bromide, or "dry" plate. Since the early 1850's, the most practicable kind of photographic material for picture taking was the collodion, or "wet" plate, which required that a darkroom be available near the camera for the manipulation of the plate both before and after exposure. A more convenient dry-plate material was avidly researched in the early 1870's, and by the end of the decade dry plates were widely available from manufacturers in Europe and the United States, providing greater convenience as well as increased emulsion speed to photographers. With the encouragement and the financial support of their father, in 1882 Louis and Auguste entered into the production of an improved dry plate, and in 1883 a company with the name Antoine Lumière et Ses Fils (Antoine Lumière and sons) began operating at 21 Chemin de Saint Victor in Lyons. The initial daily production of sixty dozen plates increased dramatically as Louis' "blue label," plate became famous; in 1886, the factory produced nearly 1.5 million of them, and by 1894 annual production had reached 15 million.

The individual contributions of Louis and Auguste to the family enterprises are seldom easy to distinguish during this early period. It is clear that both brothers had a considerable knowledge of organic chemistry, which formed the basis of numerous researches into the nature of photographic materials. In general, however, Louis' scientific interests inclined toward physics, while Auguste was drawn to biochemistry and medicine. Their investigations reveal strong theoretical knowledge combined with a desire to make material improvements of economic value. These traits, combined with the brothers' managerial acumen, allowed the Lumière business to thrive in its early years, setting the stage for more far-reaching advances in the 1890's.

Life's Work

From the first public appearance of photography in 1839, its monochromatic character was widely considered a shortcoming of the medium, and many researchers attempted to devise a method of generating the colors of nature on photographic plates and prints. Some approaches to the problem that were theoretically sound were impractical for widespread use, such as the method of the English scientist James Clerk Maxwell, who showed in 1861 that a photographic representation of the colors of the spectrum could be achieved by recording a scene by photographing it on three separate plates through red, green, and blue filters. The physical result of Maxwell's demonstration was a projected image, which was inadequate mostly because of the unequal sensitivity of the emulsions of the day to the various colors of light. The first successful experiments in the production of color prints, which could be viewed in a conventional manner, were carried out in 1868 and 1869 by a French investigator, Louis Ducos du Hauron. This investigator made negatives through blue, green, and orange filters and then superimposed red, yellow, and blue monochrome positives made from these to produce a color print. The foundations of color photography, which involved many other talented inventors, were well established when the Lumière brothers began to consider problems of color photography in the early 1890's. Their diverse experiments, later culminating in the Autochrome process, are chiefly notable not for their originality but for their technical refinement, which was achieved through methodical experimentation supported by the expert staff of technical personnel employed in the Lumière laboratories.

An early indicator of the brothers' involvement in exacting methodologies was their improvement of a technique introduced by the physicist Gabriel Lippmann, in which the interference property of light enabled colors to be photographed directly upon a silver halide emulsion which could be processed in a customary manner. In the summer of 1893, Auguste and Louis were the first to produce a portrait in natural colors, which was shown at the International Photographic Exhibition in Geneva, Switzerland. The Lumières' contribution to Lippmann's process, characteristically, was to apply their advanced emulsion technology to the problem, supplanting Lippmann's albumen and potassium bromide emulsion with a particularly fine-grained gelatin-bromide emulsion. Of special importance in this and subsequent color experiments was the Lumières' expertise in extending the spectral sensitivity of their plates from the inherent range of blue to green light into the yellow and red region, a virtual necessity to the future practicability of color photography.

In the midst of these successful experiments, which were conducted in an atmosphere of financial prosperity for the Lumière family, Louis and Auguste became interested in the budding technology of moving pictures. As with research in color

Auguste Lumière with his kinescope.

photography, which despite mixed successes occupied many talented individuals over a period of decades, the development of the motion picture was a goal pursued by seemingly countless inventors. No single contribution to early film technology represents a crucial advance without which the advent of the cinema would have been greatly delayed, and the technical innovations supplied by the Lumières should be ascribed more to effective technical problem solving than to theoretical or mechanical genius.

The preeminent figure in early attempts to record motion with a photographic apparatus was Eadweard Muybridge, an Englishman who had become an accomplished photographer while working as a bookseller in San Francisco, California. Muybridge's well-documented work was initially aimed at analyzing the motion of the horse and later grew to encompass the photography of humans and animals in motion. Around 1880, he developed an apparatus for projecting sequences of his instantaneous serial photographs of horses, but the dura-

2278 / THE TWENTIETH CENTURY: AUGUSTE LUMIÈRE AND LOUIS LUMIÈRE

tion of the sequence thus synthesized was limited by the placement of the photographs on the circumference of a glass disc. In the early 1880's, the charismatic Muybridge met and influenced the American inventor Thomas Edison and the French physiologist Étienne-Jules Marey, both of whom soon contributed innovations to the photography of movement. By 1889, Edison and his associates had produced his "kinetograph," a device for taking motion photographs on a continuous strip of photographic paper 35 millimeters wide; this device was joined in 1893 by a "kinetoscope" for viewing the kinetograph pictures. The kinetoscope "peep box," which accommodated only one viewer at a time, was popular but was clearly vulnerable to competition from a successful projection system.

In the summer of 1894, Louis and Auguste began their work upon the problem of the projection of moving images. Louis later stated that the main problem to be solved was that of driving the strip of film bearing the series of images. Edison's kinetoscope operated by passing a continuously moving strip of paper in front of a viewing lens, employing a slotted disk to hide the view of the paper except during the instant the images passed under the lens, an arrangement which compromised clarity for simplicity. One night when Louis was unable to sleep, the solution to this problem came to him: It was to adapt the "presser foot" mechanism of the sewing machine to the camera, permitting the photographic material to be advanced in quick steps in front of the lens and to be momentarily stationary during exposure. Louis gave sketches of his idea to the chief mechanic at the Lumière works, who built the prototype camera which was to become known as the "Cinématograph." At first, Louis used strips of photographic paper in the camera to verify the quality of his apparatus, and then as sheets of celluloid film became available from the United States they were cut, perforated for the presser foot mechanism, and sensitized in the Lumière factory for use in the camera.

Louis Lumière later stated that after he arrived at the presser-foot concept, Auguste ceased being interested in the technical side of the invention. This statement, however, does not imply any sense of antagonism between the brothers. Throughout their careers, Louis and Auguste signed jointly the work on which they reported as well as the patents they filed. On the basis of this record of collaboration, as well as upon photographs and films of the Lumière family, it appears that the brothers greatly esteemed each other. An interview with Louis, filmed for French television only months before his death, also reveals his affection for his colleagues and employees of former years.

The development of the Cinematograph was partly a leisure-time activity for the Lumière brothers, but they were not indifferent to the commercial potential of their invention and cleverly added two important features to the device: The camera was used not only to make the negative the original scene but also to print the required positive image from it, which was then projected by the camera apparatus itself. This versatility, combined with the excellence of the projections, gave the Cinematograph a competitive advantage over other systems appearing in the same period. Louis' first film, *La Sortie des ouvriers de l'usine Lumière* (*Workers Leaving the Lumière Factory*), was made at the end of the summer of 1894 and was first shown to the public in Paris before the Société d'Encouragement pour l'Industrie Nationale on March 22, 1895. The first commercial showing of the invention took place on December 28 in the Salon Indien, a basement room of the Grand Café located on the Boulevard des Capuchines in Paris. The press was initially indifferent, and the proprietor of the café, skeptical of the moneymaking potential of the show, declined the Lumières' offer of 20 percent of receipts from admissions in favor of a daily rental of thirty francs. After three weeks, the show of nine or ten brief films was earning an average of twenty-five hundred francs per day.

The success of the Cinematograph propelled the Lumières into a new business of producing, distributing, and presenting films in France and elsewhere. Louis himself was for a time an avid film photographer and showed a flair for exploiting the new and often startling properties of the medium—it was reported that when his film *L'Arrivée du train en gare* (the arrival of the train at the station) was first shown, spectators dived for cover at the rapid approach of the train, which seemed to be happening in reality and not in shadows upon a screen. Auguste also used the camera but was much less involved in this branch of their activity. As more Cinematograph machines were constructed, the conduct of the fledgling industry passed almost wholly into the hands of collaborators and employees.

As the Cinematograph and its many competitors became a commonplace, Louis again turned to researches in color photography, typically following up solid leads by earlier investigators with the intention of producing a commercially viable medium. On May 30, 1904, he presented the Autochrome process to a session of the Académie des Sciences in Paris (though the material did not become commercially available until 1907). The Autochrome process depends upon the property of minute spots of color to fuse visually, at an appropriate distance from the viewer's eye, into a gradation of intermediate colors. A glass plate was evenly coated with a thin layer of starch grains colored red, green, and blue, which was lightly rolled and then dusted with an opaque material to fill in the spaces between the grains. A gelatin-bromide emulsion, carefully sensitized to record all the colors of the visible spectrum, was then applied over the layer of starch grains. After exposure in a conventional camera, the emulsion was developed to a positive image through which the mosaic of starch grains could again be seen. The plate had to be viewed by transmitted light, as a transparency. Where the image of a red object had fallen upon the emulsion, the image was relatively clear in those areas corresponding to the red starch grains and allowed light passing through the grains to represent the color of the object. Other colors were similarly shown—violet, for example, being the blending of blue and red spots moderately exposed. Yellow, in keeping with the optical theory of the mixture of primaries of colored light, was composed of a mixture of red and green mosaic components. Thus, the entire visible spectrum was recorded with some degree of success. Most important, however, the Autochrome plate could be handled by the photographer much like any dry-plate material and made color photography widely available. The Autochrome medium was relatively expensive, required longer exposures than did most black-and-white materials, and did not prodce images of great brilliance, but it was widely accepted by professional and amateur photographers alike. For many years it was unexcelled in its class of materials, and it remained in production for more than three decades.

Summary

With many inventions to their credit, Auguste Lumière and Louis Lumière did not relax their activity in scientific and technological research. Auguste concentrated increasingly upon medical topics in tuberculosis, cancer, and pharmacology. In 1914, he was named head of the radiology department of a major hospital and in 1928 published his book *La Vie, la maladie, et la mort: Phénomènes colloïdaux* (life, illness and death: colloidal phenomena). Louis' interest in cinema and optical instrumentation continued, resulting in methods of measuring objects in relief by photographic means (1920) and relief cinematography (1935). Both brothers received public honors, Auguste being elected to the Legion of Honor like his father before him, and Louis becoming a member of the Academy of Sciences. Louis, the younger brother, died on June 6, 1948, at age eighty-three, and Auguste died six years later on April 10, 1954, at the age of ninety-one.

Auguste and Louis Lumière seem to embody the optimism of nineteenth century science, which offered apparently limitless material improvements to society. Louis was particularly comfortable in the world of daily events, and some commentators have remarked upon the rationalist, extroverted quality of his early Cinematograph films as evidence of a representative cultural sensibility embracing the materialist ethos of modern industrial society. Some critics have even described him as a kind of symbolic father of the documentary branch of the art of film and have contrasted him with his near contemporary, the theatrical filmmaker George Méliès. While one might doubt that Louis Lumière approached filmmaking with a conscious aesthetic, his brief turn as a producer of films was more than an accident of fate, and in this connection it should be noted that his father was first a painter and only later an industrialist. That both Louis and Auguste were avid photographers seems natural in view of their business interests, but the progress of their varied careers suggests that, beyond being generalists in an increasingly specialized world, they lived with the confidence that their efforts, wherever directed, would be both useful to society and profitable to them.

Bibliography

Eder, Josef Maria. *History of Photography*. Translated by Edward Epstean. New York: Columbia University Press, 1945. Although indispensable to the study of the history of photography, this largely technical treatise dating from the turn of the century is occasionally poorly organized. Eder, a contemporary of the Lumières, was a participant in many of the advances of the day, which lends flavor and authenticity to the book.

Jones, Bernard E., ed. *Cassell's Cyclopaedia of Photography*. London and New York: Cassell, 1911. This work can be consulted for a revealing glimpse of the physical and chemical complexity of the preparation of an Autochrome plate.

Lumière, Auguste, and Louis Lumière. *Letters: Inventing the Cinema*. Translated by Pierre Hodgson. London and Boston: Faber, 1997. A collection of letters by the Lumières with a preface by Louis' grandson, Maurice Trarieux-Lumière.

Lumière, Louis. "The Lumière Cinematograph." In *A Technological History of Motion Pictures and Television*, compiled by Raymond Fielding. Berkeley: University of California Press, 1967. This article is Louis Lumière's account not only of the Cinematograph apparatus but also of a monumental projection arrangement for the "Gallery of Machines" at the Paris Exposition of 1898.

Macgowan, Kenneth. *Behind the Screen: The History and Techniques of the Motion Picture*. New York: Delacorte Press, 1965. The author does a fine job of untangling the complex web of inventions leading to, and beyond, the introduction of the Lumières' Cinematograph.

Rosenblum, Naomi A. *World History of Photography*. 3d ed. New York: Abbeville Press, 1997. This beautifully illustrated volume has surprising depth for a survey of the history of photography. Particularly valuable are the reproductions of Autochrome photographs and concise accounts of early color photography methods, though the latter are not invariably clear.

Sadoul, Georges. "Louis Lumière: The Last Interview." In *Rediscovering French Film*, edited by Mary Lea Bandy. New York: Museum of Modern Art, 1982. In the absence of a translation from the French of Sadoul's book on Louis Lumière, this short but poignant article is the best introduction to Louis in the context of the art of the film.

Walter, Claude. "The Story of Lumière." In *Ciba Journal*, Spring, 1964: 28-35. Useful for its unique photographs and human anecdotes, this article consists largely of an account of the integration of the Lumière business into the Ciba Company.

C. S. McConnell

ALBERT LUTULI

Born: c. 1898; near Bulawayo, Rhodesia (now Zimbabwe)

Died: July 21, 1967; Stanger, South Africa

Areas of Achievement: Civil rights, social reform, government, and politics

Contribution: In 1960, Lutuli became the first African to receive the Nobel Peace Prize. This international honor recognized his commitment to nonviolent means to free South Africans from apartheid and to restore the honor of Africa.

Early Life

Albert John Mvumbi ("Continuous Rain") Lutuli ("Dust") was born to South African parents in Rhodesia (now Zimbabwe). Lutuli was an infant when his father died. In 1908, Lutuli's mother returned to Natal and sent her son to Groutville to live with his uncle, Chief Martin Lutuli. Young Lutuli's formal education was influenced by rural isolation and American missionaries, whose interaction gave him a slight American accent. In 1922, he accepted a faculty position at Adams Mission Station College and came under the influence of his renowned colleague, Zacharia Keodireland Matthews. In 1933, Lutuli became president of the African Teachers' Association.

Lutuli's devout Christianity led to church-sponsored trips to India in 1938 and the United States in 1948. While in the United States, Lutuli often spoke of his quest to merge Christianity with traditional African beliefs. His religion and sheltered life with his uncle helped shield him from the racist policies of South African government. These early experiences help explain why he was an advocate of nonviolence and free from bitterness when he entered politics late in life.

In 1927, Lutuli married Nokukhanya ("The Bright One") Bhengu. Their happy marriage produced three sons and four daughters and encouraged his fondness for singing, sense of humor, and ability to put people at ease. His wife supported him throughout his difficult political career and convinced him that women had a pivotal role to play in the antiapartheid movement.

Life's Work

In 1936, Lutuli exchanged his comfortable academic life for the government-paid, elected office of chief of five thousand Abase-Makolweni Zulus. From Groutville, Lutuli's position of responsibility gradually revealed vistas of government-induced suffering and deprivation. By the time he had reached his mid-forties, Lutuli realized that the government needed more than prayer; in 1945, he joined the Natal chapter of the African National Congress (ANC). Six years later, he became president of the Natal chapter. In the meantime, the national ANC was changing course.

In 1944, Nelson Mandela and Oliver Tambo helped organize the Youth League to replace ANC policies of petitions and deputations with mass mobilization. On June 26, 1952, the Defiance Campaign was launched. Discriminatory laws of apartheid were intentionally disobeyed; Lutuli and more than 8,500 protestors filled the jails. After the government dismissed Lutuli as chief in November, 1952, the ANC elected him president-general in December, 1952. Under Lutuli's leadership the Youth League's nonviolent, mass demonstration policies came of age.

In May, 1953, the government acted again. Lutuli was banned from attending public gatherings and from visiting some twenty cities for a year. Nevertheless, Lutuli's dignified, moderate speeches continued to be read. His demand of a South Africa in which all people participated in government was rejected by the government. In July, 1954, Lutuli was banned for two years and confined to a twenty-mile radius of Groutville. His popularity with South African blacks increased with each ban. ANC leaders secretly met Lutuli in the isolation of Natal's sugarcane country and reelected him president-general in 1955 and 1958.

Under Lutuli's leadership, the ANC joined other antiapartheid groups in the Congress Alliance. Together a national convention was organized to discuss South Africa's future. Recommendations from many South Africans were considered by an alliance committee responsible for drafting the Freedom Charter. Lutuli was kept informed about plans for the conference throughout the remainder of 1954, but his stroke in mid-January, a two-month period of convalescence, and his banning prevented him from contributing to the draft of the Freedom Charter or attending the convention.

From June 25 to 26 near Johannesburg, some three thousand delegates discussed and approved the Freedom Charter. Lutuli and the ANC Executive Committee endorsed it a few months later. The ten articles combined liberty, democracy, and so-

cialism. The ANC's highest award, the Isitwaland-we ("one who has fought courageously in battle"), was presented to Lutuli in absentia. Police broke up the meeting shortly before the end of the second day.

In December, 1956, Lutuli and other activists were charged with treason. The Treason Trial increased Lutuli's stature among South African blacks and gave him much international recognition. Months of interrogation only produced his release in late 1957, although the trial lasted until March 29, 1961, when the remaining defendants were acquitted. Between late 1957 and mid-1959, Lutuli enjoyed relative freedom of speech and movement. He advocated reason to prevail in race relations to a wide variety of South African audiences and sought international support for a black boycott of certain South African produce. The government responded in May, 1959, by banning Lutuli for five years.

While government bans undermined Lutuli's leadership in the ANC, the organization itself suffered a serious rift. A disgruntled faction called Africanists left and founded a new black nationalist movement in April, 1959. The Pan Africanist Congress (PAC) opposed the Freedom Charter and Lutuli's nonracial alliance policies, charged that white communists and Indians within the ANC were pursuing their own ends, and demanded black exclusiveness in their struggle to create a black-dominated South African state. Lutuli and Mandela rejected PAC's platform and argued to no avail that the real problem was apartheid.

PAC's first nonviolent mass campaign, Anti-Pass Day, was set for March 21, 1961. At Sharpeville sixty-nine men, women, and children were shot and killed while fleeing government police. Lutuli burned his passbook, urged others to do likewise, and declared a National Day of Mourning to be observed by staying at home. Government repression increased. A state of emergency was declared on March 30, the ANC and PAC were outlawed on April 5, and Lutuli and more than eighteen thousand activists were arrested by May 6. The government released Lutuli after five months' detention with a six-month suspended prison sentence. The timing was convenient.

On December 10, 1961, in Oslo, Norway, Lutuli received the Nobel Peace Prize awarded to him the previous year. The Nobel Committee had chosen Lutuli because of his courage, humanity, and nonviolent tactics to promote social reform. Lutuli was the first African to receive this honor. During his acceptance speech, Lutuli called for international sanctions against South Africa, a nonracial, democratic government, and the redemption of the honor of Africa from centuries of racist slander. The government prohibited Lutuli from addressing cheering crowds that welcomed his return and banned his autobiography. Shortly afterward, Lutuli bought two farms in Swaziland with his prize money; they would serve as havens for political exiles from South Africa. Years later, the farms were sold to fund the Lutuli Memorial Scholarships.

Without consulting Lutuli, Nelson Mandela and other ANC leaders decided in June, 1961, to adopt violent tactics. Umkonto We Sizwe ("Spear of the Nation") was created to attack strategic targets of apartheid without loss of life. Explosions damaged electric power stations and government buildings in the wake of Lutuli's return from Norway. As the president-general considered resigning over this policy change, the government in late June, 1962, prohibited Lutuli's words from being reproduced in any form. Two months later, Mandela, now underground, met secretly with Lutuli. The president-general criticized both Umkonto's announcement in December, 1961, that the period of nonviolence had ended and Mandela for neither consulting Lutuli nor the ANC grassroots membership. Mandela defended Umkonto and argued that Lutuli was not consulted, in order to protect the Nobel laureate. The next day, August 5, 1962, Mandela was captured.

On July 11, 1963, the police captured Umkonto's leadership. After they were tried and given life sentences, Lutuli proclaimed that the imprisoned leaders of Umkonto represented the highest in morality and ethics, that no one could blame them for seeking justice by using violent methods, and that the ANC had never abandoned its policy of nonviolence. The following year, Lutuli called on the United States to implement full sanctions against South Africa.

Lutuli's courageous leadership and international acclaim earned for him many honors. When the government left the British Commonwealth to become a republic, the South African Coloured People's Congress nominated Lutuli for president. Lutuli received the Christopher Gell Memorial Award (1961), a rectorship at the University of Glasgow (1962), a visit from Robert Kennedy (1966), United Nations recognition for outstanding achievements in human rights (1968), and the Organization of African Unity's tenth anniversary medal for service to humanity (1974).

On July 21, 1967, Lutuli died from multiple injuries after being struck by a train while walking across the Umvoti railway bridge in Stanger. Alan Paton, a friend and writer who gave the funeral tribute at the Groutville Congregational Church, said aptly, "History will make his voice speak again."

Summary

Albert Lutuli devoted his life to end apartheid through nonviolent methods. As a Christian, teacher, chief, and ANC leader, Lutuli relied on faith and optimism to reform South Africa and to restore the honor of Africa. In spite of being banned, charged, or imprisoned almost constantly between May, 1953, and July, 1967, Lutuli transformed the ANC into an effective, internationally recognized organization. Still, he had his critics. Some argued that Lutuli's bannings made him a figurehead and permitted the left wing to seize control of the ANC. Other critics argued that Lutuli's idealism and moral scruples precluded viable options. Still other critics argued that Lutuli wasted the ANC's limited physical resources. Critics aside, communications within the ANC were always difficult: Long hours, low wages, a dearth of room and board, an overwhelmingly illiterate, multilingual population, and government bannings of ANC leaders were all obstacles to Lutuli's leadership. In addition, region, class, Lutuli's isolation, and communist and Africanist members all contributed to the complexity of the ANC. Given these difficulties, it is a wonder that Lutuli, the humble, dignified mediator, succeeded at all. By promoting human rights, nonviolence, and democracy, Lutuli earned worldwide respect and renown. Lutuli contributed significantly to the process of social and political reform in South Africa by transforming from rhetoric into reality one of his favorite slogans—"Mayibuye Afrika" ("Come back Africa").

Bibliography

Benson, Mary. *Chief Albert Lutuli of South Africa*. London: Oxford University Press, 1963. An outstanding, early biography that is now a standard. Benson takes the best of Lutuli's autobiography, adds other sources and Paton's "Praise Song for Lutuli," and assesses the chief's contribution to events in South Africa until 1963— all in seventy-one pages.

Callan, Edward. *Albert John Luthuli and the South African Race Conflict*. Rev. ed. Kalamazoo: Western Michigan University Press, 1965. This is another outstanding, early, brief biography. Contains good analysis, Lutuli's Nobel Peace Prize address, and valuable bibliographic notes and a selected reading list for further research.

Gordimer, Nadine. "Chief Luthuli." *Atlantic* 203 (April, 1959): 34-39. This eloquent, short biographical sketch of Lutuli is superb for younger readers. Its weakness is that it was written just before he was awarded the Nobel Peace Prize.

Joseph, Helen. *Side by Side: The Autobiography of Helen Joseph*. London: Zed, and New York: Morrow, 1986. A strong, often persecuted opponent of the South African government and one of Lutuli's non-ANC allies assesses the character and impact of her "Beloved Chief." Joseph gives a recent, sympathetic interpretation of Lutuli. The work contains interesting anecdotes about Lutuli.

Karis, Thomas, and Gwendolyn M. Carter, eds. *From Protest to Challenge: A Documentary History of African Politics in South Africa, 1882-*

1964. 4 vols. Stanford, Calif.: Hoover Institution Press, 1977. These four volumes are clearly the most valuable yet compiled on the relationship between the ANC and Lutuli. Perspective and analysis are outstanding. Many of Lutuli's most important speeches are reprinted and discussed here.

Legum, Colin, and Margaret Legum. *The Bitter Choice: Eight South Africans' Resistance to Tyranny*. Cleveland, Ohio: World, 1968. The chapter on Lutuli was written just after his death and contains a balance between the Legums'

analysis and quotations from Lutuli's writings. This rather brief effort has the advantage of some hindsight.

Luthuli, Albert. *Let My People Go*. London: Collins, and New York: McGraw-Hill, 1962. Written with the help of friends, this work is a typical autobiography. While it gives readers important facts about the author's life and a perspective from the center of activity, it lacks the circumspection only an objective observer can provide.

Kenneth Wilburn

ROSA LUXEMBURG

Born: March 5, 1871; Zamość, Poland, Russian
  Empire
Died: January 15, 1919; Berlin, Germany
Areas of Achievement: Social reform, philosophy,
  and journalism
Contribution: Luxemburg was a leading figure in
  the left wing of the German Social Democratic
  Party, and she played a key role in the founding
  of the Polish Social Democratic Party and the
  German Communist Party. An able, indefatigable journalist and writer, she developed a humanistic version of Marxism that emphasized
  internationalism, mass participation, a dislike of
  violence, and opposition to gradual reformism.

Early Life

Born in 1871, Rozalia Luksenburg (her name until
1889) was reared and educated in the Polish city of
Warsaw, then a part of the Russian Empire. The
youngest child in a secular Jewish family of the
lower middle class, her personal experiences with
anti-Semitism, including a violent pogrom in 1881,
resulted in a strong aversion toward Polish nationalism. She was always an excellent, hardworking
student, and in high school she was converted to
Marxist socialism, with her academic record indicating "a rebellious attitude." Because of harassment from the Russian authorities and also because
no Polish universities were open to women, she decided in 1889 to emigrate to Switzerland to study
at the University of Zurich.

In Zurich, Luxemburg was a brilliant student of
law and political science, receiving her doctorate in
1897. Her doctoral thesis, published in book form,
was a study of the development of capitalism in
Poland, and it emphasized that because of Poland's
dependence on the Russian economy, independence was highly impractical. Zurich was a center
for radical refugees from Eastern Europe, and Luxemburg energetically participated in Socialist activities, becoming a friend of Russian Social Democrats such as Georgy Plekhanov. It was also at this
time that she began her long intimacy with Leo
Jogiches, a young revolutionary from Lithuania.

Luxemburg and Jogiches, employing Jogiches'
considerable inheritance, founded the Social Democracy of the Kingdom of Poland and Lithuania
(the nucleus of the future Communist Party of Poland), and Luxemburg worked as the chief editor of
the group's newspaper, *The Workers' Cause.* At
this time, most Polish Socialists were strong nationalists who wanted independence for their country, but Luxemburg and her followers rejected such
a goal as contrary to the principles of international
solidarity. This persistent distrust of national aspirations would remain one of the major themes of
Luxemburg's thought.

Completely fluent in the use of the German language, after graduation Luxemburg decided to
move to Germany. She was having trouble with the
Swiss authorities, and the German Social Democratic Party, the largest and most powerful Socialist
organization of the world, dominated the Second
International. To gain German citizenship, in 1898
she temporarily married Gustav Lübeck, the son of
one of her friends, and she then moved to the capital city of Berlin.

Life's Work

As Luxemburg was establishing herself in Germany, the socialist revisionist, Eduard Bernstein,
was publishing a controversial series of articles,
later translated into the book *Evolutionary Socialism.* Bernstein argued that Marx's idea of a violent upheaval was no longer necessary and that in
modern industrial countries workers could improve their conditions through a combination of
parliamentary reforms and trade union activities.
Luxemberg believed that Bernstein was attacking
the "corner-stone of scientific socialism," which
was the inevitable collapse of capitalism. Refuting his thesis in *Sozialreform oder Revolution?*
(1899; *Reform or Revolution?*, 1937), she argued
that, while reforms might be of some help in promoting the struggle, the liberation of the workers
could only occur with the radical transformation
from capitalism to socialism.

Luxemburg was one of the first to attack revisionism, and she took the position that was then
supported by Karl Kautsky and most of the leadership of the Second International. Bernstein was
generally looked upon as a heretic within the Socialist movement, although selective aspects of his
revisionism continued gradually to gain acceptance. This polemical controversy promoted Luxemburg's career, and henceforth she was recognized as a leader in the left wing of the movement.

The Russian/Polish Revolution of 1905 was one
of the central events in Luxemburg's life. Like

most Marxists, she was surprised by the uprising, since she had expected that a workers' revolution would first occur in an advanced country such as Germany. Hopeful that this would be the beginning of an international revolution, she rushed to Warsaw, where she energetically took part in the final stages of the event. Taken prisoner and charged with illegal activities, she was able to jump bail and to return to Berlin. This exciting experience, and especially the use of general strikes, helped Luxemburg to formulate her theory of revolutionary mass action, published in *Massenstreik: Partei und Gewerkschaften* (1906; *The Mass Strike: The Political Party and the Trade Unions*, 1925). Arguing that a large-scale strike was the most useful tool that the proletariat possessed, she explained that such revolutionary praxis would result from the workers' realization of their exploitation under capitalism. Such views were contrary to many of the theories of Vladimir Ilich Lenin.

Having emerged as the leader of the Bolshevik faction of the Russian Social Democrats, Lenin wanted to organize the party according to the disciplined model of the armed forces, declaring that an elitist party would be the "vanguard of the working classes." In contrast, Luxemburg minimized the necessity for a tight organizational structure and assumed that a "self-administration" of the workers would emerge from the class struggle. Contrary to what is sometimes suggested, she did not entirely eliminate the role of party leadership, but rather she wanted it to concentrate upon the work of developing the revolutionary consciousness of the proletariat. She charged that Lenin's theory, in practice, would result in a dictatorship of a small elite over the workers.

Recognized as both a serious scholar and a dynamic speaker, Luxemburg joined the teaching staff of the prestigious Social Democratic Party School in Berlin, working there from 1907 to 1914. Even with her busy schedule, she wrote and published a major work of socialist economics, *Die Akkumulation des Kapitals* (1913; *The Accumulation of Capital*, 1951). In this large and complex book, she maintained that imperialism was a consequence of the need for capitalists to find markets for their products, and, when the less developed areas would begin to disappear, capitalism would no longer be able to survive. With the perspective of time, it is generally recognized that this book greatly underestimated the ability for change and adaptation under

a capitalist system. Critics called this the "automatic collapse of capitalism" theory, but Luxemburg always insisted that revolutionary praxis would be necessary for the triumph of socialism.

Increasingly dissatisfied with the moderation of the German Social Democrats, Luxemburg incessantly pushed for militant actions to bring about the revolution, which she believed was inevitable. Kautsky and other party leaders, in contrast, became more devoted to a program of legal gradualism, often called a "strategy of attrition." When Kautsky refused to publish one of her articles in 1910, she began to criticize his leadership with the same vehemence with which she had earlier denounced Bernstein; this criticism intensified the deep split between the left and right wings of the party.

With the outbreak of World War I in 1914, the Social Democratic majority supported the military policies of the German government. Luxemburg bitterly criticized this cooperation, and, because of her antiwar activities, she spent most of the years 1915-1918 in prison, where she maintained close contact with Karl Liebknecht and other radical Socialists. Although not directly involved in the founding of the Spartacus League in 1916, she provided a theoretical defense for the new organization in *Die Krise des Sozialdemokratie* (1916; *the Crisis in the German Social Democracy*, 1918). This pamphlet, signed with the pseudonym of "Junius," castigated Social Democratic betrayal and argued that the war presented the opportunity for the workers of the world to unite to overthrow the existing regimes. The actual influence of the Spartacists remained small during the war.

With the German revolution of November, 1918, Luxemburg gained her freedom. She and the impulsive Liebknecht failed in their efforts to gain control of the newly formed Workers' and Soldiers' Councils, and they were actively involved in the founding of the German Communist Party in December. The moderate wing of the Social Democratic Party, under the leadership of Friedrich Ebert and Philipp Scheidemann, gained control of the temporary government, and, against Luxemburg's advice, the Communist Party voted to boycott the elections to a Constituent Assembly. Although she had earlier insisted that any seizure of power would fail without widespread support, she nevertheless enthusiastically participated in the so-called Spartacus insurrection of January 5-13.

While calling for a dictatorship of the proletariat in Germany, Luxemburg tried to distance herself from Lenin's policies in Russia. In her writings during this tubulent and confused period, published posthumously in *Die Russische Revolution* (1922; *The Russian Revolution*, 1940), Luxemburg chastised the Bolsheviks for their support for national self-determination, their division of agricultural lands into private holdings, their suspending of the elections to the Constituent Assembly, and their use of terror to crush the opposition. Social Democrats believed that her analysis of the Russian situation was contradictory with her part in an insurrection attempting to overthrow a democratic republic.

With the brutal crushing of the Spartacus insurrection, Luxemburg and Liebknecht went into hiding, but on January 15 they were discovered and arrested. That same day, extremist soldiers murdered both leaders without trial, throwing Luxemburg's body into the Landwehr Canal. Some of those responsible for the murders were convicted but received ridiculously light sentences.

Summary

Rosa Luxemburg inspired a generation of radicals, and, with her tragic death, she became a martyr to many people of the Left. She was a forceful personality, completely convinced of the moral correctness of her cause, and she had an unusual ability to communicate in both speeches and writings. Historically she is primarily important because of the strength and coherence of her ideas, and "Luxemburgism" represents one of the major systems of Marxist theory.

Although a radical Marxist, Luxemburg was clearly dedicated to a number of liberal and humanistic values. In spite of her actions of 1919, she was committed to the preservation of democratic institutions, writing that "the elimination of democracy as such is worse than the disease it is supposed to cure." If she believed that some violence would be necessary for the establishment of socialism, she wanted it to be limited and temporary. Although not always consistent on the topic of liberty, she insisted that she did not want to end the freedom to oppose the government, declaring that "freedom is always and exclusively freedom for the one who thinks differently." In like manner, she spoke out in favor of equality and human brotherhood. A feminist, she refused to limit her concerns to half of humanity. For those who concentrated upon oppression of the Jews, she wrote that "poor victims on the rubber plantations in Putamayo, the Negroes in Africa with whose bodies the Europeans play a game of catch, are just as near to me."

Despite her influence in leftist circles, Luxemburg was ultimately unsuccessful because of the circumstances of the time and also because of the questionable validity of some of her assumptions. Both in her tactics and in the development of her theories, Luxemburg used general principles in making logical deductions, but she tended to disregard empirical facts that did not correspond with these deductions. In spite of the evidence to the contrary, therefore, Luxemburg insisted that it was impossible for real improvement in the condition of the workers under capitalism. Tenaciously holding to an abstract view of workers committed to internationalism, she ignored manifest evidence of their patriotism and national identity. When she made the mistake of supporting a hopeless insurrection in 1919, her decision was based upon abstract theory rather than a realistic analysis of the situation.

Bibliography

Cocks, Joan. "From Politics to Paralysis: Critical Intellectuals Answer the National Question." *Political Theory* 24, no. 3 (August, 1996). Examines Luxemburg's attempt to define nationalism along with thoughts on the subject by Tom Nairn, Ernest Gellner, and Benedict Anderson.

Ettinger, Elżbieta. *Rosa Luxemburg: A Life.* Boston: Beacon Press, 1986; London: Harrap, 1987. Based upon many Polish and German sources, this scholarly book is as fascinating as any novel. Although there are summaries of her views, the emphasis is upon her personality, her conflicts, her efforts to promote revolution, and her love affairs and friendships. The best introductory account for the general reader.

Frölich, Paul. *Rosa Luxemburg: Her Life and Work.* Translated by Johanna Hoornweg. London: Gollancz, 1940; New York: Fertig, 1969. Standard Marxist biography, written by a member of the SPD opposition during World War I. Frölich minimizes the disagreements between Lenin and Luxemburg.

Kolakowski, Leszek. *Main Currents in Marxism.* Vol. 2, *The Golden Age*, translated by P. S. Falla. Oxford: Clarendon Press, 1978; New York: Oxford University Press, 1981. An erudite study of Marxist thought during the years of the Second International, with excellent chapters devoted to Luxemburg, Kautsky, Lenin, Jaures, and Bernstein.

Lim, Jie-Hyun. "Rosa Luxemburg on the Dialectics of Proletarian Internationalism and Social Patriotism." *Science and Society* 59, no. 4 (Winter 1995). Lim considers Luxemburg's socialist philosophies in comparison to Austrian-Marxists' and proposes that a more complete understanding of Luxemburg must be accompanied by freedom from nihilist labels.

Luxemburg, Rosa. *The Letters of Rosa Luxemburg.* Edited by Stephen Bonner. Boulder, Colo.: Westview Press, 1978. An excellent selection of more than one hundred letters dealing with socialist theory as well as personal relationships, including an excellent fifty-page introduction to Luxemburg's life and thought.

————. *Rosa Luxemburg Speaks.* Edited by Mary Alice Walters. New York: Pathfinder Press, 1970. The best collection of important speeches and articles, with interesting annotations written from a Leninist perspective.

Nettl, J. Peter. *Rosa Luxemburg.* 2 vols. London and New York: Oxford University Press, 1966. The most comprehensive and objective study of Luxemburg, with an emphasis on her ideas and career, making an exhaustive use of a wealth of sources.

Schorske, Carl. *German Social Democracy, 1905-1917.* Cambridge, Mass.: Harvard University Press, 1955. An excellent analysis of the conflict between the left and right wings of the SDP during some of the most active years of Luxemburg's career.

Thomas T. Lewis

DAME ENID MURIEL LYONS

Born: July 9, 1897; Duck River, Tasmania, Australia

Died: September 2, 1981; Ulverstone, Tasmania, Australia

Areas of Achievement: Government and politics

Contribution: Lyons became the first woman to sit in the Australian House of Representatives (1943-1951) and the first woman to become a federal cabinet minister (1949-1951).

Early Life

Dame Enid Muriel Lyons was born on July 9, 1897, in Duck River (now Smithton), in northern Tasmania. Her mother, née Eliza Taggett, was born in South Australia of Cornish parents; her father, William Charles Burnell, born in Devonshire, England, and an assisted immigrant, worked his way up from sawyer to mill manager. When Enid was seven, the family moved to Cooee and lived in a house with a general store attached, a means of supplementing their income. She had two sisters, Nellie and Annie, and a younger brother, Bertram. The three girls attended school at Burnie. At age fourteen, Enid followed Nellie to the Teachers' Training College in the capital, Hobart.

Teaching, however, was not to be Enid's vocation. On a visit to the state parliament with her mother and Nellie, she charmed one of the Labor members, Joseph A. Lyons, and soon a correspondence began between the two that continued throughout his lifetime. By the time she was seventeen, he was treasurer and minister for education, as well as being her fiancé. Apart from age (her father wanted her to wait until she was twenty), the most serious obstacle to marriage was religion. Enid was reared in the Methodist tradition: She taught Sunday school, sang in the church choir, and played the organ. When Joseph, thirty-five and a Roman Catholic, explained that non-Catholic ceremonies were not recognized by his church, she and her mother accepted an invitation to spend a month at the presbytery in Stanley while studying the tenets of his faith. During this time, Enid was received into the Church. On April 28, 1915, the couple exchanged vows before Father T. J. O'Donnell at St. Brigid's, Wynyard.

A few years later, the Lyonses built a house on a nine-acre plot about a mile and a half outside Devonport. Without sewerage, town water, electricity, or telephone in the early years, "Home Hill" provided a refuge from the many pressures of public life. In April, 1916, Joseph's party went out of government. When, under Lyons' leadership, Labor again lost the election in 1919, the family moved to Hobart so that Joseph could study law and improve the family's precarious finances. Soon after he became premier of Tasmania in October, 1923, however, the family again took up residence at Home Hill.

Life's Work

As her husband advanced in his political career, so did Lyons advance in her political awareness. At his wish she often accompanied him on election tours, her training in elocution proving an advantage when she appeared on the platform as one of the (rare) women speakers. She was a delegate at the momentous Tasmanian conference of the Labor Party in 1921 at which the federal socialization objective—never rescinded—was approved. Both she and her mother, an independent woman with a love of politics, were candidates, albeit unsuccessful, in the 1923 elections, following the passing of a bill (1921) entitling women to sit in the state parliament.

At the request of the federal leader, James H. Scullin, Joseph stood for and in October, 1929, carried the seat of Wilmot in national elections which Labor won handsomely. Gradually, however, Joseph became increasingly unhappy with his government's fiscal policies; he resigned from the cabinet on January 29, 1931, and then on March 13 joined the opposition in a vote of no confidence in the prime minister. A new party, the United Australia Party, accepted Lyons as leader. In the campaign that followed, his wife was, she later wrote, "one of the team." "Let every Australian feel for Australia," she would urge, "what every Englishman feels for England, and every Scot for Scotland; what every Irishman feels for Ireland."

Lyons was now widely acknowledged to be her husband's closest confidante and adviser. "They are not two people," wrote Louise Mack in the *Australian Christian World*, "They are one." After Joseph became prime minister on January 6, 1932, his first act was to write, "Whatever honours or distinctions come are *ours* not mine."

When Lyons arrived at the prime minister's lodge in Canberra she was thirty-five, a rather plump matron who wore little makeup and dressed to suit her husband's conservative tastes. The difference in their ages was thus less apparent: She fitted easily into the mother role assigned by most politicians to women. Privately, she was torn between the needs of her husband and those of their ten children. Four accompanied her to Canberra, six were in boarding school, and their twelfth (one died of pneumonia at age ten months) and last child was born in October of the following year. During these years, as in earlier ones when he was studying law in Hobart, Joseph helped with the care of their children, allowing her to retreat to Home Hill from time to time.

The highlights of his prime ministership for her were their two visits to London—in 1935 for the Royal Jubilee and in 1937 (the year she became Dame Grand Cross of the Order of the British Empire) for the coronation of King George VI—and the two days she and her husband spent at the White House as guests of Franklin D. and Eleanor Roosevelt. On April 7, 1939, however, their wonderful partnership ended. At age fifty-nine, Joseph Lyons was dead.

Such was her standing in the political world that Lyons was offered the nomination of his vacant seat of Wilmot, which she refused. Instead, the electors of Darwin (now Braddon) sent her to Canberra in her own right several years later. This was the seat for which Joseph had once stood—the only time he was unsuccessful—and it encompassed the state seat her mother had contested. Urged on by her own daughter and namesake, and at age forty-six still young enough for a career of her own, Lyons set up campaign headquarters in Devonport. There were seven candidates, three from the United Australia Party, which balked at putting all of its efforts behind a woman. The year was 1943, Australia was at war, and John Curtin's Labor government had introduced many austerity measures affecting the family. Yet it was the postal vote of the men on active service that put Lyons ahead by 816 votes—they had decided, one reportedly said, to give women a go. For the first time since the inauguration of the Commonwealth in 1901, a woman won election to the House of Representatives. At the same time, another of the less populous states, West Australia, sent Dorothy Tangney, an unmarried Catholic schoolteacher, to Canberra as the first woman senator.

The House was crowded on the occasion of Enid Lyons' maiden speech. Nelson T. Johnson, a career diplomat serving as United States Minister to Australia, that night (September 29, 1943) recorded in his private diary that it was "a very fine speech," an opinion shared by all who heard it. During her first three years, she became knowledgeable about matters concerning her constituents: agriculture, potato marketing, mining, and (as Tasmania is an island state) shipping problems. She acted independently in the matter of a bill to set up an aluminum industry in her home state, ensuring the Tasmanian parliament a say in its disposition and risking her party's displeasure by voting with the Labor government. On another occasion she gave the best speech of her parliamentary career when opposing a section of the Stevedoring Industry Bill which smacked of industrial conscription.

Lyons held her seat after the election of 1946 gave Curtin's successor, J. B. Chifley, a resounding victory. Dressed in her usual simple black dress with white detachable collar, she continued to live up to her reputation as the champion of the family, both in Parliament and in the party room. The determination of the prime minister to pursue his party's socialization objectives, especially the nationalization of banking, lost for him popular support, and in December, 1949, Robert G. Menzies formed a government coalition of the Liberal (in 1944 the successor to the United Australia Party) and Country parties. Lyons won in Darwin by more than four times her original majority. Offered a place in the cabinet, she believed as a public relations exercise, she served in the prestigious post of vice president of the Executive Council for fifteen months. During a bout of ill health (from which she suffered intermittently throughout her life), she reluctantly resigned. Parliament was dissolved shortly afterward and she decided to retire.

Highly regarded as a public speaker and broadcaster, in 1951 Lyons was appointed to the board of the Australian Broadcasting Commission, the national radio service inaugurated in 1932 by Joseph Lyons. During the next eleven years, the American Broadcasting Company's historian (Professor Kenneth Stanley Inglis) says, successive chairmen valued her calm and knowledgeable contribution.

From the early 1920's, when *Woman's Day* published a series of her articles on life as a politician's wife, Lyons wrote occasionally for the press. At the end of her parliamentary career, she produced a twice-weekly syndicated column and several books, the first, as Joseph had wished, an account of their marriage and another about her career in Parliament. On September 2, 1981, Lyons was reported to be seriously ill in a hospital at Ulverstone in northwestern Tasmania, having suffered a series of strokes. She died that day at the age of eighty-four. Her much-loved Home Hill has been preserved for the nation by the National Trust.

Summary

Women in the Australian colonies were among the first in the world to receive the vote. By 1884, those with property, only a small minority to be sure, could participate in municipal elections. In 1896, South Australian women got the right both to vote and to sit in Parliament; West Australian women won the franchise three years later. Under the Australian Constitution (1901), these women were automatically eligible to vote in national elections and to stand for Parliament. The Commonwealth Electoral Act of 1902 extended the same rights to women in all states of the Commonwealth.

The first woman elected to a state parliament was Edith Cowan, who became a member of the legislative assembly in Western Australia in 1921, the year after women became eligible to stand there. When Dame Enid Muriel Lyons entered the House of Representatives in 1943, no woman had yet sat in her state's parliament. New South Wales, Queensland, and Victoria had had women Parliamentarians. Seen in this context, Lyons' achievement is all the greater, since she did not succeed her husband but contested and won a seat in her own right.

Lyons was not the first woman appointed to cabinet rank; that honor again goes to a member of the Western Australian parliament, Dame Florence Cardell-Oliver, in 1947. Yet Lyons was the first woman minister in the national Parliament, thus distinguishing herself at that level.

Bibliography

Encel, Sol, Norman Mackenzie, and Margaret Tebbutt. *Women and Society: An Australian Study.* London: Malaby Press, 1975. See part 5 on "Public Life," especially chapter 15, for background to women in Parliament.

Hetherington, Mollie. "Dame Enid Lyons." In *Famous Australians.* Rev. ed. Melbourne: Hutchinson, 1983. A collection of sixty biographies.

Lyons, Dame Enid. *So We Take Comfort.* London: Heinemann, 1966. Described by Lyons as "the story of our marriage," this autobiographical account of her life ends with his death in 1939.

———. *Among the Carrion Crows.* Adelaide: Rigby, 1972. Continues the story of her career, covering her term in Parliament and as cabinet minister, as well as her life after politics.

Ward, Russel. *A Nation for a Continent: The History of Australia, 1901-1975.* Melbourne: Heinemann, 1977. A useful account of the whole period.

White, Kate. *A Political Love Story: Joe and Enid Lyons.* Melbourne: Penguin, 1987. An interesting account for the general reader, concluding at the death of Joe Lyons.

Annette Potts
E. Daniel Potts

JOSEPH ALOYSIUS LYONS

Born: September 15, 1879; Stanley, Tasmania, Australia

Died: April 7, 1939; Sydney, New South Wales, Australia

Areas of Achievement: Government and politics

Contribution: Winning a reputation as the "financial recovery" leader, first in the Tasmanian state parliament and then at the national level, Lyons broke away from the Australian Labor Party to lead the newly formed United Australia Party to victory in December, 1931, giving the Commonwealth seven years of stable government.

Early Life

Joseph Aloysius Lyons was born on September 15, 1879, in Stanley, Tasmania. His mother, née Ellen Carroll, and father, Michael Henry Lyons, were both born in Ireland. One of eight children, Joseph attended St. Joseph's convent school at Ulverstone. After his father's health failed, he worked for three years to help support the family before resuming his education at the Stanley state school, from which he qualified as a teacher in 1901. He later (1907) achieved the second highest marks for the year among those awarded a certificate in teacher training at the Hobart Teachers' Training College.

While teaching at Smithton in 1906, Lyons became active in the Workers' Political League, the Tasmanian forerunner to the Australian Labor Party. As a member of the State School Teachers' Union, he also publicly criticized the state education system. On March 12, 1909, he resigned from the teaching service to contest the state legislative seat of Wilmot. In October, he became minister for education in the first Labor government in Tasmania; it lasted only a week, but within five years he was again minister for education (as well as treasurer and minister for railways), after a no-confidence vote in April, 1914, brought down the existing government.

These were especially fiery years in Australian politics. Support for Great Britain in the war against Germany was strong, and volunteers of the Australian Imperial Force were fighting in Europe. Determined to bring in conscription for overseas service, however, Labor Prime Minister William Morris Hughes held a referendum and lost. The Labor Party expelled him and many other conscriptionists for contravening party policy opposing compulsory overseas military service. After

elections on May 5, 1917, Hughes, now leader of the Nationalist Party, resumed the prime ministership, called another referendum, and again lost. Vice president of the Hobart United Irish League, Lyons vigorously campaigned for a no-vote. Both times, however, Tasmanians supported conscription, although by a reduced margin the second time.

Labor lost the state election in April, 1916, and shortly afterward Lyons became leader of the opposition. In October, 1923, an internal dispute among the Nationalists resulted in Labor's return, with Lyons as premier and treasurer. His efforts in reforming state finances were rewarded at the polls in 1925 but were not quite enough to retain government in 1928, on the eve of the Depression.

On April 28, 1915, Lyons married Enid Muriel Burnell, a trainee teacher almost eighteen years his junior. A "pretty, blue-eyed cheeky kid," to use his words, she converted to her husband's Catholic faith, though he always liked to listen to her sing the hymns of her Methodist forebears. On November 13, 1916, the first of their twelve children, Gerald Desmond, was born.

A blond and blue-eyed man of amiable appearance, likened by some to a cuddly koala, who walked with a limp following an almost fatal car accident, Lyons was an effective speaker. His voice had a high, slightly nasal quality, more obvious on radio, a medium he soon learned to use skillfully. He was not at ease behind the wheel, preferring that his wife drive the car given to him by sympathetic admirers, though he later unhesitatingly took advantage of plane travel to cover Australia's vast distances when electioneering. He liked people and, his wife said, enjoyed dropping in on friends unannounced.

Life's Work

Although in December, 1919, Lyons failed in an attempt to win the federal seat of Darwin (later Braddon), he continued to find the idea of a larger stage attractive. At the request of the national leader, James H. Scullin, in 1929 he stood for Wilmot, which since 1906 had returned a non-Labor federal member. The people gave Labor the reins, ousting Hughes's replacement, Stanley M. Bruce, for six and a half years leader of a Nationalist-Country Party coalition government. Lyons went to Canberra as a senior member of Scullin's cabinet, having the trust of both the Labor caucus, which selected the ministers, and the prime minister, who allotted the portfolios.

Only prime ministers carried enough weight at imperial conferences, so in 1930 Scullin departed by ship for London, hoping to find the means for alleviating the effects on Australia of the world-wide depression. During his absence, Lyons served as acting treasurer, earning a national reputation for honesty and tenacity. The chairman of the Commonwealth Bank, like Lyons a believer in balanced budgets, refused to extend credit unless government expenditure was also curbed. Unwilling to agree to the Tasmanian's push for pension and other cuts, caucus radicals proposed legislation to postpone redemption of maturing Commonwealth bonds. Lyons threatened to resign. In frequent radio-telephone contact, Scullin supported him and the acting prime minister, James Fenton, accepting their argument for a conversion loan. That it was subscribed within a month was largely a result of the energy with which Lyons conducted the national appeal. On his return, however, Scullin reinstated as treasurer E. G. Theodore, who had temporarily stepped down while allegations of corruption were being investigated. Rather than resume the positions of postmaster general and minister of works and railways, an outraged Lyons resigned from the cabinet.

While the prime minister also instituted stringent financial measures and struggled to contain a party faction still favoring overseas debt repudiation, Lyons accepted leadership of the newly formed United Australia Party (UAP). Incorporating the Nationalists and other non-Labor groups, but excluding the Country Party, the UAP won an absolute majority in Australia's national elections of December, 1931. For the next seven years, until his death, Lyons served as prime minister. It was his government which defused the debt-repudiation issue, bringing about the dismissal of its controversial leader, New South Wales Premier John Thomas Lang.

Lyons was, as Bruce later said, somewhat disparagingly, "a wonderful election winner and a helluva nice bloke," but he was more than that. He preferred to work as part of a team, delegating where necessary, loyally supporting his ministers in their decisions. When after the election in 1934 it became necessary to form a coalition with the Country Party, he worked well with its leader, Sir Earle Page, who admired him immensely.

Using the prime minister's lodge in Canberra as a family residence, Mrs. Lyons (from 1937 Dame Enid and after his death the first woman elected to the House of Representatives) became a national mother figure to the people. To her husband she was much more: She became his closest adviser and shared election platforms with him.

Winning his third successive federal election on October 23, 1937, Lyons began to think seriously about retirement. His health was deteriorating, and he was unhappy about his long separations from Dame Enid, whose chronic ill health forced her to retire periodically from public life. The UAP rejected Robert G. Menzies as a candidate because he lacked Lyons' appeal to the electorate as well as his ability as a conciliator. When Lyons died suddenly on April 7, 1939, however, it was Menzies who eventually succeeded him.

The Australian Broadcasting Commission broadcast nationally the Requiem Mass for the dead prime minister on April 11, 1939, afterward in a moving sequel transmitting the sounds of the horses' hooves and the wheels of the gun carriage carrying his coffin through Sydney streets to the harbor, where HMAS *Vendetta* waited to carry it in state to Tasmania for burial at Devonport. Parliamentary tributes were many. Hughes, another man too big for the inflexible discipline of the Labor Party, captured the essence of the man: "He was a true patriot, he never posed nor boasted of his service. Not for him the tinsel and the glitter that served the pinchbeck patriot and poseur. He served his country zealously but without ostentation." Lyons' estate amounted to a mere £344. After much petty bickering, Parliament provided for his widow and eleven surviving children.

Summary

Joseph Aloysius Lyons preferred to devote himself to domestic matters. Yet he availed himself, during trips abroad in 1935 and 1937, of opportunities to promote the country's trade and defense interests. He incurred the criticism of Jay Pierrepont Moffatt, United States consul general in Sydney, for permitting a trade diversion policy which during 1936-1937 restricted the importation of American goods through high tariffs and increased the margin of preference for British imports. This program was only announced when efforts, including personal representations to President Franklin D. Roosevelt by the prime minister, failed to bring about a reciprocal trade treaty with the United States. Lyons was ruled by the need to overcome a large trade imbalance, mostly in favor of the United States and Japan, both countries maintaining high tariffs against Australian goods.

Lyons and his minister for external affairs were inclined to leave foreign affairs to Bruce, from October, 1933, high commissioner in London and also principal representative at the League of Nations. In 1936, however, Lyons himself agreed that Australia should have its own representative in Washington, having discussed the possibility the year before with President Roosevelt while he and his wife were staying at the White House on their way home from the Royal Silver Jubilee. Furthermore, on March 30, 1939, he advised Great Britain of his decision to upgrade representation in Washington from counselor attached to the British Embassy to legation level, though it was Menzies who made the decision public.

Lyons also took the initiative at the Imperial Conference in London in 1937, personally proposing that a nonaggression pact be made among all the major powers of the Pacific. While appreciating that its neutrality policies precluded American participation, he had taken the idea up with President Roosevelt in 1935 and pursued it with the former Japanese ambassador to the United States during Katsuji Debuchi's visit to Australia the same year. Only China showed enthusiasm. Lacking any positive response from Great Britain or Japan, the proposal lapsed.

After the 1937 elections, Lyons made Hughes minister for external affairs, a surprising choice for one whose religious beliefs inclined him to pacifism and who encouraged the British prime minister, Neville Chamberlain, to use the Italian dictator Benito Mussolini as an intermediary with Adolf Hitler. Opposed to compulsory military training, Lyons instructed Hughes to double the strength of the volunteer militia and increased expenditure on defense. These actions suggest that he realized that Chamberlain's appeasement policies were only delaying tactics. Death spared Lyons from another confrontation with the conscription issue. Instead, his reputation remains that of a popular peacetime leader who brought honesty, stability, and regularity to government in difficult economic times.

Bibliography

Edwards, P. G. *Prime Ministers and Diplomats: The Making of Australian Foreign Policy, 1901-1949.* Melbourne and New York: Oxford University Press, 1983. Discusses Lyons' role in the opening of a diplomatic mission in the United States and includes a useful bibliography.

Esthus, Raymond A. *From Enmity to Alliance: U.S.-Australian Relations, 1931-1941.* Seattle: University of Washington Press, 1964. Good coverage on Australia's trade diversion policy and Lyons' Pacific Pact.

Hart, P. R. "Lyons: Labor Minister, Leader of the U.A.P." *Labor History* 17 (1970): 37-51. Based on Hart's unpublished doctoral thesis, this article covers the period from Lyons' move to Canberra in 1929 up to his becoming prime minister.

Hart, P. R., and C. J. Lloyd. "Joseph Aloysius Lyons." In *Australian Dictionary of Biography*, edited by Bede Nairn et al., vol. 10. Melbourne: Melbourne University Press, 1986.

Lake, Marilyn. *A Divided Society: Tasmania During World War I.* Melbourne: Melbourne University Press, 1975. A competent study of the community's attitude toward conscription.

Lyons, Dame Enid. *So We Take Comfort.* London: Heinemann, 1966. Described by Dame Enid as "the story of our marriage," this book provides an important insight into Lyons the man.

MacIntyre, Stuart. *The Succeeding Age: 1901-1942.* Melbourne and New York: Oxford University Press, 1986. A good general account of the period.

Robertson, John. *J. H. Scullin: A Political Biography.* Nedlands: University of Western Australia Press, 1974. An important aid to understanding the role Lyons played in the Scullin cabinet.

White, Kate. *A Political Love Story: Joe and Enid Lyons.* Melbourne: Penguin, 1987. An interesting account for the general reader, concluding with Lyons' death.

Annette Potts
E. Daniel Potts

DOUGLAS MacARTHUR

Born: January 26, 1880; Little Rock, Arkansas
Died: April 5, 1964; Washington, D.C.
Area of Achievement: The military
Contribution: MacArthur had a greater impact on American military history than virtually any other officer in the twentieth century. Variously gifted, he was a hero to much of the American public but a center of controversy on several occasions.

Early Life

Douglas MacArthur, the son of Captain Arthur MacArthur and Mary Pinckney "Pinky" Hardy, was born on January 26, 1880, at an army post in Little Rock, Arkansas. MacArthur and his older brother (another had died early) led gangs of young army brats, growing up in a succession of forts scattered throughout the United States as his father, a Civil War veteran of distinction, climbed to the highest ranks of the army before running afoul of civilian authorities and ending his career in bitterness in 1909.

In 1899, Douglas MacArthur entered the United States Military Academy in West Point, New York. Nearly six feet tall, he was slender—as a plebe he weighed less than one hundred and forty pounds—but gave the impression of Western ruggedness. Pushed to excel by his devoted mother, who resided in the West Point area during his four years there, MacArthur finished first in his class academically, rivaling the record compiled by Robert E. Lee more than half a century before. Also like Lee, MacArthur achieved the signal honor of being chosen cadet first captain in recognition of his leadership and military bearing.

Yet he also exhibited some of the character traits that were to make his later years so controversial. One cadet found that it was impossible to be neutral about MacArthur. If one knew him at all well, another cadet concluded, one ended up either admiring him to the point of adulation or hating him. So extreme was MacArthur's sense of honor that he threatened to resign over an interpretation of the rules in a mathematics class. He won the confrontation with his professor, a lieutenant colonel, but jeopardized his career in doing so.

Life's Work

The army in which MacArthur was commissioned as a second lieutenant in June, 1903, had outgrown its post-Civil War doldrums, but it was still a small force by European standards. Promotion was accordingly slow, and he did not gain the rank of captain until 1911. As an engineer officer, the branch to which the top-ranking graduates of West Point were usually assigned, he saw service in Wisconsin, Kansas, Michigan, Texas, Panama, and the Philippines. On detached duty, he accompanied his father on a lengthy tour of the Orient in 1906, and in 1914 he undertook a risky intelligence mission in Mexico during the American occupation of Vera Cruz.

Before and after his assignment in Mexico, MacArthur had staff duty in Washington and proved of great value in public relations. MacArthur, who could be as genial as he could be arrogant and supercilious, excelled in this role and also performed important work in setting up and selling to Congress and the public the selective service law when it was enacted after the United States entry into World War I. Unlike some career army officers who disliked relying on the National Guard in wartime, MacArthur believed in it and in its public relations value and suggested that National Guard units from several states be combined into a division for duty in France. MacArthur, who requested a transfer to the infantry, was promoted to colonel and designated by the secretary of war to be chief of staff of this new division.

MacArthur remained with the Forty-second "Rainbow" Division from its arrival in France in October, 1917, until the end of the war. He showed himself to have both the administrative talent required of a capable staff officer and an unusual flair for leadership. Although his duties did not require it, he paid frequent visits to the trenches and accompanied troops on several raids. His unconventional dress, highlighted by sweaters and scarves, also won for him much attention. Promoted to brigadier general in the summer of 1918, MacArthur received command of a brigade. Twice wounded in combat, he led his brigade throughout the Meuse-Argonne campaign, moving up to acting divisional commander shortly before the Armistice. For his exploits, he received a Distinguished Service Medal, two Purple Hearts, several other decorations from his own government, and many more from Allied nations, emerging from the war as one of the army's brightest young officers.

The postwar demobilization, however, would cause many other officers of equal merit to wait years between promotions. Good luck and good timing enabled him to retain his brigadier's rank, and, after service with the American contingent stationed in the Rhineland, he became superintendent of West Point in June, 1919. He went there at a time when West Point's image had been tarnished by excessive hazing and an outdated curriculum. Although in politics he would be identified with conservative Republicans, MacArthur (as he proved over twenty-five years later when commander of the occupation of Japan) could also be a champion of progressive ideas, and he brought about some liberalization of cadet life and improvement in the curriculum.

Between 1922 when he left West Point and 1930 when he became chief of staff, MacArthur served two tours of duty in the Philippines and was twice assigned corps commands in the United States. In 1922, he married Henrietta Louise Cromwell Brooks, a wealthy divorcée. They had no children and were divorced in 1929. He married Jean Marie Faircloth in 1937; they had one son.

Promoted to major general in 1925, the youngest man to hold the rank at that time, MacArthur was named chief of staff by President Hoover in 1930. The position carried with it the rank of general. His five years in the post were difficult. The Depression made it difficult to accomplish much in the way of the modernization the army required; his outspoken advocacy of preparedness at a time of financial austerity and antiwar sentiment earned for him much criticism, as did his linking of pacifism with Communism as a threat to American security. His identification with the dispersal of the Bonus Army of unemployed veterans, who had come to Washington in 1932 to seek financial relief, also was controversial. Despite the understanding he frequently showed in public relations and his oft-demonstrated ability to use the media for his own advantage, in this case MacArthur misjudged the situation. He disregarded the advice of his assistant, Dwight D. Eisenhower, that he remain in the background and instead dressed in full uniform and, wearing his decorations, proceeded personally to lead the troops sent to evict the veterans from the old federal building they had been occupying. Ignoring the instructions sent from the secretary of war by messenger, MacArthur ordered the marchers to be forced back to their encampment, which went up in flames. Exactly who was responsible for setting the fires was not ascertained, but the affair proved to be a public relations disaster both for the Hoover Administration and for MacArthur personally, and it helped attach an authoritarian image to him.

MacArthur continued to serve as chief of staff during the first two years of the New Deal, making a genuine contribution to its domestic program. Instructed to do so, he effectively utilized army personnel to organize the camps of the Civilian Conservation Corps, one of the New Deal's most popular and productive agencies.

At the request of the new Philippine Commonwealth government, MacArthur was named military adviser to the Philippines in 1935 with the duty of developing its armed forces. It was then anticipated that the Philippines would become an independent nation in 1944, at which time it would have to provide for its own security. MacArthur performed essentially the same role for about six years, first as adviser to the Philippine Commonwealth, then, from 1937 on, when he retired from the army, as a field marshal in Philippine service.

In the summer of 1941, with war between the United States and Japan becoming more and more likely, President Roosevelt recalled MacArthur to active service. Given the command of United States Army Forces Far East, he was quickly promoted to lieutenant general and led both the Filipino troops, whose training he had directed, and a small but slowly growing contingent of American forces.

When war struck the Philippines in December, 1941, neither the training of Filipino forces nor the buildup of American troops had advanced far enough to avert disaster. MacArthur's initial troop dispositions only compounded the difficulties—defending the beachheads with inexperienced personnel, failing to move adequate supplies to the strategic Bataan Peninsula, where MacArthur soon ordered a delaying action, allowing his air power to be caught on the ground and largely destroyed even though he had ample warning of the strike upon Pearl Harbor. Yet perhaps because of his command's forward position, he ironically emerged from the debacle as a hero and was promoted to full general in late December.

The gallant though doomed defense of Bataan and Corregidor increased MacArthur's heroic stature, which his staff at headquarters was careful to enhance with laudatory press communiqués then and throughout the war. As the campaign on Bataan ground along, estrangement grew between MacArthur and his superiors in Washington, who were unable to send the reinforcements for which he kept pleading and which he kept promising his increasingly embittered troops. In March, 1942, MacArthur and his family left their Corregidor quarters under orders to proceed to Australia. In April, he was named commander of the Southwest Pacific Area, a newly formed theater of war. On his arrival in Australia, he had made the dramatic statement, "I shall return," fostering the image of resolute leadership that would characterize his strategy throughout the war.

Eventually, MacArthur's forces did return to the Philippines, but first it was necessary to augment his troop strength, halt the Japanese advance in his theater in late 1942, and then begin the laborious process of advancing northward along the coast of New Guinea and nearby islands. Relying on a strategy of using the superior air and sea power that he had begun to achieve by mid-1943, MacArthur was able to bypass enemy strong points. In cooperation with Admiral William Halsey's forces operating in the Solomon Islands, troops under MacArthur and his able air, naval, and ground commanders moved throughout 1943 from the Papuan region of New Guinea to Salamaua, Lae, and Finschhafen in the Huon Gulf area. In 1944, his forces advanced more than one thousand miles, into and beyond Hollandia in New Guinea to Morotai in the Molucca Islands. In doing so, his ground forces suffered fewer than two thousand combat casualties.

While operations were still being conducted by other troops on Leyte, in the central Philippines, which had been invaded in October, 1944, General Walter Krueger's Sixth Army landed at Lingayen Gulf on Luzon in January, 1945, initiating the largest American ground campaign of the entire war in the Pacific. With the campaign on this strategic northern island progressing satisfactorily, units from the Eighth Army made numerous amphibious landings to liberate islands in the central and southern Philippines. Many of these operations were conducted without explicit approval from the Joint Chiefs of Staff, continuing MacArthur's long-standing habit of ignoring instructions he did not like and undertaking campaigns in advance of firm directives.

By the spring of 1945, American forces were converging on Japan itself, and the division of the Pacific into Southwest Pacific and Pacific Ocean areas had become meaningless. Admiral Chester Nimitz, previously the commander of the Pacific Ocean area, would henceforth command all United States naval forces. As the newly appointed head of all United States army forces in the Pacific, MacArthur, who now held the five-star rank of general of the army, would have overall command of the ground phases of Operations Olympic and Coronet, the planned invasions of the Japanese home islands of Kyūshū and Honshū scheduled to take place in November, 1945, and early 1946, respectively.

The announcement of Japan's surrender in August, 1945, following the dropping of the atomic bombs on Hiroshima and Nagasaki and the Soviet declaration of war on Japan, abrogated these plans, and President Truman designated MacArthur Supreme Commander, Allied Powers (SCAP). As such he conducted the surrender ceremonies on board the battleship *Missouri* on September 2, 1945, and commanded the Allied occupation of Japan itself.

MacArthur's years as SCAP have often been regarded as his finest and most enduring accomplishment. The Japanese armed forces were demobilized with little difficulty. Democratic advances were made in land ownership, education, labor relations, and the structure of government, and antitrust legislation directed against the prewar holding companies, the *zaibatsu*, was promulgated. The actual story was more complicated, for some of the reforms were more cosmetic than real and many could not be credited solely to MacArthur but to a complex interplay between Japanese elites and various American authorities. MacArthur's most conspicuous failure was what his most informed biographer has termed his "quixotic" attempt to promote evangelical Christianity in Japan: The people simply did not want it.

Some of MacArthur's actions were undoubtedly carried out with his own presidential ambitions in mind—he would gladly have accepted the Republican nomination in 1944, 1948, or 1952, had it been forthcoming—but for whatever motives, MacArthur's tenure as SCAP was in general a success. In his final years, he seems to have recognized that it was his most lasting contribution to world peace.

The war that broke out in divided Korea in June, 1950, brought MacArthur new military laurels followed by an abrupt end to his long career. After initial retreats, the forces under MacArthur's command recovered following the Inch'ŏn landings which reprised the best of his World War II operations for audacity and success, and by October, victory seemed at hand. Tensions instead mounted between the general and President Truman following the Communist Chinese entry into a war that settled down into one of attrition. In April, 1951, MacArthur was relieved of all of his military responsibilities following the publication of a letter the general had sent to an influential Republican politician making clear his disagreement with the president's policies of limiting the warfare in Korea until a negotiated peace could be had. In a way, the very success of Inch'ŏn could be blamed for his unceremonious relief, for it made the aging general more certain than ever of the correctness of his own judgments and by the same token made it more difficult for President Truman and the Joint Chiefs of Staff to question his recommendations and to make clear that he was insubordinate when he issued policy statements, as he clearly had in a letter to the Veterans of Foreign Wars in August, 1950.

Within a week after his dismissal, MacArthur was being greeted as a hero in the several stops he made en route to Washington, D.C., where he spoke to a joint session of Congress. His remarks critical of Truman's policies were applauded, but in the Senate hearings held about his dismissal, the enthusiasm of many for MacArthur's views on the Korean conflict cooled.

MacArthur still had political aspirations and gave the keynote address at the 1952 Republican National Convention. It was a poor speech and helped neither the cause of Senator Robert Taft, whom MacArthur supported, nor his own chances for a draft should Taft falter and the convention delegates look elsewhere for a nominee. Eisenhower received the nomination.

MacArthur lived twelve more years, residing in New York City, discharging his nominal duties as chairman of the board of Remington Rand and making only infrequent public appearances, one of them a visit to the Philippines in 1961. He died at Walter Reed Army Hospital in Washington on April 5, 1964, only a few months after he had completed writing his memoirs.

Summary

Douglas MacArthur served in the United States Army for almost fifty years, achieving his country's highest honors, leading his forces to memorable victories after appalling defeat, only to have his career end amid controversy. Throughout, he was an actor almost as much as a soldier, a characteristic which was recognized by many who observed him closely. His use of distinctive attire, his often brilliant if theatrical speeches, his seeking of the headlines, all added to the aura of a larger-than-life personality. Was it because of his flamboyance that he never achieved the presidency, a position he would have liked but preferred not to seek openly? Unlike Eisenhower, whose unassuming mannerisms made him the perfect citizen-soldier, MacArthur always seemed too removed from the people of the United States to become their president. Perhaps he was indeed, as one of his biographers has put it, the "American Caesar."

Bibliography

Breuer, William B. *MacArthur's Undercover War: Spies, Saboteurs, Guerrillas and Secret Missions*. New York: Wiley, 1995. Exciting account of the activities of MacArthur's Allied Intelligence Bureau, based on first-hand interviews with participants.

Duffy, Bernard K., and Ronald H. Carpenter. *Douglas MacArthur: Warrior as Wordsmith*. Westport, Conn.: Greenwood Press, 1997. In-depth study of MacArthur's oratory in two sections: analysis of MacArthur and his many speeches; and the text of the speeches.

James, D. Clayton. *The Years of MacArthur*. 3 vols. Boston: Houghton Mifflin, 1970-1985. Magnificent study of MacArthur. Critical of the general's weaknesses but also shrewd in appreciating and evaluating his many strengths. Not likely to be surpassed as the definitive work.

Kenney, George C. *General Kenney Reports: A Personal History of the Pacific War*. New York: Duell Sloan, 1949. An example of a memoir written by one of the able field commanders who joined MacArthur in Australia. Kenney built and led a superb air arm for MacArthur to use on the road back.

MacArthur, Douglas. *Reminiscences*. New York: McGraw-Hill, and London: Heinemann, 1964. A memoir that is a fine example of selective memory in writing. Better for MacArthur's perception of himself than as historical record.

Manchester, William. *American Caesar: Douglas MacArthur, 1880-1964*. Boston: Little Brown, 1978; London: Hutchinson, 1979. Not very well received as history, certainly not in a class with James's study, but readable and the best extant one-volume biography.

Petillo, Carole M. *Douglas MacArthur: The Philippine Years*. Bloomington: Indiana University Press, 1981. Reveals one of the more questionable episodes in MacArthur's life, his acceptance of a large cash payment from the Philippine Commonwealth early in 1942. The author speculates: Was it a bribe to ensure that MacArthur would see that Philippine leaders were evacuated to safety, or was it in the Filipino tradition of gift-giving? Mainly concerned with establishing the psychological impact on MacArthur of the many years he spent in the Philippines at various intervals in his career. (His father had also served in the islands.) Belongs to the genre of psychobiography, the controversial but sometimes rewarding use of psychoanalytic theory in the writing of biography.

Schaller, Michael. *The American Occupation of Japan: The Origins of the Cold War in Asia*. New York: Oxford University Press, 1985. A study of American occupation policy in Japan, revisionist in nature and laudable in its effort to place the occupation in the context of the Cold War.

Smith, Robert Ross. *Triumph in the Philippines*. Washington, D.C.: Office of the Chief of Military History, 1963. One of several detailed books in the official series, "The United States Army in World War II," that together provide a comprehensive view of MacArthur's campaigns from Bataan to the triumphant return to Luzon. Indispensable on the subject of MacArthur's campaigns. A similar series is available for the Korean conflict.

Willoughby, Charles A., and John Chamberlain. *MacArthur, 1941-1951*. New York: McGraw-Hill, 1954; London: Heinemann, 1956. Members of MacArthur's staff in the Philippines, the so-called Bataan Club, many of whom remained with him throughout the war and on into his service as SCAP, generally wrote memoirs. This is an example.

Lloyd J. Graybar

JOSEPH R. McCARTHY

Born: November 14, 1908; Grand Chute, near Appleton, Wisconsin

Died: May 2, 1957; Bethesda, Maryland

Area of Achievement: Politics

Contribution: McCarthy was the key figure in what came to be labeled "McCarthyism"—a national furor of divisive concern and suspicion regarding alleged Communists in American government. For four years, he was a dominant figure in American political life, striking fear into his opponents and confusion into the public mind.

Early Life

Joseph Raymond McCarthy was born November 14, 1908, in Grand Chute, a farming community near Appleton, Wisconsin. He was the fifth child of Tim McCarthy, a farmer of Irish-German background, and Bridget Tierney McCarthy, of Irish stock. The family was devoutly Roman Catholic and poor. Despite some conflict, the family members remained close to one another throughout McCarthy's life.

As the youngest son, and an ungainly one at that, McCarthy was subject to some mistreatment by his brothers, worked hard by his father, and doted upon by his mother. McCarthy early developed his lifelong traits of combativeness, respect for hard work, and extroversion. He attended the local public school only until age fourteen.

McCarthy's interests were not academic, however, nor were they agricultural. He wanted to escape his family's traditional poverty and do so in a manner that would make him independent of the rest of the family. He first worked at farming, then, at age sixteen, he began his own chicken business, which prospered for a while but ultimately failed. At age twenty, McCarthy left his hometown to manage a grocery store in Manawa, Wisconsin. By virtue of extremely hard work and real promotional talent, he did very well in the grocery business. While working full-time as a grocer, he also completed in only one year's time the four years of high school he had missed.

McCarthy then moved on to Marquette University in Milwaukee, where he majored in law. Never scholarly or intellectual, he thrived by dint of industriousness and a prodigious memory, which left him able to ignore work until the last minute, and then to cram successfully. He had numerous jobs while at the university and also augmented his in-come with gambling, particularly poker, at which he was extremely aggressive and successful. He was also an active amateur boxer, ungraceful but determined, bullying his way past opponents.

Following his graduation in 1935, McCarthy practiced law and big-money poker in small Wisconsin towns and became active in politics as a pro-New Deal Democrat. In 1939, he was elected to the nonpartisan office of circuit court judge; the campaign was bitter, and McCarthy, though victorious, was accused of dishonesty and questionable tactics. He was an equally controversial and unorthodox judge, but most observers believed that he did a fairly good job at it. McCarthy held on to his judicial position when he entered the Marines in 1942.

McCarthy's military career is a source of much controversy, since he made his military prowess (as "Tail Gunner Joe") such a key part of his later political campaigns. He may have had some combat experience, but most of it was surely invented, with a view toward its future political usefulness. He went on leave in 1944, in order to seek the Republican senatorial nomination (when he became a Republican is not clear, but he realized that his prospects were clearly better, in the mid-1940's, in that party). He failed in that year, but tried again in 1946, when he narrowly defeated longtime Republican senator Robert M. La Follette for the nomination and then easily won the general election.

Life's Work

The early years of McCarthy's Senate career were undistinguished. Beyond gaining a reputation for brashness and general unscrupulousness, he made little impression on his colleagues or on the press. At the start of 1950, however, facing the likelihood of not being reelected in the 1952 campaign, he took up the increasingly popular issue of Communists in government. The reasons for his adopting this issue, and the degree to which he was sincere about it, remain unclear. The era started with his famous Wheeling, West Virginia, Lincoln's Day speech, which alleged that 205 federal employees were "known to the Secretary of State . . . who nevertheless are still working and shaping the policy of the State Department." Before it ended, more than four years later, he had become one of the most powerful figures in American national life.

Within a few months of the Wheeling speech, McCarthy was a national figure. Dismissed by many in government and the press as a charlatan, he also had numerous supporters among political conservatives and a general public which was truly impressed with the Communist danger to American influence and institutions. Soviet atomic power, the fall of Chiang Kai-shek in China, and the coming of the Korean War in mid-1950 all contributed to a mood of apprehension.

Working from his position on previously unimportant senate committees, McCarthy used his shrewd sense of public relations to exploit these fears, in the process focusing attention on himself. By accusing his senatorial opponents and press critics such as Drew Pearson of Communist sympathies, he gradually silenced criticism. When questions were raised relative to the substance of his charges, McCarthy would respond, not with evidence, but with even stronger accusations—accusations which overwhelmed his opponents and kept his name in the headlines.

In 1951, on the Senate floor, he announced "a conspiracy so immense and an infamy so black as to dwarf any previous venture in the history of man." Included in the alleged conspiracy was George C. Marshall, general of the Army in World War II and secretary of state under President Harry S Truman. The actual allegations, as was true throughout McCarthy's career, were nonsubstantive.

McCarthy's power by 1952 was such that General Dwight D. Eisenhower, running for president, had to swallow his distaste for the senator and support his reelection. McCarthy won renomination and reelection, but the constant tension of his career was beginning to affect him. His health was not good, and he was drinking constantly and heavily.

The pressure was now on McCarthy to provide substantive proof of the charges he had been making for more than two years, or else lose his influence. He had the advantage of chairing the Committee on Government Operations, whose Permanent Subcommittee on Investigations he could use for the furthering of his personal interests. From this vantage point, McCarthy began the extremely emotional investigations of subversion in government that brought him to the pinnacle of his power and then led to his downfall.

In 1953, McCarthy began with highly publicized and televised investigations of two branches of the

International Information Agency—the Voice of America and the Overseas Library Program—alleging subversion and "un-Americanism" in both. He then began his attack on the United States Army, in his fall, 1953, investigation of the Army Signal Corps. Also in the fall of 1953, the bachelor senator married his longtime aide, Jean Kerr.

The Eisenhower Administration, finding the senator's attacks increasingly dubious and hurtful to the Administration, was frequently trying to persuade Senator McCarthy to let up on his attacks on public figures, but to no avail. McCarthy's opponents began, also, to counterattack, especially in the case of favors allegedly exacted from the Army for G. David Schine, a friend of the McCarthy committee's general counsel, Roy Cohn, and an unpaid aide on the senator's staff.

McCarthy was not dissuaded by either persuasion or confrontation, and he continued on the attack, most notably in the televised Army-McCarthy hearings of 1954. In these hearings, with the Army ably represented by private attorney Joseph N. Welch, McCarthy suffered the severest defeat of his career. The national television audience saw both sides, in effect, on trial, but McCarthy was the focus of the whole affair. His coarseness, bullying tactics, and lack of meaningful evidence for his manifold charges came across convincingly. More and more of those who had been afraid to oppose McCarthy previously now did so. Most important, this included members of the Eisenhower Administration. The senator's public approval rating also dropped precipitously. The hearings were a disaster for him.

By August, 1954, the Senate was holding hearings relative to a censure of McCarthy. In December, it voted censure by a vote of sixty-seven to twenty-two. McCarthy lost interest in public affairs at this point, neglecting his Senate duties and drinking heavily. His health suffered accordingly. On May 2, 1957, he died.

Summary

There was much debate among contemporaries—a debate continued among historians—as to McCarthy's true motives in public life. Overall, scholars agree, he was more of an opportunist than anything else. Lacking intellectual depth and any real ideology, McCarthy ever sought the main chance, which he found, ultimately, in politics. A smaller number of McCarthy defenders, on the other hand, insist that he was sincere in his efforts and was besmirched by a liberal press and intellectual community that was unsympathetic to his aims.

The traits he developed as a youth—the capacity for hard work, ambition, deviousness, and brute force of personality—served him throughout his life. Ultimately, however, they also defeated him, because there was no real substance to the man or his movement. The problems he addressed were real enough, although there is no hard evidence that their reality or unreality mattered to McCarthy. Rather, they were issues which he could use for his own personal aggrandizement. Thus, the issues were exaggerated and contorted, until they no longer represented real problems or real people. In the process, an entire nation went through anguished soul-searching, bitter suspicion, and animosity. It is difficult to find any national benefit deriving from four years of McCarthy and McCarthyism.

Bibliography

Buckley, William F., Jr., and L. Brent Bozell. *McCarthy and His Enemies: The Record and Its Meaning*. Chicago: Regnery, 1954. A generally sympathetic study by two contemporaries; its nature reflects their strong anti-Communism. While not entirely uncritical of McCarthy, the authors are most impressed with the reality of the Communist menace at the time.

Cohn, Roy. *McCarthy*. New York: New American Library, 1968. By one of McCarthy's closest collaborators, the book is both a McCarthy biography and a Cohn autobiography, focusing on the years of their association. Not uncritical, but overall a sympathetic account.

Crosby, Donald F. *God, Church, and Flag: Senator Joseph R. McCarthy and the Catholic Church*. Chapel Hill: University of North Carolina Press, 1978. A study by a Roman Catholic priest, focusing on the interrelationship between McCarthy and McCarthyism, on the one hand, and the Church and the Roman Catholic public, on the other.

Griffith, Robert. *The Politics of Fear: Joseph R. McCarthy and the Senate*. Lexington: University Press of Kentucky, 1970; London: Eurospan, 1987. A scholarly study, focusing on McCarthy's senatorial activities and relations with other members of the Senate. Valuable for understanding the effects of McCarthy and McCarthyism on American political life.

Oshinsky, David M. *A Conspiracy So Immense: The World of Joe McCarthy*. London: Macmillan, and New York: Free Press, 1983. A scholarly biography, well researched and as objective as McCarthy studies are likely to be. Thorough and reasonably complete.

Reeves, Thomas C. *The Life and Times of Joe McCarthy: A Biography*. London: Blond and Briggs, and New York: Stein and Day, 1982. The largest and most complete McCarthy biography. Very well researched and extensively annotated. Balanced and fair in its analysis.

Rovere, Richard H. *Senator Joe McCarthy*. New York: Harcourt Brace, 1959; London: Methuen, 1960. The first major McCarthy biography; popular rather than scholarly. Quite anti-McCarthy in tone, but perceptive and valuable for an understanding of the man.

Schrecker, Ellen. "Immigration and Internal Security: Political Deportations during the McCarthy Era." *Science and Society* 60, no. 4 (Winter 1996). Examines the effects of McCarthyism on immigrants and foreign-born U.S. citizens and residents.

Thomas, Lately. *When Even Angels Wept: The Senator Joseph McCarthy Affair—A Story Without a Hero*. New York: Morrow, 1973. A journalistic biography, without documentation and bibliography. Well written, informative, and well balanced.

Walker, Richard L. "China Studies in McCarthy's Shadow: A Personal Memoir." *National Interest*, no. 53 (Fall 1998). Discusses the effects of McCarthyism on Chinese affairs and studies in the United States.

John M. Allswang

MARY McCARTHY

Born: June 21, 1912; Seattle, Washington
Died: October 25, 1989; New York, New York
Areas of Achievement: Journalism and literature
Contribution: The most prominent woman among what came to be called the New York intellectuals, notorious for her acerbic tongue and for rather stormy relations with her male colleagues, McCarthy brought great vigor and insight and an uncompromising set of standards to American criticism and fiction.

Early Life

Mary Therese McCarthy's earliest years took their color from her charming alcoholic father and her devoted, beautiful mother. Her secure childhood in Seattle, in the home of a father who had apparently reformed for love of his wife, and within the environs of an influential, wealthy family, graced by the rather romantic figure of her vibrant Jewish grandmother, was shattered during the flu epidemic of World War I. McCarthy lost both of her parents at the age of six and was wrenched from the comfort of Seattle to live in Minneapolis, taken care of by relatives who apparently pocketed most of the funds intended for the support of Mary and her brother Kevin. She describes this period with chilling effectiveness in *Memories of a Catholic Girlhood* (1957).

In her memories of her earliest years, McCarthy would often put a high gloss on her father's figure, refusing to see the flaws that were painfully apparent to family members who had had to support him during his drinking bouts. Something of a loner, McCarthy demonstrated an intense interest in literature at Vassar College (she was graduated in 1933) but no remarkable talent. She first found work as a book reviewer for *The Nation* and *The New Republic*, but it was not until the mid-1930's, after a series of affairs which culminated in a short marriage to theater director Harold Johnsrud and a liaison with the critic Philip Rahv, that she began to develop her own literary style and point of view.

These male figures served as mentors, especially the truculent Rahv, one of the editors of *The Partisan Review*, which was arguably the most influential intellectual journal of its time. The journal had begun as a Marxist, pro-Soviet organ, but by the late 1930's it had adopted an anti-Stalinist position and championed the work of the great modernist writers. In this feisty, combative milieu, McCarthy honed her skills as drama editor and critic, exciting the interest of Edmund Wilson, the dean of American literary critics. McCarthy's stormy marriage to Wilson lasted eight years (1938-1946). With his encouragement, she wrote her first fiction, *The Company She Keeps* (1942), an incisive portrayal of a bohemian, intellectual young woman.

Rahv, McCarthy later admitted, would never have encouraged her to write novels, and he was incapable of removing her from the intense but curiously provincial milieu of New York intellectuals who spent too much of their time in sectarian fights among liberals, Stalinists, anti-Stalinists, Trotskyites, and so on. Yet Rahv seemed to love McCarthy for herself, a quality she evidently found rare in the men who were attracted to her.

Life's Work

Mary McCarthy is best known for her astringent critical writing and her best-selling novel *The Group* (1963), which details the lives and sexual affairs of eight Vassar College graduates. She often reviewed films and plays and was notorious for her negative reviews. In private life, she had an equally sharp tongue that made her a fearsome presence on the New York literary scene. She was also a much-admired debunker of the fashionable and facile products of American culture.

McCarthy began to hit her stride in the late 1940's and the 1950's. She married Bowden Broadwater, who catered to her love of gossip, often supplying the background for scenes that would become a part of *The Group*. During her marriage to Broadwater (1946-1961), she published three novels that reflect her critical and imaginative grasp of the canvas of American Life. *The Oasis* (1949) is a sharp, satiric portrayal of a utopia established by a group of intellectuals on a mountaintop. It reveals her witty grasp of group dynamics, of the way intellectuals feed upon and destroy one another as ideas are perverted by warring personalities. *The Groves of Academe* (1952) is another satire set in her favorite territory, a liberal arts college for women. Similarly, *A Charmed Life* (1955) takes place in an artist's colony in which the putative creators become destroyers. In much of her fiction, McCarthy dramatizes the inability of intellectuals to sustain a cohesive community; the acid of their intellectuality seems to corrode their humanity.

The Group exemplifies McCarthy's expertise at delineating social manners and the ideas of her time. It is perhaps her most ambitious work because it essays an interpretation of a whole generation. Yet it has also been faulted for its shallow characterizations. One of her biographers, Carol Brightman, contends that only in memoirs such as *Memories of a Catholic Girlhood* was McCarthy able to concentrate on a character (herself) who grew over time and developed in depth and complexity.

Brightman also suggests that McCarthy was adept at fastening on real-life characters, exaggerating and combining the aspects of several personalities, dressing them up in fiction, so to speak, but ultimately proving unable to transcend her real-life models, who often recognized themselves and were hurt by her biting sarcasm. McCarthy thus failed the test of the greatest novelists: She could not create transcendent characters, selves independent of their creator and their roots in reality. Yet the fact that McCarthy stayed close to her real-life models also made the novels extraordinarily authentic as documents of their age, and her fiction remains valid as a brand of social history.

Perhaps because criticism by its nature does not demand warmth and charity (although some critics have been known to be kind), McCarthy's scathing attacks have been accepted more readily in her criticism than in her fiction, where her assaults on intellectuals and opinion makers wear thin because human character seems to be manipulated merely to serve the points she wants to make. What the novels lack is psychological profundity, a certain mystery or ambiguity that would enliven and complicate her characters. Instead, too many of those characters are contemptible.

As a cultural and political critic, however, critics agree that McCarthy deserves a very high place in America literature. Her theater reviews, collected in *Sights and Spectacles, 1937-1956* (1956) and in *Mary McCarthy's Theatre Chronicles 1937-1962* (1963), demonstrate a discriminating, if severe, standard for American drama. They are often characterized as witty, a quality that often makes them more interesting than the plays they criticized.

McCarthy's later works—particularly *Vietnam* (1967), *Hanoi* (1968), and *The Mask of State: Watergate Portraits* (1974)—show her courage in taking on controversial political events. She was a fierce critic of the American government, and she opposed the Vietnam War and the policies created in its aftermath as steadfastly as she had castigated

the hypocrisy of intellectuals. She also turned to fiction again in *Cannibals and Missionaries* (1979), an uneven novel about the hijacking of a plane carrying a motley group to the Shah's Iran. Once again, McCarthy was focusing on the dynamics of group behavior, seeing in the group a metaphor for the politics that she saw pervading human interaction. Similarly, she continued to examine generational conflicts in her novel *Birds of America* (1971), which depicts the strained relations between a mother and her son.

Almost all of McCarthy's writing has been about a clarification of values and an exposure of those who purvey false precepts. By the mid-1930's, McCarthy had jettisoned a brief fascination with Marxism, realizing that Stalin's Moscow trials (in which the founders of the Soviet state were accused of treason) were a sham and that the communists would not be able to deliver on their promise of a new and democratic free world based on human equality. When many writers of her generation persisted in their Stalinism, they confirmed her skeptical view of intellectuals and the dishonest uses to which they put their dialectical skills.

Less important are her travel books, *Venice Observed* (1956) and *The Stones of Florence* (1959), which show a more relaxed, appreciative side of McCarthy's character. They are a product of her extensive travels, continued during her last and enduring marriage in 1961 to the diplomat James West. It was a happy union, but McCarthy was restless, constantly on the move from New York to Paris to Castine, Maine (where she and West had a summer home), to various parts of Italy, and to Saigon and Hanoi during the Vietnam War, when she made herself extremely unpopular with the U.S. government.

Her last autobiographical books, *How I Grew* (1987) and *Intellectual Memories* (1993), continue the story of *Memoirs of a Catholic Girlhood*, but they do not have that volume's verve and do not rank with it as classics of American autobiography. *Ideas and the Novel* (1980) is an impressive recapitulation of her long-held views on the nature of fiction and its potential as an intellectual instrument.

Summary

Mary McCarthy was not a standard-definition feminist. She belonged to a generation growing up in the 1920's and 1930's that took for granted and ignored the advances achieved by late nineteenth and twentieth century feminists. As she moved beyond the college campus and the boundaries of conventional marriage, McCarthy sought her freedom in the city among intellectuals and bohemians. She was influenced by powerful male mentors, but she soon developed an independent viewpoint and outspoken positions on literary and political matters.

McCarthy would have disliked the tag woman writer, for like many of her generation she wanted to be considered a writer first and to be judged by her work, not by her sex. Yet her very ability to compete with and often surpass her male colleagues made an impact on other women, showing them what could be accomplished even in the fiercely competitive milieu of New York male intellectuals. She was an outsider, by virtue of her sex and her sharp tongue, yet she was a part of this group. This simultaneous inside/outside perspective of hers gave her great insight into how groups define themselves and choose their members. By virtue of her sex, she was a minority member, yet her superiority as a critic gave her an edge in assessing the peculiar characteristics of the group she had joined. Perhaps her greatest gift to women was to show that they could be thoroughly absorbed in the culture of their times and yet remain intact and independent.

Bibliography

Brightman, Carol. *Between Friends: The Correspondence of Hannah Arendt and Mary McCarthy, 1949-1975*. London: Secker and Warburg, and New York: Harcourt Brace, 1995. A collection of letters exchanged by McCarthy and Arendt. Includes a good deal of information on the eclectic mix of poets, lovers, and other characters that populated their literary worlds.

————. *Writing Dangerously: Mary McCarthy and Her World*. New York: Potter, 1992; London: Lime Tree, 1993. A full-length, sensitive, well-balanced account of McCarthy's life and work. A friend of McCarthy, Brightman is very sympathetic toward her subject, but she does not overlook the faults of her work and her character. A biographical glossary, extensive notes, and an index are included.

Gelderman, Carol. *Mary McCarthy: A Life*. New York: St. Martin's Press, 1988; London: Sidgwick and Jackson, 1989. Written with McCarthy's cooperation, this is a solid and reliable full-length biography. Includes extensive notes and a bibliography.

Hardwick, Elizabeth. *A View of My Own: Essays in Literature and Society*. New York: Noonday Press, 1963; London: Heinemann, 1964. Contains a chapter on McCarthy which is an excellent, succinct appraisal of her character and her work by a close friend.

McKenzie, Barbara. *Mary McCarthy*. New Haven, Conn.: Yale University Press, 1966. An introductory study with chapters on McCarthy's life, intellectual development, fiction, and nonfiction. Includes a chronology, notes, an annotated bibliography, and an index.

Stock, Irvin. *Mary McCarthy*. Minneapolis, Minn.: University of Minnesota Press, 1968. A long biographical and critical essay emphasizing McCarthy's fiction. A selected bibliography is included.

Stwertka, Eve, and Margo Viscusi. Twenty-Four *Ways of Looking at Mary McCarthy: The Writer and Her Work*. Westport, Conn.: Greenwood Press, 1996. A collection of essays by critics, writers, and scholars who discuss McCarthy's years with the New York intelligentsia and her views on feminism and politics.

Carl Rollyson

CARSON McCULLERS

Born: February 19, 1917; Columbus, Georgia
Died: September 29, 1967; Nyack, New York
Area of Achievement: Literature
Contribution: A Southern novelist and short-story writer, Carson McCullers presented in her fiction a world of alienated adolescents, misfits, and outcasts, treating themes of human isolation with great sensitivity.

Early Life

Carson McCullers was born Lula Carson Smith, the daughter of Lamar Smith, a watchmaker, and Marguerite Waters Smith. For generations, Smith's family had been Southerners, so her family history, as well as her own childhood and adolescence, deepened her relationship with the South. It was in ramblings through Columbus' streets and the disparate quarters of African Americans, millworkers, and the wealthy that she gained the many impressions that enrich her fictional world. Carson was recognized as an odd, lively girl with artistic talents, and her passion for music and writing was encouraged. She studied the piano assiduously and as an adolescent wrote some violence-filled plays (patterned after those of Eugene O'Neill), a novel, and some poetry. An early short story, "Sucker," about a sixteen-year-old boy whose first friendship causes him to reject the affection of a younger brother, demonstrates her precocity. She changed her name, read voraciously, and earned a reputation for having a phenomenal memory. Although in all her work Carson McCullers focuses on alienated individuals, she herself grew up in a harmonious family that accepted her eccentricities and extended her their affection.

At eighteen, Carson traveled to New York, purportedly to attend the Juilliard School of Music, but she lost the tuition and was forced to work at several jobs. She did, however, register for creative writing courses at Columbia University and New York University. One of her teachers, Whit Burnett, liked one of her stories, "Wunderkind" (1936), about a self-critical child musical prodigy who abandons her music, and he had it published in *Story Magazine.* Because of frail health resulting from childhood illnesses, Carson took trips home to Georgia for recuperative purposes. On one such trip, she met a Georgia soldier named Reeves McCullers, and in 1938 she was married to him. For two years, they lived happily in Charlotte,

North Carolina, where she wrote a novel outline called "The Mute," earning a Houghton Mifflin Fiction Fellowship and a book contract. The editor changed the title to *The Heart Is a Lonely Hunter,* and the book appeared in 1940 to generally enthusiastic reviews. For a twenty-two-year-old writer to probe so perceptively into adult characters was a startling achievement.

Life's Work

Characteristically, *The Heart Is a Lonely Hunter* is set in Georgia. Filled with impressions of Carson McCullers' childhood, it creates a richly detailed view of a Southern mill town. At the center of the novel is a deaf-mute surrounded by four lonely characters who are unable to connect with the world. One is a thirteen-year-old girl who is burdened with frustrated musical ambitions. Through her, McCullers deals with the individual's compulsion to revolt against enforced isolation, and she presents love as the only anodyne.

When her first novel was published, the author and her husband settled in New York, where she was lauded as the literary discovery of the year. She was invited to be a Fellow at the Bread Loaf Writers Conference in Vermont. That fall, *Reflections in a Golden Eye,* a hastily written story of infidelity, murder, and perversion at a Southern army base, appeared in installments in *Harper's Bazaar* before it was published as a book in 1941. Although it may have contributed to McCullers' image as a writer of Southern gothic fiction, it disappointed serious readers who were expecting as careful and sympathetic a delineation of character and situation as that contained in her first novel. The critical response was unenthusiastic.

McCullers' disappointment at the second novel's reception was matched by domestic misfortune and divorce. For the next five years, McCullers lived sporadically in Columbus and at Yaddo, an artists' colony in Saratoga, New York, but mostly amid a legendary gathering of artists and writers at February House, in Brooklyn Heights. The old brownstone rented jointly by McCullers and George Davis, editor of *Harper's Bazaar,* harbored celebrated artists and writers, including Christopher Isherwood, W. H. Auden, Richard Wright, Oliver Smith, Benjamin Britten, and Gypsy Rose Lee. Many famous guests dropped by. February House provided spirited company and singular material for novels

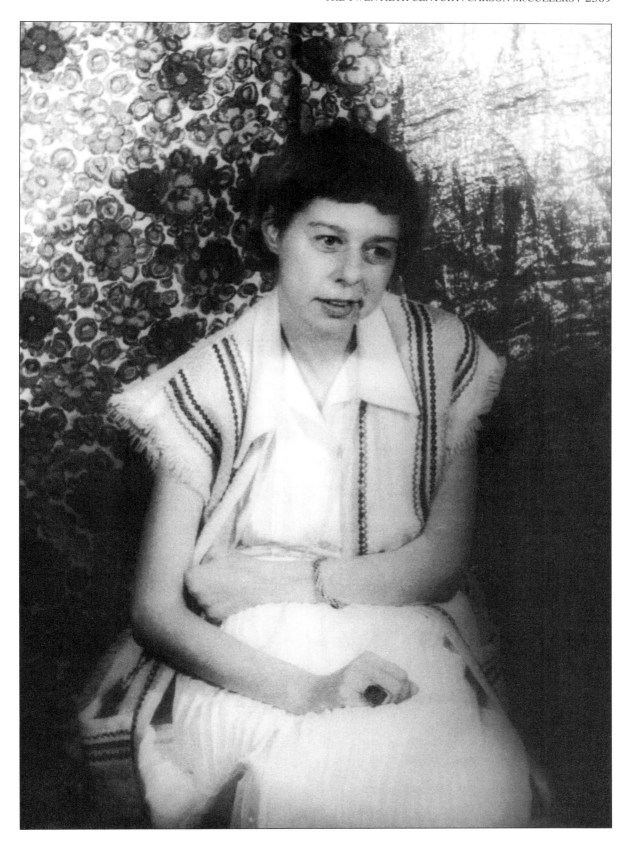

and stories. The irregular life did exhaust McCullers, however, and she returned to Columbus to recuperate. While there, she suffered the first in a series of strokes that were to plague her the rest of her life. On regaining her health, she composed the short story "A Tree, a Rock, a Cloud," which was published in *Harper's Bazaar* (1942) and selected for the anthology *O. Henry Prize Stories of 1942*. She also received a Guggenheim Fellowship that year.

After her father's death in 1944, she moved with her mother and sister to Nyack, New York. She resumed a correspondence with her former husband after his reenlistment, and they remarried after his discharge in 1945 for war wounds.

The early 1940's were McCullers' most productive period. Her third major work, a novella, *The Ballad of the Sad Café*, the story of a grotesque love affair between a giantess and a hunchback, appeared in *Harper's Bazaar* in 1943. A thousand-dollar grant from the American Academy of Arts and Letters, along with various other grants and fellowships, encouraged her. *The Member of the Wedding* (1946), the most directly autobiographical of all her works, which explores a teenage girl's feelings of isolation and longing, was immediately both popular and critically successful. Playwright Tennessee Williams was so impressed by its remembrance of childhood memories that he persuaded McCullers to rework it into a play. Spending some weeks at Williams' cottage on Nantucket, she finished the play by the end of the summer of 1946. A second Guggenheim Fellowship was given to her that same year.

For the next three years, McCullers fought failing health and tried to find a producer for *The Member of the Wedding*. In 1947, she experienced two serious strokes that impaired her vision and partially paralyzed her. Her recuperation was slow. At the same time, her husband underwent treatment for acute alcoholism. The decade, however, ended triumphantly: In 1950, *The Member of the Wedding*, starring Julie Harris and Ethel Waters, opened in New York to the praise of audience and critics. It won three awards, including the New York Drama Critics' Circle Award, and after it had received 501 performances, it was made into a film by Stanley Kramer. The successful Broadway production, together with the enthusiastically received collected edition of her work by Houghton Mifflin in 1951, established her literary reputation in America and Europe.

If her literary reputation was secure, her health and domestic security were not. In 1951, she and her husband bought a house near Paris, where they lived on and off for two years. He drank heavily and had fits of depression. She returned alone to Nyack by 1953, planning a divorce. He committed suicide in France. Between 1952 and 1953, McCullers published two short stories in *Mademoiselle* and some of her poems in *Botteghe Oscure*. In 1954, she made lecture appearances with Tennessee Williams and worked at Yaddo. Her mother, who had been a great help to her, died suddenly in 1955.

The play McCullers produced in 1957 and the novel she published in 1961 were triumphs of will but artistic failures. The play *The Square Root of Wonderful*, an autobiographical attempt to re-create and understand her mother and her husband, closed after forty-five Broadway performances. It lacks the dramatic purpose and compelling characterizations necessary to make it work on stage. Discouraged by its failure, she returned to the unfinished manuscript of *Clock Without Hands*, which she completed for publication in 1961. An uneven work treating a central character's preparations for death and unsuccessfully attempting a comic allegory of the ways in which the 1950's had changed the South, it was her last novel.

Despite her illness, McCullers achieved remarkable success between the ages twenty-three and thirty. Although she continued writing as an invalid until her death at fifty of a massive cerebral hemorrhage, her creative activity between 1958 and 1962 was necessarily lessened. She underwent surgery for breast cancer and for an atrophied hand muscle, and psychiatric care for depression. In 1964, she underwent hip surgery, and a long critical illness in 1965 led to her death in 1967. Despite her later artistic disappointments, McCullers' early work continued to be widely read and appreciated. Adapters were eager to translate her work into other media. Edward Albee dramatized *The Ballad of the Sad Café* in 1963, and the play ran for 123 performances on Broadway. John Huston cast Marlon Brando and Elizabeth Taylor in a film version of *Reflections in a Golden Eye* in 1967, and a film version of *The Heart Is a Lonely Hunter*, with Alan Arkin, appeared in 1968.

McCullers' sister, Margarita C. Smith, published *The Mortgaged Heart* (1971), a posthumous collection of McCullers' short stories, essays, and poems. In several essays, McCullers discusses the methods and concerns of her own writing. She states her belief that good prose must be both realistic and poetic, and admits her reliance on the

South of her childhood for locales. Furthermore, she reports that her technique of creating characters involves getting entirely within those characters so that their motives become her own: "I become the characters I write about," she wrote. If her vision is one of alienation, it is a vision that is imbued with sympathy; her isolated eccentrics and disturbed children are portrayed as human beings who are not, in the final analysis, extremely different from the rest of humanity.

Summary

Although frail health plagued Carson McCullers throughout her life and limited her productivity, she achieved critical and popular success in four genres in her twenties. Her first three novels, all of which were best-sellers, appeared within a six-year period, and her award-winning play *The Member of the Wedding* appeared four years later.

McCullers is an accomplished portrayer of character who presents in her novels a richly detailed world of lonely and often unlovable misfits with a need for love that they find difficult to satisfy. They embody such major themes of the author as human isolation and loneliness caused by inability to love, communicate deep feeling, or find one's identity. Although her works are outwardly realistic, they often move into a symbolic or allegorical dimension without allowing their characters to lose their humanity. Commonly rendering fiction as parable, McCullers accents truths about human nature. She displays virtuosity in her language, mixing the poetic and the prosaic to her advantage. Musical and metaphysical perspectives blend, for example, with ordinary sounds of life in a Southern town. Music pervades her work, sometimes lending it structure, as in *The Member of the Wedding*, in which the themes are suggested, stated, and restated, sonata fashion, throughout the three distinct parts of the story.

That McCullers has become a significant figure in the study of women's literature is no surprise. Her compelling portraits of women and adolescents such as Frankie Adams in *The Member of the Wedding* are memorable, and they reflect an uncommon compassion for hidden suffering. In her brief lifetime, this richly talented and diversely gifted writer left a distinctive legacy to American fiction.

Bibliography

Bloom, Harold, ed. *Carson McCullers*. New York: Chelsea House, 1986. An excellent collection of criticism encompassing all of McCullers' fiction. Essay authors include Marguerite Young, Tennessee Williams, Gore Vidal, Oliver Evans, Richard M. Cook, Lawrence Graver, and Margaret B. McDowell. Includes a bibliography, a chronology, and an index. Gives readers a helpful perspective on critical writing about McCullers.

Cook, Richard M. *Carson McCullers*. New York: Ungar, 1975; London: Lorrimer, 1982. This biography also contains insightful writing about McCullers' five novels. Included are a chronology, a bibliography, and an index. Cook considers McCullers' compassionate insight into hidden suffering her greatest achievement.

Evans, Oliver. *The Ballad of Carson McCullers: A Biography*. New York: Coward-McCann, 1966. A biography that includes incisive comments on McCullers' work, emphasizing its allegorical aspect. Includes eight photographs, index, and McCullers' outline of "The Mute," later published in book form as *The Heart Is a Lonely Hunter*. Valuable for detailing connections between McCullers' life and fiction.

Graver, Lawrence. *Carson McCullers*. Minneapolis: University of Minnesota Press, 1969. A forty-eight-page biography with an interesting discussion of each major work. Offers a helpfully condensed yet substantial view of the author's life and work. Graver places McCullers in a quartet of accomplished Southern women writers consisting of McCullers, Eudora Welty, Katherine Anne Porter, and Flannery O'Connor.

Hannon, Charles. "'The Ballad of the Sad Café and Other Stories of Women's Wartime Labor.'" *Genders*, no. 23 (Spring 1996). Examines McCullers' short story "The Ballad of the Sad Café," which deals with the roles of women in the workforce during and after World War II.

McDowell, Margaret. *Carson McCullers*. Boston: Twayne, 1980. A comprehensive study that contains summaries and well-detailed analyses of her major works, including short stories, poems, and her second play, *The Square Root of Wonderful*. Included are a chronology, the author's photograph, and a bibliography of primary sources and annotated secondary sources.

Whitt, Jan. "The Loneliest Hunter." *Southern Literary Journal* 24, no. 2 (Spring 1992). Examines McCullers' novel *The Heart Is a Lonely Hunter* and its theme of loss in people's lives. The author discusses the role of the protagonist as a Christ-like figure.

Christian H. Moe

RAMSAY MacDONALD

Born: October 12, 1866; Lossiemouth, Morayshire, Scotland
Died: November 9, 1937; at sea
Areas of Achievement: Government and politics
Contribution: The most significant figure in the development of the Labour Party, MacDonald
guided it through his voluminous political writings, his organizational acumen and skills, and
his actions as prime minister of its first two governments. The party became in practice more reformist than Socialist. It grew as a broad-based
party aspiring to govern rather than a small pressure group within Parliament; it tapped trade
union strength but rebuffed trade union control.

Early Life

James Ramsay MacDonald was born on October
12, 1866, in the small fishing village of Lossiemouth, in Morayshire, Scotland, the illegitimate
son of a ploughman and a farm servant. His mother, Anne Ramsay, a determined but warmhearted
woman, never married and supported herself and
her son as a seamstress. Influenced by an exciting
schoolteacher, MacDonald became a pupil-teacher
for four years (1881-1885), developing skills in
analysis, speaking, leadership, and organization in
his teens. Because class distinctions were of less
significance in the Scottish Highlands, MacDonald
was rising on his own merits. As a young man, he
had already developed both his romantic and pragmatic tendencies, had an inquiring mind (he always loved geology and biology and once thought
of becoming a chemist), and had become a local
public speaker. He was impressive physically:
handsome with wavy hair (and he was soon to
wear a mustache), tall and trim, with a dignified
though rugged bearing. Although throughout his
career he constantly returned to Lossiemouth, almost as a second home, the adventurous Mac-
Donald left it at age nineteen for opportunities
elsewhere: He headed to Bristol in 1885 and
moved to London in 1886.

Life's Work

Personable, eager, and articulate, MacDonald immediately joined political clubs (the Social Democratic Federation branch in Bristol and the Fabian
Society in London). He served as the private secretary of a radical Liberal parliamentary candidate
from 1888 to 1892 and also worked as a journalist.

The young, late Victorian Socialist lived in a world
of politics, ideas, and middle-class surroundings.
After a frustrating association with the Liberal Party, MacDonald joined the new Independent Labour
Party (ILP) in 1894 but was defeated in the parliamentary elections the following year. In 1896, he
married Margaret Gladstone, an upper-middle-
class Socialist and social worker, with whom he
eventually had four children. In their closely knit
family, Margaret provided MacDonald great emotional and political support. After MacDonald's
wife, younger son, and mother all died in 1911, he
was often lonely and moody.

In 1896, MacDonald joined the ILP's national
administrative committee; he served until 1909 and
kept close links with it until the late 1920's. Selected secretary at the founding of the Labour Representation Committee in 1900 (the precursor of the
Labour Party), the thirty-three-year-old Mac-
Donald contributed vitally to its success. The party
was composed primarily of trade unions and Socialist organizations (such as the ILP). Careful to
nurture union support, MacDonald nevertheless
steered it away from merely being either a union-
dominated parliamentary pressure group or a
working-class party. Personally advocating socialism, MacDonald ensured that the party itself became a nondoctrinaire, broadly based party. He
called it a party of "opinion" (that is, of attitudes,
goals, and concepts), not a party of class. Mac-
Donald also chiefly determined Labour's relationship with Liberals, helping to arrange the secret
Labour-Liberal pact of 1903 by which the two parties agreed not to compete against each other in selected constituencies in 1906 (which helped Mac-
Donald and some other Labourites be elected) and
cooperating with Liberals in Parliament, especially
when from 1910 to 1914 the minority Liberal governments needed Labour support in the House of
Commons. MacDonald championed Great Britain's constitutional and parliamentary process as
the only way to produce changes—both immediate
ameliorative measures and basic structural Socialist ones. He was an excellent parliamentarian: a superb debater skilled in parliamentary procedure
and usually astute in determining parliamentary
tactics for his party, even though the Labourites
were acknowledged as an unwieldy group.

MacDonald was an exciting, effusive speaker
and a prolific writer of pamphlets, articles, and

books. Generally stressing social justice and social democracy, his works deeply influenced the Labour movement and installed MacDonald as the party's leading theoretician. Yet his greatest status came through Parliament (serving as M.P. for Leicester, 1906-1918; Aberavon, 1922-1929; Seaham, 1929-1935; and the Scottish Universities, 1936-1937). In 1912, he relinquished the party secretariat to Arthur Henderson after becoming the first effective leader of the parliamentary Labour Party (1911-1914 and 1922-1931). Although rivals rather than friends, Henderson and MacDonald complemented each other in organizational work and political direction of the party. MacDonald resigned the party leadership in August, 1914, when Labour supported British entry into World War I. He did not leave the party; he continued as its treasurer and as a member of its national executive committee. Not a pacifist, he sought a negotiated peace and a postwar organization to prevent future wars. Vilified during the war, he was not reelected M.P. in 1918 and was further distressed by the harshness of the 1919 Treaty of Versailles. Always a Socialist internationalist, he helped establish the Labour and Socialist International (basically a reincarnation of the older prewar Second International) and rebuffed Lenin's attempt to destroy Democratic Socialist parties through his rival Communist International.

By 1922, MacDonald's wartime stance and concern for international harmony had become more acceptable, and he was returned to Parliament and reelected party leader. In the December, 1923, election, the ruling Conservative Party lost its majority, and surprisingly, Labour (now the second largest party) took office, though it needed Liberal support. As prime minister, MacDonald succeeded in demonstrating that Labour had become one of the two major parties and that this professed Socialist Party could capably administer the government. Serving also as foreign minister, he inaugurated full diplomatic relations with the Soviet Union, championed the new League of Nations, and sought to link disarmament and arbitration of disputes with France's desire for security. As anticipated, Labour lost office later in 1924, and MacDonald's status declined. His qualms about the 1926 General Strike proved to be correct; thus the merits of his parliamentary approach seemed greater. Reasserting his mastery over the party by the late 1920's, he led it in 1929 to victory as the largest party, though still without a majority in Parlia-

ment, and as prime minister formed a second minority Labour government, in power from 1929 to 1931.

While forced to appoint Henderson as foreign secretary, MacDonald asserted his own responsibility for improving relations with the United States. Strengthened Anglo-American ties were demonstrated as the two countries extended their naval disarmament program at the 1930 London Conference. MacDonald's friction with Henderson, though, jeopardized other British actions, especially Henderson's attempt for a coherent policy toward improved Franco-German relations.

On domestic matters, MacDonald wanted again to demonstrate Labour's capability to govern and to improve conditions for those adversely affected by Great Britain's decade of high unemployment (approximately ten percent throughout the 1920's, spiraling during the world depression to sixteen percent in 1930 and twenty-two percent in 1931). The party lacked acceptable bold ideas on how to reduce the rate, even though MacDonald immediately upon taking office created an unemployment committee of four cabinet members to devise a strategy. Recognizing its failure, MacDonald replaced it with one he himself chaired, but it, too, foundered. Expanding unemployment discredited the Labour Party, which was based on working-class support and which had strongly criticized the preceding government's inaction. Unemployment benefits costs also increased, much of which came from the general treasury. While not as inflexible as the obdurate Chancellor of the Exchequer, Philip Snowden, MacDonald shared Labour's fiscal tenets of a balanced budget, free trade, and the existing gold standard. Thus, while advocating a future Socialist reorientation of society, MacDonald and Labour sought to govern within the existing economic system. When in August, 1931, an international financial crisis led to a British gold drain, orthodox views insisted that confidence abroad in Great Britain would be restored if the government displayed fiscal restraint. The cabinet agreed with a recent alarming official report that the most practical immediate governmental cuts in expenditures must be primarily in unemployment benefits.

Half the cabinet members (strongly backed by leaders of the Trades Union Congress) hesitated to make major reductions affecting the unemployed, so the Labour government resigned. MacDonald then shocked his party by forming a coalition National Government, including the Conservative and Liberal parties. Although realizing that the bulk of the Labour Party would go into opposition, MacDonald was nevertheless disappointed when only a few followed him.

MacDonald's premiership of the National Government, 1931-1935, was the most controversial period of his career. The National Government's reduction of unemployment payments did not restore sufficient confidence abroad to end the gold drain, so Great Britain left the gold standard in September. He accepted Conservative Party demands for a new election in October, and his former party (which had now expelled him from membership) was decimated in Parliament. The next year, the Conservatives persuaded Great Britain to abandon free trade and institute wide-ranging protective tariffs, which caused some free-trade Liberals to leave the coalition. The National Government was no longer national: With only a small "National Labour" contingent and a rump "National Liberal" party, it was dominated by the Conservatives with their vast parliamentary majority. With little influence (except on some international and imperial issues), MacDonald lingered in the pre-

miership, unwilling to resign either to protest publicly over any governmental action or to acknowledge his declining influence. In his late sixties, rapidly aging, suffering from glaucoma, and often mentally confused, he finally resigned as prime minister only to continue in the cabinet impotently as lord president of the council. Decisively defeated in 1935 by Labour in his mining constituency, he returned to Parliament early the next year in a by-election at a safe seat. Finally retiring from the cabinet in 1937, the septuagenarian MacDonald died at sea on vacation on November 9, 1937. After a public funeral in Westminster Abbey, his ashes were buried beside his wife's at Lossiemouth.

Summary

Ramsay MacDonald's career bridged Labour's transition from a loose band of small, struggling organizations to a major party forming the government of Great Britain. For more than three decades, he was the single most significant individuals in defining and guiding the party's development. He held each of its major offices and served on its national executive committee. A radical and a Socialist, he sought attainable goals, many of which involved governmental programs for collective action to help the common people. Fundamentally a democrat, MacDonald championed Great Britain's constitutional and parliamentary process. His main contribution was by words and action to shape the political efforts of Great Britain's radical Socialist workers' movement into an effective parliamentary party.

Vain and ambitious, MacDonald thrust himself to national influence and power, yet he was fundamentally a man of principle. While never resigning from the party, he nevertheless twice gave up its leadership, not knowing whether it meant political suicide. He refused to accept the party's decisions to support the war in 1914 and oppose unemployment cuts in 1931. Both times the trade unions opposed him, although the Socialist ILP supported him the first time. Yet in both cases (and both were sudden, unplanned responses to crises), he followed his conscience in his perception of the national interest.

MacDonald's commitment to socialism continues to be questioned. His two Labour governments made no new bold Socialist initiatives. The lack of a parliamentary majority, the weakened British economy, and the caution of most other cabinet members were contributing factors, but Mac-

Donald himself was also responsible. He was more interested in providing acceptable governments than Socialist ones. Rather than betraying socialism as some critics charged, MacDonald had never been primarily interested in a basic restructuring of society in the immediate future, a goal which he considered unattainable. Social democracy and international affairs were his great interests, and his socialism essentially pertained to social justice, that is, to social and economic reforms in the distribution of goods within society. To obtain these reforms, the party needed wider electoral support and cooperation with the Liberal Party, especially prior to World War I. He abhorred any sudden revolution, be it Communist or syndicalist. He helped prevent the new Communist International from dominating the international Socialist movement, and as prime minister and foreign minister, he sought to improve Franco-German relations.

MacDonald died unwanted by his new allies and despised by his old party, his policies of the 1930's in shambles: Great Britain was by then off the gold standard, applying protective tariffs, maintaining social welfare programs unsuited to the scope of the Depression's serious unemployment, and unwilling to work with Communist Russia against a rearming Nazi Germany. Intact, though, was the Labour Party, with the composition that he helped forge, determined both to be an independent party and to stay within the constitutional system, although this time determined to develop coherent plans for major programs when it next took office. It was a party which identified its goals as being national ones, not class ones. MacDonaldism, though not MacDonald, survived within the party.

Bibliography

Bassett, Reginald. *1931: Political Crisis.* London: Macmillan, and New York: St. Martin's Press, 1958. The August crisis was meticulously researched (except for the MacDonald papers, which were then not available and except for interviews of participants still living) to produce this exhaustive study. Complex and detailed as it sorts out the chronology among contradictory sources, it demonstrates the confusion and resulting bitterness and frustration of that controversial episode in MacDonald's career.

Bealey, Frank, and Henry Pelling. *Labour and Politics, 1900-1906: A History of the Labour Representation Committee.* London: Macmillan, and New York: St. Martin's Press, 1958. This thorough and seminal work demonstrates MacDonald's enormous political and organizational skills. Only in his thirties, he, as secretary, perceived that the newly formed Labour Representation Committee could become an independent party but only by cooperating with Liberals in parliamentary elections and in Parliament itself, all of which was accomplished, primarily through MacDonald's organizational abilities.

Carlton, David. *MacDonald versus Henderson: The Foreign Policy of the Second Labour Government.* London: Macmillan, and New York: Humanities Press, 1970. This fine work demonstrates that even during deteriorating world conditions, the government tried valiantly to pursue the party's general international aspirations supporting international law, mutual disarmament, and international harmony. Complicating matters was the personal (not policy) tension between the prime minister and foreign minister, which actually is only a minor theme of the book.

Lloyd, Trevor. "James Ramsay MacDonald." In *British Prime Ministers in the Twentieth Century,* edited by John P. Mackintosh, 2 vols. London: Weidenfeld and Nicolson, and New York: St. Martin's Press, 1977-1978. In this fine essay focusing on MacDonald as prime minister, Lloyd considers that portion of his career anticlimactic after his great contributions in Labour theory and organization. Sensitive but critical, Lloyd describes the aloof MacDonald unable to work well with backbenchers or cabinet members and too interested in external affairs while too little informed on economics.

Lyman, Richard W. *The First Labour Government, 1924.* London: Chapman and Hall, 1957; New York: Russell and Russell, 1975. This standard work examines all three parties, the 1923 and 1924 elections, and Labour in office. Lyman is basically favorable to MacDonald and the Labour Party, approving their decision to form a temporary government to demonstrate their moderation and acceptability.

MacDonald, Ramsay. *Ramsay MacDonald's Political Writings.* Edited by Bernard Barker. London: Allen Lane, and New York: St. Martin's Press, 1972. Barker's perceptive introductory essay warns against the traditional biological emphasis on MacDonald's concept of "evolutionary socialism." Instead, he stresses the theme of social justice in an expanding industrial society. All or major portions of MacDonald's most significant works are represented: *Socialism and Society* (1905), *Socialism* (1907), *Socialism: Critical and Constructive* (1921), *Parliament and Revolution* (1919), and *Parliament and Democracy* (1920).

McKibbin, Ross. *The Evolution of the Labour Party, 1910-1924*. London and New York: Oxford University Press, 1974. Focusing on the party organization outside of Parliament, McKibbin recognizes MacDonald's key role in structuring it during the early 1910's, even after he resigned as secretary in 1911. MacDonald (and Henderson) wanted to run parliamentary candidates only where they had a chance of victory and to create constituency parties not dominated by trade unions.

Marquand, David. "In Defence of the Class Traitor." *New Statesman* 126, no. 4347 (August 15, 1997). Discussion of MacDonald's role in the history of modern Britain.

———. *Ramsay MacDonald*. London: Cape, 1977. This impressive, sympathetic, and massive biography captures the very complex public and private MacDonald, often through pertinent, extensive quotations from his diary and letters. Marquand stresses MacDonald's consistency in advocating that the party (and MacDonald) should not be dominated by trade unions or be class-bound but rather be directed toward the entire society's interests.

Oborne, Peter. "For Labour, There's No Such Thing as Society." *Spectator* 281, no. 8886 (November 28, 1998). Compares Prime Minister Tony Blair and MacDonald.

Sacks, Benjamin. *J. Ramsay MacDonald in Thought and Action: An Architect for a Better World*. Albuquerque: University of New Mexico Press, 1952. Extracting from MacDonald's voluminous writings, Sacks weaves together MacDonald's views and analyses around five major headings: politics, social issues, industry, imperialism, and international relations. Most of it in MacDonald's own words, this book demonstrates his tremendous contribution to formulating a Labour perspective.

Skidelsky, Robert. *Politicians and the Slump: The Labour Government of 1929-1931*. London: Macmillan, 1967. Highly critical of MacDonald and the second Labour government, Skidelsky considers them out of their element in attempting to cope with the widening economic and financial crises, which the author considers the major governmental issues.

Jerry H. Brookshire

SAMORA MOISÈS MACHEL

Born: September 29, 1933; Chilembene,
  Mozambique
Died: October 19, 1986; Mbuzini, near Komati-
  poort, Lebombo Mountains, South Africa
Areas of Achievement: The military, government,
  and politics
Contribution: Machel is mostly remembered for
  his able leadership as commander of the guerrilla army of the Mozambique Liberation Front,
  which fought against the stronger Portuguese
  army from 1964 to 1974. He was also the first
  President of the People's Republic of Mozambique, from 1975 to his death in 1986.

Early Life

Samora Moisès Machel was born in the Shangaan
district, Chilembene village, Gaza Province,
Mozambique, on September 29, 1933, of well-to-
do peasant parents who owned land in the Limpo-
po River Valley. His family was known and quite
respected in the district, as some of its members
had participated in the resistance against the Portuguese at the turn of the century. Despite the fact
that Machel's family was Protestant, his father sent
him to study at a Catholic mission, where he was
baptized a Catholic. Following completion of his
four years of primary school, he decided to work in
Lourenço Marques (modern Maputo) and attend
classes at a nurses' training school, while at the
same time pursuing private secondary school
courses, all at his own expense.

In 1962, the Mozambique Liberation Front
(FRELIMO) was created in Dar es Salaam, Tanzania, under the leadership of Eduardo Mondlane, a
scholar educated in the United States. Revolutionary change was at the time sweeping through Africa, and Machel, a nurse who was then serving under a female Portuguese doctor at Lourenço
Marques, decided to abandon his career and join
FRELIMO. He was eventually made a trainer of
new military recruits and commander of the campaigns against the Portuguese in the Niassa Province. In this capacity, he was in charge of the Center of Political and Military Training at
Nachingwea, earning the respect of his revolutionary colleagues. Soon, while Mondlane essentially
became the political leader of FRELIMO, and
Marcelino dos Santos (member of the Central
Committee) the socialist ideologue, Machel was
clearly the promising military tactician.

Machel assumed the position of secretary of the
Department of Defense of FRELIMO, thus qualifying to be a member of the Central Committee.
He soon became the number-one man in command
of the Forcas Populares de Libertacao de Moçam-
bique (Popular Forces for the Liberation of
Mozambique). Not only did Machel lead the war
of liberation in the north of Mozambique but also
he established people's committees in the growing
liberated zones in an effort to educate the people,
provide them with the rudiments of health, improve the peasants' plight, and prepare them for
eventual independence.

Life's Work

During the 1967-1970 period, now in his thirties,
Machel became a seasoned military leader and succeeded, region after region, in slowly driving the
well-equipped Portuguese army as far down as
Tete Province by 1974. His determination and
sound military judgment continued to earn for him
the respect of all guerrilla leaders and fighters. At
the same time, he was developing in his mind and
formulating publicly his social philosophy, which
was in part based on his Marxist training in Algeria
and his experience at the hands of the Portuguese
colonialists. He embraced a Marxist-Leninist philosophy in an attempt to see the elimination of the
"petty" bourgeoisie which, in his view, exploited
the African masses along with the Portuguese, and
to advance the cause of the peasants and the workers. The assassination of Mondlane in February,
1969, preceded and followed by the most serious
leadership crisis FRELIMO ever experienced,
emerged as an opportunity for him to become both
FRELIMO's highest military commander and its
political leader. By 1969, his radical philosophy,
supported by Marxist ideologue Marcelino dos
Santos, had triumphed. Following the assassination
of Mondlane, Machel and dos Santos, instead of
letting moderate Urias Simango—the vice president of FRELIMO—succeed to the Front's presidency, conspired and created instead a triumvirate
dominated by Machel. After the ouster of many
party members and the defection of others to the
Portuguese (Simango eventually followed this
path), in May, 1970, the Central Committee appointed Machel president of FRELIMO.

Meanwhile, despite its internal problems,
FRELIMO was still making progress on the war

front. Unexpectedly, on April 24, 1974, the Portuguese army, tired of an irrational dictatorship at home and the protracted fighting in three colonies (Angola, Mozambique, and Guinea-Bissau), overthrew its own government in Lisbon and initiated independence negotiations with the liberation movements. As a result of the formal talks held in Lusaka, Zambia, a transitional government was installed to lead the colony to full independence, scheduled for June 25, 1975. Joaquim Chissano, a member of the Central Committee, assumed the position of prime minister of the transitional government, while Machel remained in Tanzania, assured that the latter would not upstage him. In June, 1975, Machel was officially appointed President of Mozambique by FRELIMO's Central Committee. Almost immediately, the new president embarked upon fully implementing his socialist program. By the end of 1977, following FRELIMO's III Congress (February 3-7, 1977), education, health, justice, property, and major business establishments had been nationalized. FRELIMO was transformed into a vanguard party for the workers and the peasants, following a Marxist-Leninist philosophy; membership requirements were tightened and many old members were purged—only those embracing the socialist ideology who exhibited accepted moral behavior could apply for membership, and collective villages, farms, and people's shops were established throughout the country. The immediacy of the radical changes caused a stir in the country and worsened the fragile political and economic situation.

In April, 1983, Machel was reelected president of the republic and continued to hold his position as president of the party and commander in chief of the Popular Forces. A man of medium height, bearded, and fearing no one, Machel became a charismatic leader and accumulated considerable personal power—a move away from previous collective leadership. No one could question his authority, and those few who did ended up in jail or in reeducation camps, or lost their lives. He praised the Soviet Union and castigated the West as a group of imperialist racists and selfish capitalist nations. He signed a Treaty of Friendship with the Soviet Union in 1977. He also closed the Mozambique border to goods from the white regime in southern Rhodesia (now Zimbabwe) and provided bases to Robert Mugabe's Zimbabwe African National Union (a move that cost the country $550 million between 1976 and 1980). He stepped up

his rhetoric against the apartheid regime and spearheaded the creation of the Southern Africa Development Coordination Conference, established in 1980 by nine frontline states to break South Africa's hegemony in the subcontinent.

Machel's problems at home, however, were formidable. Immediately after he assumed power, several reactionary elements opposed the regime. At the same time, the Mozambique National Resistance (RENAMO) emerged in Southern Rhodesia, supported by the white regime and by South Africa after Zimbabwe's independence in April, 1980. RENAMO systematically aimed at paralyzing the country by destroying the infrastructure and eliminating FRELIMO supporters in order to force the government to abandon its Marxist-Leninist socialism and accept the concept of free elections, free enterprise, and the principle of a multiparty state.

Unfortunately, RENAMO was actively assisted by South Africa, partly because Machel had allowed the African National Congress to have bases in southern Mozambique. The West, particularly the United States, refused to provide any financial assistance to Mozambique as long as the country was strengthening its ties with the Soviet Union, while blasting the "imperialist capitalist West." The socialist steps taken at home were failing, as European technicians, managers, farmers, and professionals began a massive exodus out of the country, frightened by the new rhetoric and the nationalization policies. By 1983, some 200,000 Portuguese had left the country. The economy, worsened by RENAMO's attacks and by droughts and floodings in the south, was in shambles, plagued by inflation, unemployment, and a drop in agricultural and industrial productivity by almost 50 percent in some sectors.

The deteriorating national situation compelled the president to take several drastic measures. He began a diplomatic offensive to garner economic and military support from the West through his visits to Portugal, France, Great Britain, and Belgium in 1983, while toning down his rhetoric against the United States. He invited foreign entrepreneurs and investors to start businesses in the country, returned some of the nationalized property to individuals, put up for sale some of the people's shops and began reconciliation with the churches to which he had shown only contempt. The most dramatic move of his new pragmatism was the signing of the Nkomati Accord with South Africa on March 16, 1984. In a pompous ceremony at which Machel appeared in his field marshal's outfit, the President of Mozambique and Pieter Botha, then Prime Minister of South Africa, pledged not to interfere in each other's internal affairs. While South Africa would stop supporting RENAMO, Mozambique would curtail the ANC's activities. Thus, by October, 1984, Mozambique had forced the departure of close to one thousand ANC members from the country, allowing only ten staff members to remain in Maputo. South Africa, however, never kept its part of the pact.

In addition, to end corruption and inefficiency, the new Machel shuffled and reshuffled his cabinet, as he did in April, 1986, when he created the position of prime minister (given to Mario Da Graca Machungo) in order for him to concentrate on the military situation, and appointed four members of the Politburo to supervise the activities of government ministers.

Frustrated by South Africa's continued assistance to RENAMO, Machel requested military assistance from Prime Minister Robert Mugabe at a Harare summit attended by the two leaders and Julius Nyerere of Tanzania. In October, 1986, Machel visited President Hastings Banda in an attempt to persuade him not to allow free access to RENAMO through Malawi. Yet Machel received only vague promises from Banda. Despite the involvement of Zimbabwean and, later, Tanzanian troops in the Mozambique civil war, RENAMO continued to devastate the country, and the economy did not improve. The West promised assistance, but it was not forthcoming in significant amounts, while the Soviet Union continued its supply of military hardware but not of food and funds. As is common when things are in disarray in developing countries, rumors of assassination plots against the president spread, and Machel became, indeed, a besieged man. On October 19, 1986, returning from a minisummit in Zambia where a new strategy against RENAMO was plotted, Machel's Tupolev-134 crashed against the Libombo Mountains in South African territory, only three miles from Namaacha, Mozambique, as apparently the Soviet pilots were unable to reach Maputo airport. South Africa was accused of having engineered the crash, although an international board of inquiry, of which Mozambique was a participant in the early stages, blamed pilot error for the tragic incident. Two weeks later, Joaquim Chissano, the minister for foreign affairs, was appointed President of Mozambique by the Central Committee.

Summary

Samora Moisès Machel was doubtless a self-made man. In spite of the little formal education he had, he was able to rise to the ranks of the modern military and statesmen. Seasoned by his own experience and propelled by an unswerving will, the former nurse was able to defy any personal shortcomings resulting from five hundred years of Portuguese colonial rule and became one of the most important revolutionaries of the Third World. As a guerrilla leader, he successfully waged a war that drove the Portuguese out of Mozambique. As a statesman, however, Machel became too dogmatic and too impatient with the pace of change and with those who served under him. The atmosphere of his cabinet meetings, for example, is only now being discussed openly. It is reported that Machel often humiliated ministers, was prone to sudden outbursts of anger, and displayed a disregard for protocol that sometimes bordered on the insane. His hasty socialist policies, barely understood by the people of Mozambique and those who were supposed to implement them, fell on deaf ears. Ultimately, his economic policies hurt more than helped the country.

His ascension to power was premature, as FRELIMO and most observers expected a long, protracted war against the Portuguese. The collapse of the Portuguese colonial state in 1974 surprised everyone, including Machel, who had not been prepared to lead a new country. As the years passed, however, the president became a pragmatist of sorts, but this pragmatism was forced upon him by the country's miserable state and the questionable future of his own leadership. Tragic is the fact that Machel was unable to see the result of his change of diplomatic emphasis and the country's new economic direction. If Machel had some major victories as a statesman, however, the accelerated improvements in education and literacy in the country top the list, followed by his implementation of a nonracial policy as president, in spite of the fact that earlier, as a radical Marxist on the Central Committee, Machel sounded antiwhite and antimestizo.

On the other hand, among his major failures stand the Nkomati Accord, which was covertly opposed by Presidents Julius Nyerere of Tanzania and Kenneth Kaunda of Zambia. Evidently, Machel and his advisers had failed to see that the Pact was a South African trap. The fact that Machel made the signing of the pact a momentous occasion, with himself standing in colorful uniform side by side with the perpetuator of the apartheid regime, made the mistake even more regrettable to most observers and analysts.

Regardless of his mistakes, one thing seems to be clear about Machel: He was genuinely concerned with the plight of the peasants and the workers. Unfortunately, the concern was couched either in the wrong developmental philosophy or in a sound philosophy that adopted the wrong strategies. His premature death prevented him from completing the implementation of his ideals, leaving the question of the outcome of his government unanswered. Overall, by 1986, Machel had fewer victories to celebrate. Whether his policies and tactics as President of Mozambique will be repudiated by his successors remains to be seen.

Bibliography

Azevedo, Mario. "A Sober Commitment to Liberation? Mozambique and South Africa." *African Affairs* 79, no. 317 (1980): 567-584. The article highlights the dilemmas that Machel encountered in his relations with South Africa in the spheres of trade, railways, harbors, tourism, technical assistance, and employment of Mozambicans, all of which influenced his pragmatism.

Chilcote, Ronald H. *Portuguese Africa*. Englewood Cliffs, N.J.: Prentice-Hall, 1977. A general work on the former Portuguese colonies that also looks objectively at the liberation leaders.

Duffy, James. *Portugal in Africa*. London and Baltimore: Penguin, 1962. One of the best succinct studies of the Portuguese colonial system. Duffy's sympathy goes to the nationalist movement; he could not foresee how the new leaders would fare as statesmen.

Hanlon, Joseph. *Mozambique: The Revolution Under Fire*. London: Zed Press, and Totowa, N.J.: Biblio, 1984. This is probably the best account of the successes and failures of FRELIMO's policies in Mozambique and the evolution of Marxist thinking within the Front.

Isaacman, Allen, and Barbara Isaacman. *Mozambique: From Colonialism to Revolution, 1900-1982*. Boulder, Colo.: Westview Press, and Aldershot, Hampshire: Gower, 1983. An excellent work on the history of Mozambique that enlightens any reader on the conditions that brought about the nationalist movement in Mozambique.

Mondlane, Eduardo. *The Struggle for Mozambique*. London and Baltimore: Penguin, 1969. One of the best sources on the development of the nationalist movement in Mozambique, imbued with the personal insights of the first president of FRELIMO.

Serapiao, Luis, and Mohamed El-Khawas. *Mozambique in the Twentieth Century: From Colonialism to Independence*. Washington, D.C.: University Press of America, 1979. Although reviews of the book have been mixed, Serapiao and El-Khawas provide insightful information about FRELIMO and Machel's leadership style. One of the authors, however, a Mozambican, does not hide his disapproval of Machel's leadership and FRELIMO's policies in Mozambique.

Mario Azevedo

SIR HALFORD JOHN MACKINDER

Born: February 15, 1861; Gainsborough, Lincoln-
shire, England
Died: March 6, 1947; Parkstone, Dorset, England
Areas of Achievement: Geography, politics, and
education
Contribution: Mackinder's contributions in the
academic discipline of geography gained early recognition, and significant institutions
were created for which he was credited. Mackinder is most noted for the Heartland theory
of geopolitics.

Early Life

Halford John Mackinder initially hoped to follow
the occupation of his father, a medical doctor. Later he shifted his studies to science, then history and
strategy, then law, which he actually practiced for a
time, and, finally, he began lecturing on "the New
Geography."

Mackinder was the eldest son of Draper and Fanny Anne Hewitt Mackinder, who were both of
Scottish ancestry. His education was at Epsom
College and at Oxford, where he first gained a junior studentship at Christ Church in 1880. In 1883,
he was president of the Oxford Union, and in 1884
he gained the Burdett-Coutts science scholarship.
Later, he was called to the bar at Inner Temple and
also began lecturing in the university extension
system, eventually delivering more than six hundred lectures, mostly in the North and West between 1885 and 1893.

Mackinder was asked to give his lecture on
"Scope and Methods of Geography" to the Royal
Geographical Society in January, 1887, thus stimulating the revival of the academic discipline of geography in Great Britain. In 1892, he traveled to
the United States and lectured at a number of major universities, including Johns Hopkins, Harvard,
and Chicago.

Mackinder always involved himself in a number
of endeavors simultaneously. Extension lecturing
led him into university administration, where he
was to make significant contributions at several institutions. During the 1890's he was director of
what evolved into the University of Reading. Between 1903 and 1908 he served as the second director of the newly formed London School of Economics and Political Science. Between 1895 and
1925 he was lecturer and then professor of geography at the University of London. At the same time

he was instrumental in the creation of the first institute, and then school, of geography, officially
formed at Oxford in 1899. His readership in geography at Oxford, the first such appointment in a
British university, was from 1887 to 1905.

In 1889, Mackinder married Emilie Catherine
Ginsburg, the daughter of an Old Testament scholar. Emilie Mackinder often lived abroad, and, although she survived her husband, there is rarely
any mention of her in Mackinder's obituaries.

Life's Work

At the same time that Mackinder was accomplishing so much in university administration and in the
academic institutionalization of the discipline of
geography, he was also formulating innovative theories on political geography, later known as geopolitics. He had already impressed academic authorities, especially leaders of the Royal
Geographical Society, with his early lectures on
the New Geography and the scope and methods of
geography.

The discipline of geography in Great Britain had
been declining, and many considered it unworthy of
academic study. Oxford University, influenced by
Mackinder, began the most significant steps of the
subject's rehabilitation. During his formative years,
Mackinder was influenced by Sir Bartle Frere, president of the Royal Geographical Society in the
1870's. While working as an administrator, Mackinder published basic texts in geography. Most important was *Britain and the British Seas* (1902).
This book became the standard regional guide and
was considered a classic of modern geographical
literature. Other texts followed, including guides
on India and the Rhine area of Europe.

Mackinder's close association with the Royal
Geographical Society provided a platform for the
development of his geopolitical theories. In 1904,
Mackinder presented a paper, "The Geographical
Pivot of History," in the *Geographical Journal*.
This was the first statement of his geopolitical theories. The second major statement of his theories
appeared in a book, *Democratic Ideals and Reality*,
published in 1919, in which the famous Heartland
thesis is found in full. *Democratic Ideals and Reality* was addressed to the peacemakers at the Paris
Peace Conference after World War I. Mackinder
continued to refine his views in an article published
in *Foreign Affairs*, a journal of interest to experts

in the foreign policy of the United States. The article, "The Round World and the Winning of the Peace" (July, 1943), was written during World War II and incorporates concepts associated with the rapid, dramatic industrial and technological advances of the past several decades.

The essence of Mackinder's theory is his famous dictum or triptych, first published in *Democratic Ideals and Reality:*

> Who rules East Europe commands the Heartland:
> Who rules the Heartland commands the World-Island:
> Who rules the World-Island commands the World.

Mackinder was never consistent about the precise location of the Heartland; presumably it was an area about twenty-five hundred miles across and the same up and down, and included Western Asia and Eastern Europe. At one point he described the southern Ural mountain region as "the very pivot of the pivot area."

In the variations of his theory, Mackinder speculated about possible controllers of the Heartland: Russia, Germany, a combination of those two, or a number of small states. The first three possibilities

would definitely threaten the hegemony of British or Anglo-American interests, among others, and Mackinder obviously favored a unified British imperial and naval influence; he feared, however, that these interests would be overwhelmed by a powerful land-based axis, especially by the feared combination of Russia and Germany. He anticipated that after further technological advances, such as the railway and air power, sea-based or peripheral powers would decline. In various ways, Mackinder perceived the potential of railroads and of air power, of the rise of Japan, and of some powerful political combinations such as those of Russia and Germany and Great Britain and the United States.

There is much debate about the influence of Mackinder and his geopolitical theories. At worst he has been accused of directly encouraging the expansionist and racist machinations of Adolf Hitler and the Nazis, and of causing the Cold War, the ultimate confrontation over the Heartland and global domination. At a more academic and less emotional level, scholars have debated his influence upon other geopolitical theorists, such as Alfred Thayer Mahan and Friedrich Ratzel. Most commentary focuses upon Mackinder's influence on the German geopolitician Karl Haushofer of the University of Munich. Presumably, a case can be made that Haushofer taught his student, Rudolf Hess, who later instructed his superior, Adolf Hitler. There is no question that Haushofer and his school of German *Geopolitik* made important contributions to the Nazi cause, supplying a pseudo-scientific rationalization for Hitler's policies of expansion and racism.

It should be noted that Mackinder made a definite effort to distance himself from any association with Haushofer. He pointedly avoided the use of the term "geopolitics," preferring instead "geostrategic" to describe his own methodology. In a note in the 1942 edition of *Democratic Ideals and Reality*, Mackinder specifically renounced any links to Haushofer and his school.

In his native Great Britain, Mackinder received belated recognition. Only at the end of his life, in 1945, did he receive the Patron's Medal, the highest award from the Royal Geographical Society. In 1971, Oxford University finally honored the founder of academic geography by establishing the Halford Mackinder Professorship of Geography.

For all of his academic status, however, Mackinder did not confine himself solely to scholarly concerns. In addition to academic geography and political geography, Mackinder was an explorer, elected politician, diplomatic official, public servant, activist, and intellectual. In 1899, Mackinder led an expedition to East Africa and was the first to climb the seventeen-thousand-foot-high Mount Kenya successfully. As early as 1900, then a Liberal Imperialist, Mackinder became interested in pursuing politics. Unfortunately, he was ahead of his time. As his political center of gravity moved to the right, to the Unionists and then the Conservatives, the Liberals united and achieved a spectacular victory in the election of 1906. Finally, in 1910, Mackinder won a seat in the House of Commons, in the industrial district of Camlachie, Glasgow. His political career lasted until 1922, when he was defeated by a Labour Party candidate. He was consistently an advocate of imperialism, tariff reform, colonial preference, and a unified empire. He was a member of the Tariff Reform League and Victoria League.

It was during his time in the House of Commons that Mackinder entered the somewhat murky situation of Allied intervention in Russia. In 1920, he was appointed British High Commissioner for South Russia. Mackinder was the obvious choice for the decision makers. Lord Curzon became Foreign Secretary in October, 1919. He was president of the Royal Geographical Society and was advised by two other associates of Mackinder, Lord Milner and L. S. Amery. Mackinder had just presented recommendations to the Versailles peacemakers on the disposition of Eastern Europe and Western Asia—the Heartland. As commissioner, Mackinder was to lead a team of political and economic experts to evaluate the situation, contact influential leaders, and report to the cabinet.

The team departed on December 4, 1919, traveled to Warsaw, Bucharest, Sofia, Constantinople, and, via the Royal Navy, into the Black Sea. Among the prominent leaders interviewed was Anton Denikin, the White Russian leader in the Russian civil war. Mackinder made his report and recommendations to the cabinet on January 29, 1920. Unfortunately, the situation in the cabinet was rapidly changing: The Allies were withdrawing from Eastern Europe and the position of the White Russians was deteriorating. Great Britain had already announced that no further direct aid would go to them.

Mackinder's team had concocted various schemes with the anti-Bolshevist leaders of the region. He warned that Russia under Bolshevism would make the world "an uncomfortable place for democracies" and that there was a threat of "a new Russian Czardom of the proletariat." As a boundary commissioner he recommended establishing another tier of states east of the *cordon sanitaire* set up at Versailles (the Baltic states, Poland, Hungary, Romania). This new set of buffer states might include White Russia, the Ukraine, Georgia, Armenia, and Byelorussia.

The cabinet rudely rejected Mackinder's recommendations, one cabinet member declared them "absurd." Even Winston Churchill opposed them. In addition, such blatantly anticommunist declarations caused his working-class constituents of Glasgow to react negatively. Mackinder resigned as commissioner and was soon defeated for reelection.

Mackinder pursued other opportunities for public service. He was knighted in 1920 and made privy councillor in 1926. During World War I he was instrumental in recruitment in Scotland and served prominently on the National War Savings Committee. He is credited with formulating the process of saving by stamps. From 1920 to 1945 he served as chairman of the Imperial Shipping Committee (at two thousand pounds per year) and from 1925 to 1931 he was chair of the Imperial Economic Committee.

Prior to World War I, Mackinder was a founding member of an extraordinary group of intellectuals, the Coefficients Club. The club's primary concern was the reversal of a perceived loss of national efficiency. At about the same time, Mackinder helped found the Compatriots, a small group which dedicated itself to "promote the wider patriotism of the Commonwealth."

Mackinder, growing deaf, increasingly withdrew from world affairs during the 1930's. He collected papers, subsequently deposited in the School of Geography at Oxford, for an autobiography, but only fragments survive. He died on March 6, 1947.

Summary

Sir Halford John Mackinder was always ahead of his time and insufficiently appreciated at home. To some extent he has been unfairly maligned, especially for his alleged influence on developments in Nazi Germany and in the Cold War. His political and diplomatic careers seemed plagued by anachronisms, in these cases futuristic and not past. Recognition and credit were often late and distant, fully arriving only after his death because of the global and interdisciplinary nature of his treatises. Few critics had the breadth of vision to appreciate him.

Nevertheless, Mackinder's contributions are major ones, particularly in the fields of academic geography and geopolitics. He was a leader in reviving the discipline of geography in the late nineteenth century, and his theory of the Heartland has become a geopolitical axiom.

Bibliography

Blouet, Brian W. *Halford Mackinder: A Biography.* College Station: Texas A&M University Press, 1987. The long-awaited full biography. The bibliography, which is comprehensive, lists 111 works by Mackinder from 1887 to 1945. Explains some of the personal aspects of Mackinder's activities, such as the lack of close friends, the absence of dedicated students, and the failed marriage.

———. "Sir Halford Mackinder as British High Commissioner to South Russia, 1919-1920." *Geographical Journal* 108 (1976): 228-236. A step-by-step presentation of the notorious commission sent into Eastern Europe and Russia in 1919-1920, headed by Mackinder, which effectively laid the foundation of an anti-Bolshevik alliance. Incorporates previously secret files from the Public Record Office. The failure affected Mackinder politically and personally.

Gilbert, Edmund W., and W. H. Parker. "Mackinder's *Democratic Ideals and Reality* After Fifty Years." *Geographical Journal* 135 (June, 1969): 228-231. An appreciation of Mackinder's major book after fifty years. Gilbert concludes that the book was too far ahead of its time, and its relevance has increased with time.

Hall, Arthur B. "Mackinder and the Course of Events." *Annals of the Association of American Geographers* 45 (June, 1955): 109-126. A thorough and scholarly assessment of Mackinder's geopolitical theories from the perspective of American scholars. Hall concludes that Mackinder set out to create "a geographical formula into which you could fit any political balance."

Parker, W. H. *Mackinder: Geography as an Aid to Statecraft.* Oxford: Clarendon Press, and New York: Oxford University Press, 1982. An intellectual history. Parker analyzes the Mackinder-Haushofer link and the criticism of the Heartland thesis. Not a biography.

Eugene L. Rasor

CATHARINE A. MacKINNON

Born: 1946; Minneapolis, Minnesota

Areas of Achievement: Law and women's rights

Contribution: A pioneer in the development of feminist legal theory, MacKinnon formulated the argument that sexual harassment should be viewed as a form of sex discrimination—an argument that later became embedded in law.

Early Life

Catharine Alice MacKinnon was born in Minneapolis, Minnesota, in 1946, the daughter of George E. and Elizabeth V. (Davis) MacKinnon. George MacKinnon was a leading figure in Minnesota politics during Catharine's childhood; he was an adviser to the Eisenhower and Nixon presidential campaigns, served as a U.S. congressman from Minnesota and as Republican nominee for governor, and was appointed by President Richard M. Nixon to serve on the U.S. Court of Appeals for the District of Columbia.

Like her mother and her maternal grandmother, Catharine MacKinnon attended Smith College. She graduated magna cum laude in 1969 with a bachelor of arts degree in government. She went on to study at Yale University, where she did graduate work in political science before being accepted at Yale Law School, where she received her law degree in 1977. (She was awarded the Ph.D. in political science from Yale in 1987.) While at Yale, MacKinnon created the first course in the university's women's studies program, and was active in radical politics, working with the Black Panthers and in the campaign against the Vietnam War.

It was while still a law student that she conceived her now-famous argument that sexual harassment is a form of sex discrimination. Since its initial publication, her book *Sexual Harassment of Working Women* (1979) has been considered to be the definitive work on the subject.

While feminist legal theory has become a firmly established part of the curriculum at most American law schools, this was not the case when MacKinnon first set out; indeed, her pathbreaking work was one of the main influences on the development of this new discipline. The basic premise of feminist legal theory, as advanced by MacKinnon and others, is that the law, as a social institution in a male-dominated (patriarchal) society, reflects the viewpoints, and represents the interests, of men rather than women. According to MacKin-

non and other feminist legal scholars, laws against rape are based on men's conceptions of what constitutes nonconsensual sex, obscenity laws reflect men's conceptions of offensiveness, and so forth.

During the 1980's, MacKinnon was a guest lecturer at a number of leading universities, including Chicago, Harvard, Stanford, and Yale. Despite widespread acknowledgment of the significance of her work, however, MacKinnon was not offered a full-time teaching position until 1990, when she obtained a position as tenured professor at the University of Michigan Law School.

Life's Work

Catharine MacKinnon's first book was the pioneering study, *Sexual Harassment of Working Women*. The book contains her analysis of harassment, which was taken up by a U.S. Court of Appeals in *Barnes v. Costle* (1977), and thus provided the theoretical basis for viewing harassment as an offense that transgresses the law. Her basic idea was simple: Sexual harassment is a kind of behavior to which a person is subject because of her sex, and therefore it can be seen as a form of discrimination under Title VII of the Civil Rights Act of 1964, which forbids differential treatment in the workplace on the basis of group membership (race, sex, religion, or other classification).

Barnes was a landmark decision: for the first time, a high-level court went on record as opposing the popular notion that harassment is an inevitable fact of life and that for the law to try to protect against such treatment is equivalent to tampering with the laws of nature. A typical feature of pre-*Barnes* cases as documented by MacKinnon was the courts' insistence that what plaintiffs had argued was abusive treatment was merely a normal expression of male sexuality ("boys will be boys," in effect), where "normal" is assumed to mean something like "natural." Another typical feature of such cases was the courts' assumption that harassing behavior was a feature of the unique dynamics of the relationship between two individuals, rather than as a pattern that was made possible by the fact that the harasser is in a position of power vis-à-vis the harassed and so should be seen as an expression of that power.

Thus MacKinnon's argument, basically endorsed by *Barnes*, involved two steps: recognizing that certain typical expressions of male sexuality may be abusive despite their being typical; and recognizing the workplace as an environment in which men will tend to harass women because they have the power to do so.

While *Barnes* was significant, feminists such as MacKinnon considered that its definition of what constituted harassment—basically, "sleep with me or you're fired" or variations of this sort of quid pro quo—was too narrow. Then, in 1986, the U.S. Supreme Court unanimously decided, in *Meritor Savings Bank v. Vinson*, that harassment as a legal offense is committed whenever unwanted sexual remarks or behaviors create a "hostile environment" for workers. MacKinnon was part of the plaintiff's legal team in this case. She wrote Vinson's brief to the Court, helped her attorney prepare for oral argument, and appeared as co-counsel before the Court. What was at issue was whether Title VII covered only tangible losses—such as if an employee were fired for not sleeping with the boss—or whether psychological damage was also covered. Vinson's employer conceded that her supervisor harassed her—by fondling her, for example—but that such behavior was not illegal. MacKinnon's argument was again quite simple: Does the court require that a person "bring intensified injury upon herself"—quit or be fired—"in order to demonstrate that she is injured at all?" The Court responded unanimously: No!

In *Harris v. Forklift Systems* (1993), the Supreme Court took a further step along the course charted by *Vinson*, when it decided unanimously that the criteria for deciding whether a hostile environment exists should depend on the quality of the environment—specifically, on whether it could be reasonably perceived as hostile or abusive—and not on the psychological or other effects it has on its victims. Otherwise, a harassed individual who did not break down under the pressure of harassment would, in effect, be punished for having summoned the emotional resources to survive the experience. This argument is basically the same as the "intensified injury" argument MacKinnon made in the *Vinson* case.

Since the early 1980's, MacKinnon has been involved in a campaign against another normal expression of male-dominant sexuality that she perceives as harmful to women: pornography. She notes that in the video age the harm done is direct and immediate: What is depicted in visual pornography as rape, coercion, and torture, actually occur as rape, coercion, and torture in the making of the pornography. MacKinnon implies that there are at least two reasons why most people fail to recognize this obvious fact about pornography (and why, as a result, her views on the subject are considered outrageous by many commentators). First of all, pornography depicts women as enjoying what is done to them. Second, even if they are not enjoying themselves, it is assumed that these women are participating voluntarily. To take the second assumption first: MacKinnon argues that women are in most cases coerced into making pornography by their boyfriends or pimps or drug suppliers (who may, of course, be the same person). Once this coercion becomes apparent, the first defense of pornography falls by the wayside: If you can be forced to make pornography, you can be forced to appear to enjoy it. Furthermore, MacKinnon argues that pornography is an indirect cause of tangible harms to women in the sense that abusers and rapists are often inspired to abuse and rape by the scenes of abuse and rape they have seen, and been turned on by, in pornography.

In the mid-1980's, MacKinnon and feminist writer and activist Andrea Dworkin embarked on a campaign to make it possible for victims of pornography to sue their victimizers. In the fall of 1983, MacKinnon and Dworkin framed a civil antipornography ordinance for the city of Minneapolis; it was passed by the city council, but was vetoed by the mayor before being passed and vetoed again. In 1984, a similar law was passed by the city of Indianapolis and was signed by Mayor William Hudnut. This ordinance was struck down by a district court shortly thereafter; and the district court's decision was upheld by a federal court of appeals in 1986. It agreed with the lower court that the ordinance violated the First Amendment guarantee of free speech—even while conceding, for the most part, the harms pornography does to women.

Despite these legal setbacks, MacKinnon has continued to campaign tirelessly against the pornography industry. Over the years, she has further refined her argument against pornography. In her 1993 book, *Only Words*, she continues to treat pornography, like harassment, as sex discrimination, and points out the tension between the First Amendment guarantee of free speech, which has so far protected the pornography industry, and the Fourteenth Amendment guarantee of equal protection of the laws, which MacKinnon believes ought to apply to victims of pornography. But then she adds a new argument, which would, if accepted, resolve this tension, at least in the case of pornography: While the defenders of pornography assume that pornography is "merely speech," the reality of pornography is what it does.

MacKinnon's views on pornography have made her a frequent target of attacks in the press; reviews of *Only Words* in major publications ranged from the politely dismissive to the crude and badgering. The review that appeared in *The Nation* was so abusive that it elicited a written protest from her publisher. She has been ridiculed by Katie Roiphe, in her book *The Morning After*, as an "anti-porn queen." Many feminists oppose MacKinnon's "obsession" with pornography, which they claim diverts attention from more significant issues of economic and political equality (though MacKinnon believes these issues are all related) and depicts women as helpless victims in need of protection by the state (as if demanding equality does not normally involve seeking protection from the state, as in the case of civil rights legislation).

Despite these criticisms, MacKinnon has become a popular speaker on college campuses and at academic conferences, and is widely regarded as a charismatic teacher who has profoundly influenced an entire generation of law students—not to mention influencing the law itself.

Since 1993, MacKinnon has been involved in publicizing the sexual atrocities perpetrated by the Bosnian Serbs as part of their ethnic cleansing campaign, and providing legal assistance for the victims.

MacKinnon's other books include *Feminism Unmodified* (1987) and *Toward a Feminist Theory of the State* (1989), both published by Harvard University Press.

Summary

There is perhaps no other feminist of her generation who has had as direct and profound an impact on society as Catharine MacKinnon. Her views on sexual harassment have become the law of the land; she continues to struggle, however, to achieve the same recognition for her views on pornography. That the law has begun to recognize certain normal expressions of male sexuality as violative of women's dignity and women's rights is an astonishing development—as astonishing as court decisions striking down segregation must have seemed in their day. Her crusade against the victimization of women raises the same painful question: Is society ready for equality? The development of case law in the areas of sexual harassment and pornography is largely the result of the influence of feminist legal theory, of which MacKinnon is widely acknowledged to be the foremost representative.

Bibliography

Cornell, Drucilla. *Transformations: Recollective Imagination and Sexual Difference*. New York: Routledge, 1993. A respectful yet critical assessment of MacKinnon's analysis of sex inequality. Situates MacKinnon's views within the context of contemporary feminist theory.

Fineman, Martha A., and Nancy S. Thomadsen, eds. *At the Boundaries of Law*. New York: Routledge, 1991. This collection of essays in feminist legal theory includes detailed analysis of MacKinnon's work.

Lacayo, Richard. "Assault by Paragraph." *Time* 143 (January 17, 1994): 62. Provides an account of MacKinnon's war of words with book critic Carlin Romano, whose review of *Only Words* opened with a provocative statement about rape that offended MacKinnon deeply. Although brief, this article does provide insight into MacKinnon's thesis concerning the representation of an assault as inciting real acts of discrimination and rape.

MacKinnon, Catharine A. *Only Words*. Cambridge, Mass.: Harvard University Press, 1993; London: HarperCollins, 1994. MacKinnon's presentation of her views on freedom of expression and pornography. Explosive, controversial, and well-written.

MacKinnon, Catharine A., and Andrea Dworkin, eds. *In Harm's Way: The Pornography Civil Rights Hearings*. Cambridge, Mass.: Harvard University Press, 1997. This volume includes the first publication of the full transcripts of the pornography hearings held in cities such as Los Angeles, Indianapolis, and Boston, which led to the drafting of anti-pornography civil rights law by MacKinnon and Dworkin. Also provides information from both authors on their particular reasons for involvement in this issue.

Rhode, Deborah L. *Justice and Gender*. Cambridge, Mass.: Harvard University Press, 1989; London: Harvard University Press, 1991. A prominent law professor at Stanford University, Rhode surveys a wide range of issues bearing on women and the law. Includes pertinent discussion of MacKinnon's views on harassment and pornography.

Stoltenberg, John. *Refusing to Be a Man: Essays on Sex and Justice*. Portland, Or.: Breitenbush, 1989; London: Fontana, 1990. A collection of essays by a leading antipornography activist. Stoltenberg's detailed discussion of the Minneapolis civil rights ordinance drafted by MacKinnon and Andrea Dworkin provides insights into how the ordinance came to be written, how its provisions were expected to be implemented, and why the issues raised by this ordinance are central to the struggle for gender equality.

Sunstein, Cass R. *Democracy and the Problem of Free Speech*. New York: Free Press, 1993. A professor at the University of Chicago, Sunstein is a widely respected expert on constitutional law. Because it contains a detailed argument that is in close accord with MacKinnon's position on pornography, Sunstein's work provides a noteworthy signal of the gradual mainstream acceptance of MacKinnon's views.

Jay Mullin

JOHN J. R. MACLEOD

Born: September 6, 1876; Cluny, Perthshire, Scotland

Died: March 16, 1935; Aberdeen, Scotland

Areas of Achievement: Biochemistry and physiology

Contribution: As the leader of a physiology research laboratory at the University of Toronto in Canada, Macleod shared the 1923 Nobel Prize in Physiology or Medicine for the discovery of insulin as a treatment for diabetes.

Early Life

John James Rickard Macleod was born in Cluny, a village near Dunkeld, Perthshire, Scotland. His father, Reverend Robert Macleod, served a church in the area but soon after John's birth received a call to serve in Aberdeen. It was in Aberdeen that the younger Macleod attended Marischal College, Aberdeen University, to study medicine. He graduated with distinction in 1898.

In 1900, he accepted a teaching position at the London Hospital Medical College. Macleod's reputation as a teacher and researcher attained international status, and in 1903, with his new wife, Mary Watson McWalter, he traveled to Cleveland, Ohio, where he was appointed professor of physiology at what is now Case Western Reserve University. In 1918, he moved to Canada to accept a position as professor of physiology at the University of Toronto.

While he was at Toronto, Macleod published a book on diabetes and how it functions as a human disease. In the text he suggested that the disease was brought about by mental stress, such as that experienced by locomotive engineers, captains of ocean liners, and workers who are frequently under severe strain. He also recognized that individuals with diabetes showed high levels of sugar in their blood (hyperglycemia), high levels of sugar in the urine (glycosuria), and sometimes both. This was a manifestation of carbohydrate metabolism, one of Macleod's longtime research interests.

Life's Work

A biographer describes Macleod as reserved in manner and perhaps a trifle shy, especially around strangers. The results of his research were reached not by flashes of brilliance but rather by steady, well-directed work. Contemporary photographs show Macleod with crisp dark hair, a strong nose and chin, a steady direct gaze, and a full upper-lip moustache.

Macleod was a good—if not sometimes brilliant—laboratory theoretician and researcher. His association with Frederick G. Banting is a good example of this function. Banting, a Canadian surgeon in private practice in London, Ontario, had an idea for a possible treatment for diabetes. An article in medical literature suggested a link between the pancreas gland and the onset of the disease. His idea was to surgically interfere with the pancreas of laboratory dogs and study the effects on the animals' metabolism of sugar. Because his experience had largely been as a clinician, Banting sought a mentor and laboratory space in which to carry out his research. Banting discussed his research proposal with Macleod, a respected scientist fifteen years Banting's senior.

Macleod was not thoroughly convinced that Banting was on the right track but evidently thought enough of the concept to at least give the younger man some support. He provided laboratory space, an assistant, and ten dogs as experimental animals. The procedure Banting proposed was to surgically interfere with the functioning of a dog's pancreas and isolate the precise pancreatic function that induced diabetes. Macleod offered Banting one of two recent graduates to serve as an assistant. The choice was actually made by the candidates, according to legend, on the basis of a coin toss. The assistant was to be Charles H. Best, a recent graduate in physiology and chemistry.

Macleod left Canada for a summer sojourn in Scotland, leaving the two junior workers to carry on the research. Evidently, Macleod was impressed by what he found on his return to Canada. After evaluating the success of what Banting and Best had discovered, Macleod abandoned his own research and applied all the resources of his laboratory to the new work. In addition, Macleod invited another researcher to become part of the team. James B. Collip, a biochemist on leave from the University of Alberta, joined them in December, 1921.

Their first patient was a fourteen-year-old boy named Leonard Thompson whose physician expected him to live only a few weeks more. The initial treatment of Thompson with the insulin extract on January 11, 1922, proved inconclusive. Apparently, there were impurities in the extract. More

purified preparations were made available, and Thompson underwent a series of treatments. His condition soon improved. He gained weight and began to act like a healthy boy his age. (Unfortunately, Thompson died eleven years later from complications following a motorcycle accident.) News of the discovery spread in the scientific literature as well as in newspapers and popular magazines. Diabetics who formerly faced a certain death from the disease clamored for treatment with this new, miraculous "silver bullet."

More patients were successfully treated with the revolutionary medication. The production of insulin improved, and soon commercial quantities were available. It became obvious that the injections of insulin did not cure diabetes but rather controlled it. With daily injections of the substance, diabetic patients were able to live a reasonably active lifestyle and enjoy a more or less reasonable life span. To many people—diabetics, health care professionals, and the general public—the discovery of insulin and its application to route out what had previously been a surely fatal disease was a miracle. The crowning recognition for the discovery of insulin came in 1923 when Macleod and Banting were nominated for the Nobel Prize in Physiology or Medicine. The nominating committee recommended a joint award based on the respective roles of the two scientists. The committee noted that whereas Banting had the basic idea and the initiative to carry out the research, Macleod had been the advisor and senior leader of the project.

Banting was furious at having to share the prize with Macleod. According to Banting, Macleod's only contribution was to provide laboratory space. He wrote that his young assistant, Charles Best, was more deserving of a share. Accordingly, Banting shared his prize money with Best. In similar fashion, Macleod elected to share his portion of the prize money with the chemist, James Collip.

The research team soon disbanded, each pursing his own interests. For his efforts, Macleod was made a fellow of the Royal Society. In addition, he received honorary degrees from the University of Toronto, Case Western Reserve, and other universities. After returning to Scotland in 1928, he was appointed regius professor of physiology at Aberdeen University. Advancing age, and no doubt the climate of Scotland, brought on crippling arthritis, and he was forced to retire from active laboratory research. He died in Aberdeen on March 16, 1935.

Summary

In a world grown used to the medical miracles of antibiotics immunization and seemingly "magic bullets" against disease, it may be difficult to imagine the impact of the discovery of insulin. Diabetes had been known since antiquity, and up until the time of Macleod and his colleagues, the treatments were nearly on the order of bleeding and purging. Near starvation of the diabetic patient was a common approach, as was forcing fluids or withholding fluids. In almost all cases, however, the diabetic patient ultimately died from the disease.

The global impact of diabetes is not well known because in some areas the condition may not be recognized. However, it is estimated that there may be as many as ten million diagnosed cases in the United States and 1.5 million cases in Canada. The actual number of cases in 1922 is not known.

The work that came out of Macleod's laboratory paved the way for research by others on diabetes. Later workers recognized three forms of diabetes: type I (insulin dependent), sometimes termed "juvenile onset diabetes" because most of the patients are children and young adults; type II (non-insulin-dependent), where the disease symptoms can be controlled by diet; and secondary diabetes, resulting from diseases that destroy the pancreas gland or otherwise interfere with its functioning. The results of their work gave hope to the more than 100 million diabetics in the world that theirs was a chronic but treatable disease, not a death sentence.

Bibliography

Bliss, Michael. *The Discovery of Insulin*. Chicago: University of Chicago Press, 1982; London: Macmillan, 1987. Discusses in detail the history of diabetes and the search for a cure. Describes the pathways of medical research that culminated in the discovery of insulin by Macleod and his colleagues, and also discusses the personal and professional conflicts among members of the research team.

————. "J.J.R. Macleod and the Discovery of Insulin." *Quarterly Journal of Experimental Physiology* 74, no. 2 (1989): 87-95. Describes Macleod as a research physiologist and the role he played in advising and directing the research that led to the use of insulin as a treatment for diabetes. Bliss, a professional historian, places Macleod's participation in the research in an understandable context.

————. "Rewriting Medical History: Charles Best and the Banting and Best Myth." *Journal of Medical History* 48, no. 3 (1993): 258-274. A biographical sketch of Banting and his place in the discovery of insulin. Reviews some of the controversy and ill will that developed among the members of Macleod's research team.

Harris, Seale. *Banting's Miracle: The Story of the Discoverer of Insulin*. Philadelphia: Lippincott, 1946. A favorable biography of Banting as part of Macleod's research group. Places Banting as the major contributor to the discovery of insulin as a treatment for diabetes.

Macleod, J. J. R. "History of the Researches Leading to the Discovery of Insulin." *Bulletin of the History of Medicine* 52 (1978): 295-312. This document was allegedly suppressed for more than fifty years by officials of the University of Toronto. The reason for doing so is not clear but is perhaps linked to the controversy that arose among the members of Macleod's research team during their discovery of insulin.

Rafuse, Jill. "Seventy-five Years Later, Insulin Remains Canada's Major Medical-research Coup." *Canadian Medical Journal* 155, no. 9 (1996): 1306-1308. This brief review of the history of the discovery of insulin and the roles played by Canadian scientists describes some of the modern impacts of the disease on a regional as well as a global scale.

Saudek, Christopher D. *The Johns Hopkins Guide to Diabetes: For Today and Tomorrow*. Baltimore: Johns Hopkins University Press, 1997. A detailed text for the nonprofessional that explains diabetes and how to control the disease. Includes information on lifestyle changes to cope with the condition, complications, sexual activities, and, for women, risks during pregnancy. Illustrations and diagrams help explain some of the technical aspects.

Albert C. Jensen

MARSHALL McLUHAN

Born: July 21, 1911; Edmonton, Alberta, Canada
Died: December 31, 1980; Toronto, Ontario, Canada
Area of Achievement: Communications theory
Contribution: With a cryptic, maddeningly epigrammatic style, McLuhan provided the twentieth century with its most provocative critique of the way technology, specifically electronic media, has shaped the modern view of what it means to be human.

Early Life

Herbert Marshall McLuhan was born in western Canada on July 21, 1911, to religious, Scotch-Irish parents; his father earned his livelihood by selling real estate and insurance, while his mother worked in theater as an actress and monologuist. His family moved to Winnipeg during his youth, and in his adolescence, McLuhan began his lifelong infatuation with electronic media, building his own crystal radio set at the age of ten. He later enrolled at the University of Manitoba, intending to become an engineer but, in his own words, eventually "reading his way out of engineering into English literature"; he was graduated from the university in 1933 with a B.A. in literature. The following year he earned an M.A. in the same field and took a vacation to Europe, acquainting himself with Continental scholarship.

Soon after this trip, McLuhan decided to study further in England, enrolling at Cambridge University and attending the lectures of such famous British scholars as I. A. Richards and F. R. Leavis. Eventually McLuhan took a second B.A. and M.A. at Cambridge and remained long enough to complete a brilliant graduate career with a Ph.D. in medieval and Renaissance studies in 1942. In the midst of his graduate study, McLuhan had begun a teaching career in the United States, where he was first exposed to the power of popular culture in Western society, as he noticed the hold that the relatively new media of cinema and radio had on young American students. It was also during this period that he met his wife, Corinne Keller Lewis, and converted to Roman Catholicism—the latter an event that undoubtedly influenced his critique of the morality of technology.

After having taught at various colleges and universities in the United States and Canada between 1937 and 1946, McLuhan accepted a professorship at the University of Toronto, where he spent most of his teaching career and where he enjoyed his most fruitful and provocative years of scholarship. In the early 1950's, surrounded by evidence that the popular culture of film and television had begun to displace centuries of traditional literary values and preoccupations, McLuhan began his incisive inquiry into the nature of media. In particular, McLuhan focused on the effect of advertising on human behavior, a subject which he pursued in his first book, *The Mechanical Bride: Folklore of Industrial Man* (1951). Influenced by his colleague at the University of Toronto, economist Harold Innis, McLuhan continued to enlarge his critique of mass media and reached the zenith of his productivity and notoriety in the early 1960's.

Life's Work

To appreciate McLuhan's impact on and contribution to the twentieth century's understanding of communication and communications media, one must examine not only particular events or achievements in his life but the substance of his ideas as well. In 1962, McLuhan published *The Gutenberg Galaxy: The Making of Typographic Man*, a far-reaching analysis of the effect of the printing press on the culture of Western Europe, a book which earned for him the Governor-General's Award for Critical Prose, Canada's equivalent of the Pulitzer Prize. In this book, McLuhan argued that the fixed, linear nature of typeset texts affected the way sixteenth century writers, musicians, and scientists thought about their disciplines and about the meaning of humanness, thus forging a radical change in the values and modes of perception in Western culture. The eye displaced the ear as the primary sensory organ, and, McLuhan claimed, this alteration of perception encouraged a self-reflectiveness or narcissism. This in turn led, McLuhan believed, to a fragmentation in society that sharply divided literates from nonliterates, creating a new underclass.

Sociologists had long debated the effect of industrialization—of the machine—on society's members and their modes of perception, but McLuhan was one of the first to identify the printed word as a unique technology that altered perception, value, and authority in a culture. He, in effect, made a "thing," or a "machine," out of the printed word, so that it could be seen as the powerful and thus disruptive influence it was in human society. By objectifying the technology of writing, he empowered communications theorists to recognize and explain the burgeoning gap between the highly technologized cultures of the West and the undertechnologized cultures of the third world and elsewhere.

In 1963, McLuhan established, at the University of Toronto, the Center for Culture and Technology, an institution devoted to the investigation of the social consequences of the new technological media (telephone, television, and radio). This led to his next book, *Understanding Media: The Extensions of Man* (1964), an elaborated discussion of how the next wave of media had influenced civilization by creating a "global village" that linked all cultures through an electronic circuitry, potentially uniting and stabilizing the world community. McLuhan's most important and most enduring generalization was that "the medium is the message." In other words, the "content" of any electronic message is in part defined by the medium itself. He further extended his point by characterizing print media (books, newspapers, and magazines) as "hot" media that saturated the reader with information and demanded his direct attention, while categorizing electronic media (television, film, and radio) as "cool" media that required little audience involvement and encouraged passivity. The linearity and logical thought processes fostered by printed matter were undermined by the more "immediate," less structured thought process implicit in viewing television programming. The implication was that television especially was creating a new orality in society that would restore a sense of community and solidarity which had been lost to literacy after the birth of the printing press.

The publication of these two books brought McLuhan immediate celebrity—both wide adulation and wide disparagement—and have earned for McLuhan his somewhat notorious place in twentieth century communications theory. In 1964, McLuhan was elected a Fellow of the Royal Society of Canada, but critics have ever since diverged widely in their appreciation for McLuhan's broad dichotomies and characteristically elusive style. In essence, McLuhan's books serve as cogent examples of one of his main tenets, that the medium is the message. By deliberately undermining the accepted conventions and standards of typical scholarship (clarity, linearity, and cohesiveness), McLuhan served notice that the next century would be

dominated no longer by learned professors who proved their learnedness in dry, deliberative tomes, but by media-sensitive provocateurs who would communicate as much with their mastery of the medium as they would with their selection of words.

McLuhan's prescient, prophetic analyses of the effect of technology, especially electronic media, on human society immediately became an important contribution to a number of fields, among them journalism, rhetoric, anthropology, and the philosophy of science. The gnomic quality of his work, and the appearance it has of deliberate eccentricism, however, also undermined, to some extent, the scholarly appreciation of McLuhan's basic insights into what it means to be a human being and the foundations of human society. The sheer quotability of the Canadian professor's early maxims distracted and dismayed professional media scholars, while pleasing social pundits who were anxious to exploit McLuhan's sudden fame by linking their own critiques with his punning, anti-academic style. McLuhan retained his connections with the University of Toronto until his death on December 31, 1980.

Summary

In the words of admirer and critical protégé Hugh Kenner, "though McLuhan's pronouncements on the electronic age and its global village made him briefly famous, what he really knew was literacy, and what he developed most fully was his insight into its consequences." Marshall McLuhan's exposition of the changes the printing press had wrought in destroying the older, less linear, oral Western culture and his further delineation of how more recent media such as film and television have altered consciousness and have effectively restored humankind to a new, "secondary orality," are only beginning to permeate scholarly citadels.

McLuhan's legacy to the twenty-first century, finally, is a sharpened realization that no medium or technology is neutral or value-free, that the very tools by which we attempt to communicate, build, and structure human relationships and define their nature affect those relationships and become part of their definition. Because of McLuhan, wielders of words, cameras, and microphones can no longer disguise the effects that their technologies foist upon their audience in the garb of objectivity. In the McLuhanesque universe there are no neutral corners, only the recognition that what and who we are as human beings is in part determined by the lenses and earphones—the technologies—with which we choose (or which are chosen for us) to perceive and negotiate the world at large.

Bibliography

Benedetti, Paul, and Nancy DeHart, eds. *Forward through the Rearview Mirror: Reflections on and by Marshall McLuhan*. Cambridge, Mass.: MIT Press, 1997. A collection of essays resurrecting McLuhan's philosophies in the age of e-mail and electronic communications.

Curtis, James M. *Culture as Polyphony: An Essay on the Nature of Paradigms*. Columbia: University of Missouri Press, 1978. A densely written but ultimately illuminating volume, which uses the work of McLuhan and his most famous student, Walter J. Ong, to posit a coherent definition of culture and those forces which effect cultural change. This volume effectively weaves together the many strands of McLuhan's critique of media and explains the role of media in redefining humankind and human relationships at the end of the twentieth century.

Duffy, Dennis. *Marshall McLuhan*. Toronto: McClelland and Stewart, 1969. A brief overview of McLuhan's life and work by a Canadian author whose purpose is to delineate the essential ideas for which McLuhan became notorious. Of particular merit is Duffy's terse but provocative discussion of the influences on McLuhan's thought: James Joyce, Wyndham Lewis, and Harold Innis, the latter a fellow Canadian.

Finkelstein, Sydney. *Sense and Nonsense of Marshall McLuhan*. New York: International, 1968. An early, surprisingly harsh attack on McLuhan's views as a new utopianism and a kind of benign totalitarianism. Provides a more cynical view of McLuhan than most treatments contemporary with it and thus is a useful counterpoint to the adulation McLuhan engendered in the late 1960's.

Kroker, Arthur. *Technology and the Canadian Mind*. New York: St. Martin's Press, 1985. The chapter on McLuhan in this volume may be the single most helpful exposition of the sources and impact of his ideas available. In discussing the ways in which Canadian intellectuals have understood the impact of technology on Western culture, the author helpfully compares McLuhan with colleague Harold Innis in articulating McLuhan's vision of a new technological humanism. Especially valuable is the author's perceptive elucidation of the impact of McLuhan's Catholicism on his view of humankind.

Miller, Jonathan. *Marshall McLuhan*. New York: Viking Press, 1971. Miller's early assessment of McLuhan's importance as a media critic/philosopher holds up well as perhaps the most useful short introduction to the main themes of his work. This work captures, as well as any extant volume, the tantalizing and elusive quality of McLuhan's analysis of media and the paradox of using print media to convey the news that books were passé.

Neill, S. D. *Clarifying McLuhan: An Assessment of Process and Product*. Westport, Conn.: Greenwood Press, 1993. Analysis of the impact of McLuhan's work. The author is not in agreement with McLuhan's basic premise that "the medium is the message" but argues for McLuhan as an artist.

Rosenthal, Raymond, ed. *McLuhan Pro and Con*. New York: Funk and Wagnalls, 1967. Uneven collection of brief, popular essays and reactions to McLuhan's ideas. Valuable chiefly for the contributions of such renowned rhetoricians and media critics as Hugh Kenner, Anthony Burgess, Theodore Roszak, and Kenneth Burke, who assess McLuhan's notions and contrast them with the older rhetorical tradition of literacy founded in print media.

Stearn, Gerald E., ed. *McLuhan: Hot and Cool.* New York: Dial Press, 1967; London: Penguin, 1968. The best compendium of the wide range of early scholarly reactions to McLuhan, especially enlightening in that it includes McLuhan's response to his early critics. A helpful though somewhat dated volume that assists the reader in understanding what impact McLuhan initially had as a "media prophet." The volume's bibliography offers a nearly complete list of McLuhan's most important essays and books from 1934 to 1967, his most productive periods.

Bruce L. Edwards

EDWIN MATTISON McMILLAN

Born: September 18, 1907; Redondo Beach, California

Died: September 7, 1991; El Cerrito, California

Area of Achievement: Physics

Contribution: McMillan discovered the first transuranic element, neptunium, and was codiscoverer of plutonium, an artificially made element which is fundamental to nuclear power and nuclear bombs. He also discovered the important principle of phase stability, which made possible the high-energy accelerators of the late twentieth century producing fundamental advances in man's understanding of the nature of matter.

Early Life

Edwin Mattison McMillan was born in Redondo Beach, California, on September 18, 1907, of American-Scottish parents. Medicine was a tradition on both sides of the family, but Edwin's interests turned at an early date to the physical world. His family moved to Pasadena when he was only a year old, and he subsequently was educated in the public schools there. Since the family home was only about a mile from the California Institute of Technology, young Edwin spent considerable time attending public lectures and being around the laboratories.

In this environment he developed his powers of observation, attention to detail, and a sense of self-reliance, qualities that would serve him well in future scientific work. He later majored in physics at the Institute and obtained his bachelor's and master's degrees with an outstanding record. His curiosity led him to pursue much more chemistry than is typical for a student of physics; in fact, his first publication, "An X-ray Study of Alloys of Lead and Thallium," was in this field. This work was done under the direction of Linus Pauling and was published in the *Journal of the American Chemical Society*.

He again earned an enviable record as a Ph.D. student at Princeton. Subsequently he was awarded a coveted National Research Fellowship for postdoctoral study. With this fellowship he elected to go to the University of California, Berkeley.

After his fellowship ended, McMillan was awarded a research assistantship in Ernest O. Lawrence's laboratory working with Lawrence's new idea for a particle accelerator, the cyclotron. In 1935 he was appointed as an instructor in the phys-

ics department at Berkeley, becoming a full professor of physics in 1946.

Life's Work

When he arrived in Berkeley in 1932, McMillan set out to measure the magnetic moment of the proton, a difficult experimental task. Just as his apparatus was getting to working order, he learned that Nobel laureate Otto Stern had successfully completed the measurement. This was quite a blow, but not unusual in a field that moves forward quickly, as does physics. McMillan rapidly recovered and decided to change his field of research to nuclear physics. He soon began to make a large impact on Lawrence's Radiation Laboratory. His keen experimental ability led to improvements in the cyclotron: a method for "shimming" the magnetic field to permit acceleration of the particles, development of an external particle beam, and designing its control system. He also was active in the laboratory's experimental program. With Stanley Livingston, he discovered the isotope oxygen-15, which is now used in medical physics to diagnose disease. With Samuel Ruben, he discovered a long-lived isotope of beryllium, beryllium-10, which now has important applications in the dating of geological and archaeological materials.

McMillan's early broad training, not only in physics but also in chemistry, was of great value in his discovery of the transuranic elements. After the discovery of fission in Germany in 1939, McMillan quickly began to investigate this new phenomenon. He was interested in the range that the fission fragments would have. To do this, he put a thin coating of uranium oxide on a cigarette paper and then put, adjacent to it, more sheets of cigarette paper to form a stack. The stack was then placed in a neutron beam formed by the cyclotron in order to produce fissions in the uranium. He reasoned correctly that the fission fragments would have enough energy to penetrate several layers of the paper. Paying attention to detail, however, he noticed that after the neutron bombardment, the original uranium oxide had a new radioactivity.

He suspected that this activity might be from a new element, element 93, since a fission fragment would not stay in the target foil. According to the then current chemical theories, the new element should have had properties similar to the element rhenium. Tests showed that the new activity did not behave like rhenium. McMillan remained puzzled by this enigma and a year later decided to try the investigation once more with a colleague, Philip Abelson, who was visiting Berkeley. The hypothesis this time was that the new observed radioactivity came from element 93, but its chemistry was different from that supposed by current theories. This proved correct after exhaustive chemical tests. Before this discovery there were only ninety-two known elements. With the discovery of element 93, McMillan had opened a new field of transuranic elements.

McMillan named the new element neptunium in analogy to the naming of uranium, which was named after a planet. Furthermore, Neptune is the planet just beyond Uranus in the solar system.

McMillan immediately started experiments directed at finding element 94, using deuterons from the sixty-inch cyclotron. He found new patterns of radioactivity, but before he could complete the work he was called to the Massachusetts Institute of Technology to do radar research for the War Department. With McMillan's permission and notes, Glenn T. Seaborg and co-workers Arthur C. Wahl and Joseph W. Kennedy took up the research and obtained definitive proof that element 94 had indeed been made in the cyclotron. It was named plutonium by McMillan, for the next planet in the solar system after Neptune, which is Pluto. This research on plutonium was of crucial importance to the Manhattan Project, for it turned out that plutonium is a fissionable material suitable for fabrication of a nuclear bomb. In fact, the bomb used at Nagasaki in the final days of World War II was made of plutonium. In the early work on the Manhattan Project, the cyclotron-produced plutonium was of critical importance in establishing design criteria for the bomb and for the reactors that would produce the plutonium in the quantities needed.

For his work in the transuranic field, McMillan (jointly with Seaborg) received the Nobel Prize for Chemistry in 1951—quite an unusual achievement for a physicist.

McMillan continued his research for the war effort at the United States Navy's Radio and Sound Laboratory in San Diego, California, investigating sonar. He finished his war work at the Los Alamos Laboratory of the Manhattan Project. It was there at the conclusion of the war that his thoughts turned to the problem of the energy limitation to 100 million electron volts for particles produced by

prewar cyclotrons. This limitation was produced by the special theory of relativity, which requires that as a particle increases its velocity, it also increases its mass. Therefore, during the particle's acceleration in the cyclotron, it fell out of synchronism with the radio frequency field and eventually failed to gain energy from it.

McMillan showed theoretically that if one used a new principle of phase stability, the relativistic limitation could be overcome. This was done by changing either the magnetic field holding the particles in orbit or the frequency of the accelerating electric field in such a way that if a particle were too slow compared to the electric field, it was speeded up, or slowed down if it were too fast. In this manner, a particle was "stable" as it was accelerated and remained in synchronization with the accelerating electric field, thereby continually gaining energy.

McMillan's concept of phase stability was immediately put to the test in an electron synchrotron, as he named it, which was constructed at the Berkeley laboratory. It performed as the theory predicted. Electrons were accelerated to 335 million electron volts of energy. At that energy they had more than six hundred times their rest mass—a clear proof that the relativistic limitation had been removed.

The principle of phase stability was soon applied to dramatically increase the energy available from cyclotrons, the first such application being to the 184-inch cyclotron at the Berkeley laboratory. With the new design this accelerator easily produced deuterons of 200 million volts—more than twice the energy that itself would have been extraordinarily difficult to achieve with a conventional design. Soon a number of synchrocyclotrons, as they came to be called, were built at nuclear laboratories throughout the world.

The phase stability concept is central to all large modern accelerators. For example, the Bevatron was constructed at Berkeley to accelerate protons to six billion electron volts—more than six times their rest mass. With this energy available, antimatter consisting of antiprotons and antineutrons was subsequently discovered.

It is remarkable, but not an uncommon coincidence in scientific history, that the principle of phase stability was discovered independently by another scientist. In this case it was a Russian, Vladimir I. Vexler, working in isolation in the Soviet Union during World War II. For their joint discovery McMillan and Vexler shared the prestigious Atoms for Peace Award for 1963, which had a prize of seventy-five thousand dollars.

In July of 1958, an ill Lawrence appointed McMillan Deputy Director of the Berkeley Radiation Laboratory, as it was then called. Upon Lawrence's death soon thereafter, McMillan was named director of the laboratory. It grew and prospered under his leadership on a broad front in materials science, nuclear chemistry, biology, and medicine, and in high-energy and nuclear physics. An eighty-eight-inch cyclotron was constructed and elements 103, 104, and 105 were discovered—continuing the expansion of knowledge of the transuranic elements. In the first decade of McMillan's directorship, more than four thousand scientists and graduate students from abroad worked at the laboratory for various periods of time. In addition, there were normally about four hundred graduate students and 125 faculty in various fields doing research at the laboratory.

McMillan has been recognized in many ways for his service to science and his country. From 1954 to 1958 he served on the important General Advisory Committee of the Atomic Energy Commission, and from 1960 to 1966 on the Commission on High Energy Physics of the International Union of Pure and Applied Physics. He served in 1972 as vice president of the American Association for the Advancement of Science and was a member of the National Academy of Sciences, having achieved this honor at the early age of thirty-nine. He was also a member of the American Philisophical Society and a fellow of both the American Physical Society and the American Academy of Arts and Sciences.

Summary

Both of Edwin McMillan's seminal discoveries have had a major impact on science. The discovery of neptunium opened the field of the transuranic elements. The element plutonium, which he codiscovered, is of profound importance to the nuclear fuel cycle and is, along with uranium-235, the fissionable material that makes a nuclear bomb possible. It is remarkable that this artificially made element assumed such a formidable place in the modern world in the few decades after McMillan's discovery.

The principle of phase stability led to a whole new generation of accelerators and is still a fundamental element in the design of "atom-smashers," such as the Superconducting Supercollider, which was designed to produce twenty-trillion-volt protons. The synchrocyclotron at Berkeley was used to produce the first artificial mesons, up to that time only observed in cosmic rays. Again, in the 1980's, the W and Z particles were discovered at the European Center of Nuclear Research, CERN, with an accelerator designed on the principle of phase stability. The mesons are important constituents of the nucleus of the atom, and the W and Z particles are intimately associated with the new theory that combines electromagnetism and the weak interactions, such as beta radioactivity. These advances in the fundamental knowledge of matter owe a large debt to the principle of phase stability discovered by McMillan.

Bibliography

Lambert, B. "Edwin McMillan, Nobel Recipient and Chemistry Pioneer, Dies at 83." *New York Times* 140, no. 48718 (September 9, 1991). A profile and obituary of McMillan.

Livingood, John J. *Principles of Cyclic Particle Accelerators.* Princeton, N.J.: Van Nostrand, 1961. A chapter of this book is devoted to the idea of phase stability and the associated betatron oscillations of the particle beam. Applications to electron synchrotrons, fixed frequency cyclotrons, and alternating gradient accelerators are given. The latter are the accelerators of choice for producing the highest energy proton or antiproton beams at present, such as the accelerators at Fermilab, near Chicago, and at CERN, near Geneva, Switzerland.

Livingston, M. Stanley. *High-Energy Accelerators.* New York: Interscience, 1954. Livingston discusses high-energy accelerators as tools for research in nuclear and particle physics. He gives the principles of acceleration to higher energies, including orbital stability and phase stability. He gives some detail on the development of the electron synchrotron of McMillan's design as well as the design of synchrocyclotrons that also operate on the principle of phase stability and permit the acceleration of heavy particles, such as protons and deuterons. He discusses the application of phase stability to accelerators with magnets placed in a ring, which permits protons to be accelerated to billions of electron-volts.

McMillan, E. M. "Synchrotron: A Proposed High Energy Particle Accelerator." *Physical Review* 68 (September 1 and 15, 1943): 143-144. In this short and seminal paper, McMillan sets forth the principle of phase stability and argues physically why it should occur under proper conditions in an accelerator. He derives an equation of motion for the phase and also gives a preliminary design for an accelerator which would produce an electron beam of 300 million electron volts of particle energy. This accelerator was subsequently constructed at the Berkeley laboratory. McMillan gave it the name "synchrotron."

McMillan, E. M., and P. H. Abelson. "Radioactive Element 93." *Physical Review* 57 (June 15, 1940): 1185-1186. This paper announces the discovery of element 93, the first transuranic element. Transuranic elements had been claimed to have been discovered before, but further investigations showed the claims to be false. This publication shows conclusively that a 2.3-day radioactive period is formed when a thin uranium foil is activated with neutrons from the cyclotron. The activity remains in the uranium, whereas fission products would have enough energy to leave the uranium foil. (It was known that neutrons induce fission in uranium.) Investigation of chemical properties of the 2.3-day activity showed that it had a much closer resemblance chemically to uranium, rather than to rhenium, which had been predicted by the then-current chemical theories. Element 93 was then identified as beginning a second series of "rare earths" starting with uranium. The investigators also proved that the neptunium was a daughter product from the decay of twenty-three-minute uranium-239, which is formed by neutron capture in the uranium-238 target.

Seaborg, Glenn T., and Joseph J. Katz, eds. *The Chemistry of the Actinide Elements.* 2d ed. London and New York: Chapman and Hall, 1986. This large and definitive volume has a detailed chapter on the nuclear properties of plutonium. It describes the importance of the cyclotron-produced plutonium that was made by bombardment of deuterons on uranium (according to the original discovery described by Seaborg and his colleagues in the citation that follows) to the Manhattan Project. Microgram quantities and later milligram quantities of plutonium from this source were used to study the chemical and nuclear properties of plutonium, making possible the design of nuclear reactors for large-scale production of plutonium. These properties were also essential for the design of the atomic bomb from the plutonium so produced. There are several chapters on the chemistry of plutonium, neptunium, and other transuranic elements, as well as a discussion of how alpha-particles and fissions were detected.

Seaborg, G. T., E. M. McMillan, J. W. Kennedy, and A. C. Wahl. "Radioactive Element 94 from Deuterons on Uranium." *Physical Review* 69 (April 1 and 15, 1946): 366. McMillan in earlier work suspected that plutonium was formed by deuteron bombardment of uranium in the cyclotron. Seaborg, Kennedy, and Wahl continued this work using McMillan's notes after he was called away to do war research. They observed alpha particles that were identified as arising from the 2.3-day decay of neptunium-239. The alpha-particle activity was different chemically from neptunium or uranium, indicating that element 94 was formed. It was subsequently named plutonium. This paper was originally submitted January 28, 1941, but voluntarily withheld during World War II because of its importance to the Manhattan Project, which produced the first atomic bomb.

J. A. Jungerman

HAROLD MACMILLAN

Born: February 10, 1894; London, England
Died: December 29, 1986; Birch Grove, Sussex, England
Areas of Achievement: Government, politics, and publishing
Contribution: As British prime minister from 1957 to 1963, Macmillan witnessed a period of unprecedented affluence combined with a diminished role in world affairs for Great Britain. Committed to improving the lot of the average Englishman, to granting independence to the British possessions, and to strong economic policies, he ended his career as prime minister in the wake of ill health, divisions within his party, and scandal.

Early Life

Maurice Harold Macmillan was born in London on February 10, 1894, the son of Maurice Macmillan and his American-born wife, Helen Bolles. His education followed the pattern in the Macmillan family, which was noted for its scholarship as well as its business acumen; Harold's grandfather had founded in 1844 the publishing house bearing the family name. At the age of nine, the boy was sent to an exclusive boarding school, Summer Fields at Oxford; from there he went to Eton, leaving an undistinguished record. In 1912, he entered Balliol College, Oxford, and it was as an undergraduate there that he initially became involved in politics. He became a member of that training ground for future politicians, the Oxford Union. His speeches before the Union were indicative of the politician of later years, showing careful preparation and love of epigram. His allegiances at this time wavered between Liberal and Labour, but more important, his education and Union membership provided young Macmillan with a well-trained mind, one able to penetrate and resolve difficult problems.

Macmillan joined the army at the outbreak of World War I, initially serving in the King's Royal Rifles and then joining a guards regiment, the Grenadier Guards. Although not decorated for his military service, he gained a reputation as one of the bravest officers in any of the five Guards Regiments. He was wounded three times, the last being a severe pelvic wound received during the Battle of the Somme (1916), which incapacitated him for the remainder of the war. His wound did not finally heal until 1920, and it left him in pain and with a

shuffling walk for the remainder of his life. It was a result of his wartime experiences that Macmillan sought to compensate for his academic background by assuming an exaggerated military manner, symbolized by his mustache, which, along with his drooping eyebrows, gave him a rather odd appearance, in keeping with high Tory manners. More significant, these wartime experiences changed his outlook on life. He emerged more pessimistic, more practical, and more confident of his own capabilities: He had experienced the horrors of mass warfare and was imbued with a real concern for the quality of life of ordinary Englishmen.

At the end of the war, Macmillan chose not to return to the family publishing house and accepted an appointment as aide to the Duke of Devonshire, Governor General of Canada. This appointment was Macmillan's first close association with the English aristocracy and encouraged that quality in the young man. This relationship was important also in that he met the duke's daughter, Lady Dorothy, to whom he was married in April, 1920, at Saint Margaret's, Westminster. This marriage into the established, eccentric, and wealthy Cavendish family undoubtedly spurred Macmillan's political ambitions, and when he finally entered the House of Commons he found himself, as a result of this match, related to sixteen members of the lower chamber.

Macmillan was working in the family firm in 1923, when he decided to run for Parliament. He approached the Conservative Party Central Office and was assigned to Stockton-on-Tees, a community he had never seen before. At this time, Stockton was experiencing the full impact of the industrial slump characteristic of the old English industries, and Macmillan's discovery of the misery of the city's populace renewed his wartime concern over the average Englishman's lot and provided a focus for his vague radicalism. Although he lost his first attempt for a parliamentary career, the Labour government fell the next year (1924) and in the subsequent general election Macmillan (now aged thirty) entered the Commons.

Life's Work

When he entered the House of Commons for the first time in October, 1924, Macmillan quickly linked himself with a number of young Tories with similar experiences, service in the trenches during the war, which left them all with a sense of mission to remedy evils in England, all representing industrial towns, and shocked by the quality of life among the electorate. Macmillan and his fellow Conservatives became convinced that the economic structure of the land must be changed to avert revolution. Yet although he had had his radical moments in the past, he was never tempted to become a Socialist and cross the aisle to join the Labour Party. With the exception of the Labour years of 1929 to 1931, he was to represent Stockton until 1945. Although Macmillan soon was regarded as one of the more promising younger Conservative members of the Commons, ministerial appointment eluded him (Anthony Eden, three years his junior, was made an undersecretary at the Foreign Office in 1931). Thus, during the 1930's, Macmillan settled into a routine, combining politics with the family publishing business. In Parliament, he gained the reputation of being a clever, if impractical, idealist, a rather dull and nervous speaker with too much of the "Oxford manner" about him. With the passing of time, he became somewhat disillusioned with Parliament and traditional conservatism, which he believed was adhering too strictly to laissez-faire attitudes and deviating from its tradition of nineteenth century paternalism for the lower classes.

The main concern of the Tory Member of Parliament during the years from 1924 to the outbreak of World War II was domestic affairs: the quality of life, economic and industrial policy, unemployment. Macmillan was probably more influential outside Parliament than he was within, which may partially explain his disillusionment. As early as 1927 he and three other members of the Commons—Oliver Stanley, Bob Boothby, and John Loder—had published a book, *Industry and the State*. The four authors condemned socialism for its denial of individual freedom but were equally harsh in their judgment of laissez-faire capitalism, and they advocated increased governmental intervention to encourage business mergers, and guidance for industry and finance. The work also promoted an extension of property ownership, employee shareholding in business, and worker partnership in public industries. In 1933, Macmillan published his first book under his own name, *Reconstruction: A Plea for a National Policy*, advocating the same policies and procedures set forward earlier. Five years later, he published *The Middle Way* (1938), his prewar political testament,

a study once again of the problem of social and economic development within a free and democratic system. Although a restatement of earlier ideas, *The Middle Way* was a prophetic statement of policies to be implemented a quarter of a century later when he became prime minister: nationalization of coal and other essential industries, as well as of the Bank of England; the formation of a national board to oversee the distribution of food throughout the land; and other forms of governmental intervention.

As Europe moved closer to war, Macmillan was one of those who increasingly lost confidence in Stanley Baldwin's and Neville Chamberlain's leadership of the nation and the Conservative Party; his disenchantment with this leadership increased after the outbreak of hostilities in 1939. He was one of a group voting against Chamberlain's leadership in the debate of May 7-8, 1940, and when Winston Churchill was made prime minister, Macmillan received his first ministerial appointment, the modest post of parliamentary secretary to the Ministry of Supply, where he was able to put into operation some of his ideas on planning. In June, 1942, he was moved to the Colonial Office as undersecretary.

The real turning point in Macmillan's career, however, came in November, 1942, when he was sent to Algiers as British Resident Minister following the Allied invasion of North Africa. The next year, he was appointed Resident Minister for the Central Mediterranean, with the task of handling Italian affairs for the Churchill government. In both of these tasks, Macmillan gained his initial experience with diplomacy and discovered that he enjoyed its challenge and had a certain flair for it. He established a comfortable relationship with General Charles de Gaulle, whom he considered a friend, and the Allied overall commander, General Dwight D. Eisenhower. Macmillan always believed that as a result of these experiences he and the British had a "special relationship" with the future American president and the American people. These wartime experiences were also instrumental in altering Macmillan. Before the war, he had been essentially an intellectual, theorizing, pleading, and waiting for his time to come. Now he found himself in a succession of situations in which his actions and decisions could affect people: His theories were converted into reality, and he had become a man of action.

In the national election of July 5, 1945, Macmillan was the first cabinet minister to be a casualty of Labour's victory; subsequently, a safe Conservative seat was found for him at Bromley, Kent, which he represented for the remainder of his time in the Commons (to 1964). From 1945 to 1951, Macmillan was a member of the Shadow Cabinet as spokesman for the Tories on such matters as industrial policy, fuel and power, and European unity. In the Conservative victory of 1951, Churchill was returned as prime minister, and Macmillan accepted a post in the Ministry of Housing. Superficially, his attainments were outstanding. Two million people were waiting for houses, and in 1952 a pledge was made to construct 300,000 units a year, a goal that was attained during the next twelve months and was considered a great success for the party and for the minister personally. In October, 1954, he moved to the Ministry of Defence, and in the Sir Anthony Eden cabinet of 1955 he was Foreign Secretary and later Chancellor of the Exchequer; in none of these posts did he have the success that had come his way in the Ministry of Housing.

The opportunity for which he had been waiting a lifetime finally came his way in 1957. Although Macmillan had initially urged intervention in Egypt to block that nation's seizure of the Suez Canal, he shifted course quickly when it became obvious that the international community was opposed to the joint Anglo-French intervention there (which contributed to Eden's resignation of the premiership in January). Macmillan was asked to assume the office of prime minister; the Conservative Party was in disarray, and Great Britain's credibility was low. Macmillan was expected to be only a stopgap prime minister, but to everyone's surprise he remained in office for seven years. Perhaps the chaotic conditions worked to his advantage; things could only get better. From the beginning, Macmillan gave every indication that he enjoyed the ultimate power in the land—he seemed to be ten years younger: The atmosphere of crisis seemed to suit his temperament and style.

As prime minister, Macmillan's achievements may be summarily listed. His major interest had become by this time international relations, and he saw himself as a twentieth century "honest broker," playing the role of an elder statesman, a mediator between the Soviet and the American superpowers, keeping the lines of communication open when these two states seemed on the brink of nuclear conflict. His personal friendship with President Eisenhower eased Anglo-American tensions following the Suez debacle. He worked hard for a big power summit to be held in Paris in 1960, but this came to nought as a result of the U-2 incident. The lessened position of Great Britain was clearly indicated by both Macmillan and his countrymen being mere spectators at the time of the Cuban Missile Crisis of 1962.

More positive was Macmillan's role in the process of decolonization that swept through the Third World after 1945. Despite reservations within his own party, from 1957 Macmillan actively advocated granting independence to British colonies, a policy he believed preferable to rebellion and violence. It was his hope that by granting independence, strong economic ties would be maintained between Great Britain and the former possessions. These ideas were contained in a speech he made to the South African Parliament in 1960, urging them to heed the "wind of change" sweeping across Africa, a wind that could not be resisted. South Africa rejected Macmillan's advice, proclaiming herself to be an independent republic and withdrawing from the Commonwealth.

Economically, Macmillan now had the opportunity to put into practice his dreams from the 1920's and 1930's. The National Economic Development Council (nicknamed "Neddy") established an advisory body of appropriate economic ministers and representatives from the trade unions and Confederation of British Industries to undertake the sort of planning that had been so successful on the Continent.

By 1963, however, conditions had begun to change. The Conservative political position had started to deteriorate, unemployment was on the rise, that winter was a severe one, and the sex scandal involving Secretary of State John Profumo was taking its toll on the Macmillan government. Although Macmillan was not personally involved in the scandal, he was blamed for not keeping a closer watch on his associates. Additionally, his health was deteriorating, and he resigned in October, 1962. He rejected the almost conventional offer of an earldom and the Order of the Garter, saying that nothing could match his term as prime minister. He returned to the Macmillan publishing house and relaxed his normal fifteen-hour-a-day work schedule. He did find time, however, to write the six volumes of his memoirs, books which remain a basic source of information about the man.

He finally accepted the peerage on his ninetieth birthday in 1984, taking the title Earl of Stockton, in honor of his first parliamentary constituency. After his retirement from the Commons, he filled the largely honorary position of Chancellor of Oxford University. Macmillan died at his home, in Birch Grove, Sussex, on December, 29, 1986, after a brief illness.

Summary

Harold Macmillan's life of ninety-two years spanned an era of fundamental change in Great Britain's world position, and these changes prompted his flexible and adaptive nature. As a young man he enjoyed the experiences of the pampered upper classes, but during World War I witnessed the destruction of the old European order and the beginning of a steady decline in Great Britain's position in the world. Still, his premiership from 1957 to 1963 witnessed the height of British affluence after the devastation wreaked by World War II. By the 1950's, although poverty still existed, the mass of the population was better fed, better housed, better amused than ever before, and there was talk of a new Elizabethan Age (inaugurated by the coronation in June, 1953, of Queen Elizabeth II). This spirit was echoed in the cartoonist's image of Macmillan as "Supermac" and the election boast of 1959 that "most of our people have never had it so good." This positive image is in sharp contrast to the lessened status of the land internationally, perhaps best illustrated by Macmillan's recognition that Great Britain could not survive alone in the modern nuclear world, the 1960 cancellation of their "Bluestreak" missile program, and the acceptance of American Polaris missiles to arm British submarines. Great Britain had become virtually dependent on the United States.

Bibliography

Bartlett, C. J. *A History of Postwar Britain, 1945-1974*. London and New York: Longman, 1977. A general history in which three chapters are devoted to the Macmillan era, but with the emphasis on the deeds of the prime minister and very little attention paid to the personal side of the Tory statesman.

Evans, Stephen. "The Earl of Stockton's Critique of Thatcherism." *Parliamentary Affairs* 51, no. 1 (January, 1998). Examines Macmillan's 1984 critique of Margaret Thatcher and the government's conservative policies.

Macmillan, Harold. *Winds of Change, 1914-1939*. London: Macmillan, and New York: Harper, 1966.

―――. *The Blast of War, 1939-1945*. London: Macmillan, and New York: Harper, 1969.

―――. *Tides of Fortune, 1945-1955*. London: Macmillan, and New York: Harper, 1969.

―――. *Riding the Storm, 1956-1959*. London: Macmillan, and New York: Harper, 1971.

―――. *Pointing the Way, 1959-1961*. London: Macmillan, and New York: Harper, 1972.

―――. *At the End of the Day, 1961-1963*. London: Macmillan, and New York: Harper, 1973. The six volumes of Macmillan's memoirs are basic to an understanding of the man and his age. Six volumes, almost thirty-eight hundred pages, will naturally be of an inconsistent quality. All provide fascinating anecdotes for the reader, but should be carefully scrutinized in the light of subsequent material made public. All show the care for exact language and the subtle and cynical mind evident in his parliamentary speeches.

Ovendale, Ritchie. "Macmillan and the Wind of Change in Africa, 1957-1960." *Historical Journal* 38, no. 2 (June, 1995). Discusses the shift in

British policy in Africa as foreshadowed in Prime Minister Macleod's 1960 speech to the South African parliament.

Pollard, Sidney. *The Development of the British Economy, 1914-1967.* 4th ed. London and New York: Arnold, 1992. The final chapter treats postwar Great Britain, covering industry, foreign trade, banking, economic policy, and wealth and poverty; generally notes an upward leveling and greater consumption throughout the entire population but against a background of positive decline in the old industries or relative decline against foreign competition in new industries.

Sampson, Anthony. *Macmillan: A Study in Ambiguity.* London: Allen Lane, and New York: Simon and Schuster, 1967. Seeks to relate the stresses within Macmillan's character to the various strands of his experience as publisher, radical intellectual, guards officer, and duke's son-in-law. Published four years after his resignation as prime minister and still the only general study of Macmillan.

Theobald, Robert, ed. *Britain in the Sixties.* New York: Wilson, 1961. A collection of articles from American and British periodicals concerned with Macmillan's England and its world position; important for the contemporary impressions of the land's position and conditions within Great Britain.

Winkler, Henry R., ed. *Twentieth-century Britain: National Power and Social Welfare.* New York: Watts, 1976. The final four chapters evaluate the legacy of the Macmillan years: the future of the welfare state, Great Britain's decreasing world position, and the national elections.

Ronald O. Moore

FRANCISCO MADERO

Born: October 30, 1873; Parras, Coahuila, Mexico
Died: February 22, 1913; Mexico City, Mexico
Areas of Achievement: Government and politics
Contribution: Madero ushered in the first phase of the Mexican Revolution of 1910. Through his book, political organizing, and his campaign of opposition, he provided the leadership for the opposition to the dictator Porfirio Díaz. When Díaz fell, Madero became the president of Mexico.

Early Life

Francisco Indalécio Madero, the oldest of the fifteen children of Francisco Madero and Mercedes González Treviño, came from a wealthy and distinguished landowning family of northern Mexico. The Madero family was large, close-knit, paternalistic, and patriarchal. Grandfather Evaristo began the family fortune by operating wagon trains between northern Mexico and San Antonio, Texas, during the American Civil War. He broadened the family economic interest to include cotton and *guayule* (rubber) haciendas, textile factories, wine distilleries, copper mines, and refineries with rolling mills in Monterrey, Tampico, and Mérida. He founded the first bank in northern Mexico. By 1910, Evaristo had amassed one of the ten largest fortunes in Mexico.

Madero was educated at home until the age of twelve. In 1886 he and his brother Gustavo enrolled in St. Mary's College in a suburb of Baltimore, Maryland, and from 1887 to 1892 continued their education in France, first at the Lycée of Versailles and then at the School of Advanced Commercial Studies in Paris. Madero's courses were primarily commercial and business. He was impressed with the equality accorded foreigners in the French schools. In Paris, Madero was introduced to spiritism and later to Asian religions. He accepted spiritism because he believed it promoted the welfare and progress of the human race. He later became a vegetarian and a practitioner of holistic medicine.

Madero returned to Mexico, and, after summer vacation, he and Gustavo went to California to attend the University of California at Berkeley. For eight months he studied agriculture, and he also became an admirer of U.S. democracy. Now twenty years old, his formal education had ended, and he returned to Mexico to manage family proper-

ties. His father assigned him properties in the semi-arid Laguna area near San Pedro de las Colonias. Madero introduced modern machinery, American cotton seed that produced a much higher yield, and a more efficient irrigation system. He was recognized as a modern agriculturalist and earned a fortune for himself at the same time. He also provided the laborers on the Madero properties with fair treatment, good housing, higher wages, schooling, and medical attention.

In 1903 Madero married Sara Pérez, daughter of a large landowner. Shortly afterward, Madero began his political career. Sara was a faithful supporter of his political activities and accompanied him on his campaigns.

Life's Work

In nearby Monterrey, a peaceful demonstration in favor of an opposition candidate was broken up by agents of the government using gunfire. The public outcry against the actions of the state government convinced Madero that public spirit and democracy were not dead. He and some of his friends decided to organize a political club called the Benito Juárez Democratic Club. The stated purpose was to exercise their right at the state level with the objective of eliminating tyranny.

The club's candidate for the municipal elections in San Pedro in 1904 was defeated by another candidate. Undiscouraged, the club began preparing for the 1905 gubernatorial election. Madero travelled around the state organizing other political clubs, wrote articles, and subsidized a weekly newspaper but was again defeated. For three years he organized political clubs all over Mexico, encouraged independent journalists, and corresponded with other dissidents. The two objectives of Madero were effective elections and one-term limits. The Porfirio Díaz administration felt that Madero was unimportant and did not molest him.

In 1908, Díaz, dictator since 1876, stated in an interview that he would not be a candidate in the next election and that he would accept an opposition party. Although the interview was published in the United States, it was soon known in Mexico. The reaction was widespread. Political literature critical of the administration poured forth, and political organization began on a major scale. Madero published a book, *La sucesion presidencial en 1910* (1908; *The Presidential Succession in 1910,*

1960), that summarized the history of Mexico, discussed the tyranny of absolute power with a description of the accomplishments and faults of the Díaz regime, and proposed the formation of a democratic party to include all independents. Although the book had no literary, social, or intellectual merit, it did propel Madero into national prominence and enabled him to assume leadership of the opposition movement he was advocating.

Opposition parties were organized in 1909, the most important of which supported General Bernardo Reyes. When President Díaz exiled Reyes, Madero became the undisputed leader of the opposition, and he travelled around Mexico promoting his book and gaining support for his party. To crystallize popular sentiment and attract independent support, Madero published a booklet, *El partido nacional Antireeleccionista y la proxima lucha* (1910; the antireelectionist party and the next electoral struggle), in which he described the program and goals of the party and the democratic reform needed to permit the people to accomplish the changes they wanted. During the nominating convention in April, 1910, the party nominated Madero. The platform contained planks for one-term limits, impartial justice, education, and social programs.

Although he was not an impressive campaigner, Madero demonstrated courage, sincerity, and good faith. As Madero attracted more and more support, Díaz became concerned. In June of 1910, Madero was arrested along with other leaders of the party, and the opposition press was closed. Madero and his running mate were imprisoned. The presidential elections were held, and Díaz was declared the victor. On October 6, Madero escaped and fled into exile in Texas, where he began to prepare for revolution. Even though he felt that revolutions did more harm than good, he stated that only through revolution could Díaz be overthrown and democracy be established. Madero called the elections fraudulent and proclaimed himself provisional president.

The military phase of the revolution began in November, 1911, when several uprisings occurred. Most were in northern Mexico and, with the exception of one in Chihuahua, were easily suppressed. Madero entered Mexico in February, 1912, and assumed leadership of the revolution. Most of the fighting continued to take place in northern Mexico. The federal forces were initially successful, but the tide of battle turned against the government by April. Mexico was in turmoil everywhere, and disturbances broke out in all but five states. By May, the revolutionaries controlled two-thirds of Mexico. Despite strenuous opposition by most of the revolutionaries, Madero accepted an agreement by which the Díaz government would resign and a provisional president would assume control until elections could be held. Díaz resigned on May 25 and left the country. The revolution had succeeded, but the problem of implementing the changes remained.

During the interim period, divisions between the revolutionary leaders emerged and adversely affected Madero. Rural disorders continued in some areas, part of the revolutionary army was undisciplined, and the now-free press showed no restraint or concern for the truth. As expected, Madero was elected president in October of 1912 in one of the most honest elections in Mexican history. He was inaugurated in November. President Madero maintained civil rights in spite of the attacks upon him. He moved slowly in implementing a program, and his critics charged him with relying too heavily on former officials of the old regime and upon his family. He regarded his victory as a triumph for democracy and said other changes would follow later. However, he failed to see the urgency of reform and lost support.

In preserving civil rights, Madero allowed the conservative opposition to organize against him. Honest elections in the states resulted in opposition candidates winning control of the national senate. Madero refused to do anything to change the elections. During his fifteen months in office, he was challenged by several small and two major rebellions. All were put down, but they required expenditures from the limited federal budget and distracted Madero's attention away from reform.

On February 9, 1913, a revolt by conservatives began in Mexico City. Against his better judgement, Madero appointed General Victoriano Huerta commander of the federal troops. After ten days of fighting, Huerta revolted, seized Madero and his vice president, and imprisoned them. On February 22, late in the evening, the two prisoners were transferred from the presidential palace to the federal penitentiary, but they were shot before they entered the prison. Huerta then seized power for himself. Although there is no definite proof, almost everyone believed that Huerta was involved in the murders. Madero's death justified a united war against Huerta that ended with his overthrow. Unity could not be maintained, and violence on a greater scale erupted. However, a revolutionary program eventually emerged out of the chaos.

Summary

Madero had moved from obscurity to leadership of the Mexican Revolution of 1910. Through his books, political organizing, correspondence, and campaigning, he awakened the people of Mexico and led them in the drive to achieve democracy. His administration was brief and difficult, perhaps because the people were not yet ready for democracy or because it was not their most pressing need. What they really wanted was economic reform.

In spite of his limitations and the political reality of the times, Madero accomplished some significant gains. Labor enjoyed freedom to organize and strike, agrarian reform was studied, education was promoted, and democratic principles were implemented. These gains were considerable when one considers the difficulties that confronted the administration: a hostile press that exaggerated or invented charges, entrenched conservatives who continued to control the economy, foreigners who distrusted Madera's program, and revolutionaries who were divided and who demanded special favors. Armed rebellions wasted resources and diminished the creditability of the government. Yet Madero was beginning to surmount the problems and was moving to initiate the programs incorporated in the revolution. In death, Madero accomplished what he had been unable to do while he was alive. As a martyr, his faults, errors, and limitations were forgotten, and his ideals, virtues, and sacrifices were remembered.

Bibliography

Cumberland, Charles C. *Mexican Revolution: Genesis Under Madero*. Austin: University of Texas Press, 1952. Cumberland covers the life of Madero and the influence of his family, education, and philosophy. The emergence of Madero as a leader of the revolution and the problems of his administration are described. An evaluation of Madero is sympathetic yet recognizes the faults and limitations of the man.

Knight, Alan. *The Mexican Revolution: Vol 1. Porfirians, Liberals and Peasants*. Cambridge and New York: Cambridge University Press, 1986. The author devotes approximately one-third of the volume to describing the background and the popular agrarian base of the Mexican Revolution. The remainder describes Madero as the leader of the revolution and as president.

Meyer, Michael C., and William L. Sherman. *The Course of Mexican History*. 6th ed. New York: Oxford University Press, 1999. This one-volume history of Mexico is one of the best available. The brief but excellent background and account of the revolution is highly readable and nicely illustrated.

Meyers, Williams K. *Forge of Progress, Crucible of Revolt: Origins of The Mexican Revolution in La Colmarca Lagunera, 1880-1911*. Albuquerque: University of New Mexico Press, 1994. The author describes the development of the Laguna area and the leadership of Madero in promoting its agricultural development. He explains the problems that accounted for the dissatisfaction that provided support for Madero and the revolution.

Ross, Stanley R. *Francisco I. Madero: Apostle of Democracy*. New York: Columbia University Press, 1955. This book is the most widely recognized biography of Madero. It is very well documented and well written. The author gives a complete and unbiased account of Madero's life and accomplishments. He recognizes the limitations of Madero and places him in perspective in the history of Mexico.

Robert D. Talbott

RENÉ MAGRITTE

Born: November 21, 1898; Lessines, Belgium
Died: August 15, 1967; Brussels, Belgium
Area of Achievement: Art
Contribution: Magritte was the most prominent Belgian associated with the modern art movement known as Surrealism. While his concept of the art of painting increasingly diverged from Surrealist theory, the integrity and fascination of his large body of work won for him an extended and devoted audience in the latter part of his career.

Early Life

René François Ghislain Magritte was born to Léopold and Régina Magritte on November 21, 1898, in Lessines, a small town in the province of Hainaut, part of the Walloon, as distinct from the Flemish region of Belgium. Magritte was the eldest of three children. His brother Raymond, born two years later, became a successful businessman, and in adulthood there was little contact between the two. In childhood, Magritte was devoted to his youngest brother, Paul, who later pursued interests in music and poetry and remained on close terms with Magritte.

In 1899, Magritte's father, who was a wholesale merchant, moved the family to nearby Gilly, where a peculiar event became fixed in Magritte's imagination. Though it may have been remembered more through his parents' retelling than directly in René's memory—he was a year old when it happened—the unexpected landing of a hot-air balloon on the roof of the family's house became a touchstone of his childhood experience, helping to prepare the ground for his sense of poetic wonder. Another early formative experience was stressed by Magritte in his account of his artistic origins. Around 1906, at a period when the Magritte children spent summer vacations with relatives in Soignies, Magritte played frequently in an old cemetery, where he and a young girl would lift iron gates and go down into the underground burial vaults. One day, climbing out into the sunlight, he found a painter at work among some broken stone columns. The artist, Magritte believed, seemed to be performing magic. The young boy's impression may well have been tempered by his own first attempts at drawing, as he had begun to study sketching with other local children.

In 1912, while the Magritte family was living in Châtelet, Magritte's mother was found drowned in the Sambre River. There is little doubt that her death was a suicide. When her body was found, the nightgown that she had been wearing when she disappeared had become wrapped around her face, a circumstance that has been remarked upon by writers because a not uncommon element of Magritte's imagery is the shrouding of the human face, and other forms, with light-colored cloth. Magritte's only remembered reaction to this catastrophic event was a feeling of pride in the attention given him as the son of the dead woman. As a child, Magritte seems to have enjoyed unusual pastimes, such as dressing up as a priest to perform somber masses in front of an altar he made up himself. Practices like these often seemed intended to shock the family's servants.

The year following his mother's death, Magritte's father moved the family to Charleroi. One day, on a carousel at the town fair, he met and became a close friend of a thirteen-year-old girl, Georgette Berger, who would later become his wife. Magritte was initially a student at the Athénée, the Charleroi high school, but in 1916 his father allowed him to begin art studies at the Académie des Beaux-Arts in Brussels. Despite his enthusiasm for painting and drawing, his attendance at the academy was intermittent and the results of his studies mediocre, but he was rapidly acquiring knowledge, ideas, and artistic acquaintances. After a brief period in which he painted in the Impressionist style widely popular since the 1880's, he discovered cubism, a radical development in art that had originated about a decade earlier in Paris with Pablo Picasso and Georges Braque. In 1919, another new development in the arts called Futurism captured his attention. Futurism, like cubism, was based intuitively upon new concepts of space and time, but unlike cubism it had a pronounced technological and political element. Despite the profound attraction of these new ideas, Magritte continued to paint eclectically, absorbing a variety of other influences and allowing a degree of eroticism to remain in his partly abstract images.

In 1920, on a visit to the botanical gardens in Brussels, Magritte met Berger again by chance, and from that day to the end of his life he was rarely apart from her. The couple, whose earlier friendship had been interrupted by the war and

Magritte's move to Brussels, married in 1922 following Magritte's compulsory military service. By this time he had exhibited his work in Brussels, but he took a number of jobs as a commercial artist in order to support himself and his wife. Freedom from financial cares was still many years in the future, though he was to achieve artistic, though not critical, success within a few years.

Life's Work

A crucial turning point in Magritte's conception of painting occurred in 1922 when he saw a reproduction of a painting, *The Song of Love*, by the Italian artist Giorgio De Chirico. This work, dating from the years 1913-1914, is the representation of several seemingly unrelated objects—a plaster cast of an ancient Greek sculpture, a surgeon's glove, and a ball—placed in an imaginary urban space. Rather than having an arbitrary effect, the juxtaposition of these unrelated objects evoked in Magritte a powerful response. He felt that a new kind of poetry had been revealed to him which was based on the mysterious resonance of objects. *The Song of Love* revealed the unsuspected affinities of objects and their capacity to command attention when freed of their functional roles and enabled Magritte to envision a fresh starting point for his painting.

A second vital influence of the early 1920's began in Magritte's association with Belgian writers and poets sympathetic to the activities of the avant-garde Dada movement, which had arisen in 1916 as a high-spirited defiance of the cultural norms implicated in the catastrophe of World War I. Dada was conceived as "anti-art" and was inherently self-limiting, but in its brief heyday it served as a liberating force for many artists; more important, it was the seed-bed of Surrealism, a more complex and influential movement, with a wide range of artistic and political ambitions. Surrealism is an elusive concept, but the words of the author Louis Aragon serve as a capsule description: "Reality," stated Aragon, "is the apparent absence of contradiction. The marvelous is the eruption of contradiction within the real." Thus, Surrealism is "the marvelous"—the chance event that reveals the weakness of the narrowly rational view of the world. Though in common usage the term has come to denote something crazy and dreamlike, Surrealism as a distinct cultural episode includes much sophisticated speculation, experimentation, and cultural criticism, as well as many episodes of leftist political activity.

Surrealism emanated from Paris, but one of the foremost groups of Surrealist artists was Belgian and included Magritte's friends E. L. T. Mesens, Camille Geomans, Marcel Lecomte, and others. The "Pope of Surrealism," as he has been called, was the French writer André Breton, with whom Magritte had a long and occasionally uncomfortable relationship. Among the Belgian Surrealists, Magritte was perhaps the leading figure, but because the movement was in large part a French literary matter, Magritte's unique contribution to it was slow to be acknowledged.

The emergence of explicit Surrealist content in Magritte's painting occurs in works dated 1926, during a period of intense activity in which Magritte often painted a picture a day. In the previous year, he had acquired a contract with a new gallery in Brussels, "Le Centaure," which in 1927 presented his first one-man exhibition. Filled with novel and disturbing material, the show was not favorably received. Among the works shown were *Le jockey perdu* (the lost jockey), which for Magritte was a breakthrough to the new kind of painting that he had envisioned years earlier under the spell of De Chirico's *The Song of Love*. It shows a jockey whose mount seems to have frozen in mid-stride while passing through a strange forest of trees possessing trunks in the form of giant balustrades. The suspension of time, the juxtaposition of logically unrelated objects, and the cold tonality of the picture are hallmarks of Magritte's imagery both early and late in his career.

In August, 1927, Magritte and his wife moved to Paris, where Magritte played an active role in the circle of Surrealists around Breton and the poet Paul Éluard. Magritte's painting of the late 1920's and early 1930's adopted a central Surrealist notion, valid for poetry and painting alike, of challenging everyday consciousness by allowing dissonant objects, images, or ideas to confront one another. With the intention of undermining stereotyped attitudes toward art and life, the shock provoked by the Surrealist object, painting, or poem was viewed less as an artistic than as a moral gesture. In the period just following *The Lost Jockey*, Magritte's imagery had been bizarre, somber, and often inclined to suggestions of violence, but as he drew closer to the Parisian Surrealists his imagery became more philosophical and, almost paradoxically, more disturbing. Magritte found that a powerful poetic result could be obtained by objectively representing familiar objects in unexpected surroundings or by creating inspired marriages of objects that moved the viewer by their mysterious alliance. Fantasy and exotic narrative increasingly gave way to imagery that deliberately posed the deepest problems of interpretation. One of Magritte's most popular themes, formulated in several variations, embodies these problems in a highly refined form. *La Condition humaine I* (1930) shows a canvas on an easel standing by an open window, which superimposes upon the landscape seen through the window a painted representation of the landscape in identical detail. In a 1940 statement, Magritte observed that for the viewer, the tree in the painting was both inside the room and outside in the real landscape, a situation that embodies the process of vision, in which the object is both outside ourselves, in the real world, and within us, as a representation. Paintings such as this may be subject to what Magritte termed more or less adequate description, and even to metaphorical expression, but as with virtually all of is images, words may complement the poetry of the image but cannot displace it. Explanation, in the usual sense, was abhorrent to Magritte, who believed that the image should surpass one's ability to interpret it. In his view, an "inspired" visual image was one embodying a thought that could be presented in no other way. He made a determined effort to distance himself and his work from the Surrealist enthusiasm for psychoanalytical interpetation, although some critics have made plausible interpretations of some of his paintings along psychoanalytic lines.

After three years in Paris, Magritte's enthusiasm for the Parisian Surrealist milieu waned, and he returned to Brussels, where, except for occasional travels, he lived the rest of his life. During the 1930's, he was represented in all the major international exhibitions of Surrealist art, but his paintings were still not avidly sought after. New associates entered his life, foremost among them the writer Louis Scutenaire, who became an indispensable friend and supporter. Magritte was indifferent to promoting himself in art circles, insisting that his images served not the world of painting but that of thought, but he occasionally wrote and lectured on his own work in a fashion that was labored but occasionally inspired. His writings and the accounts of his friends reveal him as a perceptive and sophisticated person with a lively appreciation of philosophy, literature, and music (his wife was a talented pianist and would often play for him works of the French composers Claude Debussy,

Maurice Ravel, and Erik Satie). Magritte lived and worked in modest rented accommodations until, late in life, he purchased a house. He and his wife remained childless but had a succession of Pomeranian dogs.

Before the end of the decade, Magritte's work had been seen in the United States and England, but the broadening of his audience was cut short in 1939 by the beginning of World War II. Following the German invasion of Belgium, Magritte spent three months in Carcassonne, France, before returning to Brussels. His painting continued along familiar channels for a time and then temporarily underwent a dramatic change in which he adopted the technique of the Impressionists, especially that of Auguste Renoir. Magritte's stated intention in these works was to defy the wartime gloom and adapt Surrealism to open air and sunlight, but it can be doubted that he meant this experiment in anything but an ironic sense. He was roundly criticized by his friends and critics alike for this manner of painting, and he soon abandoned it. Another such essay in irony and, one suspects, defiance, was a series of twenty paintings done in raucous imitation of the Fauvist painters of the first decade of the century. These works, too, found few defenders when they were exhibited in Paris in 1948.

The final two decades of Magritte's life were highly productive, but the work did not differ in fundamental character from the work of the previous two decades. His skill in representing objects, including the selection and application of colors to produce illusions of depth and volume, reached extraordinary heights in some of the later works. The 1952 painting *Valeurs personelles* (personal values) is reminiscent of the works of great Flemish masters of the fifteenth century in its sense of light and densely filled interior space. In it Magritte has enlarged several commonplace objects—a comb, a match, a shaving brush, a glass, and a bar of soap—to gargantuan size, putting on trial the logic of perception in much the same way as the author/mathematician Lewis Carroll had done three quarters of a century earlier in his *Alice's Adventures in Wonderland*.

Magritte's powers of thought and execution never waned, but beginning in the late 1950's his health and stamina declined. In his later years, he took some pleasure, though little intellectual comfort, from the great respect he had gained throughout the world for his determined and productive career. On August 15, 1967, after seeming to have recovered from a serious illness, he unexpectedly died in Brussels.

Summary

One authority on René Magritte has accurately characterized the artist's mature work by the phrase "pictures as problems," but this should not be allowed to suggest that he conceived of painting as a theoretical act, or that his work is systematic or doctrinaire. In personal appearance, Magritte was resolutely bourgeois, somewhat resembling in middle age the bowler-hatted man he often placed in his paintings; yet he was an essentially subversive artist, seeking to break through conventions of thought that were obstacles to knowledge. Within his skillful and attractive paintings lie traps for the mind. When Magritte launched, in 1929, his image consisting of a pipe and the inscription "This is not a pipe," he began, in the words of Breton, "the systematic trial of the visual image, emphasizing its shortcomings and indicating the dependent nature of the figures of language and thought." With this and a succession of related images, Magritte brought painting into a close relation to linguistic philosophy and contributed directly to subsequent phases of modern art such as Pop Art and Conceptual Art. The wide popularity of Magritte's art in the years immediately following his death may not often reflect an appreciation of the complexities of his art, but his own words express conviction that his work would, in the end, have its due effect: "Women, children, men who never think about art history," he said, "have personal preferences just as much as aesthetes do."

Bibliography

Gablik, Suzi. *Magritte*. London: Thames and Hudson, and Greenwich, Conn.: New York Graphic Society, 1970. The author befriended Magritte in the latter years of his career, and this book, originally published in 1970, is both an homage to the artist and a serious attempt to place Magritte in a broad cultural and intellectual context. Gablik's approach is to focus on thematic constellations in Magritte's work; consequently the selection of plates is more purposeful than in most other sources. The text sometimes lapses into jargon but is nevertheless highly recommended.

Hammacher, A. M. *René Magritte*. Translated by James Brockway. London: Thames and Hudson, and New York: Abrams, 1974. This volume belongs to a series of art books of uniform design, a circumstance that creates a sense of tidiness in Magritte's production that can be misleading. The text, however, is solid, and the chronological presentation of plates is as welcome as it is rare in books on Magritte's painting.

Magritte, René. *Rene Magritte*. Text by René Passeron. Translated by Elisabeth Abbott. Chicago: O'Hara, 1972. The brief text is perceptive but the layout of the book is peculiar and claustrophobic. An introductory interview with Magritte's widow is of more than sentimental interest.

Noël, Bernard. *Magritte*. Translated by Jeffrey Arsham. New York: Crown, 1977. The text of this book is a flawed translation from an original French edition. The author attempts to be breezy and sophisticated, but instead he sows confusion. The plates are adequate in quality but not in number.

Ollinger-Zinque, Gisele, and Frederik Leen, eds. *Magritte, 1898-1967*. New York: Abrams, 1998. More than 500 black-and-white and color illustrations testify to Magritte's success in creating what he referred to as "disturbing poetic effects."

Soby, James Thrall. *René Magritte*. New York: Museum of Modern Art, 1965. This slim volume features an agreeable but impressionistic essay accompanying illustrations of paintings seen in a celebrated 1965 American exhibition of Magritte's work. The witty and lyrical elements of the artist's work tend to come to the fore both in the text and in the images reproduced. Includes a bibliography.

Spitz, Ellen H. *Museums of the Mind: Magrittes's Labyrinth and Other Essays in the Arts*. New Haven, Conn.: Yale University Press, 1994. The author argues that art's significance is in its impact on the mind of its audience. Examines the works of Magritte and others from this perspective.

Sylvester, David. *René Magritte, 1898-1967*. New York: Praeger, 1969. In this catalog of a 1969 Magritte retrospective exhibition at the Tate Gallery, London, the author manages to offer stimulating commentaries on the paintings without transgressing Magritte's injunction against "interpretation," which the painter believed would obscure the poetry of his images.

Torczyner, Harry. *Magritte: Ideas and Images*. Translated by Richard Miller. New York: Harry Abrams, 1977. The author, a lawyer and American friend of Magritte, is a dedicated servant of the painter rather than a scholar, and this large book is a superb compendium of commentary, documentation, and illustrations.

Waldberg, Patrick. *René Magritte*. Translated by Austryn Wainhouse. Brussels: André de Rache, 1966. Produced with the painter's blessing, this is an indispensable resource for the study of Magritte's life and work. Some of Magritte's most celebrated images do not appear in it and must be found elsewhere, but of more importance, much pertinent visual material is found only here.

C. S. McConnell

NAGUIB MAHFOUZ

Born: December 11, 1911; Cairo, Egypt

Areas of Achievement: Literature, social reform, government, and politics

Contribution: Mahfouz is Egypt's foremost writer and the premier man of letters for the entire Arabic-speaking world. He began publishing in 1939, and his literary output since then can only be described as astounding. In recognition of his contribution to world literature, Mahfouz was awarded the 1988 Nobel Prize in Literature, becoming the first Arab writer to be so honored.

Early Life

Naguib Mahfouz was born in the traditional Cairene quarter of Jamaliyya, a densely populated neighborhood composed of mazelike alleys and cul-de-sacs that was home to the popular classes then as it is today. Many of his best works are set within the confines of this quarter, which has provided Mahfouz with a rich, variegated human landscape made up of petty artisans, tradesmen, street vendors, and social marginals. His family, however, enjoyed a more elevated social status than most of their neighbors, since Mahfouz's father held a minor bureaucratic post within the British-dominated government. The period from the eve of World War I until the 1919 Paris Peace Conference, convened by the European victors to determine, among other things, the political fate of the Middle East, was a tumultuous era for Egypt. The country had suffered British occupation since 1882, and in 1914 Egypt was officially declared a British protectorate. The occupation had been opposed by Egyptian nationalists from its inception; after the war, increasingly militant demands for independence were voiced by all strata of Egyptian society. Because his family resided in Jamaliyya, the center of political unrest, Mahfouz as a young boy witnessed bloody street clashes between the British police and protestors demonstrating against Egypt's continued protectorate status. Moreover, Mahfouz's father was himself a dedicated nationalist, and these experiences naturally had a profound impact upon Mahfouz. The Egyptian National Revolution of March, 1919, figures in several of his novels and short stories.

When Mahfouz was twelve, his family left the crowds and noise of Jamaliyya for the newer, more Europeanized suburb of Abbassia. Despite the move to a very different social environment, Mah-fouz never lost his deep attachment for the neighborhood of his birth. Mahfouz continues to frequent the cafés and Islamic monuments of Jamaliyya, which he has always regarded as his real home. Both of Mahfouz's parents were devout Muslims. Thus, at an early age, he was sent for education to the mosque school, where he developed an interest in religion, especially in Sufism or Muslim mysticism. After completing high school, he was sent to the University of Cairo in 1930. Although his parents encouraged him to specialize in medicine or engineering because of his aptitude for science, Mahfouz chose rather to study philosophy in order to "solve the mystery of existence."

Life's Work

Graduating second in his class at the Faculty of Arts in 1934, Mahfouz began work on a master's thesis in aesthetics only to renounce this enterprise two years later to devote his energies fully to literature. While studying at the University of Cairo, he had begun writing articles devoted to philosophical topics, publishing them in journals such as *al-Majalla al-Jadīda* (the new review). In order to support himself and pursue his beloved writing, he joined the civil service in 1939, accepting first a modest administrative position at the University of Cairo and later an appointment at the Ministry of Waqf (religious endowments). The experience of working for years in humble, often dismal, bureaucratic posts furnished Mahfouz with ample material about another dimension of Egyptian life—the daily servitude suffered by thousands of civil servants, most of them holding university degrees yet condemned to a stifling existence because suitable employment was lacking elsewhere. The dreary life of the lower-level Egyptian bureaucrat has been a theme of many of Mahfouz's works.

The year that Mahfouz entered the labyrinth of the Egyptian bureaucracy saw the publication of his first novel, ʿ*Abath al-aqdār* (1939; play of fate), which appeared in a special number of the monthly *al-Majalla al-Jadīda;* the year before, he published his first collection of short stories. ʿ*Abath al-aqdār* and its two successor novels, *Radūbīs* (1943) and *Kifāh Tība* (1944; Theban struggle), were historical romances set in the Egypt of the Pharaohs, but inspired by historical works of fiction by Alexandre Dumas, *père,* and Sir Walter Scott. The backdrop for these three novels was the ancient Nile Valley,

yet the underlying message and plots were directly tied to Egypt's modern political woes of the 1940's. While the formal British Protectorate had ended by then, foreign domination was very much in evidence, particularly in the Suez Canal Zone, still under joint Franco-British occupation, much to the distress of the nationalists. Worse still was the irresponsible rule of Egypt's last king, Farouq, a weak, pleasure-loving monarch, who increasingly alienated his countrymen, thus leading to the Revolution of 1952.

Egyptian society of the 1930's and the World War II era had undergone immense, rapid social changes: inflation, rural-to-urban migration, high unemployment, corruption in government, and unrest among both the peasantry and the urban poor. The five novels that Mahfouz wrote between 1945 and 1949 signal another stage in his writing. Realistic rather than romantic, they ruthlessly exposed the misery of the lower middle classes in Cairo during the late 1930's and the war years. Social conflict, upheaval, and tragedy in the lives of relatively powerless members of society are portrayed with such sensitivity and realism that these early

novels have won for their author the sobriquet "Balzac of the Arabs." One in particular, *Zuqāq al-Midaq q* (1947; *Midaq Alley*, 1966), brought him national recognition and has remained one of his best-loved works. Furthermore, Mahfouz's own social philosophy regarding the nature and function of literature emerged clearly in this period. The novel was not only a form of entertainment but also a potent vehicle for achieving moral reform and enlightenment.

In the late 1940's, Mahfouz undertook a more ambitious project—a massive fifteen-hundred-page trilogy published in 1956-1957. *Al-Thulathiyya* (trilogy) was a bold work in terms of both the social themes it dared to address and its complex literary construction. Tracing the fortunes of a wealthy merchant clan from the Jamaliyya quarter over three generations from 1917 to 1944, the trilogy examines in painstaking detail and remarkable authenticity the disruptions wrought by large-scale political and social changes upon all the clan's members. In addition to focusing national attention upon his earlier novels, many of which were subsequently republished several times, the work won lavish praise by Egyptian critics; it also brought Mahfouz a state prize (the *ja'izat al-dawla lil-adab*) in 1957.

As the various parts of the trilogy first appeared in serialized form, momentous transformations shook Egyptian society; these had an impact upon Mahfouz's personal life as well as upon his professional development. In July of 1952, the Free Officers Revolution, led by Muhammad Nagib and Gamal Abdel Nasser, toppled the *ancien régime:* Egypt was declared a republic the next year. Because of his growing literary fame, Mahfouz was transferred to the newly created Ministry of Culture, in which he joined the higher ranks of the arts administration. Nevertheless, Mahfouz did not write for seven years following the 1952 Revolution, perhaps because of disenchantment with the growing excesses of Nasser's rule. Moreover, Mahfouz's social vision was experiencing significant shifts as were his writing techniques. When he did publish again, in 1957, he had clearly abandoned the naturalism of his earlier novels for more experimental forms.

Awlād hāratinā (1959; *Children of Gebelawi*, 1981), published serially in the leading Egyptian newspaper, *Al-Ahrām*, was his most controversial work and aroused the opprobrium of Muslim clerics of the Azhar Mosque-University in Cairo. Allegorical and rather pessimistic in its view of humanity's unending struggle to regain paradise lost, the construction of *Children of Gebelawi* resembles the Koran, having the same number of chapters—114—as the Muslim Book of Revelations. Moses, Jesus, and Mohammad are portrayed as the leaders of the dispossessed in conflict with the oppressors, some of whom might be interpreted as part of the traditionalist religious establishment. Equally distressing to the Egyptian *'ulamā* (Muslim scholars) was the fact that the novel dealt in a thinly disguised manner with the modern dilemma of the "death of God." Because representations of the Prophets are not permitted in works of fiction, cinema, or drama, *Children of Gebelawi* remained unpublished in book format in Egypt. Nevertheless, a Lebanese edition eventually appeared in 1967. The work's reception appears to have disheartened Mahfouz to the point that he ceased writing for several years.

When he did publish again in 1961, coming out with *Al-Liss wa al-kilāb* (*A Thief in Search of His Identity*, 1979), he chose to deal with less religiously sensitive topics, although by this time his literary technique had changed fundamentally to include "stream of consciousness" and impressionism, perhaps to avoid censure. *A Thief in Search of His Identity* was followed by five other short novels, which, taken as a group, are regarded by many as his finest work. Now the psychological dimensions of his characters—their thoughts and subliminal motivations—were probed in richly suggestive and at times hallucinatory language. Most of the novels in this series courageously paint a frankly distressing picture of the intellectual's benighted situation under the repressive Nasserist regime, in which hopes for true political and social reforms had been dashed by the late 1960's. By this period, Mahfouz had achieved such national and international acclaim that he was largely immune to attacks from political authorities. Moreover, many of his works had been adapted for television, film, and theater presentations not only in Egypt, the cultural and media center of the Middle East, but also in much of the Arabic-speaking world.

Nasser's sudden death in 1970, while provoking a great outpouring of grief in Egypt, subsequently brought a more liberal intellectual climate for the country's writers and artists, at least for a while. In 1970, Mahfouz was awarded Egypt's National Prize for Letters; two years later, in 1972, he re-ceived his nation's most coveted decoration, the Collar of the Republic. In this period, Mahfouz, then adviser to the Minister of Culture, retired from the civil service at age sixty; he was subsequently appointed to the honorary post of resident writer at the semiofficial *Al-Ahrām* newspaper. He continued to publish a short novel or collection of stories as an almost annual event, and in the late 1960's and early 1970's he began experimenting with one-act plays, for him a literary departure. These plays were published collectively under the title of *Taht al-mazalla* (1969; the bus shelter). Mahfouz has stated repeatedly that writing for him represents life itself and only death will put an end to his literary endeavors.

His most recent works are set once more in the now mythical *hāra*, or small, partly enclosed urban neighborhood, where his earliest novels and most memorable characters were conceived, born, and grew to maturity. Note should be made of his *Ḥikāyāt hāratinā*, which appeared in 1975 in Arabic and was translated into English as *Fountain and Tomb* (1988). The stories, some seventy-eight in number, are related by a young boy whose social universe is circumscribed by an alley, the favored locus for so many of Mahfouz's works.

Mahfouz has always shunned the limelight, preferring a private existence that allowed him to produce so prodigiously while haunting popular spots in old Cairo to observe daily life amid the "swirling hem of change." The awarding of the Nobel Prize in Literature in October of 1988 was the first time that he had achieved international recognition of this magnitude and represents long overdue worldwide appreciation of the mature state of modern Arabic literature in general. Because of his frail health and distaste for celebrity, Mahfouz did not attend the awards ceremony in Stockholm, Sweden, but rather sent his two daughters, Umm Kalthoum and Fatima, to accept the medal and diploma on his behalf. In addition, he requested that Mohammad Salmawi from the Egyptian Ministry of Culture deliver for him the Nobel lecture—in Arabic—to the Swedish Academy in December of 1988.

In 1994 Mahfouz, diabetic and nearly blind, was attacked in a Cairo street. No one claimed responsibility for the attack, but police blamed Muslim militants seeking to destabalize the government and install Islamic rule. Mahfouz said the attack provided an opportunity for prayers for the defeat of Islamic extremism.

Summary

More than any other single Arab writer of the present century, Naguib Mahfouz has profoundly influenced the field of Arabic literature in general and that of fiction in particular. While he belongs to the second generation of Egyptian novelists rather than to the pioneering school of the 1930's, Mahfouz's works, taken collectively, display the various stages in the evolution of the novel as a literary form in Egypt and the Arab world. An imported European genre, the novel in Mahfouz's hands went through three identifiable "moments": historical romanticism; social realism; and postrealism, with its multiplicity of forms and voices and emphasis upon the surreal or the psychological. During his half-century of literary production, Mahfouz has not only achieved a maturity and sophistication in the conventions of novel-writing comparable to the best European novelists but also transformed a borrowed genre into a new, yet characteristically indigenous, art form. His decisive impact upon intellectuals and writers in the Arab world can, in part, be measured by the large number of dissertations and literary studies devoted to Mahfouz's oeuvre. Nevertheless, this impact reaches far beyond the educated, middle classes of Egyptian or Arab society. Because of film and television productions of his novels and stories, many of Mahfouz's memorable characters, whether heroes or antiheroes, have been introduced to all strata of society, becoming part of popular lore. Because of his finely calibrated depictions of the humble and the highborn and his moral commitment to social justice, Mahfouz has changed the way that Egyptians look at themselves. Therein lies his greatest contribution.

Bibliography

Allen, Roger. *The Arabic Novel: An Historical and Critical Introduction.* Syracuse, N.Y.: Syracuse University Press, 1995. This is an in-depth analysis of eight Arabic novels, beginning with Mahfouz's *Tharthara fawq al-Nīl* (1966; chatter on the Nile), by one of the leading scholars of modern Arabic literature in general and Mahfouz's oeuvre in particular.

———. *"Mirrors* by Nagib Mahfuz." *Muslim World* 62 (April, 1972): 115-125. A descriptive analysis of Mahfouz's *Al-Marāyā* (1972; *Mirrors*, 1977) that points out the autobiographical nature of the work since the story's narrator resembles the author in many ways.

———, ed. *Modern Arabic Literature.* New York: Ungar, 1987. This is an exhaustive compilation of literary criticism by leading Arab and non-Arab critics, some thirteen pages of which are devoted to evaluations of Mahfouz's works.

Altoma, Salih J. *Modern Arabic Literature: A Bibliography of Articles, Books, Dissertations, and Translations in English.* Bloomington: Indiana University Press, 1975. For those wanting additional information on Mahfouz, this seventy-three-page bibliography is indispensable. Many entries are devoted to Mahfouz.

Hartman, Michelle. "Re-Reading Women in/to Naguib Mahfouz's *al-Liss wa'l kilab* (The Thief and the Dogs)." *Research in African Literatures* 28, no. 3 (Fall 1997). Analysis of Mahfouz's *al-Liss wa'l kilab* with emphasis on the roles of his female characters.

Kilpatrick, Hilary. *The Modern Egyptian Novel: A Study in Social Criticism.* London: Ithaca Press for the Middle East Centre, St. Anthony's College, 1974. This study surveys the Egyptian novel from 1914 until 1968, mainly from the perspective of social criticism, yet provides a solid, detailed discussion of the historical context in which the novel as a genre developed.

Moosa, Matti. "Naguib Mahfouz: Life in the Alley of Arab History." *Georgia Review* 49, no. 1 (Spring 1995). Examines Mahfouz's early career as an essayist in philosophy. Discusses his ideal society and his views on science and religion, which angered Islamic theologians.

Moussa-Mahmoud, Fatma. "Depth of Vision: The Fiction of Naguib Mahfouz." *Third World Quarterly* 11 (April, 1989): 154-166. This is a first-rate, comprehensive study of Mahfouz's life and work by a professor of English at the Universities of Cairo and Riyadh.

Sakkut, Hamdi. *The Egyptian Novel and Its Main Trends from 1913 to 1952.* Cairo: American University in Cairo Press, 1971. The author surveys the romantic, historical, and realistic evolution of the novel in Egypt from 1913 until 1952, devoting a large section to Mahfouz's output of the 1940's and early 1950's.

Julia A. Clancy-Smith

GUSTAV MAHLER

Born: July 7, 1860; Kalischt, Bohemia, Austrian Empire

Died: May 18, 1911; Vienna, Austria

Area of Achievement: Music

Contribution: Mahler had parallel careers as conductor and composer, in each of which he was regarded by many of his contemporaries as the leading musical figure of his generation. His ten symphonies and other varied compositions represent the culmination of romanticism and the beginnings of modern music.

Early Life

Gustav Mahler was born on July 7, 1860, in Kalischt, Bohemia, a small town which now lies in the Czech Republic but which was then part of the Austrian Empire.

His father, Bernhard Mahler, had married Marie Hermann three years earlier, and a son was born in 1858, but he died in infancy. Bernhard, a coachman who had become the owner of a small distillery and tavern, was thirty at the time of his marriage and ten years older than his bride. Marie may have agreed to marry beneath her social station because she was lame from birth, for there is no evidence of affection between her and the ambitious Bernhard.

In the sixteen years following Gustav's birth, his mother bore twelve more children, of which six died in infancy. Though this rate of infant mortality was not uncommon at the time, in an emotionally ambivalent household it could not fail to affect a sensitive child like Gustav. It is reported that when he was asked, at an early age, what he would like to be when he grew up, he replied: "A martyr." Fortunately, his love of music soon became a refuge from the brutality of his home life: At age four he could play folk tunes on a small accordion, and at five he was discovered in his grandparents' attic playing a piano. By the age of ten, he gave his first public piano recital, which took place in the Moravian town of Iglau (now Jihlava), where the family had moved in late 1860.

In the Austria of Mahler's youth, there had been a liberalization in the laws governing the activities of members of the Jewish faith, to which all Gustav's forebears belonged (though perhaps with varying degrees of orthodoxy). Gustav's father, who read widely and fancied himself a scholar, was devoted to the hope that his children would take advantage of the situation and improve their lot in life. Bernhard hoped that Gustav would excel in music, but he also insisted that Gustav continue his general education; in 1870, Gustav was sent to Prague to study. When it was discovered that Gustav was being mistreated in the home where he boarded and received piano lessons, his father brought him back to Iglau.

Mahler's growing local reputation as a pianist caused him to be taken by a benefactor to play for Julius Epstein, a professor at the Vienna Conservatory of Music. On September 20, 1875, the fifteen-year-old Mahler was enrolled at the conservatory, where he remained for nearly three years studying harmony, composition, and piano. Perhaps as significant as the instruction that he received was his exposure to the artistic life of Vienna, the musical capital of Europe, and the home of successive generations of great composers. In June, 1876, Gustav's single-minded devotion to his studies won for him the conservatory's first prize in piano for a performance of a sonata by Franz Schubert, a Viennese predecessor whose influence can be seen in Mahler's mature work. Another piano prize followed in 1877, and in the same year he won a prize for the composition of a chamber music work. When Mahler left the conservatory with a diploma in 1878, he possessed a fine general musical education. At his father's insistence, however, Gustav immediately returned to Iglau to continue his general studies, and in the summer he passed his final examinations, apparently not without difficulty. Although his father has been unsympathetically treated by the composer's biographers, Mahler's broad range of intellectual interests may be credited partly to Bernhard's persistent influence.

Life's Work

Returning to Vienna in the autumn of 1878, Mahler was enrolled at the university to study philosophy and art history. At about the same time, he began to write the text of a cantata, *Das klagende Lied* (the song of lament), his earliest surviving large-scale composition, which he composed during the following months and completed on November 1, 1880. Mahler's main source of support had been his earnings from teaching piano, an occupation that he had begun nearly ten years earlier, but in the summer of 1880 he gained summer employment as a conductor at a resort. In the following year, he obtained a longer-term appointment as

conductor at Laibach (now Ljubljana), and in January, 1883, a position at Olomouc, which he held for only a few months. In the midst of his modest but rising conducting career, Mahler continued to compose. In 1881, Mahler had unsuccessfully placed *Das klagende Lied* in competition for the Beethoven Prize, offered by a Vienna musical group. He later reflected that had he won the prize, he would not have had to remain in the world of the stage as an opera director, but much evidence points to the immense creative advantages that Mahler derived from his experiences as a conductor. In any event, his career continued to advance. In August of 1883, he started work as assistant at the Court Theatre of Kassel, Germany, and in August of the following year he moved to the German Theatre in Prague, the leading city of his native Bohemia, where he was successful as an interpreter of the operas of Richard Wagner and Wolfgang Amadeus Mozart.

While still at Kassel, Gustav fell in love with a singer, Johanna Richter. When their relationship ended with Richter leaving Mahler for another man, Gustav composed a memorial to the affair, *Lieder eines fahrenden Gesellen* (1884; *Songs of a Wayfarer*). This cycle of four songs for soprano and orchestra, widely regarded as the composer's first masterpiece, reveals with great force the emotional world of the twenty-three-year-old Mahler. His love of nature and capacity for grief are communicated in a strikingly original musical language that weds elements of folk song to unorthodox harmony and highly colorful orchestration. *Lieder eines fahrenden Gesellen* reflects Mahler's devotion to a famous collection of traditional poems and songs known as *Des Knaben Wunderhorn* (youth's magic horn), from which he was to draw much inspiration in composing both songs and symphonies.

Mahler's first four symphonies, completed between 1887 and 1900, are appropriately referred to as the "Wunderhorn" symphonies, since they incorporate verses and melodies from the original *Wunderhorn* sources and Mahler's adaptations of them. Mahler's conception of the symphony—that it "must be like the world" and embrace everything—allowed him to expand its scope by including vocal elements and by greatly lengthening the works. In Mahler's works, the traditional form of the symphony is superseded by the composer's expressive ambitions. Mahler sought a mastery of symphonic form but defined it more flexibly; unity was a matter not only of rational musical architecture but also of mood and philosophical intention.

In August, 1886, Mahler took up an appointment as second conductor at Leipzig, Germany, where he remained until May of 1888. His departure from Leipzig because of a conflict with the director sounds a characteristic note in Mahler's subsequent conducting career; his standards were uncompromising and his methods were sometimes nearly tyrannical, and could not have been tolerated in any case had Mahler not been a musician of the highest caliber. His next position, begun on October 1, 1888, was as musical director at the Royal Budapest Opera; he remained there until March of 1891, immediately moving to Hamburg, Germany's largest city, as chief opera conductor. During this period, the personal circumstances of Mahler's life changed considerably; in 1889, his father, mother, and a married sister died within months of one another, and he had to assume responsibility for his brothers and sisters. Although he was well paid for his conducting, his finances were rarely in good order. Nevertheless he succeeded in completing many works, seeing to their performance as circumstances allowed. His success as a composer was not immediate. Only with the presentation in 1895 of his second symphony—at his own expense and under his direction—did Mahler achieve unquestioned recognition as a composer.

As Mahler's fame as a conductor grew, he began to hope that he might be appointed to direct the Vienna Court Opera, which was the leading opera institution of its day. Although in his composing Mahler was a visionary, he approached his conducting career with a mastery of musical politics. One necessary step on the way to becoming director in Vienna was his conversion to Roman Catholicism; it might be doubted if a Protestant, let alone a Jew, could then have served in that capacity. Much has been said about Mahler's conversion, but there is a consensus that it was practical rather than cynical and accorded with an important element in Mahler's personality—his receptivity to many varieties of spiritual experience.

On October 8, 1897, Mahler was named director of the Vienna Court Opera, a post that he held with distinction for most of ten years. It was a powerful but troublesome position, and Mahler was incapable of much compromise on artistic matters. Nevertheless, he succeeded in revitalizing the institution and was once congratulated by the Emperor Francis Joseph I for "having made himself master of the situation" at the opera, where egos daily clashed in the pursuit of the often contradictory goals of personal fame and artistic integrity. Mahler became known as an advocate of clarity and the realization of the composer's intentions, which sometimes led him to alter the musical scores of famous and popular works—a practice that caused much criticism. He was for a time the elected leader of the Vienna Philharmonic Orchestra, where he conducted memorable performances of symphonic works, including his own symphonies. Mahler's great specialty, however, was the work of Richard Wagner, whose operas were the foundation of the operatic repertoire throughout Europe.

Unfortunately for subsequent generations, Mahler's career antedates the era of widespread sound recording, but a fair notion of his conducting style can be gained from written accounts, which are almost unanimous in their praise. Many photographs, drawings, and caricatures of Mahler have been preserved, as well as a famous bust of the composer by the French sculptor Auguste Rodin. Mahler was a slightly built but athletic man; pictures of him show an almost gravely intelligent face with a high forehead and somewhat unruly hair. In conversation with friends and on the conductor's podium, he seemed charismatic, but when he walked on the boulevards of Vienna people noticed a peculiar gait, which is now thought to have been a habit involuntarily recalling his mother's lameness.

The last decade of Mahler's life is a mixture of triumph and despair, but never of defeat. In 1901, he met Alma Schindler, at twenty-two perhaps the most beautiful woman in Vienna, and within a few months they were married. Late in 1902 their first daughter, Maria Anna, was born, followed in 1904 by another daughter, Anna Justine. Mahler's yearly cycle of work consisted of conducting in Vienna and elsewhere through the winter, followed by composing in the summer in a modest cabin near the family's lakeside summer home at Maiernigg in the Tyrol Mountains. Mahler's circle of friends, which included many of the most talented and interesting people in Austria, extended to Paris and other major European centers. He was financially secure—enough to sacrifice a substantial part of the royalties from the publication of his work to assist his publisher in printing Anton Bruckner's symphonies. Yet having gained hard-won worldly success, he continued to pursue creative projects that can only be called gargantuan, especially in

view of the limited time he could allot to them. More ominously, his inner creative life began to exact a toll both on his health and on his family life. Alma, at first a lively and adoring wife, began to believe that she was married to an abstraction; a musician herself, she had made a personal sacrifice when she married Mahler. In the summer of 1907, Mahler's world came close to total collapse. His elder daughter, Maria, died of diphtheria, precipitating Alma's breakdown from exhaustion. Then, on being examined by the doctor summoned to help Alma, Mahler was diagnosed as having a serious heart problem, which required a drastic curtailment of his activities.

Mahler's personal suffering had been prefigured in much of his work of the preceding six years. In 1901 he had begun his *Kindertotenlieder* (songs on the death of children), published in 1905 as five songs to verses by the poet Friedrich Rückert; it is easy to believe Alma when she states that she reproached her husband for thus tempting fate. Mahler's Sixth Symphony, completed in 1904, is an explicitly tragic musical essay in which the "hammer-blows of fate" fall upon the creator-protagonist as cruelly as they were soon to do in real life.

Mahler's fortunes at the Vienna Court Opera were in decline when, in mid-1907, his resignation was announced. Although his departure was brought about in behind-the-scenes maneuvers by court officials, Mahler had been convinced for some time that his withdrawal would be to his own advantage, and he had been reviewing offers from New York for some time. Beginning on January 1, 1908, Mahler directed the Metropolitan Opera, leaving there to accept a three-year contract with the New York Philharmonic Orchestra. Both ventures were ill-advised on the grounds of his health and artistic prospects, and neither turned out particularly well, but as Mahler's conducting career was coming to a conclusion he was at work on some of his finest compositions. His last major work to be performed in his lifetime, the Eighth Symphony, was first heard in Munich, Germany, in early September of 1910. This massive work, which requires for its performance hundreds of instrumentalists and several choirs, was enthusiastically acclaimed at its premiere in a manner reserved for a very few works of art. By this time Mahler had already completed *Das Lied von der Erde* (*The Song of the Earth*), a song-cycle in essentially symphonic form, and his ninth symphony

(1909). The Tenth Symphony, which was to remain incomplete, was begun in the summer of 1910.

More personal difficulties awaited Mahler as he prepared for the premiere of the Eighth Symphony and worked on the composition of the Tenth Symphony at Toblach. In June, Alma had gone, on her physician's advice, to a spa near Tobelbad, Austria; in addition to rest, the doctor had prescribed dancing. There Alma met the young architect Walter Gropius and had an affair with him, which came to Mahler's attention when Gropius accidentally, as he later claimed, addressed to "Director Mahler" a letter intended for Alma. In August, Mahler sought out Sigmund Freud, and in a few brief hours, according to Freud, was able to comprehend the harm that his obsession with music had done to his marriage. A break with Alma was averted, though a true reconciliation seems to have been impossible.

Mahler was perceptibly weakening, but he went on with a rigorous conducting schedule. In New York on February 21, 1911, critically ill with a streptococcal infection, he conducted his last concert. Upon returning to Europe, he sought treatment first in Paris and then in Vienna, but his heart was irreparably damaged. He died on May 18 in the Loew Sanatorium, at the age of fifty.

Summary

The dominant quality of Gustav Mahler's music is its intensity of expression, through which the composer hoped to address the highest philosophical concerns. This ambitious program, which unfolds relentlessly in Mahler's symphonies, remains a controversial one because of widely diverging concepts of the nature and limits of art. Mahler was the heir of Romanticism, which often valued the artist's subjectivity above the conventions of art, and consequently his music has had limited appeal to those listeners who view art as ideally an expression of the intellect.

From his earliest works, Mahler's music is full of extremes of emotion ranging from unbearable loneliness to religious transcendence. In achieving this richness of expression, Mahler drew upon a vast store of musical experience in which the most influential voices were those of Ludwig van Beethoven, Schubert, Bruckner, and Wagner. From Beethoven and Bruckner he drew a sense of the possibilities of symphonic form and content, and from Schubert the lyric capacity of song. Wagner's influence upon Mahler and his generation was so profound that of all of Wagner's contributions to late Romanticism, his extension of the limits of harmony is the only one that can be placed well above the rest. All of this and more Mahler grasped and transformed into a new musical language which is instantly recognizable. The clarity and inventiveness of his counterpoint and instrumentation are acknowledged even by those who do not especially care for his work as a whole: *Das Lied von der Erde*, in particular, shows Mahler's genius for sparseness of orchestration and delicacy of instrumental color, and in a technical sense, at minimum, the work belongs to the small group of compositions that define the transition from Romanticism to modern music.

In the view of the American composer Aaron Copland, Mahler was the "focal point" of an age; he amplified the psychological tensions of nineteenth century European culture and helped to forge the "violent patterns" of modern music. Mahler's profound influence upon twentieth century music has been profound, diverting too much attention, in the view of Deryck Cooke, from the composer's own creative achievement. Mahler was a generous mentor to Arnold Schoenberg, Alban Berg, and Anton von Webern, each of whom drew in some way upon the master's example. After Mahler's death, there was a period of decades during which his works were seldom performed, but beginning with the 1960's his popularity increased immensely, doubtless aided by the availability of his music on long-playing recordings. Composers as diverse as Dmitri Shostakovich, Benjamin Britten, and Karlheinz Stockhausen acknowledge debts to him, and the controversy surrounding his works has diminished. Mahler's music seems likely to endure many cycles of fashion, and, at a distance of many decades, for some listeners it has taken on an almost archetypal status.

Bibliography

Blaukopf, Kurt. *Gustav Mahler.* Translated by Inge Goodwin. London: Allen Lane, and New York: Praeger, 1973. This book provides a well-integrated account of Mahler's dual career and gives a sense of his music without recourse to a single musical quotation.

————. *Mahler: A Documentary Study.* Compiled and edited by Kurt Blaukopf. London: Thames and Hudson, and New York: Oxford University Press, 1976. Much of the material presented here will come alive only to those who already know the outlines of Mahler's life, but this is a well-produced study with substantial content and not merely a coffee-table book.

Cooke, Deryck. *Gustav Mahler: An Introduction to His Music*. 2d ed. Cambridge and New York: Cambridge University Press, 1988. This book consists of a chronological presentation of the composer's major works, framed by an introductory essay, "Mahler as Man and Artist," and a postscript, "Mahler's Report on Experience." Most of the texts that Mahler employed are printed in German and English. Cooke's opinions display his deep personal as well as scholarly commitment to Mahler's music.

Franklin, Peter. *The Life of Mahler*. Cambridge and New York: Cambridge University Press, 1997. A study of the often-misunderstood Mahler, his thoughts, his style as a conductor, and his traditionalist approach.

Gartenberg, Egon. *Mahler: The Man and His Music*. London: Cassell, and New York: Schirmer, 1978. With the division of this book into two main sections, the author seems to acknowledge that his account of Mahler is overextended; his embellishment of the social and historical background of the composer's time is interesting but often distracting.

Hefling, Stephen E., ed. *Mahler Studies*. Cambridge and New York: Cambridge University Press, 1997. A collection of ten essays by several experts who consider Mahler from a number of perspectives. Includes previously unavailable documents and family letters.

Holbrook, David. *Gustav Mahler and the Courage to Be*. London: Vision Press, 1975; New York: Da Capo Press, 1982. Originally published in a series of books entitled "Studies in the Psychology of Culture," this is a sincere and extremely demanding attempt to probe Mahler's psychological and spiritual world with the insights of psychoanalysis and existentialist philosophy.

Kennedy, Michael. *Mahler*. 2d ed. London: Dent, 1990. The modest dimensions of this book, a volume in the Master Musicians series, are made up for by the efficiency with which the author presents the truly essential information on Mahler's life and works.

Lebrecht, Norman. *Mahler Remembered*. London: Faber, 1987; New York: Norton, 1988. This collection of accounts of Mahler by his friends, associates, enemies, and survivors is indispensable for understanding his role and status in European culture around the turn of the century.

Mitchell, Donald. *Gustav Mahler: Songs and Symphonies of Life and Death*. London: Faber, and Berkeley: University of California Press, 1985. This is the third volume of Mitchell's series of studies of Mahler's music and, like its predecessors, it is aimed at the patient specialist rather than the general reader. Within the labyrinthine text, however, are found some of the keenest and most detailed insights into Mahler's art.

Werfel, Alma Schindler Mahler. *Gustav Mahler: Memories and Letters*. Edited and with an introduction by Donald Mitchell. Translated by Basil Creighton. 4th ed. London: Cardinal, 1990. Mahler's widow has been judged a frequently unreliable source of information and opinions, but her book makes fascinating reading.

C. S. McConnell

NORMAN MAILER

Born: January 31, 1923; Long Branch, New Jersey
Area of Achievement: Literature
Contribution: One of the most controversial literary figure of his generation, Mailer redefined the art of literary journalism and became one of the most prominent and unpredictable novelists and social critics in the United States.

Early Life

Norman Kingsley Mailer was born in Long Branch, New Jersey, to Isaac Barnett Mailer and Fanny Schneider Mailer. He was an only child. After his family moved to Brooklyn, New York, in 1927, Norman had a calm childhood playing neighborhood sports, building model airplanes, and excelling in public schools. His innate intelligence (an intelligence quotient measured at 165 in school and about 150 later in the Army) propelled him to college. At age sixteen, he applied to the Massachusetts Institute of Technology (MIT) for study in aeronautical engineering, but the university suggested he take a year of college elsewhere. Norman enrolled at Harvard University, where he received his engineering degree with honors in 1943.

At Harvard, Mailer had become attracted to the career of a writer. He began writing in earnest, contributing pieces to the *Harvard Advocate* and winning a national collegiate fiction award in 1941. Emulating his literary hero, Ernest Hemingway, Mailer sought some life experience to bolster his writing, which approached one million words before his first novel appeared. He hitchhiked through the South and worked at a mental hospital to gather material. In 1944 he married Beatrice Silverman, his college girlfriend and the first of his six wives. Induction into the Army followed. At first, Mailer had telephone lineman and clerk positions, but he volunteered for combat as a rifleman. He was part of a reconnaissance platoon in the Philippines and the occupation army in Japan before his discharge in 1946.

Life's Work

Mailer burst onto the American literary scene in 1948 with a bold, big first novel, *The Naked and the Dead*. Fame came quickly to the twenty-five-year-old as the sweeping war adventure became a best-seller and won critical acclaim. His second novel, *Barbary Shore* (1951), however, was a failure, a claustrophobic debate of the Cold War in a Brooklyn boardinghouse. The third novel, *The Deer Park* (1955), an examination of sex and power and spiritual failure in Hollywood, was a mixed success and deepened Mailer's fear that he had expended his talents on his first book. Not for another decade did he write another novel, but by the time *An American Dream* (1965) appeared, Mailer had already resecured his career with his nonfiction essays.

From the outset, Mailer threw himself into the intellectual and political currents of his day. *The Naked and the Dead* had criticized the war, and by extension American culture, as totalitarian. In 1948 he studied in Paris at the Sorbonne and established a long friendship with Marxist philosopher Jean Malaquais. Mailer began to envision the role of the writer as one of political commitment and activism rather than isolated retreat from society. Later that year, he worked for Progressive Party presidential candidate Henry Wallace. Throughout the 1950's, Mailer moved toward more extreme positions of cultural radicalism. His first marriage ended, and in 1954 he married Adele Morales, a painter he met in Greenwich Village. He became associated with the Beat movement and helped found *The Village Voice* as an alternative to the mainstream press. He experimented with drugs and drank heavily. In 1957, in *Dissent*, he published *The White Negro*, praising the hipster—what he called a "psychic outlaw"—as vital for a free society. Two years later, he collected his *Village Voice* columns and other pieces into his first prose collection, *Advertisements for Myself* (1959).

These forays into journalism reenergized Mailer. He decided to run for mayor of New York in 1960. However, his private life remained tumultuous. In November of that year, after a drunken party, Mailer stabbed Adele with a penknife. This led to incarceration at Bellevue mental hospital and eventually to divorce. After a short marriage to his third spouse, British journalist Lady Jeanne Campbell, he wed actor Beverly Bentley. Some domestic stability ensued, but with an expanded family of five children from his marriages, Mailer relied on journalism for financial security. In 1963, he published *The Presidential Papers* (1963), undoubtedly one of his best collections of prose. In "Superman Comes to the Supermarket," he covered the 1960 Democratic National Convention, and, with his

vivid portrait of John Kennedy, Mailer found his forte in the style of political coverage that would sustain him throughout the rest of his career.

Emboldened with his success, Mailer returned to fiction. In *An American Dream*, a novel much underrated by critics, he took the reader on a phantasmagoric trip through murder, lust, power, and Las Vegas, turning Theodore Dreiser's classic *An American Tragedy* (1925) inside out, as the hero escapes prosecution. In this novel, Mailer sought to illuminate what he labeled in *The Presidential Papers* the "dream life of the nation," a "subterranean river of untapped, ferocious, lonely, and romantic desires, that concentration of ecstasy and violence." Next Mailer delivered his most experimental novel, *Why Are We in Vietnam?* (1967), a story of a bear-hunting trip to Alaska symbolic of the United States' approaching debacle in Southeast Asia. In this book, Mailer told the tale through the hipster dialect of a teenager, one of the sons along on the hunt. The novel received a National Book Award nomination.

As fine as those novels were, Mailer was about to embark on his most productive period of literary journalism. In *Cannibals and Christians* (1966), he widened his scope to explore all sorts of topics from politics to architecture, plastics to cancer. The next year, however, he focused his attack on the Vietnam War and produced a Pulitzer Prize winner, *The Armies of the Night* (1967). Embracing the "new journalism" techniques employed by Tom Wolfe and others, Mailer jettisoned any attempt at complete journalistic objectivity and described his interior feelings as a participant in a major antiwar rally at the Pentagon in October, 1967. Writing of himself in the third person in the first part, "History as a Novel," Mailer fashioned a persona caught up in the protest and the subsequent arrest. In the second part, "The Novel as History," he wove together newspaper accounts, other eyewitness accounts, and other sources to narrate the story of the incident.

Hitting full stride as a literary reporter, Mailer next covered the 1968 presidential conventions in *Miami and the Siege of Chicago* (1969), the 1969 Apollo 11 moonshot in *Of a Fire on The Moon* (1970), and the Muhammad Ali-Joe Frazier heavyweight boxing match in *King of the Hill: On the Fight of the Century* (1971). With the last, he continued his literary and personal interest in boxing dating from a 1962 piece, "Ten Thousand Words a Minute." He then published a rebuttal to the Women's Liberation Movement and feminist attacks on his fiction in *The Prisoner of Sex* (1971). The next year brought another prose miscellany, *Existential Errands* (1972), and political reportage on the 1972 presidential campaign, *St. George and the Godfather* (1972). In 1973, he put together a stunning biography and photographic study of actress Marilyn Monroe. *Marilyn* (1973) allowed Mailer to indulge in his fantasies for the blond bombshell and speculate on her death as a possible murder. Indeed, at a self-organized fiftieth birthday party that year, Mailer announced an effort to start a watchdog organization to watch the Central Intelligence Agency (CIA) and other federal agencies. Ever the gadfly, his next prose work, *The Faith of Graffiti* (1974), contended that graffiti, instead of being an ugly defacement of property, was a vibrant expression of individualism. In mid-decade, he delivered another piece of boxing coverage, *The Fight* (1975), and an annotated collection of Henry Miller's fiction, *Genius and Lust* (1976).

For the next four years, Mailer retreated from the limelight. In 1979, however, he astonished the literary world with the Pulitzer Prize-winning book

The Executioner's Song (1979). Submerging his own ego to near invisibility (no mean feat for Mailer), he recounted the story of Gary Gilmore, who had murdered two people in Utah in 1976 and then refused to appeal his execution the next January. The tale provided Mailer a chance to explore the place of personal and institutional violence in American culture. Two years later, he became involved in a bizarre spinoff when he helped arrange the publication of Utah convict Jack Henry Abbott's letters from prison and supported his release, a few weeks after which Abbott stabbed a New York waiter to death. On a more peaceful plane, Mailer resolved his marital situation in 1980 by divorcing Beverly, quickly marrying and divorcing Carol Stevens (a singer with whom he had lived in the 1970's to legitimize their nine-year-old daughter), and marrying his sixth wife, Norris Church, an Arkansas artist and the mother of his eighth child. He also published another prose ensemble, *Pieces and Pontifications* (1982).

Mailer then entered another stretch of literary waning. *Ancient Evenings* (1983), a long and sluggish disquisition on reincarnation, preceded a murder mystery, *Tough Guys Don't Dance* (1984), which in turn preceded another large-scale novel on CIA intrigue, *Harlot's Ghost* (1991). Critics found little to cheer in these three works. Mailer returned to nonfiction, cranking out his own interpretation of part of the Kennedy assassination in *Oswald's Tale: An American Mystery* (1995) and a study of another artist with whom he likely identified, Pablo Picasso, in *Portrait of Picasso as a Young Man* (1995). Two years later, he published a quirky small novel, *The Gospel According to the Son* (1997), a retelling of the life of Jesus from Christ's vantage point. The following year, he published a reprise of some of his more famous essays and some unpublished prose in *The Time of Our Time* (1998).

Summary

More than any other writer since Ernest Hemingway, Norman Mailer has merged his pugilistic personality and ebullient persona with his writing. Alternately belligerent and contrite, Mailer has explored the intersection of experience and fiction as an activist writer. Always predictably unpredictable, he has rarely shied away from the confrontational and aggressive theories about American culture that have won him many admirers and earned him probably an equal number of detractors. Sometimes a lightning rod for the crackpot and the harebrained, Mailer has nonetheless patrolled areas of violence, lust, power, and greed that unsettle most Americans. His public image, his thrust for celebrity and brushes with notoriety, however, distract from an appreciation of how solid and professional his written work has been. With his virtuoso versatility, arguably no other author has seized on so many topics, spiritual and material, in his literary quest to explain modern American life. Undoubtedly one of America's major prose stylists, Mailer helped elevate the craft of writing during an era of the visualization of American popular culture. He may never deliver his promised blockbuster "Great American Novel," but Mailer's thirty or so works have ensured him a secure place as one of the most ferocious social critics of late twentieth century America.

Bibliography

Hitchens, Christopher. "Norman Mailer: A Minority of One." *New Left Review*, no. 222 (March-April, 1997). Interview with Mailer in which he discusses his work *The Naked and the Dead*, violence in men, racism, Presidents Kennedy and Clinton, and capital punishment.

Lennon, J. Michael, ed. *Conversations with Norman Mailer*. Jackson: University Press of Mississippi, 1988. A fine collection of interviews from 1948 to 1987.

Lucid, Robert F., ed. *Norman Mailer: The Man and His Work*. Boston: Little Brown, 1971. A good assemblage of pre-1971 literary criticism that places Mailer in historical context.

Mailer, Adele. *The Last Party: Scenes from My Life with Norman Mailer*. London: Blake, and New York: Barricade, 1997. Mailer's second wife, Adele, offers a glimpse into her life with the often-abusive man who eventually stabbed her nearly to death, ending their ten-year relationship.

Manso, Peter. *Mailer: His Life and Times*. New York: Simon and Schuster, and London: Viking, 1985. A "biography" composed of excerpts and remembrances from Mailer's friends, acquaintances, and enemies.

Merrill, Robert. *Norman Mailer Revisited*. New York: Twayne, 1992. An updated version of Merrill's 1970 literary study of Mailer with more emphasis on his work than his life.

Mills, Hilary. *Mailer: A Biography*. New York: Empire, 1982. A standard, straightforward biography covering Mailer's life and career to 1982.

Rollyson, Carl. *The Lives of Norman Mailer*. New York: Paragon House, 1991. This full-scale biography is probably too sympathetic to Mailer.

Solotaroff, Robert. *Down Mailer's Way*. Urbana: University of Illinois Press, 1974. A thoroughly academic but spirited critique of Mailer's literature and nonfiction.

Wenke, Joseph. *Mailer's America*. Hanover, N.H.: University Press of New England, 1987. A competent analysis and summation of Mailer's work to the late 1980's with some attempt at relating it to his times.

Thomas L. Altherr

JOHN MAJOR

Born: March 29, 1943; London, England

Areas of Achievement: Government and politics

Contribution: After a rapid rise through the ranks of the Conservative Party, John Major succeeded Margaret Thatcher as prime minister of England in November, 1990, and through quiet but pragmatic leadership, kept the party in power for another seven years.

Early Life

John Roy Major's father, Tom, was born in 1879 and spent part of his early life in the United States, after which he returned to England and started his own business. In 1921 he married the much younger Gwen Coates. John, the couple's third child, was born in 1943. The family was poor, and the children were sometimes lonely. In 1955 the Majors were in Brixton, and John was enrolled at the Rutlish Grammar School. At sixteen he left school to help support his family, but he had already developed an interest in politics and was dreaming of a seat in Parliament.

Major found work in the accounting department of a bank. He was quickly promoted and, from 1965 to 1979, was an executive at the Standard Chartered Bank. He also became an associate of the Institute of Bankers. His interest in politics lingered, and in 1968 he won a place on the Lambeth Borough Council, becoming vice chairman of the Housing Committee. Major considered a run for Parliament in 1970 but decided against the effort for fear that the Conservative Party would reject him. It was an important year in his life, however, for he met Norma Johnson, who was to become his wife. His political chance came in 1974, but in a typical British party arrangement, he was chosen to contest St. Pancras North—a safe Labour Party seat. The parties often expect newcomers to be sacrificial lambs during their first elections. If individuals show that they can carry their share of the political burden, a seat with better prospects is offered during the next election. So it was with Major.

Life's Work

In the 1979 election, Major was surprisingly offered Huntingdon, a safe seat for the Tories. He was thirty-six that year and not particularly distinguished in appearance. Slender and bespectacled with short hair, he seemed a cliché of a banker. Despite his lack of flair, however, he was embarking on a political career that would take him to the top of British government. His performance in the 1979 election was impressive, for despite serious competition, he significantly increased the Conservative majority in Huntingdon.

Major's rise in the Conservative Party began soon after he reached Westminster, for he had already attracted the eye of Margaret Thatcher, who became prime minister with the Tory victory of 1979. He became an assistant government whip in 1983 and lord commissioner of the Treasury in 1984. The next year he was appointed parliamentary undersecretary of state in the Department of Health and Social Security and, following the general election of June, 1987 (another Conservative victory), chief secretary to the Treasury. Major was a hard worker, frequently putting in very long hours but never seeming to exhaust his energy. Despite his relatively limited education, he was increasingly respected in the ranks of government financial specialists.

In July, 1989, Prime Minister Thatcher surprised the public and even some in her own party by appointing Major foreign secretary. Her move seemed to have surprised even him. Although his new position was one of the highest in British government, a public opinion poll taken at the time suggested that few people even recognized his name. The promotion showed Major's growing connection to Thatcher, who had become one of the most powerful politicians of the day. It was perhaps fortunate for Major's career that his tenure at the Foreign Office was only three months, for he showed less skill there than in jobs connected to financial matters.

Financial problems for the government arose during the late 1980's. Thatcher was continuing to press her conservative economic philosophy, which at that time was causing an economic slow-down. The party was also split over involvement in the European Economic Community (EEC). Both Nigel Lawson, the chancellor of the Exchequer, and Geoffrey Howe, then foreign minister, had threatened to resign before the Madrid Summit of June, 1989, unless Thatcher strengthened the British commitment to join the Exchange Rate Mechanism (ERM). This precipitated the cabinet reshuffle that resulted in Major replacing Howe at the Foreign Office. Thatcher was concerned that British sovereignty would be undermined by a sort of super state of Europe, but many Conservatives feared that the euro (the common currency adopted by the EEC) would be imposed with London having no control over the situation. On October 26, 1989, Lawson, faced with inflation, rising overseas interest rates, and continuing disagreements with Thatcher, resigned.

Although her position was, in fact, weakening, Thatcher responded to the resignation of her chancellor decisively by restructuring her cabinet. Douglas Hurd went to the Foreign Office, David Waddington replaced him at the Home Office, and Major became the new chancellor of the Exchequer. Major was now in the office that is traditionally held by the heir apparent to the prime ministership. He was also in a position to make maximum use of his financial expertise. One result of the shift in personnel was that Thatcher's handling of ERM and other matters concerning the EEC was shared with Major and Hurd, and she was less influenced by outside advisors. With Major as a leading influence, Thatcher agreed to British commitment to ERM.

The new cabinet and compromise by Thatcher failed, however, to heal the rifts within the Conservative Party. Long known for iron-fisted control, Thatcher was increasingly indecisive. There were riots over poll taxes at home, the economic decline continued, and she was unable to develop any agreement over European commitments within the party. In the fall of 1990, Michael Heseltine challenged her in the election for party leader. Thatcher won, but only by 204 to 152, and absolute victory required both a majority of the 372 Tory members of Parliament and a 15 percent margin. She was four votes short of the required margin. It was a devastating result for a party leader. After first vowing to fight, she resigned.

Major's friends pressed him to put his name forward for the leadership, but he was initially reluctant, not wanting to appear disloyal to Thatcher, who had done so much to advance his career. In the end he did so, resulting in a three-way contest with Hurd and Heseltine. On November 27, 1990, Major got 185 votes—two short of an outright majority—and his opponents withdrew their names from further consideration. The next day John Major officially became prime minister of the United Kingdom.

As prime minister, Major was almost immediately embroiled in the Gulf War in support of the

United States. Hostilities began January 17, 1991, and ten days later opinion polls showed Major the most popular prime minister since Winston Churchill. In March he had a summit meeting with Mikhail Gorbachev, leader of the Soviet Union. It seemed like a promising beginning, and party faithful began to think the glory days of Thatcher's tenure were returning. There were troublesome signs, however. In March, 1991, the Labour Party, for the first time in many years, was more popular in opinion polls than the Conservatives. Refusing an early election, Major went to the Maastricht summit in the Netherlands concerning the economic union of Europe on December 9, 1991. Taking Britain further into the union, Major proclaimed Maastricht a triumph.

Once again seeming to be on top, Major announced elections for April, 1992. Despite recent gains of the Labour Party, the Conservatives won a majority of twenty-one in the House of Commons and retained control of the government. Over the next several years Major continued the Conservatives' economic change with such policies as the privatization of British Rail, and he had to deal with the unpleasant scandals and ultimately the divorce of the heir to the throne, Prince Charles, and his wife, Princess Diana. Politically, the question of Europe continued to dog his party. He was also criticized for his blandness. In June, 1995, he was challenged for party leadership by John Redwood, who opposed the economic union. Major won comfortably and reshuffled his cabinet to oust Redwood. He was still in control, but such challenges to successful prime ministers with reasonable majorities in the House of Commons are unusual. In this case it reflected the continuing divisions in the Conservative Party.

With the Conservatives in disarray, the Labour Party, now led by Tony Blair, rejected parts of its socialist heritage, moved to the political center, and exploited the popular support for full membership in the European Economic Union. Major was also struggling with negotiating an end to the violence in Northern Ireland. Again his lack of flair was criticized, though given the history of that bitter and bloody conflict, it seems unlikely that many could have done better, for progress toward a peaceful resolution was made. In 1997, Major, unable to hold his party together on the European question and increasingly criticized for lack of charisma, headed into elections. Blair, the dynamic Labour leader, offered a centrist platform with promises not to reverse popular Conservative tax policies and support for the economic union. On May 1, 1997, the Labour Party won a convincing electoral victory. Major held his own seat in Parliament but resigned as Conservative leader within a few weeks. He turned to writing his memoirs and making speaking tours.

Summary

Considering his social background and limited education, John Major was hardly the typical Tory leader. He rose because of his ability and built a reputation that provided the foundation for his eventual assumption of leadership. Major came to prominence during a difficult time. The economic policies of the Conservatives had not proven consistently successful, and the question of participation in the European Economic Union was strongly debated. He rose in politics with the patronage of Margaret Thatcher, the first woman prime minister and an extremely popular and successful politician. Although her reputation suggested a lack of tolerance for independence, let alone opposition, Major was never merely a "yes man." As chancellor he influenced her policy in favor of the economic union and showed his independence by making it known that she had not seen his first speech prior to delivery.

As prime minister, Major reconnected his party just as it seemed that it would split over the question of the EEC. He dealt effectively with a number of major problems, including the divorce of the prince and princess of Wales, and although the party's consensus over the EEC ultimately failed, Major did handle the negotiation that brought Britain into agreement with the rest of Europe. It cannot be denied that he lacked flash as a politician, but with Britain facing financial problems, his knowledge of banking and commerce and his pragmatic, diligent efforts were effective. He is not likely to be considered one of Britain's greatest prime ministers, but he is equally unlikely to be listed among the worst.

Bibliography

Cradock, Percy. *In Pursuit of British Interests: Reflections on Foreign Policy under Margaret Thatcher and John Major.* London: Murray, 1997. Although Major's expertise was domestic policy, foreign policy, especially relations with the EEC and the aftermath of the Cold War, was significant in his period of power. This study helps set that aspect of his government into context.

Crowley, Philip, and John Garry. "The British Conservative Party and Europe: The Choosing of John Major." *British Journal of Political Science* 28, no. 3 (July, 1998). Examines the second ballot in the 1990 Conservative Party leadership battle that made Major prime minister.

Dorey, Peter, ed. *The Major Premiership: Politics and Policies under John Major, 1990-97.* New York: St. Martin's Press, 1999. Provides an indepth analysis of Major as head of the government and of the Conservative Party. This work is a major contribution to political history.

Holmes, Martin. "The Conservative Party and Europe: From Major to Hague." *Political Quarterly* 69, no. 2 (April-June, 1998). Compares the attempts of Major and conservative leader William Hague to unite the Conservative Party.

Howe, Geoffrey. *Conflict of Loyalty.* London: Macmillan, and New York: St. Martin's Press, 1994. Howe, a Conservative minister and supporter of the EEC, discusses Major's involvement in the party and his rise to power. His firsthand accounts of behind-the-scenes political activity are insightful.

Reitan, Earl. *Tory Radicalism: Margaret Thatcher, John Major, and the Transformation of Modern Britain, 1979-1997*. Totowa, N.J.: Rowman and Littlefield, 1997. Reitan provides a thorough account of Conservative policy and its impact on Britain. Major's importance in extending Thatcher's heritage is a significant theme in the book.

Seldon, Anthony. *Major: A Political Life*. London: Weidenfield and Nicolson, 1997. A complete biography based in significant part on oral history, Seldon's book portrays Major as neither purely saint nor purely sinner. It is the best of the current biographies.

Thatcher, Margaret. *The Downing Street Years*. London and New York: HarperCollins, 1993. This second volume of Thatcher's memoirs describes Major's rise to power and discusses Conservative and national politics at the time.

Fred R. van Hartesveldt

MALCOLM X

Born: May 19, 1925; Omaha, Nebraska
Died: February 21, 1965; New York, New York
Areas of Achievement: Civil rights and social reform
Contribution: Born Malcolm Little, Malcolm X rose from life as a criminal hustler to become the national minister of the Nation of Islam and a popularizer of black nationalism, which emphasized self-defense for African Americans and independence from white America. Malcolm X's separatism served as a political alternative to Martin Luther King, Jr.'s advocacy of nonviolence and desegregation.

Early Life

In his best-seller *The Autobiography of Malcolm X* (1964), Malcolm described his father, Baptist preacher Earl Little, and his mother, Granada native M. Louise Norton, as dedicated followers of Marcus Garvey. Garvey, founder of the United Negro Improvement Association, argued that black people in the Western Hemisphere could achieve political freedom only by returning to the African homeland and could win economic independence by developing black-owned businesses. According to the autobiography, Louise was pregnant with Malcolm when Ku Klux Klan nightriders, angered at Earl's preaching, appeared at the Little home and warned them to move out of Omaha.

Nineteen months after Malcolm was born, the family left Omaha, eventually settling in Lansing, Michigan. According to the autobiography, a local white hate group called the Black Legion became alarmed about the "uppity" Earl Little, suspecting him of spreading unrest in the African American community. In late 1929, a deliberately set fire broke out at the Little home. The family escaped unharmed, but Earl was forced to build a new home outside of East Lansing. On September 28, 1931, Earl died after being struck by a streetcar. Malcolm later claimed that the Black Legion murdered his father.

Alone, Louise had eight children to raise. Worried about her family and embarrassed by having to accept welfare, she suffered a nervous breakdown eight years after her husband's death. The courts divided the Little children among several foster families. Often hungry as he grew up during the Great Depression, Malcolm still did well in school through the eighth grade. He made the highest grades among his peers and became class president in the seventh grade even while enduring condescending, racist comments from teachers and his peers. A previously supportive white English teacher asked Malcolm what he wanted to do for a living. When Malcolm said he wanted to become a lawyer, the teacher told him, "that's no realistic goal for a nigger," and advised him to become a carpenter. Disillusioned, Malcolm withdrew from white society and committed petty thefts before spending time in a detention home. Malcolm's problems prompted his move to Boston, Massachusetts, in 1941, where he lived with his half-sister Ella.

Malcolm accepted several low-paying jobs, including work as a busboy, dishwasher, and shoe shiner. He also drifted to the fringes of Boston's underworld and spent his years in Boston and New York as "Detroit Red"—a zoot-suit-wearing dope dealer, con artist, and pimp who organized a burglary ring. In February, 1946, while reclaiming a stolen watch he left at a Boston jewelry store for repairs, police arrested Malcolm for several felony charges, including illegal breaking and entering. The court sentenced him to a seven-year sentence.

Life's Work

While in prison, Malcolm began an intense self-education program, copying a dictionary word for word and voraciously reading at Charleston Prison library. By the time he was transferred to a prison in Concord, Massachusetts, his brothers Philbert and Reginald had exposed him to the teachings of the Nation of Islam religious sect led by Elijah Muhammad. The Nation of Islam (NOI), founded in Detroit around 1930, taught that white people were an inherently evil race created in ancient times by a dissident black scientist named Yacub. The white slave trade destroyed the great African civilizations, stripped black men and women of their culture, and deceived them with a Christian religion that left them vice-ridden and subservient. The NOI taught that political reform was futile in an innately evil world. Only the final judgment of the NOI deity, Allah, against the white race could bring justice. Until then, black people should redeem themselves by surrendering vices such as alcohol, avoiding impure foods such as pork, and rediscovering past achievements of the black race. Rather than integration into a white society poi-

soned with racism, black people needed separation from the white world and the creation of a financially independent black homeland.

Muhammad's teachings explained for Malcolm his past experiences with racial injustice. Released from prison in 1952, Malcolm replaced his last name with "X," which represented the African family name lost under slavery. After working briefly in Michigan as a furniture salesman and auto assembly worker, he soon devoted himself full-time to the Muslim ministry and became Muhammad's most effective recruiter and spokesman.

An imposing figure, Malcolm stood about 6 feet 5 inches tall with a lanky physique, light skin, closely cropped reddish hair, and grayish eyes that peered intensely through horn-rimmed glasses. Despite his intense appearance, he often surprised audiences and visitors with his politeness and charm. He rose quickly through NOI ranks, becoming an assistant minister at Detroit Temple Number 1 in late 1953, then holding minister's posts in Boston, Philadelphia, and, in June, 1954, at New York Temple Number 7. It was there that he met his future wife Betty Saunders. Malcolm and Betty married in January, 1958, and eventually had six daughters.

Malcolm acquired high visibility when New York City police beat and jailed NOI member Hinton Johnson in April, 1957. Malcolm led a contingent of fifty Muslims who gathered outside the Harlem police station where Johnson was being held. Malcolm insisted that Johnson be transferred to a hospital for medical treatment. When police complied, the incident prompted front-page coverage by the black-owned Amsterdam News and inspired closer police surveillance of the Muslims and their charismatic minister.

Malcolm gained national exposure with the July, 1959, New York broadcast of "The Hate That Hate Produced," a television report by journalist Mike Wallace. Malcolm boldly denounced not only white people but also middle-class black leaders, who he dismissed as Uncle Toms. Malcolm called Martin Luther King, Jr., a "chump" for advocating integration and insisted that "an integrated cup of coffee was insufficient pay for 400 years of slave labor." Malcolm rejected the vision of brotherhood in King's "I Have a Dream" speech during the 1963 March on Washington as a nightmare. At times straying from NOI's doctrine, Malcolm called for a global "black revolution" aiming at independence, not the integration sought by King's "Negro revolution."

By 1964, Malcolm's flamboyant rhetoric had made him the second most sought after speaker on college campuses, after Republican presidential candidate Barry Goldwater. Many within the NOI considered him Muhammad's heir apparent. Under Malcolm, the NOI grew from a few hundred adherents to 100,000 or more members during the early 1960's. Malcolm's successes sparked jealousy within the NOI even as Malcolm found himself frustrated with the NOI's apolitical approach. For all its rhetoric of self-defense and autonomy, the NOI stood on the sidelines while the Civil Rights campaign directly challenged white authority.

Reports that the married Muhammad had affairs with several secretaries and fathered six illegitimate children further alienated Malcolm. Corrupt NOI officials may have also feared that Malcolm, if he succeeded Muhammad, would crack down on financial improprieties. When Malcolm described the recent assassination of President John F. Kennedy as a case of "chickens coming home to roost" at a New York rally in December, 1963, Muhammad feared a backlash and suspended Malcolm from his ministry for ninety days. The breach, however, proved permanent.

On March 8, 1964, Malcolm announced a formal break with the Nation of Islam. He sought closer ties with the mainstream Civil Rights movement, saying that he and King both sought black freedom. Malcolm urged black people to make their voting rights a reality. He hoped to link the struggle of African Americans with the liberation struggles fought by people of color around the globe. He soon formed Muslim Mosque, Inc. and the Organization of Afro-American Unity, which aimed to make the rights of African Americans an international issue. Malcolm completed his transformation that April when he undertook the journey to Mecca, Saudi Arabia, required of traditional Muslims. There he encountered Muslims of all colors who were experiencing spiritual brotherhood. He no longer saw all white people as devils but would judge white individuals by their actions. Concluding that the racist theology of the NOI conflicted with traditional Islam, he converted to the Sunni branch of Islam and took the name el-Hajj Malik el-Shabazz.

Malcolm sought a United Nations hearing on the suppression of black human rights in the United States, a goal never realized. His New York home, rewarded to him for his ministerial work, was firebombed on February 14, 1965, four days before the NOI evicted him. On February 21, at the start of a speech at the Audubon Ballroom in New York, Malcolm was shot repeatedly by Talmadge Hayer. A grand jury later indicted Hayer, Norman 3X Butler, and Thomas 15X Johnson for Malcolm's murder. All three held ties with the Nation of Islam and were convicted the next year. One day after the murder, Muhammad denied involvement with the assassination.

Summary

Malcolm X's influence increased after his death with the publication of his autobiography. As racism and black poverty persisted even with the signing of major civil rights legislation by Lyndon Johnson in 1964 and 1965, Malcolm's rage rang true for increasingly radicalized youth in organizations such as the Student Nonviolent Coordinating Committee (SNCC). The "black is beautiful" slogans of the 1960's and the development of black studies programs at universities and public schools echo Malcolm's emphasis on black pride and knowledge of the African past. The Black Panther Party, founded in Oakland, California, in 1966, acknowledged their ideological debt to Malcolm X and his emphasis on self-defense and the economic roots of racism. Transformed into a merchandising franchise by director Spike Lee's 1992 film biography *Malcolm X*, Malcolm's image haunts rap music videos, while rap recordings sample his speeches. In popular culture, Malcolm X now serves as both antihero and hero in the guise of the street-smart hustler and the self-educated minister who redeemed himself from an intellectual ghetto.

Bibliography

Burrows, Rufus, Jr. "Malcolm X Was a Racist: The Great Myth." *Western Journal of Black Studies* 20, no. 2 (Summer 1996). Examines Malcolm X's views on racial integration and what the author views as Malcolm's misunderstood rhetoric against the treatment of blacks by whites.

Dyson, Michael Eric. *Making Malcolm: The Myth and Meaning of Malcolm X*. New York: Oxford University Press, 1995. At 215 pages, this work explores the political uses (and abuses) to which Malcolm's memory is subjected. The book includes analysis of previous biographers and provides a helpful overview of the scholarly literature on Malcolm X, summarizing academic disagreements about the man, his life, and his cultural impact.

Gallen, David. *Malcolm X as They Knew Him.* New York: Carroll and Graf, 1992. Gallen's book includes vivid reminiscences of Malcolm from friends and associates, a *Playboy* interview of Malcolm by Alex Haley before they worked together on the autobiography, and lively essays from writers as diverse as Black Panther Eldridge Cleaver and Southern novelist and poet Robert Penn Warren.

Malcolm X. *The Autobiography of Malcolm X.* New York: Ballantine, 1964; London: Hutchinson, 1966. This autobiography contains both the eloquent oration that actor Ossie Davis delivered at Malcolm's funeral and Haley's illuminating epilogue, which captures the pressures, fears, and hopes of Malcolm's last months. Compellingly written, this remains the definitive text on Malcolm's life.

Perry, Bruce. *Malcolm: The Life of a Man Who Changed Black America*. Barrytown, N.Y.: Station Hill Press, 1991. Aggressively revisionist, Perry suggests that a childhood of physical abuse and guilt over an ambiguous sexual orientation partly drove Malcolm's rage and the sudden shifts in his identity. Critics complain that Perry carelessly evaluates the quality of his evidence.

Saldana-Portillo, Maria J. "Consuming Malcolm X: Prophecy and Performative Masculinity." *Novel* 30, no. 3 (Spring 1997). Considers the public and private Malcolm X.

Sales, William W., Jr. *From Civil Rights To Black Liberation: Malcolm X and the Organization of Afro-American Unity*. Boston: South End Press, 1994. Sales seeks to shift attention from Malcolm the emotionally powerful icon to Malcolm the political and economic thinker. He sees the post-NOI Malcolm as an almost Marxist revolutionary who clearly articulated the relationship of capitalism and colonialism to the oppression of black people.

Michael Phillips

GEORGI M. MALENKOV

Born: January 8, 1902; Orenburg, Russia
Died: January 14, 1988; Moscow, U.S.S.R.
Areas of Achievement: Government and politics
Contribution: Malenkov was a close associate of
Joseph Stalin in his bloody terror against the
Communist Party of the Soviet Union and Soviet
society in general. In 1953, he was Stalin's im-
mediate successor as prime minister of the gov-
ernment and first secretary of the Communist
Party, positions that he soon lost in the power
struggle with Nikita S. Khrushchev.

Early Life

Georgi Maksimilianovich Malenkov was born in
the Ural Mountains region of southeastern European Russia traditionally inhabited by Cossacks. The
city of his birth is now called Chkalov. Little is
known of Malenkov's childhood. His family appears to have been of the lower white-collar class.
Official biographical notes about Malenkov never
included personal data about him, as was the custom for political figures of the years of Stalin's
rule.

While still in his teens Malenkov became active
in politics during the civil war that followed the
Bolshevik seizure of power in 1917. In 1919, he
was appointed an officer in charge of political affairs (commissar) in a unit of the Bolshevik Red
Army fighting in Turkestan. He became a member
of the Communist Party at the age of eighteen. After the Bolsheviks had secured their power by tri-
umphing over the assorted "white" armies of their
opponents, Malenkov was enrolled in a technical
institute in Moscow. While still in school, he married Valeria Alekseevna Golubtsova, a worker in
the office of the Central Committee of the Party.
Through his wife, Malenkov established connections that permitted him to gain employment by the
committee after his graduation in 1925. In a short
time, he became a personal secretary to Stalin at a
time when Stalin was nearing his victory in the
contest for supreme political power.

By 1930, Malenkov had taken up the work that
was to bring him the great influence that he exercised in Soviet politics. He became chairman of
the Organization Bureau of the party in the city of
Moscow, and in 1934 he became chief of the department, supervising party organizations
throughout the Soviet Union. Thus Malenkov
commanded the Party's personnel network that
stretched over the country and facilitated Communist control of the economic and governmental
structures of the Soviet Union. From 1936 through
1940, he was chief editor of the Party journal devoted to organizational work, *Partiinoe stroitel'st-
vo* (party structure).

Life's Work

Malenkov parlayed the information that he acquired through his responsibilities for Party organizational work into arbitrary control over the lives
of tens of thousands of Communists. In 1934, he
became chief aide to Nikolai Ezhov, chairman of
the disciplinary arm of the Party, the Control Commission. Ezhov soon was to assume the top post in
the political police and give his name to the worst
months of Stalinist terror, the Ezhovshchina, or
"the evil era of Ezhov," by which the period of
1936-1938 often is named. In that time, Malenkov
remained at Ezhov's side. After Khrushchev exposed the crimes of the purge years, one party offical reported that Malenkov personally had participated in the interrogation under torture and
eventual elimination of as many as thirty-five hundred Armenian Communists in 1937. He and
Ezhov were partners in a similarly brutal and thorough purge of the Belorussian party organization.

Malenkov continued his speedy ascent in the
Party power hierarchy even after Ezhov was executed and replaced by Lavrenti Beria. In 1939,
Malenkov was appointed to the party secretariat,
retaining his responsibility for party personnel. At
this time an important debate began over principle
that was to govern an intense personal rivalry between Malenkov and Andrey Zhdanov. Malenkov
advocated close practical supervision by the party
over economic activity, while Zhdanov argued for
governmental supervision of the economy with the
Party's efforts devoted to ideological education of
society. By early 1941, it was evident that Malenkov
had won this contest, for the time being, when he
emerged from the shadows of the Party apparatus
to make his first important public speech before the
Party. At the Nineteenth Party Conference in February, he pronounced a harsh criticism of government officials who supervised economic matters
but were themselves incompetent for their offices.
In the aftermath of the speech, a number of apparently influential Communist politicians were demoted, and Malenkov was promoted to nonvoting

(candidate) membership in the Politburo, the small committee that exercised effective power in the country.

After German armies invaded the Soviet Union on June 22, 1941, Malenkov was made one of the five members of the Committee of State Defense, headed by Stalin. Malenkov demonstrated considerable managerial skill as the chief of aircraft and tank manufacturing in the country. The armed force that his planes and tanks were able to direct against the Germans in a very short time was one important factor in the Soviet Union's being able to recover from the devastating blow initially delivered by Adolf Hitler's forces. In little more than two years, the invaders were turned back by Soviet mechanized might. As they retreated, it became Malenkov's duty to supervise the economic rehabilitation of liberated regions, a task in which he exercised enormous authority over all aspects of citizens' lives.

In March, 1946, Malenkov became a full voting member of the Politburo, and in October he was appointed one of eight deputy premiers of the country. In 1947, however, his ascent to the pinnacle of power was halted temporarily as he neared the top. Intense rivalry for the favor of the aging Stalin as he marked his successor resulted in Malenkov's being relieved briefly of his seat on the secretariat. For a time, the influence of Zhdanov dominated, a situation signaled by the name often given to the years 1947-1948, "Zhdanovshchina," a period of severe cultural repression in the Soviet Union and expansion of Stalinist control in Eastern Europe. Although he remained on the Politburo, Malenkov's influence waned, and he was saddled with the apparently thankless task of supervising the perpetually deficient agricultural sector of the economy.

Malenkov demonstrated his ability to play the ruthless game of Party politics, with the support of Beria. Together they manufactured the "Leningrad affair," which resulted in the arrests of thousands of Communists who were associates of Zhdanov in the Leningrad Party organization. Zhdanov himself died in August, 1948. An element of mystery surrounded the death which remains to be cleared up. What is certain is that Zhdanov's demise led to Malenkov's emergence as one of Stalin's two most intimate associates in power (along with Viacheslav Molotov). The aggressively anti-Semitic Malenkov accused Jewish physicians of poisoning Zhdanov, a lie that was exposed after the death of Stalin, whose own hatred of Jews Malenkov manipulated to his own advantage.

That Malenkov had won the status of heir-apparent to Stalin seemed especially clear when in 1952 he was given the responsibility of planning the Nineteenth Party Congress, the first convocation of this highest formal authority of the Party to have been made since 1939. Malenkov delivered the principal speech of the congress in October. When Stalin died less than five months later, in March, 1953, Malenkov reaped the fruits of his status by assuming the supreme offices in government and Party which Stalin had held.

After only ten days, Malenkov surrendered his post of first secretary of the Party and remained the premier. His power as leader of the government was contested by Beria, but Malenkov eventually eliminated the police chief, who was executed in June. Thereupon Malenkov promoted his "new course," a combination of a conciliatory posture toward the West, symbolized in the ending of armed conflict in Korea and a shift of some industrial resources away from production of heavy equipment into consumer goods and housing.

Khrushchev soon emerged as Malenkov's chief rival. Khrushchev pried power out of Malenkov's hands, in part by placing upon him blame for the "Leningrad affair" and for enormous failures in Soviet agriculture. On January 25, 1955, Malenkov resigned the premiership, fatuously citing his "lack of experience." He retained for a time some influence within the Party because he was a member of the Presidium of the Central Committee, a body that substituted for the Politburo between 1952 and 1966. Khrushchev forced him to surrender this position in 1957 after Malenkov joined an unsuccessful conspiracy to oust Khrushchev from his post of first secretary.

Malenkov was exiled to the job of managing a hydroelectric plant in Kazakhstan. Such a fate for one who had lost a bold political gambit was far more merciful than the vengeance that he had visited upon thousands of Communists. Four years later he resigned, complaining about the insubordination of his underlings. Almost simultaneously he was expelled from the Communist Party after the public de-Stalinization of the Twenty-second Party Congress of 1961. Malenkov was punished for his participation in an "antiparty group," namely those who had sought to remove Khrushchev from his secretaryship in 1957. For the next twenty-seven years Malenkov lived in idle obscurity in a comfortable Moscow apartment. Persistent rumors circulated that he became a regular frequenter of Orthodox churches, but confirmation of these is lacking. His funeral in January, 1988, was a very private affair.

Summary

Because the brutality of the Stalinist regime is one of the salient features of the twentieth century and because Georgi M. Malenkov was closely implicated in that brutality, he must be recognized as an important figure of the time. It cannot be said that Malenkov made an identifiable contribution to humanity or that he even had the personal ability to do so. What he did, he did because he was Stalin's intimate. It seems that he excelled only as an agent for the leader to whom he gave total devotion. Although he manifested some hints of possessing real managerial skill, in actual practice, when Stalin was gone, Malenkov proved unable to retain the enormous power that had passed into his hands as holder of the highest offices of the second most powerful country of the world. Some observers have suggested that his "new course" set important precedents for the de-Stalinization that Khrushchev began and Mikhail Gorbachev brought to fruition. Such a claim carries only tentative conviction and probably represents the best that can be said of a man whose record of inhumanity would require much more to redeem it.

Bibliography

Hahn, Werner G. *Postwar Soviet Politics: The Fall of Zhdanov and the Defeat of Moderation, 1946-1953.* Ithaca, N.Y.: Cornell University Press, 1982. A study that portrays Malenkov as more brutal than Zhdanov and explains his triumph over him. This interpretation is somewhat at variance with the more common view that Malenkov was more of a moderate pragmatist than the ideological dogmatist that Zhdanov was.

McNeal, Robert H. *Stalin: Man and Ruler.* New York: New York University Press, and London: Macmillan, 1988. Because no book-length biography of Malenkov is available in any language, information about him can be gleaned most successfully from biographies of his mentor, of which this one is among the best.

Medvedev, Roy. *All Stalin's Men.* Translated by Harold Shukman. Oxford: Blackwell, 1983; New York: Doubleday, 1984. Chapter 6, "G. M. Malenkov: The 'Heir' that Never Was," is the most detailed biography of Malenkov in English, written by a man who has been the most outspoken anti-Stalinist Soviet historian of the 1970's and 1980's.

————. *Let History Judge.* Translated by George Shriver. Rev. ed. Oxford: Oxford University Press, and New York: Columbia University Press, 1989. The most detailed and authoritative history of the Stalinist era of Soviet history. The first edition of the book, published in New York in 1971, was denied publication in the Soviet Union in the Brezhnev era. The second, considerably enlarged, edition benefited from the liberalization of the Gorbachev era.

Rush, Myron. *Political Succession in the USSR.* 2d ed. New York: Columbia University Press, 1968. A political science comparison of the way successors to Vladimir Ilich Lenin, Stalin, and Khrushchev emerged which casts light on the failure of Malenkov to retain power.

Young, Gordon. *Stalin's Heirs.* London: Verschoyle, 1953. A dated, but useful, account from the period in which Malenkov emerged to the exercise of political power in his own right.

Paul D. Steeves

ANDRÉ MALRAUX

Born: November 3, 1901; Paris, France
Died: November 23, 1976; Paris, France
Areas of Achievement: Literature, government, and politics
Contribution: Malraux was a multifaceted twentieth century intellectual who had significant accomplishments in three worthy pursuits: As a novelist he produced some of the best fiction written in French during the century; in politics, he functioned successfully as a right-hand man to French President Charles de Gaulle; as an art critic, collector, and theorist, he also made noteworthy advancements.

Early Life

Georges André Malraux was born in the Montmartre section of Paris on November 3, 1901, to Fernand Malraux and Berthe Lamy Malraux, middle-class parents who were ill-matched. When Malraux was four years old, his parents permanently separated and later divorced. At that time, the child and his mother went to Bondy to live with Andrienne Romania, his Italian maternal grandmother. Generally, he was reared by these two women and had minimal contact with his father. Perhaps the best part of his childhood was his frequent visits to Dunkerque, a coastal town in northern France, where he visited his grandfather, Alphonse Émile, a working-class industrialist with various seafaring business interests.

His education was received almost entirely in Bondy. Reportedly, he was quite bored most of the time in school, finding little in the curriculum to challenge his acute mind. In 1915, he applied for a scholarship at a private institution, the École Turgot, in Paris; this pursuit was successful, and he attended school there until 1918. Again, he was not entirely happy, although he did rather well. His interests, aptitudes, and energies were usually directed toward the study of literature and art, and he displayed a fascination with world history, civilizations, and cultures as well. Perhaps his dissatisfaction with educational institutions explains why he did not attempt to obtain a college degree.

Between 1918 and 1923, he worked for a bookseller in Paris, an activity that gave rise to his later editing and publishing, which, in turn, accounts for his early contact with numerous influential writers in Paris at the time, such as André Gide. During these years, he often attended lectures, visited and studied at museums and art galleries, and began to circulate in literary and art circles. In 1921, he published his first book, *Lunes en papier* (1921; paper moons), a work of fantasy written as a prose poem. During this same year, he married his first of three wives, Clara Goldschmidt, a well-to-do Jew who was in many respects his intellectual equal; subsequent to the marriage they traveled to Italy.

Life's Work

In 1923, Malraux and his wife traveled to Indochina, where they expected to find artifacts of the ancient Khmer civilization. During their search in Cambodia, Malraux, following the example of accepted precedent and practice, removed several figures from ancient stone ruins. The action was illegal and, as it happened, Malraux was caught by local authorities before the remnants were removed from the country. The twenty-two-year-old Malraux was arrested and went through a series of trials and appeals before the matter was finally dropped some six to eight years later. During this first trip to Indochina, Malraux learned about more than the ancient ruins that he sought: He saw at first hand the corruption of the French in their control of Indochina, and in 1925 he helped found a short-lived newspaper, *L'Indochine*, which was quite severe in its criticism of those in power in the colony.

For the rest of his life, Malraux displayed success after success in his pursuits of literature, art, and politics. To him, these areas were all different focuses of an overriding belief about the nature of man. Discovery of an existential self required expression in literature and art as well as action to right social wrongs and corrupt, even faulty, systems of government. He lived primarily as a radical and revolutionary yet almost always at the center of the influential figures and powerful leaders, not only in France but also throughout the world.

In retrospect, it is clear that his most outstanding contributions are in literature. His greatest novels were recognized as such at their initial publication: *Les Conquérants* (1928, 1949; *The Conquerors,* 1929, 1956), *La Condition humaine* (1933; *Man's Fate,* 1934; also as *Storm in Shanghai,* 1934), and *L'Espoir* (1937; *Days of Hope,* 1938; also as *Man's Hope,* 1938). In each of these novels, he deals with the connection between identity and meaning for mankind in a context of revolution, which becomes the means of self-expression and assertion that can possibly transform one's life from being meaningless to meaningful. Collectively, these three novels established Malraux as chief communist spokesman in Europe, although he later renounced and abandoned communist social and political theory. These novels were never communist propaganda pieces, as their conception and execution transcend matters of the state so as to dwell on the individualistic purposes of the main characters; specifically, characters try to escape their mortality by coming to terms with it—thus revolution in China, for example, as is the case for *Man's Fate*, provides an appropriate setting and backdrop. Malraux never received the Nobel Prize, but he was awarded the Prix Goncourt in 1933 for *Man's Fate.*

In matters of art, Malraux, while deeply engrossed in contemporaneous productions, was more caught up with accomplishments of earlier civilizations. He joined or conducted several archaeological explorations, wrote numerous reviews, and befriended the most important artists of his time, including Pablo Picasso. Malraux held that all forms of art, whether painting, photography, stone cuttings, or voodoo dolls, were all expressions of some sort of unified whole wherein lay truth and wherein it became possible for one human being to communicate with another. Accordingly, he found common qualities and characteristics in all art, and he discounted fashionable explanations that saw differences in art as explainable in terms of differences in time and culture. He also applied this understanding to literature, finding common features in totally different works. For him, literature was one form of artistic expression and merely one part of a coherent, unified wholeness.

Malraux believed that political beliefs require action more than study, just as in literature and art he argued that appreciation required production. Accordingly, he was politically active throughout his life for one cause or another; yet, his pursuits were always intelligent, defensible ones. He served as a soldier, diplomat, spokesman, speech writer, and speech giver, among other things, never really turning down an opportunity to be politically involved. As a close friend to Charles de Gaulle, he always found such opportunities available.

A chronology of Malraux's life demonstrates these various endeavors and accomplishments. From 1923 to 1926, he was involved with archaeological studies and political intrigue in French In-

dochina. In 1926, he returned to Paris to write of his experiences in Asia and published *The Conquerors* in 1928. For the next three years, he and Clara traveled extensively throughout the world, visiting Iran, Afghanistan, India, Japan, China, and the United States. He organized art exhibitions of Gothic, Buddhist, Greek, and Hindu works, placing these various works beside one another in the same showings. In 1931, Leon Trotsky and he debated *The Conquerors.* In 1933, Malraux wrote a preface for William Faulkner's *Sanctuary* (1931), his daughter Florence was born, and he was subsequently divorced from Clara.

In 1934, Malraux used the money from the Prix Goncourt to search for the location of the kingdom of the Queen of Sheba in the Middle East. He became president of the World Committee against War and Fascism and gave a speech at the first Congress of Soviet Writers in Moscow, where he met Boris Pasternak, Maxim Gorky, and Joseph Stalin. Two years later, he became active in the Spanish Civil War, where he organized and led the Escuadrilla España; he participated in dozens of military operations in the air and was wounded twice. After recovering from these wounds, he went to the United States to raise money for the Republican cause in Spain; in the United States he met Ernest Hemingway, Albert Einstein, and Robert Oppenheimer.

At the outset of World War II, Malraux joined the French Tank Corps as a private and was again wounded in battle. He was taken prisoner and escaped five months later. During the war, his second wife, Josette Clotis, also a writer, was killed in a train accident. (His two children by this marriage, Gautier and Vincent, were killed in an automobile accident in 1961.) In 1944, now serving in the army under the pseudonym "Colonel Berger," he was wounded and captured a second time to be interrogated by the Gestapo, which threatened to kill him. After the war, he met and befriended Charles de Gaulle, for whom he served as minister of information. He received an award from the Legion of Honor, and he completed his film *Espoir* (1947; *Man's Hope*), which won the Prix Louis Delluc.

During the next thirty years, Malraux continued to be relentlessly active in every way. He gave dozens of speeches, both political and literary; he wrote dozens of reviews and published another twelve or so book-length studies and works of fiction; he traveled extensively both on behalf of the French government and in pursuit of his own inter-

ests. His third marriage (1950) was to Marie-Madeleine Lioux, a concert pianist and widow of his half-brother Roland, who had been killed in the war. Most noteworthy of his sundry accomplishments during these years include his service as minister of information (1958) and minister for cultural affairs (1959-1969) during de Gaulle's second administration. He visited two American presidents: John F. Kennedy in 1963 and Richard Nixon in 1972 before Nixon's visit to China. (In 1965 Malraux had gone to China to meet Chou En-lai and Mao Tse-tung.) His most important work from these later years was *Antimémoires* (1967; *Anti-Memoirs*, 1968). He died in Paris in 1976 of pulmonary congestion, having just turned seventy-five years old.

Summary

André Malraux's life and accomplishments are exemplary of the struggle to find meaning in life in the twentieth century and formed a prelude to coming historical events and intellectual thought. His multifaceted activities well served his beliefs about action being necessary to give meaning to study and thought. In his greatest work, *Man's Fate*, Malraux has the main character say "What am I? A kind of absolute, the affirmation of an idiot: an intensity greater than that of all the rest." The character, like Malraux himself as representative of modern man, recognizes his existential limitations and the requirements placed upon him if he is to escape idiocy by becoming more intense than others who suffer the disease of idiocy. In another place, the character comments that "his mythomania is a means of denying life, don't you see, of denying, and not of forgetting. Beware of logic in these matters. . . ." That man exists as a madman is commonplace enough in modern literature, but perhaps only in the works and life of Malraux is there such possibility of hope for escaping the madness through understanding it and taking purposeful action—if that can be defined. Malraux believed that only in art, literature, and activity could man transcend the bounds of futile existence. As in the literature of other leading twentieth century figures, characters and people are alone; yet through art and literature this entrapment in aloneness can be meaningfully lived with if not escaped. Malraux believed that the fact of alienation is the source of mythomania and idiocy and that the mythomania is the source of whatever salvation from it there may be.

Bibliography

Blumenthal, Gerda. *André Malraux: The Conquest of Dread.* Baltimore: Johns Hopkins University Press, 1960. Blumenthal's scholarly study focuses on the darkness and alienation of modern life as it appears in Malraux's major works. She traces the theme of the dread of death as an impetus for finding creativity and meaning in life.

Courcel, Martine de, ed. *Malraux: Life and Work.* London: Weidenfeld and Nicolson, and New York: Harcourt Brace, 1976. This book is a collection of essays written by people who knew well Malraux's life and works. It is perhaps the best available overall guide to his work and life, as the essays have a bent toward the biographical and treat the various aspects of his pursuits.

Dorenlot, Françoise, and Micheline Tison-Braun, eds. *André Malraux: Metamorphosis and Imagination.* New York: New York Literary Forum, 1979. The essays collected in this volume focus on the matter of "transformation of life into art." In so doing, "imagination" is held as the common denominator in the production of literature and art. The work contains a most useful chronology of Malraux's life and a bibliography of secondary sources.

Frohock, W. M. *André Malraux and the Tragic Imagination.* Stanford, Calif.: Stanford University Press, 1952. This study focuses primarily upon Malraux's actions and productivity within the context of the intellectual. The criticism is highly biographical and political; Frohook's discussion of the three main novels is valuable.

Hartman, Geoffrey H. *André Malraux.* London: Bowes and Bowes, and New York: Hillary House, 1960. Hartman discusses the "adventure" aspects of Malraux's life, arguing that he was something of a universal, timeless man. The treatment of his political activities is not in-depth.

Hewitt, James Robert. *André Malraux.* New York: Ungar, 1978. This study is an amalgam of approaches to Malraux's life. Criticism, biography, theory, and fact are all joined to interpret the meaning of Malraux's life and accomplishments.

Horvath, Violet M. *André Malraux: The Human Adventure.* New York: New York University Press, 1969. Horvath's rather well-written book focuses upon Malraux's art and politics and does not emphasize the literature. The chapter on the *Anti-Memoirs* is especially lucid.

Jenkins, Cecil. *André Malraux.* New York: Twayne, 1972. Jenkins argues that Malraux's greatest accomplishments were in literature; thus, the writer's pursuits of art, politics, journalism, and so forth are all treated as of lesser import.

Kline, Thomas Jefferson. *André Malraux and the Metamorphosis of Death.* New York: Columbia University Press, 1973. Kline analyzes the style and structure of Malraux's works in order to comment about their philosophical and moral meanings. The bibliography is especially thorough.

Lebovics, Herman. *Mona Lisa's Escort: André Malraux and the Reinvention of French Culture.* Ithaca, N.Y.: Cornell University Press, 1999. Lebovics examines Malraux's career and efforts as a cultural diplomat for France.

Lewis, R. W. B., ed. *Malraux: A Collection of Critical Essays.* Englewood Cliffs, N.J.: Prentice-Hall, 1964. This collection brings together much of the valuable pieces of criticism on Malraux, including selections from Leon Trotsky, Edmund Wilson, and Maurice Blanchot.

Tame, Peter. *The Ideological Hero in the Novels of Robert Brasillach, Roger Vailland, and André Malraux.* New York: Lang, 1998. Tame discusses the ideological hero in the works of Malraux, Robert Brasillach, and Roger Vailland, arguing that their concepts have much in common.

Carl Singleton

NELSON MANDELA

Born: July 18, 1918; Mvezo, Umtata district, Transkei, South Africa

Areas of Achievement: Civil rights and social reform

Contribution: Mandela dedicated his life to the struggle to end racial segregation and white minority rule under the apartheid system in South Africa. His contribution to the political education, mobilization, and organization of millions of people against the apartheid system has been unparalleled. In the 1990's the South African government moved to abolish apartheid, and Mandela was elected president in 1994.

Early Life

Nelson Rolihlahla Mandela was born in Transkei, South Africa, in a village called Mvezo on July 18, 1918. Although born of royal parentage, Mandela was reared in the traditional African setting among the Thembu. In addition to his mother, who was very strong-willed and dignified, Mandela's father had three other wives. Along with his peers, Mandela was inculcated with a tremendous sense of responsibility to his family and community, reflected in some of his childhood duties such as ploughing land, herding cattle, and tending sheep.

An important element that contributed to the political consciousness of Mandela during his youth was his listening to the elders of his village discuss the history of their people. Mandela learned of the noble traditions of his people before the European colonial invasion and the gallant struggles of resistance to European colonial rule. Mandela's insatiable thirst for knowledge was partially satisfied when he attended mission school as a child and then later while studying at Clarebury, a nearby training college. He learned much about some of the atrocities experienced by his people under European colonial rule. Mandela's desire to study law emanated from his observations of the paramount chief conducting court in his village and from his commitment to helping to end minority rule in South Africa.

Perhaps the most significant event that raised Mandela's political consciousness while still a teenager was the series of laws that were passed by the white-controlled, minority government in 1936. In the face of massive African opposition, the entire African population was effectively disenfranchised, the pass laws that restricted the movement and daily lives of Africans were extended throughout the country, and the increased expropriation of African land left the African majority population (80 percent) with only 12.7 percent of South African land. Like most South Africans, Mandela was deeply affected by these events.

Mandela's initiation into political activism began in 1940 while he was working on his bachelor of arts degree at Fort Hare College in the Eastern Cape. As a member of the Student's Representative Council, he was suspended from school for participating in a boycott to protest the reduction of the council's powers by authorities. After returning home briefly, he soon left for Johannesburg to avoid an arranged marriage and being trained for chieftainship.

Mandela found a small room in Alexandra, an overcrowded township on the edge of Johannesburg. With the encouragement of Walter Sisulu, in 1941 he joined the African National Congress (ANC), a multiracial, antiapartheid organization founded in 1912. This marked the beginning of Mandela's enduring struggle to establish justice and equality throughout South African society.

Life's Work

Along with Oliver Tambo, his former schoolmate at Fort Hare College, and Sisulu, who provided Mandela with work and financial assistance to finish his B.A. by correspondence, Mandela helped to revitalize a faltering ANC. By 1944, Mandela was instrumental in founding the Youth League, which became an integral part of the ANC. As the most radical element within the ANC, the Youth League helped to turn the ANC into a mass movement. In 1949, Mandela was elected secretary of the Youth League and helped to develop its Program of Action, which it submitted to the ANC executive officers. The Program of Action called for a series of boycotts, strikes, and other forms of civil disobedience designed to end white minority rule in South Africa. As a newly elected member of the ANC national executive board, Mandela worked hard to ensure that the ANC would adopt the Program of Action and implement it on May Day of 1950. Despite brutal repression by the South African government, the Program of Action gained considerable support from African workers.

Near the end of 1950, with the apartheid system fully intact, Mandela was elected the national president of the Youth League. His natural charisma

and dauntless personality contributed significantly to his outstanding leadership ability. As president, Mandela helped to formulate a plan to intensify the ANC's antiapartheid activities, called the Defiance Campaign. In 1952, he was appointed the campaign's national volunteer-in-chief, which required that he travel throughout South Africa visiting the many black townships in order to explain and win mass support for the campaign. During this period, Mandela played a leading role in forming the first significant alliance between the Africans, Asians, and so-called coloreds of South Africa against the apartheid system.

On June 26, 1952, the official start of the campaign, Mandela was arrested for the first time by South African police for violating the curfew restrictions imposed on Africans at that time. He was soon released and observed the rapid spread of the campaign throughout the country. Within a month, he, Sisulu and others were arrested once again, charged with "furthering the aims of communism," under the Suppression of Communism Act. Their arrest merely fueled the antiapartheid movement across the country. Nevertheless, the South African government remained intransigent as it eventually crushed the movement.

Although Mandela was released after a few months in jail, his freedom of movement was severely restricted, and he lived under the constant threat of imprisonment for life. Nevertheless, he was able to qualify as an attorney—after several years of studying law part-time at the University of Witwatersrand—and he and Tambo, also an attorney, established a partnership in 1953. They practiced together during the mid-1950's, handling as many as seven cases a day, at times, in a country with one of the highest arrest rates and prison populations in the world.

Once again, however, because of his continued ANC activity, Mandela was arrested shortly before 1957. He, along with Sisulu, Tambo, and others, was charged with high treason. Their trial, which gained worldwide attention, took more than four years to complete, during which time they spent two years in prison under very harsh and intolerable conditions. While in prison and during this celebrated trial, Mandela was elected spokesperson for the accused. His brilliant testimony in court in their defense is regarded as one of the most profound antiapartheid commentaries ever made. On March 29, 1961, the judge found Mandela and the other defendants not guilty.

After his release, and with the ANC officially banned by the South African government, Mandela's freedom of movement was restricted more than ever before. As the newly elected leader for the ANC, he was now faced with the formidable task of building the ANC underground. Mandela soon violated his restriction and the government issued a warrant for his arrest. It would be another seventeen months before he was captured. During the interim, he was able successfully to evade being arrested through the use of a series of disguises and with the help of close friends and associates. These efforts by Mandela were very inspiring to his people, as he secretly toured the country meeting with people, giving advice, and directing certain efforts.

As the South African government intensified its efforts to destroy every manifestation of peaceful resistance to apartheid, Mandela began to question the ANC's long-standing policy of unconditional nonviolent resistance. By mid-1961, in the face of several more brutal government attacks against peaceful demonstrations, Mandela led a group of ANC loyalists in forming Umkhonto we Sizwe (Spear of the Nation), the armed wing of the ANC. He began reading the writings of armed struggle strategists such as Mao Tse-tung and Che Guevara. When Mandela was smuggled out of South Africa in January of 1962 to visit other countries in Africa, he learned considerably more about armed struggle, especially from the Algerians who were engaged in an armed struggle against the French in Algeria. After secretly returning to South Africa, Mandela resumed his duties of building Umkhonto we Sizwe. He was finally captured, however, by South African police on August 5, 1962.

After being found guilty for inciting workers to strike and leaving the country without appropriate travel documents, Mandela was sentenced on November 7, 1962, to five years' hard labor. He was tried again, along with Sisulu and several other defendants, for recruiting persons for sabotage and guerrilla warfare and several other charges relating to a supposed violent overthrow of the South African government. Rather than deny guilt in any legal sense, Mandela convinced his codefendants that the trial should be used as an opportunity to espouse their antiapartheid beliefs. They did, and in June of 1964 they were found guilty and sentenced to life in prison. Rather than appeal the decision, they simply left the court with dignity.

Between 1962 and 1982, Mandela was confined to the maximum security prison on Robin Island, where he lived and labored under very harsh conditions. In April of 1982, he and his comrades were transferred to Pollsmoor Prison, another maximum security prison on the mainland. In response to domestic and international pressures, South Africa placed Mandela under minimum security in 1988 and, after almost thirty years, finally released him on February 11, 1990.

Despite his ordeal, Mandela's spirit and commitment to ending apartheid had not diminished. He spoke to throngs of people in Cape Town and Soweto and stressed his unequivocal loyalty to the ANC and his continued support for armed struggle and for an international campaign of divestment and economic sanctions against South Africa. Additionally, after his release, Mandela traveled extensively outside South Africa, including a visit to the United States in June, 1990, during which he stressed the importance to his cause of maintaining sanctions against the apartheid-supporting government.

In 1993, Mandela and South African president F. W. de Klerk announced an agreement by which the ANC and the National Party would form a transitional government, ending apartheid and opening the political process to all South Africans. In 1994, Mandela was elected president. The economic sanctions that many nations had established against South Africa were lifted, and trade and tourism increased under his presidency.

Summary

The impact of Nelson Mandela's life on South Africa in particular and the world in general has been and continues to be tremendous. The extreme sacrifices that he has made, the unflinching courage that he has exemplified, and the dogged commitment that he has maintained have all served to move millions of people around the world against the apartheid system. Mandela's numerous trials in South African courts, for example, always received the watchful eye of the world community. On each occasion, his renowned defense of the ideals of freedom and democracy for his people helped to raise the consciousness of the world against the daily injustices experienced by the South African masses.

Furthermore, Mandela lent his outstanding talent as a charismatic leader to rebuilding the ANC into a liberation movement with a huge mass following inside South Africa and with international respect-ability abroad. The ANC has been regarded as the organization most representative of the South African people; a large part of this accomplishment is the result of Mandela's successful efforts at working with the Indian, colored, and European populations toward common aims in the struggle against apartheid. As the human embodiment of this struggle, Mandela served for almost thirty years as the quintessential political prisoner. Now, the daily challenges that the people of South Africa face as they try to heal the wounds of apartheid will require all of President Mandela's hard-won courage, strength, and charisma as he continues to galvanize the energies of millions of people toward the establishment of a just and democratic order in South Africa.

Bibliography

Benson, Mary. *The African Patriots: The Story of the African National Congress of South Africa.* London: Faber, 1963; Chicago: Encyclopaedia Britannica Press, 1964. This book provides a historical account of the ANC from its beginning in 1912 until the turbulent years of the early 1960's, just prior to Mandela's arrest and imprisonment on Robin Island. It is replete with information on Mandela's contribution to building the ANC. Includes an index and several pages of illustrations.

———. *Nelson Mandela: The Man and the Movement.* London: Hamilton, and New York: Norton, 1986. This book provides a fairly comprehensive biographical account of Mandela's life from his childhood to his elder years in prison. It benefits immeasurably from private interviews and personal letters of Mandela, his family, and his close friends. Includes a bibliography and an index.

Bratton, Michael. "After Mandela's Miracle in South Africa." *Current History* 97, no. 619 (May, 1998). Bratton considers the possible future of South Africa after the retirement of Mandela.

Derrida, Jacques, and Mustapha Tlili, eds. *For Nelson Mandela.* New York: Seaver, 1987. This book contains more than twenty entries from popular creative writers from around the world. Each essay pays tribute to the exceptional character of Mandela and to the courageous struggle of the South African people. Provides the reader with a passionate discourse on the meaning of Mandela's life and the emotional impact it has had on the world at large.

Feit, Edward. *Urban Revolt in South Africa, 1960-1964: A Case Study.* Evanston, Ill.: Northwestern University Press, 1971. This book provides an in-depth examination of the factors that led to the armed phase of the antiapartheid struggle. Mandela's role in the development of the ANC's armed wing, Umkhonto we Sizwe, is given considerable attention. Includes an index and an appendix with a list of acts of sabotage carried out by the South African resistance movement.

Gibson, Richard. "South Africa (Azania)." In *African Liberation Movements: Contemporary Struggles Against White Minority Rule.* London and New York: Oxford University Press, 1972. This chapter is one of the most extensive and sophisticated analyses of the organized resistance struggle against apartheid rule. Focuses primarily on the origin and development of the ANC and the Pan-Africanist Congress (PAC). It provides a critical look at some of the major conflicts between the ANC and the PAC and the role of Mandela in the context of these differences. Includes a bibliography and an index.

Glad, Betty, and Robert Blanton. "F. W. de Klerk and Nelson Mandela: A Study in Cooperative Transformational Leadership." *Presidential Studies Quarterly* 27, no. 3 (Summer 1997). The authors examine the traits of Mandela and de Klerk that made possible a smooth transition in South African government.

Mandela, Nelson. *No Easy Walk to Freedom.* Edited by Ruth First, with a foreword by Ahmed Ben Bella. London: Heinemann, and New York: Basic, 1965. Contains some of Mandela's most important speeches and articles. Includes accounts and transcripts of the trials in which Mandela was the chief defendant and speeches and papers from Mandela's fugitive years.

Mandela, Winnie. *Part of My Soul Went with Him.* Edited by Anne Benjamin. New York: Norton, 1985. Contains vital information on life under apartheid for Nelson and Winnie Mandela. Includes many firsthand accounts of events in the Mandelas' lives. Also contains an appendix of important events and photographs.

Michael W. Williams

WILMA P. MANKILLER

Born: November 18, 1945; Tahlequah, Oklahoma
Area of Achievement: Government and politics
Contribution: By becoming the first woman to be the principal chief of the Cherokee Nation, or of any major American Indian tribe, Wilma Mankiller renewed a long tradition of female leadership in Cherokee affairs.

Early Life

Wilma Pearl Mankiller was born on November 18, 1945, in the W. W. Hastings Indian Hospital in Tahlequah, Oklahoma. Her father, Charley Mankiller, a full-blooded Cherokee, married her mother, Clara Irene Sitton, of Dutch-Irish descent, in 1937. Wilma was the sixth of their eleven children. The family lived on Mankiller Flats in Adair County, northeastern Oklahoma. Mankiller Flats was an allotment of 160 acres that had been given to John Mankiller, Charley's father, in 1907, when Oklahoma became a state. The name "Mankiller" was the Cherokee military title of Wilma's great-great-great grandfather, Mankiller of Tellico, in the eighteenth century. Tellico, in eastern Tennessee, was part of the original Cherokee Nation. The Mankillers and most other Cherokee were forcibly moved to the Indian Territory, later the state of Oklahoma, on the infamous Trail of Tears in 1838 and 1839.

The first eleven years of Wilma's life were spent on Mankiller Flats and in traditional Cherokee culture. In 1956, however, the Mankiller family moved to San Francisco, California, as part of a government relocation plan to move American Indians to large cities and into mainstream American life. Life in San Francisco was a culture shock, especially for the Mankiller children, but they soon adjusted to their new life.

On November 13, 1963, Wilma Mankiller was married to Hugo Olaya, a member of a wealthy Ecuadorian family, who was then a student in San Francisco. Two daughters, Felicia and Gina, were born to the couple before differences in lifestyles led to a divorce in 1975. During the years of her first marriage, Wilma earned a degree from San Francisco State College.

Wilma's Cherokee background was revived, and her activist work was initiated, in 1969, when a group of American Indians occupied Alcatraz Island, in San Francisco Bay, to gain support for American Indian rights. Wilma and many others in her family participated in that occupation.

Charley Mankiller, who had become a longshoreman and a union organizer in California, died in 1971. His body was returned to his native Adair County, Oklahoma, for burial. That burial seemed to be a signal for the Mankillers to return, one by one, to Oklahoma. Wilma returned after her divorce in 1975. Only two older brothers remained in California.

After living in two worlds, Wilma Mankiller was able to emulate Nancy Ward, an eighteenth century Cherokee woman who had also lived in both worlds. Like Ward, Wilma was able to combine the best of Cherokee tradition with the best of European-American civilization. Her balanced philosophy enabled Wilma to contribute greatly to the welfare of the Cherokee Nation.

Life's Work

Wilma Mankiller began her work to improve American Indian life before she left California. In 1974, with Bill Wahpapah, she cofounded the American Indian Community School in Oakland. Her return to Oklahoma in 1975, however, marked the beginning of her full-time service to the Cherokee Nation.

The Cherokee Nation, with 55,000 acres of northeastern Oklahoma and a population of about 67,000 people, ranks second only to the Navajo in size among American Indian tribes in the United States. When Oklahoma became a state in 1907, the traditional tribal government of the Cherokee was dissolved. This created a unique political organization, neither a reservation nor an autonomous government, with unique political and social problems. Wilma Mankiller now began directing her energy toward solving those problems.

Wilma's first regular job with the Cherokee Nation began in 1977, when she was hired as an economic-stimulus coordinator. Her job was to guide as many people as possible toward university training in such fields as environmental science and health, and then to integrate them back into their communities. Wilma soon became frustrated with the slow-moving male-dominated bureaucracy of the Cherokee Nation.

Before Europeans came to North America, Cherokee women such as Nancy Ward occupied leadership roles in tribal affairs. The title of Beloved Woman was given to those who performed extraordinary service. The first Europeans to contact the Cherokee accused them of having a "petticoat government." After this contact, the influence of Cherokee women began to decrease. In her autobiography *Mankiller: A Chief and Her People* (1993), Wilma Mankiller declared her belief that the Trail of Tears in 1838 and 1839, combined with the tremendous strain of relocation in the West, was the final step in the development of a more subservient position for women.

A very significant development in 1971 helped to open the way for a return to more female participation in Cherokee affairs. A revision of the tribal constitution provided that, for the first time since Oklahoma statehood in 1907, the principal chief would be elected by the people of the tribe rather than be appointed by the president of the United States. An entirely new constitution in 1976 solidified that change and provided for the election of a new fifteen-member tribal council.

In 1979, after working for two years as an economic-stimulus coordinator, Wilma Mankiller was made a program-development specialist and grant writer. Her immediate success in this position, especially in writing grant proposals, brought her to the attention of the tribal council and Principal Chief Ross Swimmer. This phase of Wilma's work was soon interrupted by tragedy. On November 9, 1979, she was seriously injured in a head-on collision on a country road. The driver of the other car was Sherry Morris, a white woman who was a very close friend of Wilma Mankiller. Morris was killed. In *Mankiller: A Chief and Her People*, Wilma gives an extremely moving account of that tragedy.

Within a year of the accident, Wilma was afflicted with a rare form of muscular dystrophy. These back-to-back experiences caused her to reach more deeply into her Cherokee background and led to a change in her philosophy of life.

In 1981, although still undergoing physical therapy, Wilma was able to return to her work with the Cherokee Nation, and she did so with her old energy. In that year, she helped to establish the Cherokee Nation Community Development Department and became its first director.

The next step in Wilma's career came in 1983, when Chief Ross Swimmer asked her to join his re-election ticket as his deputy chief. This request, by which Chief Swimmer recognized Wilma's potential, was very unusual because Swimmer was a conservative Republican and Wilma Mankiller was a liberal Democrat. After first declining, Wilma accepted the offer as a way to help her people.

One of Wilma's opponents for deputy chief was Agnes Cowan, the first woman to serve on the tribal council. Wilma was surprised when gender became an immediate issue in the campaign. The hostility toward Wilma ranged from having her car tires slashed to death threats. She fought that negative campaigning by conducting a very positive and cheerful campaign based primarily on her past service to the Cherokee people. The victory for the Swimmer-Mankiller ticket meant that, on August 14, 1983, Wilma Mankiller became the first female deputy chief in Cherokee history.

In 1984, Deputy Chief Mankiller participated in a very significant meeting—a reunion between the Cherokee Nation of Oklahoma and the Eastern Band of the Cherokee from North Carolina. The Eastern Band had descended from those who escaped the Trail of Tears by hiding in the mountains. This meeting, the first full tribal council since 1838, was held at Red Clay in Tennessee, the last capital of the original Cherokee Nation. In her autobiography, Wilma emphasized the tremendous historical impact that this event had on the Cherokee people.

A major career surprise for Wilma Mankiller came in 1985, when President Ronald Reagan nominated Chief Swimmer as Assistant Secretary of the Interior for Indian Affairs. This meant that, on December 14, 1985, Wilma Mankiller was inaugurated as the first woman principal chief of the Cherokee Nation.

Chief Mankiller immediately declared that economic growth would be the primary goal of her administration. She described her guiding theory as bubble-up economics, in which the people would plan and implement projects that would benefit the tribe in future years, even though the present generation might not benefit. Until the next scheduled election in 1987, however, Chief Mankiller had to govern without a mandate from the people. She faced strong opposition that limited her real power.

In October of 1986, while considering whether to run for a full term, Chief Mankiller married Charlie Soap, a full-blooded Cherokee whom she had first met in 1977. She described her new husband as the most well-adjusted male she had ever known. It was Charlie Soap who persuaded her to run in 1987, and she won in a runoff election. Because the Cherokee had now returned to the strong female leadership of their past, Chief Mankiller described her election as a step forward and a step backward at the same time.

Although Chief Mankiller's first full term was successful in terms of economic progress, her level of personal involvement was influenced by a resurgence of kidney disease, from which she had suffered for many years. This difficulty led to a kidney transplant in June, 1990. The donor was Wilma's older brother Don.

Summary

The early years of Principal Chief Wilma P. Mankiller produced many significant results, both tangible and intangible. The most important of the former is the Department of Commerce, which was created soon after Mankiller's 1987 victory. This department coordinates the business enterprises of the tribe and tries to balance tribal income with the needs of tribal members, creating jobs and producing a profit. The intangible results include a renewed spirit of independence for all Cherokee and a renewed confidence that Cherokee women can once again influence the destiny of the tribe.

In 1990, Chief Mankiller signed a historic self-governance agreement that authorized the Cherokee Nation to administer federal funds that previously had been administered by the Bureau of Indian Affairs in Washington. The same year saw a revitalizing of tribal courts and tribal police as well as the establishment of a Cherokee Nation tax commission.

The impact of Chief Mankiller was soon recognized far beyond the borders of the Cherokee Nation. In 1988, she was named Alumnus of the Year at San Francisco State College. This was followed, in 1990, by an honorary doctorate from Yale University.

The most outstanding proof of Chief Wilma Mankiller's impact on the Cherokee Nation was her reelection victory in 1991, one year after her kidney transplant, with more than 82 percent of the votes. The same election put six women on the fifteen-member tribal council. The Cherokee Nation, with a resounding voice, had returned to its past.

Bibliography

Mankiller, Wilma. *Mankiller: A Chief and Her People*. New York: St. Martin's Press, 1993. This autobiography is by far the best source available for the life, career, and philosophy of Mankiller. Includes many excellent photographs of the Mankiller family, other key individuals, and major events in Wilma Mankiller's life.

Nabokov, Peter, ed. *Native American Testimony: A Chronicle of Indian-White Relations from Prophecy to the Present, 1492-1992*. New York: Viking, 1991. A collection of essays and personal accounts. Gives an emotional vision of the sufferings and the sacrifices of American Indians, including the Cherokee. No reference to Wilma Mankiller.

Van Viema, David. "Activist Wilma Mankiller Is Set to Become the First Female Chief of the Cherokee Nation." *People Weekly* 24 (December 2, 1985): 91-92. Based on an interview with Mankiller by Michael Wallis, this article conveys the initial impression she had of her new job as chief. Reveals Mankiller's identification with her Cherokee roots.

Verhovek, Sam Howe. "The Name's the Most and Least of Her." *New York Times* 143, no. 49505 (November 4, 1993). Interview with Mankiller in which she discusses her duties as chief, her book *Mankiller: A Chief and Her People,* and her family.

Wallace, Michele. "Wilma Mankiller." *Ms.* 16 (January, 1988): 68-69. Wallace emphasizes the role of women in Cherokee history. Also covered is Mankiller's philosophy of leadership and her influence on women's rights in general. Includes Mankiller's plans for future Cherokee progress.

Woodward, Grace Steele. *The Cherokees*. Norman: University of Oklahoma Press, 1963. This author presents a close look at the Cherokee tradition to which Mankiller sought to return. Covers Nancy Ward and refers to Mankiller of Tellico but makes no reference to Wilma Mankiller.

Yannuzzi, Della A. "A New Voice." *New Moon* 4, no. 4 (March-April, 1997). Profile of Mankiller discussing her election as chief in 1985 and her accomplishments in that capacity.

Glenn L. Swygart

THOMAS MANN

Born: June 6, 1875; Lübeck, Germany
Died: August 12, 1955; Zurich, Switzerland
Area of Achievement: Literature
Contribution: Mann wrote in the tradition of nineteenth century realism, depending upon depth and breadth of treatment rather than stylistic innovation for his effectiveness. After receiving the Nobel Prize in Literature in 1929, he was widely regarded as a sage as well as a great artist.

Early Life

Thomas Mann was born in Lübeck, Germany (later West Germany), an important city since the days of the Hanseatic League, on June 6, 1875. His father, Johann Heinrich Mann, was an apparently prosperous grain merchant, who operated a family business dating back to the eighteenth century. His mother, Julia da Silva-Bruhns, was from Rio de Janeiro, a half Portuguese Creole. Johann Heinrich Mann was a senator and twice was mayor of Lübeck, while Frau Mann was romantic, temperamental, and musically gifted. He would serve as the prototype for the phlegmatic, psychologically healthy burghers and she for the sensitive, neurotic Latin artists who populate Thomas Mann's fiction.

Thomas Mann was the second of five children. His elder brother Heinrich would also become a renowned writer. Thomas had a younger brother and two younger sisters, both of whom eventually committed suicide. He was not a good student. Like his fictional character Tonio Kröger, Mann was a romantic youth with artistic tendencies, who disliked the scientific emphasis at his *Gymnasium.* Not until his father's death in 1890 was it apparent that the family business was failing. The next year, the rest of the family left the Baltic and relocated in Munich. After having to repeat two years, Mann received his certificate and left school to rejoin them. The year was 1894, and Mann became an unsalaried apprentice with a fire insurance firm. After a year of copying out accounts, he realized that a future in business was not what he desired. He was eventually able to terminate the apprenticeship and free himself to attend university lectures in the arts, history, and political economy.

During his brief business career, Mann had been writing, sometimes at the desk where he was supposed to be copying accounts. The result was his first story, "Gefallen" ("Fallen"), published in 1896. It attracted the attention of the poet Richard Dehmel, who praised it. Mann then joined his brother Heinrich in Rome. He remained in Italy until 1898, reading voraciously and writing. His first book was published by the prestigious Berlin house of Fischer during this period. His literary career had auspiciously begun.

Life's Work

For about a year, Mann served on the staff of the periodical *Simplicissimus.* Upon returning to Munich, he had turned his attention to a huge manuscript he had begun in Italy. His publisher was understandably nervous about the long autobiographical novel, *Buddenbrooks: Verfall einer Familie* (1901; English translation, 1924). It was published in two expensive volumes, and, when it appeared in the closing days of 1900, its little-known author was only twenty-five years of age. The novel sold well, however, and almost thirty years later would be cited prominently by the Swedish Academy as it presented Mann with the Nobel Prize. *Buddenbrooks* traces the decline of a family through several generations from bourgeois self-confidence and adaptability to self-doubt and enervation as aesthetic and artistic elements are introduced into the family. For the next decade, in the novellas *Tonio Kröger* (1903; English translation, 1914) and *Der Tod in Venedig* (1911; *Death in Venice*, 1925) and in short stories such as "Tristan" (1903; English translation, 1925), Mann—himself the child of a Nordic father and a Latin mother—explored the conflicts between Northern European stolidity and Southern European passion, between the robust Philistinism of the middle class and the morbid sensitivity of the artist. Also during this period, he wrote the comic novel *Königliche Hoheit* (1909; *Royal Highness*, 1916).

During the early years of his career, Mann was heavily influenced by the pessimistic philosophy of Arthur Schopenhauer and by Friedrich Nietzsche's reevaluation of all values. His own life, however, entered a protracted period of happiness. He was lionized as the author of *Buddenbrooks*, which was eventually to sell more than a million copies in Germany alone. In February, 1905, he married Katja Pringsheim, the only daughter of a wealthy Munich family. On November 9 of that year, Erika Julia was born (she became an actress, journalist, author, and the wife of Wystan Hugh Auden, the English poet). On November 18, 1906, Klaus Heinrich was born (he became a novelist, essayist, and playwright). In all, six children were born to Mann and his wife. This happy period in the author's life was marred in 1910 by the suicide of his beloved sister Carla and in 1914 by the outbreak of war in Europe. The youngest Mann child was born in the same year that his book of essays, *Betrachtungen eines Unpolitischen* (1918; reflections of a nonpolitical man), appeared. Mann, who supported his country in World War I, was widely criticized for the perceived conservatism and nationalism of this book.

Up until 1933, Mann lived the life of the author who is both critically and financially successful. He lectured throughout Northern Europe and took holidays in the South. As well as a fine home in Munich, he had a summer home and a vacation cottage. His second major masterpiece was *Der Zauberberg* (1924; *The Magic Mountain*, 1927), on which he had been working since 1912. The novel, in which Mann again explores the conflicts within the middle-class German mind, has been called an epic of a civilization in decay. His much praised novella *Unordnung und frühes Leid* (1926; *Disorder and Early Sorrow*, 1929) was inspired by his favorite daughter, Elizabeth. On December 10, 1929, Mann received the Nobel Prize in Literature. His only reservation about the award was that the Swedish Academy had virtually ignored *The Magic Mountain* in its citation. By this time, also, Mann had entered the battle against Fascism. His "Mario und der Zauberer" (1929; "Mario and the Magician," 1936) explores the appeal and the inherent evil of this form of dictatorship. In 1933, Mann was lecturing in Holland and completing the first volume of his tetralogy, *Joseph und seine Brüder* (1933-1943; *Joseph and His Brothers*, 1934-1944), when events in Germany persuaded him not to return to his homeland.

Mann settled in Zurich. There he took up the editorship of the periodical *Mass und Wert*. Another three years passed before he publicly denounced the Nazi regime. When he finally did so—in the most unambiguous of terms—Adolf Hitler's responses were swift and sweeping: Mann was stripped of his German citizenship, his honorary doctorate from the University of Bonn was rescinded, and *Buddenbrooks* (which the Nobel committee had praised as representative of the German people) was banned.

In 1938, Mann emigrated to the United States. He lived for several years in Princeton, New Jersey, where he lectured at Princeton University. He was named a Fellow of the Library of Congress, a consultant in German literature. Over the years, he had moved politically from the authoritarianism he seemed to advocate in *Betrachtungen eines Unpolitischen* to an endorsement of democracy in *The Coming Victory of Democracy* (1938). He gave anti-Fascist lectures all across America. In 1941, he built a home in Santa Monica, California.

Mann became an American citizen in 1944 but returned to Switzerland in 1947. During his decade of residence in the United States, he published two short novels—*Lotte in Weimar* (1939; *The Beloved Returns*, 1940), based upon incidents in the life of Johann Wolfgang von Goethe, and *Die vertauschten Köpfe: Eine indische Legende* (1940; *The Transposed Heads: A Legend of India*, 1941)—and another major work, *Doktor Faustus* (1947; *Doctor Faustus*, 1948), simultaneously the fictional biography of a contemporary German composer and a retelling of the Faust legend. Here Mann returns to one of his favorite themes, the artist's role in the world.

Mann's last novels were *Der Erwählte* (1950; *The Holy Sinner*, 1951) and *Bekentnisse des Hochstaplers Felix Krull* (1954; *Confessions of Felix Krull, Confidence Man*, 1955). The genesis of the latter work was a short story, "Felix Krull" (first published in 1911 and translated into English in 1936). Mann had always viewed the humorous tale of a happy, unrepentant confidence man as a fragment of a novel. In fact, he conceived it to be in its final form a multivolume work. After the completion of the first volume, however, Mann turned his attention to a proposed book on Friedrich Schiller. Before he could complete this project, Mann, who had been healthy and productive to the very end of his life, developed phlebitis and died on August 12, 1955, in Zurich, Switzerland.

Summary

Thomas Mann was only four years younger than Marcel Proust and only seven years older than James Joyce, but, unlike these innovators in narrative form and language, he wrote novels which were superficially like their nineteenth century predecessors. By minutely examining his characters' behavior and thought processes, he gave his work a seriousness of purpose which has demanded attention ever since the publication of *Buddenbrooks*. The air of profundity in Mann's work is lightened by frequent flashes of humor, which are as much a part of his makeup as his philosophic turn of mind. His tendency to explore every nuance, to examine each incident in a narrative passage from every conceivable angle, has caused him to be compared to Henry James, the Anglo-American novelist. This tendency has also caused some readers to complain that Mann's style is at times static and boring.

Still, Mann's characters wrestle with the central problems of family, social, and political life. He was first praised as the master interpreter of German life. Later, he was viewed as a spokesman for the best of European values during a savage period. By his last years, he had become a world figure, whose books were required reading for the student of Western man. Many of Mann's protagonists are artists. One could even argue that, in practicing his art of deception without regard to any moral or societal restraints, Felix Krull is the complete artist or, conversely, that every artist is something of a confidence man. Mann was fascinated by the function of the artist in society and devoted several books to the subject. Few writers have explored as effectively as he the mixed blessing and curse that is the artist's patrimony.

Bibliography

Bauer, Arnold. *Thomas Mann*. Translated by Alexander and Elizabeth Henderson, New York: Ungar, 1971. This short study points up each of the major phases in the subject's life. It is an entry in the Modern Literature Monographs series and was originally published by Colloquium Verlag, Berlin. It contains a bibliography and is indexed.

Bergsten, Gunilla. *Thomas Mann's Doctor Faustus: The Sources and Structure of the Novel*. Translated by Krishna Winston. Chicago: University of Chicago Press, 1969. This close examination of the genesis of Mann's masterpiece emphasizes the author's refugee status at the time of composition. Bergsten notes the paradox that this most German of all Mann's novels was written in the United States while his adopted country was at war with his native country.

Brennan, Joseph Gerard. *Thomas Mann's World*. New York: Columbia University Press, 1942. This work takes as its point of departure Mann's questions about the nature of the artist and applies them to Mann himself. It contains an annotated bibliography and a very thorough index.

Breuer, Stefan. "Between 'Conservative Revolution,' Aesthetic Fundamentalism and New Nationalism: Thomas Mann's Early Political Writings." *History of Human Sciences* 11, no. 2 (May, 1998). Discusses Mann's political writings and their liberal tendencies.

Feuerlicht, Ignace. *Thomas Mann*. New York: Twayne, 1968. This entry in the Twayne's World Authors series will give the general reader a concise introduction to Mann. It contains a chronology, a selected bibliography, and an index.

Hamilton, Nigel. *The Brothers Mann: The Lives of Heinrich and Thomas Mann 1871-1950 and 1875-1955*. London: Secker and Warburg, 1978; New Haven, Conn.: Yale University Press, 1979. In sixteen chapters the author explores the interlinked lives of what he calls the most distinguished literary brotherhood in modern history. While noting that no definitive biography of either brother has yet been done in English, Hamilton seeks to do justice to both. The book, which was first published in England in 1978, is thorough and welldocumented, running to more than four hundred pages of text, with extensive notes and a bibliography arranged chronologically within categories.

Hatfield, Henry, ed. *Thomas Mann: A Collection of Critical Essays.* Englewood Cliffs, N.J.: Prentice-Hall, 1964. These twelve essays include at least one on each of the major works, as well as a discussion of Mann's use of humor and irony. A chronology of important dates and a selected bibliography is included.

Kahler, Erich. *The Orbit of Thomas Mann.* Princeton, N.J.: Princeton University Press, 1969. Some of these essays were originally written in German, some of them in English. One is a revised and enlarged version of a lecture. They deal with Mann's environment—both the outer, physical environment and the inner, spiritual or metaphysical environment.

Kaufmann, Fritz. *Thomas Mann: The World as Will and Representation.* Boston: Beacon Press, 1957. This book, by a professor of philosophy, devotes its first two chapters to Mann's philosophy and its last six to how this philosophy is adapted to fiction in the major works.

Lukács, Georg. *Essays on Thomas Mann.* Translated by Stanley Mitchell. London: Merlin Press, 1964; New York: Grosset and Dunlap, 1965. The essays in this book were written over a period of many years and under a variety of circumstances. They profit from Lukács' personal relationship with Mann.

Prater, Donald A. *Thomas Mann: A Life.* Oxford and New York: Oxford University Press, 1995. Excellent account of the life and times of Mann by celebrated biographer Donald Prater. The author pays particular attention to Mann's politics and his role in Nazi Germany.

Patrick Adcock

CARL GUSTAF MANNERHEIM

Born: June 4, 1867; Louhisaari, villnas, near
Turku, Finland
Died: January 27, 1951; Lausanne, Switzerland
Areas of Achievement: The military, government,
and politics
Contribution: Mannerheim dominated the political
and military history of Finland from the time
Finland became independent in 1917 until his retirement in 1946. He fought in both world wars
as a military general. As a political figure, he
served as president of his nation during a critical
period of the 1940's.

Early Life
Carl Gustaf Mannerheim, of Swedish descent, was
born into a prominent Finnish family. He entered
military school at Hamina as a cadet in 1882 to
prepare for a career in the Finnish army. Expelled
in 1886, he succeeded in entering the prestigious
Nicholas Cavalry School in St. Petersburg and was
graduated in 1889. Fortunate assignments eventually placed him in the czar's Chevalier Guards, and
he participated in the coronation ceremonies of
Czar Nicholas II. He married the daughter of a
Russian general in 1892 and fathered two daughters but separated from his wife in 1902.

Following service in the guards and another intermediate assignment, Mannerheim took command (1903) of a squadron of the Officers' Cavalry School in St. Petersburg. During the Russo-
Japanese War of 1904-1905, Mannerheim eventually obtained reassignment to the Asian front and
served in Manchuria in several campaigns before
the Russian surrender. He finished the war with the
rank of colonel. His next assignment was to embark on a two-year expedition across central Asia
and northern China, a journey of approximately
eighty-five hundred miles. His task was to observe
and report on the potential for military activities as
well as on the political conditions in those regions.
This ambitious and grueling journey (1906-1908)
added to his reputation as an audacious and enterprising officer and showed his skill in gathering information about geographical features, archaeological information, and anthropological observations.
(The copious records of the journey were published in 1940.)

Between 1909 and 1911, Mannerheim commanded the Thirteenth Vladimir Cavalry Regiment
stationed in Poland. He was promoted to the rank

of major general in 1911 and took command of another important cavalry unit based in Warsaw. He
seems to have enjoyed his Polish experience, noting the problems that Poland and his native Finland
had as subject regions within the Russian Empire.
He anticipated the war and worked to prepare his
forces for that possibility. In the campaigns of
1914-1915, he commanded units at various levels
(brigade, division, and corps levels), primarily on
the Polish front facing Austrian forces. His leadership and military successes, in what generally were
Russian defeats and withdrawals, increased his
reputation and led to significant military awards. In
1916, he was promoted to lieutenant general and
commanded the Sixth Cavalry Army Corps, located on the Romanian front.

His support for the Russian army and government surprised many of his Finnish friends and relatives, but he felt a sense of loyalty to the Russian
monarchy to whom he had taken the oath of service. He disagreed with the revolutionary elements
that finally overthrew the monarchy in the winter
of early 1917 and culminated in the victory of the
Bolsheviks in the capital in November, 1917. In
these deteriorating conditions, Mannerheim terminated his military service and decided to return to
his native Finland, which was entering the throes
of dissension and potential civil war. Finnish nationalists saw the chaotic period as the opportune
time (December, 1917) to declare independence
from Russia. The factions varied between socialists
and Marxists on the Left and conservative elements
on the Right. Mannerheim's return coincided with
this confusion in Helsinki and elsewhere in the
country, and the Finnish senate commissioned
Mannerheim to restore order by commanding the
Finnish Civil Guards. This assignment began his
famous career as a prominent figure in Finnish political and military affairs. At the age of fifty, a new
and important future lay before him.

Life's Work
The story of the Finnish War for Independence
from Russia, and the battles between Mannerheim's "White Guards" and the Finnish "Red
Guard" sympathetic to Vladimir Ilich Lenin's Bolsheviks, gave him the opportunity to show his
qualities of leadership and careful planning. The
so-called War of Liberation lasted from January to
May, 1918, and included the use of Finnish forces

trained in Germany during World War I. The capital city of Helsinki was finally recaptured in April from the Red Guards, thanks to German military efforts and their Finnish allies. Mannerheim entered Helsinki in May as a national hero but resigned as commander of the Civil Guards in a dispute over German control of Finnish military forces.

During October and November, 1918, Mannerheim carried out several diplomatic missions to Western European nations, seeking recognition and food supplies. In December, 1918, he was named Regent of Finland, with virtually absolute civil and military power. He held this position until July, 1919, during the period of the final independence of Finland, the writing of a new constitution, and the holding of parliamentary elections. Mannerheim ran for office as president under the new constitution but was decisively defeated (July, 1919) by Kaarlo Juho Ståhlberg. At age fifty-two, Mannerheim decided to return to private life. He gained a positive reputation for his civic and humanitarian efforts, which included the formation of a child welfare program (1920) using his name and financial support and his becoming the chairman of the Finnish Red Cross (1922).

Mannerheim began to resume his political interests in the early 1930's, supporting the Lapua movement for a time before its prohibition by the government for alleged Fascist and totalitarian activities. At the same time, he accepted military and defense responsibilities upon being named the Chairman of the Finnish Defense Council (1931). This assignment included the responsibility to act as commander in chief of Finnish forces in wartime. The government promoted him to the rank of field marshal in 1933. He oversaw the steady but slow improvements in the Finnish military, especially important in 1938, and a major defense line between the Gulf of Finland and Lake Ladoga was named in his honor.

Relations with the Soviet Union began to deteriorate in the later 1930's, resulting in the Winter War (1939-1940). This war grew primarily out of Soviet demands for strategic portions of Finnish territory, including essential defense positions, but also resulted from the fundamental hostility that the Soviet Union felt toward its small independent neighbor that had once been a part of the Russian Empire for more than a century. The Soviet attack began in November, 1939, and Mannerheim took command of all Finnish forces. A nation of four

millon faced an enemy of 180 million. The outcome was never seriously in doubt, as overwhelming Soviet forces eventually overcame the Finns. Yet the unexpected duration of Finnish resistance shocked the Russians and gained the admiration of many Western governments and populations. The March, 1940, peace treaty with the Soviet Union ceded Finnish territory and also led to other restrictions on Finnish sovereignty. The Soviet Union also indicated its determination that Mannerheim should not be allowed to become the leader of the Finnish government in the future.

Finland's peace was short-lived, however, with the Nazi invasion of the Soviet Union in June, 1941. In this new crisis, Finland took the opportunity to attempt to regain Karelia and other regions taken previously by the Soviet Union. Mannerheim considered moving farther into Soviet territory but eventually decided not to do so. These limited war aims are further revealed by his refusal to implement German orders for coordinated attacks, especially the order to attack Leningrad during the German siege of that city in the Nine Hundred Days (1941-1944). This new phase of a Russo-Finnish war, known as the Continuation War, also brought Finland into conflict with other nations. Great Britain declared war on Finland in December, 1941.

Mannerheim's forces were generally successful in regaining territory lost in the 1939-1940 Winter War. The Finns also had to contend with getting German forces out of Finland, as the tide of battle turned against the Nazis on the Eastern Front. Major efforts to achieve this goal occurred in 1944, as Finland attempted to withdraw from involvement in the Russo-German War. (A curious side-note on German-Finnish relations is that Adolf Hitler traveled to Finland on the occasion of Mannerheim's seventy-fifth birthday in June, 1942, providing a rare instance of the German leader acknowledging the leadership, stature, and importance of one of the European figures whom he had met.)

Finland finally withdrew from the war with the Soviet Union in September, 1944, which once again led to the loss of Finnish territory to its neighbor. Mannerheim in this period attempted to follow a course with the Soviets and Germans that would be least injurious to his nation's independence and territorial integrity. It was a no-win situation, but at that time and since Mannerheim and his associates have been given credit for achieving the best solution possible under the circumstances.

On the eve of the September, 1944, armistice with the Soviets, Mannerheim succeeded Risto Heikki Ryti as president in August, 1944. The preliminary peace and the official treaty (December) occurred during Mannerheim's presidential term. At the time that he assumed the presidency, Mannerheim was seventy-seven years old. He held the position for nineteen months (to mid-March, 1946). During Mannerheim's tenure as president, the Soviet Union required the Finns to hold war crimes trials for prominent Finnish leaders accused of pro-German collaboration or cooperation. Several former officials were sentenced to prison terms in what was an extraordinarily difficult period for the Finnish nation and its people.

After the trials had been completed, Mannerheim resigned in what was widely perceived as a sign of his sympathy with the accused. At seventy-eight, his age and failing health also were factors in his decision to resign before completing his term of office. Juho Kusti Paasikivi succeeded Mannerheim and continued the efforts to find a neutral course for Finland in the post-World War II years, especially in the light of Finland's awkward geographic location adjacent to the Soviet Union.

Mannerheim spent most of his last years in Switzerland, working with associates on his memoirs (first published in 1952), until his death in 1951 at the age of eighty-three.

Summary

Carl Gustaf Mannerheim's ambivalence toward his Finnish homeland (sources indicate he did not learn to speak Finnish until he was in his fifties, relying instead on Swedish and Russian) in the first five decades of his life makes his later determination to serve his homeland during very difficult times even more remarkable and commendable. He did not seem to be driven by an irrational passion for power but certainly assumed power easily and used his leadership opportunities to full advantage. He steadfastly remained confident that his political and military contributions had to be respected and appreciated. Those close to Mannerheim saw him as an aloof and private person but also generous in his time and efforts to serve his nation when called to do so.

His relation to the history of Finland coincided with several of the most trying and critical points in that nation's history in the twentieth century. In times of crisis, many looked to Mannerheim for leadership that was both stabilizing and inspirational in a small nation suffering from scarce resources and manpower. His enemies have characterized Mannerheim as the "White Butcher" (based on the 1918 War of Liberation events), and many of the Finnish Left saw him as an authoritarian conservative with few redeeming features as a national leader.

Today, he is buried in a place of prominence in a Helsinki military cemetery surrounded by those whom he led and those who served him. The main street in Helsinki is named in his honor, and a large equestrian statue of Mannerheim is a prominent sight in downtown Helsinki. Given the challenges that Finland faced, most agree that Mannerheim was a worthy leader of his nation.

Bibliography

Borenius, Tancred. *Field-Marshal Mannerheim.* London: Hutchinson, 1940. The author personally knew Mannerheim and used this knowledge in part as a basis for this laudatory biography. Includes some revealing letters from Mannerheim's sister Sophie about her brother as well as numerous Mannerheim addresses and "Orders of the Day" to his armed forces in the War of Liberation and the Winter War.

Gellermann, Josef Egmond. *Generals as Statesmen*. New York: Vantage Press, 1959. Assessment of famous military figures to see the personal qualities of leadership. Overall the reader gets the message, not the author's intention, that military generals are likely to be ineffective in political roles. The coverage of Mannerheim's life is barely adequate, lacking sufficient detail or depth.

Jägerskiöld, Stig Axel Fridolf. *Mannerheim, Marshal of Finland*. London: Hurst, and Minneapolis: University of Minnesota Press, 1986. The most recent English biography of Mannerheim, excellently balanced in description and assessment. Based on extensive work in the Mannerheim archives and abridged from the author's eight-volume biography of the marshal. The best recent and complete biography in English.

Mannerheim, Carl Gustaf. *Memoirs*. Translated by Eric Lewenhaupt. London: Cassell, and New York: Dutton, 1954. Mannerheim's recollections, written in his later years in retirement. Provides detailed coverage of military and political topics but does not include some of the more controversial aspects of his leadership and outlook. Virtually all English language accounts refer to this volume as an important source of information.

Rintala, Marvin. *Four Finns: Political Profiles*. Berkeley: University of California Press, 1969. Biographical account of four major figures (Mannerheim, Paasikivi, Ståhlberg, and Väinnö Alfred Tanner) in a brief but readable and informative book. Good assessment of political issues during the decades of the twentieth century in which Mannerheim was a player.

Rodzianko, Paul. *Mannerheim: An Intimate Picture of a Great Soldier and Statesman*. London: Jarrolds, 1940. Based on interviews with Mannerheim associates plus use of some of Mannerheim's papers. A good example of biography written in the form of hero-worship. Chatty account, with some assumed conversations and thoughts from Mannerheim's earlier life. Covers the period from his origins to the end of the Winter War.

Screen, John Ernest Oliver. *Mannerheim: The Years of Preparation*. London: Hurst, 1970. This work is short in length but is a very detailed biography of Mannerheim from his earliest years to the end of his service in the Russian army at the end of 1917. Good coverage of his military training and command responsibilities. Includes World War I and the Russian Revolution. Unusual in that the author does not deal with the later period (1918 on) which is the most famous part of Mannerheim's life and career.

Warner, Oliver. *Marshal Mannerheim and the Finns*. London: Weidenfeld and Nicolson, 1967. A more than adequate biography of Mannerheim, covering his entire life from a very sympathetic viewpoint. Based on interviews and relevant documentary archival materials. Good balance of Mannerheim's life and the conditions of Finland during this period of the twentieth century. A good introduction to the man and the marshal.

Taylor Stults

MAO TSE-TUNG

Born: December 26, 1893; Shaoshan, Hunan Province, China

Died: September 9, 1976; Peking, China

Areas of Achievement: The military, government, and politics

Contribution: Mao, Chairman of the Chinese Communist Party, led the People's Liberation Army to victory over the Chinese government headed by Chiang Kai-shek, leader of the Kuomintang, or Nationalist Party; established the People's Republic of China; and was the key figure in both party and government during most of his remaining years. He also adapted Marxist-Leninist theory and practice to Chinese conditions and, in effect, created a new doctrine that he later viewed as valid on a world scale.

Early Life

Mao Tse-tung was born into a peasant family of some means. His father, seeing little value in education, forced him to leave school at thirteen to work on the farm. Mao, however, had acquired a taste for reading, and novels about heroic bandits, peasant rebels, and notable rulers had fired his imagination. Continuing his reading, he came upon a book calling for the modernization of China and constitutional government. It motivated him to leave home and continue his studies. At sixteen, he entered primary school, where he became acquainted with Western liberal thought. A book on heroes led him to admire nation-building military men and respect the martial virtues. A short stint in a revolutionary army led to his first encounter with the ideas of socialism.

In time, Mao settled on becoming a teacher and entered normal school in 1913, graduating in 1918. He acquired an effective writing style and ideas to write about. In short, he came to believe in the goodness of man, the malleability of human nature, the power of the human will, the potential inherent in the Chinese peasantry, and the need to adapt Western ways to Chinese culture. He was also involved in radical organizations and thus in laying a foundation for future political action.

In 1918, Mao was at the University of Peking, where he found enthusiasm for the Bolshevik Revolution and Marxism. Back in Hunan Province in 1919, he was a leader in the anti-Japanese, anti-government May Fourth Movement. The following year, he became a primary school director and thereby attained status and influence. By 1920, he considered himself a Marxist and in July, 1921, was present at the founding of the Chinese Communist Party.

Russian insistence on controlling the Chinese party split it into factions. Mao accepted Russian leadership and the official Party position, including Communist membership in the Kuomintang and support for a bourgeois nationalist revolution. In 1924, illness sent him back to Hunan, where a new peasant militancy convinced him that the poor peasantry was the true revolutionary class. After his failure to spark a revolt in 1927, Mao took his ragtag army to the Chingkangsan Mountains. He lost his major Party positions, but he built his peasant army. Beginning in 1930, the Kuomintang, now his enemy, began a series of attacks against Mao's new base area in Kiangsi, leading to the six-thousand-mile Long March that began in late 1934. By 1935, Mao was chairman of the Party's politburo. A new phase had begun.

Life's Work

Mao had bested the Soviet-backed so-called Twenty-eight Bolsheviks, whom he had fought politically for control of the Party. Of elite background, these members lacked an understanding of the masses. The relationship between the Chinese and Soviet parties would remain strained thereafter, especially since the Soviets backed the Kuomintang in their own strategic interests and were willing to sacrifice the Chinese Communist Party accordingly. When Japan invaded China in 1937, the Soviets, concerned about their eastern territories, called for a Kuomintang-Communist United Front, even though Mao's Yen-an base area was under Kuomintang attack. Necessity, however, dictated such an alliance. The alliance was effected, both parties aware that it was but a temporary partnership.

During the Yen-an period, Mao developed what became Maoism. Contrary to Marxist-Leninist orthodoxy, he stressed the role of the peasantry over that of the proletariat. Similarly, his goal was to conquer the countryside through guerrilla warfare and encircle the cities, which would later be taken by conventional warfare. He also set forth the basis for his theory of "permanent revolution," holding that change is perpetual and conflict will continue even under communism. He also expounded his doctrine of the "mass line." In a protracted war, the zeal of the masses must be maintained by the Party cadres. The masses being infallible, it was the task of the cadres to gather their scattered ideas, synthesize them, propagate them among the masses until they accept them as their own, and then test them through action.

Meanwhile, Mao won over the peasants through fair treatment. People of all classes were called to join the anti-Japanese war, with the national (middle and patriotic) and petty bourgeoisie, and even the landlords, assured of retaining their property, at least for the moment. A clash with the Kuomintang in 1940-1941 ended the United Front. This necessitated the rectification campaign of 1942-1944, as Mao believed that the recruits needed disciplining through studying Marxism-Leninism. Also, as Mao's Sinification of Marxism was being ignored, he believed that it needed emphasizing. The tool was the so-called cult of Mao—Mao was supreme in matters of ideology and was proclaimed infallible. In 1945, "Mao Tse-tung Thought" was incorporated into the Party constitution.

The final phase of the civil war began in late 1948. The Kuomintang, having lost both American military aid and the confidence of the Chinese, were weakened enough for the Communist People's Liberation Army to take the major cities. On October 1, 1949, the People's Republic of China was officially inaugurated. The revolution was not a socialist revolution but a "New Democratic Revolution." The government was a coalition of four elements defined as "the people": the proletariat, the peasants, and the national and petty bourgeoisie. The Communists, however, would exercise hegemony over these classes through force and exercise a dictatorship over elements designated as "reactionary." Thus landlords and corrupt merchants were subject to severe punishment, including death. Corrupt bureaucrats met the same fate. Lack of enthusiasm for Chinese involvement in the Korean War led to millions of executions.

Rapid economic development was Mao's immediate goal. In early 1952, he inaugurated the First Five-Year Plan, which was meant to be the first step on the road to socialism. In July, 1955, he began the rapid nationalization of remaining private enterprises and the collectivization of agriculture. The peasants lost their recently acquired lands and were merged into agricultural collectives.

Aware that enthusiasm for his policies was weak among intellectuals, but convinced that they were true believers after years of thought reform, Mao sought to involve them with his "Let a Hundred Flowers Bloom" campaign. In 1956, intellectuals were encouraged to air their views. So vehement was the criticism of both the Party and Mao that the campaign was ended in 1957, and the offenders were punished through hard and humiliating labor.

Convinced that being "red" was more productive than being "expert" and at odds with the Soviet Union over Nikita S. Khrushchev's de-Stalinization speech and Eastern European policies, Mao set out to prove that China could become a great power on its own and attain communism before the Soviet Union. Certain that the Chinese people could accomplish anything through sheer willpower, he launched his "Great Leap Forward" in 1958. Steel was produced in backyard furnaces, mines were worked as never before, and regimented agricultural communes were inaugurated. People and machines were pushed beyond endurance. Millions died, the soil was depleted, and the economy was wrecked for years to come.

Mao's prestige within the Party was at its nadir. He blamed the local officials for the failures, but the Party blamed him. He resigned his chairmanship of the republic, but he retained the Party chairmanship and his public image was kept intact. He fended off a move to topple him by a Party faction led by Defense Minister P'eng Te-huai in 1959, but the intensity of the verbal attack returned him to the realm of mortality.

The years 1960 and 1961 saw Mao in seclusion as Party leaders openly criticized him and reversed his economic policies. By 1963, with the aid of the army headed by Lin Piao, he was attempting to weaken the Party bureaucracy and prepare for his restoration. He returned to seclusion from 1964 to mid-1966, supposedly dying but actually preparing for a spectacular return. It came with a swim in the Yangtze River and a pronouncement of good health.

Mao, formerly a distant figure with a cultivated air of mystery, now appeared in public, as did his wife Chiang Ch'ing, making her political debut. The cult of Mao was pushed to new heights. The army had been thoroughly indoctrinated, and the Red Guard, composed of Chinese youth directly under Mao, made its appearance. So, too, did their "bible," the so-called little red book, which contained selections from Mao's writings. Formerly the Chinese were encouraged to study all of Mao's writings; now they had short excerpts from them. Their thinking had been done for them. All these events were linked to the Cultural Revolution. An-

ticipating another Great Leap Forward, Mao opted to eliminate his critics beforehand. Moreover, Mao held that each generation must experience revolution firsthand. Accordingly, the Red Guard was turned loose on the bureaucracy. Educational institutions were devastated and a multitude of historical sites destroyed. Ultimately the army intervened to restore order.

By 1968 the Party was being reconstructed and its primacy proclaimed. Lin Piao was designated as Mao's successor. Mao came to suspect Lin of plotting against him, however, and Lin died under mysterious circumstances in 1971. Mao remained largely in the background from 1972 to his death in 1976. Still, he led the criticism of elitist Confucianism, with which he linked Lin, and later of the bourgeois Right. The radical Left remained dominant because of Mao's presence. His death brought factional conflict into the open and left the future uncertain.

Summary

Piecing together the life and writings of Mao Tse-tung is akin to trying to solve a Chinese puzzle.

While his life's story as told to Edgar Snow and related by him in *Red Star over China* (1937) is a vital source, scholars have found discrepancies that need explaining. Moreover, Mao's writings were repeatedly revised during his lifetime to support his claims to infallibility. Clearly, then, they were flawed, and his claims to be an original thinker of great import must be at least partially rejected. His theory and practice of guerrilla warfare, however, must be given due respect. His place in history as a military leader who withstood every conceivable adversity but survived to conquer power is secure. Later military ventures against China's neighbors were a different story. The wars with India and Vietnam were less than successful, and successes in the Korean War less than hoped for.

Mao's major claim to historical significance is his unification of China into a nation. From what amounted to a conglomeration of feudal principalities ruled by warlords, he fashioned a China that was more than a place on a map. Yet his brutality in forging and maintaining that unity, together with his megalomania and military aggressiveness, made him one of the great mass murderers of history. The China that he left was one devoid of much of its cultural heritage, destroyed in the name of progress. Oppression, repression, and suppression sum up much of his immediate legacy to China.

Bibliography

Breslin, Shaun. *Mao.* London and New York: Longman, 1998. Breslin places the People's Republic of China and the Cultural Revolution in historical context, considering Mao as a general, a leader, and a political manipulator. Includes a biographical essay, comprehensive chronology, and a glossary.

Chai, Winberg, ed. *Essential Works of Chinese Communism.* Rev. ed. London and New York: Bantam, 1972. A history of Chinese communism told largely through key documents and writings, including the most important of Mao's. Arranged into seven chronological chapters, a commentary on each plus an introduction by the editor makes this a genuine historical presentation. A three-page chronology gives the reader an excellent overview.

Ch'en, Jerome, ed. *Mao.* Englewood Cliffs, N.J.: Prentice-Hall, 1969. Part of the Great Lives Observed series, this book contains a series of excerpts from the writings of Mao, his contemporaries, and historians. In addition, the editor has written a lengthy introduction that can stand by itself as a short biography. A detailed chronology of Mao's political activities can be a valuable aid.

Huang, Yu, and Xu Yu. "Broadcasting and Politics: Chinese Television in the Mao Era, 1958-1976." *Historical Journal of Film, Radio and Television* 17, no. 4 (October, 1997). Examines the development and use of the media during Mao's rule.

Karnow, Stanley. *Mao and China: From Revolution to Revolution.* Introduction by John K. Fairbank. New York: Viking Press, 1972; London: Macmillan, 1973. An account that puts Mao into historical perspective by including a short chapter on Chinese history. While Mao's entire life is included, the major emphasis is on the period of the Cultural Revolution and its aftermath. A large book that is invaluable for the reader who wants detail.

Leys, Simon. *Chinese Shadows.* New York: Viking Press, 1977. An enlightening set of observations by a China specialist made during his 1972 visit to China, with an occasional note on his 1976 stay. Leys was able to visit places and people unavailable to most observers and presents an extraordinary account of the destruction of China's cultural heritage and an intimate account of the continuing oppression.

North, Robert C. *Chinese Communism.* London: Weidenfeld and Nicolson, and New York: McGraw-Hill, 1966. An excellent historical study that concentrates on Mao's early years in the context of the development of the Communist Party. The last chapter is a fine summary of China through the early 1960's, including the early stages of the Sino-Soviet dispute. A chronology, maps, and numerous illustrations are included.

Schram, Stuart. *Mao Tse-tung.* London and Baltimore: Penguin, 1966. Probably the best biography of Mao to the beginning of the Cultural Revolution. Very good on questioning the accuracy of points in earlier accounts and reporting on the continual revisions of Mao's writings. Schram's examination of the formative influences that helped shape the future Mao is particularly well done.

Snow, Edgar. *Red Star over China.* Introduction by John K. Fairbank. Rev. ed. London: Gollancz, and New York: Grove Press, 1968. Snow was the first Westerner to observe the Chinese Communists and interview Mao. The book is thus the essential starting point for a serious study of Mao. Its flaws have been noted by later authors, some even in this edition by Snow himself. Includes additional interviews with Mao, a chronology, and ninety-three short biographies, including one of Mao.

Robert W. Small

FRANZ MARC

Born: February 8, 1880; Munich, Germany
Died: March 4, 1916; near Verdun, France
Area of Achievement: Art
Contribution: Known for symbolic paintings of horses and other animals and as a founder of the Blue Rider group of German expressionist artists, Marc contributed to the development of modern abstract art.

Early Life

Franz Marc was born in Munich on February 8, 1880, to Wilhelm Marc, a minor Bavarian landscape painter and lawyer, and Sophie Maurice Marc. He studied theology at the Luitpold Gymnasium, where he made his *Abitur* in 1899. Introverted and melancholy even as a youth, he possessed an acute intelligence and a disquieted and searching mind. Spiritual affinities with German Romanticism led him not only to such nineteenth century writers and painters as E. T. A. Hoffmann and Caspar David Friedrich but also to the writings of Friedrich Nietzsche and to the ideas and music of Richard Wagner. Uncertain about his future, he first contemplated studying philosophy, but, following a year of compulsory military service, he entered the Munich Academy of Fine Arts. Early works, perceptive portraits of his parents as well as landscapes, evince the naturalism of this conservative training. While a brief sojourn in Italy scarcely affected Marc's artistic development, he christened a visit to Paris and Brittany in 1903, which had allowed him to see Impressionist canvases by Édouard Manet, Claude Monet, and Camille Pissarro, among others, a turning point in his life. These works, the first among the many by contemporary French artists who would so decisively influence Marc's art, helped free him from his academic schooling while disclosing the possibilities inherent in color.

Between 1903 and 1907, years of liberating visits to Paris, Marc experienced a profound depression. Likely resulting from a deep-seated individual crisis that paralleled the spiritual malaise of his time and from misgivings about his vocation as an artist, this depression would be transformed in his mature art into a semireligious quest for innocence and for the truth concealed beneath material appearances. Marc's restlessness led him to spend the summers of 1905 and 1906 in the mountains near Kochel am See, from which a number of land-scapes resulted, and to journey in the company of his elder brother Paul to Salonika and Mount Athos in the spring in 1906. His first animal paintings date from these years, with some, such as *The Dead Sparrow* (1905), attesting his mood of morbid sentimentality. Marc's depression reached its depths in the spring of 1907. In April, his father died following a debilitating illness, and Marc entered an ill-conceived marriage with Marie Schnür, from whom he fled on his wedding night to Paris. There Marc viewed works by Paul Cézanne, Paul Gauguin, and Vincent van Gogh, artists, especially van Gogh, in whom the captivated Marc perceived a spiritual kinship and whose brilliant canvases stimulated him to experiment with color.

Life's Work

Marc's break with the naturalism of his academic training was all but complete by 1907, and he embarked upon a search for a visual vocabulary suited to the expression of his innermost concerns and ideas. For the remaining seven years of his artistic career, he would grapple ceaselessly with pictorial styles and techniques, especially with those of the French avant-garde, gaining an ever greater mastery over form and color as he adopted and just as abruptly discarded representationalism, symbolism, and cubism, embracing finally, on the eve of World War I, an almost completely abstract style. From these experiments came memorable paintings, pictures important not only as works of art but also as portents of the mood that would mislead Marc, together with so many of his contemporaries, into welcoming World War I.

Once the emotional crisis of 1907 had passed, Franz Marc's depiction of animals and nature became more complex. Desirous of capturing the harmony of animals and nature, he still worked within the conventions of representational art, making detailed anatomical studies. Images of animals, especially horses, he believed, evoked an innocent and serene nature, one uncorrupted by the man he increasingly disliked. A well-received one-man exhibit at the Brackl Gallery in February of 1910 amounted to a retrospective for this style, which he was about to abandon. Receptive to new influences, Marc now came under the sway of Wassily Kandinsky, whose works he saw at the exhibit of the New Artists' Federation in December, 1909. In January of 1910, he met August Macke and his relative

Bernhard Köhler, who purchased paintings from Marc and who later provided him with a much-needed monthly stipend. Also during 1910, Marc saw works by Henri Matisse and Gauguin, further influences on his ideas about color.

Encouraged by these diverse encounters to think deeply about the meanings that color could convey, Marc continued to paint animals within natural settings. Yet, as the red horse in *Horse in Landscape* of 1910 or *Yellow Cow* of the next year make evident, they became less representational and more symbolic. Marc now sought to integrate his animals with nature and, by using pure expressive colors as well as simplified nonnatural forms, to make them carry the outpourings of his imagination and intellect. The symbolic and emotional values that Marc attached to different colors were explained in a letter of December, 1910, to Macke.

In September of 1910, the second exhibit of the New Artists' Federation opened, featuring works by Kandinsky, cubist paintings by Pablo Picasso and Georges Braque, and canvases by the French Fauves. Scornful comments in the local press prompted Marc to publish a vigorous defense of the new art. He then joined the federation in January of 1911, making the all-important personal acquaintance with Kandinsky the following month. Soon, however, the federation began to disintegrate, with disputes over the acceptability of nonobjective art serving as the catalyst for the departure of Kandinsky, Marc, and others in December, 1911. Meanwhile, the dissidents had already laid plans for a new exhibition, the first of two by the newly founded Blue Rider group, and for the publication of *Der Blaue Reiter* (1912; *The Blaue Reiter Almanac*, 1974), a celebrated manifesto of German expressionism.

To the first Blue Rider Exhibit, an international collection of modern art which opened at the Galerie Thannhauser in Munich on December 18, 1911, Marc sent *Yellow Cow* and *Deer in the Woods I;* in the second and last exhibit of February, 1912, he placed five works alongside contributions from France and from "Die Brücke" (the bridge), the Berlin group of German expressionists. *The Blaue Reiter Almanac*, edited jointly by Kandinsky and Marc, appeared in May, 1912, and it contained theoretical essays by Marc, Kandinsky, Arnold Schoenberg, and others, as well as an eclectic assemblage of illustrations that ranged from paintings by the Blue Rider group, Die Brücke, and the French artists Picasso and Robert Delaunay, to folk art from Bavaria and Russia, to primitive art from Africa and Asia. Uniting these works, the editors asserted, was the aspiration to depict symbolically the nature of spiritual reality.

Marc's art of 1911-1912 reveals new directions in style and mood, changes attributable both to renewed spiritual restlessness on his part and to a sequence of crises that threatened Europe repeatedly with war. Replacing the earlier harmony and serenity was an emphasis on energy and discord, on power and the potential for violence, concerns manifest in *The Tiger* of March, 1912, a picture in which Marc combined the techniques of the cubists with the color of the expressionists. Equally apparent was the influence of Delaunay, who had shown *St. Séverin* (1909) and *Tour Eiffel* (1910) at the first Blue Rider Exhibit and who now worked with abstract color as well as intersecting geometric lines. In such enigmatic paintings as the lost *Tower of Blue Horses* (1913), Marc began to overlap both forms and colors, a technique that allowed him to make his animals one with nature.

During 1913, the last year of peace before World War I, Marc painted his great apocalyptic canvases, several of which, including the hauntingly prophetic *Fate of Animals*, were shown at the first Herbstsalon (autumn salon) in Berlin that same year. Common to them is the theme of the catastrophic conflagration that necessarily precedes redemption, surely the same spiritual apocalypse that Kandinsky anticipated in *Improvisation No. 30 (Cannons)*, also of 1913. These paintings also partook of a more general mood, one that, although engendered in the immediate instance by persistent threats of a major war, was widespread in both prewar expressionist art and literature; the mood anticipated the destruction of Wilhelmine Germany as well as bourgeois Europe as a prelude to a universal spiritual regeneration. When sent a reproduction of *Fate of Animals* in 1915, Marc responded from the Western Front that "it is like a premonition of this war." Marc's longing for spiritual transformation by apocalyptic act led him to embrace the war when it arrived in August, 1914.

By late 1913 and early 1914, Marc's art had once again shifted course. In paintings such as *Fighting Forms* (1914), where recognizable objects have given way to relations among swirling lines and colors, he almost reached pure abstraction. Marc's subject nevertheless remained the apocalypse that he believed imminent, although he turned on occasion, as in an unfinished series of woodcuts for the

Book of Genesis, to its corollary, the theme of new creation.

This latest verge in Marc's artistic evolution ended abruptly in 1914, for, immediately after the outbreak of war, he entered the army, serving until killed in March, 1916. During his military service, Marc ceased to paint, but he wrote numerous letters to his wife and friends, and he continued to sketch. His wartime drawings depict neither military life nor the horrors of trench warfare but rather abstract concepts of destruction and rebirth. Before his death, however, Marc had begun to question his earlier enthusiasm and to see in the war little more than the meaningless sacrifice of friends such as Macke, who had been killed in 1914.

Summary

Throughout the twentieth century, interest in the work of Franz Marc has remained high, especially in Germany. Not long after his death, a memorial exhibition was mounted at the Sturm Gallery in Berlin in November of 1916, and, in 1920, an important collection of his letters and notes was published. When the Nazis confiscated *Fate of Animals* and displayed it in 1937 as "degenerate art," a public outcry forced its removal. Since the end of World War II, exhibits in Germany and elsewhere have made both Marc's art and his writings more widely known. As a founder of the Blue Rider movement and an artist who borrowed artistic techniques from his avant-garde contemporaries in France in his search for ways to express his spiritual cravings, Marc had a pivotal role in the evolution of pre-World War I expressionism toward abstraction. His contribution to the development of modern art is accordingly patent but still underappreciated in the United States. Marc's enduring influence is discernible in the work of his friend Paul Klee, in the Blue Four, founded in 1924 by Klee, Kandinsky, Alexei von Jawlensky, and Lyonel Feininger, and in the aspirations of artists attached to the Bauhaus. The expressionist tradition, to which Marc made such important contributions, has also inspired such painters as Piet Mondrian and the American abstract expressionists Mark Rothko and Barnett Newman.

Bibliography

Herbert, Barry. *German Expressionism: Die Brücke and Der Blaue Reiter.* London: Jupiter, and New York: Hippocrene, 1983. Two readable essays on the Brücke and the Blue Rider movements, excellent color and black-and-white illustrations, and appendices listing expressionist exhibitions make this a useful introduction.

Kandinsky, Wassily, and Franz Marc, eds. *The Blaue Reiter Almanac.* Edited with an introduction by Klaus Lankheit. London: Thames and Hudson, and New York: Viking Press, 1974. A translation of this important expressionist manifesto together with reproductions of the original illustrations. Lankheit's introductory essay and notes recount the history of the almanac's publication; a useful bibliography concludes the volume.

Levine, Frederick S. *The Apocalyptic Vision: The Art of Franz Marc as German Expressionism.* New York: Harper, 1979. Since few of Marc's writings have been translated into English, Levine's work, with its suggestive readings of individual paintings, extensive notes, and comprehensive bibliography, is a convenient introduction; it should, however, be used with caution.

Marc, Franz. *Franz Marc: Watercolors, Drawings, Writings.* Text and notes by Klaus Lankheit. Translated by Norbert Guterman. London: Thames and Hudson, and New York: Abrams, 1960. A searching essay by Lankheit, one of the few available in English, on Marc's artistic development complements good reproductions of his watercolors.

Rosenblum, Robert. *Modern Painting and the Northern Romantic Tradition: Friedrich to Rothko.* London: Thames and Hudson, and New York: Harper, 1975. An always stimulating study, which is excellent on the Romantic traditions within which Marc worked and on those artists whose works have been shaped by it.

Rosenthal, Mark. *Franz Marc, 1880-1916.* Berkeley: University Art Museum, University of California, 1979. This exhibition catalog offers, in addition to color and black-and-white reproductions of paintings by Marc, four essays on Marc and his art; of special interest are the translated excerpts from his wartime letters.

Selz, Peter. *German Expressionist Painting.* Berkeley: University of California Press, 1957; London: University of California Press, 1974. This essential study of expressionism, which focuses on Die Brücke and the Blue Rider group between 1905 and 1914, establishes the context in which Marc worked. Discussions of his career and art, together with comprehensive notes and a bibliography, make this a work to consult.

Robert W. Brown

GABRIEL MARCEL

Born: December 7, 1889; Paris, France
Died: October 8, 1973; Paris, France
Areas of Achievement: Philosophy and literature
Contribution: Marcel was a major figure in the
mid-twentieth century development of French
philosophy, as well as a significant dramatist. He
was the first French thinker to explore phenomenological and existential themes in depth and,
along with Maurice Merleau-Ponty, Jean-Paul
Sartre, and Albert Camus, became a key influence on the post-World War II French intellectual scene.

Early Life

Gabriel Marcel was born on December 7, 1889,
into a Parisian bourgeois family. His father had a
distinguished career as a government official, diplomat, and curator, holding the rank of councillor
of state and eventually holding posts in the Biblio-
thèque National and the Musées Nationaux. Marcel's mother died when he was four, an event that
had a powerful formative influence on him in regis-
tering both the irrevocability of death and the mystery of abiding presence. His upbringing took place
in an atmosphere essentially devoid of religious experience, his father being a cultured agnostic and
his stepmother (his mother's sister) a nonreligious
Jew who converted to a liberal humanist Protestantism. Young Marcel was thus reared in an environment whose basic values reflected those of the
French Third Republic—reason, science, and ethical conscience.

Marcel was an early and brilliant academic
achiever, passing his *agrégation* in philosophy at
the very early age of twenty in 1910. This qualified
him to teach at the *lycée* level in the French educational system, which he later did sporadically. He
never earned a doctorate, however, or became a
university professor. Part of the reason for this was
the impact of World War I. He worked for the
French Red Cross, with the job of locating missing
soldiers and communicating information concerning them to their relatives. As for so many other
young men during World War I, Marcel's experiences were a great shock, disturbing the securities
of the rational bourgeois universe of his early years
and bringing home starkly to him the tragic character of human existence. After this, his prewar
philosophical training, highly abstract in character,

came to seem arid and mechanical, and he now
sought a more concrete mode of philosophy, better
able to do justice to the intimacies of human experience not touched by abstract forms of thought.

If World War I was the occasion for a philosophical conversion for Marcel, the decade of intense
intellectual searching that ensued after the war's
end culminated in the decisive event in his spiritual
life—his conversion to Roman Catholicism on
March 23, 1929. Marcel had for years been concerned with philosophical investigation of the character of personal existence and the experience of
faith so that his conversion was a culmination of,
rather than a turn from, the spiritual quest occasioned by his philosophical conversion. It also
placed him in the company of a number of other
distinguished French intellectuals who converted
to Catholicism in the years of the Third Republic,
among them Paul Claudel, Charles Péguy, and
Jacques Maritain.

Marcel's struggle against that systematic spirit
that had characterized much of French philosophical inquiry after René Descartes built upon the
anti-Cartesian turn in French thought associated
with the work of Henri Bergson. Three of Marcel's
writings of the period 1925 to 1933 signaled his
emergence as a major new intellectual voice in
French philosophy: "Existence et objectivité"
(1925; "Existence and Objectivity," 1952); *Journal
métaphysique* (1927; *Metaphysical Journal*, 1952);
and "Position et approches concrètes du mystère
ontologique" (1933; "On the Ontological Mystery," 1948). All the major themes of his mature
work are adumbrated in these texts. Variations on
the themes that Marcel had begun to articulate
within the framework of his emerging philosophical viewpoint received exposition in a series of
nine plays that he wrote in the years between 1914
and 1933. He later insisted on the intimacy of his
philosophical and dramatic works, through which
the concrete examples on which much of his philosophical reflection rested received theatrical embodiment in dramatic characters.

Life's Work

Marcel called one of his books *Homo Viator: Pro-
légomènes à une métaphysique de l'espérance*
(1945; *Homo Viator: Introduction to a Metaphysic
of Hope*, 1951), and the title captures several en-

during themes of his mature work. *Homo viator* means man en route, or man the journeyer. The phrase reveals Marcel's belief both that the task of the philosopher is always an exploratory one, a searching along the paths of human experience for those key themes that he must patiently explore, and that the philosopher's task itself mirrors the life situation of every human individual. Hope was one of those crucial experiences—faith, exile, fidelity, trust, witness, and despair were others—that Marcel conceived it to be the purpose of the philosopher to interrogate because they had been dismissed by the dominant schools of modern philosophy as inaccessible to or unworthy of philosophical scrutiny.

Marcel's method in approaching philosophical questions was always open, probing, and intuitive, what he called "concrete." Rather than publish systematic treatises, he published his philosophical workbooks, his daily journals of philosophical investigations, and his philosophical diaries—thinking in process. Later these "drillings" into the depth of human experience could be worked up into philosophical essays and given extended development, perhaps finally to receive fully organized treatment, as in his Gifford Lectures in 1949-1950, *Le Mystère de l'être*, published in two volumes, *Réflexion et mystère* and *Foi et réalité* (1951; *The Mystery of Being*, 2 vols., 1950-1951), or his William James Lectures at Harvard in 1961-1962, *The Existential Background of Human Dignity* (1963). Yet always Marcel's concern was to deny that the detached, disembodied *cogito* of Descartes could be the appropriate beginning for philosophy as he conceived it. For him philosophy began more in wonder and astonishment than in curiosity and doubt, and the exploratory texts that constitute the bulk of his philosophical oeuvre were better vehicles than systematic treatises for capturing these foundational philosophical experiences.

A distinction crucial to Marcel's philosophical stance is the one that he made between primary and secondary reflection. Primary reflection is the realm of abstraction, objectivity, and universality; this is the world of the analytically verifiable, best exemplified in modern scientific and technological thought. The great threat from primary reflection for Marcel was that the spirit of abstraction was too likely to become imperialistic, tyrannizing over all domains of human experience. Hence, he opposed primary reflection to secondary reflection, the latter being the realm in which emphasis falls on the intuitive, on participation, and on dialogue. Herein Marcel emphasized over and over the possibility of human beings' penetrating the mystery of existence through confrontation with "presence" and "mystery" rather than with the "object" of primary reflection. He rejected any relationship of the philosopher to reality that could be described as that "of an onlooker to a picture." Rather, Marcel developed a "concrete philosophy" in which secondary reflection, approaching the world, the self, and other human beings through love, or fidelity, or hope, or another "concrete approach," could yield a knowledge that would illuminate human life as it is lived, although a kind of knowledge not verifiable by the techniques of primary reflection.

It is appropriate to characterize Marcel's sense of the necessity for a full, open relationship between beings, or between a person and what he or she confronts—a mystery or a presence—as dialogical. It is a relationship well characterized in the terms "I" and "thou," made popular through the work of the Jewish philosopher Martin Buber. To establish such a dialogical relationship with others and with the world demands a *disponibilité*, an availability or readiness of the self toward others and the world, as well as an involvement or engagement with the world. The origin of such a relationship lies in the experience of the body, of human incarnation. The self projects into the world its sense of bodily presence as it becomes aware of its own body, and this bodily experience becomes the prototype for the way the world exists for the self. Just as the self cannot be separated from the body, so too it is inseparable from its situation in the world. It is impossible to abstract completely from those concrete situations that are constitutent of the human self, although one of the great temptations of primary reflection is to accomplish just such a complete separation of self from situation. Thus, a self that is open to the world, that can establish dialogical relations with it and with others, can develop a participant knowledge of great ontological depth, something denied to the self that treats others as objects to be manipulated.

Marcel's sensitive probing of existential experiences revealed to him a deep-seated "exigence," or impulse, at the base of all human life, which he described as an impulse to transcendence. He was convinced that this "ontological exigence" in human beings testified to the existence of an inexhaustible presence that he called "being." His analyses of human experiences convinced him of the presence of this inexhaustible being, although it could only be approached obliquely through phenomenological description. Thus Marcel's mature philosophy came to rest on the assurance that through openness to such crucial human experiences as love, fidelity, and hope it was possible to approach God in a fashion identical with the approach of his concrete philosophy to other persons. Through concrete human experience, being itself could be approached and the human "ontological exigence" proven to be more than what the French existentialist thinker Jean-Paul Sartre had called it: a "useless passion."

In one sense, Marcel's thinking was a call to restore simple human values—faith, trust, comradeship, love—in a world threatened increasingly by technological abstractions and political alienation. In *Les Hommes contre l'humain* (1951; *Men Against Humanity*, 1952), he brought his philosophical views to bear upon an analysis of the social and political world of immediate postwar Europe. He worried that the dominance of technology was leading to a world ruled by despair, without hope; he blamed the increasing violence of the contemporary world on that spirit of abstraction, against which he had conducted a long philosophical struggle. While he never developed anything like a fully articulated social philosophy, his essays on social and political themes exhibit a marked congruence with his more speculative work. In both there are the consistent effort to give meaning and depth to central human experiences, the deep sadness at the varieties of human grief, and the desire to bring together the metaphysical certainty of the convinced Christian with the concrete awareness of real human relationships of the phenomenologist, which characterized Marcel's life work from beginning to end.

Summary

Gabriel Marcel is often characterized as an existentialist, although he himself rejected that term. Such a characterization usually sees him as a theistic existentialist as opposed to the atheistic existentialism of Jean-Paul Sartre or Martin Heidegger. While the differences between and among the various existentialist philosophers were many, and Marcel was certainly right to reject any term that served to conflate his views and those of people such as Sartre, whom he vehemently opposed, there is, nevertheless, a grain of truth in applying the label "existentialist" to him. He shared with other existentialist thinkers a passion to engage philosophically with the world of lived human experience, a profound distrust with the abstractions of scientific and technological thought, and a sensitivity to literature and art as perhaps more powerful tools than philosophy for the analysis of human existence. In his essay "Existence and Objectivity" and in his *Metaphysical Journal*, Marcel was deeply involved with many of the ideas that later became central to existentialism, and these texts were published before Karl Jaspers, Heidegger, and Sartre had published any of their major works. Thus, Marcel is rightly characterized as the first French existentialist.

Marcel's thought also demonstrates affinities with other important twentieth century European thinkers. His philosophical method, based on the intuitive approach of his concrete philosophy, in many respects parallels the work of the German phenomenologist Edmund Husserl, although Marcel worked independently of him. Similarly, Marcel's dialogical approach to existential concerns is reminiscent of the work of Buber, although here again his work began and was pursued independently of influence from Buber. Marcel's concern with the philosophical description of bodily experience anticipates as well some of the major emphases in the work of the French thinker Merleau-Ponty. Marcel is also appropriately characterized as the first French phenomenologist.

Marcel belongs to that distinguished group of twentieth century French thinkers whom the historian H. Stuart Hughes has called "philosophers who were Catholics." Like Péguy and Maritain, Marcel was a convert to Catholicism; like them, he lived in and wrote out of an ambiguous situation in which the society around him opposed the spiritual values to which he was committed. Writing against the grain of his world, Marcel developed a highly personalized, even idiosyncratic, philosophical stance, one he communicated best through essays, diaries, and other fragmentary forms. He himself provided the best descriptive term for his work when he called it neo-Socratic, for, like his chosen Greek forebear, Marcel as a thinker was concerned to show how important it is to pose problems correctly before even attempting their solution. In invoking the person of Socrates, Marcel associated his work with the constant questioning, risk-taking, and ongoing dialogical approach of an earlier *homo viator* like himself.

Bibliography

Blackham, H. J. *Six Existentialist Thinkers.* London: Routledge, and New York: Macmillan, 1952. The chapter on Marcel situates him in the wider currents of existentialist thought.

Cain, Seymour. *Gabriel Marcel.* London: Bowes, and New York: Hillary House, 1963. This is a short introduction to the major themes of Marcel's thinking and proves a good starting point for further study.

Cain, Seymour. *Gabriel Marcel's Theory of Religious Experience.* New York: Lang, 1995. Cain studies Marcel's theories on human existence and their religious implications.

Gallagher, Kenneth T. *The Philosophy of Gabriel Marcel.* New York: Fordham University Press, 1962. Good overall study of Marcel's philosophical work, with an introduction by Marcel.

Hanley, Katherine Rose. *Dramatic Approaches to Creative Fidelity: A Study in the Theater and Philosophy of Gabriel Marcel (1889-1973).* Lanham, Md.: University Press of America, 1987. This is the most extensive attempt in English to relate Marcel's philosophical and dramatic works.

Heinemann, F. H. *Existentialism and the Modern Predicament.* London: Black, and New York: Harper, 1953. Another good survey of existentialist thinking, with a chapter devoted to Marcel.

Hughes, H. Stuart. *The Obstructed Path: French Social Thought in the Years of Desperation, 1930-1960.* New York: Harper, 1968. An excellent intellectual history with a chapter on Marcel and other French Catholic thinkers.

Keen, Sam. *Gabriel Marcel.* London: Carey Kingsgate Press, 1966; Richmond, Ky.: John Knox Press, 1967. This work is a good short survey of Marcel's philosophical work.

Polk, Danne W. "Gabriel Marcel's Kinship to Ecophilosophy." *Environmental Ethics* 16, no. 2 (Summer 1994). Polk evaluates Marcel's thoughts on technology and religion and compares his philosophies with those of contemporary movements.

Schilpp, Paul Arthur, and Lewis Edwin Hahn, eds. *The Philosophy of Gabriel Marcel.* La Salle, Ill.: Open Court, 1984. A book in the important Library of Living Philosophers series. Contains a number of essays on Marcel's work, as well as his own 1969 "Autobiographical Essay."

Michael W. Messmer

ROCKY MARCIANO

Born: Sept. 1, 1923; Brockton, Massachusetts
Died: August 31, 1969; near Newton, Iowa
Area of Achievement: Sports
Contribution: Marciano retired as the only undefeated heavyweight champion in boxing history. The son of poor Italian immigrants, he dignified the legendary belt and brought great pride to the Italian American community.

Early Life

The first born of Pierino and Pasqualena Marchegiano, Rocco Francis Marchegiano survived a life-threatening bout with pneumonia in March, 1925. The experience presaged the determination that he would later show in the ring. The doctor who was attending eighteen-month-old Rocco advised the mother that if the youngster had the spirit to survive, he would be a strong boy. The crisis passed, and the doctor's prediction came true.

First, however, Rocco had to overcome the temper of the times and the circumstances of his family's poverty. When Rocco was born, the shadow of the Red Scare hung over the Italian American community. United States Attorney General Alexander Mitchell Palmer directed raids against immigrant groups and deported many. Based on what many felt was circumstantial evidence, two Italian anarchists, Nicola Sacco and Bartolomeo Vanzetti, were tried, convicted, and executed for allegedly murdering a payroll guard in Braintree, Massachusetts. Rocco's father, a frail, hard-working laborer in a shoe factory, resented the anti-Italian sentiment. He had been gassed while serving in the United States Army on the western front during World War I and was proud of his service to his country. Rocco's mother, a homemaker, set a good table of mostly simple fare of pasta, soup, and vegetables. She was further kept busy by the births of five more children between 1925 and 1939. With the onset of the Great Depression, factory pay remained low, and the Marchegianos, like a lot of families, struggled to survive.

Rocco's first love was baseball. Growing up in the shadow of James Edgar playground, he and his buddies dreamed that they would one day make the major leagues. As a catcher for the Saint Patrick's Church baseball team, he helped them to an archdiocese championship. At fifteen he was also the starting linebacker on the Brockton High School football team. Never a serious student, he quit school at sixteen in order to work while continuing to pursue his dream of playing professional baseball.

What marked Rocky from his earliest sports endeavors through the end of his fight career was his intense dedication to training to make himself a better athlete. He was self-conscious about his small and short arms, so he began lifting homemade weights and doing development exercises. He lacked a strong throwing arm, so every evening he practiced for hours just throwing from home plate to second base. He was clumsy and slow, so every evening after throwing he ran hills and did wind sprints in the park. He developed into a powerful hitter, but his other limitations denied him a professional baseball career.

Rocky took various jobs, but the one he hated most was a stint in the shoe factory. He swore he would not do factory work for a living. Much later he commented, "I couldn't stand the smell of wet leather—it nauseated me—but I had to have a job. Whenever a boxing match isn't going my way, I can smell my sweat on my opponent's leather gloves. . . . I then give the fight that extra effort and I win." In March, 1943, he was drafted into the U.S. Army and sent to Wales to ferry supplies across the English Channel. After the end of World War II, he was sent back to Fort Lewis, Washington, where he found the path leading to the world's heavyweight championship.

Life's Work

At Fort Lewis, Rocky fought to avoid having to work undesirable details and also played on the baseball team. While home on leave in April, 1946, Rocky impressed his uncle, Mike Piccento, with stories about his fight prowess in the Army. Through a local booking agent, Generosa "Gene" Caggiano (who later sued Rocky for breech of a management contract), Piccento arranged Rocky's first local bout on April 15, 1946, against a former New England Golden Gloves heavyweight champ named Henry Lester. Overweight and out of shape from rich home cooking, Rocky was through by the second round. Sensing defeat, he kneed his opponent in the groin and was disqualified. It would be the only disqualification of his career.

He returned to Fort Lewis and began serious training for the Amateur Athletic Union (AAU)

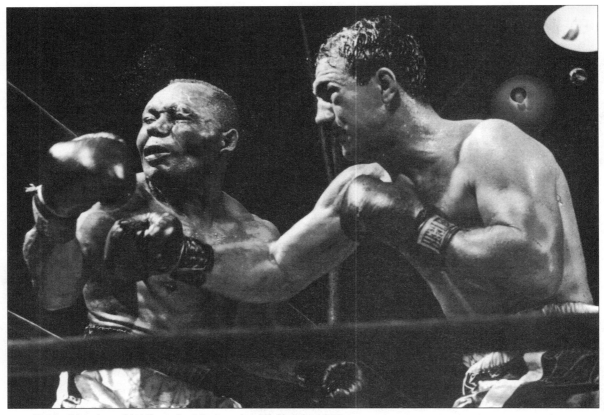

Rocky Marciano (right) against Jersey Joe Walcott in 1952.

championships in Portland, Oregon. Needing to win three fights, he took the first two with dramatic first-round knockouts. He had, however, painfully dislocated a knuckle in the second fight. Fighting one-handed, the 5 foot 10 inch Rocky lost to 6 foot 3 inch Joe De Angelis of Chelsea, Massachusetts, in the decisive bout.

Honorably discharged, Rocky returned to Brockton in the summer of 1946. He also returned to his first love, baseball. He played for a regionally famous semipro team, Taunton Lumber Company. He also took a quick fling at professional boxing. Trained and managed by his boyhood friend Allie Colombo, Rocky agreed to fight a four-rounder in Holyoke, Massachusetts, against a local favorite named Lee Epperson. To protect his amateur status, Rocky fought under the pseudonym Rocky Mack. It was March 17, 1947 (St. Patrick's Day). He began his professional career with a third-round knockout. The purse was thirty-five dollars. Then he accepted an invitation from a baseball scout from the Chicago Cubs to a tryout in Fayetteville,

North Carolina. After a three-week trial, he was rejected because of his weak throwing arm.

His throwing arm would, however, never affect his punching power. He returned home and, despite his mother's misgivings, embarked on a training regimen in order to become a professional boxer. He worked the bags, sparred, and ran eight miles per day in specially weighted training boots. In January of 1948, Rocky entered the Golden Gloves tournament in Lowell, Massachusetts, and quickly recorded three straight knockouts. Hurting from a bad knuckle, he lost to Bob Girard but went on to win the New England championship before losing to Coley Wallace in the Eastern championships. It would be his last loss inside a ring. He completed his amateur career of twelve fights with a record of eight wins and four losses.

Rocky was twenty-five, engaged to be married, and smallish for a heavyweight when a New York manager named Al Weill came calling. Weill introduced him to the famous trainer Charley Goldman, and Rocky's professional career began in earnest.

On July 12, 1948, in Providence, Rhode Island, Rocky faced twenty-one-year-old Haroutune "Harry" Bilazarian of Bolyston, Massachusetts, who had been the Army light heavyweight champ in Sapporo, Japan, in 1947. Rocky knocked him out during the first round. It was Weill who turned Rocky Marchegiano to Rocky Marciano and booked the rest of his pro career.

After wading through a series of lesser opponents, Rocky's big break came when Weill matched him against unbeaten Roland LaStarza at Madison Square Garden on March 24, 1950. The crafty LaStarza countered the powerful Rocky until, after ten rounds, it was up to the judges to award a split decision to Rocky. One year later, Rocky knocked out the legendary Joe Louis, who was attempting a comeback at age thirty-seven.

Meanwhile, Rocky had married his longtime sweetheart, Barbara Cousins, on December 31, 1950, at St. Coleman's Church in Brockton. She was a tall, athletic, dark-haired Irish girl of twenty-two. The marriage produced a daughter, Mary Anne, born in Brockton on December 6, 1952. The couple also adopted an infant, Rocky Kevin, who was only seventeen months old when Rocky died in 1969.

Rocky's career was now in its ascendancy. The Louis bout led to a title fight in Philadelphia on September 23, 1952, against thirty-eight-year-old champion "Jersey Joe" Walcott. Overcoming a first round knockdown, Rocky came back to claim the title with a thirteenth-round knockout. The following May in Chicago, Rocky took Walcott out in the first round.

Rocky would successfully defend his crown once against Roland LaStarza, twice against former champ Ezzard Charles, and once against Don Cockell. In his final fight against light heavyweight champion Archie Moore, Rocky recovered from an early knockdown to knock down Moore three times en route to a ninth-round knockout.

As a fighter, Rocky was known for his crowding style and aggressiveness, complemented by a good left hook and a devastating overhand right. He could take a hard punch but had a penchant for bleeding. He almost lost the second Ezzard Charles fight because his corner was unable to staunch the bleeding from a split nose. Rocky had to summon his reserves to knock out Charles in the eighth round before the referee could stop the fight.

On April 28, 1956, Rocky retired from the ring with a record of forty-nine wins (forty-three of which were knockouts) and no losses. He cited the need to spend more time with his family. Other reasons may have been more compelling. He distrusted Weill, whom he thought shorted him on purses. He also had a bad back from years of almost fanatical training. He had made more than four million dollars during his professional career and had spent very little of it. After his retirement, Rocky settled in Fort Lauderdale, Florida, but never spent much time with his family. He bounced around the country making public appearances and hanging out with celebrities. He could be generous to friends (especially former pugilists) but was secretive and miserly with his money. He usually let hangers-on pick up the tabs for the parties.

In 1957, in conjunction with Charley Goldman, Rocky lent his name to a book, *Rocky Marciano's Book of Boxing and Bodybuilding*. He did a couple of bit parts in motion pictures and, in the summer of 1969, agreed to a simulated match with Muhammad Ali in which they sparred over several days while a computer picked the winner. Rocky shed fifty pounds and actually got himself into some semblance of fighting shape. Rocky won the ersatz bout.

On Sunday, August 31, 1969, Rocky was a passenger with one other man on a flight in a small plane from Chicago to Des Moines. He was to attend a birthday party as a favor to a friend. Stormy weather and an inexperienced pilot contributed to the plane crashing near Newton, Iowa. The three men aboard were killed on impact. It was the day before Rocky's forty-sixth birthday.

Summary

As a heavyweight boxer, Rocky Marciano was a transitional figure between Depression-era greats, led by Joe Louis, and the greats of the 1960's, led by Muhammad Ali. He is the only heavyweight champion to retire undefeated, but some claim he was aided by weak competition. However, no one can doubt his punching power.

As a public figure, Rocky was idolized for his ethnic background and also as something of a "Great White Hope." At his zenith, at the same time that the modern Civil Rights movement began to break down Jim Crow laws, he was lauded in some circles for his victories over black boxers. His fame was also abetted by being the first heavyweight champion to benefit from television exposure. His brawling, bleeding, bombastic style played well to the camera.

Bibliography

Marciano, Rocky. *Rocky Marciano's Book of Boxing and Bodybuilding.* Englewood Cliffs, N.J.: Prentice-Hall, 1957. Includes photographs of Rocky training.

Nack, William. "The Rock." *Sports Illustrated* 79, no. 8 (August 23, 1993). Nack discusses the life of Marciano, including his risk-taking nature, his financial activities, and the plane crash that took his life.

Nelson, Allan. "The Scent of Failure." *American Heritage* (February-March, 1997): 56. A personal anecdote about Marciano's aversion to leather work.

Skehan, Everett. *Rocky Marciano: Biography of a First Son.* Boston: Houghton Mifflin, 1977. Assisted by two of Rocky's brothers and his daughter, this is a definitive account of his life and career.

Brian G. Tobin

GUGLIELMO MARCONI

Born: April 25, 1874; Bologna, Italy
Died: July 20, 1937; Rome, Italy
Areas of Achievement: Invention and technology
Contribution: Marconi, who shared the 1909 Nobel Prize in Physics with Karl Ferdinand Braun,
was recognized for his pioneering work in physics that led to the invention of devices for sending signals wirelessly, thereby revolutionizing
telegraphic and radio transmission over long
distances.

Early Life

By age six, Guglielmo Marconi had spent half of
his life in Italy and half in England. His father,
Giuseppe Marconi, was a comfortably fixed landowner in northern Italy, who, when his first wife
died, married Guglielmo's mother, Annie Jameson,
a British subject and the daughter of a well-to-do
family in the liquor-distilling business that had left
Ireland to settle in England. In 1864, defying parental admonitions, Annie married Giuseppe. She
was twenty-one, her husband thirty-eight.

When Guglielmo was three, his mother took him
and his nine-year-old brother, Alfonso, to England
for a three-year visit. Upon their return, their father
employed a teacher, who came to their home, Villa
Grifone, to help them catch up on their Italian.
Their mother taught them English and the Bible.
When Guglielmo finally went to school in Florence, the experience was miserable for him. His
Italian was bad, and he was rebellious. He stayed
in constant trouble. The only positive benefit he derived from attending that school was that there he
met Luigi Solari, his lifelong, highly influential
friend.

At thirteen, in Leghorn (Livorno), to which his
mother often took him and his brother to escape
northern Italy's winter, Marconi attended the Technical Institute. In the same year, 1888, Heinrich
Hertz discovered that electricity could be transmitted through space from one point to another and
that when an electric spark leaped the gap between
two metal spheres, periodic oscillations, now
called Hertzian waves, occurred. Marconi believed
that these oscillating waves could carry signals.

His autocratic father was intolerant of what he
considered his son's idle, directionless dallying. He
envisioned a naval career for his son, whom he
gave little encouragement to follow his natural bent

toward chemistry and physics, subjects that intrigued the boy.

When Marconi failed his entrance examinations
for the University of Bologna, his mother interceded with the Marconis' neighbor, Professor Augusto
Righi, who finally permitted Marconi to use laboratory facilities and equipment at the university on
an unofficial basis. Marconi, excited at the possibility of wireless telegraphy, shared this excitement
with Righi. The professor discouraged him, cau-
tioning the twenty-year-old Marconi that he did not
have the scientific background to succeed at work
that for years had baffled experimental physicists,
including Righi.

Marconi, however, was undaunted. Overcoming
paternal disapproval, he set up his experiments in
the attics of Villa Grifone and labored tirelessly to
prove his theory of the wireless transmission of
signals. Although he knew that others much better
trained than he were working on the same problem,
he was determined to succeed. Perhaps his innocence of theory and his emphasis on the practical
outcomes of his experiments made his successes
possible. Marconi proceeded in relative ignorance
to try things that more seasoned scientists knew
theoretically could not work; sometimes, remarkably, these things succeeded.

Life's Work

Marconi began his life's work in earnest when he
was barely more than twenty and began to seques-
ter himself for long hours in his attic workshop. He
irritated his father by asking him for money to buy
apparatuses. His neighbor Righi lent him some of
the equipment he needed, and Marconi, ever talented at working with his hands, constructed many of
his own apparatuses.

Using a Hertz oscillator and a Branly coherer
(named for Édouard-Eugène Branly) that could detect the oscillations that the Hertzian apparatus impelled, sometimes working theoretically but more
often working intuitively and succeeding by patient trial and error, Marconi finally, early in 1895,
achieved his end in one simple application: With
the minimal equipment he had available, he made a
bell ring by capturing the Hertzian oscillations and
converting them into energy, which he sent across
the expanse of his attic workshop.

By a fortuitous stroke, Marconi one day placed
one of his terminals on a rise in the ground and dis-

covered that the signal increased. He then experimented with burying a transmitter deep in the ground, first horizontally, then vertically, and elevating the receiver. By the middle of 1895, Marconi had gone farther and farther afield, finally sending a signal one and a half miles. He sent signals from one side of a hill to the other, making him think that perhaps Hertzian waves penetrated solids and exited the other side; he later learned that they circumvent them. By this time, even Marconi's skeptical father was beginning to acknowledge that his son's work was important.

It was time for Marconi to market his idea. He first turned to the Italian government for help but was rebuffed. He took his equipment to England, where his cousin, Henry Jameson Davis, set to work helping Marconi get his patent application for radiotelegraphy into acceptable form. Despite a delay occasioned by custom officers' smashing some of his transmitting equipment when he tried to import it, Marconi quickly made replacements, improving his terminals and vacuum tubes to the extent that by September, 1896, he was able to transmit a signal a distance of two miles.

In 1897, just as he was perfecting his invention and finding financial backing for it, Marconi was called upon to meet the three-year military obligation imposed on all Italian males when they reached their majority. Marconi considered renouncing his Italian citizenship and declaring himself a British subject, which he could have done. Instead, through the intervention of Italy's Minister of Marine, Benedetto Brin, Marconi became a naval cadet stationed in London as an attaché in the Italian embassy. Because his appointment involved no duties, he donated the pay he received from the government to an orphanage.

Henry Jameson Davis helped Marconi form the Wireless Telegraph and Signal Company in July, 1897, to finance continued experiments. Before that, Marconi had gained considerable attention by sending a signal across Bristol Channel, a distance of nine miles. Marconi, realizing that he could increase his range by increasing the number of antennae he used and by increasing their length, constructed a string of antennae 150 feet high across the English Channel, fixing them to lighthouses and naval vessels, enabling him to send a signal the twenty-eight miles to France.

The next step was clearly a dramatic one: Marconi, who by 1900 had sent signals almost two hundred miles, was determined to send a signal across the Atlantic. Preparatory to this transmission, a huge, high receiver was erected on Cape Cod off the Massachusetts mainland and a transmitter—the most powerful Marconi had yet built—was placed on England's Cornwall coast. When a windstorm destroyed the receiver, Marconi sailed to St. John's, Newfoundland. There he launched a receiver on a kite, taking a page from his boyhood reading in the works of Benjamin Franklin.

By the end of 1901, with Solari at the transmitter and Marconi more than two thousand miles away flying the receiver in the air, the wireless transatlantic transmission was made. Solari tapped in the three telegraphic dots of "S" in Morse code, and Marconi received it. The next year, Marconi sent the first wireless signal back to England.

Only twenty-eight years old, Marconi, a handsome Italian of olive complexion and chiseled Roman features, saw his name become a household word. The inventor, lacking the usual academic credentials of physicists, was well on the way to receiving the Nobel Prize in Physics that he would share in 1909.

Marconi's patent 7777, granted in 1900, gave its holder great control over the communications industry of his day. He spent much of his remaining years expanding Marconi's Wireless Telegraph Company and perfecting his basic invention. He continued to patent his inventions of such implements as the directional aerial and improved transmission devices.

In 1905, Marconi married Beatrice O'Brien, who, like his mother, was Irish. They had three children, but Marconi's relationship with his family, both wife and children, deteriorated because of his life-style, which included considerable womanizing. The marriage was annulled in 1924. In 1927, Marconi married the Countess Maria Bezzi-Scali, by whom he had one daughter.

Marconi served Italy in several military capacities during World War I, finally serving as a commander in the Italian navy, ironically fulfilling his father's early preference. He was in charge of telegraphy for all of Italy's armed forces and rose to a position of sufficient prominence that he was Italy's plenipotentiary delegate to the Paris Peace Conference, where he was signatory to the peace treaties Italy entered into with Austria and Bulgaria.

By 1921, Marconi had redesigned his yacht, *Elettra*, into a combined home and laboratory, conducting most of his corporate business from that base. His experimentation continued, focusing now on shortwaves. His corporation assumed immense international proportions, the United States branch becoming the influential Radio Corporation of America (RCA).

His activities hampered by a heart condition that resulted in several severe attacks, Marconi worked as steadily as his health permitted. On July 19, 1937, having reconciled somewhat with the three children from his first marriage and two days after having an audience with the pope, Marconi saw his wife and young daughter off for a seaside resort, promising to join them there the next day. He went home to prepare for an evening appointment with his friend, Benito Mussolini, for whom he had made broadcasts supporting Italy's rising Fascism. He was never to keep that appointment. Shortly before he was to leave for it, he was stricken with a heart attack that proved fatal in the early hours of July 20.

Summary

Guglielmo Marconi was the sort of original genius whose name is inextricably attached to wireless communication, particularly to the radio. He, along with Thomas Alva Edison, Samuel F. B. Morse, and Alexander Graham Bell, helped to bring about the modern age in communication. Edison perfected the power sources required for the inventions of the others, each of whom helped to shrink the world by making it possible for people to communicate with speed across great distances.

The political implications of Marconi's invention are particularly significant, because his invention brought the whole world into one's own living room or bedroom. People in the remotest venues could now be as well informed about world events as those who lived in thriving metropolises. Politicians throughout the world quickly took advantage of the new medium that Marconi developed to disseminate their ideas to hundreds of times more people than they would have been able to reach through making whistle stops throughout their constituencies. Although Marconi lived for many years after his initial invention of the wireless, it is with this invention that his name is generally connected.

Bibliography

Donaldson, Frances. *The Marconi Scandal.* London: Hart-Davis, and New York: Harcourt Brace, 1962. The book provides details about the fall of Godfrey Isaacs, managing director of Marconi's Wireless Telegraph Company, who was charged with corruption in his aggressive handling of the company's affairs, particularly of the so-called imperial wireless scheme, which was generally known as the "Marconi scandal." Donaldson's report of this convoluted proceeding is filled with all the intrigue of a mystery novel.

Jacot, B. L., and D. M. B. Collier. *Marconi—Master of Space: An Authorized Biography of the Marchesa Marconi.* London: Hutchinson, 1935. Although much additional information about Marconi became available to biographers after his death in 1937, Jacot and Collier uncovered valuable information about the inventor, particularly about his early experiments at Villa Grifone and later in England. Less enlightening about his later personal life than some of the later books are.

Jolly, W. P. *Marconi.* London: Constable, and New York: Stein and Day, 1972. Jolly's biography is one of the most comprehensive to date. It is well written, objective in its presentation of a man whose life was filled with contradictions, and well illustrated with carefully chosen pictures of its subject. The index is not always as thorough as it might be, but it is generally serviceable.

Marconi, Degna. *My Father, Marconi.* London: Muller, and New York: McGraw-Hill, 1962. In this book, Marconi's daughter by Beatrice O'Brien, alienated from her father until shortly before his death, when they had a most satisfying reconciliation, tries more than two decades after his death to sort out her feelings about him. The book is more valuable for the personal information it provides than for detailed work about Marconi's scientific contributions, although these are treated. Marconi's life is the stuff of which novels are made, and this book provides a base for any writer inclined in that direction.

Rhoads, B. Eric. "Who Really Invented Radio?" *Audio* 79, no. 12 (December, 1995). Discusses the various people who made discoveries in wireless communication, including Marconi, Tesla, and Hertz.

Riley, John Powell. "The Man Who Started Ripples in the Ether." *Electronics World + Wireless World* 100, no. 1702 (September, 1994). Riley provides information on Marconi's patent for his telegraphic system, his first transatlantic transmission, and other accomplishments.

Schueler, D. G. "Inventor Marconi: Brilliant, Dapper, Tough to Live With." *Smithsonian* 12

(March, 1982): 126. Discusses Marconi in terms of his intellectual independence and insights, pointing out the more flamboyant side of his personality that led to his divorce, his womanizing, and his frequent breaks with his children.

R. Baird Shuman

FERDINAND E. MARCOS

Born: September 11, 1917; Sarrat, Philippines
Died: September 28, 1989; Honolulu, Hawaii
Areas of Achievement: Government and politics
Contribution: Marcos was regarded in the 1960's as a reformer dealing with long-standing national problems, such as corruption, smuggling, and poverty. Marcos was regarded throughout the 1960's as a staunch American ally, even sending Philippine troops to fight in Vietnam. His increasingly autocratic style of governing from 1972 onward, combined with his family's extravagant corruption, began to erode his popularity to the point at which he had to flee the country in February, 1986.

Early Life

Ferdinand Edralin Marcos was born in Sarrat, Ilocos Norte, on the main Philippines island of Luzon on September 11, 1917, the eldest son of Mariano R. Marcos and Josefa Edralin. Both of Marcos' parents were teachers, and, as their assignments changed, the family moved about the country. Marcos' father was a strict disciplinarian and stressed sports and physical toughness in addition to academic study. Marcos also acquired his oratorical skills from his father, achieving fluency in Tagalog, English, Spanish, and Ilocano.

When Mariano Marcos was elected to the Philippine Congress in 1925, the family moved to Manila, which provided Ferdinand with educational opportunities unavailable elsewhere. Marcos studied in the University of the Philippines High School from 1929 to 1933. Following his graduation, he was given a scholarship and was enrolled in the liberal arts program of the University of the Philippines in Manila. While there he was commissioned as a third lieutenant in the Philippine Constabulary Reserve. Marcos captained the school's rifle and pistol team.

While Marcos' future seemed bright, a political incident involving his father now threatened to detail his ambitions. Mariano Marcos had been elected as a congressman for the Second District of Ilocos Norte in 1924 and 1928 but had been defeated in the 1932 election. When the Philippines received self-government as a commonwealth in 1935, the electorate not only had to choose a president but also had to reelect the national assembly. Julio Nalundasan, a member of the new president's Nacionalista Party, won the Ilocos Norte seat. On September 20, 1935, Nalundasan was murdered, and suspicion eventually fell on Ferdinand Marcos. In 1939, while at the University of the Philippines College of Law, he was tried and convicted for Nalundasan's murder, while studying for his bar examinations. During the trial, Marcos took his bar examinations and scored the highest grade of those taking the test in 1939, receiving his bachelor of laws cum laude. Marcos' scores on the written examinations were so high that suspicious officials subsequently examined him orally, and he again succeeded in scoring very high. The case made the front pages of all Philippine newspapers.

In 1940, the Philippine Supreme Court overturned Marcos' conviction. Marcos subsequently began practicing in his father's law firm. In November, 1940, Marcos joined the Philippine Army as a third lieutenant, leaving the service with the rank of colonel in February, 1946. Marcos was present at the final defense of Bataan and endured harsh treatment at the hands of his Japanese captors. After his escape, Marcos organized a resistance group, the Ang Ma Maharlika. In the confused atmosphere of the Philippines under occupation, many exploits were accredited to the group.

Life's Work

Marcos' war record brought him new prominence and controversy. Depending on contradictory Philippine governmental reports, Marcos received thirty-two to thirty-four decorations for distinguished service. None of Marcos' awards was received in the immediate aftermath of battle; Marcos received two American medals and many of his Philippine awards on the basis of affidavits.

The United States gave the Philippines independence and a new constitution on July 4, 1946. Marcos had begun working in March in the law firm that had defended him in his murder trial, Vincente Francisco. In 1947, Marcos served as the Technical Assistant to the Philippine president, Manuel Roxas y Acuña; among his activities, Marcos visited the United States as a member of the Philippine Veterans Mission, which pushed through support for Filipino veterans to have access to the opportunities of the American GI Bill of Rights. As a prelude to his political ambitions, Marcos established his residency in his home province, Ilocos Norte, winning his first election in 1949. Marcos, as a member of the Liberal Party, ran for the newly formed House of Representatives on the slogan "Elect me a Congressman now, and I pledge you an Ilocano President in twenty years." At age thirty-two, Marcos was the youngest member of the House of Representatives. Marcos authored the Import Control Law and subsequently became chairman of the committee implementing the ordinance.

In April, 1954, Marcos met a beauty queen from Tacloban, Leyte, Imelda Romualdez, and proposed on the spot. On May 1, 1954, Marcos married the twenty-three-year-old Imelda following a hectic eleven-day courtship. In 1957, Marcos was elected for a second time, serving as minority floor leader and acting temporary president of the Liberal Party.

After three successful terms in congress, in 1959 Marcos was elected a senator. Marcos quickly became the minority floor leader of the Philippine senate, and on April 6, 1963, was elected senate president, taking over from the elderly Eulogio Rodriguez, president of the Nacionalista Party. Marcos in 1961 had supported as Liberal Party candidate Diosadado Macapagal, serving as his campaign manager in return for a promise of reciprocal support in 1965. As this arrangement fell through, Marcos changed sides; as Macapagal refused to honor his 1961 agreement with Marcos to step aside, in April, 1964, Marcos was sworn in as a Nacionalista candidate by José Laurel. In November, 1964, Marcos won the Nacionalista Party presidential nomination; Imelda Marcos managed the campaign.

The November, 1965, presidential campaign was one of the most expensive and sordid in Philippine political history. Both candidates traveled widely, and used increasingly harsh rhetoric. Marcos accused Macapagal of ineptitude, and Macapagal in turn labeled Marcos a "murderer, a thief, a swindler, a forger, and a threat to the country." Marcos won the contest by 670,000 votes, replacing Macapagal and becoming the sixth President of the Philippines on December 30, 1965. Marcos attempted at this point to portray himself as a "man of the people," listing his total assets as $30,000 and his annual salary as president as $5,600. In his January, 1966, "State of the Nation" address, Marcos vowed to be a "leader of the people," reaffirming his promise to "make this nation great again." Campaigns were undertaken to reduce crime and corruption, while in the countryside a limited program of land reform was inaugurated to reduce insurgent influence.

While Marcos had run on a platform of no Filipino aid to American forces in Vietnam, he now changed his mind. Noncombatant construction teams were sent in late 1966, an action which in turn generated increased support for Marcos in Washington. In October, 1966, Marcos hosted a seven-nation conference of countries allied in defending Vietnam, winning wide praise for his statesmanship.

Philippine problems began to mount; in 1968, the Communist Party of the Philippines (CPP) was organized, taking over from the older Partido Komunistang Pilipinas (PKP), whose leadership had been decimated by arrests. In 1969, the CPP allied itself with the remains of the military arm of the PKP; the resultant amalgam was named the New Peoples Army (NPA). In the midst of this growing threat, Marcos won his second term as president.

In 1970, a constitutional convention began rewriting the country's constitution; the president attempted to influence the convention, an action which created an outcry among student groups. Marcos attempted to persuade the delegates to the convention to include a provision that would allow an incumbent president to run for a third term. In January, riot police were set upon student demonstrators, who fought back and suffered bloody reprisals. The ensuing wave of protest was known as the "First-Quarter Storm."

Throughout 1972, unrest continued to grow. A bad monsoon season devastated the country's rice crop, and urban terrorist bombings were on the increase. A vehicle carrying the defense minister, Juan Ponce Enrile, was attacked in September, which led Marcos to declare martial law. Enrile later stated that the attack was staged to allow Marcos to implement his plans. As Marcos' second term was ending, he was unable to stand for a third term; his assumption of emergency powers allowed him to evade these constitutional niceties.

Martial law was announced to the nation on September 23, 1972, and was repealed only in January, 1981. To counteract the unfavorable publicity, Marcos called for the formation of a "new society," in which a "democratic revolution" would abolish the oligarchy's control of the nation. The underlying idea was that connections would no longer matter, but the optimism and goodwill generated by the gestures were short-lived. Marcos labeled his actions "constitutional authoritarianism."

Marcos declared in General Order Number One that he would "govern the nation and direct the operation of the entire government. . . ." A second general order allowed the minister of defense broad powers to detain individuals deemed dangerous by the government. Senator Benigno Aquino was picked up and the newspapers, radio, and television were shut down while the government determined their loyalty. Congress was shut down, and the constitution suspended.

In his address to the nation Marcos stated that he was acting in accordance with the 1935 Philippine constitution. Marcos rejected all subsequent criticism, expanding the police powers of the military. A number of delegates to the constitutional convention were arrested. The rump convention's activities were ordered by the president to be hurried along; on November 29, 1972, a draft constitution was approved.

The single event that galvanized the country against the Marcos regime was the assassination of Benigno Aquino on August 21, 1983, at Manila International Airport. Aquino was the country's leading dissident and had returned to Manila after several years in exile in the United States. The official government version of the attack stated that a lone gunman was responsible, who was then killed by governmental security forces. On October 24, 1984, the Agrava Board, which had been charged with investigating the murder, concluded that there had been a military plot. The political frustration caused by Aquino's assassination, combined with growing anger at Imelda's extravagance, caused a surge of unrest in the country.

On November 3, 1985, Marcos announced the holding of presidential elections, in response to American pressure. Aquino's widow, Corazon, announced her candidacy. Following the February 7, 1986, election, both sides claimed victory; on February 25 each group held inauguration ceremonies. Foreign observers, a group that included a number of American congressmen, believed that Marcos' claims of victory were built on the blatantly fraudulent tactics used by his supporters. Cardinal Jaime Sin, long a prominent oppositionist, urged Catholics to go into the streets and protect the rebel army units that were disassociating themselves from the regime. Later that evening, crowds estimated to number more than a million surged into the streets of Manila and began making their way to the Malacanang Palace.

The Marcos entourage hurriedly departed the palace and were taken by helicopter to Clark Airfield. The Marcoses first flew to Guam and then to Hawaii. In Manila, the excesses of the departed regime were symbolized by the discovery of 1,060 pairs of Imelda's shoes, along with 580 ballroom gowns. Medical equipment, including a dialysis machine, left in the palace confirmed the poor state of Marcos' health.

The Marcos entourage was immediately charged with gross corruption by Corazon Aquino's government, which began to use the courts in an attempt to recover the billions that they claimed Marcos had stolen. Marcos died of cardiac arrest complicated by kidney and lung failure early in the morning of September 28, 1989. Aquino's government has denied a family request to allow his remains to be returned to the Philippines for burial.

Summary

For a leader who embodied such hopes when he first became president, Ferdinand E. Marcos' fall from grace has been extraordinarily complete. On his election to president in November, 1965, the Philippines seemed poised to enter a new era. Marcos vowed to right some of the more blatant abuses of the system, and a number of his actions, among them land reforms, eased life for the poorer segments of Philippine society. Marcos also proved himself a loyal ally of the United States during this period, sending Philippine troops to South Vietnam, a decision that was not popular at home.

Marcos' second term was more turbulent, with Marcos declaring martial law in September, 1972, to repress a Communist insurgency. While the crackdown was extended to include a wide field of antigovernment critics, Marcos proclaimed a "new society" that, despite the political harshness, included national benefits such as a drop in the inflation rate and increased government revenues.

As Marcos continued his "constitutional authoritarianism," the country grew slowly more disenchanted with its ruler. The increasingly opulent lifestyle of the Marcoses offended many in a country with one of the lowest levels of per capita income in the world, while the increasingly harsh repression of all political dissent blocked any legitimate outlets for the people's frustration. The blatant as-sassination of Benigno Aquino in August, 1983, proved the final straw for many Filipinos. Marcos' war record has been challenged by historians, journalists, and politicians. Marcos died accused of plundering his country of billions of dollars. Aquino would not allow his body to be returned to the Philippines for burial, though flags were flown at half-mast. Perhaps Marcos is best summed up in his own words: "I do not care how brave a President is. . . . If he violates the will of the people, he shall be eliminated."

Bibliography

Celoza, Albert F. *Ferdinand Marcos and the Philippines: The Political Economy of Authoritarianism.* Westport, Conn.: Greenwood Press, 1997. Celoza examines Marcos' fourteen-year authoritarian rule of the Philippines. Analyses are provided concerning opposition to his rule, support by the United States, and support by Filipino business and military interests.

Ellison, Katherine. *Imelda: Steel Butterfly of the Philippines.* New York: McGraw-Hill, 1988. Ellison visited the Philippines several times and interviewed Imelda there. She was present in Manila during the last days of the Marcos regime, and her account is vivid and informal.

McDougald, Charles C. *The Marcos File: Was He a Philippine Hero or Corrupt Tyrant?* San Francisco: San Francisco Publishers, 1987. For Marcos' war record and the controversy surrounding his military honors, this is an incisive (and skeptical) work. McDougald made use of numerous contacts in the Philippines, including Cardinal Sin. While the work's commentary on Marcos' alleged military exploits is quite harsh, extensive use is made of both primary source records and personal interviews.

Mamot, Patricia R. *People Power.* Quezon City, Philippines: New Day, 1986. Mamot gives an arresting, immediate account of the last days of the Marcos dynasty.

Shaplen, Robert. *A Turning Wheel.* London: Deutsch, and New York: Random House, 1979. Shaplen spent three decades as a correspondent covering Asian affairs. Shaplen met Marcos several times, and his work is a good accounting of the successes and failures of the Marcos regime.

Spence, Hartzell. *For Every Tear a Victory: The Story of Ferdinand E. Marcos.* New York: McGraw-Hill, 1964. This book was a campaign biography assembled by Spence in an uncritical atmosphere; it is of slight historical value but of interest as an artifact of the Marcos regime.

Steinberg, David Joel. *The Philippines: A Singular and a Plural Place.* 3d ed. Boulder, Colo.: Westview, 1994. Steinberg provides an overview of the problems besetting the Philippines during and immediately after martial law. His coverage of the Communist insurgency and the regime's failure to deal with it is especially useful.

Thompson, Mark R. *The Anti-Marcos Struggle: Personalistic Rule and Democratic Transition in the Philippines.* New Haven, Conn., and London: Yale University Press, 1995. Thompson considers the peaceful transition from the authoritarian rule of Marcos to democracy under Corazon Aquino. The author makes use of 150 personal interviews and previously unpublished materials collected during his trips to the Philippines.

John C. K. Daly

JACQUES MARITAIN

Born: November 18, 1882; Paris, France
Died: April 28, 1973; Toulouse, France
Areas of Achievement: Religion, theology, and philosophy
Contribution: Perhaps the most influential Catholic philosopher of the twentieth century, Maritain spearheaded a Catholic revival in France and, more broadly, the revival of philosophical Thomism in Europe and the United States. Although a traditionalist, philosophically speaking, he was one of the century's foremost proponents of Christian democracy, and his work helped pave the way for the reforms of Vatican II in the early 1960's.

Early Life

The story of Jacques Maritain's formative years is one of the oft-told legends of Catholic rebirth in the twentieth century. Born in Paris on November 18, 1882, Maritain was the son of Paul Maritain, a prosperous lawyer, and Geneviève Favre, granddaughter of a founder of France's Third Republic. Reared in an atmosphere of liberal Protestantism, he entered the Sorbonne in 1901, by which time he considered himself an unbeliever and a revolutionary socialist; he was, in short, the very embodiment of French secularism at the turn of the century.

At the Sorbonne, however, Maritain encountered Charles Péguy, who, having been a dedicated defender of left-republican ideals during the infamous Dreyfus affair of the 1890's, was in the process of severing his ties with the victorious Dreyfusards. The ideals of the affair, in Péguy's view, had degenerated into cynical parliamentary alliances and assaults on the Church. Péguy also attacked the Sorbonne—a "positivist Church" as he called it—for its new scientific curriculum, which he deemed barren and amoral. Under Péguy's influence, Maritain and Raissa Oumansoff, a Russian Jewess whom the latter had met at the Sorbonne, underwent a profound spiritual crisis. Unwilling to live with the determinism and moral relativism imparted to them by their scientific training, the two formed a suicide pact in 1902.

Yet Péguy had also introduced his young followers to the views of Henri Bergson, then the most celebrated lecturer at the Collège de France and the perfect philosophical antidote for the Sorbonne's materialism. Bergson's message was clear and therapeutic: Neither scientific method nor rational analysis, he asserted, is appropriate to the study of man; authentic human experience can be grasped not through the intellect's spatial categories, but rather through an intuitive union with life's natural flow, *la durée*. Thus freed from positivism by Bergson, Maritain married Raissa in 1904, and shortly thereafter fell under the spell of Léon Bloy, a Catholic poet and self-proclaimed "pilgrim of the absolute." A paradoxical figure, Bloy combined a socialist's egalitarianism with the intransigent faith of a convert, which he was. Attracted by Bloy's certainty and fervor, the Maritains both converted in 1906. Péguy followed suit shortly thereafter, as did quite a number of elite young Frenchmen before the war. Thus, Maritain is often said to have paved the way for a generation's conversion from secular and even anticlerical republicanism to the Catholic church.

Life's Work

As important as Maritain's conversion was the broad historical context within which it took place. Far from signaling the end of clerical influence in France, the separation of church and state in 1905 created a powerful Catholic backlash, which was enhanced after 1907 by the so-called modernist crisis within the Church. Responding to the ongoing attempt of reforming clergymen to reconcile Catholicism with the modern world, Pope Pius X issued a series of condemnations reaffirming the Church's opposition to secular science and liberalism. The pope's "integral Catholicism" repudiated individualism, laissez-faire capitalism, and socialism, embracing instead the vision of a universal Christian community publicly regulated by the Church under a Thomist orthodoxy.

It is no surprise, then, that Maritain's budding Catholicism was nurtured by an integral Catholic, the Père Humbert Clérissac, whom he encountered in 1908. Clerissac was an admirer of the neo-royalist Charles Maurras, a pro-Catholic agnostic who in 1899 had formed the reactionary, anti-Semitic league Action Française, in response to Dreyfusard liberalism. The young Maritain, who disdained politics and would later claim never to have read Maurras' works, nevertheless mirrored the belief of his spiritual mentor that only the Action Française could prepare France for the reestablishment of an integral Christian order.

More important to Maritain than Clérissac's politics were the priest's philosophical views: He was a Thomist. It was under Clérissac's guidance that Maritain fashioned his first philosophical works. In 1914, he published *La Philosophie bergsonienne* (*Bergsonian Philosophy and Thomism*, 1955), a comprehensive assault on the reigning monarch of French philosophy from the vantage point of Thomism. This work not only made a name for the young philosopher and set him on an intellectual path for life but also marked the beginning of the Thomist revival in the twentieth century.

Maritain's argument was twofold. First, while lauding Bergson for the "genuinely liberating effect" of his philosophical assault on positivism, Maritain faulted him for his repudiation of those basic Aristotelian categories of subject and object, cause and effect, mover and moved, without which Christian theology is impossible. Second, Maritain focused on Bergson's critique of the intellect. Thomism, he argued, while rejecting with Bergson the "perverted intellect" of the modern mechanists, does not "rend the living unity of the mind," as does Bergson, into the realms of intellect and

intuition, but rather posits the "integrity of body and soul." Thus, from the Sorbonne's intellectualism, which had left him feeling psychologically fragmented and morally uncommitted, Maritain had passed through the Bergsonian critique of the intellect to a new Thomistic intellectualism which left him feeling psychologically integrated and authentically Catholic.

Maritain's prolific writings between 1914 and his death bear the mark of this second, Thomist conversion. In such works as *Art et scholastique* (1920; *Art and Scholasticism*, 1962), *Science et sagesse* (1935; *Science and Wisdom*, 1940), *Scholasticism and Politics* (1940), and *Court Traité de l'existence et l'existant* (1947; *Existence and the Existent*, 1957), he continued to apply his neo-Thomist analysis to the realms of aesthetics, politics, science, and philosophy. He was at least equally successful at spreading the Thomist gospel by word of mouth: A professor of philosophy at the Institut Catholique in Paris between 1914 and 1933, at Toronto's Medieval Institute between 1933 and 1945, and at Princeton and various other American universities thereafter, Maritain also began in 1919 a Thomist study-circle at Meudon which would become a famous meeting place for Catholic intellectuals from around the world.

Whatever controversy remains over Maritain's career, however, revolves around his early association with the Action Française and his break with the reactionary league following its condemnation by Pope Pius XI in 1926. That Maritain was deeply involved with the movement is beyond question. A founding member in 1919 of the pro-Maurrasian journal, *La Revue universelle*, he also authored two works in the early 1920's, *Antimoderne* (1922) and *Trois réformateurs: Luther, Descartes, Rousseau* (1925; *Three Reformers: Luther, Descartes, Rousseau*, 1936), which reflected a passionate hostility toward secular individualism and liberal democracy. In the latter work, for example, he renounced the three reformers in question for having severed reason from faith, fostered the growth of relativism and subjectivism, and created a cult of the individual. Indeed, notwithstanding a certain ambivalence concerning Maurras' stress on secular politics, as well as his agnosticism and anti-Semitism, it was the royalist's critique of secular liberalism that attracted the young philosopher.

Yet, while he initially hoped to save Maurras from the papal ax, once the decision was made, Maritain supported it actively. In 1927, he published *Primauté du spirituel* (*The Things That Are Not Caesar's*, 1930), which repudiated Maurras' notion that the religious transformation of society must be preceded by its political transformation, and his own political views seem to have undergone a marked shift thereafter. During the 1930's, Maritain became one among several important French Catholic voices to speak out against Francisco Franco, Benito Mussolini, and Adolf Hitler. Indeed, Maritain's positions and works of his epoch earned for him, in some quarters, the epithet "Christian Marxist." In *Humanisme intégral* (1936; *Integral Humanism*, 1968), he assaulted the "anthropocentric humanism" of modern capitalism, which, he argued, dehumanized rich and poor alike through its materialism and competitive individualism. Eschewing, however, both revolutionary Marxism and reactionary royalism, he advocated a Christian approach to social justice, a "spiritual revolution" based on the moral recognition of the individual human being as an intrinsically social and spiritual reality rather than as an isolated material atom.

Impressed by the political atmosphere of the United States, where he resided during and after World War II, Maritain continued to evolve toward Christian Democracy in such works as *Christianisme et démocratie* (1943; *Christianity and Democracy*, 1944), *La Personne et le bien commun* (1947; *The Person and the Common Good*, 1947), and *Man and the State* (1951). Apart from expressing his horror of Fascism and totalitarianism in these works, Maritain argued that democracy, purified of bourgeois materialism and infused with a sense of the sacredness of the human person, is nothing more than a secular name for the Christian ideal.

In 1945, Maritain became the living link between French democracy and the Church, accepting, at Charles de Gaulle's insistence, the post of French ambassador to the Vatican, where he served for three years. Maritain's relations with the Church during the final years of his life, however, were ambiguous at best. On the one hand, his post-1926 works, as well as his high profile as a symbol of "left Catholicism," had an undeniable influence on the reforms of the Second Vatican Council in 1962. Yet, in his final work, *Le Paysan de la Garonne* (1966; *The Peasant of the Garonne*, 1968), Maritain scandalized Church reformers by raging against their excesses. Embracing the council's declarations in favor of religious liberty and Christian democracy as well as its repudiation of racism

and anti-Semitism, he nevertheless reaffirmed doctrinal orthodoxy and firmly warned the Church against accommodation with the modern world. Thus Maritain, who had been formed in the context of one modernist crisis, ended his career perhaps fittingly, by protecting the Church against what appeared to be another.

Summary

Seeking a single thread which unites Jacques Maritain the young revolutionary socialist, Maritain the Maurrasian Catholic and Thomist, and Maritain the Christian democrat and humanist is a daunting task from which most scholars have understandably shied away. He is typically cast either as a great humanitarian who was politically indiscreet in his youth, or as a weak soul caught in the gravity of stronger ones, ultimately tying himself to the ever-shifting party line of the Church. Certainly Maritain's series of powerful mentors—Péguy, Bergson, Bloy, and Clérissac—as well as his obedient response to the condemnation of Action Française in 1926, give some credence to the latter interpretation.

Yet, one fact does seem to reconcile the philosopher's many faces: Whether of the socialist left, the Catholic right, or the Christian democratic center, Maritain was ever and always opposed to bourgeois liberalism. Indeed, he refused for most of his life to be placed on the scale of secular politics: "To be neither left nor right," he wrote in 1967, "means simply that one intends to keep his sanity." Despairing of the scientific materialism and soulless individualism of secular liberalism, he dreamed instead of a transcendent spiritual community. Through his capacity to transform that vision, employing the tools of Thomist philosophy, into a powerful critique of modernity, Maritain was able to revitalize Catholic thought in the twentieth century.

Bibliography

Amato, Joseph. *Mounier and Maritain: A French Catholic Understanding of the Modern World.* University: University of Alabama Press, 1975. An examination of Maritain and his disciple Emmanuel Mounier, a Catholic thinker and social egalitarian of the 1930's and 1940's, in the context of French politics and Catholic revival in the twentieth century. Amato offers a good historical backdrop for understanding Maritain's work and influence.

Doering, Bernard. *Jacques Maritain and the French Catholic Intellectuals.* Notre Dame, Ind.: University of Notre Dame Press, 1983. An in-depth account of Maritain's relations with such important French intellectuals as Charles Maurras, Henri Massis, and Georges Bernanos. This work tends toward apologia but is again useful in placing Maritain into historical context. Extensive citation of Maritain's private letters, but no bibliography.

Evans, Joseph W., ed. *Jacques Maritain, the Man and His Achievement.* New York: Sheed and Ward, 1963. An eclectic collection of essays on Maritain covering such topics as his aesthetic views, his moral philosophy, his politics, and his impact on Thomism in the United States. Most of the essays are short and easily accessible.

Gallagher, Donald, and Idella Gallagher. *The Achievement of Jacques and Raissa Maritain: A Bibliography, 1906-1961.* New York: Doubleday, 1962. While obviously dated, this still represents an excellent starting point for the English reader beginning research on Maritain.

Kraynak, Robert P. "The Christian Democracy of Glenn Tinder and Jacques Maritain." *Perspectives on Political Science* 27, no. 2 (Spring 1998). Discusses the philosophies of Maritain and Tinder, focusing on their views on the relationship between Christianity and democracy.

Maritain, Raissa. *We Have Been Friends Together.* Translated by Julie Kernan. New York: Longman, 1942.

———. *Adventures in Grace.* Translated by Julie Kernan. New York: Longman, 1945. These two volumes of memoirs, written by Maritain's wife, span the period between 1900 and World War II. While obviously biased, these graceful and moving recollections are indispensable for students of Maritain's life and times.

Smith, Brooke Williams. *Jacques Maritain, Antimodern or Ultramodern?* New York: Elsevier, 1976. A concise analysis of Maritain's philosophy of history, which has the virtue of providing synopses of several of his most important works. Also provides a biographical sketch and an excellent bibliography of works both by and about Maritain.

Paul M. Cohen

GEORGE C. MARSHALL

Born: December 31, 1880; Uniontown, Pennsylvania

Died: October 16, 1959; Washington, D.C.

Area of Achievement: Government and politics

Contribution: General Marshall created the United States Army of World War II, picked the commanders who led it to victory, and exemplified the best in the American military tradition: civilian control, integrity, and competence.

Early Life

George Catlett Marshall, Jr., was born in 1880, the second son of George C. Marshall, a businessman, and Laura Bradford Marshall. He was an enterprising boy who enjoyed history and who, possibly because of his reading, became interested in a military career. After attending Uniontown's public schools, he went to the Virginia Military Academy at Lexington. By this time, young Marshall had grown to just under six feet in height and was tough; despite weighing only 145 pounds, he starred in football. His bearing became very military, and he gained self-confidence along with military skills; as first captain, he made his voice heard across the length of the parade ground. Marshall's manner grew austere, and his "cold blue and seldom smiling eyes" were piercing to those who did less than their best. Despite his bony face, under a thatch of sandy hair, he was becoming a formidable person.

Upon his graduation, Marshall married the beauty of Lexington, Elizabeth "Lily" Coles, on February 11, 1902. Three years after her death, in 1927, he married Katherine Tupper Brown.

Life's Work

Marshall was commissioned a second lieutenant of infantry in the United States Army in January, 1902, with date of rank from 1901. He was immediately assigned to the newly conquered Philippine Islands, where he was often on his own with troops, and where he revealed the abilities to learn rapidly and to discover and put to best use his subordinates' talents. He served in Oklahoma and Texas before being assigned, in 1906, to the Infantry and Cavalry School at Fort Leavenworth. Promoted to first lieutenant that year, he stood first in his class and came to the notice of General J. Franklin Bell, the commandant, who kept Marshall on as an instructor. Displaying unusual talent as an instructor, Marshall also learned to watch several maneuvers at once in war games. Returned to the Philippines in 1913, he was made chief of staff for one side in maneuvers, despite his junior rank, effectively commanding five thousand troops. He also visited Japan and Manchuria to learn how the Japanese had won the Russo-Japanese War (1904-1905).

Reassigned as aide to General Bell, Marshall was promoted to captain in August, 1916. As the United States entered World War I, in April, 1917, Bell became commander of the Eastern Department. Marshall virtually ran the office during Bell's illness, learning how to cut red tape in the hasty mobilization. Because of his now great reputation as both a thinker and a doer, Marshall was sent to France with the First Division, becoming its chief of operations. He became a major in November, 1917, and a lieutenant colonel in December. By July, 1918, he was an acting colonel at General John J. Pershing's headquarters, already famous for his gifts of organization and improvisation and nicknamed Wizard. There, and as chief of operations for the First Army, Marshall learned how to maneuver large bodies of troops and how to solve the many problems that arise in war.

At the end of World War I, reduced to his permanent rank of major, Marshall became Pershing's aide. Because of Pershing's trust in him, Marshall's duties were broad; he took part in inspections of many army posts and in Pershing's dealings with Congress, coming to know intimately the army he would command after 1939. Also serving in China, the Pacific Northwest, the Midwest, at the Army War College, and as assistant commandant of the Infantry School, he came to know well some 150 future generals of World War II. A colonel again by 1933, he became a brigadier general in 1936. In 1938, he was assigned to Washington, D.C., first as chief of war plans and then as deputy chief of staff of the army.

On September 1, 1939, as World War II began in Europe, Marshall became chief of staff of the United States Army, with the temporary rank of four-star general. President Franklin D. Roosevelt named him to the post because of his breadth of experience, his ability to organize and to train troops, and his ability even to be unorthodox, qualities desperately needed in the building of the army.

Marshall took command of an army that was small, poorly equipped, and poorly trained. He built a reputation for truth with both the president and Congress, won their respect and support, and slowly obtained the money to build a modern army. He was aided by a new secretary of war, Henry L. Stimson, who, after 1940, used his own considerable influence on Marshall's behalf. The task was formidable, for World War II brought with it the blitzkrieg, the "lightning war" of tanks and mobility. Marshall had not only to argue for money but also to find commanders who would use resources effectively. He promoted such men as Dwight D. Eisenhower, Omar N. Bradley, Henry H. Arnold, Mark W. Clark, George S. Patton, and Matthew Ridgway. Marshall was also tireless in supervising the development of new weapons and equipment and of training and maneuvers.

When the United States entered the war after the Pearl Harbor attack of December 7, 1941, Marshall also had to work with allies, especially the British, but also the Russians, Free French, and Nationalist Chinese. He had to deal with British Prime Minister Winston Churchill, who saw himself as a military genius, and British reluctance to attack Adolf Hitler's strong fortifications in Western Europe. Britons were afraid of such trench warfare as had decimated the armies of World War I. Marshall agreed with reasonable British ideas, such as clearing North Africa of Axis forces, but kept the focus on plans for the invasion of France and the defeat of Nazi Germany. He personally chose Eisenhower to command the North African invasion, worked with FDR and Stimson to limit later Mediterranean operations to Italy, and built an ever larger American army for invading Europe. From less than 200,000 men in 1939, the army and its air force grew to some 8,300,000 by early 1945, Marshall also building an air force which was capable of destroying German industry. While accomplishing all this, he never forgot that soldiers are human beings and constantly guarded their welfare, from making sure that they received needed medical treatment and their mail, to explaining the reasons for the war to Americans who had to fight thousands of miles from home.

Marshall wanted to command the invasion of France in 1944 but revealed no disappointment when FDR insisted that he remain as chief of staff, saying that he could not sleep well with Marshall out of the country. Marshall then gave Eisenhower the command, supporting him in every possible way. Marshall's own job became one of keeping supplies flowing and mediating between General Douglas MacArthur and the navy's commanders in the Pacific. Marshall supported the navy's strategy of a direct attack on Japan itself, via the Pacific islands, rather than MacArthur's longer route through Southeast Asia.

Named a five-star general of the army on December 15, 1944, Marshall retired as chief of staff on November 26, 1945. President Harry S Truman soon asked him to try to bring peace to China, then torn by civil war. Marshall spent almost a year seeking some agreement between Nationalists and Communists but ultimately failed. Truman then appointed him secretary of state on January 21, 1947, and he served until January, 1949, when ill health forced his retirement. As secretary of state, he helped devise the Marshall Plan, massive economic aid to Western Europe which literally rebuilt that region, and helped Truman find ways to deal with the Cold War. He was awarded the Nobel Peace Prize in 1953 because of the Marshall Plan. He served as head of the American Red Cross from 1949 to 1950 and as secretary of defense from September, 1950, to September, 1951. His task was again organizing mobilization, this time for the Korean War, and finding a new commander for Korea and Japan when Truman fired the insubordinate MacArthur. He chose Matthew Ridgway, whose World War II record was superb. Marshall last served his country as its representative at the coronation of Queen Elizabeth II of Great Britain in June, 1953.

Summary

Marshall represented the best in the American military tradition: belief in civilian control; uncompromising integrity; quiet competence. Able to learn from the broad experience of a long career, he put what he had learned to work in the United States' most significant and dangerous war, that against the Axis powers. A superb organizer, he created the army of World War II, saw that it was competently commanded, kept it well supplied, and never forgot the welfare and morale of the troops in the field. He was able to deal with foreign politicians and military officers with both tact and force, ultimately putting his own stamp on the winning strategies. Indeed, Winston Churchill described Marshall as "the true organizer of victory."

Marshall's devotion to his country permitted President Truman to call on him repeatedly for further service, despite the general's advancing age and worsening health. Marshall attempted an impossible mission in China, led the State Department for two years with an impressive record of realism regarding the Soviet Union, helped rebuild Western Europe, and, as secretary of defense, turned the chaos of sudden remobilization into order.

Bibliography

Alperovitz, Gar, et al. "Marshall, Truman, and the Decision to Drop the Bomb." *International Security* 16, no. 3 (Winter 1991). The author considers the roles of Marshall and Harry Truman in the decision to use the atomic bomb in Hiroshima and Nagasaki.

Ferrell, Robert H. *George C. Marshall.* In *The American Secretaries of State and Their Diplomacy*, vol. 15. New York: Cooper Square, 1966. The only major work on Marshall as secretary of state, it was written before many documents were declassified. Gracefully written and well balanced.

Marshall, George Catlett. *The Papers of George Catlett Marshall.* Vol. 1, *"The Soldierly Spirit," December, 1880-June, 1939.* Edited by Larry I. Bland and Fred L. Hadsel. Baltimore: Johns Hopkins University Press, 1981. This is the first in a series of volumes containing letters, speeches, and other revealing documents.

Marshall, Katherine T. *Together: Annals of an Army Wife.* Atlanta: Tupper and Love, and London: Blandford Press, 1946. An affectionate but useful memoir.

Morrow, Lance. "George C. Marshall: The Last Great American?" *Smithsonian* 28, no. 5 (August, 1997). Discusses Marshall's achievements as Army Chief of Staff in World War II and his Marshall Plan for the reconstruction of Europe after the war.

Mosley, Leonard. *Marshall: Hero for Our Times.* New York: Hearst, 1982; as *Marshall: Organizer of Victory,* London: Methuen, 1982. The best full biography, covering Marshall's army career and postwar civilian appointments. Especially good on the controversies surrounding Pearl Harbor, Marshall and MacArthur, and the World War II summit meetings.

Pogue, Forrest C. *George C. Marshall: Education of a General, 1880-1939.* New York: Viking Press, 1963; London: MacGibbon and Kee, 1964. The first volume of the definitive biography, based on exhaustive research. Covers Marshall's boyhood, education, and army career to his appointment as chief of staff.

————. *George C. Marshall: Ordeal and Hope, 1939-1942.* New York: Viking Press, 1966; London: MacGibbon and Kee, 1968. Second volume of the definitive biography. Tells of Marshall's creation of the United States Army of World War II, his search for new leadership, and the early war years.

————. *George C. Marshall: Organizer of Victory, 1943-1945.* New York: Viking Press, 1972. The third volume of the definitive biography carries the tale to victory in Europe in May, 1945, including summit conferences and the invasion of France in June, 1944.

Robert W. Sellen

THURGOOD MARSHALL

Born: July 2, 1908; Baltimore, Maryland
Died: January 24, 1993; Bethesda, Maryland
Area of Achievement: Law
Contribution: As an advocate and jurist, Marshall has had a sustained commitment to equal justice under the law.

Early Life

Thurgood Marshall was born July 2, 1908, in Baltimore, Maryland. His father, William Canfield Marshall, was employed as a waiter and came to be head steward at the affluent Gibson Island Club on the Chesapeake Bay by the time Marshall reached school age. Marshall's mother, née Norma Arica Williams, taught in the Baltimore schools for more than thirty years. Both of their families had resided in Maryland for some time. The Marshall family enjoyed a comfortable, stable, middle-class existence. The achievement of this status by a black family less than forty years after the abolition of slavery in the United States is remarkable. Although Maryland, in general, and Baltimore, in particular, were quite well-known for their relatively large free black populations, even modest financial legacies were the exception rather than the rule for most blacks in those decades following the Civil War.

One of Marshall's great grandfathers had been a slave, and little is known about him. Marshall's paternal grandfather, Thoroughgood Marshall, served in the United States merchant marine for many years, and his maternal grandfather, Isaiah Olive Branch Williams, also spent a number of years traveling abroad. Both gave up a life at sea to settle in the Baltimore area; also, both owned and operated grocery stores.

Marshall grew up in a world of books, opera, and tales of adventure. He came into contact with black men who were important and influential in their own communities, and, consequently, he lived in a world of conversation, debate, curiosity, and political and racial awareness. He enjoyed a supportive, extended family network which protected and encouraged in him the growth and development of an independent, well-adjusted, and assertive personality.

Two ambitious, disciplined, and playful young men grew up in the Marshall household. Both sons earned undergraduate degrees at Lincoln University in Oxford, Pennsylvania. Opened in 1856, the historically black university offered the two Marshall youths unique educational and social opportunities. In addition to employing an all-white, essentially Princeton-trained faculty, the college attracted a variety of individuals from throughout the black community. Marshall's classmates included, for example, Kwame Nkrumah, president of Ghana between 1960 and 1966, and Nnamdi Azikiwe, who served as president of Nigeria between 1963 and 1966. Marshall's older brother, William Aubrey, chose medicine as his profession and became a surgeon. Only a quarter of a century before Marshall's graduation there were only 1,734 black doctors in the United States and even fewer black lawyers—only 728.

Before he was graduated from Lincoln, the gregarious Marshall married Vivian Burey and became more focused in his academic interests. He was graduated at the top of his class and chose to attend Howard University Law School in Washington, D.C.

Marshall's school years do not, at first glance, seem to have anticipated his participation in a more equal, more fully integrated society. He grew up in an essentially segregated community, attended segregated public schools, a black university, and a predominantly black professional school. Clearly, this environment reflected the legacy of racism, yet Marshall's experiences during this period helped him to secure his racial identity, his long-standing principles, and his tendency to work and to fight for those things in which he believed. During this period, too, he came into contact with faculty members of vision who recognized his talent, challenging and directing the lanky, brash, and assertive young man in his preparations for a highly competitive profession. Particularly important was Marshall's association with Charles H. Houston, a Phi Beta Kappa at Amherst and a Harvard Law School graduate. Under Houston's tutelage, Marshall excelled as a law student; later, when Houston became counsel to the National Association for the Advancement of Colored People (NAACP), he hired Marshall as assistant counsel.

Life's Work

Marshall began his law career when he was graduated from the Howard University Law School at the head of his class in 1933. His career began inauspiciously in Baltimore, Maryland, as the Great

Depression hung over the nation. Marshall was not immune to the hardships most Americans were experiencing and found it necessary to supplement the meager income he earned in his law practice with money he earned by acting as counsel to the local NAACP branch. The young lawyer unknowingly took the first step in an association through which he would reach the top of his profession.

In 1936, Marshall's former law professor and mentor, Charles Houston, invited him to accept the position of assistant special counsel to the NAACP in New York. The regularity of the small salary attached to the position was attractive to Marshall, and he was happy to renew his association with Houston, one of the top black attorneys in the United States.

Significantly, Marshall moved from being a practicing attorney to being a politician-lawyer, from counselor to advocate. In 1940, he became director-counsel of the NAACP Legal Defense Fund. In this capacity, he came to be known as a "pioneer civil rights lawyer" and the "legal champion of black Americans." He was, from his earliest involvement with the NAACP, an important figure in what was emerging as a remarkable alteration of the legal position of blacks in the United States.

Although the NAACP's legal team enjoyed a number of successes and victories under Marshall's leadership, his greatest legal triumph was in 1954, when he successfully argued before the Supreme Court in *Brown v. Board of Education of Topeka*, and the Court decided unanimously that school segregation violated the equal protection provision of the Fourteenth Amendment to the Constitution. Thereafter, in addition to enjoying greater prominence in his profession, Marshall, as President Lyndon B. Johnson would remark at a later date, had "already earned his place in history."

Marshall's nomination, in 1961, to a federal judgeship on the United States Court of Appeals by President John F. Kennedy was almost anticlimactic given Marshall's earlier victory. He agreed to serve, however, and after lengthy debate by the United States Senate, he won confirmation.

Citing competence, wisdom, and courage, President Johnson selected Marshall to become solicitor general of the United States. He was speedily confirmed by the Senate and became the government's chief legal spokesperson. At the same time, Marshall became the first black person to hold that position. Marshall, thanks to the interest of Presidents Kennedy and Johnson, was becoming more broadly engaged in the legal profession and less narrowly identified with the Civil Rights movement. In 1967, only two years after Marshall was appointed solicitor general, President Johnson, in perhaps the most dramatic appointment of his administration, named Marshall as his candidate to fill the vacancy created on the United States Supreme Court by the retirement of Justice Tom Clark.

Johnson's political instincts were never better or his moral leadership more pronounced. As the nation anguished over urban unrest and the Civil Rights movement began to crest, Johnson chose Marshall and others—Robert Weaver, the first black to hold a cabinet post; Andrew Brimmer, federal reserve board governor; Patricia Harris, ambassador to Luxembourg; Walter Washington, mayor of Washington, D.C.—to assume significant public offices. In his autobiography, *The Vantage Point* (1971), Johnson said that he had not chosen these leaders for the color of their skin:

But I also deeply believed that with these appointments Negro mothers could look at their children and hope with good reason that someday their sons and daughters might reach the highest offices their government could offer.

Johnson personally announced the appointment of Marshall on June 14, 1967. The American Bar Association (ABA) found the president's nominee "highly acceptable," and the Senate voted sixty-nine to eleven for confirmation on August 30, 1967.

Marshall's credentials were extraordinary, but when an old friend of the new justice was asked to account for his success, he observed that Marshall was a tolerant person who could relax in his interpersonal relationships, had an unusual ability to put people at ease, and was earnest about finding solutions to human problems.

On the Supreme Court, Marshall proved to be a skilled and practical jurist who had special concern for the plight of the poor and disadvantaged. Ramsey Clark, former attorney general of the United States and son of Justice Tom Clark, has argued that Marshall's full power as a jurist and his concern for humanity were most clearly demonstrated in his application of the principles of the Constitution to the death penalty.

Summary

Marshall had a far-reaching, direct, and dramatic impact on American life. He was a pioneer in the Civil Rights movement, successfully argued the case of *Brown v. Board of Education* and numerous other cases before the Supreme Court, served on the United States Court of Appeals for the Second Circuit, served as solicitor general of the United States, and was appointed to the Supreme Court.

Born black early in the twentieth century, he overcame the restrictions of a segregated society and worked to advance the cause of blacks in the United States. Marshall has become both a symbol of equal opportunity under the law and of the commitment to the rule of law. Marshall urged blacks to use the courts to secure their legal rights, successfully arguing their cases before the Supreme Court. These cases established milestones in the areas of voting rights, fair housing, and integration. As an attorney, he worked tirelessly to obtain factual data to improve the existence of racism and its negative impact upon the lives of the powerless. Marshall brought to the Supreme Court an understanding of the consequences of unequal justice under the law, and he extended this understanding to the elderly, the poor, women, and those on death row.

In poor health, Marshall retired from the bench in 1991.

Bibliography

Bland, Randall W. *Private Pressure on Public Law: The Legal Career of Justice Thurgood Marshall.* Rev. ed. Lanham, Md.: University Press of America, 1993. An examination of the judicial behavior of Marshall before his appointment to the Supreme Court. Emphasizes Marshall's conservatism in interpreting the law.

Fax, Elton C. *Contemporary Black Leaders.* New York: Dodd Mead, 1970. Contains a short biographical sketch of Marshall, emphasizing his contributions to the cause of desegregation.

Friedman, Leon, ed. *The Justices of the United States Supreme Court: Their Lives and Major Opinions.* Vol. 5. New York: Chelsea House, 1978. Contains an excellent essay by Ramsey Clark which focuses upon questions regarding Marshall's confirmation and his role on the Court.

Johnson, Lyndon Baines. *The Vantage Point: Perspectives of the Presidency: 1963-1969.* London: Weidenfeld and Nicolson, and New York: Holt Rinehart, 1971. Very few references to Marshall but useful for background information and a presidential perspective of the Civil Rights movement.

Kluger, Richard. *Simple Justice: The History of Brown v. Board of Education and Black America's Struggle for Equality.* New York: Knopf, 1976; London: Deutsch, 1976. An excellent history of *Brown v. Board of Education*, including an invaluable account of Marshall's role in that landmark decision. One full chapter is devoted to Marshall.

Sitkoff, Harvard. *A New Deal for Blacks: The Emergence of Civil Rights as a National Issue.* New York: Oxford University Press, 1978; Oxford: Oxford University Press, 1981. A comprehensive account of the emergence of the Civil Rights movement. Only mentions Marshall but excellent for understanding the forces which operated on those who were early leaders in the civil rights field.

Tushnet, Mark V. *Making Civil Rights Law: Thurgood Marshall and the Supreme Court, 1936-1961.* New York: Oxford University Press, 1994. Covers Marshall's early career and his battles in concert with the NAACP that led to U.S. civil rights law.

————. *Making Constitutional Law: Thurgood Marshall and the Supreme Court, 1961-1991.* New York: Oxford University Press, 1997. Covers the Marshall's Supreme Court career. Includes Marshall's work in areas such as the death penalty, civil rights, and abortion.

Witt, Elder. *A Different Justice: Reagan and the Supreme Court.* Washington, D.C.: Congressional Quarterly, 1986. A portrait of the contemporary Court. Questions how the Court may change in the future. Contains a short discussion of Marshall's role on the Court.

Woodward, Bob, and Scott Armstrong. *The Brethren: Inside the Supreme Court.* New York: Simon and Schuster, 1979. A resourceful account of the contemporary Court. Contains useful and interesting information regarding Marshall's relationship with other members of the bench.

Michael J. Clark

AGNES MARTIN

Born: March 22, 1912; Maklin, Saskatchewan, Canada

Area of Achievement: Art

Contribution: A leading American artist of the style of minimalism in the 1960's and 1970's, Agnes Martin persevered in her commitment to art as a means of spiritual expression to become one of the few women artists of the twentieth century to achieve recognition and success.

Early Life

Born on a farm in Maklin, Saskatchewan, Canada, on March 22, 1912, Agnes Bernice Martin grew up in a pioneer family in Vancouver, British Columbia, and moved to Bellingham, Washington, in 1919, where she attended high school and college. She went on to receive a degree from the Teachers College of Columbia University in New York City, majoring in fine arts and art education. After working for four years as an art teacher, she moved to New Mexico looking for new opportunities and the environment to pursue her own work, away from the complexities of city life. She taught in a number of art programs in high schools and colleges in New Mexico and received early recognition for her own work with the receipt of scholarships and awards. In 1950, Agnes Martin became a United States citizen.

The experience of living in the beauty and open spaces of the West would always be inspirational to her work, despite a number of return trips to New York to complete her education and earn a Masters of Arts degree in 1952. Although her early work was dominated by landscapes and floating abstract shapes, in the period of postgraduate study, she was finally ready to understand and accept the stylistic achievements of the avante-garde painters working in New York. Finding it too difficult and expensive to live in New York, she returned to Taos, New Mexico, for five years. Beginning in 1957, Agnes Martin lived and worked in New York City. It was a dynamic period for art, dominated by the New York school of abstract expressionists and action painters. For the next ten years, a critical phase of development in her early life as an artist, she would become part of the movement of many of her contemporaries to respond to the painterly aggression of the abstract expressionists. Seeking new solutions to the pictorial problems inherent in painting, she would progress from painting simple biomorphic shapes in open spaces to the tranquil geometric canvases of her own personal and mature vision of art.

In December of 1958, Agnes Martin had her first one-artist exhibition at the Betty Parsons Gallery in New York City and received critical acclaim for her work, a significant accomplishment for a woman artist at that time.

Life's Work

The decade of the 1960's in New York was definitive in the formulation of Agnes Martin's personal aesthetic. Based on the total distillation of geometric forms to pure translucent surfaces, this aesthetic was quiet and simple. It appeared to be totally contrary to the brash and gestural painting techniques practiced by the abstract expressionists beginning in the 1940's and much more structured than those of their followers, the color field painters, who reduced their canvases to freely formed areas of color. After many years of working with abstract shapes floating in space, Martin realized that geometry was the most appropriate vehicle for her to express the spiritual content that was implicit in her paintings. Taking the "expressionist" definition of modern painting seriously, she sought the means to express the inspirational views of nature that had so affected her for many years in the West. Inspired by the Greeks, who had also used the perfection of mathematical geometric forms as the basis of Classical art, her canvases used mathematics in their underlying organizational structure. In the middle of the twentieth century, however, the representational subject matter that was so important to the Greeks was no longer necessary; it had been rejected in favor of the purity of mathematical forms. Over monochromatic color surfaces painted in thin washes of oils, Agnes Martin penciled in geometrics as a series of grids of different sizes and arrangements within the rectangle of the picture frame.

In 1964, Agnes Martin changed her technique from oils to acrylics painted in a limited palette on white-gessoed canvases. With the graphite grids dematerializing beneath the muted colors, the paintings were simplified to the bare minimum. Acrylics also allowed her to create misty background effects that would enhance the spiritual and emotional content of her works. Requiring the utmost concentration, these canvases lured the viewer into their very being and acted as meditational devices. They created a transcendental reality in paint. With nature as the source of inspiration, the paintings of Agnes Martin went beyond the simple forms favored by other artists of the 1960's known as minimalists.

Although hailed as a minimalist artist during her entire career, Agnes Martin was inspired to produce simple geometric shapes for reasons that were quite different in concept from the minimalist school. Minimalism, with Agnes Martin in its midst, was introduced to the American public in 1966 at an exhibition at the Guggenheim Museum in New York titled "Systemic Painting." True minimalist artists avoid expressive painting devices and representational subjects and concentrate on the repetition of simple shapes and forms which can be extended indefinitely. The repetitive grids played out in infinite series of variations by Agnes Martin appear to reflect such ideas. Nevertheless, her work was full of personal meaning and human expression, while minimalism was purely objective and lacking in sentimentality. Actually, Martin was far more of an abstract expressionist according to its true definition and saw herself as such, rather than as a minimalist totally devoid of expressive feeling. Abstract expressionism embraces a number of styles that reveal emotional content, its "expression" revealed through "abstract" means. Agnes Martin also expresses herself, but with quiet sublime means based on the reductive abstract principles of geometry. These principles are closer to abstract expressionism than minimalism.

Agnes Martin's personal philosophy emerged from a number of sources which were popular in the intellectual communities of the 1950's and 1960's. The teachings of Taoism and Zen Buddhism joined those of the Bible as inspiration for artists looking beyond mundane earthly reality for their subject matter. Asserting that enlightenment could be attained through self-contemplation and inner awareness, these Asian philosophies directed an entire generation to participate in the tranquillity of meditation. The paintings of Agnes Martin assist in the meditative process, affecting the viewer with the chant of their subliminal atmospheric vibrations.

The personal content of Agnes Martin's work demanded spiritual isolation and a level of quietude that was impossible in the vibrant life of the New York art world. In 1967, she announced her retirement from painting and left the constant inter-ruptions of the city to find solitude in New Mexico. She settled on an isolated mesa near the village of Cuba, built an adobe and log house, and abandoned the distractions of the world for an existence without even a telephone. It was not until 1974, after several offers by gallery dealers and museum directors to organize exhibitions of her work, that she built a studio adjacent to her home and resumed painting.

At the age of sixty-two, Agnes Martin began another phase of her painting career. The translucent canvases with their wide variety of pencil grids barely visible through the dominantly white color field were replaced by paintings featuring broad stripes of lightly modulated colors. As if merely washed with bands of pale colors, her canvases of the late 1970's and 1980's are as luminous as the perfect harmony found in nature. The graphite markings are less conspicuous and washes of color are dominant. Still contained within the geometric construction of the canvas and defined by ordered and ruled markings, the broad color bands shimmer and tremble as if induced by a meditative state.

In the early 1990's, Agnes Martin has continued to work in solitude, surrounded by the desert beauty of the American West. True to her belief that art involves an awareness of perfection to achieve beauty and happiness, she has maintained a personal and unique vision during a lifetime of work. In a field of achievement where many women have failed to receive proper recognition, Agnes Martin deserves a place as a major figure in the history of American art.

Summary

The history of modern art follows two major paths of artistic stylization: expressionism and abstractionism. Beginning at the end of the nineteenth century, artists have followed these paths in an effort to create a visual language significant to modern life. Agnes Martin determined that she could do both: express her own personal concepts about art and its meaning as a universal phenomenon created by human beings from their own instincts and formalize these concepts within the perfect structures of geometry. As a woman working outside of the commercial environment and demands of the New York art world, she was prevented from receiving the popular acclaim and recognition given to so many of her male contemporaries, despite critical praise from writers. The highly personal and intellectual nature of her art often demanded more than the ordinary art viewer was willing to invest in order to comprehend its meaning fully. Agnes Martin determined her own path as an artist and maintained her vision throughout her long career. It was a vision of sublime perfection incorporating deceptively simple imagery and the tenets of modernism as understood and successfully executed by very few artists. For this perfect association of personal expression and abstraction, Agnes Martin stands as one of the masters of twentieth century modern art.

Bibliography

Arnason, H. H. *History of Modern Art*. 4th ed. New York: Abrams, 1998. History of modern art includes section on minimal art and the work of Agnes Martin. Excellent basic survey of modern art.

Cotter, Holland. "Agnes Martin: All the Way to Heaven." *Art in America* 81, no. 4 (April, 1993). Examines the works of Martin and their reflection of her lifestyle.

Gruen, John. "Agnes Martin: 'Everything, Everything Is About Feeling . . . Feeling and Recognition.'" *ARTnews* 75 (September, 1976): 91-94. Review of exhibition of Agnes Martin's paintings at The Pace Gallery and Robert Elkon Gallery.

Haskell, Barbara. *Agnes Martin*. New York: Whitney Museum of American Art, 1992. The catalog for the major retrospective exhibition of Agnes Martin's works organized by the Whitney Museum in 1993. Includes essays by Barbara Haskell, Rosalind Krauss and Anna C. Chave and quotations from writings by the artist. It is the only monograph to date on the artist.

Hunter, Sam, and John Jacobus. *Modern Art*. 3d ed. Englewood Cliffs, N.J.: Prentice-Hall, 1992. Overview of modern painting, sculpture, and architecture that includes chapter on minimalism and brief commentary on works of Agnes Martin.

Simon, Jean. "Perfection Is in the Mind: An Interview with Agnes Martin." *Art in America* 84, no. 5 (May, 1996). Interview with Martin in which she discusses her techniques and career.

Carol Damian

TOMÁŠ MASARYK

Born: March 7, 1850; near Göding, Moravia, Austrian Empire (now Hodonín, Czechoslovakia)

Died: September 14, 1937; Lány, Czechoslovakia

Areas of Achievement: Government, politics, and philosophy

Contribution: Masaryk was a professor of philosophy, an author, and a statesman who was the principal founder and first president of Czechoslovakia. He secured the support of the Western liberal powers during World War I for the Czechoslovakian cause and was awarded numerous honors including a D.C.L. from the University of Oxford in 1928.

Early Life

Tomáš Garrigue Masaryk was born in Moravia in 1850 to a Slovak father and a German-speaking Czech mother. His homeland was part of Austria-Hungary and his father was employed as a coachman on an imperial estate. Because of the low social position of his parents, it was difficult for him to receive an education. His father encouraged him to enter a trade and for a while he worked as a blacksmith. He was finally able to attend school in Brno and completed his secondary education in Vienna in 1872. He supported himself by tutoring wealthy students, and in appreciation their parents helped him to further his education. He entered the University of Vienna and completed his doctorate in 1876. Following his graduation, he spent a year studying at the University of Leipzig, where he met an American student of music, Charlotte Garrigue. They were married in New York in 1878. She was a major influence in his life, causing him to have a greater understanding of international affairs than most Czech leaders of his day. In order to symbolize the closeness of this relationship, Masaryk adopted his wife's maiden name and thus became known to the world as Thomas Garrigue Masaryk. Charlotte also influenced his religious views. He had already left the Roman Catholic faith in which he was reared, and now he adopted many of the Unitarian views of his wife. Not only did his marriage change his religious outlook, but also it led him to adopt English as his third language after Czech and German.

In 1879, Masaryk became a lecturer at the University of Vienna, and in 1882 he was appointed professor of philosophy at the Czech university in Prague. His position gave him the opportunity to become one of the leaders of the rising nationalist movement among his people. Masaryk's mind had a practical bent, causing him to use his philosophic training to try to solve the problems of life and to work toward a more just society. He had little interest in problems of epistemology or cosmology. In the early stages of his career, he reacted against German philosophy, accepting British empiricism and logical positivism. His philosophical position can be described as realism, an outlook that accepts not only reason but also the will, the emotions, and the senses. His main interest, however, began to concentrate on sociology and the philosophy of history. These preoccupations were reflected in his book *Der Selbstmord als sociale Massenerscheinung der modernen Civilisation* (1881; *Suicide and the Meaning of Civilization*, 1970) and several other works on the Czech Reformation and the early nineteenth century Czech nationalist revival.

Life's Work

Masaryk became one of the most popular teachers in the university at Prague, and he used his academic role to attack political and social injustices. As he elaborated his views they came to include a search for scientific truth, a pragmatic approach to life, a rejection of force and extremism in human affairs, and an emphasis on morality. As the author of numerous books and as a muckraking journalist, he entered into debates on the important social issues of the day.

Masaryk demonstrated his devotion to his ideals by exposing two ostensibly early Czech poems that were regarded as the Slavic counterparts to the *Nibelungenlied* but were in reality early nineteenth century forgeries. He also challenged the anti-Semitism of his homeland by proving the innocence of Leopold Hilsner, a Jew accused of the ritual murder of a Christian in 1899. Despite his involvement in these practical issues, Masaryk found time to publish several volumes including *Česká otázka; Snahy a tužby národního obrození* (1895; the Czech question), *Die philosophischen und sociologischen Grundlagen des Marxismus* (1899; the philosophical and sociological foundation of Marxism), and *Russland und Europa* (1913; *The Spirit of Russia*, 1919). These works assigned a key role in the improvement of the human condition to the Czech nation through the transmission of its ancient ideals as embodied in the Hussites and the Bohemian Brethren. Such an outlook, Masaryk believed, could be an effective antidote to the materialism, selfishness, and alienation of modern society. His writings and teachings were meant to educate the Czech people in their own tradition. As he interpreted their history, it was an enduring defense of democracy in church and state.

Masaryk believed that Hussite ideals would give his people an orientation toward the ethical and democratic outlook of Western civilization, and he was suspicious of the Pan-Slavism and communist ideology emanating from Russia. His book on Russia dealt with the philosophy, religion, and literature of his great Eastern neighbor. He was extremely critical of Russia, characterizing the land as preserving the childhood of Europe through the mass of ignorant peasants. Russian nobles were no better, he stated, because they were half-educated, immoral, boorish, cruel, and reactionary. Their example had set the pattern for the entire society. Those such as the Marxists who wanted revolution were suggesting a cure little better than the illness. On occasion he would refer to the Bolsheviks as the "new Jesuits" because of their opposition to religion and accepted standards of Christian morality.

In 1890, Masaryk entered politics as a member of the young Czech Party, and in 1891 he was elected to the Austrian Reichsrat (parliament). His disagreements with some of the emotional outbursts of his fellow party members led him to resign in 1893. In March, 1900, he started the Realist Party, which more accurately expressed his aim for reform within the imperial framework. He was returned to the Reichsrat in 1907 and served until 1914. As a member of the Reichsrat, he represented the leftist position among the Slavs and tried to achieve greater autonomy for them within the empire. He also wished to end the alliance between Germany and Austria-Hungary and to stop the imperialistic policies of Austria in the Balkans. The tension between the empire and the Slavs in the Balkans led to the Agram (now Zagreb) Treason Trials in 1908, during which Masaryk exposed the weak case of the Austrians against a group of Serbs. He proved that the government's charges rested upon forged documents. As a result, the Viennese historian, Heinrich Friedjung, was sued for libel. Masaryk demonstrated that Friedjung had accepted documents in good faith that were fabricated in the office of the Austrian foreign ministry.

His fearless stand for the truth in this case further enhanced his worldwide reputation.

The outbreak of World War I was a decisive event in Masaryk's life. Austrian involvement in the conflict led him to believe that the time had come to work for an independent Czech nation. He left Austria in December, 1914, and lived for the next few years in various places in Western Europe and the United States including Geneva, Paris, London, Chicago, and Washington. In 1915, he founded the Czechoslovak Council with Edvard Beneš and Milan Stefanik. The council had two aims: first, to bring together various groups of Czech and Slovak émigrés and, second, to secure Allied recognition of the council as the representative of the Czechoslovakian people. More than 120,000 Czech troops fighting on various fronts for the Allied cause recognized the council as their government.

Relying on his reputation and the aid of such eminent authorities on Eastern Europe as Ernest Dennis, Wickham Steed, and R. W. Seton-Watson, Masaryk began a propaganda campaign to convince the Allies of the necessity of breaking up

Austria-Hungary so that the various people of that polyglot empire would be able to control their own destinies. As part of this program of self-determination, Masaryk wanted to establish a democratic Czech and Slovak confederation along with a number of new Eastern European states founded on ethnic principles which would act as a bulwark against German imperialism. He also tried to focus Western attention on the courageous activities of the Czech legion fighting on the crumbling Eastern Front. Between May, 1917, and March, 1918, he was in Russia trying to work out an alliance with the provincial government that had come to power following the overthrow of the czarist regime. After the Bolshevik Revolution, he left Russia and went to the United States. The large Czech and Slovak population greeted him warmly. These immigrants were an important factor in his success because of their political and economic support for his organization. Also, Masaryk met with President Woodrow Wilson and with Secretary Robert Lansing and succeeded in securing the Lansing Declaration of May, 1918, which recognized the independence of Czechoslovakia. In addition, the new nation's existence was made one of Wilson's Fourteen Points, an important document on which the peace settlement was based. After receiving the firm support of the American government, Masaryk came to terms with the Slovak immigrants in the United States though the Pittsburgh Pact of May 30, 1918. This document promised a large measure of home rule to the Slovak element of Czechoslovakia and was to lead to considerable tension in the future.

The new republic was proclaimed in October, 1918, and Masaryk returned to Prague as president on December 21, 1918. He was reelected to the presidency in 1920, 1927, and 1934. The country had problems not only with relations between the Czechs and the Slovaks but also with the large German and Hungarian population. Masaryk did his best to respect the rights of the minorities under Czech control, but he was forced to deal with economic problems caused by the Great Depression and with a growing Nazi movement among the German citizens. After a prolonged illness, he resigned in 1935 and died at his residence near Lány in 1937.

Summary

The life and ideals of Tomáš Masaryk were shaped by the age in which he lived. The nineteenth and early twentieth centuries were a period when liberalism and nationalism triumphed. Consequently Masaryk's desire for political freedom and national independence reflect this background. Not only was Masaryk a scholar and theorist but also he was a man able to apply his ideas to practical politics. During the years in which he served as President of Czechoslovakia, although his position was constitutionally weak he brought peace and stability to the land and guided it in a democratic direction. He also established friendly relations with Austria and Germany and to a certain extent even with Poland and Hungary. His humanitarian outlook on social and political problems, combined with his humble yet dignified manner, endeared him to his fellow countrymen and to many people in the Western liberal democracies. Of all the new nations created by the Peace of Versailles, Czechoslovakia came closest to reflecting the hope of a just world envisioned by Woodrow Wilson. Much of the credit for this achievement belongs to Masaryk.

During the closing years of his life, however, Masaryk was troubled about the future of his country. His philosophic training and democratic outlook led him to realize the danger to Central Europe because of the rise of the Nazi movement in Germany. The heir to his political legacy, Beneš and Masaryk's son Jan were to be confronted with the ravages of their homeland brought on by World War II and the subsequent Soviet domination of Eastern Europe.

Bibliography

Čapek, Karel. *Masaryk on Thought and Life.* Translated by M. Weatherall and R. Weatherall. London: Allen and Unwin, and New York: Macmillan, 1938. Another volume of Čapek's interviews with Masaryk. This one is concerned with his thoughts rather than his actions and includes chapters on epistemology, metaphysics, religion, the problems of culture in the modern world, politics, and nationalism. As with the volume on Masaryk's life, this one is scrupulously careful in presenting an accurate presentation of the material.

—————. *President Masaryk Tells His Story.* London: Allen and Unwin, 1934; New York: Putnam, 1935. Masaryk spent several weeks with Čapek over the period of many years while the president recounted his life. He reminisced about his childhood, education, and the tumultuous events involved in the creation of Czechoslovakia.

Selver, Paul. *Masaryk: A Biography*. London: Joseph, 1940; Westport, Conn.: Greenwood Press, 1975. A general study of Masaryk's life based upon excellent sources. Contains material that had never been available in English before. Selver has written an excellent book that is notable for the frequent quotations from Masaryk.

Seton-Watson, R. W. *A History of the Czechs and Slovaks*. London and New York: Hutchinson, 1943. This general history of the Czechoslovakian people is a thoughtful introduction in English to many of the problems with which Masaryk was forced to deal. Written by one of the first professors of Czechoslovak studies at the University of London and an acquaintance of Masaryk.

Thomson, S. Harrison. *Czechoslovakia in European History*. Princeton, N.J.: Princeton University Press, 1943. A scholarly, readable volume that makes the story of Masaryk's nation accessible to English students. Thomson has provided his readers with the main themes of Czech history in a sympathetic yet fair manner. Probably the finest one-volume introduction to the land of Masaryk.

Woolfolk, Alan. "Thomas Garrigue Masaryk: Science and Politics as a Vocation." *Society* 33, no. 3 (March-April, 1996). Considers Masaryk's contributions as one of the founders of sociology, an area often obscured by his political activities.

Zeman, Zbynek. *The Masaryks: The Making of Czechoslovakia*. London: Weidenfeld and Nicolson, and New York: Barnes and Noble, 1976. This dual biography of Tomáš and Jan Masaryk gives a variety of interpretations of the legacy of these two individuals. Some looked on Tomáš Masaryk as a "philosopher-king," while others regarded him as a "scholar-saint," but in reality his legacy was more ambiguous. Zbynek discusses some of the Marxist criticisms of Masaryk, among them that he plotted against Vladimir Ilich Lenin and Joseph Stalin, was supported by international bankers, and that his presidency was a very expensive affair.

Robert G. Clouse

WILLIAM FERGUSON MASSEY

Born: March 26, 1856; Limavady, County Londonderry, Ireland
Died: May 10, 1925; Wellington, New Zealand
Areas of Achievement: Government and politics
Contribution: Massey's tenure as prime minister marked the coming-of-age and domination of the small farmer in New Zealand politics. Steadfastly steering his country through the trials of World War I, he combined conservative social values and fierce anti-Labour attitudes with a continuation of policies based on the intervention of the state to develop New Zealand as a prosperous outlying farm of the British Empire.

Early Life

William Ferguson Massey was born March 26, 1856, at Limavady, County Londonderry, Ireland, the eldest son of a small Ulster freeholder, John Massey, and his Scottish wife, Marianne, née Ferguson. Educated at the local National School and a private secondary school, Massey emigrated to New Zealand at the age of fourteen in December, 1870, to join his father in farming at Tamaki, near Auckland. Between 1872 and 1876, he was a ploughman on John Grigg's Longbeach Estate, Canterbury, where the most advanced agricultural techniques were being implemented. Massey received a valuable practical education at a time when New Zealand's economy, formerly based on wool and gold, was being supplemented by intensive grassland farming, supplying refrigerated products for the British table.

Returning north, Massey leased and subsequently purchased a small farm at Mangere (near the present Auckland International Airport), operated a lucrative portable threshing business, and married Christina Allen Paul (1863-1932), by whom he had three sons and two daughters. Christina Massey's public services were recognized when she was created New Zealand's first Dame Commander of the British Empire. Two sons subsequently became rural Members of Parliament.

Markedly successful, Massey joined a Farmers' Club, revived the Auckland Agricultural and Pastoral Society and, in 1891, became the driving force behind the quasi-political Auckland National Association formed to combat radical liberalism, advocate freehold land tenure, and, through roads and bridges policies, drag the rising numbers of small bush farmers in the Auckland Province out of the mud. In 1894, he entered Parliament as M.P. for Waitemata, after acceding to a requisition from electors, presented to him on a pitchfork while he was building a haystack. Massey was the acknowledged champion of the small farmers, and the leader of the new groups that were emerging to challenge the Liberal hegemony of Richard John Seddon that had emerged following the shattering of the old conservatives during the economic depression.

A born organizer and party manager, Massey became Leader of the Opposition in 1902, undisputed head of the new Reform Party in February, 1909, and Prime Minister of New Zealand on July 6, 1912, when, after a confused election result the previous year, he defeated the Liberals on the floor of Parliament. This office he retained until his death.

Massey's character and beliefs were fixed by his youthful Ulster farming experiences. Strong-framed and portly in his later years, Massey was instantly recognizable. With a round, red, jowly face dominated by piercing blue eyes and a large white mustache, "Old Bill," as Massey was universally called, was a cartoonist's delight. Initially underestimated by senior politicians—the intellectual Fabian William Pember Reeves thought him to be "merely a decent country member; what we called a 'roads and bridges' man"—Massey's prodigious industry, ability to master detail, and expert grasp of the principles of legislation and of parliamentary procedure made him a formidable, indeed dominant, debater. Drawing his precepts and examples from the Old Testament, his deep Presbyterian faith and his attachment to British Israelism's notion of the divine mission of the scattered British people, Massey epitomized the virtues and limitations of his farming fraternity.

Life's Work

Massey's career as prime minister was troubled by the fact that only once, in 1919, did he have an adequate majority. "Never try to carry on a Government with a majority of only two or three; it is hell all the time," he said. Yet he did have an inbuilt electoral advantage in that a twenty-eight percent "country quota" was automatically added to rural electorates at the expense of voters in the larger towns and cities. Nevertheless, he vigorously embarked on his policy of giving freehold tenure to

Crown leaseholders at original valuation, thereby presenting farmers with the unearned increment. He maintained populist expenditure on rural public works and reformed the patronage system riddling the civil service. Privately profoundly Orange (Protestant Irish) in outlook, he shared the sectarian views of Protestant extremists but was too astute to endorse publicly their fulminations against the Catholic minority. A moderate whiskey drinker, he contained the socially divisive Prohibition movement, which, but for the soldiers' votes, would have had New Zealand following the United States' experiment in 1919.

Continual crises marked his years in office, reflecting emerging fissures and new conflicts in New Zealand and overseas. In 1912, miners at the Waihi gold mine struck under the influence of the "Red" Federation of labor. Massey smashed the strike by deregistering the union, employing scab labor and using the police. The following year the waterfront, mines, railways, and processing plants—all elements in New Zealand's rural export trade upon which the country lived—were hit by further strikes and similarly crushed, this time by "Massey's Cossacks," special constables of young farmers on horseback. Increasingly, Massey saw organized urban labor and its political representatives as tools of syndicalist agitations and later as Bolshevik revolutionaries and unpatriotic wreckers. His detestation was reciprocated by his opponents.

A new trial fell upon Massey in August, 1914. Upon Great Britain declaring war on Germany, Massey declared with almost universal approval that "All we have and all we are are at the disposal of the Imperial Government." In August, 1915, Sir Joseph Ward's Liberals joined Massey in a coalition government which lasted until July, 1919; conscription was imposed in 1916, Labour leaders were jailed for sedition, primary products were commandeered and shipped to England at regulated prices, and all efforts were directed at winning the war. Massey himself was frequently overseas, attending several meetings of the Imperial War Cabinet in London and signing, on behalf of New Zealand, the Treaty of Versailles in 1919. New Zealand casualties were horrific—nearly seventeen thousand men were killed and forty-one thousand wounded. This represented one in every three New Zealand males aged between twenty and forty. More than $160 millions, 36.4 percent of the total, had been added to the public debt of the Dominion.

Although Ward, as treasurer, had great domestic influence, Massey easily won the 1919 election, resumed borrowing for public works, attempted (disastrously in the event) to settle former servicemen on the land, and combatted rising social weariness and unrest culminating in the sharp recession of 1921-1922. Massey moved the state, in cooperation with the farmers, into regulated marketing schemes for dairy products and meat, thus demonstrating that he was not a traditional conservative but a politician firmly entrenched in this key aspect of New Zealand's social life and economic history.

Although he had participated in imperial wartime decisions concerning the empire as a whole, Massey, while holding little if any faith in the League of Nations, declined to seize, or indeed accept, after 1918 the new opportunities offered for New Zealand's developing independence in world affairs. He reverted to the subservient empire loyalty of his past. Yet he had threatened resignation in 1914 if the Admiralty did not provide adequate escorts for the New Zealand troopships. He secured formerly German Western Samoa as a New Zealand mandate, and, by a brilliant coup, obtained a share in the phosphates of Nauru Island for his fellow farmers. Massey regarded moves toward independence as unique, and the Royal Navy and the Singapore naval base as New Zealand's only sure shield.

Massey barely survived the 1922 election. Worried by the rise of Labour and the difficulty of making old remedies effective, fearful of burgeoning agrarian protest and well aware of New Zealand's almost total dependence on the British market, Massey adopted new versions of developmental policies. He initiated electrification schemes, raised rural production through promoting intensive farming on artificial pastures, and pursued urban wage restraint. Yet these remedies could not cure "the instability of a dependent economy." Worn out by work and political cares and suffering from intestinal cancer from 1923, Massey died at Wellington on May 10, 1925, and was buried at Point Halswell, where a substantial memorial was erected. Massey University at Palmerston North honors his memory.

Summary

William Ferguson Massey's career encapsulated many of the enduring verities of New Zealand political life between 1890 and 1929. His life marked the coming of political and social power to the

small farmer, particularly in the North Island. An Ulster Presbyterian migrant, he brought many of the virtues and flaws of that tribe to his adopted country as his cultural baggage. Personally hearty and genial, often bigoted, of limited vision as the world shifted under his feet, he was, beneath an apparently uncaring demeanor when challenged, intensely sensitive to criticism. His mind seldom expanded to meet the new challenges after 1918 that his political abilities—tactical perception and a capacity to work with talented lieutenants of superior formal education—had thrust before him. The parliamentary equal of Seddon, many of whose populist approaches and astute distributions of political largesse he continued, Massey lacked Seddon's wider visions and more appealing humanity. Yet, as his young, radical opponent J. A. Lee observed, "I can truthfully say every member [of Parliament] listened, some to cheer, some to jeer, but they listened. . . . He was master and the class knew he was." Lee continued to relate how the normally taciturn and phlegmatic Massey had burst into tears when cheered by limbless New Zealand soldiers at Twickenham and how he had later insisted

in traversing the "nightmare ward" of the physically shattered at Brockenhurst, England.

The foundations of Massey's values—the Bible, the virtues of thrift, hard work, rural toil, self-denial, and loyalty to the Mother Country, Great Britain—were simple. So, too, was his political objective of fulfilling what seemed to be New Zealand's destiny as the ever-productive dairy farm of the Empire. Yet his character was more complex than his simple tenets suggested, and his virtues of loyalty, steadfastness, self-improvement and conformity reflected those of so many of his adopted fellow countrymen.

Bibliography

Burdon, R. M. *The New Dominion: A Social and Political History of New Zealand, 1918-1939.* London: Allen and Unwin, 1965. The standard account of Massey's last years in politics and the new forces that were ultimately to overwhelm many of his values, assumptions, and political structures.

Chapman, Robert M. *The Political Scene, 1919-1931.* Auckland, New Zealand: Heinemann, 1969. A seminal monograph based on original research critical of Massey but candidly analyzing his difficulties and his manifest success in surmounting many of them.

Gardner, William J. *The Farmer Politician in New Zealand History.* Palmerston North, New Zealand: Massey University, 1970.

———. *William Massey.* Wellington, New Zealand: Reed, 1969. While there is no full-scale biography of Massey, Gardner is the acknowledged expert on his life. Sympathetic yet scholarly, he has restored Massey to his rightful place in New Zealand history while recognizing his subject's limitations.

Macdonald, Barrie. *Massey's Imperialism and the Politics of Phosphate.* Palmerston North, New Zealand: Massey University, 1982. A fascinating analysis of Massey's success in securing the spoils of war in the form of cheap Nauruan phosphate for New Zealand's artificial pastures partly at the expense of Australian and British interests—and those of the indigenous people.

O'Connor, Peter S. *Mr. Massey and the American Meat Trust: Some Sidelights on the Origins of the Meat Board.* Palmerston North, New Zealand: Massey University, 1973. A detailed monograph examining Massey's shrewd use of the "conspiracy notion" in politics. In this case the American meat packers, Armours, were the villains and the South Americans the rivals. Massey's exploitation of economic fears and uncertainties ultimately led to producer control and government regulation of New Zealand's meat export trade to the United Kingdom. Other exports were similarly dealt with.

Oliver, William H., ed., with B. R. Williams. *The Oxford History of New Zealand*. Oxford: Clarendon Press, and New York: Oxford University Press, 1981. Chapters 8 and 9 covering Massey and his times by Len Richardson ("Parties and Political Change") and Tom Brooking ("Economic Transformation") convey the results of recent research and soften earlier and harsher judgments of Massey's policies and personality.

Scholefield, G. H. "William Ferguson Massey." In *A Dictionary of New Zealand Biography*. Vol. 2. Wellington, New Zealand: Department of International Affairs, 1940. A useful entry based on the author's privately circulated *W. F. Massey, a Personal Biography*.

Sinclair, Sir Keith. *A Destiny Apart: New Zealand's Search for National Identity*. Wellington, New Zealand: Allen and Unwin, 1986.

———. *A History of New Zealand*. 4th ed. New York: Penguin, 1991. Readable, penetrating accounts, often critical of Massey's ideology and imperial sentiments, by New Zealand's leading historian of unashamedly social democratic and nationalist beliefs.

Stewart, W. Downie. *Sir Francis Bell, His Life and Times*. London: Butterworth, 1937. Both the biographer and his subject served in Massey's cabinets, the latter as Massey's indispensable alter ego in finance and legislation. Includes lively and anecdotal portraits of Massey by a younger, crippled, returned soldier contemporary.

Duncan Waterson

LÉONIDE MASSINE
Leonid Fyodorovich Miassin

Born: August 8, 1895; Moscow, Russia
Died: March 16, 1979; Cologne, West Germany
Area of Achievement: Dance
Contribution: Massine's career as a performer and creator of dance changed the nature of the art. His stage presence and dance style made a powerful impression in Europe and the United States and helped to establish the companies with which he worked as the leading forces in the renewal of ballet. His choreography was especially innovative in its collaboration with music and depth of characterization.

Early Life

Leonid Fyodorovich Miassin (his name was changed to Léonide Massine by Sergei Diaghilev when he joined the Ballet Russe company) was born in Moscow in 1895. He was the youngest of five children, four boys and one girl, in a closely knit, warm family. His father played French horn in the Bolshoi Theater orchestra, and his mother was a soprano in the Bolshoi Theater chorus. Although his parents were both artists, they never assumed that Massine would have a career in the arts. His elder brothers studied mathematics and engineering. The eldest, Mikhail, became a professional soldier; Gregori became an engineer; and Konstantin died after a hunting accident when he was twenty-one. Raissa, the only sister, was closest to Massine in age and was his frequent playmate. They especially enjoyed dancing folk dances and playing games with the children of a family that worked as household servants for their parents. Often Massine would amuse himself on the mouth organ. As an adult, he recalled the happiness of this time and commemorated it by incorporating his childhood games and dances in his ballets.

A friend of his mother observed Massine dancing alone and suggested that his parents enroll him in the Moscow Theater School to be trained as a dancer. He underwent the entrance examination, which included a physical examination to judge if he could develop into a dancer. He was admitted on a one-year trial basis and, after the year, he was accepted as a permanent student.

Massine fell in love with the world of the theater. His slight build, dark coloring, and skill awarded him his first role. He portrayed the dwarf, Cherno-mor, in *Russlan and Ludmilla*, by the Russian composer Mikhail Glinka. Although wearing an exotic costume and an immense beard was the most required of him, it was his first character role and the beginning of a series of professional appearances as a child actor. He made hundreds of performances at the Maly and the Bolshoi theaters in Moscow. He also appeared in ballets at the Bolshoi, but, by age fifteen, Massine began to think he would be happier in the theater than in ballet. He found the plays more interesting, the actors more intelligent, and, except for that of Peter Ilich Tchaikovsky, the ballet music second rate. Typical of his lifelong dedication to broadening his education, he began to study the violin and painting while a teenager. His parents retired to a country home, and Massine moved into a room near the theater school. He delved into reading works by Fyodor Dostoevski, an exceptional pursuit for a dancer.

At this time, the leading choreographer for the theater was Alexander Gorsky. Massine admired his personality but believed that he could not transmit his ideas to his dancers, move big groups across the stage, or choreograph dances in authentic foreign styles. These were all to become central concerns of Massine's mature work. Massine was graduated from the Moscow Theater School in 1912 and joined the Bolshoi company.

In 1913, Massine danced the Tarantella in *Swan Lake*. Diaghilev, director of the Ballet Russe company, was in the audience. Michel Fokine, the leading choreographer of Diaghilev's company, was to create a ballet, *La Legende de Joseph*, based on the biblical story; Diaghilev selected Massine as Joseph. After an interview with Fokine, Massine was offered the role and a position in the company, but he would have to leave Moscow in two days. His friends advised him not to go, as it would abruptly end his blossoming theater career. Massine himself decided to reject the offer. When he met Diaghilev again, however, he suddenly said yes and thus created an entirely new life for himself.

Life's Work

As a choreographer and dancer, Massine always sought the most encompassing expression by including the finest work not only in dance but also in music, painting and design, and literary and philosophical thought. A fusion of the arts was the ideal of Diaghilev's ballet. By taking an immediate interest in the education of Massine, Diaghilev helped to develop Massine's already broad curiosity and learning. Even as a young man, Massine was never content to be only the instrument of his mentors. His artistic contributions went beyond the strictures laid out by Diaghilev to different areas of art, especially in his use of major symphonic works, as Diaghilev had a preference for obscure music. Massine also developed his work further by his precise use of traditional dance from various cultures. Scholarly in his preparation, Massine differed from other choreographers by his interest in and knowledge of arts other than dance and his willingness to study.

Massine's role as Joseph had been a success though the ballet was not. Performed in Paris in 1914, it elevated Massine to sudden stardom. He still wanted to improve his technique, however, and studied with ballet master Enrico Cecchetti. He found that the academic ballet he had learned in the Moscow Theater School was not enough to meet the demands of Fokine's style, inspired by the freer movement of Isadora Duncan.

When World War I broke out in Europe, in 1914, Diaghilev's leading male dancer, Vaslav Nijinsky, and much of the company was in the United States. This gave Massine the opportunity to work with composer Igor Stravinsky and designer Mikhail Larionov and to experiment in new work with Diaghilev. In 1915, Massine created his first ballet, *Soleil de nuit* (midnight sun), in which the Russian dances and games of his childhood appear as the basis of the choreography. The music was by Nikolay Rimsky-Korsakov.

In only four years, Massine produced masterpieces of ballet. In each one, he pushed the art form into new areas. In 1917, he premiered *Les Femmes de bonne humeur* (the good-humored ladies), with music by Giuseppe Scarlatti, and *Parade*, a collaborative work with costumes and sets by Pablo Picasso and Jean Cocteau and music by Erik Satie. *Les Femmes de bonne humeur* incorporated the Italian *commedia dell'arte* style of masked characters representing personality types. Massine created the first of many parts no one has adequately been able to fill after him because of his stage presence and precisely choreographed characterization.

La Boutique fantasque (1919), Massine's next work, is the story of a shop whose toys come to life. The characterization of the shopkeeper, assistant, Russians, Americans, dolls, and even poodles is presented in careful detail. Massine appeared with Lydia Sokolova in a can-can, which became one of the celebrated dances in ballet history. *Le Tricorne* (the three-cornered hat) premiered in 1919 in London. It was the result of Massine's wartime studies in Seville of Spanish classical and folk dance. Massine's accomplishment was to take the true movement and rhythm of the dances and put them into ballet without giving them a false prettiness.

Massine's last work for Diaghilev's company at this time was a reproduction of *The Rite of Spring*. The ballet for Stravinsky's music had been originally choreographed by Nijinsky. When Diaghilev was angered by Nijinsky's marriage, Nijinsky left the Ballet Russe. Massine rechoreographed the controversial piece. The primitive-sounding music with its complicated and jagged rhythms supported the creation of modern movements to express an ancient story of a community sacrificing a young woman. Latter-day dance enthusiasts have engaged in pointless debate over which was the superior version of the dance. Massine's was not adequately recorded, and Massine himself would not involve himself in such a debate. His version was a great success when performed. The chief choreographic element was the use of the dancers' weight to create an earth-bound look and shape to the movement. This was the opposite of the ethereal look of classical ballet and its appearance of airborne lightness. The use of weighted movement was a basic element of modern dance, and Massine understood its usefulness in creating dramatic tension and expression.

A personal dispute with Diaghilev led Massine to quit the company in 1921. In only six years, he had created a body of work that made major changes in ballet. He formed his own company and produced several works for the "Soirées de Paris" organized by Le Comte Étienne de Beaumont. These included *Salade*, music by Darius Milhaud, *Mercure*, music by Satie and decor by Picasso, and *Le Beau Danube*, music by Johann Strauss; all appeared in 1924. Diaghilev convinced Massine to rejoin his company after these successes; the second engagement with Diaghilev lasted from 1925 to 1928.

Massine's second time with the Ballet Russe produced still more experiments with movement, themes, and the adventurous use of music. *Zéphere et Flore* (1925) had costumes and decor by the cubist artist Georges Braque and music by Dukelsky. *Les Matelots* (1925) was the first of an ongoing tradition of lighthearted dances about three sailors on the town. *Les Pas d'acier* (1927), with music by Sergei Prokofiev, started another tradition in dance—that of the dancers taking on the angular, abrupt movement style of machinery, expressing fear of automation and the encroaching "steps of steel" of the title. During this same period, Massine worked as dancer-choreographer for the London Cochrane Revues and as solo dancer and ballet master of the Roxy Theater of New York. In 1930, he revived *The Rite of Spring* for Martha Graham. He also choreographed for the Rubinstein company from 1929 to 1931.

In 1932, Colonel de Basil began his own Ballet Russe de Monte Carlo, and Massine joined the company as ballet master in 1933. In this period, Massine choreographed three of his symphonic ballets: *Les Présages* (1934), for Tchaikovsky's fifth symphony; *Choréartium* (1934), for Johannes Brahms's fourth symphony; and *Symphonie fantastique* (1936), for music by Hector Berlioz. Although these works are among Massine's greatest achievements, they are also perhaps the least appreciated. They demonstrated his mastery of music of the greatest scope and complexity and his interest in themes of the broadest human concerns. It is rare for ballet reviewers to know music well or for music reviewers to know ballet. Massine's fusion of art forms reached for a unity of art and understanding on a scale as grand as human aspirations.

Massine choreographed more than one hundred ballets. He worked with other companies including New York's Ballet Theater in 1942-1943. In 1945-1946, he toured his own company, Ballet Russe Highlights. His work continued to grow by using the best of music and the widest variety of human concerns and expressions from the frivolity of *Gaîté parisienne* (1938) to the religious inspiration of *Laudes Evangelii* (1952). In keeping with his interest in innovations, he made three notable films: *The Red Shoes* (1948), *Tales of Hoffman* (1951), and *Carosello Napoletano* (1953; *Neapolitan Carousel*). He continued his dedication to the study and presentation of dances of specific cultures by studying the dances of American Indians and presented lecture-demonstrations on the subject throughout the world. He devoted much of his later life to the study of the theoretical essentials of choreography and wrote a book on the subject while a teacher at the Royal Ballet School in London.

Summary

As a dancer, Léonide Massine's greatest accomplishments were his own performances, celebrated for not only his technique but also the delicate and precise characterizations that no one has been able to duplicate. As a great performer, it will be possible to memorialize him only through the accounts of his audience. He was best known for his character roles in lighthearted ballets, and he captured the imaginations of all who saw him. His greatest contributions, however, were in his unification of the arts of the actor, dancer, and musician. His reputation suffered sometimes in commentary by those who preferred the discrete categorization of the arts or those who were displeased when he left Diaghilev, but his curiosity, energy, and restless self-education made him a great artist. His gifts of understanding several art forms and his willingness to study outside his own cultural sphere allowed his work to transcend more narrow outlooks and encompass the broadest sense of the human comedy.

Bibliography

Antony, Gordon. *Massine*. London: Routledge, 1939. Excellent black-and-white photographs of Massine in his most famous roles. Sitwell's commentary credits Massine for a unique greatness combining the skills of both dancer and choreographer, and for his unusually fine intelligence, especially in identifying great artists in other fields and bringing them to the public.

Grigoriev, S. L. *The Diaghilev Ballet, 1909-1929*. Edited and translated by Vera Bowen. London: Constable, 1953; New York: Dance Horizons, 1970. The memoirs of one of Diaghilev's company who was with the company from beginning to end. There is much discussion of Massine.

Gruen, John. *The Private World of Ballet*. New York: Viking Press, 1970. A collection of descriptions and interviews. Gruen interviewed Massine while he was in New York working with the Joffrey Ballet. He includes information from an interview with Eugenia Delarova Doll, a ballerina who had been married to Massine.

Haskell, Arnold. *Diaghileff: His Artistic and Private Life*. London: Gollancz, and New York: Simon and Schuster, 1935. Places Massine at the center of the rebuilding of Diaghilev's company and portrays him as a key figure of the renaissance of ballet; this is a thorough history of the Ballet Russe and its founder.

Hunt, Marilyn. "Massine Wins a New Generation of Admirers." *Dance Magazine* 66, no. 1 (January, 1992). Discussion of the revival of Massine's symphonic ballet *Choreartium* by the Birmingham Royal Ballet of England.

Kochno, Boris. *Diaghilev and the Ballets Russes.* Translated by Adrienne Foulke. New York: Harper, 1970; London: Allen Lane, 1976. Kochno became Diaghilev's private secretary in 1921, edited programs, and composed ballet librettos. His is an insider's look at the company, dancers, and ballets. This is a large-format book with illustrations and photographs.

Massine, Leonide. *Massine on Choreography: Theory and Exercises in Composition.* London: Faber, 1976. Massine considered this study the crowning achievement of his life's work and a way to transmit what he had learned through experience to successive generations.

―――. *My Life in Ballet.* London: Macmillan, and New York: St. Martin's Press, 1968. An autobiography that narrates family life as well as artistic accomplishment. Massine reflects on the relationship within the ballet world and the vagaries of his personal fortune and maintains a generous attitude toward all of his colleagues and a consistent modesty about himself.

Leslie Friedman

HENRI MATISSE

Born: December 31, 1869; Le Cateau-Cambrésis, France

Died: November 3, 1954; Nice, France

Area of Achievement: Art

Contribution: Matisse became the leader of the French expressionists called Les Fauves, or wild beasts. When the artists of that unofficial movement dispersed, he steadfastly and daringly simplified painting to the point of abstract decoration.

Early Life

Henri-Émile-Benoît Matisse was born in extreme northern France at Le Cateau-Cambrésis, the town of his grandparents, but spent his youth in nearby Bohain-en-Vermandois, where his father Émile had financial interests in a drugstore and a grain elevator. Little is known of the boy's early youth, but not long after the age of ten Matisse was sent to Saint-Quentin, some distance to the south, to study Latin and Greek. Up to age eighteen, Matisse moved dutifully from one school to the next without exhibiting an inclination toward any particular profession. In 1887, however, he went to Paris to study law and did so with his father's blessing. In three years he completed legal coursework, passed the required examinations, and returned to Saint-Quentin, where he began a monotonous existence as a clerk in a lawyer's office.

That type of life might have continued for many years had Matisse not attended morning classes in 1889 at the École Quentin Latour, where he drew from sculpture casts, and had he not had appendicitis, necessitating a long convalescence that was alleviated by his mother's gift of a box of paints, brushes, and an instruction manual. The latter changed Matisse's life. Within two years, he abandoned law and traveled to Paris to prepare for entrance exams to the École des Beaux-Arts, the official, state-supported school for the arts in France. His preparation took place at the respectable Académie Julian under the well-established painter Adolphe William Bouguereau. Disagreeing with Bouguereau's insistence upon conservative modes of painting, Matisse became disillusioned, left the school, and failed his first entrance examination to the École des Beaux-Arts.

Frustrated, but not defeated, Matisse fortunately met Gustave Moreau, a symbolist painter and a new instructor at the École des Beaux-Arts, who allowed him to enter his class unofficially upon seeing some of his drawings. In addition to Moreau's instruction, the teacher encouraged Matisse to copy artworks in the Louvre, which he did diligently during 1893 and 1894. By the winter of 1894, he passed the entrance exam into the École des Beaux-Arts and then officially entered Moreau's painting class. Moreau was an important key to Matisse's development. He inspired Matisse through his enthusiastic teaching, lavish attention, and his encouragement to grow independently, free of dogma or pressure for stylistic conformity. Moreau also encouraged Matisse and other students to go into the streets to study actual life and to seek out new works by painters at the galleries.

In 1895, Matisse began to paint outdoors, first in Paris and over the next few years in Brittany as well. There he met the Australian Impressionist painter John Russell, who as a friend of Claude Monet and the late Vincent van Gogh, passed on their emphasis on remaining independent in one's development. Coinciding with his new interest in plein air painting, Matisse became aware of Impressionism on a grand scale when the Gustave Caillebotte Bequest Collection was exhibited at the Musée Luxemburg, Paris.

A modicum of success came to Matisse in 1897 when he exhibited the painting *La Desserte* at the Salon de la Nationale after having been elected an associate member of the Société Nationale the previous year. Encouraged, his next several years were marked by intense drawing, painting, more study at the École des Beaux-Arts, the Académie F. Carrière, the studio of La Grande Chaumière, plus much travel. Those same years up through 1903 were also marked by financial hardships, yet bright spots too, such as viewing the van Gogh retrospective show at the Galérie Bernheim-Jeune. The faith that Matisse had in his independent stance, his receptivity to new currents, his great capacity for work, and his affinity for color as structure coalesced, and Matisse's name and work were soon known with thunder.

Life's Work

By the first years of the twentieth century, Matisse's explorations in color and painting structure gained momentum. His canvas *Luxe, Calm, et Volupté* of 1904-1905 was executed almost entirely in the Neo-Impressionist manner of dots and small

bars of bold colors. Its imagery alluded to an arcadian existence, its setting to the Mediterranean coast, and its title to Charles Baudelaire's "L'Invitation au voyage."

Matisse understood Neo-Impressionism with its near-scientific approach to optics and perception, but with this painting he mostly derived a mosaic effect which definitely pointed him closer to abstraction. By 1905, when Matisse was in his midthirties, his work was still not unequivocally his in style or content. Yet, a trip the same year with painter and friend André Derain to the Mediterranean fishing village of Collioure changed his art forever.

From his collaboration with Derain and his immersion into the sundrenched vibrant colors of southern France, Matisse reworked older paintings of Collioure and the immediate environs. In these paintings, tree trunks were painted with bold strokes and equally bold, arbitrary shots of color. Actual or descriptive colors were sacrificed for an intuitive, spontaneous approach in which each color stroke was related to all other color marks in the composition. When Matisse returned to Paris that fall, he used his new Collioure approach in a portrait of his wife entitled *Woman with the Hat*. Utilizing the standard society portrait mode, Matisse again disregarded actual colors and applied those reflecting his feelings of the moment.

The French public first viewed *Woman with the Hat* and four other Matisse paintings in the same manner at the Salon d'Automne that same year. These were joined by a number of other vigorous color experiments by his academy friends Derain, Henri Manquin, Charles Camoin, and Albert Marquet. Salon organizers assumed a new movement was forming and hung all paintings by the above men in the same room. Art critic Louis Vauxcelles, noticing that the paintings surrounded a statue in the conventional academic style, lamented that the scene reminded him of Donatello, a Renaissance sculptor, surrounded by *les fauves*, or wild beasts. Upon appearing in a printed review, the name stuck to a movement that was not intended, had no agreed upon theories, no manifesto, and no regular meetings or organization.

Vauxcelles' reaction of shock was equaled by that of the general public, which was not impressed by unrepressed colors and did not comprehend such color as a direct expression of the joy of life. Instead most viewers were bewildered, aghast, and believed that the Fauve paintings were insulting and a hoax. By contrast, the intended messages of color for color's sake and painting as a physical act of exhilaration were not lost on young European painters. Color became synonymous with expressionism—Fauvism in France and Die Brücke and Der Blaue Reiter in Germany.

The Salon d'Automne of 1905 brought Matisse to the attention of wealthy collectors of modern art and patrons including Leo and Gertrude Stein, Michael and Sarah Stein, the Cone sisters Etta and Claribel, as well as Sergei Shehukin. Soon Matisse was pursuing even bolder color schemes and more radically simplified structure resulting in the landmark paintings *Harmony in Red* (1908-1909) and the monumental diptych *Dance and Music* of 1910. This pair explored music and athletic rhythmic responses to it in a universal, timeless distillation. *The Red Studio* of 1911 was even more advanced in its reductive color space, yet it is touched with whimsy—viewers are invited symbolically to pick up one of the painted crayons on a foreground table and participate in the picture.

Matisse's appreciation of Muslim culture resulted in working voyages to North Africa in 1911-1913. In Tangier, Morocco, he conceived and developed a triptych involving a local model named Zorah, Muslim architecture and the tropical sun reflecting on both. This immersion into a non-Western environment had a long-standing impact on Matisse, for, during the war years 1914-1918 and throughout the 1920's, he was increasingly engrossed in an exotic visual dialogue with models in his studios whether in Paris or southern France at Nice. Typical of his oriental themes is *Decorative Figure* (1927), which exudes relaxed detachment and indolent luxury.

Noteworthy activity later in life included his decoration of the Dominican Chapel of the Rosary at Vence and his extraordinary cut paper collages. The clinically white spartan interior of the Vence Chapel is barely relieved by Matisse's calligraphic murals of the *Stations of the Cross* on one wall near the altar and equally large *Madonna and Child* and *St. Dominic* compositions on the adjacent walls. The compositions were rendered in black outlines only.

Matisse's collage work was composed of prepainted sheets of paper cut with scissors and glued to a support, often a white wall. When declining health in the 1940's forced the artist to work in bed, paper cut-outs did not represent a withdrawal from art. Through this medium, Matisse masterfully summed up themes and experiments covering a sixty-year career. Yet his compositions were anything but redundant, especially not those devoted to jazz and Caribbean rhythms. The cut-outs blaze with color, energy, and a celebration of life understandable by connoisseurs and children alike. Matisse's celebration of life came to a close at his death on November 3, 1954, in Nice, after which he was buried at Cimiez.

Summary

Coming late to art, Henri Matisse was nevertheless blessed by two factors: a tremendous capacity for work and a long life to see that energy mature. He came to painting from a preparation in law but seemed to possess an independent nature wary of influences and a willingness to explore directions even though the way was paved with doubt and disappointment.

Matisse's innate gifts in painting revolved around color and design. He was quite content to produce near abstractions with a cross-referential color structure. His imagery was always approximately representational, and his spaces were never overly rational or splintered like those of Cézanne. His art reflected the attitude that painting is a superior distraction. It was his diary, his mistress, his labor, and his intellectual stimulation. Matisse's worlds of the studio, indolent models, Mediterranean environments, and chromatic geometry were part of an aloof existence.

Basically apolitical, Matisse worked with almost total indifference through two world wars while maintaining his own world of balanced opposites, security, and comfort. Matisse believed that the audience for fine art is relatively small and comes from the educated bourgeoisie. Thus, for that audience, he strove to produce art that would have the same soothing effect as a good armchair for tired business professionals.

Bibliography

Barr, Alfred H., Jr. *Matisse: His Art and His Public.* New York: Museum of Modern Art, 1951; London: Secker and Warburg, 1975. Considered the standard work on Matisse for decades, though it is seriously challenged now by Pierre Schneider's monograph of 1984. Terrific organization of data is matched by an uncomplicated writing style and indulgent notes on the text, and thoughtful appendices far outweigh the value of the eight color plates and too many poor quality black-and-white illustrations.

Elderfield, John. *The Drawings of Henri Matisse.* London: Thames and Hudson, 1984; New York: Thames and Hudson, 1985. A long overdue examination of the role played by drawing for an artist known as one of the major colorists of the twentieth century. The text was sensitively researched, bringing to readers rarely explored ideas and frames of reference by Matisse. Contains notes and a catalog of 159 drawings.

Escholier, Raymond. *Matisse: A Portrait of the Artist and the Man.* Translated by Geraldine and H. M. Colvile. London: Faber, and New York: Praeger, 1960. A good biography that contains a small, selected bibliography and several reproductions.

Jacobus, John. *Henri Matisse.* London: Thames and Hudson, and New York: Abrams, 1973. A monograph from a series on major twentieth century European modernists. The too-brief biographical overview is, however, punctuated with well-chosen drawings and well-known paintings. The main section comprises forty color plates of key paintings, each preceded by a page of interpretation.

Matisse, Henri. *Henri Matisse: Drawings and Paper Cut-outs.* Introduction by Raoul Jean Moulin. Translated by Michael Ross. London: Thames and Hudson, and New York: McGraw-Hill, 1969. Moulin's thesis is that Matisse drew with scissors and prepainted cut paper as well as he did with a lithographic crayon.

————. *Matisse: Fifty Years of His Graphic Art.* Text by William S. Lieberman. New York: Braziller, 1956; London: Thames and Hudson, 1957. A survey of Matisse's prints that reveals his lifelong fascination with the female image mystique.

O'Brian, John. *Ruthless Hedonism: The American Reception of Matisse.* Chicago: University of Chicago Press, 1999. A study of Matisse's calculated approach to self-promotion in America.

Russell, John. *The World of Matisse, 1869-1954.* New York: Time-Life, 1969. A cultural-historical approach to art, this is a frank, entertaining, and well-illustrated work. Russell brings to light valuable data regarding the artist's friendships with other Fauve painters. The chapter on the early collectors and patrons is admirable in its depth.

Schneider, Pierre. *Matisse*. Translated by Michael Taylor and Bridget Strevens Romer. London: Thames and Hudson, and New York: Rizzoli, 1984. Herein Matisse is documented in a sumptuous and exhaustive fashion. Schneider covers every aspect of Matisse's life and career and illustrates brilliantly the importance of drawing for an artist revered as a colorist. Stresses the importance of women in Matisse's painting. Contains a biographical appendix and several photographs.

Spurling, Hilary. *The Unknown Matisse: Life of Henri Matisse, Volume One: 1869-1908*. London: Hamilton, and New York: Knopf, 1998. Spurling explores the reasons behind Matisse's "dark period," attributing it to a scandal involving the artist's in-laws.

Tom Dewey II

KONOSUKE MATSUSHITA

Born: November 27, 1894; Wasa, Wakayama Prefecture, Japan

Died: April 27, 1989; Osaka, Japan

Areas of Achievement: Business and industry

Contribution: Matsushita was an energetic manufacturing and marketing genius who built the world's biggest multinational electric home appliance industry—Matsushita Electric Company. In the process, he developed a revolutionary management system that has influenced industry worldwide.

Early Life

Konosuke Matsushita was born in Wasa, Wakayama Prefecture, south of Osaka, on November 27, 1894. The youngest of eight children, he had two brothers and five sisters. His father, Masakusu, was a well-to-do farmer but became impoverished because of his loss in speculative investments in the rice market. Losing all fortunes, including house and land, Matsushita's parents were forced to leave the village and move to Wakayama City, where they started a small shop selling wooden clogs (*geta*). Matsushita was then four years old. The clog business did not go well and worse, Matsushita's two brothers and a sister died of influenza. In desperation, Matsushita's father left home for Osaka looking for a job and eventually found one. When Matsushita was ten, his father found him an apprentice job in a *hibachi* (charcoal brazier) shop in Osaka. Matsushita was then in his fourth year at the local elementary school, but his formal education had to be terminated, and he had to start practical training as an apprentice, learning about careful work and sound business practices. Three months afterward, Matsushita moved on to a bicycle shop, where he worked as an apprentice. Repair work was not a matter of simply replacing parts but producing new parts. Matsushita worked for the shop for five years, acquiring needed skills that would later prove to be most essential for producing the electrical devices that would make him Japan's richest man. In 1910, foreseeing the potential opportunity in growing electric power and technology, fifteen-year-old Matsushita left the bicycle shop to join the Osaka Electric Light Company as an assistant wiring technician. After one year of hard work, he was promoted to foreman of the installation technicians—the youngest foreman on the payroll. For the next few years, he would gain the invaluable experience of managing people and making decisions, which would later prove to be most indispensable in his managerial career in one of the top corporations in the world.

In September, 1915, Konosuke married Mumeno Iue, who would play a vital role in establishing Matsushita Electric Company as cofounder and faithful supporter throughout their seventy-four years of marriage. In 1917, Matsushita left Osaka Electric Company to manufacture an electrical light socket that he had designed. His entire capital for the venture was about one hundred dollars. The first experiment was a failure. After persistent efforts, Matsushita succeeded in making an electric attachment plug that brought him a profit of about forty dollars. Encouraged by this success, Matsushita decided to establish Matsushita Electric Company with his wife and her brother. The company was established on March 7, 1918, in the Matsushita's small tenement house in Osaka, which would afterward be developed into Japan's largest electric and home appliance industry.

Life's Work

The three hardworking members of the Matsushita Electric Company gave everything to improve the quality of attachment plugs and two-way sockets, which Matsushita designed. The sales of the plugs escalated quickly, because the products were attractive and of high quality. Moreover, Matsushita's plugs were considerably lower in price than others on the market. Toward the end of 1918, the sales of the plugs increased sharply, and, consequently, Matsushita had to increase the number of his employees to twenty. The company was now producing five thousand plugs a month. By this time, Matsushita had learned many lessons in business and management. He was firmly convinced that the major ingredients for success in business were establishing a solid plan, making steady and consistent effort, winning complete loyalty of employees, giving careful training to employees, manufacturing a product one believes in, and winning the trust and confidence of customers and suppliers. These elements would later be incorporated into the governing principles of management in the Matsushita Electric Company.

In 1923, Matsushita's company took a major step by designing and manufacturing a battery-powered lamp for bicycles, the major mode of transportation for commuting workers, who were forced to travel on risky roads after dark. Matsushita was confident that the new product would sell well because it would replace the troublesome, old-fashioned candle-lit lanterns. Moreover, the battery lamp was more economical than candles and was much easier to operate. To Matsushita's surprise, sales of the lamp did not go well at all, because retailers were distrustful of dry-cell batteries. Matsushita, therefore, adopted a revolutionary sales campaign. He decided to convince the retailers that his lamp would shine for thirty hours by placing a battery lamp in each one of the skeptic retailers' stores and turning on the switch. The plan worked, and soon the orders for the lamp poured in. His bold salesmanship successfully gained the great confidence and trust of his retailers and customers. By 1929, the Matsushita Electric Company had three hundred employees and produced electric irons and heaters, in addition to the plugs and battery lamps. In 1929, the Matsushita Electric Company's sale of lamps hit 1.8 million a year.

In December, 1929, the Matsushita Electric Company, like all other companies in Japan, was critically affected by the worldwide depression. The Japanese newspapers were filled with reports of factory closings and labor disputes resulting from wage cuts and layoffs. At this critical time, Matsushita made a significant decision that would become his company's governing policy—the policy was that of lifetime job security. The company would not dismiss or lay off any worker. This policy of giving complete job security to his employees brought about very positive and beneficial results. The employees were more loyal to the company and worked harder, and the company's operations quickly revived. By February, 1930, the company thrived despite the fact that the depression dragged on. The company business went so well that Matsushita had to build two new factories during the first half of that year.

The year of 1932 was an important landmark for Matsushita. In this year, his philosophy of life was clearly defined and firmly crystallized. One day, he visited a temple, where he witnessed a large number of the Buddhist congregation building their temple diligently and with profound devotion. Matsushita vividly realized that religious groups had a well-defined purpose in life, a fact which makes them different from others. This realization prompted him to define his own mission: As an industrialist he was to serve society, and his duty was

to produce and supply useful goods to improve living conditions of people in the society. He believed that material abundance was an important precondition for creating a prosperous, happy, and peaceful society.

In the same year, the Employee Training Institute was established to educate young employees to become core members of the company. The institute offered them a three-year course of electrical engineering and business curriculums. The students would study four hours and receive four hours of practical training. This program was established based on Matsushita's firm belief that the success or failure of the company depended entirely on its employees, and the high standards of the company must be maintained by the high caliber of employees.

In 1933, Matsushita established the divisional management system, dividing the company operations into three main product groups—radios, storage batteries and lamps, and electric fixtures. The major aim of the system was clearly to evaluate performance and achievement of each division and to develop capable managers who would be able to manage their own division by themselves. By the end of 1936, the Matsushita Electric Company was producing more products, including radio sets, electric heating appliances, phonographs, batteries, fans, stoves, and other electric appliances. The company's sales volume was estimated at about 4.7 million dollars. The scope of the company's business grew, and it expanded further. By 1940, it had thirty plants with ten thousand employees.

During World War II, the Matsushita Electric Company, like all other major companies, was drafted for military production. It produced two-hundred-ton wooden transport ships and airplanes. Immediately following the war, the Matsushita Electric Company quickly resumed the manufacturing of home appliances with a work force of fifteen thousand. Its operations were abruptly suspended, however, by the American Occupation authorities. The Occupation authorities designated Matsushita a *zaibatsu* (financial clique) and froze all of his assets. The Occupation authorities saw that the *zaibatsu* system, made up of a dozen giant families, had controlled 80 percent of the country's industrial and financial enterprises and such excessive concentration of economic power was a serious obstruction to the democratization of Japan. In fact, the Matsushita Electric Company was not a *zaibatsu*, although it had grown to a giant size and had the look of a powerful combine, and that led to the misconception of the Occupation authorities. In October, 1950, after four years of appeals, Matsushita's people, including the company labor union, managed to convince the Occupation authorities that the Matsushita Electric Company was not a *zaibatsu*, and Matsushita's name was finally lifted from the purge list.

In the beginning of 1951, the Matsushita Electric Company resumed its production operations with its work force of thirty-eight hundred employees. With Japan's speedy economic recovery, partly the result of the Korean War, the Matsushita Electric Company enjoyed a rapid growth. Now the Japanese could afford Matsushita's newly manufactured washing machines, refrigerators, and televisions. The sales of the company rose from 17 million dollars in 1951 to 186 million dollars in 1961. In that year, the company's empire swelled to eighty-nine plants, employing forty-nine thousand workers. The company added a startling array of products, including television sets, tape recorders, electric pencil sharpeners, freezers, and computers. Matsushita's products would rapidly change the Japanese life-style. In January, 1961, Matsushita, with gratifying conviction that the company was soundly established with his management philosophy, resigned as its president, assuming the role of chairman of the board. He was succeeded by his son-in-law and adopted son, Masaharu. (Matsushita's only son died when he was two years old.) Matsushita remained as chairman until 1977. Thereafter, he served the company as executive adviser until his death on April 27, 1989. At the age of ninety-four, he died of pneumonia in a hospital that he had founded.

Summary

Konosuke Matsushita indeed was one of the most successful industrial and managerial tycoons of the twentieth century. He rose from near-poverty to establish the world's largest manufacturing empire of home appliances. In 1986, the Matsushita empire had a work force of 165,000 and had 101 overseas subsidiary companies and plants engaging in productions in thirty-eight countries. In the same year, the total annual sales of the sixty-five Matsushita Group companies in Japan were estimated at 40 billion dollars. The Matsushita employees were producing more than fourteen thousand varieties of products to be distributed to every corner of the world.

The impact of Matsushita products upon the social life of people during the second half of the twentieth century was great. An abundance of Matsushita's products not only raised the standard of living for millions but also radically changed their life-styles. Matsushita's products also considerably liberated millions of women from long days of household drudgery and gave them more leisure time to engage in creative activities. In the early 1960's, when Anastas Mikoyan, then the Soviet Union's vice premier, was boastfully explaining to Matsushita how the Bolsheviks had liberated the Russians from exploitation, Matsushita braggingly declared that he was instrumental in liberating Japanese women from the heavy burden of labor in their households.

Matsushita made many significant contributions in the business and managerial sectors. He was the first employer in the modern business world to implement the policy of lifetime employment and to found a welfare system that provided workers with housing, gymnasiums, hospital care, and wedding halls. He was the first Japanese employer to institute the five-day work week and was also the first one to establish an employee training institute to train young workers. He was also the first man to establish the divisional management system in order to facilitate efficient performance of company operations. It is not surprising to find that some of the best-managed corporations in the United States, including International Business Machines (IBM) and Delta Air Lines, have already adopted the Japanese model of management instituted by Matsushita.

Bibliography

"Background to PHP—30 Years." *PHP Intersect*, September, 1976: 75-80. An invaluable interview article by the staff of the Peace, Happiness, and Prosperity (PHP) Institute for *PHP Intersect*, its monthly magazine. Gives an excellent background account of PHP Institute told by Matsushita, the founder of the institute. The article discusses the founding of the institute in 1946, the goals of the institute, and how those goals are to be achieved.

"Following Henry Ford." *Time* 79 (February 23, 1962): 93-97. This article covers Matsushita's success story. Shows how the Matsushita Electric Company was established and how it expanded to become the biggest home appliance industry in the world.

"Konosuke Matsushita of Matsushita Electric, Interview." *Nation's Business* 59 (January, 1971): 32-37. Matsushita responds to many questions about his early apprentice years, the founding of his company in 1918, the establishment of his division system, the post-World War II period, and his success. A brief but valuable account of Matsushita's life.

Kotter, John P. "Matsushita: The World's Greatest Entrepreneur?" *Fortune* 135, no. 6 (March 31, 1997): 104:8. Discussion of Matsushita's management techniques and life.

"Matsushita." *Harvard Business School Bulletin*, February, 1983: 8-9, 49-116. This work, a very informative account of Matsushita's life, philosophy, and contributions, consists of four parts: Part 1 traces the historical development of Matsushita's industrial complex in Osaka from 1918 to the early 1980's; part 2 describes the success story of Matsushita Industrial Canada; part 3 provides comprehensive details of the founding of the Matsushita School of Government and Management in 1979; and part 4 recounts the personal story of the lifelong friendship between Matsushita and Shozo Hotta, an honorary chairman of the Sumitomo Bank. Matsushita is depicted as an idealist and a great achiever.

Matsushita, Konosuke. *Quest for Prosperity: The Life of a Japanese Industrialist.* Tokyo: PHO Institute, 1988. An excellent autobiography—the last of Matsushita's major works—written in 1988, one year prior to his death. The author relates many interesting and invaluable anecdotes of his many years of experience. Contains a good chronology and a bibliography.

Pascale, Richard Tanner, and Anthony G. Athos. *The Art of Japanese Management: Applications for American Executives.* New York: Simon and Schuster, 1981; London: Allen Lane, 1982. This book is well worth reading for those who wish to study and learn about the ways in which many Japanese industries are more successful than American industries. The authors use the Matsushita Electric Company as a Japanese example.

Won Z. Yoon

VLADIMIR MAYAKOVSKY

Born: July 19, 1893; Bagdadi (now Mayakovsky), Georgia, Russian Empire
Died: April 14, 1930; Moscow, U.S.S.R.
Area of Achievement: Literature
Contribution: Mayakovsky was the poet laureate of the Russian Revolution. Celebrating the modern technological age, he became the voice of the masses. Combining propaganda and innovative poetic techniques, he created sweeping epics, mass spectacles, and dramatic slogans that brought a vibrant literature to the people in the streets.

Early Life

Vladimir Vladimirovich Mayakovsky, born in Bagdadi, Georgia, was an unpromising student who became involved in revolutionary activities early in his life. When his family moved to Moscow, the young Mayakovsky became fascinated with the spectacle of the 1905 Revolution. At the age of fourteen, he joined the Bolshevik Party and was arrested for revolutionary activities. In prison, he started to write poetry and to learn the power of literature. Mayakovsky eventually rechanneled his revolutionary zeal in the direction of creating socialist art and enrolled in the Moscow Institute of Painting, Sculpture, and Art, where he was introduced to modern art by David Burlyuk, an expressionist turned cubist. He also joined the Futurist movement, whose principles he was to embrace for the rest of his life. Mayakovsky supported the Futurists in their call for a dynamic art that would separate itself from the literature of the romantic past and celebrate the urban landscape. Dressed in conspicuous outfits, Mayakovsky went on tour reciting his poetry and giving lectures on art. These performances provided excellent training for his future role as an artistic ambassador for the Soviet Union. In his early poetry, he experimented with unmelodious sounds, distorted syntax, unusual words, bizarre figures of speech, and hyperbolic images. In 1913, he wrote, directed, and acted in his first drama, *Vladimir Mayakovsky* (1913; English translation, 1968). The play is a monodrama in which there is essentially only one character—Mayakovsky, the suffering poet; all the other characters are dreamlike reflections of various elements of his ego. A plotless series of long interior monologues written in fractured verse, this early drama introduced some of the themes and techniques that

he would develop in his later works. It calls for the destruction of past cultures, concentrates on images of urban technology, presents a future-oriented vision, introduces the themes of martyrdom and suicide, and hints at a revolution to come.

In 1913, Mayakovsky also became associated with the literary theorist Osip Brik and fell in love with Osip's wife Lili. The Briks aided him in his career as a Futurist poet, and his love for Lili inspired many of his poems. In fact, she inspired his first epic poem, *Oblako v shtanakh* (1915; *A Cloud in Pants*). In this poem, the poet starts with an incident of rejected love and builds to scenes of crucifixion and martyrdom. In "Chelovek" ("Man"), published in 1916, Mayakovsky explores cosmic themes in the form of a parody of the life of an orthodox saint. This poem paved the way for the cosmic sweep of his later poetry. Mayakovsky was already a poet with a mission, and the Russian Revolution gave him a platform from which to convey his message.

Life's Work

Mayakovsky was a poet of the Revolution. From propaganda slogans to epic poems, from poetry readings to mass spectacles, Mayakovsky was imbued with the ideas of the Revolution. He even called it "my Revolution." During the Revolution, he joined in the Futurists' program to take art into the streets and to bring it directly to the masses. Between 1918 and 1921, he created poster art with poetic captions.

In order to reach the people more effectively, he turned to theater. On November 7, 1918, in collabration with the avant-garde director Vsevolod Meyerhold, Mayakovsky commemorated the first anniversary of the Revolution with his second play *Misteriya-buff* (1918; *Mystery-Bouffe*, 1933). In this play, he parodies a medieval mystery cycle. In true propaganda style, Mayakovsky caricatures the enemies of Communism: the greedy capitalist, the compromising Mensheviks, the inactive intellectuals, and the Soviet merchants. Along with Meyerhold, Mayakovsky helped to transform the stage from a two-dimensional, photographic representation of reality into a constructivist circus.

During this period, Mayakovsky continued to create moving epic poetry. In *150,000,000* (1920; English translation, 1949), Mayakovsky pits the giant Ivan, a symbol for 150,000,000 cold, hungry, desperate Russians, against the grotesque capitalist warrior, Woodrow Wilson, who sinks to the bottom of the sea. In *Pro eto* (1923; *About That*, 1965), he transforms a story of rejected love into an agon on his martyrdom and his resurrection in a futuristic world. This love poem shows his ability to elevate personal tragedy to the level of the messianic. In his greatest epic, *Vladimir Illich Lenin* (1924; English translation, 1939), he mixes comic and epic styles to celebrate the sweep of history. The use of cosmic imagery, the archetypal pattern of death and resurrection, the visions of futuristic worlds, and the interweaving of hard-hitting polemics with intricate poetry won for Mayakovsky national fame as an epic poet.

Mayakovsky soon became the artistic ambassador for the Soviet Union. In this capacity, he traveled throughout Germany, France, Eastern Europe, and the United States promoting Communism, speaking out for his brand of Soviet art, and writing travelogues and poems. He also established several journals and organizations to promote his own artistic programs. In his journal *Lef*, he proclaimed the need to slough off the decadent bourgeois culture and to create a proletarian art. His line "Time Forward March!" became the battle cry for the revolutionary art that would lead humanity into a new age of technology. When *Lef* went out of circulation, Mayakovsky created *New Lef* to restate his position. Again, he called for an art that was utilitarian but still avant-garde, attacking Maxim Gorky and other noted Soviet authors for their return to heroic and realistic depictions of Soviet life.

Mayakovsky also tried to move theater away from psychological realism. By 1927, however, the tide of Soviet politics was changing. Soviet society was searching for stability, and revolutionary art was giving way to Socialist Realism. Critics attacked Mayakovsky's art as bombastic and bohemian and accused him of lacking sincerity and concern for individual human problems. He met his critics head on with the production of *Klop* (1929; *The Bedbug*, 1931), a play in which the enemies of socialism are depicted as grotesque caricatures. In the character Oleg Bayan, Mayakovsky lampooned Vladimir Sidorov and other reactionary poets of his time, who not only saw their doubles on stage but also demanded an apology. He also satirized the Soviet program of modified capitalism (the so-called New Economic Policy) in his depiction of a beauty parlor and in his caricatures of

hawking merchants peddling everything from lampshades to sausage balloons. In *The Bedbug*, Mayakovsky emphasized overt theatricalism over realism. In the Meyerhold production, actors marched through the audience hawking bras while the set consisted of everything from kitsch art to multimedia scenery. Mayakovsky had created a theater of public spectacle that included everything from temperance propaganda to clown acts. *Banya* (1930; *The Bathhouse*, 1963), Mayakovsky's last play produced within his lifetime, was his most vicious attack on his contemporaries, especially those in the Soviet bureaucracy. Everywhere in the play there were official bureaus with lengthy acronyms, but nothing ever got done. In the third act, he used the play-within-a play device to satirize the realistic school of the Moscow Art Theater as well as the poetic style of the Russian ballet theater. Mayakovsky reduced the objects of his satire to grotesque types, broke with fourth-wall realism, and tried to jar his audience into the action. Again Mayakovsky tried to create a theater of spectacle that would magnify, notmirror reality. The play angered many in the literary establishment and closed after three performances.

In his last great poem, *Vo ves golos* (1930; *At the Top of My Voice*, 1940), Mayakovsky depicted himself as he had always depicted himself: as a poet of the future, a poet of the people, and a poet of the Communist Party, loyal to the cause. Having been refused an exit visa, despondent over the boycott of a retrospective exhibition of his work, and disillusioned over the failure of *The Bathhouse*, Mayakovsky shot himself on April 14, 1930. In his suicide note, he wrote that he did not want to list his grievances; instead, he proclaimed: "Night has imposed a starry tribute on the sky/ It is in such hours that one rises and speaks to/ the ages, history, and the universe." To the end, Mayakovsky was a poet with a revolutionary vision.

Summary

Vladimir Mayakovsky was indeed the poet of the Revolution. As a member of the Futurist movement, he broke with the heroic literature of the past and the sentimentality of bourgeois realism to fight for a democratic art that would allow the free word of the creative personality to be "written on the walls, fences, and streets of the cities." He wanted a new form of poetry that would cry out to the people, abandon traditional imagery, praise the urban landscape, and hail the coming of the utopian com-

mune. To accomplish this artistic revolution, Mayakovsky created a literature that eschewed the notion of absolute value and eternal beauty and spoke directly to the masses—a literature that produced poetic devices that were based more on their ability to propagandize than on their ability to create aesthetic embellishments.

As a dramatist, Mayakovsky, with the aid of the director Vsevolod Meyerhold, revolutionized modern theater. He brought the action of the drama into the audience, breaking the bonds of keyhole realism. He also replaced realistic characters with grotesque figures—slapstick clowns bouncing across constructivist three-dimensional sets composed of ropes, grids, and platforms. In essence, he created a theater of spectacle.

Upon his death, Mayakovsky was accorded a state funeral; he was widely mourned. In 1938, Joseph Stalin proclaimed him one of the most important socialist poets. In the Soviet Union, both a town and a square were named for him. Today, he is one of the most highly acclaimed Soviet poets, and his influence has reached beyond the Soviet Union.

Bibliography

Brown, Edward J. *Mayakovsky: A Poet in the Revolution.* Princeton, N.J.: Princeton University Press, 1973. The first major critical biography of Mayakovsky in English. The book shows a close connection between Mayakovsky's life and his works. It provides close readings of Mayakovsky's major and minor works and even focuses on his didactic verse. Most important, it examines Mayakovsky's work in context with the social, political, and artistic revolutions that helped to structure his artistic vision. Contains an annotated bibliography of works by and on Mayakovsky.

Lahti, Katherine. "Vladimir Mayakovsky: A Dithyramb." *Slavic and East European Journal* 40, no. 2 (Summer 1996). Lahti discusses Mayakovsky's "Vladimir Mayakovsky: A Tragedy," and its similarity to the Greek dithyramb.

Mikhailov, Alexander. "At the Feet of a Giant." *New Literary History* 23, no. 1 (Winter 1992). Examines the changing assessment of Mayakovsky over time.

Shklovskii, Viktor. *Mayakovsky and His Circle.* Edited and translated by Lily Feiler. New York: Dodd Mead, 1972; London: Pluto Press, 1974. A tribute to Mayakovsky by a close associate and intimate friend. The book not only covers the relationship between Shklovsky and Mayakovsky but also focuses on the other figures in the Futurist movement in Russia. Although it promotes Shklovsky's Formalist bias, it is a good firsthand account of Mayakovsky's development as a poet as well as a history of the artistic revolutions in Russia from 1910 to 1930.

Stapanian, Juliette R. *Mayakovsky's Cubo-Futurist Vision.* Houston, Tex.: Rice University Press, 1986. An analysis of Mayakovsky's poetry in the light of developments in the fine arts during the early part of the twentieth century. Stapanian shows a correlation between Mayakovsky's poetic techniques and the artistic styles of the cubist and the Futurist painters. She demonstrates how the images in his poems mirror the fractured and multidimensional images in Cubo-Futurist art.

Terras, Victor. *Vladimir Mayakovsky.* Boston: Twayne, 1983. An excellent critical introduction to Mayakovsky. The book provides a clear, well-organized biographical sketch of Mayakovsky's life followed by a close analysis of his major works. Terras defines critical terms, traces the history of artistic movements, and provides a clear critical assessment of Mayakovsky's works. The book also contains a comprehensive checklist of Mayakovsky's work and an annotated bibliography of secondary sources.

Woroszylski, Wiktor. *The Life of Mayakovsky.* Translated by Boleslaw Taborski. New York: Orion Press, 1970; London: Gollancz, 1972. A translation of a 1966 work by a Polish poet. The book is an encyclopedic compendium of documentary sources on Mayakovsky's life and work, including police reports, personal letters, impressions of close associates, and interviews with intimate friends—all interspersed with samples of Mayakovsky's poetry. It is a good reference work for someone looking for primary source material, but it does not present a clear perspective for the reader who is unfamiliar with Mayakovsky's work.

Paul Rosefeldt

WILLIAM J. MAYO and CHARLES H. MAYO

William J. Mayo

Born: June 29, 1861; Le Sueur, Minnesota

Died: July 28, 1939; Rochester, Minnesota

Charles H. Mayo

Born: July 19, 1865; Rochester, Minnesota

Died: May 26, 1939; Chicago, Illinois

Area of Achievement: Medicine

Contribution: In 1889, William W. Mayo and his two sons, William J. Mayo and Charles H. Mayo, with the Sisters of St. Francis founded St. Mary's Hospital in Rochester, Minnesota. From the "cooperative group clinic" which began at the hospital, the Mayo doctors founded the Mayo Clinic and, subsequently, the Mayo Foundation for Medical Education and Research, a part of the University of Minnesota Graduate School in Rochester.

Early Lives

William James Mayo, older brother of Charles Horace Mayo, was born June 29, 1861, in Le Sueur, Minnesota, to Dr. William Worall Mayo, who had immigrated to the United States from England in 1845, and Louise Abigail (née Wright). Charles Horace Mayo was born July 19, 1865, in Rochester, Minnesota, the second son of five children.

Despite their father's renown and financial success, the two boys spent a relatively ordinary youth on the Mayo farm in Rochester. They attended public and private high schools, performed customary chores at home, and, after finishing school, worked to learn the various skills necessary for their future profession. After finishing school, for example, Charles worked as a clerk-apprentice in an apothecary, where he was expected to learn the various aspects of making as well as dispensing medication.

Two significant differences, however, distinguish their youth from mere ordinariness: the education they received at home from their parents, and their years at the Rochester Training School, where they were required to study Latin, art, and the classics. At home, their introduction to science began in a broad and personal way. Mrs. Mayo taught them about botany as they walked and studied the plants and trees on their farm. She had a telescope built on the roof of the farmhouse so that the boys could develop one of their favorite pastimes: stargazing. Dr. Mayo kept a large medical and scientific library in his office, and as the boys did their chores at home or in the office, they were instructed in both the application of medical knowledge and its precepts in general chemistry, anatomy, and physics. In addition to their education at Rochester Training School, Dr. and Mrs. Mayo maintained a personal library of classical and literary works from which the boys were encouraged to read. Works by Charles Dickens and James Fenimore Cooper were of particular interest. From Dickens, the boys gained a better understanding of social conscience, which was esteemed and nurtured in the Mayo family. From Cooper, because of his regional appeal, they deepened their respect for the land and the humanity which shared it. To these stories, Dr. and Mrs. Mayo added their own experiences of the Sioux Outbreak (1862) and of the Civil War, for which Dr. Mayo was an induction physician. They taught their children about the horrors and casualties of prejudice and armed conflict. They taught them, above all, about the joys of working together, and it can be said of the boys, although starkly contrasted in appearance and temperament, that they were always "together."

From their childhood to the time of Dr. Mayo's death in 1911, they would be reminded of their father's belief that no man existed independently from others. In these early years, the Mayo brothers developed the keen sense of equality, individualism, and humanitarianism that would define one of the world's most famous and beloved medical institutions, the Mayo Clinic.

Life's Work

The professional lives of the young Mayo doctors began when they returned to join their father's already respected, thriving practice in Rochester. After the death of their father, William Worral Mayo, on March 6, 1911, the Mayo brothers carried on the work of the clinic as a partnership. From this partnership developed the "cooperative group clinic" which later became the Mayo Clinic.

The first major event in the professional lives of the young men occurred in 1883, only a few months after William received his medical degree

William J. Mayo

from the University of Michigan: A tornado devastated Rochester. In response to the catastrophe, the Mayos and the Sisters of St. Francis, under the leadership of Mother Alfred, proposed a new hospital to care for the immediate as well as long-term needs of the destitute. This occurred at a time in American history when hospitals were regarded as objectionable facilities which housed the infectious and chronically ill poor. Until the late nineteenth century, preferred medical care was administered by private physicians and nurses or in special clinics most often associated with medical schools. Similarly, major institutions were not Catholic. Thus, it was not without opposition that the new St. Mary's Hospital, a Catholic institution, opened its doors with thirteen patients on October 1, 1889. From this hospital, in affiliation with the Mayo's private practice, the network which was to become the Mayo Clinic and Foundation was born.

In 1888, when Charles had received his medical degree from the Chicago Medical College (later Northwestern University Medical School), he re-

turned to Rochester to join his older brother and his father at St. Mary's Hospital. Because neither brother had served an internship, both Charles and William practiced general medicine with an emphasis in surgery. William eventually specialized in the surgery of the abdomen, pelvis, and kidneys, which he practiced until his retirement in 1928. Charles, unlike his brother, had broader talents for surgery. So broad, in fact, were Charles's surgical interests and skills that he has been recognized as the originator of special procedures in thyroid, neurologic, cataract, and orthopedic surgeries. To honor his achievement, the American Medical Association elected him president in 1906. During World War I, William and Charles, both with the rank of colonel, rotated as the chief consultants for all surgery to the United States Army.

From 1907 until his death in 1939, William was a member of the Board of Regents of the University of Minnesota. Similarly, Charles, who had retired from surgery in 1930, was professor of surgery at the University of Minnesota Medical School from 1919 to 1936 and professor of surgery at the graduate school from 1915 to 1936. After retiring from their surgical duties, the two brothers purchased adjoining homes in Tucson, Arizona. Although they remained actively involved on the board of the clinic and the foundation, they preferred the warmth of the Arizona sun to the cold winters of Minnesota.

In the spring of 1939, William Mayo returned to the clinic for a checkup to learn that he had stomach cancer. He was operated on immediately and recovered quickly from the surgery. Unfortunately, the surgery was not successful in removing the cancer. William returned to his home in Rochester, where he died in his bed on July 28, 1939.

To be with his brother during the operation and the recuperative period, Charles Mayo returned early from his home in Tucson. Because his brother was recuperating rapidly, Charles decided to visit his tailor in Chicago. During his stay, he developed pneumonia and died on May 26, 1939, only two months before his brother.

Summary

Although the principal legacy of the Mayo brothers is the Mayo Clinic and the Mayo Foundation, modern medicine has been provided with more than a prototypical clinic. Through their mutual devotion and generosity, the Mayo brothers provided practical guidelines for the division of labor

Charles H. Mayo

within the hospital; they developed cooperative partnerships between surgical and medical specialties without the loss of individualism. The Case Records Division and the library allow comprehensive clinical and historical record keeping and analysis. Its resources are open to medical professionals worldwide. Consistent with the idea that no man is independent from another, the Mayo brothers intended their knowledge to be shared. The Mayo Clinic and Foundation, the first major institution of its kind in the United States, does just that—achieving a balance between the specialized and humane care to patients and the specialized and humane training and research equally needed by medical professionals.

Bibliography

Braasch, William F. *Early Days in the Mayo Clinic*. Springfield, Ill.: Thomas, 1969. Historical perspective on formation of the Mayo Clinic; particular interest on the development of cooperative specialties; written by a celebrated urologist affiliated with the clinic.

Clapesattle, Helen B. *The Doctors Mayo*. Minneapolis: University of Minnesota Press, 1941. The most popular, comprehensive and authoritative biography, based on historical documents and interviews, many of which are available in the archives of the clinic; includes comprehensive research bibliography.

Garrison, Fielding H. "A Medical Tour of the West." In *Contributions to the History of Medicine*, 685-692. New York: Hafner, 1966. An overview of the beginnings of the Mayo Clinic; collection of documents providing historical and international perspective on medical ideas and practices between 1925 and 1935.

Johnson, Victor. *Mayo Clinic: Its Growth and Progress*. Bloomington, Minn.: Voyageur Press, 1984. Concise historical overview of the clinic from the turn of the century to the 1980's.

Mayo, Charles Horace. "Early Days of the Mayo Clinic." *Proceedings of the Mayo Clinic* 7 (October, 1932): 584-587. Personal notes on the ideas behind the Mayo Clinic, by one of the founding brothers.

Mayo, Charles William. *Mayo: The Story of My Family and My Career*. New York: Doubleday, 1968. Important inside view of the family and the clinic, based on family letters, anecdotes, and historical documents, by the son of Charles Horace Mayo, who was a member of the Board of Governors of the clinic and chairman of the Mayo Association.

Mayo Clinic. *Sketch of the History of the Mayo Clinic and the Mayo Foundation*. Philadelphia: Saunders, 1926. A chronological history of the clinic; foreword by William J. and Charles H. Mayo.

Shryock, Richard Harrison, ed. *Medicine in America: Historical Essays*. Baltimore: Johns Hopkins University Press, 1966. Background readings in the social history of American medicine; important scholarly work.

Wilder, Lucy. *The Mayo Clinic*. New York: Harcourt Brace, 1936. Written by the wife of Mayo clinician Dr. Russel M. Wilder. Includes a letter to the University of Minnesota from Dr. William J. Mayo, 1934.

Clinton A. Gould

MARGARET MEAD

Born: December 16, 1901; Philadelphia,
Pennsylvania
Died: November 15, 1978; New York, New York
Area of Achievement: Anthropology
Contribution: Through her best-selling books, her
public lecturing, and her column in *Redbook*
magazine, Mead popularized anthropology in
the United States. She also provided American
women with a role model, encouraging them to
pursue professions while simultaneously championing their roles as mothers.

Early Life

Margaret Mead credited her parents, Emily Fogg
and Edward Sherwood Mead, and her paternal
grandmother, Martha Ramsay Mead, as her primary childhood influences. They were all educators;
her mother was a teacher and sociologist who was
pursuing graduate work when Margaret was born,
her father was a professor of economics at the University of Pennsylvania, and her grandmother, who
was primarily responsible for teaching Margaret,
was a retired school principal. As a child, Margaret
received only sporadic formal education, attending
two years of kindergarten, one year of half days in
fourth grade, and six years at a variety of high
schools during which she was given supplemental
instruction by her grandmother. Her inherent love
of ritual found expression in religion when, at the
age of eleven, Mead joined the Episcopalian
church. She sustained her faith throughout her life.

Her mother and grandmother were the principal
role models for Mead. Both were able women who
had married and borne children but also had attended college and pursued careers. From them she
learned to enjoy reading and to observe and record
the world around her.

Mead anticipated finding a rich intellectual and
social life in college. Instead, she suffered isolation during her freshman year at DePauw University in the Midwest, where she experienced the
trauma of exclusion by college sororities. She was
also profoundly affected by her discovery that
"bright girls could do better than bright boys" but
"would suffer for it." She departed after one year,
convinced that coeducation disadvantaged wom-
en, and subsequently entered Barnard College,
where she found intellectual stimulation in the
company of several intelligent young women. Her
ordeal shaped her preference for her life's work:

She decided "not to compete with men in male
fields, but instead to concentrate on the kinds of
work that are better done by women." In anthropology, Mead found such a niche investigating
families and child-rearing practices.

Initially, Mead studied psychology, but in her senior year she was influenced by the Columbia University anthropologist Franz Boas and his graduate
student Ruth Benedict, who inspired her by the urgency with which they pursued their work. Boas,
the founder of modern American anthropology,
recognized that cultures rapidly were being cor-
rupted by world contact and was busily orchestrat-
ing the ethnographic description of as many cultures as possible with the limited number of field
workers available to him. Both Boas and Benedict
were responsible for convincing Mead that she
could make a contribution in anthropology.

Life's Work

Margaret Mead first traveled to the field in 1925,
when Boas dispatched her to American Samoa,
where she was to observe adolescence as an aid in
determining whether it was universally a time of
stress. The science of anthropology was in its infancy when Mead departed for Samoa. Methods
for gathering and deciphering information were yet
to be defined, and Mead invented techniques while
in the field. She lived with adolescent girls in a Samoan village, becoming the first American to use
the participant observer method developed by the
British anthropologist Stanislaw Malinowski.

Upon returning to the United States, Mead
earned her Ph.D. and simultaneously achieved
fame by publishing *Coming of Age in Samoa*
(1928). In her work, she described a culture that
was free of the *Sturm und Drang* of American adolescence and in which girls as well as boys were
taught to value and cherish their sexuality.

Between 1925 and 1939, Mead zealously performed field work, observing seven Pacific cultures
as well as the American Omaha Indians. After her
initial trip to Samoa, she never again worked alone,
choosing instead to collaborate with others, thereby making possible a more thorough analysis of
cultures. She focused on women and children who
were inaccessible to her male colleagues. Throughout her career, she was concerned with character
formation and the influence of cultural and biological determinants of behavior.

During three months of intensive discussion among Mead, her husband and collaborator Reo Fortune, and the British anthropologist Gregory Bateson, with whom they lived in New Guinea, Mead developed her theories of character formation. In *Sex and Temperament in Three Primitive Societies* (1935), she formalized her inferences regarding the process by which cultures established behavioral norms for men and women. She also provided explanations for deviance. Mead observed among the Iatmul, Arapesh, and Mundugumor peoples widely diverging behavioral patterns for men and women which she determined were culturally defined rather than biologically mandated. Traits that were considered feminine in one culture—the nurturing of children, for example—could as easily be considered masculine in another. In 1949, Mead explored more fully the interactive nature of cultural and biological determinants of gender in *In Male and Female: A Study of the Sexes in a Changing World.*

In 1935, Mead and Fortune divorced, and Mead married Bateson, with whom she also collaborated. In two exceptionally productive years during which the pair worked in Bali, Mead pursued her work on character formation while Bateson continued his theorizing regarding the nature of human nonverbal communications. Together, they pioneered the use of photographs and films as tools for anthropological research. Whereas previously anthropologists had taken still photographs for the purpose of illustrating their books, Mead and Bateson used film as a technique for studying nonverbal behavior. They shot an unprecedented 22,000 feet of film and 25,000 still photographs and edited and released several films, including *Balinese Character* and *Trance and Dance in Bali.* Their use of photography was a major innovation in anthropological methodology.

During World War II, Mead, along with other social scientists throughout the country, contributed her expertise to the war effort through work in government intelligence agencies. Some efforts were destructive in nature. Gregory Bateson, for example, at the Office of Strategic Services, forerunner to the CIA, developed methods of psychological warfare and ways of using propaganda to unnerve the Japanese. For her part, Mead lectured in England for the Office of War Information in 1943, attempting to facilitate relations between American troops and wartime Britons. She also served as the executive secretary of the Committee on Food Habits and in 1942 joined the National Research Council. Her principal contribution, however, occurred in the development of national character studies that provided techniques for analyzing the cultural characteristics of nations that could not be directly studied, such as Japan and Germany. Techniques for studying "culture at a distance" in which numerous sources, including movies, fiction, and interviews with immigrants, were employed to determine the nature of complex cultures in which the war inhibited fieldwork but which were strategically significant. In her 1942 book *And Keep Your Powder Dry*, Mead utilized her skills to analyze American society. At war's end, Mead continued to work as a Cold War intellectual at Columbia University's Research in Contemporary Cultures (RCC), which was funded by the Office of Navy Research. Initially the director of research, Mead replaced Ruth Benedict as director of the council after Benedict's sudden death.

Mead never, except peripherally, entered the male bastion of academe, choosing instead to work for the American Museum of Natural History in New York City. There she was appointed assistant curator of ethnology in 1926, promoted to associate curator in 1942, and promoted to curator in 1964. She retired from the museum in 1969 as curator emeritus.

In the last twenty-five years of her life, Mead focused extensively on teaching, becoming an adjunct professor at Columbia in 1954. She also served in a variety of visiting professorships. Among other positions she held were the presidencies of the World Federation of Mental Health (1956-1957), the American Anthropological Association (1960), and the American Association for the Advancement of Science (1975). She received several honorary degrees and was awarded posthumously the Presidential Medal of Freedom.

In 1962, Mead was invited to contribute a monthly column to *Redbook* magazine, and through it she developed a vast popular readership. She wrote to women about social problems, the future of the family, and child-rearing practices. In return, she used the letters she received from her readers as a source of information regarding the concerns of American women.

Summary

For American women, one of Mead's most salient achievements was her reevaluation of gender roles while she simultaneously championed tradition and ritual. She wrote and worried about the future of the American family, condemning the isolation imposed on women in modern suburbia and mourning the loss of the community of extended families. Mead envisioned a world in which women's and men's unique skills and contributions would be valued equally. Women would have options for contributions outside the traditional domestic sphere, but maternal and domestic roles also would be valued.

Mead's numerous contributions to the field of anthropology included her field work in seven Oceania cultures, her innovations in the use of film, and the development of national character studies. Mead also was instrumental in popularizing anthropology through her best-selling books, which were written for a public as well as for a scholarly audience, and through her column in *Redbook*. She provided insights and advice to women in her roles as anthropologist and mother.

To her lengthy list of achievements may also be added that of role model for American women. She was a successful and famous professional in an era in which the professions were virtually closed to women.

Bibliography

Bateson, Mary Catherine. *With a Daughter's Eye: A Memoir of Margaret Mead and Gregory Bateson.* New York: Morrow, 1984. Bateson, who is also an anthropologist, provides her own intimate recollections of her parents' lives. Illustrated.

Cassidy, Robert. *Margaret Mead: A Voice for the Century.* New York: Universe, 1982. Because of its brevity (156 pages) and lack of obvious footnotes (there are synopses for all chapters at the end) this book may seem appealing. It should, however, be viewed with caution, because it is uncritical and often simplistic. It does provide a useful chapter on Mead's views and contributions to feminism.

Cote, James E. "Much Ado about Nothing: The 'Fateful Hoaxing' of Margaret Mead." *Skeptical Inquirer* 22, no. 6 (November-December, 1998). Examines Professor Derek Freeman's unsuccessful attempts to discredit Mead's Samoan research.

Foerstel, Lenora, and Angela Gilliam, eds. *Confronting the Margaret Mead Legacy: Scholarship, Empire, and the South Pacific.* Philadelphia: Temple University Press, 1992. This is a compilation of ten articles critiquing Mead's anthropological achievements. Foerstel and Gilliam's "Margaret Mead's Contradictory Legacy" is particularly useful in its discussion of her entire career, including her long service in American intelligence agencies.

Holmes, Lowell D. *Quest for the* Real *Samoa: The Mead/Freeman Controversy and Beyond.* South Hadley, Mass.: Bergin and Garvey, 1987. In 1954, anthropologist Holmes traveled to Samoa to re-create the conditions and reexamine the conclusions of Mead's Samoan research. He challenged Derek Freeman, whose scathing and well-publicized critique of Mead, *Margaret Mead and Samoa: The Making and Unmaking of an Anthropological Myth* (1983), engendered fierce debate regarding the value of her work. While Holmes's conclusions differ in several details from Mead's, he finds that the validity of her research is "remarkably high" but that it was prone to such exaggerations as are commonly found in the work of novice fieldworkers.

Howard, Jane. *Margaret Mead: A Life.* London: Harvill, and New York: Simon and Schuster, 1984. Although Howard uses numerous interviews with people who knew Mead, she is uncritical in her sources. Mead's former husbands are quoted extensively along with colleagues, friends, and critics. The author's frequently florid language and her inclusion of gratuitous observations are disconcerting. Contains an extensive bibliography.

Mead, Margaret. *An Anthropologist at Work: Writings of Ruth Benedict.* Boston: Houghton Mifflin, 1959. Because their professional lives were intertwined, Mead's collection of Benedict's papers, in which she includes five biographical essays, provides invaluable biographical data on Mead's own career, including, notably, her training with Franz Boas and her World War II intelligence work.

———. *Blackberry Winter: My Earlier Years.* New York: Simon and Schuster, 1972; London: Angus and Robertson, 1973. In many ways the most useful work on Mead's life, this book contains three parts detailing her early personal life, professional work, and experiences as a mother and grandmother. Illustrated with photographs.

Metraux, Rhoda. "Margaret Mead: A Biographical Sketch," *American Anthropologist* 82 (June, 1980): 262-269. Metraux, Mead's friend and collaborator from the American Museum of Natural History, provides a concise but detailed biography of Mead which organizes her contributions into four distinct periods.

Newman, Louise M. "Coming of Age, but Not in Samoa: Reflections on Margaret Mead's Legacy for Western Liberal Feminism." *American Quarterly* 48, no. 2 (June, 1996). Discusses Mead's theories and work in evolutionary anthropology.

Mary E. Virginia

GOLDA MEIR

Born: May 3, 1898; Kiev, Ukraine, Russian Empire
Died: December 8, 1978; Jerusalem, Israel
Areas of Achievement: Government and politics
Contribution: Meir was a leading Zionist and inspirational figure for world Jewry who rejected life in the United States to immigrate to Palestine in 1920. She became a major role player in Zionist organizations there, eventually rising to become Israel's first ambassador to the Soviet Union (1948), minister of labor (1949), foreign minister (1956), and prime minister (1969).

Early Life

Golda Meir was born in Kiev, Russian Empire, on May 3, 1898. Her father was Moshe Yitzhak Mabovitch, who was a carpenter by training. Moshe and his wife had three children: Sheyna, Golda, and Zipke. The family moved from Kiev to their ancestral town of Pinsk after Golda's birth but ultimately sought to leave Russia because of the violent attacks that threatened Jewish life there. In 1906, the family immigrated to Milwaukee, Wisconsin. Golda worked with her sisters in the family's grocery store. Sheyna became involved in 1915 in the Poale Zion movement, a labor- and socialist-oriented branch of the Zionist movement, which in turn became an inspiration for Golda. Poale Zion aspired to national and social equality of the Jewish people in their own homeland through labor.

Golda fled home in 1912 at age fourteen and moved to Denver to live with Sheyna, who had gone there earlier for treatment of tuberculosis. Four years later (1916), she returned to Milwaukee under extreme parental pressure. While in Denver, she met Morris Meyerson (the name was Hebraized to "Meir" in 1956), whom she married in 1917. For a short time after her return to Wisconsin, Golda was enrolled in Milwaukee Normal School for Teachers. The idea of living and working in the United States did not have much appeal for Golda, who was more attracted to the Poale Zion leaders A. D. Gorden, Nachman Syrkin, and Shmaryahu Levin. She was instrumental in organizing the first Midwest marches in Milwaukee to protest the 1919 pogroms against the Jews in the Ukraine. On May 23, 1921, the Meyersons departed for Palestine on the SS *Pocahontas*. They arrived in Egypt and then transferred by train to Tel Aviv. During the fall of 1921, the Meyersons joined Kibbutz Merhavia (a collective farm based on egalitarian principles). The kibbutz placed Golda face-to-face with issues relating to feminism and female emancipation. Golda, however, never considered herself a feminist. She worked in the fields picking almonds, planting trees, and taking care of chickens. On kitchen duty, she became famous for introducing oatmeal and glasses in an otherwise Spartan environment.

In 1922, the Meyersons left Merhavia because of Morris' health and because of his unwillingness to have a child reared by the collective methods of the kibbutz. Their first child, Menachem, was born in November, 1923. The Meyersons moved to Jerusalem to work for Solel Boneh, a government-owned company that was at that time in poor financial standing. A second child, Sarah, was born during the spring of 1926. Meir later lamented that if she could do things over again, she would have remained on the kibbutz. In this period, Meir believed that the application of Jewish labor to Palestine would also improve the quality of life for the Arabs. She always believed that had been the case, justified by the rise in the Arab population during the period of the British mandate over Palestine.

Life's Work

During 1928, Meir became secretary of Moezet ha-Poalot, the Women's Labor Council of the Histadrut (Jewish labor union of Palestine/Israel) and supervised training of immigrant girls. In 1932, she was sent back to the United States as a representative to the Pioneer Women's Organization, where she would remain until 1934. Around this time her marriage broke up, but there was never a divorce. Morris continued to live in Israel and died there in 1951.

In 1934, Meir became a member of the executive committee of the Histadrut and head of the political department, which allowed her advancement into higher circles. In 1938, she was a Jewish observer to the Evian Conference, which failed to solve the problem of Jewish emigration from Europe in the face of Nazi brutality. During World War II, Meir was a member of the War Economic Advisory Council set up by the mandatory government in Palestine. In 1946, Meir was made acting head of the Jewish agency after the British mandatory authorities arrested the leaders of the Jewish community following outbreaks of violence in the country. She later commented that her failure to be arrested was a minor insult of sorts because the British apparently believed she was unimportant. In fact, she was one of the most important negotiators for the Jewish community of Palestine during the last two years of the mandate. Meir remained as head of the Political Department until statehood.

During the last years of the mandate, Meir was an active opponent of Ernst Bevin, British foreign secretary, who favored the position of the Palestinian Arabs. Meir was indignant over powerlessness imposed on Jews by the white paper of 1939. She also expressed regret with the boundaries for a Jewish state proposed by the United Nations Special Committee on Palestine (UNSCOP) in 1947, which excluded Jerusalem and parts of Galilee from the Jewish zone. In November, 1947, the United Nations proclaimed the partition of Palestine. In January, 1948, Meir visited the United States in the hope of raising between $25 and $30 million from American Jews for the State of Israel's survival. In fact, she raised more than $50 million.

Meir visited King Abdullah of Transjordan twice in an attempt to avert war between Jews and Arabs. The first time was November, 1947, when Meir, acting as head of the political department of the Jewish Agency, met the king in a house at Naharayim, near the Jordan River. At this meeting, Abdullah indicated his desire for peace and that the two shared a common enemy, Hajj-Amin al Husseini, the Mufti of Jerusalem and leader of the Palestinian community. On May 10, 1948, the two again met in Amman after Meir crossed into Transjordan in disguise, hoping to avert a Jordanian invasion of Palestine. Abdullah asked her not to hurry in proclaiming a state. She responded that Jews had been waiting for two thousand years. Abdullah requested that the Jews drop their plans for free immigration. Later, rumor had it that Abdullah blamed the war on Meir, as she was perceived as being too proud to accept his offer.

Meir was one of the twenty-five signators of the Declaration of Independence on May 14, 1948. Shortly thereafter, she was again dispatched to the United States for additional fund-raising. She again raised millions of dollars which helped the state survive. Meir, however, did not have time to savor the fruits of statehood and was immediately dispatched to Moscow in 1948 as Israel's first ambassador to the Soviet Union. She arrived in Moscow on September 3, 1948, and established the Is-

raeli mission there. She became the center of a famous demonstration outside the Moscow synagogue on Rosh Hashanah, 1948, which was one of the first indications that Zionist aspirations still existed among Soviet Jews. More than fifty thousand Soviet Jews came to see the first Israeli delegation in Moscow, which provided the first hint of the potential of a large exodus of Jews to Israel and the West.

After departing Moscow in 1949, Meir served in the Israeli Knesset (parliament) until 1974 and rose to many top governmental positions. As a member of the Mapai (labor) Party, she was elected to the First Knesset in 1949 and was appointed minister of labor. In charge of the large-scale immigration of Jews from Arab lands, particularly Iraq and Morocco, she was responsible for settling newcomers in tents and later in permanent housing. More than 680,000 Jews from Arab lands arrived in Israel during the period of her ministry. She had running battles with Minister of Finance Levi Eshkol about financial allocation for housing. All newcomers, however, were placed under shelter when they arrived in Israel, although conditions were very poor from 1950 to 1952. Meir's theory was that all new immigrants had to be employed and get paid for their work. This employment came through huge public works projects, focusing on road building.

Meir herself believed that the most significant thing she did in politics was the work connected with the Ministry of Labor, because it symbolized social equality and justice. She was instrumental in the presentation of Israel's first National Insurance Bill in 1952 which came into effect in 1954; the establishment of vocational training for adults and youngsters by allying the Ministry of Labor with older voluntary Jewish organizations such as the Histadrut (labor union), Organization for Rehabilitation Through Training (ORT), Hadassah (women's organization), and Women's International Zionist Organization (WIZO); and the development town projects, which were of only modest success.

In 1955, Meir attempted to become mayor of Tel Aviv but was defeated when the religious bloc in the Israeli Knesset refused to vote for a woman. In 1956, Meir became foreign minister, succeeding Moshe Sharett. She flew to France in 1956 with Shimon Peres and Moshe Dayan to plan a joint attack on Egypt as an ally of Great Britain and France. She gave a speech at the United Nations General Assembly in March, 1957, in which she announced the Israeli military withdrawal from the Si-

nai Peninsula and Sharm-el-Sheik, which had been occupied by Israel in October, 1956, as a response to Gamal Abdel Nasser's blockade of the Gulf of Aqaba, and in which she called for all states of the Middle East to join in peaceful endeavors.

As foreign minister, Meir developed an energetic development program with emerging African nations. Part of this strategy was to obtain votes at the United Nations, but the bottom line on Israeli-African policy was the common history of suffering. Oppression against the Jews, in Meir's mind, was similar to African slavery and European imperialism. During the late 1950's, Meir traveled to Ghana, Cameroon, Togo, Liberia, Sierre Leone, Gambia, Guinea, the Ivory Coast, and other states. African leaders often found her honest in her appraisals of the possibilities of development and the problems of instant solutions. The African policy, however, collapsed during and after the 1973 War, when most African states bowed to Arab oil pressure and severed relations.

In 1965, Meir retired as foreign minister and became secretary-general of the Labor Party (Mapai).

This was a critical period in the development of the center-left Israeli political parties, as part of the Labor Party had split with David Ben Gurion to establish Rafi, while Achdut Ha Avodah represented another position of labor. Meir believed that unification was necessary to ensure the future of the Labor Party. During the crisis before the Six-Day War, Meir was brought into the government and supported a hesitant Eshkol. After the war, she participated in the unification of the three labor parties into the new Israel Labor Party.

When Prime Minister Eshkol died on February 16, 1969, Meir was chosen as prime minister (March 7, 1969) as a means to avoid an open struggle between Moshe Dayan and Yigal Allon. On matters involving peace with the Arabs, Meir was often said to possess hard-line bargaining positions. She believed that the only alternative to war was peace and the only way to peace was negotiations. She indicated her willingness to go anywhere to talk peace and to negotiate anything except national suicide. She was never willing to talk with the Palestine Liberation Organization (PLO), however, which she viewed as a terrorist organization.

Late in 1969, Meir went to the United States to meet with President Richard Nixon, as well as to fill a shopping list for weapons, especially a specific request for twenty-five Phantom and eighty Skyhawk jet aircraft. It was a warm meeting with the American president, and Meir stayed on for an extended speaking tour. In January, 1973, Meir met with Pope Paul VI, the first Jewish head of state to do so.

The October, 1973, Yom Kippur War was a watershed in Israeli history and a horrible period in Meir's life. She became aware of plans for an Egyptian and Syrian attack against Israel but held off mobilization of reserves. Israel won the war but with substantial casualties. Meir also had a rift with General Ariel Sharon over disposition of the Egyptian Third Army, which had been surrounded by Israeli forces in Sinai. Meir, in order to save Sadat's position as possible negotiator, ordered Sharon not to move against the Third Army. Meir also had ambivalent feelings about United States Secretary of State Henry Kissinger, who threatened economic retaliation against Israel during ceasefire and disengagement negotiations. In the end, Meir believed that she had been correct in rejecting a preemptive strike against the Arab states, as the

Arab attack ensured American aid, which, she believed, saved lives.

The Labor Party again prevailed in elections held on December 31, 1973, but Meir resigned less than four months later, on April 11, 1974. She became a casualty of the Yom Kippur War, so to speak, after the Agranat Commission's report indicted the general staff, the military intelligence, the Sinai field commanders, and David Eleazar, who was the commander in chief, but not the minister of defense, Moshe Dayan. Meir left office June 4, 1974, at age seventy-six. She continued as a spokesperson for Israel in academic and public circles.

Summary

Golda Meir was one of the most beloved of Israel's leaders but unfortunately left office after what became a national disaster—the Yom Kippur War. Still, she was highly regarded, even by her former enemies. In November, 1977, when President Anwar el-Sadat of Egypt went on a peace mission to Israel, Meir was at the airport to greet him; Sadat regarded her as "the tough old lady." Meir was generally considered a tough and often stubborn politician, holding onto views that had a foundation deep in her Zionist ideology, which was influenced by memories of atrocities against the Jews in Eastern Europe during her childhood and the Holocaust of World War II. This quality was useful for Israel as an embattled people but became problematic once peace initiatives appeared, for Meir often believed such initiatives were insincere.

Meir helped create certain problems in the peace process that continued beyond her tenure as prime minister. She failed to establish any specific position about the occupied territories—the West Bank and Gaza Strip. She insisted upon direct negotiations with the enemy and opposed any form of mediation by outsiders. She refused, perhaps correctly, any interim withdrawal before a peace treaty was signed. Her most serious misjudgment was probably the failure to take up Sadat's explorations for peace in 1971. Yet she was an exponent of peace and held a consistent view. Meir died in Jerusalem on December 8, 1978, of leukemia, which she had known about since the early 1970's but managed to hide from public view.

Bibliography

Martin, Ralph. *Golda Meir: The Romantic Years.* New York: Scribner, 1988; London: Piatkus, 1989. An examination of Meir's personal life, with less emphasis on the politics of the Middle East.

Meir, Golda. *My Life.* London: Weidenfeld and Nicolson, and New York: Putnam, 1975. The most valuable work for understanding the life and accomplishments of Meir. This is not a diary but rather an exposition of what Meir believed were her most important accomplishments. Includes some texts of her more important speeches.

Rafael, Gideon. *Destination Peace: Three Decades of Israeli Foreign Policy.* London: Weidenfeld and Nicolson, and New York: Stein and Day, 1981. An examination of Israeli foreign policy from the perspective of an individual who served as Israeli ambassador to London, permanent representative to the United Nations, and director-general of the Israeli Foreign Ministry. Contains many insightful references to the career of Golda Meir.

Sachar, Howard M. *A History of Israel.* 2 vols. 2d ed. New York: Knopf, 1996. A comprehensive history of Zionism and the state of history, with particular references to Meir's prime ministry.

Shenker, Israel. "Golda Meir: Peace and Arab Acceptance Were Goals of Her Years as Premier." *The New York Times*, December 9, 1978: 7. This is an article that appeared as part of an extensive obituary of Meir, summarizing her main approaches to the peace process.

Syrkin, Marie. *Golda Meir: Israel's Leader.* New York: Putnam, 1969.

―――. *Golda Meir: Woman with a Cause.* New York: Putnam, 1963; London: Gollancz, 1964. Two early and sympathetic portraits by a fellow American Zionist. Syrkin's father, Nachman Syrkin, was a leading labor Zionist and strong influence on Meir during the 1930's. These portraits are, therefore, based on a very close friendship between two women Zionist leaders. Neither of the works, however, gives a full picture of Meir's life, as they were completed before her tenure as prime minister was completed.

Stephen C. Feinstein

LISE MEITNER

Born: November 7, 1878; Vienna, Austro-Hungarian Empire

Died: October 27, 1968; Cambridge, England

Area of Achievement: Physics

Contribution: Working as a pioneer in a field to which few women were drawn—nuclear physics—Meitner's joint research with chemist Otto Hahn (and later Fritz Strassmann) yielded the discovery of new radioactive elements and their properties and paved the way for the discovery of uranium fission.

Early Life

Lise Meitner was the third of eight children born to Hedwig Skovran and Philipp Meitner, a Viennese lawyer. Meitner had a very marked bent for mathematics and physics from a young age but did not begin her schooling immediately. This was partly because of prevailing attitudes in Vienna regarding the education of women. In order to regain the several years she had lost, she was tutored privately. After receiving a matriculation certificate from the Academic *Gymnasium* (high school) in Vienna, Meitner went on to the University of Vienna where, from 1901 until the end of 1905, she studied mathematics, physics, and philosophy. She decided early to concentrate on physics, realizing that she did not want to be a mathematician. During this time, she met with some rudeness from her fellows, since a female student was then regarded as something of a freak. In 1902, however, she had the good fortune to begin her study of theoretical physics under the stimulating and inspiring tutelage of Ludwig Boltzmann, who was a zealous advocate of atomic theory (the idea that all matter is composed of tiny, invisible, and, at that time at least, indivisible components). This was by no means generally accepted by physicists of the day, but in Boltzmann's view the discovery of radioactivity supplied the experimental proof that tiny particles, or atoms, formed the building blocks of all things.

In 1905, Meitner finished her doctoral thesis on heat conduction in non-homogeneous bodies and became the second woman to receive a doctorate in science from the University of Vienna. She soon became familiar with the new field of radioactivity and was ready to enter the realm of atomic physics at the beginning of a promising new period in that branch of science.

Life's Work

Though Meitner had no intention of making the study of radioactivity her specialty, this would become her life's work. After graduation, she persuaded her parents to allow her to go to Berlin to study with the theoretical physicist Max Planck for a few terms, but the intended short stay became a thirty-one-year period of research pushing back the frontiers of atomic physics and radioactivity.

Meitner arrived in Berlin in 1907 and enrolled in Planck's lectures. He was one of the world's most notable scientists, having developed the theory of thermal radiation (or quantum theory) in 1900 and having been one of the first to recognize and stress the importance of Albert Einstein's special theory of relativity. Meitner spoke of him not only with respect and admiration but also with much affection. Yet as important as Meitner's association with Planck was, it was her friendship and her long and productive collaboration with Otto Hahn that would change the course of atomic science.

Meitner and Hahn also met in 1907, and, finding that she had the opportunity for experimentation, Meitner decided she wanted to work with Hahn and keep to the study of radioactivity. After some persuasion, they finally received permission from Emil Fischer, the director of the Chemical Institute of Berlin where Hahn was working, to become a research team with the provision that Meitner promise not to go into the chemistry department, where the male students did their research and where Hahn conducted his chemical experiments. For the first few years, their joint research was confined to a small room originally planned as a carpenter's shop. When women's education was officially sanctioned and regulated in Germany in 1909, Fischer gave permission at once for Meitner to enter the chemistry department. In later years, he was most kind to and supportive of Meitner, eventually helping her to establish and become head of the new department of radiation physics in the Kaiser Wilhelm Institute for Chemistry in 1917.

In 1912, the Kaiser Wilhelm Institute for Chemistry was opened as a part of the University of Berlin, and Hahn became a member. Meitner became an assistant to Max Planck at the university's Institute for Theoretical Physics. Far from ending their cooperative effects, this development meant that the Meitner-Hahn partnership could continue with greater facilities and an enlarged staff. Their collaboration was a fruitful one for both of them. Hahn, a future Nobel laureate, brought to the team a splendid knowledge of organic chemistry; Meitner brought an expertise in theoretical physics and mathematics. Together they would be responsible for some important advances, including their 1917 discovery of the rare radioactive element 91, protactinium.

Though World War I did not dramatically affect her in a personal way, Meitner maintained that physics during World War I changed decisively because of Niels Bohr's work on the structure of the atom. In her opinion, his research on the atomic nucleus gave an extraordinary impetus to the development of nuclear physics itself, finally leading to the fission of uranium. She first met Bohr in 1920 and got to know him personally a year later. Her respect and gratitude stemmed not only from her opinion that no one—not even the great Ernest Rutherford—had such a worldwide influence on physicists as Bohr but also from the great efforts extended by him to regain for Germans admittance to scientific conferences, from which they had been strictly excluded in the postwar years. In the years following their first meetings, Meitner took part in many of Bohr's famous conferences, which were held at almost annual intervals in Copenhagen and at which were discussed new advances in physics and neighboring fields.

From 1917 to 1926, Meitner continued to conduct her own research on the nature of beta rays. The interpretation of the physical properties of radioactive substances continued to be an area of personal interest. She was the first to maintain that, in the process of disintegration of radioactive materials, the emission of radiation follows rather than precedes the emission of the particles. During this time, she won considerable acclaim for herself and in 1926 was named professor extraordinary at the University of Berlin. This was a position she would be able to retain only until Adolf Hitler's anti-Semitic decrees forced her to leave the post. Although all the children in Meitner's family had been baptized, and Lise herself had been reared as a Protestant, both of her parents were of Jewish background and this brought upon her the condemnation of the Nazis. For a few years after Hitler came to power in 1933, however, the change in government did not affect Meitner's collaboration with Hahn.

Meitner never invented a laboratory instrument or experimental technique of her own, but she rapidly adopted any new methods to her research and used them in innovative ways. From 1926 to 1933, Meitner became a pioneer in the use of a device called the Wilson cloud chamber for Charles Thomson Rees Wilson. In 1926, she was able to use it to measure the track length of slow electrons. In 1933, she was also one of the first to photograph in a chamber and to report on the tracks of positrons formed from gamma radiation.

In the early 1930's, nuclear physics made profound and dramatic advances when the neutron was discovered by Sir James Chadwick and artificial radioactivity was discovered by Frédéric Joliot and Irène Joliot-Curie. New techniques in experimentation were now possible, and in 1934 Meitner and Hahn began to follow up the work of a group of scientists in Italy headed by Enrico Fermi, who had bombarded uranium with neutrons and found several radioactive products thought to be transuranic elements (elements with an atomic number higher than 92, or uranium). Meitner and Hahn soon found a new group of radioactive substances that could not be identified with any of the elements just below uranium in the periodic table. Only one assumption was possible—that they were higher. Still, unanswered questions and puzzling results remained, even though another scientist, Fritz Strassmann, had joined Meitner and Hahn.

As the spring of 1938 arrived and Austria was occupied by the Nazis, Meitner was forced to leave Germany. Robbed now of protection owing to her foreign (Austrian) nationality and with the enforcement of Nazi policies regarding individuals of Jewish origin, Meitner knew that it was only a matter of time before she would face even graver choices. She went first to The Netherlands, then to Copenhagen as a guest of Niels Bohr and his wife, and finally to Stockholm to work in the new Nobel Institute, where a cyclotron was being constructed.

Meitner was sixty years old when she went to Sweden. Nevertheless, she continued her hard work, built up a small research group, and did experiments on the properties of radioactive elements formed with the cyclotron. Yet her most famous contribution to physics came shortly after she arrived in Stockholm.

In Berlin, Hahn and Strassmann had continued their work after Meitner left. She wrote to Hahn for data on the properties of the substances produced by their experiments. Hahn and Strassmann conducted more tests to prove the existence of radium but could only identify products resembling

barium isotopes. Meitner discussed this new information with her nephew, the physicist Otto Frisch, who was working in the laboratory of her friend Bohr. Meitner and Frisch concluded that the uranium nuclei had split into two fragments and that a large amount of energy had been released. Meitner actually used Einstein's mass-energy equivalence equations to do the calculations. Immediately, Meitner and Frisch prepared a communication for the British science journal *Nature*, in which they introduced the term "nuclear fission" to elucidate scientific principles previously thought to be impossible. For a short time after 1939, Meitner continued to investigate the nature of fission. In 1950, independently of others doing similar research, Meitner advanced accepted ideas concerning the asymmetry of fission fragments and worked on various aspects of the shell model of the nucleus.

Meitner's residence in Stockholm eventually became permanent. In 1947, after having spent half a year as a visiting professor at Catholic University in the United States, she became a citizen of Swe-

den, retired from the Nobel Institute, and went to work in a small laboratory that the Swedish Atomic Energy Commission had established for her at the Royal Institute of Technology. In 1960, Meitner left Sweden and retired to Cambridge, England, to travel, lecture, and enjoy her lifelong love of music. She had lived a full life, but her strength gradually deteriorated and she died a few days prior to her ninetieth birthday.

Summary

Lise Meitner was a true pioneer. She helped revolutionize the science of physics and its concepts. Her active participation in nuclear research resulted in the discovery of new elements and paved the way for the discovery of atomic fission, a term she helped coin and a process she helped interpret correctly. She entered her field at a time when women in science were not only a rarity but also an oddity. This is nowhere better demonstrated than at the first meeting between Meitner and Rutherford, who stopped in Berlin in 1908 to see his pupil Hahn on his way home from Stockholm after receiving the Nobel Prize in Chemistry. When he saw Meitner he said in great astonishment: "Oh, I thought you were a man!" It was no mean task to overcome some of the prejudices and preconceptions that were far less harmless than Rutherford's mistake. Yet she overcame these attitudes, and Meitner's contributions to nuclear physics are acknowledged to be of the highest rank.

Honors came to Meitner from all quarters throughout her long life. She earned a distinguished reputation in the 1920's, receiving, in 1924, the Liebnitz Medal of the Berlin Academy of Sciences and, in 1925, the Lieber Prize of the Austrian Academy of Sciences. In 1947, she was awarded the Prize of the City of Vienna and in 1949 the Max Planck Medal. Meitner was elected a foreign member of the Royal Society of London in 1955 and of the American Academy of Arts and Sciences in 1960. In 1966, she shared the United States Atomic Energy Commission's Fermi Award with Hahn and Strassmann. In addition, four American educational institutions (Syracuse, Rutgers, Smith, and Adelphi) bestowed upon her honorary doctorates in science. The list of awards is impressive, but they are simply a by-product of Meitner's love of science. Perhaps that is why she continued her work well beyond the years when most others have stopped.

Bibliography

Crawford, Elizabeth, et al. "A Nobel Tale of Postwar Injustice." *Physics Today* 50, no. 9 (September, 1997). Examines the reasons for the Nobel judges' failure to include Meitner and Fritz Strassmann in the Nobel Prize for their work on nuclear fission.

Frisch, O. R. "Lise Meitner." In *Dictionary of Scientific Biography*, edited by Charles C. Gillispie, vol. 9. New York: Scribner, 1972. This compact but thorough article was authored by Meitner's colleague and nephew, who participated in the events surrounding the discovery and naming of the fission process. Contains a detailed bibliography. Very accurate scientifically but not for the layperson.

Graetzer, Hans G., and David L. Anderson. *The Discovery of Nuclear Fission: A Documentary History.* New York: Van Nostrand, 1970. This short volume is an invaluable source. Provides reprints of the original papers and reports by scientists who first uncovered the problem and meaning of nuclear fission. Includes several of the original papers that provided a basis for the application of nuclear fission to military or peaceful purposes.

Hahn, Otto. *My Life: The Autobiography of a Scientist.* Translated by Ernest Kaiser and Eithne Wilkins. New York: Herder, 1970. Because this volume presents the life of Meitner's collaborator in great detail, much information is contained about Meitner throughout. Engaging reading that presents a detailed background of the long partnership as well as an account of the discovery of fission and its interpretation by Meitner.

Meitner, Lise. "Looking Back." *Bulletin of the Atomic Scientists* 20 (November, 1964): 2-7. The most complete autobiographical account of Meitner's life that is available in the English language. With clarity and charm, Meitner discusses her life from her youth through the discovery of atomic fission.

Rife, Patricia, and Lise Meitner. *Lise Meitner and the Dawn of the Nuclear Age.* Birkhauser Boston, 1998. The author assesses the life and times of Meitner and considers why Meitner did not share in the Nobel Prize related to the discovery of nuclear fission.

Sparberg, Esther B. "A Study of the Discovery of Fission." *American Journal of Physics* 32 (1964): 2-8. Reviews the history of the discovery of fission and succinctly discusses Meitner's place in that history. Contains some interesting statements made by Meitner.

Yost, Edna. "Lise Meitner: Physicist." In *Women of Modern Science.* New York: Dodd Mead, 1959. Written before Meitner's death, this chapter is one of the most readable accounts of her life yet published. Particularly good at discussing the professional associations made by Meitner during her life. Relates her work to that of other famous scientists and emphasizes the honors that came to her.

Andrew C. Skinner

ANDREW MELLON

Born: March 24, 1855; Pittsburgh, Pennsylvania
Died: August 26, 1937; Southampton, New York
Area of Achievement: Business
Contribution: Through a combination of caution and shrewd investment, Mellon became one of the three richest men in the United States. He was called "the greatest Secretary of the Treasury since Alexander Hamilton."

Early Life

Andrew William Mellon was born March 24, 1855, in Pittsburgh, Pennsylvania. His mother, née Sarah Jane Negley, was the daughter of a distinguished landed family in the Pittsburgh area. His father, Thomas Mellon, the son of an Ulster immigrant, started life as a poor farm boy and ended it as a millionaire. Andrew was the fourth son, one of six brothers and two sisters. The children were all educated, according to the dictates of their father, in a private school on the Mellon estate. Andrew's education trained him solely for business. In 1870, he attended Western University in Pittsburgh. At the age of eighteen, Andrew and his brother Richard were able to set up in the real estate business. In the Panic of 1873, the family bank, T. Mellon and Sons, survived on its founder's reputation for rectitude. In the period that followed, the family interests were swollen by vigorous foreclosures. By this time at work in the bank, Andrew met Henry Clay Frick, whom Thomas had stood by in the Panic and who was, by 1878, the undisputed king of coke. The two young men became friends and set off on a grand tour of Europe in 1879. Together, they visited Ireland, London, Paris, and Venice. Andrew's views were broadened. On his return, his father handed over to him the running of all of his affairs—his interests in real estate, traction, coal, foundries, and the bank.

By the 1880's, Mellon was short and slight, elegant in appearance and manner. The most striking feature about the man was his deep-set, chilly blue eyes. While he has been called handsome by his biographers, Mellon was painfully shy. Because of his withdrawn temperament, Mellon abhorred public occasions and jealously guarded his privacy. People who spoke to him found him polite, even courtly. When he spoke, which he did rarely, he stammered slightly and spoke so softly that his listeners had to strain to hear his words. Throughout his business career, he was content to let his younger brother and partner Richard take care of the personal contacts whenever possible, while he played the role of strategist, planner, and ultimate arbiter. He was a lonely man, and a certain wistfulness surrounded him. He was probably never close to anyone, not even the coke king, whom he always addressed as "Mr. Frick."

Life's Work

Through the 1880's, Mellon steadily expanded the businesses established by his father. T. Mellon and Sons increasingly became the bank for industry in the Pittsburgh area.

In 1889, Mellon's first big opportunity came when he was asked for a loan for a new industrial process. In return for the loan, Mellon took a substantial share in the company—and financial control. The Pittsburgh Reduction Company would become the Aluminum Company of America (ALCOA), and, as a result of its exclusive patent rights, tariff walls, the ever-expanding uses for the product, and a phalanx of subsidiary companies engaged at all levels and in all spheres of aluminum marketing, production, and uses, came to exercise a total monopoly of the market in North America and a share in the division of the world market. Mellon became extremely rich.

Other parts of the Mellon portfolio were developed. Andrew formed Union Trust in 1899. Within ten years, the financial power of Pittsburgh was centered in it. From 1898 to 1902, there came a flood of mergers in the city, many of them engineered by Mellon, almost all of them financed by him. He garnered fees, shares, and huge new bank deposits. With the crash of 1903, many of the Mellon-promoted mergers failed. Mellon held the mortgage bonds and foreclosed. Thus, even in times of economic adversity, he increased his fortune.

In 1899, following Frick's resignation from Carnegie Steel, Mellon and he created Union Steel and made it into a vertically integrated company, with its own ore supply, transportation, furnaces, rod and wire mill, and associated companies in shipbuilding, railroad car construction, and structural steel. The Mellon-Frick steel interests were used as a lever against the attempt by United States Steel to establish dominance in the steel industry. These efforts paid off when United States Steel offered the outrageous price of seventy-five million dollars to acquire its menacing rival.

In January, 1901, at Spindletop, near Beaumont, Texas, the largest oil gusher in history to that time burst out of the ground. The claim was owned by a Pittsburgh company. The oil strike was so large that the company ran out of money and went to Mellon for help. He agreed to finance the new J.M. Guffey Petroleum Company and retained forty percent of the stock. The company was later renamed Gulf Oil. By 1904, the company had become the largest independent oil company in the world, controlling pipe lines, a tanker fleet, and oil refineries. In 1906, Guffey was ousted and W.L. Mellon, Andrew's nephew, was named to serve as head of Gulf's diverse oil interests.

The year 1914 saw the completion of the inner core of the Mellon portfolio. It came with the acquisition of the Koppers Gas and Coke Company and was accompanied by patents for coke by-products that were extremely important for war production. Fifty-seven subsidiary companies were spawned from this one concern, including control over utilities up and down the East Coast.

Besides these important and very wealthy companies directly controlled by Mellon, family interests were powerful in the Pullman companies, Bethlehem Steel, Westinghouse, and many other major concerns. By 1920, Mellon family interests were estimated at $1.69 billion.

In 1920, Mellon underwrote a $1.5 million deficit in the campaign fund of the Republican National Committee. For this, President Warren G. Harding named Mellon to his new cabinet as secretary of the treasury. Thus began a political career for Mellon. At the time, Mellon's name was virtually unknown outside Pittsburgh.

Tax reform was needed. In 1923, the Mellon Plan was unveiled. It envisaged huge tax cuts for the wealthy. Stocks boomed on Wall Street, but the plan was emasculated in Congress and became the major issue of the 1924 presidential election. With the sweeping victory of Calvin Coolidge, Mellon's prestige was never higher. In February, 1926, a tax measure was signed that set taxes for the wealthy at a lower rate even than that envisaged in the Mellon Plan. Andrew Mellon was dubbed "the greatest Secretary of the Treasury since Alexander Hamilton." A period of rapid expansion in industry and escalating stock speculation followed. In 1927, Mellon was even thought of as a possible candidate for president and was referred to by Democrat leader John Garner as "the most powerful man in the world today. . . . He has dominated the finan-

cial, economic and fiscal relations of the United States for the past five years."

When the Mellon political machine in Pennsylvania faltered, however, his presidential aspirations were thwarted. Instead, Herbert Hoover was nominated and became president, though Mellon retained his position at the Treasury. When the Wall Street Crash came in 1929, the glamour of the Mellon name was lost, as he predicted a swift end to the recession and was blamed, along with Coolidge and Hoover, for the catastrophe that had overcome the country. In 1932, there was a move to impeach Mellon, and embarrassing revelations were made about his tax returns and the practices of his companies. Reluctantly, he accepted the post of ambassador to the court of St. James and headed for London. The Mellon Plan was discarded.

Following Hoover's defeat in the presidential election that same year, Mellon was reduced once more to private citizenship. He spent his time quietly in Pittsburgh but had to make frequent trips to Washington to defend himself against continuous attack by supporters and officials of Franklin D. Roosevelt's New Deal administration.

Mellon's charitable bequests were few indeed. In 1914, he set up the Mellon Institute, which served principally as a set of useful laboratories dealing in practical research projects for his numerous companies and for others who paid the appropriate fees. In 1936, he donated his art collection to the nation and built the National Gallery of Art in Washington, District of Columbia, to house it. He died August 26, 1937, while visiting his daughter at Southampton, New York.

Summary

Andrew Mellon's major achievement was the creation of a fortune that was to be largely self-sustaining and self-increasing. The key to this accomplishment was diversity. As a banker with access not only to his father's millions but also to the deposits of companies in the nation's leading heavy industrial district, Mellon was able to greet eagerly yet cautiously each opportunity placed before him. He used money to make money, he speculated discreetly, he manufactured and manipulated stocks, and he used the legal system to further his interests. Moreover, Mellon supervised minutely the growth of his infant enterprises and had the gift for selecting able subordinates whom he trusted to manage his corporations. His executive ability was unquestionably outstanding.

The question of why, at the age of sixty-five—when he was among the three richest men in the country and still shrank from the hurly-burly of human contact—Andrew Mellon should have chosen to embark on a political career must remain something of a mystery. For nine of the twelve years he spent in office, his prestige and reputation were enormous. He represented business control over the political system at a time when business could do no wrong. For his last three years as secretary of the treasury, and for the remainder of his life, Mellon suffered from public opprobrium, vilified as the embodiment of corporate greed, one of the principal culprits responsible for the Wall Street Crash.

Bibliography

Finley, David Edward. *A Standard of Excellence: Andrew W. Mellon Founds the National Gallery of Art at Washington, D.C.* Washington, D.C.: Smithsonian Institution Press, 1973. This is the account of Mellon's only truly altruistic public gesture, begun only a year before his death. Written by the first director of the gallery.

Holbrook, Stewart H. *The Age of the Moguls.* New York: Doubleday, 1953; London: Gollancz, 1954. Contains one chapter on Mellon, chapter 4 in part 4. Best brief account of Mellon's life; owes much to O'Connor's work. Best on the inner core of Mellon's business interests.

Koskoff, David E. *The Mellons: The Chronicle of America's Richest Family.* New York: Crowell, 1978. Mellon's life is covered in the first three sections of the book. Suffers from too close an identification with the subject matter, as when opponents of Mellon are described as the "villains of the story." Yet the book is readable and contains much information (much of it taken from O'Connor), not all of it showing Mellon in a favorable light. Best modern discussion of Mellon in a very sparse field.

Love, Philip H. *Andrew W. Mellon: The Man and His Work.* Baltimore: Coggins, 1929. First biography of Mellon, written at the height of his public career before the Wall Street Crash ruined his reputation. Highly favorable to its subject and tends to treat all opposition to Mellon, all politics and politicians, as vindictive and sacrilegious.

Mellon, Andrew William. *Taxation: The People's Business.* New York: Macmillan, 1924. Published to explain and popularize the Mellon Plan for tax reductions. Mellon attempts to answer his critics and to explain why it is in the nation's interest to cut by half surtaxes on the wealthy and to base all other taxes on this group not on their ability to pay but on their willingness. Good for Mellon's thought.

O'Connor, Harvey. *Mellon's Millions, the Biography of a Fortune: The Life and Times of Andrew W. Mellon.* New York: Day, 1933. Written before Mellon's death, this biography infuriated its subject. Well researched; tries to follow all of Mellon's myriad financial dealings and their effects, a supremely difficult task. O'Connor's work has formed the basis of much of what little has been written about Mellon since. Upon publication of the book, the author, a radical journalist, was arrested at his home in Pittsburgh as a "suspicious character," apparently at the bidding of Mellon or that of a zealous subordinate. Still the best account available.

Stephen Burwood

H. L. MENCKEN

Born: September 12, 1880; Baltimore, Maryland
Died: January 29, 1956; Baltimore, Maryland
Area of Achievement: Journalism
Contribution: Mencken, in his roles as editor, writer, and critic, kept an ever-watchful eye on American politics, letters, language, and ideas. He argued eloquently for an indigenous and independent American literature, and he encouraged and nurtured the authors who were striving to create it.

Early Life

Henry Louis Mencken was born to Anna Margaret (née Abhau) and August Mencken on September 12, 1880. His early years were remarkable only for their unusual comfort and security. August Mencken managed a thriving cigar factory, and by Henry's third year, he had moved the Mencken family into a charming three-story brick house at 1524 Hollins Street in Baltimore. This would be the home where Henry would spend all of his life, with the exception of five years of marriage to Miss Sara Powell Haardt (1930-1935).

August was a responsible family man and had a special interest in his sons, taking them to Washington with him on his weekly business trips; buying them a Shetland pony, conveniently stabled in their ample backyard; removing them to the cooler and more rustic Ellicott City for their summers; and providing Henry, on the Christmas of 1888, with an almost prophetic self-inker printing press.

Much of the character of the mature H. L. Mencken can be traced to these early years and to the influence and encouragement of his father. As an example, when Henry showed an interest in photography, August immediately helped him to set up a developing room on the third floor of their home. Henry, fascinated as much by the chemistry as the artistry of the new medium, wrote his first factual article about a new toning solution he had perfected.

Henry was also given piano lessons, which proved to be the happy genesis of a deep and sustaining love of music. His participation in the "Saturday Night Club," a quasi-musical organization, was a lifetime social and musical outlet for him.

When, at eight years old, Henry became a curious reader, he found in his own home a wide variety of periodicals and newspapers. Even more important, he discovered his father's small collection of well-worn books, including the novels of Mark Twain. Henry read *The Adventures of Huckleberry Finn* (1884) with great fervor, and then rushed on to read the rest of Twain. Subsequently, he became a voracious reader and, as an adult, a major critical champion of Twain's work.

When Henry was about to graduate from Polytechnic Institute, it became clear that with a concerted effort, he could graduate with distinction, and so August offered him a purse of one hundred dollars if he could graduate at the head of his class. On June 23, 1896, Henry proudly delivered the school's valedictory address. He was almost sixteen, and one hundred dollars to the good.

In Henry's early years can be seen the seeds of almost all of his later habits and ideas. That the son of a German cigar manufacturer at the turn of the century should be an inveterate smoker, devoted to his family, economically conservative, responsive to social Darwinism, proud of his European ancestry, enamored of middle-class values and comforts, suspicious of Puritans and uplifters, and cheerfully agnostic is perhaps to be expected; that he should turn away from his family's manufacturing business to be a journalist was an understandable disappointment to his father, and a lucky turn of events for American literature.

Life's Work

Mencken's journalistic career began at the Baltimore *Morning Herald* in 1899, with a five-line story about a horse-stealing rumor circulating in the suburbs of Baltimore. By 1903, Mencken was city editor of the paper, and was working on his first book: *George Bernard Shaw: His Plays*, published in 1905. In 1906, Mencken switched his allegiance to the Baltimore *Sun* to manage its Sunday edition. From 1911 to 1915, he wrote his Free Lance column for the *Evening Sun*, an editorial endeavor that eventually gave way to a regular Monday column. Typical of his writing in this period is this description of America: " . . . here, more than anywhere else that I know of or have ever heard of, the daily panorama of human existence . . . is so inordinately gross and preposterous . . . that only a man who was born with a petrified diaphragm can fail to laugh himself to sleep every night, and to awake every morning with all the eager, unflagging expectation of a Sunday-school superintendent touring the Paris peep-shows." His bombastic, vituperative, and productive association with the *Sun* lasted until 1948, when his last newspaper editorial, "Mencken's Last Stand," appeared on November 9.

In 1908, at the request of the publishers of his book on Shaw, Mencken completed *The Philosophy of Friedrich Nietzsche*. It was an arduous task, undertaken in a time when only a few of Nietzsche's works had been published in English.

In 1919, Mencken completed his opus *The American Language*, probably the most important contribution to American language studies since Noah Webster's revolutionary *A Compendious Dictionary of the English Language* (1806), which declared for the first time America's linguistic independence from Great Britain. Mencken's enormous tome was followed by two equally wide-ranging supplements, still definitive works in their field.

By 1909, Mencken was writing regular book reviews for *The Smart Set*, a magazine that he was soon to coedit with George Jean Nathan. His associations at *The Smart Set*, with Nathan and the distinguished publisher Alfred A. Knopf, eventually culminated in the founding of *The American Mercury* in 1924. While *The Smart Set* had embodied the dual personalities of Nathan and Mencken, *The American Mercury* primarily projected the inimitable character and style of H. L. Mencken. One can almost see Mencken's round cherubic face, ever-present cigar, and neatly parted hair, as he intones the objectives of the new review: "The editors are committed to nothing save this: to keep common sense as fast as they can, to belabor sham as agreeably as possible, to give civilized entertainment." *The American Mercury* quickly became one of the major journalistic and literary phenomena of the 1920's.

Amid a mountain of correspondence (which was always graciously answered within twenty-four hours), between national presidential conventions and lesser political caucuses, interspersed with cut-and-paste research for his nearly twenty books, Mencken managed to complete, by the end of 1943, his three-volume autobiography: *Happy Days* (1940), *Newspaper Days* (1941), and *Heathen Days* (1943).

By his own estimate, Mencken's writings embrace some five million words. He wrote, on the average, between two and three thousand sensible and amusing words a day. If that were his only accomplishment, it would be enough to sustain his reputation as a great American man of letters. In addition to his own incredible productivity, however, he was also, as an editor and a critic, a fine judge of literary talent and a warm and helpful mentor for the young authors of his day.

Mencken printed the first plays of the controversial new playwright Eugene O'Neill. He was the first to recognize the excellence of Sinclair Lewis' *Main Street* (1920), and he perceptively encouraged Lewis to write a novel about a typical American businessman and booster, which became *Babbitt* (1922). Mencken befriended and provided an appreciative audience for Edmund Wilson, F. Scott Fitzgerald, Sherwood Anderson, and Willa Cather.

As a journalist and a writer himself, Mencken was also a staunch upholder of First Amendment rights. He was quick to come to the defense of Theodore Dreiser when his novel *The "Genius"* (1915) was singled out for censorship by the New York Society for the Suppression of Vice. He also came to the aid of James Branch Cabell, whose novel *Jurgen* (1919) met similar well-intentioned opposition. Mencken's instinct for quality, and his intense loyalty, made him a great patriarch of American Letters.

Summary

Although Mencken was not in any way a systematic thinker, he did maintain a stable set of values, or prejudices, through many decades of change in American society. The natural consequence of his consistency was a continual waxing and waning of his reputation, which he accepted philosophically.

For example, Mencken's social Darwinist views were understandably more popular in the free-for-all 1920's than they were in the imposed austerity of the Great Depression. His convivial attitude toward drinking was more accepted at the turn of the century than during the era of Prohibition. His pro-German pride and bilingualism were a great help in his early Nietzsche studies but were a considerable encumbrance during World War II. His humorous attitude toward politics, which was seen as unpatriotic during the world wars, came into vogue again in the early 1950's.

What is saliently American about H. L. Mencken is that, while he reserved the right to criticize with great gusto the entire panorama of American life— from William Jennings Bryan to Calvin Coolidge, from Fundamentalist religion to the New Deal, from Thorstein Veblen's *The Theory of the Leisure Class* (1899) to his favorite invention, the Ameri-

can "booboisie"—he also embodied the best that America has to offer. He was a man of tremendous character, writing with a white-hot intensity about the things he cared about. It would be a fine thing if every age and every nation had its gadfly, its H. L. Mencken, to expose hypocrisy and defend the rights of common sense against thoughtless men and ideologies.

Bibliography

Bode, Carl. *Mencken.* Carbondale: Southern Illinois University Press, 1969; London: Johns Hopkins University Press, 1986. An extensive, well-documented, and readable biography of Mencken. Illustrated with numerous, carefully chosen photographs.

Cain, William E. "A Lost Voice of Dissent: H. L. Mencken in Our Time." *Sewanee Review* 104, no. 2 (Spring 1996). Discusses Mencken's impressionistic approach to criticism and his belief that criticism must be honest, forthright, and unencumbered by conventional pretense.

Hobson, Fred C., Jr. *Serpent in Eden: H. L. Mencken and the South.* Chapel Hill: University of North Carolina Press, 1974. This is an investigation into the interesting relationship between Mencken and the South. It discusses his strident criticisms of the South, such as his essay "Sahara of the Bozart," as well as examining his respect for some of the South's best writers and small-review editors.

Hobson, Fred, et al, eds. *Thirty-Five Years of Newspaper Work: A Memoir by H. L. Mencken.* Baltimore: Johns Hopkins University Press, 1994. This is the first publication of highlights from Mencken's memoirs, *Thirty-five Years of Newspaper Work,* written from 1941 to 1942 and finally released in 1991. Excellent new information on Mencken's coverage of presidential candidates from 1912 to 1940 and of the Scopes trial.

Manchester, William. *Disturber of the Peace: The Life of H. L. Mencken.* New York: Harper, 1951. This engaging biography has the advantage of having been written with Mencken's cooperation, by a man who knew Mencken personally. Manchester has a lively, anecdotal style, and his book is only slightly limited by its date of publication, which was five years before Mencken's death.

Mencken, H. L. *A Carnival of Buncombe: Writings on Politics*. Edited by Malcolm Moos. Baltimore: Johns Hopkins University Press, 1956. A selection of Mencken's political writings spanning the fertile period from February, 1920, to November, 1936, with a concise and provocative foreword by Joseph Epstein.

————. *A Choice of Days*. Edited by Edward L. Galligan. New York: Knopf, 1980. A one-volume abridgment of the author's autobiographical works: *Happy Days*, *Newspaper Days* and *Heathen Days*. It was published on the hundredth anniversary of his birth.

————. *H. L. Mencken: The American Scene*. Edited by Huntington Cairn. New York: Vintage Books, 1982. This is a well-organized compilation of Mencken's writing. It explores his ideas on politics, religion, morals, and American journalism, letters, and English. It is an excellent introduction to the full range of Mencken's prose.

————. *A Mencken Chrestomathy*. New York: Knopf, 1949. A chrestomathy is a collection of choice passages from an author, and this book lives up to its name. It consists primarily of sections from Mencken's out-of-print writings, such as the Prejudices series, *A Book of Burlesques*, and *In Defense of Women*, as well as magazine and newspaper articles which never found their way into any of Mencken's many books. An essential anthology of Mencken's prose.

————. *The Vintage Mencken*. Edited by Alistair Cooke. New York: Vintage, 1955. A rather eclectic assortment of Mencken pieces, put together just before his death by Alistair Cooke with the help of the editors of the *Sunpapers* and Mencken's publisher Alfred Knopf. It includes some enduring classics, among them "The Lure of Beauty," "The Hills of Zion," and "Mencken's Last Stand."

Stenerson, Douglas C. *H. L. Mencken: Iconoclast from Baltimore*. Chicago: University of Chicago Press, 1971. A well-documented, modern biography, with an emphasis on Mencken's place in American journalism and the history of American ideas.

Cynthia Lee Katona

ERICH MENDELSOHN

Born: March 21, 1887; Allenstein, Germany
Died: September 15, 1953; San Francisco, California
Area of Achievement: Architecture
Contribution: Mendelsohn did at least as much as such better-known contemporaries as Le Corbusier, Walter Gropius, and Ludwig Mies van der Rohe to develop and popularize modern architecture. Even more fully than the other founders of the so-called International Style, Mendelsohn was the representative architect of modern world industrialism—of machine, steel, concrete, and glass.

Early Life

Erich Mendelsohn was born March 21, 1887, in the town of Allenstein in East Prussia, Germany (now Olsztyn, Poland). His father was a well-to-do Jewish businessman of Russian-Polish background. His mother was a talented musician, and Mendelsohn's lifelong interest in musical rhythms and forms (with Johann Sebastian Bach his favorite composer) had a major impact on his architecture. As early as the age of five, Mendelsohn appears to have resolved to be an architect. After a year at the University of Munich studying economics, he switched in 1908 to the Berlin Technische Hochschule to begin work in architecture. Two years later, he transferred to the Technische Hochschule at Munich, where he obtained his degree in architecture in 1912. Shortly after the outbreak of World War I, he enlisted for military service in the engineers. He served on the Eastern (Russian) Front until late 1917; then he was transferred to the Western Front, where he remained until the war's end. In 1915, he married Luise Maas, a talented cellist; they had one daughter. The surviving Mendelsohn letters show a young man filled with restless energy and a strong creative drive. "Everywhere," he wrote in 1913, "new ideas, new achievements. How can one possibly look on idly, and not, with every fibre of one's being, desire to take a part?" As it was for so many others of his generation, the experience of World War I was an emotional and cultural watershed. "As few before us," he would recall, "we felt the meaning of living and dying, of end and beginning—its creative meaning in the midst of the silent terror of no-man's land and the terrifying din of rapid fire."

Mendelsohn had a lifelong interest in, and enthusiasm for, Greek art, the classical simplicity of which would inspire him. Yet the most important influence shaping his early architecture was his association with the Blaue Reiter (Blue Rider) group of expressionist painters led by Wassily Kandinsky. The keynote of the application of the expressionist aesthetic to architecture was that the character of a building should be determined by its purpose. The sketches that Mendelsohn did between 1914 and 1918 (many done while he was serving in the trenches) show his fascination with themes that would characterize his mature work: his attraction to steel, concrete, and glass; his fascination with the horizontal and broad plain surfaces; his juxtaposition of curved forms with straight lines; and his conception of a building as not simply a machine fulfilling its purpose but an organic unit, with each part belonging to the whole and each form growing out of another.

Life's Work

Immediately after his demobilization, Mendelsohn started his own architectural practice. An exhibition of his sketches entitled "Architecture in Steel and Concrete" at the famous avant-garde art gallery of Paul Cassirer in Berlin created a sensation. What catapulted him into sudden fame was his design of the Einstein Tower (1919-1924) at Potsdam, a suburb of Berlin; it was a combination of cupola observatory and astrophysical laboratory for further research into Albert Einstein's theory of relativity. Although conceived in reinforced concrete, the main body was built in brick with a cement façade because of the postwar shortage of cement. The rounded shapes that compose the building, both in general mass and details, coupled with the deep window recesses are expressive of optical instruments while simultaneously conveying an aura of the mysteries of the universe. Further evidence of Mendelsohn's virtuosity was furnished by his next two major projects. The first was a hat factory at Luckenwalde (1919-1921) consisting of four long sheds made up of a series of triangular concrete arches curved at the springing with brick walls and rubberoid roofing. The second was his addition to the *Berliner Tageblatt* newspaper building (1921-1923), done in collaboration with Richard Neutra. The structure consisted of a steel frame encased in concrete, with its long horizontal lines and horizontal windows in contrast to the vertical emphasis of the nineteenth century main building.

A major turning point in Mendelsohn's development was his contact with the Dutch painters and architects of the De Stilj school, most importantly J. J. P. Oud. Mendelsohn took as his goal the fusion of the romantic free-form impulses of expressionism with the geometrically inspired rationalism of the De Stilj group. Perhaps even more influential was his visit to the United States in 1924, during which he met Frank Lloyd Wright and was deeply impressed by Wright's call for an architecture reflecting the organic structure of natural forms. After his return, he published *Amerika: Bilderbuch eines Architekten* (1926; America: picturebook of an architect), containing seventy-seven photographs of the more important buildings he had seen, accompanied by his personal commentaries. Trips in 1925 and 1926 to the Soviet Union to oversee construction of his design for a factory for the Leningrad Textile Trust resulted in the publishing in 1929 of *Russland, Europa, Amerika: Ein Architektonischer Querschnitt*, a comparative appraisal of new developments in architecture in the three places. The finest expressions of Mendelsohn's mid- and latter-1920's architectural work were his department store designs: the Herpich Fur Store in Berlin (1924); the Schocken stores in Nürnberg (1926-1927), Stuttgart (1926-1928), and Chemnitz (1928-1929); and the Petersdorff store in Breslau (1926-1927). The distinguishing features of those stores was his making the front outer wall a screen of chiefly glass to maximize the natural light during daytime plus his typical emphasis on long horizontal lines.

Mendelsohn's last five years in Germany, 1928-1933, were ones of intense activity, during which he had as many as forty assistants and draftsmen working for him. Many of his projects remained unbuilt, but the completed work included three outstanding designs. One was Berlin's Universum motion picture theater (1927-1928), with an elongated horseshoe interior and curved balcony front that maximized the number of seats with an undistorted view of the screen. The second was his own home on a slope overlooking Havel Lake on the outskirts of Berlin (1929-1930); it is a masterful arrangement externally and internally of plain rectangular forms that succeeded in blending harmoniously with its site. The third was Columbushaus (1929-1931), a twelve-story office building at Postdamer-platz, Berlin, featuring a technically innovative steel skeleton with a façade of horizontal bands of glass and polished cream travertine.

In 1932, Mendelsohn was elected a member of the Prussian Academy of Arts, but in March, 1933, following Adolf Hitler's takeover of power, he left Germany and settled in Great Britain. He first entered into a partnership in London with Serge Chermayeff; in 1936 he set up an independent practice. He became a naturalized British subject in 1938, and, in February, 1939, he was elected a fellow of the Royal Institute of British Architects. The most distinguished of his British buildings is the De la Warr Pavilion at Bexhill-on-the Sea (1933-1935). A longish, low horizontal steel-and-glass building, the pavilion admirably fits in with the adjacent sea. Another typical Mendelsohn touch was his breaking of the long horizontal movement of the building by two semicircular glass projections enclosing staircases at either end of the central block.

After 1937, Mendelsohn's principal work was done in Palestine. In February, 1939, he left Great Britain to make Palestine his home. Architecture in Palestine presented new problems for the northern Europe architect, such as keeping out rather than letting in the sunlight and handling the extremely wide variations in temperature between day and night. Mendelsohn's success in adapting European modern architecture to this new environment is shown by the Chaim Weizmann house in Rehovot, near Tel Aviv (1935-1936); the Salman Schocken house and office/library in Jerusalem (1935-1936); the Government Hospital in Haifa overlooking the Bay of Acre (1936-1938); and the Anglo-Palestine Bank in Jerusalem (1937-1939). His most important work was the Hadassah University Medical Center (1936-1938) on Jerusalem's Mount Scopus, a complex of three reinforced concrete buildings faced with cream Jerusalem limestone arranged in narrow panels and narrow vertical windows. Perhaps the most striking features of his Palestine work were the orientation of the buildings to take advantage of the prevailing breezes coupled with the painstaking design of the surrounding gardens to complement the building masses.

The outbreak of war led to a halt in further building in Palestine. After unsuccessful efforts first to join the British army and then to obtain a war job, he left for the United States in March, 1941. Shortly after his arrival, New York City's Museum of Modern Art presented an exhibition of his work, and he received invitations to lecture at universities across the country. Lectures that he delivered at the University of California-Berkeley in April, 1942, were published two years later as *Three Lectures on Architecture*. With America's entry into the war, new building came to a standstill. Fortunately, Mendelsohn was awarded in 1943 a Guggenheim Fellowship for two years. From May, 1943, to October, 1945, he lived at Croton, thirty miles north of New York City in a house overlooking the Hudson River; then he moved to San Francisco, where he resumed the practice of architecture. The first of his American buildings to be completed was the Maimonides Hospital in San Francisco (1946-1950). Its outstanding feature was the balconies with white balustrades that swung out in rhythmic curves to give the effect of lacy ribbons. Most of his American work consisted of designs for Jewish synagogues or temples combined with community centers. Four of these designs were built—one in St. Louis (1946-1950), one in Cleveland (1946-1952), one in Grand Rapids, Michigan (1948-1952), and one in St. Paul, Minnesota (1950-1954), which was completed after Mendelsohn's death to a partially altered plan. Mendelsohn died September 15, 1953, from cancer in a San Francisco hospital. He was cremated and, according to his wishes, his ashes were scattered in an unrecorded place.

Summary

Erich Mendelsohn was given to philosophizing in rather ponderous Germanic fashion upon the nature of architecture. In his 1942 lectures at the University of California, he took as his major target architecture that, "instead of being in plan and appearance the true expression of a building's utility, material, and structure, tried to hide its own life behind the lifeless ornamental features of a bygone society." He identified as "the main issue of building: to simplify life in accordance with and in consequence of the technical inventions and scientific discoveries of our age." The hallmark of that simplification was the quest for an organic unity.

Mendelsohn's achievements were the more remarkable given that he lost one eye in 1921 because of cancer and the remaining one was weak. He was one of the fathers of the International Style, but he avoided the boxlike monotony that became associated with that school. A major reason for his success in doing so was his juxtaposition of curvilinear forms to temper his use of long horizontal and rectangular spaces. One example was his repeated use of the semicircular projection to break the horizontal movement of his buildings; another was his fondness for the spiral staircase. A second recurring theme is his adaptation of the structure not simply to the building's purpose but to the natural environment of its site—including the climate as well as the physical terrain. The most distinctive feature of his work, however, is genius for achieving an organic unity in which there is a oneness of exterior and interior, in which each part has a definite function in relation to the other parts, and in which there is the rhythmic continuity of the different parts appearing to flow into one other as an integrated whole.

Mendelsohn is less well known than most of the other founders of modern architecture. One reason is that his inflexible and uncompromising attitude toward his designs antagonized would-be clients. Yet the major reason appears to be, simply, bad luck. Many of his most imaginative designs never got beyond the paper stage, and many of his most outstanding completed buildings were done in the backwater of Palestine. He also died at a relatively young age compared to such contemporaries as Le Corbusier, Gropius, and Mies van der Rohe.

Bibliography

James, Kathleen. *Erich Mendelsohn and the Architecture of German Modernism*. Cambridge and New York: Cambridge University Press, 1997. The author examines Mendelsohn's modernism through analysis of his department store, cinema, and office building designs.

Mendelsohn, Erich. *The Drawings of Eric Mendelsohn*. Edited by Susan King. San Francisco: California Print, 1969. This catalog of an exhibition of 133 of Mendelsohn's drawings is invaluable for understanding his work methods and tracing the evolution of his architectural style. King's introduction provides useful background. Included is a listing of Mendelsohn's own published writings and unpublished lectures, writings about him, and exhibitions on him.

———. *Eric Mendelsohn: Letters of an Architect*. Edited by Oskar Beyer. Translated by Geoffrey Strachan. London and New York: Abelard-Schuman, 1967. These letters—mostly to Mendelsohn's wife before and after their marriage—span the years 1910 to 1953 and constitute an invaluable source, illuminating Mendelsohn's intellectual, emotional, and aesthetic development. An introduction by the distinguished architectural historian Nikolaus Pevsner briefly but judiciously appraises Mendelsohn's contribution to modern architecture.

———. *Three Lectures on Architecture*. Berkeley: University of California Press, 1944. These lectures—presented at the University of California-Berkeley in April, 1942—constitute the fullest expression of Mendelsohn's philosophical reflection on the nature of architecture. Required reading for students wishing insight into the intellectual presuppositions shaping and undergirding Mendelsohn's work.

Pehnt, Wolfgang. *Expressionist Architecture*. Translated by J. A. Underwood and Edith Küstner. London: Thames and Hudson, and New York: Praeger, 1973. The volume has only a brief chapter directly on Mendelsohn, but it is the fullest available account of the expressionist impulse/movement in European architecture and, thus, important for placing Mendelsohn's early work in context.

Von Eckardt, Wolf. *Eric Mendelsohn*. New York: Braziller, 1960; London: Mayflower, 1961. Von Eckardt's brief text for this volume in the Braziller Masters of World Architecture series is on the superficial side but provides a helpful introduction for the beginning student. The volume includes approximately eighty pages of illustrations, half of which are reproductions of sketches and models that were never built. Includes a chronological listing of Mendelsohn's buildings and projects plus a bibliography.

Whittick, Arnold. *Eric Mendelsohn*. 2d ed. London: Hill, and New York: Dodge, 1956. Whittick is an enthusiastic Mendelsohn booster and had access to Mendelsohn's still unpublished letters, sketches, and plans. The text is written for the nonspecialist. There are 75 black-and-white photographs and 109 reproductions of drawings, sketches, plans, elevations, and sections.

Wong, Janay Jadine. "Synagogue Art of the 1950s: A New Context for Abstraction." *Art Journal* 53, no. 4 (Winter 1994). Wong examines synagogue art and architecture in the 1950s and 1960s.

Zevi, Bruno. *Erich Mendelsohn*. London: Architectural Press, and New York: Rizzoli, 1985. One of the leading architects of the present day, Zevi is a strong admirer of Mendelsohn. The volume consists of a brief overall appraisal, "Mendelsohn and the Path from Expressionism to the Organic," followed by brief descriptions/analyses of his more important designs. Contains excellent accompanying illustrations.

John Braeman

PIERRE MENDÈS-FRANCE

Born: January 11, 1907; Paris, France

Died: October 18, 1982; Paris, France

Areas of Achievement: Economics, government, and politics

Contribution: Mendès-France was a Left-leaning French politician of the Radical Party who is best remembered for negotiating an armistice with the Vietminh in 1954, which ended the French Indochina War, and for opening the negotiations which led to Tunisian independence. More generally, he acted as the conscience of the democratic non-Communist Left in France during the Fourth and early Fifth republics.

Early Life

Born into an assimilated Jewish family in Paris in January, 1907, Pierre Mendès-France received a secular republican education at the Lycée Turgot and the Lycée Louis-le-Grand, followed by studies at the Faculty of Law and the École Libre des Sciences Politiques. In 1924, he helped found the Ligue d'Action Universitaire Républicaine et Socialistes (LAURS), an anti-Fascist student organization.

The early renown of Mendès-France was a result of his expertise in economics and finance. His thesis for the doctor of law degree, submitted in 1928, was entitled "La Politique financière du gouvernement Poincaré." A 1929 article, "Les Finances de l'état démocratique," and a 1930 book, *La Banque internationale,* focused on the central role of economics in the modern world and argued that the effective solution to practical difficulties required international solutions and, therefore, international organizations. These early publications, boldly critical of individualist law, were very well received and made Mendès-France a well-known figure, though in 1930 he was only twenty-three years old.

Life's Work

The active political career of Mendès-France lasted for forty years. In 1932, he was elected deputy for the city of Louviers (Eure département); at twenty-five, he was the youngest deputy in the National Assembly. Though a member of a Radical Party, he was considered a "Young Turk," along with Jacques Kayser, Pierre Cot, Gaston Bergery, Jean Zay, and Gaston Mannerville. In May, 1935, he was elected mayor of Louviers, a position he held,

except for the interruption of the war, until 1958. He devoted himself to financial and economic matters: In the National Assembly, he spoke in favor of government loans to farmers and was a member, then chair, of the Customs Committee; as a lawyer, he defended peasants; as mayor in Louviers, he oversaw the installation of public utilities and the provision of social welfare.

A strong proponent of the Popular Front strategy, Mendès-France was reelected to the National Assembly in 1936. He was critical of the delayed devaluation of the franc by the Blum government, favoring instead immediate devaluation, and he opposed the policy of nonintervention in the Spanish Civil War. He nevertheless remained a vocal supporter of the government's record of reform, and in 1938 entered Léon Blum's second government as under-secretary of the Treasury. With Georges Boris, he authored the first French planning program, but in less than a month, and before implementation could proceed, the government fell.

With the outbreak of World War II, Mendès-France joined the air force. He was first assigned to the Levant but was on leave in Paris when the invasion of France began. He traveled to Louviers (he was still the elected mayor), witnessed the flight of French refugees fleeing the German army, and himself returned to Paris after receiving a shrapnel wound in the shoulder on June 9. He traveled southward as the Germans advanced and gained passage to Casablanca on the ship *Massilia.*

This "flight" became one portion of the charge of desertion trumped up by the Vichy government. Arrested on August 31, 1940, Mendès-France was transferred to Clermont-Ferrand where he was tried, convicted, and sentenced to six years in prison. After a failed appeal, Mendès-France escaped from prison (on June 21, 1941). He lived underground for several months, mostly in Grenoble, and then escaped, via Geneva and Lisbon, to London on March 1, 1942, to join Charles de Gaulle and the Free French. Between October, 1942, and November, 1943, he rejoined his squadron at Hartfordbridge, England, and flew about a dozen bombing operations.

In November, 1943, Mendès-France moved to Algiers and became the Commissioner of Finance in the French National Liberation Committee (CFLN). In this capacity, he prepared for reconstruction and represented Free France at the inter-

national meeting at Bretton Woods (June, 1944) that established the World Bank and the International Monetary Fund (IMF). Following liberation, he was appointed minister of national economy in Charles de Gaulle's first government. He urged a policy of austerity, including the reduction of the volume of inflated currency in circulation; the restriction of consumption; wage and price controls; the freezing of bank accounts; a tax on capital gains; and state-imposed discipline on some production and exchange. De Gaulle rejected his advice in favor of the more laissez-faire policy advocated by minister of finance René Pleven, and as a result Mendès-France resigned in April, 1945.

Mendès-France returned to his duties as mayor of Louviers and was elected deputy, first to the Constituent Assembly in 1946, and then to the National Assembly in 1951. His various roles in formulating economic policy were arguably even more important: He taught courses at the École Nationale d'Administration on the fiscal and budgetary problems posed by planning and reconstruction, was a member of the Executive Committee of the IMF and World Bank, and became France's

representative, from 1947 to 1951, to the Economic and Social Council of the United Nations.

The issue that catapulted Mendès-France to the center of French politics was not economic policy, however, but colonial policy. After 1950, he became a vocal public advocate of a negotiated settlement in Indochina that would entail the gradual evacuation of French troops and called for free elections and national independence for Vietnam. This campaign, coupled with his calls for dialogue with North Africa and his program for fiscal and economic reform, made Mendès-France the statesman of choice for many young technocrats and intellectuals.

His brief tenure as premier began on June 18, 1954, in the midst of the debacle of Dien Bien Phu. Mendès-France moved quickly to open direct negotiations with the Vietminh in Geneva, and he succeeded in arranging the armistice that halted the fighting. Simultaneously, he traveled to Carthage to set in motion the negotiations that led to the internal autonomy of Tunisia. Finally, Mendès-France oversaw, after the French rejection of the European Defense Community, the London Agreements that led to German rearmament and English attachment to continental security. While Mendès-France was occupied with foreign policy issues, economic policy was left in the hands of the more moderate Edgar Faure, and by the time Mendès-France himself took over control of the Finance Ministry, on January 20, 1955, opponents were preparing to bring down the government.

The government fell on February 2, 1955, during a debate on the Maghreb. Many analysts believe that the underlying cause was too much success: Mendès-France had succeeded in the politically delicate tasks for which he had been given political power—of extricating France from Vietnam and establishing a Western European union. Once achieved, Mendès-France was viewed as expendable by more traditional politicians of the Fourth Republic.

Mendès-France turned his attention to a consolidation of power for his progressive faction within the Radical Party. He was instrumental in forming the Republican Front, which brought together the parties of the non-Communist Left. The coalition won the elections of December, 1956, and Mendès-France served briefly as minister without portfolio in the government of Guy Mollet. He resigned in May, 1957, because of his opposition to the hard-line Algerian policy of the Socialist Party leader. Mendès-France became spokesman for the democratic opposition on the Left: He was critical of government policy in North Africa; he almost alone warned against the consequences of the Suez adventure; he voted against the Treaty of Rome establishing the Common Market; and he opposed de Gaulle's return to power in 1958. He was so out of step with national opinion that he lost the support of his constituency in Louviers in the elections of November, 1958. The following year, Mendès-France, now fifty-two years old, broke with the Radical Party, declared himself a socialist, and adhered to a splinter party of the Socialist party that was attempting to distance itself from the policies of Mollet.

His brief return to the center of national politics occurred in 1967-1969. In March, 1967, he was elected deputy for Grenoble. During the crisis of 1968, he sympathized with the striking workers and students, attended the demonstration in Charléty, and even suggested (during de Gaulle's dramatic disappearance) that he might lead a provisional government. In the Gaullist landslide that followed, he lost his assembly seat (by 132 votes). In 1969, he and Gaston Defferre ran a campaign against Georges Pompidou and the Gaullist system. They were badly beaten, and for all practical purposes Mendès-France passed from active political life. He died on October 18, 1982.

Summary

Pierre Mendès-France was probably the most influential figure in postwar French political life after Charles de Gaulle, despite the fact that he headed a government for only 245 days. His early renown came in the field for which his academic work best prepared him—economics. At the age of twenty-one, he published a refutation of Henri Poincaré's stabilization program, which made him famous. At thirty-one, he coauthored the first French planning program with a member of Léon Blum's Popular Front cabinet. At thirty-seven, he was the interlocutor of John Maynard Keynes at Bretton Woods. At thirty-eight, he called on de Gaulle to stabilize the economy in liberated France. Known for his rigor and his scrupulous attention to economic facts, he was the hardheaded conscience of a French Left which, too often in Mendès-France's opinion, allowed flights of utopian fancy to obscure reality.

The event for which Mendès-France will be best remembered is the ending of French involvement in Indochina during his premiership between June, 1954, and February, 1955. Perhaps no European colonial power has withdrawn from its colonial possessions with greater human costs. It was Mendès-France who began the painful process of extricating France from its colonial past. Not only did he end the French war in Vietnam but also he began the negotiations in relatively friendly circumstances that led to the independence of Morocco and Tunisia.

For many in France, Mendès-France restored hope that reason and politics did not necessarily exclude each other; he represented a politics that was neither useless nor corrupt. In the words of François Mitterrand, "Pierre Mendès-France awakened our consciences."

Bibliography

Lacouture, Jean. *Pierre Mendès France*. Translated by George Holoch. New York: Holmes and Meier, 1984. This political biography is the best available book on Mendès-France. It describes with a sure hand the French political world to which Mendès-France not only reacted but also helped to shape.

Mendès-France, Pierre, and Gabriel Ardant. *Economics and Action*. New York: Columbia University Press, 1955. The essential book on Mendès-France's economic thought.

Rioux, Jean-Pierre. *The Fourth Republic, 1944-1958*. Translated by Godfrey Rogers. Cambridge and New York: Cambridge University Press, 1987. The history of the French Fourth Republic, written by a French expert.

Werth, Alexander. *The Strange History of Mendès-France and the Great Conflict Over French North Africa*. London: Barrie, 1957. Published during the final crisis of the French Fourth Republic, this book provides a sense of the drama of this period by a close observer. The greatest part of the book deals, as the title indicates, with the crisis of the French North African Empire.

Williams, Philip M. *Crisis and Compromise: Politics in the Fourth Republic*. London and New York: Longmans, 1964. A standard history of the Fourth Republic by a British expert.

K. Steven Vincent

GIAN CARLO MENOTTI

Born: July 7, 1911; Cadegliano, Italy

Area of Achievement: Music

Contribution: Menotti is known primarily for his opera compositions, for which he composed the music and wrote the libretti. He is also a composer of ballets, concerti, and orchestral music.

Early Life

Gian Carlo Menotti was born in Cadegliano, Italy, on July 7, 1911, to wealthy parents who were able by their financial and cultural backgrounds to nurse his immense musical interests. At the early age of four, Menotti began studying piano, and, by the age of six, he had progressed to the point of composing his own melodies and simple accompaniments. On his ninth birthday, Menotti was given a puppet theater by his parents. This was a source of great fun and learning for Menotti, as he not only wrote and directed his own plays but also composed his own music for the productions. His first full-length opera was written in 1922, when he was eleven years old.

In 1923, the Menotti family moved to Milan, where Gian Carlo was enrolled in academic school, in which he displayed very little interest. At this same time, however, he also began studying at the Milan Conservatory of Music, where he was a regular student from 1923 to 1928. During this time, he composed a second full-length opera entitled *The Death of Pierrot*, the last act of which sees all the characters kill themselves. While studying at the conservatory, Menotti was also in demand as a pianist. Handsome, intelligent, and musically gifted, he was proudly exhibited in the most fashionable Milanese salons and was so spoiled that he refused to practice as he should have.

His mother was wise enough to realize that the musical growth of her son was somewhat stunted in Milan. Compelled to travel to South America to untangle some of her husband's interests following his death, she took her son with her in hopes of stopping off in New York City on the return trip. Menotti was seventeen at the time and enjoyed visiting the different cultures of the Western world. On the return trip to Italy, they did stop in New York to visit an old friend of the family, Tullio Serafin, then conductor at the Metropolitan Opera House. Serafin introduced the Menottis to Rosario Scalero, an eminent composition teacher at the Curtis Institute of Music in Philadelphia. To

Scalero, Menotti seemed to be only an undisciplined boy, in spite of his talents, but through a solemn promise by Menotti, Scalero consented to teach him the fine points of composition. Menotti's mother returned to Italy, leaving the young man in a strange new country, where he not only had to work hard and practice but also had to learn a new language—English. This he did by attending the motion picture show four times a week.

Life's Work

By the time he reached the age of twenty-two, Menotti was able to graduate from writing contrapuntal class exercises and began working on his first mature opera, *Amelia Goes to the Ball*. This one-act comic opera was produced in Philadelphia and New York by students and faculty of the Curtis Institute and was conducted by Fritz Reiner in 1937. Menotti's operas are important as theatrical spectacles. Their greatest significance does not lie in the musical score, as it does with most operas. His music is sometimes more functional than inspired. Menotti draws from every available style and idiom to cater to his dramatic needs: from the popular to the esoteric, from the lyrical to the dissonant, from the romantic to the realistic. For the operas of Menotti, music is never an end but a means, and the end is realized in projection of effective theater.

Because of the necessary flow of the music to provide the listener with something substantial, portions of Menotti's operas are seldom heard in the concert setting. The music loses its appeal when not heard in sequence of the story. Within the theater, however, his music carries tremendous impact and serves to tie the production together, provide a continual flow, and enhance the other artistic qualities of the productions.

Menotti had written his first libretto in Italian, but henceforth he would write all his opera libretti in English. The musical format for *Amelia Goes to the Ball* is in traditional style, with solo arias, duets, trios, and recitatives. The style is happy and tuneful, although at times spiced with a touch of discord or polytonality. The impressive nature of this work led to a commission by the National Broadcasting Company (NBC) to write an opera exclusively for radio production. On April 27, 1939, NBC introduced the work *The Old Man and the Thief*, also written in a comic vein.

Meanwhile, in 1938 Menotti received word that his opera *Amelia Goes to the Ball* had been accepted by the Metropolitan Opera Company for its 1938 season. It was played seven times during that and the following season. Several years later, in 1942, the Metropolitan Opera commissioned an opera by Menotti, entitled *The Island God*. This opera, unfortunately, was not well received by the public.

Menotti became determined to compose a successful serious opera, as he had thus far only seen success with his comic operas. *The Medium*, first heard in New York City in May of 1946, proved to be the work that opened to public view Menotti's far-reaching dramatic powers. Since the first performance of *The Medium*, it has become one of the most famous American operas. It has been given more than one thousand performances in the United States, London, Paris, and Italy, and has also been made into a stirring motion picture.

Between 1948 and 1958, Menotti continued to compose, write, produce, and direct operas, sometimes as commissioned works, sometimes at his own pleasure, but always intelligent, quality productions. In 1958, Menotti founded the Festival of the Two Worlds in Spoleto, Italy. As founder and president, he has been responsible for the presentation of several provocative contemporary operas.

On Christmas Eve, 1951, the production of *Amahl and the Night Visitors* was seen for the first time. This very popular work of Menotti is unique in that it is the first opera produced expressly for television transmission. The broadcast was repeated the following Easter and Christmas by NBC and has since been staged by many opera companies, including the New York City Opera.

Like Richard Wagner, Menotti is a one-man theater. He not only writes his own text and music but also is his own stage director and casting director and has a general command of every other aspect of the production, much like he did at age nine with his puppet theater, only on a much grander scale. Menotti seems to have an extraordinary sixth sense for finding small details that may enhance good drama. His ability to see clearly all details of the production even before rehearsals have begun, combined with his sense for what he desires to see in his opera in spite of popular opinion, has led him often to select many comparatively inexperienced and unknown singers and performers for his works.

Menotti is known first and foremost as an opera composer, and though Italian born and reared (re-

taining his Italian citizenship), he is considered to be America's greatest composer of opera, because of his training in Philadelphia and his residency in New York City. He has also written a concerto for piano and orchestra, another concerto for violin and orchestra, some pieces for orchestra, and some ballet music. These pieces, however, have not seen the publicity or the public acceptance of his operas.

His orchestration usually requires small groups of instruments in balance with small casts. His operas very seldom use the chorus so popular with other composers, and he relies on his solo singers to carry the work. This combination of relatively small performing forces has made his operas approachable by small opera companies and even school production groups. Especially popular with school-age students is *Amahl and the Night Visitors* because of its familiar message of Christmas and because the lead character is a young boy.

Menotti uses the standard orchestral instruments for the most part. Very seldom does he venture into the lures of uncommon instrumental techniques for the sake of effect. He prefers, instead, when special effects are called for, to create them on the stage rather than in the orchestra pit. Although his music is spiced with twentieth century composition techniques such as polytonality and discords, the audience generally feels at ease as the music begins near and never strays very far from the tonal center. His melodic structure may not always be singable to the average listener, but it is always listenable and pleasant to the ear.

Amahl and the Night Visitors is probably Menotti's most popular opera. The music ranges from tender to exciting as the story of the three wise men following the star of the Christ child unfolds. During their travels, they come upon the poor home of Amahl, a crippled beggar boy, and his mother. When Amahl learns of the wise men's purpose, he gives his set of small crutches to the Magi as a present to the Holy Child. As Amahl goes forth to present his gift to the kings, he discovers that a miracle has taken place and that he is able to walk. This work thrives on beautifully flowing arias and angelic choruses. The emotion of the opera can only be felt when the entire production is presented. Therefore, it does not break down into concert sections well. Although *Amahl and the Night Visitors* was written for and introduced by the television screen, it has also been presented with immense success on stage.

Summary

Gian Carlo Menotti's eclecticism carries him from a Puccini-like lyricism to the most advanced composition idioms. He can be romantic or dissonant, lyrical or mystic. Yet he never seems to sacrifice unity of concept or coherence of viewpoint. Menotti is above all else a man of the theater. He writes his own libretti and music and commands full control of the production of his operas. His operas are not only a vehicle for musical expression but also a vibrant and pulsating stage experience. Perhaps for this reason Menotti has commanded a larger and more varied audience than any other composer in the twentieth century.

Bibliography

Austin, William W. *Music in the Twentieth Century: From Debussy Through Stravinsky.* London: Dent, and New York: Norton, 1966. This book discusses the student/teacher relationships of twentieth century composers such as Menotti. It also discusses Menotti's works in relationship to music of other composers.

Drummond, Andrew H. *American Opera Librettos.* Metuchen, N.J.: Scarecrow Press, 1973. Drummond lists all Menotti's operas and quotes the poetic text of each. This book allows the reader the opportunity to see Menotti's creative literary work.

Ewen, David. *David Ewen Introduces Modern Music.* Rev. ed. Philadelphia: Chilton, 1969. Ewen, a highly respected music historian, offers an indepth discussion of Menotti's life, works, and contributions to music and opera as well as brings to the light his ability as a theater director and his staging genius.

Honig, Joel. "Passing Time in Spoleto: A Festival Alumnus Returns after Thirty Years and Looks into the Future." *Opera News* 58, no. 16 (May, 1994). Discusses Menotti's unpleasant split with the Spoleto Festival.

Howard, John Tasker, and Arthur Mendel. *Our Contemporary Composers.* New York: Crowell, 1941. This source quotes music critics in discussing Menotti's operas. There is also a list of the few works by Menotti that were not written for the opera stage but for concert settings.

Myers, Rollo H., ed. *Twentieth Century Music.* New York: Orion Press, and London: Calder and Boyars, 1968. This book gives a brief description of the performing elements that make up Menotti's operas and lists each of his operas in chronological order. A good description of Menotti's work without in-depth details.

Pniewski, Tom. "Menotti Reminisces." *World and I* 11, no. 7 (July, 1996). Profile of Menotti including his contributions in opera, chamber, and symphonic music; Pulitzer Prizes won; and his ideas on the artistic process.

Reis, Claire R. *Composers in America.* Rev. ed. New York: Macmillan, 1947. Following a brief synopsis of Menotti's career, Reis offers a complete list of works, dates, and publishers of Menotti's works.

Salzman, Eric. *Twentieth Century Music: An Introduction.* 3d ed. Englewood Cliffs, N.J.: Prentice-Hall, 1988. Salzman compares Menotti's theater talent to that of Puccini, describing how it goes beyond music and enters the areas of drama, stage usage, and function of characters among other things.

Robert Briggs

ROBERT GORDON MENZIES

Born: December 20, 1894; Jeparit, Victoria, Australia

Died: May 15, 1978; Melbourne, Victoria, Australia

Areas of Achievement: Government and politics

Contribution: As the leading conservative politician of Australia for more than a third of a century, and as prime minister from 1939 to 1941 and from 1949 to 1966, Menzies forged critical, lasting international commitments and national policies.

Early Life

Robert Gordon Menzies was born on December 20, 1894, at Jeparit, Victoria. His parents, James Menzies and Kate Sampson Menzies, ran a general store and served as agents for farm implement manufacturers; their fourth child's middle name came from the popular imperial martyr, General Charles "Chinese" Gordon. Robert Menzies began his education in public schools and later studied at private schools in Ballarat and in Melbourne after his father's election to the Victorian Parliament. At eighteen, Menzies entered Melbourne University to study law. With its small size and elite reputation, Melbourne University at the time offered talented, proper, and ambitious young men a stepping-stone to prominence within the city's social and political establishments.

Menzies was graduated in 1916; although trained in the university officer program, Menzies declined service for personal and family reasons. Later attempts to discredit him on these grounds generally backfired, but they may have stung Menzies sufficiently to determine, by way of compensation, his subsequent approval of conscription, military alliance, and intervention: During his administrations, Australia committed troops to international forces in World War II, Korea, and Vietnam.

Life's Work

In 1918, Menzies began his law practice. In 1920, he married Pattie Maie Leckie, a politician's daughter, who remained with him throughout his life. As his reputation in constitutional law grew, his political career began to develop. In 1928, he won a seat in the Victorian Parliament. By 1932, he was deputy premier and attorney general of Victoria. In 1934, Prime Minister Joseph Lyons asked Menzies to run for the national Parliament as a candidate of the United Australian Party (UAP). Menzies won the seat for Kooyong, Melbourne, which he retained for thirty-two years. He served the Lyons government until March, 1939, when he resigned in a dispute over national insurance which split Lyons' UPA-Country Party coalition. Lyons died a month later, and Menzies ascended to head the UAP on behalf of its liberal (that is centrist) faction. Supporting the National Insurance Act perhaps more for political placement than on principle, Menzies became Prime Minister of Australia on April 29, 1939, in a UAP government without coalition.

With World War II approaching, Menzies' suspicion of Japanese intentions found little support in London but was not enough to force Menzies to seek an independent national agenda; his testimony also conflicted with his previous criticism of Australian union protests against shipping iron to Japan. He defended the Munich appeasement of Adolf Hitler even after Germany invaded Czechoslovakia, the point of crisis for most other observers. Nevertheless, Menzies reverted to imperial loyalties when the war began: Australia declared war on Germany as a result of Great Britain's declaration. This postcolonial obligation left Australia in a dangerously straddled position: The bulk of Australian forces were committed to the British campaign in North Africa, while Australian forces in the Pacific were essentially confined to coastal defense and to the ill-fated garrisons of such British ports as Hong Kong and Singapore. His insistence that British motives coincided exactly with Australian interests reduced Menzies' parliamentary majority after the 1940 elections, but he relied upon personal visibility and external recognition to carry him through: In 1941, he departed for London and the Middle East. Menzies returned to a government in deep division, which eventually resulted in the disbanding of the UAP and eight years of power for the Australian Labor Party (ALP).

If Menzies gave the government to Labor in 1941, the ALP returned the gift in 1949, by failing to recognize the polarization of Cold War thought. Like other countries, Australia had long accommodated a large amount of Socialist sentiment and a highly vocal, if small, Communist Party; these elements historically overlapped the left wing of the ALP and were not renounced despite the swing of postwar public opinion. Menzies countered with a new Liberal Party organization, drawing in many of the former UAP and Country Party factions, including conservative veterans' groups, and swept the elections of 1949 on an anti-Socialist platform: While Labor proposed to nationalize the banks, Menzies proposed to outlaw the Communist Party.

Although Menzies probably knew that his proposed restriction would be ruled unconstitutional, he caught the tone of the electorate. Tall and portly, with trademark bushy black eyebrows, an orator in a league with Churchill, Menzies looked the part of the statesman. His demeanor, matched with his ability to gauge the public and his quickness to profit from others' missteps, may in fact help account for Menzies' long tenure as prime minister. His attention to international affairs thrust Australia into the flattering appearance of global leadership: Menzies was a major voice in urging Commonwealth cooperation; he asserted Australia's role in the United Nations; and he led the nation to war on behalf of alliances that he had fostered in accordance with his own vision of the domino theory. In an example of his public forcefulness, Menzies was able to turn the 1954 defection of a Soviet agent, Vladimir Petrov, into a further indictment of the Labor Left, rather than permitting it to signal lapses within his own intelligence staff. In 1956, he led a team which attempted to negotiate international jurisdiction of the Suez Canal. His mission failed, but he retained popularity at home by supporting the subsequent British and French invasion of Egypt.

In his domestic policies, similarly, Menzies succeeded largely through well-timed visibility and by taking fewer false steps than his opponents. He consistently supported Australian federalism (as opposed to centralization), both as a matter of states' rights in principle and as a means of playing one state's interests against those of another. Some of the institutions that he sustained or created, such as national insurance, free tertiary education, and the development of the national capital of Canberra, read almost like a Labor platform. That, in fact, is how many of his positions originated: Menzies consistently adopted liberal social policies just before or immediately after elections, alternately throwing Labor into confusion and appeasing restive elements within his own party. When he retired in 1966, after seventeen years in office, the extent to which Menzies had governed through personal insight and individual forcefulness was clear: No

real heir had been groomed among the Liberals, and no cohesive ALP policy was prepared to fill the void.

Summary

Robert Gordon Menzies' style of government was both consistently motivated by tradition and curiously ad hoc. He aggressively sought international recognition and alliance at a time when Australia might have reverted to isolationism and restriction. Yet many of his policies might well be called reactionary or neocolonial: It is difficult to view Menzies' Australia as more than a secondary partner in the relationships he forged, and difficult to ignore his commitments to the British monarchy, to American industry, and, at home, to large-scale edifices and performances. Those commitments represented ties, in short, to an unquestioned concept of a fundamentally metropolitan Anglo-Saxon tradition. Menzies' record on social welfare, aborigine rights, and immigration standards is mediocre at best and potentially self-defeating in the long run. Menzies abandoned to his successors any possible visions of a truly independent Australia in the world arena, as a political and cultural force in the Pacific and Indian basins, as a power having affinities with developing nations in black Africa and South America, and as a domestic realm demanding strong diversification and interstate cooperation. Perhaps the most telling summary of Menzies' tenure came in the virtual explosion of Australian culture in the early 1970's, under the Labor government of Gough Whitlam. It was as if Australia had suddenly thrown off the blankets of English sentiment and American realpolitik. With strong state support and public encouragement, a vast amount of literature, film, social history, and commentary emerged, much of it directed at examining, perhaps for the first time in the postwar age, the possibilities of modern Australian identity and to asserting, at last, both the cultural autonomy and political self-direction of an independent Australia.

Bibliography

Barclay, Glen St. J. *Friends in High Places: Australian-American Diplomatic Relations Since 1945*. Melbourne and New York: Oxford University Press, 1985. Barclay portrays Menzies as consistently outmaneuvered by American leaders, Lyndon Johnson in particular. Traces the process of Australian involvement in Vietnam and the development of American communications bases in the Australian outback.

Crowley, F. K., ed. *A New History of Australia*. Melbourne: Heinemann, 1974. G. C. Bolton's chapter, "1939-1951," deals with Menzies' first term, including the Australian entry into World War II, and with the evolution of the postwar Liberal Party. W. J. Hudson's chapter, "1951-1972," covers Menzies' domestic strategies.

Day, David. *Menzies and Churchill at War*. New York: Paragon House, 1988; Oxford: Oxford University Press, 1994. Through extensive research of private papers and diaries, Day presents a detailed study of the struggle between Menzies and Winston Churchill over the running of the war and the protection of the Empire.

Hazlehurst, Cameron. *Menzies Observed*. Sydney: Allen and Unwin, 1979. Illustrated with official publicity shots—Menzies with Churchill, Menzies with Nasser—and laden with extensive quotation of Menzies' papers and speeches; highly critical of policies and "accomplishments."

Holt, Edgar. *Politics Is People: The Men of the Menzies Era*. Sydney: Angus and Robertson, 1969. At the opposite pole from Hazlehurst: A highly sympathetic chronological appreciation, with personal anecdotes regarding major figures and events.

Menzies, Robert Gordon. *Afternoon Light: Some Memories of Men and Events*. London: Cassell, 1967; New York: Coward-McCann, 1968.

———. *The Measure of the Years*. London: Cassell, 1970. Both works contain long quotations from his own speeches, with little new analysis, and anecdotal reminiscences of famous statesmen; Menzies knew them all. Elaborate, if not quite convincing, arguments in favor of monarchist sentiment and South African domestic policy.

Millar, T. B. *Australia in Peace and War: External Relations 1788-1977*. London: Hurst, and New York: St. Martin's Press, 1978. Extensive and technical, presumes prior knowledge of the main contours of events. Heavily documented with charts of foreign aid appropriations, editorial cartoons, and quotations from documents. Particularly strong on Australian relations to nonaligned and Third World nations.

Perkins, Kevin. *Menzies: Last of the Queen's Men*. London: Angus and Robertson, 1968. A criticism of Menzies' policies. Contains a series of complaints in short, jabbing paragraphs but lacks real development. Hazlehurst makes similar evaluations, but his strategy of damnation by quotation works better.

Reese, Trevor R. *Australia in the Twentieth Century: A Political History*. New York: Praeger, 1964. Dated and inconclusive; Menzies was still in office when this work was published. Valuable, nevertheless, as a straightforward chronology and as a working critique of Menzies' policies in the midst of their enactment.

John Scheckter

MAURICE MERLEAU-PONTY

Born: March 14, 1908; Rochefort, France
Died: May 4, 1961; Paris, France
Area of Achievement: Philosophy
Contribution: Merleau-Ponty, French philosopher and man of letters, was one of the most original and profound thinkers of the postwar French movement of existential phenomenology.

Early Life

Maurice Merleau-Ponty's father died before his son was seven years old, and Maurice, his brother, and his sister were reared in Paris by their mother, a devout Catholic who gave her children a strongly religious upbringing. It was not until the 1930's that Merleau-Ponty eventually became discontented with the established Church and ceased to practice his faith. At one point in his life, he even admitted to being an atheist but then altered his position to one of agnosticism. His final position with regard to religion is not known; what is clear, however, is that some degree of reconciliation with the Church of his early years must have occurred prior to his sudden death in May of 1961, since a Catholic Mass was said at his funeral.

According to the testimony of his own writings, Merleau-Ponty's childhood was happy, so happy that his adult years never quite provided him with the same sense of complete fulfillment. The death of his father while the boy was still very young is thought to have affected the boy immeasurably, and as a result he became extremely close to his mother and remained completely devoted to her until her death only a few years prior to his own.

Merleau-Ponty received his secondary education at the Lycée Louis-le-Grand, and then studied at the École Normale Supérieure in Paris. After taking his *agrégation* in philosophy in 1931, he taught in a *lycée* at Beauvais for the next five years. He then held a research grant from the Caisse de la Recherche Scientifique for a year and subsequently took up teaching again, this time at the *lycée* in Chartres. In 1935, he returned to Paris as a junior member of the faculty at the school he had attended, the École Normale.

Life's Work

In the winter of 1939, after the Nazi invasion of Poland, Merleau-Ponty entered the army and served as a lieutenant in the infantry. While in the army, he wrote his first major work, *La Structure du comportement* (1942; *The Structure of Behavior*, 1963). Although the work was completed in 1938, when he was thirty years old, because of the war, the book was not published until 1942. Perhaps the most important thesis of this work is Merleau-Ponty's reinterpretation of the distinctions between the physical, the biological (or vital), and the mental dimensions of existence. These dimensions were treated by him as different levels of conceptualization at which human behavior could be studied, and they were distinguished by the degree to which the concepts used were useful and meaningful. While Merleau-Ponty was very insistent upon the irreducibility of these distinctions, he also maintained that they were logically cumulative, such that biological concepts presuppose physical concepts, and mental concepts presuppose both. Yet, at the same time that he defended this thesis of the logical interdependence of the physical and the mental, Merleau-Ponty rejected in principle all attempts to explain this relationship in causal terms. Merleau-Ponty's first work, then, was both a sustained and powerful attack on behaviorism in psychology as well as a new philosophical interpretation of the experimental work of the Gestalt psychologists.

After the demobilization of France and during the German Occupation, Merleau-Ponty again returned to teaching and writing. Continuing his critique of traditional psychology, in 1945 he published what was to become his masterwork: *Phénoménologie de la perception* (1945; *Phenomenology of Perception*, 1962). This second book examined what he viewed as traditional prejudices regarding perception in order to advance a "return" to things themselves. According to Merleau-Ponty, understanding the body itself involves a theory of perception. One is able to know oneself only through relationships with the world, and the world is not what one thinks it is but what one lives through. Drawing heavily upon, but also modifying, the phenomenological techniques of Edmund Husserl as well as the existential threads in the thought of Gabriel Marcel and Martin Heidegger, Merleau-Ponty, in this work, begins to construct a personal synthesis, an original philosophical interpretation of human experience. For this reason he is considered to be one of the originators of contemporary existential philosophy and, in the opinion of one of his notable colleagues, Paul Ricoeur, "was the greatest of the French phenomenologists."

After the Occupation of France ended, Merleau-Ponty joined the faculty of the University of Lyon and at the same time (in 1945) became coeditor of the existentialist periodical *Les Temps modernes* with Jean-Paul Sartre, a former schoolmate and longtime friend. By 1950, Merleau-Ponty's reputation was established, and he took a position at the Sorbonne as professor of psychology and pedagogy. He was to remain in this post for only two years. Then, in 1952, he was appointed to a chair at the Collège de France. This was the chair that had been left vacant by the death of Louis Lavelle and that had previously been occupied by Henri Bergson and Édouard Le Roy. Merleau-Ponty, in fact, was the youngest philosopher ever to hold this position—one of the more prestigious in French academic life—and he retained it until his death in May, 1961. Merleau-Ponty was happily married to a woman prominent in her own right as a physician and psychiatrist in Paris, and they had one child, a daughter.

All Merleau-Ponty's work demonstrates a familiarity with both current scientific research and with the history of philosophy, a combination that gives his work a more balanced character than that of the other existentialists. Another of his major concerns was with political and social philosophy as well as the problems of everyday politics. Consequently he wrote numerous newspaper articles on contemporary events and problems. His more sustained essays on Marxist theory and leftist politics, however, were gathered in two collections: *Humanisme et terreur* (1947; humanism and terror) and *Les Aventures de la dialectique* (1955; the adventures of the dialectic).

In the former work, Merleau-Ponty leaned so far in the direction of Marxist historicism as to argue that historical undertakings are to be judged retroactively by their success or failure and that to act "historically" is inevitably to submit oneself to this "objective" judgment of events, in which personal intentions, good or bad, are irrelevant. Simultaneously, however, he rejected the orthodox Marxist view that a scientific theory of the logic of historical development is accessible as a basis for such action. The latter work, exhibiting a new direction in the philosopher's social thought, contains a powerful critique of the French Communist Party, with which he had earlier sympathized. Marxism, in his opinion, was a timely device for thinking

about human needs and contingencies in modern industrial society; he, however, rejected its dogmatic rigidity, particularly its claims to predictive power and historical mission, and the nonliberating, totalitarian features that had become associated with it.

Well to the left of Sartre during the 1940's, Merleau-Ponty was close to the Communists from 1945 to 1950 and played a crucial role in linking existentialist and Marxist thought during that period; by 1955, however, he was no longer engaged in Marxist politics. From 1950 on, Sartre, on the other hand, was moving closer to Marxism. For some years after 1955, Sartre was occupied almost exclusively with the existentialism-Marxism debate, which since 1945 had continued to be an explosive issue in French intellectual and political life. The ideological split with Sartre led to an open break with him and to Merleau-Ponty's resignation from the editorship of *Les Temps modernes*. Nevertheless, Merleau-Ponty's political views remained decisive for Sartre, as the latter freely admitted in a memoir published after Merleau-Ponty's death.

Essays and articles on language, literature, the aesthetics of film, and painting were also undertaken by Merleau-Ponty in the busy final decade of his life. In these essays, published as collections entitled *Sens et non-sens* (1948; *Sense and NonSense*, 1964) and *Signs* (1960; English translation, 1964), he sought to work out some of the implications of his thesis on the primacy of perception using Husserl as his fundamental reference point for epistemological grounding and dialogue. Merleau-Ponty had hoped to conclude his analysis of the prereflective life of consciousness with a survey of the major modes of reflective thought in which he would seek to determine their criteria for validity and truth. At the time of his sudden death from a coronary thrombosis in 1961, he had written only incomplete fragments and sketches.

Summary

Maurice Merleau-Ponty's career included two principal aspects. He was, first, a professional philosopher and teacher of philosophy whose main body of work was done in the field of philosophical psychology and phenomenology. In addition, he was a man of letters who wrote extensively on political and aesthetic subjects and actively participated in the intellectual life of his time. Despite the fact that Merleau-Ponty is sometimes viewed as a kind of junior collaborator of Sartre, both his philosophical work and his more general writings reveal a mind and a mode of thought that developed in a fully independent manner and that are at once very different from Sartre's and, in terms of intellectual rigor and elegance, often demonstrably superior.

As in the case with other "existentialist" philosophers, there are no "disciples" of Merleau-Ponty in the strict sense of the word, since his method was his life. To adopt his method then, would be to begin to experience the world in a new way, with a new philosophy, and not with a continuation of Merleau-Ponty's life and thought. Thus it is not by virtue of his existentialism, Marxism, or phenomenology that he has made his greatest contribution, but rather by the extent to which, through each of these, he has been able to illuminate the lived human quality of existence. It is in and through his uniqueness that his impact will be felt most strongly.

Bibliography

Bannan, John F. *The Philosophy of Merleau-Ponty.* New York: Harcourt Brace, 1967. The aim of Bannan's excellent and very thorough work is not to locate the thought of Merleau-Ponty among the classic positions in the history of philosophy but to focus upon his more immediate context—his relations with Husserl's work, with Sartre, and with Marxism. Contains a very brief biographical note on the philosopher.

Dillon, M. C. *Merleau-Ponty's Ontology.* 2d ed. Evanston, Ill.: Northwestern University Press, 1997. This well-documented, scholarly work approaches Merleau-Ponty in the historical context out of which Merleau-Ponty's ontology, his alternative to Cartesian knowledge, arose. This lengthy work also contains an excellent bibliography and extensive notes.

Mallin, Samuel B. *Merleau-Ponty's Philosophy.* New Haven, Conn.: Yale University Press, 1979. In this lengthy and scholarly work, the author's purpose is to provide a unified and comprehensive interpretation of Merleau-Ponty's philosophy. His method is to analyze extensively the concepts that are central and original to Merleau-Ponty's philosophy and the way in which they form an integrated whole. The work also contains a bibliography of primary and secondary sources and an appendix consisting of a table of contents of the philosophy of perception and its integration into the text.

Rabil, Albert, Jr. *Merleau-Ponty: Existentialist of the Social World.* New York: Columbia University Press, 1967. In this well-respected and lengthy work, Rabil suggests that in Merleau-Ponty more than any other philosopher a dialectical tension exists in his existentialist preoccupation with self-understanding and the social orientation of the politically minded and the reformer. The author analyzes the sources, the vision and the viability of this "social philosophy." Contains a bibliography and extensive notes.

Spurling, Laurie. *Phenomenology and the Social World: The Philosophy of Merleau-Ponty and Its Relation to the Social Sciences.* London and Boston: Routledge, 1977. Spurling argues that Merleau-Ponty's philosophy can be understood as a dialectic between a discipline and a transcendental impulse and that it is this overall dialectical relationship that offers a coherent perspective on being in the world, especially on those areas of thought often considered to be the exclusive domain of the social sciences. Contains a bibliography and extensive notes.

Vasseleu, Cathryn. *Textures of Light: Vision and Touch in Irigaray, Levinas, and Merleau-Ponty.* London and New York: Routledge, 1998. The author offers a new view of light as metaphor for truth and objectivity through analysis of the philosophies of Merleau-Ponty, Levinas, and Iriguaray.

Whitford, Margaret. *Merleau-Ponty's Critique of Sartre's Philosophy.* Lexington, Ky.: French Forum, 1982. Rather than presenting a straightforward comparison of the two philosophers' thought, the author of this brief but illuminating book focuses upon the limits of Merleau-Ponty's critique of Sartre. Cogito, freedom, temporality, others, ontology, phenomenology, and dialectic are the categories discussed.

Genevieve Slomski

OLIVIER MESSIAEN

Born: December 10, 1908; Avignon, France
Died: April 28, 1992; Paris, France
Area of Achievement: Music
Contribution: Messiaen was the most important French composer of the twentieth century's second half. His catalog of compositions (which numbers more than seventy works) includes pieces for solo keyboard, chamber ensemble, electronic media, orchestra, oratorio, art song, and opera. He was the most significant composer for the organ since Johann Sebastian Bach.

Early Life

Olivier-Eugène-Prosper-Charles Messiaen was born in Avignon, France, on December 10, 1908, the son of parents well known in French literary circles. His mother was the poetess Cécile Sauvage, and his father, Pierre, was an English teacher respected for his critical translations of Shakespeare. Recognizing the young Messiaen's musical gifts (by eight he had taught himself piano), Pierre encouraged him with gifts of scores to Hector Berlioz's *Damnation of Faust* and Wolfgang Amadeus Mozart's *Don Giovanni.* After a move to Nantes in 1918, Messiaen, now ten years old, began formal studies in harmony with the local teacher Jehan de Gibon. Soon after the boy began his studies, Gibon presented Messiaen with the score to Claude Debussy's opera *Pelléas et Mélisande.* Later, the mature composer described that gift as "a real bombshell . . . probably the most decisive influence of my life."

In 1919, the family moved to Grenoble. In the fall of that year, Messiaen was enrolled in the Paris Conservatoire, where he studied under France's leading musicians (Maurice Dupré taught him organ and Paul Dukas tutored him in composition). The student flourished. In 1926, Messiaen took first prize in fugue and in 1928 first prize in piano accompaniment. Firsts in music history and composition followed in 1929 and 1930. The year of his prize in fugue also saw the appearance of his first publication, the organ work *Le Banquet céleste* (the heavenly banquet). In 1929, Messiaen's final complete year at the Conservatoire, he published a set of eight preludes for piano. While the preludes particularly showed the influence of Debussy, in both of these early publications the characteristics of Messiaen's mature style were present. Both used chromatic scales (or "modes")

of the composer's own invention (as opposed to culturally received scales, such as G minor or D major). Both used nontraditional rhythms, Messiaen stretching note values in *Le Banquet céleste* to the point at which meter was lost within the six minute (but only twenty-five measure) piece. In both works, much of their interest and significance lay in Messiaen's musical exploitation of instrumental color. Finally, and here the preludes were somewhat atypical, aspects of Christianity sparked Messiaen's imagination and served as programmatic titles.

Life's Work

Messiaen left the Conservatoire in 1930, having won twice as many "firsts" as Debussy and with two publications already before the public. He was appointed principal organist at the Church of La Trinité (one of Paris' most important liturgical positions) in 1931. Teaching responsibilities at the École Normale Supérieure and at the Schola Cantorum were added five years later. In 1936, he married the violinist Claire Delbos (the dedicatee of his first song cycle, *Poèmes pour Mi*). A year later their son Pascal was born. Through these years, Messiaen composed for organ as well as for chamber ensembles and even for a new electronic instrument, the ondes martenot.

All of this work was broken off by World War II. Although thirty-one (and therefore beyond the reach of general conscription), Messiaen volunteered for the army, serving as a hospital attendant. Overtaken by the Germans near Nancy in June, 1940, the composer was imprisoned in a prisoner of war camp near Görlitz in Silesia. There in the prison camp, Messiaen wrote what was universally to be regarded as one of the century's most remarkable works, the *Quatuor pour la fin du temps* (quartet for the end of time). Finding a clarinetist, violinist, and cellist among his fellow prisoners, Messiaen wrote the piece for himself and this ensemble, premiering it before the five-thousand-member camp on January 15, 1941.

The quartet began the fully mature period of Messiaen's work. A highly evocative series of meditations upon the Apocalypse (its title has a double meaning, referring both to Revelations 10:5-6 and to Messiaen's own new rhythmic character), Messiaen here made extensive use of bird calls for the first time (the quartet's first movement, "Liturgie de Cristal," opens with the calls of a blackbird on the clarinet and the nightingale on the flute). Herein Messiaen first used "nonretrogradable" rhythms, or complex rhythmic patterns that whether read from left to right or right to left remain the same. This kind of rhythmic device (and others derived from his studies of Hindu ragam) continued Messiaen's movement toward completely nonmetric rhythm first seen in *Le Banquet céleste*.

Repatriated in 1942, Messiaen returned to Paris, where he was appointed professor of harmony at the Conservatoire. During the next decades, he began to be seen as a leader of the avant-garde, some of the next generation's leading composers seeking out his teaching in Paris and elsewhere (both Pierre Boulez and Karlheinz Stockhausen were his students). He continued to compose in the manner established in the *Quatuor pour la fin du temps*.

Those characteristics, however, began to burden many of Messiaen's listeners. His works' lengths and almost hyper-baroque textures offended musicians increasingly influenced by Anton von Webern's terse severity. The Christian themes and unabashed emotionalism of Messiaen's works seemed both hopelessly naïve and out of step with postwar materialism. For the first time since the brouhaha that had greeted Igor Stravinsky's *Rite of Spring* in 1913, the Parisians rioted at the premiere of Messiaen's *Trois Petites Liturgies* on April 21, 1945. The press followed the performance with a sustained, critical barrage.

While surprised by the critics' ferocity (one writer later called it a "dance of glory and death around Messiaen"), the composer appeared undisturbed. He followed *Trois Petites Liturgies* with even more challenging works, between 1944 and 1948 completing major pieces for piano, voice, and orchestra. A symphony was commissioned by Serge Koussevitzky for the Boston Symphony and was premiered by Leonard Bernstein on December 2, 1949. In this symphony, entitled *Turangalîla*, Messiaen continued his interest in Hindu music, both constructing its title from two Hindi words ("Lîla," meaning game, and "Turanga," meaning time) and employing again Hindu and symmetric rhythms. Messiaen was at his most adventurous in his 1949 piano work *Mode de valeurs et d'intensités*. Here he systematically ordered thirty-six pitches, twenty-four note values, twelve kinds of articulation, and seven dynamic levels. This kind of "total serialization," while only experimental for

Messiaen, was to have a profound impact upon younger composers.

In 1943, when Messiaen had been privately teaching a class in analysis and composition, he met Yvonne Loriod. Impressed by her virtuosity, Messiaen wrote his major piano works of the period—*Visions de l'amen* (1943), *Reveil des oiseaux* (1953), and *Catalogue des oiseaux* (1958)—for her. Loriod and Messiaen were married in 1962, his first wife Claire having died three years earlier after a ten-year illness.

Messiaen's energies in the years 1960 to 1980 were channeled primarily into the creation of six huge ensemble compositions: *Chronochromie* (1961), *Couleurs de la cité céleste* (1963), *Et exspecto resurrectionem* (1964), *La Transfiguration de Notre Seigneur Jesus-Christ* (1969), *Des canyons aux étoiles* (1974), and *Saint François d'Assie* (1983). *Chronochromie* (literally "time-color") was a sixty-minute, seven-movement work for full orchestra with a greatly enlarged percussion section. Its sixth movement ("Epôde") was remarkable for its evocation of bird song performed by solo strings in eighteen individual parts. *Couleurs de la cité céleste* was premiered by Boulez in 1963, three years after *Chronochromie*'s completion. It was another hour-long work but for an ensemble reduced from the earlier piece's heroic dimensions (thirteen winds and seven percussionists).

In 1964, Messiaen fulfulled a commission from the French government for a work memorializing the two world wars' dead with *Et exspecto resurrectionem*. This composition for large woodwind, brass, and percussion ensemble (the composer even required three different sets of gongs) was premiered the following year in Paris' St. Chappelle, with repeated performances throughout France. *La Transfiguration de Notre Seigneur Jesus-Christ* was begun in 1965 and premiered in Lisbon four years later. For the first time since the 1945 *Trois Petites Liturgies*, Messiaen returned to writing for chorus and solo singers. For the fourteen-movement oratorio, he drew texts from the Bible, Saint Thomas Aquinas' *Summa*, and from the Roman rite for the Feast of the Transfiguration. After a visit to Utah in 1970, Messiaen completed a twelve-movement orchestral piece, *Des canyons aux étoiles* (premiered in New York on November 20, 1974).

Saint François d'Assie is Messiaen's only dramatic work. Commissioned by the Paris Opéra in 1975, Messiaen himself composed both the libretto and the score in a labor that lasted eight uninterrupted years. The resulting opera, although not without its detractors, was perhaps his masterpiece. A synopsis of his entire creative life, requiring extraordinary forces (a two-hundred-member chorus, three antiphonal ondes martenots, a huge orchestra, and a length of four and a half hours), it has received repeated performances since its Paris premier in 1983.

Summary

Although his work itself is not at all traditional, Olivier Messiaen's view of himself as a Catholic artist placed him firmly within the tradition of Christians whose art served primarily theological and propagandistic purposes. Thus the anonymous sculptors of Chartres, Michelangelo, Heinrich Schütz, Bach, and Dante, are all Messiaen's forebears. Indeed, of nineteenth century composers, the one Messiaen most closely resembles is Anton Bruckner, although without that Austrian's provincialisms.

As a youth Messiaen did not participate in the cynical witticisms of Francis Poulenc and Darius Milhaud. Interested in Indian music, he became neither an ethnomusicologist nor an Eastern mystic. Although his work was crucial to the development of totally serialized music, Messiaen's work was never an exercise in the cerebral. One of the era's most important teachers, he founded no "school," nor were his students united by any particular characteristic. Thus, while his aesthetic can be seen as a continuation of at least a fifteen-hundred-year-old tradition, within the twentieth century Messiaen was unique. Stylistically, his work stands apart from any of the movements that characterized (and polarized) modern music.

Bibliography

Griffiths, Paul. *Olivier Messiaen and the Music of Time.* London: Faber, and Ithaca, N.Y.: Cornell University Press, 1985. A significant and highly detailed study of Messiaen largely intended for the specialist but useful also to the general reader.

Gurewitsch, Matthew. "An Audubon in Sound: Messiaen's Radiant Birdsongs, the Crown of His Creation, Belong as Much to the Artist as to Nature." *Atlantic Monthly* 279, no. 3 (March, 1997). The author considers the influence of Catholicism, color, rhythm, and birdsong on the works of Messiaen.

Hold, Thomas. "Messiaen's Birds." *Music and Letters* 3 (1971): 113. An important essay on the composer's quotation and employment of bird calls.

Johnson, Robert Sherlaw. *Messiaen.* London: Dent, and Berkeley: University of California Press, 1975. A thorough but dated study of Messiaen's work. Johnson includes charts that are helpful in untangling the relationships in some of Messiaen's larger compositions.

Machlis, Joseph. *Introduction to Contemporary Music.* 2d ed. New York: Norton, 1979; London: Dent, 1980. Machlis is one of his generation's best writers on music. A man of broad cultural understanding (he is the translator of at least sixteen operas), he is able to clearly draw this century's significant lines of musical changes. Helpful also is his concluding "dictionary," which presents brief biographies of several hundred contemporary composers, including Messiaen.

Messiaen, Olivier. *The Technique of My Musical Language.* Translated by John Satterfield. New York: American Biographical Service, 1987. Any study of Messiaen should begin with this apologia for his musical style. Messiaen's frequently poetic descriptions of his ideas are of particular interest to the nonspecialist reader.

Nichols, Roger. *Messiaen.* 2d ed. Oxford and New York: Oxford University Press, 1986. The best introduction to the composer in English. Highly readable and sympathetic to Messiaen's work, Nichols provides a vivid portrait of the artist and his art in his eighty-seven-page text.

Samuel, Claude. *Olivier Messiaen: Music and Color—Conversations with Claude Samuel.* Translated by E. Thomas Glasow. Portland, Ore.: Amadeus Press, 1994. A comprehensive English language version of Samuel's conversations with Messiaen. Includes a thorough analysis of the opera *St. Francois d'Assise,* a comprehensive listing of works (some with complete instrumentation), an updated bibliography, and a thorough index.

Michael Linton

REINHOLD MESSNER

Born: September 17, 1944; Bressanone, Italy

Areas of Achievement: Exploration and sports

Contribution: The first man to climb all fourteen mountains in the world over 8000 meters high, Messner revolutionized mountaineering through his advocacy of a climbing style that relied upon minimal equipment and his refusal to use bottled oxygen at high altitudes.

Early Life

Reinhold Messner—the son of Josef Messner (a schoolteacher) and Maria Troi—was born in the South Tyrol, a mountainous region in northern Italy. Always fascinated by mountains, Messner accompanied his parents and brother Helmut on the ascent of a 10,000-foot peak at the age of five. Although Messner worked on the family chicken farm and attended public school, he spent his free time honing his mountaineering skills. At age fourteen, Messner finished a difficult climb alone after his father refused to continue, a decision that evidenced his growing confidence in his abilities. By age twenty, he had made approximately five hundred climbs, excelling in both rock and ice climbing. He later looked back at this period as the most exciting in his life.

In the mid-1960's, Messner turned to some of the great climbs in the Alps, including the infamous Eiger in Switzerland. He made the first solo ascent of the north wall of Les Droites, considered to be one of the most difficult Alpine rock faces. Word of his exploits spread among members of the climbing community, and Messner's reputation as a mountaineer grew. In 1969, he made his first climb outside Europe, reaching the summit of the 21,709-foot Yerupaja Grande in the Peruvian Andes on a nighttime ascent. In 1970, he received an invitation to join a Himalayan expedition committed to climbing the 26,660-foot Nanga Parbat by way of the unclimbed Rupal face, a massive wall over 14,000 feet high. To prepare, Messner abandoned his studies in civil engineering, took a job as a schoolteacher, and engaged in a strenuous training program in his free time.

Life's Work

Messner's first Himalayan experience was both a triumph and a tragedy. Messner and his brother Gunther scaled the Rupal face and reached the summit of Nanga Parbat. Ill with altitude sickness and exhausted from the climb, Gunther feared that he could not climb down the Rupal face. The brothers then completed an amazing feat by crossing Nanga Parbat to descend on an easier but unfamiliar route. During the descent, however, they were separated. Reinhold searched but could not find his brother, who in all likelihood had been swept to his death in an avalanche. Reinhold arrived at the base camp ten days later, his toes so severely frostbitten that several had to be amputated.

The Nanga Parbat expedition established a pattern that Messner would repeat again and again during his career. On the one hand, he received praise for his successful and daring climb. However, critics charged that Messner's thirst for glory led him to take unnecessary risks and ignore his own safety and that of his fellow climbers. For his part, Messner claimed that his experiences on Nanga Parbat strengthened him, improved his judgment of mountaineering hazards, and provided him with a greater appreciation of life. After the expedition, Messner turned to mountaineering full time and financed his climbs through articles, books, and public lectures.

In 1971, Messner traveled the world and completed climbs in such places as Europe, Africa, and New Zealand. Tragedy and controversy struck again in 1972 on Manaslu, a 26,760-foot peak in Nepal. Messner's partner, who could no longer climb, urged Messner to continue to the summit alone. The partner and two other team members were caught in a blizzard in which two men died. Messner reached the summit but again found his success marred by contentions that he should have remained with his fellow climbers.

In 1968, Messner had argued that while the use of artificial climbing aids such as pitons (metal pegs hammered into rock) allowed mountaineers to scale peaks and rock faces once believed unclimbable, the overuse of these aids diminished their achievements. He challenged his peers to reach summits using only the minimal equipment necessary. He expanded upon his climbing philosophy in his book *The Seventh Grade: Most Extreme Climbing* (1973), in which he argued that alpine-style climbing (small teams of skilled climbers carrying minimal equipment) could achieve the same successes on the world's highest mountains that huge expeditions hauling tons of equipment had achieved. Critics regarded Messner's claim that he

and a gifted partner could climb high peaks without major expedition support as evidence of his arrogance and foolhardiness.

Messner set out to prove his contentions, teaming up with Peter Habeler, an outstanding climber from the South Tyrol. In 1974, the two men climbed the north face of the Eiger, a wall that most teams complete in several days, in a mere ten hours, an accomplishment that astounded the climbing world. Messner, however, had his sights set on greater accomplishments. The following year, avalanches thwarted his attempt to summit Lhotse, a 27,890-foot mountain, but later that year he and Habeler climbed the 26,470-foot Gasherbrum I (also known as Hidden Peak) in Pakistan with just over two hundred pounds of climbing gear. The Hidden Peak ascent confirmed Messner's argument regarding the ability of small teams to scale major peaks and secured his place as a mountaineering pioneer.

Messner now prepared to go one step further and challenge a long-standing belief among mountaineers regarding the use of bottled oxygen. Having summitted Hidden Peak without the use of bottled

oxygen, he announced his intention to scale Mount Everest, the world's tallest peak at 29,028 feet, without supplemental oxygen. Skeptics argued that the limited oxygen available at such an extreme altitude was insufficient for human needs. Anyone attempting to climb Everest without bottled oxygen would surely die.

Undaunted by the criticism, Messner and Habeler accompanied the Austrian Everest Expedition to the Everest base camp in March, 1978. Expedition members spent the next several weeks preparing a series of camps high on the mountain. On April 21, Messner and Habeler made their first summit attempt, reaching camp 3 two days later with the assistance of porters. When food poisoning felled Habeler the following morning, Messner went ahead with two Sherpa climbers, but winds reaching 125 miles per hour turned the climbers back. The entire party returned to the base camp, where Messner and Habeler agreed to try one more time before abandoning the project. On May 6, 1978, they set forth from the base camp and reached camp 4 at 26,200 feet on the afternoon of May 7. On the early morning of May 8, they made their final push, reaching the summit after eight hours of arduous climbing. Messner was stricken with snow blindness on the descent, but both climbers safely reached the base camp on May 10 after climbing the world's highest peak and, in the process, revolutionizing high-altitude mountaineering.

Not content to rest upon his laurels, Messner completed a solo ascent of Nanga Parbat by way of a new route only months after his Everest triumph. The following year, he and a small party climbed 28,251-foot K2, the second highest mountain in the world and regarded by many climbers to be far more difficult than Everest. In response to detractors who pointed out that Messner had relied upon assistance from climbers using oxygen during the Everest climb, Messner soloed the mountain in three days without oxygen in 1980. In 1982, he climbed Kangchenjunga, Gasherbrum II, and Broad Peak. With these successes, Messner had climbed nine of the fourteen peaks over 8000 meters (26,246 feet) high. Messner achieved the goal of climbing all fourteen in 1986, when he summitted Lhotse, the fourth-highest mountain in the world, with partner Hans Kammerlander.

After climbing Lhotse, Messner declared that he would no longer climb into the "death zone," the heights above 8000 meters at which the human body can only survive for short periods. However, he had not abandoned his commitment to mountaineering. He hoped to be the first person to climb all "Seven Summits," the highest mountain on each of the seven continents. With the ascent of the 16,067-foot Mount Vinson in Antarctica in December, 1986, he reached his seventh summit, but another climber had beaten him to the record by two months. Eager for new challenges, Messner used his visit to Antarctica to plan another adventure: a crossing of the southernmost continent.

After three years of preparation, Messner and his partner, Arved Fuchs, set out from the Ronne Ice Shelf on November 19, 1989. Committed to a "fair means" crossing, the two men did not use mechanized sleds or dogs to carry their gear. Each man pulled a 48-pound sled containing camping equipment, cooking gear, and supplies. On windy days, they used kite sails to help with the hauling. Committed to preserving the environment, Messner and Fuchs carried out all their trash. However, they did receive supplies twice during the journey, once from an airplane and once at the research station at the South Pole. They successfully completed their journey in ninety-two days.

Messner's exploits made him a sports superstar and a best-selling author in Europe. However, his fame came at a cost. His marriage to Ursula Demeter ended in 1977, in part because of the stress that mountaineering placed on the relationship. Following their 1978 Everest climb, Messner and Habeler had a falling out caused by differences in their published accounts of the event. Messner had a similar public dispute with Fuchs after the Antarctic traverse. He earned a reputation for arrogance and tactlessness. Some people argued that his personality changed because of brain damage brought on by oxygen deprivation, while others claimed that Messner found his popularity too stressful. Messner dismissed stories about his personality as media fabrications.

During the 1990's, Messner mounted a failed expedition to the North Pole. In 1996, he returned to Gasherbrum I, which he had first climbed over twenty years earlier, but left when he encountered a large number of climbers at the base camp. Although he declared that he would always seek adventure, Messner admitted in 1995 that parenthood—he had two daughters—made him more willing to remain at his home, a renovated castle in South Tyrol.

Summary
Reinhold Messner forever changed high-altitude mountaineering. His success with alpine-style climbing on 8000-meter peaks led to increased criticism of large expeditions as costly, environmentally damaging, and lacking in grace and style. However, because alpine climbing allowed for no margin of error, it increased the risks mountaineers took on high peaks. Climbers who did not possess Messner's skill and judgment faced great danger when they applied his philosophy on their attempts to scale the world's highest mountains.

Bibliography
Bonington, Chris. *The Climbers: A History of Mountaineering.* London: BBC Books, 1992. Written by a world-class mountaineer, this history places Messner's achievements in historical context. The book includes black-and-white and color photographs, a chronology of important mountaineering events, a glossary, and a select bibliography.

Messner, Reinhold. *Antarctica: Both Heaven and Hell.* Ramsbury, Great Britain: Crowood Press, and Seattle, Wash.: Mountaineers, 1991. This book examines the history of Antarctic exploration and Messner's transcontinental journey. The volume includes black-and-white and color photographs, a map, and an appendix detailing the gear Messner carried.

—————. *Everest Expedition to the Ultimate*. London: Kaye and Ward, and New York: Oxford University Press, 1979. Messner's account of the 1978 Everest climb includes black-and-white and color photographs, maps, and a chronology of Everest ascents from 1953 to 1978.

Roberts, David. *Moments of Doubt and Other Mountaineering Writings*. Seattle: Mountaineers, 1986. This collection of essays includes an insightful discussion of Messner's relationship with climbing partner Peter Habeler.

Rowell, Galen. *In the Throne Room of the Mountain Gods*. London: Allen and Unwin, and San Francisco: Sierra Club Books, 1977. Rowell's comprehensive history of climbing on K2 includes a discussion of Messner's career and his 1975 climb of Hidden Peak, quality color plates, and a bibliography.

"Top Dog." *The Economist* 331, no. 7869 (June 25, 1994). A short profile of Messner, his accomplishments, and his climbing techniques.

Thomas Clarkin

VSEVOLOD YEMILYEVICH MEYERHOLD
Karl Theodor Kasimir Meyergold

Born: February 9, 1874; Penza, Russia
Died: February 2, 1940; Moscow, U.S.S.R.
Areas of Achievement: Theater and acting
Contribution: Meyerhold departed from the powerful naturalistic influences of Constantin Stanislavsky and the Moscow Art Theatre to experiment with more abstract forms of theater. Representing the other side of the universal duality in theater—expressionistic versus naturalistic—he dared to experiment with an ingenious stage language of his own invention and devised the constructivist principles of set design and the biomechanical approach to actor training.

Early Life

Born Karl Theodor Kasimir Meyergold and of German parentage, Vsevolod Yemilyevich Meyerhold converted to the orthodox faith and adopted Russian nationality in 1895, thereby avoiding conscription into the Prussian army. In Moscow ostensibly to study law, he began to frequent the theater, where he was often disappointed by the mediocrity and pointlessness of the fare. In 1896, he joined the Moscow Philharmonic Society's drama school, auditioning for the well-known Vladimir Nemirovich-Danchenko with a speech imitated in gesture and style from Stanislavsky's Othello. On graduation, he was invited to become a member of the Moscow Art Theatre, which had been formed by Nemirovich-Danchenko and Stanislavsky in 1898.

From the outset, Meyerhold's work at the Moscow Art Theatre came in conflict with the central mission of Stanislavsky and Nemirovich-Danchenko. He believed that he had discovered the limitations of the realistic acting style and held strong opinions against the aesthetic value of naturalism in the production of such playwrights as Anton Chekhov and Henrik Ibsen. His leadership of the Theatre-Studio, a branch of the Moscow Art Theatre, was the beginning of his departure from the tradition (however young) of naturalism.

For four years, Meyerhold was a member of the Moscow Art Theatre's acting company, playing some eighteen roles in a wide range of characterizations. His gaunt, angular face prevented his complete metamorphosis into the more romantic fictive characters, although he did play Treplev in Chekhov's *Chayka* (1896; *The Sea Gull*, 1909).

According to his notes during these four years, he was even then in search of new forms; his first attempts at a stylized approach to the stage came in 1905, with *La Mort de Tintagiles* (pb. 1894; *The Death of Tintagiles*, 1899), by Maurice Maeterlinck, a Belgian playwright writing what Meyerhold termed "The New Theatre," a passive, actor-oriented, nonhistrionic dramatization of a silent moment in the tragedy of quotidian life.

A brief association with Vera Komissarzhevskaya's Dramatic Theatre in St. Petersburg from 1906 to 1908 served as a transition for Meyerhold from the Moscow Art Theatre to the less protective environments of commercial theater. Meyerhold's apprenticeship ended in 1908, when he accepted a position at the St. Petersburg Imperial Theatres, where, from 1908 to the October Revolution of 1917, he was to explore the possibilities of his unique theatrical vision in the unlikely venues of commercial enterprise, working at a series of "official" St. Petersburg theaters.

Life's Work

"The essence of stage rhythm is the antithesis of real, everyday life," declared Meyerhold as early as 1909, referring to his production of Richard Wagner's opera *Tristan and Isolde* at the Mariinsky Theatre but stating at the same time one of the principles on which he built his theatrical style. Even during the years of his commercial acting successes, Meyerhold experimented in the private theaters of St. Petersburg, especially the intimate theater style of The Interlude House, run by a fellowship of actors and artists. In order to avoid contractual complications, he adopted the pseudonym Dr. Dapertutto, under which name he created many of his most imaginative stage pieces. His contribution to an evening of pieces in October, 1910, which he called *Columbine's Scarf*, was a haunting, chillingly grotesque pantomime based on Arthur Schnitzler's *Der Schleir der Pierrette* (1910; the veil of Pierrette) but turned the romantic story into a tragedy. It was typical of Meyerhold's attempts at this time to treat traditional stage literature with a new interpretation.

By 1912, Meyerhold was splitting his theater career between a hectic acting and directing schedule at the Mariinsky Opera in St. Petersburg and a company of actors and artists in Terioki, under his artistic leadership, living in a communal environment. He still had time to write and publish his theories on theater in 1913. The smaller theater gave him several opportunities to experiment with a minimalist stage set, almost devoid of realistic setting, more a platform and background for action than an integral part of the play itself. These attempts solidified his theories about the function of the stage set, not as a photographic reproduction of real space but as an environment for the machinery of the stage action to be magnified, moved from site to site, and explored.

While his experiments were being well received in the smaller theater community, his "extravagances" in the larger theater were beginning to be criticized by a more and more vocal "popularist" political body. Meyerhold began to be characterized in the press as decadent and megalomaniacal. Scholars regard this production (*Masquerade*) as the culmination of Meyerhold's St. Petersburg career; it was to be revived repeatedly after the Revolution by Meyerhold himself as well as by his successors.

The 1917 Revolution transferred all artistic endeavors into state control. Theater, the most public art, saw many changes, but Meyerhold's own "reforms" continued to progress as a kind of parallel to the revolutionary changes around him. He started a theater school in what was now called Petrograd, under the Theater Department of the Commissariat of Englightenment. The real question was how the repertory would change with the new political overview; after World War I, theater, according to the *Petrograd Pravda*, needed to be "born of that same Revolution, which we all look upon as our own great mother." Meyerhold's futurist ideas, in tandem with Italian theater developments around the same time, were received with mixed reaction from the press. It soon became clear that Meyerhold's theatrical activities would always be viewed as a political statement, interpreted by each side (the conservative reformists and the radicalists) according to its own lights.

Meyerhold enjoyed the strongest support for the juxtaposition of his art form and the Communist Party ideology when, in 1921, he was appointed director of the State Higher Theatre Workshops in Moscow. It was a theater school, complete with courses in history and theory. By now "Master," Meyerhold could formulate his acting theories into an actual course of study. A highly physical approach to acting, his "biomechanics" grew out of a series of physical fitness exercises, coupled with stage combat techniques. Awarded the title of "People's Artist" in 1923 for twenty years of service to the theater, Meyerhold was free to examine the productive results of long years of experimental uncertainty in a series of highly publicized productions matching his acting theories to his staging style in a theatre in Moscow named after himself.

In 1926, probably the height of Meyerhold's career, the play by Nikolai Gogol entitled *Revizor* (1836; *The Inspector General*, 1890) finally brought together all the potential of Meyerhold's theories in a highly successful stage production, seen today as a model of alternative theatrical presentation. Too controversial, however, was a play by Sergei Tretiakov whose thesis was contradictory to the Soviet "line" on the importance (or nonimportance) of family life; this and similar experiments eventually were to undermine Meyerhold's popularity with the bureaucracies under whose authority he worked. On the other hand, Meyerhold and the playwright Vladimir Mayakovsky were particularly productive partners during this period, working together in some ten works, including *Klop* (1929; *The Bed-bug*, 1931) and *Banya* (*1930; The Bathhouse*, 1963).

The Soviet government, entering the period of repressive measures that is now called the Stalin era, was not always happy with Meyerhold's view of the world as expressed on stage. Meyerhold himself, in what can only be seen as a heroic defiance of good sense, continued to insist on the autonomy of the artist over the wishes of the social system, refusing to acknowledge any demands of the state to use his stage as a propaganda platform and ignoring the growing tensions and the clear signs of his incipient disfavor. In 1939, the government-controlled press had damned Meyerhold's "decadent" work, primarily for failure to reduce his chaotic productions down to the Socialist Realism seen by the government as the proper sphere for theater. An anti-intellectual bias was working against him from 1930 to his death in 1940. Claims that he had ruined his theater were nothing more than excuses for closing it down in 1939. A victim of the paranoia of the Soviet government on the eve of World War II, Meyerhold was arrested shortly thereafter and shot in 1940.

Summary

Over a long career, Vsevolod Yemilyevich Meyerhold established a distinct ideology of theatrical presentation characterized by rapidly changing "loci" simply suggested by a montage of set alterations on a central "plateau," or general acting area (sometimes referred to as "cinefication"), a method of physical preparation for actors (called biomechanics) complementing or rivaling that of Stanislavsky, and a style of visual spectacle celebrating the rise of industrial and technological invention, called "constructivism," that today informs virtually all scenic design. His mature work, itself iconoclastic and irreverent, in so many ways the theatrical equivalent of the Bolshevik Revolution and its ideologies, and in other ways antithetical to the Socialist Realism embraced by its less imaginative political leaders, is responsible for the strength of the continuing combative dichotomy that still gives live performance its viability in an age of mass media: the dialectic between theater as hyperrealization of actual life and theater as an independent language whose vocabulary is larger than mere representational photographic replication and closer to the abstract spirit of theater handed down to Western civilization from the Greeks.

In the wide-ranging reexamination of aesthetic principles begun after World War II, modern theater practitioners found themselves more indebted to Meyerhold's vision and daring and more comfortable with the stage vocabulary that he had designed and implemented than his Soviet executioners could have imagined; Bertolt Brecht, the East German director of presentational, propagandistic, "alienation" theater, acknowledged a considerable debt to Meyerhold's innovations, as have such highly regarded modern experimental directors as Jerzy Grotowski and Peter Brook. In fact, every experimenter in theatrical forms from 1950 on owes a debt to Meyerhold, who turned his back on the invidious and ultimately self-defeating naturalism of his peers and tutors to discover theater's unique power to communicate directly.

Bibliography

Braun, Edward. *The Theatre of Meyerhold: Revolution on the Modern Stage.* London: Methuen, and New York: Drama Book Specialists, 1979. An important critical biography and a thorough examination of Meyerhold's entire career, taking advantage of Braun's thirteen years of study on the same figure. Deliberately avoids comparisons with contemporaries and successors, concentrating instead on the details of Meyerhold's own contributions. Includes many illustrations, strong notes, a bibliography, and an index.

Eaton, Katherine Bliss. *The Theater of Meyerhold and Brecht.* Contributions in Drama and Theatre Studies 19. Westport, Conn.: Greenwood Press, 1985. Defends the idea that the main source of inspiration was Meyerhold. The interchange of ideas between Germany and Russia, an exchange that went both ways, culminated in Brecht's visit to Russia in 1936, three years into his own exile and three years before Meyerhold's arrest and execution. A sturdy critical comparison, leaning slightly toward an over-enthusiastic appraisal of Meyerhold. Includes a bibliography and an index.

Hoover, Marjorie L. *Meyerhold: The Art of Conscious Theater.* Amherst: University of Massachusetts Press, 1974. A full-length scholarly study coinciding with the one hundredth anniversary of his birth, and, excepting Braun's compilation of primary material, the first critical account in English of Meyerhold's work.

Meyerhold, V. E. *Meyerhold on Theatre.* Edited and translated by Edward Braun. London: Methuen, and New York: Hill and Wang, 1969. The first, and for years the only, study of Meyerhold in English, these excerpts from his theoretical writings are woven together with Braun's commentaries to present a unified documentary record that validates his respected reputation in Europe and the United States. Includes more than fifty illustrations.

Piette, Alain. "Crommelynck and Meyerhold: Two Geniuses Meet on the Stage." *Modern Drama* 39, no. 3 (Fall 1996). Discusses Meyerhold's Moscow production of Fernand Crommelynck's play *The Magnanimous Cuckold* in 1992, including his approach to production and his techniques.

Rudnitskii, Konstantin. *Meyerhold the Director.* Translated by George Petrov. Ann Arbor, Mich.: Ardis Press, 1981. Generated from archives hidden by the filmmaker Sergei Eisenstein, Meyerhold's former student, and used here for the first time, this authoritative study concentrates on the artist as a director who worked in many contradictory styles. The more than two hundred illustrations include heretofore unpublished production stills and diagrams of Meyerhold's stage blocking. Includes an index.

Sayler, Oliver M. *Inside the Moscow Art Theatre.* New York: Brentano's, 1925. For years, this definitive study of the Moscow Art Theatre has been interesting for comparisons between the traditional realism of Stanislavsky and the "cubist," "Futurist," "theoretical" Meyerhold, who is mentioned only five times, always as a foil for Sayler's real subject. Index.

Schechner, Richard. *Environmental Theater.* New York: Hawthorne, 1973. As a highly visible successor of the experimental styles of previous "anti-illusion" stage directors, Schechner pays homage to Meyerhold's overwhelming influence by citing whole passages of his theories throughout this study of the Performance Group. A clear example of how Meyerhold's work broke ground for the next generations of presentational theater practitioners. Bibliography and index.

Thomas J. Taylor

ANDRÉ MICHELIN and ÉDOUARD MICHELIN

André Michelin

Born: January 16, 1853; Paris, France   *Died:* April 4, 1931; Paris, France

Édouard Michelin

Born: June 23, 1859; Clermont-Ferrand, France   *Died:* August 25, 1940; Orcines, Puy-de-Dôme, France

Areas of Achievement: Business, industry, invention, and technology

Contribution: The Michelin brothers pioneered the use of pneumatic tires on automobiles and were also leaders in the development of the radial-ply tire as well as steel-reinforced tire construction. They founded a motorist's travel guide company that produces handbooks for numerous tourist destinations throughout the world.

Early Lives

André Jules Michelin was born in Paris in 1853. During childhood, he showed a talent for art and, on completion of elementary school near Clermont-Ferrand, entered the Académie des Beaux-Arts in Paris to study architecture. He left before obtaining his degree to learn the art of map-making at the French Ministry of the Interior. André subsequently opened several shops in Paris, where he produced and sold locks for wrought-iron gates and metal picture frames of his own design.

Édouard was born six years after his brother in Clermont-Ferrand and also went to Paris, where he pursued painting at the École des Beaux-Arts and opened a studio in the Montparnasse area of Paris. Édouard painted portraits, landscapes, and biblical and battle scenes for sale and began developing a talent for free-hand drawing.

Art was not to be the lifelong vocation of the Michelin brothers. Édouard returned to Clermont-Ferrand in 1888 to assist with a small rubber business. The enterprise had been started in the mid-nineteenth century by a maternal grandfather and a cousin who was related by marriage to Charles MacIntosh, the Scottish chemist who experimented with the rubberization of textiles and whose name became synonymous with raincoats. The shop had originally produced farm equipment, but later, as a result of the indirect association with MacIntosh, added rubber products such as balls, tubes, valves, and elastic bands. When the founders of the business died, it passed to the Michelin brothers, and

their careers focused increasingly away from Paris toward Clermont-Ferrand.

Life's Work

The first pneumatic bicycle tires were produced by the English in 1888 and facilitated a considerably more agreeable ride than the earlier solid rubber and iron-clad types. Yet because the tire was glued to the rim, blow-outs were time-consuming to repair, severely inhibiting the widespread application of pneumatics to wheeled travel. The Michelins' first contact with pneumatic tires came with a cycling Englishman who brought his vehicle to the shop in Clermont-Ferrand for a puncture repair. The task took hours, largely because of the time required for the glue to dry. Édouard recognized the potential of pneumatics and began developing a removable bicycle tire that could be changed in minutes. By 1891, he had perfected such a system and entered the Paris-Brest-Paris 750-mile bicycle race to test and publicize the demountable pneumatic tire. The Michelins' tire was the only one of its type among the 211 participants, and their rider won the race by an eight-hour lead. In the following year, more than ten thousand bicycles were equipped with Michelin tires, and the company became the unquestioned leader in the bicycle tire business.

During the mid-1890's, France was a front-runner in the incipient world automotive industry. A major obstacle to the development of that industry lay in speeds. Automobile tires, which at that time were either ironclad or solid rubber, tended to come apart at speeds exceeding thirteen miles per hour. Even at lower velocities, the ride remained less than pleasant. André Michelin rode as a passenger in the 1894 motor car race from Paris to Rouen, an experience that persuaded him that the future of the automobile industry lay with the more comfortable and quiet pneumatic tire. The Michelin brothers pioneered the application of pneumatic tires to automobiles, testing and introducing them in the 745-mile Paris-Bordeaux-Paris race in June,

1895. Of the forty-six participants who entered the race, the Michelin car survived the race with nine others, demonstrating that the demountable pneumatic tire offered a viable option to its ironclad and solid rubber predecessors. By 1896, more than three hundred taxis in the city of Paris ran on air-filled Michelins.

André and Édouard continued improvements on tires, testing innovations in subsequent races. By 1901, an electrically driven car on Michelin tires had set a record of sixty-two miles per hour. Two years later, tires with anti-skid treads were introduced, and, in 1906, Michelin became one of the first companies in Europe to market an automobile tire with a detachable rim. During 1908, Michelin experimented with the principle of dual-pneumatic tire sets for trucks, and, after four years of experimentation, the first Michelin truck tires appeared on the market. In 1923, low-pressure balloon tires were introduced, providing a smoother ride, increased load capacity, higher speed capability, and longer tire life. The company began research in 1929 on the application of rubber tires to railroad travel. In order to support the increased weight associated with railcars, the Michelin Company augmented the tires with steel bands. Experience with rail tires gave the firm a considerable lead over other manufacturers in the application of steel reinforcements, and the Michelin Company eventually produced the first steel-belted radial tires for automobiles in 1948. Another by-product of the research into suitable pneumatic rail tires was the Micheline, a lightweight railcar produced in several models by the Michelin Company. The Micheline inaugurated service between Paris and Deauville in 1931, achieving an average speed of sixty-five miles per hour. By 1938, the Micheline averaged five million miles of service annually. Because of the heightened traction problems associated with the use of rubber on steel tracks, new research into tread designs was undertaken, resulting in enhanced wet traction tires.

Apart from tires, the Michelin brothers contributed most significantly to automobile travel by a series of guidebooks to assist motorists. In 1900, André added a road map department to the business, and later the company began publishing a travel guide that amplified the maps with listings of gas stations, repair shops, and Michelin tire dealers. Ultimately, hotels and restaurants were included with quality ratings, and Michelin Guides evolved into the most well-known and widely used

handbooks of automobile touring. In 1908, André created a Car Traveler's Information Bureau in Paris, which furnished itineraries and road information, and further promoted automobile travel in France by embarking on a campaign to number routes and by donating road signs and posts. In 1927, the brothers financed the placement of concrete pillars along the Paris-Nice route featuring letters formed of enameled lava, which could be seen from a distance day or night. The French government subsequently approved these signs for use elsewhere in France.

The Michelin brothers also instituted progressive practices in employee relations. In 1901, they established a health center that provided medical care to Michelin employees at a fraction of the normal cost. The company later provided a maternity hospital, an anti-tuberculosis dispensary, a ninety-bed sanatorium, a sixty-bed hospital, and a dental clinic. The brothers began building settlements of low-rent housing for workers in 1909. Swimming pools, theaters, playing fields, gardens, and cinemas were added over the years, and eventually there were seventeen settlements totaling 865 buildings that contain 3,698 apartments available to employees of Michelin enterprises.

Édouard recognized early in the company's development that workers in the shop understood obstacles to tire improvement best. Employee participation in problem-solving and innovation was encouraged from the outset, and Édouard praised and rewarded workers who challenged his opinions and decisions for the betterment of the company.

The Michelin penchant for innovation extended to the nascent aviation industry as well. The brothers encouraged distance and speed achievements in French aircraft development by offering a 100,000 franc prize to the first pilot to set a speed record flying a predetermined route that circled the Arc de Triomphe. André was particularly interested in the potential military applications of aviation, working before World War I to persuade France that its military future lay in air power and, after the war, to motivate the French and their allies to deal with the threat of aerochemical attack by Germany.

Summary

André Michelin died on April 4, 1931, and was followed by his younger brother, Édouard, on August 25, 1940. The outstanding contribution of the Michelin brothers to modern transportation derived from their ability to anticipate the future of the automobile industry and to create the breakthroughs that would make travel safe, convenient, and accessible for the average person.

The company founded by André and Édouard continued under the direction of younger Michelin family members. In the early 1950's, the firm became a holding company, and by the 1970's the Michelin enterprise employed more than 100,000 workers in facilities throughout Europe, in Africa, and in the United States. Michelin is known for its tight family control, its secretive management and marketing practices, and its assiduous guarding of technical know-how. The company has always been and remains among the top world producers of tires.

Bibliography

Coates, Austin. *The Commerce in Rubber: The First 250 Years*. New York: Oxford University Press, 1987. Coates's chapter on the advent of rubber products in Europe includes a respectable treatment of the early years of the professional lives of the Michelin brothers, extending through their first application of pneumatic tires to the motor car.

Day, John. *The Bosch Book of the Motor Car*. New York: St. Martin's Press, 1976. Day's chapter entitled "Wheels, Tyres, and Brakes" offers a concise description of the development of plys, treads, and detachable pneumatic rims, and the Michelin contribution to these developments.

Levy-LeBoyer, Maurice. "Innovation and Business Strategies in Nineteenth and Twentieth Century France." In *Enterprise and Entrepreneurs in Nineteenth and Twentieth Century France*, edited by Edward C. Carter et al. Baltimore: The Johns Hopkins University Press, 1976. LeBoyer provides a concise but quite sufficient description of the dynamics affecting the economic environment into which French entrepreneurs came during the early years of the Michelin tire business.

Norbye, Jan P. *The Michelin Magic*. Bridge Summit, Pa.: Tab, 1982. This volume provides an excellent history of the Michelin Company from its inception until the early 1980's. It includes considerable information on the lives of André and Édouard Michelin and their contributions to the tire industry. This is the outstanding resource for the story of Michelin research and development.

Rowand, Roger. "Early Tires Were as Primitive as Early Cars." *Automotive News*, Special Issue (June 26, 1996). Short discussion of the development of the pneumatic automobile tire including the contributions of André and Édouard Michelin.

Setright, L. J. K. *Automobile Tyres*. London: Chapman and Hall, 1972. Setright discusses all aspects of tires, including the history of their development and the Michelin role in that process. The focus of this work is on the modern legacy of tire research.

Margaret B. Denning

JAMES A. MICHENER

Born: February 3, 1907 (?); New York, New
   York (?)
Died: October 16, 1997; Austin, Texas
Area of Achievement: Literature
Contribution: Michener was a prolific writer who
   became known for his epic novels that explored
   the landscape, history, and culture of specific
   geographic regions in the United States and
   around the world.

Early Life

James Albert Michener was born in 1907. His
place of birth is unknown but was probably New
York City or Doylestown, Pennsylvania. Very little
is known of his early life since he was an orphan
raised by a Quaker widow from Doylestown
named Mabel Michener. He never discovered the
identity of his biological mother and father. His
family was poor, but Michener managed to expand
his horizons by traveling through forty-five states
during the summer of 1921. That fall, he enrolled
in Doylestown High School, where, according to at
least one teacher, he did not work very hard because he did not have to, being brighter than most
students. He became a good basketball player for
Doylestown High and later gained scholarship to
play on the basketball team of Swarthmore College. Besides playing basketball at Swarthmore,
Michener focused on English, history, and philosophy in a rigorous honors program.

After his graduation from Swarthmore College
with a bachelor of arts in English and history,
Michener taught English at the Hill School in
Pottstown, Pennsylvania, from 1929 to 1931. From
1931 to 1933, he studied at St. Andrews in Scotland on a Lippincott Fellowship, visited London
and Italy, toured part of Spain, and served for a
time in the British Merchant Marine. In 1935, he
married his first wife, Patti Koon, and from 1936 to
1939, he taught English at the George School, a
Quaker institution in Bucks County, Pennsylvania.
From 1936 to 1939, Michener taught at the Colorado State College of Education, where he completed a master of arts degree in 1937. He then
taught education at the Harvard Graduate School
as a visiting lecturer in 1939 and 1940. In 1940,
Michener joined the Macmillan Publishing Company as the social studies editor, a position he held
until 1949.

His editorship, however, was interrupted by
World War II, and despite both his age and his
Quaker background, Michener joined the U.S.
Navy in 1942, arriving in the South Pacific as a
lieutenant in the spring of 1944. His position as an
aviations inspector and publications director led
him to visit some fifty islands, an experience that
he translated into *Tales of the South Pacific*, which
he began writing during his term of service. In late
1945, Michener returned to his position at Macmillan. *Tales of the South Pacific* was published in
1947, and the book won Michener the Pulitzer
Prize in fiction in 1948. It was turned into a very
popular Broadway musical in 1949 and a film in
1958, both titled *South Pacific*. In 1949, having
achieved financial independence, Michener left his
job at Macmillan and embraced writing full time.

Life's Work

During the 1950's, Michener continued to write
about the world of the Pacific. These works included *Return to Paradise* (1951), a collection of essays coupled with stories about the islands of the
South Pacific, Australia, and New Zealand. In 1953
he published *The Bridges at Toko-Ri*, a novel featuring an American pilot and set during the Korean
War. Michener then took up the theme of interracial relationships in the novel *Sayonara* (1954), in
which two American servicemen who develop relationships with Japanese women face official and
unofficial obstacles. By this time, Michener had
been married and divorced twice: His first marriage, to Patti Koon, ended in 1948; his second
marriage, to Vange Nord, lasted from 1948 to
1955. He then met Mari Yoriko, a Japanese American who had been held in a U.S. internment camp
with her parents during World War II. They were
married in 1955, a union that lasted until Mari's
death in 1994. Her influence led Michener toward a
greater emphasis on the need for tolerance, and the
order she gave to his personal life was an indispensable aid in the production of his many books.

A decade of writing about the world of the Pacific culminated in 1959 with Michener's massive
novel *Hawaii*. In it, he established the basic pattern
for later historical novels, each centered on the geography, history, and people of places that he visited and studied: Hawaii, Afghanistan, Israel, Spain,
Poland, and others. Michener also turned to his
own nation's development in novels such as *Cen-

tennial (1974), *Chesapeake* (1978), *Texas* (1985), and *Legacy* (1987). In *Hawaii*, Michener begins with a description of the land and the geographic forces that shaped it. He then describes four successive waves of settlement on the island: Polynesians, American missionaries and sailors, Chinese peasants, and Japanese settlers. In an interview during the last years of his life, Michener described the basic message of this novel and those that followed: "I've testified to the fact that people of different climates and nationalities and religions and skin color can be delightful people—just like your next door neighbors. And I have never deviated from that."

During the 1960's and 1970's, novels similar in format to *Hawaii* continued to pour from Michener. His work regimen was simple, and he stuck to it: He worked each morning from a manual typewriter and read or conducted research every afternoon. He spent much of his time visiting the places he wrote about. In preparation for his novel *Poland* (1983), for example, Michener journeyed to Poland eight times between 1977 and 1983, visiting and later revisiting sites that he would write about in the novel, consulting with experts in various fields of Polish history, and getting to know many Poles from all walks of life. Moreover, in such novels, which spanned vast periods of time, Michener was also able to explore serious historical themes that resonated with his nonacademic audience. For example, in *The Source* (1965), which chronicles an archaeological dig at the mythical site of Tell Makor in Israel, Michener brings each of the several levels that the archaeologists excavate to life with interesting stories featuring complex characters and relationships. Each tale, which is centered around a single artifact, develops larger themes: how monotheism and Judaism emerged, why Jews were so often persecuted during this long historical process, and whether the three great religions of the West can ever truly coexist peacefully.

While establishing and extending his literary reputation, Michener was also very politically active. A staunch opponent of communism, he covered the Soviet invasion of Hungary in 1956 for *Reader's Digest* and actually helped some Hungarian refugees over the border into Austria. Soon after, his interest in U.S. politics led him to work for the election of John F. Kennedy as president in 1960. Moreover, Michener sought a political career for himself: In 1962, he ran for the U.S. Congress as a Democrat from the conservative eighth district in Pennsylvania. Michener lost, but he remained

politically involved, serving as secretary of the Pennsylvania Constitutional Convention in 1967 and 1968, investigating and writing about the Kent State shooting in 1970, and serving as a correspondent during President Richard M. Nixon's historical trips to the Soviet Union and China in 1972.

During the second half of his life, Michener won an increasing number of awards and honors. He was granted honorary degrees by more than thirty colleges and universities. In addition, he was awarded the Medal of Freedom in 1977 by President Gerald Ford and was named Outstanding Philanthropist in 1996 by the National Society of Fund-Raising Executives. During this period, Michener also donated large sums of money to various institutions. These grants included $7.2 million to Swarthmore College, $9.5 million to the James A. Michener Art Museum, and $64.2 million to the University of Texas at Austin. Michener also patronized the visual arts—in 1994, he pledged $5 million each to art museums in Doylestown, Pennsylvania, and Texas.

During the 1980's, Michener faced a number of physical problems but continued to write prolifically. Indeed, some of Michener's most popular novels were published in the 1980's, such as *Space* (1982) and *Caribbean* (1989); between 1986 and 1992, he wrote and published eleven books. After the death of his wife Mari in 1994 from cancer, Michener's own health began to deteriorate. His death eventually came because of renal failure; dependent on kidney dialysis to stay alive, Michener ordered doctors to disconnect him, and he died in Austin, Texas, on October 16, 1997.

Summary

James Michener deserves to be remembered as one of the most prolific and widely read of American novelists in the twentieth century. By the time of his death, his fame as a writer of fiction had been secured by the early success of such works as *Tales of the South Pacific* and *The Bridges at Toko-Ri* and by a later series of historical novels in which fact and fiction from the past were blended with contemporary themes and issues. These long and complex novels followed a pattern of development that became familiar and beloved to millions of readers around the world, despite some professional criticism. Michener's more than forty books sold more than seventy-five million copies.

Despite Michener's great success as a best-selling novelist, he should also be remembered for many works of nonfiction, which focused on such diverse topics as the role of social studies in public education, the history of Japanese art, the dangers of U.S. electoral politics, the reasons for the killing of students at Kent State University in 1970, and the importance of sports in American life. Moreover, Michener became a major philanthropist, giving away over $100 million to universities, libraries, and museums. Michener's life experiences were quite varied: a Naval lieutenant during World War II, a journalist, a teacher at every level from elementary to graduate school, and a candidate for the U.S. Congress. Yet through a life packed with so much activity that it might seem incoherent, certain themes remained constant: a concern for America's young people and a commitment to education, a belief in human dignity and freedom, a recognition of the need for intercultural tolerance and understanding, and a conviction that people everywhere and in all times share basically the same desires, needs, and struggles.

Bibliography

Becker, George J. *James A. Michener*. New York: Ungar, 1983. Becker's book duplicates much of the information contained in Day's biography of Michener, but it covers the years from 1978 to 1983.

Day, A. Grove. *James A. Michener*. 2d ed. Boston: Twayne, 1977. This book is written from the point of view of someone who knew and worked with Michener. Its excellent bibliography is limited, naturally, to materials published before 1977.

Hayes, John P. *James A. Michener: A Biography*. London: Allen, and Indianapolis: Bobbs-Merrill, 1984. Hayes conducted more than twenty-five interviews with Michener, providing rich biographical material for this meticulous work that was ten years in the making. Covers his prolific writings, from *Tales of the South Pacific* to *Space*, and praises *Centennial*, even though it was rejected by the literary community. Most useful for background information and anecdotes on Michener.

Michener, James A. *Literary Reflections: Michener on Michener, Hemingway, Capote, and Others*. Austin, Tex.: State House Press, 1993. A collection of literary commentary by Michener on several authors, including Margaret Mead, Truman Capote, and Ernest Hemingway. Also includes several poems and Michener's first published short story.

———. *This Noble Land: My Vision for America*. New York: Random House, 1996. This is Michener's assessment of problems in the United States and how to solve them. Included are issues such as race relations, health care, and the redistribution of wealth. Straightforward and passionate account of the writer's feelings on the country he loves.

———. *The World Is My Home*. London: Secker and Warburg, and New York: Random House, 1992. A memoir of Michener's life and writing.

Severson, Marilyn S. *James A. Michener: A Critical Companion*. Westport, Conn.: Greenwood Press, 1996. Contains critical commentaries on all of Michener's major works.

Straub, Deborah A., ed. *Contemporary Authors*. New Revision Series 21. Detroit: Gale Research, 1985. Chronicles the storytelling talents of Michener, the "master" reporter who has gone on to become a brand name author of epic proportions, and mentions his major novels. An excellent source for a variety of extracts of book reviews many of which grudgingly give praise to Michener's painstaking research. Includes a bibliography.

Robert Harrison

LUDWIG MIES VAN DER ROHE

Born: March 27, 1886; Aachen, Germany
Died: August 7, 1969; Chicago, Illinois
Area of Achievement: Architecture
Contribution: One of the greatest architects and architectural educators of the twentieth century, Mies van der Rohe left a legacy of famous buildings and a legacy in furniture design unmatched by any other member of the Modern Movement.

Early Life

Born Ludwig Mies to Michael Mies, a master mason, and his wife, Amalie, both German, Ludwig Mies van der Rohe was to add a version of his mother's maiden name to his own in adulthood, believing that *mies*, which in German means "bad" or "poor," was professionally a liability. He was, however, known to intimates as "Mies" throughout his life.

His father owned a stone-cutting shop, and Mies van der Rohe got his first experience with building materials while helping his father. He was educated in the Aachen Cathedral School, which could trace its existence back to the time when Aachen (formerly Aix-la-Chapelle) had been the first capital of Charlemagne's Holy Roman Empire. In his childhood, much of the medieval city was extant (much of it was lost during World War II), and he spoke of its architecture as an important influence on him in his formative years.

At the age of thirteen, he became a student in the local trade school, studying there for two years, during which time he was also a part-time apprentice to a brick mason. With a natural talent for drawing, at the age of fifteen he joined an interior decorating firm specializing in stucco ornamentation, soon becoming their designer. In 1904, he entered a local architect's office, and a year later, he moved to Berlin. He had, by then, some deep knowledge of stone, but knew little about how to use wood; he took employment with Bruno Paul, who had a distinguished reputation for his use of wood in both his architecture and his furniture design.

In 1907, Mies van der Rohe left Paul to work on a private commission. His first house, designed in the popular eighteenth century German style, possessed an air of proportion and a fineness of detail which were to be common aspects of his architecture. The next year, the prestigious Peter Behrens firm hired him, and during his time there, two other young architects, who were, like Mies van der Rohe, to have important careers, passed through the firm: Walter Gropius and Le Corbusier. Behrens carried on the tradition of the early nineteenth century architect Karl Friedrich Schinkel (1781-1841), who had advocated the sensitive use of fine materials, gracious space and balance in design, and careful and fastidious concern for detail. The Behrens group was committed to the union of engineering and architecture, accepting the facts of industrialization and mass production without presuming that beauty had to give way to utility. AEG, the German equivalent of General Electric in America, used Behrens to design their buildings, their building fixtures, and even the letterhead for their stationery. Mies van der Rohe was involved in the building of the Turbine factory for AEG which Behrens had designed with interesting anticipations of later architectural ideas, and Behrens put him in charge of the construction of the German Embassy in St. Petersburg, Russia.

On his own by 1913, Mies van der Rohe designed some intriguing domestic buildings, still, albeit, in the old tradition, but showing a sensitive and original grasp of space and proportion. He served in World War I in the German army as an engineer, supervising the building of roads and bridges. A solidly built young man with the bland good looks of the German burgher, it would have been difficult to tell by looking that he possessed the imagination, energy, and will to impose his ideas of architecture and design upon the entire Western world.

Life's Work

After the war, Mies van der Rohe committed himself as a designer to the architecture of what has been called the "Modern Movement," and he became a prominent member of the group of German architects and designers determined to make a new kind of building using the materials of twentieth century industrial technology: steel, glass, and reinforced concrete. The German economy was so disastrously affected by the war that little major building took place, but Mies van der Rohe exhibited five major projects which were to establish his reputation. These plans, the "Glass Skyscrapers" (1919-1921), the "Concrete Office Building" (1922), the "Brick Country House" (1923), and the "Concrete Country House" (1924), exemplify, in

part in their titles, the new direction taken by their creator. Uninterested in politics, he accepted, nevertheless, the proposition that architecture should be a sign of a society's vitality, that it was an important expression of its own time. He was a member of several organizations supporting the new movement in the arts, and the director of several exhibitions of contemporary architecture during the 1920's.

By the mid-1920's, Mies van der Rohe had established his reputation as an innovator but had constructed very few buildings. During this lean period, he put his experience in the crafts to the problem of designing furniture which would be consistent with the new architecture, and it was to be this work which would result in his development of the famous tubular steel chair that was to bear his copyright.

In 1928, he was awarded a commission for the German Pavilion at the International Exposition to be held in Barcelona, Spain. Although the building was to exist only during the period of the fair, it was to be remembered by photographs and drawings as one of the most important buildings of the Modern Movement and was to become a touchstone building in modern architecture. Although he had revealed bits and pieces of his ideas in previous buildings during the 1920's, this was the first time that he was free to express his ideas without the limitations and impositions of ordinary contracts. The building itself was simply to be a showpiece unwedded to any particular function, the funds were generous, and he was allowed the use of first-class materials and first-class artisans.

The trademarks of his career were displayed with astonishing success: roof weight was to be carried not by walls but by steel columns, and the walls, as a result, were to function as aesthetic planes and screens in space, with as little enclosed area as possible, so that the whole structure had an open-aired aspect. He managed to join the austerity of modern design, the materials of twentieth century industry, to the traditional materials of the past builders, such as marble and onyx. He showed in one simple building that technology, the skeletal design, and modern materials could be used aesthetically.

In 1929-1930, his Tugendhat House in Brno, Czechoslovakia, applied the same principles to a private dwelling. Again, he freed the walls from load-bearing, refused to box in anything save service areas such as bathrooms and kitchens, used an abundance of glass walls as exteriors, and only loosely distinguished living areas by the steel columns carrying the roof and curved planes of richly polished onyx and ebony. As in the Barcelona building, the furniture was specially designed to complement, and compliment, the light, airy openness.

In 1930, Mies van der Rohe became the director of Germany's famous Bauhaus, the school founded by Walter Gropius to teach art and design in the modern mode, and in which the fusion of the functional and the beautiful was explored in the production of everything from cutlery to plans for entire towns. There had been continual conservative criticism of the school since its inception in 1919, and in the early 1930's, the Nazis, on coming to power, closed it down. Mies van der Rohe resisted for a few months, received permission to reopen, but on unacceptable terms, and gave it up in 1933. Out of favor with the Fascists, who suspected the intellectual community in general, Mies van der Rohe received few commissions and lived on royalties from his furniture designs.

In 1938, he left Germany and took the post of Director of Architecture at the Armour (later Illinois) Institute of Technology in Chicago. He became an American citizen in 1944.

Welcomed to Chicago by Frank Lloyd Wright, whose work he deeply admired (and who was later to complain about Mies van der Rohe's "flat-chested" architecture), he brought the best aspects of the Bauhaus into conjunction with American architectural education, putting emphasis, as always, upon the symbiotic relationship of modern technology and modern design. Fully committed to the steel skeleton as aesthetically valid, he led his school away from "façade" architecture. He had always been an articulate spokesman for the new ideas, and in his role of educator and practitioner he continued to express the theories of the Modern Movement with gnomic attractiveness.

He was to remain at the school until 1958, and during that period, he was to work away at the design of an entirely new campus for the institute, using his ideas of variations on the skeletal steel configuration to build a campus of artistic oneness, even for buildings which in the hands of past architects were considered too special for such treatment. By 1947, he was so firmly established as a major figure that the Museum of Modern Art in New York held an exhibition of his work (as they did again in 1986).

His career, however, has not been without resistance, even from those who admired him. His Farnsworth House, designed and built between 1945 and 1950, won the important Twenty-five-year Award from the American Institute of Architects in 1981. Its owner complained about getting an expensive one-room glass box and was sued for its payment, but she was not far from the truth in the sense that Mies van der Rohe had designed a simple, glass-walled box with the roof and the floor riding on cantilevered supports—in a sense, a transparent house through which the natural setting (it was a country retreat) flowed. For good or ill, it was to have an important influence on house design.

The same can be said for his work in urban, high-rise apartment design. His Lake Shore Drive apartments (1948-1951) were to be the first of the high-rise city dwellings made almost solely of glass and steel, and they were to be the prototype for the new age of urban architecture. He also provided a model for the urban housing development with his Lafayette Park project in Detroit (1955-1963), in which he mixed one-story, two-story, and high-rise apartment complexes in a garden and park setting with special attention to keeping the parking areas on the perimeters of the property.

His Seagram Building in New York City is one of the best examples of the application of his design theories to the needs of the corporate world. Facing on Park Avenue, it occupies one of the most expensive pieces of real estate in the world, yet Mies van der Rohe preserved half the site as open space, using it as a jeweled base for the building by the tasteful addition of greenery, pools, pink granite paving, and marble benches. The building itself is an uncompromising exercise in his use of steel and glass, but the steel is bronze-clad, the glass is topaz-gray, and the incidental furnishings are of comparable richness. It set a new standard not only in design but also in siting and in dressing a building which the business world has insisted on imitating ever since, sometimes with success (if they could get Mies van der Rohe to do the work), and sometimes with less happy results.

His own buildings have, in the main, been formidable variations on the Seagram theme, and examples of his work can be seen in cities all over the world. In his later years, Mies van der Rohe confined himself almost exclusively to corporate projects with the emphasis on high-rise offices and apartment buildings. His thrusting, concrete-cased structures lapped in steel and glass, both richly colored, decorated by equally handsome I-beam mullions, are visual confirmations of the power of the industrialized world. Since his death in 1969, that enthusiasm for his work or for the work of his followers has continued, and his influence on renewed or revived or rebuilt city and town centers is ubiquitous.

Summary

If credit for the revolution of modern architecture must be shared by Mies van der Rohe with Le Corbusier, Walter Gropius, and Frank Lloyd Wright, and if Gropius anticipated everyone with the matchbox style in his famous Fagus Werke in 1911, it was Mies van der Rohe who was eventually to dominate (indeed, almost corner) the market in urban center planning and particularly in post-World War II skyscrapers.

He became the most international of architects, who tended, in the past, to be confined in their commissions to their native land, although their influence might transcend space and time. Mies van der Rohe, like Gropius, straddled the Atlantic, Mies van der Rohe taking the Bauhaus to Chicago, Gropius taking it to Harvard. As a practitioner, however, Mies van der Rohe is everywhere in the Western world, and his work is standing in major and minor cities often cheek-to-jowl with that of his followers.

There is the rub: Mies van der Rohe, with no expense spared, using rich materials, brought together with craftsmanlike skill and fastidiousness, produced buildings of stunning aesthetic clarity and simplicity. Standing alone, they are often great works of art. Surrounded by equally tall imitations, they can lose that power simply because their creator is one of those artists who is easily emulated. The copies, less lavish materially, less lovingly constructed, often parodic in their determination to be like the original, are a principal reason for the monotony of late twentieth century city cores. The clutter of glass-and-steel monoliths, reflecting one another across narrow streets and looking alike from town to town, is the sad legacy of Mies van der Rohe's domination of urban architecture.

Bibliography

Blaser, Werner. *Mies van der Rohe*. 6th ed. Boston: Verlag, 1997. Originally published in 1965, this book is particularly interesting because it is based upon conversations with Mies van der

Rohe and allows him to discuss the development of his ideas in relation to specific buildings.

Carter, Peter. *Mies van der Rohe at Work*. London: Pall Mall Press, and New York: Praeger, 1974. Divided into chapters dealing with technical aspects of Mies van der Rohe's work but easily understood by the lay reader. A helpful chart shows the number of projects and their progression toward the big building.

Henderson, Justin. "Mies Lives." *Interiors* 153, no. 6 (June, 1994). Discussion of the renovation and restoration of Van Der Rohe's penthouse to its original form and structure.

Hilberseimer, L. *Mies van der Rohe*. Chicago: Theobald, 1956. A bit short on text but the commentary is succinct nevertheless. Includes generous photographs.

Johnson, Phillip C. *Mies van der Rohe*. 3d ed. London: Secker and Warburg, and New York: Museum of Modern Art, 1978. Published on the occasion of the 1947 Exhibition and prepared with the help of Mies van der Rohe himself, this volume offers a well-written, illustrated account of his career until the time of the show.

Pawley, Martin. *Mies van der Rohe*. London: Thames and Hudson, and New York: Simon and Schuster, 1970. Pawley, quite properly, claims only to write an introduction and notes to what is really a book of pictures (some in color), but these pictures are by an excellent photographer, Yukio Futagawa. The best way to understand Mies van der Rohe is to see the buildings in person, but good photographs help.

Reif, Rita. "Furniture from the Mind of an Architect." *New York Times* 146, no. 50726 (March 9, 1997). Examines the auction of five pieces of Van Der Rohe furniture, their styles, and their expected going prices.

Spaeth, David A. *Mies van der Rohe*. London: Architectural Press, and New York: Rizzoli, 1985. Popular critical biography, taking Mies van der Rohe through his entire career. Ample use of his own statements, with technical jargon kept to a minimum. Well illustrated with excellent photographs and generous use of drawings.

Speyer, A. James. *Mies van der Rohe*. Chicago: Art Institute of Chicago, 1968. Published at the time of the Retrospective Exhibition at the Institute, the book concentrates on specific projects, bringing photos, plans, and short, sensible commentaries together.

Charles H. Pullen

DARIUS MILHAUD

Born: September 4, 1892; Aix-en-Provence, France

Died: June 22, 1974; Geneva, Switzerland

Area of Achievement: Music

Contribution: Perhaps the most famous composer of the mythical "Les Six," Milhaud was undoubtedly the most prolific, his published works running to nearly 450. He did highly original work in such areas as polytonality and percussion music. His best work is characterized by a Gallic lyricism.

Early Life

Born on September 4, 1892, in Aix-en-Provence, France, Darius Milhaud belonged to a well-to-do Jewish family for centuries settled in Aix and in close touch with the region's cultural life. His father was an amateur pianist, his mother an amateur singer. Piano lessons from his father were followed at age seven by violin lessons from a former Paris Conservatoire prizewinner, Léo Bruquier. In 1902, Milhaud was enrolled at the local *lycée*, where he distinguished himself academically. By the time he was twelve, he was playing second violin in a string quartet with his teacher, taking harmony lessons, and writing a violin sonata. Léo Latil and Armand Lunel, both promising young writers, were his closest friends; later, Milhaud was strongly influenced by friendship with such writers as Francis Jammes, Paul Claudel, and Jean Cocteau. The many friends he made among writers and painters would influence him as much, if not more, than his contemporaries in music.

After passing his baccalaureate examinations at the age of sixteen, Milhaud entered the Paris Conservatoire primarily as a violin student, though he soon came to see composing as his true vocation. In addition to taking the orchestral class of Paul Dukas, he studied harmony with Xavier Leroux and composition with André Gédalge. Milhaud began to travel widely at this time, a habit he would continue throughout his life, despite a severely disabling case of rheumatoid arthritis, which eventually kept him in a wheelchair. He visited Spain in 1911 and Germany in 1913.

Life's Work

Milhaud began composing his first major works while at the Conservatoire. In 1910, he began work on an opera, *La Brebis égarée*, to a libretto by Jammes, for whom he had the opportunity to play and sing the first act. Beginning in 1913, he was engaged in writing the incidental music to Claudel's *Protée;* he composed three different versions of this music during the next six years as he tried to suit it to changing plans for production. The year 1913 also found Milhaud at work on *Agamemnon*, the first of an operatic trilogy based on Claudel's translation of Aeschylus' *Orestia*. He avoided the traditional techniques of incidental music in this work; instead, he employed a novel type of transition from speech to song, one he would also employ in the other two parts of the trilogy.

Milhaud was declared unfit for service on medical grounds when World War I broke out in August of 1914. Returning to the Conservatoire, he was awarded a prize for his two-violin sonata—the only prize, he noted in his 1949 autobiography, that he ever won. In 1915, Milhaud composed *Les Choëphores*, the second part of the *Orestia* trilogy. This work is especially notable for its utilization of a speaking chorus with percussion and for the introduction of polytonality—the simultaneous use of two or more keys—which would remain a distinctive feature of Milhaud's style. In two scenes of *Les Choëphores*, a woman narrator declaims the text against a backdrop of pitchless percussion while the chorus whistles, groans, and shrieks.

In the autumn of 1916, Milhaud entered the propaganda wing of the government; given military standing, he was assigned to the photographic service. Shortly afterward, Claudel, then better known as a diplomat than as a poet and newly appointed ambassador to Brazil, invited Milhaud to accompany him to Rio de Janeiro as his secretary. In 1917, Milhaud began work on the third part of the *Orestia* trilogy, *Les Euménides* (completed in 1922). The sights and native music of Brazil, where he would remain for two years, made an indelible impression on Milhaud. The ballet *L'Homme et son désir* (1918), the two dance suites *Saudades do Brasil* (1920-1921), and random parts of many later works all bear witness to the enormous and productive impact that Milhaud's Brazilian sojourn had upon his work. An encounter with the dancer Vaslav Nijinsky had led to *L'Homme et son désir*, but Nijinsky was no longer able to dance by the time it was completed.

When he returned to Paris in November of 1918, Milhaud was drawn into the Cocteau circle of writers, artists, and composers. Reviewing a concert that included songs by Louis Durey and Milhaud's fourth string quartet, Henri Collet dubbed these two, along with Georges Auric, Arthur Honegger, Francis Poulenc, and Germaine Tailleferre, "Les Six," apparently an arbitrarily chosen French counterpart to the Russian "Five." Their differences in temperament and aesthetic outlook precluded them from working together as a unit for very long. Nevertheless, this rather ill-assorted group decided to capitalize on the "Les Six" designation before eventually going their several ways. They collaborated on a Cocteau ballet, *Les Mariés de la tour Eiffel* (1921), without Durey, and staged a two-year series of Saturday *soirées*. Milhaud wrote the music for another Cocteau ballet, *Le Bœuf sur le toit* (1919), named after a popular Brazilian song and produced on a program that included Erik Satie's *Pièces montées*, Auric's *Fox-Trot*, and Poulenc's *Cocardes*. The press found it all very amusing, and the following year, it was put on as a part of a music-hall show at London's Coliseum.

Milhaud's collaborations with "Les Six" and works of his own such as *Le boeuf sur le toit* soon caused the music public to brand him as an unprincipled and flippant exploiter of fashionable music curiosities. His standing was by no means redeemed by the *Rite of Spring*-like reception of the first performances of the *Protée* symphonic suite in 1920 and of the *Cinq études* for piano and orchestra in 1921. The long-postponed *L'Homme et son désir*, danced by the Ballet Suedois in 1921, occasioned a similar uproar. Even a relatively conventional piece as *La Brebis égarée* caused a riot when it was staged in 1923 at the Opéra-Comique. To make matters worse, critics refused to take seriously, as Milhaud intended them to be, the song cycles *Machines agricoles* (1919), composed of extracts from a catalog of agricultural machinery set to music, and *Catalogue de fleurs* (1920), musical settings to poems by Lucien Daudet inspired by a florist's catalog.

Billy Arnold and his band provided Milhaud's first exposure to jazz when Milhaud visited London in 1920 for a performance of *Le Bœuf sur le toit*. He soon began to steep himself in all of the American popular music he could find. His friends Clément Doucet and Jean Wiener played a variety of transatlantic blues and ragtime imports. In 1922, Milhaud embarked on a tour of the United States. In addition to making his podium debut as conductor of the Philadelphia Orchestra for a program he chose, appearing as a pianist, and lecturing at various colleges, he was taken to Harlem to hear jazz firsthand. His announcement to reporters that jazz was the American music that most stimulated him became front-page news. Fired by his exposure to authentic black jazz, Milhaud composed the ballet *La Création du monde* (1923), which is certainly one of his masterpieces.

Milhaud continued to travel restlessly during the early 1920's; in addition to the United States, he visited Italy, Sardinia, Palestine, Turkey, and Russia. Part of this travel involved his honeymoon; he had married his cousin, Madeline, an actress. *La Création du monde* was followed in 1924 by two more ballets: *Salade* and *Le Train Bleu*. *Salade* eventually became *Le Carnaval d'Aix* for piano and orchestra. In 1925, Milhaud completed the comic opera *Esther de Carprentras*, which was commissioned by the Princess de Polignac, the heiress to the Singer Sewing Machine fortune. Also in 1925, he completed *Les Malheurs d'Orphée*, with a libretto by Lunel. This was the first of several chamber operas that were counterparts to his six chamber symphonies composed between 1917 and 1923. Relatively short in duration, each is scored for a minimum of instrumentalists and singers.

Christophe Colomb, the most imposing collaboration between Milhaud and Claudel, was completed in 1928. Partly expressionistic and partly symbolic, it is an opera on a vast scale. It contains references to the Wagnerian leitmotif, the medieval mystery play, and the Greek chorus. An offstage orchestra, forty-five vocal soloists, numerous nonsinging actors, and a huge chorus were necessary for its execution. The opera was successfully produced in Berlin in 1930—complete with film inserts—but it would not be taken up again for thirty years. Almost every facet of Milhaud's musical personality can be found in this work. The same concentrated musical vitality is not to be found in his later large-scale stage works.

Christophe Colomb was quickly followed by another ambitious opera, *Maximilien*, which was completed in 1930 and staged in Paris in 1932. In 1929, Milhaud had also begun a career as a writer of film scores. He would eventually write more than twenty-five, but none of them was a major success. In 1932, Milhaud also returned to writing incidental music for the theater, eventually providing scores for thirty-odd dramas.

By the 1930's, Milhaud had attained international prominence and respect. He was regularly asked to appear at big music festivals, world's fairs, and other important occasional events. Continuing to combine frequent composition with extensive traveling during the 1930's, Milhaud often appeared as both conductor and pianist at, for example, the Florence and Venice music festivals. He participated in a congress of music critics convened by the government of Portugal in 1932. The year 1937 saw Milhaud making a number of contributions to the International Exposition, including music for Claudel's *Fête de la musique*.

Milhaud had suffered bouts of illness on several occasions during his travels. Always notably overweight, he began to suffer increasingly from rheumatoid arthritis. In an effort to relieve his pain, Milhaud tried such things as acupuncture and faith healing in addition to consulting conventional physicians. Nothing worked, and he was doomed to suffer pain, which was often severe, for the rest of his life. While he was ailing in 1930, Milhaud's son Daniel was born.

Milhaud was bedridden at home in Provence during the first year of World War II. After the fall of Paris, he and his wife realized that they had to leave France. Reaching New York in July of 1940, Milhaud and his wife, after recuperating at the home of friends, bought a second-hand automobile and drove cross-country to Oakland, California, where Milhaud was to teach at Mills College. He taught there for the next thirty-one years.

Before fleeing France, Milhaud had begun the first of a series of twelve symphonies for full orchestra. Of these, No. 3 (1946) is a choral hymn of thanksgiving for victory, No. 4 (1947) is an epic of the 1848 Revolution in Europe, and No. 8 (1957) is a portrait of the Rhone River. Milhaud was seriously ill during 1946, but, by the end of the summer of 1947, he was well enough to return to France. There, he suffered a relapse and was forced to spend much of his time indoors. After August of 1947, despite indifferent health, he combined his post at Mills College with that of professor of composition at the Paris Conservatoire. Among his successful pupils were Morton Subotnick, Steven Reich, Dave Brubeck, Howard Brubeck, William Bolcom, Ben Johnston, Seymour Shifrin, and Betsy Jolas. Together with his wife Madeline, he became a prime mover at the music school connected with the summer festival at Aspen, Colorado.

During the latter part of his career, Milhaud received many commissions and composed as prolif-

ically as before. In 1952, he composed the opera *David*, with a libretto by Lunel, for the Festival of Israel in honor of the three-thousandth anniversary of King David's founding of Jerusalem. Milhaud made a special journey to Israel as part of his preparation for this work. In spite of his ill health, he continued an active schedule of composing and teaching until long after his seventieth birthday, which was marked by a number of new recordings and enthusiastic celebrations in France. Ill health finally forced him to resign his post at Mills College and move to Geneva in 1971. Tribute was paid to him in Brussels, Aix, Rome, Nice, and elsewhere on his eightieth birthday. His last work was *Ani maamin, un chant perdu et retrouvé*, a cantata written for the 1973 Festival of Israel. Milhaud died in Geneva on June 22, 1974.

Summary

Darius Milhaud composed his most enduring works while he was still a comparatively young man. Undoubtedly, his best work was done by the beginning of World War II. After the war, the distinct decline in quality, if not in quantity, may be attributed in part to increasing age, infirmities, and professional commitments. Nevertheless, the real cause of this decline was the war, which cut him off from one of the two primary sources of his inspiration—the Provençal landscape of France and its popular music (the other source of his inspiration being his Jewish heritage). Milhaud's unselfconscious and spontaneous utilization of folk materials give his best work a freshness and an element of Mediterranean lyricism that is conspicuously absent elsewhere. As a folklorist, Milhaud successfully crossed the borderline between popular culture and high art.

In Milhaud's Provençal landscapes, no less than in those of Paul Cézanne, there is the imprint of the familiar features of the Provençal scene: the dry air, the harsh light, the jagged shape of rocks and trees, and the noisy blend of colors. Both Milhaud and Cézanne achieved a remarkable combination of earthy solidity and rustic simplicity. This achievement would not have been possible in Milhaud's case were it not for the new dimension of polytonality that he added to the harmonic language of his time. As he saw it, polytonality was a melodic, tonal antidote to the disintegration of the diatonic system. It was not an end in itself, but rather a means of creating the unique atmosphere in which Milhaud created his best music, in which he captured the Mediterranean spirit of Provençal better than any other composer.

Bibliography

Bolcom, William. "Reminiscences of Darius Milhaud." *Musical Newsletter* 7 (Summer, 1977): 3-11. An affectionate memoir by one of Milhaud's students, who was later an important composer in his own right.

Brody, Elaine. *Paris: The Musical Kaleidoscope, 1870-1925.* New York: Braziller, 1987; London: Robson, 1988. This excellent study chronicles an important chapter in French musical history. Particularly good on the growth of a specifically French musical nationalism and on the new importance of ballet and its function as a focus for artists, writers, musicians, and impresarios.

Collaer, Paul. *Darius Milhaud.* San Francisco: San Francisco Press, 1988. Edited and translated by Jane Hohfeld Galante. This work is valuable for its complete catalog of Milhaud's works, editions, discography, writings, and translations.

Harding, James. *The Ox on the Roof: Scenes from Musical Life in Paris in the Twenties.* London: Macdonald, and New York: St. Martin's Press, 1972. In this book about "Les Six," Harding maintains that the group, even though it did not found a school or stimulate disciples, contributed much to the musical flavor of the 1920's.

Mawer, Deborah. *Darius Milhaud: Modality and Structure in Music of the 1920s.* Aldershot: Scolar Press, and Brookfield, Vt.: Ashgate, 1997. The first comprehensive analysis of a large selection of Milhaud's works that focuses on pitch structure and places the works in historical context.

Milhaud, Darius. *Notes Without Music.* Edited by Rollo H. Myers. Translated by Donald Evans. London: Dobson, 1952; New York: Knopf, 1953. On the first page of this autobiography, Milhaud proclaims the mainsprings of his musical inspiration: He is a Frenchman from Provence and a Jew in religion.

Palmer, Christopher. *Darius Milhaud.* London, 1976. The standard treatment in English of Milhaud and his work.

Teachout, Terry. "Modernism with a Smile." *Commentary* 105, no. 4 (April, 1998). Teachout considers the historical linking of Milhaud and Poulenc and suggests that they should now be evaluated based on their own merits.

L. Moody Simms, Jr.

EDNA ST. VINCENT MILLAY

Born: February 22, 1892; Rockland, Maine
Died: October 19, 1950; Austerlitz, New York
Area of Achievement: Literature
Contribution: Edna St. Vincent Millay was a symbol and spokeswoman for women's sexual liberation, particularly during the Roaring Twenties, and continues to be regarded as a pioneering American feminist.

Early Life

Edna St. Vincent Millay was born in Rockland, Maine, on February 22, 1892. Her parents were divorced in 1900, and her strong-minded mother reared her three girls by working as a practical nurse. Cora Millay encouraged her daughters to be independent individualists like herself and supported any intellectual or artistic interest they displayed. Her mother's example was the most important influence in Millay's childhood; it was largely responsible for her uninhibited behavior and the autonomous attitude expressed in her writing.

Millay displayed musical talent at an early age. She took piano lessons for several years and planned on a musical career, but decided in favor of becoming a writer when her poem "Renaissance" was published in *Lyric Year* in 1912 and received enthusiastic praise. Her musical talent and musical education contributed to her remarkable sense of harmony and rhythm, which were the features of her poetry that made her celebrated during the 1920's and 1930's. She was also interested in drama as a young girl; this interest continued throughout her life and led to her writing a total of six dramatic works.

Millay was educated at Vassar College, one of the leading American institutions of higher education for women. She studied Latin, French, Greek, Italian, Spanish, and German while continuing to write poetry and to act in amateur theatrical productions. When she was only twenty years old, she was already establishing a reputation as a writer. She experimented with all the literary forms she would work in for the rest of her life. Her first collection of poetry, *Renascence and Other Poems*, was published in the fall of 1917.

The most significant event in Millay's early life came when she moved to Greenwich Village in New York City. The Village was considered by many to be the center of American intellectual and cultural life, and Millay responded to life there with enthusiasm. She met people whose names would become famous in American art and literature, including Theodore Dreiser, Dorothy Day, Paul Robeson, E. E. Cummings, Hart Crane, Wallace Stevens, Susan Glaspell, Eugene O'Neill, and Edmund Wilson.

For many years, Millay had a hard time surviving financially. Despite these challenges, she was sustained by a zest for life, for nature, for beauty, for love, and for art that was expressed in all of her writing. She supported herself by turning out stories, light verse, and personal articles under the pen name of Nancy Boyd. She also did some professional acting, but received little pay.

The year 1923 was a turning point in her life. That year she became the first woman ever to receive the Pulitzer Prize for Poetry. In 1923, Millay also was married to Eugen Jan Boissevain, a wealthy importer who adored her and was willing to provide her with financial security for the rest of her life.

Life's Work

Edna St. Vincent Millay will always be identified with the rebellious, hedonistic, iconoclastic, crusading, and often self-destructive spirit of the Roaring Twenties, the era when America came of age as a world power and a unique cultural force with its jazz, uninhibited dances, motion pictures, comic strips, bizarre slang, shocking feminine fashions, cheap mass-produced consumer goods, awesome skyscrapers, gaudy automobiles, potent cocktails made from bootleg gin and whiskey, and sometimes shocking plays and novels.

Millay was popular with men because of her beauty, wit, talent, and vivacious spirit. She had many love affairs, even after her marriage to the tolerant Boissevain, and wrote about them candidly in her poetry. She shared the hedonism of the 1920's, believing that life is a short, essentially meaningless but endlessly fascinating phenomenon that should be lived to the fullest. Her most often-quoted lines are:

My candle burns at both ends;
It will not last the night;
But ah, my foes, and oh, my friends—
It gives a lovely light.

In contrast to the flippant attitude Millay affected in much of her poetry, she was actually a studious and hard-working person. During her lifetime, she turned out an impressive body of work. In addition to her many volumes of poetry, she wrote six plays, including the widely popular *Aria da Capo* (1919) and the highly original *Conversation at Midnight* (1937), a great many short stories, essays and sketches, and collaborated on *Flowers of Evil* (1936), an English translation of Charles Baudelaire's *Les Fleurs du mal* (1857). She also carried on an extensive correspondence and was always in demand for readings and lectures all over the United States. She frequently complained that importunate strangers made such demands on her time with requests for advice and criticism that they prevented her from turning out even more original work.

Millay was one of the most popular American poets of all time. Critic Louis Untermeyer explained the reason for the success of her poetry as follows: "Plain and rhetorical, traditional in form and unorthodox in spirit, it satisfied the reader's dual desire for familiarity and surprise."

Millay received an honorary doctorate from New York University and another from Colby College in 1937, and in 1940 she was elected to the American Academy of Arts and Letters. After the 1930's, however, her reputation faded because literary tastes were changing. The Great Depression of the 1930's, World War II in the 1940's, and the Cold War which followed all made the cavalier tone of much of the art of the 1920's seem hopelessly trivial and irrelevant.

Highly influential Modernist critics and poets such as T. S. Eliot were totally out of sympathy with romanticists such as Millay, who wrote personal, lyrical poetry addressed to the general reader. Modernists generally felt that poetry should sound almost like conversation. Hostile critics pointed out that Millay often used unnatural constructions purely for the sake of rhyme or meter. An example can be drawn from the opening lines of one of her most famous poems:

> What lips my lips have kissed, and where, and why,
> I have forgotten, and what arms have lain
> Under my head till morning; but the rain
> Is full of ghosts tonight, that tap and sigh
> Upon the glass and listen for reply,
> And in my heart there stirs a quiet pain
> For unremembered lads that not again
> Will turn to me at midnight with a cry.

The natural way of expressing the thought contained in the last three lines might be: "A quiet pain stirs in my heart for forgotten lads who will never turn to me again at midnight with a cry." This change, however, would destroy the rhyme and meter entirely.

After her husband's death in 1949, Millay continued living at their rural retreat in upstate New York and went on working in increasing loneliness and solitude until her death of a heart attack on October 19, 1950.

Summary

Edna St. Vincent Millay's greatest impact came as a result of her outspoken advocacy of sexual freedom for women. She shocked American by repudiating the so-called "double standard" both in her writings and in her personal life. The double standard, which had existed since time immemorial, was tolerant of men's sexual experimentation, but expected women to be chaste, monogamous, and virtually asexual. Millay was responsible for challenging social restrictions and prejudices against women's freedom of self-expression. She ignored the boundaries of conventional subject matter for women writers, and revealed the range of depth of the feminine character.

As a poet, Millay was influenced by the style and subject matter found in works by the English Cavalier poets of the seventeenth century, particularly by Andrew Marvell. Yet sexual freedom was only one part of the total freedom that women of Millay's generation were demanding. Millay's flippant, sophisticated poetry—so modern and yet so reminiscent of the Cavaliers—conveyed the implicit message that the subject of sex could be amusing and was not necessarily the fire-and-brimstone affair that had been traditionally made of it. The rigid self-censorship that had always existed in the publishing world began to relax with the evolution of public opinion.

Millay, although never a militant feminist, was in wholehearted sympathy with the women's rights movement. She belonged to Alice Paul's National Woman's Party, which agitated for woman suffrage and later for an Equal Rights Amendment, but Millay did not participate in demonstrations. Her unique contribution to feminism was in assuming she already possessed the rights other women were fighting to obtain.

Millay was not cut out to be a follower or crusader; when she tried writing propaganda poems during World War II, she was unsuccessful and injured her literary reputation. She will always be re-

membered as a courageous individualist; she contributed more by her personal example than by marching or passing out leaflets. Writing about her shortly after her death, John Ciardi summarized her career in the following words: "It was not as a craftsman nor as an influence, but as the creator of her own legend that she was most alive for us. Her success was as a figure of passionate living."

Bibliography

Brittin, Norman A. *Edna St. Vincent Millay.* Rev. ed. New York: Twayne, 1982. An excellent study of Millay full of valuable reference material. Discusses some of her most important works in a scholarly but not overly difficult manner. Part of Twayne's excellent United States Authors series. Contains many pages of endnotes, a chronology, and an annotated bibliography.

Cheney, Anne. *Millay in Greenwich Village.* University: University of Alabama Press, 1975. A psychological biography of Millay focusing on her liberated lifestyle and relationships with men during her days of experimentation with free love in Greenwich Village. Contains a good bibliography of books, articles, and interviews.

Daffron, Carolyn. *Edna St. Vincent Millay.* New York: Chelsea House, 1989. This short biographical and critical study, part of the American Women of Achievement series, was written especially for young readers. Contains many photographs and direct quotations from Millay's poetry. Daffron does a good job of making younger readers appreciate the political and intellectual climate of Millay's time.

Gurko, Miriam. *Restless Spirit: The Life of Edna St. Vincent Millay.* New York: Crowell, 1962. This biography is addressed to readers of high school age. It does an effective job of bringing Millay to life as a real person—idealistic, contradictory, romantic, rebellious. Analyzes the role she played in the intellectual and cultural life of the early twentieth century. Contains excellent bibliography.

Johnson, R. "Six, Alas." *Chicago Review* 37, no. 1 (Winter 1990). A tribute to six women writers who are largely disregarded in contemporary times, including St. Vincent Millay, Stevie Smith, and others.

Millay, Edna St. Vincent. *Collected Poems.* Edited by Norma Millay. New York: Harper, 1956. This large volume contains a selection of poems representing Millay's range of subject matter and technical versatility, drawn from many of her previously published volumes.

————. *Letters of Edna St. Vincent Millay.* Edited by Allan Ross Macdougall. New York: Harper, 1952. A generous selection of letters written to Millay's many friends, acquaintances and admirers from earliest childhood until the last days of her life. Extensively footnoted.

Newcomb, John Timberman. "The Woman as Political Poet: Edna St. Vincent Millay and the Mid-Century Canon." *Criticism* 37, no. 2 (Spring 1995). Examines the negative criticism of St. Vincent Millay and suggests that it has historically been offered by individuals more concerned with technical matters than with valuable social discourse.

Sheean, Vincent. *The Indigo Bunting: A Memoir of Edna St. Vincent Millay.* New York: Harper, 1951. Written by a personal friend who was himself a noted journalist, biographer, and novelist, this sensitively written memoir focuses on Millay's life at Steepletop during the 1940's and her long interest in birds and bird imagery.

Bill Delaney

ARTHUR MILLER

Born: October 17, 1915; New York, New York
Areas of Achievement: Theater and entertainment
Contribution: Considered one of the foremost dramatists in the United States, Miller has penetrated the American consciousness and gained worldwide recognition for his probing dramas of social awareness.

Early Life

On October 17, 1915, Arthur Miller, son of Jewish immigrants, was born in Manhattan in New York. His father, Isadore, ran a prosperous garment business, and his mother, Augusta Barnett, was at one-time a school teacher. When Isadore's firm began to fail in 1928, the Millers moved to Brooklyn, an area that would be the model for the settings of *All My Sons* (1947) and *Death of a Salesman* (1949). He inherited a strong sense of mysticism from his mother that would inform his later work. As a young boy, Miller came to resent his father's withdrawal from failure. The figure of the failed father would play a significant role in Miller's plays.

The young Miller came of age during the Great Depression, and seeing once-prosperous people on the streets begging for work deeply affected him. To Miller, the Depression signified the failure of a system and the tragedy of a generation of people who would blame this failure on themselves. The Depression's impact on the aspects of personal success and failure would lead Miller to probe into individuals' relations to their work and the price they had to pay for success or lack of it.

Like Biff Loman in *Death of a Salesman*, Miller was more of an athlete than a scholar. He read mostly adventure novels and some Charles Dickens. Unable to get into college, he worked for his father and became moved by the sad plight of salesmen. After a series of odd jobs, Miller worked in an auto parts warehouse, where he was able to save $500 for college on a $15-per-week job. He recreated this experience in *A Memory of Two Mondays* (1955). While working, Miller became an avid reader and was especially impressed with Fyodor Dostoevski's *Bratya Karamazovy* (1879-1880; *The Brothers Karamazov*, 1912), a novel that focuses on a failed father, fraternal rivalry, and a trial motif, themes that would repeatedly occur in Miller's works.

After much convincing, Miller finally got accepted into the University of Michigan, where he be-came interested in social causes and began to form his liberal philosophy. He studied playwriting under Kenneth Rowe and won two Hopwood Awards, in 1936, for "No Villain" and in 1937, for "Honor at Dawn." In 1938, he won the Theater Guild National Award for "They Too Arise." Following the style of the 1930's, Miller's early plays focus on young idealists fighting to eliminate social injustice. After college, he worked for the Federal Theater Project and wrote radio scripts. In 1944, he tried to recreate the feelings of the ordinary soldier in his screenplay for *The Story of G. I. Joe* but was thwarted by motion-picture executives who wanted him to romanticize his work. That same year, he had his first Broadway production, *The Man Who Had All the Luck* (1944). This drama of a man dismayed by his incredible success was a flop.

Life's Work

After this initial failure, Miller rose up to become one of the United States' leading playwrights and gained an international reputation. In 1947, Miller achieved his first success with *All My Sons*, the tragedy of Joe Keller who, in order to save his business, sells defective airplane parts to the military and leaves his partner to bear the blame. He indirectly becomes responsible for the death of his own son, who condemns his father's action and flies a suicide mission. Faced with the guilt for many deaths, Keller kills himself.

In 1949, *Death of a Salesman* achieved unprecedented critical acclaim and established Miller as a significant American playwright. Willy Loman, an unsuccessful salesman, relives his past, trying to discover the reasons for his failure. Unable to accept failure, he pressures his son into far-fetched business schemes and commits suicide in order to leave his son the legacy of his insurance. In 1949, *Death of a Salesman* won the New York Drama Critics Circle Award and the Pulitzer Prize. The play ran for 742 performances. In 1966, the television production played to seventeen million people. In 1975, it was successfully produced at the Circle in the Square with George C. Scott in the lead; in 1984, it played Broadway again with Dustin Hoffman in the lead. In 1985, Hoffman was featured in a new television production of the play. Furthermore, *Death of a Salesman* has been acclaimed and produced around the world. In his book *Salesman in Beijing* (1984), Miller documents an unprecedented Chinese production. The play still appears in most college anthologies and continues to be taught as an American classic.

Disturbed by the repressive climate of the 1950's Cold War, the scare tactics of Senator Joseph McCarthy, and the betrayal by his one-time liberal friends who cited names before the House Committee on Un-American Activities, Miller wrote *The Crucible* (1953), which connected the witch hunts of seventeenth century Salem with the hunt for Communists of the 1950's. In *The Crucible*, Miller shows how an ordinary individual living in a repressive community gains tragic stature by sacrificing his life rather than betraying his conscience. *The Crucible* opened on Broadway in 1953 to a lukewarm reception but was later revived Off-Broadway with more success. Jean-Paul Sartre wrote the screenplay for the French film version of *The Crucible, Les Sorcieres de Salem* (1955). In 1961, *The Crucible* was converted into an opera, and, in 1967, it was adapted for television with George C. Scott in the lead role. In 1997, it was made into a motion picture with Miller writing the screenplay. According to Miller, *The Crucible* is his most frequently produced work both in the United States and abroad.

His next works were two one-act plays: *A Memory of Two Mondays* (1955) and *A View from the Bridge* (1955). An expanded version of *A View from the Bridge* (1956) told the story of Eddie Carbone, a longshoreman who is driven by incestuous desires for his niece to inform on his niece's boyfriend and other illegal immigrants living with him.

During the mid-1950's, Miller entered a troubled period of his life. After divorcing his first wife, Mary Grace Slattery, Miller married film star Marilyn Monroe and became involved in her turbulent career. He was also cited for contempt of Congress for refusing to name names before the House Committee on Un-American Activities. Although acquitted on appeal, this ordeal took a financial and emotional toll on him. In 1961, his marriage to Monroe ended in divorce; in 1962, he married photographer Ingeborg Morath.

After a nine-year hiatus from the American stage, Miller wrote *After the Fall* (1964) and *Incident at Vichy* (1964). Both plays dealt with the universal guilt associated with the genocide of the Jews. Miller returned to the form of family drama with *The Price* (1968), a drama depicting the rivalry of two brothers. Continuing to experiment, Miller wrote *The Creation of the World and Other Business* (1972), a comedy based on Genesis; *The American*

Clock (1980), a montage view of the Depression focusing on the trials of one family; *The Archbishop's Ceiling* (1984), a play about power and oppression in a European Communist country; and *Danger: Memory!* (1986), two short, symbolic dramas exploring the mysteries hidden in past actions.

In the 1990's, Miller experienced a resurgence. *The Ride Down Mt. Morgan* (1991) captures the gaudy materialism and egotistical self-absorption of 1980's America. As scenes from his life pass before him in his hospital room, an insurance magnate and bigamist lives for the unabated gratification of his pleasures as he struggles with the phantom of death. In *The Last Yankee* (1991), Miller examines the marital relationships of two women confined to a mental institution—one who cannot adjust to her husband's apparent failure to achieve the American Dream and the other isolated by the success of a husband who can only give her material comforts. In this play, Miller critiques the immigrant dream of unbridled success and issues a plea for self-acceptance. In *Broken Glass* (1994), Miller probes the indifference to the Nazi's persecution of the Jews by exploring the psyche of a Jewish woman in New York who undergoes hysterical paralysis when confronted with both an impotent, demanding husband and a world on the brink of chaos. *Mr. Peters' Connections* (1998) captures the inner world of a retired and ailing airplane pilot sitting in a broken-down saloon watching the phantoms of his past inexplicably parade before him. In Mr. Peters's inability to find continuity in the events of his life, Miller focuses on the alienation of modern humans in an ever-changing world. In the plays of the 1990's, Miller continued to examine private relationships in light of social criticism.

Between 1997 and 1998, Miller saw the revival in New York of *All My Sons, The American Clock, I Can't Remember Anything* (a part of *Danger: Memory!*), *The Last Yankee*, and *A View from the Bridge*, which won Broadway's Tony Award for Best Revival. Miller continued producing new plays, and the continuous revivals of his dramas both onstage and on television and his burgeoning international reputation have kept Miller in the forefront of American theater.

Miller, a serious dramatist who believes in drama's ability to effect change, explores the social as well as the psychological aspects of his characters. For him, individual dilemmas cannot be removed from their social contexts. His dramas attempt to go beyond simple protest pieces or self-absorbed psychological studies to deal with moral and ethi-

cal issues. He is interested in how ordinary individuals can live in unity and harmony with their fellow humans without sacrificing their individual dignity.

Although labeled a realist, Miller has experimented with a number of innovative dramatic techniques. Also, Miller's poetic use of idiomatic speech and his subtle deployment of dramatic symbols show that his drama has moved beyond photographic realism. Using a variety of approaches, Miller most often puts characters in confrontation with their past actions so that they may define themselves not only in terms of their social situation but also in terms of their moral convictions. Miller's ability to probe the human psyche as well as to question the social fabric of the United States has made him a towering presence in the American theater.

Summary

Arthur Miller examines both the psychological and sociological makeup of his troubled characters. His heroes are common men who relentlessly pursue either their firm convictions or their misguided illusions. Using family relationships as a starting point, Miller's plays confront contemporary moral dilemmas and focus on people's responsibility to be true to themselves as well as their responsibility to be a part of the human race. In showing how individuals confront their past actions, Miller employs a variety of dramatic forms, including flashbacks, stream-of-consciousness monologues, direct narration, and dynamic symbols. His concern with the struggle to define oneself in a troubled world has made him a popular American playwright and has also gained him worldwide attention.

Bibliography

Bigsby, Christopher, ed. *Arthur Miller and Company.* London: Methuen, 1990. A series of impressions on Miller's works from noted writers and theater personalities. Presents a variety of insights into Miller and his work.

————, ed. *The Cambridge Companion to Arthur Miller.* Cambridge and New York: Cambridge University Press, 1997. An introduction to Miller's work that analyzes his fiction and plays and places his works in historical and social context.

Carson, Neil. *Arthur Miller.* London and New York: Macmillan, 1982. A good introductory work to Miller's major plays with chapters on his early work and nontheatrical writings.

Murphy, Brenda C. W., and Susan Abbotson. *Understanding "Death of a Salesman": A Student Casebook to Issues, Sources and Historical Documents.* Westport, Conn.: Greenwood Press, 1999. A collection of historical, cultural, and social documents (with commentary) designed to assist the reader in better understanding Miller's *Death of a Salesman.* All materials shed light on conflicts in society that are the basis for the play.

Schlueter, June, and James K. Flanagan. *Arthur Miller.* New York: Ungar, 1987. Contains a detailed analysis of Miller's major and minor plays, a concise biography that includes his political activity, a detailed chronology of his life and works, and a bibliography of his primary works, including radio plays and unpublished manuscripts.

Welland, Dennis. *Arthur Miller: The Playwright.* 3d ed. London and New York: Methuen, 1985. A thorough analysis of Miller's major work, including a detailed list of American and British premieres of Miller's plays and films and a short bibliography.

Paul Rosefeldt

KATE MILLETT

Born: September 14, 1934; St. Paul, Minnesota
Area of Achievement: Women's rights
Contribution: Since the 1970 publication of her book *Sexual Politics*, a manifesto of the feminist movement, Millett has been an acknowledged leader of the modern women's movement.

Early Life

Katherine Murray Millett was born on September 14, 1934, in St. Paul, Minnesota. Her father, James Albert Millett, was an engineer, and her mother, Helen Feely Millett, was a teacher. The family's background was Irish Catholic, and Kate attended several parochial schools. When Kate was fourteen, her father deserted the family. After attending parochial schools with dwindling faith and increasing rebelliousness, Kate Millett attended the University of Minnesota, where she received her bachelor's degree in English, magna cum laude and Phi Beta Kappa, in 1956. A rich aunt, who was disturbed by Kate's increasing tendency to defy convention, offered to send her to Oxford University for graduate study. For two years, Kate Millett studied English literature at Oxford, and she received first-class honors in 1958. Returning to the United States, she obtained her first job, teaching English at the University of North Carolina. In mid-semester, she quit her position and moved to New York City to paint and sculpt. In New York, she rented a loft to serve as her studio and living quarters, and to support herself she worked as a file clerk in a bank and as a kindergarten teacher in Harlem.

From 1961 to 1963, Kate Millett sculpted and taught English at Waseda University in Tokyo, Japan. She had her first one-woman show at the Minami Gallery in Tokyo. While in Japan, she met her future husband, Fumio Yoshimura, also a sculptor. In 1968, she returned to academic life, working for her Ph.D. degree in English and comparative literature at Columbia University while teaching English in the university's undergraduate school for women, Barnard College.

Life's Work

At Columbia University, Kate Millett's concern with politics and women's rights began to develop and deepen. After returning from Japan, she joined the Congress of Racial Equality (CORE) and the peace movement. In 1965, the campaign for women's liberation attracted her attention and energies. At Columbia, she was a vocal organizer for women's liberation and a militant champion of other progressive causes, including abortion reform and student rights. On December 23, 1968, because her activism made her unpopular with the Barnard College administration, she was relieved of her teaching position.

In its original form, *Sexual Politics* was a short manifesto that Millett read to a women's liberation meeting at Cornell University in November of 1968. In February of 1969, however, Millett began to develop the manifesto into her doctoral dissertation. Working on it with undivided attention, Kate Millett finished it in September of 1969 and successfully defended it to receive her doctorate in March of 1970. She was awarded the degree "with distinction."

Few doctoral dissertations are published outside the academic community, and fewer still become bestsellers, but Millett's *Sexual Politics* (1970) was a huge success, going through seven printings and selling 80,000 copies in its first year on the market. Although some reviews of *Sexual Politics* were decidedly hostile, most critics have judged the book to be a reasonable and scholarly political analysis of gender tensions.

Sexual Politics is divided into three sections. The first, which deals with theories and examples of sexual politics, establishes the fundamental thesis that sex is a political category with status implications. Millett argues that what is largely unexamined in the social order is an automatically assumed priority whereby males rule females as a birthright. In monogamous marriage and the nuclear family, women and children are treated primarily as property belonging to the male. Lower-class women are exploited and reduced to a source of cheap labor, while middle-class and upper-class women are forced into a parasitical existence, dependent for food and favor upon the ruling males. When the system is most successful, Millett says, it results in an interior colonization—the creation of a slavelike mentality in which women are devoted to their masters and the institutions that keep them in bondage.

The second part of *Sexual Politics* discusses the historical background of the subjugation and liberation of women. The section begins with an account of the first phase of the sexual revolution, which started about 1830 and ended, abortively, in reform rather than revolution, when women in the United States gained suffrage. Going on to analyze the counterrevolution, Millett identifies Sigmund Freud as its archvillain. She dismisses as a male supremacist bias Freud's theory that "penis envy" is the basis for women's masochism and passivity and that fear of castration is the basis for men's greater success at repressing instinctual drives and therefore attaining higher cultural achievement. She also examines and rejects Erik Erickson's theory of womb envy, among other versions of anatomy-is-destiny thought.

In the third and final section, Millett examines four major modern writers insofar as they reflect the sexual politics of our society. D. H. Lawrence sees women at their most womanly as willing subjects and sacrifices to male creative power. Henry Miller sees women only as sexual partners and sees the ideal sexual partner not as a person but as an object, a genital playground designed solely to fulfill male needs. Norman Mailer is a prisoner of the cult of virility, to whom sexuality means sadism, violence, and usually sodomy as well. Only in Jean Genet, the French chronicler of the homosexual underworld, does Millett find a sympathetic understanding of the position of women. She sees in Genet's portrayal of the hatred and hostility directed at homosexual "queens" a mirror image and intentional parody of relations between the sexes in heterosexual society.

Since the publication of her book, Kate Millett has been involved in a wide range of feminist activities. In 1970, she partially financed and directed an all-woman crew in the production of a low-budget documentary film about the lives of three women. Although *Three Lives* was intended for college and other noncommercial audiences, it was premiered at a commercial New York City theater late in 1971 and received generally excellent reviews. Millett then taught a course on the sociology of women once a week at Bryn Mawr College.

Kate Millett is an activist and supporter of a full range of women's liberation groups, from the National Organization for Women to the Radical Lesbians. She has been involved in attempts to organize prostitutes, and in August of 1970 she took part in the symbolic seizing of the Statue of Liberty in celebration of the passage of the Equal Rights Amendment, prohibiting discrimination because of sex, by the House of Representatives. (The amendment ultimately failed to be ratified by enough states to become law.)

Sexual Politics removed Millett from the anonymity of the New York art world and established her as a widely interviewed spokesperson for the women's movement. Within months, however, the author realized that she could not control the image of herself that was projected by the press and on television. In the midst of her excessive celebrity, Millett found herself unsuited to life as a talk-show exhibit, but she did not quit the scene. Once recognized as an articulate member of the women's movement, she had somehow ceased to be a free agent. In her uncomfortable new spokeswoman status, she was urged by other women to do her duty in speaking out on their behalf, while, at the same time, being browbeaten and harassed for her arrogance and elitism in presuming to do so. Millett's book *Flying* (1974) details her struggle to remain self-aware, personally happy, and productive in the face of all the publicity she was receiving as a result of *Sexual Politics*. The central theme of *Flying*, as well as that of her 1977 memoir *Sita*, is her avowed lesbianism and the effect that her honest admission of lesbianism had on her public and private life. The extent of the publicity attached to Millett was so intense that her greatest desire after the publication of *Sexual Politics* was to reconstruct some sort of private personality for herself after the glare of the cameras had begun to fade.

With her two autobiographical works finished, Millett turned to a topic that had haunted her for more than ten years—the brutal torture and murder of an Indianapolis teenager named Sylvia Likens. *The Basement*, released in 1980, offers a chilling chronology of Sylvia's last months, from her point of view as well as her killers'. The book combined reporting, the various consciousnesses of those involved in the crime, and a feminist analysis of power to follow human realities wherever they might lead. What emerges is not only the story of an isolated incident but also that of the powerlessness of children, the imposition of sexual shame on adolescent girls, and the ways in which a woman is used to break the spirit and body of younger women. Clearly, the fourteen years that Millett spent pondering Sylvia's fate and how to detail it enhance the book's value. Quite apart from any feminist polemics, *The Basement* can stand alone as an intensely felt and movingly written study of the problems of cruelty and submission. *The Loony-Bin Trip* (1990) recounts the ordeals Millett experienced after her involuntary hospitalizations in psychiatric wards for manic- depression, her divorce from sculptor Fumio Yoshimura, and the painful efforts she made to reconstruct her personal and public identities despite her illness. Millett now spends most of her time at a farm she owns where an art colony of other like-minded artists and activists reside.

Summary

Kate Millett will be remembered primarily as the author of *Sexual Politics*. *Sexual Politics* is an impressively informed, controlled analysis of the patriarchal order by a young radical sensibility that is challenging the confinements of cultural stereotypes and institutions in order to envision possibilities for refashioning power relationships between the sexes. With its phenomenal success, *Sexual Politics* provided the women's movement with a theoretical background for its struggles against male domination. It also pioneered academic feminist literary criticism, which has since influenced heavily the teaching and research on literature in many American colleges and universities. In addition, by avowing and celebrating first her bisexuality and later her lesbianism, Kate Millett has become an articulate and influential spokesperson in the struggle for gay and lesbian rights. Combining feminist ideals with careful and controlled analyses of the limitations and abuses of patriarchal social control, she has emerged as a champion of human rights.

Bibliography

Charvet, John. *Feminism*. London: Dent, 1982. Traces the evolution of feminism from its beginnings in eighteenth century thought to the twentieth century. The chapter "Radical Feminism" includes a summary of the major arguments of *Sexual Politics*.

Donovan, Josephine, ed. *Feminist Literary Criticism*. 2d ed. Lexington: University Press of Kentucky, 1989. A series of essays examining the impact of feminist literary criticism on the academy. The first essay places *Sexual Politics* in the context of other works that analyze images of women created by male authors.

Lawson, Kate. "Imagining Eve: Charlotte Brontë, Kate Millett, Helene Cixous." *Women's Studies* 24, no. 5 (June, 1995). Lawson compares works by Millett, Charlotte Brontë, and Helene Cixous with respect to their examination of women's lives and roles in society.

Millett, Kate. *Flying*. New York: Knopf, 1974; London: Hart-Davis, 1975. After the phenomenal success of *Sexual Politics*, Kate Millett found herself both canonized and reviled as the near-mythical leader of the women's movement. This book recounts the relationship between a writer's life and her art, and her attempts to salvage a believable, productive woman out of the uproar surrounding the publication of her first book.

―――. *The Loony-Bin Trip*. New York: Simon and Schuster, 1990. An autobiographical account of Millett's thirteen-year struggle with manic-depression, her treatment with the drug lithium, and her decision in 1980 to stop taking the drug. Her account is an indictment of psychiatric treatment as a form of social control that she resolutely challenges and opposes.

―――. *Sita*. London: Virage, and New York: Ballantine, 1977. Millett's autobiographical account of her first diagnosis as a manic-depressive, her divorce from her husband, and the road to recovery she journeyed when she met and fell in love with Sita, a woman ten years older than Millett, artistic, witty, seductive, and strong. The memoir recounts the successes and despairs of a deeply felt lesbian relationship.

Millett, Kate, and Betsy Hinden. "Adventures of a Feminist." *Women and Therapy* 17, no. 3-4 (Winter 1995). An interview with Millett in which she discusses her views on feminist therapy and psychiatry's oppression of women and its lack of care standards.

Roberta M. Hooks

ROBERT ANDREWS MILLIKAN

Born: March 22, 1868; Morrison, Illinois
Died: December 19, 1953; Pasadena, California
Areas of Achievement: Physics, education, and administration
Contribution: As a skilled and meticulous experimenter, Millikan made major contributions to twentieth century physics; as a textbook author, university teacher, and supervisor of research, he greatly influenced the way that physics was studied in the United States; as an administrator, he was responsible for the rise to prominence of the California Institute of Technology.

Early Life

Robert Andrews Millikan was born in Morrison, Illinois, on March 22, 1868, the son of Silas Franklin Millikan, a Congregational preacher, and Mary Jane (Andrews) Millikan, a graduate of Oberlin College and former dean of a small college in Michigan. When Robert was five years old, the family, which was to include three sons and three daughters, moved westward to Iowa, where they settled permanently in Maquoketa two years later.

Robert began his education at home under his mother's tutelege, continuing in the local public schools through high school. He recalled his childhood experience as being typical for a Midwestern American boy of the late nineteenth century, with plenty of work, thrift, fun, healthy exercise, and little formal exposure to science.

He entered Oberlin College in 1886 and initially embarked on a classical course of study, later shifting to physics, in which he was largely self-taught. After receiving an M.A. from Oberlin in 1893, he enrolled as the sole graduate student in physics at Columbia University, where he came under the strong influence of Michael Pupin, a self-made scientist who had arrived in the United States virtually penniless from Eastern Europe in 1874. (Pupin's autobiography, *From Immigrant to Inventor*, published by Charles Scribner's Sons in 1923, is well worth reading as illustrative of the period.) Encouraged and financially aided by Pupin, Millikan set off for a year of study in Europe after completing his Ph.D. in 1895. A year later he was invited to come to the University of Chicago as an assistant in physics by Albert A. Michelson, America's best-known experimental physicist at the time and under whom Millikan had taken a summer course in 1894.

Early photographs show Millikan to have been a handsome young man of good stature and athletic build. As he aged, his hair turned white and he gave the appearance of a confident elder statesman of science. He was outgoing and sociable and enjoyed interacting with persons on all levels. His marriage in 1902 to Greta Blanchard produced three sons and endured until she predeceased him by a few weeks in 1953.

Life's Work

Millikan was given heavy teaching responsibilities at Chicago, the more so because Michelson did not enjoy working with students. Millikan took his duties seriously, throwing himself into classroom teaching and laboratory instruction, and writing textbooks and laboratory manuals in physics. These ventures into text writing, usually in collaboration with others, were highly successful. The books were revised many times and widely used for decades. It is interesting to note that Millikan was one of the first authors to incorporate historical material as background into physics texts. When the History of Science Society was formed in 1923, he was a founding member.

By dint of working twelve hours a day, six days a week, at the University of Chicago, Millikan also embarked on a research program, achieving notable success in two areas. Through his "oil drop" method he showed that electric charge always occurs in exact multiples of a fundamental unit quantity whose numerical value he was able to calculate. His second area of success was the photoelectric effect, an action that occurs when electrons are emitted from the surface of certain metals under illumination by light of suitable wavelength. The results obtained by Millikan in 1916 exactly confirmed the theoretical prediction made by Albert Einstein in 1905. Einstein had based his theory on a belief in "quanta," units of energy first introduced by Max Planck in 1899. It is curious to note that Millikan, despite his experimental confirmation of Einstein's equation, could not bring himself to accept the existence of quanta until several years later, since these new entities were so much at variance with the ideas of classical physics. In 1923, Millikan was awarded the Nobel Prize for Physics for these experiments. By that time he had moved to the California Institute of Technology and declined to make the journey to

Stockholm for the ceremony, pleading the urgency of his research and teaching. (It should be remembered that, in those days, such a trip would have required him to be away from California for more than a month.)

In 1915, Millikan was elected to membership in the National Academy of Sciences, the prestigious body established during the Civil War to provide scientific assistance to the federal government. A year after Millikan's election, that organization moved to form the National Research Council for the purpose of mobilizing for defense the nation's scientific talent. Millikan was a member of the organizing committee of the council and subsequently was named its executive officer and director of research. Among the areas of concern were submarine detection and chemical warfare. When the United States became actively involved in World War I, Millikan moved to Washington for the duration of the war, donning an army uniform and becoming a lieutenant colonel in the Signal Corps.

After the war, Millikan was instrumental in having the National Research Council expand its function to establish and supervise a program of postdoctoral fellowships for young Americans entering scientific professions. Funding for the program was provided by the Rockefeller Foundation. The aim of the program was twofold: The individual National Research Council Fellow could engage in research unencumbered by heavy teaching duties (as Millikan had been), and the institutions where they chose to take their fellowships would benefit from their presence. As a result of this program, American scientific competence was strengthened.

Following Millikan's return to the University of Chicago in 1919, he found himself being sought after by the Throop College of Technology in Pasadena, California, having come to their attention through contacts he had made while in Washington, D.C. Initially, Millikan served at Throop only in a visiting capacity, but by 1921 he had moved there permanently as professor of physics and chairman of the Executive Council. Although he refused the title of president, he insisted that the name of the institution be changed to the California Institute of Technology. He convinced a group of wealthy and influential Californians that "Caltech," as it became known, was a unique state asset, well worthy of the support of businessmen, philanthropists, and ordinary citizens.

Until his retirement in 1945, at the age of seventy-seven, Millikan worked tirelessly to enhance the

prestige of Caltech, not only in the United States but also worldwide. One way of achieving this was to have an eminent European physicist as guest lecturer nearly every year. Among such visitors were Niels Bohr, Max Born, Albert Einstein, H.A. Lorentz, Erwin Schrödinger, and Arnold Sommerfeld. The generous funding provided by the trustees of Caltech made it possible for such visitors to lecture at other academic institutions as well, on their way to or from Pasadena, thereby benefiting the entire American physics community. Furthermore, each year a group of National Research Council Fellows found Caltech a stimulating place to be.

In addition to his administrative duties, Millikan continued an active research program, usually in collaboration with his doctoral candidates or postdoctoral fellows. A new area of study that attracted him was cosmic rays, those mysterious rays that caused electroscopes to lose their charge spontaneously. Millikan devoted great attention to this phenomenon during the 1920's and early 1930's. His research made it clear that these rays were of extraterrestrial origin, but he failed to recognize their true nature. For years, Millikan argued, often acrimoniously and in public, that the rays were electromagnetic—that is, similar to light but at invisible wavelengths. Other investigators, notably Arthur H. Compton, another American recipient of the Nobel Prize for Physics, had evidence that the rays consisted of charged particles, namely protons. Millikan was eventually proved wrong in this case.

Summary

Robert A. Millikan, a proud and dedicated man, was a leading figure in the American scientific community during the first half of the twentieth century, a period during which science in the United States rapidly rose to worldwide preeminence. Millikan traveled often to Europe, where he was well-known and respected in scientific circles as early as 1912. His success as an experimenter was widely recognized, but there were others, such as Michelson, of whom this could be said. What distinguished Millikan was his unswerving devotion to the *promotion* of science, not only in his personal laboratory but also in its institutional context and in the development of first-class educational opportunity for America's young scientific talent. He viewed science as a positive, vital element in the growth of America as a nation, a growth that had taken place dramatically in his own lifetime. He never failed to respond to critics of science who argued that science was inimical to religion or was responsible for human misery through loss of employment when resulting technology eliminated some jobs. As an advocate of the scientific component of modern society, he epitomized a man of science for the general public. He was described by *Time* magazine as "a man of twinkling blue-gray eyes and sparkling wit who knows how to make scientific complexities charming as well as awesome."

After his death in 1953, Millikan was eulogized by a colleague, L. A. DuBridge, as a contributor to knowledge, a creator of a scientific institution, and an inspiration to hundreds of students as well as a contributor to the maturing of science in America.

Bibliography

Compton, Arthur H. *The Cosmos of Arthur Holly Compton*. Edited by Marjorie Johnston with an introduction by Vannevar Bush. New York: Knopf, 1968. A collection of scientific and humanistic essays by a younger fellow physicist of Millikan, his adversary in the cosmic ray controversy. Contains a number of references to Millikan's work and a book review of Millikan's autobiography, listed below.

DuBridge, L. A., and Paul S. Epstein. "Robert Andrews Millikan." *National Academy of Sciences Biographical Memoirs* 33 (1959): 241-282. Written by two of Millikan's colleagues at the California Institute of Technology, this article surveys his life, work, and personality. Includes a full bibliography of Millikan's writings.

Kargon, Robert H. *The Rise of Robert Millikan: Portrait of a Life in American Science*. Ithaca, N.Y.: Cornell University Press, 1982. A carefully written, fully documented critical study of Millikan's life as illustrative of science in America during his lifetime—not a full biography. Kargon has drawn heavily on the Millikan papers deposited in the Archives of the California Institute of Technology. Contains a number of photographs not previously published.

Kevles, Daniel J. *The Physicists: The History of a Scientific Community*. New York: Knopf, 1978; London: Harvard University Press, 1995. Written by a contemporary historian of science, with documentation, this work contains significant coverage of Millikan's activities.

Millikan, Robert A. *The Autobiography of Robert A. Millikan*. New York: Prentice-Hall, 1950. Written when the author was nearly eighty years old, it present a firsthand account of how life and science had changed in America during his lifetime; narrates the details of his own career as he saw it. Includes photographs of Millikan, family members, and colleagues.

————. *The Electron: Its Isolation and Measurements and Determination of Some of Its Properties*. Edited with an introduction by Jesse W.M. DuMond. Chicago: University of Chicago Press, 1917. A facsimile edition of Millikan's original account of his electron studies as published in 1917. The editor, a friend and colleague of Millikan, has provided a valuable biographical study of Millikan and his work.

————. "The Electron and the Light-Quant from the Experimental Point of View," in *Physics*. New York: Elsevier, 1965. Millikan's Nobel Prize address describing his own investigations and discussing their significance in relation to the work of others.

————. *Electrons (+ and -), Protons, Photons, Neutrons and Cosmic Rays*. Rev. ed. Chicago: University of Chicago Press, 1947. Essentially an updating of *The Electron*. In both these volumes, Millikan addressed himself to the educated layman, putting the more mathematical passages at the end as appendices.

————. *Evolution in Science and Religion*. New Haven, Conn. and London: Yale University Press, 1927. Three invited lectures given at Yale University some years earlier dealing with the compatibility of science and religion, a favorite theme with Millikan.

Sopka, Katherine R. *Quantum Physics in America, 1920-1935*. Edited by I. Bernard Cohen. New York: Arno Press, 1980. Includes some discussion of Millikan's work and influence on physics in America.

Katherine R. Sopka

A. A. MILNE

Born: January 18, 1882; London, England
Died: January 31, 1956; Hartfield, Sussex, England
Area of Achievement: Literature
Contribution: Milne wrote light comedy and drama but was most successful with his stories and poems for children, especially those featuring Winnie-the-Pooh.

Early Life

Alan Alexander Milne was born in London in 1882 the third and youngest son of a school headmaster. Milne won a highly competitive scholarship to Westminster school in 1893 and entered Trinity College, Cambridge, in 1900. Although he was supposed to study mathematics, he devoted his time and energy to writing. In 1902 he was appointed editor of *Granta*, a prestigious literary magazine at the university.

On graduation in 1903, Milne went to London and became a freelance journalist, publishing mostly sketches and pieces of light humor. Milne sold several dozen poems and short items to *Punch*, the leading British humor magazine. In 1906 these brought him to the attention of *Punch*'s new editor, Owen Seaman, who offered him an assistantship. Milne accepted and, as a staff writer over the next eight years, published a constant stream of witty and charming trifles that established his reputation. Many of his pieces were collected and reappeared as books—*The Days Play* (1910), *The Holiday Round* (1912), and *Once a Week* (1914). In 1913, capping his growing success, he married his editor's goddaughter, Dorothy de Selincourt.

Shortly after the outbreak of World War I, Milne took a leave of absence from the magazine and enlisted in the Royal Warwickshire Regiment. Serving as a signals officer, he was sent to the front in France in late July, 1916, for the great battle of the Somme, where the British army suffered its most severe casualties in a long and bloody war. By early November, after three and one-half months in the trenches around the Mametz Woods, Milne was lucky to be sent home as an invalid with a severe case of trench fever. This probably saved his life.

After some months recuperating, he did the rest of his military service in Britain turning out propaganda for the War Office. He used his free time in the army to write plays. In the face of endless casualty lists, it seemed inappropriate to continue pub-

lishing his usual collections of amusing material from *Punch*. He did, however, allow a "fairy tale for adults," *Once on a Time*, to appear in 1917. That year, his friend J. M. Barrie, one of the most successful playwrights of the day, had Milne's short farce *Wurzel-Flummery* produced with some success in the West End (the London equivalent of Broadway) as part of an evening of his own short plays. On being demobilized from the army early in 1919, Milne gave up his editorial position at Punch to take up his own independent writing career full time.

Life's Work

Milne's first play after returning to civilian life, *Mr. Pim Passes By* (1919), was quickly produced on the West End to great acclaim and launched his career as a major writer for the London stage for the following decade. *Mr. Pim Passes By* was soon followed by seven other plays through 1924, including *The Dover Road* (1922) and *The Great Broxapp* (1923). In addition, Milne wrote a bestselling "whodunit," *The Red House Mystery* (1922), a novelized version of Mr. Pim, and published several new collections of his short humorous pieces and poems from *Punch, Vanity Fair*, and elsewhere titled *Not That it Matters* (1919), *If I May* (1920), and *The Sunny Side* (1922). In the midst of this flood of productivity, in August, 1920, the Milnes had their first and only child, a little boy they named Christopher Robin.

Milne was rather shy and reserved, as his father had been. Though Christopher Robin was usually looked after by a nursemaid, Milne began to write poems and songs to amuse him when they spent time together. His wife suggested that these should be published. After some had appeared individually, Milne had them collected as *When We Were Very Young* (1924), which rapidly became a considerable success. Though Milne continued to turn out a generally well received drawing-room comedy for the West End stage every year or two for the rest of the decade, the poems, songs, and stories written for his son began to overshadow his other work.

As Christopher Robin grew a little older, his father made him and his teddy bear the leading characters in a series of short stories. They appeared in 1926 as *Winnie-the-Pooh*, with delightful illustrations by an old colleague from *Punch*, E. H. Shepard. The book immediately captured the hearts of children and adults alike across the English-speaking world. This double success in the children's market was soon followed by another equally popular volume of songs and poems, *Now We Are Six* (1927), and a second book of Pooh stories, *The House at Pooh Corner* (1928), which added the wise owl, Piglet, Kanga, Eeyore the gloomy donkey, and the assertive Tigger to the cast of characters. Milne's fertile whimsy and Shepard's graceful line drawings used the real Christopher Robin as a model for the literary one. The physical surroundings of the Milne weekend cottage in the Sussex countryside were turned by Shepard's sketches into the enchanting woodland of Christopher and Pooh's adventures.

In 1930 Milne, capitalizing on his triumph as a gentle entertainer of young children, adapted Kenneth Grahame's delightful nursery classic *The Wind and the Willows* (1908) for the stage as *Toad of Toad Hall*. This added to his sweeping success in writing for children.

For Milne and his son, Christopher Robin the literary creation and his teddy bear became something of a burden. As he grew older, the shy boy did not care to be teased by his schoolmates about being a literary icon. His father had to suppress his displeasure that his writing for children had eclipsed the rest of his career. At the same time, the taste for his kind of amusing drawing-room comedies, mysteries, and fanciful romances began to fade.

In the 1930's, economic depression and the rise of the Nazi dictatorship cast a shadow over Europe. Milne had no further great successes in the West End, though he continued to write plays that were produced, among them *Michael and Mary* (1930) and *Miss Elizabeth Bennett* (1936), an adaptation of Jane Austen's 1813 novel *Pride and Prejudice*. He also turned out a novel, *Two People* (1931), and two collections of stories, *The Secret* (1929) and *The Magic Hill* (1937).

In the darkening political climate, Milne became active in public affairs by raising an articulate voice against the folly of another war in *Peace with Honour* (1934). As a veteran of the trenches he had earned the right to be heard respectfully and became a figure of some importance in the antiwar movement. At the decade's end he worked on his *Autobiography* (1939; published in Britain as *It's Too Late Now*), which appeared just as the dam burst and World War II began.

Milne published little during the war, though he bitterly denounced Nazism in several widely circulated pieces that justified the conduct of the war against fascism. He published a volume of poetry, *Behind the Lines* (1940), on life on the home front. The Milnes watched anxiously as a grown-up Christopher Robin went off to war as an officer in the Royal Engineers in 1942. Their son served in the Middle East, Tunisia, and Italy, where, in October, 1944, he was wounded in the head. Christopher recovered and returned home safely.

Milne's career did not revive after the war, though Winnie-the-Pooh insured his continuing prosperity. He published a novel, *Chloe Marr* (1946); two collections of short stories, *Birthday Party* (1948) and *A Table Near the Band* (1950); *The Norman Church* (1948), a long philosophical poem; a collection of essays called *Year in Year Out* (1952); and a final play, *After the Flood* (1951). His audience for light comedy had vanished.

In October, 1952, Milne suffered a severe stroke. An operation that he endured in December failed, leaving him partially paralysed. This normally sunny-tempered if shy man spent the last years of his life in a wheelchair as a difficult patient, worrying about his estranged relationship with his son. He died in January, 1956. Christopher Robin's teddy bear, however, had been sent to the United States where Milne's American publisher engaged him to promote the continuing sales of the children's books before he was eventually retired to a place of honor on display at a branch of the New York Public Library.

Summary

A. A. Milne's career as a leading dramatist of the 1920's, as a craftsman of drawing-room comedies and whimsical romances (a label he hated), was eventually eclipsed by his brilliantly imaginative writing for children. His creation, Winnie-the-Pooh, has taken his place in the world of classic children's literature alongside Lewis Carroll's *Alice's Adventures in Wonderland* (1865), Beatrix Potter's *The Tale of Peter Rabbit* (1900), J. M. Barrie's *Peter Pan* (1904), and Kenneth Grahame's *The Wind in the Willows*. At the time of Milne's death, his American publishers estimated they had sold seven million copies of the Pooh stories in various editions. The stories have continued to sell steadily since then and have been translated into twenty-five foreign languages, from Bulgarian to Japanese. Even a Latin version, *Winnie Ille Pu*, was successful in 1960. Milne's bear became the subject of a satire on literary criticism, *The Pooh Perplex* (1963) by F. C. Crews, and the star of a Walt Disney animated film (1966). If the author is largely forgotten, his creation remains a long-lived best-seller and a recognizable icon in toy shops and cartoons across the industrial world.

Bibliography

Connolly, Paula. *Winnie-the-Pooh and the House at Pooh Corner: Recovering Arcadia*. New York: Twayne, 1995. A literary study by an academic tightly focused on Milne's output as a writer for children. Connolly treats his work seriously, putting it in historical and critical context with other classics for young readers.

Haring-Smith, Tori. *A. A. Milne: A Critical Bibliography*. New York: Garland, 1982. This provides a thorough and extensive guide both to Milne's own work and to the writing about him. It is indispensable for any extensive research project.

Milne, A. A. *Autobiography*. New York: Dutton, 1939; as *It's Too Late Now: The Autobiography of a Writer*, London: Methuen, 1939. Milne's informative account of himself spends more time on his childhood and youth than on his years of success, about which he is disarmingly modest. There is relatively little theater gossip, and he treats his frontline service in World War I briefly, underplaying the grim realities. His impatience with the overshadowing of his work by the writing for children is only touched on. As in all his work, the principal intention is to entertain and amuse.

Milne, Christopher. *Enchanted Places*. London: Methuen, 1974; New York: Dutton, 1975. Christopher Robin's own memoir on what his early life was like presented his father as a cool and rather detached figure. *The Path Through the Trees* (1979), his subsequent memoir about his adult life, adds a few details about his father but is warmer in tone and is dedicated to his memory.

Swann, Thomas Burnett. *A. A. Milne*. New York: Twayne, 1971. A literary study by an academic who reviews all of Milne's output systematically, arranged by category, and, within each, chronologically. Swann summarizes the individual works and offers a brief chronology of Milne's life and literary career. His critical judgements reinforce the conventional view that the writing for children was brilliant and the balance is rather deservedly forgotten.

Thwaite, Ann. *A. A. Milne: His Life*. London and Boston: Faber, 1990. This full and careful study of Milne's life is closely based on his personal and literary papers and on interviews with his surviving extended family. This is a sympathetic work by a writer of children's literature herself and is the only large-scale biography.

———, ed. *A. A. Milne: The Man Behind Winnie-the-Pooh*. New York: Random House, 1990. Interesting biography of Milne's life and desire for success, which put him ever in the shadow of his creations and eventually estranged him from his son, Christopher.

S. J. Stearns

JOAN MIRÓ

Born: April 20, 1893; Barcelona, Spain
Died: December 25, 1983; Palma, Majorca, Spain
Area of Achievement: Art
Contribution: The work of Miró, Spanish painter, sculptor, and ceramist, is acclaimed for its highly individualistic style, abstract as well as figurative, and is characterized by its vivacious fantasy. Many critics regard Miró as the greatest artist of the Surrealist movement.

Early Life

Born in Barcelona, Joan Miró was the first son of Michel Miró Adzirias and Dolores Ferrá. Descending from a strong family tradition of craftsmanship, Miró's father was a prosperous goldsmith and watchmaker, his paternal grandfather a blacksmith, and his maternal grandfather a cabinetmaker. The young Miró, although a poor student at school, began to draw at the age of eight and announced soon thereafter that he wished to become a painter. In 1907, he was enrolled at the Escuela de Bellas Artes (school of fine arts), the same official academy in Barcelona where, some twelve years earlier, Pablo Picasso had studied. Modesto Urgell and José Pascó, his teachers at the school, recognized Miró as a promising pupil and encouraged his interest in primitive painting.

Miró's family, convinced that an artist's life was too precarious, insisted that he take an office job; he obediently accepted a job as a store clerk in 1910, when he was seventeen years old. Bored, depressed, and demoralized by the position, however, he suffered a nervous breakdown, and his father sent him to recuperate at a farm overlooking the coastal plain, south of Tarragona. This farm and the nearby hill town of Montroig (red mountain) were to become places of great importance and inspiration in Miró's life.

The artist's parents eventually realized that they had no choice but to allow their son to pursue an artistic career, and in 1912 he was enrolled in a Barcelona art school operated by the architect Francesc Galí. During his years at Galí's school, where he painted his first canvases, Miró discovered the work of Claude Monet, Vincent van Gogh, Paul Gauguin, and Paul Cézanne, as well as the Fauves and cubists. In 1915, however, dissatisfied with traditional art instruction, Miró established himself in a studio that he shared with his friend, E. C. Ricart. During this time, Miró's paintings, influenced by van Gogh and the Fauves, and later by the expressionists, were already marked by a hint of humor. Among these early canvases were his first *Self-Portrait, Portrait of Ricart*, and *The Chauffeur*, all dating from 1917, some expressionist nudes, and *Landscape with a Donkey*. The dealer José Dalmau took an interest in his work and gave Miró his first showing at the Galeria Dalmau in Barcelona in 1918.

Life's Work

After his first exhibition in Barcelona, Miró's work exhibited a dramatic change. He began a series of paintings that combined minutely realistic detail with light and subtle color. Critics have compared the earliest of these, *Montroig Landscape* (1919), with works by the Italian primitives. Among Miró's neoprimitive yet sophisticated Catalan landscapes is *The Olive Grove* (1919).

In 1919, Miró briefly visited Paris, to which he would return every year from then on. There he was welcomed by Picasso, whom he had seen previously in Barcelona, but whom he had never dared to approach. Picasso, who in 1921 purchased Miró's second *Self-Portrait*, introduced him to the avant-garde poets Pierre Reverdy, Max Jacob, and the Dadaist Tristan Tzara. It was during this Paris visit that Miró also became acquainted with the work of Henri Rousseau. After his return to the Barcelona area later in 1919, his works, though still faithful to reality, began to show cubist influences, especially in his basic drawing style, which became more angular and formalized, with greater emphasis on planes. A series of still lifes, among them *Still Life with Toy Horse* and *Table with Rabbit*, both completed in 1920, combine cubist influences with colorful imagery inspired in part by Catalan folk art and the Catalan landscape. These still lifes were shown in Miró's first Paris exhibition, held in 1921 at the Galérie La Licorne.

The outstanding work of Miró's early career, and later referred to by Miró as "the crowning work" of his life, was *The Farm*, completed in 1922, a painting on which he had worked for nine months. (It was later purchased by Ernest Hemingway.) The work possesses Miró's typical freshness of approach, and, while it reflects his admiration for Rousseau, it also reveals an intricate calculation of compositional effect. It marks the end of Miró's "poetic realist" period.

Several months of doubt and self-searching followed the completion of this work. The artist finally emerged from his despair after meeting in Paris with the painter André Masson, and the writers Jacques Prévert and Henry Miller, among others. In *The Farmer's Wife* and *The Carbide*, both of 1922-1923, realism blends with a strong element of fantasy and greater intensity of mood.

By the early 1920's, Miró had become acquainted with the Dadaist poets. During this period, he also met the painter Max Ernst and the poet André Breton and through them was introduced to Surrealism. In 1923, during a stay in Montroig, Miró worked on two canvases (completed in 1924) that determined the future course of his art: *The Tilled Field* and *Catalan Landscape* (*The Hunter*). In the former there is still Miró's favorite sunshine-yellow tonality, but there is also a wild, almost Boschlike transposition of images and animal shapes loosely derived from nature. In the latter canvas, Miró moved closer to a kind of Surrealist abstraction, his imagery sometimes suggesting organic forms observed through a microscope, sometimes evoking the sense of realistic objects through symbolic shapes. Among the signers of Breton's "Surrealist Manifesto" of 1924, Miró was hailed by the poet as "the most 'surrealist' of us all." One of Miró's most engaging paintings of 1924-1925 (and one of his most significant works) was *The Harlequin Carnival*, with its tiny allusive figures, more "signs" than forms, and its playful poetic fantasy and festive color.

In 1925 Miró participated in the first Surrealist group exhibition, held at the Galérie Pierre, Paris. There he was impressed by the work of Paul Klee. The following year Miró, in collaboration with Max Ernst, worked on costumes and settings for Serge Diaghilev's production of *Romeo and Juliet*. This concession to so-called "bourgeois" modernism, however, infuriated Breton and the orthodox Surrealists, who condemned him for his lack of seriousness. Miró's essentially intuitive approach was indeed far removed from the more rigid, intellectual attitude of Breton, although the two were able to maintain a friendly relationship. Miró painted one of his most celebrated and impressive pictures in 1926—*Dog Barking at the Moon*. Sometimes interpreted as symbolizing the link between the physical and the intellectual world, the painting has also been regarded as an almost absurdist statement about the human condition.

In 1928, Miró was married to Pilar Jonosca and traveled to Holland. His admiration for Jan Vermeer and the intimate realism of the Dutch genre paintings led to a series of works entitled *Dutch Interiors*. Next, Miró deliberately sacrificed elegance of line and festiveness of color in such subsequent works as *Spanish Dancer* (1928) and his series of dream-vision "Imaginary Portraits." In the early 1930's, he began to experiment with collages, *papiers collés*, lithography, and etchings, and, in years to come, he illustrated many books with color lithographs. He exhibited his first Surrealist "Sculpture-objects" at the Galérie Pierre in 1931. They were characterized, like his paintings, by great freedom of form and mocking fantasy. The best known of these sculptures of the 1930's is *Object poétique* (1936), a construction of found objects, including a derby hat, a toy fish, a doll's leg, and a map, topped by a stuffed parrot.

Miró exhibited with the Surrealist painters in the Paris Salon des Indépendents in 1932, and in 1933 produced some of his most masterful paintings, including *Composition*, a large elegant canvas in which silhouetted free forms, analogous to some of Jean Arp's reliefs of the same period, were executed in rich black against subtle background tones. Like others of Miró's best paintings of the early 1930's, this work contains an intense primitivism that links it to the prehistoric cave-paintings of northern Spain.

A brutal eroticism accompanied by monstrous forms invaded Miró's work beginning from about 1934, accompanied by a note of intense anxiety—reflecting his awareness of the imminence of civil war in Spain—that appeared in his paintings of 1935-1936. Although rarely overtly political, Miró, like Picasso and unlike Salvador Dalí, supported the Spanish Republic in its resistance of Fascism. In 1937, the year of Picasso's *Guernica*, Miró worked for five months on *Still Life with an Old Shoe*, a painting in which he expressed his anguished feeling for his country and the poverty of the Spanish people. His large mural, *The Reaper*, painted for the Pavilion of the Spanish Republic at the Paris Exposition of 1937 was an anguished and savage protest, as was his anti-Franco poster of that year, *Aidez l'Espangne* (help Spain). In *Nocturne* (1938), Miró's favorite yellow-colored earth is overwhelmed by a stark, black sky, relieved only by some amorphous stellar shapes.

Between 1936 and 1940, Miró lived in France and did not return to Spain. In 1939, when residing in the village of Varengeville, Normandy, he abruptly turned away from his so-called "wild" paintings and the horrors they evoked and began a series of small lyrical paintings on burlap. These were followed by a group of twenty-three gouaches entitled *Constellations*, on which he was working when the Nazis approached Paris in 1940. At this time, Miró managed to get himself, his wife, and their one child, Dolores, on the last train leaving for the Spanish border. The family went first to Montroig, then settled in Palma, Majorca, with Miró's wife's family.

From 1942 to 1944, Miró, having returned to Barcelona, painted almost entirely on paper. In 1944, he began to work in ceramics, in collaboration with the Catalan ceramist Joseph Lloréns Artigas. Miró divided his time between Barcelona and Paris from 1944 on. His painted compositions became more elaborate, often containing repetitious and self-perpetuating imagery. Such paintings as *Woman* and *Little Girl in Front of the Sun* (1946), however, did exhibit much of his former energy and exuberance.

In 1947, Miró, now world famous, went to the United States for the first time and was impressed by the country's vitality. He received commissions for two large murals, one of which was eventually hung in the Cincinnati Art Museum, and the other, executed in 1950, was commissioned for the Graduate Center at Harvard University in Cambridge, Massachusetts. In 1956, Miró settled once again in Palma, Majorca, where he lived and worked until his death. In 1957-1958, he designed two walls for the garden of the United Nations Educational, Scientific, and Cultural Organization headquarters in Paris. A series of large painted mural compositions followed in 1961-1962; the unifying motif of these was the development of a single line on a monochrome ground.

Following his ceramic sculpture of the early 1950's, some of which displayed a primitive totemic quality, sculpture in bronze played an important role in Miró's work in the 1960's and 1970's. His sculptures were included in a large Miró show at the Galérie Pierre Matisse, Paris, in the spring of 1973.

Summary

Although Joan Miró himself rejected any attempt to categorize his art, especially disdaining the label "abstract," the artist is, nevertheless, most often identified with the abstract Surrealist movement, of which he was one of the most original and sensitive exponents. His highly personalized idiom, replete with great charm and wit comparable in a general way to the art of Klee, remained entirely and recognizably his own.

Miró's free-form, associational, highly colored, and decorative art has influenced countless other artists in both the fine and the applied arts, who have profited from the imaginative possibilities of his artistic language. A Catalan who always clung proudly to the language, culture, and landscape of his native province, Miró worked forms of nature into his own personal vocabulary of sign images.

Many future currents of painting were anticipated in Miró's work. Several critics have even maintained that it is Miró, and not Henri Matisse or Picasso, who was the most visionary of the early modern masters. The beauty of nature, rustic folklore, symbols of age-old fertility cults, subtle psychological experiences, and highly sophisticated literary concepts were all embraced within Miró's cosmic scope. What is likely to assure the artist's immortality is his irony, risqué puns, humor, vitality, and the fascinating realm of assorted creatures that were produced by his inexhaustible imagination and reproduced upon his canvases.

Bibliography

Greenberg, Clement. *Joan Miró.* New York: Quadrangle Press, 1948. In this 133-page work containing a list of exhibitions, a bibliography, and numerous monochrome reproductions, Greenberg ranks Miró with Matisse, Picasso, and others as one of the formative masters of modern painting. He describes the artist's early years, the influences of cubism and Surrealism, his mastery of Art Nouveau, and his reach beyond Surrealism to comedy and hedonism in his later years.

Lubar, Robert S. "Miró's Defiance of Painting." *Art in America* 82, no. 9 (September, 1994). Examines the art of Miró and its rebellious aspects.

Meisler, Stanley. "For Joan Miró, Poetry and Painting Were the Same." *Smithsonian* 24, no. 8 (November, 1993). Discusses Miró's life and works.

Miró, Joan. *Joan Miró: Selected Writings and Interviews.* Edited by Margit Rowell. Translated by Paul Auster and Patricia Mathews. Boston: Hall, 1986; London: Thames and Hudson, 1987. Rowell, in this work, offers the reader a fascinating firsthand account of the complex weaving together of the life and work of an artist. Through the artist's letters, statements, interviews, notebook entries and poems, Miró is allowed to speak for himself. The lengthy work contains photos of the artist, some monochrome reproductions, and a biographical chronology.

Penrose, Roland. *Miró*. London: Thames and Hudson, and New York: Abrams, 1970. A biography of Miró that is interspersed with critical commentary and numerous reproductions, both in color and black-and-white. Includes a bibliography, a list of the illustrations contained in the book, and an index.

Perucho, Joan. *Joan Miró y Cataluña*. New York: Tudor, 1968; London: Fine Arts Collection, 1988. Perucho succeeds admirably in analyzing the impact of Miró's native land on the artist's life and work in this book. The work, written in interfacing Spanish, English, French, and German text, contains a chronology of the artist's life and work, an index of works, a bibliography and many black-and-white and color plates.

Soby, James Thrall. *Joán Miró*. New York: Museum of Modern Art, 1959. Soby maintains, in this somewhat dated book, that Miró was one of the most instinctively talented artists of his generation and that he advanced the art of his predecessors (such as Picasso) in a new and valid direction. Although brief, this interesting book also contains a list of exhibitions, a bibliography, and numerous black-and-white and color reproductions.

Stich, Sidra, ed. *Miró: The Development of a Sign Language*. St. Louis, Mo.: Washington University, 1980. The aim of this well-written exhibition catalog is to clarify the origins of the many elements of Miró's style and subject matter. It examines the sources of the artist's neoprimitivism and clarifies the nature and consequences of his contribution to a sign language, a pictorial element envisioned at a primary sensory level. This very brief work also contains numerous monochrome reproductions of the artist's works.

Genevieve Slomski

YUKIO MISHIMA
Kimitake Hiraoka

Born: January 14, 1925; Tokyo, Japan
Died: November 25, 1970; Tokyo, Japan
Area of Achievement: Literature
Contribution: Mishima was a writer of great power, whose life became a performance, ultimately a tragic performance. At the time of his suicide, he was widely regarded as a leading candidate for the Nobel Prize in Literature.

Early Life

Yukio Mishima was born Kimitake Hiraoka in Tokyo, Japan, on January 14, 1925. His father was Azusa Hiraoka, a senior official in the Ministry of Agriculture. His mother was Shizue (Hashi) Hiraoka. Because of his father's position, the boy was able to attend the prestigious Gakushuin (the Peers' School). He proved a fine scholar and was cited for excellence by the emperor himself. During his schoolboy days, his complex nature was already evident. He was a gentle, bookish child, with a delicate constitution. Nevertheless, he was drawn to stories that portrayed the valiant deaths of warriors or their ritual suicides. This fascination with ritualized death persisted throughout his work and life.

Mishima began to write at an early age and was publishing short stories in the magazine *Bungei Bunka* (literary culture) before the age of sixteen. In 1944, he entered the University of Tokyo to undertake the study of law. He was graduated in 1947, but his education was briefly interrupted by his conscription into the army in February, 1945. He saw no action in the closing months of the war, and his period of active service was short. Still, it was to affect him profoundly in the years to come. In *Taiyō to tetsu* (1968; *Sun and Steel*, 1970), he describes the process by which his personal philosophy of physical prowess and the beauty of violent death began to emerge as he underwent the rigors of military training. In 1947, he received a position in the Ministry of Finance, but he resigned it in the following year to devote himself exclusively to writing.

Life's Work

While he was still a schoolboy, Mishima met Yasunari Kawabata, who was to receive the Nobel Prize in Literature in 1968. The elder writer not only served as a literary influence but also became a lifelong friend. Mishima's decision to use a pseudonym may have been prompted by the subject matter of his first, and very successful, novel, *Kamen no kokuhaku* (1949; *Confessions of a Mask*, 1958), an autobiographical tale of a shy, sensitive young man who is wrestling with his homosexual and sadomasochistic impulses. Critics have suggested that this novel set the tone for the rest of Mishima's fiction: He had adopted not only a new name but also a new personality. Henceforward, he would mask his timidity, vulnerability, and aestheticism with an arrogant, even a provocative, persona. While retaining the love for fine prose and for the Japanese and Western classics that he had shared with Kawabata, he began to affect a strident manliness. He sought the ideal of male beauty and, through a regimen of weight lifting, transformed his puny physique. He studied boxing and karate until he achieved proficiency in both. He made himself into an excellent swordsman and imbibed deeply the tradition of the samurai.

Throughout the 1950's and 1960's, Mishima produced a succession of critically acclaimed novels, including *Shiosai* (1954; *The Sound of Waves*, 1956), *Kinkakuji* (1956; *The Temple of the Golden Pavilion*, 1959), *Utage no ato* (1960; *After the Banquet*, 1963), and *Gogo no eikō* (1963; *The Sailor Who Fell from Grace with the Sea*, 1965). On June 1, 1958, he married Yoko Sugiyama. He eventually became the father of two children—a daughter, Noriko, and a son, Iichiro.

Mishima was prolific in genres other than the novel. He wrote many short stories, most of which are uncollected or collected in Japanese editions only. A collection in English translation, *Death in Midsummer and Other Stories*, appeared in 1966. Among the stories in this volume is one of Mishima's most celebrated, "Yūkoku" ("Patriotism"), the haunting and prophetic story of a young army officer and his wife. When a group of his close friends rebel against their military command, he is torn by his loyalty to them and to the nation. As an honorable alternative, he chooses a warrior's form of suicide. His wife assists him before killing herself. Every detail of the preparations and of the acts themselves is graphically described.

Mishima also became one of Japan's leading playwrights. By his early thirties, he had published some thirty plays, several of which are available in English. His modernized versions of traditional Japanese No plays were very popular. These can be sampled in the 1957 collection in English, *Five Modern Nō Plays*. His play *Sado kōshaku fujin* (1965; *Madame de Sade*, 1967) employs the Western setting of revolutionary France. When many of his plays were produced, Mishima himself directed them.

He grew increasingly versatile in his work, while he grew increasingly flamboyant in his life. He became a motion picture actor, screenwriter, and director—even appearing in a gangster film. He became a recording artist. For a time, he achieved more fame as a television celebrity than he had gained from his many literary prizes and awards. He built an Italianate villa in Tokyo and filled it with English antiques. He enrolled his wife in classes in Western cooking. His writing began to contain more allusions to French literature than to Japanese literature. Yet he came to oppose the Westernization of Japan, even to hate it. In a stream of essays and articles, he advocated a return to the samurai tradition. He organized a small private army made up of young apostles from the university. Mishima named this group the Tate No Kai (Shield Society). His elitism, his militancy, and his idealization of the old Japan disturbed many people. The Shield Society stirred memories of the military adventurism that had led Japan into World War II. Still, Mishima's charismatic personality and provocative behavior made him fine copy for journalists and a much sought-after guest for television shows.

He ended his life with a *beau geste*. On November 25, 1970, he and four members of the Shield Society invaded the headquarters of the Eastern Ground Defense Forces, took the commanding officer hostage, and demanded that the troops be assembled. Japan's constitution, forced upon her at the end of the war by the victorious Allies, was for Mishima the codification of the pernicious Westernizing of his country. From a balcony, he harangued the twelve hundred soldiers for their failure to rise in rebellion against the constitution. The men responded to his speech with laughter and derision. He then knelt and, in the traditional seppuku ceremony, committed suicide. He disemboweled himself with a dagger, and one of his followers beheaded him with a sword.

Mishima completed his tetralogy *Hōjō no umi* (*The Sea of Fertility: A Cycle of Four Novels*) on the last day of his life. The novels in the tetralogy are *Hara no yuki* (1969; *Spring Snow*, 1972), *Homba* (1969, *Runaway Horses*, 1973), *Akatsuki no tera* (1970; *The Temple of Dawn*, 1973), and *Tennin gosui* (1971; *The Decay of the Angel*, 1974). Critical opinion on this work remains divided, some critics seeing the tetralogy as the summation of Mishima's career while others see a decline from his earlier achievements.

Summary

Yukio Mishima had written his own death scene in his 1960 story "Patriotism." He had later dramatized his death by adapting "Patriotism" as a film, which he directed and in which he acted the leading role. So prophetic was the suicide scene that Mishima's family had the film suppressed after his death. The form of suicide Mishima chose, seppuku, is significant. It tests the warrior's courage and tenacity because, after driving the knife into his belly, he must draw it slowly from one side of his abdomen to the other until his intestines spill out of his body. The act requires physical strength as well as strength of purpose. That seppuku is incomprehensible to the Western mind is precisely the point Mishima was making.

It could be argued that, with the few exceptions which immediately come to mind (for example, Miguel de Cervantes, Ernest Hemingway), the lives of writers are no more dramatic than those of the general population. As a class, writers are more likely to be observers and commentators than active participants. Mishima is, however, such a striking exception to this rule of thumb, that his fascinating life and horrifying death may tend to overshadow the fact that he is probably Japan's greatest postwar writer.

Bibliography

Keene, Donald. *Dawn to the West: Japanese Literature of the Modern Era, Fiction.* New York: Holt Rinehart, 1984. A massive study of the fiction produced since the Japanese "Enlightenment" in the nineteenth century. The last fifty-eight pages of the text are devoted to Mishima.

———. "Mishima in 1958." *Paris Review* 35, no. 134 (Spring 1995). Examines the life of Mishima, his views on his own works (including his surprise that his novels were popular beyond Japan), and his suicide in 1970.

———. *Modern Japanese Literature: An Anthology.* London: Thames and Hudson, and New York: Grove Press, 1956. Pieces compiled by Keene from various genres. His last selection is "Omi," extracted from *Confessions of a Mask.* The evaluation of Mishima in Keene's long introduction is of historical interest, because it was made so early in the novelist's career.

"The Man Japan Wants to Forget." *The Economist* 337, no. 7940 (November 11, 1995). Considers Mishima's work as a writer and political activist who challenged Japan's evolution after World War II.

Nathan, John. *Mishima: A Biography.* Boston: Little Brown, 1974; London: Hamilton, 1975. The author of this biography, a translator and professor of Japanese literature, was acquainted with Mishima. He provides a full and detailed account of Mishima's life. Includes illustrations and a selected list of Mishima's principal works.

Petersen, Gwenn Boardman. *The Moon in the Water: Understanding Tanizaki, Kawabata, and Mishima.* Honolulu: University Press of Hawaii, 1979. Pages 201-336 are devoted to Mishima. A partial chronology and a general bibliography are provided.

Pronko, Leonard C. *Guide to Japanese Drama.* 2d ed. Boston: Hall, 1984. An entry in the Asian Literature Bibliography series. Here, Mishima is considered exclusively as a dramatist. Pronko devotes several pages to discussions of *Five Modern Nō Plays* and *Madam de Sade.*

Ueda, Makoto. *Modern Japanese Writers and the Nature of Literature.* Stanford, Calif.: Stanford University Press, 1976. A study of eight major writers of modern Japan. Pages 219-261 are devoted to Mishima. Although many of the novels are discussed, Ueda places special emphasis upon *The Temple of the Golden Pavilion.*

Yamanouchi, Hisaaki. *The Search for Authenticity in Modern Japanese Literature.* Cambridge and New York: Cambridge University Press, 1978. Chapter 6, "A Phantasy World: Mishima Yukio," argues essentially that Mishima's alienation from the external world drove him to create a world not only for his literature but also for his life.

Yourcenar, Marguerite. *Mishima: A Vision of the Void.* Translated by Alberto Manguel in collaboration with the author. Henley-on-Thames: Ellis, and New York: Farrar Straus, 1986. In this short work, first published in French in 1980, the distinguished novelist Yourcenar explores Mishima's life and works, with the emphasis on the latter.

Patrick Adcock

WILLIAM MITCHELL

Born: December 29, 1879; Nice, France
Died: February 19, 1936; New York, New York
Area of Achievement: The military
Contribution: An advocate of air power in the armed forces, Mitchell worked to create a separate air force and to develop strategic doctrines that would utilize its potential in the conduct of modern war.

Early Life

William Lendrum Mitchell was born during his parents' visit to France in 1879. His paternal grandfather, Alexander Mitchell, was born in Scotland, migrated to Wisconsin, and became a successful businessman and investor. His grandfather served in Congress, a path followed by his father, John Lendrum Mitchell, who served in both houses of Congress as representative of Wisconsin. Mitchell, one of nine children, attended private schools in Wisconsin and received his college degree from George Washington University after his military enlistment.

"Billy" Mitchell's military career began with the declaration of war against Spain in 1898. He enlisted as a private with the Wisconsin volunteers and was quickly commissioned a lieutenant in the Signal Corps. He served on the staff of General Fitzhugh Lee, and when Cuba fell to American troops, he transferred to the Philippines, where the war continued in 1899 against Philippine nationalists led by Emilio Aguinaldo. There, he served on the staff of General Arthur MacArthur, whose son, Douglas, later served on the courtmartial board that convicted Mitchell of insubordination and ordered his five-year suspension from active military duty.

After the war in the Philippines ended in 1902, Mitchell returned to the United States with the army Signal Corps. He was assigned to duty in Alaska, where he commanded units charged with laying three thousand miles of telegraphic lines connecting the territory with the United States. In 1912, he was sent to the army's General Staff School as a young and promising officer. His first real encounter with the untried but intriguing flying machine was in 1908, when he served as an army representative to a demonstration flight of a Wright brothers airplane at Fort Myer. He later learned the fundamentals of piloting from Orville Wright and

soloed in 1914. Always sensitive to technological changes that modified traditional doctrines of warfare, Mitchell quickly appreciated the tactical uses of manned flight.

As a young officer serving outside the United States, Mitchell gained new insights into the geopolitical implications of modern warfare. His experiences in Cuba, the Philippines, and Alaska focused Mitchell's attention on the strategic significance of the Pacific area. Before the United States entered World War I, he was sent to Spain as an observer and then to France in 1917. After the war, he traveled in Europe, and he toured the Pacific and Far East in 1923 and 1924. He understood the significance of the growing power of Japan better than many of his military contemporaries, leading him to argue forcefully for air power as America's first line of defense, especially in the Pacific. He formed close relationships with the important early air-power spokesmen abroad and after World War I was awarded not only the Distinguished Service Cross but also France's Croix de Guerre, as well as special commendations by the British and Italian governments.

Life's Work

After 1900, the potential development of motorized air power for military purposes struggled for recognition and adequate financial support. The War Department, through the Board of Ordinance and Fortification, believed that dirigibles were of greater value than fixed-wing aircraft for military use, especially for reconnaissance. It was not until 1909 that Orville and Wilbur Wright produced a test aircraft for the army's Signal Corps. Mitchell agreed with other military strategists that air power should be used not for tactical support for ground troops or strategic bombing, but for observation, in part because technological problems prevented the production of fast, large, and reliable aircraft capable of sustained air operations. The First Aero Squadron, composed of Curtiss biplanes, was activated for service in Mexico in 1916 to support "Black Jack" Pershing's expedition into northern Mexico to pursue Pancho Villa's revolutionary force. Mechanical and maintenance problems, however, soon grounded all aircraft. Between 1916 and 1918, American intervention in World War I provided the new advocates of air power with ample opportunities to perfect superior aircraft and to develop new strategies for the deployment and use of winged aircraft.

The Air Service of the American Expeditionary Forces (AEF), under the direction of the Signal Corps, initially asked for five thousand pilots and planes to accompany the ground forces to France. The Army Air Service grew rapidly under the supervision of three ambitious young officers, operating very much on their own: Brigadier General Mitchell, Brigadier General Benjamin D. Foulois, and Colonel Reynal C. Bolling, soon joined by a senior officer, Major General Mason M. Patrick. Mitchell assumed the position of air combat commander and chief advocate of the AEF's air-power contribution to the war in France. Mitchell argued for a separate role for American pilots at the front: to observe and to protect the separate operational front assigned to the American land forces under the command of General John J. Pershing by the joint Allied command. A combined attack of air and land forces was planned for the St. Mihiel salient in September, 1918. Mitchell was given the command of six hundred aircraft—a combined force of American, French, Italian, and Portuguese air forces—and coordinated assault operations with a joint attack by American and French ground forces, successfully reducing the salient and capturing more than fifteen thousand prisoners. The victory not only established the integrity of American infantry forces but also proved the success of combined air-land operations.

With the return of peace in 1919, American advocates of air power returned to the United States prepared to lobby for public and governmental support for the establishment of a permanent and well-financed commitment to military aviation. Mitchell was the most enthusiastic advocate for a new role for air operations in modern warfare. The debate on air power after 1919 involved both the army and the navy, often focusing on the activities of Mitchell and creating a sharp split between the two services on the future of air power in the United States military. While both services acknowledged the essential usefulness of air operations, the navy rejected the proposition that air power alone could win future wars. Mitchell's advocacy of aerial warfare both antagonized and threatened the navy's efforts to build adequate public support in the postwar era. Mitchell defined four basic functions for the new air service: to destroy the enemy's air effectiveness, to destroy enemy ground targets, to

demoralize enemy ground forces, and to gather information. The suggestion by Mitchell that adequate air power was the key to coastal defense irritated naval strategists. Focusing on the Pacific as an area of future military operations, Mitchell suggested that air power was the most efficient substitute for naval power; aircraft development thus warranted adequate congressional support and a separate institutional identity. In 1920, the reorganization of the army elevated the Air Service to an equal rank with other military services.

Never adept at mediating interservice arguments over the role of air power in the armed forces, Mitchell planned a dramatic demonstration. He secured a role for the Air Service in bombing tests planned by the navy in 1921 to test the vulnerability of battleships to air attack. The captured German battleship *Ostfriesland* was anchored near Chesapeake Bay, and Mitchell's pilots sent it to the bottom with heavy bombs, in disregard of the rules set by the navy for the demonstration. Mitchell's success strengthened his congressional supporters, but alienated his colleagues in the military. This incident led the army to remove Mitchell from the center of political debate over appropriations and reorganization by sending him to Europe, where he consulted with other primary architects of modern aerial warfare: General Sir Hugh Trenchard of Great Britain's Royal Air Force and General Giulio Douhet of the Italian air force, author of *Command of the Air* (1921). Mitchell agreed with Douhet that strategic bombing, when directed against enemy urban centers and their civilian populations, could effectively diminish morale and support for a war; nevertheless, Mitchell still viewed strategic air power as a substitute for naval power and the key to the coastal defense of the United States. American strategic bombing in World War II later proved Douhet's vision to have been more accurate.

Mitchell's return to the United States did nothing to further the creation of a separate air force. Tired of his constant lobbying efforts, Major General Mason M. Patrick transferred Mitchell to a field position and reduced his rank to colonel. Mitchell's outspoken accusations of negligence on the part of American military leaders prompted President Calvin Coolidge to appoint a special review board to investigate charges that the neglect of air power bordered on "treason," and Dwight W. Morrow was selected to head the special panel of inquiry. While the review board endorsed increased attention to aviation development, the army moved to silence Mitchell's criticisms of incompetence, negligence, and "almost treasonable administration" of national defense, accusations Mitchell had directed not only against the navy but also against the army itself. President Coolidge personally ordered a court-martial hearing, which to no one's surprise found Mitchell guilty and ordered his suspension from military service for five years. He resigned his commission in January, 1926, but continued to speak and write extensively in favor of separate and coequal status for the air service. His ideas of strategic air operations were later tested extensively by American operations in the European theater under American air general Henry H. Arnold, although with mixed results.

Mitchell's unrelenting and impolitic advocacy of a separate and independent air arm may have dissuaded more effective and influential supporters from aiding his cause. His critics referred to him as the "General of the Hot Air Force." He called his army critics the "longbowmen." While the Morrow board recommended changing the Army Air Service to the Army Air Corps (AAC) and increasing its strength to eighteen hundred planes, the air force remained under the command of the General Staff of the Army. In the 1920's, Congress, concerned with tax and budget reductions, generally ignored pleas to increase allocations for AAC personnel and equipment. The most pressing need of the air force was the development of a heavy bomber to accomplish the type of strategic bombing Mitchell continued to advocate.

By 1930, Mitchell was the most persuasive spokesman for Douhet's "morale" warfare. The proper targets in future wars were the "vital centers," areas of civilian population where transport, food supplies, and material support were located. He defended the destruction of such civilian centers as the key to short and decisive wars, avoiding the horrible trench warfare of World War I. While many Americans could not accept the strategic destruction of civilian populations as humane warfare, Mitchell intellectually "prepared them to accept it." The intensive bombing of centers of civilian populations such as Hamburg, Dresden, and Hiroshima in World War II was the outcome of his writings, although he never advocated "throwing the strategic bomber at the man in the street." His emotional and partisan defense of an independent air arm coequal with surface forces made him the martyr of the modern Air Force.

Summary

What Alfred Thayer Mahan did for naval strategy at the turn of the century, Mitchell did for strategic air-power development in the 1920's and 1930's. Based on his firsthand observation of the futility of land warfare in World War I, he believed that the proper development and deployment of specialized aircraft and the targeting of civilian centers could shorten future wars by destroying an enemy's industrial capabilities. He envisioned military aircraft capable of many tasks—pursuit, attack, bombardment, reconnaissance, and the delivery of airborne troops behind enemy lines, an idea he first proposed in 1919. His vision of a separate role for military aircraft was not unique; his writings and lectures were refined by exchanges with his counterparts in the emergence of the new air age, Trenchard and Douhet being only two of his well-known colleagues.

Mitchell understood that modern warfare required the destruction of the weak and the old, women and children, and that air power "put a completely new complexion on the old system of making war." He set forth his ideas by lecture and by book. He published *Winged Defense* in 1925 and *Skyways* in 1930. His refusal to work through a bureaucratic system of conservative procurement and governmental reluctance to finance innovative weapon systems in the 1920's led directly to his court-martial in 1925. As a civilian, he continued to espouse the strategic use of air power until his death in 1936. He lectured, he wrote, he testified before Congress, and he used the press to push his particular views. Indifference he found impossible to tolerate. The irony of Mitchell's career was that the real systemization of his thoughts on strategic warfare and "vital centers" came after 1926, when he joined the ranks of civilians.

Bibliography

Craven, Wesley Frank, and James Lea Cate, eds. *The Army Air Forces in World War II.* 7 vols. Chicago: University of Chicago Press, 1949-1958. The standard history of the use of air power, deployment of forces, theater of operation, and air power development during World War II.

Dupuy, R. Ernest, and Trevor N. Dupuy. *The Encyclopedia of Military History.* Rev. ed. London: Jane's, and New York: Harper, 1977. The standard reference source for students of military history, containing sections on strategy, tactics, weaponry, and war and battle chronologies.

Earle, Edward Mead, ed. *Makers of Modern Strategy: Military Thought from Machiavelli to Hitler.* Princeton, N.J.: Princeton University Press, 1943. This anthology contains a well-written, if slightly dated, essay on three great architects of aerial warfare: Douhet, Mitchell, and Alexander de Seversky. Douhet's doctrine influenced American air-power theory through Mitchell's interpretation and popularization of his arguments.

Glines, Carroll V. "Air Power Visionary Billy Mitchell." *Aviation History* 8, no. 1 (September, 1997). Profile of Mitchell, his military career, his court-martial in 1925, and his ideas for change in the Air Force.

Hurley, Alfred F. *Billy Mitchell: Crusader for Air Power.* New York: Watts, 1964. A biographical portrait of Mitchell that is considered the most factual and objective. It has been reprinted by Indiana University Press (1975) and should be used to balance Mitchell's often exaggerated claims for his own ideas and the superiority of air-power.

Millett, Allan R., and Peter Maslowski. *For the Common Defense: A Military History of the United States of America.* Rev. ed. New York: Free Press, 1994. The best single history of America at war. The authors integrate naval and air force developments with the conduct of war by conventional surface forces. Mitchell's contributions are balanced by adequate attention to the navy's assessment of the role of military aircraft in the post-World War I era.

Mitchell, William. *Memoirs of World War I: "From Start to Finish of Our Greatest War."* New York: Random House, 1960. Mitchell's memoirs were first published in 1960, twenty-four years after his death.

————. *Winged Defense: The Development and Possibilities of Modern Air Power, Economic and Military.* New York and London: Putnam, 1925. To understand the development of Mitchell's thought and the development of strategic air-power doctrines, there is no better place to start than this work.

Weigley, Russell F. *The American Way of War: A History of United States Military Strategy and Policy.* New York: Macmillan, 1973. Weigley's excellent study of the evolution of American military strategy devotes a chapter to Billy Mitchell's thought, writings, and advocacy of directing air-power to the destruction of the "vital centers." He also traces the interpretation of Mitchell's doctrines as they were applied to strategic bombing in World War II, where its results often fell short of those promised by its advocates, including Alexander de Seversky.

Ronald M. Benson

FRANÇOIS MITTERRAND

Born: October 26, 1916; Jarnac, France
Died: January 8, 1996; Paris, France
Areas of Achievement: Government and politics
Contribution: Elected President of France in 1981 and again in 1988 with the backing of a coalition of the Left, which he had played a strong role in forging, Mitterrand was also a minister of several governments in the Fourth Republic and a Resistance leader in World War II.

Early Life

François Maurice Adrien Marie Mitterrand was born and spent his early life in Jarnac, a town of five thousand people not far from Cognac in southwest France. He was the fifth of eight children in a close-knit family. His mother, Yvonne, was devoutly Catholic. His father, Joseph, was the stationmaster of the town of Angoulême. Joseph inherited his wife's father's vinegar-making business and became president of the Union of Vinegar-Makers of France.

At age nine, Mitterrand was sent to a boarding school run by priests of the Diocese of Angoulême. There he was a loner and often sick. A devout Catholic, he sometimes thought about becoming a priest. He enjoyed reading philosophy and the French classics. At the Facultés de Droit et des Lettres in Paris in 1934, he enjoyed lengthy student discussions about literature. In 1938, at age twenty-one, he published in a small student journal an attack on the French and British governments for appeasing Adolf Hitler.

In September, 1938, newly graduated, Mitterrand was called up for compulsory military service. He was a sergeant in September, 1939, when France declared war on Germany and spent that winter manning a section of the Maginot line. Wounded in May, 1940, he was taken prisoner by the German army. His third attempt at escape succeeded in December, 1941. He worked for a period in a Vichy department servicing French prisoners of war and received a Vichy decoration which was later controversial. When the Germans occupied all of France in November, 1942, Mitterrand began the full-time Resistance work for which he later received several decorations.

In 1943, Mitterrand resisted Free French efforts to pressure him to merge his network with a similar one headed by General Charles de Gaulle's nephew. A meeting with de Gaulle in Algiers ended in hostility. Mitterrand became a lifelong virulent critic of de Gaulle. In March, 1944, when the three main Resistance organizations to help escaped prisoners of war were merged, Mitterrand became the leader of the unified group. Nominated by de Gaulle to be temporary secretary general in charge of prisoners of war and deportees, from August 19, 1944, he was briefly part of an ad hoc government for France.

Mitterrand then became editorial director of a publishing house and resumed his legal studies. He wrote articles for the journal of the Federation of Ex-Prisoners of War, wrote a pamphlet, and joined with left-wing Resistance leaders to stop a Communist takeover of the Resistance. Although he was more in the Center than the Left, from then on he made common cause with the Left. In 1945, he married Danielle Gouze. They had two sons. A third child died soon after he was born in 1945.

Life's Work

From 1945 to 1957, Mitterrand was in and out as a minister in eleven of the many governments of the Fourth Republic. In November, 1946 he became deputy for Nièvre in central France. His first position as a minister was in 1946. He was information minister in 1948 at the start of television transmissions, but most of his several ministerial posts dealt with colonial affairs, in which he tried to hold on to the empire by giving more internal autonomy to the colonies. Intermittently, he was out of the government.

Mitterrand became a friend of Pierre Mendès-France when they both collaborated with the new weekly journal, *L'Express*. When Mendès-France was premier (1954-1955), Mitterrand became minister of the interior. As such, he favored keeping Algeria for France, while proposing some reforms. In February, 1956, under Socialist Premier Guy Mollet, Mitterrand was minister of justice. He left the government in June, 1957, and did not hold office again until he was elected president in 1981. In 1957, he was called to the bar.

In September, 1958, the public voted to abolish the Fourth Republic. When Mitterrand lost his seat in the Gaullist 1958 election landslide, he was president of his party and one of the recognized leaders of the Left. From March, 1959, until 1981 Mitterrand held the position of elected mayor of Château-Chinon and other local offices. In April,

1959, he was elected a member of the senate. His career seemed back on track until autumn, 1959, when events made it seem as if he had contrived a fake attempt to assassinate him, in order to discredit Algerian hard-liners. The facts never were made clear.

In bad repute as a politician, Mitterrand began practicing law and wrote a short book, *La Chine au défi,* published in 1961. Throughout the de Gaulle administration he scathingly criticized de Gaulle's policies. Under a new electoral process begun in 1962, Mitterrand once more became deputy for Nièvre. He wrote regularly for *L'Express*, contributed to *Le Monde*, and in 1964 published a book, *Le Coup d'Etat permanent* criticizing the de Gaulle regime and its constitution. In 1965, when the Communist Party decided not to run a candidate against de Gaulle, Mitterrand ran. His first move was to form the Federation of the Democratic and Socialist Left, grouping the Socialist Party, the Radical Party, and a paper organization that Mitterrand headed. In the final round in December, 1965, Mitterrand received 44.8 percent of the votes.

In the summer of 1966, Mitterrand created a shadow cabinet. In December, 1966, his organization signed an electoral pact with the Communist Party. By the end of the March, 1967, elections, the Left had 193 seats in the National Assembly. In February, 1968, the two wings of the Left agreed on a common policy platform. What put Mitterrand in political limbo was his televised announcement, during the height of the student-worker rebellions in May, 1968, proposing to form a ten-member caretaker government. His bid for power offended many people, and the Left lost one hundred seats in the June elections. In 1969, Mitterrand's book, *Ma part de vérité, de rupture à l'unité*, was published. In it, he who had been such an anti-communist in the Fourth Republic, openly embraced Marxist concepts. At the same time, he attacked the Soviet Union's intervention in Czechoslovakia. In 1970, Mitterrand published a short book, *Un Socialisme du possible*. In the summer of 1971, he was elected first secretary of the Socialist Party. In 1972, the Socialist and Communist parties signed a formal agreement on what was termed a Common Programme. Mitterrand ran for president in 1974, receiving wide support. In 1973, he called for direct elections to the European parliament.

Mitterrand made a number of trips to various parts of the world. His meetings with political

leaders in the United States and the Soviet Union in 1975 were described in detail in his book, *L'Abeille et architecte: Chronique* (1978; *The Wheat and the Chaff,* 1982). He put his faith in Eurosocialism as an antidote to the excessive power of American capitalism. In 1977, the Union of the Left was ruptured. In his book *Ici et maintenant* (1980), Mitterand charged that the rupture was the result of a change of policy by the Communist Party in the Soviet Union. The Right won comfortably in the 1978 elections.

Despite efforts to replace him, he retained his hold on the Socialist Party. In 1981, he ran again for president. This time he won, with "110 propositions for France," including nationalization, a wealth tax, increase of public service jobs, abolition of the death penalty, increased rights for women, criticisms of both the Soviet Union and the United States, support for more aid to Third World countries, decentralization of French government and pluralization of television and radio, more rights and benefits for workers, and unified secular public education. He also hoped to scale down the nuclear program.

President Mitterrand appointed a very moderate government led by the Center-Right of his party, but he also included four Communists, in relatively minor posts. Pierre Mauroy, social-democratic mayor of Lille, became premier. While nationalizations of industry were put into effect, the minimum wage was raised, a wealth tax was added, and strong support was given to the arts, the government soon had to cope with rising inflation and unemployment. The first reactions were Keynesian policies of massive public spending and easier credit. Large street demonstrations against the government's efforts to weaken the autonomy of Catholic schools forced it to back down. In mid-1982, Mitterrand announced a plan to devalue the franc, freeze wages and prices, and cut his budget. He lowered domestic interest rates. By 1984, his popularity had dropped sharply, but the economy was better by 1985. While having problems of his own in the South Pacific, Mitterrand was critical of the Latin American policy of the United States and provided weapons to the Sandinistas in Nicaragua. In Paris, new projects were aimed at developing the workers' East Side. Eventually a new concert hall was built at Parc des Vincennes, and a new opera house was built on the site of the old Bastille prison. Controversy arose over the design by Chinese-American I. M. Pei for a seventy-foot-high glass pyramid as the new entrance to the Louvre.

In 1986, when the Right won the elections for National Assembly, Mitterrand made Jacques Chirac premier. The French called it cohabitation and liked it. Few changes were made in foreign policy. Chirac aimed to privatize many of the sixty-five state-owned companies and began the process, but problems multipled. The extreme Right wanted more restrictions on immigrants. Students revolted when efforts were made to make admission to the state-run universities more difficult. French competitiveness in world markets was declining. Chirac bore the brunt of popular discontent. Mitterrand stayed above the fray and became more popular than ever.

In 1988, at the age of seventy-two, Mitterrand ran again for president, promising to privatize some industries and to move to the Center. He won. The new premier was Michel Rocard, who fellow Socialists believed was an apologist for capitalism. He was Mitterrand's main rival in the Socialist Party. Mitterrand has been hopeful about greater economic unification of Europe, expecting Paris to be the center. In 1988, the French economy was booming, but unemployment was still high.

In 1991 Mitterrand appointed the first woman to be prime minister of France, Edith Cresson. Two years later the conservative opposition regained control of the parliament. In addition to his political struggles, Mitterrand also battled cancer during the remainder of his term. He died in 1996, shortly after leaving office.

Summary

François Mitterrand developed the French Socialist Party into a large, broadly based, national party aimed at social justice and brought it to national power after years of Gaullist rule. This accomplishment entailed a short-term collaboration with the Communist Party that helped him in the latter's decline. Then Mitterrand moved toward the center, while still embracing Socialist principles. Unlike his three predecessors as president, Miterrand is a veteran politician. In this capacity, he is tough and clever as well as ambitious and vain. As a private person, he is intellectual, almost mystic, a solitary dreamer. His inconsistencies have made some people distrust him. By 1988, though, many French people saw him as a father figure.

A long-term critic of de Gaulle and of the constitution of the Fifth Republic, once president himself he made no move to diminish the constitutional power of the presidency. He has been more of a friend of a unified Europe than the Gaullists had been. By 1988, his government seemed pro-American. He has always been a man of ambiguities, but then France itself is a country of ambiguities. Whereas de Gaulle was known in some circles as a monarch, some have called Mitterrand "the prince."

He has been all his life an indefatigable traveler, going to China to meet Mao Tse-tung in 1961. A learned man, he has read deeply and written extensively, hoping to provide a testament for Socialists everywhere in the world. He has written many articles and books, which may turn out to be his most lasting testament.

Bibliography

Balassa, Bela. *The First Year of Socialist Government in France*. Washington, D.C.: American Enterprise Institute, 1982. A pamphlet analyzing the Mitterrand government's first-year achievements from an American point of view. *Le Monde* is cited as a major source.

Cole, Alistair. *Francois Mitterrand: Study in Political Leadership*. 2d ed. London: Routledge, 1997. Cole offers a comprehensive study of Mitterrand's career and an assessment of his presidency based on an analysis of his policies.

MacShane, Denis. *François Mitterrand, a Political Odyssey*. London: Quartet, 1982. This biography gives a readable, thorough account of Mitterrand's career up to 1981 and includes the 110 Propositions as an appendix.

Mazey, Sonia, and Michael Newman, eds. *Mitterrand's France*. London and New York: Croom Helm, 1987. The two principal authors are lecturers at the Polytechnic of North London. The chapters analyze promises and accomplishments of the Mitterrand administration. Each chapter has a bibliography related to the policy discussed in the chapter. The "conclusion" credits Mitterrand's government up to 1986 with some modest achievements but also with some serious failures. Appendices give election results for 1981 and a chronology of major political events in France from 1981 to 1986.

Morray, Joseph P. *Grand Disillusion: François Mitterrand and the French Left*. Westport, Conn.: Greenwood Press, 1997. Examines the life and career of Mitterand with emphasis on his abandonment of leftist socialism for capitalism.

Nay, Catherine. *The Black and the Red: François Mitterrand and the Story of an Ambition*. Translated by Alan Sheridan. San Diego: Harcourt Brace, 1987. Written in a more novelistic style than many biographies, this book contains references that readers outside France might find puzzling. The book has notes with references but no bibliography.

Ross, George, et al., eds. *The Mitterrand Experiment: Continuity and Change in Modern France*. Oxford: Blackwell, and New York: Oxford University Press, 1987. This book evaluates Mitterrand's achievements before he was reelected in 1988.

Singer, Daniel. *Is Socialism Doomed? The Meaning of Mitterrand*. New York: Oxford University Press, 1988. As the title indicates, this book evaluates Mitterrand's policies. Analysts have frequently expressed the opinion that Mitterrand was originally more Right than Left. In the early postwar years, he was strongly anticommunist. To some, his embrace of the Left was political opportunism.

Williams, Stuart, ed. *Socialism in France: From Jaurès to Mitterrand*. London: Pinter, and New York: St. Martin's Press, 1983. This book puts Mitterrand's socialism in perspective.

Corinne Lathrop Gilb

MOBUTU SESE SEKO

Born: October 14, 1930; Lisala, Belgian Congo
  (now Zaire)
Died: September 7, 1997; Rabat, Morocco
Areas of Achievement: The military, government,
  and politics
Contribution: Mobutu was one of the first major
  African leaders to come to power since the early
  1960's. His Pan-Africanism gained for him
  much power in the Third World and his anticommunism pleased major Western powers. His long
  authoritarian presidency, however, ended in a
  coup.

Early Life

Mobutu Sese Seko, christened Joseph Désiré
Mobutu, was born into the Bangala People in
Équateur Province in the northern Belgian Congo.
He came from middle-income parents who sent
him to good primary (Léopoldville Mission
School) and secondary (Coquilhatville Mission
School) schools in the provincial capital. After finishing secondary school in Coquilhatville, he went
to Brussels to attend the Institut d'Études Sociales
de l'État in 1948. He was selected by the Belgian
authorities to attend the institute because of his
good grades and superior intellect. When he returned to the Congo in 1949, he enlisted in the
Belgian-controlled colonial army, the Force Publique. During his enlistment, he was sent to Lulua-
bourg to receive training in clerical, accounting,
and secretarial work at the École des Cadres. Sev-
en years later, in 1956, Mobutu was honorably discharged from the Force Publique. At that time he
held the rank of sergeant major, the highest rank a
Congolese could hold in the colonial military.

Earlier, while Mobutu was in the army, he was a
free-lance writer. After he was discharged, he obtained employment with a left-wing newspaper in
Léopoldville (now Kinshasa). The Belgian Socialists supported this paper called *L'Avenir.* His writings were rather moderate, despite the politics of
the paper. He later moved to another paper, *Actual-
ités africaines*, where he became an assistant editor. He was promoted to chief news editor and then
editor in chief in 1958. Mobutu's journalism career
reached its apex when he attended the World's Fair
in Brussels in 1958 as a representative of Belgian
colonial newspapers. When he returned to the Congo, he briefly worked for Inforcongo, the official
government information agency.

Over the course of several years, Mobutu became increasingly interested in politics and affairs
of the state. He rose quickly in a new national party, the Mouvement National Congolais (MNC),
founded in 1958. He was a supporter of Patrice Lumumba, the leader of the militant faction of the
MNC. When the party split in 1959, Lumumba appointed Mobutu as head of the party office in Brussels. This position allowed him to be a delegate to
the Round Table Constitutional Conference held in
the Belgian capital in January, 1960. Later he was a
delegate to the Round Table Economic Conference
in Brussels in April and May, 1960. Soon thereafter, these appointments would help him in his rise
to the presidency of Zaire. Mobutu is regarded as
one of the founding fathers of modern-day Zaire.

Life's Work

Mobutu rose to prominence in the newly decolo-
nized Congo as a military leader. He was appointed
secretary of state for national defense in Lumumba's cabinet in 1959. He was quickly demoted,
however, to the rank of colonel as a result of the
Congolese army revolting against its Belgian officers, only eight days after independence had been
declared on June 30, 1960. Lumumba trusted
Mobutu and wanted him as a colonel so he could
try to preserve the new government from the field.
He served under General Victor Lundula and was
relatively successful in commanding some authority over the rebellious Congolese forces. He did this
by obtaining for them food and pay and enlisting
their allegiance to their homeland.

Though Mobutu was successful in this new endeavor, the country was still in chaos. A new civil
war had erupted because several groups wanted
their own forms of independence, separate from
Lumumba. The situation further deteriorated when
Belgium sent troops to the Congo to protect Belgian nationals from the army mutineers. Lumumba
then, in turn, asked the United Nations to intervene, because he feared that the Belgians would reassert their authority over the government as a result of the civil war. Lumumba then admitted
several groups of Soviet and Czechoslovakian
technicians. Moreover, there was much disagreement between Premier Lumumba and President Joseph Kasavubu, the post-independence leaders.

During this time, Lundula had been ousted from
command of the army, and Mobutu took full con-

trol. It is then that he led a *coup d'état* on September 14, 1960, in which he ousted both Kasavubu and Lumumba from their positions. He announced that the army would rule while trying to "achieve a political agreement between the factions." He also promised that his army would try to guarantee the security of the people and their property. As a result of Mobutu's strong action, he was immediately condemned by the Soviet Union and Czechoslovakia. He then deported all Eastern Bloc technicians. His actions, however, were praised by the Western press and Western governments, because he presented a welcome alternate to Lumumba's Socialist tendencies. As a result of this coup, Mobutu emerged as a leader. The world recognition that he received remains, and his position of prominence is almost unmatched by any other modern-day African leader.

Meanwhile Mobutu backed Kasavubu over Lumumba, because he feared Lumumba's Socialist leanings would destroy his homeland. Mobutu seemed to hold a joint power seat with Kasavubu, because Mobutu made it well known that he would not tolerate any challenges to his authority by either Lumumba's followers or the U.N. forces still present in the Congo. Mobutu and Kasavubu further consolidated their power by issuing a warrant for Lumumba's arrest, charging him with having misused his powers while he was premier. The United Nations objected, but Mobutu had Lumumba kidnapped and taken to an outlying province and killed, many say with the complicity of the U.S. Central Intelligence Agency (CIA). In 1961, Kasavubu promoted Mobutu to major general and appointed him commander in chief of all Congolese forces. Thus, Mobutu wielded considerable power and let Kasavubu work with the politicians while he ran the nation's army.

Several years later, in June, 1964, the U.N. troops were withdrawn from the Congo. Nevertheless, another power struggle erupted in the Congo, this time between Kasavubu and Moise Tshombe, the new premier. Again, Mobutu staged a coup on November 25, 1965, and took over the government as new president for not more than five years. He declared that the "race for the top is finished . . . our political leaders had engaged in a sterile struggle to grab power without consideration for the welfare of the citizens." There was no opposition to the takeover, and there were no arrests. Mobutu, at age thirty-five, was president of a major African nation. After 1965, the year of his

ascension to power, Mobutu consolidated his power and made the lives of his potential adversaries very difficult. One such man, a former politician, Nguza Karl I Bond, has described Mobutu as a man of state who keeps secrets. He also describes him as a tyrant and a dictator who runs a reign of terror. In addition, he accused Mobutu and his family of raiding the country's coffers to build their own personal fortunes. Some earlier men who resisted Mobutu's rule tried to assassinate him in 1966 and were later hanged. It is apparent that once Mobutu had tasted power, he would take all steps to get rid of any threat to his power. He was once overheard to say concerning the severe death sentences he imposed on enemies, "I have no lessons to receive from humanity."

Even though it was known that Mobutu did not like political parties or anyone deviating from his idea of the "best Zaire," he still had to try to legitimize his power in the highly politicized bastions of the Zairian cabinet and government. He at first proceeded with caution until he had built up his loyal forces; then, he rewarded them for their loyalty by letting it be known that opposition would be dealt with very severely. This was further enforced by his desire for a single-party system that would help routinize and institutionalize his consolidated power. It was a presidential system, but many labeled Mobutu's government as nothing short of a monarchy.

In economic terms, Mobutu brought Zaire, with its rich deposits of minerals and copper, to the forefront of African nations. Mobutu was criticized for exploiting his country to some Western economic interests and in response nationalized copper production in the country—a radical step that angered many world leaders. It showed, however, that Zaire, Africa, and the Third World in general were tired of being manipulated by multinational corporations of the Western world and that Zaire could stand up to the rest of the world. This, along with his "authenticity campaign" in 1972, gained for him wide respect in both Africa and the Third World.

By the late 1970's, however, failed economic policies and corruption had severely damaged the country's infrastructure and resulted in widespread hunger and poverty. Mobutu weathered attacks on his administration from the Catholic church and the United States and suppressed opposition led by popular candidate for prime minister Etienne Tshisekedi. In the 1990's cancer weakened Mobutu

physically, and when a rebel army led by Laurent Kabila advanced through Zaire, no support from his former Western allies was forthcoming. He fled to Morocco, where he died in 1997.

Summary

Mobutu Sese Seko was a powerful, egotistical, domineering, ruthless man who loved his country, but more so, his great power. He was one of the most powerful men in Africa, with great wealth. He was once called "the [Ferdinand] Marcos of Africa." Mobutu was one of the first modern-day African leaders to advance the idea of rejecting European names and culture. In 1972, he called for all Zairians who had European names to adopt African names. Similarly, the previous year, the Congo was renamed Zaire in what he called a "national authenticity" campaign to Africanize Africa. He came onto the political scene at the right time—at the end of colonial rule—and was in the diplomatic limelight almost until his death. Mobutu had a Pan-African style of rule in that he tried to do what was best for Africa on the whole; he believed that whatever was good for Zaire was good for Africa. He controlled through economic aid in an attempt to limit the sphere of influence that industrialized nations seek to have over Africa.

Mobutu chose to be more in the Western sphere than the Soviet and aligned himself with the United States. Mobutu was vehemently anticommunist; thus he was seen by the West as a "safe" African leader and was given both military and economic support. His appetites, however, were huge, and eventually he was driven almost undefended from his own capital. Authoritarianism and corruption had so eroded Mobutu's reputation that he fled with little support from any quarter.

Bibliography

Bohannan, Paul, and Philip Curtin. *Africa and Africans.* 4th ed. Prospect Heights, Ill.: Waveland Press, 1995. The book focuses on African history, colonialism, and independence. The section on Africa since independence covers the circumstances under which Joseph Mobutu changed his name to Mobutu Sese Seko, and the country's name from the Congo to Zaire. It also discusses his insistence that his people change their names to "authentic" African forms.

Callaghy, Thomas M. *The State Society Struggle: Zaire in Comparative Perspective.* New York: Columbia University Press, 1984. This book is very theoretical and analytical. It examines the concept of the nation of Zaire and the politics of its leaders. The author explores the development of Mobutu's absolutism and its effective utilization.

Gran, Guy, ed. *Zaire: The Political Economy of Underdevelopment.* New York: Praeger, 1979. An excellent book on Zaire in the realm of political economy and the role that Zaire plays in the game of international politics and its relation to the Western world and the African continent. It also deals with factionalism and internal political struggles.

Parker, Frank J. "From Mobutu to Kabila: An Improvement?" *America* 177, no. 14 (November 8, 1997). Looks at Kabila's possibilities for resolving problems in the Democratic Republic of Congo after Mobutu and in the face of Kabila's part in the deaths of thousands of refugees.

Rieff, David. "Realpolitik in Congo: Should Zaire's Fate Have Been Subordinate to the Fate of Rwandan Refugees?" *The Nation* 265, no. 1 (July 7, 1997). Considers future prospects for Zaire after the fall of Mobutu.

Taylor, Sidney. "Lt.-General Joseph Mobutu." In his *The New Africans: A Guide to the Contemporary History of Emergent Africa and Its Leaders.* London: Hamlyn, and New York: Putnam, 1967. The book includes biographies of important men in the Congo Democratic Republic. Examples of other leaders listed are Jean-Marie Kikangala and Felicien Kimvoy. Each biography contains the major contributions and other information about the leaders.

Young, Crawford, and Thomas Turner. *The Rise and Decline of the Zairian State.* Madison: University of Wisconsin Press, 1985. Young and Turner shed new light on Mobutu's political policies at the time of Zaire's revolt from Belgian control. In addition, they examine the economic decline as well as the purported corruption of the Mobutu family.

Alphine W. Jefferson

MOHAMMAD REZA SHAH PAHLAVI

Born: October 26, 1919; Tehran, Iran
Died: July 27, 1980; Cairo, Egypt
Areas of Achievement: Government and politics
Contribution: Mohammad Reza ruled Iran from 1941 to 1979. His reign coincided with major changes in the social and economic life of Iran, although his despotic rule, sustained by brutal repression, and the corruption that accompanied his modernizing program contributed directly to the Islamic Revolution of 1979.

Early Life

Mohammad Reza was the eldest son of the preceding ruler, Reza Shah Pahlavi, and was born when the latter, then known as Reza Khan, was a colonel in the Cossack Brigade of the last ruler of the Qajar Dynasty. In 1921, Reza Khan participated in a *coup d'état* aimed at introducing much-needed reforms and reducing foreign (especially British) influence in the country's internal affairs. In 1925, he had himself proclaimed shah, taking the dynastic name of Pahlavi. As heir-apparent, Mohammad Reza underwent strict training under the eagle eyes of his harsh and overbearing father. Although Reza Shah himself had no experience of the world outside Iran, he sent his heir abroad to complete his education.

In 1936, Mohammad Reza was summoned home to enter the Military Academy in Tehran and to continue his apprenticeship as his father's heir. It was also arranged that he should marry Princess Fawzia, the sister of King Farouk I of Egypt. They were married in 1939, and a daughter, Shahnaz, was born in 1940; but Fawzia returned to Egypt in 1947, and there was a divorce in the following year. In 1951, Mohammad Reza married Soraya Esfandiari, daughter of one of the Bakhtiyari Khans and a German woman. The couple were said to be very much in love, but no heir was produced and Soraya had to compete for her husband's affections against Mohammad Reza's relatives and courtiers in a court riddled with intrigue and backbiting. A divorce was announced in 1958. In 1959, Mohammad Reza married a commoner, Farah Diba, who presented him with two sons and two daughters.

Life's Work

Reza Shah shared with his countrymen deep-seated suspicions of both Great Britain and Russia, and during the course of the 1930's he had leaned increasingly in the direction of the Third Reich, which sedulously wooed him and flattered his vanity. At the outset of World War II, therefore, the British and the Russians demanded an end to Iran's German connection. Unwilling to comply, Reza Shah was compelled to abdicate and was taken into enforced exile in South Africa, where he died in 1944.

Initially, the British contemplated restoring the former Qajar Dynasty, but, in the end, the Allies decided that Mohammad Reza would do as well as any other puppet. He was, therefore, permitted to succeed to the throne, although for the duration of the war the real rulers of the country were the British and Soviet ambassadors. As soon as the war was over, the occupying British troops were withdrawn, but the Soviet Union showed an obvious unwillingness to withdraw Red Army units stationed in the northwest of the country. The prime minister, Ahmad Qavam, one of the ablest Iranian statesmen of the twentieth century, maneuvered the Soviet government into recalling its forces, but he was then compelled to call upon the Iranian army to reintegrate the dissident provinces by a show of force (undertaken with excessive brutality), which inevitably brought the Shah, as supreme commander, to the fore. The so-called liberation of Azarbaijan (August, 1949) greatly boosted the public image of both the Shah and the army. Shortly afterward, Qavam was forced to resign the premiership under pressure from the hostile Majlis (the Iranian parliament, established by the constitution of 1906).

Mohammad Reza had always hated and feared Qavam, and it was with undisguised pleasure that he now saw him leave the political stage. Henceforth, he would begin to participate more actively in politics. He appointed General Ali Razmara as prime minister (June, 1950-February, 1951), but the latter almost immediately became embroiled in controversy over the status of the Anglo-Iranian Oil Company, regarded by virtually all Iranians as a symbol of quasi-colonial domination. When the new premier was assassinated by a religious fanatic, his opponents openly rejoiced. Nevertheless, there were those who whispered that the order for his death had emanated from somewhere within the palace.

Following Razmara's assassination, the issue of oil nationalization came to dominate both Iran's in-

Mohammad Reza Pahlavi (left), the shah of Iran, meeting with U.S. president Franklin D. Roosevelt.

ternal politics and its international relations, leading to the emergence to prominence of Mohammad Mosaddeq and to his stormy premiership (March, 1951-August, 1953). Despite his antecedents as a descendant of the former Qajar Dynasty and as an old-style landowner and bureaucrat, Mosaddeq was an object of intense popular adulation, especially among the more politically sophisticated people of Tehran who shared his animus against both the Pahlavi Dynasty and the British. For a short while, it seemed that Mosaddeq would become the charismatic leader of a new, forward-looking, and progressive Iran; as he proceeded, in the face of hostile world opinion, with the nationalization of the Anglo-Iranian Oil Company, his authority and influence grew accordingly. The British reacted by persuading the United States' government (at the height of the Cold War) that Mosaddeq was becoming dependent upon the support of the Communist-led Tuda Party, itself seen as the cat's-paw of the Soviet Union. Mohammad Reza had long sensed the threat to the monarchy posed by Mosaddeq's popularity, and so he and a palace

clique, together with a number of senior generals, entered into a conspiracy, masterminded by the Central Intelligence Agency (CIA), which led to Mosaddeq's ouster, despite the fact that he was the country's duly constituted prime minister. Mosaddeq was put on trial, imprisoned, and later exiled to one of his estates, where he died in 1967.

The Shah began to assume a greater direction over the day-to-day running of the government. By 1960, underlying discontent with the regime for its failure to address fundamental social and economic concerns was being openly aired, despite the ever-increasing ruthlessness of the secret police. To head off opposition, Mohammad Reza ordered the creation of two political parties, one to head the government and the other to serve as a loyal opposition; while each vied with the other in fulsome flattery of the ruler, the elections of 1960 were so blatantly rigged and the public outcry so vociferous that even the Shah was forced to denounce them. Under pressure from the Kennedy administration, which wanted a program of liberalization and reform for Iran, Mohammed Reza appointed as prime minister in May, 1961, a former Iranian ambassador to Washington, Ali Amini. An economist by training, Amini had experience in government going back to the time of Qavam.

Like Qavam and Mosaddeq, Amini was a statesman of vision whose premiership offered the last chance for prerevolutionary Iran to evolve along the lines of a liberal parliamentary democracy, but his period in office (1961-1962) proved tragically brief. He prepared a far-reaching program of reforms, and it was under him and his able Minister of Agriculture, Hasan Arsanjani, that the government promulgated its first land reform decree of January, 1962, the opening phase of a program of land redistribution later co-opted by the Shah in a relentless propaganda campaign in which he was represented as the emancipator of the peasantry. Amini could never overcome the liability that he lacked the nationwide support that Mosaddeq had undoubtedly enjoyed, and he suffered from the additional disadvantage that Mohammad Reza disliked and mistrusted him. The two were bound to part company, sooner or later. The break, when it came, was over military expenditure. Amini the economist knew that the military budget was excessive when the country was in the midst of a grave fiscal crisis, but, to the Shah, the army was sacrosanct. Amini resigned in July, 1962.

Between 1962 and 1977, Mohammad Reza's rule became increasingly despotic: His will was law, his policies were not to be questioned, and any form of opposition or criticism was regarded as treason, to be stamped out without mercy by the secret police. Isolated from reality by his obsequious entourage and flattered and cajoled by Western leaders, who regarded Iran as an island of stability in the turbulent Middle East, he grew megalomanic in his ambition and his delusions of grandeur.

After Amini, no prime minister possessed the moral courage or the independence to challenge the Shah's will. Asadollah Alam (prime minister from 1962 to 1964) was a close confidant and a born courtier, who in 1963 presided over the savage repression of opposition to the Shah's so-called White Revolution. His successor, Hasan Ali Mansur, was assassinated in January, 1965. Mansur was followed by Amir Abbas Hoveyda, a technocrat who was to hold the premiership longer than any other Iranian prime minister of the twentieth century (January, 1965-July, 1977). Dismissed in response to mounting criticism of the government and imprisoned for alleged corrupt practices, he

was still incarcerated when the revolutionaries seized power in 1979 and duly had him executed.

Amid increasing repression, Mohammad Reza had celebrated in 1971 what was styled "Five Thousand Years of Iranian Monarchy" in tawdry ceremonies at Persepolis. Even then, some otherwise friendly foreign journalists had commented unfavorably on the obvious signs of Napoleonic delusions of grandeur. Thereafter, with Iran replacing Great Britain as "policeman" of the Persian Gulf, with the Nixon administration agreeing to provide Iran with unlimited military hardware (short of nuclear weapons), and with the steep rise in the world price of oil, the Shah—engaged in an incredible buying spree, especially of the latest weaponry—was boasting that by the year 2000, Iran would be a power of world class, economically and militarily second to none save the superpowers. In reality, by the late 1970's Iran was suffering from an overheated economy, staggering inflation, massive social dislocation, the breakdown of public services, a monstrous military budget out of all proportion to the country's needs, and mounting fury against the regime and its foreign supporters, especially the Americans, who were in large measure blamed for these developments, since most Iranians since the overthrow of Mosaddeq in 1953 regarded their ruler as an American puppet.

As successive governments between 1977 and 1979 lost control of the situation, Mohammad Reza found that, since he had killed, imprisoned, or driven into exile his liberal or democratic critics, leadership of the opposition had passed to the implacably hostile Muslim clergy, and especially to the charismatic figure of Ayatollah Ruhollah Khomeini. By the end of 1978, the Shah's government had, quite literally, disintegrated, and on January 16, 1979, he fled the country, never to return. He died in Egypt on July 27, 1980, an exile like his father.

Summary

A man of limited imagination and serious character flaws, Mohammad Reza Shah Pahlavi pursued with vigor his father's goal of subverting the spirit of the constitution of 1906 in the interests of Pahlavi dynasticism and a twentieth century version of monarchical absolutism, which was, in effect, dictatorship. In achieving this goal, he undoubtedly benefited from the circumstances of the Cold War, which enabled him to convince the United States and its allies that he was indispensable as a stabilizing factor in the Middle East. As in the case of other Western-backed dictators, it was to be his own people, driven to desperation by the excesses of the regime, who would eventually overthrow him.

Coinciding with a peculiarly challenging and volatile period of modern Iranian history, involving wrenching social and economic changes that would have occurred with or without the Shah's leadership, the reign of Mohammad Reza brought great material benefits to the urban-based elite and to sections of the burgeoning middle class, while creating uncertainty, dislocation, and often new forms of economic hardship among those at the lower end of the social ladder. A ruthless foe to genuine democratic institutions and to the free expression of opinion, Mohammad Reza directed his security forces to eliminate all semblances of legitimate oppositional activity, which they did with extraordinary brutality. In consequence, the only effective leadership left to defy the regime came from the ideologically conservative but well-organized and widely respected Muslim clergy. The Islamic Revolution of 1979 was a direct consequence of the Shah's determined elimination of all other forms of opposition during the preceding two decades. In retrospect, Mohammad Reza's career may be viewed as a monumental failure and a classic object lesson in the limitations of dictatorship.

Bibliography

Abrahamian, Ervand. *Iran Between Two Revolutions*. Princeton, N.J.: Princeton University Press, 1982. This is an important and in some respects definitive account of the period between the Constitutional Revolution of 1905 and the Islamic Revolution of 1979. The greater part, however, deals with the reign of Mohammad Reza and is especially detailed regarding the years 1946 to 1953 and the politics of the Mosaddeq premiership.

Hambly, Gavin R. G. "The Reign of Muhammad Riza Shah." In *The Cambridge History of Iran*, edited by Peter Avery and Gavin R. G. Hambly, vol. 7. Cambridge: Cambridge University Press, 1989. This narrative account of the period 1941-1979 argues that only under the leadership of the three independently minded and charismatic prime ministers—Ahmad Qavam, Mohammad Mosaddeq, and Ali Amini—was there any hope of Iran evolving along the path envisaged in the constitution of 1906.

Hoveyda, Fereydoun. *The Fall of the Shah*. Translated by Roger Liddell. London: Weidenfeld and Nicolson, and New York: Wyndham, 1980. Fereydoun Hoveyda was brother to Amir Abbas Hoveyda. Fereydoun was Permanent Representative of Iran to the United Nations between 1971 and 1979. His assessment of the factors that contributed to the collapse of the Shah's regime are based upon an insider's knowledge and experience.

Katouzian, Homa. *The Political Economy of Modern Iran: Despotism and Pseudo-Modernism, 1926-1979*. London: Macmillan, and New York: New York University Press, 1981. This constitutes the best detailed account of the Shah's reign available. In this penetrating study, Katouzian shows the Shah's modernization program to have been a facade masking brutal repression and the staggering corruption of a venal elite.

Keddie, Nikki R. *Roots of Revolution: An Interpretive History of Modern Iran*. New Haven, Conn.: Yale University Press, 1981. This is an outstanding work of synthesis, an interpretation of recent Iranian history from the beginning of the nineteenth century down to the Islamic Revolution of 1979. Especially useful in the perspective that it provides for the Pahlavi period.

Radji, Parviz C. *In the Service of the Peacock Throne: The Diaries of the Shah's Last Ambassador to London*. London: Hamilton, 1983. Parviz Radji was the Iranian ambassador to Great Britain between 1976 and 1979. In his diaries, he conveys with considerable frankness his growing dismay at the crass stupidity and lack of vision that characterized the *ancien régime* in its last days.

Rafizadeh, Mansur. *Witness: From the Shah to the Secret Arms Deal, An Insider's Account of U.S. Involvement in Iran*. New York: Morrow, 1987. Rafizadeh was a member of the notorious Iranian secret police, in which he rose to be station chief in the United States. From this vantage point, he obtained insights into the working of the Iranian government and the court enjoyed by few other outsiders.

Reeves, Minou. *Behind the Peacock Throne*. London: Sidgwick and Jackson, 1986. Reeves was an Iranian woman who, after employment in the foreign service and in Empress Farah's Organization for the Protection of Children, served in the empress' private office from 1976 until 1979. Her memoirs provide an insider's impression of life in the Pahlavi court.

Samii, Abbas William. "The Shah's Lebanon Policy: The Role of SAVAK." *Middle Eastern Studies* 33, no. 1 (January, 1997). Discussion of the Shah's policy towards Lebanon from 1957 to 1978 and his use of SAVAK, the National Intelligence and Security Organization.

Zonis, Marvin. *Majestic Failure: The Fall of the Shah*. Chicago: University of Chicago Press, 1991. The author considers several of the Shah's personality traits from a psychological perspective.

Gavin R. G. Hambly

VYACHESLAV MIKHAILOVICH MOLOTOV

Born: March 9, 1890; Kukarka, Vyatka Province, Russia

Died: November 8, 1986; Moscow, U.S.S.R.

Areas of Achievement: Diplomacy, government, and politics

Contribution: As one of Joseph Stalin's most loyal subordinates, Molotov played a major role in the development of the Soviet Union's domestic and foreign policies, particularly the creation of the centralized command economy and the establishment of Soviet domination of Eastern Europe.

Early Life

Vyacheslav Mikhailovich Molotov was born Vyacheslav Mikhailovich Skryabin in the village of Kukarka, approximately five hundred miles northeast of Moscow. He was the third son of Mikhail Skryabin, a middle-class merchant who was prosperous enough to afford a good education for his children. Vyacheslav was attending secondary school in Kazan at the time of the revolution of 1905. He began reading Marxist tracts and joined the Russian Social Democratic Labor Party the following year, gravitating toward Vladimir Ilich Lenin's Bolshevik faction. Like many revolutionaries in czarist Russia, he employed a number of pseudonyms in an effort to conceal his true identity from the police. He first used the name "Molotov," which is derived from the Russian word for "hammer," in 1918 and kept it for the remainder of his life.

Molotov's early revolutionary activity foreshadowed the important but subordinate role that typified his later career. A friend from his Kazan school days recruited him to join the staff of *Pravda*, the Bolshevik Party's newspaper in St. Petersburg. Molotov published a few minor articles in *Pravda*, but he did not establish a name for himself as a Marxist thinker or writer. He was arrested twice for revolutionary activity but resumed his editorial work on *Pravda* after the February Revolution of 1917 overthrew Czar Nicholas II. In the absence of the more prominent Bolsheviks, most of whom were in Siberian or foreign exile at the time the revolution broke out, Molotov became a member of the party's Central Committee. With the return of Lenin and other leading Bolsheviks, however, Molotov was relegated to a secondary role, distinguishing himself with his clerical skills and

capacity for paperwork. He was a consummate bureaucrat rather than an inspiring leader in the revolution and ensuing civil war.

Life's Work

Molotov's rise to political prominence began shortly after the end of the civil war. In March, 1921, at the Tenth Congress of the Russian Communist Party (as the Bolshevik Party had been renamed in 1918), Molotov became executive secretary of the party's Central Committee, a candidate (nonvoting) member of the Politburo, and head of a new bureaucratic organization, the Secretariat, which was in charge of party records and correspondence. The following year, the Secretariat was reorganized, with Joseph Stalin assuming the title of general secretary and Molotov once again reduced to a subordinate role. This change, however, marked the beginning of Molotov's close political collaboration with Stalin.

For nearly three decades, Molotov was Stalin's most faithful supporter. A short, stocky man who wore a mustache and pince-nez eyeglasses, Molotov supported Stalin against his rivals in the struggle for power after Lenin's death in January, 1924. Becoming a full member of the Politburo in 1925, Molotov also supported Stalin's efforts to create a highly centralized "command economy" during the 1930's. Stalin sought to achieve this goal through a series of "five-year plans" that forced most peasants to join collective farms and based rapid industrial growth on government fiat rather than on market forces. Stalin, recognizing Molotov's bureaucratic skills, had him named to the post of chairman of the Council of People's Commissars (the Soviet equivalent of premier) in 1930 to oversee the governmental bureaucracy during this period of internal upheaval. Molotov was also deeply involved with Stalin's Great Purge of the Communist Party in the later 1930's, cosigning arrest warrants and execution orders that sometimes contained hundreds, even thousands, of names. Molotov never wavered in his conviction that Stalin's policies, which caused the deaths of several million Soviet citizens and inflicted enormous hardship on the country, were absolutely necessary for the defense of the Soviet Union against its capitalist enemies.

In May, 1939, Molotov suddenly replaced Maxim Litvinov as people's commissar of foreign affairs (the revolutionary title of "people's commissar" was replaced by "minister" in 1946). Litvinov had strongly promoted a policy of "collective security," which meant that the Soviet Union sought cooperation with the capitalist states of Western Europe against the common threat of Nazi-ruled Germany. Litvinov's replacement by Molotov, who had virtually no foreign policy experience, was a signal that Stalin was willing to abandon collective security in favor of a separate deal with Nazi Germany. After several weeks of hesitation, Nazi leader Adolf Hitler sent his foreign minister, Joachim von Ribbentrop to Moscow to negotiate what became known as the Molotov-Ribbentrop Pact, which the two foreign ministers signed on August 23, 1939. The Soviet Union promised to remain neutral in the upcoming conflict in exchange for territorial concessions (including eastern Poland, Estonia, and Latvia) that were spelled out in a secret protocol attached to the treaty. Lithuania and Moldova were later added to the Soviet Union's sphere of influence. The Molotov-Ribbentrop Pact bought a twenty-two month respite from World War II for the Soviet Union (not counting the invasion of Poland in September, 1939, and its Winter War against Finland in 1939-1940), but Stalin did not wisely use this time to prepare his country for war with Germany.

Stalin assumed the title of premier in May, 1941, but Molotov continued to supervise the day-to-day operations of the government as his first deputy. It was Molotov, not Stalin, who addressed the Soviet people on June 22, 1941, breaking the news that Germany had invaded the Soviet Union that morning. He also authorized the mass production of a weapon consisting of a bottle filled with an inflammable liquid; German soldiers called these primitive antitank weapons "Molotov cocktails." After the German invasion, Molotov's diplomatic role changed from trying to placate Germany to negotiating with the Soviet Union's allies, Great Britain and the United States, and securing a Soviet sphere of influence in Eastern Europe. He took part in the four major wartime conferences (Moscow in 1942, Tehran in 1943, and Yalta and Potsdam in 1945) at which the Allied powers discussed coordination of their war efforts and the postwar settlement. Since Stalin traveled only to places occupied by Soviet troops, such as Tehran and Potsdam, Molotov also represented the Soviet Union in negotiations held in the United Kingdom or the United States, including the San Francisco Conference, which created the United Nations in April, 1945.

Allied cooperation, however, did not long survive the defeat of Germany and Japan. Stalin was determined to keep control of the territories that the Molotov-Ribbentrop Pact had gained for the Soviet Union and insisted that only governments friendly to the Soviet Union could rule in the neighboring countries of Eastern Europe. The Western Allies, on the other hand, favored self-determination for Eastern Europe. This disagreement over the future of Eastern Europe produced the Cold War. Fearing that free elections would threaten Soviet security interests in Eastern Europe, Stalin imposed obedient Communist governments in 1947 and 1948. Molotov rigidly defended these policies at the United Nations and during negotiations with the Western powers.

By 1949, Molotov was losing Stalin's favor. Stalin ordered the arrest of Molotov's wife, Polina Zhemchuzhina, who was Jewish, on the spurious charge of being a Zionist; she remained imprisoned until after Stalin's death. When the Central Committee debated and rubber-stamped the arrest, Molotov did not defend her and abstained from voting rather than violate party discipline. In March, 1949, Andrei Vyshinsky, the notorious prosecutor in the show trials of the late 1930's, replaced him as foreign minister. According to Nikita S. Khrushchev, Stalin, who was becoming increasingly suspicious in his last years, believed that Molotov had become an "agent of American imperialism." At the Nineteenth Party Congress in October, 1952, Stalin sharply criticized Molotov, who was not reelected to the Presidium (which replaced the Politburo from 1952 to 1966). Molotov probably would have been one of the principal victims of a new blood purge that Stalin was preparing, but he was saved by the dictator's death on March 4, 1953.

Following Stalin's death, Molotov was restored to the Presidium and regained the post of foreign minister but had little impact on policy. He supported Khrushchev against Lavrenti Beria and Georgy Malenkov in the power struggle to succeed Stalin but strongly disagreed with the new Soviet leader's departures from Stalinist orthodoxy in both domestic and foreign affairs. Molotov was removed from the foreign ministry in June, 1956, after the Twentieth Party Congress, at which Khrushchev denounced Stalin's terror against the party and his blindness regarding Hitler, policies with which Molotov was closely associated. After a

in World War II seemed to achieve this goal. At the time of his death, Molotov had no inkling that the Soviet Union would survive him by only five years. Yet the system that he had done so much to create contained the seeds of its own demise. The centralized command economy favored military needs and heavy industry over consumer goods and concern for the environment. The collective farm system emphasized political control over the production and sale of agricultural goods rather than efficiency or innovation. The Communist Party's dictatorship necessitated the suppression of both political opposition and the free flow of information. The Soviet Union's sphere of influence in Eastern Europe could be maintained only by force. Faced with economic stagnation, declining living standards, serious environmental problems, and recurring unrest in Eastern Europe, a new generation of Soviet leaders, headed by Gorbachev, decided that it was necessary to implement radical changes in the system that Molotov had done so much to build.

Bibliography

Chuev, Felix. *Molotov Remembers: Inside Kremlin Politics; Conversations with Felix Chuev.* Edited by Albert Resis. Chicago: Dee, 1993. These reminiscences, recorded by a Soviet journalist over a period of several years, show that even in his last years Molotov remained an unrepentant Stalinist who was proud of his accomplishments.

Lih, Lars T. *Stalin's Letters to Molotov, 1925-1936.* New Haven, Conn.: Yale University Press, 1995. The first publication of this previously top secret correspondence offers insight into Stalin's control of the government, his dealings with his enemies, and his plans for the future. The letters are accompanied by annotations and supplementary materials placing the letters in context.

Mastny, Vojtech. *The Cold War and Soviet Insecurity: The Stalin Years.* New York: Oxford University Press, 1996. This detailed investigation of Soviet foreign policy during the years 1947-1953 argues that Stalin's insatiable quest for security and control made the Cold War inevitable.

———. *Russia's Road to the Cold War: Diplomacy, Warfare, and the Politics of Communism, 1941-1945.* New York: Columbia University Press, 1979. Although it was published before the collapse of the Soviet Union and the opening of Soviet archives, this book remains a classic study of Soviet foreign policy during World War II.

failed attempt by Molotov and other members of the so-called Anti-Party Group to overthrow Khrushchev in June, 1957, Molotov was removed from the Presidium and the Central Committee. The former foreign minister served in the comparatively minor post of ambassador to Mongolia until 1960, then as Soviet representative to the International Agency on Atomic Energy in Vienna, Austria. Amid another round of de-Stalinization in 1962, Molotov was expelled from the Communist Party. He spent the remainder of his life living obscurely, though comfortably, in Moscow. In 1984, two years before his death, Molotov was readmitted to the Communist Party during the brief neo-Stalinist rule of Konstantin Chernenko. It was a last symbolic victory of the Stalinist system before the onset of the reforms of Mikhail Gorbachev, the collapse of the Soviet Union's East European empire, and the end of the Soviet Union itself in 1991.

Summary

Stalin and Molotov wanted to turn the Soviet Union into one of the world's great powers, and the economic transformation of the 1930's and victory

Medvedev, Roy. *All Stalin's Men: Six Who Carried Out the Bloody Policies*. Translated by Harold Shukman. Oxford: Blackwell, 1984; New York: Anchor Press/Doubleday, 1985. This volume contains biographical studies of Molotov and five other members of Stalin's inner circle written by a prominent Soviet-era dissident historian.

Miner, Steven Merritt. "His Master's Voice: Viacheslav Mikhailovich Molotov as Stalin's Foreign Commissar." In *The Diplomats, 1939-1979*, edited by Gordon A. Craig and Francis L. Loeweneim. Princeton: Princeton University Press, 1994. Concentrating on Molotov's first period as Soviet foreign minister (1939-1949), Miner argues that Molotov was Stalin's faithful servant in carrying out Soviet foreign policy but played a minor role, at best, in shaping policy.

Tucker, Robert C. *Stalin in Power: The Revolution from Above, 1928-1941*. New York: Norton, 1990. This magisterial history of the internal transformation of the Soviet Union illuminates Molotov's role in domestic politics.

Vizulis, Izidors. *The Molotov-Ribbentrop Pact of 1939: The Baltic Case*. New York: Praeger, 1990. Vizulis studies the historical causes and consequences of the Molotov-Ribbentrop Pact of 1939 and the protocols in the treaty that led to fifty years of Soviet occupation of the Baltic States.

Zubok, Vladislav, and Constantine Pleshakov. *Inside the Kremlin's Cold War: From Stalin to Khrushchev*. Cambridge, Mass.: Harvard University Press, 1996. This study of Soviet foreign policy toward the West from 1945 to 1962, written by two Russian historians, contends that Molotov played a significant role in formulating, not merely implementing, Soviet foreign policy under Stalin.

Richard D. King

PIET MONDRIAN

Born: March 7, 1872; Amersfoort, The Netherlands
Died: February 1, 1944; New York, New York
Area of Achievement: Art
Contribution: Mondrian was of paramount importance to the initiation of geometric abstraction for modern art during World War I. He was the principal voice and exemplar of neoplasticism in Dutch painting as well as one of the founders of the Dutch modern movement in architecture and design known as de Stijl, a movement that influenced the International style in building construction during the 1920's and 1930's.

Early Life
Pieter Cornelis Mondriaan, Jr. (Piet Mondrian), was born in Amersfoort, a central Netherlands town, where his father was headmaster at a Dutch reformed grammar school. Piet Mondrian, as he was known, lived only eight childhood years in Amersfoort, after which his family moved east to Winterswijk near the German border. There his father began duties as headmaster of a Calvinist primary school. Mondrian finished early formal education at that school by 1886. Of special importance for his future, he developed an interest in drawing there as a student, from self-training plus guidance from his father, who was a competent draftsman. He received his first painting instruction from an uncle, Fritz Mondriaan, a professional painter of land- scapes who, though based at The Hague, spent numerous summers at his brother's home in Winterswijk. Not surprisingly, early lessons for Mondrian from his uncle included landscape composition. Other documented training in art was received from the Doetinchem artist Johan Braet van Ueberfeldt.

By age fourteen, young Piet Mondrian (he shortened his first name and dropped the second "a" from his last name by 1912) was already consumed with the notion of becoming a painter. His father did not concur and initially prevailed, insisting that his son prepare for a stable profession. Mondrian worked diligently toward, first, a diploma to teach drawing at grammar school levels and then an additional certificate as a secondary school drawing teacher. By 1892, he taught briefly in Winterswijk but less thereafter. Still, his teaching certificates served as exemptions from preparatory courses when he was enrolled at the National Academy in Art in Amsterdam in 1892. There he joined all-day classes in painting and in 1894 added night classes in drawing.

Frustrated by the academy's curriculum and his own money problems, Mondrian withdrew from school for a year. During 1895-1896 and for several years afterward, Mondrian intensified his interest in landscape studies, notably undramatic rural scenery. In Mondrian's early years of academy training his approach was patient, sober, neutral, and objective regarding figuration, a manner that Mondrian carried over to his landscapes. All in all, his was hardly an early life prophetic of a brilliant career as a major figure in twentieth century modernism.

Life's Work
Mondrian's naturalistic paintings and his life remained relatively undistinguished from 1898 until about 1908. During this period, the channel of success for a picturesque landscape painter such as Mondrian included joining various art organizations in cities such as Amsterdam and submitting works to their frequent exhibitions. Mondrian did so, occasionally faring well, but by 1908 other forces were stirring within him and around him that began to change his painting interests forever.

That year he met the painter Jan Toorop, an exponent of Art Nouveau. Mondrian was not swayed by the sinuous excess and thick symbolism in Toorop's work, but his light palette and immersion into theosophy intrigued Mondrian. Soon considerations about the mystical apprehension of God caused the artist to clarify his painting goals. He realized that his current search for an imitation of the divine, present in his naturalistic, or luminist, paintings, actually lay within himself. Slowly but progressively Mondrian set about painting the divine absolute without references to externalized objects.

This procedure required a different pictorial language, one faithful to his new direction yet intelligible to the art-viewing public as well. The direction was one of liberation, exploration, experimentation, and a brighter palette, and it continued up to World War I. From 1908 to 1911 and again in 1913 and 1914, Mondrian painted for long periods during summers at Domburg in the coastal area of The Netherlands called Zeeland. There he continued a preference for single motifs such as mills, lighthouses, church towers, dunes, beaches, and individual stemmed flowers. These paintings were composed of a minimum of strokes, some wide, most gestural, and, again, almost all in brighter, stronger color, leaving behind for good the dark, rather brooding spell of his previous works.

Between 1909 and 1912, at least a dozen paintings and watercolors evidence a metamorphosis wherein a flowering tree is interpreted first in the Fauve manner, next with arbitrary smoldering color, and then as a type of turgid, brittle expressionism, followed by a version as a formalized system with curving webs of crisscrossing branches with spaces infilled with flat color. The last paintings in this series were completed during a trip to Paris in 1912. In them, the tree motif was simplified still more radically into a lattice of laterally repeated branches, some ellipsoidal. At that point, what seemed a conclusion of natural synthesis became an altered visual problem begging further resolution; that is, object representation changed to a schematicized incomplete grid on a flat background.

Part of this transformation from object-oriented art to linear abstraction was the result of Mondrian's exposure to the laboratory-like Paris development of analytical cubism by Pablo Picasso and Georges Braque between 1909 and 1911. Yet Mondrian's own development may not have needed such contact. Whatever the case, world events affected his next potential spheres of influence. A trip home to The Netherlands in 1914 for the impending death of his father was prolonged for four years by the outbreak of World War I. The involuntary detention nevertheless had beneficial ramifications for Mondrian. He grew distant from cubism, believing that its experimental progress stopped prematurely and that it could have advanced to the logical elimination of all subject matter. In The Netherlands from 1914 to 1915, Mondrian resumed his experimental synthesis of form in sparse compositions of varied colors and line-enhanced rectangles. His goal was to achieve what he termed "pure reality" and to represent ideas by pure plastic means—hence neoplasticism, in which all visual information is reduced to activities coded by colors to shapes. Reality now meant, not the picture as an open hole in the wall, but picture making, that is, line, color, shape, texture, composition, rhythm, balance, and the like.

Slowly formulating that position, Mondrian refined it into the concept of dynamic movement of color and shape and then enlarged upon it with the idea of balanced but unequal opposition. The latter was realized by almost exclusive use of rectilinear planes rendered in primary colors and divided by black borders of right angles. *Oval Composition with Bright Colors* (1914) is typical of this radical approach, although a few curved lines remained. Within a year, even curvilinear marks had been eliminated, and the resolution of Mondrian's compositions from then on reflected the rectangle of the picture plane, with architectonic structure dominant.

During this same period, Mondrian met Bart van der Leck, a painter exploring problems related to his own. Through Leck, Mondrian met artist and critic Theo van Doesburg, who was eager to launch both a new architecture and design movement and a journal to promote it. Both he called *de stijl*, meaning "the style." De Stijl championed machine forms and simplicity. Essays by Mondrian were published in the journal.

Possessing nearly obsessional concentration in his search for spiritual expressions of dynamic grid oppositions, Mondrian spent the rest of his career exploring their possibilities. Much of that life (1919 to 1938) was spent in Paris, where Mondrian's presence and active career seemed to encourage the spread of abstraction. His work in general saw the black grid simplified and become bolder, wider, and filled with a reduced palette of the primary colors plus white and gray. The archetypical example of this phase of his work remains *Composition in Red, Yellow, and Blue* (1930).

In 1938, sensing the approach of another war in Europe, Mondrian left Paris and sailed to London, where he lived and worked for two years. With the onset of the Blitzkrieg, the artist changed countries for the last time to the United States, specifically New York City, and did so with no regrets.

In 1941, Mondrian's work experienced another change: The black line network was exchanged for one in yellow and, in some work, for a yellow grid containing small bars of primary colors. Mondrian enthusiasts attribute the transformation to the artist's admiration for the dense but dynamic horizontal and vertical structure of Manhattan, particularly when it is illuminated at night. Additional stimuli proved to be the accelerated pace of life and, above all, the syncopation of jazz, a music form both new and intoxicating to the artist. So fond was Mondrian of the new music that he named his last two major paintings, *Broadway Boogie Woogie* and *Victo-*

ry Boogie-Woogie, both from 1942-1943, in its honor.

During this same brief time span, Mondrian was given his only one-person exhibition, thanks to the Valentine Dudensing Gallery in New York City. In late January of 1944, Mondrian developed pneumonia, and, though medically treated, he died early on February 1 at Murray Hill Hospital.

Summary

In probably no other single artist can the metamorphosis of specific naturalistic motifs into geometric abstraction be traced and studied more clearly than through Piet Mondrian. What is more important, the transformation of his motifs was not the result of clinical deductive reasoning as they may appear, but the search for spiritual equivalents and a universal language for natural form. In his patient, methodical way, he quietly launched one of the most important arms of twentieth century nonobjective painting, that of geometric abstraction.

As a founding member of de Stijl, his ideas regarding neoplastic painting as well as geometric abstraction in sculpture and architecture were published in the Dutch post-World War I journal *De Stijl*. Consequently, Mondrian's ideas were extended to Germany, where they were eagerly received by Walter Gropius during his formation of the Bauhaus. During the heyday of that astounding school of architecture, design, and art, Mondrian's ideas were indirectly spread throughout much of Western civilization.

Reared in a milieu of landscape and cityscape painting, Mondrian had turned away from those genres by 1909. Yet his move to New York in 1940 subsequently witnessed interpretations of Manhattan important as a heroic finale to his career and highly significant in the ongoing development of abstract painting. Mondrian's work and presence in the United States during the early 1940's inspired emerging young painters soon to launch the major movement of abstract expressionism. Finally, Mondrian's influence impacted still later twentieth century painting movements such as color-field abstraction and hard edge abstraction (or, minimal art) as well as optical painting (or, op art).

Bibliography

Blotkamp, Carel. "Mondrian's First Diamond Compositions." *Artforum* 18 (December, 1979): 33-39. The article responds to data and opinions in the catalog of a 1979 exhibition at the National Gallery of Art in Washington, D.C. Blotkamp convincingly refutes catalog author E. A. Carmean's contention as to the sources for Mondrian's diamond, or lozenge, paintings, saying that they were likely based on Mondrian's wartime conversations with de Stijl artists and not on Postimpressionism and the slightly later cubism.

Champa, Kermit S. "Mondrian's Broadway Boogie Woogie." *Arts Magazine* 54 (January, 1980): 170-176. An in-depth examination of Mondrian's most important painting from the artist's New York period.

Cotter, Holland. "Abstraction and the True Believer." *Art in America* 83, no. 11 (November, 1995). Covers an exhibit of 160 of Mondrian's works, many in his abstract period. Comments on the spiritual nature of the works.

Friedman, Mildred, ed. *De Stijl, 1917-1931: Visions of Utopia*. Oxford: Phaidon Press, and New York: Abbeville Press, 1982. This catalog's essays reveal the planned interconnectedness of de Stijl's total design and its prophecy of machine form, efficiency, and dignified simplicity.

Jaffe, Hans Ludwig C. *Piet Mondrian*. London: Thames and Hudson, and New York: Abrams, 1970. The book combines an overview of the artist's life, including biographical photographs, student-era paintings, and an in-depth discussion of a key series in which the tree motif evolves into a nonobjective painting mode. It includes description and analysis for most of Mondrian's major paintings.

Mondrian, Piet. *Piet Mondrian, 1872-1944: Centennial Exhibition*. New York: Solomon R. Guggenheim Foundation, 1971. The catalog lists 131 works dated from 1889 to 1944 and illustrates the most familiar pieces. Also includes an interview with one of Mondrian's closest friends.

Rembert, Virginia Pitts. "Mondrian's Aesthetics, as Interpreted Through His Statements." *Arts Magazine* 54 (June, 1980): 170-176. Art historian Rembert maintains that Mondrian's aesthetic reasoning was not only the operative beginning of his paintings but also valid art in itself and equal to the paintings.

Rosenblum, Robert, and Mel Bochner. "Plastic Made Perfect: Measuring Mondrian." *Artforum* 34, no. 2 (October, 1995). Analysis of Mondrian's use of basic color and geometric shapes and his influence on modern abstract painting.

Seuphor, Michel. *Piet Mondrian: Life and Work.* London: Thames and Hudson, and New York: Abrams, 1957. A monographic study composed of a poignant text interspersed with appropriate illustrated works, most in acceptable color. The book is valuable as an explanation of Mondrian's concepts of neoplasticism and his identification with theosophy and as an exploration of his major painting themes.

Welsh, Robert P. *Piet Mondrian's Early Career: The "Naturalistic" Periods.* New York: Garland, 1977. This published dissertation addresses the artist's art training in the 1880's, when he came under the spell of painting styles in contemporary France. Exhaustive research is evident, covering Mondrian's long gestation as a painter of humble landscape imagery.

Tom Dewey II

CLAUDE MONET

Born: November 14, 1840; Paris, France
Died: December 5, 1926; Giverny, France
Area of Achievement: Art
Contribution: Monet is central to the development of Impressionist painting in the 1870's. In the 1890's, Monet developed the concept of multiple views of one subject, and in the 1940's and 1950's the abstract Impressionism of Monet's late water lily paintings provided a stimulus for the American abstract expressionists.

Early Life

Although Claude Monet was born in Paris, he grew up on the Normandy coast at Le Havre. Yet the first intimations of his future vocation came not with landscape paintings but with a series of caricatures of local personalities which earned for him a considerable reputation by age sixteen. His direction changed after meeting the marine painter Eugène Boudin in 1858. Boudin, who was already a devotee of working outdoors, introduced Monet to plein air painting, which would eventually become the touchstone of the Impressionist landscape approach.

Monet used the proceeds from his lucrative caricature business to finance his first art studies in Paris in 1859, where he met the future Impressionist Camille Pissarro at the Académie Suisse. A photograph of Monet at age twenty suggests a romantic sensitivity, but later photographs portray a more rugged, stockier individual, with a square-cut, curly beard emphasizing his square face. Monet's studies were interrupted in 1861 by obligatory military service, but in 1862 he became ill and was sent home, after which his parents bought an exemption from his remaining service.

Returning to Paris, Monet enrolled in the studio of the academic painter Charles Gleyre. His year there was notable only because three of his future colleagues and friends, Pierre-Auguste Renoir, Alfred Sisley, and Frédéric Bazille, were fellow students; all four quickly became disillusioned with the academic curriculum. Henceforth they developed on their own, discovering for themselves the Forest of Fontainebleau and the Barbizon landscapists who had worked there since the 1830's.

In the spring of 1865, Monet had two large landscapes of the Normandy coast accepted by the salon (the official government-sponsored exhibi-

tions), achieving considerable success with them, as well as with the figure painting sent the next year, although some reviewers confused Monet with the slightly older painter Édouard Manet, who was creating scandals with the exhibition of such precedent-shattering paintings as *Déjeuner sur l'herbe* (1863; luncheon on the grass). Manet's revolutionary technique, which aimed, by the elimination of halftones, to produce the effect of forms seen in a blaze of light, was an additional stimulus toward Monet's development as an Impressionist.

Life's Work

Those early successes at the salon were almost the only official ones for Monet. As he became more individualistic, his paintings were increasingly refused by the tradition-bound salon juries. The first refusal was in 1867 of a major work, *Women in the Garden*, which has since been hailed as the first large whole-figure composition to be painted entirely outdoors. Though not a true Impressionist painting, since the treatment of light is static, it represents a major milestone in the stages leading toward the development of Impressionism.

The Impressionist movement actually began when Monet and Renoir painted together in the summer of 1869 at a suburban pleasure spot on the Seine, la Grenouillère, where the moving current of the river sparked the new approach and vocabulary of Impressionism, with its interest in transitory effects of light, color, and atmosphere. To capture these effects, the painters developed a broken technique of swift, small, separate strokes of pure color. Monet and Renoir also began developing the so-called rainbow palette, eliminating earth tones and bitumens to enhance the effects of prismatically refracted light. Throughout the 1870's, this interest in capturing the moment was of paramount interest for the Impressionists. To achieve the effect they wanted, they required the plein air approach and subjects which lent themselves to a casual treatment, such as riverbank scenes, fields, the railway, and the crowded, newly created great boulevards of Paris.

In 1870, Monet went to London to escape the Franco-Prussian War and had a chance to study at first hand the paintings of John Constable and J. M. W. Turner, whose interests in atmosphere prefigured those of the Impressionists. Upon his return,

Monet moved with his family to Argenteuil, a Paris suburb on the Seine, where many of his most famous Impressionist landscape paintings were produced. Although Monet and his friends were now mature artists, the problem with salon juries did not improve, and the precarious financial situation of most of them was exacerbated by the depression that began in 1873. Therefore, in 1874, Monet, Pissarro, Renoir, and Edgar Degas executed a plan they had been considering for some time: to bypass the salon altogether and mount their own juryless Exhibition, to which each would contribute a sum for expenses. Thirty artists, not all of them Impressionists, took part in what has come to be known as the First Impressionist Exhibition, which was held from April 15 to May 15. There would be eight Impressionist exhibitions, the last one held in 1886; Monet took part in all but three. While at first the exhibitions were greeted mainly with derision (indeed, the name "Impressionism" comes from a sneering remark in a satirical review by the critic Louis Leroy, commenting on a Monet painting entitled *Impression, Sunrise*), this approach finally proved to be the most viable way for avant-garde artists to get their work shown.

Monet painted many views of the St. Lazare station in 1877, showing eight of them together at the Third Impressionist Exhibition that April; the simultaneous showing may have provided the germ for his later series paintings. In the early 1880's, all the Impressionists went through a crisis in reaction to all the criticism of "carelessness" and "formlessness." While Monet does not seem to have reacted as much as Renoir, he was nevertheless affected by the criticism and attempted henceforth a more fully actualized treatment.

In 1890, Monet began to paint his first deliberate series of paintings: views of haystacks. These were produced at different seasons of the year and from different points of view, with different aspects of light, but in 1891 he showed fifteen of them in an exhibition at the dealer Paul Durand-Ruel's; the series proved to be surprisingly successful. In 1892 and 1893, Monet painted the famous sequences of views of the façade of Rouen Cathedral, in which his serial procedure is fully developed. For these paintings, Monet worked on several canvases during the course of one day, moving from one to another as the light changed. To appreciate fully this serial progression, one must see several of the canvases in sequence.

After 1900, the majority of Monet's paintings were done in and around Giverny, on a tributary of the Seine halfway between Paris and Rouen, where he had lived since 1883. Monet gradually acquired the status of the dean of living painters, and Giverny became a mecca, especially for two types of visitors: young American Impressionists and young Symbolist writers, such as Gustave Geffroy, who became Monet's biographer, and Octave Mirbeau, who elucidated one of the major reasons for Symbolist interest in later Monet works when he praised Monet for expressing the inexpressible and seizing the unseizable. Perhaps even more significant were Monet's numerous contacts with the great Symbolist poet Stéphane Mallarmé, beginning in the mid-1880's.

Once Monet had created his Japanese water garden on his Giverny property, he began, in 1899, to produce the stunning series of paintings of the pond that formed his chief endeavor in the twentieth century. Most of the sequences show the surface of the pond, its water lilies, its overhanging willows, and its reflections. These paintings, which Monet called "waterscapes," tend increasingly toward a form of abstract Impressionism, partly because of Monet's treatment of the entire surface of the canvas, which negates the idea of focus, and partly because of his elimination of the horizon line in his paintings after 1905, which meant that he painted the surface of the pond only, providing no clear sense of direction. A further impetus toward abstraction may have been provided by Monet's increasing eye problems (cataracts in both eyes were diagnosed in 1912; in 1923, he underwent a partially successful operation on his right eye), which necessitated greater breadth of technique and the use of stronger color. Yet these bold, free strokes are still intended to record the specific nuances of Monet's visual impressions of light and color.

The greatest of all the water lily series is the huge cycle housed in two large oval rooms in the Orangerie in Paris, a project originally suggested to Monet by Georges Clemenceau during World War I and intended as a donation to the state. Much of the painting was done during World War I, but Monet continued to rework and revise the sequence until close to his death in 1926. The cycle was dedicated in May of 1927, a fitting tribute to one of the most extraordinary artists of the modern era. The viewer, standing in the middle of each oval space engulfed by the huge size of the panels, is himself put into the picture. It is, as André Masson described it in 1952, the "Sistine Chapel of Impressionism . . . one of the summits of French art."

Summary

Through the years, Claude Monet has come to be considered the leading Impressionist painter, a position which is strengthened by the fact that he, unlike Renoir or Pissarro, who had periods when they retreated from the Impressionist approach, remained largely faithful to the Impressionist goal of transcribing every nuance of changing optical sensations for the whole of his exceptionally long career, which spanned a full sixty years. This mammoth oeuvre, consisting of approximately two thousand paintings, was not codified until the 1970's and 1980's in a definitive four-volume *catalogue raisonné* by Daniel Wildenstein, *Claude Monet, biographie et catalogue raisonné* (1974-1985). Monet's vision remained remarkably consistent throughout the developments in his style.

It is, rather, outside judgments that have varied: Supporters in the 1870's stressed the element of di-rect observation; Symbolist champions of the late 1880's and 1890's sensed an affinity with their aims in the infinitely nuanced transcription of his series paintings. In the wake of formalist movements of the early twentieth century, Impressionism was often judged as a short-lived, limited phenomenon and late Monet paintings, in particular, as a dead end. That was before the large "action paintings" of artists such as Jackson Pollock suddenly revealed the relevance of the late Monet works. Somewhat later, the interpretations of social historians stressed the contemporaneity of Impressionist themes in the 1870's, such as the railroad, and questioned the famous judgment of Paul Cézanne, who became one of the foremost challengers of Impressionism, that "Monet is only an eye . . . but what an eye." Most scholars, however, continue to stress the aspect of observation over interpretation, emphasizing that the Impressionists never comment on what they observe. In Monet's case, the central importance of his essentially visual focus is amply supported by many of his own statements. Whether one's interest in Monet centers on pure observation, on social concerns, or on the affinities with Symbolism, Monet's central position in the late nineteenth century seems secure, and Giverny, refurbished and restored, has once again become a mecca for pilgrims.

Bibliography

Belloli, Andrew P. A., ed. *A Day in the Country: Impressionism and the French Landscape*. Los Angeles: Los Angeles County Museum of Art, 1984. This scholarly exhibition catalog provides a considerable treatment of Monet which enables one to see his work in the context of the Impressionist movement. Consists of a series of articles on different aspects of Impressionism, notes on each of the paintings exhibited, a bibliography, and an index.

House, John. *Monet: Nature into Art*. New Haven, Conn.: Yale University Press, 1986; London: Yale University Press, 1989. An excellent, detailed study of aspects of Monet's themes, composition, techniques, and the like, as well as a discussion of the evolution of his series concept. Includes a chronology, footnotes, bibliography, and index. Amply illustrated.

Isaacson, Joel. *Claude Monet: Observation and Reflection*. Oxford: Phaidon Press, 1978. This study consists of a succinct essay chronicling the major phases of Monet's career and stylistic development, followed by individual notes on each of the plates, a chronology, a bibliographical note, and an index.

Rewald, John. *The History of Impressionism.* Rev. ed. New York: Museum of Modern Art, 1973. This exhaustively detailed chronological treatment of Impressionism remains the most essential work on the movement. The treatment of Monet is interwoven throughout the volume to give a thorough presentation of his place in the Impressionist group. Excellent footnotes, a chronology, a superlative chronological bibliography, and an extensive index are included. Contains many plates.

Stuckey, Charles F., ed. *Monet: A Retrospective.* New York: Park Lane, 1985. Consists of seventy-seven selections from a series of books and articles on Monet (dating from 1865 to 1957), a number of them eyewitness accounts, some translated from the French for the first time. Includes an index and plates.

Dorathea K. Beard

JEAN MONNET

Born: November 9, 1888; Cognac, France
Died: March 16, 1979; Montfort-l'Amaury, France
Areas of Achievement: Diplomacy, economics, government, and politics
Contribution: Monnet has justly been called "the father of Europe," in recognition of the importance of his role in the foundation of the European Coal and Steel Community, Euratom, and the Common Market. He worked primarily as an adviser rather than as the holder of powerful political positions; his ideas and plans have been instrumental in shaping Europe's postwar moves toward economic and political integration.

Early Life

Jean Monnet was born on November 9, 1888, into a family of winegrowers in Cognac, a small town set amid the vineyards of the Angoulëme region of France. In contrast to other European leaders of his generation, his formal education was minimal. He left school at the age of sixteen, never to return. Instead, he spent the next decade traveling the world selling his family's brandy. Long stays in the United States and Canada left him fluent in English and cosmopolitan in outlook as well as increasingly prosperous. During this period, he also began to form the network of friendships and contacts among leading figures in all areas of public life around the world that would serve him so well throughout his career.

A short, compact, highly animated and energetic man, Monnet was never a towering intellect who dazzled people with the brilliant originality of his ideas. Nor was he an imposing physical presence or an impressive public speaker. He had instead solid common sense, enormous tact and discretion, and a remarkably clear vision of what he wanted to accomplish and how to go about realizing his goals most efficiently.

Life's Work

During World War I, Monnet advised both his own government and that of Great Britain on economic matters. The experience convinced him of the importance of rational economic planning and of the necessity of countries cooperating with one another rather than trying to achieve their economic goals unilaterally. His success in coordinating economic aspects of the Anglo-French war effort, particularly shipping, led to his being given the post of Deputy Secretary-General of the League of Nations after the war ended in 1918.

In 1923, problems in the family brandy business led Monnet to resign his position with the League of Nations and return to private life. After reorganizing the family concern, he began working in investment banking. His career as a businessman took him to Sweden, China, and the United States over the following decade and a half. Then, in 1938, the gathering clouds of World War II led Monnet back into public service. Working in the United States on behalf first of the French and then of the British government, he was instrumental in convincing American leaders of the importance of shifting American economic resources over to military production even before the war began. He is credited with coining the phrase "arsenal of democracy" to describe the role that the United States would have to play in defeating the challenge of Fascism and with helping to prepare it to play that role successfully.

In the spring of 1940, with the deadly thrust of the Nazi war machine spreading despair throughout France, Monnet seized upon a bold idea to prevent an ignominious French surrender to Adolf Hitler and keep the French people in the war even after their homeland had fallen. He suggested that France and England merge, that their people share a common citizenship, and that the war be carried on under the direction of a cabinet composed of French as well as English leaders. Winston Churchill, the English prime minister, quickly agreed and formally extended an offer of joint citizenship to the French. This breathtakingly bold idea for submerging ancient national rivalries and loyalties in a new supranational entity was not to come to pass, however, as the French government opted for surrender instead.

Throughout the remainder of the war, Monnet used his diplomatic skills to smooth relations between the English and Americans on the one hand, and the French forces of resistance to Hitler on the other. This proved to be a difficult task, as the most important French leader was the proud and prickly General Charles de Gaulle, whose single-minded French nationalism was a striking contrast to Monnet's broadly international outlook.

At war's end, with France prostrate and impoverished, Monnet was able to convince its government that economic recovery would require careful plan-

ning and direction. He worked out a system of planning in which leaders of government, business, and labor unions would sit down together and decide where resources and investments could best be utilized. Monnet became the first director of France's enormously successful postwar planning commission in 1947 and did much to launch France on the road to the prosperity of the second half of the twentieth century. Under his guidance, resources were used not only to relieve current suffering but also to rebuild, reshape, and modernize the entire French economy.

After World War II, all over Europe there was much sentiment in favor of some sort of European unification. Such unification, it was argued, could help strengthen Europe against the Russian menace, could promote the more rational and efficient development of Europe's economic resources, and, most important, could help defuse the murderous national resentments and ambitions that had so often led to war in the past. A number of approaches to unification were proposed and even attempted in the late 1940's and early 1950's, but none succeeded in overcoming the tremendous psychological,

political, economic, and military obstacles that blocked the path.

Monnet, long an enthusiastic advocate of supranationalism, argued that the best way to overcome the hatreds and divisions of the past was to unite the peoples and nations of Europe around mutual striving toward a common goal. In this they could begin to see that they had common interests and could form the habit of working together to further them. A common goal required a common institution to coordinate and direct the peoples' efforts. Monnet had few illusions about the possibility of eliminating greed or aggression from human nature. He was convinced, however, that the experience of living and working together under common institutions and common rules could slowly create habits of cooperation and of the peaceful settlement of disputes. His example was the civilized, peaceful lives shared by people within each sovereign country. His goal was to build common institutions for all Europe.

In the spring of 1950, Monnet presented his friend, the French Foreign Minister Robert Schuman, with a plan for beginning the economic integration of Europe. It called for the establishment of a supranational authority to coordinate, direct, and plan the coal and steel production of Europe. The member nations would have to agree to yield some of their sovereign authority over their most significant resources and industries. Monnet argued that in doing so, they not only would ease the staggering task of rebuilding Europe's blasted economies but also would deprive themselves of the independent power to arm against and strike at their neighbors, since coal and steel are the indispensable sinews of modern warefare. Individual governments, he pointed out, would no longer have the ability to control these parts of their nations' economies.

Here at last was a viable proposal for beginning the process of European integration. Monnet's plan quickly led to a treaty between France, West Germany, Italy, Belgium, The Netherlands, and Luxembourg, forming the European Coal and Steel Community. This community, which went into effect in 1952, stripped away all the members' quotas, tariff restrictions, artificial monopolies, discriminatory freight rates, and other nationalistic regulations—regulations that had long strangled the heavy industry of the members in the name of protecting each from the competition of the others. Monnet, as the first president of the Community's High Authority, directed it through its formative years. As he had predicted, economic integration was an enormous success. Trade between the six member countries rose dramatically as did overall production and prosperity.

During the early 1950's, Monnet also attempted to further European integration by advancing a plan for military unification in the form of an integrated army known as the European Defense Community. His hopes, however, were dashed in 1954 when the government of France rejected the project. In 1955, convinced that the Coal and Steel Community was functioning well, Monnet resigned from its High Authority. Its presidency was the last significant political office that he would ever hold, but its abandonment was far from the end of his career. Indeed, the influence that he had on events in Europe continued to be enormous. Throughout his career, he was most comfortable, and most effective, standing slightly in the background, acting as an adviser, allowing others to put his ideas into effect and take the credit for them, rather than doing it himself.

Upon leaving the Coal and Steel Community, he founded the Action Committee for the United States of Europe, which he would lead from 1955 until its dissolution twenty years later. The Action Committee was a group of experts, labor leaders, and political figures who shared Monnet's dream of a united Europe and his conviction that the path to the achievement of this goal lay in the building of institutions that would accustom the Europeans to working together. It became a veritable cornucopia of ideas, suggestions, and plans designed to further the integration of Europe. The work of Monnet's Action Committee, combined with his own tireless lobbying, was indispensable in laying the groundwork for the treaties forming Euratom and the Common Market in 1957. These new organizations extended the Coal and Steel Community into the development of nuclear energy and into far more ambitious economic integration of the six, creating a real European Community.

By the end of the 1950's, the integration of Europe was an irreversible reality but was far from complete. Monnet was highly disappointed by the refusal of the other European nations, particularly Great Britain, to join the six nations of the European Community. In addition, the economic integration represented by the Common Market fell far short of the political and cultural unification that was Monnet's ultimate goal. During the 1960's and 1970's, Monnet continued to advance the cause of

European unification through his Action Committee, through his writings and speeches, and above all through his quiet but effective work of advising and persuading. By the time of his death in 1979, Great Britain, Ireland, and Denmark had all joined the European Community, and the negotiations for the addition of Portugal, Spain, and Greece were virtually completed. Meanwhile such developments as a European Monetary System for the community and direct elections of delegates to its legislature appeared to justify Monnet's optimism about the future of European unification.

Summary

Throughout his life, Jean Monnet believed in the ability of human beings to address their problems successfully through rational planning and through the building of institutions that would in turn build habits of cooperating with one another in the pursuit of common goals rather than fighting against one another. Rarely holding any office that gave him power, Monnet worked by preference through advising and persuading others to make such plans and to build such institutions. The economic planning that he suggested helped to lead the Western democracies to victory in the two world wars of the first half of the twentieth century. After World War II, he went on to play a key role in reviving and reshaping the economy of France. His tact and his negotiating skills were instrumental in convincing French businessmen, labor leaders, and politicians to accept the idea of a planned economy.

Monnet's most important role was his leadership in the movement toward European integration. He was able to translate what appeared to be hopelessly idealistic dreams of overcoming deeply embedded nationalistic prejudices into solid, workable plans. No less important, he inspired others with his vision and his enthusiasm. The Common Market and its success are, in a real sense, the offspring of Monnet.

Bibliography

Beloff, Max. "Jean Monnet's Europe and After." *Encounter* 48 (May, 1977): 29-35. In large part a response to the criticisms of Monnet presented by Douglas Johnson (see entry below), this article emphasizes the important and constructive role played by Monnet in European affairs throughout his life.

Bromberger, Merry, and Serge Bromberger. *Jean Monnet and the United States of Europe.* New

York: Coward-McCann, 1969. The Brombergers, French journalists, admire Monnet enormously and present a full and sympathetic picture of his career in this popular biography. Despite the authors' advantage of having Monnet's cooperation, however, their work is not very accurate or even well written. The lack of a bibliography, citations of sources, or an index further limits the volume's scholarly usefulness.

Featherstone, Kevin. "Jean Monnet and the 'Democratic Deficit' in the European Union." *Journal of Common Market Studies* 32, no. 2 (June, 1994). Reevaluates the economic philosophy of Monnet and its role in the development of the European Coal and Steel Community.

Hitchcock, William I. "France, the Western Alliance, and the Origins of the Schuman Plan, 1948-1950." *Diplomatic History* 21, no. 4 (Fall 1997). Discusses Robert Schuman's 1950 plan, written by Monnet, for consolidating European coal and steel resources.

Johnson, Douglas. "A Certain Idea of Europe." *Times Literary Supplement* (December 10, 1976): 1530-1531. Johnson, in this review article occasioned by the publication of Monnet's autobiography, makes it plain that he does not share Monnet's faith in the potential advantages of European integration. Johnson attacks him harshly for being unrealistic and egotistical, both in his writing and throughout his career.

Mayne, Richard. "Gray Eminence." *American Scholar* 53 (August, 1984): 533-540. A brief, sympathetic examination of Monnet's importance behind the scenes in the movement to unify Europe. Mayne stresses Monnet's remarkable ability to get what he wanted done while allowing others to take the credit.

———. *The Recovery of Europe, 1945-1973.* Rev. ed. New York: Anchor Press, 1973. This book, by an English journalist who knew Monnet well and admired him intensely, contains an excellent scholarly account of Monnet's role in Europe's most significant economic and political events following World War II. Meticulous notes and a good bibliography and index enhance the value of this volume.

Monnet, Jean. *Memoirs.* London: Collins, and New York: Doubleday, 1978. Monnet presents a readable and extremely detailed account of his public career, but there is little about his private life here. Indeed, Monnet shows himself to be too tactful and reserved even to make strong judgments about the figures with whom he wrestled in politics. The book is well indexed.

"What Jean Monnet Wrought." *Foreign Affairs* 55 (April, 1977): 630-635. This anonymous article reviewing Monnet's *Memoirs* stresses his role in the founding of the European Community. It also raises serious questions about whether Monnet's approach, centering on the building of supranational economic institutions while leaving national governments intact, will ever produce the true European unity of which Monnet dreamed.

Garrett L. McAinsh

MARILYN MONROE

Born: June 1, 1926; Los Angeles, California
Died: August 4, 1962; Los Angeles, California
Area of Achievement: Film
Contribution: Monroe rose from poverty to become one of the most famous film stars of the twentieth century. Despite the skepticism of studio executives, her Cinderella story touched filmgoers, and their reactions made her a cult figure rivaling Elvis Presley and the Beatles.

Early Life

Marilyn Monroe was born as Norma Jeane Mortenson, daughter of Gladys Monroe Baker Mortenson and an unknown father. Her mother had married Martin Edward Mortenson in October, 1924; he filed for divorce in May, 1925. Norma Jeane sometimes used the name Baker, since Gladys had been previously married to Jasper Baker and had borne two other children, Berniece and Jackie. Both lived in Kentucky with Jasper and a stepmother while Gladys, in California, worked as a film cutter. Lacking financial resources, Gladys boarded Norma Jeane with neighbors Albert and Ida Bolender until, in 1933, she could afford a house. Gladys and her friend Grace McKee, later Goddard, encouraged Norma Jeane to dream of a film career modeled on that of early blonde star Jean Harlow.

The financial situation, lengthy work hours, motherhood, and other problems led to Gladys's mental breakdown. She was institutionalized. Grace McKee took charge of Gladys and Norma Jeane; the child lived in the Los Angeles County Children's Home from September 13, 1935, to June, 1937, when Grace's petition for guardianship was granted. Perhaps because of sexual overtures from "Doc" Goddard, Grace's new husband, Norma Jeane lived with relatives in Compton, California, from late 1937 until August, 1938, when she returned to Los Angeles to live first with Grace and then with Ana Lower, Grace's aunt, a Christian Science practitioner for whom Monroe expressed lasting affection. She lived there until her marriage, on June 19, 1942, to James Dougherty.

Monroe herself, as well as publicists and some biographers, later exaggerated this already turbulent life into a saga of abusive foster parents and orphanage life. Without these exaggerations, however, the insecurities of Monroe's childhood were enough to cause her lifelong problems. She began to draw attention with tight clothes and bright makeup and dropped out of high school during her second year. Her marriage, at sixteen, was a normal way for young working-class girls of her time to seek security. Such girls rarely attended college, and few careers were open to them.

With World War II raging, Dougherty joined the Merchant Marines. When he was sent overseas, Norma Jeane moved in with his mother. The war created unprecedented job opportunities for women, and Norma Jeane found work at the Radioplane Company in Burbank. In 1944, army photographers arrived at the company to take pictures of women on the job. Norma Jeane attracted the attention of photographer David Conover, who encouraged her to become a model. By 1945 she had been accepted by the Blue Book Agency for models, had begun attending the school's training sessions, and had moved out from her mother-in-law's house. By spring, 1946, she had appeared on thirty-three magazine covers. She was divorced from Dougherty later that year.

Life's Work

With her hair lightened and her name changed to Marilyn Monroe, the young actor won her first screen test at Twentieth Century-Fox Studios on July 17, 1946. She received a contract. Her first role was as a high school girl barely visible in the background of *Scudda-Hoo! Scudda-Hay!* (1948), a film about a farm family raising mules. In the same year, she made three brief appearances in *Dangerous Years*, a film concerning juvenile delinquency. After the two motion pictures were released, her contract was not renewed.

While unemployed, Monroe began studies at the Actors Laboratory, a showcase for playwrights, actors, and directors, where Monroe hoped to compensate for her limited training and education. She met actor John Carroll and his wife Lucille Ryman, director of the Metro-Goldwyn-Mayer (MGM) talent department, who became her sponsors, as did Fox's executive producer Joseph Schenck and, later, powerful agent Johnny Hyde. Schenck's friend Harry Cohn, head of Columbia Studios, offered her a six-month contract. At Columbia, she appeared briefly in *Ladies of the Chorus* (1948). After this contract expired, she played small roles in the Marx Brothers comedy *Love Happy* (1950) and in *A Ticket to Tomahawk* (1950). During this period,

Marilyn Monroe and Yves Montand in the film Let's Make Love.

she posed nude for photographer Tom Kelley; his calendar shots, "New Wrinkle" and "Golden Dreams," became famous three years later.

Public response to Monroe's appearance and to a promotional tour for *Love Happy* was quick and positive, but, as Monroe realized, she appealed to a poor and working-class audience. With her sexy walk and overly tight clothes, she was joining the pre-1934 censorship tradition of seductive and sexy blondes such as Mae West and Jean Harlow. In the 1950's, however, working under rigid censorship codes, major Hollywood studios tended to reinforce the religious and family values emphasized under that code with stars such as Betty Grable, who projected a more wholesome image than did West and Harlow. The seductive blonde was now automatically cast as dumb, evil, or both. Even newspaper and magazine reports often ridiculed Monroe's desire for serious dramatic roles.

In 1950, she signed a seven-year contract with Twentieth Century-Fox, but the contract did not immediately improve her roles. She portrayed one of several girls attracted to a roller-skating star in *The Fireball* and a dumb but aspiring actor in *All About Eve*, both released in 1950. She had small roles in *Right Cross* (1950), *Hometown Story* (1951), and *As Young As You Feel* (1951), and slightly more important roles in *Love Nest* (1951) and *Let's Make It Legal* (1951). Her first major role was as part of the criminal underworld in *The Asphalt Jungle* (1950). She played light comedy in *We're Not Married* (1952) and *Monkey Business* (1952), and dramatic roles in *Clash by Night* (1952) and *Don't Bother to Knock* (1952). In the latter, she played a mentally disturbed babysitter. Other films of the period included *O. Henry's Full House* (1952) and *Niagara* (1953).

Monroe's fame grew, despite her limited roles. News that she had posed nude for Kelley's photographs frightened studio employees but actually enhanced her reputation when she publicly explained that she had posed because she needed the money. With her combined sexiness and childlike vulnerability, she had come to embody the Cinderella myth for millions of Americans, especially when she began to be seen with baseball great Joe DiMaggio, whom she married in 1954. (She filed for divorce later that year.) In view of this popularity, Monroe began to refuse roles she considered demeaning.

The series of major films for which she is best known began with the musical *Gentlemen Prefer Blondes* (1953) and the comedy *How to Marry a Millionaire* (1953). In both, she played a vulnerable girl who seeks security through a wealthy marriage. An intelligent and likeable mind is visible behind the dumb blonde facade. These were followed by major roles in the Western *River of No Return* (1954) and in *There's No Business Like Show Business* (1954), and, more important, lead roles in *The Seven Year Itch* (1955) and *Bus Stop* (1956), in which she played perhaps her finest role as a pathetic saloon singer who dreams of Hollywood stardom.

By this time, she had broken with Twentieth Century-Fox, formed her own production company called Marilyn Monroe Productions (MMP), established a base in New York, and begun studying with Lee Strasberg, famed head of the Actor's Studio, which fostered serious acting talent. She began psychotherapy, which she would continue to the end of her life, sometimes falling prey to manipulative therapists. Her difficulties in appearing on film sets on time, sometimes caused by serious illness and sometimes by insecurity, increased, and she also became addicted to prescription drugs, sometimes in combination with alcohol. Her problems were not solved by her 1956 marriage to Arthur Miller, the Pulitzer Prize-winning playwright best known for *Death of a Salesman* (1949) and *The Crucible* (1953). They were divorced in 1961.

Monroe made only four films between 1957 and 1961. Of these, the most important was the comedy *Some Like It Hot* (1959). *The Prince and the Showgirl* (1957) and *Let's Make Love* (1960) were critical and popular failures. Monroe's last film, *The Misfits* (1961), has gained lasting fame for its all-star cast. It was the final completed film of legendary star Clark Gable; the script was written by Miller. Footage from the unfinished *Something's Got to Give*, filmed in 1962, has been praised by Monroe fans, but Monroe was fired from the film after problems variously attributed to illness, behavior, and addiction.

Monroe's death on the night of August 4, 1962, was officially listed as suicide but has since become the material of various legends, some fostered by the deliberate fictionalizations of novelist Norman Mailer and some by numerous exploitational books and media programs. Donald Spoto, in the afterword to his 1993 *Marilyn Monroe*, discusses the growth of these myths and their sources. While Spoto presents a reasonable theory of her death, the facts are now obscured by myths, lies, and even forged letters. Even the facts of Monroe's life were further clouded by the posthumous publication, in 1974, of her "autobiography," *My Story* (actually ghostwritten), which reemphasized the Cinderella legend that continues to appeal to the public.

Summary

While Marilyn Monroe was capable of brilliant acting, her role in American culture transcends her importance as an actor. The events of her life are important for an understanding of the role of women in the post-World War II world, as women who had learned independence and experienced freedom were urged back to the home in the world after the war. The response to Monroe illuminates the contradictory attitudes of Americans toward female sexuality; while she was publicly condemned for her walk, her revealingly tight clothes, and her blatant sexuality, the condemnations served only to increase the audiences for her films, and, despite them, she gained a measure of social importance denied to the earlier West and Harlow. In 1962, for example, wearing a particularly revealing form-fitting gown, she sang "Happy Birthday to You" to President John F. Kennedy before fifteen thousand people in New York's Madison Square Garden. She possibly had a brief affair with the president.

In addition, reactions illuminate the attitudes of middle-class media and corporate executives toward the working class and its values and toward women of that class. Like Elvis Presley and the Beatles, she attracted enormous media and corporate attention, but, during her lifetime and for many years afterward, that attention was often tinged with condescension and contempt. Finally, the mythologizing of Monroe's life reveals the lasting importance of the Cinderella story, while the various conspiracy theories surrounding her death show the vague fears of corporate, criminal, and governmental manipulation that haunt the American popular consciousness.

Bibliography

Cohen, Lisa. "The Horizontal Walk: Marilyn Monroe, CinemaScope, and Sexuality." *Yale Journal of Criticism* 11, no. 1 (Spring 1998). Discusses perceptions of Monroe and how CinemaScope was used to enhance her features.

Guiles, Fred Lawrence. *Legend: The Life and Death of Marilyn Monroe.* New York: Stein and Day, 1984. Guiles provides a readable and complete biography, but facts should be compared with those presented in Donald Spoto's Monroe biography.

Mailer, Norman. *Marilyn: A Biography.* London: Hodder and Stoughton, and New York: Grosset and Dunlap, 1973. This fictionalized biography by well-known novelist Mailer became the source of many stories surrounding Monroe and her death.

Mellen, Joan. *Marilyn Monroe.* New York: Pyramid, 1973. This feminist reading of Monroe's life and films provides an unconventional critique of her acting career.

Mereyman, Richard, and Allan Grant. "Marilyn Monroe: The Last Interview." *Life* 15, no. 8 (August, 1992). Monroe's last interview (July, 1962) in which she discussed her turbulent childhood, her career, loves, and more.

Miracle, Berniece Baker, and Mona Rae Miracle. *My Sister Marilyn: A Memoir of Marilyn Monroe.* Chapel Hill, N.C.: Algonquin, and London: Weidenfeld and Nicolson, 1994. Monroe's half sister and niece offer a poignant account of a poor and dysfunctional family struggling against their environment during Monroe's early years.

Monroe, Marilyn. *My Story.* New York: Stein and Day, 1974; London: Allen, 1975. Published after the deaths of both Monroe and ghostwriter Ben Hecht, this autobiography may have been compiled by several hands, although it does contain some genuine autobiographical material.

Rollyson, Carl. *Marilyn Monroe: A Life of the Actress.* Ann Arbor, Mich.: UMI Research Press, 1986; London: Souvenir Press, 1987. While repeating many biographical myths, Rollyson's book is the most readable of the serious studies of Monroe's acting and films.

Spoto, Donald. *Marilyn Monroe: The Biography.* New York: HarperCollins, and London: Chatto and Windus, 1993. This is essential reading. Spoto provides information based on thousands of new documents—including government documents—and two hundred new interviews. The book traces sources of myths surrounding Monroe's life and death.

Steinem, Gloria. *Marilyn.* New York: Holt, 1986; London: Gollancz, 1987. This feminist interpretation is illustrated with photographs by George Barris.

Wagenknecht, Edward, ed. *Marilyn Monroe: A Composite View*. Philadelphia: Chilton, 1969. This book contains two 1962 interviews with Monroe and important essays by photographer Cecil Beaton, Lee Strasberg (Monroe's acting mentor), critic Diana Trilling, British poet Edith Sitwell, and others.

Zolotow, Maurice. *Marilyn Monroe*. Rev. ed. New York: Harper, 1990. Many facts are questionable, but Zolotow presents a vivid picture of social and film culture by a Hollywood insider of Monroe's time.

Betty Richardson

EUGENIO MONTALE

Born: October 12, 1896; Genoa, Italy
Died: September 12, 1981; Milan, Italy
Area of Achievement: Literature
Contribution: Montale is the foremost Italian poet of the twentieth century and the recipient of the Nobel Prize in Literature in 1975. With his contemporaries Giuseppe Ungaretti and Salvatore Quasimodo, Montale created a modern Italian poetry of international significance: honest, poignant, serious, and wise.

Early Life

Eugenio Montale was born in Genoa, Italy, on October 12, 1896. His father owned an import firm and would take the family—Montale's mother and his three elder brothers and one elder sister—to his native place of Monterosso on the Ligurian coast every summer. Montale returned there each summer through his first thirty years. He loved both the lonely splendor of the Italian coastline and the activity of turn-of-the-century Genoa. While he knew the local dialects and grew familiar with the typical mix of rich and poor in the city, he also became entranced by the beauty of the small coastal villages. The formative influences of these places would later color his poetry.

Montale did not attend a university. He was drawn toward a musical career as a singer, but the death of his teacher and his father's objections dissuaded him. Montale went through his early life with no clear idea of a career. His mother died, and he was, as the youngest, the favorite son. He was called up to serve in the army for two years in 1917. He went to Parma for training and then to the front in Trentino.

After World War I, he returned to Genoa and stayed there until 1927, cofounding the Turin review *Primo tempo* (1922) and becoming acquainted with the writers and critics of the day. Being unemployed for most of the time, he read voraciously: Poets such as Stéphane Mallarmé, Paul Valéry, and Charles Baudelaire, as well as the "prose-poet" Maurice de Guérin, Henry James, and philosophers such as Henri Bergson and Benedetto Croce captured his attention. Montale used the libraries, held long discussions with friends, and began to send out poems, essays, and reviews to the literary and popular press. He was quick to appreciate the quality of Italo Svevo, writing an "Omaggio" (homage) in 1925 that virtually created Sve-

vo's Italian reputation. Montale became famous with the publication of his first book, *Ossi di seppia* (1925; *Bones of the Cuttlefish*, 1984). In 1927, he left Genoa for Florence, where he remained for some twenty years before going on to Milan and a full-time appointment as a literary editor for the newspaper *Corriere della sera.*

Life's Work

Montale's poetry draws upon the stark, rocky coastal landscapes of his youth. The poetry flourished throughout his career as a journalist and developed along with his interest in music and painting. *Ossi di seppia* gathered these interests and fused them in a mature, poised, stylish poetry of compact and passionate lyricism, bringing together evocations of youthful energy, the vivid landscapes of Monterosso, and the sense of an inimical world. It was a unique, unrepeatable achievement, mixing tones of longing and loneliness, isolation and love, in acknowledgment not only of the remorselessness of material existence but also of human care and hope for the safety of others. Montale is unflinching in his understanding of human vulnerability on the cosmic scale and is reminiscent of the grim, visionary Italian poet Giacomo Leopardi in his tenacity and depth. Memories, suspended emotions, symbolic presences of sea and coastline—Montale shares certain tonalities with T. S. Eliot. He resolutely refuses easy consolations and brings himself to terms with a world between the wars, in which living is compared to following a wall "with bits/ of broken bottle glass on top" ("Meriggiare pallido e assorto"). Correspondingly, Montale's versification surprises, with lines suddenly extending or contracting and with dissonant half-rhymes and old rhythmic effects. He departs from traditional prosody as he draws upon his memories of youth. Yet, the knowledge that the period of youthful innocence is over and that prosodic traditions have been broken as well lends a startling immediacy and a resilient vitality to his first book.

Upon arriving in Florence in 1927, Montale began work for the publisher Bemporad, but a year later was made director of the famous and prestigious literary and scientific library, the Gabinetto Vieusseux. He was the only candidate for the post not a member of the Fascist Party. In 1938, when Fascism had become much more powerful, his abstention from overt political life worked against him. He resigned from his post at that time rather than be coerced into joining the Party. He married, and throughout World War II, he lived in occupied Florence. He was by then writing for various important Florentine journals, and Einaudi published his second book of poems, *Le occasioni* (1939; the occasions). Here, Montale's most famous poems ("Dora Markus," "Motetti," "La casa dei dogani-ari," and "Eastbourne") reveal a great personal depth, focused on the love of a woman Montale's persona names Clizia. She is both a real, suffering person and a symbolic force crystallizing life and poetry, transforming fiction and reality. The volume marks the increased extent of the autobiographical aspect in Montale's poetry. Separation and loss, reunion and longing are the fundamental areas of experience explored in the most poignant and intimate fashion. Montale does not romanticize, but he maintains a deeply satisfying fusion of the experience of love with the moral and political dilemmas of the time. His poetry is attentive to the zeitgeist, but it is made more human, more sensitive, and more credible by the strength of love that runs through it. The language is spare; the certainties of Europe and his love are threatened by war and adversity. A number of actual women are given Beatrice-like significance in the poems, but the fragmented sense of their actuality and vulnerability illuminates the atmosphere of incipient tragedy. Underlying the poems runs a tone of anger and protest against human destruction.

If Montale's early life in Liguria, Monterosso, and Genoa had encouraged his introspection and self-absorption, the two decades he passed in Florence fostered his cultural awareness of humanism, literary ideas, and intellectual traditions. He was at this time writing reviews and essays on various literary subjects, and he translated into Italian Christopher Marlowe's *The Tragicall History of Dr. Faustus* (1604), William Shakespeare's *The Comedy of Errors* (1592-1593), *Julius Caesar* (1599-1600), *Hamlet* (1600-1601), *The Winter's Tale* (1610-1611), and other works. As his literary taste expanded and the range of his cultural appreciation widened, Montale was also producing poetry that was to appear in his third book. Between 1940 and 1942, he produced a sequence published in Lugano, Switzerland, in 1943 entitled "Finisterre." In 1948, on January 30, an opportune meeting with Guglielmo Emanuel, the editor of the national daily *Corriere della sera*, resulted in Montale being asked to provide immediately an article on the as-

sassination of Mahatma Gandhi, which had just occurred. In two hours, Montale had the piece ready, and it appeared (anonymously) the next day. As a result, Montale was offered a permanent post on the paper, and he moved to Milan.

Montale's third volume, *La bufera e altro* (1956; *Eugenio Montale: The Storm and Other Poems*, 1978), gathers work written throughout the 1940's, in which lyrical and autobiographical qualities are mixed with political and historical concerns. He regarded it as his best book, and poems such as "L'anguilla" ("The Eel") and the "Finisterre" cycle are brilliantly realized. "Primavera hitleriana" ("The Hitler Spring") is an evocative and sinister depiction of Adolf Hitler and Benito Mussolini meeting in Florence. A sequence of poems sprang from Montale's visits to England and Scotland, as his attention to his immediate location, in Ely or Glasgow or Edinburgh, is disturbingly haunted by the vision of the woman he loves and his craving to rejoin her. Montale visited the Middle East (with his wife), and as his love poetry deepened and grew in poignancy and poise, his resolute refusal to engage directly in political life was reconfirmed.

The book ends with two "provisional conclusions": "Piccolo testamento" (small testament) and "Il sogno del prigioniero" (the prisoner's dream), in which Montale's stoical adherence to spiritual independence rejects all recourse to the securities of either the Catholic church or Communism, the two political regimes then dominant in Italy. The mature restraint in these poems is a register of Montale's historical as well as his spiritual condition.

Montale's volume *Satura* (1971) contains poems previously published as "Xenia" (1964-1967), written on the death of his wife, Drusilla Tanzi, and published in translation in 1970, together with miscellaneous other poems. The elegies are profoundly moving and reminiscent of Thomas Hardy in their hallucinatory power. They were written when Montale was in his seventies. The honorary degree of doctor of letters was awarded to Montale by the Universities of Rome, Milan, and Cambridge. In 1967, he was made a life-senator. The Nobel Prize, awarded in 1975, was a recognition of his life's achievement in poetry, which, though limited to a handful of books, has been compared to that of T. S. Eliot and Ezra Pound. He died in Milan, an elder statesman of Italian literature, in 1981.

Summary

Throughout his working life, Eugenio Montale was a professional journalist as well as a major poet. His published criticism includes work on modern Italian, British, and American literature, as well as essays on Dante, Giovanni Boccaccio, and a wide range of others. He published a book of stories, *La farfalla di Dinard* (1956; *Butterfly of Dinard*, 1971), and collections of essays and articles have also appeared. His achievement as a critic of literature and music and as a storyteller has added to his stature as a man of letters, but it is as a poet of lyric depth and lonely honesty that his moral and political significance is to be found. No one has written so well of the common ground between solitude and love. Concurrently, Montale's intellectual experiences brought about a cultured wisdom that tempered the oblique idiosyncrasies of his style. The intensity of Montale's poetry, its quartzlike beauty, suggests the strength of his character. In contradistinction to T. S. Eliot, Montale consistently refused to come to a point of certainty: His conclusions are deliberate and arrived at with difficulty, but if they are tempered, they are always provisional. Throughout a long life spanning both world wars and the Italian experience during the twentieth century, Montale exerted an immense influence on contemporary poets. As a critic and journalist, a senior figure in the Italian literary world, and a very modest man of great skeptical intelligence, he came to be seen as "the poet" of modern Italy.

Bibliography

Franke, William. "In the Interstices between Symbol and Allegory: Montale's Figurative Mode." *Comparative Literature Studies* 31, no. 4 (Fall 1994). The author examines symbol and allegory in Montale's poetry.

Gatt-Rutter, John. "Manichee and Hierophant: Montale's Negative Epiphany." In *Writers and Politics in Modern Italy.* London: Hodder and Stoughton, and New York: Holmes and Meier, 1978. A useful discussion of the poem "Nel silenzio" from *Satura* (1971) brings out the relation of Montale's rhetorical devices to the "political structure" of his poetry, determining its "oracular force" as a consequence of its "metaphysical affirmative."

Huffman, Claire. *Montale and the Occasions of Poetry.* Princeton, N.J.: Princeton University Press, 1983. Six interconnected essays offer close discussions of individual poems, drawing upon Montale's essays, interviews, and letters. Much Italian literary criticism of Montale is also made available in this extremely helpful book. Includes copious annotations and an index.

————. "T. S. Eliot, Eugenio Montale, and Vagaries of Influence." *Comparative Literature* 27 (1975): 193-207. A carefully judged comparative study of poetic influence. Montale wrote with great sympathy on Eliot and translated his poetry.

Leavis, F. R. "Xenia." *The Listener* (December 16, 1971): 845-846. The great English moralist and critic appraises Montale's elegaic poems in this highly astute and sensitive critique.

Praz, M. "Eliot and Montale." In *T. S. Eliot: A Symposium,* compiled by Richard March and Tambimuttu. London: Editions Poetry, 1948; Chicago: Regnery, 1949. An early comparative study of the vision and understanding demonstrated by two of the greatest twentieth century poets.

Singh, G. "Eugenio Montale." In *Italian Studies,* edited by E. R. Vincent. Cambridge: Heffer, 1962. An essay providing a general overview of Montale's work and achievement.

————. *Eugenio Montale: A Critical Study of His Poetry, Prose, and Criticism.* New Haven, Conn.: Yale University Press, 1973. An indispensable, full-scale study of Montale's work, discussing his biography, literary background, affiliations, and influences, and providing critical analysis of the poems in each of Montale's books. Contains a bibliography and indexes.

Williams, Mary Francis. "Poetic Seacoasts: Montale's 'I morti' and Propertius 3.18, 1.11, 3.5." *Classical and Modern Literature: A Quarterly* 17, no. 2 (Winter 1997). Discusses the influence of Roman poet Sextus Propertius on Montale's "I morti."

Katherine Kearney Maynard

MARIA MONTESSORI

Born: August 31, 1870; Chiaravalle, Italy

Died: May 6, 1952; Noordwijk aan Zee, The Netherlands

Areas of Achievement: Education, science, and social reform

Contribution: The first woman to earn a medical degree and to practice medicine in Italy, Montessori became a spokesperson for human liberation and a pioneer in "scientific pedagogy." She developed an educational theory based upon children's spontaneous desire to learn in a prepared, free, child-centered environment that won international acclaim during her lifetime and enjoyed continued success after her death.

Early Life

Maria Montessori was born in the town of Chiaravalle, Italy, on August 31, 1870, the year of Italian unification. She was the only child of Renilde Stoppani Montessori, an educated, patriotic daughter of a landed family, and Alessandro Montessori, a conservative civil servant. The family moved to Rome in 1875. There Montessori attended a public elementary school and, at age thirteen, elected to study mathematics at a technical school. After graduating from technical school with high marks, Montessori attended a technical institute from 1886 to 1890. Then, to the shock of her father and the Italian academic community, she decided to study medicine and to become Italy's first female medical doctor. Montessori's ultimate graduation from the Medical College in Rome as a doctor of medicine and surgery in 1896 was a triumph of self-discipline, persistence, and courage.

Upon graduation, Montessori was chosen to represent Italian women at an international women's congress in Berlin, where her speeches on behalf of educational opportunity and equal pay for women won much praise. In November, 1896, Montessori was appointed a surgical assistant at a hospital for men, a medical assistant at the university hospital, and a visiting doctor at a women's and a children's hospital, all in Rome; in addition, she opened a private practice. She also continued her research at the psychiatric clinic of the University of Rome. As a voluntary assistant there, Montessori visited mental asylums to select patients for treatment at the clinic. Sorely troubled by the neglect of retarded children in the city's asylums,

Montessori increasingly directed her research toward possible treatment of these children. Her determination that the best treatment was not medical, but pedagogical, turned Montessori's gaze to the study of educational theory and method.

Montessori undertook this new project with her customary energy and thoroughness, auditing education and physical anthropology courses at the university in 1897-1898 and reading all the pedagogical theory advanced over the last two hundred years. Ultimately, Montessori combined the century-old pedagogical ideas of Johann Heinrich Pestalozzi and Friedrich Froebel (both of whom stressed the interrelationship of sensory, intellectual, and moral education and the need to move from the concrete to the abstract) with the early nineteenth century reformer Édouard Séguin's graduated exercises in sensory and motor development for retarded children and the new measurement techniques of physiology and anthropology. She tested her ideas about special education for retarded children at the psychiatric clinic, at national medical and teachers' conferences, on public lecture tours around Italy, and finally, in 1900, as the director of a new Roman medical-pedagogical institute for teachers of retarded children. In the demonstration school attached to this institute, Montessori experimented with new teaching methods and materials to foster sensory, motor, and intellectual skills in retarded kindergarten and primary students. The results were impressive: Under Montessori's care, many of the supposedly unteachable children mastered basic skills, learned to read and write, and even passed the examinations given to all Italian elementary-school students. In two short years, Montessori had become the most successful and famous educator of retarded children in Rome. At last she was ready to devote her attention to the education of all children.

Life's Work

In 1901, at the age of thirty-one, Montessori resigned her directorship of the medical-pedagogical institute, gave up her medical practice, and launched a new career. She reasoned that if her classes of retarded children could outperform normal children on standard tests, there had to be something dreadfully wrong with normal elementary education. Simultaneously reading voracious-

ly in educational philosophy and observing in local primary schools, Montessori was struck by the disjunction between the two: While educational theorists preached the need for individual development and freedom to learn, educators practiced a deadening rote instruction, physical restraint and silence, and reliance on external rewards and punishments. Montessori became convinced that her new methods and materials, if "applied to normal children, would develop or set free their personality in a marvelous and surprising way." As a lecturer in the Pedagogic School of the University of Rome from 1904 to 1908, she refined her view that education should develop from the nature of the child rather than the other way around, as in traditional elementary education. She called this innovative approach "scientific pedagogy," but it was at least as concerned with spiritual/moral development and human autonomy as with scientific observation and prediction. Montessori was increasingly certain that her scientific/mystical pedagogy could reform not only the schools but also all of society.

Montessori won the opportunity to prove her theory's worth in 1907. A group of bankers had recently renovated a tenement house in a poor section of Rome and wished to establish a day-care center in the building, to keep the children of working parents from destroying the property. They turned to Montessori to direct the children's center. To the surprise and dismay of her faculty colleagues, she accepted the challenge with alacrity and transformed the empty room and fifty undisciplined, culturally disadvantaged, preschool children into a research laboratory and subjects. There she would observe the children's natures, test various approaches and materials, and ultimately develop the Montessori method.

In this unusual laboratory, Montessori quickly discovered that the children possessed a natural desire to learn and actually preferred challenging educational materials to frivolous toys. The previously unruly children developed tremendous powers of concentration and displayed great contentment when they were permitted to work with interesting, self-correcting materials, such as blocks or cylinders of graduated size, bells along a scale, or colors arranged according to the spectrum. Moreover, learning became joyful and easy when these didactic materials and exercises were introduced in an order that logically developed and coordinated sensory, motor, and intellectual skills. The teacher had only to demonstrate (never to preach) the proper use of the materials to a few children and then stand back and watch them teach themselves and one another. With special child-sized furniture, cupboards, dishes, and washstands, the children eagerly learned to choose and put away their own materials, fix their own lunches, and wash up. Even more impressively, these four- and five-year-olds painlessly and happily "exploded into writing and reading" in less than two months, through the carefully designed sequence of graduated exercises. In her Children's House in the slums of Rome, Montessori demonstrated that children's "spontaneous activity in a prepared environment" was more effective than the traditional coercive methods and rote instruction. Her respect for children's autonomy, desire to learn and grow, and inner dignity yielded rich rewards.

From the very start of the experiment at the Children's House, Montessori had encouraged community involvement. Uniquely at the time, she invited the working-class parents to visit the school often and confer about their children's progress. In an inaugural address at the opening of a second Children's House only three months after the first, Montessori stressed the community's ownership of the school, which she hoped would not only free working mothers from undue stress but also transform the local environment and thus redeem "the entire community." Montessori did not rest there. She also invited the attention and support of the wider community of educators, journalists, philanthropists, and religious and political leaders. Particularly after the children's miraculous initiation into writing and reading gained highly favorable press notices, a group of dedicated young women encircled Montessori and gradually relieved her of many daily operations in the schools. They also frequently served as missionaries for her method, setting up new Children's Houses in other Italian cities and towns. Meanwhile, convinced of the educational and social value of her work, Montessori began a lifelong campaign to publicize and spread her method.

This campaign was truly launched with the publication of Montessori's first book about education, *Il metodo della pedagogia scientifica applicato all' educazione infantile nelle case dei bambini* (1909; *The Montessori Method*, 1912). In her book she outlined the history of her "scientific pedagogy" and its realization in the Children's Houses, described her noncoercive methods and self-correcting materials in detail, postulated the existence of "sensitive periods" or stages of development in young children, and restated her basic belief in education as spontaneous self-development in a prepared but free environment.

This mixture of pedagogical theory and practical details also marked Montessori's other books in these years: *Dr. Montessori's Own Handbook* (1914), originally published in English as a concise summary of her theory and method, and *L'autoeducazione nelle scuole elementari* (1916; *The Advanced Montessori Method*, 2 vols., 1917), which introduced materials for teaching grammar and mathematics to older primary students. These books enjoyed great popularity in more than twenty languages; *The Montessori Method* alone sold five thousand copies in four days in the United States and became the second nonfiction bestseller of 1912.

Montessori's true genius for promotion, however, was manifested in her personal appearances to deliver public lectures and give teacher-training institutes around the world. Her deep conviction in the worth of her method and her charming personality led many who came to hear a celebrity leave converted to the Montessori movement. At the age of forty, Montessori decided to devote all of her time to foster that movement. Over the next forty years, she traveled intensively and extensively, to reach those who could not attend her teacher-training institutes in Italy. Everywhere the pattern followed that of her triumphal visit to the United States in 1913: Enthusiastic advance publicity drew huge crowds to Montessori's public lectures and institutes, which in turn sparked the formation or growth of Montessori societies and schools. With or without government sponsorship, Montessori schools were established in the United States, Great Britain, Italy, The Netherlands, Spain, Switzerland, Sweden, Austria, France, Australia, New Zealand, Hawaii, Mexico, Argentina, Japan, China, Korea, Syria, and India, and the movement continued to gain momentum and scope throughout Montessori's life. At the age of sixty-nine, Montessori spent the years of World War II in India, where she personally trained more than one thousand new teachers. Her striking success in this region that was new to her simply redoubled her energy; she returned to India in 1947 and Pakistan in 1949. Montessori was just planning a lecture tour in Africa, when she died suddenly at Noordwijk aan Zee in The Netherlands on May 6, 1952, at the age of eighty-one.

Summary

Wherever she went and whomever she addressed over a long and phenomenally active career, Maria Montessori stressed two interrelated themes: the desperate need for educational reform to develop the true potential of all children and the equally important need for human liberation around the world. While she believed fervently in the power of education to transform individuals and society, she never neglected other social issues and approaches to her desired goals. From her early advocacy of women's rights as a young medical doctor, through her proposal for an international "White Cross" to nurse and teach the children of war in 1917, to her frequent calls for recognition of the rights of children in the family and the dangers of international competition in the 1920's and 1930's, Montessori proved herself to be a tireless and determined spokesperson for the powerless. While she refused to politicize her educational method and movement—and accepted simultaneous support from the Italian government, the Viennese socialist government, and the Dutch liberal government in the 1920's—there was never any doubt about Montessori's fundamental respect for human dignity. She was invited to speak to the League of Nations in Geneva in 1926 on "Education and Peace" and lectured on the same subject at the United Nations Educational, Scientific, and Cultural Organization (UNESCO) in 1947. Her long insistence on the interdependence of humanity won for Montessori the French cross of the Legion of Honor in 1949 and a nomination for the Nobel Peace Prize in 1949, 1950, and 1951.

These were fitting tributes, for Montessori was, throughout her life, a bridge between worlds. Her equal faith in science and spirituality allowed her to translate between the early nineteenth century visions of moral education of Pestalozzi and Froebel and the twentieth century cognitive psychology of Jean Piaget (who was an active sponsor of the International Montessori Association). That special combination of scientific pragmatism and spiritual mysticism also permitted Montessori to appeal to an extraordinarily wide audience, ranging from the British Psychological Society of the Royal Society of Medicine to the Theosophical Society of India. She moved easily between the academic and nonacademic worlds, addressing scholars, teachers, social reformers, and working-class parents with equal success. Above all, Montessori's determination to achieve order and harmony without sacrificing freedom in education, society, and her own life served as an inspiration for advocates of human liberation, social justice, and peace around the world.

Bibliography

Hainstock, Elizabeth G. *Teaching Montessori in the Home.* Rev. ed. New York: Plume, 1997. This clear, attractive book introduces the Montessori method to parents and provides recipes for Montessori materials and exercises to develop practical skills, finger dexterity, and sensory and intellectual abilities.

Kocher, Marjorie B. *The Montessori Manual of Cultural Subjects: A Guide for Teachers.* Minneapolis: Denison, 1973. This is a well-organized and clearly written guide to the Montessori method and materials, designed for teachers. The large quantity and fine quality of the illustrations (photographs and drawings) is especially helpful.

Kramer, Rita. *Maria Montessori: A Biography.* New York: Putnam, 1976; Oxford: Blackwell, 1978. Chicago: University of Chicago Press, 1976. Part of the Radcliffe biography series, this is a densely packed, long, critical biography. Kramer devotes roughly a third of the book to Montessori's "Early Struggles," a third to "The Children's House," and a third to "The Method and the Movement."

Orem, R. C. ed. *Montessori: Her Method and the Movement: What You Need to Know.* New York: Putnam, 1974. This collection of essays by various Montessori teachers and advocates summarizes the essentials of the Montessori method in readable style and argues for the "relevance of Montessori to contemporary America."

Plekhanov, A., and Anthony Jones. "The Pedagogical Theory and Practice of Maria Montessori." *Russian Social Science Review* 33, no. 4 (July-August, 1992). Examines the theories of Montessori with respect to the upbringing of preschool children.

Schapiro, Dennis. "What if Montessori Education is Part of the Answer?" *Education Digest* 58, no. 7 (March, 1993). Short profile of the Montessori Method of education and its success in spite of virtually no support from government or the educational community.

Standing, E. M. *Maria Montessori: Her Life and Work.* London: Hollis and Carter, and Fresno, Calif.: Academy Library Guild, 1957. This was the authorized, first biography of Montessori, by one of her followers. While the descriptions of the life and work are highly appreciative and uncritical, the book contains many firsthand observations. The final comparison of Montessori and Froebel is especially illuminating.

Eve Kornfeld

BERNARD LAW MONTGOMERY

Born: November 17, 1887; London, England
Died: March 24, 1976; near Alton, Hampshire, England
Area of Achievement: The military
Contribution: Montgomery will be remembered as Great Britain's best field general during World War II and one of the great military leaders of the twentieth century.

Early Life

Bernard Law Montgomery was born on November 17, 1887, in Kennington (a district in the south of London), England, the fourth of nine children born to Henry and Maud Montgomery. His father was an Episcopal minister, and his mother was the daughter of Frederic Farrar, a well-known and controversial clergyman in England. When he was but two years of age, Montgomery's family moved to Tasmania, his father having been appointed to serve as bishop in that country. The family returned to England in the summer of 1901, at which time Montgomery and his brother Donald became students at St. Paul's School. Montgomery compiled a less than enviable academic record at St. Paul's, developed no close friendships with his peers, and cultivated no outside interests or hobbies. Only when warned that his poor performance might preclude his pursuing a career in the military did he begin to apply himself intellectually.

Choosing the military over the Church was a decision which further alienated Montgomery from his mother, with whom he had never had, nor ever would have, a satisfactory relationship. In fact, when she died in 1949, he did not even attend her funeral. He entered the Royal Military College at Sandhurst in January of 1907, where he felt very much out of place in this "stronghold of privilege" and social snobbery. Nevertheless, it was there that Montgomery first exhibited the rigid self-discipline and determination which would enable him to master the art of soldiering and prepare for the responsibility of command.

Life's Work

Montgomery was graduated from Sandhurst in 1910, roughly in the middle of his class, and joined the Warwickshire Infantry, which had been assigned to duty in India. The battalion returned to England in early 1913 and, with the outbreak of World War I in August of the following year, was mobilized for war. Not having fought a major war in almost a century, the British army was in no way prepared for the type of conflict it now faced. At age twenty-seven, Montgomery got his first taste of combat during the battles of the Marne and the Aisne and later at the first Battle of Ypres. During the latter engagement, he was wounded and actually left for dead on the battlefield for some time. He recovered from his wound and returned to France in 1916, having been awarded the Distinguished Service Order (DSO) and holding the rank of captain.

Montgomery emerged from the war convinced that the technology of modern warfare required drastic changes in strategy and tactics as well as in the training of the men who might be called upon to fight such wars in the future. He did not believe that Great Britain could survive another war in which the gap between technology and tactics would be bridged by the expenditure of human life on a scale comparable to that which he had witnessed in France. These ideas fundamentally shaped Montgomery's military thinking and undoubtedly contributed to his reputation as a very methodical, if somewhat unimaginative, field commander.

By his own admission, it was only after World War I that Montgomery began seriously to apply himself to mastering all the details and skills required of his profession. He persisted, for example, in having his name included on the roster of officers selected to attend the Staff College at Camberley in 1920 and apparently did quite well during his two years there. He was obviously pleased when in 1927 he was assigned to Camberley as an instructor—an appointment he regarded as "his first important advance in the military hierarchy."

Prior to returning to Camberley, Montgomery served a tour of duty in Ireland and then returned to England as a general staff officer with the Forty-ninth West Riding Division at Yorkshire. It was here that he had a fortuitous meeting with Francis de Guingand, who would later become his chief of staff in the Western Desert and in Normandy. He returned to Camberley in 1926 and, approximately a year later, married Betty Carver, the widow of an army officer who had been killed in the Gallipoli campaign.

Montgomery was devoted to his wife, and the next ten years were to prove very rewarding to him, particularly insofar as his personal life was concerned. In 1928, Betty gave birth to their only child, David, who, like his father, spent very little of his early childhood in England. Montgomery served tours of duty in Palestine and Egypt in the early 1930's and then returned to India, where, in June, 1934, he was appointed senior instructor at the Army Staff College at Quetta. When the family returned to England in the summer of 1937, Montgomery, now a brigadier general, was given command of the Ninth Infantry Brigade at Portsmouth.

With Europe apparently moving inexorably toward yet another and possibly much more devastating world war, Montgomery suffered a great tragedy in his personal life. His wife died in October from septicemia following the amputation of her leg, which had become infected from the sting of an insect. He went into seclusion for a brief period of time but soon returned to duty, exhibiting as much drive and determination as ever. The magnitude of his loss manifested itself more in his personal than in his professional life. He and his son began to grow apart and were never again very close, and he never evidenced any interest in another woman throughout the rest of his life.

Following another brief tour in Palestine in October, 1938, Montgomery was, in August, 1939, selected to command the Third Division—one of the few combat-ready divisions in Great Britain and thus part of the British Expeditionary Force. As in World War I, however, neither the British nor the French were prepared for what Adolf Hitler had in store for them. Hitler may never have imagined, however, that among that mass of bodies which huddled along the beaches at Dunkirk in June, 1940, was the future leader of Operation Overlord.

Back in England, Montgomery was elevated to corps command, and then in December, 1941, was selected to head the South-Eastern Command. In this capacity, he played a role in planning the disastrous Dieppe raid in August, 1942, though his professional career did not suffer unduly as a result. Indeed, he had been called to duty elsewhere when the ill-fated mission was carried out on August 19.

On August 8, the assignment for which Montgomery had prepared himself was presented to him, albeit by a set of untoward and unfortunate circumstances. On the previous day, Lieutenant General W. H. E. Gott, who had just been named as the new commander of the British Eighth Army, had been killed, and Montgomery had been cho-

sen as his successor. He assumed command in mid-August and continued preparations for what promised to be a decisive battle with Erwin Rommel's famed Africa Corps. The Battle of El Alamein, which began on October 23, was the type of set-piece engagement at which Montgomery excelled. His victory there represented the crowning achievement of his military career and shattered the mythical invincibility of the German army. With his "Desert Rats" in pursuit of the "Desert Fox," the world was soon to become familiar with the Montgomery image.

Locked inside his small wiry frame was a reservoir of energy and an abundance of self-confidence which, to many, bordered on arrogance. The thin, stern-looking face, accentuated by the high cheekbones, the steely blue eyes, the rather prominent nose, and the famous black beret, were indelibly etched in the minds of those who followed Montgomery's exploits.

After the North African theater was cleared in May, 1943, Montgomery led his forces in the invasion of Sicily (July, 1943) and later in the invasion of Italy (September, 1943). During the course of the Italian campaign, however, he was recalled to England to assist in the planning of the Normandy invasion, over which he was given tactical command. He directed Allied ground forces during the Battle of Normandy and assumed command of Twenty-first Army Group in August when Dwight D. Eisenhower became operational commander of Allied forces in Europe. Such a change in command had been agreed upon prior to the invasion, but Montgomery did not accept it well. Nor were his feelings assuaged by his subsequent elevation to the rank of field marshal. He became and remained personal friends with Eisenhower, but his professional relationship with the supreme commander was, to say the least, a rather stormy one. Eisenhower's chief of staff, Walter Bedell Smith, probably expressed the sentiments of many individuals at Supreme Headquarters when he told Montgomery: "You may be great to serve under, difficult to serve alongside, but you sure are hell to serve over!"

When the war in Europe came to an end, Montgomery was placed in charge of the British zone of occupation in Germany—a post he held until February, 1946, when he succeeded General Alan Brooke as chief of the Imperial General Staff. He was in the view of some "kicked upstairs" in 1948 when he was named chairman of the Western Union Commanders-in-Chief Committee and ironically found himself once again in a subordinate role to Eisenhower when the North Atlantic Treaty Organization was created in April, 1949.

Montgomery retired from active service in 1958 and became something of an international statesman, traveling to the Soviet Union, China, and South Africa. He proved to be a rather prolific writer as well. His most interesting and certainly most controversial work was his memoirs, which appeared in 1958. Other works included *A History of Warfare* (1959), *An Approach to Sanity* (1959), *The Path to Leadership* (1961), and *Three Continents* (1962). Montgomery withdrew from the public view in 1968. He died eight years later, on March 24, 1976, near Alton, Hampshire at the age of eighty-eight.

Summary

In 1946, Bernard Law Montgomery was made a Peer of the British Empire. His official title was Field Marshal Lord Montgomery of Alamein, but in the hearts of most Britishers he remained simply "Monty." He was a gifted and inspirational battle-field commander whose meticulous planning and methodical tactics, though often criticized, proved to be extremely effective in the set or prepared battle. Characterized by those who knew him as being pompous, arrogant, abrasive, and dogmatic, Montgomery was granted considerable leeway because of his significant military talents.

Opinion remains divided as to Montgomery's place in history. It would seem safe to say that he was England's greatest field commander in World War II, though his greatest distinction may lie in his being viewed as the last great military leader to direct the armed forces of Great Britain as a major world power.

Bibliography

Barnett, Correlli. *The Desert Generals.* 2d ed. Bloomington: Indiana University Press, 1982; London: Pan, 1983. A narrative portrait of five leading British generals, including Montgomery. This work takes a somewhat critical view of the latter as a battlefield commander.

Chalfont, Alun. *Montgomery of Alamein.* London: Weidenfeld and Nicolson, and New York: Atheneum, 1976. Relying heavily on psychological factors to explain Montgomery's personal and professional life, this work offers a very narrow view of the field marshal and fails to assess fully his contributions as a military leader.

Clark, Ronald William. *Montgomery of Alamein.* London: Phoenix House, and New York: Roy, 1960. Written as part of the Living Biographies series, this work would appeal more to younger readers. It is a flattering, though not interpretive, account of Montgomery and his career.

Hamilton, Nigel. *Monty: The Making of a General, 1887-1942; Master of the Battlefield: Monty's War Years, 1942-1944; Monty-Field-Marshal: The Final Years, 1944-1976.* New York: McGraw-Hill, and London: Hamilton, 1981-1986. Based largely on Montgomery's private papers and diaries, this three-volume work is meticulously researched and well-written. It must be regarded as the definitive account of Montgomery's life.

Lewin, Ronald. *Montgomery as Military Commander.* London: Batsford, and New York: Stein and Day, 1971. Lewin's work generally supports the idea of Montgomery as a great British general despite his numerous personal shortcomings.

Montgomery, B. L. *The Memoirs of Field-Marshal the Viscount Montgomery of Alamein.* London:

Collins, and New York: World, 1958. Written by Montgomery himself, this controversial study should be read for its historical value as well as for what it reveals about the character and personality of the author.

Moorehead, Alan. *Montgomery*. London: Hamilton, and New York: Coward-McCann, 1946. Though now dated, this work remains a useful and informative account of Montgomery's life through the period of World War II.

Murray, G. E. *Eisenhower vs. Montgomery: The Continuing Debate*. Westport, Conn.: Greenwood Press, 1996. Examines postwar memoirs and the official histories of the United States, Canada, and Britain with respect to the information they provide on the conflict between Eisenhower and Montgomery.

Thompson, R.W. *The Montgomery Legend*. London: Allen and Unwin, 1967; New York: Lippincott, 1968. Concentrating on the period between August, 1942, and December, 1943, Thompson has produced a revisionist account of Montgomery's desert campaign. The author downplays the "crisis" situation in the desert as well as the importance of El Alamein.

Kirk Ford, Jr.

G. E. MOORE

Born: November 4, 1873; London, England
Died: October 24, 1958; Cambridge, England
Area of Achievement: Philosophy
Contribution: With his meticulous and uncompromising analytic technique, Moore helped lead the movement away from the dominance of Idealism, establishing Analytic philosophy as a major methodology in modern philosophical thought.

Early Life

George Edward Moore was born November 4, 1873, the fifth of eight children, in Upper Norwood, a suburb of London. His father, Daniel Moore, was a medical doctor; his mother, the former Henrietta Sturge, a member of a prominent Quaker family. The Moore home was situated down the hill from the Crystal Cathedral, that landmark of protomodern architecture and symbol of nineteenth century faith in progress through science, technology, and trade—an optimism characteristic of the nonaristrocratic educated professional class to which Moore belonged and which was by then an important political and intellectual force in England.

The family had moved to Norwood so that Moore and his two older brothers could attend Dulwich College, a highly respected boy's school. When he was eight years old, Moore entered Dulwich and soon showed an aptitude and preference for the study of classics, excelling in both Greek and Latin. He also studied piano and voice. At that time the study of classics was considered a primary avenue to literacy which, of itself, constituted a complete education for a gentleman, and consequently Moore studied very little mathematics or science. It is, therefore, remarkable that Moore's later work had the influence that it did on the development of philosophical movements which owed much of their inspiration and subject matter to science and mathematics.

A lonely boy, Moore seems to have been content to spend his time doing the prescribed translating of English verse into Latin and Greek, and, though he was exposed to some Greek philosophy, he showed no inkling of his later passion for philosophy or of his characteristic style of philosophical analysis with its demand for a rigorous accounting of the basis for one's beliefs.

Indeed, when Moore was twelve years old, he was converted by an evangelical sect which believed that an individual faced with a moral dilemma should ask what Jesus would do in that situation. For a time, the young Moore forced himself to act in a manner consistent with this view, and though it caused him great internal conflict and embarrassment, he stood on the promenade at a seaside resort and handed out pamphlets to passersby, among whom were some of his fellow schoolmates. Before he left Dulwich, however, he had become, and remained for the rest of his life, an agnostic.

In 1892, Moore entered Trinity College, Cambridge, modestly expecting to put the finishing touches on his already thorough classical education, obtain a position at a boys' school as a master in his own right, and spend a comfortable life preparing other boys for the rigors of translating English verse into Latin and Greek. This was not to be: In his first year as an undergraduate, he was invited by an upperclassman named Bertrand Russell to a discussion given by a man who said that time was unreal.

The man was John McTaggert Ellis, a proponent of the then-fashionable Idealist philosophy of George Wilhelm Friedrich Hegel which held that the picture of the world given by science and common sense of a multiplicity of objects which have an existence independent of the mind is false, and that, in fact, nothing has independent reality except the whole, or "Absolute." Moore considered the idea that time is unreal monstrous and argued strenuously against it, earning the respect of Russell, who later encouraged him to pursue philosophy. McTaggert, too, was impressed enough to recommend Moore for membership in the Apostles, a kind of undergraduate debating society with a long and distinguished history of membership by some of the leading intellectuals in England.

Moore's debut as an Apostle was said to have been electrifying. Unlike most newly elected members, he spoke without nervousness and with the greatest earnestness and enthusiasm. All were impressed with the passion and purity of his character, a feeling which did not fade—and, if anything, grew to the point where Moore's friendship with his contemporary Apostles became an important avenue, independent of his published work, for the wide dissemination of his ideas.

Taking Russell's advice, Moore began a formal study of philosophy at Cambridge, attending lectures given by Henry Sidgwick, James Ward, G. F. Stout, and McTaggert. For a time, Moore himself fell under the spell of Idealism. Yet even then his independence showed itself in his choice of the ethics of Immanuel Kant for his dissertation topic. While Kant was honored by the Idealists, who considered him the starting point for any study of their hero Hegel, Kant was not himself an Idealist. Though he believed that the individual's experience of the phenomenal world was a construction of the mind and that one could never know the "thing-in-itself," he rejected the view that reality was therefore mental.

Moore's dissertation was rejected, and it was only after he had worked another year and added a second part that it was accepted and he was elected to a six-year fellowship at Trinity College, Cambridge.

Life's Work

Moore's fellowship was unconditional, which meant that for a period of six years he would receive two hundred pounds per year no matter what he did or where he lived. Moore chose to live at Cambridge, where he would receive free room and board, and work at philosophy. He had already reached the turning point in his philosophical thinking in his dissertation. The natural restraints on critical independence of the undergraduate were gone, and he had soon published the second half of his dissertation as a separate paper in the journal *Mind* under the title "The Nature of Judgment." The Idealists had held that there are no facts independent of one's experience of them. Moore argued against this view, holding that the objects of mental acts and perception have an existence wholly independent of a person's mind; thus, as Russell acknowledged, he took the lead in developing a new direction for philosophy which Russell himself soon followed.

As a new fellow Moore became involved in a number of projects. He contributed to James Mark Baldwin's *Dictionary of Philosophy and Psychology* (1901-1905), and he joined the Aristotelian Society of London, which, because of its frequent requests for papers, led to the production of many of Moore's published works. He also undertook to give a series of lectures on Kant's ethics, and on ethics in general. The notes from these lectures served as the basis for the elaboration of Moore's

own ideas about ethics, which he developed slowly and painstakingly over the six years of his fellowship and which were finally published in 1903 as *Principia Ethica.*

The importance of this work was immediately recognized by both philosophers and educated laymen. Biographer and critic (and fellow Apostle) Lytton Strachey hailed it as "the beginning of the Age of Reason," and Russell called it a "triumph of lucidity."

Again, turning against a long philosophical tradition, Moore argued that "good" is a simple and unanalyzable, nonnatural quality (a natural quality would be something such as a color or an emotion). Those who tried to say that good is identical with pleasure or with what one desires or approves of—or anything else in the world—were committing what Moore called "the naturalistic fallacy." Thus, one of the tasks of ethics is to determine the most important "goods" for man. Moore maintained that "personal affection and aesthetic enjoyments include all the greatest, and by far the greatest goods with which we are acquainted." Moral and ethical rules, as well as obligations and duties, are to be judged by whether they promote the greatest amount of good in the universe, a view called "Ideal Utilitarianism." The views expressed in *Principia Ethica* influenced an entire generation of writers, artists, and intellectuals through their impact on the Bloomsbury Group, a literary coterie whose membership overlapped with that of the Apostles and included Strachey, Virginia and Leonard Woolf, E. M. Forster, Roger Fry, and Clive Bell.

The year 1903 also marked the publication of "The Refutation of Idealism," a paper in which Moore's opposition to Idealism reached its most confident formulation. He attacked what he considered to be the cornerstone of all Idealist systems, succinctly formulated by Bishop George Berkeley in the Latin phrase, "esse est percipi" (to be is to be perceived), from which it was concluded that all reality was inescapably mental. Moore argued that this formula failed to distinguish the act of awareness in perception and the object of awareness. Once this distinction is recognized, the problem of the continued existence of unobserved objects disappears. Moore later lost confidence in this argument, and he continued throughout the rest of his life to struggle with the problem of the relationship between perception and reality. He later confessed that he thought himself better at the precise formulation of philosophical questions than at answering them, and his work after 1903 became increasingly fragmented and inconclusive. With the publication of these works, Moore was at the height of his powers, his reputation established. Slender and handsome, he had achieved acceptance, even leadership, in one of the foremost intellectual debating societies in England.

Despite his achievements, however, when Moore's fellowship came to an end in 1904, he was unable to obtain a research fellowship to continue at Cambridge. He had, however, recently inherited enough money on which to live comfortably. He did not stay at Cambridge, though he could have. Instead, Moore moved to Edinburgh, where he lived with his friend Alfred Ainsworth. For six years, at Edinburgh, and later at London, he continued to work at philosophy, studying Russell's *The Principles of Mathematics* (1903) and writing reviews. During the period from 1903 to 1904, Moore and Russell had had frequent discussions on philosophy, and Russell in his introduction to that work credited Moore with a breakthrough that had cleared up many difficulties which had seemed insoluble. During that period away from Cambridge, Moore also wrote a small book titled *Ethics* (1912), which he personally preferred to *Principia Ethica*, primarily because he believed that it was clearer and had fewer invalid arguments.

In 1911, largely because of the lobbying of John Maynard Keynes, Moore was offered a lectureship at Cambridge, which he accepted gladly. He remained at Cambridge for the next twenty-eight years. He first lectured in psychology, partly because there were no positions in philosophy proper available, but also because psychology was then still closely connected with philosophy, having only recently emerged as a separate discipline, and Moore was well qualified to teach all but its experimental aspects. Later, as a result of retirements and gracious adjustments by other faculty members, Moore was able to replace psychology with metaphysics and a course called "Elements of Philosophy." Moore was a popular lecturer who made a point of leaving time for open discussion. When he lectured, he felt compelled to think his subject through over again rather than rely on his lecture notes from the previous year. He believed this gave his lectures more life because the lecture then centered on problems that currently interested him.

It was while he was lecturing on psychology that Moore met Ludwig Wittgenstein, the famous Aus-

trian philosopher. Wittgenstein told Moore bluntly that his lectures were very bad because Moore did not express his own views. Like his relationship with Russell, Moore's relationship with Wittgenstein was a peculiar mixture of professional admiration and conflict. They experienced periods of frequent and fruitful discussions. Unfortunately, they also had a series of petty quarrels followed by long periods during which they would not even speak to each other. Despite their difficulties, however, Moore maintained that both Russell and Wittgenstein were more profound thinkers and had made more important contributions to philosophy than he. The people who knew Moore remarked on his total lack of professional vanity and on a kind of innocence or childlikeness in his personality. Wittgenstein, in a letter to Norman Malcolm, admitted this about Moore, but then went on to eviscerate the compliment by adding

> As to its being to his 'credit' to be childlike—I can't understand that: unless it's also to a child's credit. For you aren't talking of the innocence a man has fought for, but of an innocence which comes from a natural absence of a temptation. . . .

In 1916, at the age of forty-three, Moore was married to Dorothy M. Ely, a woman who had attended his lectures that year. They had two sons, Nicholas, who became a well-known poet, and Timothy. Moore continued to work in philosophy throughout his life, though he never again produced a full-length work such as *Principia Ethica*. His many papers were published in a series of anthologies under the titles *Philosophical Studies* (1922), *Some Main Problems of Philosophy* (1953), and the posthumously published *Philosophical Papers* (1959) and *Commonplace Book, 1919-1953* (1962). In these works Moore continued to support common sense over the extravagantly metaphysical view of the world and insisted that the solution to philosophical problems required proper framing of the question and careful analysis of the meaning of the words and concepts involved.

From 1921 to 1947, he was the editor of the philosophical journal *Mind*, in which his own essay "The Nature of Judgment" had appeared. During his life, he received numerous honors, including the Litt.D. from Cambridge (1913), the honorary degree of LL.D. from the University of St. Andrews (1918), election as a Fellow of the British Academy (1918), and appointment to the Order of Merit (1951).

In 1939, Moore reached the mandatory retirement age for professors at Cambridge. He continued, however, to lecture and hold discussions with students at Oxford and later at universities in the United States. Until the end of his life, he continued writing and revising his earlier work. Moore died in Cambridge in 1958, shortly before his eighty-fifth birthday.

Summary

G. E. Moore was not a man of action in the conventional sense. His life was without significant outward conflict or change. He never suffered from financial worries or came up against serious obstacles to his goals, and he spent the major portion of his life doing exactly what he wanted to do, working in philosophy at Cambridge.

He has been called a "philosopher's philosopher," a characterization that is accurate both with respect to the esteem in which he is held by other philosophers and with respect to the difficulty that his writings present to the lay reader, based as they often are on the minute and critical examination of the positions of other philosophers. Yet Moore's writings account for only a part of his influence. His impact on his many students and contemporaries, his personal force in conversation both in and out of the classroom, and his pure and intense pursuit of the truth have caused him to be compared to Socrates. Moore's commitment to clear thinking affected not only the narrow technical confines of academia but also, through their influence on members of the Apostles and the Bloomsbury Group, such diverse fields as economics, politics, literature, and art criticism.

Bibliography

Levy, Paul. *Moore: G. E. Moore and the Cambridge Apostles.* London: Weidenfeld and Nicolson, 1979; New York: Holt Rinehart, 1980. A detailed account of Moore's life and connection with the Apostles through World War I. An excellent reference based on primary sources.

Moore, G. E. *Ethics.* London: Williams and Norgate, and New York: Oxford University Press, 1912. Moore's own choice as the best presentation of his ethical views.

———. *Philosophical Studies.* London: Routledge, and New York: Humanities Press, 1922. A selection of Moore's papers written between 1903 and 1920, including "The Refutation of Idealism."

———. *Principia Ethica.* Rev. ed. Cambridge and New York: Cambridge University Press, 1993. Probably Moore's most influential work. The last chapter should be of particular interest to those interested in Moore's influence in art and literary circles.

Nelson, John. "George Edward Moore." In *The Encyclopedia of Philosophy.* Edited by Paul Edwards. Vols. 5-6. New York: Macmillan, 1967. A helpful starting point before attempting to read Moore's actual writings, which can be quite daunting.

Schlipp, Paul Arthur, ed. *The Philosophy of G. E. Moore.* Evanston, Ill.: Northwestern University Press, 1942; London: Cambridge University Press, 1968. A book of critical essays on Moore to which Moore himself contributes a reply. Especially notable because it contains Moore's only autobiography.

Shaw, William H. *Moore on Right and Wrong: The Normative Ethics of G. E. Moore.* Boston: Kluwer Academic, 1995. Reconstruction of Moore's thoughts on normative theory and moral conduct, areas often neglected in deference to his work in ethics.

Stroll, Avrum. *Moore and Wittgenstein on Certainty.* New York: Oxford University Press, 1994. This book discusses the philosophical relationship between the views of Moore and Ludwig Wittgenstein through analysis of their differing approaches to several epistemological problems.

Urmson, J. O. *Philosophical Analysis, Its Development Between the Two World Wars.* Oxford: Clarendon Press, and New York: Oxford University Press, 1956. Provides background in the Analytic philosophy movement to which Moore belonged.

Scott Bouvier

HENRY MOORE

Born: July 30, 1898; Castleford, Yorkshire, England
Died: August 31, 1986; Much Hadham, Hertfordshire, England
Area of Achievement: Art
Contribution: Through an elemental understanding of form and materials, Moore created sculpture of archetypal significance, universally recognized yet uniquely his.

Early Life

From the beginning, earth and stone were an important part of Henry Moore's life. After years of sculpting outdoors in Hertfordshire, Moore reflected that it was the landscape of Yorkshire, where he grew up, which inspired him to do sculpture in the open air. The moors of the northern countryside, a monumental rock formation near Leeds, and the slag heaps of the Yorkshire mining villages educated his eye on natural forms.

At an early age, Moore knew that he could work in three dimensions. At home, he would whittle wooden game pieces and other small carvings. Outside, Moore was acutely aware of the Gothic sculpture at the nearby cathedrals of Adel and Methley. Their archaic stone forms shaped his imagination. A Sunday school story about Michelangelo named his dream: sculptor. From that moment, Moore claimed, he knew what he wanted to do, and ardently applied himself.

It was in the Yorkshire mining village of Castleford that Moore was born on July 30, 1898. He was the seventh of eight children born to a miner father of Irish descent, Raymond Spencer Moore, and to a mother from Staffordshire, Mary Baker.

Mary Baker Moore suffered from arthritis. While Moore was growing up, it was his chore in the evening to rub her back with ointment. As a daily ritual, this provided the sculptor's hands with an exercise in the contours of the body.

For inspiration in academic exercises, Moore looked to his father, a self-educated man. Raymond Moore was a stern presence in the home, but he was also a loving father, ambitious for his children not to end up in the mines.

When young Moore announced his intentions to pursue art, his father, though not against the notion, insisted that he be qualified to teach. At the age of twelve, Henry Moore won a scholarship to Castleford Grammar School, where he trained to be a teacher. Nevertheless, a teaching position, he knew, would not be his ultimate achievement.

In his studies at the grammar school, Moore was encouraged by Alice Gostick, the art teacher, to pursue his artistic interests. He was chosen to carve the wooden memorial scroll to commemorate alumni enlisting in the war effort. Having completed the course of study, Moore returned as a student teacher to his elementary school.

His teaching days were cut short by World War I. In February, 1917, he joined the Fifteenth London Regiment and was stationed in France for the summer. In the Battle of Cambrai, he was gassed, and subsequently he was sent back to England. A photo of Moore from this period, looking very young and dressed in military garb, shows a serious countenance. The high forehead curves in an oval above bushy brows that shadow deep-set blue eyes. The nose is a triangular volume; its lines extend to a sraight, thin-lipped mouth. Later photos focus on the hands: long fingers on well-used hands, attached to strong arms and a sturdy frame that show the strength of a man who carved stone.

In February, 1919, Moore resumed teaching. By September, he had secured an ex-serviceman's grant to study at the Leeds School of Art. As the only full-time sculpture student in the Leeds program, Moore received a thorough grounding in technique. The first year he spent in drawing. Though the whitewashed antique Roman copies of Greek sculpture he was required to copy offered little inspiration, the disciplines of drawing and sculpting academically gave Moore the skills for his later work. He devoted the following year to sculpture, completing the examination course in half the usual time and winning a scholarship to the Royal College of Art.

His examination piece for the Royal College of Art, a drawing of a pair of hands, proved so satisfactory that it circulated to other art schools as an example for all other students applying to the Royal College of Art.

By the time he got to London, Moore was well versed in the basics of his craft and had read Roger Fry's *Vision and Design* (1920), which had a profound influence on his work. The book is a collection of essays on art, including several devoted to understanding archaic sculpture from Mexico, Africa, and assorted islands. Moore found in this

Henry Moore in the marble quarry in Querceta.

writing and in the accompanying illustrations a touchstone for aesthetics.

With Fry's book as a guide, Moore would spend afternoons in the British Museum, visiting first the Egyptian exhibit, which seemed more accessible to the Western eye accustomed to art with Hellenistic origins. As he grew accustomed to the ancient works, he inspected the galleries of other ancient civilizations. He found the rough stone and elongated wood sculpture of these "primitives" superior, in their truth to material, to Western works. That is, the sculptures did not obscure the qualities of their media. Moore also admired the way the forms were conceived and executed as full volumes.

The primitive art influence which began to appear in his work prompted strong, though not always approving, reactions from the art department. Nevertheless, in 1925 the Royal College appointed Moore a lecturer in sculpture, and the following year he won a traveling scholarship to Paris, Rome, Florence, Venice, and Ravenna. He was most impressed by Giotto and the later work of Michelangelo. As for classical art, he called Praxiteles "the first hack." When Moore returned to London, the college offered him a seven-year appointment as an instructor. This job put Moore in an environment in which he could meet some talented, creative people, and gave him the time and means to carve his early sculptures in stone and wood.

Life's Work

Sculpture defines space, and one of Moore's goals was to teach his audience, through sculpture, how to appreciate three-dimensional space. His first commission, however, was not a sculpture in the round. In 1928, the new headquarters of the London Underground Railway needed a relief carving of the North Wind. Moore was one of several artists selected. His *North Wind*, though grounded in the wall, suggests the forms of his reclining figures. Moore's figure of the North Wind looks forward, as if in motion. The legs, though massive, appear to float effortlessly behind.

In addition to his first commission, Moore also presented his first one-man show in 1928 at the Warren Gallery in London. He exhibited ninety-three works, presenting subjects which he would further develop over the years. Most often, at these early shows, it was the drawings that sold, and Moore found satisfaction in the number bought by other artists.

The sculptures in his early shows were small, compared to his later work. Nevertheless, photographs of the early works, many of them female figures or mother-and-child configurations, show a monumental quality. His *Mother and Child* from 1925 is less than two feet tall, yet not diminutive. The solemn expression of the mother's face, the roundness of the rock, and the unity of the mother with the baby on her shoulders could accommodate a much larger scale.

Following his professional debut, Moore married the painting student Irina Radetzky, internationally educated and graceful as a dancer. During this era Moore's reclining-figure sculptures emerged. Carved in stone or wood, these solid, benevolent earth mothers lounge like great mountains in assorted positions. For these sculptures, Moore worked with easily available stones, carving out the shape "imprisoned" inside a particular piece of rock.

Although World War II severely curtailed Moore's activities, the War Artists Advisory Committee commissioned him to sketch the Underground shelters. Critics compare these drawings to William Blake's illuminations. Moore's illustrations are sculptural in feeling, and the combination of dark crayons and bright paints lends these works a surreal quality. The sketches provided themes which Moore would continue to develop in later works. The many mother-and-child groupings wrapped in blankets foreshadow Moore's draped figures, and also his leaf figures. The sleepers' open mouths, reminiscent of the legend of souls that leave the body through open mouths to roam at night, influenced Moore's 1950's helmet heads. The subway shelters themselves offered an emblematic study of the earth mother as a shelter, a cave.

Moore entered the caves of the coal miners for the committee, as well. Moore's drawings of coal miners are a rarity in his opus, because they record men at work. Men became part of Moore's sculptural repertory only after his daughter, Mary, was born in 1946. Though he continued to develop his mother-and-child motif, he also worked on a series of family-group arrangements which included a father figure. For these he used bronze, a sculptural medium which he had largely neglected because, in the artist's view, there could be no such thing as "truth to bronze." Bronze, however, offered the artist freedom to move into the vertical mode of the family groupings and the series of seated and standing figures. Bronze also allowed Moore to direct the way light would interact with the form, reflecting off the smoothed curves and shadowing in the etched areas.

Around this time, the Moores moved to a seventeenth century farmhouse in Much Hadham, Hertfordshire. At the farmhouse, Moore was able to undertake large-scale works, and though he summered in Italy and traveled widely, he would call the farmhouse home for the rest of his life. In fact, as the property grew, Moore built nine studios to accommodate his casting of small bronzes, photographing of completed works, printmaking, drawing, and sculpting. The studios became a village, with a small group of neighbors working as staff.

The staff attended to correspondence and the growing responsibilities of shipping sculpture all over the world for exhibit at galleries and museums. Meanwhile, Moore worked on an increasing number of large-scale commissions, including Moore's *Reclining Figure* for the United Nations Educational, Scientific, and Cultural Organization (UNESCO) headquarters in Paris (1957), the two-piece *Reclining Figure* for Lincoln Center for the Performing Arts in New York (1965), and *Double Oval Bronze* (1967) for the Chase Manhattan Bank in New York, a sculpture through which the public could walk.

Even during his final years, Moore continued to explore the possibilities of the reclining figure. His *Draped Reclining Mother and Baby* (1983-1984) is a bronze of 104 inches. The attention to texture contrasts the shadows with the smooth, rounded surfaces. The heart is hollowed out, and the lower arm and leg have sharp angles, forming a protective pen for the baby. The baby itself looks like a small reclining figure, supported by the mother's arm as the mother looks up and off into the infinite vista.

Summary

Depending on the critic, there are different estimations of Henry Moore's aristic accomplishments. According to John Read, Moore's greatest contribution to sculpture was a "blending of human and natural form [in the *Reclining Figure* sculptures], this ability to see figures in the landscape, and landscape in the figures." Other critics cite the emotional impact of his works. Still others commend Moore's sculpture of the vitality inherent in each piece. These assessments are not particularly amazing. The wonder comes from Moore himself, whose vision for sculpture turned rock into beauty and bronze into form. The sculptor's vision was so strong that the critics seem merely to echo his intentions when appraising his work.

In his own life, Moore mirrored the liveliness of his sculpture with his vigor as a citizen. He was not an artist who withdrew from society or held people in disdain. When both world wars called, he answered with action. He served as a trustee for the Tate Gallery, on the Royal Fine Arts Commission, and on the Arts Council of Great Britain, among other organizations. He received several honorary doctorates and awards. Though he moved to the country, it was not as an escape. Rather, the move allowed him to make large sculpture; to work in the natural English light, to which he attributed truth-telling powers; and to gain the perspective of distance for his work.

Moore refused to criticize publicly other artists. He cooperated with writers, filmmakers, and book publishers, providing photographs, spending time with interviewers, and making needed materials available to all. This characteristic cooperation mirrors the technique of the carving sculptor. Whether Moore was working with available stone or stone specially selected for a project, he sculpted in harmony with the material itself.

Sculpture, he thought, should be in harmony not only with its materials but with its location and purpose as well. For the *Madonna and Child* commission at the Church of St. Matthew in Northampton in 1943, Moore strove to make a sculpture which would transcend the usual mother-and-child works. The final effect he described as "a sense of complete easiness and repose as though the Madonna could stay in that position for ever (as, being in stone, she will have to do)."

While submitting to the qualities of the materials and the specifics of commissions, Moore was still able to create sculpture of a highly original quality. Moore's brand of modern art was not merely a reaction to classicism. It reestablished the line of an archetypal style by which sculpture accomplished its own reality, rather than imitating real life.

Bibliography

Doan, Laura. "Wombs of War: Henry Moore's Repositioning of Gender." *Genders*, no. 17 (Fall 1993). Examines several of Moore's works that were influenced by the consequences of war.

Fry, Roger. *Vision and Design*. London: Chatto and Windus, and New York: Meridian, 1920. This is the book credited with giving Moore an understanding of archaic sculpture. Of particular significance are the essays "The Art of the Bushmen," "Negro Sculpture," and "Giotto."

Grohmann, Will. *The Art of Henry Moore*. London: Thames and Hudson, and New York: Abrams, 1960. A wonderful collection illustrating Moore's drawing and sculpture. Though this book at times frustrates the reader with belabored prose and poor identification of photos, the author has done the research to make this a good introduction to the man and his work.

Lieberman, William S. *Henry Moore: Sixty Years of His Art*. New York: Thames and Hudson, 1983. Probably among the best published photographic reproductions of Moore's work, accompanied by a well-organized introduction and excellent labeling of the collection.

Moore, Henry. *Energy in Space*. Photographs by John Hedgecoe. Greenwich, Conn.: New York Graphic Society, 1974. A visual and artistic delight. Shows works in progress, works on location, and works superimposed on photographic backgrounds.

———. *Henry Moore on Sculpture*. Edited by Philip James. Rev. ed. New York: Viking Press, 1971. Comprehensive. Incorporates statements made by Moore over the years with biographical notes and commentary on the sculpture and its inspirations.

Neumann, Erich. *The Archetypal World of Henry Moore*. Translated by R. F. C. Hull. London: Routledge, and New York: Pantheon, 1959. When the author sent the sculptor a copy of the newly published book, Moore put it aside after the first chapter. "It explained too much about what my motives were and what things were about," he wrote in *Henry Moore on Sculpture* (see above). All psychological analysis aside, this book contains some very good work on the themes inherent to Moore's sculpture.

Read, John. *Portrait of an Artist: Henry Moore*. London: Whizzard Press, 1979. Well-written, though biased, introduction to the life of the sculptor. The author is the son of Sir Herbert Read, a friend and biographer of Henry Moore.

Sweeney, James Johnson. *Henry Moore*. New York: Museum of Modern Art, 1946. This book offers a fine summary of the man and his art. One wishes only that Sweeney could follow it up with a book on the next forty years of Moore's life.

Ellen Clark

MARIANNE MOORE

Born: November 15, 1887; Kirkwood, Missouri
Died: February 5, 1972; New York, New York
Area of Achievement: Literature
Contribution: An early leader in Modernist poetry, Moore eventually gained recognition as one of the half-dozen major poets in English of the middle twentieth century.

Early Life

Marianne Craig Moore was born on November 15, 1887, in Kirkwood, Missouri, near St. Louis, where her mother had moved after a breakdown had permanently institutionalized her father. Her mother's brother, pastor of the Presbyterian Church, provided all Marianne knew of a father during her first years. Upon his death in 1894, Marianne, an older brother, and her mother moved to be with friends at Carlisle, Pennsylvania. Here Marianne attended the Metzger Institute, where her mother took a part-time teaching position. Another Presbyterian pastor, George Norcross, involved young Marianne in the life of the mind and the spirit.

Marianne next enrolled at Bryn Mawr College, where she struggled, especially during the first two years, gradually finding a home in the biology laboratory and at the literary magazine, although literature courses daunted her. To contribute to the household income after receiving her degree in 1909, she took a business and secretarial course at Carlisle Commercial College. This gained her a job at the Carlisle Indian School, at the time a center for assimilating American Indians into the common culture. Here she taught classes in English and business skills, maintained the typewriters and stenographic equipment, and coached both boys and girls in field sports for four years. She also sent out poems for publication, placing pieces in the most prestigious and progressive journals of the time: *Egoist* (London) and *Poetry* (Chicago).

In 1916, mother and daughter moved first to Chatham, New Jersey, and then two years later to New York, where Marianne lived for the rest of her life. At first supporting herself by tutoring, Moore eventually obtained a part-time position with the New York Public Library, but she quickly decided to devote her life to literature. Without her knowledge, some of her editors and readers at *Egoist* published her first book, *Poems*, in 1921. Her subsequent volume *Observations* (1924), however, proclaimed her entry into the literary lists. Besides containing some of her finest and most reprinted poems, it declared her dedication to the literary life. Editing *Dial*, another pioneering journal, from 1925 to 1929 confirmed her decision. When that journal ceased publication, Moore resolved to devote the rest of her life solely to writing.

Life's Work

For the next forty years, Marianne Moore supported herself as a freelance reviewer, essayist, and poet, proving it possible to make money by writing: By the time she "retired," she had put enough away so that she could live comfortably on the interest, even in a sickbed. She also gained recognition, though quietly. Throughout her publishing career, every new work earned both acclaim and merit; her list of literary prizes was longer, the weight of her medals heavier, than those of her more celebrated colleagues. She may look at first like a token "female representative" among the writers, but a second look reveals that if there was prejudice against women writers, Moore deserves more credit for having broken through the barriers. Besides, her male peers were the first to acknowledge her eminence.

At least some of her lack of celebrity stems from her own withdrawn habits, her failure to promote herself. Still, within her own limits, she outperformed all of her rivals. She alone succeeded at supporting herself entirely by writing—the only professional among amateurs. Moreover, she is the only world-class poet to have thrown out the first pitch of the season for both the Brooklyn Dodgers and New York Yankees, just as she is the only one to have held a conference on poetry with then-heavyweight boxing champion Muhammad Ali. Late in life, she even gained a semipopular following, especially after being seen about New York conspicuously garbed in billowing cape and tricorn hat. In the 1960's, the picture magazines made regular copy of her. Yet she never found the audience she deserved.

What is called her early work was hardly early; she was in her mid-thirties before her publications gained much currency. Still, many of her best-known poems and several signature techniques appeared in her first two books. Her fascination with animals, especially with exotic and bizarre forms, stands out, as do her jagged lines, quirky rhythms,

and metaphorical tangents. Still, although she gained positive reviews, she had not yet found herself. Editing *The Dial*, however, introduced her to the leading writers of the time, and she made much of her contacts. Several of those writers urged her to publish more widely, and her *Selected Poems* (1936) was introduced by T. S. Eliot (1888-1965). From that point on she did not lack readers.

Selected Poems did not so much break new ground as expand established colonies. It also demonstrated one of Moore's most ingrained habits, variously considered irritating or refreshing. Several touchstone poems reappeared here in altered form; the poet had improved them, even after publication. Such constant tinkering is typical of Moore. For her a poem is constantly in process, in the act of being brought about, rather than a product fixed and definite. In her final volume, *The Complete Poems of Marianne Moore* (1967), she perfected this process, paring down her best-known poem, "Poetry," to a three-line distillation of the original thirty-four. In doing so, she deprived many readers of lines they cherished. At the same time, again typically, she made amends by reprinting the original version in the notes appended to the text of the poems—another characteristic gesture of playfulness.

That habit of concentration, of reducing poems to their metaphorical essence, is at the core of Moore's poetic practice, although this was not at first recognized. Partly because of her fascination with depicting unusual animals in minute detail, partly because her second book was titled *Observations*, she was long considered a visual poet, distinguished as much by what she saw as by her techniques of reporting and reconstructing. Thus a catalog of typical titles reads much like the roster of a peculiar zoo: "The Fish," "No Swan So Fine," "The Frigate Pelican," "The Pangolin," "The Jerboa," "To a Snail," "Sojourn in the Whale," "The Basilisk," "Elephants," "Peter" (about a cat), and many more. Even poems ostensibly dealing with unrelated topics regularly modulate—by Moore's methods—to images of animal behavior. Furthermore, this pseudopictorial mode carries the animal images over into other scenes, so that reading Moore often seems like touring a splendid museum.

Ultimately, however, Moore's work strikes home because of technique, structure, and imaginative wit, qualities that rule her major publications: *The Pangolin and Other Verse* (1936), *What Are Years?* (1941), and *Nevertheless* (1944). Although Moore

had experimented early with free verse and Imagist formulas, in these works she developed her idiosyncratic forms and verbal techniques. She derived these from the wordplay of certain sixteenth and seventeenth century English prose masters: Lancelot Andrewes, John Donne, Francis Bacon, and Sir Thomas Browne. Her poetry begins, as her contemporary and friend Ezra Pound had prescribed, as good prose—that is, it exemplifies precision, conciseness, weight, poise, and exactness. This gives her work hard edges, definite lines, a felt presence; her poems display rather than decorate. Often they seem to be sculpted.

Moore developed poetic forms and techniques to complement these prose-based virtues. Although her metrics are basically conventional, she considered the stanza rather than the line as the formal center of the poem. Her poems began with an individuating stanzaic form, chosen ordinarily by working with a found or invented verbal pattern—more often than not a quotation from something essentially prosaic: a guidebook, a review, a memo. Completing the poem meant fashioning further stanzas on identical linear patterns, so that the rhymes and line divisions all occurred at precise points and each poem had a unique pattern. Furthermore, because the line divisions do not control the shapings of the phrase, Moore was free within the formal strictures to exploit the phrase rhythms characteristic of prose. The cross-patterns thus generated often seem abrupt and jagged, even crude, at first, but they allow her wit and playfulness to sport within them, and occasionally break free. An early poem, "The Past Is the Present," established this aesthetic objective for all of her work: "Ecstasy affords/ the occasion and expediency determines the form."

Summary

Despite making a living out of writing and gaining some late recognition, Marianne Moore cannot be termed a female pioneer or even a successful role model in a conventional sense. She lived almost as a recluse, acquiring fame only as a caricature of the female poet, grotesquely caped, bonneted, and caparisoned. Far from asserting her sexual independence, she spent most of her life caring for her increasingly infirm mother and her minister brother; clearly, she was the hero in the family. She carried Victorian reticence about sexuality around with her as if it were a veil. As the editor of *The Dial*, she rejected some overt sexual references in a submission by Hart Crane, prompting him to call her a hysterical virgin; and, asked late in life for her opinion about current poets, she complained about their sexual frankness.

Nevertheless, she deserves credit as the truest liberator. At a time when almost no one in a remarkable generation of poetic genius could make literature pay, she did. Furthermore, she showed that women could compete on equal terms with men in one of the most intensely combative arenas anywhere: that of professional literature. What better demonstration could anyone ask of the potential of women? As daringly as any explorer into uncharted regions, she blazed her own trails, established her own range, and gained the respect and admiration of the men who walked beside—but never before—her. She continues to hold the territory she staked out.

Bibliography

Goodridge, Celeste. *Marianne Moore and Her Contemporaries.* Iowa City: University of Iowa Press, 1989. In some respects a study for specialists, this work does document the interactions between Moore and her more conspicuous male colleagues T. S. Eliot, Wallace Stevens, Ezra Pound, and William Carlos Williams. It is fully documented and indexed, and contains a selected bibliography.

Holley, Margaret. *The Poetry of Marianne Moore: A Study in Voice and Value.* Cambridge and New York: Cambridge University Press, 1987. This mainstay standard scholarly commentary on Moore's poetry is more readable and useful than most. It provides insights and persuasive interpretations. The biographical sketch is separate and concise, and the text also includes a chronology of publication, notes, an accurate bibliography, and an index.

Martin, Taffy. *Marianne Moore: Subversive Modernist.* Austin: University of Texas Press, 1986. Martin attempts to integrate Moore into the women's movement, with some success but also some strain. The study combines biography and commentary, and includes notes and an index.

Miller, Cristanne. *Marianne Moore: Questions of Authority.* Cambridge, Mass.: Harvard University Press, 1995. Analysis of the work of Moore through new readings and previously unpublished correspondence revealing Moore as a radical oppositionist concerned in many cases with the unfortunate power relationships occasioned by culture.

Molesworth, Charles. *Marianne Moore: A Literary Life.* New York: Atheneum, 1990. Molesworth's work is the major literary biography, massive in scholarship and compiled from total immersion in all available sources. Meticulous in its detailed reconstruction of Moore's life, it has been criticized for failing to bring its subject to life. It includes full scholarly apparatus.

Moore, Marianne. *The Selected Letters of Marianne Moore.* New York: Knopf, 1997; London: Faber, 1998. A stunning selection from the thirty thousand focused, exquisitely detailed letters of Moore including correspondence with Ezra Pound and T. S. Eliot.

Phillips, Elizabeth. *Marianne Moore.* Modern Literature Series. New York: Ungar, 1982. Intended as an introduction to the poet and woman for the general reader, this work achieves its objectives. Although the biographical material is dated and superficial, Phillips' work remains the first reference of choice. It is fully noted and indexed.

Tomlinson, Charles, ed. *Marianne Moore: A Collection of Critical Essays.* Englewood Cliffs, N.J.: Prentice-Hall, 1969. Although it is badly dated, this work contains indispensable material not readily available elsewhere: letters, an interview, early reviews about and by Moore, and particularly essays by leading critics of the mid-century: Kenneth Burke, John Crowe Ransom, Stevens, Williams, Randall Jarrell, and various major scholars.

Willis, Patricia C., ed. *Marianne Moore: Woman and Poet.* Orono, Maine: National Poetry Foundation, University of Maine, 1990. This major work is invaluable for making possible an uncluttered view of the poet. It collects essays about Moore's life and writings from a kaleidoscopic array of perspectives and by a formidable battery of scholars. It also contains a complete and useful annotated bibliography.

James Livingston

THOMAS HUNT MORGAN

Born: September 25, 1866; Lexington, Kentucky
Died: December 4, 1945; Pasadena, California
Area of Achievement: Genetics
Contribution: Through his ability to work closely with colleagues in unselfishly pursuing a scientific problem, Morgan's *Drosophila* research pioneered modern chromosome theory and genetic research.

Early Life

Born September 25, 1866, in Lexington, Kentucky, Thomas Hunt Morgan was the son of Charlton Hunt Morgan and Ellen Key Howard. His paternal uncle was General John Hunt Morgan, commander of Morgan's Raiders, under whom his father served during the Civil War. Through his mother's family he was related to Francis Scott Key, author of "The Star-Spangled Banner."

Morgan's boyhood was spent in Kentucky and in the mountains of western Maryland. During his childhood vacations in the mountains, he spent much of his time collecting fossils, birds, and bird's eggs. He continued in his scientific interests during his college years at the University of Kentucky, from which he was graduated in 1886. In the summer after his college graduation, he worked at the Boston Society of Natural History's marine laboratory in Annisquam, Massachusetts, prior to entering graduate school at The Johns Hopkins University in Baltimore.

At The Johns Hopkins University, his major professor was William Keith Brooks, by whom he was influenced to study embryology, especially in marine organisms. Since Brooks's research was on how an organism's parts went together or how these parts developed, it was to be expected that Thomas Hunt Morgan's early work was descriptive. His 1890 doctoral dissertation on sea spiders was entitled "A Contribution to the Embryology and Phylogeny of the Pycnogonids."

Among the influential factors shaping his life was his introduction to the marine laboratory at Woods Hole, Massachusetts. He spent his first summer there in 1888, while still a graduate student. So conducive was this environment to research that Morgan spent nearly every summer there for the remainder of his life, even after he moved to California in the late 1920's. During his teaching days in the East, he would actually pack all of his experimental specimens, whether plant or animal, and ship them on the train to the marine laboratory.

Morgan's first academic teaching appointment came in 1891, when he was named associate professor of biology at Bryn Mawr. There he remained until 1904, working closely with his faculty colleagues R. G. Harrison and Jacques Loeb. Among his outstanding students were Nettie M. Stevens, who worked in regeneration and cytology, and Lilian V. Sampson, whose research was in embryology and regeneration. Morgan and Sampson were married in 1904, the same year that he accepted a position as professor of experimental zoology at Columbia University, in New York.

Life's Work

The twenty-four years spent at Columbia would be the most productive period in Morgan's life. By the time of his arrival in New York, he was addressing the research issue of genetics, which would lead him to his greatest achievements. Sex determination was one of the first topics of investigation in this area, a subject whose literature he reviewed in 1903: "Recent Theories in Regard to the Determination of Sex." Work on honeybees, phylloxera, and aphids during the next five years led him toward the chromosome interpretation of sex determination. As one of his students wrote:

> This was one of Morgan's most brilliant achievements, involving great skill and patience in the collecting and care of the animals, insight in seeing what were the critical points to study, and ability to recognize and to follow up unexpected facts. The results were of importance in serving to demonstrate the role of the chromosomes in sex determination, at a time when that importance was seriously questioned by many biologists.

Before adopting the uniquely suitable *Drosophila* as a laboratory animal for genetic research, Morgan had worked for a time with both mice and rats. By 1910, however, he published his first paper on *Drosophila*: "Hybridization in a Mutating Period in *Drosophila.*" The particular strain about which he reported had been started in 1909, although Morgan had been supervising a graduate experimenting with breeding *Drosophila* in the dark even before that time.

The fruit fly was ideal for genetic work because it produced a new generation every two to three weeks, was virtually immune to disease, and, perhaps most important, had only four pairs of chromosomes, compared to the usual plus or minus twenty-four in most mammals.

By 1910, the so-called fly room at Columbia University had come into being. Into a rather small room were crowded eight desks—some were assigned permanently, others went to visiting researchers—where, for the next seventeen years, Thomas Hunt Morgan and his colleagues—undergraduates, graduates, faculty, and visitors from around the world—would work to lay the foundations of the modern chromosome theory of heredity. All this would be learned from a small fly which would breed in a milk bottle that was provided with a piece of rotting fruit.

The first of the major discoveries based on the *Drosophila* research was announced in July, 1910, in a paper in which Morgan revealed the sex-linked inheritance of white eyes. The next major step came as a second sex-linked characteristic, rudimentary wings, appeared as a mutant in one of the cultures. When white eyes and rudimentary wings were crossed, there was evidence for a new step in the development of chromosome theory:

> White and rudimentary happen to lie far apart in the X chromosome, with the result that it was not apparent in this first cross that they were linked. . . . But in 1911 cases of linkage had been recognized—most obvious in the relation between yellow body and white eyes— and Morgan then laid down the essence of the modern chromosome theory of heredity. The basis of linkage is nearness together in chromosomes, and recombination between linked genes is due to exchange of parts between homologous chromosomes. . . .

Five years later, Thomas Hunt Morgan and three of his fly-room colleagues published *The Mechanism of Mendelian Heredity* (1915). Here for the first time appeared an attempt to interpret the field of genetics in terms of chromosome theory. From this landmark publication came scientific vindication for Gregor Mendel and a foundation upon which all future chromosome research could be built.

Despite the sophistication of Morgan's research and its results, he insisted on working with the simplest of equipment. His early cultures of *Drosophila* were cultivated in an odd assortment of milk bottles. In each bottle it was customary to place a piece of paper for identification purposes; Morgan often used the envelopes torn from correspondence which he had just opened. Flies were ultimately examined with a hand lens. According

to one of his students and collaborators, Morgan was always generous with his own personal funds (to the point of lending money to students), but rather miserly with budgetary allotments for which he was responsible.

Another unique characteristic of the research done in Morgan's laboratory at Columbia was the unselfish cooperation on the part of all those who worked there. As one of the participants (A. H. Sturtevant) explained:

> This group worked as a unit. . . . What mattered was to get ahead with the work. There can have been few times and places in scientific laboratories with such an atmosphere of excitement and with such a record of sustained enthusiasm. This was due in large part to Morgan's own attitude, compounded of enthusiasm combined with a strong critical sense, generosity, open-mindedness, and a remarkable sense of humor.

The slender, bearded Morgan was always ready to contribute boundless energy and an incisive mind to the solution of any problem.

However important Morgan's fly work may have been in opening new approaches to chromosome theory research, his methods of research were fundamental to the changes which would come in twentieth century biology. Morgan and his generation of biologists had studied under professors who, by training and practice, were descriptive biologists, to whom the more important focus was on structure rather than on function. Morgan's success in his *Drosophila* work through quantitative and experimental analysis would encourage others to free themselves from the shackles of descriptivism.

At Johns Hopkins, Thomas Hunt Morgan had worked with W. K. Brooks, a descriptive biologist. Fortunately, he had also encountered H. Newell Martin and W. H. Howell, who helped him appreciate physiological approaches. Even more powerful influences on his future research strategies had been brought to bear by two European trained scientists, Jacques Loeb and Hans Dreisch. From his training the Prussian-born Loeb had concluded that the methods of physics and chemistry were the only way that research could advance knowledge about life.

> Loeb concluded that behavior, like all events in nature, was deterministic. . . . Analysis on the physical or chemical level demanded synthesis on the biological level. The use of quantitative methods, analysis, and experimentation offered the best means, . . . of raising biology to the status of a rigorous science.

Morgan and Loeb met in 1891, when the two joined the faculty at Bryn Mawr. Loeb's stay at Bryn Mawr was brief, because he moved to the University of Chicago in January of 1892, but the two men had become fast friends and sympathetic scholars. Every summer for many years at the Woods Hole marine lab, the two men worked in collaboration, often disagreeing about conclusions but never about methodology. Once Loeb moved to the Rockefeller Institute in 1910, the two scholars could enjoy interchanges of ideas almost year-round.

Morgan's second influential European friend was Hans Driesch, whom he met when he spent some time doing research at the Naples Zoological Station in 1894-1895. These sojourns were not only academically stimulating but also personally pleasant, since Morgan's father was revered by the Italians for his service as American consul at Messina when he befriended the Italian patriot Giuseppe Garibaldi.

Driesch believed that biology, like physics and chemistry, should be made quantitative and mechanical; indeed, thought Driesch, the indispens-able tools of biology were math and physics. Morgan's leanings toward the value of experimentation and quantification were encouraged by his friendship and collaboration with Driesch. They worked together at Naples, traveled in Europe, and published papers on ctenophore development in 1895.

From his inspiring experiences at the Naples Zoological Station, Morgan concluded that American biology would remain relatively stagnant until there was a comparable marine laboratory facility in the United States. A library, outstanding facilities, an immediate source of marine organisms, freedom to work, and, perhaps most significant of all, a place to exchange ideas, were the elements which made Naples such a fruitful place to work. These would be the conditions which Morgan would seek to incorporate into the Woods Hole Marine Biological Laboratory, especially after he became a trustee there in 1897.

Summary

According to the Nobel Prize presentation speech in 1933, Morgan's greatness lay in his ability "to join two important methods in hereditary research, the statistic-genetic method adopted by Mendel, and the microscopic method. . . . " Morgan was fortunate also in his choice of an object for his experiments and in the brilliance of the students and collaborators he gathered about him in the fly room. "With perfect justice we speak about the Morgan school, and it is often difficult to distinguish what is Morgan's work and what is that of his associates. But nobody has doubted that Morgan is the genuine leader." Morgan's work, concluded the Nobel committee, can be expressed in four rules: "the combination rule, the rule of the limited number of the combination groups, the crossing-over rule, and the rule of the linear arrangement of the genes in the chromosomes." Without Morgan's investigations in human hereditary research, modern human genetics would be impractical. "Morgan's discoveries are simply fundamental and decisive for the investigation and understanding of the hereditary diseases of man."

In addition to Morgan's impact on biological study through his *Drosophila* research, he was similarly influential in his role as coeditor of a series of biological monographs published by the Lippincott Company. Morgan, along with Loeb, and W. J. V. Osterhout, intended to further the progress of science in the United States along the lines of scientific investigation favored by the three editors.

Although Loeb was European by birth and training, and Morgan was European-influenced, the two were trying to break away from the domination of European speculative biology. The Lippincott series was conceived by its editors as a fresh start in the direction of quantitative and mechanistic biology. During the critical decade after 1918, the three men labored to choose monographs which they believed would be instrumental in shaping a new American biology. Morgan ultimately would accept the directorship of a new Division of Biology at the California Institute of Technology in order to establish his ideas firmly within the framework of a great university. Morgan is regarded in the West as one of the fathers of modern genetics. His work helped make possible the great strides in hereditary research leading to our modern understanding.

Bibliography

Allen, Garland E. "T. H. Morgan and the Emergence of a New American Biology." *The Quarterly Review of Biology* 44 (June, 1969): 168-187. A useful analysis of the factors instrumental in shaping Morgan's attitudes and methodology. It should be used in conjunction with the Sturtevant memoir listed below.

Crow, James F., et al. "Anecdotal, Historical and Critical Commentaries on Genetics." *Genetics* 149, no. 4 (August, 1998). The author discusses his experiences with Morgan and how he was influenced by them. Includes a detailed look at Morgan's love of experimentation.

Horowitz, Norman H. "T. H. Morgan at CalTech: A Reminiscence." *Genetics* 149, no. 4 (August, 1998). Horowitz, a biologist, discusses several personal meetings with Morgan.

Mayr, Ernst. *The Growth of Biological Thought: Diversity, Evolution and Inheritance.* Cambridge, Mass. and London: Harvard University Press, 1982. A history of ideas in biology which is fundamental for understanding the context and impact of Morgan's scholarly contribution.

Moore, Ruth E. *The Coil of Life: The Story of the Great Discoveries in the Life Sciences.* London: Constable, and New York: Knopf, 1961. A popular account ranging from Antoine-Laurent Lavoisier's experiments to developments in DNA research. Less formidable for the average reader than the volume by Mayr.

Morgan, T. H., A. H. Sturtevant, H. J. Muller, and C. B. Bridges. *The Mechanism of Mendelian Heredity.* Rev. ed. New York: Holt, 1922. Under Morgan's leadership, these inhabitants of the Columbia fly room demonstrated how their *Drosophila* research illustrated chromosome theory.

Nobelstiftelsen [the Nobel Foundation]. *Physiology or Medicine, 1922-1941.* Amsterdam: Elsevier, 1965. The official source for remarks made by the Nobel Prize Committee about the award winners and the speech written by the recipient.

Sturtevant, A. H. *A History of Genetics.* New York: Harper, 1965. Sturtevant, T. H. Morgan Professor of Biology, Emeritus, from the California Institute of Technology, writes from the perspective of a founding father on the history of genetics from Mendel to World War II. Interesting intellectual pedigree charts included as an appendix.

————. *Selected Papers of A. H. Sturtevant: Genetics and Evolution.* Edited by E. B. Lewis. San Francisco: Freeman, 1961. An edition of thirty-three Sturtevant papers from 1913-1956, edited by an intellectual grandson of Thomas Hunt Morgan, E. B. Lewis, who worked at the California Institute of Technology as a research fellow from 1931 to 1936.

————. "Thomas Hunt Morgan." *Biographical Memoirs, National Academy of Science* 33 (1959): 283-325. An indispensable account by one of Morgan's students who assisted in writing *The Mechanism of Mendelian Heredity* (1915). This is the source to which most general accounts refer.

James H. O'Donnell III

AKIO MORITA

Born: January 26, 1921; Nagoya, Japan

Areas of Achievement: Business and industry

Contribution: Together with his mentor and business partner, Masaru Ibuka, Morita turned a tiny precision-instrument factory into the Sony Corporation, one of the largest industrial firms in the world and home of one of the best-known brand names in the world of business.

Early Life

Akio Morita was born in 1921 of a prominent family in Nagoya, the fifteenth-generation heir to one of Japan's oldest sake-brewing families. He grew up in an affluent household that mixed native traditions with an easy familiarity with Western ways. While the family was devoutly Buddhist, holding religious services at home, the young Morita could play tennis on the family court, go for Sunday outings in an open Model T Ford, and listen to Western classical music on an imported Victrola. In his autobiography, Morita writes that as a youngster he was intrigued by electrical devices such as the vacuum tube, which could take old scratchy, hissing records and turn them into beautiful sounding music.

Before long the intrigue turned into an obsession, and he was making his own crude radio and electric phonograph as well as a primitive voice-recording device. His scientific tinkering may have been responsible for his somewhat spotty academic record: While he excelled at mathematics and science, he received less than average grades in other studies. Still, by dint of a determined effort during a year of intense study with tutors, he managed to gain admission to the prestigious Eighth Higher School. With a mixture of self-mockery and pride, he relates that he became the lowest-ranking graduate of his middle school ever to be admitted to the science department at the Eighth Higher School.

Morita continued to develop his scientific skills, from 1940 to 1944, as a disciple of Tsunesaburo Asada, a distinguished specialist in applied physics at Osaka Imperial University. Upon graduation in 1944, Morita entered the navy as a technician-lieutenant and engaged in research on heat-seeking devices in the one year that remained in the Pacific War. It was during that period that he met a brilliant electronics engineer, Masaru Ibuka, thirteen years his senior.

Ibuka, though working on the same military project, was a civilian and owned his own precision-instrument company. Those who know both men frequently comment on their differing personalities. Ibuka is invariably described as shy, retiring, and more typically Japanese, while Morita is a dynamic super-salesman, bold and outspoken. Nevertheless, the two were to become the closest of friends, colleagues, partners, and cofounders of the Sony Corporation.

Life's Work

The story of Sony begins when Morita and Ibuka set up a shop repairing radios and making vacuum-tube voltmeters on the seventh floor of the charred, gutted ruins of a department store in Tokyo's Ginza shopping district in the grim days immediately after the end of the war. With a total capitalization of five hundred dollars—a loan from Morita's father—the business was formally incorporated as Tokyo Tsushin Kogyo (Tokyo Telecommunications Engineering Company) in May, 1946. The world-famous name "Sony" would come later.

There were false starts in the early years—experiments with manufacturing an electric rice cooker proved a failure, for example. In the meantime, when it became necessary to vacate their Ginza premises in 1947, they moved to the Gotenyama district on the southern edge of Tokyo, an area still devastated from the wartime bombing but once renowned for its cherry blossoms. The headquarters of the Sony Corporation remains to this day in Gotenyama.

The first major breakthrough product that Morita and Ibuka produced was a tape recorder, manufactured for the domestic market in 1950. When sales for the machine proved disappointing, it was Morita who decided to bypass the powerful trading companies, which customarily acted as middlemen, and instead set up the company's own distribution system. Morita himself personally visited Japanese schools to show how the product, then virtually unknown in Japan, could be used as a teaching tool, and before long nearly a third of Japan's elementary schools had purchased the devices. More important, the gamble to ignore traditional marketing practices had paid off and from then on it was the company's policy to manage its own sales, a factor that business analysts regard as crucial to Sony's later success.

The next milestone in the company's history has turned into one of the enduring legends of Japanese business history. In 1952, Ibuka (as president of the company) went to the United States to explore the possibilities of obtaining a patent owned by the Western Electric Company (WEC). When prospects for a deal seemed worth pursuing, the task was delegated to Morita, the more business-savvy vice president, who traveled to the United States for the first time in 1953. The negotiations with WEC—and with the Japanese government to take valuable currency out of the country to pay for patent rights—took a year to complete, but by 1954 Morita had successfully completed the deal. For twenty-five thousand dollars—a princely sum in a Japan which had yet to commence its "economic miracle"—Tokyo Telecommunications purchased a license to the transistor. WEC had used the transistor to make hearing aids; Ibuka and Morita had another idea that would tap a much larger consumer demand: a transistorized radio.

One year later, after much work to modify the newly acquired transistor for use in a radio, Morita and Ibuka put the first transistor radio on the market in Japan. Though the new product sold well, they were not satisfied; only the radio tubes had been transistorized. After successfully applying the new technology to the loudspeaker and transformer, the company introduced the world's first pocket-sized transistor radio in 1957.

It was about this time that Tokyo Telecommunications changed its name. Morita insisted that the firm's name was cumbersome in either Japanese or its English version. Someone looked up the Latin word for sound. "Sonus" sounded nice, but they were searching for something that was a little more catchy. Briefly Morita and Ibuka toyed with "Sonny," but the overtones of mischievous little boys did not seem appropriate. The word "Sony" was selected, first as the name for the transistor radio and then in January, 1957, as the name of their firm.

The tiny device was an instant success, and for the first time Sony was able to establish a market in the United States, a major turning point in the fortunes of the company. Morita considered offers from an American firm to market the miniaturized radio in the United States under an American brand name. It was tempting for the still tiny Japanese firm to rely on a large American firm to sell the radios in the unfamiliar American market, but Morita rejected the offer, calculating that it was time for Sony to establish its own name abroad no matter how great the obstacles might be.

Accordingly, in 1960, Sony America was established. From its first show-room on Fifth Avenue in Manhattan and very soon from Sony retailers all across the country, Americans gradually became familiar with the company's product line, which soon expanded into transistorized (solid-state) television. It took a decade for the American operation to become profitable, but by the end of the 1960's Sony had sold more than a million micro-televisions in the United States. The 1970's would see the introduction of the Trinitron color television, followed by a succession of other products, including the Betamax videocassette recorder and the Walkman portable stereo.

Morita also guided the establishment of Sony's first major joint-venture agreement, with the American television network CBS in 1966. Other joint ventures and cross-licensing agreements followed, bringing the Japanese firm more and more deeply into both North America and Europe. Further integration occurred when Sony began not only to sell but also to manufacture in the United States—in 1972, Morita presided over the groundbreaking ceremonies of its San Diego, California, television plant, which soon employed more than one thousand workers.

As president of Sony America, Morita took up residence in New York City with his wife and three children in 1962. This allowed him not only to directly manage the affairs of Sony in the United States but also to immerse himself in Western society and deepen his understanding of Western culture. One of his sons was graduated from Georgetown University. Regarding education, Morita noted that, contrary to Japan, many of the business elite in the United States did not possess a university education, an observation that prompted him to write, in 1966, a book entitled *Gakureki Muyouron* (college education is not always necessary). It became a best-seller in Japan.

In the course of his residence abroad, Morita accumulated a wide circle of friends not only in the business world, but among the leaders of the world political and cultural communities as well. He is always in great demand as a speaker and is known for his lively wit and the frank expression of his views. In an era when "trade friction" has dominated American-Japanese economic relations, Morita is an articulate spokesman for the prevailing Japanese view that the declining competitive position of the United States in world markets can best be explained not by unfair Japanese practices but by shortcomings in the American economy. While praising the innovative accomplishments of American science and technology, Morita faults the way American business is mesmerized by short-term profits to the neglect of long-term growth. Morita served as president of the Sony Corporation from 1971 to 1976 and has served as chairman of the board and chief executive officer since 1976.

Summary

Akio Morita is one of the best-known businessmen in the world, and the Sony label, established by Morita and Ibuka, is one of the best-known commercial names in the world. The two built the Sony empire from nothing in 1946 to its first billion-dollar sales year in 1973, and then to a five-billion-dollar year in 1984. In doing so, they made a major contribution in changing the image enjoyed by Japanese manufactured products throughout the world. At the time when Sony was first introduced to the West, Japanese goods invariably evoked adjectives such as "cheap" and "shoddy" among the consuming public outside Japan. In 1969, after only a decade of experience in international markets, Sony could take pride that the American Apollo mission carrying the first men to the moon carried Sony tape recorders.

By emphasizing reliability and quality and by producing attractive consumer merchandise at highly competitive prices, Sony, along with a few other companies, caused the "Made in Japan" label to become a symbol of excellence. In addition, Sony proved false the stereotype of Japanese industry as imitators. Its modification and improvement of the transistor and its discovery of radically new uses of that invention proved that the Japanese were skilled at innovation and adaptation.

Bibliography

Abegglen, James C., and George Stalk, Jr. *Kaisha: The Japanese Corporation*. New York: Basic, 1985; London: Tauris, 1986. Though not exclusively devoted to Morita or Sony, this book does discuss them in the course of explaining how marketing, money, and manpower strategy made the Japanese world pacesetters.

Frailey, Fred, with Mary Lord. "Sony's No-Baloney Boss." *U.S. News and World Report* 101 (November 17, 1986): 57. A brief profile of Morita and Sony that gives some background of the company and of Morita. Morita is quoted about his future plans for Sony.

Kamioka, Kazuyoshi. *Japanese Business Pioneers*. Union City, Calif.: Heian, 1988. In addition to general comments on characteristics of business and management styles in Japan, this book includes chapters devoted to eight corporate leaders in Japan, including Morita.

Lyons, Nick. *The Sony Vision*. New York: Crown, 1976. An informal company history that is made interesting because Lyons interviewed key Sony figures including Morita and Ibuka. The book, however, suffers from the fact that the author has little or no specialized expertise concerning Japan. Contains interesting illustrations.

Morita, Akio. "Building Bridges East and West: The Opening of Minds." *Vital Speeches* 60, no. 5 (December 15, 1993). Transcript of a speech by Morita concerning the role of Japanese-Americans in changing the traditional Japanese isolationist mindset.

Morita, Akio, and David Rockefeller. "Capitalism East and West: A Dialogue." *New Perspectives Quarterly* 9, no. 1 (Winter 1992). Transcript of discussions between Morita and David Rockefeller concerning the history and economic relations of the United States and Japan, differences in their cultures, and the reconstruction after Pearl Harbor.

Morita, Akio, Edwin M. Reingold and Mitsuko Shimomura. *Made in Japan: Akio Morita and Sony.* New York: Dutton, 1986; London: Collins, 1987. A highly personalized account of the life and times of Morita and Sony. The book, in addition to autobiographical information, includes extensive commentaries by Morita on such topics as management, the difference between American and Japanese business styles, and world trade.

Weymouth, Lally. "Meet Mr. Sony: How the Japanese Outsmart Us." *The Atlantic* 244 (November, 1979): 33-34. Although brief and somewhat dated, this is a fine interpretive examination of the importance of Sony and Morita.

John H. Boyle

TONI MORRISON

Born: February 18, 1931; Lorain, Ohio

Area of Achievement: Literature

Contribution: Morrison was the first African American woman to win the Nobel Prize in Literature. Her work includes some of the most engaging contributions to American literature in the last hundred years.

Early Life

Toni Morrison was born Chloe Anthony Wofford in Lorain, Ohio, on February 18, 1931. She was the second of four children born to George Wofford and Ramah Willis Wofford. Her father's occupations included car washing, steel mill welding, road construction, and shipyard work, which typified the eclectic labor lifestyle of African American men living during the Great Depression of the late 1920's and 1930's. Her mother worked at home and sang in church. Both parents had strong Southern roots. Morrison's father was from Georgia and had vivid memories of racial violence in his childhood, while her mother's parents were part of the migration of African Americans from Alabama, via Kentucky, who sought to find a better life in the North.

Morrison's parents taught her much about understanding racism and growing up in predominantly white America. Her father was not very optimistic about the capacity of whites to transcend their bigotry toward blacks and remained acutely untrusting of all white people. Her mother's judgment about whites was less pessimistic, although she adhered to the thinking that strength and hope in the black community had to be secured from within that community and not from without. These community values—values of the village—have become the cornerstone of Morrison's literary and political thinking. Her focus is consistently directed within the black community, a focus that reflects her confidence in the tangible culture of black America and its crucial role in shaping strong and talented people.

In her childhood, Morrison's eclectic literary tastes introduced her to such literary works as Gustave Flaubert's *Madame Bovary* and the works of Leo Tolstoy, Fyodor Dostoevski, and Jane Austen. Morrison was quite aware of the disparity that existed between the largely white worlds of these works and her own black female experience. Her reading enabled her to understand the value of cultural specificity in literature and the universality of the particular. It also demonstrated that her own culture, values, dreams, and feelings were not being represented in the literature she was reading. In many ways, her movement toward writing fiction was spurred by a need to redress what she felt was a woeful silence about black experience in the literature she read.

After completing high school in Lorain, Morrison went on to receive her B.A. from Howard University. She became involved with theater and had the opportunity to travel through the South performing before black audiences. Those trips gave her a better understanding of the geographical reality of the black American experience, a grounding that would be reproduced in her fiction. In 1953, she went on to Cornell University, where she completed her master's degree, studying suicide in the work of William Faulkner and Virginia Woolf. These writers were fitting figures against which she could react as a writer. Faulkner, because of his white vision of the Southern experience, and Woolf, because of her white treatment of the female experience in a male-dominated world, provided Morrison with models upon which she would later improvise.

Morrison taught at Texas Southern University for two years and then taught at Howard. There she honed her political views on black America, arguing against the current desegregation rhetoric by suggesting that blacks needed greater economic independence and needed to be wary of distorting their own culture and values through assimilation.

At Howard she married Harold Morrison, a Jamaican architect with whom she had two sons. The marriage was not a positive experience for Morrison; it left her feeling powerless and unsatisfied. She left Howard in 1964, divorced her husband, and assumed a post at Random House in New York City as an editor. Morrison continued her teaching career despite her intense work with Random House as a senior editor for so many years. She has taught at Yale University, Bard College, the State University of New York campuses at Purchase and Albany, and Princeton University.

Life's Work

In 1993, Toni Morrison was awarded the Nobel Prize in Literature in recognition of her achievements as a novelist of outstanding talent. The award represented the culmination of a series of accolades that have followed Morrison after the publication of each of her six novels. These novels have become classics in American literature and have been the subject of extensive critical study. Morrison has also published remarkably intelligent discussions of her works in numerous interviews and essays. She forces literary critics to reevaluate their innate suspicion of writers who write and speak about their own works. The combination of the novels and Morrison's engaging commentaries produces an insight into the deeply committed psyche and spirit of this woman. Her reviews and critical articles published in *The New York Times* and its *Review of Books* (to which she has been a regular contributor for years) constitute a significant body of critical approaches to literature and culture. Her commitment is to her African American experience, and her goal has been to evolve a literary aesthetic that is intrinsically African and American.

Morrison wrote her first novel, *The Bluest Eye*, during her painful marriage. The instinct to write was shaped by a need to read something with which she could identify. In this regard, Morrison identifies with the discourse of the postcolonial writer who seeks to evolve a voice that will articulate her experience in a way that allows it to overwhelm the domination of the culture of the colonizer. In *The Bluest Eye*, Morrison deftly treats the issues of identity and race with language and poetics that echo the writing of Frantz Fanon. At the core of the novel is the psychological trauma of Pecola, a black girl's experience of her racial identity in a predominantly white society. Her desire to have blue eyes represents the painful refutation of her own sense of self-worth as a black child. The novel is posited as a parable—a tale that painfully explores issues of incest, maturation, friendship, racism, and sexual violence through poetic language that is at once simple and startlingly complex. Morrison's achievement with this first novel was to contribute a series of vivid images and literary insights (complete with their paradoxes and complexities) to the raging debate around the Black Power movement of the late 1960's. Morrison provided a grounding for these ideas.

Her commitment to the black experience continued in her second novel *Sula* (1973), in which she makes the community that she describes a living character. In this community, the individuals are distinctive and complex. They range from the schizophrenic war veteran Shadrack to the doggedly independent and mysteriously explosive Eva, a virtual matriarch who commits an act of violence in the work. The central, character, Sula, is posited as a dangerous figure. She does not fit easy stereotypes but is, ultimately, associated with evil. Many black critics appear to share the view that *Sula* is one of Morrison's best works because of its deconstruction and reconstruction of myths surrounding motherhood, race, gender, and class in American society.

Morrison's third novel, *Song of Solomon* (1977), has a male protagonist, Macon, or "Milkman," who embarks on a journey South to discover a lost family treasure. His mammon-centered quest becomes a quest for self-discovery and a discovery of his ancestry. Morrison structures this narrative around a series of folktales. The work climaxes in the dramatic and magical flight of Macon—a flight associated with the African slave's narrative of escape from the drudgery of slavery, which has been passed down through African American culture. *Song of Solomon* established Morrison's reputation as a writer. The work was awarded the National Book Critics' Circle Award and the National Book Award for best novel. Critics and reviewers commended the work for its narrative force and its complex examination of the history of the African American community.

In *Tar Baby* (1981), her fourth novel, Morrison expands her geographical boundaries, setting part of the novel in a fictional Caribbean island. The novel is a complex treatment of theories of sexuality and race that is couched in the African folktale of the "tar-baby." Morrison also includes in this text some examination of the traditions of black rebellions, as demonstrated in the Maroon lifestyle of Caribbean blacks during slavery.

In 1987, Morrison published *Beloved*, a frightening narrative about a slave woman who murders her child to prevent the child from becoming a slave. This horrifying act becomes a challenge for Morrison, who tries to articulate the realities that could make such an act possible. *Beloved* is layered with images and ideas that demonstrate Morrison's commitment to using actual historical "texts" as the basis for her consistently mythic approach to fiction writing. *Beloved* was awarded the Pulitzer Prize in 1988 and became a critically acclaimed film in 1998. In this work, as in all her novels, Morrison demonstrates a desire to speak to her own community or from that community. Mor-

rison bluntly states that she writes for a black audience because she is writing for the village.

She demonstrates this trend most vividly in her novel *Jazz* (1992), in which she uses the most fascinating elements of this African American music form to shape her work. In *Jazz*, which is set in the 1920's during the heyday of jazz music and black innovation in the arts, Morrison applies the discipline and classical grounding of the music, its capacity to evoke the blues-like lament of black experience and history, and its improvisational nature to create a novel that is not explicitly about jazz music but is in fact jazz. The Nobel Prize in Literature was awarded to Morrison largely on the strength of this, her sixth novel.

Summary

Toni Morrison has done in her fiction writing what August Wilson has achieved in drama since the 1970's. These writers share the distinction of providing American literature with an insight into the dignity and richness of African American culture in a manner that both chronicles the history of this culture and celebrates its uniquely brilliant ethos

through the use of language, folk forms, and narrative traditions. As a commentator on her own work, Morrison has brilliantly analyzed her lyrical sensibility and has managed to contextualize the experience of the African American artist in American literature. Her work represents possibility and legitimizes the inclination of African American artists to delve into the African American experience without fear of being deemed irrelevant, inaccessible, or parochial. She has also demonstrated this commitment in her editorial work. Her crucial role in the publication of Middleton Harris' *The Black Book* (1974) demonstrates her concern for preserving images of African culture in America's collective consciousness.

Apart from her talent as an artist, Morrison brings an intensely political engagement to her art. She constantly speaks of the irrelevance of work that is not political. Politics, for her, embraces the elements of relevance, accountability, and truth. She is a leading voice among African American women writers who are not afraid to emphasize their political discourse. Others who share this ethos and who speak of Morrison's leadership in this regard include Toni Cade Bambara, Ntozake Shange, Alice Walker, and Maya Angelou.

Morrison has worked as a teacher and an editor for most of her adult life, and she continues to bring these skills to bear on her own work. She is a committed defender of the rights of women and speaks up against injustices against women. More important, she has supplied intelligent and cogent criticism of the white feminist movement from the perspective of an African American woman.

Bibliography

Bell, Roseann P., Betty J. Parker, and Beverly Guy-Sheftall, eds. *Sturdy Black Bridges: Visions of Black Women in Literature*. New York: Anchor Press, 1979. An eclectic compilation of critical essays, prose pieces, and creative work from Africa and the African diaspora which places Morrison squarely and comfortably in the evolving milieu of writers whose roots are in Africa.

Christian, Barbara. *Black Feminist Criticism: Perspectives on Black Women Writers*. New York: Pergamon Press, 1985. A wide-ranging examination of black women's writing which contains an intelligent examination of the politics of Toni Morrison's early works.

Evans, Mari, ed. *Black Women Writers, 1950-1980: A Critical Evaluation*. London: Pluto

Press, and New York: Anchor Press/Doubleday, 1984. Contains Morrison's seminal essay "Rootedness: The Ancestor as Foundation," as well as several insightful critical discussions of Morrison's writing.

Holden-Kirwan, Jennifer L. "Looking into the Self That Is No Self: An Examination of Subjectivity in 'Beloved.'" *African American Review* 32, no. 3 (Fall 1998). Analysis of Morrison's novel *Beloved* and its treatment of slaves as victims of repression.

Rice, Herbert W. *Toni Morrison and the American Tradition: A Rhetorical Reading.* New York: Lang, 1996. Rice examines the similarities and differences in Morrison's works when compared to writers such as William Faulkner.

Ruas, Charles. *Conversations with American Writers.* New York: Knopf, 1984; London: Quartet, 1986. Contains an enlightening interview with Morrison in which she defines her place in American letters.

Tate, Claudia, ed. *Black Women Writers at Work.* New York: Continuum, 1983. This book is made up of interviews with Morrison and other black women writers. The Morrison interview contains some of her most cogent and forthright expressions of her commitment to politics in writing and a black or Afrocentric aesthetic.

Wilentz, Gay. *Binding Cultures: Black Women Writers in Africa and the Diaspora.* Bloomington: Indiana University Press, 1992. Wilentz writes informatively about Morrison's use of African folklore and folk patterns in the generation of her literary work.

Kwame Dawes

GAETANO MOSCA

Born: April 1, 1858; Palermo, Sicily

Died: November 8, 1941; Rome, Italy

Areas of Achievement: Political science, government, and politics

Contribution: Mosca was one of the founders of modern political science. His writings on the concept of elite rule were crucial contributions to a modern theory of government. Mosca combined a university position with an active political life, serving in the Italian parliament for fifteen years and eventually opposing Benito Mussolini and Fascism.

Early Life

Gaetano Mosca was born in Palermo, the capital city of the island of Sicily, on April 1, 1858. He was one of seven children in a middle-class family; his father was an administrator in the postal service. Mosca's Sicilian background played a crucial role in his later intellectual development. Sicily entered the Kingdom of Italy in 1861 with hopes for the island's resurgence as part of a newly unified country; however, the northern rulers proved to be every bit as harsh and corrupt, and as insensitive to Sicily's needs, as their Bourbon predecessors. Indeed, for much of the 1860's, and occasionally over the next two decades, Sicily rebelled against northern rule and was placed under martial law. Elections, when held, were fraudulent, results falsified, and coercion openly practiced.

All of this imbued the young Mosca, a bright and energetic student, with the strong distrust of politics common to most Sicilians. In the late 1870's, Mosca entered the University of Palermo, where he studied law. His degree, awarded in 1881, was based on a thesis whose central theme was nationalism. Mosca argued that national identity was largely a political myth of less real importance than people's regional or even local allegiances. This emphasis on the true rather than the apparent in politics remained with Mosca for the rest of his life.

In 1883, Mosca moved to Rome to take up advanced study in politics and government administration. The following year, he published a treatise on the theory of government, which was quite well-received and established something of a name for the young and clearly talented Mosca. Though he hoped for a position in the national university system, Mosca had to return home to Palermo for financial reasons and spent one year teaching history and geography in a local secondary school.

The call to the university, however, came soon afterward, and in 1885 Mosca became a lecturer in constitutional law in Palermo. He stayed two years, publishing monographs on constitutional issues while at the university. Disappointed at not receiving a full professorship, Mosca competed in a national civil service examination and won a position as editor of the official publications of the Italian Chamber of Deputies. He moved to Rome in 1887, took up his new duties, and embarked on further, direct study of the operation of government within the halls of parliament itself. This experience culminated in the publication of his first major work, *Elementi di scienza politica* (elements of political science), in 1896. In this book he outlined both a theory of government and a scientific methodology for the study of politics. These two issues would remain constant features in Mosca's later writings.

Life's Work

The most productive period of Mosca's life coincided with one of the most turbulent periods of European history: 1895 to 1925, the years of *la belle époque*, its disintegration in World War I, and the rise of Fascism on the Continent. A single concept informed all of Mosca's adult work—the existence and importance of minority rule in government and politics. Indeed, for the forty years of his active intellectual life, Mosca continued to elaborate and expand on this one idea.

Underlying his work was a simple and profoundly modern conception of the purpose of political science: to examine government, not as the state appears or according to what it claims to do but rather as it really operates. In particular, Mosca maintained that modern governments, behind the appearance of majority rule and representative democracy, were really the expression of the power of a small, well-organized minority.

Mosca embarked on a detailed historical investigation into government in the past to see if minority rule was a constant feature in human societies. He insisted on grounding all political theory in actual history rather than on subjective impressions. This approach marked the first serious effort to give the study of politics a real methodology akin to that of the natural sciences. Mosca, first in the 1896 *Elementi di scienza politica* and then as a university professor in Turin from 1898 to 1923, looked at government over a wide sweep of time, starting with the Greek city-states, and then studying the Roman Empire, European feudal societies, absolutist monarchies on the Continent, representative government in England, and finally ending with considerations on democracy in the United States. His conclusion was simple and profound: "Everywhere and in every time," Mosca wrote in *Elementi di scienza politica*, "all that is called government, the exercise of authority, command and responsibility, always belongs to a special class that always forms a small minority." Mosca labeled this minority the "political class," though it is better known today as a ruling elite.

In his teaching at the University of Turin and also at Italy's most prestigious private academy, the Bocconi in Milan, Mosca developed his ideas on the "political class." His mature writings focused on the formation and organization of elite rule in modern society. Mosca maintained that the concentration of power in the modern state and its vast influence over the lives of its citizens made elite rule the most important single issue for contemporary political science.

Initially, Mosca's contention that minority rule was a permanent feature of society made him a strong critic of what he considered to be the democratic pretensions in modern representative government. Most people, he believed, had neither the resources nor the education to rule adequately; as a result, they were thoroughly unqualified to govern themselves. Indeed, Mosca, as a Deputy to the Italian Chamber from 1909 to 1919, was one of only two representatives to vote against the extension of the suffrage to all adult males shortly before World War I.

Mosca offered an original and telling criticism of modern democracies with the assertion that the electors' free choice among candidates—an essential foundation of democratic theory—was quite simply "a lie." He pointed out how various groups in society—politicians, influential social and economic figures, and trade unions—had a determinate voice in the selection of those candidates who would appear before the electorate. The influence of these groups guaranteed the reproduction of the already established ruling elite.

Mosca also argued that increasingly complex technology was an important element in maintaining elite rule in contemporary societies. Knowledge of such technology and mastery of certain vi-

tal productive skills, what Mosca referred to as both "personal merit" and "special culture," gave certain individuals and social groups great influence in the political affairs of society. Additionally, Mosca noted that the consent of the governed was crucial to the maintenance of minority rule. Governing elites justified their position in society by developing and disseminating "political formulas," which legitimized their rule and gave their power a "moral and legal base." Mosca left this potent insight undeveloped, turning his attention instead to how elites organize themselves. Modern political and social theorists have used Mosca's conception of political formulas as a springboard for their own work on the social function of ideology.

Mosca found nothing morally objectionable in his assertion that all societies were governed by a ruling minority—for him, this was merely a statement of historical fact. Mosca did distinguish between good and bad forms of elite rule. Minority government was good when it blocked the emergence of disruptive elements and deviant behavior, both of which threatened society's existence; the political class was also "good" when it allowed for a gradual renewal of the ruling elite without violent clashes or revolutionary change. Minority rule was bad when it tended to confer too much power in the hands of one social group, leading to despotic or even dictatorial rule.

Mosca most clearly revealed the prejudices that underlay his claim to an objective theory of government. Mosca was a social and political conservative, a middle-class gentleman and intellectual who mistrusted both the masses and the privileged. Mosca's ideal government was one in which other middle-class, university-trained intellectuals (men like himself) would manage the state. World War I demolished the possibilities for this kind of enlightened elite rule. Mass politics were the order of the day after 1919, and Italy was the first European country to experience the rise of Fascism out of the ruins of a representative democracy.

Mosca was a senator in the Italian parliament from 1919 to 1925, and directly witnessed the destruction of parliamentary rule at the hands of Mussolini. This experience led Mosca to a final development in his theory of government—the advocacy of a mixed form of political rule. The second edition of his *Elementi di scienza politica*, published in 1923 (and issued in an English translation in 1939 with the title *The Ruling Class*), included Mosca's writings on the need to include in the governing minority members of all the major "social forces" in society. Mosca was most concerned to keep political power separate from clerical influence and to avoid mixing politics with either military or economic strengths. Mosca maintained that only a balance of social forces would ensure that elite rule would tend toward social stability and block the drift toward dictatorship. Therefore, Mosca ended his academic and political career strongly supportive of one interpretation of a classic element in democratic theory—the separation of powers.

Summary

The tragedy of World War I and, immediately afterward, the rise of Fascism in Italy forced many European intellectuals, Gaetano Mosca included, to choose among the alternatives outlined in their academic studies. Despite his constant focus on elite rule, Mosca, to his great credit (and unlike the other elite theorists Vilfredo Pareto and Robert Michels), moved increasingly toward an acceptance, albeit a reluctant one, of mass parliamentary democracy. In 1925, Mosca opposed a law granting Mussolini full executive and legislative powers; he then resigned his seat in the senate and spent the rest of his active life teaching political theory at the University of Rome. He retired from teaching in 1933 and in 1937 published a collection of his lectures, *Storia delle dottrine politiche* (history of political theory), which included a strong criticism of the Fascist racial theory of government. Mosca died at his home in Rome late in 1941.

With his theory of a "political class" and elite rule and the outlines of a historical methodology for the study of government, Mosca offered the beginnings of a truly modern science of politics. The real significance and fuller development of political science along the lines sketched out by Mosca waited another decade after his death, but modern political theorists of elite rule and democracy owe much to the work of Mosca.

Bibliography

Albertoni, Ettore A. *Mosca and the Theory of Elitism*. Translated by Paul Goodrick. Oxford and New York: Blackwell, 1987. A good introduction to the work of Mosca, written by one of the foremost Italian specialists. Includes a bibliography of Mosca's principal works, a list of critical studies in English and Italian, a summary of the major interpretations of Mosca's theories, and a brief biography.

Bellamy, Richard. *Modern Italian Social Theory: Ideology and Politics from Pareto to the Present*. Cambridge: Polity Press, and Stanford, Calif.: Stanford University Press, 1987. Bellamy presents a concise treatment of several major Italian social theorists, including Mosca. The combination of intellectual history and political theory gives this book strengths that few others in the field achieve.

Bobbio, Norberto. *On Mosca and Pareto*. Geneva: Librairie Droz, 1972. A short paper on the two major Italian theorists of elite rule in modern societies, written by the leading contemporary political philosopher in Italy. Bobbio contrasts the political implications (and actions) of these two men whose understanding of elite theory was so similar.

Finocchiaro, Maurice A. *Beyond Right and Left: Democratic Elitism in Mosca and Gramsci*. New Haven, Conn.: Yale University Press, 1999. This is the first thorough study comparing the political thought of Mosca, a conservative, and Antonio Gramsci, a Marxist. The author suggests that Gramsci's views are actually constructive critiques of Mosca's theories.

Hughes, H. Stuart. *Consciousness and Society: The Reorientation of European Social Thought*. New York: Knopf, 1958; London: MacGibbon and Kee, 1959. One of the best and most succinct accounts of Mosca's work in English. Of particular value is Hughes's approach, which situates Mosca in the context of general intellectual trends and social theory in Europe from 1890 to 1930.

Meisel, James H. *The Myth of the Ruling Class: Gaetano Mosca and the "Elite."* Ann Arbor: University of Michigan Press, 1958. This was the one of the first critical studies in English. Meisel's book contains detailed treatments of Mosca's work and thought.

David Travis

GRANDMA MOSES

Born: September 7, 1860; Washington County, near Greenwich, New York
Died: December 13, 1961; Hoosick Falls, New York
Area of Achievement: Art
Contribution: A self-taught artist, Grandma Moses developed a distinctive style of painting, a form of Primitivism also referred to as naïve art or folk art.

Early Life

Anna Mary Robertson, of Scotch-Irish descent, was born on September 7, 1860, on a farm in Washington County, in eastern New York. Her parents were Russell King Robertson, a flax grower, and Margaret Shannahan. Anna Mary was the third of ten children. Her parents called her Sissy, her siblings, Molly, and her husband, Mary, but to the world she was known as Grandma Moses.

In her autobiography, she described the pleasures of her childhood and the work on the farm. Her memories of these happy days, as she called them, were the resources upon which she drew for her art. She learned early to express herself in a creative way. She remembered how her father liked to see his children occupy themselves with drawing. He would buy large sheets of white blank newspaper that cost only a penny. Paper was cheaper than candy and lasted longer.

Her school days were limited. At the age of twelve, Anna Mary left home to earn her living as a hired girl, working neighborhood farms for the next fifteen years. In November of 1887, she married Thomas Salmon Moses, a hired man who worked on the same farm. On their wedding day, they left New York to settle on a dairy farm in Staunton, Virginia. They had ten children, only five of whom survived.

In December, 1905, the family returned to eastern New York and bought a farm at Eagle Bridge. For the next twenty-two years, Anna Mary's main occupation was to work on the farm, care for the family, and keep up their house. On one occasion, she was wallpapering the parlor when she ran out of paper. Her solution became her first known painting. She applied some white paper to the empty space and painted a landscape, the *Fireboard* (1918). It is housed in the Bennington Museum.

When her husband died in 1927, her youngest son, Hugh, and daughter-in-law Dorothy took over the farm. She now had fewer responsibilities. She enjoyed embroidery, creating worsted yarn landscape pictures that she composed herself. When her rheumatism made embroidering difficult, she turned to painting. These were mainly done for amusement and given as gifts to friends. Sometimes she sold a few with her homemade preserves and jams in the Women's Exchange in the W. D. Thomas Pharmacy in Hoosick Falls.

Life's Work

The turning point in Grandma Moses' artistic career came in 1938. Louis J. Caldor, an art collector and engineer, is credited with discovering her talent. He had stopped in Hoosick Falls while on vacation. As he walked by the Thomas Pharmacy, he noticed the Moses paintings in the window. He bought three and inquired where he could buy more. The prices were reasonable, usually between $3 and $5. Moses priced her paintings according to size. When Caldor left for New York the next day, he had an additional ten pictures, some painted and some embroidered in yarn.

The subjects of Moses' paintings were memories of scenes and events she knew well. Landscape paintings of the four seasons dominate: white for winter paintings, light green for spring, deep green for summer, and brown and yellow for fall. Her early paintings were strongly influenced by illustrations, such as Currier and Ives lithographs, which she found in magazines. Sometimes she cut out figures that she moved around to find a composition that pleased her. Her usual practice was to work from memory, without a preliminary sketch.

Caldor tried for a year to interest someone in the Moses pictures. When he heard about the exhibition "Contemporary Unknown American Painters" at the Museum of Modern Art, New York City, from October 18 to November 18, 1939, Caldor entered three paintings: *Home, In the Maple Sugar Days,* and *The First Automobile.*

In 1940, these paintings were included in the artist's first solo exhibition. Caldor had finally located an art dealer, Otto Kallir, who was interested in folk art and who agreed to arrange an exhibition. Kallir selected thirty-three paintings and one worsted picture. The exhibition "What a Farm Wife Painted" was held at Kallir's gallery, St. Etienne, in New York, from October 9 to October 31,

1940. The artist, who had just turned eighty, did not come to the opening; as she said, she knew all the paintings.

An art critic in the *New York Herald Tribune*, on October 8, 1940, noted that in Washington County the artist was known as Grandma Moses. This was the first time the name appeared in print.

The reaction to her work was overwhelmingly positive. Requests came from everywhere for her paintings, in the beginning mainly for copies. This explains why so many paintings have the same or similar names, such as *Sugaring Off* or *Turkey Hunt*.

Before the exhibition closed, plans were under way for the next exhibition. The Gimbels Department Store in New York City invited Grandma Moses to show her work from November 14 to November 25, 1940. She was also asked to attend the opening. She accepted and appeared with complete self-confidence before an audience of more than four hundred people.

Now began a long series of exhibitions in the United States, including the New York State Art Show, where *The Old Oaken Bucket* (1941) received the State Prize. Her works were also shown abroad, first in 1949 in Canada and then in traveling exhibitions to Europe. In Grandma Moses' lifetime, her paintings were shown in about eighty exhibitions.

Grandma Moses' reputation continued to grow as she received other honors. On May 14, 1949, she accepted the Achievement Award of the Women's National Press Club in Washington, D.C., and received a standing ovation from seven hundred dinner guests when she entered the hall. President Harry S Truman presented the award to her and five other women, including Eleanor Roosevelt. The president, who was much impressed by Grandma Moses and her lively conversation, arranged to meet her the next day at Blair House. Later, Grandma Moses' mentor and friend Otto Kallir offered the White House her painting *July Fourth* (1951).

More recognition came to Grandma Moses. She was the recipient of two honorary doctorate degrees: in 1949, from Russell Sage College, Troy, New York, and, in 1951, from the Moore Institute of Art, Philadelphia. A documentary film about her, completed in 1950, received a Certificate of Nomination for Award from the Academy of Motion Picture Arts and Sciences. Edward R. Murrow, a well-known broadcast commentator, interviewed her for the CBS *See It Now* television series. The interview aired on June 29, 1955.

In the film, Grandma Moses explained and demonstrated her work method. Neither a heat wave nor the hot camera lights bothered the almost ninety-five-year-old artist. The CBS film crew followed the creation of a painting from the beginning to the end. The subject that Grandma Moses chose was one of her favorites: a sugaring-off scene.

She selected a Masonite board. With a broad house painter's brush, she applied flat white paint for the ground. When the surface was dry, she penciled in the horizon to see how high it would be. Then she indicated trees, bushes, and houses. Her painting began with the sky. A winter sky, she explained to the camera crew. She worked steadily, occasionally closing her eyes as if to conjure up the scene in her mind. Sometimes she put a dab of bright red or blue on the board. This would soon turn into a recognizable figure. When she finished painting the white snow, she sprinkled glitter over it, ignoring those who said that glitter was inappropriate for a painting. She argued that anyone who had seen snow in sunlight knew it glittered.

One exception from her practice to paint only from memory was the painting of the *Eisenhower Farm* (1956). To honor President Eisenhower on the anniversary of his inauguration, the president's cabinet wanted to give him a Grandma Moses painting. Working from numerous photographs of the farm, she accomplished her task to the president's satisfaction. She was paid $1,000, the largest amount she ever received for a painting.

Grandma Moses completed almost 1,600 paintings, of which some twenty-five were done after her one-hundredth birthday. After she entered a nursing home in July of 1961, she was not allowed to paint. This was a great disappointment to her. Her death, on December 13, 1961, was announced on all radio networks and reported on the front pages of newspapers nationwide.

The Bennington Museum in Bennington, Vermont, holds the largest public collection of Grandma Moses' work. The old schoolhouse from Eagle Bridge, now moved to the museum grounds, exhibits memorabilia from her life.

Summary

Grandma Moses, a talented untrained artist, created a unique style of painting. Unlike those of most nonacademic artists, especially in the nineteenth century, her artistic career was successful. She received international fame during her lifetime and furthered the cause of nonacademic art in both the United States and Europe. She helped to increase critical appreciation and popular acceptance of primitive, or naïve, art, the genre to which her works are usually thought to belong. In her art, she celebrated the virtues of American rural life, and through her example she taught thousands of people the value of a simple and uncomplicated manner of living. At an age in life when most people are retired, she started to work professionally and thereby became an inspiration to senior citizens. She demonstrated that age need not be a hindrance to a fulfilled life. In connection with Senior Citizens Month, in May of 1969, honoring all older Americans, the U.S. government issued a stamp to commemorate Grandma Moses, a distinction given to few artists. The commemorative stamp depicts a detail of *July Fourth*, 1951, the painting that hangs in the White House, Washington, D.C. Interest in Grandma Moses has not declined. In 1989, Cloris Leachman played Grandma Moses in a play, *American Primitive*, covering the years from 1905, when Grandma Moses moved back to New York, until 1960. The play, which was on tour from April 26 to July 9, 1989, went to fourteen major cities across the country.

Bibliography

Biracree, Tom. *Grandma Moses: Painter.* American Women of Achievement Series. New York: Chelsea House, 1989. With an introduction by Matina S. Horner, president of Radcliffe College, the book gives a clear account of the artist's life and career. It has a good selection of black-and-white photographs and eight pages of color reproductions, and it should be useful to high school students as well as to general readers.

Kallir, Jane. *Grandma Moses, The Artist Behind the Myth.* New York: Potter, 1982; Bristol: Art-line, 1989. The writer, granddaughter of Otto Kallir, see below, discusses several other nonacademic artists contemporary with Grandma Moses, such as John Kane and Joseph Pickett. Describes Grandma Moses' personal growth and artistic development and notes that the artist did not adopt any established style but invented her own.

Kallir, Otto. *Grandma Moses.* New York: Abrams, 1973. This is the major work on Grandma Moses. It contains valuable biographical information and a catalog of all of her nearly 1,600 paintings, her worsted pictures, and her tiles. The book includes 253 large illustrations, of which 135 are in color, plus 1,203 documentary illustrations.

————. ed. *Grandma Moses: American Primitive.* Introduction by Louis Bromfield. New York: Doubleday, 1947. Grandma Moses' autobiographical comments, reproduced in her own handwriting, accompany the forty reproductions (two in color) of her paintings. Gives a clear description of how an untrained person came to take up painting.

Moses, Anna Mary (Robertson). *Grandma Moses: My Life's History.* Edited by Otto Kallir. New York: Harper, and London: Deutsche, 1952. Encouraged by Kallir, Grandma Moses wrote several autobiographical sketches focusing on her early childhood and her married years. Includes photographs and reproductions of sixteen paintings in color.

Oneal, Zibby. *Grandma Moses: Painter of Rural America.* Women of Our Time Series. New York: Viking, 1986. A brief (58 pages), illustrated, very readable text written to interest children seven to eleven years of age. Focuses on Grandma Moses' country childhood and hard work as a farm wife. She is presented as an independent woman who found the time to be creative.

Elvy Setterqvist O'Brien

JOHN R. MOTT

Born: May 25, 1865; Livingston Manor, New York
Died: January 31, 1955; Orlando, Florida
Area of Achievement: Religion
Contribution: The central figure in at least four worldwide Christian movements, Mott combined missionary zeal and personal piety with administrative efficiency. Cowinner of the Nobel Peace Prize in 1946, he is widely regarded as the father of the ecumenical movement, the most significant religious movement of the twentieth century.

Early Life

John Mott was born May 25, 1865, in the farming community of Livingston Manor, New York, the third of four children and the only son of John Stitt Mott and Elmira Dodge Mott. When he was only four months old, his father, a farmer, moved the family to Postville, Iowa, where he entered the lumber business and soon became the leading lumber and hardware dealer in town. While working in his father's lumberyard, Mott learned to keep meticulously accurate and detailed records, which he continued to do throughout his life. John Mott expressed his individuality early when, at age eleven, on his own initiative he added the initial "R" (for "Raleigh") to his name.

Mott acquired from his mother much of his personal piety, together with an almost insatiable desire for knowledge. Elmira was an earnest Methodist and subscribed regularly to such magazines as *Harper's Weekly, The Youth's Companion, The Christian Advocate*, and *The Guide to Holiness*, all of which were eagerly devoured by young Mott. The family also had a relatively large library, and his mother told him much about European history and public affairs, both absorbing interests of his in later years. At the age of thirteen, Mott came under the influence of an Iowa Quaker evangelist, J. W. Dean. Shortly thereafter, a young circuit-riding Methodist pastor, the Reverend Horace E. Warner, not only instilled in him the desire and purpose to obtain a college education but also convinced his parents to make it possible for him to do so.

In the fall of 1881, Mott, at age sixteen, enrolled in Upper Iowa University, a small Methodist preparatory college at nearby Fayette. His primary interests in his years there were English literature, history, and philosophy, with special emphasis on politics, constitutional law, and logic. He joined the Philomathean Society, a debating club, and won prizes in historical and political oration and debate. Mott's debates and orations, in preparation for a political career, were to prove highly useful to him in later years, as did his nearly complete mastery of *Robert's Rules of Order* (1876).

During his years at Upper Iowa, Mott was not particularly religious, although he did become a charter member of the local Young Men's Christian Association (YMCA). His decision to transfer to Cornell University in Ithaca, New York, seems to have been motivated primarily by a need for wider horizons in his preparation for a career in politics and law, but also by a desire to attend a large secular institution in hopes of escaping religious influences. Such was not to be. On Friday evening, January 15, 1886, Mott attended a lecture by J. E. K. Studd, famous English cricketer from Cambridge (later to be knighted and become Lord Mayor of London), and heard Studd utter three sentences which changed his life. As Mott took his seat, having arrived late, Studd announced his text: "Seekest thou great things for thyself? Seek them not. Seek ye first the kingdom of God." Mott later wrote, "These words went straight to the springs of my motive life. I have forgotten all else that the speaker said, but on these few words hinged my life-investment decision. I went back to my room not to study but to fight." Following an interview with Studd the next day, Mott wrote his parents of his decision "to devote my whole life and talents to the service of Jesus."

Mott immediately began a period of intensive Bible study and prayer, along with holding religious services in the local jail. He was elected vice president of the Cornell YMCA, whose membership rapidly grew from forty to 150. In the summer of 1886, he was selected to represent Cornell at the first international and ecumenical Christian Student Conference, a gathering of 251 young men from eighty-nine colleges and universities in the United States and Canada, at Mount Hermon, Massachusetts, under the leadership of the evangelist Dwight L. Moody. Mott returned to Cornell from Mount Hermon determined to complete his education and to devote his life to missionary work. He was elected president of the Cornell YMCA and its membership rapidly grew to 290. He also was instrumental in raising the money for a building for the Cornell YMCA. In 1888, he was graduated with degrees in philosophy, history, and political science, along with membership in Phi Beta Kappa.

Life's Work

Rejecting several opportunities for further study and travel, Mott agreed to a trial period of one year as student secretary of the International Committee of the YMCA. This involved extensive traveling to college campuses and coordination of campus Christian activities. Mott was to remain in this position not one year but for the next twenty-seven years until 1915, at which time he became the committee's general secretary until 1931. Only four months into his new job, however, Mott also accepted the additional responsibility of chairman of the newly organized Student Volunteer Movement for Foreign Missions, the missionary branch of the YMCA, the YWCA, the American Inter-Seminary Missionary Alliance, and the Canadian Intercollegiate Missionary Alliance. This post Mott would hold until 1920, and he continued to solicit funds for it most of his life. Its slogan, The Evangelization of the World in This Generation, was the title of one of his most important books (1900). Mott had an almost uncanny ability to seek out other capable leaders and to inspire them by his own contagious enthusiasm and zeal. In addition to Mott's extensive travels, he sent out others to work with student Christian groups on various campuses. By 1925, his efforts had resulted in the recruitment of more than ten thousand American and Canadian student volunteers for various mission boards.

In November of 1891, Mott married Leila Ada White, an English teacher and graduate of Wooster College, at her family home in Wooster, Ohio. Leila accompanied him in much of his travel and was a devoted wife and partner for nearly sixty-one years, until her death in 1952. The Motts had four children: John Livingstone, Irene, Frederick Dodge, and Eleanor, all of whom grew up in Montclair, New Jersey, while their father commuted to offices in New York City when not traveling elsewhere. Mott is described by his biographers as six feet tall, with handsome features and an impressive bearing. His reddish-brown hair, gray in later years, topped a large, finely molded head. Photographs indicate his most impressive facial feature to have been his thick, shaggy eyebrows. His entire physique suggested strength: square shoulders and square head, firm mouth, and dark brown, piercing eyes. Small wonder that at least one student is said

to have emerged from a conference with Mott and commented, "It was like being in to see God!"

Mott defined his life's work as one of weaving together Christian movements—particularly among students—all over the world. In 1893, he organized the Foreign Missions Conference of North America in an effort to unite missionary work on that continent. He was repeatedly elected to its executive committee and was made an honorary life member in 1942. Mott also was one of the leaders in founding the World's Student Christian Federation in Badstena, Sweden, in 1895, and he became its first general secretary. In this role, he organized student movements in China, Japan, India, New Zealand, and Australia, as well as in Europe and the Near East. International meetings were held in such unlikely places as Tokyo, Constantinople, Jerusalem, Peking, and Madras. By 1925, the WSCF claimed the membership of more than 300,000 young men and women in more than three thousand colleges and universities in twenty-seven different nations. Mott served as chairman of its executive committee from its inception until 1920, then as general chairman until 1928.

A high point in Mott's career came in June of 1910, when he was elected chairman of the World Missionary Conference, attended by more than twelve hundred delegates, in Edinburgh, Scotland, which Mott himself called "the most notable gathering in the interest of the worldwide expansion of Christianity ever held, not only in missionary annals, but in all Christian annals." Mott was also made chairman of a "continuation committee" to carry on the work of the Edinburgh conference until the next one. He toured the Far East in this role and organized regional missionary councils in various nations, including India, Japan, Korea, and China. Mott spent his days organizing these councils and his evenings addressing huge throngs of students. Although he spoke through interpreters, his impassioned words were interrupted time and again by applause. Mott deserves much of the credit for the leading role assumed by the "younger churches" in later missionary conferences throughout the world. Against strong opposition, he recruited Roman Catholic and Eastern Orthodox Christians into ecumenical groups. The "continuation committee" was succeeded by the International Missionary Council in 1921, with Mott as its chairman. In 1942, when he retired from that position, he was named its "honorary chairman."

Mott's travels on behalf of various Christian causes were prodigious. Following extensive trips throughout the United States and Canada, he made his first visit to Europe in 1891. For the next sixty years, he crossed the Atlantic both ways almost annually, occasionally twice or three times, and the Pacific at least fourteen times, in all logging well over two million miles and visiting eighty-three countries. One indication that these travels were far from pleasure junkets is that Mott was often afflicted by motion sickness—not only on sea travels, but on trains as well. When he accepted the Nobel Peace Prize in 1946 (after his first intercontinental flight), this "world citizen" received congratulatory messages from seven chiefs of state and numerous other world leaders. He died January 31, 1955, a few months before his ninetieth birthday, and was buried in the Washington Cathedral. Among his last recorded words were these: "While life lasts I am an evangelist."

Summary

For many years, Mott was the central figure in at least four major world Christian movements: president of the World's Alliance of YMCAs, general secretary and later chairman of the World's Student Christian Federation, chairman of the International Missionary Council, and the first honorary president of the World Council of Churches. As an American Methodist layman, he was awarded an honorary doctor of divinity degree by the (Russian) Orthodox Theological Institute of St. Sergius, in 1940. He declined many prestigious opportunities during his career, including President Woodrow Wilson's offer to become United States Ambassador to China and offers of the presidencies of Princeton University, Oberlin College, and Yale Divinity School. At President Wilson's request, he served on the Mexican Commission in 1916 and the Special Diplomatic Mission to Russia (the "Root Mission") in 1917, utilizing the latter as an opportunity to bring the Russian Orthodox Church into the ecumenical network. Mott was awarded the Distinguished Service Medal for his fund-raising work and other service during World War I, at the conclusion of which he also made significant contributions to the peace conferences at Versailles. In addition to the Nobel Peace Prize, which he shared with the pacifist Emily Greene Balch in 1946, he was the recipient of seven honorary degrees, the Imperial Order of Meija from Japan, the Order of the Saviour from Greece, the Order of the Holy Sepulchre from Jerusalem, the Prince Carl Medal from Sweden, the Order of the White Rose from Finland, the Second Order of the Crown from Siam, the Order of Polonia Restituta from Poland, the Order of the Italian Crown, and he was made a chevalier, and later an officer, of the French Legion of Honor. He raised more than $300 million for his various Christian causes, most of it for World War I relief work.

Although a brilliant organizer and fund-raiser, Mott was also a man of deep spiritual strength. "Organize as though there were no such thing as prayer," he said, "and pray as though there were no such thing as organization." President Wilson once called him "the world's most useful man."

Mott was typical of much of early twentieth century American religious thought. An evangelical liberal, he eagerly embraced the "social gospel" and applied it to missions and other burning issues of his day. Mott was probably influenced as well by the "social Darwinism" of the period; there was unbounded optimism in the popular slogan The Evangelization of the World in This Generation. This slogan did not originate with Mott, although he made it his own. Yet it is also clear that he knew the difference between the "evangelization" of the world and its "conversion." He simply wanted the Christian Gospel to be preached to the entire world and sincerely believed it could be done in a single generation. Perhaps in part because of his lack of a seminary education, Mott was not deterred by theological niceties in urging ecumenical cooperation. He made the words of Jesus, "that they all may be one," into an ecumenical rallying cry.

In his speech responding to the 1946 Nobel Peace Prize, Mott characterized his career: "My life might be summed up as an earnest and undiscourageable effort to weave together all nations, all races, and all religious communions in friendliness, in fellowship, and in cooperation." In its 1965 tribute to him, on the one hundredth anniversary of his birthday, the General Board of the National Council of Churches called Mott "the greatest missionary statesman since the Apostle Paul." If anyone ever deserved the title of father of one of the most important religious movements of the twentieth century, the ecumenical movement, it was John R. Mott.

Bibliography

Fisher, Galen M. *John R. Mott: Architect of Cooperation and Unity*. New York: Association Press, 1952. Written shortly before his death, this volume is very positive throughout in its analysis of Mott's many contributions. The book contains many quotations from distinguished churchmen in praise of Mott's work. The concluding chapter compares Mott's service with that of Saint Paul.

Hopkins, Charles Howard. *John R. Mott, 1865-1955: A Biography*. Grand Rapids, Mich.: Eerdmans, 1979. The definitive biography of Mott, by an emeritus professor of history at Rider College, Philadelphia, this is a detailed, straightforward, and well-documented account of Mott's career and influence. The result of fifteen years of research, this volume tends to emphasize Mott's social concern and the details of his travels, perhaps to the neglect of his Evangelicalism and churchmanship.

Mackie, Robert C. *Layman Extraordinary: John R. Mott, 1865-1955*. London: Hodder and Stoughton, and New York: Association Press, 1965. A brief monograph of nearly unbridled praise and enthusiasm on behalf of Mott and his accomplishments.

Mathews, Basil. *John R. Mott: World Citizen*. New York: Harper, and London: SCM Press, 1934. This book was authorized by Mott to describe the principles and experiences of his life as examples for young people. An excellent portrayal of his personality and character written some twenty years before his death, this volume portrays Mott as one who applied the principles of business to the work of Christian Missions.

Mott, John R. *Addresses and Papers*. 6 vols. New York: Association Press, 1946-1947. Mott wrote at least sixteen books himself, as well as many shorter works, which are included in these volumes. His personal papers and his comprehensive archives of the World's Student Christian Federation are in the Mott Collection of the Yale Divinity School Library, New Haven, Connecticut.

Rouse, Ruth. *John R. Mott: An Appreciation*. Geneva: World's Student Christian Federation Press, 1930. A well-balanced portrayal of Mott in mid-career by an admirer and historian of the ecumenical movement.

———. *The World's Student Christian Federation: A History of the First Thirty Years*. London: SCM Press, 1948. Mott wrote the foreword to this volume, which traces the WSCF from its origins prior to Vadstena, Sweden, in 1895, to High Leigh, England, in 1924, with appropriate attention to Mott's contributions.

C. Fitzhugh Spragins

LOUIS MOUNTBATTEN

Born: June 25, 1900; Frogmore House, Windsor, England

Died: August 27, 1979; off Mullaghmore, on Donegal Bay, Ireland

Areas of Achievement: Government and the military

Contribution: A naval hero and military leader during World War II, the last viceroy of imperial India, and the first and only governor-general of an independent India, Mountbatten was a figure of great achievement, the most enduringly significant of which was perhaps the example of leadership he provided for his nephew and surrogate son Prince Philip, Duke of Edinburgh, and for his great-nephew and surrogate grandson Charles, Prince of Wales.

Early Life

His Serene Highness, Prince Louis of Battenberg (christened Louis Francis Albert Victor Nicholas), the great-grandson of Queen Victoria, was born at Frogmore House, near Windsor Castle, on June 25, 1900, the youngest of four children. His mother was the queen's favorite granddaughter, Princess Victoria of Hesse, later the Marchioness of Milford Haven. His father was Prince Louis of Battenberg, a German prince who chose England as his adopted country. At that time a captain in the Royal Navy, through concerted effort he rose to its apex as First Sea Lord. Related to most of Europe's royal families, Mountbatten, or Dickie as he became familiarly known during his childhood, spent his early years in close association with many of their members. Especially memorable were his summer holidays at Heilegenberg with his aunt and uncle, Tsarina Alexandra and Tsar Nicholas II, and their children. Indeed, he claimed to have fallen in love with his female Romanov cousins and intended to marry the ill-fated Grand Duchess Maria. The young prince was deeply influenced during his youth and throughout much of his life by his exceptional mother, who herself was broadly socialistic in instincts and convictions, and who trained her son to work amicably and effectively with those of conflicting political convictions. This training was to be of immense value to him later, especially in his activities in preparing India for independence. His mother took charge of his education early in his youth. Indeed, Mountbatten was educated primarily at home, although he later attended Osborne Naval Training College, the Royal Naval College, Dartmouth, and, briefly, Christ's College, Cambridge. Although the elder Prince Louis remained a rather distant and aloof figure to the young boy, he nevertheless was held in a position of near idolatrous regard and was to influence his son profoundly in his choice of career and in his obsessive concern with the rehabilitation of his family's name and honor.

The halcyon days of young Mountbatten's youth were suddenly interrupted with the outbreak of World War I in the summer of 1914. The war had an unanticipated and permanent impact on Mountbatten. The hysterically paranoid fringe of the British public, regarding anything German as suspect, lobbied successfully for his father's resignation as commander of the Royal Navy. This event broke the father emotionally and convinced the son of the necessity that he succeed his father as First Sea Lord to rehabilitate and enhance his family's name and honor. At a time when the royal family sought to minimize its German connections with the adoption of the surname of Windsor, the Battenbergs anglicized theirs to Mountbatten. Lord Mountbatten became so obsessed with his anglicized name that he encouraged his nephew and surrogate son Prince Philip to take his name and eventually succeeded in the addition of his surname to that of Windsor for the children of Queen Elizabeth II and Prince Philip.

His father's example and his own inclinations led Mountbatten to a naval career, and during World War I, he saw naval action in the North Sea, attaining the rank of sub-lieutenant. Following the war, Mountbatten attended Christ's College, Cambridge, and engaged in a whirlwind of social activities in Cambridge, London, and in the great houses of Great Britain. By this time, he had acquired the striking handsomeness, aristocratic mien, and approachability and engaging personality which he retained throughout his life. Unfortunately, those attractive qualities were often diminished by an irritating vanity, undoubtedly caused by the indulgences of his youth. In 1920 and 1921, he accompanied his cousin the Prince of Wales (later Edward VIII) on two extensive empire tours on HMS *Renown*. During the trips, a close friendship was cemented between the young men which survived the Abdication Crisis of 1936. The second tour was most momentous since it included a four-month sojourn in India, the jewel in the British imperial crown. Mountbatten often claimed that three of his lifelong loves resulted from this stay in India. One was India itself; another was polo, a passion which he instilled in his nephew, Prince Philip and in his great-nephew Prince Charles. The third was his future wife, Edwina.

Shortly before the beginning of the second tour, in July, 1921, Mountbatten met Edwina Ashley, the granddaughter and sole heiress of Sir Ernest Cassel, an enormously wealthy international banker. Edwina had the wit, beauty, and youthful energy which complemented Mountbatten's aristocratic bearing, decisiveness, ambition, and competitiveness. She and Mountbatten's mother shared a variety of interests; each enjoyed a superior intelligence and pragmatic outlook, and, although born into families with a conservative outlook, they shared broadly socialistic views about domestic and world problems. Penniless (her grandfather had died leaving her as sole heiress, but with the stipulation that she was to receive only three hundred pounds a year until she was twenty-one or until she married), she borrowed one hundred pounds from a relative, booked passage on the cheapest ship she could find, and sailed to India, under conditions of considerable discomfort and privation, to see Mountbatten, with whom she had corresponded throughout his tour with the Prince of Wales. Arriving in Bombay with almost no funds, the future vicereine traveled by land to Delhi, where the young couple became engaged. They were married on July 18, 1922, almost exactly a year after their first meeting, with the Prince of Wales serving as best man. "The Wedding of the Century," as it was hailed by the tabloids, was followed by a six-month honeymoon in Europe and the United States.

Life's Work

The effect of the marriage on Mountbatten was threefold. The match brought him not only supreme happiness but also a personal fortune and extensive property holdings that allowed him to indulge his expensive tastes and gave him the free time and financial security to advance his naval career. Most important, Mountbatten acquired a partner who offered him indispensable aid and advice in the various assignments that he later accepted and who enhanced his reputation as well as her own through her untiring services to humanitarian causes, especially, though by no means exclusively, during World War II and as the last vicereine of India. Although she, with her husband, indulged her appetite for pleasure, especially during the first decade of her marriage, and although this marriage was unconventional (Edwina was rumored to have had numerous extramarital affairs, notably with India's first prime minister, Jawaharlal Nehru, to which Mountbatten inexplicably did not object), Edwina had a deep commitment to using her energy, talents, and wealth for humanitarian purposes and helped to associate the Mountbatten name with causes of social concern. She traveled constantly, especially during the last two decades of her life, often suffering from pain and nearly total exhaustion, and in her travels developed a sincere empathy with the problems of the world's poor, injured, suffering, and dispossessed which was often translated into direct action. Although the rigors of travel and service contributed to her early death, she helped to establish for herself and her husband a deep affection in Great Britain and throughout the former British Empire, especially in India.

During the 1920's and 1930's, Mountbatten continued to advance in his naval career and build a family. Ever anxious to emulate his father's career, Mountbatten was happiest and proudest following his appointment in 1927 to Great Britain's prestigious Mediterranean Fleet. Stationed in Malta, where he had visited his father many years earlier, he and Edwina both enjoyed the possibilities for service and activity afforded them. Their first of two daughters, Patricia (later Countess Mountbatten of Burma), was born in 1924; a second daughter, Pamela (later Lady Pamela Hicks) was born in 1929. Unknowingly, Mountbatten's most significant achievement during this was his assumption of partial responsibility for the rearing of his nephew Prince Philip of Greece, the future Duke of Edinburgh. Prince Philip, the youngest of several children of Mountbatten's sister, Princess Alice of Greece, and Prince Andrew of Greece, had become an exile in his infancy when his parents escaped a revolution in Greece in 1922. By 1926, his emotionally unstable mother and passive father had drifted apart. Philip's siblings were old enough to function independently, but Philip, only five years of age, was turned over to relatives, namely to Mountbatten, his mother, and his brother, George. Initially, George assumed the greatest responsibility, but when George died in 1938, Mountbatten assumed full responsibility, and he and Edwina treated Philip as the son they never had. Philip was to reciprocate with unbounded filial loyalty, respect,

British vice admiral Louis Mountbatten (right) in 1943, with British prime minister Winston Churchill between meetings at the Casablanca conference.

and affection. Mountbatten instilled in Philip a sense of commitment and an approachability which have contributed to his popularity as a member of the royal family. Mountbatten naturally took great pride in Prince Philip's marriage to the Princess Elizabeth and in the birth of their children, especially Prince Charles. Because of Prince Philip's close attachment to his uncle, who became a surrogate father and whose name he adopted, the young Prince of Wales also came to regard his great-uncle and godfather as asurrogate grandfather, confidant, and adviser. All three remained extremely close until Mountbatten's death, and Mountbatten has been credited with shaping their character and style, especially that of the Prince of Wales, who has impressed all with his curiosity, intelligence, and gregariousness.

Mountbatten became a figure of international prominence during World War II. His early wartime exploits became widely known primarily because of his friend Noël Coward's internationally proclaimed film *In Which We Serve* (1942), which,

though fictional, was based upon Mountbatten's command of the destroyer *Kelly*, which was sunk during the Battle of Crete in the Mediterranean on May 23, 1941. The men Mountbatten commanded on the *Kelly* revered him. Indeed, the Reunion Association which has remained active is the only one of its type run by the survivors of a destroyed ship's company. A favorite of Prime Minister Winston Churchill, who also sought to please King George VI by utilizing the services of his cousin, Mountbatten served between 1941 and 1943 as Chief of Combined Operations and member of the British Chiefs of Staff. He worked as an intermediary between Churchill and President Franklin D. Roosevelt, who also liked him and respected his opinions. Thus, Mountbatten helped to achieve harmony in war between the two allies. The disastrous Dieppe raid of August 19, 1942, which Mountbatten played a major role in preparing, was the low point of his wartime career. The high point was his appointment, under Churchill's auspices, as supreme allied commander for Southeast Asia in August, 1943. Thus began a two-year period which was to prove for Mountbatten one of the most strenuous but rewarding of his life. Under Mountbatten's leadership, Burma and Malaya were won back from the Japanese. Mountbatten's services in Southeast Asia culminated in his acceptance of the formal Japanese surrender on September 5, 1945. Mountbatten's wartime experiences in Asia bred in him a lifelong hatred of the Japanese. Indeed, Japan was the only major nation intentionally not invited to Mountbatten's funeral, excluded from a list he had prepared before his death.

In March, 1947, Mountbatten undertook what he personally regarded as his greatest achievement: his service as the last viceroy of India for the purpose of effecting a transfer of power from Great Britain to an independent Indian government. Although Mountbatten was politically identified with Conservative prime minister Churchill, it was Churchill's successor, Labour Party prime minister Clement Atlee, who convinced Mountbatten to assume this thankless task despite Churchill's disapproval. Mountbatten accepted it only with the understanding that he would enjoy plenipotentiary powers in dealing with the Congress Party, led by Nehru; its rival Muslim League, led by Mohammed Ali Jinnah; and the scores of princes and maharajahs bound to Great Britain by treaties. Originally setting a deadline of fourteen months for completing the negotiations necessary for independence, Mountbatten succeeded in arranging a transfer of power in less than five. On August 15, 1947, India became an independent nation, which Mountbatten served for ten months as governor-general.

The price of independence, however, was high. It had been achieved quickly only by accession to Jinnah's demand for the partition of India and the creation of an independent Muslim nation, Pakistan. The immediate tragedy was the uprooting of thousands of people on both sides of the border and the starvation and massacres that followed. The long-term effect was the creation of an Indian-Pakistani enmity which continues to plague the region. Although Mountbatten and many others have regarded his work as the last viceroy as his greatest achievement, others have disagreed. Churchill felt that India had been scuttled by Mountbatten's transfer of power, and others have come to believe that Mountbatten's actions were hasty and reckless, although, in fairness to Mountbatten, these as-

sessments are the products of hindsight, and Mountbatten had good reason to believe that his quick actions would avert bloodshed rather than cause it. Perhaps testimony to his labors and to his respect for the nationalist aspirations of imperially dominated peoples is the fact that Lord and Lady Mountbatten continued until their deaths to be held in nearly reverential regard by Indian leaders and by the Indian people in general.

Following several years of additional service in the Royal Navy and a series of promotions, Mountbatten finally attained the summit of his naval career in April, 1955, with his appointment as First Sea Lord, and shortly after as Admiral of the Fleet. Finally, he had attained the rank for which he had worked since his youth. The family name had been fully vindicated. In his new position, which he held for three years, Mountbatten thoroughly modernized the Royal Navy. After serving as Chief of the United Kingdom Defence Staff and Chairman of the Chiefs of Staff Committee, he retired in 1965. The remaining years of his life were devoted to membership in various organizations, to an active role as the first president of the International Council of United World Colleges, to appearances at various official functions, to the preparation of a television series on his career, to serving as an adviser to various members of the royal family, especially to Prince Charles, and to spending time with his daughters and their families (Edwina died in 1960 while visiting Borneo). On August 27, 1979, Mountbatten was assassinated by the Provisional Irish Republican Army. He, along with one of his grandsons, a neighbor boy, and the Dowager Lady Brabourne, the mother-in-law of Mountbatten's daughter Patricia, were killed when a gelignite bomb exploded the family's twenty-nine-foot converted fishing boat, Shadow V, soon after they had left the harbor of the village of Mullaghmore, near the family retreat, Classiebawn Castle, County Sligo, in the Republic of Ireland not far from the Ulster border. The worldwide respect and affection which he had won were reflected in the size of Mountbatten's funeral at Westminster Abbey and in the international media coverage of the event. In those countries of his best-known achievements, expressions of sympathy were notable. In Rangoon, a line of mourners filed through the British Embassy for four days to sign a book in tribute to Mountbatten. In New Delhi, every shop and office was cosed and a week's state mourning was declared.

Summary

Louis, first Earl Mountbatten of Burma, Chief of Combined Operations and Supreme Allied Commander, Southeast Asia, Viceroy of India, First Sea Lord, and Admiral of the Fleet, played a vital role in world affairs for more than four decades. His tangible achievements are clear, including, especially, his role in Southeast Asia in World War II, his labors in India in 1947, and his modernization of the Royal Navy and the other armed services. Of equal importance, however, are his less tangible contributions. Although Mountbatten had his faults, not the least of which were excessive vanity and ambition, his many virtues far outweighed them. His vanity was balanced by his ability to admit his errors, his ambition by his achievements and by his sincere warmheartedness. Loyal, courteous, genuinely friendly, tolerant, and respectful of the views of others, and always energetic and enthusiastic in his myriad undertakings, he was the paragon of enlightened modern aristocracy. He also intuitively realized that in order to survive and flourish in the twentieth century royalty must serve its subjects and command their respect within the constraints of constitutional government. He rewarded the British people and the peoples of Great Britain's former empire with a life of service for the privileges they had allowed him to enjoy. Perhaps his most enduring contribution will prove to be the example of leadership he provided for Prince Philip and especially for Prince Charles. The intense popularity of the British royal family and the institution of the monarchy in the late twentieth century is to a not insignificant degree, though by no means exclusively, the product of the examples set by Lord and Lady Mountbatten.

Bibliography

Campbell-Johnson, Alan. *Mission with Mountbatten.* London: Hale, 1951; New York: Dutton, 1953. A superb firsthand account of Mountbatten's tenure as India's last viceroy and its first and only governor-general by his press attaché in 1947-1948.

————. "Mountbatten and the Transfer of Power." *History Today* 47, no. 9 (September, 1997). Discusses Mountbatten's role in India's transition to independence.

Collins, Larry, and Dominique Lapierre. *Freedom at Midnight.* London: Collins, and New York: Simon and Schuster, 1975. An outstanding popular history of the final year in the struggle for Indian independence from Great Britain, an event in which Mountbatten, as the last viceroy, played a role of major significance. This volume benefits especially from more than thirty hours of taped interviews of Mountbatten by the authors and his extensive collection of documents and papers which he made accessible to them.

Hough, Richard. *Edwina: Countess Mountbatten of Burma.* London: Weidenfeld and Nicolson, 1983; New York: Morrow, 1984. One in a series of books by the author on the Mountbatten family. This is an ideal companion volume to Hough's biography of Mountbatten, although Lady Mountbatten's greatness was achieved through her own endeavors and not simply as a by-produce of her marriage.

————. *Mountbatten.* London: Weidenfeld and Nicolson, 1980; New York: Random House, 1981. First published in the United Kingdom on the anniversary of Mountbatten's death, this volume was nearly completed while Mountbatten lived. As a result of his longtime association with the author, who had previously been selected by Mountbatten to prepare a joint biography of his parents (*The Mountbattens*, 1975) Mountbatten himself served as a source of much of the information in this volume. Nevertheless, Hough has maintained his objectivity and produced a balanced, complete biography of this extraordinary personality.

Masson, Madeleine. *Edwina: The Biography of the Countess Mountbatten of Burma.* Rev. ed. London: Hale, 1960. A well-written, useful account of the woman whose sincere and active concern for the plight of the powerless complemented her husband's talent as a political compromiser.

Rasor, Eugene L. *Earl Mountbatten of Burma, 1900-1979: Historiography and Annotated Bibliography.* Westport, Conn.: Greenwood Press, 1998. A guide to the available literature on Mountbatten, including general histories, dissertations, biographies, and more.

Swinson, Arthur. *Mountbatten.* New York: Ballantine, 1971; London: Pan, 1973. A useful account on the subject in the War Leader Books series.

Terraine, John. *The Life and Times of Lord Mountbatten.* London: Hutchinson, 1968; New York: Holt Rinehart, 1980. An unusual volume: Not truly a biography, it is based on a twelve-part television series in which Mountbatten actively participated and is primarily a compilation of

Mountbatten's own observations about himself and others given continuity with transitional passages by Terraine.

Ziegler, Philip. *Mountbatten*. London: Collins, and New York: Knopf, 1985. The official biography of the subject and the product of Ziegler's unrestricted access to Mountbatten's personal archives, perhaps the most important private archives of the twentieth century in Great Britain. Although massive in length, this volume is eminently readable, balanced, and well-organized.

J. Stewart Alverson

ROBERT MUGABE

Born: February 21, 1924; Kutama, Southern Rhodesia (now Zimbabwe)

Areas of Achievement: Government and politics

Contribution: Mugabe rose rapidly in the struggle for independence in southern Africa during the 1960's to become a prominent nationalist leader and statesman during the later part of the 1970's and the 1980's. Mugabe participated actively in the Lancaster House negotiations that led Rhodesia (Zimbabwe) to majority rule in April, 1980, and became the first black prime minister of Zimbabwe and its first executive president.

Early Life

Robert Gabriel Mugabe was born in Kutama, near Salisbury (modern Harare), in Sinoia district, Southern Rhodesia, in 1924 (some biographers cite the year 1928 for his birth). His father was a Catholic mission-trained carpenter who also owned a considerable number of cattle, which the young Mugabe tended with his friends. Although a gentle and quiet boy, Mugabe is said to have loved boxing and wrestling. He completed his primary education in such Catholic schools as Empandeni and a Jesuit institution in Matabeleland. In 1950, he continued his studies in South Africa and was graduated as a schoolteacher from Fort Hare University College. Immediately following his graduation, Mugabe taught school in Zimbabwe from 1952 to 1955 and then moved to Northern Rhodesia (now Zambia), in 1955, and to Ghana, during its transition to independence (1956-1960), continuing his teaching career in both British colonies.

Developing an interest in politics, Mugabe returned to his fatherland in 1960 and became information and publicity secretary of the (African) National Democratic Party, which had initiated negotiations toward independence with the British government. Yet as the self-governing whites banned the party in 1961, Mugabe joined Joshua Nkomo's Zimbabwe African People's Union (ZAPU), becoming his deputy. As a result of political differences and perhaps leadership styles, however, Mugabe defected from the party and joined Ndabaningi Sithole's Zimbabwe African National Union (ZANU) based in Tanzania. Before escaping to Tanzania in 1963, however, Mugabe was accused of calling the Rhodesian Front "a bunch of cowboys" and was arrested and imprisoned in 1962-1963. In Tanzania, he became secretary general of ZANU. In August, 1963, he dared to return to Southern Rhodesia but was arrested in December and spent the next ten years in and out of jail, in a permanent state of detention. In jail, Mugabe found time to take advanced courses in business and law through correspondence and received six degrees, including a master's and a bachelor's degree in law and a bachelor's degree in public administration.

Life's Work

Since 1965, Southern Rhodesia had become independent following a unilateral declaration of independence by the white population. The rebel colony, however, did not receive international recognition. Meanwhile, the white regime, under severe United Nations (U.N.) sanctions, imprisoned most nationalist leaders. In 1974, Ian Smith, the rebel white prime minister, declared a general amnesty and freed all political prisoners, including Mugabe. Mugabe took refuge in Mozambique and assumed leadership of ZANU's guerrilla wing, the Zimbabwe African National Liberation Army (ZANLA), which, along with ZAPU (based in Lusaka, Zambia), began inflicting severe casualties and economic and political damage on the Rhodesian white regime, particularly after Mozambique gained its independence in mid-1975. By 1976, it looked as if international pressure and nationalist guerrillas had succeeded in convincing the white minority regime to negotiate toward majority rule. In fact, the British government arranged such negotiations in Geneva, which Mugabe and Nkomo attended as leaders of their newly formed Patriotic Front (PF). Of the two, Mugabe was the more outspoken critic of the Smith regime at the conference. Unfortunately, the talks ended, and Mugabe returned to Mozambique convinced that only military action could bring down the white regime in Rhodesia.

Inside the former British colony, however, several black political leaders were willing to compromise with Smith. Thus, in 1978, Smith (and his Rhodesian Front) and Bishop Abel Muzorewa (leader of the United African National Council), as well as Sithole, agreed on the formation of a government that would lead to majority rule. Mugabe and Nkomo did not participate in the negotiations and therefore condemned them and their outcome. Notwithstanding their objections, elections followed, making Muzorewa the winner and the Prime Minister of Zimbabwe-Rhodesia. In 1979, however, Muzorewa and Smith repudiated their "internal political settlement" and accepted a new round of negotiations sponsored by the British government at Lancaster House in London from September to December, 1979. Both Mugabe and Nkomo, urged by the frontline states, attended the talks, which endorsed national elections and a bicameral assembly—a house of parliament with one hundred seats, twenty of which would be reserved for the white minority, and a forty-member senate. Following the talks, however, Mugabe announced that he and his followers would run independent of the ZAPU wing of the PF as candidates for parliament. ZANU's political strength was such that it captured fifty-seven of the eighty seats reserved for the black parties in the February, 1980, elections. Nkomo's party won twenty, while Muzorewa's secured only three seats. On April 18, 1980, Mugabe became prime minister and immediately formed a coalition government that included five ZAPU members in a cabinet of twenty-five ministers.

Thereafter, Mugabe followed a policy of reconciliation with both white and African political opponents, particularly Nkomo, and slowed down the implementation of his socialist goals and the breakup of the large white farms. Abroad, he followed a nonaligned policy, reserving his harshest criticism for South Africa. The attempt to merge and disband ZANU and ZAPU guerrilla forces, however, proved to be an almost impossible task. ZAPU military elements were accused of terrorizing the countryside in southwest Matabeleland Province through intimidation and murders of white settlers. The ZAPU cabinet ministers, including Nkomo, were allegedly plotting to overthrow Mugabe and his government and were therefore dismissed in 1982. Nkomo became an outspoken critic of ZANU, but in the 1985 elections, Mugabe demonstrated his strength by winning sixty-six seats. He also won two extra seats when a white member of the Conservative Alliance of Zimbabwe (successor to the Rhodesian Front) and a ZAPU delegate switched sides. Tensions between Mugabe and Nkomo were so high that the latter's passport was confiscated as he tried to leave the country in 1985. (He eventually escaped to Great Britain through Botswana but returned home soon thereafter.) The murder of fifteen white missionaries in November of 1987 in Matabeleland, however, compelled the government to arrest several ZAPU members, including some ministers who were subsequently exonerated and released by the High Court. In spite of all the political turmoil, ZANU's leadership was so strong that on December 3, 1987, after a change of the constitution, Mugabe became the first executive President of Zimbabwe, forcing President Canaan Banana to step down. In September of that year, the president had also succeeded in compelling parliament to rescind the provision guaranteeing the twenty seats for the white minority. Meanwhile, reconciliation talks between ZANU and ZAPU had been going on since 1986, after Nkomo condemned the murders in Matabeleland. As a result, on January 2, 1988, a new cabinet, representing all ethnic groups in the country, was announced and, in April, 1988, the two parties fused into ZANU-PF, making Mugabe president and first secretary of the new front and Nkomo and Simon Muzenda co-vice presidents and second secretaries, while agreeing to work toward a one-party state based on Marxist-Leninist principles.

In late 1988 and early 1989, however, the stability of Mugabe's government was threatened by corruption charges involving the selling of state cars at a profit by government officials, including five ministers. Eventually, all of them resigned and one of the officials committed suicide from an overdose of an insecticide, after Mugabe forced all of them to appear before a judicial inquiry commission. The inquiry was embarrassing to the government, and critics of Mugabe accelerated their inflammatory rhetoric. Despite the formation of a new party in 1989, the Zimbabwe Unity Movement (ZUM), by a founding member of ZANU, former Secretary-General Edgar Tekere, whose platform was "anti-corruption, anti-one-party state, and pro-economic growth," Mugabe consolidated his pwers and ruled Zimbabwe throughout the 1990's.

Summary

Robert Mugabe's popularity, despite his autocratic rule in Zimbabwe, is based on many factors. As elsewhere in revolutionary Africa, former guerrilla leaders become extremely popular when they turn statesmen. In fact, his leadership of the ZANU military wing based in Mozambique during the war of liberation has been given much more credit for weakening the Smith regime than ZANU, in spite of the fact that the latter was led by a more seasoned politician, Nkomo. Nkomo, however, was perceived as being manipulated by and the favorite

THE TWENTIETH CENTURY: ROBERT MUGABE / 2649

of the West, particularly during the last years of the struggle, in spite of his party's assistance from the Soviet Union. Mugabe, on the contrary, notwithstanding his ties with China, was viewed in the country as a determined "man of his own," with Zimbabwean black people's welfare as his uncompromising goal. His stature was enhanced by the fact that ZANU was predominantly a party of the Shona, who constitute 75 percent of the country, while ZAPU received more of its support from the Ndebele, who make up only 20 percent of the country's population.

Mugabe is, furthermore, one of the most educated African leaders in Africa and the most educated among the frontline presidents. He understands the workings of the capitalist system and the impact of socialist principles and objectives. Thus, his pragmatic approach, mixing capitalism (liberalization of the economy) with socialism (slow and extremely careful nationalization), has been able to maintain an acceptable level of productivity not lower than that of the preindependence period. This method has attracted investors while reducing the flight of needed skilled manpower.

Mugabe's unending emphasis on reconciliation, his strong support for and participation in the Southern Africa Development Coordinating Conference, and his tough stand on South Africa, which advocated "punitive sanctions" against apartheid before South Africa democratized in the early 1990's, made him a popular president. His foreign policy has mostly been nonaligned. The United States has been uncomfortable with Mugabe's Marxist-Leninist philosophy. His pragmatic approach, however, has made him a more acceptable statesman than, for example, António Agostinho Neto, Joao dos Santos, Samora Moises Machel, or Joaquim Chissano.

Mugabe's problems have come from the corruption of his government officials, the military assistance to the Mozambique Liberation Front against the Mozambique National Resistance (an assistance that has become costly in human and economic resources), his insistence on a one-party state, and his feud with Nkomo. Yet, he has faced these problems squarely, as he and President Daniel arap Moi of Kenya, for example, decided to mediate the Mozambique conflict in 1989. He settled his differences with Nkomo in early 1988 and showed his integrity when he ordered an inquiry of the corruption charges. It seemed likely, however, that his survival would be determined by the do-

mestic economic conditions and the rapidly changing situation in southern Africa. Mugabe is a quiet man; his personality has been shaped by Catholic discipline and influenced by his readings of the works of Karl Marx and his encounter with the philosophy of the African National Congress in South Africa as well as by his admiration for Ghana's Kwame Nkrumah.

Bibliography

Astrow, Andrén. *Zimbabwe: A Revolution That Lost Its Way?* London: Zed Press, and Totowa, N.J.: Biblio, 1983. One of the best accounts of the Zimbabwe revolutionary movements, although it portrays Mugabe as one who compromised his principles to accommodate imperialist capitalism in the former British colony.

Gifford, Prosser, and Wm. Roger Louis, eds. *Decolonization and African Independence.* New Haven, Conn.: Yale University Press, 1982; London: Yale University Press, 1988. The chapter on Zimbabwe outlines the context in which Mugabe assumed power. It provides a sympathetic account of Mugabe's leadership of ZANU.

Lipschutz, Mark R., and R. Kent Rasmussen. *Dictionary of African Historical Biography.* 2d ed. Berkeley: University of California Press, 1986; London: University of California Press, 1989. An impartial, nonanalytical treatment of Mugabe.

Martin, David, and Phyllis Johnson. *The Struggle for Zimbabwe.* London and Boston: Faber, 1981. One of the most important sources for the understanding of the war of liberation in Zimbabwe and the crucial role Mugabe played as leader of ZANLA, the military wing of ZANU.

Meldrum, Andrew. "Mugabe Crosses the Rubicon: Whites Are Forced off the Land." *African Business*, no. 228 (January, 1998). Examines Mugabe's plan to nationalize almost five million hectares of white-owned farmland and the concerns of the plan's opponents.

———. "Rubber-Stamp Parliament." *Africa Report* 40, no. 3 (May-June, 1995). Considers the faux democracy of Zimbabwe where the actual situation is a one-party authoritarian state in which Mugabe controls the government, the media, and campaign funding.

Rasmussen, R. Kent. *Historical Dictionary of Rhodesia/Zimbabwe.* 2d ed. Metuchen, N.J.: Scarecrow Press, 1990. A quick and easy reference source on the historical, political, and economic development of Rhodesia/Zimbabwe, including a biographical sketch of Mugabe.

Stoneman, Colin, and Lionel Cliffe. *Zimbabwe: Politics, Economics, and Society.* London and New York: Pinter, 1989. One of the most comprehensive recent works on Zimbabwe and a good analysis of Mugabe's Marxist philosophy. The work is part of Pinter's series on Marxist regimes.

Ungar, Sanfor J. *Africa: The People and Politics of an Emerging Continent.* Rev. ed. New York: Simon and Schuster, 1986. Here Mugabe is described as "quiet, pensive, austere . . . and probably the best-educated head of any government in Africa, aloof, undecided, [a man] whose style looks less like caution than like a failure of leadership."

Mario Azevedo

HERMANN JOSEPH MULLER

Born: December 21, 1890; New York, New York
Died: April 5, 1967; Indianapolis, Indiana
Area of Achievement: Genetics
Contribution: The first scientist to induce mutations with X rays and the founder of the field of radiation genetics, Muller became a crusader for radiation protection.

Early Life

Hermann Joseph Muller was a third-generation American born to H.J. Muller, Sr., and Frances Lyons. His paternal grandparents emigrated from Koblenz, Germany, after the unsuccessful revolution of 1848. Muller's father was a partner in a family-owned brass artworks shop in New York City. Muller was reared a Unitarian, his father being a freethinker with Socialist sympathies who had abandoned the family's Catholic ancestry. Muller's mother was of partly Jewish and Congregationalist English ancestry. When Muller was ten, his father died of a stroke and his mother supported the family on a meager income from the shop. Muller was a gifted student, receiving scholarship support to study at Columbia College, obtaining his bachelor's degree in 1910. Muller's love for science settled in the new field of genetics, which he explored in course work with Edmund Beecher Wilson and later with Thomas Hunt Morgan. Joining Muller in this enthusiasm for genetics were two students who entered Columbia two years after he did, Calvin Blackman Bridges and Alfred Henry Sturtevant. These five men were the major contributors to the development of classical genetics, the theory of the gene, and the field of cytogenetics.

Muller was a diminutive five feet, two inches tall, but this boyish height was counterbalanced by his pattern baldness and muscular physique. Although Muller had to support himself and his mother with many outside jobs, he maintained contact with "the fly lab," as the group called itself. After receiving a master's degree in physiology in 1912, Muller succeeded in having Morgan serve as his dissertation supervisor. Until 1910, Morgan had not made a major discovery with fruit flies. Between 1910 and 1915, when Muller completed the work for his Ph.D., the fly lab had introduced the concepts of sex-linked inheritance and crossing over, the mapping of genes, and the relation of genes to character formation. Some of the work involved individual discovery, but much of it was a cooperative effort in what was one of the first research teams, a model that is now characteristic of modern science.

Muller's role in the fly lab was that of a zealot. He believed that all biological phenomena ultimately stemmed from the activity of genes, and he tried to interpret all heredity through this model. Morgan and Muller differed both in personality and in scientific style, Morgan favoring experimental data that forced a theory to emerge and Muller favoring the reasoning that generated experiments and tossed out weak hypotheses. Muller, as a theoretician, provided abundant models and insights into the new discoveries, but Morgan rewarded credit and authorship to the careful execution of experiments. Muller felt resentful that Sturtevant and Bridges were financially supported through Morgan's efforts while he had to support himself with time-consuming jobs that were unrelated to his research. This incompatibility of temperament eventually led to Muller's estrangement from the fly lab and a lifelong reputation as a difficult man, preoccupied with issues of priority.

Life's Work

Muller's major theoretical contributions to genetics were in gene theory. He pointed out that genes were the only molecules that had the property of copying their errors and that, thus, the copying property must be a fundamental feature of life. He clarified the concept of mutation, which then included numerous different abnormal processes, by restricting it to a change within the individual gene or what is now called a gene mutation. He extended the primacy of the gene to evolution and asserted that the gene was the basis of life, life having originated with the first replicating molecule capable of copying its variations. These ideas, developed between 1920 and 1926, were frequently resisted as fanciful or naïvely speculative by many of his contemporaries, but they gradually gained acceptance after the molecular revolution of the 1950's when the chemical structure of genes proposed by James Dewey Watson and Francis Harry Compton Crick provided a material basis for these views.

Muller was also a gifted experimenter, and he designed complex genetic stocks that enabled geneticists to repeat the work of others and to use them as tools for genetic studies, theoretical and applied. In 1916, after receiving his Ph.D., Muller was recruited by Julian Sorell Huxley to join the faculty at the newly founded Rice Institute. He returned to Columbia in 1920, while Morgan was on leave, and then secured a position at the University of Texas, where he worked from 1920 to 1932. During these years, Muller pursued the study of the gene and mutation. He demonstrated that mutation frequency was measurable and that temperature affected the frequency. He proved that gene mutation was not restricted to the process of sperm or egg formation but could occur throughout the life cycle. He studied environmental effects by comparing the behavioral and physical traits of a pair of identical twins reared apart, concluding that it would take an army of experts to tease apart the genetic and environmental components in human behavior.

In 1926, Muller made the most important experimental contribution of his career. He reasoned, after a thorough review of the literature on biological effects of radiation, that X rays might damage individual genes. With his carefully designed stocks, he proved that ionizing radiation produced mutations. He demonstrated this fact quantitatively for a class of mutations that kills half the sons of the mothers who carry the induced mutation on a sex chromosome. This work he reported in 1927 to the International Congress of Genetics in Berlin. The work was rapidly confirmed by many geneticists, and Muller found himself an international celebrity and the leading authority on radiation genetics. In the years that followed, Muller and his students showed that gene mutation frequency rises proportionally to the dose received; that there is no apparent threshold dose, the low or attenuated doses spread out over a month having the same amount of mutations induced as the identical dose when administered over a short interval of time. Muller also demonstrated that ionizing radiation induced breakage of chromosomes, and this breakage resulted in many changes such as rearrangements of the sequences of genes, losses of chromosomes, and fatal early abortion of the embryos receiving such damaged sperm or eggs. By 1945, Muller and his students applied these findings to interpret the mechanism of radiation sickness among the victims of the first atomic bombings in Hiroshima and Nagasaki.

Muller's political views shifted from Socialist to Communist. He supported the Bolsheviks and visited the Soviet Union in 1922 to set up research programs in fruit fly genetics. He attracted postdoctoral students from the Soviet Union to his Texas laboratory. In 1932, he helped edit and distribute an underground newspaper, *The Spark*, and the FBI kept him under surveillance. He criticized the American eugenics movement as racist, sexist, and misguided in a paper he delivered at the third and last International Congress of Eugenics. That same year, he left Texas for Berlin on a Guggenheim fellowship, but the Nazis came to power before the year was over and Muller accepted an invitation to set up a laboratory in the Soviet Union. Between 1933 and 1937, at Leningrad and then in larger quarters in Moscow, Muller had a flourishing research school that studied problems of gene size, shape, boundaries, and number. This work was interrupted in 1936 by the arrest and execution of two of Muller's students and by the growing antigenetic movement of Trofim Denisovitch Lysenko, who secretly had the Communist Party's support to replace genetics with a curious theory of environmental modification or training of heredity. Muller and Lysenko clashed in public debate, and by 1937 Muller realized that the cause was lost and he escaped by volunteering to fight in the Spanish Civil War. After the siege of Madrid, Muller was helped by Huxley, who recommended him for a job in Edinburgh.

Once again, Muller established a productive laboratory with graduate students from many Commonwealth nations, only to find his work interrupted by the onset of World War II. In 1940, Muller returned to the United States as an interim professor at Amherst, but he relinquished the job when the war ended in 1945. Because of his erratic past, many universities were not interested in hiring him, but Indiana University took that chance, and the following year, 1946, Muller was awarded the Nobel Prize for Medicine. Muller continued to speak out on the importance of genetics to the future of mankind until his death, on April 5, 1967.

Summary

Muller was unusual in speaking out on issues related to genetics; this frequently embroiled him in controversy. He was a staunch critic of those who attacked the teaching of evolution in public schools. He advocated the teaching of biology free of religious or supernatural interpretation. He denounced Lysenko as a gangster at a time when more liberal scientists looked upon the genetics

controversy in the Soviet Union as a clash between two worldviews. He criticized the medical profession for not protecting its own practitioners and for taking too paternalistic an attitude when using radiation excessively on patients. He fought hard for radiation protection at a time when the United States Atomic Energy Commission tried to hide the occurrence and the effects of fallout from weapons testing. He was often mistrusted and misinterpreted because of his past. He believed in a strong national defense, including weapons testing, during the years of the Cold War and only came to support the international move to ban atmospheric testing when the quantity of fallout began to reach dangerous levels. Although he denounced the cruder eugenics of his generation, he championed differential breeding and favored the breeding of more intelligent, more cooperative, and healthier people as a response to the increasing load of mutations that he identified as a concern in the industrial nations. He was an idealist who believed in education and the use of knowledge to transform mankind outwardly and inwardly. At the same time, he rejected coercion as a basis for bringing about

change. As a critic and a crusader, he was an exemplar of a vital American tradition.

Bibliography

Carlson, Elof Axel. *Genes, Radiation, and Society: The Life and Work of H. J. Muller.* Ithaca, N.Y.: Cornell University Press, 1981. This is the first full account of Muller's life and his scientific accomplishments. It is based on more than thirty thousand letters, his 375 published articles, and numerous interviews with his students, colleagues, and critics. Carlson was Muller's student, and his view of his subject is essentially sympathetic.

Crow, James F., and Seymour Abrahamson. "Seventy Years Ago: Mutation Becomes Experimental." *Genetics* 147, no. 4 (December, 1997). Discusses the career of Muller and his lifelong crusade against exposure to high-energy radiation.

Ludmerer, Kenneth M. *Genetics and American Society.* Baltimore: Johns Hopkins University Press, 1972. This study deals largely with the eugenics movement and the failure of many of the United States' leading geneticists to criticize many of the false claims made by advocates of compulsory sterilization laws and restrictive immigration. Muller's views are downplayed in the otherwise informative and scholarly work.

Medvedev, Zhores. *The Rise and Fall of T. D. Lysenko.* New York: Columbia University Press, 1969. The criminality and self-deception that characterized the Lysenkoist movement are revealed in this account by a dissident critic of political and scientific repression in the Soviet Union. Medvedev did not know Muller; he was a youth when the controversy broke out.

Morgan, T. H., A. H. Sturtevant, H. J. Muller, and C. B. Bridges. *The Mechanism of Mendelian Heredity.* Rev. ed. New York: Holt, 1923. This summation of the fly lab's contributions to classical genetics established the now-prevailing theory of inheritance, replacing contending views in Europe and the United States. It led to an American dominance in genetics throughout the rest of the twentieth century.

Muller, H. J. *Out of the Night: A Biologist's View of the Future.* New York: Vanguard Press, 1935; London: Gollancz, 1936. This was Muller's only venture into popular writing. He was still communistic in spirit, and the book's eugenic utopia reveals a Socialist bias. The book presents a proposal for sperm banks and eugenic breeding which was superseded by his articles after 1957, when he recognized the importance of what he termed "germinal choice," the freedom to choose the genetic worth that one wishes for one's children.

―――. "The Problem of Genic Modification." In *Proceedings of the Fifth International Congress of Genetics: Berlin, 1927*. Berlin: International Congress of Genetics, 1928. Muller's original paper on the artificial induction of mutations is one of the classics of science. In it, Muller spells out his research program for the next twenty years of his life.

Elof Axel Carlson

BRIAN MULRONEY

Born: March 20, 1939; Baie-Comeau, Quebec, Canada

Areas of Achievement: Government and politics

Contribution: Mulroney served as prime minister of Canada, won two general elections for the Progressive Conservative Party, and negotiated a significant free trade agreement with the United States.

Early Life

Martin Brian Mulroney was born of Irish ancestry in the remote company town of Baie-Comeau, Quebec, on March 20, 1939. His parents, who strongly believed in education, allowed him to leave Baie-Comeau to attend St. Thomas High School in Chatham, New Brunswick, and then St. Francis Xavier University in Antigonish, Nova Scotia. While at the university, he became active in Progressive Conservative Party politics and made a name for himself as a sound organizer and tireless worker. Following graduation, he returned to Quebec province to study law at Laval University. During his university days, he established a wide network of loyal friends who were to serve him well later in his career. He was also fluently bilingual, and his knowledge of colloquial French was to be of enormous value in advancing his political career.

Upon leaving Laval University, he joined the large and prestigious Montreal law firm of Ogilvy, Renault. Beginning in 1966, he represented management's side in its troublesome dealings with longshoremen on the Montreal waterfront. It was during this period that he established a reputation as a skilled negotiator and deal maker and learned the advantage of conciliation instead of confrontation, something that would serve him well when he became prime minister. In 1973, he married Mila Pivnicki, a Yugoslavian by birth, who also served as his close political confidant and valuable campaigner. The following year, he was invited to serve on the Cliche Commission, a royal inquiry into corruption and violence in the Quebec construction industry. This helped transform him into a public figure. By this time, Mulroney was well established in Progressive Conservative circles as an organizer and fund raiser in Quebec, and in 1976 he was encouraged to run for the party leadership despite the fact that he had never been elected to political office. His campaign, perhaps a trifle showy and flashing too much money, alienated large numbers of delegates, and he lost to Joe Clark. Following this depressing defeat, he became vice president of the Iron Ore Company of Canada in 1976; the following year, he was named president of the company, which finally made his future financially secure. He was successful as president and was noted for establishing harmonious relations with labor. These relations were tested when he eventually had to close operations and shut down the company town of Schefferville, Quebec, which he managed to do without damage to his political career.

Life's Work

In June, 1983, Mulroney made another run for the party leadership. This time, his well-organized and low-key campaign defeated Joe Clark. During the leadership contest, Mulroney emphasized his Quebec connection and claimed that he alone could revive Conservative fortunes in his native French-speaking province. In August, he won a by-election in Central Nova, Nova Scotia, which meant that he could lead the Conservatives from the House of Commons. In a general election held in November, 1984, Mulroney ran a smooth and well-funded campaign against the disorganized Liberal Party and won one of the largest landslides in Canadian history by capturing 211 seats, including fifty-seven out of seventy-five seats in Quebec.

Mulroney soon ran into trouble in office. His government was seen as launching an assault on the costly but popular Canadian social welfare program. His government was also perceived as racked by cronyism and incompetence, as evidenced by the resignations of six cabinet ministers during his first two years in office. On the positive side, he abolished the National Energy Program, which was widely hated in western Canada, and also abolished the Federal Investment Review Agency, creating in its place Investment Canada, whose purpose, unlike its predecessor, was to ease and facilitate foreign investment in the country. This led to more than a doubling of foreign investment in the country. To solve Canada's outstanding domestic constitutional issue—the failure of Quebec province to accede to the new constitution adopted in 1982—he brokered an agreement with the ten provincial premiers, called the Meech Lake Accord, to grant Quebec a number of concessions, including recognizing Quebec as a "distinct society" and giving it a veto over future constitutional amendments. To become effective, it had to be ratified by the provincial legislatures by June, 1990. In foreign policy, he pushed for better relations with the United States, a country he personally admired, and established a close, friendly relationship with President Ronald Reagan. He also began a vigorous antiapartheid campaign against the racist regime in South Africa.

Perhaps his greatest accomplishment was a free trade agreement with the United States. Although Mulroney had initially been opposed to the idea, Canada was alarmed by the increasingly protectionist-minded American Congress of the 1980's. Canada was heavily dependent upon the U.S. market, which accounted for over 75 percent of Canadian exports. Serious negotiations concluded in the autumn of 1987, and the lengthy text was initialled by Mulroney and Reagan on January 2, 1988. The pact called for the gradual elimination of tariff barriers and unfettered access to financial and service industries of both countries, and established a dispute settlement mechanism. The pact deeply divided Canadians in almost equal numbers. Many Canadians, believing that their smaller economy might be unable to compete with the economic powerhouse to the south, feared job losses and the eventual surrender of their political sovereignty as well as their cultural identity. It became the major issue in the general election of 1988, which Mulroney won, thanks in large measure to strong support from the business community and the province of Quebec, where the Conservatives actually increased their number of seats. However, his majority in the Commons was reduced in size: The Progressive Conservatives took 166 seats, the Liberals won 101, and the New Democratic Party settled for 40 seats. Following the election, the Free Trade Agreement (FTA) was passed by Parliament and became law. In the early 1990's, the North American Free Trade Agreement (NAFTA) in effect expanded the provisions of the FTA to include Mexico.

Almost immediately after the election, Mulroney's popularity began to dive. A highly unpopular "goods and services" tax was passed, which was essentially a national sales tax of 7 percent. His government also cut budgets for costly but popular pan-Canadian institutions, including VIA railways, Canada Post, and the Canadian Broadcasting Corporation. Unemployment crept up past the 11 percent level. He also appeared to be too accommodating to the United States in foreign policy—he supported the United States in its invasion of Panama, the drug war against Latin America cartels, and the Gulf War—and joined the Organization of American States, a body perceived to be dominated by the United States. All this gave the appearance of a prime minister who poorly defended Canadian institutions and the country's economy while being servile to the national interests of the United States.

Further adding to Mulroney's woes was the failure of all the provinces to approve the Meech Lake Accord, which, by the time it died, had simultaneously alienated much of English-speaking Canada and Quebec. Mulroney tried hard to repair the damage. He negotiated a new agreement with the provincial premiers and other leaders called the Charlottetown Accord, which once again recognized Quebec as a distinct society and gave it a veto over future constitutional amendments but also added concessions favorable to other Canadian provinces and to aboriginal people to make it more acceptable to the country. However, in provincial referendums held on October 26, 1992, only four provinces approved it, while six voted it down, including Quebec, which felt the concessions did not go far enough. The total national vote showed that 54 percent had voted against it. The accord died because most Canadians felt it had made excessive concessions to Quebec and would have seriously weakened the federal government and because the unpopular Mulroney had been too closely identified with it.

By 1993, public opinion polls showed that Mulroney had the lowest popular approval rating of any prime minister in Canadian history, and he announced his intention to resign on February 24 of that year. He was eventually replaced by Kim Campbell, a former minister of justice and minister of defense, who became the first female prime minister in Canadian history. In the election of 1993, Campbell, who was initially popular but lost much of her support because of blunders, inexperience, and the Mulroney legacy, suffered a stunning defeat: Her party won only two seats, while the Liberals captured 177. Although Campbell was technically the loser, most political observers felt the election had actually been a referendum on the Mulroney years.

Summary

During his public career, Mulroney aroused fierce emotions in people. His critics claim that he lacked a national vision, possessed no grand ideas, and had no personal ideology to guide him, but was merely carried along by his personal ambition. He has been accused of not adequately defending the interests of Canada's national government and being too willing to surrender power to the provinces, particularly Alberta and Quebec, in order to stop constitutional bickering. These critics further claim that he never did solve the country's economic problems, presiding instead over a growing public debt and rising unemployment. In foreign policy, he has been charged with slavishly following the United States and, in the process, jeopardizing the country's fragile cultural and economic independence. In the end, his policies ruined the once-proud Progressive Conservative Party, dooming it (at least temporarily) to the margins of Canadian politics.

Mulroney's defenders assert that he honorably and courageously tried to resolve the country's vexed constitutional crisis but could not overcome the reluctance of Canada's anglophone population to compromise with their French-speaking fellow citizens in Quebec. He also tried to modernize the Canadian economy and put Canada in step with the economic forces of the age: globalization, free trade, and a reduction of government interference in the economy. Supporters also claim that he did not share many of his fellow Canadians' biases against the United States but believed that their southern neighbor was on the right side of many issues, including the struggle against totalitarian communism, Middle Eastern aggression, and drugs. Much of the bad press that Mulroney received sprang from the intellectual and media elites who resented his probusiness, pro-United States, and pro-Quebec policies. Thus, there was little consensus on the Mulroney legacy in Canada when he left office.

Bibliography

Cameron, Steve. *On the Take: Crime, Corruption and Greed in the Mulroney Years.* Toronto: MacFarlane Walter and Ross, 1994. Details the corruption in the Mulroney government and why the voters eventually punished the Conservative Party for it. Largely undocumented.

Curtis, Douglas. "Canadian Fiscal and Monetary Policy and Macroeconomic Performance 1984-1993: The Mulroney Years." *Journal of Canadian Studies* 32, no. 1 (Spring 1997). Curtis discusses Canada's monetary policies during Mulroney's tenure as Prime Minister.

Frizzell, Alan, and Anthony Westell. *The Canadian General Election of 1984.* Ottawa, Ontario: Carleton University Press, 1985. Excellent study of the issues, candidates, campaign, and statistical results of the 1984 election. The authors have written a similar account of the 1988 election.

MacDonald, L. Ian. *Mulroney: The Making of the Prime Minister.* Toronto: McClelland and Stewart, 1984. Written by a Montreal political columnist, this widely respected biography details Mulroney's career up to his election as prime minister in 1984. Valuable for detailing Mulroney's intricate network of friends from the worlds of politics, business, and law.

McDonald, Marci. *Yankee Doodle Dandy: Brian Mulroney and the American Agenda.* Toronto: Stoddart, 1995. An account of the Mulroney administration's policies toward the United States. Seriously marred by a pronounced bias against Mulroney.

Morton, Desmond. *A Short History of Canada.* 3d ed. Toronto: McClelland and Stewart, 1997. Places the Mulroney years within the larger context of Canadian history.

Mulroney, Brian. *Where I Stand.* Toronto: McClelland and Stewart, 1983. A collection of writings and speeches by Mulroney prior to his election as prime minister.

Sawatsky, John. *Mulroney: The Politics of Ambition.* Toronto: MacFarlane Walter and Ross, 1991. Entertaining biography filled with anecdotes emphasizing Mulroney's personal ambition.

Wilson-Smith, Anthony. "Revenge: Ottawa Folds Its Cards and Apologizes to Mulroney." *Maclean's* 110, no. 3 (January 20, 1997). A discussion of Mulroney's libel suit against the Canadian government, the history of the scandal, and the government's 1997 settlement and apology to Mulroney.

David C. Lukowitz

EDVARD MUNCH

Born: December 12, 1863; Løten, Norway
Died: January 23, 1944; Ekely, Norway
Area of Achievement: Art
Contribution: The dramatic paintings and graphics of Munch not only reflected his inner torments and emotions but also proved highly influential on artistic developments in the late nineteenth and early twentieth centuries. In addition to becoming his native country's most famous artist, Munch served as one of the main progenitors of expressionism.

Early Life

Born December 12, 1863, in Løten, Norway, Edvard Munch was the second of five children born to Christian Munch and his wife Laura Cathrine Bjølstad. Munch's father was a doctor who in 1864 moved his family to Oslo, then called Christiania, where he earned a fairly meager living in one of the city's poorer districts. A sickly, lonely child, Munch experienced two early tragedies that haunted the rest of his life—the deaths of his mother in 1868 and of his beloved elder sister Sophie in 1877, both victims of tuberculosis. His mother's sister Karen moved into the household to care for the children, and she provided Munch with a degree of warmth and encouragement that his strict and deeply religious father failed to do. All the Munch children grew accustomed to drawing as a means to pass the long winter nights. Recognizing her nephew's talents, Karen Bjølstad encouraged his interest and bought him painting materials.

Munch's father decided that his son's abilities would enable him to pursue a career in engineering, so Munch was enrolled at the Technical College in 1879. Poor health prevented his attending regularly, and the young Munch became determined to follow a career in painting, a decision that a family friend, C. F. Dirike, helped convince the elder Munch to accept.

In 1880, Munch left the technical school and began painting seriously. The following year, he was enrolled in the School of Design to take classes in drawing and modeling under the direction of sculptor Julius Middlethun. With six other young aspiring artists, Munch rented a studio in Christiania's art district in 1882 and soon became the prize pupil of Christian Krogh, a naturalist painter who was the leader of the town's artistic community. During these years, Munch was also befriended by a dis-

tant relative, Frits Thaulow, who had close connections with many French painters. Thaulow provided financial support that allowed the young Munch to make his first trip to Paris in 1885. During his three weeks there, he studied the masterpieces in the Louvre and the salons and found himself particularly impressed by the landmark works of Édouard Manet.

As early as 1883 Munch had participated in a group exhibition in Oslo and had managed to sell a few works, but his early career remained hampered by his environment. Norway in the late nineteenth century remained culturally conservative and unreceptive to the new trends then revolutionizing the art world. Local critics attacked Munch's work as sloppy, unfinished, and unrealistic.

During this period, Munch fell under the influence of the bohemian movement in Oslo, led by the anarchist writer Hans Jaeger. This group of young writers and artists deliberately shocked bourgeois society with their unconventional ideas and behavior and their attack on nearly all sacred traditions. Munch never embraced their program totally, but he was nevertheless influenced by their avant-garde attitudes.

Life's Work

In 1885, shortly after his return from Paris, Munch began work on three paintings that became hallmarks of his mature style: *The Morning After, Puberty,* and *The Sick Child.* The last of these three, clearly inspired by memories of his sister's death, created an uproar when shown at the Annual State Exhibition in 1886. Critics assailed his works as laughable and the product of a madman. Still, during the years 1889-1891, Munch received three grants from his government that enabled him to escape the narrow cultural confines of Norway and study abroad.

Following his first one-man show in Oslo in 1889, Munch utilized the first of his state grants to leave for study in Paris. The death of his father later in the year, coupled with this move, opened a new era in Munch's life, a peripatetic existence in which he absorbed many of the dramatic new ideas of late-nineteenth century European culture. He initially was enrolled in the Parisian art school of Léon Bonnat, who was a strict academician. Munch soon quarreled with Bonnat, whose commitment to realism he found unchallenging. He moved to St. Cloud, where he shared a room with Danish poet Emmanuel Goldstein. There he developed a new artistic commitment to abandon his earlier naturalism in favor of mood painting, depicting themes such as suffering and love.

Munch returned to Norway periodically and in 1892 held his second one-man show there, which resulted in his receiving an invitation from the Berlin Artists' Union to exhibit his works in the German capital. The resulting show created such an uproar that conservatives in the union forced it to close after one week. Nevertheless, the 1882 Berlin exhibition made Munch famous throughout Germany and a hero to the more avant-garde artistic community there. He spent much of the next sixteen years in Germany and became associated with Berlin's bohemian circles.

From 1892 until 1908, Munch embraced a restless life-style, living mainly in hotel rooms and traveling constantly. His artistic output remained prolific, and dozens of exhibitions of his work were held in major cities across Europe. During the 1890's, he began work on graphics, a field he found both challenging and rewarding, enabling him to reach a wider audience and give new expression to some of his familiar themes. He eventually mastered all graphic techniques, with his greatest output being in lithographs.

Beginning in 1893, Munch embarked upon an artistic project that he called *The Frieze of Life*, conceived as a series of paintings to present a picture of life, love, and death. Many of the works were inspired by his early childhood experiences and reflected his preoccupation with illness, anxiety, and emotional trauma. He worked on this series periodically for more than thirty years and hoped to have all of it eventually collected in one great hall, an aspiration that remained unfulfilled.

Munch's mature style, which developed throughout the 1890's, followed his determination to make his works explore man's inner psyche. He kept notes of his visual experiences and most often drew from memory. Mood dominated Munch's paintings and graphics more than any other artistic element; he frequently gave his works a bold simplicity that enabled them to convey his emotional reactions. Sometimes he went weeks without painting and then would work in a frenzy of activity late into the night, rapidly putting on the canvas visual images that had been building in his mind.

Certain themes and subjects consistently appeared in Munch's work throughout his long career, many of them reflecting his traumatic childhood and his own introverted nature. Many dealt with death, illness, and isolation. Others were blatantly erotic in nature. Munch became a revealing portraitist and also produced a remarkable series of self-portraits between 1880 and 1943. Other Munch paintings concentrated on the landscape of his beloved Norway. In the early 1900's, he turned to a new theme, depicting members of the working class. Throughout the entire era he was never totally committed to a single style, and he refrained from joining any one of the numerous schools of art that developed during his lifetime. He remained a supreme individualist, letting his art convey his attitudes and emotions.

Although Munch remained devoted to his aunt and sisters, he deliberately avoided permanent entanglements in his personal life. A lifelong bachelor, he early decided against marriage, citing his family history of tuberculosis and mental illness and also fearing that a wife and children would hinder his artistic development. His most serious affair, with Tulla Larsen, ended disastrously, when she threatened suicide and accidentally shot Munch in the hand, permanently paralyzing one of his fingers.

In the early 1900's, Munch's nomadic life-style, coupled with overwork and excessive drinking, threatened his mental stability and led to irrational behavior. He became quarrelsome and consumed by feelings of persecution, an emotion perhaps fed by the continued rejection of his work by Norwegian critics. Despite increasing financial security and a growing reputation in Germany, Munch suffered a nervous breakdown in Copenhagen in late 1908 and voluntarily checked himself into a clinic run by Dr. Daniel Jacobsen. After eight months of treatment, he emerged fully recovered physically and mentally. He abandoned his wandering life in favor of a more stable existence in Norway. Munch's new self-confidence and more optimistic attitude were reflected in his subsequent works, which were less somber and violent.

Although he occasionally traveled throughout Scandinavia and the continent, Munch spent most of his time after 1908 in Norway. One of his major projects during the initial years after his return concerned a series of murals he painted for the Great Hall of the University of Oslo, an undertaking that caused a fierce controversy in which his designs were initially rejected and only approved five years after he entered the competition. These strikingly modern murals consumed most of Munch's time until their completion in 1916.

Munch eventually bought or rented several manors in Norway to provide himself with sufficient space for his work. In 1916, he purchased Ekely, an estate on the outskirts of Oslo, which remained his principal home until his death.

Gradually his native country extended official recognition for his accomplishments, purchasing several of his works for the National Gallery and subsequently awarding him the Grand Cross of the Order of Saint Olav on his seventieth birthday. Yet in spite of his growing prominence, Munch preferred to live a hermitlike existence at Ekely. He saw only a few friends and lived a spartan life surrounded by his paintings and graphics, which he called his children.

In 1930, a blood vessel burst in Munch's right eye, which prevented him from working for almost a year. He had troubles with his vision for the rest of his life. Nevertheless, Munch continued to work twelve hours or more a day. In 1937, the Nazi regime in Germany included Munch on a list of "degenerate" artists and confiscated eighty-two of his works on exhibit in German museums. After the Nazi occupation of Norway in 1940 Munch was left alone. He continued painting and printmaking and refused all contact with the invaders.

Munch died of complications resulting from bronchitis on January 23, 1944. In his will he unconditionally bequeathed all of his work in his possession to the city of Oslo. This collection formed the basis for the museum in his honor that opened in Oslo in 1963.

Summary

During a career that spanned six decades, Edvard Munch produced a remarkable collection of paintings, drawings, and graphics that made him one of the leading figures of modern European art. His works were highly personal, reflecting his inner torments and anxieties and providing glimpses into the psychological aspects of man's nature. His most famous painting, *The Scream* (1893), foreshadowed the horrors that awaited mankind amid the brutality and existential dilemmas of the twentieth century.

In contrast to his tragic contemporary, Vincent van Gogh, Munch managed to survive despite threatened sanity and emerge a stronger figure who vigorously continued to work into his eighties. His bold use of lines and colors, combined with the psychological implications of his work, clearly made him one of the chief influences on the emerging artistic movement called expressionism. His influence, first greatest in Germany, spread throughout Central and Eastern Europe and was eventually recognized throughout the Continent and the United States.

In his writings, Munch maintained that art resulted from man's desire to communicate with others, and throughout his long life his profoundly personal paintings and other artistic works reflected his desire to share his own grief and joys with his fellowman. His monumental body of work always retained the integrity of his purpose and provided the twentieth century with a poignant glimpse into the dilemmas and perplexities that confronted humanity in an increasingly unsettled and threatening world.

Bibliography

Amman, Per. *Edvard Munch*. Thornbury, England: Artlines UK, 1987. This monograph contains a brief introductory essay on Munch's life and significance, a chronological table of major events in his life, and more than eighty pages of enlarged reproductions of his major works.

Berman, Patricia G. "(Re-) Reading Edvard Munch: Trends in the Current Literature." *Scandinavian Studies* 66, no. 1 (Winter 1994). The author notes that studies of Munch have moved past the historical fixation on his works as the products of a troubled mind and that his place in art history can now be more clearly understood.

Dunlop, Ian. *Edvard Munch*. London: Thames and Hudson, and New York: St. Martin's Press, 1977. Dunlop provides a biographical sketch of Munch's life and forty color prints of the Norwegian artist's key works, accompanied by commentary.

Hagen, Charles. "Dark Mirror: The Photographs of Edvard Munch." *Aperture*, no. 145 (Fall 1996). Considers Munch's use of photographs as sources for his paintings and in particular the photographs he took of himself after suffering a nervous breakdown.

Heller, Reinhold. *Munch: His Life and Work*. London: Murray, and Chicago: University of Chicago Press, 1984. This recent, well-researched biography is thoroughly documented and contains copious excerpts from Munch's letters and other writings. It includes a select bibliography and 180 illustrations.

Hodin, J. P. *Edvard Munch*. London: Thames and Hudson, and New York: Praeger, 1972. A volume in Oxford's respected World of Art series, this monograph by an author noted for his Munch studies provides a sympathetic account of the artist's life and works. The format is basically chronological, with separate chapters devoted specifically to Munch's graphics and his general style. Contains a short bibliography and 168 illustrations.

Stang, Ragna. *Edvard Munch: The Man and His Art*. Translated by Geoffrey Culverwell. New York: Abbeville Press, 1979. Probably the most impressive and comprehensive survey of Munch's life and works, lavishly illustrated. The text is accompanied by numerous quotations from Munch's writings as well as comments by his contemporaries. The author played a key role at the Munch museum in Oslo.

Tom L. Auffenberg

EDWARD R. MURROW

Born: April 25, 1908; Greensboro, North Carolina
Died: April 27, 1965; Pawling, New York
Area of Achievement: Broadcast journalism
Contribution: The pioneer of news broadcasting, Murrow set the standard for objective reporting while warning against the potential for manipulation by electronic journalism.

Early Life

Egbert Roscoe Murrow was born April 25, 1908, in Greensboro, North Carolina. Called "Egg" by family and friends, he changed his name to the more acceptable "Edward" as a young man. When he was still a child, his family moved to the Pacific Northwest, where Murrow spent summers working in the logging camps. In high school, he was a superachiever on several levels: a successful athlete, valedictorian of his class, student body officer, and, prophetically, star of the debate team. Following his graduation, the rangy, six-foot, two-inch young man returned to the logging camps. In 1926, after one year of this hard labor, he had saved sufficiently to enroll at Washington State University.

His popularity continued in college, enhanced by his dark, handsome looks—a physical appearance which would prove useful in his final career choice. In college, he majored in speech, honing his communication skills; he also added acting to his list of credits and began to cultivate the taste for elegant, expensive clothes for which he would later be known.

As the president of the student government, Murrow was a delegate to the annual convention of NSFA, the National Student Federation of America, of which he was elected president. Immediately following his graduation with a B.A. in speech, he moved to New York City to undertake his new, unpaid responsibilities. His tenure with NSFA afforded him travel throughout Europe, where he began to establish a network of friends and acquaintances that would eventually encompass the most influential people of the time. During these early Depression years, he also traveled frequently within the United States; these experiences were to affect his developing social and political conscience. Murrow resigned from NFSA in his second year as president (1931) to take a salaried position with the Institute of International Education.

In this position, he was assistant to Stephen Pierce Duggan, director of the institute, a reformer who believed in the betterment of mankind and in the principle of noblesse oblige. Duggan and the Eastern Establishment, to whom he introduced his young protégé, further contributed to Murrow's political development as well as adding to his list of valuable contacts.

In 1934, Murrow married Janet Brewster. He was earning five thousand dollars a year, a comfortable sum by Depression standards, when he accepted a position at Columbia Broadcasting System (CBS) Radio. Eventually, he was made European director for CBS in London. This posting marked the beginning of the CBS wartime news team and Murrow's own beginning as the major influence in broadcast journalism.

Life's Work

For an energetic, talented, and idealistic young reporter, there could have been no better vantage point from which to view the ensuing struggle than prewar London. By 1939, Murrow had established a crew which included Eric Sevareid, Bill Henry, William Shirer, and Cecil Brown, among others. Murrow charged them to report the human side of the news, not only the facts but also how the average person reacted to the facts. He also urged them to speak naturally, to be honest, and to be neutral. One of his greatest achievements was the training of this impressive group of reporters, who could communicate over the air a sense of the drama unfolding around them. For the first time, broadcast journalism eclipsed print in popularity. Without endless rewrites, copy editors, layouts, and printings, it was demonstrated that the electronic medium could accurately report the news and do so faster.

As radio's most recognizable personality, Murrow himself did not realize the extent of his influence or his huge listenership until a 1941 trip to the United States. At a banquet in his honor, the poet Archibald MacLeish, commenting on Murrow's reports on the attack of London, acknowledged his achievement:

> You burned the city of London at our doors and we knew that the dead were our dead . . . were mankind's dead . . . without rhetoric, without dramatics, without more emotion than need be . . . you have destroyed . . . the superstition that what is done beyond 3,000 miles is not done at all.

Never content to sit back and be the London bureau chief, Murrow needed to face danger, to be present to absorb the flavor of the events he reported. He stood on a rooftop and watched the bombing of London. He flew twenty-five bombing missions, refusing even the president of CBS's plea that he cease such a dangerous practice. He was in Vienna when the city was occupied by the Nazis and saw at firsthand the atrocities of which they were capable. He walked among the half-dead inmates of the concentration camp at Buchenwald soon after it had been liberated. His harrowing broadcast describing this experience was reprinted in the media and replayed over and over on the air.

Many years previously, Murrow had begun smoking. As early as 1942, this pleasure had become an addiction; he was smoking up to three packs of unfiltered cigarettes a day. He was already exhibiting a "weak chest" and other pulmonary problems. His restless nature, probing mind, need for experience, and inability to relax all led him to periodic exhaustion, requiring hospitalization.

On November 6, 1945, Janet Murrow, at age thirty-five, gave birth to a son, Charles Casey Murrow. With the war over, it was time for the family to return to New York. Murrow took the position of vice president and director of public affairs for CBS.

This was a difficult period of adjustment. Postwar New York was brash and wealthy, in stark contrast to war-torn London; Murrow missed his old friends and colleagues and the excitement of covering the war. After eighteen months in the position, Murrow resigned to return to broadcasting the news. He settled into a comfortable life, doing what he knew and loved best at a salary of $125,000 a year, an amount necessary for a man who enjoyed fine clothes, a good address, fast cars, and the best restaurants.

Augmenting this income were royalties from the *Hear It Now* recordings. This record was the brainchild of Fred Friendly, a colleague whose partnership would span the remainder of Murrow's broadcast career. Released in 1948, the record brought together the actual recorded speeches of such personalities as Winston Churchill, Franklin D. Roosevelt, Adolf Hitler, Huey Long, Will Rogers, and Edward VIII, with Murrow narrating. A quarter of a million copies were sold in the first year.

See It Now, the documentary program that established Murrow's reputation as a television journalist, debuted on November 18, 1951, the result of another partnership with Fred Friendly. A precursor to the present-day documentary, the program was improvised and rife with technical problems: blackouts, loss of picture, and so on. The show explored contemporary issues: from what it was like underground with coal miners in West Virginia to the experience of riding a school bus following desegregation in the South. A particularly moving segment was on Korea at Christmas. Rather than focus on military strategies, Murrow interviewed average soldiers and their reactions to the war. Before being canceled, this show won three Peabodys, four Emmys, and various other awards from *Look, Saturday Review*, the New York Newspaper Guild, and others.

Along with *See It Now*, Murrow's other venture into television was *Person to Person*, a program which took cameras into the homes of the rich and famous while Murrow interviewed them by remote from the studio. *Person to Person* was an enormous commercial success, widening his audience to include millions of viewers who would never have watched *See It Now*. Through *Person to Person*, Murrow became as familiar as the celebrities he interviewed, vastly increasing his credibility. The show also served to document an era, featuring interviews of such diverse subjects as Marilyn Monroe, Fred Astaire, Fidel Castro, and John F. Kennedy and his new wife, Jacqueline.

In early 1953, Murrow was targeted by the House Committee on Un-American Activities. He had been too consistently critical of Joseph McCarthy; he was prominent and, through his activities in the 1930's, he was vulnerable. Murrow fought back with a segment of *See It Now* entitled "A Report on Senator Joseph R. McCarthy." His strategy was to catch McCarthy in his own contradictions by splicing together his various speeches with Murrow's voice-over narration. Murrow ended with a speech spoken directly to the camera, not read as was his normal practice:

> He [McCarthy] didn't create this situation of fear, he merely exploited it; and rather successfully. Cassius was right. "The fault, Dear Brutus, is not in our stars, but in ourselves."

By the following morning, CBS had received one thousand telegrams applauding the telecast. Murrow, returning from lunch the next day, was mobbed on Fifth Avenue. *Variety* labeled him "practically a hero." McCarthy's power was beginning to wane.

In 1961, exhausted from his years in broadcasting and disillusioned with CBS, Murrow accepted the directorship of the United States Information Agency in the Kennedy Administration. His tenure ended after three years, after surgery for cancer of the lung. Awarded the Presidential Medal of Freedom in 1964, Murrow died at his farm in New York on April 27, 1965, at the age of fifty-seven.

Summary

Edward R. Murrow spent his life following the dictates of his conscience: struggling with the top executives at CBS, with Kennedy, with McCarthy, and even with his adoring public. With a profound commitment to fair reporting, Murrow set the standard for broadcast journalism.

He became a dedicated anti-Fascist in the early 1930's, working with the Emergency Committee to bring out of Europe ninety-one scholars whose lives and works were endangered. These activities would figure prominently in smear tactics made against him by the House Committee on Un-American Activities. Although his head-on collision with McCarthy was considered by many to be television's "finest hour," Murrow himself agonized over its production. His objectivity and his dedication to balanced presentation were lacking. He called it a "half hour editorial."

In a career-long relationship, flawed at times with serious bitterness, CBS found the perfect vehicle in Murrow. Not only had nature bequeathed him a mellifluous baritone voice and dark good looks, but he was also a trained and skillful debater. His speaking ability, his passionate social conscience, and his dedication to providing the truth infused his broadcasting with a rare vitality. Yet Murrow was taxed by television in a way that his audiences would never guess: He was incredibly camera shy. He had been nervous on the radio, but television added the dimension of the camera. His hands trembled, the heat of the lights made him perspire and squirm; under the table, his nervous leg jumped.

Murrow's most enduring battle was with broadcasting itself, to see that it upheld its integrity. Repeatedly—to colleagues, in speeches, and in articles—he warned of the potential of broadcasting to manipulate the news and the public. At the same time, he believed that broadcasting had the potential to be "a real aid in keeping the light of Western Civilization burning." In his lifetime, he saw that light burn dangerously low.

Bibliography

Cloud, Stanley, and Lynne Olson. "The Murrow Boys—Broadcasting for the Mind's Eye." *Media Studies Journal* 22, no. 2 (Spring 1997). Cloud considers the unique reporting style of Murrow and those on his CBS team, which was designed to create mental pictures for listeners.

———. "The Murrow Brigade." *Vanity Fair*, no. 429 (May, 1996). Examines the relationship between CBS wartime reporters Murrow and William L. Shirer. Includes background information on Murrow.

Friendly, Fred W. *Due to Circumstances Beyond Our Control*. London: MacGibbon and Kee, and New York: Random House, 1967. In this occupational memoir of his sixteen years at CBS, Friendly presents a critical, disturbing picture of commercial television. He also discusses *See It Now* from a production point of view.

Kendrick, Alexander. *Prime Time: The Life of Edward R. Murrow*. Boston: Little Brown, 1969; London: Dent, 1970. Kendrick was one of the so-called Murrow Boys, trained in his tradition. This training gives him an insider's view in this profusely illustrated and anecdote-rich biography. Often insightful, he captures Murrow's involvement and his conscience but stops short of any criticism. Good for an overview of the sins of commercial television.

Murrow, Edward R. *In Search of Light: The Broadcasts of Edward R. Murrow, 1938-1961*. Edited by Edward Bliss, Jr. New York: Knopf, 1967; London: Macmillan, 1968. These selections were made from five thousand broadcasts, which spanned Hitler's seizure of Austria to Kennedy's inaugural address. Bliss, a longtime CBS staffer, has chosen broadcasts which add dimension to history or show Murrow's perspective on the development of his style.

———. *This Is London*. London: Cassell, and New York: Simon and Schuster, 1941. Texts of his London radio broadcasts from August, 1939, to December, 1940, when he was chief of the European bureau for CBS. The broadcasts read well because Murrow was not only a good speaker but also a sensitive writer with a good grasp of the language. An excellent source for a historical perspective.

Paley, William S. *As It Happened: A Memoir*. New York: Doubleday, 1979. This autobiography by the founder and president of CBS describes the heyday of radio and television programming, including controversies with Murrow, Daniel Schorr, and the CIA. Often pretentious, he presents a one-sided view without attempting to be analytical. Important for the corporate view of broadcasting.

Sperber, A. M. *Murrow: His Life and Times*. New York: Freundlich, 1986; London: Joseph, 1987. Exhaustive biography. Almost obsessive in its documentation of each detail of Murrow's life. In this well-balanced, critical presentation, Sperber penetrates the reasons for Murrow's actions and the sources of his beliefs while communicating Murrow's passion for proper news reportage. The definitive biography.

Terrill Brooks

BENITO MUSSOLINI

Born: July 29, 1883; Predappio, Italy
Died: April 28, 1945; Giulino di Mezzegra, near
   Dongo, Italy
Areas of Achievement: Government and politics
Contribution: Mussolini was the first Fascist dicta-
   tor. He founded the Fascist Party in 1919 and led
   it to power in Italy in October, 1922.

Early Life

Benito Amilcare Andrea Mussolini was born on
July 29, 1883, outside the village of Predappio, fifteen miles from Forli in the region of Romagna. His
mother, Rosa, was a schoolteacher and a devout
Catholic, who was able to provide modest support
for the family. His father, Alessandro, had a much
greater influence upon Mussolini's character and
outlook. His father, a blacksmith who drank more
frequently than he worked, was a passionate character who was committed to an anarchistic non-
ideological vision of socialism. Life in the Mussolini household was tumultuous, and young Benito
received harsh discipline but little affection. He later expressed pride in the fact that he was a loner
who did not make friends. He assuaged his own
deep inferiority complex by dominating others.

In imitation of his father, Mussolini became an
instinctive and perpetual rebel. He was expelled
from a Catholic boarding school at the age of ten
for stabbing a fellow student. He continued his
schooling, despite additional disciplinary interrup-
tions, until he received his educational diploma in
1901. Apart from his rhetorical skill, his academic
performance was rather mediocre.

After leaving school, Mussolini's reputation as a
promiscuous and brutal misanthrope flourished,
but he accomplished little else. In 1902, at the age
of eighteen, he fled to Switzerland to avoid induction into the army and worked intermittently as a
laborer. He came into contact with exiled Russian
Marxists and, under their influence, became a
Marxist, though an eclectic one. His most consistent and persistent idea, the use of violence as a political weapon, predated his Marxism. In 1905, he
took advantage of a general amnesty to perform his
military service so that he could return to Italy.

After leaving the military in 1906, Mussolini
passed a test to teach French on the secondary level
and earned the title "professor." He taught at several places without much success. In 1909, he was
hired to edit a socialist weekly in the Austrian

province of Trentino, but his intemperate writing
landed him in jail, an experience with which he
was not unfamiliar. Expelled from Austria, he returned to Forli where he edited a socialist weekly.

In 1910, he married Rachele Guidi, the daughter of his father's mistress. Rachele was a simple
peasant, completely uninterested in politics and
her husband's subsequent career. Though he and
Rachele had five children, he was notoriously
unfaithful.

Mussolini's extreme radicalism and opposition
to reformism isolated him from the leaders of the
Italian Socialist Party, but he gained notoriety
when he was jailed for his violent opposition to Italy's 1911 war against Turkey for Libya. After his
release from prison, he led the left wing in an attack against the party's moderate leaders and, with
their expulsion, became a member of the party directorate and editor of the national Socialist newspaper, *Avanti!*

Life's Work

In *Avanti!* Mussolini derided parliamentary activity
and advocated revolution. In private, he expressed
his desire to be the "man of destiny," who would
dominate the passive people. He was disillusioned
when he failed to win the support of the people of
Forli in the parliamentary race in 1913 and when
the Socialist Party did not seize the opportunity
provided by the massive but disorganized unrest of
"Red Week" in June, 1914. The outbreak of World
War I a few weeks later led to his break with the
party if not with a vague idea of socialism. Believing that the war itself could be the catalyst for
change, on October 18, 1914, without consulting
the other party leaders or his coeditor, he published
an editorial in *Avanti!* calling for Italian entry into
the war.

Unable to win the party over to his new position,
Mussolini was expelled and forced to give up the
editorship of *Avanti!* On November 15, he
launched his own paper, *Il Popolo d'Italia.* The paper was financed by France and other belligerents,
but money also came from the Italian government
and rich industrialists. Money, however, played no
part in Mussolini's defection.

Italy's entry into the war in May, 1915, against
the wishes of the parliamentary majority, through
the damage done to Italy's political, economic, and
social stability, ultimately provided the conditions

that contributed to the rise of Fascism. Mussolini's political activities, however, were interrupted when he was conscripted in September, 1915, and sent to the front. After recovering from wounds received in February, 1917, when a mortar exploded, he was discharged, and he returned to his newspaper. His politics remained very fluid and opportunistic but were permeated with a hypernationalism.

At a meeting in Milan on March 23, 1919, Mussolini formally established the movement that would in November, 1921, become the Fascist Party. The miserable performance of the nascent party in the November, 1919, election and the failure of the sit-down strikes of 1920 led Mussolini to change his tack. Repudiating the remnants of his socialism, Mussolini recruited a militia of black-shirted hooligans who, with the avowed purpose of saving Italy from Bolshevism, terrorized the Left. Consequently, he received strong financial support from industrialists and large landowners frightened by the specter of social revolution. The Fascists won their first parliamentary seats in the May, 1921, election. With only thirty-five seats, however, their real strength was in their use of terror.

The anarchy created by the Fascists paved their way to power. The weakness of the government coupled with the collapse of the Left created a vacuum. Only the king, Victor Emmanuel III, and the army stood in Mussolini's way. Many generals sympathized with the Fascists, but to preclude the opposition of those who did not, Mussolini unequivocally expressed his support for the monarchy.

Confident that there would be no opposition, Mussolini mobilized his Blackshirts on October 27 to march on Rome and seize power. The twenty-six thousand badly armed and disorganized Fascists would have been no match for the army, and Mussolini, himself, remained close to the Swiss border in case the coup miscarried. Victor Emmanuel, however, fearing that a divided army might not be able to resist successfully and that he might be replaced as king by his pro-Fascist cousin, the Duke of Aosta, changed his mind about approving Premier Luigi Facta's declaration of martial law. In the face of this weakness, Mussolini would accept nothing less than the power to form a government. When the king submitted and confirmed this with a telegram, Mussolini made his "march" on Rome in a sleeping car on October 29.

Mussolini moved toward his goal of a one-party state gradually. His initial cabinet included representatives from all the parties except the Socialists and the Communists. After Mussolini promised to respect the law, his cabinet was not only confirmed by the parliament but also given the power to rule by decree for a year. Mussolini then proceeded to purge the police and the bureaucracy. A Fascist Grand Council, which in 1928 officially became the supreme organ of state power, was established as a shadow government and the Blackshirts were transformed into a state militia. The Acerbo Law, passed by parliament in July, 1923, promised the party with a plurality of the vote two-thirds of parliament's seats, but it was unnecessary. Through terror and intimidation the Fascists, in April, 1924, were able to win 65 percent of the vote.

When the Socialist leader, Giacomo Matteotti, denounced the tactics of the Fascists, he was murdered in June by associates of Mussolini. The crime left Mussolini vulnerable, but the failure of his opponents to seize the initiative allowed him to move against them. In 1925, Mussolini abolished political liberties and, finally, outlawed the Socialist Party. By the end of the year, he had reduced the parliament to impotence by making himself head of the government, answerable only to the king, and had replaced elected officials throughout the peninsula with administrators appointed by himself. In October, 1926, he outlawed all anti-Fascist parties and then set up a secret police organization to cow the nation. By 1928, in fact and in law, Mussolini, as leader of the Fascist Party, had become the omnipotent head of the Italian state.

As he consolidated his power, Mussolini ushered in a transformation of Italian society that he labeled the corporate state. The interests of the state were dominant. Strikes were banned, and the interests of workers and capital were supposedly mediated through organizations called corporations. The party, however, dominated the corporations and the interests of workers received short shrift. With the Fascists supporting the interests of capital, the standard of living of Italian working people declined after 1922. Mussolini claimed that a Chamber of Corporations would eventually replace the old flawed parliament, but the project was not implemented until 1939 and even then was only window dressing for his dictatorship.

Mussolini pursued an adventurous and aggressive foreign policy. He conquered Ethiopia in 1936, supported the Nationalists in the Spanish Civil War, and took control of Albania in April,

1939. Alienated from the British and the French over Ethiopia and cooperating with Adolf Hitler in Spain, Mussolini signed the Axis Pact with Germany in October, 1936. The association with Nazi Germany eventually led to the importation of anti-Semitic laws into Italy, a military alliance, the May, 1939, Pact of Steel, and, finally, defeat.

Mussolini's fate was sealed when he entered the war on June 10, 1940. He erroneously believed that a German victory was inevitable and wished to participate in the division of the spoils. The war, however, continued, and a series of humiliating Italian defeats in Greece, on the Mediterranean, and in North Africa led to the supplanting of Italy in those theaters by the Germans. Increasingly the Germans transformed Italy itself into a fiefdom. Mussolini's dynamism had faded with time, and it was now sapped by defeat and a recurrent ulcer.

The defeat of the Axis forces in North Africa and massive labor unrest in the north of Italy led to a rupture in the Fascist movement. Hoping for a separate peace, leading Fascists began plotting against Mussolini. The court circle, too, began working to replace Mussolini with Marshal Pietro Badoglio. The king's hesitation vanished with the Allied invasion of Sicily and bombing of Rome. The Grand Council of the Fascist Party, attempting to retain control of the government, on the night of July 24 and the early morning of July 25, revolted against Mussolini. That morning, Victor Emmanuel removed Mussolini from office but replaced him with Badoglio.

Mussolini, whose exit was welcomed by most Italians, was held in police custody until his rescue by German rangers on September 12. Flown to Hitler's headquarters, Mussolini denounced Italy's September 8 surrender to the Allies and, reverting to the socialist sentiments of his earliest Fascism, attempted to rally the working class to a new social Fascist regime. Mussolini was escorted back to Italy, where he proclaimed an Italian Social Republic for the north of Italy, headquartered at Salò on Lake Garda. Mussolini was a largely impotent puppet of the Germans, but he was able to revenge himself against five of the Fascist leaders who had revolted against him. Among them was his son-in-law and former foreign minister, Galeazzo Ciano, who was executed on January 11, 1944.

In April, 1945, the end was in sight. The Allies were advancing, partisan activity was increasing, and German forces in Italy were attempting to ar-

range terms with the Americans. Mussolini was incapacitated by indecisiveness. He met with leaders of the resistance in Milan but decided against surrender. He headed toward his vaunted but nonexistent Valtelline redoubt, and his vacillations cost him any chance that he might have had to cross into Switzerland. On April 27, he and his mistress, Clara Petacci, finally joined a German column headed for Austria. At Dongo, near the head of Lake Como, the Germans were stopped by a partisan brigade and Mussolini, disguised as a German, was discovered. When the partisans sought instructions from the indecisive National Liberation Committee in Milan, the Communists seized the initiative. Walter Audisio was dispatched from Milan to carry out the death sentence. Mussolini and Clara Petacci, who had insisted on being with her lover, were stood against a low wall at Giulino di Mezzegra and shot on April 28. Their bodies, along with those of fifteen other executed Fascist leaders, were brought back to Milan, where the corpses of Mussolini and Petacci were hung by their feet from a girder on the Piazalle Loreto for public display and excoriation.

Summary

Benito Mussolini's egotistical quest for personal power led to a regime of which the only coherent themes were power and violence and finally resulted in the execution of the dictator and the defeat of Italy. Mussolini and his movement left behind some architectural remains and the Lateran Pact of 1929, a rapprochement between the Catholic church and the Italian state, with which it had been at odds since the Italian kingdom seized the Papal States in 1870. The onetime revolutionary, however, did not transform the class structure or the distribution of wealth in Italy but, rather, reinforced it. He left behind him conditions and structures that would promote class antagonism and produce, after his demise, Western Europe's largest Communist Party.

Mussolini's movement had, at best, an ad hoc program. More than anything it was his personal vehicle to power. Unfortunately, in his egotistical quest, he was able to play on the emotions and fears that many Italians experienced in the turmoil following World War I. Many believed that Italy had been inadequately rewarded for its war effort, but, after Mussolini's enterprise, Italy was stripped of all its colonies and was smaller than it had been when he came to power. Mussolini did temporarily crush the Left and, perhaps more permanently, cemented Italy's class structure in place, but when defeat loomed, the Italian establishment deserted him and sought a new protector against the Left in the conquering Americans.

Bibliography

Bosworth, R. J. *The Italian Dictatorship: Problems and Perspectives in the Interpretation of Mussolini and Fascism.* London and New York: Arnold, 1998. An in-depth study of Mussolini and fascism including analyses of writings and historical accounts between 1917 and 1997.

Cannistraro, Philip V. "Mussolini, Sacco-Vanzetti, and the Anarchists: The Transatlantic Context." *Journal of Modern History* 68, no. 1 (March, 1996). Examines the support given by Mussolini to Nicola Sacco and Bartolomeo Vanzetti, which varied and was calculated based on Mussolini's political needs.

Cassels, Alan. *Fascist Italy.* 2d ed. Arlington Heights, Ill.: Harland Davidson, 1985. This is a short but balanced and cogent study of Fascist Italy and Mussolini. Contains a very useful critical bibliography.

Gregor, A. James. *Young Mussolini and the Intellectual Origins of Fascism.* Berkeley: University of California Press, 1979. A flawed revisionist work by a political scientist whose enthusiasm for intellectually formulated political constructs or models here takes precedence over the evidence of historical data. Gregor views Mussolini as the creative formulator of a theory of modernization rooted in, but transcending, Marxism.

Halperin, S. William. *Mussolini and Italian Fascism.* New York: Van Nostrand, 1964. This is an excellent brief treatment supplemented by key documents. It is well written and clearly developed. Halperin, a respected academic, offers sound and insightful observations.

Joes, Anthony James. *Mussolini.* New York: Watts, 1982. This book, written by a historian for a popular audience, is a revisionist approach to Mussolini. Joes attempts to offer a positive assessment of Mussolini, depicting him as the leader who saved Italy from Bolshevism and restored order, prosperity, and self-respect to the country.

Mack Smith, Dennis. *Mussolini.* London: Weidenfeld and Nicolson, 1981; New York: Knopf, 1982. This book, written by a prominent English historian of Italy, is an excellent source. Although it presumes a certain amount of contextual knowledge, it is the best comprehensive biography of Mussolini written in English. Mack Smith convincingly portrays Mussolini as a violent and demagogic opportunist bent on attaining and retaining personal power.

Bernard A. Cook

GUNNAR MYRDAL

Born: December 6, 1898; Gustafs, Dalecarlia, Sweden
Died: May 17, 1987; Stockholm, Sweden
Areas of Achievement: Economics and sociology
Contribution: Myrdal, who received the Nobel Prize in Economic Sciences, is among the most important intellectual figures of the twentieth century. He was one of the primary forces responsible for the development of the welfare state in his native Sweden, and his study of American racial relations contributed to the dismantling of legal segregation in the United States. His analyses of the Third World—its poverty and other problems—have been equally influential.

Early Life

Gunnar Myrdal was born in the rural parish of Gustafs, in the province of Dalecarlia in central Sweden on December 6, 1898. His father was a farmer and a railroad employee. The eldest of four children, Myrdal, a brilliant and an ambitious student, attended Stockholm University, where he received a degree in law in 1923. Finding the practice of law in itself unsatisfactory, he returned to the university to study economics and received a doctorate in that discipline in 1927. His abilities being obvious, he was retained at the university after graduation, becoming first a lecturer and then, in 1931, a professor. In 1933, he became the Lars Hierta Professor of Political Economy at Stockholm, a position he held for many years.

In 1924, he married Alva Reimer, a fellow student at Stockholm University. Alva Reimer Myrdal had an equally distinguished academic and public career, and the Myrdals often worked together on various social and economic subjects. In 1934, they published *Kris i befolkningsfrågan* (crisis in the population question), which analyzed the reasons for the low birth rate in their native Sweden. Their recommendations included government loans and subsidies to married couples in order to encourage them to have children, as well as the building of public housing and provisions for child care. Since they believed that children should be desired by their parents, however, they also urged the necessity of sex education and family planning. Soon the Myrdal name became famous, so famous that a home planned for large families was known as a Myrdal house, a long couch was a Myrdal so-

fa, and, used as a verb, the name became a slang term for the procreative act itself. The Myrdals eventually had three children.

Life's Work

Although trained in economics and deeply interested in mathematical models and their application to economic issues, Myrdal early came to believe that too often pure economic theory ignored the more important cultural, historical, political, and societal influences. He became a leading advocate of the multidisciplinary and multicausational approach in the analysis of society, and he is considered to be a major proponent of the institutionalist school. A strong believer in stating his own value premises, Myrdal argued that it was impossible to approach any study without values and preconceptions and that it was thus necessary that the student or observer make those values and preconceptions explicit. Pretensions to simple empiricism or objectivity—an impossibility to Myrdal—could only result in chaos. Intellectually a child of the eighteenth century Enlightenment, Myrdal had great faith in human reason and rationality, and he believed that such reason must be used for the general improvement of society. Never simply an academic, Myrdal regularly served the Swedish government in various executive and legislative capacities and is considered one of the formative influences on the development of the welfare state in that country. During the worldwide economic depression of the 1930's, Myrdal urged additional government spending to combat its effects, a position often popularly associated with the ideas of John Maynard Keynes.

Myrdal was a recipient of a Rockefeller Foundation Fellowship in 1929, beginning a long, fruitful, and sometimes contentious relationship with the United States. He was a great admirer of Presidents Thomas Jefferson and Abraham Lincoln, and he spent much time in the United States. Myrdal approved of American idealism and openness, but he was not uncritical of various institutions and practices which he believed perverted those positive values. In 1938, he was chosen by the Carnegie Corporation to direct a study of the plight of blacks in the United States. The result was *An American Dilemma: The Negro Problem and Modern Democracy* (1944). It was a work which was not only an analysis of the black community but also a profound commentary on the conflict and tensions between the ideals of equality as expressed in the Declaration of Independence and the discrimination that blacks suffered in American society. Myrdal was selected to lead the project in part because of his previous academic and political accomplishments, in part because, as an outsider, he had the appearance of being more objective; thus, the study's findings would be more acceptable.

It was several years before the fourteen-hundred-page work was finally published, in 1944. Its appearance had been delayed by the outbreak of World War II, which prompted Myrdal to return to Sweden for a time. *An American Dilemma* was never a best-seller. Its initial printing was only twenty-five hundred copies. Yet it eventually went through more than thirty editions. More important, it was a major influence on the emerging civil rights movement, culminating in the landmark case of *Brown vs. the Board of Education of Topeka, Kansas*, which saw the United States Supreme Court ban segregation in public schools. In its unanimous decision, rendered in 1954, the court specifically cited Myrdal's work as supporting the argument that the separation of races was inherently unequal and much to the detriment of black students. When *An American Dilemma* first appeared, Myrdal expressed opptimism regarding the future relations of the races in the United States. Because of the slow pace of integration and the intractable problems of economic deprivation, Myrdal later became more pessimistic regarding America's dilemma.

Toward the end of World War II, Myrdal traveled throughout the United States as an economic adviser to the Swedish government. As did many other economists, Myrdal predicted the return of the Depression of the 1930's once the war concluded. In his opinion, the depths of the new economic crisis would be compounded as a result of the lack of government planning in the United States. In 1945, Myrdal was appointed minister of commerce in the first postwar Swedish government. His great faith in planning and his reputation for seeking solutions in extensive government actions made his term as minister of commerce controversial. Also, Myrdal pursued a policy of increased trade with the Soviet Union, a move resented in some quarters, including the United States. Yet, as American idealism and self-interest led to the development of the Marshall Plan in 1947, trade with the Soviet Union became of less consequence, and Myrdal resigned

from the Swedish cabinet, accepting instead a position in the United Nations as the secretary general of the European Economic Commission. Here, too, however, the Cold War dogged Myrdal: Europe remained divided, and the commission proved to be of less consequence than he had hoped.

In 1953, Myrdal spent six weeks in Southeast Asia and was struck by the various economic problems in the region. Alva Myrdal, who had also worked for the United Nations, was appointed Sweden's ambassador to India in 1955. Although husband and wife were often apart because of their separate careers, Myrdal was able to spend some time in India with Alva. His Asian visits led to a deep interest in the poverty endemic in Asia. In 1958, he published *Rich Lands and Poor: The Road to World Prosperity.* That work proved to be a preliminary study of Third World poverty, a study which culminated ten years later in a monumental three-volume, twenty-three-hundred-page work entitled *Asian Drama: An Inquiry into the Poverty of Nations* (1968), the subtitle suggesting a comparison with Adam Smith's eighteenth century classic, *Inquiry into the Nature and Causes of the*

Wealth of Nations (1776). Like his earlier *An American Dilemma*, *Asian Drama* saw many years of gestation and the contributions of many scholars before its publication.

Consistent with his multicausational analysis of societies and their institutions, and expressing his belief in the need for Southeast Asia to modernize through rational planning and development, social discipline, and changed attitudes, Myrdal criticized earlier theories and programs that had posited that Asia could easily adopt and adapt to Western models of development. Although Myrdal urged more capital investment by the West, *Asian Drama* was more descriptive than prescriptive and caused its reviewers considerable difficulty. While all recognized its scope and its analytic significance, many claimed that Myrdal had become both discouraged and pessimistic. The magnitude of the problems was so profound—a rapidly increasing population, inefficient agricultural and unsuitable educational systems, and the lack of effective governments to make the necessary changes—that Myrdal seemed to be saying that little could be usefully done by the industrialized nations of the West in assisting the East. Others noted that Myrdal's own stated values were perhaps too Western for the varied Asian cultural experience, and still others pointed out that *Asian Drama* failed to discuss the more encouraging experiences of Japan, Taiwan, and South Korea. Nevertheless, the work was a milestone in its discussion of the problems of poverty that faced one-quarter of the earth's population.

Summary

Two years later, in *The Challenge to World Poverty: A World Anti-Poverty Program in Outline*, published in 1970, Gunnar Myrdal returned to the subject matter of *Asian Drama*. Some modern observers of the Third World had expressed optimism over indications of increased food production through the introduction of new and hybrid crops and the possibility of population reduction through birth-control programs. Myrdal was not convinced and reiterated his demand for structural changes in the developing world: land and educational reform and attitudinal and social changes. The so-called Green Revolution and Western programs to limit births were, in his opinion, too ephemeral, too transient, and too superficial. Myrdal, with his multidisciplinary and multicausational approach, had long doubted the efficacy of simple solutions. He agreed with the Keynesians

and their belief in deficit funding, but only during times of crisis. Over the long run and for more permanent solutions, structural changes in the economy and society were required, an argument he had earlier made in *Challenge to Affluence*, an analysis of the economy of the United States, published in 1963.

In the late 1960's and the 1970's, Myrdal pleaded publicly for massive increases in spending to solve the combined urban and poverty problems of the United States. The programs of Lyndon Johnson's Great Society and its successors were simply inadequate. He hoped to revise and update *An American Dilemma*, expressing both optimism regarding American idealism and pessimism over the slow rate of change in solving the crucial problem of American racism. Yet his major work was done. By 1975, his health had declined, although he continued to speak and lecture in the United States and Sweden for many years. In 1974, he shared the Nobel Prize in Economic Sciences with his antithesis, the conservative Austrian economist Friedrich von Hayek. Later Myrdal said that he should have rejected the award because economics was not a science, what with its many value judgments, a position he had maintained for many years. Although wealthy from his many writings, he continued a rather simple life-style until his death in Stockholm in 1987 at the age of eighty-eight.

Myrdal's legacy is a rich and varied one. In the United States, perhaps his most enduring contribution is in the area of race relations. *An American Dilemma* not only influenced policymakers and fellow scholars but also, as Myrdal's ideas were disseminated in textbooks and popular studies, helped to shape the attitudes of several generations of American students. Myrdal's massively documented study of racial discrimination thus played a significant part in forcing American society to acknowledge a great injustice and begin to redress it.

Bibliography

Dykema, Eugene R. "No View Without a Viewpoint: Gunnar Myrdal." *World Development* 14 (1986): 147-163. The author of this study of Myrdal's intellectual approach discusses the latter's belief in the importance of stating one's values before attempting any analysis of social problems. Dykema, while sympathetic to Myrdal's positions, also argues that Myrdal perhaps too often reflects the Western belief in human rationality, sometimes at the expense of differing value systems from other cultures.

Maddison, Angus, ed. *"Myrdal's Asian Drama": An Interdisciplinary Critique.* Liège, Belgium: Ciriec, 1971. This volume is a collection of articles devoted to Myrdal's *Asian Drama.* Originally presented at a conference in Montreal, the papers reflect the diverse background of their authors, all of whom had varied responses to Myrdal's long analysis of the many problems of Southeast Asian societies.

Myrdal, Gunnar. *Against the Stream.* New York: Pantheon, 1973; London: Macmillan, 1974. Myrdal never wrote his autobiography, arguing in the preface to this collection of articles that his life had focused more on the problems that interested him than on his experiences and on persons he knew. He stated that this volume should be read as a substitute for his memoirs.

Sherman, Howard. "Gunnar Myrdal: Economics as Social Relations." *Journal of Economic Issues* 10 (June, 1976): 210-214. This article announced that Myrdal had received the Veblen-Commons Award. Sherman, a Marxist scholar, praises Myrdal for his critique of the neoclassical economists and his work on American racism but criticizes Myrdal for not making use of the concepts of class conflict and socialist revolution.

Syll, Lars Palsson. "Myrdal's Immanent Critique of Utility Theory." *History of Political Economy* 30, no. 3 (Fall 1998). The author explains Myrdal's critique of utility theory.

Thernstrom, Abigail, and Stephan Thernstrom. "The Prescience of Myrdal." *Public Interest,* no. 128 (Summer 1997). Discussion of Myrdal's "An American Dilemma" (1944), which considered racism in the United States.

Walsh, Francis P. "The Most International Swede." *Contemporary Review* 224 (March, 1974): 113-120. In this venerable British journal, the author, in the year that Myrdal received the Nobel Prize, summarizes, in an interesting and readable fashion, Myrdal's long and varied career.

Eugene S. Larson

VLADIMIR NABOKOV

Born: April 23, 1899; St. Petersburg, Russia
Died: July 2, 1977; Montreux, Switzerland
Area of Achievement: Literature
Contribution: Nabokov established himself as one of the greatest novelists of the twentieth century. During the first half of his life, he wrote in Russian, while in his later years, he turned out a series of English-language masterpieces.

Early Life

Vladimir Nabokov was born into a wealthy, aristocratic Russian family. In his cosmopolitan home, he learned to read and write in English, Russian, and French. By the time he was fifteen, he had read all of the works of William Shakespeare in English, all of Gustave Flaubert in French, and all of Leo Tolstoy in Russian.

Nabokov's father was a courageous fighter for individual freedom, and his liberalism caused him to be imprisoned first by the czarist government and then by the Bolsheviks. In 1917, when the czar was overthrown, Nabokov's father and other liberals fought to build a democratic state, but the Bolsheviks quickly took over and established a dictatorship. The family fled to Western Europe, and Nabokov never returned to his homeland. Although his family was financially ruined, Nabokov did not become embittered by his losses. He took with him what he valued most: his family, culture, and language.

His mother's jewelry financed Nabokov's two years at Cambridge University, from which he graduated in 1922. He wrote poetry, short stories, and plays at a fever pitch and, under the pseudonym Vladimir Sirin, established himself as a major figure in the émigré community centered in Berlin, Germany. In March, 1922, his father was killed trying to protect a friend from attack by two czarist sympathizers. Nabokov survived financially by writing, tutoring, translating, and lecturing. Despite the losses and hardships he suffered, Nabokov never lost the feeling that life was an exciting gift, an endless source of wonder and joy.

Life's Work

In April, 1925, Nabokov married Vera Slonim, a beautiful and cultured Jewish woman. Over their long life together, Vera acted as Nabokov's secretary, editor, business manager, teaching and research assistant, chauffeur, and translator. She, an observer wrote, allowed Nabokov to put his genius into his work, while she managed their life. In 1934 Dmitri, their only child, was born.

In 1926 Nabokov published his first novel, *Mashenka* (*Mary*, 1970), which was followed in 1928 by *Korol', dama, valet* (*King, Queen, Knave*, 1968). These first two books were greeted with excitement in the émigré community, but it was *Zashchita Luzhina* (1930; *The Defense*, 1964), *Priglashenie na kazn'* (1938; *Invitation to a Beheading*, 1959), and *Dar* (1952; *The Gift*, 1963) that placed him among the major writers in twentieth century Russian literature.

Seldom has loneliness and obsession been more compellingly portrayed than in *The Defense*. Luzhin is a withdrawn, clumsy boy who sits like a lump when his doting mother and father try to communicate with him and writhes in silence at the torment of his schoolmates. However, he discovers a genius for chess and retreats into a safe world of harmony and abstraction. As an adult, Luzhin becomes a world chess master, but Nabokov portrays his torturous descent into a mental breakdown. His slow recovery requires his absolute abstention from chess, but then Luzhin begins to believe that his entire life is composed of moves in some monstrous chess game against an unknown opponent. He decides that he can avoid the game in only one way: by dropping out. He plunges out of an apartment window, and, as he falls to his death, the courtyard below resolves itself into a gigantic chessboard.

Nabokov always maintained that his books had no political or social message, but read against the backdrop of the Nazi and Soviet regimes, *Invitation to a Beheading* makes its political point by portraying the cruelty and crudity of the type of leaders that totalitarianism inevitably draws upward into power. In *The Gift*, Fyodor, a young émigré writer, struggles to find his calling. He contemplates writing a biography of his famous explorer father, and, through Fyodor's musings, Nabokov is able to pay a tribute to his own father. Fyodor then decides to write a biography of Nikolay Chernyshevsky, whose writings had a freeing impact on Russian political thinking but whose crude aesthetic principles helped cripple Soviet literature. The Chernyshevsky biography is incorporated into *The Gift*, allowing Nabokov to make his point about the vulgarity of Soviet culture. Fyodor finally discov-

ers his gift by writing a love story for a woman named Zina, which is the book in the reader's hands, *The Gift*.

Nabokov angered some critics because he frequently proclaimed that art had no value for society. He had no concern with moral messages or social improvement. "I don't give a damn for the group, the community, the masses," he said. He detested Freudianism and Marxism. He had no use for organized religion; he believed Darwinism could not account for the world's wonderful diversity. He was a scientist and a lepidopterist, but he believed that science could never explain life's deepest mysteries.

Nabokov's work did carry a moral message made not by preaching but by his attention to the details of specific lives: the loneliness of a young misfit, the cruelty of the strong toward the weak, and the moral crime of an older man robbing a young girl, Lolita, of her childhood. He often explored the mind of characters to find why they were unable to grasp the joy the world offered them. The world was a place of wonder and mystery. "Every day, every instant all this around me

laughs, gleams, begs to be looked at, to be loved," he said. "The world stands like a dog pleading to be played with." Consciousness allowed humans to partake of all the wonders the world had to offer, yet consciousness was strictly limited by, above all, death: "The cradle rocks above an abyss," Nabokov wrote, "and common sense tells us that our existence is but a brief crack of light between two eternities of darkness." Nabokov rebelled against this limitation and explored the possibility of escape through love and art.

As Nazi leader Adolf Hitler tightened his grip on Germany, Vera, a Jew, was in danger. In 1937 the Nabokovs moved to France, now the center of émigré life. When Hitler's forces invaded France, the Nabokovs again were threatened. Sensing where his future lay, Nabokov wrote his first English-language novel, *The Real Life of Sebastian Knight* (1941). A friend arranged a summer position for him at Stanford University, and in 1940 Vladimir, Vera, and Dmitri left for the United States.

Nabokov stitched together a career in the United States. He got temporary appointments at several American universities and a part-time position at a Harvard natural history museum; he tutored, wrote reviews, and established a lucrative relationship with *The New Yorker*. In 1948 he got a tenured position at Cornell University, giving him economic security for the first time since 1917.

Despite the pressures of teaching, Nabokov continued to write. He completed a major study of Nikolay Gogol and began his translation of and commentary on Alexander Pushkin's *Evgeniy Onegin* (1831; *Eugene Onegin*, Nabokov translation, 1964). He published the novel *Bend Sinister* (1947), a brilliant study of the banality of totalitarian rule. In 1950 he finished his autobiography, which was later reworked into *Speak, Memory* (1966), regarded as one of his masterpieces.

In 1953 he finished writing *Lolita* (1955), a study of obsession and cruelty. Humbert Humbert is consumed with his desire for the twelve-year-old Lolita. He marries her mother to have access to the girl and after her mother's death holds Lolita captive through psychological manipulation, moving her back and forth across the United States from one dreary motel to another. Humbert tells his own story so persuasively and contritely that it seduced many readers into accepting his version of himself as a victim. Nabokov had little patience for that view; Humbert was an enslaver, rapist, and murderer who victimized a young orphan girl. Publishers realized that *Lolita* was a masterpiece but feared the legal consequences of publishing it. It was finally released in the United States in 1958, where it won critical acclaim and became a best-seller; it was twice made into major films and, by the mid-1980's, had sold fourteen million copies.

Nabokov's next novel, *Pnin* (1957), also became a best-seller. Publishers brought out translations of virtually all of his Russian writing, and his new wealth allowed him to quit teaching and devote the rest of his life to literature.

In 1959 Nabokov and Vera left the United States and moved to Montreux, Switzerland, where they began to put Nabokov's life's work in order, especially by supervising translations of his early writing. He also finished four more novels, including *Pale Fire* (1962), which biographer Brian Boyd called the most perfect novel in form ever written. *Pale Fire* is narrated by Kinbote, a madman, who tells the story of the poet John Shade, a pairing that allows Nabokov to summarize many of his old concerns: love and isolation, healthy creative sanity and perverted inward-dwelling madness, and death and the possibility that it can be transformed into something more.

As he approached his seventieth year, Nabokov continued to write and translate his earlier works. In 1974 he began a new novel, but in 1975 he developed a series of health problems and died on June 30, 1977, without finishing his book. Vera died in 1991.

Summary

Vladimir Nabokov's self-assurance and aristocratic manner veiled the losses he suffered in his life from public view. Forced to flee from the Bolsheviks and then the Nazis, he sometimes wrote while listening to the sounds of gunshots and rioting in the streets. He, with Vera's help, carved out a space for artistic serenity in the midst of political turmoil and economic deprivation. Toward the end of his life, he told Dmitri that he had achieved all of his important dreams and that his life had been marvelously happy.

By the mid-1960's, Nabokov was often referred to as the world's greatest living writer. He had achieved success with literary critics and had a large and devoted group of readers. Some critics found his work too cerebral, but Nabokov trusted his readers and wanted them to feel the excitement of untangling his meaning and following his shifts in thought.

By the mid-1970's, Nabokov enjoyed the acclaim of literary critics, but his books were not selling well. Many readers had probably been attracted by the controversy surrounding *Lolita* and were disappointed when they searched for explicit sex scenes that were not there. In addition, with the translations of his Russian works, twenty-nine of Nabokov's books hit the market in fourteen years, too many for readers and critics to absorb. By the 1990's, however, the quality of his body of work was again becoming apparent, and Nabokov was recognized as one of the greatest writers of modern times.

Bibliography

Boyd, Brian. *Vladimir Nabokov: The Russian Years*. Princeton, N.J.: Princeton University Press, 1990; London: Vintage, 1993. In this excellent biography, Boyd traces Nabokov's idyllic childhood and follows him into exile, first from the Bolsheviks and then from the Nazis. It ends in 1940 with his flight to the United States.

―――. *Vladimir Nabokov: The American Years*. Princeton, N.J.: Princeton University Press, 1991; London: Vintage, 1992. Boyd worked closely with Vera and Dmitri Nabokov and was able to use sources unavailable to most researchers. He intersperses his biographical chapters with brilliant chapters of analysis of each of Nabokov's novels.

Nabokov, Vladimir. *Speak, Memory: An Autobiography Revisited*. New York: Putnam, 1966; London: Weidenfeld and Nicolson, 1967. Considered one of Nabokov's masterpieces, this autobiography described, in unforgettable vignettes, his life in Russia and in European exile.

―――. *Strong Opinions*. New York: McGraw-Hill, 1973; London: Weidenfeld and Nicolson, 1974. This book contains some of Nabokov's letters and essays but is especially valuable for its inclusion of over two hundred pages of transcripts of interviews with him.

Shapiro, Gavriel. *Delicate Markers: Subtexts in Vladimir Nabokov's "Invitation to a Beheading."* New York: Lang, 1998. This is the first multidimensional analysis of Nabokov's novel *Invitation to a Beheading*. It reflects the complexity of the writer's "American years."

Shrayer, Maxim D. "Mapping Narrative Space in Nabokov's Short Fiction." *Slavonic and East Eu-*

ropean Review 75, no. 4 (October, 1997). Discusses Nabokov's cartographic style of describing space.

Wood, Michael. *The Magician's Doubts: Nabokov and the Risks of Fiction.* London: Chatto and Windus, 1994; Princeton, N.J.: Princeton University Press, 1995. Wood's close reading of the Nabokovian texts shows the power and beauty of his language and the subtly of his art, and it uncovers an ethical and moral foundation of his work that Nabokov denied existed.

William E. Pemberton

RALPH NADER

Born: February 27, 1934; Winsted, Connecticut
Areas of Achievement: Government and politics; law; and social reform
Contribution: Using a variety of methods, including speech-making, writing, testifying before congressional committees, and establishing numerous public interest organizations, Nader has been the nation's leading advocate for the public interest in opposition to concentrations of unaccountable corporate and bureaucratic power.

Early Life

Ralph Nader, the youngest of four children, grew up speaking English and Arabic, the native language of his immigrant parents, Nathra and Rose Bouziane Nader, who came to the United States from Lebanon. Nathra owned and operated a restaurant in Winsted, Connecticut, and did well enough to provide his family with a comfortable ten-room house. He also taught his children to think for themselves, to abhor injustice, and to take action to promote justice. He taught them that one person could make a difference. Lively discussions of political and social issues were commonplace in the Nader home and in the restaurant.

The Nader children's formal education began in Winsted public schools. Ralph enjoyed learning. While still a small child, he would go to the courthouse to listen to the lawyers argue. As he grew older, he enjoyed reading the works of early twentieth century "muckrakers" such as Upton Sinclair, Ida Tarbell, and Lincoln Steffens. After high school, he enrolled in the Woodrow Wilson School of Public Affairs at Princeton University and graduated magna cum laude in 1955. Nader enjoyed his Princeton years but found his years at Harvard Law School less enjoyable. Since he did not own a car, he did a good deal of hitchhiking during his student years and, while doing so, witnessed automobile accidents and the terrible injuries they caused. From these experiences, Nader developed an interest in automobile safety, took a medical-legal seminar, and began to do serious research on the subject. This research became the basis of a paper that he wrote in his third year at Harvard. He graduated from Harvard Law School in 1958.

After completion of his formal education, Nader did not immediately become America's foremost consumer advocate, but he did have a variety of life experiences. He joined the Army reserve and spent six months as a cook at Fort Dix in New Jersey. He seemed to enjoy the experience. He was a freelance writer and, in April of 1959, published "The Safe Car You Can't Buy" in *The Nation*. That same year, he established a general legal practice in Hartford, Connecticut. From 1961 to 1963, he was an adjunct faculty member at the University of Hartford, where he taught history and political science.

Life's Work

Nader's career as a consumer advocate got under way when, at age thirty, the lean, somewhat shy, six-feet four-inch-tall bachelor went to Washington, D.C., in 1964. Daniel Patrick Moynihan, assistant secretary of labor in the administration of President Lyndon B. Johnson, hired him as a consultant on highway safety for fifty dollars per day. His next opportunity came when Democratic senator Abraham Ribicoff of Nader's home state of Connecticut, then chairperson of the Senate Subcommittee on Executive Reorganization, prepared to hold a hearing on automobile safety and had to do background preparation. When Nader found out about it, he went to see the staff director, Jerome Sonosky, who found several reasons for desiring Nader's participation: He was very knowledgeable about automobile safety, he would work for nothing, and he would let the politicians have all the credit. In addition to the background work, Nader testified at the hearing.

It was while Ribicoff's hearing was in progress that Nader's first book, *Unsafe at Any Speed* (1965), was published. Although it briefly made the best-seller list, it was much less the book than the attempt by General Motors executives to discredit Nader that catapulted him to prominence. They employed a private investigation firm to investigate Nader. On the pretext that their client—unidentified—was considering hiring Nader for an important position, the private investigators questioned people who knew him about his sex life, his political activity, and any prejudices he might have. Because of his Lebanese background, they particularly inquired about possible anti-Semitism. They found nothing to discredit him, but when the investigation was discovered, some members of the subcommittee were outraged at the attempt to smear Nader.

James Roche, the president of General Motors, appeared before the subcommittee and testified

that he had not authorized the investigation or had even known of it prior to its initiation. As president of the company, however, he accepted responsibility and apologized to Nader. Thereafter, he proceeded to deny that most of the things Nader complained of had been any part of General Motors' investigation. The denials virtually negated the apology. Senator Ribicoff asked the Justice Department to investigate possible criminal violations related to the harassment of a congressional witness. The Department of Justice brought no criminal charges; however, Nader brought a civil action against General Motors for invasion of privacy. In 1970, the suit was settled out of court for $425,000.

Nader's public advocacy took off in 1968, even before the settlement of his suit against General Motors. Several young, bright, and energetic law students who shared Nader's values came to Washington, D.C., to work with him at their own expense. They could afford to do so because they were from affluent families that could be described as pillars of the establishment. One was a great grandson of former President and Chief Justice

William Howard Taft, and another later married one of the daughters of President Richard M. Nixon. They fit Nader's vision of aroused citizens taking action to make things better. This group of seven law students came to be known as "Nader's Raiders." Their project was the Federal Trade Commission (FTC). They wrote a report indicting the FTC as a "do-nothing" agency and recommended reforms. Some of their recommendations were implemented during the Nixon administration. Other Raiders, young lawyers rather than law students, staffed the Center for the Study of Responsive Law, which Nader established in June of 1969. These young lawyers received $500 of expense money for the entire summer, but only if they could not afford to pay their expenses from other sources. The Raiders turned out reports critical of the Interstate Commerce Commission and the Food and Drug Administration. Groups of Raiders came and went.

In July of 1970, using $280,000 from the settlement of his civil suit against General Motors, Nader established the Public Interest Research Group (PIRG) and supported it with funds derived from his speaking engagements. The lawyers Nader hired were paid low salaries but were responsible to no one but him. Like Nader, these lawyers believed that helping to reform the economic and political systems was more important than the higher salaries they could earn in profit-making law firms. At PIRG they filed petitions with regulatory agencies, conducted investigations, and provided information and advice to members of Congress who sought it. Next, as a result of a conversation with a college student on an airplane, Nader began the creation of a network of PIRGs on college campuses. Students and local professionals, both lawyers and nonlawyers, would become citizen activists in the local arena, taking up causes such as consumerism and environmentalism. Moreover, these college PIRGs would constitute a national network to support reform. They were funded by students voting to pay a small amount as part of their student fees.

In 1971, Nader established Public Citizen, which engaged in public interest lobbying and litigation; however, the main reason for its creation was to raise money. Most of Nader's organizations were primarily funded by the fees he received from his speaking engagements. His speeches took him all over the United States, which meant constant travel, and the speeches with question and answer sessions afterward averaged two and one-half hours each. It was very tiring, and he could not increase the number of his speaking engagements. He tried mass mailings to raise funds but was less successful than he had hoped. He was able to restructure the organization, separating its educational and political arms. In this way, he was able to get some funding for the educational functions of Public Citizen from nonprofit foundations. Nader resigned as president of Public Citizen in 1980, but his ideals continued to permeate the organization. For example, in 1988 it took on the educational function of warning consumers of dangerous drugs and dangerous drug interactions.

By the 1990's, Nader was still working eighty-hour weeks even though much of his dark hair had become thin and gray. In 1992, he spoke of the deterioration of American democracy and campaigned in the New Hampshire presidential primaries of both the Democratic and Republican parties as a write-in candidate, although he was himself an independent. He was not really running for president but was critical of the electoral process. He said that a write-in vote for him should be construed as a vote for "none of the above" and called for an official "none of the above" option on ballots. In 1996, he again entered presidential politics, this time as the nominee of the Green Party, although he was not a member of the party and did not endorse its platform. He accepted no contributions and said he would spend no more than $5,000 of his own money. Some interpreted this as simply an angry response to President Bill Clinton's signing of legislation ending the fifty-five-mile-per-hour speed limit on the nation's highways.

The 1990's were not congenial to several of Nader's positions. He unsuccessfully supported reform of the health care system. He unsuccessfully opposed the North American Free Trade Agreement (NAFTA) and the General Agreement on Tariff and Trade (GATT). In 1998, Nader fought against tort reform legislation supported by many conservative members of Congress. Nader believed it would take away or at least seriously blunt civil litigation, the most effective weapon Americans had against dangerous consumer products; therefore, Nader was compelled to fight it.

Summary

Ralph Nader symbolizes the public interest movement. As such, he has received criticism from conservatives and liberals. Conservatives have criticized him for being hypocritical and practicing the same kind of secrecy in the operation of his organizations, particularly in regard to funding, that he has criticized in government. He has not answered the charge. Liberals have criticized Nader for failing to include racial issues among his many causes. His response has been that minorities and the poor are among those who are most hurt by the kind of corporate behavior that he fights. Other liberals have been critical of his consumerist politics that treat even environmental issues as consumer issues. These critics claim that by considering people only in the capacity of consumers in a capitalist society, Nader encourages demand for even more consumer products, which puts greater strain on the environment. Nader has not addressed this criticism. However, critics from both sides of the political spectrum concede that Nader has been instrumental in the passage of important consumer legislation and governmental reforms. Many Americans believe that he has contributed greatly to the public interest, which he has never attempted to define.

Bibliography

Burt, Dan M. *Abuse of Trust: A Report on Ralph Nader's Network*. Chicago: Regnery, 1982. A report of a conservative public interest organization critical of Nader's secrecy. Contains a bibliography.

Holsworth, Robert D. *Public Interest Liberalism and the Crisis of Affluence: Reflections on Nader, Environmentalism, and the Politics of a Sustainable Society*. Boston: Hall, 1980. A work critical of, but not hostile to, Nader from the perspective of environmentalism. Contains an extensive bibliography on Nader and his work.

Litwak, Mark. *Courtroom Crusaders*. New York: Morrow, 1989. Contains one chapter on Nader. No bibliography.

McCarry, Charles. *Citizen Nader*. London: Cape, and New York: Saturday Review Press, 1972. A balanced treatment of Nader's early life and career. Contains a useful chronology of major events but no bibliography.

Nader, Ralph, and Wesley J. Smith. *No Contest: How the Power Lawyers Are Perverting Justice in America*. New York: Random House, 1996. Nader and Smith take on attorneys for firms that serve large corporations, contending that these attorneys have abandoned their responsibilities to the public.

Rowe, Jonathan. "The Most Dangerous Man in America." *Rolling Stone*, no. 721 (November 16, 1995). An interview with Nader in which he discusses the evils of large, powerful organizations such as the government, the media, and the mega-corporations formed through mergers.

Whiteside, Thomas. *The Investigation of Ralph Nader: General Motors vs. One Determined Man*. New York: Arbor House, 1972. Reports on the investigation by private investigators hired by General Motors into the private life of Nader. An appendix contains a transcript of relevant portions of the hearing before Senator Ribicoff's subcommittee.

Patricia A. Behlar

SAROJINI NAIDU

Born: February 13, 1879; Hyderabad, India
Died: March 2, 1949; Lucknow, India
Areas of Achievement: Government, politics, women's rights, education, and literature
Contribution: Naidu demonstrated that strong-willed women can develop the statesmanship necessary to assume leadership of a nation. Her poetry, while overlooked in the West, is regarded as some of the most important in India.

Early Life

Sarojini Chattopadhyay was born in Hyderābād, the capital of the princely state of Hyderābād (Deccan) in the south-central part of India, on February 13, 1879, to Aghorenath Chattopadhyay and Vardha Sundari. Her parents were members of an old priest-caste (Brahman) family in the northeast province of East Bengal (now called Bangladesh). Her parents migrated to Hyderābād because of a teaching position that Sarojini's father, who had received a doctor of science degree from the University of Edinburgh, had obtained. Her father, an ardent educationist, considered radical by his contemporaries because of his advocacy of education for women, hired private tutors to teach English, French, and, later, Persian to his daughter. Sarojini proved to be a child prodigy. She was graduated from one of the toughest school systems in the country with a first class education when she was eleven years old and won a scholarship from the King of Hyderābād (the Nizam) to continue her college education in England. England found the sixteen-year-old too young for college, so Sarojini was asked to attend classes in King's College, London, for a year; later, she was formally admitted to Girton College of the University of Cambridge.

Sarojini's life in England was far from happy. She was uncomfortable with the English image of her as an exotic—almost extraterrestrial—girl, quiet and rather aloof. She enjoyed, however, the opportunity of meeting Arthur Symons, a member of the Rhymers' Club founded by William Butler Yeats in 1891, and Sir Edmund Gosse, a prominent literary figure of the day. The former introduced Sarojini to the English world through his introduction to the first volume of her poems, *The Golden Threshold* (1905), while the latter offered practical advice on how to express her unique poetic sensibility.

Life's Work

Sarojini had changed her name from Chattopadhyay to Naidu when the English reviewed her poems favorably and the Indians exultantly in 1905, the year of their first publication. The very next year saw the need for a new impression, which was followed by two more, in 1909 and 1914, respectively. In the meantime, Naidu was busy rearing her four children and putting together a new volume of poetry. *The Bird of Time* (1912), with new editions in 1914 and 1916. A third volume, *The Broken Wing*, was published in 1917, and a fourth, *The Feather of the Dawn*, was posthumously issued in 1961.

Naidu was apologetic about the songlike nature of her poetry. "I sing just as birds do," she wrote to Symons, without a "voice," probably implying the awesome prophetic voice of a God thundering through a burning bush—a voice that, presumably, alone can transmute the flimsy material of a song into the weighty substance of great poetry. In her self-effacing humility, she forgot the tradition, exemplified by the Old Testament Song of Solomon and Walt Whitman's "Song of Myself," great poetry in the form of song. Her songs, after all, are songs of life, love, death, and destiny—themes the human race has always considered substantial. Further, they add a new note to the repertoire of poetry as song through a harmonious fusion of otherwise intransigent traditions, their "Eastern-ness" meticulously transposed into the Western medium of English prosody. Such a fusion is evident in the way she weaves magical strands around her themes "like a pearl on a string" ("Palinquin-Bearers") or elevates them to mystical heights "And scale the stars upon my broken wing!" ("The Broken Wing"). In these songs, it looks as if, in P. E. Dustoor's words, "an English garden has exotically put out the most dazzling tropical blooms."

The dazzling English garden of Naidu's consciousness slowly started turning into a blighted one with the fast-changing historical events under the leadership of Mahatma Gandhi and his satyagraha movement. In Sanskrit, *satya* means "truth" and *graha* is the act of "grasping." Satyagraha is a blanket term that Gandhi used for all forms of peaceful efforts to gain independence from the British rule organized through the Indian National Congress, one of the major political parties in India. Naidu joined the party wholeheartedly. She represented the people of India in negotiating with the British government in England as a member of the Home Rule League (1919) and the Round Table Conference for Indian-British cooperation (1931). She also led demonstrations against the government policies at home and was imprisoned three times: in 1930, 1932, and 1942. She visited the major sections of the African continent in 1924, 1929, and 1931, lending the imperial subjects moral support and political guidance. In 1928-1929 she visited the United States to mobilize American support for the independence struggle.

Fighting the battle outside the country, Naidu realized, would not be productive if she did not address the problems inside it. As a woman, she knew of social injustices to women that tradition had helped institutionalize, such as prohibition of remarriage for widows, child marriage, polygamy, and deprivation of education for all women. She organized women's groups, especially for the promotion of education, and raised the consciousness of the women she addressed as speaker to a wide range of women's groups. Curiously enough, she found it harder to convince the "civilized" English about women's rights than the "primitives" at home.

Above all, Naidu gave her full attention to the most sensitive issue of her day: the crisis between the Hindu religious majority and the Muslim minority. A Hindu herself, she was singularly equipped with a heightened awareness that helped her appreciate the experiences of both as one. She did not arrive at this ability because she was a mystic, although three of her poems were included in *Oxford Book of English Mystical Verse* (1927), but because she had retained the resilience of the truly primitive imagination that is able to take consciousness back to its undifferentiated origins. Past and present were copresent in her consciousness, not with the discrete linearity of two neighbors but rather like the commingling of waters. It was this unifying consciousness that gave her the courage to be a friend to Mohammad Ali Jinnah, the Muslim leader who was a devout follower of the Congress but, later, had to dissociate himself from it and espouse the cause of the rival political party, the Muslim League. She remained his friend without losing her loyalty to the Congress at a time when Jinnah came to be looked upon as intransigent and fanatical by the leaders of the Congress. In 1947, when she became the governor of the United Provinces (now Uttar Pradesh) in north-

central independent India, her inauguration ceremony was blessed by the representatives of all the religions of India. During her governorship, she restrained the majority from treating the minority as a poor relation, especially on issues concerning language, which took on epic proportions in the first decade of India's independence.

Although a dynamic woman, Naidu, strangely enough, had always been physically ill. Her health started deteriorating close to her birthday in 1949 and worsened in March. On March 2, 1949, she asked the nurse attending her to sing a song for her. As the nurse's song ended, Naidu breathed her last. It is ironical that her active public life began with the publication of a book of songs and ended with a song. Perhaps she saw life itself as a song.

Summary

Sarojini Naidu led a full and successful life. It was full because it was authentic in the Sartrean existential sense of choosing freely and accepting the consequences of one's choice. Such behavior is unlike that of the multitude who let externals—social constraints for example—choose for them; consequently, they live the lives of others, which creates emptiness instead of adding fullness. One glorious example of an authentic choice in Naidu's life is her choice of husband: Govindarajulu Naidu, a person of a non-Brahman caste. This act alienated her from family, friends, and society—especially the Indian society of her time—yet she wore her choice with pride all through her life. Her life was successful not only because she made it through these "outrageously" authentic choices but also because she produced spectacular, though "mundane," results because of them. She won the Kaisar-i Hind award from the Nizam of Hyderābād in 1908, became a fellow of the Royal Society of Literature in 1914, was elected president of the Indian National Congress—the first woman to hold that elective office—and finally became, in 1947, the governor of the most politically active state in India, another first for a woman. Today she is known as the "Nightingale of India." February 13, her birthday, is celebrated as women's day throughout the country.

Bibliography

Azad, Abul Kalam. *India Wins Freedom: An Autobiographical Narrative*. Introduction and explanatory notes by Louis Fischer. New York: Longman, 1960. Ghost-written by Humayun Kabir. Contains little discussion of Naidu but gives useful insights into the political controversies of the time by a contemporary who, like herself, fought for India's freedom with heart in pain and mind in conflict.

Baig, Tara Ali. *Sarojini Naidu*. New Delhi: Publications Division, Ministry of Information and Broadcasting, Government of India, 1974. A smaller version of the biography by Padmini Sengupta, cited below, this source is slightly different because of the author's personal reminiscences of Naidu. Included are interesting but defensive comments on the place of women in India and a few citations about Naidu from the police records of British India.

Gandhi, Mahatma. *An Autobiography: The Story of My Experiments with Truth*. Translated by Mahadev Desai. London: Phoenix Press, 1949; Boston: Beacon Press, 1957. Almost a classic for a student of the freedom movement in India. A "spiritual" profile of its ethos, excellent for understanding popular Indian philosophy and the soul-searching that accompanies political activity.

Marx, Edward. "Sarojini Naidu: The Nightingale as Nationalist." *Journal of Commonwealth Literature* 31, no. 1 (Spring 1996). Examines the career of Naidu and the artistic adjustments she was forced to make in order for her work to be heard in English poetic circles.

Morton, Eleanor. *The Women in Gandhi's Life*. New York: Dodd Mead, 1953. The women surrounding Gandhi are portrayed as they figure in his life chronologically. Naidu appears six times. Tara Ali Baig and Padmini Sengupta, two other women writers cited in the bibliography, are amiably critical of Indian society's treatment of women, as was Naidu herself. Useful sourcebook for feminist connections to the Indian freedom movement.

Sengupta, Padmini. *Sarojini Naidu*. London and New York: Asia Publishing House, 1966. A well-written and more comprehensive biography of Naidu than the one by Baig, cited above. Follows the life of the subject chronologically but fails to convey her dynamism as effectively as one might expect from a book of this length. Provides useful bibliographical footnotes and a fairly comprehensive bibliography. A must for the researcher on Naidu.

Srinivasa Iyengar, K. R. *Indian Writing in English*. 2d ed. London and New York: Asia Publishing House, 1973. A pioneering work, this comprehensive study of Indian writing in English is almost a definitive work on the subject. Very useful for a study of the poetic talents of Naidu. Contains a good bibliography and well-organized index.

Abdulla K. Badsha

FRIDTJOF NANSEN

Born: October 10, 1861; Store-Frøen, Norway
Died: May 13, 1930; Polhøgda, Norway
Area of Achievement: Exploration
Contribution: Nansen was a major Arctic explorer, an accomplished scientist, an outstanding statesman, and world-renowned for his humanitarian services to advance the rights of the oppressed and war refugees.

Early Life

Fridtjof Nansen, with his brother Alexander and a number of half brothers and sisters, grew up several miles from Christiania in a rural paradise, one with wooded areas, near lakes where they learned to swim and where, in the winter, they skated on the ice. His father, Baldur Nansen, was a lawyer of unswerving integrity, reputed to have been slender, precise, and gentle in manner, firm and honorable in character. His mother, Adelaide Wedel Jarlsberg Nansen, was a tall, industrious, and stately woman who was an accomplished snowshoer and skier, introducing her son to snowshoeing when he was four. Nansen was most like his mother, tall and large of frame, with strongly marked features and boundless energy, inheriting his mother's love of outdoor sport.

As a young man, Nansen won the national cross-country skiing championship twelve times in succession, and at eighteen he broke the world record for one-mile skating. As he grew older, it became apparent that he had acquired from his father a strong sense of obligation, a gentle manner, thoughtful sympathy for others, a careful, accurate habit of work, and a strict firmness of character. Though Nansen's family was relatively wealthy, he learned at a young age the value of hard work, discipline, and frugality. Interestingly, his very name, Fridtjof, means a Viking, or more properly speaking a "thief of peace."

As a young man Nansen became intimately knowledgeable of Daniel Defoe's *Robinson Crusoe* (1719), Peter Christian Asbjørnsen's Norwegian fairy tales, and young fishermen bare-legged in the icy Frogner River with their bait of worms. From an early age, he never tired of boating and sailing or of boarding the sealing and whaling boats as they lay in Christiania harbor. Nansen possessed an insatiable desire for reading and asking questions—so persistently, so continually, that one friend said, "It made us absolutely ill." In later years, Nansen wrote, with a homesick longing, of the "unspeakably dear and happy home."

Life's Work

A brilliant scholar, Nansen matriculated in 1880 with honors in all natural science subjects, mathematics, and history, and in the same year entered the University of Christiania to study zoology. In the spring of 1882, while still at the university, he was asked to participate in collecting zoological specimens on an expedition to the Arctic Ocean aboard the sealer *Viking*, a six-month adventure hunting saddleback seals and one that had a momentous influence on his future career. It was during this cruise that he observed bits of driftwood and deposits of fine earth on the ice; he asked himself whether, since there were no trees in Greenland, the polar ice moved from east to west—from Siberia to Greenland—and perhaps touched the North Pole. Upon his return he was offered a position at the Bergen Museum as curator of natural history, where he spent six years.

In 1888, immediately after defending his pioneering Ph.D. dissertation in zoology, on the histology of the central nervous system of the hagfish (1887), Nansen with a party of five (including two Norwegian Lapps) made a memorable journey on skis across Greenland's inland ice sheet from east to west, which he described in his *First Crossing of Greenland* (1890). When Nansen returned home on May 30, 1889, he was greeted as a hero, having established his international reputation as a resourceful and successful Arctic explorer.

However, some explorers and scholars maintain that his major contribution to polar exploration was his expedition of 1893-1896, when he attempted to drift across the Arctic Ocean aboard the indestructible *Fram*, therefore demonstrating a water route across the polar basin. The *Fram* ("forward") was undoubtedly the most famous Arctic exploration ship, which Nansen, along with the Scottish naval architect Colin Archer, designed for its unique task of avoiding being crushed by sea ice, which was the fate of most Arctic-going vessels. This famous and unique polar vessel was a 400-ton, fore and aft iron-clad, barkentine-rigged ship, one with rounded ends that allowed the ship to rise with any increased pressure of sea ice. From earlier experience in Greenland, where Nansen observed icebound driftwood, he was also aware that wreckage from the *Jeannette*, of George W. De Long's ill-fated 1879-1881 expedition which had foundered off Siberia, eventually was found along Greenland's east shore. Nansen correctly posited, from his experience on the *Viking*, that there existed a trans-Arctic ice drift. Between 1893 and 1896, Nansen's *Fram* drifted icebound from the East Siberian Sea across the Arctic basin as he had hoped, though somewhat to the left of the North Pole. He took soundings—often two miles in depth—providing a profile that dispelled the popular notion that the Polar Sea was a shallow basin.

On March 14, 1895, Nansen and his most durable skier, Lieutenant Hjalmer Johansen, left the *Fram* at 84 degrees north latitude and made a desperate attempt for the pole by dog sled and skis over the ice. In early April, at 86 degrees, 12 minutes north latitude, they gave up and turned south, arriving in Franz Josef Land, where they wintered after five months and a three-hundred-mile journey. They were rescued the following spring by a British expedition sent out to explore Franz Josef Land, led by Frederick Jackson. Two months later, on August 13, 1896, Jackson deposited Nansen and Johansen at the port of Vardø in north Norway. Unbeknown to them, the *Fram* had the same day shaken off the last of the pack ice near Spitsbergen and was steaming south for the first time in three years. Only one week after Nansen and Johansen's arrival, the *Fram* cast anchor in the far north port of Skjervøy. Nansen had now attained the status of an oracle, for this austere, self-possessed, and enigmatic Titan proved his hypothesis about a westward drift of polar currents.

Nansen consequently exerted considerable influence upon Antarctic and Arctic explorers when he advocated the use of dogs and skis, and he recommended emulating the adaptive technology and diet of the Inuit of the Arctic. His experiences laid the basis for nearly all Arctic and even Antarctic explorations, as well as establishing him as a scholar in the relatively new fields of ethnology, nutrition, oceanography, and meteorology. These accomplishments led to his appointment as professor of zoology (1897) and professor of oceanography (1908) at the University of Christiania (now Oslo). During this period he edited a six-volume account, *The Norwegian North Polar Expedition* (published between 1900 and 1906). As a scientist, Nansen made numerous contributions, including published monographs, based on his extensive fieldwork, particularly after 1901, when he was ap-

pointed director of an international commission to study oceanographic subjects. He also made several scientific expeditions (1906-1908), mainly to the North Atlantic.

Nansen's considerable influence on the Norwegian government, in its internal affairs discussions regarding the uneasy union with Sweden, commenced his career as a statesman, for in 1905 he negotiated Norway's peaceful separation from Sweden after almost a century of Swedish rule and, before that, four centuries under Denmark. In recognition of his efforts, Nansen was appointed Norway's first ambassador to Britain (1906-1908). Nansen's international reputation was enhanced through his numerous significant contributions of informative articles to the world press and his reputation for integrity and devotion to humanitarian causes. Although Nansen wanted to continue his explorations, particularly to the South Pole, demands by his country, and later by millions of helpless World War I refugees abroad, became increasingly pressing. His strong sense of citizenship, compassion, and obligation forced Nansen to forgo his own personal ambitions in order to assist those many refugees less fortunate than himself and to perform acts of mercy without regard to his own inclinations, convenience, and even his health.

After World War I, Nansen became known internationally as a humanitarian, mainly through his services to famine-stricken Russia as well as his work in the repatriation of prisoners of war. In 1921 he was appointed as League of Nations High Commissioner for Refugees, and he was able to save millions of destitute Armenians, Greeks, and Russians, for which he received the 1922 Nobel Peace Prize, which, characteristically, he donated to international relief efforts. The League of Nations again honored him in 1931 by creating the Nansen International Office for Refugees, which won the 1938 Nobel Peace Prize. Nansen continued his work in the League of Nations, working in the Assemblies of 1925 to 1929, in which capacity he played a major role in securing the adoption of a convention against forced labor in colonial territories, and in preparations for a disarmament conference.

Summary

Fridtjof Nansen was the most famous Arctic explorer, greatly influencing both Arctic and Antarctic explorers. In time, he was fairly judged by most explorers as one of the most successful, dedicated, innovative, and influential, if not inspirational, of all polar explorers. Much of Nansen's success in exploration was that he possessed the unique ability to plan the needs and logistics of an expedition, to choose good men, and to inspire them through his own example of dedication. Nansen's success as an explorer was based on his thorough understanding of oceanographic circulation patterns, climatology, navigation, astronomy, and Eskimo culture (especially their clothing, shelter, diet, and transportation). However, many scholars and biographers of Nansen believe that his greatest skills and contributions were demonstrated in the fields of diplomacy and politics, and of course in his tireless efforts in directing humanitarian aid to refugees.

Remarkable about Nansen are the numerous academic, literary, political, and humanitarian contributions he made. To this day, Nansen epitomizes for Norwegians a strength, integrity, and sense of both personal and national independence. His writings, in addition to those works already mentioned, included *Eskimo Life* (1958), *In Northern Mists: Arctic Exploration in Early Times* (1975), *Closing-Nets for Vertical Hands and for Vertical Towing* (1915), *Russia and Peace* (1923), and *Armenia and the Near East* (1976). In addition, Nansen wrote numerous scientific reports and journal articles, particularly in the fields of biology and zoology.

Bibliography

Bain, J. Arthur. *Life and Explorations of Fridtjof Nansen*. London and New York: Scott, 1897. An excellent biography by an Arctic explorer who knew Nansen intimately and who effectively conveys the strong sense of Norwegian nationalism evoked by Nansen's many accomplishments.

Berton, Pierre. *The Arctic Grail: The Quest for the North West Passage and the North Pole, 1818-1909*. New York: Penguin, 1988. A thorough and exceptionally well written account that critically compares Nansen's philosophy and techniques of exploration with those of Robert McClure, Charles Francis Hall, William Parry, Robert Peary, and Roald Amundsen.

Cherry-Garrard, Apsley. *The Worst Journey in the World*. London: Constable, and New York: Doran, 1922. Perhaps the best-written account of the Scott Expedition to the South Pole, also containing invaluable information regarding Nansen's solution for scurvy and his innovation of arctic equipment.

Christopersen, A. R. *Fridtjof Nansen: A Life in the Service of Science and Humanity*. Oslo: Cultural Office of the Norwegian Ministry of Foreign Affairs, 1961. A brief but succinct monograph that presents an in-depth and relatively detailed essay on Nansen's successful efforts in the areas of politics and diplomacy, particularly his role in the repatriation of prisoners of war and his contributions to assisting refuges of the Russian famine.

Hall, Anna Gertrude. *Nansen*. New York: Viking Press, 1940. The book presents important biographical information from Nansen's unpublished diaries, mostly on his youth and period of exploration, particularly his time aboard the *Viking* and the *Fram*.

Huntford, Roland. "Hero of the Arctic." *Geographical Magazine* 70, no. 4 (April, 1998). Examines Nansen's attempt to reach the North Pole in 1893.

————. *Scott and Amundsen*. London: Hodder and Stoughton, 1979; New York: Putnam, 1980. A brilliant and well-researched account of previously unknown material dealing with Nansen's professional and personal relation with two famous explorers, Roald Amundsen and Robert Scott.

Mirsky, Jeannette. *To the Arctic! The Story of Northern Exploration from Earliest Times to the Present*. New York: Knopf, 1948; London: Wingate, 1949. A complete survey that provides a thorough understanding of the ineradicable effect that Nansen had on both Arctic and Antarctic exploration.

Nansen, Fridtjof. *Adventure and Other Papers*. London: Woolf, 1927; Freeport, N.Y.: Books for Libraries Press, 1957. A collection of papers that dwell mostly on Nansen's exploration, with excellent accounts of his preparations, strategies, and the logistics of his explorations.

————. *Farthest North: Being the Record of a Voyage of Exploration of the Ship "Fram" 1893-96 and of a Fifteen Months' Sleigh Journey by Dr. Nansen and Lieut. Johansen*. 2 vols. London and New York: Harper, 1897. An honest and even humble account of Nansen's early childhood, personal training, and devotion to his many pursuits, which were critical to his political ambitions and success as an explorer.

Ryne, Linn. *Fridtjof Nansen*. Oslo: Norwegian Ministry of Foreign Affairs, 1996. A brief but valuable account of information usually available only in untranslated books and articles.

John Alan Ross

PAUL NASH

Born: May 11, 1889; London, England
Died: July 11, 1946; Boscombe, England
Areas of Achievement: Art and book illustration
Contribution: Nash's landscape paintings, aptly depicting the destruction of World Wars I and II, are among the best in the English tradition.

Early Life

On May 11, 1889, Paul Nash was born in the Kensington district of London, England. His father, William Harry Nash, was a lawyer whose family had for generations been involved in agriculture. Paul's mother was Caroline Maud Nash, the daughter of a naval captain. The Nash family would later include another son and a daughter; Paul's younger brother, John N. Nash, was also to enjoy a successful career as a painter.

Paul Nash was an imaginative child who loved both the natural world and the descriptions of it which he found in fairy tales, such as those by Hans Christian Andersen and the Brothers Grimm. These early impressions of nature were reflected in his artwork throughout his career. Interestingly, Nash was concerned primarily with places and the inanimate things he found there (especially trees and rocks); he seldom included people in his drawings and paintings. Only some evidence of man's existence was seen in his art, such as fences, paths, walls, and later the machinery of war.

Nash's formal education began in January of 1898, when he enrolled at Colet Court, a preparatory school for boys, wishing to enter St. Paul's School eventually. He was an anxious and nervous child, a disposition he inherited from his mother. A target for bullies at school, he disciplined himself in adulthood to display a confident, almost diffident, demeanor, sometimes mistaken for aloofness.

Because Nash's mother was in very poor health, the family moved from London to a country home, Iver Health, near Langley, at the end of 1901. Nash would live there for many years, later drawing on the natural scenery of the heath for imagery in his paintings. In the fall of 1903, he entered St. Paul's School, but deficiencies in mathematics hurt his progress as a student. His interest at this time was in school theatrical productions, for which he designed some stage scenery. He was also proficient at expressing himself in writing. When Nash was

graduated in July of 1906, he was still undecided about a future career.

Since Nash had always enjoyed art, his father encouraged him to enroll in an art school. Nash first attended the Chelsea Polytechnic School in December of 1906, where he began illustrating his favorite books in order to practice his drawing. In the fall of 1908, he transferred to the London County Council School to prepare for employment as a commercial artist. He studied there for the next two years.

Through the influence of a prominent art scholar, William Rotenstein, Nash was encouraged to attend the prestigious Slade School of Art at the University of London, which he entered in the fall of 1910. There he became friends with a fellow student, Ben Nicholson, who would also have a successful career as an artist. During his tenure at the Slade School, Nash fell under the powerful influence of the works of two great artists and writers, Dante Gabriel Rossetti and William Blake. Nash was especially fascinated with the imagery each man used in his works; the sun, the moon, and stars began to loom large in his own imagination.

Life's Work

Nash's first drawings as a maturing artist were of landscapes that have a poetic and sometimes haunting atmosphere about them. Some of these works are *Vision at Evening* (1911), in which a face peers out of the sky, and *Pyramids in the Sea* (1912), in which a decorative style of painting is employed, predominantly in blue tones.

The most important influence on Nash's early works, however, came when World War I began. Although he first enlisted as a home guard (for service in England only), Nash was sent to France in early 1917 as an official war artist. Early in the war, on December 17, 1914, Paul had married Margaret Theodosia Odeh, the daughter of an Anglican minister. His letters to her from the front, in 1917, display his great ability as a descriptive writer; they abound in startling details of war scenes. These same horrifying scenes were to become the substance of Nash's first important paintings and drawings. All of his works from World War I on display exceptional merit in their depiction of the phantasmagoric imagery of its battle. Among Nash's very best pieces from this era are *Sunrise:*

Inverness Copse (1918), *Dawn: Sanctuary Wood* (1918), and *Landscape: Year of Our Lord 1917* (1918).

The powerful impact that trench warfare made on Nash actually hurt his ability to depict other subjects in his paintings upon his return to England. Art critics often consider the 1920's to be one of his least successful decades as an artist. The landscapes he then produced tended to focus on Dymchurch, an area of England he visited often. Nash's interests, however, were also diversified in this decade; he was employed as a designer of stage scenery and costumes, primarily by his good friend, the playwright Gordon Bottomley. Nash also worked as a book illustrator at this time, drawing for Ford Madox Ford's *Mr. Bosphorus and the Muses* (1923).

Unfortunately, Nash's private life was affected by severe trauma all through the 1920's. His wife was almost constantly in poor health, and his father failed in strength and died in 1929. Nash himself was to suffer from debilitating asthma for most of his adult life. Attacks of breathlessness would leave him deeply fatigued, and he consulted many doctors to find a cure for his suffering. There was no cure, however; he would have to conserve his strength and periodically rest at nursing homes. Throughout all of these personal trials, Nash maintained some sense of humor. He had a sharp wit that could hurt his enemies, but a kindly and generous nature was at his core. He was a very hard worker despite his illness.

The 1930's marked some new developments in Nash's life. He and his wife moved to a new home in Rye in December of 1930. In the next year they traveled to the United States, where Nash was a judge for the annual art awards presented by the Carnegie Institute of Pittsburgh. Despite his severe asthma attack in 1933, Nash remained active in several areas of the art world. In early 1933, he founded a group of painters, sculptors, and architects known as Unit One. They were a selection of some of England's finest artists of the era, all working outside the mainstream of their fields. The membership of Unit One included Edward Wadsworth, Edward Burra, John Bigge, Ben Nicholson, Barbara Hepworth, Henry Moore, and Wells Coates. In April of 1934, they held their first exhibition of works at the Mayor Gallery in London; these pieces later toured major English cities. The great diversity of interests and of artistic styles that the members of Unit One pursued, however, soon led them to disband, in early 1935.

Nash also worked as an art critic throughout the 1930's and after. In December of 1930, he became the art critic of the *Week-end Review*, and in April, 1931, he first wrote for *The Listener*, alternating his essays with those of Herbert Read. Nash was a successful practitioner of journalistic writing. His fastidiousness in all areas of his life led him to choose his words with great care so as to use their fullest meanings.

Besides being meticulous in the details of his work, Nash was an impeccably elegant dresser with an eye for fine apparel. Consequently, he cut a handsome, aristocratic figure. His eyes were intensely blue, his mouth full and expressive.

From the late 1920's and continuing into the 1930's, Nash had also been involved in producing patterns for several commercial projects. He designed book jackets for publishers, printed fabrics for clothiers, and did glass and ceramic designs for china companies. Nash made his greatest contribution to the decorative arts with his book illustrations of this period; his drawings for a one-volume set of Sir Thomas Browne's *Urne Buriall* and *The Garden of Cyrus*, issued in 1932, are considered to be particularly outstanding.

Nash even found time in the 1930's to begin a new hobby, photography. He used his camera to record and recall the scenes in nature that he wished to employ in his art. Nash had usually first sketched the scenes that he would later develop into oil paintings or watercolors. With his camera, he could instead photograph places or items from which he would work at length in his studio. During this period, Nash became fascinated by stones and used them as images in his paintings. He also seems to have felt some influence from surrealism. He even exhibited in the Surrealists' first international show, held in London in 1936. The Surrealists moved Nash to use poetic elements and his own fantasies in his paintings; he also was much taken by folklore and myths during this period. All these various influences resulted in such pictures as *Forest* (1932), *Strange Coast* (1934), and *Wood Sea* (1937).

When World War II began in 1939, Nash was again asked to paint as an official war artist. He was assigned to the air force, but his asthmatic condition was so debilitating that doctors repeatedly refused him permission to fly. Consequently, all of his depictions of combat flying and aerial warfare were made from the ground. Nevertheless, Nash produced a very powerful, moving group of battle pictures in the early 1940's. His relentless pursuit of detail caused him to study in earnest all the pictures and designs of British and German airplanes that his government provided for him.

As was the case in World War I, Nash's perception of the terrible waste and destruction of war resulted in some very impressive works during World War II. Among his best paintings on this subject are *The Battle of Britain* (1941) and *Totes Meer* (1941). The latter was the result of his close observation of a large dumpsite for wrecked airplanes near Oxford. It is an evocative picture that shows man's deadly power at work, without any men being present in the scene; only their violent, broken machinery evokes their presence for the viewer.

Among Nash's last works are some landscapes that concentrate on his favorite images of the sun and the moon, but with a new element added. Nash was interested in fungi late in his career. He painted a series of pictures centering on the fungus, which are regarded by critics as among his best pieces. These works include *Landscape of the Red Fungus* (1943), *Landscape of the Brown Fungus* (1943), and *Landscape of the Puff Ball* (1943). The symbolic effect in these landscapes is twofold: The fungi are living, like all plant life, but they also have a death-bearing quality, perhaps evoked by the poison they produce. Nash was, at this time, facing his own death: His asthmatic condition had steadily worsened in the 1940's. In the last winter of his life he suffered from pneumonia, and he died in the night, on July 11, 1946.

Summary

Paul Nash produced a rather wide range of works during his career. He painted some of the finest and most innovative landscapes in a nation that reveres such painting. These pieces alone would be sufficient to secure for him a permanent place in British art history.

Nash was also an advocate of better economic opportunities for artists. He was conscious of the harsh struggles many of his fellow artists had to face, and his concern led to his involvement, albeit briefly, in Roger Fry's Omega Workshops and his own Unit One. Allied to this commitment was his interest in promoting the integrity of the arts in daily life in England. He worked with bookbinders, poster printers, glassblowers, china makers, and clothing manufacturers (among others) to advance the design and quality of products in his native land.

Bibliography

Bertram, Anthony. *Paul Nash: The Portrait of an Artist*. London: Faber, 1955. Bertram provides a very detailed discussion of Nash's life and career. He draws on Nash's letters and biographical writings to a great extent. He also discusses the influences on and the products of each of the artist's various periods. A listing of Nash's paintings is included.

Causey, Andrew. *Paul Nash*. Oxford: Clarendon Press, and New York: Oxford University Press, 1980. Causey emphasizes the eclectic aspects of Nash's style and discusses the greatness of his landscapes. This thorough study also shows how personal events and other influences affected Nash's art. Includes color photographs and a bibliography.

Corbett, David Peters. "'The Third Factor': Modernity and the Absent City in the Work of Paul Nash, 1919-36." *Art Bulletin* 74, no. 3 (September, 1992). Discusses Nash's paintings of British urban life, their themes, and other such paintings by British artists.

Eates, Margot, ed. *Paul Nash: Paintings, Drawings, and Illustrations*. London: Humphries, 1948. This book contains several essays on Nash's art by such scholars as Herbert Read, John Rothenstein, and Richard Seddon. Eates also provides a chronology of Nash's life and a bibliography. The text is amply illustrated by twenty color pictures and more than one hundred in black and white.

Friedenthal, Richard, ed. *Letters of the Great Artists, from Blake to Pollock*. London: Thames and Hudson, and New York: Random House, 1963. In this second volume of a two-volume set, the author has included two of Nash's letters to his wife from the front in 1917. A biographical sketch of Nash also appears here, as well as some of his war pictures.

Hendon, Paul. "Paul Nash: 'Outline'—The Immortality of the 'I.'" *Art History* 20, no. 4 (December, 1997). Hendon considers Nash's autobiography, which includes information on his development as an artist.

Nash, Paul. *Outline: An Autobiography and Other Writings*. London: Faber, 1949. Nash began writing this book in 1938, but he died before he could complete his life story; the narrative ends in 1913. His wife added to this, mainly selections from Nash's wartime letters to her. Herbert Read provides a good preface and several of Nash's pictures are reproduced here, too.

Ritchie, Andrew C. *Masters of British Painting, 1800-1950*. New York: Museum of Modern Art, 1957. This is a catalog of paintings that accompanied an exhibition in the fall of 1956. Ritchie provides a brief but informative text discussing the excellent pictures here, including some by Nash. Ritchie also discusses Nash's life and the influences on his art.

Rothenstein, John. *Modern English Painters: Lewis to Moore*. Rev. ed.: London: Macdonald and Jane's, and New York: St. Martin's Press, 1976. Rothenstein, a major British art scholar, gives a very good analysis of Nash's career. Rothenstein's style is lively, penetrating, and clear; his analyses are complemented by revealing anecdotes.

Patricia E. Sweeney

GAMAL ABDEL NASSER

Born: January 15, 1918; Alexandria, Egypt
Died: September 28, 1970; Cairo, Egypt
Areas of Achievement: The military, government, and politics
Contribution: Nasser was a member of the Free Officers Society that came to power in Egypt in 1952 via a military coup. Subsequently Prime Minister and President of Egypt, Nasser was a major player in the Arab-Israeli conflict.

Early Life

Gamal Abdel Nasser's father, Abdel Nasser Hussein, was born of a fairly well-to-do family from the village of Beni Murr near Assyut, was educated in a Western primary school in Assyut, and eventually became district postmaster in Alexandria. Little is known about Nasser's mother except that she was the daughter of a local contractor and died young. Nasser was the first of four sons, born in Alexandria. His father remarried, and consequently Gamal was reared for a good part of his life by an uncle in Beni Murr. He attended nine different schools, most in Cairo, spent a term at the University of Cairo (1936) in the law curriculum and then was accepted into the military academy after a first-time rejection. He was graduated at age twenty. During his high school years, he took part in many demonstrations and was wounded by a bullet at age seventeen. He was also known to like American motion pictures. Politically, he was an admirer of Napoleon I and Kemal Atatürk and possessed an extreme dislike of the British army, whose presence in Egypt he never accepted. He married a woman who was from a Persian-Egyptian family.

The students at the military academy during the 1930's found themselves involved in intense discussions about Egypt's problems and destiny. Grievances about poverty, imperialism, and the power of the landed aristocracy occupied much of their time. In fall, 1938, Nasser began to plan a revolutionary organization which, by 1942, had many cells across Egypt. Because of a heavy-handed British policy over Egypt during World War II, many of the military-revolutionaries favored Germany, although no serious plans for an alliance ever materialized. Close relations were also established with a religious fundamentalist group known as the Muslim Brotherhood. Eventually, the Egyptian and general Arab failures in preventing the partition of Palestine in 1947 and then being defeated by Israel in 1948 led to the formation of a larger Free Officers Society. In 1948, Nasser was a lieutenant colonel of infantry and was wounded during the First Palestine War.

Life's Work

In 1950, General Muhammad Neguib, who was regarded as a military hero, was chosen by the young officers as their leader, largely to convey a sense of legitimacy to their organization. On July 23, 1952, after a period of restlessness and demonstrations in Cairo, eleven members of the Free Officers Society staged a bloodless coup against King Farouk I. A revolutionary executive committee was formed, later to be called the Revolutionary Command Council (RCC). Neguib became prime minister, war minister, commander in chief, and RCC chairman in September, 1952, and appeared to be the leading figure. Nasser, however, played a significant role as he represented the views of the younger and less affluent officers. Nasser was the recipient of three million dollars of clandestine support from the United States' Central Intelligence Agency before the July 23 coup, as he was viewed as pro-Western and democratic, yet this was not to be the case.

Nasser believed that democracy had to be established in Egyptian life, which, in particular, focused on social democracy, meaning the uprooting of class distinctions, wealth, and privilege. Nasser's vision of the state also focused on suppressing "sensational" dissent. As a result, most of the press was censored and eventually nationalized in 1960.

During 1953, Nasser and Neguib found themselves in direct opposition over the future of Egypt. Nasser wanted revolutionary reforms, while Neguib stuck to a more reformist line. In January, 1953, Nasser was instrumental in forming the Liberation Rally, an organization designed to mobilize the masses and a forerunner of the Arab Socialist Union. Egypt was declared a republic on June 19, 1953. In February, 1954, Nasser's and Neguib's forces almost forced violence into the streets, but Nasser prevailed and Neguib resigned. Nasser became prime minister and imposed a series of laws restricting opposition to his regime. Political parties were banned and even groups that had supported the Free Officers Society, such as the Muslim Brotherhood, were broken up.

Egyptian president Gamal Nasser addresses air force cadets during the Suez Crisis in 1956.

The RCC came more under Nasser's domination as he began the process of creating an authoritarian-mobilizational regime that would feature frequent popular rallies and referenda to demonstrate popular support. Islam also came under the control of Nasser within Egypt, with religious leaders being reduced to mouthpieces for the government, while Pan-Islamism was preached as part of an anti-imperialist foreign policy.

In January, 1956, Nasser presented a new constitution that proclaimed the abolition of imperialism, feudalism, monopoly, and capitalist influence. Egyptians were given basic human rights, but the ban on political parties continued. Nasser and three RCC officers had the right to nominate members to the 350-seat National Assembly. The assembly had a useful life of only two years, until February, 1958, when it was suspended because of unification with Syria. Power actually centered on Nasser's National Union, which provided the ideology for Egypt's future.

In February, 1958, Syria and Egypt agreed to form a single country, called the United Arab Republic (UAR), of which Nasser was president. At first this was desired by the Syrian Baathists out of regard for the principles of Arab unity and the desire to see rapid economic development. Real unity, however, never materialized, as the Syrians came to object to the heavy-handed attempt to implement Nasser's reforms in Syria. The UAR broke apart in September, 1961. Afterward, the power of the National Union was increased to include elements from various social groups, and its name was changed in 1962 to the Arab Socialist Union, representing a form of "one-party democracy," modeled probably on Turkey before 1945. Nasser, however, was not an Eastern Bloc-type socialist, as indicated by the dissolution of the two Communist parties of Egypt in 1965.

One of Nasser's most significant reforms in theory was found in agriculture. In September, 1952, Nasser sponsored the land reform that confiscated land from estates of more than two hundred acres and distributed it to poor peasants. The shortage of arable land and Egypt's increasing population since the turn of the century made it difficult to provide land for all who needed it. Only one in five who needed land received it. The Nasser government continually reduced maximum acreages of individual ownership, from two hundred to one hundred acres in 1961 and down to fifty acres in 1969. These reforms, however, did destroy the material base for the two thousand wealthiest landlords in Egypt.

Nasser envisioned many big industrial projects for Egypt, which were to be largely state-directed, as extensive restrictions on private enterprise, even nationalization, was part of his economic policies (Egyptianization). The focal point of these projects was the plan for the Aswan High Dam, which was conceived as a symbol of the 1952 Revolution as well as a source of hydroelectric power for industry and land reclamation in agriculture.

Nasser's anti-Western attitude foreclosed the possibility of Western aid for the dam's construction. After nationalization of the Suez Canal in July, 1956, as a means to obtain capital for construction, and an invasion from Great Britain and France during the Suez War of October, 1956, the funding for the dam eventually came from the Soviet Union, which loaned Egypt $300 million for construction costs and supplied a corps of advisers. The artificial lake created by the construction of the dam was named for Nasser.

The anti-imperialist position adopted by Nasser lent itself naturally to support from the Soviet Union. Nasser, after seizing power, moved away from any pro-Western military agreement. On the other hand, he opposed the North Atlantic Treaty Organization (NATO) policy of trying to contain Soviet expansion in the Middle East. He attended the first meeting of the Afro-Asian excolonial states meeting in Bandung, Indonesia, in April, 1955, which marked the beginning of the "nonaligned movement." Nasser became acutely interested in Soviet support as he saw Soviet interests in Asia parallel his own: support of anti-imperialism, nonalignment, and Third World independence.

In September, 1955, the first arms agreement between Egypt and Czechoslovakia was announced, with the latter acting as a surrogate for the Soviet Union. Before 1958, Nasser's biggest ideological enemy in the Middle East was the Hashemite regime in Iraq, which was supported by the United States and was a member of the Baghdad Pact Organization. In July, 1958, King Faisal II and his government were overthrown in a pro-Nasser coup, and Iraq moved toward a revolutionary position.

The Soviet Union became more interested in Egypt after 1960, when the Sino-Soviet split led Albania to close a Soviet naval base there. Major arms agreements were made during 1964, and Nasser visited Moscow in August, 1965.

The Palestine/Israel problem was one of Nasser's obsessions. He indicated that "when the Palestine crisis loomed on the horizon, I was firmly convinced that the fighting in Palestine was not fighting on foreign territory. Nor was it inspired by sentiment. It was a duty imposed by self-defense." He viewed the issue of Palestine through the prism of colonialism. Israel had been successful, Nasser believed, only because it was a neocolonialist state. Through liberation of Palestine, however, Nasser saw the possibilities of uniting the Arab peoples and restoring some of the greatness of the medieval Arab past, when Arab civilization was dominant on a worldwide basis.

Nasser often deceived himself and was subject to hyperbole regarding the basis of the conflict and the results. After blockading the Strait of Tiran and Gulf of Aqaba to Israeli shipping during 1955 in addition to nationalizing the Suez Canal, Egypt was invaded by Great Britain, France, and Israel. Israel captured the Sinai Peninsula, while France and England occupied the Suez Canal zone. Nasser's interpretation of the defeat in Sinai during October, 1956, was that Egypt withdrew its forces before the actual fighting began. Nasser convinced himself that whatever success Israel achieved in 1956 was the result of air defenses provided by the French. Hence, by May, 1967, Nasser was willing to take new risks to defeat Israel, impelled by the belief that Israel was now alone.

On May 14, 1967, Nasser began moving his forces into the Sinai Peninsula and on May 16 demanded that United Nations Emergency Forces stationed in the Sinai and at Sharm el-Sheik be removed. Secretary General of the United Nations U Thant complied without debate, thus ushering in the crisis leading to the Six-Day War. Nasser was convinced that Israel was about to attack Syria. Nasser created a military alliance with Syria, Jordan, and Iraq, and prepared for war. A blockade was reintroduced at the Strait of Tiran. In his May, 1967, speeches, Nasser constantly raised the issue of the destruction of Israel: "The battle will be a general one and our basic objective will be to destroy Israel."

Israeli forces staged a preemptive strike against Egypt, Syria, and Jordan on the morning of June

5, 1967, destroying the combined air forces of the three states and defeating the Arab alliance in six days. Israel emerged occupying all of the Sinai, the West Bank and Gaza Strip, and the Golan Heights, taken from Syria. Nasser, in response to this overwhelming defeat, resigned in a national radio broadcast on June 9. He blamed the Egyptian defeat on collusion between Israel and the United States. A massive outpouring of Egyptian public support, partially engineered by the Arab Socialist Union, made Nasser's resignation short-lived, indicating that the resignation speech was not serious and merely a tactic for maintaining popular support.

In October, 1962, Nasser had introduced Egyptian troops into Yemen to support the Yemeni Arab Republic, an effort which had a destabilizing effect on the Arabian peninsula as well as inter-Arab politics. The campaign in Yemen was very costly for Egypt, as one-third of the Egyptian army eventually became engaged in the conflict. Nasser used Yemen as a training ground of sorts for his troops. After his defeat in the Six-Day War, Nasser was forced, in September, 1967, to remove all Egyptian forces from Yemen.

The disengagement in Yemen allowed Nasser to step up his confrontation with Israel along the Suez Canal, which began again in the summer of 1968 and eventually matured into the War of Attrition. Nasser's theory was to wear down Israel by manpower losses and perpetual mobilization. Egyptian losses were significant, however, as Israel staged aerial raids on Egyptian bases and cities, with the result being the virtual abandonment of Egyptian cities along the Suez Canal. During the course of these confrontations, Nasser consistently rejected plans for phased Israeli withdrawals. He insisted on his interpretation of United Nations Security Council Resolution 242, which called for the withdrawal of Israeli forces from occupied territories.

From the mid-1950's until his death, Nasser was a strong supporter of the Palestinian cause, although he held the Palestinian resistance movement in check until after his defeat in 1967. The Palestine Liberation Organization (PLO) was created under Egyptian auspices in 1964 but became independent of Egyptian control only after 1967. Late in 1967, Nasser took Yasir Arafat, PLO leader, with him to Moscow. During September, 1970, Nasser negotiated preliminary arrangements for the removal of Palestinian guerrillas from Jordan into Lebanon.

Nasser had sensitive health problems from the fall of 1969 until his death a year later. On September 11, 1969, he suffered a heart attack and was incapacitated thereafter. During his last year of life, he became increasingly cranky and mistrustful and refused to take advice from his staff. He appointed Anwar el-Sadat as vice president on September 20, 1969, who succeeded him as president upon Nasser's death of a second heart attack on September 28, 1970. He was survived by his wife and four children.

Summary

Gamal Abdel Nasser had an enigmatic political career. He had many political setbacks yet was durable as the President of Egypt. He seemed to defy the laws of political gravity, especially after defeats in 1956 and 1967 at the hands of Israel. He was known in the West for a biting and belligerent rhetoric. Before his unexpected death, however, he was viewed as a likely candidate to make peace with Israel. Nasser was in such a position because of his legacy from the 1950's, when Egyptians began to regard him as the savior of the Egyptian Revolution by his nationalization of the Suez Canal.

In the realm of foreign policy, Nasser has been criticized for having opened Egypt and the Middle East to Soviet penetration. The ultimate reason for such penetration may be linked to the failures of the American administration to understand Third World frustrations as embodied in Nasser. The involvement of the Soviet Union in Middle East politics, however, guaranteed Nasser and his successors that Israel could never absolutely "win" a Middle East war because of the threat of Soviet intervention.

Nasser reestablished the long-held Middle Eastern idea of Arab unity, epitomized in the union established between Syria and Egypt in 1958. This union, however, failed after three years. Nasser's attempt to bring Yemen under his control also failed. He did establish links with Gaafar Nimeiry's Sudan and Muammar Quaddafi's Libya, both regarded as left-wing regimes of the late 1960's.

Nasser left Egypt in poor financial condition, racked by losses connected with the Arab-Israeli wars. He succeeded, however, in several areas, including the building of schools and medical clinics around the country and making fresh water more easily available. His socialism was effectively ended in 1968, when the difficulties of war began to erode the Egyptian economy, and by the Sadat regime, which restored contacts with Western countries.

Bibliography

Baker, Raymond. *Egypt's Uncertain Revolution Under Nasser and Sadat.* Cambridge, Mass.: Harvard University Press, 1978. A useful institutional examination of Egypt's difficulties under two regimes.

Copeland, Miles. *The Game of Nations.* London: Weidenfeld and Nicolson, and New York: Simon and Schuster, 1969. This work focuses on foreign policy before 1967 and identifies Nasser as one of the authors of terrorism in the Middle East.

Dekmejian, R. Hrair. *Egypt Under Nasir.* Albany: State University of New York Press, and London: University of London Press, 1971. A study of Nasser that examines issues such as myth in politics, charismatic leadership, and the theory of routinization of charisma within the Egyptian revolution.

Goldschmidt, Arthur, Jr. *Modern Egypt: The Formation of a Nation-State.* Boulder, Colo.: Westview Press, and London: Hutchinson, 1988. An important general work that embodies the latest historiography on the subject.

Gordon, Joel. "Secular and Religious Memory in Egypt: Recalling Nasserist Civics." *Muslim World* 87, no. 2 (April, 1997). The author discusses the continuing influence of Nasserism in Egypt.

Laqueur, Walter, and Barry Rubin, eds. *The Israel-Arab Reader.* 5th ed. New York: Penguin, 1995. This work contains significant speeches by Nasser related to the Arab-Israeli wars.

Lesch, David W. "Gamal Abd al-Nasser and an Example of Diplomatic Acumen." *Middle Eastern Studies* 31, no. 2 (April, 1995). Lesch examines Nasser's handling of the U.S.-Syrian crisis of 1957.

Mansfield, Peter. *Nasser's Egypt.* Rev. ed. London and Baltimore: Penguin, 1969. A straightforward account of Nasser's policies through 1965.

Rubinstein, Alvin Z. *Red Star on the Nile: The Soviet-Egyptian Influence Relationship Since the June War.* Princeton, N.J.: Princeton University Press, 1977. A very useful, detailed study of Soviet-Egyptian relations, with particular emphasis on Nasser's foreign policy.

Vatikiotis, P. J., ed. *Egypt Since the Revolution.* London: Allen and Unwin, and New York: Praeger, 1968. This work contains articles that deal with the economy, politics, and culture under Nasser. Although a bit dated, it is still useful as it represents a diversity of views.

Waterbury, John. *The Egypt of Nasser and Sadat: The Political Economy of Two Regimes.* Princeton, N.J.: Princeton University Press, 1983. This is a technical analysis of the performance of the Egyptian economy, with useful evaluations of development projects.

Stephen C. Feinstein

GIULIO NATTA

Born: February 26, 1903; Imperia, Italy
Died: May 2, 1979; Bergamo, Italy
Areas of Achievement: Chemistry, education, and technology
Contribution: Natta was awarded the Nobel Prize in Chemistry in 1963 for his work on macromolecular synthesis with total control of the relative spatial orientation of groups of atoms that are bonded to the polymer chain. This important development revolutionized the plastics industry and made possible the use of polymers in widespread applications, such as plasticware, laundry detergents, and antiknock admixtures to high-octane fuels.

Early Life

Giulio Natta was born on February 26, 1903, in Imperia, on the Italian Riviera, to Francesco Natta, a prominent attorney and judge, and Elena (Crespi) Natta. He was educated in the nearby city of Genoa. Natta claimed that his interest in chemistry began at the age of twelve, when he found that he could not put his chemistry book aside: "From then on, chemistry was my love," he said. He was graduated with honors from Genoa's high school of science in 1919, at the age of sixteen. Initially, he was enrolled in the pure mathematics course at the University of Genoa but found that mathematics was too abstract. As his father had taken up the challenge of putting the ideals of justice into practice, so also was Giulio attracted by the application of the concepts of chemical theory to the solution of practical questions, and this led him to transfer to the Polytechnic Institute of Milan, where he studied chemical engineering. He received his doctorate degree in chemical engineering from the Polytechnic Institute in 1924, five years after his high school graduation.

In his Nobel presentation on December 12, 1963, Natta stated that he first became interested in the spatial relationships of atoms and in structural chemistry in general while he was still a student and apprentice of a Professor Bruni in 1924. It was then that Natta learned the techniques of structure elucidation by X-ray analysis. This analytical procedure was complemented by his study of analysis by electron diffraction at Freiburg, Germany. While in Freiburg, Natta came to know Hermann Staudinger, who was pioneering the analysis of polymers by chemical methods, and he was so influenced by Staudinger that he resolved to investigate the structure of polymers using electron diffraction and X-ray techniques.

On April 25, 1935, Natta married Rosita Beati, a literature teacher at the University of Milan. They had two children, Franca and Giuseppe. He remained close to his wife throughout his life, and it was through her influence and background in literature that the word "isotactic" was coined to describe the structure of the particular form of polypropylene that he had prepared and that marked the beginning of his prizewinning research. Natta's need to combine theory with practical applications was a basic driving force throughout his life. He utilized the techniques of X-ray analysis and electron diffraction, both of which he had learned at a very early stage in his career, throughout his research.

Life's Work

After obtaining his doctorate in chemical engineering in 1924, Natta remained at the Polytechnic Institute of Milan as an instructor. His talents as an educator were quickly recognized and marked by his rapid rise through the academic ranks. In 1925, he was made assistant professor of analytical chemistry and was promoted to professor of general chemistry in 1927. During this period, Natta's research centered on the application of X-ray analysis to the structure elucidation and crystallinity of inorganic substances. He used X-ray analysis to investigate the properties of industrial catalysts. In 1932, he visited the University of Freiburg in Germany to learn the new technique of electron diffraction and immediately began to utilize this new method in his work. His interaction with Hermann Staudinger inspired his idea to apply these analytical techniques to the investigation of macromolecular structure.

Natta returned to Milan in 1933 and then accepted a position as professor and director of the Institute of General Chemistry at the University of Pavia, where he remained for two years. He became professor of physical chemistry at the University of Rome in 1935, professor and director of the Institute of Industrial Chemistry at the Turin Polytechnic Institute in 1937, and then professor and director of the Industrial Chemistry Research Center at the University of Milan in 1938.

Because of his close ties to industrial applications of chemistry research, Natta was asked by the Italian government, under Benito Mussolini, to initiate research and development on the production of synthetic rubber, and he successfully implemented the industrial production of butadiene-styrene rubbers at Ferrara during World War II. His earlier work on industrial catalysts also led at this time to his development of catalytic processes for production of methanol and other alcohols, as well as formaldehyde and butyraldehyde. After the war, Montecatini, a large Italian chemical company in Milan, funded much of Natta's research. The low cost and availability of petroleum stimulated his work in the use of petroleum as a raw material base for industrial chemicals and monomers used in plastics production.

Natta became immediately interested in the work of Karl Ziegler, who had succeeded in preparing high molecular weight polyethylene using transition metal compounds as catalysts, in 1952. Since Ziegler was working on ethylene polymerization, Natta turned his attention to propylene, which has one more carbon than ethylene. Propylene had the advantage of being much cheaper than ethylene, as it was a by-product of the petroleum and propane refining processes.

All Natta's previous research knowledge and industrial experience came to bear on this effort. In 1954, Natta announced that he had succeeded in preparing a new polypropylene that was far superior in physical properties than previous methods could produce. He used X-ray and electron diffraction techniques to show that his polymer had a greater degree of crystallinity than could be obtained previously. In fact, all the methyl groups, which are bonded to the backbone of the polymer chain, where shown to be oriented so that they were all on the same side of the chain. The new class of polymers, where the stereochemistry (the relative spatial arrangement of atoms and groups) could be controlled, were called stereoregular polymers. Further research with a variety of vinyl polymers and catalyst systems led to the total control of macromolecular stereochemistry during the polymerization process. Isotactic polymers, with pendant groups all on the same side of the chain, and syndiotactic polymers, with pendant groups alternating from side to side with each monomer unit, could now be prepared readily and inexpensively.

Natta became a member of the National Academy of Sciences of Italy in 1955. He visited the United States in 1956, and showed several articles made from isotactic polypropylene, including a cup, a washing-machine agitator, and pipes, at a press conference. Montecatini was producing the polymer on an industrial scale in 1957, and the patented process was licensed throughout the world.

He continued research in the area of polymer science and made many other notable contributions. These included the stereospecific polymerization of butadiene to give polybutadiene, which had a configuration analogous to natural rubber. The copolymerization of ethylene with other monomers gave unusual rubber materials in that no double bonds were present in the macromolecule. He also developed the asymmetric synthesis of polymers, where an optically active macromolecule can be produced from optically inactive monomers. To mimic biological processes in this way was a remarkable and insightful achievement. In the 1960's, Natta was continuing this extensive work with the polymerization of nonhydrocarbon monomers, such as benzofuran, and vinyl ether.

Numerous gold medals were awarded to Natta in recognition of his scientific contributions, including the First International Gold Medal of the Synthetic Rubber Industry (1961), the Society of Plastics Engineers Gold Medal (1963), the Lavoisier Medal from the French Chemical Society (1963), and the Perkin Medal (1963). He also received honorary degrees from the University of Turin (1962) and from the University of Mainz (1963). Natta was awarded the Nobel Prize in Chemistry, jointly with Ziegler, in November, 1963. Arne Fredga of the Royal Swedish Academy of Sciences observed, during the formal presentation, that nature's monopoly on stereospecific and asymmetric polymerization had been broken.

In the last twenty years of his life, Natta became increasingly limited in his activities by Parkinson's disease. He could still go for long walks in the woods and hunt for mushrooms with his wife, but his other hobbies, mountain climbing and skiing, were impossible. Natta also had an interest in fossils and kept a collection of petrified fish. He continued his impact on chemistry education as coeditor of the book *Stereoregular Polymers and Stereospecific Polymerizations* (1967) and was coauthor of *Stereochimica: Molecole in 3D* (1968; *Stereochemistry*, 1972) with Mario Farina; he retired in 1972. Natta died in Bergamo, Italy, on May 2, 1979, following complications from surgery for a broken femur.

laid the foundations for understanding the relationships between polymer structure and the resulting physical properties of polymers. These discoveries influenced the development of the entire plastics industry. The advancement of technology in many other fields, such as the aerospace industry, computers, and the automotive industry, are directly related to the availability of inexpensive, lightweight materials that outperform metals, wood, and paper in terms of strength, durability, heat resistance, and other physical properties.

Summary

The driving force in Giulio Natta's scientific achievements was the desire to apply the theories of chemistry to practical applications. His background in engineering and chemistry provided him with the intellectual tools required to transform ideas into reality. He was known as "the wizard of plastics" and was one of the foremost personalities in leading the world into the age of plastics. The explosive expansion of the plastics industry and the use of plastics in every facet of life brought about an environmental stress as the result of the quantities of durable waste accumulating in dump sites. Legislation has been aimed at limiting the type and quantities of plastics waste. Many industrial projects in the plastics industry have been initiated to develop product biodegradability and the recyclability of polymers.

The impact of Natta's contributions can hardly be overstated. Much of the plasticware used in household goods, scientific and medical laboratories, microwavable containers, detergents, pipes, and antiknock additives are a direct result of his work. He

Bibliography

"Giulio Natta." In *Contemporary Authors*, edited by Hal May, vol. 113. Detroit, Mich.: Gale Research, 1985. Contains an obituary notice with a brief overview of Natta's contributions to science.

"Giulio Natta." In *Current Biography Yearbook 1964*, edited by Charles Moritz. New York: Wilson, 1964. Contains much of the biographical material available on Natta. The article mentions some of his coworkers by name and lists the early trade names of some of the plastics produced industrially by Montecatini and others. References at the end of the article provide a few other sources.

McGraw-Hill Modern Scientists and Engineers. Vol. 2. New York and London: McGraw-Hill, 1980. The section on Giulio Natta summarizes Natta's scientific achievements and lists a reference on Hermann Staudinger, who influenced Natta's interest in high polymers, as well as references to the polymerization process in general, to rubber, and to stereochemistry.

Natta, Giulio, and Ferdinando Danusso, eds. *Stereoregular Polymers and Stereospecific Polymerization.* Oxford and New York: Pergamon Press, 1967. This book is a compendium of the publications by Natta. Since most of Natta's research was published in Italian, or languages other than English, the book is an invaluable source to anyone wishing access to Natta's original work.

Natta, Giulio, and Mario Farina. *Stereochemistry.* Translated by Andrew Dempster. London: Longman, 1972; New York: Harper, 1973. An excellent source on the technical aspects of stereochemistry for a college-level student. Many parts can be read with a minimal background in chemistry. Shows the clarity of thought that Natta had in visualizing molecules in three dimensions and contains many illustrations. Discusses the entire field of stereochemistry and is not limited to the polymer aspects. Biological considerations are extensively treated.

Wasson, Tyler, ed. *Nobel Prize Winners*. New York: Wilson, 1987. The chapter on Natta gives the English translation of the formal presentation speech made by Arne Fredga of the Royal Swedish Academy of Sciences as well as Natta's Nobel lecture. An extensive list of references are cited at the end of the lecture, and these are followed by a condensed biographical sketch, which details the awards and honors received by Natta.

Massimo D. Bezoari

MARTINA NAVRATILOVA

Born: October 18, 1956; Prague, Czechoslovakia

Area of Achievement: Sports

Contribution: As a leading figure in women's tennis since the mid-1970's, Martina Navratilova was one of the first women athletes to demonstrate that women's sports could be as exciting as men's and that professional women athletes deserved comparable financial rewards.

Early Life

Martina Navratilova was born Martina Subertova in Prague, Czechoslovakia, on October 18, 1956. Her parents were divorced a short time after her birth, and her mother married her second husband, Mirek Navratil. Martina lived a robust outdoor life in the Krkno_e Mountains until the age of five, when her family moved to Revnice near the capital city of Prague. She started skiing before she was three years old and became an excellent skier by the time she was five. She preferred to play rough games such as soccer with the boys rather than playing with girls. From earliest childhood she exhibited exceptional strength and athletic ability. Her mother and stepfather were concerned about her "unfeminine" behavior, but were impressed by her physical gifts; they believed she would become a champion if she could find the right sport on which to focus her energies.

In the densely populated urban environment near Prague, Martina found that opportunities for vigorous physical activity were limited. Nevertheless, the city offered ample facilities for playing tennis. Her whole family played the game. Her maternal grandmother, Agnes Semanska, had been a national champion before World War II. Both of Martina's parents competed in amateur tournaments and served as tennis administrators for the Czech government. They were on the courts practically every day and brought Martina with them. Her stepfather cut down an old racket for Martina to use, and he became her first tennis instructor. She immediately became enthusiastic about the game and was competing in junior tournaments by the age of eight. Soon she was beating players five and six years older than herself.

By age sixteen, Martina had won three national women's championships with her aggressive play. She was ecstatic when selected by the Czechoslovakian Tennis Association to tour the United States in 1973 with a team of the best men and women play-ers. She was enchanted by the freedom she found in the United States, which was so much different from the repressed spirit of her Communist-dominated homeland. Fascinated by American music, American fashions, and American food, she was twenty pounds heavier when she returned home. Her first trip to the United States made an impression that changed her life. She realized that many of the bad things she had heard about the United States were merely Communist propaganda.

Martina became pregnant when she was seventeen and had an abortion. She later said that she regretted the whole affair because she had not truly been in love. She eventually acknowledged that she felt a strong sexual attraction to women. After being granted American citizenship, she would become candid about her homosexuality, something that would have been impossible to acknowledge in ultraconservative Czechoslovakia.

While still a teenager, Martina asked the American government for political asylum and applied for citizenship. For years she lived in fear of being kidnapped by her government's secret police because her act created bad publicity for the whole Communist system. In defecting, Martina knew she was cutting herself off from home and family, because she would not be allowed to visit her homeland after becoming an American citizen. She bravely faced the future in a strange new land with only a limited knowledge of the English language.

Life's Work

Martina Navratilova is universally referred to as "Martina." In her autobiography, *Martina*, she explains that her last name should be pronounced *Nav-RAH-tee-low-VAH*, with emphasis on the second and last syllables. She prefers to be called by her first name because Americans, including sports announcers, have so much trouble pronouncing her surname.

Once Martina discovered tennis, she devoted her life to it with the intensity that is her outstanding characteristic. Women's tennis had been a game of finesse until Martina burst upon the scene. She turned it into a game of speed and power—one that was less "ladylike" than it had been in the past, but far more interesting to spectators. Martina brought to professional tennis a cannonball serve that was clocked at a higher speed than the serves of some of the better professional male players. She was left-handed, which is considered an asset in tennis, and was noted for her powerful forehand as well as her aggressive charges to the net.

Her rivalry with Chris Evert became legendary. For years, the two women battled for first place at the world's most important tournaments: the Australian Open, the U.S. Open, the French Open, and Wimbledon in England. Martina won so many titles on the grass courts of the historic All English Lawn Tennis and Croquet Club that people said she owned Wimbledon. Despite their rivalry, Chris and Martina became good friends and often played as partners in doubles matches. Martina's record at doubles became almost as impressive as her singles record.

Martina was not a popular player when she entered professional tennis. Because she possessed a steely determination and demeanor unmatched since Helen Wills Moody was champion, spectators thought of Martina as an iceberg. Her limited knowledge of English made it difficult for her to communicate with the press, and she had a subtle sense of humor that did not translate easily into English. Because of her size and strength, she gave the impression that she beat other women players simply by overpowering them. This was not true, although she could hardly be blamed for making the most of her physical assets.

Martina quickly became wealthy from prize money and endorsements. She brought her parents to the United States and gave them a beautiful house near her own home in Texas. She continued to pursue an active professional schedule into the 1990's, one which included travel, public appearances, and all sorts of athletic activities. Martina also began exploring other interests, and signed a contract with a New York publisher to write mystery novels.

Martina has established an example for women who are not considered "feminine" in the conventional sense; she has proved that there are as many different types of women as there are different types of men, and that each woman has the option to develop to her fullest potential. She has always loved America because it is the one country that offers opportunity to everyone and has led the world in promoting women's rights.

In the twilight of her professional tennis career, Martina Navratilova had become one of the most popular personalities in the game. It was a tearful crowd that saw her play her tennis matches at Wimbledon in 1993. She made it to the semifinals,

but had to bow to talented younger players, such as Monica Seles and Steffi Graf, who were only half her age and had learned to play her aggressive style of tennis. Success had made Martina feel more relaxed and amiable, while at the same time the public had come to understand that her impassive exterior concealed a sensitive temperament. Like Jimmy Connors and John McEnroe, two of the greatest men tennis players of all time, she was disliked at the beginning of her career, but came to be adored for courage and dedication to excellence.

As an international superstar, Martina's personal life has been a subject of great media interest. She soon realized that it was impossible to conceal her homosexuality or her intimate relationships with various women. One of the biggest news stories had to do with her so-called "palimony" legal battle with Judy Nelson, who sued Martina for half of the money she had earned during the years they had lived together. The suit was finally settled out of court, with Nelson receiving an expensive house in Aspen, Colorado, and an undisclosed amount of cash.

In 1994, shortly before Martina announced her retirement from professional tennis, she had won her 167th singles title by defeating Julie Halard of France in the $400,000 Paris Women's Open. This set an all-time record for career singles championships for both women and men. Martina had also earned more money in prizes than any other male or female tennis player in history. In addition to the nearly $20,000,000 in prize money she had won during her professional career, she had received a huge amount of additional money for sponsoring various products. This was a fantastic achievement, considering that when she entered professional tennis the lion's share of the big prizes as well as the lucrative advertising fees went to men.

Summary

Martina Navratilova contributed greatly to women's tennis and to women's sports in general by demonstrating that women could compete just as fiercely as men and could play with as high a degree of technical excellence. Many sportswriters suggested that she was sufficiently strong and aggressive to compete with the best male players. Shrugging off such speculations, she helped to popularize women's tennis as a spectator sport, thereby attracting larger attendances as well as much broader television coverage.

Martina also had a tremendous impact in the area of gay rights because she was one of the few public figures who lived openly as a homosexual and was outspoken in her views on the subject of homosexuality. Particularly offended by a growing trend in the United States to pass discriminatory legislation targeting the homosexual community, Martina called for greater public understanding and tolerance.

The publicity generated by Martina Navratilova on and off the tennis courts naturally increased the value of professional women athletes as endorsers of products such as tennis racquets and tennis shoes, further motivating more and more women to compete in sports. Martina's stardom helped to strengthen the case for professional women athletes being compensated at the same level as men. Her fame and fortune set an example for young girls to follow, helping to encourage more young women to enter professional sports and women in general to lead vigorous, healthy lives.

Bibliography

Faulkner, Sandra, with Judy Nelson. *Love Match: Nelson vs. Navratilova.* New York: Carol, 1993. A full-length book about the notorious "palimony" suit brought against Martina by her live-in lover, Judy Nelson. Brings out much information about Martina's character outside the public view.

Henry, William A., III. "The Lioness in Winter." *Time* 140 (November 30, 1992): 62-63. A brief retrospective article on Martina's career and her feelings about professional sports, gay rights, and life in general as she was approaching the end of her illustrious tennis career.

Jacobs, Linda. *Martina Navratilova: Tennis Fury.* St. Paul, Minn.: EMC Corporation, 1976. A short book covering Martina's childhood and tennis career up until the day in 1975 when she defeated the world's number-one women's tennis player, Chris Evert. Contains many interesting photographic illustrations.

Kort, Michele. "Martina Navratilova: 1982 The First Female Athlete to Earn More Than a Million Dollars in One Year." *Working Woman* 21, no. 11 (November-December, 1996). Short profile of Navratilova including her contributions to women's tennis and her openness regarding her sexual orientation.

———. "Ms. Conversation." *Ms.* 16 (February, 1988): 58-62. An interesting interview with both Martina Navratilova and another great tennis player, Billie Jean King, who discuss their views on women's tennis, their personal lives, and other subjects.

Navratilova, Martina, with George Vecsey. *Martina.* New York: Knopf, 1985. A frank and revealing autobiography in which Martina describes her unhappy childhood and conflicts over homosexuality. Portrays her as a very sympathetic and human personality, in dramatic contrast to the ice-cold, aggressive image she projected on the tennis courts.

Price, S.L. "The Last Hurrah." *Sports Illustrated* 81, no. 2 (July 11, 1994). Price focuses on significant matches in the careers of Navratilova and Pete Sampras.

Vecsey, George. "Martina's Last Bow? (1993 Wimbledon)." *Tennis* 29 (July, 1993): 90-97. Discusses Martina's forthcoming appearance in the 1993 Wimbledon tennis tournament and the unsurpassed record she established at this prestigious event, beginning in 1974. Paints a word picture of historic All England Lawn Tennis and Croquet Club. Illustrated with photographs.

Bill Delaney

LOUIS-EUGÈNE-FÉLIX NÉEL

Born: November 22, 1904; Lyons, France
Area of Achievement: Physics
Contribution: By applying revolutionary viewpoints to old ideas of physics, Néel discovered new forms of magnetism, including antiferromagnetic and ferrimagnetic materials. His work greatly strengthened modern magnetic theory and has added fundamentally to computer-memory techniques and to the use of high-frequency waves. For his scientific zeal, he was awarded the Nobel Prize in 1970. Additionally, he has had tremendous importance in the establishment of various research centers in Europe.

Early Life

Louis-Eugène-Félix Néel was born in Lyons, France, on November 22, 1904. He was quite precocious as a child, and his exceptional ability in mathematics became evident early in his schooling. As a result of his outstanding examination scores and teacher comments, he was admitted to the École Normale Supérieure in Paris, which he attended from 1924 to 1928. In the latter year, he received a lectureship at the school, during which time he further developed his abilities in mathematics and physics, and began formulating his ideas on magnetism. In 1932, he obtained his doctorate of science from the University of Strasbourg.

Working in the laboratory of Pierre Weiss at Strasbourg, Néel started his original research in 1928 on basic problems of magnetism, a subject which would consume his interests until 1939. While working on his doctoral thesis, he had found extremely original possibilities in the works of Werner Heisenberg on ferromagnetism and in Heisenberg's idea that the field was a result of actions over small distances between neighboring atoms. Néel's work suggested that there should also be interactions between closely packed atoms that would cause an antiparallel alignment of the magnetic moment of individual atoms. In a series of papers published from 1932 to 1936, he described the characteristics of those materials he would name "antiferromagnets" (originally he had called the phenomenon constant paramagnetism). For that excellent series of researches, he was appointed professor of physics at the faculty of science at Strasbourg, where he served until 1945. For a brief period, his tenure was interrupted by World War II, during which he served the government as an in-vestigative scientist. His main topic of research was the means of defending ships from floating German magnetized mines. To counteract them, he invented a new method of protection, known as neutralization, which gave the ship a permanent magnetization in a direction opposite to the terrestrial magnetic field.

In 1947, he became professor of physics at the University of Grenoble. In 1940, he had gone there, being the principal agent in establishing the Laboratoire d'Électrostatique et de Physique du Métal. He served as director of the Polytechnic Institute until 1956, when he created and formed the Centre d'Études Nucléaires de Grenoble. Subsequently, he represented France at the Scientific Council of the North Atlantic Treaty Organization.

Life's Work

During his tenure at Pierre Weiss's laboratory, Néel came into contact with the current theory for the properties of matter, that of ferromagnetism's being a result of a uniform imaginary molecular field resulting from interactions of individual atoms. No origin for this field had been discovered, so Néel introduced the idea of local molecular fields, resulting from close neighboring atoms, abandoning the notion of a general field. Accompanying this idea with that of time-varying fluctuations in the heat energy of the field, Néel found that he could account for constant paramagnetism, in elements such as manganese and chromium, changing to a temperature-dependent paramagnetism, via an interaction that would cause an antiparallel alignment of the magnetic moments of closely spaced atoms. He referred to this as antiferromagnetism. He considered that, at low temperatures, atomic moments within a crystal lattice would couple together, dividing the atoms in a typical crystal into two types, one with magnetic moment pointing in the reverse direction of the other set. The atoms in these sublattices, as they were called, were opposite in orientation to their neighbors. When the temperature increased, Néel found, this ordered orientation of magnetic moments seemed to disappear, the temperature where the disruption becomes complete being known now as the Néel temperature. Néel noted that, from his analysis, two conditions for ferromagnetism had to occur: Atoms must have a net magnetic moment, a result of unfilled electron shells, and the quality known as the exchange integral between nearby atoms must be positive. Néel argued that, for nonferromagnetic materials that did contain magnetic atoms, the exchange integral would be negative, and the maximum number of antiparallel moments would have the lowest available energy state. He called these materials antiferromagnetic. Above the Néel temperature, the susceptibility, or ability to hold a magnetic field, of an antiferromagnet, behaves according to the well-established CurieWeiss law for magnetic susceptibility-temperature interactions of molecular regions.

While developing his theory of antiferromagnetism, Néel also became interested in the properties of very fine-grained ferromagnets, the material of a size necessary to be resolved with a microscope. In 1941, he set out to explain, based on his understanding how these minute particles must act in a magnetic field, the "magnetic memory" exhibited in diverse forms found in nature, including lavas, both granitic and basaltic. He found that the locked-in memory tied the time of cooling of the sample below the temperature necessary to keep the magnetic atoms totally disrupted in orientation to the absolute age of the sample. This type of memory allows geologists and archaeologists to retrace the history of paleomagnetism, or how the nonconstant earth's field varies with the passage of four billion years.

While working on the memory idea, Néel discovered a new class of permanent magnets, whose properties are a result of the very fine grains enclosed together. Materials of this sort he called "ferrimagnets," the term describing such compounds as the ferrites, a class of compounds with a general structural formula of divalent metals, such as copper, magnesium, nickel, or iron, combined with oxygen in the form $MOFe(2)O(3)$. These compounds exhibit a spontaneous magnetization at room temperature of a low value; that is, they develop a field by themselves without any outside influence. Above the Curie point, where materials lose their ability to hold a magnetic field, the magnetic susceptibility does not obey a simple Curie-Weiss law but rather follows a nonlinear curve when susceptibility is plotted against temperature. Néel resolved the problem by developing an unbalanced antiferromagnetic structure he called a "ferrimagnet."

In 1956, Néel's concepts were used by others on the garnet ferrites of the rare earths, which were found to be extremely useful in technological applications in high-frequency engineering. Equally important today is the discovery that ferromagnetic oxides and spinels can be tailored to suit the job based on the theoretical descriptions of the magnetic properties as proposed by Néel. Such materials are fundamental to core memories in computers, magnetic tapes, and the ideas of domain memories.

In the 1950's and 1960's, Néel was concerned primarily with theoretical problems, which have formed the main subjects of more than 150 publications. One series of his researches derived from the importance of the role of the internal demagnetizing fields in the properties of ferromagnetic substances. Néel developed a theory of magnetization for monocrystals based on the idea of the existence of various modes and phases of sublattices and interacting atoms. He showed that, in a perfect crystal, a number of phases coexist, the number being based on external conditions. He suggested that each phase was composed of what are known now as elementary domains, whose spontaneous counteractions, such as magnetizations, are aligned parallel. In simple cases, Néel was able to detail the subdivision of a ferromagnetic substance into those domains. The domain formation was found to have a special form, known as "Néel's spikes," around inclusions or cavities within the mineral, and a different form within very thin layers of walls of separation between the elementary domains (called Néel walls). Néel also published numerous papers on the theory of Rayleigh's laws, magnetic viscosity, internal dispersion fields, superantiferromagnetism, and hysteresis.

Besides his great discoveries in magnetism and solid-state physics, for which he received the Nobel Prize in Physics, Néel has also been of tremendous importance in the establishment of great research centers in Europe. In 1940, he went to Grenoble and established the world-famous laboratory there, which, in 1946, became one of the external laboratories of the Centre National de la Recherche Scientifique, expanding rapidly and giving rise to several new laboratories. Since 1946, he has been professor at Grenoble and the director of the laboratory, during which time Néel's school has become internationally recognized for excellence in magnetism research. Néel has been the director of the Centre d'Études Nucléaires de Grenoble, which he founded in 1956, and which has strong programs in neutron diffraction, crystal growth, Mossbauer studies, high-

tronic high-frequency oscillatory controls, transference of information at exceedingly high rates of data turnover, and the development of magnetic "memory cores" for modern computer technology.

Outside the area of physics proper, his hand has guided the development of successful laboratories in France, enhancing national prestige with developments in fields ranging from cryogenics to nuclear technology to the education of new generations of scientists. For his many contributions, he has been awarded numerous awards and honors, all graciously received, including his being named a Nobel laureate in physics.

strength magnetic fields, high-level pressure studies, and very low-temperature physics. In 1967, he was one of the principals in the decision to install the Franco-German high-flux reactor in Grenoble. He has been the director of the Polytechnic Institute of Grenoble, a member of the Consulting Committee on Higher Education, and a director of the Centre National de la Recherche Scientifique.

Summary

Louis-Eugène-Félix Néel's contributions to physics have been numerous and innovative; he has virtually rewritten the knowledge of how magnetic fields are generated, maintained, and modified in diverse natural materials. From his studies of permanent magnetism in ferromagnets, his discoveries have led to the understanding of how antiferromagnetism and ferrimagnetism work, and to further work on more quantum-related topics such as superantiferromagnetism. In physics alone, his ideas have made possible the development of a modern, quantum-level understanding and theory of atomic magnetism, a perception that has led to further advances in such diverse fields as aircraft and elec-

Bibliography

Burke, Harry. *Handbook of Magnetic Phenomena for Electronic Engineers.* New York: Van Nostrand, 1986. Providing an excellent overview, this book covers all the known phenomena associated with magnetism. Burke explores the diverse relationships between magnetism and the particles of nature. Measurement techniques are detailed. Thorough discussions, with well-conceived illustrations.

Cotterill, Rodney. *The Cambridge Guide to the Material World.* Cambridge and New York: Cambridge University Press, 1985. Providing a comprehensive survey, this work details the physics and chemistry of the crystalline and non-crystalline worlds on an atomic and superatomic level. The role of magnetism is intertwined throughout the text, being an integral element in explaining such topics as crystals, ceramics, conductors, and electrical interactions in living matter. Well illustrated, and well written.

D'Abro, A. *The Rise of the New Physics: Its Mathematical and Physical Theories.* New York: Dover, 1951. A detailed history of the rise of twentieth century physics, this two-volume set covers all the developments of physics in the twentieth century. Contemporaries of Néel, and developments in magnetism, are related to electrical and solid-state physics. Some difficult mathematics.

McKeehan, Louis W. *Magnets.* New Jersey: Van Nostrand, 1967. Deals with the history of magnets, from their first use in the ancient world to the sophisticated developments of modern times.

Massey, Harrie S. W. *The New Age in Physics.* 2d ed. London: Elek, and New York: Basic, 1966. Deals with the major topics explored in physics throughout the twentieth century. A detailed section on electrons views the magnetic properties of matter, with well-written descriptions of paramagnetism and ferromagnetism, and the science of magnetic properties of matter at low temperatures. Well written, with a wide range of interlocking topics.

Schneer, Cecil J. *The Evolution of Physical Science: Major Ideas from the Earliest Times to the Present.* New York: Grove Press, 1960; London: University Press of America, 1984. This work illustrates how science is performed, how scientific discoveries are made to bring order out of disorder. Provides a chapter on magnetism, giving basic reading for understanding Néel's ideas. Supplemental readings provided for each major scientific theme.

Arthur L. Alt

JAWAHARLAL NEHRU

Born: November 14, 1889; Allahabad, India
Died: May 27, 1964; New Delhi, India
Areas of Achievement: Government and politics
Contribution: Nehru led India through the difficult transition from colony to independence, providing the critical political skills for his close friend and mentor, Mahatma Gandhi. Upon India's being granted independence on August 15, 1947, Nehru became India's first prime minister. Following Gandhi's assassination in January, 1948, Nehru placed India firmly in a nonaligned, democratic path, ruling the country until his own death on May 27, 1964.

Early Life

Jawaharlal Nehru was born into an affluent, prominent Kashmiri Brahman family on November 14, 1889. Nehru's father was both a barrister and prominent politician, and Jawaharlal was groomed for a similar role from an early age. Given the family background, young Nehru was reared in an Anglophile atmosphere, tutored by a succession of British nannies and teachers.

At thirteen, under the influence of his tutor, Ferdinand Brooks, Nehru joined Annie Besant's Theosophical Society. In May, 1905, Nehru arrived at Harrow School in London to prepare for college. Following three years of study at Harrow, Nehru began his studies in 1907 at Trinity College, Cambridge. Following completion of his undergraduate studies, in 1910 Nehru moved to London to begin his bar studies at the Inner Temple.

Nehru returned to India in September, 1912. Given his family interests in Congress Party politics, young Nehru soon became involved in Allahabad's political scene, though at the time the Congress Party was fairly obscure. Nehru attended the Congress Party's Bankipore meeting as a delegate in October, 1912. He worked as a junior barrister under his father's supervision, but he was not drawn to the practice of law as a profession.

Nehru married Kamala Kaul, the daughter of an orthodox Brahman Kashmiri family, on February 8, 1916. In November, 1917, their daughter Indira was born, who would herself later become Prime Minister of India.

Life's Work

Despite India's contributions to the Allies in World War I, the nation was disappointed by Britain's subsequent Government of India Act of December 23, 1919, feeling that it fell far short of Indian desires for home rule. Nehru by this time had determined to work with Gandhi, who had returned to India from South Africa in January, 1915. Gandhi's satyagraha (nonviolence) campaign began in March, 1919, and Nehru fully supported it. Nehru believed that Gandhi's policies offered "a method of action which was straight and open and possibly effective." The relevance of Gandhi's policies was highlighted by the massacre on April 13, 1919, at Amritsar, when troops under General Reginald Dyer opened fire, killing hundreds of unarmed civilians. Nehru's father had continued to rise in Indian politics; in November, 1919, he was elected to the presidency of the Congress Party.

In June, 1920, Nehru met with a crowd of peasants who had marched fifty miles to Allahabad to acquaint the politicians with the appalling conditions of their lives. Nehru was sufficiently moved by their tales of exploitation by the large landowners that he began to interest himself in the plight of the peasantry. Nehru began to understand that in the countryside might be built a base of political support for a national movement, rather than largely relying on the cities. He quickly became very popular among the peasantry as a politician who, despite a background of affluence, was genuinely concerned with their problems. Nehru now busied himself with spreading Gandhi's satyagraha policies throughout the countryside.

British authorities were sufficiently vexed by the Nehrus' activities that on December 6, 1921, they took father and son into custody. Jawaharlal was released in March, 1922, when it was discovered that he had been wrongly convicted. Upon his release he worked to urge Indians to boycott foreign goods, resulting in his rearrest and sentencing on May 19, 1922, to a twenty-one-month prison term. Nehru was again released early, in January, 1923. Nehru was arrested yet again in September, 1923, but given a suspended sentence.

Nehru now believed that Congress Party policies needed a body of regular, disciplined volunteers; he accordingly founded the Hindustan Seva Dal in December, 1923, a body under congressional control that was to recruit and train patriotic Indians. Within the month, Nehru was formally elected General Secretary of Congress.

Nehru's wife's health began to deteriorate; she was diagnosed as having tuberculosis. In March, 1926, the entire family moved to Switzerland in order to facilitate her recovery. The Nehrus settled in Geneva; while Kamala underwent medical treatment, Jawaharlal busied himself observing the International Labor Office and the League of Nations, both headquartered in the city.

Nehru was a keen political observer of the European political scene and during his twenty-month stay in Europe, visited a number of the European capitals. During the summer of 1926, he visited Italy, observing the effects of Fascism there. During September he again went to England, while that autumn a trip to Berlin impressed him with German industrial might. In February, 1927, Nehru went to Brussels as an Indian National Congress Party representative to attend the International Congress of Oppressed Nationalities Against Imperialism. Nehru pursued some academic interests while in Switzerland, becoming enrolled in the University of Geneva's International Summer School. During November, 1927, Nehru and his family went to Moscow for the tenth anniversary celebrations of the establishment of Soviet power, giving Nehru a chance to observe firsthand the workings of a socialist state.

Upon his return to India in December, 1927, Nehru threw himself into Congress political work, immersing himself in it for the next two years. In answer to the hotly debated question of whether India should seek either dominion status within the British Empire or complete independence, Nehru at the Madras Congress in December, 1927, forwarded a resolution that this "Congress declares the goal of the Indian people to be complete National Independence." The same month he formed the first of his pressure groups within Congress, the Republican Party of Congress. Nehru contributed extensively to the popular press, particularly the *Hindu* and *Tribune*. His untiring efforts were rewarded with election to the presidency of Congress in 1929. At Congress' annual meeting that December, Nehru moved the main resolution, that Congress now stood for complete Indian independence. The resolution passed overwhelmingly.

Nehru's predicament was that he was drawn to both Gandhian principles of nonviolence and socialism. His interest in socialism had been strengthened by his visit to the Soviet Union, which he saw as a nonimperialist nation attempting to implement true equality. His closeness to Gandhi, however, made him constantly aware of the ethical strength embodied in his nonviolent principles.

Direct conflict with the British government erupted with Gandhi's famous March, 1930, "March to the Sea" to manufacture salt in violation of a government monopoly. Both Gandhi and Nehru spent much of the next few years in and out of British jails; Nehru served nearly four years during the period 1930-1935. While in prison he wrote *Glimpses of World History* (1934-1935), a series of letters to his daughter Indira that contemplated the entire sweep of human history. Nehru also wrote *Jawaharlal Nehru: An Autobiography* (1936) and many articles during this period of confinement. Nehru was to spend nearly nine years total in prison between 1921 and 1945, but he never allowed himself to become embittered by the experience; instead, he tried to put his time to good use.

A great personal loss was the death of his father on February 6, 1931. As his wife's health deteriorated, Nehru became more and more concerned; following an early release from prison in September, 1935, he flew immediately to Europe to be with his wife, who had earlier gone there for medical treatment. His wife died in Lausanne on February 29, 1936. With his wife's death, Nehru threw himself into political work. Following his return to India, by February, 1937, he had visited every province in India, giving him a broad perspective of the country's problems. Subsequent elections strengthened Congress' power. Congress now faced growing unrest from the Muslim League, led by Mohammad Ali Jinnah.

The next major issue facing Congress was the declaration by Great Britain on September 3, 1939, of Indian belligerency in the war against Adolf Hitler without Indian consent. As a member of the Working Committee, Nehru drew up a protest, but this was contrary to the emergency acts passed by the government, and on October 31, 1940, Nehru was immediately arrested and sentenced to four years' imprisonment. Despite the severity of the British crackdown, Nehru and five hundred Congress colleagues were released in early December, 1941.

Given the seriousness of the British position in the Far East with the Japanese advances since December, 1941, Churchill's government began to deal seriously with India. Sir Stafford Cripps arrived in India on March 22, 1942, with a compromise offer from His Majesty's government. In return for wholehearted Indian support of the war effort, India would achieve independence after the war. Nehru and Gandhi were arrested after rioting erupted in August, 1942, after the proposal was rejected. Nehru wrote *The Discovery of India* (1946) during this period of confinement, which lasted from August, 1942, to June, 1945.

Upon release, Nehru continued to agitate for complete independence. Clement Atlee's government had declared in December, 1945, its support for Indian independence, but increasing Muslim resistance to inclusion in a Hindu state made negotiations increasingly difficult. Nehru in August, 1946, was invited as the president of Congress to form an interim cabinet. In early 1947, the British government declared its intention to quit India by June, 1948, and the friction between the Muslim League under Jinnah and Congress increased.

India was formally granted independence on August 15, 1947. Fighting between the areas assigned to an independent Muslim Pakistan and a Hindu India forced a migration of hundreds of thousands and resulted in many deaths. Prime Minister Nehru and Gandhi attempted to stanch the bloodshed but were largely unsuccessful. Gandhi himself was assassinated on January 25, 1948.

Nehru's troubles as prime minister were immediately increased in 1947-1948 by the problem of conflicting Indian-Pakistani claims to Kashmir, with firefights occurring along the disputed frontier. India also experienced increasing tension with China, especially after China's invasion of Tibet in October, 1950. After a revolt in Tibet failed in 1959, the Dalai Lama with 100,000 followers found sanctuary in India. Chinese and Indian troops subsequently fought a series of fierce border skirmishes in the autumn of 1962.

India's postcolonial domestic problems were immense. In order to improve the economy, Nehru's government on April 1, 1951, inaugurated its first Five Year Plan, with an emphasis on increasing agricultural output. The government also instituted a Community Development Program to raise the living standard of the countryside. In 1955, the Untouchability Act was passed to attempt to ease life for India's most degraded citizens.

Nehru's popularity remained high; he was reelected in March, 1957, and to a third five-year term in March, 1962. Nehru's nonaligned stance slowly won for him grudging admiration, even in the fiercely anticommunist United States. He visited the United States in 1949 and 1956; President

Dwight D. Eisenhower returned the courtesy in 1960. His emphasis on India's need for both democracy and socialism has increasingly proven a model for the Third World since Nehru's death on May 27, 1964. With brief exceptions, his descendants ruled India up until 1989.

Summary

Jawaharlal Nehru had an influence far outside India's borders. In pursuing democratic, nonaligned policies, Nehru's India provided a pattern for the newly emerging postcolonial nations of Africa and Asia. With Gandhi's untimely death, Nehru was the one Indian political leader who had been sufficiently closely associated with the Mahatma to be accepted as his most capable disciple and successor. In the postwar, postcolonial era, Nehru, as leader of the world's largest democracy, faced the staggering problems brought about by the ending of the British Raj. Despite Nehru's cosmopolitan background and his close friendship with many Englishmen, he did not want to turn an independent India into an Asian replica of Great Britain.

Nehru's acute observations of both the European and Soviet political systems led him to attempt to combine the best features of both in India. Given India's industrial weakness, Nehru believed that a centrally planned economy would provide the most immediate results. In politics, Nehru believed that the British parliamentary system and a multiparty structure provided a better model for India than the Soviet one-party state. Nehru was also an innovator in international relations. Nehru attempted to draw closer to other Asian states attempting to maintain an equal distance between the American and Soviet blocs, believing that India's immense size made it the natural leader in south Asia.

The political dynasty that Nehru founded remained remarkably stable in Indian politics. When his grandson, Rajiv Gandhi, resigned as prime minister, on November 29, 1989, a Nehru had ruled India for all but five of its forty-two years of independence from Britain. While Rajiv was not able to carry on that heritage, his mother, Indira Gandhi, governed India from January, 1966, with a brief break in 1977-1979, until her assassination by Sikh extremists on October 31, 1984. For whatever future direction the nation may take, many of Nehru's values continue to guide the country's destiny.

Bibliography

Brecher, Michael. *Nehru: A Political Biography.* London and New York: Oxford University Press, 1959. A massive, scholarly examination of Nehru's life and political philosophy. The work is especially valuable for its setting of Nehru's life in the larger context of India's resurgent nationalism under British rule from the nineteenth century onward.

Collins, Larry, and Dominique Lapierre. *Freedom at Midnight.* Rev. ed. New York: HarperCollins, 1997. Based on extensive use of both primary and secondary sources, this work is a very readable account of India's push toward independence and the immediate postindependence era. The book succeeds in putting Nehru's accomplishments in the larger perspective of twentieth century Indian politics, though the account ends with Gandhi's assassination.

Gopal, Sarvepali. *Jawaharlal Nehru: A Biography.* 3 vols. London: Cape, and Cambridge, Mass.: Harvard University Press, 1976-1984. As one of India's most respected historians, Gopal was chosen to write Nehru's official biography and enjoyed access to Nehru's papers and associates. While the work is extremely thorough, it suffers from a slight lack of relative objectivity about its subject.

Nanda, B.R. *Jawaharlal Nehru: Rebel and Statesman.* Oxford and New York: Oxford University Press, 1995. A balanced profile of Nehru.

―――. "Nehru and the British." *Modern Asian Studies* 30, no. 2 (May, 1996). Nanda focuses on Nehru's life, India's independence, and the nation's relations with the British empire.

Nehru, Jawaharlal. *Jawaharlal Nehru: An Autobiography.* London: Bodley Head, 1937; New York: Oxford University Press, 1985. The bulk of this work was written by Nehru during his confinement June, 1934-February, 1935, with additional material added later by the author to cover events up to 1940. The tone is both thoughtful and reserved, and is marked by a remarkable lack of rancor toward the British.

Pandey, B. N. *Nehru.* London: Macmillan, and New York: Stein and Day, 1976. Pandey, a member of the University of London's School of Oriental and African Studies, conducted extensive interviews in India with members of Nehru's family, friends, and fellow politicians.

Shorter, Bani. *Nehru: A Voice for Mankind.* New York: Day, 1970. A fairly intimate biography of Nehru that serves as an introduction to the man, his work, and the history of India. Includes an index and photographs.

John C. K. Daly

WALTHER HERMANN NERNST

Born: June 25, 1864; Briesen, Prussia
Died: November 18, 1941; near Bad Muskau,
  Germany
Area of Achievement: Chemistry
Contribution: Nernst won the Nobel Prize in
  Chemistry in 1920 for his statement of the third
  law of thermodynamics. Yet his equation for the
  electrode potential of a voltaic cell is his best-
  known contribution and appears in nearly all
  general chemistry texts.

Early Life

Walther Hermann Nernst, born in 1864, in the
town of Briesen, in what was then Prussia, was not
from a family of scientists. In fact, he displayed a
talent for the arts and maintained a lifelong interest
in the theater. Yet he was inspired by the chemistry
master at the *Gymnasium*, where he finished at the
top of his class, to become what is now called a
physical chemist. During his early school and undergraduate years, the German chemical industry
became world-dominant in dyestuffs and pharmaceuticals. The discovery by Friedrich Wöhler in
1828 that urea could be synthesized from inorganic
materials had inspired German scientists to design
chemical processes to manufacture products previously obtainable only from biological sources.
There developed a strong relationship between
German industry and the universities to foster this
revolutionary notion of basic research aimed at the
creation of new products. Industry established and
maintained its own research laboratories for the development of these products. The professors from
these technical universities did consulting work,
which furthered the opportunities for graduating
scientists and engineers. Capital was provided and
controlled by the various German governments
through ministers of higher education, who believed strongly in this emerging pattern. It was in
this atmosphere that Nernst began his career in
higher learning.

It is important to note that there was an increased
emphasis on basic research as Nernst began his undergraduate education. Otherwise, Nernst might
never have been able to devote almost his entire career to the fundamental research that brought him
to such important discoveries. Much freedom was
enjoyed by university students of that time. They
attended lectures and laboratory sessions at a variety of institutions, if they chose, until they believed
themselves to be qualified to sit for examinations.
Nernst was no exception to this practice. He attended lectures at Zurich, Berlin, Graz, and
Würzburg, and he was attracted to the outstanding
scientists of the day. Nernst first began research at
Graz in 1886 under Ludwig Boltzmann, a champion of the atomistic viewpoint. Nernst soon moved
to Würzburg, where he continued his research under Friedrich Kohlrausch on electrical currents in
solutions.

Life's Work

Ultimately Nernst was to become the world's authority in the field of electrical currents in solution.
Michael Faraday had suggested in his publications
of the mid-nineteenth century that ions were produced by electric currents in solution. Svante Arrhenius, however, suggested that these ions could
be produced by the dissociation of a salt in forming
a solution. These ions then were free to move between electrodes as current carriers, suggesting an
electrical nature of salts before dissociation. That
is, the nature of chemical bonds was somehow
electrical. At the invitation of Friedrich Ostwald,
Nernst accepted a position at the new Physico-
Chemical Institute in Leipzig. He continued to
study the nature of ions in solution, but he now began to include the ideas of Hermann von Helmholtz and Rudolf Clausius and to investigate the
behavior of ions in a chemical reaction in solution.
Helmholtz and Clausius had clarified the concept
of spontaneity in a physical process as related to
the external work capability of the system. Nernst
realized that the idea of external work capability of
a chemical system is related to the electrode potential of the reaction embodied in the configuration
of a voltaic cell. A voltaic cell is superbly adapted
to demonstrate this relation of external work and
the electrical potential generated between ions in
relation to an electrode. The electrode either do-
nates or accepts the electron charge while, perhaps,
it is even involved in the reaction. Nernst supplied
the equation that related the concentrations of ions
to the external work capability of a cell, which is a
means of separating a reaction into donating and
accepting cell halves. The overall cell potential, as
a combination of these half-cell potentials, is a
measure of the chemical potential of the reaction
and hence the external work capability. This external work capability has since become known as

free energy. The free energy change in a chemical reaction is related to the equilibrium constant for the reaction, or the point of quilibrium as it was then known.

This research earned for Nernst a lectureship at Leipzig. In a few years, however, he accepted a lectureship at Göttingen. The attraction was a promise of his own department and eventually an assistant professorship. Göttingen had a very high reputation among German universities. More offers prompted the creation of a chair of physical chemistry at Göttingen for Nernst, and Nernst accepted in 1894. During his time at Göttingen, Nernst wrote a physical chemistry text entitled *Theoretische Chemie vom Standpunkte der Avogadroschen Regel und der Thermodynamik* (1893; *Theoretical Chemistry from the Standpoint of Avogadro's Rule and Thermodynamics*, 1895), which was widely used and went through ten editions. He remained there for fifteen years, during which time he also met and married Emma Lohmeyer, the daughter of a local physician, and together they had five children. They eventually settled into a mansion that was provided by the Ministry of Education. Directly connected was a new electrochemical laboratory of which Nernst became the director. The Nernsts hosted many social functions, many of which were for the research assistants at the laboratory. There were as many as forty young people there working for doctorates, and an extension was eventually added to keep up with the work in progress.

Nernst was compelled to leave Germany because of a war-crimes scare following World War I. After returning to Germany, he moved to Berlin, where new labs were under construction from the rubble left after the war. The prominence of Germany in academics was manifested by a succession of Nobel Prizes in the years following the war. This dominance was to last for many years. A revolution was taking place, and Nernst was at the center of it.

Alfred Bertholet's explanation of chemical spontaneity in 1867, although of profound impact, was not complete. Bertholet said that spontaneous chemical reactions are those that are exothermic. This theory required much additional work to define the concepts that made it possible to formulate a complete statement of chemical spontaneity. Statements by Sadi Carnot (1824) and Clausius (1850) were crucial to the equations of Helmholtz and Oliver Gibbs. Carnot's cycle defines a heat engine, operating between two specified tempera-

tures, that converts a given amount of heat into the maximum amount of useful work possible. This heat engine applies to physical as well as chemical processes. Clausius introduced the entropy term S, which is a disorder function that defines the unavailable energy in the process of heat energy conversion to useful work. The equations of Helmholtz and Gibbs were to follow. They state that this maximum amount of useful work is the difference between the total heat energy and that amount that is unavailable for useful work. Nernst's heat theorem states that, in the equations of Helmholtz and Gibbs, the total heat energy in a chemical reaction and the maximum work available are identical at the absolute zero of temperature. Nernst stated that the specific heat of substances in the condensed phases would become zero at the absolute zero of temperature and therefore S would become zero. With a better understanding of absolute zero, the heat theorem became the third law of thermodynamics: The entropy, S, of a substance (in a perfect crystalline state) may become zero at the absolute zero of temperature, if the absolute of temperature can be reached. S means disorder and thus it is what goes to zero at the absolute zero of temperature instead of energy. It follows, then, that S has a finite positive value at temperatures above absolute zero. Chemists were then able to determine the free energy changes for chemical reactions ata variety of temperatures. This permits the calculation of the equilibrium distribution of mass between reactants and products.

After having received the Nobel Prize for his heat theorem, Nernst spent two years as president of the National Physical Laboratory. He did not like this assignment and returned to the academic life as head of the physics department at the University of Berlin. During his last years, he purchased a one-thousand-acre estate at Zibelle. He held bird shoots and began to raise carp in some of the ponds available on the grounds. The Nernsts permanently retired to Zibelle in 1933, though Nernst maintained an apartment in Berlin for use during his frequent attendance at university functions. He suffered a heart attack, from which he never recovered, and died on November 18, 1941.

Summary

The impact of Walther Nernst on the evolving science of physical chemistry cannot be overemphasized. His contribution to thermodynamics is well established. A knowledge of the equilibrium distribution constants for chemical reactions is of inestimable value to the design of commercial manufacturing processes. Nernst also wrote the equation for predicting the potential of a voltaic cell in terms of ion concentrations. This equation is essential to the prediction of spontaneity of chemical reactions that can be expressed as electron exchange.

Nernst also sponsored a discussion group every Friday afternoon in his laboratory in the University of Berlin. The group included world-class physicists and chemists such as Albert Einstein as well as research students. Recent publications and new research findings were brought in for discussion. Nernst's sponsorship of these weekly colloquia may be his one under-recognized contribution to the revolution in physics and chemistry in the early twentieth century.

Bibliography

Atkins, P. W. *The Second Law.* New York: Freeman, 1984. This book is excellent for the lay reader, outlining the physical meaning of entropy and its relation to chemical reactions. The author uses the steam engine as an example of the workings of the second law of thermodynamics.

Glasstone, Samuel. *Thermodynamics for Chemists.* New York: Van Nostrand, 1947. Author provides the reader with an excellent reference to the third law of thermodynamics that is closer to that of the chemists of Nernst's time.

Mahan, Bruce H. *Elementary Chemical Thermodynamics.* New York: Benjamin, 1963. This text contains an excellent mathematical discussion of the second law of thermodynamics. Discusses the molecular interpretation of the third law and its relation to the specific heat of substances. The reader is introduced to the voltaic cell as the vehicle for illustrating the second law as Nernst did in his Nobel address.

Mendelssohn, Kurt. *The World of Walther Nernst: The Rise and Fall of German Science, 1864-1941.* London: Macmillan, and Pittsburgh: University of Pittsburgh Press, 1973. Provides a thorough portrayal of Nernst's life against the background of the spectacular growth of German science. The development of the university-industry reciprocal relationship is examined.

Pimentel, George C., and Richard D. Spratley. *Understanding Chemistry.* San Francisco: Holden Day, 1971. Chapter 9 offers an excellent step-by-step derivation of the first law of thermodynamics. The voltaic cell is used as a means of introducing the second law. Chapter 10 describes the relationship between free energy and equilibrium.

Robert E. Whipple

PABLO NERUDA
Neftalí Ricardo Reyes Basoalto

Born: July 12, 1904; Parral, Chile
Died: September 23, 1973; Santiago, Chile
Area of Achievement: Literature
Contribution: Neruda is the greatest modern poet to have combined a personal and lyrical mode with a political voice in a way that spoke to and for a popular mass readership. Rooted in Chile, his poetry has a universal human significance marked by the award of the Nobel Prize in 1971.

Early Life

Pablo Neruda was born Neftalí Ricardo Reyes Basoalto, in the small town of Parral in southern Chile, on July 12, 1904, the son of José del Carmen Reyes and Rosa de Basoalt. His mother, a school-teacher, died of tuberculosis not long after he was born. Neruda began writing poetry at the local schools but kept it hidden from his schoolmates and his relations, who were mainly agricultural or manual workers, and his father, a tough railroad worker. The family moved to Temuco in 1906, and Neruda grew up in a frontier atmosphere, becoming familiar with the forests and the native Indians who inhabited them. His father remarried, and Neruda grew close to his stepmother, a quiet, unassuming peasant woman named Trinidad Candia Marverde. The headmaster of the local school was the poet Gabriela Mistral, who encouraged the literary talent she saw in the boy. Neruda's reading at this time was eager and indiscriminate. He grew to be a tall, slim youth and began translating Baudelaire and winning various local poetry prizes.

In 1921, he left high school and went to the teachers' college in Santiago (the capital of Chile) but much preferred talking about literature in the cafés to studying French. He had submitted his earliest poems for magazine publication when he was only fifteen, signing himself "Pablo Neruda." His range of literary acquaintances widened, but his early poetry, *Crepusculario* (1923), remained provincial and sentimental. At twenty, however, he published *Veinte poemas de amor y una canción desesperada* (1924; *Twenty Love Poems and a Song of Despair*, 1969, 1976) and established his reputation as a love poet.

Neruda worked fanatically, earning money writing articles for newspapers and journals and writing translations. He edited his own magazine,

wrote short stories and an immature episodic novel, and began work on a larger sequence, *Residencia en la tierra* (3 vols., 1933, 1935, 1947; *Residence on Earth and Other Poems*, 1946, 1973). Yet his love affairs left him unhappy, and he remained poor. It was not until 1927 that Neruda successfully gained an appointment with Chile's Ministry of Foreign Affairs and became the honorary consul to Rangoon, Burma. He was neither a trained diplomat nor an outstanding linguist, but, as a gregarious, charismatic, presentable, and accomplished writer who had a proven ability to move his readers, he fulfilled the requirements of an ambassador for his country.

Life's Work

The sense of political solidarity that Neruda came to affirm was gained through years of isolation and a continuous balancing of powerful emotions of love, with rich, dark, sometimes surreal journeys of the imagination. Personal loneliness and a fond memory of his home were counterpointed in his verse. He traveled to various parts of the world on his first trip to the East and sent articles back to the Santiago daily newspaper *La Nación*. In Burma he encountered professionally the remnants of ancient cultures and the continuing exploitation of colonial occupation, and his personal anxieties found a counterpart in society at large. He attempted to maintain contact with friends and writers in Chile and was published in Spain, but in Burma he was depressed.

While visiting India to cover a political meeting in Calcutta in 1929, the enormous crowds that he encountered in the subcontinent brought him to greater depths of despair. He continued writing the *Residence on Earth* poems. In 1930, Neruda became Consul to the Dutch East Indies and married a Dutch woman, Maria Antonieta Haagenar. In 1932, they returned, briefly, to Chile. Though Neruda's poems were by now being published and re-published, they would not bring him a living wage. In 1933, he took up another consular appointment in Buenos Aires and in 1934 yet another in Barcelona. His bureaucratic experience had not made him a happy man, but now things were to change. He moved on to Madrid, where the Spanish poet Federico García Lorca (whom he had met in Bue-

nos Aires) introduced him to a new public. He separated from his first wife and later was happily married to Delia del Carril, with whom he remained until the 1950's. His great work *Residence on Earth* was now published, and an international audience was responding to Neruda with vital enthusiasm. Concurrently, Neruda was becoming more thoroughly intellectually politicized, as he was introduced to the social struggles that underlay the Spanish Civil War. García Lorca, who had become a friend of Neruda, was murdered by the Fascists, and Neruda found comradeship with the French left-wing Surrealist writers Louis Aragon and Paul Éluard, and with the Peruvian Cesar Vallejo. He allied himself with the political struggle of the Spanish Republic.

Neruda returned to Chile, and through 1937 and 1938 supported the struggle of the Spanish Republic and the left-wing Chilean government, giving lectures and readings. He began work on a long poetic sequence that was to comprise his greatest work, *Canto general* (1950). In 1939, he traveled to Paris to assist the Spanish Republican refugees in flight to Chile.

Neruda's life continued to be peripatetic. He returned to Chile in 1940 and went on to Mexico. He became more deeply acquainted with meso-America, traveling throughout the Caribbean, Guatemala, and Cuba. Though he wrote a "Song to Stalingrad" in 1942, he became fascinated by the fate of man in the Americas, and a climb to the ruined Inca city of Machu Picchu, on October 22, 1943, resulted in one of the most profound meditative poems of the century, a key poem in the *Canto general* sequence: "Alturas de Machu Picchu" (1946; "The Heights of Machu Picchu," 1966). When the poem was written, in 1945, Neruda had returned to Chile, been elected a senator, won the National Literary Prize, and officially joined the Communist Party. The political forces of the right were growing more powerful, and the leftist President González Videla became a puppet for international monopolists. Neruda, who had at first supported Videla, was now seen as a dangerous rebel. The Communist Party was made illegal and Neruda, to avoid arrest, took refuge among the rural and urban proletariat of the country before fleeing on horseback to Mexico. The poetry of *Canto general* that was written through 1948-1949 exhibits much of the rage and protest of the persecuted poet.

Neruda made his way to Paris and the Soviet Union. His poetry had by now been published in countries throughout the world. He was internationally honored. He returned to Mexico, where *Canto general* was published (with illustrations by the great mural artists Diego Rivera and David Alfaro Siqueiros), and though he was awarded global public recognition (the Soviet edition of *Canto general* ran to 250,000 copies), he was still banned in his native Chile. He met Matilde Urrutia in Mexico, and a stunning series of love poems, *Los versos del Capitán* (1952; *The Captain's Verses*, 1972), followed. After a worldwide reading tour, Neruda and Matilde heard that he was no longer under arrest in Chile. He returned there in 1952.

His poetry turned now to the commonplace and everyday objects of the *Odas elementales* (1954; *The Elemental Odes*, 1961), simple poems of praise and delight that pleased critics and general readers of his work alike. He was equally acclaimed in capitalist and communist worlds. He separated from Delia del Carril in 1955 and remained in love with Matilde Urrutia for the rest of his life. He did not stop traveling: to South America, the Soviet Union, China, and elsewhere. His vanity was appealed to wherever he went, and his gregarious love of life was indulged alongside his enthusiasm for collecting things. Royalties from book sales at last began to bring him some money, and he built a house on Isla Negra that became his favorite retreat, filled with the books and things he had collected over the years. He continued to produce poetry of great tenderness and exquisite sensuality, such as *Estravagario* (1958; *Extravagaria*, 1974) and *Cien sonetos de amor* (1959; *One Hundred Love Sonnets*, 1986). He also began work on his autobiographical *Confieso que he vivido: Memorias* (*Memoirs*, 1977), published posthumously in 1974.

In the late 1960's, Neruda began writing for the theater, with a Spanish translation of William Shakespeare's *Romeo and Juliet* and *Fulgor y muerte de Joaquín Murieta* (1967; *Splendor and Death of Joaquin Murieta*, 1972). He also maintained his political activities, becoming the Communist candidate for the presidency of Chile. He renounced his candidacy, however, to campaign in support of his friend Salvador Allende. After Allende's victory, Neruda, although suffering from cancer of the prostate, agreed once again to act as Chilean ambassador to France.

Neruda was awarded the Nobel Prize in 1971, and his acceptance speech presents a moving vision of a future world free of exploitation. He was seriously ill, though, and returned to Chile for the last time in 1972, to find his country poised upon disaster. Opposition to Allende from both outside and inside Chile was growing, and Neruda himself was becoming weaker. He attempted to rally friends abroad to support the Chilean government and wrote a vehement diatribe calling for the extermination of Richard M. Nixon. He was also working on his memoirs and the eight books of poetry he had planned to publish on his seventieth birthday. Disaster overtook the country, however, with Allende assassinated, the government broken, and a military dictatorship instated under Augosto Pinochet Ugarte. Neruda died in a hospital in Santiago, on September 23, 1973.

Summary

Since his involvement with the Republicans during the Spanish Civil War in the 1930's until his death, Pablo Neruda's political commitment and personal sincerity were constant, unwavering even as the popularity of his work developed internationally. His loneliness drove him into himself, to explore his own imagination and his past, while the solidarity that he felt with other living things drove him to celebrate life with an infectious enthusiasm and an effusive sense of riotous abundance. Poetry was not the pursuit of an elite for Neruda. In *Canto general*, he took his beginnings and his bearings from Chile but opened out to hymn the Americas in general, in all their detail, animals, flowers, history, and politics, and opened further to consider their place in the global context.

A hugely prolific poet, Neruda was the most magniloquent Latin American writer to span the literature of the century, beginning in provincial Chile, centering on Europe, then returning to take his place on the global stage. Even those who consider his political beliefs misguided or naïve grant the earthly vitality and vivacious sensuality of his celebrations and the profundity of his meditations.

Neruda believed that poetry was as essential for human life as bread and that it was not the property of scholars or booksellers but the inheritance of humanity. In the end, his accommodative vision contemplated the certainty of his own death, but he continued to write, leaving numerous posthumous works. He was a love poet, a public poet, and a poet of the natural world. He identified himself with his native place, but he aligned himself with all mankind.

Bibliography

Boraiko, Allen A. "A Poet's Sea Wrack." *Sea Frontiers* 39, no. 5 (September-October, 1993). Discusses Neruda's fascination with the sea, which is evident in his work and his life.

Costa, René de. *The Poetry of Pablo Neruda.* Cambridge, Mass.: Harvard University Press, 1979. A good introductory critical study of Neruda's poetic achievement as a whole.

Durán, Manuel, and Margery Safir. *Earth Tones: The Poetry of Pablo Neruda.* Bloomington: Indiana University Press, 1981. A detailed survey of individual books of Neruda's poems, including the posthumous works. Separate areas covered include Neruda as a poet of nature and of the erotic, the public, and the personal.

Gallagher, D. P. "Pablo Neruda." In *Modern Latin American Literature.* London and New York: Oxford University Press, 1973. A judicious essay discussing Neruda's relation to modernism, his love poetry, and his communism that suggests a link between *The Elemental Odes* and the mode of "magic realism" favored by other Latin American writers.

Riess, Frank. *The Word and the Stone: Language and Imagery in Neruda's "Canto general."* London: Oxford University Press, 1972. An extremely useful in-depth study of the forms and imagery in Neruda's most ambitious poetic sequence.

Rodman, Selden. "Pablo Neruda's Chile." In *South America of the Poets.* New York: Hawthorn, 1970. A helpful essay, with illustrations by Bill Negrón, introducing Neruda's native land.

Willard, Nancy. *Testimony of the Invisible Man: William Carlos Williams, Francis Ponge, Rainer Maria Rilke, Pablo Neruda.* Columbia: University of Missouri Press, 1970. This book is particularly useful as it considers Neruda in the company of three other internationally respected modern authors and thereby highlights his individual characteristics.

Young-Moo, Kim. "Pablo Neruda and Today's Korean Poetry." *Korea Journal* 36, no. 2 (Summer 1996). Focuses on Neruda and the influence his poetry had on Koreans in the 1980s, many of whom became poets in order to comment on social issues and government corruption.

Katherine Kearney Maynard

PIER LUIGI NERVI

Born: June 21, 1891; Sondrio, Italy
Died: January 9, 1979; Rome, Italy
Area of Achievement: Architecture
Contribution: Nervi was actually an engineer, but one whose goal was to create aesthetically pleasing structures. His importance lies in the fact that he was among the first in modern times to re-unite architecture and engineering.

Early Life

Pier Luigi Nervi was born in the village of Sondrio in the Italian Alps to the local postmaster and his wife. Nervi remained thoroughly Italian throughout his life, and his work symbolizes the confluence of two major factors: his upbringing amid the aesthetic richness of Italy and his engineering education. Significantly, some of Nervi's first major works were large domes that may be said to have been influenced by earlier domes such as St. Peter's in Rome and the dome of the cathedral of Santa Maria del Fiore in Florence. As a youngster, he attended the Ginnasio-Liceo Muratori in Modena. In 1913, Nervi was graduated from the Civil Engineering School of Bologna, where he learned the basic principles of structures (and at the same time satisfied his childhood fascination with mechanical things). His schooling, however, treated art and science as two distinct endeavors—an approach that seemed illogical to Nervi.

Upon graduating from Bologna, Nervi gained employment as a civil engineer with the Societa per Costruzioni Cementizie. The Societa provided him with much experience in reinforced concrete, a structural material that he would eventually master. Nervi remained with the Societa until 1923 (his tenure having been interrupted by World War I when he served with the Italian Army's Engineering Corps), when he left in order to work full-time in a firm he had founded in 1920. As a partner in this firm, Nervi and Nebbiosi, he built several structures that drew international attention for their originality and beauty.

It is significant that Nervi began his career just as new materials and a new architectural movement were gaining momentum. During the first decade of the twentieth century, reinforced concrete gained recognition as an important new structural material through the works of François Hennebique, Auguste Perret, Robert Maillart, and others. Furthermore, by the early 1920's the outlines of the modern architectural movement were being clarified by pioneers such as Walter Gropius, Ludwig Mies van der Rohe, and Le Corbusier. In April, 1924, shortly after joining Nervi and Nebbiosi on a full-time basis, Nervi married Irene Calosi, and they eventually had four sons, Antonio, Mario, Carlo, and Vittorio.

Life's Work

One of Nervi's first major works was the Municipal Stadium in Florence. As with all of Nervi's work, the stadium design began with a concern for economy, and Nervi won the design competition because of the low cost of his project. The outstanding feature of the stadium is the grandstand roof: a shell extending over the seating on cantilevered beams. It clearly demonstrates, at an early point in Nervi's career, his ability to achieve both beauty and economy with reinforced concrete.

In 1932, Nervi joined with a cousin to form a new firm. This firm won a competition announced by the Italian Air Force in 1935 to build a series of airplane hangars. The hangars, as designed by Nervi, were to become landmarks of reinforced concrete construction. The problem posed by the hangars was how to span an area 330 feet by 135 feet with no internal supports. Nervi chose to make a vaulted roof with concrete ribs, which were cast in place and then covered with tiles. One problem with this type of construction was the vast amount of timber required for the concrete forms. Nervi solved that problem in a second series of hangars that he built beginning in 1940, by using precast concrete ribs for much of the roof's span. Driven by the need for greater economy in both material and timbers, Nervi had thus created a light but incredibly strong vaulted structure, which only required a roof covering and walls in order to make a hangar. When the Germans destroyed these hangars by demolishing the supporting columns, many of the roofs remained intact after they fell.

In the mid-1940's, Nervi developed an important new type of reinforced concrete, which he called "ferro-cement." Ferro-cement consists of several layers of fine steel mesh sprayed with a cement mortar. For heavier uses, it sometimes has reinforcing rods between the mesh layers. Ferro-cement is very thin—slightly thicker than the mesh itself—and its great strength and elasticity make it ideal for constructing thin shells and slabs. Since the mortar can be sprayed directly onto the mesh, structures can often be built of ferro-cement without the use of forms. In cases in which Nervi did use forms, he made them of ferro-cement instead of wood, thus giving him greater flexibility in shaping cast concrete pieces.

In the late 1940's, Nervi was faced with a new challenge: to build Salone B, 243 feet by 310 feet, for the Turin Exposition Hall of 1948-1949. Again, Nervi's was the most economical proposal submitted. He had only eight months in which to complete the building, and he used ferro-cement to help him meet that demanding schedule. To form the roof vaulting, he made prefabricated sections of corrugated ferro-cement, which were then lifted into place. The troughs and peaks of the corrugated pieces were then filled with cast-in-place reinforced concrete to form integral ribs—the main load-bearing structural members. Thus, the roof vaulting was a combination of ferro-cement and reinforced concrete.

For the half-dome at one end of the hall, Nervi introduced another innovation. He used precast, panlike units made of ferro-cement, which created troughs between them when laid side by side. The units had been cast in concrete molds, which had been built from a model of the half-dome. The precast units, in the shape of diamonds, were then lifted into place and supported by scaffolding while the roof was completed. Into the troughs between the units, Nervi laid reinforced concrete in order to form the supporting ribs of the half-dome. Thus, the reinforced concrete ribs together with the precast units formed the entirety of the half-dome. Nervi also used this system on Salone C of the Turin Exposition Hall and later on a number of other domes, vaults, and ceilings. In addition to being light, strong, and easy to build, the crossing ribs and diamond-shaped panels created a pleasing visual effect.

In addition to his busy schedule with these and other projects, Nervi began teaching in 1947. He joined the faculty of architecture at the University of Rome and remained there until 1961. During the academic year 1961-1962, he was the Charles E. Norton Professor at Harvard. Nervi's diligence allowed him to maintain this demanding schedule. He always started work promptly at 8:30 A.M. and only took time out to teach or to visit one of his building sites.

In 1952, Nervi devised yet another construction technique for use in building the Tobacco Factory

in Bologna. The five-story building was to be large in measure and thus represented a significant challenge. Nervi once again won the design competition on the basis of the great economy of his design, which was, in turn, based on movable forms. Avoiding a costly timber framework, Nervi made ferro-cement forms that resembled inverted rectangular pans. The forms rested on wheeled scaffolding that could be raised and lowered by hydraulic jacks. The troughs between adjacent forms created strengthening ribs in the floor, when filled with cement. After the concrete pillars for a given floor were in place, the builders raised the ferro-cement forms into place and poured the reinforced concrete floor on top of them. Once the concrete had hardened sufficiently, the builders lowered the forms and wheeled them to the next bay. Nervi carried this time- and money-saving technique one step further in the Gatti wool factory in Rome. In this building, the forms were shaped so as to locate the strengthening ribs along the lines of greatest stress. This technique added to both the efficiency and the beauty of the building.

The 1960 Olympics in Rome created for Nervi the opportunity to achieve some of his most spectacular structural engineering—but not at the cost of aesthetics. Nervi designed three structures for the Olympics: the Palazzetto dello Sport, the Palazzo dello Sport, and the Stadio Flaminio. The Palazzetto, though smallest, has perhaps the strongest impact from both inside and outside. The flute-edged roof of the Palazzetto was constructed in typical Nervi style. He used precast, diamond-shaped units to form the shell of the roof. As in some of his earlier structures, these pieces were joined by cast-in-place ribs that gently curved outward from the center in left- and right-handed curves, thus intersecting to create the diamond pattern. The ceiling's visual effect was one of a light and elegant webbing. The ribs carry their load to Y-shaped buttresses, which also carry the line of the shell to the ground. The outside view of the larger Palazzo is spoiled, however, by a gallery all the way around it which conceals the lines of the structure. Inside, however, Nervi created a much different look from that in the Palazzetto by using precast, corrugated sections (resembling those in the Turin Exhibition Hall) which radiate out from the center. As in the Turin Exhibition Hall, he filled the troughs and peaks in the corrugation with cast-in-place concrete. Although the outside surface of the corrugations have been covered in order to create a smooth surface, the inner view is quite striking.

Pier Luigi Nervi received many honorary degrees and awards during his lifetime, including honorary membership in the American Academy and National Institute of Arts and Letters (1957). He died at the age of eighty-seven in his home in Rome.

Summary

The two primary motivating factors in Pier Luigi Nervi's designs were economy and art. He produced his first major work during the Great Depression and remained quite busy throughout World War II and after. The resultant search for economy not only won many design competitions but also produced new construction techniques and forms. His concern for art probably stemmed from his upbringing in Italy and his consciousness of the many beautiful structures to be found there.

Nervi achieved his desired economic and aesthetic ends largely through the repeated use of three structural elements: precast corrugated beams, precast ceiling panels, and ferro-cement. Using these elements in combination with techniques of his own device (such as forms on movable scaffolding), Nervi avoided the use of expensive timber forms and framework, speeded construction time, and gave himself much freedom in shaping the lines of a structure. In the process, he also created very light but strong roof spans, enclosing and beautifying large indoor spaces. By always striving for economy and beauty, Nervi reached a high point in building with concrete. Although trained as an engineer, he did not let mathematics and scientific theories dominate his work. Through his buildings, he proved that structure can be art.

Bibliography

Huxtable, Ada Louise. "Geodetic and Plastic Expressions Abroad." *Progressive Architecture*, June, 1953: 111-116. This brief article summarizes Nervi's contributions to the field of structural engineering, emphasizing ferro-cement. It also summarizes some of his most important works (as of 1953) and illustrates one of his hangars, the Gatti wool factory, and Salone B of the Turin Exposition Hall.

———. *Pier Luigi Nervi.* London: Mayflower, and New York: Braziller, 1960. Part of the Masters of World Architecture series, this short book provides a concise, yet thorough account of Nervi's life, work, and place among the world's architects. Roughly one-half of the book is devoted to photographs and drawings of his major works, both in progress and completed. The book contains a complete list of his works and bibliographies of books and articles written by and about him.

Nervi, Pier Luigi. *Structures.* Translated by Giuseppina and Mario Salvadori. New York: Dodge, 1956. In this book, Nervi explained in his own words, clearly and simply, the principles behind the structures that he built. He also pointed out why he thought beauty was unavoidable in finding a solution to structural problems. The reader will also find discussions of the role of economy in design, the advantages and behavior of reinforced concrete, and a separate chapter on ferro-cement (with photographs of several boats that Nervi built with hulls of ferro-cement).

———. *The Works of Pier Luigi Nervi.* Translated by Ernest Priefert. London: Architectural Press, and New York: Praeger, 1957. With a preface by Nervi and an introduction by Ernesto N. Rogers, this is probably the best illustrated book available on the work of Pier Luigi Nervi. The bulk of the volume (almost 140 pages) consists of black-and-white photographs and line drawings of Nervi's works. Useful explanatory notes accompany many of the illustrations.

"Pier Luigi Nervi." *Architectural Forum* 99 (November, 1953): 141-148. This article highlights Nervi's structural innovations—precast corrugated beams, precast ceiling panels, and ferrocement forms—and then illustrates their use in Nervi's projects.

Smith, G. E. Kidder. *Italy Builds: Its Modern Architecture and Native Inheritance.* London: Architectural Press, and New York: Reinhold, 1955. This work begins with a brief and very general overview of the influences in Italian architecture. The remainder of the book is then devoted to a discussion of modern architecture in Italy. Most of Nervi's major works, as of the date of publication, are included. Reasonably well illustrated; includes an index and a useful bibliography.

Brian J. Nichelson

JOHN VON NEUMANN

Born: December 28, 1903; Budapest, Hungary
Died: February 8, 1957; Washington, D.C.
Areas of Achievement: Mathematics, mathematical physics, and computer science
Contribution: A brilliant mathematician who laid the mathematical foundations of modern physics and computer science, von Neumann affirmed the importance of autonomous scientific research during the anti-Communist McCarthy era.

Early Life

The eldest of three boys, John von Neumann was born in Budapest on December 28, 1903. In the United States, he came to be known universally as Johnny, perhaps because he was already known by the Hungarian Jancsi. Von Neumann belonged to the group of Hungarian mathematicians and physicists including Eugene Wigner, Edward Teller, Leo Szilard, and Dennis Gabor, who have substantially contributed to twentieth century science. In addition to knowing one another, some of them even attended the same high school, Budapest Lutheran.

Von Neumann's father, Max von Neumann, was a successful banker who had been elevated to the nobility. The Hungarian honorific "Margittai" was later Germanized to "von." The family was Jewish and bilingual in Hungarian and German. When John entered the gymnasium at age ten, he came into contact with László Rátz, a teacher who perceived his mathematical talents and arranged with his father for special tutoring. Von Neumann worked concurrently on a degree in chemical engineering, awarded by the Eidgenössische Technische Hochschule of Zurich in 1926, and a doctorate in mathematics, which was awarded by the University of Budapest, also in 1926.

Although von Neumann then held positions at the University of Berlin and at the University of Hamburg, he also visited Göttingen, where there was an amazing group of physicists and mathematicians, including David Hilbert, Werner Heisenberg, Max Born, and Erwin Schrödinger. The visitors included Albert Einstein, Wolfgang Pauli, Linus Pauling, J. Robert Oppenheimer, and Norbert Wiener.

After coming to the United States as a visiting professor at Princeton University in 1930, he accepted a permanent position in 1931. In 1933, he was invited to join the permanent faculty of the Institute for Advanced Study, also located at Princeton University, and became the youngest faculty member at the institute. He married Marietta Kövesi in 1930; she was Catholic, and he at least nominally became a Catholic during his first marriage. His daughter, Marina, was born in Princeton in 1935. The marriage ended in divorce in 1937. In 1938, he visited Hungary and married Klára Dán, who joined him in Princeton.

Von Neumann was one of the rare men of extraordinary scientific genius who was as engaging personally as he was brilliant mentally. Colleagues relate anecdotes concerning his foibles, but all with a touch of nostalgia because his charm as well as his intelligence endeared him to those who knew him best. Von Neumann was of medium size, slender as a young man, plump as he grew older. His colleagues teased him about dressing like a banker—perhaps because he was the son of a banker; he habitually wore three-piece suits with a neatly buttoned coat and a handkerchief in his pocket. Cheerful and gregarious, he was a great raconteur. Not at all athletic, he had to watch his appetite for rich gravies, sauces, and desserts. He drove erratically, regularly acquiring speeding tickets and wearing out approximately a car a year. According to his friends, he was not mechanical enough to change a tire on his car, but his wife attributed to him a great skill at releasing zippers.

Because of his powers of concentration, he could appear absentminded. He would sometimes start out on a trip and then have to call home to find out with whom he had an appointment and where it was to be. He loved off-color limericks and repeated them at parties. Especially fond of children, he enjoyed their toys so much that friends would give him toys as gifts on special occasions. Von Neumann's associates described him as sociable, witty, and party-loving.

History intrigued von Neumann. He had systematically read and learned most of the names and facts in the twenty-one volumes of the *Cambridge Ancient History* (1923-1939). During World War II, his colleagues were amazed at how frequently his forecasts were borne out by later events. Once asked by his colleague Herman Goldstine to recite Charles Dickens' *A Tale of Two Cities* (1859), von Neumann continued for so long that it was clear that he was prepared to recite from memory the entire book, even though he had read it twenty years before. While he had a photographic memory of books he had read decades earlier, he was quite capable of forgetting what his luncheon menu had been. When his wife once asked him to get her a glass of water, he came back and asked her where the glasses were—even though they had lived in the same house for seventeen years.

Life's Work

Von Neumann's first group of mathematical papers involved presenting an axiomatic treatment of set theory. Related to this concern with set theory was the problem of the freedom of contradiction of mathematics. Bertrand Russell and Alfred North Whitehead, in *Principia Mathematica* (1910-1913), contended that all mathematics derives from logic and is without contradiction. In 1927, following David Hilbert, who wanted to separate number from experiential logic, where seven is related to seven objects, von Neumann argued that all analysis could be proved to be without contradiction. Three years later, the German mathematician Kurt Gödel upset these theories by showing that "in any sufficiently powerful logical system, statements can be formulated which are neither provable nor unprovable within that system unless the system is logically inconsistent." Von Neumann was entirely comfortable with theoretical issues of this kind.

In a series of important papers, culminating in his book entitled *The Mathematical Foundations of Quantum Mechanics* (1944), von Neumann showed that two different theories, Erwin Schrödinger's wave mechanics and Werner Heisenberg's matrix mechanics, are equivalent. His work on the mathematical foundations of quantum theory had brought him into the small, closely knit circle of theoretical physicists, and so he shared from the beginning an awareness of the technological possibilities of the energy which could be generated by nuclear fission.

The first self-sustaining nuclear chain reaction was produced by a group of physicists headed by Enrico Fermi in Chicago on December 2, 1942. It was not until spring of 1943 that physicists and mathematicians were summoned to Los Alamos, New Mexico, where the Manhattan Project, charged with developing an atom bomb, had established a research laboratory. Von Neumann was already engaged in scientific defense work, particularly in connection with the motions of compressible gases, but he did not arrive at Los Alamos until the fall of 1943. His contributions to

the work at Los Alamos were substantial. He assisted in the development of a method of implosion and a means of calculating the characteristics of nuclear explosions.

Prior to and during the Manhattan Project, von Neumann became interested in problems of turbulence, general dynamics of continua, and meteorological calculation. Because these problems took too long to calculate even with the assistance of desk calculators, he became convinced that progress in developing electronic computing machines was essential.

The issue of who deserves the credit and patents for inventing the computer is complex and hotly debated. According to his colleague Stanislaw Ulam, von Neumann's contribution to the development of the computer was that he formulated the methods of translating mathematical procedures into a language of instructions for a computing machine. He developed the idea of a universal set of circuits in the machine, "a flow diagram," and a "code," or fixed set of connections which could solve a great variety of problems. Prior to that, each problem required a special and different set of wiring in order to perform operations in a given sequence. When von Neumann was awarded the Fermi Prize of the Atomic Energy Commission, he was especially cited for his work on using electronic computing machines.

After World War II, von Neumann was increasingly called upon to act as an adviser to the government. From the perspective of the peace movement of the 1960's and 1970's, the arms race between the United States and the Soviet Union seemed irresponsible and inhumane. In the 1940's and 1950's, the very vivid memories of World War II contributed to the intense anti-Soviet atmosphere of the Cold War. After the Soviet Union tested its own atom bomb, von Neumann supported work on the hydrogen bomb in order to maintain American ascendancy in the arms race. Unlike the physicist Edward Teller and Lewis Strauss, one of the commissioners of the Atomic Energy Commission, von Neumann insisted upon limiting his role to that of a technical expert; he resisted pressures to join scientists who publicly supported banning nuclear tests; he also engaged in political lobbying in support of development of the hydrogen bomb.

In 1954, when J. Robert Oppenheimer, formerly the director of the Manhattan Project, was attacked as a security risk and hearings concerning his loyalty were conducted, von Neumann expressed complete confidence in Oppenheimer's integrity and loyalty. He acknowledged that their views concerning the importance of developing the hydrogen bomb differed, but he unequivocally opposed the political harassment of scientists. In October, 1954, the president offered von Neumann a position on the United States Atomic Energy Commission. According to his friend Stanislaw Ulam, von Neumann was flattered and proud that he, even though foreign-born, would be entrusted with such responsibility, but he was concerned about the Oppenheimer affair. Convinced that work on the commission was of great national importance, he accepted the post. In a written statement prepared for the hearing before the Special Senate Committee on Atomic Energy, which took place on January 31, 1946, von Neumann stated that "science has outgrown the age of independence from society." Observing that the combination of politics and physics could render the earth uninhabitable, he commented that regulation is necessary in both spheres. Restricting himself as a scientist to the scientific, he supported health and safety measures and protection by government police power, but

unequivocally asserted the importance of freedom of information: "There must, however, be no restriction in principle on research in any part of science, and none in nuclear physics in particular, and absolutely no secrecy or possibility of classification of the results of fundamental research."

A proponent of armament during the Cold War, von Neumann incorrectly predicted a massive war between the United States and the Soviet Union immediately after World War II; still, he accurately foresaw that the Soviet Union would take control of Eastern European countries, including his native Hungary, and crush all opposition to Communism.

In the summer of 1955, von Neumann slipped in a corridor and injured his left shoulder. Diagnosis of the injury revealed that he had bone cancer. During this illness, he surprised his Jewish colleagues by consulting a Catholic priest, but it is likely that he had received instruction in Catholicism at the time of his first marriage. Until the last, he continued to function as a member of the Atomic Energy Commission; he also worked on a number of projects, including the texts for the honorary Silliman lectures to be given at Yale. The painful nature of his illness prevented him from concentrating with his accustomed intensity. He was forced to leave the lectures entitled *The Computer and the Brain* unfinished, but they were published posthumously in 1958.

Summary

When von Neumann answered a questionnaire in 1954 distributed by the National Academy of Science, which asked him to name his three most important contributions to mathematics, he identified his work on the rigorous formulation of quantum theory as one of those three. His papers on this topic represent one-third of his total work. As his most important contributions, von Neumann selected his work on the mathematical foundations of quantum theory and ergodic theorems and his theory of operators. In making this selection, von Neumann may have been motivated by a keen desire to maintain the importance of mathematics on a conceptual level in solving the problems of the physical sciences. Von Neumann's interest in the development of the electronic computing machine was prompted in part by the need for swift answers to problems in mathematical physics and engineering. Later, he pioneered in the use of computing machines to assist in weather prediction. In addition to working on the mathematics of weather prediction, he believed that control over climate might one day be possible.

Von Neumann was essentially the creator of game theory, a new branch of mathematics. He later coauthored a treatise with Oskar Morgenstern, *Theory of Games and Economic Behavior* (1944), which attempts to schematize mathematically the economic exchange of goods and to solve problems concerning monopoly, oligopoly, and free competition.

In his theory of automata, an area of study in which von Neumann was a pioneer, he effectively demonstrated that in principle it is possible to build machines which can reproduce themselves. His posthumously published lectures, *The Computer and the Brain* (1958), return to these problems and draw upon ideas and terminology from mathematics, electrical engineering, and neurology to outline a theory of representation of logical propositions by electrical networks or nervous systems.

Bibliography

Goldstine, Herman. *The Computer from Pascal to von Neumann*. Princeton, N.J.: Princeton University Press, 1972. A history of the computer, written by a very close and loyal friend of von Neumann.

Heims, Steve J. *John von Neumann and Norbert Wiener: From Mathematics to the Technologies of Life and Death*. Boston: MIT Press, 1980. A biased attack on von Neumann which uses his life as a means of editorializing in favor of a ban on nuclear tests.

Leonard, Robert J. "From Parlor Games to Social Science: von Neumann, Morgenstern, and the Creation of Game Theory, 1928-1944." *Journal of Economic Literature* 33, no. 2 (June, 1995). The author offers profiles of Neumann and Oskar Morgenstern.

Nagy, Dénes, and Ferenc Nagy. "Neumann János." In *Magyarok a természettudomány és technika történetében*, edited by Ferenc Nagy and Dénes Nagy, 215-218, 407-415, 423-449. Budapest: Omikk, 1986. Accurate and useful biographical treatment.

Neumann, John von. *Collected Works*. Edited by A. H. Taub. 6 vols. Oxford and New York: Pergamon Press, 1961-1963. Standard edition of the works of von Neumann.

Shurkin, Joel. "John von Neumann." In *Engines of the Mind: A History of the Computer*. New York: W. W. Norton and Co., 1984. A survey of the difficulty in ascertaining who deserves credit for the development of the computer, inaccurate concerning von Neumann's life. Opposes Goldstine's view.

Stern, Nancy. "John von Neumann's Influence on Electronic Digital Computing: 1944-1946." *Annals of the History of Computers* 2 (1980): 349-361. Discussion of von Neumann's contribution to the development of the computer.

Stewart, Ian. "Rules of Engagement." *New Scientist* 159, no. 2149 (August 29, 1998). Stewart discusses Neumann's discovery of cellular automata and its scientific applications.

Ulam, Stanislaw. "John von Neumann." *Bulletin of the American Mathematical Society* 64, no. 3, pt. 2 (1958): 1-49. Biography and highly mathematical assessment of von Neumann's career.

Wigner, Eugene. *Symmetries and Reflections*. Bloomington: Indiana University Press, 1967; London: MIT Press, 1970. Autobiography of Wigner, and friend and colleague of von Neumann.

Jeanie R. Brink

LOUISE NEVELSON

Born: Early Autumn of 1899 (possibly September 23 or October 16); Kiev, Russia
Died: April 17, 1988; New York, New York
Area of Achievement: Art
Contribution: Louise Nevelson's original and unusual view of sculpture as environmental and transforming, as well as her innovative use of materials, made her a leading sculptor of the twentieth century and a major role model for twentieth century women artists.

Early Life

Louise Nevelson was born Leah Berliawsky in 1899 in Kiev, Russia. She was the second child of four born to Isaac and Zeisel Berliawsky. Isaac Berliawsky immigrated to America in 1902, and his family joined him in 1905; they settled in the small coastal town of Rockland, Maine. Isaac had been involved in the family lumber business in Russia. After settling in the United States, he supported his own family by selling "junk," building houses, and buying and selling properties.

As a working-class Jewish immigrant family, the Berliawskys were viewed as outsiders by the predominantly Protestant population of Rockland. From the beginning, Leah, now called Louise, felt a sense of isolation and alienation. Forced to change her name and to abandon her mother tongue in favor of English, she found her refuge in the arts. Both of Louise's parents enjoyed the arts, especially music. Louise's mother was interested in fashion and made her own unusual and extravagant clothes. Louise also enjoyed wearing her own "creations," and by the age of seven she was expressing a desire to become an artist. As a young girl, Louise took private voice lessons and piano lessons, drew, and painted in oil and watercolor.

After her graduation from high school in June of 1918, Louise became engaged to a wealthy shipowner from New York named Charles Nevelson, who was descended from Lithuanian Jews. In 1920, they married in Boston, settled in New York, and Louise began to live the lifestyle of an upperclass, socially elite lady. Louise's only child, Myron Irving Nevelson, was born in 1922.

At the same time Louise was functioning as a New York socialite, wife, and mother, she was unable to forget her interest in the arts. She continued to wear flamboyant fashions of her own creation, and by 1924 she was studying voice with Metropolitan Opera coach Estelle Liebling, attending Saturday afternoon drawing classes at the Art Students League, and taking private drawing lessons with the well-known artist William Meyerowitz. In 1926, she began studying acting at the International Theater Arts Institute in Brooklyn under the Italian actress, Princess Norina Matchabelli.

Throughout her life, Louise Nevelson was to retain a deep interest in theater and music, as well as dance; but the visual arts were to become her lifetime passion. She began her first serious, full-time study of art in 1929 at the Art Students League in New York, where she studied painting and drawing with the distinguished artist and teacher Kenneth Hayes Miller.

Almost from its inception there was strife in Louise's marriage to Charles Nevelson. Charles was a conservative businessman who desired his wife to play a more traditional role in family and social life. After the family business suffered losses during the mid-1920's, Charles moved the family to modest housing and expected his wife to help economize. She chose instead to develop her creative interests. Although she cared deeply for her son, Louise ultimately decided to dedicate her life exclusively to art. In 1931, she separated from her husband and left their son in his custody. She later divorced Charles in 1941.

Louise Nevelson went to Munich in 1931 to study with Hans Hofmann, who was one of the most influential avant-garde artists and teachers of the period. In Munich, she expanded her understanding of cubism, but because of general disappointment with Hofmann's program, she left after about three months. She traveled to Berlin and Vienna, where she played small roles in several films. After spending a few weeks in Italy and Paris, she returned to New York.

In 1932, Nevelson became an assistant on a series of frescos executed by the famous Mexican artist Diego Rivera at the New Worker's School in New York. She returned to the Art Students League to study drawing and painting with Hans Hofmann, who had moved to New York. She also began her long study of modern dance at this time, and took up the study of sculpture under the sculptor Chaim Gross.

Life's Work

It was in 1934 that Louise Nevelson began to make the transition from art student to professional artist. She rented an artist's studio in New York and exhibited paintings in her first gallery showing at Alfred Stieglitz's Secession Gallery. From 1935 to 1939, she taught art for the government-subsidized Works Progress Administration.

Although Nevelson continued to paint and draw throughout her life, by 1934, she was directing most of her artistic energy into sculpture, the art form for which she would become famous. Her early sculptures were primarily human, animal, or abstract forms made out of plaster or clay. She exhibited a sculpture for the first time at the Brooklyn Museum show entitled "Sculpture: A Group Exhibition by Young Sculptors" (1935).

In the 1930's and 1940's, two of the most influential avant-garde art styles were cubism and surrealism. Nevelson was inspired by both. In the 1940's, her work became increasingly more geometric, abstract, and complexly layered and was to reveal subtle metaphysical and surrealist tendencies in her creation of sculpture which included movable parts, viewer participation, and later, the erection of total, theatrical environments. By the 1940's, she was also constructing or assembling sculpture, in the manner that was becoming a major sculptural method of the twentieth century, rather than carving or modeling. Sculptural assemblage would become Nevelson's primary means of artistic expression.

During the 1940's, Louise Nevelson experienced severe financial difficulties. Although she exhibited widely at the Karl Nierendorf Gallery and elsewhere, her work received mixed reviews and rarely sold. It was not until Nevelson was in her fifties that her mature sculptural style developed and she began creating the enormous abstract environmental sculptures for which she became well known.

By 1955, Nevelson's work was being represented by the important but nonprofit Grand Central Moderns Gallery in New York. "The Royal Voyage" (1955), Nevelson's second solo exhibition at the Grand Central Moderns Gallery, was the first in a series of Nevelson's theme exhibitions that consisted of assembled wood painted entirely black. "The Royal Voyage" was an environmental installation created from dozens of large, rough wood pieces arranged to symbolize a king and queen (represented by huge beams) embarking on a mysterious, mystical sea journey.

After "The Royal Voyage" show, Nevelson presented other theme exhibitions in black wood at the Grand Central Moderns. "Moon Garden + One" (1958) was a huge black theatrical environment which featured her first wall, *Sky Cathedral*, a structure more than eleven feet high and ten feet long that was constructed out of boxes filled with a variety of wooden forms and objects arranged in a complex and abstract manner. The exhibition was lit dramatically in blue and emanated a mood of otherworldliness.

"Moon Garden + One" was highly applauded by critics and the national media. The show marked the beginning of Nevelson's critical success and her recognition as a major twentieth century sculptor. By this time, Nevelson had collected huge warehouses and storerooms full of "junk" and "odds and ends," mostly wood, that she assembled in large walls constructed of boxes or into immense environmental installations, most of which were painted uniformly in one color, usually black, white, or gold.

In 1960, Nevelson created her first totally white environment at the Museum of Modern Art in

New York, in a show entitled "Sixteen Americans." Nevelson was given the biggest gallery for the installation of her "Dawn's Wedding Feast," which consisted of walls constructed of filled boxes, intricately constructed columns, hanging sun and moon assemblages, a nuptial pillow, a wedding chest, and a wedding cake made from Victorian finials and chair legs. The marriage theme was to be a recurrent one in Nevelson's work and can be seen as symbolizing traditional marriage ceremonies, marriage to life, or marriage to one's work.

By 1961, Nevelson was being represented by the prestigious Martha Jackson Gallery in New York and was receiving a guaranteed income. Fascinated by the allure of gold, she made a golden environment out of her walls of assemblage boxes called "The Royal Tides" (1961). Toilet seats, furniture parts, tools, and junk in abstract arrangements glowed in shimmering gold and were meant to evoke the mood of royalty, another of Nevelson's recurrent themes.

By the early 1960's, Nevelson had become an extremely famous and highly respected sculptor. In 1962, she was selected as one of the three artists to represent the United States at the important international exhibition, the XXXI Biennale, Internazionale d'Arte in Venice, Italy. She was awarded the grand prize in the First Sculpture International at the Torcuato di Tella Institute's Center of Visual Arts, Buenos Aires, in the same year. In 1963, she was given a Ford Foundation grant to work on printmaking at the Tamarind Lithography Workshop in Los Angeles, California. In 1964, Nevelson began her official affiliation with the important Pace Gallery in New York, which sold her work regularly and gave her a guaranteed income. The Whitney Museum of American Art gave Nevelson a retrospective exhibition in 1967, and she was elected to the National Institute of Arts and Letters in 1968.

Nevelson began to make large metal sculptures for public spaces in the late 1960's. She worked primarily with cor-ten steel, out of which she created immense abstract forms generally meant for permanent outdoor display. Princeton University commissioned the first of these, *Atmosphere and Environment X* (1969). In 1972, *Night Presence IV* (22 feet high) was installed on Park Avenue in New York and *Atmosphere and Environment XIII: Windows to the West* (15 feet high) was erected in Scottsdale, Arizona.

In the late 1960's, Nevelson also began to work with plastics, plexiglas, and Lucite. She assembled these materials into abstract forms in the manner of the wood constructions, but these were smaller and more delicate in appearance. Sculptures such as *Ice Palace I* (1967) and *Canada Series I* (1968) featured overlapping transparencies and reflection of light.

The interior of the Chapel of the Good Shepherd in Saint Peter's Church, New York, was entirely designed by Louise Nevelson in 1977. Again taking on a large-scale project, Nevelson designed benches, vestments, and constructed wall sculptures in white, and created another of her total environments. In the same year, *Mrs. N's Palace* was being shown at the Pace Gallery, an installation of massive wooden forms which symbolized Nevelson's dream home or environment.

By the time of Louise Nevelson's death, she had become a major media celebrity and was recognized as a leader in twentieth century sculpture. Her vision of sculpture as environmental and transforming, and her incorporation of old, found objects and "junk" into works of art was highly innovative and daring. Nevelson received many honors and awards in the later part of her life. In 1978, Legion Memorial Square in Manhattan was renamed Louise Nevelson Plaza. In 1979, she was elected to the American Academy of Arts and Letters and was awarded their gold medal for sculpture in 1983. She was presented with a National Medal of the Arts by President Ronald Reagan in 1985.

Louise Nevelson continued to work as an artist almost to the end of her life. In 1988, after undergoing radiation treatment, she died of a brain tumor at her home in New York. A memorial service was held for her in the Medieval Sculpture Hall of the Metropolitan Museum of Art in New York.

Summary

Louise Nevelson was a truly independent woman whose life was entirely dedicated to her art. While her mode of dress was feminine and extravagant, she proved, through her art, that there was no limit to what a woman could accomplish or create if she was seriously dedicated. The materials, methods, and size of Nevelson's art were highly nontraditional for women. Early in her career, Nevelson was criticized for her choices, but she commanded her art so well that she eventually even overwhelmed and impressed most of her critics. Ultimately, she came to be acknowledged internationally for her originality and contribution to the history of sculpture, primarily because of her constructed environments and innovative use of materials.

Throughout her life, Nevelson identified herself as a feminist many times. She refused to be controlled by any strictures put upon her merely because she was a woman. During the 1940's, she came to associate more and more with other women artists in an effort to gain strength against the sexist attitudes which were predominant in the art world of the time. She participated in women artist exhibitions and was elected to the National Association of Women Artists in 1952. In 1979, Nevelson was chosen to be the New York Feminist Art Institute's guest of honor at the benefit given at the World Trade Center.

By the end of the 1970's, Louise Nevelson, because of her highly public presence, had become a major role model for women, and for women artists in particular. She was an example of a powerful woman who was able to claim her life for her own, mold it, control it, and devote it to the thing she cared about most deeply. She was flamboyant, outspoken, energetic, and resilient, and her art was daring, innovative, and supremely her own. She stopped at almost nothing to express her innermost self through her art and she always believed that what she had to express was important and valid. Since the time of Louise Nevelson, women artists have begun working widely in large-scale forums and nontraditional materials such as metals, plastics, and wood. Nevelson provided women artists with a truly inspiring example of female strength, creativity, and courage.

Bibliography

Gardner, P. "'Diana Was Always There.'" *Art News* 89, no. 10 (December, 1990). Short account of the legal battle between Diana MacKown, Nevelson's friend and assistant, and Nevelson's son, Mike, over the ownership of 37 of Nevelson's works after her death.

Glimcher, Arnold B. *Louise Nevelson*. London: Secker and Warburg, and New York: Praeger, 1972. Written by the director of the Pace Gallery, New York, who was Nevelson's friend and dealer. This book serves as an excellent introduction to her life and work up to 1972. Includes a list of major exhibitions and collections, as well as more than one hundred black-and-white and color photographs of her work. No bibliography.

Lipman, Jean. *Nevelson's World*. New York: Hudson Hills Press, 1983. With an introduction by the art critic, Hilton Kramer and an afterword by Louise Nevelson. This book focuses on the art of Nevelson with thorough discussions of her early work, wood sculpture, transparent and metal sculpture, as well as works on paper. Includes a bibliography and more than one hundred color and black-and-white reproductions.

Lisle, Laurie. *Louise Nevelson: A Passionate Life*. New York: Summit, 1990. An important, thorough examination of Nevelson's life, career, and work. This is an interesting, well-researched biography which analyzes Nevelson's development, from birth to death. Includes an excellent bibliography and black-and-white photographs.

Nevelson, Louise. *Dawns and Dusks*. New York: Scribner, 1976. Based on taped conversations between Nevelson and her assistant, Diana MacKown, with whom Nevelson discusses her life and art. The focus of the book is on her career and her sculpture. Includes black-and-white photographs of Nevelson, family, and friends, as well as reproductions of art. Introduction by art historian John Canaday

———. *Louise Nevelson: Atmospheres and Environments*. New York: Potter, 1980. A beautiful catalog published in conjunction with a 1980 exhibition of Nevelson's sculpture at the Whitney. Includes an introduction by Edward Albee and excellent color photographs of some of Nevelson's most important environmental exhibits, including "Moon Garden + One," "Dawn's Wedding Feast," and "The Royal Tides." With bibliography.

Wilson, Laurie. *Louise Nevelson, Iconography and Sources*. New York: Garland, 1981. Based on a Ph.D. dissertation finished in 1978, this book is an important contribution to the study of the meanings and background behind Nevelson's imagery. Wilson seeks the sources of Nevelson's symbolism, particularly of marriage, royalty, and death, in her life, studies, travel, and philosophy. Includes a bibliography and 191 black-and-white illustrations.

Nannette Fabré Kelly

BEN NICHOLSON

Born: April 10, 1894; Denham, Buckinghamshire,
England
Died: February 6, 1982; London, England
Area of Achievement: Art
Contribution: Influenced by such Continental in-
novators as Piet Mondrian, Joan Miró, and Pablo
Picasso, Nicholson became the foremost expo-
nent of abstract painting in twentieth century
Great Britain.

Early Life

Ben Nicholson was born on April 10, 1894, in
Denham, Buckinghamshire. Both his father, Sir
William Nicholson, and his mother, Mabel (née
Pryde), were painters, as was his uncle, James
Pryde. The eldest of four children, Nicholson at
first attempted to resist the family tradition and
sought to become a writer. After receiving his primary education at Heddon Court School (Hampstead) and the Gresham School (Holt), however,
he decided to follow his natural inclinations and
attended the Slade School of Art (London) in
1911. Although Nicholson only completed a single semester at the Slade School, he did produce
his first oil painting there, a still life of a jug sitting
on a table, and thereby launched a productive career that would continue into the 1980's.

After leaving the Slade School, Nicholson continued his education in Europe, studying in Tours
during 1911-1912 and Milan in 1912-1913. During
this period, he found himself attracted to such
painters as Giotto, Paolo Uccello, Paul Cézanne,
and Henri Matisse, but he was especially impressed by the Cubist works of Picasso. His own
paintings from this period remained rather traditional, consisting mainly of still lifes and romanticized landscapes, but the seeds of his future abstract work had been planted.

At the outbreak of World War I in 1914, Nicholson volunteered for military service but was turned
down for reasons of poor health. He spent the war
years in England and married Winifred Dacre Roberts, a fellow writer and painter, in 1917. They took
an extended honeymoon to Pasadena, California,
and, upon returning to England in 1918, split their
time between homes in Switzerland, Cumberland
(in northern England), and London. They were divorced in 1932.

The postwar years were a period of "fast and furious experimentation," according to Nicholson. In
his first one-man show, held at the Adelphi Gallery
in London in 1922, his paintings, still mainly still
lifes and landscapes, attempted to re-create the
simplicity of British folk art and impressed viewers
with their "brilliant, innocent coloring and lively
surface variations." Nicholson also included some
portraits in this exhibition, but they failed to attract
the same favorable attention as his other work.

Descriptions and photographs of Nicholson from
this formative period depict a small, almost fragile
man, once described as "a smaller and more delicate Picasso." His hair, originally dark, turned
white rather early in life and gave him a serious
and distinguished demeanor. He did have a lighter
side, however, and was noted by his friends and acquaintances for his good humor, his expertise at
puns, and his skill at Ping-Pong and tennis.

Life's Work

Although Nicholson produced a few abstract paintings in the immediate postwar period, it was not
until the early 1930's that he began to devote himself entirely to this new area of art. Various influences determined this growing interest in abstract
art. Primary among them was Nicholson's exposure to the pioneering work of Picasso, Miró, and
especially Mondrian. He met Mondrian for the first
time in Paris in 1932, and this meeting permanently changed the direction of Nicholson's work. The
overwhelming simplicity and power of Mondrian's
geometric shapes had a tremendous impact on
Nicholson and transformed his latent interest in abstraction into a lifelong mission. Another influence
was the work of Barbara Hepworth, an abstract
sculptor whom he took as his second wife in 1933.
Her interest in expressing emotion through pure
form can be observed in many of Nicholson's later
abstract paintings.

This new direction in Nicholson's work first
came to public attention at a one-man show held at
the Lefevre Gallery (London) in October, 1933.
The show demonstrated Nicholson's obsession
with absolute form and consisted of textile designs,
collages, plaster canvases, figure drawings, and
paintings composed of nothing more than a few apparently random lines or circles scattered on a
blank surface. His best-known work from this
show is *1933 (painting)*, composed of several free-
floating red circles against a light background. Reaction to his radical departure from the mainstream

of British art was mixed. Some condemned Nicholson's work as superficial and a spatial disaster. Others, however, admired the simplicity and impression of silent power that his works conveyed and drew parallels between Nicholson's clean and straightforward geometric shapes and the work of the best of the twentieth century's architects and industrial designers.

In 1937, Nicholson helped found an artistic journal, *Circle: International Survey of Constructive Art*, to promote those qualities he was trying to express in his art. Co-edited by Nicholson, Naum Gabo, and J. L. Martin, the first issue included articles by Mondrian, Charles-Édouard Corbusier, Walter Gropius, Lewis Mumford, Henry Moore, and Nicholson himself. Although the journal folded shortly thereafter, it did provide at least a temporary forum for the adherents of "Constructionism" (as abstraction was often termed) and marked Nicholson as the foremost advocate of that art form in England.

Nicholson lived in London with his second wife until 1940, when their marriage ended in divorce. He then moved to the coastal town of St. Ives in Cornwall and lived there until shortly before his death in 1982. He never remarried, but he did often enjoy the company of his six children: two sons and a daughter by Winifred Roberts and triplets (one son and two daughters) by Barbara Hepworth.

Although he had met with some critical resistance during his pioneering Lefevre Gallery show, Nicholson remained completely devoted to abstract art and, as time went on, he won over many of his former critics as well as the majority of the sophisticated art public. Beginning in the late 1930's, many of his works were purchased by some of the most important art museums and galleries in the world, including the Tate Gallery in London, the Ottowa National Gallery of Canada, the Ohara Museum in Japan, and the National Gallery of New South Wales in Australia. Several of Nicholson's paintings were included in the British exhibit at the 1939 World's Fair in New York City, and he also received prestigious commissions to create murals for the Festival of Britain (1951) and the new Time-Life Building in London (1952). In 1956, he was honored by being included in the "Masters of British Painting: 1800-1950" show put on by the Museum of Modern Art in New York.

Nicholson reached the peak of his career in the 1950's. In addition to the honors and commissions mentioned above, he was also the recipient of numerous prizes and awards during this decade. These included first prize at the Carnegie's Thirty-ninth International Exhibition in Pittsburgh in 1952; the Ulissi Award at the Venice Biennale in 1954; the Governor of Tokyo Award at the Third International Exhibition in Japan in 1955; the Grand Prix Award in the 1956 Fourth Mostra Internazionale di Bianco e Nero in Lugano, Switzerland; and first prize for non-Brazilian painters at the Fourth São Paulo Bienal in Brazil in 1957.

His most important achievement during this fruitful period, however, was an award of ten thousand dollars from the Guggenheim Foundation for the outstanding contemporary painting of 1955-1956. Entitled *August 1956*, the painting consisted of a pattern of blue, gray, brown, and red geometric shapes and portrayed a subtle mood of tranquillity and peace. Some criticized the selection and claimed that it was not equal to Nicholson's earlier works. They may have had a point, but the Guggenheim nevertheless represented recognition for Nicholson's long devotion to abstract art and, in this sense, was richly deserved.

Nicholson's productivity diminished dramatically in the 1960's and 1970's as he spent more and more time with his family, pursuing his hobbies of Ping-Pong and golf, and enjoying the scenery of his beloved Cornwall. His health, never strong to begin with, began to fail in the 1970's and, late in the decade, he moved back to London in order to be near increasingly necessary medical facilities. Nicholson died in that city on February 6, 1982, at the age of eighty-seven.

Summary

British artists never achieved the stature and renown of their French, Italian, German, and even American counterparts in the various schools of modern art that appeared during the twentieth century. In many ways, British art during this century seems somewhat derivative and unimaginative compared to the work of such Continental and American innovators as Picasso, Miró, Marc Chagall, Jackson Pollock, Mondrian, and Wassily Kandinsky. Ben Nicholson, however, represents an important exception to this generalization. Although Continental abstractionists such as Miró and Mondrian had a strong impact on the direction of his painting after 1920, Nicholson filtered their influence through his unique personality to create original and exciting works that received international recognition.

One of Nicholson's best paintings, *Vertical Seconds* (1953), illustrates this point very well. It is a large, rectangular canvas filled with various lines and geometric shapes. The influence of Mondrian, with his emphasis on the power of straight lines and rectangular relationships, is clear. Yet one would never mistake this painting for one by Mondrian. Demonstrating a beautiful sense of balance and proportion, the painting presents an airy, almost mystical, mood and gives the viewer the impression that he is looking at something distinctly British.

It was Nicholson's subtle blending of Continental influences and his own British artistic inheritance that gave his work its special flavor and its own importance. He may not have been at the same level as a Mondrian or a Miró, but he cannot be dismissed as merely being a less talented imitator. The best of his work exposed Great Britain to the potential and beauty of abstract art and provided an example for younger artists who were seeking a means of expression that transcended the confines of traditional British art without completely losing touch with it. In this important sense, Ben Nicholson represents a pivotal figure in the evolution of modern art in twentieth century Great Britain.

Bibliography

De Sausmarez, Maurice, ed. *Ben Nicholson*. London and New York: Studio International, 1969. Although the text is meager, this book includes an outstanding series of color plates covering the entire span of Nicholson's career.

Gaunt, William. *A Concise History of English Painting*. London: Thames and Hudson, and New York: Praeger, 1964. A very brief survey of British art from the Middle Ages to the 1960's. Nicholson receives only a few paragraphs in this study, but this brief discussion does a good job of placing his work within the context of British artistic traditions.

Hodin, Josef Paul. *Ben Nicholson: The Meaning of His Art*. London: Tiranti, 1957. A rather sophisticated, almost philosophical, discussion of what Nicholson was trying to achieve through his art. Hodin also includes an excellent section on Nicholson's impact on younger generations of British artists.

Micucci, Dana. "St. Ives Modernists." *Architectural Digest* 54, no. 8 (August, 1997). Micucci focuses on the St. Ives Modernists.

Nash, Steven A. "Ben Nicholson: An Historical Perspective." In *Ben Nicholson: Fifty Years of His Art*. Seattle: University of Washington Press, 1978. Includes abundant prints from the various stages in his artistic evolution and a balanced assessment of his contribution to modern art in the twentieth century.

Rothenstein, John. *Modern English Painters: Lewis to Moore*. 2 vols. London: Eyre and Spottiswoode, and New York: Macmillan, 1956. A fussy, eccentric analysis of modern art in Great Britain by the former director of the Tate Gallery in London. The chapter on Nicholson contains some good insights, but it is weakened by a long and rather pointless diatribe against the philosophy behind abstract art.

Soby, James T. *Masters of English Painting, 1800-1950*. New York: Museum of Modern Art, 1956. A catalog prepared to accompany the show of the same title that was presented by the Museum of Modern Art in 1956. Nicholson was one of many artists featured in this show, and Soby includes a concise and sympathetic analysis of Nicholson's place in British art.

Summerson, John. *Ben Nicholson*. London: Penguin, 1948. Summerson was a close friend of Nicholson and an admirer of his work. This book is based on Nicholson's correspondence with the author and provides an excellent portrayal of the former's motivations, influences, and goals.

Christopher E. Guthrie

REINHOLD NIEBUHR

Born: June 21, 1892; Wright City, Missouri
Died: June 1, 1971; Stockbridge, Massachusetts
Areas of Achievement: Theology and social and political ethics
Contribution: The leading American formulator of Neoorthodox theology, Niebuhr used the political and social arenas to place the Christian faith in the center of the cultural and political world of his day.

Early Life

Reinhold Niebuhr was born June 21, 1892, in Wright City, Missouri, the fourth child of Lydia and Gustav Niebuhr. Lydia was the daughter of an Evangelical Synod missionary, and Gustav was a young minister for the denomination. Reinhold later said that his father was the first formative religious influence on his life, combining a vital personal piety with a complete freedom in his theological training. This combination reflected the stance of the German-originated Evangelical Synod with its "liberal" de-emphasis of doctrine and its stress on heartfelt religion. Although he never exerted pressure, Gustav began early to talk to his son about the ministry, and by the time he was ten Reinhold had made the decision to be a preacher.

In 1902, the Niebuhr family moved to Lincoln, Illinois, where Gustav became pastor of St. John's Church. It was there that Reinhold experienced an incident which he was later to recount as a great influence on his thinking about the nature and destiny of humankind. During a recession, a local grocer for whom Reinhold worked, Adam Denger, had extended considerable credit to a number of unemployed miners. Embarrassed by his generosity and unable to pay him back, many of them moved away without even saying good-bye. Despite Denger's belief that God would protect him if he did what was right, he went bankrupt, and his young assistant, Reinhold, grew up to preach against sentimentality and reliance on special providence.

Niebuhr attended Elmhurst College in Elmhurst, Illinois, and Eden Theological Seminary in St. Louis, Missouri, both Evangelical Synod schools, but he found himself uninterested in any specific academic discipline. While Niebuhr was at Eden in April, 1913, his father, Gustav, suffered an attack of diabetes and died. Niebuhr went on to Yale Divinity School and received his M.A. in 1915, but rather than continue his graduate studies, he chose to accept a parish of the Evangelical Synod.

Life's Work

The board of the Evangelical Synod chose for Niebuhr a newly organized parish in Detroit, Michigan, the location of the Ford Motor Company. That institution came to have a powerful impact on the thinking and actions of Niebuhr taking on symbolic proportions and illustrating the tyranny of power.

Niebuhr experienced the problems common to all young ministers, many of which are told in his delightful *Leaves from the Notebook of a Tamed Cynic* (1929), a kind of diary of his years as parish minister. This book marked the beginning of a transition in Niebuhr's thought which eventually led to a rejection of all the liberal theological ideals with which he had ventured forth in 1915.

He said that the theological convictions he later came to hold began to dawn on him in Detroit

> because the simple little moral homilies which were preached in that as in other cities, by myself and others, seemed completely irrelevant to the brutal facts of life in a great industrial center. Whether irrelevant or not they were certainly futile. They did not change human actions or attitudes in any problem of collective behavior by a hair's breadth.

The problems of collective behavior to which he refers were the extreme working conditions and financial insecurity of the mass of industrial workers, especially employees of the Ford Motor Company, contrasted with the complacency and satisfaction of the middle and upper classes. People from all these groups were found among the membership of Niebuhr's church. He began to agonize about the validity and practicability of the optimistic liberal ideals which he was preaching each week.

Niebuhr's sermons began to contain more and more references to social and political issues, and he became more involved in social activity, speaking on behalf of the industrial workers in Detroit and other cities and lobbying for the formation of labor unions. Although he was not directly involved in World War I, the tragedy of that event led him to join and ultimately to become the head of the pacifist Fellowship of Reconciliation. He was also instrumental in organizing the Fellowship of Socialist Christians in the late 1920's.

In 1928, Henry Sloane Coffin, then president of Union Theological Seminary, offered Niebuhr a teaching post at Union. Although he considered himself inadequately prepared for teaching, particularly theology, he accepted Coffin's offer to teach "just what you think," with his subject area labeled "Applied Christianity." The thin, eagle-eyed, balding minister soon became one of the most sought-after professors on the Union campus as he brought his experiences with world political and religious figures to the campus. He continued to preach, traveling every weekend to colleges and universities around the country, and he continued to take part in an ever-increasing number of religious and secular organizations, besides his full-time teaching.

In 1931, Niebuhr married Ursula Keppel-Compton, daughter of a doctor and niece of an Anglican bishop, who was a student at Union. Ursula shared her husband's political interests and became a great help and collaborator with him in his work. He later acknowledged that his wife was the more diligent student of biblical literature (she taught courses in biblical literature at Barnard College) and that she was responsible for many of his viewpoints.

Niebuhr's theology compelled him to become involved in an extraordinary range of activities. He was a pioneer in the movement for racial justice, strongly supporting the Tenant Farmers' Union and the Conference of Southern Churchmen. He was involved in the work of a cooperative farm in Mississippi, an effort to enable the sharecroppers in the South to improve their conditions. He participated in the World Conference on Church, Community, and State in Oxford in 1937. Later, he worked on the United States Federal Council of Churches. After World War II, he was a key member of the World Council of Churches Commission on a Just and Durable Peace. He made hundreds of transatlantic trips, and his influence became strong in other countries, especially in Britain, where he had many ties.

Just before a worship service during the summer of 1934, Niebuhr casually jotted down a short prayer and used it in the worship. The prayer was, "O God, give us serenity to accept what cannot be changed, courage to change what should be changed, and wisdom to distinguish the one from the other." After the service Niebuhr gave the notes

to Chandler Robins, dean of the Cathedral of St. John the Divine, and the "serenity prayer" gradually made its way into the religious folklore of America.

Because of his strenuous schedule in connection with war activities, Niebuhr was near nervous collapse at the end of each school year from 1938 to 1940. Contrary to his doctor's orders, he kept up the pace. His Neoorthodox theology, which he called Christian Realism, led him to conclude that because of humankind's freedom to sin, true sacrificial love could never triumph in history. Nevertheless, it was his belief that this sacrificial love was ultimately right and true, and that this love might be approximated in history to divert or stop the abuse of power.

In February, 1952, Niebuhr suffered several small strokes. He was hospitalized for several weeks, being partially paralyzed on his left side. At last his rigorous schedule was curtailed; he was unable to do any work at all. He spent much of the rest of his nineteen years as an invalid or semi-invalid. Niebuhr continued his writing and made what appearances he could. He officially retired from teaching in 1960, becoming Professor Emeritus at Union and Research Associate at Columbia University's Institute for War and Peace Studies. He died June 1, 1971, one of the most influential thinkers of the twentieth century.

Summary

From the naïve liberalism of 1915 Niebuhr moved toward what he called Christian Realism. The events in which he had become involved forced him to recognize not only the effects of power in society, like that of Ford Motor Company over its thousands of helpless workers, but they also made him painfully aware of the corruption that had been imposed on the Christian norm. When confronted with the brutal realities of the industrialized city of Detroit, he came to realize the inadequacy of liberal thought with its naïve belief in the ultimate goodness of humankind to deal with evil in society. He began first to express his opposition to liberal viewpoints in terms of Marxist politics, but came to the conclusion that Marxism had essentially all the same illusions, again maintaining the ultimate goodness of human beings once capitalism was destroyed. Gradually he articulated his search for an alternative to liberal and orthodox theologies and ethical views. In *Beyond Tragedy* (1937), he focused on the symbol of the Cross of Christ as pivotal in understanding the human situation. While on the surface it appeared that evil had triumphed over the sacrificial love of Jesus, from the eschatological, or "beyond history," vantage point available to Christians, the Cross transcends tragedy.

Perhaps Niebuhr's clearest statement of Christian Realism is found in *The Nature and Destiny of Man* (1949). There he explains the paradox of self-less love, a divine attribute, coming into human society. While the inherent evil of human society prevents the triumph of love in this world, in historical existence, it will triumph in the end. Niebuhr's emphasis is not on a future vindication, although that is essential for his thought. Rather, he focuses on the acting out of sacrificial love by humans. While that love can never be fully embodied in any human motive or action, it was the ultimate standard. Niebuhr saw the possibility of divine love having an impact on history only in a life which ends tragically, the ultimate example being that of Jesus Christ. He threw himself into the exercise of divine love, trying to rectify social and political evils, and in many ways he ended his own life tragically in that pursuit. Theologically there was no preexisting group that fully agreed with him; his ideas were too orthodox for the liberals and too liberal for the orthodox.

Bibliography

Bingham, June. *Courage to Change: An Introduction to the Life and Thought of Reinhold Niebuhr.* New York: Scribner, 1961. A biographical study of Niebuhr's life as well as a thorough examination of his theology. Bingham, a close friend of Niebuhr, tends to be less than critical, and the lack of footnotes reduces the utility of the volume as a reference work. Nevertheless, an excellent introduction to Niebuhr's life and thought, containing much material not found elsewhere.

Fackre, Gabriel J. *The Promise of Reinhold Niebuhr.* Rev. ed. Lanham, Md.: University Press of America, 1994. A brief (less than one hundred pages) overview of Niebuhr's life and thought, synthesizing many of his views and concepts into a manageable and coherent whole. May serve as a starting point, but too abbreviated to function as a comprehensive account of Niebuhr's life and thought.

Fox, Richard Wightman. *Reinhold Niebuhr: A Biography.* New York: Pantheon, 1985; London: Cornell University Press, 1996. An extremely well-written biography, reading at times like a good novel yet thorough and critical. Makes extensive use of unpublished materials; meticulously documented throughout. By far the best historical treatment of Niebuhr, though not as strong on theology.

Hofmann, Hans. *The Theology of Reinhold Niebuhr.* New York: Scribner, 1956. Hofmann traces the development of Niebuhr's theology first by examining his major writings in chronological order, then by structuring his thought into a logical system. Uses lengthy quotations from Niebuhr's works. Marred by failure to relate Niebuhr's thought to his life experiences; still very useful for a clear and comprehensive understanding of his ideas.

Kegley, Charles W., and Robert W. Bretall, eds. *Reinhold Niebuhr: His Religious, Social and Political Thought.* New York: Macmillan, 1956. A collection of essays which critically interpret all phases of Niebuhr's work. Also contains an important intellectual autobiography by Niebuhr himself. Particularly significant for American studies is Arthur Schlesinger, Jr.'s "Reinhold

Niebuhr's Role in American Political Thought and Life." Indispensable volume for Niebuhr studies.

Patterson, Bob E. *Reinhold Niebuhr.* Waco, Tex.: Word, 1977. Part of Word's "Makers of the Modern Theological Mind" series, this concise and well-written biography gives a positive interpretation of Niebuhr's thought from a moderate Evangelical viewpoint.

Rice, Daniel F. *Reinhold Niebuhr and John Dewey: An American Odyssey.* Albany: State University of New York Press, 1993. Rice compares and contrasts the views of these two American philosophers.

Robertson, D. B. *Reinhold Niebuhr's Works: A Bibliography.* Boston: Hall, 1979. The most complete listing available of Niebuhr's published works, including both books and articles. Also contains a full listing of books about Niebuhr, as well as a large number of articles and dissertations.

Stone, Ronald H. *Reinhold Niebuhr: Prophet to Politicians.* Nashville: Abingdon Press, 1972. Carefully traces and analyzes the stages of Niebuhr's political ethics. Well organized and documented, although tedious at points. Perhaps the best treatment of the development of Niebuhr's theology of Christian Realism as it both shaped and was shaped by his political thought and activities.

Weaver, Jace. "Original Simplicities and Present Complexities: Reinhold Niebuhr, Ethnocentrism, and the Myth of American Exceptionalism." *Journal of the American Academy of Religion* 63, no. 2 (Summer 1995). The author discusses Niebuhr's views on American history which Weaver considers incongruous.

Douglas A. Foster

OSCAR NIEMEYER

Born: December 15, 1907; Rio de Janeiro, Brazil

Area of Achievement: Architecture

Contribution: Perhaps the most widely known of Brazilian architects, Niemeyer is one of a key group of architects who gave a distinctly Brazilian flavor to the modern international architectural style.

Early Life

Oscar Niemeyer Soares Filho (commonly known as Oscar Niemeyer) was born to a well-to-do Rio de Janeiro family. Little has been written of his childhood, but it is clear that his early career was an undistinguished one. At the age of twenty-three, after completing Barnabitas College, he entered the National School of Fine Arts in Rio de Janeiro to study architecture. While still a student, he insisted upon joining the office of Lucio Costa, a well-known architect and city planner. Niemeyer continued in Costa's office after completing his architectural studies (in 1934), but prior to 1936 his work drew little notice.

In 1936 a dramatic transformation occurred in Niemeyer's career. He joined a group under Costa's direction that had been formed in order to design a new building for the Brazilian Ministry of Education and Health. When the group submitted its design in May, 1936, Costa suggested that Le Corbusier be invited to Brazil in order to evaluate the design. Le Corbusier stayed for nearly a month, working in close cooperation with Costa's group. During that time he had a profound impact on Niemeyer and the other architects in the group. Many consider his 1936 visit to Brazil to be the launching point for modern architecture in that country.

In 1939, Costa left the design group for the Ministry of Education and Health building, and the remaining architects then elected Niemeyer to take Costa's place as head of the group. This sign of acclaim, in addition to several projects that Niemeyer had undertaken on his own, signaled the start of a promising career—a career that was to afford Niemeyer unusual opportunities for developing and expressing his creativity.

Life's Work

The first project of Niemeyer actually to be built was a maternity clinic and day nursery he designed for a philanthropic institution known as "Obra de Berco." The design problem was complicated by the need to accommodate a number of diverse functions—medical care, staff areas, nursery—but Niemeyer handled the problem in a way that reflected the modest means of the Obra de Berco, while maintaining a friendly, almost anti-institutional atmosphere. On the northern side of the building, Niemeyer put vertical louvers on the outside of the building as protection from the sun. Several years after completion of the building, Niemeyer found that the louvers were not working as designed, so he replaced them at his own expense.

Niemeyer remained involved with the Ministry of Education and Health building through its completion in 1943. The design team finally adopted a variation of a plan proposed by Le Corbusier, and it proved quite successful. The building drew worldwide attention as the first public building to embody the concepts of the modern architecture movement. The design team, sensing that this building was to be a proving ground for modern architecture in Brazil, spent many years perfecting the design, and it is generally conceded that they were successful.

After completing the Ministry of Education and Health building, Niemeyer began to experiment with different forms more widely. He began to break out on his own, away from what had by then become the conventional "new" architecture. Rather than striving for austere and highly rational designs, Niemeyer became more preoccupied with aesthetics. The first example of his new direction comes from a group of buildings that he built on the shores of Lake Pampulha: a casino, a yacht club, a restaurant, and a church. In these buildings, Niemeyer continued to use plastic forms but, in a major departure, not always for functional elements. His use of contrasting room heights, floating ramps, and a variety of means for modulating light all indicated his break from the functionalism and rationalism of the natural sciences.

The church at Lake Pampulha, named for Saint Francis of Assisi, was both the most striking and the most controversial building of the group. Niemeyer chose paraboloid vaults as the main structural elements of the church. By thus creating walls and ceiling with one continuous structural component, he created both a unified and an economical structure. Although criticized roundly by some observers, Niemeyer refused to be inhibited by this subject. The Church of Saint Francis of Assisi is quite in keeping with his style of this period.

Niemeyer's commissions increased after World War II, and with them his fame. The Boavista Bank building marked his return to downtown Rio de Janeiro and clearly illustrates the influence of Le Corbusier (in the cubism of the building's exterior) as well as the freely curving forms of Brazilian architecture. One striking feature of the building in which many elements of Niemeyer's style come together is a two-story, undulating wall of glass blocks. This wall forms the backdrop for the main banking floor and is stunning in its structural and visual effect.

By 1950, Niemeyer had firmly established himself as one of the world's premier architects. By the middle of the decade, he had more than sixty commissions on the drawing board at one time. Some of his projects dating from this period include the United Nations Building in New York (he was a member of an international team of architects), the Sul American Hospital in Rio de Janeiro, the Aeronautical Training Center in São José dos Campos, and the Museum of Modern Art in Caracas. In September, 1956, Niemeyer embarked upon perhaps the largest and most important project of his career: creating a new capital city for Brazil.

In 1955, Juscelino Kubitschek had been elected President of Brazil, and he quickly set out to accomplish a number of reforms. One of those reforms was to be the relocation of Brazil's capital to the interior of the country. This new capital was to be built from scratch and was to be called Brasilia. Kubitschek and Niemeyer had formed a close relationship years earlier and so Kubitschek came to his architect friend for help in this massive undertaking. By 1957, Niemeyer had been appointed chief architect for the Authority for the New Capital of Brazil (NOVACAP). In that capacity, he was responsible for the design of all the important federal buildings. With the help of Lucio Costa and sixty young architects, Niemeyer completed the final drawings in only two years. Construction also proceeded at a hectic pace, and, on April 21, 1960, Brasilia became the capital city of Brazil.

The scale of the project is hard to imagine: to design and build a city and government center with an initial population of 500,000. Laid out on Costa's plan based on the form of a curved cross, the city was intended to be a fully working metropolis from the start. Niemeyer was directly involved in all the major projects, including the congress buildings, the supreme court and presidential offices, the Cathedral and Chapel of Our Lady of Fatima, the presidential residence (Alvorada Palace), the foreign office, the Brasilia Palace Hotel, and the National Theater.

Brasilia did not come cheap, however, and the city took a political toll on Niemeyer's patron, President Kubitschek, who decided against seeking reelection in the October, 1960, election. In the meantime, Niemeyer had been injured in an automobile accident. After a lengthy recovery, he continued his work around the world, having lived in Israel, Paris, and again returning to Rio de Janeiro.

Summary

Oscar Niemeyer and other Brazilian architects were influenced by Le Corbusier, but they built upon that foundation in order to establish a clearly Brazilian style of achitecture—one held in high esteem in international architectural schools. Niemeyer found new, highly imaginative (hence, not strictly rational) uses for freely curving architectural forms. He also took conventions of the modern style, such as lifting buildings off the ground, and gave them his own form as seen in the stylistic "V" shaped stilts he often used.

Another important aspect of Niemeyer's work is his ability to adapt his buildings to the climatic, physical, and economic setting of Brazil. He used the *brise soleil* (literally "sun breakers") in a variety of ways that enhanced both a building's appearance and the comfort of its occupants. Not only was such a solution more economical than air conditioning but also it served as a minimum barrier between the indoors and the outdoors. Breezes were allowed to enter Niemeyer's buildings, where they were channeled through the building to create a more comfortable environment. Niemeyer did not neglect Brazil's history either. Many observers see a baroque influence from Brazil's colonial period. Furthermore, Niemeyer capitalized upon a suggestion by Le Corbusier to use the traditional Portuguese blue ceramic tile (normally associated only with colonial-era buildings) as a finishing material. Niemeyer used these *azulejo* tiles, as they were known, extensively, and on some buildings, notably the Church of Saint Francis of Assisi, created striking murals. In this manner, Niemeyer adapted the international modern style of architecture to his native and beloved Brazil.

Bibliography

Bailby, Edouard. "Oscar Niemeyer Talks to Edouard Bailby." *UNESCO Courier* 45, no. 6 (June, 1992). Interview with Niemeyer in which he discusses architectural styles and his articles and books.

Dixon, John Morris. "Women, Clouds and Oscar Niemeyer." *Progressive Architecture* 75, no. 12 (December, 1994). Dixon discusses the work of Niemeyer with architectural historian David Underwood.

Joedicke, Jürgen. *A History of Modern Architecture*. Translated by James C. Palmes. London: Architectural Press, and New York: Praeger, 1959. Joedicke establishes the setting of the architectural world within which Niemeyer worked. He discusses the intellectual and social factors behind the modern movement, new materials, the early pioneers and later masters, and a summary of contributions to the movement from countries around the world (including Brazil).

Mindlin, Henrique E. *Modern Architecture in Brazil*. London: Architectural Press, and New York: Reinhold, 1956. Mindlin's book is most useful in providing a historical overview of Brazilian architecture in general, with a focus on modern architecture. The reader thus gains a good feel for Niemeyer's place among the architectural exuberance evident in Brazil. The bulk of the book examines the work of Brazilian architecture, classified by building type.

Niemeyer, Oscar. *Oscar Niemeyer*. Introduction and notes by Rupert Spade. London: Thames and Hudson, and New York: Simon and Schuster, 1971. The strength of this book is that it allows the reader to see Niemeyer's work. The almost one hundred pages of glossy plates include photographs (many in color) and drawings of the plan and elevations of many of the buildings. In addition, useful explanatory notes accompany the illustrations for each project, thus interpreting Niemeyer's work. Spade's introductory comments also shed light on Niemeyer's life and work.

—————. *Oscar Niemeyer: Works in Progress*. Edited by Stamo Papadaki. New York: Reinhold, 1956. A continuation of the work cited below, this book covers what was perhaps Niemeyer's most fertile period: 1950 to 1956. It clearly demonstrates how busy he was during the 1950's. Plentifully illustrated with photographs (often of scale models, since many of the projects were not complete at the time of publication) and drawings, this book is an important visual record of this period of Niemeyer's career. Unfortunately, it stops before he became involved with Brasilia.

—————. *The Work of Oscar Niemeyer*. Edited by Stamo Papadaki. New York: Reinhold, 1950. After a few introductory remarks by Papadaki and a foreword by Lucio Costa, the bulk of this book is devoted to chronicling all of Niemeyer's projects through 1950. The Obra de Berco nursery and day-care center, the buildings at Lake Pampulha, the Boavista Bank, and many other buildings that contributed to Niemeyer's rise to fame are illustrated (with both photographs and drawings) and interpreted here.

Papadaki, Stamo. *Oscar Niemeyer*. New York: Braziller, 1960; London: Mayflower, 1961. One of the books in the Masters of World Architecture series, Papadaki's book is a concise account of Niemeyer's life and work. It puts him in proper context within both Brazil and the international modern architecture movement. Roughly half the book is devoted to photographs and drawings of Niemeyer's projects. The chronology and bibliographies of works by and about Niemeyer are all quite useful.

Brian J. Nichelson

MARTIN NIEMÖLLER

Born: January 14, 1892; Lippstadt, Germany
Died: March 6, 1984; Wiesbaden, West Germany
Areas of Achievement: Church reform and social reform
Contribution: Niemöller, a leading religious opponent of the National Socialist regime, helped to organize the Confessing church in 1934, a body within the German Evangelical church that formed the center of Protestant resistance in the Third Reich. After his liberation from eight years in a concentration camp, he became a prominent figure in the restored German Evangelical church and the World Council of Churches, best known for his outspoken opposition to West German rearmament, nuclear armament, and his advocacy of pacifism.

Early Life

Friedrich Gustav Emil Martin Niemöller was born in Lippstadt, Westphalia, on January 14, 1892, as the second of six children of a Lutheran pastor. He was educated in public schools, first in Lippstadt and, after age eight, in Elberfeld, where his father moved to a new parish. In the Niemöller family the practice of the Protestant religion went hand in hand with German nationalism. Following an early fascination with the sea, young Niemöller joined the imperial navy upon graduation from the Elberfeld Gymnasium, an academic secondary school, in 1910. Talented, ambitious, and imbued with the teaching from home that a good Christian is a good citizen and as such a good soldier, he quickly advanced in his naval career. After first being trained on a battleship, he was transferred to submarine service in 1915. Two years later he was put in command of a submarine and led several missions against the British and the French. During his submarine service, he was awarded the Iron Cross First Class. After the war, he resigned from the navy in March, 1919.

Disillusioned by Germany's defeat and antagonistic to the democracy of the Weimar Republic, Niemöller briefly tried farming but soon concluded that the postwar inflation made the purchase of a farm impossible. He married Else Bremer, who was to be his supportive wife and mother of seven children until her death in a car accident in 1961. Having repeatedly faced the meaning of life and death in war, drawing on his religious upbringing, and hopeful that the church could help regenerate German spiritual life, he began to study theology in 1920 with the intention of entering the ministry. At the same time, he remained captivated by right-wing political sentiments. In March, 1920, he and other nationalist students formed the Academic Defense Corps during the monarchist Kapp Putsch against the Weimar government. After the failure of the coup, Niemöller and his compatriots battled communist insurgents in the Ruhr region before resuming their studies. Throughout much of his life, Niemöller saw himself both as a good Christian and as a supreme German patriot.

While a student and then during his mandatory service as a curate, he helped supplement his family income by working as a platelayer and accountant on the German railroad. Once he got closer to finishing his studies, he was reluctant to take a parish of his own because of the difficult economic conditions in Germany. Instead, late in 1923, he became manager of the Inner Mission of Westphalia and was thus put in charge of the administration of church social welfare for an entire province. Over the next seven years, this work gave him invaluable organizational experience as well as heightened awareness of the meaning of the "social gospel."

Life's Work

By 1931, Niemöller was eager to accept a church of his own. He was appointed third pastor to a church in Berlin-Dahlem, one of the richest and most fashionable parishes in Germany. Within months he became senior pastor upon the death of the incumbent, and two years later he found himself a national figure in Germany. The two sides of his personality continued to show: He was a committed Christian caring for the souls of his parishioners and a man of deep political convictions. He identified most closely with nationalist conservatives who loathed the Weimar Republic and, on several occasions from 1924 to 1933, even voted for the National Socialist Party. He was impressed with a part of the National Socialist program that advocated freedom for all religious denominations and the idea of "positive Christianity." Adolf Hitler, however, upon becoming chancellor in January, 1933, attempted to achieve dominance over the Evangelical Church (Lutheran and Reformed) by promoting the neopagan movement of the German Christians and the appointment of Pastor Ludwig

Müller, a National Socialist follower, as Reich bishop.

Disillusioned by such blatant interference in church affairs, Niemöller attacked the religious policies of the government. In September, 1933, he and others established the Pastors' Emergency League to assist non-Aryan pastors or those married to non-Aryans, such as Christian Jews, who were threatened with dismissal, and to serve as an organizational network for the clergy, who resisted the inroads of the regime in church work. In the following year, Niemöller and his allies set to work creating a new church structure by adding lay support to the efforts of the clergy. At two synodal meetings at Barmen and Berlin-Dahlem, they organized free synods, in opposition to those dominated by the Reich bishop, and thus laid the groundwork for the Confessing church. Informed by Karl Barth's theological declaration that drew a sharp distinction between the true church and the German Christians, the Confessing church claimed to be the duly constituted Protestant church in Germany. It managed to maintain itself as the sole coherent opposition among Protestants to the religious policies of the Third Reich.

Niemöller's outspoken criticism of National Socialist religious policies and fearless defense of the independence of the church focused national attention on his person and earned for him Hitler's personal wrath. Disagreement with the regime's religious policies and racial measures as they affected Christian Jews, albeit much less so Jews in general, did not lead Niemöller to dissent from the government's political and foreign policies. In the fall of 1933, he sent a congratulatory telegram to Hitler, on behalf of the Pastors' Emergency League, when Germany left the League of Nations. He also approved of German rearmament. In the following year, he authored his autobiographical *Vom U-Boot zur Kanzel* (1934; *From U-boat to Pulpit*, 1936), which revealed his singular patriotism, bringing him considerable fame in Germany and abroad. None of this, however, saved him from repeated arrest by the Gestapo and permanent imprisonment starting in July, 1937. Early in 1938, he was tried on charges of violating the law and engaging in treasonous activity. He mounted a defense stressing his patriotic service in war and peacetime, which resulted in a reduction of charges and a minimal sentence. Expecting to be released, he was immediately rearrested and sent to the Sachsenhausen concentration camp near Berlin as Hitler's personal prisoner. In June, 1941, he was transferred to the Dachau concentration camp near Munich. At the end of the war, he escaped execution and was freed while on transport to the Austrian Tyrol.

Having become aware of the full magnitude of the crimes committed by the Hitler regime only after his release, Niemöller concluded that the renewal of the German church and its acceptance by foreign churches required unconditional penance. He became a driving force behind the Stuttgart Declaration of Guilt issues in October, 1945. In the presence of ecumenical representatives, twelve leaders of the German Evangelical church confessed that the church shared with the German people responsibility for the endless suffering caused to many peoples and countries and accused themselves of not acting more courageously to prevent it. In sermons and speeches, especially before student audiences, Niemöller explicitly asserted that his confession included responsibility for the murder of five to six million Jews, but he rejected the political conception of collective guilt. Because of his international reputation, he was named president of foreign affairs of the German Evangelical church in 1945. Very soon he became an active participant in the emerging World Council of Churches and was appointed its copresident in 1961. In addition, he also served as president of the Evangelical church of Hesse and Nassau from 1947.

The concentration camp experience and contact with foreign inmates at Dachau had broadened Niemöller's narrow German vistas. The ecumenical work that he engaged in and the regular contact with non-Germans both in occupied Germany and on his frequent travels abroad completed his development from a German nationalist into an internationalist. Taking the role of the church as a moral force in society very seriously, he felt an obligation as one of its leaders to speak out boldly on current issues of concern. In 1946, he was among the first prominent Germans to criticize the treatment of German prisoners of war in British camps. He clashed with the occupation authorities over their policies of denazification and dismantling. He actively worked for the release of Waffen Schützstaffeln Gestapo officers and several prominent Nazis when he believed that their sentence outweighed their alleged crimes. Fearing that the division of Germany might become permanent, he opposed the creation of the Federal Republic of Germany in 1949. He vehemently objected to Ger-

2744 / THE TWENTIETH CENTURY: MARTIN NIEMÖLLER

man rearmament in the early 1950's, incurring the wrath of Chancellor Konrad Adenauer, who called him an enemy of the state.

While the Cold War raged, Niemöller met with the patriarch of Moscow in 1952 and soon joined the communist dominated World Peace Council. He angered many in the West with his contacts in East Germany and his insistence that the vitality of Christianity was much greater there under communism than in materialist West Germany. His attack on racism as a threat to world peace won for him wide support, but his antinuclear stance raised much objection. Having learned from Otto Hahn that nuclear weapons could extinguish higher life on the planet, he declared himself a convinced pacifist in the mid-1950's. His controversial if not iconoclastic pronouncements tended to lose friends for him and to diminish his organizational influence. In 1956, he was removed as head of the church's foreign affairs office. In 1964, he retired from the presidency of the Hesse and Nassau church, and in 1968 he relinquished his leading position on the World Council of Churches. He continued his active involvement in the German and European peace and antinuclear movement in sermons, speeches, and writing until only a few years before his death in 1984.

Summary

Martin Niemöller, who never really liked theology and considered philosophy useless, was a practical man of action. Imbued with strong religious convictions, he had boundless energy and demonstrated remarkable commitment applying Christian principles to life in society. He once remarked that he developed from an ultraconservative into a revolutionary and, if he were to live to be a hundred, he might become an anarchist. He never fully internalized a Western liberal worldview and regarded West German democracy as imperfect. Much of his life his commitment was that of a Christian and a German nationalist; after World War II it became that of a Christian and an internationalist who continued to love his homeland deeply. Above all, he came to believe that Christian spirituality transcended national boundaries and could unite believers under different political systems.

Niemöller's most notable historical achievement was the dedication to Christian ideals that he showed and the leadership role that he performed during the early years of National Socialist rule in Germany—one of the most troubled times for modern Christianity. He committed his life to creating the German Protestant church's resistance to the Hitler regime. His courage and fearless defense of Christian beliefs inspired others to carry on when he was incarcerated and gave him a reputation much beyond Germany's borders. The moral prestige that he commanded as a Protestant resister and imprisoned martyr enabled him to play a prominent role during the aftermath of the war, when the German Evangelical church was struggling to reconstitute itself and restore its moral prestige. He is remembered for his untiring effort to establish ecumenical ties with churches in the West and the East. His relentless promotion of international peace and antinuclear campaigns helped to shape in no insignificant way the climate of public opinion in West Germany and Europe for the concrete steps toward nuclear disarmament taken by the United States and the Soviet Union during the 1970's and 1980's. It was indicative of Niemöller's international stature that he was honored for the promotion of world peace by being awarded both the Lenin Peace Prize in 1967 and the Grand Cross of Merit, West Germany's highest recognition, in 1971.

Bibliography

Bentley, James. *Martin Niemöller, 1892-1984*. Oxford and New York: Oxford University Press, 1984. This definitive biography draws on archival sources and also relies heavily on information obtained from interviews with Niemöller. It is well written and covers all phases of his life and career. Its principal weakness lies in the absence of an adequate historical context for its subject.

Helmreich, Ernst Christian. *The German Churches Under Hitler: Background, Struggle, and Epilogue*. Detroit: Wayne State University Press, 1979. The most important scholarly treatment of German churches during the Third Reich. It also summarizes developments before and after the National Socialist era. Essential for putting Niemöller in the broader context of church history.

Schmidt, Dietmar. *Pastor Niemöller*. Translated by Lawrence Wilson. London: Odhams Press, and New York: Doubleday, 1959. An informed journalistic account of Niemöller's life and work through the late 1950's by a close associate. It offers insights into its subject's complex personality but does not purport to be a completely impartial biography. Contains a short bibliography.

Spotts, Frederic. *The Churches and Politics in Germany*. Middletown, Conn.: Wesleyan University Press, 1973. Based on unpublished sources, this detailed study of the West German churches in the postwar period analyzes such issues as denazification, reunification, and political attitudes of church leaders. Niemöller's role is put in the broader context of German church development.

Start, Clarissa. *God's Man: The Story of Pastor Niemöller*. New York: Washburn, 1959. A more captivating journalistic partial biography than Dietmar Schmidt's book noted below. Davidson met Niemöller and his family and presents a sympathetic portrait of a man whom she much admires. Includes a bibliography.

George P. Blum

VASLAV NIJINSKY

Born: March 12, 1890; Kiev, Ukraine, Russian
Empire
Died: April 8, 1950; London, England
Area of Achievement: Dance
Contribution: With the impresario Sergei Diaghilev, who enlisted him as a premier dancer in the
Ballet Russe company, Nijinsky established the
popularity of Russian ballet throughout the
Western world in the second decade of the twentieth century. As a choreographer, he was also
very instrumental in adapting dance movements
to the new music of the twentieth century, especially that of Russian composer Igor Stravinsky.

Early Life

Vaslav Nijinsky was born in Kiev when his dancer
parents were on tour in the Ukraine. Both of his
parents, Eleonora Nikolayevich and Thomas, were
Polish, and when young Vaslav was two they took
him to Warsaw for baptism in the Catholic religion.
Vaslav was the second of three children. An elder
brother, Stanislav, was mentally retarded following
a fall at age six. The youngest was Bronisława,
who became a celebrated ballerina in St. Petersburg. After Thomas deserted the family, Eleonora
took the children to St. Petersburg and enrolled
Vaslav, then age nine, in the Imperial School of
Ballet. The celebrated dancer Nicholas Legat noticed his athleticism and recommended his admittance. He began his studies there in 1898, graduating in 1907. He quickly caught the eyes of the
critics with his exceptional leaping ability. Aside
from dance, Nijinsky was a poor student and was
teased by other boys for his Tatar-like features.
Young Nijinsky never made a real friend there.

In 1902, Nijinsky's dance instructor was
Mikhail Obukhov, who protected him from the
cruelty of the other boys. During these years
Nijinsky also learned how to play the piano, flute,
balalaika, and accordion. In January, 1905, Nijinsky was caught in the crowds during the demonstrations against the government when Cossacks
attacked. On this "Bloody Sunday," Nijinsky was
bloodied by a knout from one of the Cossacks. He
was not politically inclined and spent most of his
hours devoted to music. He was not an avid reader
but was absorbed by Charles Dickens' *David Cop-
perfield* (1849-1850), which he and his sister read
together. He also read Fyodor Dostoevski's *Idiot*
(1868; *The Idiot,* 1887). He was very moved by

the main character in this last story, Prince Mysh-
kin, a Christ-like simpleton with whom he apparently identified. His favorite composers were the
Russian Nikolay Rimsky-Korsakov and the German Richard Wagner.

Life's Work

When American dancer Isadora Duncan visited the
Russian capital, Nijinsky was fascinated by her.
The choreographer Michel Fokine decided to stage
a short ballet in her honor and chose Nijinsky for a
small part. His manner and style were very appealing to the St. Petersburg critics, who were more attracted by the dramatic abilities of dancers than by
their technique. Famed dancer Tamara Karsavina
was so attracted by the splendor of his leaps that
she promised to dance with him. His first real applause came on January 31, 1906, during a special
dance for eight people inserted into the Mozart opera *Don Giovanni* at the Mariinsky Theater. Nijinsky was the only one who had not yet graduated,
but he stole the short dance to take his first solo
bow. Weeks later the program was repeated, and
this time the dancers included the acclaimed Anna
Pavlova.

Several small parts followed that year, and, after
his graduation performance on April 29, even the
most celebrated Mathilde Kchessinskaya expressed a desire to dance with him. He was readily
admitted to the Imperial Ballet Company, and that
summer he vacationed at Krasnoe Selo, where he
danced with Kchessinskaya before the military
troops. Following a solo dance before Czar Nicholas II, the emperor presented him with a gold
watch. Before autumn he was contacted by his father and visited him in Nizhni Novgorod. They
danced together and had a very friendly reunion.
That was to be the last time that they met.

Back in St. Petersburg, the family moved to a
well-to-do district near the Hermitage. Nijinsky
was only a member of the Corps de Ballet, but he
accepted offers to instruct children in the art of
dance, for which he received one hundred rubles an
hour. When his first season began he had opportunities to dance solo pieces and a *pas de deux* with
Karsavina. In the winter, his roles increased in importance and frequency, and he soon found a patron in Prince Pavel Dmitryevich Lvov. The prince
introduced him to Diaghilev in the early winter of
1908.

Vaslav Nijinsky with his daughter in 1916.

It was not until Nijinsky first danced with the Diaghilev company in the Russian season in Paris in 1909 that audiences noticed his greatness. He soon became the showcase for Russian dance throughout Europe and South and North America. He was the "Favorite Slave" in *Le Pavillon d'Armide*, the "Poet" in *Les Sylphides*, the "Golden Slave" in *Schéhérazade*, "Harlequin" in *Carnaval*, and the transformed "Puppet" in *Petrushka*. Nijinsky developed a reputation for being exotic and otherworldly. Critics found his dancing technically perfect and his performances highly dramatic. Diaghilev saw in him also a choreographer and trained him as such. Their relationship became intimate, and, after Nijinsky became seriously ill with typhoid fever, Diaghilev nursed him back to health.

Nijinsky returned from Paris to dance the season with the Imperial Ballet Company, but when he danced in a shocking costume designed by Alexander Benois for the ballet *Giselle*, the theatrical authorities demanded that he alter it. When he refused, they gave him the option of apologizing or resigning from the company. He resigned. There is some suspicion that the affair was staged by Diaghilev to free the dancer from his five-year contract with the Imperial Ballet Company. Following his resignation in January, 1911, he returned to France that spring to join the next season with Diaghilev full-time. On April 9, the company abandoned its summer status, and at Monte Carlo Diaghilev formed the permanent Ballet Russe. Fokine's *Specter of a Rose* was first performed there as Nijinsky's most famous role of a phantom was danced opposite Karsavina. Upon reaching Paris, the company thrilled French audiences with marvelous tableaux of Russian life in Fokine's choreography of Stravinsky's *Petrushka* with Nijinsky as the puppet. So popular were the dancers that the company was invited to London to celebrate the coronation of King George V.

The Ballet Russe was equally popular in the following year, but in Paris Nijinsky the dancer also became Nijinsky the choreographer. Fokine's work had worn thin with Diaghilev, and the famed dancer choreographed Claude Debussy's *Afternoon of a Faun*. He reversed many of the classical postures as he struggled to create new dance forms, consciously breaking with the past. These new movements themselves were controversial, but the closing scene displayed an erotic episode that scandalized the audiences. Nevertheless, the reaction was a mixture of damnation and enthusiastic praise. Among the latter was a newspaper letter of sculptor Auguste Rodin. If the controversy over the Debussy piece was well known, it was soon eclipsed by one of greater dimensions. This was the reaction to Nijinsky's choreography of Stravinsky's *The Rite of Spring*, in which Nijinsky danced the leading role. The spasmic and frenzied motions were ill understood even by his followers, and audiences were repelled by the cacophonous rhythms of the composer. When it was first performed in Paris on May 29, 1913, it produced a near riot in the theater. That season, Nijinsky also choreographed *Jeux*, a ballet performed in modern dress that was never popular.

There followed tours to London and to South America. A year earlier, when the company was in Budapest, Nijinsky met Romola de Pulszky, a famous actress and daughter of the founder and first director of the National Gallery of Hungary, Karoly de Pulszky, a Pole whose family had long resided in Hungary. Attracted to Nijinsky, she was determined to become a member of the Ballet Russe. She took dancing lessons and, using her family influence, persuaded Diaghilev to take her to South America as a student dancer. En route to Argentina she and Nijinsky fell in love, and four days after landing they were married in Buenos Aires. So enraged was Diaghilev that he dismissed his famous star.

An independent Nijinsky and his bride went to London, where he started his own short-lived company. They then returned to Budapest, where their daughter Kyra was born. While in Hungary, they were caught in the maelstrom of World War I. As a Russian citizen, Nijinsky was declared a prisoner of war and detained. Nevertheless, Diaghilev, who was planning an American tour for the Ballet Russe, had a change of heart and negotiated for his release. When the couple arrived in New York early in 1916, the impresario met them with flowers, and a reconciliation took place. In autumn the company took a second tour of the United States, and the Nijinskys simply stayed there between tours. It was during the second American season that Nijinsky choreographed his last ballet, *Tyl Eulenspiegel*, at the Metropolitan Opera House in New York. In 1917, Nijinsky embarked on a four-month dancing tour of the United States and joined Diaghilev in Spain by June. There they planned another tour of South America, where Nijinsky last danced with the Ballet Russe on September 26 in Buenos Aires.

One year later in St. Moritz, Nijinsky fell into severe depression. In 1919, he was diagnosed as an incurable schizophrenic. Romola stayed close to him for the next thirty-one years while he was in and out of asylums. In 1928, the Nijinskys sat in Diaghilev's box to watch the Ballet Russe perform in Paris. When World War II began, the couple was again stranded in Hungary, and Nijinsky rejoiced upon seeing Russian armies arriving in 1945. Two years later, the couple moved to London, where Nijinsky died after a kidney illness on April 8, 1950, at age sixty. Nijinsky was given a Roman Catholic funeral and buried outside London. Three years later, Serge Lifar arranged for the transfer of the body to Paris, at which time Bronisława Nijinska insisted upon a new funeral in the Russian Orthodox rite.

Summary

An assessment of Vaslav Nijinsky's impact necessarily includes both his dancing and his choreography. Parisian audiences were astonished by the gracefulness of his leaps. Until he performed with the Ballet Russe, Western audiences were unaccustomed to admiring the beauty of male dancers such as Nijinsky and others in the troupe. Nijinsky and his generation of dancers had already changed the image of the male dancer at home in St. Petersburg with the Imperial Ballet Company. Before this time, it was not unusual for females to assume male dancing roles. At other times, the male was expected to render mere support for the female star. After Nijinsky's era, the female was not eclipsed, certainly, but the famed Polish dancer made it possible for later male stars such as Rudolph Nureyev and Mikhail Baryshnikov to emerge.

Nijinsky was equally innovative in choreography, but his contribution here was more by design than by instinct. A keen student of music, he was one of the first to appreciate the direction in which modern rhythms should take the art of dance. Hence Nijinsky choreographed *Afternoon of a Faun, Jeux, The Rite of Spring*, and *Tyl Eulenspiegel* in the new style for the Diaghilev company. These may have been the first truly creative ballets of the twentieth century. He surely surpassed his rival, Fokine, by using a bolder and more daring style. There was a sense of mystery to his dance and choreography that seemed to suit the new music of Igor Stravinsky and other modern composers. Nowhere was this match so evident as in Stravinsky's *The Rite of Spring*, a ballet that has become standard fare throughout much of the world.

Bibliography

Buckle, Richard. *Diaghilev*. London: Weidenfeld and Nicolson, and New York: Atheneum, 1979. Especially useful in the section entitled "The Fokine-Nijinsky Period" in this, the latest and most definitive biography yet written of Diaghilev.

———. *Nijinsky*. London: Weidenfeld and Nicolson, and New York: Simon and Schuster, 1976. This work presents the basic information about the subject and is the standard, reliable work.

Gelatt, Roland. *Nijinsky: The Film*. New York: Ballantine, 1980. Gelatt wrote the text, and the book has sixty-two pages of photographs from the film. Other photographs are of Nijinsky himself.

Kopelson, Kevin. *The Queer Afterlife of Vaslav Nijinsky*. Stanford, Calif.: Stanford University Press, 1997. Kopelson considers Nijinsky's career, emphasizing the less-than-masculine elements of his life and performances.

Krasovskaia, Vera. *Nijinsky*. Translated by John E. Bowlt. New York: Schirmer, 1979. First published in Russia in 1974, this is the first Russian account of Nijinsky to be translated into English. Somewhat anecdotal and without a bibliography, the narration is a revealing portrait by another well-known dancer. Contains many photographs.

Nijinska, Bronislawa. *Bronislava Nijinska: Early Memoirs*. Edited and translated by Irina Nijinsky and Jean Rawlinson. New York: Holt Rinehart, 1981; London: Faber, 1982. A charming, readable account of her brother's life as well as her own. The work reveals a magnificent eye for detail.

Nijinsky, Vaslav. *The Diary of Vaslav Nijinsky*. Edited by Joan Acocella and translated by Kyril FitzÎlyon. New York: Farrar, Straus, 1999. This is the "unexpurgated" English-language edition of Nijinsky's diary, which he kept between January 19 and March 4, 1919, and which provides a clear indication of the onset of psychosis.

Philip, Richard, and Mary Whitney. "The Living Legend of Nijinsky." In *Danseur: The Male in Ballet*. New York: McGraw-Hill, 1977. Containing an easy-to-read summary of Nijinsky's career, this narrative stresses his innovations and influence. The text also contains twelve full-page photographs of the dancer and a bibliography.

John D. Windhausen

CHESTER W. NIMITZ

Born: February 24, 1885; Fredericksburg, Texas
Died: February 20, 1966; San Francisco, California
Area of Achievement: The military
Contribution: Nimitz commanded American forces in the Pacific during World War II and played a crucial role in winning the important and difficult Battle of Midway. After the war, he became Chief of Naval Operations.

Early Life

Chester William Nimitz was born on February 24, 1885, in the German immigrant community of Fredericksburg, Texas, the son of Chester B. Nimitz and Anna Henke Nimitz. Although his father had died before he was born and the family was never well-off financially, he enjoyed a happy childhood with his cherished and hardworking mother and his not-so-hardworking but happy-go-lucky stepfather (who was also his uncle), William Nimitz. Perhaps the most important male influence on the boy, however, was that of his grandfather, Charles Henry Nimitz, who filled his mind with tales of nautical adventure. Despite such talk of the sea, Nimitz's ambition as a teenager was to become a soldier, so impressed was he by officers from the Army post at Fort Sam Houston. There were no vacancies at West Point, however, so he attended the United States Naval Academy instead, and was graduated on January 30, 1905, seventh in a class of 114.

Blond and handsome, kindly and humorous, above all capable of laughing at himself when the need arose, young Nimitz was prime material for a happy marriage; yet nuptials did not occur until April 9, 1913, when he wed Catherine B. Freeman of Wollaston, Massachusetts. They had four children: Catherine (born 1914), Chester (born 1915), Anna (born 1919), and Mary (born 1931).

Life's Work

Nimitz's early interests were in engineering and submarines. During World War I, he served on an oiler and also with the submarines, ending the war as a lieutenant commander. In the postwar period, he had the usual kinds of assignments that rising officers enjoyed: attendance at the Naval War College, teaching in ROTC, service with battleships, and command of a cruiser. He never became an aviator, a fact that might have caused problems for a lesser man during World War II, when he was called upon to command an aircraft carrier-orient-

ed fleet. Nimitz became an admiral in 1938 and in 1939 took charge of the Bureau of Navigation, the office that controlled personnel assignments.

This latter post gave him access to President Franklin D. Roosevelt, who, along with almost everyone else, took a liking to the new admiral. In early 1941, Roosevelt offered Nimitz command of the Pacific Fleet, but he declined because of lack of seniority—a lucky move: Had he accepted the offer, he, instead of Admiral Husband E. Kimmel, might have had to take the blame for the disaster at Pearl Harbor later that same year.

After the invasion at Pearl Harbor, Kimmel was dismissed and Nimitz was named to replace him as Commander in Chief Pacific (CINCPAC), as of December 31, 1941. From his desk in Pearl Harbor, Nimitz would lead all the American forces, Army as well as Navy and Marines, in the North, Central, and South Pacific areas; he also was in direct command of all naval units in those areas by virtue of wearing a different hat. Thus, in a sense, he was his own boss, being both theater commander and theater naval chieftain. This arrangement worked well, but did not eliminate all command problems in the war against Japan.

One of Nimitz's difficulties was with General Douglas MacArthur, commander of the Southwest Pacific Area (SWPA). MacArthur wanted his theater to be the scene of the principal thrust against Japan, even if that meant reducing Nimitz's activity to nothing. Probably MacArthur would have been happiest if Nimitz and his theater had been put under SWPA command. The Navy Department would never have allowed either the lesser or the greater of MacArthur's ambitions to come true, but Nimitz had to operate throughout the war with the knowledge that the Army in general, and MacArthur in particular, wanted a greater share of material and command.

Nimitz also had to contend with his own boss, Admiral Ernest J. King, Chief of Naval Operations and Commander in Chief of all American warships around the world. King was a ferocious man, just as harsh as Nimitz was kindly, and he worried about CINCPAC's aggressiveness. King thought that Nimitz might not be willing to dismiss those who fell short of perfection; he also wondered at first about Nimitz's willingness to take enormous risks in fighting the Japanese. Perhaps the real problem was that King could not resist the temptation to become personally involved in running the Pacific war. Another thing that bothered King about Nimitz was the latter's reluctance to do battle against MacArthur. King was responsible for upholding the Navy's prerogatives in the face of demands from his equals in the highest councils of war—the British, the Army, and the Army Air Forces; therefore, he could not afford to be affable, or so he seems to have reckoned. Nimitz, on the other hand, outranked all the generals and admirals in his own theater and was not in a position to thwart MacArthur's plans directly; he, therefore, could approach the war in a more genial frame of mind. For all that, King and Nimitz made a good team, each compensating for the other's rare moments of bad judgment.

Since Nimitz was tied for the most part to his desk, the battles in his theater were conducted either by commanders at sea or on the invaded islands: Admirals Frank Jack Fletcher, William F. Halsey, and Raymond A. Spruance, and Marine Generals A. Archer Vandegrift and Holland M. Smith, among others. Nevertheless, as Commander in Chief, Nimitz bore the ultimate responsibility for their campaigns, except insofar as King himself sometimes determined the overall strategy—and except for the times when Halsey's services were lent to MacArthur.

Undoubtedly, the most important battle in which Nimitz's role was most personal and crucial was that fought near the island of Midway. The Pacific Fleet was much inferior to that of Japan, and so it was vital for the Americans, if they were to hold Midway, to know what the Japanese intended to do. Fortunately, Nimitz could tap the resources of a brilliant cryptologist, Lieutenant Commander Joseph J. Rochefort, Jr., who had recently broken the Japanese naval code and thereby was able to predict the enemy's plan. It was Nimitz himself, however, who had to decide whether to believe Rochefort's evidence, and it was also Nimitz who next had to convince a headstrong King that Rochefort was right. Even after that, there were plans to be made and risks to be taken. It was Nimitz who decided not to use the United States' elderly battleships in the coming fight because they would only get in the way; a nonaviator, he nevertheless put his faith in his aircraft carriers. It was Nimitz who decided on the deployment of those carriers, although Fletcher and Spruance were in command afloat. The result of all these plans and decisions, along with the skill and luck of those on the scene, was

an overwhelming American victory, one of the great turning points of the war.

Nimitz was farther removed from the controls during the battles on and around Guadalcanal in August and November, 1942. These were King's pet projects, and conducted on the scene by the South Pacific commanders, who reported to Nimitz. Though close victories, they served to confirm the verdict of Midway: From then on, it was not a question of whether the United States would win the war against Japan but of how soon and at what cost. If Nimitz took too long or spent too much American blood, the public might demand that MacArthur be given the lion's share of men, material, and tasks. Nimitz was responsible more than any other single person for the fact that his forces moved ahead as rapidly as they did and, for the most part, with no more bloodshed than necessary. His campaigns in the Gilberts, the Marshalls, the Marianas, Iwo Jima, and Okinawa were all successful. During the reconquest of the Philippines, however, Nimitz was in general an onlooker: Halsey still reported to him but was operating according to MacArthur's plan. Thus, there was no unity of command during the

Battle of Leyte Gulf (October 23-26, 1944); the only common commander of all American forces at Leyte was President Roosevelt himself. Nimitz did intervene once in order to correct an unfortunate move by Halsey.

World War II ended with Nimitz and MacArthur accepting Japan's surrender, both of them now wearing the five stars of the new American ranks, respectively Fleet Admiral and General of the Army; this was an honor shared by only five other officers as of V-J Day.

On December 15, 1945, Nimitz succeeded King as Chief of Naval Operations. It was a time of demobilization, but the biggest issue facing the new chief was that of unification of the services. Although CINCPAC's joint command had worked well, and although command disunity had bedeviled the Leyte Gulf campaign, Nimitz nevertheless agreed with most Navy men in objecting to unification on the national level. Sailors feared that the new Air Force might try to take over the Navy's aerial component, while the Army, having lost its airplanes, might attempt to seize control of the Marine Corps as compensation. Yet when Congress "unified" the services in 1947, the Navy Department retained its airplanes and the Marines. Nimitz deserves some of the credit for his department's victory: He had made himself welcome at the White House of President Harry S Truman, a man who, unlike Roosevelt, had originally favored the Army.

Although five-star officers do not retire in the usual sense, Nimitz nevertheless went off active duty in December, 1947. In 1949, however, Truman offered to reappoint him as Chief of Naval Operations in the wake of the so-called Admirals' Revolt against the Defense Department, an incident touched off by Navy—Air Force rivalry. What Truman wanted was a conciliator, but Nimitz declined the offer. Instead, he spent his retirement as regent of the University of California, as United Nations plebiscite administrator for Kashmir (1949-1950), and as roving ambassador for the United Nations (1950-1952). In the late 1950's, he helped E. B. Potter edit an important textbook of naval history, *Sea Power: A Naval History* (1960).

By 1965, Nimitz was suffering from osteoarthritis and pneumonia; the latter had bothered him off and on for many years despite his generally robust condition. Strokes and heart failure followed, and he died in San Francisco on February 20, 1966.

Summary

Despite King's occasional misgivings, Nimitz's career proves that nice guys do not necessarily finish last. He fully deserved his elevation to five-star rank for his all-important role in the Battle of Midway and his more distant but still vital part in subsequent American Pacific victories. His postwar services also justified the honor. Although he disliked controversy, and therefore did not subsequently write his memoirs or even allow a biography in his lifetime, he nevertheless was able to carry out the duties of a great commander without inordinate displays of ego or temper. Whether such a pleasant man could have held off the War Department and the British in Washington during World War II is another question, but perhaps the American Joint Chiefs of Staff and the Anglo-American Combined Chiefs of Staff would have benefitted from his reasonable and amiable presence. He was too quiet a man to make good "copy" for the press, as was the case with some other famous World War II commanders, but he achieved as much greatness or more.

Bibliography

Bergstrom, Robert W. "A Former Naval Officer Asserts General Douglas MacArthur Was Wrongly Credited with America's Island-Hopping Strategy." *World War II* 13, no. 7 (March, 1999). Considers Nimitz's concept of "island-hopping," which has incorrectly been attributed to MacArthur.

Buell, Thomas B. *Master of Sea Power: A Biography of Fleet Admiral Ernest J. King.* Boston: Little Brown, 1980. This book does not rank with Potter's biography of Nimitz (see below), but it is quite worthwhile and helps the reader to see Nimitz from the point of view of Washington and London.

Dull, Paul S. *The Imperial Japanese Navy, 1941-1945.* Annapolis, Md.: Naval Institute Press, 1978. This is a highly successful attempt to see the war in the Pacific from the Japanese Navy's viewpoint.

James, Dorris Clayton. *The Years of MacArthur: Volume II, 1941-1945.* Boston: Houghton Mifflin, 1970. A gigantic, brilliant biography. James accomplishes the nearly impossible: He provides a balanced, fair treatment of one of America's most controversial leaders.

McIntyre, Edison. "War in the Pacific." *Cobblestone* 15, no. 1 (January, 1994). The author discusses the Pacific conflicts of World War II including Nimitz's contributions.

Morison, Samuel E. *The Two-Ocean War: A Short History of the United States Navy in the Second World War.* Boston: Little Brown, 1963. Admiral Morison, himself a professional historian, oversaw the production of the Navy's multivolume official history of World War II; this is a one-volume distillation of that effort.

Potter, E. B. *Nimitz.* Annapolis, Md.: Naval Institute Press, 1976. This is a long but well-written, authoritative, and masterful biography by an eminent naval historian. It is by far the most important source for any sketch of Nimitz's life.

Potter, E. B., and Chester W. Nimitz, eds. *Sea Power: A Naval History.* Englewood Cliffs, N.J.: Prentice-Hall, 1960. A useful textbook covering all the history of naval warfare.

Prange, Gordon W., Donald M. Goldstein, and Katherine V. Dillon. *Miracle at Midway.* London and New York: Penguin, 1983. One of Prange's posthumous books, perhaps a bit flawed because it was put together after his death; nevertheless, it provides interesting and dramatically told insights concerning Nimitz's most famous battle.

Spector, Ronald H. *Eagle Against the Sun.* London: Viking, and New York: Free Press, 1985. A well-balanced, well-written, and up-to-date account of the Pacific war by a highly respected, rising young historian.

Karl G. Larew

KITARŌ NISHIDA

Born: May 19, 1870; Unoke, near Kanazawa, Japan
Died: June 7, 1945; Kamakura, Japan
Areas of Achievement: Philosophy and religion
Contribution: Nishida is widely considered to be the foremost philosopher of modern Japan. He created his own highly original and distinctive philosophy, based upon his thorough assimilation of both Western philosophy and methodology and the Zen Buddhist tradition.

Early Life

Kitarō Nishida was born on May 19, 1870, in the Mori section of the village of Unoke in Ishikawa Prefecture, located near Kanazawa on the Sea of Japan. He was the eldest son, the middle child out of five. Nishida's family moved to Kanazawa in 1883. There Nishida entered the local school, the prefectural normal school, which boasted an enterprising Western-style school system. Typhus forced his withdrawal from the school one year later, and he studied privately with several teachers for the next two years. In July, 1886, Nishida entered the Middle School attached to the Ishikawa Prefectural College. After completing his preparatory work there, Nishida entered the Fourth Higher School in July, 1889. While attending the Fourth Higher School, Nishida lived in the home of the mathematician Hōjō Tokiyoshi. His interest in Zen Buddhism, of which his mathematics teacher was an adept, dates to this period of his life.

Despite the urging of Hōjō that he become a mathematician, Nishida specialized in philosophy. He left the Fourth Higher School shortly before his graduation in 1890. The circumstances surrounding his departure remain mysterious. Lack of formal graduation from high school forced Nishida to enter the philosophy department of Tokyo Imperial University as a special student in September of 1891. There he was exposed to contemporary European thought. Nishida was graduated from Tokyo Imperial University in 1894. He encountered difficulties in finding employment because of his irregular academic background and was unemployed for nearly a full year after graduation. He took a room in the house of a painter named Tokuda Kō; during this time he wrote a study of Thomas Hill Green, a British Hegelian. He then obtained a position with a meager salary at a prefectural middle school on remote Noto Peninsula.

Nishida married the daugher of Tokuda Kō, Tokuda Kotomi, in May of 1895. His first daughter, Yayoi, was born in March of 1896. Together, Nishida and Kotomi had eight children: six daughters and two sons. Shortly after his marriage, Nishida's religious interests deepened. Upon returning to Kanazawa in 1896 to take a teaching position at the Fourth Higher School, Nishida began Zen meditation. A diary begun in 1897 provides an account of his rigorous introspective regimen. This spiritual discipline intensified in 1897 to 1899, when Nishida was alone in Yamaguchi, separated from his wife as a result of a serious disagreement with his father.

Life's Work

After teaching as a part-time professor at Yamaguchi Higher School from 1897 to 1899, Nishida returned to teach again at the Fourth Higher School in Kanazawa. There he taught psychology, ethics, German, and logic for ten years, from 1899 to 1909; at this time, he developed the basic philosophical views that he would broaden and deepen for the rest of his life but never abandon. In addition to teaching, Nishida was active in establishing extra-curricular literary groups. His most ambitious project was the establishment of a student residence and study center called San San Juku. San San Juku served as a meeting place for students to discuss problems of religion and literature with invited lecturers from various religious sects and denominations. This institution became a lasting one of the Fourth Higher School in Kanazawa.

In January of 1907, Nishida's daughter, Yūko, died of bronchitis. In June of that same year, another daughter, only one month old, died. Nishida himself fell ill. In the face of these tragedies, Nishida encouraged himself toward greater self-reliance. He also disciplined himself to increase the level of his intellectual output. The fruit of this discipline was the publication of his first book, *Zen-no-kenkyū (A Study of Good,* 1960), in January of 1911. Nishida's lifelong concern was to provide a Western philosophical framework for Zen intuition. *A Study of Good* launched this project. It included a theory of reality, a study of ethics, and the skeleton of a philosophy of religion. One of Nishida's most central philosophical concepts, that of "pure experience," is introduced in this first major work. Nishida defines "pure experience" as direct experience without deliberative discrimination and without the least addition of one's own fabrications. Unlike many practitioners of Zen, Nishida does not give the impression of being anti-intellectual. "Pure experience" is not in opposition to thought and intellect but rather lies at the base of all the oppositions produced by the mind, such as those of subject and object, body and mind, and spirit and matter. Nishida was inspired by the American philosopher William James and found in Henri Bergson a kindred spirit, but if he borrowed anything from either, it became thoroughly assimilated into his own philosophy. The publication of *A Study of Good* in 1911 was hailed as an epoch-making event in the introduction of Western philosophy into Japan. The academic world perceived it to be the first truly original philosophic work by a Japanese thinker in the modern period (which began in 1868 with the Meiji Restoration). All prior attempts at combining traditional Japanese thought with Western philosophy had been patently eclectic.

Following one year at Gakushūin University in Tokyo, Nishida was appointed assistant professor of ethics at Kyōto Imperial University in 1910. In August of 1914, he was relieved from his chair of ethics in the Faculty of Letters and called to the first chair of the history of philosophy in the philosophy department of the University of Kyōto. There he taught until his retirement in 1928. Many brilliant students flocked to his classes. Together with Hajime Tanabe, he established what has come to be known as the Kyōto, or Nishida-Tanabe, school of philosophy. Around 1910, Nishida's philosophy was influenced by his study of Bergson and the German Neo-Kantians, especially Wilhelm Windelband, Heinrich Rickert, and Hermann Cohen. His thorough assimilation of the logical epistemology of Neo-Kantian transcendentalism and his own critique of its fundamental principles enabled Nishida to discover a deeper significance in Immanuel Kant's philosophy and the transcendental method of German idealism. This achievement enabled him to bring his earlier concept of "pure experience" to a higher level. In his second major work, *Jikaku ni okeru chokkan to hansei* (1917; intuitions and reflection in self-consciousness), Nishida strove to eliminate psychologism from his thinking. In this work, he defined the ultimate character of self-consciousness as "absolute free will." "Absolute free will," when genuine, transcends re-

flection. it cannot be reflected upon, for it is that which causes reflection.

In August of 1918, Nishida's mother died; disaster struck again when his wife, Kotomi, suffered a brain hemorrhage in September of 1919. Kotomi was paralyzed for the remaining six years of her life. In June of 1920, Nishida's eldest son, Ken, died of peritonitis at the age of twenty-two. During the next several years, three more of his daughters fell ill with typhus. In January of 1925, Kotomi died after a prolonged period of suffering. She was fifty years old. Nishida's diary reveals that these personal tragedies affected him deeply. Nevertheless, he disciplined himself to maintain his philosophical activity. His next two works, *Ishiki no mondai* (1920; problems of consciousness) and *Geijutsu to dotoku* (1923; *Art and Morality*, 1973), offered progressive refinements of the concepts of "pure experience" and "absolute free will."

The epoch-making *Hataraku-mono kara mirumono e* (1927; from the acting to the seeing self) formulates the concept of *basho no ronri* ("logic of place"). It is Nishida's notion of "place" and his "logic of place" that distinguish him in the history of philosophy. In this work, he discusses a realm of reality that corresponds to his own mystical experience. Indeed, with his concept of "place," Nishida provided a conceptual and logical framework for a philosophical position that is usually categorized as mysticism in the West. According to Nishida, the "true self" is revealed in the "place" of "absolute nothingness." The concept of "absolute nothingness" has clear roots in Buddhist tradition. This "nothingness" is not relative nothingness, nothingness as contrasted with phenomenal existence; rather, it is absolute nothingness, that wherein all phenomenal existences appear as determinations of it. "Absolute free will" emerges from creative nothingness and returns to creative nothingness.

Retirement from his teaching position at the University of Kyōto in 1928 did not slow Nishida's productive pace. His postretirement works include *Ippansha no jikakuteki taikei* (1930; the self-conscious system of the universal), *Mu no jikakuteki gentei* (1932; the self-conscious determination of nothingness), *Tetsugaku no kompon mondai* (2 vols., 1933-1934; *Fundamental Problems of Philosophy*, 1970), and *Tetsugaku rombunshu* (7 vols., 1937-1946; philosophical essays). In this last stage of his philosophical development, Nishida was concerned with "the self-identity of absolute contradiction," or "the unity of opposites." This concept was discovered through his investigation of the relationship between the self and the world. Nishida used this concept to probe what he considered to be one of the fundamental problems of a philosophy of religion: the contradictions of an existence in which the satisfaction of desire means the extinction of desire and in which the will makes its own extinction its goal. These contradictions undergird religious experience, for it is only in the awareness of the absolute contradictoriness and nothingness of the self's existence that human beings are able to touch God and the absolute.

Nishida's first grandchild was born in October of 1928. He married again in December of 1931; his second wife's name was Koto. For perhaps the first time in his life, Nishida's family life became serene. The retired professor enjoyed the visits of his children and grandchildren immensely. There were no further deaths in the family until February of 1945, when his favorite daughter, Yayoi, died suddenly. Nishida found World War II to be a profoundly distressing event. He managed, however, to continue his philosophical writings at his home in Kamakura despite the destruction in Tokyo and other major Japanese cities. He died suddenly in early June of 1945, only two months before Japan's surrender.

Summary

Kitarō Nishida is widely recognized as the first genuinely original Japanese philosopher of the modern period. He departed from the crude eclecticism of his predecessors and almost singlehandedly created an indigenous Japanese philosophy. His true significance will probably not be determined until a comprehensive, global history of modern ideas is written. Nishida is the only Japanese philosopher of recent times around whom a philosophical school has been formed. Most of the leading philosophers of twentieth century Japan were influenced by him, either as a result of being his student or through assimilation of his thought.

Since the late 1950's, Nishida's works have begun to be known outside Japan. Although his thought has been severely criticized by Marxist and other antimetaphysical thinkers, on the whole Nishida's philosophy has been favorably received by the Western world. He is recognized as one of the first philosophers to offer a system that transcends the distinctions between Eastern and Western philosophy. He is further credited with having given Oriental thought a logical foundation with his "logic of nothingness."

Bibliography

Abe, Masao. "Nishida's Philosophy of 'Place.'" *The International Philosophical Quarterly* 28 (December, 1988): 355-371. Abe's intended audience is composed of professional philosophers. Nishida's concept of "place" distinguishes him in the history of philosophy.

Elwood, Brian D. "The Problem of the Self in the Later Nishida and in Sartre." *Philosophy East and West* 44, no. 2 (April, 1994). Compares the philosophies of Nishida and Jean-Paul Sartre as they concern death and self-realization.

Knauth, Lothar. "Life Is Tragic—The Diary of Nishida Kitaro." *Monumenta Nipponica* 20 (1965): 335-358. A study of Nishida's life, based on his diary. Discussions of Nishida's personal and family life, his professional life, his reading interests, and the development of his philosophical ideas are included.

Masao, Abe, and James L. Fredericks. "The Problem of 'Inverse Correspondence' in the Philosophy of Nishida: Comparing Nishida with Tanabe." *International Philosophical Quarterly* 39, no. 1 (March, 1999). Compares the philosophies of Nishida and Hajime Tanabe with respect to religion and the achievement of a state of "absolute nothingness."

Merton, Thomas. "Nishida: A Zen Philosopher." In *Zen and the Birds of Appetite*. New York: New Directions, 1968. A brief introduction to Nishida's philosophy for Westerners. It would be helpful to know something about Western philosophy and have some knowledge of Zen before reading this article.

Piovesana, Gino K. "The Philosophy of Nishida Kitarō, 1870-1945." In *Recent Japanese Philosophical Thought, 1862-1962: A Survey*. 3d ed. Richmond, Surrey: Japan Library, 1997. An introduction to Nishida's thought, with some helpful introductory comments that suggest how to approach the demanding aspects of Nishida's works. Includes an index and a bibliography.

Piper, Raymond Frank. "Nishida, Notable Japanese Personalist." *Personalist* 17 (1936): 21-31. The only English-language article on Nishida written while he was still alive, it is a study of

Nishida's philosophy based on the author's acquaintance with *A Study of Good*.

Shibata, Masumi. "The Diary of a Zen Layman: The Philosopher Nishida Kitaro." *The Eastern Buddhist* 14 (1981): 121-131. A study of what can be learned about Nishida's Zen practice and his thoughts about Zen from the pages of his diary.

Shimomura, Torataro. Introduction to *A Study of Good*, by Kitarō Nishida. Translated by V. H. Viglielmo. New York: Greenwood Press, 1988. Nishida's thought is related to the Japanese philosophy that preceded him. This article also contains brief overviews of Nishida's life and of his later philosophical development.

Viglielmo, Valdo Humbert. "Nishida Kitarō: The Early Years." In *Tradition and Modernization in Japanese Culture*, edited by Donald H. Shively. Princeton, N.J.: Princeton University Press, 1971. A detailed account of Nishida's early life, from birth to approximately thirty-three years of age. Viglielmo is a noted Nishida scholar, and this well-written work does nothing to detract from his reputation.

Ann Marie B. Bahr

RICHARD M. NIXON

Born: January 9, 1913; Yorba Linda, California
Died: April 22, 1994; New York, New York
Area of Achievement: Government and politics
Contribution: A realist in foreign policy, Nixon renewed American relations with the People's Republic of China, achieved détente with the Soviet Union, and ended the United States' involvement in Vietnam. Ironically, because of his "Watergate coverup," he aroused public and congressional opposition to the "imperial presidency."

Early Life

Richard Milhous Nixon was born in Yorba Linda, in Southern California, on January 9, 1913, the son of Francis A. Nixon and Hannah Milhous Nixon. "Frank" Nixon was a small businessman, and Richard as a boy worked in the family store, driving into Los Angeles early each morning to buy fruits and vegetables and then going on to school. He attended public schools, was graduated from Whittier College in 1934, and from Duke University's law school in 1937. As a young man Nixon was above average in height, strong, but slender, weighing a little more than 150 pounds. His most prominent physical characteristics were a "ski-slide" nose, a dark beard despite frequent shaving, and a rather stiff manner. Despite a good record in law school, he found no job in New York City or even with the Federal Bureau of Investigation, which may have made him wary of the "Eastern Establishment." He practiced law in California from 1937 to 1942, in 1940 marrying Thelma Catherine "Pat" Ryan. They had two daughters, Patricia and Julie. Soon after the United States entered World War II, Nixon, a Quaker, became a lawyer with the Office of Price Administration but in the summer of 1942 joined the United States Navy and served as a transportation officer in the South Pacific. He was released from active duty as a lieutenant commander.

Life's Work

In 1946 Nixon ran as a Republican for United States representative from the Twelfth District of California, winning after a harsh campaign. Re-elected in 1948, in 1950 he sought a senate seat from California, defeating the popular Helen Gahagan Douglas after another controversial campaign. In both house and senate, Nixon's record was one of moderate conservatism but also one of strident anticommunism, which fitted America's mood in the early Cold War. He helped secure the conviction of Alger Hiss for perjury in a case which made Nixon famous. He won the Republican nomination for vice president in 1952 largely because his youth, his "hard line" position, and his being from the West balanced the presidential candidate, General Dwight D. Eisenhower. Nixon found himself to be vice president in charge of the Republican Party because of Eisenhower's wish to remain above partisan politics. He relished his trips abroad for Eisenhower, to Asia, Latin America, and the Soviet Union. He was again a controversial campaigner in 1956 because of his harsh attacks on opponents. Admired by party regulars because of his faithful partisan services, Nixon easily secured the Republican nomination for president in 1960. Nixon lost to Senator John F. Kennedy, probably because of televised debates in which Nixon showed his exhaustion from campaigning while Kennedy gained an image of vigor and competence. The margin of defeat was extremely narrow in the popular vote—119,000 out of 68,838,000 cast—but 303 to 219 electoral votes.

Nixon then practiced law in California, seeking the governorship in 1962 but losing to Edmund G. Brown. He again became controversial by bitterly attacking the press after the election, in effect accusing its people of deliberately defeating him. Moving to New York, he joined a Wall Street law firm, becoming a partner in 1964. With the overwhelming defeat that year of Senator Barry Goldwater, Nixon again became a major contender for the presidential nomination. He continued to travel widely abroad, meeting important leaders, and maintained his political contacts, campaigning for many Republican candidates in 1966. In 1968 he again won the presidential nomination and defeated Vice President Hubert Humphrey by 510,000 popular votes out of 63,160,000 cast for the two men, and by 301 to 191 electoral votes, probably because of public disillusionment with the Democrats' handling of the Vietnam War and their catastrophically divided presidential convention.

As president, Nixon was most interested in foreign policy, commenting that a competent cabinet could look after the country. Reflecting his moderate conservatism, his administration did nothing about civil rights except to oppose some laws already enacted, sought to win Southern segregationists into the Republican Party, stressed "law and order" issues, tried to shift some emphasis to state and local government through revenue sharing, sought reform of the welfare system, and took some steps toward environmental protection. Strangely, it did not cut down "big government" much or reduce tax burdens. Vice President Spiro T. Agnew and Attorney General John Mitchell became especially controversial because of Agnew's attacks on the "media" and Mitchell's recommending one questionable nominee for the Supreme Court and then one unsuitable one. The Senate rejected both. The administration was also hurt by its changing responses to "stagflation," a new term for a slowing economy with continued inflation, a situation created by the Vietnam War and then by a sudden oil price rise because Arab states were angry at the American-aided Israeli victory in the Yom Kippur War of 1973. Nixon's task was made no easier by his facing a Congress controlled by Democrats.

Nixon revealed his foreign policy position by appointing as his chief adviser Dr. Henry A. Kissinger of Harvard University. Kissinger, a student of *Realpolitik*, fitted Nixon's own wish for realism. Nixon had shed his earlier bitter anticommunism and also recognized the fact that because of the Vietnam War Americans would no longer support endless intervention abroad. Seeking to end United States involvement in Vietnam without South Vietnam's collapsing, he bombed and invaded Cambodia, helped a South Vietnamese invasion of Laos, and tried "Vietnamization," a massive buildup of South Vietnam's armed forces accompanied by the withdrawal of many thousands of United States troops. He later intensified United States bombing of North Vietnam and ordered the mining of its major harbors, all this to apply sufficient pressure for a peace settlement. His reelection in 1972 left North Vietnam only Nixon to deal with, and in January, 1973, the United States and North Vietnam signed an agreement which ended the United States' involvement in Vietnam but which was so loosely worded that the war never really ended and South Vietnam fell in 1975.

With the Soviet Union Nixon concluded agreements for grain sales and, most important, arms limitation. A 1972 agreement, called the "strategic arms limitation treaty" (SALT I), limited antiballistic missiles and, in effect, granted to two superpowers equality in nuclear weapons. By warning the Soviet government and ordering a middle-level

alert of United States armed forces, Nixon may also have kept the Soviet Union from intervening in the Middle East during the Yom Kippur War. Nixon's major foreign policy triumph was his 1972 trip to Beijing, China, and meetings with Mao Tse-tung and Chou En-lai. While Nixon and Kissinger could not solve all the problems between the two countries, the renewal of contact led ultimately to the renewal of Chinese-American diplomatic relations, which had ended in 1949. Nixon also paved the way for a renewal of American trade with China, which aided China in its modernization. Chinese-American relations may also have restrained some Soviet actions. The only exceptions to a record of sound diplomacy were Nixon's aiding the overthrow and murder of Chilean President Salvador Allende in 1973 and his support for Pakistan despite its murderous behavior toward its own people in East Pakistan as the latter broke away to become Bangladesh.

Nixon was overwhelmingly reelected in 1972, defeating Senator George McGovern by 520 to 17 electoral votes and by 47,170,000 to 29,170,000 popular votes. Public opinion polls revealed massive approval of Nixon's foreign policy, especially detente and relations with China, but fairly strong disapproval of his handling of domestic matters. Unfortunately, high officials in the Nixon campaign sponsored or allowed a burglary of the national Democratic headquarters in the Watergate building. This was probably a symptom of the Administration's atmosphere, one of near siege, of feeling surrounded by enemies and of sharing Nixon's demand for overwhelming reelection as a vindication of himself. There was also a rejection by "Middle America" of everything that McGovern allegedly stood for: left-wing liberalism and the "counterculture" of the 1960's. When others tried to cover up their roles in "Watergate," Nixon himself became involved in the "cover-up." Tape recordings made of conversations in the president's office, intended to be the basis of a historical record, proved Nixon's role in attempted deception. About to be impeached by the House of Representatives, Nixon resigned the presidency on August 9, 1974; he was the first president in the United States' history to do so. Earlier, Vice President Agnew, himself under indictment, had resigned, and under the new Twenty-fifth Amendment, Nixon had appointed Representative Gerald R. Ford, who thus became president after Nixon.

In retirement, first at San Clemente, California, and later at Saddle River, New Jersey, Nixon was quiet for a time and then began to travel again, to Europe and twice to China. With the help of able assistants, he produced four books in addition to his memoirs: *The Real War* (1980), *Leaders* (1982), *Real Peace* (1984), and *No More Vietnams* (1985). He also took part in a number of televised interviews, entertained members of the press, and with other former presidents represented the United States at the funeral of assassinated Egyptian President Anwar el-Sadat in 1981. He was in general silent on President Gerald Ford, critical of President Jimmy Carter, and supportive of President Ronald Reagan. His books reveal a mixture of a wish for lasting world peace and a hard-line approach toward the Soviet Union.

Summary

In some ways, Nixon represented millions of post-World War II Americans: Well educated, he was a professional man and also a veteran who wanted to succeed in life and also build a better world for his family. He was highly ambitious, driven by the example of his father, who never really succeeded, but also controlled by his mother's example of piety and manipulativeness. He thus created the public image of a patriotic young man of ambition but decency. As such, he was repeatedly elected to public office but was sometimes defeated and was always suspect to millions of voters. Behind the public image remained the real man who revealed himself occasionally: remote, lonely, under tremendous stress in his drive to succeed, and angry at those who opposed him. When, during the Watergate crisis, this inner person was revealed, there was public shock and his defenders melted away. He had built up presidential power and prestige, and there arose opposition to what was named the "imperial presidency." His legacy, aside from foreign policy successes, was one of increased public distrust of government.

Bibliography

Aitken, Jonathan. *Nixon, A Life*. Washington, D.C.: Regnery, and London: Weidenfeld and Nicolson, 1993.

Brodie, Fawn M. *Richard Nixon: The Shaping of His Character*. New York: W. W. Norton and Co., 1981. The best attempt at a "psychobiography," based on exhaustive interviews with relatives, classmates, and others; connects Nixon's character with his behavior in office.

Evans, Rowland, Jr., and Robert D. Novak. *Nixon in the White House: The Frustration of Power*. New York: Norton, 1971. A critical but penetrating analysis of the Nixon Administration's early successes and errors, on a case-by-case basis, ranging from appointments to legislative strategy.

Hoff, Joan. *Nixon Reconsidered*. New York: Basic, 1994.

Kissinger, Henry A. *White House Years*. Boston: Little Brown, and London: Weidenfeld and Nicolson, 1979.

————. *Years of Upheaval*. Boston: Little Brown, and London: Weidenfeld and Nicolson, 1982. These two volumes form a highly personal account of Nixon's foreign policy by his chief adviser and secretary of state. Egocentric, reluctant to admit errors or even his ignorance of parts of the globe, Kissinger subtly places himself ahead of the president.

Kotlowski, Dean J. "Richard Nixon and the Origins of Affirmative Action." *Historian* 60, no. 3 (Spring 1998). The author argues that Nixon's approval of the Philadelphia Plan marked the beginning of affirmative action, in contrast to the popular belief that this policy originated with the Democrats who preceded him.

Morris, Roger. *Richard Milhous Nixon: The Rise of an American Politician*. New York: Holt, 1990.

Nixon, Richard M. *Leaders*. London: Sidgwick and Jackson, and New York: Warner, 1982. A superb example of Nixon's later writings, highly egocentric and revealing Nixon's wish to be seen as a pragmatist with ideals, who knew and dealt with so many great men. Especially revealing is Nixon's treatment of Winston Churchill and Charles de Gaulle.

————. *RN: The Memoirs of Richard Nixon*. New York: Grosset and Dunlap, and London: Sidgwick and Jackson, 1978. Revealing even when they try to conceal, as in refusing to admit guilt for Watergate or the cover-up, these offer Nixon's version of what he wants as his public image. Emphasizes his parents' positive qualities, his own struggles, but above all the presidency, Nixon overstating his administration's achievements.

————. *Six Crises*. New York: Doubleday, and London: Allen, 1962. Memoirs of Nixon in the Congress and the vice presidency, including the Checkers speech, trips abroad, and defeat for the governorship of California.

Safire, William. *Before the Fall*. New York: Doubleday, 1975. An "insider's account" which covers such conversations as Nixon's comments on trips to China and Russia, and internal struggles within the Administration.

Schwartz, Barry, and Lori Holyfield. "Nixon Postmodern." *Annals of the American Academy of Political and Social Science* 560 (November 1998). The authors consider the eulogies given at Nixon's funeral and comment on the media's responsibility to provide balanced information.

White, Theodore H. *Breach of Faith: The Fall of Richard Nixon*. New York: Atheneum, and London: Cape, 1975. The best account of Watergate, the cover-up, and Nixon's resignation, based on interviews as well as the presidential tape recordings, and revealing of who in the Administration was how deeply involved.

Wicker, Tom. *One of Us: Richard Nixon and the American Dream*. New York: Random House, 1991.

Wills, Garry. *Nixon Agonistes: The Crisis of the Self-Made Man*. Boston: Houghton Mifflin, 1970. Nixon as the self-made man who built flaws in himself, the classical liberal believing in competition, a representative of America itself, placed in the setting of the disorderly decades of the 1950's and 1960's.

Robert W. Sellen

KWAME NKRUMAH
Francis Nwia Kofi

Born: September 21, 1909; Nkroful, Gold Coast
Died: April 27, 1972; Bucharest, Romania
Areas of Achievement: Government and politics
Contribution: Nkrumah was the first statesman to lead an African country to independence after World War II. As the first major proponent of Pan-Africanism, he gained both continental and international stature. He served as Prime Minister of the Gold Coast, Prime Minister of Ghana after its independence, and President of Ghana. After the coup that deposed him, he was named titular copresident of Guinea, a recognition of his status as an international leader and world statesman.

Early Life
The man who would one day be internationally known as Kwame Nkrumah was born in Nkroful in the British West African colony of Gold Coast on September 21, 1909. Although he was christened Francis Nwia Kofi, his African name, Kwame, is indicative of the day on which he was born as was the local custom. Despite the fact that he was his mother's only child, he grew up in a large family of fourteen people, including children of his father by other wives. Nkrumah's father was a goldsmith and jeweler; his mother was a retail trader. He was baptized a Roman Catholic, and at his mother's insistence he attended the nearby Roman Catholic mission schools at Esima and Sekondi-Takoradi. Nkrumah did so well in school that he was sent to the Government Training School in Accra. He was graduated from Achiomota College, where he was trained as a teacher, in 1930 and taught at Catholic junior schools and a seminary until 1935. While at school, Nkrumah met Kwegyir Aggrey, the school's first African staff member. It was Aggrey who guided Nkrumah's mind toward the issues to which he would later devote his life. At the same time, another major influence came into Nkrumah's life. Nnamdi Azikiwe, a Nigerian journalist, who would later become Nigeria's first president, fired Nkrumah's enthusiasm for nationalist struggle. He would also have a direct impact on the next phase of Nkrumah's life. He suggested that Nkrumah attend Lincoln University in the United States. From Lincoln, Nkrumah received a bachelor of arts degree in economics and sociology in 1939, a bachelor of theology degree in 1942, and an honor-

ary law degree in 1951. In addition, Nkrumah received a master's degree in education from the University of Pennsylvania in 1942 and a master of arts in philosophy from the same school in 1943. He finished all the requirements for the doctoral degree except the dissertation. After having worked his way through school for ten years, exhausted and homesick as well as excited about the political stirrings in Africa and Europe, Nkrumah decidd to return to Africa via Europe.

In May of 1945, Nkrumah left the United States for Europe. Landing in England, he decided to continue his studies by enrolling at University College and the London School of Economics, but, having become radicalized politically, abandoned this pursuit in order to devote his energies full-time to a publication he had founded called *The New African.* Moreover, his increasing revolutionary consciousness made the liberation of Ghana specifically and Africa generally his primary goals. Thus, he joined several Pan-African groups in London. Because of his political activities in the United States (where he had been president of the African Students' Association of North America) and Europe (where he was a leader in the West African National Secretariat), Nkrumah was invited to return to the Gold Coast in 1947 as general secretary of the United Gold Coast Convention (UGCC), the nationalist party popular throughout the land. Nkrumah heeded the call of his people and returned to Ghana.

Life's Work
When Nkrumah returned to the Gold Coast, the colony was experiencing very bad economic conditions and the social situation was in chaos. These difficulties would eventually help him into power. The main source of these problems rested with the coca tree disease "swollen shoot." The government considered this a major issue because coca was the main export. The government's solution to the problem was to cut out the diseased trees to protect the others. Farmers resented this policy because it threatened their whole livelihood. This policy was particularly offensive because the price of coca was rising after a long period of low prices during the 1930's. The economic result of the government's farm policies was severe inflation and high prices while wages remained low. In addition,

there were other problems associated with the presence of both European and Syrian merchants dominating retail and commercial trade. Moreover, soldiers returning from overseas were disillusioned with the government's failure to fulfill its promises of better housing and more jobs. Indeed, the government's failure to pay attention to these issues and the problems they engendered caused the people to resent further the British and their colonial leaders, including the UGCC.

The failure of the older leaders of the UGCC to address these issues and their continued association with the British led Nkrumah to form his own party in June of 1949. Indeed, the Convention People's Party (CPP) was an attempt by the young leaders, including Nkrumah, seen by the people as the "petit bourgeois," to overcome the soft and satisfied image of the older elite, which was identified as the "grand bourgeois." Nkrumah's charisma, speaking ability, and charm had pulled many people into the UGCC; when he formed his own party, they followed him, as did most of the colony's activists and local leaders. The CPP elected Nkrumah president and life chairman; from that position he stressed West African unity at first and then called for the unity of the entire African continent, or Pan-Africanism. With the UGCC weakened by Nkrumah's departure, the CPP emerged as the colony's main political organization. The planks in its political program were indicative of its ability to articulate the hopes and needs of the people. The party's goals were to achieve "self-government now" as well as to end all forms of oppression and establish a democratic government. The party also called for the complete unity of the colony by ensuring the rights of local chiefs and all ethnic groups. The CPP appealed to workers and soldiers by advocating the interests of the trade union movement as well as the right of the people in the Gold Coast to live and govern themselves. Its final goal, the realization of West African unity, reflected Nkrumah's Pan-African ideals.

In an effort to coerce the government to accept constitutional reform, the CPP called a general strike in 1948. Nkrumah and the other leaders were arrested. The British allowed an election and used trucks with sound systems to drive about the colony and denounce the CPP. Despite these and other tactics, Nkrumah's party won thirty-three of thirty-eight seats in the governing body. Thus, he and the leaders were released from jail. In some ways, this election became Nkrumah's mandate to lead his people to independence. The CPP continued to gain power and popularity under limited British self-government. In his first speech after the election, Nkrumah called himself "a friend of Great Britian" and spoke of the Gold Coast becoming a dominion within the Commonwealth. During this period of limited self-government, internal rivalries caused accusations against Nkrumah and his party. Some called him a Communist, others hailed him as a puppet of the British. Nkrumah was in a difficult position as he tried to work with the British while keeping the trust and support of his people. Nkrumah continued to enjoy the support of the youth groups and the military as well as many local factions. He appealed to the Africans because he continued to remind them of their own glorious history and their dignity.

Nkrumah's rise to power was swift. After a second arrest and imprisonment in 1950, he rose from leader of government business to prime minister. While still prime minister in the British colonial government, Nkrumah made his date with destiny when he called for the independence of the Gold Coast within the British commonwealth on July 10, 1953. Nkrumah would serve as prime minister for the Gold Coast from 1952 to 1957 and then of Ghana from 1957 to 1960. He changed the name of the colony to Ghana in an attempt to move away from British influences and English titles. In 1957, he married Fathia Halen Ritzk, and the couple eventually had three children. In 1960, he became president of the independent republic and was granted the title *ossaggeto*, which means redeemer.

Having achieved the independence of Ghana, his first political goal, Nkrumah turned his energies toward a second major issue, the unity of Africa. In April of 1958, he convened a conference of eight states, and from this group, the Organization of African Unity (OAU) was born. In turning his attentions away from the problems of Ghana, Nkrumah let too much responsibility be taken by his ministers. In turn, several of his closest friends had to be dismissed for corruption, graft, and mismanagement. In addition, there were demonstrations by the soldiers, displeasure at his policies in the farming sector, and ethnic tensions. The people of Ghana were so displeased that they formed an organization, Ghana Shifimo, to address their concerns. The group's inception was unlawful, and its threatened violence and bombing of indiscriminate areas presented major problems. Nkrumah's reponse was repression. He had its leaders detained under the

Preventive Detention Act of 1958. By 1960, more than 318 detention orders had been issued, and this act was extended to the Ghana Shifimo.

Many people believed that Nkrumah had responded properly to the growing violence, social unrest, bombings, and assassination attempts on his life. Others believed that he had lost touch with the people. Frustrated and depressed, Nkrumah withdrew more and more from public life. Much of the political unrest was the result of general dissatisfaction with the CPP and its monopoly on power. In dismissing some of his ministers, Nkrumah addressed some of the peoples' complaints; however, the task of bringing a colony into the world body of nations as a free and equal partner proved harder than Nkrumah had realized. Ghana was independent, but it was not free of the problems of nationhood.

When Ghana first became independent, its economy was strong. As in times before, it relied heavily on the export of coca. In his attempt to make Ghana more self-sufficient, Nkrumah forced farmers to diversify their crops. The growing unhappiness with his farm policies, a chronic shortage of trained personnel, and the breakdown of the tradi-

tional British civil service all undermined many of his reforms. The decline in the world price of coca, large-scale smuggling, and the recently minted cedi, Ghana's currency, which had no attachment to the international standard, combined to make Ghana unable to pay its debts to various international bodies. This caused Ghana additional problems, and cries of incompetence and mismanagement arose. In some ways, Nkrumah was the appropriate person to lead his African country to independence; however, many speculate that he was not the best choice to handle the day-to-day operations of a fragile government.

On February 24, 1966, a long-planned military coup deposed Nkrumah. At the time, Nkrumah was in North Vietnam attempting to create a peaceful solution to the conflict there. Many speculate that he was aware of the coup before he left Ghana. He was deliberately out of the country both to avoid what would have been a very bloody civil war and to protect his good name and international stature. In some ways, he let the coup occur in recognition of his failure to address the problem of a crumbling economy and massive unrest as well as political turmoil over his increasingly repressive measures. After the coup was announced, Nkrumah continued his travels throughout the Eastern Bloc and accepted exile in Conakry, Guinea, where President Ahmed Sékou Touré named him copresident in a gesture of solidarity and in recognition of his status as the redeemer not only of Ghana but also of much of Africa.

Summary

Kwame Nkrumah was an international statesman, politican, and philosopher. He was a visionary who led a nation and influenced a continent toward independence. His two main goals were the independence of Ghana and the liberation of Africa. At some level he was able to achieve both. Nkrumah was a very intelligent and articulate man who was able to formulate a strategy that was appropriate for both the time and place to achieve his lifelong goals. His insistence on nonviolent civil disobedience as well as his appeal to the righteousness of political freedom for African people were good tactics in the context of the colonial regime. Like most great statesmen, Nkrumah appeared to be the right man for the right time. In some ways he was profoundly affected by the injustices he witnessed as a small child while the British controlled his people. His intelligence and willingness to leave home and study in the United States and Europe made him ripe for the roles he would later occupy in life. His vast knowledge and his reading of a variety of political philosophies were to become the tools he used to orchestrate his people's independence. Nkrumah was a farsighted man who brought free education, health care, and other social services to his nation. In addition, he repaired the physical infrastructure of roads, bridges, and dams in an attempt to assist Ghana in claiming its place among the modern nations in the world. His most important role was his insistence on the unity of Africa and the creation of the OAU. His basic philosophies and approach became a model for the rest of emerging Africa and the globe. In many ways, he is the father of modern political struggle.

Bibliography

Ames, Sophia Ripley. *Nkrumah of Ghana.* New York: Rand McNally, 1961. This short biography contains interesting anecdotes about and insights into the personal side of Nkrumah, the statesman and politician. It also looks at the development of his philosophy.

Bretton, Henry L. *The Rise and Fall of Kwame Nkrumah: A Study of Personal Rule in Africa.* London: Pall Mall Press, and New York: Praeger, 1966. This work presents a rather critical look at both the personal and political Nkrumah. The author examines what he calls Nkrumah's "political machine" and the effects of his personality cult on the government and politics of Ghana.

Hodgkin, Thomas. *Nationalism in Colonial Africa.* London: Muller, 1956; New York: New York University Press, 1957. In this political analysis of Africa, Hodgkin looks at Africa's many different political organizations and documents their evolution. He takes a close look at Ghanian leaders such as Danquah and Nkrumah and examines how their views and visions of Ghana differed.

Hountondji, Paulin. "From the Ethnosciences to Ethnophilosophy: Kwame Nkrumah's Thesis Project." *Research in African Literatures* 28, no. 4 (Winter 1997). Examines the origin of the term "ethnophilosophy," which has been attributed to Hountondji and Marcien Towa but was used by Nkrumah in earlier writings.

Nkrumah, Kwame. *Africa Must Unite.* London: Heinemann, and New York: Praeger, 1963. In this work, Nkrumah discusses African history and the evolution of its distinct political institutions. Nkrumah also gives insight into the governmental systems of Ghana and other African nations. He examines how colonialism affected Africa negatively and asserts that Ghana will redeem the entire continent.

———. *The Autobiography of Kwame Nkrumah.* Edinburgh and New York: Nelson, 1957. In this balanced and expressive autobiography, Nkrumah presents in detail his life from birth to the declaration of Ghana's independence. It also gives much insight into the various local and international personalities who admired both the man for his charisma and the politician for his skill.

———. *Revolutionary Path.* London: Panaf, and New York: International Press, 1973. This work was compiled during the last two years of the author's life. It was written as a result of a request for a single book that would contain documents relating to the development of Nkrumah's thoughts. It is very informative for understanding Nkrumah's political motivations and his vision for Africa.

Omari, T. Peter. *Kwame Nkrumah: The Anatomy of an African Dictatorship.* London: Hurst, and New York: Africana, 1970. This work looks at the rise and fall of Nkrumah as well as critiques his use of power and the treatment of his political adversaries.

Powell, Erica. *Private Secretary (Female)/Gold Coast.* London: Hurst, and New York: St. Martin's Press, 1984. This is a unique biography of Nkrumah written by the white female British private secretary who worked for Nkrumah for more than a decade. She brings to her story the insight of a loyal assistant and the criticisms of a trusted friend. It has interesting personal anecdotes and political insights about Nkrumah and the people he knew.

Rooney, David. *Kwame Nkrumah: The Political Kingdom in the Third World.* London: Tauris, 1988; New York: St. Martin's Press, 1989. This work is the story of Nkrumah's life from birth to death. The author's goal is to provide an objective account of Nkrumah's life in view of recent developments in Africa and the history of Ghana. It presents a detailed discussion of the complex cultural, psychological, sociological as well as political factors that influenced Nkrumah's development.

Yoda, Lalbila. "The Influence of the USA on the Political Ideas of Kwame Nkrumah." *Round Table*, no. 326 (April, 1993). Yoda discusses the political philosophy of Nkrumah and the impact of U.S. ideas on him.

Alphine W. Jefferson

MAX NORDAU

Born: July 29, 1849; Pest (now Budapest), Hungary
Died: January 22, 1923; Paris, France
Areas of Achievement: Art, government, politics, and literature
Contribution: Nordau analyzed negative tendencies in late nineteenth century industrial society and its culture in terms understandable to the popular readers of his day. He also seconded Theodore Herzl in developing the World Zionist Organization, preparing international opinion for the rebirth of a Jewish state in Palestine.

Early Life

Max Simon Nordau was born Simon Maximilian Südfeld in 1849 in the Pest division of Budapest. He was registered in the synagogue as Simcha Meir and known in his family as Simi. His father, Gabriel Südfeld, was a private tutor and had been a rabbi in Posen, Prussia. A widower with four children, he married Rosalie Sarah, née Nelkin, of Riga, who became the mother of Max and his sister Charlotte. Raised in poverty, young Max enrolled in the Pest German-language Jewish elementary school in 1854, the Catholic *Gymnasium* in 1859, and the Calvinist *Gymnasium* in 1863. In addition, he was instructed by his father in Greek, Hebrew, Ladino, and religion.

In 1867 Max enrolled in the University of Pest premedical program. He did his military service as an army physician at Vienna in 1873, at the same time adopting Max Nordau as his legal name. He received his medical diploma at Pest in January of 1876 and proceeded to the University of Paris to study gynecology. Nordau's first practice in Pest in 1878 did not satisfy his career plans. In 1880 he moved with his mother and sister to Paris, where he opened an office as a gynecologist and obstetrician in 1882.

Nordau's medical studies were financed by his journalism. He began writing as a boy for school newspapers and at age eighteen was a regular contributor to *Pester Lloyd*. His specialty was news sidelights written to be both informative and entertaining. In 1873 *Pester Lloyd* sent him to cover the Vienna World Exposition and followed this with a travel assignment that took Nordau to Russia, Germany, Denmark, Sweden, Scotland, England, Iceland, France, and Spain. His travel articles made him well known and provided material for two books, *Aus dem Wahren Milliardenlande* (1878;

Paris Sketches, 1884) and *Vom Kreml zur Alhambra* (1879; from the Kremlin to the Alhambra). *Paris unter der Dritten Republik* (Paris under the Third Republic) followed in 1880. By 1881, he was a Paris correspondent for the prestigious *Frankfurter Zeitung* and the leading Berlin liberal paper, *Vossische Zeitung*, as well as *Pester Lloyd*. He also published short stories, plays, novels, and various articles, in addition to his growing medical practice. As Nordau's scientific and rationalistic outlook came to supersede many of his earlier religious beliefs, his friendships grew across lines of both religion and nationality. Short statured, he cultivated a full beard that whitened prematurely and gave him a patriarchal appearance. Athletic, his hobbies included swimming and fencing. As Nordau was a bachelor for many years, his mother and sister—both religiously observant—managed his Paris household.

Life's Work

Nordau gained a worldwide reputation with the 1883 publication of *Die Conventionellen Luegen der Kulturmenschheit* (*The Conventional Lies of Our Civilization*, 1906) which went through seven printings in seven weeks. He attacked religious promises of individual immortality as improbable, monarchism and aristocracy as relics of a dead past, democratic politics as a deceit, economics as a swindle, and marriage as materialistic. The pope denounced the book, Russia and Austria-Hungary banned it, and U.S. publishers put "prohibited in Europe" on the book's cover. *Paradoxe* (1885; *Paradoxes*, 1885) examined the counterplay of optimism and pessimism, the social problem of love, and the baneful influence of prejudice. Nordau followed this with a few novels and plays before his next major success, *Entartung* (1893; *Degeneration*, 1895), in which he argued that art during the classical era, the Renaissance, and the Enlightenment was natural and healthy, and played a positive role in society, while late nineteenth century culture was dominated by negative attitudes and pathological tendencies that reflected the nervous exhaustion of industrialized society. The Romantic movement had opened the door to mysticism, egomania, and other forms of individual escapism. Among the examples he analyzed were Dante Gabriel Rossetti, Henrik Ibsen, Leo Tolstoy, Oscar Wilde, Richard Wagner, Charles Baudelaire, Émile

Zola, and Friedrich Nietzsche. Nordau maintained that in varying ways and degrees, all of these people had a negative, twisted, or unnatural view of humankind and society.

Degeneration, translated into many languages, was widely read and discussed, and not always calmly. Historian Brooks Adams "enormously admired" the book, and *New York Sun* literary editor Mayo Hazeltine found it "brilliant." However, Columbia University's Nicholas Murray Butler called Nordau "a pathological type," and psychologist William James diagnosed Nordau as "a victim of insane delusions." Certainly, *Degeneration* was a stimulating cultural analysis suited to popular readers rather than to academic specialists. Of course, the book did nothing to arrest modernism. Indeed, it brought popular attention to some of the previously obscure Decadents, and Nordau's assertion that "the aberrations of art have no future" was an inaccurate forecast for the twentieth century.

Nordau long claimed to regard himself as "only German," but ties of family and friendship clearly connected him to the Jewish community, and he was quick to notice and denounce instances of anti-Semitism. He also took a constructive interest in a plan for a Jewish colony in Argentina. In the summer of 1893, while vacationing at Borkum, he received anonymous and threatening anti-Jewish letters on a daily basis. He was deeply disturbed by this experience, and, once back in Paris, he found himself reporting on the 1894 trial of Captain Alfred Dreyfus. Convinced of Dreyfus's innocence, Nordau was also impressed by the breadth and depth of anti-Semitic feeling that the case evoked in France and Europe. His friendship with another Hungarian-German-Jewish correspondent in Paris, Theodore Herzl, took a significant turn in November, 1895, when Herzl described his ideas for creating a Jewish state in Palestine. Nordau agreed to support him in this project and henceforth felt that Zionism gave his life "purpose and content."

Nordau's Zionist writings analyzed nineteenth century Jewish legal "emancipation" as hollow and "assimilation" as destructive of Judaism. He urged physical fitness clubs to develop "muscle Jews" capable of rebuilding Zion in Palestine. When Herzl summoned a Zionist Conference of delegates to meet in Basel, Switzerland, in 1897, Nordau gave an eloquent "state of the Jews" keynote speech, wrote most of the statement of goals, and became vice president of Herzl's new World Zionist Organization.

However, while Zionism was almost an integral part of Judaism during the diaspora, it was far from uniform or organized. Spiritual Zionists such as Ahad Ha-am saw political Zionism as potentially irreligious. The Russo-Polish Zionists of Leo Pinsker had already held their first conference in Cattowitz, Poland, in 1884, represented the congregations most likely to emigrate, and were doubtful about Western "diploma chasers" such as Herzl and Nordau. Herzl spent eight years contacting world leaders, but the best he could manage was a tentative offer of Uganda as a Jewish colony under British rule. Nordau reluctantly supported Herzl's recommendation to investigate the possibilities of Uganda, but the hostile reaction of the 1903 conference in fact killed the plan, and shortly thereafter an agitated young Zionist in Paris shot at Nordau in an unsuccessful assassination attempt.

Upon Herzl's premature death in 1904, Nordau was offered the leadership of the World Zionist Organization, but he felt compelled to decline. In 1898 he had married Anna Dons-Kaufman, a Danish protestant widow. With their daughter, Maxa Nordau, he now had increased family obligations in addition to his medical practice, journalism contracts, and Zionist writings, which of course took time away from preparing his more popular social criticism publications. Further, Chaim Weizmann and the practical Zionists were already challenging Nordau's direction of policy. Weizmann later complained that Nordau was "a heldentenor, a prima donna. . . . Spade work was not his line." However, this seems a little ungenerous in view of Weizmann's consistent opposition to Nordau's leadership. In fact, Nordau continued to contribute articles to the Zionist cause and continued to keynote conferences as late as 1911. Thereafter, as the practical Zionists dominated meetings, he ceased to attend and by then had resumed his cultural criticism studies.

Nordau's *Der Sinn der Geschichte* (1909; *The Interpretation of History*, 1910) examined the role and psychology of historians who collect fragmentary evidence, arrange it according to their own personal views, and believe they write objective history when, in fact, they describe their own imaginary versions of the past without any relation to the real world. Nordau suggested that most men who write history are unsuited to make history because the historian's fact-collecting cast of mind tends to inhibit his capacity to act. He may have had himself in mind. In *Die Biologie der Ethik*

(1920; *Morals and Evolution of Man*, 1922), Nordau examined the conflict between the egoistic instinct to survive and succeed, and rational social conscience. World War I, he felt, was proof that the courage and self-sacrifice of the soldiers was a moral force that needed to be put to constructive purposes. Nordau's last and unfinished book, *Esencia de la Civilization* (1932; the meaning of civilization), dealt with the relationship between personal morality and community ethics.

During World War I, the French interned Nordau as an enemy alien, confiscated his property and savings, and deported him to Spain. He was thus in reduced circumstances while Chaim Weizmann of the practical Zionists obtained Britain's 1917 Balfour Declaration favoring a Jewish homeland in Palestine. Invited to attend a Zionist conference at London in 1920, Nordau called for recruitment of 500,000 Jews from among Europe's refugees to form the controlling majority in Palestine. Weizmann knew this was more than the British would concede or the Jews could accomplish in 1920. Nordau's arguments for the necessity of a Jewish majority in Palestine would become more relevant to Israel after 1948. After the London conference, Nordau's health declined, curtailing his Zionist activities and forcing cancellation of a planned lecture tour of the United States. He died in Paris on January 23, 1923, and was reburied in Tel Aviv in 1926.

Summary

Max Nordau was, to a great extent, a self-made man of the nineteenth century trained in medicine, gynecology, and obstetrics but also abreast of developments in neurology and psychiatry. At the same time, he was one of Europe's leading newspaper columnists and a prolific author of short stories, novels, and plays. In addition, he was world famous as a readable critic of nineteenth century life and culture and an advocate of "a philosophy of human solidarity." Finally, there was "the other Nordau," cofounder of the World Zionist Organization, chief author of the Basel Program, compelling orator, and prolific writer on Jewry, anti-Semitism, and the aims and tactics of Zionism.

In such a wide field of activity and achievement, there were bound to be imperfections. The chief posthumous charge appears to be that in *The Conventional Lies of Our Civilization* and *Degeneration* he wrote as a liberal antinationalist but then
endorsed a nationalistic Zionism. This view overlooks the conservative morality of Nordau's criticism and misunderstands his concept of Jewish nationalism. In Nordau's words, "My ideal is to see a Jewish people in the land of the fathers, ennobled by its two-thousand-year-old fortitude of character, respected for its honest and fruitful cultural endeavors, an instrument of wise progress, and a champion of justice, proclaiming and practicing brotherly love."

Bibliography

Aschheim, Steven E. "Max Nordau, Friedrich Nietzsche and 'Degeneration.'" *Journal of Contemporary History* 28, no. 4 (October, 1993). Compares and contrasts the philosophies of Nordau and Nietzsche and presents each man's opinions of the other's views.

Averini, Shlomo. *The Making of Modern Zionism.* London: Weidenfeld and Nicolson, and New York: Basic, 1981. Includes a chapter on Nordau.

Baldwin, P. M. "Liberalism, Nationalism and Degeneration: The Case of Max Nordau." *Central European History* 131 (June, 1980): 99-120. An analysis of Nordau's ideas that finds an irreconcilable contradiction between Nordau's liberalism and his Zionism.

Ben-Horin, Meir. *Common Faith, Uncommon People.* New York: Reconstructionist Press, 1970. Includes a chapter on Nordau's human solidarity as related to Zionism.

—————. *Max Nordau, Philosopher of Human Solidarity.* New York: Conference on Jewish Social Studies, 1956. Views Nordau's positive message—human solidarity—as essentially consistent in his general and Zionist writings. Also provides useful biographical information.

Mosse, George L. "Max Nordau, Liberalism and the New Jew." *Journal of Contemporary History* 27 (October, 1992): 565-581. Mosse calls Nordau "a child of his times" and contends that "his Zionism did not run counter to his liberalism."

Nordau, Anna Dons, and Maxa Nordau. *Max Nordau.* New York: Nordau Committee, 1943. An affectionate and admiring biography by his widow and daughter. An intimate picture of the man, but not a systematic account of his career.

Soder, Hans-Peter. "Disease and Health as Contexts of Modernity: Max Nordau as a Critic of Fin-de-siecle Modernism." *German Studies Review*, Fall, 1991, 473-487.

K. Fred Gillum

JESSYE NORMAN

Born: September 15, 1945; Augusta, Georgia
Area of Achievement: Music
Contribution: Gifted with an extraordinary voice, Norman has established herself as one of the leading figures on the opera stage and as a recording artist with an unusually broad repertoire.

Early Life

Jessye Norman was born on September 15, 1945, one of the five children of Silas and Janie Norman. The Normans were a prosperous, middle-class black family from Augusta, Georgia, whose children were expected to attend college. Norman grew up hoping to become a doctor or a nurse. Although she admired the singing of Leontyne Price, whom she recalls hearing when she was very young, and Marian Anderson, whom she saw on television when she was about eleven, she did not think that a person could simply decide to become a singer. Her family was quite musical—her father sang in church, her mother played piano, and she and all of her siblings took piano lessons from an early age. Norman spent her childhood singing at church and in school; although people often commented on her ability, she thought nothing of it.

When Norman was thirteen it was suggested to her parents that she start voice lessons, but they refused. Norman later commended her parents for what she saw as their good judgment in this area. She was convinced that too much training too early would have resulted in damage to such a heavy voice as her own. Norman sang as often as she could, performing for the Girl Scouts, in Sunday school, and at PTA meetings. She began learning arias with the help of her high-school music teacher and listened to Metropolitan Opera radio broadcasts on Saturday afternoons.

When Norman was sixteen, she entered the Marian Anderson Foundation scholarship auditions in Philadelphia, at the encouragement of her music teacher. She did not win anything, but on the way back from the auditions she was introduced to Carolyn Grant, a voice teacher at Howard University. Grant was so impressed with Norman's voice that she asked the university to offer Norman a full four-year scholarship to Howard. The offer was made immediately, even though Norman was not be able to take advantage of it until her graduation from high school, a year and a half later. Norman began matriculating at Howard in the fall of 1963.

Life's Work

Although Jessye Norman had not had formal voice lessons prior to her years at Howard University, her voice had been well exercised and developed during high school. Her teachers in later years encouraged her to specialize in a single voice classification, but she soon expanded her repertoire. Mezzo-soprano, spinto, dramatic soprano, and lyric soprano—most of these labels were applied to her vocal range at different times. At the beginning of her career she was most commonly identified as a mezzo, but her upper range was developed enough to allow her to sing roles few mezzos would even attempt. In Berlin, from 1969 to 1975, Norman was expected to be able to perform in roles that ranged from high coloratura to dramatic parts. By the early 1990's, she was generally recognized as a dramatic soprano, although she continued to perform other roles.

Howard University provided Norman with a community that allowed her to grow musically and personally. Besides her formal vocal training under Carolyn Grant, Norman became a paid soloist at two churches in the Washington, D.C., area; she also served as president of her sorority and as a member of various student government and music organizations. Upon her graduation in 1967, Norman went to study with Alice Duschak at the Peabody Conservatory in Baltimore. She was not happy there, however, and transferred after only one semester to the University of Michigan, where she studied with Pierre Bernac and Elizabeth Mannion. Her work with Bernac, especially, let to her development of a large repertoire of art songs, focusing particularly on the French chanson.

During both her undergraduate and graduate years, Norman participated in several vocal competitions. In 1965, she won first place in the National Society of Arts and Letters competition. She helped to fund her graduate study by auditioning for William Mathews Sullivan Music Foundation. In 1968, she entered and won the International Music Competition in Munich. This honor resulted in several professional offers to work in Germany, and Norman moved to West Berlin in 1969. She signed a three-year contract with the Deutsche Oper Berlin and made her operatic debut that same year as Elizabeth in Richard Wagner's *Tannhäuser.* The Berlin opera, like most European operas, expected its singers to fill in as needed on various

parts. During her time in Berlin, Norman expanded her repertoire to include the unusually large number of operas Berlin considered standard. Upon the completion of her first contract, Norman re-signed for another three years, but she did not complete this contract. Unhappy with her lack of freedom to choose her own roles, she resigned from the Deutsche Oper Berlin in 1975.

While working with the Berlin opera, Norman had made debuts all over the world. In 1970 she appeared in Florence, Italy, singing George Friedrich Handel's *Deborah*, and in 1972 she sang as Aïda at La Scala in Milan. Also in 1972, Norman made her American opera debut in the same role, at the Hollywood Bowl under the direction of James Levine. A few months later, she debuted at the Royal Opera House at Covent Garden in London, singing a role which later won her even greater acclaim, that of Cassandra in *Les Troyens* by Hector Berlioz.

Despite the glowing reviews of her performances in these years, Norman was not satisfied. Although she is known for the wide variety of works she performs, in both style and vocal range, Norman has

been exceedingly careful in avoiding roles she believes are unsuitable for her. The expectation that she act as a useful fill-in soprano at the Berlin opera went against the grain, and upon her resignation, Norman left opera altogether until 1980. From 1975 to 1980, she performed recitals of lieder and chanson, orchestral concerts, and opera excerpts throughout Europe and North and South America.

Norman has consistently recorded much of her repertoire, and it continues to be her recordings that earn for her the most critical acclaim. Not willing to limit herself to the tried and true, Norman has recorded opera, spirituals, the songs of Francis Poulenc, Erik Satie, and Jean-Philippe Rameau, lieder by composers from Gustav Mahler to Gabriel Fauré to Igor Stravinsky, and the work of contemporary composers often ignored by other musicians. In 1971, Norman signed an exclusive recording contract with Philips Classics, which expanded to include London and Deutsche Grammophon when the companies joined under one label.

Eventually Norman decided to return to opera. In 1983, she finally made her Metropolitan Opera debut in New York, once again as Cassandra in *Les Troyens*. She alternated this role with that of Dido in the same opera, switching off with Tatiana Troyanos throughout the season. On one memorable night during the first season, Norman ended up singing both roles in a single performance when the singer scheduled as Dido had to cancel. After her Met debut, Norman continued her concert tours and expanded her roles each year. She sang the French national anthem, *La Marseillaise*, before a television audience of millions for the French bicentennial. She is widely respected for her acting ability and her capacity to communicate on many levels through her music. Each summer she appears at prestigious music festivals such as Tanglewood and Salzburg. She has been awarded honorary doctorates from such universities as Howard, Michigan, Harvard, Sewanee, and Brandeis, as well as the Boston Conservatory. She is said to have been the inspiration for the French film *Diva* (1980) by Jean-Jacques Beineix, based on the obsession of a French fan, and released in the United States in 1982. This fan spent his entire income to attend Norman's concerts throughout Europe and to send her armloads of flowers. The Museum of Natural History in Paris has even named an orchid in Norman's honor.

Norman continues to maintain her family ties, returning to visit her mother (her father is deceased) in Georgia when she can. She has homes in London and in Westchester County, New York. Although Norman is careful to keep her private life private, she devotes much time to charitable work, raising money for black colleges, the Save the Children campaign, and the Girl Scouts. She performs regularly for the Metropolitan Opera in New York City and made history at that venue with her performance of Schoenberg's *Erwartung*, the company's first one-character production, in 1989. She was a recipient of the *Kennedy Center Honors* Lifetime Achievement Award in 1997.

Summary

Jessye Norman's career has continued to rise, but it is clear that she has already made a lasting impression on the music world. She has the rare quality of refusing to conform to the images others have of her. Her 1989 recording of Bizet's *Carmen*, for example, is not the standard interpretation of the part that most performers try to duplicate. Although she says she did not deliberately try to be different, her aim was to interpret the role so as to make it a com-

fortable role for herself. Her independence, both in interpretations and in her choice of music to perform and record, has helped to broaden the offerings to the musical public.

Norman is reticent about her life outside of music, but she has stated that she needs to feel connected to the world around her. She is concerned about political and social issues, remembering experiences from her childhood in the South before the Civil Rights movement. She has said that being an African American artist has not made any difference to her during her career. Although her identity as an African American clearly has shaped Norman's musical interests and opportunities to some degree, it is interesting to note that her statement, made less than two decades after Marian Anderson's debut as the first African American to sing at the Metropolitan Opera, clearly rejects the notion that racial identity has imposed any significant limitations on Norman's career.

Norman enjoys her reputation as an iconoclast. She dislikes being referred to as a diva—although, in the true sense of the word, no one would deny her the title— because of the connotations of temperament and pettiness that have come to be associated with that term. Although she takes great pride in her accomplishments, Norman also has a reputation for always arriving on time for rehearsals and for being fully prepared, unpretentious, and friendly—the epitome of professionalism.

Jessye Norman's persistent individuality and consummate musicianship are impressive. As she continues to shine on the opera stage, her example and her financial support have encouraged others to strive to achieve their dreams and to do their best at the work they love.

Bibliography

Daniel, David. "Norman Conquest." *Vogue* 183, no.3 (March, 1993). Profile of Norman focusing on her work ethic, background, and need to balance career and personal life.

Garland, Phyl. "Jessye Norman: Diva." *Ebony* 43 (March, 1988): 52. Focusing on Norman's life outside music, this short article provides more information on her childhood than any other source. Of limited value otherwise, it has a few interesting quotes about growing up black in the South that reveal aspects of Norman's character not seen elsewhere.

Livingstone, William. "Jessye Norman." *Stereo Review* 54 (October, 1989): 102. This well-written article is composed from interviews with Norman and includes Norman's assessment of various roles and how she interprets them.

Mayer, Martin, "Double Header." *Opera News* 48 (February 18, 1984): 8-11. Although it includes little biographical material, this excellent article provides interesting critical commentary (bordering on the snide at times) on Norman's stage and recording careers.

Mordden, Ethan. *Demented: The World of the Opera Diva*. New York: Watts, 1984. Although this work mentions Norman specifically only a few times, it gives a picture of the world of opera unequaled elsewhere. Mordden's explanation of the types of voices and the operatic roles written for these voices is especially helpful for anyone trying to assess Norman's career. Knowledge of the opera repertoire is assumed. Bibliography and index included.

"Perennial Diva," *New Yorker* 71, no. 25 (August 21, 1995). Short piece on Norman's love of gardening.

Story, Rosalyn M. *And So I Sing: African-American Divas of Opera and Concert*. New York: Warner, 1993. A history of African American women singers in the world of classical music, this work considers Norman in the perspective of other black artists. Index and bibliography included.

Margaret Hawthorne

JULIUS NYERERE

Born: March, 1922; Butiama, Tanganyika (now Tanzania)

Areas of Achievement: Government and politics

Contribution: Nyerere peacefully brought an end to the British United Nations Trusteeship of Tanzania and became the founding father of independent Tanzania. Throughout the 1960's, 1970's, and 1980's, he opposed racial oppression and discrimination of all types.

Early Life

Julius Kambarage Nyerere was born in the village of Butiama in Zanakiland, Tanganyika, in March, 1922. He was named for his father, Chief Nyerere Burito, who ruled the surrounding area. Nyerere grew up in the sheltered, peaceful, safe world of the Zanaki. He learned Zanaki traditions and was initiated into manhood. His basic values are African and never changed, though he added Western values and skills to this foundation later in life. Nyerere's father sheltered him from the humiliations and dehumanization of the colonial system until he was certain that his son had developed self-assurance that no insult or mistreatment could destroy. His father believed that this was important for a man destined to lead his people.

Nyerere took Zanaki values to school with him, such as the notion that a leader's first duty is to serve his people; that group interests are more important than individual interests; and that social welfare depends on cooperation, not competition. He attended Mwisenge Elementary School, Tabora High School, and Makerere College. While at Makerere, he discovered political science. He stated that "John Stuart Mill's essays on representative government and on the subjection of women . . . had a terrific influence on me." He won an essay contest by applying Mill's ideas to his own society. He was graduated from Makerere in 1946 and wanted to continue his education but did not have an opportunity to do so until awarded a scholarship to the University of Edinburgh in 1949.

While seeking opportunities to continue his studies, Nyerere taught school and worked as a political organizer for the Tanganyika African Association (TAA). Simple, clear explanations came naturally to him, and this earned for him the title *mwalimu*, meaning teacher. When he combined this skill with politics, he became the "fighting professor of Tanzania."

Nyerere arrived in Edinburgh in 1949 and was impressed by Scottish politicians' ability to overcome clan divisions, thereby uniting their people. He used much of what he learned from the Scots later to unify Tanganyika's Africans. Pursuit of an arts degree at Edinburgh allowed Nyerere to formulate his own philosophy. His studies convinced him that only independence could remove the menace of colonialism.

Life's Work

Shortly after returning to Tanganyika in 1952, Nyerere married Maria Gabriel. They moved to Zanakiland, and Nyerere made a house for his new bride using traditional building techniques. To neighbors who were shocked that a university graduate would perform such work, he replied that "everyone who has an education must work." Nyerere assumed teaching duties at St. Mary's and tried to ascertain the political consciousness of his fellow Africans. He learned that, in 1951, Europeans had taken large tracts of land from Meru tribesmen and evicted them. This caused bitter resentment and protest. Fear that the British would treat other tribes as callously spread. Nyerere saw in this crisis an opportunity to organize Africans and unite them.

Nyerere was elected president of the TAA in 1953, and by July 7, 1954, he had organized the TAA into a political party known as the Tanganyika African National Union (TANU). *Saba saba*, or the seventh day of the seventh month, is celebrated as a national holiday that rivals independence day. A few months after its formation, TANU voted to send Nyerere to the United Nations to address the United Nations Trusteeship Council on the Meru Land Case and on independence. Upon his return from the United Nations, Nyerere resigned his teaching position and began to work full-time for TANU. His career as a national and international politician had begun.

He argued for prohibition of land alienation, cessation of foreign immigration, expansion of education and technical training, and encouragement of trade unions and cooperatives. His logical, reasoned arguments won wide support for his position and the restoration of Meru land to the Meru people. Nyerere stated that he believed in the brotherhood of the races and that any European or Asian who accepted the principle of "one man, one vote"

would be welcomed as a citizen of an independent Tanganyika.

Nyerere admired Mahatma Gandhi and wanted to achieve independence without bloodshed. *Uhuru na kazi*, meaning freedom and work, became TANU's slogan and rallying cry. The party's ranks swelled as peasants joined forces with the educated elite. Nyerere soon headed a popular grass-roots movement capable of mobilizing mass support for its policies. Without doubt dissension existed—the militants wanted to abolish the office and power of the chiefs; wealthy Africans clashed with egalitarian idealists. In the early days, however, the dream of *uhuru* was enough to keep them together. Nyerere was convinced that a national movement had to represent all interests. TANU was fighting to build a democratic state in which each person had one vote and in this regard everyone would be equal. Since most Tanganyikans spoke Swahili, communication was not a major problem and this helped unify Tanganyika.

When it became clear to the British that Nyerere had emerged as the spokesman for Tanganyika's African majority, they tried to silence him by appointing him to the legislative council on a temporary basis. He surprised everyone by using this opportunity to attack the government's educational policy. He declared the policy inadequate, because 64 percent of school-aged African children were not in school, and no provision was made for their education. He also attacked a proposed increase in civil servant salaries, stating that salaries should be frozen and the difference applied toward the education of African youth. As rejected patrons, the British were bitter toward Nyerere, but the African masses hailed him as their champion. He became a folk hero, and the more the British attacked him the more popular he became.

By 1957, Ghana had become the first African nation to achieve independence from Great Britain. Kenya was embroiled in the Mau Mau Rebellion, and most whites in Tanganyika resigned themselves to the inevitability of majority rule. The "winds of change" were sweeping across Africa. Thus, no one was surprised that, when the colonial government called for elections in 1958, every candidate nominated by TANU won. Nyerere's party gained control of the legislature, so Great Britain began immediate preparation to hand over power without bloodshed. By 1961, Tanganyika had achieved internal self-government and full independence. Nyerere predicted that independence did not mark the end of his nation's problems. He began to work on his greatest challenge: eliminating poverty for the majority of Tanganyikans.

A dedicated Pan-Africanist, Nyerere convinced Karume, the leader of revolutionary Zanzibar, to combine Tanganyika and Zanzibar into a single nation now known as Tanzania. In 1963, he helped form the East African Community, which had a common currency, postal service, and airline. Irresolvable differences caused the community to collapse in 1976. Thus, the dream of transforming Kenya, Uganda, and Tanzania into one large nation died too.

Nyerere emerged as a spokesman for Africa's oppressed. He financed refugee camps for displaced Africans and settled them on their own farms. Nyerere backed the Mozambique Liberation Front (FRELIMO) for fourteen years while Mozambicans fought to overthrow Portuguese colonial rule. He provided school and training facilities for the African National Congress (ANC) of South Africa as it struggled to end apartheid and usher in power sharing in South Africa. As part of this effort, he inspired the formation of the Southern African Development Coordination Council (SADCC), an organization of the frontline African nations that border South Africa. Nyerere was one of the most outspoken opponents of apartheid and used a very high proportion of Tanzania's income to defeat this system.

Nyerere coined the slogan *uhuru na kazi*. He also devised the policy of *ujamaa*, or African socialism, which he used to organize and mobilize the masses. Nyerere's socialism is based upon the African concept of the extended family. Land is owned collectively by the state, and individuals lease it as long as they demonstrate that they are improving it or productively using it. This policy also encourages collective production of wealth and the collective pursuit of prosperity. More than 80 percent of all Tanzanians have been moved into nucleated villages so that the government can provide them with clean water, health care, agricultural advice, and other services. Difficulties in gaining voluntary compliance caused this *ujamaa vijijini*, or collective village, scheme to be abandoned.

Nyerere teaches Tanzanians that they cannot rely upon money to develop their country, because they are poor. Money, he argues, "is the weapon of the rich." He advises Tanzanians to learn to work intelligently and to combine this with much hard work to develop their country. Education is a key factor to this development, and it is free up through university level for those who qualify. Yearly Nyerere educates quadruple the number of Africans that were educated annually by the former colonial regime.

By encouraging Tanzanians to modernize agriculture and grow enough food crops to feed themselves as well as manufacture cloth and other items used often, Nyerere is teaching self-reliance. Compulsory military service has been used to instill discipline and has made Tanzania a formidable regional power, as the country's easy victory over Uganda in the 1977-1978 Uganda-Tanzania War proved. Nyerere has taught Tanzanians to value sharing, education, hard work, and honesty and to fight all forms of discrimination. This has provided Tanzania a stable foundation on which to build their future. Perhaps the greatest lesson that Nyerere taught Tanzanians was not to covet power. In 1985, he voluntarily stepped down, making way for Ali Hassan Mwinyi to become, democratically, the second head of state of Tanzania. This proved that a *coup d'état* is not necessary to effect a transfer of power in Africa. It also demonstrated that a former head of state can live out the balance of his life in peace in his own nation if he managed it well.

Summary

Julius Nyerere peacefully achieved independence for Tanzania in 1961. Using a unique form of socialism based upon traditional African values and the close bonds of the family, he instilled a spirit of close cooperation, sharing, and love that he called *ujamaa*. Because he led by persuasion rather than force, he is affectionately known as *mwalimu*, or the teacher. Unlike Gandhi, he used peace wherever possible but force without fear where needed, as demonstrated by his support for African freedom fighters from Mozambique, Angola, Zimbabwe, Namibia, and South Africa for more than a decade. His calm, humor, self-control, and personal honesty and integrity, and his devotion to the education, freedom, and development of Africa and Africans assure Nyerere pride of place in African and world history. The development of humans remains his guiding star and the highest ideal of independent Tanzania.

Bibliography

Duggan, William Redman, and John R. Civille. *Tanzania and Nyerere: A Study of Ujamaa and Nationhood.* Maryknoll, N.Y.: Orbis, 1976. Contains substantial biographical information on Nyerere. Follows the emergence of an independent Tanzania and Nyerere's part in that emergence. Includes an extensive bibliography, index, notes.

Graham, Shirley. *Julius K. Nyerere: Teacher of Africa.* New York: Messner, 1975. An inspiring picture of a man born to privilege who risked everything to champion the rights of all and to build a nation where all share equally its benefits and shoulder its responsibilities.

Hatch, John. *Two African Statesmen: Kaunda of Zambia and Nyerere of Tanzania.* London: Secker and Warburg, and Chicago: Regnery, 1976. Contains little-known facts about the British Labor Party's role in the independence of both Zambia and Tanzania. A sympathetic portrait by a British Labor Party official who knew both leaders.

Kaiser, Paul J. "Structural Adjustment and the Fragile Nation: The Demise of Social Unity in Tanzania." *Journal of Modern African Studies*

34, no. 2 (June, 1996). Kaiser considers Tazmanian social instability under the Economic Recovery Program, a situation foreseen by Nyerere.

Melfrum, Andrew. "Julius Nyerere: Former President of Tanzania." *Africa Report* 39, no. 5, (September-October, 1994). An interview with Nyerere in which he discusses colonial rule prior to 1961 and the improvements seen in education and literacy since Tazmanian independence.

Nnoli, Okwudiba. *Self Reliance and Foreign Policy in Tanzania.* New York: NOK, 1978. An in-depth look at Tanzania's foreign affairs that places Nyerere in context. The president is discussed in a very favorable way. Includes an index.

Smith, William Edgett. *We Must Run While They Walk: A Portrait of Africa's Julius Nyerere.* New York: Random House, 1972; as *Nyerere of Tanzania*, London: Gollancz, 1973. A warm, endearing portrait of the man behind Tanzania's freedom movement. The influence of his father, his brother Edward, Oscar Kambona, Rashidi Kawawa, Abeid Karume, and others on Nyerere is assessed. It is enjoyable and easy to read.

Dallas L. Browne

HERMANN OBERTH

Born: June 25, 1894; Hermannstadt, Siebenburgen, Transylvania
Died: December 29, 1989; Nürnberg, West Germany
Area of Achievement: Aeronautics
Contribution: Oberth is one of the three great pioneers of the sciences of astronautics and modern rocketry. Along with Konstantin Tsiolkovsky and Robert Goddard, he is credited with developing the principles behind rocket-powered flight beyond Earth's atmosphere, liquid-fueled rockets, a manned Earth orbital space station, and manned interplanetary flight.

Early Life

Hermann Julius Oberth was born on June 25, 1894, in Hermannstadt, Siebenburgen, Transylvania, a part of what is modern Romania. His father, Julius, was a physician who stressed learning to his son from an early age. The younger Oberth attended elementary and high school in the town of Schaessburg until 1913, when he entered the University of Munich to study medicine, as had his father. Oberth, like fellow rocketry pioneers Konstantin Tsiolkovsky in Russia and Robert Goddard in the United States, was heavily influenced in his formative years by the emerging genre of science fiction in the late nineteenth and early twentieth centuries that detailed possible methods of traveling into space. Indeed, in his later years Oberth acknowledged that his mother's gift of Jules Verne's books in his eleventh year helped shape the course of the rest of his life.

When World War I started in 1914, the twenty-year-old Oberth joined the German army's medical service. This experience gave him a strong distaste for the healing arts and convinced him to pursue another area of endeavor as his life's work. Turning to his childhood fascination with the concept of spaceflight, he chose mathematics and physics to be his new fields of study.

After leaving the army medical service, Oberth returned to the University of Munich and began his studies. He also studied at Göttingen and Heidelberg before receiving his schoolmaster's diploma in July, 1923. Returning to Siebenburgen, he began work as a fifth-grade teacher of mathematics and physics. Later he taught in the German town of Mediasch, where he made his home until 1938. He later took German citizenship. It was during his service in Germany in World War I that he unsuccessfully proposed that the German government build liquid-fueled bombardment missiles, the forerunners of the modern Intercontinental Ballistic Missiles.

Oberth continued to read and theorize about the prospects of rocket-powered space flight. This avocation led to the publication of his first and most well known work on astronautics, *Die Rakete zu den Planetenräumen* (1923; the rocket into interplanetary space). It was this seminal work's worldwide popularity that gave Oberth an international reputation as an expert in astronautics.

Life's Work

Oberth's *Die Rakete zu den Planetenräumen* and an expanded version of the book published in 1929, *Wege zur Raumschiffahrt* (*Ways to Spaceflight*, 1972), put forth numerous ideas that were to form the basis of the German missile program in World War II and the ongoing American and Soviet manned and unmanned space programs. These included the theory that a liquid-fueled rocket could propel an object through the airless void of space and that the vehicle could develop sufficient velocity and centrifugal force to counterbalance Earth's gravity and remain in orbit around the planet. He also theorized that the vehicle could move quickly enough to break free of Earth's gravity and move into interplanetary space.

Moving beyond the theory of propulsion, Oberth hypothesized the potential effects of space travel on the human body and was the first to coin the phrase "space station" to mean a permanent manned facility in Earth orbit. Although he developed his theories independently of his peers, Oberth's two books confirmed both Tsiolkovsky's theoretical work on rocket propulsion and Goddard's practical experience in rocketry, and moved Oberth to the pinnacle of the rapidly developing field. Both before and after the publication of his first books he maintained active correspondence with both men until their deaths.

In 1928, Oberth was given the chance to put the theories he had developed into practice when he became the technical adviser to the famous film director Fritz Lang and the Ufa film company for the motion picture *Die Frau im Mond*. As part of his

service to Ufa, he was asked to build and fly a liquid-fueled rocket to promote the film. Unfortunately, the rocket Oberth constructed was unable to fly, and the film company ran out of development funds before he was able to correct the design. Oberth was, however, able to test-fire a rocket engine successfully in 1930 as part of the project.

An active and vocal proponent of space exploration, Oberth helped found in 1929 the Verein fur Raumschiffahrt (VfR), Germany's first society for space travel. In addition to Oberth, who was elected the society's first president, the group's first members included such pioneers of aeronautics and rocketry as Willy Ley and an eighteen-year-old student of Oberth by the name of Wernher von Braun. The VfR's development paralleled the founding of similar groups elsewhere in the world, including the Moscow Group for the Study of Reactive Propulsion, whose members included the future chief designer of the Soviet space program, Sergei Korolev, and aircraft designer Andrei Tupolev. The VfR and other of these groups both built and flew rudimentary rockets and sponsored public displays on rocketry such as the one built by

Oberth and von Braun in a Berlin department store to educate the public about their work.

In 1930, the VfR was given a parcel of land outside Berlin to conduct practical experiments in rocketry. This empty field, which was once an ammunition dump for the German army, was called Raketenflugplatz Berlin (rocket field Berlin). Oberth and the VfR spent the next two years conducting experiments there before the German army developed an interest in their work and recruited several of the VfR's members into service developing ordnance. During this period, Oberth supported himself by teaching mathematics and physics at the technical universities in Vienna and Dresden, as well as by publishing his research in astronautics in numerous books and articles. In 1941, he went to work for his former student von Braun as a member of the team of scientists at the German rocket-development center in Heeresversuchsstelle, Peenemünde.

At Peenemünde, von Braun and Oberth developed and then successfully launched the Vengeance weapons, the V-1 and V-2 rockets. The V-1 "Buzz Bomb" was a short-range, rocket-powered winged bomb, while the V-2 was a powerful ballistic missile able to span hundreds of miles to deliver its deadly payload. With the approval in June, 1943, of Adolf Hitler, the V-2 went into mass production. The first operational V-2 missile was launched on September 8, 1944, at London, England, from The Hague, The Netherlands.

In 1943, Oberth transferred to the Rheinsdorf aircraft facility near Wittenberg, Germany, where he remained for the duration of World War II. After the war, he left Germany unnoticed by the Allies and moved to Switzerland, where he lived in seclusion until 1949. Oberth's research into rocketry resumed in 1949 at Oberried am Brienzer Lake and, later, for the Italian navy at La Spezia, Italy. During these years, he also gained considerable recognition from the growing international community of rocket scientists. His theories were being put to use by both the United States with its early V-2 tests and its own Viking rocket, and by the Soviet Union under Sergei Korolev and his larger, more powerful rockets.

During these years and later, Oberth continued to publish both technical materials and popular treatises on practical concepts of space travel. His later books and articles, including *Menschen im Weltraum* (1954; men into space) and *Stoff und Leben* (1959; matter and life), were well received both by the scientific community and by the general public. He was the recipient of numerous awards during his long career, including the REP Hirsch Award of the Société Astronomique de France, of which he was the first to be so honored in 1925, and the coveted Galabert Prize in 1962. As one of the pioneers of space travel, he was also invited to lecture and participate in many international conferences and programs on astronautics and rocketry. One of the honors he is known to have most prized, however, was having been invited to participate in the realization of his dream of interplanetary space travel as a witness to the launch of Apollo 11, the first manned landing on the moon, in 1969.

In 1955, Oberth again went to work for his former student von Braun at the Technical Feasibility Studies Office of the Ordnance Missile Laboratories in the United States. In 1956, he transferred to the Army Ballistic Missile Agency with von Braun to assist in the development of the Redstone Rocket, one of the United States' first liquid-fueled boosters and the backbone of the early U.S. space program. Two years later, Oberth returned to Germany in semiretirement.

Summary

Hermann Oberth was one of the first great idealists of space travel in the modern age. He, along with his contemporaries Tsiolkovsky and Goddard, had the knowledge and the passion to take the fantasy of science fiction and turn it into the reality of science fact. Through their vision, they forged a new understanding of their world. Oberth's theories, enumerated in his books, showed how the laws of physics could be put to use to conquer the heavens. He theorized about the first space station and gave a detailed, startlingly accurate account of how microgravity would affect the human body on long space voyages. These writings, along with his seminal works about reaction propulsion of a space vehicle and liquid-fueled rockets, gave future engineers and scientists a path to follow in making space travel a reality.

While his work at Peenemünde helped develop weapons of destruction, he was a man who believed deeply in the peaceful pursuit of space. He urged international cooperation between the United States and the Soviet Union in the early days of the space race, even going so far as asking Nikita Khrushchev to allow him to work with Sergei Korolev in the development of the Soviet space program. One of Oberth's most direct contributions to the progress of space travel was the encouragement he gave to the rocketry enthusiasts of his day, such as Wernher von Braun. Von Braun took the knowledge he gained from Oberth, expanded upon it, and made space travel a reality by developing the launch vehicles that carried men to the moon and the unmanned probes that traveled beyond the solar system.

Bibliography

Braun, Wernher von, and Frederick I. Ordway III. *The History of Rocketry and Space Travel.* 3d ed. New York: Crowell, 1975. As one of the unequaled giants in modern rocketry, von Braun brings to this well-written and easily understandable compendium a unique and fascinating perspective. An excellent starting point for the layperson for information on the early days of the American space program.

Freeman, Marsha G. "The Father of Spaceflight." *World and I* 9, no. 12 (December, 1994). Profile of Oberth that includes information on his book *The Rocket into Interplanetary Space* and the scientific community's reaction to it.

Hurt, Harry, III. *For All Mankind.* New York: Atlantic Monthly Press, 1988; London: Queen Anne Press, 1989. Gives an overview of the American space program through the Apollo lunar landings. An accompanying volume to a documentary on the men who flew the lunar landing missions.

Huzel, Dieter K. *Peenemünde to Canaveral.* Englewood Cliffs, N.J.: Prentice-Hall, 1962. This insider's account of the German rocket program during World War II is fast-paced and reads like a novel. Of interest to anyone who wishes to learn more about the proving ground for much of the technology in use in the modern space race.

McAleer, Neil. *The Omni Space Almanac: A Complete Guide to the Space Age.* New York: World Almanac, 1987. A compendium of information about the major developments of the space age, with emphasis on the modern years and their import for the future.

Neufeld, M.J. "Weimar Culture and Futuristic Technology: The Rocketry and Spaceflight Fad in Germany, 1923-1933." *Technology and Culture* 31, no. 4 (October, 1990). Focuses on the German interest in spaceflight in the 1920s and 1930s, including contributions by Oberth.

Oberth, Hermann. *Man into Space: New Projects for Rocket and Space Travel.* Translated by G. P. H. De Freville. London: Weidenfeld and Nicolson, and New York: Harper, 1957. This book, one of Oberth's last, is a scholarly approach to space travel, written on the eve of the modern space age. While it contains some technical information, the book is written in easily understandable language for the layperson or amateur space enthusiast.

Stuhlinger, Ernst, et al., eds. *Astronautical Engineering and Science: From Peenemünde to Planetary Space, Honoring the 50th Birthday of Wernher von Braun.* New York: McGraw-Hill, 1963. Written by von Braun's colleagues from Peenemünde, the U.S. Army missile program, the Marshall Space Center, and Cape Canaveral, this collection of essays on space technology and exploration is excellent. Oberth contributed a paper on an electrical rocket engine that is well written and informative.

Eric Christensen